Fodor's **up**CLOSE

D0069310

EUROPE

the complete guide, thoroughly up-to-date

SAVVY TRAVELING: WHERE TO SPEND, HOW TO SAVE

packed with details that will make your trip

CULTURAL TIPS: ESSENTIAL LOCAL DO'S AND TABOOS

must-see sights, on and off the beaten path

INSIDER SECRETS: WHAT'S HIP AND WHAT TO SKIP

the buzz on restaurants, the lowdown on lodgings

FIND YOUR WAY WITH CLEAR AND EASY-TO-USE MAPS

Previously published as *The Berkeley Guide to Europe*
FODOR'S TRAVEL PUBLICATIONS, INC.
NEW YORK • TORONTO • LONDON • SYDNEY • AUCKLAN
www.fodors.com/

FODOR'S UPCLOSE™ EUROPE

EDITOR: Christine Cipriani

Editorial Contributors: Robert Andrews, Eleanore Boyse, Jennifer Brewer, Emmanuel Briand, Jacqueline Brown, Jules Brown, Martha de la Cal, Jeffrey Carson, John Chapple, Kim Conniff, Nancy Coons, Daniel Cooper, Pippa Craig, Bonnie Dodson, Jon Eldan, Robert Fisher, Gerri Gallagher, Brent Gregston, Gregory Hedger, Simon Hewitt, Aaron Hicklin, Anto Howard, Gareth Jenkins, Andres Kahar, Suzanne Kelleher, Margaret Kemp, Natasha Lesser, Richard Lewis, Alexander Lobrano, Andrew May, Marius Meland, Jennifer Paull, Tim Perry, Ian Phillips, Karina Porcelli, Caragh Rockwood, Pam Rolfe, Mar Roman, Jürgen Scheunemann, George Semler, Eric Sjogren, Wif Stenger, Donna Stonecipher, Michelle Sweeney, Roger Thomas, Robert Tilley, Julie Tomasz, Nancy van Itallie, Stuart Wade, Annie Ward, Diana Willensky

Editorial Production: Linda K. Schmidt

Maps: David Lindroth, *cartographer*; Steven Amsterdam, *map editor*

Design: Fabrizio La Rocca, *creative director*; Allison Saltzman, *cover and text design*; Jolie Novak, *photo editor*

Production/Manufacturing: Robert B. Shields

Cover Art: Allan Montaine/Photonica

CONTENTS

2. AUSTRIA 26

3. BALTIC REPUBLICS 56

4. BELGIUM 69

5. BULGARIA 94

6. CZECH REPUBLIC 108

7. DENMARK 129

8. FINLAND 154

9. FRANCE 174

10. GERMANY 262

11. GREAT BRITAIN 337

12. GREECE 416

13. HUNGARY 459

14. IRELAND 487

15. ITALY 511

16. LUXEMBOURG 586

17. MOROCCO 593

18. THE NETHERLANDS 617

19. NORWAY 647

26. SWITZERLAND 849

27. TURKEY 877

INDEX 909

FORGET^{TO} PACK ENOUGH MONEY?

MoneyGram^{SM} can help you, NOW!

- Your money arrives in just minutes to any of our 3,300 locations throughout Europe

- Customer Service Representatives available 24 hours a day who can inform you where the closest MoneyGram^{SM} money transfer location is.

So, if the money you need to see Europe has seen its last days, call us and we'll direct you to a MoneyGram^{SM} Agent close to you.

Spain	900-96-1218	**Belgium**	0800-7-1173
Germany	0130-8-16629	**Croatia**	99-385-0111 then
Greece	00-800-119293-0309		dial 1-800-592-3688
Netherlands	06-022-3392	**Hungary**	00-800-12249
Czech Republic	00-41-00-101	**For any other country in Europe**	
	dial 1-800-592-3688	**call collect to the US** 303-980-3340	

MoneyGram^{SM}
MONEY IN MINUTES WORLDWIDE.^{SM}

TRAVELING UPCLOSE

Take an overnight train. Shop for a picnic. Hike the Alps. Have a coffee. Prowl a flea market. Go to a festival. Commune with nature. Memorize the symphony of the streets— then get lost. And if you want to experience the heart and soul of Europe, whatever you do, don't spend too much money.

The deep and rich experience of Europe that every true traveler yearns for is one of the things in life that money can't buy. In fact, if you have it, don't use it. Traveling lavishly is the surest way to turn yourself into a sideline traveler. Restaurants with white-glove service are great—sometimes—but they're usually not the best place to find the perfect kebab. Doormen at plush hotels have their place, but not when your look-alike room could be anywhere from Düsseldorf to Detroit. Better to stay in a more intimate place that truly gives you the atmosphere you traveled so far to experience. Don't just stand and watch— jump into the spirit of what's around you.

If you want to see Europe up close and savor the essence of the continent and its people in all their various glory, this book is for you. We'll show you the local culture, the offbeat sights, the bars and cafés where tourists rarely tread, and the B&Bs and other hostelries where you'll meet fellow travelers—places where the locals would send their friends. And because you'll probably want to see the famous places if you haven't already been there, we give you tips on losing the crowds, plus the quirky and obscure facts you want as well as the basics everyone needs.

OUR GANG

Who's are we? We're artists and poets, slackers and straight arrows, and travel writers and journalists, who in our less hedonistic moments report on local news and spin out an occasional opinion piece. What we share is a certain footloose spirit and a passion for all things Euro, which we celebrate in this guidebook. Shamelessly, we've revealed all of our favorite places and our deepest, darkest travel secrets, all so that you can learn from our past mistakes and experience the best part of Europe to the fullest. If you can't take your best friend on the road, or if your best friend is hopeless with directions, stick with us.

A SEND-OFF

Always call ahead. We knock ourselves out to check all the facts, but everything changes all the time, in ways that none of us can ever fully anticipate. Whenever you're making a special trip to a special place, as opposed to merely wandering, always call ahead. Trust us on this.

And then, if something doesn't go quite right, as inevitably happens with even the best-laid plans, stay cool. Missed your train? Stuck in the airport? Use the time to study the people. Strike up a conversation with a stranger. Study the newsstands or flip through the local press. Take a walk. Find the silver lining in the clouds, whatever it is. And do send us a postcard to tell us what went wrong and what went right. You can e-mail us at: editors@fodors.com (specify the name of the book on the subject line) or write the upClose Europe editor at Fodor's upClose, 201 East 50th Street, New York, NY 10022. We'll put your ideas to good use and let other travelers benefit from your experiences. In the mean time, bon voyage!

EUROPE

0 ——— 400 miles
0 ——— 600 km
N

NORWAY
Bergen

Skagerra

SCOTLAND

NORTHERN
IRELAND
Edinburgh

North
Sea

DENMARK

Belfast
IRELAND   Irish
Sea   GREAT
BRITAIN
Dublin
Cork   WALES
Hamburg
ENGLAND   THE
NETHERLANDS
Cardiff   Amsterdam
The Hague
London   Rotterdam   GER
Brussels   Bonn
BELGIUM
Frankfurt
Paris
LUXEMBOURG

ATLANTIC
OCEAN

English Channel

FRANCE
Zürich   Muni
Bern   Salzbu
SWITZERLAND
Lyon   LIECHTENST
Milan   Ve

Nice
Marseille   Monte Carlo
PORTUGAL   Florence
Madrid   ANDORRA
Corsica
Lisbon
Barcelona
SPAIN
Sardinia
Sevilla   Granada
Balearic   Tyrrhen
Islands
Gibraltar   Mediterranean Sea
Tangier
Rabat
MOROCCO   ALGERIA   TUNISIA
Fès

FINLAND

Gulf of Bothnia

Oslo

SWEDEN

Helsinki

Gulf of Finland

St. Petersburg

Tallinn

Stockholm

ESTONIA

Tartu

Göteborg

RUSSIA

Rīga

Moscow

Kattegat

LATVIA

Copenhagen

LITHUANIA

Baltic Sea

RUSSIA

Kaunas

Vilnius

Kaliningrad

Minsk

Berlin

POLAND

BELARUS

Dresden

Warsaw

RMANY

Kraków

Kiev

nich

Prague

UKRAINE

CZECH REP.

urg

SLOVAKIA

Vienna

Bratislava

AUSTRIA

Budapest

MOLDOVA

TEIN

HUNGARY

Kishinev

SLOVENIA

Ljubljana

Zagreb

enice

CROATIA

ROMANIA

BOSNIA AND HERZEGOVINA

Belgrade

Bucharest

Black Sea

Rome

Sarajevo

SERBIA

ITALY

MONTENEGRO

Pristina

BULGARIA

Adriatic Sea

Podgorica

Skopje

Sofia

Naples

Tirane

F.Y.R of MACEDONIA

İstanbul

ALBANIA

Ankara

nian Sea

GREECE

TURKEY

Aegean Sea

Palermo

Ionian Sea

Sicily

Athens

MALTA

Crete

CYPRUS

Mediterranean Sea

BASICS

Contacts and Savvy Tips to Make Your Trip Hassle-Free

f you've ever traveled with anyone before, you know that there are two kinds of people in the world—the planners and the nonplanners. Travel brings out the worst in both groups. Left to their own devices, the planners will have you goose-stepping from sight to sight, with no more noble aim than crossing each one off a list; while the nonplanners will have you sitting on a bench in the train station, waiting for a missed connection. This chapter suggests a middle ground; we hope it provides enough information to help you plan your trip to Europe without nailing you down. Be flexible, and hold on to your sense of humor—the most hair-pulling situations abroad can turn into the best travel stories back home.

AIR TRAVEL

MAJOR AIRLINE OR LOW-COST CARRIER?

Most people choose a flight based on price, yet there are other issues to consider. Major airlines offer the greatest number of departures; smaller airlines—including regional, low-cost, and no-frill airlines—usually have a limited number of flights daily. Major airlines have frequent-flyer partners, which allow you to credit mileage earned on one airline to your account with another. Low-cost airlines offer a definite price advantage and fewer restrictions, such as advance-purchase requirements. As a group, low-cost carriers have the best safety record, but **check the safety record before booking a flight** with one; call the Federal Aviation Administration's Consumer Hotline (*see* Airline Complaints, *below*).

MAJOR AIRLINES • American (tel. 800/433–7300). **Continental** (tel. 800/525–0280). **Delta** (tel. 800/221–1212). **Northwest** (tel. 800/225–2525). **TWA** (tel. 800/221–2000). **United** (tel. 800/241–6522). **USAirways** (tel. 800/428–4322).

NATIONAL AIRLINES • Austria: **Austrian Airlines** (tel. 800/843–0002). Belgium: **Sabena Belgian World Airlines** (tel. 800/955–2000). The Czech Republic and Slovakia: **Czech Airlines** (CSA, tel. 212/765–6022 or 800/223–2365). Denmark: **Scandinavian Airlines** (SAS, tel. 800/221–2350). Finland: **Finnair** (tel. 800/950–5000). France: Air France (tel. 800/237–2747). Germany: **Lufthansa** (tel. 800/645–3880). Great Britain: **British Airways** (tel. 800/247–9297). **Virgin Atlantic** (tel. 800/862–8621). Greece: **Olympic Airways** (tel. 212/838–3600 or 800/223–1226). Holland: **KLM Royal Dutch Airlines** (tel. 800/374–7747). Hungary: **Malév Hungarian Airlines** (tel. 212/757–6446). Iceland: **Icelandair** (tel. 800/223–5500). Ireland: **Aer Lingus** (tel. 212/557–1110 or 800/223–6537). Italy: **Alitalia**

(tel. 800/223–5730). Norway: **Scandinavian Airlines** (SAS, tel. 800/221–2350). Poland: **LOT Polish Airlines** (tel. 212/869–1074). Portugal: **TAP Air Portugal** (tel. 800/221–7370). Romania: **Tarom Romanian Air Transport** (tel. 212/687–6013). Spain: **Iberia Airlines** (tel. 800/772–4642). Sweden: **Scandinavian Airlines** (tel. 800/221–2350). Switzerland: **Swissair** (tel. 800/221–4750). Turkey: **THY Turkish Airlines** (tel. 212/339–9650).

FROM CANADA • Every major U.S. airline flies between the United States and Canada, as does **Air Canada** (tel. 800/776–3000).

FROM THE U.K. • Contact **British Airways** (156 Regent St., London W1R 5TA, tel. 0345/222111), **British Midland** (tel. 0181/745–7321 or 0345/554–554), or **Air UK** (tel. 0345/666777). **Britannia Airways** sells charter flights only through travel agents; you should also ask about the new no-frills scheduled airlines. **Ryanair** (tel. 0541/569569) serves Dublin, Cork, and Knock from London's Stansted airport, and Dublin also from Luton and Gatwick. **EasyJet** (tel. 0990/292929). When you're quoted a price, **ask your agent if the price is likely to get any lower.** Good agents know the seasonal fluctuations of airfares and can usually anticipate a sale or fare war. However, waiting can be risky: The fare could go *up* as seats become scarce, and you may wait so long that your preferred flight sells out. A wait-and-see strategy works best if your plans are flexible; but if you must arrive and depart on certain dates, don't delay.

GET THE LOWEST FARE

The least expensive airfares to Europe are priced for round-trip travel. Major airlines usually require that you **book far in advance and stay between 7 and 30 days** to get the lowest fares. Ask about "ultrasaver" fares, which are the cheapest; they must be booked 90 days in advance and are nonrefundable. A little more expensive are "supersaver" fares, which require only a 30-day advance purchase. Remember that penalties for refunds or scheduling changes are stiff for international tickets, usually about $150. International flights are also season-sensitive: **plan to fly in the off season** for the cheapest fares. If your destination or home city has more than one gateway, **compare prices to and from different airports.** Flexibility is the key to getting a serious bargain on airfare. If you can play around with your departure date, destination, and return date, you will probably save money. Ask which days of the week are the cheapest to fly on—weekends are often the most expensive. Even the time of day you fly can make a big difference in the cost of your ticket. Other possible discount sources are student- and budget-travel organizations (*see* Students, *below*).

To save money on round-trip flights originating in the United Kingdom, **look into an APEX or Super-PEX ticket.** APEX tickets must be booked in advance and have certain restrictions. Super-PEX tickets can be purchased at the airport on the day of departure—subject to availability.

CHECK WITH CONSOLIDATORS

Consolidators (sometimes known as bucket shops) buy tickets for scheduled flights at reduced rates from the airlines, then sell them at prices that beat the best fares available directly from the airlines—and usually without advance restrictions. Sometimes you can even get your money back if you need to return the ticket. Read carefully the fine print detailing penalties for changes and cancellations, **confirm your consolidator reservation with the airline itself,** and be sure to check restrictions, refund possibilities, and payment conditions.

CONSOLIDATORS • **Airfare Busters** (5100 Westheimer, Suite 550, Houston, TX 77056, tel. 713/961–5109 or 800/232–8783, fax 713/961–3385. **Globe Travel** (507 5th Ave., Suite 606, New York, NY 10017, tel. 212/843–9885 or 800/969–4562, fax 212/843–9889.). **United States Air Consolidators Association** (925 L St., Suite 220, Sacramento, CA 95814, tel. 916/441–4166, fax 916/441–3520). **UniTravel** (1177 N. Warson Rd., St. Louis, MO 63132, tel. 314/569–2501 or 800/325–2222, fax 314/569–2503). **Up & Away Travel** (347 5th Ave., Suite 202, New York, NY 10016, tel. 212/889–2345 or 800/275–8001, fax 212/889–2350).

CONSIDER A CHARTER

Charters usually have the lowest fares but are not entirely dependable. Schedules are often strange; departures are infrequent and seldom on time; check-in can be chaos; and flights can be delayed for up to 48 hours, or can be cancelled for any reason up to 10 days before you're scheduled to leave. Moreover, itineraries and prices can change after you've booked your flight, so you must **be very careful to choose a legitimate charter carrier.** Read the fine print regarding refund policies, and if you can't pay with a credit card, **make your check payable to a charter carrier's escrow account** (unless you're dealing with a travel agent, in which case his or her check should be made payable to the escrow account). The name of the bank should be in the charter contract.

CHARTER CARRIERS • DER Tours (Box 1606, Des Plains, IL 60017, tel. 800/782–2424). **Travel CUTS** (187 College St., Toronto, Ont. M5T 1P7, tel. 416/979–2406). Reputable charter airlines to contact directly include **MartinAir** (tel. 800/627–8462) and **Tower Air** (tel. 800/348–6937).

GO AS A COURIER

Courier flights are simple: You sign a contract with a courier service to babysit some packages (usually without having seen them first), and the courier company pays half or more of your airfare. On the day of departure, you arrive at the airport a few hours early, meet someone who hands you a ticket and customs forms, and off you go. You need not deal with the package at that point. After you land, you simply clear customs with the courier luggage and deliver it to a waiting agent.

Flying as a courier is cheap and easy, but there are restrictions. Flights are usually booked only a week or two in advance—often only a few days in advance—and you are allowed carry-on luggage only, because the courier uses your checked-luggage allowance to transport its shipment. You must return within one to four weeks, and flight times and destinations are limited. If you plan to travel with a companion, you'll probably have to travel a day apart. And you may be asked to pay a deposit, to be refunded after you have completed your assignment.

COURIER CONTACTS • Discount Travel International (169 W. 81st St., New York, NY 10024, tel. 212/362–3636, fax 212/362–3236). **Now Voyager** (tel. 212/431–1616, fax 212/334–5243).

AVOID GETTING BUMPED

Airlines routinely overbook planes, assuming that not everyone with a ticket will show up, but occasionally everyone does. When this happens, airlines ask for volunteers to give up their seats. In return these volunteers usually get a certificate for a free flight and are rebooked on the next flight out. If there are not enough volunteers, the airline must decide who will be denied boarding. The first to get bumped are passengers who checked in late and passengers flying on discounted tickets, so **get to the gate and check in as early as possible,** especially during peak periods.

Always **bring a photo ID to the airport.** You may be asked to show it before you are allowed to check in.

ENJOY THE FLIGHT

For better service, **fly smaller or regional carriers,** which often have higher passenger-satisfaction ratings. Sometimes you'll find leather seats, more legroom, and better food.

For more legroom, **request an emergency-aisle seat**; do not, however, sit in the row in front of the emergency aisle or in front of a partition, where seats may not recline.

If you stick to a specific diet, such as vegetarian, low-cholesterol, or kosher, **ask for a special meal when you reserve.**

To avoid jet lag, try to maintain a normal routine while traveling. Once your plane takes off, set your watch to the time at your destination, and start thinking accordingly. At night (destination time), **get some sleep.** During the day, **eat light meals, drink water (not alcohol), and move about the cabin** to stretch your legs.

Some airlines prohibit smoking on all flights; others allow smoking only on certain routes or even certain departures from that route, so **contact your airline for its smoking policy.**

WITHIN EUROPE

Flying from one European city to another is often costly, but it can save you heaps of time on trains, buses, and ferries if you're traveling to a remote area. In countries such as Sweden, Norway, Greece, and to some extent the United Kingdom, air service is a vital link between cities and remote island or mountain communities and is often subsidized by the government. In Greece, for example, you can fly very inexpensively between Athens and the islands (though not *between* the islands).

For budget travelers, the best news in years has been the birth of a handful of **no-frills airlines.** On the Continent, Brussels-based **Virgin Express** (tel. 02/752–0505) has the field virtually to itself, flying from Brussels to Milan, Rome, Nice, Vienna, Madrid, Barcelona, Copenhagen, London Heathrow, and London Gatwick, with Stockholm and German destinations likely to be added. Additional flights go from Rome to Barcelona and Madrid. The eccentrically spelled **easyJet** (tel. 0990/292929 or 01582/445555) flies from London's Luton airport to Amsterdam, Nice, and Barcelona, and plans to add routes to Geneva and Oslo. **Ryanair** (tel. 0541/569569) serves Dublin, Cork, and Knock from London's Stansted airport.

These airlines are not part of international reservations systems and thus do not show up on U.S. travel agents' screens. You call them direct, get a reservation number, and pick up your boarding pass at the airport. The only fare you're likely to see advertised is the lowest; to get it, book two weeks ahead of time and be prepared to be flexible about your travel dates. On board, service is limited to a soft drink and a smile; your reward is a one-way fare of $60–$100.

A number of **mid-priced airlines** have also appeared, and thanks to lower overhead and pay scales, these are able to undersell nationals by a considerable margin while continuing to offer standard airline services. **British Midland** has established itself in Europe as a credible, cheaper alternative to British Airways. Others include Britain's **Air U.K.** and **Debonair,** Germany's **Deutsche BA,** France's **TAT** and **Air Liberté,** Sweden's **Transwede** and **Malmoe Aviation,** Italy's **Air One,** and Spain's **Spanair.**

On **national airlines,** the most reasonable fares have long been nonrefundable and nontransferable round-trips (APEX fares, in Eurospeak), which require a Saturday-night stay at the destination. Ask about new, less restrictive fares. If you're under 25, you may be in for a bonus, as many European airlines offer bargain tickets one day in advance or standby tickets to travelers 25 and under; always ask about youth discounts when booking with a European airline.

COMPLAIN IF NECESSARY

If your baggage goes astray or your flight goes awry, **complain right away.** Most carriers require that you file a claim immediately.

AIRLINE COMPLAINTS • U.S. Department of Transportation **Aviation Consumer Protection Division** (C-75, Washington, DC 20590, tel. 202/366–2220). **Federal Aviation Administration (FAA) Consumer Hotline** (tel. 800/322–7873).

BUS TRAVEL

International bus travel is just catching on in Europe in a major way, and it caters mostly to travelers under 35. The **Eurolines Group** consists of 28 motorcoach operators with scheduled international service; starting in 1998, these companies will also have the right to transport passengers within each country. The 25-nation network serves 1,500 cities, with services ranging from twice weekly to five times daily. Eurolines has its own coach stations in Paris (28 avenue du Général de Gaulle at Bagnelot; Métro: Gallieni), Brussels (80 rue du Progrès, next to the Gare du Nord), and Amsterdam (adjacent to the Amstel Railway Station); in London it uses the Victoria Coach Station (adjoining the railway station). In other cities, coaches depart from railway stations or municipal bus terminals. If you're planning to hit a lot of countries, check out the new **Eurolines Pass,** which buys you unlimited travel between 20 European cities; a 30-day pass costs $339 ($299 for those under 26 or over 60), a 60-day pass $409 ($369). They're available from Eurolines offices and travel agents in Europe, or from **Rebel Tours** (2405 Kearney Ave., Valencia CA 91355, tel. 805/294–0944) or **DER** (9501 Devon Ave., Rosemont IL 60018, tel. 847/692–4141) in the United States.

Eurobus operates "hop-on, hop-off" service on three different (but linked) one-way circuits in northern, central, and southern Europe, plus a London/Paris link. Passes are valid for four months from the first day of travel. Passes range from $225 for one zone, for those ages 27–38 ($210 for those under 26) to $525 ($470) for all three zones. You can get them from STA or Council (*see* Students, *below*).

CAR RENTAL

Rental rates in London begin at $39 a day and $136 a week for an economy car with air-conditioning, manual transmission, and unlimited mileage; rates do not include the tax on car rentals, which is 17.5%. Rates in Paris begin at $60 a day and $196 a week, with an additional car-rental tax of 20.6%. Rates in Madrid begin at $37 a day and $132 a week; the tax is 16%. Rates in Rome begin at $49 a day and $167 a week; the tax is 19%. Rates in Frankfurt begin at $18 a day and $91 a week; the tax is 15%. Check out the Hertz Affordable Europe program, which offers a one-week rental, including drop fee, from $201.

Your own driver's license is acceptable in Europe, but it's still a good idea to get an International Driver's Permit for universal recognition (*see* Driving, *below*).

CUT COSTS

You can save as much as 30% if you reserve a car before leaving home, rather than renting one on the spot abroad. To get the best deal, **book through a travel agent who is willing to shop around.**

Be sure to **look into wholesalers,** companies that do not own fleets but rent in bulk from those that do, and frequently offer better rates than traditional car-rental companies. Prices are best during off-peak periods. Rentals booked through wholesalers must be paid for before you leave the United States.

Ask your travel agent about a rental company's customer-service record. How has the company responded to late plane arrivals and vehicle mishaps? Are there often lines at the rental counter, and, if you're traveling during a holiday period, does a confirmed reservation guarantee you a car?

No matter who rents you the car, remember to ask about required deposits, cancellation penalties, and drop-off charges if you're planning to pick up the car in one city and leave it in another.

MAJOR AGENCIES • Alamo (tel. 800/879–2847 in Canada). **Budget** (tel. 800/527–0700, 0800/181181 in the U.K.). **Dollar** (tel. 800/800–4000; 0990/565656 in the U.K., where it is known as Eurodollar). **Hertz** (tel. 800/654–3001, 800/263–0600 in Canada, 0345/555888 in the U.K.). **National InterRent** (tel. 800/227–3876; 0345/222525 in the U.K., where it is known as Europcar InterRent).

RENTAL WHOLESALERS • Auto Europe (tel. 207/842–2000 or 800/223–5555, fax 800/235–6321). **Europe by Car** (tel. 212/581–3040 or 800/223–1516, fax 212/246–1458). **DER Travel Services** (9501 W. Devon Ave., Rosemont, IL 60018, tel. 800/782–2424, fax 800/282–7474 for information or 800/860–9944 for brochures). The **Kemwel Group** (tel. 914/835–5555 or 800/678–0678, fax 914/835–5126).

NEED INSURANCE?

When driving a rented car you are generally responsible for any damage to or loss of the vehicle. Before you rent, **see what insurance coverage you already have** under the terms of your personal auto-insurance policy and/or credit cards.

Collision policies that car-rental companies sell for European rentals typically do not cover stolen vehicles. Before you buy additional coverage for theft, find out if your own auto insurance or credit card will cover the loss. All car-rental companies operating in Italy require that you buy a theft-protection policy.

BEWARE SURCHARGES

Before you pick up a car in one city and leave it in another, **ask about drop-off charges or one-way service fees,** which can be substantial. Note, too, that some rental agencies charge extra if you return the car before the time specified on your contract. To avoid a hefty refueling fee, **fill the tank before you turn in the car,** but be aware that gas stations right near the rental outlet may overcharge.

CHANNEL TUNNEL

Short of flying, the "Chunnel" is now the fastest way to cross the English Channel: the ride takes 35 minutes from Folkestone to Calais, 60 minutes from motorway to motorway, or three hours from London's Waterloo Station to Paris's Gare du Nord. Foot passengers take the passenger trains operated by Eurostar. Drivers take the car train known as Le Shuttle; one-way tickets go for 490F (395F if purchased 15 days in advance). However, prices fluctuate depending on the time of day, week, and year, so be sure to check prices before you make your plans, and if you're driving a rental car, remember the drop-off charges.

EUROSTAR • In the United States, **BritRail Travel** (tel. 800/677–8585; in New York City, 212/575–2667) or **Rail Europe** (tel. 800/942–4866). In the United Kingdom, **Eurostar** (tel. 0345/881881) or **InterCity Europe** (tel. 0990/848848).

CAR TRANSPORT • Le Shuttle (0990/353535 or 1303/273300 in the United Kingdom).

CONSUMER PROTECTION

Whenever possible, **pay with a major credit card** so you can cancel payment if there's a problem—just remember to keep documentation. Plastic is a good idea whether you're buying in advance or shopping at your destination.

If you're doing business with a particular travel company for the first time, **contact your local Better Business Bureau and the attorney general's offices** in your state and in the company's home state. Has the company received any complaints?

LOCAL BBBS • Council of Better Business Bureaus (4200 Wilson Blvd., Suite 800, Arlington, VA 22203, tel. 703/276–0100, fax 703/525–8277).

Finally, if you're buying a package trip, always **consider travel insurance** that includes default coverage (*see* Insurance, *below*).

CUSTOMS & DUTIES

When shopping, **keep receipts** for all of your purchases. Upon returning home, **be ready to show customs officials what you've bought.** Have everything in one easily accessible place—and don't wrap gifts. If you feel a duty is incorrect, appeal the assessment. If you object to the way your clearance was handled, get the inspector's badge number. In either case, first ask to see a supervisor, then write to the port director at the address listed on your receipt. Send a copy of the receipt and other appropriate documentation. If you're still not satisfied, you can take your case to customs headquarters in Washington.

ENTERING AUSTRALIA

If you're 18 or older, you may bring back A$400 worth of souvenirs and gifts, including jewelry. Your duty-free allowance also includes 250 cigarettes or 250 grams of tobacco and 1,125ml of alcohol, including wine, beer, or spirits. Residents under 18 may bring back A$200 worth of goods.

RESOURCES • Australian Customs Service (Regional Director, Box 8, Sydney, NSW 2001, tel. 02/9213–2000, fax 02/9213–4000).

ENTERING CANADA

If you've been out of Canada for at least seven days, you may bring in C$500 worth of goods duty-free. If you've been away for fewer than seven days but more than 48 hours, the duty-free allowance drops to C$200; if your trip lasts only 24–48 hours, the allowance is C$50. You may not pool allowances with family members. Goods claimed under the C$500 exemption may follow you by mail; those claimed under the lesser exemptions must accompany you.

Alcohol and tobacco products may be included in the seven-day and 48-hour exemptions but not in the 24-hour exemption. If you meet the age requirements of the province or territory through which you reenter Canada, you may bring in, duty-free, 1.14 liters (40 imperial ounces) of wine or liquor *or* 24 12-ounce cans or bottles of beer or ale. If you are 16 or older you may bring in, duty-free, 200 cigarettes and 50 cigars; these items must accompany you.

You may send an unlimited number of gifts worth up to C$60 each to Canada duty-free. Label the package UNSOLICITED GIFT—VALUE UNDER $60. Alcohol and tobacco are excluded.

INFORMATION • Revenue Canada (2265 St. Laurent Blvd. S, Ottawa, Ontario K1G 4K3, tel. 613/993–0534, 800/461–9999 in Canada).

ENTERING NEW ZEALAND

If you're 17 or older, you may bring back NZ$700 worth of souvenirs and gifts. Your duty-free allowance also includes 200 cigarettes, 250 grams of tobacco, or 50 cigars, or a combo of all three up to 250 grams; 4.5 liters of wine or beer; and one 1,125-ml bottle of spirits.

RESOURCES • New Zealand Customs (Custom House, 50 Anzac Ave., Box 29, Auckland, New Zealand, tel. 09/359–6655, fax 09/309–2978).

ENTERING THE UNITED KINGDOM

If your journey was wholly within European Union (EU) countries, you needn't pass through customs when you return to the United Kingdom. If you plan to bring back large quantities of alcohol or tobacco, check on EU limits beforehand.

From countries outside the EU, you may import, duty-free, 200 cigarettes or 50 cigars; 1 liter of spirits or 2 liters of fortified or sparkling wine or liqueurs; 2 liters of still table wine; 60 ml of perfume; and 250 ml of toilet water; plus £136 worth of other goods, including gifts and souvenirs.

INFORMATION • HM Customs and Excise (Dorset House, Stamford St., London SE1 9NG, tel. 0171/202–4227).

ENTERING THE UNITED STATES

You must declare everthing you bought abroad, but you don't have to pay a duty unless your foreign loot is worth more than $400—as long as you've been out of the country for at least 48 hours and haven't already used the $400 allowance or any part of it in the past 30 days. For purchases between $400 and $1,000, you have to pay a 10% duty. You also have to pay tax if you exceed your duty-free allowances:

1 liter of alcohol or wine; 100 non-Cuban cigars, 200 cigarettes, or 2 kilograms of tobacco; and one bottle of perfume. Prohibited: meat products, seeds, plants, and fruits.

If you're 21 or older, you may bring back 1 liter of alcohol duty-free. In addition, regardless of your age, you are allowed 200 cigarettes and 100 non-Cuban cigars. (At press time, a federal rule restricting tobacco access to persons 18 years and older did not apply to importation.) Antiques, which the U.S. Customs Service defines as objects more than 100 years old, enter duty-free, as do original works of art done entirely by hand, including paintings, drawings, and sculptures.

You may also send packages home duty-free: up to $200 worth of goods for your own use, with a limit of one parcel per addressee per day (and no alcohol or tobacco products or perfume worth more than $5); label the package PERSONAL USE, and attach a list of its contents and their retail value. Do not label the package UNSOLICITED GIFT, or your duty-free exemption will drop to $100. Mailed items do not affect your duty-free allowance on your return.

INFORMATION • U.S. Customs Service (Inquiries, Box 7407, Washington, DC 20044, tel. 202/927–6724; complaints, Commissioner's Office, 1301 Constitution Ave. NW, Washington, DC 20229; registration of equipment, Resource Management, 1301 Constitution Ave. NW, Washington DC, 20229, tel. 202/927–0540).

CRIME AND PUNISHMENT

DRUGS • Drug consumption and possession are almost always punishable by fines or a jail sentence, and trying to transport drugs across borders is just asking to be extradited or imprisoned. Keep in mind that border officials don't do random searches—they specifically select the scruffier backpackers. But even if you dress to the hilt specifically to cross the border, you never know when there will be dogs waiting to nail you. Drug *sale* is also a big no-no—if you're caught, you *will* go to jail. If you get busted for drugs (or for breaking any other law), your embassy might say a few sympathetic words but cannot give you one iota of legal help. You're on your own.

DISABILITIES & ACCESSIBILITY

ACCESS IN EUROPE

While awareness of the needs of travelers with disabilities increases every year, budget opportunities are harder to find. Always ask if discounts are available, either for you or for a companion. In addition, plan your trip and make reservations far in advance, as companies that serve people with disabilities go in and out of business regularly.

Most trains and train stations in Western Europe are wheelchair-accessible, though many in more remote locations are not. Call **Rail Europe** (tel. 800/438–7245) for more information about accessibility where you will be traveling.

TIPS AND HINTS

When discussing accessibility with an operator or reservationist, **ask hard questions.** Are there any stairs, inside *or* out? Are there grab bars next to the toilet *and* in the shower or tub? How wide is the doorway to the room? To the bathroom? When possible, **opt for newer accommodations,** which are more likely to have been designed with access in mind. Be sure to **discuss your needs before booking.**

COMPLAINTS • In the U.S., call the **Disability Rights Section** (U.S. Department of Justice, Box 66738, Washington, DC 20035–6738, tel. 202/514–0301 or 800/514–0301, fax 202/307–1198, TTY 202/514–0383 or 800/514–0383) for general complaints, the **Aviation Consumer Protection Division** (*see* Air Travel, *above*) for airline-related problems, and the **Civil Rights Office** (U.S. Department of Transportation, Departmental Office of Civil Rights, S-30, 400 7th St. SW, Room 10215, Washington, DC, 20590, tel. 202/366–4648) for problems with surface transportation.

TRAVEL AGENCIES

Some agencies specialize in travel arrangements for individuals with disabilities.

BEST BETS • Access Adventures (206 Chestnut Ridge Rd., Rochester, NY 14624, tel. 716/889–9096) is run by a former physical-rehabilitation counselor. **Flying Wheels Travel** (143 W. Bridge St., Box 382, Owatonna, MN 55060, tel. 507/451–5005 or 800/535–6790, fax 507/451–1685) specializes in European cruises and tours. **Hinsdale Travel Service** (201 E. Ogden Ave., Suite 100, Hinsdale, IL 60521, tel. 630/325–1335) offers advice from wheelchair traveler Janice Perkins. **Wheelchair Journeys**

(16979 Redmond Way, Redmond, WA 98052, tel. 206/885–2210 or 800/313–4751) makes general travel arrangements.

DISCOUNTS & DEALS

While your travel plans are still in the fantasy stage, start studying the travel sections of major Sunday newspapers; you'll often find listings for good packages and incredibly cheap flights. Surfing the Internet can also give you some great ideas. Travel agents are another obvious resource; agencies on or near college campuses, accustomed to dealing with budget travelers, can be especially helpful.

Always **compare all your options before making a choice.** A plane ticket bought with a promotional coupon may not be cheaper than the least expensive fare from a discount ticket agency. (For more on cheap airfares, *see* Get the Lowest Fare *in* Air Travel, *above*.) When evaluating a package, keep in mind that what you get for the money is just as important as what you save. Just because something is cheap doesn't mean it's a good value.

CREDIT CARDS & AUTO CLUBS

When you use your credit card to purchase transport or lodging, you may get free travel-accident insurance, collision-damage insurance, and medical or legal help, depending on the card and the bank that issued it. **Get a copy of your credit card's travel-benefits policy.** If you are a member of the American Automobile Association (AAA) or a road-assistance plan sponsored by an oil company, always **ask hotel or car-rental reservationists about auto-club discounts;** some clubs offer additional discounts on admission to attractions. And don't forget that auto-club membership entitles you to free maps and trip-planning services.

DISCOUNTS BY PHONE

Don't be afraid to **check out "1-800" discount reservations services,** which use their buying power to get better prices on hotels, airline tickets, and even car rentals. Always ask about special packages. When shopping for the best car-rental deals, **look for guaranteed exchange rates,** which protect you against a falling dollar. With your rate locked in, you won't pay more even if the price goes up in the local currency.

CHEAP AIRLINE TICKETS • Tel. **800/FLY–4–LESS.**

CHEAP HOTEL ROOMS • **Hotels Plus** (tel. 800/235–0909). **Hotel Reservations Network (HRN)** (tel. 800/964–6835). **International Marketing & Travel Concepts (IMTC)** (tel. 800/790–4682). **Steigenberger Reservation Service** (tel. 800/223–5652).

SAVE ON COMBOS

Packages and guided tours can both save you money, but don't confuse the two. When you buy a package, your travel remains independent, just as though you had planned and booked the trip yourself. Fly/drive packages, which combine airfare and car rental, are often a good deal. In cities, ask the local visitors bureau about hotel packages, which often include tickets to major museum exhibits and other special events you'd be going to anyway. If you **buy a rail/drive pass** you'll save on train tickets and car rentals. All Eurail and Europass holders get a discount on Eurostar fares through the Channel Tunnel. A German Rail Pass is also good for selected routes aboard KD River Steamers and on certain bus routes operated by Deutsche Touring/Europabus. Greek Flexipass options may include sightseeing, hotels, and plane tickets.

DRIVING

In Europe, trains and buses are so efficient and rental cars are so expensive that few budget travelers rent cars. If you're traveling with a group, however, and trying to cover an area poorly served by public transportation, you might find that renting a car is the easiest and even the cheapest way to go (even though gas can cost $5 a gallon). Timid drivers should be wary of driving in Europe, however; signs and traffic rules vary from country to country, and navigating a country where you don't even know the language on the signs, much less the lay of the land, can bewilder the hardiest of drivers. If you accept the challenge, invest in some good road maps and seek out alternative main roads (to help avoid speed-demon drivers and the hefty tolls charged on many main thoroughfares).

If you plan to rent or buy a car abroad, you should **get an International Driver's Permit (IDP) before leaving home.** To qualify for an IDP, you must be 18 years old and hold a valid U.S. driver's license. The IDP is available from the American Automobile Association (AAA) for $10 and two passport-size photos.

Some offices can issue an IDP on the spot in about 15 minutes, but be sure to call ahead; during the busy season IDPs can take a week or more.

AUTO CLUBS • In the United States, **American Automobile Association** (tel. 800/564–6222). In the U.K., **Automobile Association** (AA, tel. 0990/500600), **Royal Automobile Club** (RAC, membership tel. 0990/722722; insurance 0345/121345).

ELECTRICITY

Before tossing a hair dryer into your bag, remember that European electrical outlets pump out 220 volts, enough to fry American appliances. **You'll need a converter** that matches the outlet's current and the wattage of your dryer, and you'll need an adapter to plug it in; wall outlets in Europe take several different types of plugs. In the United States, Radio Shack sells a complete line of this paraphernalia; the package indicates which converters and adapters function in which countries. You can get by with just an adapter if you bring a dual-voltage appliance, available from travel-gear catalogues (*see below*). Most laptop computers operate equally well on 110 and 220 volts and need only an adapter. Be careful not to use 110-volt outlets—marked FOR SHAVERS ONLY—for high-wattage appliances (like your hair dryer).

FERRY TRAVEL

Ferry routes for passengers and vehicles link the countries surrounding the North Sea, the Irish Sea, and the Baltic; Italy with Greece; and Spain, France, Italy, and Greece with their respective islands in the Mediterranean. If you're driving, longer ferry routes—between, for instance, Britain and Spain or Scandinavia—can help you reduce fatigue and save time. A number of modern ships offer improved comfort and entertainment ranging from one-armed bandits to gourmet dining. Mini-cruises, including a few days ashore, can be a good option if you're moderately opulent and feel like lazing about.

The growing popularity of the Channel Tunnel—which now has the largest share of the Channel-traffic market—has caused a furious price war across the English Channel. Some companies offer round-trip fares so low that they're a bargain even if you don't use the return ticket. Catamarans, monocraft, and hovercraft make the crossing as fast as the car-carrying Le Shuttle, which uses the tunnel, so you can choose your worst-case scenario: a sick-bag or a short spell of claustrophobia.

GAY & LESBIAN TRAVEL

Although many European cities, such as Amsterdam and Paris, have visible and happening gay scenes, most of Europe has a view of homosexuality similar to what you might find outside major cities in the United States. Homosexuality is technically illegal in a few countries, but for the most part, openly gay travelers will face no worse than a frosty reception.

GAY- AND LESBIAN-FRIENDLY TRAVEL AGENCIES • **Advance Damron** (1 Greenway Plaza, Suite 800, Houston, TX 77046, tel. 713/682–2002 or 800/695–0880, fax 713/888–1010). **Club Travel** (8739 Santa Monica Blvd., West Hollywood, CA 90069, tel. 310/358–2200 or 800/429–8747, fax 310/358–2222). **Islanders/Kennedy Travel** (183 W. 10th St., New York, NY 10014, tel. 212/242–3222 or 800/988–1181, fax 212/929–8530). **Now Voyager** (4406 18th St., San Francisco, CA 94114, tel. 415/626–1169 or 800/255–6951, fax 415/626–8626). **Yellowbrick Road** (1500 W. Balmoral Ave., Chicago, IL 60640, tel. 773/561–1800 or 800/642–2488, fax 773/561–4497). **Skylink Women's Travel** (3577 Moorland Ave., Santa Rosa, CA 95407, tel. 707/585–8355 or 800/225–5759, fax 707/584–5637) serves lesbian travelers.

HEALTH

There are few serious health risks associated with travel in Europe. For up-to-the-minute information about health risks and disease precautions in all parts of the world, you can call the U.S. Centers for Disease Control's 24-hour **International Travelers' Hotline** (tel. 404/332–4559), which dispenses recorded information, and receives faxes of current reports. The ITH does warn travelers of insect-transmitted diseases, such as tick-borne encephalitis, Lyme disease, and yellow fever, but none is a huge concern in Europe today; just beware of any flying or crawling bloodsuckers, as you would anywhere else. Many travelers do suffer from mild diarrhea and nausea during their travels, but these are more often caused by stress and changes in diet than by nasty bacteria. In general, common sense prevails.

Get plenty of rest, eat balanced meals, don't drink unpasteurized milk or water from a river, don't stay in the sun too long—do we sound like your mother yet?

FIRST-AID KITS

A first-aid kit may add nothing to your trip but extra bulk. However, in an emergency you'll be glad to have even the most basic medical supplies. Prepackaged kits are available, but you can pack your own from the following list: bandages, cortisone cream, antiseptic, tweezers, an antacid such as Alka-Seltzer, something for diarrhea (Pepto-Bismol or Imodium), waterproof surgical tape and gauze pads, a thermometer in a sturdy case, and, of course, aspirin. Depending on the health conditions in your destination, you might also ask a doctor for a general antibiotic. If you're prone to motion sickness or are planning to use particularly rough modes of transportation in your travels, take along some Dramamine. Women: If you're prone to yeast infections, over-the-counter medications, such as Monistat or Gynelotrimin, can save you grief on the road.

INSURANCE

Many private health-insurance policies do not cover you outside the United States. If yours is among them, consider buying supplemental medical coverage, available through several private organizations. It's worth noting that the ISIC card (*see* Students, *below*) includes health-and-accident coverage.

Citizens of the United Kingdom can buy an annual travel-insurance policy valid for most vacations during the year in which it's purchased. If you are pregnant or have a preexisting medical condition, make sure you're covered.

TRAVEL INSURERS • In the United States, **Access America** (6600 W. Broad St., Richmond, VA 23230, tel. 804/285–3300 or 800/284–8300), **Carefree Travel Insurance** (Box 9366, 100 Garden City Plaza, Garden City, NY 11530, tel. 516/294–0220 or 800/323–3149), **Travel Guard International** (1145 Clark St., Stevens Point, WI 54481, tel. 715/345–0505 or 800/826–1300), **Travel Insured International** (Box 280568, East Hartford, CT 06128-0568, tel. 860/528–7663 or 800/243–3174). In Canada, **Mutual of Omaha** (Travel Division, 500 University Ave., Toronto, Ontario M5G 1V8, tel. 416/598–4083, 800/268–8825 in Canada). In the United Kingdom, **Association of British Insurers** (51 Gresham St., London EC2V 7HQ, tel. 0171/600–3333).

LAUNDRY

Hotel rooms are the cheapest place to do laundry, but hotels don't always approve of the practice; you may want to ask first. A bring-your-own laundry service includes: a plastic bottle of liquid detergent (powder doesn't break down as well), about 6 ft of clothesline, and some plastic clips (bobby pins or paper clips can substitute). Failing a clothesline, porch railings, shower-curtain rods, bathtubs, and faucets can all serve as wet-laundry hangers, and plain old bar soap, dishwashing liquid, or liquid soap will clean clothes in a pinch. A hair dryer can double as a last-minute clothes dryer, at least making damp things wearable. In case of plugless sinks, stuff a sock or plastic bag in the drain. Be sure to bring an extra plastic bag or two for still-damp laundry and dirty clothes.

LODGING

Lodging will probably be your second-largest expense after transportation, but in most places your options are wide open. European lodging is a far cry from that in the United States, where your only choices are usually a bland motel or a posh hotel. If you'll be arriving in Europe during high season, you may want to **reserve your first few nights' lodging in advance** to avoid the stress of looking for a room on a few hours of sleep. If you're in a bind, the local tourist office can usually book rooms, sometimes for a small fee, but they can't work miracles in high season and are sometimes less than enthusiastic about catering to budget travelers.

HOTELS, PENSIONS, AND B&BS

Hotels usually aren't a bad deal if you have one or two traveling companions. Double rooms at budget hotels are rarely more than $60, even in more expensive countries like Great Britain and Switzerland. In the least expensive countries, like Turkey, doubles are closer to $15 a night. Don't expect to have your bed turned down and your every whim catered to; most budget hotels are small places with simple facilities. The least expensive rooms usually don't have a shower or toilet attached; you'll have to share the bathroom down the hall with everyone else, and will sometimes have to pay a few dollars to take a shower. In this book, "with bath" means that a hotel room has an attached toilet and bath or shower. The price refers to a double room, without bath (if available).

Here are a few examples of special deals on lodging. If you're 65 or older you qualify for a percentage-point discount equal to your age at most European **Radisson SAS Hotels** (especially helpful in Germany and Scandinavia). This means that if you're, say, 70 years old, you and your partner can stay in the lap of luxury for about $100. You may be eligible for special rates at other hotels as well; always mention your senior status up front.

At the other end of the scale, if you're between 18 and 26, the **Ibis hotel chain** will give you a room for $50 or less, provided you show up after 9 PM and they have a vacancy. Your chances are best on week-ends. There are 410 Ibis hotels in Europe, most of them in France, where there isn't a town without one. Get a list of locations at the first one you try.

For a smaller, family-run place, look for signs advertising a pension, guest house, private room, bed-and-breakfast, or any foreign-language equivalent (*see* Where to Sleep *in* Basics *section of each country*). These are generally (but not always) cheaper than hotels and can offer a more intimate experience. In general, though, budget B&Bs tend to be pretty utilitarian and not the cozy, chintz-decorated homes you may be imagining.

If you want a quality guarantee and prefer to know the people who are hosting you, check out **American International Homestays** (Box 1754, Nederland, CO 80466, tel. 800/876–2048). Their network covers most of central and parts of Eastern Europe, but not the Mediterranean countries. B&B rates start at $49.

HOSTELS

If you want to scrimp on lodging, **look into hostels.** In some 5,000 locations in more than 70 countries around the world, Hostelling International (HI), the umbrella group for a number of national youth-hostel associations, offers single-sex, dorm-style beds and sometimes double rooms and family accommodations. Membership in any HI national hostel association, open to travelers of all ages, allows you to stay in HI-affiliated hostels at member rates (one-year membership about $25 for adults; hostels about $10–$25 per night). Members also have priority if the hostel is full and are eligible for discounts around the world, even on rail and bus travel in some countries. HI publishes two international hostel directories, one covering Europe and the Mediterranean, the other covering Africa, the Americas, Asia, and the Pacific ($13.95 each).

Hostels are particularly good values for solo travelers, as single rooms can be expensive and difficult to find. On the down side, hostels are sometimes overrun with groups of vacationing children, are sometimes on the outskirts of town, and frequently have strict curfews (often around midnight) and daytime lockouts (particularly oppressive in cities like Barcelona, where nightlife doesn't even begin until the wee hours).

The usual hostel setup consists of single-sex dorms with 4–40 beds, in anything from an atmospheric Renaissance castle to a cinderblock building. Breakfast (usually just bread or a pastry and coffee) is often included in the price. Some hostels also serve dinner, and occasionally lunch, at a small extra charge; the food may be bland and institutional, but often a hostel dinner is the cheapest hot meal in town. In Scandinavia, where hotels tend to be astronomically expensive, hostels tend to be nicer than in other countries, often providing double and triple rooms as well as dorm beds; here you'll find more families and adult travelers than in hostels in the south.

At least half the hostels you'll run across are affiliated with Hostelling International, designated in this book with the abbreviation HI. Many of these hostels require guests to be members of a national hostel organization, and others require nonmembers to pay a small supplement. While some hostels will sell you a hostel membership on the spot, many won't, so if you plan to stay in hostels, pick up an HI card at a budget travel agency (*see* Student IDs and Services, *below*) before leaving home. There are no age restrictions for buying hostel cards or staying in hostels, though travelers under 26 might get priority if the hostel is full.

Hostels that are not affiliated with Hostelling International are as varied as the affiliated ones. They sometimes have the advantage of not enforcing a curfew or lockout, and sometimes the disadvantage of being a bit dirtier or less organized than HI hostels.

ORGANIZATIONS • Hostelling International—American Youth Hostels (HI–AYH; 733 15th St. NW, Suite 840, Washington, DC 20005, tel. 202/783–6161, fax 202/783–6171). **Hostelling International—Canada** (HI–C; 400-205 Catherine St., Ottawa, Ontario K2P 1C3, tel. 613/237–7884, fax

613/237–7868). **Youth Hostel Association of England and Wales** (YHA; Trevelyan House, 8 St. Stephen's Hill, St. Albans, Hertfordshire AL1 2DY, tel. 01727/855215 or 01727/845047, fax 01727/844126). **Australian Youth Hostels Association** (YHA; Level 3, 10 Mallett St., Camperdown, New South Wales 2050, tel. 02/565–1699). **Youth Hostels Association of New Zealand** (YHA; Box 436, Christchurch 1, tel. 3/379–9970).

CAMPING

Some Europeans seem to have an affinity for camping in shady parking lots on the outskirts of town. If you don't mind camping with several dozen families and their dogs, you can save a bundle on urban travel by staying in campgrounds, which generally cost $1–$20 a night, depending on the country. If you prefer to camp among more trees than people, all is not lost; families tend to stick pretty close to the cities, so a foray into the wilderness should grant you the serenity you crave.

Before packing loads of camping gear, seriously consider how much camping you will actually do versus how much trouble it will be to haul around your tent, sleeping bag, stove, and assorted other junk. Unless you have some great backwoods adventures in mind, camping may not be worth it.

MAIL

When sending letters or postcards home, mark them with the words "air mail" and the local equivalent (*par avion* in French, *mit Luftposte* in German, *por avion* in Spanish); *par avion* will do if you don't know the local phrase. A growing number of countries have only two classes of mail: A (first class) and B (second class). You can get blue A stickers and green B stickers free at the local post office; blue stickers are mandatory for airmail. Your mail can take anywhere from a few days to a few weeks to reach the homestead; mail from the U.S. to Europe usually arrives in about a week.

RECEIVING MAIL

In most countries you can receive mail in major post offices. Have your loved ones address mail to Your Name, the name of the city, the postal code, and the words POSTE RESTANTE. Add the local equivalent of *poste restante* if possible; it's *lista de correos* in Spanish, *fermo posta* in Italian, and *postlagernde briefe* in German. Whenever you want to pick up held mail, take your passport or other photo ID and some money; you'll usually you have to pay a small, per-letter fee to pick up mail. Some postal codes and other country- or city-specific information is covered in the Basics section of each chapter.

If you are an American Express cardmember, it may be easier for you to pick up mail at the nearest AmEx office. They, too, might charge a small fee each time you ask for mail. Pick up a copy of the "American Express Traveler's Companion" for a list of all of AmEx's locations abroad.

MONEY

ATMS

Before leaving home, to increase your chances of happy encounters with cash machines in Europe, **make sure that your card has been programmed for ATM use there**—ATMs in Europe accept PINs of four or fewer digits only. If your PIN is longer, try to change it. If you know your PIN as a word, learn the numerical equivalent, since most Europe ATM keypads show numbers only. You should also have your credit card programmed for ATM use (note that Discover is rarely accepted abroad); a Visa or Master-Card can be used for a cash advance at certain ATMs, though fees may be steep and the charge may begin to accrue interest immediately, even if your monthly bills are paid up. Despite best efforts, local bank cards often do not work overseas or may access only your checking account. **Ask your bank about a MasterCard/Cirrus or Visa debit card**—long popular in Europe, these cards work like bank cards but can be used at any ATM displaying a MasterCard/Cirrus or Visa logo, and at many stores as well. They may also access only your checking account; check with your bank.

ATM LOCATIONS • Cirrus (tel. 800/424–7787). A list of **Plus** locations is available at your local bank.

COSTS

Even in the most expensive European countries (France, Germany, Great Britain, Switzerland, and the Scandinavian countries), budget travelers will rarely spend more than $60 a day, less if they're willing to rough it a bit. But if you have a Eurailpass in hand, all it takes is a few hours on a train to go somewhere much cheaper. Although prices in Eastern Europe are rising steadily, you can stay in cities such as

Prague and Budapest for about $20–$30 a day. Greece and Turkey are also big travel bargains; you may spend 24 hours on a bone-jarring bus or train to get there, but once you arrive you're unlikely to spend more than $20–$25 a day in Turkey, $35–$45 in Greece. In each chapter, we've given a ballpark figure of how much it costs to travel in that country, as well as the exchange rate for that country's currency at press time. **Check the financial section of a major newspaper or call your local bank for the latest exchange rates.**

CURRENCY EXCHANGE

You'll get a better deal buying local currency in Europe than at home. Nonetheless, it's a good idea to change a bit of money into local currency before you fly, in case the exchange booth at the train station or airport you enter is closed or has a long line. Once abroad, for the most favorable rates, **change money at banks.** Although fees charged for ATM transactions may be higher abroad than at home, Cirrus and Plus exchange rates are excellent, because they are based on wholesale rates offered only by major banks. You won't do as well at exchange booths in airports, rail and bus stations, hotels, restaurants, or stores, although you may find their hours more convenient.

EXCHANGE SERVICES • International Currency Express (tel. 888/842–0880 on the East Coast; 888/278–6628 on the West Coast for telephone orders). **Thomas Cook Currency Services** (tel. 800/287–7362 for telephone orders and retail locations).

TRAVELER'S CHECKS

Whether or not to buy traveler's checks depends on where you're headed. You should **bring cash to rural areas** and small towns, traveler's checks to cities. If a thief makes off with your checks, they can usually be replaced within 24 hours; just remember to **keep the address(es) and phone number(s) of your check issuer separate from the checks themselves.** Always pay for your checks yourself—don't delegate—otherwise there may be problems if you need a refund later on.

PACKING FOR EUROPE

You've heard it a million times; now you'll hear it once again—pack light. The weight of your luggage is directly proportional to the length of time you've been carrying it around. At the very least, bring comfortable, easy-to-clean clothes. Black hides dirt but also absorbs heat. Artificial fabrics don't breathe and will make you grimier than you'd ever thought possible, so go with light cotton instead. If you're traveling in the summer, bring several t-shirts and one sweater for cooler nights. Socks and undies don't take up too much room, so throw in a few extra pairs.

Packing light does not mean relying on a pair of cutoff shorts and a tank top to get you through any situation. Shorts, if not frowned upon, will almost certainly brand you as a foreigner in most countries, as will sneakers. In general, Europeans dress a bit more formally than Americans, even if that only means scruffy shoes and casual trousers or skirts rather than sneakers and jeans. Travelers who plan to visit churches, especially in southern Europe, should take at least one modest outfit; Italians in particular sometimes insist that women cover their shoulders and arms.

A sturdy pair of walking shoes or hiking boots (broken in before your trip) and a spare pair (perhaps sandals) allow you to switch off and give your tootsies a rest. Plastic sandals or thongs protect feet on hostile shower floors and are also useful for camping or beach-hopping.

Use a separate, waterproof bag for your toiletries; the pressure on airplanes can cause lids to pop off and create instant slicks inside your luggage. If you wear contact lenses, bring all the accompanying paraphernalia. Bring some toilet paper with you and have some in your pockets at all times (trust us). Bring deodorant, soap, shampoo, toothpaste, tampons/pads, and any prescription drugs you might need, as well as insect repellent, sunscreen, and lip balm. And note that hostels require that you use a sleep sheet; some include them, and some don't.

Bring an extra pair of eyeglasses or contact lenses in your carry-on luggage, if possible, and if you have a health problem, **pack enough medication** to last the entire trip or have your doctor write you a prescription using the drug's generic name; brand names vary from country to country. It's important that you **do not put prescription drugs, your passport, or other valuables in luggage that will be checked**: it might go astray. To avoid problems with customs, carry medications in their original packaging.

Other stuff you might not think to take but might be really glad to have: a travel alarm clock; a pocket knife for cutting fruit, spreading cheese, and opening wine bottles; a water bottle; sunglasses; several

The trouble with "reliable travel gear" is that it's so hard to find

Hint: call 1-800-688-9577

J20 Eagle Creek World Journey Backpack

We're in the "reliable travel gear" business - our latest catalog not only features a variety of backpacks and over 100 exciting products, but you'll also find just about every **rail pass** you can imagine.

Backpacks - The Eagle Creek World Journey backpack shown here is a tough high quality travel pack with a capacity of 4,950 cubic inches of storage for your clothing and gear. It even includes an expandable zip-off day pack! Best of all the World Journey is available in either a man's or a woman's fit.

BACKPACK-RAIL SPECIAL: Receive $25 off your entire merchandise purchase and FREE shipping when you buy your **Eurail-Europass** plus a **Jansport "Fiji"** backpack from Bitter Root. The "Fiji", a large capacity travel pack expandable to 6,700 cubic inches, includes a zip-off day pack, hidden shoulder straps and padded waist belt.

 Travel Gear - If you're looking for a **money belt, sleep sack, or even laundry gear**, we have what you need! Buy your backpack from us and shipping is free for your entire order. Look our catalog over, it's free

 Eurail, Europass, or individual country passes - There's no delivery charge with your Eurail or Europass and we'll even include a FREE 500 page Eurail guide book to help you plan your trip

 International Student Exchange Cards - Receive discounts on lodgings, museums and attractions - includes basic medical insurance

 Hostelling International - With nearly 5,000 accommodations worldwide, we can help you join the Hostelling International Network

 Just call any time day or night 1-800-688-9577 Most orders are shipped within 24 hours anywhere in the U.S.A. Just leave your name and address, and we'll send you a catalog immediately. You can also visit us at our web site www.brtravelgear.com

The Backpack Traveler *by Bitter Root*

P.O. Box 3538, Dana Point, CA 92629

www.brtravelgear.com or call 1-800-688-9577

large, zip-type plastic bags, useful for wet swimsuits, leaky bottles, and rancid socks; a needle and thread; a miniature flashlight; extra batteries, if you're wired to a Walkman; a good book; and a day pack.

LUGGAGE

In general, you are entitled to check two bags on international flights from the United States. You can carry a third piece on board, but it must fit easily under the seat in front of you or in the overhead compartment. If your carry-on is too porky, you may be forced to check it at the last minute, so **keep your carry-on bag small and fill it with essentials.**

If you're flying between two foreign destinations, note that baggage allowances may be determined not by piece but by weight—generally 88 pounds (40 kilograms) in first class, 66 pounds (30 kilograms) in business class, and 44 pounds (20 kilograms) in economy. If your flight between two cities abroad *connects* with your transatlantic or transpacific flight, the piece method still applies. Here, too, your carry-on must be small enough to be carried on.

Airline liability for baggage is limited to $1,250 per person on flights within the United States. On international flights it amounts to $9.07 per pound or $20 per kilogram for checked baggage (roughly $640 per 70-pound bag) and $400 per passenger for unchecked baggage. Insurance for losses exceeding these amounts can be bought from the airline at check-in for about $10 per $1,000 of coverage; note that this coverage excludes a rather extensive list of items, which is shown on your airline ticket.

At check-in, **make sure that each bag is correctly tagged** with the destination airport's three-letter code. If your bags arrive damaged or not at all, file a written report with the airline before leaving the airport. If you're traveling with a backpack, tie all loose straps to each other or onto the pack itself so they don't get caught in luggage conveyer belts.

PASSPORTS & VISAS

Citizens of Australia, Canada, New Zealand, the United Kingdom, and the United States need a valid passport to enter the countries covered in this guide. Once your travel plans are confirmed, **check the expiration date of your passport.** If you lose your documents on the road, it's a real pain to get new ones, so **make photocopies of the data page**; leave one copy with someone at home and keep another with you, separate from your passport. If you lose your passport, promptly call the nearest embassy or consulate and the local police; having a copy of the data page can speed replacement.

Visas—government passport stamps that authorize your stay in the country for a certain period of time—are not usually required for visitors from the United States, Canada, the United Kingdom, Australia, or New Zealand who are staying in any one European country for less than three months. (Exceptions are noted in the Basics sections of the appropriate chapters, along with possible restrictions on the length of your stay.) Countries that require visas will sometimes issue them upon entry; with other countries, you have to apply to the relevant consulate several weeks before leaving home. Eastern European countries keep flip-flopping on their visa requirements, so talk to the appropriate embassy or consulate in your home country well before you take off.

INFORMATION • Australian Passport Office (tel. 008/131282). **Canadian Passport Office** (tel. 819/994–3500 or 800/567–6868). The **London Passport Office** (tel. 0990/21010) can also issue emergency passports. **U.S. Office of Passport Services** (tel. 202/647–0518).

SAFETY

Money belts and neck pouches can be uncomfortable, but it's better to be a little itchy than broke. You'd be wise to carry all cash, traveler's checks, credit cards, and your passport there or in some other inaccessible place. Keep a *copy* of your passport somewhere else. Waist packs are safe *if* you keep the pack part in front of your body. All of these vessels are sold in luggage or camping-supply stores. Keep your carry-on bag attached to you if you plan to nap on the train.

When is it safe to take your valuables off your body? Hostels and even hotel rooms are not necessarily safe; don't leave anything valuable out in the open. When sleeping or leaving your room, keep what you cherish on your person, or at least inside your sleep sheet (if you're in it). And it may go without saying, but *never* leave your pack unguarded or with a total stranger in train or bus stations or any other public place, even if you're only planning to be gone for a minute—it's not worth the risk. If you're carrying a smaller bag with a strap (or a camera), sling it crosswise over your body and try to keep your arm down over the bag in front of you. Back pockets are fine for maps, but don't keep your wallet back there; you might attract the wrong kind of attention.

PRECAUTIONS FOR WOMEN

Women traveling in Europe get mixed reactions. To generalize grossly, women are treated fine in the north. In the south, and especially in Greece, Turkey, Morocco, and southern Italy, where Western women traveling alone are considered easy, men will often hiss or whistle at women or follow them for short distances. As well as taking common-sense precautions (not walking in isolated areas at night, not telling men where they're staying), women should not advertise their singleness; you may want to say you're meeting a boyfriend later. Some hotels have floors reserved for women travelers, but these tend to fall in the pricier categories.

PEOPLE OF COLOR

The attitudes that people of color will face in Europe vary widely from country to country. In more cosmopolitan areas, people of color will rarely attract attention, and in more remote locations, curiosity far outweighs prejudice. The attention can be annoying, but it usually doesn't blossom into antagonism. An African-American traveler in Romania wrote, "Out in the country, I was like someone from Mars; people were too amazed to be upset."

In countries where racism toward African immigrants is common, some locals may not understand or care that you haven't immigrated from Africa, and a small minority may be somewhat antagonistic. If you find yourself in a sticky situation, it may be best to emphasize that you are an American (or a Brit, etc.) traveling through the country.

STUDENTS

To save money, **check in with student-oriented travel agencies** and the various other organizations dedicated to helping student and budget travelers. You'll typically find discounted airfares, rail passes, tours, lodgings, and other travel goodies, and **you don't always have to be a student to qualify.**

The big names in the field are STA Travel, with some 100 offices worldwide, and the Council on International Educational Exchange (CIEE or "Council" for short), a private, nonprofit organization that administers work, volunteer, academic, and professional programs worldwide and makes travel arrangements through its own agency, Council Travel. (Council has a helpful Web site at http://www.ciee.org) Travel CUTS, strictly a travel agency, sells discounted airline tickets from offices on or near college campuses. The Educational Travel Center (ETC) books low-cost flights to destinations within the continental United States and around the world. And Student Flights, Inc., specializes in student and faculty airfares.

Most of these organizations also issue student identity cards ($10–$20), which entitle the bearer to special fares on local transportation, discounts at museums, theaters, sports events, and other attractions, and a handful of other benefits, all listed in the handbook accompanying most cards. Major cards include the International Student Identity Card (ISIC) and the Go 25: International Youth Travel Card (GO25), available to non-students as well as students age 25 and under. The ISIC, when purchased in the United States, comes with $3,000 in emergency medical coverage and a few related benefits. Both the ISIC and GO25 are issued by Council Travel and STA in the United States, Travel CUTS in Canada, student unions and student-travel companies in the United Kingdom, and STA in Australia. The International Student Exchange Card (ISEC), issued by Student Flights, Inc., is available to faculty members as well as students, and the International Teacher Identity Card (ITIC), issued by Travel CUTS, provides similar benefits to teachers of all grade levels, from kindergarten through graduate school.

STUDENT IDS AND SERVICES • Council on International Educational Exchange (CIEE): 205 E. 42nd St., 14th floor, New York, NY 10017, tel. 212/822–2600 or 888/268–6245. **Council Travel in the U.S.:** Tel. 800/226–8624. **Council Travel in Europe:** In London, 28A Poland St., Oxford Circle, tel. 171/287–3337; in Paris, 66 av. des Champs-Elysées, tel. 01-46-55–55–65; in Dusseldorf, Graf Adolf Strasse 64, tel. 089/395022. **Educational Travel Center (ETC):** 438 N. Frances St., Madison, WI 53703, tel. 608/256–5551 or 800/747–5551. **STA in the U.S.:** Tel. 800/777–0112. **STA elsewhere:** In London, tel. 171/361–6262; in Frankfurt, tel. 69/979–07460; in Auckland, tel. 0800/100–677; in Melbourne, 3/9349–2411; in Johannesburg, 11/447–5551. **Student Flights:** 5010 E. Shea Blvd., Suite A104, Scottsdale, AZ 85254, tel. 602/951–1177 or 800/255–8000. **Travel CUTS:** 187 College St., Toronto, Ontario M5T 1P7, tel. 416/979–2406 or, in Ontario, 800/667–2887.

TELEPHONES

European phone systems range from the state-of-the-art to the barely functional. To call Europe from the United States or Canada, dial 011 (indicating an international call), then the country code (listed for each country in its Basics section), then the area code and phone number. In most cases, you should omit the first number of the area code (often a 0, 1, or 9); these first digits are usually used only for long-distance calls within that country. When calling from Great Britain, follow the same procedure, but substitute 010 for the 011; in Ireland, use 16; in Australia, 0011; and in New Zealand, 00.

CALLING HOME

The country code for the United States and Canada is 1; for Great Britain, 44; for Ireland, 353; for Australia, 61; and for New Zealand, 64. In most Western European countries you can call home by dialing an AT&T, MCI, or Sprint operator. Access codes and directions are given in the Basics sections of each chapter; **note that access codes vary depending on where you are.** You can also call collect, or buy a phone card to insert in a public phone. Calling collect is the most expensive route; you'll pay almost $6 just to set up the call. Often the easiest method is finding a telephone office (often located in or near the post office), where you can call from a phone booth assigned to you and pay after you hang up (occasionally even with a credit card). In less developed countries, you'll probably get through, but you may have to wait hours to get a connection and suffer through frequent disconnections and bad sound quality. The ins and outs of each country's phone system are detailed in the Basics section of each chapter.

Be warned that you may find the local AT&T, MCI, or Sprint access number blocked in many hotel rooms. If this happens, first ask the hotel operator to connect you. If the hotel operator balks, ask for an international operator, or dial the international operator yourself. One way to improve your odds of getting connected to your long-distance carrier is to travel with more than one company's calling card. If all else fails, call your phone company in the United States collect, or make your call from a pay phone in the hotel lobby.

TO OBTAIN ACCESS CODES • AT&T Direct (800/435–0812). **MCI** WorldPhone (800/444–4141). **Sprint** International Access (800/877–4646).

TOUR OPERATORS

A vacation package can make your trip to Europe less expensive. The tour operators who put such trips together may handle several hundred thousand travelers per year and can use their purchasing power to give you a good price. Their high volume may also indicate financial stability. Small companies, however, provide more personalized service; and because they tend to specialize, they may be more knowledgeable about a given area.

A GOOD DEAL?

The more your package includes, the better you can predict the ultimate cost of your vacation. Make sure you know exactly what is covered, and **beware of hidden costs.** Are taxes, tips, and service charges included? Transfers and baggage handling? Entertainment and excursions? These add up.

If the package you are considering is priced lower than in your wildest dreams, **be skeptical.** Ask detailed questions about the hotel's location, room size, beds, and amenities.

BUYER BEWARE

Each year consumers are stranded or lose their money when tour operators—even large ones with excellent reputations—go out of business. **Check out the operator.** Find out how long the company has been in business, and ask for references that you can check. And **don't book unless the firm has a consumer-protection program.**

Members of the National Tour Association and United States Tour Operators Association are required to set aside funds to cover your payments and travel arrangements in case the company defaults. Non-members may carry insurance instead. Look for the details, and the name of an underwriter with a solid reputation, in the operator's brochure. And when it comes to tour operators, **don't trust escrow accounts.** Although laws govern escrow accounts for charter-flight operators, no law prevents tour operators from raiding the till. For more information, *see* Consumer Protection, *above.*

TOUR-OPERATOR RECOMMENDATIONS • National Tour Association (NTA, 546 E. Main St., Lexington, KY 40508, tel. 606/226–4444 or 800/755–8687). **United States Tour Operators Association** (USTOA, 342 Madison Ave., Suite 1522, New York, NY 10173, tel. 212/599–6599, fax 212/599–6744).

USING AN AGENT

A good travel agent is an excellent resource. When shopping for one, **collect brochures from several sources** and remember that some agents' suggestions may be skewed by promotional relationships with tour and package firms that reward them for a high sales volume. If you have a special interest, **find an agent with expertise in that area** (*see* Travel Agents, *below*).

SINGLE TRAVELERS

Remember that prices for vacation packages are usually quoted per person, based on two sharing a room. If traveling solo, you may be required to pay the full double-occupancy rate.

PACKAGES

The companies listed below offer vacation packages in a broad price range.

AIR/HOTEL • **American Airlines Fly AAway Vacations** (tel. 800/321–2121). **Celtic International Tours** (1860 Western Ave., Albany, NY 12203, tel. 518/862–1810 or 800/833–4373). **CIE Tours** (Box 501, 100 Hanover Ave., Cedar Knolls, NJ 07927-0501, tel. 201/292–3899 or 800/243–8687). **Continental Vacations** (tel. 800/634–5555). **Delta Dream Vacations** (tel. 800/872–7786). **DER Tours** (11933 Wilshire Blvd., Los Angeles, CA 90025, tel. 310/479–4140 or 800/937–1235). **Five Star Touring** (60 E. 42nd St., #612, New York, NY 10165, tel. 212/818–9140 or 800/792–7827, fax 212/818–9142). **4th Dimension Tours** (7101 S.W. 99th Ave., #105, Miami, FL 33173, tel. 305/279–0014 or 800/644–0438, fax 305/273–9777. **TWA Getaway Vacations** (tel. 800/438–2929). **United Vacations** (tel. 800/328–6877).

FLY/DRIVE • **American Airlines Fly AAway Vacations** (tel. 800/321–2121). **Delta Dream Vacations** (tel. 800/872–7786). **United Vacations** (tel. 800/328–6877). Also contact **Budget WorldClass Drive** (tel. 800/527–0700, 0800/181181 in the U.K.) for self-drive itineraries.

THEME TRIPS

Travel Contacts (Box 173, Camberley, GU15 1YE, England, tel. 1276/677217, fax 1276/63477) represents over 150 tour operators in Europe.

ADVENTURE • **Adventure Center** (1311 63rd St., #200, Emeryville, CA 94608, tel. 510/654–1879 or 800/227–8747, fax 510/654–4200). **Himalayan Travel** (110 Prospect St., Stamford, CT 06901, tel. 203/359–3711 or 800/225–2380, fax 203/359–3669). **Mountain Travel-Sobek** (6420 Fairmount Ave., El Cerrito, CA 94530, tel. 510/527–8100 or 800/227–2384, fax 510/525–7710). **Uniquely Europe** (2819 1st Ave., Suite 280, Seattle, WA 98121-1113, tel. 206/441–8682 or 800/426–3615, fax 206/441–8862). **Wilderness Travel** (801 Allston Way, Berkeley, CA 94710, tel. 510/548–0420 or 800/368–2794, fax 510/548–0347).

ART AND ARCHITECTURE • **Archeological Tours** (271 Madison Ave., Suite 904, New York, NY 10016, tel. 212/986–3054, fax 212/370–1561). **Endless Beginnings Tours** (12650 Sabre Springs Pkwy., Suite 207-105, San Diego, CA 92128, tel. 619/679–5374 or 800/822–7855, fax 619/679–5376). **Esplanade Tours** (581 Boylston St., Boston, MA 02116, tel. 617/266–7465 or 800/426–5492, fax 617/262–9829). In the U.K., contact **Prospect Music & Art Tours Ltd.** (454–458 Chiswick High Rd., London W4 5TT, tel. 0181/995–2151) and **Swan Hellenic Art Treasure Tours** (77 New Oxford St., London WC1A 1PP, tel. 0171/800–2300).

BALLOONING • **Buddy Bombard European Balloon Adventures** (855 Donald Ross Rd., Juno Beach, FL 33408, tel. 561/837–6610 or 800/862–8537, fax 561/837–6623). **Virgin Balloon Flights** (54 Linhope St., London NW1 6HL, tel. 0171/706–1021) runs balloon trips in the U.K. and elsewhere in Europe.

BICYCLING • **Backroads** (801 Cedar St., Berkeley, CA 94710-1800, tel. 510/527–1555 or 800/462–2848, fax 510-527–1444). **Classic Adventures** (Box 153, Hamlin, NY 14464-0153, tel. 716/964–8488 or 800/777–8090, fax 716/964–7297). **Europeds** (761 Lighthouse Ave., Monterey, CA 93940, tel. 800/321–9552, fax 408/655–4501). **Rocky Mountain Worldwide Cycle Tours** (333 Baker St., Nelson, BC, Canada V1L 4H6, tel. 250/354–1241 or 800/661–2453, fax 250/354–2058).

CRUISES • **EuroCruises** (303 W. 13th St., New York, NY 10014-1207, tel. 800/688–3876, fax 212/366–4747). **KD River Cruises of Europe** (2500 Westchester Ave., Purchase, NY 10577, tel. 914/696–3600 or 800/346–6525, fax 914/696–0833). **Le Boat** (10 S. Franklin Turnpike, Ramsey, NJ 07446, tel. 201/342–1838 or 800/922–0291). In the U.K., **Top Deck Travel** (131–135 Earls Court Rd., London SW5 9RH, tel. 0171/244–8641) offers tours to Europe, with activities including flotilla sailing and a variety of water sports, such as rafting.

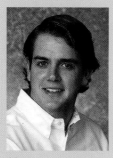

OUR BEST SELLERS

THE #1 TOP SELLER

EURAIL YOUTHPASS

For maximum flexibility and convenience.

2ND CLASS*

15 days	$376
21 days	$489
1 month	$605
2 months	$857
3 months	$1,059

A close 2nd – travel almost anywhere and anytime.

EUROPASS YOUTH

(France, Germany, Italy, Spain, Switzerland)
Less flexible but maximum value.

2ND CLASS*

Any 5 days in 2 months **$216**

Call for additional countries and extra rail days, 1-888-RAIL-444.

Not recommended for spontaneous types, but great for tight budgets and itineraries.

* You must be **under** 26 on your first date of rail travel.

EURAIL YOUTH FLEXIPASS

For maximum flexibility and value.

2ND CLASS*

Any 10 days in 2 months . . . **$444**
Any 15 days in 2 months . . . **$585**

HONORABLE MENTION

EUROPASS *(price per person)*
(France, Germany, Italy, Spain, Switzerland)
Great value for two people traveling together.

	2 ADULTS † 1ST CLASS	1 ADULT 1ST CLASS
Any 5 days in 2 months	$261	$326

Call for additional countries and extra rail days, 1-888-RAIL-444.

† *Price per person based on 2 people traveling together at all times.*

EURAILPASS

The grand-daddy of them all – travel in style.

1ST CLASS

15 days	$538
21 days	$698
1 month	$864
2 months	$1,224
3 months	$1,512

EURAIL FLEXIPASS

For maximum flexibility and style.

1ST CLASS

10 days in 2 months	$634
15 days in 2 months	$836

Prices valid to December 31, 1998 and subject to change.

TRAVEL TRICK™

Flexipass holders who board a train after 7:00 p.m. and arrive at their destination the next day only use up one day on their pass. You save money on accommodation by sleeping on the train and valuable rail days aren't eaten up by the long trip. Make sure you board after 7:00 p.m. to save that extra day.

We also sell many other passes including Eurail Saverpass, Eurail Saver Flexipass, point-to-point, individual country passes, multi-country passes, Eurostar and more!

Call 1-888-RAIL-444 for details.

NO HANDLING FEES • NO BUSY SIGNALS • NO LINE

COMMON QUESTIONS

DOES EVERYBODY SELL EURAIL PASSES AT THE SAME PRICE?

Yes. Unlike airfares which can fluctuate dramatically, Eurail Passes are the same price everywhere. Please note though, many travel agents charge up to a $20 "handling" fee. The Rail Connection <u>does</u> <u>not</u> charge a handling fee!

WHAT IS PASS PROTECTION AND SHOULD I GET IT?

It's a good idea. In the event that your pass is lost or stolen, you are reimbursed for 100% of the <u>unused</u> portion of your pass. We highly recommend purchasing pass protection, it costs only $10 and has saved many of our clients hundreds of dollars.

WHAT IS THE DIFFERENCE BETWEEN A FLEXIPASS AND A CONSECUTIVE DAY PASS?

Both passes are excellent, but many young travelers prefer the Flexipass because when they come across a great place (like The Pink Palace), they don't want to worry about their pass "ticking" away. Unlike a consecutive day pass, the Flexipass allows for non-consecutive days of travel, which means that you can make stopovers for as long as you want without losing time on your pass. In effect, you are only paying for the days you travel on.

WHERE IS MY PASS VALID?

The Eurail Youth Flexipass, Eurail Youthpass, Eurailpass, Eurail Flexipass and Saverpass are valid within the following 17 countries: *Austria, Belgium, Denmark, Finland, France, Germany, Greece, Hungary, Italy, Luxembourg, Netherlands, Norway, Portugal, Republic of Ireland, Spain, Sweden and Switzerland.* Call us for details on the Europass and Europass Youth at 1-888-RAIL-444.

For answers to all your Eurail Pass questions call 1-888-RAIL-444.

ORDER NOW!

Your Eurail Pass is shipped within one business day – it's out-the-door in 24™ – along with the best FREE discount certificates on museums, attractions, shopping, restaurants and more; plus, you get one free night at The Pink Palace – The World's Largest Youth Resort.

CALL 1-888-RAIL-444

The Rail Connection™

SUPER BONUS!*
One Free Night at the Pink Palace including breakfast and dinner.

* Certain restrictions may apply. Offer good while supplies last.

FOOD AND WINE • Cuisine International (Box 25228, Dallas, TX 75225, tel. 214/373–1161 or fax 214/373–1162). In the U.K., **Winetrails** (Greenways, Vann Lake, Ockley, Dorking RH5 5NT, tel. 01306/712111) has leisurely walks through wine regions of Europe, with accommodations in family hotels, wine estates, and chateaux.

HISTORY • Herodot Travel (775 E. Blithedale, Box 234, Mill Valley, CA 94941, tel./fax 415/461–1409).

HORSEBACK RIDING • Equitour FITS Equestrian (Box 807, Dubois, WY 82513, tel. 307/455–3363 or 800/545–0019, fax 307/455–2354).

MOTORCYCLE • Beach's Motorcycle Adventures (2763 W. River Pkwy., Grand Island, NY 14072-2053, tel. 716/773–4960, fax 716/773–5227).

MUSIC • In the U.S., **Dailey-Thorp Travel** (330 W. 58th St., #610, New York, NY 10019-1817, tel. 212/307–1555 or 800/998–4677, fax 212/974–1420) runs opera trips. In the U.K., **Travel for the Arts** (117 Regent's Park Rd., London NW1 8UR, tel. 0171/483–4466) arranges individual and group holidays to musical highlights throughout Europe. **Prospect Music & Art Tours** (see Art and Architecture, above) has tours to many of the famous annual festivals, including Verona, Savonlinna, Prague, Bregenz, and Munich.

NATURAL HISTORY • Questers (381 Park Ave. S, New York, NY 10016, tel. 212/251–0444 or 800/468–8668, fax 212/251–0890). **Earthwatch** (Box 9104, 680 Mount Auburn St., Watertown, MA 02272, tel. 617/926–8200 or 800/776–0188, fax 617/926–8532) runs research expeditions.

SINGLES AND YOUNG ADULTS • Club Europa (802 W. Oregon St., Urbana, IL 61801, tel. 217/344–5863 or 800/331–1882, fax 217/344–4072). **Contiki Holidays** (300 Plaza Alicante, #900, Garden Grove, CA 92640, tel. 714/740–0808 or 800/266–8454, fax 714/740–0818).

SPAS • Custom Spa Vacations (1318 Beacon St., Brookline, MA 02146, tel. 617/566–5144 or 800/443–7727, fax 617/731–0599). **Great Spas of the World** (630 Fifth Ave., New York, NY 10111, tel. 212/599–0382 or 800/772–8463, fax 212/599–0380). **Spa-Finders** (91 Fifth Ave., #301, New York, NY 10003-3039, tel. 212/924–6800 or 800/255–7727). **Spa Trek Travel** (475 Park Ave. S. New York, NY 10016, tel. 212/779–3480 or 800/272–3480, fax 212/779–3471). In the U.K., **Moswin Tours Ltd.** (21 Church St., Oadby, Leicester LE2 5DB, tel. 0116/271–9922) counts spa resorts and city breaks among its programs.

SPORTS • Championship Tennis Tours (7350 E. Stetson Dr., #106, Scottsdale, AZ 85251, tel. 602/990–8760 or 800/468–3664, fax 602/990–8744). **Sportstours** (Box 191072, Miami Beach, FL 33119, tel. 800/879–8647, fax 305/535–0008). **Steve Furgal's International Tennis Tours** (11828 Rancho Bernardo Rd., #123-305, San Diego, CA 92128, tel. 619/675–3555 or 800/258–3664).

VILLA RENTALS • Eurovillas (1398 55th St., Emeryville, CA 94608, tel./fax 707/648–2066). **Villas International** (605 Market St., San Francisco, CA 94105, tel. 415/281–0910 or 800/221–2260, fax 415/281–0919).

WALKING • Above the Clouds Trekking (Box 398, Worcester, MA 01602-0398, tel. 508/799–4499 or 800/233–4499, fax 508/797–4779). **Backroads** (see Bicycling, above). **Country Walkers** (Box 180, Waterbury, VT 05676-0180, tel. 802/244–1387 or 800/464–9255, fax 802/244–5661). **Europeds** (see Bicycling, above). In the United Kingdom **Ramblers Holidays Ltd.** (Box 43, Welwyn Garden City, Hertfordshire AL8 6PQ, tel. 01707/331–133) arranges walking tours within Europe with guides who point out natural features of interest.

TRAIN TRAVEL

High-speed trains (often referred to as TGV, for *Trains à Grande Vitesse*) are revolutionizing travel in Europe. Eurostar, linking London with Paris and Brussels via the Channel Tunnel, has had the most publicity. But the French TGV system is the real pioneer, serving virtually all major cities in France as well as Geneva, Lausanne, and Milan. The TGV has also been first to introduce double-decker coaches; seated on the upper deck, you have the impression of low-level flying. Thalys TGV trains go from Paris to Brussels, Amsterdam and Liège, and by 1998 they'll serve Cologne as well. Germany's equally fast ICE trains run on a special track from Hamburg to Frankfurt and Munich. In Italy, the "tilting" Pendolino trains link Rome with Milan and operate international routes from Turin to Lyon and from Milan to Geneva. The flip side to all this progress is a reservation and pricing system that seems to have been copied from the airlines. You must have a reservation (though it can often be made at the station just before departure), and although great bargains are available, they include conditions like a Saturday-night stay and apply only to round trips.

In central and northern Europe, trains are almost unfailingly clean and punctual. The farther south and east you go, however, the more unreliable and crowded trains generally get. In certain places in Greece, Turkey, and Eastern Europe, taking a bus is often a better choice. Prices generally correspond to efficiency. You'll pay about $50 to travel a few hundred miles in France, about $10 to travel the same distance in Hungary. For the most part, though, European trains are a budget traveler's godsend, toting passengers across the continent in good time at relatively good prices.

Most trains have first- and second-class compartments, but the difference in comfort is generally minimal. Get second-class tickets unless you feel the need to hang out with the business crowd. If you're taking an overnight train rather than a TGV, be prepared to pay about $20 for a *couchette,* or second-class bunk. *Couchettes* are usually six to a compartment. It's not the Ritz, but six to eight hours of sleep in the prone position can do wonders for your disposition the next day.

Before you leave home, consider buying a rail pass (*see* Rail Passes, *below*). An oft-overlooked option for young travelers *without* a rail pass is the **Billet International de Jeunesse** (International Youth Ticket), usually known as a **BIJ** ticket. Here's how it works: Travelers under the age of 26 can purchase a second-class ticket between two far-flung European cities at a 30% savings, then make unlimited stops along the way for up to two months. Subject to availability, BIJ tickets can be purchased throughout Europe at rail stations and budget-travel agencies; try the European offices of STA and Council Travel (*see* Students, *above*).

RAIL PASSES

If you plan to ride the rails, **compare costs for rail passes and individual tickets.** If you plan to cover a lot of ground in a short period, rail passes may be worth your while; they also save you the time of waiting in ticket lines. For individual ticket costs, ask a travel agent or call Rail Europe, Railpass Express, or DER Tours. If you're under 26 on your first day of travel, you're eligible for a youth pass, valid for second-class travel only (like Europass Youth, Eurail Youth Flexipass, or Eurail Youthpass); if you're older, you must buy one of the more expensive regular passes, valid for first-class travel, and in that case it might cost you less to buy individual tickets, especially if your budget calls for second-class travel. If you're going the Eurail route, be sure to buy your pass *before* leaving the United States; Eurailpasses are not available in Europe (though you might find one for an inflated price at some questionable European travel agencies).

Don't assume that your rail pass guarantees you a seat on every train—seat reservations are required on some trains, particularly express, overnight, and high-speed trains (Eurostar, TGV, Thalys, and others). See your travel agent or call Rail Europe to reserve in advance; failing that, stop at a ticket window when you enter the city you'll be departing. Note that high-speed trains will charge you a supplement. Many rail passes also entitle you to free or reduced fares on some ferries—but you should still make seat reservations in advance.

Rail Europe (tel. 800/438–7245), **Railpass Express** (tel. 800/722–7151), **DER Tours** (tel. 800/782–2424), and **The Rail Connection** (888/724-5444), are four agencies that sell rail passes over the phone.

If you decide that you'll save money with a rail pass, ask yourself whether you want a Eurailpass, an InterRail pass, or a national or regional pass (*see below*). The Eurailpass is a good deal if you plan to tackle several countries. InterRail is a real bargain, but it's available only to European residents and those who have lived in an EU country for longer than six months.

EURAIL • Help is at hand in the form of the **Guide to European Rail Passes,** by Rick Steves, available free from Europe Through the Back Door (Box 2009, Edmonds, WA 98020, tel. 206/771–8304, fax 206/771-0833). You can order passes from Back Door as well. **Eurailpasses** provide unlimited first-class rail travel for the duration of the pass in 17 European countries: Austria, Belgium, Denmark, Finland, France, Germany, Greece, Hungary, the Irish Republic, Italy, Luxembourg, the Netherlands, Norway, Portugal, Spain, Sweden, and Switzerland (but not the United Kingdom). This may sound expensive, and it is: 15 days cost $522, 21 days $678, one month $838, two months $1,188, and 3 months $1,468. If you're under 26, the **Eurail Youthpass** is a much better deal. One or two months of unlimited second-class train travel costs $598 and $832, respectively. For 15 consecutive days of travel you pay $418.

Unlike the Eurailpass and Eurail Youthpass, which are good for unlimited travel for a certain period of time, the **Eurail Flexipass** allows you to travel for 10 or 15 days within a two-month period. The Flexipass is valid in the same 17 countries as the Eurailpass and costs $616 for 10 days, and $812 for 15 days. If you're under 26, the second-class **Eurail Youth Flexipass** is a better deal. Within a two-month period it entitles you to 10 days ($438), or 15 days ($588) of travel.

For travel in France, Germany, Italy, Spain, and Switzerland only, consider the **Europass** (first-class) or **Europass Youth** (second-class). The basic Europass is good for five, six, or seven days of travel in any three of the above-named countries, as long as they border one another. The five-day pass costs $316 (first-class) or $253 (second-class). The 8-, 9-, and 10-day passes are good in four of the five countries. The eight-day pass costs $442 (first-class) or $297 (second-class). The passes good for any number of days from 11 to 15 are valid in all five countries. The 11-day pass costs $568 (first-class) or $384 (second-class). In all cases the days of travel can be spread out over two months. Call Rail Europe or ask a travel agent for the brochures "1997 Europe On Track" or "Eurailpass and Europass" for details on adding extra travel days, buying a discounted pass for your companion, or expanding the reach of your Europass to Austria, Belgium, Greece, Luxembourg, and Portugal.

The very first time you use any Eurailpass, you must **have the pass validated.** Before getting on the train, go to a ticket window and have the agent fill out the necessary forms—a painless but important procedure that could save you being fined or kicked off the train. Another pitfall to avoid is having your pass stolen or lost; the only real safeguard is Eurail's "Pass Protection Plan," which costs $10 and must be arranged at the time of purchase. If you buy the protection plan and your pass mysteriously disappears, file a police report within 24 hours and keep the receipts for any train tickets you purchase. Then, upon your return home, send a copy of the report and receipts to Eurail. For your trouble you get a 100% refund on the *unused* portion of your stolen or lost pass.

INTERRAIL • European citizens and anyone who has lived in the EU for at least six months can purchase an **InterRail Pass,** valid for one month's travel in Austria, Belgium, Bulgaria, Croatia, the Czech Republic, Denmark, Finland, France, Germany, Great Britain, Greece, Hungary, Italy, Luxembourg, Morocco, the Netherlands, Norway, Poland, Portugal, the Republic of Ireland, Romania, Slovakia, Slovenia, Spain, Sweden, Switzerland, and Turkey. InterRail works much like Eurail, except that you only get a 50% reduction on train travel in the country where you buy the pass. Be prepared to prove EU citizenship or six months of continuous residency. In most cases you'll have to show your passport for proof of age and residency, but sometimes a European university ID will suffice. To prove residency, old passport entry stamps may do the trick, but be forewarned that each time passes are presented, the ticket controller has the option of looking at passports and confiscating "illegitimate" passes. InterRail can only be purchased in Europe at rail stations and some budget-travel agencies; try the European branches of STA or Council Travel (*see* Students, *below*).

NATIONAL AND REGIONAL PASSES

As well as the above passes, which are good in a number of countries, there are dozens of other passes for travel within a single country—the United Kingdom, for instance, where you'll need a **BritRail Pass** to travel by train for any substantial length of time (*see* Chapter 11)—or within a certain region (Scandinavia or Eastern Europe, for example). Information on these passes is given in the Basics section of individual chapters. Call the country's tourist office in your own country (*see* Visitor Information, *below*) to find out how to buy these passes.

TRAVEL AGENTS

A good travel agent puts your needs first. **Look for an agency that specializes in your destination, has been in business at least five years, and emphasizes customer service.** If you're looking for an agency-organized package, choose an agency that's a member of the National Tour Association or the United States Tour Operator's Association (*see* Tour Operators, *above*).

LOCAL AGENT REFERRALS • **American Society of Travel Agents** (ASTA, 1101 King St., Suite 200, Alexandria, VA 22314, tel. 703/739–2782, fax 703/684–8319). **Alliance of Canadian Travel Associations** (Suite 201, 1729 Bank St., Ottawa, Ontario K1V 7Z5, tel. 613/521–0474, fax 613/521–0805). **Association of British Travel Agents** (55–57 Newman St., London W1P 4AH, tel. 0171/637–2444, fax 0171/637–0713).

TRAVEL GEAR

Travel catalogs specialize in nifty items that can save space when packing. They also offer dual-voltage appliances, currency converters, and foreign-language phrase books.

MAIL-ORDER CATALOGS • **Magellan's** (tel. 800/962–4943, fax 805/568–5406). **Orvis Travel** (tel. 800/541–3541, fax 540/343–7053). **TravelSmith** (tel. 800/950–1600, fax 800/950–1656).

U.S. GOVERNMENT

The U.S. government can be an excellent source of inexpensive travel information. When planning your trip, **find out what government materials are available.**

ADVISORIES • U.S. Department of State American Citizens Services Office (Room 4811, Washington, DC 20520); enclose a self-addressed, stamped envelope. Interactive hot line (tel. 202/647–5225, fax 202/647–3000). Computer bulletin board (tel. 202/647–9225).

PAMPHLETS • Consumer Information Center (Consumer Information Catalogue, Pueblo, CO 81009, tel. 719/948–3334) for a free catalog that includes travel titles.

VISITOR INFORMATION

For general information on specific countries, contact the national tourism offices below. Scandinavian Tourism Inc. provides general information for Denmark, Finland, Iceland, Norway, and Sweden.

AUSTRIAN NATIONAL TOURIST OFFICE • U.S.: Box 1142, Times Square Station, New York, NY 10108-1142, tel. 212/944–6880, fax 212/730–4568. Canada: 2 Bloor St. E, Suite 3330, Toronto, Ontario M4W 1A8, tel. 416/967–3381, fax 416/967–4101; 1010 Ouest Rue, Sherbrooke, Ste. 1410, Montréal, Québec, H3A 2R7, tel. 514/849–3709, fax 514/849–9577; U.K. (phone, fax, and written inquiries only): 30 St. George St., London W1R 0AL, tel. 0171/629–0461, fax 0171/499–6038.

BELGIAN NATIONAL TOURIST OFFICE • U.S.: 780 3rd Ave., New York, NY 10017, tel. 212/758–8130, fax 212/355—7675. Canada: Box 760 NDG, Montréal, Québec H4A 3S2, tel. 514/484–3594, fax 514/489–8965. U.K.: 29 Princes St., London W1R 7RG, tel. 0891/887–799, fax 0171/629–0454; calls cost 50p per minute peak rate or 45p per minute cheap rate.

BRITISH TOURIST AUTHORITY • U.S. Nationwide: 551 5th Ave., Suite .701, New York, NY 10176, tel. 212/986–2200 or 800/462–2748, fax 212/986–1188; 24-Hour Fax Information Line (call *from a fax machine,* listen to a menu, and receive instant information by fax): 310/820–4770. Chicago: 625 N. Michigan Ave., Ste. 1510, Chicago, IL 60611; walk-in service only. Canada: 111 Avenue Rd., Suite 450, Toronto, Ontario M5R 3J8, tel. 416/961–8124, fax 416/961–2175. U.K.: British Travel Centre, 12 Regent St., London SW1Y 4PQ (no information by phone) or Thames Tower, Black's Rd., London W6 9EL, tel. 0181/846–9000.

BULGARIAN NATIONAL TOURIST OFFICE • U.S. and Canada: Balkan Tourist (authorized agent), 20 E. 46th St., Suite 1003, New York, NY 10017, tel. 212/822–5900, fax 212/822–5910. U.K.: contact Balkan Holidays, 19 Conduit St., London W1R 9TD, tel. 0171/491–4499.

CYPRUS TOURIST OFFICE • U.S. and Canada: 13 E. 40th St., New York, NY 10016, tel. 212/683–5280, fax 212/683–5282. U.K.: 213 Regent St., London W1R 8DA, tel. 0171/734–9822 or 0171/734–2593, fax 0171/287-6534.

CZECH CENTER • U.S. and Canada: 1109 Madison Ave., New York, NY 10028, tel. 212/288–0830. U.K.: 30 Kensington Palace Gardens, London W8 4QY, tel. 0171/243–7981, fax 0171/727–9589.

DANISH TOURIST BOARD • U.S. and Canada: Scandinavia Tourism Inc., Box 4649 Grand Central Station, New York, NY 10163–4649, tel. 212/949–2333, fax 212/885–9710. U.K.: 55 Sloane St., London SW1X 9SY, tel. 0171/259–5959 or 0891/600109 for 24-hour brochure line, fax 0171/259–5955; calls to the brochure line cost 50p per minute peak rate or 45p per minute cheap rate.

FINNISH TOURIST BOARD • U.S. and Canada: Scandinavia Tourism Inc., Box 4649 Grand Central Station, New York, NY 10163–4649, tel. 212/949–2333, fax 212/885–9710. U.K.: 30–35 Pall Mall, London SW1Y 5LP, tel. 0171/839–4048, fax 0171/321–0696.

FRENCH GOVERNMENT TOURIST OFFICE • U.S. Nationwide: tel. 900/990–0040; calls cost 50¢ per minute. New York City: 444 Madison Ave., New York, NY 10022, tel. 212/838–7800. Chicago: 676 N. Michigan Ave., Chicago, IL 60611, tel. 312/751–7800. Beverly Hills: 9454 Wilshire Blvd., Beverly Hills, CA 90212, tel. 310/271–6665, fax 310/276–2835. Canada: 1981 Ave., McGill College, Suite 490, Montréal, Québec H3A 2W9, tel. 514/288–4264, fax 514/845–4868; 30 St. Patrick St., Suite 700, Toronto, Ontario M5T 3A3, tel. 416/491–7622, fax 416/979–7587. U.K.: 178 Piccadilly, London W1V 0AL, tel. 0891/244–123, fax 0171/493–6594; calls cost 50p per minute peak rate or 45p per minute cheap rate.

GERMAN NATIONAL TOURIST OFFICE • U.S. Nationwide: 122 E. 42nd St., New York, NY 10168, tel. 212/661–7200, fax 212/661–7174. Los Angeles: 11766 Wilshire Blvd., Suite 750, Los Angeles, CA 90025, tel. 310/575–9799, fax 310/575–156. Canada: 175 Bloor St. E, Suite 604,

Toronto, Ontario M4W 3R8, tel. 416/968–1570, fax 416/968–1986. U.K.: Nightingale House, 65 Curzon St., London W1Y 8NE, tel. 0171/493–0081 or 0891/600100 for brochures, fax 0171/495–6129; calls to the brochure line cost 50p per minute peak rate or 45p per minute cheap rate.

GIBRALTAR INFORMATION BUREAU • U.S. and Canada: 1156 15th St. NW, Ste. 1100, Washington, DC 20005, tel. 202/452–1108, fax 202/872–854). U.K.: Arundel Great Court, 179 The Strand, London WC2R 1EH, tel. 0171/836–0777, fax 0170/240–6612.

GREEK NATIONAL TOURIST ORGANIZATION • U.S. Nationwide: 645 Fifth Ave., New York, NY 10022, tel. 212/421–5777, fax 212/826–6940. Los Angeles: 611 W. 6th St., Suite 2198, Los Angeles, CA 90017, tel. 213/626–6696, fax 213/489–9744. Chicago: 168 N. Michigan Ave., Suite 600, Chicago, IL 60601, tel. 312/782–1084, fax 312/782–1091. Canada: 1233 Rue de la Montagne, Suite 101, Montréal, Québec H3G 1Z2, tel. 514/871–1535, fax 514/871–1498; 1300 Bay St., Toronto, Ontario M5R 3K8, tel. 416/968–2220, fax 416/968–6533. U.K.: 4 Conduit St., London W1R 0DJ, tel. 0171/734–5997, fax 0171/287–1369.

HUNGARIAN NATIONAL TOURIST OFFICE • U.S. and Canada: 150 E. 58th St., New York, NY 10155, tel. 212/355–0240, fax 212/207–4103. U.K.: Embassy of the Republic of Hungary, Commercial Section, 46 Eaton Place, London SW1X 8AL, tel. 0171/823–1032 or 0171/823–1055, fax 0171/823–1459.

IRISH TOURIST BOARD • U.S.: 345 Park Ave., New York, NY 10154, tel. 212/418–0800 or 800/223–6470, fax 212/371–9052. Canada: 160 Bloor St. E, Suite 1150, Toronto, Ontario M4W 1B9, tel. 416/929–2779, fax 416/929–6783. U.K.: Ireland House, 150 New Bond St., London W1Y 0AQ, tel. 0171/493–3201, fax 0171/493–9065.

ITALIAN GOVERNMENT TOURIST BOARD (ENIT) • U.S.: 630 Fifth Ave., New York, NY 10111, tel. 212/245–4822, fax 212/586–9249. Chicago: 401 N. Michigan Ave., Chicago, IL 60611, tel. 312/644–0990, fax 312/644–3019. Los Angeles: 12400 Wilshire Blvd., Suite 550, Los Angeles, CA 90025, tel. 310/820–0098, fax 310/820–6357. Canada: 1 Pl. Ville Marie, Suite 1914, Montréal, Québec H3B 3M9, tel. 514/866–7667, fax 514/392–1429. U.K.: 1 Princes St., London W1R 8AY, tel. 0171/408–1254, fax 0171/493-6695.

LUXEMBOURG NATIONAL TOURIST OFFICE • U.S. and Canada: 17 Beekman Pl., New York, NY 10022, tel. 212/935–8888, fax 212/935–5896. U.K.: 122 Regent St., London W1R 5FE, tel. 0171/434–2800, fax 0171/734–1205.

NETHERLANDS BOARD OF TOURISM • U.S. and Canada: 225 N. Michigan Ave., Suite 1854, Chicago, IL 60601, tel. 312/819–1500, fax 312/819–1740; for brochures, tel. 888/464–6552. Canada: 25 Adelaide St. E, Suite 710, Toronto, Ontario M5C 1Y2; mailing address only. U.K.: 25–28 Buckingham Gate, London SW1E 6LD, tel. 0891/717777, fax 0171/828–7941; calls cost 50p per minute peak rate or 45p per minute cheap rate.

NORWEGIAN TOURIST BOARD • U.S. and Canada: Scandinavia Tourism Inc., Box 4649 Grand Central Station, New York, NY 10163-4649, tel. 212/949–2333, fax 212/885–9710. U.K.: Charles House, 5–11 Lower Regent St., London SW1Y 4LR, tel. 0171/839–6255, fax 0171/839–6041.

POLISH NATIONAL TOURIST OFFICE • U.S. and Canada: 275 Madison Ave., Suite 1711, New York, NY 10016, tel. 212/338–9412, fax 212/338–9283. U.K.: Remo House, 1st floor, 310–312 Regent St., London W1R 5AJ, tel. 0171/580–8811, fax 0171/580–8866.

PORTUGUESE NATIONAL TOURIST OFFICE • U.S.: 590 5th Ave., 4th floor, New York, NY 10036, tel. 212/354–4403, fax 212/764–6137. Canada: 60 Bloor St. W, Suite 1005, Toronto, Ontario M4W 3B4, tel. 416/921–7376, fax 416/921–1353. U.K.: 22–25A Sackville St., 2nd floor, London W1X 2LY, tel. 0171/494–1441 or 0891/600370 (24-hour brochure line), fax 0171/494–1868; calls to the brochure line cost 50p per minute peak rate or 45p per minute cheap rate.

ROMANIAN NATIONAL TOURIST OFFICE • U.S. and Canada: 342 Madison Ave., Suite 210, New York, NY 10173, tel. 212/697–6971, fax 212/697–6972. U.K.: 83A Marylebone High St., London W1M 3DE, tel. 0171/224–3692, fax 0171/224–3692.

SLOVAKIA • U.S.: Slovak Information Center, 406 E. 67th St., New York, NY 10021, tel. 212/737–3971, fax 212/737–3454. Canada: Slovak Culture and Information Center, 12 Birch Ave., Toronto, Ontario M4V 1C8, tel. 416/925–0008, fax 416/925–0009. U.K.: Embassy of the Slovak Republic, Information Department, 25 Kensington Palace Gardens, London W8 4QY, tel. 0171/243–0803, fax 0171/727–5821.

TOURIST OFFICE OF SPAIN • U.S. Nationwide: 666 5th Ave., 35th floor, New York, NY 10103, tel. 212/265–8822, fax 212/265–8864. Chicago: 845 N. Michigan Ave., Chicago, IL 60611, tel. 312/642–1992, fax 312/642–9817. Los Angeles: 8383 Wilshire Blvd., Suite 960, Beverly Hills, CA 90211, tel. 213/658–7188, fax 213/658–1061. Miami: 1221 Brickell Ave., Suite 1850, Miami, FL 33131, tel. 305/358–1992, fax 305/358–8223. Canada: 2 Bloor St. W, 34th floor, Toronto, Ontario M4W 3E2, tel. 416/961–3131, fax 416/961–199). U.K.: 57–58 St. James's St., London SW1A 1LD, tel. 0171/499–0901 or 0891/669920 (24-hour brochure line), fax 0171/629–4257; calls to the brochure line cost 50p per minute peak rate or 45p per minute cheap rate.

SWEDISH TRAVEL AND TOURISM COUNCIL • U.S. and Canada: Scandinavia Tourism Inc., Box 4649 Grand Central Station, New York, NY 10163-4649, tel. 212/949–2333, fax 212/885–9710. U.K.: 73 Welbeck St., London W1M 8AN, tel. 0171/935–9784, fax 0171/935–5853.

SWISS NATIONAL TOURIST OFFICE • U.S.: 608 5th Ave., New York, NY 10020, tel. 212/757–5944, fax 212/262–6116. El Segundo: 222 N. Sepulveda Blvd., Suite 1570, El Segundo, CA 90245, tel. 310/335–5980, fax 310/335–5982. Chicago: 150 N. Michigan Ave., Suite 2930, Chicago, IL 60601, tel. 312/630–5840, fax 312/630–5848. Canada: 926 The East Mall, Etobicoke, Ontario M9B 6KI, tel. 416/695–2090, fax 416/695–2774. U.K.: Swiss Centre, 1 New Coventry St., London W1V 8EE, tel. 0171/734–1921, fax 0171/437–4577.

TURKISH TOURIST OFFICE • U.S. Nationwide: 821 UN Plaza, New York, NY 10017, tel. 212/687–2194, fax 212/599–7568. Washington D.C.: 1717 Massachusetts Ave. NW, Suite 306, Washington, DC 20036, tel. 202/429–9844, fax 202/429–5649. Canada: 360 Albert St., Ste. 801, Ottawa, Ontario K1R 7X7, tel. 613/230–8654, fax 613/230–3683. U.K.: Egyptian House, 1st floor, 170–173 Piccadilly, London W1V 9DD, tel. 0171/629–7771, fax 0171/491–0773.

VOLUNTEERING

A variety of volunteer programs are available in Europe. Council (*see* Students, *above*) is a key player, running its own roster of projects and publishing a directory that lists other sponsor organizations, *Volunteer! The Comprehensive Guide to Voluntary Service in the U.S. and Abroad* ($12.95 plus $1.50 postage). Service Civil International (SCI), International Voluntary Service (IVS), and Volunteers for Peace (VFP) run two- and three-week workcamps; VFP also publishes the *International Workcamp Directory* ($12). WorldTeach, run by Harvard University, arranges year-long teaching stints in subjects ranging from English and science to carpentry, forestry, and sports.

RESOURCES • **SCI/IVS** (5474 Walnut Level Rd., Crozet, VA 22932, tel. 804/823–1826). **VFP** (43 Tiffany Rd., Belmont, VT 05730, tel. 802/259–2759, fax 802/259–2922). **WorldTeach** (1 Eliot St., Cambridge, MA 02138, tel. 617/495–5527 or 800/483–2240, fax 617/495–1599).

WHEN TO GO

Most travelers descend on Europe in the summer, when school is out and the weather is warm. Although summer may be the best time to come if you want to bask on the beach or hike around the north, you will be faced with crowds, the highest prices of the year, and possibly the hostility of locals who are tired of the tourist packs. Winter means relative solitude everywhere except at winter resorts, but services may be less readily available, daylight hours are distressingly few in the north, and bad weather can leave you huddling by the radiator in your hotel room (if your hotel room *has* a radiator). If you can choose when to travel, **you can't beat late spring and early fall** for a happy balance; crowds and prices are moderate, and the weather is generally good.

CLIMATE

FORECASTS • **Weather Channel Connection** (tel. 900/932–8437), 95¢ per minute from a Touch-Tone phone. On the Web, www.weather.com.

AUSTRIA

any travelers have only hazy images of Austria: Alpine villages, Mozart operas, and Arnold Schwarzenegger. Austrians are always appalled to learn of their relative obscurity in the world's collective consciousness. They take their cosmopolitanism quite seriously and yearn to be considered a cultural superpower. There's no denying their credentials: classical music flourishes year-round in festivals all over the country, drama and dance in Vienna are some of the world's best, and opera thrives not only in the capital, but also in Salzburg, Innsbruck, Graz, and Linz.

Austria's worldly outlook is not surprising when you consider that it was once the center of the mammoth Austro-Hungarian Empire, which stretched as far east as Transylvania in the 18th century. The Dual Monarchy with Hungary gave Austria a taste of imperialism, with a sizable chunk of the empire's resources going into monumental Renaissance and baroque architectural projects in Vienna. The Austro-Hungarian Empire collapsed in 1918, and prodigal son Adolf Hitler returned home in 1938 to proclaim Austria a member of a different kind of imperial league. Hitler gave his Anschluß (annexation) speech to a jubilant Vienna and an already widely National Socialist country.

Austria's political influence was severely restricted when its leaders signed the Treaty of Permanent Neutrality in 1955 to end the Allied occupation. Though undoubtedly a better deal than the one East Germany got, it nonetheless made joining the EC (European Community) impossible. Vienna, which had been a center of world culture into the 1920s, slid to the status of cultural backwater, in limbo between East and West. With the dismantling of the Iron Curtain, however, Austria joined the embryonic EU (European Union) and reestablished important ties with old eastern friends. The promise of cultural renewal and economic prosperity brought a flood of new art galleries, restaurants, and immigrants, but today, the lagging fulfillment of that promise has produced rumblings of dissatisfaction with the EU.

Austria is still best known for its traditional attractions, but lest you fear that all your days here must be spent in museums or concert halls, know that the country's natural splendor rivals its artistic sophistication. Bike trails trace the route of the Danube (Donau) River, Alpine slopes provide plenty of powder for die-hard skiers, and scads of Dörfer (villages) offer stunning scenery and down-home hospitality.

AUSTRIA

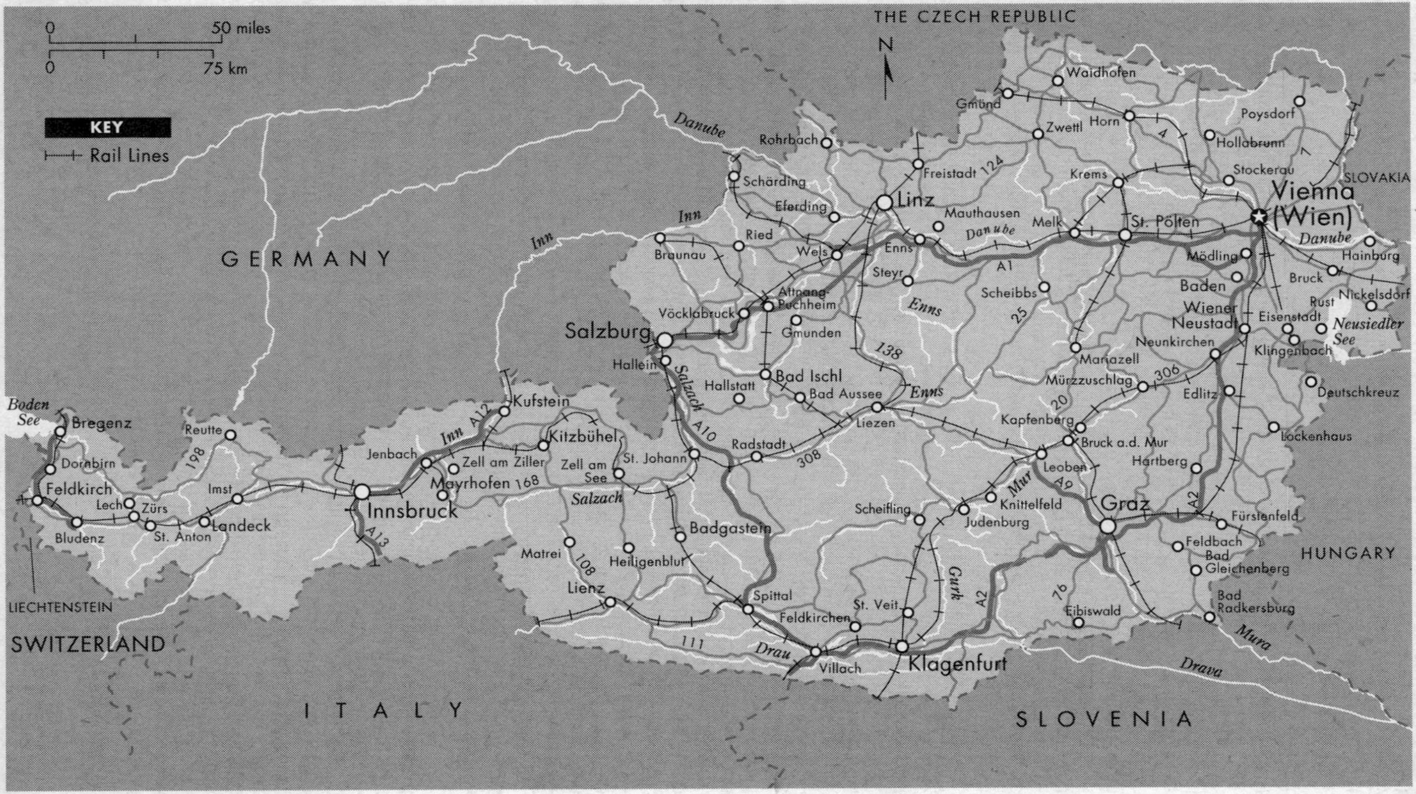
0 50 miles
0 75 km
KEY
Rail Lines
N
GERMANY
THE CZECH REPUBLIC
SLOVAKIA
HUNGARY
SLOVENIA
ITALY
SWITZERLAND
LIECHTENSTEIN
Boden See
Danube
Inn
Salzach
Enns
Mur
Gurk
Drau
Drava
Mura
Neusiedler See
Vienna (Wien)
Linz
Salzburg
Innsbruck
Graz
Klagenfurt
St. Pölten
Bregenz
Dornbirn
Feldkirch
Bludenz
Lech
Zürs
St. Anton
Landeck
Imst
Reutte
Jenbach
Mayrhofen
Zell am Ziller
Kufstein
Kitzbühel
Zell am See
St. Johann
Matrei
Lienz
Heiligenblut
Badgastein
Hallein
Hallstatt
Bad Ischl
Bad Aussee
Radstadt
Liezen
Gmunden
Vöcklabruck
Attnang-Puchheim
Braunau
Ried
Schärding
Eferding
Wels
Rohrbach
Freistadt
Steyr
Enns
Mauthausen
Scheibbs
Melk
Gmünd
Zwettl
Waidhofen
Horn
Krems
Poysdorf
Hollabrunn
Stockerau
Mödling
Baden
Hainburg
Bruck
Rust
Nickelsdorf
Eisenstadt
Wiener Neustadt
Klingenbach
Neunkirchen
Mariazell
Mürzzuschlag
Edlitz
Deutschkreuz
Kapfenberg
Bruck a.d. Mur
Leoben
Lockenhaus
Hartberg
Knittelfeld
Judenburg
Scheifling
Fürstenfeld
Feldbach
Bad Gleichenberg
Bad Radkersburg
Eibiswald
St. Veit
Feldkirchen
Spittal
Villach
A1
A2
A9
A10
A12
A13
1
4
20
25
76
108
111
124
138
168
198
306
308

BASICS

MONEY

US$1 = 12.75 Austrian Schillings and 1 Austrian Schilling = 7.8¢. The Austrian Schilling (AS) is subdivided into 100 Groschen and is pegged to the Deutsche Mark at a constant 7-to-1 ratio (i.e., 7 AS = DM 1). Austrian banks are generally open weekdays from 8:30 or 9 until 3 or 4. Banks, along with many other businesses in Austria, frequently shut their doors for 1–1½ hours between noon and 2 PM. Bank commissions on traveler's checks are atrocious—you're better off exchanging your money at an AmEx or post office. Train stations in all major cities have *Geldwechsel* (money change) offices that offer reasonable, standardized rates similar to those at post offices. ATMs are fixtures in almost all Austrian cities; look for the green and blue B signs. Many accept Visa, MasterCard, and PLUS- and Cirrus-affiliated bank cards.

HOW MUCH IT WILL COST • Vienna, Salzburg, and Innsbruck, in that order, are Austria's most expensive cities, but even they aren't outrageous. Throughout Austria a hostel bed costs 150 AS–250 AS (nonmembers usually pay 40 AS more). *Privatzimmer* (private rooms) cost 150 AS–500 AS per person. Pension prices generally start around 250 AS per person. Cheap restaurant lunches start around 50 AS, dinners around 80 AS. In resort towns, ask at your hotel or the tourist office about the **Guest Card** (called *Gastkarte*), which gets you a discount of 10%–20% at some museums and attractions.

GETTING AROUND

Eurail and InterRail passes are valid on all Austrian trains. For information on reduced airfares within Austria and throughout Europe, contact **Ökista** (tel. 01/401–480, fax 01/401–482290) in Vienna.

BY BIKE • Austria is criss-crossed with well-kept bike paths on some gorgeous routes (the **Donauradweg** along the Danube River is the most popular). Austrians are known for their love of cycling, and even urban drivers will go out of their way to avoid crushing the two-wheeled. Many Austrian train stations rent bicycles (usually for 100 AS per day, less with valid ticket), and many trains and some postal buses will take bikes as baggage at no additional charge.

BY BUS • Although buses are slower and generally less convenient than trains, you might need them in Austria's forested interior. In most towns, bus routes begin and end at the train station, making transfers a breeze. Ask at tourist offices, train stations, or bus stations for a *Fahrplan BundesBus,* which lists schedules for the unmistakably orange regional buses. Buy tickets at the ticket window, from ticket machines, or from your neighborhood bus driver.

BY TRAIN • The **Austrian Railpass** ($111 second class, $165 first class), available only outside Austria, provides four days of rail travel within a 10-day period, half off Danube riverboat tickets, and discounts on bike rentals at Austrian train stations. Those planning an extended stay in Austria should consider the **Vorteilscard** (1,190 AS), which gets you half-price train fares in both first and second class, among other deals, for a year. Buy one at any major train station in Austria. Austrians are generally not forthcoming with information (of any kind), so if you're buying a ticket to a destination outside the country, be sure to ask if you'll need to pay a supplement on board the train.

WHERE TO SLEEP

Austria has some of the nicest *Jugendherbergen* (youth hostels) anywhere. Showers and sheets are often included, though breakfast usually is not. Most hostels are overseen by two independent associations, **Österreichischer Jugendherbergsverband (ÖJHV)** (tel. 01/533–5353, fax 01/535–0861) and **Österreichisches Jugendherbergswerk (ÖJHW)** (tel. 01/533–1833, fax 01/533–1885). **ÖJHV** charges 240 AS per person; **ÖJHW** charges 200 AS for those over 26, 150 AS for ages 19–26. Both belong to Hostelling International (HI).

For an edge on the masses, call or fax your reservation up to a month in advance. Privatzimmer are common in touristed towns, fairly cheap, and a great way to meet Austrians; unfortunately, they're also often in the boonies. The rates range from 150 AS to 300 AS per person, usually including breakfast. Make reservations through local tourist offices. A Gasthof or Gasthaus is a simple country inn that usually serves breakfast and often serves other meals. A *Frühstückspension* (bed-and-breakfast) is a little cheaper since only breakfast is served. Plain old pensions are cheaper still.

FOOD

Most of Austria is still dining in the 19th century. Beef, pork, and sausages are everywhere, most cheaply at *Würstel* stands (sausage vendors). *Imbiß* stands (snack bars), often found at city markets, are cheap places for soup, kebabs, burgers, and other greasy goodies. University *Mensen* (cafeterias) are generally the cheapest spots for a meal, and most of their chow is even edible. Meats are often breaded and fried as schnitzel, the most famous version of which is Wiener schnitzel, traditionally made with veal. Aside from Wiener schnitzel, Austrian specialties include *G'röstl* (potato and onion hash with sausage or bacon, topped with an egg), *Palatschinken* (crêpes filled with fruit or jam), *Kaiserschmarren* (chopped pancakes with fruit topping), *Sachertorte* (dense chocolate cake with apricot-jelly filling and chocolate topping), *Bosna* (grilled sausage with curry spices and pickle relish), and *Salzburger Nockerl* (a giant dessert dumpling). Restaurants have a nasty habit of serving bread or appetizer plates without telling you that a *Gedeck* (charge) will apply—ask before you dig in. For dessert, *Strudel* (thin pastry wrapped around a filling) comes in all varieties, including apple (*Apfelstrudel*), cream cheese (*Topfenstrudel*), and cherry (*Kirschstrudel*). Be aware that if you order water, you will be served mineral water; to keep the bill down, ask for *Leitungswasser* (tap water).

Cafés are a huge part of Austrian life, though their food can be a rip-off. The popular *Portion Kaffee* is a small pot of coffee served with a thimbleful of milk or cream and a glass of water; java addicts will feel at home with a *Großer Brauner,* a large coffee that borders on espresso-strength. You can sit in a café all afternoon if you'd like, but don't expect free refills. Finally, wine lovers may find themselves spending lots of time in *Heurigen,* Austria's answer to the pub, where you can get light meals to go with Austrian white wines.

PHONES
Country Code: 43. For local telephone information, dial 1611; for long-distance information, dial 1613. A local call costs 2 AS for one minute. Coin-operated phones, which take 1, 5, 10, or 20 AS coins, are still everywhere, though using *Kartentelefone* (card phones) is a much easier affair. Buy your *Telefonkarte* (phone card) at any post office or tobacco shop; they come in

A tip of 10% is generally included in restaurant and taxi bills, though it is customary to round the bill up to the nearest multiple of 10 schillings.

values of 48 AS and up. A green sign on a phone booth means you can receive calls there. Austria is in the process of computerizing its phone system by district, so some numbers listed here may change.

Post offices have booths for call-now, pay-later international calls. Look for the window marked FERNGE-SPRÄCHE and simply tell them you want to telephone; they'll give you a booth number. To phone first and pay *much* later, dial **AT&T** Direct Access^SM (tel. 022/903011), **MCI** (tel. 022/903012), **Sprint** (tel. 022/903014), or **Canada Direct** (tel. 022/903013). If you're dialing from a pay phone, you must insert 2 AS for these numbers, as well as for emergency numbers.

EMERGENCIES
First, deposit at least 2 AS; then dial 133 for the **police,** 144 for an **ambulance,** and 122 for the **fire department.** To find out which of the city's pharmacies (*Apotheken*) is open 24 hours, consult a newspaper or the door of any pharmacy, or, in Vienna, dial 1550.

MAIL
Post offices are generally open weekdays 8–noon and 2–6, Saturday 8–10. The German term for poste restante is *Postlagernde Briefe.* Have your letters sent to the main post office in any town, and flash some ID within 30 days to pick them up. It costs 13 AS to send a postcard abroad and at least 13 AS for international airmail. Remember to ask for airmail stickers (*Flugpost*) for each item you're mailing—without them your postcard might end up inching across the ocean.

LANGUAGE
Ninety-eight percent of all Austrians are ethnic Germans and speak a German dialect. Throughout the country, *Grüß Gott* (formal) and *Servus* (informal) replace *Guten Tag* as a greeting, and *Auf Wiederschauen* is a more common "Good-bye" than *Auf Wiedersehen.* Most Austrians in the tourist industry speak English, though some do so grudgingly.

VIENNA

Vienna (Wien) is considered by its fashionable residents to be *der Nabel der Welt* (literally, the belly button of the world). Outside the Nabel, however, Vienna is sometimes written off as a living, breathing fossil, a wedding-cake city that once shared the spotlight with London, Paris, and Rome but has since

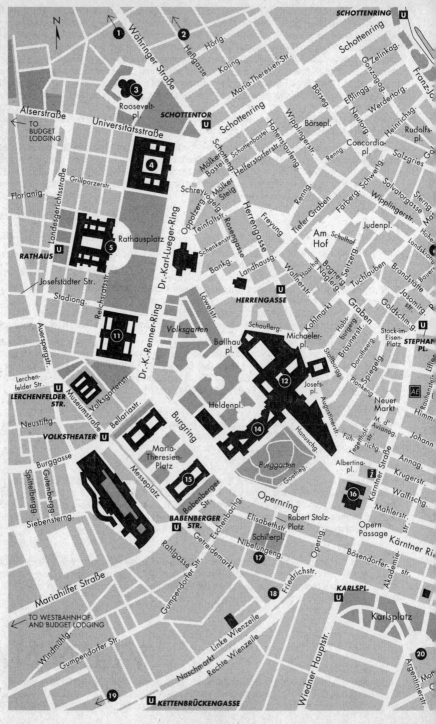

N

SCHOTTENRING U

① Währinger Straße ②

Heßgasse Hörlg.

Koling.

Maria-Theresien-Str.

Schottenring

Schottenring

Zelinkag.

Gonzaga-g.

Börseg.

③ Roosevelt-pl.

SCHOTTENTOR U

Schottenring

Börsepl.

Wipplingerstr.

Eßlingg.

Neutorg.

Werdertorg.

Heinrichsg.

Rudolfs-pl.

Alserstraße

TO BUDGET LODGING

Universitätsstraße

Schottengasse

Mölkerbastei

Hohenstaufeng.

Renng.

Concordia-pl.

Salzgries

Florianig.

Grillparzerstr.

Schreyvogelg. Mölker Steig

Oppolzerg.

Helferstorferstr.

Renng.

Renng.

Färberg.

Salvatorgasse

Sterng.

Landesgerichtsstraße

④

Schreyvogelg.

Teinfaltstr.

Rosengasse

Herrengasse

Freyung

Tiefer Graben

Am Hof Schulhof

Judenpl.

Wipplingerstr.

RATHAUS U

⑤ Rathausplatz

Schenkenstraße

Bankg.

Landhausg.

Wallnerstr.

Bognerg.

Seitzerg.

Tuchlauben

Brandstätte

Jasomirg.

Goldschm.g.

Josefstädter Str.

Reichsratsstr.

Löwelstr.

HERRENGASSE U

Kohlmarkt

Graben

Stock-im-Eisen-Platz

U

Stadiong.

Dr.-Karl-Lueger-Ring

Volksgarten

Schauflerg.

Michaeler-pl.

Habsburgerg.

Bräunerstr.

Spiegelg.

STEPHAN PL.

⑪

Auerspergstr.

Ballhaus-pl.

Stallburgg.

Dorotheerg.

Plankeng.

Neuer Markt

Himm.

Lerchen-felder Str.

LERCHENFELDER STR. U

Museumstraße

Volksgartenstr.

Bellariastr.

Burgring

Heldenpl.

⑫

Josefs-pl.

Augustinerstr.

Führ. richg.

Tegetthoff-str.

M. d.-Avianog.

Johann

Neustiftg.

VOLKSTHEATER U

⑭

Hanusch-g.

Tegetthoffstraße

Annag.

Krugerstr.

Burggasse

Messeplatz

Maria-Theresien-Platz

⑮

Babenberger Str.

Burggarten

Goetheg.

Albertina-pl.

i

⑯

Walfischg.

Mahlerstr.

Gutenbergg.

Spittelbergg.

Siebensterng.

BABENBERGER STR. U

Getreidemarkt

Eschenbachg.

Elisabethstr.

Schillerpl.

Nibelungeng.

Opernring

Robert Stolz-Platz

Opern Passage

Akademiestr.

Bösendorfer-str.

Kärntner Rir

Mariahilfer Straße

⑰

Friedrichstr.

KARLSPL. U

Karlsplatz

TO WESTBAHNHOF AND BUDGET LODGING

Rahlgasse Str.

Gumpendorfer Str.

⑱

Wiedner Hauptstr.

⑳

Windmühlg.

Gumpendorfer Str.

Naschmarkt

Linke Wienzeile

Rechte Wienzeile

Argentinierstr.

⑲

U KETTENBRÜCKENGASSE

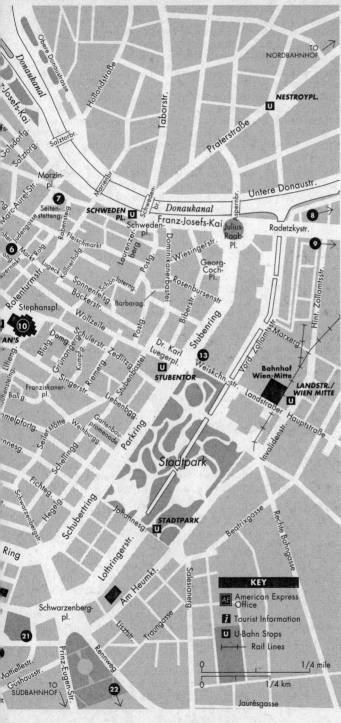

Akademie der bildenden Künste, **17**

Beethoven Haus Museum, **1**

Historisches Museum der Stadt Wien, **21**

Hofburg, **12**

Karlskirche, **20**

KunstHaus-Wien, **9**

Kunsthistorisches Museum, **15**

Museum für Angewandte Kunst (MAK), **13**

Neue Hofburg, **14**

Parlament, **11**

Prater, **8**

Rathaus, **5**

Schönbrunn Palace, **19**

Schloss Belvedere, **22**

Secession Building, **18**

Staatsoper, **16**

Ruprechtskirche, **7**

Sigmund Freud Haus Museum, **2**

Stephansdom, **10**

Underground Roman ruins, **6**

Universität, **4**

Votivkirche, **3**

KEY

AE American Express Office

i Tourist Information

U U-Bahn Stops

⊢ Rail Lines

0 — 1/4 mile

0 — 1/4 km

slipped into peaceful obscurity. This longtime center of the Hapsburg Empire and the pet project of the medieval Babenberg dynasty does boast some magnificent baroque and Gothic architecture, yet the city is much more than a collection of monuments. Even during Vienna's most stagnant days under Emperor Franz Joseph I, Viennese writers such as Arthur Schnitzler were feeding voraciously on the city's corpse, producing works of death and decline that used Vienna as both setting and metaphor.

Today, alongside imperial palaces and 12th-century cathedrals, you'll find Art Nouveau by Otto Wagner and whimsically colorful, undulating designs by Friedensreich Hundertwasser. The Vienna Opera House still packs them in, but the feature could just as easily be Natalie Cole as Puccini. And in cafés where Trotsky, Loos, and Lenin once debated art and revolution, new generations discuss rising taxes and membership in the EU. Vienna has always been the site of contradictions and change; over the years, it's hosted the religious reformations of Empress Maria Theresa (whose own husband was notoriously unfaithful), Freud's liberalism and rationalism, the antitraditional Jugendstil (Art Nouveau) movement, and the summit between Kennedy and Khrushchev.

As Eastern Europe becomes more popular, and travel there easier, Vienna finds itself in the familiar position of a gateway city—a role it hasn't played since the Allies left Austria on the East–West fence after World War II. Visitors and young explorers passing through on the way to Budapest and Prague will find a Vienna in transition—a city still relying on its amazing past while staking out a place as a modern European metropolis.

BASICS

VISITOR INFORMATION

The **Central Tourist Office** (tel. 01/211140) is for phone inquiries only. Walk-ins should go to **Tourist Information**, at 1010 Kärntner Straße 38, at Philharmonikerstraße, open daily 9–7; take the U-Bahn to Karlsplatz. If you plan to stay more than one day, be sure to get **The Vienna Card** for 180 AS, available at the Kärntner Straße Tourist Office and the information offices at Stephansplatz, Karlsplatz, Westbahnhof, and Landstraße/Wien-Mitte; it gets you discounts on museums, sightseeing tours, and theater tickets, plus it's good for 72 hours of unlimited use on the U-Bahn. **Jugend-Info Wien** (1010 Dr.-Karl-Renner-Ring, underground in Bellaria Passage, tel. 01/1799; open weekdays noon–7, Sat. 10–7) doles out information on Vienna events and can score cut-rate tickets for those under 27. Contact **Rosa Lila Villa Gay and Lesbian Community Center** (1060 Linke Wienzeile 102, tel. 01/586–8150 or 01/587–1778; open weekdays 5 PM–8 PM) for the dope on the *Szene* in Vienna or anywhere else in Austria.

AMERICAN EXPRESS

1010 Kärntnerstr. 21–23, tel. 01/51540. U-Bahn to Stephansplatz. Open weekdays 9–5:30, Sat. 9– noon.

BUREAUX DE CHANGE

The exchange windows at the main post office (*see below*) are open 24 hours. The window at the Westbahnhof is open 7 AM–10 PM, and the one at the Südbahnhof is open 7 AM–10 PM (until 9 PM Nov.–Apr.).

DISCOUNT TRAVEL AGENCIES

Go to **Ökista** for plane, train, and bus tickets—cheap. *1090 Türkenstr. 6, or 1010 Reichsratstr. 13, next to Rathaus, tel. 01/402–1561.*

EMBASSIES

Australia: *1040 Mattiellistr. 2–4, next to Karlskirche, tel. 01/512–8580178. Open Mon.–Thurs. 9:30– 1 and 2–5:30, Fri. 8:30–1:15.* **Canada:** *1010 Laurenzerberg 2 (3rd floor of Hauptpost building complex), tel. 01/5313801. Open weekdays 8:30–12:30 and 1:30–3:30.* **Ireland:** *1030 Landstraßer Hauptstr. 2, 16th floor of Hilton Center, tel. 01/715–4246. Open weekdays 9:30–11:30 and 1:30– 4:00.* **United Kingdom:** *1030 Jaurèsgasse 10, near Schloß Belvedere, tel. 01/71613–5151. Open weekdays 9:15–noon and 2–4.* **United States:** *1010 Gartenbaupromenade 2, in Marriott building off Parkring, tel. 01/31339. Open weekdays 8:30–noon and 1–3:30.*

MAIL AND PHONES

When calling Vienna from outside Austria, insert the city code, 1, after the country code. The **Hauptpostamt** (main post office; 1010 Fleischmarkt 19) has a bureau de change, a fax desk, international phone booths, and photocopiers, all available 24 hours. Have poste restante sent to Your Name, Postlagernde Briefe, Hauptpostamt, Fleischmarkt 19, 1010 Wien. There are additional post offices next to the Franz-Josefs-Bahnhof, Westbahnhof, and Südbahnhof.

COMING AND GOING

BY BUS

Most international buses pass through **Busbahnhof Wien-Mitte,** next to Bahnhof Wien-Mitte on the east side of town; head there for schedules and routes.

BY FERRY

DDSG Blue Danube Schiffahrt (1020 Handelskai 265, tel. 01/72750–222) sends ferries up the Danube, organizes a *Hundertwasser Tour* (140 AS) of the Vienna area on a special boat refashioned by the artist himself, and operates express boats to Bratislava (1½ hrs, 210 AS) and Budapest (5 hrs, 750 AS). Alas, they don't accept Eurail or InterRail passes. In summer, ferries leave daily at 8 AM (off season, 9 AM) from Vienna's **ferry terminal** (Reichsbrücke Schiffahrtszentrum; U1 to Vorgartenstr.). Reservations are wise, though not required.

BY PLANE

International flights arrive at **Wien-Schwechat Flughafen** (tel. 01/70070), about 20 km (12 mi) southeast of the city. To reach the airport from Wien-Nord or Landstraße/Wien-Mitte, take the twice-hourly S7 train, a 35-minute ride (34 AS). The S7 is also the cheapest way into town *from* the airport, leaving twice hourly. Follow the signs picturing a train to the basement of the airport. The 34 AS one-way ticket is good for transfers on the U-Bahn to your destination in town. **Airport buses** (tel. 01/5800–33369; 70 AS) make the 35-minute trek between the Südbahnhof and Westbahnhof and the airport at least hourly 5:40 AM–midnight; they leave every 20 minutes 6:30 AM–11:30 PM from the City Air Terminal next to the Hilton Hotel (U4 to Stadtpark). To find these buses, look for a yellow airplane on an orange sign. C&K Airport Taxi has the cheapest set fare (tel. 01/1731; 270 AS) from anywhere in Vienna, but you must book ahead.

BY TRAIN

Vienna has two major train stations. The **Westbahnhof,** west of the center on the U3 and U6, sends trains to Munich (4½ hrs, 722 AS), Salzburg (3 hrs, 436 AS), Zürich (10 hrs, 1,106 AS), Budapest (3 hrs, 358 AS), and Frankfurt (7½ hrs, 1,232 AS). The station closes 1:15 AM–4 AM. Destinations from the **Südbahnhof** include Venice (8 hrs, 944 AS), Prague (4 hrs, 412 AS), Graz (2½ hrs, 336 AS), Bratislava (1 hr, 114 AS), and Berlin (10 hrs, 926 AS). The station closes 1 AM–4 AM. The smaller **Franz-Josefs-Bahnhof** runs local trains to destinations like Krems, as well as a couple of trains daily to Prague. **Bahnhof Wien-Meidling** provides service to smaller towns east of Vienna. **Bahnhof Wien-Mitte** (U-Bahn or S-Bahn to Landstr./Wien-Mitte), in the middle of town, handles commuter trains and shuttles to the airport.

RIDES

Mitfahrzentrale (1080 Daungasse 1A; tel. 01/408–2210) offers rides with registered drivers for about half the price of a train ticket. Vienna to Innsbruck costs 270 AS, Vienna to Munich, 310 AS, Vienna to Paris, 790 AS. You need to reserve three days in advance. Take Tram 5, 43, or 44 to Alserstraße.

GETTING AROUND

Vienna is as neatly laid out as a box of sweets and is best explored on foot. The city is divided into 23 *Bezirke* (districts). The first district, where you'll find most of the city's attractions, cafés, and bars, consists of the densely packed pedestrian area encircled by the 7-km (4½-mi) **Ringstraße.** Districts 2–9 circle the first district clockwise, while districts 10 and up edge outward toward the *Wienerwald* (Vienna Woods). Most addresses in this chapter include the district number before the street address (1010 refers to the first district, 1020 to the second, all the way up to 1230 for the 23rd).

BY BIKE

The West, Süd, and Nord train stations rent bikes for 100 AS per day. The Ringstraße has wide bicycle lanes and is accessible from the train stations via cycling routes. Wien Nord is convenient to the Prater amusement park and is a good departure point for hooking up with the main Danube cycling road. *Logbuch Radwege Wien* (100 AS), available in bookstores, is a detailed map of all 460 km (276 mi) of bike roads that run past Vienna's main sights.

BY PUBLIC TRANSPORT

If the spirit is willing but the feet are weak, make use of Vienna's safe and efficient public transportation system, **Wiener Linien** (Vienna Lines, tel. 01/790–9105). The system includes the U-Bahn (subway), S-Bahn (commuter trains), buses, and trams. Vienna's **U-Bahn** covers most of the major routes in the city, while the **S-Bahn** system covers outlying areas and connects the train stations. Public transport starts running around 5 AM, and the whole system goes into cardiac arrest shortly after midnight. After that, you can either take a cab or try a **night bus** (25 AS, special passes not valid). These operate nightly 12:30 AM–4 AM, are designated by an N, and depart from Schwedenplatz (near the Bermuda Triangle), Schottentor, and Oper on the Ringstraße before traveling to various parts of Vienna. Route maps and schedules are posted at each bus stop.

Single tickets, valid for a one-way ride including connections on all public transport (except express buses and the S-Bahn beyond the city limits), cost 20 AS, or 17 AS if purchased in advance from a ticket machine, a ticket office (in most major U-Bahn stations), or a tobacconist. Passes include the 24-hour or 72-hour **Rover Ticket** (50 AS and 130 AS, respectively) and the eight-day network ticket (265 AS), valid for any eight days, consecutive or not. All are available from ticket machines. Yet another option is the **Wochenkarte** (142 AS), valid from Monday 9 AM to the following Monday 9 AM. If you have a Eurailpass, you can ride the S-Bahn for free.

BY TAXI

Taxis in Vienna aren't cheap, but they may be your only convenient option late at night. The basic rate is 24 AS plus 12 AS per kilometer, and up to four people can ride for one fare. To call a cab, dial 01/31300, 01/40100, or 01/60160.

WHERE TO SLEEP

Lodging in Vienna is substantially more expensive than elsewhere in Austria. Many of the city's hostels and budget pensions are clustered around Mariahilfer Straße, near the Westbahnhof, in districts 6, 7, and 8, and most listings give directions from that station. Private rooms start at 250 AS per day without breakfast, but they're usually far from the city center.

UNDER 600 AS • Pension Fünfhaus. Step into an enormous, uncarpeted room with a sofa, right near the Westbahnhof. Singles start at 390 AS, doubles at 560 AS, without bath, breakfast included. This area can get sketchy at night; plan accordingly. *1150 Sperrgasse 12, tel. 01/892–3545. From Westbahnhof, west on Mariahilfer Str., right on Sperrgasse. Closed Jan.–Feb.*

Pension Mahal. Close to the museums, Mahal is one of the best deals in the city. Rooms are cheery, and some face the quaint St. Ulricht's Platz, which looks like a set from a 1930s Hollywood movie. Doubles are 560 AS, triples 840 AS, without bath, breakfast included. No singles. *1070 Neustiftgasse 31, tel. 01/523–6202 or 0663/910–1356 (mobile phone). Take U2 or U3 to Volkstheater; skirt around the right side of the theater, then go up Neustiftgasse.*

Quisisana. This old, well-kept building has simple, quiet rooms with cheesy landscape paintings. Singles are 320 AS, doubles 540 AS, without bath, breakfast included. *1060 Windmühlgasse 6, tel. 01/587–3341, fax 01/58771–5633. Take U3 (or Bus 13A from Südbahnhof) to Neubaugasse; go east on Mariahilfer Str., then right on Capistrangasse to Windmühlgasse.*

UNDER 750 AS • Hotel Hospiz. The simple, clean rooms have sinks in this quiet YMCA five minutes from the Westbahnhof. Singles start at 380 AS, doubles 680 AS, triples 960 AS, quads 1,280 AS, all including breakfast. *1070 Kenyongasse 15, tel. 01/523–1304, fax 01/523–130413. From Westbahnhof, walk left and cross Neubaugürtel onto Stollgasse, then left on Kenyongasse.*

Kraml. You'll find this classy, family-run establishment in an alley near the Westbahnhof. Singles start at 310 AS, doubles at 620 AS, triples at 820 AS; hearty breakfast included. *1060 Brauergasse 5, tel. 01/587–8588, fax 01/586–7573. Take U3 to Zieglergasse; head down Otto-Bauer-Gasse, left on Königseggasse, and right on Brauergasse. Closed Feb.*

Pension Reimer. Extremely friendly and comfortable, Reimer has doubles with high ceilings and large windows (610 AS–830 AS) and singles for 380 AS–500 AS, breakfast included. *1070 Kirchengasse 18, tel. 01/523–6162, fax 01/524–3782. Take U3 (or Bus 13A from Südbahnhof) to Neubaugasse; go east down Mariahilfer Str., left on Kirchengasse.*

UNDER 1,000 AS • Pension Grun. There's a minimum stay of three nights here, but you can't beat the five-minute walk to the city center. Rooms are spacious, and there's a comfy sitting room. Singles are 500 AS and doubles 950 AS, without breakfast. *1010 Gonzagagasse 1/3/19, tel. 01/533–2506. Take U1 or U4 to Schwedenplatz; walk along Franz-Josefs-Kai to Marc Aurel-Str., turn right and go to Morzinplatz, then turn left on Gonzagagasse.*

Pension Riedl. These rooms occupy the upper floors of a lovely 19th-century building overlooking the Postsparkassenamt, a Jugendstil building designed by Otto Wagner. Singles start at 550 AS, doubles at 920 AS, full breakfast included. *1010 Georg-Coch-Platz 3/4/10, tel. 01/512–7919, fax 01/512–79198. Take U1 or U4 to Schwedenplatz; walk 5 mins in the direction of Julius Raab Platz, and turn right on Stubenring, then right on Georg-Coch-Platz.*

UNDER 1,300 AS • Hotel-Pension Altstadt. This gem of a small hotel was once a patrician home. Rooms are large and have all the modern comforts, but they retain an antique feel. The English-style lounge has a fireplace and plump floral sofas. Buffet breakfast included. Singles start at 1,080 AS, doubles at 1,280 AS. *1070 Kirchengasse 41, tel. 01/526–33990, fax 01/523–4901. Take U2 or U3 to Volkstheater and exit on Burggasse; walk up Burggasse and turn left on Kirchengasse.*

HOSTELS

Gästehaus Ruthensteiner (HI). A five-minute walk from the Westbahnhof, this place is super-friendly, curfew-free, and equipped with kitchen facilities. Dorm beds start at 139 AS. Breakfast is 25 AS extra. *1150 Robert-Hamerling-Gasse 24, tel. and fax 01/893–2796. From Westbahnhof, go right on Mariahilfer Str., left on Haidmannsgasse, and right on Robert-Hammerling-Gasse. Reception open 24 hrs.*

Hostel Zöhrer. Here's a central, sunny hostel with a courtyard rose garden. Beds go for 170 AS, and you get breakfast, sheets, and kitchen access in the bargain. There's no curfew. *1080 Skodagasse 26, tel. 01/406–0730, fax 01/408–0409. Take Tram 5 to Florianigasse, or from Südbahnhof, Bus 13A to Skodagasse. Laundry (60 AS).*

Jugendgästehaus Wien Brigittenau (HI). This is the largest hostel in town, which means way too many school groups. There is a flexible midnight curfew. Beds cost 160 AS. *1200 Friedrich-Engels-Platz 24, tel. 01/3328–2940, fax 01/330–8379. Take U6 to Dresdner Str. (from Südbahnhof, S-Bahn to Traisengasse); then Tram N to Friedrich-Engels-Platz. Reception open 24 hrs, lockout 9–1.*

Jugendherberge Myrthengasse und Neustiftgasse (HI). These two extremely popular, central hostels are right next to one another. Reserve a few days ahead or show up for their 7 AM–11:15 AM reception hours (Sun. until 10:30 at Neustiftgasse); actual check-in is 2 PM–10 PM (from 3:45 at Neustiftgasse). Although there's a 1 AM curfew, a key is available. Beds are 200 AS. *1070 Myrthengasse 7 and 1070 Neustiftgasse 85, tel. 01/523–6316, fax 01/523–5849. Take U3 to Neubaugasse, then Bus 13A to Kellermanngasse; go left down Neustiftgasse 2 blocks, then round corner to left. Laundry (50 AS).*

Schloßherberge am Wilhelminenberg (HI). Transportation here is less than convenient, but this beauteous hostel on Vienna's green outskirts is well worth the effort. There's a midnight curfew (key available). Beds in cheery quads, with breakfast, go for 220 AS. *1160 Savoyenstr. 2, tel. 01/4585–03700, fax 01/4585–03702. Take U6 to Thaliastr. (from Südbahnhof, Tram D to Dr.-Karl-Renner-Ring); then Tram 46 (direction: Joachimsthalerplatz) to Ottakring, then Bus 46B or 146B to Schloß Wilhelminenberg. The hostel is down a wooded path to the left of the large white hotel. Reception open 7 AM–midnight, lockout 9–4. Laundry (60 AS).*

FOOD

Most of the restaurants listed below are in the first Bezirk, where you'll most likely spend your days. Even in this historic district, you can find cheap eats at places like the **Anker** bakery chain (there's one across from the Opera House). For groceries, head to supermarkets like **Billa** (Singerstr. 6), just around the corner from Stephansdom. The city's largest open-air market, **Naschmarkt** (open weekdays 7–6, Sat. 7–1; U4 to Kettenbrückengasse), has cheap eats and fresh produce, as well as Eurojunk with lots of souvenir potential. Scarf Mensa meals weekdays (7:30 AM–3 PM) at the **Hochschule für Musik.**

UNDER 80 AS • Einstein. With lots of outdoor tables, this student hangout behind the Universität serves everything from continental breakfasts (42 AS) to Wiener schnitzel with potato salad (60 AS) and beers on tap. *1010 Rathausplatz 4, tel. 01/422626. U2 to Rathaus. Open Mon.–Sat. until 2 AM, Sun. until midnight.*

UNDER 100 AS • Ma Pitom. In one of Vienna's loveliest, quietest courtyards, the biggest and best salad bar in the district draws a young, well-heeled crowd. At night, candlelit tables are crowded with

VIENNA BOYS' CHOIR

The Hofburg palace's Hofburgkapelle (Hofburg Chapel) is home to the famous Wiener Sängerknaben (Vienna Boys' Choir). From late September to June, the choir sings its famous Sunday mass here at 9:15 AM. Limited standing room is available for free; get to the chapel by 8:30 (at least) for a shot at a spot. For seats (60 AS–280 AS), write at least eight weeks in advance to Hofmusikkapelle, Hofburg, 1010 Wien (or fax 01/5339–92775). Any leftover tickets go on sale each Friday at the chapel at 5 PM.

the arty and upscale. *1010 Seitenstettengasse 5, next to Ruprechtskirche, tel. 01/535–4313. U-Bahn to Schwedenplatz. Open Sun.–Thurs. 11:30–3 and 5:30–1, Fri. and Sat. 11:30–3 and 5:30–2.*

Plutzer Bräu. In the hip Spittelberg area, this brew pub offers everything from main-course salads to schnitzels to accompany the beer brewed on the premises. The interior is sleek and modern, and in summer you can sit outdoors, just off the cobblestone street. *1070 Schrankgasse 2, tel. 01/526–1215. Take U2 to Volkstheater and exit on Burggasse; go up Burggasse and left on Schrankgasse. Cash only.*

UNDER 130 AS • Brezl Gwölb. Housed in a medieval pretzel factory, this snug restaurant fills up quickly at night. Try the scrumptious *Tyroler G'röstl* (a tasty potato hash with chunks of pork), served in a blackened skillet, or the *Kasnockerl*, spaetzle in a pungent cheese sauce. Get a table downstairs in the real medieval cellar, which looks like a set from *Phantom of the Opera*. *1010 Ledererhof 9, tel. 01/533–8811. U-3 to Herrengasse, exit Herrengasse and walk through passageway opposite post office (Fahnen-Haarhf.-Irisg.) to Am Hof. Ledererhof is a tiny street between Farbergasse and Drahtgasse.*

UNDER 200 AS • Neu Wien. This trendy, upscale eatery has a new slant on traditional Austrian cooking. Try the crispy *Zanderfilet* (pike-perch) in a basil-oil sauce, or the free-range chicken in a mushroom sauce. *1010 Bäckerstr. 5 (behind Stephansdom), tel. 01/512–0999. Closed weekends in July and Aug. Cash only.*

CAFES

Not just a caffeine fix, the café is a classic Viennese institution—a meeting place for artists, writers, and radicals since the turn of the century. Stop in at **Café Central** (1010 Herrengasse 14, in the Palais Ferstel, tel. 01/533–3763; closed Sun.) for the traditional Viennese-café experience. Everyone—from students to tourists to people who may have been here with Robert Musil or Trotsky—comes here to read newspapers and chat with friends. **Demel** (1010 Kohlmarkt 14, tel. 01/535–17170) is a 200-year-old Viennese institution, and in a city famous for its pastries, their Senegal torte takes the cake. The elegant **Café Landtmann** (1010 Dr.-Karl-Leuger-Str. 4, tel. 01/532–0621) is where Freud hung out. In summer, sit outside facing the Burgtheater.

WORTH SEEING

The first district, roughly outlined by the Ringstraße, contains the oldest part of town and most of Vienna's major sights. Buy *Vienna From A to Z* (50 AS) from the tourist office for a concise, building-by-building guide to more than 300 attractions.

ALTSTADT (OLD TOWN)

In the 1st century AD the Romans built a fort, called Vindobona, by the Danube; Marcus Aurelius wrote his famous *Meditations* here while directing the military abuse of Germanic tribes. For a glimpse of ancient history, descend the stairs inside the bakery at Hoher Markt 3 to the **underground Roman ruins** (tel. 01/535–5606; admission 25 AS; open Tues.–Sun. 9–12:15 and 1–4), where the excavated remains of two Roman houses are on display. In 799, a revived Roman military outpost guarded the eastern edge of Charlemagne's empire here, and in 1156 Vienna became the seat of the Babenberg family, who ruled the up-and-coming duchy of Austria before the arrival of the Hapsburgs. One of the few visible remnants of the Babenberg era is the humble but well-preserved 11th-century **Ruprecht-skirche** (1010 Judengasse, in the Bermuda Triangle near Schwedenplatz), Vienna's oldest church.

HOFBURG

The palace of the ruling Hapsburgs from 1278 until their fall in 1918, the Hofburg grew to become as sprawling and confused as the empire over which it presided. Exploring the 2,600-odd rooms would take quite a while; if you don't have a lot of time, skip the famous but rather glum **Kaiserapartements** (Imperial Apartments), which aren't worth the 70 AS admission. However, *don't* skip the **Schatzkammer** (Treasury Room; tel. 01/533-7931; admission 70 AS), which holds a millennium's worth of crowns, relics, and vestments. Room 11 features the duds that Napoléon wore when he crowned himself emperor in 1804. Less traditional treasures include the 96-inch Horn of the Unicorn (actually the tusk of a narwhal), which has been housed here for more than 500 years. *1010 Michaelerplatz, tel. 01/533-7570. U3 to Herrengasse. Kaiserapartements open daily 9–4:30. Schatzkammer open Wed.–Mon. 10–6 (Thurs. until 9).*

Catch the intricate prancing of the Lipizzaner stallions during training sessions at the **Spanische Reitschule** (1010 Burgring, tel. 01/533-9032; admission 100 AS). The horses of the Spanish Riding School are away July and August, but otherwise they can usually be seen Tuesday–Friday (sometimes Saturday) at 10 AM. Actual performances (250 AS–900 AS, standing room 200 AS) sell out months in advance; write to Spanische Reitschule, Hofburg, 1010 Vienna. The AmEx office (*see above*) sometimes has a few last-minute tickets, but they'll add a 22% service charge.

At KunstHausWien, watch the short film on Friedensreich Hundertwasser, which shows the eccentric artist painting in the buff.

The astounding collections of the **Nationalbibliothek** (National Library) include musical manuscripts by the masters and the hefty *Globensammlungen* (globe collections), with 199 ancient globes—well worth the 15 AS admission. Hapsburg book collections were first gathered together under Emperor Karl VI in the library's **Prunksaal** (admission 60 AS), a magnificent baroque showpiece of a library. *1010 Josefsplatz 1, tel. 01/534-100. Open May–Oct., Mon.–Sat. 10–4; Jan.–Feb., Mon.–Sat. 10–2; Mar.–Apr. and Nov.–Dec., Mon.–Sat. 10–noon; year-round, Sun. and holidays, 10–1.*

A young and impressionable Hitler lived in Vienna just before World War I, when the **Neue Hofburg,** the newest wing of the palace, was being completed. A quarter of a century later, in 1938, Hitler chose the balcony of the Neue Hofburg to announce to an enthusiastic (and carefully orchestrated) crowd that Austria had become a part of the Third Reich. Today, this behemoth houses four excellent collections: the **Ephesus Museum,** with artifacts excavated from this famous lost city by the Aegean Sea (entrance behind the Prince Eugene monument); the **Museum of Musical Instruments,** including pianos belonging to Beethoven, Brahms, and Schumann; the **Collection of Weapons** (admission to all three, 30 AS); and the vast ethnological museum, the **Museum für Volkerkunde** (separate admission 30 AS). *1010 Neue Burg, Heldenplatz, no phone. Open Wed.–Mon. 10–6. Museum für Volkerkunde, tel. 01/534-300. Open Wed.–Mon. 10–4.*

KARLSKIRCHE

Emperor Karl VI celebrated the end of a plague in 1713 by commissioning an extraordinary baroque church (on Karlsplatz) in honor of St. Charles (Karl) Borromeo, famous for his work with plague victims. Charles shows up all over the church—on the exterior twin pillars, the high altar, and the ceiling frescoes (which also show an angel setting fire to a copy of Luther's Bible). Gustav and Alma Mahler exchanged rings and said "Ja" here in 1902. *U-Bahn to Karlsplatz.*

KUNSTHAUSWIEN

If you're getting queasy at the thought of another baroque or Renaissance painting, check out this bizarre museum, designed by contemporary Austrian artist and architect Friedensreich Hundertwasser. The exterior, which caused quite a ruckus when it went up, is a hodgepodge of crooked tiles, black and white checkers, and colored windows. Inside is an equally entertaining collection of Hundertwasser's works. To see Hundertwasser's architectural philosophy in action, head to the nearby **Hundertwasserhaus** (Kegelgasse at Löwengasse). This seriously funky apartment building can only be viewed from the outside, as for some reason the residents aren't into herds of looky-loos stampeding through their home. *1030 Untere Weißgerberstr. 13, tel. 01/712–0491. U-Bahn to Schwedenplatz, then Tram N to Radetzkyplatz; walk under tracks, then left toward river. Admission 60 AS. Open daily 10–7.*

RINGSTRAßE

This ambitious piece of city planning, based around a single street that encircles the center of Vienna, was the Hapsburg Empire's extravagant final effort to buy off the grumbling middle class with great gobs of Kultur while, behind the scenes, tightening the autocratic screws loosened by the revolution of 1848. One of the first buildings to go up, the elaborate **Votivkirche,** set the aren't-we-lucky-to-have-the-Hapsburgs tone implicit in Ringstraße monumentalism. Within 30 years, costly buildings for virtually all the major cultural and political institutions had been erected on the Ringstraße, each a revival of some earlier architectural style considered symbolic of the building's function. Thus the **Staatsoper** (State Opera House) is neo-Italianate, the **Universität** neo-Renaissance, the **Parlament** neoclassical, the **Rathaus** (City Hall) neo–medieval guild.

How the Haps decided to organize the Ringstraße is not clear; most of the buildings look like they were randomly plunked down. Still, artists soon found the Ring's heavy emphasis on tradition oppressive, and in 1898 the **Secession Building** (1010 Friedrichstr. 12, tel. 01/587–5307; admission 60 AS; open Tues.–Fri. 10–6, weekends 10–4) began to display controversial modern works by Gustav Klimt and other artists in direct defiance of Ringstraße taste. Within only a few years, Klimt's Jugendstil became the new orthodoxy. Today the Secession Building displays Klimt's *Beethoven Frieze* and unusual rotating exhibitions.

Housing one of the world's great art collections, the 19th-century **Kunsthistorisches Museum** (Museum of Fine Arts) is home to centuries of Hapsburg artistic acquisitions and is Vienna's best-preserved example of budget-busting Ringstraße architecture. The extravagant central staircase alone, smothered by priceless works, sums up the museum's grand and essentially retrospective view of art. Its **Gemäldegalerie** (Painting Gallery) includes major works by the Old Masters, while the **Kunstkammer** (Art Chamber), under restoration until 1998, boasts an enormous collection of ornate miniature sculptures, metalwork, and specially commissioned artistic objects such as Cellini's dizzyingly elaborate *Saliera*, a golden salt cellar. The **Antikensammlung** (Collection of Greek and Roman Antiquities) is one of the world's leading collections of classical stuff. *Maria-Theresien-Platz, tel. 01/525–240. U2 to Babenburgerstr. Admission 60 AS–95 AS. Open Tues.–Sun. 10–6, Thurs. 10–9. Wheelchair entrance at Burgring 5.*

SCHÖNBRUNN

Schönbrunn palace, Austria's answer to Versailles, has grounds so vast that occupying armies have used it as a headquarters. Admission to the park, which has a nice hilltop view and lots of wooded pathways, is free, and the grounds are open daily from 6 AM to dusk. A six-year-old Mozart played for Maria Theresa in the **Hall of Mirrors.** In the **Blue Chinese Salon,** Emperor Karl I made history (or, rather, ended it) when he signed his abdication and resigned the crown in 1918, ending the 640-year Hapsburg domination of Austria. *Tel. 01/81113. Admission 80 AS to visit 20 rooms, 110 AS for 40 rooms (140 AS with tour). Open daily 8:30–5 (Nov.–Mar. until 4:30), tours (1¼ hrs) every other hour in English.*

Inside the palace, the **Wagenburg** (Imperial Coach Collection; tel. 01/877–3244; admission 30 AS; open Apr.–Oct., daily 9–6, Nov.–Mar., Tues.–Sun. 10–4) displays all kinds of royal wheels: coaches, carriages, sleighs, and the imperial hearse. The **Schmetterlinghaus** (Butterfly House, tel. 01/877–5087–421; admission 30 AS; open May–Sept., daily 10–4:30, Oct.–Apr., daily 10–3) is also way cool; flit in and check it out (entrance at Hietzing U-Bahn station).

STEPHANSDOM

In 1258, Ottokar II of Bohemia, having just conquered Vienna, ingratiated himself to his new subjects by ordering the construction of a new and much-improved Gothic version of the Stephansdom (formerly a small, fire-prone Romanesque church). The Hapsburgs gave Ottokar the boot in 1279 but continued the construction he had begun. The cathedral was never officially completed, and in 1579 the **North Tower** was capped with a makeshift Renaissance spire (by then, Gothic was passé). You can take an elevator (40 AS) up the North Tower, hike to the top of the Stephansdom's 450-ft **South Tower** (admission 25 AS), or, on a guided tour only, visit the **catacombs.** The latter have graves filled with enormous heaps of bones from plague victims, not to mention little bronze cases containing the innards of notable Hapsburgs. Note the "O5" carved into the stone to the right of the outer massive front door; the *5* is for the fifth letter of the alphabet, translating into OE (the *E* indicates an umlaut over the *O*) for Österreich (Austria). It was a covert sign of resistance to the Nazi takeover. *1010 Stephansplatz 1, tel. 01/5155–2526. Guided tours of the catacombs (40 AS) Mon.–Sat. every half hour 10–noon and 2:30–4:30, Sun. 2–4:30. English tours July and Aug., or by reservation.*

OTHER MUSEUMS

Akademie der bildenden Künste (Academy of Fine Arts). The impressive Old Masters collection includes the bizarre *Last Judgment,* by Hieronymus Bosch. *1010 Schillerplatz 3, tel. 01/5881–6225. U-Bahn to Karlsplatz. Admission 30 AS. Open Tues., Thurs., and Fri. 10–2, Wed. 10–1 and 3–6, weekends 9–1.*

Historisches Museum der Stadt Wien (Vienna Historical Museum). Take advantage of this excellent intro to the city, with archaeological finds, paintings by leading artists, and objects ranging from toys to weaponry. *1040 Karlsplatz, tel. 01/505–8747–021. Admission 50 AS. Open Tues.–Sun. 9–4:30.*

Museum für Angewandte Kunst/MAK (Museum of Applied Arts). Here lies everything from Oriental carpets to antique furniture to installations by contemporary artists. *1010 Stubenring 5, tel. 01/711–360. Admission 90 AS. Open Tues.–Sun. 10–6, until 9 on Thurs.*

Museum Beethoven-Haus. Beethoven inhabited several dozen dwellings around Vienna, but he spent most of his summers at 1190 Probusgasse 6, where in 1802 he wrote his *Heiligenstädter Testament* in poignant rage at his increasing deafness. The house now contains a small commemorative museum. Take Tram 37, and stop on the way at Pokornygasse to check out the **Eroicahaus** (1190 Döblinger Hauptstr. 92), where the big guy composed most of his Third Symphony. *Tel. 01/375408. Admission to each 25 AS. Both open Tues.–Sun. 9–12:15 and 1–4:30.*

Museum Sigmund-Freud-Haus. The father of modern psychoanalysis lived and worked here from 1891 until 1938, when he was persuaded to flee from the Nazis. Beyond a few pieces of original furniture, the only attractions are the scores of minute original documents and photographs affixed to the walls. *1090 Berggasse 19, tel. 01/319–1596. U2 to Schottentor. Admission 60 AS. Open July–Sept., daily 9–6, Oct.–June, daily 9–4.*

> *The Akademie der bildenden Künste twice denied admission to prospective art student Adolf Hitler.*

Schloß Belvedere. Prince Eugen of Savoy hung his hat in this former baroque palace. The Lower Belvedere houses Gothic art, while the Upper Belvedere has 19th- and 20th-century Austrian art and features the work of Gustav Klimt. *1030 Prinz-Eugen-Str. 27 (near the Südbahnhof), tel. 01/795–570. Admission 60 AS. Open Tues.–Sun. 10–5.*

CHEAP THRILLS

Every summer night around 9, the Rathaus becomes the stage for free **opera films.** Lots of cheap food and drink stands are set up nearby, and it's plenty of fun, even if you don't watch the opera. If you're dead serious about your classical music, take Tram 71 to Tor II and the **Zentralfriedhof** (Central Cemetery; open May–Aug., daily 7–7; shorter hrs off-season), where Beethoven, Schubert, Gluck, Hugo Wolf, Brahms, and Strauss the Elder and Younger all rest in section 32A. Schönberg is in section 32C.

Believe it or not, the Danube is clean enough to swim in, and the banks east of town host a major beach scene. On the south end of **Donauinsel** (U1 to Donauinsel) you'll find waterskiing, the world's longest water slide, and lots of topless sunbathers. Rent bikes and in-line skates below the Donauinsel U-Bahn stop. The huge, shady **Prater** park (U1 to Praterstern) is great for strolling or relaxing, and also has an amusement park. There's a huge **flea market** Saturdays 9–6 (9–3 or 4 during winter months) on Rechte Wienziele, south of Karlsplatz—a huge gathering of junk, cheap clothes, and cool antiques, and Ground Zero for cheesy souvenirs.

FESTIVALS

Music festivals take place almost year-round in Vienna. The biggie, worth planning a vacation around, is the **Wiener Festwochen** (tel. 01/589220), during May and June, when plays, operas, exhibitions, and other events seem to fill every hall in town.

AFTER DARK

BARS

To sample Vienna's bar scene, head to the **Bermuda Triangle,** the area between Hoher Markt and Franz-Josefs-Kai (U-Bahn to Schwedenplatz). **Kaktus** (1010 Seitenstettengasse 5, tel. 01/533–1938) is the most boisterous of the Triangle's nightspots, packed until 4 AM on weekends with a diverse twentysomething crowd. **Krah Krah** (1010 Rabensteig 8, tel. 01/533–8193) serves more than 50 different types of beer to college students listening to Euro power pop. Near Stephansplatz, the smoke-filled **Café**

Alt Wien (1010 Bäckerstr. 9, tel. 01/512–5222), one of Vienna's best, serves up beer and wine to a friendly crowd of intellectuals, students, and young professionals.

CLUBS

Jazz has a large following in Vienna; consult the journal *Falter* (28 AS) for the latest. **Jazzland** (1010 Franz-Josefs-Kai 29, tel. 01/533–2575), the granddaddy of Vienna jazz clubs, is still going strong. Black lights, red curtains, and deep throbbing beats shake one section of the **U4** (1120 Schönbrunner Str. 222, tel. 01/815–8307; open daily until 5 AM)—the other has fewer club kids, more tourists, and a slightly funkier beat. Either way you'll pay 50 AS–150 AS cover and 79 AS for mixed drinks, 57 AS for a beer. Take the U4 to Meidling Hauptstraße. **Volksgarten** (1010 Heldenplatz, tel. 01/533–0518; cover 70 AS–130 AS) is a major disco with a retractable roof. Get your fix of rock and blues at **Roter Engel** (Rabensteig 5, tel. 01/535–5368; cover 60 AS), where the mixed crowd is as likely to be sipping chardonnay as chugging beer.

CLASSICAL MUSIC AND OPERA

The 19th-century **Staatsoper** (1010 Opernring 1, tel. 01/514–440) stages major operas. The renowned Vienna Philharmonic can be heard at both the Staatsoper and the **Musikverein** (1010 Karlsplatz 6, tel. 01/50586–8194), but most seats belong to season-ticket holders; aim for standing room. The Vienna Symphony Orchestra appears most often at the **Konzerthaus** (1010 Lothringerstr. 20, tel. 01/712–1211). You can also watch first-rate opera at the **Volksoper** (1090 Währinger Str., tel. 01/51444–3318) and musicals (100 AS–1,000 AS) at **Theater an der Wien** (1060 Linke Wienzeile 6, tel. 01/587–0550) and **Raimund-Theater** (1060 Wallgasse 18, tel. 01/599770). *Stehplätze* (standing-room tickets; 20 AS–50 AS) are available at all national halls.

THEATER

Vienna's theater is rivaled only by that of London and Berlin, and cheap tickets abound. Inquire about current shows at the traditional **Burgtheater** (1010 Dr.-Karl-Lueger-Ring, tel. 01/514440), the more modern **Akademietheater** (1030 Lisztstr. 1, also 01/514440), the **Volkstheater** (1070 Neustiftgasse 1, tel. 01/523–2776, ticket window 01/523–3501), and the **Theater in der Josefstadt** (1080 Josefstädter Str. 24–26, tel. 01/402–5127). All four take July and August off. Year-round, you'll find avant-garde theater (most tickets 120 AS–300 AS) at **die theater Künstlerhaus** (1010 Karlsplatz 5, tel. 01/587–0504) and anything organized by **WUK** (1090 Währinger Str. 59, tel. 01/401–2142). If you want to see a play in English, go to the rococo **Vienna's English Theater** (1080 Josefsgasse 12, tel. 01/402–1260). Consult *Falter* for other venues.

NEAR VIENNA

BADEN

Thirty minutes from downtown Vienna, this serenely elegant spa town, with its lovely, sloping Kurpark gardens, gives you an idea of how 19th-century Viennese high society took the waters. To pamper yourself in grand style, stay at the regal Hotel Sauerhof, or just go for a day to get the full body treatment at their Beauty Farm. Doubles start at 2,500 AS. *Weilburgstr. 11–13, A-2500 Baden, tel. 02252/412510, fax 02252/48047. Take the blue tram or bus leaving frequently from the corner of Kärntnerstr. and Opernring, opposite the Opera House; 54 AS.*

THE DANUBE VALLEY

Austria's Danube (*Donau*) Valley has been producing world-famous wine for millennia. Starting with the nectar-loving Celts, the tradition continued after the Romans moved in, and today locals still tend lovingly to their grapes. Throughout the valley, vineyards cascade from hill to bank, and marvelous castles and abbeys appear suddenly behind every river bend. Don't leave the valley without indulging in a little vino and regional culture at the many Heurigen, where vintners open up their gardens and serve the latest vintage.

For a more aerobic take on the valley, rent two wheels and hit the **Donauradweg.** Austria's most famous bike trail starts in Passau (Germany) and runs through Linz, Melk, Krems, and Vienna all the way to Bratislava, in Slovakia. Many cyclists take advantage of it, so don't be surprised to see everyone from kiddies with belt packs to grandmas in black Spandex shorts. The **Donauuferbahn** (Danube train) also follows the river from Vienna's Franz-Josefs-Bahnhof upstream to St. Valentin, 20 minutes short of Linz. With a single Vienna–Salzburg ticket, you can make as many stops as you want for up to four days; with a round-trip ticket, you can do the same for up to two months. Probably the loveliest, and easily the most romantic, way to view the area is from a ferry; the stretch from Krems to Melk is especially well-endowed with natural and man-made gems. Bother **Blue Danube Schiffahrt** (1020 Handelskai 265, Vienna, tel. 01/72750–222) for boat information.

LINZ

Austria's third-largest city and the home of large steel and chemical industries, Linz is underrated, but its appealing position straddling the Danube makes it an ideal stopping point for cyclists along the river valley. With a well-preserved Altstadt and excellent museums, Linz may be the best place outside Vienna to dip into urban Austrian culture.

Linz also holds the dubious distinction of having produced both Adolf Eichmann and Adolf Hitler. However, the city has quietly made significant positive contributions to the nation's culture and heritage. Astronomer Johannes Kepler lived here during his years as court mathematician for Upper Austria, trying to figure out what makes the world go 'round; composer Anton Bruckner played the organ at Linz's Alter Dom; writer Rainer Maria Rilke attended the Handelsschule on Rudigierstraße; and philosopher Ludwig Wittgenstein attended the Realschule (a year after Hitler dropped out).

BASICS

The staff at **Freudenverkehrszentrale** (Hauptplatz 5, tel. 0732/7070–1777) has maps and lodging information. The **American Express** office (Bürgerstr. 14, tel. 0732/669013; open weekdays 9–5:30, Sat. 9–noon) changes currency and books excursions.

COMING AND GOING

Linz lies roughly halfway between Vienna (2 hrs, 294 AS) and Salzburg (1¾ hrs, 212 AS), on the rail line. Linz's main strip, **Landstraße,** runs north from the Hauptbahnhof to **Hauptplatz,** the focal point of town. You can walk there in 20–30 minutes, or take Tram 3. Buses and trams cost 18 AS, or 35 AS for a day pass. Rent a **bike** from the station or call a **taxi** at 0732/6969.

WHERE TO SLEEP

There are no Privatzimmer in Linz. The smallest, most central, and nicest hostel in town is the **Jugendherberge Linz (HI)** (Kapuzinerstr. 14, tel. 0732/782720; beds 160 AS), where there's no curfew or lockout. From the station take Tram 3 to Taubenmarkt and walk down Promenade (which becomes Klammstr.) to Kapuzinerstraße. There's an on-site bar (and an 11 PM curfew) at the more remote **Jugendgästehaus Linz (HI)** (Stanglhofweg 3, tel. 0732/664434), where singles are 310 AS, doubles 420 AS; to get there, walk through the park in front of the station and take Bus 19, 22, 27, or 45 to Leondinger Straße, then backtrack a block and turn left. The simple **Goldenes Dachl** (Hafnerstr. 27, tel. 0732/675480) has some huge, modern doubles with showers from 515 AS. The **Gasthof Wilder Mann** (Goethestr. 14, tel. 0732/656078; doubles from 750 AS) is close to both the station and Hauptplatz; from the Hauptbahnhof, take Tram 3 to Hauptplatz and turn left on Hofgasse. **Zum Schwarzen Bären** has a prime location in the center of the Altstadt and plain, comfortable rooms. Singles are 680 AS and doubles 880 AS, including breakfast.

FOOD

Creative types crowd **S'Kistl** (Altstadt 17, tel. 0732/784545; closed Sun.) until 2 AM for the finger-food buffet and more than 25 different beers. Artists and lefties munch on cheap, healthy grub at **Gelbes Krokodil** (Dametzstr. 30, tel. 0732/784182), open weekdays 11 AM–1 AM, weekends 5 PM–1 AM; look for it in the Theater Moviemento complex near Mozartstraße. Just off Landstraße, **Kasper-Keller** (Spittelwiese 1, tel. 0732/773692; closed weekends) serves traditional Austrian fare (under 98 AS) in a cozy cellar restaurant. Do-it-yourselfers can visit the supermarket **Billa** (Landstr. 44, near Rudigierstr.). For a taste of café culture, kick back in **Jentschke** (Landstr. 24, tel. 0732/770089; closed Sun.), an intimate lookout on the pedestrian zone.

WORTH SEEING

A trip to Linz would be wasted without stops in at least a few of the city's museums. In the castle up the hill from Hauptplatz is **Schloßmuseum Linz,** an earthy and appealing collection spanning all aspects of daily life along the Danube from the early Middle Ages to the turn of the century. Displays on folk art, pottery, musical instruments, medieval weapons, domestic architecture, and 18th-century science all have their own rooms. *Tummelplatz 10, just west of Alstadt, tel. 0732/774419. Admission 50 AS. Open Tues.–Fri. 9–5, weekends 10–4.*

Picking up where the Schloßmuseum leaves off, the **Neue Galerie der Stadt Linz** is across the river, on the second floor of a shopping mall. The modern Austrian gang's all here, including Klimt, Kubin, and Albin Egger-Lienz. *Blütenstr. 15, tel. 0732/7070–3600. Admission 40 AS. Open weekdays 10–6 (Thurs. until 10), Sat. 10–1.*

Composer Anton Bruckner was cathedral organist for a dozen years at the 17th-century **Alter Dom** (open daily 7–noon and 3–7), the main cathedral in town during Linz's heyday. On the other side of the main drag, the Promenade, take a peek at the three lovely courtyards of the **Landhaus** and look for the **Planetenbrunnen** (planet fountain) showing the five-planet solar system. Hey, it was the 16th century. Further south on Herrenstraße, you can't miss the **Neuer Dom.** The 19th-century bishop who commissioned this huge Gothic structure bowed to Vienna and ordered that the cathedral not stand higher than the Stephansdom (at 440 ft, it's 10 ft shorter). Just up the hill from the Schloßmuseum is the small, well-restored **Martinskirche,** which dates back to AD 799 and may be the oldest church in Austria.

AFTER DARK

Linz is a pretty hopping town at night, with the scene conveniently centered around the **Bermuda Triangle,** bordered by the Hauptplatz, Hofgasse, Altstadt, and Klostergasse—the idea being that people who venture into this area end up having too much fun to come out again. Head to the underground **17er Keller** (Hauptplatz 17, tel. 0732/779000) for cool jazz tunes and a relaxed student atmosphere. Go through the arch on Hauptplatz and look for the poster-plastered door.

NEAR LINZ

MAUTHAUSEN

Adolf Hitler planned to make his native Linz a center of German culture, but he had no qualms about building Austria's main *Konzentrationslager* (concentration camp) only half an hour down the Danube in Mauthausen. The site includes a small museum and memorials to the more than 110,000 people murdered here, but the value of a visit lies more in the significance of the space than in the quality of the displays. The camp is a 5-km (3-mi) signposted walk from the Mauthausen train station; local buses drop you 3 km (2 mi) closer to the camp. From the Linz Busbahnhof, the ride takes 50 minutes (56 AS), and the last bus heads back around 6 PM—check the schedule. *Tel. 07238/2269. Admission 25 AS. Open Apr.–Sept., daily 8–6, Oct.–Mar., daily 8–4. For more information, call the Jewish Welcome Service in Vienna, tel. 01/533–8891 or 01/533–2730.*

MELK

If it had not been for an architect by the name of Jacob Prandtauer, Melk probably wouldn't even be mentioned in most European history books. The town got off to a great start as the imperial residence of the first five Babenberg rulers, but it was cast aside in favor of Klosterneuburg and, eventually, Vienna. It would have seemed natural for Melk to slip into the background and become an unremarkable, albeit quaint, town on the banks of the Danube. In 1700, however, Herr Prandtauer began his transformation of a former 11th-century fortress into the magnificent baroque **Benediktinerstift** (Benedictine Abbey). Now one of the Continent's finest examples of baroque architecture, it attracts hundreds of thousands of visitors annually.

A permanent exhibit entitled *The Monastery at Melk, Past and Present* has been established in the abbey's imperial chambers, which once accommodated such guests as Pope Pius VI, Maria Theresa, and Napoléon. All of the objects on display were culled from the monastery's treasury, archives, and library, but the centerpiece of the collection is the famous **Melk Cross,** encrusted with precious stones and said to hold a piece of the holy cross inside. At the heart of the abbey is the beautiful **baroque church.** The art here alone is reason enough to visit Melk, and includes an inspiring ceiling fresco by Salzburg master Michael Rottmayr as well as altar paintings by Troger and Beduzzi. Impossible to over-look is the radiant high altar designed by Antonio Beduzzi, representing the connection between God, Melk, and the Benedictine Order. *Tel. 02752/2312–232, admission 55 AS. Abbey open Apr.–Oct., daily 9–5, Nov.–Mar. only on guided tours at 11 and 2.*

BASICS

Melk's **tourist office** (Babenbergerstr. 1, tel. 02752/2307–32; open daily July and Aug., shorter hrs off season) stocks the useful Melk *Stadtplan* (city map) and a list of accommodations. Trains depart Melk hourly for Vienna (1 hr, 140 AS) and Linz (1½ hrs, 160 AS). To reach Krems, take Bus 1451 from the front of the train station (1 hr, 70 AS). Ferries leave the **DDSG ferry station** (tel. 02752/25900) daily May–September for Krems (238 AS), Vienna (530 AS), and Linz (328 AS). To reach the station, take Kremser Straße, cross the bridge, and continue to the end.

WHERE TO SLEEP AND EAT

Book a room at the friendly **Gasthof Goldener Stern** (Sterngasse 17, tel. 02752/2214), a favorite with cyclists. Rooms are 270 AS–300 AS for singles, 440 AS–520 AS for doubles. The newly renovated **Jugendherberge Melk (HI)** offers 104 comfortable beds in clean quads, each with its own shower and a price tag of 160 AS. *Abt-Karl-Str. 42, tel. 02752/2681. From Bahnhof, head down Bahnhofstr. and turn right at Abt-Karl-Str. Reception open 5 PM–10 PM. Closed mid-Oct.–Mar.*

For traditional Austrian dishes, seat yourself at one of the outdoor tables in front of **Goldener Stern** (Sterngasse 17, near Rathausplatz, tel. 02752/2214) and try the *Semmelknodel* (dumpling) with mush-room sauce. Grab coffee and cake at **Café Bäckerei** (Hauptstr. 1, tel. 02752/2350).

KREMS

In the heart of the Wachau—the Danube Valley's loveliest and most historic stretch—Krems is a 1,000-year-old town of winding cobblestone lanes brimming with medieval gems. The lovingly restored Alt-stadt, bisected by the east–west Landstraße, sits in the shadow of the Gothic **Piaristenkirche**; Martin Johann "Kremser" Schmidt, the town's most famous artist, created all the altarpieces here, as well as the frescoes in the nearby baroque **Pfarrkirche St. Veit** (Pfarrplatz). **Dominikanerkirche** (Theaterplatz 8–9, tel. 02732/84927), no longer used as a church, houses the truly excellent **city historical museum** and has information on the region's wine culture in the **Weinbaumuseum** (admission to both 40 AS; open Mar.–Nov., Tues. 9–6, Wed.–Sat. 1–6). Alas, one cannot live by sights alone; after you've satisfied your cultural needs, grab a *Heurigenkalender,* which lists the local wine taverns.

Krems is a mere train ride from Linz (2 hrs, 210 AS). Crash at **Radfahrjugendherberge Krems (HI)** (Ringstr. 77, tel. 02732/83452; beds 190 AS; closed Oct.–Mar.) or take one of the attractive rooms in the **Hotel Alte Post** (Obere Landstr. 32, tel. 02732/82276; doubles from 580 AS; closed Jan. and Feb.). The **tourist office** (Undstr. 6, tel. 02732/82676) may have dirt on other accommodations.

GRAZ

Native son Arnold Schwarzenegger hasn't managed to give Graz quite the cultural cachet that Mozart bestowed on Vienna and Salzburg, so this second-largest Austrian city (and capital of the province of Styria) has to work harder to grab the spotlight. The Styriarte summer music festival has become one of the most prestigious cultural events in the country, and Graz's opera house now attracts top companies like the Bolshoi. With its skyline dominated by the squat 16th-century clock tower, the city has a well-preserved medieval center in the Italian Renaissance style, creating a scene rather more Mediterranean than Austrian.

BASICS

The **main tourist office** (Herrengasse 16, tel. 0316/80750) has information on Graz and surroundings, books rooms (30 AS fee), and sells bus/tram tickets. A day pass is 40 AS; otherwise you'll pay 20 AS per ride. For the best currency-exchange deals, hit the post office or **Die 1rste Bank** (Hans-Sachs-Gasse 5; open weekdays 8–12:30 and 1:30–3:30, Thurs. until 5:30, and Fri. until 2:30 PM).

COMING AND GOING

Graz is 2½ hours by train from Vienna (296 AS). The **Hauptbahnhof** is a 30-minute walk or a short tram ride (Tram 3, 6, or 14) west of downtown; Hauptplatz and Herrengasse mark the very center. The university area starts just up the hill, on the other side of Glacisstraße. For a **taxi,** dial 0316/878.

WHERE TO SLEEP

The doubles (from 980 AS) at **Hotel Grazerhof** (Stubenberggasse 10, tel. 0316/824358) are the best deal in the Altstadt, but the management can be unpleasant. If you want to stay in the Altstadt and don't mind laying out some money, go to the classy **Hotel Erzherzog Johann** (Sackstr. 3, tel. 0316/811–616, fax 0316/811–515). Rooms (doubles from 1,900 AS) are spacious and furnished in Biedermeier style; a huge buffet breakfast is included. Five minutes from the train station is the **Hotel Strasser** (Eggenberger Gürtl 11, tel. 0316/913977), with doubles from 560 to 690 AS. Near Schloß Eggenberg (i.e., far from everything else) is **"Alt Eggenberg" Wagenhofer** (Baiernstr. 3, tel. 0316/586615), with doubles and triples for 280 AS per person; from the station, take Tram 1 to Alt Eggenberg. The local **hostel** (Idlhofgasse 74, tel. 0316/914876) has newly renovated singles (380 AS), doubles (330 AS per person), and quads (270 AS per person); from the station, walk down Annenstraße 3 blocks and turn right on Idlhofgasse (20 mins).

FOOD

Styrian specialties such as the tart, pale-orange *Schilcher* wine and intensely nutty *Kurbiskernöl* (pumpkin-seed oil) give Graz a flavor of its own. The areas around the university (Zinzendorfgasse, east of the Stadtpark) and the Hauptplatz have a wealth of eateries for the not-so-wealthy. Typical Austrian dishes at reasonable prices can be found at **Glockenspiel Keller** (Mehlplatz 3). For tasty, cafeteria-style veggie fare, head to **Mangold's Vollwertrestaurant** (Griesgasse 10, near Südtirolerplatz, tel. 0316/918002; closed Sat. evening and all day Sun.). Cozy and romantic **Stainzerbauer** (Burgergasse 4, tel. 0316/821106) offers Styrian specialties like *Schinkenfleckerl,* a ham-and-noodle dish, and, for heartier appetites, pork ribs with garlic bread. Be sure to try the crispy salad tossed with Kurbiskernöl and yogurt dressing.

WORTH SEEING

Graz's main attractions all lie in or near the Altstadt. The tourist office's *Old Town Walk* brochure (10 AS) gives a brief history of most sights. The **Hauptplatz,** with its daily produce market, is within walking distance of the majority of Graz's museums and shops. Northwest of the Hauptplatz you'll find the late-Gothic **Dom.** A faded 15th-century fresco in the cathedral depicts the horrors of life at the time (the plague, the locusts, the Turks); inside, the drab cathedral is surprisingly rich and ornate. Across from the Dom are the ruins of the former **Burg** (imperial palace), including the **Burgtor** (castle gate), which leads into the Stadtpark, and the striking double-spiral **Gothic staircase.** To reach the **university,** trek east through the park to Heinrichstrasse, then go 3 blocks and look to your right.

Founded in 1811 by Archduke Johann, the Landesmuseum Johanneum is the oldest public museum in Austria. The museum has several branches. The **Landzeughaus** (armory; Herrengasse 16, tel. 0316/8017–4810; admission 80 AS; open Tues.–Sun. 9–5) houses more than 32,000 pieces of heavy artillery, swords, and other deadly pointy things used against the Turks. All kinds of art from Romanesque to late baroque are displayed in the **Alte Gallerie** (Neutorgasse 45, tel. 0316/8017–4770; admission 60 AS; open Tues.–Sun. 10–5). Ponder more recent artistic endeavors, including an interesting sculpture made of acrylic, formaldehyde, and sausage, in the **Neue Gallerie** (Sackstr. 16, Palais Herberstain, tel. 0316/829155; admission 60 AS; open Tues.–Sun. 10–6, Thurs. 10–8).

The most beautiful addition to the Landesmuseum is **Schloß Eggenberg** (admission 80 AS), on the western outskirts of Graz. Its magnificent rococo **Prunkräume** (State Rooms) include the large **Planetensaal** (Planet Hall), so named for the cycle of paintings depicting the terrestrial powers, celestial constellations, seven planets, and zodiac signs. The rooms of the Prunkräme can only be seen on the hourly tours given April–October 9–noon and 2–5. *Eggenberger Allee 90, tel. 0316/5832640. Tram 1 to Schloß Eggenberg, or Tram 7 to Franzsteinergasse.*

SALZBURG

Against the dramatic backdrop of the medieval fortress on the Mönchsberg, Salzburg gives you a better idea of what Wolfgang Amadeus Mozart experienced than Vienna's 19th-century pomp does. Salzburg features exquisite baroque and Gothic churches, real Alpine scenery, and a rich musical tradition. From the end of July through August, the **Salzburger Sommer Festspiele** fills the town with music, much of it composed by Salzburg's most famous resident. Salzburg's other cash cow is *The Sound of Music*, which was filmed here in the '60s. When you see just how many tourists swarm Salzburg to see Mozart/*Sound*iana, you won't wonder why Salzburgers have a reputation, even among other Austrians, of being aloof. If you want to see the real Salzburg, you'll have to come during the off season, when the locals come out of hiding; otherwise, take a long walk along the banks of the Salzach River, visit the local bars and hangouts, and check out the university area and its students.

BASICS

Call the **Central Office** (tel. 0662/889870; open Mon.–Thurs. 8–4, Fri. 8–2) for general phone inquiries. **Information Hauptbahnhof** (Bahnsteig 2A, in Hauptbahnhof, tel. 0662/88987 ext. 340; open daily 8:15 AM–8:30 PM; shorter hrs off season) stocks brochures and books rooms (30 AS fee). Ditto for **Information Mozartplatz** (Mozartplatz 5; open daily 9–8; shorter hrs off season), which also sells concert tickets. While you're here, take care of your **American Express** (Mozartplatz 5, tel. 0662/8080; open weekdays 9–5:30, Sat. 9–noon) needs. Next door, **Information der Salzburger Land Tourismus** (tel. 0662/ 422232) has hiking and mountain-biking information. For postal biz 24 hours a day (including currency exchange), hit the **Bahnhofpost,** next to the train station (Südtiroler Platz 17, tel. 0662/88970; postal code 5020).

COMING AND GOING

Frequent trains leave Salzburg's **train station** (tel. 0662/1717), a 20-minute walk north of the center, for Vienna (3 hrs, 396 AS), Munich (2 hrs, 286 AS), Zürich (6 hrs, 846 AS), Venice (6½ hrs, 484 AS), and Prague (8 hrs, 486 AS). From the **Bundesbus** station, in front of the Hauptbahnhof, you can hop buses to Kitzbühel (Bus 3060, 2¾ hrs, 116 AS) and the Salzkammergut lake region (*see* Near Salzburg, *below*).

GETTING AROUND

Part of Salzburg's charm is the rushing Salzach River, which splits the town in half. On the eastern side of the river are the Hauptbahnhof and the not-so-new Neustadt. Close to the river's edge is the green oasis of **Mirabellgarten** and the Neustadt's central square, **Mirabellplatz.** On the west side of the Salzach is the Altstadt, which backs up against the towering cliffs of the Mönchsberg—easily ascended via the Mönchsbergaufzug, an elevator inside the mountain. The Altstadt's main thoroughfare is the pedestrian-only **Getreidegasse.** Still farther south along the river is **Nonntaler Hauptstraße,** just below which is the main transfer point for city buses, at the foot of the Staatsbrücke (State Bridge). Late at night, **taxis** congregate on the Neustadt side of the Staatsbrücke and at the Hauptbahnhof; call 0662/8111 to order one.

BY BIKE

Fantastic paths run along the **Salzach,** and everyone in Salzburg turns out on a sunny day. Rent a bike at the Hauptbahnhof (Window 3) for 100 AS per day (50 AS with valid rail ticket).

BY BUS

Buses 1, 2, 5, 6, 51, and 55 travel between the Hauptbahnhof, Mirabellplatz, and the Altstadt 6 AM–11 PM. Tickets cost 19 AS on board, 17 AS from a ticket machine at major bus stops; you can also get a day pass (38 AS) or a week pass (100 AS) from the machine or a tobacco shop. When you get on, stamp your ticket in one of the blue boxes.

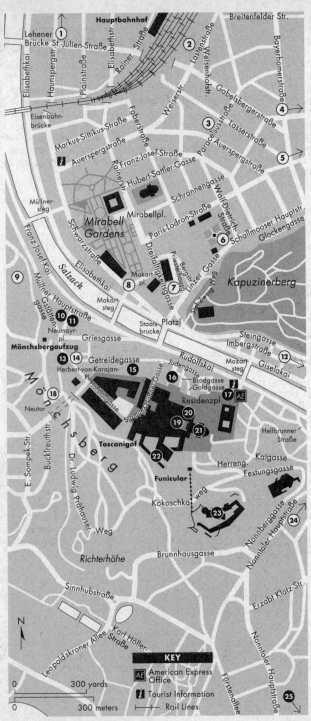

SALZBURG

Sights ●

Alter Markt, **16**

Bürgerspital
Spielzeug-
museum, **13**

Dom, **21**

Franziskaner-
kirche, **19**

Haus der Natur, **10**

Hohensalzburg
Fortress, **23**

Mozart's
Geburtshaus, **15**

Mozartplatz, **17**

Museum Carolino
Augusteum, **11**

Residenz, **20**

Schloß Hellbrun, **25**

Stiftskirche
St. Peter, **22**

Lodging ○

Bergland, **5**

Blaue Gans, **14**

Camping
Gnigl/Ost, **4**

Gasthaus
Bürgerwehr, **18**

Haunspergstraße
(HI), **1**

Hotel Bristol, **8**

International Youth
Hostel, **3**

Jugendherberge
Aigen (HI), **12**

Jugendgästehaus
Nonntal (HI), **24**

Junger Fuchs, **6**

Sandwirt, **2**

Schloß
Mönchstein, **9**

Schwarzes
Rössl, **7**

WHERE TO SLEEP

Because so many visitors pass through Salzburg, there are plenty of well-run accommodations. The tourist office has lists of Privatzimmer and will book you into a pension or hotel for a 30 AS fee. The numerous hostels are your best bet for a central location at a decent rate; many also book *Sound of Music* and salt-mine tours at a discount. If everything listed below is full, **Schwarzes Rössl** (Priesterhausgasse 6, tel. 0662/874426) has doubles for 640 AS. **Camping Ost/Gnigl** (Parscher Str. 4, tel. 0662/643060; closed mid-Sept.–mid-May) is the nearest campground, readily accessible via Bus 29 from Mirabellplatz (direction: Langwied). Sites run 50 AS per person plus 20 AS per tent.

UNDER 500 AS • Junger Fuchs. This clean pension is a 10-minute walk from the Altstadt; just watch out for the narrow halls and low ceilings. Singles are 260 AS, doubles 380 AS, triples 480 AS, and showers 15 AS extra. *Linzer Gasse 54, tel. 0662/875496. From Hauptbahnhof, bus 1, 2, 5, 6, 51, or 55 to Makartplatz. Reception open 10–7.*

Sandwirt. The place is a little old, but it's clean, well-maintained, and right behind the train station. Better still, guests have free laundry rights. Singles start at 280 AS, doubles at 440 AS, and triples at 600 AS, breakfast included. *Lastenstr. 6a, tel. 0662/874351. Cross to back of Hauptbahnhof, take footbridge over tracks, left on Lastenstr. Reception open 7 AM–8 PM.*

UNDER 600 AS • Bergland. The friendly owner pours drinks in the cozy bar, serves a complimentary breakfast buffet, and maintains 18 tip-top rooms. Reserve ahead if possible. Singles with shower are 440 AS, doubles 580 AS, triples with bath 960 AS. *Rupertgasse 15, tel. 0662/872318, fax 0662/8723188. Turn left out of Hauptbahnhof and left under tracks to Gabelsbergerstr., right on Bayernhamerstr., left on Rupertgasse (20 mins). Closed Nov.–Dec.*

UNDER 800 AS • Blaue Gans. Just down the street from Mozart's birthplace, these rooms are simple but utterly adequate and the best deal for the location, so try to book ahead. Singles without bath are 400 AS; doubles without bath are 750 AS. Breakfast included. *Getreidegasse 43, tel. 0662/841317, fax 0662/842491.*

HOSTELS

Gasthaus Bürgerwehr. Salzburg's smallest hostel has a magnificent mountaintop view of the city. You can reserve only one day in advance, and the place is always booked by noon; but you can call after 4 PM and pray for a no-show. There's a 1 AM curfew. Beds go for 120 AS, showers 10 AS. *Mönchsberg 19c, tel. 0662/841729. From Hauptbahnhof, Bus 1, 2, or 15 to Mönchsbergaufzug; take Mönchsberg elevator (17 AS, 27 AS round-trip), follow signs downward (right) through stone arch, and make sharp loop left uphill. Reception open 8 AM–9 PM, closed mid-Oct.–Apr.*

Haunspergstraße (HI). It's sparkling and quiet, but it's only open in July and August. Beds are 160 AS, including sheets, shower, and breakfast. There's a midnight curfew. *Haunspergstr. 27, tel. 0662/875030, fax 0662/883477. From Hauptbahnhof, go straight up Kaiserschützenstr. (which becomes Jahnstr.), then right on Haunspergstr.*

International Youth Hotel. Experience threadbare rooms stuffed with Americans and Australians. There's a free *Sound of Music* screening daily at 1:30 PM. Beds go for 130 AS–150 AS, doubles 340 AS; Breakfast (30 AS–55 AS). You can also shower (10 AS), stash your luggage (1 AS–10 AS), and exchange money here. The curfew is 1 AM. *Paracelsusstr. 9, tel. 0662/879649, fax 0662/878810. Cross to back of Hauptbahnhof, take footbridge over tracks, left on Lastenstr., right on Merianstr., left on Paracelsusstr. Reception open 24 hrs. Laundry (50 AS).*

Jugendgästehaus Nonntal (HI). Salzburg's largest hostel has a café and a tame disco on the premises, as well as a midnight curfew. Per person, beds in dorms are 160 AS, doubles 260 AS, and quads 210 AS, including breakfast, shower, and sheets. They'll accept reservations in writing or by fax only. *Josef-Preis-Allee 18, tel. 0662/8426700 or 0662/846857, fax 0662/841101. From Hauptbahnhof, Bus 5 or 55 to Nonntaler Hauptstr./Justizgebäude, continue on Nonntaler Hauptstr., left on Josef-Preis-Allee. Lockout 9 AM–11 AM. Laundry (30 AS).*

Jugendherberge Aigen (HI). This newly renovated hostel is a 30-minute walk from the Altstadt. Beds cost 160 AS, including breakfast, sheets, and shower, and they'll store your luggage if need be. There's a midnight curfew. *Aigner Str. 34, tel. 0662/623248, fax 0662/6232–4813. From Hauptbahnhof, Bus 1 or 2 to Hanuschplatz, or Bus 5, 6, 51, or 55 to Mozartsteg, then Bus 49 to Finanzamt. Reception open 7–9 and 5–midnight.*

SPLURGE

Hotel Bristol. Elizabeth Taylor and Richard Burton holed up here in the '60s, during the filming of *Where Eagles Dare*, and you can see why. Recently revamped, each room is decorated in a different sumptuous style. The hotel's Polo Lounge restaurant offers nouvelle Austrian cuisine. Doubles start at 2,800 AS, buffet breakfast included. *Makartplatz 4, tel. 0662/873557, fax 0662/873557–6. From the Altstadt, take the Makart-Steg footbridge across the river, cross Schwarzstr. to Makartplatz; from the train station go down Rainerstr. past the Mirabell to Makartplatz. Closed Jan.–Feb.*

Schloß Mönchstein. This palatial mountain retreat is in its own little world, complete with gardens and hiking trails, yet it's minutes from the center of Salzburg. The award-winning Paris Lodron is considered the finest restaurant in the city. Doubles start at 2,900 AS, breakfast included. *Mönchsberg Park 26, tel. 0662/848555–0, fax 0662/848559. From the Altstadt, take the Mönchberg lift and follow the signs along the wooded trail to the Schloß.*

FOOD

Steer clear of the Altstadt if you're tight on cash, and join the locals at the cheaper joints across the river. Three blocks from the train station, **Steierischen Weinstuben** (St.-Julien-Str. 9, tel. 0662/874790) serves working-class Salzburgers hot meals (80 AS–145 AS) and hosts live traditional music until 3 AM. Hit **Uni-Café** (Sigmund-Haffner-Gasse 11, near Staatsbrücke, tel. 0662/8044–6909) weekdays for filling cafeteria-style lunches (40 AS–56 AS) in slick art-deco surroundings. The **Schrannemarkt,** on Schrannengasse in the Neustadt, is the place to come for fruits and veggies every Thursday until 1 PM; otherwise, head to the open-air **Grünmarkt** on Universitätsplatz, open weekdays 6–6, Saturday 6–1.

UNDER 110 AS • Zum Fidelen Affen (at the Faithful Ape). Across the river from the Altstadt, this small brew pub serves up tasty Austrian dishes to go with its house beer. Open daily 5–11 PM. *Priesterhausgasse 8, tel. 0662/877361. Cash only.*

Zwettler's Gastwirtschaft. On a quiet plaza in the Altstadt, this comfortable student bistro serves cheap daily specials like spinach dumplings in garlic-ham sauce. *Kaigasse 3, tel. 0662/840044.*

UNDER 150 AS • Goldener Zirkel. Please your insides with good, solid, cheap Austrian fare in the Altstadt. *Papagenoplatz, tel. 0662/841106. Closed Sat. night and all day Sun.*

UNDER 180 AS • Stiftskeller St. Peter. People don't come here for the food, which is only so-so; but you can't beat the atmosphere, especially if you're lucky enough to get a table in the courtyard, with its stone archways and vine-covered trellises. *St. Peter Bezirk 1/4, across from Franziskanerkirche, tel. 0662/8482680.*

Zum Eulenspiegel. Here's a warren of cozy rooms decorated in a variety of charming antique styles. Try the potato goulash with chunks of sausage and beef in a creamy paprika sauce, or the house specialty, fish stew Provençal (served at lunch, or all day in the bar downstairs). *Hagenauerplatz, 2, tel. 0662/843180. Closed Sun. except during the music festival.*

CAFÉS

A favorite among Salzburgers is **Niemetz** (Herbert-von-Karajan-Platz 11, tel. 0662/843367; closed Sun.), where you can while away the hours amid sugarplum kitsch. **Café Tomaselli** (Alter Markt 9, tel. 0662/844488), established in 1705, is the oldest café in Salzburg; it's got a plush interior and a view of the Alter Markt and Mozartplatz. Directly across from Tomaselli is **Café Fürst** (Brodgasse 13, tel. 0662/843759), which offers a greater variety of pastries and gets credit for the original *Mozartkugel,* a dark-chocolate ball stuffed with marzipan. Take the Mönchsberg elevator to **Hotel Schloß Mönchstein** (Mönchsberg Park 26, tel. 0662/8485550), where every Sunday between 3 and 4 you can sip your coffee to the tune of a free harp concert. In fine weather the concert is held outdoors in the garden, overlooking the rooftops of Salzburg.

WORTH SEEING

In the pristine Altstadt, south of the Salzach River, the brooding hill-top Hohensalzburg Fortress and the airy Italianate **Residenz** of the archbishops, below, compete for aesthetic dominance. Since Salzburg was long an archbishopric, it's not surprising that the Altstadt is dominated by religious buildings. The recently restored **Franziskanerkirche,** dating from the 8th century, hosts a steady stream of concerts beneath its bright burgundy roof. **Stiftskirche St. Peter,** a luxurious Romanesque-turned-rococo church, marks the site of St. Rupert's 7th-century monastery, which grew to become the city of Salzburg. If you're planning a whirlwind tour of the sights, consider the **Salzburg Card** (24 hrs for 190 AS, 48 hrs for 270 AS, or 72 hrs for 360 AS), which entitles you to free transportation in the city and free admission to most museums.

DOM

Gazing at the restored baroque interior and breathtaking arched roof of Salzburg's Dom, you'd never know that a bomb dropped right through the huge central dome during World War II. Check out the massive 13th-century baptismal font in the corner, used to baptize an infant Wolfgang Mozart in 1756. The composer was the Dom's organist for three years, and many of his early pieces were first performed here. Check the schedules out front for organ concerts (150 AS) and *Domkonzerte* (choral concerts; 260 AS); buy tickets at the door. *Domplatz 1, tel. 0662/841162. Admission free. Open daily 7–7.*

HOHENSALZBURG FORTRESS

Although a recent scrub has restored its pristine white color, the fortress overlooking Salzburg was never the place to be swept away by Prince Charming. It was actually enlarged by Archbishop Leonhard "The Turnip" von Keutschach to keep pace with modern techniques of warfare and torture. The fortress supposedly provided Salzburg's less-than-popular ruling archbishops with a siege-proof hideout, though the 50-minute tour (30 AS extra) shows you where angry peasants catapulted a cannonball into the main room. Also inside, the **Burg-Museum** (30 AS including tour) has nifty torture devices, armor, and weapons. To reach the *Festung* (fortress), take the *Festungsbahn* (69 AS round-trip; open May–Sept., daily 9–9; Oct.–Apr., daily 9–5), a funicular railway launched from behind Friedhof St. Peter, or make the steep 15-minute walk up Festungsgasse. *Mönchsberg 34, tel. 0662/8042–2133. Admission to Festung 35 AS. Open July–Sept., daily 8–7; Apr.–June and Oct., daily 9–6; Nov.–Mar., daily 9–5. Daily tours in English Apr.–Oct., 9:30–5; Nov.–Mar., 10–4:30.*

> *It was in the white gazebo on the grounds of Hellbrunn that a suspiciously mature-looking Liesl and Rolf professed their adolescent love.*

MOZART'S GEBURTSHAUS

Mozart complained that audiences in his native city were no more responsive than tables and chairs, but of course that's mostly what you'll see in his birthplace. Still, home is home, and this was Mozart's (when he wasn't away delighting foreign gentry) until he was 17. The child prodigy's 1760 clavichord is here, as is the 1780 pianoforte he preferred later on. *Getreidegasse 9, tel. 0662/844313. Admission 65 AS. Open daily 9–6 (July–Aug. 9–7).*

SCHLOß HELLBRUNN

This summer palace 4 km (2½ mi) south of the Altstadt was built in the early 1600s by Archbishop Markus Sitticus. The highlight of any visit to Salzburg is Hellbrunn's **Wasserspiele** (Water Garden), which the merry archbishop used to amuse and humiliate his guests; the 40-minute tour gives you a taste of his tactics (tip: wear a raincoat). Hourly evening tours are offered in July and August 6 PM–10 PM (minimum five people). Tickets for the tour also include admission to the bright-yellow **Schloß,** which houses a fair collection of 17th- and 18th-century artwork. *Tel. 0662/820372. From Hauptbahnhof or Altstadt, Bus 55 to Schloß Hellbrunn. Admission to Wasserspiele 70 AS; admission to Schloß 30 AS; combined ticket 90 AS. Open daily 9–4:30 (9–5 in summer).*

SOUND OF MUSIC TOURS

The manicured **Mirabellgarten,** just off the river and bordering the Altstadt, was the site of both prince-archbishop intrigues and goofy games of do-re-mi; today, *Sound of Music* tours (330 AS) use it as their point of departure. The two major companies offering the roughly four-hour tour are **Panorama Tours** (Mirabellplatz, tel. 0662/874029) and **Salzburg Sightseeing** (Mirabellplatz 2, tel. 0662/881616), both of which strike out daily at 9:30 AM and 2 PM. If you just want the highlights, Schloß Leopoldskron and Schloß Frohnburg, the houses used in the movie, are an easy bike ride south of the city center.

MUSEUMS

Bürgerspital Spielzeugmuseum (Bürgerspitalgasse 2, tel. 0662/847560; open Tues.–Sun. 9–5), Salzburg's toy museum, displays a remarkable collection of toys from the pre-Nintendo age. Look for Professor Anton's *Spielen mit Physik* (Playing with Physics), an exhibit for today's little brainiacs. Admission is 30 AS. **Haus der Natur** (Museumsplatz 5, tel. 0662/842653; open daily 9–5), Salzburg's natural history museum, includes a largish aquarium, a big reptile zoo, several ethnographic collections, and plenty of (real) stuffed animals. Admission is 55 AS. Exhibits in the classy **Museum Carolino Augusteum** (Museumsplatz 1, tel. 0662/843145; open Tues. 9–8, Wed.–Sun. 9–5) include everything from Iron Age artifacts to 19th-century paintings by native son Hans Makart. Don't miss the Roman mosaics depicting Olympic wrestlers or the section on antique musical instruments, featuring a horn shaped like a dragon and an ornate 17th-century cembalo. Admission is 40 AS. The **Rupertinum** (Wiener-Philhar-moniker-Gasse 9, tel. 0662/8042–2336; open Tues.–Sun. 10–5 [10–6 in summer], Wed. 10–9) displays a broad range of 20th-century art on its three floors. Check out works by Chagall, Kollwitz, and Klimt. In the lobby, old exhibit posters cost 50 AS a pop. Basic admission is 40 AS, but in summer special exhibits bump the price to 50 AS.

AFTER DARK

For mainstream fun and cheap beer, join the party animals at the International Youth Hotel's bar. Cough up 80 AS cover to hear the best jazz in town at **Urban Keller** (Schallmooser Hauptstr. 50, tel. 0662/870894; closed Sun.). Green velour couches, loud bands, micro-brewed beer, and the coolest cats in Salzburg mix every night at **Schneitl-Music Pub** (Bergstr. 5–7, tel. 0662/878678). At the **Augustiner Bräu/Müllner Stübl** (Augustinergasse 4 in Kloster Mülln, tel. 0662/431246), you can choose from several different stands to concoct your meal and, in summer, sip some of the delicious house beer in the garden. In winter, plank tables create a beer-hall atmosphere.

NEAR SALZBURG

SALZBERGWERK

Located 16 km (10 mi) south of Salzburg, Hallein's Salzbergwerk is the oldest Austrian salt mine open to the public. At the height of the salt-trade era, Archbishop Wolf Dietrich monopolized the industry by controlling Hallein, and he used the sizable revenue to transform Salzburg architecturally into the pala-tial city it is today. The mine was used for almost 3,000 years, until its retirement in 1989. Today it still rakes in the bucks as a full-scale tourist attraction. Sign on for the 4-hour tour and you'll toboggan down-hill on polished tree trunks to view the underground salt chambers, cross a salt lake on a raft, and career through tunnels in miners' trucks. Hallein is best reached via train from Salzburg (20 mins, 34 AS). To reach the mine, take the Salzbergbahn **cable car** (tel. 06134/852–8522), which leaves from Zatlokalstraße 3, off Hallein's Gampertorplatz; round-trip fare is 100 AS. *Admission to Salzbergwerk (including cable car): 240 AS. Open daily 9–5, Nov.–Mar. 11–3, Jun.–mid-Sept. until 5:30).*

THE SALZKAMMERGUT AND HALLSTATT

The district just east of Salzburg is known for stunning lakes, Alpine scenery, and the curative proper-ties of its salt baths. When the baths in Bad Ischl received the stamp of approval from the Austrian impe-rial family in the 19th century, nearby towns started emphasizing their own saline characteristics, and eventually every town within 50 km (30 mi) was grouped under one name, the Salzkammergut. Trains travel hourly to Bad Ischl from both Vienna (4 hrs, 376 AS) and Salzburg (2 hrs, 180 AS). From here you can connect to **Hallstatt** (30 mins, 34 AS).

Not only does Hallstatt, the jewel of the Salzkammergut, have the world's oldest salt mines, it's also the most drop-dead gorgeous lakeside village in the region. You'll have to cross the Hallstätter See on a ferry (40 AS round trip) to reach the village from the station; the last ferry in either direction leaves at about 6 PM. Hallstatt's lakeside location means that its **Salzbergwerk tour** (135 AS; open June–Sept. 20, daily 9:30–4:30; May and Sept. 21–mid-Oct., daily 9:30–3) is arguably the most scenic in the Salzkam-mergut. From the ferry dock, walk left along Seestraße, turn right at the Salzbergwerk sign, and follow the path to the **Salzbergbahn**, a cable car that will take you to the mines for 97 AS round trip. The **Prähis-torisches Museum** (Markt 56, tel. 06134/8202; admission 40 AS; open daily 10–6) has tools, coins, and Iron Age artifacts unearthed in the area. Perhaps the most bizarre sight in Hallstatt is the **Beinhaus** (char-nel house; Kirchenweg 40, behind church in Hallstatt-Markt; admission 10 AS), a small room filled with an amazing collection of skulls and bones that were dug up to make room in the tiny graveyard.

WHERE TO SLEEP

The **Tourismus Verband** (Seestraße 169, tel. 06134/8208) will book you a room for free. **Pension Sarstein** (Gosaumühlstr. 83, tel. 06134/8217; closed Nov.), on the main road five minutes north of the

If you're stuck for cash on your travels, don't panic. Western Union can transfer money in minutes. We've 37,000 outlets in over 140 countries. And our record of safety and reliability is second to none. Call Western Union: wherever you are, you're never far from home.

WESTERN UNION | MONEY TRANSFER®

The fastest way to send money worldwide.

We'll give you a $20 tip for driving.

See the real Europe with Hertz.

It's time to see Europe from a new perspective. From behind the wheel of a Hertz car. And we'd like to save you $20 on your prepaid Affordable Europe Weekly Rental. Our low rates are guaranteed in U.S. dollars and English is spoken at all of our European locations. Computerized driving directions are available at many locations, and Free Unlimited Mileage and 24-Hour Emergency Roadside Assistance are standard in our European packages. For complete details call 1-800-654-3001. Mention PC #95384 So, discover Europe with Hertz.

Offer is valid at participating airport locations in Europe from Jan.1 – Dec.15,1998, on Economy through Full size cars. Reservations must be made at least 8 hours prior to departure. $20 will be deducted at time of booking. Standard rental qualifications, significant restrictions and blackout periods apply.

ferry terminal, has quaint, rustic rooms—most with garden balconies and jaw-dropping views of the lake—for 210 AS and up, breakfast included.

INNSBRUCK

Visitors to Innsbruck should be prepared for a lot of neck strain. Everywhere you go in this city, your eyes are constantly being drawn upward to icy white peaks set against the deep blue of the sky. Not that there's nothing to see at ground level—a focal point of the Austrian Renaissance, sometime imperial residence after the coronation of Maximilian I in 1493, and political capital of the quintessentially Alpine region of Tirol, Innsbruck came to world attention in 1964 and 1976 as host of the Winter Olympics. Since then, travelers have awakened to the fact that this is one of the most beautifully situated and exciting cities in Austria. Traditional Tyrolean culture, evident in the excellent Tirol Folk Museum and in the streets of the almost completely preserved Altstadt, is supplemented by an opera house, a major university, and frequent, if slightly wacky, events like candle-carrying scuba divers in the Inn River or a carefully choreographed concert using all the church bells in the Inn Valley.

BASICS

The train station has a **Hotel Information** office (tel. 0512/583766; open daily 9–9) that specializes in room bookings (40 AS fee). **Innsbruck Information** (Burggraben 3, tel. 0512/5356, 0512/535638 for hotel reservations; open Mon.–Sat. 8–7, Sun. 9–6) books rooms and handles event tickets. Be aware that the exchange window closes an hour earlier than the information window. For big savings, buy the **Innsbruck Card** (200 AS for 24 hours, 280 AS for 48 hours, and 350 AS for 72 hours), which gets you free admission to all museums, mountain cable cars, the zoo, and Schloß Ambras, plus free bus and tram transportation. **Tirol-Information** (Maria-Theresian-Str. 55, tel. 0512/7272, fax 0512/7272–7) has a mountaineering expert to answer questions daily 9–noon. The **American Express** office (Brixner Str. 3, A-6020, tel. 0512/582491) is open weekdays 9–5:30 and Saturday 9–noon. The **Hauptpostamt** (Maximilian Str. 2, tel. 0512/500–6500) is open 24 hours.

COMING AND GOING

Frequent train destinations from Innsbruck include Munich (2 hrs, 372 AS), Salzburg (2 hrs, 376 AS), Vienna (7 hrs, 690 AS), and Zürich (4 hrs, 558 AS). The Altstadt, where historic attractions are clustered, is a 10-minute walk from the train station. Local bus or tram tickets cost 21 AS; four tickets cost 54 AS. The 32 AS **Tageskarte,** good for a day of travel in central Innsbruck, and the 34 AS version, good for 24 hours, are both great deals; pick 'em up at the train station, the tourist office (where you can also pick up a route map for 10 AS), or a tobacco shop. For a **taxi,** dial 0512/1718. After 9 PM, women can call **Frauen Nachttaxi** (tel. 0512/5311) and be taken anywhere within Innsbruck for 40 AS. The Hauptbahnhof is a good bet for **bike rentals.**

WHERE TO SLEEP

The tourist office has a complete list of Privatzimmer, but Innsbruck's pensions and guest houses are more convenient. For cheap lodging in July and August, call the **Internationales Studentenhaus** (Rechengasse 7, tel. 0512/501912, fax 0512/50115) for the scoop on the more than 600 rooms available in student dorms.

Gasthof Innsbrücke. The riverside location is so pleasant that you might forget about the street noise. Singles are 350 AS, doubles 520 AS. *Innstr. 1, tel. 0512/281934. From Bahnhof, Bus A or K across river to first stop (Innstr.).*

Pension Paula. Paula's is a cheap and friendly pension in the hills. Singles cost 340 AS–440 AS, doubles 500 AS–640 AS. Reserve ahead in summer and December. *Weiherburggasse 35, tel. 0512/292262. From station, Bus K (direction: St. Nikolaus) to Schmelzergasse; then uphill and right on Weiherburggasse.*

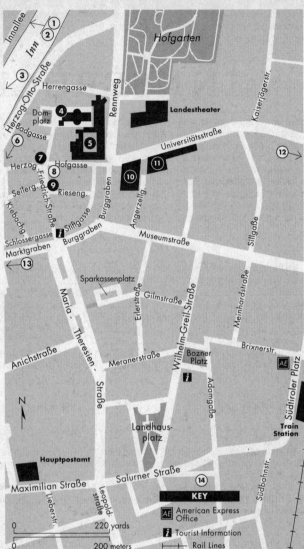

INNSBRUCK

Sights ●
Dom zu St. Jacob, **4**
Goldenes Dachl, **7**
Hofburg, **5**
Hofkirche, **10**
Stadtturm, **9**
Tiroler Volkskunst-museum, **11**

Lodging ○
Alpotel Tirol, **13**
Gasthof Innsbrücke, **3**
Internationales Studentenhaus, **6**
Jugendherberge Innsbruck, **12**
Jugendherberge St. Nikolaus, **2**
Pension Paula, **1**
Pension Stoi, **14**
Weisses Kreuz, **8**

KEY

AE American Express Office
i Tourist Information
├──┼── Rail Lines

Pension Stoi. Only five minutes' walk from the station, these rooms are quiet and spotless. Triples and quads have great balconies. Singles start at 450 AS, doubles at 660 AS. *Salurner Str. 7, tel. 0512/585434. From Hauptbahnhof, head down Salurner Str., turn left on Adamgasse, then make an immediate right.*

Weisses Kreuz. Mozart stayed here as a teenager. Newly renovated rooms exude Tyrolean charm, and you're in the heart of the Altstadt. Singles are 440 AS without bath, 710 AS with; doubles are 820 without bath, 1,120 AS with. Buffet breakfast included. *Herzog-Friedrich-Str. 31, tel. 0512/59479, fax 0512/594–7990. Tram 1, 3, 6 or Bus O, L, K, N to Altstadt.*

HOSTELS

To reach Innsbruck's oldest, cheapest hostel, **Jugendherberge Innsbruck** (Reichenauer Str. 147, tel. 0512/346179; beds 145 AS), walk 1 block north and west from the train station and take Bus O (direction: Olympisches Dorf) to Jugendherberge. **Jugendherberge St. Nikolaus** (Innstr. 95, tel. 0512/286515; beds 115 AS) is more convenient to the Altstadt and the hills, but the owner is rude and the carpets threadbare. Take Bus K to Schmelzergasse.

SPLURGE

Alpotel Tirol. Some of the Tirol's modern and extremely comfortable rooms have balconies overlooking the quiet garden and mountains, and there's a sauna in the hotel. The complimentary buffet breakfast includes homemade whole-grain bread. You're only a five-minute walk from the Altstadt. Singles start at 900 AS, doubles at 1,400 AS. *Innrain 13 (Ursulinenhof), tel. 0512/577931–15, Tram 1, 3, 6 or Bus O, L, K, N. From Marktgraben, go left on Innrain.*

FOOD

The cheapest lunch in Innsbruck is at the **University Mensa** (Herzog-Sigmund-Ufer 15, at Josef Hirn Str.; open Mon.–Thurs. 11–2, Fri. 11–1:30), open to all. You'll find plenty of grocery stores on Maria-Theresien-Straße and a huge indoor farmer's market in the **Innrain Markthalle** (Innrain and Markt-graben), open Monday–Saturday 7 AM–1 PM. Austrian-Italian joints tend to offer the best food for the price, as do the numerous ethnic restaurants near the university.

Gasthof Sailer. A block from the train station, this quaint restaurant in the Hotel Sailer was assembled from the rooms of 17th-century Tyrolean farmhouses. Try the *Tyroler G'röstl* (115 AS) or the pillowy spinach spaetzle with ham and melted cheese (92 AS). *Adamgasse 6–10, tel. 0512/5363.*

Ottoburg. Just down the street from the Goldenes Dachl, Ottoburg is housed in a medieval gray-stone townhouse with charming red and white shutters. Sit in a bay window in one of the upstairs rooms over-looking the Altstadt. The lunch menu changes daily, but look for Tyroler G'röstl with a side order of bacon-studded sauerkraut (110 AS). *Herzog-Friedrich-Str. 1, tel. 0512/574652. Open 10 AM–midnight, closed Tues.*

Philippine. As in Philippine Welser, morganatic wife of Archduke Ferdinand II. This vegetarian restau-rant has a friendly staff, healthy food, and enormous pots of tea. Nosh on unusual spaghetti dishes or hit the salad bar for under 100 AS. *Corner of Müllerstr. and Templstr., tel. 0512/561636. Closed Sun.*

Schwarzer-Adler. The rustic Tyrolean decor creates a romantic setting. Specialties include lobster ragout with tagliatelle in a red-wine tomato sauce and grilled fresh-water trout. It's expensive (main courses around 260 AS), but worth it. *Kaiserjägerstr. 2, in Romantikhotel Schwarzer-Adler, tel. 0512/587109.*

Tiroler Stuben. Known for some of the best food in town, the Tiroler Stuben has a broad seasonal menu, including lots of vegetarian choices. Try the *Schlutzkrapferln*—Tyrolean ravioli stuffed with cheese, pota-toes, and spinach and topped with melted butter and parmesan (170 AS)—the roast chicken and potato salad (160 AS), or the Tyrolean braised beef in a bacon-and-onion cream sauce (190 AS). There's a cover charge for the bread and crudités with a variety of dips (26 AS). *Innrain 13 (Ursulinen-hof), in Alpotel Tirol, tel. 0512/577931.*

CAFÉS

The outdoor tables at **Katzung** (Herzog-Friedrich-Str. 16; closed Sun.) buy you a great view of the Gold-enes Dachl (*see* Worth Seeing, *below*) to go with your coffee and pastry. **Ebi's Uni Café Bistro** (Innrain 55, tel. 0512/573949) is a premier student café, complete with cheap drinks, snacks, and a balcony facing the university. The best place for live music, day or night, is **Treibhaus** (Angerzellgasse 8, tel. 0512/586874); the cover charge varies.

WORTH SEEING

The principal sight in Innsbruck is the medieval Altstadt. The 185-ft high **Stadtturm** (City Tower; Her-zog-Friedrich-Str.; admission 22 AS) affords a real panoramic view, if you can see over the heads of the other travelers. The **Hofburg** (Rennweg 1; admission 55 AS), where the imperial family lived off and on after 1493, was completely renovated in the 18th century; inside you'll find the awe-inspiring Giant Hall, and much less worthy rooms with no appeal beyond their color schemes. The Hofburg is once again undergoing extensive renovations, so check with the tourist office for opening hours. **Dom zu St. Jakob** (open Sat.–Thurs. 6–noon, Fri. 2–5), behind the palace, features an impressive facade of dark pudding stone and light marble. On the high altar is Lukas Cranach's painting of the Madonna.

Perhaps the artistic highlight of Innsbruck's medieval Altstadt is the **Goldenes Dachl** (Golden Roof), which was built in 1500 to celebrate Emperor Maximilian I's second marriage. Below the gilded copper are frescoes and reliefs, including two flagbearers holding the banners of Tirol and the Holy Roman Empire. Inside this building is the new **Maximilianeum Museum** (Herzog-Friedrich-Str. 15, tel. 0512/581111; admission 60 AS), dedicated to Hapsburg Emperor Maximilian and open daily 10–6.

ALPENZOO ·

Here's a unique opportunity to see 150 species of Alpine animals in their natural habitat; some are extinct outside this zoo. *Weiherburggasse 37, tel. 0512/292323. Admission 70 AS. Tram 1, Hunger-burgbahn or Bus 0, N, D, E, 4, Shuttle from Maria-Theresien-Str. (Alter Landhaus) and Hofburg.*

HOFKIRCHE

Emperor Maximilian wrote prolifically on the importance of building monuments to oneself, and the Hofkirche is the practice of his preaching. Built by Max's grandson Ferdinand I between 1553 and 1563, the church contains an impressive marble cenotaph decorated with scenes from Maximilian's life. The tiny Silver Chapel upstairs contains the tomb of Archduke Ferdinand II (the pious kneeling position was his own idea) and his wife. Next door, the Tiroler Volkskunstmuseum (admission 40 AS) displays Tyrolean cultural artifacts, including dowry furniture, period clothing, and enormous cowbells. *Universitätsstr. 2, tel. 0512/584302. Admission 20 AS. Open Mon.–Sat. 9–5.*

SCHLOß AMBRAS

Tyroleans begrudgingly allowed Archduke Ferdinand II's morganatic marriage to Philippine Welser, but the thought of the ill-matched couple living within the city limits was more than they could take, so Ferdinand fixed up a little 10th-century château for his honey outside town. The upper castle, completed in 1556, now houses a collection of Hapsburg portraits. The Kunst und Wunderkammer rooms contain the archduke's personal collections, including what looks like an early forerunner of the disco ball, an iron chair with shackles, and portraits of an astonishingly hairy man and his children. *Schloßstr. 20, tel. 0512/348446. Tram 3 to Ambras or Tram 6 (direction: Igls) to Tummelplatz; keep walking in direction of the tram; or shuttle (30 AS round-trip; leaves on the hour) from Maria-Theresien-Str. 45. Admission 60 AS; guided tour 25 AS extra. Open Apr.–Oct., Wed.–Mon. 10–5. Check with the tourist office for winter hours.*

AFTER DARK

A full schedule of opera and other classical music, dance, and drama is performed at the **Tiroler Landestheater** (Rennweg 2, tel. 0512/520744).

Innsbruck's bar and club scene happens almost exclusively in the Viaduktbogen, the brick structure under the train tracks along Ingenieur-Etzel-Straße—all of the bars are built into its arches. If you feel the earth move, don't run for the doorway; it's just a train passing overhead. Metal, reggae, and classical music, depending on the night, all pour from **Bogen 13** (Viaduktbogen 13, tel. 0512/562463). Near the university, the warm-sounding **Café Fuzzy** (Universitätsstr. 19, tel. 0512/561072; closed Sat.) is a relaxed and friendly café-bar. Alternative tunes and likable folks hold court at **Weli** (Viaduktbogen 26, tel. 0512/581254), open daily until 1 AM.

OUTDOOR ACTIVITIES

SUMMER SPORTS

Innsbruck's combination of rushing rivers and towering mountains makes for excellent hiking, mountain biking, mountain climbing, and river rafting. Take note: if you stay a minimum of three nights at any hotel, pension, or hostel, you can join the **Mountain Hiking Program,** which includes free guided mountain hikes, equipment, and transportation. For more information, pick up the *Mountain Hiking Program* pamphlet at any tourist office. Summer skiers can get the best deals on all-inclusive packages to Stubaier Glacier from Innsbruck Information. **Österreichischer Alpenverein** (Wilhelm Greil-Str. 15, tel. 0512/59547–34, fax 0512/575528) has tips on mountaineering and Alpine huts.

To explore the **Nordkette,** mountain bikers should cross the Innbrücke to Höttinger Gasse and take a right on Höhenstraße to Hungerburg near the Hungerbahn gondola. Mountain bikes aren't allowed on this gondola or on any buses or trains in the city, but you can pedal up the mountain from here via Rosnerweg. Hikers can take the Hungerbahn and Nordkettenbahn gondolas to Höttinger Seegrube

(Olympic wanna-bes can walk two hours uphill), then hike up to **Langer Sattel** (1½ hrs), where on a good day you can see all the way to Germany. Pick up a free trail map at any tourist office.

WINTER SPORTS

A two-time Olympic host, Innsbruck packs in the winter crowds with its 52 lifts and 112 km (67 mi) of groomed Alpine ski runs. The **Club Innsbruck** card gets you discounts on ski passes and mountain railways; be sure to grab one from your hotel or hostel. For serious skiers, Innsbruck offers the **Super Ski Pass** (1,690 AS with Club Innsbruck card), which is valid for four of six days and entitles you to free rides on all cable cars and lifts in Innsbruck, the Stubaier Glacier, Kitzbühel, and Arlberg (including all bus transfers). Downhill and cross-country equipment rental starts at 250 AS per day in high season. In the off season, it's cheaper to get equipment and lift tickets at the ski lodges than at the ski shops in town.

NEAR INNSBRUCK

KITZBUHEL

An erstwhile mining village and a health resort since the 19th century, Kitzbühel has built a reputation as one of the best ski locations on the planet. This compact little valley town, a one-hour train ride east of Innsbruck (125 AS), is also one of the world's more efficient operations for extracting money from wealthy ski bunnies and celebrities. Fortunately, a network of mostly Australian ski bums devoted to the place supports a small network of cheap hotels and restaurants. Ride Austria's first cable car, the **Hahnenkamm** (tel. 05356/58510; 160 AS), to the start of several runs and hikes. The local **Tourismusverband** (Hinterstadt 18, tel. 05356/21550–2272) can make lodging suggestions. The Australian contingent runs **House Mahlknecht** (Sportfeld 10, tel. 05356/72034), with dorm beds for 140 AS and doubles for 400 AS. For food, drinks, company, or the latest on what's happening in Kitzbühel, head for **La Fonda** (Hinterstadt 13, tel. 05356/73673), a popular pub among Australians.

LIENZ

Lienz may not have all the dazzle of Austria's hot ski spots or the mystique of a remote Alpine village, but it calls out to ski fanatics and is not nearly as touristy as Kitzbühel. Sprawled at the base of the Italian Dolomites, Lienz is said to be the sunniest city in Austria. Day passes to the **Lienzer Dolomiten Ski-Region** go for 290 AS, and two-day passes start at 560 AS (prices lower off season); they're available at the lift a few kilometers north of town. In winter, free buses run regularly from town to the Zettersfeld gondola and Hochstein lift (*see below*).

There are three main hiking areas in Lienz. To the immediate west is the forest **Edenwald,** which engulfs the entire mountain Hochstein except for the very top. The **Hochsteinbahn lift** (next to Schloß Bruck) will take hikers as far as the 4,950-ft Sternalm (60 AS one-way, 100 AS round-trip), from which you can climb another 3,300 ft to the *Böses Weibele* (Evil Wench) overlook. The breathtaking panorama of the Dolomites and the Puster Valley is worth the trek. Directly to the north, the **Zettersfeld gondola** (100 AS round-trip) leads to another ski area and hiking cornucopia with awe-inspiring views of the mighty Hohe Tauern. Finally, to the south rise the bald craggy peaks of the **Lienz Dolomites**; this rugged, less accessible range offers more serious mountaineering opportunities.

The helpful staff at Lienz's **Tourismusverband** (Europaplatz 1, tel. 04852/65265; closed Sun.) books rooms for free and sells good hiking maps (89 AS). Lienz is four hours (264 AS) from Innsbruck by train. If you're crashing here, head to **Frühstückspension Gretl** (Schweizergasse 32, tel. 04852/62106), where all doubles (450 AS–500 AS) have private bathrooms and showers.

BALTIC REPUBLICS

E stonia, Latvia, Lithuania: These three small countries in northeastern Europe have weathered centuries of domination by Germans, Swedes, Russians, and Poles; fought countless battles to preserve, if nothing else, their dignity; and won their independence twice in this century alone—only to lose it again and again at the hands of travel guides (like this one) that invariably cram them together under the narrow rubric "Baltic states." Of course, in some ways it makes sense; the three countries do share a common terrain, history, and visa zone. Nevertheless, since breaking free of the Soviet Union in 1991, the Baltics have been quietly reconstructing their individual national identities, societies, and economies, and each is quite resolute about its distinction from the others.

The good news for travelers is twofold: The Baltics are cheap compared with Scandinavia and even with Warsaw and Prague, and they aren't yet overrun with tourists. While you won't find too many world-famous attractions in the Baltics, the region's obscurity and remoteness may actually be the best thing about it. Another plus for the English-speaker is that it is becoming increasingly easy to roam the three Baltic capitals of Tallinn, Rīga, and Vilnius without encountering language barriers. The landscape itself is also free of barriers; everywhere in the Baltics you'll find unspoiled forests and beaches, and people whose initial aloofness toward strangers often gives way to genuine friendliness.

BASICS

For country-specific details (money, phones, etc.), see the appropriate sections below; the following is general information on all three Baltic Republics.

VISA AND ENTRY REQUIREMENTS

American, Australian, British, Canadian, Irish, and New Zealand citizens can stay in Estonia visa-free for up to 90 days. Citizens of New Zealand and Ireland need visas to enter Lithuania; take $20, your passport, and a photo to a consulate outside Lithuania, because visas aren't available at the border. Australians, Canadians, and New Zealanders need visas for Latvia; a 90-day visa ($15) can be purchased from consulates outside Latvia, and 10-day visas can be purchased at the airport upon arrival.

FINLAND

★ Helsinki

Gulf of Finland

Kohtla-Järve Narva Ivangorod

Tallinn ★ Rakvere *Narvskoe Vdchr.*

TO STOCKHOLM

Kärdla Haapsalu ESTONIA Jõgeva RUSSIA

Hiiumaa Käina Rohukula Paide Põltsamaa *Peipsi järv*

Orjaku Heltermaa Lihula

Baltic Sea Trigi Virtsu Vändra *Vörtsjärv* Tartu

Saaremaa Orissaare Sindi Viljandi

Kihelkonna Pärnu *Pskovskoe ozero* Pskov

Kuressaare Võru Valga Ostrov

Sääre *Gulf of Riga* Valmiera

Ventspils Gauja National Park Cēsis Gulbene Balvi

TO KIEL Talsi Līgatne Sigulda

Kuldīga Jūrmala ★ Rīga Madona Kārsava

Tukums LATVIA

Jelgava *Lielupe* Jēkabpils Rēzekne

Liepāja *Venta* Bauska *Daugava* Subate Krāslava

Palanga *Vaduva* ■ Rundāle Palace Daugavpils

TO KIEL Šiauliai

Smyltinė Telšiai Panevėžys *Aukštaitiyos National Park*

Klaipēda

Juodkrante LITHUANIA

Courland Spit Nida Ukmergė

Nemunas Kaunas *Neris* N

Kaliningrad Sovetsk Rumšiškės Trakai Vilnius ★

RUSSIA Marijampolė BELARUS

Šeštokai

KEY Minsk ★

Suwałki

Rail Lines

Ferry Lines

POLAND

0   100 miles

0   150 km

WHERE TO SLEEP

Quality varies, but **private rooms** are your best bet; book them through tourist offices. The few **hostels** in the Baltics (most are in Latvia) are not always the cheapest choice. In summer, **camping** is a good option, and rough camping is generally okay, as long as you're not sleeping in someone's cabbage patch. Bring your own camping supplies.

FOOD

Baltic cuisine is the standard fare of Eastern and Central Europe, and the predictable *karbonades* (grilled meats), *beefsteaks* (fried meats), and *stroganoff* (sauced meats) can get tedious. Latvia's national dish is *zirņi* (peas with pork fat); Lithuania's is *cepelinai* (hollowed potatoes filled with beef). You'll find *blini* (pancakes) everywhere, but the best are in Lithuania. The best beers are Estonia's Saku, Latvia's Aldaris, and Lithuania's Utenos.

VISITOR INFORMATION

Estonia has tourist offices in nearly every sizable town; unfortunately, the same cannot be said of Latvia or Lithuania. If you have Internet access, tune into the news group soc.culture.baltics or subscribe to BALT-L, the Baltic Listserv exchange. For glossy brochures, write to one of the embassies or consulates:

Estonian Consulate: *630 5th Ave., Suite 2415, New York, NY 10111, tel. 212/247–7634.* **Latvian Embassy:** *4325 17th St. NW, Washington, D.C. 20011, tel. 202/726–8213.* **Lithuanian Consulate:** *420 5th Ave., 3rd floor, New York, NY 10018, tel. 212/354–7840.*

HEALTH AND SAFETY

Though crime is low, wandering alone at night in big cities like Rīga and Vilnius isn't the brightest idea. Also, avoid drinking tap water, particularly in Rīga.

ESTONIA

Estonia has a sometime rep as a nation of frosty pseudo-Scandinavians who compete with the Finns for the title of "Most Reserved Europeans." It's said that you can get Lake Peipsi to crack in winter before you can get an Estonian to crack a smile. While it's true that centuries of Soviet oppression didn't help Estonians to relax, you'll discover a genuine warmth if you get to know them. And with a couple of heady Sakus under their belts, their capacity to party rivals even that of their close linguistic cousins the Finns. Though recent infusions of foreign investment have revved Estonia's economy, the national culture remains profoundly rural, a celebration of peasant life in the countryside.

BASICS

MONEY

US$1 = 12 EEK and 1 EEK = 8¢. Estonia's official currency is the *kroon* (crown), abbreviated EEK and equal to 100 senti. National *panks* (banks), with branches in all major and most minor cities, change cash and traveler's checks at fair commissions; most also give advances on a Visa or MasterCard. Credit cards are accepted at some upscale venues and in most grocery stores.

PHONES

Country code: 372. Most pay phones (except the free ones in Tallinn) accept 10- or 20-senti coins. For long-distance calls, go to **Eesti Telefon,** the national telephone company, or buy a *telefoni kaart* (phone card) in 16-EEK, 40-EEK, 95-EEK, or 190-EEK denominations. You can also buy phone cards for domestic calls. For **AT&T** or **MCI** calls, dial 07 and ask to be connected to the desired service. For additional telephone information in English—or almost any other tourist information—call Ekspress Hotline (tel. 631–3222).

COMING AND GOING

Flying into Helsinki and catching a ferry to Tallinn is probably the cheapest way to reach Estonia. There are also daily ferries from Stockholm. **Finnair, SAS,** and **Lufthansa** make frequent trips. **Trains** are the best way to enter the country from Russia or elsewhere in Eastern Europe, but Eurailpasses aren't accepted here.

GETTING AROUND

Only if you're atoning for unconfessed sins should you try to travel by rail within Estonia. Trains are infrequent, uncomfortable, and twice as slow as buses (though only slightly cheaper), and service on board can be less than friendly.

BY BUS • Domestic bus trips rarely cost more than 90 EEK, though prices vary widely between bus companies. Schedules are posted in every *bussijaam* (bus station); go to the *kassa* (ticket window) with your destination written down. Unless you're into seeing rural Estonia, take *ekspress* (express) or *kiirliin* (not quite as fast) buses. If you're not getting on at the beginning of the line, your bus will be marked PILETID AUTOBUSSIST, which means you buy a ticket from the driver.

TALLINN

It's often said that Tallinn walks with a limp. It limped through several centuries of German, Danish, and Swedish control and then hobbled through the 18th and 19th centuries under Russian domination before emerging as the capital of an independent state in 1918. Just as it was beginning to right itself, the Nazis, rapidly followed by the Soviets, descended. When Estonia regained independence in 1991, Tallinn wasted no time in westernizing, and today it has the highest economic growth rate of any major Baltic city. This, combined with its wealth of soaring Gothic spires, tucked-away cellar cafés, and winding cobblestone streets, makes it one of the most enjoyable cities in Northern Europe.

Come in early July to catch top acts at the Rock Summer music festival (350 EEK).

BASICS

Get maps (10 EEK) at the **main tourist office** (Raekoja pl. 18, tel. 631–3940; open June–Aug. weekdays 9–7, weekends 10–5; shorter hrs off season). The main **Estravel** office (Suur-Karja 15, tel. 631–3313; open weekdays 9–6, Sat. 10–3) provides AmEx services. Change cash and traveler's checks (1% fee) or get Visa cash advances (3% commission) at **Virumaa Kommerstpank** (Vana-Viru 14; open weekdays 9–6, Sat. 10–4); there are also numerous *valuutavahetus* (bureaux de change) around Tallinn, but the rates are lousy near the center. Pick up poste restante (addressed Poste Restante, Your Name, Main Post Office, Narva mnt. 1, Tallinn EE0001) at Window 31 of the **main post office** (Narva mnt. 1); the entrance to the **phone office** is on the west side.

EMBASSIES • Canada: *Toomkooli 13, 2nd floor, tel. 2/449–056. Open weekdays 9–4:30.* **United Kingdom:** *Kentmanni 20, upstairs from U.S. embassy, tel. 631–3463. Open weekdays 10–noon and 2–4.* **United States:** *Kentmanni 20, tel. 631–2021. Open weekdays 8:30–5:30.*

COMING AND GOING

Trains breeze into **Balti Jaam** (Baltic Station; Toom pst. 35, tel. 2/446–756) from St. Petersburg (11 hrs, 201 EEK) and Moscow (16 hrs, 482 EEK). The popular Balti Ekspress travels nightly to Warsaw (change in Šeštokai; 20 hrs, 716 EEK), stopping in Rīga around midnight. Catch buses at the **autobussijaam** (Lastekodu 46, tel. 641–0100), southeast of the Old Town; take Tram 2 or 4 down Tartu maantee. Destinations include Rīga (6 hrs, 96 EEK), Vilnius (12 hrs, 190 EEK), and Haapsalu (2 hrs, 30 EEK). The **main ferry terminal** (Sadama 25, tel. 631–8002) is north of town. Tallink (Terminal A, tel. 2/601–960) has five daily ferries (3½ hrs, 220 EEK–350 EEK) and six daily hydrofoils (1½ hrs, 360 EEK–675 EEK) to Helsinki. Estline (Terminal B, tel. 631–3636) has ferries to Stockholm (15 hrs, 840 EEK).

GETTING AROUND

Comprehensive trams, buses, and trolleys operate 6 AM–midnight; punch-as-you-board tickets (3 EEK) are available from drivers and at select kiosks. Ten-day passes are also available at kiosks for a cost of 60 EEK. Taxis are expensive around hotels and ferry, bus, and train stations, cheaper within the city center; most taxis don't have meters, but the official fare is 4 EEK per km (½ mi). For some of the comfiest cab rides in the Baltics, hunt down Tulika (tel. 2/603–044) or Esra (tel. 641–0440).

WHERE TO SLEEP

Hotel Central (Narva mnt. 7, tel. 633–9800) is, as the name suggests, ideally located in the center of Tallinn. Crash in a double for 992 EEK.

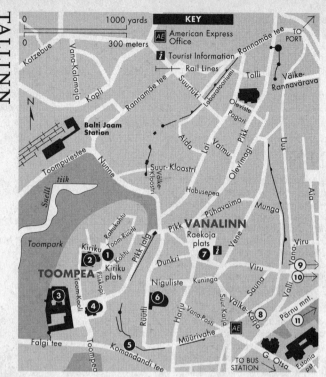

KEY

AE American Express Office

i Tourist Information

Rail Lines

Sights ●

Estonian National Art Museum, **1**

Kiek-in-de-Kök, **5**

Niguliste Church, **6**

Raekoda (Town Hall), **7**

St. Alexander Nevsky's Cathedral, **4**

Toomkirik, **2**

Toompea Castle, **3**

Lodging ○

The Barn, **8**

Hotel Central, **9**

Hotel Stroomi, **11**

Vikerlase 15 Hostel, **10**

Hotel Stroomi (Randla 11, tel. 630–4200) is only 7 km (4 mi) from the airport and 4 km (2½ mi) from the city center. Doubles are 488 EEK.

For a smaller outlay of EEK, **CDS Reisid** (Raekoja pl. 17, tel. 2/445–262; open mid-May–Aug., daily 9–5; closed weekends off season) and the **Family Hotel Service** (Mere pst. 6, at Inseneri, behind Chinese restaurant, tel. 2/441–187) arrange doubles (200 EEK–335 EEK) in local homes.

The Barn (Väike-Karja 1, tel. 2/443–465; beds 150 EEK) has clean bathrooms and is only a minute's walk from the Old Town. Or grab a bed (100 EEK, 90 EEK with HI card) at the **Vikerlase 15 Hostel** (Vikerlase 15, tel. 632–7718); the office is open 9–9, but if you call ahead they'll make sure someone waits up. From Narva maantee, take Bus 19, 35, or 44 to Puistee Pinna, walk north on Tchaikovskii, and turn right on Vikerlase.

FOOD

Tallinn has a variety of ethnic restaurants, as well as traditional *kohviks* (cafés) serving cold appetizers. **Contravento** (Vene 12, tel. 2/440–470) serves outstanding Italian cuisine (pizza 35 EEK–60 EEK) and Tallinn's best cappuccino (16 EEK). Head to **Vanaema Juures** (Grandma's Place; Rataskaevu 10/12, tel. 2/441–081) for traditional Estonian cooking in a family atmosphere. If it's North American you crave, try **Ervin's Tex-Mex Restaurant** (Tartu mnt. 50, tel. 631–2736), which is run by a former American basketball player and features live music in the evening. Irish bars have caught on in the Baltics, and **Hell Hunt** (Pikk 39)—which means "gentle wolf" in Estonian—was the first, serving up hearty Irish meals and Irish brews amid live music from the Emerald Isle. For cheaper fare, try the small *poods* (stores) or markets like the one on the first floor of the **Tallinna Kaubamall** (Aia 7, near Vana-Viru; open Mon.–Sat. 9–8, Sun. 10–6) department store.

WORTH SEEING

Two distinct areas comprise Tallinn's center. The stately, sedate **Toompea** (Upper Town), site of the original Estonian settlement, is now the seat of Estonia's government. Two steep stone streets, the **Pikk Jalg** (Long Leg) and the **Luhike Jalg** (Short Leg)—hence the saying "Tallinn walks with a limp"—lead down the hills into the bustling, colorful **Vanalinn** (Old Town), which has been home to Tallinn's merchants and artisans since the Middle Ages.

VANALINN • Like all good town squares, **Raekoja plats** (Town Hall Square) has a long, illustrious history of intrigue, executions, and salt (Tallinn's main export in the Middle Ages). Head to the **Raekoda** (open weekdays 10–4), Tallinn's town hall, for a guided tour (25 EEK) of the meticulously restored council hall. South of Raekoja plats, you'll spy the tall spire of the 15th-century church **Niguliste** (Niguliste 13, tel. 2/449–903; admission 7 EEK; open Thurs.–Sun. 11–6, Wed. 2–9), which holds Bernt Notke's chilling frieze *Danse Macabre.* The **Estonian National Art Museum** (Kiriku pl. 1, tel. 2/441–478; admission 7 EEK; open Wed.–Sun. 11–6) has a fine cross-section of Estonian art from the past 200 years. At the southern end of the Old Town looms the magnificent 1,475-gun tower **Kiek-in-de-Kök** (Komandandi 1, tel. 2/446–686; admission 5 EEK; open Tues., Wed., Fri. 10:30–5:30, weekends 11–4); its name means "peek into the kitchen," so called because during the 15th century you could peer into neighboring living spaces from up here. A stone's throw from the Old Town are the **Estonia Concert Hall** (Pueiestee 4, tel. 2/442–901) and the regionally renowned **Estonia Theatre** (box office on Estonia 4, tel. 626–0215, open daily noon–7), both good bets for first-rate chamber music, opera, ballet, and theater at reasonable prices.

TOOMPEA • Rising above the end of Pikk Jalg is the Lutheran **Toomkirik** (Toom-Kooli 6, tel. 2/444–140; open daily 9:30–4:30-ish), the first church ever erected on Toompea, a collection of fortifications originally built by the Danish. Tallinn's newest church, **St. Alexander Nevsky's Cathedral** (Lossi pl. 10, tel. 2/443–484; admission free; open daily 8–7:30), dominates Lossi plats with its onion-dome roof and redbrick walls; inside hangs the largest bell in Estonia.

NEAR TALLINN

SAAREMAA

The island of Saaremaa has been inhabited since around 4000 BC, supporting an indigenous population until the 8th century AD. Later it was conquered by the Germans, Danes, Swedes, and finally the Russians—leaving it with a varied stockpile of sights and architectural relics. In **Kuressaare**, Saaremaa's capital, check out the labyrinthine floor plan and interesting Saaremaa Museum at the **Bishop's Castle**, built in 1830, the massive Gothic pile at the end of Lossi (Lossihoovi 3, tel. 45/57–542; admission 20 EEK; open daily 11–7). If you just want to kick back and relax, bike (or bus) out to one of the several warm, sandy beaches near Kuressaare: Try **Mändjala** or **Järve**, about 10 km (6 mi) west of town.

BASICS • The **tourist office** (Tallinna 2, Kuressaare, tel. 45/55–120; open weekdays 9–5, Sat. 10–5), in the Raekoda (Town Hall), books rooms for 10 EEK. Buses run from Tallinn (4½ hrs, 90 EEK) to Kuressaare's **autobussijaam** (Pihtla tee 2, tel. 45/57–380); to reach the center, veer left toward Tallinna maantee and follow it south toward the tall building with the antenna. Local buses are infrequent, so consider renting a car (350 EEK per day) at **Steady Ltd.** (Rohu 5, Kuressaare, tel. 45/57–294; open daily 9–7) or a bike (10 EEK per hr, 60 EEK per day) at **Bicycle Rental** (Kraavi 1, Kuressaare, tel. 45/55–242; open daily 9–6).

WHERE TO SLEEP AND EAT • You can **camp** all over the island, but be sure to get a map and suggestions from the tourist office (*see above*). Otherwise, book ahead for **Hotell Mardi Öömaja** (Vallimaa 5A, Kuressaare, tel. 45/57–436; closed early Sept.–late June), with clean doubles (120 EEK) and a short walk from the center; the restaurant downstairs, **Kass,** is excellent. To get here from the Raekoda, turn right on Kohtu, right on Garnisoni, and left on Vallimaa.

TARTU

Estonia's second city, Tartu may lack the cosmopolitan flash of Tallinn, but as Estonian writer Bernard Kangro puts it, "The heart of the Estonian nation beats in Tartu." As the home of **Tartu University,** which was founded by Swedish King Gustav Adolph in 1632, Tartu offers lively cafés and nightlife. Bus here (66 EEK–70 EEK, 2½ hours) from Tallinn.

PARNU

Pärnu, Estonia's third-largest city, feels like a small town. A famous resort during the 1920s and '30s, this seaside town is eager to reclaim its former status as Estonia's capital of tourism. Playing on the market for "health tourism," Pärnu advertises golden beaches, sanatoriums, and mud baths galore. The two-hour bus ride from Tallinn (56 EEK–65 EEK) hugs the Baltic coast.

LATVIA

Although Latvia has had six years to enjoy its independence, it is still, in a sense, dominated by Russia. Ever since Stalin began relocating Russians to this then–Soviet republic, Latvians have been a minority in their own cities—less than 40% in Rīga—and this issue promises to dominate Latvian politics well into the 21st century. On the bright side, the ethnic mix contributes to the Latvian capital's more cosmopolitan air; Rīga's residents are of a decidedly multicultural mindset. If industrial Rīga is your (unfortunate) first stop in Latvia, just remember that the key to enjoying this country is getting out of the capital and off its beaten paths.

BASICS

MONEY

US$1 = 0.6 Ls and 1 Ls = 1.7 US$. The official currency in Latvia is the lat (Ls), equal to 100 santimi (s). Credit cards and traveler's checks are widely accepted in Rīga but not in rural areas. Many large hotels in Rīga also have ATMs that accept Visa, MasterCard, and Cirrus cards. It might be said that Rīga aspires to be the Switzerland of the Baltics, so currency exchanges are easy to come by.

PHONES

Country code: 371. Lattelekom is currently digitizing the country's phone system, and it's a bit confusing. If you're dialing a six-digit number from a pay phone, dial 2 first; if you're dialing a seven-digit number, no prefix is necessary. For general phone information, dial 079 from any phone. For phone information (or entertainment and transportation listings) in English call Latvia's 24-hour Ekspress Hotline (tel. 777–0777). The new card phones have worldwide access, but local calls on these cost 4s. Get tokens or *a telefona karte* (phone card) in 2 Ls, 5 Ls, or 10 Ls denominations at telephone offices and most kiosks. To reach **AT&T** Direct Access^{SM} from Rīga, dial 700–7007; outside Rīga dial 8, wait for a tone, then dial 2/700–7007.

COMING AND GOING

The **Balti Ekspress** stops in Rīga on the way from Warsaw (14–23 hrs, 25 Ls–39 Ls) to Tallinn (7 hrs, 6.45 Ls). Of all the Baltic Republics, Latvia is probably the cheapest to fly directly into. From the United States, try **FinnAir** (tel. 800/950–5000), **Air Baltic** (tel. 800/548–8181), or **British Airways** (tel. 800/247–9297).

GETTING AROUND

The electric **trains** serving Rīga and beyond are just as cheap as buses and more convenient, and—hallelujah—they run on time. By **bus**, it's hit or miss: Tickets don't guarantee seats, and "long-distance" buses often become stop-at-every-corner city buses about 30 km (18½ mi) from your destination. Also, a "t" or TRANZĪT tag on the schedule means that the bus makes a stop but does not terminate in the town you're in—buy your ticket on board and fight for a seat.

RIGA

Once known as the Paris of the North, Rīga has long been the Baltics' largest and most energetic city. Its denizens are the most urbane in the Baltics. Long avenues of art-nouveau facades hint at a grand past; Rīga was once the Russian Empire's main port, and it's still the commercial center of the Baltics, with the most active airport, expensive hotels, and hordes of American, Scandinavian, and Western European businessfolk. But Rīga is also where you'll see the most homeless and unemployed, the most crime, and the most menacing Russian mafiosi. With all its newfound wealth, Rīga offers much to its visitors—restaurants, bars, galleries—and by the year 2000, it might even have a cutting-edge telecommunications network. Maybe by then the water will be potable as well.

BASICS

Pick up the useful *Rīga in Your Pocket* (50s) from kiosks or hotel desks. **Latvia Tours** (Kaļķu 8, tel. 721–3652; open weekdays 9–6) offers AmEx services. Change money at stores with VALŪTAS MAIŅA signs. Make calls and pick up poste restante (addressed to Your Name, Poste Restante, Rīga 50, LV–1050,

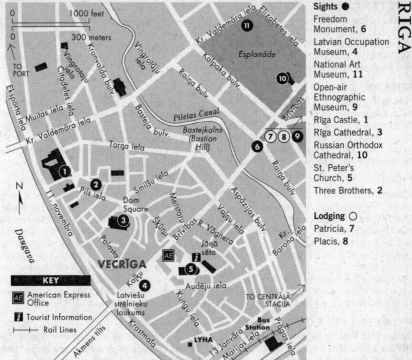

Sights ●

Freedom Monument, **6**

Latvian Occupation Museum, **4**

National Art Museum, **11**

Open-air Ethnographic Museum, **9**

Rīga Castle, **1**

Rīga Cathedral, **3**

Russian Orthodox Cathedral, **10**

St. Peter's Church, **5**

Three Brothers, **2**

Lodging ○

Patricia, **7**

Placis, **8**

KEY

AE American Express Office

i Tourist Information

├──┼ Rail Lines

Latvia) at the 24-hour **main post office** (Brīvības 21, tel. 722–4155), catercorner from the Independence Monument. The **Tourist Club of Latvia** (Skārņu 22, behind Pētera baznīca, tel. 722–1731; open daily 8–6) can help with accommodations.

EMBASSIES • Canada: *Doma laukums 4, tel. 722–6315. Open weekdays 10–1.* **United Kingdom:** *J. Alunāna 5, tel. 733–8126. Open weekdays 9:30–noon.* **United States:** *Raiņa 7, tel. 722– 0367 or 721– 0005. Open weekdays 9–noon and 2–5.*

COMING AND GOING

BY BUS • The **autoosta** (bus station; tel. 721–3611) is just southwest of the train station, next to the market. Buses to Vilnius (6 hrs, 5 Ls–6 Ls) and Tallinn (6 hrs, 5 Ls–6 Ls) depart from the platforms marked on the schedule; look on the wall to the right and ignore the inaccurate color map. Also ignore the troll at the information window, who charges 4s for each question you ask. For international routes, it's easiest to take a private bus; **Eurolines** (Dzirnavu 113, tel. 728–1356) and **Nordeka** (in autoosta, tel. 2/468–814; open 8–4) are faster, far more comfortable, and only marginally more expensive.

BY PLANE • The Baltics' major airport, **Lidosta Rīga** (tel. 720–7009), is 8 km (5 mi) southwest of the center. It's served by **Air Baltic** (tel. 720–7401), with flights to Helsinki ($264); **Transaero** (tel. 720–7738), with flights to Moscow ($329); and **British Airways** (tel. 720–7096), with flights to London ($250).

BY TRAIN • Rīga's **Centrālā Stacija** (Stacijas laukums, tel. 2/233–095), with its bewildering layout, can be a harrowing experience. To make the experience even more memorable, try a *belaši,* the Russian version of the hamburger. They're sold outside the train station, often by gruff, formidable matrons. *Atiešanas* (departures; marked in green) and *pienākšanas* (arrivals; marked in red) are in big numbers on the wall, next to the *ceļa* (platform number). For international tickets, enter on the left side (as you face the station), where you'll find the **Dzelzcela Kases** (International Railway Office; tel. 2/232–134; open daily 8–1 and 2–7). Trains from the main station run to Tallinn (7 hrs via Balti Ekspress, 7.30 Ls), Vilnius (8 hrs, 12 Ls), and Moscow (16 hrs, 25 Ls).

GETTING AROUND

Buses and **trams,** which run 5 AM–midnight, cost 14s; buy tickets at kiosks or on the buses. Have your ticket handy in case one of the humorless controllers boards your bus. Local maps of Rīga (50s), available at kiosks, list all lines. Taxis will rip you off unless you agree on a rate beforehand; **state-run taxis** (tel. 070) supposedly charge 25s per km (½ mi), and private taxis, which have green lights, charge whatever they want. A taxi from the airport to the city center costs 7 Ls–8 Ls.

WHERE TO SLEEP

Patricia (Elizabetes 22/6, tel. 728–4868; open weekdays 9–6, Sat. 10–1) books private rooms in the Old Town; doubles with breakfast start at 10 Ls. Thanks to the **Latvian Youth Hostel Association (LYHA)** (Minsterejas 8/10, tel. 755–1271; open weekdays 9–5), Latvia now has the best hostel system in the Baltics. **Placis** (Laimdotas 2A, tel. 755–1824; beds 3 Ls–5 Ls) has semiluxurious furnishings and a helpful staff; to get here from the station, take Trolleybus 4 north to Teika, walk back diagonally across the small park, and head down Laimdotas.

FOOD

Vincent's (Elizabetes 19, tel. 733–2830) is run by a charismatic Latvian-English chef and specializes in Latvian, nouvelle, and California cuisine. For Latvian-meets-Mexican food, make your way into the Old Town to **Citrons** (Vagnēra 3, tel. 721–2301). **Paddy Whelan's** (Grēcinieku 4, tel. 722–5908) serves big Irish breakfasts (1.7 Ls) and possibly the best coffee (Irish coffee, too) in the Latvian capital, and doubles as a popular bar at night. Try the cheap, veggie Indian cuisine at **Rama** (Kr. Barona 56, at Ģertrūdes, tel. 2/274–134), then head down the street to **Andalūzijas Suns**—"Andalusian Dog" in Latvian—(Elizabetes 83/85, at Kr. Barona), one of Rīga's best cafés. Andalūzijas Suns also houses an elegant cinema that hosts several international film festivals. For uncooked grub, stop at an **Interpegro** convenience store (there's a 24-hour newly renovated branch across from the train station) or browse the *tirgus* (market; open Tues.–Sat. 8–5, Sun.–Mon. 8–3) behind the bus terminal.

WORTH SEEING

Vecrīga (Old Rīga) is conveniently divided by Kaļķu into northern and southern portions. The central **Brīvības Piemineklis** (Freedom Monument; at Brīvības and Raiņa), a 1935 statue whose upheld stars represent Latvia's united peoples (the Kurzeme, Vidzeme, and Latgale), was the rallying point for many a nationalist protest during the late 1980s and early 1990s. Latvia's newly restored 18th-century **Opera House,** where Richard Wagner once conducted early in his career, is an imposing sight just off Freedom Square. Take in an opera or chamber-music performance for 6 Ls–25 Ls (box office at Teatra 10/12, tel. 722–5747). The Soviet-era **Riflemen's monument,** a memorial to the Latvian soldiers who fought on Lenin's side, lies at the southern end of the Old Town. Directly behind the Riflemen is the **Blackheads House,** which is currently being reconstructed for Rīga's 800th anniversary in 2001.

NORTH OF KALKU • **Mazā Pils** is one of Old Rīga's most photogenic streets; note the houses at Nos. 17, 19, and 21 (the three oldest), known collectively as the **Three Brothers.** At the end of Mazā Pils, the two museums within the 14th-century **Rīga Pils** (Rīga Castle) are worth a look: the **Latvijas ārzemjumākslas muzejs** (Latvian Foreign Art Museum; tel. 722–6467; open Tues.–Sun. 11–5) and the **Latvijas vēstures muzejs** (Latvian History Museum; tel. 722–1357; open Wed.–Sun. 11–5). Admission to each is 50s. Head south from the castle for cobbled **Doma laukums** (Dom Square) and the stately 1210 **Rīgas doms** (Rīga Cathedral; admission 20s); the highlight is the massive, 6,718-pipe organ. Concert schedules are posted outside.

SOUTH OF KALKU • Head south from Doma laukums on Šķūņu, cross Kaļķu, and continue down Skārņu toward towering **Pētera baznīca** (St. Peter's Church; open Tues.–Sun. 10–7), originally built in 1209; check out the view from the **observation deck** (admission 1 Ls) of the church's 200-ft spire; young Latvian couples traditionally propose marriage here. Just west of St. Peter's is the **Latvian Occupation Museum** (Strēlnieku laukums 1, tel. 721–2715; admission free; open Tues.–Sun. 11–5), which details the devastation of Latvia at the hands of the Nazis and Soviets during World War II.

BEYOND VECRIGA • Brīvības runs east from Old Rīga across the Pilsētas Canal and past the Independence Monument before spilling past the **Russian Orthodox Cathedral** (open daily 7:30 AM–8 PM). Behind the cathedral, the sprawling **Esplanade** is home to the **Valsts mākslas muzejs** (National Art Museum; at Kr. Valdemara and Elizabetes, tel. 732–5021; admission 40s; open Wed.–Mon. 11–5), with loads of 19th- and 20th-century Latvian art. The **Brīvdabas muzejs** (Open-air Ethnographic Museum; Brīvības 440, tel. 799–4510; admission 50s; open daily 11–5) is well worth the 9-km (5½-mi) bus trek from downtown; catch Bus 1 anywhere on Brīvības and get off at the first stop after Jugla Lake. In early June the museum hosts a great **crafts fair,** a major Baltic event.

NEAR RIGA

JURMALA

Jūrmala literally means "seaside," and that's exactly what you get in this cluster of towns: 20 km (12 mi) of glorious, sandy beach. **Majori,** the biggest and most tourist-friendly town, is the best place to start any lengthy stay in Jūrmala. The **tourist office** (Jomas 42, tel. 27/64–276; open weekdays 10–6), just 2 blocks from the train station, has free maps and books rooms (6 Ls–12 Ls). You can rent bikes (1 Ls per hour) at **Veloviss** (Jomas 75; open Tues.–Sun. 11–7) to ride along the water. Every half hour, trains leave Rīga for Majori via the Tukums II line (40 min, 50s); weekend trains are often standing-room-only.

WHERE TO SLEEP AND EAT • Though most people visit Jūrmala towns on day trips, the lovely **Marienbāde** (Meirovica 43, tel. 27/62–518) has a sauna and clean doubles with bath for 15 Ls. The cozy **Barbara: Spanish Restaurant** (Jomas 66, tel. 27/62-201) has semi-authentic Spanish cuisine (entrées 2.50 Ls–7 Ls).

LITHUANIA

The most outwardly friendly of the Baltic Republics, Lithuania is also unpredictable and eclectic. A list of its citizens' affections—Frank Zappa, basketball, and God—would sound like a Mad Lib. This heterogeneity isn't surprising when you consider Lithuania's unique history: Within just a few generations, Lithuania went from being pagan, defending its "sacrilegious" ways longer than any other European nation, to being ultra-Catholic. The shift occurred when Lithuania's King Jogaila married a Polish princess in 1386, took on a nice Christian name (Ladislaus V), and begat the Polish-Lithuanian commonwealth, which lasted for nearly 4 centuries. Having once co-chaired an empire, Lithuanians still, from time to time, exude the pride of former regional rulers. In 1990, Lithuania was the first Baltic Republic to declare independence from the Soviets, but since then it has been slower than its neighbors to embrace capitalism, leaving the country more ramshackle in places but also a lot more human. The Lithuanians are by far the most rural people of the Baltic, which may explain their anticapitalist and anti-urban streaks.

BASICS

MONEY

US$1 = 4 Lt and 1 Lt = 25¢. The official currency in Lithuania is the litas (Lt), equivalent to 100 centų (c). Credit cards are accepted at better hotels and restaurants and many grocery stores. Most towns have a bank that gives cash advances on credit cards and exchanges traveler's checks (3% fee).

PHONES

Country code: 370. Lithuania is revamping its phone system, so don't panic if you see phone numbers with anywhere from five to seven digits. To make calls, deposit coins or a žeton (token; 56c), good for three minutes, then dial 8, wait for the tone, and dial the number. Telefono korteles (phone cards; 7 Lt–30 Lt) for the blue phones found at post offices and kiosks are available everywhere. To call abroad from Lithuania, dial 8, wait for the tone, dial 10, then dial the country code and number. For **AT&T,** dial 8, wait for the tone, then dial 196. You can dial international calls directly from older coin-operated Lithuanian phones.

COMING AND GOING

Trains are the best way to reach Vilnius from Rīga or Warsaw. If you're coming from Warsaw and don't want to pay $30 for a Belorussian transit visa, take the Balti Ekspress to Kaunas, where you can transfer to one of numerous Vilnius-bound trains (2 hrs, 8.70 Lt). International **buses** are slow but cheap if you're coming from Berlin or Warsaw, and less of a bargain from Tallinn or Rīga. For cheap **flights,** check with Vilnius's student travel shop, **LSJKB** (Basanavičiaus 30/13, tel. 2/22–09–80; open weekdays 9–6, Sat. 10–2).

GETTING AROUND

Train travel is iffy in Lithuania; sometimes you're stuck on an old clunker with wooden benches, sometimes you're in a compartment with cushioned seats. Buses tend to be quicker and cheaper than trains.

VILNIUS

Founded by Lithuanian Grand Duke Gediminas in the 14th century, Vilnius was an important center of Lithuanian, Polish, and Jewish culture until World War II. Now this former "Jerusalem of the East" is Lithuania's bustling capital—a national symbol to extradited Poles, a ghost town to the 150,000 Jews who once lived here, and home to 100,000 displaced Russians. With museums, lush parks, a wealth of baroque churches, and myriad courtyards, many of which have been converted into cafés and jazz clubs, there's also plenty for tourists to enjoy.

BASICS

Lithuanian Tours (Šeimyniškiŭg., 18-2005 Vilnius, Lithuania, tel. 2/72–41–56; open weekdays 9–6) offers AmEx services (but can't cash checks). **Vilniaus Bankas** (Gedimino pr. 12, tel. 2/61–07–23; open Mon.–Thurs. 9–1:30 and 2:30–4:30, Fri. 9–4) changes traveler's checks and cash, and gives Visa cash advances. Send mail, make calls, and change money at the **Centrinis Paštas** (central post office; Gedimino pr. 7, tel. 2/61–67–59; open weekdays 8–8, weekends 11–7). For operator-assisted or direct-dial calls (from a phone in the main hall), head to the 24-hour **Central Telephone and Telegraph Office** (Vilniaus 33, at Islandijos, tel. 2/61–96–14).

EMBASSIES • Canada: *Didžioji 8-5, tel. 2/22–08–98. Open weekdays 10–1.* **United Kingdom:** *Antakalnio 2, tel. 2/22–20–70. Open weekdays 9–5:30.* **United States:** *Akmenų 6, tel. 2/22–30–31. Open weekdays 8:30–5:30.*

COMING AND GOING

The 24-hour **Geležinkelio stotis** (train station; Geležinkelio 16, ½ km (⅓ mi) south of Old Town, tel. 2/63–00–86) serves Kaunas (1¼–2 hrs, 7.30 Lt–8.70 Lt), Rīga (8–9 hrs, 27 Lt–39 Lt), Moscow (12 hrs, 78 Lt–128 Lt), and Warsaw (12 hrs, 110 Lt) via Grodno, Belarus; the **information booth** (tel. 2/69–28–52; open weekdays 9–7) sells the handy "Vilnius In Your Pocket" (4 Lt) and reserves rooms. Buses from the 24-hour **Autobusų stotis** (Sodų 22, tel. 2/26–24–82), just west of the train station, go to Kaunas (2 hrs, 7 Lt), Klaipėda (5 hrs, 30 Lt), Tallinn (10 hrs, 45 Lt), and Warsaw (10 hrs, 75 Lt). **Tranzito Centras** (Giedraičių 85, tel. 2/72–37–10) arranges shared rides to Western Europe.

GETTING AROUND

Tram and **bus** tickets (60c–75c) are sold at newsstands and kiosks. Most lines run 6 AM–midnight (some stop earlier). **Taxis** (tel. 2/228–888) charge about 1 Lt–1.30 Lt per km. As a general rule, cabbies in Vilnius are the most affable and honest cabbies in the Baltics.

WHERE TO SLEEP

LJNN (Kauno 1A/407, 1,000 ft from train station, tel. 2/26–26–60; open weekdays 8:30–6) is a good place to get information. The friendly **Litinterp** (Bernadinų 7, tel. 2/22–32–91; open weekdays 9–6, Sat. 9–4) books rooms in the Old Town (doubles 100 Lt) and with families (25 Lt per person). The LJNN hostel, **Filaretai** (Filaretų 17, SW of Kalnų Park, 1 km (⅔ mi) from Old Town, tel. 2/69–66–27), charges 28 Lt per person the first night, 24 Lt each additional night. From the train station, take Bus 34 seven stops to Filaretų, cross the street, and go down 415 yds. The **Teachers' University Hostel** (Vivulskio 36, tel. 2/23–07–04) has cheap, drab doubles for 56 Lt.

FOOD

For traditional Lithuanian cuisine, try **Aludi Stikliai Taverna** (in the Old Town, Gaono 7, tel. 2/62–79–71), which resembles a cheery Bavarian beer hall. **Ritos Smuklė,** a Chicago-style pizza joint run by a Lithuanian-American, serves just about the best pizza in the Baltics. For a quick, cheap bite, try **Pilies Menė** (Pilies 8), famous for its *miėsa* (meat-filled) or *sūriu* (cheese-filled) *blynai* (pancakes; 3 Lt). Even locals consider the expat hangout **Prie Parlamento** (Gedimino pr. 46, tel. 2/62–16–06) one of the best in Vilnius; try the fantastic shepherd's pie (10 Lt). The most convenient Visa-accepting grocery store is **Naktigonė** (Jogailos 12; open daily 8 AM–10 PM). At night, try the **Langas Music Club** (Ašmenos 8), which draws some of the hottest jazz and blues acts in the Baltics.

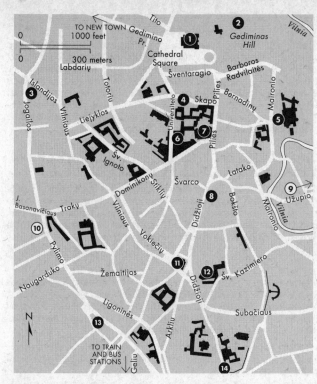

Sights ●

Arkikatedra Bazilika (Cathedral), **1**

Aušros Vartai (Gates of Dawn), **14**

Gedimino Tower, **2**

Lithuanian Art Museum, **11**

Observatory, **6**

St. Anne's Church, **5**

St. Casimir's Church, **12**

St. John's Church, **7**

Synagogue, **13**

State Jewish Museum, **3**

Vilnius Art Gallery, **8**

Vilnius University, **4**

Lodging ○

Filaretai, **9**

Teachers' University Hostel, **10**

WORTH SEEING

The most fascinating sight in the New Town is the **KGB Museum** (Aukų 4, tel. 2/62–24–49; admission 2 Lt; open daily 10–5), whose guides are all former prisoners and exiles.

SENAMIESTIS (OLD TOWN) • The **Aušros Vartai** (Gates of Dawn), the main entrance to the Old Town, is the only one remaining of Vilnius's nine 16th-century gates. Beyond it to the right, a door leads to the **Chapel of Our Lady of Vilnius** (Aušros Vartų 12), a heart-covered room with an icon of the Virgin Mary renowned for its healing powers. A short walk away is the 17th-century **Šv Kazimiero bažnyčia** (St. Casimir's Church; Didžioji 34, tel. 2/22–17–15), named after the city's patron saint Prince Casimir Jagiellon. Where Šv Jono collides with Pilies, enter the main square of **Vilnius University,** founded by the Jesuits in 1570; if you're lost, look for **St. John's Church** (open Wed.–Sun. 10–6). The archway opposite the church leads to the **observatory.** Don't miss the amazing Gothic façade of the 16th-century **St. Anne's Church** (Maironis 8, at Bernidinų). Art fanatics should browse the excellent **Vilniaus Paveikslų galerija** (Vilnius Art Gallery; Didžioji 4, tel. 2/22–08–41; admission 2 Lt; open Tues.–Sun. noon–6), which displays fine 16- to 19th-century art, and the **Lietuvos dailės muziejus** (Lithuanian Art Museum; Didžioji 31, tel. 2/62–86–79; admission 1 Lt; open Tues.–Sun. noon–6), which features early 20th-century Lithuanian art, including several colorful Cubist pieces by Kaririūkštis.

GEDIMINO KALNAS AND KATEDROS AIKSTE • During the Middle Ages, **Gediminas Hill** and **Cathedral Square** were graced with two castles, but thanks to ongoing restorations, there's not much to see now. Vilnius's main cathedral, **Arkikatedra Bazilika** (closed Sun.), has been a major national symbol for centuries; step inside and take a peak at the dazzling 17th-century **Chapel of St. Kazimieras** in front on the right. Stroll up from Cathedral Square through Kalnų Parkas, and you'll wind through woods, past an old funicular, to the entrance of 13th-century **Gedimino bokštas** (Gedimino Tower), once part of the city's fortifications. Check out the view from the tower's **Vilniaus pilies muziejus** (Vilnius Castle Museum; admission 2 Lt; open Wed.–Sun. 11–6). From there, you can see the three white crosses in **Kalnų Park,** which are said to commemorate seven Franciscan monks killed on the hill by pagans; four of them were thrown into the river below (hence the three crosses). Not too far away, **Šv Petro ir Povilo** (Church of Saints Peter and Paul) has an astounding baroque interior.

JEWISH QUARTER • In the early 1900s, Vilnius was Europe's major center of Yiddish education and literature. By the end of World War II, all but 6,000 of Vilnius's 100,000 Jews had been killed, most of them at the nearby Paneriai death camp. Today the Jewish Quarter contains almost no trace of the once-thriving culture. The single remaining **synagogue** (Pylimo 39) survived only because the Nazis used it as a medical-supply warehouse. The best way to learn about Vilnius's Jewish heritage is to visit the **Valstybinis ăydų muziejus** (State Jewish Museum; Pylimo 4, tel. 2/61–79–17; open weekdays 11– 5; donations accepted) and the **Holocaust Museum** (Pamėnkalnio 12, tel. 2/62–07–30; open weekdays 9–5; donations accepted), with photographs and documents from the Holocaust.

NERINGA (COURLAND SPIT)

This 100-km-long (62-mi-long) fingernail of land (Kuršių nerija in Lithuanian) is by far the most beautiful natural attraction in the Baltic Republics. Tourists flock here in summer, but there are plenty of dense forests, empty beaches, and sand dunes to explore on your own. The **Kuršių Nerija National Park** (admission 2 Lt) covers most of the spit. Camping is illegal, so base yourself in **Juodkrantė,** one of the two main towns (the other is Nida, which is less scenic and more touristed, though better equipped with hot water and comfy hotels).

JUODKRANTE

Juodkrantė is the place to get away from it all. One of the best hikes in the area is to **Raganų kalnas** (Witches' Hill), accessed via a 1-km (⅔ mi) trail lined with wooden sculptures of devils, trolls, goblins, and mythic Lithuanian kings; if your interest flags halfway through, several additional trails branch off toward the beach. The trailhead is on the main road, Liudviko Rėzos, ½ km (¼ mi) south of the bus stop. The bus stop is in the center of town, just south of **Gintari jlanka** (Amber Bay).

Several daily **buses** and a few daily trains make the trip from Vilnius to Klaipėda (5 hrs, 22 Lt), where you can catch a ferry over to Smiltynė (80c). From Smiltynė, bike or hop a bus (3 Lt) or *maršrutini* (a buslike taxi; 5 Lt) to Juodkrantė (20 km; 13 mi.).

WHERE TO SLEEP AND EAT • Friendly **Alano Stonenė** (Liudviko Rėzos 20, tel. 59/53–181) rents beds in her house (10 Lt–20 Lt per person) and can help you find accommodations elsewhere if she's booked. For some of the best home cooking anywhere, grab a table on **Raimonda Norkienė**'s front porch (Liudviko Rėzos 34, tel. 59/53–369).

BELGIUM

T he most obvious difference between Belgium's two very distinct population groups—the Flemish in the north and the Walloons in the south—is language: Northerners speak Dutch, and southerners speak French. But you'll notice further differences in everything from architecture to politics. The two regions don't even share a common history; each has been controlled by different ruling families (from France, Spain, Austria, and elsewhere) at various times. Belgium was born after a mild war of independence with the Netherlands in 1830, but it has yet to develop a national identity that supersedes regional loyalties. The country recently modified itself into a federation of three separate regions—Flanders, Wallonie, and Brussels—and a number of Flemish and Walloons would like to see it split into independent nations.

In the past few years, Belgians have been shaken by several cases of missing children, which were exacerbated by inefficiency and corruption among the investigators. Widespread demand for greater accountability has resulted in plans for a European center to coordinate the search for missing children. As a result of these highly publicized tragedies, Belgians have experienced a new unity that may ultimately benefit the fragile federal structure.

It is ironic that a country with such long-standing internal conflicts should be home to the European Commission, the governing body of the European Union and the heart of the effort to unify Europe. Most Belgians would honestly like to see their EU neighbors come together; World Wars I and II, in which Belgium was ravaged, convinced them that the only secure future lies in a unified Europe.

Belgium's most appealing city and the darling of the tourist industry is old-fashioned Brugge, in the west. The nation's capital, Brussels, in the center of the country, is home to the most powerful EU institutions, while Antwerp, the heart of Flanders, beats with live music and the legacy of Peter Paul Rubens. And the southeast corner of Belgium, though thick with memories of World War II, is graced with the beautiful hills and forests of the Ardennes, where nature still reigns supreme.

BASICS

MONEY

US$1 = 34 Belgian francs and 10 Belgian francs = 29¢. The Belgian franc (BF) is accepted in both Belgium and Luxembourg. Banks, generally open weekdays 9–noon and 2–4, offer the best exchange

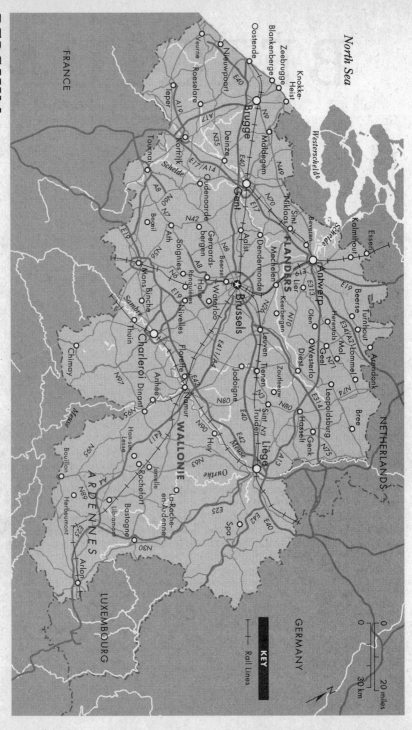

BELGIUM

North Sea

FRANCE

FLANDERS

WALLONIE

ARDENNES

LUXEMBOURG

NETHERLANDS

GERMANY

KEY
Rail lines

0   20 miles
0   30 km

Oostende
Blankenberge
Zeebrugge
Knokke-
Heist
Nieuwpoort
Veurne
Roeselare
Ieper
Brugge
Middegem
Deinze
Kortrijk
Tournai
Oudenaarde
Gerards-
bergen
Ath
Beveren
Soignies
Mons
Binche
Thuin
Chimay
Renquelles
Halle
Nivelles
Waterloo
Gent
Sint-
Niklaas
Lier
Antwerp
Essen
Kalmthout
Beveren
Dendermonde
Mechelen
Aalst
Brussels
Leuven
Tienen
Zoutleeuw
Sint-
Truiden
Hasselt
Diest
Olen
Westerlo
Geel
Mol
Herentals
Turnhout
Beerse
Lommel
Asgodonk
Bree
Leopoldsburg
Genk
Liège
Spa
Huy
Namur
Florette
Dinant
Anhée
Arlon
Bouillon
Herbeumont
Libramont
Bastogne
La-Roche-
en-Ardenne
Rochefort
Jemelle
Han-sur-
Lesse
Jodoigne
Zoutleeuw
Keerbergen
Beersel
Bergeil

Schelde
Westerschelde
Schelde
Sambre
Meuse
Ourthe
Lesse
Maas

E40
A17
N9
N35
E40
E17/A14
A8
N60
N7
N42
N35
A8
N6
N35
E19
N97
N5
N53
N8
N70
E17
N16
E313
N10
N19
E34/A21
N71
N74
N75
A13
E314
N3
N80
E40
E42
E25
E411/A4
N4
N89
N85
N63
N30
E25
N30
N29
E19
A19
N49
N3

70

rates, but Thomas Cook and American Express are also competitive. ATMs are a good option if you have a credit card or bank card on the Cirrus system. Bureaux de change and exchange windows at most train stations will change your money after hours, but they offer lower rates and charge fees.

HOW MUCH IT WILL COST • Belgium's food and lodging are expensive (hotel doubles start at 1,200BF), but low transportation costs balance them out. If you stay in hotels, figure at least $45 a day to get by; if you sleep in hostels and shop at grocery stores, you can keep it under $35.

GETTING AROUND

Because it's so small, travel within Belgium is generally quite cheap. Trains run almost everywhere, except in the Ardennes, where you'll have to use the bus.

BY BIKE • Biking is a good way to get around the country, though it's tougher in the bigger cities. Outside the cities, many roads have bike lanes, and the terrain is easy to tackle almost everywhere but in the Ardennes. Many train stations rent bicycles for 150BF per day to travelers with rail tickets, but they're not your state-of-the-art mountain bikes.

BY BUS AND TRAM • Two Belgian companies handle travel within and between cities: **DeLijn** (tel. 02/526–28–28) in Flanders and **TEC** (tel. 081/72–08–40) in Wallonie. Tickets for one system are not valid on the other. DeLijn one-day passes (450BF) are good in *any* city in Flanders. TEC's one-day pass (200BF) covers travel around Wallonie; you can buy it from the driver.

BY TRAIN • If you plan to spend more than a couple days here and don't have a Eurailpass, national rail passes can help keep fares low. The **Belgium Tourrail Pass** (2,060BF) is good for five days of unlimited travel in Belgium within a month; the **Go Pass** (1,390BF), the best deal for people under 26, is valid for 10 one-way trips anywhere in Belgium and can be shared by two or more people. The **Benelux Tourrail Pass** is good for five days of unlimited train travel in Belgium, the Netherlands, and Luxembourg within a 30-day period and costs 4,220BF (2nd Class), or 3,160BF if you're under 26.

WHERE TO SLEEP

Most of Belgium's extremely popular **hostels** have bars, are well-run, and are good places to meet European travelers. Ask at any HI hostel for the free booklet listing all HI hostels in Belgium. The privacy of a **hotel** double will run you at least 1,200BF, including breakfast and shower. Some **universities** rent out rooms in the summer, especially in Gent. **Camping** is also cheap and popular throughout Belgium, but campgrounds are rarely centrally located. A number of campgrounds in Flanders (and in southern Holland) can rent you a *trekkershutte*, a small chalet that sleeps four, for 960BF; these come equipped with kitchenette and utensils, and are intended primarily for hikers and bikers. **Toerisme Kempen** handles central reservations (Grote Markt 44, 2300 Turnhout, tel. 014/43–61–11, fax 014/42–88–01). For custom holidays in Wallonie, contact **Belsud Reservations** (rue du Marché–aux–Herbes 61, 1000 Brussels, tel. 02/504–02–80, fax 02/514–53–35).

FOOD

National specialties like *moules* (mussels) or *waterzooi* (chicken stew) are served in budget restaurants for about 400BF. Service charges are always included, so don't worry about tips. Even if you're not a slave to your sweet tooth, don't pass up the chocolates this country is famous for; do as the Belgians do, and go for the half-price Leonidas. Belgium is also a nation of brewers. Hundreds of beers are available, the cheapest starting at around 40BF and the best going for about 75BF; the Trappist Rochefort, brewed by the Trappist monks, and *kriek*, a cherry-flavored beer, are well worth a try.

PHONES AND MAIL

Country code: 32. Some of Belgium's phones accept coins, but most only take cards, available in different denominations at newsstands and post offices. Local calls cost 20BF. For credit card or collect calls, dial 0–800–100–10 for **AT&T**; 0–800–100–12 for **MCI**; 0–800–100–14 for **Sprint.**

Mail service in Belgium is reliable. It costs 34BF to mail a postcard or letter to the United States; slap a blue A PRIOR sticker on the envelope for speedy airmail delivery.

LANGUAGE

Most Flemish people speak English, as do French-speakers employed in the service industries. For a crash course in handy French and Dutch phrases, *see* Language *in* Chapters 9 *and* 18.

BRUSSELS

Given that Brussels (Bruxelles in French, Brussel in Flemish), the Belgian capital and headquarters of both NATO and the European Union, is a bustling center for diplomats, lobbyists, and Europoliticians, you'd think it would have plenty of sights and a lively cultural scene. It does, but you have to look for them; this city values privacy and doesn't flaunt its charms. Thus Brussels rarely ranks as a top sight-seeing destination, and it's not a particularly cool place to hang out. Look beyond the glamorous world of international diplomacy and you'll find a city with some serious social problems.

But Brussels *is* worth seeing, if only for its history: Everyone from the French to the Spanish to the Austrians has helped shape this city. One of Brussels' most beautiful sights, the Grand' Place, is ringed with 15th- and 17th-century buildings that you could gaze at for hours. There are also enough museums to fill a couple days, including two designed by Victor Horta, a pioneer of the Art Nouveau style 100 years ago: one dedicated to his own work, and another with a terrific collection of comic-strip art.

BASICS

VISITOR INFORMATION

You may find a long line at the **Tourism and Information Office of Brussels** (Hôtel de Ville, Grand' Place, tel. 02/513–89–40; open daily 9–6), but their comprehensive city guide/map (100BF) is worth the wait. If you have no place to stay, the staff here won't rest until they've found you one. Brussels also has a **Tourist Office** (rue du Marché-aux-Herbes 63, tel. 02/504–03–09; open daily 9–7; shorter hours off season) with general information on the rest of Belgium.

AMERICAN EXPRESS

Pl. Louise 2, tel. 02/676–21–21 or 02/11–76–32 for 24-hour traveler's check refunds. Metro: Louise. Open weekdays 9–5, Sat. 9:30–noon.

CHANGING MONEY

The best place to change money at great rates with no commission is **Petercam Securities** (Pl. Ste-Gudule 19, tel. 02/229–65–70; open weekdays 9–5). For late-night exchange, you'll have to resort to the awful rates at the train stations or the bureaux de change (usually open until midnight) near the Grand' Place.

EMBASSIES

Australia: *Rue Guimard 6, tel. 02/231–05–00; open weekdays 9–noon and 2–4:30.* **Canada:** *Ave. Tervuren 2, tel. 02/735–60–40; open weekdays 9–noon and 2–4.* **United Kingdom:** *Rue d'Arlon 85, tel. 02/287–62–17; open weekdays 9:30–12:30 and 2:30–4:30.* **United States:** *Blvd. du Regent 25, tel. 02/513–38–30; open weekdays 9–noon.*

MAIL

For 24-hour postal service, go to the **Gare du Midi post office** at Avenue Fonsny 48A. Poste restante is held in the **post office** (open weekdays 8:30–5:30) at the Gare Centrale; have mail sent to Your Name, Poste Restante, Brussels 22, 1000 Brussels, BELGIUM.

COMING AND GOING

BY BUS

Eurolines operates up to three daily express services from and to Amsterdam (4 hrs, 600BF), Berlin (10 hrs, 2,200BF), Frankfurt (6½ hrs, 1,100BF), Paris, (4 hrs, 900BF) and London (8 hrs via Calais–Dover ferry, 1,850BF). The Eurolines Coach Station adjoins the Gare du Nord (Rue du Progrès 80, tel. 02/203–0707).

BY PLANE

Brussels National Airport is in the suburb of Zaventem, 14 km (8½ mi) northeast of the city center. Getting into Brussels from the airport is a snap: Between 6 AM and 11:30 PM, take the train (20 min, 85BF) to Gare du Nord or Gare Centrale. Buy a ticket before you get on or they'll slap you with extra fees. A cab into town runs about 1,000BF.

BY TRAIN

Brussels is served by three main stations, all of which store luggage, change money, and hook up with the Metro. **Gare du Nord** (rue du Progrès 85) handles northern and eastern destinations, including Antwerp (30 min, 190BF), Amsterdam (3 hrs, 1,100BF), and Cologne (3 hrs, 1,080BF), as well as the Brussels airport. The station's in a seedy part of town, but it's within walking distance of the main shopping streets and most hostels. **Gare du Midi** (rue de France 2) is the busiest of the three, handling southern and western destinations like Paris (2 hrs, 1,750BF by TGV) and London (3¼ hrs by Eurostar via the Channel Tunnel, 3,680BF; 7 hrs via Oostende–Ramsgate catamaran, 2,540BF), Gent (30 min, 285BF), Brugge (1 hr, 360BF), and Oostende (1¼ hr, 440BF). From the station, Trams 52 and 55 will take you to Bourse (50BF), near the Grand' Place. **Gare Centrale** (carrefour de l'Europe 2) is served mostly by commuter trains that also stop at Midi and/or Nord, but Centrale is right by the Grand' Place and is perfect for luggage storage (60BF–100BF; open 4:30 AM–1 AM). For all Brussels train information, dial 02/203–36–40.

GETTING AROUND

Try to cover Brussels by instinct and you're bound to get lost. Pick up a map and use a combination of walking and the extensive public-transit system (information: 02/515–20–00). Metros, trams, and buses all run on the same tickets. A single ticket costs 50BF, but the day pass (130BF) and the 10-trip card (320BF) are great deals, and you can buy all three at any Metro station. On buses you can buy only single tickets. The information offices at Rogier, Porte de Namur, and Gare du Midi Metro stations are open weekdays 8:30–5; the Rogier and Porte de Namur offices are also open Saturday 9:30–5:15. All three give out free Metro maps. Taxis (02/349–49–49) are expensive, but necessary after most public transit closes down around midnight. Call one or pick one up at a cab stand.

WHERE TO SLEEP

Brussels offers everything from international chains to sleazy one-nighters to friendly hostels. Try one of two main lodging areas: the **city center** in the Grand' Place area, or **St-Gilles** to the south of the center. **BTR** (Belgian Tourist Reservations, Blvd Anspach 111, tel. 02/513–74–84) handles hotel reservations free of charge. **Acotra** (Rue de la Madeleine 53, tel. 02/512–86–07) will find you rooms in hostels.

CITY CENTER

Stay in the city center if you want to be close to sights and shopping. The area near the Gare du Nord is a red-light district, where women should not walk alone at night, but the Old City is generally safe.

UNDER 2,000BF • Galia. Right on the flea market in the (slowly gentrifying) old working-class area of Marolles, Galia boasts a lively, skylighted tavern just behind the reception desk, and a small terrace in front. Rooms are small, but all have showers, and the elevator shudders but gets you there. Doubles are 1,600BF, less on weekends. *Place du Jeu de Balle 16, tel. 02/502–42–43, fax 02/502–76–19. Metro: Porte de Hal. NW 2 blocks on blvd du Midi, NE on rue Blaes.*

Hôtel à la Grande Cloche. The lobby and breakfast area may be less than inviting, but rooms are airy and light. The cheapest rooms have washbasin and bidet, with hair dryer in the corridor. Doubles start at 1,750BF; triples with bath are good values at 3,300BF. Breakfast is included and weekend rates possible. Across the square is Brussels' most famous restaurant, Comme Chez Soi. *Place Rouppe 10–12, tel. 02/512–61–40, fax 02/512–65–91. Metro Anneessens. From blvd. Lemonnier, 1 block SE on rue de Tournai.*

Sabina. The carpets are well-worn and the wallpaper musty, but the Sabina remains a favorite among travelers susceptible to its old-fashioned charm. Doubles start at 1,700BF. Weekend rates negotiable. *Rue du Nord 78, tel. 02/218–26–37, fax 219–32-39. From Metro Botanique, walk SW on rue Royale, SE on rue de la Sablonnière, and across the handsome pl. des Barricades.*

SPLURGE • Hôtel Mozart. If you're going to splurge, do it right: This hotel's rooms and decor, including ancient oak beams and gorgeous 18th-century artwork, elegantly echo the feel of the Grand' Place, about 200 ft away. All rooms have private baths. Doubles are 3,000BF; and the split-level triple is a bargain at 4,000BF. *Rue du Marché aux Fromages 15A, tel. 02/502–66–61, fax 02/502–77–58. Metro: Bourse.*

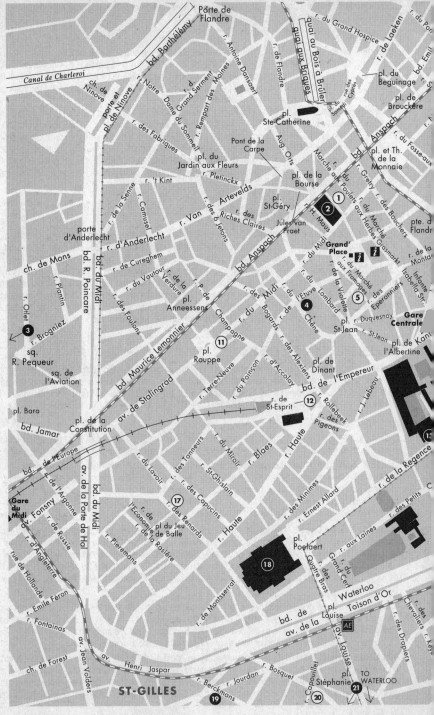

Canal de Charleroi

Pörte de Flandre

bd. Barthélémy

r. du Grand Hospice

r. de Laeten

ch. de Ninove

porte et bd. de Ninove

pl. de Ninove

r. Notre Dame du Sommet

r. d. Grand Serment

r. Antoine Dansaert

r. de Flandre

quai aux Bois à Brûler

quai aux Briques

pl. du Beguinage

pl. de Brouckère

r. des Fabriques

r. du Rempart des Moines

pl. Ste-Catherine

Aug. Orts

bd. Anspach

r. du Fossé-aux-

pl. du Jardin aux Fleurs

Pont de la Carpe

Marché aux Poulets aux Herbes Gassmarkt

r. Grétry

r. des Bouchers

pl. et Th. de la Monnaie

r. 't Kint

r. Pletinckx

pl. de la Bourse

r. de la Senne

r. Van Artevelds

r. des Riches Claires

pl. St-Géry

Jules van Praet

r. H. Maus

pte. d Flandr

porte d'Anderlecht

r. d'Anderlecht

r. Camusel

r. à Jelons

Grand' Place

r. de la Monta

r. de Cureghem

bd. Anspach

r. du Marché aux Fromages

Infante r. Isabella Str

r. Plantin

r. du Vautour

r. de la Verdure

p. de

r. des Midi

r. de l'Étuve Lombard

r. du Chêne

r. des Eperonniers

Gare Centrale

ch. de Mons

bd. du Midi

bd. R. Poincare

r. des Foulons

pl. Anneessens

Champagne

r. du Bogards

r. des Alexiens

pl. St-Jean

r. Duquesnoy

r. St-Jean

pl. de Kan l'Albertine

r. Ollier

r. Brogniez

sq. R. Pequeur

sq. de l'Aviation

bd. Maurice Lemonnier

pl. Rouppe

r. Terre-Neuve

r. du Poinçon

r. d'Accolay

pl. de Dinant

bd. de l'Empereur

r. Lebeau

pl. Bara

bd. Jamar

pl. de la Constitution

av. de Stalingrad

r. de St-Esprit

Rollebeek

r. des Pigeons

bd. de l'Europe

av. de la Porte de Hal

r. du Lavoir

r. des Tanneurs

r. du Miroir

r. St-Ghislain

r. Blaes

r. Haute

r. de la Regence

Gare du Midi

av. Fonsny

av. de l'Argonne

r. de Russie

bd. du Midi

r. des Capucins

r. de l'Economie

r. des Renards

pl. du Jeu de Balle

r. de la Rasière

r. Haute

r. des Minimes

r. Ernest Allard

r. des Petits

rue de Hollande

r. d'Angleterre

r. Emile Féron

r. Pieremans

pl. Poelaert

r. aux Laines

Grand Cerf

r. des Quatre Bras

r. Fontainas

r. de Montserrat

pl. Poelaert

Waterloo

ch. de Forest

av. Jean Volders

av. Henri Jaspar

r. Berckmans

r. Bosquet

r. Jourdan

pl. Toison d'Or

av. de la Louise

av. Louise

r. des Chevaliers

r. des Drapiers

pl. Stéphanie

r. Capouillet

TO WATERLOO

ST-GILLES

AE

① ② ③ ④ ⑤ ⑪ ⑫ ⑰ ⑱ ⑲ ⑳ ㉑

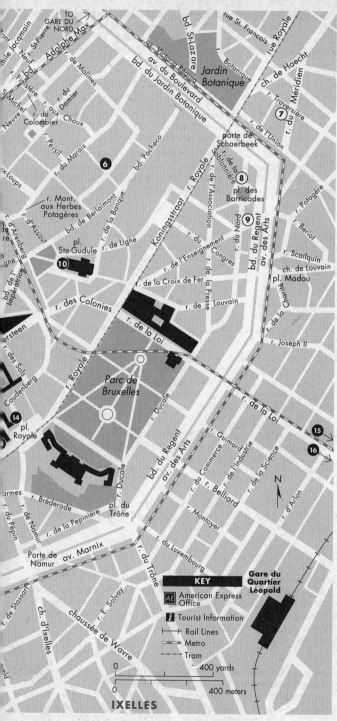

Sights ●

Autoworld, **16**

Belgian Comic Strip Center, **6**

Bourse, **2**

Cathédrale St-Michel, **10**

Manneken-Pis, **4**

Musée d'Art Ancien, **13**

Musée d'Art Moderne, **14**

Musée Gueuze, **3**

Musée Horta, **21**

Musée Royal de l'Afrique Centrale, **15**

Palais du Justice, **18**

Lodging ○

Bruegel (HI), **12**

Centre Vincent Van Gogh-Chab, **7**

Hôtel les Bluets, **19**

Hôtel Galia, **17**

Hôtel á la Grande Cloche, **11**

Hôtel Matignon, **1**

Hôtel Mozart, **5**

Hôtel Sabina, **9**

Jacques Brel (HI), **8**

Résidence Duke of Windsor, **20**

Matignon. Across the street from the Bourse, the Matignon is an all-new (1993) family-owned hotel behind its Belle Epoque facade. Rooms are on the small side but have generous beds, and there is a large and lively brasserie on the ground floor. A double with bath comes to 3,100BF; suites sleeping four are bargains at 4,100BF. *Rue de la Bourse 10, tel. 02/511–08–88, fax 02/513—69–27. Metro: Bourse.*

ST-GILLES

You'll need the Metro to reach most sights from this residential area just south of the city center. The hotels here are often family-owned and a little more personal than those downtown.

Hôtel les Bluets. The 10 rooms vary greatly in price; those with shower but no toilet are great values. Classical music is in the air, and you feel more like a house guest than a hotel client. Doubles start at 1,250BF. *Rue Berckmans 124, tel. and fax 02/534–39–83. Metro: Hôtel des Monnaies.*

Résidence Duke of Windsor. All five rooms have 19th-century furnishings and private baths, and all are worth the splurge. The friendly sixtysomething proprietress strives for a family atmosphere, but if you don't follow house rules, she'll kick you out. No smoking. Minimum stay 2 nights. Call to reserve and confirm in writing. Doubles go for 2,000BF. *Rue Capouillet 4, tel. 02/539–18–19. Metro: Hôtel des Monnaies. Cash only.*

B&B

Bed & Brussels. This upscale B&B chain arranges accommodations with 90 host families, most of them with room to spare after children have flown the coop. Most charge much less than hotels. Twenty-odd are close to the center; the rest are a tram or bus ride away. Breakfast with the hosts is included. Call during office hours to reserve. *Rue Victor Greyson, 1050, tel. 02/217–2300, fax 02/218–0220. Cash only.*

HOSTELS

Bruegel (HI). A stone's throw from the Manneken-Pis and Gare Centrale, this modern hostel has a TV room with MTV and CNN. Dorm beds cost 395BF (sheets 125BF), doubles 1,100BF. No age limit; nonmembers 100BF extra. Luggage storage is an option. There's a 1 AM curfew. *Rue du St-Esprit 2, tel. 02/511–04–36, fax 02/512–07–11. Metro: Gare Centrale. Lockout 1 PM–2 PM. Cash only.*

Centre Vincent Van Gogh (CHAB). Van Gogh did stay here, before it became a privately owned youth hotel with a pool table and sculpted-frog fountains in the spacious common area. You're walking distance from the city center and Gare du Nord. Nine new rooms with access to a private garden were added in 1997. Dorm beds are 300BF (sheets 100BF), doubles 1,040BF. Guests must be under 35. Luggage storage is available. *Rue Traversière 8, tel. 02/217–01–58, fax 02/219–79–95. Metro: Botanique. Lockout 10–4. Laundry.*

Jacques Brel (HI). The quiet location and cozy courtyard make this hostel a welcome retreat, and it's only a 15-minute walk from Grand' Place and Gare du Nord. Beds go for 395BF, sheets for 120BF; doubles are 1,100BF (nonmembers 100BF extra). *Rue de la Sablonnière 30, tel. 02/218–01–87, fax 02/217–20–05. Metro: Botanique. Lockout noon–3. Laundry.*

CAMPING

Camping Veldkant. Fifteen kilometers (9 miles) north of town, Veldkant has tent sites for 100BF plus 100BF per person. *Veldkantstr. 64, tel. 02/269–25–97. From Gare du Nord, Bus G to Grimbergen (45 min, 100BF; last bus from station 11:30 PM).*

FOOD

Brussels has tons of restaurants, but most serve small portions at steep prices. Your best bet is to stick to restaurants with an ethnic twist. Two good areas for cheap eats are the *city center* and the *Ixelles* neighborhood, southeast of the center. To free up some cash for the evening, lunch on a *baguette* (French-bread) sandwich, a meal in itself (60BF–95BF); you'll find them in snack bars everywhere. Or try *frites* (french fries) in a twist with your choice of sauce; some of the best *fritures* are on Place Sainte-Catherine downtown and Place Flagey in Ixelles.

CITY CENTER

After strolling down the famous **rue des Bouchers** and ogling the expensive seafood, head to one of the pita joints along **rue du Marché aux Fromages** (1 block south of Grand' Place). For cheap crêpes, try **La Fleur de Blé Noir** (rue de l'Enseignement 55, east of cathedral, tel. 02/218–55–06), where a meal costs about 250BF. Delicious open sandwiches on farm-style bread (150–200BF), served at a communal table, are the specialty of **Le Pain Quotidien,** a chain of bakeries-cum–snack bars, open from from 7 AM to 7 PM. *Rue Antoine Dansaert 16, tel. 02/502–23–61 (Metro: Sainte-Catherine); Rue des Sablons 11, tel. 02/513-51-44 (Metro: Porte de Namur), and other locations.*

Restaurants must display menus and prices outside; for the best bargain, examine the price of a prix-fixe menu and the *plat du jour* (daily special). By choosing wisely you can eat for less than 500BF in some of the best-known restaurants around the Grand' Place, like **La Roue d'Or** (Rue des Chapeliers 26, tel. 02/514–25–54, closed mid-July–mid-Aug.), with Magritte-inspired paintings; **Chez Jean** (Rue des Chapeliers 6, tel. 02/511–98–15; closed Sun., Mon., and June), where neither the decor nor, it seems, the menu has changed since 1931; and **Vincent** (Rue des Dominicains 8, tel. 02/511–26–07; closed mid-July–mid-Aug.), with 100-year old ceramic-tile murals, where red meat rules.

Among many Vietnamese restaurants, **Da Kao,** near the Bourse, serves large portions of Asian specialties, such as fried chicken with lemongrass (250BF). *Rue Antoine Dansaert 38, tel. 02/512–67–16. Metro: Bourse. Closed Sun. lunch.*

IXELLES

Locals come to this artsy neighborhood to eat, shop, and escape the tourist crowds. Head south from the Porte de Namur Metro stop, past McDonald's, and you'll find all kinds of restaurants.

Le Campus. A student hangout next door to the university, this huge restaurant features "democratic" prices, starting with a plat du jour at 240BF, and a great selection of pasta and pizzas. *Ave. de la Couronne 437–439, tel. 02/648–53–80. Bus 71, stop Cimitière d'Ixelles.*

Restaurant Indochine. Enjoy good, cheap Vietnamese specialties (350BF) among hanging plants and bamboo decor. *Rue Lesbroussart 58, tel. 02/649–96–15. From Porte de Namur Metro, south on chaussée d'Ixelles 20 min to pl. Flagey; or Bus 71. Closed Sun.*

Shezan. Traditional Indian and Pakistani food is served amid Indian art and music. Tandoori dishes start at 300BF. *Chaussée de Wavre 120, tel. 02/512–94–95. Metro: Porte de Namur. Closed for lunch Mon.*

WORTH SEEING

Brussels has plenty of museums, many with adjoining parks that are great for picnics. Some of the city's most famous landmarks are the **Cathédrale St-Michel,** with its gleaming white Gothic towers; the 19th-century **Palais du Justice**; and the **Bourse,** a magnificent stock exchange built in 1871 on a scale that Brussels' stock trading has never quite justified. Perhaps the most famous sight in all of Brussels, though, is the **Manneken-Pis,** a statue of a little boy peeing his heart out a few blocks off the Grand' Place (down rue Charles Buls, which becomes rue de l'Etuve).

GRAND' PLACE

Some fans insist that the Grand' Place, surrounded by enormous gilded buildings, is the most beautiful square in Europe. Legend has it that the **Hôtel de Ville**'s 15th-century architect committed suicide when he saw that the tower on the finished building was off-center. Most of the other buildings on the Grand' Place were built between 1695 and 1700, after Louis XIV of France bombarded and destroyed earlier structures. In No. 9, nicknamed **Le Cygne** (The Swan—you'll see one above the door), Karl Marx and Friedrich Engels dashed off the *Communist Manifesto* in 1848. The **Musée de la Ville de Bruxelles** (tel. 02/279–43–50; admission 80BF; open weekdays 10–12:30 and 1:30–5, weekends 10–1) traces the city's evolution and displays artwork by less-than-famous locals, as well as a room full of Manneken-Pis costumes—look for the little Elvis bell-bottoms.

When you've had enough sightseeing, join the crowds for a drink at a café on the square. From late April to early October, the Grand' Place brightens with nightly entertainment—**light shows** (just after sunset), rock, jazz, and folklore.

MUSEES DES BEAUX-ARTS

Two adjoining museums of fine art display early and modern works. The **Musée d'Art Ancien** houses works from the 15th to 19th centuries, including tons of Rubens's paintings and sketches, and an entire room devoted to Bruegel. Don't miss the surreal devils and demons in the early Dutch religious paintings. *Rue de la Régence 3, tel. 02/508–32–11. Metro: Parc. Admission free. Open Tues.–Sun. 10–noon and 1–5.*

The ingeniously designed, underground **Musée d'Art Moderne** covers 20th-century art and features Belgian works, including Magritte's enigmatic canvases and Delvaux's nudes and skeletons. Sports fans will enjoy the portrait of Wayne Gretzky by Andy Warhol. *Pl. Royale 1–2, tel. 02/508–32–11. Metro: Parc. Admission free. Open Tues.–Sun. 10–1 and 2–5.*

BELGIAN COMIC STRIP CENTER

This unique museum, housed in a splendid Art Nouveau building from 1903, celebrates such famous Belgian graphic artists as Hergé, Tintin's creator, and Morris, the progenitor of Lucky Luke. *Rue des Sables 20, tel. 02/219–19–80. From Botanique Metro, go northwest on Blvd. du Jardin Botanique and southwest on Blvd. Pacheco to the flight of stairs leading down to rue des Sables. Admission 180BF. Open Tues.–Sun. 10–6.*

MUSEE HORTA

Victor Horta, the master of Art Nouveau, designed this building for his own use. From cellar to attic, every detail of the house flaunts the exuberant curves of the new style. Horta tried to put nature and light back into daily life, and here his floral motifs create opulence and spaciousness despite the limited quarters. *Rue Américain 25, tel. 02/537–16–92. Bus 91 or 92, stop Ma Campagne. Admission 120BF (weekends 200BF). Open Tues.–Sun. 2–5:30.*

AUTOWORLD

This mecca for vintage-car aficionados presents 450 vehicles. The surprise star of the show is the Belgian-made Minerva, a luxury car from the early '30s. *Parc du Cinquantenaire 11, tel. 02/736–4165. Open daily 10–6 (until 5 Nov.–March).*

MUSEE GUEUZE

This family brewery is the last traditional brewer of Gueuze, a beer that takes three years to make. They only brew in the winter, but you can always go on the self-guided tour, which ends with the all-important free samples. *Rue Gheude 56, tel. 02/520–28–91. From Clemenceau Metro, north on chaussée de Mons. Admission: 70BF. Open weekdays 8:30–4:30, Sat. 10–1 (until 6 mid-Oct.–June).*

MUSEE ROYAL DE L'AFRIQUE CENTRALE

King Leopold II (1835–1909) hired the explorer Henry Stanley to help him map out the huge domain, now Zaire, of which he became sole owner. This museum outside Brussels houses some 250,000 objects looted in Africa. It is now a leading research center for African studies, with 13 specialized libraries. Pick a nice day, bring lunch, and enjoy the magnificent park. *Leuvensesteenweg 13, tel. 02/769–52–11. From Montgomery Metro station, take Tram 44 to Tervuren. Admission: 80BF. Open Tues.–Sun. 9–5:30; shorter hrs off season.*

AFTER DARK

Brussels is not exactly a hopping city. Most public transportation stops at midnight, drinks and covers are expensive, and the bars seem built for comfort rather than speed. Many, however, stay open until the last customer leaves, and while you're in Brussels, you *must* sample Belgium's world-renowned beer. There's a tavern on every corner, but the most sociable ones are on and around the **Grand' Place.**

Falstaff (rue Henri Maus 17, across the street from the Bourse, tel. 02/511–98–77) stays open from noon until 5 AM, changing character all the time. The prix-fixe lunch is a great value. The interior is perfectly preserved Art Nouveau, but you can also chug beer out on the covered terrace. **Henry J. Beans's** (rue du Montagne-aux-Herbes-Potagères 40, near the Cathedral, tel. 02/219–28–28) is a fifties-style bar-and-grill. For dancing, try **Le Magasin 4** (rue du Magasin 4, Metro Yser), a huge brick warehouse popular with the grunge crowd, open Friday and Saturday from 10 PM. Brussels' African immigrants congregate at **Interface** (chaussée de Wavre 72, tel. 02/502–40–54; Porte de Namur Metro), which has live music Thursday–Saturday 11 PM–4 AM (no cover). The best jazz in town is at **Travers** (rue Traversière 11, Metro Botanique, tel. 02/218–40–86).

NEAR BRUSSELS

WATERLOO

Yes, it was a popular Abba song, but Waterloo was originally known as the site of Napoléon's final battle on June 18, 1815. Some 48,000 soldiers died when the Duke of Wellington and Field Marshal von

Blücher led their troops to victory over the French. The unexpected rain may have turned the tide of war that day by delaying the arrival of French reinforcements, so if Belgium's temperamental skies go gray during your visit to Waterloo, take heart in the fact that you're not staring down a bayonet.

You can visit the battlefield and several monuments and museums here, but the trek is only worth it if you're a serious history buff. **Musée Wellington** (chaussée de Bruxelles 147, tel. 02/354–78–06), is in the building where the general established his headquarters. The collections include maps and models of the battle and military memorabilia. From here you can head out to the battlefield itself, where the best view, including the quadrangular fortified farms where British troops broke the French assault, is from the **Butte du Lion** (rte. du Lion 254, tel. 02/385–19–12); you have to scale 226 steep and narrow steps to get to the top. In defiance of the rules, sightseers still manage to pick up bullets and buttons in the fields. Just below the hill is the **Visitors' Center** (Rte. du Lion 252–254, tel. 02/385–1912; open daily 9:30–6:30, shorter hrs in winter), which has an audiovisual presentation of the battle. Don't miss the **Grand Panorama,** a circular painting of the battle, 360 ft in circumference. Before there were movies, there were panoramic paintings, yet only a very few have survived (Rte. du Lion 256, same tel. and hrs. as Visitors' Center). Every five years, the battle is reenacted by a cast of thousands; the next battle is in mid-June 2000.

If you want to make a day of Waterloo, buy the combination ticket (385BF), which covers all attractions. Otherwise, individual museum admission costs about 120BF. If you get hungry, there are several touristy restaurants at the battlefield. In town, **Mezzanina Da Toni** (rue du Couvent 11, tel. 02/354–00–28, across from the tourist office) has pizza for 270BF.

COMING AND GOING • Nivelles-bound trains leave Brussels' Gare Centrale every hour and stop in Waterloo (30 min, 90BF). Waterloo's **tourist office** (chaussée de Bruxelles 149, tel. 02/354–99–10) is a 1-km (½-mi) walk east of the station toward town. To get to the battlefield, 5 km (3 mi) south of the center, take Bus W (across the street from the Musée Wellington) to Le Lion (40BF).

LEUVEN

For a taste of the ongoing political struggle between the Flemish and the Walloons, consider the recent history of the 570-year-old Catholic University of Leuven (Louvain). Although it's in the Flemish province of Brabant and most students are Flemish, lectures were once delivered in both Flemish and French. In 1968, when student protests and riots swept through Europe, Flemish students in Leuven demanded that the French hit the road, and eventually they did, founding a French-speaking university town called Louvain-la-Neuve, south of the linguistic borders. Today classes at Leuven are taught only in Flemish, and students have settled back down to drinking the locally brewed Artois beer and hanging loose in this cheerful and architecturally beautiful town.

The train ride from Brussels (110BF) takes only 20 minutes. To get to town from the station, walk west on Bondgenotenlaan, and look for the signs to the **tourist office** (L. Vanderkelenstr. 30, tel. 016/21–15–39; open weekdays 9–5, weekends 10–1 and 1:30–5; Nov.–Feb., closed Sun.). The cheapest beds in town are across from the train station at **Hotel Mille Colonne** (Martelarenplein 5, tel. 016/22–86–21, fax 016/22–04–34), where doubles with showers are 1,700BF. For more comfort and a central location, try **Jackson's** (Brusselsestr. 110–112, tel. 016/20–24–92, fax 016/23–13–29)—family-owned, a bit old-fashioned, and open to negotiating a lower weekend rate than the standard 2,950BF for a double with bath. **Schoolbergen** (Sneppenstr. 58, Kessel-Lo, tel. 016/25–59–69) is an unaffiliated hostel-cum-campground where two people with a tent pay 345BF, and beds in summer camp–style dorm rooms are 315BF (180BF for sheets). From the station, take Bus 2 (40BF) towards Holsbeek and tell the driver you're heading for Schoolbergen.

WORTH SEEING • Every Flemish town prides itself on its ornate, medieval Town Hall, and Leuven's **Stadhuis,** on the central Grote Markt, is one of the finest. It celebrates its 550th anniversary in 1998. Guided tours are given weekdays at 11 and 3, weekends at 3. **St. Peter's Collegiate Church** (Grote Markt; admission free; open Mon.-Sat. 10–noon and 2–5, Sun. 2–5, closed Mon. in winter) is remarkable for the purity of its Gothic nave. The ambulatory and choir are closed for restoration, but some of their treasures, including the 15th-century *The Last Supper,* by Dirk Bouts, are on temporary display in the nave. Also worth checking out is the **Stedelijk Museum Vander Kelen-Mertens** (Savoyestr. 6, tel. 016/22–69–06; open Tues.–Sat. 10–5, Sun. 2–5), with restored Renaissance, baroque, and rococo salons.

Walking south from Grote Markt on Naamsestraat you pass a number of colleges (the American College is at No. 100), and at the end of the street is the **Groot Begijnhof** (beguinage), a city-within-a-city of tiny, whitewashed houses, formerly inhabited by members of a Christian sisterhood dating from the 13th century. The last nun died in 1988, and all but one of the houses are now occupied by faculty members. The immense 16th-century **Arenberg Castle,** also university-owned, is a 20-minute walk south of town on Kardinaal Mercierlaan, with perfect grounds for Frisbee and picnics. Before you go, stock your backpack with groceries from **Match** (Bondgenotenlaan, at Jan Stasstr.).

FLANDERS

Flanders is flat. Its big-sky topography has served as a convenient thoroughfare for invading armies en route to France, and for French troops pushing north into the troublesome Low Countries. Fortunately, the Flemish are not as flat as their land; most are very friendly and enjoy speaking English with travelers (though, as always, you should ask first). Actually, most Flemish can chat with you in English, French, Flemish, or German, but French would be their last choice—a strong separatist movement has developed here, perhaps as a result of the region's recent economic prosperity. Historically, Flanders has been the poorest part of Belgium, but since World War II its industrial base has helped it surpass Wallonie in wealth and population. And as for sightseeing, this area contains Belgium's most interesting sights, especially in Brugge and Antwerp.

BRUGGE

Brugge (Bruges), an hour from Brussels by train (360BF), offers a taste of pre–World War II Europe— the Europe many travelers imagine when their trips are still in the planning stages. Canals and cobblestone streets snake everywhere, and almost every building looks like it dates from the 15th or 16th century, even when it doesn't. Simply put, Brugge is one of the most beautiful cities in Europe. If you have time for only one stop in Belgium, make this it. And if possible, go in the spring.

Brugge is definitely a tourist town—you may feel like you're in a medieval theme park—but that means there's a lot to take advantage of. Guided tours, though they may seem cheesy, are one of the best ways to learn about the history of Brugge and Flanders; several agencies in town (*see* Worth Seeing, *below*) make them lots of of fun. But don't spend too much time staring at the back of your tour guide's head; strike out on your own to explore Brugge's incredibly picturesque streets, squares, and canals.

BASICS

You can change money at **Kredietbank (KB)** (Steenstr. 38, tel. 050/44–45–11; open weekdays 9–12:30 and 1:30–4:15, Sat. 9:15–noon) and other banks. Nights and Sundays you'll have to resort to the **GWK** bureau de change (Steenstr. 2; open daily 9–9), where you'll pay a minimum 150BF commission on traveler's checks. The **post office** (Markt 5, tel. 050/33–14–11; postal code 8000) is open weekdays 9–7 and Sat. 9–noon.

The **tourist office** is open year-round and sells city maps for 25BF. *Burg 11, tel. 050/44–86–86. Open Apr.–Sept., weekdays 9:30–6:30, weekends 10–noon and 2–6:30; Oct.–Mar., weekdays 9:30–5, Sat. 9:30–1 and 2–5:30.*

GETTING AROUND

Brugge is centered around the **Markt,** which is encircled by bustling streets and canals. The town itself is skirted by a series of forgotten parks—good escapes from the sightseeing masses. The best one is **Minnewater** (Lake of Love), in the southern part of town. Romantics might want to row through Brugge's canals à deux, but the waterways are reserved solely for tourist boats, so you'll have to resort to biking or walking alongside them. Both are a cinch, as Brugge, like all of western Flanders, is as flat as a board. **Buses** cost 40BF; there's a DeLijn information booth in the **train station** on Stationsplein, about 2 km (1 mi) south of the town center.

BY BIKE • Biking through town is great. Private cars are banned from the town center; just beware of dazed tourists, psycho bus drivers, and one-way streets. You can rent a one-speed bike at the train station, or a three-speed at **Eric Popelier** (Hallestr. 14, near Markt, tel. 050/34–32–62; open 9–9), for 250BF a day, or 150BF for a half-day.

WHERE TO SLEEP

Most of Brugge's lodging is packed into the central and western parts of town. The very best deals are the hostels, but the hotels listed below offer more privacy for just a bit more money. Hotel reservations

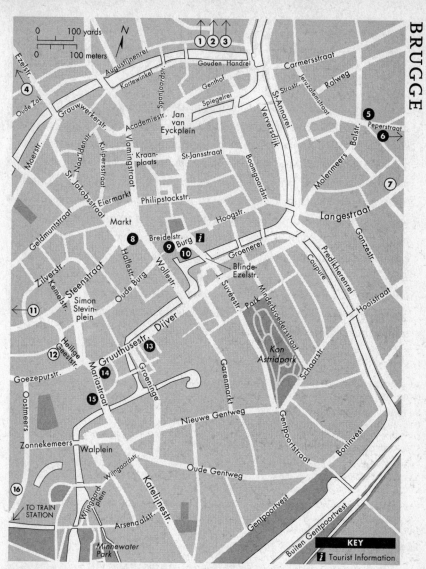

Sights ●

Belfort, **8**

Groeninge
Museum, **13**

Heilig-Bloed
Basiliek, **9**

Kantcentrum, **5**

Memling
Museum, **15**

Onze-Lieve
Vrouwkerk, **14**

Stadhuis, **10**

St-
Janshuysmolen, **6**

Lodging ○

Bauhaus
International Youth
Hotel, **7**

De Pauw, **2**

Fevery, **3**

Het Geestelijk
Hof, **12**

Jacobs, **1**

Passage, **11**

Snuffel, **4**

't Keizershof, **16**

FLANDERS VS. WALLONIE, AND THE WINNER IS . . .

In 1993, the Belgian Parliament officially made Belgium a three-part federalist state composed of French-speaking Wallonie, Flemish-speaking Flanders, and bilingual Brussels. As many separatists—especially from Flanders—pushed for an out-and-out split, King Baudouin I, whom both sides liked and respected, provided a stabilizing force. A few weeks after Parliament set up the federalist state, however, Baudouin died. His brother Albert has since assumed the throne and promised continuity of the federal state. Tensions run high at times, but future Flemish-Walloon conflicts will likely remain within the realm of economic policy and center around such issues as national health-care funding. Both Flemings and Walloons are (at least nominally) Catholic, so the flames are not fanned by religious differences, and physical clashes are nonexistent. Some people claim that the dispute is artificial, and is kept alive by fewer than a thousand politicians and journalists.

are strongly advised in July and August (call a week or two ahead to be safe), but most hostels are first come, first served.

De Pauw. At this spotless, family-run hotel, the warmly furnished rooms have names rather than numbers, and breakfast comes with cold cuts, cheese, and six different kinds of bread. The two rooms that share a shower down the hall are super values at 1,750BF; doubles with shower are 2,300BF. *St. Gilliskerkhof 8, tel. 050/33–71–18, fax 050/34–51–40.*

Fevery. You won't see much from the outside, but once inside, you'll feel like a personal guest. They'll even collect you from the train station on request. Doubles with showers start at 2,000BF. *Collaert Mansionstraat 3, tel. 050/33–12–69, fax 050/33–17–91.*

Het Geestelijk Hof. Some guests cram all of their buddies into these huge rooms when no one is looking. The area is quiet, but close to major sights. Doubles start at 1,490BF, breakfast included. *Heilige Geeststr. 2, tel. 050/34–25–94.*

Jacobs. A handsome, step-gabled house with an abundance of flowers on the window sills, Jacobs excels in ambience and is only a seven-minute walk from the Markt. There's an agreeable bar for a nightcap with friends. Doubles start at 1,650BF. *Baliestr. 1, tel. 050/33–98–31, fax 050/33–56–94. Closed Jan.*

'T Keizershof. These pleasant rooms with flower boxes in the windows are just three minutes from the station. Ask to meet the dog. Doubles are 1,300BF. *Oostmeers 126, tel. 050/33–87–28. Laundry.*

HOSTELS • Bauhaus International Youth Hotel. The location is so-so, but the prices are fetching: dorm beds from 300BF, doubles 950BF, breakfast included. You can also change money, rent bikes (300 BF per day), and do laundry nearby. Rooms are clean, and there's always a party in the bar. *Langestr. 135–137, tel. 050/34–10–93, fax 050/33–41–80. From station, take Bus 6 or 16 to Bauhaus. From Markt, follow Breidelstr., which becomes Hoogstr. and then crosses canal to become Langestr.*

Passage. Dynamic duo Sabine and Steve take care of your every need, even free maps. Passage is comfortable, tidy, and conveniently located between the town center and the train station. The restaurant/bar serves large, delicious portions. Beds are 310BF–375BF, 5% off with HI card or your *upCLOSE* guide. If you're craving privacy, get a double (1,550BF) at the ritzier annex, **Hotel Passage** (tel. 050/33–90–14), next door. Both will guard your luggage. *Dweerstr. 26, tel. 050/34–02–32, fax 050/34–01–40. From station, north (left) on Buiten Begijnenvest (becomes Koning Albertlaan); at 't Zand, turn right on Zuidzandstr., then left on Dweersstr.*

Snuffel. A hostel with a cause: All profits go to a local homeless shelter. Whip up a meal in the kitchen and save your money for the bar downstairs. Ten minutes from the town center, Snuffel is near a laundromat, a supermarket, and great restaurants (*see* Food, *below*). Dorm beds go for 275BF–315BF, doubles 800BF, quads 1,320BF, and sheets 80BF. *Ezelstr. 47–49, tel. 050/33–31–33, fax 050/33–32–50.*

CAMPING • Both campgrounds are a half-hour hike from town, but bus service continues until 11 PM. The closest to the station is **St-Michiel** (Tillegemstr. 55, tel. 050/38–08–19), where sites cost 130BF plus 110BF per person. From the station, take Bus 7 (40BF), or walk south on Koning Albertlaan for 20 minutes. If St-Michiel is full, try the prettier **Camping Memling** (Veltemveg. 109, 3 km/2 mi east of town, tel. 050/35–58–45), which has comparable rates; take Bus 11 from the station (40BF). Both campgrounds have on-site restaurants and are near big grocery stores.

FOOD

Affordable meals are scarce in Brugge. The central supermarket **Nopri** (Noordzandstr. 4; open Mon.–Sat. 9–6) is a little pricey; for better deals, try the **GB** (Scheepsdaelelaan 3; open Mon.–Sat. 9–6), just northwest of the canal that rings the town. To get there, follow Ezelstraat, which becomes Scheepsdaelelaan. Avoid restaurants on or near the Markt at dinnertime; cheaper and more authentic cuisine is further from the center, especially around Ezelstraat to the north and Langestraat to the east. During the day, though, many expensive restaurants in the center turn into tearooms, setting up outside tables where you can join other travelers and shoppers for a drink and maybe a waffle. Fresh fruit and vegetable markets set up shop Wednesday morning on the Burg and Saturday morning on 't Zand and Beursplein, on the west side of town.

Because this city is in Flemish-speaking Flanders and not French-speaking Wallonie, its correct name is Brugge (pronounced brooheh), not Bruges (broozh). If you call it Bruges in front of a Flemish separatist, you'll surely get your pronunciation corrected, and possibly a political lecture to boot.

You can also try the hostels listed above for a meal; all have restaurants with good food at budget prices. The meals at Passage are particularly good.

Breydel–De Coninck. The sole distinction of this no-nonsense bourgeois restaurant is its ample and wonderfully fresh food. Order mussels, and they serve you 3 pounds plus fries for 525BF. Everyone born in Brugge knows this place but tries to keep it a secret from the tourists. *Breidelstr. 24, close to the Markt, tel. 050/33–97–46. Open until 9:30 PM. Closed Wed. and June.*

L'Estaminet. Locals rave about the filling spaghetti, potent drinks, and blues music. Interesting variations on the *croque* (grilled-cheese sandwich) start at 150BF, and the covered terrace faces Koningin Astridpark. Zap the late-night munchies; this place stays open until 7 AM on weekends. *Park 5, tel. 050/33–09–16. Closed Mon., Thurs., and Nov. Cash only.*

Restaurant Ganzespel. On a quiet side street, owner and chef Nicky whips up a different Flemish menu every day. This is a good place to try *waterzooï*, a rich vegetable-and-chicken stew that's a meal in itself (360BF). When the menu's meaty, vegetarians can ask for a special omelette (200BF). Menus 245BF and 400BF. *Ganzestr. 37, near Langestr., tel. 050/33–12–33. Closed Mon. and Tues. Cash only.*

Taverne Oud Handbogenhof. Here's an authentic Flemish inn, complete with a big courtyard and barbecue shaded by linden trees. It's near the Jacobs, Fevery, and De Pauw hotels—and the food? Simple but succulent, and favored by locals. Menus from 350BF. *Baliestr. 6, tel. 050/33–19–45. Closed Mon., no dinner Sun.*

WORTH SEEING

For a great view of Brugge, climb to the top of the 13th-century **Belfort**—366 steps!—(admission 100BF; open daily 9:30–5; shorter hrs off season), on the Markt in the town center. On the nearby Burg, you can enter the Gothic hall of the gleaming-white **Stadhuis** (Town Hall) and the **Brugse Vrije,** which is part of the old county hall and includes a carved-oak mantelpiece depicting the Emperor Charles V, for 100BF (combination ticket). Also on the Burg is the extravagant **Heilig-Bloed Basiliek** (Basilica of the Holy Blood; closed daily noon–2), built to enshrine the vial containing Christ's blood. The lower chapel is pure 12th-century Romanesque; the upper has been twice destroyed and rebuilt. The reliquary is kept in a small museum (admission 40BF).

Brugge may have loads of churches, but the **Onze-Lieve Vrouwkerk** (Church of Our Lady; corner of Mariastr. and Gruuthusestr.; closed daily 11:30–2:30), built between the 13th and 15th centuries, offers the rare chance to see a Michelangelo masterpiece—the exquisite *Madonna with Child*—without trekking all the way to Italy. Art lovers should get to the **Memling Museum** (Mariastr. 38; admission 100BF; open Apr.–Sept., daily 9:30–5; shorter hrs off season), in the former St-Jans Hospital, which showcases the brilliant work of 15th-century local Hans Memling; and to the nearby **Groeninge Museum** (Dijver 12; admission 200BF; open Apr.–Sept., daily 9:30–5; shorter hrs off season), which houses a compact but exquisite collection of Flemish art from the 15th to 20th centuries, including stunning paintings by Jan Van Eyck, Hieronymus Bosch, Pieter Bruegel, and others less widely known but almost equally brilliant. When you get tired of staring at paintings, climb the rickety **St-Janshuysmolen windmill** (Kruisvest, on east edge of town; admission 40BF; open Apr.–Sept., daily 9:30–12:30 and 1:15–5). As the wind picks up, the wooden gears spin faster, and you fear that the whole thing is about to fly away. Dial 050/44–87–11 for information on all museums in Brugge.

TOURS • Boat tours of the town (35 min, 170BF) leave from jetties at the corner of Wollestraat and Dijver, from Blinde Ezelstraat, and from Mariastraat. For a refreshing and informative tour of the countryside around Brugge, take off with the **Back Road Bike Co.** (tel. 050/34–30–45), run by energetic Aussie Sharon. Tours (400BF–450BF) last two to three hours and include mountain-bike rental. **Quasimodo Tours** (Leenhofweg 7, tel. 050/37–04–70) runs two day-long bus trips: "Flanders Fields" (a tour of famous World War I battlefields) and "Triple Treat" (a chocolate, waffle, and beer tour). They're a bit pricey (1,300BF), but well worth the francs. To learn more about the Belgian art of brewing, sign up for a brewery tour with **Straffe Hendrik** (Walplein 26, tel. 050/33–26–97), which runs five tours (120BF) daily from 11 to 5.

AFTER DARK

When the shops close at about 6 PM, the city seems to die. Hard-core partyers can seek out a few lively nighspots on **Eiermarkt,** near the Markt, but the crowd here is pretty young—as in "junior high." Try **Vino Vino** (Grauwwerkersstr. 15, north of Markt), a cool blues bar, or hang with locals and choose from more than 300 beers at **'t Brugs Beertje** (Kemelstr. 5, off Steenstr.). The Passage, Bauhaus, and Snuffel hostels (*see* Where to Sleep, *above*) also have bars, each with a different scene; locals favor Passage.

NEAR BRUGGE: THE COAST

The Belgian coast is short, but it's home to several remarkably distinct small towns. Cosmopolitan Oostende draws an upscale international crowd, while ritzy Knokke-Heist is a local favorite. Knokke-Heist can intimidate the hell out of a budget traveler, but it's worth a stop if only to marvel at Belgian beach culture. For a quieter beach experience, try the tiny industrial town of **Zeebrugge,** good for shy types who don't like to flaunt their stuff in front of all Belgium.

None of these towns is more than a 20-minute train ride (100BF) from Brugge; in fact, many budget travelers bike from Brugge to the coast (about 1 hr) and between the individual towns. Otherwise, a single tram runs the length of the Belgian coast, making it easy to visit at least a few towns in a day. Tram trips start around 40BF.

OOSTENDE

This coastal city in western Flanders tries to do it all and nearly succeeds. It's a medieval European town, Florida's Palm Beach, Amsterdam's Red Light District, and a bit of Atlantic City, all mixed up and thrown onto the Belgian shore. Mostly older Belgians and Brits hang out at the luxurious hotels overlooking the ocean. Families flock to the beach, and you'll see parents taking romantic walks on the promenade while their kids scamper in the sand. And at night, as the elderly lock themselves away and the parents put the kiddies to bed, the younger set hits the bars.

Oostende started as a humble fishing village, but by the 19th century the Belgian royal family had chosen it as their second residence, and since then the town has been a first-rate seaside resort. The best thing to do here is bum around the streets, parks, and beach, preferably on a warm, sunny day. But if your sunny day gets too warm, find cool relief in **St-Petrus-en-Pauluskerk** (Sts. Peter and Paul Church), facing the train station; built early in the 20th century, this church has beautiful, quasi-cubist stained glass. The **Museum voor Schone Kunsten** (Wapenplein, tel. 059/80–53–35; admission 50BF; closed Tues.), on the main square between the station and the beach, holds an admirable collection of etchings and paintings by the fiercely Expressionist Oostende native James Ensor, along with temporary exhibits of local artists' work. The **tourist office** (Monacoplein 2, 15 min NW of station, tel. 059/70–11–99; open June–Sept., Mon.–Sat. 9–7, Sun. 10–7; shorter hrs off season) can help you out with the rest of Oostende's museums. Trains from Brugge (15 min, 105BF) roll into Oostende's **train station** (at SE corner of town, tel. 059/70–08–81) thrice daily. The station is next to the port, where the ferries have been replaced by fast catamarans carrying both cars and foot passengers to Ramsgate in two hours.

WHERE TO SLEEP AND EAT • Oostende's restaurants cater to wealthy vacationers, so get to know the streetside *frituurs* (french-fry stands). The burgers look questionable, but the locals seem to love them. Another cheap option is to stock up on groceries at **Maenhout** (on Groentemarkt, east of Wapenplein). You can get dinner for 250BF and a bed for 440BF at the busy and friendly HI hostel **De Ploate** (Langestr. 82, near Wapenplein and nightlife, tel. 059/80–52–97, fax 059/80–92–74, curfew at midnight), or try the **Polaris Hotel** (Groentemarkt 19, just east of Wapenplein, tel. 059/50–16–02), which has gorgeous doubles (1,450BF, 1,800BF with shower) and rents bikes (150BF per day).

KNOKKE-HEIST

Knokke-Heist is actually a conglomeration of five small towns: Heist, Duinbergen, Albertstrand, Knokke, and Het Zoute. Together, the towns offer 5 km (3 mi) of beautiful beach, with the street Zeedijk and a boardwalk running the entire length. As far as Belgians are concerned, Knokke-Heist is the beach with the most. Here local entrepreneurs turn sunbathing into an art, sectioning off their bits of sand with spikes and canvas and charging a steep price for the use of a deck chair. From the boardwalk, it's quite entertaining to see a beach so neatly partitioned into a grid. Closer to the water, you can simply throw your towel down on the beach; just be sure it's not invading your neighbor's personal sand swatch.

At the Kantcentrum *(Peperstraat 3; admission 40BF; open Mon.–Sat. 10–noon and 2–6; Sat. until 5), watch lacemakers toil away at their delicate craft (afternoons only). Lace is expensive here, but the cheaper stuff sold on the streets probably isn't handmade.*

Trekking along the boardwalk is the best way to get around, but if you're foot-weary you can take the coastal **tram** (about 40BF), which follows **Elizabetlaan** through Knokke-Heist. Tourism is the main industry here, and the streets are packed with hotels, restaurants, and shops. The entire area is overpriced, but generally the cost of food and lodging rises as you move from Heist toward Knokke. Get free maps and lodging information from the **tourist office** in Knokke (Zeedijk 660, tel. 050/63–03–80), and rent bikes at the **train station** (tel. 050/60–33–14).

Het Zwin, just north of Knokke, is a 375-acre nature preserve and bird sanctuary. From the top of the dike there's a splendid view of the dunes and inlets. Bring indestructible shoes if you think you'll want to wander around. Storks nest in the aviary, which also holds a large variety of aquatic birds and birds of prey. The best times to visit are in spring, for the bird migrations, and after mid-July, for the flowers. *Ooievaarslaan 8, Bus 788 from the train station, tel. 050/607086. Admission 150BF. Open daily 9–7 (9–5 Oct.–Mar.).*

WHERE TO SLEEP AND EAT • Doubles with bath are 1,600BF–2,400BF (breakfast included) at the beachfront **Ter Heis** (Zeedijk Heist 210, off Heldenplein, tel. 050/51–78–84, fax 050/42–98–08; closed Oct.–Easter). At **De Kubus** (Vlamingstr. 15, Heist, tel. 050/51–54–42), basics such as spaghetti are 190BF.

GENT

Gent's old town may be small, but its castle, romantic canals, and stunning cathedral adorned with a Van Eyck masterpiece make this one of Belgium's more rewarding stopovers. The Flemish pronounce the name of their city "khent"; the English pronounce and spell it "Ghent," and the French "Gand." The festive atmosphere, generated by the hordes of students streaming through the cafés along St-Pietersnieuwstraat, will probably make you want to stay a while. The wildest time to visit is during the last 10 days in July, when the town explodes in its annual **Gentse Feesten** festival; the circuslike party starts daily at noon, and revelers press on until 5 AM.

BASICS

Seek **visitor information** at the Town Hall (Botermarkt, near Korenmarkt north of Belfort, tel. 09/224–15–55; open Apr.–Nov., daily 9:30–6:30; shorter hrs off season). Send mail to the **main post office** (Korenmarkt 16, tel. 09/225–20–34; open weekdays 8–6, Sat. 9–noon; postal code 9000).

GETTING AROUND

To get to the center of town from the train station, take Tram 1, 10, or 11 (40BF) to Korenmarkt (or Veerleplein, for the hostel). With your free map from the visitor information center (*see* Basics, *above*) in hand, navigate the flat and walkable town using the central Three Towers and the many river crossings as landmarks. DeLijn also runs trams 5:30 AM–11:30 PM.

WHERE TO SLEEP

Hotels aren't that pricey if you're traveling with a partner—doubles cost about 1,300BF—but single travelers will probably want to stay at the hostel. The town's best hotels and the hostel are near the Three Towers; university housing is closer to the train station.

Flandria Hotel. These elegant rooms are in a great location (near St-Baafs) that has turned into an international meeting place. Check out the manager's aquarium. Doubles start at 1,500BF. Other rooms sleep up to five. *Barrestr. 3, tel. 09/223–06–26, fax 09/233–77-87. From Town Hall, go south on Hoogpoort, left on Kwaadham, and then right on Barrestr.*

Hotel De IJzer. The cheapest hotel in Gent has squeaky doors, but otherwise rooms are okay. Traffic outside is heavy, and an elderly crowd plays billiards in the smoky bar below. Doubles are 1,150BF, but you still have to report back for the 2:30 AM curfew. *Vlaanderenstr. 117, tel. 09/225–98–73. From Town Hall, go south to St-Baafspl., then southeast on Limburgstr. (becomes Vlaanderenstr.).*

SPLURGE • Erasmus. Gent has no hotel more pleasant. From the flagstone-and-wood-beam library/lounge to the stone mantels in the bedrooms, every inch of this noble 16th-century home has been scrubbed, polished, and bedecked with period ornaments. Even the tiny garden has been carefully manicured. Doubles with bath will set you back 3,675BF. *Poel 25, tel. 09/224–2195, fax 233–4241. Poel is back of Korenlei on the left bank of the river. Closed mid-Dec.–mid-Jan.*

HOSTEL • De Draecke (HI). In a great location near the castle, De Draecke offers a private toilet and shower in each room. Ask for the card-key if you'll be out past 11 PM. Beds are 365BF, sheets 120BF. *St-Widostr. 11, tel. 09/233–70–50, fax 09/233–80–01. From Korenmarkt, go north on Korte Munt, cross bridge to Veerlepl., and turn left over smaller bridge, right on Gewardstr., then right on St-Widostr. Checkout 10 AM.*

FOOD

The cheapest meals in town are on the student strip, south of the city center along St-Pietersnieuwstraat, which turns into Overpoortstraat. One of the best places is **La Rustica** (St-Pietersnieuwstr., tel. 09/233–07–08; closed Sat. lunch and Sun.), with filling pastas and pizzas from 150BF. A student ID will get you into the cafeteria **Octopus** (Overpoortstr. 49, no phone), where you can eat for 150BF and meet local students. The nearby pizzerias and french-fry stands are also good places for a quick fix. Vegetarians should make the trek to **De Appelier** (Citadellaan 47, tel. 02/221–67–33; closed Sat.), where meals go for as little as 250BF; to get there from St-Pietersplein, walk south on Overpoortstraat and turn left on Citadellaan.

De Pomp. This place is at the back of a courtyard; look for the brass pump and the pink-and-strawberry facade. Take your pick of eight ultracompetitively-priced dishes. *Drapstraat 34A, tel. 09/233–07–36. Turn off Korenlei where it changes name to Jan Breydelstr. Cash only.*

Taverne Keizershof. *Keizer* means Emperor, and this restaurant's gabled facade is crowned by a bust of Gent-born Emperor Charles V of Spain. It's heads and shoulders above the tourist-hungry eateries that surround it. Enjoy copious salads, brochettes, and steaks for 300BF–500BF. *Vrijdagmarkt 47, tel. 09/223–44–46. Closed Sun.*

WORTH SEEING

Most of Gent's tourists are drawn to its landmark Three Towers. The most important of these is the 14th-century bell tower, the **Belfort** (between E. Braunpl. and St-Baafspl., tel. 09/233–39–54; admission 80BF; open daily 10–12:30 and 2–5:30), which has a great view of the city and a room filled with old bells. **St-Niklaaskerk** (between Korenmarkt and E. Braunpl.; open daily 10–11:45 and 2–5) has sustained the most damage over the years as a result of wars and fires but has been meticulously restored.

St-Baafskathedraal (St-Baafspl.; open Mon.–Sat. 9:30–noon and 2–6, Sun. 1–6; shorter hrs off season) houses Van Eyck's breathtaking *The Adoration of the Mystic Lamb* (admission to painting 50BF), as well as a Rubens and a magnificent oak-and-marble pulpit.

The **Gravensteen castle** (St-Veerlepl., north of Korenmarkt, tel. 09/225–93–06; admission 200BF; open daily 9–6; off season until 5) has been so well restored that even the torture devices sparkle. Grab a beer on the Veerleplein, the adjacent square. How often do you have a leisurely drink in the shade of a 12th-century castle?

AFTER DARK

Bad news for summer travelers: Most of Gent's bars close for the summer vacation (July–Aug. 15). The rest of the year, you'll find reasonably priced bars everywhere, especially around St-Pietersnieuwstraat, where each bar seems to attract a different type of scholar. Two of the best are **De Sloef** (St-Pietersnieuwstr. 226, tel. 09/224–22–05), your basic friendly dive, and **Pole Pole** (St-Pietersnieuwstr. 158, tel. 09/233–21–73), a hopping club with an African theme. In the old town center, try the relaxing and intimate **Rococo** (Corduwanierstr. 57, in the Patershol area behind the castle, tel. 09/224–30–35) or the **Lazy River Jazz Club** (Stadhuissteeg 5, behind the Town Hall, tel. 09/222–23–01), with live music that takes you back (way back) to Dixie.

ANTWERP

If you're searching for the cosmopolitan side of Belgium, you'll find it in Antwerp, Belgium's second-largest city. It's fitting that the home of the world's first stock exchange should be a rich city; money rolls into Antwerp via the diamond business (the city produces half of the world's finished diamonds) and the thriving port, which ranks among Europe's busiest and most prosperous. But Antwerp hasn't always been so successful. It went through two centuries of poverty when rival nations closed its port in the 17th and 18th centuries, and it suffered heavily during the Napoleonic Wars. But even through hard times, Antwerp remained culturally exciting. As the home of Peter Paul Rubens, Antwerp lays claim to many of the artist's best works, as well as a beautiful cathedral and the Grote Markt. Today, the friendly people and the live music in bars, in cafés, and on the streets make Antwerp an exciting place to visit.

Vooruit (St-Pietersnieuwstraat 23, tel. 09/225–10–44) used to be a Socialist Party meeting place. Today it's just a theater and music hall with a cool café where you can watch Gent's culture hounds come and go.

BASICS

Get free maps at the **visitor information office** (Grote Markt 15, tel. 03/232–01–03, fax 03/231–19–37), open weekdays 9–5:45 and weekends 9–4:45. To find the **American Express** office (Frankrijklei 21, tel. 03/232–59–20; open weekdays 9–5:30, Sat. 9–noon) from the station, take De Keyserlei and turn left on Frankrijklei. The **post office** (Pelikaanstr. 16) is just south of the train station.

GETTING AROUND

Antwerp is a 40-minute train ride from Brussels (145BF). Although the city sprawls out along the Scheldt River and into the countryside, all the sights are crammed into the Oude Stad (Old Town), so you won't need the tram and bus much, except to get to some budget lodging. The **train station** (tel. 03/204–20–40) is east of the city center—take the Metro (Line 3–10–11) from the station (Diamant) to reach Groenplaats, just south of the Grote Markt.

BY BUS AND TRAM • As always, **DeLijn** (tel. 03/218–14–06) runs a comprehensive system of buses and trams, which are referred to as the Metro when they run underground. Buy regular tickets (40BF) on board, and get 10-trip cards (270BF) and route maps at a DeLijn office—the most convenient two are at Groenplaats and at Diamant.

WHERE TO SLEEP

The **Antwerp City Tourist Office** (*see* Basics, *above*) is extraordinarily helpful in making reservations and cutting deals; they also have a list of recommended B&Bs. Not surprisingly, the office is often mobbed. Solo travelers get a better deal here than in most cities: Single rooms often cost less than 800BF. Doubles tend toward 1,200BF. If you're in a bind, the 100-room **Internationaal Zeemanshuis** usually has space; it's north of the Old Town in the port area, frequented by seamen from all over the world (Falconrui 12, tel. 03/227–54–33; Bus 86; doubles 1,720BF).

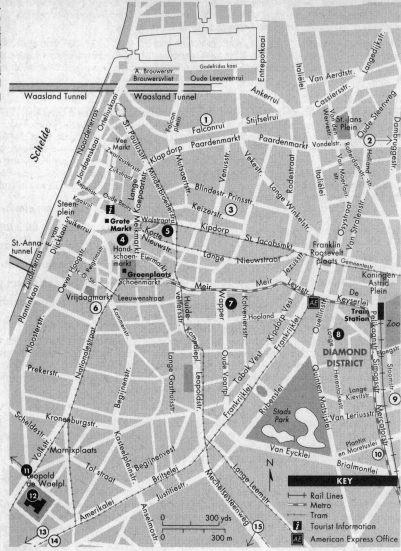

ANTWERP

KEY

- Rail Lines
- Metro
- Tram
- **i** Tourist Information
- **AE** American Express Office

Sights ●

Hendrik
Conscienceplein, **5**

Koninklijke Musea
voor Schone
Kunsten, **12**

MuHKA
Contemporary Art
Museum, **11**

Onze-Lieve
Vrouwekathedraal, **4**

Provinciaal
Diamantmuseum, **8**

Rubenshuis, **7**

Lodging ○

Globetrotter's
Nest, **2**

International
Zeemanshuis, **1**

New International
Youth Hotel, **10**

Op Sinjoorke
(HI), **15**

Pension
Cammerpoorte, **6**

Prinse, **3**

Rubenshof, **14**

Scotel, **9**

Sleep Inn, **13**

New International Youth Hotel. This clean hotel, a 15-minute walk from the station, must have been designed for a Minotaur; just hope you don't have to find your way out in an emergency. Doubles start at 1,320BF; dorm beds are 430BF, sheets 120BF. *Provinciestr. 256, tel. 03/230–05–22, fax 03/281–09–33. From the station, go south on Pelikaanstr. along the tracks, then left on Lamorinierestr.*

Pension Cammerpoorte. Rooms in this cheerful budget hotel (some with a view of the cathedral) are decorated in bright pastels and sad-clown art. A buffet breakfast, included in the price, is served in the tidy brick-and-lace café downstairs and helps drive up the price to 2,450BF, but you won't need any lunch. *Steenhouwersvest 55, a block south of Groenplaats, tel. 03/231–2836, fax 03/226–2968.*

Rubenshof. Once a cardinal's residence, the Rubenshof is now owned by a friendly Dutch couple. You can see remnants of its former glory in its mixture of turn-of-the-century styles. Rooms (most without bath) have recently been freshened up and the facade given a new coat of paint. You're near the Fine Arts Museum. Doubles cost 1,400BF–2,400BF. *Amerikalei 115-117, tel. 03/237–0789, fax 03/248–2594.*

Scoutel. It may be a plastic prefab hotel near the station, but its double and triple rooms all have toilets and showers. Breakfast and sheets are included, towels can be rented, and guests are provided with front-door keys. Doubles are 1,580BF (1,380BF if you're under 25). *Stoomstr. 3, tel. 03/226–46–06 or 03/232–63–92. From station, left on Pelikaanstr., left at Lange Kievitstr., right on Stoomstr. Check-in until 6 PM; 8 PM weekends.*

Sleep Inn. The Sleep is the cheapest, friendliest hotel in town, a short distance from the Fine Arts Museum and a downtown-bound tram. The chatty old proprietor's family has been here since the Hapsburg era. Rooms are 500BF per person, 600BF with bath. *Bolivarpl. 1, tel. 03/237–37–48, fax 03/248–02–48. From station, follow De Keyserlei to Frankrijklei and take Bus 1 to Bolivarpl. Laundry.*

SPLURGE • Prinse. Set well back from a street in the Old Town, this 400-year-old landmark with an interior courtyard opened as a hotel in 1990 and is a member of the Relais du Silence (Quiet Inns) group. Rooms are Nondescript Modern, with black leather chairs, soft blue curtains, and tile baths. Exposed beams give top-floor rooms more character. Doubles start at 4,100BF. *Keizerstraat 63, tel. 03/226–4050, fax. 03/225–1148.*

HOSTELS • Globetrotters' Nest. Small and super-friendly, this nine-bed dorm was created to give budget travelers a break from anonymous-feeling hostels. Bring a sleeping bag, or rent sheets by the week. There are bikes for rent, a common room with TV and games, a garden with barbecue, and a cook-it-yourself kitchen. Beds 390BF, including breakfast; sheets 60BF per week. *Vlagstr. 25, opposite Stuivenberg Hospital (Bus 23 from station), tel. 03/236–99–28. Kitchen. Cash only.*

Op Sinjoorke (HI). Modern and youthful, the Op Sinjoorke rests on the site of former city defenses, and the beautiful surroundings include a partial moat. Dorms and doubles are 365BF per person and sheets are 120BF, but the package is not as cheap as it seems, since bus fare into town is 40BF. There's a midnight curfew. *Eric Sasselaan 2, tel. 03/238–02–73, fax 03/248–19–32. From station, Bus 18 to C. Huysmanslaan. Lockout 10–4. Laundry. Closed mid-Dec.–early Jan.*

CAMPING • Camping De Molen. You have a great view of Antwerp from this campground on the west side of the river, and Sint-Anna Strand is where the Antwerpers themselves go to sunbathe, though not to swim. (Thonetlaan, Sint-Anna Strand, tel. 03/219–60–90, fax 03/261–91–17). Facilities are few, but there are plenty of eateries nearby, including the reasonably priced **De Molen** (Jachthavensweg 2, tel. 03/219–32–08), great for mussels.

FOOD

Antwerp's Oude Stade is the best place in the city to grab a meal. Although Antwerp serves some of the country's best food at premium prices, budget ethnic joints abound, even in the Oude Stade. You'll find lots of places on **Oude Koornmarkt,** off Grote Markt. Antwerp also has a great café scene, and many of its coffeehouses become roaring bars at night. For groceries, head to **Super GB** (on Schoenmarkt in Grand Bazar, just east of Groenplaats).

Kiekekot. Hordes of twentysomethings satisfy their cravings for spit-roasted chicken and frites at this no-frills "chicken coop," which offers a juicy, golden half-chicken for little more than its retail price (250BF) from 6 PM to 4 AM, Friday and Saturday until 6 AM. *Grote Markt 35, tel. 03/232–15–02. Closed Tues.*

Pasta. The smell of pesto grabs you as soon as you enter. The upstairs section (entrance on Pelgrimsstr.) has a cheaper menu and a partial glass ceiling with an awesome view of the cathedral. All pasta dishes (around 400BF) come with scrumptious Italian bread. *Oude Koornmarkt 32, off Grote Markt, tel. 03/233–17–76. No lunch on weekends.*

't Hofke. Visit for the situation alone: Here in the Vlaeykensgang alley, time stands still. There's a large selection of salads and omelettes for less than 500BF, as well as more substantial fare. *Oude Koornmarkt 16, tel. 03/233–86–06. Closed Mon.*

Ulcke van Zurich. This trendy dinner spot occupies an old building where the young and young-at-heart enjoy chicken salad, spareribs, or chicken-liver mousse (entrées from 400BF) with port every night from 6 PM until late. *Oude Beurs 50, just north of Grote Markt, tel. 03/234–04–94.*

Zuiderterras. A stark pile of glass and black steel, this avant-garde riverside café and restaurant draws an avant-garde crowd. A light meal is about 500BF and includes a view of the river traffic on one side and the cathedral and old town on the other. *Ernest Van Dijckkaai, tel. 03/234–12–75.*

WORTH SEEING

Entering Antwerp means entering the world of Rubens. In the 14th-century **Onze Lieve Vrouwekathedraal** (Handschoenmarkt, tel. 03/231–30–33; admission 60BF; open weekdays 10–6, Sat. 10–3, Sun. 1–4), you can see what are arguably Rubens's best works: the two triptychs *The Raising of the Cross* (1610) and *The Descent from the Cross* (1612). These huge paintings and many other treasures make this cathedral one of Belgium's greatest marvels.

For more Rubens, visit the **Koninklijke Museum voor Schone Kunsten** (Leopold de Waelpl. 1–9, tel. 03/238–78–09; admission 150BF; open Tues.–Sun. 10–5), which has an entire velvet-walled room filled with the painter's dramatic visions of Christ. Other Northern Renaissance stars, such as Van Eyck, get lots of wall space as well. To round off your Rubens experience, wander around the **Rubenshuis** (Wapper 9, tel. 03/232–47–47; admission 75BF; open Tues.–Sun. 10–4:45), the artist's home for the last 25 years of his life. If you're still itching for more, the tourist office has a "Rubens Walk" pamphlet and map (30BF) that direct you to buildings containing his works.

But there's more to Antwerp than Rubens. The streets of the Oude Stad are packed with sights and incredible architecture, most notably around the **Grote Markt.** The Diamond District, near the train station, harbors one of the largest Hasidic Jewish communities in the world; at the **Provinciaal Diamantmuseum** (Lange Herentalsestr. 31–33, tel. 03/202–4890; admission free, except for special exhibits; open daily 10–5), you can view mounds of diamonds and exhibits on every aspect of diamond-processing. Watch diamond-cutting demonstrations on Saturday from 1:30 to 4:30. Old Antwerp renews itself in the exuberant contemporary-art museum **MuHKA** (Leuvenstr. 16-30, near the Fine Arts Museum, Bus 23, admission free, tel. 03/238–59–60; open Tues.–Sun. 10–5.), and in the superexpensive boutiques south of Groenplaats you can ogle the latest creations of the **Antwerp Six,** who gave the world the grunge look.

CHEAP THRILLS

A great place to relax is on the peaceful square **Hendrik Conscienceplein,** which faces the magnificent facade of the church of St-Carolus Borromeus. Another beautiful spot is the peaceful sculpture garden in the suburb of Mortsel; from Groenplaats, take Bus 26. For a really cheap thrill, walk through Antwerp's **red light district,** a few blocks northeast of the Grote Markt.

AFTER DARK

Antwerp has a fantastic nightlife. It's such a musical city that you can almost always find a live show, especially after 10 PM, when most people hit the bars. Cover charges are rare, and the cheapest beers are about 50BF. **De Muze** (Melkmarkt 15, near Grote Markt, tel. 03/226–01–25) is a great place for live or recorded jazz and De Koninck beer. (Natives call this Antwerp brew Bolleke, or "small bowl," after the glass it's usually served in.) **De Muziekdoos** (Lange Nieuwstr., east of Grote Markt, tel. 03/231–28–55) has a stage for street performers. Homesick rockers should head to **Kids Rhythm and Blues Danskaffee** (Grote Markt 50, tel. 03/227–35–85), where people start dancing at about midnight on Friday and Saturday, and live bands perform every Sunday.

WALLONIE

The people of Wallonie speak French and share much of their cultural heritage with their French neighbors to the south. Fortunately, they don't share the mythical French 'tude; Walloons are nearly as hospitable as the Flemish to English-speaking travelers, though fewer Walloons actually speak English. Still, they're patient and probably won't laugh at your wounded French. You have to give the Walloons a break—they're still trying to deal with their relatively new position of political and financial inferiority to Flanders. Walloon cities don't have half the allure of Antwerp or Brugge, but the hills and forests of the Ardennes make Wallonie a hotspot for outdoor thrill-seekers.

LIEGE

Liège's prince bishops presided over an ecclesiastical state for 1,000 years, after which the city became a leading center for steelmaking. But its most famous claim is native son Georges Simenon, the prolific crime writer. Liège is far from being Belgium's most exciting city, but it's worth a visit on your way to Germany or into the Ardennes. Most of the sights are concentrated in the small area known as **Le Carré**, on the left bank of the River Meuse.

Eglise St-Jean (pl. Xavier Neujean, tel. 041/23–70–42; open Fri.–Wed. 10–noon and 2–5, Thurs. 2–5) has several amazing 13th-century wood sculptures. Duck into **Eglise St-Jacques** (pl. St-Jacques), a Bénedictine abbey built between the 12th and 16th centuries, to see its exuberant decoration; the nave vaulting is covered with intricate patterns of blue and gold, like frozen fireworks. A treasury full of silver, gold, and ivory sculptures is the best reason to visit **Cathédrale St-Paul** (pl. de la Cathédrale; admission to treasury 50BF; open daily 10:45–11:45 and 2–4). To round out your church tour, check out the **baptismal font** in the Romanesque **Eglise St-Barthélemy** (pl. St-Barthélemy, tel. 041/23–49–98; admission 80BF; open Mon.–Sat. 10–noon and 2–5, Sun. 2–5); this beautifully decorated brass piece, with its many baptismal scenes in high relief, was the work of Renier de Huy, one of a small group of 12th-century silversmiths whose work can be found in churches along the Meuse River. To experience Wallonie's rich arts-and-crafts tradition, head to **Musée de la Vie Wallonne** (Cours des Mineurs, tel. 041/23–60–94; admission 80BF), which displays old marionettes and lacework, as well as a guillotine used as recently as 1824.

Risk traveling in the Ardennes on Sunday and the sleepy little town you dreamed about becomes a tourist hell, complete with a Harley-Davidson convention in the main square.

VISITOR INFORMATION

Get free maps from the **tourist office** (Féronstrée 92, tel. 041/21–92–21; open weekdays 9–6, Sat. 10–4, Sun. 10–2), in the center of the old town.

COMING AND GOING

Liège isn't hard to cover on foot, but getting to the city center can be a pain. Most trains roll into the **Liège-Guillemins** station at the south end of town, near the cheap hotels but not much else; trek 20 minutes to the center or take Bus 4 (40BF). **Liège-Palais** and the **TEC bus station** (tel. 04/361–94–44) are at the north end of the city, much closer to the sights but a 15-minute walk from lodging. The train ride from Brussels (1 hr 20 min) costs 200BF.

WHERE TO SLEEP AND EAT

The huge, new **HI Hostel "Georges Simenon"** (rue Georges Simenon 2, tel. 04/344–56–89, fax 04/344–56–87; no curfew), on the right bank of the Meuse only 15 minutes south of downtown, has dorm beds (450BF) and doubles (550BF per person); to get there from Liège-Guillemins, take Bus 4 to place du Congrès and head west. **Hotel le Simenon,** in the same area (blvd. de l'Est 16, tel. 04/342–86–90, fax 04/344–26–69) honors the creator of Commissaire Maigret, with each room named for one of his novels. Doubles start at 2,000BF.

Pont-d'Avroy, rue St-Gilles, and rue du Pot d'Or are packed with restaurants. If you find yourself starving at some ungodly hour, turn to **Le Vaudree II** (rue St-Gilles 149, tel. 041/23–18–80), which is open all night and offers 42 beers on tap and 980 bottled. Full meals cost about 450BF, but a hearty sandwich with fries is only 175BF. Liège has nocturnal habits, and its specialty is the café chantant, where everyone is welcome to burst into song and frequently does; try **Les Caves de Porto** (En Féronstrée 144, tel. 04/223–07–08). The huge grocery store **Central Cash** (blvd. de la Constitution 32, tel. 041/44–28–28) is just 1 block north of the hostel.

MONS

The quiet cobblestone streets of Mons, an hour from Brussels by train (100BF), are a refreshing change of pace from the rest of industrialized Wallonie, and a few of its sights are worth checking out. At the **Collégiale Ste-Waudru,** a Gothic church begun in 1450, a copper reliquary above the altar holds the body of the patron saint. In the church waits the **Golden Chariot,** in which the reliquary is carried on a Trinity Sunday procession. Also worth a visit is the (some say) hideous **belfry,** which Victor Hugo proclaimed was redeemed only by its intimidating size.

Buses don't run through the center (with the one exception of Bus U, for *urbain*), but everything worth seeing in Mons is easy to reach on foot. The **train station** is northeast of and downhill from the center; to get to Grand' Place and the extremely helpful **tourist information office** (Grand' Place 22, tel. 065/33–55–80), walk south on rue de la Houssière past Ste-Waudru Church and follow rue des Clercs from there.

WHERE TO SLEEP AND EAT

Cheap sleeps are few. (A hostel is nearing completion.) In July and August, **M. et Mme. Rousseau** (rue des Belneux 5 and blvd. Kennedy 61, tel. 065/33–80–72) offer 1,200BF doubles in two houses near the center. Your cheapest option is **Camping du Waux-Hall** (av. St-Pierre 17, tel. 065/33–79–23), where two people can camp for 203BF; to get there from Grand' Place, walk south on rue de Havre for 10 minutes and look for signs. The streets surrounding Grand' Place are packed with restaurants and cafés. For local cuisine and murals that celebrate Mons's history and culture, go to **No Maison** (Grand' Place 21, tel. 065/34–74–74), where meals start at 350BF. Mons has three universities, which means it has a nightlife of sorts. Get your french fries at **Friterie Billy** (rue d'Enghien 5), and munch them with a beer at **Au Doudou** (Grand-Place 34, tel. 065/35–19–20).

THE ARDENNES

Every summer, campers and caravans from Brussels and points north descend upon the villages of the Ardennes in droves. They don't necessarily come for the quiet; with kayak trips, cave tours, hiking, World War II monuments, and hilltop citadels, there's plenty to do and explore. Trains don't get very far here, though **TEC** (tel. 081/72–08–40) has extensive bus service to all but the smallest villages. A dozen of the most attractive hamlets have banded together to form **Les Plus Beaux Villages de Wallonie** (rue Pieds d'Alouette 18, 5100 Naninne, tel. 081/40–80–10, fax 081/40–80–20); you can find a *gîte* (rural guest room) in any of these, and local guides arrange walks to show off their charms.

NAMUR

The gateway to the beautiful Belgian southeast, Namur sits at the confluence of the Sambre and Meuse rivers, under cliffs that support a 2,000-year-old **Citadelle** (tel. 081/22–68–29). You're free to explore the expansive grounds surrounding the fortress, but to get inside the buildings and network of tunnels, you'll have to fork over 195BF. If you're too lazy to hike up to the citadel, the *téléférique* (cable car) will whisk you there in just 15 minutes for 160BF. Don't miss the **Musée Félicien Rops** downtown (rue Fumal 12, tel. 081/22–01–10; admission 100BF; open Tues.–Sun. 10–6), devoted to the brilliant painter and printmaker who shocked the 19th-century bourgeoisie (while winning the admiration of Baudelaire and his friends) with his wittily erotic and satirical illustrations. The town's **tourist office** (sq. de l'Europe Unis, just east of train station, tel. 081/22–28–59; open daily 9–6) has free maps, extensive brochures, and transport options for the area.

COMING AND GOING • Namur is a one-hour train ride from Brussels (175BF). To get into the Ardennes from Namur, hop a train to Libramont (2 hrs, 410BF) or Jemelle (1½ hrs, 330BF), and then a bus to Bouillon or Rochefort (*see below*).

WHERE TO SLEEP AND EAT • The **Auberge de Jeunesse de Namur "Félicien Rops" (HI)** (8 av. Félicien Rops, tel. 081/22–36–88, fax 081/22–44–12; dorm beds 365BF; curfew 1 AM) is a hike from town, but its riverfront location and friendly staff make up for the distance. The hostel offers dinner (270BF) in a communal atmosphere and 10% discounts on kayaking trips. To get here, walk the 3 km (2 mi) south along the River Meuse, or take Bus 3 or 4 (40BF) and tell the driver where you're going. If you want a meal in town, try one of the restaurants on the streets around Eglise St-Jean. At **Au Passé Simple** (33 rue Fossés-Fleuris, tel. 081/23–14–31), salads and meals run about 350BF.

BOUILLON

Set aside some time to explore every dark, damp passageway of Bouillon's **château** (tel. 061/46–62–57; admission 140BF). The castle was once home to Godfrey of Bouillon, the legendary crusader who became ruler of Jerusalem. The **tourist office** (tel. 061/46–62–57) at the castle sells trail maps (100BF) of the surrounding hills and forests. To get to Bouillon from Libramont's train station, take Bus 8 (120BF) to Pont de France for the campground or to Dépot TEC for the hostel.

WHERE TO SLEEP • The **HI hostel** (rte. du Christ 16, tel. 061/46–81–37, fax 061/46–78–18) has dorm beds for 365BF and does laundry for 100BF. The **Moulin de la Falize** campground (Vieille rte. de France 33, tel. 061/46–62–00, fax 061/46–72–75) has tent sites for 200BF plus 60BF per person. There are also bike rentals (700BF per day) and a bowling alley; ask for a bike-trail map. Both options are long uphill walks from the bus stop; just follow the signs.

ROCHEFORT

While hordes of tourists steamroll through the choreographed cave tour in Han-sur-Lesse, you can opt for the rougher, more rugged caves at **Grotte de Rochefort** (rue de Lorette, 10 min east of bus stop, tel. 084/21–20–80; open Thurs.–Tues. 10–4:30). Bats, stalactites, stalagmites, and chambers that induce head-spinning vertigo and claustrophobia all at once make the obligatory guided tour (daily Apr.–mid Nov. except Wed. at the beginning and end of the season) well worth the 190BF fee. As if that's not enough, the trappist monks of Rochefort brew a formidable and potent beer. To get to Rochefort from Jemelle's train station, take Bus 29 (40BF); most days, the last bus leaves Jemelle just after 6 PM, so plan ahead.

For 900BF a day, you can rent a double kayak from the Moulin de la Falize campground and paddle it down the River Semois.

WHERE TO SLEEP • The best deal in town is the hostel-like **Gîte d'Etape** (rue du Hableau 25, tel. 084/21–46–04, fax 084/21–46–04), where a bed with dinner and breakfast is 575BF. Follow the signs from the bus stop.

BULGARIA

In most Westerners, Bulgaria inspires shrugs and blank looks. Much about the country adds to its mystery: Virtually everything is written in Cyrillic (a script designed by saints Cyril and Methodius in the 9th century to help preserve the Slavic language and culture), the minarets of ancient Ottoman mosques rise above Eastern Orthodox towns, and the people nod to indicate "no" and shake their heads to indicate "yes." Both modern and medieval, Bulgaria is a place where Western sports cars speed down cobblestone streets past farmers leading donkey-drawn carts laden with produce.

An ancient proverb warns, "God forbid you live in an interesting time," and Bulgaria's history has been anything but dull. The First Bulgarian Empire was founded in 681 by the Bulgars, a Turkic tribe who settled alongside the Slavs in the southern Balkans. By the 10th century, the thriving Bulgarian Empire had adopted Orthodox Christianity (courtesy of the looming Byzantium) and spread as far west as the Adriatic Sea. After falling entirely into Byzantine hands during the 11th century, it reemerged as the Second Bulgarian Empire—a wealthy kingdom comprising present-day Albania, Macedonia, Serbia, Bulgaria, and parts of Greece—which finally surrendered completely to the Turks in 1396. Under the Ottoman thumb for the next five centuries, Bulgaria's religion, language, and culture survived only in a few remote monasteries. During the National Revival of the early 19th century, however, Bulgarian culture flourished, sparking the patriotic fervor that, with Russia's help, led to liberation in 1878.

After decades of Communist dictatorship, Bulgaria is currently struggling to advance a market economy and implement the economic policies required for aid from the International Monetary Fund. Having watched six different governments come and go since the first free elections in 1990, Bulgarians have developed a thick skin of political skepticism. Recently, hyperinflation, massive unemployment, and rampant corruption ignited them: Apathy gave way to outrage, and in January of 1997, Sofia exploded with a political uprising that soon spread to other cities. After storming the National Assembly and paralyzing the country with a full month of nationwide protests and strikes, the opposition succeeded in ousting the Socialist cabinet from parliament before the end of its term. The legacy of Communism is formidable here—a stagnant economy, rising environmental problems, and deep ethnic distrust—and reform has been slow. But, politics aside, visitors to this relatively undiscovered country will be amazed at how beautiful and inexpensive it is. It's easy to retreat from the cities to medieval villages set in lush mountain ranges, and you'll never have to fight for a spot on the Black Sea's sandy beaches.

BULGARIA

KEY
— Rail Lines

SERBIA

FORMER YUGOSLAV
REPUBLIC OF
MACEDONIA

ROMANIA

GREECE

TURKEY

Black
Sea

N

0   80 miles
0   120 km

BASICS

MONEY

US$1 = 1,850 leva and 1,000 leva = 54¢. The value of the lev fluctuates madly; most prices in this chapter are given in dollars so that you can budget with some confidence. You may find it difficult to exchange traveler's checks even at banks (the best bets are the ubiquitous and reliable **Bul Bank** and **TSBank**). Some tourist offices and major hotels will do it, usually for a 2%–5% commission. Credit cards can occasionally be used for cash advances (5% fee) at banks in larger cities, but ATMs are still a nonentity. Generally, banks are open weekdays 9–4 and Saturday before noon. Private **bureaux de change,** open on weekends, give the best rates for cash, so don't bother looking for a better deal in the street. Counterfeiting is a recent phenomenon, so bring new, clean bills; otherwise, a suspicious teller may turn down your dollars. Change only what you need, as selling leva back is problematic.

HOW MUCH IT WILL COST • Prices are rising, but the lev is falling, which means you can still eat well for a few dollars a day. Lodging will be your biggest expense; museum-admission and entertainment costs are negligible. You can live pretty well here for less than $30 a day.

VISA AND ENTRY REQUIREMENTS

U.S. citizens can stay for up to 30 days visa-free. For longer visits, purchase a visa (US$68 in hard currency) at the border, the airport, or the Bulgarian embassy (1621 22nd St. NW, Washington, DC 20008, tel. 202/387–7969). Processing takes about two weeks. U.S. citizens also pay a $20 border tax when entering Bulgaria. Be careful: Bulgarian border guards *will* attempt to overcharge you. All other travelers need a visa (available at the border) to travel in Bulgaria. For details, contact the Bulgarian consulate in the **United Kingdom** (186 Queensgate, London SW7 5HL, tel. 0171/584–9400); **Canada** (65 Overlea Blvd., Suite 406, Toronto, Ont. M4H 1P1, tel. 416/696–2420); or **Australia** (Carlotta Rd., Double Bay, Sydney NSW 2028, tel. 02/327–7592). Finally, everyone entering Bulgaria receives a statistical card to keep track of where they're sleeping. Stamp the card everywhere you stay the night, and present it as you leave the country (no stamps mean a $30 fine). If you're not given a statistical card, get your passport stamped instead.

COMING AND GOING

The cheapest way to get to Bulgaria is by train from Romania or Greece, or by bus from Turkey. Inter-Rail passes (but not Eurailpasses) are accepted here, and the Bulgarian Flexipass is new on the rail scene, though train fare is still so cheap (a cross-country trek costs $6), that it's not yet worth the hassle. Sofia is the main rail hub, sending **trains** to Bucharest ($7), Budapest ($42), İstanbul ($16), and Athens ($28). Private **buses** run daily from Sofia to most major European cities, including İstanbul ($20), Budapest ($35), and Prague ($40). **Balkan Airlines** (tel. 212/573–5530 in the United States), the Bulgarian state carrier, has flights to Sofia from various European hubs, but fares vary widely. Most western airlines serve Sofia.

GETTING AROUND

Buses are convenient for local trips and travel along the Black Sea coast. State-run buses usually cover regional destinations, while private companies send air-conditioned buses on longer trips. Except in Sofia, both private and state-run buses operate out of the same *avtogara* (bus station). Buy your *bilet* (ticket) a day in advance for popular trips, such as those from Sofia to Plovdiv or Varna. **Trains** cost about the same as buses. There are three classifications of trains: *expresni* (express), *burzi* (fast), and *puticheski* (slow). Take the fastest train, and, for pennies more, go *purva clasa* (first class). Buy domestic tickets at the *zhelezoputna gara* (train station) and international tickets in advance at **Rila Railway Bureau** offices in larger towns. Timetables are posted in every station, listing *pristigashti* (arrivals), *zaminavashti* (departures), and *kolovoz* (track) numbers. Look for the new, useful *sukrateno razpicanie* (railway timetable; 500 leva) at ticket windows.

WHERE TO SLEEP

When possible, stay in a *chastna kvartira* (**private room**) in either a family home or a private hotel. (Such lodgings rarely accept credit cards; ask up front.) Most cities have agencies that will find $20 doubles in private homes. **Hostels** are grungier, and almost as costly as private rooms. About 100 **campgrounds** ($2–$5 per night) are scattered throughout Bulgaria, mostly on the Black Sea coast.

FOOD

Grocery stores carry only staples, such as *hlyab* (bread). Guess what? The Bulgarian diet is meat-heavy, with *kebapche* (pork sausage) topping the list; be wary, and consider requesting your food *dobre opechen* (well-done). Vegetarians should try *bop* (lentil soup), and can find a *shopska* salad—tomato, cucumber, and *sirene* (like feta, but tastier)—in most restaurants. For dessert, order *palachinka* (a delicious crêpe with nut filling). Bulgarian tap water is generally potable. Even better, Bulgarian wines (both red and white) are delicious and usually cost less than $2 a bottle. Your *smetkata* (bill) won't come until you ask; always check the math.

VISITOR INFORMATION

Orbita, the national student-travel organization, books private homes and hostels for all travelers. They also operate their own hotels, of which quality and prices vary. **Balkantourist** arranges rooms in private homes and campgrounds; don't let them steer you to an expensive, government-owned hotel.

PHONES

Country Code: 359. Local calls cost 2 leva. Post offices sell two types of cards for the two types of card phones: Use the black cards for domestic calls on the orange-color *Bulfon* phones; use the small decorative cards for domestic and European calls on the silver-color *Betkom* phones. To call outside Europe, use the post office, or try dialing 0123 from a major hotel to reach an international operator (you can't dial direct from public phones). Placing collect calls (by saying "*zatiachna smetka telefonen razgovar*") is next to impossible. Calling cards work a bit better (dial 00–800–0010 for **AT&T** Direct Access[SM]), but only from private phones. Outside Sofia (the only place where you *can* dial direct from a post office), post-office attendants place international calls for you. Calls to the U.S. cost about $3 per minute; to Europe, about $2 per minute.

MAIL

Post offices are open late. Letters to Europe (400 leva) take a week; letters to the United States and Australia (800 leva) take one to two weeks. Drop letters in any red box marked with a horn.

CRIME AND PUNISHMENT

As a rule, Bulgarians are not a gregarious bunch, so if you're approached by any particularly chummy locals, maintain a healthy cynicism. Crime is on the rise.

LANGUAGE

Bulgarian, a Slavic language, uses the Cyrillic alphabet. Russian is the nation's second-most-common language, with German coming in third. English is not widespread, so learn these key Bulgarian words: *dobur den* (hello); *dovizhdane* (goodbye); *molya* (please); *blagodarya* (thank you); *da/ne* (yes/no); *izvinete* (excuse me); *govorite li angliyski?* (do you speak English?); *ne razbiram* (I don't understand); *kolko struva?* (how much does it cost?); *kude e . . .?* (where is . . .?).

SOFIA

Sofia is ripe for discovery. Compared with those in other European capitals, prices are low, and people are friendly. And despite its largely bland, Soviet-inspired architecture, Sofia has Roman churches, Byzantine and Ottoman mosques, and yellow-brick roads crowded with characters—even the occasional dancing bear led by a mandolin player. Lucky for outdoorsy types, Sofia is ringed by two mountain ranges, and Mt. Vitosha is a year-round playground right in the city's backyard. The Communists left Sofia with some awful monuments and a decaying urban infrastructure, but Sofia has endeavored with capitalist zeal to recapture its former charisma: These days, sidewalk cafés with colorful umbrellas will distract you from the less pleasing aesthetics. New businesses, restaurants, and theaters are popping up all over, and the nightlife is inexhaustible. The moral of the story? Visit now, before Sofia is overrun with hipsters in search of another Prague to exploit.

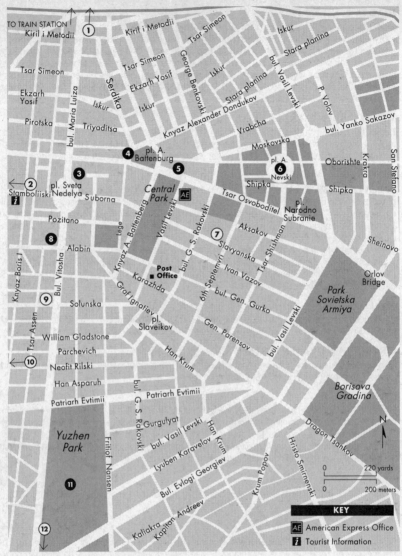

TO TRAIN STATION
Kiril i Metodii

Kiril i Metodii

Tsar Simeon

Tsar Simeon

Tsar Simeon

Iskur

Stara planina

Ekzarh Yosif

Iskur

bul. Vasil Levski

George Benkovski

Tsar Simeon

Serdika

Ekzarh Yosif

Iskur

P. Volov

Ekzarh
Yosif

Iskur

Stara planina

Stara planina

bul. Yanko Sakazov

Pirotska

bul. Maria Luiza

Triyaditsa

Knyaz Alexander Dondukov

Vrabcha

Moskovska

Oborishte

Krakra

San Stefano

pl. A.
Battenburg

pl. A.
Nevski

Shipka

Shipka

Sheinovo

pl. Sveta
Nedelya

Suborna

Tsar Osvoboditel

pl.
Narodno
Subranie

Stamboliiski

Central
Park

AE

Pozitano

lege

Vasil Levski

Aksakov

Orlov
Bridge

Alabin

Knyaz A. Battenberg

bul. G. S. Rakovski

Slavyanska

Tsar Shishman

Park
Sovietska
Armiya

Bul. Vitosha

Karazhda

6th Septemvri

Ivan Vazov

bul. Vasil Levski

Post
Office

Graf Ignatiev

bul. Gen. Gurko

Solunska

pl.
Slaveikov

Gen. Parensov

Borisova
Gradina

William Gladstone

Parchevich

Han Krum

Neofit Rilski

bul. G. S. Rakovski

Patriarh Evtimii

Dragon Tsankov

Han Asparuh

Gurgulyat

Han Krum

Patriarh Evtimii

bul. Vasil Levski

Yuzhen
Park

Fritiof Nansen

Lyuben Karavelov

Bul. Evlogi Georgiev

Krum Popov

Hristo Smirnenski

N

Kaliakra

Kapitan Andreev

0   220 yards
0   200 meters

KEY

AE American Express Office

i Tourist Information

Knyaz Boris I

Tsar Assen

Sights ●

Alexander Nevski
Memorial Church, 6

National Art
Gallery, 5

National Museum
of History, 8

National Palace of
Culture (NDK), 11

Party House, 4

St. George's
Church, 3

Lodging ○

Business Repos, 1

Cherniya Kos, 12

Hotel Baldzhieva, 9

Hotel Niky, 10

Slavyanska
Beseda, 7

Tourist Hotel
Yubileina, 2

BASICS

VISITOR INFORMATION

Balkantourist charges $16 per person and $18 per double for clean, centrally located private rooms. They also provide hiking and camping information, currency exchange, and the handy *Sofia Quick Guide,* an English guide to the city. *Bul. Alexander Stamboliiski 27, 2 blocks west of pl. Sveta Nedelya, tel. 02/87–72–33, 02/88–52–56, or 02/88–06–55. Open daily 8:30 AM–7 PM.*

Pirin (bul. Alexander Stamboliiski 30, 3 blocks west of pl. Sveta Nedelya, tel. 02/87–05–79; open weekdays 9–5:30) books hostels and provides camping information. Two blocks west of Pirin, **Orbita** (bul. Hristo Botev 48, tel. 02/80–01–02; open weekdays 9–5:30) arranges $20 doubles in its own hotel. **Markella Company** (bul. Maria Luiza 17, just north of pl. Sveta Nedelya, tel. 02/81–52–99; open weekdays 9–8, Sat. 9–4), located in a kiosk off the street, charges $12 a person for private rooms.

AMERICAN EXPRESS

Inside **Megatours,** Sofia's helpful, full-service AmEx desk changes traveler's checks (4% commission) and hands out the *Sofia City Info Guide. Vasil Levski 1, 1000 Sofia, tel. 02/981–42–01, fax 02/981– 21–67. Open weekdays 9–6, Sat. 9–12:30.*

EMBASSIES

United Kingdom. Brits, Canadians, Australians, and Kiwis *must* register here to stay in Bulgaria longer than a month. *Bul. Vasil Levski 38 (not Vasil Levski St.), 2 blocks east of Yuzhen Park, tel. 02/88–53– 61. Open Mon.–Thurs. 8:30–12:30 and 1:30–5:30, Fri. 8:30–12:30.*

United States. The **embassy** (Suborna 1, tel. 02/980–52–41; open weekdays 9–5) handles emergencies only. The **consulate** is open to Americans for travel information, and prefers that Yanks register here upon arrival. *Consulate: Kapitan Andreev 1, tel. 02/963–20–22. Walk down Fritiof Nansen; after it turns into Cherni Vruh, continue 2 blocks and turn left. Open weekdays 9–1 and 2–4:30.*

EMERGENCIES

Look on tourist maps to find an *apteka* (pharmacy) in Sofia. **Apteka No. 7** (pl. Sveta Nedelya 5, on west side of square, tel. 02/87–50–89) is open daily 7 AM–9 PM. For emergencies, go directly to the 24-hour **Piragov Emergency Hospital** (bul. General Totleben, near bul. General Skobelev, tel. 02/515–31); it's just past the Russian Monument.

PHONES AND MAIL

Local calls cost 2 leva at coin phones. You can also make local calls at the **central post office** (bul. General Gurko 2, near Central Park), and pick up poste restante mail at Window 8 (open weekdays 8–8); have mail addressed to Your Name, c/o Poste Restante, 1000 Sofia, Bulgaria. Half a block west of the post-office entrance is the **phone office** (open 24 hrs), where you can place international calls.

COMING AND GOING

BY BUS

Down the street from Gare Centrale Sofia (*see above*), the parking lot at Hotel Novotel Europa and another parking lot across the street serve as a **stations** for both private and public buses. For most destinations, private buses are the way to go. The kiosks here have information and sell tickets: Buses run frequently to Plovdiv (2 hrs, $2), Veliko Turnovo (3 hrs, $3), Varna (6 hrs, $5), Burgas (6 hrs, $4.50), and Sozopol (7 hrs, $6). Otherwise, try the state-run **international bus station** (Damyan Aruev 23, tel. 02/52–50–04); take bul. Alexander Stamboliiski to Hristo Botev, turn left, continue two blocks, and turn right. State buses are less comfortable than private ones, and not much cheaper. For regional destinations including Rila Monastery, go to **Ovcha Kupel** (Tsar Boris III, tel. 02/55–30–47); take Tram 5 (30 min) from ploshtad Sveta Nedelya.

BY PLANE

Sofia's **airport** (tel. 02/72–06–72 for international flights, 02/72–24–14 for domestic flights), 13 km (8 mi) northeast of the city, has a pharmacy, post office, and Balkantourist office. From outside the terminal, take Bus 84 (20 min, 100 leva) to downtown Sofia. Avoid the official taxi kiosk, which hawks rides for $17, an outrageous fare. Choose from the taxis lined up outside, and agree on the price ($6–$8) beforehand.

BY TRAIN

The behemoth **Gare Centrale Sofia** (bul. Maria Luiza, tel. 02/311–11) is a good time: Destination signs are in Cyrillic, platform numbers are in Roman, and track numbers are in Arabic. To reach the city center, take Tram 1 or 7 south (10 min); buy tickets from one of the many vendors. On the station's main level, **Balkantourist** (open daily 7 AM–10:30 PM) changes money and arranges accommodations. Buy domestic tickets upstairs for northern destinations, on the lower level for southern destinations; make international reservations downstairs or at the **Rila International Travel Office** (bul. General Gurko 5, tel. 02/87–07–77; open Sun.–Fri. 7–7, Sat. 7–3). For more information or reservations, try the **Travel Office** (tel. 02/59–31–06; open weekdays 7–7, Sat. 7–3) in the National Palace of Cultures (*see* Worth Seeing, *below*), by the lower main entrance.

GETTING AROUND

Sofia's main artery, **bulevard Maria Luiza,** runs south from the train station to **ploshtad Sveta Nedelya** (Holy Sunday Church Square), where it turns into bulevard Vitosha and continues south past the popular **Yuzhen Park,** home to the NDK (National Palace of Culture). To the west of ploshtad Sveta Nedelya, **bulevard Alexander Stamboliiski** is where you'll find the tourist offices, and to the east lies Central Park. Though most of Sofia is walkable, public transportation is cheap and easy: Frequent **buses** and **trams** (which run 4:30 AM–midnight) cover the city extensively. Buy tickets (100 leva, 340 leva for a day pass) from street vendors or the driver, and punch them on board—or risk a 1,000-lev fine. **Official taxis,** designated by a TAKCU sign, charge 300 leva per km (⅔ mi); rides in the city center should cost no more than 4000 leva.

WHERE TO SLEEP

The best bargains are private accommodations arranged through Balkantourist and Markella Company (*see* Visitor Information *in* Basics, *above*); for about $18 you'll score a centrally located double in far better shape than those in the city's cheap hotels. Brush up on your universal sign language, though; most hosts speak little English, if any at all.

CENTRAL SOFIA

Hotel Baldzhieva. Although they have no showers, the newly renovated $40 doubles in this hotel are spacious and clean. Breakfast is $3 extra. *Tsar Assen 23, tel. 02/87–37–84 or 02/87–29–14. From pl. Sveta Nedelya; walk up bul. Vitosha and turn right on Solunska, then right on Tzar Assen. Reservations advised. Cash only.*

Hotel Niky. A few blocks from Vitosha, this family-run hotel has a pool table and café. Some of the $40 doubles have showers, and the manager speaks English. Reception is open 24 hours. *Neofit Rilski St. 16, tel. 02/51–19–15. From pl. Sveta Nedelya, walk down Vitosha, then right on Neofit Rilski. Reservations advised. Cash only.*

Slavyanska Beseda. This hotel's austere $40 doubles aren't a bad deal given that they all have baths and phones. *Slavyanska St. 3, on the corner of Rakovski, tel. 02/88–04–41. Reservations advised.*

NEAR GARE CENTRALE SOFIA

Business Repos. This private hotel, across from the expensive Hotel Novotel Europa, offers doubles for $30. The stairway may be gloomy, but the rooms are pleasant and clean and have private baths. Reception is open 24 hours. *Klokotnitza 1, tel. and fax 02/31–46–12 or 02/310–77–85. From train station, walk 1 block south on bul. M. Luiza and turn right after Hotel Novotel Europa. Reservations advised.*

DIRT CHEAP

Tourist Hotel Yubileina, (Rizhki Prohod St. 1, tel. 02/20–49–91 or 02/20–50–14) is just a place to rest your head, but at $8 a bed, it's worth the 20-minute trip on bus 77 from the train station.

CAMPING

To reach **Cherniya Kos** (Hwy. E79, tel. 02/57–11–29), take Tram 5 to the last stop, then Bus 57, 58, or 59 until you see the large white statue. The $5 sites are 11 km (7 mi) from Sofia, at the foot of Mt. Vitosha.

FOOD

Eating out in Sofia can be a cross-cultural culinary adventure. Influenced by both East and West, the fast-food scene on bulevards Vitosha, Graf Ignatiev, and Alexander Stamboliiski provides an exotic mixture of Parisian pastries, Middle Eastern kebabs and falafel, and Mediterranean fruits and vegetables. Whatever you do, though, don't neglect the local cuisine; Bulgarians love to eat. Leisurely dining over *shopska* salads, grilled meats, and shots of *rakia* (a potent grape brandy), is a popular recreational activity. Check out a crowded *mehana,* or tavern, where you can taste the local culture by doing as the Bulgarisn do: Eat slowly, drink lots, and stay late.

Bai Gencho. A favorite with locals, this traditional restaurant is on the elegant end of Bulgarian *mehana*s. At about $10 for a three-course meal, it provides classic food and the essential tavern experience with the added allure of candles, flowers, and a fireplace. Make reservations. *Dondukov, 15, tel. 02/81-74-54.*

Tio Pepe's Cocina Espanola. Decorated with photos of the motherland, this charming Spanish restaurant boasts delicious gazpacho (50¢), spicy calamari ($3), paella ($2), and a long list of veggie tapas ($1-$2). Wash it all down with a fine Rioja ($5). *Murgash 8, at Evlogi Georgiev, next to the canal, tel. 02/72-64-88.*

Pizzeria Venezia. There's an honest reason for this restaurant's overwhelming popularity: the excellent, wood-oven-baked pizzas ($2-$5). *Benkovski 12, north of National Science Museum, tel. 02/87-63-64.*

Catch weekend soccer games for $1.50 at the Vasil Levski stadium in Borisova Gradina (Boris's Garden), southeast of the city center.

WORTH SEEING

In a pinch, Sofia can be covered in a single hectic day, but there's plenty to fill up a longer stay. North of Central Park, look for the former **mausoleum** of Georgi Dimitrov, Bulgaria's first Communist leader. In Central Park, the **Sofia City Gallery** (bul. General Gurko 1, tel. 02/87-21-81; admission free; open Wed.-Sun. 10:30-1 and 2-6) shows contemporary art and pieces from its permanent collection of Bulgarian masters. East of ploshtad Alexander Nevski, the **Union of Bulgarian Artists** (Shipka 6; admission free; open Mon.-Sat. 10-6) houses several galleries with eclectic exhibits featuring past and contemporary Bulgarian artists.

ALEXANDER NEVSKI MEMORIAL CHURCH

The domed, neo-Byzantine Hram-Pametnik Alexander Nevski (Alexander Nevski Memorial Church) was completed in 1912 as a memorial to the 200,000 Russian soldiers who died fighting for Bulgaria's liberation from the Turks in 1878. More recently, the Church, strategically located just north of the National Assembly (home of Bulgaria's on-again/off-again parliament), was the site of the January 1997 uprising. Over 40,000 demonstrators assembled around the Church and in the adjacent plaza, causing members of parliament to barricade themselves inside the National Assembly throughout the night, until armed guards surrounded the building and the riots subsided. Catch an evening service when the choir—which includes members of the National Opera—sings from the balcony. Also check out the 170 icons in the **crypt** (admission 200 leva). *Pl. A. Nevski. Cathedral open daily 4:30-7 (Sat. service 6 PM). Crypt open Wed.-Mon. 10:30-12:30 and 2-6:30.*

Just behind the cathedral is the **Cyril and Methodius International Art Gallery** (admission 300 leva; open Wed.-Mon. 11-6:30), run by the daughter of former dictator Todor Zhivkov. The collection of contemporary art, focusing on Eastern European and socialist artists, is well worth a look.

NATIONAL PALACE OF CULTURE

Known to Sofians as the NDK (Naroden Dvorets Na Kulturata), this monstrous cultural center in Yuzhen Park is dominated by a modern sculpture commemorating the 1,300th anniversary of Bulgaria's nationhood. The building is used for public gatherings; in the basement, you'll find a sprawling bazaar, cafés, discos, and the remnants of a bombed fountain destroyed in a Mafia dispute. Take the elevator to the top for great views from the **Panorama Café.** *Bul. Vitosha, tel. 2/5-15-01.*

NATIONAL MUSEUM OF HISTORY

The Natsionalna Historicheski (National Museum of History) has the country's most complete collection of ancient Bulgarian art and artifacts. The dark marble interior and sparse lighting accent Thracian treasures in the main room and seem to capture the depth of Bulgaria's history. *Bul. Vitosha 2, tel. 02/88–15–55. Admission: $2. Open weekdays 9:30–5:15.*

NATIONAL ART GALLERY

The Natsionalna Hudozhestvena Galeria (National Art Gallery), housed in a neo-baroque palace, hosts traveling exhibits as well as its own collection of mainly Bulgarian works. Also inside is the drab National Ethnographic Museum. *Pl. A. Battenburg, tel. 02/88–35–59. Admission: 500 leva. Open Tues.–Sun. 10:30–12:30 and 1:30–6.*

PARTY HOUSE

The mammoth Partiyniyat Dom (Party House), a legacy of the Stalin years, now houses the administrative offices of Bulgaria's parliament. You can still see the black scars of a fire that broke out during a 1990 student rally. *Pl. A. Battenburg. Open weekdays 9–5.*

ST. GEORGE'S CHURCH

Hidden in the Sheraton Hotel's courtyard is one of the oldest structures in Sofia, Sveti Georgi Rotonda (St. George's Church). Built during the 4th century, it was first a Roman rotunda; after destruction by the Huns and restoration by Justinian, it was turned into a Turkish mosque before being restored as a church. You'll find remains of other Roman buildings nearby. *Pl. Sveta Nedelya 2.*

SHOPPING

From Italian shoes and fine perfumes to antique Russian weapons and hand-crafted lace, Sofia has much to offer both the bargain hunter and the quality-conscious. The most enlightening shopping experience in Sofia is a stroll through Zhenski Market (near Gare Centrale, between bul. Slivnitsa and Ekzarh Yosif St.; open Mon.–Sat. 10–7, Sun. 10–2), where villagers come daily to hawk produce, clothes, pottery, baskets, and even used electronic equipment. The market's rock-bottom prices reflect the subsistence-level incomes of many of the villagers; even locals don't often bargain for better deals. Large, hand-crafted wooden bowls are less than $6, and a six-piece set of handmade ceramic mugs can be had for $5. Homemade lace is traditional, plentiful, and competitively priced; caps, globes, and trim are $1, and large tablecloths are under $30. Under Communism, Bulgaria was well-known for its quality textiles; browse through the shops lining bul. Vitosha and bul. Graf Ignatiev for clothes by modern Bulgarian designers at one-third the price of comparable items in the U.S. For better deals and often better quality, hit the side streets surrounding Zhenski Market; whether you're looking for leather, silk, cashmere, or cotton, shops hawk vintage clothes by the kilo here, and the prices are unbeatable. For amateur antiquers, the touristy arts-and-crafts market next to the Nevski Cathedral has former Soviet Union knickknacks, old paintings, and rare books. It's more acceptable to haggle here, but watch out for scams; some of the "antiques" are mass productions aimed at naive Westerners. Experts will want to forage in the city center's many curiosity shops for the real finds. Sofia's one department store, the drab and monstrous TsUM (Plaza Sveta Nedelya; open weekends 10–7, Sat. 10–2), sells a wide range of useful items and is navigable by English-speakers, but it lacks the surprises and local charm of the markets and small shops.

AFTER DARK

In the evening, throngs of young people mill about the cafés on the southern end of bul. Vitosha, near the NDK; and Yuzhen Park is packed with strolling families, skateboarders, and hip Sofians in romantic repose on the lawn. For more upscale action, head for the library. No joke: One of the most fashionable destinations in Sofia is the basement of the **National Library of Cyril and Methodius** (bul. Vasil Levski, on the corner of Shipka, next to the University). Here, twentysomethings sing karaoke in the outer room, and a stylish crowd including local politicians and celebrities congregates inside for live music. Don't be shocked if you're frisked at the door; any crowded venue in Sofia is bound to be popular with the omnipresent Mafia, called the *Mutri*.

DANCING

Most clubs are open from 10 PM until dawn and charge a 75l cover. Old standby the **Yalta Club** (Aksakov 31, opposite university) is still popular, but many people have moved on to newer, more cutting-edge environments, such as techno haven **Ecstasy** (Suborna 3, next to the American Embassy), or the more upscale **Jazzy** (bul. Tsarigradsko Shose 33, at the corner of San Stefano, tel 02/943–38–03).

MUSIC

Classical-music concerts are held at 7:30 PM in the **Bulgaria Concert Hall** (Aksavkov St. 1, at Benkovski, 1 block east of Central Park, tel. 02/87–40–73), and at the **NDK** (*see* Worth Seeing, *above*). Don't miss the excellent **National Opera and Ballet** (Vrabcha 1, north of pl. Alexander Nevski, tel. 02/887–70–11). For tickets, go to the ticket offices in concert halls and on the first floor of the NDK. Rock and blues? **Funky's** (Shandor Petyofi 24A, tel 02/54–33–26) usually lives up to its name. For more sophistication, **La Strada** (6th of September St., 4) is an arty jazz club that draws an international clientele.

NEAR SOFIA

RILA MONASTERY

Tucked into the imposing Rila Mountains 100 km (60 mi) south of Sofia, the famous **Rila Monastery** sits atop a steep ascent through a forested valley. Built during the 10th century by Ivan of Rila (876–946), it remains the largest monastery in Bulgaria. The oldest part of the fortresslike structure is **Hreylu's Tower** (1335), adjacent to the church. Inside, you'll find a sarcophagus containing Ivan's embalmed body and a collection of religious artifacts spanning more than 1,000 years. The monastery **museum** (admission 1,000 leva; open daily 8–5) features the Rila Cross, a 16-inch wooden piece with more than 1,500 minute figurines carved into it. Legend has it that a monk named Raphael spent 12 years carving the cross, then went blind. Open daily, Rila has services at 6 AM and 4:30 PM; guided tours in English cost $1.50.

COMING AND GOING • Sofia's Ovcha Kupel station (*see* Coming and Going *in* Sofia, *above*) sends two daily buses to the monastery: The direct bus (3 hrs) leaves at 6:30 AM; the other leaves at 10:30 AM and connects in Rila. From the monastery, buses leave for Sofia at 10:20 AM (direct) and 2 PM (via Rila). The last bus from the monastery leaves at 5:15 PM and drops you in Rila; from here, take the 6 PM bus to Blagoevgrad, then a train to Sofia.

WHERE TO SLEEP • Accommodations near the monastery are limited, so reserve ahead in summer. The monastery itself offers cozy $7 beds; register in Room 170. Lockout is at 9 PM sharp. Or follow signs behind the monastery to **Camping Bor** (⅔ km/½ mi away), with $11 double bungalows and a café that's open late. Just down the road, the **Riletz Hotel** (tel. 2106) has large, mountain-view doubles for $36, and a good restaurant.

CENTRAL BULGARIA

Some travelers, shooting across Bulgaria on an express train from Sofia to the Black Sea coast, wistfully contemplate the fields of roses and rugged mountains in the center of the country. Follow your instincts, and don't be afraid to forsake a Black Sea suntan in favor of exploring **Plovdiv** or **Koprivshtitsa**. If you're bent on seeing the coast, consider a brief stop in the ancient village of **Veliko Turnovo**.

PLOVDIV

Beyond the bland high-rise apartment blocks on the edge of town is **Old Plovdiv**, a well-preserved 19th-century neighborhood at the top of the three hills that inspired the town's Roman name, Trimontium. Old Plovdiv has become Bulgaria's center of bohemian chic: Home to a cosmopolitan university and winding cobblestone streets, the area is a perfect spawning ground for art galleries, bars, and antique shops. Wandering Old Plovdiv, you'll encounter museums, churches, ancient fortified walls, and restored houses from the National Revival period. Some of Plovdiv's Roman ruins have been excavated and put to modern use, rather adding to the town's old-town ambience.

BASICS

Prima Vista (bul. General Gurko 8, just north of central square, off Knyaz Alexander Battenburg, tel. 032/27–27–78; open daily 10–1:30 and 2–6) has maps, an English-speaking staff, and $20 doubles in private homes. The Balkantourist office, **Puldin Tourist** (bul. Bulgaria 102, tel. 032/55–38–48, fax 032/55–51–42; open weekdays 9–noon and 1–5:30), also books private $16 doubles; from the stations, take Trolleybus 102 or 2 and look for the office on the left at the first roundabout after the river.

COMING AND GOING

Bulgaria's second-largest city, Plovdiv is easily accessible by bus and train. The **train station** (tel. 032/22–27–29) has frequent service to Sofia (2½ hrs, $1) and Burgas (4½ hrs, $2.50). The nearby **bus station** (tel. 032/77–76–07) has connections to Sofia (2 hrs, $2) and Burgas (3½ hrs, $3). Both stations are a 15-minute walk from the center; in front of the train station, cross Hristo Botev, walk to the turnabout on bulevard Ruski, and turn right on Ivan Vazov, or take buses 2, 20, and 26 to the central square.

WHERE TO SLEEP

Plovdiv is short on cheap sleeps, especially during local festivals in May, September, and October. Situated between the main drag and old town, the brand-new, private **Hotel S&M** (Hristo Duckmedjiev St. 28, tel. 032/26–01–35) has airy doubles with bay windows for $48 (cash only). The excellent hostel **Touristcheski Dom** (Slaveikov 5, tel. 032/23–32–11), in a restored mansion in Old Plovdiv, is a steal at $16 a double (cash only); from the tunnel on Tsar Boris III Obedinitel, walk uphill two blocks. The **Leipzig Hotel** (bul. Ruski 70, tel. 032/23–22–50) has little to recommend it except reasonable $27 doubles and a convenient locale; four blocks from the train station, cross Hristo Botev, then head up bulevard Ruski.

FOOD AND MUSIC

The best traditional Bulgarian restaurants here are in Old Plovdiv. The superb **Puldin Restaurant** (Tseretelev 3, tel. 032/23–17–20) offers an assortment of salads (50¢–$1) and grilled meats and fish ($3–$4); from Knyaz Alexander Battenburg, take Suborna to Tseretelev and turn right. Pizza at the spotless **Verdi** (Ponkovnik Bonev, 1, tel. 032/65–03–69), on a side street off Aleksandrovska, is a cheaper alternative. After dark, the liveliest place to catch a band is in the subterranean beer hall **Yctata** (Aleksandrovska, 30).

WORTH SEEING

Head behind the post office near the central square to see the **Forum of Philoppolis** and other Roman ruins. At the end of Knyaz Alexander Battenburg is the 14th-century **Mosque of Djoumaya Djamiya,** built by order of Sultan Murad II. It's open from first to last prayer, except during services; leave your shoes at the door. The 2nd-century **Roman amphitheater** was discovered in the 20th century, when a landslide removed part of the hill. Opened to the public in 1980, the 3,000-seat amphitheater is the largest in Bulgaria and hosts opera and symphony performances in summer. Buy tickets at the symphony office, next to the Hotel Trimontium. In a beautiful old National Revival home in Old Plovdiv, the **Ethnographic Museum** (at end of Suborna, tel. 032/22–56–56; admission free; open daily 9–noon and 2–5) has a large collection of local cultural artifacts, including costumes, jewelry, furniture, and musical instruments.

VELIKO TURNOVO

Built along the banks of the Yantra River, the old homes of Veliko Turnovo are carved deep into a hillside under the shadow of dramatic limestone cliffs. Since the town's layout follows the twisting Yantra River, getting around can be confusing. Orient yourself using two major landmarks: the triangular **Maika Bulgaria Square** on the west side of town, and **Tsarevets Hill** to the east. Buy a map (500 leva) from the Etur or Yantra hotel.

Almost nightly from May through October, a spectacular **light show** starts at 10 PM on Tsarevets Hill. Colored lights symbolize each stage of Bulgarian history: Pink for the newborn nation; flashing lights for war; violet for the grandeur of the Second Bulgarian Empire; and darkness for the repression under the Turks. Finally, the hill is bathed in violet (a return to the greatness of the Second Kingdom). Inquire at the Interhotel Veliko Turnovo (behind post office, tel. 062/305–7) about show dates, and buy tickets (25¢) just outside Tsarevets Gate.

COMING AND GOING

Veliko's tiny **train station** (off Magistralna, tel. 062/200–65) is near Sveta Gora Park, across the Yantra River from the city center. From here, buses 4 and 13 head downtown every 20 minutes, and taxis downtown cost less than $2. Trains from Veliko go to Sofia (4 hrs, $2.50) and Tulovo (2 hrs, $1.50), where you can transfer for Kazanluk and Koprivshtitsa. The town of **Gorna Oryahovitsa,** 13 km (8 mi) north, has a larger station and handles most travelers headed to Veliko Turnovo; minivans waiting outside the station whisk people to Turnovo in minutes (500 leva). Buses also run frequently between the two towns; they'll drop you at the **bus station** (Nikola Gabrovski, SW of town, tel. 062/408–09), but you can also ask to stop at ploshtad Maika Bulgaria, in the center of town. From the bus station, buses 7, 10, and 11 run regularly to the center.

WHERE TO SLEEP

Consider private-room offers at the stations, but don't pay more than $10 per person. In the old, picturesque part of town, **Hotel Komfort** (Panayat Triptografev 5, tel. 062/287–28) has pleasant $24 doubles with beautiful views. From Stefan Stambolov, take Rakovski to ploshtad Maika Bulgaria; Panayat Triptografev begins on the far side of the square. Otherwise, try **Hotel Trapezitsa** (Stefan Stankolov 79, north of post office, tel. 062/220–61), where it's $16 (cash only) for a sparse room for two. Though grim, **Orbita Hotel** (Hristo Botev 15, off pl. Maika Bulgaria, tel. 062/220–41) has beds for a mere $4 (cash only).

FOOD

The popular **Starata Kushta** (Lyuben Karavelov 1, no phone), where you can sample traditional Bulgarian fare on a shady patio, is off the east end of Gabrovski. The **Yantra Hotel Restaurant** (Opalchenska, at Stefan Stambolov, tel. 062/203–91) has great food (pork kebabs $2, desserts under $1) and unrivaled views. At night, you may have to pay extra for a perfect view of the Tsarevets light show.

WORTH SEEING

Veliko Turnovo's most prominent landmark is **Tsarevets Hill** (admission 75¢; open daily 8–7), with its fort, church, and palace, and a summit dominated by **Ascension Patriarchal Church.** The hill is almost completely enclosed by a loop in the Yantra; you reach it via a narrow 17th-century stone bridge. Head down the road behind the Etur Hotel and cross the footbridge to **Asenoutsi Park** to check out the **State Art Museum** (admission 50¢; open Tues.–Sun. 10–6), with modern Bulgarian art.

KOPRIVSHTITSA

Koprivshtitsa is perhaps the most significant of Bulgaria's museum towns: The first shots in Bulgaria's war for independence against the Turks were fired here on April 20, 1876. More than a century later, the town remains virtually unchanged, and exhibits the various styles developed during the National Revival period in half a dozen noted homes (now open as museums). Koprivshtitsa can be seen in a day, but if you're tempted by the town's fairy-tale charm, stay the night in one of its period-piece houses.

COMING AND GOING

The **train station** lies on the Sofia–Burgas line, but not all trains stop; ask first. A bus (20¢) meets trains at the station and carries passengers to town. The **bus station** (tel. 07184/2133), a block south of the town square, posts a schedule for all trains and buses.

WHERE TO SLEEP

For about $18 a double (cash only), you can stay at the charmless **Hotel Koprivshtitsa** (tel. 07184/2182), across the bridge (near the bus stop) and up the stairs. Better yet, for only $16 (cash only), stay in a double room at traditional **Hotel Byaloto Kouche** (Generilo 2, uphill from town square, tel. 07184/2250), with timber floors and woven rugs; request the room with the fireplace in winter. For **private rooms,** at $12 a double, inquire at the first souvenir shop on the right side of the town square.

WORTH SEEING

One ticket ($1)—available at any museum house or the ticket office on the town square—gets you into all the National Revival museum houses. The houses are open Wednesday–Monday 9–noon and 1:30–5:30. **Georgi Benkovski House** (Jako Dorosiev 5), built in 1831, is worth seeing for its National Revival architectural touches. The **Lyuben Karavelov House** (bul. Anton Ivanov 39) contains an exhibit on the writing career of Lyuben Karavelov (1843–1876), with copies of his revolutionary works, such as *Svoboda* (Freedom). **Todor Kableshkov House** (Todor Kableshkov 8), built in 1845, is now a museum documenting the activities of Todor Kableshkov and his fellow revolutionaries.

BLACK SEA COAST

Bulgaria may be shaped by the collision of East and West, but locals claim that the Black Sea coast has been shaped by Balkantourist alone. Happily, it's possible to avoid the expensive, flashy resorts and head for picturesque seaside towns, such as **Sozopol,** which date from Roman times. **Varna,** in the north, and **Burgas,** in the south, are the only coastal towns with train service; therefore, they serve as transit hubs for coastal resorts and small, undiscovered fishing villages like **Balchik.**

VARNA

Bulgaria's third-largest city, Varna (population 300,000) has dominated the Black Sea coast for almost three millennia. Throughout this time, sailors have lent Varna a cosmopolitan air, enhanced these days by a throng of summer tourists and a growing international renown—the nearby coast subbed for Romania in the recent American remake of *Dracula.* Like any big city, Varna can be overwhelming, but respite can be found in the long beach and oceanfront garden. Varna is a good base for exploring nearby resorts, such as Albena and Zlatni Pyasutsi.

BASICS

The city center has many *kvartino byuro* (private accommodation offices). **Varnenski Bryag** books private $20 doubles at two offices: one catercorner from the train station (pl. Slaveykov 6, tel. 052/22–22–06; open daily 8–6), the other next to Hotel Musala (tel. 052/22–55–24; open in summer, daily 7 AM–8 PM; off season, weekdays 8–6). **Megatours Inc.** (Slivnitsa 3, at bul. Knyaz Boris I, in Hotel Cherno More, tel. 052/22–00–47; open weekdays 9–6:30, Sat. 9–noon) has an English-speaking staff and offers AmEx services.

COMING AND GOING

The train station, **Gare Centrale,** is near the harbor on the southern edge of town. The center is a minute's walk up Tsar Simeon I to ploshtad Nezavisimost. Destinations include Sofia (8 hrs, $6), Veliko Turnovo (4 hrs, $3), Burgas (4 hrs, $2.50), and Plovdiv (6 hrs, $3.50). From the **bus station** (Vladislav Varnenchik 159, NW side of town, tel. 052/44–83–49), Bus 1, 22, or 41 will drop you just north of ploshtad Nezavisimost (5 min, 15 leva). Varna's passenger **port** (tel. 052/22–23–26) is a 20-minute walk (or $1 taxi ride) from the train station: Cross Plaza Slaveikov and walk east on bul. Primorski to the hydrofoil-station pier, just before the beach starts. From June to September, boats go to İstanbul (6 hrs, $90) and Balchik via Zlatni Pyasutsi (3 hrs, $4).

WHERE TO SLEEP AND EAT

Near the beach, **Hotel Odessa** (bul. Slivnitsa 1, tel. 052/22–83–81) is the nicest of the bargain hotels, at $66 a double (breakfast included). Nestled in a quiet, private courtyard by the port, **Bistro Rimski Termi** (8th of Noemvri 4, tel. 052/22–95–73) has grilled kebabs ($1), salads (50¢), and wine ($2 per bottle). In the winter, Rimski Termi is prone to odd hours, but the restaurant next door, **Starata Kushta,** is a fine alternative. After dark, head to **Bonkers** (Hristo Botev, just before the Asparuhov Bridge, tel. 052/23–50–09) to shoot pool and listen to local bands. For an older crowd and a more central location, **Horizont** (Morska Gradina, tel. 052/88–45–30), by the main entrance to the beach park, has Greek-style music and food.

WORTH SEEING

Don't miss the **Archeological Museum** (bul. Maria Luiza 41, in park, tel. 052/212–41; admission $1; open Tues.–Sun. 10–5), with graveyard artifacts from a 3rd-century BC necropolis discovered in 1972 near Varna. Also worth a visit are ancient baths at **Roman Thermae** (Han Krum, between Tsar Kaloyan and San Stefano; admission $1; open Tues.–Sun. 9–5; closed winter weekends); built at the end of the 2nd century AD, the baths were in use until the end of the 3rd.

NEAR VARNA

BALCHIK

A scenic old fishing village nestled at the base of stark, white cliffs, Balchik is a good place to escape the coastal crowds and still soak up some rays. Just 40 km (25 mi) north of Varna, Balchik retains an unhurried, small-town air, even in the height of summer. Be sure to visit **Dvorets** (admission $1.50; open daily 8–8), once the summer home of Romania's former queen Marie. Built in 1931, it features a minaret and extensive manicured gardens—all perched directly above a beautiful beach. From town, walk south on Primorska for about 20 minutes; at the top of the hill, turn left onto the road lined with vendors. From 8 AM to 7 PM, frequent buses run between Varna and Balchik (1 hr, 1,000 leva).

Crash at the private **Hotel Esperanza** (Cherno More 16, past square, tel. 0579/5148), where a cheerful owner offers $16 doubles (cash only). For the best meal and view in town, climb the stairs at the base of Cherno More to **Emona** (Emona 14, tel. 0579/2269) to indulge in great salads (75¢), fried perch ($2), and a tasty chardonnay.

BURGAS

The youngest city on the Black Sea coast (the town center and port date from the early 20th century), Burgas has few historical sights but a pleasant main street for strolling. **Menabria Tours** (Aleksandrovska 2, tel. 056/472–75; open in summer, daily 8–7; in winter, Mon.–Sat. 8–6), opposite the stations, changes money and accepts traveler's checks (4% commission); they also arrange private $16 doubles. To change money after hours, try the office (open 7 AM–midnight) in the **Bulgaria Hotel** (Aleksandrovska 21, tel. 056/428–20).

COMING AND GOING

From the centrally located **train station** (pl. Garov, tel. 056/450–22), frequent trains run to Sofia (7 hrs, $3), Plovdiv (5 hrs, $2.50), and Varna (5 hrs, $2.50). From the *Yug* (south) **bus station** (tel. 056/456–31) next to the train station, buses run to towns along the coast, including Varna (3 hrs, $2). To reach the center, take Aleksandrovska to bulevard Bogoridi, which heads east to the gardens and beaches.

WHERE TO SLEEP AND EAT

Private rooms through **Menabria Tours** are the best option; try to arrive when the office is open. Otherwise, say the magic words *chastna kvartira* (private room) to taxi drivers and they might be able to set you up. More concerned with ease than affordability? Try the **Hotel Primorets** (Lilyana Dimitrova, 1, tel. 056/441–17), by the sea; though less charming than a private home, your $40 double gets you privacy and a view. Escape the tourist track for a relaxing dinner at **Cheren Peter** (Gurko St. 26, no phone), where salad, moussaka, dessert crêpes, and wine can be had for $6 a head.

WORTH SEEING

Pick up the free English pamphlet and browse the **Archeological Museum** (bul. Bogoridi 21; admission 500 leva; open weekdays 9–noon and 2–5), a treasure chest of ancient Thracian and Greek relics. Don't be daunted by the graffiti on the museum's dilapidated facade; the collection inside is top-notch. One block south, the city **Art Gallery** (Mitropolit Simeon; admission 400 leva; open Tues.–Fri. 9–noon and 3–6) has colorful modern paintings on the first floor, works by Burgas artists on the second, and paintings of religious icons on the third. Again, don't be fooled by the facade.

NEAR BURGAS

SOZOPOL

With National Revival–style homes lining cobblestone alleys and with a nice stretch of beach, ancient Burgas is distinctly Old World. Thirty-five kilometers (21 miles) south of Burgas, Sozopol is haunted mostly by fishermen, artists, and Bulgarian tourists, so it's not as crowded as other Black Sea towns. From 6 AM to 8 PM hourly buses run between Burgas and Sozopol (45 min, 800 leva), arriving at the southern edge of the old town. From Sozopol, three to four buses daily head farther south to Tsarevo and Ahtopol. From the bus station, turn left to reach Apolonia (which bisects the old town), or turn right onto Republikanska for the new town.

The family-run **Hotel Radik** (Republikanska 4, 5 min south of bus station, tel. 05514/1706) offers spacious doubles with kitchen, beach view, and bath for $24 (cash only). Tourist agency **Lotos** (Ropotamo 1, at end of Republikanska, tel. 05514/429; open daily 8–7) books $7 beds in private homes. Reserve ahead for August.

CZECH REPUBLIC

A h yes, the Czech Republic, where the angry wails of police sirens are as rare as vowels, and the kindness of strangers is as abundant as the quality beer that floods the countless pubs. But the borders of this newborn nation haven't always been this inviting. For hundreds of years the lands of Bohemia and Moravia have been in dispute, and until quite recently, the Czech people have had little say in the matter.

Since the 5th century AD, tribes of Czechs have considered the lands of Bohemia and Moravia their divinely ordained home, and centuries of foreign domination, first by the Holy Roman Empire and later by the Nazis and the Soviets, only intensified Czech nationalism. When the Catholic Church set Jan Hus, a Czech priest, ablaze in 1415 for his heretical beliefs, his followers rose in revolt and Bohemia became the earliest battleground of the Reformation. After World War I, Bohemia, Moravia, and Slovakia spliced themselves together to form Czechoslovakia, one of the most prosperous nations in Europe until Hitler took over. The "Prague Spring" of 1968 was a relatively peaceful attempt to birth a brand of "socialism with a human face," but it was promptly squashed by the Soviets. Widespread protests and strikes finally led to the expulsion of the Communists in 1990. Finally, on New Year's Day, 1993, the Czech Republic became an autonomous political entity when the Slovaks, tired of being second-class citizens in a country ruled by Czechs, seceded to form Slovakia in the bloodless "Velvet Divorce."

In the early 1990s, Prime Minister Václav Klaus, together with Václav Havel, president and dissident playwright from the Prague Spring era, implemented an aggressive plan for a market-driven economy, boosting the Czech Republic into the international marketplace. As joint-venture capital washes across the borders, unemployment drops, slick new shops appear, and prices rise dramatically.

Despite the country's headlong rush toward capitalism, the Czech spirit lies in the soft green hills of Bohemia and Moravia, where rivers and hiking trails lace their way through forests and fields of wildflowers. The magnificence of Prague's cobblestone streets and spired skyline refuses to be diminished by a few McDonald's franchises, and some of the best beer in the world ensures that the country remains infused with levity.

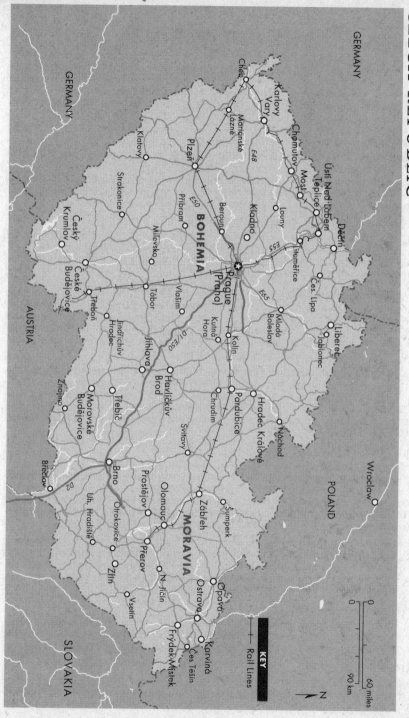

GERMANY

GERMANY

Cheb

Karlovy
Vary

Mariánské
Lázně

Klatovy

Strakonice

Český
Krumlov

České
Budějovice

Třeboň

Plzeň

Příbram

Milevsko

Beroun

Tábor

Vlašim

Jindřichův
Hradec

Znojmo

Morovské
Budějovice

Třebíč

Jihlava

Havlíčkův
Brod

Chomutov

Most

Teplice

Ústí Nad Labem

Louny

Kladno

E48

E50

E55

BOHEMIA

Prague
(Praha)

Kuná
Hora

Kolín

Chrudim

Svitavy

Pardubice

Brno

Uh. Hradiště

Otrokovice

Prostějov

Olomouc

Přerov

Zlín

Vsetín

N. Jičín

Frýdek-Místek

Čes. Těšín

Karviná

Ostrava

Opava

Šumperk

Zábřeh

Náchod

Hradec Králové

Mladá
Boleslav

Ces. Lipa

Jablonec

Liberec

Děčín

Litoměřice

E65

D1/E50

D2

MORAVIA

Břeclav

AUSTRIA

SLOVAKIA

POLAND

Wroclaw

KEY

Rail Lines

N

0   60 miles

0   90 km

BASICS

MONEY

US$1 = 29 Kč and 1 Kč = 3½ cents. The unit of currency in the Czech Republic is the *koruna* (crown), abbreviated Kč; it's divided into 100 *haléřu* (hellers). To change money, your best bet is to brave the lines on weekdays at state banks, which charge 2% commission and sometimes give cash advances on credit cards. **Komerční Banka** and **Československá Obchodní Banka** offer similar rates; the former gives cash advances on major credit cards. Most banks also have ATMs linked to Cirrus or PLUS systems. Exchange companies, such as Chequepoint, offer poor rates and charge commissions, but some are open 24 hours. Hotels are likely to rob you of even more. Hold onto receipts if you want to change 5,000 Kč or more into foreign currency upon departure.

HOW MUCH IT WILL COST • Prices in the Czech Republic are catching up with those in the West, but they still have a long way to go. By seeking cheap lodging—rooms in private homes (300 Kč–500 Kč per person) and hostels (200 Kč–400 Kč)—you can keep your daily budget well below US$40 in the cities, and significantly less outside the cities. Although Czech train fares tripled in the early '90s, a trip from one side of this small country to the other still won't cost you more than 150 Kč.

VISA AND ENTRY REQUIREMENTS

U.S. citizens may enter the Czech Republic for 30 days without a visa; Canadians and Brits get six months visa-free. Australians and New Zealanders can either apply for 30-day visas ahead of time or get them at the border, though Kiwis must pay about $22 for them. Border guards may ask you to show that you have ample funds for your stay.

COMING AND GOING

Trains are the most common means of entering the Czech Republic. You can use Eurail and InterRail passes to get to the Czech border, but be prepared to pay in Czech currency once inside. The **European East Pass** covers the Czech Republic, Slovakia, Poland, Hungary, and Austria, but it isn't much of a bargain at $195 for five days' travel over a 15-day period or $300 for 10 days' travel over a 30-day period. Call Rail Europe, in the U.S. (tel. 800/438–7245), for details.

If you're headed straight to the Czech Republic from the United States, you might save some aggravation and money by flying directly to Prague or Bratislava. **ČSA** (1350 Sixth Ave., New York, NY 10019, tel. 212/765–6022), the state airline, has direct flights from New York to Prague six times a week (US$900) and from Toronto and Montréal (more than US$1,000) every Saturday. You'll probably get a better deal with one of the European airlines currently serving Prague, which include **British Airways, KLM,** and **Air France.**

GETTING AROUND

The government runs **ČD** (the railways; formerly known as ČSD) and ČSAD (the bus system). Barring only express lines, trains give painstaking attention to every town between you and your destination; some are vintage steam trains that are an experience unto themselves. Schedules are posted on all train and bus platforms; *odjezd* and *příjezd* are departures and arrivals, respectively. *Rychlík* (express trains) are listed in red, *osobný vlak* (domestic trains) in black. In larger train stations, domestic and *mezinárodní* (international) tickets are sold at separate windows. Travelers under 26 are eligible for discounts.

Buses are often crowded and slightly more expensive than trains, but they're more direct and will thus get you there faster. Even small towns have a bus terminal with a ticket office, numbered platforms, and an inordinately complex schedule for every route. Remember that a crossed-hammer logo above a bus itinerary means "work days only" (no weekend service); *S* means the bus runs on Saturday; *N* indicates Sunday service.

WHERE TO SLEEP

Your cheapest options are **private rooms**; look for ZIMMER FREI and PRIVAT ZIMMER signs, or inquire at tourist agencies. Hostelling International (HI) runs more than 20 **hostels** with beds that go for as little as 150 Kč with an HI card (a few crowns more without a card). All hostels have showers and kitchen facilities.

FOOD

Czechs have one of the highest rates of meat consumption in the world, and the menus in their restaurants reflect this (although vegetarianism is beginning to take hold). When eating out, budget travelers should look for HOSTINEC, PIVNICE, or HOSPODA signs, indicating beer halls that serve filling meals for less than 100 Kč—cheaper than a *restaurace* or *vinárna*. For lunch, *bufets* or *lahůdky,* where *chlébiček* (open-face sandwiches) are dirt cheap, can't be beat. On menus, *předkrmy* are appetizers and *polévky* are soups. *Jídla na objednávku* are main dishes: *Ryby* is fish; *kuře,* chicken; *vepřový,* pork; *hovězí,* beef; and *kachna,* duck. *Masa* is a general term for meats; *bez masa* means "without meat." Meat comes *grilovaný* (baked) or *pečený* (roasted); *roštu* (grilled); and often *smažený* (breaded and fried). *Brambory knedlíky* (potato dumplings) make frequent appearances, as does *zelí* (pickled cabbage). After dinner, head to a *cukrárna* (sweet shop) for cheap cones of *zmrzlina* (ice cream). *Potraviny* are grocery stores, where you can get *chléb* (bread), *ovoce* (fruit), and *zeleniny* (vegetables).

For drinks, you can pick up a bottle of Moravian *víno* (wine) for about 100 Kč. Half-liters of *pivo* (beer) cost about 15 Kč. The most popular aperitifs are *slivovice* (plum brandy), *Becherovka* (herb liqueur), and Slovakia's *borovička,* a ginlike drink derived from juniper berries. You're not likely to find the de-caffeinated versions of *káva* (coffee), *presso* (espresso), or *čaj* (tea).

BUSINESS HOURS

Most banks are open weekdays from 8 to 4. Private and hotel exchange offices are open daily, often late into the evening. Post offices are generally open weekdays 8–5:30. Tourist offices hold regular weekday hours but may not open or close early on weekends. Museums are generally open Tuesday–Sunday 9–5, though some are closed November through April. Stores are open weekdays 9–6 (grocery stores often open at 6 AM); most close at noon on Saturday and almost all are closed Sunday.

VISITOR INFORMATION

Čedok is your best resource for information on accommodations before you leave home, but once here, you'll find that this outfit is more interested in setting up package tours. Ask the offices in New York and London for brochures. *10 E. 40th St., New York, NY 10016, tel. 212/689–9720; 49 Southwark St., London SE1, tel. 0171/378–6009.*

Cestovní Kancelář Mládeže (CKM), the youth travel bureau, will help you find budget accommodations and point you to inexpensive activities, but not every town has a branch. Look instead for the **Městské Informační Středisko** (Town Information Service), guaranteed to be within a stone's throw of the *radnice* (town hall). It's usually open daily 9–6, closes around 4 at the earliest on weekends, has lots of maps, and can arrange inexpensive accommodations in private flats.

PHONES

Country code: 420. Purchase phone cards in various increments up to 100 units (3 Kč per unit, which lasts about six minutes) at most *tabák*s (tobacco shops), some shops, and post offices. It's difficult to find a coin-operated phone, which requires 3 Kč for local calls. When using the gray phones, place the coin in the holding slot, but do not let it drop. Dial, and when you hear an answer, drop the coin in. When making intercity calls, be prepared to insert more coins when you hear the tone. You can call the United States collect or with a calling card by dialing **AT&T** Direct Access[SM] (tel. 00–420–00101) or **MCI** World-Phone (tel. 00–420–00112). You can also reach English-speaking operators through **Canada Direct** (tel. 00–420–00151) and **BT Direct** (tel. 00–420–04401). For direct-dial international calls, dial 00 + country code + phone number. If you can't find a working pay phone, check the post office.

MAIL

The Czech mail system is inexpensive and fairly efficient. Letters (7 Kč) and postcards (5 Kč) to European destinations take about five days; outside Europe, they'll cost a bit more (8 Kč and 6 Kč, respectively) and will take a week to 10 days.

EMERGENCIES

Dial 158 for the **police,** 155 for an **ambulance,** and 150 for the **fire department.**

LANGUAGE

Czech (*český*) is the official language. Many older Czechs speak German, and English is on the rise among the younger generations. Enough people are familiar with the basics of English that you won't often have to struggle with Czech, but you'll want to pack some key phrases to help you get by: *prosím* (excuse me/please); *děkuju* (thank you); *dobrý den* (hello); *na shledanou* (goodbye); *ano* (yes); *ne* (no); *pardon* (sorry); *kde je . . .?* (where is . . .?); *kolik to stojí* (how much is it?); and *nerozumím* (I haven't the slightest clue what you're saying to me).

PRAGUE

Legions of foreigners, Americans mostly, have recently decided that Prague (Praha in Czech) is one of the most amazing cities on earth. The daily parade of musicians, sword-swallowers, marionettes, and artists along its romantic bridges and cobblestone streets creates an aura of magic. Unlike many European capitals, Prague survived World War II undamaged, and the city is a testament to European architectural history, with a medieval center, Communist outskirts, and buildings from every period and style in-between. Baroque palaces recall prosperous days under the Catholic Hapsburgs, and ominous government bureaus from the Communist era seem to have come straight from the stories of Kafka, a German-speaking Jew but Prague's most famous writer. *Pražens* (citizens of Prague) have always had a knack for absorbing the best of foreign influences: It was here, for instance, not in his native Austria, that Mozart won his greatest acclaim. The latest influx of foreigners has started to wear out its welcome, however, as prices rise so high that Pražens can only watch while tourists feast in restaurants they used to frequent.

BASICS

VISITOR INFORMATION

Čedok has a counter staff of English-speakers, who distribute information on lodging, tours, and car rentals. (To rent a **Škoda,** you must be 21, have a valid driver's license, and about 1,500 Kč a day; you have to be 23 to rent anything else.) They also sell bus, train, and concert tickets. For other Čedok locations, *see* Where to Sleep, *below. Na příkopě 18, near nám, tel. 02/2419–7111, fax 02/2422–2300. Open weekdays 8:30–6, Sat. 9–1. Metro: Republiky.*

CKM sells youth-hostel maps of Europe and organizes bus trips to major European cities. *Jindřišská 28, tel. 02/268–532. From the train station, walk north along Růžová, then right on Jindřišská. Open Mon.–Thurs. 9:30–5; Fri. 9:30–4.*

Prague Information Service (PIS) can update you on events and sell you concert tickets and city maps (45 Kč) from two locations. *Staroměstské nám. 1, Staré Město, tel. 02/544–444; Na příkopě 20, tel. 02/26–40–22. Both open weekdays 9–6, weekends 9–5.*

AMERICAN EXPRESS

The AmEx office in Wenceslas Square cashes personal checks, replaces lost or stolen traveler's checks, and holds mail (30 Kč fee for nonmembers). Commissions are 2% for changing cash, 8% for changing crowns, and 4%–6% for changing traveler's checks into dollars. With an AmEx card you can withdraw cash from the 24-hour ATM outside; there's another AmEx ATM at the airport. *Václavské nám. 56, tel. 02/2421–9992, fax 02/2422–7708. Open weekdays 9–6, Sat. 9–2; exchange open daily 9–6. Metro: Muzeum.*

CHANGING MONEY

After hours, you'll pay a higher commission (4%–8%) to change money at large hotels like the central **Ambassador** (Václavské nám. 5, tel. 02/2419–3111). In a pinch you can also try **Thomas Cook** (Národní 28, tel. 02/2110–5276; Národní třída metro; open weekdays 9–7, Sat. 9–6, Sun. 10–6), which is cater-corner from AmEx. **Československá Obchodní Banka** (Na příkopě 14; open weekdays 8–5) charges a 1% commission at the counter but only 1% if you use their Exact Automatic Exchange machine, which takes cash only. **Bank Austria** (Havelská 19) also has a cash-only Exact Automatic Exchange machine, but it's open 24 hours.

Komerční Banka charges a 2% commission to change cash and traveler's checks, but no fee to use the 24-hour ATM outside, which accepts Visa, American Express, MasterCard, Eurocard, Plus System, and Cirrus. *Na příkopě 33. Metro: Nám. Republiky. Open weekdays 8–5. Other locations: Na příkopě 5; Metro: Můstek. Václavské nám. 42.*

EMBASSIES

Canada: *Mickiewiczova 6, Hradčany, tel. 02/2431–1108. Tram 22 or 18 uphill to Chotkovy Sady; follow Mickiewiczova to Canadian flag. Open weekdays 9–noon and 2–4.* **United States:** *Tržiště 15, Malá Strana, tel. 02/5732–0063. Metro: Malostranská, or Tram 22 to Malostranské nám. Open weekdays 9–noon and 2–3.*

United Kingdom. Aussies and New Zealanders should bring their questions here. *Thunovská 14, Malá Strana, tel. 02/5732– 0355. Open weekdays 9–noon.*

ENGLISH-LANGUAGE BOOKS AND NEWSPAPERS

The American-published weekly *Prague Post* (40 Kč) covers local news; it's also a great source for restaurants, clubs, and cultural events. The *Prague Guide* lists sights, restaurants, and services. *Cultural Events* covers theater and nightlife. **Program** has weekly listings of club venues, theaters, television, radio, and film. **Bohemian Ventures** (Nám. Jana Palacha 2, tel. 02/231–9516; Metro: Staroměstská; open weekdays 9–5), in Charles University's Philosophy Department, sells classics, history, and philosophy texts.

The Globe. The Globe's American owners have created a relaxed atmosphere with reading lamps and cozy chairs, and the clerks pulling cappuccinos (30 Kč) in the next room happily offer tips on cool Prague activities. *Janovského 14, tel. or fax 02/6671–2610. From Vltavská metro, left on Antonínská, continue 2 blocks, turn right. Open daily 10 AM–midnight.*

PHONES AND MAIL

Prague's area code is 02. If you're calling from outside the Czech Republic, omit the zero. For telephone assistance, dial 120 (outside Prague dial 121). International calls can be made 24 hours a day from the **main post office** (*see below*). For tips on international dialing, *see* Phones *in* Basics, *above.*

The **main post office** (Jindřišská 14, off Václavské Náměs tí, tel. 02/2422–9051, fax 02/2423–0303) is open 24 hours and handles direct international phone calls; you can also send or receive a fax (11 Kč per page) or telex (121726VDSC). Have poste restante addressed to Poste Restante, c/o Last Name, First Name, Jindřišská 14, 11–000 Prague 1, Czech Republic, and pick it up at Window 17. The post office at **Hlavní nádraží,** Prague's main train station, is open weekdays 8–7 and Saturday 8–1.

COMING AND GOING

BY BUS

Buses leaving from **Florenc Bus Terminal** serve most domestic and international destinations; head to the **information counter** (open daily 8–8) to assess the complicated schedules. Buses are preferable to trains for travel to other Bohemian cities. Tickets to Karlovy Vary (2½ hrs) are 85 Kč; Brno (2½ hrs) 85 Kč; and Plzeň (1.5 hrs) 60 Kč. *4–6 Křižíkova, tel. 02/2421–1060. Open daily 5 AM–11 PM. Metro: Florenc.*

BY PLANE

Ruzyně Airport (tel. 02/2011–4433 or 02/2011–4533), 15 km (9 mi) northwest of the center, always has long lines, so get here early. **AVE Ltd.** (open daily 7 AM–10 PM) helps travelers find lodging; rent a pricey car here from Budget (tel. or fax 02/316–5214), Hertz (tel. 02/312–0717), or Europcar (tel. 02/2481–1290). Between 8:30 AM and 7 PM daily, a ČSA bus departs every half-hour from the front of the terminal for the Dejvická metro station and Náměstí Republiky. Bus 119 from Dejvická (10 Kč), Bus 108 from Hradčanská, and Bus 179 from Nové Butovice make the trip more frequently but stop more often. Taxis usually charge 400 Kč from the airport to the city center.

BY TRAIN

Two small stations, **Masarykovo nádraží** (corner of Hybernská and Havlíčkova; Metro: Nám. Republiky) and **Smíchovské nádraží** (Křížová ul.), serve destinations in Bohemia and Moravia.

The city's main station, **Hlavní nádraží,** is an international hub. Second-class tickets to Amsterdam are 4,700 Kč; Paris 5,350 Kč; Vienna 700 Kč; Berlin 1,400 Kč; Bucharest 3,320 Kč; Budapest 1,100 Kč; and Kraków 450 Kč. Reservations for international travel are highly recommended: Head to **ČD** (tel. 02/2421–7062; open weekdays 9–noon and 1–6, weekends 9–noon and 1–3), located just outside the main building; they accept AmEx, MasterCard, and Visa. Check baggage in lockers for 10 Kč, or at the 24-hour luggage desk, down the ramp on the bottom floor (follow the suitcase signs), for 15Kč. *Wilsonova 80, tel. 02/2422–4200.*

HOLESOVICE • International trains not terminating in Prague often deposit you here rather than at Hlavní nádraží. Several accommodation services have desks in the station; try **AVE Ltd.** (open until 10 PM). If you need to catch a connecting train at Hlavní nádraží, take Metro Line C. *Arnoštovská ul. Metro: Nádraží Holešovice. Luggage lockers (10 Kč).*

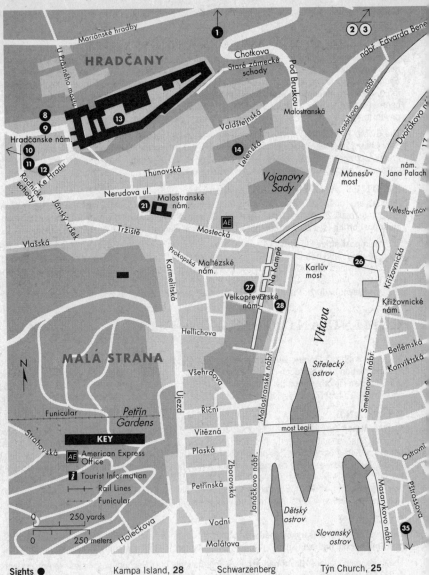

PRAGUE

Sights ●

Anežský Klášter, **7**

Arcibiskupský palác, **9**

Belvedere Summer Palace, **1**

Chrám sv. Mikuláše, **21**

Church of the Nativity of Our Lord, **11**

John Lennon Wall, **27**

Kampa Island, **28**

Karlův Most, **26**

Kostel sv. Mikuláše, **23**

Loreto Church, **10**

Národní Muzeum, **39**

Kongresový Centrum, **38**

Pinkas Synagogue, **18**

Pražský Hrad, **13**

Schwarzenberg Palace, **12**

Staroměstská radnice, **24**

Staronová Synagóga, **17**

Starý Židovský Hřbitov, **15**

Státní Židovský Muzeum, **16**

Šternberský Palác, **8**

Troja Palace and Zoo, **4**

Týn Church, **25**

Vojenské Muzeum, **12**

Vyšehrad, **35**

Wallenstein Palace, **14**

Lodging ○

Accommodation
Service, **19**

Autocamp Trojská, **5**

AVE Ltd. Travel
Agency, **32**

Bonsai Privat, **2**

Camp Dana, **6**

Charles
University, **33**

CKM
Juniorhotel, **37**

Grand Hotel
Evropa, **34**

Hostel Podoli, **40**

Hotel Axa, **20**

Hotel Garni, **42**

Hotel Kafka, **44**

Libra Q, **29**

Pension City, **43**

Pension
Krokodýl, **41**

Penzion Triska, **30**

Penzion Troja, **3**

Pension Unitas, **31**

RHIA Tours, **36**

Toptour, **22**

GETTING AROUND

The Vltava River (Moldau in German), Prague's spine, runs south–north with a single sharp curve to the east at Josefov. Prague was originally five independent towns, represented today by **Hradčany** (Castle Area), **Malá Strana** (Little Side), **Staré Město** (Old Town), and **Josefov** (the Jewish Quarter), neighborhoods that today make up Prague 1. South and east of Prague 1, the creatively named Prague 2 comprises **Nové Město** (New Town) and **Vinohrady.** Hradčany, the seat of Czech royalty for hundreds of years, is centered around **Pražský hrad** (Prague Castle), overlooking the city from its hilltop west of the Vltava. **Karlův most** (Charles Bridge) spans the Vltava, joining Malá Strana and Staré Město. East of the bridge is **Staroměstské náměstí** (Old Town Square), the focal point of Staré Město.

Pick up the bargain *Plán Města* (city map) from any bookstore or *tabák* for 40 Kč; it's an indispensable guide to transportation and the city streets. The metro, bus, and tram lines serve the city thoroughly and cheaply. For 6 Kč you can buy a ticket for one 15-minute tram or bus ride or four stations on the metro; for 10 Kč you get 60 minutes unlimited travel (weekdays 5 AM–8 PM) or 90 minutes unlimited travel (daily 8–5). Yellow vending machines dispense single tickets in metro stations; you can also buy them at *tabáks* and some newsstands. Long-term passes are sold at the information booths in the I.P. Pavlova and Náměstí Míru metro stations on weekdays and at the information booths in the Muzeum and Můstek stations all week. Passes come in the following increments: one-day (50 Kč), three-day (130 Kč), seven-day (190 Kč), 15-day (220 Kč), and one-month (320 Kč; bring your passport and a photo).

BY BUS AND TRAM

Buses and trams run 24 hours, but service is reduced after 11 PM. Every stop has a map of the *noční provoz* (night routes) and a fairly reliable schedule.

BY SUBWAY

The Metro consists of three lines, which form a triangle around the center of the city. **Line A** (the green line) runs east–west; **Line B** (the yellow line) runs southwest–northeast; and **Line C** (the red line) connects the two biggest railway stations and extends far to the south. The Metro opens at 5 AM, and the last trains leave terminal stations at midnight. Punch your ticket before entering; each metro ticket is valid for one hour. If you're caught without a valid ticket by one of the growing troop of plainclothes inspectors, your fine is 200 Kč.

WHERE TO SLEEP

The area around **Hlavní nádraží** is not rich in historical sights, but it's well connected by metro and tram to Staré Město, Malá Strana, and Hradčany. The **Strahov** district west of Malá Strana offers a number of hostels in converted university dorms along Vaníčkova, at the foot of the enormous Strahov stadium. **Nové Město** has the plushest hotels in the Czech Republic, so it's difficult to find affordable lodging there, and the same could be said of central **Staré Město,** where the few existing rooms are quite dear. A better budget bet is **Žižkov,** northeast of Hlavní nádraží, home of Prague's raunchiest, smokiest pubs.

ACCOMMODATION SERVICES

Most accommodation services will set you up in a private home for 300 Kč–800 Kč (depending on location and bath facilities). If the first price is too high, ask for something cheaper.

Accommodation Service offers doubles in private homes for 1,260 Kč to 1,710 Kč. *Haštalská 7, Staré Město, tel. 02/231–0202 and 02/231–6663, fax 02/231–6640. Open daily 9–1 and 3–7.*

AVE Ltd. Travel Agency has eight offices in Prague; all accept AmEx, MasterCard, and Visa. *Hlavní Nádraží, tel. 02/2422–3226 or 02/2422–3521, fax 02/2422–3463 or 02/2423–0783. Open daily 6 AM–10 PM. Other locations include: Holešovice train station, tel. 02/6671–0514; open daily 7 AM–10 PM. Ruzyně airport, tel. 02/316–4266 and 02/2011–3106; open weekdays 7–10 (9 in winter). Křížová 59 (booking office), tel. 02/2461–7133 or 02/549–744, fax 02/542–239 and 02/2461–7113; open daily 8–6.*

Čedok has three accommodation offices in Prague. They don't make advance reservations, but they will make last-minute bookings. *Na Příkopě 18, tel. 02/2419–7111; open weekdays 8:30–6, Sat. 9–1. Other locations: Rytířská 16, tel. 02/262–790; open weekdays 9–6, Sat. 9–noon. Ruzyně Airport, tel. 02/367–802; open weekdays 8–9, weekends 8–8.*

RHIA Tours. *Školská 1, tel. or fax 02/294–843. Open daily 10–8.*

Toptour can find accommodations in private homes for groups of up to five. *Rybná 3, tel. 02/232–1077, fax 02/2481–1400. Open weekdays 9–8 (until 7 in winter), weekends 10–7.*

HOTELS

Hotel reservations are imperative if you want to sleep within a stone's throw of the city center in summer. In the Troja neighborhood north of the center, many pensions line the quiet streets above the main road to the Troja Chateau. Take Bus 112 from the Nádraží Holešovice metro station to the Trojská stop, then go right uphill and left on Nad Kazankou and look for PENSION or PRIVAT signs. Among the old villas are **Bonsai Privat** (Nad Kazankou 21, tel. 02/689–0863), a very homey bed-and-breakfast with a beautiful dark-wood interior (450 Kč per person), and **Penzion Troja** (Nad Kazankou 26, tel. 02/688–1081) across the street, decorated with antlers and hunting knives (500 Kč per person).

UNDER 1,200 Kč • Libra Q. Near Hlavní nádraží, the Libra Q doubles as a pension and a hostel. Doubles without shower are 810 Kč; with shower, 1,250 Kč. Plain ol' beds are 290Kč. *Senovážné nám. 21, tel. 02/2423–1754 or 02/22210–5536, fax 02/2422–1579. Go through courtyard, and enter in back.*

Pension Krokodýl. This small, family-run pension has a comfortable, easy-going atmosphere. Doubles start at 1,100 Kč, and each has a small kitchen. *Bělehradská 26, tel. 02/259–9908. From Muzeum metro, take Tram 11 four stops (pension directly across street).*

UNDER 2,000 Kč • Hotel Kafka. This renovated building offers a clean, almost sterile environment with nothing Kafkaesque about it, except perhaps the neighborhood—you're in poor, sooty Žižkov. Doubles are 1,100, 1,600, or 1,900 Kč, depending on the season. *Cimburkova 24, tel. and fax 02/273101. From Hlavní nádraží, take Tram 5, 9, or 26 to first stop; walk up 2 blocks and turn left on Cimburkova.*

Hotel Nusle Garni. The long, single-story Garni has small, decent rooms for 1,780 Kč (double). Bring earplugs for the traffic noise. *Závišova 30, tel. or fax 02/691–0240. From Muzeum metro, take Tram 11 south 4 stops; hotel down about 2 blocks on right.*

Pension City. Clean rooms are just a few minutes walk from Náměstí Míru, in the quiet central neighborhood of Vinohrady. Doubles are 1,396 Kč, or 2,070 Kč with private bath. Breakfast is served. *Belgická 10, tel. or fax 02/6911–334. From Nám. Míru metro, turn left at bottom of square (away from church) and walk 2 blocks. Reception open 8–10.*

Pension Unitas/Cloister Inn. Originally a convent, this central pension/inn was converted to a prison (which once held Václav Havel) in 1948 before becoming a hotel. Pension doubles are 1,800 Kč, hotel doubles 2,700 Kč; some have baths. *Bartolomějská 9, tel. 02/232–7700, fax 02/232–7709. Metro: Národní třída. Reception open 24 hrs (ring bell), checkout 2 PM. At pension, cash only.*

Pension Tříska. The rooms are spare but clean and bright and the staff is friendly and accommodating at this pension in the pretty neighborhood of Vinohrady. Doubles are about 1,400 Kč. *Vinohradská 105, tel. and fax 627–0662. Metro: Jiřího z Poděbrad (exit Vinohradská).*

SPLURGE

Grand Hotel Evropa. The Art Nouveau Evropa is an anomaly among the five-star hotels in Nové Město. Doubles are 2,160 Kč, 3,400 Kč with bath; triples are 2,790 Kč, 4,350 Kč with bath. It ain't budget, but scoring a room in Prague's center for less than US$200 is unheard of. Reception is open 24 hours, and bonuses include currency exchange and medical service. *Václavské nám. 25, tel. 02/2422–8117, fax 02/2422–4544.*

HOSTELS

CKM Hotel Junior. Not just for students, this hotel is clean and only one block from Karlovo náměstí. It also has a restaurant and snack bar. For summer, reserve about three months in advance. Doubles with bath are 2,200 Kč, triples with bath 2,820 Kč. Dorm beds are 500 Kč. Breakfast and use of the on-site nightclub are included. *Žitná 12, tel. 02/2422–2811, fax 02/2422–3911. Metro: Karlovo nám.*

Hostel Podoli. Local music students hang out at the small basement bar in these attractive turn-of-the-century buildings in quiet Vyšehrad. The English-speaking staff knows what's up in Prague, serves breakfast, and guards your luggage. Doubles are 600 Kč. Reservations advised. *Na Lysině 12, tel. and fax 02/6431–105. From the Pražskeho povstání metro, exit left onto Lomnického and turn left on Pod Děkankou to narrow street Na Lysině (follow signs to Bldg. B). Reception open 8–noon and 12:30–10.*

CAMPING

Most campgrounds—many little more than glorified backyards—are open April through October. Reservations are advised for bungalows. The brochure "Praha Camping" lists sites around the city. There's a series of small campgrounds—such as **Autocamp Trojská** (tel. 02/688–6036, fax 02/854–2945) and **Camp Dana** (tel. or fax 02/689–0630), both 90 Kč plus 90 Kč per person—along Trojská ulice, easily reached by Bus 112 from the Holešovice metro station.

FOOD

Vinárny (wine cellars) and *pivnice* (beer halls) serve snacks and sometimes full meals and are popular gathering places from 6 PM to 10 PM. *Lahůdky* (delicatessens) usually offer delicious open-face sandwiches; for fresh produce, try the open-air **market** (open daily 9–6) on Havelská in Staré Město. You'll find everything you need in the **Krone Supermarket** (Václavské nám., at Jindřišská; Můstek metro; open daily).

STARE MESTO

Alehouse Radegast. An easy haul from Old Town Square, this watering hole serves award-winning Radegast beer (20 Kč) with goulash (54 Kč), a plate of meat and potatoes (65 Kč), or a full meal (around 120 Kč). *Templová ul. From Old Town Square, head down Celetná, left on Templová through passage. Open daily 11 AM–midnight.*

Góvinda. Better known as "that Hare Krishna place," Góvinda is cheap, delicious, and vegetarian; curried vegetable stew with soup, salad, unleavened bread, and fruit compote is 50 Kč. Chant and be happy. *Soukenická 27, tel. 02/2481–6016. From nám. Republiky, take Na Poříčí to Zlatnická and turn left. Open Mon.–Sat. 11–5.*

Pizzeria Kmotra. Delicious foot-wide pizzas (56 Kč–145 Kč) ensure a long wait for a seat in the cozy cellar. *V Jirchářích 12, tel. 02/2491–5809. From Národní třída metro, left on Národní, left on Voršilská. Open daily 11 AM–1 AM. Reservations advised.*

U Vejvodů. This classic Czech restaurant and beer hall serves spicy and commendable *Ďábelský Kotlík* (Devil's Goulash; 75 Kč) and *polévka* (soup; only 15 Kč). Staropramen beer, *černa* (black) or *bílá* (white), is also 15 Kč. *Jílská 4, tel. 02/2421–0591. Open daily 11–11. Metro: Můstek.*

NOVE MESTO

Akropolis. At this popular hangout between the Žižkov and Vinohrady neighborhoods, aqua walls and funky decor make you feel as if you're hallucinating underwater. Cheap beer, chicken and fish dishes (40 Kč–70 Kč), and meat dishes (about 65 Kč) will help you regain your equilibrium. *Kubelíkova 27, at Vita Nejedlého, tel. 02/271–269. Open daily 4 PM–2 AM. Metro: Jiřího z Poděbrad.*

Radost. The passel of American expats will make you feel ill at ease or right at home at this small, sassy hangout above the FX nightclub and next to the FX Lounge. Great salads, Mexican and Italian food, and a wide range of vegetarian options are all 90 Kč–130 Kč. *Bělehradská 120, tel. 02/2425–4776. Open daily 11:30 AM–6 AM. Metro: I.P.*

U Mázlů. At this small, quiet restaurant and wine bar (Moravian and Slovakian whites 84 Kč–240 Kč) pot roast, Wiener schnitzel, and vegetable dishes start at 80 Kč. *Jungmannova 26, tel. 02/261–272. Open daily 11–11. Metro: Národní třída.*

Velryba. The underground "Whale" restaurant has been branded as one of Prague's intellectual hot spots. Good pasta dishes and crêpes can be had for less than 60 Kč. *Opatovická 24, tel. 02/241–2391. From Národní třída metro, exit left onto Ostrovní (small side street) and go left on Opatovická. Open daily 11 AM–2 AM.*

HRADCANY

U Černého Vola. Light meals start at 40Kč at this genuine Czech beer hall with great prices, lively atmosphere, quasi-medieval murals, and Velkopopovické beer (14 Kč). *Loretánská 1, at Loretánské nám., west of castle. Open daily 10–10.*

Všebaráčnická Rychta. Drink reasonably-priced beer in a large auditorium complete with filthy tablecloths and red-eyed regulars—distinctly nontouristy. Supplement your ales with traditional potato pancakes (15 Kč, fixins a little extra). *Břtislavova. Up unnamed alley across from American Embassy. Open daily 11–11. Metro: Malostranská.*

CAFES

Kavárny (cafés) serve a variety of coffees, alcoholic drinks, light dishes, and indulgent desserts. **Espreso U tří králů** (Nerudova ul. 48, at Ke Hradu; open daily 11–9), just below the castle in Malá Strana, is perfect for a quiet break. The **FX Lounge,** behind the Radost restaurant (*see above*), has overstuffed couches and is a low-key place for an aperitif or espresso. The tiny **La Chiave d'Oro Caffe** (Nerudova 27, Malá Strana, up hill from Malostranskě nám.) serves up wine, spirits, espresso, and snacks. One of the more obvious choices is **The Globe** (see English-Language Books and Newspapers, *above*), with cappuccinos as big and smooth as the ones in Seattle.

WORTH SEEING

PRAZSKY HRAD

Surrounded by museums and monuments, Pražský Hrad (Prague Castle) presides serenely over Prague's medieval core like royalty surveying the color guard. Its ensemble of sharp spires and rooflines is the city's defining landmark and the symbolic center of the country. At any of the ticket offices, you can buy a three-day inclusive ticket (100 Kč) to the cathedral crypt, choir, and tower; the old Royal Palace; and the Basilica of St. George. Inquire at the information booth near the Hradčanské náměstí entrance about guided tours in English. Most of the castle's attractions are open daily 9–5 (9–4 in winter).

You can enter the enormous castle complex at **Hradčanské náměstí** (Castle Square), accessible via Nerudova ulice, or by taking the **Nove zámecké schody** (New Castle steps), which lead up from Thunovská. Crowds gather daily at the imposing main gate to watch the hourly changing of the guard. Inside the gate is the first of three courtyards around which the castle is arranged. On the opposite side of the complex, the **Staré zámecké schody** (Old Castle steps) lead down to the Malostranská metro station; you can beat the hordes of tourists and enter the castle here (turn left after you exit the metro, walk past Valdštejnská ulice, then turn left again). This route leads you past the **Lobkovický Palác** (Jiřská 3), now a museum of Czech and Moravian history.

Tucked into the southeast corner of the courtyard is the simple, elegant Kaple **svatého Kříže** (Chapel of the Holy Cross). A passage leads from this courtyard to the **Powder Bridge** and magnificent **Royal Gardens.**

CHRAM SV. VITA • St. Vitus's Cathedral, begun during the 14th century but not finished until the early 1900s, dominates the castle complex's third courtyard, and its Gothic and neo-Gothic buttresses and towers dwarf the rest of Prague's 100 spires. Inside, fight the crowds for a look at the brilliant **Chapel of Václav,** built over the remains of its eponymous 10th-century duke, who would become the nation's patron saint; and the crypt, where several other Czech kings and queens are buried. In the main hall, note the spectacular stained glass, particularly the window designed in 1931 by Alfons Mucha in the **New Archbishops Chapel.** You can also climb the cathedral's tower for a view of the city. *Open daily 9–5; last admission 4 PM.*

STARY KRALOVSKY PALAC • The seat of Czech political power since the 9th century, Starý Královský Palác (Royal Palace) sits high on a ridge that has protected it for more than 1,000 years. Wide Romanesque fortifications were added during the 12th century and are now the setting for the **Garden on the Ramparts** and summer concerts. In the 15th century King Vladislav ordered the construction of the most memorable addition, the immense **Vladislavský sál** (Vladislav Hall). This late-Gothic hall was built with a wide staircase that enabled knights to bring their horses up for jousting sessions. The **defenestration room** is where imperial governors rebelling against Catholic rule were tossed out the window by Czech nobility in 1618, sparking the Thirty Years' War.

BAZILIKA AND KLASTER SV. JIRI • Across the courtyard from Královský Palác is the 10th-century St. George's Basilica and Convent, the first convent in Bohemia. The Romanesque interior dates from the 1140s, when it was rebuilt after a devastating fire. The church often holds concerts, and the **National Gallery** next door has a permanent display of Bohemian art from the Gothic to baroque eras.

After St. George's, head down Jiřská to the **Zlatá ulička** (Golden Lane), where a row of tiny houses was built into the castle walls in 1541. These houses have been home to artists and artisans over the centuries, and one of them quartered Franz Kafka briefly (it's well marked). At the end of the lane is **Daliborka,** the castle dungeon.

HRADCANY

This neighborhood surrounding Pražský Hrad is packed with sights and tourists. Among the well-preserved buildings outside the Hrad on Hradčanské náměstí are the baroque **Arcibiskupský palác** (Archbishop's Palace) and the **Šternberský Palác** (admission 50 Kč; open Tues.–Sun. 10–6), with paintings from the Middle Ages to the 18th century. The Vojenské Muzeum (Military Museum; admission 20 Kč; open Tues.–Sun. 9:30–4:30; closed Nov.–Apr.), in the 16th-century section of the **Schwarzenberg Palác,** shows the development of weapons until 1918.

West of Hradčanské náměstí is the **Loreto Church** (Loretanské nám. 7; admission 40 Kč), named for the Italian town to which angels supposedly transported the Virgin Mary's house from Nazareth to save it from infidels. Behind the church is the opulent, baroque **Church of the Nativity of Our Lord**; upstairs is the dazzling Loreto treasury, with relics from the 17th and 18th centuries.

BELVEDERE SUMMER PALACE

A short hike from Hradčany, in the gardens east of Prague Castle, is the Belvedere Summer Palace, with its "singing fountain": You can hear voicelike sounds when you sit under its metal bowl. Designed by Italian architects during the 1550s, the palace was Prague's first taste of Renaissance architecture and is now used as a gallery space for changing art exhibits. *Mariánské hradby ul., tel. 02/2437–1111. Admission: about 30 Kč (changes with exhibits). Open Tues.–Sun. 10–6.*

MALA STRANA

Below the Prague Castle lie the Renaissance and baroque palaces of Malá Strana, home primarily to museums and government offices. The center of Malá Strana is the square **Malostranské náměstí,** dominated by **Chrám sv. Mikuláše** (Church of St. Nicholas). Built in 1755, the church is one of the best examples of baroque architecture in Prague.

The magnificent 17th-century **Wallenstein Palace** contains an art gallery and peaceful gardens with bronze casts of statues (the Swedes carted off the originals at the end of the Thirty Years' War). Frescoes decorate the immense baroque stage, focal point of the gardens and the setting for summer concerts. *Entrance gate at Letenská 10. From Malostranská metro, walk south and turn right. Gardens open May–Sept., daily 9–7.*

KARLUV MOST

Built during the 14th century by Charles IV, Karlův Most (Charles Bridge) was the only bridge in Prague for almost 500 years (there are 17 today). Used in earlier centuries as a marketplace, the bridge is now a busy pedestrian zone filled with tourists, musicians, artists, and vendors. At the west end of Karlův Most (down the stairs at the Malostranská end of the bridge) is **Kampa**, an island separated from Malá Strana by a narrow channel of the Vltava River. Between Kampa and Maltézské náměstí (just past the Maltese Embassy) is a graffiti-covered wall that began as a billboard for dissidents of the Communist regime. It's been known as the **John Lennon Wall** ever since someone painted his portrait here after 1989; but alas, John is vanishing bit by bit, as tourists remove pieces of his face as souvenirs.

STARE MESTO

The Staré Město (Old Town) radiates from **Staroměstské náměstí,** an enormous, lively square. Every hour a crowd gathers beneath the clock tower of the 14th-century **Staroměstská radnice** (Old Town Hall; open daily 9–5) to watch its mechanical parade of figures. Behind the hall is the grand **Kostel sv. Mikuláše** (St. Nicholas's Church; open Tues.–Sun. 10–5). Across the square is another church, the somber Roman Catholic **Týn Church,** housing the tomb of the astronomer Tycho Brahe. Next door is the Renaissance House of the Stone Bell, which offers art exhibits by day and concerts by night.

At the other end of Staré Město, close to where Revoluční meets the river, is the **Anežský Klášter** (St. Agnes's Convent). This meticulously restored early-Gothic convent was founded in 1233. Aside from the architecture, the convent is worth visiting for its collection of 19th-century Czech paintings and drawings. *Anežská ul., tel. 02/2481–0628. Metro: Nám. Republiky. Admission: 50 Kč. Open Tues.–Sun. 10–6.*

JOSEFOV

If you follow swanky Pařížská ulice in the direction of the Vltava River, you'll soon come upon **Josefov,** Prague's Jewish ghetto. The area was the center of the Jewish community from the 10th century through World War II, but almost all of Prague's Jews fled or were murdered during the Holocaust. Even today, with only a few museums and synagogues and a cemetery to commemorate one of Europe's oldest Jewish ghettoes, the streets are somewhat somber, the mood hushed in contrast to the baroque flair of Prague's Old Town.

The **Staronová Synagóga** (Old-New Synagogue; Maiselova ul. and Bílkova) was built in 1270 in the early-Gothic style and called "New." In the 16th century, when other synagogues were being built in Prague, it was given the name "Old-New" to distinguish it from newer synagogues. Either way, it's the oldest standing synagogue in Europe. Across the alley are the rich collections of the **StátníŽidovský Muzeum** (State Jewish Museum; tel. 02/2481–0099). Farther down the street is the **Starý Židovský Hřbitov** (Old Jewish Cemetery), where almost 12,000 tombs were laid between 1439 and 1787; as available space diminished, new graves were as many as 12 layers deep. In the nearby the **Pinkas Syn-**

agogue (Sinoka ul., just south of cemetery) are inscribed the names of more than 77,000 Bohemian and Moravian Jews who were murdered by the Nazis. *Admission to all sights in Josefov: 360 Kč. Admission to museum (Pinkas Synagogue and cemetery included): 200 Kč. All sights open Sun.–Fri. 9–12:30 and 1–5:30; 1–5 in winter.*

NOVE MESTO

The Nové Město (New Town) is predominantly commercial, with busy shopping and business areas. Its focal point is **Václavské náměstí** (Wenceslas Square), a long, broad boulevard that has been a center of political action, including the Prague Spring of 1968 and the 1989 Velvet Revolution.

Národní Muzeum. The National Museum is a stately neo-Renaissance structure with exhibits on history, zoology, and mineralogy. The interior alone is worth a peek for its frescoes and statues. *Václavské nám. 68, tel. 02/2449–7111. Metro: Muzeum. Admission: 40 Kč (free first Mon. of month). Open Wed.–Mon. 10–6.*

VYSEHRAD

Perched atop a sheer rock face rising from the bank of the Vltava River, **Vyšehrad** is a medieval citadel 4 km (2½ mi) south of the Staré Město. This is where the Přemyslid tribe founded the first Czech dynasty during the 11th century. The Romanesque **Rotunda of St. Martin** and extensive walls are reminders of Vyšehrad's former prominence. Many important Czech cultural figures are buried here in the **Slavín Cemetery,** including the composers Dvořák and Smetana. *Soběslavova 1, no phone. Metro: Vyšehrad. Open daily 9:30–6:30.*

Next to the Vyšehrad metro station lies the modern **Kongresové centrum** (Congress Center), a sprawling complex of concert halls, restaurants, and a movie theater. Ask at the box office about the jazz festivals and dramas performed here. *5. Května 65, tel. 02/6117–2711. Information booth open 8 AM–10 PM. Box office open weekdays 9–1 and 2–7:30, weekends 1 hr before performance.*

Since the Renaissance, Czechs have had a strange way of settling a score—they simply throw you out the window. Thus there was the Defenestration of 1419, which led to the Hussite Revolution. The most recent incident went down (oops) in 1948.

TROJA PALACE AND ZOO

Across the Vltava, on the northern outskirts of Prague, lies the quiet, provincial neighborhood of **Troja.** A 17th-century frescoed palace surrounded by a formal garden, Troja Palace now contains an exhibit of 18th- and 19th-century Czech paintings. Across the street from the palace is the extensive Troja Zoo. *U trojského zámku. From Holešovice metro, Bus 112 to end. Palace admission: 40 Kč. Open Tues.–Sun. 10–5. Zoo admission: 30 Kč. Open daily 9–7.*

CHEAP THRILLS

Immerse yourself in the pool (1 Kč per minute) or sauna (2 Kč per minute) at the **Hotel Axa.** Beat travel weariness by treating yourself to a massage (tel. 02/232–6656 for appointments) for 4 Kč per minute of therapeutic bliss. *Na Poříčí 40. Pool open weekdays 5 PM–10 PM, Sat. 9–6, Sun. 9–8. Sauna open weekdays 8 AM–10 PM (Tues. and Sat. 10–6), Sun. 10–8.*

The Radost's (*see* Food, *above*) **FX Lounge** shows films, usually American, for free on Monday night. If you feel compelled to see just how insular the expat community gets, attend the Beefstew open-mic readings held on Sunday night at 7 PM.

Check the *Prague Post* for film listings; most films shown are in English with Czech subtitles (s českými titulky).

If you're looking for clothes or East-bloc curios, head for the bustling **flea market** (open weekdays 8–6, Sat. 8–noon) in Holešovice. There's plenty of junk to keep you busy all afternoon. *From Vltavská metro, take any tram heading left from exit for 1 stop, then follow crowds.*

On a nice enough day, head to **Klub Lávka** (Novotného lávka 1, tel. 02/2421–4797), on the eastern shore of the Vltava just south of Karlův Most. You can rent a boat here for 50 Kč per hour, so wipe off the seat and see Prague from a new perspective. Or pack a picnic and lounge by the **Jan Hus Monument,** in Staroměstská náměští; the popular monument is the heart and soul of Prague, if not all of the Czech Republic.

AFTER DARK

Your best sources for the latest nightlife information are Prague's English-language newspapers. The *Prague Post* covers a broad range of the city's cultural activities. You can buy tickets at individual theaters, at ticket outlets such as **Bohemia Ticket International** (Salvátorská 6, tel. 02/2422–7832; Staroměstská metro), or through **Ticketpro** (tel. 02/2481–4020) with your handy Visa.

BEER HALLS

For good beer and tables full of merry foreigners, try **U sv. Tomáše** (Letenská 12, Malá Strana) or **U Fleků** (Křemencova 11, Staré Město), Prague's most famous beer hall. In general, beer halls close at 10 or 11 PM, so start early.

ROCK AND JAZZ

AghaRTA Jazz Centrum. Catch live acts here, including some of Prague's best jazz. Check out the adjoining music shop and café. *Krakovská 5, tel. 02/2221–1275. Metro: Muzeum or I.P. Pavlova. Cover: 80 Kč and up. Open daily 9 PM–midnight.*

Radost. This club completes the restaurant–bar–lounge triumvirate. The young crowd à la mode drops an 80 Kč–120 Kč cover charge to join the quirky moves of go-go dancers to techno tracks. For directions, *see* Food, *above.*

Roxy. A perennial favorite experimental space, the Roxy has changed with the times. Once a roomy alternative club that took occasional stabs at artsy events, the Roxy is now bursting at the seams with Prague's exploding population of young, cool technoheads. Sleek sunglasses are de rigueur. *Dlouhá 33, tel. 2481–0951. Cover 50 Kč and up, significantly more on nights with guest DJs. Hours vary depending on event.*

Lucerna Music Bar. In one of Prague's poignantly neglected *pasáže* (passages), you can hear classic rock, blues, reggae, and jazz in this all-purpose club. *In the Lucerna pasáž, Vodičkova 36, tel. 2421–7108. Cover 70 Kč. Open daily 8 PM–3 AM. Metro Můstek.*

CLASSICAL MUSIC

Chamber music and other classical concerts are held in churches throughout the city, most notably the **Kostel sv. Míkuláše** (St. Nicholas' Church) and **Dům U kamenného zvonu** (House at the Stone Bell), both on Staroměstské náměstí. The newly renovated Dvořák Hall in the **Rudolfinum** (nám. Jana Palacha, tel. 02/2489–3111; Staroměstská metro) is the home of the renowned Czech Philharmonic, as well as the host for visiting orchestras; tickets cost 110 Kč–350 Kč. Opera, drama, and ballet lovers should check out the **Národní Divadlo** (National Theater; Národní třída 2, tel. 02/2491–3437; Národní třída metro) and the **Státní Opera** (Wilsonova 4, tel. 02/2422–7693; Muzeum metro). Tickets at both venues start at 100 Kč. The newly restored Art Nouveau treasure **Obecní dům** (Náměstí Republiky 5, tel. 02/22–00–21–11, Nám. Republiky metro) is the home of the Prague Symphony.

NEAR PRAGUE

KUTNA HORA

From the 1400s to the 1700s, this town prospered as a silver-mining center and as an occasional headquarters for kings. Visit the magnificent Gothic **Church of St. Barbara** (20 Kč; open Tues–Sun. 9–4), with its flying buttresses, three spires, and numerous coats of arms decorating the ceiling. Signposts on every corner in Kutná Hora point you to the town's other attractions, such as the **Museum of Mining** in the old castle. There are also beautiful walking paths in the valley just below the old part of town; walk down one of the many trails from the cathedral walls, or take the path by the Mining Museum. To reach Kutná Hora, take the train from Hlavní nádraží to Kolín (45 min), then change trains to Kutná Hora (10 min). They'll sell you one ticket all the way to Kutná Hora for 32 Kč. Don't be dismayed by the lonely look of the train depot in Kutná Hora; a half-hour ride on Bus 2 or 4 will bring you to the old part of town.

For a uniquely ghoulish experience, visit the **Kostnice** (Bone Church) in Sedlec, a suburb of Kutná Hora about 2 km (1 mi) northeast of town (near the train station). A handful of dirt from Golgotha (the reputed site of the Crucifixion) sprinkled here in the 12th century made this an extremely popular place to be buried. A quick glance at the diminutive graveyard reveals why the government turned to František Rint, a woodcarver, in 1870 to contend with the bones of the 40,000 people buried here. Rint's ghastly solutions—four giant bells, a chandelier, and a Czech coat of arms, all made of human bones—are on display in the grotto beneath the church. *Admission: 20 Kč. Open Tues.–Sun. 9–noon and 1–4.*

BOHEMIA

Take the slow train through Bohemia. The region's soft hills are wrapped in thick pine forests and brilliant fields of wildflowers, punctuated with medieval villages and castles. Even four decades of Communism touched Bohemia lightly, leaving behind few concrete boxes and smokestacks. Free love and nudism once flowered here among the Adamites, a Hussite (anti-Catholic) splinter group. Their shenanigans furnished the Pope with plenty of material for anti-Czech propaganda, and over time the word "bohemian" became synonymous with "flake" in several languages. Most people today, unaware of the word's origins, use "bohemian" to describe anyone leading an unconventional life and harboring artistic or intellectual aspirations.

KARLOVY VARY

Set in a winding river valley, the world-renowned spa town Karlovy Vary (Karlsbad in German) exudes cosmopolitan confidence. The town has always boasted an impressive clientele: Peter the Great, J.S. Bach, Casanova, and Karl Marx have been some of its more illustrious visitors. Open for business since 1401, the town still receives as many patients as tourists at its 12 hot springs. Every July the city also hosts an **international film festival** that draws a few stars.

BASICS
Komerční Banka changes money at a fair rate; there's a branch at Tržíště 11 and another at Náměstí Republiky 1. Otherwise, **Čedok** exchanges money and arranges lodging. *Dr. Davida Bechera 23, near stations, tel. 017/322–7837 or 017/322–3335. Open Mon. 9–6, Tues.–Fri. 9–5, Sat. 9–noon.*

COMING AND GOING
The main **train station** is across the River Ohře; take Bus 2 to reach downtown, or walk 550 yds south. A smaller station, which serves Mariánské Lázně, is closer to the center and near the major **bus station** on Západní, at Náměstí Republiky. Buses offer better service than do trains between Karlovy Vary and Plzeň or Prague (2½ hrs, 85 Kč). The center of town is within easy walking distance; as you leave the station, head up the main driveway and veer away from the river to the right. Along the way you'll pass the Tržnice **city bus center** on Varšavská.

WHERE TO SLEEP
CKM's extremely comfortable **Juniorhotel Alice** (Hamerská 1, tel. 017/248–489, fax 017/993–89; doubles 1,800 Kč) in the wooded hills south of town is the nicest budget double your crowns can buy; take the infrequent Karlovy Vary–Březova bus from the stop outside Varšavská 6. Otherwise, it's a beautiful 45-minute walk. About 550 yds closer to town is **Geizerpark Pupp Motel Autocamping** (Slovenská 9, tel. 017/251–0102, fax 017/25–225), a well-equipped campground with tent sites (95 Kč per person) and bungalows (doubles 570 Kč; triples 855 Kč). For private accommodations, try one of the pensions along the main pedestrian corridor: **Penzion Kučera,** in the U Tří Mouřenínů building (Stará Louka 2, tel. 017/252–34, fax 017/252–35), has doubles for 1,300 Kč. High on the hill behind the Hotel Thermal is the charming **Pension Amadeus** (Ondřejská 37, tel. 017/272–54, fax 017/271–79), with doubles for 1,400 Kč, breakfast included. The excellently located **Pension Kosmos** (Zahradní 39; tel. 017/322–3168), closer to the train and bus stations, offers doubles without bath for 660 Kč, with bath for 1,200 Kč.

WORTH SEEING
The areas flanking the **Teplá River** are the major attraction here. To get a feel for the town and its opulent Art Nouveau architecture, stroll along the riverbanks between the concrete high-rise sanitarium Thermal, at one end, and Grandhotel Pupp, at the other. On the hill above Thermal is a thermal pool (25 Kč per hour); package spas include two hours access to pool and sauna for 90 Kč or two hours in the fitness center and pool for 60 Kč. Inquire at Thermal's reception desk. Wander down the river from Thermal to sample the bubbling waters at various springs. At the central spring, **Vřídlo,** you can watch the geyser shoot skyward or join patients filling their *bechers* (special spouted spa cups) from taps in the adjacent hall. Those wanting further treatments should ask at one of the spa hotels; massages start at 500 Kč. Also sharing the waterfront are the 1736 **Kostel sv. Maří Magdaleny** (Church of Mary Magdalene) and the 1701 **Grandhotel Pupp** (Mirové nám., off Stará louka), a remarkable, white, ornate sprawl, the site of centuries of personal and political intrigue. The hills above the Teplá River are dotted

with tiny chapels and monuments, and you can take any of the smooth color-coded **trails** to explore them. Or, for a few crowns, let the **funicular railway** behind the Grandhotel Pupp do the work.

MARIANSKE LAZNE

Set in a forested valley, Mariánské Lázně (better known as Marienbad) retains the peace and elegance that bewitched the great German poet Goethe, who came here 13 times to enjoy the mineral waters and his mistress. Start a walk around town at the impressive **colonnade,** a wrought-iron extravaganza dating from 1889, where patients fill their *bechers* with mineral water every morning and afternoon. At one end, a musical fountain plays its heart out every odd hour from 7 to 7, then every hour until 10. See it after dark, when colored lights make this otherwise silly spectacle worthwhile. If you've got mineral-spring madness, visit the newly renovated **Křížový pramen** (Cross Spring) at the upper end of the colonnade, or walk through the park to **Rudolph and Ferdinand's Springs,** named after King Rudolph II and King Ferdinand V. To complete your cure, take a marked **spa walk,** following one of several color-coded trails through the forested hills above the town.

If you're a serious spa-goer, the **Ustřední Lázně** (Masarykova 22) will arrange a treatment for you. Otherwise, take a dip at the indoor pool at **Ředitelství Kadeřník Solárium** on Tyršova, 2 blocks off Hlavní, for 50 Kč an hour. Massages are an extra 50 Kč.

BASICS

Infocentrum on the main strip sells maps and arranges accommodations in hotels and pensions. *Hlavní třída 47, tel. 0165/622–474, fax 0165/5892. Bus 5 to* CITY SERVICE *stop; walk up street. Open weekdays 9–6, Sat. 9–5, Sun. 10–5.*

COMING AND GOING

Depending on which **train** you take from Prague, you'll be whisked through beautiful ravines and tunnels in about three hours (80 Kč). To reach town from the station, catch Bus 5 out front or use your feet; turn right outside the station, left on Hlavní třída, and continue for 30 minutes to the center.

WHERE TO SLEEP

Two hotels, the **Kossuth** (Ruská 77, tel. 0165/622–861, fax 622–862) and the preferable **Evropa** (Třebízského 101, tel. 0165/622–064), are both former workers' spas and charge 600 Kč and 980 Kč for doubles with and without bath, respectively. The best deal in town is CKM's hunting lodge, **Junior-hotel Krakonoš** (Zádub 53, tel. 0165/2624), on a tree-lined ridge above town. A double here is only 870 Kč; take Bus 12 (infrequent service) from downtown to the end of the line. Near Infocentrum, **Penzion Oradour** (Hlavní 43, tel. 0165/3059) may not be a five-star haven, but at 180 Kč a bed, who's sneezing?

PLZEN

Plzeň has two claims to fame. The first you can experience fully in 45 minutes: The enormous Gothic **Chrám sv. Bartoloměja** (St. Bartholomew's Church) stands alone in náměstí Republiky, boasting catacombs and, at more than 328 ft, the highest steeple in the country. You can climb up through the tower's bells and clock to a platform once used as a lookout point (17 Kč; open daily 10–6). Access the city's underground catacombs through the **House of Perlová** (Dům V Perlové, Perlová 65, tel. 019/225–214; admission 30 Kč, open Wed.–Sun. 9–4:30).

How long it takes you to see Plzeň's second attraction depends on how well you hold your brew. Known in Czech as *Plzensky Prazdroj,* the Pilsner Urquell brewery (U. Prazdroje 7, near train station; admission 30 Kč) gives tours starting at the main gate weekdays at 12:30. For weekend tours, dial 019/706–2017. The **Pivovarské muzeum** (Brewery Museum; Veleslavínova 6; admission 40 Kč), in a former 16th-century pub, has a variety of historical implements as well as an authentic, chilly cellar; it's open Tues.–Sun. 10–6.

COMING AND GOING

Frequent trains connect Prague with Plzeň (1¾ hrs, 48 Kč). From the **train station,** the center is less than 1 km (½ mi) northwest; take Tram 1 (direction Bolevec). The **bus station** is about a ½ km (¼ mi) west of the center; head into town by walking to the tram stop along Přemyslova and taking Tram 2 (direction Světovar). Tram tickets (6 Kč) are available in the station and at tabáks in town.

WHERE TO SLEEP AND EAT

The elegant **Slovan** (Smetanovy sady 1, tel. 019/722–7256; doubles from 900 Kč) is the best deal of the three central hotels. Arrange private rooms (from 350 Kč per person) at **Městské Informační Středisko** (nám. Republiky 41, tel. 019/723–6535, fax 019/7224–473; open weekdays 10–5, weekends 9–5) on the main square next to the town hall, or just outside the train station at **No. 59** (tel. 019/722–3435; open daily 8–7). Drop by the information counter in the train station for maps to nearby hostels. Camp near a lake in a northern suburb at **Intercamping Bílá Hora,** with four-bed bungalows (800 Kč–900 Kč) and tent sites (70 Kč); take Bus 20 or 39 from downtown to the terminus. Several snack bars offer inexpensive Czech food—try the **Bistro,** with outside seating on the main square. **Pivnice na Parkánu** (Veleslavínova 4), next to the brewery museum, is a no-nonsense beer hall where you can down mugs of Pilsner Urquell (14 Kč) and fill up on goulash and potato dumplings (33 Kč).

CESKY KRUMLOV

None of the surrounding towns and villages will prepare you for the stunning beauty of Český Krumlov's majestic, haunting castle or its narrow, twisting streets interwoven with the swirling Vltava River. Although it's now undergoing extensive renovation and a deluge of German tourists, Ceský Krumlov still has a powerful allure. Visit the **Městské Muzeum** (City Museum; Horní 152) for a crash course in the town's history; above the museum are the Gothic **St. Vitus Church** and the Renaissance **Jesuit School,** both excellent examples of Bohemian craftsmanship.

Perched on a crag, the proud **Rožmberk Castle** rivals any castle in the country in size and splendor. Follow the winding carriage passage to the ticket office, where tours (100 Kč) begin. Connected to the castle by a covered bridge is the 1760 rococo **Bellaria Summerhouse,** one of the oldest in Europe. In the adjacent garden, next to the Bellaria Pavilion, musicians and dancers perform for a revolving grandstand in summer. *Castle open May–Aug. 9–noon and 1–5; shorter hrs off season.*

BASICS

Český Krumlov is an easy 45-minute train or bus ride from České Budějovice (less than 30 Kč). To reach town from the train station (about ½ km/¼ mi north of town), walk downhill to the right and head over the bridge (10 minutes). The bus station is immediately east of the center; take the footpath uphill at the far end of the station and follow the street as it curves down to the right. In the center you'll find **Infocentrum** (Nám. Svornosti 1, tel. or fax 0337/711–183; open weekdays 9–6, Sat. 9–4, Sun. 10–3), where the staff has scads of information on current events and lodging.

WHERE TO SLEEP AND EAT

Hotels here are expensive and full in summer. Doubles at the central, homey **Krumlov** (Nám. Svornosti 14, tel. 0337/711–565, fax 0337/711–195) are 1,500 Kč. Fortunately, private rooms are also plentiful near the center. Look for the Czech signs UBYTOVNA (rather than the German ZIMMER FREI signs), especially on **Rooseveltova,** a street near the bus station. Off Rooseveltova is the hostel **U Vodnika** (Po vodě 55, tel. 0337/711–935), where the atmosphere is, well, relaxed. Beds are 180 Kč; from the bus station, head toward the center and look for sign on the left.

Na Louži (Kájovská 66) serves surprisingly tasty food; try "Smith's Fire," a spicy pork dish with potatoes, for 109 Kč. **Cikánská jizba** (Dlouhá 31) pours the cheapest half-liters of the local brew Eggenburg (12 Kč) and dishes out heaping platters of traditional Czech food.

CESKE BUDEJOVICE

České Budějovice, the major city of southern Bohemia, is home to Budvar beer—better known by its German name, Budweiser—and much of the town is devoted to the beer's production. The large, drab **Budvar brewery** is accessible only to groups; you can join one through Čedok (Nám. Přemysla Otakara II 39, tel. 038/63538–87; open weekdays 8–6, Sat. 9–1), but you'll need to reserve two weeks in advance. At its heart, České Budějovice is pretty much the same town that was built during the 13th century. At the southwest corner of the main square, **náměstí Přemysla Otakara II,** stands the baroque city hall, with its striking dragon rainspouts. A few steps from the central **Samson Fountain,** look for the **Bludny Kámeň** (Wandering Stone), a small, five-side stone with a cross etched into it. Legend has it that anyone who steps over the stone after 9 PM will get lost at night. A short walk west of the square brings you to the 14th-century **Dominican Monastery,** the oldest preserved building in town. Northeast of the square is the 17th-century **Kostel sv. Mikuláše** (St. Nicholas's Church) and the neighboring **Černá Věž** (Black Tower; nám. Přemysla Otakara II; admission 6 Kč; open Mar.–June 10–6 daily except Mon.; July and Aug. 10–7 daily; Sept.–Nov. 9–5 daily except Mon.). For a view, climb the 252 steps of the tower, blackened by the great fire of 1641.

COMING AND GOING

České Budějovice has excellent train connections to Prague (2½ hrs, 72 Kč) and all southern-Bohemian destinations. The **bus terminal** across the street from the train station sends several buses a day to Prague (2½ hrs, 72 Kč). From the **train station,** take the underground passageway to Žižkova and follow it to the main square (15 minutes).

WHERE TO SLEEP AND EAT

Most hotels are expensive. In a pinch, the drab **Hotel Grand** (Nádražní 27, tel. 038/565–03), across from the train station, always has rooms available (doubles 800 Kč). **Pension Garni** (Na Mlýnské stoce 7, tel. and fax 038/635–34–75) has doubles for 950 Kč but is small and often full. **CKM** (Lannova 63, tel. 038/245–05), near the train station, arranges private accommodations weekdays 9–6. **Informační centrum** (nám. Přemysla Otakara II 2, tel. and fax 038/594–80; open fall–spring, weekdays 9–5 and weekends 9–noon, and summer, weekdays 9–7 and weekends 9–3) will set you up in pensions and hotels.

Down a half-liter of Budvar beer (14 Kč) and a heavy plate of pork (80 Kč) at **Masné Krámy** (Krajinská 13, at Hroznova, tel. 038/326–52). Get relief from the usual pork and dumplings at **Snack Bar Krijcos** (Na Mlýnksé stoce 11), serving pizza and atmosphere.

MORAVIA

Like the intricate theories of its most famous native son, Sigmund Freud, Moravia's vitality lies buried beneath the obvious. From the rural villages of the mountainous Jeseníky region in the north to the smooth, fertile vineyards of the south, Moravia's subtleties await the more inquisitive traveler. The local urban experience, Brno, with a bustling inner city, has enough sights to occupy tourists for several days; in fact, Brno is sopping up some of the overflow of expatriates from Prague.

BRNO

Moravia's capital and the Czech Republic's second-largest city, Brno buzzes with activity. During the 18th and 19th centuries, it became the industrial center of the Austrian empire, and during the First Czechoslovak Republic (1919–1938), outstanding avant-garde architects—including Adolf Loos, Johann Pieter Oude, and later Ludwig Mies van der Rohe—designed buildings throughout the city. Besides their works, the downtown area is filled with whimsical architecture, from the "Ninnies" on the town square to the gargoyle who appears to be mooning the square from atop the cathedral at Jakubské náměstí. If you can resist the temptation to compare Brno to Prague, you'll find that it has its own gritty charm.

BASICS

The English-speaking staff at **Kulturní a Informační Centrum (KIC) Města Brna** arranges private rooms (200 Kč and up) for a 10% commission. *Radnická 4, 8, 10, tel. 05/4221–1090, fax 05/4221–4625. Open weekdays 8–6, weekends 9–5.*

COMING AND GOING

The **train station** just south of the city center has frequent service to Prague (2 hrs, 110 Kč), Bratislava (1½ hrs, 72 Kč), and Olomouc (1½ hrs, 44 Kč). To reach the center, follow the tram lines north up Masarykova ulice. An overhead walkway connects the train station to the **bus station** (at Plotní and Zvonařka). Several buses run daily to Prague (2½ hrs, 95 Kč), Bratislava (2 hrs, 75 Kč), and Olomouc (1½ hrs, 60 Kč).

WHERE TO SLEEP

Most hotels are central and pricey. Cheap options include private rooms or summer dorms arranged by KIC (*see* Basics, *above*). **Interservis** (Lomená 38, tel. 05/4332–1335 ext. 281) is a quiet hostel 10 minutes by tram from the center; from the train station, take Tram 12 to Komárov. With beds for 150 Kč, **Komárov** (B. Zůzků 5, tel. 05/4332–1342; Tram 12 to Komárov) is the cheapest hotel in town; doubles (390 Kč) all have toilets and showers. Just north of the main square, **U Jakuba** (Jakubské nám. 6, tel. 05/4221–07–956, fax 05/4221–0797) has plain and clean rooms; doubles are 1,290 Kč.

FOOD

Founded in 1552, **Stopkova** (Česká ul. 5, off nám. Svobody) serves filling dinners of sausage, kraut, and potatoes (80 Kč); walk upstairs for ritzier fare. **Černohorská pivnice** (off Masarykova, at Kapucínské nám.) is an aged Czech beer hall with vaulted ceilings, solid wooden tables, and tons of locals and expats guzzling different kinds of *černý* (dark beer) on tap. **Čínská Restaurace** (Průchodní 1, across from Staré radnice) has all the requisite chicken and pork Chinese dishes (about 100 Kč) plus a fair selection of tofu dishes (60 Kč). Line up at Aida (Orlí 4, off Masarykova) for great ice cream that costs all of 4 Kč a scoop.

WORTH SEEING

Masarykova ulice runs north–south through the central square Náměstí Svobody. The Gothic **Katedrála sv. Petr a Pavla** (Cathedral of Sts. Peter and Paul) sits on Petrov Hill, overlooking the city from the southwest corner. Next door is the **Kapucínský Klášster** (Capuchin Monastery), with a 17th-century crypt in which bodies were buried and dried by air channeled through 60 vents; enter through the door marked KAPUCÍNSKÁ HROBKA (admission 20 Kč; open Mon.–Sat. 9–noon and 2–4:30, Sun. 11–11:45 and 2–4:30. Immediately north is the **Zelný trh** (Cabbage Market), filled with vendors hawking produce, flowers, and whatever else they can get their hands on. Just off Zelný trh is **Staré radnice** (Old Town Hall, Radnická ul.; tower admission 2 Kč; open daily 9–5). Legend has it that in 1510 the town council refused to pay architect Anton Pilgrim the agreed sum of money, so he built the portal's central spire, above the statue of Justice, crooked.

Originally constructed for Přemysl King Otakar II in the 13th century, **Špilberk hrad** (Spilberk Castle) still broods over Brno. The prisoners' cells in the casement jail are open and unlighted, so you can climb in and contemplate life in the slammer, then gawk at reproductions of torture devices used here. For a self-guided tour, ask for a pamphlet in English. *Admission: 20 Kč. Open June–Sept., Tues.–Sun. 9–6; Oct.–May, Tues.–Sun. 9–5.*

CHEAP THRILLS

One of Brno's best features is its location in the midst of wine country. Try to visit one of the small villages nearby—Bzenec, Strašnice, Mikulov, and Velká Pavlovice are a few—where people make their own wine and store it in cellars called *sklepy*, recognizable by doors buried in hillsides. Try knocking on a few; if someone is home, they'll invite you in to sample and buy. September and October, harvest months, are especially festive. In **Mikulov** (1½ hrs, 33 Kč by bus), you can buy a bottle from one of the *sklepy* that tunnel into the Holy Hill, then climb to the top (about 1½ km/¾ mi) for a view of the town to the west and Austria to the south.

OLOMOUC

One of the most attractive and lively towns in northern Moravia, Olomouc is the home of the highly regarded **Palacký University,** the Czech Republic's second-oldest university, established in 1573. The town is known both for Palacký and for its superb annual horticulture exhibition, **Flora Olomouc,** held in April or May. The city center is filled with well-preserved historical monuments, fortress walls, and churches, all within walking distance of one another.

BASICS

In summer, **CKM** arranges accommodations in hotels and dorms. *Denisova and Univerzitní, west of nám. Republiky, tel. 068/522–3939. Open weekdays 9–5.*

The excellent, English-speaking staff at **Informační Středisko Olomouce** books private accommodations (300 Kč and up) and hands out maps (20 Kč). *Horní nám., in town hall to right of clock, tel. 068/551–3385. Open daily 9–7.*

COMING AND GOING

The **train station** (Jeremenkova ul.) is at the eastern end of town. Frequent trains depart southward toward Brno and Prague (4 hrs, 120 Kč). Just southeast of the train station is the **bus depot** (Sladkovského ul.), from where you can depart to small villages in Moravia. Trams 4 and 5 connect both stations with town.

WHERE TO SLEEP

You'll get a better deal in Olomouc's dorms, private rooms, or hostel than in the shabby hotels. The clean rooms at the new **Hotel Gol** (Legionářská 12, tel. 068/286–17; doubles 660 Kč) are built right into the grandstand of the local soccer club's stadium, a 10-minute walk from the city center. From either station, take Tram 4 or 5 to Náměstí Národních hrdinů, then walk north past the Legionnaires building, turn right before the ticket offices, turn left on the paved road, and follow the road toward the grandstand. In the complex at the far side of the swimming building, **Hostel Stadion** (Plavecký Stadión, Legionářská 11, tel. 068/413–181) has beds for 180 Kč, doubles for 380 Kč, and triples for 420 Kč. They're often booked, so reserve ahead. In July and August the cheapest beds are in student dorms (beds are 259 Kč); make arrangements at the **Vysokoškolská** office (17 Listopadu 54, tel. 068/522–6059). To reach the office, take Tram 4 or 5 to Žižkovo and turn right on 17. Listopadu; it's the second building on the left. The dorms are a 15-minute walk southeast of the center.

FOOD

Hanácká Restaurace (Dolní nám., at Lafayettova, tel. 068/522–5296) is the place to go for Moravian specialties in a smoke-free environment. **Caesar** (Horní nám., tel. 068/522–9287; open Mon.–Sat. 9 AM–1 AM, Sun. until midnight), next to the art gallery of the same name (*see* Worth Seeing, *below*), serves excellent pizzas for about 70 Kč. The **U Musea** (Třída 1. máje 8, tel. 068/522–3201) is a student pub where you can trade pocket change for sausages and catch the occasional caterwaul of big guitars.

WORTH SEEING

The Horní náměstí (Upper Square) is dominated by the large, fairy-tale town hall, which was built as a merchant's house in 1261; its newly restored tower dates from 1607. Don't miss the marvelous Socialist astronomical clock, a Communist makeover from 1954, where glorious workers clang out the hours with their hammers. Concerts are held in the hall's courtyard; buy tickets and get schedules at the adjacent art gallery, **Caesar** (Horní nám., tel. 068/522–5587; open weekdays 9–noon and 12:45–5, Sat. 9–1). North of the square, off Opletalova ulice, is the Gothic **Chrám sv. Mořice** (Cathedral of St. Moritz; ul. 8. května). The baroque interior was crowned by the Czech Republic's largest organ (2,311 pipes) in 1745; the annual International Organ Festival ensures its skillful abuse every September. One block north of St. Moritz stands the **Church of the Immaculate Conception,** whose frescoes, which date from 1500, were discovered during its 1983 restoration. Massive, neo-Gothic **Dóm sv. Václava** (St. Wenceslas Cathedral; Václavské nám.) is noteworthy for its three aisles and the astral decoration covering its vaulted ceiling; it also holds the remains of Olomouc's champion of Catholicism, Jan Sarkandu, who was tortured for treason during an uprising in 1618. The stairs to the left of the altar lead to the **crypt.** Be sure to take a stroll through the **gardens** between the old town walls and the Mlýnský Canal, accessible from a number of spots along the east side of the town center.

DENMARK

P erched inconspicuously between the rest of Scandinavia and the Continent, with just over 5 million people spread among 90 of its 406 islands, Denmark is a tiny country with one of the friendliest populations in the world. Although most foreigners know little about Denmark (other than of its pastries and Vikings), Danes exhibit no resentment or inferiority complex. In fact, Danes cherish their relative anonymity—it keeps their country *hyggeligt* (pronounced *hoog*-ly), which translates roughly as "small and cozy." Still, the Danes have a distinct affinity for the English-speaking world, and it shows up in everything from their command of the English language to their music, fashion, and movie preferences.

That everyone must be heard is Denmark's golden rule, and it's embodied most obviously in the country's economic policies. A large portion of Denmark's GNP goes to social services, and generous unemployment benefits ensure that you'll see very few down-and-out Danes. The system also enforces strict labor regulations: a 37-hour workweek and five weeks of paid vacation per year. Thanks to their wealth of leisure time, Danes can concentrate on the really important things in life, like soccer. When Denmark's soccer team won the European Cup in 1992, the streets of Copenhagen were more crowded than they had been on the day Denmark was liberated from the Germans during World War II.

Still, the state of their nation is of utmost importance to Danes, and the zealous debate over what's best for Denmark seems never-ending. When Great Britain joined the European Community in 1973, Denmark followed suit, in hopes of stimulating its agricultural and industrial exports. Almost 20 years later, though, the country sent the EU into a panic, with 50.7% of its voting public rejecting union with Europe. However, in 1993, 57% of Denmark's voters turned around and approved an amended treaty to allow the country to join the EU. In the years that have followed, however, it seems many Danes still question what they are getting out of the deal: While Denmark is considered a part of the European community, it maintains its own set of laws and policies concerning tax regulation, social welfare, and the environment—three of the Danes' hottest-button issues.

BASICS

MONEY

US$1 = 6.4 kroner and 1 krone = 100 øre = 15.6¢. Changing money in Denmark can be expensive: The average exchange fee for traveler's checks at either banks or currency exchange offices is a per-check

DENMARK

TO KRISTIANSAND · TO STAVANGER · TO OSLO

Skagerrak

TO GREENLAND
TO FAROE ISLANDS

Hirtshals
Skagen
Göteborg
SWEDEN
Hjørring
Frederikshavn
Brønderslev
Sæby
Hanstholm
Thisted
LÆSØ
Limfjord
Limfjord
Aalborg
Varberg
North Sea
Nykøbing
Aalborg Bugt
Kattegat
Hobro
Hadsund
Lemvig
Skive
ANHOLT
Struer
Viborg
Holstebro
Randers
JYLLAND
Grenå
Herning
Silkeborg
Ringkøbing
Skjern
Skanderborg
Arhus
Ebeltoft
TO ICELAND, FAROE ISLANDS
Grindsted
Vejle
SAMSØ
Horsens
Tisvileleje
Hornbæk
Nykøbing
Helsingør
Hillerød
Humlebæk
Frederikssund
Fredensborg
Kalundborg
Holbæk
Copenhagen
Billund
Fredericia
Storebælt
Jyderup
Roskilde
Esbjerg
Holsted
Middelfart
Dragør
TO ENGLAND
FANØ
Kolding
Kerteminde
Odense
Slagelse
SJÆLLAND
AMAGER
Ribe
Vojens
Assens
FYN
Korsør
Ringsted
Køge
Køge Bugt
RØMØ
Haderslev
Ringe
Nyborg
Næstved
St. Heddinge
Skærbæk
Åbenrå
Fåborg
Kværndrup
Karrebæksminde
Tønder
Svendborg
LANGELAND
Troense
Sønderborg
Søby
Rudkøbing
Vordingborg
Stege
Flensburg
Ærøskøbing
Nakskov
MØN
ÆRØ
Marstal
Nykøbing
FALSTER
TO BORNHOLM
Rødby
Maribo
Ostsee
LOLLAND
Nysted

GERMANY

N

KEY
Rail Lines
Ferry Lines

0 ___ 50 miles
0 ___ 75 km

Baltic Sea
SWEDEN
BORNHOLM
Rønne

charge (usually 35kr for the first check and less for additional checks) or it is a percentage of the total amount plus a 25kr transaction fee. Fortunately, there are a few exceptions to the rule: If you're an American Express cardholder, you can cash traveler's checks for free at Copenhagen's American Express office (*see* American Express *in* Copenhagen Basics, *below*). The currency exchange service Forex charges a measly 10kr per check to change travelers checks, or 20kr to change up to $500 cash. Keep your receipt and they'll even change your kroner back to dollars for free. There are several Forex offices in Copenhagen, including one at the main train station. The cheapest option, however, is to use ATMs, found in all of Denmark's cities and many larger towns. ATMs typically accept Visa, MasterCard, and Cirrus cards, and Jyske Bank machines accept Plus cards.

HOW MUCH IT WILL COST • Despite high prices and taxes, Denmark is not impossibly expensive if you stick to modest hotels, or the even cheaper hostels and campgrounds, and if you don't overdo it at cafés and restaurants. Hostels usually cost 70kr–85kr, campgrounds 44kr per person. Train rides within Denmark run 130kr–250kr without a Eurailpass, and intracity buses rarely cost more than 10kr. All-you-can-eat lunch specials go for 30kr–60kr, an average dinner 50kr–100kr (tips are always included). Beers cost 15kr–30kr; live music is often free, but cover charges at most clubs hover around 40kr. Credit cards are usually accepted only for purchases over 100kr.

COMING AND GOING

DSB (Danish State Railways) honors Eurail and InterRail passes. For those without rail passes, buses and even planes are sometimes cheaper. Your best bet is to call a reputable discount travel agency and let them fill you in on the cheapest mode of travel to your chosen destination.

Fail-safe ways to make Danish friends: Offer a beer, criticize the Swedes, or compliment the Danish Soccer League.

BY BUS • Danish buses are more crowded and much less comfortable than trains, but they're cheap and usually not much slower. **Eurolines** (Reventlowsgade 8, Copenhagen, tel. 33–25–95–11), has buses to Hamburg (6 hrs, 240kr), London (20 hrs, 595kr–675kr), and most other cities in Europe. Reserve seats one week in advance. Rail passes are not valid on buses, and bicycles aren't allowed on international buses.

BY FERRY • Ferries, which connect most of Scandinavia, are a part of almost all train rides in and around Denmark—and trains drive right on board. ScanRail passes include many free or half-price ferry crossings; Eurail and InterRail passes include a few free crossings and some 20%–30% discounts. The ferry is a popular way to travel from Denmark to Malmö, Sweden (45 min, 40kr–87kr); Stockholm (9 hrs, 435kr, train fare included); Oslo, Norway (16 hrs, 450kr–615kr, 100kr–300kr extra for cabin); London (26 hrs, 1,210kr, train fare included); and Świnoujście, Poland (10 hrs, 310kr, 75kr–135kr extra for cabin). However, international flights are sometimes cheaper than the ferries. Contact DSB's travel agency (tel. 33–14–11–26) for more information on ferry travel.

BY PLANE • If you don't mind spending some time comparison-shopping, bargains abound. Check out charter specials and weekend fares, as well as "Jackpot" discount tickets offered by the Scandinavian airline **SAS**. If you're under 26, you can find laughably cheap flights through discount travel agencies (*see* Discount Travel Agencies *in* Copenhagen Basics, *below*). If you are going to be traveling extensively in Scandinavia (usually a very expensive endeavor) find out about SAS's "Visit Scandinavia" program. Cost is $80 for one coupon, or $480 for six, and each coupon is good for one flight to anywhere in Scandinavia. Coupons are valid year-round but must be used within a three-month period. You must purchase the coupons before arriving in Scandinavia; contact your local travel agent for details.

BY TRAIN • Trains in Denmark are comfortable and usually on time, and all DSB stations in Denmark come equipped with storage lockers (10kr–20kr per day). The main route to Copenhagen is via Hamburg (6 hrs, 410kr); you can also get there via Berlin (8 hrs, 395kr). Reservations (42kr) are required for second-class travel on international-bound Danish trains; you do not need a reservation with a first-class ticket. The **ScanRail** pass, valid on DSB, entitles you to unlimited train travel in Scandinavia for three weeks (2,000kr), or five days of unlimited train travel within 15 (1,300kr). You can buy ScanRail passes in Scandinavia, but they're 20% cheaper in your home country; check with your local travel agency. If Denmark is the only Scandinavian country you'll visit, though, the ScanRail pass probably isn't worth it.

GETTING AROUND

You can travel almost everywhere in Denmark by train. Some areas in Jylland, including Billund (home of Legoland), are accessible only by bus or plane.

BY BIKE • Extensive bike paths, miles of rural roads, and plenty of flat terrain make Denmark ideal for cycling. Bikes are allowed on most regional trains for free, and on interregional trains and ferries for a

HOW TALL IS YOUR SMØRREBRØD?

The best-known Danish delicacy is smørrebrød, an open-face sandwich. Ages ago, fishermen craving a quick, cheap meal piled sild (herring) and some accompaniments on bread. During a wood shortage in the 1770s, the government urged all Danes to eat cold lunches, and smørrebrød quickly became the people's choice. Since then it has become increasingly elaborate, piled high with smoked salmon, marinated cucumbers, eggs, pickled beets, remoulade (relish), and every other conceivable foodstuff.

small charge; on interregional buses it's a good idea to reserve bike space in advance. You can rent bikes all over Denmark for 35kr–50kr per day or 200kr–250kr per week; to avoid heavy fines, make sure your bike's front *and* rear lights are working. Before hitting the roads, contact **Dansk Cyklist Forbund** in Copenhagen (Rømersgade 7, tel. 33–32–31–21, fax 33–32–76–83; open summer, Mon.–Thurs. 10–6:30, Fri. 10–7, and Sat. 10–2; off season, weekdays only) for excellent bike maps, tour information, and equipment. Also, stop by Copenhagen Tourist Information (*see* Visitor Information *in* Copenhagen Basics, *below*) and pick up a copy of the helpful *Cykel CORT* (95kr), which includes maps and a listing of hostels, campgrounds, and bicycle shops around the country.

BY TRAIN • Hourly trains link Sjælland with Fyn and Jylland. Rail passes cover ferry crossings on state-run lines, but not on private ones. Even with a pass, seat reservations (20kr domestic, 42kr international) are mandatory for all second-class ticket holders; you do not need a seat reservation with a first-class ticket. The speediest trains are the IC-3 (InterCity) trains. Daily between 9 AM and noon you can travel anywhere within Denmark on a local train (no IC trains) for just 139kr.

WHERE TO SLEEP

A *vandrerhjem* (hostel; literally, wanderers' home) or campground is often the best option for lodging. Hostels here are used by people of all ages—families, students, young adults, and even business travelers—and most offer private rooms as well as dorms. However, Danish hostels slap nonmembers with an extra 25kr "one-day membership" fee; save money by buying a 125kr six-stamp membership, valid for five nights of hostel stays (hostels rarely cancel stamps, though, so stretch that 125kr as far as you can). Throughout Denmark, rooms in private homes rent for about 200kr–300kr. Hotels usually cost more than 450kr per double (although prices are often negotiable off season). A *sømandshjem* (seaman's hotel) is a cheap and pleasant alternative: These simple, homey, secure hotels once catered exclusively to sailors, but as the sailor population has declined they've been adopted by travelers who seek value over luxury.

FOOD

Restaurants here often exist more for the sake of tourists than for Danes, who typically prefer to eat at home. The most affordable restaurants are ethnic: Italian, Greek, Chinese, Middle Eastern, and Indian; Indian restaurants are the best option for vegetarians. Look for *tilbud* (fixed-price specials, usually a main course and side dish), *aftensmenu* (50kr–75kr dinner specials), and midweek half-price specials. For some typical Danish grub, try *smørrebrød* (an open-face Danish sandwich) or *sild* (marinated herring) on *rugbrød* (dark, thinly sliced rye bread), and wash it down with beer or schnapps. For really cheap eats, venture to your friendly neighborhood Netto, Superbrugsen, or Irma grocery stores, or sniff out any one of Denmark's ubiquitous *pølse* stands and sample the Danes' tasty version of the hot dog (10kr–18kr). Most Danish restaurants are shuttered from Christmas Eve (Dec. 24) through New Year's Day (Jan. 1).

BUSINESS HOURS

Banks are generally open Monday–Wednesday 9:30–4, Thursday 9:30–6, and Friday 9:30–4. Museums are open Tuesday–Sunday from 10 to 4 or 5. Stores are open Monday–Thursday from 9 or 10 to 5:30 or 6, Friday from 9 or 10 to 7 or 8, and Saturday from 9 or 10 to noon or 2 (some as late as 5).

FESTIVALS

Major annual festivals include the 10-day **Copenhagen Jazz Festival** (early July), the four-day **Roskilde Festival** of rock music (late June or early July), the **Århus International Jazz Festival** (mid-July), and Ringe's **Mid-Fyn Festival** of folk and rock music (late June). Tickets for major cultural events can be purchased throughout Denmark at BILLETnet counters in post offices, and at some tourist information offices. Call ahead for hotel reservations if you plan to visit during one of Denmark's major festivals.

PHONES

Country code: 45. Cities in Denmark don't have telephone codes, so just dial the eight-digit number. At public phones, brief local calls cost 1kr–2kr (insert money after the call is answered); long-distance calls cost 5kr–10kr. Since coin-phones are becoming obsolete in many places, it's often easiest to buy a phone card (20kr minimum) from any DSB kiosk, and some small stores. Local rates are half-price Monday–Saturday 7:30 PM–8 AM and all day Sunday. For local directory assistance dial 118.

To call other parts of Europe, dial 00 + country code + area code + telephone number. Directory assistance for all of Europe is 113. Calls cost 3kr per minute to Scandinavia and 3kr–6kr to the rest of Europe. To dial the United States direct or collect, call **AT&T Direct Access**^SM (tel. 8001–0010), **MCI** (tel. 8001–0022), or **Sprint** (tel. 8001–0877). Direct-dial calls to the United States cost 10kr per minute (8kr per minute 7:30PM–8 AM). To place collect calls through a Danish operator, dial 141.

MAIL

Post offices, generally open weekdays from 9 or 10 to 5 or 6, Saturday 9–noon, run a speedy mail service. Letters and postcards to the United States, Canada, Australia, and New Zealand cost 5.25kr, to anywhere in Europe and Scandinavia 4kr. You can buy stamps at DSB kiosks and post offices. Mailboxes, labeled POSTKASSE, are bright red with a yellow horn and crown.

Denmark's well-loved monarch, Queen Margrethe II, has little influence in the country's social-democratic parliament, but her presence qualifies this as the oldest monarchy in the world, dating from AD 800.

EMERGENCIES

Dial 112 for **fire, police,** or **ambulance.** You can get emergency medical treatment from the casualty wards of most hospitals 24 hours a day, free of charge. Denmark's apoteks (pharmacies) are open weekdays 9–5:30, Saturday 9–1. A few have extended hours; check the telephone directory for specifics.

LANGUAGE

Virtually all Danes (especially younger ones) speak English and are more than willing to use it. If you're intent on leaving your English at home, try German, which most Danes also speak. Or attempt a few words of Danish: *hej* (hello); *hej hej* or *vi ses* (goodbye); *tak* (thank you); *undskyld* (excuse me); *ja* (yes); *nej* (no); *hvor er toilettet?* (where is the bathroom?); *har du . . .?* (do you have . . .?); *hvor meget koster . . .?* (how much does . . . cost?); or *taler du engelsk?* (do you speak English?).

GAY AND LESBIAN TRAVELERS

Denmark was the first country to legalize domestic partnerships for gays and lesbians, and the spirit of tolerance lives on. **LBL,** also known as the **National Danish Organization for Gays and Lesbians** (Teglgaardstræde 13, Copenhagen, tel. 33–13–19–48), owns and runs the Pan Club chain of gay bars and cafés throughout Denmark; it also publishes Pan *Bladet* (free in gay bars and cafés), a magazine with articles on gay issues and listings of gay bars, discos, and organizations throughout the country. For information on general women's issues, contact the national women's organization **Dansk Kvindesamfund** (Niels Hemmingens Gade 10, 3rd floor, Copenhagen, tel. 33–15–78–37).

COPENHAGEN

With more than a fifth of Denmark's population and half of the country's businesses, schools, and museums, Copenhagen—in Danish, København, meaning "Merchants' Harbor"—is a booming cosmopolitan center. The city's liberal laws, sizzling nightlife, and well-established café culture make it a

KEY

AE American Express Office

i Tourist Information

—|— Rail Lines

----- Ferry Lines

N

NØRREBRO

SLOTSHOLMEN

VESTERBRO

Ostre Anlæg

Botanisk Have

Kongens Have

Ørsteds Parken

Tivoli

Central Railway Station (Hovedbanegården)

Vesterport Station

Nørreport Station

Christiansborg Slotsplads

Rådhus Pl.

Gammel torv

Nytorv

Amagertorv

Abenrå

0 _____ 440 yds

0 _____ 400 m

Norre Al.
Tagensv.
Blegdamsv.
Dossering
Farimagsg.
Dag Hammarskjölds Al.
Guldbergsg.
Mølleg.
Elmeg.
Skt. Hans Torv
Fælledv.
Ryesg.
Sortedam Dossering
Sortedam
Søndre Søg.
Øster Søg.
Øster Søg.
Stockholmsg.
Sølvg.
Rigensg.
Griffenfeldsg.
Nørrebrog.
Ravnsborgg.
Sortedams
Øster Farimagsg.
Sølvg.
Sølvg.
Kronprinsessg.
Blågårdsg.
Dronning Louises Bro
Venderg.
Øster Farimagsg.
Gothersg.
Øster Voldg.
Aboulevard
Peblinge Dossering
Nørre Søg.
Frederiksborgg.
Abenrå
Kronprinsensg.
Gothersg.
Rosenørns A.
Gyldenløvesg.
Nørre Farimagsg.
Nansensg.
Rømersg.
Israels Pl.
Linnésg.
Nørreg.
Købmagerg.
Vognmagerg.
Gammel Mønt
Ny Østerg.
Vodroffsv.
Vester Søg.
Nørre Voldg.
Fiolstr.
Krystalg.
Landemærket
Pilestræde
Store Kannikestr.
Kr. Bernikows g.
Østerg.
Jørgens Sø
Kampmannsg.
Vester Farimagsg.
H.C. Andersens Blvd.
Vester Voldg.
Teglgårds
Studiestr.
Larsbjørns str.
Vestergade
Niels Hemmingsens G.
Skinderg.
Voldendorffsg.
Niels Hemmingsens
Hyskenstr.
Vimmelsk.
Nyg.
Knabrostr.
Badstuestr.
Læderstr.
Gammel Strand
Helgo
Brenterhorn
Sankt
Nyropsg.
Axelterv.
Frederiksberg g.
Gammel
Kattesundet
Frederiksbg.
Farverg.
Kompagnistr.
Rådhusstr.
Vindebrog.
Christians Brygge
Svineryggen
Vodroffsv.
Vesterport
Vesterbrog.
Bernstorffsg.
Reventlowsg.
Tietgensg.
Stormg.
Ny Vesterg.
Frederiksholms Kanal
Tøjhusgade
Gammel Kongev.
Vesterbrog.
Svendsg.
Niels Brocks G.
H. Dantes Pl.
H.C. Andersens Blvd.
Vester Voldg.
Langebro
Absalonsg.
Istedg.
Holmtorvet
Colbjørnsensg.
Hambrosg.
Amager Blvd.
Lange

Søo

Fredensg.
Blegdamsv.
Blegdamsv.
Fredensbro

③ ④ ⑤ ⑥ ⑦ ⑧ ⑩ ⑪ ⑫ ⑭ ⑮ ⑯ ⑰ ⑳ ㉑ ㉒ ㉓ ㉔ ㉕ ㉖

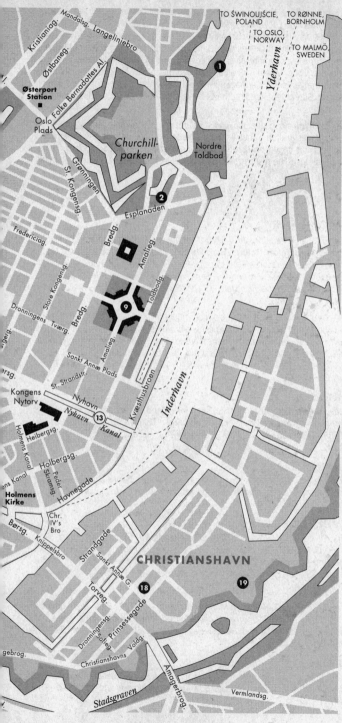

Sights ●

Amalienborg
Plads, **9**

Carlsberg
Brewery, **25**

Christiania, **19**

Christiansborg
Slot, **15**

Erotica Museum, **12**

Frihedsmuseet, **2**

The Little
Mermaid, **1**

National Museet, **16**

Ny Carlsberg
Glyptotek, **20**

Rosenborg Slot, **5**

Rundetårn, **10**

Strøget, **14**

Tivoli, **17**

Vor Frelsers
Kirke, **18**

Lodging ○

Absalon
Campground, **21**

Bellahøj Camping, **4**

City Public
Hostel, **22**

Copenhagen
Danhostel, **26**

Hotel Cab Inn, **11**

Hotel Jørgensen, **8**

Ibsens Hotel, **6**

KFUM's YMCA
Soldaterjhem, **7**

Missionhotellet
Nebo, **23**

Saga Hotel, **24**

Sømandshjemmet
Bethel, **13**

Vandrerhjem
Bellahøj, **3**

haven for the young at heart and for those who embrace more alternative lifestyles. Particularly in summer, the city comes alive with Danes who flock outdoors to enjoy their few months of sunshine. Indeed, whenever the sun appears, the Strøget (the pedestrian-only mall in the city center), the Nyhavn Canal, and many smaller pedestrian-only streets quickly fill with Danes and their bicycles, boats, and beers. Copenhagen's summer music scene is also impressive, with several annual summer festivals, and regular live bands in cafés and parks. Copenhagen isn't all about beer and music, however; the city has a soulful side as well. Search out the genteel Copenhagen in its old-fashioned pastry shops and among the pews of its historic churches. Spend time feeding the birds in King's Garden, or strolling along the elegant rose beds in Tivoli Gardens.

In many ways, Copenhagen, Denmark's capital since 1443, still retains the intimate feeling of a small harbor town. Its 17th-century palaces and churches lie alongside canals filled with rickety fisherman's boats, while elsewhere, a 12th-century castle, timbered houses, ancient street signs, and cobbled sidewalks all evoke the city's medieval past. The restless sea, brisk air, and charming streetscapes all make Copenhagen lovely.

BASICS

VISITOR INFORMATION

Pick up the free monthly information/entertainment guide, *Copenhagen This Week,* from the helpful English-speaking staff at **Copenhagen Tourist Information.** For 17kr they'll book you a private room. *Bernstorffsgade 1, across from Hovedbanegården, tel. 33–11–13–25. Information hot line: tel. 38–38–30–25, fax 33–93–49–69. Open May–June and late Sept., daily 9–6; July–mid-Sept., daily 9–8; shorter hrs off season. Accommodation service: tel. 33–12–28–80, fax 33–12–97–23. Open May–mid-Sept. 9–9; shorter hrs off season.*

Use It is the budget traveler's best friend. It provides free accommodation services, a message and ride board, poste restante, one-day baggage storage (50kr deposit), brochures, and *Play Time,* a free guide to budget services and activities in Copenhagen. The offices are located in the Huset building (a cultural/youth center with a café, cinema, and music) *Rådhusstræde 13, east of Rådhus Pl., tel. 33–15–65–18, fax 33–15–75–18. Open mid-June–mid-Sept., daily 9–7; mid-Sept.–mid-June, Sat.–Thurs. 10–4, Fri. 10–2.*

AMERICAN EXPRESS

Card- and check-holders can receive poste restante mail, send faxes, and exchange traveler's checks for free (there's a 15kr fee for nonmembers). All cash exchanges carry a 15kr fee. *Amagertorv 18, 1160 Copenhagen K, tel. 33–12–23–01, fax 33–12–29–80. Open May–Aug., weekdays 9–5, Sat. 9–noon; shorter hrs off season.*

CHANGING MONEY

Bureaux de change line the Strøget, but they rarely have good exchange rates. Banks change money for a steep 40kr fee. For cash withdrawals, use any of the ubiquitous red Kontanten ATMs, or the 24-hour Unibank ATMs.

DISCOUNT TRAVEL AGENCIES

Spies (Nyropsgade 41, tel. 70–10–42–00; weekdays 8–8, weekends 10–5) and **Star Tours** (H.C. Andersens Boulevard 12, tel. 33–11–88–88; weekdays 9–7, weekends 10–5) offer excellent prices on charter trips to sights around Denmark. If you just want travel advice and assistance, try **Skibby Rejser** (Vester Voldgade 10, tel. 33–11–15–01; weekdays 9–5, Sat. 10–2).

EMBASSIES

Australia: *Kristianiagade 21, tel. 35–26–22–44. Open Mon.–Thurs. 8:30–4:50, Fri. 8:30–3:25.* **Canada:** *Kristen Bernikowsgade 1, tel. 33–12–22–99. Open weekdays 8:30–4.* **United Kingdom:** *Kastelvej 40, tel. 35–26–46–00. Open weekdays 9–5.* **United States:** *Dag Hammarskjölds Allé 24, tel. 31–42–31–44. Open weekdays 8:30–5.*

PHONES AND MAIL

Make long-distance calls and photocopies, or send telegrams and faxes at the **Telecom Center** in the central train station. T*el. 33–14–20–00. Open weekdays 8 AM–10 PM, weekends and holidays 9–9.*

Main post office. *Pick up poste restante mail here. Tietgensgade 35–39, behind Hovedbanegården, tel. 33–33–89–00. Open weekdays 10–6, Sat. 9–1. Postal code: 1500.*

COMING AND GOING

A new rail link, which will connect Copenhagen to the European continent for the first time, is scheduled to open in summer, 1998. The nine-year project has involved building a bridge and tunnel to the mainland, and will cut the travel time between Copenhagen and Århus to less than three hours. Contact the train station or tourist office for more information.

BY BUS

Few buses go directly from Copenhagen to outlying towns, so it's easiest to take the train. However, from the Lyngby station (take train lines A, B, or E north from Hovedbanegården) you can catch buses to Humlebæk, Helsingor, and Roskilde. Get information at the HT bus information office in Rådhuspladsen.

BY FERRY

The ferry to **Oslo, Norway** (16 hrs, 405kr–555kr, 540kr–830kr for cabins) leaves daily at 5 PM from Kvæsthusbroen 1, near Nyhavn. Buy tickets the day of departure at the ferry building (tel. 33–11–22–55; open daily 8:30–5); take Bus 28 from the city center. Hourly catamarans to **Malmö, Sweden** (45 min) depart daily 6 AM–1 AM from the corner of Nyhavn and Havnegade; cost is 87kr one way with Flyvebåden (tel. 33–12–80–88) or 60kr round trip with Pilen (tel. 33–32–12–60). Ferries to the island of **Bornholm** (7 hrs, 148kr–189kr) leave from Kvæsthusbroen 2 (tel. 33–13–18–66) daily at 11:30 PM (also at 8:30 AM in summer). Ferries to **Świnoujście, Poland** (10 hrs, 315kr, 70kr–140kr extra for cabins) leave five times per week from Nordre Toldbod 12A (tel. 33–11–46–45); it's 500 yards north of Amalienborg, the Queen's castle.

BY PLANE

Copenhagen's **Kastrup Airport** is 10 km (6 mi) from the capital's center. The main carrier is **SAS** (Scandinavian Airlines System) (tel. 32–32–68–68), offering international and domestic flights. British Airways (tel. 33–14–60–00), Icelandair (tel. 33–12–33–88), and Delta (tel. 33–11–56–56) also serve Copenhagen. To reach the airport, take Bus 9, 13, or 36 (30 min, 15kr) from Rådhuspladsen, or the direct SAS bus (20 min, 35kr) from Hovedbanegården.

BY TRAIN

All trains stop at the central train station, **Hovedbanegården** (tel. 33–14–30–88 for reservations, 33–14–88–00 for domestic travel information, or 70–13–14–16 for international travel information), across from the Tivoli Gardens' west entrance and a few blocks southwest of Rådhuspladsen, where the Strøget begins. Domestic trains head to Århus (4½ hrs, 220kr), Odense (2½ hrs, 158kr), Fredericia (3 hrs, 183kr), and most other parts of Denmark. International trains go to Stockholm (9 hrs, 435kr, ferry fare included); Oslo, Norway (16 hrs, 450kr–615kr, plus 100kr–300kr extra for cabin); Hamburg (5 hrs, 452kr), and most major European cities. Seat reservations (20kr domestic, 42kr international) are required for second-class travel on all trains within Denmark. Copenghagen's main station has luggage storage (20kr) and showers (15kr).

GETTING AROUND

Though Copenhagen is easily explored on foot or by bike, its public transportation system is also efficient. The S-tog (subway) serves central destinations, and buses travel the city's outskirts. The **Copenhagen Card** entitles you to free bus and S-tog travel within Copenhagen, plus discounts on ferries to Sweden, and free admission to most museums and sights. A one-day pass costs 140kr, a two-day pass 230kr, and a three-day pass 295kr. Buy them at the airport, tourist offices, hotels, travel agencies, or train stations.

BY BIKE

Borrow bikes from **City Bike** racks at train stations and tourist attractions for a 20kr deposit (refunded upon return to any City Bike rack), but check the bike thoroughly before you take off—the last ones on the rack are often the broken ones. Buy a bike permit (one-time 11kr fee) and you can bring your bike along on subways weekdays 6:30 AM–8:30 AM and 3:30 PM–5:30 PM, and all day weekends. **Dan Wheel** (Cølbjornsensgade 3, 2 blocks west of Hovedbanegården, tel. 31–21–22–27; open daily 8–noon and

4–7) rents bikes for 35kr per day or 165kr per week, with a 200kr deposit; come in the morning because they only rent bikes until noon. Use It (*see* Visitor Information, *above*) publishes a handy free booklet titled "Copenhagen by Bicycle."

BY BUS

Bus and S-tog tickets are interchangeable, so don't buy separate tickets. Although buses are slower than the S-tog, their routes are more extensive, and some lines run all night (tickets double in price 1 AM–4:30 AM). Most buses stop at Rådhuspladsen or Hovedbanegården. Route maps (5kr) are available at all S-tog stations.

BY S-TOG

Rail passes (Eurail, InterRail, ScanRail) entitle you to free travel on S-tog trains, which run every three to five minutes 5:30 AM–12:30 AM. Tickets (10kr for two zones, 15kr for three), from machines marked BILLETAUTOMAT at every station, are valid for one hour on both the buses and the S-tog. *Klippekorts* (clip cards; 75kr for 10 two-zone tickets, 100kr for 10 three-zone tickets, or 65kr for 24-hour pass) are available at subway stations and on the bus; be sure to stamp your card in the yellow metal boxes on the platform as you board the train or bus, or risk paying a 500kr fine. Get S-tog maps and information at Hovedbanegården.

WHERE TO SLEEP

The cheapest lodging options (hostels and campgrounds) are far from the city center, but generally easily reached by train, bus, or bike. Most budget hotels are south and west of Hovedbanegården. Another option is to rent a room in a private house (280kr per night), which usually requires a 10- to 15-minute trek from the city center; book rooms through the tourist office for a 17kr fee.

UNDER 500KR • Hotel Cab Inn. A huge hotel with small, sterile rooms and convenient location, it has doubles with bath for 495kr, 575kr with breakfast. *Vodroffsvej 55, off Gledenløvesgade across Jørgens Sø, tel. 35–36–11–11, fax 35–36–11–14. From Rådhus Pl., Bus 2 Bronshøj to Rosenørns Allé.*

Hotel Jørgensen. Across from Israel Plads you'll find a hotel with cozy, old-fashioned doubles (480kr, 580kr with bath) as well as dorm beds (100kr, plus 30kr sheet rental). Ask for a room on the sunny south side. Breakfast is included with all rooms and dorms. The hotel offers luggage storage, and there's a laundry service nearby. *Rømersgade 11, tel. 33–13–81–86, fax 33–15–51–05. Lockout 10:30–3.*

Missionhotellet Nebo. Despite its location—between the main train station and Istedgade's row of porn shops—this prim hotel offers comfortable, well-maintained rooms and a friendly staff. Doubles cost 550kr or 770kr with shower, breakfast included. The breakfast room opens onto a small courtyard. *Istedgade 6, tel. 31–21–12–17, fax 31–23–47–74.*

Saga Hotel. It's in a gritty part of town, but near lots of restaurants and a short walk from Hovedbanegården. Doubles cost 350kr–520kr, 550kr–800kr with bath. Luggage storage is available. *Colbjørnsensgade 18–20, tel. 31–24–49–44, fax 31–24–60–33.*

UNDER 650KR • Ibsens Hotel. This family-run place offers friendly proprietors and charming, homey rooms. Doubles cost 600kr, 800kr–950kr with bath (breakfast included). *Vendersgade 23, near Nørreport S-tog, tel. 33–13–19–13, fax 33–13–19–16. Closed mid-Dec.–early Jan.*

Sømandshjemmet Bethel. Ask for a room overlooking Nyhavn Canal at this seaman's hotel with excellent views. Doubles with bath are 595kr, breakfast included. *Nyhavn 22, tel. 33–13–03–70, fax 33–15–85–70. From Hovedbanegården, Bus 500S.*

HOSTELS

City Public Hostel. The most conveniently located hostel in town is a 10-minute trek from Hovedbanegården. Dorm beds cost 100kr (120kr with breakfast) plus 30kr for sheet rental. The hostel's lounge is a cosy place with an alpine-lodge look. *Absalonsgade 8, tel. 31–31–20–70, fax 31–23–51–75. Kitchen. Cash only. Closed Sept.– April.*

Copenhagen Danhostel. In a big, beautiful park, a 15-minute bus ride from the center, you'll find a hostel with plenty of amenities: kitchen, laundry, and cafeteria. Dorm beds are 70kr. *Vejlands Allé 200, tel. 32–52–29–08. From Hovedbanegården, take Bus 46 or 10 to Mozarts Plads and transfer to Bus 37. Cash only. Closed mid-Dec.–mid-Jan.*

KFUM's YMCA Soldaterhjem. The Y offers 10 private, basic rooms (doubles 340kr), two shared bathrooms, and a public lounge area. Rooms on the south side have views of Rosenborg Castle. *Gothersgade 115, 1 block south of Nørreport S-tog, tel. 33–15–40–44. Cash only.*

Vandrerhjem Bellahøj (HI). Take a 15-minute bus ride from the city center to find this hostel, next to a prime picnic area with grassy hills and a pond. Beds are 80kr (70kr in winter) plus 30kr sheet rental. Luggage storage is available. *Herbergvejen 8, tel. 38–28–97–15. From Rådhus Pl. Bus 2 Bellahøj (not Bus 2 Brønshøj Plads) to Hvildevej. Lockout 10 AM–1 PM. Laundry. Cash only. Closed last 2 wks in Jan.*

CAMPING

Absalon Campground. This campground lies 9 km (5½ mi) from the city center. It offers a miniature golf course, kitchen, market, showers, and laundry facilities. Choose from tent sites (45kr per person) and cabins (200kr). The campground is next to a highway and housing projects, so prepare to leave your visions of the great outdoors behind. *Korsdalsvej 132, tel. 36–41–06–00, fax 36–41–02–93. From Hovedbanegården, S-tog B or L to Brønbyøster; cross Nygårds Plads, turn right on Nykæ, and left on Brønbyøstervej.*

Bellahøj Camping. Not exactly a pine-scented, rustic camping experience, this is simply a cheap spot to sleep 4 km (2½ mi) from the city center. Bonuses include a café, kitchen, and store. Camp sites cost 47kr per person. The reception is open 24 hours. *Hvidkildevej 66, tel. 31–10–11–50. From Hovedbanegården, Bus 11. Showers. Cash only. Closed Sept.–June.*

FOOD

Restaurants that serve good, typical Danish food tend to charge extra for their efforts, and even a humble meal of **smørrebrød** (*see box, above*) can be expensive. But Copenhagen has loads of cheap ethnic restaurants and atmospheric cafés, especially in Nørrebro and Vesterbro. Try one of the many **pølse** (hot dog) or falafel and gyro stands for a quick meal costing less than 30kr. **Feinsmäckker** sandwich bars have excellent sandwiches and Belgian waffles with ice cream; most items cost under 30kr. Copenhagen's largest **outdoor market** (closed weekends), a great place to pick up fresh produce, is at Israels Plads, just west of the Nørreport station.

UNDER 50KR • Govinda. This Hare Krishna–run, cafeteria-style vegetarian restaurant offers unbelievably delicious food. The all-you-can-eat buffet costs 45kr. *Nørre Farimagsgade 82, near Nørreport S-tog, tel. 33–33–74–44. Closed Sun. Cash only.*

UNDER 75KR • Café Krasnapolsky. Here is a trendy café-and-bar with an ultradiverse crowd of fashion models, tourists, and down-to-earth regulars. Try the lasagna or smørrebrød (40kr). Dancing takes place Thursday–Saturday nights. *Vestergade 10, 1 block north of Rådhus Pl., tel. 33–32–88–00. Cash only.*

Færgecaféen. For Danish food and a Danish crowd, right on the Christianshavn Canal, head to Færgecaféen. Sunday's all-you-can-eat feast (59kr) consists of a huge smørrebrød "kolt bord" set up on a pool table. *Strandgade 50, tel. 31–54–46–24. Cash only.*

Kashmir Indian Restaurant. The all-you-can-eat Indian lunch buffet costs a mere 39kr. It's a pretty good deal at night, too, with tantalizing tandoori dishes and curries. Even Queen Margrethe II has supped here. *Nørrebrogade 35, near Dronning Louises Bridge, tel. 35–37–54–71. Cash only.*

Pasta Basta. This is a classy Slotsholmen eatery well loved by all Copenhageners. The all-you-can-eat cold-pasta bar costs 69kr; warm pastas and other entrées cost more. *Valkendorffsgade 22, tel. 33–11–21–31. Cash only.*

UNDER 90KR • El Mexicano. This lively, slightly out-of-the-way place serves up tasty enchiladas, quesàdillas, and icy margaritas. *Gammel Kongevej 41, tel. 33–25–25–77. Cash only. No lunch.*

Peder Oxe. All of Copenhagen loves this bustling bistro. Delicious burgers cost 69kr, but an extra 20kr buys the city's best salad bar: fresh whole tomatoes, feta cheese, olives, sprouts, the works. *Gråbrødretorv 11, tel. 33–11–00–77. No breakfast.*

WORTH SEEING

With baroque palaces, beer breweries, canal communities, and one-of-a-kind museums to choose from, you couldn't ever be bored in Copenhagen. Most attractions are in or near the center, so you can either walk or take Bus 6, which swings past the major sights. Canal tours are another pleasant way to see the city; **Netto Boats** (Groendalsvej 67, tel. 31–54–41–02) has the best price: 20kr for one hour. From May to September boats leave two to five times every hour, daily 10–5, from the corner of Holmens Kirke and Nyhavn. Buy your ticket at the dock.

AMALIENBORG PLADS

This octagonal plaza with four palaces—one each for the queen (a flag hangs in front when she's in residence), her mother, the prince, and the guards—was never intended as a royal address. It was built in 1754 for the four wealthiest families of Copenhagen, but when a fire destroyed Christiansborg Palace at the end of the 18th century, the royalty took over Amalienborg as "temporary housing"—and never left. The changing of the guard (daily at noon) is most elaborate in winter, when the queen is usually at home.

CARLSBERG BREWERY

The Carlsberg tour gives you background on J. C. Jacobsen, founder of the original Carlsberg Brewery in 1847, and his son Carl, who founded the more modern Ny Carlsberg Brewery in order to meet the public's growing demand for beer. On the tour you'll see both breweries, which merged in 1906, and the world's largest beer-bottle collection (10,473 unique bottles). At the tour's end, you can sample the Carlsberg product. *Ny Carlsbergvej 140, tel. 33–27–13–14. From Rådhus Pl., Bus 6. Admission free. Tours weekdays at 11 and 2.*

CHRISTIANSBORG SLOT

Christiansborg Castle looms above Copenhagen's first building, a fortress constructed by Bishop Absalon in 1167. The original fortress, **Ruinerne af Absalons Borg** (entrance on Christiansborg Slotsplads, tel. 33–92–64–94; admission 20kr; open May–Sept., daily 9:30–3:30; closed Mon. and Sat. off season) is now a vast jumble of crumbling rocks, but posted signs offer detailed explanations of the castle's history.

Christiansborg Slot once served as the royal residence and now houses the Parliament, the Supreme Court, and the Royal Reception rooms, all accessible to the public. See the country's first three constitutions and the meeting rooms of the *Folketing* (People's Parliament) at the **Parliament chambers** (enter from Ny Vestergade and turn right; admission free). July through August, hourly tours happen daily 10–4 (in English at 1 only); September through June, tours are only on Sunday. Tours fill up fast and are limited to 35 people; arrive by 9 AM to reserve a space.

You'll need to don special nonscuff slippers before trekking across the wooden floors of the **Kongelige Repræsentationslokaler** (Royal Reception Rooms), where you'll see the queen's throne, rows of royal portraits, and 16 of the 600 or so *rooms. Enter from Ny Vestergade and turn left. Admission: 30kr. 40-min tours in English June–Aug., Tues.–Sun. at 11, 1, and 3; fewer off season.*

THE LITTLE MERMAID

You must be in a poetic frame of mind to appreciate the little lump of bronze that sits at the entrance to Copenhagen's harbor. Dedicated to the city in 1913 by Carl Jacobsen (of Carlsberg Breweries fame), **Den Lille Havfrue** (The Little Mermaid) is the legendary subject of Hans Christian Andersen's tale about a mermaid who wants to be human, because she's in love with a prince. Sadly, she only partially succeeded: Now she's stuck with legs and feet but no voice, forever doomed to be the object of fawning tourists, Kodak moments, and the occasional act of vandalism (her original head, severed and stolen in 1964, has never been recovered).

ROSENBORG SLOT

This Dutch Renaissance castle is a treasure chest of royal Danish history. Conceived as a summer home, the castle was constructed over four periods between 1605 and 1633, its last additions courtesy of King Christian IV, Denmark's architect-king. By the end of the 17th century, however, the castle was deemed old-fashioned; King Frederick III only lived here when he wasn't ensconced in Christiansborg Slot (*see above*) or Fredensborg Slot farther north. Now a museum, Rosenborg displays the crown jewels and a few castle rooms; the best is the king's "winter room," one of the oldest art galleries in Europe. *Øster Voldgade, tel. 33–15–32–86. Admission: 40kr. Open daily 10–4 ; shorter hrs off season.*

RUNDETARN

The view of Copenhagen from the Rundetårn (Round Tower) is reason enough to ascend this circa-1642 astronomical observatory—the oldest functioning observatory in Europe. Look for the king's monogram and motto, REGNA FIRMAT PIETAS (PIETY STRENGTHENS EMPIRE), in the famous wrought-iron balustrade.

Købmagergade 52A, tel. 33–73–03– 73. Admission: 15kr. Open June–Aug., Mon.–Sat. 10–8, Sun. noon–8; shorter hrs off season.

TIVOLI

Inspired by the 18th-century pleasure gardens of London, Paris, and Vienna, Tivoli is a summer-only miniature city offering concert pavilions, manicured gardens, rides, and restaurants. It's frequently the setting for free outdoor music and drama performances. The rides (8kr–16kr each) range from roller coasters to theme rides built around characters from Hans Christian Andersen's fairy tales. Fireworks light up the gardens on Wednesday and Saturday nights. *Vesterbrogade 3, across from Hovedbanegard, tel. 33–15–10–01. Admission: 30kr–40kr. Open May–mid-Sept., daily 10 AM–midnight.*

NEIGHBORHOODS

CHRISTIANIA

Ten minutes from the center of what brochures call "Wonderful, Wonderful, Copenhagen" is a commune of people who don't find it so wonderful. That's why they created the self-governed, free-living community now called Christiania. It started in 1971, when squatters discovered the abandoned military barracks near the island of Amager; they tore down the walls, constructed houses, and moved in. They also organized their own government, and made their own rules, one of which was to legalize drugs. For many years Copenhagen refused to supply the community with electricity or water, but Christianians thrived, using wood stoves, importing water, and creating workshops to produce everything they needed. Today Christiania is an organized, fully recognized commune with grocery stores, cafés, a theater, day-care centers, and a local radio station. Indeed, in many ways it's an establishment not so different from the one that its founders sought to escape. The city no longer opposes Christiania's existence, especially since the commune instituted its own cleanup of hard drugs in 1979.

Christiania's residents are surprisingly tolerant of visitors. Free guided walking tours regularly parade through the car-free community, but you're better off striking out on your own if you want to meet the locals. Tours (which occur daily at 3 PM, depending on how many people show up) leave from just inside the main entrance on **Prinsenssegade**; for a self-guided tour, pick up the free *Christiania Tourist Guide* at Use It (*see* Visitor Information, *above*).

CHRISTIANSHAVN

Occupying the small island between Copenhagen and Amager, Christianshavn has a look and mood all its own. The area was nothing but water until 1618, when King Christian IV commissioned Dutch engineers to build a commercial harbor here. The result is a rampart-enclosed, Dutch-style canal community (nicknamed "Little Amsterdam") with some of the city's best-preserved 17th-century houses and courtyards. Walk along **Strandgade,** the waterfront promenade, to see Christianshavn's oldest, most beautiful homes. **Vor Frelsers Kirke** (Our Savior's Church; Sankt Annæ Gade 25, tel. 31–57–92–48; open weekdays 9–3:30, Sun. 11:30–1:30; shorter weekday hrs off season) has an exterior spiral staircase (admission 20kr; closed Sept.–April), a live carillon demonstration (listen for the bells Saturday at 5 and Sunday at noon), and the largest organ in Copenhagen. In July the church puts on free organ concerts; call ahead for times.

NYHAVN

Now a picturesque canal community, Nyhavn, or "New Harbor," was once the sailors' red-light district, full of taverns and tattoo parlors. When booze was rationed in Sweden during the early- to mid-20th century, Swedes flocked here to get their fill of cheap, legal liquor. Nyhavn was also the favorite residence of Hans Christian Andersen. A walk along Nyhavn's canal-side houses is an unbeatable people-watching experience, especially on sunny days when cafés roll out their portable bars and the beer starts flowing.

OLD COPENHAGEN

Sometimes called the Latin Quarter, the oldest and liveliest part of Copenhagen lies within the streets Nørre Voldgade, Vester Vøldgade, Gothersgade, and Østergade. The district's prominent **Rådhuspladsen** (Town Hall Square), built in 1900, sports a distinct neo-Renaissance style; look for the bust of Bishop Absalon, the founding father of Copenhagen, over the main door of the Rådhus. A few blocks up the Strøget are Gammeltorv and Nytorv, the twin squares that dominate the heart of medieval Copenhagen. If you want to take a stroll through Old Copenhagen, head down Købmagergade, a pleasant pedestrian avenue with fewer crowds than the other nearby streets.

MUSEUMS

EROTICA MUSEUM
This museum, housing a collection of sex toys and wax figures, as well as erotic paintings, photos, and videos, is absolutely not for the bashful. The images of erotica in antiquity that adorn the stairwell are only a warm-up for the two floors of increasingly graphic exhibits that follow. *Købmagergade 24, tel. 33–12–03–11. Admission: 49kr. Open May–Sept., daily 10–9; Oct.–Apr., daily noon–6.*

FRIHEDSMUSEET
Built in the 1950s by the Danish Resistance Movement, this museum documents Denmark's unsuccessful attempt to stay neutral during World War II, as well as the Danes' efforts to hide Jews until they could be transported to safety in Sweden. The multimedia exhibits are in English, as are most tours (June–Aug., Tues., Thurs., Sun. at 2; May, Thurs. and Sun. at 2). *Churchillparken, tel. 33–13–77–14. Admission free. Open May–mid-Sept., Tues.–Sat. 10–4, Sun. 10–5; shorter hrs off season.*

NATIONAL MUSEET
Housed in an 18th-century palace, this museum has a huge collection of prehistoric artifacts—from Bronze Age tools and weapons to Viking longboats, as well as a permanent children's section, where big and little people can get up close and personal with the exhibits. *Ny Vestergade 10, between Christiansborg Slot and Tivoli Gardens, tel. 33–13–44–11. Admission: 30kr. Open Tues.–Sun. 10–5.*

NY CARLSBERG GLYPTOTEK
The museum boasts one of the world's finest collections of Etruscan art outside Italy, as well as Europe's finest collection of Roman portraits. In addition to these classical treasures, the museum (founded by Carl Jacobsen of Carlsberg Brewery) has a sizable collection of Impressionist art, including several works by Degas and Gauguin. *Dantes Plads 7, east of Tivoli Gardens, tel. 33–41–81–41. Admission: 15kr; free Sun. and Wed. Open May–Aug., Tues.–Sun. 10–4, Sept.–Apr., Tues.–Sat. noon–3, Sun. 10–4.*

SHOPPING

The Strøget's pedestrian streets offer glorious shopping for Danish-design home furnishings, from kitchen gadgets to armchairs. Sadly, there aren't many bargains. Wander away from the city center, toward Vesterbro and Nørrebro, to find quirky second-hand shops and flea markets. The flea market at **Israels Plads** (just off Frederiksborggade, near Nørreport Station; open May–Oct., Sat. 8–2) is equal parts antiques and junk. Bargaining skills are essential. The slightly smaller market behind Frederiksberg Rådhus (May–Aug., Sat. morning) offers lower prices and more junk.

AFTER DARK

Most of the city's bars, cafés, and clubs are just west of the Strøget and in Nørrebro. There's often free music in parks and cafés throughout the city. For the latest on city happenings, peruse *Gaffa, Nat og Dag, The Neon Guide,* or *Copenhagen This Week*; these are available free in many cafés and hotels, as well as at tourist information centers. At Use It (*see* Visitor Information, *above*), pick up free copies of *Musik Kalenderen,* with information on concerts, and Film Kalenderen, with listings of theaters featuring English-language and European art films. Though Copenhagen prices, for both cover charges and drinks, are only slightly outrageous (a half-liter of beer averages 35kr) a late night with lots of drinks can get very expensive.

Copenhagen's annual 10-day **jazz festival** begins on the first Friday in July and showcases some of the best jazz musicians in the world. Sessions take place on street corners, in cafés, along the water, and in parks; ticket prices range from 40kr to 350kr, though many performances are free. For information and tickets, call the festival office (Kjeld Langesgade 4A, tel. 33–93–20–13).

CAFES AND BARS
When Copenhagen's first Parisian-style café opened in 1976, its success inspired myriad others to follow. **Café Sommersko** (Kronprinsensgade 6, off Købmagergade, tel. 33–14–81–89), an enduring

favorite, has a Mediterranean atmosphere and terrific homemade sandwiches. A cutting-edge pack hangs out on the outdoor patio at **Café Rust** in Nørrebro (Guldbergsgade 8, tel. 35–37–72–83; cover 25kr–75kr Thurs.–Sat.); live rock is free on Tuesday. Nearby, tiny **Café Funke** (Skt. Hans Torv, tel. 31–35–17–32) offers a variety of free live music, from funk to acoustic guitar; get there early if you want a seat. There's free live jazz Sunday at 3:30 PM at **Krut's Karport** (Øster Farimagsgade 12, near Botanical Gardens, tel. 35–26–86–38), where you'll find 65 varieties of whisky (25kr–125kr). For moderately priced drinks and a mellow atmosphere, duck into **Kul Kaféen** (Teglgårdsstræde 5, near Nørreport S-tog, tel. 33–32–17–77), which hosts everything from evening healing sessions to stand-up comedy to all kinds of live acoustic music. The café's volunteer staff are excellent resources for information on current and upcoming cultural events.

The gay and lesbian **Pan Café** (Knabrostræde 3, off the Strøget, tel. 33–11–37–84) has five floors of coffee-and-cocktail bars; Pan's disco is open Wednesday through Saturday nights (40kr cover). Nearby, the ultrapopular **Sebastian Café** (Hyskenstræde 10, tel. 33–32–22–79) has art exhibits upstairs and a bulletin board with gay news and announcements.

LIVE MUSIC AND DANCING

Live music fans, rejoice—Copenhagen's nightlife can fulfill your every desire. **A/S BananRepublikken** (Nørrebrogade 13, near Dronning Louises Bridge, tel. 35–36–08–30; cover 30kr–40kr), a Caribbean-style café/bar/restaurant, serves its diverse crowd excellent world music, reggae, and salsa. **Sabor Latino** (Vester Voldgade 85, tel. 33–11–97–66; cover 30kr; closed Mon.–Wed.) is like a UN of discos, with an international crowd dancing to salsa and other Latin rhythms.

Christiania's concert house, **Loppen** (Loppehygningen, Christiania, tel. 31–57–84–22; Bus 8 from city center) is a good choice for rock, jazz, pop, and fusion; free concerts take place every Wednesday and Thursday at 9 PM. The **Stereo Bar** (Linnésgade 16A, tel. 33–13–61–13) on Israel Plads is the newest hot spot with a house- and hip-hop music bar upstairs, and deejay spinning '70s tunes downstairs.

For something a bit more old-fashioned, head to **Søpavillionen** (Gyldenløvesgade 24, tel. 33–15–12–24), between St. Jørgen and Peblinge lakes. There's pleasant dinner-dancing music nightly 7–10; dinners are expensive, but cover charge without dinner is just 30kr. At the **Røde Pimpernel** (Hans Christian Andersen Blvd. 7, tel. 33–12–20–32) an adult audience gathers for dancing to live orchestras, trios, and old-time sounds.

For powerful jazz, try the **Copenhagen Jazz House** (Niels Hemmingsens Gade 10, 2 blocks south of Rundetårn, tel. 33–15–16–00; cover 60kr–300kr for jazz, 40kr for disco; closed Sun. and Mon.), a huge venue that hosts some of the biggest names in jazz; get ready to shift gears at midnight, though, when they start up the disco 'til dawn. Another must for jazz lovers is **La Fontaine** (Kompagnistræde 11, tel 33–11–60–98; cover 40kr; closed Mon.–Tues.). It's a quintessential jazz dive, with sagging curtains, impenetrable smoke, and sizzling Scandinavian jazz talent.

Copenhagen also has a regular schedule of free outdoor concerts during summer—the sort of happy events that bring folks of every generation for good music, a clear sky, and lots of beer. Do as the Danes do, and bring along a picnic supper. At **Fælledparken** (in Østerbro; from Hovedbanegården, take Bus 10) jazz and rock bands play Thursday–Saturday from 8 PM to 10 PM; some shows are free. Afterward, the 100-year-old **Pavilionen Café** in the middle of the park becomes a late-night disco. More *hyggeligt* concerts happen June–August, every other Saturday 2 PM–7 PM at 5'Øren (tel. 31–59–79–33), a seaside park in Amager, 20 minutes from Copenhagen via Bus 9, 12, or 37.

NEAR COPENHAGEN

HELSINGOR

It's hard to say who holds more sway in this idyllic port town—Prince Hamlet or Holgar the Dane. Legend has it that Hamlet killed his mother in **Kronborg Slot** (tel. 49–21–80–88; admission 30kr; open May–Sept., daily 10:30–5; shorter hrs off season), the alleged model for Elsinore Castle in Shakespeare's *Hamlet*. In the castle's dungeon, there's a massive stone statue of Holgar the Dane, the heroic Viking who supposedly walked all the way from France to return to his homeland. According to legend, Holgar will rise from the dead if ever Denmark should need him in battle. Lesser known, but still worthwhile, is **Sankt Maria's Kirke** (Sankt Annagade 38, tel. 49–21–17–74; open daily noon–3; 10kr guided tours at 2), said to be the best-preserved monastery in northern Europe. Its gently humorous frescoes are sure to win over even avowed atheists. Helsingør's **tourist information office** (tel. 49–21–13–33; open mid-June–Aug., weekdays 9:30–7, Sat. 10–6; shorter hrs off season) is across from the train station at Havnepladsen 3.

Helsingør is practically within swimming range of Sweden. Two ferry lines make the 25-minute crossing to Helsingborg every 20 minutes. **Sundbusserne** (tel. 49–21–35–45; 14kr one way, 7.50kr extra for bikes) is the cheapest, but **Scandlines** (tel. 49–26–26–40; 19kr one way, 28kr round trip, bikes included) operates all night long. Helsingør's **train station** (tel. 49–21–12–55) is a one-hour ride (35kr) from Copenhagen.

WHERE TO SLEEP AND EAT • Once a count's summer home, **Helsingør Vandrerhjem** (Nørdre Strandvej 24, tel. 49–21–16–40; cash only) is now a first-rate, HI-affiliated hostel with family-size rooms (doubles 228kr), dorm rooms (beds 87kr), and a backyard beach. From Copenhagen take the train to Marienlyst station (45 min, 28 kr); from there it's a short, well-marked walk to the hostel. If you're coming from the Helsingør station, take Bus 340. The **Kammer Kafféen** (Havnepladsen 1, tel. 49–28–20–52; cash only), next to the tourist office, has a lively atmosphere and good, cheap food.

HILLEROD

Visiting **Frederiksborg Slot** (tel. 42–26–04–39; admission 30kr; open May–Sept., daily 10–5; shorter hrs off season) is like being transported back to the decadent age of Romanticism, when bigger was better and architecture was dictated by royal whimsy. Built by Frederick II and his son Christian IV, this Dutch Renaissance extravaganza was first the favorite residence of Danish kings, later the site of royal coronations, and is now a museum of Danish national history. Sunday services are held for the public in the lavishly ornamented baroque chapel, and organists give free concerts on the famous Compenius organ Thursday at 1:30. Hillerød's **tourist information office** (Slotsgade 52; tel. 42–26–28–52; open June–Aug., weekdays 9–6, Sat. 9–5; shorter hrs off season) is just outside the castle, a 15-minute walk west of the train station through the old town. The train ride from Copenhagen (30kr) takes 40 minutes.

Though Hilleroø's sights can be seen in a single day, **Hillerød Campground** (Blytækkervej 18, tel. 42–26–48–54; open May–mid-Sept.), a 15-minute walk south of town, has campsites for 44kr per person. **Torvets Pizza Kebob** (in Torvecentret, tel. 42–26–11–19; closed Sun.) serves falafel sandwiches, pastas, and pizzas, all under 50kr.

HUMLEBAEK

The **Louisiana Museum of Modern Art** (Gammel Strandvej 13, tel. 46–19–07–19; admission 49kr; open daily 10–5, Wed. until 10), in Humlebæk, has a stunning collection of unconventional modern sculptures and paintings by Henry Moore, Max Ernst, Alberto Giacometti, and others. The museum is itself a masterpiece: Glass walls give gorgeous views of the sea and surrounding lush countryside, blurring the distinction between nature and art. Humlebæk is about 35 km (21 mi) north of Copenhagen (40 min, 35kr); save by buying a combination round-trip train ticket and museum admission from the Copenhagen DSB for 98kr. You can also take the train from Helsingør (13 min, 15kr) or Bus 733 from Hillerød (15 min, 20kr).

KLAMPENBORG

For those who want to take a relaxing day trip out of the city, Klampenborg has dual appeal. Just two minutes from the train station is crowded but beautiful **Bellevue** beach, where Danes and tourists alike come to soak up the summer sun. A 15-minute walk in the opposite direction takes you through **Dyrehaven** (Deer Park), the old royal hunting grounds, to the world's oldest amusement park, **Bakken** (tel. 39–63–73–00; admission free, rides 20kr; open Apr.–Aug., daily 2–midnight), with a wooden roller coaster built in 1932. Klampenborg is a 20-minute train ride (20kr) from Copenhagen.

ROSKILDE

Roskilde's role as the medieval capital of Denmark is evidenced today by its many ancient churches and monasteries. Most impressive is the huge cathedral **Roskilde Domkirke,** whose architecture, which evolved over five centuries, is as varied as the royal tombs inside. The most ornate tomb belongs to Denmark's favorite king, Christian IV; it's surrounded by life-size murals and a Thorvaldsen sculpture. The cathedral is frequently closed to the public for special events and masses, so call ahead to confirm hours. *Domkirkepladsen, tel. 46–35–27–00. Admission: 10kr. Open mid-June–Sept., weekdays 9–4:45, Sat. 9–noon, Sun. 12:30–4:45; shorter hrs off season.*

As intriguing as the cathedral is the **Vikingskibshallen** (Viking Ship Museum), which displays five Viking wrecks unearthed near Roskilde in 1962 and then expertly pieced together. Don't miss the 15-minute film (in English) that shows how the painstaking excavation process was completed. To test your sea legs, the museum lets you help sail modern copies of Viking ships from its collection (40kr; late July–mid-Aug., daily 11–3:30). Strandengen, tel. 46–35–65–55. Admission: 30kr. Open Apr.–Oct., daily 9–5; Nov.–Mar., daily 10–4.

The last weekend of June, Roskilde hosts a four-day **music festival**; big acts like Bob Dylan, The Cranberries, and Red Hot Chili Peppers have performed in the past. Tickets (US$130) sell out months in advance; for information, contact **clubroskilde** (tel. 33–15–62–64, fax 33–15–62–70) in Copenhagen. The friendly, helpful staff at Roskilde's **tourist information office** (Gullandstræde 15, tel. 46–35–27–00; open Apr.–June, weekdays 9–5, Sat. 10–1; July–Aug., weekdays 9–6, Sat. 9–3, Sun. 10–2; shorter hrs off season) can answer questions about the festival, as well as provide general information on Roskilde. To get here, take the train from Copenhagen (40 min, 35kr), or Bus 600S from Hillerød (50 min, 35kr).

WHERE TO SLEEP AND EAT • At the **Roskilde Campground** (Baunehøjvej 7, tel. 46–75–79–96; closed mid-Sept.–Mar.) you can camp (50kr per person), or rent a six-person cabin (225kr plus 50kr per person) or plush apartment (350kr plus 50kr per person). Sandwiched between a beach and green fields just 4 km (2½ mi) north of town, it feels like a vacation resort. Take Bus 603 to get here. At the **HI hostel** (Hørhusene 61, tel. 46–35–21–84, fax 46–36–66–90; lockout noon–4; closed Jan.; cash only) beds are 80kr and doubles are 200kr. The hostel is 3 km (2 mi) east of town; take Bus 601 or 604. If you're coming for the Roskilde music festival, make reservations no later than May or try the festival campground, which is free for ticket holders. For cheap eats, try the pizza and kebab places along **Skomagergade,** the central pedestrian street.

The tourist offices of Aalborg, Århus, Odense, and Roskilde offer a free "Meet the Danes" program: With 24-hour notice, they will set you up with some friendly, English-speaking Danish folk for an evening.

FYN

The island of Fyn (Funen in English) is said to be the most Danish part of Denmark: small, farm-filled, friendly, and tranquil. The main city, Odense, is a far cry from a metropolis, though it does tout itself as the birthplace of Hans Christian Andersen. Fyn's tiny, castle-covered islands are magical, and the Danish sun seems to shine more often here than anywhere else, making it the most popular part of Denmark for biking and camping. Pick up a copy of *Cykelguide Fyn* (75kr), a helpful guide featuring detailed cycling maps and route descriptions, at the tourist information office in Odense (*see below*) or at a local bookstore.

ODENSE

Named in honor of Odin, the Nordic god of hospitality, the biggest city on Fyn is an odd cross between a provincial village and mecca for the alternative and avant-garde. Tucked among its redbrick streets (many of which are decked with strands of kitschy plastic flags depicting Hans Christian Andersen) are several surprisingly progressive art museums, theaters, and cafés. Still, if you can't stomach quaintness and quietude, you might very well find this town as underwhelming as Andersen did. A couple of days here is plenty.

BASICS

To find the Odense **tourist information office** (tel. 66–12–75–20; open mid-June–Aug., Mon.–Sat. 9–7, Sun. 11–7; Sept.–mid-June, weekdays 9:30–4:30, Sat. 10–1), housed in the Rådhuset, walk south on Jernbanegade from the train station and turn left on Vestergade. The office books accommodations for a 25kr fee. The town's main **post office** (tel. 65–42–02–00) is at Dannebrogsgade 2, but the one at Lille Gfbrøøderstræde (tel. 65–42–02–00) is closer to the center of town.

COMING AND GOING

The main train station, **Odense Bånegards Center** (Østre Stationsvej 27, tel. 70–30–14–15), is on the northern edge of town, a 10-minute walk from the city center. IC trains offer the fastest service from Copenhagen (2½ hrs, 158kr); the train passes through the Great Belt tunnel.

GETTING AROUND

Although most of the town can easily be seen on foot, several sights and most budget accommodations are best reached by bus or bike. The two main bus-departure points are at the train station and on Klingenberg, the city hall square. Buses, which you pay for as you board, generally cost 5kr–10kr (exact change required). The **Adventure Pass** (90kr two days, 50kr one day), available at the train station, tourist office, and hostels, gets you free public transportation within Odense, as well as free admission or discounts to most museums. For general **bus information,** dial 66–13–13–72 ext. 2929. Rent bikes at **City Cykel** (Vestergade 27, tel. 66–13–97–83) for 50kr per day.

WHERE TO SLEEP

Del Lille Hotel. On a quiet street a 10-minute walk from the train station, this quaint hotel has the cheapest rooms in town. Doubles are 350kr, 450kr with bath (breakfast included). *Dronningensgade 5, tel. 66–12–28–21. Cash only.*

Hotel Ydes. This bright, colorful hotel is basic, but a nice change from barracks-style accommodations. The plain, white, hospital-style rooms are clean and comfortable. Doubles cost 360kr, 450kr with bath. *Hans Tausensgade 11, tel. 66–12–11–31. 984 ft from main train station; right from station, left onto Hans Tausensgade.*

Odense Vandrehjem. In a quiet neighborhood just 2 km (1 mi) from the city center you'll find a manor house-turned-hostel offering kitchen (bring your own plates and utensils), laundry, and TV room. Dorm beds are 75kr, doubles and quads 200kr–320kr, breakfast 40kr, sheets 40kr. *Kragsbjergvej 121, tel. 66–13–04–25, fax 65–91–28–63. From bus or train station, Bus 61 or 62 to Kragsbjergvej. Lockout noon–4. Cash only. Closed Dec.–mid-Jan.*

CAMPING • DCU Camping. This place is near idyllic Fruens Bøge park and the Fyn Village Museum—but far from everything else. Grass and trees compensate for highway noise. Sites are 40kr per person, cabins 165kr–195kr. Amenities include a kitchen, laundry, store, and swimming pool. *Odensevej 102, tel. 66–11–47–02. From Klingenberg, Bus 41 or 81 to Fruens Bøge. Showers. Closed mid-Oct.–mid-Mar.*

FOOD

Most cafés and restaurants are on or near Vestergade and Brandt's Passage.

Babylon. Good, fast, cheap Middle Eastern and Italian food is served in this cute café with outdoor tables. Kebabs are under 40kr. *Klaregade 14, tel. 66–14–82–99. Cash only.*

Cafe Cuckoo's Nest. This popular, relaxed place—with an extra-friendly staff and an outdoor patio—serves sandwiches and omelets for less than 50 kr. *Vestergade 73, next to Brandt's Passage, tel. 65–91–57–87. Cash only.*

Den Grimme Ælling. The "Ugly Duckling" is a homey place with pine furnishings. It's popular with tourists and locals alike for its all-you-can-eat, hot and cold buffet: Lunch (70kr) includes unlimited beer, wine, and soft drinks. Dinner is 100kr plus drinks. *Hans Jensens Stræde 1, tel. 65–91–70–30.*

Grøn Mad i Kærnehuset. This funky vegetarian cooperative offers whatever's in the stars that day; dinner (40kr) is served only one hour a night, from 6 to 7. *Nedergade 6, no phone. Closed Mon. Closed July.*

WORTH SEEING

The **Hans Christian Andersen Hus** (Hans Jensens Stræde 37–45, tel. 66–13–13–72 ext. 4611; admission 25kr; open June–Aug., daily 9–6; shorter hrs off season) fancies itself a "literary museum," but its collection of Andersen's personal effects don't shed much light on the author or his work. At the **H. C. Andersens Barndomshjem** (Munkemøllestræde 3–5, tel. 66–13–13–72 ext. 4611; admission 5kr; open June–Aug., daily 10–4; shorter hrs off season), Andersen's childhood home, the highlight is a brief tour of three tiny rooms. To the rescue comes **Brandt's Klædefabrik** (Brandt's Passage 37–43, tel. 66–13–78–97; open July–Aug., daily 10–5; closed Mon. off season). Once a cloth mill, it now houses three museums: the **Danske Presse Museet** (Danish Printing Museum; tel. 66–12–10–20; admission 20kr), the **Museet for Fotokunst** (Museum of Photographic Art; tel. 66–13–78–16; admission 20kr), and **Kunst-hallen** (Art Gallery; tel. 66–13–73–10; admission 25kr), all of which boast first-rate exhibits. A discount ticket good for admission to all three museums costs 40kr.

The **Fyns Kunstmuseum** (Jernbanegade 13, tel. 66–13–13–72 ext. 4611; admission 15kr–25kr; open July–Aug., daily 10–5; closed Mon. off season) houses modern and abstract art pieces, as well as works by the Fyn group, the nationally famous artists who favored natural renditions of the local landscape and people, 1900–1930. At the Møntergarden (Overgade 48–50, tel. 66–13–13–72 ext. 4611; admission 15kr; open July–Aug., daily 10–5; closed Mon. off season), or city museum, explore eclectic exhibits on Odense's urban and cultural history from the Viking age to the 20th century. The museum is in a complex that dates from the 16th to the 18th centuries. The **Tidens Samling** (Brandt's Passage 29, 2nd floor, tel. 65–91–19–42; admission 25kr; open daily 10–5) is a small museum where you can view clothes and furnishings of the past. It's particularly popular with families, since children are allowed to play with some of the antique toys.

AFTER DARK

Odense's nightlife has a decidedly cosmopolitan flair. **Musikhuset** (Vestergade 68, Arkaden, tel. 66–14–09–01; cover free) plays rock, jazz, and blues Thursday–Saturday, and holds tipsy karaoke sessions Monday and Wednesday at 10, and Friday and Saturday at 10:30. **Frederik's Café** (Brogade 3, tel. 65–91–20–91) draws a mostly gay crowd for cocktails and chatter. The lively café/theater **Café Biografen** (Brandt's Klædefabrik, tel. 66–13–16–16) shows quality American and European films.

NEAR ODENSE

EGESKOV SLOT

The difficulty of getting to the isolated Egeskov Slot, the so-called "floating castle," only adds to its allure. The 100kr admission fee is unusually high, but worth every øre if you have a passion for castle architecture, hunting trophies, labyrinthine gardens, or vampire lore. Egeskov means "oak forest" in Danish and refers to the stand of trees felled in about 1540 to form the piles on which the rose-stone structure was erected in the middle of a lake. One ticket gives you access to all the gardens, and a museum, which houses historical airplanes, cars, motorcycles, and carriages. You also get to see a few unoccupied castle rooms, but you can't wander around the parts of the castle still inhabited by Count and Countess Ahlefeldt-Laurvig-Bille. To reach the castle, take the Odense–Svendborg train to Kværndrup (40 min, 38kr). From the station, turn right and walk 2 km (1 mi) down Bøjdenvej (follow the signs), or wait for the hourly bus. *Egeskovgade 18, tel. 62–27–16–25. Open May–Sept., daily 10–5.*

AERO

If you spend much time on the island of Ærø, you'll come to believe that the tiny town of **Ærøskøbing** occupies the most delectable corner of Denmark, with fresh sea air, indigo water, and deep-green fields. The town's present claim to fame is the internationally renowned **Flaskeskibsmuseet** (Smedegade 22, tel. 62–52–29–51; admission 20kr; open May–Oct., daily 10–5; Nov.–Apr., Tues.–Thurs. 1–3, Sat. 10–2, Sun. 10–1), which houses an amazing collection of ships in bottles—all pieced together by a sailor, Peter "Bottle" Jacobsen. Make sure you leave enough time to scan the tons of museum fan mail, and the tombstone Jacobsen designed for himself, but, alas, was never laid beneath.

The **tourist office** (Vestergade 1B, tel. 62–52–13–00; open mid-June–Aug., weekdays 9–5, Sat. 10–3; shorter hrs off season) will direct you to the small beachside **hostel** (Smedevejen 15, tel. 62–52–10–44; beds 74kr; closed Oct.–Mar.), which rents bikes for 40kr, or to the scenic **Ærøskøbing Campingplads** (Sygehusvej 40B, tel. 62–52–18–54; 42kr per person; closed Oct.–Mar.). They'll also help you find a cheap B&B—expect to pay 250kr per double. At the **Waffelbageriet** (Vestergade 21), join the line of people waiting to buy the "Ærøskøbing special" (16kr)—a waffle cone of walnut ice cream topped with maple syrup and whipped cream. At night head for the harborside bar, **Arrebo** (Vestergade 4, tel. 62–52–28–58), which has billiard tables and free live music (mainly blues and '70s tunes) most summer nights.

COMING AND GOING

Svendborg and **Faaborg,** each an hour from Odense by train (44kr), are the most practical departure points for Ærø Island. From Svendborg's harbor—located just east of the train station on Frederiks-

FOLLOW THE LEGO-BRICK ROAD

Lego means "play well" in Danish, and happy children all over the world have grown up with Lego sets. Hop the train to Vejle, then Bus 912 to Billund (30 min, 30kr) to revel in scaled-down versions of cities, towns, villages, working harbors and airports (complete with sound effects), even a tiny Statue of Liberty—all built with millions of tiny, brightly colored Lego bricks. Admission to Legoland is 100kr–110kr; open April–September, daily 10–8. For information, dial 75-33-13-33.

gade—the ferry takes you to Ærøskøbing (1¼ hr, 61kr one way, 107kr round trip). Another option is the ferry that connects Faaborg with Søby (1 hr, 61kr one way, 107kr round trip), which is timed to meet the hourly bus to Ærøskøbing. It's a good idea to ask your skipper to notify the bus driver that there's a passenger on board, since the ferries sometimes run late. Expect to pay an extra 18kr (30kr round trip) to bring your bike on the ferry. If you're only planning a day trip to Ærø from Odense, consider a **one-day bus-and-ferry pass** (150kr), available at Odense's train station. Plan ahead—ferries only run a few times each day.

JYLLAND

The Jylland (Jutland) peninsula, the only part of Denmark attached to mainland Europe, is the largest of Denmark's regions, home to two-thirds of its population. The landscape is more dynamic and diverse than that of any other part of Denmark, with vast fjords, moors, and sand dunes, the country's best beaches and highest "mountains" (hills, really), and the famous meeting point off Skagen of the Baltic and North seas. The countryside is thoroughly accessible by bicycle; never-ending bike paths crisscross all of Jylland, and two-wheelers are allowed on nearly all public transport systems. There's a Viking flavor to Århus, Denmark's second-largest city, and a jovial atmosphere to Aalborg, which has the longest stretch of bars and discotheques in the country. Best of all, Jylland is less touristed than Sjælland and Fyn, giving you the chance to hang with **jyderne** (locals) and discover the true meaning of *hyggeligt*.

Jylland is also a popular jumping-off point for Norway, Sweden, England, and the Faroe Islands. From **Frederikshavn,** you can hop a Læsø Færgen (tel. 98–42–83–00) catamaran to Göteberg, Sweden (1¾ hrs; weekdays 50kr, weekends 60kr); a Stena (tel. 96–20–02–00) ferry to Oslo, Norway (8½–12 hrs, 200kr); or a Color Line (tel. 99–56–20–00) ferry to Kristiansand, Norway (6 hrs, 226kr–274kr). From **Esbjerg,** DFDS Scandinavian Seaways (tel. 79–17–79–17) goes to Harwich (19½ hrs, 550kr–1090kr; lower prices in winter); Smyril Line (tel. 33–16–40–04) sails to the Faroe Islands (2 days, 1,260kr) and Iceland (4 days, 1,980kr); and DSB (tel. 75–12–33–77) takes you to Fanø (12 min, 22kr).

ARHUS

Århus, home to a major university, has cafés and bars that buzz with activity; it also hosts two popular annual festivals, one for jazz in early July and one for civic pride (and beer drinking) in mid-September. Thanks to its ripe old age—Århus was first settled by Vikings, who called it "Aros," an Old Norse word meaning "river mouth"—the city has two 13th-century cathedrals, an Old Town whose streets and buildings date from the 16th century, and one of Denmark's best prehistory museums. The **tourist office** (in Rådhuset, tel. 86–12–16–00; open mid-June–Aug., weekdays 9:30–6, Sat. 9:30–5, Sun. 9:30–1; shorter hrs off season), provides free maps and B&B listings. The **post office** (postal code 8000) is at Banegårdspladsen 1A, next to the train station.

COMING AND GOING

The **train station** (tel. 86–18–17–78), on the city center's southern edge, has trains to Copenhagen (4½ hrs, 220kr), Odense (2 hrs, 134kr), Aalborg (1½ hrs, 108kr), and Silkeborg (1 hr, 54kr). The **bus station** (Fredensgade 45, tel. 86–12–86–22), east of the train station, serves Copenhagen (4½ hrs, 280kr), Aalborg (2 hrs, 99kr), and Silkeborg (1 hr, 43kr). You can also jet out of Århus's airport, Billund Lufthavn (tel. 76–50–50–50).

GETTING AROUND

You can catch most local buses in front of the train station or along Park Allé, near the Rådhus; enter buses at the rear and buy your ticket (13kr), valid for two hours, from the automatic machine on board. The **tourist multiride ticket** (45kr), valid on all buses for 24 hours, gets you free sightseeing tours, and the **Passport** (110kr for two days, 155kr per week) allows unlimited bus travel and free admission to most major attractions; for information on both, dial 89–46–56–00. Better yet, throw on a pair of comfortable shoes and walk, or rent a bike (50kr first day, 35kr per each additional day) at **Asmussen G Cykelsportcenter** (Fredensgade 54, near train station, tel. 86–19–57–00).

WHERE TO SLEEP

Århus City Sleep-In. This place is a good choice if you're short on cash, as its central, cheap, and pleasant, and offers bike rental (50kr) and luggage storage to boot. Dorm beds are 75kr, 105kr with sheets; doubles are 180kr, 240kr with bath. *Havnegade 20, tel. 86–19–20–55, fax 86–19–18–11. Kitchen, laundry. Cash only.*

Eriksen's Hotel. Look for this clean and cosy hotel about a block west of the train station. Doubles are 420kr, 480kr with breakfast. *Banegårdsgade 6–8, tel. 86–13–62–96, fax 86–13–76–76.*

Plaza Hotel Århus. This recently rebuilt hotel includes a steak restaurant on the ground floor. Most of the rooms have been renovated; all have colorful interiors. Doubles cost 660kr, including breakfast. *Banegårdsplads 14, tel. 86–12–41–22, fax 86–20–29–04. Restaurant.*

HOSTEL • Århus Vandrerhjem. The idyllic wooded setting near the beach makes up for the 3-km (2-mi) trek north of the city center. Beds are 70kr in dorm-style rooms and 106kr in semiprivate rooms. They'll even store your luggage here; just ask. *Marienlundsvej 10, tel. 86–16–72–98, fax 86–10–55–60. From train station, Bus 1 to last stop. Reception open daily 7:30 AM–10 AM and 4 PM–10 PM. Kitchen, laundry. Closed mid-Dec.–mid-Jan.*

CAMPING • Blommehaven Campground. Four kilometers (2½ miles) south of town is a nature lover's dream, set in the heart of the Marselisborg Forest. Rent a bike (50kr) to explore the deer park, wooded trails, and a beach. The pretty campsites, hedged by rose bushes, cost 46kr per person; cabins cost 190kr–320kr plus 46kr per person. The campground offers clean, modern bathrooms, a minimarket, and a kitchen. *Orneredevej 35, tel. 86–27–02–07. From train station, Bus 19. Closed mid-Sept.–Mar.*

FOOD

As a university town, Århus is loaded with affordable, atmospheric eating spots, cafés, and good ethnic restaurants, especially in the Latin Quarter, northwest of Domkirkepladsen, or along Frederiksgade, north of Rådhuspladsen. There's also a **farmer's market** (Wed. and Sat. mornings) at Domkirkepladsen.

Café Smagløs. The "Tasteless Café" has a popular 14kr breakfast, a 38kr–48kr brunch, and light meals, as well as a funky assortment of knickknacks, mismatched chairs, and customers. *Klostertorv 7, tel. 86–13–51–33. Cash only.*

Gyngen Restaurant. The restaurant's friendly staff are part of a government-funded social project for the unemployed. A diverse lunch menu includes Indian dal with rice, hummus plate, and sandwiches. Dinner menu limited to a single daily special (55kr), often followed by live music. *Mejlgade 53, tel. 86–19–22–55. Closed Sun. Cash only.*

Rådhus Kafeen. If you're looking for Danish food, this is the place to visit. Smørrebrød and other light meals are served for less than 50kr. *Sønder Allé 3, near Rådhus, tel. 86–12–37–74. Cash only.*

WORTH SEEING

Don't leave Århus without visiting **Huset** (Vesterallé 15, tel. 86–12–27–95; open Mon.–Thurs. 9 AM–10:30 PM, Fri. until 9, Sun. 10–4), a cultural center with live music, art exhibitions, and an arts-and-crafts studio, where you can practice woodworking, batik, and photography for a small fee. **Århus Koncerthus** (Thomas Jensens Allé, tel. 89–31–82–10; open daily 11–9) hosts musical performances (50kr–350kr, free weekends) and free art exhibits. The brewery **Ceres Bryggerierne** (Ceres Allé 1, tel.

AS AMERICAN AS APPLE PIE

Since 1912, Aalborg's Danish-American Association has annually hosted the largest Fourth of July celebration outside the United States. The highlight, at sprawling Kilde Park in Rebild (20 km/12 mi south of Aalborg), draws thousands of picknickers for a full day of bluegrass music and fireworks, and occasionally there's a celebrity Yank handy to slice the apple pie. Special buses (30 min, 70kr round trip) transport tourists to Kilde Park from Aalborg's tourist office (tel. 98–12–60–22).

86–12–58–55; closed Dec.) offers 5kr guided tours (mid-June–Aug., Tues. and Thurs. at 9, Wed. at 2; off season, Wed. at 2 only) with free beer at the end; book tickets through the tourist information office.

ARHUS KUNST MUSEUM • There's a little of everything here: classical paintings from the Danish golden age, Danish works from the 1900s, some German canvases, a decent modern art collection, and a few Warhols. *Vennelystparken, tel. 86–13–52–55. From Park Allé, Bus 1, 6, 9, 56, or 58. Admission: 30kr, 40kr special exhibits. Open Tues.–Sun. 10–5.*

DEN GAMLE BY • You could spend all day exploring Århus's **Old Town,** a reconstructed village that features 75 half-timbered houses, shops, and a mill, all meticulously re-created with period interiors. It's also right next to the **Botanic Gardens,** a good place to relax with a beer. *Warmingsvej 2–6, tel. 86–12–31–88. Bus 3, 14, or 25. Admission: 50kr (Apr.–Dec.), 40kr (Jan.–Mar.). Open June–Aug., daily 9–6; shorter hrs off season.*

KVINDEMUSEET • The "Women's Museum" has rotating exhibits on women's international history, issues, and roles in society. The café upstairs serves light lunches (under 50kr) and has piano concerts some Sunday afternoons. *Domkirkepladsen 5, tel. 86–13–61–44. Bus 1, 2, 3, 6, 7, 9, 11, 14, or 16. Admission: 15kr. Open June–mid-Sept., daily 10–5; mid-Sept.–May, Tues.–Sun. 10–4.*

MOESGARD FORHISTORISK MUSEET • Among Denmark's innumerable prehistory museums, this one stands out for its possession of the Grauballe Man, whose skin and hair have been miraculously preserved since his death in 80 BC. He was found in 1952 in a peat bog, where tannic acids prevented his decay; now he lies in a case, looking somewhat prunelike, but nonetheless human. The museum's other highlight is its 6-km (4-mi) "prehistoric trackway"—a scenic path that winds through the woods along a river, with Viking burial sites and a Stone Age temple at some of the stopping points. *Moesgaard Allé 20, tel. 89–42–45–45. From station or center, Bus 6. Admission: 30kr. Open May–mid-Sept., daily 10–5; mid-Sept.–Apr., Tues.–Sun. 10–4.*

AFTER DARK

The pamphlet "What's On in Århus," available at the tourist office, and the flyer "Ugen Ud," found in most cafés, list local clubs and discos. Cover charges at most live music joints hover around 40kr–50kr, but can soar up to 100kr when big names perform. Thursday often means cheap drinks and/or free covers. **Café Paradis** (Paradisgade 7–9, tel. 86–13–71–11), is better known as *Den Sidste,* "The Last," because of its late hours (until 6 AM). Århus's biggest discotheque is **Blitz** (Klostergade 34, tel. 86–19–10–99; cover 20kr–50kr; closed Sun.–Wed.), with a regular disco on the ground floor, an alternative disco (mostly hip-hop) below, and live bands rocking the upstairs bar. If you want to hear excellent jazz and blues in a more sophisticated atmosphere, head to **Glazz Huset** (Clemensborg/Strøget, tel. 86–12–13–12; cover 40kr; closed Sun).

If you're a café rat, head for the streets around Studsgade and Rosensgade, the area known as the Latin Quarter; the farther north you venture in this neighborhood, the more alternative the cafés and bars become. The local favorites are **Café Jorden** (Badstuegade 3A, tel. 86–19–72–22) and the artsy **Casablanca** (Rosensgade 12, tel. 86–13–82–22). The **Pan Café** (Jægergårdsgade 42, tel. 86–13–43–80) is the local gay and lesbian hangout. The **Pan disco** is open Wednesday and Thursday cover-free, Friday and Saturday for 45kr cover.

NEAR ARHUS

SILKEBORG

Silkeborg, in the heart of Denmark's Lake District, is paradise for outdoorsy folks. Just one hour (54kr) by train (tel. 86–82–32–00) from Århus, it offers one of the most scenic forests in Denmark, a river great for canoeing, an annual riverboat jazz festival (tel. 86–82–20–00 for information) in mid-June, and a sailing regatta in early August. Visit the town's helpful **tourist information office** (Åhavevej 2A, tel. 86–82–19–11; open weekdays 9–5) for tips on hiking and biking routes. **Cykel Klubben** (Frederiksggade 1, tel 86–82–26–33; closed Sun.) rents mountain bikes for 70kr per day. In Silkeborg's city center, the **Silkeborg Museum** (Hovegårdsvej, tel. 86–82–14–99; admission 20kr; open daily 10–5; shorter hrs off season) is the resting place of Grauballe Man's two peat-bog contemporaries, the Tollund Man and the Elling Woman, plus a host of Iron Age artifacts.

Leave the city behind by renting a canoe (50kr per hour) from **Silkeborg Kanocenter** (Åhave Allé 7, tel. 86–80–30–03), then floating down the **Remstrup Å River.** Row ashore at **Himmelbjerg,** Denmark's tallest "mountain," which affords a dramatic view of lakes and pine forests. The river runs between the trail-filled Dronningstolen Forest and Indelukket Park, where you'll find the **Silkeborg Museum of Art** (Gudenåvej 7–9, tel. 86–82–53–88; admission 30kr; open Apr.–Oct., Tues.–Sun. 10–5; shorter hrs off season), with exhibits of European and Danish art. Almost too idyllic and convenient to be true, the **Silkeborg Hostel** (Åhavevej 55, tel. 86–82–36–42, fax 86–81–27–77; beds 60kr–85kr; closed Dec.–Feb.) has dorm rooms overlooking the river, and lots of smaller 240kr–340kr family rooms. **Indelukkets Camping** (Vejlsøvej 7, tel. 86–82–22–01; 48kr per person) is on the river in a beautiful setting.

Sandy beaches run north and south from Århus, but the best is Moesgård Beach, 20 minutes south of the city in Dyrehaven (Deer Park). Take Bus 19 (summer only) to the end of the line.

AALBORG

Aalborg has a charming 16th-century atmosphere, a placid fjord-side setting, and a hearty nightlife—so hearty, in fact, that according to local lore the city installed a direct pipeline from the breweries to the pubs and bars along Jomfru Ane Gade to keep them from running dry. If you're thirsty, you might want to make a one-night stop here on your way to Norway, Sweden, or Limfjord, northern Jylland's famed waterway. Aalborg's main draw is north of the city in Nørresundby: **Lindholm Høje** (Vendilavej 11, tel. 98–17–55–22; admission 20kr; open Easter–mid-Oct., Tues.–Sun. 10–5, shorter hrs off season), a Viking burial ground and museum, is a must for anyone even remotely interested in the Vikings. Here you'll find 700 ancient graves marked by stones that form triangles, ovals, and ships, and great archaeological displays illustrating the Vikings' lifestyle, work habits, and burial customs. From the train station or city center, take Bus 6. In the **Rådhus Torv** (Town Hall Square), the elaborate, five-story **Jens Bangs Stenhus** (Jens Bang's Stone House) stands as a testament to the egotism of the 17th-century bourgeoisie. Despite his wealth and politicking, Bang was never elected to the town council, so a stone mason was instructed to add a sculpture on the house's south facade (facing town hall) of Bang sticking out his tongue.

COMING AND GOING

The **train station** (John F. Kennedy Pl. 3, tel. 98–16–16–66) offers service to Copenhagen (7 hrs, 246kr), Århus (1½ hrs, 108kr), and Frederikshavn (1 hr, 60kr). The adjacent **bus station** (tel. 98–11–11–11) has buses to Copenhagen (5½ hrs, 180kr; reservations required) and Esbjerg (3½ hrs, 165kr; buy tickets on the bus).

GETTING AROUND

Most of Aalborg is walkable; a network of pedestrian streets branches off Østerågade, which runs from the city center toward the train station, where it becomes Boulevarden. The **tourist office** (Østerågade 8, tel. 98–12–60–22; open June–Aug., weekdays 9–6, Sat. 9–5; shorter hrs off season) hands out free maps, and books rooms in private homes (doubles 240kr) for a 25kr fee. The famous **Jomfru Ane Gade,** where you'll find most restaurants, bars, and discotheques, is just off Bispensgade in the city center. Within Aalborg, most local buses (tel. 98–11–11–11) leave from Nytorv (the central square); drivers sell tickets (11kr), valid for one hour.

WHERE TO SLEEP AND EAT

The **HI Fjordparken Hostel and Campground** (Skydebanevej 50, tel. 98–11–60–44, fax 98–12–47–11; cash only) is in a beautiful area next to Limfjord, 2 km (1 mi) northwest of the center. The hostel has dorm beds (70kr–85kr) and family-size rooms with bath (170kr–410kr); the campground has sites for 44kr per person and family-size cabins for 175kr–235kr plus 44kr per person. Campers can use all of the hostel facilities, including the cafeteria, kitchen, laundry, and minimarket. From the bus station, take Bus 8. Aalborg's cheapest hotel is the **Aalborg Somandshjem** (Østerbro 27, tel. 98–12–19–00, fax 98–11–76–97), where clean doubles cost 475kr, 575kr with bath (breakfast included). From the bus station or city center, take Bus 1, 7, or 38. Far from the madness at Jomfru Ana Gade is **Cafe Kloster Torvet** (C. W. Obel Plads 4, tel. 98–16–86–11; cash only) a Parisian-style bistro with an under-50kr menu including lasagna, quiche, and desserts.

SKAGEN

Skagen lies at the northernmost tip of Jylland, where the Skagerrak and Kattegat seas meet and the mighty North Sea winds blow. Until the 19th century, only the hardiest Skagen fishermen eked out a fragile living here, battling the wind-whipped sands that destroyed their farmlands, wrecked ships, and even buried a church. In the early 1900s, new rail lines and a harbor transformed the town, and Scandinavian artists poured in, lured by the rugged beauty of the dunes, moors, and water. Today Skagen is a holiday resort full of first-rate museums, second-rate galleries, picturesque yellow houses, and the same craggy shoreline that withstood the sea's punishment for centuries. It is also home to a much-loved folk music festival held the last weekend in June; contact the tourist office (*see below*) for information.

Skagen's best attraction, the landscape, is free. For a wet and wild experience, walk north along the beach to the point where the two seas meet in an endless clashing of waves. But do not let the sirens lure you in—a careless soul drowns offshore almost every year. To sample Skagen-inspired art, visit the **Skagen Museet** (Brøndumsvej 4, tel. 98–44–64–44; admission 40kr; open June–Aug., daily 10–6; shorter hrs off season). In July and August, the museum hosts a series of musical concerts (60kr) Thursday at 8 PM.

BASICS

You can get to Skagen only via Frederikshavn on privately owned trains (40 min) and buses (1 hr). Both cost 35kr, and rail passes are not valid. The **tourist office** (Sankt Laurentii Vej 22, tel. 98–44–13–77; open June–Aug., Mon.–Sat. 9–7; shorter hrs off season), conveniently located inside the train-and-bus station, will book you a room in a private home (doubles 250kr–300kr) for a 35kr fee. Rent bikes (60kr) at **Cykeludlejning** (outside station, tel. 98–44–10–70).

WHERE TO SLEEP

The **Gammel Skagen Hostel** (Højensvej 32, tel. 98–44–13–56, fax 98–45–08–17; beds 85kr, doubles 220kr–250kr; closed Dec.–Jan.; cash only), 4 km (2½ mi) from town in Gammel Skagen, takes phone reservations daily 9–11 and 4–8; from the train station, take Bus 79. Infinitely more convenient, though, is **Skagens Ny Vandrerhjem** (Rolighedsvej 2, tel. 98–44–22–00, fax 98–44–22–55; dorm beds 75kr–85kr, no doubles, quads 320kr–340kr; cash only), just 1 km (⅔ mi) south of the train station; take Bus 79 if you don't want to walk. It's usually fully booked in summer, so call ahead; it also offers kitchen and laundry facilities. The home and art gallery of Orla Andersen (Oddevej 11, tel. 98–45–16–48) doubles an informal **sleep-in.** Andersen lets travelers pitch a tent on his lawn or lay a sleeping bag on his floor for 75kr, kitchen facilities and shower included. He also has four doubles (350kr each). Payment by cash only. The cheapest of Skagen's nice hotels is **Skagen Sømandshjem** (Østre Strandvej, near harbor, tel. 98–44–25–88, fax 98–44–30–28), where doubles go for a whopping 490kr, 595kr with bath (breakfast included). To rent a room in a **private home** (doubles from 200kr), look for VÆRELSER signs. The most accessible campground, **Grenen Camping** (Fyrvej 16, tel. 98–44–25–46; closed Sept.–Apr.; cash only), is 1½ km (¾ mi) north of town; take Bus 79. Tent sites cost 49kr, cabins 140kr plus 49kr per person. You'll find cheap pizza and kebab eateries along Havnevej between Sct. Laurenti Vej and Østre Strandvej. If you crave a romantic meal, head to the harbor; the tiny red cottages along the water are actually fish shops! Pick up a bag of fresh shrimp or some fish and chips, buy a bottle of wine at a local grocery, and settle down to watch your ship come in.

RIBE

Founded by Vikings around AD 705, Ribe is the oldest town in Denmark; it's also one of the best-preserved, despite several major floods and a fire that destroyed a third of the town in 1580. With a cathedral, a striking monastery, and a slew of old inns and houses lining the narrow, cobbled streets, Ribe is a charming place to pass a few days. For an unbeatable view, you can climb the redbrick tower (admission 7kr) of the 12th-century **Ribe Domkirke** (Torvet, tel. 75–42–06–19; open June–Aug., Mon.–Sat. 10–6, Sun. noon–6; shorter hrs off season). Outside the cathedral, in the main square, is Denmark's oldest inn, **Weis' Stue** (tel. 75–42–07–00), with rough-hewn farmer's tables, biblical frescoes, and pewter mugs dating back to 1700. From here you can join the night watchman on his rounds (June–Aug. at 8 PM and 10 PM, May and Sept. at 10 PM); by lantern light he rambles through Ribe, singing and stopping at various points to spill a little town history in Danish and English. Although you could wander Ribe's medieval streets all day, save time for the 13th-century **Sankt Catherine's Kirke and Abbey** (Sankt Catherine Plads, tel. 75–42–05–34; open daily 10–noon and 2–5), one of few Danish churches to survive the Reformation; admission to the cloister court is 2kr (free for the church). Across from the train station, the new multimillion-kroner **Ribes Vikinger** (Odin Plads, tel. 75–42–22–22; admission 40kr; open mid-June–mid-Sept., Tues.–Sun. 10–5; shorter hrs off season) houses an impressive collection of Viking artifacts and historical exhibits on Ribe.

Ribe's **tourist information office** (Torvet 3–5, tel. 75–42–15–00) has a free brochure with a map, and information on rooms in private homes (doubles 200kr). The **train station** (Dagmarsgade 16, tel. 75–42–00–46) serves Esbjerg (35 min, 32kr) and other destinations throughout Denmark via Bramming (20 min, 19kr) and Fredericia (1 hr 12 min, 82kr).

WHERE TO SLEEP AND EAT

Ribe's **HI hostel** (Sankt Pedersgade 16, tel. 75–42–06–20, fax 75–42–42–88; closed Dec.; cash only), on a quiet street two minutes' walk from the city center, has 85kr beds and rents bikes (50kr per day). The **campground** (Farupvej 2, tel. 75–41–07–77, fax 75–41–00–01; closed Nov.–Easter), in the woods 1½ km (¾ mi) from town, has campsites (49kr per person) and cabins (85kr plus 49kr per person); from train station take Bus 715. **Ribe's Café Nicolaj** (Sankt Nicolajgade 6, tel. 75–42–42–03; cash only) is where locals come to play backgammon, listen to jazz, or while away a few hours in the riverside garden. **Firenze** (Skolegade 6, tel. 75–42–42–11) serves up pastas and Ribe's best pizza (47kr–65kr).

FINLAND

C hances are, your idea of a prototypical Finn has ice cubes for eyes and all the personal charm of granite. True, there's no fawning affection among Finns, and their characteristic disdain for wasting words may leave you feeling somewhat chilled. But try to forgive the honest, hard-working Finns their curtness, for these are a people who have endured a tumultuous history: six centuries of Swedish rule (1155–1809), another 100 years under Russia's czars, a bloody civil war in 1918, and, of course, six months of darkness every winter. Despite such hardships, Suomi (Finnish for "Finland") has emerged a self-sufficient and prosperous nation. Indeed, the Finns have made the philosophy of *sisu*—grim perseverance and inexhaustible stamina—a sort of national credo.

When the Bolsheviks wrested the Russian Empire from Czar Nicholas II in 1917, they granted Finland independence, and the Russian Grand Duchy of Finland was nevermore. Ever since, Finland has attempted to practice neutrality, with varying degrees of success. A notable slip-up occurred during World War II, when Finland briefly joined forces with the Nazis to reclaim land from Russia. To their credit, the Finns refused to participate in Nazi atrocities, and ousted the Nazis from Lapland in 1945. After fully paying off its war debts (the only European country to do so), Finland has settled comfortably into an era of peace, and hasn't strayed far from the postwar Scandinavian political mold of commitment to UN peacekeeping missions, minimal crime, and a generous social-welfare system. These days, however, the social umbrella is contested, as the strain of providing relief to Finland's unemployed 16% prompts conservatives in the *eduskunta* (parliament) to urge a diminished role for government.

Although Finns are proud of their unique culture and heritage—Finland is one of the few countries that shared a border with the Soviet Union in 1939 and retained its independence—visitors will also detect traces of the Swedish and Russian cultures here, including a small Swedish-speaking population in the Åland Islands and a number of Russian Orthodox churches dotting the land. The country also offers excellent museums, lively clubs and bars, and unique festivals. But it's the landscape that will truly hook you, for Finland possesses Europe's last great tracts of wilderness. The country is 70% forest and boasts 187,000 glassy lakes. Nothing in the world is as stunning as a tree-fringed Finnish lake under summer's midnight sun, or in the dancing northern lights of winter.

BASICS

MONEY

US$1 = 5.1 markkaa and 1 markka = 20¢. The Finnish unit of currency is the markka (FIM), consisting of 100 penniä. You can exchange traveler's checks and cash at airports, train stations, and big hotels, but banks offer the best rates. ATMs in Finland widely accept Visa or MasterCard, and most towns have at least one 24-hour ATM.

HOW MUCH IT WILL COST • A cheap meal runs about FIM 40, a beer at a bar FIM 15–FIM 30, a 100-km (62-mi) train trip roughly FIM 45, and a double in a mid-range hotel about FIM 300. If you stay in hostels, you can get by on $55–$60 per day (not including transportation and museums), or even less if you take advantage of the kitchens in hostels and hotels. You're not expected to tip for services, but if your cab driver lugs your bags around or the waiterperson is wonderful, an extra FIM 5–FIM 10 is plenty.

COMING AND GOING

Although Finland is in the far northeastern quadrant of Europe, getting here doesn't have to be a Herculean task. The quickest, most direct route is to cross the Baltic Sea by ferry from Stockholm, Sweden. You can get to Finland with a Eurailpass, but traveling strictly by train will mean a long, roundabout journey through northern Sweden, which is poorly served by trains.

The ships that sail the Baltic are modern, comfortable, festive, and, if you pay for a seat rather than a cabin, cheap. **Silja Line** (tel. 08/222–140 in Stockholm; 09/180–4555 or 09/800–526–82 toll-free in Helsinki) sails twice daily from Stockholm to Turku (11 hrs, FIM 110), once daily from Stockholm to Helsinki (14 hrs, FIM 200), and once daily between Helsinki and Tallinn, Estonia (3½ hrs, FIM 100). **Viking Line** (tel. 08/452–4200 in Stockholm or 09/123–577 in Helsinki) sails frequently from Stockholm to Helsinki (15 hrs, FIM 115) and Turku via Mariehamn (12 hrs, FIM 69, free with ScanRail). Railpass holders get discounts, and prices often drop more than 50% when boats are underbooked; check with the ferry office for specifics.

Flying directly to Finland will save you from days and hours of travel by train and boat. **Finnair** serves Helsinki from London (FIM 2,000), Copenhagen (FIM 1,880), Amsterdam (FIM 1,530), Stockholm (FIM 1,030), Berlin (FIM 1,600), and St. Petersburg (FIM 1,350).

GETTING AROUND

Finland's train service is brisk and punctual, but the railway is inadequate for extensive travel. Fortunately, the highways are well maintained, and buses travel 90% of them. Hitchhiking is also safer and easier than in many European countries.

BY TRAIN • **Valtion Rautatiet (VR)** (Vilhonkatu 13, Helsinki, tel. 010–0121), the national railway, is clean and high-tech. Especially good are connections along the Helsinki–Tampere–Turku triangle. One of the three main lines can get you as far north as Kolari or Kemijärvi in Lapland (via Oulu from Helsinki). VR sends one "Sibelius" train daily to St. Petersburg (FIM 265). The Eurailpass is good for unlimited travel in Finland, and you can buy a **Finnrail pass** at all major stations, entitling you to unlimited train use for three days (FIM 540), five days (FIM 730), or 10 days (FIM 995). The **ScanRail pass** allows you five days of travel in 15 (FIM 1,080) or three weeks of unlimited travel (FIM 1,650).

BY BUS • Buses, a must for any traveler hoping to get off the beaten track in Finland, are also good for reaching St. Petersburg (3 per day; 8 hrs, FIM 234). Eurail and Finnrail passes aren't valid on buses, but the discount **Coach Holiday Ticket** (FIM 350) is good for 1,000 km (620 mi) of travel in Finland within two weeks. Buy tickets at the station or on board. Dial 9600–4000 (FIM 3.80 per minute) for information on long-distance bus travel.

BY PLANE • Some domestic fares on **Finnair** (tel. 09/800–34–66 toll-free) are quite cheap, especially in July. One option is the Finnair Holiday Ticket (US$500), which allows 10 domestic flights in one month. If you want to visit northern Lapland but don't fancy traveling 1,200 km (720 mi) over land, inquire about the Helsinki–Ivalo airfare (from FIM 1,060 round trip, FIM 530 one way).

BY BIKE • Bicycles are ideal for touring Finland. The main roads are excellent, the minor roads are deserted, the camping regulations are liberal (though most people use the plentiful wilderness huts), and June and July offer extended daylight hours. Best of all, Finland is essentially mountainless, and you can usually rent a bike for about FIM 30–FIM 50 per day and bring it on board trains and most long-distance buses.

FINLAND

NORWAY

Nuorgam
Utsjoki
Näätämö
Karigasniemi
Inarijärvi

Kilpisjärvi
Nakkälä
Inari
Ivalo
Raja-Jooseppi

Enontekiö
Hetta
*Porttipahdan
tekojärvi*
RUSSIA

Palojoensuu
Ommasjoki
*Lokan
tekojärvi*
E4/E75

Muonio

Kittilä
Sodankylä
Kemijoki

SWEDEN
E69
LAPLAND
Kemijärvi

Arctic Circle
Rovaniemi
Joutsijärvi
Arctic Circle
*Karhunkierros
Trekking Route*

Perä-Posio
Juuma
Kuusamo
Posio

Tornio
Kemi
20

E4/E75
5

Pudasjärvi

Oulu
Hailuoto
Raahe
Oulujoki
Puolanka
Suomussalmi

22
E63

8
Oulujärvi
Kajaani

Kalajoki
Pulkkila
Nivala
85
Otanmäki
Kuhmo

Kokkola
Kärsämäki
E63
Nurmes

Haapajärvi
E4/E75
Iisalmi
Pielinen

Vaasa
16
Kyyjärvi
5
Kuopio
Ilomantsi

8
Äänekoski
Kallavesi
17
Joensuu

Seinäjoki
Rieksämäki
Orivesi
N

12
23
Jyväskylä
23
Varkaus
Savonlinna

23
Parkano
E63
14
Punkaharju

Pori
Näsijärvi
Mikkeli
Kokonselkä
Parikkala

Rauma
11
Päijänne
Tampere
Ristiina
Saimaa

8
Hämeenlinna
Heinola
Imatra
*Lake
Ladoga*

12
Lahti
9
Lappeenranta

*Åland
(Ahvenanmaa)*
Turku
3
Kouvola
RUSSIA

2
Kotka
1

Salo
E18
Porvoo

Mariehamn
Baltic Sea
Hanko
(Hangö)
Tammisaari
(Ekenäs)
Helsinki
Gulf of Finland

Gulf
of
Bothnia

KEY
Rail Lines

0   50 miles
0   50 km

WHERE TO SLEEP

The cost of sleeping in Finland varies greatly, depending on your needs. Most **hotels** offer weekend discounts, and **hostels** cost FIM 70–FIM 120. The Finnish youth-hostel association, **Suomen Retkeilyma-jajärjestö (SRM),** is a member of Hostelling International. Prices for all HI hostels listed below are for members; nonmembers should expect to pay FIM 15 more. Technically, though, you could get away without paying a penni, since Finland's "everyman's right" grants legal permission to pitch a tent anywhere that's not obstructive (try the abandoned farms all over the countryside). **Campgrounds** (FIM 25–FIM 80 per person) have reasonably priced cottages (FIM 400–FIM 600 for a four-bed version), and throughout Lapland you'll find cheap or free **wilderness huts** with bunk beds and even firewood (replace what you use), where you can come and go as you please.

FOOD

International grub like pizzas, burgers, and sausages are among the cheapest options. Take advantage of breakfast deals (FIM 20–FIM 30) at your hotel or hostel, get your authentic-cuisine fix at lunch (FIM 35–FIM 45), and self-cater dinner to avoid paying FIM 50–FIM 60 at a restaurant. Specialties include *poro* (reindeer), *graavi lohi* (salt-cured salmon), *kalakukko* (freshwater fish baked with pork in a rye crust), and *karjalanpiirakka* (little rye knishes filled with potatoes or rice). Small pizzas (FIM 30–FIM 50) and salad bars (FIM 25–FIM 45) are vegetarian standards, and outdoor markets are common. *Olut* (beer) is big in Finland and comes in three classes: Class I is the cheapest and weakest; Class III, equal to U.S. beer, is the strongest beer sold in markets; and Class IV A and IV B are the most potent, sold only at state-run liquor stores called Alko. Outside Helsinki, beer usually costs less than FIM 20. The drinking age in Finland is 18 (beer and wine), or 20 to purchase vodka or hard alcohol.

> *With a population density of 16 people per square km, Finland is home to 50% of all people living above latitude 60° N.*

BUSINESS HOURS

Shops are generally open weekdays 9–5 and Saturday 9 to 1 or 2, and many department stores stay open weekdays until 6 or 8. Banks are open weekdays 9:15–4:15, post offices weekdays 8–5 and Saturday 10–5. Travel agencies are open weekdays 9–5. Alko, the state-run chain of liquor stores, is open Monday–Thursday 10–5, Friday 10–6, and Saturday 9–2. Almost everything is closed Sunday, but R-kioskis, which sell only basics (phone cards, cigarettes, soda, cookies), are usually open daily until 11 PM.

FESTIVALS AND HOLIDAYS

Finns hold a slew of festivals during their short summer. The **Pori Jazz Festival,** the **Savonlinna Opera Festival,** and the **Turku Ruisrock Festival,** all in July, have attracted international attention, but folks in every town find something to raise their glasses to. You should plan ahead if you're going to be in town during any festivities, and especially during the **Midsummer** weekend (around summer solstice in late June), when all of Finland effectively shuts down—the natives escape to the countryside and bus and train tickets become scarce.

PHONES

Country code: 358. Dial 118 for information. Many pay phones accept coins, but more accept only credit cards and phone cards, which you can buy at post offices and R-kioskis. Rates are constant on public phones; a two-minute local call costs FIM 2. From residential phones, international rates are lowest 10 PM–8 AM; during these hours a call to the United States or Australia costs FIM 3.89 per minute (dial 00 + country code + area code + phone number). For international information, dial 0100–0999. Access **AT&T** Direct Access[SM] (tel. 9800–100–10), **MCI** (tel. 9800–102–80), or **Sprint** (tel. 9800–102–84) from any phone.

MAIL

Postcards and letters (under 20 grams) sent abroad cost FIM 3.40; label your international mail PRIORI-TAIRE. You can receive mail at post offices all over Finland; have it sent to Your Name, Poste Restante, postal code, city, FINLAND.

EMERGENCIES

Dial 112 for an **ambulance** or the **fire** department, and 100–22 for **police.** Most towns have at least one 24-hour *apteekki* (pharmacy).

LANGUAGE

Finnish is a Finno-Ugric language, related closely to Estonian and distantly to Hungarian and Sami. As citizens of a bilingual state, Finns are required to learn Swedish, the primary language in some areas along the western coast, and most also speak English. If you're up for a challenge, try using these handy Finnish phrases: *hyvää päivää* or *hei* (good day or hello); *näkemiin* (goodbye); *olkaa hyvä* (please or you're welcome); *kiitos* (thank you); *missä on vessa?* (where is the bathroom?); *onko teillä . . .?* (do you have . . .?); *kyllä* (yes); *ei* (no); *puhutko englantia?* (do you speak English?); *anteeksi* (excuse me); and *paljonko . . . maksaa?* (how much does . . . cost?).

GAY AND LESBIAN TRAVELERS

Of the Scandinavian countries, Finland is the least accepting of homosexuality, though violence and threats rarely occur. Few establishments openly catering to gays and lesbians exist outside Helsinki. For more information, contact the helpful nonprofit gay and lesbian association **Seta** (Oikokatu 3, tel. 09/612–3233) in Helsinki, and ask about Seta chapters in Finland's other major towns.

HELSINKI

To the denizens of this friendly, safe, and cosmopolitan city, Helsinki is Finland. With 1 million residents in the city and its sprawling suburbs, Helsinki lays claim to one fifth of the total Finnish population, most of whom, it seems, chat incessantly on cellular phones or tap manically away on their laptops. Though Finland's love affair with technology is most obvious in Helsinki, the city's glamour stems as much from its magnificent neoclassical buildings lining elegant plazas as from its smartly attired businesspeople and students.

Around 1550, when King Gustav I, ruler of the Swedish-Finnish empire, uprooted a humble market town from the muddy mouth of the Vantaa River and replanted it on the Gulf of Finland (hoping to create a bustling trade mecca), Helsinki was born. In 1812, after Russia annexed Finland, Czar Alexander I declared Helsinki Finland's new capital and asked German architect Carl Ludvig Engel to bestow the city with a more appropriate stately style. In the 1950s, led by Alvar Aalto, architects began to fill the capital with outstanding modernist buildings. As a result of this long, passionate commitment to cutting-edge architecture, Helsinki has been called the last European city to be built as art.

BASICS

VISITOR INFORMATION

The **City Tourist Office** sells the invaluable **Helsinki Card** (one-day FIM 105, two-day FIM 135, three-day FIM 165), good for unlimited local transport, admission to about 50 citywide museums, and discounts at bars, restaurants, and theaters. *Pohjoisesplanadi 19, tel. 09/169–3757. Open June–Aug., weekdays 9–5, Sat. 9–3; shorter hrs off season.*

The **Finnish Tourist Board** (Eteläesplanadi 4, tel. 09/417–6911; open June–Aug., weekdays 8:30–5 and weekends 10–2; Sept.–May, weekdays 8:30–4), across from the City Tourist Office, has information on tours, long-distance travel, and camping and biking routes. **Hotellikeskus** (in train station's west wing, tel. 09/171–133; open June–Aug., Mon.–Sat. 9–7 and Sun. 10–6; shorter hrs off season) will book you a room in a hotel or hostel for FIM 12; it also sells the Helsinki Card.

AMERICAN EXPRESS

As in every other Finnish town, member services are handled by **Area Travel.** They'll cash personal checks, hold mail, and replace lost cards. *Mikonkatu 2D, 2nd floor, tel. 09/628–788. Open weekdays 9–1 and 2:15–4:30. Postal code: 00100.*

CHANGING MONEY

You'll get competitive rates at the airport, at banks, or at one of the numerous exchange offices, particularly **Forex** (expect to pay FIM 30 per transaction when changing traveler's checks). After hours, hotels and their stiff commissions may be your only choice.

EMBASSIES

Canada: *Pohjoisesplanadi 25B, tel. 09/171–141. Open weekdays 8:30–4:30.* **Great Britain:** *Itäinen Puistotie 17, tel. 09/2286–5100. Open weekdays 9–noon.* **United States:** *Itäinen Puistotie 14B, tel. 09/171–931. Open weekdays 9–noon.*

PHONES AND MAIL

The **main post office,** next to the train station, has poste restante, pay-after-you-call booths (which typically have long queues and poor connections), currency exchange, phone cards, and stamps. *Mannerheimintie 11, tel. 09/9800–7100 or 09/9800–8353. Open weekdays 9–5. Telephone center open weekdays 9 AM–10 PM, Sat. 10–4. Poste restante office open weekdays 7 AM–9 PM, Sat. 9–6, Sun. 11–9. Postal code: 00100.*

COMING AND GOING

The **train station** (tel. 010–0121) is in the city center, next to the main post office. Eight trains travel daily from Helsinki to Turku (2¼ hrs, FIM 90) and Tampere (2¾ hrs, FIM 90). **Kilroy Travels** (Mannerheimintie 5, tel. 09/680–7811), near the train station, helps with all budget booking needs. The **long-distance bus station** (tel. 09/613–681), on Salomonkatu across Mannerheimintie from the post office, sends buses from Helsinki to Turku (FIM 98). Helsinki is linked to Stockholm by two ferry lines: **Viking** (Katajanokan Terminaali, tel. 09/123–577) and **Silja** (Olympia Terminaali, tel. 09/180–4555 or 09/800–526–82 toll-free), which also goes to Travemünde, Germany (from FIM 470 in summer, FIM 300 in winter).

During summer, Finns delight in downing rapu (crayfish). Traditionally, you drink a shot of frosty schnapps for each rapu tail you munch; after 10 crayfish you'll be crawling around like a mud bug yourself.

The **Helsinki-Vantaa airport** (tel. 09/9600–8100) is about 20 km (12 mi) from Helsinki in Vantaa. Bus 615 (FIM 15) runs between the airport and Platform 12 in front of the train station. Quicker Finnair buses (FIM 24) run between the airport and the Finnair City Bus Terminal, next to the train station.

GETTING AROUND

Most hotels, restaurants, and sights are clustered on a single peninsula. The main street, **Mannerheimintie,** runs roughly north–south and intersects the other major street, **Aleksanterinkatu,** one block south of the train station. Most sights are concentrated within a few blocks of these streets and around the **Esplanadi** strolling park, off the south end of Mannerheimintie.

Hill-free Helsinki is perfect for walking. **Trams** and **buses** will help when you tire—trams are best in the city center, and buses are more helpful in the outskirts and suburbs. Tram 4 takes you north up Mannerheimintie, or east of the city center to the Katajanokka neighborhood. Tram 3T is a tourist tram (free June–Aug.) whose route carves a big figure eight through Helsinki, making it a great way to get oriented. Helsinki's one **Metro** line is more useful to commuters than travelers, and **taxis** are expensive. There are cheap, frequent **ferries** to the nearby islands, notably Suomenlinna and Pihlajasaari.

Each bus and tram line has its own schedule, but most lines run from about 5:30 AM or 6 AM to around midnight; get maps and schedules from the tourist office or from the Rautatientori Metro station under the train station. Tickets on all city transport lines cost FIM 9 and are valid for one hour; buy tickets from drivers or from automatic dispensers at metro stations. You can also purchase tourist passes good for one day (FIM 25), three days (FIM 50), or five days (FIM 75) of unlimited travel on all lines; passes are sold at the Rautatientori Metro station, tourist office, and R-kioskis.

WHERE TO SLEEP

Helsinki offers plain hotels, posh ones, and little in-between. The lower-end places may be bland, but they're not grimy, and most are less than 10 minutes' walk from the train station and city center. Many hotels also offer FIM 40–FIM 80 weekend discounts and may negotiate prices when uncrowded.

HELSINKI

Taivallahti

Taivalsaari

Sibeliuksen puisto ❶

Merikannontie

Mechelink.

Topeliuksenk.

Töölönk.

Sibeliuksenk.

Runebergink.

Mannerheimintie

Töölönlahti

Eläintarhantie

Kaisa

Pohjoinen Hesperiank.

Etelainen Hesperiank.

Caloniuksenk.

Apollonk.

Museok.

❹

Mannerheimintie

Kaisa

Hietaniemi Cemetery

Mechelinink.

Temppelik.

❸

Lutherink.

Nervanderink.

Kaisaniemenkatu

It. Teatterik.

Vilhonka

❻

Hietaniemenk.

Arkadiank.

❺

Train Station

City Stati

Lapinlahti

Mechelinink.

Hietaniemenk.

❽

Pohj. Rautajtiek.

Etel. Rautatiek.

Long-Distance Bus Station

Salomonk.

Kaivok.

Mannerheimintie

❾

Keskusk.

Alek

Länsiväylä

Lapinlahdentie

Lapinlahdenk.

Lapinrinne

Malmink.

Urho Kekkosenk.

Simonk.

Fredrikink.

Pohjoisesp.

AE

Yrjönk.

Porkkalank.

Lastenkodink.

❶❸

Eerikink.

Kalevank.

❶❹

Lönnrotink.

Albertink.

Annank.

❶❺

Uudenmaank.

P

Rool

Itämerenk.

❶❽

Ruoholanranta

Ruoholahdenk.

Abrahamink.

Hietalahdenk.

Köydenpunojenk.

Hietalahdenranta

Bulevardi

Iso

Mallask.

Punavuorenk.

Roobertink.

Merimiehenk.

Pursimiehenk.

Sepänk.

Jääkärink.

Ruoholahti

Hietalahti

Munkkisaarenk.

Hernesaarenk.

Telakkak.

Tehtaankatu

Rehbinderintie

Ehrensvärdintie

Merikatu

Me

❶❾

Sights ●

Ateneum, **9**

Eduskuntatalo, **5**

Kaapelitehdas, **18**

Kansallismuseo, **4**

Kauppatori, **16**

Pihlajasaari Island, **19**

Presidentinlinna/ Päävartio, **11**

Seurasaari, **1**

Suomenlinna, **17**

Temppeliaukio kirkko, **3**

Tuomiokirkko, **10**

Uspenskin katedraali, **12**

Lodging ○

Gasthaus Omapohja, **6**

Hostel Academica, **8**

Hostel Erottajanpuisto, **15**

Hotel Lönnrot, **14**

Kallion Retkeilymaja, **2**

Kongressikoti, **7**

Satakuntatalo, **13**

KEY

AE American Express Office

i Tourist Information

Rail Lines

0 _____ 1/4 mile

0 _____ 1/4 km

UNDER FIM 250 • Kongressikoti. The owner rents cozy doubles (FIM 240) in a narrow old building but usually leaves at 5 PM, so call ahead if you'll be late and need her to wait. All rooms share bath and kitchenette. *Snellmaninkatu 15, tel. 09/135–6839. Cash only.*

UNDER FIM 300 • Gasthaus Omapohja. This is Helsinki's oldest inn, and also its nicest budget option. Clean doubles with tall French windows cost FIM 280–370. Luggage storage is available. *Itäinen Teatterikuja 3, tel. 09/666–211. From train station, walk east on Vilhonkatu, left on tiny Itäinen Teatterikuja just past Finnish National Theatre. Laundry.*

Hotel Lönnrot. The Lönnrot offers small, clean rooms in a prime location, with good vistas of Lönnrotinkatu. Doubles cost FIM 280. *Lönnrotinkatu 16, tel. 09/693–2590. From train station, walk south on Mannerheimintie, right on Lönnrotinkatu, continue 3 blocks. Cash only.*

HOSTELS

Hostel Academica. All 115 nonsmoking rooms (dorm beds FIM 75, doubles FIM 290) at this part-time student dormitory come with toilets, kitchenettes, and refrigerators. Showers are an extra FIM 5. A buffet breakfast (FIM 28) is available at Perho Mechelin (*see* Food, *below*). Frills at Academica include a disco, pool, and sauna. *Hietaniemenkatu 14, tel. 09/1311–4334. From train station, follow Arkadiankatu, left on Runeberginkatu, right on Hietaniemenkatu. Reception open 24 hrs, checkout noon. Laundry. Closed Sept.–May.*

Hostel Erottajanpuisto (HI). This hostel is centrally located. There are only 15 rooms, but they've all got color TVs. Chat with other travelers in the lounge or ask questions of the extra-friendly staff. Dorm beds are FIM 115, doubles FIM 240, breakfast FIM 25–FIM 35. *Uudenmaankatu 9, tel. 09/642–169. From train station, walk south on Mannerheimintie, right on Erottajankatu, right on Uudenmaankatu. Reception open 24 hrs. Kitchen, laundry.*

Kallion Retkeilymaja. Despite a 10 AM–3 PM daily lockout, the 35 beds (in single-sex rooms) at this slightly cramped and creaky hostel are often full. Beds (all with lockers) cost FIM 60, sheets FIM 10, breakfast FIM 20. It's a social place, with a TV room, cafeteria, and bike rentals (FIM 30). *Porthaninkatu 2, tel. 09/7099–2590. Metro: Hakaniemi. Curfew 2 AM. Reception open 8 AM–11 PM. Kitchen, laundry. Closed Sept.–mid-June. Cash only.*

Satakuntatalo. You'll love this place for its on-site cafeteria and sauna (FIM 20 per hr), but its noon–2 PM daily lockout isn't so convenient. Suites (FIM 230) with three to five rooms share shower, toilet, phone, and kitchen. Dorm beds cost FIM 70, breakfast FIM 25. *Lapinrinne 1A, tel. 09/695–851. Metro: Kamppi; walk SW on Salomonkatu (becomes Lapinrinne). Reception open 24 hrs. Laundry. Closed Sept.–May.*

FOOD

If you require anything more than fresh fish, you'll find it hard to forage cheaply in Helsinki. If not, **Kauppatori** (Market Square) is jammed with umbrella-covered stands selling all kinds of sea creatures, raw and cooked. The market is open daily until early afternoon, though in summer it also has evening hours. Here you can also test your Finnish on vendors selling fresh vegetables and fruit, danishes, and cheese- or fruit-filled crêpes (both FIM 15), *lihapiirakka* (a beef- and rice-filled pastry; FIM 12), and strong coffee (FIM 6). Other smart food-shopping ideas include the discount markets **Alepa** and **Pirkka** underneath the train station. The deli cases in the basement of the behemoth department store **Stockmann** (Aleksanterinkatu 52, tel. 09/1211) also have tasty, surprisingly cheap eats.

UNDER FIM 45 • Kaspian. Order delicious Persian specialties or try the salmon topped with applesauce. *Albertinkatu 7, tel. 09/664–431. From train station, walk south on Mannerheimintie, right on Lönnrotinkatu, left on Albertinkatu, continue 6 blocks. Closed Sat. Cash only.*

Perho Mechelin. Specialties at this culinary school and restaurant include pasta *à la mechelin* (pasta with broiled salmon and reindeer; half-portion FIM 42). They brew their own thick beer and also carry a large selection of international brands. *Mechelininkatu 7, tel. 09/493–481. From Mannerheimintie, walk west on Arkadiankatu, left on Mechelininkatu. Cash only.*

UNDER FIM 55 • Konstan Möljä. Delicious à la carte dishes at this popular Finnish restaurant include baked salmon in mushroom sauce and spicy reindeer stew. The buffet of meat or fish, salad, bread, soup, and drink costs FIM 45 weekdays, FIM 59 weekends. *Hietalahdenkatu 14, tel. 09/694–7504. From Mannerheimintie, walk down Kalevankatu, right on Hietalahdenkatu. Cash only.*

Ryan Thai. The fiery vegetable curry at this small, authentic eatery will reawaken your taste buds from spiceless Finnish fare. *Pohjoinen Makasiinikatu 7, on Kasarmintori, tel. 09/629–600. From Manner-heimintie, walk up Etaleesplanadi, right on Kasarmikatu, left on Pohjoinen Makasiinikatu. Cash only.*

Zucchini. For vegetarian lunch or just coffee and dessert, try this cozy hideaway with soothing music and sidewalk tables. The pizzas, soups and salads are delicious. *Fabianinkatu 4, between Etale-esplanadi and Kasarmintori, tel. 09/622–2907. Closed weekends.*

WORTH SEEING

Get a feel for the city by walking along **Pohjoisesplanadi,** cruising through **Kauppatori** (Market Square), or strolling along the harbor. Most sights are within 3 km (2 mi) of the train station. For background information on all the sights, take along the tourist office's detailed booklet "See Helsinki on Foot."

SENAATINTORI

The graceful Senaatintori (Senate Square) is dominated by the **Tuomiokirkko** (tel. 09/656–365; open June–Aug., weekdays 9–5, Sat. 9–7, Sun. 9–8; shorter hrs off season), a Lutheran cathedral originally designed by Carl Ludvig Engel in 1830 and later augmented with four conical green towers to support the weight of its bells. Hike up its steep stairs for a glimpse at the cathedral's mighty organ. In summer, the cathedral hosts organ concerts Sunday at 8 PM (FIM 20) and Wednesday at 12:15 PM (free). The university and state-council buildings around Senaatintori, also neoclassical creations by Engel, give the square a distinct Russian feel, and you'll see other signs of Russian influence, such as the statue of Czar Alexander II in front of the cathedral. So Eastern is the setting here that several Hollywood films, including *Reds, Gorky Park,* and *White Nights,* featured the Senaatintori in their "Russian" scenes.

CHURCHES

Besides the cathedral on Senaatintori (*see above*), Helsinki has two other houses of worship that are worth a look. The otherworldly **Temppeliaukion Kirkko** (Lutherinkatu 3, tel. 09/494–698; open weekdays 10–8, Sat. 10–6, Sun. varied hrs), designed by Timo and Tuomo Suomalainen, is set into a hill of granite and is topped with a copper dome. Trek up to the **Uspenskin katedraali** (Kanavakatu 1, tel. 09/634–267; open weekdays 9:30–4, Tues. until 6, Sat. 10–4, Sun. noon–3) for huge colorful icons and gold-trimmed frescoes. Built in 1868, it remains the Nordic region's largest Orthodox church, with distinctly Russian spires and a view of the city from the upstairs terrace.

GOVERNMENT BUILDINGS

The 200 members of Finland's *eduskunta* (parliament) meet, quarrel, and make laws in the austere **Eduskuntatalo** (Parliament House; Mannerheimintie 30, tel. 09/432–2027), built entirely by hand in 1930. Free tours are given year-round on Saturday at 11 and noon, and Sunday at noon and 1, with additional tours June–August weekdays at 2 PM. The 1818 **Presidentinlinna** (President's Palace; tel. 09/641–200), at Pohjoisesplanadi 1, was once the Czar's dwelling when he'd visit his duchy; it became the official home of the Finnish president in 1919. (The current chief, Martti Ahtisaari, lives in the ultra-modern Mäntyniemi residence near Seurasaari and uses the Presidentinlinna as his office.) Just around the corner from the Presidentinlinna is the **Päävartio** (Main Guard Post). Catch the changing of the guard and a small parade Tuesday and Friday at 1.

MUSEUMS

Helsinki has more than 50 museums, and the Helsinki Card (*see* Visitor Information *in* Basics, *above*) gets you into most of them for free. The **Kansallismuseo** (National Museum), with a collection ranging from tools and art of the region's nomadic Sami people to souvenirs of Russia's reign over Finland, is closed for renovation until December 1999. The building is a vintage example of the National Romantic style by Eliel Saarinen and partners. *Mannerheimintie 34, tel. 09/405–0470.*

The **Ateneum,** or Finnish National Gallery, Finland's largest art museum, contains Finnish and foreign art from the 18th century to the present. The works of national greats—from the frightening mythical scenes of Hugo Simberg to the moody, anonymous portraits of Helène Schjerfbeck—are on the second floor. *Kaivokatu 2–4, tel. 09/173–361. Admission: FIM 10. Open Tues. and Fri. 9–6, Wed. and Thurs. 9–9, weekends 11–5.*

The **Kaapelitehdas** (Cable Factory) is an enormous, recently renovated industrial complex that boasts numerous avant-garde galleries and performance-art spaces. The permanent galleries (open Tues.–Fri. noon–6, Wed. 6 PM–8 PM, weekends noon–5) include the Photography Museum (tel. 09/6866–3621),

FINLAND, LAND OF SAUNAS?

When Finns want to hold a power lunch, they take it to the sauna. Saunas (pronounced "sow-nuhz") have always been important to the Finns: In bygone days, the sauna was usually the first building to be constructed on a new farm. Babies were delivered within saunas' sterile walls, and the dead were bathed and dressed in them before burial. Even in modern Finland there's an average of one sauna for every three people. Though it would be a shame to visit Finland without spending a few hours naked and contemplative in one of these sweltering little wooden cabins, the activity is definitely not for the faint of heart. Saunas are generally heated to 80°C–100°C (175°F–212°F), and Finns like to heighten the experience with a few quick, well-timed plunges into ice-cold lakes. If you choose to visit a sauna, keep in mind that the temperature near your feet can be 11°C (20°F) lower than it is up around your ears—if you start feeling woozy, duck down low, or hit the showers.

the Theatre Museum (tel. 09/694–5088), and the Hotel and Restaurant Museum (tel. 09/693–1774). *Tallberginkatu 1F. Metro to Ruoholahti; or Tram 8 to end. Admission to each gallery: FIM 10.*

SEURASAARI

This island west of the city is ideal for a picnic, a stroll, or a lazy afternoon with a favorite novel. If you're up for it, bushwhack your way to the beach on the island's western edge for sunbathing in the buff. At the **Seurasaaren Ulkomuseo** (Open-Air Museum; tel. 09/484–712; admission FIM 15; open mid-May-Aug., daily 9–3, Wed. until 5), you can explore transplanted Finnish country dwellings and farmsteads. Tours are given daily at 11:30 and 3:30. Tuesday, Thursday, and weekend evenings in summer, the island hosts folk dances (tel. 09/484–234 for times; admission FIM 20). Nearby, FIM 15 gets you into **Tamminiemi Villa,** President Urho Kekkonen's home during his term in office (1956–1981). The house is full of typical Finnish furniture, and you can see the famous sauna where pressing international issues were settled. *From corner of Mannerheimintie and Esplanadi (Swedish Theater), Bus 24 to end; cross footpath.*

SUOMENLINNA

The fortifications of Suomenlinna (tel. 09/668–154), built on a series of small adjoining islands in Helsinki's harbor, formed an active military installation from 1748 until 1973. They are now part of a city park. Suomenlinna makes an ideal day trip, with six museums; the retired World War II submarine *Vesikko* (tel. 09/161–5295); a summer theater (tel. 09/718–622); a public beach; and endless catacombs, bunkers, and rusting artillery. If you're not a military-history buff, bring along some vittles and head for the island's easternmost tip to watch the huge ferries pass. Ferries for Suomenlinna (15 min, FIM 9) leave from Market Square every 20–30 minutes from 6:20 AM to 1:30 AM.

CHEAP THRILLS

If you've whizzed through the tourist office's "See Helsinki by Foot," take a trip to **Kaivopuisto,** a waterside park south of the city center (take Tram 3T). In summer, the park hosts frequent outdoor concerts. If you're visiting in the dead of winter, you can amuse yourself by walking from tiny island to island on the frozen sea by the park. In summer, after the ice has melted, hop a boat to **Pihlajasaari** (FIM 20) for a day on the nude beach; boats depart daily every half hour 9–6 from the pier near the Carusel Café (Merisatamaranta 2).

AFTER DARK

Summer's perpetual light doesn't prevent Helsinki from having a boisterous nightlife. Just about any restaurant with a liquor license and outdoor patio turns into a nightspot after 10 PM; the most lively streets on weekends are Iso Roobertinkatu, Pohjoisesplanadi, Kluuvikatu, Aleksanterinkatu, and Mikonkatu. To avoid stiff beer prices, swing by one of the state-run **Alko** liquor stores (Mannerheimintie 1 or Salomonkatu 1; closed Sun.), and then join jovial locals at Suomenlinna or on the cathedral steps. For the latest on the city's nighttime scene, pick up the free magazines *Helsinki Happens* and *City*, available at hotels, restaurants, and shops citywide.

Bar H2O/Blue Boy. Of these two side-by-side gay, mostly male bars, Bar H2O is for outgoing swingers and Blue Boy is for the more subdued. Both bars play hip-hop music. *Eerikinkatu 14, tel. 09/608–826. From Mannerheimintie, head SW on Simonkatu, left on Annankatu, right on Eerikinkatu.*

Café Engel. Named after the architect responsible for the Senaatintori, across the street, Engel serves cappuccino, espresso, beer (FIM 13.50), pastries, and salads. In winter, the café puts up therapeutic light panels to help patrons chase away the seasonal blues. *Aleksanterinkatu 26, across from Tuomiokirkko, tel. 09/652–776.*

Café Ursula. At the southern tip of Kaivopuisto, this place serves up gorgeous Baltic views with its FIM 22 half-liter brews. A young, fashionable crowd throngs the glass-bubble room and outdoor patio. *Ehrenströmintie 3, tel. 09/652–817. Tram 3B to Kaivopuisto; walk down Iso Puistotie.*

Kaarle XII. The Carl the Twelfth dance club has been hot ever since it opened for business in the '70s. There's no cover, even though it's a 24-and-up crowd that comes to dance its heart out. An *iso tuoppi* ("big mug") of Class III beer is FIM 23. *Kasarmikatu 40, tel. 09/171–353. From Mannerheimintie, walk up Eteläesplanade, right on Kasarmikatu. Closed Sun. and Mon.*

Tavastia. Helsinki's primary venue for live music draws big Finnish acts (such as Electric Sauna) and international stars; the schedule is posted outside. The minimum age is 18, the minimum cover FIM 40, but both vary. Under the same ownership two doors down, Semifinal hosts lesser-known bands, but be ready for high testosterone and noise levels. *Urho Kekkosenkatu 4–6B, SW of bus station, tel. 09/694–8511. From Mannerheimintie, walk west on Simonkatu, right on Annankatu, left on Urho Kekkosenkatu. Closed Sun. and Mon.*

THE SOUTHWEST

The southwest is Finland's hard-working agricultural region, dotted with farms and fields. Cities along the Gulf of Bothnia have become industrialized since World War II, but the rest of the region remains steadfastly rural. The liveliest town is Turku, one of Finland's major ports and the site of two universities. West of Turku, the beautiful Åland Islands offer great outdoor activities, especially for cyclists.

TURKU

The proud citizens of Turku might feel a little envious of Helsinki—after all, Turku was the capital of Finland from the 13th century until the early 19th century. It was also home to the country's first university and to Michael Agricola, the bishop who brought Lutheranism to Finland. Beginning in 1812 the city's luck turned, and over the span of just a few years it suffered several mortal blows: It lost its status as the capital to Helsinki, it lost its university (also to Helsinki), and then in 1827 it suffered a catastrophic fire. Today things look brighter for Turku; its port, the number-one gateway to Finland from the Baltic, is thriving, and students at two local universities breathe life into the town. In summer the city's pace slows, but the July **Ruisrock Festival** and the August **Turku Music Festival** liven things up.

BASICS

The **tourist office** (Aurakatu 4, tel. 02/233–6366; open weekdays 8:30–5, weekends 9–4) has plenty of maps and brochures in English. There's an **American Express** desk at Area Travel (Kauppiaskatu 110, tel. 02/610–611; open weekdays 8:30–5), half a block north of the market square. The **post office** (Humalistonkatu 1, tel. 02/920–4511) contains a tiny phone center. You can reach Turku's **train**

station (Ratapihankatu 37, tel. 02/632–21) from Helsinki (2¼ hrs, FIM 90). **Viking Line** (Linnansatama, tel. 02/633–11) and **Silja Line** (Käsityöläiskatu 4, tel. 02/652–211) sail twice daily to Turku from Stockholm; for more information *see* Basics, *above*.

GETTING AROUND

The city is walkable, though the Turku Castle is about a 30-minute hike from downtown. The **Museum Bus Pass** (FIM 8), available at the tourist office, entitles you to 24 hours of city bus rides plus a 50% discount at the museums. Bikes, however, are the preferred mode of transportation here; rent one for FIM 50 per day at the hostel (*see* Where to Sleep, *below*).

WHERE TO SLEEP

Hotel Astro (Humalistonkatu 18, tel. 02/251–7838; doubles FIM 260) has clean, modern rooms near the town center; prices include breakfast and sauna. **Majatalo Kupittaa** (Käsityöläiskatu 11, tel. 02/233–4484; cash only) offers smaller doubles for FIM 180. Turku's only hostel is the excellent **Turun Kaupungin Retkeilymaja (HI)** (Linnankatu 39, near the ferry terminals, tel. 02/231–6578; cash only), with FIM 60 dorm beds and FIM 160 doubles; breakfast is FIM 20. From the train station, walk down Käsityöläiskatu and turn right on Linnankatu, or from the bus station, take Bus 3 or 1. Bus 8 makes the 10-km (6-mi) trek twice hourly to Ruissalo Island, site of **Ruissalo Campground** (tel. 02/258–9249; closed mid-Aug.–May; cash only), which has tent spots for FIM 45 per person and is surrounded by beaches (including a nude one) and trim forests.

FOOD

For fish, bread, fruits, and vegetables head to the outdoor **kauppatori** (market square; corner of Humalistonkatu and Eerikinkatu; closed Sun.) or **kauppahalli** (market hall; corner of Linnankatu and Aurakatu; closed Sun.). The lunch spot **Verso** (Linnankatu 3, 2nd floor, tel. 02/251–0956) dishes out vegetarian and macrobiotic Finnish plates for about FIM 35 each. **Pinella** (Porthanin puisto, above Tuomiokirkko bridge, tel. 02/251–7557) has a pleasant patio overlooking the river; the Finnish menu ranges from pancake meals (FIM 45) to salmon plates (FIM 74).

WORTH SEEING

Turku's attractions include several excellent museums. The **Turun Linna** (Turku Castle) is situated at the mouth of the Aurajoki River. A dull exterior masks the historical significance and complex design of this 13th-century structure. Inside is a small **historical museum** (FIM 15) with medieval icons, goblets, and golden knickknacks. *Between Linnankatu and Nuottasaarenkatu. Admission: FIM 30. Open Tues.–Sun. 10–6; shorter hrs off season. Tours at 11, 1, and 3.*

Even if classical music doesn't normally send you into fits of joy, you'll probably enjoy the sleek **Sibelius Museum,** named after Finland's national composer, Jean Sibelius (1865–1957). Among the hundreds of musical instruments on display are a 19th-century Parisian piano-violin hybrid once owned by Czar Alexander III, and a balalaika (Russian instrument with three strings and triangular body), a gift from Soviet premier Khrushchev. *Piispankatu 17, catercorner to Turun Tuomiokirkko, tel. 02/265–4494. Admission: FIM 15. Open Tues. and Thurs.–Sun. 11–3, Wed. 11–3 and 6–8.*

The Art Nouveau **Turku Art Museum** houses a permanent collection of modern and turn-of-the-century Finnish art, second in size to that of Helsinki's Ateneum. The special exhibits of contemporary art are the museum's best, and in summer impromptu concerts are held in the adjoining park. *Aurakatu 26, tel. 02/233–0954. From market square, follow Aurakatu 2 blocks north. Admission: FIM 30. Open Apr.–Sept., Tues., Fri., and Sat. 10–4, Wed. and Thurs. 10–7, Sun. 11–6; shorter hrs off season.*

In the 16th century, Bishop Agricola so enjoyed his chats with Martin Luther in Germany that he took up Luther's Reformation movement in Finland. Agricola's venue for proclaiming Evangelical Lutheranism, **Turun Tuomiokirkko,** was actually founded during the 13th century, and the church is the resting place of medieval Finnish royalty and knights. The adjacent cathedral museum houses relics and a photo essay tracing the church's development. Free organ concerts are held on summer Tuesdays at 8 PM. *From market square, follow Eerikinkatu to Aninkaistenkatu, turn right, and cross bridge.*

AFTER DARK

Most of Turku's nightlife is concentrated in the market square/market hall area or along the Aurajoki River, where bar boats float. **Apteekki** (Kaskenkatu 1, tel. 02/250–2595) is a friendly pub in a former apothecary shop, with all the orginal pharmacist's drawers intact. At **Café 57** (Eerikinkatu 12, tel. 02/251–9574) you can catch Finnish rock or jazz nightly. A few doors down is **Börs Club** (Kauppiaskatu 6, tel. 02/337–381; cover FIM 40 Sat.), Turku's hottest dance club, playing disco and hip-hop.

RAUMA

UNESCO named Rauma's **old town,** full of wooden medieval dwellings and shops, a World Heritage Site in 1991. Rauma is Finland's third-oldest city (it was founded in 1442), and today its income comes from the paper and pulp industries as well as tourism. Just north of Market Place in the old town's center is the 15th-century **Church of the Holy Cross,** with carefully retouched frescoes and a big polished organ. Its tower was built with stones from the 14th-century **Church of the Holy Trinity,** destroyed by fire along with the rest of the village in 1682; the somber ruins are worth a peek. From Market Place, go right on Vaharaastuvankatu and right on Vanhankirkonkatu. Skip Rauma's four dull history museums and head instead to the town's **Art Museum** (Kuninkaankatu 37, tel. 02/822–4346; admission FIM 20; open weekdays 10–6, Sat. 10–4, Sun. noon–6), which hosts summer-long contemporary art exhibitions. Ten buses a day make the 92-km (55-mi) trip (1 hr, 40 min) north from Turku's bus station to Rauma (FIM 50, express service FIM 71). Rauma's **tourist office** (tel. 02/834–4552) is at Valtakatu 2; from the bus station, head south on Luoteisväylä and turn left on Valtakatu.

The town's best budget-lodging options are **HI Poroholman Retkeilymaja** and the **Poroholman Leirintäalue campground** (2 km/1⅓ mi from bus station, tel. 02/822–4666; closed Sept.–mid-May), both of which share a reception area. Dorm beds cost FIM 40, doubles without electricity FIM 200, and campsites FIM 30 per person. From the tourist office, take Valtakatu west, cross the tracks and go left on Syväraumankatu, then left on Urheilukatu. Join locals at **Buena Vista** (Kanalinranta 5, tel. 02/822–7757) for authentic Finnish and mediocre Mexican food (FIM 40—FIM 80). The old town's rustic **Café Kantio** (Kuninkaankatu 9, tel. 02/822–1422; cash only) serves good coffee, pastries, and *lihapiirakka* (meat pie, FIM 6).

MARIEHAMN AND THE ÅLAND ISLANDS

Comprising more than 6,500 islands—most smaller than the ferry boats that sail around them—the Åland (pronounced OH-land) Islands lie in the Baltic Sea midway between Finland and Sweden. The Åland are officially Finnish, but residents speak Swedish and identify culturally with Sweden. Most businesses accept both the Finnish markka and the Swedish krona.

Named by Czar Alexander II in honor of his wife, Maria, **Mariehamn** (population 11,000), the only town in the island group, is situated along a narrow peninsula on the southern tip of the main island, Åland. The Storagatan/Norra Esplanaden, graced with linden trees, connects the harbors on the eastern and western sides of town. The **Åland Museum** (Stadshusparken, tel. 018/254–26; admission FIM 15; open Wed.–Sun. 10–4, Tues. until 8) presents the area's history and culture. The **Åland Art Museum** is in the same building. A few minutes east of the museums lies **Lilla Holmen,** a beach and park accessible by footbridge and renowned for its flock of peacocks.

Biking is the best way to tour the terrestrial portions of the archipelago, and you don't have to be an Olympic medalist to cruise the flat islands via well-maintained bike paths and bridges. With a passenger ticket for a Viking or Silja ferry, there is no additional charge to bring a bike on board. For bike-route maps and ferry schedules, visit Mariehamn's **tourist office** (Storagatan 8, tel. 018/221–00; open June–Aug., daily 9–6; Sept.–May, weekdays 10–4). The office can also help you find accommodations.

COMING AND GOING

Mariehamn is a port of call for the daily **Silja Line** (Norragatan 2, tel. 018/167–11) ferries from Stockholm (5½ hrs; FIM 80, FIM 50 off-season) and Turku (6 hrs; FIM 50). **Viking Line** (Storagatan 2, tel. 018/260–11) also sails to Mariehamn from Stockholm (FIM 50) and Turku (FIM 115, FIM 55 off season). Viking and Silja give 50% discounts to rail-pass holders. The ferry service **Eckerö Linjen** (Storagatan 8, tel. 018/280–00) will get you to Stockholm (under FIM 50) in two hours.

In Mariehamn, **RO-NO Rent** (Österhamn, eastern harbor, tel. 018/128–20; Västerhamn, western harbor, tel. 018/128–21) rents basic bikes (FIM 30 per day, FIM 150 per week), mountain bikes (FIM 70 per day, FIM 350 per week), and mopeds, canoes, and dune buggies. Local buses depart from Mariehamn's **bus station** (Strandgatan and Styrmansgatan), near the eastern harbor.

WHERE TO SLEEP AND EAT

Swedish and Finnish tourists flock to the Åland Islands in summer, especially in July, so make reservations. The travel agency **Ålandsresor** (Torgatan 2, tel. 018/280–40) will help you find budget lodging on the islands. **Botel Alida** (Mariehamn, anchored at Osterleden and Styrmansgatan, tel. 018/137–55) is a boat with closet-sized but character-filled double berths for FIM 140. **Strandnäs Hotel** (Godbyvägen, tel. 018/215–11) and **Adlon Sleepover** (Hamngatan 7, tel. 018/153–00) are plain hotels that won't break the bank, with doubles for FIM 360. The **Pensionat Solheim** (Lökskärsvägen, tel. 018/163–22) offers FIM 300 doubles. There are campgrounds all over the islands. On Åland, **Camping Gröna Uddens** (Östernäsvägen, tel. 018/190–41; closed Sept.–mid-May), 1 km (⅔ mi) south of Storagatan and Lilla Holmen, has beach sites for FIM 20 per person and FIM 15 per tent.

For budget snacks, hit the markets in Mariehamn; **Mathis Hallen** (Ålandsvägen 42, tel. 018/281–9980) is one option. The town is full of cafés—don't miss **Cha Shoo Tropical** (Torggatan 10, tel. 018/140–07) for enormous pizzas, crêpes, or pastas (each 40 FIM with salad). **Hotel Arkipelag** (Strandgatan 31, tel. 018/240–20) has FIM 30 lunch buffets and for dinner serves Åland delicacies such as grilled whitefish with goat cheese and potato pancakes. The restaurant becomes a dance club after 11 PM.

THE LAKE REGION

More than 180,000 lakes and a seemingly endless series of rivers, canals, and inlets break up the forested landscape of southeast Finland. This area, wildly popular with thousands of Finnish vacationers, is dotted with tiny lakeside cabins and summer resorts, perfect for weekend relaxation. Somehow the railways of the Lake Region weave between the waterways, connecting a garland of larger cities: Tampere, Jyväskylä, Kuopio, Savonlinna, and Lahti. In addition to regular buses and trains, water buses and cruise ships are common means of transportation, and hiking, biking, and canoeing are good bets for leisurely exploration. The Lake Region is heavily visited, but odds are you'll find a canoe route, hiking path, or cove to call your own.

TAMPERE

On the Lake Region's western edge, 175 km (105 mi) north of Helsinki, Tampere languished for years as a tiny trading post, on a 4-km (2½-mi) stretch of land between Lake Näsijärvi to the north and Lake Pyhäjärvi to the south. The town's big break came in 1820, when itinerant Scottish businessman James Finlayson harnessed the raging Tammerkoski rapids, which run through the city, to power his spinning mill. His enterprise turned Tampere into the country's industrial center, specializing in textiles and garnering the dubious title "the Manchester of Finland." Communism flourished in Tampere during the early 20th century, in part because Lenin resided in Finland during 1905. Tampere served as the Reds' capital during the 1918 Finnish Civil War, and though the Reds were defeated that year, the town continued to prosper. Today, Tampere battles Turku for recognition as Finland's second-largest city.

Nowadays, the fabled Tammerkoski rapids are lined with fishing boats, shopping malls, and factories. The only real traces of communism remain at the **Lenin-Museo** (Hämeenpuisto 28, 3rd floor, tel. 03/212–7313; admission FIM 15; open Tues.–Fri. 9–5, weekends 11–4), housed in the building where Lenin first met Stalin in 1905, during a revolutionary conference. The **Amurin Työläiskorttelimuseo** (Makasiininkatu 12, tel. 03/219–6690; admission FIM 10; open mid-May–mid-Sept., Tues.–Fri. 9–5, weekends 11–6) presents 100 years of well-preserved workers' housing. **Kaleva Church** (in park at corner of Sammonkatu and Teiskontie), designed by Reima and Raili Pietilä, is a house of worship in the shape of a fish.

At the **Särkänniemi** recreation area (2 km/1⅓ mi NW of the train station, tel. 03/248–8111), a small peninsula jutting into Lake Näsijärvi, make tracks for the intimate **Sara Hildén Art Museum** (tel. 03/214–3134; admission FIM 25; open daily 11–6) to see the modern exhibits. Also on park grounds are an amusement park, an aquarium, and a planetarium. At the other end of town, Lake Pyhäjärvi's **Viikinsaari Island** (open June–Aug. 25, Tues.–Thurs. 10 AM–11:30 PM, Fri. and Sat. 10 AM–12:30 AM, Sun. 10–7:30) has beaches and raucous dancing on summer evenings. Catch the boat (30 min, FIM 20) just south of Kehräsaari across the rapids from Koskikeskus.

BASICS

The **tourist office** (Verkatehtaankatu 2, tel. 03/212–6652; open May–Sept., weekdays 8:30–5, Sat. 8:30–6, Sun. 11–6), on the eastern shore of the Tammerkoski south of Hämeenkatu, clarifies confusing lake-cruise schedules, rents bikes (FIM 100 deposit), and sells 24-hour bus passes (FIM 25). **American Express** (Area Travel, Hämeenkatu 7A, tel. 03/223–5100) provides limited services to members.

COMING AND GOING

Frequent trains run to Tampere from Helsinki (2¾ hrs, FIM 90) and Turku (2 hrs, FIM 80). The **train station** is east of the Tammerkoski rapids at the end of Hämeenkatu. Crammed with shops and banks, Hämeenkatu runs 1½ km (1 mi) between the train station and Hämeenpuisto, and crosses the Tammerkoski rapids at Hämeensilta Bridge. All local buses (FIM 9) stop at Keskustori, the central square, ¾ km (about ½ mi) west of the train station on Hämeenkatu.

WHERE TO SLEEP

Try the pleasant **Hotel Victoria** (Itsenäisyydenkatu 1, tel. 03/242–5111; doubles FIM 380) or the passable **Hotel Kauppi** (Kalevanpuistotie 2, tel. 03/253–5353; doubles FIM 340). Tampere also has three spacious hostels. The popular **Camping Härmälä** (Leirintäkatu 8, 5 km/3 mi south of town, tel. 03/613–8311) offers cottages (FIM 120) with beach access; the campground's summer-only **hostel** (closed Sept.–May) has FIM 230 doubles. Take Bus 1 south to its terminus.

Ålanders, descended from Swedes, harbor no love for mainland Finns. They're Finnish citizens, but the islands' government devises its own laws, prints it own stamps, and flies its own flag.

Domus (HI). This is a combination hostel and hotel. The hotel rooms are equipped with kitchen and bath and provide free access to sauna, laundry, and bikes (FIM 100 deposit required for bikes). Dorm beds in the hostel are FIM 75, doubles FIM 150. *Pellervonkatu 9, tel. 03/255–000. From train station, walk east on Itsenäisyydenkatu (becomes Sammonkatu) and turn left on Joukahaisenkatu; or Bus 25 east. Closed Sept.–May.*

NNKY Retkeilymaja (HI). This YWCA-affiliated hostel is close to the train station and as clean as can be. Beds cost FIM 70, doubles FIM 170, sheets FIM 25, and breakfast FIM 25. *Tuomiokirkonkatu 12A, tel. 03/225–5446. From station, take Hämeenkatu, then first right on Tuomiokirkonkatu. Reception open daily 8–10 and 4–midnight. Kitchen. Cash only. Closed Sept.–May.*

Uimahallin Maja (HI). A friendly staff and social dorms are the outstanding features at Uimahallin Maja. Dorm beds go for FIM 95, doubles for FIM 250. *Pirkankatu 10–12, tel. 03/222–9460. From station, take Hämeenkatu, go right on Hämeenpuisto, left on Pirkankatu. Cash only.*

FOOD

Tampere's famous regional dish is *mustamakkara* (black sausage), a meal of pork cooked with milk and flour and served with sweet lingonberry jam. Buy sausage, produce, and other foodstuffs at the **kauppahalli** (market hall; Hämeenkatu 14; closed Sun.) or the **kehräsaari** (market square; from train station, left on Hämeenkatu, left on Kirkkokatu to water). Amid the galleries and shops in a converted factory, **Fall's Café** (tel. 03/223–0061; lunch only) has a variable menu; try the FIM 35 Hungarian goulash or the beef burgundy. Crowded **Pub Rosendahl** (Pynikintie 13, tel. 03/244–1504; Bus 27 from train station), in hilly Tenniskenttä Park overlooking Lake Pyhäjärvi, has salads, sandwiches, and FIM 15 beer.

SAVONLINNA

Savonlinna (population 28,000) is just small and elegant enough to make you and a slew of summering Finns feel like exclusive guests. Boasting the Nordic area's best-preserved medieval fortress, this town packs 'em in, particularly during July's annual **Opera Festival,** a month of evening performances at locales in and around the city. You can order tickets (FIM 100–FIM 480) by mail or phone; contact the Opera Festival staff (Olavinkatu 27, 57130 Savonlinna, tel. 015/576–750). The more expensive concerts take place in the open-air theater at **Olavinlinna Castle** (Olavinlinna Island, tel. 015/572–1164; admission FIM 20; open June–mid-Aug., daily 10–5; off season, daily 10–3), built in 1475 to protect the Swedish-Finnish empire's eastern border. Get there by way of a 164-ft bridge that spans Lake Pihlajavesi, southeast of the city center. The **Savonlinna Provincial Museum** (tel. 015/571–712; admission

WHO ARE THE SAMI?

The Sami are the indigenous people of Lapland, nomads who once followed reindeer herds across Norway, Sweden, Finland, and Russia. When Finland and Sweden joined the European Union in 1995, however, it became difficult for the Sami to range with their herds. Some continue to farm reindeer using snowmobiles and mobile phones; others live in traditional villages with reindeer-skin shelters called "kota" and open fires. The majority have forsaken their old ways to assimilate into mainstream culture.

FIM 15; open Tues.–Sun. 11–5), on the Riihisaari peninsula near Olavinlinna Castle, displays an anthropological history of the Lake Region's inhabitants. The **Retretti Art Center** (Punkaharju, tel. 015/644–253; admission FIM 65; open June–Aug. daily 10–5) displays modern art in a cave—an ironically appropriate venue for work ranging from Matisse to inscrutable contemporary painters. The art center is a 20-minute train ride from the city center.

Check with the **tourist office** (Puistokatu 1, off Olavinkatu, tel. 015/273–492; open June and Aug., daily 8–6; July, daily 8–10; Sept.–May, weekdays 9–4) for information on the entire region and lake-cruise schedules. The best cruise is the Heinävesi route, which leaves Savonlinna's port and calls at Punkaharju (FIM 130). Savonlinna lies off the main rail lines; to get here, take one of the four daily trains to Joensuu from Helsinki, get off in Parikkala, and transfer to Savonlinna (5 hrs, FIM 184). The **Savonlinna-Kauppatori station,** one stop before the central station (tel. 015/573–4111), is near the tourist office, a block north of the main artery Olavinkatu.

WHERE TO SLEEP AND EAT

In July, prices for all accommodations jump FIM 50–FIM 100, and rooms go fast. Happily, the tourist office (*see above*) makes reservations. The most central hostel, **HI Vuorilinna** (Kylpylaitoksentie, behind casino, tel. 015/739–5495; closed Sept.–June; dorm beds FIM 110, singles FIM 170), is a short walk from the train station across a footbridge. **HI Malakias** (Pihlajavedenkuja 6, tel. 015/533–283; closed mid-Aug.–June) offers comfortable, clean doubles (FIM 270); from the tourist office, take Bus 2 or 3. Snooze in luxury at the family-run **Hospits Hotel** (Linnankatu 20, tel. 015/515–661; doubles FIM 300) near Olavinlinna Castle.

Cheap souvenirs, fresh produce, and cooked fish are peddled at the **kauppatori** (market square), south of Olavinkatu next to the Haapasalmi canal. Across the street, **Terassi** (Kauppatori 4–6, 6th floor of Hotelli Seurahuone, tel. 015/573–1) serves up a FIM 35 lunch of fish, salad, and baked potato. Its outdoor tables have appealing lake vistas. Around the corner, **Majakka** (Satamakatu 11, tel. 015/531–456) serves FIM 38 dishes of reindeer, oxen, and seafood. Afterward, soothe your tastebuds at **Nelson Pub** (Olavinkatu 31, tel. 015/576–910).

NORTHERN FINLAND

Northern Finland is often called Europe's last great wilderness, a region of vast forests, steep fells, and profound silences. The Arctic Circle bisects the area; south of the circle lie the port town of Oulu, surrounded by farmland, and the town of Kuusamo, near the Russian border. North of the circle is the icy tundra of Lapland. Intrepid visitors to Northern Finland leave the train behind at the town of Kemijärvi, and hike north to experience the surreal midnight sun of summer and the magical, dancing aurora borealis.

The city of Rovaniemi provides the best access to western Lapland, as well as to Sweden and Norway. Farther north lie the tiny villages of Ivalo and Inari, set on Lake Inarinjärvi. North of these two villages, the trees thin out and then disappear, and you'll see why Lapland is often referred to as "the other Finland"—the plowed-and-planted south simply bears no resemblance to the sparse and isolated north.

The trekking is difficult in Finland's most mountainous region, along the Norwegian border in western Lapland. Before you strap on your trekking boots, contact **Metsähallitus** (Etiäinen, Napapiiri, 96930 Rovaniemi, tel. 016/362–526) in Santa Claus Village for maps or referrals to specific park information centers. The **Finnish Forest and Park Service** (Box 36, 99801, Ivalo, tel. 016/663–601) also has tips.

OULU

The port town of Oulu makes a worthwhile stop for its provocative science museum and eclectic, university-driven nightlife. Founded by Sweden's King Carl IX in 1605, Oulu was highly industrialized by the 1820s, producing much of the world's tar as well as great quantities of leather, turpentine, beer, and lumber. The **Ainola Provincial Museum** (Ainola Park, tel. 08/375–200; admission FIM 10; open June–Aug., Mon.–Thurs. 10–6, Sat. 10–4, Sun. 11–5) shows the history of the town's diverse industries. The **Zoological Museum** (Linnanmaa, tel. 08/553–1011; admission free; open June–Aug., Sun.–Fri. 11–3; Sept.–May, weekdays 8:30–3:30, Sun. 11–3), north of the city near the university (take Bus 4, 6, 7, or 16), houses photo and taxidermy displays on Finnish wildlife; it's adjacent to "Romeo and Juliet," the two glass pyramids of the **botanical gardens** (open Tues.–Fri. 8–5). Oulu's biggest draw is **Tietomaa** (Nahkatehtaankatu 6, tel. 08/377–911; admission FIM 50; open Apr.–Aug., daily 10–6; shorter hrs off season), a hands-on science center full of aerodynamic, electronic, and magnetic gizmos.

Trains from Helsinki (6½–9 hrs, FIM 260) and Turku (4½–9 hrs, FIM 262) run to Oulu six to eight times daily. Within town, a bike does the trick—rent one at the train station (FIM 30 per day). You'll need a bus only to reach the campground at Nallikari or **Turkansaari,** an island 14 km (8½ mi) from Oulu on the Oulujoki River; take the M.S. *Lempi* water bus (tel. 049/854–642) for FIM 70 round-trip. The island features a 17th-century church, 19th-century buildings, an open-air museum of industry, and plenty of summer festivals, including Tar-Burning Day (Midsummer's Eve), a celebration of Oulu's industrial beginnings. Usually held in late June, the festival, an entire week of folk music and dancing, is the busiest time of the year for Oulu's **tourist office** (Torikatu 10, tel. 08/314–1295; open weekdays 9–4).

WHERE TO SLEEP AND EAT

The **HI Välkkylä** (Kajaanintie 36, tel. 08/311–8060; closed Sept.–May) offers beds in two-room, four-bed suites (shared kitchen and bath) for FIM 85; doubles are FIM 260. To get here from the train station, turn right onto Rautatienkatu and right again on Kajaanintie. **HI Otokylä** (Haapanatie 2, tel. 08/530–8413; closed mid-Aug.–mid-May) offers FIM 60 dorm beds and FIM 180 doubles, plus FIM 25 breakfasts; take Bus 11 south. Closer to town, the clean, spacious **Kesähotelli Oppimestari** (Nahkatehtaankatu 3, tel. 08/313–0527; beds FIM 100, doubles FIM 200) is across the street from Tietomaa (*see above*). Bus 5 will take you a few kilometers northwest to **Nallikari Camping** (tel. 08/554–1541; closed mid-Oct.–Apr.), where you can sleep next to lovely Gulf of Bothnia beaches for FIM 45 per person (single cabins from FIM 140, doubles FIM 200).

At **Rock Club 45** (Saaristonkatu 12, tel. 08/373–886), enjoy a sandwich (FIM 15), a side of Cajun fries, and a cold beer while listening to live music. **Jumpru** (Kauppurienkatu 6, tel. 08/373–776) serves a decent, all-you-can-eat, soup-and-salad lunch and stays crowded into the wee hours. For a dose of reggae, try the tiny **Never Grow Old** (Valkealinnankulma, tel. 08/311–3936), with a wide beer selection (FIM 17–FIM 22) including Czech Budvar.

ROVANIEMI

Rovaniemi, the largest town in Northern Finland, lies almost precisely along the Arctic Circle. Though it's 300 km (180 mi) south of any Sami village, it's frequently called the "Gateway to Lapland." Indeed, the town's wealth of information about Sami culture, plus its convenient rail connections to the south (12 hrs, FIM 295 to Helsinki), make it the best jumping-off point for trips into Lapland. First settled during the 11th century, Rovaniemi is a drab but friendly town that was rebuilt in the 1950s and '60s after retreating German troops left destruction in their wake in 1945. You won't be able to tell just by wandering around, but architect Alvar Aalto gridded the streets in the shape of reindeer antlers.

TREKKING THE BEAR'S RING

The grandest of Finland's trekking routes, the 95-km (57-mi) Karhunkierros (Bear's Ring) offers a five- to seven-day ramble through stunning wilderness. The trail zigzags along the Kitkajoki and Oulankajoki rivers and skims the Russian border. The Karhunkierros is often crowded, but it's good practice for the more-demanding treks in western Lapland, and you'll find plenty of campsites and wilderness huts along the way. These free and sometimes crowded huts are scattered every 10–15 km (6–9 mi) along the route; some lack cots, so bring a sleeping pad. If they're full, tent camping is also popular in summer, despite the mosquitoes. For a shorter hike, try Little Bear's Ring (12 km/7 mi) or Ristikallio Trail (30 km/18 mi).

The village of Juuma makes a great trekking base, with hotels, restaurants, a post office, and phones. You can get here by bus (FIM 60) from Kuusamo, which is connected to Helsinki by rail. The Kuusamo tourist office (Torangintaival 2, tel. 08/850-2910) can provide trekking information and a map with Karhunkierros wilderness huts clearly marked.

The staff at the **tourist office** (Koskikatu 1, tel. 016/346–270; open June–Aug., weekdays 8–6, weekends 11:30–4; shorter hrs off season) has plenty of information on travel throughout Lapland. **Arctic Adventure Treks** (Lamperontie, tel. 016/399–244) leads hiking, rafting, canoeing, and camping trips for up to five days in the vicinity of Rovaniemi. If you're interested, call in advance to set something up, and plan to pay about FIM 150 for night hiking and FIM 400 for a day of rafting. **Lapland Safaris** (Harrikatu 4, tel. 016/331–1200) runs gentler, more tourist-oriented trips to points north of Rovaniemi. Boat cruises to the reindeer farm (*see below*) go for FIM 270; rafting on the Raudanjoki rapids is FIM 295; a three-hour mountain-bike excursion costs FIM 240 (bikes included); and a romantic summer-night cruise is FIM 145.

Tacky **Santa Claus Village,** 9 km (5½ mi) north of Rovaniemi, is the destination of more than half a million children's letters annually. Take Bus 8 or 10 from the Rovaniemi train station. Seven kilometers (5 miles) northwest of Rovaniemi is a **reindeer farm** (admission FIM 30) where tourists can pet the indigenous beasts and get pulled along on a sleigh (in winter); call 016/384–150 for an appointment. Buses don't serve the farm; a taxi there costs about FIM 70.

WHERE TO SLEEP AND EAT

For FIM 180–FIM 200 doubles, try one of two small guest houses: **Matka Borealis** (Asemieskatu 1, tel. 016/342–0130) or **Outa** (Ukkoherrantie 16, tel. 016/312–474; cash only). Doubles at the larger, centrally located **Aakenus** (Koskikatu 47, tel. 016/342–2051) are FIM 260. Rovaniemi's **HI Tervashonka** (Hallituskatu 16, tel. 016/344–644; beds FIM 75; cash only) is dull and smoky, with hallway bathrooms, basement showers, and a FIM 26 breakfast; turn right outside the train station and walk down Hallituskatu to Rovakatu. Check-in is 6:30 AM–10 AM and 5 PM–10 PM. **Ounaskoski Camping** (Jäämerentie 1, tel. 016/345–304 or 049/692–421; closed Sept.–May) has FIM 90 sites on the banks of the Kemijoki River.

Fill up on a traditional ham, potato, and salad lunch at **Ruokahuone Mariza** (Ruokasenkatu 2, tel. 016/319–616; cash only). At the pleasantly divey **Torikeidas** (Lapinkävijäntie 3, tel. 016/342–3630), you'll finally get to sample reindeer casserole (FIM 52). **Rio Grande** (Korkulonkatu 13, tel. 016/313–211; cash only), the "Arctic Circle Rock Pub," has pool tables, loud music, and FIM 20 pizzas.

LAPLAND

The largest of Finland's 12 provinces, Lapland is a vast wilderness of tundra and trees, covering a third of the country. In summer you'll have to brave swarms of mosquitoes (hit a Finnish pharmacy for repellent) and endure the midnight sun (north of Rovaniemi the 24-hour day starts around June 6), but you'll be rewarded with excellent trekking, fishing, and canoeing.

From Rovaniemi, the region's transport hub (*see above*), two daily buses (FIM 180) run north along the Swedish border and then head 30 km (18 mi) inland to **Enontekiö**; one bus continues north across the border to Kautokeino for connections to Norwegian bus lines. Enontekiö's **tourist office** (tel. 016/521–215) can direct you to the popular 26-km (16-mi) trek to the Sami village of **Näkkälä,** and also has the scoop on canoe rentals for one- to seven-day journeys down the Ounasjoki River.

Further north is **Kilpisjärvi,** with the highest terrain in Finland and fantastic multiday treks. You can reach the town by bus every day from Enontekiö (change in Palojoensuu) or from Rovaniemi (6½ hrs, FIM 230) via Kittilä. The trekking center **Kilpisjärven Retkeilykeskus** (tel. 016/537–771; open Apr.–Sept., daily 8 AM–10 PM) brings hikers together and provides maps. Ask the staff about the limited lodging in the **HI Peeran Retkeilykeskus** (tel. 016/532–659; beds FIM 75; cash only; closed Jan.–Feb.), about 20 km (12 mi) south of town.

Route E75 rambles north from Rovaniemi to the villages of Ivalo (5 hrs, FIM 168) and Inari (6½ hrs, FIM 180), both on the shores of Lake Inarinjärvi. Several buses a day (and plenty of hopeful hitchhikers) travel this road. On the way, 30 km (19 mi) south of Ivalo, you pass through Saariselkä, which is home to **Urho Kekkonen National Park,** one of Finland's most popular trekking areas. The routes are well traveled, clearly marked, and laden with wilderness huts. Get more information at the **Pankavaara Information Center** (tel. 016/626–251; open summer, daily 10–7; winter, daily 10–4) inside the park.

Northern Lapland's major town is **Ivalo.** Get regional information at **Lapponia Tours** (Uhdustie 14, tel. 016/663–050) or the bus terminal at the airport. Forty kilometers (24 miles) north is **Inari,** a town with Finland's best museum on Lapland, **Saamelaismuseo** (Sami Museum). Inari's **tourist office** (tel. 016/671–194) is next to the bank, across from the bus depot, and ½ km (⅓ mi) from **HI Ahopää** (Tunturikeskus, Kiilopää, tel. 016/667–101; beds FIM 100; cash only). Continue along Route E75 to reach **Karigasniemi** (7 hrs, FIM 230 from Rovaniemi), on the Norwegian border, and the adjacent **Kevo Natural Park.** A 70-km (42-mi), four-day (minimum) trek runs through the Kevo River Gorge. There's a **tourist office** (tel. 016/676–811; open summer, daily 10–6) at the bus stop in Karigasniemi. Stay at rooms let by the **Kalastajan Maja** eatery (tel. 016/676–188; beds FIM 60, doubles FIM 160; cash only) before or after your trek.

FRANCE

France sits squarely in the middle of Western Europe; according to many of the French and assorted Francophiles, it might just as well be the center of the universe. The country has been the locus of European intellectual life ever since the founding of the Sorbonne in Paris in the 13th century. During the next few centuries, the entire Western world began to adopt the French language and aspects of French culture. Then, with the French Revolution of 1789 and Napoléon's frolic over the European continent, France established itself as a world political, as well as cultural, power—a fact the proud French have not forgotten, and are always eager to remind you about.

In more recent years, the tables have turned, and foreign cultures have been invading France. Young French people often emulate foreigners in the way they dress, the music they listen to, and even in their manner of speaking. Levi's go for $80 a pair and can be seen gracing the legs of any slick twentysomething, buskers sing Bob Dylan tunes in the streets, and teenagers hang out in the local MacDo (MacDonald's to the French) not in the corner café. And though they curse American movies to the death, the French love-hate relationship with Yankee films has let Hollywood win over the big screen.

But the French also fear the movement toward what they call *mondialisation* (globalization), which to many is a synonym for Americanization. The older generation in particular sees the infiltration of American fads and the country's integration into the European Union (EU) as eroding traditional French ways of life. Many grumble about the universality of the English language, which is commanding World Wide Chats across the Internet and is the common parlance in international business deals. The Académie Française, tireless preserver of French culture, even set about to strike English words (like "le weekend" and "le parking") from the French vocabulary and establish 66% French music quotas for radio stations. The proposed changes stuck like wet Velcro when cultural minister Jacques Toubon accidentally slipped an English word into his announcement speech. But even with the trend toward mondialisation, French culture remains, well, distinctly French. Paris is still the world center of the ultrastylish, and its cafés continue to be the breeding ground for smoking, coffee-drinking, armchair intellectuals. And in the French provinces, with their pastoral landscapes, stunning architecture, and delicious cuisine, there remains a determination to keep old-world charm uncompromised.

It is also, however, important to remember that there is not just one France: the country's geography is as diverse as the people who inhabit it. The Riviera attracts an international jet-set crowd to its famous strips of sand. In the south you'll find an influx of recent immigrants and a myriad of cultures to match, a phenomenon that has met hostility from the steadily expanding Front National, France's ultraright party. In Provence, the soil yields many gifts, and sunny pride blends with Spanish influence and Roman history to create an intriguing culture. In the southwest, along the Spanish border, the Basque people struggle to preserve their culture and their unique language, Euskera, in the face of trends toward centralization. Alsace-Lorraine, on the eastern edge of France, is almost as German as it is French. And in Brittany, one of the last regions to be incorporated into France, people still occasionally speak Breton and celebrate their Celtic heritage.

To really see France, you obviously must travel outside of Paris. In the country's small villages, you'll be surprised at how relaxed the pace is and at how much care goes into preparing a meal (and how much time is spent enjoying it). Venture off the Eurailpass trail, and head to the Pyrénées at the Spanish border and the Alps at France's eastern edge to ski or mountain bike. Or head north through rolling farmland where you might not be awed by dramatic vistas, but where you will find plenty of locals willing to listen to your fumbling French and show you what "la belle vie française" is all about.

BASICS

MONEY

US$1 = 5.5 francs and 1 franc = 18¢. The units of currency in France are the franc and the centime (1 franc = 100 centimes). Banks are usually open on weekdays from about 9:30 to 4:30 (and sometimes Saturdays), and most close for an hour or two between noon and 2. Some banks are open on Saturday instead of Monday. Bank exchange rates are usually pretty good (Banque de France is the best), but check to see if they charge a commission (sometimes 10F–20F). The rates at bureaux de change vary widely, but are sometimes as good as those at the bank. ATM machines are found in towns all over France and many take regular credit cards as well as bank cards. If you're going to be in rural areas, though, it's better to bring cash.

HOW MUCH IT WILL COST • You can do France for about $50 a day less if you're really frugal, more if you want to splurge on French goodies or plan on spending a few days in Paris. Hotels are not a big problem for budget travelers; singles in one- or no-star hotels cost 120F–250F, doubles 200F–500F. Hostels cost anywhere between 50F and 170F per night and charge 20F–50F for a meal. A three-course meal at a cheap but good restaurant usually costs 60F–100F; lunch prices are toward the lower end. In most cafés, brasseries, and restaurants the service is *compris* (included), so they can be as rude to you as they want and still not get stiffed. Cover charges for nightclubs range from 70F to a steep 140F and usually include one drink. Drinks in clubs are outrageously expensive—about 50F each—but a beer or a glass of wine in a bar goes for 12F–20F.

GETTING AROUND

BY BUS • Buses, which are slightly less expensive and significantly slower than the trains, are generally used only to fill in the gaps left by the rail lines.

BY CAR • If you want to explore some of the tiny hills above the Riviera or delve into the traditional lifestyles in remote areas of Brittany, renting a car is a good idea. Though these more out-of-the-way areas are sometimes covered by bus companies, service tends to be infrequent. It's a good idea to reserve a car before you leave home, as you can usually get a better deal and the major car rental agencies (Avis, Budget, Hertz) sometimes offer airline, train, and/or hotel packages.

Keep in mind that gas is costly, especially on expressways and in rural areas. Don't let your tank get too low—you can go for many miles in the country without passing a gas station—and keep an eye on pump prices as you go. These vary enormously; from 5.80 to 6.80 francs per liter. The cheapest gas can be found at *hypermarchés* (super stores).

You may use your own driver's license in France, but you must be able to prove you have third-party insurance. Drive on the right and yield to drivers coming from the right if there is no solid white line. Seat belts are obligatory for all passengers, and children under 12 may not travel in the front seat. Speed limits are 130 kph (80 mph) on expressways, 110 kph (70 mph) on divided highways, 90 kph (55 mph) on other roads, 50 kph (30 mph) in towns. French drivers break these limits and police dish out hefty on-the-spot fines with equal abandon.

France's roads are classified into five types, numbered and prefixed *A, N, D, C,* or *V.* Roads marked *A* (Autoroutes) are expressways. There are excellent links between Paris and most French cities, but poor ones between the provinces (the principal exceptions being A26 from Calais to Reims, A62 between

FRANCE

ENGLAND

La Manche
(English Channel)

Calais
Boulogne

NOR
PICAR

Cherbourg
Fécamp Dieppe
Etretat Amiens
Le Havre
Arromanches Honfleur Rouen B
Bayeux Caen
NORMANDY Giverny
Seine
IL
FR
Versailles

Ile de
Bréhat

Mont
St-Michel
St-Malo

Ile
d'Ouessant Perros-Guirec
Roscoff

Brest Morlaix
St-Brieuc Dinan
BRITTANY Fougères Chartres
Quimper Rennes Orlé
Concarneau Vitré Le Mans
Lorient Vannes
Quiberon Angers Chambor
Saumur Blois
Belle-Ile Nantes Tours
Loire LOIRE
PAYS-DE- VALLEY
LOIRE

ATLANTIC
OCEAN

Niort Poitiers
Ile de Ré
La Rochelle

Bay of Biscay Saintes Limoges
Angoulême LIMOUSIN

Périgueux AUVER
Bordeaux Sarlat Brive-la-
Gaillarde A
Dordogne Rocamadour
Langon Cahors

Montauban
AQUITAINE Albi
Bayonne
Biarritz Pau Toulouse
Tarbes LANGUE
St-Jean-Pied- ROUSSIL
de-Port
MIDI- Carcassonne
PYRÉNÉES

N

Rail Lines
0   50 mi
0   75 km

S P A I N

ANDORRA

176

Calais
gne
BELGIUM

**NORTH
PICARDY**
Lille

Arras

Cambrai

Amiens
St-Quentin

LUXEMBOURG

Beauvais

uen
**CHAMPAGNE
ARDENNES**

Seine
**ILE DE
FRANCE**
Reims

Metz
ALSACE-LORRAINE

lles
Paris
Châlons-sur-
Marne
Nancy
Saverne

Rhine

Troyes
Strasbourg
GERMANY

Orléans
Calmar

hambord
Auxerre
Mulhouse

Bourges
Vézelay
Belfort

Clamecy
Dijon
Besançon

Nevers
Beaune
**FRANCHE
COMTE**

SWITZERLAND

BURGUNDY

Montluçon
Saône

Mâcon
Bourg-en-
Bresse

OUSIN
Rhône
Chamonix

Clermont-
Ferrand
Lyon
Annecy

AUVERGNE
ALPES

Vienne
Voiron
Chambéry

la-
arde
Aurillac
ITALY

adour
Le Puy
Grenoble

**RHÔNE
VALLEY**
Rhône

Rodez
Montélimar

Millau
Orange

Albi
Avignon

an
Nîmes
PROVENCE
Nice
Menton

se
Arles
RIVIERA
MONACO

ANGUEDOC
Montpellier
Aix-en-Provence
Monte Carlo

OUSSILLON
Cannes
Antibes

sonne
Narbonne
Marseille
St-Raphaël

Perpignan
Toulon
St-Tropez

Mediterranean Sea
Corsica

Bordeaux and Toulouse, and A9/A8 the length of the Mediterranean coast). It is often difficult to avoid Paris when crossing France—just try to steer clear of the rush hours (7–9:30 AM and 4:30–7:30 PM). A *péage* (toll) must be paid on most expressways: The rate varies but can be steep. The *N* (Route Nationale) roads—which are sometimes divided highways—and *D* (Route Départementale) roads are usually wide and fast, and driving along them can be a real pleasure. Don't be daunted by smaller (*C* and *V*) roads, either. The yellow regional Michelin maps—on sale throughout France—are invaluable.

If your car breaks down on an expressway, go to a roadside emergency telephone and call the breakdown service. If you have a breakdown anywhere else, find the nearest garage or contact the police (dial 17).

Parking is a nightmare in Paris and often difficult in other large towns. Meters and ticket machines (pay and display) are common: Make sure you have a supply of 1-, 2-, and 5-franc coins. Parking is free during August in most of Paris, but be sure to check the signs. In smaller towns, parking may be permitted on one side of the street only—alternating every two weeks—so pay attention to signs.

HITCHING • For organized (and expensive) hitching, contact **Allo Stop Provoya,** an organization that links up hitchers and drivers for a membership fee (about 250F for two years, or 30F–70F each time) plus 20 centimes per kilometer to the driver. Contact the main office in Paris (tel. 01–53–20–42–42) for information and locations of branch Allo Stop offices.

BY TRAIN • The railway system in France is fast, extensive, and efficient. For long distances, it's better to take the lightning-fast TGVs (*Trains à Grande Vitesse,* or Very Fast Trains). They require a reservation, which can cost anywhere from 19F to 90F to make. All French trains have first- and second-class cars; second-class cars are perfectly comfortable.

Eurailpasses are good in France, but if you're staying within the country, the **French Railpass** is a better deal. The three-day pass ($185 in first class, $145 in second) is valid for one month; added days (up to six allowed) cost $30. The France Railpass isn't available once you arrive, so be sure to pick one up before leaving home. Another good deal is the **France Rail 'n Drive Pass**; for only a bit more than the plain ol' train pass ($219 in second class, and you can add car days for $39 each and rail days for $30 each per person), you get three days of train travel and two days of Avis car rental within one month. Car-rental reservations must be made directly with Avis at least seven days in advance (tel. 800/331–1084 in U.S.), and drivers must be age 24 or older.

SNCF offers various **Prix Découverts,** discounted fares based on certain restrictions. If you're under 26 you can get a 25% discount by showing a valid ID; if you know you're going to be traveling around the country quite a bit consider purchasing the 270F **Carte 12–25,** which gets you unlimited 50% reductions for one year (provided that there are seats available at this price). The **Prix Découverts à Deux** will get two people traveling together (you don't have to be a couple) a 25% reduction during a "période bleu" (blue period; weekdays and non-holidays). The **Carte Vermeil** is a good value if you're over 60; ask about the various options for discounts of 30% to 50%. If you don't qualify for any of these reductions, you can get discounts if you buy your ticket well in advance, travel only during blue periods, or go at least 1000 km (620 mi) roundtrip (even with several stops) using a **Billet Séjour.**

WHERE TO SLEEP

The French rate their **hotels** by the star system, ranging from no stars to four. The number of stars indicates the percentage of rooms equipped with bath or other amenities but may not be a good indication of how nice the place is. Room prices should be listed near the hotel's front door or on the wall behind the reception desk. Rooms marked *e.c.* offer only running water; rooms marked *douche* have a shower in the room; rooms marked *lavabo* have only a sink; and rooms marked *douche/WC* or *bain/WC* have a shower and a toilet, or a bath and toilet, in the room. *Petit dejeuner compris* means that breakfast is included in the price of the room.

Hotels are a good deal if you are traveling in twos or threes, but **hostels** are often a better deal for solo travelers. Hostels tend to be inconveniently on the edge of town, but a few are housed in spectacular old abbeys or châteaux and are worth the trek. Most hostels charge 50F–170F per night and about 16F for sheets. Another cheap alternative, especially in rural areas, is the *gîte d'étape* (rural hostel). Like hostels, gîtes usually feature dorm rooms and community showers, occasionally housed in cool, rustic buildings. Although they are often technically reserved for hikers, budget travelers can often wheedle their way in. **Camping** in France is not for you if you're seeking peaceful seclusion among trees and streams; campgrounds are often filled with family caravans in shady parking lots on the outskirts of towns. Campgrounds charge 30F–100F per person.

In case you want to be welcomed there.

We're here to see that you're always welcomed at establishments everywhere. That's why millions of people carry the American Express® Card — for peace of mind, confidence, and security, around the world or just around the corner.

And just in case.

We're here with American Express® Travelers Cheques and Cheques *for Two.*® They're the safest way to carry money on your vacation and the surest way to get a refund, practically anywhere, anytime.
Another way we help you...

do more ®

AMERICAN
EXPRESS

Travelers
Cheques

FOOD

It's not by chance that France is known as one of the culinary capitals of the world. Whether it's a 15F crêpe from a sidewalk stand at 2 AM or a 100F menu at the traditional 8 PM dinner hour, food in France is a gastronomic delight.

When eating out, look for the words *menu* or *prix fixe,* which generally point you to three- or four-course meals served at a special rate, often 50F–100F. The biggest money-saver, though, is eating your big meal in the middle of the day, when prices are often reduced by about a third. Restaurants operate in two shifts: lunch is served around noon–2 and dinner around 8–10. To avoid paying 15F for bottled water, which the waiter will inevitably try to serve, order simply a *carafe d'eau* (tap water). Don't forget wine, which comes by the bottle, by the *pichet* (pitcher), or by the glass. It usually costs 50F–80F a bottle in budget restaurants.

Supermarkets are plentiful and have the best prices for the basics. Small *boucheries* (butcher shops) and *fromageries* (cheese shops) will sell you *jambon* (ham) and all kinds of cheeses by the piece for about the same price, and you can always pick up a baguette at the local *boulangerie* (bakery). *Charcuteries* and *epiceries* are the French equivalent of a deli, with fresh salads and take-out stuff such as quiche or lasagna sold by weight for pretty good prices.

HOLIDAYS AND FESTIVALS

Bastille Day, celebrated on July 14, is France's biggest national celebration. Parades and fireworks mark the anniversary of the storming of the famous state prison in 1789, in the early days of the French Revolution. Other days when you can expect most businesses to close are: January 1, Easter Monday, May 1 (Labor Day), May 8 (World War II Armistice Day-a new holiday that's not observed as widely as the others), Ascension Day (five weeks after Easter), the Monday after Pentecost, August 15 (Assumption Day), November 1 (All Saints' Day), November 11 (Armistice Day), and December 25.

BUSINESS HOURS

Most museums are closed one day a week (usually Monday or Tuesday) and on national holidays. Normal opening times are from 9:30 to 5 or 6, often with a long lunch break between noon and 2. Many of the large museums have one *Nocturne* opening per week when they close at 9:30 or 10:00 PM. Large stores in big towns are open from 9 or 9:30 in the morning until 6 or 7 in the evening, without a lunch break. Smaller shops often open an hour or so earlier and close a few hours later, but they often close for a lengthy lunch break. Banks are open weekdays, generally from 9:30 AM to 4:30 or 5 PM.

PHONES

Country Code: 33. French phone numbers have 10 digits (the first two are the regional codes): all Paris numbers start with 01, all numbers in the northwest start with 02, in the northeast 03, in the southeast 04, and in the southwest 05. Nationwide numbers begin with 08. To call anywhere in France, while in the country, dial the whole 10-digit number. To make a call *to* France from another country, dial France's country code (33), drop the initial zero from the telephone number, and then dial the remaining nine digits.

Public phones are never far away in France; you will find them at post offices and often in cafés. Almost all French phones nowadays accept only the **Télécarte,** a handy little card you can buy at *tabacs* (tobacco shops), post offices, or métro stations; it costs 41F for 50 units or 96F for 120 units. The digital display on the phone counts down your units while you're talking and tells you how many you have left when you hang up. For local and national directory assistance, dial 12 on any phone.

To use an **AT&T** calling card or to talk to their international operators, dial 0–800–99–00–11. For **MCI,** dial 0–800–99–00–19; for **Sprint,** dial 0–800–99–00–87. Within France, you can call collect by dialing 12 for the operator and saying *"en PCV"* ("on pay say vay").

MAIL

France's postal system is relatively efficient; mail takes about 4 to 10 days to make its way to the United States and it costs about 4F40 to send a letter or postcard there. Buy stamps in tabacs unless you're already headed toward a post office. Most local post offices also hold mail that is marked POSTE RESTANTE for up to 15 days.

EMERGENCIES

Dial 17 for the **police,** 15 for an **ambulance,** and 18 for the **fire department.** For nonemergency situations, look in the phone directory for the number of the *commissariat* or the *gendarmerie,* both referring to the local police station. Most pharmacies close at 7 or 8 PM, but the commissariat in every city has the list of the *pharmacies de garde,* the pharmacists on call for the evening. Pharmacies de garde are also often printed in the newspaper or posted on the doors of closed pharmacies.

LANGUAGE

The French study English for a minimum of four years at school, so you can almost always find some-one with a good grasp of the language. Start every conversation with a few polite phrases in French and people will be happier to speak to you in English. Following are a few helpful phrases: *bonjour* (hello); *au revoir* (good-bye); *Parlez-vous anglais?* (Do you speak English?); *s'il vous plaît* (please); *merci* (thank you); *où est/où sont . . .?* (where is/where are . . .?); *C'est combien?* (How much does it cost?).

PARIS

Paris is one of the most written about, raved about, and spat upon cities in the entire world. Droves of people have come for hundreds of years looking to inject their lives with beauty, glamour, culture, scan-dal, and romance. They have sung about Paris, painted her, found themselves, lost their religion, and learned how to eat well and smoke too much.

Paris is a city for sensualists. The gargoyles leering down from medieval walls, the smell of freshly baked croissants, the pulse of jazz through overcrowded streets, the young and old couples making out along the Seine, and that first sip of wine to start off the evening all are part of the Parisian obsession with the physical world. Paris voluptuaries explore the city during the late-night and early morning hours, when the boutiques are blessedly dark and the footsteps of party stragglers echo through the streets. When day breaks, though, Paris puts her face on. Fashionable 85-year-old matrons parade their freshly coifed Pekingese pooches past boutique windows, spruced-up facades of medieval buildings, and artfully arranged *pâtisserie* (pastry shop) displays. Cafés fill up, and the strong, dark coffee starts to pour, wiring up the professionals seated at little bitty tables packed along the sidewalks. All the while, tourists sweep through town, trying to see in a week what locals haven't seen in a lifetime.

All this action can be overwhelming, and you might feel this is a place where people were meant to shop, not live. But whatever Paris's shortcomings, you and a few hundred thousand other travelers will come to her in awe and admiration again this year, and will revel in an atmosphere as heady and full-bodied as a good French wine.

BASICS

VISITOR INFORMATION

Paris's main tourist office, the **Office de Tourisme de Paris** (127 av. des Champs-Elysées, 8e, tel. 01–49–52–53–54; open daily 9–8), sells phone cards and all sorts of guides and passes; they'll also book you rooms for a fee of 8F–25F. The branch offices, at the Eiffel Tower (7e, tel. 01–45–51–22–15; open May–Sept., daily 11–6) and all the main-line train stations apart from St-Lazare (open daily 8–8), also book rooms and distribute brochures. For 24-hour information in English on the week's cultural events, dial 01–49–52–53–56.

AMERICAN EXPRESS

Both members and nonmembers can pick up mail (5F per pickup for nonmembers) and buy traveler's checks. *11 rue Scribe, 9e, tel. 01–47–77–79–50, métro Opéra; open weekdays 9–6:30, Sat. 9–5:30. 38 av. de Wagram, 8e, tel. 01–42–27–58–80, métro Ternes; open weekdays 9–5:30. 5 rue de Chail-lot, 16e, tel. 01–47–23–72–15, métro Iéna; open weekdays 9–5.*

CHANGING MONEY

During business hours you can get good rates at the banks around Opéra Garnier and the Champs-Elysées. The bureaux de change at the train stations, open until 8 PM or 10 PM, have slightly worse rates. More and more **ATMs** taking American bank cards and credit cards can be found throughout the city, including the ATM at **Crédit Mutuel** (13 rue des Abbesses, métro Abbesses), which takes Cirrus cards, and the ATM at **Bred Bank** (33 rue de Rivoli, métro Hôtel de Ville), which takes PLUS. Before you leave, ask your bank for a list of other Cirrus or PLUS locations. For late-night transactions, use one of the 24-

hour automatic cash-exchange machines at **Crédit du Nord** (24 blvd. Sébastopol, 1er); **CCF** (115 av. des Champs-Elysées, 8e); or **BNP** (2 pl. de l'Opéra, 2e).

DISCOUNT TRAVEL AGENCIES

Council Travel. *6 rue de Vaugirard, 6e, tel. 01–46–34–02–90, métro Odéon; open weekdays 9:30– 6:30, Sat. 10–5. 22 rue des Pyramides, 1er, tel. 01–44–55–55–65, métro Pyramides.*

Nouvelles Frontières. *5 av. de l'Opéra, 1er, tel. 08–03–33–33–33, métro Opéra; call for hours and other locations.*

Wasteels. *113 blvd. St-Michel, 5e, tel. 01–43–26–25–25, RER Luxembourg; 5 rue de la Banque, 2e, tel. 01–42–61–53–21, métro Bourse; both open weekdays 9–7.*

EMBASSIES

Australia: *4 rue Jean-Rey, 15e, tel. 01–40–59–33–00. Métro: Bir-Hakeim. Open weekdays 9–5:30.* **Canada:** *35 av. Montaigne, 8e, tel. 01–44–43–29–16. Métro: Franklin D. Roosevelt. Open weekdays 8:30–11.* **New Zealand:** *7 ter rue Léonard-de-Vinci, 16e, tel. 01–45–00–24–11. Métro: Victor Hugo. Open weekdays 9–1 and 2–5:30.* **United Kingdom:** *35 rue du Faubourg-St-Honoré, 8e, tel. 01–42– 66–91–42. Métro: Madeleine. Open weekdays 9:30–1 and 2:30–6.* **United States:** *2 rue St-Florentin, 1er, tel. 01–40–39–84–11. Métro: Concorde. Open weekdays 9–4.*

EMERGENCIES

Dial 17 for the **police,** 15 for an **ambulance,** and 18 for the **fire department.** Regular pharmacy hours are about 9 AM to 7 or 8 PM, but **Pharmacie Dhéry** (84 av. des Champs-Elysées, 8e, tel. 01–45–62– 02–41, métro George V) is open 24 hours. There are 24-hour emergency centers at the **Hôpital Améri- cain** (63 blvd. Victor-Hugo, Neuilly-sur-Seine, tel. 01–46–41–25–25), which takes Blue Cross/Blue Shield, and the **Hôpital Anglais** (3 rue Barbès, Levallois, tel. 01–46–39–22–22). Both are about a 45- minute ride outside Paris.

ENGLISH BOOKS AND NEWSPAPERS

Pick up a copy of the monthly *The Free Voice,* available at English-language bookstores, some restau- rants, and L'Eglise Américaine (American Church; 65 quai d'Orsay, 7e, tel. 01–47–05–07–99). English-language bookstores carry the free *France USA Contacts* (also known as FUSAC), which has all sorts of classified listings in English and French. *Pariscope* (3F) has an invaluable English-language section listing cool things to do in the city, as well as the usual lists of movies, clubs, and other weekly events (in French).

Find new and used books for as little as 15F at **Shakespeare & Company** (37 rue de la Bûcherie, 5e, tel. 01–43–26–96–50). The **Village Voice Bookshop** (6 rue Princesse, 6e, tel. 01–46–33–36–47) is easily the best English-language bookstore in Paris. Also try the larger bookstore chains, including **Brentano's** (37 av. de l'Opéra, 2e, tel. 01–42–61–52–50, métro Opéra) and **W. H. Smith** (248 rue de Rivoli, 1er, tel. 01–44–78–88–89, métro Concorde).

MAIL

The central post office, the **Hôtel des Postes** (52 rue du Louvre, at rue Etienne-Marcel, 1er, tel. 01–40– 28–20–00, métro Sentier) is open 24 hours for limited services, such as buying stamps, using the phones, or receiving poste restante. All post offices in Paris accept poste restante mail, but this is where your mail will end up if it's simply addressed: LAST NAME, first name, Poste Restante, 75001 Paris.

COMING AND GOING

BY BUS

Eurolines offers international service only. Popular routes are to London (8 hrs, 330F), Barcelona (16 hrs, 530F), and Berlin (14 hrs, 490F). *28 av. du Général-de-Gaulle, Bagnolet, tel. 01–49–72–51–51. Métro: Gallieni. Open daily 9–6.*

BY PLANE

Paris has two international airports: **Orly,** 16 km (10 mi) south of town, and **Charles de Gaulle** (also called **Roissy**), 26 km (16 mi) northeast. The easiest way to get to town from either airport is by bus, with departures from the terminals for Paris every 15 minutes 6 AM–11 PM. The **Roissybus** from Charles de Gaulle (45–60 mins, 40F) stops at rue Scribe, next to the Opéra; the **Orlybus** (30–40 mins, 30F) runs to place Denfert-Rochereau. You can pick up the métro or RER from both these drop-off points. Signs near the baggage pickup at both airports list many other transportation options, including taking the **RER** (50 mins, 30F–55F) train directly into the city or taking a **taxi** (150F–200F).

BY TRAIN

Six train stations serve Paris; most have tourist offices, and all have cafés, newsstands, bureaux de change, and luggage storage, although be aware that automatic lockers (15F–30F for 72 hrs) may have been sealed off for security reasons. Each station connects to the métro system. **Gare d'Austerlitz** serves southwest France and Spain, including Barcelona (9–12 hrs, 510F), and Madrid (12 hrs, 744F). **Gare de l'Est** sends daily trains to eastern France, Frankfurt (6 hrs, 467F), Prague (14 hrs, 911F), and Vienna (13½ hrs, 1,023F). From **Gare de Lyon**, catch a train to Milan (6½ hrs, 550F), Rome (13 hrs, 807F), and destinations in the south of France, such as Lyon (2 hrs, 254F–298F). Trains leave **Gare Montparnasse** for Brittany and southwestern France; daily trains travel to Bordeaux (3 hrs, 340F), Rennes (2 hrs, 260F), and Biarritz (5½ hrs, 410F). From **Gare du Nord** regular trains head to northern France (Calais and Lille), Amsterdam (5½ hrs, 385F), Copenhagen (14 hrs, 1,345F), and London (3 hrs, 395F–645F) via the Channel Tunnel. **Gare St-Lazare,** the only major station without a tourist office, serves Normandy. Dial 08–36–35–35–35 for all train information and reservations (note, however, that there is a 2F32 charge per minute).

GETTING AROUND

The **Rive Gauche** (Left Bank) refers to the part of the city roughly south of the Seine and includes the Sorbonne, Quartier Latin, and many other bustling neighborhoods full of young people. The **Rive Droite** (Right Bank), north of the Seine, is traditionally more elegant and commercial; it's home to ritzy shopping districts and most big-name sights. Between the two banks you have the two islands, the Ile de la Cité and the smaller Ile St-Louis.

Once you have the Left and Right Banks figured out, move on to the ***arrondissements,*** or districts, numbered 1 through 20. Arrondissements 1 through 8 are the most central and contain most of the big tourist attractions, while 9 through 20 gradually spiral out toward the city's outskirts. Practically essential is the ***Plan de Paris par Arrondissement,*** a booklet of detailed maps. For information on all public transport, dial 08–36–68–77–14 daily 6 AM–9 PM.

BY BOAT

In summer, hordes of *Bateaux Mouches* travel the Seine shining their lights on buildings on the riverbanks and offer a running commentary in five languages. The lights make people living along the river mad as hell, but they do show off the city at its glitziest. Board the boat for a 40F, one-hour tour at the Pont de l'Alma. From April to September, a less touristy but more expensive alternative is **Bateaux Parisiens** (tel. 01–44–11–33–55), a small boat-bus that runs between Pont de la Bourdonnais at the Eiffel Tower and the Hôtel de Ville. There are five stations along the way, and you'll pay 20F for the journey from Hôtel de Ville to the Eiffel Tower; 60F gets you a day pass to the whole line. The boats leave about every half hour daily 10 AM–9 PM.

BY BUS

There are maps of the bus system at all bus stops; all 63 lines run Monday–Saturday 6:30 AM–8:30 PM, with limited service until 12:30 AM and all day on Sunday. The **Noctambus** service runs 10 lines every hour on the half hour 1:30 AM–5:30 AM; all lines start at métro Châtelet, and all Noctambus stops have a yellow-and-black sign with an owl symbol.

Métro tickets are accepted on the buses. Theoretically you need one to three tickets, but you probably won't get caught if you travel with only one. Stamp your ticket in the machine at the front of the bus. But don't stamp a Carte Orange—just flash it to the driver.

BY METRO

Except for the fact that it closes at 1:15 AM, with last trains from some stations soon after midnight, the métro is the epitome of convenient public transportation. Thirteen métro lines crisscross Paris, and you'll almost never be more than 10 minutes' walk from a stop. The métro starts up at 5:30 AM and trains run every 3–5 minutes during weekdays, and every 5–8 minutes after 8 PM and on Sundays. You can get a métro map at any station or tourist office. métro lines are marked in the station both by line number and by the names of the stops at each end of the line; find the line number and the name of the terminus toward which you want to travel, and follow the signs. To transfer to a different line, look for orange CORRESPONDENCE signs and for the new line number you need. The blue-and-white SORTIE (exit) signs will lead you back above ground. Individual tickets cost 8F, but *carnets* (books of 10) are only 46F. For longer stays, consider getting a **Carte Orange,** either for a week, the *coupon semaine* (weekly pass; 72F) or for a month, the *coupon mensuel* (monthly pass; 243F); buy these at any métro station or at tabac stores with a RATP sign on the window.

RER • Several métro stations also double as **RER** (Réseau Express Régional) stations; the higher-speed RER rail system extends into the suburbs and passes through Paris. You can use normal métro tickets on the RER system within Paris, but you must buy a separate, more expensive ticket if you plan to leave the city boundaries.

BY TAXI

Hailing a taxi on the street is difficult; try to get one at a major hotel or a makeshift taxi stand in a well-traveled part of the city. Per-kilometer rates are about 8F; after dark they might go up 50 centimes or so. To call for a taxi, try **Taxis Radio 7000** (tel. 01–42–70–00–42) or **Taxis Bleus** (tel. 01–49–36–10–10).

WHERE TO SLEEP

Unless you have well-placed friends, Paris isn't the cheapest place to spend a night. Nonetheless, soaking up the City of Light doesn't have to break the bank. It's possible to get a nice (if not huge), immaculate double room for 500F or less. Expect to pay a minimum of 250F for a dead-simple, clean but perhaps slightly threadbare double with toilet and shower. If you don't mind sharing facilities, you can land equally spartan quarters with only a sink for about 200F. But for that price you

To figure out zip codes in Paris, tack the arrondissement number onto the digits 750. For example, for the fifth arrondissement, 5e, the five-digit zip code would be 75005—turning 5 into 05.

may be better off in one of the nicer hostels (*see below*). Most hotels reviewed below accept credit cards, unless otherwise stated. Many serve breakfast (20F–40F), but you're better off going to the nearest café.

ARC DE TRIOMPHE AND MONCEAU

The genteel, residential 16th and 17th arrondissements, extending out from the Etoile and the Parc Monceau, aren't packed with budget finds. But staying here will put you within footsteps of the ultimate in Parisian elegance.

UNDER 350F • **Hôtel des Deux Acacias.** This fin de siècle hotel was modernized in the early '90s, though some of the Belle Epoque details remain. Singles with shower are 310F and doubles with shower are 350F; you'll pay more for the luxury of a tub. *28 rue de l'Arc de Triomphe, 75017, tel. 01–43–80–01–85, fax 01–40–53–94–62. Métro: Charles-de-Gaulle Etoile. 50 rooms with toilet and shower or bath.*

UNDER 400F • **Keppler.** Near the Champs-Elysées, this small hotel in a 19th-century building is a cut above other budget options in the neighborhood. The spacious, airy rooms are simply decorated with wood furniture and bright fabrics, and have satellite TV. Singles and doubles with toilet and shower go for 400F. *12 rue Keppler, 75016, tel. 01–47–20–65–05, fax 01–47–23–02–29. Métro: George V. 31 rooms with toilet and bath, 18 with toilet and shower. Bar.*

BASTILLE

Spreading over the 11th and 12th arrondissements on the Right Bank, the Bastille is all about cool cafés, cheap restaurants, and more hip bars than you could visit in a lifetime. It's the only area in Paris still humming at 4 AM.

DIRT CHEAP • **Hôtel de l'Europe.** This small but impersonal hotel is popular with German tourists. It has roomy, clean, basic doubles. The cheapest rooms without showers go for 185F. Ask for one with a balcony. *74 rue Sedaine, 75011, tel. 01–47–00–54–38, fax 01–47–00–75–31. Métro: Voltaire. 6 rooms with toilet and shower, 10 rooms with shower only, 6 rooms with sink only.*

Hôtel de la Herse d'Or. The "Golden Gateway," right off the place de la Bastille, is popular with young travelers and backpackers. Rooms are basic and spotless. Those off the street are infinitely quieter, but darker. A double with no shower is only 200F; rooms with shower or tub are more. Singles are 160F. *20*

PARIS METRO

N

Seine

Gabriel Péri
(Asnières-Gennevilliers) ⑬ Météor

Carrefour Pleyel ⑬
Mairie de St-Ouen
St-Denis
Porte de Paris
St-Ouen
Garibaldi
Porte de Clignancourt ④
Mairie de Clichy
Jules Joffrin
Lamarck-Caulaincourt
Porte de St-Ouen
Porte de Clichy
Guy Môquet
Abbesses
Brochant
Pigalle
Pont de Levallois-Bécon ③
La Fourche
Blanche
Anvers
Anatole-France
Place de Clichy
Notre-Dame-de-Lorette
Saint-Georges
Louise-Michel
Wagram
Malesherbes
Rome
Liège
Trinité
Cadet
Le Peletier
Richelieu-Drouot
R. Montmartre
Porte de Champerret
Pereire
Villiers
St-Lazare
Europe
Chaussée-d'Antin
La Fayette
Havre-Caumartin
R. Montmartre
4 Septembre
Monceau
Auber
Opéra
Bourse
Courcelles
St-Augustin
Pyramides
Charles de Gaulle Etoile
Ternes
St-Philippe-du-Roule
Miromesnil
Madeleine
Palais-Royal
Musée du Louvre
Grande Arche de La Défense
Esplanade de La Défense
RER LINE A
① George V
F.D. Roosevelt
Champs-Elysées-Clemenceau
Concorde
Tuileries
Pont de Neuilly
Les Sablons
Porte Maillot
Argentine
⑥ Victor Hugo
Alma-Marceau
Seine
Musée d'Orsay
Porte Dauphine ②
Kléber
Boissière
Iéna
Invalides
Assemblée Nationale
St-Germain-des-Prés
Av. Foch
Rue de la Pompe
Trocadéro
Varenne
Solférino
Av. Henri Martin
Passy
Pont de l'Alma
Rue du Bac
La Muette
Boulainvilliers
Kennedy Radio France
Bir-Hakeim
La Tour-Maubourg
St-François Xavier
Sèvres-Babylone
Mabillon
Ranelagh
Champ-de-Mars
Tour Eiffel
Duroc
Rennes
Vaneau
St-Sulpice
Jasmin
Michel-Ange Auteuil
Eglise d'Auteuil
Ségur
Saint-Placide
Porte d'Auteuil
Duplex
Ecole Mil.
Cambronne
Sèvres-Lecourbe
Falguière
Boulogne Jean-Jaurès
Javel
⑩ Michel-Ange-Molitor
Chardon-Lagache
Mirabeau
Javel André Citroën
Av Emile Zola
Charles Michels
Commerce
La Motte-Picquet-Grenelle
Volontaires
Pasteur
Montparnasse Bienvenüe
Edgar Quinet
Exelmans
Boulogne-Pt. de St-Cloud
Félix Faure
Vaugirard
Gaîté
Boulevard Victor
Boucicaut
Pernety
Porte de St-Cloud
Lourmel
Convention
Plaisance
Marcel Sembat
⑧ Balard
Porte de Versailles
Porte de Vanves
Malakoff-Plateau de Vanves
Billancourt
Issy Plaine
Corentin Celton
Malakoff-Rue Etienne Dolet
⑨ Pont de Sèvres
RER LINE C
⑫ Mairie d'Issy
Châtillon-Montrouge ⑬

PARIS METRO

St-Denis-Basilique

RER LINE B

7 La Courneuve 8 Mai 1945

5 Bobigny Pablo Picasso

Porte de la Chapelle

12 Simplon

Marx Dormoy

Fort d'Aubervilliers

Bobigny-Pantin Raymond Queneau

Aubervilliers-Pantin 4 Chemins

Eglise de Pantin

Porte de la Villette

Hoche

Marcadet-Poissonniers

Crimée

Corentin Cariou

Porte de Pantin

Mairie des Lilas

11

Château-Rouge

Stalingrad

Riquet

Ourcq

Barbès-Rochechouart

Jean Jaurès

Laumière

Danube

Pré St-Gervais

Bolivar

Porte des Lilas

La Chapelle

Louis-Blanc

Buttes-Chaumont

Botzaris

St-Fargeau

3 Gallieni

Gare du Nord

Colonel Fabien

Jourdain

Place des Fêtes

Télégraphe

3b

Porte de Bagnolet

Gare de l'Est

Château-Landon

Pyrénées

Belleville

Pelleport

Poissonnière

Gambetta

Château-d'Eau

Jaques Bonsergent

Goncourt

Couronnes

Mairie de Montreuil

9

Bonne-Nouvelle

Strasbourg St-Denis

Ménilmontant

Père-Lachaise

Croix-de-Chavaux

Bonne-Nouvelle

Temple

St-Maur

Philippe-Auguste

Robespierre

Vincennes

Réaumur-Sébastopol

République

Parmentier

Porte de Montreuil

Sentier Etienne Marcel

Filles du Calvaire

Oberkampf

Alexandre Dumas

Maraichers

Château de Vincennes

Arts et Métiers

St-Ambroise

Charonne

Avron

Buzenval

1

Châtelet-Les Halles

Rambuteau

Richard-Lenoir

Voltaire

Boulets-Montreuil

2 Nation

Bérault

Les Halles

St-Sébastien-Froissart

Bréguet-Sabin

Faidherbe-Chaligny

6

St-Mandé-Tourelle

Louvre Rivoli

Hôtel de Ville

St-Paul

Chemin Vert

Bastille

Picpus

Pont Neuf

11 Châtelet

Ledru-Rollin

Reuilly-Diderot

Porte de Vincennes

Cité

Pont Marie

Sully-Morland

Bel-Air

St-Michel Notre Dame

Quai de la Rapée

Daumesnil

Michel Bizot

St-Michel

Maubert-Mutualité

Jussieu

Gare de Lyon

Montgallet

Dugommier

Porte Dorée

Odéon

10 Gare d'Austerlitz

Bercy

Cluny-La Sorbonne

Cardinal Lemoine

Luxembourg

Place Monge

Dijon

Porte de Charenton

St-Marcel

RER LINE C

Quai de la Gare

Notre-Dame-des-Champs

Censier-Daubenton

Campo Formio

Liberté

Vavin

Port-Royal

Lac de Tolbiac

Les Gobelins

5

Charenton-Ecoles

Denfert-Rochereau

Nationale

Chevaleret

Tolbiac

Boulevard Masséna

Raspail

pl. d'Italie

Port d'Ivry

Porte de Choisy

St-Jacques

Glacière

Corvisart

Tolbiac

Porte d'Italie

Pierre Curie

Alfort-Ecole Vétérinaire

Mouton Duvernet

Maison-Blanche

Alésia

Cité Universitaire

Le Kremlin Bicêtre

7 Mairie d'Ivry

Maisons Alfort-Stade

4 Porte d'Orléans

Villejuif Léo Lagrange

Maisons Alfort-Les Juilliottes

RER LINE B

Gentilly

Villejuif Paul Vaillant Couturier

Créteil-l'Echat (Hôpital Henri Mondor)

Créteil Université

Villejuif Louis Aragon

7

Créteil Préfecture

8

Seine

185

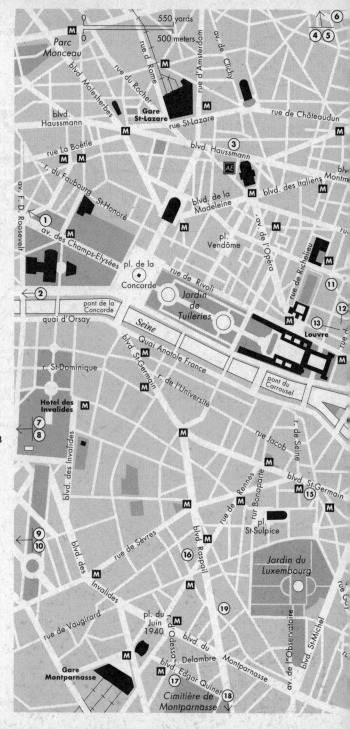

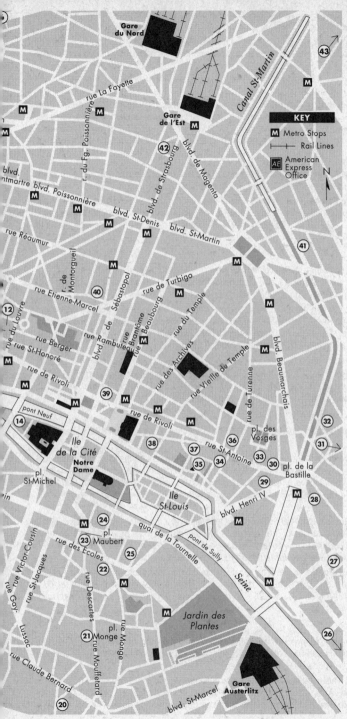

(MIJE) Hôtel le Fauconnier, **35**

(MIJE) Hôtel le Fourcy, **37**

(MIJE) Hôtel Maubuisson, **38**

Parc Montsouris, **17**

Pax Hôtel, **32**

Place des Vosges, **33**

Pratic, **36**

Regyn's Montmartre, **4**

Tiquetonne, **40**

Tour Eiffel Dupleix, **10**

Utrillo, **5**

Young and Happy Youth Hostel, **21**

KEY

M Metro Stops

Rail Lines

AE American Express Office

N

Gare du Nord

Gare de l'Est

Canal St-Martin

rue La Fayette

r. du Fg. Poissonnière

blvd. de Magenta

blvd. de Strasbourg

blvd.
ontmartre blvd. Poissonnière

blvd. St-Denis

blvd. St-Martin

rue Réaumur

r. de Montorgueil

rue Etienne-Marcel

rue de Turbigo

rue du Louvre

rue Berger

rue St-Honoré

rue de Rivoli

Sébastopol

blvd. de

rue Rambuteau

rue Brantôme

rue Beaubourg

rue des Archives

rue du Temple

rue Vieille du Temple

blvd. Beaumarchais

rue de Turenne

pont Neuf

Ile de la Cité

Notre Dame

rue de Rivoli

rue St-Antoine

pl. des Vosges

pl. de la Bastille

pl. St-Michel

Ile St-Louis

blvd. Henri IV

rue des Ecoles

pl. Maubert

rue Victor-Cousin

quai de la Tournelle

pont de Sully

Seine

rue St-Jacques

rue Descartes

rue Gay-

Lussac

Jardin des Plantes

rue Monge

rue Mouffetard

rue Claude Bernard

blvd. St-Marcel

Gare Austerlitz

rue St-Antoine, 75004, tel. 01–48–87–84–09, fax 01–42–78–12–68. Métro: Bastille. 23 rooms with toilet and shower, 12 with sink only.

UNDER 300F • Pax Hôtel. The Pax is no palace, which the 1970s-style lobby will clue you into right away. But it is in a great location near the clubs and galleries and has meticulously maintained rooms with TV. Doubles with shower go for 290F; singles with sink only are 210F. *12 rue de Charonne, 75011, tel. 01–47–00–40–98, fax 01–43–38–57–81. Métro: Bastille. 37 rooms with toilet and shower, 10 with sink only.*

UNDER 350F • Jules-César. Open since 1930, this hotel has a rather glitzy marble lobby and, thankfully, more subdued rooms. Ask for one facing the street, they are larger and sunnier. For 345F you'll get a double (with bath or shower). *52 av. Ledru-Rollin, 75012, tel. 01–43–43–15–88, fax 01–43–43–53–60. Métro: Gare de Lyon, Ledru-Rollin. 4 rooms with toilet and bath, 44 with toilet and shower.*

GARE DE L'EST

This part of Paris, surrounding the train station, isn't one of the city's most beautiful (or quietest) spots. But it's a convenient place to stay if you're on your way in or out of the city.

DIRT CHEAP • Hôtel de France. This modest, turn-of-the-century hotel is the biggest bargain near the Gare de l'Est. Don't expect frills: just a clean room with inoffensive pastel decor for 250F. *3 rue Jarry, 75010, tel. 01–45–23–50–00, fax 01–45–23–30–65. Métro: Gare de l'Est. 35 rooms with toilet and shower. In-room safes.*

LES HALLES

Lively and a bit more downscale than the rest of central Paris, Les Halles makes for a cheap but not necessarily quiet place to get some sleep. It's also steps from the Centre Pompidou and the Louvre. But steer clear of rue St-Denis, a sleazy (though fairly safe) pocket of prostitution and sex shops.

DIRT CHEAP • Andréa. You can get a relatively spacious double at this modest hotel, but insist on a room away from noisy rue de Rivoli. For the five smallish, bargain 200F doubles (with sink only) be sure to book months in advance; the others are more. *3 rue St-Bon, 75004, tel. 01–42–78–43–93. Métro: Hôtel de Ville or Châtelet. 21 rooms with toilet and shower, 5 with sink only.*

Tiquetonne. If all you need is a simple, clean room on a quiet street near Les Halles, then this place is for you. If you're traveling solo, singles cost under 140F. Doubles (with private bathrooms) are 225F. *6 rue Tiquetonne, 75002, tel. 01–42–36–94–58, fax 01–42–36–02–94. Métro: Etienne Marcel. 35 rooms with toilet and shower, 12 with sink only.*

LOUVRE AND OPERA

You can't get any more central than this—smack in the historic heart of the city amid Paris's grandest monuments.

DIRT CHEAP • Hôtel Henri IV. Despite the bleak lobby and narrow, creaky hallway, the place, just steps from Notre-Dame, has rustic charm. Rooms with just a sink go for under 200F; the two with toilet and shower go for 250F. The place is almost consistently full, so book well ahead. *25 pl. Dauphine, 75001, tel. 01–43–54–44–53. Métro: Pont Neuf. 2 rooms with toilet and shower, 20 with sink only. Cash only.*

UNDER 300F • Hôtel Haussmann. Right behind the Opéra and near the big department stores you'll find this clean, small, professional place. The clientele is mainly French (so be prepared for smokers). Book ahead; at 285F for a double, rooms go fast. *89 rue de Provence, 75009, tel. 01–48–74–24–57, fax 01–44–91–97–25. Métro: Havre-Caumartin. 34 rooms with toilet and bath.*

UNDER 400F • Louvre Forum. This centrally located hotel has an eager-to-please staff and clean, comfortable, well-equipped rooms (with satellite TV) starting at 350F. *25 rue du Bouloi, 75001, tel. 01–42–36–54–19, fax 01–42–33–66–31. Métro: Louvre. 11 rooms with toilet and bath, 16 with toilet and shower. Bar.*

LE MARAIS

The Marais is Paris's answer to Greenwich Village, a Seine-side neighborhood sandwiched between Les Halles and the Bastille. It brims with Revolution-era architecture, fun shops, a clutch of kosher delis, an active gay community, and myriad wine bars and cafés.

UNDER 350F • Castex. This hotel in a Revolution-era building has rooms (300F–340F) that are low on frills but squeaky clean. A big plus are the friendly owners. It's often booked months ahead, so reserve early. There's no elevator, and the only TV is on the ground floor. *5 rue Castex, 4e, tel. 01–42–*

72–31–52, fax 01–42–72–57–91. Métro: St-Paul. 4 rooms with toilet and bath, 23 with toilet and shower.

Pratic. Just a block from the place des Vosges, this hotel has rooms in a casual, mix-and-match style. Count on paying 340F for a double with toilet and shower, 290F for one with a shower only. A caveat: if you go for one of the showerless rooms (245F), you may have to descend as many as four flights to bathe. *9 rue d'Ormesson, 75004, tel. 01–48–87–80–47, fax 01–48–87–40–04. Métro: St-Paul. 5 with toilet and shower, 10 with shower only, 7 with neither toilet nor shower.*

UNDER 450F • Hôtel du 7e Art. The theme of this hip Marais hotel is Hollywood from the '40s to the '60s. Rates start at 410F (but go as high as 650F), so ask for one of the cheaper rooms. It will be small and spartan, but clean, quiet, and equipped with cable TV. There's no elevator. *20 rue St-Paul, 75004, tel. 01–42–77–04–03, fax 01–42–77–69–10. Métro: St-Paul. 9 rooms with toilet and bath, 14 with toilet and shower. Bar, in-room safes.*

SPLURGE • Place des Vosges. An eclectic and loyal clientele swears by this small, historic hotel just off place des Vosges. Splurge on a top-floor room with a view (460F); the least expensive rooms (400F) are the size of walk-in closets. *12 rue de Birague, 75004, tel. 01–42–72–60–46, fax 01–42–72–02–64. Métro: St-Paul. 11 rooms with toilet and bath, 5 with toilet and shower.*

MONTPARNASSE

Montparnasse expands across the sprawling 14e arrondissement and nudges its way into neighboring Left Bank districts, including the Quartier Latin and St-Germain.

DIRT CHEAP • Hôtel de l'Espérance. Book well ahead for a 190F double with toilet or one with a sink only for 140F at the "Hotel of Hope," on a small street in the southern part of Montparnasse. Rooms either look shabby or hopelessly romantic, depending on your disposition, but the proprietress is eager to please. *1 rue de Grancey, 75014, tel. 01–43–21–41–04, fax 01–43–22–06–02. Métro: Denfert-Rochereau. 6 rooms with toilet, 4 with toilet and shower, 4 with sink only.*

UNDER 300F • Beaunier. A friendly welcome, a flower-filled patio, satellite TV, and well-kept, if basic, rooms make this hotel a good choice. Doubles go for 260F. *31 rue Beaunier, 75014, tel. 01–45–39–36–45, fax 01–45–39–33–55. Métro: Porte d'Orléans. 23 rooms with toilet and bath.*

UNDER 350F • Parc Montsouris. This modest hotel in a 1930s villa (really more of a small house) is on a quiet street next to the Parc Montsouris. You can expect your room to be small but tastefully done and to have satellite TV. Rooms with shower are 320F; tubs cost an extra 60F. *4 rue du Parc-Montsouris, 75014, tel. 01–45–89–09–72, fax 01–45–80–92–72. Métro: Montparnasse-Bienvenue. 28 rooms with toilet and bath, 7 with toilet and shower.*

MONTMARTRE

Perched on the northern edge of the city, Montmartre epitomizes Paris's bohemian alter ego. Most major attractions are just 10 minutes by métro, making it a good bet if you're budget-minded and into experiencing more than just the main sights.

UNDER 250F • Grand Hôtel de Turin. Although it's on the seedy side of Montmartre near the Moulin Rouge, this hotel has clean, surprisingly spacious rooms with comfortable beds. Doubles go for 245F. *6 rue Victor-Massé, 75009, tel. 01–48–78–45–26, fax 01–42–80–61–50. Métro: Pigalle. 14 rooms with toilet and bath, 37 with toilet and shower.*

UNDER 450F • Regyn's Montmartre. Rooms here (starting at 430F) are smallish, but comfortable. Each floor is dedicated to a Montmartre artist, and poetic homages by local writers feature in the hallways. Ask for a room on the top two floors for great views of the Eiffel Tower or the Sacré-Coeur. *18 pl. des Abbesses, 75018, tel. 01–42–54–45–21, fax 01–42–23–76–69. Métro: Abbesses. 14 rooms with toilet and bath, 8 with toilet and shower. In-room safes.*

Utrillo. For 440F you get fabulous views *and* a sauna at this hotel on a quiet side street near colorful rue Lepic. The impressionist prints and marble-top breakfast tables in every room make rooms feel charmingly old-fashioned. Two rooms (numbers 61 and 63) have views of the Eiffel Tower. *7 rue Aristide-Bruant, 75018, tel. 01–42–58–13–44, fax 01–42–23–93–88. Métro: Abbesses. 5 rooms with toilet and bath, 25 with toilet and shower. Sauna.*

NEAR THE EIFFEL TOWER

This is the Left Bank at its poshest. Stately apartment buildings line the wide, tree-lined avenues of the 7e arrondissement, often invisible to the hordes of tourists rushing to the Eiffel Tower and Les Invalides.

UNDER 300F • Family. This well-run hotel has clean rooms and an efficient staff. For 290F you'll get a spic-and-span if basic double equipped with a kitchenette—a great way to save a few francs by cooking at "home." *23 rue Fondary, 75015, 01–45–75–20–49, 01–45–77–70–73. Métro: Dupleix. 1 room with toilet and bath, 20 with toilet and shower. Kitchenettes.*

UNDER 400F • Champ de Mars. Only a stone's throw from the rue Cler market and the Eiffel tower, this little gem has comfortable rooms in cheery blue-and-yellow French country-house style. They're also equipped with satellite TV and CNN. Doubles with shower are 360F. *7 rue du Champ de Mars, 75007, tel. 01–45–51–52–30, fax 01–45–51–64–36. Métro: Ecole Militaire. 19 rooms with toilet and bath, 6 with toilet and shower.*

Grand Hôtel Lévêque. On one of Paris's best market streets, this immaculate hotel has an eager-to-please staff, comfortable rooms, and satellite TV. There's no elevator. Doubles are 380F, but five singles without private bathrooms go for 225F. *29 rue Cler, 75007, tel. 01–47–05–49–15, fax 01–45–50–49–36. Métro: Ecole Militaire. 45 rooms with toilet and shower, 5 with sink only. In-room safes.*

Tour Eiffel Dupleix. Ask for one of the rooms with a view of the Eiffel Tower at this comfortable hotel. All have modern bathrooms and cable TV. Doubles with shower are 460F, but in July and August they're 390F. The buffet breakfast is a bargain. *11 rue Juge, 75015, tel. 01–45–78–29–29, fax 01–45–78–60–00. Métro: Dupleix. 30 rooms with toilet and bath, 10 with toilet and shower. Laundry.*

QUARTIER LATIN

The Quartier Latin is one of the most heavily visited districts in the city, but it still delivers a very real, laid-back, Paris experience.

DIRT CHEAP • Marignan. A friendly French-American couple owns this modest hotel with functionally decorated rooms. A double with shared facilities is 220F, and with a private bathroom 270F. *13 rue du Sommerard, 75005, tel. 01–43–54–63–81. Métro: Maubert-Mutualité. 10 rooms with toilet and shower, 20 with sink only. Laundry.*

UNDER 400F • Familia. Rooms start at 380F, then climb to above 450F if you want a walk-out balcony on the second or fifth floor (well worth the price). Or ask for a room with a sepia fresco depicting a celebrated Paris monument; others are furnished with fine Louis XV-style furnishings. *11 rue des Ecoles, 75005, tel. 01–43–54–55–27, fax 01–43–29–61–77. Métro: Cardinal Lemoine. 14 rooms with toilet and bath, 16 with toilet and shower.*

SPLURGE • Grandes Ecoles. Okay, so we're cheating: rooms here cost 510F, but it's worth splurging to feel like you're staying at a country cottage. Louis-Philippe-style furnishings, lace bedspreads, and the absence of TV all add to the rustic ambience. *75 rue du Cardinal Lemoine, 75005, tel. 01–43–26–79–23, fax 01–43–25–28–15. Métro: Cardinal Lemoine. 45 rooms with toilet and bath, 6 with toilet and shower.*

ST-GERMAIN-DES-PRES

This Left Bank district bordering the Seine cradles the oldest church in Paris (Eglise St-Germain) and has some of the most captivating and romantic streets in the city.

UNDER 300F • Jean Bart. You can't beat this hotel's location right near the Jardin du Luxembourg. Rooms are clean and old-fashioned, with sturdy armoires and comfy beds. Doubles with shower are 280F; tubs are 30F extra. *9 rue Jean-Bart, 75006, tel. 01–45–48–29–13. Métro: St-Placide. 17 rooms with toilet and bath, 17 with toilet and shower.*

UNDER 350F • Hôtel du Globe. At this tiny hotel in the heart of the 6e arrondissement, French floral fabrics, wood beams, and, if you're lucky, a canopy bed give it a rustic feel. Though the cheapest rooms (340F) are very small, you'll feel like you're in your own little garret. Reserve at least two weeks ahead. *15 rue des Quatre-Vents, 75006, tel. 01–46–33–62–69. Métro: Mabillon. 6 rooms with toilet and bath, 9 with toilet and shower. Closed Aug.*

UNDER 450F • Acacias St-Germain. If you book early enough, you can snag one of the least expensive rooms (doubles start at 400F but go up as high as 700F). Everything is done up in *style anglais*, with sturdy pine furniture and summery upholstery. Ask about weekend discounts. *151 bis rue de Rennes, 75006, tel. 01–45–48–97–38, fax 01–45–44–63–57. Métro: St-Placide. 33 rooms and 4 apartments with bath, 8 rooms with shower. In-room safes, laundry.*

HOSTELS AND FOYERS

At 100F–170F a night for a bed in a clean room with free showers and breakfast, hostels are not only a bargain but they're placed in some of the city's prime locations. Furthermore, they're great places to meet young foreign people, find travel companions, get tips, and hear about other travelers' adventures (or misadventures).

In summer, you should reserve *in writing* (or by fax) a month in advance. You'll probably have to provide a credit card number or fork over a deposit for the first night, so don't forget to get written confirmation in case of a mix-up. It's a good idea to check in as early as 7 AM.

Although hostels tend to house young students, they often have dormlike accommodation for travelers of all ages. Many hostels have fairly strict rules regarding curfews, late-night carousing, and alcohol intake, but be prepared for the occasional rowdy group making your night a sleepless hell.

HI HOSTELS • All three HI hostels are run by the Fédération Unie des Auberges de Jeunesse (FUAJ), the French branch of Hostelling International. First you'll need a hostel card, which you can buy for 100F at any of the following four FUAJ offices: **FUAJ Beaubourg** (9 rue Brantôme, 3e, tel. 01–48–04–70–40, métro Châtelet); **FUAJ Ile de France** (9 rue Notre-Dame-de-Lorette, 9e, tel. 01–42–85–55–40, métro Notre-Dame-de-Lorette); **FUAJ République** (4 blvd. Jules-Ferry, 11e, tel. 01–43–57–02–60, fax 01–40–21–79–92, métro République); and **FUAJ Centre National** (27 rue Pajol, 18e, tel. 01–44–89–87–27, métro La Chapelle).

For 130F, you'll get a bed, sheets, shower, and breakfast. Most rooms are single-sex. To reserve a space ahead of time at the Cité des Sciences or d'Artagnan hostels, call the HI-AYH office in Washington, DC (tel. 202/783–6161) and give them your credit card number; they'll charge you for the price of a night's stay plus a $6 booking fee. The third HI hostel is at 84 blvd. Jules Ferry and doesn't take reservations. Show up before 10 AM to secure a spot. Be sure to note the afternoon lockout hours (noon–3 PM). Many will store your luggage for the day for around 10F.

Auberge de Jeunesse d'Artagnan. This clean, enormous hostel is only steps from Père-Lachaise. It gets loud and packed in summer. A bed in a three- or four-bed dorm costs 110F (including sheets and breakfast); beds in double rooms go for 121F (130F with private shower). Three meals are served daily (menus for 28F–50F) at the very social bar and cafeteria. *80 rue Vitruve, 75020, tel. 01–43–61–08–75, fax 01–40–32–34–55. Métro: Porte de Bagnolet. 411 beds. Reception open 8 AM–midnight, lockout noon–3. Laundry.*

Auberge de Jeunesse Cité des Sciences. Although technically in the suburbs, this hostel is well served by métro, so you can be smack in the center of Paris in less than 20 minutes. A mellow staff welcomes you to standard four- to six-bed dorm rooms. Though the rooms close every day noon–3PM, the reception desk and a small common room stay open 24 hours. Beds cost 110F per night. *24 rue des Sept-Arpents, 93000 rue du Pré-St-Gervais, tel. 01–48–43–24–11, fax 01–48–43–26–82. Métro: Hoche. 128 beds. Reception open 24 hrs. Laundry.*

Auberge de Jeunesse Jules-Ferry. Come early and be ready to socialize. This hostel is extremely popular with friendly and rowdy backpackers. It's also well located, close to place de la République and the Bastille. Bed and breakfast in a dorm runs 110F (115F per person for the few doubles). *8 blvd. Jules-Ferry, 75011, tel. 01–43–57–55–60, fax 01–40–21–79–92. Métro: République. 100 beds. Reception open 24 hrs, lockout noon–2.*

PRIVATE HOSTELS • **Young and Happy Youth Hostel.** Well located among the cafés, shops, and restaurants of the Quartier Latin, the hostel is no stranger to American and Japanese travelers. The two- to six-bed rooms are spotless but basic and cost 97F per person, including breakfast. Sheets rent for 15F, towels 5F. Arrive before 11 AM or reserve with a deposit for the first night. *80 rue Mouffetard, 75005, tel. 01–45–35–09–53. Métro: Monge. 75 beds. Curfew 2 AM, lockout 11–5.*

BVJ FOYERS • These foyers for travelers aged 16–35 are in great locations. The immaculate rooms hold up to 10 people. You'll get a bed, breakfast, sheets, and a shower for 120F, plus access to kitchen facilities, 10F lockers, and a 24-hour reception desk. Unfortunately you can't make reservations, so show up early in the morning. Singles cost 10F more in the Latin Quarter. The Louvre location has a restaurant where guests at any of the four foyers can eat for 55F. There's also a shuttle service to Orly (59F) and Charles de Gaulle (69F), which you can reserve at the desk. *BVJ de Paris/Louvre, 20 rue J.-J. Rousseau, 75001, tel. 01–42–36–88–18, fax 01–42–33–82–10. Métro: Palais Royal. BVJ de Paris Quartier Latin, 44 rue des Bernardins, 75005, tel. 01–43–29–34–80, fax 01–42–33–40–53. Métro: Maubert-Mutualité.*

MIJE FOYERS • In a trio of medieval palaces and 18th-century Marais townhouses, Maisons Internationales des Jeunes Etudiants (MIJE) foyers are more comfortable than many budget hotels. The catch is that you must be between the ages of 18 and 30. The 125F rate includes a bed, sheets, breakfast, showers, and free luggage storage. Doubles with private bath cost 150F. They don't accept reservations, so show up between 7 and 8:30 AM for one of the 450 beds. There's a seven-night maximum and a 1 AM curfew. A restaurant in the Fourcy location offers meals to visitors (menus are 32F to 52F). The lockout is between noon and 4 PM. *Hôtel le Fauconnier, 11 rue de Fauconnier, 75004, tel 01–42–74–23–45, fax 01–42–74–08–93. Métro: St-Paul. Hôtel le Fourcy, 6 rue de Fourcy, 75004, tel 01–42–74–23–45, fax 01–42–74–08–93. Métro: St-Paul. Hôtel Maubuisson, 12 rue des Barres, 75004, tel. 01–42–72–72–09, fax 01–42–74–08–93. Métro: St-Paul or Hôtel de Ville.*

Auberge Internationale des Jeunes. If you're a swinging youth, this impeccable, modern hostel is for you. It's right next to place de la Bastille and in the heart of all the nighttime action. The friendly (albeit hectic) management accepts reservations. Rooms for two to six people rent for 81F-91F per person, breakfast included. *10 rue Trousseau, 75011, tel. 01–47–00–62–00, fax 01–47–00–33–16. Métro: Bastille or Ledru Rollin. 240 beds. Reception open 24 hrs, lockout 10–3. Laundry.*

Maison des Etudiants. This fabulous house with a flower-filled courtyard has beds in a double for 140F and singles for 160F (150F if you stay three weeks or more). There's a four-night minimum stay and breakfast is included. The maison accepts students year-round and tourists of all ages in summer. *18 rue J.-J. Rousseau, 75001, tel. 01–45–08–02–10. Métro: Palais Royal. 52 beds.*

FOOD

To truly experience life in Paris, it's imperative that you indulge in at least one slightly drunken, drawn-out meal and treat the event as religiously as the French do. When the high price of Parisian cuisine gets you down, do like the Parisians do and stop by the pâtisseries, boulangeries, boucheries, charcuteries, and fromageries found in every residential area of the city. Unless otherwise noted, assume all places take credit cards.

BASTILLE

This great nighttime area has a number of affordable dining options as well as a huge selection of restaurants to cure late-night snack attacks. Take-out joints of all stripes line **rue de la Roquette**; on the rue's first block off place de la Bastille, homesick Americans take comfort in the thick pizza at **Slice.** As you get farther from place de la Bastille toward **place de la République** and along **boulevard Voltaire,** prices drop and ethnic eateries pop up more often.

UNDER 50F • Le Bistrot du Peintre. This popular café and bar serves food until midnight. The standard French cuisine includes a great *soupe à l'oignon* (onion soup; 30F) and the city's best *salade au chèvre chaud* (warm goat-cheese salad; 35F). *116 av. Ledru-Rollin, 11e, tel. 01–47–00–34–39. Métro: Ledru-Rollin.*

UNDER 75F • Le Petit Keller. Though many of Paris's good budget places dish up foreign cooking, this unprepossessing spot near the Bastille serves food that's resolutely French—and surprisingly good for the money. Your best bet is the 70F, three-course menu. *13 rue Keller, 11e, tel. 01–47–00–12–97. Métro: Ledru-Rollin. Closed Sun., Aug.*

Restaurant Sarah. At this Persian delight, the 30F plat du jour is always a good bet, as is the excellent lunch menu (55F) that includes specialties like *tchelo kebab koubidee* (beef, onion, grilled tomatoes, and saffron rice). The dinner menu is a deal at 65F. *10 rue Oberkampf, 11e, tel. 01–43–57–83–48. Métro: Oberkampf. Cash only.*

UNDER 100F • Chez Paul. A modest sign welcomes you to a reliably good splurge. Try the delectable grilled salmon (80F), rabbit with goat-cheese sauce (75F), and escargots (40F). Spring for a bottle of wine (100F) and whip out that credit card. Reservations are essential. *13 rue de Charonne, at rue de Lappe, 11e, tel. 01–47–00–34–57. Métro: Bastille.*

UNDER 150F • Au Camelot. Book as soon as you get into town—this tiny bistro only seats 20 and is hugely popular for its outstanding 130F menu. You'll start with soup, go on to separate fish and meat courses, then cheese and dessert— all delicious. Though it's a bit of a splurge, it's worth it. *50 rue Amelot, 11e, tel. 01–43–55–54–04. Métro: Chemin-Vert. No lunch Mon. and Sat. Closed Sun. Cash only.*

BELLEVILLE

Belleville's African, Asian, and Eastern European restaurants—on **rue de Belleville, rue des Pyrénées,** and the streets stretching south from them—are a refreshing alternative to standard Parisian cuisine. Sephardic Jews have opened up kosher shops; try the **Maison du Zabayon** (122 blvd. de Belleville, 20e, tel. 01–47–97–16–70), a kosher bakery with good pastries (8F–10F).

UNDER 100F • Le Vieux Byzantin. On a street packed with sorry-looking stands of greasy Greek food, this restaurant stands above the rest with its Greek and Turkish delicacies. Daily specials such as chicken *tagine* (braised in a clay pot) are only 35F; the 50F lunch menu is a deal. Fancier dinner menus run 70F to 95F. *128 rue Oberkampf, 11e, tel. 01–43–57–35–84. Métro: Ménilmontant. Closed Sun. lunch. Cash only.*

CHAMPS-ELYSEES

Though it's one of Paris's best-known boulevards, the area around it is a tough place to find a decent meal for under 200F. Hunt around **rue La Boétie** and **rue de Ponthieu** for your most reasonable options.

UNDER 100F • Chicago Pizza Pie Factory. Come here to watch sports and chow on pizzas—84F for two-person cheese, 200F for four-person with everything. Happy-hour drinks (Monday–Saturday 6–8) are 50% off. *5 rue de Berri, 8e, tel. 01–45–62–50–23. Métro: George V.*

LES HALLES AND BEAUBOURG

On sunny days stroll through the daily market on **rue Montorgueil** and picnic in the park next to the Eglise St-Eustache. Les Halles has the worst crêpe stands in town, but the restaurants stay open late, including **Pizza Pino** (open daily 11 AM–5 AM) on place des Innocents.

UNDER 50F • Le Café. A young, goateed crowd munches on zucchini and cheddar tarts (45F) and *croques* (grilled ham-and-cheese sandwiches) with side salads (40F) at this mellow place. *62 rue Tiquetonne, 2e, tel. 01–40–39–08–00. Métro: Etienne Marcel. Cash only.*

Dame Tartine. This restaurant-cum-art gallery next to the Centre Pompidou specializes in *tartines* (hot or cold open-faced sandwiches). Chow down on *poulet aux amandes* (chicken with almonds; 30F). *2 rue Brisemiche, 3e, tel. 01–42–77–32–22. Métro: Rambuteau or Châtelet–Les Halles. Cash only.*

UNDER 75F • Entre Ciel et Terre. The focus at this happy, crunchy place is healthy meals of fruits and veggies. Try the veggie lasagna (55F) with a 15F glass of organic grape juice. *5 rue Hérold, 1er, tel. 01–45–08–49–84. Métro: Les Halles or Louvre-Rivoli. Closed weekends.*

LOUVRE TO OPERA

Good lunch deals can be found on **rue du Faubourg-St-Honoré.** For Japanese food, check out **rue Ste-Anne** and, across avenue de l'Opéra, **rue St-Roch.** Excellent sushi is served at **Foujita** (41 rue St-Roch, 1er, tel. 01–42–61–42–93), where a sampler costs 100F.

UNDER 75F • Le Gavroche. Loyal locals come for the 70F menu of provincial specialties like foie gras and *pot au feu* (beef and vegetable broth). *19 rue St-Marc, 2e, tel. 01–42–96–89–70. Métro: Richelieu-Drouot. Closed Sun. and Aug.*

L'Incroyable. Sit in the rustic interior or on the front patio and enjoy the 75F (lunch 67F) traditional French menu, with *blanquette de veau* (veal cooked in butter and stock) and dessert. *26 rue de Richelieu, 1er, tel. 01–42–96–24–64. Métro: Palais Royal–Musée du Louvre. No dinner Mon or Sat. Closed Sun. Cash only.*

LE MARAIS

Thanks to its strong Jewish community, the Marais has a variety of kosher restaurants, delis, and bakeries. The falafel stands on **rue des Rosiers** are amazing. The Marais's other main contingent, the hip gay crowd, means you'll also find more expensive, artsy, trendy joints; try the primarily gay restaurants, cafés, and bars on **rue Ste-Croix-de-la-Bretonnerie** and **rue Vieille-du-Temple.**

UNDER 25F • L'As du Fallafel. Get the best falafel in town for 20F at this cramped hole-in-the-wall. Shell out an extra 5F for the deluxe with grilled eggplant, hummus, tahini, and hot sauce. *34 rue des Rosiers, 4e, tel. 01–48–87–63–60. Métro: St-Paul. Closed Sat. Cash only.*

UNDER 50F • Sacha et Florence Finkelsztajn. Eastern European and Russian snacks and specialties are served here. A small *pirojki* (pastries filled with fish, meat, or vegetables) cost 10F (20F for a large). Hefty sandwiches are 30F–40F. *Sacha: 27 rue des Rosiers, 4e, tel. 01–42–72–78–91. Métro: St-Paul. Closed Mon., Tues., and July. Florence: 24 rue des Ecouffes, 4e, tel. 01–48–87–92–85. Métro: St-Paul. Closed Tues., Wed., and Aug.*

UNDER 100F • Baracane. This pleasant, easygoing place serves first-rate southwestern French food. If you're careful with the wine, you'll be able to come and go for less than 100F, especially at lunch when they serve a 50F menu (at night it runs 80F). *38 rue des Tournelles, 4e, tel. 01–42–71–43–33. Métro: Bastille. Closed Sun.*

MONTMARTRE

Don't buy a thing near the Sacré-Coeur and place du Tertre. Try going behind the church to **rue Lamarck** and **rue Caulaincourt** for relatively cheap French fare. Better yet, head down the stairs toward **rue Muller,** where the food is less expensive.

UNDER 50F • Le Fouta Toro. Get a whole day's worth of food for 50F. The Senegalese dishes are terrific—try the *mafé au poulet* (chicken in peanut sauce) for 47F. *3 rue du Nord, 18e, tel. 01–42–55–42–73. Métro: Marcadet-Poissonniers. Closed Tues.*

Rayons de Santé. The entirely vegetarian menu features 20F–30F appetizers like vegetable pâté and artichoke mousse. Main courses (30F–35F) include spicy couscous with vegetables and soy sausage or veggie goulash. *8 pl. Charles-Dullin, 18e, tel. 01–42–59–64–81. Métro: Abbesses. No dinner Fri. Closed Sat. Cash only.*

UNDER 100F • Au Refuge des Fondus. Waiters ask "*viande ou fromage?*" (meat or cheese?) and "*rouge ou blanc?*" (red or white wine?), then set you up with an aperitif, appetizers, fondue, dessert, and wine for 87F. Reservations are essential. *17 rue des Trois-Frères, 18e, tel. 01–42–55–22–65. Métro: Abbesses.*

La Bouche du Roi. West African cuisine meets traditional French cooking at "The Mouth of the King." On weekday nights there is often live music; Friday nights an African *conteuse* (storyteller) weaves her tales. The lunch menu is 55F, the dinner menu 80F. *4 rue Lamarck, 18e, tel. 01–42–62–55–41. Métro: Abbesses or Château-Rouge. Closed Mon.*

MONTPARNASSE

Boulevard du Montparnasse marks the line between bourgeois St-Germain-des-Prés and working-class Montparnasse. Meals range from cheap and filling to expensive and froufrou. But you can always get a good crêpe around **rue d'Odessa** or **rue Daguerre.**

UNDER 50F • Chez Papa. Rowdy waitresses serve southwestern French food. Mongo salads, called *boyardes,* packed with potatoes, egg, ham, cheese, and tomato cost 35F. Escargots "Papa" (49F) come piping hot. Set menus are 50F until 1 AM. *6 rue Gassendi, 14e, tel. 01–43–22–41–19, métro Denfert-Rochereau. Other location: 206 rue La Fayette, 10e, tel. 01–42–09–53–87, métro Louis Blanc.*

Mustang Café. It's the most popular of the many Tex-Mex café/bars in Montparnasse and it's open from 9 AM–5 AM daily. Taco salads run 50F, quesadillas 40F, and Dos Equis 30F. Weekdays 4–7 margaritas and cocktails are half-price. *84 blvd. du Montparnasse, 14e, tel. 01–43–35–36–12. Métro: Montparnasse.*

NEAR THE EIFFEL TOWER

The restaurants in this area cater primarily to diplomats and politicians, stray tourists, and a few solemn locals. **Rue de Sevres** is a promising place to look for a moderately priced lunch.

UNDER 75F • Chez l'Ami Jean. One good bet in the area is this Basque restaurant that dishes up pâté *campagne* (country-style; 25F), and trout meunière (55F); equally tempting desserts run 25F–40F. *27 rue Malar, 7e, tel. 01–47–05–86–89. Métro: Latour-Maubourg. Closed Sun.*

SPLURGE • Au Bon Acceuil. It's imperative that you make reservations at this bustling bistro because the 120F menu is one of the best deals in Paris. Depending on the season, you'll get baked St-Marcellin cheese on salad, tender veal filet, or pot au feu. *14 rue de Monttessuy, 7e, tel. 01–47–05–46–11. Métro: Ecole Militaire. Closed Sun.*

QUARTIER LATIN

Competition is high among French, Greek, and Tunisian joints on **rue de la Huchette.** For more upscale dining, try the area behind **square René-Viviani.** Head to **rue Mouffetard** for a 13F crêpe at a stand; you'll also find many French, Greek, and Mexican places serving full meals for 50F–70F.

UNDER 50F • Cousin Cousine. This spacious crêperie picks up on the French fetish for old flicks, with *galettes* (buckwheat pancakes) named L'Ange Bleu (walnuts, blue cheese, crème fraîche; 35F) and Mad Max (ground beef, cheese, ratatouille; 41F). *36 rue Mouffetard, 5e, tel. 01–47–07–73–83. Métro: Monge. Cash only under 150F.*

UNDER 75F • Le Boute Grill. Maghrebian expats say this Tunisian restaurant serves the best couscous in Paris. Enormous servings come with choice of 14 kinds of meat. A huge three-course menu is 72F. *12 rue Boutebrie, 5e, tel. 01–43–54–03–30. Métro: Cluny–La Sorbonne. Closed Sun. Cash only.*

Le Jardin des Pâtes. Fresh, organic-grain pastas (43F–73F) lavished with sauces like mixed vegetables with ginger and tofu are served. For the carnivores there is smoked duck with cream and nutmeg. *4 rue Lacépède, 5e, tel. 01–43–31–50–71. Métro: Monge. Closed Mon.*

ST-GERMAIN-DES-PRES

Beyond the chichi galleries and boutiques of St-Germain are plenty of substantial dining options, although the classic French fare here often falls flat. **Rue Monsieur-le-Prince** is one of the best restaurant streets in the city, featuring Asian spots with three-course menus for as little as 50F. **Rue des Canettes** and the surrounding small streets are best for crêpes and other fast eats.

UNDER 50F • Cosi. At this chic sandwich shop order your choice of ingredients—chèvre, spinach, salmon, mozzarella, curried chicken, or others—on a fresh, flat bread for 30F–50F. Get a glass of wine (20F) and enjoy the background opera music. *54 rue de Seine, 6e, tel. 01–46–33–35–36. Métro: Odéon. Cash only.*

UNDER 75F • Le Coffee Parisien. Popular with St-Germain's young leisure class, this place serves *real* brunch—like eggs Benedict (70F), pancakes (50F), and eggs Florentine (70F)—all day. *5 rue Perronet, 7e, tel. 01–40–49–08–08. Métro: St-Germain-des-Prés.*

CAFES

Along with wine and the three-course meals, the café remains one of the basic necessities of life in Paris. Avoid tourist areas, and step into the smaller, less flashy establishments for a feeling of what real French café life is like. Cafés are required to post a *tarif des consommations,* a menu that includes two prices: for food or drinks *au comptoir* (at the counter), and for food or drinks *à terrasse* or *en salle* (seated at a table). Below we give the seated prices. If you just need a cup of coffee, have it at the counter and you'll save a lot of money.

Relax under ceiling fans in a tattered leather chair, and stare at old movie posters at **Les Enfants Gâtés** (43 rue des Francs-Bourgeois, 4e, tel. 01–42–77–07–63, métro St-Paul) while you enjoy your café (15F), flavored tea (25F), or pastry (40F). Afterward hit the nearby bars and restaurants on place des Vosges. The shop up front at **Mariage Frères** (30 rue du Bourg-Tibourg, 4e, tel. 01–42–72–28–11, métro Hôtel de Ville or St-Paul), the most reputable teahouse in Paris, sells hundreds of varieties of loose leaves by the gram. A pot of *thé* (tea) will run you 45F, desserts 45F–55F. **La Mosquée** (19–39 rue Geoffroy-St-Hilaire, 5e, tel. 01–43–31–18–14, métro Censier-Daubenton), a salon de thé inside Paris's main mosque, is intricately tiled and decorated with Moroccan wood carvings and tapestried benches. Coffee or a teeny (but potent) glass of sweet mint tea is 10F; baklava and other pastries cost 11F–15F. The music's just loud enough to keep conversations private at the dimly lit, gay **Amnésia Café** (42 rue Vieille-du-Temple, 4e, tel. 01–42–72–16–94, métro St-Paul or Hôtel de Ville). The cool **Café de l'Industrie** (16 rue St-Sabin, 11e, tel. 01–47–00–13–53, métro Bastille or Bréguet-Sabin) has large, smoky rooms where you can hang out all afternoon or until 2 AM with hip Frenchies schmoozing at the bar; beers are 16F. **La Palette** (43 rue de Seine, 6e, tel. 01–43–26–68–15, métro Mabillon) an old, muted café amidst rue de Seine's galleries, lets you sip coffee (12F) or wine (20F) outside under the cherry trees.

MARKETS

Two large chain stores, **Monoprix** and **Prisunic,** house low-priced supermarkets. Monoprix is all over and usually open until 8 or 9; the Prisunic just off the Champs-Elysées (109 rue de La Boétie, 8e, tel. 01–42–25–10–27) is open Monday–Saturday until midnight. **Ed l'Epicier** (84 rue Notre-Dame-des-Champs, 6e, métro Notre-Dame-des-Champs) is the cheapest supermarket in Paris. Selection varies, but you can always find the basics for way less than anywhere else. Bring your own grocery bags. Two other stores are at 80 rue de Rivoli, 4e (métro Hôtel de Ville), and 123 rue de Charonne, 11e (métro Bastille).

WORTH SEEING

Proudly bearing the scars of a 2,000-year history, and now home to 2 million people, Paris could take you multiple lifetimes to explore from top to bottom—and that's not counting the Louvre. The métro system is extremely efficient for hit-and-run sightseeing, but getting around on the bus—and your feet—is the only way to get a real feel for Parisian street life: its action, its glamour, its pooper-scoopers. The center of town is especially walkable.

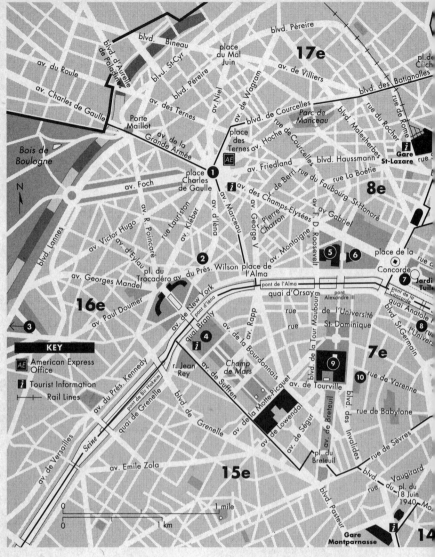

ARC DE TRIOMPHE

Commissioned by Napoléon, the Arc de Triomphe remains the largest triumphal arch in the world. The sculpture on the sides includes François Rude's famous *La Marseillaise,* depicting the uprising of 1792. Climb the 164-ft arch for one of the better views of Paris, highlighting the city's unmistakable design; radiating out from the arch are 12 avenues. Gaze along the precise lines to La Défense, and down the Champs-Elysées to place de la Concorde, and on to the Louvre. *Pl. Charles de Gaulle–Etoile, tel. 01–43–80–31–31. Métro: Charles de Gaulle–Etoile. Admission 35F. Open Apr.–Sept., daily 9:30–6, (Fri. until 10); Oct.–Mar., daily 10–5:30.*

BASILIQUE DU SACRE-CŒUR

This garish white concoction was dreamt up by overzealous Catholics specifically to "expiate the sins" of the citizens participating in the Paris Commune of 1871, massacred by government troops that same year. The Romanesque-Byzantine structure looks so white because the stones secrete calcite when wet; the more it rains, the more the Sacré-Cœur gleams. The 15F admission fee to the 367-ft **bell tower** will get you a magnificent view of the city, but you can get almost the same view for free in front of the basilica. *35 rue du Chevalier-de-la-Barre, tel. 01–42–51–17–02. Métro: Anvers. Basilica open daily 6:45 AM– 11 PM. Tower open daily 9–7 (until 6 off-season).*

CATHEDRALE DE NOTRE-DAME

For centuries Notre-Dame (built between 1163 and 1361) has watched Paris go through all sorts of phases, riding out periods of neglect and hostility like a patient parent. All its waiting has paid off: it is one of the best-known houses of worship in the world. The intricate sculpted portals depict (from left to right) the Virgin (to whom the cathedral is dedicated), the Last Judgment, and St Anne, Mary's mother. Above is a row of statues depicting 28 kings of Judah and Israel, all of which lost their heads during the French Revolution, when the cathedral became a Temple of Reason (the heads were replaced once the fuss died down). Climb the cathedral's **towers** (around to the left as you face the building) for a terrific view of Paris. *Pl. du Parvis Notre-Dame, 4e, tel. 01–42–34–56–10. Métro: Cité. Admission to tower 28F. Open daily 8–7. Towers open daily 9:30–6:30.*

CENTRE GEORGES-POMPIDOU

Also known as Beaubourg, the Centre Pompidou is one of Paris's biggest tourist attractions: fire-eaters, jugglers, and caricaturists cover the large plaza out front, and inside a museum, library, theater, and cinema act as the "laboratory" envisioned when the Centre was first conceived in the early 1970s. What wasn't envisioned was that the center would need renovating a mere quarter-century after being built: the aim is to revamp the whole complex by December 1999. In the meantime, various sections of the museum will be closed; call for information.

The building is easy to recognize: it's the huge structure that looks like someone turned it inside out, then went to town on it with crayons. The building displays all the machinations that are usually safely hidden away; the water mains are green, the air-conditioning ducts blue, and the electricity cables yellow, just as they appear on architectural drawings. The building itself became a working model for architecture classes everywhere and its museums soon defined the Centre's role in Parisian life. The **Centre des Créations Industriel (CCI),** the interactive part of the center, hosts all sorts of performances, including music, computer-generated videos, dance, drama, lectures, and debates. On the fifth floor the **Grande Galerie** holds big temporary exhibitions.

The major draw is the **Musée National d'Art Moderne,** usually referred to as the Pompidou. The Pompidou's collection picks up around 1906, where the Orsay leaves off. Encompassing more than 40,000 works—including pieces by Matisse, Duchamp, Mondrian, and Pollock—it is the largest gathering of modern art in the world. *Pl. Georges Pompidou, 4e, tel. 01–44–78–12–33 or 01–42–77–11–12. Métro: Rambuteau. Admission to center free; permanent collection 35F, Sun. 10–2 free for everyone; Grande Galerie 35F; Galeries Nord and Sud 27F; all galleries and permanent collection 70F. Open Wed.–Mon. 10–6 (Fri. until 10).*

HOTEL DES INVALIDES

The Invalides was commissioned by Louis XIV to house soldiers wounded during his many military campaigns. The **Musée de l'Armée** inside has Napoléon's death mask, plus mildly interesting displays of armor, weapons, maps, and models of soldiers in war garb. Admission to the museum includes a visit to Napoléon's tomb, housed in the **Eglise du Dôme.** Here the mighty general lies ensconced in five coffins, one inside the next. *Esplanade des Invalides, 7e, tel. 01–44–42–37–67. Métro: Latour-*

Maubourg or Varenne. RER: Invalides. Admission (valid for 2 days) 37F, 27F on Sun. Open Apr.–Sept., daily 10–6; Oct.–Mar., daily 10–5.

LOUVRE

The Louvre is the grandest museum in the world—and not only because recent renovations have made it the largest, nor because it is the oldest and most visited. The Louvre is the queen of museums because it displays the most stunning artwork in the most elegant of settings. It also possesses an overwhelming collection of art and artifacts from almost all ages, cultures, and regions. Before you skip down the escalator and turn into the first wing you see, remember that the Louvre is *enormous*. There's French art, Greek art, Renaissance sculpture, Egyptian artifacts, art from Germany, art from . . . you get the idea. To plan your visit—and avoid spending several days wandering in search of the exit—pick up a visitors' guide in the bookstore. Lines can be long, especially during the midday tourist rush. *Rue de Rivoli, 1er, tel. 01–40–20–53–17. Métro: Palais Royal–Musée du Louvre. Admission 45F, 26F daily after 3 PM and all day Sun., first Sun. each month free. Open Wed. 9 AM–10 PM, Thurs.–Mon. 9–6 (Richelieu open Mon. until 10 PM).*

MUSEE D'ORSAY

The Musée d'Orsay has a spectacular collection, encompassing art produced between 1848 (where the Louvre drops off) and about 1906 (where the Pompidou picks up). Of course, most of the work of any worth created during this time, at least according to Parisians, was French, and most was painted by the impressionists. But this artistically tumultuous time also saw the rise and fall of literary salons and the creation of the concept of the avant-garde. The Orsay explores all of these aspects of early modern art, including an exhaustive collection of impressionist paintings. The museum shop sells excellent guides to the collection, and free maps are available at the information desk. If you're itching to see a van Gogh, Monet, Toulouse-Lautrec, or Renoir, this is the place. *62 rue de Lille, 7e, tel. 01–40–49–48–14. Métro: Solférino. RER: Musée d'Orsay. Admission 39F; separate admission for temporary exhibits. Open Tues.–Sat. 10–6 (Thurs. until 9:45), Sun. 9–6; in summer, daily from 9 AM.*

The Musée de la Sculpture en Plein Air (Open Air Sculpture Museum) at the edge of the Jardin des Plantes near the Pont d'Austerlitz is an ideal place to hang out among modern sculptures and contemplate the murky depths of the Seine.

OPERA GARNIER

The Opéra Garnier is rich, velvety, and gaudy, with an army of gilt statuettes and a ceiling repainted by Marc Chagall in 1964. Spring for the 30F fee and you'll be allowed to climb the ornate stairway and check out the plush auditorium and small museum. Call or stop by to reserve seats (60F–610F); for the 60F cheapie seats, you must come in person. You can also try to get rush tickets 45 minutes before a performance. *8 rue Scribe, 9e, tel. 01–47–42–57–50. Métro: Opéra. Open daily 11–4:30.*

PERE-LACHAISE

The world's most celebrated necropolis, Père-Lachaise Cemetery is the final stop for luminaries like Oscar Wilde, Alice B. Toklas, Gertrude Stein, Frédéric Chopin, Edith Piaf, Marcel Proust, and Georges Seurat, to name a few. The oldest residents at Père-Lachaise are the celebrated lovers **Abélard** (1079–1142) and **Héloïse** (1101–64). But let's face it, you're probably tromping out here to see lizard king **James Douglas Morrison** (1943–71). A gendarme is now posted to keep crowds from committing all those rowdy acts that Doors fans are capable of, and the grave site is periodically cleaned of all messages left by well-intentioned devotees. Free photocopied maps of famous gravesites are occasionally available at the cemetery office, or you can buy a detailed map (10F) from surrounding florists. *Blvd. de Ménilmontant, 20e, tel. 01–43–70–70–33. Métro: Père-Lachaise or Gambetta. Open daily 8 AM–6 PM.*

TOUR EIFFEL

It's funny to think that a construction so abhorred by the French public upon its conception could become the monument most closely associated with the country. In 1885, the city held a contest to design a 984-ft tower for the 1889 World Exposition, and Gustave Eiffel won. It was slated for the junkyard even as it was being built, but somewhere along the way people realized it might actually have a practical use or two; the tower, which bristles with television and radio transmitters, has gone on to help decipher German radio codes during World War I, capture Mata Hari, and serve as the chosen place of suicide for more than 350 people. This 10,000-ton dark metal structure was the world's tallest building

LA MOSQUÉE

Behind the Jardin des Plantes, La Mosquée (pl. du Puits-de-l'Ermite, 5e, tel. 01–36–68–70–05; admission 15F, gardens free; closed Fri.) is both the religious and the intellectual center of the Parisian Muslim community. Built in the 1920s as a monument to North African Muslims who died fighting for France in World War I, its white walls enclose colorful, intricately tiled courtyards, which surround the prayer room, a tearoom (see Cafés, above), and a hammam *(bath; 39 rue Geoffroy-St-Hilaire, 5e, tel. 01–43–31–38–20; admission 85F, towel rental 12F, rubdown 50F; men Tues. and Sun., women Mon. and Wed.–Sat.).*

until New York's Chrysler Building took over that title in 1930. Nowadays, it's simply a source of wonder for legions of visitors, especially at night when it's lit up. The hour-long lines to ascend the tower in summer are decidedly less wonderful; to avoid them, try visiting early in the morning or late at night. The best view, though, is on a clear day an hour before sunset, when visibility from the top extends 90 km (56 mi). To save money, walk up to the second level and take the elevator from there to the top. *Champ de Mars, 7e, tel. 01–44–11–23–23. Métro: Bir-Hakeim. RER: Champ de Mars. Admission elevator 20F to 1st level, 42F to 2nd level, 57F to top; stairs 14F to 2nd level. Open daily 9 AM–11 PM (until midnight July–Aug.).*

MUSEUMS

Paris has so many museums, you could spend all your time indoors. In addition to the biggies, the city has many small, quirky museums devoted to a single artist, writer, or deviant strain of thought. The **Espace Montmartre–Dalí** (11 rue Poulbot, 18e, tel. 01–42–64–40–10, métro Abbesses; admission 35F) houses more than 300 works by the wacked-out master of surrealism. The **Musée des Arts d'Afrique et d'Océanie** (293 av. Daumesnil, 12e, tel. 01–44–74–84–80, métro Porte Dorée; admission 30F) has excellent displays of South Pacific and African cultures and artwork; downstairs there is an aquarium and crocodiles from the Nile. The enormous collection of religious and secular artwork from China, Japan, India, Indochina, Indonesia, and central Asia at the **Musée National des Arts Asiatiques–Guimet** (6 pl. d'Iéna, 16e, tel. 01–47–23–61–65, métro Iéna) is closed through 1999 for an ambitious rebuilding program; in the meantime, some exhibits can be seen at the nearby annex at 19 avenue d'Iéna (admission 16F), which also explores the Buddha in images from China and Japan.

Museums aren't cheap, but if you're under 26 or a student, you may be able to get a discount—bring all kinds of ID and hope for the best. Another option is the **Carte Musées et Monuments,** which gets you into most of Paris's museums. The pass—valid for one day (70F), three days (140F), or five days (200F) and sold at participating museums and most major métro stations—is only a deal if you both (a) don't qualify for any discount admissions and (b) have the stamina of a marathon runner. You might be better off looking out for special discounted (or free) visiting days or hours.

CITÉ DES SCIENCES ET DE L'INDUSTRIE

A mammoth orgy of everything industrial and scientific—play with, test out, or just marvel at its many exhibits. Give yourself half a day here. Exhibits (including futuristic musical instruments, a simulated space voyage, and cutting-edge photography) are in several languages. The second-floor **planetarium** is well worth a stop. The magnificent steel sphere behind the exhibit building is the **Géode** (tel. 01–40–05–80–00), a cinema that claims to have the largest projection screen in existence; tickets for films (usually nature flicks) are 57F. *Parc de La Villette, 30 av. Corentin-Cariou, 19e, tel. 01–40–05–70–00. Métro: Porte de la Villette. Admission 50F. Open Tues.–Sun. 10–6.*

GRAND PALAIS AND PETIT PALAIS

These domed extravaganzas, intended to be temporary structures for the 1900 World Exposition, dodged the wrecking ball to become full-time tourist attractions. The Grand Palais is now an exhibition hall for major art exhibitions; its landmark glass-roofed main hall is closed for restoration, but the wings continue to host art shows. The rich, vaulted halls of the Petit Palais, across the street, feature 17th-century Flemish and 19th-century French works, and impressionist-era pieces, including paintings by Courbet and Cézanne. *Grand Palais, 3 av. du Général-Eisenhower, 8e, tel. 01–44–13–17–17, métro Champs-Elysées–Clemenceau. Admission 25F–40F, depending on exhibit. Open Thurs.–Mon. 10–8, Wed. 10–10. Petit Palais, Av. Winston-Churchill, 8e, tel. 01–42–65–12–73. Admission 27F; temporary exhibits 20F–45F extra. Open Tues.–Sun. 10–5:40.*

INSTITUT DU MONDE ARABE

More than a museum, this is a monstrous multimedia cultural center. Built with funds from the French and most Arab governments, the institute is attempting to become a "cultural bridge" between Europe and the Arab world. In addition to its huge library and audiovisual center and traveling exhibitions, the institute has a **permanent collection** (admission 40F), a combination of the institute's and some of the Louvre's Arabic artifacts, with works dating from the pre-Islamic era to the present. Films (25F), all in their original language with French subtitles, are shown in the **cinema** on weekends. *1 rue des Fossés-St-Bernard, 5e, tel. 01–40–51–38–38. Métro: Jussieu or Cardinal-Lemoine. Open Tues.–Sun. 10–6.*

If you want to do the Louvre for tourists, here it is: da Vinci's La Joconde (a.k.a. the Mona Lisa), under her protective layer of plastic and surrounded by many more layers of tourists, is in the Denon wing, section five on your map.

MUSEE DE CLUNY

This museum, built upon the remains of some Roman baths, features medieval stained glass, furniture, jewelry, carvings, music manuscripts, and some exquisite tapestries. One of the finest tapestry series—found half-eaten by rats before being brought here—is *The Lady and the Unicorn,* comprising six panels in which a refined lady demonstrates the five senses to a unicorn. The museum recently acquired the stone heads of the kings of Judea, removed from Notre-Dame during the Revolution and thought lost until they turned up in a bank vault in 1977. *6 pl. du Paul-Painlevé, 5e, tel. 01–43–25–62–00. Métro: Cluny–La Sorbonne. Admission 27F, 18F Sun. Open Wed.–Mon. 9:15–5:45.*

MUSEE MARMOTTAN CLAUDE MONET

A couple of years ago this museum tacked "Claude Monet" onto its official name—and justly so; this has to be the best collection of his work anywhere. A sampling of works by fellow impressionists and portraitists like Louis-Léopold Boilly fills out the wall space not claimed by Claude. The big Monet display is down in the basement; among other well-known works, you'll find *Impression: Soleil Levant* (1873), now recognized as the first impressionist painting. *2 rue Louis-Boilly, 16e, tel. 01–42–24–07–02. Métro: La Muette. Admission 40F. Open Tues.–Sun. 10–5:30.*

MUSEE DE L'ORANGERIE

This small but rewarding collection of impressionist and postimpressionist paintings sits peacefully at one end of the Jardin des Tuileries. Below generous rooms of Renoirs and thorough displays of Cézanne, Manet, and Modigliani is the museum's most popular room: a magical, watery oval space lined with Monet's huge *Nymphéas* (Water Lilies), perhaps the best-known of his "series" works—continuous studies of the effects of different lighting on the same subject. *Pl. de la Concorde, 1er, tel. 01–42–97–48–16. Métro: Concorde. Admission 30F, 20F Sun. Open Wed.–Mon. 9:45–5:15.*

MUSEE PICASSO

To house the large number of Picasso's works donated by the artist's family (to settle taxes on his estate), the government created a museum in the beautiful 17th-century Hôtel Salé in the heart of the Marais. The Musée Picasso is one of the most popular museums in Paris, largely because of its pleasant, tailored setting. The collection, arranged chronologically and accompanied by biographical information (in English), represents a sampling of every stage of Picasso's work. *5 rue Thorigny, 3e, tel. 01–42–71–25–21. Métro: St-Sébastien. Admission 30F, 20F Wed. Open Wed.–Mon. 9:30–6.*

MUSEE RODIN

The Musée Rodin is possibly the most beautiful museum in all of Paris. The undisputed master of 19th-century French sculpture left his house, the early 18th-century Hôtel Biron (with the second-largest garden in the neighborhood, after the prime minister's), and all the works in it to the state when he died. In addition to the garden and Rodin's personal collection of impressionist and postimpressionist paintings, you can view works by **Camille Claudel** (1864–1943); Rodin's mistress, Claudel was a remarkable sculptor in her own right. *77 rue de Varenne, 7e, tel. 01–47–05–01–34. Métro: Varenne. Admission 28F, 18F Sun., gardens only 5F. Open Tues.–Sun. 9:30–5:45.*

PARKS AND GARDENS

If you're beginning to feel trapped by Paris's bustling streets, more than 350 green spots come to the rescue, complete with kids floating boats in fountains, gossiping old ladies, poodle-walkers, and randy French men preying on tourists. Most parks are open daily, dawn–dusk.

BOIS DE BOULOGNE

The Bois de Boulogne is such a pleasant reprieve from the urbanity of Paris that only the Eiffel Tower has more annual visitors. Boating on **Lac Inférieur** is an integral part of a Parisian Sunday; you can rent a boat for 45F per hour (200F deposit). Or pack a picnic and take the ferry (7F round-trip) to the lake's islands. You can also rent **bikes** (30F per hour) at the stand northwest of the lake. Other attractions include the **Jardin d'Acclimatation,** a children's park/zoo/playground at the north end of the park, and to the northwest the exuberant flower display in the **Parc de Bagatelle,** especially stunning in springtime.

The métro stops at the perimeter of the sprawling woods. From métro: Porte d'Auteil, Bus 52 or 241 traverse the park. You can also take Bus 244 from Porte Maillot. Avoid the park after dark; the Bois is Paris's prostitution center, and an estimated 5 million francs change hands here nightly.

JARDIN DU LUXEMBOURG

The Jardin du Luxembourg possesses all that is unique and befuddling about Parisian parks: swarms of pigeons, cookie-cutter trees, ironed-and-pressed dirt walkways, and not-quite-perfect lawns that until recently could not be trodden upon. Now look for signs telling you which lawns can be walked upon and which are off limits. It's an ideal place to plant yourself on a bench and discover the breed of adorable toddlers, dotty old women, and smooching university students who once found their way into Doisneau's photographs. Surrounded by well-armed guards, the 17th-century **Palais du Luxembourg,** at the park's northern boundary, is home to the French Senate. Be sure to catch the **Théâtre des Marionnettes**' classic *guignols* (puppet shows; 22F) on Wednesday and weekends at 3 and 4 PM. *6e. RER: Luxembourg.*

JARDIN DES PLANTES

Louis XIII commissioned this park in 1626 as "The King's Garden of Medicinal Herbs." Today it's the city's official botanical garden and it houses more than 10,000 varieties of plants (all tidily arranged in little rows and labeled, of course), a zoo, an aquarium, huge collections of rocks and insects, the **Musée National d'Histoire Naturelle,** and lots of students playing hooky from the nearby Ecole Normale Supérieure. *5e. Métro: Jussieu, Monge, or Gare d'Austerlitz. Admission to museums 15F–40F.*

JARDIN DES TUILERIES

A stroll around this stately (albeit dusty) onetime royal garden is like a monument tour: you'll see the Louvre, place de la Concorde, the Musée d'Orsay, the Eiffel Tower, and the Seine. In one direction you can see straight down the Champs-Elysées all the way to the Arc de Triomphe; in the other, you see a long, orderly expanse of garden between you and the Louvre. Besides a series of sculptures by **Aristide Maillol** (1861–1944), the Tuileries has a thriving, gay pick-up scene on the Seineside. Walk through the park, then take refuge in the two art museums at the west end: the **Orangerie** (*see* Museums, *above*) or the **Jeu de Paume** (Pl. de la Concorde, 1er, tel. 01–47–60–69–69; admission 35F; closed Mon.), a contemporary art museum. *1er. Métro: Tuileries or Concorde.*

NEIGHBORHOODS

BASTILLE

The only storming of the Bastille that you'll see today is that of opera-goers lining up for seats and hip Parisians out on the town. The area around the former prison at **place de la Bastille** has been gentrified and galleries, shops, theaters, cafés, restaurants, and bars now exist in the formerly decrepit buildings and alleys. Especially good streets for exploration are **rue de la Roquette** and **rue de Charonne,** which lead you into areas largely inhabited by African and Arab Parisians. A myriad of small streets between the two, such as **rue Keller** and **rue des Taillandiers,** hide a surprising number of cool art galleries, and funky clothing and music shops.

BELLEVILLE

Subject to Paris's urban renewal frenzy, Belleville is undergoing dramatic transformations. Although not the most aesthetically pleasing area of the city, Belleville, roughly bordered by rue de Ménilmontant, rue de Pyrénées, rue de Belleville, and boulevard de Belleville, still warrants rambling. One refreshing change here is the recent influx of artists, musicians, and young people who can still afford this part of town. The arrival of waves of immigrants in the 20th century, most fleeing persecution in their homelands, has contributed to Belleville's international esprit: Polish, Russian, German, and Sephardic Jews; Armenians; Greeks; Spanish Republicans; Africans; Eastern Europeans; Chinese . . . all have brought their specialties to shops, markets, and restaurants throughout the district.

CHAMPS-ELYSEES

What was once an aristocratic pleasure park is now a commercialized tourist trap living off its reputation. Although there's a certain thrill about strutting down the world's most famous avenue in the shadow of the Arc de Triomphe, the abundance of characterless shops and restaurant chains (and the lack of actual Parisians) makes the experience feel suspiciously like a mall. Lots of French kids and tourists cruise around, scoping each other out. The only exclusive things left in the area are the power-lunch bistros, the private nightclubs, and the haute-couture shops on the surrounding streets, particularly **avenue Montaigne.**

On the west end of the Jardin des Tuileries, the place de la Concorde is where Louis XVI lost his head (literally)—as did Marie-Antoinette, Robespierre, and Danton. The Egyptian obelisk in the middle was given to France by the Pasha Mohammed Ali in 1831.

GARE DE L'EST AND GARE DU NORD

You may breeze through this down-to-earth quarter on your way from the center up to Montmartre; if you stop, you'll get a more satisfying taste of Paris than you could soak up from 38 portrait sittings on place du Tertre. Many of the city's old *passages* (covered walkways) are here, but unlike the spruced-up ones in the center, these passages are old and crumbling, housing Indian restaurants or used-book vendors. The area right around the train stations can get a little sleazy, but if you head south toward rue du Château-d'Eau or east toward quai de Valmy, you'll find the best parts of this neighborhood.

Come to the 9th and 10th arrondissements to hit some of Paris's hottest clubs and to eat. A large Jewish population sustains kosher restaurants and bakeries, especially in the area above métro Rue Montmartre, and Indian and Eastern European joints crowd the 10th. **Rue d'Enghien** hosts a great marketplace. But don't come here alone at night; it's one of Paris's worst areas for theft.

LA DEFENSE

With sleek modern buildings and urban art, La Défense is Paris's version of Futureland. About 2 km (1¼ mi) outside Paris proper, La Défense does not exactly fit the traditional idea of a "neighborhood." High-rise complexes house 35,000, and the business and shopping towers employ more than 110,000. The **Grande Arche de La Défense,** an enormous arch that hides an office building within its walls, draws thousands of tourists daily. The **esplanade,** the wide concrete promenade extending along the axis, is lined with big-name art, including a sculpture by Joan Miró that sparked furious controversy over its bizarre shape; Yaacov Agam's *Waterfall,* a fountain powered by 50 computer-controlled jets; and Takis's neat-o fountain filled with traffic signal-like lights. Visit the information center by the Grande Arche to pick up a map outlining all the sculptures and architectural details, including information about the history of La Défense. *Métro: Grande Arche de La Défense or Esplanade de La Défense.*

LES HALLES AND BEAUBOURG

Northern Les Halles has evolved into one of Paris's hotter hot spots; a city project to redo the streets has proven successful, and hip cafés surround **rue Montorgueil,** lined with food markets and restaurants. In the other direction, to the south of the Forum, you have the **Fontaine des Innocents**—the public square here is filled day and night with Rasta bongo players, hair weavers, French skate rats, and truckloads of tourists. Farther south are small streets filled with jazz clubs and trendy shops until you hit place du Châtelet and its facing theaters. A couple blocks northeast is the best-known landmark of the neighborhood: the **Centre Georges-Pompidou** (*see* Worth Seeing, *above*). Around the corner on **place Igor-Stravinsky,** beneath the elegantly Gothic **Eglise St-Merri,** is a wild and wonderful fountain designed by Jean Tinguely and Niki de St-Phalle.

ILE DE LA CITE

Beyond its appeal as the city's ancient heart, the Ile de la Cité is home to two of the finest Gothic buildings anywhere: **Ste-Chapelle** and **Notre-Dame** (*see* Worth Seeing, *above*). The **Crypte Archéologique** (tel. 01–43–29–83–51; admission 28F), in the place du Parvis in front of the cathedral, became a museum after ruins were discovered in 1965. Among the excavated details are parts of the 3rd-century wall of Lutetia; a Merovingian cathedral (Notre-Dame's predecessor) from AD 600; and bits of Roman and medieval houses.

For the most tranquil moment you are likely to have on the Ile de la Cité, head to the square du Vert-Galant at the island's western tip for a view out over the Seine, or picnic nearby on shady place Dauphine. The small garden behind Notre-Dame is another verdant spot, where you can gaze at flying buttresses all day long. From the back of Notre-Dame head across the street and down the steep granite stairs to the **Mémorial de la Déportation,** a striking tribute to the 200,000 French sent to death camps by the Vichy government during World War II.

ILE ST-LOUIS

If Ile St-Louis weren't sitting directly behind Notre-Dame, attached by a bridge, you probably wouldn't go to the island or its **rue St-Louis-en-l'Ile,** possibly the most charming street in Paris. On warm days and clear evenings, plenty of locals will join you here, most of them standing in line at the island's best-known feature: **Berthillon** (31 rue St-Louis-en-l'Ile, 4e, tel. 01–43–54–31–61), hands-down Paris's most famous ice creamery. As you wander around the Ile St-Louis, keep an eye out for building plaques describing who lived where and when. The **Hôtel de Lauzun** at 17 quai d'Anjou was one of Baudelaire's haunts. An especially somber reminder adorns 19 quai de Bourbon: "Here lived Camille Claudel, sculptor, from 1899 to 1913. Then ended her brave career as an artist and began her long night of internment." Claudel's family committed her to an insane asylum where she was forbidden to practice her art until her death. Some of her works are displayed in the Musée Rodin (*see* Museums, *above*).

LOUVRE TO OPERA

It's expensive, snobbish, and packed with tourists, but it also has the centers of the Western art, theater, and music worlds all within a 15-minute walk. The **Louvre** (*see* Worth Seeing, *above*), originally a royal palace, is the biggie here. Just a block above it is the **Comédie Française**—a bastion of traditionalism tacked onto another royal residence, the Palais Royal—which points the way up the avenue de l'Opéra to the **Opéra Garnier** (*see* Worth Seeing, *above*). Off the avenue de l'Opéra, you'll find the famous restaurants, age-old bistros, and upscale shops that form the opulent heart of the quarter. Recently, a sizable Japanese population has moved in, bringing restaurants, bookstores, and specialty shops. North of the Jardin du Palais Royal is **rue des Petits-Champs,** one of the neighborhood's best spots for roaming. The street ends in the intimate place des Victoires, which, along with the stately and refined place Vendôme, on the other side of avenue de l'Opéra, was designed in 1685 by Versailles architect Hardouin-Mansart.

West of the Louvre and Opéra is the decadent **Eglise de la Madeleine**; the surrounding area is where rich French do their shopping. To stroll among the well-heeled of Paris, head to its version of Rodeo Drive, **rue du Faubourg-St-Honoré,** lined with ridiculously expensive boutiques. While you're in the area, stop in and say hello to the president—the **Palais de l'Elysée** on place Beauvau has been the official residence of the head of state since 1873.

LE MARAIS

The Marais covers the third and fourth arrondissements, and though its narrow streets get crowded in summer, this is one of Paris's best neighborhoods for eating, drinking, singing, and walking. The last 20 years have seen the transformation of the Marais into a trendy, artsy neighborhood, with a good mix of artists' studios and working-class folk. The **Jewish quarter,** centered on rue des Rosiers and rue des Ecouffes, adds to the Marais's bustling, sometimes bizarre, character: Hasidic Jews with beards and yarmulkes emerge from the kosher stores, passing young men in tight shirts heading to gay bars. You can't visit the inside, but walk past the **1913 synagogue** (10 rue Pavée, 4e) designed by art nouveau-great Hector Guimard. The **Mémorial du Martyr Juif Inconnu** (Memorial of the Unknown Jewish Martyr) and, in the same building, the **Centre de Documentation Juive Contemporaine** (17 rue Geoffroy-l'Asnier, 4e, tel. 01–42–77–44–72) house temporary art and history expositions, as well as the ashes of concentration camp victims; the center is a great resource for Jewish studies.

Rue Ste-Croix-de-la-Bretonnerie and rue Vieille-du-Temple are the center of gay life in Paris, with bars, bookstores, and cultural information. Rue des Francs-Bourgeois is another great street, full of sleek cafés and homey restaurants. Just north of it are a couple of the city's best museums: the **Musée Picasso** (*see* Museums, *above*) and the **Musée Carnavalet** (23 rue de Sévigné, 3e, tel. 01–42–72–21–13; admission 27F; closed Mon.), a museum on Parisian history. At the end of rue des Francs-Bourgeois is the elegant square, place des Vosges, lined with stately arcades and, at one corner, the **Maison de Victor Hugo** (6 pl. des Vosges, 4e, tel. 01–42–72–10–16, métro St-Paul; admission 27F; closed Mon.). Weekend afternoons, sporadic free classical music concerts add to the royal atmosphere. Between the Seine and the rue de Rivoli is the calmer part of the Marais, packed with beautiful old hôtels and green patches; in particular look for the tiny garden behind the **Hôtel de Sens.** Wander along rue St-Paul for cool shops and antiques.

MONTMARTRE

Rising above the city on the highest hill in Paris is Montmartre, site of the **Basilique du Sacré-Cœur** (*see* Worth Seeing, *above*) and home to a once-thriving artistic community. Even now, after many of the artists have headed for cheaper quarters and tour buses deliver hordes to its minuscule streets, Montmartre remains first and foremost a village where a special breed of Parisian lives and drinks. A trip through the streets of this neighborhood affords you glimpses of gardens, small cafés filled with locals, and perhaps the sound of a practicing violinist. For details on the history and illustrious personalities of Montmartre, visit the **Musée de Montmartre** (12 rue Cortot, 18e, tel. 01–46–06–61–11; admission 25F; closed Mon.), in the building where Renoir once had his studio.

Ste-Chapelle (blvd. du Palais, 1er; admission 32F) is regularly touted as one of the most stunning churches in Paris. Ascending to the upper chapel is like climbing into a jewel box: brilliantly colored windows fill the interior with light.

Today, the aggressive second-rate painters clustered around place du Tertre, one of the most tourist-attacked spots in the entire city, are the only reminders of Montmartre's artistic heritage. Real artists live behind the hill, in million-dollar homes on avenue Junot or the picturesque villa Léandre just off it. To the east, on rue des Saules, the last remaining vineyard in Paris produces 125 gallons of wine per year.

In eastern Montmartre, demarcated by rue Doudeauville to the north and boulevard de la Chapelle to the south, is the **Goutte d'Or** (Drop of Gold), named after the white wine the vineyards here used to produce. A bastion of the Algerian independence party (the FLN) during the Algerian-French war, the area has absorbed constant waves of immigrants, most recently from the Antilles and Africa. This multiethnic working-class quarter gets most festive on Sunday; streets are often blocked off for markets, and shops stay open late.

MONTPARNASSE

The name Montparnasse is burdened with images of all kinds of brilliant expatriates doing silly drunken things in the years surrounding World War I. Acting as an intellectual counterweight to all of the artistry going on up in Montmartre, a quartet of cafés on the corner of boulevard du Montparnasse and boulevard Raspail—La Coupole, Le Dôme, Le Sélect, and La Rotonde—became the stomping grounds for American writers. Montparnasse is a typical Paris neighborhood, though the huge commercial center, finished in 1973, detracts from the neighborhood's charm, as does the towering **Tour Montparnasse,** one of the tallest structures (690 ft) in Europe. Along boulevard du Montparnasse and tucked into off-shoots of avenue du Maine you'll find the latest American-inspired developments—the restaurants and bars frequented by the many students in the area.

A few old sights are still worth visiting: The **Parc Montsouris** and **Cité Universitaire** area is a great place to meet other foreigners in Paris. The **Cimetière du Montparnasse** has been packing them in for years, and the entrance to the network of **catacombs** (admission 27F; closed Mon.), Paris's principal ossuary and most disturbing collection of human remains, is at place Denfert-Rochereau. This maze of tunnels was used by Resistance fighters during the German occupation. Montparnasse also has scores of tiny streets and cul-de-sacs lined with ivy-covered houses reminiscent of a country village. **Villa Adrienne,** off avenue du Général-Leclerc, and **villa Hallé,** off avenue René-Coty, are especially picturesque.

QUARTIER LATIN

The center of French intellectual life for more than 700 years, the Quartier Latin has drawn the meta-physically restless, the politically discontent, the artistically inspired, and those who like to hang out with them to the neighborhood's universities, cafés, and garrets. The presence of several institutions of higher learning, including the prestigious **Sorbonne,** keeps the quarter youthful, creative, and relatively liberal. Down toward the Seine, the confusing maze of streets surrounding **rue de la Huchette** is the ultimate test in crowd tolerance. Just to the west, **place St-Michel** and its fountain act as a meeting/pickup spot for tourists year-round. In the evening many students from the Ecole Normale Supérieure—"normaliens"—come out to eat and socialize on winding **rue Mouffetard,** and eventually converge at the fountain at **place de la Contrescarpe.**

A good place to get lost is in the labyrinthine streets between place Maubert and the Seine; these streets manage to retain their medieval feel despite the presence of fast-food stops and expensive homes (François Mitterrand's private residence was 22 rue de Bièvre). The **square René-Viviani,** just east of the Huchette madness, is a pleasant little park with the oldest tree in Paris, sprouted in 1601. **Shakespeare & Company** (*see* English Books and Newspapers, *above*), a handy refuge for Anglophones, is next door. **Rue de la Montagne-Sainte-Geneviève,** winding between the **Panthéon** and place Maubert, is one of the oldest streets in Paris, with a number of buildings dating from the Middle Ages. Make sure to check out the *bouquinistes* (book stalls) along the Seine, where you can rummage through rare books, posters, postcards, and plastic Eiffel Towers.

ST-GERMAIN-DES-PRES

The venerable tower of **St-Germain-des-Prés,** the oldest church in Paris, anchors a neighborhood of bookstores, art galleries, designer boutiques, and cafes where Picasso, Camus, Sartre, and de Beauvoir spent their days and nights. The cynical and the nostalgic bemoan that the area has relinquished its spirit to the hands of the mainstream, the upscale, and the comfortable—and it's true that in summer you'll encounter many tourists in the shops and cafés. But wander off the traffic-clogged boulevard St-Germain and you'll find winding streets, ancient facades, and hidden courtyards that defy the onrush of modernity.

A short walking tour: Start at Eglise St-Germain, where monks who set up camp here infused the area with its initial intellectual flair; continue on rue Bonaparte toward the river and you'll soon reach the once-great **Ecole Nationale Supérieure des Beaux-Arts.** Turn right at the river and walk past the **Palais de l'Institut de France** (at the corner of quai de Conti and Pont des Arts), the seat of the Académie Française, which Richelieu created in 1635 in an attempt to supervise the activities of Parisian intellectuals. Walking along the Seine toward the Louvre, you pass **rue des Grands-Augustins,** where at No. 5–7 Picasso enjoyed his last—and most luxurious—Parisian home from 1936 to 1955. Also check out **rue de Tournon,** whose 18th-century *hôtels particuliers* (mansions) have housed too many celebrities to mention, among them Casanova (No. 27) and Balzac (No. 2). **Rue St-André-des-Arts,** a pedestrian street between place St-Michel and carrefour de Buci, is lined with crêperies and postcard shops. The nearby **cour du Commerce St-André** (an alley between rue St-André-des-Arts and boulevard St-Germain), opened in 1776, saw all sorts of revolutionary activity, including the printing of Marat's *L'Ami du Peuple* at No. 8, the invention of the guillotine at No. 9, and the daily life of Danton in his apartment at No. 20.

AFTER DARK

Whether you're a jazz fiend or a dance freak, a patron of the arts or a lounge lizard seeking refuge in a dark smoky bar, Paris is your place. For events information, consult the ubiquitous ad boards or check in the weekly *Pariscope* (3F at newsstands) or *L'Officiel des Spectacles* (2F), both of which list concerts, theater, movies, and bars. You can still find free music in Paris: **Eglise St-Merri** (78 rue St-Martin, 4e, tel. 01–42–71–93–93) hosts free classical concerts Saturdays at 9 PM and Sundays at 4 PM. The gay and lesbian scene in Paris isn't as active as in many American cities, though the Marais is definitely the place to be. Contact the **Centre Gai et Lesbien** (3 rue Keller, 11e, tel. 01–43–57–21–47) or check the free monthly *Illico,* found in gay bars and café, for information on events.

BARS

Banana Café. A hip gay crowd gathers at this flamboyant Les Halles bar, which welcomes a mixed crowd and serves 30F beers. The interior is sleek and slim, while the terrace is prime people-watching territory. *13 rue de la Ferronnerie, 1er, tel. 01–42–33–35–31. Métro: Châtelet.*

La Baraka. All bars should be like La Baraka: it's laid-back, friendly, and serves tapas and cheap beer (10F–13F before 10 PM, 13F–16F after). It's the spot of choice for artsy types. *6 rue Marie Stuart, 2e, tel. 01–42–36–10–56. Métro: Etienne Marcel.*

Boca Chica. This tapas bar is one of the most talked-about new places in Paris. Sit on high stools and wash a selection of tapas (15F–40F) down with a glass of beer (10F) or sangria (15F). The twice-weekly concerts all have a distinctly Latin feel (Brazilian music, tango and Latin jazz). *58 rue de Charonne, 11e, tel. 01—43—57—93—13. Métro: Ledru-Rollin.*

Cannibale Café. With its large mirrors, old-fashioned chairs and tables, and long curved bar, this cool café has a distinctly popular feel to it. Sip a *demi* (from 11F) while you listen to a great selection of world music. At 6:30 PM on Sundays, there are live concerts—from acoustic guitar and lute music to gypsy, tango, and Celtic melodies. *93 rue Jean-Pierre Timbaud, 11e, tel. 01—49—29—95—59. Métro: Couronnes.*

La Chaise au Plafond. A heterosexual haven in the gay Marais, this bar has a nice old Parisian feel to it. Have a beer (17F) or an excellent glass of wine (around 20F), or even go for a light meal. Don't leave without checking out the futuristic metal toilets downstairs. *10 rue du Trésor, 4e, tel. 01—42—76—03—22. Métro: Hôtel de Ville.*

Le Frog & Rosbif. This English pub has everything you could want from a "local." Beers are brewed on premises (22F a half-pint, 35F a pint, and 25F a pint during happy hour, 6–7 PM weekdays). On Sunday there's a jazz brunch. *116 rue St-Denis, 2e, tel. 01—42—36—34—73. Métro: Etienne Marcel.*

Next to the Eglise de la Madeleine you'll find the most beautiful pay toilets in Paris—a stunning display of art deco and porcelain. Using this luxurious loo costs a mere 2F.

Le Moloko. All kinds, from sophisticated models to giggly high schoolers, fill this *branché* (hip) bar/boîte until 6 AM. Admission is free (though there's a charge for live music on Saturdays) and drinks start at 30F. The three rooms include a dance floor, a red-velvet sitting room, and a "salon." *26 rue Fontaine, 9e, tel. 01-48-74-50-26. Métro: Pigalle.*

Le Piano Vache. University students come here in groups to rest elbows on the tables, chain-smoke, and solve the world's problems. The bar is dark enough and the music angst-inspiring enough to keep you from feeling too optimistic. Beer is 20F–30F. *8 rue Laplace, 5e, tel. 01-46-33-75-03. Métro: Cardinal Lemoine.*

Les Scandaleuses. This bar has quickly established itself as one of the hippest lesbian hangouts in Paris. Men are also allowed in (in small numbers) as long as they are accompanied by a number of "scandalous women." A beer will set you back 20F. During happy hour (6–8 PM), you get two for the price of one. *8 rue des Ecouffes, 4e, tel. 01—48—87—39—26.*

DANCE CLUBS

Les Bains. This former Turkish bath has been Paris's hottest nightspot for the past 15 years. Stars and models regularly have private parties here and the new ownership is once again attracting a younger, trendier crowd. Cover is 100F. It's hard to get in the door, so do yourself up. *7 rue du Bourg-l'Abbé, 3e, tel. 01—48—87—01—80. Métro: Etienne Marcel. Closed Monday.*

L'Entr'acte. Paris has a serious dearth of lesbian clubs and L'Entr'acte is the most happening place at the moment for gay women. Music ranges from house and techno to groove and rock, with free tapas and sangria on Friday. Cover is 50F (with a drink) on weekends. After that, you can count on 50F per beer. *25 blvd. Poissonière, 2e, tel. 01—40—26—01—93. Closed Mon.–Weds.*

Les Folies Pigalle. This small, red-hot gay club plays techno and hip-hop for a crowd crammed onto the two-level dance floor. Lately they've been trying to bring in more women with male strip shows (for women only) on Wednesday nights. Admission is free during the week, 100F on weekends, and 150F for shows. On weekends the party goes on until noon. *11 pl. Pigalle, 9e, tel. 01-48-78-25-56. Métro: Pigalle.*

Le Queen. This high-profile, super-cool gay nightclub admits women if they're accompanied by a man. Thursdays are strictly men-only. Everyone gyrates to house music on the vast dance floor (Monday is '70s night), and the whole scene is outrageous and definitely very image-conscious. There's no cover during the week (except on Mondays, when it's 50F), but it's 100F on the weekend. *102 av. des Champs-Elysées, 8e, tel. 01-42-89-31-32. Métro: George V.*

Rex Club. The Rex's decor is about as '70s as it gets, with a roller-rink dance floor and mirrored backdrop. The club now devotes itself almost exclusively to techno and house music. The cover varies from 50F to 100F. Beer is always 30F. *5 blvd. Poissonnière, 2e, tel. 01–42–36–83–98. Métro: Bonne-Nouvelle. Closed Sun.–Tues.*

LIVE MUSIC

Most jazz clubs are in Les Halles, St-Germain, or the Quartier Latin. You can usually stay all night for the price of a drink—a 50F–100F drink, that is. For cheaper shows (occasionally free), keep an eye on some of the museums and cultural centers around town (the Institut du Monde Arabe, for example). The free monthly *Paris Boum-Boum* (available at cafés) has a section on world music happenings around town. For most thrash and punk shows look to the Pigalle area. **Elysée Montmartre** (72 blvd. de Rochechouart, 18e, tel. 01–42–52–25–15) is one of the better venues for alternative bands. Big international stars usually take to the stage at either **Palais Omnisports Paris Bercy** (8 blvd. Bercy, 12e, tel. 01–44–68–44–68) or **Le Zenith** (211 blvd. Jean-Jaurès, 19e, no phone).

Au Duc des Lombards. Quality European blues and jazz acts regularly fill up this Les Halles club for 10 PM shows. Admission varies between 50F and 80F and beers only cost 24F (12F before 10 PM). *42 rue des Lombards, 1er, tel. 01–42–33–22–88. Métro: Châtelet.*

Le Baiser Salé. This bar's small, upstairs room is the perfect venue for small, potentially hot jazz ensembles. Shows are at 8 PM and 10:30 PM every night; cover charges are 30F–90F. Beers cost about 25F. *58 rue des Lombards, 1er, tel. 01–4–33–37–71. Métro: Châtelet.***Le Caveau de la Huchette.** This classic *caveau* (underground club) has been serving up swing and Dixieland to hepcats since the 1950s. Entrance is 60F, 70F weekends. *5 rue de la Huchette, 5e, tel. 01–43–26–65–05. Métro: St-Michel.*

New Morning. This is Paris's big-time jazz club. All the greats (Dizzy Gillespie, Miles Davis, and more) have sweated on its stage at one time or another. Entrance to the dark, 600-seat club is 110F–130F. Drinks are 30F. *7–9 rue des Petites-Ecuries, 10e, tel. 01–45–23–51–41. Métro: Château d'Eau.*

L'Opus Café. Run by a bunch of young French hipsters, L'Opus is one of the coolest hangouts for twentysomethings who look like they were born smoking in the back of a blues bar. Cover swings from nada to 100F. *167 quai de Valmy, 10e, tel. 01–40–34–70–00. Métro: Louis-Blanc.*

CINEMA

Almost all foreign films are played in the *version originale* (original language) with French subtitles, marked "v.o." in listings; the abbreviation "v.f." (*version française*) means a foreign film is dubbed in French. Both of Paris's entertainment weeklies, *L'Officiel des Spectacles* and *Pariscope,* have comprehensive film listings that include prices (35F–50F). Different theaters also offer price breaks on certain days of the week, most often Monday. Two cinema events to look out for are **18 heures/18F** in February, when you only have to pay 18F for screenings at 6 PM; and the **Fête du Cinéma** in June, when you pay the normal price for the first film and are then given a card that allows you entrance to an unlimited number of screenings for just 10F a film.

Paris's small, funky cinemas are mostly found in and around the Quartier Latin. Two of the bigger, flashier cinemas are **Gaumont Grand Ecran** (30 pl. d'Italie, 13e, tel. 01–45–80–77–00) and **Max Linder Panorama** (24 blvd. Poissonnière, 9e, tel. 01–48–24–88–88), both of which have immense screens and seat hundreds of people. The Champs-Elysées is also a good spot to go for new screenings. **Cinémathèque Française** (tel. 01–47–04–24–24) is a world-famous cinephile heaven, with different classic French and international films playing daily at two locations: Palais de Chaillot at Trocadéro (16e, métro Trocadéro), and République at 18 rue du Faubourg-du-Temple (11e, métro République). Tickets are 20F–30F.

OPERA AND CLASSICAL MUSIC

The performing arts scene in Paris is overwhelming, with two of the world's greatest opera houses, more than 150 theaters, and a daily dose of at least a dozen classical concerts. Scan *Pariscope* or *L'Officiel des Spectacles* each week for listings, and look for the words *entrée gratuite* or *entrée libre* (i.e., "freebie"). The posters and notices pasted on the walls of métro stations are also good ways to keep up with goings-on.

Go to the **Opéra Bastille** (120 rue de Lyon, 12e, tel. 01–44–73–13–99 for information or 01–44–73–13–00 for reservations; box office open Mon.–Sat. 11–6:30) to experience its "perfect" acoustics and the clear sight lines available to all 2,700 of its democratically designed seats. The opulent **Opéra Garnier** (*see* Worth Seeing, *above*) has an extraordinary number of gilt statuettes and a ceiling repainted by

Marc Chagall in 1964. **Théâtre Musical de Paris** (1 pl. du Châtelet, 1er, tel. 01–40–28–28–40, métro Châtelet) tickets cost 80F and up; 50F rush tickets are available 15 minutes before curtain time to students with ID or those under 20. Its "Midis Musicaux" (Musical Noons; Mon., Wed., and Fri. 12:45) series costs 50F.

ILE-DE-FRANCE

If Paris starts feeling tourist-infested, muggy, and much too urban, an ideal escape might just be the Ile-de-France—with its rural pace, peaceful villages, and grandiose châteaux. On summer weekends, Parisians flock to the forests and small towns of the Ile-de-France, while tourists head to its more famous sights: the palace at Versailles, the cathedral at Chartres, and Disneyland Paris. Prices for food and lodging can be expensive, but you can get by if you picnic—one of the best ways to enjoy the countryside—and stay in the few inexpensive hotels or the hostels that have sprung up in towns like Chartres and Vernon (near Giverny).

VERSAILLES

Louis XIII originally built the château at Versailles as his hunting lodge in 1631, but when Louis "Sun King" XIV converted it from a weekend retreat to the headquarters of his government, he didn't cut any corners. Between 1661 and 1710, architects Louis Le Vau and Jules Hardouin-Mansart designed everything his royal acquisitiveness could want, including a throne room dedicated to Apollo, the king's mythical hero. An opera house was later added so Louis XV could be entertained at home. Efforts to restore the entire estate to how it looked when the Sun King lived here will continue for the next couple of decades.

At the Petit Fer à Cheval (30 rue Vieille-du-Temple, 4e), a venerable wine-bar opened in 1903, old wooden seats—from former métro cars—and a U-shaped bar provide a faded, nostalgic backdrop for sipping wine at 16F–25F per glass.

It's hard to tell which is larger at Versailles—the tremendous château that housed Louis XIV and 20,000 courtiers, or the mass of tour buses and visitors standing in front of it. Arrive at 9 AM sharp, when the château opens, to avoid the 90-minute wait for a tour. The hard part is figuring out where you're supposed to go once you arrive: there are different lines depending on tour, physical ability, and group status. To figure out the system, pick up the brochure available at the tent at the château gates or consult the information desk at the ticket center. *Tel. 01–30–84–76–18. Admission 45F, 35F Sun. Tours 25F–50F. Open Tues.–Sun. 9–6:30 (Oct.–Apr. until 5:30).*

If you don't feel like dealing with crowds, or if you don't have any money left but still want to say that you've been to Versailles, head straight behind the château to the **gardens.** The section of the garden nearest the château is regimented and ordered in typical 17th-century French fashion—designer André Le Nôtre demonstrating his command over Mother Nature. The gardens are where you'll find Versailles's hundreds of famous fountains, which spout only on Sundays (when admission to the garden is 20F), and on certain Saturday nights for the **Fêtes de Nuit,** when the fountains come to life with music and lights. Ask at a tourist office for dates and ticket prices (70F–185F). Move farther away from the château to discover 250 acres of less formal gardens, and lose the less adventurous tourists huddling around the fountains. *Gardens open daily 7–sunset.*

In the northwest corner of the gardens are the smaller châteaux, the **Grand Trianon** and the **Petit Trianon,** which have been used as guest houses for everyone from Napoléon I to Richard Nixon. Visiting them is particularly anticlimactic if you've just toured the big château. Behind the Petit Trianon is the **Hameau de la Reine** (Queen's Hamlet), an idealized village of cute cottages around a small lake, where Marie-Antoinette came to play peasant. *Admission to Grand Trianon 25F, 15F Sun.; Petit Trianon 15F, 10F Sun. Combined ticket 30F. Both open May–Sept., daily 10–6:30; Oct.–Apr., Tues.–Fri. 9–12:30 and 2–5:30, weekends 10–5:30.*

COMING AND GOING

The easiest way to reach Versailles from Paris is via the **yellow RER Line C** that runs along the Left Bank of the Seine to Versailles–Rive Gauche (30–40 mins, 13F), 400 yards from the palace. Otherwise, trains from Paris's Gare St-Lazare arrive at the Gare Rive–Droite near place du Marché de Notre-Dame, 10 minutes' walk from the palace; and trains from Paris's Gare Montparnasse stop at Gare des Chantiers (rue des Etats-Généraux), leaving you with a 15-minute walk.

CHARTRES

Religious pilgrims, who began coming to Chartres more than 1,000 years ago, paved the way for travelers who come here to see the **Notre-Dame de Chartres** cathedral today. In the late 9th century, King Charles the Bald presented Chartres with the *sacra camisia* (sacred tunic) of the Virgin Mary, turning the city into a hot spot for the Christian faithful. The magnificent Gothic cathedral was built in the 12th and 13th centuries in appreciation of the miraculously unsinged state of Mary's tunic after the original church burned to the ground in 1194.

The cathedral and its 21,500 square ft of glass—including 38-ft-high stained-glass windows—have survived seven centuries of wars. The oldest window is *Notre Dame de la Belle Verrière* (Our Lady of the Beautiful Window), in the south choir. Fabulous tours (25F) in English are given daily at noon and 2:45. For an additional 20F (probably better spent elsewhere), you can climb the northern tower for a view of the city. Free organ recitals take place July–October on Sunday at 4:45 PM. Chartres's **Office de Tourisme** (pl. de la Cathédrale, tel. 02–37–21–50–00; open weekdays 9:30–6:30, Sat. 9:30–6, Sun. 10:30–12:30 and 2:30–5:30) reserves hotel rooms and sells helpful guides (10F) to the town and cathedral.

Like the cathedral, the old part of town has been preserved in its cloak of mellowing old stone. The sign-posted **route touristique** behind the cathedral takes you along cobblestone streets past rivers used by old wash-houses, stone buildings, and a bridge all but demolished by World War II bombing. But stray from the path and you'll be slapped by modern apartment buildings and whizzing traffic.

COMING AND GOING

Hourly trains make the 60-minute, 140F round-trip from Paris's Gare Montparnasse to Chartres's **train station** (pl. Pierre Sémard, tel. 02–37–28–50–50), within walking distance of the cathedral; a map in the station shows you exactly where to go. Check your bags here 8 AM–7:30 PM for an extortionate 20F, or put them in equally expensive lockers.

WHERE TO SLEEP AND EAT

Cheap hotels in Chartres are almost nonexistent; your best bet is **Le Chêne Fleuri** (14 rue de la Porte-Morard, tel. 02–37–35–25–70; closed mid-Sept.–mid-Oct.) in the old town; rooms run 140F–240F; book well ahead. The most affordable option is the **Auberge de Jeunesse** (23 av. Neigre, tel. 02–37–34–27–64; closed mid-Dec.–mid-Jan.) where beds are 70F, including breakfast; its ugly exterior belies the clean and comfortable interior. Go to the bottom of the old town, across the river from the cathedral—it's a well-marked, 20-minute walk from the train station, or a five-minute trip on Bus 3.

For food, avoid the area surrounding Notre-Dame and stick to the old town south of the cathedral—**rue Noël Ballay, rue du Cygne,** and **rue du Bois-Merrain Marceau** are good bets for grocery stores and inexpensive restaurants. **Feu Follet** (21 pl. du Cygne, tel. 02–37–21–24–06) is the best place for cheap hamburgers (13F) and crepes. For more substantial meals, head for the restaurants on **rue de la Porte Morard**; **Au P'tit Morard** (25 rue de la Porte-Morard, tel. 02–37–34–15–89) has 80F and 100F menus.

GIVERNY

From 1883 until his death in 1926, Claude Monet painted some of his most famous works in (and of) the gardens at Giverny, 80 km (50 mi) outside Paris. The gardens themselves are a work of art; Monet spent several years perfecting them before he began recreating them on canvas. He planted colorful checkerboard gardens, installed a water lily pond, put up a Japanese bridge, and finally decorated the interior of his house to match it all. For the full effect, come mornings midweek to avoid the crush. *Tel. 02–32–51–28–21. Admission to gardens 25F; gardens and house 35F. Open Apr.–Oct., Tues.–Sun. 10–6.*

Trains leave Paris's Gare St-Lazare every two or three hours for Vernon (50–80 mins, 66F), where buses meet the trains and whisk you away to Giverny (12F). The last bus back to Vernon from Giverny leaves around 5 PM—check with the driver before you settle down for a late-afternoon pastis. You can also walk the nice, flat 6-km (4-mi) stretch from Vernon to Giverny. The **Office de Tourisme** (36 rue Carnot, Vernon, tel. 02–32–51–39–60; open Tues.–Sat. 9:30–noon and 2:30–6:30, Sun.–Mon. 10–noon) has brochures on Monet's stay at Giverny and trail maps for hiking and biking in the surrounding forest.

DISNEYLAND PARIS

It's controversial, it's expensive, and it's a lot of fun. At this meticulously conceived fantasy world, the grounds are spotless, the lines endless, and the rides detailed, right down to the smell of bread coming out of Snow White's kitchen window. *Star Tours, Captain Eo, It's a Small World, Peter Pan* . . . they're all here, and more state-of-the-art than ever. Other stuff includes *Space Mountain, Indiana Jones and the Temple of Peril,* with Disney's first-ever roller-coaster loop, and *Alice's Curious Labyrinth,* a trippy maze of hedges and Wonderland characters.

Time your visit carefully. Rates fluctuate based on school and national holidays, weekends, and tourist season; standard entry fee is 195F, but call ahead to verify prices for specific dates—going a day later could make a huge difference. Food is expensive, so you may want to smuggle some into the park, but a few restaurants—**Café Hyperion** (inside Videopolis in Discoveryland) or **Cowboy Cookout Barbeque** (Frontierland)—actually have affordable menus (from 40F). *Tel. 01–60–30–60–30. Take RER Line A to Marne-la-Vallée/Chessy (38F). Admission 195F–250F. Open daily 9–7 (until 11 in summer).*

THE LOIRE VALLEY

If Brittany is stubbornly independent and Paris is arrogantly cosmopolitan, then the Loire Valley is France, pure and simple. Joan of Arc's first battleground, the playground of Valois kings, and the center of French Renaissance architecture: the region is a living reminder of France's glory days. Dotting this fertile 300-km-long (186-mi-long) valley, the famous châteaux range from medieval fortresses like Chinon to Renaissance country homes like Azay-le-Rideau, with everything in between. Builders, digging into hillsides to create these Renaissance homes for dukes and counts, left in their wake these other unique Loire Valley sights: *caves champignonnières* (mushroom cellars), where more than 60% of France's edible fungi grow on the walls; *caves de vin* (wine cellars), where the constant 14°C temperature ages wines to perfection; and *maisons troglodytiques,* dwellings scooped out of the cliffs. These odd houses, along with the mushrooms, the wine, and the fairy-tale splendor of the hundreds of châteaux, lure swarms of tourists yearly to the poppy-covered hills along the Loire.

The region's dearth of train and bus lines means that it's *possible,* but extremely difficult, to reach the châteaux by public transport. To visit lots of châteaux in little time without your own wheels, you might have to deal with day-long tours with the private bus companies out of **Tours** and **Blois.** If you're traveling with two or three friends, it might be worthwhile to rent a car, but the best way to get around the valley is by bike; the countryside is fairly flat, the châteaux are within easy reach, and you can usually take your bike on trains and buses. Rent in cities to avoid the high prices in smaller towns. A good map like *Michelin 64* will steer you away from congested main routes.

THE HUNDRED YEARS' WAR

Most of the châteaux in the Loire Valley were built during the Hundred Years' War, which actually spanned 116 years. All this self-destructive fervor between 1337 and 1453 was inspired by a continuing conflict over who belonged on which throne and who owed allegiance to whom. King Edward III of England kicked off the war by making a claim to the French throne. After Edward's death in 1377, the fighting died down until Joan of Arc appeared on the scene in 1429, claiming God had told her to deliver Orléans from the English. The French whipped the weary English at Orléans, then proceeded to beat them all over the country.

ORLEANS

Much of Orléans is consecrated to the *pucelle d'Orléans* (maid of Orléans), Joan of Arc, the 18-year-old shepherdess who came in 1429 to liberate the city from the English during the Hundred Years' War. Her statue, her name, her presence are everywhere, from a Center for Joan of Arc Studies to a Jeanne d'Arc Dry Cleaners down the block. Joan aside, the main reason to visit is to use the town as a base for exploring the nearby châteaux. Still, while you're here, you might as well visit the **Cathédrale Ste-Croix** (open daily 9–noon and 2–6) where Joan prayed for the lifting of the English siege; the stunning stained-glass windows tell her life story.

COMING AND GOING

Trains run frequently from Paris's Gare d'Austerlitz (65 mins, 110F), Blois (30 mins, 51F), and Tours (1 hr, 89F). The **train station** (pl. Albert-Ier), four blocks from the center of town, is connected to local and regional bus services and the **tourist office** (pl. Albert-Ier, tel. 02–38–24–05–05). To catch trains that depart from the **Les Aubrais** station (10 minutes away), go to the Orléans station 30 minutes early and catch the free *navette* (shuttle).

WHERE TO SLEEP

Rue Bannier (off rue Cappon, southwest of the train station) has a decent selection of hotels. A 15-minute walk from the station, the bright **Hôtel Coligny** (80 rue de la Gare, tel. 02–38–53–61–60) has 130F doubles with shower. Or reserve ahead for the always popular **Hôtel de Paris** (29 rue du Faubourg-Bannier, tel. 02–38–53–39–58), which has clean doubles for 140F–160F. The cheapest beds (40F, plus 14F for sheets and 18F for breakfast) are at the **Auberge de Jeunesse (HI)** (14 rue du Faubourg-Madeleine, tel. 02–38–62–45–75); take Bus B toward Paul Bert to Jean Jaurès.

FOOD

Orléans's main dining area is the lively pedestrian **rue de Bourgogne,** where traditional French cooking rubs elbows with African, Middle Eastern, and Asian cuisines. At the **Crêperie Bretonne** (244 rue de Bourgogne, tel. 02–38–62–24–62) a full meal with salad, ham and cheese galette, dessert, and cider is only 48F. The town's best-loved bar, the **George V** (in Les Halles-Châtelet, tel. 02–38–53–08–79), is near place du Châtelet, but most of Orléans's not-quite-hopping nightlife takes place near the train station.

NEAR ORLEANS

Thirty kilometers (19 miles) downriver from Orléans, in the yet-untouristed village of **Beaugency** you'll find the Château Dunois and magnificent views of the valley. The castle's not much from the outside, but it houses the **Musée Régional de l'Orléanais** (mandatory French tour 21F), which displays an interesting assortment of local crafts. Ask the cheery ladies at the **tourist office** (pl. du Docteur-Hyvernaud, tel. 02–38–44–54–42; open Mon.–Sat. 9:30–12:30 and 2:30–6:30, Sun. 10–noon) for maps and more information about the town. Several daily trains make the trip from Orléans (29F).

BLOIS

For all its size, Blois is a pretty sleepy town. Other than the château, there's little else to do or see here. The surrounding area, however, is dense with châteaux—ask the staff at the **tourist office** (3 av. Jean-Laigret, tel. 02–54–74–06–49; open Mon.–Sat. 9–7, Sun. 10–7; shorter hours off-season) to arrange transportation.

The architecturally jumbled **Château de Blois** sports every major style from Gothic to 17th-century classicism. The dramatic **staircase** and the **François I wing** are adorned with his famous salamander logo, chosen because the salamander was believed to spit forth the fires of good and extinguish the fires of evil. Notice also his mother's emblem (the crossed wings), and his wife's: the swan, the symbol of purity, pierced by an arrow, the symbol of sin.

COMING AND GOING

About 15 trains a day stop at Blois's **station** (pl. de la Gare) from Orléans (30 mins, 51F) and Tours (35 mins, 71F). To reserve a bike rental, call **Cycles Leblond** (44 levée des Tuileries, tel. 02–54–74–30–13; open daily 9–9) or **Yamaha Sports-Moto-Cycles** (6 rue Henri Drussy, tel. 02–54–78–02–64); rentals cost 30F–60F per day plus passport deposit.

WHERE TO SLEEP

Reserve early for the **Hôtel du Bellay** (12 rue des Minimes, tel. 02–54–78–23–62), a popular place with modern rooms and CNN from 150F; from the station, take avenue Jean-Laigret, turn left on rue Gallois after the church, left again on rue du Bourg-Neuf, and left on rue des Minimes. The cheery **Hôtel St-Jacques** (7 rue Ducoux, tel. 02–54–78–04–15) is five seconds from the station; rooms run 120F–210F. The rustic **Auberge de Jeunesse (HI)** (18 rue de l'Hôtel-Pasquier, tel. 02–54–78–27–21) is 5 km (3 mi) outside Blois, so don't miss the last bus out (Bus 4 to Eglise) at 7:30; beds are 40F.

FOOD

Avoid the tourist traps immediately around the château; instead, head one block closer to the river to **rue St-Lubin** for good, cheap food. At **La Jeune France** (62 rue Denis-Papin, near pl. Victor-Hugo, tel. 02–54–78–07–44), a mere 40F gets you an *océne* (seafood salad with clams). **La Garbure** (36 rue Saint Lubin, tel. 02–54–74–32–89) serves a 79F *garbure,* a traditional duck and vegetable soup.

NEAR BLOIS

The bus company **Transports du Loir-et-Cher (TLC)** (2 pl. Victor-Hugo, tel. 02–54–78–15–66) starts running its châteaux circuit out of Blois the second week of June; it costs about 110F to see three châteaux. Fortunately, most châteaux around Blois are within biking distance, and two-wheel rentals are plentiful (*see* Coming and Going, *above*); for good maps, pick up the free pamphlet "Effeuillez Blois" at Blois's tourist office. Pack a picnic lunch and plan to return to Blois for the night; rooms in château towns are expensive.

CHATEAU DE CHAMBORD

One hour's bike ride upriver from Blois, Chambord is the Loire Valley's largest château. It's hard to believe that it was built as a hunting lodge—all 440 rooms, 365 fireplaces, and 5,500 acres of it. François I started work on Chambord in 1519 and never took a break, even when he was so broke that he couldn't ransom his sons out of Spain, and had to resort to confiscating and melting down his subjects' silverware. The 5F brochure does little to help you navigate the massive château, but try to find the **terrace** upstairs, where hundreds of chimneys form a veritable city skyline, and the funky double-helix **staircase,** which many believe was designed by Leonardo da Vinci. *Tel. 02–54–50–40–18. Admission 40F. Open daily 9:30–5:45; shorter hours off-season.*

CHATEAU DE CHEVERNY

Perhaps best remembered as Capitaine Haddock's mansion from the *Tintin* comic books, the château grounds include a hunting reserve, an orangerie where the *Mona Lisa* was hidden during World War II, a kennel of 70 hounds, and a trophy room with 2,000 antlers. The inside, however, is warm and homey, and despite priceless Delft vases, Gobelin tapestries, and Persian embroideries, it feels lived in. You can check out the photos of the count's family by the entrance to prove it; the real-life versions are just upstairs. *On D765, 20 km (12 mi) south of Blois, tel. 02–54–79–96–29. Admission 32F. Open daily 9:15–6:45; shorter hours off-season.*

TOURS

Though much of Tours was destroyed during World War II (it was bombed by both German *and* Allied troops), some imposing buildings—notably the train station and the Hôtel de Ville—do remain. The cobblestone streets in the pedestrian-only old town were also spared, and today they're packed with young people streaming through the many cafés, bars, and restaurants. A quarter of this commercial city's population is made up of students, giving Tours a lively, hard-edged nightlife as well as affordable room and board.

Housed in an impressive palace that used to be the archbishop's residence, the **Musée des Beaux-Arts** (18 pl. François Sicard, tel. 02–47–05–68–73; admission 30F; open daily 9–12:45 and 2–6) holds a few goodies, including a tiny Rembrandt hardly visible behind thick security glass. Tours's real gem, the **Musée du Gemmail** (7 rue du Mûrier, tel. 02–47–61–01–19; admission 30F, 20F students; open mid-Apr.–mid-Nov., daily 10–noon and 2–6:30) displays stunning artworks of backlit layers of broken colored glass.

BASICS

Trains run frequently from Paris (65 mins, 203F), Orléans (65 mins, 89F), Bordeaux (2¾ hrs, 223F), and Nantes (1¾ hrs, 156F). The **tourist office** (78 rue Bernard-Palissy, tel. 02–47–70–37–37; open Mon.–Sat. 8:30–6:30, Sun. 10–12:30 and 3–6; shorter hours off-season) is across from the train station. Tickets on the city bus service **Fil Bleu** (tel. 02–47–66–70–70) cost 7F and are good for an hour. Most buses pass **place Jean-Jaurès** and run until 8 PM. Rent mountain bikes in summer at **Amster Cycles** (20 blvd. Heurteloup, tel. 02–47–61–28–48) for 70F per day with a passport deposit.

WHERE TO SLEEP

The central **Hôtel Berthelot** (8 rue Berthelot, tel. 02–47–05–71–95) has immaculate, garden-view rooms with balcony and shower for 155F. **Hôtel Voltaire** (13 rue Voltaire, tel. 02–47–05–77–51) has 130F doubles with balcony and shower. Otherwise, big, comfy doubles (65F per person) await you at the central **Le Foyer** (16 rue Bernard Palissy, off pl. de la Gare, tel. 02–47–60–51–51); arrive early, especially in summer. Even if you can't get a room (65F per person in double, 100F for a single), excellent cafeteria privileges are worth the 15F membership fee.

FOOD

Tons of cheap restaurants with outdoor seating congregate around **place Plumereau** (place Plume to locals). Choose from the enormous pan-Asian selection at **Palais de Laido** (12 rue de la Rôtisserie, tel. 02–47–20–85–16), where hearty menus start at 37F (lunch) and 45F (dinner). The young staff at **Le Steven** (102 rue du Commerce, tel. 02–47–64–72–68; closed Mon. lunch) will serve you large salads (30F–40F) and delicious crêpes (from 10F).

NEAR TOURS

Welcome to the Land of the Big-Name Châteaux. Many of the châteaux can be reached from Tours via regular SNCF trains. Even if you hate bus tours, **Les Circuits Chateaux de la Loire** (in Tours train station, tel. 02–47–05–46–09; open Mon.–Sat. 8–11 and 3:30–7, Sun. 8 AM–11 AM) is worth a go. Cheap accommodations around here are hard to find, so stick to Tours as a home base.

Three people renting a car can often beat bus prices and make their own schedule to boot. **Calypso** (6 rue George-Sand, tel. 02–47–61–12–28) rents cars from 230F a day (630F for five days), insurance included. The catch: You must have $800 available on your credit card for the deposit, and you must reserve early because it's the cheapest rental company in town. There's also an **Avis** (pl. Général-Leclerc, tel. 02–47–93–11–04) in Tours.

CHINON

Once a favorite home of English kings, the **Château de Chinon** (tel. 02–47–93–13–45; admission 27F) is now an old and crumbling shell of a fortress overlooking Chinon's centre ville. This imposing château was almost done in by jealous Cardinal Richelieu, who gutted Chinon and robbed it of stones to build his own château 20 km (12 mi) away. The state has since reconstructed a couple of rooms, but their efforts at authenticity are pretty sorry. One original piece is the Marie-Javelle, a bell that has been rung every half hour since 1399, and, legend says, rang of its own accord at each of Joan of Arc's victories.

COMING AND GOING • SNCF trains (46F) and **buses** (45F) leave for Chinon from Tours's train station at least three times a day. From Chinon's **station** (av. Gambetta, tel. 02–47–93–11–04), make a left, follow the quay to the Rabelais statue, and head to your right for the city center. The **tourist office** (12 rue Voltaire, tel. 02–47–93–17–85; open Mon.–Sat. 9–12:15 and 2–9, Sun. 10–12:30; also during lunch mid-June–mid-Sept.) has lots of information on Chinon's yearly festivals.

WHERE TO SLEEP AND EAT • The only cheap hotel in town is **Hôtel le Point du Jour** (102 quai Jeanne-d'Arc, tel. 02–47–93–07–20), where doubles go for 155F (with showers) and 125F (without). The **Auberge de Jeunesse/Maison des Jeunes (HI)** (60 rue Descartes, tel. 02–47–93–10–48; beds 45F) is five minutes from the train station. The French **La Bonne France** (4 pl. Victoire-de-Verdun, tel. 02–47–98–41–41) and the Italian **La Grappa** (50 rue Voltaire, tel. 02–47–93–19–29) both serve large lunch menus for less than 60F. Place Jeanne-d'Arc and place du Général-de-Gaulle both hold Thursday **markets.**

USSE

The Château d'Ussé is the kind you imagined when you read fairy tales as a kid (perhaps because Charles Perrault based his *Sleeping Beauty* on Ussé and its setting). The dwindled forest of today may have lost its enchantment, but the well-kept château (tel. 02–47–95–54–05; admission 60F; open daily 9–noon and 2–5; shorter hours off-season; closed mid-Nov.–mid-Mar.) still provides an enticing picture. It hosts a different historical-costume exhibition every year; you can also ascend the tower, where life-size dolls tell the story of Aurora and that nasty witch who cursed her. If you have a car, it's a cinch to get here. If you don't, the best way is to rent a bike for 50F a day from Chinon (*see above*), 14 km (9 mi) south. Follow the route de Tours near the Chinon castle, turn left at the roundabout to Huismes (D16), and follow the signs to Rigny-Ussé; the ride to the romantic castle is hilly but beautiful.

CHATEAU D'AZAY-LE-RIDEAU

This state-owned, 16th-century château (tel. 02–47–45–42–04; admission 32F; open daily 9–6; shorter hours off-season) represents the model of Renaissance design. Built on an island and surrounded by trees, the castle is such a gorgeous sight that it's hard to believe an angry Charles VII once destroyed it—the people of Azay had called him a bastard, and in revenge he killed every one of the 350 guards and burned down the surrounding forest. Don't miss the astounding fireplace sculpted by Rodin or the famous 12th-century tapestries in the **Grande Salle** (Great Reception Hall). Every summer evening, walks are given through the exquisite gardens. Several daily buses roll 30 km (19 mi) down the Loire from Tours to Azay, and drop you right by the château.

CHATEAU DE CHENONCEAU

The graceful facade, the string of delicate, sunlit galleries overlooking the water, and the airy apartments have given **Chenonceau** (tel. 02–47–23–90–07; admission 45F; open daily 9–7; shorter hours off-season) a reputation as the prettiest château in the Loire. Known as the Château des Dames (Château of the Ladies) because the design was entirely overseen by women, this beautiful monument has an undeniably feminine history. After the first lady of the château, Catherine Briçonnet, built the main body from 1513 to 1521, Henri II's mistress, Diane de Poitiers, ordered gardens and a bridge across the River Cher for easy access to her hunting grounds. Henri's wife, Catherine de' Médici, then kicked Diane out, ordered her *own* gardens, and tacked galleries onto the bridge. In 1589, the château passed to Henri III's widow, Louise de Lorraine, who, in mourning until the day she died, did her second-floor room in black and gray and decorated it with shovels, skulls, and thorns.

COMING AND GOING • Three **trains** arrive from Tours (35 mins, 33F) daily; the château is a well-marked kilometer from the train station. From Tours's gare routière (pl. du Général Leclerc, tel. 02–47–05–30–49), **Fil Vert** also has a 10 AM bus to Chenonceau (30 mins, 37F).

ANGERS

Despite its skyscrapers and industrial complexes, the western gateway to the Loire Valley is worth a day's exploration, if only for its intriguing museums, its medieval fortress, and its good restaurants. The **Château d'Angers** (tel. 02–41–87–43–47; admission 35F; open daily 9–7; shorter hours off-season) looks like a photo negative: the forbidding black walls are made of *ardoise*, a strong slate usually saved for château rooftops, and the towers are topped with the white tufa stone usually seen in château walls. With a guide, you can tour the **Logis Royal** (Royal Chambers), which shelter some fine 14th- to 17th-century tapestries. But these are just a warm-up for the stunning **Tenture de l'Apocalypse,** housed next door in a 20th-century addition. The oldest preserved tapestry in the world, this 300-ft, 14th-century, wool- and gold-thread masterpiece depicts John the Evangelist's narration of the *Book of Revelations*. The **tourist office** (tel. 02–41–23–51–11; open Mon.–Sat. 9–7, Sun. 10–1 and 2–6; shorter hours off-season) is next to the château on place Kennedy.

COMING AND GOING

Several daily **trains** arrive from Tours (65 mins, 86F) and Nantes (45 mins, 72F), and the **TGV** shoots straight from Paris (1 hr 30 mins, 232F). From the station, take rue de la Gare and veer right at place de la Visitation to the city center. You'll only need to use the bus system, **COTRA,** to go outside the city; buy your 6F50 ticket from the driver if there's no machine by the stop.

WHERE TO SLEEP

You should have no problem finding a room in Angers year-round. The **Hôtel des Lices** (25 rue des Lices, tel. 02–41–87–44–10) is clean and comfortable; doubles start at 120F. The cozy **Hôtel du Centre** (12 rue St-Laud, tel. 02–41–87–45–07) is above a lively brasserie; it has old-fashioned rooms for 130F–165F (with shower). Right on the lush Lac de Maine, the **Centre d'Accueil/Camping** (av. du Lac de Maine, tel. 02–41–22–32–32) has beds (81F including breakfast) in quads, and campsites (tel. 02–41–73–05–03; 63F for two people and a tent, 77F in summer) near the water; take Bus 6 across the bridge. Beds are 60F at the modern **Foyer de Darwin/Auberge de Jeunesse (HI)** (3 rue Darwin, tel. 02–41–22–61–20), 5 km (3 mi) from town; from Gare Marengo, take Bus 1 or 8 to EFFCA and follow the signs.

FOOD

Angers's pedestrian quarter around **place du Ralliement** is chock-full of restaurants, crêperies, and cafés. Get two-person deep-dish pizzas (60F–70F) at **California Street Line** (13 rue des Poëliers, tel. 02–41–87–18–42). Or go to **La Ferme** (pl. Freppel, tel. 02–41–87–09–90) for huge meals, such as the fabulous *magret de canard* (duck breast; 64F). Your best bet for cheap eats, though, is the indoor market **Les Halles** (rue Plantaganêt).

NEAR ANGERS

SAUMUR

This little town's restored **château** (tel. 02–41–51–30–46; admission 35F) has been converted into three well-kept museums. Saumur is also known for its wines, mushroom and wine caves, and the monumental cavalry school, the **Ecole Nationale d'Equitation** (tel. 02–41–53–50–50; closed Nov.–Mar.). The school puts on popular 60F demonstrations throughout the summer; Monday–Saturday at 9:30 AM (30F) and 2:30 PM (20F), you can visit the school and watch students train in the arena (9:30 AM only). Saumur's **tourist office** (pl. de la Bilange, tel. 02–41–40–20–60) can direct you to **Musée du Champignon** (tel. 02–41–50–31–55), where you can learn how mushroom spores ripen to make that tasty fungi.

COMING AND GOING • Eleven **trains** arrive daily from both Angers (21 mins, 42F) and Tours (65 mins, 86 F). Saumur makes an easy day trip, but you can stay at the **Hôtel de Bretagne** (55 rue St-Nicolas, tel. 02–41–51–26–38), in the center of town, where clean doubles go for 140F (without shower) and 160F (with). The hostel selection is more appealing: at the modern **Centre de Séjour/Auberge de Jeunesse** (rue de Verdun, tel. 02–41–40–30–00) beds go for 80F–120F. Head into the side streets behind **quai Carnot** for decent cafés and crêperies.

BRITTANY

You can get an idea of what Brittany is all about just by looking at a map of France. A rugged peninsula jutting out into the Atlantic off the western coast, Brittany has wave-battered crags and smooth, sunny beaches, all accessible by hundreds of windswept footpaths. Off the coast, dozens of islands lure you into unexpectedly long stays. Inland, what was once a huge forest is now a world of rolling farmland and forgotten villages.

Brittany's geographic isolation mirrors its cultural separateness from the rest of France. Brittany wasn't even part of France until 1532, when Anne de Bretagne, duchess of Brittany, keeled over after having linked Brittany to France by marrying two French kings in succession. Since then, the relationship between France and Brittany has been rocky. The Bretons, descendants of 5th-century refugee Celts, have resisted the pull of French culture, preserving a language and customs all their own.

RENNES

Only a handful of medieval streets survived Rennes's disastrous 1720 fire. Austere gray granite and tufa buildings gradually replaced many of the original colorful, wood-beamed houses. Since the 1980s, however, the city has brightened, thanks to the construction of more modern edifices. The city is also enlivened by the 40,000 students who populate it during the school year. Near the **quartier medieval** and looming over one end of rue des Portes Mordelaises, the **Cathédrale St-Pierre** is a gloomy but visually rich 19th-century church. Full of twisting paths, grottos, tree-lined alleys, and manicured lawns, the **Jardin du Thabor** cajoles you away from Rennes's mean streets with the promise of picnics, promenades, and naps (on the benches, that is—lounging on the tempting green grass is frowned upon).

A traditional Breton dish is the galette, a thin buckwheat pancake usually filled with butter or eggs and sausage. Crêpes are just flimsier galettes, made of wheat flour and usually filled with sweeter things: sugar, butter, honey, or chocolate.

VISITOR INFORMATION
Pont de Nemours, tel. 02–99–79–01–98. Train station branch, tel. 02–99–53–23–23.

COMING AND GOING
Trains leave from the **Gare SNCF** (pl. de la Gare, tel. 02–36–35–35–35 for reservations) for Paris (2 hrs, 270F), Nantes (2 hrs, 134F), and St-Malo (1 hr, 68F). Regional buses leave from the **bus station** (blvd. Magenta, tel. 02–99–30–87–80) just up the street. **City buses** are plentiful, though most of Rennes is walkable. Buy single tickets for 6F from the driver or carnets (books of 10 tickets) for 46F from the stand (tel. 02–99–79–37–37) on place de la République.

WHERE TO SLEEP
Many cheap hotels are clustered around the train station. **Hôtel de Léon** (15 rue de Léon, tel. 02–99–30–55–28), in a quiet residential area down down the quai Richemont, has quiet doubles for 130F–180F. **Hôtel d'Angleterre** (19 rue du Maréchal Joffre, tel. 02–99–79–38–61) has comfortable rooms for 120F–145F and is in an ideal location. On a busy boulevard, the **Hôtel Tour d'Argent** (20 blvd. de la T. d'Auvergne, tel. 02–99–30–84–16) has doubles (some with balconies) for 140F–170F. Beds at the **Auberge de Jeunesse** (10–12 canal St-Martin, tel. 02–99–33–22–33) go for 80F–130F; from the station, take Bus 18 or 20 to Coëtlogon and follow the signs.

FOOD
Rennes has tons of ethnic restaurants (including Polish, Moroccan, and Lebanese), and crêperies abound, particularly around place Ste-Anne. The elaborately decorated **Crêperie Ar Billig** (10 rue d'Argentré, tel. 02–99–79–53–89) has galettes for 11F–40F and crêpes for 11F–34F. **The Cosmo** (14 rue St-Malo, tel. 02–99–79–57–27) serves up international fare in a kitschy environment; try the Scandinavian plate (64F) along with a delicious iced vodka (20F).

NEAR RENNES

In the area around Rennes you'll discover remnants of Brittany's medieval past: many of France's best fortress towns are clustered here, glaring suspiciously out over the rolling farmland. **Vitré,** just 30 minutes from Rennes by train, has a castle with massive towers and a well-preserved medieval walled town that spreads out from the castle's gates. **Fougères's** enormous 12-towered castle, surrounded by a loop of the Nançon River, is in ruins after having been used as a quarry by 18th-century builders. Buses make the trip from Rennes hourly (1 hr, 64F). A few minutes farther away by bus or train, the northern coast makes an easy day trip from Rennes.

ST-MALO

Although most of Brittany remains proudly detached from tourism, St-Malo makes up for it. With its long stretch of gorgeous beach and famous *intra muros* (within the walls), a fortified section of town on a near-island, St-Malo is one of those places that tour-buses attack every morning. At low tide you can easily walk to the **Fort National,** a massive fortress accessible only by guided tour, and the **Grand Bé,** an island where the French author Châteaubriand was entombed.

COMING AND GOING • Trains arrive from Rennes (1 hr, 68F) at the **train station** (sq Jean Coquelin), a 15-minute walk from the walled town. **Buses,** run by several different companies, leave from the gare routière, immediately outside the intra muros. Next door to the gare routière, the **Office de Tourisme** (Port des Yachts, tel. 02–99–56–64–48) gives out information on bus and ferry schedules.

WHERE TO SLEEP AND EAT • In summer call ahead, even to the hostel. **Hôtel de l'Europe** (44 blvd. de la République, tel. 02–99–56–13–42) has rooms starting at 170F. In the Courtoisville quarter, at the **Hôtel Les Charmettes** (64 blvd. Hebert, tel. 02–99–56–07–31), some seaside doubles go for 180F. Beds at the comfortable **Auberge de Jeunesse** (37 av. du Père Umbricht, tel. 02–99–40–29–80) are 67F with the obligatory HI card. From the station, take Bus 5 to "Auberge." The intra muros restaurants are overpriced and touristy, except for a few that are slightly off the beaten track. The specialties at **L'Art Caddy** (7 rue des Petites Degrès, tel. 02–99–40–82–78) are endangered species, such as a plate of thin slices of alligator for 89F. For a less adventurous meal, **Teddy Bears** (22 rue de la Herse, tel. 02–99–56–03–80), just around the corner, serves steak tartare (65F) and a good selection of Bordeaux wines.

DINAN

Dinan is one of the best-preserved medieval towns in Brittany. Seven-hundred-year-old ramparts tower on steep hillsides that slope down to the Rance River, and medieval buildings line rue de l'Apport, place des Merciers, place des Cordeliers, and rue de la Poissonnerie. Climb the **Tour de l'Horloge** (Clock Tower), at the intersection of rue de l'Horloge and rue de l'Apport, for a view of the big picture. The **Office de Tourisme** (6 rue de l'Horloge, tel. 02–96–39–75–40) is just down the street from the Tour de l'Horloge.

COMING AND GOING • Trains arrive at the art deco **train station** (pl. du 11 Novembre 1918) from Rennes via Dol (50 mins, 70F) and other major towns in Brittany. **CAT** (tel. 02–96–39–21–05) and **TAE** buses (tel. 02–99–50–64–17) connect Dinan to St-Malo, Rennes, and other nearby towns.

WHERE TO SLEEP AND EAT • **Hôtel du Théâtre** (2 rue Ste-Claire, tel. 02–96–39–06–91), right next to the tourist office, has one single for 90F and doubles for 105F–160F. A 30-minute walk from the train station or the center of town, the friendly **Auberge de Jeunesse** (Vallée de la Fontaine des Eaux, Moulin de Méen, tel. 02–96–39–10–83) has beds for 48F, and cots in a tent outside for 26F. Sites at the **campground** next door are also 38F. From the station, turn left onto rue Clos du Hètre, turn left across the tracks, and follow the signs. Many of Dinan's restaurants and good crêperies line **rue du Petit Fort,** from the Porte du Jerzual down to the riverbank. For wood-burning oven-cooked pizzas (40F–50F), try **La Lumachelle** (80 rue du Petit Fort, tel. 02–96–39–38–13), a relaxed local hangout. **Chez Flochon** (24 rue du Jerzual, tel. 02–96–87–91–57) serves a great 49F menu that includes salad, galette du jour, dessert crêpe, and a glass of cider.

COTES D'ARMOR

To the west of Dinan along Brittany's northern coast, the tourist towns fall behind, and the coastline gets wilder and weirder. Visit the Côtes d'Armor, the long stretch of Brittany's northern coast, to witness the dramatic struggle between sea and granite shore. The coastline is loosely divided into two parts: the

Côte d'Emeraude (Emerald Coast), stretching westward from Concale, where tough, old cliffs are punctuated by golden, curving beaches and chin-high forests of ferns; and the peaceful Côte de Granit Rose (Pink Granite Coast), where Brittany's granite glows an otherworldly pink and the beaches themselves seem out of a dream. This area isn't cheap and transportation can be horrific, so advance planning is needed wherever you go. But once you get there and dive into those crystal waters, you'll agree it's well worth the trouble.

Perros-Guirec is the best place to scope out the pink granite boulders of the region and lounge on an idyllic crescent of white sand encircled by plunging hills. About five daily buses arrive from Lannion near the coast—a town on the Paris–Brest rail line that has one of the region's few hostels (tel. 02–96–37–91–28). The Sentier des Douaniers footpath leads from Perros-Guirec through fern forests, past cliffs and amazing pink granite boulders, to the beach at Ploumanac'h.

BREST

Allied bombs flattened Brest during World War II, and the city was rebuilt in the tacky, concrete-building style of the '50s and '60s. Brest is a working town, made famous by its port and naval base. But there are plenty of beaches and museums around this city of about 200,000. Océanopolis (Port de Plaisance, tel. 02–98–34–40–40), a huge aquarium and museum, is worth your time. Cough up the 50F and you'll painlessly learn all sorts of things about marine life and ocean dynamics. Brest's other main draw is that it's the pickup point for ferries to the windswept Ile d'Ouessant (*see below*) and the Crozon peninsula. The tourist office (8 av. Georges Clémenceau, tel. 02–98–44–24–96) can help you unravel ferry schedules.

COMING AND GOING

TGV and regular trains travel to Brest's Gare SNCF (pl. du 19ème R.I.) from Paris several times a day (4 hrs, 360F). Trains also connect Brest to Morlaix (40 mins, 56F), Rennes (2 ¼ hrs, 170F), and Quimper (1 hrs, 80F). The regional bus station (tel. 02–98–44–46–73) is across from the train station. From the Port de Commerce, the Penn ar Bed ferry company (tel. 02–98–80–24–68) runs ferries to the Ile d'Ouessant and other islands. Most of the local bus lines radiate from place de la Liberté. An hour-long trip costs 6F.

WHERE TO SLEEP AND EAT

Lodging is cheap, easy to find, and generally uninspiring. The rooms at the Hôtel Bar du Musée (1 rue Couédic, tel. 02–98–44–70–20) are a little frayed, but basically comfy; doubles go for 110F. The airy, modern Auberge de Jeunesse (rue Kerbriant, Port de Plaisance du Moulin Blanc, tel. 02–98–41–90–41) has lots of amenities and 68F beds, and it's close to a beach. Take Bus 7 from the train station to the end, turn left uphill, and follow signs. Head up the rue Jean Jaurès and you'll be bombarded with food options. If you want to do the full crêpe thing, swing by Crêperie Les Goelettes (9 rue de la Porte; closed Mon.) in the Recouvrance quarter for the 49F lunch menu.

NEAR BREST

ILE D'OUESSANT • The Ile d'Ouessant, isolated from the mainland by 20 km (12 mi) of waves and treacherous tides, resembles many other Breton islands: it's small, windswept, and rocky. You can bike around the island and admire its craggy coast, compact farmhouses, and thousands of sheep. The trip out to the far western point rewards you with a view of wave-torn boulders, several ruined outposts, and glimpses of the island's seals and rare birds.

Penn ar Bed ferry company (*see* Brest, *above*) charges 180F for a round-trip ticket from Brest. Ferries leave on this 2½-hour jaunt daily from the dock in Brest at 8:30 AM, and pull away from the island at 5 PM, 7 PM on Sundays and in summer. Since the ferry only gives you six hours on the island, consider staying overnight. Hotels cluster in Lampaul, the town at the island's center, a 10F bus ride from the port. Try the Hôtel Roc'h Ar Mor (tel. 02–98–48–80–19) or the Hôtel de la Duchesse Anne (tel. 02–98–48–80–25), both with doubles from 140F. At the entrance to Lampaul, the tourist office (pl. de l'Eglise, tel. 02–98–48–85–83) has maps and ferry information.

SOUTHERN COAST

From Quimper to Nantes, Brittany's kaleidoscopic southern coast is one of the most popular vacation spots in France. Traditional crowd-pullers, the twisting streets and tottering medieval houses of Quimper furnish rich postcard material. At the northern edge of the Golfe du Morbihan, **Vannes** draws tourists like flies to its considerable vieille ville, bordered by a long stretch of ramparts, towers, and gates. The coast's sunny beaches, though, especially those at Quiberon, are the real reason to come here. Nothing beats Belle-Ile's sea-bound beauty: the island's sandy beaches and tormented coast have inspired more than one poet. Neolithic menhirs sprinkle the whole region, but the densest concentration lines the fields outside **Carnac.**

QUIMPER

Quimper has all the amenities of a standard Breton tourist town: a medieval town center, a soaring cathedral, and a pleasant river. The requisite **vieille ville** extends from the doorsteps of the St-Corentin church along rue Kéréon to place Terre-au-Duc, and north toward place avenue Beurre. The vast 13th- to 15th-century **Cathédrale St-Corentin** (pl. St-Corentin) remains very much in use by fervent *Quimperois*, giving the candlelit vaults a meditative air. To the side of the cathedral, the **Palais des Evêques** (1 rue du Roi Gradlon, tel. 02–98–95–21–60) leads to a small garden and the extremely modest remains of the town's ramparts. The helpful staff at the **Office de Tourisme** (pl. de la Résistance, tel. 02–98–53–04–05) leads summertime guided tours of Quimper for 30F.

COMING AND GOING
Several trains daily leave for Brest (1¼ hrs, 80F), Nantes (2½ hrs, 167F), and Paris (4½ hrs, 360F by TGV) from the **train station** (av. de la Gare). **CAT** and **Transports Caoudal** run regional buses. Schedules are posted in the train station parking lot. Most of the local bus lines converge near the Odet river next to the vieille ville, and a ticket costs 6F.

WHERE TO SLEEP AND EAT
Few hotels in Quimper are cheap; those that are, are quickly booked. The **Hôtel de l'Ouest** (63 rue le Déan, tel. 02–98–90–28–35) and **Hôtel Celtic** (13 rue de Dournenez, tel. 02–98–55–59–35) both have doubles for around 150F. The mediocre **Auberge de Jeunesse** (6 av. des Oiseaux, tel. 02–98–64–97–97) has beds for 55F to 80F. Directly behind it, the **Camping Municipal** (tel. 02–98–55–61–09) costs 16F per site plus 4F per tent. A few great bars and crêperies stay open late on rue Ste-Catherine; **Pub Le Watson** (11 rue Ste-Catherine, tel. 02–98–53–31–75) is a good place for beer or crêpes on the second floor (the 50F, three crêpe meal is the best deal in town). A completely different option is the **Le Flamboyant** (32 quai Odet, tel. 02–98–52–94–95), serving spicy dishes from the Réunion Island such as chicken samosas (32F), and the famous *boudins créoles* (blood sausages; 29F). The permanent covered market, **Les Halles,** is bordered by rue St-François and rue Astor. **Pâtisserie Boule de Neige** (12 rue des Boucheries, tel. 02–98–95–88–22; closed Mon.) is one of the best pastry shops in France.

QUIBERON

The Presqu'ile de Quiberon is a 15-km (9-mi) stretch of rough coastal cliffs and beaches joined to the mainland by a hairs-breadth of sand. Though in many ways similar to other crowded and pricey beach towns, Quiberon's spectacular coast and its port, with departures for the islands of Belle-Ile, Hoëdic, and Houat, draws outdoorsy types, who come to bike along the spectacular coast and stay at one of the 15 campgrounds or the rustic youth hostel. An 18-km (11-mi) footpath follows the dramatic western coast, dubbed the **Côte Sauvage** (Savage Coast). Beaches ring the coast like pearls, and the **Grande Plage** is the most popular. The **Office de Tourisme** (7 rue de Verdun, tel. 02–97–50–07–84) has information on walking trails and rentals of Windsurfers and kayaks.

COMING AND GOING
Trains only make it to Quiberon July–September. **Cariane Atlantique** (tel. 02–97–47–29–64) and **SA Autocars Le Bayon** (tel. 02–97–24–26–20) run several buses daily from Carnac (25 mins, 21F), and Auray (30 mins, 35F). Buses stop at the train station.

WHERE TO SLEEP AND EAT
Cheap hotels are hard to come by. The **Hôtel Bon Acceuil** (6 quai de Houat, tel. 02–97–50–07–92) has decent doubles for 145F–185F, and the **Auberge de Jeunesse** (45 rue du Roch-Priol, tel. 02–97–50–15–54) has 30 beds for 48F. Most of Quiberon's restaurants post a nearly identical 49F menu of mussels, fries, and beer. Or you can try **Armor Express** (tel. 02–97–30–42–26), across from the station, which serves a fish dish for 45F.

NANTES

The writer Stendhal remarked of 19th-century Nantes, "I hadn't taken 20 steps before I recognized a great city." Since then, the river that flowed around the wealthy Ile Feydeau has been filled in and replaced with a rushing torrent of traffic and major highways that cut through the heart of the town. Despite the traffic jams, the **vieille ville** retains a special character with medieval buildings and tottering 18th-century mansions built with wealth from Nantes's huge slave trade. The 15th-century **Château des Ducs de Bretagne** (pl. Marc Elder, tel. 02–40–41–56–56), a heavily fortified castle built by the dukes of Brittany, is also still in relatively good shape, despite having lost an entire tower during a gunpowder explosion in 1800. The 15th-century **Cathédrale St-Pierre** (pl. St-Pierre) has had a tougher time of it. It was damaged during the Revolution, had its windows blown out from the château's 1800 gunpowder explosion, was bombed by Allies in 1944, and had its roof completely burned off in 1972. Despite all this abuse, its immense height and airy interior make it one of France's best. Nantes's many museums are skippable, though the **Musée des Beaux-Arts** (10 rue Georges Clemenceau, tel. 02–40–41–65–65) is notable for the huge Rubens hanging above the sinks in the bathroom. West of the centre ville on Bus Route 21, the **Musée Jules Verne** (3 rue de l'Hermitage, tel. 02–40–69–72–52) is heavy on pictures and light on facts about Verne, who spent his life in Nantes.

VISITOR INFORMATION

Pl. du Commerce, tel. 02–40–20–60–00.

COMING AND GOING

Nantes's **train station** (27 blvd. Stalingrad) is a 10-minute walk from the vieille ville. Trains leave several times a day for Paris (2½ hrs, 278F by TGV), Rennes (2 hrs, 113F), and Bordeaux, Gare St-Jean (4 hrs, 239F). **Cariane Atlantique** (5 allée Duquesne, off cour 50 Otages, tel. 02–40–20–46–99) runs regional buses. Trams and local buses tote you around town, though all the major sights and most of the cheap lodging are clustered within the vieille ville. The ticket stand at the Commerce tram stop has free maps of the bus and tram systems. One ticket, good for an hour on both tram and bus, is 8F; five tickets are 34F; and 10 are 55F.

WHERE TO SLEEP AND EAT

Nantes has lots of cheap hotels around the centre ville. The **Hôtel Surcouf** (41 rue Richebourg, tel. 02–40–74–17–25) is a stone's throw from the château; doubles run 110F–175F. At the **Hôtel St-Daniel** (4 rue du Bouffay, tel. 02–40–47–41–25), the large doubles (140F) overlook a garden behind the Ste-Croix church. The modern and antiseptic **Auberge de Jeunesse** (2 pl. de la Manu, tel. 02–40–29–29–20), a 30-minute walk from the sights, charges 87F–100F a night. From the train station, turn right on boulevard Stalingrad, then left on rue de Manille.

The pedestrian areas around **place du Bouffay** and **place Ste-Croix** are the best places to look for restaurants. Place du Bouffay is also home to a market that dates back to the 16th century. Sit elbow to elbow with a local Nantais at **La Ciboulette** (9 rue St-Pierre, tel. 02–40–47–88–71) and enjoy the copious 41F lunch menu or the 71F four-course dinner menu and a 10F glass of wine. For a sampling of oysters from the Atlantic Coast, stop by **Chez L'Huitre** (5 rue des Petites Ecuries, tel. 02–51–82–02–02) and order l'Apperi-huitre, a half dozen oysters served with a glass of white wine (27F–29F). **Rue Scribe,** near place Graslin, is the spot par excellence for late-night bars.

NORMANDY

Every summer, tourists swarm to Normandy's medieval city of Rouen, the magnificent rock island of Mont St-Michel, and popular northern coast seaside resorts. All three areas merit the attention, but they have little in common with the rest of isolated and inward-looking Normandy. Away from the hordes of vacationing Brits and Parisians, you can happily lose yourself in the region's cliff-lined coast, apple orchards, and green countryside, where a crowd is a Norman farmer with his herd of brown-and-white cows.

ROUEN

With many monuments, churches, and medieval streets, Rouen is a living, open-air museum as well as a busy industrial port city of about a half-million people. Corneille and Flaubert both lived here, and Victor Hugo nicknamed Rouen the "City of One Hundred Spires," referring to its cathedral-filled skyline. The city was heavily bombed during World War II, but parts of the medieval town of the Rive Droite (the right bank of the Seine) miraculously survived, and the rest has been reconstructed.

BASICS

The English-speaking staff at the **Office de Tourisme** (25 pl. de la Cathédrale, tel. 02–32–08–32–40) dispenses free maps and brochures. The **American Express** office (1–3 pl. Jacques Lelieur, tel. 02–32–08–19–20) is the only one in Normandy. Pick up poste restante mail at the central **post office** (45 rue Jeanne-d'Arc, tel. 02–35–08–73–73). The postal code is 76000.

COMING AND GOING

The **Gare SNCF** is on place Bernard-Tissot at the far northern end of rue Jeanne d'Arc, about a 10-minute walk north of the center of town. Trains travel to and from Paris's Gare St-Lazare (108F), Caen (116F), and Le Havre (92F). **Compagnie Normande d'Autobus (CNA)** runs regional buses from the **bus station** (25 rue des Charettes, tel. 02–35–52–92–29) on the north bank of the Seine.

Like Paris, Rouen is divided by the Seine. The medieval section of town is on the Right Bank. The old town is relatively compact and walkable. Bus and métro tickets cost 7F50 each and a carnet is 56F. Buy single tickets from the driver or from the platform dispensers, carnets from a tabac. Call **Allô le bus** (tel. 02–35–52–52–52) for information about bus and métro routes.

WHERE TO SLEEP

Prices on the Left Bank are not particularly cheap, so go ahead and stay on the right, closer to all the sights. The **Hôtel Normandya** (32 rue du Cordier, tel. 02–35–71–46–15), five minutes from the station, has great views of greater Rouen and doubles for 140F–150F. Also convenient is **Hôtel du Sphynx** (130 rue Beauvoisine, tel. 02–35–71–35–86), just north of the town center, with doubles for 100F. **Hôtel St-Ouen** (43 rue des Faulx, tel. 02–35–71–46–44), in the heart of the medieval quarter, has simple but charming doubles (110F–130F). On the Rive Gauche, the institutional and generally unpleasant **Auberge de Jeunesse, Centre de Séjour** (118 blvd. de l'Europe, tel. 02–35–72–06–45) has beds for 60F. Take the métro, direction Hôtel de Ville/Sotteville, to the Europe stop.

FOOD

Most Rouen restaurants are pricey, but there's always the **open-air market,** held Tuesday and Friday–Sunday at place St-Marc, for cheap produce. Just off place de la Cathédrale, **Natural** (3 rue du Petit Salut, tel. 02–35–98–15–74) serves vegetarian specials (38F) and tartes (43F), lunch only. **Au Temps des Cerises** (4–6 rue des Basnages, tel. 02–35–89–98–00) features filling dishes made with Normandy cheeses. Menus are 60F for lunch or 88F for dinner.

WORTH SEEING

The most important sights are close together between place du Vieux Marché and St-Maclou and can be covered on a walking tour. The **Cathédrale de Notre-Dame** (pl. de la Cathédrale) was built and rebuilt between the 12th and 16th centuries. The cast-iron steeple added in the 19th century is the tallest in France. In the courtyard to the left is the **Portail des Libraires** (Booksellers' Portal), illustrating scenes from the Resurrection. Try to escape the tourist hordes on rue du Gros Horloge, by climbing to the belfry of the **Gros Horloge** where you'll see a small clockworks museum and a knockout view of the city. The magnificent Gothic **l'Abbatiale St-Ouen** (pl. du Général-de-Gaulle) is all that remains of an ancient abbey founded by Benedictine monks during the Carolingian era. The aesthetic merits of the odd **Eglise Jeanne d'Arc** (pl. du Vieux-Marché, tel. 02–35–88–02–70) are debatable; the shape of the roof is *supposed* to evoke the flames of Joan's funeral pyre, but it takes a lot of imagination. Built in 15th-century Flamboyant Gothic style, the **Eglise St-Maclou** (pl. Barthélémy) has beautifully carved wooden doors from 1552. Across the street and to the left is the fantastically decorated **Aître St-Maclou** (186 rue Martainville), a 16th-century, half-timbered house that originally served as a charnel house, a building where they dump the bodies of the dearly departed. The more-interesting-than-it-sounds ironworks museum, **Musée Le Secq des Tournelles** (rue Jacques-Villon, tel. 02–35–71–28–40), displays intricate wrought-iron objects like keys, coffeemakers, and weapons.

AFTER DARK

The super-popular **Café Leffe** (36 pl. des Carmes, tel. 02–35–71–93–30), in the medieval quarter, has outdoor tables that spill across the square. Locals go to **La Taverne St-Amant** (11 rue St-Amand, tel. 02–35–88–51–34) in an old, half-timbered house. At **l'Espace Bleu** (13 rue de Crosne, tel 02–35–15–27–33; no cover) you can hang out and watch either silent, black-and-white films on video screens or a trendy young crowd flailing around to loud rock.

NEAR ROUEN

If you travel northwest from Rouen through the lush Seine valley, you pass through the almost-undisturbed ruins of abbeys and churches in the towns along the **Route des Abbayes,** a passage that includes six abbeys, two priories, three châteaux, and six museums. Regional buses from Rouen will drop you off in most of these tiny towns. Continuing farther northwest you reach the coast, with its white chalk cliffs and popular fishing and resort towns. In the 19th and early 20th centuries, these French versions of British bathing resorts attracted writers and artists like Maupassant, Proust, and Monet.

Etretat is perhaps the most attractive of the towns along the "Alabaster Coast," which stretches from Le Havre to Dieppe. Although the promenade along the pebbly beach is congested with seedy cafés and *frites* (french fry) stands, the town is justly famous for its magnificent cliffs arching into the sea. The price of food and hotels in Etretat means it works best as a day trip; buses traveling from Fécamp, Dieppe, and Le Havre make frequent stops here.

Joan of Arc once asked the question, "Oh Rouen, art thou then my final resting place?" In short, yes it was. She was held captive in the still-standing Tour Jeanne d'Arc and was burned at the stake on May 30, 1431, on place du Vieux-Marché.

FECAMP

Although best known as the home of Benedictine, Fécamp's easy atmosphere, friendly locals, and reasonable restaurants and hotels (for a seaside resort, that is) make it a great place to visit. As well as its chalk cliffs and rocky beaches, the town has its fair share of sights. The neo-Gothic **Palais de la Bénédictine** (110 rue Alexandre-le-Grand, tel. 02–35–10–26–10) is the distillery that produces the sharp, sweet Benedictine liqueur. Tours—complete with a sample—are 27F. The **Maison de Tourisme** (113 rue Alexandre-le-Grand, tel. 02–35–29–16–34) is across the street from the Benedictine Palace.

COMING AND GOING • Several trains daily run to Le Havre (1 hr, 38F), Rouen (1 hr, 80F), and Paris (2½ hrs, 145F) from the **train station** (blvd. de la République, tel. 08–36–35–35–35). **Auto Car Gris** (8 av. Gambetta, tel. 02–35–27–04–25) runs buses to Etretat several times a day for 45F.

WHERE TO SLEEP AND EAT • Most of Fécamp's inexpensive hotels are around place St-Etienne. Try the **Hôtel-Restaurant Martin** (18 pl. St-Etienne, tel. 02–35–28–23–82; closed Sun.–Mon., and first 2 wks in Mar. and Sept.), where the rooms are clean and comfortable (doubles are 135F–155F) and there's a great restaurant downstairs. Also try the **Hôtel Moderne** (3 av. Gambetta, tel. 02–35–28–04–04, where doubles go for 150F–200F. Look along the quay for relatively inexpensive brasseries. **Brasserie des Halles** (3 pl. Bellet, tel. 02–35–28–62–03) serves salads, sandwiches, and fish soup for 12F–24F, and larger menus for around 55F.

DIEPPE

Dieppe is your typical seaside resort, filled with French and British weekenders who sunbathe, shop on the Grande Rue, or have a go at the card tables in the **casino** (3 bd. de Verdun, tel. 02–35–82–33–60). Although the town was largely rebuilt after World War II, it still has some historic neighborhoods, especially around the **Eglise St-Jacques,** a mossy 14th-century building with Renaissance carvings. The beach is where Allied troops attempted a landing on August 19, 1942, and lost more than half their 6,000 troops. Overlooking town from the cliffs to the northwest, the 15th-century **château** is the place for a view of Dieppe's guano-covered rooftops; inside, a worthwhile museum (tel. 02–35–84–19–76; admission 13F) houses paintings, maps, and African ivory carvings. For more information, talk to the friendly folks at the **Office du Tourisme** (quai du Carénage, tel. 02–35–84–11–77).

COMING AND GOING • The **train station** (blvd. Clemenceau, tel. 08–36–35–35–35) runs 10 daily trains to Rouen (50 mins, 55F), Paris via Rouen (2½ hrs, 143F), and Le Havre via Rouen or Malaunay (2½ hrs, 92F). **Stena Line** (tel. 02–35–06–39–00) ferries make the 2–4 hour, 180F–220F run to

Newhaven in England from the *gare maritime* (harbor) at quai Henri IV. You can reach the main sights in town on foot, but buses can save you a long uphill haul to the youth hostel. The **Société des Transports Urbains Dieppois** (tel. 02–35–84–49–49) distributes bus schedules at 1 place Ventabren, off quai Duquesne.

WHERE TO SLEEP AND EAT • Hotels here are not cheap and are crowded in July and August. **Hôtel de la Jetée** (5 rue de l'Asile Thomas, tel. 02–35–84–89–98) has clean, attractive rooms (140F–195F), some with a bit of an ocean view. If it's full, try to snag one of the seven rooms (110F–142F) at **Hôtel de L'Entracte** (39 rue du Commandant Fayolle, tel. 02–35–84–26–45). The **Auberge de Jeunesse** (48 rue Louis Fromager, tel. 02–35–84–85–73) is southwest of town (66F a night). Take Bus 2 to the Château Michel stop. Café and brasserie prices tend to be cheaper farther away from the quay. **Restaurant les Tourelles** (43 rue du Cdt. Fayolle, tel. 02–35–84–15–88) serves good seafood and traditional Norman cuisine; lunch and dinner menus start at 65F. On the beach, **Club House** (tel. 02–35–84–59–22; closed Oct.–Apr.) has a large variety of *moules* et frîtes (mussels and fries) starting at 50F.

CAEN

Like many towns in the region, Caen was reduced to rubble by artillery and bombing in 1944 when the Allied troops descended on the town to recapture it from the Germans. Still, two magnificent abbeys survived the war. When William the Conqueror blew his chance to get into heaven by marrying his cousin, Mathilda of Flanders, he had the **Abbaye aux Hommes** (Men's Abbey, tel. 02–31–30–42–01) constructed to atone for his sins. The nave and towers remain from the original 11th-century abbey church, **Eglise St-Etienne.** Mathilda promised to do her part in the expiation process when she married her cousin, and so founded the **Abbaye aux Dames** (Women's Abbey; off blvd. de la République, tel. 02–31–06–98–98). It's less ornate than the Men's Abbey, but it's still a fine example of Romanesque architecture. Normandy war museums are legion, but **Mémorial: Un Musée pour la Paix** (Esplanade Eisenhower, tel. 02–31–06–06–44; admission 65F), its one *peace* museum, is special; one gallery is dedicated to Nobel Peace Prize winners. For more information on Caen's sights, stop by the **Office du Tourisme** (pl. St-Pierre, tel. 02–31–27–14–14).

COMING AND GOING

The **train station,** south of town on place de la Gare, has trains to Paris (2 hrs, 172F), Rouen (108F), and Bayeux (50F). Regional buses leave from the **Bus Verts** station (tel. 02–31–44–77–44) right next to the train station. Caen's centre ville is easy to get around on foot; hop on the city's **bus system, CTAC** (11 blvd. Maréchal-Leclerc, tel. 02–31–15–55–55), for 6F. They also have an information booth near the train station.

WHERE TO SLEEP AND EAT

Head up avenue du 6 Juin and look for hotels around place de la Résistance. The **Hôtel Auto-Bar** (40 rue de Bras, tel. 02–31–86–12–48), near the town's museums, has clean, no-frills doubles for 115F. The **Central Hôtel** (23 pl. Jean-Letellier, tel. 02–31–86–18–52) lives up to its name—it's in the center of town and near the château; doubles are 130F. The **Auberge de Jeunesse** (68 rue Eustache Restout, tel. 02–31–52–19–96) is a hassle to get to, but the two- and four-person rooms (beds 60F) are nice; take Bus 5 or 17 from the station or the centre ville to Fresnel. Cafés and brasseries cluster around **place Courtonne** and the south part of **rue Vaugueux. La Petite Auberge** (17 rue des Equipes d'Urgences, off rue St-Jean, tel. 02–31–86–43–30) serves delicious Norman specialties with menus for 70F and 85F.

NEAR CAEN

Northeast of Caen stretches the **Côte Fleurie** (Flowered Coast), a string of ritzy resort towns between Honfleur and Cabourg. The population of the small beach towns here triples in summer, when French and foreign tourists come to spend money on overpriced cocktails and luxury hotels. West of the Côte Fleurie, the beaches attract travelers for another reason: here thousands of Allied troops arrived in the 1944 D-Day landings, a turning point of World War II.

HONFLEUR

Honfleur is one of the prettiest and most interesting of the little seaside towns along the Côte Fleurie. Unlike many towns in Normandy, it was untouched by World War II and much of its Renaissance architecture remains intact. Buses from Caen, Le Havre, and many towns in between arrive at Honfleur's **Bus Verts** station (tel. 02–31–89–28–41). The **Office du Tourisme** (pl. Arthur Boudin, tel. 02–31–89–23–30) might be able to find you a less-than-extravagant spot in a guest house.

BAYEUX

Most travelers to Bayeux don't pay much attention to the town's magnificent **Gothic cathedral** or historic houses of the vieille ville. They're too busy making a beeline for its famous 11th-century **tapestry** (Centre Guillaume le Conquérant, tel. 02–31–92–05–48), which depicts William the Conqueror's invasion of England. Actually a linen embroidery, the work narrates Will's trials and victory over his cousin Harold in 58 amusing, embroidered scenes. Admission is 37F. Consult the **Office de Tourisme** (Pont St-Jean, tel. 02–31–92–16–26) for information on Bayeux's lesser-known attractions, and for help in arranging a visit to the nearby D-Day landing beaches.

COMING AND GOING • Trains run to Caen (20 mins, 50F) and Paris (3 hrs, 186F) from Bayeux's **train station** (pl. de la Gare). **Bus Verts** (tel. 02–31–92–02–92) runs buses to Caen and Arromanches. To reach the centre ville from the station, head straight onto rue de Crémel and turn right on rue St-Jean.

WHERE TO SLEEP AND EAT • The 100F doubles at **Hôtel de la Gare** (26 pl. de la Gare, tel. 02–31–92–10–70) are small and a little dingy but generally comfortable. Jean-Marc, the owners' son, leads informative tours to the D-Day beaches in English. **Hôtel d'Argouges** (21 rue St-Patrice, tel. 02–31–92–88–86), in an 18th-century manor in the old center of town, is more luxurious at 200F–400F for rooms. The **Auberge de Jeunesse/Family Home** (39 rue Général Dais, tel. 02–31–92–15–22) has beds for 90F and up. From the station, follow the FAMILY HOME signs (15 mins). Crêperies surround the cathedral; brasseries and pizzerias are on rue St-Jean. **Le Printanier** (pl. aux Pommes, tel. 02–31–92–03–01) has a 60F lunch menu and a typical 90F Norman menu; the light desserts are exceptional.

D-DAY BEACHES

In the predawn darkness of June 6, 1944, thousands of U.S. and British paratroopers dropped from the sky along an 80-km (50-mi) stretch of coast west of Cabourg during "Operation Overlord." Their mission was to blow up river crossings, sever enemy communications, and distract the Germans so they would be unable to attack the seaborne assault troops due to land later that morning on five beaches: Omaha, Utah, Sword, Gold, and Juno. After successfully gaining control of Normandy, the Allied troops swept through France. The events and consequences of this momentous invasion are immortalized in many museums and cemeteries in Arromanches and on the nearby beaches.

Arromanches, a town on Gold Beach, is the best place to see the remains of Port Winston, one of the concrete ports where Allied troops unloaded their supplies during the invasion. The **Musée du Débarquement,** overlooking the ocean, provides a detailed account of the construction of Port Winston, as well as the usual collection of Allied invasion paraphernalia. West of Arromanches, overlooking Omaha Beach, the somber but beautiful **American cemetery** is covered with endless rows of white crosses and stars of David. West of Omaha Beach is **Pointe du Hoc,** where American Rangers scaled the 100-ft cliffs to destroy the German artillery that threatened troops landing on the Omaha and Utah beaches.

COMING AND GOING • Unless you have a car, the D-Day beaches are best visited on a bus tour from Bayeux. **Bus Fly** (tel. 02–31–22–00–08) leaves from the tourist office or the hostel, and the smaller **Normandy Tours** (tel. 02–31–92–10–70) leaves from Bayeux's Hôtel de la Gare (*see* Bayeux, *above*). Both tour companies charge about 100F–160F per person and conduct tours in French and English.

MONT ST-MICHEL

Acting as a homing signal to every traveler in France, Mont St-Michel is a 264-ft mound of rock topped by a delicate abbey that looms a few hundred yards off the coast in dramatic contrast to the bay and grasslands that surround it. The causeway from the mainland leads over a flat, sandy bay bed at low tide, but the waters roll almost to the causeway's edge when the tide rises. You approach the Mont's maze of chambers and spires via a single winding street that seethes with human activity. Try to visit off-season; the crowds are almost unbearable in July and August.

A lively guided tour (tel. 02–33–60–14–14; 40F) takes you through the impressive abbey and the abbey church, as well as the **Merveille,** a 13th-century, three-story collection of rooms and passage-ways. Another tour, which is longer and costs 60F, takes you through the delicate **Escalier de Dentelle** (Lace Staircase) and **pre-Roman church.** The **tourist office** (tel. 02–33–60–14–30) on the left behind the first gate as you enter town can give you more information.

COMING AND GOING

STN buses (tel. 02–33–50–08–99) run from Pontorson (15 mins, 21F20 round-trip), the nearest town served by train. To avoid crowds on the way up to the abbey, go through the Gendarmerie gateway to the left of the main entrance.

WHERE TO SLEEP

Reserve, reserve, reserve, or sleep in a nearby town like Pontorson or Avranches. The simple, clean doubles at the **Hôtel du Mouton Blanc** (Grande Rue, tel. 02–33–60–14–08) are the cheapest on the Mont, starting at 200F, but are usually booked far in advance. The **Hôtel St-Aubert** (Le Mont St-Michel, tel. 02–33–60–08–74) is 2 km (1 mi) from the Mont; doubles run 150F–350F. The nearest camp-ground, **Camping du Mont** (tel. 02–33–60–09–33; closed mid-Nov.–mid-Feb.), is also 2 km (1 mi) away, and it's often crowded in summer. In Pontorson, try **Hôtel l'Arrivée** (14 rue du Docteur Tizon, tel. 02–33–60–01–57), right across the street from the train station, or stay at the spartan **Auberge de Jeunesse** (rue Patton, tel. 02–33–60–18–65; beds 41F), in a small farmhouse 10 minutes from the train station.

CHAMPAGNE AND THE NORTH

A history of bickering monarchies, two world wars, and wafts of industrial smoke have left northern France lacking in the easy charm that most of the country enjoys. This region seduces relatively few tourists away from Paris and the rest of France, but the millions of bottles of bubbly maturing in chalky tunnels, carved under towns like Reims, make Champagne worth a visit. Even if you can't snag a bottle for a good price, at the very least you'll get a complementary glass at the end of a tour.

REIMS

The capital of the Champagne region, Reims has been at the center of champagne production for cen-turies, stocking the cellars of its many conquerors—Napoléon, Tsar Nicholas I, and the Duke of Welling-ton. Today, most champagne houses give tours (about 25F) of their *caves* (cellars), complete with a sample and informative lectures. **Mumm** (29 rue du Champ-de-Mars, tel. 03–26–49–59–70) is the closest to the centre ville; other caves are just southeast of the center. Make reservations to tour **Veuve-Clicquot Ponsardin** (1 pl. des Droits-de l'Homme, tel. 03–26–89–54–41); their introductory film isn't as soporific as some. The slide show at **Pommery** (5 pl. du Général Gouraud, tel. 03–26–61–62–55) gives a tour of its ancient Roman chalk pits and tunnels, where the widow Pommery had friezes sculpted for the viewing pleasure of her workers. **Taittinger** (9 pl. St-Niçaise, tel. 03–26–85–45–35) has some of the best tunnels.

When you're done at the champagne houses, stagger over to Reims's huge **Cathédrale de Notre-Dame** (pl. du Cardinal-Luçon; open daily 7:30–7:30); tours are 15F. Thirty-four French kings and eight queens were crowned under the cathedral's ethereal heights, but you wouldn't know it by the more fan-ciful features of its facade—giggling angels, stern saints, and a grinning bovine. Devoid of the video-camera crowd that infests the cathedral, the sober **Basilique St-Rémi** (53 rue St-Rémi, tel. 03–26–85–31–20) modestly displays its Gothic curves. For your daily art fix, visit the **Musée de Beaux-Arts** (8 rue Chanzy, tel. 03–26–47–28–44; admission 10F), with a small but stimulating col-lection that includes a room of Corot and David's *La Mort de Marat* (Death of Marat).

VISITOR INFORMATION

The **Office de Tourisme** has good maps and complete lists of the day's champagne-house tours. *2 rue Guillaume-de-Machault, next to cathedral, tel. 03–26–47–25–69. Open July–Aug., Mon.–Sat. 9–8, Sun. 9:30–7; shorter hours off-season.*

COMING AND GOING

The **train station** (blvd. Joffre, tel. 03–26–65–17–07; open daily 5:30 AM–11:30 PM), about a 10-minute walk from the center of town, sends trains to Paris's Gare de l'Est (90 mins, 118F), Epernay (20 mins, 52F), and Dijon (4 hrs, 206F). **STDM Trans-Champagne** (tel. 03–26–65–17–07) and **RTA** (tel. 03–23–50–68–50) provide bus transportation around the region; catch STDM buses at place du Forum or in front of the train station, and RTA buses at rue St-Symphorien, one block behind the cathedral. **Transports Urbains de Reims** (6 rue Chanzy, tel. 03–26–88–25–38) runs the checkered city buses (5F); most stop in front of the train station.

WHERE TO SLEEP

Place Drouet-d'Erlon and **rue de Thillois,** across the park from the train station, harbor a number of cheap hotels. It's a good idea to reserve ahead. The **Hôtel Linguet** (14 rue Linguet, tel. 03–26–47–31–89) is in a quiet location minutes from the cathedral; doubles are 125F–135F. At **Hôtel St-André** (46 av. Jean-Jaurès, tel. 03–26–47–24–16), only 20 minutes from the station, the bright rooms with floral decor start at 105F. Reserve a few days in advance for a 67F bed at the **Auberge de Jeunesse/Centre International de Séjours** (Esplanade André-Malraux, near Parc Leo-Lagrange, tel. 03–26–40–52–60). If they're full, call the **Foyer AREPJ** (66 rue de Courcelles, tel. 03–26–79–16–16), which has 61F dorm singles and gives priority to students with ID. From the train station, go right on boulevard Louis Roederer, and right again on rue de Courcelles.

FOOD

At dinnertime, and into the night, **place Drouet-d'Erlon** is the happening spot. The romantic **Le Chamois** (45 rue des Capucins, off rue de Vesle, tel. 03–26–88–69–75) cooks your choice of meat on a volcanic rock and serves it with cheese and dessert for 75F; it's enough food for two, at least. If you want to dance, **Le Tigre** (2 bis av. Georges Clemenceau, tel. 03–26–82–64–00) plays Top-40 tunes and serves a discreet gay clientele. The cover, which is 40F weekdays and 60F Saturday, includes a drink.

TROYES

Though it falls within the Champagne region geographically, Troyes's medieval character differs vastly from the flamboyant 19th-century spirit of Reims or Epernay. The famous half-timbered houses in the Vauluisant and St-Jean districts have been meticulously maintained, creating a central core of pleasantly rambling narrow walks. The **Office de Tourisme** (16 blvd. Carnot, tel. 03–25–73–00–36; open daily 10–noon and 2–5), on the square in front of the station, changes money when the banks are closed.

Oodles of churches and fine museums add to Troyes's appeal. Most impressive is the **Cathédrale St-Pierre–St-Paul** (pl. St-Pierre)—flamboyant flames lick its outlandish facade, but the nave is classic Gothic. The truly first-class **Musée d'Art Moderne** (pl. St-Pierre, tel. 03–25–80–57–30; admission 30F; open Wed.–Mon. 11–6) displays works by modern masters such as Degas and Braques. A 60F pass gets you into this and all other city-run museums; all are free on Wednesday.

COMING AND GOING

About nine daily trains run from Paris (1½ hrs, 135F) to Troyes's **train station** (cour de la Gare, tel. 03–25–70–41–40). To avoid a detour through Paris, take an **STDM Trans-Champagne** bus (tel. 03–26–65–17–07) to Reims (2 hrs, 101F) and other towns in the region.

WHERE TO SLEEP

In the heart of the old town, the half-timbered **Les Comtes de Champagne** (54–56 rue de la Monnaie, tel. 03–25–73–11–70) has clean singles and doubles from 120F. The **Hôtel Butat** (50 rue Turenne, tel. 03–25–73–77–39) has immaculate singles (120F) and doubles (140F). The **Auberge de Jeunesse** (Chemin Ste-Scholastique, Rosières, tel. 03–25–82–00–65; beds 48F, campsites 25F), bordering a modest forest, is 7 km (4½ mi) from Troyes. From the tourist office, take Bus 6 to the end of the line,

THE RIDDLER KNOWS

Dom Pérignon, a blind 17th-century Benedictine monk, was reputedly the first to discover the secret of bubbly, which hasn't changed much today. Chardonnay, Pinot Noir, and sometimes Pinot Meunier grapes are fermented separately, then mixed and bottled. The bottles, left slanting down in chilly underground tunnels, are turned by "riddlers" who's job it is to nudge the sediment into the neck. After turning, the bottle necks are frozen, the caps taken off, and the sediment shoots out. A small quantity of liqueur is then added, and the corks are tied down with wire. Three years of fermentation produces the proper level of fizz, alcohol, and taste.

turn right on rue Pasteur, walk 30 minutes, turn left on rue Jules Ferry, continue for another 10 minutes, and then go left on Chemin Ste-Scholastique.

FOOD

Reasonable restaurants dot Troyes's old town, and the outdoor tables of pricey crêperies and pizzerias clog the pedestrian streets around Eglise St-Jean. Strains of sitar music and incense drift from **Soleil de l'Inde** (33 rue de la Cité, down the street from the cathedral, tel. 03–25–80–75–71), where spicy Indian menus are about 60F. At **Le Bouchon Champenois** (1 cour du Mortier d'Or, between ruelle des Chats and rue des Quinze-Vingts, tel. 03–25–73–69–24; closed Sun. dinner, Mon.), the four-course 70F menu of French fare is well worth the investment.

CALAIS

If you're planning to take the three-hour train ride through the Channel Tunnel from London to Paris, you and millions of British visitors will end up passing through Calais. There's little here to tempt you to stay long; the town's sole claim to fame is the Rodin bronze, *The Burghers of Calais,* which graces the front of Calais's Hôtel de Ville.

If you get stuck here for the night, try the **Hôtel du Littoral** (71 rue Aristide Briand, tel. 03–21–34–47–28), where doubles go for 120F–150F. Or try the cheery, new **HI hostel** (av. du Maréchal-de Lattre-de Tassigny, tel. 03–21–34–70–20; beds 80F–90F), 15 minutes from the train station and town center. At **Crêperie la Bigoudène** (22 rue de la Paix, tel. 03–21–96–29–32), choose among 30 kinds of crêpes (24F) or the 36F–70F menus.

If want to cross the channel, talk to the folks at **Sealink** (tel. 03–21–46–80–00) or **P&O Ferries** (tel. 03–21–46–04–40), both at the Car-Ferry Terminal, or **Hoverspeed** (Hoverport, tel. 03–21–46–14–14). Sealink and P&O send ferries to Dover (1½ hrs, 180F), and Hoverspeed sends Hovercrafts (200F), which are twice as fast. Compare prices, as competition with the Channel Tunnel sometimes leads to extremely cheap deals.

BOULOGNE

A hop, skip, and a hydroplane from the south coast of England, Boulogne suffers from an overload of British day-trippers. Still, the town's fine, walled **vieille ville,** high above the port, is worth a visit. For a dizzying panoramic view, wheeze your way up the 13th-century **belfry** (open weekdays 8–5:30); access is free through the **Hôtel de Ville.** The **Office de Tourisme** (quai de la Poste, tel. 03–21–31–68–38; open July–Aug., daily 9–8; shorter hours off-season) adeptly dispenses information about the town.

COMING AND GOING

Boulogne has two train stations: the **Gare Boulogne-Ville** (blvd. Voltaire, tel. 03–21–80–48–44), a good walk from the center of town, sends trains to Calais (40 mins, 42F) and Paris (3 hrs, 179F) via Amiens; the **Gare Maritime** (quai Thurot, near ferry terminal) has a service to Paris timed to coincide with ferry arrivals. From the ferry terminal, across the river from central Boulogne, **Hoverspeed** (tel. 03–21–30–27–26) sends sleek Seacats to Folkestone (200F) February–Christmas. **Cariane Littoral** (tel. 03–21–34–74–40) runs buses Monday–Saturday from boulevard Daunou, at rue Belvalette, to Calais (1 hr, 28F).

WHERE TO SLEEP AND EAT

Hôtel Hamiot (1 rue Faidherbe, tel. 03–21–31–44–20) has 20 singles and doubles (120F–210F) above a popular dockside bar and restaurant. **Hôtel Sleeping** (18 blvd. Daunou, tel. 03–21–80–62–79) also has comfy singles (105F) and doubles (160F). At the **Auberge de Jeunesse** (pl. Rouget-de-Lisle, tel. 03–21–32–61–61), across from the Boulogne Ville train station, 67F (16F for sheets) and an HI card get you a bed in a triple. **Place Dalton** and the surrounding streets have a few so-so bistros; one of the liveliest is **Chez Jules** (pl. Dalton, tel. 03–21–31–54–12), where generous pizzas run 40F–55F. The square also hosts a Wednesday and Saturday **market**. **Le Doyen** (11 rue du Doyen, tel. 03–21–30–13–08) is a small, friendly restaurant in the center of town serving fresh caught seafood; menus are 90F and 125F.

ALSACE-LORRAINE

Although the two regions are almost always grouped together, Alsace and Lorraine actually have distinct personalities. Alsace is more German, more exciting, and more popular, with welcoming towns that cater to tourists without being touristy. Most Lorraine towns are poorer than their Alsace neighbors and hardly know what to do with tourists; they're fine if you want to get a taste of everyday village life, but otherwise they don't have much to offer.

STRASBOURG

Edged right up to the German border among mountains and vineyards, Strasbourg is one of the most happening cities in France. If you visit only one city in Alsace-Lorraine, this should be it. The capital of Alsace, Strasbourg has changed hands between the French and the Germans about four times in the last 300 years, leaving a mix of German half-timber architecture and very French cafés. Looming above it all is the ultramodern, super-sleek tram system that runs through Strasbourg—a system worthy of Disneyland. Middle Eastern markets, museums filled with French impressionist paintings, and the presence of the Council of Europe and European Parliament complete Strasbourg's pan-European scene.

BASICS

The main **Office de Tourisme** (17 pl. de la Cathédrale, tel. 03–88–52–28–28) and the **branch office** (pl. de la Gare, tel. 03–88–32–51–49) at the train station have similar services. The **American Express office** (31 pl. Kléber, tel. 03–88–75–78–75) has the best exchange rates in town. The main **post office** (5 av. de la Marseillaise, tel. 03–88–52–31–00) also exchanges money at fair rates.

COMING AND GOING

Trains speed from the **Gare SNCF** (20 pl. de la Gare) to Lyon (5 hrs, 272F), Frankfurt (2½ hrs, 236F), and Paris's Gare de l'Est (4 hrs, 285F) by way of Nancy (1½ hrs, 128F). You can cover most of the town on foot, but local **buses** leave from the train station. Tickets are 7F, good for one hour, and can be used on the tram.

WHERE TO SLEEP

An easy walk from the train station, the **Hôtel le Colmar** (1 rue du Maire Kuss, tel. 03–88–32–16–89) has spiffy, sometimes noisy rooms starting at 150F. Closer to the center of town, the **Hôtel Michelet** (48 rue du Vieux Marché aux Poissons, tel. 03–88–32–47–38) is regularly swamped by budget travelers; doubles run 135F–170F. The **Auberge de Jeunesse "René Cassin"** (9 rue de l'Auberge de Jeunesse, tel. 03–88–30–26–46), 2 km (1 mi) from the train station, charges 68F–147F per bed; camping out back costs 41F. From the train station, take Bus 3 or 23. The **CIARUS dorm** (7 rue Finkmatt, tel. 03–88–32–12–12) isn't cheap (beds are 75F–177F), but it's filled with cool people from all over the world. From the train station, take Bus 10 toward Tribunal.

FOOD

You can find cheap eats in the winding streets behind the cathedral. **Place Austerlitz** has an outdoor vendor scene as well as some nice cafés and restaurants. **Flam's** (20 rue des Frères, tel. 03–88–36–36–90) does *tarte flambées,* thin-crusted pizzalike things, for 30F and up. **Pfifferbrieder** (9 pl. du Marché aux Cochons de Lait,,tel. 03–88–32–15–43) is a warm, tiny place loved by locals. They serve hearty traditional meals including a delicious *tarte à l'oignon* (onion quiche; 30F) and a filling 55F menu. Just off the central island, **Restaurant du Petit Pêcheur** (3 pl. du Courbeau, off quai St-Nicolas, tel. 03–88–36–11–49) serves Alsatian cuisine at reasonable prices; three-course menus start at 50F.

WORTH SEEING

At the heart of Strasbourg, the red-stone **Cathédrale de Notre-Dame** impresses even Parisians. The spire reaches 471 ft, making it the highest in France and the second-highest in Europe. Every day at 12:30 PM little apostles march past a likeness of Christ and a rooster crows in the **astronomical clock** (4F for the show) at the cathedral's far right end. Most of Strasbourg's other major sights radiate from the cathedral. The seat of the **European Parliament** (av. de l'Europe; open daily 9–4:30) is a paragon of modern European design, and the flags, guards, and luxury automobiles outside are an indication of the heavy-duty business that goes on inside. You can arrange a free weekday visit (in English or French) of the **congressional halls** by calling 03–88–41–20–29. The adjacent **Orangerie** is a vast expanse of formal gardens, fountains, and flowers. The **Palais Rohan** (2 pl. du Château, tel. 03–88–52–50–00), built in the 1700s as a royal residence, is worth visiting in its own right, but it also houses three fun museums: the **Musée Archéologique,** the **Musée des Arts Décoratifs,** and the **Musée des Beaux-Arts.** A ticket to all museums costs 40F or buy individual tickets for 20F. Right next to the Palais Rohan and near the cathedral is the **Musée de l'Oeuvre Notre-Dame** (3 pl. du Château, tel. 03–88–52–50–00). Artists working on the cathedral during the 14th and 15th centuries used this building as a workshop; the statues and stained-glass windows that didn't make the cut stayed here, including a lion with a halo holding a Bible, and several cross-eyed saints. The terrace up top gives you a rooftop view of La Petite France. Both are free and open daily 9–8.

AFTER DARK

Most bars are cover-free, but expect to pay 20F–25F for a beer and up to 50F for mixed drinks. **Place du Marché Gayot** is a cheery square with several good bars, among them **Le Perroquet Bleu** (13 rue des Soeurs, tel. 03–88–24–22–00), with expensive specialty drinks that are worth the splurge. **Café des Anges** (5 rue Ste-Catherine, tel. 03–88–37–12–67) is a popular live-music joint that showcases local reggae, funk, and country groups.

NANCY

West of Strasbourg on the other side of the Vosges mountains, Nancy once enjoyed a noble period as the long-time capital of the powerful dukes of Lorraine. The last duke of Lorraine, Stanislas of Poland, ordered the creation of **place Stanislas,** one of the few breathtaking sites of Nancy. Unfortunately, outside the magnificent plaza, Nancy's architecture and ambience are fairly urban, in a drab sort of way. Art nouveau buildings do help to perk up the duller parts of town, though; Nancy was one of the movement's centers in the early 20th century.

Life revolves around the huge place Stanislas, which is bordered by the spacious **Musée des Beaux-Arts** (tel. 03–83–85–30–72; admission 20F, free Wed.), the **Hôtel de Ville,** the **Opéra,** outdoor cafés, fountains, and a triumphal arch. Ask at the **Office de Tourisme** (14 pl. Stanislas, tel. 03–83–35–22–41) for information about Nancy's myriad museums and free listings of goings-on around town.

COMING AND GOING

Lots of trains arrive from Paris (3 hrs, 223F) and Strasbourg (1½ hrs, 128F) at the **Gare SNCF** (3 pl. Thiers, tel. 03–83–22–15–15). Nancy is fairly spread out, but the central area is manageable on foot. **Allô bus** (tel. 03–83–35–54–54) runs buses (7F) all over the city.

WHERE TO SLEEP

The best place to stay is near place Stanislas. The **Hôtel de la Poste** (56 pl. Mgr. Ruch, tel. 03–83–32–11–52) edges right up to the cathedral; doubles are 185F. Closer to the train station, **Hôtel Foch** (8 av. Foch, tel. 03–83–32–88–50) has a shabby reception area but okay rooms that go for 145F–190F. The **Auberge de Jeunesse/Château de Remicourt** (149 rue de Vandœuvre, Villers, tel. 03–83–27–73–67; beds 70F) is in a castle 4 km (2 mi) southwest of town. Take Bus 4 or 26 to the St-Fiacre stop, walk downhill, turn right on rue de Vandœuvre, and follow the signs.

FOOD

Reasonably priced restaurants line **rue des Maréchaux** and **Grande Rue.** An open-air **market** is held Tuesday–Saturday at place Henri Mengin. Just one of the many great restaurants on Grande Rue, **La Gavotte** (47 Grande Rue, tel. 03–83–37–65–64) features good crêpes from the simple buttered (13F) to the smoked duck with mushrooms (45F). The art nouveau brasserie **Excelsior** (50 rue Henri Poincaré, tel. 03–83–35–24–57) is an essential stop for coffee (7F) or beer (12F), and the 100F "*faim de nuit*" (night hunger) menu, served past midnight, includes three courses and wine.

BURGUNDY

Burgundy's landscape is curvaceous, swelling with the fertility that gives rise to its world-renowned wine. Covered with intermittent patches of hills, lakes, forests, vineyards, and the occasional cow clinging to 30° inclines, this region attracts more ramblers than city slickers. In Burgundy, people have their noses shoved deep into wine glasses, not high into the stratosphere. Head to **Dijon** to set up camp—and do a little mustard-tasting—before tackling the winery circuit in towns south of the city. If nature is what you're seeking, there's the 3,500-square-km (1,260-square-mi) **Parc Naturel Régional du Morvan** (Morvan Regional Park), with 1,001 ways to work yourself into a sweaty delirium.

AUXERRE

On slow summer days, Auxerre, with its colorful shop awnings, friendly, unhurried locals, and tourists wearing khaki and sunglasses, feels almost like a beach town without the beach. But the seductive **Cathédrale St-Etienne** looming above a cascade of rambling medieval streets and red-tile roofs reminds you that you're in Burgundy. Slip in among the stone houses and laid-back Auxerrois reading newspapers in the cafés, and don't expect to see vampires roaming the city—Auxerre goes to bed early.

BASICS

The **tourist office** (1–2 quai de la République, near cathedral, tel. 03–86–52–06–19; open Mon.–Sat. 9–1 and 2–7, Sun. 9:30–1 and 3–6:30; shorter hours off-season) has free town maps, and books rooms (15F). The **train station** (rue Paul Doumer, east of Yonne River) sends daily trains to Paris (2½ hrs, 118F) and Dijon (2 hrs, 118F). The **bus station** (rue des Migraines, northwest of centre ville, tel. 03–86–46–90–66) serves local towns; call **Les Rapides de Bourgogne** (rue des Fontenottes, tel. 03–86–46–90–90) for tickets.

WHERE TO SLEEP

The central **Hôtel de la Renommée** (27 rue d'Egleny, off pl. Charles Lepère, tel. 03–86–52–03–53) has simple doubles (from 160F) off a quiet courtyard. Picturesque, vine-covered **Hôtel Normandie** (41 blvd. Vauban, tel. 03–86–52–57–80, fax 03–86–51–54–33) occupies a grand-looking building in the center of town, a short walk from the cathedral. Singles (240F–280F) and doubles (280F–360F) with bath or shower are spanking clean, but it is the amenities that you are paying for. The best deals in town are the coed hostels, both near the centre ville. Crash in 76F singles (breakfast included) at the **Foyer des Jeunes Travailleurs** (16 av. de la Résistance, tel. 03–86–46–95–11); from the station, cross the tracks to rue St-Gervais and continue along avenue de la Résistance. If they are full, ask about rooms in the other Foyer one block away. For a quiet evening, venture 10 km (6 mi) into truffle-speckled countryside and stay at **Domaine de Montpierreux** (in Venoy, on the D695 route to Chablis, tel. 03–86–40–20–91, fax 03–86–40–28–00), a 19th-century manor with delightful doubles (260F–320F). Reservations are advised and they take cash only.

FOOD

Chow down on fantastic salads and hearty pizzas at **Le Toon's** (82 rue de Paris, tel. 03–86–51–32–71; closed Mon.), where fixed menus cost 32F–70F. Or try traditional Burgundian cuisine (menus from 68F) at **Hôtel-Restaurant du Commerce** (5 rue René Schaeffer, tel. 03–86–52–03–16).

WORTH SEEING

Buy a pass (28F) at any of the museums, good for all sights, or wait until Wednesday when all the museums are free. Start your exploration at the 13th- to 15th-century **Abbaye St-Germain** (pl. St-Germain; open Wed.–Mon. 10–6:30; closed noon–2 off-season), whose star attractions are the crypts and their superb 9th-century Carolingian frescoes; the 20F admission includes a tour and entry to most other museums in town. The abbey's beautiful **Musée St-Germain** has exhibits of prehistoric, Gallo-Roman, and modern art. A bit farther south, the **Cathédrale St-Etienne** (pl. St-Etienne; open daily 8–7) features a flamboyant Gothic facade with slightly damaged (but still interesting) portal carvings depicting Bible stories. For 8F you can see manuscripts and enamels from the 12th–13th centuries in the **treasury,** as well as a rare fresco of Christ on horseback in the medieval **crypt** (open daily 9–6; closed noon–2 off-season).

DIJON

Dijon is a placid mix of historical monuments, art, gardens, gastronomy, and university students. The mayor, once the Minister of the Environment, keeps the air clean and the trees flourishing, but the town's tranquillity can be eerie. Cigarette butts don't litter the streets here, dogs don't bark out of place, and the Dijonnais look more weary than peaceful—perhaps as a result of tourism and high mustard intakes. On the up side, the city has great restaurants and the vineyards to the south are only a hop, skip, and a jump away.

For centuries an insignificant Roman colony called Divio, Dijon became the capital of the duchy of Burgundy in the 11th century and acquired most of its important art treasures during the 14th and 15th centuries; today the city's churches, the ducal palace, and one of the finest art museums in France evidence the Burgundian dukes' patronage of the arts. For brochures, or to peruse the city guide *Divio,* go to the **tourist office** (pl. Darcy, tel. 03–80–44–11–44; open daily 9–9; shorter hours off-season).

COMING AND GOING

Several daily trains zoom to the **station** (end of av. Foch) from Paris (3 hrs, 215F), Lyon (2 hrs, 132F), and Strasbourg (3 hrs, 220F); the **TRANSCO bus station** (rue des Perrières, tel. 03–80–42–11–00) is adjacent. Dijon's centre ville is walkable, but you can rent bikes at **Bourgogne Tour** (11 rue de la Liberté, tel. 03–80–30–49–49) for 80F per day (plus 1,000F or passport deposit).

WHERE TO SLEEP

The centre ville is safe and full of cheap hotels; reserve ahead in summer. **Hôtel le Chambellan** (92 rue Vannerie, tel. 03–80–67–12–67, fax 03–80–70–00–61) is a shade nicer than most budget hotels; doubles start at 120F. In a pretty stone house near the train station, **Hostellerie du Sauvage** (64 rue Monge, tel. 03–80–41–31–21, fax 03–80–42–06–07) has modern rooms for 180F–450F. Its restaurant serves delicious Burgundian cuisine for 100F–150F. An HI card and 68F get you a clean dorm bed at the **Centre de Rencontres Internationales (HI)** (1 blvd. Champollion, tel. 03–80–72–95–20), 4 km (2 mi) outside town; from the train station, take Bus 9 to rue des Godrans, then Bus 5 (Bus A at night) to Epirey. **Foyer des Jeunes Travailleurs** (9 rue Aubriot, near hospital, tel. 03–80–43–00–87, fax 03–80–42–03–31) rents doubles (115F) to men or women. From the station, walk right along rue de l'Arquebuse past place 1er Mai.

FOOD

Dijon has plenty of good restaurants, especially on rue Jeannin. Also try **avenue Foch** for crêperies and pizzerias, and **place Emile Zola** for ethnic food or for **Les Moules Zola** (3 pl. Emile Zola, tel. 03–80–58–93–26), where mussels prepared a half dozen ways are served; the 60F lunch menu is the cheapest option; à la carte dinner starts at 80F. **La Vie Saine** (29 rue Musette, tel. 03–80–30–15–10) is a sunny, vegetarian place with an all-you-can-eat buffet (55F). The cozy atmosphere at **L'Bout d'la Rue** (52 rue Verrerie, tel. 03–80–71–37–92) lures locals to its tables every night for 50F–70F dishes, including salads and seafood.

WORTH SEEING

The museums are free for everyone on Sunday. On other days, a one-year pass (20F) gets you into all of them. Buy the pass at the **Musée des Beaux-Arts**, which is housed in the 17th-century **Ancien Palais des Ducs de Bourgogne** (pl. de la Libération, tel. 03–80–74–52–70; admission 18F; open Wed.–Mon. 10–6). The museum has a well-displayed collection of cubist art, and its spectacular *salle des gardes* (guard room) contains the richly decorated tombs of Burgundy bigwigs. The **Musée Archéologique** (5 rue Docteur Maret, tel. 03–80–30–88–54; admission 15F; open Wed.–Mon. 9–6) is the most impressive in the region, with a collection of pottery and rare wood and stone sculpture in excellent condition.

Three churches in town really merit a visit. Dating from the 13th–14th centuries, the **Cathédrale St-Bénigne** (pl. St-Bénigne) presents an austere facade, but a colorful roof pattern and a 300-ft, 19th-century spire lighten the effect. Inside the **Eglise St-Michel** (pl. St-Michel), check out the choir, which has some fine 18th-century wood carvings. The Gothic **Eglise Notre-Dame,** north of the ducal palace, houses an 11th-century statue of the *Vierge Noire* (Black Virgin) and a tapestry commemorating Dijon's 1944 liberation from German occupation.

NEAR DIJON

Burgundy's most famous **vineyards** stretch south of Dijon all the way to Mâcon. Throughout the countryside, small towns with big wine names attract tourists to their cellars for wine tastings. You can visit the whole area by TRANSCO bus or by bike, but if you're simply looking for cheap or free wine tastings, go straight to Beaune.

Believe it or not, people come to southern Burgundy for things other than wine—namely spectacular church architecture. The tiny town of **Cluny** revolves around its famous abbey (tel. 03–85–59–12–79; admission 32F; open daily 9–7; shorter hours off-season), founded in AD 909. The basilica, a symbol of the order's vast wealth and power, was built between 1088 and 1130 and was the world's largest church before St. Peter's was built in Rome. It was ransacked during the 16th-century Wars of Religion between the Protestants and Catholics, and today, visitors from all over the world often leave grumbling in various languages, "Is this all that's left?" But informative guided tours, leaving from the Musée Ochier, give you an idea of the abbey's original enormous size, and the surrounding town is a great place to spend a mellow afternoon.

BEAUNE

People come to Beaune (20 mins from Dijon by train) for two reasons: to buy wine and to see **Hôtel Dieu** (rue de l'Hôtel Dieu, tel. 03–80–24–45–00; admission 29F; open daily 9–6:30; shorter hours off-season) with its colorfully patterned roof tiles and medieval courtyard. In 1443, chancellor and tax collector Nicolas Rolin founded this hospital, hoping to get a ticket to heaven; today the Hôtel Dieu houses several large galleries and art treasures. Across the street, at the **Marché aux Vins** (tel. 03–80–22–27–69; open daily 9:30–noon and 2–6), 50F buys you a *tastevin* (wine-tasting cup) and free rein among 25 bottles of the best Burgundian wine. If you want to do the wine thing full force, either stop by the **tourist office** (pl. de la Halle, tel. 03–80–26–21–30) for a handout describing the various caves and what they offer, or wander around on your own and check out all the places with a DÉGUSTATION (tasting) sign.

LYON

Lyon's history stretches back to 43 BC, when the invading Roman army found its position at the confluence of the Rhône and Saône rivers an ideal site for Lugdunum, the future capital of Roman Gaul. During the Renaissance, Lyon became a center of silkworm cultivation; evidence of this prosperous era is still visible in the Croix-Rousse district, where a maze of *traboules* (covered passageways) protected the precious silk as it was carried from place to place.

Including the surrounding suburbs, Lyon's population exceeds 2 million, making it the second-largest city in France. Lyon continues to prosper from industry, particularly metallurgy and chemical production. Easy access to the Alps and to the Beaujolais is what may tempt you to set up camp here: the pristine Alps are only an hour away by train, and the city is the best place in the region to catch trains and planes, visit museums, and enjoy lively nightlife and superb food.

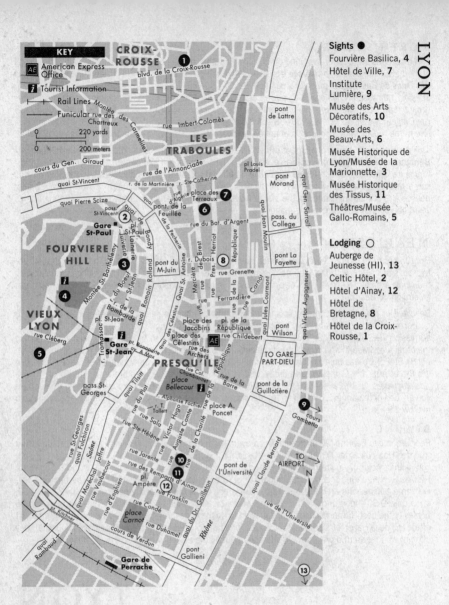

BASICS

VISITOR INFORMATION

The main **Office de Tourisme** has an SNCF booth where you can buy train tickets and make reservations. Branches in Vieux Lyon near St-Jean Cathédral on Fourvière Hill and in Gare de Perrache have the same weekday hours; the St-Jean branch is the only one open on Sunday. For nitty-gritty information on local events and films pick up the 7F, weekly, *Lyon Poche* at any tabac. *Pl. Bellecour, tel. 04–72–77–69–69. Open mid-June–mid-Sept., weekdays 9–7, Sat. 9–6; shorter hours off-season.*

AMERICAN EXPRESS

AmEx will cash their own traveler's checks at slightly better rates than the banks. *6 rue Childebert, 2e, tel. 04–72–77–74–50. Open weekdays 9–12:30 and 2–6 (currency exchange until 5:30); also May–Sept., Sat 9–noon.*

MAIL

The **main post office** is the best place (after the AmEx office) to exchange traveler's checks. *Pl. Antonin Poncet, off pl. Bellecour. Open weekdays 8–7, Sat. 8–noon.*

COMING AND GOING

Across the Rhône from the Presqu'île, the modern **Gare de la Part-Dieu** serves Paris (2 hrs, 330F by TGV), Nice (3½ hrs, 293F by TGV), and major destinations in Italy; to get here, take Bus 28 from Vieux Lyon. The smaller, more central **Gare de Perrache** serves most of the same towns as Part-Dieu. Both stations have a Thomas Cook change bureau, an SOS Voyagers office, luggage storage, and showers. More fashion than function, the art-deco **Gare St-Paul** is at the base of Fourvière Hill in Vieux Lyon.

Lyon is divided into three sections by the Rhône and the Saône rivers. **Vieux Lyon** is on the west side of the Saône at the bottom of Fourvière Hill. Between the two rivers is the **Presqu'île,** which can be covered on foot. The northern part of the Presqu'île ascends steeply through run-down streets to the **Croix-Rousse** district. The city is subdivided into nine arrondissements; the first and second are on the Presqu'île, the third is east of the Rhône, and Vieux Lyon is in the fifth.

Four métro lines (which run 5 AM–midnight) traverse the city in a tick-tack-toe grid. Automated dispensers in each station spit out 8F tickets and carnets (67F). Lyon's **TCL buses** (tel. 04–78–71–70–00 for information), however, are more efficient and cost the same. When boarding the bus or métro, stamp your ticket in the orange machine. Pick up bus maps at the TCL office across from Gare de la Part-Dieu or on the ground floor of Gare de Perrache.

WHERE TO SLEEP

Most hotels are within walking distance of sights and nightlife. They often fill up with business travelers on weeknights, making it easier to find weekend accommodations. In last-ditch situations, you can usually find a room north of **place des Terreaux.** The Croix-Rousse district is mostly residential, as a result hotels are less-known and often quieter than those in the centre ville.

UNDER 175F • Hôtel d'Ainay. These basic, clean, well-lit rooms (130F, 165F with shower) are conveniently located two blocks north of place Carnot, across from a laundry, and a few doors down from a market. *14 rue des Remparts d'Ainay, off rue Victor Hugo, tel. 04–78–42–43–42. Métro: Ampère. Closed early–mid-Aug.*

UNDER 200F • Celtic Hôtel. In Vieux Lyon, with a common terrace overlooking place St-Paul, this is one of Lyon's best deals. Most rooms (130F–150F, 180F with shower) have private balconies. *10 rue François Varnay, tel. 04–78–28–01–12. Métro: Vieux Lyon.*

UNDER 250F • Hôtel de Bretagne. Above a bar, this newly renovated little hotel is definitely worth the splurge. Singles run 180F–190F, doubles are 210F–230F, and all come with shower. *10 rue Dubois, tel. 04–78–37–79–33. Métro: Cordeliers.*

UNDER 275F • Hôtel de la Croix-Rousse. On colorful place de la Croix-Rousse, this relaxed hotel is in the hip residential part of town. Cheerful singles (185–260F) and doubles (260–275F), and a friendly front desk make staying here a pleasure. *157 blvd. de la Croix-Rousse, tel. 04–78–28–29–85, fax 04–78–27–00–26. Métro: Croix-Rousse. 34 rooms, all with bath.*

HOSTEL

Auberge de Jeunesse (HI). It's too bad that this great, clean hostel has to be in an industrial suburb a half hour from town. It has a sunny common area, TV room, rooftop deck, and bar. Rooms 12–28 are quietest. The last bus leaves Part-Dieu at 11:35 PM, but a special bus leaves bus stop No. 53 at Parilly métro at 12:07 AM. Beds are 48F, breakfast is 18F. *51 rue Roger Salengro, Vénissieux, tel. 04–78–76–39–23. From Part-Dieu, Bus 36 to Vivani-Joliot-Curie; walk left under PARIS/MARSEILLE freeway sign (hostel is on right). Flexible 11:30 PM curfew, lockout 10 AM–5:30 PM. Reception open 7–noon and 5–12:30. 116 beds. Kitchen, laundry.*

FOOD

Dining is Lyon's most popular pastime and the city's *bouchons* (bistros) are known for gastronomic goodies like *andouillette* (tripe sausage), *quenelles* (dumplings made with flour, eggs, and fish or veal), and salad *lyonnaise* (with bacon, croutons, and a poached egg on top). **Rue Mercière, rue St-Jean, and rue des Marronniers** are full of small bouchons. Stands selling *donner-kebabs* (spicy lamb and yogurt sauce in a pita) are all over town. At the morning **market** along quai des Célestins on the east bank of the Saône you'll find fresh meat, produce, and cheese Tuesday–Sunday.

UNDER 100 • Brasserie les Halles. Come here for heaping bowls of moules served with frîtes and salade (55F), a three-course menu including fresh salmon and salad lyonnaise (69F), and 30 kinds of beer. Jazz trios liven the terrace bar scene after 11 PM. *4 rue du Palais de Justice, Vieux Lyon, tel. 04–78–42–54–43.*

La Mère Jean. This bouchon has been dishing out traditional Lyonnais fare since 1923. The lunch menu is 61F; various dinner menus are 72F, 85F, and 132F. *5 rue des Marronniers, 2e, tel. 04–78–37–81–27. Closed weekends.*

Le Pâtisson. This vegetarian restaurant uses only organically grown produce and grains; a heaping plate of grub with dessert is 55F (lunch) or 80F (dinner). *17 rue Port-du-Temple, tel. 04–72–81–41–71. Closed weekends.*

UNDER 150F • Brasserie Georges. Established in 1836, this immense brasserie is one of the oldest restaurants in Europe. Big and simple is the name of the game here. The portions of traditional dishes are very hearty. Menus start at 71F. *30 cours de Verdun, (330 ft behind the gare de Perrache), tel. 04–72–56–54–54.*

Mister Higgins. Come here for top-notch salads (50F–70F), mouth-watering entrees like salmon in light curry sauce (70F), and desserts to charm any sweet tooth. Sundays, there's a big brunch. *16 rue Dumenge, tel. 04–78–30–10–20. No lunch Sat., dinner Sun. Closed Mon.*

WORTH SEEING

Get a feel for the city by walking through the narrow cobblestone alleys and beautiful courtyards of Vieux Lyon; most sights are here or on the Presqu'île. **Traboules,** covered passageways originally built to protect silk from the elements as silk weavers traveled around the city, connect streets within the Croix-Rousse and Vieux Lyon. Many are just run-down alleys with roofs, but others pass through beautiful Renaissance courtyards. The classier traboules lie along **rue St-Jean** and **rue Juiverie.** Many young people hang out on the southern part of the Presqu'île, especially on **place Bellecour**; another fun hangout, **place des Terreaux,** is home to the **Hôtel de Ville.** Many museums (*see below*) sell day passes (30F) valid for most other museums in town.

FOURVIERE HILL

The sinister-looking Roman Catholic church (open daily 9–noon and 2–6) atop Fourvière Hill is relatively young (built in 1870), but what it lacks in age, it makes up for in ornate detail: note the red marble lining the base of the walls and doors, and the rich mosaics on the basilica walls. South of the church are the **Théâtres Gallo-Romains**—the oldest Roman theaters in France, built in 15 BC by Emperor Augustus. Overlooking the theaters, the **Musée Gallo-Romain** (17 rue Cléberg, tel. 04–72–38–81–90; admission 20F; closed Mon.–Tues.) takes you through Lugdunum's history.

MUSEUMS

The **Musée des Beaux-Arts** contains France's largest collection of art after the Louvre, and is housed in a 16th-century abbey. The collection of Egyptian artifacts discovered by local archaeologists is almost worth a museum in itself. Even if you don't go inside, check out the Rodin sculptures in the inner courtyard. *Palais St-Pierre, pl. des Terreaux, tel. 04–72–10–17–40. Admission 25F. Open Wed.–Sun. 10:30–6.*

The **Musée Historique des Tissus** (Fabric History Museum) has information on every aspect of silk, from worms to weaving, focusing on Lyon's former monopoly on the silk world. Next door (and on the same admission ticket), the **Musée des Arts Décoratifs** chronicles the development of Lyon's decorative arts. *Musée Historique des Tissus: 34 rue de la Charité, 2e, tel. 04–78–37–15–05. Admission 28F, free Wed.*

The **Institute Lumière** (25 rue du Premier-Film, tel. 04–78–78–18–95; admission 15F; open Tues.–Sun. 2–7), in the former home of the Lumière brothers, displays loads of funky projection inventions, old stereoscopes, and some of the first animated cartoons. Films are shown on-site October–June. Of the two museums inside the 16th-century **Hôtel Gadagne** (pl. du Petit-Collèe, Vieux Lyon, tel. 04–78–42–03–61), the **Musée de la Marionnette** and the **Musée Historique de Lyon,** the former is more impressive by far. This incredible collection includes marionettes created by puppet pioneer Laurent Mourguet, as well as other exotic, costumed puppets from Great Britain, Indonesia, Cambodia, and the Czech Republic. It's open Wednesday–Monday 11–6; admission is 20F.

AFTER DARK

Bars and clubs get going around 11 PM and don't stop until the roosters crow. Bars in the alleys around **place des Terreaux** fill up with young people; the "alternative" scene is north from here, on the way up the Croix-Rousse hill. At **Café Prosper** (10 rue Mulet, south of pl. des Terreaux, tel. 04–78–28–05–48), drunken Frenchmen sing songs by Cyndi Lauper and the Commodores. Don't miss **La Plantation** (9 rue Port du Temple, off pl. des Jacobins, tel. 04–78–42–03–47) for good punch, great Caribbean music, and dancing till dawn. Lyon's best gay club, **Le Mylord** (112 quai Pierre-Scize, at north end of Vieux Lyon, tel. 04–72–41–72–92), has the requisite disco lights and go-go boys. For a romantic night, stop in the intimate, wood-paneled **Métro Club** (2 rue Stella te. 04–78–42–58–46). *Lyon Poche* (available at tabacs for 7F) is your guide to Lyon's great movie scene.

NEAR LYON

LE BEAUJOLAIS

About 32F for a northbound train and another 100F for a bike puts the whole Beaujolais wine region at your feet. The best place for dégustation is near **Belleville,** in the northern section of the Beaujolais, where the *Grands Crus* (the region's 10 best wines) come from. Literally hundreds of caves lie in this area, and you can taste 10 different appellations of wine, ranging from the light Fleurie to the coarser Morgon. Twenty kilometers (12 miles) south, near **Villefranche-sur-Saône,** the concentration of caves gives way to medieval villages built of *pierre dorées,* soft, gold-colored stones quarried from the local hillsides. From Lyon, trains head to Belleville (50 mins, 44F) and Villefranche-sur-Saône (20 mins, 32F); rent a bike in Villefranche, then get to Belleville to start exploring.

THE ALPS

One of the world's most important mountain ranges, the Alps should not be left out of any French itinerary. Studded with tiny, unfrequented towns and surging from one billowy mountaintop to another, the Alps manage to overrun the borders of eight European countries in a gallant sweep from the tip of the Riviera to Germany in the north, Austria to the northeast, and Italy and Slovenia to the east. This area can be a little difficult to explore, but any difficulties you encounter traveling in the Alps will be immediately forgotten when you experience their overwhelming beauty.

Some of the best **skiing** in the world is done at Chamonix, at the foot of Mont Blanc (Europe's highest peak at 15,863 ft), Les Arcs, and Val d'Isère, but big prices (at least 150F for a lift ticket) reflect the big operations. For better prices (about 100F), head to a smaller station like Valloire or St-Véran. **Cross-country skiing** might be the most enjoyable way to really see the Alps. All it takes is equipment (75F–100F per day) and a strong set of lungs. In the summer, **mountain bikers** take over the cross-country ski trails. Look for the little yellow bicycle sign pointing you toward a VTT Circuit (mountain biking trail), or ask for maps at any local bike shop, where bikes go for 80F–120F a day. For those truly short of funds, **hiking** is the best way to see the Alps. Two major routes, the Grande Randonnée (GR) and the Grand Traversée des Alpes (GTA), lead from town to town.

GRENOBLE

At the confluence of the Isère and Drac rivers, Grenoble, the capital of the Dauphiné (lower Alps) region, lies nestled within three *massifs* (mountain ranges): La Chartreuse, Le Vercors, and Belledonne. Home to five different universities, Grenoble is a cosmopolitan city that gets its energy and terrific nightlife from its large, international student population. The major nuclear research station perched on the banks of the Drac and the Hewlett-Packard aircraft company headquarters also contribute a diverse business class to the population.

Native Grenoblois, known for their down-home friendliness, consider themselves mountain people. The ancient village of St-Hugues, once a separate community and now filled with antiques shops and art galleries, is considered part of Grenoble's vieille ville. But the *real* old town, across the river from St-Hugues and once enclosed by a Roman wall, is a collection of small squares—place de Gordes, place St-André, and place aux Herbes—filled with open markets in the morning and beer-drinking folks in the evening. The 19th-century writer and music critic Stendhal remains the town's most celebrated citizen, although people are generally surprised if you know who he is. The **Office de Tourisme** (14 rue de la République, tel. 04−76−42−41−41) distributes an itinerary that directs you to all the town's Stendhal-related sights. Hiking enthusiasts should make a beeline for the **Info-Montagnes** (at the tourist office, 14, rue de la République, tel. 40−76−42−45−90) to find out about the many day hikes from Grenoble.

COMING AND GOING

The **train station** (pl. de la Gare), on the western edge of town, serves the Alps region and sends frequent trains to Paris (3 hrs, 348F by TGV), Lyon (1¼ hrs, 94F), and Nice (10 hrs, 291F). Regional buses leave from the **bus station** (tel. 04−76−87−90−31), right next to the train station. The 21 efficient lines of Grenoble's **TAG buses** (8F) cover every corner of the city; most leave from place Victor Hugo. TAG also runs **trams** that take the same tickets. Flat Grenoble is perfect for biking. The **Mistral Shop** (13 pl. Ste-Claire, tel. 04−76−51−11−50), across from the tourist office, rents bikes for about 120F a day.

WHERE TO SLEEP

Cheap hotels cover the area between the train station and place Victor Hugo, but most near the station have jacked-up prices. **Hôtel de la Poste** (25 rue de la Poste, tel. 04−76−46−67−25) has well-kept rooms (120F−160F) in a 17th-century apartment house on a hip pedestrian street. From the station, take either tram to the Felix-Poulat stop. **Hôtel des Alpes** (45 av. Félix-Viallet, tel. 04−76−87−00−71) offers solid (if 70s-style) comfort for 240F to 290F, and it's a block from the gare. Twelve minutes south of town, at the well-equipped **Auberge de Jeunesse (HI)** (10 av. Grésivaudan, Echirolles, tel. 04−76−09−33−52), you'll have to put up with shoe-box-size dorm rooms and the 11 PM curfew, cut shorter by the 9 PM last bus from town. Take Bus 1 or 8 to Quinzaine.

FOOD

The small streets between **place Notre-Dame** and **place St-André** are littered with hole-in-the-wall restaurants that fix filling sandwiches for less than 25F. Across from the tourist office, Grenoble's large **covered market** is open 8−noon Tuesday through Sunday. **Le Valgo** (2 rue St-Hugues, off pl. Notre-Dame, tel. 04−76−51−38−85) serves up specialties of the Hautes Alpes (Upper Alps) family-style in a cozy wooden room or outside. The *oreilles d'ânes* (donkeys' ears) ravioli are well worth the 45F. The upscale **Café de la Table Ronde** (pl. St-André, tel. 04−76−44−51−41) is supposedly the second-oldest café in France, established in 1739. Stendhal used to come here for coffee, which today is about the only affordable thing on the menu. **La Hotte de Père Joël** (8 bis rue du Vieux-Temple, by the cathedral; tel. 04−76−42−04−00) serves hearty old-time menus with wine included (lentils, pigs' feet, and Beaujolais are 85F).

WORTH SEEING

For great views of the surrounding mountains (on a clear day you can see Mont Blanc), head up to the **Bastille**, a maze of walls and stairways at the foot of the Chartreux Mountains. It was constructed at the beginning of the 19th century to replace a decaying hillside fortress. Travel up to the Bastille via the 20F *téléphérique* that runs daily 10 AM−midnight, and walk back down along the path through the Jardin Dauphinoise.

On the hill below the Bastille, housed in the ancient convent of Ste-Marie-d'en-Haut, the terrific **Musée Dauphinois** (30 rue Maurice Gignoux, tel. 04−76−85−19−01) has changing exhibits and permanent displays on life in the Alps. It's open Wednesday−Monday 10−6 (until 7 May−October); admission is 20F and free Wednesday afternoon. The slick **Musée de Grenoble** (5 pl. de Lavalette, tel. 04–76–63–44–44) houses some worthy pieces by Matisse, de la Tour, Delacroix, and Picasso, as well as a smattering of contemporary paintings and sculptures. Admission is 25F and it's open Wednesday 11–10, and Thursday–Monday 11–7. The 12th-century **Cathédrale Notre-Dame** (pl. Notre-Dame), updated to mediocrity in the 19th century, adjoins the **eveché** (bishop's house), where you'll find an excellent new museum of Grenoble history opening in mid-1998; called the tourist office for information.

CHEAP THRILLS

The **Chartreuse distillery** (10 blvd. Edgar Kofler, tel. 04–76–05–81–77), 20 minutes north in Voiron, is the only place in the world where the famous green 110-proof liqueur is produced; only three monks are entrusted with the secret formula, which Marshall d'Estrées originally gave to the monastery in 1605 as a "health elixir." Tours are in French, but you don't need any language skills to taste the potent stuff. You *do* need 40F for round-trip bus fare to Voiron on Bus 715.

CHAMONIX

In the Haute-Savoie between the Swiss and Italian borders, this rugged mountain town laden with tourists has the highest peak in the Alps—the 15,863-ft Mont Blanc. The complex transportation infrastructure takes people up to peaks like the Aiguille du Midi via téléphériques, gondolas, chairlifts, and narrow-rail train cars. The **Maison de la Montagne** (190 pl. de l'Eglise, tel. 04–50–53–00–88) will help you with maps, weather reports, and other information on hiking. The **Office de Tourisme** (45 pl. du Triangle de l'Amité, tel. 04–50–53–00–24) is better for information on Chamonix itself.

COMING AND GOING

Chamonix's centrally located **train station** (pl. de la Gare, tel. 08–36–35–35–35) serves Grenoble (4 hrs, 161F), Geneva (3½ hrs, 112F), and Annecy (2½ hrs, 103F). Once you're in Chamonix, transportation is easy on foot or by local 7F buses that loop around town.

WHERE TO SLEEP AND EAT

Chamonix is chock-full of cheapish hotels, but the best place to stay is outside town away from the tourist throngs. The **Auberge de Jeunesse (HI)** (127 monté Jacques Balmat, tel. 04–50–53–14–52), south of town in Les Pèlerins at the foot of the Bossons glacier, has dorm beds, showers, and breakfast for 74F. If you aren't up to the 15-minute walk, Les Pèlerins is on the train line. **Le Chamoniard Volant** (45 rte. de la Frasse, tel. 04–50–53–14–09) and **Le Vagabond** (365 av. Ravanel-le-Rouge, tel. 04–50–53–15–43) both have dorm beds for 65F in chalets within walking distance of the train station. The small, newly refurnished **El Paso Hôtel** (37 impasse des Rhododendrons, tel. 04–50–53–64–20), run by an outgoing Australian, has wood-lined rooms with splashes of color for 150F–220F. The bar downstairs served Mexican food (60F–100F) at night.

FOOD

Almost every bar and restaurant in Chamonix seems to serve "authentic" fondue or *raclette* (a round of cheese melted over potatoes and ham) for 70F–100F per person. One local favorite, **Le Fer à Cheval** (pl. du Poilu, tel. 04–50–53–13–22), has traditional meals for 40F–70F and a great bar. **Le Chaudron** (79 rue des Moulins, tel. 04–50–53–40–34) serves *tartiflette* (cheese, bacon, and potato casserole) and other Savoie treats in a romantic setting of old wood and stone.

ANNECY

Everything about Annecy—from its overpriced restaurants to the paddleboat vendors that try to outcharm each other for your business—says "touristville." But it's so picturesque, with its flower-lined canals and stunning lake, that it's still a good place to dawdle awhile. Summer brings a very international, bacchanalian crowd and light shows on the lake. From mid-September to July you'll pretty much have the place to yourself, which makes it more charming by day but a bit lonely at night. There *are* two constants in this extremely seasonal town: the funky, asymmetric, added-on, squished-in buildings, and the sheer limestone cliffs and jagged peaks behind the lake.

When you're ready for some sights, head up to the **Château d'Annecy,** which houses an observatory (with a nice aquarium and underwater archaeology display) and a regional art display. Or go to the old

prisons in the Palais de l'Isle with exhibits on town history. Annecy's biggest attraction is the **lake.** Swim from the beach south of the vieille ville along quai Bayreuth, rent a paddleboat (35F per half hour) along quai Napoléon III, or take one of the boat tours (57F per person per hour), which leave from Pont de la Halle. The high-tech **Office de Tourisme** (Centre Bonlieu, 1 rue Jean Jaurès, tel. 04–50–45–00–33) leads daily tours of town for 32F.

COMING AND GOING

Trains run regularly to Chamonix (2½ hrs, 103F), Grenoble (2½hrs, 87F), and Lyon (3½ hrs, 112F) through Annecy's centrally located **Gare SNCF** (pl. de la Gare). **Frossard** (tel. 04–50–45–73–90), **Crolard** (tel. 04–50–45–08–12), and **Francony** (tel. 04–50–45–02–43) run regional buses from the gare routière right across from the train station.

WHERE TO SLEEP AND EAT

Near the train station is **Hôtel les Terraces** (15 rue Louis Chaumontal, tel. 04–50–57–08–98), which has beautiful, modern rooms for 150F–180F. A worthy splurge is **Hôtel de Savoie** (1 pl. St-François, tel. 04–50–45–15–45), smack in the heart of the vieille ville; doubles run 200F–280F. From the station, take rue de la Poste and follow the canal upstream. The super-duper **Auberge de Jeunesse** (16 rte. de Semnoz, tel. 04–50–45–00–33) is a bit out-of-the-way (take Bus 91 from the train station), but a clean, modern dorm room costs 69F. You'll find fondue and raclette in almost every restaurant in the vieille ville, with sandwich stands and pizza joints for those who want something cheaper. The **Buck John Grill** (1 passage des Clercs, tel. 04–50–51–87–68) has steaks at bargain prices on its two-course (59F) and three-course (67F) menus. **Le Petit Zinc** (11 rue du Pont-Morens, tel. 04–50–51–12–93), a cozy, beamed vielle-ville bistro (the oldest in town), serves Savoie specialties like *diots* (sausage cooked with onions and white wine), and *frikacoffe* (a pork fricasse with onion- and red-wine sauce).

PROVENCE

What many visitors remember best about Provence is the light. The sunlight here is vibrant and alive, bathing the vineyards, olive groves, and fields full of lavender and sunflowers with an intensity that captivated Cézanne and van Gogh. Bordering the Mediterranean and flanked by the Alps and the Rhône River, Provence attracts hordes of visitors, especially during frequent summer festivals. Fortunately, many of the tourists are siphoned off to the beaches along the Riviera, which is a part of Provence but whose jet-set image doesn't fit in with the tranquil pace of the rest of the region.

AVIGNON

Nestled in the fertile valley of the Rhône River, Avignon served as the papal residence in the 14th century—a detail the city capitalizes on to the hilt. Within the city walls, all signs herd the endless swarms of tourists to the pope's former abode, the posh **Palais des Papes.** The French-born Pope Clement V shifted the seat of the papacy from Rome to Avignon in 1309, and it remained the capital of Christendom until 1377. This period was known as the "Babylonian Captivity" by its detractors, although it helped spark a cultural blossoming in Avignon.

Away from the main sights, Avignon's cobbled streets become narrow and serene. Though the holy fathers are long gone, the arts still flourish; Avignon is most exciting in July and August, when the **Festival d'Avignon** brings opera, ballet, theater, dance performances, and music to nearly every street corner. Outside of festival months, the city remains calm and a bit cheaper than many of its Provençal neighbors (although it's a bit more urban than you might expect), and it makes a perfect base for exploring the surrounding Vaucluse region.

VISITOR INFORMATION

The multilingual staff at the **main tourist office** (41 cours Jean-Jaurès, tel. 04–90–82–65–11) will happily load you down with shiny brochures; the annex is at the entrance to the Pont St-Bénézet.

COMING AND GOING

From Avignon's **train station** (blvd. St-Roch), trains go all over Provence and to Paris (4 hrs on the TGV, 349F). The **bus station** (5 av. Monclar, tel. 04-90-82-07-35), right next door, sends buses to most nearby towns. Walking is the best way to traverse Avignon's narrow streets, but **Vélomania** (1 rue Amelier, tel. 04-90-82-06-98) rents bikes for 70F-100F per day.

WHERE TO SLEEP

Most of the cheap hotels are bunched on two streets, **rue Perdiguier** and **rue Joseph Vernet.** The popular, central **Hôtel du Parc** (18 rue Agricol Perdiguier, just off cours Jean-Jaurès, tel. 04-90-82-71-55) has airy rooms starting at 145F. **Hôtel Angleterre** (29 blvd. Raspail, tel. 04-90-86-34-31) is snazzier than most; doubles start at 170F. **Hôtel de Mons** (5 rue de Mons, tel. 04-90-86-57-16) is in a former chapel that was once part of the Palais des Papes; stay in a double for 230F. The cheapest deal in Avignon is the huge **Foyer and Camping Bagatelle** (Ile de la Barthelasse, tel. 04-90-86-30-39; beds 60F), a 15-minute walk from the center of town. Take Bus 10 from the main post office to the Ile de la Barthelasse.

FOOD

For affordable food, look beyond the shiny tourist traps near the Palais des Papes. **Rue des Lices** and **rue des Teinturiers,** which extend from rue Bonneterie, are cobblestone pathways dotted with tiny restaurants, bars, and bistros. You can buy produce at the large **indoor market** on place Pie (Tues.-Sun. mornings). Schmooze with Avignon's actors and dancers at **La Tache d'Encre** (22 rue des Teinturiers, tel. 04-90-85-46-03), which has creative dishes like pineapple on basmati rice for 60F-90F and jazz on weekends. Cozy **Le Table de Patrick** (20-22 rue du Chapeau Rouge, tel. 04-90-86-10-46) has a delicious 50F-60F menu of Provençal specialties and a salad bar. For some after-dinner intoxication, **Le Blues** (25 rue Carnot) and **Pub Z** (58 rue Bonneterie) are popular hangouts.

WORTH SEEING

Avignon's character is best defined by the colossal **Palais des Papes** (pl. du Palais, tel. 04-90-27-50-74; admission 35F) where six Avignon popes held court. The **Grand Court** (Great Court), where visitors arrive, forms a link between the severe Palais Vieux (Old Palace) built by Pope Benedict XII, a member of the Cistercian order, and the more decorative Palais Nouveau (New Palace), courtesy of the artsy Pope Clement VI. Guides conduct tours of the austere interior in English daily at 10 AM and 3:30 PM for 43F. Near the Palais des Papes, the mostly Romanesque **Cathédrale Notre-Dame des Doms** has had many incongruous extras layered on throughout the centuries. The immense statue of the Virgin Mary flying above the cathedral's bell tower was added in 1859. For a quick change of scenery, go beyond the cathedral to the **Rocher des Doms,** a large park with great views of the area as well as swans and ducks in a somewhat fake-looking fenced lake. Built in the 14th century, the **Petit Palais** (pl. du Palais, tel. 04-90-86-44-58; admission 30F, free Sun. off-season) used to be a residence for cardinals and archbishops, but now it's a museum housing an outstanding collection of Italian paintings and Avignonais sculpture and painting. Worship both modern art and Greek antiques in the **Musée Calvet** (65 rue Joseph Vernet, tel. 04-90-86-33-84; admission 30F), housed in an 18th-century mansion.

NEAR AVIGNON

To taste of some of the world's most renowned wine, head to **Châteauneuf-du-Pape,** a small hillside town just a half hour bus ride (18F) from Avignon. The 13 million bottles produced here each year can be very expensive, but you can sip for free in the caves de dégustation on practically every street.

ORANGE

Orange is cradled in the heart of the Côte du Rhone vineyards in northern Provence. It is a compact, vibrant town, with most of the activity focused around the narrow, cobbled streets of the centre ville. The enormous, semicircular **Théâtre Antique** (pl. des Frères Mounet, tel. 04-90-51-17-60; admission 30F) in the center of town looks like it was transplanted from a different world. The back wall of the Roman theater's stage dominates the town—King Louis XIV called it the finest wall in his kingdom. On the northern side of town, the magnificent **Arc de Triomphe** was built in the 1st century AD on the ancient Via Agrippa, the road that used to link Lyon with Arles. Dedicated to Julius Caesar's triumph over the Gauls, the monument is composed of three archways and decorated with images of war (Caeser's naval victories in particular).

BASICS • Orange is only 30 minutes and 28F away from Avignon by train, so there's not much point in spending the night. But if you do want to stay here, the **main tourist office** (cours Aristide Briand, tel. 04–90–34–70–88) has an English-speaking staff and can provide maps and lodging information. Try **Hôtel Fréau** (3 Ancien Collège, tel. 04–90–34–06–26), where the quiet 115F rooms have views of the surrounding hills.

ARLES

Arles's small vieille ville is filled with residential pockets where time seems to have stood still since 1888, the year Vincent van Gogh immortalized the city in his paintings. Arles actually manages to live up to the beauty of van Gogh's swirling renditions (and capitalizes on them with ubiquitous "Vince" T-shirts), but the town's biggest tourist attractions are the Roman theater and amphitheater, built by Roman colonists who came to Arles in 46 BC.

COMING AND GOING

The **train station** (av. Paulin Talabot) harbors a **tourist office annex.** The **main tourist office** (tel. 04–90–18–41–20) is on esplanade Charles de Gaulle. The **bus station** (tel. 04–90–49–38–01) faces the train station on avenue Paulin Talabot. All you need to get around the vieille ville is your feet, but you can rent bicycles at **Peugeot** (15 rue du Pont, tel. 04–90–96–03–77; 80F a day) or at the train station.

WHERE TO SLEEP

Many well-maintained hotels in the vieille ville have singles and doubles for 100F–200F. A 250-year-old ivy-covered building awaits you at **Hôtel la Galoubet** (18 rue Dr. Fanton, 1 block north of pl. du Forum, tel. 04–90–96–25–34), where doubles run 120F–240F. **Le Cloître** (16 rue du Cloître, tel. 04–90–96–29–50), a few steps from the Théâtre Romain, has open, airy rooms in warm Provençal colors; singles and doubles start at 265F. An uptight staff presides over the **Auberge de Jeunesse (HI)** (20 av. Maréchal Foch, tel. 04–90–96–18–25; beds 75F the first night, 64F thereafter), a five-minute walk from the center of town. From the train station, take Bus 4 and transfer to Bus 3 on boulevard des Lices.

FOOD

Stay away from the overpriced restaurants on the central boulevard des Lices; **place du Forum, place Voltaire,** and the narrow streets leading away from them are better bets for lively cafés and restaurants. At **Restaurant d'Arlaten** (7 rue de la Cavalerie, tel. 04–90–96–24–85), a rustic eatery with a terrace, you can get a three-course meal for a mere 69F. For a quick fix of crêpes or pizza, go to **rue Hôtel de Ville.**

WORTH SEEING

A 55F ticket, available at all the attractions, buys you access to all of Arles's sights. **Les Arènes** (Rond-Point des Arènes; admission 15F), a 2nd-century Roman amphitheater, holds up to 20,000 spectators during the bullfights and concerts that take place here in summer. On the quiet edge of town behind the amphitheater is the **Théâtre Antique** (rue due Cloître; admission 15F), a Roman theater built during Augustus's reign in the 1st century BC. The semicircular seating tiers still stand, but only two columns and a few stumps remain of the stage. The ruins of the **Thermes de Constantin** (rue Dominique-Maisto, near rue du 4 Septembre; admission 12F), 4th-century Roman baths, weren't just for bathing; they were the equivalent of the modern gym, lecture hall, and social club all in one, combining physical and mental conditioning.

Enter through a 17th-century chapel to the **Cryptoporticus** (rue Balze), an eerie maze of cold, underground galleries that were discovered when the church was built. The Provençal poet Frédéric Mistral used his 1904 Nobel Prize money to establish the **Museon Arlaten** (29 rue de la République; admission 20F), a richly informative museum of Provençal ethnography where attendants garbed in traditional costume provide commentary on the exhibits. The **Musée Reattu** (rue du Grand Prieurè; admission 15F) houses a collection of contemporary works, including photography displays and sketches by Picasso.

AIX-EN-PROVENCE

If you come to Aix, bring your credit cards and nice clothes—is an upscale Provençal town. The city does have impressive architecture and elegant fountains, and many fashionable folks for whom café-going and boutique-shopping are a way of life. But if you're trying to avoid snobbery and Parisian prices, Aix is probably not for you. The museums and churches in Aix are overshadowed by the beautiful city itself; the **tourist office** (2 pl. du Général de Gaulle, tel. 04–42–16–11–61) shows off the town with guided tours in English or French for 45F.

COMING AND GOING

The **train station** (pl. Victor Hugo, tel. 08–36–35–35–35 for information and reservations) runs hourly trains to Marseille (30 mins, 38F). One block west of la Rotonde, the **bus station** (rue Lapierre, tel. 04–42–27–17–91) is filled with a zillion independent bus companies that service the surrounding region. Most of the sights are within central Aix, where walking is the best way to get around.

WHERE TO SLEEP

The lodging situation is frustrating; only a handful of hotels cost less than 200F, and the hostel is inconvenient. The **Villages Hôtel** (av. Arc de Meyran, tel. 04–42–93–56–16) is a sparkling-new chain hotel with singles and doubles for 150F. In the heart of the quartier Mazarin, the antique-filled **Hôtel Cardinal** (24 rue Cardinale, tel. 04–42–38–32–30) is in an 18th-century building; doubles are 290F. The staff at the **Auberge de Jeunesse (HI)** (3 av. Marcel Pagnol, tel. 04–42–20–15–99) is rigid and humorless, but beds with breakfast are only 79F (HI card required). Take Bus 12 from la Rotonde (last bus at 8 PM) or walk down avenue de l'Europe and follow the signs.

FOOD

Medium-priced ethnic restaurants of all stripes are on **place Ramus, rue Van Loo,** and the adjacent **rues de la Verrerie, Félibre Gaut,** and **des Marseillais.** Or splurge Aixois-style on a three-course meal at **Chez Maxime** (12 pl. Ramos, tel. 04–42–26–28–51), where 95F will get you a delectable lunch of southwestern French cuisine. Cheerful decor is the backdrop to creative vegetarian meals and a three-course menu for 75F at **L'Arbre à Pain** (12 rue Constantin, tel. 04–42–96–99–95). Fresh produce is available Tuesday, Thursday, and Saturday mornings at the open-air **market** on place Richelme.

WORTH SEEING

The leafy boulevard **cours Mirabeau** is lined with 17th- and 18th-century hôtels particuliers, which now house banks and private offices. Luxurious fountains grace every square; the main one is the **Fontaine de la Rotonde** on place du Général de Gaulle, at the west end of cours Mirabeau. If it's a rainy day, visit the **Atelier Paul Cézanne** (9 av. Paul Cézanne, tel. 04–42–21–06–53; admission 10F), the house and studio where Aix-born impressionist Paul Cézanne lived in the 1890s. It's amazing how much energy Aix puts into touting its affiliation with Cézanne, as he was literally laughed out of town when he was alive. Fans can pick up a map of **Cézanne's "footsteps"** at the tourist office. Gold studs in the pavement chronicle where the painter worked, went to school, and got married. The 17th-century Archevêché (Archbishop's Palace) is home to the **Musée des Tapisseries** (28 pl. des Martyrs de la Résistance, tel. 04–42–23–09–91; admission 10F). A striking series of 17 tapestries made in Beauvais illustrates the adventures of Don Quixote.

MARSEILLE

A large city, Marseille occupies twice the amount of land as Paris and is Europe's second-largest port. Many cultures meet in Marseille, and it is this heterogeneous population that keeps the city lively and interesting (though it has also made for racial tensions). After visiting the rest of France, you may be taken aback by Marseille's realness: there is a grittiness here that is not found elsewhere. Marseille has little regard for those in search of the picturesque, but it also distinguishes itself from other French cities through its colorful, almost defiant spirit. As in any big city, you should look out for yourself here.

BASICS

The **visitor information** annex at the train station shares duties with the main office (4 la Canebière, tel. 04–91–13–89–00). Nearby, the **American Express** office (39 la Canebière, tel. 04–91–13–71–21) has the usual services. Pick up poste restante mail at the main **post office** (1 pl. Hôtel des Postes, corner rues Colbert and Henri-Barbusse, tel. 04–91–15–47–00; postal code 13001).

COMING AND GOING

Marseille's enormous **train station** (esplanade St-Charles), at the northern end of the centre ville, is a 20-minute walk from the Vieux Port and about a 10-minute walk from most budget hotels. The **bus sta-**

tion (tel. 04–91–08–16–40) is at the east end of the train station. **SNCM** (61 blvd. des Dames, tel. 04–91–56–32–00) sends ferries to Corsica, Sardinia, and North Africa. The **Aéroport Marseille Provence** is 25 km (15½ mi) from Marseille. **Transports Routiers Passagers Aériens** runs frequent buses between the airport and the train station for 42F.

GETTING AROUND

Marseille is divided into 16 *arrondissements* (districts). The Vieux Port, the surrounding centre ville, and the main street, **la Canebière,** make up the city's nerve center. La Canebière also separates the poorer areas to the north from the more chic neighborhoods to the south. Many of the points of interest are clustered around the Vieux Port, but you'll have to use public transportation to get from one end of town to the other. Pick up a map of bus and métro lines at the tourist office or at the RTM (Réseau de Transport Marseillais) **information desk** (6–8 rue des Fabres, tel. 04–91–91–92–10). Tickets, available at bus terminals and métro stations, cost 8F and are valid for both bus and métro trips.

WHERE TO SLEEP

Stay away from the really seedy and dilapidated hotels on rue du Théâtre Français (off la Canebière, 1 block east of boulevard Garibaldi) and the intersecting rue Mazagran. North of Canebière, you'll find a number of cheap hotels clustered around **allées Léon Gambetta,** off boulevard d'Athènes between the centre ville and train station. The **Hôtel Gambetta** (49 allées Léon Gambetta, tel. 04–91–62–07–88) has simple, spotless rooms (170F–235F). The **Hôtel Little Palace** and the adjoining but nicer **Hôtel d'Athènes** (37–39 blvd. d'Athènes, tel. 04–91–90–03–83), near the train station, have rooms for 130F–195F. The **Auberge de Jeunesse Bonneveine (HI)** (47 av. Joseph-Vidal, tel. 04–91–73–21–81) is a five-minute walk from the beach; bed and breakfast is 74F. From the train station, take the métro to rond point du Prado, then take Bus 44 to place Bonnefon. A 19th-century château has been converted into the beautiful **Auberge de Jeunesse de Bois-Luzy** (Allée es Primevères, tel. 04–91–49–06–18; beds 45F). Take Bus 6 (last bus at 9 PM) to Marius Richard.

FOOD

Eats are cheap in Marseille, but the food-stand fare is greasier and staler than elsewhere in France. The largest concentration of restaurants and cafés is at the Vieux Port. Restaurants on **quai de Rive Neuve** offer good deals, and many feature the city's fish-stew specialty, bouillabaisse. For sandwich and produce stands, go to **rue de Rome** and the side streets to the east. South of la Canebière and east of boulevard Garibaldi is **cours Julien,** lined with fashionable restaurants and cafés. **Chez-Angèle** (50 rue Caisserie, parallel to quai du Port, tel. 04–91–90–63–35; closed for lunch on Sat. and Sun.) has great pasta (65F) and pizza (50F). **L'Ecailler** (10 rue Fortia, tel. 04–91–54–79–39) specializes in all types of fish, shellfish, and bouillabaisse; what distinguishes it from the others is its Victorian decor and 65F menu. The happening bar scene is at **cours Honoré d'Estienne d'Orvès** and **place de Thiars,** by the Vieux Port, and **cours Julien,** near the train station.

WORTH SEEING

You won't see the spirit of Marseille behind a glass case in a museum or under the vaulted dome of a church, but rather in its crowded streets and markets. The cultural center, the **Centre de la Vieille Charité** (2 rue de la Charité, tel. 04–91–14–58–80), in a restored 17th-century hospice, is probably the sight most worth your time. Here you'll find the **Musée d'Archéologie Méditerranéenne** (admission 25F) and its collection of primarily Egyptian and Celto-Ligurian artifacts. The 17th-century Hôtel de Montgrand houses the **Musée Cantini** (19 rue Grignan, tel. 04–91–54–77–75; admission 10F), which has an excellent collection of modern art. The permanent display includes works of the fauvist, cubist, and surrealist movements.

The most imposing structure of Marseille's cityscape, the 19th-century **Basilique de Notre-Dame de la Garde** (blvd. A. Aune), overlooks the city from a limestone cliff. The Virgin Mary guards Marseille from atop the tower and the building's interior is colorfully adorned with murals and mosaics. Take Bus 60 from cours Jean Ballard, just south of quai des Belges. In the spooky underground crypt of the **Basilique St-Victor** (between rue Sainte and av. de la Corse), you can see what's left of the 11th-century abbey's 5th-century foundations, as well as pagan and Christian sarcophagi. If you can stand the smell, the chaotic **morning fish market** on quai des Belges is a real lesson in Marseillaise culture.

NEAR MARSEILLE

CASSIS

When you have to start scraping Marseille's urban grime from under your fingernails, it's time for a day trip to Cassis, the town Virginia Woolf referred to as paradise on earth. Originally a coral fishing village, the tiny port is now an upscale beach town filled with restaurants, tourist shops, and expensive villas. Climb the white cliffs down to the spectacular *calanques* (coves), then reward yourself with a snooze on one of the cove's small beaches.

BASICS • The best way to get to Cassis is by bus, because the train station is 3 km (2 mi) from town. The ride from Marseille takes 40 minutes and costs 21F. If you plan to stay overnight, spring for a room (185F–280F) in town at the simple **Hôtel le Laurence** (rue de l'Arène, tel. 04–42–01–88–78) or hike out to the **Auberge de Jeunesse** (tel. 04–42–01–02–72; beds 45F with HI card), a one-hour, uphill walk from Cassis. It's in the middle of nowhere and there are no buses, so you'll need to get a map from the **tourist office** (pl. Baragnon, tel. 04–42–01–71–17) to get there.

THE RIVIERA

Also known as the Côte d'Azur, the French Riviera is a narrow stretch of Mediterranean coastline extending from St-Tropez to the Italian border. For decades the Riviera has been Europe's playground, conjuring up images of wealth, swanky beach resorts, and all that is chic. In reality, many beaches are small and pebbly (at least those east of Antibes), the area is overdeveloped and crowded, the movie stars have escaped to more secluded areas, and it's expensive.

Nevertheless, the sun, the sidewalk cafés, the smell of sand and sea, and the sight of aloof expatriates still hold a sublime allure. Some beaches are public and free, but on many others you have to pay a fee (up to 150F) for the right to a plot of sand and an umbrella. A closer look at the Riviera will reveal clusters of villages and small resort towns with their own distinctive character. Take time to get away from the beach and explore the winding cobblestone streets and the olive groves on the slopes above the sea, and you'll get a whole different feel.

ST-TROPEZ

One of the ritziest French vacation spots, St-Tropez has become such a byword for wealth, sun, and glitter—the yachts are among the biggest in Europe and countless stars (like Brigitte Bardot) own homes here—that you might be surprised it's so small and secluded. Though it's warm and beautiful, the town is far from budget friendly: the restaurants and hotels are outrageously priced, the beaches are hard to get to, and there's nowhere to store luggage if you come for just a day to gawk at the jet-setters.

Still, if you've always dreamed of going to St-Tropez, make it happen. The long beaches associated with St-Tropez are around the cape, far from town, and mostly private. However, **Plage de la Bouillabaisse** is a nice sand beach only 10 minutes by foot; just walk west from the port. In the other direction you'll reach **Plage des Cannebiers.** From here you can take a path that passes **Plage des Salins** (4 km/2 mi from St-Tropez) and ends up at **Plage de Pampelonne** (8 km/5 mi from St-Tropez); these beaches have their own atmosphere and particular clientele, and are divided into alternating private and public plots of sand. **Plage de Tahiti,** at the north end of Pampelonne, is supposed to be a favorite among movie stars. The most convenient way to find your little corner of paradise is to rent a moped (*see* Coming and Going, *below*). In July and August, SODETRAV buses bound for Plage de Pampelonne (15 mins, 15F) leave the station three times a day Monday–Saturday. The two **tourist offices** (open daily 10–9; shorter hours off-season) have tons of brochures, maps, and a hotel-reservation service. One office faces the port on quai Jean Jaurès (tel. 04–94–97–45–21), and the other is at the bus station (23 av. du Général-Leclerc, tel. 04–94–97–65–53).

COMING AND GOING

The closest you'll get to St-Tropez by train is St-Raphaël, about 25 km (15½ mi) away. From St-Raphaël, either take a scenic but crowded 1½-hour ride on a **SODETRAV** bus (sq. Régis, St-Raphaël, tel. 04–94–95–24–82) for 47F50 one-way, or a shorter, more reliable boat ride with **Les Bateaux St-Raphaël**

(Vieux Port de St-Raphaël, tel. 04–94–95–17–46) for 50F one-way. St-Tropez's **bus station** (tel. 04–94–97–88–51) is on place Banqui, west of the town center. To get around town, rent a scooter (210F per day) at **Espace 83 Yamaha** (2 av. Général-Leclerc, across from station, tel. 04–94–97–00–11). **Location Vélos-Motos, Louis Mas** (5 rue Quaranta, near pl. des Lices, tel. 04–94–97–00–60) rents mountain bikes (70F per day) and scooters (165F per day). Both places are open April–September and require a credit-card or 2,000F–5,000F deposit.

WHERE TO SLEEP AND EAT

Sleep elsewhere and visit St-Tropez for the day. If you must stay here, try the recently renovated **Hôtel Les Chimères** (Port du Pilon, tel. 04–94–97–02–90), near the bus station; they advise reserving two months in advance in the summer; doubles start at 260F. The vieille ville is a better option than the port for almost affordable sandwiches, salads, and the like. The **Crêperie Grand Marnier** (rue des Remparts, tel. 04–94–97–07–29) makes 30F–60F crêpes with the liqueur and even sells little bottles to go. **L'Artichaut Barigoule** (pl. Grammont, tel. 04–94–97–02–73) serves great, creative deli food for 20F–30F. There's also an outdoor **market** on place des Lices every Tuesday and Saturday morning.

ST-RAPHAËL

Between the red cliffs of the Massif de l'Esterel and the high, rocky Massif des Maures, St-Raphaël is a simple town with sandy beaches, marinas, and a casino. Although it lost many of its opulent belle époque mansions and buildings during World War II, the bombs couldn't destroy the sunny days and beautiful coastline. St-Raphaël is also a good base for exploring the surrounding area since it's well-served by public transportation and has more affordable hotels than other places along the Riviera. The **Office de Tourisme** (rue Waldeck-Rousseau, facing train station, tel. 04–94–19–52–52; open Mon.–Sat. 8:30–12 and 2–6:30), has a wealth of information.

COMING AND GOING

Nine daily trains to Paris (9½ hrs, 430F), including the TGV (7 hrs), and almost as many to Lyon (4½ hrs, 267F), Dijon (6 hrs, 349F), and Marseille (1½ hrs, 111F), leave the St-Raphaël-Valescure **train station** (pl. de la Gare, tel. 04–94–91–50–50). St-Raphaël is the western terminus of the TER line that runs along the Riviera. To get to towns farther west on the Riviera, you have to go by bus. The **bus station** is directly behind the train station. **Forum Cars** (tel. 04–94–95–16–71) goes to Cannes (1¼ hrs, 33F) and **SODETRAV** (tel. 04–94–95–24–82) to St-Tropez (1½ hrs, 48F). **Les Bateaux de St-Raphaël** (Vieux Port, tel. 04–94–95–17–46) ferries head to St-Tropez (100F round-trip), Iles-de-Lérins (150F round-trip), and the Calanques des Roches Rouges de l'Esterel (Red Rock Cliffs; 50F round-trip).

WHERE TO SLEEP AND EAT

St-Raphaël's budget hotels tend to be pretty dingy, but you can find a few nice places. **Hôtel des Pyramides** (77 av. Paul-Doumer, tel. 04–94–95–05–95), southeast of the train station and within view of the beach, has a garden patio where you can have breakfast; singles are 145F and doubles start at 200F. **Hôtel Provençal** (197 rue de la Garonne, tel. 04–94–95–01–52), also near the beach, has a homey yet modern rooms; singles and doubles run 255F (less off-season). The **Centre International du Manoir** (chemin de l'Escale, tel. 04–94–95–20–58) is near the beach in Boulouris, 5 km (3 mi) from St-Raphaël; beds are 70F and rooms are 170F in July and August and 115F at other times. From July to mid-August, the hostel only accepts people aged 18–35. Buses and trains go to Boulouris every 30 minutes from St-Raphaël.

FOOD

St-Raphaël has a buffet of fine restaurants, snack stands, crêperies, and late-night pizzerias along its oceanfront. Across from the train station, **Cristie's Pâtisserie** (40 rue Waldeck-Rousseau, tel. 04–94–40–55–30) has delicious sandwiches (22F). For a cozy atmosphere and outstanding regional food, go to **La Grillade** (32 rue Boetman, tel. 04–94–95–15–16), where for 79F you can have minestrone *au pistou* (with basil and garlic), homemade ravioli, and chocolate mousse. At the morning outdoor **market** (rue de la République, behind bus station; open Tues.–Sun.) nuts, olives, and nougat are sold, as well as the usual produce. Head to **Aux Ambassadeurs** (171 quai Albert Ier, tel. 04–94–95–10–65) for beer (25F), cocktails (50F), and live music on weekends.

CANNES

Cannes has been attracting the sapphire-and-sunglasses set since the mid-1800s. The city is best known for the celluloid parade that flocks to the **Festival International du Film** (International Film Festival) every May, when Hollywood luminaries come to party with the best of the intellectual, black-clad European filmmakers. Even though Cannes largely deserves its reputation as a playground for the rich and famous, there's a lot more to Cannes than you'll encounter promenading in front of the palatial hotels on the main drag, la Croisette. Its vieille ville is a less-touristed tangle of streets with bars and restaurants, and its music and performing arts scene is appealing year-round.

If you decide to visit the beaches on La Croisette, expect to pay at least 70F to enter the territory of the neo-aristocrats. Better to go public on **Plages du Midi, Plages de la Bocca, and Plage Gazagnaire,** east of the new casino, and then dip into the private sector for a comparably inexpensive 30F coke. The modern **Palais des Festivals,** a summer casino, and the **Vieux Port,** sit at the end of the Plages de la Croisette, nearest town; the winter casino and modern harbor occupy the other end. All along the promenade you'll find chichi cafés, expensive boutiques, and luxury hotels. Cannes's old quarter, **Le Suquet,** rises on a hill above the Vieux Port. Wind your way up the narrow streets for a great view of the glitz below.

BASICS

The biggest and best **tourist office** (esplanade Georges Pompidou, tel. 04–93–39–24–53; open July–Aug., daily 9–8; shorter hours off-season) is in the Palais des Festivals et des Congrès on blvd. de la Croisette. The branch office (tel. 04–93–99–19–77), above the café to the left of the train station, will give you a list of hotels and make reservations. If you're under 25, go to the **Cannes Information Jeunesse** (5 quai St-Pierre, tel. 04–93–06–31–31; open weekdays 9–12:30 and 2–6) for information on excursions, hostels, and camping. Change money at the 24-hour exchange machine at **Crédit Lyonnais** (corner of rue Jean de Joffre and av. d'Antibes) or **AmEx** (8 rue des Belges, tel. 04–93–38–15–87; open weekdays 9–6, Sat. 9–1), which also offers lost-card and mail service.

COMING AND GOING

The St-Raphaël–Ventimiglia train passes through Nice (25 min, 31F) and Antibes (11 min, 13F) and arrives at Cannes's **train station** (rue Jean Jaurès, tel. 04–93–99–50–50) every half hour. Don't get off at the "Cannes-la-Bocca" stop or you'll be stranded in the suburbs. You can also take the TGV from Paris (6½ hrs, 430F), with a stop in Marseille (sometimes there is a change of trains). The **bus station** (tel. 04–93–39–31–37) next to the train station sends buses inland, and the one on place de l'Hôtel-de-Ville (tel. 04–93–39–18–71) offers local and coastal service. You can rent 10-speeds and mountain bikes (60F–80F for 24 hours with a 1,000F–1,500F deposit) or scooters (150F for 24 hours with a 2,000F deposit) from **Holiday Bikes** (16 rue du 14 juillet, tel. 04–93–94–61–00), open everyday 9–12:30 and 3–7.

WHERE TO SLEEP

Festival times aside, Cannes has lots of budget hotels within walking distance of the train station. The very tidy **Le Florian** (8 rue du Commandant André, tel. 04–93-39–24–82, fax 04–92–99-18–30) has rooms for 200F–300F, and boisterous M. Florian loves to cater to the traveler on a shoestring. The **Hôtel Atlantis** (4 rue de 24-Août, 2 blocks from train station, tel. 04–93–39–18–72) gives *UpClose Europe* readers a discount; get here early during the busy season for the modern singles with shower starting at 165F, and doubles with shower from 230F (July and August the rates go up 20%). At **Hôtel Cybelle** (12 rue de 24-Août, tel. 04–93–38–31–33), worn but cheery singles and doubles start at 120F. Spacious, luxurious accommodations (by hostel standards) await you at the **Auberge de Jeunesse de Cannes** (35 av. de Vallauris, tel. 04–93–99–26–79; beds 80F with HI card); from the train station, take the underground passage, turn right on boulevard d'Alsace, left on boulevard de la République, and then right on avenue de Vallauris.

FOOD

Prices are always high in Cannes, but the cafés and restaurants farthest from the beach are usually the cheapest and the ones in **Le Suquet** are the most fun. You can buy sandwiches and crêpes along the beach and in the pedestrian zone, **rue Meynadier**; but the *best* sandwiches (25F) are at the sandwich kiosk at place Marché Gambetta. **La Crêperie** (66 rue Meynadier, tel. 04–92–99–00–00) serves big salads and crêpes from a true Breton, all in the 50F range. For a filling calzone (48F) and a free aperitif go to the popular **Papa Nino** (15 blvd. de la République, tel. 04–93–38–48–08). Try **Le Papille** (38 rue Georges Clemenceau, tel. 04–93–39–27–28) for real Provençal cooking on the 93F menu. There's a morning outdoor **market** (open Tues.–Sun.) on rue Forville, north of Le Suquet.

AFTER DARK

A bit out of town, but popular with young hipsters, is the **Whisky à Gogo** (115 av. de Lérins, tel. 04–93–43–20–63). Locals swear that **Le Queens** (48 blvd. de la République, tel. 04–93–68–13–13) is the best place to groove. The 100F cover includes a drink, and the music varies from funk to disco and house. The funky **Disco 7** (7 rue Rouguière, off rue Félix-Faure, tel. 04–93–39–10–36) is a predominantly gay hangout. European and American films (49F, 32F on Wed.) are shown at **Les Arcades** (77 rue Félix-Faure, tel. 04–93–39–00–98); **Olympia** (16 rue de la Pompe, tel. 04–93–39–13–93); and **Star** (98 rue d'Antibes, tel. 04–93–68–18–08).

NEAR CANNES

ANTIBES

There isn't much that distinguishes Antibes from other Riviera towns if you don't venture further than the new town and the beach. But if you lose yourself in the maze of streets in the vieille ville, you'll find that Antibes is layered with history and overflowing with Provençal culture. Wander to the little **Commune du Safranier** where local culture is preserved along the tiny cobblestone streets and flower-boxed windowsills. Or take a walk to the **Cap d'Antibes** peninsula, where you can check out the spectacular views and million-dollar homes immortalized by F. Scott Fitzgerald in *Tender Is the Night*. And be sure to get to the **Musée Picasso** (pl. Marisol, tel. 04–92–90–54–20; admission 20F; closed Mon.) at the seaside site of the old Château Grimaldi, where the artist spent six prolific months. In July and August, the town explodes with festivals, street artists command the public squares, and sports take over the beautiful beaches.

COMING AND GOING • Twenty minutes and 23F from Nice, Antibes's **train station** (av. Robert-Soleau, tel. 04–93–99–50–50) is on the far east end of town. Signs lead you from the train station to the well-stocked **Maison du Tourisme** (11 pl. du Général-de-Gaulle, tel. 04–92–90–53–00). Regional buses leave from the **bus station** (1 pl. Guynemer, tel. 04–93–34–37–60). To get to Cannes (13F), Nice (25F), Juan-les-Pins (7F), or to catch local buses, wait at the stop on **place du Général-de-Gaulle.**

WHERE TO SLEEP AND EAT • If you're going to spend the night, spring for a large room with marine decor (280F and up) at the **Hôtel de l'Etoile** (2 av. Gambetta, tel. 04–93–34–26–30). Or go to the wonderful, cheap, but out-of-the-way **Relais International de la Jeunesse "Caravelle 60"** (rue de l'Antiquité, off rte. de la Garoupe, tel. 04–93–61–34–40; beds 70F). It's in Cap d'Antibes near the beach; Bus 2A makes the trip from Antibes (30 mins, 7F) almost hourly 9 AM–7 PM. For an authentic Provençal meal, seek out the sunny patio and 58F menu at the **Taverne le Safranier** (1 pl. du Safranier, tel. 04–93–34–80–50). Antibes has plenty of fruit stands, grocery stores, and sandwich shops, and a lively **outdoor market** (cours Masséna; open daily 6 AM–1 PM in summer).

NICE

If a quiet beach escape is what you're looking for, then Nice is not the place for you. But if you're after top-notch museums, a charming old quarter, scads of ethnic restaurants, and a raging nightlife (not to mention an overabundance of tourists), then you'll have a blast. With nearly 450,000 residents and over 3 million visitors annually, Nice is the Riviera's largest, most dynamic city. In summer, its boulevards are jam-packed and the pebbly beaches along the Promenade des Anglais are swarming with scantily clad bodies; in winter, Nice remains active while other Riviera towns snooze. Because of the budget options available, Nice makes an excellent base for day trips to nearby towns. The most exciting time to visit Nice is for **Carnaval,** during the two weeks before Lent, when the streets are filled with parades, feasting, music, dancing, and general debauchery.

BASICS

The **tourist office** (tel. 04–93–87–07–07) next to the train station will reserve you a hotel room and give you maps and brochures. Other offices are near the **beach** (5 Promenade des Anglais, tel. 04–92–14–48–00); at **Nice-Ferber** (Promenade des Anglais, near airport, tel. 04–93–83–32–64); and at the **airport** (Terminal 1, tel. 04–93–21–44–11). The **American Express** office (11 Promenade des Anglais,

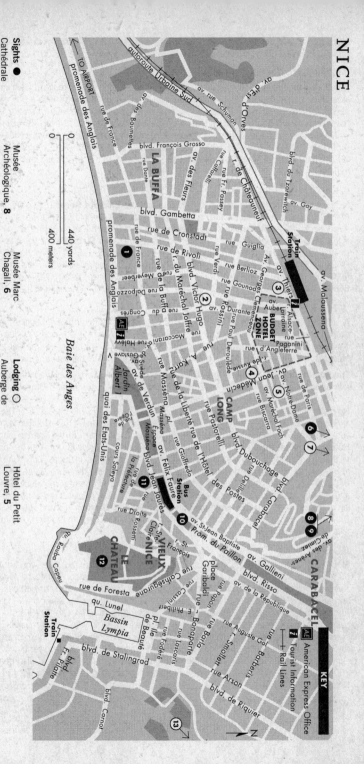

NICE

KEY

- **AE** American Express Office
- **_i_** Tourist Information
- → Rail Lines

Sights ●
Cathédrale
Ste-Réparate, **11**
Colline du
Château, **12**
Musée
Archéologique, **8**
Musée Marc
Chagall, **6**
Musée d'Art
Moderne et d'Art
Contemporain
(MAMAC), **10**
Musée Matisse, **9**
Palais Masséna, **1**

Lodging ○
Auberge de
Jeunesse
de Nice, **13**
Hôtel Belle
Meunière, **3**
Hôtel Lyonnais, **4**
Hôtel du Petit
Louvre, **5**
The Little Palace, **2**
Relais International
de la Jeunesse
"Clairvallon", **7**

TO AIRPORT
promenade des Anglais

autoroute Urbaine Sud

440 yards
400 meters

Baie des Anges

at rue du Congrès, tel. 04–93–16–53–53) has the best traveler's check exchange rates. Pick up mail at the **post office** (23 av. Thiers, tel. 04–93–82–65–00; postal code 06000).

COMING AND GOING

Nice's **train station** (av. Thiers, tel. 04–93–87–50–50) is on the north edge of town and serves all lines along the Riviera. Trains to Paris take more than 10 hours overnight (reserve a 90F overnight sleeping car, or *couchette*). Or zip to Paris via Marseille in about seven hours (430F) on the TGV. Buses leave Nice's **bus station** (Promenade du Paillon, on edge of Vieux Nice, tel. 04–93–85–61–81) regularly for points all along the Riviera. More than 30 airlines serve the international **Aéroport Nice-Côte d'Azur**; call **Air France** (tel. 04–93–18–89–89) or **Air Inter** (tel. 04–93–14–84–84) for information on flights. **Bus 23** or **Bus 24** (8F), toward St-Laurent-du-Var, runs between the airport and the train station every 30 minutes.

GETTING AROUND

Nice lies between the train station to the north and the **Baie des Anges** (Bay of Angels) to the south. **Place Masséna** is the main square; to the east is **Vieux Nice,** the old part of town, and to the west is the newer section. The **Promenades des Anglais,** a crowded beachfront stretch in the newer part of town, is just a 10-minute walk from the tracks; it becomes **quai des Etats-Unis** as you pass into Vieux Nice. Air-conditioned **SUN** buses run throughout the city; buy tickets (8F) at the central **station** (10 av. Félix Faure, tel. 04–93–16–52–10) or in tabacs around town. If you're willing to brave the traffic, rent a bike (120F per day plus 1,500F deposit) or moped (from 150F per day plus 4,000F deposit) at **Nicea Location Rent** (9 av. Thiers, tel. 04–93–82–42–71; open daily 9–6), across from the train station.

WHERE TO SLEEP

A proliferation of budget hotels, especially in the area just south of the train station, makes the city an excellent base for exploring the pricey Riviera. From the train station, cross avenue Thiers and walk down the stairs to get to the budget lodging zone, bounded by avenues Georges Clemenceau and Jean Médecin. If the area's packed, go north and check out **avenue Malausséna.**

The **Hôtel Lyonnais** (20 rue de Russie, tel. 04–93–88–70–74) has a bright lobby, an eager manager, and basic but clean rooms (singles from 110F, doubles from 154F). M. and Mme. Vila maintain a cheerful atmosphere at the cozy **Hôtel du Petit Louvre** (10 rue Emma Tiranty, tel. 04–93–80–15–54; closed Nov.–Jan.); singles with shower start at 165F, doubles cost 220F, and triples 270F. **The Little Palace** (9 av. Baquis, tel. 04–93–88–70–49, fax 04–94–88–78–89) is worth the extra francs if you want to treat yourself; singles and doubles run 250F–350F. Americans swarm to the spartan but clean rooms at **Hôtel Belle Meunière** (21 av. Durante, tel. 04–93–88–66–15; closed Dec.–Jan.), more of a youth hostel than a hotel; dorm beds start at 75F, doubles at 124F, breakfast included. Lots of Americans also stay at the very social **Auberge de Jeunesse de Nice** (rte. Forestière du Mont-Alban, tel. 04–93–89–23–64). At 5 PM the staff posts the number of beds available, but in summer, it's best to arrive early (it opens at 6:30 AM); bed, breakfast, and shower is 66F. Take Bus 14 from place Masséna. There's usually room left at the 220-bed **Relais International de la Jeunesse "Clairvallon"** (26 av. Scudéri, tel. 04–93–81–27–63; bed and breakfast 71F) after the other hostel is full. Check in is at 5 PM. From place Masséna, take Bus 15 to Scudéri.

FOOD

Stock up at the daily morning **market** at cours Saleya in Vieux Nice, but when you want to do your taste buds right, head for one of Vieux Nice's restaurants. They serve seafood dishes, pasta, and pizza, as well as local specialties like *socca* (a thin chickpea crêpe) and *pissaladière* (pizza with baked onions, olives, and anchovies). Branch out to the area around the budget hotels for Mexican, Middle-Eastern, North African, and Asian cuisines. **Nissa Socca** (5 rue Ste-Réparate, tel. 04–93–80–18–35) is a favorite pasta spot among Niçois locals. The house ravioli, which come with a huge basket of bread, and the beignets *d'aubergines* (eggplant) are a deal at 38F each. The romantic and inexpensive **La Brasière** (11 rue de l'Abbaye, Vieux Nice, tel. 04–93–62–32–17) serves *specialités niçoises* (such as ratatouille and eggplant beignets); your best bet is the 70F three-course menu. You could also treat yourself to the 100F menu or the 40F deals like olive oil-brushed gnocchis at **L'Escalinada** (22 rue Pairolière, Vieux Nice, tel. 04–93–62–11–71).

WORTH SEEING

Also called the Vieille Ville (Old Town), **Vieux Nice** (Old Nice) is the oldest and most interesting part of town, bounded by Colline du Château (Castle Hill) to the east, boulevard Jean-Jaurès to the north and west, and cours Saleya to the south. In Vieux Nice, the winding streets of the pedestrian zone offer a colorful market and restaurants aplenty. On **place Rosetti** you'll find the **Cathédrale Ste-Réparate,** a 17th-century church with an immense working organ and ornate stained-glass windows. The castle that once topped **Colline du Château** has long since crumbled, but the Castle Hill is well worth a climb for its stunning views of Nice and the water. Take the stairs at the turning point of the quai des Etats-Unis or the elevator (5F), which runs daily 9–6:30.

In **Cimiez,** a hilly area 4 km (2½ mi) north of the town center, are public gardens, ancient ruins, and some of the city's best museums. Amid the remains of the **Arènes de Cimiez** (the Roman arena), a 17th-century villa houses two museums: the **Musée Archéologique** (Archaeology Museum; 160 av. des Arènes-de-Cimiez, tel. 04–93–81–59–57) open December–October, Tuesday–Sunday 10–noon and 2–6; and the **Musée Matisse** (Matisse Museum; 164 av. des Arènes-de-Cimiez, tel. 04–93–81–08–08) open April–September, Tuesday–Sunday 10–6, and October–March, Tuesday–Sunday 10–5. Admission is 25F. The Musée Matisse pays homage to painter and former resident Henri Matisse, who settled here after World War I and lived in this Genoan-style villa until his death in 1954.

Marc Chagall also spent his last years on the Riviera; the **Musée Marc Chagall** (av. Dr-Ménard, tel. 04–93–53–87–20; admission 30F; open July–Sept., Wed.–Mon. 10–6; shorter hours off-season), features the artist's monumental paintings with floating visions of biblical characters in swirls of greens and blues. The spectacular **Musée d'Art Moderne et d'Art Contemporain (MAMAC)** (Promenade des Arts, tel. 04–93–62–61–62; admission 25F, July–Aug.; free Sept.–June) houses marvelous Warhol, Lichtenstein, and Yuesklein collections. The **Palais Masséna** (65 rue de France, tel. 04–93–88–11–34; admission 25F; open May–Sept., Tues.–Sun. 10–noon and 2–6; shorter hours off-season) is in a gorgeous villa that was once home to the Massénas, one of Napoléon Bonaparte's pet families. Today it's home to a museum of regional culture and history.

CHEAP THRILLS

In Nice, the cheapest thrill of all is a voyeuristic stroll along the beaches. Walk from end to end of the **Promenade des Anglais** and check out the private stretches, where people spend money to lie on what they consider to be a superior patch of pebbles. Stroll past the **Hôtel Negresco** (37 Promenade des Anglais) and peek behind the bellmen in their top hats for a view of the interior of the Riviera's most famous hotel. Cross the quai des Etats-Unis and head inland to find the **Jardin Albert I,** a great park for picnicking.

AFTER DARK

L'Exces, readily available around town, has information on concerts, disco parties, theater, and movies. The *Nuit Gay* section of *L'Exces* and the journal *Lynx* both cover Nice's gay scene. Start your night in Vieux Nice, where dozens of bars, cafés, and restaurants line **cours Saleya. Pub Oxford** (4 rue Mascoinat, tel. 04–93–92–24–54) charges no cover for the nightly, live guitar music. **Le Van Gogh** (7 rue du Pont-Vieux, tel. 04–93–80–34–44) is a low-key bar with a local crowd and a pool table. The very hip **Le Transformer** (18, rue François Guisol, tel. 04–93–56–93–10) has great music and drinks starting at 20F. Some of the most popular clubs are **Le Studio Grand Escurial** (29 rue Alphonse Karr, tel. 04-93–82–37–66); **Le B-52** (8 Descente Crotti, tel. 04–93–62–59–60); and **News** (passage Emile Négrin, tel. 04–93–87–76–30). Discos don't get started until midnight.

NEAR NICE

CAP D'AIL

The Cap d'Ail (Garlic Cape) is without a doubt the best escape east of Nice (18 mins, 20F). The beaches, though small and rocky, are perfect for stretching out and forgetting about civilization. For the more social, a sandy section has chairs and umbrellas for rent, a bar, and beachside restaurants. If you're feeling more active, there are some spectacular places to hike. Finding reasonably priced food and lodging is a challenge, but the prize of Cap d'Ail is the **Relais International de la Jeunesse "Thalassa"** (rte. de la Mer, tel. 04–93–78–18–58) a secluded hostel right on the beach, catering to people of all ages. Check in 9 AM–10 AM or at 5 PM; beds 70F the first night, 60F thereafter.

ST-JEAN-CAP-FERRAT

A 20-minute bus ride east from Nice brings you to **St-Jean,** one of the most stunning and peaceful towns on the Riviera. St-Jean sits on **Cap-Ferrat,** a jagged peninsula whose mountains rise steeply from the sea. This has long been a favorite spot for movie scenes and stars; a couple of James Bond movies were filmed here, and actor David Niven's former home is on a street bearing his name. Visit the **tourist office** (59 av. Denis-Séméria, tel. 04–93–76–08–90), then head south on the Promenade Maurice-Rouvier, which runs along the eastern edge of the peninsula leading you to the reasonably priced cafés on the promenade of **Plage de St-Jean.** Keep trekking around the peninsula's tip toward the Pointe St-Hospice and around to the lighthouse; you'll reach a wooded area, where a beautiful path leads along the outermost edge of Cap-Ferrat, and eventually to **Villefranche-sur-Mer.**

ST-PAUL-DE-VENCE

Whether you're taking the bus up the hill from Nice (35 mins, 19F) or down from Vence, St-Paul-de-Vence's red-roofed stone buildings and tiny, winding cobblestone streets perched high above the valley are an impressive sight. Art is everything in St-Paul, but most of the galleries and boutiques sell over-priced wares. St-Paul is best appreciated if you go off the main path and explore the medieval buildings, flowered gardens, and incredible views. The tourist office gives guided history tours that provide lots of information about the town's multi-layered past,

The **Fondation Maeght,** one of the world's most famous small museums of modern art, is housed in an architectural wonder designed to make the most of natural light. It sits on a lush hill northwest of the village. Joan Miró's outdoor sculpture and fountain garden labyrinth are in striking contrast to the naturally beautiful surroundings, and a courtyard full of Alberto Giacometti's elongated creations separates the two museum buildings. The rooms inside showcase the works of Miró, Georges Braque, Wassily Kandinsky, Pierre Bonnard, and Henri Matisse, as well as rotating temporary exhibitions *Follow signs to museum, tel. 04–93–32–81–63. Admission 40F (Oct.–June); 45F (July–Sept.). Open July–Sept., daily 10–7; shorter hours off-season.*

MONACO

If much of the world lives in misery, neither Monaco nor its 30,000 millionaire citizens know about it. Presided over by Prince Rainier III, Monaco is Europe's last constitutional autocracy (complete with all the fame and scandal the tabs bring in), but for travelers' purposes the tiny principality (only 474 acres) may as well be part of France. You do, however, have to dial 00–377 (plus the eight-digit number) when calling from outside the principality, and just the 8-digit number within the principality. The famed Monte-Carlo Casino used to be the principality's big breadwinner, but these days only about 4% of the government's revenues come from gambling; now banking, media, and tourism keep its coffers full. Budget travelers beware: Monaco is not the place to eat or sleep, unless you can squeeze into the exceptional hostel or one of the few budget hotels (*see below*).

BASICS

Ask at the main **tourist office** (2a blvd. des Moulins, Monte Carlo, tel. 92–16–61–16) for *Bienvenue!,* a free monthly guide of useful information; from the train station, take Bus 1 or 4 to Casino-Tourisme. The **American Express** office (35 blvd. Princesse Charlotte, Monte Carlo, tel. 93–25–74–45) holds mail; take Bus 1, 2, or 4 to Casino-Tourisme. The main **post office** (Palais de la Scala, sq. Beaumarchais, tel. 93–50–69–87) is near the casino in Monte Carlo.

COMING AND GOING

Trains run between Monaco's **train station** (av. Prince Pierre, tel. 36–35–35–35) and Nice (25 mins, 20F) every half hour. **Buses** depart from avenue Prince Pierre, right near the train station, connecting Monaco to points along the Riviera; buy tickets from the driver.

On a high, rocky promontory extending to the sea is the old town of **Monaco-Ville,** one of five sections of Monaco. Most worthwhile attractions are in this area, an easy walk from the train station. North of the promontory is **La Condamine,** the commercial harbor area with apartments and businesses. Farther north is **Monte Carlo,** the modern gambling town, and then **Le Larvatto,** a swimming resort with artificial beaches. **Fontvieille** is the industrial district by the port. Six **bus** lines travel to all the major points of interest in Monaco. The 9F fare includes a transfer good for 30 minutes; or get a four-ride (19F) or eight-ride (30F) card. Buy cards and get bus maps from **Compagnie des Autobus de Monaco** (3 av. Président J. F. Kennedy, tel. 93–50–62–41).

WHERE TO SLEEP

Perched high above the city and one block northeast of the train station, the **Centre de la Jeunesse Princesse Stephanie** (24 av. Prince Pierre, tel. 93–50–83–20; beds 70F) may be the nicest hostel on the Riviera and, not surprisingly, is often full. They don't take reservations July–mid-September; check-in begins at 11 AM but people arrive by 9AM to get a numbered ticket. The maximum stay is five nights, one night during peak periods. Also, the hostel is open only to travelers aged 16–26 and students 31 or under. If you can't get in here, you're best off sleeping in nearby Nice, Cap d'Ail, or Antibes, though there are a some almost reasonably priced places in town. Try the cramped but clean **Hôtel Cosmopolite** (4 rue de la Turbie, tel. 93–30–16–95), where doubles go for 225F–265F, or the modern (and more expensive) **Hôtel de France** (6 rue de la Turbie, tel. 93–30–24–64), where doubles start at 310F.

FOOD

Like everything in Monaco, food is served in high style at a high price. There's a daily morning **outdoor market** at place d'Armes near the station. If you miss the market, **Marché U** (35 blvd. Princesse Charlotte) can provides all your picnicking needs. A lot of the cheaper restaurants and take-out stands are in the old section of Monaco, east of the palace. La Condamine area is good for crêpe stands and cafés serving cheapish sandwiches and pizzas. Enjoy a sit-down crêpe or pizza for less than 50F at **Crêperie-Pizzeria du Rocher** (12 rue C. Félix Gastaldi, tel. 93–30–09–64). At the convivial **Restaurant Le Bacchus** (13 rue de la Turbie, tel. 93–30–19–35) dine on the generous 80F menu of traditional French cuisine. Monaco's social scene is very snobby, but **Le Jimmy's** (26 av. Princesse Grace, tel. 93–16–22–77), complete with drag queens and exotic cocktails, has more personality than other Monaco bars.

WORTH SEEING

In a carefully manicured sculpture garden, the **Casino de Monte Carlo** (pl. du Casino, tel. 92–16–21–21) is one of the most famous buildings on the Riviera. The high-rollers who frequent these ritzy joints never ask prices before ordering, so slip into something sleek and be ready for the big-time. Sport your passport to prove you're over 21, and ease on into the main gambling hall, the American Room. The *salons privées* (private rooms) require a jacket, tie, and money for admission. The casino, **Le Café de Paris** (pl. du Casino, tel. 92–16–23–00), is across the street, and the nearby **Loews Casino** (12 av. des Spélugues, tel. 93–50–65–00) has slot machines.

The **Palais du Prince** (Prince's Palace; admission 30F; open June–Sept., daily 9:30–6:30; Oct., daily 10–5) is anchored on the rock in Monaco-Ville. A 40-minute guided tour takes you through lavish state rooms furnished with priceless antiques and paintings, but the family's private apartments are off-limits. In front of the main entrance on **place du Palais,** you can watch the daily changing of the humorless guards at 11:55 AM. Nearby, the **Cathédrale de Monaco-Ville** (4 rue Colonel Bellando de Castro, tel. 04–93–30–88–13) contains the tombs of Monaco's former princes. You can also pay homage to the great Hitchcock heroine Grace Kelly at the tomb inscribed GRACIA PATRICIA.

High-rolling and royalty-gazing might provide a fleeting thrill, but the **Musée Océanographique** is the real reason to come to Monaco. Prince Albert I founded the Oceanographic Museum in 1910 to display objects he brought back from his deep-sea explorations. The museum has an amazing aquarium with nearly 3,000 fish and invertebrates, various halls of stuffed animals, exhibitions, and research laboratories. In the elegant conference hall you can watch a film by the late Jacques Cousteau, director of the museum from 1957 to 1988. Check out the view from the terrace, and come early to avoid crowds. *Av. St-Martin, tel. 04–93–15–36–00. Follow signs from vieille ville or palace. Admission 60F. Open July–Aug., daily 9–8; shorter hours off-season.*

THE SOUTHWEST

After you spend some time in this region that borders Spain and reaches up the Atlantic coast toward Brittany, the term "the south of France" takes on new meaning. This western half of France's south is less expensive and less pretentious than the Riviera and has a lot to offer the adventurous traveler in the way of natural beauty and historic sites. The region is a mix of coastal playgrounds, dry, vine-covered terrain, rolling hills in the Dordogne and Lot River valleys, and precipitous mountain slopes in the Pyrénées. Although Bordeaux bustles like the big city it is, once you head into the quiet country villages or climb into the mountains, you'll find yourself switching into a relaxed Mediterranean mode.

LANGUEDOC-ROUSSILLON

Spend a few days in this region and you'll be sipping red wine and taking endless midday meals before you know it. Dozens of beaches line the Mediterranean, from the swampy Camargue just east of Montpellier to Cap Cerbère at the Spanish border. Inland Languedoc-Roussillon, with its dry climate, may seem like one big vineyard: the vine thrives here, and its inhabitants thrive off it.

CARCASSONNE

Carcassonne's **la Cité,** the fortified upper town, looks like the greatest sand castle ever built. In July and August the 13th-century charm of la Cité is best appreciated from afar; once you enter the city walls, 20th-century tourism takes over and tourist traps flank each cobblestone street. The *ville basse* (lower town), across the Aude River from la Cité, is where you'll find the train station, several cheap hotels, and the main **tourist office** (15 blvd. Camille Pelletan, on sq. Gambetta, tel. 04–68–25–07–04).

Because the town is so tourist-oriented, signs point you in all the right directions. **La Porte Narbonnaise** is the main entrance to la Cité, and just inside the gate you'll find a **tourist office annex** (tel. 04–68–25–68–81). Walking around the ramparts and the Cité is free, but if you want a 45-minute guided tour of the **Château Comtal,** the last inner bastion, built in the 12th century, it will cost you 29F. You can find cool respite in the funky **Basilique St-Nazaire,** to the left of the château, featuring gargoyles on the outside and a stunning display of 14th- to 16th-century stained glass.

COMING AND GOING

Trains travel from the **station** (port du Canal du Midi) to Toulouse (50 mins, 85F) and Bordeaux (3 hrs, 217F). You can easily walk to la Cité in about a half hour, but the last 15 minutes uphill are hellish. Local Bus 4 (6F) runs twice an hour from the train station to la Cité, except on Sundays.

WHERE TO SLEEP AND EAT

Cheap hotels are in the ville basse; try the **Hôtel le Cathare** (53 rue Jean Bringer, tel. 04–68–25–65–92), which has 115F–155F doubles, or the **Hôtel St-Joseph** (81 rue de la Liberté, tel. 04–68–25–10–94), where doubles start at 130F. If you want to stay within la Cité, the modern **Auberge de Jeunesse** (rue de Vicomte Trencavel, tel. 04–68–25–23–16) is a good choice. Take Bus 4 from the train station and follow the signs. Inside the medieval walls, several outdoor restaurants fill **place Marcou,** just inside the Porte Narbonnaise and to the left. **Le Vieux Four** (9 rue St-Louis, tel. 04–68–47–88–80), a small restaurant on a quiet alley, has crêpes for 35F–45F.

MONTPELLIER

Montpellier is smack in the middle of the Mediterranean coastline, a five-hour train ride from Paris, Nice, and Barcelona. This is a student town (55,000 of them) with a vibrant nightlife and plenty of cultural events. From June to September, when many of the students are away, Montpellier plays host to festivals of music, theater, and dance.

The 1,000-year-old history of Montpellier is best revealed by its hodgepodge of architectural styles. The historic centre ville is characterized by 17th- and 18th-century **hôtels particuliers,** especially along rue de la Loge, rue de l'Argenterie, rue St-Guilhem, and rue des Etuves. At the intersection of rue Foch and boulevard Professeur Louis Vialleton is Montpellier's version of the **Arc de Triomphe.** It may not be as grand as the one in Paris, but then there aren't 10 lanes of traffic encircling it either. Past the arch is the **promenade du Peyrou;** the statue in the center of this park is of the Sun King, Louis XIV. Notice that the king's stirrups are missing. When the sculptor realized this blunder, he committed suicide. If you continue to the end of the park, you'll find the **Château d'Eau,** a Corinthian temple, and the terminal for **les Arceaux,** an 18th-century aqueduct made up of 53 arches.

At the center of it all is the classy **place de la Comédie,** known fondly as l'Oeuf, a reference to its egg shape. It's anchored at one end by the impressive **Opéra-Bastille.** The other end branches out into the expansive **esplanade de Charles de Gaulle** to the north and **le Triangle** to the east, where you'll find **le Polygone,** an American-style shopping center. Behind le Polygone is **Antigone,** Montpellier's official nod to the future. A neoclassical symmetrical wonder, it was designed by architect Ricardo Bofill to house low- to middle-income families. By comparing this structure with the 13th-century **Tour de la Babote,** also in the centre ville, you get a good sense of the range of historical influences in Montpellier. You can get a detailed map and take a guided tour from the **tourist office** (just off pl. de la Comédie in le Triangle, tel. 04–67–58–67–58).

COMING AND GOING

Frequent trains go to Paris (5 hrs, about 415F), Toulouse (2½ hrs, 157F), and Barcelona (5 hrs, 205F). The **train station** (pl. Auguste Gilberte) is just a few minutes' walk from place de la Comédie in the centre ville. The **bus station** (rue Jules Ferry, tel. 04–67–92–01–43) is next door to the train station. The historic centre ville is a pedestrian's paradise, but **SMTU** (23 rue Maguelone, tel. 04–67–22–87–87) runs local buses (7F) for the weary.

WHERE TO SLEEP

Just about all the budget hotels in Montpellier are in the centre ville. On a quiet street just off the main square, **Hôtel des Etuves** (24 rue des Etuves, tel. 04–67–60–78–19) has large rooms (160F–200F) at the top of a narrow staircase. The **Hôtel Plantade** (10 rue Plantade, tel. 04–67–92–61–45) is a five-minute walk from the city center; doubles run 100F–150F. Although it's in the centre ville, the **Auberge de Jeunesse** (2 impasse de la Petite Corraterie, off rue des Ecoles Laïques, tel. 04–67–60–32–22; beds 70F–90F) is kind of hard to find. Take Bus 3, 5, 6, or 7 from the train station to boulevard Louis Blanc.

FOOD

Produce is sold at the **market** on place Jean Jaurès and the neighboring Halles Castellane daily until noon. Or, hit the **Monoprix** on place de la Comédie for groceries. If you decide to take advantage of the ambience of the centre ville, go to **rue des Ecoles Laïques** where you'll find ethnic restaurants at bearable prices. A good size falafel and glass of wine cost about 35F at **Pita Plain** (50 rue de l'Aiguillerie, tel. 04–67–60–81–30). Crepe stands abound, but none are better than **Arcadie** (3 pl. Notre-Dame des Tables, tel. 04–67–52–84–02); try the 43F *saramaka* (bananas, chocolate, vanilla ice cream, and whipped cream). **Restaurant l'Image** (6 rue du Puits-des-Esquilles, tel. 04–67–60–47–79, closed Sun.) is a little hole-in-the-wall serving copious portions of authentic French food; come before 8 PM for the 59F menu; after that you'll pay 65F–130F. A first-rate pizzeria off place St-Roch, **La Table d'Angèle** (5 rue des Teissiers, tel. 04–67–60–48–76; closed Mon., lunch Sat. and Sun.) has a three-course meal guaranteed to leave you happily stuffed for 69F. If you want to hang with young folks and rabble-rousers, head to **place Jean-Jaurès:** What acts as a marketplace by day is a hopping cluster of bars and cafés by night. Especially popular is **Petit Negresco** (6 pl. Jean-Jaurès, tel. 04–67–66–02–10).

TOULOUSE

Just 97 km (60 mi) from the Spanish border, laid-back Toulouse is influenced by its warm Mediterranean neighbor. The city also has a well-preserved Roman heritage; the ubiquitous redbrick buildings have earned Toulouse its nickname, *la Ville Rose* (the pink city). To soak up the history of Toulouse, walk around its well-maintained centre ville. Built at the end of the 11th and beginning of the 12th centuries, the **Basilique St-Sernin** (pl. St-Sernin) is the largest Romanesque building in France. The church is named after the early Christian martyr Saturnin, former bishop of Toulouse. When Saturnin refused to take part in a bull sacrifice, the Romans tied him to a bull's horns. The nearby 14th-century church of **Notre-Dame-du-Taur** was built on the spot where St-Saturnin was dragged to his death. A masterpiece of southern Gothic architecture, **Les Jacobins** (pl. des Jacobins; admission 15F) usually plays second fiddle to the Basilique St-Sernin but it's really just as impressive. In summer, the cloisters provide an atmospheric setting for the city's music festival.

The city's largest museum, the **Musée des Augustins** (21 rue de Metz, tel. 05–61–22–21–82), open Thursday–Monday, 10–5 (June–Sept. until 6), and Wednesday until 9 (June–Sept. until 10), has an impressive display of Roman sculpture and religious paintings, as well as works by Murillo and Rubens. Admission is 12F. For more modern artwork, stop by the **Château d'Eau** (pl. Laganne, tel. 05–61–42–61–72), a fascinating photo gallery and research center that was built in 1822, the same year that Joseph Nicéphore Nièpce created the first permanent photographic images. Admission is 15F and it's open Wednesday–Monday 1–7. The **tourist office** (Donjon du Capitole, rue Lafayette, tel. 05–61–11–02–22) has city maps and information and gives walking tours (in French) in summer.

COMING AND GOING

Trains connect Toulouse to Carcassonne (1 hr, 79F), Perpignan (2½ hrs, 141F), and Paris (7 hrs, 352F). The **train station** (blvd. Pierre Sémard) is next door to the **regional bus station** (tel. 05–61–61–67–

67). The main square of the centre ville is **place du Capitole,** a good 15-minute walk or two métro stops from the train station. The new (and driverless) métro system has only one line, through the center of town. The 8F tickets are good for transfers onto buses as well.

WHERE TO SLEEP

Budget hotels are plentiful in Toulouse. One of the cheapest in town is **Hôtel Pays d'Oc** (53 rue Riquet, tel. 05–61–62–33–76) on a quiet street, with rooms from 60F to 100F. The rooms and hallway toilets are somewhat spartan and security is a bit lax, but the good-natured owner does his best to make your stay hassle-free. Just off the main square, the **Hôtel du Grand Balcon** (8 rue Romiguières, tel. 05–61–21–48–08) has large rooms with large windows that let in the breeze and, on the front side, urban noise. Stay in Antoine de St-Exupéry's old room for only 135F a night. On a cozy, narrow lane in the centre ville, the **Hôtel Croix-Baragnon** (17 rue Croix-Baragnon, tel. 05–61–52–60–10) has polished, modern rooms (170F) overlooking the red rooftops of Toulouse.

FOOD

Avoid the pricey café-restaurants on place du Capitole—you'll do much better if you head down one of the many alleys and pedestrian streets that fan out from it. Rue des Lois has cheap ethnic eateries, including **Resto Cool** (6 rue des Lois, tel. 05–61–21–51–77), which has Lebanese falafel sandwiches (19F), tabbouleh (12F), and hummus (24F). **La Trattoria** (2 rue Pargaminières, tel. 05–62–27–15–08) is a tiny dive with scrumptious food for 30F–60F a la carte. Get delicious African fare from the 40F menu at **Bagamoyo** (27 rue des Couteliers, tel. 05–62–26–11–36; closed Sun., Mon. lunch). It's worth seeking out **La Corde** (4 rue Jules Chalande, tel. 05–61–29–09–43; closed Sun., Mon. lunch), the oldest restaurant in town; your best bet is the 80F or 120F menu. The **market** on Boulevard de Strasbourg is bustling Tuesday–Sunday. At night, Toulouse hipsters gather in the bars on **place du Capitole** and **place St-Georges.**

BIARRITZ

This glitzy Atlantic resort isn't quite what it used to be. During the belle epoque, Spanish and French nobility graced its posh resort villas and palaces. Even after World War I, Biarritz continued to lure the likes of Charlie Chaplin and Coco Chanel, but these days it mostly caters to wealthy international tourists. If you're simply looking for a patch of sand on which to bask (no pun intended), you'll do better farther north. But for a glimpse of the high life, a day or two in Biarritz will do the trick.

After catching some rays on Biarritz's main beach, the **Grande Plage,** join the crowds on the **Rocher de la Vierge** (Rock of the Virgin), an impressive rock formation southwest. The bridge connecting it to the mainland is made out of a piece of metal left over from the Eiffel Tower. Note that before you hit the waves, you should read the signs to tell you when it's safe to swim as there are treacherous undercurrents. Just above the beach, **Casino Bellevue** sits imposingly on the hillside. You can store your belongings here, at **La Consigne** (left-luggage office; tel. 05–59–22–02–79), for 5F–15F.

COMING AND GOING

Trains travel to Biarritz from Bordeaux (2 hrs, 149F) and Toulouse (4 hrs, 205F). Biarritz's small **train station** (18 allée Moura, tel. 05–59–23–04–84), known as La Négresse, is 3 km (2 mi) southeast of the centre ville. Hop on Bus 2 to reach the centrally located Hôtel de Ville, a few blocks southeast of the main beach. The **main tourist office** (1 sq. d'Ixelles, tel. 05–59–24–20–24), up the street from the Hôtel de Ville, has hotel listings, maps, and information on surfing.

WHERE TO SLEEP

Be prepared to fight for one of the few double rooms under 250F. Warning: In July and August, most rooms are reserved weeks or months in advance. **Hôtel Barnetche** (5 bis av. Charles Floquet, tel. 05–59–24–22–25) has beds in a spick-and-span 12-person dorm for 80F each, and private doubles starting at 150F per person. In July and August, single rooms jump to 345F and private doubles peak at 460F. The **Hôtel de la Marine** (1 rue des Goëlands, tel. 05–59–24–34–09) has doubles for 175F (185F with shower) and triples for 210F; and the **Hôtel du Rocher de la Vierge** (13 rue du Port Vieux, tel. 05–59–24–11–74) has singles starting at 130F and doubles from 160F. Add 25F for a shower if you haven't taken advantage of the free ones on the beach.

FOOD

Cheap snacks and fast food are near the beach on boulevard du Général de Gaulle. For fresh produce, baked goods, and cheese, go to the covered **Les Halles Centrales** on place V. Sobradiel; it's open daily 7–1. There's a **Codec** supermarket near the same square on rue des Halles. **Le Blé Noir** (blvd. du Général de Gaulle, below pl. Bellevue, tel. 05–59–24–31–77; closed mid-Oct.–mid-June) dishes out delicious salads (40F), galettes (5F–40F), and dessert crepes (12F–32F). When you burn out on French cuisine, try the filling pizzas (40F–60F) or pasta dishes at **Les Princes** (13 rue Gambetta, tel. 05–59–24–21–78; closed Wed. and Thurs.)

BORDEAUX

The history, economy, and culture of Bordeaux have always been linked to the production and market-ing of the region's wine. The birth of the first Bordeaux winery is said to have occurred between 37 and 68 AD, when the Romans called this land *Burdigala*. Since then the wine trade in Bordeaux has pros-pered, riding out market fluctuations, the Hundred Years' War, and English domination of the wine industry in the 19th century. As big as Bordeaux is, as famous as it is, and as prosperous as it is there should be more to see and do here, but the real entertainment is just outside of town in the fields of grapevines bursting with the next season's harvest.

Although industry operates at full throttle here, Bordeaux tends to lack the vibrancy and variety of cities like Paris. An active student population, however, does manage to infuse some new and foreign char-acter into the general atmosphere of political conservatism. As the capital of the Gironde department, Bordeaux is also an important transportation hub for getting to southern France or Spain. And for wine connoisseurs, it is still the doorway to paradise: Sauternes lies to the south, flat and dusty Médoc to the northwest, and Pomerol and St-Emilion to the east. Though many of the vineyards surrounding Bor-deaux are tough to reach without a car, if you're enough of an oenophile to know that Lafite-Rothschild, Latour, and Mouton-Rothschild wines are all grown hereabouts, then the area is particularly worth your time and the price of car rental.

BASICS

The **tourist office** (12 cours du 30 Juillet, tel. 05–57–78–80–00) is near the Grand Théâtre. The **American Express** office (14 cours de l'Intendance, tel. 05–56–00–63–33) cashes checks, replaces lost cards, and changes traveler's checks without commission. The **post office** (37 rue du Château-d'Eau, tel. 05–56–44–20–29; postal code 33065) sells stamps and phone cards, and changes money at mediocre rates.

COMING AND GOING

Bordeaux is a major rail hub; trains travel from here to Paris (3 hrs, 350F by TGV), Lyon (8 hrs, 313F) via Toulouse, Nice (8 hrs, 413F), and many other French and Spanish cities. The **train station** (rue Charles Domercq) is about a 45-minute walk from the centre ville, in a scuzzy area full of sex shops and cheap hotels. Efficient city **buses** (8F) are useful for getting away from the station; take Bus 7 or 8 to the centre ville. Bus maps are available at the tourist office, the train station, or the **bus station** (8 rue Corneille, tel. 05–56–43–68–43).

WHERE TO SLEEP

There are a few decent hotels and a good hostel near the train station, but be wary of the neighborhood after dark. **Hôtel Regina** (26 rue Charles Domercq, tel. 05–56–91–66–07, fax 05–56–91–32–88), just across from the train station, is open round the clock; rooms are modern and comfortable (150F–180F). The centre ville is generally a better bet. A good choice is the **Hôtel d'Amboise** (22 rue de la Vieille Tour, tel. 05–56–81–62–67, fax 05–56–52–92–82), a clean and cheery stopover near place Gambetta where doubles are 125F. The funky **Hôtel Studio** (35 rue Lafaurie-de-Monbadon, tel. 05–56–48–00–14, fax 05–56–81–25–71) has lots of amenities crammed in the rooms (doubles 120F). The **Maison des Etudiantes** (50 rue Ligier, tel. 05–56–96–48–30; singles 50F–70F), is a much better deal than the hostel and is near the centre ville. It accepts travelers in summer—call to reserve a room. Take Bus 7 or 8 from the station to the Bourse du Travail stop and walk to rue Ligier.

FOOD

It's a cinch to eat cheaply in Bordeaux if you're not picky; sidewalk stands on **rue du Palais-Gallien** will sell you a kebab-stuffed baguette, greasy fries, and a Coke for 25F. Right next to the cathedral, the

Brasserie le Musée (37 pl. Pey-Berland, tel. 05–56–52–99–69) serves salad, roast chicken, dessert, and wine, all for 54F. Discover a local delicacy at Francs Délices (54 rue de la Devise, tel. 05–56–52–28–22), where the 65F menu includes foie gras.

WORTH SEEING

Bordeaux doesn't have too many blockbuster sights; it relies on the nearby vineyards and beaches to draw you here. Visit the Maison du Vin (1 cours du 30 Juillet, tel. 05–56–00–22–66), across from the tourist office, for an in-depth scoop on the vineyards in the area. Bordeaux's tourist world revolves around place Gambetta. Just down cours de l'Intendance from the place is the Grand Théâtre (pl. de la Comédie, tel. 05–56–90–91–60), an enormous building that inspired Charles Garnier's opulent Opéra in Paris. The tourist office's guided tour takes you up into the nosebleed seats for a look at the magnificent ceiling. Just north of the theater, near the tourist office at the esplanade des Quinconces, the massive Monument aux Girondins commemorates the bravery of the local party that fought to suppress an aristocratic counterrevolution during the French Revolution. There are no actual Girondins depicted on the statue, but Liberty is on top, the Republic is tossing out the vices of the monarchy on one side, and Bordeaux is frolicking in democratic harmony with the Garonne and Dordogne rivers on the other.

The Musée d'Aquitaine (20 cours Pasteur, tel. 05–56–01–51–02; admission 18F, free Wed.) is one of the city's best museums, taking you on a trip through human history, with an emphasis on daily life. The terrific prehistoric section reproduces the famous Lascaux cave paintings in part. Each year the cutting-edge Musée d'Art Contemporain (7 rue Ferrère, tel. 05–56–44–16–35; admission 30F; free noon–2) promotes four artists, who use the huge expanse to do anything they want.

AFTER DARK

Night owls start off around 9 PM in the cafés around place St-Pierre or place de la Victoire, where Le Plana (pl. de la Victoire, tel. 05–56–73–19–80) is the most popular spot. A lesbian crowd congregates at La Reine Carrotte (28 rue de Chai des Farines, tel. 05–56–01–26–68) for the 25F tropical "Pago Pago" drink. La Palmeraie (22 quai de la Monnaie, tel. 05–56–94–07–52) caters to Bordeaux's French-African population. Anyone hankering for English hospitality and 20 different types of whisky should slip into Dick Turpin's Bar (72 rue du Loup, tel. 05–56–48–07–57).

NEAR BORDEAUX

The Entre-Deux-Mers (Between Two Seas) region actually lies between two rivers, the Garonne and the Dordogne. Just southeast of Bordeaux, the area is dotted with tiny medieval towns and crumbling castles that overlook orderly rows of vines. Ninety kilometers (59 miles) north of Bordeaux, Pauillac is the base for visits to Château Mouton-Rothschild, its wine museum (tel. 05–56–73–24–29), and Château Latour (tel. 05–56–73–19–80). Tours require a reservation two weeks in advance, and a glass of wine can cost 70F, but it's worth it if you love wine. Since 1885, these châteaux have been known to produce two of the best red wines in the world. One of the most interesting places in Entre-Deux-Mers is the hilltop town of St-Macaire, where crumbling ivy-covered ramparts date from the 12th and 13th centuries. Tourists jostle through the narrow streets of the medieval town of St-Emilion, grabbing for the famous red wines and scrumptious macaroons that bear the town's name. Ignore the crowds and revel in the magnificent hillside views and visit the marvelous Eglise Monolithe, a church completely carved out of the side of a cliff. All three towns are accessible by Citram bus from Bordeaux.

THE DORDOGNE AND LOT RIVER VALLEYS

After its descent from the mountains in the Massif Central, the Dordogne River makes its way westward through Bordeaux before spilling into the Atlantic. The Lot River makes a similar journey about 40 km (25 mi) south. Inhabited by peasant farmers for centuries, the rolling countryside in this area is chock-full of riverside châteaux, medieval villages, and prehistoric sites. Towns like Périgueux have a smattering of Roman monuments and local history museums. The region is honeycombed with dozens of grottes (caves) that are filled with prehistoric drawings, etchings, and carvings. The green lushness of the area gives way to dry, vineyard-covered expanses, especially as the rivers approach the Atlantic Ocean. Biking is one of the most popular ways to see the region, but be prepared for a lot of hills.

SARLAT

Tucked among the hills 6 km (4 mi) from the Dordogne River, Sarlat is a bustling tourist center that, in certain areas, manages to preserve its small-town atmosphere. To get a sense of old Sarlat, venture off the main pedestrian artery, **rue de la République,** along some of the narrow paths of soft golden-colored brick lined with 16th- and 17th-century buildings. The commercial center of town lies on the east side of **rue de la République,** where there are cafés, restaurants, and a thousand or so wine and foie-gras shops. Unfortunately, in July and August, the streets are so packed with tourists that a walk through town is more like a rugby scrum. To find out about getting out of town to the surrounding châteaux, talk to the **tourist office** (pl. de la Liberté, tel. 05–53–59–27–67) off the main square.

COMING AND GOING

Trains from Bordeaux arrive at Sarlat's **station** (av. de la Gare), a half hour walk from town. Pick up a copy of "Guide Pratique" from the tourist office for information on **SNCF buses** that cover the area. The convenient **Cycles Cumenal** (8 av. Gambetta, tel. 05–53–31–28–40) rents bikes for about 80F a day.

WHERE TO SLEEP AND EAT

In summer be sure to have a reservation before setting foot in Sarlat. Superbly located on the quiet side of the vieille ville, the **Hôtel des Recollets** (4 rue Jean-Jacques Rousseau, tel. 05–53–59–00–49, fax 05–53–30–32–62) has charming rooms, attentive proprietors, and doubles for 220F–250F. The rustic, relaxed **Auberge de Jeunesse** (77 av. de Selves, tel. 05–53–59–47–59; closed Dec.–mid-Mar.) has beds for 40F. Campers pay 24F per person to pitch a tent out back. Walk 10 minutes from rue de la République to avenue Gambetta, then veer left onto avenue de Selves. The budget dining scene is disappointing, but markets and boulangeries line rue de la République. With some of the cheapest menus in town (60F, 70F, and 80F), **Le Commerce** (rue Alberic Cahuet, just off rue de la République, tel. 05–53–59–04–26) dishes up a saucy *cassoulet* (a pork and bean stew) among other regional specialties.

ROCAMADOUR

The medieval village of Rocamadour hangs dramatically on the edge of a cliff, 1,600 feet above the Alzou River gorge. Rocamadour became famous in 1166 when chroniclers recorded the miraculous discovery of the body of St-Amadour under a sanctuary; pilgrims have been coming ever since. A small number of people actually live in Rocamadour, but 1.5 million tourists and pilgrims visit each year. If you want to have a look at the seven sanctuaries and the crypt, take one of the free guided tours that leaves from the **Chapelle Notre-Dame.**

COMING AND GOING

Half the drama of Rocamadour is figuring out how to get here. The Rocamadour-Padirac **train station** connects directly with Toulouse (1½ hrs, 134F). The 40-minute walk from the station to town takes you down the steep gorge and then up to the village. Bus excursions also arrive from Souillac, Sarlat, and Brive. Between the train station and town you'll pass **L'Hospitalet,** a tourist center on a plateau about 1 km (½ mi) from Rocamadour. The **tourist office** (tel. 05–65–33–62–80) in L'Hospitalet is open April–September, and the office in the village itself (rue Piétonne, tel. 05–65–33–62–59) is open year-round.

WHERE TO SLEEP AND EAT

It's difficult to find a cheap bed in Rocamadour, and without a reservation it's nearly impossible. Not a bargain, but in the middle of the rock, **Hôtel le Globe** (rue Piétonne, tel. 05–65–33–67–73, fax 05–65–33–17–10) has doubles with shower and telephones for 190F. Farther from the village, but next to the train station, **Hôtel des Voyageurs** (tel. 05–65–33–63–19) has very basic doubles for 125F. The only commercial street, **rue Piétonne,** has everything from crêpe stands to restaurants with 180F menus. **Chez Anne-Marie** (tel. 05–65–71–80–91), on the far end of rue Piétonne, has a 65F lunch menu to enjoy on the cliff-side terrace.

LA ROCHELLE

By some miracle of climate, the coastline here gets nearly as much sun as the Côte d'Azur. But in an area where the main attractions are sun and sand, the port city of La Rochelle adds a dose of culture to an otherwise hedonistic vacation. Eighteenth-century stone houses line the **cour des Dames,** a spacious avenue that circles the historic harbor where two 14th-century towers stand sentinel. Inland, a massive stone gate marks the entrance to the narrow streets of the old town. The port's famous towers, historic houses, and museums draw visitors all year, but summer is particularly crowded because of the city's proximity to the beaches of nearby **Ile de Ré** and the popular six-day Francofolies music festival the beginning of July.

COMING AND GOING

La Rochelle is a major stop on the rail line between Nantes (1¼ hrs, 144F) and Bordeaux (2 hrs, 132F). You can also come from Paris (5 hrs, 302F) via Poitiers (1½ hrs, 116F). The hostel and campgrounds are outside town; to get there, you need to take the green **Autoplus** bus (8F). Most buses run from the main bus station on place de Verdun. You don't have to go near a bus to see the city's main sights, though, many of which encircle the old harbor. In summer, a boat service called the **Passeur Autoplus** (4F) takes you from cours des Dames to the museums near La Ville en Bois, the section of town south of the historic port. In addition, a **Bus de Mer** water bus (10F) picks passengers up from the cour des Dames and drops them in Port des Minimes, the port south of La Ville en Bois.

WHERE TO SLEEP

If you show up during the Francofolies without a hotel reservation, be prepared to sleep in the streets. The friendly managers at **Hôtel de la Paix** (14 rue Gargoulleau, tel. 05–46–41–33–44) spoil you with great rooms (150F–180F) in an 18th-century house. Smack-dab in the center of town, the **Hôtel Henri IV** (31 rue des Gentilshommes, behind Hôtel de Ville, tel. 05–46–41–25–79) opens onto a cobblestone square frequented by mimes and jugglers; doubles start at 185F. Two kilometers (1 mile) south of the train station, the **Auberge de Jeunesse** (av. des Minimes, tel. 05–46–44–43–11; beds 72F–107F) looks and feels like a factory. If you don't get a room, you might snag a 28F space in the campground behind. Take Bus 10 from avenue de Colmar (1 block from the train station) to the Lycée Hôtelier stop.

FOOD

Avoid the restaurants with expensive dockside views along cours des Dames; instead, trek inland to the pedestrian part of **rue du Temple** or **rue St-Nicolas,** or stick to the not-so-chichi quai du Gabut side of the harbor. For unbeatable sandwiches head to **L'Escapade** (rue Vieljeux); try their tasty panini kebab (26F). **Galerie du Temple** (8 rue la Ferté, tel. 05–46–41–97–09) is an art gallery/restaurant serving Armenian/Iranian/Poitou-Charentes dishes and delicious eggplant caviar (38F). A **market** is held daily on place du Marché.

WORTH SEEING

During the Renaissance, La Rochelle was one of the best-fortified ports in France. The only entrance from the sea was between the heavily guarded towers, the **Tour de la Chaîne** and the **Tour St-Nicolas**; a chain was passed between them at night to bar enemy passage. Unfortunately, that didn't keep Cardinal Richelieu from attacking this long-time Protestant stronghold in 1627, leaving 23,000 people dead from starvation after a year-long siege. The Tour St-Nicolas's labyrinthine passageways and multilayered fortifications open onto spectacular views of the port. Continue along the ramparts to the **Tour des Quatre Sergents** (also known as Tour de la Lanterne), named for four sergeants imprisoned here in the late 1800s. Admission to towers is 18F–21F.

La Rochelle's enjoyable **Musée Maritime** (Bassin des Chalutiers, tel. 05–46–28–03–00; admission 40F) displays three to five ships, depending on which ones are in port at the moment. None of them are too spruced up for the tourist trade, so you can appreciate just how messy, smelly, and cramped the quarters really are on a working ship. Keeping with La Rochelle's maritime theme, the **aquarium** (Port des Minimes, tel. 05–46–34–00–00; admission 42F) displays its eels, seahorses, piranhas, and various fish in large tanks that try to approximate the critters' natural habitats. The **tourist office** (pl. de la Petite-Sirène, tel. 05–46–41–14–68) offers a complete guide to the city and makes hotel reservations for 10F.

NEAR LA ROCHELLE

ILE DE RE

Linked by bridge to La Rochelle, Ré is an island for everyone. More than 50 km (31 mi) of beaches, an ornithological reserve, a citadel, a museum, a lighthouse, and great seafood all wait at the end of a 13F ride across the **Pont de Ré.** Vineyards sweep over the eastern part of the island, and oyster beds lie beneath the shallow waters to the west. The town of **St-Martin** is a good place to start a day trip. Stop by the **tourist office** (av. Victor Bouthillier, tel. 05–46–09–20–06) for a map of the island. The town's beach, **Plage de la Cible,** is just on the other side of the grass-covered citadel.

A few miles southwest, the town of **La Couarde** has great beaches and windsurfing. Rent boards and other equipment at **Club des Dauphins** (tel. 05–46–29–80–29) right on the **Plage du Peu Ragot.** All the way at the end of Ré, the beaches in **Les Portes** are unappealing at low tide, but you'll have them all to yourself. A better beach is the **Plage de la Conche des Baleines,** backed by dunes and pine trees. Climb the **Phare des Baleines** lighthouse for a great view of the island.

COMING AND GOING

The cheapest way to see the island is on the **Ré Bus** (tel. 05–46–09–20-15); take it from the train or bus stations in La Rochelle or any island town. The ride from La Rochelle to St-Martin takes around one hour and costs 28F. From there the fares range from 9F50 to 24F to get to any town on the island. The **Inter-îles** (tel. 05–46–09–87–27) ferries go to Oléron or Aix from the beach at Sablanceaux.

WHERE TO SLEEP AND EAT

Ré is such a convenient day trip from La Rochelle that there's little reason to stay overnight in the expensive hotels, unless you have a reservation at the adequate **Hôtel Le Sully** (19 rue du Marché, St-Martin, tel. 05–46–09–26–94), an old house in the pedestrian quarter of St-Martin where doubles go for 230F. For food, either bring a picnic or shell out megabucks for seaside seafood. **Martin's Pub** (quai de la Poithevinière, St-Martin, tel. 05–46–09–15–87) serves more than 50 different beers.

GERMANY 10

ermany defies easy generalizations. In fact, its contradictions support a cottage industry of scholars and pundits, and no other people has aired its dirty laundry quite like the Germans have in the last 20 years. From university classrooms to tabloid newspapers, they've run the question "What is German?" through the cultural Cuisinart, and disagreement continues over thorny subjects like the role of authority in the family or state, and the connection between toilet-bowl design and anal retentiveness. Travelers through this strange place will confront many of these oddities: This is the land of fairy-tale castles, pristine Alpine lakes, and cuckoo clocks, but also of radical squats and Internet cafés. And throughout Germany are always the reminders of Nazi horror and genocide. Certainly, this vivid contrast is one of the main reasons to come.

Germany united in 1871 on the basis of an aggressive militarism, and, allied with Austria, went on to terrorize Europe twice in our own century. After World War II, the Cold War and the Iron Curtain divided East and West Germany. West Germans responded either by seeking escape in conspicuous consumption or confronting the past in the angry radicalism and edgy hipness of Hamburg, West Berlin, and other cities. Meanwhile, the East German state denied its fascist past by insisting that the Nazis had all fled to (or had always been on) the other side, and that its own form of authoritarianism entailed a radical break with the past.

After the fall of the Berlin Wall in 1989, bold East German demonstrations for freedom of opinion gave way to giddy runs on washing machines, cars, and such symbols of western abundance as Barbie dolls and bananas. One year later in national elections East-Germans voted for re-unification with the West. The initial euphoria has since given way to bitterness and resentment on both sides. Easterners, whose economy collapsed and who now depend on the West for jobs and investment, often see westerners as arrogant, overbearing, and selfish. Westerners, meanwhile, have seen their tax bills rise to subsidize the living standards of the East, and often find easterners lazy, ungrateful, and demanding.

Not all of German history need inspire a Kafkaesque despair. Indeed, many of Europe's greatest thinkers and artists were born and worked in Germany, from Thomas Mann and Bertolt Brecht to Karl Marx and Albert Einstein. And if the sight of so many Gothic cathedrals, baroque castles, and other monuments results in a case of cultural indigestion, you can recuperate in the timeless beauty of Germany's natural landscape. From Alpine meadows that will make you want to sing "The hills are alive . . ." to the sheer cliffs of the dramatic Rhine Gorge, Germany offers plenty of rustic escapes.

But most of all, Germany is a modern place, and you'll be doing yourself a disservice if you come only for cutesy castles, mountain meadows, and yodeling yokels. Germany is contradiction: It is *Torte* and techno, poetry and punk, kitsch and glitz. It is Goethe, Schiller, and Brahms, but also Hitler, Eichmann, and Himmler.

BASICS

MONEY

US$1 = Deutsche Marks 1.48 and 1 Deutsche Mark = 68¢. One hundred pfennigs make up 1 mark. The Deutsche Mark (DM) is about as stable as a currency can get; in fact, the stability of other European currencies is measured against it. Banks generally give the best rates for exchanges; post offices and ATMs linked with Cirrus and Plus are other good outlets for cash.

HOW MUCH IT WILL COST • In small towns, hotel doubles can go for as low as DM 50, but in a city like Frankfurt you'd be hard-pressed to find one cheaper than DM 90. If you don't have a train pass, set aside some cash for Germany's expensive rail network. Within cities, transportation costs about DM 2.50 per ride or DM 8 for a day pass. As for tipping, service is generally included at restaurants, so simply round up to the nearest mark or two (and do the same in taxis).

Many Berliners, East and West, still avoid the other half of the city, and a popular saying has it that the Mauer im Kopf (wall in people's minds) still stands.

COMING AND GOING

The ultra-efficient trains of this country are the envy of all Europe. High-speed InterCity Express (ICE) trains connect Frankfurt and a few other big cities with other major European destinations. However, unless you have a Eurail, InterRail, or Deutsche Bahn (DB) pass, train travel is expensive.

BY PLANE • Because Frankfurt's airport is the second-largest in Europe, it's a popular first stop for many travelers. Traveling onward from Germany isn't cheap, but if your next stop is, say, Athens or Madrid, it's worth a phone call to check on the latest air fares. Try **Lufthansa** (tel. 069/6907–1222), Germany's national airline.

GETTING AROUND

InterCity (IC) and EuroCity (EC) trains connect most German cities, and all trains claim Frankfurt as their hub. The system is so extensive that you'll rarely have to turn to any other form of transport, even for tiny towns. **Eurail** and **InterRail** passes are accepted on all trains. The DB **Flexipass** is good for 5 days ($138; $178 over 26); 10 days ($188; $286 over 26); or 15 days ($238; $386 over 26) of second-class travel within a one-month period. Buy a Flexipass *before* you leave home.

Buses are marginally cheaper than trains, but less reliable. **Hitching** is popular and generally safe in Germany; just stand by the Autobahn parking areas or motel/restaurants in the direction you want to go with a sign stating your destination. Women rarely hitch alone, but it's not uncommon for women to travel in pairs. An alternative to hitching is the handy, country-wide *Mitfahrgelegenheit* (ride-share) service: Many towns have an office where you can hook up with drivers going your way. You just pitch in for gas and a few extra marks for your spot. Any tourist office should be able to direct you to the local Mitfahrgelegenheit office.

Within larger cities, the **U-Bahn** (subway) is the most useful way to get around. Tickets cost about DM 3. If you plan on riding the U-Bahn frequently in a single day, invest in a *Tageskarte* (day pass); they're available from most subway and train stations. The **S-Bahn** are commuter rail systems found in major cities, connecting the city with the surrounding suburbs and countryside. Eurailpasses are valid on the S-Bahn, but *not* on the U-Bahn. Finally, there are **trams** (Straßenbahnen) and **buses,** which often cost the same as the U-Bahn and are on the same system. You can buy tickets either from the driver or from machines marked FAHRSCHEINE at many stops. Most cities operate on an honor system; validate your ticket in one of the boxes in the station or on the bus. If anyone checks (and plainclothes agents often do), the on-the-spot fine is DM 60–DM 80—no excuses.

WHERE TO SLEEP

By far, the cheapest option is **Jugendherbergen** (youth hostels), where beds in dorm rooms go for around DM 18–DM 38, depending on the hostel and your age. Breakfast is almost always included, but

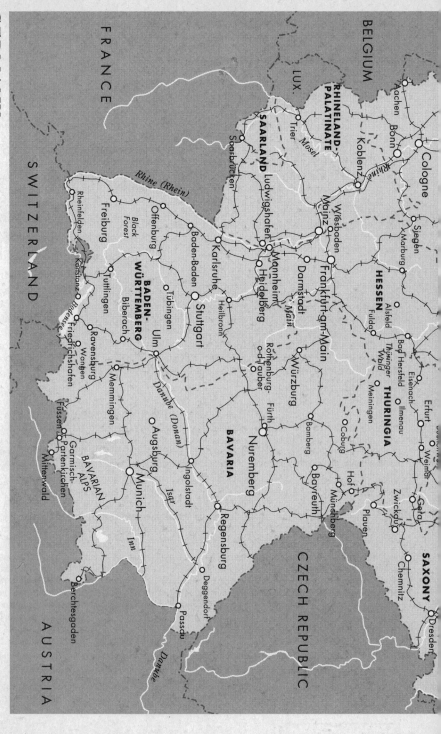

GERMANY

BELGIUM

LUX.

FRANCE

SWITZERLAND

AUSTRIA

CZECH REPUBLIC

SAXONY

THURINGIA

HESSEN

BAVARIA

BADEN-WÜRTTEMBERG

SAARLAND

RHINELAND-PALATINATE

BAVARIAN ALPS

Black Forest

Aachen
Bonn
Cologne
Siegen
Marburg
Koblenz
Trier
Mosel
Rhine
Mainz
Wiesbaden
Ludwigshafen
Saarbrücken
Mannheim
Heidelberg
Darmstadt
Frankfurt-am-Main
Main
Alsfeld
Fulda
Bad Hersfeld
Eisenach
Ilmenau
Thüringer Wald
Meiningen
Erfurt
Weimar
Gera
Zwickau
Chemnitz
Plauen
Hof
Mündelberg
Bayreuth
Coburg
Bamberg
Würzburg
Rothenburg-o-d-Tauber
Fürth
Nuremberg
Regensburg
Deggendorf
Passau
Dresden
Ingolstadt
Augsburg
Munich
Isar
Inn
Danube (Donau)
Danube
Ulm
Memmingen
Stuttgart
Heilbronn
Karlsruhe
Baden-Baden
Tübingen
Biberach
Ravensburg
Wangen
Friedrichshafen
Konstanz
Bodensee
Füssen
Garmisch-Partenkirchen
Mittenwald
Berchtesgaden
Offenburg
Freiburg
Rheinfelden
Rhine (Rhein)

Rhein

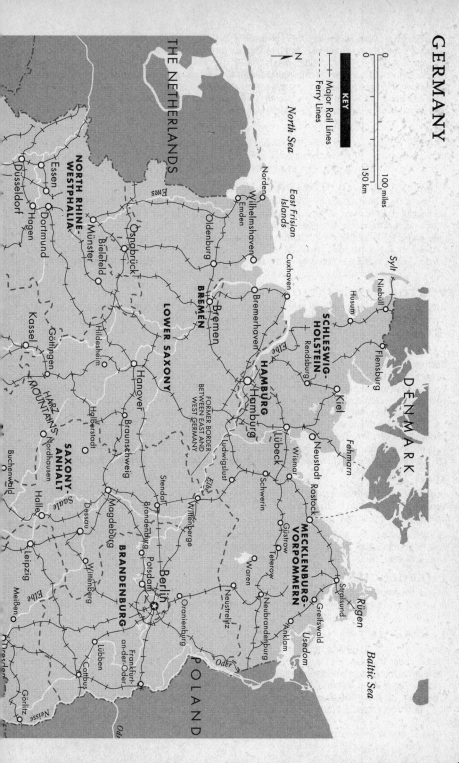

GERMANY

you might have to pay for sheets (DM 7) or showers (DM 1–DM 3). It's a little-known fact that most of Germany's youth hostels have keys that they lend out for a deposit (usually about DM 20), so you can often get around the curfew. In cities, **hotels** usually *start* at around DM 70–DM 85 for doubles, *ohne Dusche* (without shower; they're usually in the hall). A night's stay at a **Campingplatz** (campsite), found in most small towns and near most big cities, runs about DM 5 per tent plus DM 5–DM 8 per person. Almost all tourist offices can offer you a room in a **Privatzimmer** (private home), which usually require a three-day minimum stay, for DM 25–DM 50 plus a fee of about DM 5.

FOOD

One of the best ways to save money in Germany is to shop at local markets or grab a bite at a street-side *Imbißstand* (snack stand), the German equivalent of a greasy-spoon diner. Most offer *Wurst* (sausages) and fries, or ethnic specialties, such as curry and falafel, for less than DM 10.

FESTIVALS AND HOLIDAYS

If festivals are your thing, you can't go wrong in Germany. In September and October, harvest festivals bust out all over the place, especially in Munich, where the world-famous **Oktoberfest** draws hundreds of thousands of international beer-guzzlers. If you're just aching for some quaintness and happen to be in Germany in December, don't miss the **Christmas markets** in towns large and small. **Fasching**, or Karneval, is one of the most important festivals in Catholic Germany. It starts in January and rages through Shrove Tuesday in February, 48 days before Easter. In July, the **Richard Wagner Festival**—one of the major annual musical events in the world—takes place in Bayreuth.

VISITOR INFORMATION

It would take some detective work to find a German town without a tourist office; they live for organized tours and glossy brochures. Use the offices mainly to get maps and help with accommodations; they'll almost always book you a hotel room or private room for a DM 5 fee.

PHONES

Country code: 49. Germany's phone system is modern, efficient, easy to use (most phone booths have instructions in English), and *very* expensive for long-distance calls. Many phones don't accept coins, so you'd be wise to invest in a phone card (from DM 12), available at post offices and currency-exchange agencies; local calls cost 30 Pf. You can make international calls from phone booths marked with the silhouette of a receiver and, well, the word INTERNATIONAL; these phones generally accept 10 Pf, DM 1, and DM 5 coins. It's easier, though, to place international calls at the post office and pay after you phone. Rates vary from town to town, but DM 5 will usually get you about two minutes of conversation to the United States: Dial 0130–0010 for **AT&T** Direct Access℠; 0130–0013 for **Sprint**; and 0130–0012 for **MCI.** For the plain old **international operator,** dial 001188; for a **local operator,** dial 01188.

MAIL

Buy stamps from a local *Postamt* (post office) and mail your letters from any street-side postal box. Sending an airmail letter to North America costs DM 3 and takes about five days; postcards cost DM 2 apiece. Letters to European Union countries run DM 1, postcards 80 Pf.

You can receive mail at any German post office free of charge. Simply have the letter marked with your name, the address of the post office (i.e., Postamt, City Name, postal code), and the words POST-LAGERNDER BRIEF.

EMERGENCIES

In an emergency, dial 110 for the **police,** 112 for an **ambulance.** These numbers do not require coins at pay phones. There's usually one 24-hour pharmacy in each town—check the list posted on any pharmacy door to find out who's on call.

LANGUAGE

German accents and dialects vary from region to region. High German (the German spoken on TV and the radio) dominates, but in the south, east, and far north you'll encounter all sorts of variations. Most Germans in the western half of the country speak English (sometimes better than some English speakers), but fewer do in the east. Following are a few helpful German words and phrases: *guten Tag* (hello/good day); *auf Wiedersehen* (goodbye); *bitte* (please); *danke* (thank you); *wo ist . . .?* (where is . . .?); *wieviel kostet . . .?* (how much is . . .?); *sprechen sie Englisch?* (do you speak English?).

PEOPLE OF COLOR

Racially motivated hate crimes—especially outside city centers and in eastern Germany—are disconcertingly frequent. While the commercial centers of major cities and university towns are generally safe, industrial suburbs and small towns can be less so. If you're confronted, make it clear that you are a foreign tourist traveling through Germany—in most cases, you'll be left alone. If you're out after dark in unfamiliar areas, definitely grab a cab if you can afford it, and when taking public transportation, sit close to the driver.

GAY AND LESBIAN TRAVELERS

Homophobia is no more widespread in Germany than anywhere else in the western world. As could be expected, however, gays and lesbians are generally less accepted in small towns than in larger cities. If you're faced with homophobia, your best bet is simply to turn and walk away. On a more positive note, you'll find gay nightclubs and other gathering spots in most large cities, particularly Berlin and Hamburg—refer to individual sections in this chapter for specific listings.

FRANKFURT

After World War II, the old city of Frankfurt reconstructed itself out of the ashes, choosing a hyper-modern design and erecting a rash of daring skyscrapers–hence the nickname Mainhattan, a reference to the River Main, on which it stands. Fifth among German cities in size, with a population of 650,000, Frankfurt is first financially—it is home to Germany's famed *Bundesbank* (central bank) and hundreds of other commercial banks. In addition to economic clout, this steel and concrete postwar city boasts innovative cultural and nightlife scenes and a thriving student population. To take it all in, explore Frankfurt's quirky neighborhoods, like Sachsenhausen, which is packed with cafés, bars, and a slew of good modern-art museums.

BASICS

VISITOR INFORMATION

Tourist Information Römer. *Römerberg 27, tel. 069/2123–8708. Next to Römer in Römerberg Sq. Open weekdays 9–6, weekends 9:30–6.*

AMERICAN EXPRESS

Kaiserstr. 8, tel. 069/21050. From Hauptbahnhof, walk 10 min down Kaiserstr. Open weekdays 9:30–5:30, Sat. 9–noon.

CHANGING MONEY

Banks charge only 1% commission to change traveler's checks. Post offices, on the other hand, charge DM 6 per check. To change money after hours, head to the airport or train station.

CONSULATES

Australia: *Gutleutstr. 85, tel. 069/273–9090. From Hauptbahnhof, turn right on Baseler Str., left on Gutleutstr.* **United Kingdom:** *Bockenheimer Landstr. 42, tel. 069/170–0020. U6 or U7 to Westend; walk down Bockenheimer Landstr.* **United States:** *Siesmayerstr. 21, tel. 069/75350 or 069/7535–3700 for after-hours emergencies. U6 or U7 to Westend; exit Palmengarten, then right on Siesmayerstr.*

PHONES AND MAIL

The post office at the Hauptbahnhof is open until 9 PM; the one at the airport 24 hours a day. The **main post office,** near Hauptwache, has fax and poste restante services. *Hauptpostlagernd, Zeil 110, 60313, Frankfurt. Open weekdays 9–6, Sat. 9–1.*

COMING AND GOING

BY MITFAHRGELEGENHEIT

Near the Hauptbahnhof, **ADM Mitfahrzentrale** (Baseler Str. 7, tel. 069/231028 or 069/236127; closed weekends) can get you to Hamburg, Munich, or Berlin for DM 40–DM 50.

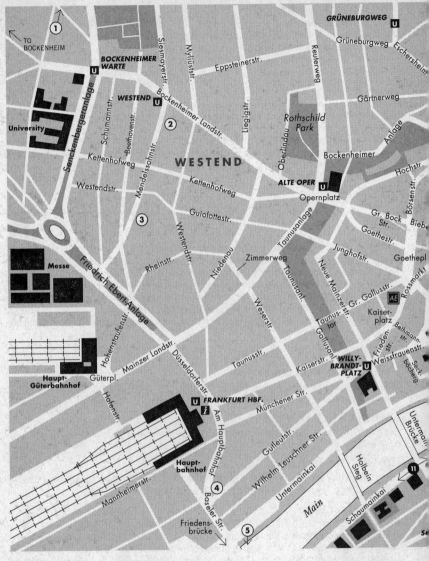

FRANKFURT

TO BOCKENHEIM

BOCKENHEIMER WARTE

GRÜNEBURGWEG

Grüneburgweg · Eschersheim

WESTEND

Eppsteinerstr.

Stresemeyerstr.

Myliusstr.

Reuterweg

Gärtnerweg

Bockenheimer Landstr.

Liegigstr.

Rothschild Park

Anlage

University

Schumannstr.

Beethovenstr.

Mendelssohnstr.

Kettenhofweg

Oberlindau

Bockenheimer

Hochstr.

WESTEND

Kettenhofweg

ALTE OPER

Gr. Bock Str.

Börsenstr.

Bieb

Westendstr.

Guiolottestr.

Opernplatz

Goethestr.

Goethepl

Messe

Westendstr.

Rheinstr.

Niedenau

Zimmerweg

Taunusanlage

Junghofstr.

Neue Mainzer Str.

Gr. Gallusstr.

Rossmarkt

AE

Kaiser-platz

Bethmann str.

Friedrich Ebert-Anlage

Hohenstaufenstr.

Güterpl.

Mainzer Landstr.

Düsseldorferstr.

Weserstr.

Taunusstr.

Taunusanl.

Taunus-tor

Gallusanl.

Kaiserstr.

Frieden- str.

Weissfrauenstr.

Seck-bächig.

WILLY-BRANDT-PLATZ

Haupt-Güterbahnhof

Hafenstr.

FRANKFURT HBF.

Münchener Str.

Untermain Brücke

Haupt-bahnhof

Am Hauptbahnhof

Baseler Str.

Gutleutstr.

Wilhelm Leuschner Str.

Untermainkai

Holbein Steg

Mannheimerstr.

Friedens-brücke

Main

Schaumainkai

11

Holbein Steg

Untermainkai

4

5

S

Sights ●

Dom St. Bartholomäus, **10**

Museum für Moderne Kunst, **7**

Museum Judengasse, **9**

Museumsufer, **11**

Römerberg, **8**

Lodging ○

Haus der Jugend (HI), **12**

Hotelschiff Peter Schlott, **5**

Hotel zur Rose, **6**

Pension Allet, **4**

Pension Backer, **2**

Pension Bruns, **3**

Sophien Hotel, **1**

MUSTERSCHULE U

Mittelweg

Oederweg

Eschenheimer Eckenheimer Landstr.

Scheffelstr.

Anlage

Friedberger Landstr.

MERIANPL. U

Merianstr.

Berger Str.

TO
BORNHEIM

Baumweg

Sandweg

Weldschmidstr.

6

Bleichstr.

Eschenheimer
Tor

Stiftstr.

Stephanstr.

Schäfergasse

K. Adenauer Str.

Seilerstr.

Friedberger

Anlage

Zoologischer
Garten

Alfred-
Brehmpl.

ZOO U Am Tiergarten

Schillerstr.

Gr. Eschenmr.-str.

Stiftstr.

Post
Office

Zeil KONSTABLER-
      WACHE

Reineckstr.

Zeil

Zeil

Haseng.

U

HAUPTWACHE

Töngesg.

Bleidenstr.

DOWNTOWN
(INNENSTADT)

Berlinerstr.

Kornmarkt

Buchg.

Bethmann
str.

Bethmannstr.

RÖMER

Mainzerg.

Alte
Mainzerg.

8

7

Domstr.

U

Braubachstr.

Fahrgasse

Fahrgasse

Allerheiligenstr.

Battonstr.

Rechneigrabenstr.

Kurt-Schumacherstr.

Langestr.

Obermainanlage

Hanauer Landstr.

Uhlandstr.

Ostendstr.

Windeckstr.

Sonnemannstr.

9

10

Weckmarkt

Mainkai

Schöne Aussicht

Oskar-von-Miller Str.

Eiserner
Steg

Sachsenhäuser Ufer

Alte
Br.

Ober-
mainbr.

Flosser
Brücke

Main

Deutschherrnufer

12

Oppenheimstr.

Walter-Kolb-Str.

Brückenstr.

Gr. Ritterg.

Kl.
Ritterg.

Paradiegasse

Dreieichstr.

Seehofstr.

Wasserweg

Gerbermühlstr.

Schweizerstr.

Gartenstr.

SACHSENHAUSEN

HWEIZER
PLATZ U

Gutzkowstr.

0   1/2 mile

0   3/4 km

N

BY PLANE

All major European cities and many U.S. cities have direct flights to **Flughafen Frankfurt,** Europe's second-busiest airport. To reach downtown Frankfurt, follow the signs (a big green dot with an "S" inside) to the S-Bahn: Take the S8 to Hauptbahnhof or Hauptwache, where you can transfer to other transit lines. It's about 15 minutes and DM 5.70 to either stop. A taxi ride from the airport into the city center costs about DM 40.

BY TRAIN

The main terminal of the Deutsche Bundesbahn (German Federal Railway), Frankfurt's **Hauptbahnhof** has connections to Munich (4½ hrs, DM 130), Hamburg (4 hrs, DM 170), Berlin (5½ hrs, DM 178), and most other European cities.

GETTING AROUND

Frankfurt is large but easily accessible. Most sights are **downtown,** on the north bank of the Main River. From here, you can cross the pedestrian bridge Eiserner Steg to reach **Sachsenhausen,** a quiet neighborhood with pubs and cobblestone streets. **Westend,** Frankfurt's financial district, is northwest of downtown and north of the Hauptbahnhof. Northwest of Westend, **Bockenheim** is a low-income area with a lively student population. And northeast of downtown is **Nordend,** a residential area spotted with hip cafés.

Frankfurt's public transportation system is complex but efficient. *Kurzstrecke* (short-distance—1 mi or less) tickets cost DM 1.90 for a single ride, DM 2.60 in rush hour (weekdays 6:30 AM–8:30 AM and 3:30 PM–6:30 PM); regular single-ride tickets cost DM 2.80, DM 3.30 during rush hour; **24-hour tickets** are DM 8.80. The U-Bahn and S-Bahn close at midnight, but some bus routes have night lines. For a **taxi,** dial 069/230033 or 069/250001.

WHERE TO SLEEP

Frankfurt caters more to wealthy businesspeople than budget travelers. If the hostel's booked, try the cheap pensions in Westend near the Hauptbahnhof.

UNDER DM 80 • Pension Backer. This is the best deal in town other than a hostel (*see below*). It's a short walk to Palmengarten in a safe residential neighborhood. Doubles are DM 60–DM 70. *Mendelssohnstr. 92, tel. 069/747992 or 069/747900. U6 or U7 to Westend; walk NW on Bockenheimer Landstr., left on Mendelssohnstr.*

Pension Bruns. Doubles go for DM 76 in this large, stoic building in the former Jewish quarter. Some rooms have hardwood floors. *Mendelssohnstr. 42, tel. 069/748896. U6 or U7 to Westend; walk NW on Bockenheimer Landstr., left on Mendelssohnstr.*

UNDER DM 100 • Hotel Zur Rose. If your nerves are easily frayed, stay in quiet, green Bornheim. It's away from the sights, but Frankfurt's super-efficient public transport gets you there and back in no time. Doubles start at DM 100. *Berger Str. 283, tel. 069/451762. U4 to Bornheim Mitte; walk NE on Berger Str.*

UNDER DM 140 • Hotelschiff Peter Schlott. The "hotel ship" is a boat anchored where the Nidda river flows into the Main. In the summer, there is a party atmosphere on deck. A room on board costs 65, doubles 115. *Bolongarostrasse in Hoechst, tel. 069/300–4643, fax 069/307671. Bus 53–55, 57, 70.*

Pension Aller. A family-run pension much favored by artists, academics, and Frankfurt trade-fairs attendees, this place has doubles for 135. *Gutleutstrasse 94, tel. 069/252596, fax 069/232330. S-Bahn 16, 19, 21 to Baseler Platz.*

Sophien Hotel. The rooms at this hotel (doubles from DM 125) are spotless and modern, yet homey. *Sophienstr. 36, tel. 069/702034, fax 069/777370. U6, U7, or Tram 19 to Bockenheimer Warte; walk up Zepellinallee, left on Sophienstr.*

HOSTEL

Haus der Jugend (HI). Clean, convenient, and Frankfurt's only true deal, this hostel is located in Sachsenhausen, near major sites and apple wine taverns. The midnight curfew isn't strict. Dorm beds are DM 23 (DM 28 over 20), doubles DM 77, quads DM 33 per person. *Deutschherrnufer 12, tel. 069/619058, fax 069/618257. From Hauptbahnhof, Bus 46 to Frankensteiner Pl. Reception open after 1, lockout 9–1.*

FOOD

This city is home to the *Frankfurter,* a smoked beef or beef-and-pork sausage, and *Grüne Soße,* herb sauce with eggs or potatoes. For your pick of specialty cheese shops, outdoor cafés, and bakeries, head over to **Freßgass'** ("Pig-out Alley"), a posh, tree-lined pedestrian zone that stretches along Große Bockenheimer Straße between Hauptwache and the Alte Oper. To find inexpensive traditional German food and apple wine, visit Sachsenhausen; look for pine wreaths above the door to indicate that apple wine is on tap. The cheapest eats of all (DM 4–DM 8) are found weekdays 11:30–2:30 at the **University Mensa** (U6 or U7 to Bockenheimer Warte); its ground floor cafeteria serves breakfast and lunch daily 7:30 AM–6 PM. You need a local student ID to get the rock-bottom prices, but it costs only a little more without one.

Café Albatros. This cheap hole-in-the-wall, adorned with funky local art, is crammed with university students at lunch. *Kiesstr. 27, Bockenheim, tel. 069/707–2769. U6 or U7 to Bockenheimer Warte; west on Bockenheimer Landstr., left on Kiesstr.*

Café Größenwahn. This cozy Nordend restaurant and bar serves a laid-back thirtysomething crowd enjoying good conversation. Try spaghetti with pesto (DM 12), Greek spinach pie with feta (DM 10), or a pricier seafood dish (from DM 15). *Lenaustr. 79, tel. 069/599356. U5 to Glauburgstr.; walk 3 blocks east to Lenaustr.*

The Frankfurt Flohmarkt (flea market) is among Germany's best. It lines the Main in Sachsenhausen every Saturday morning.

Cafe Karin. This understated café has flair and attracts an eclectic slice of Frankfurt life. This is a great place to breakfast for only a few marks. Cakes and baked goods come from the whole-grain bakery next door. *28 Grosser Hirschgraben, tel. 069/295–217. Cash only.*

Klaane Sachsenhäuser. Locals have been eating typical Frankfurt cuisine in the large beer garden here since 1886. Definitely a must. *Neuer Wall 11, Sachsenhausen, tel. 069/615983.*

Tandure. The aroma of the clay oven—called a *tandure*—wafts through the dining room in this small, affordable Turkish restaurant, decorated with kilims and Anatolian handicrafts. Lamb, marinated and cooked in the *tandure,* is the house specialty. *Wallstr. 10, Sachsenhausen, tel. 069/612–543. Open until midnight.*

Wagner. A Sachsenhausen classic that succeeds in being trendy, touristy, and traditional all at once. It serves the same hearty German dishes as other apple-wine taverns, only better. Try the *tafelspitz mit Frankfurter grüner sosse* (stewed beef with a sauce of green herbs). *Schweizer Strasse 71, Sachsenhausen, tel. 069/612–565. Cash only.*

WORTH SEEING

Most of Frankfurt's attractions lie on or near the Main in a 1-km (½-mi) belt south of Hauptwache. The few rebuilt historical buildings lie in and around the square **Römerberg,** which has been at the heart of city life for centuries: Since 1405, the Gothic three-building **Römer** (City Hall) has overlooked Römerberg's markets and fairs. Frankfurt's seven best museums line the **Museumsufer** on the river's south bank; get a one- or two-day **Frankfurt Card** (DM 10 and DM 15 respectively) at the tourist office for reduced or free admission to most museums, as well as unlimited travel on public transportation in the downtown area and to the airport. Entrance to some museums is free on Wednesday.

DOM ST. BARTHOLOMAUS

The Dom is Frankfurt's biggest church and was the coronation site for a dozen Holy Roman emperors. What really sets this church apart is the 300-ft red sandstone **tower** (DM 3; open Apr.–Oct.). *Römerberg Sq. U4 to Römer. Open daily 9–noon and 2:30–6.*

MUSEUM FUR MODERNE KUNST

The postmodern design of the Museum of Modern Art (open since 1991) provides an in-your-face presentation of the big names in post World War II art (Johns, Warhol, Rauschenberg, Beuys) in airy, angular rooms between Escheresque staircases. *Domstr. 10, north of Römerberg, tel. 069/2123–0447. Admission: DM 7. Open Tues.–Sun. 10–5 (until 7 Sat.).*

MUSEUM JUDENGASSE

This somber museum houses what was left of the old Jewish Quarter after the Nazis laid it to waste. At the center of the exhibit are excavations of homes, a *mikveh* (ritual bath), and the ancient sewer network. The **Jüdisches Museum** (Untermainkai 14–15, tel. 069/2123–5000; Theaterpl. U-Bahn; admission DM 5) documents eight centuries of Jewish life in Germany. Exhibits are in German, but the lists of Jews deported to concentration camps require no explanation. *Kurt-Schumacherstr. 10, at Börnepl., tel. 069/297–7419. From Konstablerwache, south on Kurt-Schumacherstr. Admission: DM 3 (free Sat.).*

MUSEUMSUFER

Museumsufer is the name locals have assigned the string of seven museums on the riverside street **Schaumainkai**. All are open Tuesday–Sunday 10–5 (until 8 Wednesday). Admissions are about DM 4–DM 8. The enormous **Städel** (No. 63, tel. 069/6050980) has one of the best collections of paintings in Germany with works by Rembrandt, Monet, Braque, and Picasso. The **Liebighaus Museum** (No. 71, tel. 069/212–3817) has a vast collection of sculpture displayed in a 19th-century villa and garden. A sure-fire pleaser is the fun **Deutsches Filmmuseum** (No. 41, tel. 069/2123–8830); the museum documents film history, and a theater on the ground floor shows famous and not-so-famous international films. Next door, the **Deutsches Architekturmuseum** (tel. 069/2123–8844) depicts the history of architecture in modern, white exhibition rooms.

AFTER DARK

At night *Apfelwein* (apple wine) taverns, restaurants, and discos transform Sachsenhausen into Party Central, though some locals prefer the nightlife in the city center. Frankfurt is one of Germany's big techno-pop centers, and has tons of discos to prove it. Wherever you go, beer will run about DM 3–DM 6, and the action probably won't start until at least 11 PM. The monthly magazine *Prinz* (available at any kiosk for DM 3.50) has a column called "Freies Theater," which details times and places to catch free comedy, dance, and plays; also check out one of the free monthlies, *Fritz, Strandgut,* or *Skyline.*

When you're ready to hit the discos, take the U-bahn to the world-famous **Dorian Gray** (Airport C, Level 0, tel. 069/690–22121), now part of the rave scene, or **Fantasy Garden** (Seilerstr. 34, tel. 069/285055), which hosts a gay night every Sunday. Every night is gay at **Blue Angel** (Brönnerstr. 17, tel. 069/282772). Nearby **Sinkkasten** (Brönnerstr. 5–9, tel. 069/280–385) is a great place for rock, pop, and African music. It's sometimes hard to get in but worth the effort. For the best jazz in town, head to **Der Frankfurter Jazzkeller** in Kleine Bockenheimer Straße, fondly called *Jazzgasse* (Jazz Lane). If you're in Westend or Bockenheim, check out the nighttime countercultural scene typified by **Casa Nostra** (Konrad-Broswitz-Str. 42, near Kirchpl. U-Bahn, tel. 069/772897) and **Café Exzess** (Leipziger Strasse 91, tel. 069/774670).

NEAR FRANKFURT

MARBURG

Tucked gently into the Lahn Valley about 70 km (42 mi) north of Frankfurt, Marburg boasts narrow cobblestone alleyways, medieval buildings, and a Gothic hilltop castle that escaped destruction in World War II. Philip the Magnanimous established the first Protestant university here in 1527, and ever since, students—such as the brothers Grimm—have been Marburg's driving force. Still unscathed by the blight of large-scale tourism, Marburg has a tolerant and lively atmosphere for a small town.

On the west bank of the Lahn River, Marburg's well-preserved **Oberstadt** is full of half-timbered houses, old buildings with painted posts and buttresses, and plenty of pubs and cafés. Below and north of the Oberstadt lie the coffins, altars, and colorful stained-glass windows of **Elisabethkirche** (corner of Elisabethstr. and Deutschhausstr.; admission DM 3), the oldest Gothic church in Germany. Just a *steep,* winding, 10-minute climb through the Oberstadt away is **Landgrafenschloß,** the enormous castle overlooking Marburg, and a **Museum of Cultural History** (tel. 06421/285871). For city maps (50 Pf) and lodging information, stop at the **tourist office** (Neue Kasseler Str. 1, tel. 06421/201249; open weekdays 8–12:30 and 2–5, Sat. 9:30–noon; closed Sat. off season), right outside the Hauptbahnhof. From here, it's a 20-minute walk (head down Bahnhofstraße and turn left on Elisabethstraße) or a short ride on buses 1–6 to the Oberstadt.

WHERE TO SLEEP • Gästehaus Tusculum (Gutenbergstr. 25, tel. 06421/22778) has doubles for DM 95–DM 125. From the station, take Bus 72 to Gutenbergstraße. The bright, clean **youth hostel** (Jahnstr. 1, tel. 06421/23461; beds DM 24) is on the tree-lined riverbank just 10 minutes from the Oberstadt. From Rudolphsplatz, cross the bridge and follow the path on the right down the opposite riverbank to Jahnstraße.

BADEN-WURTTEMBURG

Baden-Württemburg covers much territory that to most people epitomizes Germany, from Heidelberg's castle to the Mercedes-Benz star. Geographically and economically one of the most important German states, Baden-Württemburg also harbors a rich history (e.g., the oldest university in Germany) and diverse natural beauty: the **Neckar Valley** in the north; Germany's largest lake, the **Bodensee** (Lake Constance), in the south; the **Black Forest** in the west; and the vast, rural **Schwäbische Alb** in the east. In stark contrast are such cities as **Mannheim** and **Stuttgart**, home to many of the cutting-edge, high-tech firms at the center of industrial Germany. Striking a balance between the rural and the industrial are the lively, riverside university towns, **Tübingen** and **Heidelberg**, both of which deserve a few days' exploration. This entire region was created in 1952, when Allied forces lumped together three conservative provinces, hoping to balance the left-leaning, socialist-oriented Ruhrgebiet region to the north. Today Baden-Württemberg is still one of the more conservative regions of Germany, but its diversity—in landscape, cityscape, and people—makes it hard to categorize.

> *More than one Black Forest traveler, driven mad by the din of thousands of cuckoo clocks, has broken down and bought a wood carving of Hansel and Gretel.*

THE BLACK FOREST

Looking like something out of J. R. R. Tolkien's *Lord of the Rings,* the Schwarzwald (Black Forest) is a region of steep hills and deep valleys blanketed with fir and oak. Tourists and locals flock to the forest for its superlative hiking and skiing, and for alpine villages with the kind of jovial friendliness, or *Gemütlichkeit,* that appeals to German travel agencies. It's no surprise, then, that much of the Black Forest has gone full-tilt oompah, particularly in the central Black Forest, where Teutonic kitsch translates into major tourist dollars. Avoid the schlocky tourist towns and you'll meet some of the friendliest and most colorful characters in Germany: These are the people who gave the world some of the wackiest traditional clothing on the planet and many of the fairy tales of brothers Grimm fame. Locals also speak a dialect even Germans have difficulty understanding, and many still live in the sloping wooden houses associated with the region. Train travel through the forest is spectacular, but many towns are served only by bus (Eurail and InterRail passes accepted)—and often slowly and infrequently at that.

FREIBURG IM BREISGAU

Amidst all the German kitsch that floods the Black Forest, Freiburg emerges as a hip, sophisticated, and thoroughly fun city—thanks to the local, centuries-old university. There's also a remarkably lively cultural scene: Talented street musicians, thriving theater, and first-rate concerts are a fact of life here. Blown to bits in World War II, Freiburg has reconstructed many of its most impressive buildings and preserved the historical atmosphere of its *Altstadt* (Old Town)—today a pedestrian-friendly, medieval-meets-modern city center. As the most accessible city in the region, Freiburg is also a perfect base for exploring the villages and hills of the High Black Forest.

VISITOR INFORMATION

Rotteckring 14, 2 blocks from Hauptbahnhof, tel. 0761/388–1880. Open June–Sept., weekdays 9:30–8, Sat. 9:30–5, Sun. 10–noon; shorter hrs off season.

COMING AND GOING

Freiburg's **Hauptbahnhof** serves Frankfurt (2¼ hrs, DM 72), and Hamburg (6–7 hrs, DM 211). Buses to most of the little towns in the Black Forest leave from the **Omnibusbahnhof** (tel. 0761/36172) next to the Hauptbahnhof, and the local **Mitfahrzentrale** (Belfortstr. 55, tel. 0761/19444) is near the university. To reach the center from the station, walk up **Eisenbahnstraße** about 10 minutes. You can get to most parts of the city by **bus** or **tram** for DM 3; when public transportation stops running at 1 AM, call a **taxi** (tel. 0761/24040).

WHERE TO SLEEP

Aside from the institutional **HI hostel** (Kartäuserstr. 151, tel. 0761/67656; beds DM 24.70, DM 20.30, under 26), the cheapest option is **Camping Hirzberg** (Kartäuserstr. 99, tel. 0761/35054; DM 5 per tent plus DM 6 per person), halfway between the hostel and Schwabentor. For the hostel, take Tram 1 (toward Littenweiler) to Römerhof; for the campground, get off at Messplatz. Or try **Hotel Dionysos** (Hirschstr. 2, tel. 0761/29353; doubles DM 70–DM 75), in a beautiful neighborhood south of the center; take Tram 4 to Klosterplatz. A 15-minute walk north of the center on Kaiser-Joseph-Straße is the clean and basic **Hotel Stadt Wien** (Habsburgerstr. 48, tel. 0761/36560 or 0761/39898; doubles from DM 81).

FOOD

The area north of Schwabentor is loaded with an eclectic selection of restaurants. Just outside the Martinstor, in the **Freiburger Markthalle**, more than a dozen food stands serve Chinese, Indian, Italian, Greek, and even Afghan food, usually for around DM 10. Nearby **Freiburger Salatstuben** (Am Martinstor-Löwenstr. 1, tel. 0761/35155) serves healthy, vegetarian food prepared in creative ways—try the homemade whole-wheat noodles with cauliflower in a pepper cream. **Martin's Bräu** (Freßgässle 1, tel. 0761/387–0018) has huge regional entrées for DM 14–DM 20. Choose from 26 pizzas, salads, and pastas at **Firenze** (Friedrichring 5, northern border of city center, tel. 0761/273370). They even bring you a free glass of warm brandy with your check.

WORTH SEEING

The **Münster,** dominated by its 380-ft tower, has been Freiburg's main landmark for more than 700 years. Besides gaggles of tourists, the cathedral's dark interior contains brilliant stained-glass windows, some dating from the 13th century, and 10 richly decorated side chapels. For a view over town—and a close-up of the intricate spire—grit your teeth and climb the tower's 329 steps. On **Münsterplatz** surrounding the cathedral, a daily outdoor **market** offers the best in fresh produce, Black Forest meats and cheeses, flowers, and local handicrafts.

Freiburg's numerous city-run museums are free, with the exception of the **Augustiner Museum** (Augustinerpl., tel. 0761/201–2531; admission DM 4) and its vast collection of 14th- to 20th-century paintings, sculpture, glassware, and furniture, mostly by artists from the upper Rhine region. The nearby **Museum für Neue Kunst** (Marienstr. 10a, tel. 0761/201–2583) emphasizes modern art from southwest Germany. The **Museum für Ur-und Frühgeschichte** (Rotteckring 5, tel. 0761/201–2574; open Tues.–Sun. 9–7) has a ho-hum collection of archaeological artifacts from the area, but its location in the gorgeous neo-Gothic **Colombi Palace** makes it worth a visit. The 13th-century Schwabentor gate houses Freiburg's smallest and quirkiest museum, the **Zinnfigurenklause** (Tin Figure Collection; tel. 0761/24321; admission DM 0.50), a moderately interesting way to spend a half-hour. For a beautiful view of the city and the long valley that runs out of town, cross the overpass and walk up **Schloßberg.**

AFTER DARK

A number of bars, discos, and cafés grace the streets of the university quarter in the southwest corner of the Altstadt; Bertoldstraße, west of Werderring, is littered with alternative cafés and student-filled pubs. For information, grab a copy of *Freizeit & Kultur* at the tourist office. **Club Parabel** (Universitätstr. 3, tel. 0761/30634; closed Mon.–Tues.), one of Freiburg's many hip discos, has gay night on Sunday. **Freiburger Jazzhaus** (Schnewlinstr. 1, tel. 0761/34973) features live blues, folk, Latin, rock, or jazz nearly every night of the week; get listings and tickets (DM 10–DM 40) at the tourist office.

NEAR FREIBURG

TITISEE • A small lake sealed off from the rest of the world by a series of pine-covered hills, Titisee's mystical natural beauty makes you want to wander through the trees wearing nothing but hiking boots. Unfortunately, Never-Never land has a problem with tourists. To get away from the battling rowboats and overcrowded beaches, follow one of the several excellent hiking and biking trails that circle the Titisee;

pick up trail maps at the **tourist office** (between Seestr. and Strandbadstr., tel. 07651/980427) in the Kurhaus (the big building with all the flags). Serious cyclists can rent mountain bikes (DM 25 per day) from **Sporthaus** (Am Postpl., tel. 07651/7494), about 165 ft down Strandbadstraße from the tourist office. Trains travel twice per hour along the beautiful stretch from Freiburg to Titisee (40 min, DM 10)— for great summer hiking or winter skiing, take the train from Titisee to Feldberg-Bärrental and the **Feldberg,** the Black Forest's tallest peak (4,927 ft). The **hostel** there (Paßhöhe 14, tel. 07676/221; beds DM 22, DM 27 over 26) lies within walking distance of the ski lifts (DM 5) and hiking trails; for the hostel, take the bus to Hebelhof from the station.

TRIBERG

Deep, thickly forested valleys surround the town of Triberg, boasting some of the best hiking and biking in southwest Germany. Built on a steep hillside, the town itself has enough attractions to lure busloads of tourists. The biggest draw is the spectacular **waterfall,** which drops 540 ft in seven rocky steps. To see the cascade (DM 2.50), take the path at the top of the main drag, Hauptstraße. The **tourist office** (Luisenstr. 10, tel. 07722/953230) is in the Kurhaus, two blocks from the entrance to the waterfall. You can reach Triberg hourly by rail from Donaueschingen (40 min, DM 12), which is connected to Freiburg.

The **Schwarzwaldmuseum** (Wallfahrtstr. 4, tel. 07722/4434; admission DM 5), one block from the waterfall, possesses a quirky and fascinating collection of Black Forest culture: The museum has hundreds of cuckoo clocks, models of artisans' workshops, and a room designed to look like a mining shaft, full of minerals from the surrounding hills.

WHERE TO SLEEP AND EAT

Triberg's **HI hostel** (Rohrbacher Str. 35, tel. 07722/4110; beds DM 22, DM 27 over 26) is a steep 20-minute hike up Friedrichstraße. In the center of town, **Krone** (Schulstr. 37, tel. 07722/4524; doubles DM 70) has a restaurant serving hearty Black Forest meals. For pizza or pasta (DM 8–DM 15), head to **Pinnochio** (Hauptstr. 64, tel. 07722/4424), also near the top of the hill.

HEIDELBERG

Surrounded by mountains, forests, vineyards, and the Neckar River, Heidelberg has long been considered by travelers to embody the spirit of Germany. Home to the country's oldest university and blessed with a beautiful old town, Heidelberg has been celebrated by virtually the entire 19th-century German Romantic movement and by scores of poets, writers, and composers, such as Goethe, Mark Twain, and Robert Schumann. Far more than a mere museum piece, however, Heidelberg remains a happening college town, with scores of bars, cafés, restaurants, and shops. Its popularity as a tourist destination makes an off season (spring or fall) visit more enjoyable.

BASICS

The **tourist office** (tel. 06221/19433; open Mon.–Sat. 9–7, Sun. 10–6) is in front of the Hauptbahnhof. The **main post office** (Belfortstr. 2; postal code 69115) is also nearby. The **American Express** office (Brückenkopfstr. 1–2, at Theodor-Heuss-Brücke, tel. 06221/45050) is open weekdays 9:30–6, Saturday 10–1.

COMING AND GOING

Frequent **rail** service joins Heidelberg with Frankfurt (50 min, DM 23) and Stuttgart (1¼ hrs, DM 30). For information and schedules on the **ferries** that ply the Neckar, stop by the tourist office (*see above*). The Neckar River runs along the northern edge of the Altstadt, which is bisected by the **Hauptstraße,** a 3-km (2-mi) pedestrian zone. Most of the major attractions lie on or near Hauptstraße and especially near **Marktplatz.** From the Hauptbahnhof, hop on anything but S4 to reach the western end of Hauptstraße (at Bismarckplatz); take Bus 11 or 33 to reach the eastern end (at Kornmarkt or Karlstor). Single rides on any **bus** or **S-Bahn** within Heidelberg cost DM 3, and day tickets are DM 8.50. To take advantage of the beautiful bike paths in the surrounding countryside, head to **Fahrrad Per Bike** (Bergheimer Str. 125, tel. 06221/161148), which rents bikes for DM 15–DM 20 per day.

WHERE TO SLEEP

Trying to find a cheap room in Heidelberg—especially during the summer—is a royal pain in the butt. Get a free list of hotels and private rooms from the tourist office. If everything below is packed, consider staying in one of the small idyllic towns farther up the Neckar river—Mosbach, Hirschhorn, Neckarge-münd, medieval Bad Wimpfen—or downstream in more industrial Mannheim.

Astoria. Jovial owners run this gorgeous ivy-covered building in a tranquil neighborhood near the city's center. Splurge for doubles at DM 90–DM 110. *Rahmengasse 30, between Ladenburgerstr. and Schröderstr., tel. 06221/402929. From Hauptbahnhof, S1 to Ladenburgerstr.*

Hotel Elite. These beautiful, spacious rooms 4 blocks south of Bismarckplatz are a great deal for groups of three or four: Two people in two double beds pay DM 95, but each additional person pays only DM 15. *Bunsenstr. 15, tel. 06221/25734. From Hauptbahnhof, Bus 21 to Hans-Böckler-Str.; turn right on Bunsenstr.*

Hotel Jeske. This is the cheapest place in town, right in the heart of the Altstadt. No reservations are accepted; phone as soon as you get into town—check-in is at 11:3Q AM. Doubles, triples, or quads cost DM 24 per person. *Mittelbadgasse 2, off Marktpl., tel. 06221/23733. From Hauptbahnhof, Bus 33 to Kornmarkt. Closed late Nov.–early Jan.*

HOSTEL • Jugendherberge Heidelberg (HI). If you can score a room here, you'll get a clean, cheap night's sleep. Get a key to stay out past 11:30 curfew. Beds with breakfast are DM 19.80. *Tiergartenstr. 5, tel. 06221/412066. From Hauptbahnhof, Bus 33 to Jugendherberge (last bus 11:50 PM). Reception open 7:30–9 and 3–11:30, lockout 9–1. Laundry.*

CAMPING • There are two campgrounds facing each other across the Neckar River, about 5 km (3 mi) east of the city center: **Camping Haide** (where Ziegelhausen Landstr. becomes Kleingemünd Landstr., tel. 06223/2111) charges DM 7.50 per person, DM 6 per tent, and DM 2 per car; **Camping Heidelberg-Schlierbach** (Schlierbacher Landstr. 5, tel. 06221/802506) charges DM 10 per person, DM 6 per tent, and DM 3 per car. To get here, take Bus 35 to Orthopädische Klinik and follow the signs under the pedestrian underpass.

FOOD

Hundreds of diverse restaurants blanket the area around Hauptstraße. For cheaper food, try a supermarket chain like **Nanz** (Hauptstr. 17 and 116); or the **open-air market,** held on Marktplatz Wednesday and Saturday 7–noon, and on Friedrich-Ebert-Platz Tuesday and Friday 7–noon. Heidelberg's two Mensas are in the town center: **Marstall** (Marstallstr. 1–3, tel. 06221/542678) is the better of the two. You can get a guest coupon for DM 8.

Goldener Stern. At this no-frills Greek restaurant on the Neckar, the souvlaki (DM 13.80) and moussaka (DM 14.80) won't disappoint you. *Lauerstr. 16, west of Alte Brücke, tel. 06221/23937. Open daily 5 PM–midnight.*

Higher Taste. At midday, the Hare Krishna house restaurant has all-you-can-eat Indian buffet (DM 18). *Kurfürsten-Anlage 5 (entrance behind building), near Landhauserstr., tel. 06221/165101. Open Mon.–Sat. 11 AM–2:30 PM, Sun. 3 PM–late evening.*

Schnookeloch. This picturesque and lively old tavern dates from 1407 and is inextricably linked with Heidelberg's history and its university. Look for men both old and young, with scars on their cheeks. There is still handful of students who duel with swords, crazy as it might sound. Every evening a piano player chimes in. *Haspelgasse 8, tel. 06221/14460.*

Vetters Brauhaus. Delicious and filling German meals for less than DM 15 and strong home-brewed beer are the big draws at this unpretentious eatery. *Steingasse 9, off Marktpl., tel. 06221/16585.*

Zum Roten Ochsen. Many of the oak tables here have initials carved into them, a legacy of the thousands upon thousands who have visited Heidelberg's most famous and time-honored old tavern. Over many, many decades people as well known as Bismarck, Mark Twain, and John Foster Dulles, may have left their mark—they all ate here. *Hauptstr. 217, tel. 06221/20977. Cash only. Closed Sun., holidays, and mid-Dec.–mid-Jan.*

WORTH SEEING

ALTSTADT • Heading east on Hauptstraße toward the castle, you'll find the baroque palace housing **Kurpfälzisches Museum** (Hauptstr. 97, tel. 06221/583402; open Tues. and Thurs.–Sun. 10–5, Wed. 10–9), Heidelberg's leading museum. Most of the museum's history exhibits are in German, and there's a DM 1.50 English brochure only for the archaeology section. Admission is DM 5. Farther down Hauptstraße to the right is **Universitätsplatz,** where you'll find the oldest surviving building of the **Alte Universität,** Germany's oldest. Behind the university is the **Studentenkarzer** (Augustinergasse 2, tel. 06221/542334; open Tues.–Sat. 9–5; admission DM 1.50), where students were locked up for offenses ranging from drunkenness to distribution of political pamphlets.

The **Haus zum Ritter** (Hauptstr. 178, tel. 06221/1350) is the only renaissance building to have survived all of Heidelberg's wars and invasions intact. Across the Marktplatz, **Hercules Brunnen** (Hercules' Fountain) marks the spot where, until 1740, petty criminals were caged and whirled around in front of a taunting public—think twice before jaywalking. Also on the square is the **Heiliggeistkirche** (open Mon.–Sat. 10–5, Sun. 1–5). Originally a richly decorated Catholic church (1400), its stern interior is the product of fires, war, and the Reformation. North of Marktplatz and dwarfed by its own twin-tower gate is the stone bridge **Karl-Theodor-Brücke** (a.k.a. Alte Brücke), which was built around 1788 after eight wooden predecessors fell to various hazards. Across the Alte Brücke on Schlangenweg, the **Philosophenweg** (philosophers' path) has been trodden by the likes of Georg Hegel and Max Weber—hence the name. Gorgeous views of the river and castle, the ruins of **St. Michael's Basilica** and **St. Stephen Cloister,** and a Nazi-era amphitheater await at the top.

HEIDELBERGER SCHLOSS • Sitting on a ridge above Heidelberg, the grandiose, well-preserved ruins of the castle date from as early as the late 15th century, though most of the complex was built in Renaissance and baroque styles. In the late 17th century, French troops attacked the Schloß, leaving it in a state from which it never fully recovered.

To reach the Schloß, walk up one of the two steep paths that begin south of the Kornmarkt, or ride up the **Bergbahn** funicular (DM 4.50 round-trip), which begins in the basement of Hotel am Schloß (Zwingerstr. 22, at Burgweg). Meandering around the castle grounds is free, but admission to the courtyard runs DM 2, and it's an additional DM 4 to get into the castle proper for one of the required tours. In the basement of the Schloß is the esoteric **Deutsches Apothekenmuseum** (German Pharmaceutical Museum), with instruments and medications (e.g., dried horse testicles, Egyptian mummy hair) used by doctors and pharmacists in the 16th–19th centuries. There's also a reconstructed 18th-century apothecary's shop. *Tel. 06221/538414 for castle. Open daily 8–6.*

AFTER DARK

The magazine *Meier* (DM 2) and the less-comprehensive *Fritz* (free) list bars, restaurants, and goings on; get the publications at record shops and cafés.

BARS AND CLUBS • Heidelberg nightlife is concentrated in the area around the Heiliggeistkirche (Church of the Holy Ghost), in the Old Town. Don't miss a visit to one of the old student taverns to drink wine or beer. There are no better places to try than **Zum Roten Ochsen** and **Schnookeloch,** both of which have been in business for several centuries (*see* Food, *above*) and have the atmosphere to prove it. More modern hangouts can be found in the dozen or more bars in Untere Strasse, which runs parallel between Hauptstrasse and the Neckar river, starting from Market Square. Spots on the fringe include **Sonder Bar** (Untere Str. 13, tel. 06221/25200; closed Sun.), a small, sweaty, smoky bar with 100 brands of whiskey and Pink Floyd tunes in the background. Further afield, **Ziegler-Bräu** (Bergheimer Str. 1b, tel. 06221/25333) hosts live bands on Friday and Saturday nights (cover DM 10–DM 20) or top-of-the-charts dancing in its back room. **Cave 54** (Krämergasse 2, tel. 06221/27840) is the oldest jazz "club" in Germany; the doors open at 9 PM and there's dancing 12:30 AM–3 AM. The **Schwimmbad Music Club** (Tiergartenstr. 13, near hostel, tel. 06221/470201; cover DM 7–DM 10) is the best spot to catch underground bands.

STUTTGART

Stuttgart's star began to rise in 1883, when Gottlieb Daimler invented the gas-powered engine in a nearby suburb. The Industrial Revolution pushed the city into the machine age, through two world wars and utter destruction, and, over the past 30 years, back to prominence. Stuttgart remains one of Germany's top industrial and technological centers (i.e., it's utterly lacking in historical interest). The capital of Baden-Württemberg has used its wealth to become a center of the graphic and performing arts, compensating for its lack of historical sights with a host of excellent museums and galleries.

BASICS

The **tourist office** (Königstr. 1a, tel. 0711/222–8240; open May–Oct., weekdays 9:30–8:30, Sat. 9:30–6, Sun. 11–6; shorter hrs off season) is in front of the Hauptbahnhof. **American Express** (Lautenschlagerstr. 3, tel. 0711/18750) is open weekdays 9:30–5:30, Saturday 9:30–12:30.

COMING AND GOING

Trains connect Stuttgart with Frankfurt (1½ hrs, DM 53 Heidelberg (1 hr, DM 28), and Munich (2 hrs, DM 62). The nearby **Busbahnhof** has service only to small nearby towns.

GETTING AROUND

Exit the underground passage from the Hauptbahnhof and you'll practically be in Stuttgart's center. Ahead of you to the right lies the city's thriving business and financial district. Beginning at the tourist office and running southwest for a few miles is **Königstraße,** the city's main commercial artery. This wide pedestrian zone and its offshoots offer rows of department stores, sidewalk cafés, street performers, and strolling couples. Roughly halfway down Königstraße is Stuttgart's main square, the **Schloßplatz.**

Within the city center (zone 1), a **single-ride ticket** on trams or the U-Bahn costs DM 2.80 (DM 1.90 for "Kurzstrecke" or rides under 2 km/1 mi). A **four-ride ticket** costs DM 10.20; a **Tageskarte** (Day Card) is available for DM 18.50 and can be used by up to four persons. Between midnight and 5 AM, watch for the purple-and-yellow signs marking **Nachtbus** (Night Bus) stops. The tourist office has maps and schedules. For a **taxi,** dial 0711/566061.

WHERE TO SLEEP

If everything's booked, you can get a list of budget accommodations from the tourist office, or head to **Tramper Point** (Wiener Str. 317, tel. 0711/817–7476; U6 to Sportpark Feuerbach; open late June–Aug.); here, you can get a maximum of three nights' sleep for DM 10 in a giant tent. For city-style camping, hit **Cannstatter Wasen** (Mercedesstr. 40, 15 min east of center, tel. 0711/556696; DM 9 per person, DM 6 per tent, DM 6 per car), along the Neckar River; women traveling solo should be careful staying here. Two clean and cheap options are **Gästehaus Garni Eckel** (Vorsteigstr. 10, tel. 0711/290995; doubles DM 75–DM 90) and **Hotel-Restaurant Lamm** (Karl-Schurz-Str. 7, tel. 0711/262–2354; doubles DM 95).

HOSTELS • Jugendgästehaus Stuttgart. Impeccable rooms, pleasant atmosphere, and an unbeatable location: You'll find them all here. Beds are DM 35–DM 40. *Richard-Wagner-Str. 2, tel. 0711/241132. U15 (toward Heumaden) to Bubenbad. Laundry.*

Jugendherberge Stuttgart (HI). This is a typical hostel with the bonus of a great view. Beds are DM 27. The curfew is 11:30. *Haußmannstr. 27, tel. 0711/241583. U15 (toward Heumaden) to Eugenspl.; walk down Kernestr., right onto Werastr., up stairs on right. Reception open noon–11, lockout 9–noon.*

FOOD

If you're looking for something quick and cheap, head to the **Königstraße** pedestrian zone and keep your eyes peeled for Imbiß stands. Get groceries at the enormous indoor market, the **Markthalle** (between Marktpl. and Karlspl.; open weekdays 7–6, Sat. 7–2) or in the basement of the **Kaufhalle** department store at Königstraße 19.

Litfass bei Ali. Come here for Swabian or Turkish dishes and the best *Käsespätzle* (cheese noodles) in town. Local bands play on weekends. *Eberhardstr. 37, in Schwaben-Zentrum, tel. 0711/243031.*

Max and Moritz. Good, cheap pizzeria with outside seating. Pizzas DM 10–DM 15. *Geißstr. 3–5, tel. 0711/247818. From Schloßpl., south on Königstr., left on Fritz-Elsas-Str., left on Steinstr., right on Geißstr.*

WORTH SEEING

Postwar plans to turn Stuttgart into a hypermodern German city were countered with more conservative calls to rebuild from the blueprints of the past. The area around the **Schloßplatz**—crowned by the **Jubiläumssäule** tower and bordered by the enormous baroque government offices of the **Neues Schloß**—reflects the concessions made to both sides. Squaring off from across Königstraße is the modern, neoclassical stock exchange and shopping arcade, **Königsbau.** To the north, two contemporary art museums are housed in the 20th-century **Kunstgebäude** (tel. 0711/216–2188; admission free; closed Mon.). To the south is the bastion of Stuttgart's past, the **Altes Schloß,** whose Württembergisches Landesmuseum (tel. 0711/279–3400; admission DM 5,) stonily guards the Württemberg crown jewels and other historical artifacts.

The free **Mercedes-Benz Museum** (Mercedesstr. 136, tel. 0711/172–2578; open Tues.–Sun. 9–5) traces the history of the automobile as well as the development of ship and plane engines; take S1 (toward Plochingen) to Neckarstadion and follow the signs. Don't leave the museum without the "You Need a Mercedes" brochure. If you prefer drinking to driving, hit the **Schwäbisches Brauereimuseum** (Robert-Koch-Str. 12, tel. 0711/737–0201; U-Bahn or S-Bahn to Vaihingen), which traces the history of beer from Mesopotamian times to the present. Tastings, sadly, are not free. A must-see is the impressive **Staatsgalerie** (Konrad-Adenauer-Str. 30–32, tel. 0711/212–4050; admission DM 5; open Wed. and Fri.–Sun. 10–5, Tues. and Thurs. 10–8), one of Germany's finest art museums.

AFTER DARK

The local grunge set hangs at **Palast der Republik** (Friedrichstr. 27, tel. 0711/226–9887) until the wee hours. **Amadeus** (Charlottenpl. 17, tel. 0711/292678) is a quiet bar with an incongruous mix of button-downs and T-shirts. If you don't want to end the evening, join the grimy crew at the 24-hour **Bierteufel** (Eberhardstr. 47, near Marktpl., tel. 0711/242185).

NEAR STUTTGART

TUBINGEN

Tübingen, on a stretch of the Neckar River lined with weeping willows, has enough beautiful old buildings to make you feel like you've been transported back in time. But this cobblestoned city's university life, along with the dress and speech of its students (who make up one third of Tübingen's 75,000 residents), will jolt you back to the 20th century. Add a thriving nightlife and a gateway to the great outdoors and you've got one of the most inviting university towns in Germany. The town's two main squares are **Marktplatz** and **Holzmarkt,** both lined with timber-frame buildings, including the eye-catching **town hall.** On Münzgasse, just off Holzmarkt, are the original university buildings. Tübingen's most appealing attraction is the well-preserved **Bebenhausen Kloster** (tel. 07071/61265; admission DM 4), which creates a vivid picture of former monastic life in the rolling green hills 5 km (3 mi) north of Tübingen's center; from the Hauptbahnhof, take Bus 7955 or 7600 to Waldhorn. To get a taste of Tübingen's after-dark scene try **Pfauen** (Kornhausstr. 1, tel. 07071/23095), or dance away a theme night (African, Funk, '70s, etc.) at **Zentrum Zoo** (Schleifmühleweg 86, tel. 07071/42048) or at **Patty** (Schlachthausstr. 9, 07071/51612), a very popular club in a former factory right on the Neckar.

VISITOR INFORMATION • *An der Neckarbrücke, between the station and town center, tel. 07071/91360. Open weekdays 9–6, Sat. 9–2.*

COMING AND GOING • Tübingen is one hour from Stuttgart (DM 15) by train. From the station, head right to Karlstraße and left across the bridge. The old section of town is to your left, and the university is 2 km (1 mi) ahead.

WHERE TO SLEEP • Alongside the Neckar and a five-minute walk from the Altstadt, the **HI hostel** (Gartenstr. 22/2, tel. 07071/23002) has creaky beds for DM 24 and laundry facilities; catch Bus 11 (DM 2.60) to Jugendherberge. On the north bank of the river, west of the Altstadt, **Camping am Neckar** (Rappenberghalde 61, tel. 07071/43145) charges DM 9.50 per person, DM 5.50 per tent, and DM 5 for a car if you have one.

THE BODENSEE

Spanning some 80 km (50 mi) in length and 14 km (9 mi) in width, the Bodensee (Lake Constance), is the largest lake in the German-speaking world. Forming a natural border between Germany, Austria, and Switzerland, the lake offers warm weather, cool waters, busy resorts, and ancient cities encircled by gently sloping green hills. You can swim, boat, windsurf, waterski, or scuba dive in the lake, or hike and bike around it. Of the Bodensee towns, Konstanz is the liveliest, and Lindau and Meersburg the most picturesque. All of the beauty comes with a price tag, however, which you can slash by calling ahead and reserving a spot at one of the hostels or campgrounds.

Ships are the most pleasant and, owing to the lake's long, lanky line, sometimes most efficient way to travel around the lake. Deutsche Bundesbahn's **Bodensee-Verkehrsdienst** (tel. 07531/281389) has regular service between the Bodensee's worthwhile towns, and if you flash a Eurail or DB pass, you get 50% off the regular ticket price; with InterRail you ride free. Another great option is to rent a bike (about DM 10–DM 15 per day) and zoom around the lake on the paved bike paths. Maps for touring are available from the tourist offices, and you can throw your pack in the long-term storage available at the train stations in Überlingen, Konstanz, and Lindau.

KONSTANZ

Divided by the Rhine as it exits the western end of the Bodensee, the city of Konstanz consists of two parts: the large medieval Altstadt, on the otherwise Swiss shore of the lake, and on the narrow peninsula opposite, the primarily residential section of town dotted with scenic grassy beaches and mansions. This university city is now the lake's most popular and, by far, the hippest vacation destination. Konstanz's central monument, the 11th-century **Münster,** on the north side of the Altstadt, is topped with a spire (open Mon.–Sat. 10–6, Sun. 1–6; closed on rainy days) that affords groovy, dizzying views of the city and the Bodensee area.

The Romanesque **Stephanskirche,** a block south of the Münster, received a late Gothic facelift and contains a rococo choir and a series of early 20th-century paintings depicting the stations of the cross. On the peninsula side of town, between the main bridge connecting Konstanz's two halves, runs **Seestraße,** where the wealthy wander and the young hang out on a stately promenade of neoclassical mansions with views of the Bodensee.

Freibad Horn (Eichhornstr. 89, tel. 07531/63550), the largest and most popular beach in Konstanz (due in no small part to its nude area), is at the tip of the peninsula; take Bus 5, which runs every half hour from the post office, to the last stop. At a shack just north of the beach you can rent Windsurfers for DM 10 per hour or DM 35 per day. For city maps and information on lake cruises, stop by the **tourist office** (Konzilstr. 5, next to Hauptbahnhof, tel. 07531/284376).

COMING AND GOING

Only a few **trains** depart each day to Frankfurt (4–5 hrs, DM 105), Stuttgart (3 hrs, DM 53), and Radolfzell (15 min, DM 6); for other towns on the German side of the Bodensee, connect in Radolfzell. **Ferries** (Hafenstr. 6, tel. 07531/281373) run from the harbor behind the Hauptbahnhof to Friedrichshafen, Lindau, Mainau, Meersburg, Überlingen, and Bregenz, Austria.

WHERE TO SLEEP

HI-Jugendherberge Otto-Moericke-Turm (Allmanshöhe 18, tel. 07531/32260; beds DM 26.50) is in a decaying 10-story tower whose top-floor common room has an unbeatable view of the lake; take Bus 4 to Jugendherberge. Otherwise **Campingplatz Bruderhofer** (Fohrenbühlweg 50, tel. 07531/31388; DM 6.50 per person, DM 5.50 to 8 per tent, DM 5 per car) has 180 tightly packed sites.

MUNICH

In the midst of staunchly conservative, provincial Bavaria, Munich (*München*) towers as a paragon of serene, liberal urbanity. However, this city—founded in the 12th century by Henry the Lion—played a central role in the grim events of recent history. The Nazi party got its start here, and in 1923 Hitler led the failed Beer Hall Putsch. After gaining power, Hitler (who considered Munich the spiritual capital of National Socialism) set up the first German concentration camp at nearby Dachau (*see* Near Munich, *below*). Following the war, with Berlin isolated in the East, Munich became as much a center of cultural and financial power as was possible in the decentralized West.

In these postunification days, Munich's star is threatened as Berlin throws its replenished clout around in grand Prussian fashion. In one area, however, Munich will never be beat—beer. It is not uncommon to see 75-year-old women, clad in the gendered equivalent of Lederhosen, polishing off a second liter by 9:30 AM, and Munich's university can boast of a world-class department of beer science. If by some cruel twist of nature you detest beer, worry not. The majestic facades, the awesome cultural cachet, the merry-making, mirth, and unassuming *Gemütlichkeit* (good-naturedness) of Munich's inhabitants should make you feel more than welcome and enchanted. Munich also has some of the best museums in Germany, and the city sustains vibrant theater and eclectic clubbing and live music scenes.

BASICS

VISITOR INFORMATION

EurAide. Ostensibly for train information only, owner Alan Wissenberg speaks fluent English and will dole out other information, including a highly informative English-language pamphlet for first-time visitors to Munich. The office has a message and mail service. *Hauptbahnhof, at Track 11, tel. 089/593889. Open May–Oct., daily 7:30–noon and 1–6.*

Fremdenverkehrsamt. The "real" tourist office does tourist office–type things and has *Monatsprogramm* (DM 2.50), which lists hotels, restaurants, and social events. *Hauptbahnhof, Bahnhofpl. 2 (next to the ABR travel agency), tel. 089/239–1256. Open Mon.–Sat. 9–9, Sun. 11–7.*

AMERICAN EXPRESS
Promenadepl. 6, tel. 089/290900. Open weekdays 9–5:30, Sat. 9–12:30.

CONSULATES
Canada: *Tal 29, tel. 089/290650. Open Mon.–Thurs. 9–noon and 2–5, Fri. 9–noon and 2–3:30.* **Ireland:** *Mauerkircherstr. 1a, tel. 089/985723. Open Mon.–Thurs. 9–noon and 2–4, Fri. 9–noon.* **United Kingdom:** *Bürkleinstr. 10, tel. 089/211090. Open Mon.–Thurs. 8:30–noon and 1–5, Fri. 8:30–noon and 1–3:30.* **United States:** *Königinstr. 5, tel. 089/28880. Open weekdays 8 AM–11 AM.*

EMERGENCIES
There are international **pharmacies** at Ludwigs-Apotheke, Neuhauserstr. 11 (tel. 089/260–3021) and Europa-Apotheke, Schützen Straße 12 (tel. 089/595423).

MAIL
Have your friends address mail to: Your Name, Postamt 32 Arnulfstrasse, Poste Restante, 80321 München. *Arnulfstrasse 32, tel. 089/54540. Open weekdays 8–8, Sat. 8–noon.*

COMING AND GOING

BY BUS
Europabus, operated by **Deutsche Touring** (in Hauptbahnhof, tel. 089/591824), offers service throughout Europe: Berlin (DM 129); Paris (DM 125); Budapest (DM 110). Europabus's "Romantic Road" trip (*see* Bavaria, *below*) is free for rail-pass holders; it begins in Füssen and ends in Frankfurt, but you can hop on in Munich for free.

BY PLANE
The **Franz Josef Strauss Airport** (tel. 089/9752–1313) is 28 km (17 mi) northeast of the city and is served by many major airlines including **Lufthansa** (tel. 089/977–2544). S8 links the airport with the Hauptbahnhof.

BY TRAIN
The **Hauptbahnhof** (main train station) lies west of the city center. Destinations from Munich include Amsterdam (9 hrs, DM 231), Berlin (7 hrs, DM 171), Budapest (9 hrs, DM 138), Paris (9 hrs, DM 108), Prague (6¾ hrs, DM 86), and Vienna (5½ hrs, DM 70).

GETTING AROUND
From the Hauptbahnhof, Schützenstraße (which becomes Neuhauserstraße, then Kaufingerstraße) leads to busy Karlsplatz (also known as Stachus) and **Marienplatz,** the heart of the city. North of the center are the university and lively **Schwabing,** a former artists' and musicians' quarter now full of yuppies, outdoor cafés, and nighttime fun. The main strip cutting through the area is Ludwigstraße, which turns into Leopoldstraße past the university. Cross the Isar River at Ludwigsbrücke to reach **Haidhausen,** a lively right-bank district now rivalling Schwabing and still undiscovered by tourists.

BY BIKE
Cycling is about the most efficient way to get around town, and marked lanes are everywhere. You can rent bikes for DM 10 per two hours or DM 20 per day from **Radius Touristik** (in Hauptbahnhof, Track 31, tel. 089/596113; open daily 10–6); from **Englischer Garten** (entrance at Veterinärstr. and Königinstr., tel. 089/282500; open Wed.–Sun. 10:30–6 in good weather); or from S-Bahn stations Dachau, Herrsching, and Starnberg (reduced price with valid ticket). Pick up a copy of "Radl-Touren," a booklet with suggested biking tours, at the tourist office. **Mike's Bike Tours of Munich** (tel. 089/651–4275 to book in advance) offers a three-hour, DM 25 guided cycling tour (in English). Tours leave at 11:30 AM and 4 PM from the Spielzeug museum on Marienplatz.

BY PUBLIC TRANSIT
Tickets for all public transportation (buses, trams, U-Bahn, and S-Bahn) cost DM 3.40 for two hours, as long as you travel only in one direction and stay within one zone (only the far-lying suburbs are in the outer zone). If you take a *Kurzstrecke* (short trip), defined as four stops maximum, only two of which can be on the subway, tickets cost DM 1.70. Day passes come in two flavors: **Single-Tages-Karte** (DM 8)

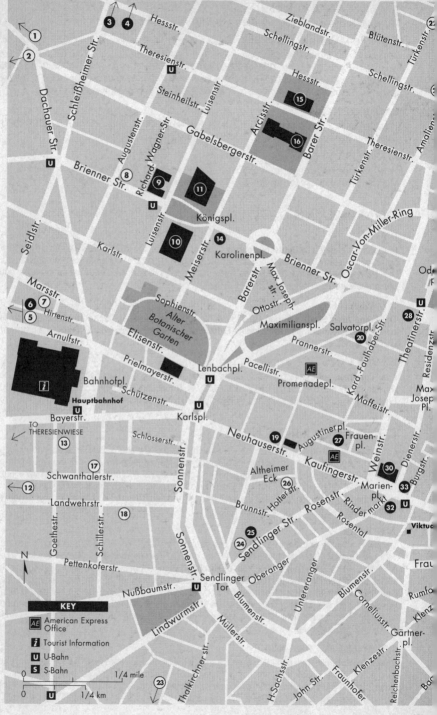

MUNICH

① ②

③ ④ Hessstr.
Zieblandstr.
Schellingstr.
Blütenstr.
Türkenstr.
②

Theresienstr. U

Schellingstr.

Steinheilstr.
Luisenstr.
Hessstr.

Arcisstr. ⑮
Barer Str.
Theresienstr.
Amalienstr.

Gabelsbergerstr. ⑯

Dachauer Str.
Schleißheimer Str.
Augustenstr.
Richard-Wagner-Str.

Brienner Str. U ⑧
⑨
⑪
Türkenstr.

Königspl.
Luisenstr. U

Karlstr.
⑩
Meiserstr.
⑭

Karolinenpl.

Oscar-Von-Miller-Ring

Brienner Str.

Od
r

Seidlstr.

Marsstr.
⑥ ⑦
⑤
Hirtenstr.

Sophienstr.
Alter
Botanischer
Garten

Barerstr.
Max-Joseph-str.
Ottostr.

Maximilianspl.

U ⑱

Salvatorpl.
⑳

Theatinerstr.
Residenzstr.

Max
Josep
Pl.

Arnulfstr.
Elisenstr.
Prielmayerstr.
Lenbachpl.
Pacellistr.

Prannerstr.
AE
Promenadepl.

Kard.-Faulhaber-Str.
Maffeistr.

Bahnhofpl.
Schützenstr.
U

Hauptbahnhof

Bayerstr. U
Karlspl.

TO
THERESIENWIESE
⑬

Schlosserstr.
Sonnenstr.

Neuhauserstr. ⑲
Augustinerpl.
⑳ ⑦
Frauen-
pl.

Weinstr.
Dienerstr.
Burgstr.

Schwanthalerstr. ⑰

⑫

Landwehrstr.

Goethestr.
Schillerstr.
⑱

Altheimer
Eck
⑳ ⑥
Brunnstr.
Hotterstr.

Kaufingerstr.
AE

Rosenstr.
Rinder markt

⑳
Marien-
pl.
⑳
⑳

Viktua

Rosental

N

Pettenkoferstr.

Sonnenstr.

⑳
⑳
Sendlinger Str.
Oberanger

Untereranger

Frau

Nußbaumstr.

Sendlinger
Tor
U
Blumenstr.

Blumenstr.
Cornelius str.
Klenzestr.
Gärtner-
pl.

Rumfo

Klenz

Lindwurmstr.
Müllerstr.

Thalkirchnerstr.
H.Sachsstr.
Jahn Str.
Fraunhofer
Reichenbachstr.

Bac

⎡ **KEY** ⎤
AE American Express
Office
i Tourist Information
U U-Bahn
S S-Bahn

0 _____ 1/4 mile
0 U _____ 1/4 km

⑳

282

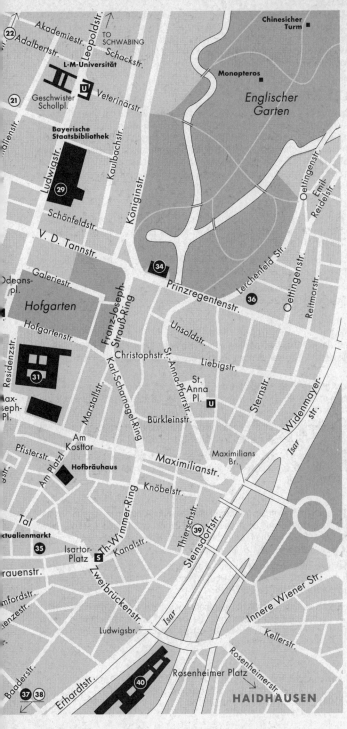

Sights ●

Alte Pinakothek, **16**
Altes Rathaus, **33**
Asamkirche, **25**
Bayerisches National-
museum, **36**
BMW Museum, **3**
Deutsches
Museum, **40**
Frauenkirche, **27**
Glyptothek, **11**
Ludwigskirche, **29**
Michaelskirche, **19**
Neue
Pinakothek, **15**
Neues Rathaus, **30**
Olympiapark, **4**
Peterskirche, **32**
Residenz, **31**
Salvatorkirche, **20**
Schloß
Nymphenburg, **6**
Staatliche Antiken-
sammlungen, **10**
Staatliche
Graphische
Sammlung, **14**
Staatsgalerie
Moderner Kunst, **34**
Städtische Galerie
im Lenbachhaus, **9**
Theatinerkirche, **28**
Tierpark
Hellabrunn, **37**
Z.A.M., **35**

Lodging ○

4 you münchen, **7**
Camping München-
Thalkirchen, **23**
Campingplatz
München-
Obermenzing, **5**
CVJM (YMCA)
Jugend-
gästehaus, **18**
Hotel Atlanta, **24**
Hotel Kurpfalz, **12**
Hotel-Pension
Beck, **39**
Jugendherberge, **2**
Kapuzinerhölzl, **1**
Marienherberge, **13**
P. am Kaiser-
platz, **22**
P. Augsburg, **17**
P. Diana, **26**
P. Frank, **21**
P. Hungaria, **8**
Y. H. Thalkirchen, **38**

and **Partner-Tages-Karte** (DM 12), which is good for two adults, three children, and one dog. The **Streifenkarten** (DM 13) is a book of 10 tickets; cross off one strip for a short trip, two for a normal fare. All tickets are available from machines and bus and tram drivers; validate them in the blue machines on station platforms. After 1 AM (2 AM Friday and Saturday nights), a limited number of night buses is available. If you need a **taxi,** dial 089/19410 or 089/21610.

WHERE TO SLEEP

The area around the Hauptbahnhof is a convenient base for exploring the city and has a large concentration of inexpensive pensions, but it's also one of the seediest parts of town. In any area, expect to pay at least DM 85–DM 100 per double (add DM 35–DM 45 for each extra person); reservations *at least* a day in advance are vital. In upscale Schwabing, try the 10 comfortable rooms of **Pension am Kaiserplatz** (Kaiserpl. 12, tel. 089/349190; U3 or U6 to Münchner Freiheit; doubles DM 75–DM 85). Both EurAide and the tourist office book rooms (DM 5–DM 6 fee). Prices below do not include breakfast or showers, usually DM 4 extra.

NEAR THE HAUPTBAHNHOF
Hotel Kurpfalz. You'll find all the amenities (TV, room service, etc.) of a high-priced hotel here. The staff is young, amiable, and English-speaking. Doubles are DM 89–DM 129. Reserve in advance. *Schwanthalerstr. 121, tel. 089/540–9860. Tram 18 or 19 or Sbahn to Hackerbrücke.*

Pension Augsburg. This cheap, plain pension just minutes from Hauptbahnhof has a three-flight climb to reception. Doubles are from DM 66, triples from DM 96. *Schillerstr. 18, tel. 089/597673.*

Pension Hungaria. In a smart neighborhood north of Hauptbahnhof, the sunny rooms at this pension come at reasonable rates. Doubles are DM 85. *Brienner Str. 42, near Augustenstr., tel. 089/521558. U2 to Königspl.*

CITY CENTER
Hotel Atlanta. Management actually likes backpackers at this little hotel. Doubles are DM 95–DM 12, including breakfast. *Sendlingerstr. 58, enter through Raab shoestore, tel. 089/263605. U1 or U2 to Sendlinger Tor.*

Hotel-Pension Beck. At Beck you'll find sleek rooms and a prime location in Munich's "museum quarter," known as Lehel. Doubles are DM 80–DM 90. *Thierschstr. 36, tel. 089/220708. S-Bahn to Isartor or Tram 17 stops outside the door.*

Pension Diana. Americans get discounts on these spacious third-floor rooms. Doubles go for DM 98, including breakfast. *Altheimer Eck 15, near Marienpl. and Karlspl., tel. 089/260–3107.*

Pension Frank. This little hotel consists of cheap rooms occupied by fashion models, student groups, and backpackers. Doubles cost DM 95; a bed in a dormitory-style room costs DM 40. *Schellingstr. 24, tel. 089/281451. U3 or U6 to Universität.*

HOSTELS
4 you münchen. This eco-hostel is two minutes from the Hauptbahnhof. Cork floors, unfinished furnishings, and organic grub make up the setting. Dorm beds are DM 25, doubles DM 35. A set of organic cotton sheets costs an extra DM 4. For a touch of luxury book a room with private bathroom; a double costs DM 99. Add DM 6 for breakfast. *Hirtenstr. 18, tel. 089/552–1660.*

CVJM (YMCA) Jugendgästehaus. Reserve at least a week in advance unless you feel lucky. Adjoining restaurant serves dinner (Tues.–Fri.) and free breakfast. Doubles cost DM 82, triples DM 42 per person. There's a 12 AM curfew. *Landwehrstr. 13, tel. 089/552–1410.*

Jugendherberge (HI). Three short subway stops from Hauptbahnhof you'll find this clean hostel, with a 1 AM curfew. Reservations by fax are required, and you must be under 27 and a member of a national youth-hostels association. Beds (including sheets and breakfast) are DM 25.50. *Wendl-Dietrich-Str. 20, tel. 089/131156, fax 089/167–8745. U1 to Rotkreuzpl.*

CAMPING
Camping München-Thalkirchen. Central and crowded, this campsite is 4 km (2½ mi) from the city center. Sites cost DM 7 per tent plus DM 7.80 per person. *Zentralländstr. 49, tel. 089/723–1707. U3 to Thalkirchen (Tierpark); then Bus 57 to end (last bus midnight).*

Campingplatz München-Obermenzing. Situated in a huge park 3,000 ft from the beginning of the Stuttgart-bound Autobahn, this camping ground has sites for DM 7.50 per tent plus DM 7.50 per person. *Lochhausenerstr. 59, tel. 089/811–2235. S-Bahn to Pasing; then Bus 76 to Lochhausener Str. (last bus 1 AM).*

Kapuzinerhölzl. Germany's Biggest Slumber Party: a spot in this circus tent with blankets and mats, plus a hot shower, costs just DM 13 per night, DM 17 with a cot. A passport is required and you might want to lock up your valuables at the station. *Franz-Schrank-Str. 8, tel. 089/141–4300. Tram 17 (toward Amalienburg) to Botanischer Garten. Open late June–Aug.*

FOOD

Bavarian specialties are the way to go in Munich. Some of the best are *Bratwurst* (grilled or fried pork sausages); *Leberkäs* (warm slabs of ground beef, bacon, and pork served with sweet mustard); *Obatzta* (cheese mixed with chopped onions, egg yolk, paprika, and other spices); *Radi* (thinly sliced white radish, dipped in salt and often eaten as a snack in a beer garden); and *Dampfnudeln* (sweet dumplings in vanilla sauce).

The cheapest places to go for food include butcher shops (for pre-made sandwiches at DM 3–DM 5.50), salad bars, and chain restaurants, especially Bella Italia, Café Rischart, Münchner Suppenküche, and Wienerwald. The colorful **Viktualienmarkt,** Munich's best-known open-air food market, is held Monday–Saturday on the square, which hosted public executions during the Middle Ages.

If you have a ticket, you can spend the night in the train station without being hassled by the fuzz, but there's no guarantee the resident weirdos won't decide you're their new best friend.

The city center boasts the densest population of typically Bavarian restaurants, a lot of them at reasonable prices. Restaurants in Schwabing tend to be pricier and chic. The university area has lots of smoky, relatively cheap, youthful restaurant-pubs; **Gaststätte Engelsburg** (Türkenstr. 51, tel. 089/272–4097) serves pizza and Bavarian fare for DM 9–DM 15 and a daily three-course lunch (DM 10–DM 13). Many ethnic restaurants line the streets of Haidhausen, although prices aren't particularly low. The *Mensas* (student cafeterias) on Arcisstraße (U2 to Königspl.) and Leopoldstraße (U3 or U6 to Universität) offer large lunches from 11 to 1:45 for a few marks. Buy the colored meal tokens before you get in line.

UNDER DM 15 • Augustiner Bräustuben. This cozy beer hall is frequented by Münchners. Try juicy *Schweineschnitzel* (pork Schnitzel; DM 9.80) and an Augustiner Weißbier (DM 4.20). Bavarian specialties run about DM 12. *Landsbergerstr. 19, at Holzapfelstr., tel. 089/507047.*

Fraunhofer. This lively, untouristy restaurant with adjoining theater is where earthy intellectuals socialize and drink over hearty meals, both vegetarian and porky. *Fraunhoferstr. 9, tel. 089/266460.*

UNDER DM 20 • Haidhauser Augustiner. This restaurant-bar with huge menu of salads, pasta, and meat dishes has a classy beer-hall feel—definitely a place to sink into. Excellent *Putenschnitzel* (turkey; DM 14.90) will fill your belly. *Wörthstr. 34, tel. 089/480–2594. U-Bahn or S-Bahn to Ostbahnhof.*

Tattenbach. Slap bang in the middle of museumland, this is the ideal place to grab a cheap, filling lunch in between gallery-browsing. Lunchtime menus (weekdays only) cost DM 11–DM 13. Prices rise in the evenings, but so does the young-crowd mood. *Tattenbachstr. 6, tel. 089/225268. U-Bahn to Lehel.*

Zum Franziskaner. Expensive but excellent Bavarian, pasta, or vegetarian dishes are available here at a decent price, (DM 14–DM 20) and wursts for (DM 7–DM 13). *Residenzstr. 9, tel. 089/231–8120.*

CAFES

Many of Munich's cafés double as bars and evening hangouts, especially on Leopoldstraße (*see* After Dark, *below*). A diverse, largely bohemian clientele descends on **Baadercafé** (Baaderstr. 47, tel. 089/201–0638; U1 or U2 to Fraunhoferstr.) for coffee and inexpensive food. Dress in black for **Café Größenwahn** (Lothringerstr. 11, tel. 089/448–5035), a café with a cool quotient almost befitting its name (Megalomania). A diverse crowd, including a gay presence enjoys the rooftop terrace of **Glockenspiel** (Marienpl. 28, enter on Rosenstr., tel. 089/126–4256).

BEER GARDENS

To keep their kegs cool during hot summers, brewers used to store them under shady chestnut trees. This practice evolved into the beer garden, where everyone shares long tables and laps up liters during dragging summer days. At most gardens, you can bring your own snacks or have a meal there. When weather permits, gardens stay open from 9 or 10 in the morning to 10 or 11 at night. A *Maß* is the standard measure (about 1 quart) of beer.

The **Hofbräuhaus** (Am Platzl 9, tel. 089/221676) doesn't need much explanation; come only to see where the "ugly American" stereotype comes from. Instead, head to **Augustinerkeller** (Arnulfstr. 52, west of Hauptbahnhof, tel. 089/594393), where you can drink the city's best brew among leafy chestnut trees, a local clientele of all ages, and brass bands. **Waldwirtschaft** (G.-Kalb-Str. 3, tel. 089/795088; S-Bahn to Großhesselohe)—called plain WaWi—was the site of the great Munich Beer Demo of 1994, when 20,000 protested a court order requiring that it close early. There certainly were grounds for protest: terrific suds, spare ribs (DM 15), and live jazz on Sunday (until 8 PM or 9:30 PM). The **Seehaus** in the Englischer Garten is Munich's most gorgeous beer garden—perfect for sunsets.

WORTH SEEING

FRAUENKIRCHE

Newly renovated for the 500th anniversary of its consecration, Munich's most famous cathedral, the Frauenkirche (Church of Our Lady), is more impressive than ever. Begun in 1468, the main body of the late Gothic brick church was built in only 20 years. The cathedral underwent a 10-year restoration after being severely damaged by wartime bombing; now the simpler, modern interior sharply contrasts with the weathered and war-scarred brick exterior. On the church's stone floor near the entrance is the imprint of a foot, known as *Der Schwarze Tritt* (the Dark Footprint). According to legend, the Devil checked out the new church right after its completion and couldn't see any of the huge 73-ft windows from where he was standing. Thinking that a building without windows was useless, he stamped his foot in triumph—leaving the print—and left. Stand at the footprint and play Satan for a moment, then take a step forward and see how architect Jörg von Halsbach outsmarted the Evil One. Even if you don't go inside, you can't miss the two bulb-top towers, added almost 75 years after the cathedral was complete. An elevator carries you to the top of one of the towers for a great view of Munich and the Bavarian countryside all the way to the Alps. *Frauenpl., near Marienpl. Tower admission: DM 4. Open Apr.–Oct., Mon.–Sat. 10–5. Closed Sunday and holidays.*

MARIENPLATZ

Named for the Mariensäule, the gilded statue of Virgin and child standing in the square's corner, Marienplatz has been Munich's main square since the city was founded in 1158. Bordering it on the north is the **Neues Rathaus** (New Town Hall), a neo-Gothic building constructed between 1867 and 1908. It's probably best known for its tower's **Glockenspiel,** Europe's fourth-largest carillon. Every day at 11 AM and noon (also 5 PM May–Oct.), tourists flock to the square to see the mechanical figures spinning around to folk-music chimes. For DM 3, tower enthusiasts can make the 281-ft climb (Mon.–Thurs. 9–4, Fri. 9–1; closed weekends).

The **Altes Rathaus** (Old Town Hall) stands in the eastern corner of the square. Destroyed during World War II, it was reconstructed according to the original 15th-century Gothic design. In its tower is the **Spielzeugmuseum** (tel. 089/294001; admission DM 5; open daily 10–5:30), exhibiting 200 years of European and American toys; unfortunately, you can't play with any of them.

RESIDENZ

For more than six centuries this palace served as the Wittelbachs' residence; it was transformed into a museum two years after the last Bavarian king, Ludwig III, abdicated in 1918. Over the centuries, the complex has gone through a number of construction phases, resulting in the mix of architectural styles you see today. The two tours of the palace cover only half the rooms and are in German; guide yourself through the beautiful rooms with the "Residenz Guidebook" (DM 5), available at the entrance. Buy a separate ticket to see the Wittelsbach treasures displayed in the **Schatzkammer** (Treasury; Residenzstr. 1, tel. 089/290671), which holds a blinding collection of jewel-studded crowns, swords, house altars, icons, and more. *Max-Joseph-Pl. 3, tel. 089/290671. U-Bahn to Odeonspl. Admission: DM 5. Open Tues.–Sun. 10–4:30.*

SCHLOSS NYMPHENBURG

The Schloß was originally a small summer villa constructed in 1663 by Prince Ferdinand Maria to pla cate his homesick Italian wife, Henriette. Some features of the complex, including the canals that wind through the grounds (meant to recall Venice for poor Henriette), date from this time, though today's palace is the result of more than 200 years of additional construction. Check out Ludwig I's **Schön- heitsgalerie** (Gallery of Beauties), which has 36 portraits of the king's pick of Munich's most beautiful women. The former royal stables, in the southern wing of the palace, have become the **Marstallmuseum** (Museum of Royal Carriages).

You could spend the whole day wandering around the beautiful 500-acre **Nymphenburg Park,** lined with classically French gravel paths and low, excessively trimmed hedges, and graced by three pavilions and a miniature palace. The **Amalienburg,** an 18th-century hunting lodge, is one of the finest examples of the rococo style; don't miss the kennels, a prime example of luxury living, doggie style. *Tel. 089/ 179080. U1 to Rotkreuzpl.; then Tram 12 to Schloß Nymphenburg. Admission: DM 6. Open Apr.–Sept., Tues.–Sun. 9–12:30 and 1:30–5; Oct.–Mar., Tues.–Sun. 10–12:30 and 1:30–4.*

TIERPARK HELLABRUN

Extending over 90 acres, Munich's world-famous zoo has enjoyed tremendous success in breeding endangered species. *Tierparkstr. 30, tel. 089/625–0824. U3 to Thalkirchen. Admission: DM 9. Open Apr.–Sept., daily 8–6; Oct.–Mar., daily 9–5.*

Do the late-night postindustrial thing at Internet-Café (Nymphenburger Str. 145, at Landshuter Allee, tel. 089/129–1120).

CHURCHES AND CHAPELS

Asamkirche, named for the two brothers who designed it, is modest on the outside, but open the door and you enter a baroque vision of paradise—complete with an overwhelming combination of intricate stuccowork, swirling frescoes, and tons of gilding. *Sendlingerstr. 62. U-Bahn to Sendlinger Tor.*

The claim to fame of the curious neo-Byzantine/early Renaissance parish church, **Ludwigskirche,** is its mammoth fresco of the Last Judgment, second in size only to Michelangelo's version in the Sistine Chapel. *Ludwigstr. 22.*

When the tower of **Michaelskirche** collapsed in 1590, only seven years after the building's completion, Duke Wilhelm V interpreted the disaster as a sign from heaven that the church wasn't big enough. He remedied that problem, and now spends his time getting dusty (along with Mad Ludwig II) in the church's **crypt.** *Neuhauser Str. 52. Open weekdays 10–1 and 3–4:45, Sat. 10–3.*

Peterskirche, built on top of an earlier church that existed 100 years *before* Munich's founding, sports a baroque interior with a late-Gothic high altar. Labor up to the top of the tower (affectionately dubbed *Alter Peter,* or Old Peter) for a view that extends as far as the Alps. On the way down, wave to Saint Munditia, the jeweled skeleton in the glass coffin with hand raised in eternal salutation. *Rindermarkt, near Marienpl. Tower admission: DM 2.50. Open weekdays 9–6, Sat. 8:30–6, Sun. 10–6.*

Salvatorkirche, a late Gothic brick church built in 1494 by the city architect Lukas Rottaler, is now the main Greek Orthodox Church of Munich. The architect Cuvilliès is buried in its yard. *Salvatorpl. 17, near Odeonspl.*

King Ferdinand Maria commissioned the building of **Theatinerkirche** to honor the birth of his and Henriette's long-awaited son and heir. The church ignited a local fascination with and emulation of the baroque style. Under the High Altar there's a crypt containing more Wittelsbachs, including Ferdinand Maria, Max Emanuel, and King Maximilian I. *Theatinerstr. 22, at Odeonspl.*

MUSEUMS AND GALLERIES

Exploring Munich's offbeat museums, you may discover you're not the only one harboring a secret fascination with chamber pots, sewing machines, or corkscrews. Many of the museums are closed Monday but open late one or two nights each week. State-run museums are free on Sunday. A number of museums are clustered together, so you can plot a museum-hopping route and see things you wouldn't normally seek out.

The ultracool, high-tech **BMW Museum** (Petuelring 130, tel. 089/3822–3307; U2 or U3 to Olympiazentrum; admission DM 5.50) uses videos, slides, and its gorgeous collection of cars, engines, and cycles to chronicle the technical development, social history, and future plans of the Bayerische Motoren Werke

̷EER IS GOOD FOR WHAT ALES YOU

In Bavaria, the beer-drinking and -producing capital of the world, beer is sometimes cheaper than bottled water, is respected as "liquid bread," is consumed by the liter, and is often brewed by monks and nuns. It is also protected by the world's most ancient food-purity law, according to which only the purest ingredients—water, hops, yeast, and barley—are acceptable for the fine art of beer brewing. The only exception is made for the delicious, light Weißbier, in which wheat is substituted for barley. When ordering the standard pale beer, ask for a "Helles"; for dark beer, "Dunkles." To toast, clink glasses at the bottom, looking your fellow drinkers in the eyes.

(Bavarian Motor Works). Call ahead for a factory tour (tel. 089/3895–3306), given weekdays at 9:30 and 1:15. Together, the **Glyptothek** (Königspl. 3, tel. 089/286100) and the **Staatliche Antikensammlungen** (Königspl. 1, tel. 089/598359) comprise Germany's largest collection of classical art. Both are closed Monday and each costs DM 6 (free Sun.); combined admission is DM 10. The **Staatliche Graphische Sammlung** (Meiserstr. 10, tel. 089/559–1490; U2 to Königspl.; closed Sat.–Mon.) has 300,000 drawings and graphics from the 14th through 20th centuries, including works by Dürer and Rembrandt. The **Zentrum für Außergewöhnliche Museen** (Westenriderstr. 26, tel. 089/290–4121; S-Bahn to Isartor; admission DM 8) includes the world's first museums devoted to the pedal car, the chamber pot, the lock, and the Easter Bunny.

ALTE PINAKOTHEK • Reopened in 1997 after extensive renovations, this first-class art gallery is now splendidly equipped to show off the old masters collected by the Wittelsbach rulers of Bavaria. Their favorite was the huge, flesh-filled canvases of Rubens, but the museum also creates a showcase for such leading German painters as Dürer and Altdorfer. *Barerstr. 27, tel. 089/2380–5195. U2 to Theresienstr. Admission: DM 7. Open Tues.–Sun. 10–5 (until 8 Tues. and Thurs.).*

BAYERISCHES NATIONALMUSEUM • This gigantic museum (under renovation until the year 2000) covers the history of Bavarian culture. You can still peruse some of the items on display, including tapestries, arms and armor, religious artifacts, and pottery. Art is displayed in rooms designed to reflect the period and style. *Prinzregentenstr. 3, tel. 089/211241. U4 or U5 to Lehel. Admission: DM 5, (free Sun.). Open Tues.–Sun. 9:30–5.*

DEUTSCHES MUSEUM • The world's largest science and technology museum (13 acres, six stories) is a playground of discovery for the kid in you. Among the 16,000 items on display are the first Mercedes-Benz, the original airplanes of the Wright brothers, and tons of hands-on gadgets. The nearby **Forum der Technik** shows IMAX films. *Museuminsel 1, tel. 089/21791. S-Bahn to Isartor or Tram 18 to Deutsches Museum. Admission: DM 10, DM 3 extra for planetarium. Open daily 9–5.*

NEUE PINAKOTHEK • This is the modern partner of the Alte Pinakothek just across the street. The low-built brick exterior hardly prepares you for the light-flooded galleries and their opulent collections of late-19th- and 20th-century art. The French impressionists are particularly well represented; you'll find Monet's famous *Waterlilies.* Even the artistically impaired will recognize Van Gogh's *Vase of Sunflowers* and *View of Arles. Barerstr. 29, enter on Theresienstr., tel. 089/2380–5195. U2 to Theresienstr. Admission: DM 7 (free Sun.). Open Tues.–Sun. 10–5 (until 8 Tues. and Thurs.).*

STAATSGALERIE MODERNER KUNST (HAUS DER KUNST) • This pillared, neoclassical building, one of Munich's few remaining Hitler-era constructions, displays works from all the major 20th-century art movements. You can see entire rooms devoted to fauvism and expressionism, cubism, surrealism, 1940s–1960s abstract art, pop art, and chromatic painting, to name just a sampling. *Prinzregentenstr. 1, tel. 089/2112–7137. U4 or U5 to Lehel. Admission: DM 6 (free Sun.). Open Tues.–Sun. 10–5 (until 8 Thurs.).*

STADTISCHE GALERIE IM LENBACHHAUS • The Lenbachhaus displays the work of the *Blaue Reiter* (Blue Rider) group. This group, which took its name from the painting *Le cavalier bleu*, by group leader Wassily Kandinsky, was a German expressionist circle (1911–1914) centered for some time in Schwabing. *Luisenstr. 33, tel. 089/2333–2000. U2 to Königspl. Admission: DM 8. Open Tues.– Sun. 10–6.*

PARKS AND GARDENS

With 14,000 plants, including orchids, cyads, alpine flowers, and rhododendrons, as well as steamy greenhouses full of cacti and exotic greens, Munich's **Botanischer Garten** (Schloß Nymphenburg, Menzinger Str. 63, tel. 089/1786–1310; admission DM 3) is one of the best in Europe. The **Englischer Garten** is the world's largest and oldest recreational city park; 5 km (3 mi) of woodland, open meadows, ponds, brooks, streams, and a willow-fringed lake, stretching from the city center to the northern city limits. It was laid out more than 200 years ago by a refugee from the American War of Independence, Count Rumford. On sunny days, the park teems with sports games, picnics, cyclists, music groups, and nude sunbathers. There's a Japanese Tea House along a tributary to the Isar, and the Greek pavilion in the southern part of the park has a nice view of the cityscape.

A completely new suburb was built for the Olympic Games in 1972 and today the **Olympiapark** (Olympiapark stop on the U3 or U8) is a popular recreation area, with all its Olympic installations still intact. Take an elevator ride up the 960-ft high Olympia Tower for a panoramic view of the site. A DM 1 ticket will get you into the empty stadium, but the best way to soak up the atmosphere is to join the local soccer fans when one of the two major teams, Bayern München or 1860 München, are playing at home.

CHEAP THRILLS

Check the *Monatsprogramm* (available at the tourist office) for classical-music performances labeled "Eintritt Frei" (free admission); you can hear some great organ concerts this way. The last Wednesday of each month, you can get into live music clubs like **Unterfahrt** (*see* After Dark, *below*) for free. Also, all state-run museums (e.g. Neue Pinakothek and Deutsches Museum) are open to the pfennig-less masses on Sunday. From the middle of September to the first week of October, Munich's world-(in)famous **Oktoberfest** rages for 15 days.

AFTER DARK

Pick up a copy of *In München* or *Munich Found* at the tourist office for comprehensive listings. For a self-guided after-dark tour of Munich, cruise Leopoldstraße in Schwabing, or, for more alternative company, try Türkenstraße and café/bars like **Türkenhof** (Türkenstr. 78, tel. 089/280–0235) or **Café Puck** (Türkenstr. 33, tel. 089/280–2280). Regardless of your sexual orientation, you should get at least a glimpse of the city's bustling gay nightlife, centered around Gärtnerplatz and on Hans-Sachs-Straße; it's one of Munich's most happening scenes. Saturday after 1 AM, practically the entire gay and lesbian population under 30 shows up to dance at **Soul City** (Maximilianpl. 5, near Karlspl., enter on Max-Joseph-Str., tel. 089/595272; cover DM 10). **Sub** (Müllerstr. 43, near Sendlinger Tor, tel. 089/595272) is both a gay resource center and groovy bar.

DANCING

Nachtwerk (Landsberger Str. 185, tel. 089/570–7390), located in a huge warehouse, is a pretension-free alternative to Munich's "exclusive" clubs. If you can look hip long enough to pass the bouncers, you can boogie to techno, house, and trance at **Parkcafé** (Sophienstr. 7, tel. 089/598313; U2 to Königspl.; cover DM 8–DM 15; closed Mon.). **Pulverturm** (Schleißheimer Str. 393, tel. 089/351–9966; U2 to Harthof; cover DM 5–DM 10; closed Mon.) leans toward hard-core, psychedelic, independent tunes, and reggae (Sat.), and is beloved for its beer garden and outdoor dance floor.

LIVE MUSIC

The center of Munich's alternative scene, **Feierwerk** (Hansastr. 39–41, tel. 089/769–3600; U-Bahn to Heimeranpl.) hosts live music and theater every night at 9. If you don't mind being body-slammed by packs of sweaty Irish rugby players you can enjoy free live Irish music every summer night at 9 at **Shamrock** (Trautenwolfstr. 4, tel. 089/331081; U3 or U6 to Giselastr.). Jazz junkies will dig **Unterfahrt** (Kirchenstr. 96, tel. 089/448–2794; U-Bahn or S-Bahn to Ostbahnhof; cover DM 10–DM 15; closed Mon.). The best deal is the jam session every Sunday at 9 PM for DM 5. Enjoy a post-dinner beer over live jazz in the stylish café-bar **Kaffee Giesing** (Bergstr. 5, tel. 089/692059; U1 or U2 to Silberhornstr.).

CLASSICAL MUSIC AND THEATER

The **Bayerische Staatsoper/Nationaltheater** (Max-Joseph-Pl., tel. 089/2185–1920) features ballet and opera; the box office (tel. 089/221316) is at Maximilianstraße 11. The **Staatstheater am Gärtnerplatz** (Gärtnerpl. 3, tel. 089/201–6767; U1 or U2 to Fraunhoferstr.) offers opera, as well as musicals and operettas. Ballet and musicals play at the **Deutsches Theater** (Schwanthalerstr. 13, near Karlspl., tel. 089/5523–4360).

CINEMA

Look for the designations "OF" and "OmU," which mean "original language" and "original language with subtitles," respectively. **Cinema** (Nymphenburger Str. 31, tel. 089/555255), **Museum-Lichtspiele** (Lilienstr. 2, tel. 089/482403), and **Theater Werkstatt-Kino** (Fraunhoferstr. 9, tel. 089/260–7250) all feature English-language films.

NEAR MUNICH

DACHAU

Although the 1,200-year-old town of Dachau attracted hordes of painters and artists from the mid-19th century to World War I, the town's name will forever be associated with Germany's first concentration camp. Opened in 1933, the camp greeted more than 206,000 political dissidents, Jews, clergy, and other "enemies" of the Nazis with the promise that ARBEIT MACHT FREI (WORK BRINGS FREEDOM). The camp's watchtowers and walls remain. Nazi authorities systematically killed and worked or starved to death more than 32,000 prisoners here before American soldiers liberated the camp in 1945; even afterward, many of the newly freed perished from disease and the effects of prolonged starvation. Through photos, letters, and official documents, the **museum** chronicles the rise of the Third Reich and the cruel working and living conditions endured by the camp's prisoners (brief English captions accompany most exhibits). A 22-minute **film** is shown in English at 11:30 and 3:30 and is sometimes repeated between these two showings. *Alte Römerstr. 75, tel. 0813/11741. Admission free. Open Tues.–Sun. 9–5.*

COMING AND GOING • From Munich's city center, take S2 (toward Petershausen) to Dachau (20 min); then take Bus 722 (DM 1.70) to *Gedenkstätte* (Memorial). The S-Bahn ride is an interzonal trip—make sure to buy the right ticket.

AROUND BAVARIA

Sprawled across some 27,000 square miles, Bavaria's diverse, romantic landscape beckons outdoorsy folks, history freaks, and those who still believe in fairy tales. Its four main cities—Nuremberg (in the northern region known as Franconia), Augsburg (in the western region of Bavarian Swabia), Regensburg (in East Bavaria), and Munich (in Upper Bavaria)—are also historic and cultural giants, making a trip to Bavaria diverse, educational, and potentially very, very long. Bavaria was ruled by the royal Wittelsbach Dynasty for seven centuries, beginning in 1180 as a duchy presented to Otto von Wittelsbach by the Emperor Barbarossa, and ending in the turbulent post–World War I period with the forced abdication of the last Wittelsbach monarch, King Ludwig III. Although the Prussian military and political strategist Otto von Bismarck yanked the land from Ludwig II, incorporating it into his Confederation of Northern German States, Bavaria held steadfastly to its distinct traditions and dialect. Even to this day, Bavaria's official name is the Free State of Bavaria.

Northerners—the so-called Prussians—consider Bavarians less refined, too loud, and provincial, whereas Bavarians describe northerners as stuffy, highfalutin, and boring. Northerners will sternly remind you that Bavaria is *not* Germany; Bavarians will say that's all right with them. Strangely enough, these most independent-minded of Germans have supplied the most common images foreigners have of the country—lederhosen, brass bands, beer gardens, castles, and Oktoberfest. Its contradictions make Bavaria the ideal place to look for all that you expect, hope for, and dread from Germany: It's got the scenery, the castles, the lingering legacy of Nazism, the Alps, beer, and history.

AUGSBURG

Founded by two stepsons of Roman Emperor Augustus in the year 15 BC and the oldest of Bavaria's cities, Augsburg is a lot like the boy in elementary school who hit puberty at age eight. The envy of the other kids, Augsburg sprouted a whisker or two, attracted all the babes and 15th-century merchants, and, with the help of sugar daddies like the Fugger clan, became *the* center of attention and continental high finance. The Fuggers were to Augsburg what the Medicis were to Florence: They bankrolled much of the Renaissance-style old town and erected in 1519 what is now the world's oldest extant welfare housing project, modestly dubbed the *Fuggerei*. Much to the city's chagrin, Augsburg is no longer a man among boys, but merely an oft-overlooked stop on the so-called Romantic Road. Come nightfall, when the tourists have cleared the streets, follow the town's students to their evening haunts, or lounge undisturbed by the fountains and think happy thoughts among the blackened monuments to Augsburg's glory days.

VISITOR INFORMATION

The main tourist office, the **Verkehrsverein** (Bahnhofstr. 7, tel. 0821/502070; open weekdays 9–6), is 990 ft from the Hauptbahnhof. Pick up the *Radwegkarte,* a free map of bicycle routes, and the indispensable English-language pamphlet "Augsburg and its Sights" (DM 1) at the **information office** (tel. 0821/502–0724; open weekdays 9–6, Sat. 10–4, Sun. 10–1; shorter hrs off season) on Rathausplatz.

COMING AND GOING

Augsburg has frequent train connections to Munich (40 min, DM 16) and Regensburg (2½ hrs, DM 36). To reach the city center, head east down Bahnhofstraße and veer left onto Annastraße. **Buses** and **trams** (in operation 5 AM–midnight) cost DM 1.70.

WHERE TO SLEEP

Rooms in decently located hotels and guest houses start at DM 65 for doubles. Try **Jakoberhof** (Jakoberstr. 39–41, tel. 0821/510030; doubles DM 75–DM 100), a simple but cozy guest house near the Fuggerei, about a 10-minute walk from the city center. **Lenzhalde** (Thelottstr. 2, tel. 0821/520745; doubles DM 75) is just behind the Hauptbahnhof. Warm showers and a washing machine await at **Campingplatz Ludwigshof** (tel. 08207/1077; closed Nov.–Mar.), which charges DM 10 per site plus DM 8 per person; take Bus 305 to Ludwigshof. Both tourist offices will also book you a room in a private house for a DM 3 fee.

Augsburg's busy **HI hostel,** a three-minute walk from the Dom, is the cheapest and easiest place to crash. Expect a 1 AM curfew. Travelers over 26 are accommodated if there's space. Beds for DM 25 include breakfast; sheets are DM 5.50. *Beim Pfaffenkeller 3, tel. 0821/33909. Tram 2 to Stadtwerke; walk toward Dom, right on Inneres Pfaffengäßchen. Reception open 2–4 and 8–10. Closed Dec. 20– Jan. 20.*

FOOD

Street stands and Imbißes line Rathausplatz and nearby Maximilianstraße. For fresh produce, meats, and cheeses, check out the **Stadtmarkt** (city market), open weekdays 7–6, Saturday 7–noon. Enter the market from Fuggerstraße, Annastraße, or Ernst Reuter Platz. **Fuggerkeller** (Maximilianstr. 40, tel. 0821/ 510031), a traditional Swabian restaurant housed in the cellars of the former Fugger family home, is good but a little expensive (around DM 20).

König von Flandern. All-you-can-eat side dishes accompany the daily *aus der Pfanne* (pan-fried; DM 9) specials; also try a colorful salad plate (DM 9.30) or *Bayernteller* (Bavarian food sampler). *Karolinenstr. 12, tel. 0821/158050. Cash only.*

Welser Kuche. If you're feeling hungry and a little lonely in Augsburg, call the Welser Kuche's number and ask if there's a place free at one of the roisterous banquets that take place most nights beneath the vaulted ceilings of this medieval-style eatery. The eight-course tuck-in, served by pretty wenches at gnarled oak tables, will last you through the following day and perhaps the one after, so it's a jolly (in every sense) good value. *Maximilianstr. 83, tel. 0821/96110.*

WORTH SEEING

Augsburg may be a large city, but its historic town center is reasonably compact and easily covered on foot. An English-language **walking tour** (DM 9) leaves from outside the Rathaus daily at 2 PM mid-May–mid-October. East of the tourist office is the 14th-century **Heilige Annakirche** (Annastr.), where

BAUHAUS IN DESSAU

Dessau's saving grace is the architectural legacy of Bauhaus design. In a nutshell, Bauhaus aimed to do away with the distinction between design (artists) and creation (craftsmen), and to make each product affordable. Its clean lines of steel, concrete, and glass were conducive to industrial and prefab construction. Star instructors were mostly abstract painters, such as Klee and Kandinsky. To visit the Bauhaus Dessau museum (Gropiusallee 38, tel. 0340/65080; admission DM 4, open Tues.–Sun. 10–5), take one of the hourly trains from Halle (50 min, DM 13) or Berlin (2 hrs, DM 28).

Martin Luther stayed while meeting with Cardinal Cajetan, the papal legate sent to convince Luther of the error of his ways. Near the northern end of Annastraße, **Rathausplatz** marks the historic heart of Augsburg. The square is dominated by the **Perlachturm** tower (admission DM 2; open Apr.–Oct., daily 10–6); the tower's Glockenspiel is played at noon and 5 PM. Adjacent to the tower is the massive **Rathaus** (City Hall). Check out the third-floor **Goldener Saal** (admission DM 2), a humongous, glittering ballroom; if you stand just outside the doorway, you can get a good peek without paying. Wander down Maximilianstraße from Rathausplatz and you'll find the **Schaezler Palace** (Maximilianstr. 46, tel. 0821/324–2175; admission DM 4; open Wed.–Sun. 10–4) and the German baroque art gallery inside.

The **Brechthaus** (Rain 7, tel. 0821/324–2779; admission DM 2.50) houses exhibits dedicated to the Augsburg-born dramatic genius Bertold Brecht, best known for his plays *Mother Courage* and *The Threepenny Opera*. It's open Wednesday–Sunday 10–4. To view relics of Augsburg's past, check out the **Maximilian Museum** (Philippine-Welserstr. 24, tel. 0821/324–2174), or mingle with the Roman artifacts in the **Römisches Museum** (Dominikanergasse 15, tel. 0821/324–2172). Each cost DM 4 and are open Wednesday–Sunday 10–4. The beautiful Jugendstil **synagogue** (Halderstr. 6–8, tel. 0821/575041; admission DM 3; open Tues.–Fri. 10–3, Sun. 10–5) documents the history of Augsburg's Jewish community.

DOM ST. MARIA • Augsburg's Dom escaped the bombing that flattened most of the city in World War II, so the town's believers erected a faux-pinecone–top tower at the cathedral's western entrance (the pinecone is the city symbol). The cathedral's real draw is the art inside: Besides five fantastic altarpieces by Hans Holbein the Elder, there's a stunning cycle of stained glass that dates from the 11th century. *Open Mon.–Sat. 7–6, Sun. noon–6.*

FUGGEREI • The Fuggerei, a 10-minute walk east of the city center, is the world's oldest subsidized housing. This tranquil complex was originally built in 1519 by the Fugger family to accommodate the city's poor, and it continues to serve that purpose. As long as you're a native of Augsburg, Catholic, and destitute by no fault of your own—*and* you agree to pray for the Fuggers on a daily basis—one of these simple but comfortable homes can be yours for the low price of "one Rheinish Guilder" per annum, set according to the 1873 exchange rate at DM 1.72. You can see an original apartment in the **Fuggerei Museum**. *Museum admission: DM 1. Open daily 9–6; in winter, weekends only.*

AFTER DARK

Once the sun sets, cruise down Maximilianstraße for a taste of Augsburg's lively café scene. For brews, your best bet is the beer garden at **Brauereigasthaus Drei Königinnen** (Meister-Veits-Gäßchen 32, tel. 0821/158405; closed Mon.). Augsburg's student pubs are concentrated in the alleys and streets behind the Rathaus. The Irish pub **Fuki's Fuchsbau** (Bei St. Ursula 1, tel. 0821/154296) has a mellow patio area in a quiet alley off Maximilianstraße. Heilig-Kreuz-Straße is another good place to check; here you'll find **Thorbräukeller** (Heilig-Kreuz-Str. 20, tel. 0821/511991), a beer garden and bar favored by locals. Black-clad hepcats head to **Liliom** (Unterer Graben 1, tel. 0821/157694). Sculpture graces the leafy beer garden, and black floors, oak furniture, great tunes, and modern art set the tone for the adjacent café-bar.

REGENSBURG

Though situated on the Danube, Regensburg is named after a smaller tributary, the Regen River. The Romans established a fortress on this site in AD 179—dubbed *Castra Regina* (Fort Regen)—as an outpost against marauding German tribes. Yet the Romans grew soft, the Germans persevered, begot and begot, and in subsequent centuries, Regensburg flowered. The city was designated the first capital of Bavaria, a *Freie Reichsstadt* (free imperial city), and later, the seat of the Holy Roman *Reichstag*, or imperial diet. Artist Albrecht Altdorfer stamped the city's intellectual life, as did astronomer, astrologer, and imperial mathematician Johannes Kepler. This formidable pedigree has bequeathed a medieval townscape modeled stylistically along lines favored by then-powerful Italian clans, and miraculously spared by wartime bombing. If you have only a day, skip the museums and wander aimlessly through Regensburg's stony byways. By nightfall, however, the turrets and pastel towers of the town's patrician homes mark out a massive party zone for every single one of Regensburg's 15,000 students, and you.

Pick up a map from the helpful **tourist office** (Altes Rathaus, tel. 0941/507–4410; open weekdays 8:30–6, Sat. 9–4, Sun. 9:30–2:30). Regensburg's **Hauptbahnhof** sits just south of the center and sends frequent trains to Munich (1½ hrs, DM 35) and Nuremberg (1 hr, DM 25). Rent a bike at **Fahrradverleih ACHT** (Furtmayrstr. 12, tel. 0941/700–0365) for DM 14 per day.

Big Bavarian bummer: Youth hostels rarely accept people older than 26.

WHERE TO SLEEP

The few cheap places in town are very popular, so call ahead. Strangely, some hotel reception desks are closed on Sunday or even the whole weekend through, so you have to check in during the week. Dial 0941/19414 day or night for information about room vacancies. The local **campground** (Weinweg 40, tel. 0941/270025; DM 7 per tent plus DM 10 per person) has kitchen, shower, and laundry facilities. Take Bus 6 from the Hauptbahnhof to Hans-Sachs-Straße and head right (Hans-Sachs-Str. turns into Weinweg); the last bus leaves at 12:30 AM.

Diözesanzentrum Obermünster. Plain but immaculate rooms in this former monastery include doubles for DM 80–DM 90. *Obermünsterpl. 7, tel. 0941/56810.*

Peterhof. Despite the old, seedy-looking facade, rooms here are in decent shape and the adjoining restaurant is good value. It's located between the Hauptbahnhof and the city center. Doubles cost DM 86–DM 114. *Fröhliche-Türken-Str. 12, tel. 0941/57514.*

HOSTEL • Jugendherberge Regensburg (HI). On an island in the Danube, a short bus ride or 35-minute walk from the Hauptbahnhof will lead you to this hostel. There's no curfew (ask for key code). Beds are DM 22, breakfast included. *Wöhrdstr. 60, tel. 0941/57402. Bus 8 to Eisstadion; or walk up Maximilianstr., cross Danube at Eiserne Brücke, right on Wöhrdstr. Closed Nov. 15–Jan. 15.*

FOOD

Tucked away in a courtyard, **Hinterhaus** (Rote-Hahnen-Gasse 2, tel. 0941/54661) has a large student clientele and cheap student fare (DM 8–DM 13). You can find classy and inexpensive pasta and pizza at **Spaghetteria** (Am Römling 12, tel. 0941/563695). Fruits and veggies fill the stalls at **Donaumarkt** (near Hunnenpl.) every Saturday 7 AM–1 PM. By the river, the lively **Historische Wurstküchl** beer garden (Thundorferstr. 3, tel. 0941/59098) has been serving its half-liter brews (DM 4.60) for 850 years. The only food option is the juicy *Schweinbratenwürste* (small pork sausages; DM 7.80) with sauerkraut. The menu is larger and the prices a bit higher in the neighboring **Salzstadel-Wirtshaus** (An der Steinernen Brücke, tel. 0941/59098), but the mood is just as lively.

WORTH SEEING

Let your mind wander as you stroll down some of Regensburg's finest and oldest relics: its alleys. Crooked **Untere Bachgasse** is one of the town's most romantic spots. And Unter den Schwibbögen still supports the original northern gate of the Roman fortress, **Porta Praetoria.** While you're exploring, check out the **patrician houses**; high towers were to rich traders what cellular phones are today.

ALTES RATHAUS • The old town hall has been converted into the **Reichstagsmuseum** (which has nothing to do with the Reichstag in Berlin), in memory of the Imperial Councils held here from 1663 to 1806. On the guided tours, you'll see the Imperial Hall and the dungeon, with some gruesomely creative torture devices. Buy tour tickets from the Rathaus tourist office. *Admission: DM 5. English-language tours May–Sept., Mon.–Sat. at 3:15. German tours Mon.–Sat. every 30 min 9:30–noon and 2–4, Sun. 10–noon.*

THE BAVARIAN FOREST

Nature lovers looking for clean air, low prices, and excellent skiing and hiking will find the Bayerischer Wald (Bavarian Forest) the perfect getaway. Other than a few Austrians and Czechs, few non-Germans make it to East Bavaria, much less to the Bavarian Forest. Here you'll encounter Bavarians in the wild, roaming their natural habitat and proving the warm Bavarian hospitality you might have thought was only a fairy tale. From Regensburg, take a train to Plattling, where you can transfer to Bodenmais or Frauenau, both small, friendly towns with hostels and scads of hiking trails. The tourist office in Bodenmais (tel. 09924/77835) is in the Hauptbahnhof; in Frauenau (tel. 09926/710), it's at Hauptstraße 12.

Gorgeous hiking trails run through just about every town in the Bavarian Forest. For invaluable info on routes and distances, pick up a Wanderkarte (trail map) at the nearest tourist office (DM 10, less with a Kurkarte [guest card] from your hotel). Bike paths also run deep; inquire at a tourist office or rental shop. Most larger towns in the forest have bike rentals for about DM 10–DM 20 a day.

From the first snowfall in December until the last patches of slush in May, the forest is a haven for German skiers, with resorts throughout.

MUSEUM OSTDEUTSCHE GALERIE • This gallery in the Stadtpark has a unique collection of 19th- and 20th-century German art from the formerly German areas of eastern Europe (highlights include Lovis Corinth), plus changing exhibits. *Dr.-Johann-Maier-Str. 5, tel. 0941/297140. Admission: DM 4. Open Tues.–Sun. 10–4.*

STEINERNE BRUECK • Built during the 12th century using Roman designs, Germany's oldest bridge was an engineering miracle in its time. As the first (and for a long time the only) bridge across the Danube, it made Regensburg a vital trading hub; bloody feuds between bishops, dukes, and traders over control of this strategic bridge raged for years. Climb up the adjoining **Brückturm** (Bridge Tower) for a splendid view.

DOM ST. PETER • St. Peter's Cathedral is widely considered Bavaria's most outstanding example of Gothic architecture. Built over six centuries, it chronicles the development of Gothic architecture; check out the different tower styles and colors of stone used. The Domspatzen, the famous boys' choir, performs during Sunday mass at 9 AM. *Dompl. Admission free. Open Apr.–Oct., daily 6:30–6; Nov.–Mar., daily 6:30–4. Tours (DM 3) Nov.–Apr., weekdays at 11 AM, Sun. and holidays at noon; May–Oct., weekdays at 10, 11, and 2, Sun. and holidays at noon and 2.*

AFTER DARK

Begin your evening at a beer garden, either under the shady chestnut trees of the **Kneitinger Keller** (Galgenbergstr. 18, tel. 0941/76680) or at the Regensburg institution **Spitalgarten** (Katharinenpl. 1, tel. 0941/84774), which overlooks the Danube from across the Steinerne Brücke. A highly chic crowd boogies at **Scala** (Gesandtenstr. 6, tel. 0941/52293) Wednesday–Sunday from 11 PM; the cover ranges from DM 3 to DM 7. Regensburg has no less than three Irish pubs, always jam-packed and jumping. Try the **Irish Harp Pub** (Brückstr. 1, tel. 0941/57268) for Guinness out of the barrel, live music, and darts.

BAVARIAN ALPS

Stretching from the Bodensee (Lake Constance) in the west to Berchtesgaden in the east, the Bavarian Alps have graced the covers of many a tourist brochure, spreading pastoral Alpine scenes and country kitsch worldwide. And the covers don't lie: You really will see milkmaids and meadows and church steeples set against snowy peaks. After a while, though, the excessive quaintness of the villages may get old and prompt you to take a hike. Luckily, with a few major exceptions (Berchtesgaden in particular), sightseeing takes a backseat to outdoorsy pleasures, such as hiking, swimming, and skiing. Be warned that the weather is totally unpredictable; on a single hike you may encounter a range of meteorological aberrations. Trains from Munich can get you to most of the main Alpine towns, but between towns you may have to use **RVO buses.** Get a free *Kurkarte* (guest card) from wherever you're staying or ask for one at the tourist office—these helpful passes often get you free or reduced admission fees.

HOHENSCHWANGAU AND NEUSCHWANSTEIN

The **Hohenschwangau palace** (admission DM 10; open Apr.–Sept., daily 8:30–5:30; Oct.–Mar., daily 10–4) is where Bavaria's famous loony king, Ludwig II, spent most of his childhood. Hohenschwangau was built by the knights of Schwangau during the 12th century, in a heavy Romanesque style. Between 1832 and 1836, the battle-ravaged castle was completely restored by Ludwig's father and transformed into an elegant palace—one that attracted the notice of composer Richard Wagner. During the few summers Wagner spent there, he became acquainted with the young Ludwig, and their friendship deepened Ludwig's already keen interest in music, theater, and mythology; it's unlikely, however, that Wagner saw Ludwig as anything more than a wealthy patron from whom he could squeeze a few gold pieces. Inside the castle is the piano Wagner played, as well as the bed he slept in. The palace also contains a dizzying *Festsaal* (festival hall), filled with gold statuettes that look like something straight out of *Dungeons and Dragons.*

If you really want to be dazzled, walk 20 minutes northeast; you won't be able to miss King Ludwig's fairy-tale castle **Neuschwanstein** (same hours and admission). Set atop a hill in the middle of a small forest, Neuschwanstein has towers, gates, battlements, courtyards, gables, spires, lookouts, spiral stairways, and just about everything else a proper castle should have. Walt Disney even used Neuschwanstein as a model for the castle you find in his theme parks. Inside the real thing, you'll find flamboyant parlors, elaborately decorated apartments, and Ludwig's tomblike bedroom, dominated by a massive Gothic-style bed. In September, chamber music concerts are sometimes held in the ornate **Minstrel's Hall,** a definite highlight. Call the Füssen tourist office at 08362/7077 for more information. After being awed by the splendor of Neuschwanstein, be sure to wander around the surrounding forest. For spectacular views, cross on **Marien Brücke** (Mary's Bridge), a vertigo-inducing span reached by few tourists. From here you can follow, at your own risk, the narrow dirt paths to the cliffs surrounding the castle.

BASICS

The easiest way to get to the two castles is from **Füssen,** 5 km (3 mi) away. To give yourself enough time (especially at Neuschwanstein, where the lines can be heinous), stay at Füssen's **HI hostel** (Mariahilferstr. 5, tel. 08362/7754; beds DM 21.20, including breakfast and "Kurkarte", giving price reductions on several Füssen attractions; closed Nov. 15–Dec. 26). From here, you can walk or catch the hourly **RVO bus** that runs from Füssen's Hauptbahnhof to Königsschlösser (DM 4.60 round-trip); it stops right at the steps that lead to Hohenschwangau, a short distance from Neuschwanstein. If you catch the bus at 8:05 AM, you'll arrive at Neuschwanstein just in time to be near the front of the line when the castle opens. Daily **trains** connect Füssen with Augsburg (hourly, 2 hrs, DM 26) and Munich (15 daily via Buchloe, 2 hrs, DM 34).

GARMISCH-PARTENKIRCHEN

Since the two separate towns of Garmisch and Partenkirchen merged for the 1936 Winter Olympics, tourism has exploded and recreational facilities of all kinds compete for your marks. The biggest high around here, in both price and altitude, is the **Zugspitze,** Germany's tallest mountain (9,778 ft). Dropping DM 39 (DM 59 round-trip) for a ride to the top of the Zugspitze by train or cable car on a dreary day is as rewarding as tossing a huge wad of currency into a fog bank, but on a clear day the view of the surrounding peaks and lowlands is priceless. Call 08821/797979 for weather conditions. The train leaves from Olympia Straße 27 (tel. 08821/7970), just east of the Hauptbahnhof, while the cable car is anchored just outside town, at Eibsee, on the main road to Austria.

If heights freak you out, perhaps you'd feel more secure surrounded by tons of rock and ice instead. Wander through the cavelike passageways of the **Partnachklamm gorge** (admission DM 3, DM 2 with Kurkarte), carved over thousands of years by the Partnach River. In the winter, bizarre ice formations dangle from the gorge's walls. The best way to get here is to take local Bus 1 or 2 (toward Kreiskrankenhaus) to the Olympic Skistadion and follow the signs for a 30-minute hike to the gorge.

COMING AND GOING

If you're coming by **train** from Munich (1½ hrs, DM 26) or Augsburg, ask at the Hauptbahnhof about a special round-trip train ticket for DM 88 that includes a free ride on the Zugspitze cable car. **RVO buses** (tel. 08821/51822) run to other Alpine villages. Rent bicycles (DM 18) and **mountain bikes** (DM 33) at Schöch (Ludwigstr. 39, tel. 08821/1230). On the western side of the town is Marienplatz, the heart of Garmisch; on the east is Ludwigstraße, Partenkirchen's main strip. Since the two halves together become an extra-large alpine town, you should use the **Ortsbus** to get around. The **tourist office** (Richard-Strauss-Pl., tel. 08821/1806; open Mon.–Sat. 8–6, Sun. 10–noon) Kurkarte gets you on free.

WHERE TO SLEEP

If the tourist office is closed, 24-hour screens outside the tourist office and above the travel agency in the Hauptbahnhof list accommodations. From the Hauptbahnhof take bus 3 or 4 to Burgrain to reach the **HI hostel** (Jochstr. 10, tel. 08821/2980; beds DM 23, including breakfast; hire of bedding costs DM 5.50; closed Nov. 15–Dec. 26), 4 km (2½ mi) outside town. Make sure you catch the last bus at 10:30 in order to make the 11:30 curfew. **Campingplatz Zugspitze** (Griesener Str. 4, tel. 08821/3180) is at the foot of the Zugspitze, between Grainau and Garmisch-Partenkirchen. Sites are DM 5 per tent plus DM 11 per person. Take the hourly blue bus (DM 3.10; last bus 8 PM) from the stop across from the Hauptbahnhof, get off at Schmultz, and follow the signs.

MITTENWALD

If you have only a day or two to kick around in the Bavarian Alps, spend your time in Mittenwald. Sandwiched between the Karwendel and Wetterstein mountains, this romantic town epitomizes every Alpine village cliché—it's got everything from snowcapped peaks to breathtaking views of lederhosen-clad villagers. Despite its awe-inspiring setting, cheery locals, and authentic small-town feel, Mittenwald is often overlooked because of its more famous neighbor, Garmisch-Partenkirchen, only 20 km (12 mi) away.

To enjoy Mittenwald's awesome views and hiking opportunities, take the cable car (tel. 08832/8480; DM 27 round-trip) that leaves from Alpenkorpsstraße 1 and runs to the **Karwendel summit** (7,405 ft). Before you go, call the weather hotline (tel. 08823/5396). Once at the top, you can take a leisurely 30-minute hike around the summit, or, for a more foresty view, take the *Sessellift* (chair lift; tel. 08823/1553; DM 9 round-trip) from the northern end of Kranzbergstraße up the Kranzberg. To reach the **Leutaschklamm gorge** and **waterfall** (open summer, daily 9–5:30), walk south on Innsbrucker Straße and veer right onto Am Köberl—it's an effortless 25-minute walk. A popular swimming destination in summer is the tiny lake **Lautersee,** an easy 40-minute walk westward on Laintalstraße, which turns into Laintal. Come winter, the Karwendel boasts Germany's longest downhill ski run (6.5 km/4¼ mi). A lift ticket costs DM 38 for one day, DM 65 for two. Rent skis at **Skischule Mittenwald** (Bahnhofstr. 6, tel. 08823/8080).

The **Geigenbau und Heimatmuseum mit Schauwerkstatt** (Ballenhausgasse 3, tel. 08823/2511; open weekdays 10–11:45 and 2–4:45, weekends 10–11:45) displays violins fashioned by Mittenwald's best. To see the violin makers in action, stop by the museum's *Schauwerkstatt* (workshop), open daily in summer and Friday–Sunday in winter. Admission is DM 2. Next door is the 18th-century church of **St. Peter und Paul,** famous for its baroque, frescoed tower. Outside the church stands a bronze statue dedicated to master violinmaker Matthias Klotz (1653–1743). West of the church extends the oldest part of town, **Im Gries,** great walking territory lined with fruit stands and other markets.

VISITOR INFORMATION

The **Kurverwaltung** will help you find a place to stay for no charge and offers excellent hiking and biking maps (DM 4) and sightseeing information. *Dammkarstr. 3, tel. 08823/33981. Open weekdays 8–noon and 1–5, Sat. 10–noon.*

COMING AND GOING

Frequent **trains** arrive from Munich (2 hrs, DM 30), Innsbruck (1 hr, DM 11), and Garmisch-Partenkirchen (20 min, DM 6). Less frequent **RVO buses** also run from Mittenwald to Garmisch-Partenkirchen (30 min, DM 5).

WHERE TO SLEEP

The 120-bed **HI hostel** (Buckelwiesen 7, tel. 08823/1701; closed Nov. and Dec.) is a one-hour hike from town on the Tonihof-Buckelwiesen trail. Beds cost DM 22.30 (including breakfast; hire of bedding is DM 5.50 extra). Call to see if space is available at the centrally located **Haus Antonia** (In der Wasserwiese 14, tel. 08823/8202); at DM 35 per person, including breakfast, it's a bargain. The nearest year-round **campground** is at Isarhorn (tel. 08823/5216; DM 8 per space), 3 km (2 mi) north of Mittenwald. From the Hauptbahnhof, take the Omnibus (DM 3) toward Krün to Campingplatz.

NUREMBERG

If you head to Nuremberg expecting Brothers Grimm–style gingerbread homes, you won't be too disappointed. Yet today, Nuremberg's cosmopolitan population of students, immigrants, tourists, and regular old Germans spills far beyond the ancient stone walls. Modernity, in the form of seedy sex shops and swank boutiques, is as much a part of northern Bavaria's industrial center as are picture-perfect footbridges and fairy-tale lanes. Nuremberg is infamous for its close association with Hitler, who drew a connection between the city's role in the Holy Roman Empire and his own projected 1,000-year *Reich.* To this day, Nuremberg is still stigmatized for its legacy of Nazism, primarily because it was chosen as the showplace of the National Socialist party rallies. The 1935 convention saw the pronouncement of the Nuremberg Laws, depriving Jews of their German citizenship and the right to marry non-Jews, and opening the gates to genocide. The *Reichsparteitagsgelände,* the original rally grounds, remain as an eerie, powerful reminder of totalitarianism. Appropriately, the Allies chose Nuremberg to host the Nuremberg War Trials, during which top-ranking Nazis were charged with and convicted of crimes against humanity.

BASICS

There's a **tourist office** in the Hauptbahnhof (tel. 0911/233–6132; open Mon.–Sat. 9–7) and another on the Hauptmarkt (tel. 0911/233–6135; open May–Sept., Mon.–Sat. 9–6 and Sun. 10–1 and 2–4). At the **American Express** office (Adlerstr. 2, tel. 0911/232397), you can get or cash traveler's checks and exchange currency commission-free, and cardholders can pick up mail.

COMING AND GOING

Train destinations include Berlin (5½ hrs, DM 119) and Munich (2 ½ hrs, DM 57). To reach the old town, take the underground passage to Königstraße and continue northwest to Lorenzer Platz. For a ride out of town contact the **Mitfahrzentrale** (Äußere Laufer Gasse 26, tel. 0911/19444).

WHERE TO SLEEP AND EAT

Sensational views of Nuremberg can be enjoyed from rooms at the city's **hostel** (Im Burg 2, tel. 0911/221024; beds DM 29, including breakfast and bedding). It's housed in the former stables and arsenal of the grand imperial castle, the Kaiserburg, which rises up over the city. If the hostel is full (as it often is during summer), head to either tourist office (*see* Basics, *above*) for an accommodations list, or try the cheery **Vater Jahn** (Jahnstr. 13, tel. 0911/444507; double DM 75–DM 95) and the central **City** (Königstr. 25–27, tel. 0911/225638; double DM 75; closed Aug. 1–14) where Fodor's readers get a discount! **Campingplatz Nürnberg** (Hans-Kalb-Str. 56, tel. 0911/811122; closed Oct.–Apr.) is near a beautiful lake. From the Bahnhof, take Tram 9 (toward Luitpoldhain) to Meistersingerhalle, and then Bus 55 (toward Langwasser Mitte) to Beuthener Straße; backtrack to Hans-Kalb-Straße and go left.

On sunny days, **Café Kiosk** (Bleichstr. 5, tel. 0911/269030) is unbeatable for beer-sipping. At **Balazzo Brozzi** (Hochstr. 2, tel. 0911/288482) you can wolf down pasta and salads (all under DM 10). On the River Pegnitz's southern bank, a few blocks east of Museumsbrücke, *Imbiß* (snack) stands are the norm, along with student-filled bars. **Roldi,** on the Hauptmarkt, stocks cheap groceries.

WORTH SEEING

Besides the castle **Kaiserburg** (admission DM 5), which looms imposingly at the northern end of Burgstraße, Nuremberg's main attraction is its colorful open-air square, the **Hauptmarkt.** During summer it overflows with street vendors and musicians; in winter it hosts all kinds of events associated with Christkindlmarkt, an enormous pre-Christmas fair that runs from November 27 through Christmas Eve.

Just west of the castle is the striking late-medieval **Albrecht-Dürer-Haus,** formerly home to Albrecht Dürer, the painter and wood engraver almost singularly responsible for the emergence of German

Renaissance art. He lived here from 1509 until his death in 1528. *Albrecht-Dürer-Str. 39, tel. 0911/ 231–2568. Admission: DM 4. Open Mar.–Oct., Tues.–Sun. 10–5; Nov.–Feb., Tues.–Fri. 1–5, weekends 10–5.*

The **Lorenzer Platz,** an open-air square a few blocks south of the Haupmarkt, is dominated by the medieval **St. Lorenzkirche,** lauded as Nuremberg's most beautiful church. Also on the square are the **Tugendbrunnen** (Fountain of Virtues), a popular spot for a summer's day water fight, and the lavish **Nassauer Haus** (Lorenzer Pl. 6), Nuremberg's oldest house.

The sprawling **Germanisches National Museum** (Germanic National Museum of Art and Culture; Kartäusergasse 1, tel. 0911/13310; admission DM 6; open Tues.–Sun. 10–5, Wed. until 9 PM) is dedicated to all aspects of German culture and history. If you don't catch one of the free English tours on the first Sunday of every month, most of this stuff may be a mystery. A more visceral exhibit of German history are the now-silent grounds of the **Reichsparteitagsgelände.** By 1938, the massive Nazi Party rallies that took place here included 750,000 participants and audiences of half a million. Behind the crumbling *Haupttribüne* (grandstands) of the Zeppelin field lies the entrance to the exhibit **Fascination and Violence** (admission DM 2; open May–Oct., Tues.–Sun. 10–6), including film clips of the rallies and anti-Semitic posters, fliers, and children's books. Take the subway U11 (toward Langwasser) to Messezentrum, and exit east onto Otto-Bärnreutherstraße, or take the tram number 9 to the terminus, Luitpoldhain.

NEAR NUREMBERG

BAYREUTH

Depending on your perspective, Bayreuth is either blessed or plagued by its annual **Richard Wagner Festival.** During this hoity-toity summer fête, the town is abuzz with 19th-century opera junkies who reserved their overpriced tickets (up to DM 300) years in advance. The influx of high-culture fiends means it becomes impossible to find a place to crash in July and August. All this can be blamed on Wagner, who designed Bayreuth's vast opera house, the **Festspielhaus** (auf dem Grünen Hügel, tel. 0921/78780; admission DM 2.50; open daily 10–4, except during the festival, late July and Aug., and Nov.). Wagner's former home, **Haus Wahnfried** (Richard-Wagner-Str. 48, tel. 0921/757–2816; admission DM 4; open daily 9–5) is now a museum with period furniture, Wagner-oriented displays, and dozens of contextual exhibits. A mini-recital of excerpts from Wagner's works is given daily at 10, noon, and 2.

BASICS • The **Gästedienst des Fremdenverkehrsvereins** doubles as a travel agency and tourist information center. Staffers at the information desk provide city maps and brochures, and make private room reservations for a DM 5 fee. *Luitpoldpl. 9, tel. 0921/88588.*

WHERE TO SLEEP • Don't bother in July or August unless you've booked months in advance. The rest of the year, Bayreuth's **hostel** (Universitätsstr. 28, tel. 0921/251262) and a very few pensions are fairly priced and located within a reasonable walk of the Altstadt. For the hostel, take Bus 4 or 18 to Kreuzsteinbad. The hostel charges DM 25. You have to be a member of a national youth hostel association. Hire of bedding costs an extra DM 5.50. Minutes from the Festspielhaus, the peaceful **Gasthof Kropf** (Tristanstr. 8, tel. 0921/26298) has doubles for DM 64–DM 130.

BAMBERG

Simply put, Bamberg is stunning. What started as a minor farming village during the late 2nd century AD was transformed into an elegant seat of power under the guidance of native son Heinrich II, an 11th-century Holy Roman emperor. He's responsible for Bamberg's impressive **Dom,** considered one of the most important medieval cathedrals in all Germany. Bamberg's old town looks like it just stepped from the pages of some medieval chronicle: Cobbled lanes meander in and out of narrow alleyways, while colorful and rickety half-timbered houses stand guard along ancient sandstone bridges. There are enough "official" sights to keep you occupied for at least a day in Bamberg, but this town was made for walking, and during summer you should stick around for the night. Bamberg's handful of beer halls grow respectably bacchanalian during the semitouristy summer season, and there are plenty of nooks along the river where you can pass time with a friend and a bottle.

COMING AND GOING • Bamberg is an easy hop from Nuremberg (50 min, DM 15). The staff at the **tourist office** (Geyerswörthstr. 3, tel. 0951/871161) arranges city tours and bus tours to nearby areas; they also book city hotels and guest houses for a DM 5 fee.

WHERE TO SLEEP • Wherever you stay, reserve ahead on summer weekends. **Hotel Garni Graupner** (Langestr. 5, tel. 0951/980400; doubles DM 90–DM 120) is a short walk from Grüner Markt and the Altstadt. At the **Bamberger Weissbierhaus** (Obere Königstr. 38, tel. 0951/25503) doubles go for DM 70–DM 80. **Fässla** (Obere Königstr. 21, 3 blocks from Hauptbahnhof, tel. 0951/22998 or 0951/126516; closed Sun.) is a joint beer tavern and guest house, with DM 98 doubles. Otherwise, Bamberg's hostel and campground are a few miles from the Altstadt. **Jugendherberge Wolfsschlucht** (Oberer Leinritt 70, tel. 0951/56002; beds, including breakfast, DM20; hire of bedding DM 5.50) is set in a large mansion, a stone's throw from the River Regnitz. Take Bus 18 (service stops at 7 PM) from ZOB's Promenadestraße depot to Rodelbahn; walk downhill and left on Oberer Leinritt. Roughly 5 km (3 mi) south of the city center, **Campingplatz Insel** (Am Campingpl. 1, tel. 0951/56320; DM 5.50–DM 11 per tent plus DM 6.50 per person) is a beautiful and popular spot along the Regnitz River. Take Bus 18 from ZOB's Promenadestraße depot to Bug; walk south along Hauptstraße.

FOOD • Bamberg is associated with a few culinary oddities. One is *Rauchbier*, or smoked beer, a deep amber brew whose unique smoky taste comes from being filtered through charred beechwood logs. Of the many beer gardens that now adorn Bamberg's hills, the **Spezial-Keller** (Oberer Stephansberg 47, tel. 0951/54887; closed Mon.) offers a stunning view and great Rauchbier for DM 3.30. Down a mushroom omelette (DM 11.50) with your Rauchbier at **Schlenkerla Brauereigaststätte** (Dominikanerstr. 6, tel. 0951/56060; closed Tues.), or veggie quiches (DM 9.50) at **Café Müller** (Austr. 23, tel. 0951/202943).

> *Bakeries all over town sell Nuremberg's famous Lebkuchen, a delicious, sweet-smelling gingerbread cake.*

WORTH SEEING • The **Diözesanmuseum** (open Tues.–Sun. 10–5; admission DM 3), with its eclectic mix of church relics, random pieces of silver and jewels, and line drawings of the Dom floor plan, lies across from the **Neue Residenz** (admission DM 4; open daily 9–noon and 1:30–5; closes one hour earlier Oct.–Mar.), a sprawling baroque palace once home to princes and electors of the Holy Roman Empire.

The tourist office leads **city tours** (in German) Monday–Saturday at 10:30 AM and 2 PM (2 PM only Nov.–Mar.; stop by to sign up and get tickets (DM 8). Don't miss out on Bamberg's unofficial sights, like **Klein Venedig** (Little Venice), the quarter huddled along both banks of the Regnitz just north of the Old Rathaus. This riverfront collection of red-roofed and brightly colored homes is pleasant to wander through, especially when the odd fishing skiff glides lazily by at dusk. The same holds true for **Maximilian Platz,** Bamberg's "other" square.

ROMANTISCHE STRASSE

In a stroke of promotional genius, Germany's National Tourism Board designated a collection of medieval villages and scenic southern towns "The Romantic Road" in 1950. Most of these spots have in common beautiful architecture, narrow cobblestone streets, strong folk traditions, and lots of "old-world charm." Today, the route has become one of the most heavily traveled regions in Germany. During the summer months, the tour buses start rolling, the hotels open their doors (and raise their prices), the souvenir stands stock up, and the hordes start coming, and coming, and coming. As well they should—many of the route's destinations rank among the most interesting and beautiful sights in Germany, if not in all Europe. The Romantische Straße runs primarily from **Würzburg,** 90 km (54 mi) northwest of Nuremberg, to **Nördlingen,** about 80 km (50 mi) southwest of Nuremberg, although the route officially ends at the foot of the Bavarian Alps, in the frontier town of Füssen. As long as you don't mind sharing its cobbled streets with a crowd of camera-wielding tourists, Würzburg makes a good day trip from Nuremberg and a convenient base for longer excursions. And from Würzburg you can also catch a bus to the justifiably popular town, **Rothenburg-ob-der-Tauber,** one of Europe's best-preserved medieval citadels.

If you don't rent a car your best option may be the **Romantische Straße Bus** (Europabus 190). This is free (except for the DM 7 daily "processing" fee) to all Eurailpass and InterRail holders, and to anyone with a Deutsche Bahn (DB) rail pass. Service runs only April–October. Every morning, one bus heads south from Frankfurt to Munich, with a connection to Füssen, and another heads north from Füssen to Dinkelsbühl, with a connection to Frankfurt; travelers are free to get on and off at any point along the route. In most towns, the bus stops only long enough to pick up new passengers; if you want to explore, you'll have to get off and pick up the bus again the next day. Final note: The Romantische Straße Bus works best as a supplement to the trains.

WURZBURG

Leafy vines shoot delicate green tendrils across the latticed hills around Würzburg, which lies along the banks of the River Main. This town that draws sighs over its stoic, weathered bridges and narrow, strollable lanes is one of the Romantische Straße's major hubs; hourly trains connect Würzburg to Nuremberg (1 hr, DM 26) and Frankfurt (1 hr 20 min, DM 41). It's also a main starting point for regional buses. Würzburg's two main sights are **Festung Marienberg** (Marienberg Fortress), and the baroque **Residenz** palace. The former sits atop a small hill on the western edge of town, dominating Würzburg's steepled skyline. It was under continuous construction between 1200 and 1600, and for more than 450 years, it provided sturdy sanctuary to the town's powerful prince-bishops. The Residenz, a short walk away on the eastern edge of the old town, became the ruler's residence upon completion in the 18th century, and is considered one of Europe's most impressive architectural monuments. Würzburg also has a student population more than 30,000 strong, harbors the three largest wineries in Germany, and—no doubt as a result of the first two—is the site of several raging annual festivals (June's **Mozart Festival** is a sedate contrast).

The main **tourist office** (Pavillon am Hauptbahnhof, tel. 0931/37436) is located just outside the Hauptbahnhof and is open Monday–Saturday 10–6; a second office (Haus zum Falken, Am Markt, tel. 0931/37398) is on the central market square and is open April–October, weekdays 10–6, weekends 10–2; November–December weekdays 10–6, Saturday 10–2. Both stock free city maps, organize guided city tours, and help you find a room in town for a DM 2 booking fee.

WHERE TO SLEEP

Würzburg's youth hostel, **Jugendgästehaus Würzburg** (Burkarderstr. 44, tel. 0931/42590; beds, DM 29, including breakfast and bedding), is below Festung Marienberg on the River Main's west bank. From the Hauptbahnhof, take Tram 5 (toward Heuchelhof) to Löwenbrüke. Follow the sign down the steps, cross the street, and go right; the hostel is on the left after the tunnel. **Hotel-Pension Spehnkuch** (Röntgenring 7, tel. 0931/54752) has tidy doubles with big, fluffy comforters for DM 90 (breakfast included).

FOOD

The central market, Am Markt, and the adjacent streets boast the usual high concentration of *Imbiß* stands, cafés, and tourist-geared beer halls. Cheapish food stands and greasy holes-in-the-wall are also around the Hauptbahnhof and in the maze of streets around Sanderstraße and Münzstraße. **Bürgerspital zum Heiligen Geist** (Theaterstr. 19, tel. 0931/13861) is a popular drinking hall where glasses of sweet Würzburger Pfaffenberg wine cost less than DM 5—a pittance for this excellent, locally grown elixir.

ROTHENBURG-OB-DER-TAUBER

Tucked along the eastern bank of the Tauber River, Rothenburg-ob-der-Tauber (literally "the red castle on the Tauber") is best known for its compact Altstadt. Preserved inside the stout city wall is, quite simply, the most impressive medieval citadel anywhere. With not one modern building in the entire Altstadt, Rothenburg is easily the most evocative Romantische Straße destination. After the Thirty Years' War (1618–48) wreaked serious havoc on the region's economic base, Rothenburg foundered for two centuries, impoverished and forgotten. But during the late 19th century it was "rediscovered" by tourism, eventually becoming one of the most visited towns in Germany. Walking down Rothenburg's medieval streets in summer, a traveler is more likely to hear English, Japanese, or Italian than German being spoken by passersby, making it seem more like Disney-ob-der-Tauber than a real medieval village. But if you just smile and accept the kitsch, you'll actually enjoy yourself.

Rothenburg is best reached by train from Nuremberg (90 min, DM 21) or Würzburg (1 hr, DM 16). Between April and October, Rothenburg is also serviced twice daily by the **Romantische Straße Bus** (*see above*). You can tour Rothenburg itself in three to four hours, but it provides a good base for exploring lesser known Romantische Straße sights, such as **Feuchtwangen** and **Dinkelsbühl**. From here you can also take walks through forests and along rivers. Ask at the **tourist office** (Marktpl., tel. 09861/40492) for its detailed walking guide. For an insightful overview of the city, join one of the tourist office's **walking tours.** Between April and October, English-language tours leave daily from Marktplatz at 11 and 2 (Nov.–Dec., 2 PM only). Especially consider the 9:30 English-language evening tour; it's led by a night watchman who hobbles through town with a lantern and a bag of stories.

WHERE TO SLEEP

The two cheapest options are **private rooms** (DM 40–DM 60), booked through the tourist office, and the youth hostel, **Jugendherberge Rothenburg** (Mühlacker 1, tel. 09861/94160; beds DM 20; closed Dec. 15–Jan. 2). From Marktplatz, walk south along Obere Schmiedgasse and turn right at the youth hostel sign just before the city wall. Campers should head straight for Detwang, a small historic village 1¼ km (½ mi) northwest of Rothenburg (exit the Altstadt at Klingentor gate and proceed straight, following the DETWANG signs). In Detwang, **Tauber-Idyll** (tel. 09861/3177; DM 6 per tent plus DM 6.50 per person) is a smaller and nicer choice than **Tauber-Romantik** (Detwang 39, tel. 09861/6191; DM 8 per tent plus DM 7.50 per person), but Romantik has a communal kitchen.

BERLIN

Berlin has always been a city on the edge. During the Cold War, the virtual island of West Berlin drew squatters, draft dodgers, and other radicals, while East Berlin's dissidents helped bring about the *Wende,* the nonviolent revolution ending communist rule—night clubs, all-night techno dance parties, a booming gay scene, avant-garde theater, and cinema continue this cultural tradition. Berlin's crowded streets will give you a glimpse of the tensions, resentments, hopes, and fears of a city in the throes of change.

The former headquarters of East Germany's secret police now houses the Museum in der runden Ecke (Dittrichring 24; tel. 0341/961–2443), with displays on 40 years of the Stasi's domestic surveillance.

Unlike other German cities dating back to Roman times, Berlin's rise to greatness did not begin until the 17th century, when the ruling Hohenzollerns made Berlin the biggest and most powerful city in northern Europe as the capital of Prussia. During the 19th century Berlin industrialized rapidly and became capital of a newly unified Germany. World War I and the victory of the Social Democrats in 1918 brought the downfall of the Hohenzollerns and the birth of the Weimar Republic, plagued from the outset by rampant inflation and continuous street battles between Communists and Fascists. Wartime bombing raids largely obliterated the city's historic center, and Berlin's division between the western Allies and the Soviets in 1945—expressed in brutally physical terms through the building of the Berlin Wall in 1961—split the city in two but did not break its spirit. In 1989 the Wall fell, and with it the GDR regime. German unification followed and in the year 2000 Berlin will again become the seat of Germany's federal government.

Caught between a traumatic past and an unknown future, a new Berlin is being born amid tense anticipation. With a burgeoning building development, the city's skyline is dominated by the towering yellow cranes of Europe's biggest construction site. By the turn of the century, more than 35 billion dollars will have been spent here. Yet Berlin maintains its youthful, dramatic, and mercurial atmosphere. Whether you prefer shopping in a busy outdoor market, scamming in a café, enjoying the quiet greenery of the city's parks, or coming home at 4:30 AM from a sweaty club, come and get it while it's hot.

BASICS

VISITOR INFORMATION

Although they're in German, the magazines *zitty, tip, prinz,* and *030* (DM 4 each, *030* is free), list all the major happenings in Berlin—and it doesn't take a genius to decipher dates, times, and addresses. The English-language monthly *Metropolis* (DM 3) can also help you figure out the scene. All are available at the tourist office, newsstands, and at clubs and movie theaters.

Berlin Touristen-Information books rooms for a DM 5 fee and has the free pamphlet "Berlin for Young People." A branch office inside the Brandenburg Gate is open daily 9:30–6. *Breitscheidpl., in Europa-Center, enter on Budapester Str., tel. 030/250025. Open Mon.–Sat. 8 AM–10 PM, Sun. 9–9.*

ARiC (Schumannstr. 5, tel. 030/280–7590, fax 030/280–7591) is a useful source of information if you have questions about safety or discrimination, or want to contact people of color in Berlin.

Schloss-
park

R. Wagner-
pl.

Schlossstr.

Quedlinburger Str.

Dovestr.

Cauerstr.

Marchstr.

Levetzowstr.

Spree

River

Altonaer Str.

Bachstr.

Grosser
Stern

Spreeweg

Str. des 17 Juni

Hofjägerallee
Tiergartenstr.
Klingelhöferstr.

CHARLOTTENBURG

Kaiser-Friedrich-Str.

Kaiserdamm

Otto-Suhr-Allee

Bismarckstr.

Ernst
Reuter
Pl.

Stein-
platz

Hardenbergstr.

Bahnhof
Zoologischer
Garten

Budapesterstr.

Kurfürstenstr.

TO
GRUNEWALD

Kantstr.

Wilmersdorferstr.

Goethestr.

Knesebeck Str.

Kantstr.

Savignyplatz

Spichernstr.

Nürnbgrstr.

Tauenzienstr.

Kleiststr.

Gervinusstr.

Kurfürstendamm

Olivaer
Pl.

WILMERSDORF

Kurfürstendamm

Leibniz Str.

Lietzenburgerstr.

Uhlandstr.

Nachodstr.

Motzstr.

Hohenstaufenstr.

Westfälischestr.

Düsseldorfer Str.

Brandenburgische Str.

Konstanzer Str.

Hohenzollern-Damm

Bundesallee

SCHÖNEBERG

Seesenerstr.

Stadtring

Berliner Str.

Berliner Str.

Grunewaldstr.

Badensche Str.

Martin-Luther-Str.

Volkspark

Mecklenburgstr.

Bundesallee

Stadtring

Hauptstr.

Ebe

KEY

AE American Express Office

ℹ Tourist Information

Hotel Transit, **35**

Jugendgästehaus
am Wannsee
(HI), **10**

Jugendgästehaus
am Zoo (HI), **9**

Jugendgästehaus
Berlin (HI), **17**

Jugendgästehaus
Central, **13**

Jugendgästehaus
Deutsche
Schreberjugend, **39**

Jugendherberge
Ernst Reuter (HI), **5**

Kladow
Camping, **11**

Krossinsee
International
Camping, **41**

Pension Alexis, **7**

Pension
Knesebeck, **3**

Pension
Kreuzberg, **33**

Riehmers
Hofgarten, **34**

Studentenhotel
Berlin, **19**

The **Jewish Community Center** (Jüdische Gemeinde zu Berlin) offers advice and information (including an events calendar) to Jewish visitors. *Fasanenstr. 79, tel. 030/880280. From Zoo station, west on Ku'-damm to Fasanenstr. Open Mon.–Sat. 10–5.*

Mann-O-Meter gives out maps (including the "Magnus Map," showing gay nightlife) and can help with accommodations. *Motzstr. 5, tel. 030/216–8008. U-Bahn to Nollendorfpl. Open weekdays 3 PM–11 PM, Sat. 3 PM–10 PM.*

AMERICAN EXPRESS

Bring your passport for money exchange. The main office also holds mail free (DM 2 nonmembers). *Main office: Uhlandstr. 173, 10719 Berlin, south of Ku'damm, tel. 030/882–7575. Open weekdays 9–5:30, Sat. 9–noon. Schöneberg: Bayreuther Str. 37, tel. 030/2149–8368. U-Bahn to Wittenbergpl. Mitte: Friedrichstr. 172, tel. 030/2017–4012. U6 to Französische Str.*

CHANGING MONEY

Most places charge DM 2–DM 4 commissions to change traveler's checks, but there's no fee (except bank fees) to get cash from ATMs. If it's late and you're desperate, most luxury hotels have bureaux de change in their lobbies. For better rates, try an American Express office (*see above*) or the branches of **Deutsche Verkehrs Bank (DVB)** at the train stations.

EMBASSIES

Australia: *Uhlandstr. 181–183, tel. 030/880–0880. From Zoo station, west on Kantstr.* **Canada: *International Trade Center, Friedrichstr. 95, tel. 030/261–1161. U-Bahn or S-Bahn to Friedrichstr.* United Kingdom:** *Unter den Linden 32–34, tel. 030/201840. U6 to Französische Str.* **United States.** For most services (8:30 AM–noon only), head for the old consulate. Hours may change—call first. *Clayallee 170, tel. 030/832–9233. U1 to Oskar-Helene-Heim.*

EMERGENCIES

Police (tel. 110); **ambulance** (tel. 112); list of **late-night pharmacies** (tel. 1141).

PHONES AND MAIL

Coin-op phones are going the way of dinosaurs; invest in a phone card, available in DM 12 and DM 50 denominations at most post offices, bureaux de change, and newsstands. There is also a **post office** inside Zoo Station (tel. 030/313–9799). Open 24 hours, it's the place to come for phone cards, to make international calls, and to send mail, a telegram, or even a fax. Poste Restante letters should be addressed: Your Name, Hauptpostlagernde Briefe, Postamt 120, Bahnhof Zoo, 10612 Berlin.

COMING AND GOING

BY BUS

Zentraler Omnibus-Bahnhof (ZOB), Berlin's grimy pit of a main bus depot, serves most major German cities. *Masurenallee 4–6, at Messedamm, tel. 030/301–8028 (office open 9–5.30). From Zoo Station, U2 to Kaiserdamm.*

BY MITFAHRGELEGENHEIT

Mitfahrzentrale Zoo (in Zoo U-Bahn station, tel. 030/19440), on the U2 platform, is open weekdays 9–7, weekends 10–6. **Citynetz** has two offices in Berlin (Ku'damm 227, tel. 030/882–7604; Bergmannstr. 57, tel. 030/693–6095).

BY PLANE

To reach Zoo Station from **Flughafen Tegel** (tel. 030/41010) take airport Bus X9 (express) or 109 (not). From eastern Berlin's **Flughafen Schönefeld** (tel. 030/60910), take S-Bahn 9 to Alexanderplatz and Zoo Station. Commuter flights coming in from West Germany usually arrive at **Flughafen Tempelhof** (tel. 030/69510).

BY TRAIN

Construction of a massive, modern main train station will be complete sometime next century. The central **Bahnhof Zoologischer Garten** (Zoo Station) is the city's busiest hub, but many trains arrive at **Lichtenberg** and **Hauptbahnhof** in eastern Berlin. All stations are served by Berlin's extensive subway network. Some popular destinations from Berlin include Hamburg (3 hrs, DM 71), Munich (8 hrs, DM 234), Amsterdam

(7½ hrs, DM 161), Prague (4½ hrs, DM 82), and Vienna (10 hrs, DM 138). Luggage lockers cost DM 2–DM 4. Pick up a *Städteverbindungen* (train timetable) at any ticket window. For German-language information, dial 030/19419.

GETTING AROUND

Even before unification, Berlin was a confusing, sprawling city that took some time getting used to. Today, unified Berlin is the largest city in Europe, so prepare to be overwhelmed. The new Berlin changes its street names like most people change their underwear, so you'll also need a detailed map, preferably the easy-to-fold *Falk Plan* (DM 13), available at tourist offices and newsstands. Zoo Station, or **Bahnhof Zoo** (pronounced TSOH) is the center of western Berlin. It's within easy walking distance of the Tiergarten, the Ku'damm, and Schöneberg, and handles six subway lines. Most western Berlin bus routes run past Zoo Station. In eastern Berlin, the busiest transit hub is **Alexanderplatz,** with easy access to the districts of Mitte, Prenzlauer Berg, and Friedrichshain.

Between the city's 150 bus routes and the subway system, you can get within walking distance of virtually every point in town. A DM 3.90 ticket covers all city districts (BVG zones A and B) for two hours; the **day card** (DM 16) is valid for 24 hours and is definitely the best deal for checking out as many sights as possible. Purchase tickets from a bus driver or from machines at subway stations, then validate them in the little red boxes on the platform or on the bus—if you're caught riding without a valid ticket, you'll be fined DM 60. You can buy a **Berlin Ticket** (30 hours for DM 15) or a **Week Pass** (DM 40), both of which allow for unlimited travel and free or reduced admission on sightseeing trips, museums, theaters, and other attractions. Buy these and other tickets at the Berliner Verkehrsbetriebe (BVG) kiosk (tel. 030/19449; open Mon.–Sat. 9–6, Sun. 10–4) on Hardenbergplatz in front of Zoo Station. The BVG office at the Kleistpark U-Bahn is open Monday–Saturday 9–6.

Since their ecstatic reunion in 1989, Ossis (Easterners) and Wessis (Westerners) have finally gotten to know each other. On the whole, either might tell you, they're not too impressed.

BY BIKE

Paths (the redbrick strips on sidewalks) are everywhere, and many corners have signals specially for cyclists. **Fahrradstation** rents bikes for DM 23–DM 25 per day, DM 40–DM 60 per weekend; leave your passport or DM 100–DM 200 as a deposit. They have five locations in Berlin, open weekdays 10–6, weekends (train station branches only) 10–2. *Bahnhof Zoo: tel. 030/2974–9319. Bahnhof Lichtenberg: tel. 030/29712798. Kreuzberg: Möckernstr. 92, tel. 030/216–9177. Mitte: Rosenthaler Str. 40–41, tel. 030/2859–9895.*

BY BUS AND TRAM

Buses (which run 4 AM–1 AM) supplement the already extensive subway system. Buses marked with an "N" run all night ("N" bus stops are recognizable by the yellow-on-green tabs atop the streetside stands). A new fleet of modern **trams,** including four night lines, operates in eastern Berlin. Their main hub is the Hackescher Markt S-Bahn station. Visitors with disabilities can contact **Telebus** (Esplanade 17, 13187 Berlin, tel. 030/478820), preferably a few weeks in advance, to take advantage of their special bus service, which runs daily 5 AM–1 AM.

BY SUBWAY

The complex subway system courses through all major sections of the city. The mostly underground **U-Bahn** is concentrated in central Berlin; the **S-Bahn** connects the city center with outlying areas and is free with a Eurailpass.

BY TAXI

BMW and Benz taxis—only in Germany. Standard fare is DM 4 plus DM 2.10 per km (½ mi; DM 2.30 after midnight). Quick trips (less than five minutes and 2 km/1 mi) cost DM 5. Add 50 Pf per bag in the trunk. Women and travelers with disabilities can have any U-Bahn announcer (the ones in the booth on the platform) call them a cab after 8 PM; to call a cab yourself, dial 030/69022, 030/261026, 030/210101, or 030/210202.

WHERE TO SLEEP

Most hotels cost DM 110–DM 150 per person per night—well beyond the reach of budget travelers. Fortunately, you can turn to Berlin's collection of pensions, which cost DM 50–DM 70 per person. Hostels are even more affordable, but they're almost all located in the western half of the city. Don't let this discourage you from staying in the east: The tourist office at Europa Center (*see* Visitor Information *in* Basics, *above*) has computerized listings of thousands of rooms in private homes (from DM 25 per night) all over Berlin. Let them know which district you want to stay in, and they'll book you a room for a DM 5 fee. Tourist offices also distribute the free German-language pamphlet *"Unterkünfte für Junge Besucher in Berlin und Brandenburg"* ("Accommodations for Young Visitors in Berlin and Brandenburg"). For DM 2, you can get an English-language version, which lists budget accommodations, youth hostels, and campgrounds.

Otherwise, try **Internationales Jugendcamp** (Ziekowstr. 161, tel. 030/433–8640; DM 10 per person), a giant tent where those under 26 can stay a maximum of three nights mid-June–late August. Take U6 to Alt-Tegel, head east on Gorkistraße, then left on Ziekowstraße. Travelers arriving late at night can crash for one night only at the **Bahnhofsmission** (Zoo Station, tel. 030/313–8088; beds DM 20).

CHARLOTTENBURG

This neighborhood is near the sight-packed Bahnhof Zoo area, but far from the raucous nightlife in Kreuzberg, Mitte, and Prenzlauer Berg.

Hotel Bialas. This is a surprisingly elegant place where most rooms have large bay windows and plush red-velvet furniture. Doubles are DM 100–DM 140. *Carmerstr. 16, off Steinpl., tel. 030/312–5025.*

Hotel Charlottenburg Pension. This classy, ornate pad has doubles for DM 100–DM 150. The owner speaks perfect English. *Grolmanstr. 32–33, tel. 030/881–5254. Cash only.*

Hotel-Pension Majesty. Rooms here are small and comfortable; doubles start at DM 75, depending on the season and the view. Breakfast is an additional DM 11. *Mommsenstr. 55, tel. 030/323–2061. Cash only.*

Pension Alexis. This quiet, family-oriented pension has spacious rooms, if a bit grandmotherly (the furniture seems too nice to sit on). Doubles are DM 95. *Carmerstr. 15, tel. 030/312–5144. Cash only.*

Pension Knesebeck. The oddball staff are the star attractions at this little hotel with small, cozy rooms. Doubles cost DM 100 (DM 150 with shower). *Knesebeckstr. 86, tel. 030/312–7255.*

KREUZBERG

The pick of the litter for the penniless party vampire is a DM 28 dorm bed in Die Fabrik, but all of the following places are close to some serious night haunts, and prices here tend to be slightly lower than in Charlottenburg.

Die Fabrik. Cool industrial meets Art Deco in this converted factory. Rooms are tidy and the location is near all the nightlife. Dorm beds are DM 30, doubles DM 94, and triples DM 120. *Schlesische Str. 18, tel. 030/611–7116. U-Bahn to Schlesisches Tor. Cash only.*

Hotel Transit. This large, upscale pension in west Kreuzberg houses a mix of German families and backpackers. Dorm beds are DM 35, doubles DM 105. *Hagelbergerstr. 53–54, tel. 030/785–5051. U6 or U7 to Mehringdamm. Cash only. Laundry (DM 7).*

Pension Kreuzberg. On a quiet, tree-lined street close to some great clubs, you'll find these comfortable double rooms for DM 95 and triples DM 126. *Großbeerenstr. 64, tel. 030/251–1362. U6 or U7 to Mehringdamm. Cash only.*

Riehmers Hofgarten. This beautifully restored late-19th-century hotel in the heart of old Kreuzberg charges slightly higher prices, but it's worth every dollar. High-ceiling rooms are comfortable, with crisp linens and firm beds. Doubles start at DM 160. *Yorckstr. 83, tel. 030/781–011. U7 to Gneisenaustr. Cash only.*

HOSTELS

In summer, hostels in Berlin fill up fast with backpackers and students. However, many of Berlin's old and worn youth hostels provide minimum comfort and sometimes dismal facilities. There are two types of hostels: **Jugendgästehäuser** (youth guest houses) and **Jugendherbergen** (youth hostels). The former tend to have higher prices and fewer beds per room, and the latter require an HI card, though in the off season they'll sometimes admit nonmembers for DM 6 extra. Note that **Hotel Transit** and **Die Fabrik** (*see above*) also have dorm beds.

Gästehaus Luftbrücke. This nice old building near mellow pubs and cafés is used by many groups and families. Beds are DM 45, breakfast included. You must check in by phone. There's no curfew. *Kolonnenstr. 10, enter on Leberstr., tel. 030/784–1037. U7 to Kleistpark.*

Jugendgästehaus am Wannsee (HI). It's a 30-minute S-Bahn ride into town from this large hostel near Wannsee Lake. Reservations are imperative in summer. Beds go for DM 41, breakfast included. There's a 1 AM curfew. *Badeweg 1, tel. 030/803–2034. S-Bahn to Nikolassee; walk west on Spanische Allee.*

Jugendgästehaus am Zoo. In the heart of the city, a five-minute walk from Zoo Station, this hostel, with no curfew, is always crowded with backpackers. Beds are DM 35, DM 40 over 27. *Hardenbergstr. 9a, 4th floor, tel. 030/312–9410.*

Jugendgästehaus Berlin (HI). With a prime location in the middle of town near Tiergarten, this place is usually packed with school classes from all over Germany. Call and reserve the minute you arrive. Beds cost DM 41. There's a midnight curfew. *Kluckstr. 3, tel. 030/261–1097. From Ku'damm, Bus 129 to Kluckstr.*

Jugendgästehaus Deutsche Schreberjugend. You'll find a few sheep, horses, and other livestock out back of this central eco-hostel with pleasant surroundings and no curfew. Beds are DM 38.50. *Franz-Künstler-Str. 4–10, tel. 030/615–1007. U-Bahn to Hallesches Tor.*

Jugendherberge Ernst Reuter (HI). A large youth hostel, particularly popular with students from western Germany, the place has a helpful staff and comfy facilities, all 45 minutes from Zoo Station. Beds are DM 33. There's a midnight curfew.

> *The subway operates 4 AM–1 AM, and on weekends the U1 and U9 run all night.*

Hermsdorfer Damm 48–50, tel. 030/404–1610. S25 to Tegel or U6 to Alt-Tegel; then Bus 125 to Hermsdorfer Damm. Reception open 24 hrs.

CAMPING

The following campsites charge DM 8.50 per person, 50 Pf–DM 1 for hot showers, and DM 5.50 for tent rentals. As a rule, the sites are quiet with clean bathrooms and flush toilets. To reserve a spot (DM 5 fee), contact **Deutscher Camping Club** (Geisbergstr. 11, 10777 Berlin, tel. 030/218–6071).

Campsite Haselhorst (Pulvermühlenweg, tel. 030/334–5955) isn't as picturesque as the others, but its location can't be beat—15 minutes from the Haselhorst U-Bahn and a 25-minute U-Bahn ride from the Ku'damm. Take U7 to Haselhorst and walk north on Daumstraße to Pulvermühlenweg. Crowded **Kladow Camping** (Krampnitzer Weg 111, tel. 030/365–2797) sits in a forest by a small lake more than an hour from the city center. From Bahnhof Zoo, take Bus 149 to Gatower Straße, then Bus 134 to Hottengrundweg; walk right on Hottengrundweg, right on Siebitzer Straße, and left on Krampnitzer Weg (a 25-minute walk). In eastern Berlin, **Krossinsee International Camping** (Wernsdorfer Str. 45, tel. 030/675–8687) lies at the edge of Krossin Lake; you're 1½ hours from the city center, but only 20 minutes from the sleepy village of Schmöckwitz. Take any S-Bahn to Ostkreuz, then S8 to Grünau, and Tram 86 (toward Alt-Schmöckwitz) to the end; walk a half hour east on Wernsdorfer Straße. The last tram leaves around 11 PM.

FOOD

Berlin is a haven for cheap eating. The **Imbiß** (snack) stand is a very German concept—plenty of these stands will serve you a *Boulette* on a *Schrippe* (a meat patty on a roll) for about DM 2. Also cheap are take-out falafel and kebabs (under DM 5) and tasty meals at Indian or Middle Eastern restaurants (DM 10–DM 15). The cheapest supermarkets are **Aldi, Plus,** and **Penny Markt;** Kaisers and **Reichelt** have better selections. Or, try your luck at Berlin's open-air markets, where everything is fresh and cheap. Neukölln's lively, so-called **Türkenmarkt** (Maybachufer, on Landwehrkanal) is held Tuesday and Friday noon–6:30, and the **Winterfeldtmarkt** on Winterfeldtplatz is open Wednesday and Saturday 8 AM–2 PM.

CHARLOTTENBURG

Buddha. Atmospheric Indian joint with specials under DM 10. The mango shakes (DM 3) are delicious. *Grolmanstr. 27, SE of Savignypl., tel. 030/883–4702.*

Pizzeria Mantovani. No-frills "self-service Italian" cafeteria offers 26 different pizzas (DM 2–DM 14) and lots of pasta (under DM 9). *Kantstr. 163, off Breitscheidpl., tel. 030/881–8516.*

Satyam. The best Indian food in the area (all-vegetarian). *Palak Paneer* (spinach and fresh cheese with rice) is DM 5.50. Subtly spiced *Natur Biriyani* (a rice dish with nuts and vegetables) is DM 6.50. *Goethestr. 5, tel. 030/312–9079. U2 or U12 to Ernst-Reuter-Pl.*

KREUZBERG

Chandra Kumari. At this fine Sri Lankan restaurant, specialties include spicy fish (DM 12.50) and *appe* (pancakes with coconut milk and curries; DM 8–DM 12). *Gneisenaustr. 4, tel. 030/694–3056. U6 or U7 to Mehringdamm.*

Diyar. One of the better affordable Turkish restaurants in town, Diyar serves a wide selection of traditional meat dishes and also has vegetarian fare. *Dresdner Str. 9, tel. 030/615–2708.*

Mangla Ashru. Dark, cavernous, fabric-draped Indian restaurant. *Biryani* (a lightly seasoned rice dish) costs a mere DM 5, so splurge on a mango *Lassi* (yogurt drink; DM 2.50). *Lausitzer Str. 6, tel. 030/612–4201. U-Bahn to Görlitzer Bahnhof.*

Rissani. Healthy and vegetarian; sit on the floor under palms. Fresh orange and carrot juices, crispy falafel (DM 4–DM 7). *Spreewaldpl. 6, tel. 030/612–4529. U-Bahn to Görlitzer Bahnhof.*

Thürnagel. This vegetarian and fish restaurant makes healthy eating fun. The *Seitan* (vegetable protein) in sherry sauce and the tempeh curry are good enough to convert a seasoned carnivore. *Gneisenaustr. 57, tel. 030/691–4800. U-Bahn to Gneisenaustr.*

MITTE

Beth Café. Run by the community of the Adass Jisroel Synagogue, this is *the* place for a bagel or a more substantial Israeli meal. Hummus, babaganoush, and tabouleh plate is DM 11. *Tucholskystr. 40, tel. 030/280–6415. S-Bahn to Oranienburger Str.*

Zur Letzten Instanz. Established in 1621, the city's oldest restaurant combines the charming atmosphere of old Berlin with a limited (but very tasty) choice of dishes. The emphasis here is on beer, both in the recipes and in the mugs. *Waisenstr. 14–16, tel. 030/242–5528.*

Zur Nolle. Elegant, carefree, '20s feel—drink and let the jazz take you back. Veggie lasagna (DM 12.80) is the cheapest menu item. Near Museumsinsel and major sights. *S-Bahnbogen 203, Georgenstr., under S-Bahn tracks, tel. 030/208–2655. U-Bahn or S-Bahn to Friedrichstr.*

PRENZLAUER BERG

Manna. Simple vegetarian/vegan Imbiß stand with outstanding food. Stand or perch on a stool. Spinach torte with feta and sesame seeds DM 3.50. *Kollwitzstr. 88/90, tel. 030/442–6451. U2 to Senefelderpl.*

Pasternak. You'll have to decipher the Cyrillic sign, but there's not much Russian cuisine in Berlin, so this place is a treat. Try *bliny* (crêpes; DM 16) or *soljanka* (thick meat and veggie soup; DM 9). Surrounded by hip bars. *Knaackstr. 22–24, tel. 030/441–3399. U2 to Eberswalder Str.*

SCHOENEBERG

Carib. One of Berlin's few honest-to-goodness Caribbean joints (expat Caribs gather here). The owner makes everyone feel welcome, even if you just want a splash of rum in your coffee. Try jerk chicken (DM 19) or grilled fish with coconut milk (DM 22). *Motzstr. 30, tel. 030/213–5381. U4 to Viktoria-Luise-Pl.*

Cascado Snack. Open 24 hours, the best Imbiß in Schöneberg. Well-spiced Turkish pizzas, super *Schafskäse mit Salat* (feta with veggies on fresh Turkish bread; DM 4). *Potsdamer Str., no phone. U2 to Bülowstr.*

Habibi. On Winterfeldplatz, the place to come for late-night falafel (from DM 4). It stays open late to catch the last bar hoppers. *Goltzstr. 24., tel. 030/215–3332. U-Bahn to Nollendorfpl.*

Rani Indischer Imbiß. Popular place on Winterfeldplatz. Try chicken *sabzi* (with spinach; DM 8.50) or Indian vegetarian plate (DM 10), both cooked fresh and served in large portions. *Goltzstr. 32, tel. 030/215–2673. U-Bahn to Nollendorfpl. or Eisenacher Str.*

WORTH SEEING

Because of Berlin's size and the sheer number of its sights, your best strategy is to target and explore a particular district completely before moving on. When you hop from one "must-see" attraction to the next, Berlin's vastness translates into incoherence. If you're short on time, you could possibly see Berlin's major sights at a frenzied pace. Generally, the S-Bahn and U-Bahn are useful for getting from one district to another, but not for traveling from sight to sight within the district—plan on walking a lot. **Berlin Walks** (Eislebener Str. 1, tel. 030/211–6663; tours DM 14) has excellent English-language tours, including "Infamous Third Reich Sites," "Jewish Life in Berlin," and "Where was the Wall?" Cruise Berlin's canals (around DM 10) with **Reederei Heinz Riedel** (Planufer 78, tel. 030/691–3782 or 030/693–4646; U-Bahn to Kottbusser Tor).

Construction and consolidation mean museum collections are moving and changing, and buildings may close for renovation. Many of Berlin's museums belong to the **Staatliche Museen Preußischer Kulturbesitz (SMPK)** and most can be visited individually for DM 4, or with a one-day combination ticket, the *Tageskarte,* for DM 8.

ALEXANDERPLATZ

Alex is genuine eastern Berlin in transition. It's easy to find, thanks to the **Fernsehturm** TV tower, rising nearly 1,320 ft above the square. From the top-floor observation deck (elevator DM 7) you get a striking 360° view of Berlin. Back on the ground, the rest of Alexanderplatz is dominated by ugly high-rises, fast-food stands, and the Kaufhof department store. Slightly southwest is the **Rotes Rathaus** (Red Town Hall), built between 1861 and 1869 to serve as the seat of Berlin's city government. Next to the Rathaus is an sexy fountain of Neptune and his foxy courtiers, and across the park to the south is the **Marx-Engels Forum,** featuring statues of the two troublemakers looking grimly into the future of socialism (or maybe at the foxy courtiers).

BRANDENBURG GATE

Those who watched the Berlin Wall crumble in 1989 will recognize the *Brandenburger Tor* (Brandenburg Gate), perhaps the most vivid symbol of German unification. When the Wall was built in 1961, ostensibly as an "antifascist protection barrier," the historic gate, built in 1791 as one of 14 other gates that once guarded Berlin, was hidden behind a 10-ft-tall barrier. On November 10, 1989, after thousands of Berliners from both East and West began smashing the wall, the Brandenburg Gate was swamped with celebrants. The most spectacular approach to the gate is along **Straße des 17. Juni,** a 2-km (1-mi) avenue that cuts through the Tiergarten's center.

CHECKPOINT CHARLIE

Between 1961 and 1989, Checkpoint Charlie (Kochstr. and Friedrichstr.) was the most (in)famous crossing point between East and West Berlin. The checkpoint itself, a wooden guard hut, was removed in 1989. Remaining are a grim, skeletal watchtower and a somber memorial slab dedicated to those killed while trying to escape. You can trace the checkpoint's history at the nearby **Haus am Checkpoint Charlie.** This small museum has hundreds of Cold War–era photographs and a fascinating exhibit on some ingenious escape attempts. *Friedrichstr. 44, tel. 030/251–1031. U6 to Kochstr. Admission: DM 7.50. Open daily 9 AM–10 PM.*

DAHLEM MUSEUMS

The West Berlin suburb of Dahlem, 15 minutes by subway from the city center, is a quiet enclave of tree-lined streets and sleepy pubs. The Dahlem Museum complex houses six world-class museums, but it would take at least two full days to see everything. Concentrate instead on the main exhibits: the **Museum für Völkerkunde,** the internationally famous ethnographic museum showcasing arts and artifacts from Africa, Asia, the Americas, and the South Seas. Equally impressive is the **Skulpturensammlung** (Sculpture Collection), which displays mostly medieval and Renaissance sculpture. *Lansstr. 8 and Arnimallee 23–27, tel. 030/83011. U1 to Dahlem-Dorf; walk right on Iltisstr., left on Lansstr. Admission: DM 8 (SMPK accepted). Open Tues.–Fri. 9–5, weekends 10–5.*

Also in Dahlem, but not part of the complex, the excellent **Brücke-Museum** houses pre–World War I examples of Berlin's expressionist movement, including works by Erich Heckel and Ernst Kirchner. *Bussardsteig 9, tel. 030/831–2029. U-Bahn to Fehrbelliner Pl.; then Bus 115 (direction Potsdamer Chaussee or Neuruppiner Str.) to Pücklerstr.; walk right on Pücklerstr., left on Fohlenweg, right on Bussardsteig. Admission: DM 5. Open Wed.–Mon. 11–5.*

FRIEDRICHSTRASSE

The once bustling "Fifth Avenue" of Berlin's pre-war days has risen from the rubble of war and communist negligence to regain its old splendor. The jewel of this street is the **Friedrichstadtpassagen,** a glitzy shopping complex, praised internationally for its daring design. At the corner of Französische Strasse is one of Berlin's most fascinating new buildings, designed by French star architect Jean Nouvel and housing the French department store **Galeries Lafayette.** Its interior is dominated by a huge steel and glass funnel surrounded by six floors of upscale shopping. *Französische Str. 23. Tel. 030/209480.*

GENDARMENMARKT

South of Unter den Linden (*see below*), you'll find one of the finest squares in all Europe. Its main features are the 18th-century **Deutscher Dom** (tel. 030/2273–2141, admission free; open daily 10–5), which houses a rather dull German history exhibit normally housed in the now-empty Reichstag (*see below*); and its twin church just opposite, the **Französischer Dom,** built in 1708 by French Protestant Huguenots fleeing persecution (its design is based on the Huguenots' original cathedral in Charenton, France). Inside is a tiny, drab Huguenot museum (tel. 030/229–1760, admission DM 3; open Tues.–Sat. noon–5, Sun. 1–5.). On the opposite side of the square is the neoclassic **Schauspielhaus,** one of the greatest works by Berlin architect Karl Friedrich Schinkel. Nowadays it's home to the **Konzerthaus Berlin** and its Berlin Symphony Orchestra.

HAMBURGER BAHNHOF

This new museum has turned Berlin into a must for *affiniconados* of modern art. Two years ago the old train station was remodeled and given a spectacular new wing, housing works by German artists Joseph Beuys and Anselm Kiefer as well as paintings by Andy Warhol, Cy Twombly, Robert Rauschenberg, and Robert Morris. *Invalidenstr. 50–51, tel. 030/3978–340. Admission 8 DM. Open Tues.–Fri. 9–5, weekends 10–5.*

KULTURFORUM

The Kulturforum (Cultural Forum), near the Tiergarten, is a series of fascinating museums, galleries, and concert halls. The newly erected **Gemäldegalerie** re-unites formerly separated collections from East and West Berlin. It is considered to be one of Germany's finest art galleries and houses an extensive selection of European paintings from the 13th to the 18th century. Several rooms are reserved for paintings by German masters, among them Dürer, Cranach the Elder, and Holbein. The exhibitions at the neighboring **Kupferstichkabinett** include European woodcuts, engravings, and illustrated books from the 15th century to the present. *Both museums are at Matthäikirchpl, tel. 030/266–2002. Admission DM 4 to each. Open Tues.–Fri. 9–5, weekends 10–5.*

Inside the new **Kunstgewerbemuseum** is a display of European arts and crafts from the Middle Ages to the present. Among its notable exhibits are the Welfenschatz (Welfen Treasure), a collection of 16th-century gold and silver plates from Nürnberg, as well as ceramics and porcelains. *Matthäikirchpl. 10, tel. 030/266–2911. Admission DM 8. Free Sun. and holidays. Open Tues.–Fri. 9–5, weekends 10–5.*

The finest attraction at the Kulturforum, however, is the **Neue Nationalgalerie.** The permanent collection leans heavily toward impressionism, but the 20th-century collection also includes some fine pieces (those made in the GDR are particularly interesting). An adjoining gallery houses works by Klee, Bacon, and Johns. *Potsdamer Str. 50, SW of Potsdamer Pl., tel. 030/266–2662. Admission: DM 4. Free first Sun. every month. Open Tues.–Fri. 9–5, weekends 10–5.*

MARX-ENGELS-PLATZ

The lavish 15th-century Berliner Schloß (Berlin Palace) once occupied this square; what was left of the palace after World War II was dynamited by the GDR to make way for the modern **Palast der Republik,** a futuristic, copper-tinted space capsule known by locals as *Palazzo Prozzo* (Show-off Palace). This once housed the GDR's parliament, but today it stands empty and is supposed to be demolished (ostensibly because of asbestos)—some dreamers even suggest rebuilding the old Hohenzollern palace in a return to royalist fantasyland. Just opposite the Palast der Republik is the 19th-century **Berliner Dom** (Am Lustgarten, tel. 030/2026–9135; open Mon.–Sat. 9–6:30, Sun. and holidays 11:30–6:30), Berlin's impressive cathedral. A short walk west across the Schloßbrücke brings you to the impressive Unter den Linden boulevard (*see below*).

MUSEUMSINSEL

Near Marx-Engels-Platz and bordered on either side by the River Spree, Museum Island houses three major museums, each of which cost DM 4 (free first Sun. every month and holidays), double for the Pergamon, and are open Tuesday–Sunday 9–5. The **Altes Museum** (Bodestr. 1–3, tel. 030/2035–5444) offers exhibits on varying periods and themes in German art. The **Alte Nationalgalerie** (Bodestr. 1–3, tel. 030/220–0381) contains Berlin's largest collection of 18th- and 19th-century paintings. To the west, the **Pergamonmuseum** (Am Kupfergraben, tel. 030/2035–5444) falls into the don't-miss category, containing one of the world's best collections of Hellenic, Egyptian, and Mesopotamian art. The museum is named for its principal display, the Pergamon altar, a dazzling 2nd-century BC Greek temple that was moved block by block from a mountaintop in Turkey. Equally remarkable in the Asia Minor section is the Ishtar Gate, which dates from the 6th-century BC reign of Nebuchadnezzar II. The island is near the Hackescher Markt S-Bahn stop; head west and left down Burgstraße.

NEUE SYNAGOGE

This lavishly restored landmark, one of Europe's largest synagogues, was built between 1859 and 1866 in an an exotic amalgam of styles. After its destruction during the infamous Kristallnacht (night of the broken glass) in 1938 and later allied bombing raids, the synagogue remained untouched until restoration began during the mid-1980s. Today, it's connected to the modern Centrum Judaicum, a center for Jewish culture and learning. Since 1989, Jewish religious and business life, which flourished here in the old Jewish **Scheunenviertel** (Stable Quarters) until 1933, is slowly finding its way back into the historic quarter around the synagogue. *Oranienburger Str. 28/30, tel. 030/280–1316. Admission free. Open Sun.–Thurs. 10–6, Fri. 10–2.*

NIKOLAIVIERTEL

The Nikolaiviertel quarter, just southwest of Alexanderplatz and bordered by the River Spree to the south, is a replica of an entire 18th- and 19th-century neighborhood, including approximated copies of the quarter's famous baroque and fin-de-siècle facades (e.g., cement, rather than marble, columns). The district is dominated by the reconstructed **Nikolaikirche** (admission DM 3), the oldest building in Berlin (1230). Opposite the church, the 17th-century **Knoblauch-Haus** (Poststr. 23, tel. 030/240020; admission DM 2; closed Mon.) traces the life of Christian Knoblauch, a wealthy silk merchant who lived here. **Zum Nußbaum,** across from Nikolaikirche at the corner of Propststraße, is a re-creation of one of Berlin's oldest inns. It still serves a hearty tankard of beer (DM 5) along with pricey German meals. Just south is Berlin's most lavish rococo house, the **Ephraim Palace** (Mühlendamm 16, tel. 030/240020; closed Mon.), built in 1764 for Veitel Ephraim, court jeweler to Friedrich II. Veitel was Jewish, so in 1933 the Nazis razed the structure and plundered its collection of rare stones.

REICHSTAG

Just northwest of Brandenburg Gate, the bulky Reichstag (Imperial Parliament) is loaded with history. Built in 1894 to house the Prussian Parliament, it performed the same function for the short-lived Weimar Republic (1919–33). On February 28, 1933, a month after Adolf Hitler had been appointed Chancellor, the Reichstag burned down under mysterious circumstances. No one's sure who actually set the fire, but the governing Nazis swiftly and vociferously blamed the Communists, using the fire as a pretext to basically suspend the constitution and outlaw all opposition parties. Currently, the Reichstag is an empty shell being renovated in preparation for the German parliament's move-in sometime around 2000.

SCHLOSS CHARLOTTENBURG

Friedrich I, the flamboyant Prussian monarch, built the Schloß Charlottenburg (Charlottenburg Palace) at the end of the 17th century for his wife, Queen Sophie Charlotte. The palace became the city residence for all Prussian rulers, and the complex evolved under the direction of each new ruler. Visits to the royal apartments are by guided tour only; tours leave every hour on the hour from 9 to 4. Also on the grounds you'll find the 18th-century **Belvedere House** (admission DM 2.50) and the **Schinkel Pavillion** (admission DM 2.50), which houses paintings by Caspar David Friedrich and some fin-de-siècle furniture. *Luisenpl., tel. 030/3209–1275. From Zoo Station, Bus 145 to Schloß Charlottenburg. Admission: DM 8 (tours and palace collections not included); palace grounds free. Open Tues.–Fri. 9–5, weekends 10–5; grounds open daily sunrise–sunset.*

Just opposite the Palace are two of Berlin's finest museums: the **Ägyptisches Museum** (Schlosstr. 70, tel. 030/320911, admission DM 8; open Mon.–Thurs. 9–5, weekends 10–5), presenting the city's most beautiful woman, the antique bust of Egyptian queen Nefertiti; and the **Sammlung Berggruen** (Schlosstr. 1, tel. 030/326–9580, admission DM 8; open Tues.–Fri. 9–5, weekends 10–5), a new museum showcasing a private collection of modern paintings, mostly Picasso and Van Gogh.

UNTER DEN LINDEN

The 1½-km (¾-mi) Unter den Linden is a sweeping, grand avenue that stretches from Brandenburg Gate in the west to Marx-Engels-Platz (*see above*) in the east. Start at **Pariser Platz,** just east of Brandenburg Gate, and walk east until you hit the 18th-century **Humboldt University,** recognizable by the statues of Wilhelm and Alexander von Humboldt, the university's founders. Across from the university is an equestrian sculpture (1851) of Friedrich II (Frederick the Great). The sculptor, Rauch, incorporated the heads of Gotthold Lessing and Immanuel Kant, two of the emperor's harshest critics, on the horse's rear end. To the right of Humboldt University is **Neue Wache,** Germany's National Memorial for Victims of Fascism and Militarism. Inside is the poignant Käthe Kollwitz statue, *Mother with Dead Son,* the memorial is still controversial for its incorporation of both dead Nazi soldiers and their victims. The area just southeast of the university is known as **Bebelplatz,** a pleasant square bordered by lime trees. Bebelplatz marks the site of the 1933 *Bücherverbrennung* (book burning), a propaganda event orchestrated by Goebbels. Works considered too "dangerous" for public consumption were thrown into the fire. Flanking the square is Berlin's main opera house, the **Deutsche Staatsoper** (Unter den Linden 7, tel. 030/2035–4494; box office open weekdays noon–5:45). Across the bridge is Marx-Engels-Platz (*see above*).

If you haven't soured on German history yet, there's an entire museum of it waiting next door the **Deutsches Historisches Museum.** This former Prussian armory houses a quirky permanent collection (including Panzer tanks, Bismarck's cane, and one of Karl Marx's flower vases), as well as an art gallery and a movie house (tickets DM 5) that shows history flicks. The gallery's rotating exhibits are generally fantastic and thought-provoking. *Unter den Linden 2, tel. 030/215020. Admission free. Open Thurs.– Tues. 10–6.*

DISTRICTS

Twenty-three distinct Bezirke (districts) make up the city. Twelve belonged to West Berlin, 11 to East Berlin, and each has its own town hall and district council. Every district in Berlin offers something of interest, be it a massive Soviet war memorial or an impressive nighttime leather scene. The most intriguing districts are those in the historic center of Berlin, namely Prenzlauer Berg, Mitte, and Kreuzberg.

CHARLOTTENBURG • Stretching west of Zoo Station, Charlottenburg is a huge and disparate district. From **Breitscheidplatz,** immediately opposite Europa-Center, the Kurfürstendamm (usually referred to as the Ku'damm) stretches 3½ km (2¼ mi) through Charlottenburg to the Grunewald (*see* Parks and Gardens, *below*). Near Europa-Center you can find people carousing and browsing at all hours of the day—a crowd evenly divided between wealthy Berliners and junkies looking to score. Here you'll find the turn-of-the-century **Kaiser-Wilhelm-Gedächtniskirche** (open Tues.–Sat. 10–4), which has been left in a war-scarred state to serve as a memorial; inside is a display of pre- and postwar photos. Charlottenburg's other thoroughfare is the less touristy Kantstraße. About 5 blocks west of Europa-Center is **Savignyplatz,** which hosts here the rich and beautiful. In some of the smaller side streets, however, you'll find crowds of students slacking off in cafés and ethnic restaurants. At night, the area's clubs keep things going until the wee hours of the morning. While in Charlottenburg, don't miss the **Käthe Kollwitz Museum** (Fasanenstr. 24, near Ku'damm, tel. 030/882–5210; closed Tues.), which contains graphics and sketches by the famous sculptor (1867–1945) despised by the Nazis for her social activism.

KREUZBERG • This is one of Berlin's liveliest quarters, home to an odd mix of progressive youth, Turkish immigrants, blue-collar workers, and yuppies. Kreuzberg has sizable gay, lesbian, and student communities, not to mention untold hordes of dropouts and junkies. The district used to be dotted with illegal squats; today many of the former squatters are upright tenants in the houses they once occupied. Kreuzberg is also *the* place for cheap dive bars and basement cafés; many cafés attract self-proclaimed bohemians and the art crowd. Though **west Kreuzberg** (check out Marheinekeplatz and Mehringdamm; U-Bahn to Mehringdamm or Gneisenaustraße) is gentrifying rapidly, Kreuzberg is, for the most part, the place to come for a nontraditional look at Berlin. At the top of Mehringdamm (U6 to Platz der Luftbrücke) is a **monument** to the Allied pilots and flight crew who died in crashes during the Berlin airlift. Thanks to its peculiar shape, Berliners call it *Hungerkralle* ("hunger claw"). The wilder, grungier **east Kreuzberg,** also known as SO36, centers around Oranienstraße and Wiener Straße; U-Bahn Görlitzer Bahnhof puts you in the middle of things.

PRENZLAUER BERG • Though Prenzlauer Berg ("Prenzlberg") was a part of eastern Berlin, you won't find bland apartment blocks here, but rather 19th-century neo-baroque tenements that are elegant in a dilapidated sort of way. Take U2 to Senefelderplatz or Eberswalder Straße; both empty onto the district's main artery, **Schönhauser Allee,** a shopping street lined with old-fashioned prewar buildings. Just north of Senefelderplatz is the **Jüdischer Friedhof** (Schönhauser Allee 23; open Mon.–Thurs. 8–4, Fri. 8–1), with its haunting, ivy-covered graves. East on Wörtherstraße is the graceful **Käthe-Kollwitz-Platz,** named in honor of the famous German artist. In the middle stands Kollwitz's sculpture *Die Mutter* (*The Mother*). Leading north from the square is one of Berlin's most beautiful streets, **Husemannstraße,** lined with trees, exquisitely restored buildings, and shops.

SCHOENEBERG • East of Charlottenburg lies the fun-loving district of Schöneberg, where residents enjoy the good life without too much pretension. At the heart of Schöneberg lies **Nollendorfplatz,** and the streets south and west of here feature the area's crowded markets, dusty bookshops, quality antique dealers, and lively bars and cafés. At the Nollendorfplatz U-Bahn station, once a cruising area for gays, is a plaque dedicated to the estimated 100,000 homosexuals murdered in Nazi concentration camps. Today, **Motzstraße,** which runs southwest from Nollendorf, is the center for the city's gay nightlife. Walking along **Maaßenstraße** past cafés and shops, you reach **Winterfeldplatz,** with its open-air market (*see* Food, *above*) and used bookstores, and the street life continues south down **Goltzstraße.**

PARKS AND GARDENS

GRUNEWALD • On the western edge of town, this 32-square-km (13-square-mi) expanse of horse trails, bike paths, beaches, and trees is Berlin's most popular weekend retreat. If you're in the mood to walk, follow the signs to **Jagdschloß Grunewald** (Hüttenweg 100, tel. 030/813–3597; closed Mon.), a 16th-century royal hunting lodge that now houses a privately owned art gallery. Another popular excursion is to **Pfaueninsel** (Peacock Island), set in a wide arm of the Havel River. The island is noted for its lush gardens—home to hundreds of wild peacocks—and its faux-ruin **castle** (tel. 030/805–3042; admission DM 2). The Grunewald is too large to cover in a single day, so if you want nothing more than beach and water take the S-Bahn to Nikolassee and follow the STRANDBAD WANNSEE signs; it's about a 20-minute walk. A more traditional starting point is one stop farther at Wannsee station, a five-minute walk to some good hiking trails.

TIERGARTEN • The Tiergarten runs from Brandenburg Gate in the east to Zoo Station in the west—a peaceful expanse of forest and lake in the otherwise urban city center. Its main feature is the sprawling 1½-km (¾-mi) **Straße des 17. Juni,** which commemorates the June 17, 1953, workers' uprising against the East German government, in which 350 people were killed by Soviet tanks and troops. In glaring contrast to this stands the **Soviet Victory Memorial,** built immediately after the war; it is flanked by two of the first tanks to enter the city in the final, bloody days of the so-called Third Reich. Much of the Tiergarten is undeveloped and attracts few tourists; the most interesting sections are the area surrounding Brandenburg Gate and the zoo, at the southwest corner of the park. In summer, Turkish families enjoy their barbecues throughout the Tiergarten.

The **Zoologischer Garten** boasts the world's largest variety of animals—more than 11,000 creatures. It's also worth the extra dough to check out the massive aquarium complex. *Enter at Hardenbergpl. or Budapester Str., tel. 030/254–010. Zoo admission: DM 11. Combined aquarium and zoo admission: DM 18. Open daily 9–6:30, 9–5 in winter; aquarium daily 9–6.*

AFTER DARK

Berlin's many nightlife districts are impossible to categorize. Kreuzberg, Schöneberg, Mitte, and Prenzlauer Berg all have every kind of bar and club and every kind of clientele imaginable. In each you'll find well-dressed yuppies, young punks, ravers, and a queer crowd, though one group or another may be more prevalent. If you want to go clubbing, check out the mags *zitty, prinz, tip,* or *030* for current listings, since offerings vary wildly at most venues. Keep your *Nachtliniennetz* (night-bus route map) handy, but remember that Berlin's most serious night owls use the night buses only to *start* their evening: By the time they go home, regular transit is up and running again.

Internationale Filmfestspiele, Berlin's International Film Festival in February, rivals those of Cannes and Venice. It features new works from an international troupe of filmmakers as well as remastered classics. Cinemas all over Berlin participate in the event, and admission runs anywhere from DM 6 to DM 50. For tickets and more information, contact Filmfestspiele Berlin (Budapester Str. 50, tel. 030/254890).

BARS

Berlin supposedly has more bars per square mile than any other city in the world, but the city's bars are notoriously short-lived, especially those in Kreuzberg and Prenzlauer Berg. The main strip in Kreuzberg is **Oranienstraße,** noted for its Turkish watering holes and offbeat cafés. German yuppies tend to gather at Charlottenburg's **Savignyplatz,** while **Winterfeldplatz** in Schöneberg attracts an odd mix of artists, long-haired dropouts, and well-dressed business types. The main drag in Prenzlauer Berg is **Schönhauser Allee** and the adjacent **Kollwitzplatz.** In Mitte, the **Oranienburger Straße** and the area around **Rosenthaler Platz** have emerged as the hippest venues for parties, clubs, and bars, attracting a mostly young and very international crowd. Bars usually open around 6 or 7 at the latest and close around 4 AM or 5 AM.

Bla Bla. Mellow yellow walls, matching music, overstuffed faux-leather couches, a friendly artsy clientele, and vampiric open hours make this a typical Prenzl joint. *Sredzkisstr. 19a, off Schönhauser Allee, tel. 030/442–3581. U2 to Eberswalder Str.*

THE BERLIN WALL

In the 1950s, the German Democratic Republic (GDR) grew increasingly embarrassed that nearly 20,000 East Germans were crossing into West Berlin every month, never to return. To stem the flow, the government decided to seal the border completely. At 1 AM on August 13, 1961, more than 25,000 GDR workers set about raising a mortar and cement-block barrier—the Berlin Wall—along the entire length of the border with the western city. The Wall, and film footage of Berliners desperately jumping from buildings and running through barbed wire (or getting shot trying), became a symbol of the Cold War. Today, a dozen or so former border guards have been sentenced to jail.

Die Krähe. This Kneipe is only one of many more similar alternative bars, clubs, and small restaurants around Kollwitzplatz. The food here is cheap but tasty. *Kollwitzstr. 84, tel. 030/442–8291. U-Bahn to Eberswalder Str.*

Dralle's. A fancy but inexpensive hang-out for upscale *Charlottenburger,* this all-red pub and bar stay open until the wee hours. *Schlüterstr. 69, tel. 030/313–5038. U1 to Ernst-Reuter-Platz or S-Bahn to Savignyplatz.*

Leydicke. A Berlin classic, the Leydicke is a must for out-of-towners. The proprietors operate their own distillery and have a superb selection of sweet wines and liqueurs. *Mansteinstr. 4, tel. 030/216–2973. S-Bahn or U7 to Yorkstr.*

Silberstein. You might pass Silberstein up at first, mistaking it for an ordinary art gallery and you wouldn't be entirely wrong; it's a gallery and one of the city's trendiest drinking holes. *Oranienburger Str. 27, tel. 030/281–2095. U-Bahn to Oranienburger Tor.*

Zosch. Some dives make you feel right at home. Live music—from speed metal to tango—is quite likely here on weekend nights. *Tucholskystr. 30, tel. 030/280–7664. S-Bahn to Oranienburger Str. or U-Bahn to Oranienburger Tor.*

DANCE CLUBS

E-Werk. *The* headquarters for techno, this massive club is in the old electric works. The place houses several bars and nonstop beats, but it'll cost you. Don't bother coming before 1 AM, later on Saturday. *Wilhelmstr. 43, tel. 030/252–2012. U2 to Mohrenstr. Cover: DM 15. Open Thurs.–Sat. U-Bahn to Mohrenstr.*

Knaack Club. Located in Prenzlauer Berg, the Knaack has three floors of nonstop dancing to '70s funk and heavy house, plus occasional live gigs and films. *Greifswalder Str. 224, tel. 030/422–7061. U2 to Eberswalder Str.*

90 Grad. This jam-packed disco plays hip-hop, soul, and some techno and really gets going around 2 AM. Mixed straight and gay crowd. *Dennewitzstr. 37, tel.030/2628–984. U1 to Kurfürstenstr.*

Sophienklub. A gathering spot for mostly former East Berliners, this cramped disco always serves up a formidable music mix. It's heavy on acid jazz. *Sophienstr. 6, tel. 030/282–4552.*

LIVE MUSIC

Eierschale (I). A variety of jazz groups appears here at the "Egg Shell," one of Berlin's oldest jazz clubs, open daily from 8:30 PM. Admission is free. *Podbielskiallee 50, tel. 030/832–7097. U1 to Podbielski-allee.*

ROCK • Franz-Club. Popular with a university-age crowd, the acts here range from jazz and rock to avant-garde Klezmer or psycho-funk. *Schönhauser Allee 36–39, tel. 030/442–8203. U2 to Eberswalder Str. Cover: DM 10–DM 15.*

Wild at Heart. Small local bands blast several nights a week for a house full of twentysomethings at this venue. The dim, red bar is like the inside of a very dark heart. *Wiener Str. 20, tel. 030/611–7010. U-Bahn to Görlitzer Bhf. Cover: DM 5.*

JAZZ • The **Jazz in the Garden** festival brings local and international talent to the Neue Nationalgalerie (*see* Worth Seeing, *above*) four Fridays in June. Many of the sessions are held outside in the gallery's lush gardens and it's all free. **Jazz in July** is Berlin's premiere jazz event, attracting big-name stars from the United States and Britain. It's sponsored by **Quasimodo** (Kantstr. 12a, tel. 030/312–8086; cover DM 5–DM 20), the festival's main venue and the club largely responsible for Berlin's jazz renaissance. Tickets, generally priced between DM 10 and DM 25, should be purchased well in advance.

A-Trane Jazzclub. The latest (and very stylish) arrival to Berlin's ever-changing scene, A-Trane has quickly found its fans among Berlin's hard-core jazz community. *Pestalozzistr. 105, tel. 030/3132–550. U2 to Ernst-Reuter-Platz or S-Bahn to Savignyplatz. Cover: DM 25.*

Flöz. Bohemian, dark, and smoky, this dive attracts local and big-name bands who play pre-1950s jazz, Dixieland, and swing. *Nassauische Str. 37, tel. 030/861–1000. U7 or U9 to Berliner Str.*

Junction Bar. A small, intimate, rough-edged club, the Junction specializes in jazz, Afro-rhythm, and piano jams. DJs spin tunes after the show Tuesday–Saturday nights. *Gneisenaustr. 18, tel. 030/694–6602. U7 to Gneisenaustr. Cover: DM 5–DM 10.*

Schloß Cecilienhof, in the Neuer Garten east of downtown, is where Truman, Attlee, and Stalin signed the 1945 Potsdam Agreement divvying up Germany.

CLASSICAL • You can find world-famous classical music at Berlin's **Philharmonie und Kammermusiksaal** (Matthäikirchstr. 1, tel. 030/254880), northwest on Bellevue Straße from Potsdamer Platz. Opera goes on at **Deutsche Oper** (Bismarckstr. 34–35, tel. 030/343–8401; U2 or U12 to Deutsche Oper) in the west and **Staatsoper Unter den Linden** (Unter den Linden 5–7, tel. 030/2035–4494; S-Bahn to Unter den Linden) in the east. Tickets usually start at DM 25.

VARIETY THEATERS

During the past few years Berlin has become Germany's prime hot spot for variety shows, presenting magic, artistic, and circus performances, sometimes combined with music and classic cabaret. The world's largest variety show is presented at the **Friedrichstadtpalast** (Friedrichstr. 107, tel. 030/2326–2474), a glossy showcase for revues and famous for its female dancers. Much smaller but classier in style is the **Wintergarten** (Potsdamer Str. 96, tel. 030/2627–070), a romantic homage to the old days of Berlin's original variety theater in the 1920s.

NEAR BERLIN

POTSDAM

No matter how short your stay in Berlin, make time for a quick visit to Potsdam, the old main garrison town of Prussia and today's capital of the German state of Brandenburg. The town's historic quarters are intensely beautiful. From Platz der Einheit, near the tourist office, Friedrich-Ebert-Straße heads north through the **baroque quarter,** noted for its colorful facades. Avoid the touristy "market" streets and head instead for the network of lanes that fan outward from the larger shopping avenues. These run through quiet residential areas, passing a few tree-lined parks on the way. On **Alter Markt,** Potsdam's central market square, check out the classical **Nikolaikirche** (1724) and the colorful facade of the city hall, and **Rathaus** (1755), recognizable by the gilded figure of Atlas atop the tower. Three blocks north of Alter Markt is **Holländisches Viertel,** the Dutch quarter. It was designed in 1732 by Friedrich Wilhelm I, who hoped to induce Dutch artisans to settle in the city. Few Dutch ever came, but the quarter's gabled, red-brick homes give the district a distinctive, very un-German feel. Continue north past **Nauener Tor,** an 18th-century city gate, to the **Alexandrowka** district, with its dense jumble of wood houses built in 19th-century Russian style. West of the tourist office, the excellent **Filmmuseum** (tel. 0331/293675; open Tues.–Fri. 10–5; weekends 10–6; admission DM 6) documents German cinema since 1895—particularly interesting are the Nazi-era propaganda films.

The stately grounds of **Sanssouci Park** spread out past the west end of Brandenburger Straße. The beautiful, rococo **Sanssouci Palace** (tel. 0331/969–4206, closed 1st and 3rd Mon. each month) is where Friedrich Wilhelm's son, Friedrich der Große (Frederick the Great), kept himself cultured by hanging out with Voltaire and the son of J. S. Bach. The palace's rich interior is shown on the DM 8 tour; pick up the English-language supplement. If you'd rather save your money, simply stroll through the garden. At its western end, you'll stumble upon Friedrich's second palace, the **Neues Palais** (admission DM 8; closed 2nd and 4th Mon. each month), and his successor Friedrich Wilhelm II's **Charlottenhof** (admission DM 6; closed 4th Mon. each month).

BASICS • Potsdam is only 30 minutes from Berlin on S3 or S7. From the Potsdam Stadt station, head up the access road and right across Lange Brücke to the **tourist office** (Friedrich-Ebert-Str. 5, tel. 0331/275680). Potsdam makes an easy day trip, but the office can book you into a private room (DM 15–DM 30) for a DM 5 fee, if you choose. If you get hungry, take your pick from the good selection of cafés and cheap restaurants on Brandenburger Straße.

BRANDENBURG

Brandenburg is one of the region's finest baroque cities, with a pleasant mix of half-timbered houses, old-style shopfronts, cobble streets, and relaxed, open-air squares in its the historic city center. The winding **Havel River** courses through town, so much of the town is given over to bridges, canals, and riverside walking paths. Brandenburg is divided into the Altstadt and Neustadt, with the **Dominsel** (Cathedral Island)—site of the city's original 10th-century settlement—in between. One of the city's many Gothic churches, **Dom St. Peter und Paul** (open Mon.–Sat. 9–6) is on the island; its towering cathedral makes a good navigating tool when exploring Brandenburg on foot. Inside, there's an unusual relief of a fox in monk's clothing, spreading the Word to a congregation of geese.

West from the tourist office and across the river is the Altstadt, where you'll find more churches and cathedrals. The old center is at Altstädtischer Markt and the **Altstädtisches Rathaus** (Old Town Hall), guarded by Roland, a 26-ft-high statue holding a sword in one hand and his pelvis (à la Michael Jackson) in the other. Inside the Rathaus is an expensive restaurant and beer garden.

BASICS • Trains arrive every two hours from Berlin's Zoo Station (1 hr, DM 15); the last train back leaves at 10:15. For detailed city maps, stop by the helpful **tourist office** (Hauptstr. 51, tel. 03381/524257; open weekdays 9–7, Sat. 9–2). Take Tram 2 or 6 to Neustädtischer Markt.

EASTERN GERMANY

If you expect eastern Germany to be *all* cement, steel, and gloom, expect to be pleasantly surprised. Thuringia, in particular, remains one of the country's most picture-perfect regions, with a dizzying array of rolling pastureland, lazy farm villages, forested mountains, forbidding castles, and lush, flamboyantly baroque palaces. The highlights here are Erfurt and Weimar, along with the Thüringer Wald (Thuringian Forest). In Saxony, Leipzig is like a mini-Berlin—great architecture, history, and nightlife without the overwhelming size. Dresden, Saxony's capital, is busily reconstructing its baroque magnificence.

The German state of Saxony-Anhalt more closely resembles what many foreigners imagine East Germany to be. It still bears the scars of overindustrialization, and its cities are wastelands of industry and cement. As former East Germans struggle with their new economy and supposed capitalist perspective, unemployment here remains the highest in Germany. To appreciate this region you need to prepare for the troublesome dichotomy of eastern Germany: unspoiled countryside countered by forests thinning from acid rain; farmland and nature as a foil for industry and pollution.

A major reason to visit this area is to soak up some history. The small towns will tell much more about an older Germany than the frenetic lifestyles of Frankfurt, Hamburg, Stuttgart, or Köln. The Communist influence here—hard-line as it was—never penetrated as deeply as did the American impact on West Germany. Instead, East Germany clung to its German heritage, proudly preserving connections with such national heroes as Luther, Goethe, Schiller, Bach, Händel, Wagner, and Hungarian-born Liszt. Today, cyclists can have a ball in these areas because the distances are not vast and the scenery—at least once you escape to the countryside—falls somewhere between rural idyllic and sylvan nirvana. Most train stations in the area rent bikes for about DM 15–DM 20 per day.

DRESDEN

Dresdeners claim they live in the most beautiful city in Germany, proudly nicknaming their home city the "Florence on the Elbe River". It's quite a bold statement—considering the city's near annihilation by brutal Allied firebombing on February 13–14, 1945, and its bleak reconstruction (with factories and cement-block housing) courtesy of the GDR. But today, the giant 17th-century baroque buildings along the Elbe are beginning to reemerge from under scaffolding and rubble as a testament to Dresden's rich past. Modern Dresden is also incredibly diverse and cultured, and the city's music halls—which long ago convinced the likes of Carl Weber, Richard Wagner, and Richard Strauss to set up shop here—now offer the visitor mainstream or experimental opera and theater side by side, while clubs and cultural centers host films and live music, from jazz to hard-core.

BASICS

The **tourist office** (Prager Str. 10, tel. 0351/491–920; open weekdays 10–6, weekends 9:30–2) books rooms (DM 5 fee), has maps (DM 1.50), and tons of information. The **American Express** office (Münzgasse 10, near Frauenkirche, tel. 0351/494–8117; open weekdays 10–6) cashes traveler's checks (10–1:30 and 2–5:30) and holds mail.

COMING AND GOING

Trains from Berlin (DM 45) and Leipzig (DM 28) arrive every hour or so at the **Hauptbahnhof**; pedestrian-only Prager Straße leads north to the Altmarkt. Many trains also stop at **Bahnhof Neustadt,** in the Neustadt on the north bank of the Elbe River. **ADM Mitfahrzentrale** (Antonstrtr. 10, tel. 0351/19440) has both short- and long-distance listings; their office is open weekdays 9–7, Saturday 9–1, Sunday 11–3.

WHERE TO SLEEP

Take Tram 11 (toward Bühlau) to Bautzner/Rothenburger Straße, continue to Martin-Luther-Straße, turn left and keep your eyes peeled for the comfy **Hotel Stadt Rendsburg** (Kamenzer Str. 1, tel. 0351/804–1551; doubles DM 95–DM 135). Otherwise, book ahead for **Jugendherberge Rudi-Arndt (HI)** (Hübnerstr. 11, tel. 0351/471–0667; beds DM 26), in a safe, quiet neighborhood near the Hauptbahnhof. Dresden's other hostel, **Jugendherberge Oberloschwitz (HI)** (Sierksstr. 33, tel. 0351/268–3672; beds DM 26), is atop a steep hill far from downtown but is definitely worth the effort. From Bahnhof Neustadt, take Tram 6 (toward Niedersedlitz) to Schillerplatz; then catch the *Schwebebahn* gondola to the hostel. The large **Jugendgästehaus Dresden** (Maternistr. 22, tel. 0351/492620, DM 38) is more expensive than other hostels, but you'll save on tram fare or long walks home. From Hauptbahnhof, take Tram 7, 9, 10, or 26 to Ammon-/Freiberger Straße, then right on Freiberger Straße, right on Maternistraße. Check in 4 PM–10 PM.

FOOD

In good weather Dresden moves its drinking and dining outside, especially to the sidewalk tables along the waterfront. For a less touristy take on the city, head to the Neustadt's pedestrian-only Hauptstraße, above Neustädter Markt.

Café aha. The vegetarian meals are made almost entirely with local organic produce. Lentil soup or nature-burger patty with salad will run DM 8–DM 11. *Kreuzstr. 7, near Kreuzkirche, tel. 0351/496–0671. Closed Mon.*

Haus Altmarkt. The choice of cuisine at the Altmarkt is enormous, but the jolly, bistro-like café and the vaulted restaurant **Zum Humpen** are the best value. The Zum Humpen boasts a midday menu with ample offerings for less than DM 20. *Am Altmarkt 1, tel. 0351/495–1212.*

Scheunecafé. Dresden's most popular student hangout serves large selections of Indian food, including lots of veggie dishes, for DM 8. Weekend brunch (DM 8) means ham, eggs, and juice. *Alaunstr. 36–40, tel. 0351/804–5532. Open weekdays 4 PM–3 AM, weekends 10 AM–3 AM.*

WORTH SEEING

Despite Allied bombing raids and the best efforts of communist city planners, the colonnaded **Altmarkt** retains much of its elegant pre-World War II grace—somewhere underneath all the scaffolding. The rich, baroque **Kreuzkirche** sits on the square's east side. If you only have one day in Dresden, focus on this square and the surrounding Altstadt.

BRÜHLSCHE TERRASSE • Brühlsche Terrasse, a tree-lined promenade overlooking the Elbe between Carolabrücke and Augustusbrücke, gives sweeping views of the new town and serves as the entrance to the excellent **Albertinum** museum. Its collection includes Flemish and Dutch art, works by German Renaissance genius Dürer, and big-name French impressionist and expressionist works. *Am Neumarkt/Brühlsche Terrasse, tel. 0351/491–4710. Admission: DM 7. Open Mon.–Wed. and Fri.–Sun. 10–6.*

NEUMARKT • Neumarkt is the heart of historic Dresden. The **Frauenkirche** was considered Germany's greatest baroque cathedral until it was ravaged by the 1945 firestorm. For a half-century the ragged walls have stood as a war memorial; today reconstruction is underway. At the northwest corner of Neumarkt is the 16th-century **Johanneum,** whose dazzling outer wall is a giant jigsaw puzzle made of 25,000 hand-painted tiles depicting more than 100 members of the royal Saxon house of Wettin. *Am Neumarkt, tel. 0351/86440. Admission: DM 4. Open Tues.–Sun. 10–5.*

SEMPEROPER • This famous opera house is in its third incarnation; earlier buildings fell victim to fire and bombings. The site has seen the premiers of Wagner's operas *The Flying Dutchman* and *Tannhäuser,* and Strauss' *Salome.* There is a guided tour (DM 8) every day at 2; meet at the entrance at your right, facing the Elbe River. *Theaterpl. 2, NE of Neumarkt, tel. 0351/491–1496.*

ZWINGER • On the south side of Theaterplatz stands the Zwinger palace complex, one of the world's finest baroque masterpieces. The bulk of the palace was built onto a section of Dresden's centuries-old fortifications. Today the palace is home to several museums. The **Gemäldegalerie Alte Meister** (Gallery of Old Masters) includes works by Raphael, Botticelli, Rembrandt, and German Romanticist Caspar David Friedrich. *Tel. 0351/491–4619. Admission DM 7. Closed Mon.*

AFTER DARK

The Altstadt is for nose-in-the-air cultural events, the Neustadt for down-and-dirty nightlife. For occasional movies and live music, head to **riesa efau** (Adlergasse 14, tel. 0351/866–0222). Live jazz can be heard in Dresden most nights of the week at the **Tonne Jazz Club** (Tzschirnerpl. 3, tel. 0351/495–1354 or 0351/496–0211); cover DM 5–DM 15. You can be sure of a very warm welcome at this friendly, laid-back haunt. Jazz and folk music are regular features of the program at the **Club Passage** (Leutewitzer Ring 5, tel. 0351/411–2665). **Disco** fans head for the **Café Prag** (Am Altmarkt 16–17, tel. 0351/495–5095), where a variety show is on the program Friday and Saturday nights. The **Schinkelwache** box office (Sofienstr., tel. 0351/491–1705) sells tickets for seasonal events, as well as opera at the Semperoper.

NEAR DRESDEN

SÄCHSISCHE SCHWEIZ

The name Sächsische Schweiz, which means "Saxon Switzerland," comes from the low-lying Elbsandstein Mountains that extend from the outskirts of Dresden to the Czech border. Here, the rock bed along the Elbe has been eroded over the millennia into curious stone columns that protrude out of the forest canopy like behemoth stacks of ash-colored poker chips. Nestled along the river or atop steep cliffs are several looming castles and quiet, well-preserved small towns—such as **Rathen** and **Bad Schandau**—perfect as bases for hikes or bike rides into the region's unspoiled nature.

COMING AND GOING • Dresden's S1 S-Bahn (toward Schöna) runs along the river every half hour, stopping in Rathen (40 min, DM 5) and Bad Schandau (50 min, DM 6). It costs less than DM 3 to hop from one town to the next. Far more scenic are the **steamships** that sail the Elbe, leaving Dresden at 8 AM, 9 AM, and noon for Rathen (4½ hrs, DM 21) and Bad Schandau (6½ hrs, DM 26); pick up schedules at a tourist office in Dresden.

LEIPZIG

It is the events of 1989 that thrust the city (eastern Germany's second-largest after Berlin) into the spotlight. The city's Nikolaikirche had been the site of *Montagsdemonstrationen* (peace prayers) for years, but as the eastern bloc began to crumble, the prayers grew into protests. Despite GDR laws forbidding unauthorized assembly, the protests attracted thousands, and despite the security forces' violent dispersion of a downtown protest in October 1989, 600,000 people marched peacefully through town on November 6, three days before the Wall came down. Leipzig's protests became a beacon for others throughout Eastern Germany. Today, Leipzig busily continues its old traditions while creating new ones. A trading center since the 12th century, Leipzig remains one of Germany's important convention cities (as it was in GDR times). The city's cabaret, theater, and exciting nightlife also keep things young and fresh.

BASICS

The enormous **Leipzig Tourist Service Center** (Sachsenpl. 1, tel. 0341/710–4260 or 0341/710–4265; open weekdays 9–7, weekends 9:30–2) has plenty of free information and a room-finding service. The **American Express** office (Dorotheenpl. 2–4, near Thomaskirche, tel. 0341/79210; open weekdays 9:30–6, Sat. 9–noon) cashes all traveler's checks for free.

COMING AND GOING

From Leipzig's elegant **Hauptbahnhof,** trains zip hourly to Berlin (DM 43) and Dresden (DM 28). Nearly all of Leipzig's sights are concentrated in its extremely small center, bordered by the Hauptbahnhof to the north and the university (Augustuspl.) to the south. If you need a **taxi,** dial 0341/921–4292 or 0341/564–0775.

WHERE TO SLEEP

Jugendherberge am Auensee. This hostel is a long ride (30 min) from city center, but a short walk to the tree-lined shore of Auensee. The four- to eight-bunk rooms are packed in summer; beds are DM 20–DM 24.*Gustav-Esche-Str. 4, tel. 0341/461–1114. From Hauptbahnhof, Tram 10 or 28 (toward Wahren) to Rathaus Wahren; follow signs.*

Jugendherberge Leipzig-Centrum. If you're planning a trip to Leipzig, make reservations for this great hostel *now.* A 20-minute walk west of the city center, beds are only DM 25, including breakfast. *Käthe-Kollwitz-Str. 64, tel. 0341/983–4507. From Hauptbahnhof, Tram 1 or 2 to Marschenerstr. Curfew 1 AM.*

If you're going to camp out, **Campingplatz am Auensee** (Gustav-Esche-Str. 5, tel. 0341/461–1977; sites DM 10) even rents tents (DM 3).

FOOD

Cafés and Imbiß stands are scattered throughout the city center, especially around Sachsenplatz, the Markt, and the side streets around Augustusplatz and the university. For a real meal, try **Paulaner** (Klostergasse 3–5, tel. 0341/211–3115), a small, intimate tavern that serves simple, satisfying grub for around DM 12. Or stop into **Auerbachs Keller** (Grimmaische Str. 2–4, in Mädlerpassage, tel. 0341/216–1040), the restaurant Goethe liked so much he worked it into his *Faust.* Nowadays an *entrée* runs DM 20–DM 40.

WORTH SEEING

Parts of the stunning **Markt,** the central market square, were severely damaged during World War II, but thanks to detailed restoration the square retains a centuries-old look. One side is taken up by the 16th-century **Altes Rathaus,** best known for its off-center tower and brilliant blue clock; inside, Leipzig's past is well-documented in the **Stadtgeschichtliches Museum** (Am Markt 1, tel. 0341/965130; admission DM 4; closed Mon.). Fanning out from the square are small streets crammed with dozens of elegant glass-roof shopping arcades; the poshest is Mädlerpassage, on Grimmaischestraße.

Bordered by university buildings and dorms, **Augustusplatz** is the place to hang out in Leipzig. The 506-ft-tall Leipzig University Tower, which resembles the business end of a fountain pen, towers over the plaza. Across from the university is the glass-and-concrete **Neues Gewandhaus** (Augustuspl. 8, tel. 0341/127–0280), home to Leipzig's renowned symphony orchestra. Opera buffs should pay a visit to the **Opernhaus** (Augustuspl. 12, tel. 0341/71680), on the square's north side, which hosts top-rate performances.

The **Museum der Bildenden Künste** (Museum of Visual Arts) is one of Germany's best, with an extensive collection of works by Old German and Dutch painters and a sizable holding of 20th-century sculpture. The building was the site of the show trial for Georgi Dimitrov, the Bulgarian communist accused of plotting the 1933 Reichstag fire in Berlin. *Georgi-Dimitroff-Pl. 1, tel. 0341/216–9914. Admission: DM 5. Open Tues., Thurs.–Sun. 9–5 and Wed. 1–9:30. Free 2nd Sun. of month.*

In the last months of 1989 thousands of East Germans gathered at **Nikolaikirche** every Monday to protest for political reform, while chanting *"Wir sind das Volk"* ("We are the people"). In the end, it was their persistent yet peaceful pressure that helped pull down the Iron Curtain. The church interior is infinitely more impressive than the bland exterior suggests. *Nikolaikirchof 3, tel. 0341/960–5270. Admission free. Open weekdays 10–6.*

J. S. Bach was choirmaster at **Thomaskirche** (Thomaskirchhof, tel. 0341/960–2855) for nearly 27 years, during which time he wrote dozens of cantatas for the church's famous Thomanerchor boys' choir. Summer Mondays at 7 PM, there are free concerts in front of the church. Across the street the **Bachmuseum** (Thomaskirchhof 16, tel. 0341/964410, admission DM 2.50–DM 4; open daily 10–5), houses an excellent display of period musical instruments.

The 1813 Battle of the Nations is commemorated by this enormous **Völkerschlachtdenkmal** (Memorial to the Battle of the Nations) on the outskirts of the city. Rising out of suburban Leipzig like some great Egyptian tomb, the somber, gray pile of granite and concrete is more than 300 ft high. Despite its ugliness, the site is well worth a visit, if only to wonder at the lengths—and heights—to which the Prussians went to celebrate their military victories, and to take in the view from a windy platform near the top (provided you can climb the 500 steps to get there). Take trams 15, 20, 21 or 25. *Prager Str., tel. 0341/878–0471. Admission DM 5. Open May–Oct., daily 10–5; Nov.–Apr., daily 9–4. Guided tours daily at 10:30, 11:30, 1:30, and 2:30.*

AFTER DARK
Your best bet is to scout the streets south of Augustusplatz and west of Nürnberger Straße, or take a 10-minute tram ride to the funky Connewitz district. Pick up a copy of *Kreuzer* (DM 2.50) to find out what's going on. Leipzig's number one student night spot is **Moritzbastei** (Universitätsstr. 9, tel. 0341/960–5191; cover DM 2–DM 8), with two music stages and a café. Or try the more exotic, 24-hour **Vis á Vis** (Rudolf-Breitscheid-Str. 33, near Hauptbahnhof, tel. 0341/980–3747), which has a mostly gay male crowd during the day. Stylish discos include the revamped **Schorsch'l** (Dufourstr. 8, tel. 0341/213–0556), where over-thirties feel at home, and the ever-popular **Esplanade** (Richard-Wagner-Str. 10, tel. 0341/282–330).

NEAR LEIPZIG
Zwickau, 100 km (60 mi) south of Leipzig, claims parentage of the Trabant car, affectionately called "Trabi," a sputtery, clanky machine with all the mechanical complexity of a wind-up clock. During the GDR era, it was one of the few car models available to the public, and out of either loyalty or insanity some masochists continue to drive it. Everyone seems to love an underdog; a postunification movie, "Go Trabi, Go!" followed the misadventures of one of the maligned little cars. The **Automobilmuseum August Horch** (Walther-Rathenau-Str. 51, tel. 0375/332–3854; open Tues. and Thurs. 9–noon and 2–5, weekends 10–5) displays nine decades of Zwickau auto history, including all things Trabesque. Zwickau's other child was Robert Schumann; visit the **Robert-Schumann-Haus** (Hauptmarkt 5, tel. 0375/215269; admission DM 5; open Tues.–Sat. 10–5).

HALLE
Halle, only a half hour from Leipzig, was an important center in the salt trade in the Middle Ages, but has been known primarily as a university town since 1694. The active student population supports a flourishing café scene, offbeat nightlife, and lots of political activity. In the *Altstadt* (Old Town) you'll find some impressive Gothic architecture and the birthplace of native son and composer, Georg Friedrich Händel (1685–1759).

VISITOR INFORMATION
Roter Turm, Marktpl.1, tel. 0345/202–3340. Open Apr.–Sept., Mon., Tues., Thurs., Fri. 9–6, Wed. 10–6, Sat. 9–1; shorter hrs off season.

COMING AND GOING
Trains arrive from **Berlin** (DM 40), **Leipzig** (DM 9), and **Erfurt** (DM 25). To reach town from the **Hauptbahnhof,** go left through the pedestrian tunnel and continue up Leipziger Straße.

WHERE TO SLEEP AND EAT
The **HI hostel** (August-Bebel-Str. 48a, tel. 0345/202–4716; beds DM 28) is a mansion of wood walls, chandeliers, and well-kept rooms. The reception desk is open 8AM–10AM and 5 PM–10 PM. Food stands circle the central Markt, but for cheap pasta head to **Café Nöö** (Große Klausstr. 11, tel. 0345/202–1651).

WORTH SEEING

Halle's central Markt is watched over by the Gothic **Marienkirche** and the **Roter Turm** (Red Tower). West of the markt is the **Dom**—probably the world's most unusual cathedral, with its Gothic design wrapped in baroque. Händel was born in the **Händelhaus** (Große Nikolaistr. 5, tel. 0345/500900), which displays the composer's original scores and piano. In the northwest corner of the Altstadt, the 15th-century **Moritzburg** (Friedemann-Bach-Pl. 5, tel. 0345/37031; admission DM 5; open Tues. 11–8:30, Wed.–Fri. 10–5.30, weekends, 10–6) houses a small but impressive art museum of mostly German Expressionist paintings.

AFTER DARK

Eisenstein (Markt 1, no phone; cover DM 5) is a superfunky joint that plays acid-jazz and house. Underneath the castle is **Turm** (Friedemann-Bach-Pl. 7, tel. 0345/202–3737; cover free–DM 5), the best student club in the city. Jazz and folk bands play in an old congregation chamber with a brick floor. The city of Händel is naturally an important music center, and Halle is famous for its opera productions, particularly for its choirs. For **opera** schedules and ticket reservations call 345/5110–0355, and for **Philharmonic Orchestra** information 0345/202–3278.

ERFURT

Although it's the cultural and political core of the state of Thuringia and one of the most visited towns in eastern Germany, Erfurt is not your typical tourist trap. Sure, its streets are crammed with luxury hotels and expensive restaurants, but Erfurt's Altstadt still looks and feels like a medieval market town, from its winding network of cobblestone alleys to the spires that crowd its skyline. As an added bonus, Erfurt's small colleges provide a critical mass of young people that makes for a hot nightlife with a little something for everyone.

VISITOR INFORMATION

Book rooms here. *Bahnhofstr. 37, tel. 0361/562–6267. Open weekdays 10–6, Sat. 10–1.*

COMING AND GOING

Trains arrive at the sleazy **Hauptbahnhof** from Berlin (3½ hrs, DM 68), Leipzig (1½ hrs, DM 27), and Frankfurt (2½ hrs, DM 66). The station is not the best introduction to Erfurt; hurry straight down Bahnhofstraße to the historic city center.

WHERE TO SLEEP AND EAT

The **hostel** (Hochheimer Str. 12, tel. 0361/562–6705; beds DM 26) is in a renovated mansion close to public transportation; take Tram 5 to Steigerstraße. Or try the small, unassuming **Pension Fiege** (Kranichfelder Str. 15, tel. 0361/413839; doubles DM 95, no credit cards); take Tram 3 or 6 to Blücherstraße. For inexpensive lunch or dinner and nightly entertainment try Wolfgang Staub's unique **Dasdie** (Marstallstr. 12, tel. 0361/646–4666) a combination of restaurant, bistro, bar, cabaret stage, and dance floor under one roof. The food is hit-or-miss, but the place is always lively and prices are low. Erfurt's oldest beer cellar, the **Restaurant zur Penne,** dates back to 1515. It has eight different beers on tap and a menu bursting with hearty Thuringian fare. *Grosse Arche 3–5, tel. 0361/643–7469.*

WORTH SEEING

Three main squares constitute the heart of Erfurt's Altstadt, 1 km (½ mi) north of the train station. **Domplatz,** a vast open-air square atop a hill, lies at the Altstadt's northwest extreme. From here Marktstraße leads east to **Fischmarkt,** another pedestrianized square. The third and arguably least attractive of Erfurt's main squares, the **Anger,** is home to the 11th-century **Kaufmann's Kirche**—Martin Luther gave a sermon here in 1522. On the square's southern side, the **Angermuseum** (Bahnhofstr., tel. 0361/562–3311; admission DM 5; open Tues.–Sun. 10–6) houses a first-rate collection of medieval relics—coins, tools, jewelry, and a huge 14th-century crossbow—along with a hodgepodge of more recent landscape paintings.

DOMPLATZ • ** This vast plaza at the western end of Marktstraße, which really comes alive on market days (Wed., Fri., and Sat.), is home to the two Gothic giants Mariendom and St. Severuskirche. Monstrous enough upon initial completion in 1154, the **Mariendom (tel. 0361/646–1265) had a choir added in front in the 14th century. The cathedral's biggest bell, the Gloriosa, is the largest free-swinging bell in the world. Cast in 1497, today, it rings only on special occasions, its deep boom sounding across the entire city. Across the courtyard stands the 13th-century **St. Severuskirche** (Church of St. Severus), whose five equal-height naves make it architecturally unique. Inside, you can pose for pictures with St. Severus's sarcophagus.

KRAMERBRUCKE • The Krämerbrücke has been home to shops and houses since 1325, when a stone bridge was constructed in place of an earlier wooden one; the current half-timbered structures (larger than the originals) were built in 1475. During the day, entertain yourself by watching the tourists scamper back and forth between shops full of expensive knickknacks; at dusk, the empty cobblestone street bridge will make you feel like you've been transported back to the 14th century.

NEAR ERFURT

EISENACH AND THE WARTBURG

People visit Eisenach mostly to see its hillside castle, the 12th-century **Wartburg,** where Martin Luther, after faking his own kidnapping, hid from the Pope in 1521. During this time, he translated the New Testament into German, thereby setting the foundation for standard written German. The main building can only be seen on a **guided tour** (DM 11) of the ornate rooms. Tour admission includes the **museum** (DM 6) and its Luther exhibit. From the grounds you get a great view of Eisenach below and the Thüringer Wald to the south. Getting to the castle involves a strenuous climb, even if you do take the bus. Steep 30-minute hiking trails start at the **Wartburg information office** (Schloßberg 2, tel. 03691/77073) and the foot of Marienstraße. Bus 10 leaves every 20 minutes (May–Sept. only) from the Hauptbahnhof and the end of Marienstraße. October–April you can catch a shuttle van (DM 4 one-way) from the Marienstraße bus stop. *Tel. 03691/77072. Open Mar.–Oct., daily 8:30–6:30 (last tour at 5); Nov.–Feb., daily 9–5 (last tour at 3:30). Wheelchair access to grounds only.*

When all the climbing around the castle wears you out, the **tourist office** (Bahnhofstr. 3–5, tel. 03691/670260) will book you a private room. Or, try the **Jugendherberge Arthur Becker** (Mariental 24, 3½ km/2¼ mi southwest of train station, tel. 03691/203613; beds DM 19), a three-story mansion perched on a forested hill. From the train station, take Bus 3 or 11 to Liliengrund (last bus at 8:30 PM) or a taxi (DM 10).

WEIMAR

Few cities illustrate the dual nature of German culture as well as Weimar. Because Leipzig and Erfurt were the traditional seats of government, Weimar developed a more liberal, even cynical, attitude that attracted thinkers, artists, and the radical fringe: Over the centuries, the city gave birth to the *Weimarer Klassik,* the art and literature of Goethe and Schiller. Others, like Nietzsche, Bach, and Liszt, were also drawn to the city's cultural legacy. In 1919, the German National Assembly met here to declare the founding of Germany's first-ever republic—the short-lived Weimar Republic. In 1925, the citizens of Weimar, outraged over what they considered a "communist" defilement of their traditions, elected a Nazi city government instead. The final irony is that one of Germany's most infamous concentration camps, Buchenwald (*see Near Weimar, below*), lies just outside the city limits. Despite such a formidable history, Weimar is surprisingly small and welcoming. In 1999 Weimar will once again be at the center stage as the long-forgotten city prepares to become the European Union's *Kulturhauptstadt,* or annual cultural capital.

VISITOR INFORMATION

The **tourist office** can sell you the WeimarCard (DM 25), which gives you 72 hours of free bus travel and disounts on the city's museums. *Markt 10, tel. 03643/24000. Open Mar.–Oct., weekdays 9–6, Sat. 9–4, Sun. 10–4; Nov.–Feb., weekdays 9–6, Sat. 9–1.*

COMING AND GOING

Weimar's **Hauptbahnhof** (tel. 03643/3330) is 1½ km (¾ mi) north of the city center; take Bus 7 or 8 (same side of the street) or Bus 1 or 6 (across the street) to Goetheplatz. Otherwise it's about a 30-minute walk down Carl-August-Allee. Destinations include Berlin (DM 64), Eisenach (DM 17), and Leipzig (DM 21).

WHERE TO SLEEP AND EAT

The tourist office arranges private rooms for a DM 5 fee. Weimar also has three youth hostels, often full of German school classes. **Jugendherberge Am Poseckschen Garten** (Humboldtstr. 17, tel. 03643/

850792; beds DM 23) is 10 minutes from the Hauptbahnhof on Bus 6. Two blocks straight out of the Hauptbahnhof, **Jugendherberge Germania** (Carl-August-Allee 13, tel. 03643/850490; beds DM 26) is clean and efficient. **Jugendgästehaus Maxim Gorki** (Zum Wilden Graben 12, tel. 03643/850750; beds DM 27) is close to a beautiful graveyard; take Bus 8 to Wilden Graben.

Near Herderplatz, you'll find a handful of quiet, smoky beer halls serving cheap pub grub. A good one is **Zum Zwiebel** (Teichgasse 6, tel. 03643/502375), 1 block west of Herderplatz. **Café Szenario** (Carl-August-Allee, tel. 03643/419640; closed Sun.) is a très cool joint for pizzas (from DM 8) and seafood pastas (from DM 11.50). For something more traditional try the **Ratskeller** (Am Markt 10, tel. 03643/64142), one of eastern Germany's most original beer cellars. The menu offers classic, hearty *Thüringen* specialties, such as wild duck in red-wine sauce.

WORTH SEEING

With rows of gorgeous buildings, Weimar's **Markt** dates from 1400, the year the city received its charter. Next to the Markt, the cobblestone **Theaterplatz** is the largest square in Weimar and the site of the neo-classical **Deutsches Nationaltheater** and the must-see **Bauhaus Museum** (tel. 03643/546161; admission DM 5; open Tues.–Sun. 10–6); the latter is home to works by Gropius and Kandinsky and their students. **Burgplatz**, by the River Ilm on the east end of town, is home to the vast **Weimar Castle** (tel. 03643/545330; admission DM 8; open Tues.–Sun. 9–5). Just north of Bergplatz, the quiet **Herderplatz** houses the 18th-century **Stadtkirche**, a baroque cathedral that contains Lucas Cranach's *Winged Altar* triptych, which depicts Christ on the cross, with John the Baptist, Cranach, and Martin Luther looking on.

Buchenwald's camp clock reads 3:15—the time on April 11, 1945 when inmates took control of the camp four days before the arrival of the American army.

Goethe, one of Europe's most renowned poets and thinkers, lived in Weimar in the three-story **Goethehaus** (Am Frauenplan 1, tel. 03643/545320; admission DM 8; closed Mon.) from 1782 until his death in 1832. Peruse letters, manuscripts, boring oil paintings of jowly noble types, and period furniture. **Schiller's** sturdy, green-shuttered home is on a tree-shaded square not far from Goethe's house. Schiller's study was tucked up underneath the mansard roof, a cozy room dominated by the desk where he probably completed *Wilhelm Tell*. (Schillerstr. 17, tel. 03643/64387; admission DM 5.).

NEAR WEIMAR

BUCHENWALD

The whole point of Buchenwald's continued existence can be summed up in two words: Never forget. At its peak in early 1945, this Nazi concentration camp 6 km (4 mi) north of Weimar interned 110,000 people, though only four months later, only 21,000 had survived. All told, 56,000 people were starved or worked to death, and camp supervisors personally tortured and executed hundreds of political prisoners. The camp—with its barbed-wire fences, ghostly barracks foundations, crematorium, and the iron gate reading mockingly "Jedem das Seine" ("To Each What He Deserves")—is indeed a monument to terror, and a sickening reminder of the human capacity for brutality.

Pick up an English-language map (50 Pf) of the camp at the **bookstore.** In the same building, a 30-minute **film** (in German) shows four times daily. The former storehouse (where prisoners' personal belongings were kept) now houses an impressive **museum** detailing the history of Buchenwald. *Gedenkstätte Buchenwald, tel. 03643/4300. From Weimar's Goethepl. or Hauptbahnhof, Bus 6 (toward Buchenwald) to end (one-way-ticket is DM 2.50). Admission free. Open May–Sept., Tues.–Sun. 9:45–5:15; Oct.–Apr., Tues.–Sun. 8:45–4:15.*

THURINGER WALD

The Thuringian Forest, with its tranquil woods, rugged trails, and sleepy villages, is one of eastern Germany's most treasured retreats. Once you breach its border there's nothing but trees, lakes, and spiny peaks—an ideal place for extended hikes. Serious hikers should consider the 168-km (105-mi) **Rennsteig** (Border Way), a mountaintop trail that extends from the outskirts of Eisenach to Blankenstein near the Czech border. The Erfurt–Ilmenau–Schleusingen train stops at an unstaffed depot named Rennsteig; from here, follow the signs ¼ km (⅛ mi) to the trail, marked with a white "R" painted on tree trunks. A few youth hostels are along the route: the **Großer Inselberg** (tel. 036259/62329) in Tabarz, near Friedrichroda; the **Wanderherberge Weidmans** (tel. 03683/604671) above Schnellbach, near Schmalkalden; and **Neuhaus am Rennweg** (Apelsbergstr. 54, tel. 03679/722862). Beds are DM 13–DM 23 (DM 28) and HI cards may be required.

If you're not up for hiking and just want to explore one of the small towns on the forest edge, consider a trip to **Ilmenau,** which is within easy reach of Thüringer Wald hiking trails. In the town center is the **Goethe-Gedenkstätte im Amtshaus** (Markt 2, tel. 03677/202667), where Goethe lived for a few years. Goethe spent much of his time roaming the hills around town; today the **Goethe-Wanderweg,** also known as "Auf Goethes Spuren" (In the Footsteps of Goethe) retraces 18 rigorous km (11 mi) of his steps. About two hours into the hike, you pass **Goethes Häuschen auf dem Kickelhahn,** the small hut where Goethe wrote one of his most famous poems, "The Wayfarer's Night Song II." The Amtshaus marks the starting point of the trail, which is posted with wood markers bearing the letter "G." Get maps from Ilmenau's **tourist office** (Lindenstr. 12, tel. 03677/62132; open weekdays 9–6, Sat. 9–noon).

WHERE TO SLEEP
Although Ilmenau has a good hostel, try one of the city's reasonably priced pensions (DM 64 doubles), the **Haus Neuschwander** (Lindenstr. 37, tel. 03677/680809). To reach the **HI hostel** (Waldstr. 22, tel. 03677/86790; beds DM 26, breakfast and sheets included), turn right from the tourist office, follow Lindenstraße to its end, and cross the tracks to Waldstraße.

NORTHERN GERMANY

HAMBURG

Hamburg is a port city through and through. Founded in 810 by Charlemagne, it has been an international trading post since the Middle Ages, and for hundreds of years it was Europe's leading port. Today, although it's fallen to third-largest port in Europe—it's still the biggest in Germany—Hamburg is again a city of enormous style, verve, and elegance. That's not to say that Hamburg is cozy, the city is too busy making money to bother with such niceties. A lot of gray- and blue-suited types, called *Hanseaten,* make their money the old-fashioned way, while another segment of the population makes its living in an even older fashion. Hamburg's **Reeperbahn** has the dubious distinction of being one of the most famous sex streets in the world. Hamburg offers less racy attractions as well, including some beautiful (and wealthy) neighborhoods, excellent museums, a lively university district, and a happening nightlife.

BASICS

VISITOR INFORMATION
The tourist office at the **Hauptbahnhof** (Kirchenallee exit, tel. 040/3005–1200) is open daily 7 AM–11 PM. Another branch is at the **harbor** (St.-Pauli Landungsbrücken, between piers 4 and 5, tel. 040/3005–1200; open daily 10–7; Nov.–Mar., daily 9:30–5:30). Both sell the **Hamburg-CARD** (DM 12.50 one-day, DM 24.50 three-day), which gives free access to public transport, free or reduced entrance to 16 museums, and discounts of up to 30% on city tours and harbor cruises. These offices can help with accommodations, and there's a central hotline for hotel and ticket reservations and general information, **HAM-Hotline** (tel. 040/3005–1300). A DM 5 fee is charged for every room reserved and then deducted from your bill at the hotel.

AMERICAN EXPRESS
Ballindam 39, tel. 040/309080. U-Bahn to Jungfernsteig. Open weekdays 9–5:30, Sat. 10 AM–1 PM.

CONSULATES
Ireland: *Feldbrunnenstr. 33, tel. 040/4418–6213. Open weekdays 9–1.* **New Zealand:** *Heimhuderstr. 56, tel. 040/442–5550. Open Mon.–Thurs. 9–noon and 1–5:30, Fri. 9–noon and 1–4:30.* **United**

Kingdom: *Harvestehuder Weg 8a, tel. 040/448–0320. Open weekdays 9–noon and 2–4.* **United States:** *Alsterufer 27–28, tel. 040/411710 or 040/4117–1211 after hours. Open weekdays 9–noon.*

MAIL

The **Hauptpost** does not exchange money. *Hühnerposten 12, across from Hauptbahnhof, tel. 040/23950. Open weekdays 8–6, Sat. 8–noon. Postal code: 20997.*

COMING AND GOING

Most trains leave from the **Hauptbahnhof** (tel. 040/19419) in central Hamburg. Long-distance destinations include Berlin (2½ hrs, DM 71) and Copenhagen (5 hrs, DM 107). The **Altona station** (Max-Brauer-Allee), west of downtown, handles domestic trains heading north. At the university, **AStA** (Von-Melle-Park 5) has a big bulletin board listing *Mitfahrgelegenheit* (ride-share) opportunities.

Most major sights and interesting neighborhoods are sandwiched in the walkable downtown area between the Elbe River and two lakes, the **Binnenalster** and **Aussenalster** (collectively just called the Alster); the Neustadt is just below the lakes, the Altstadt below that, and the river sweeps beneath it all. The **St. Pauli/Reeperbahn** area, including Hamburg's famous red-light district, is west of downtown near the harbor. The **university district** sits north of the city center and west of the Aussenalster.

HVV, Hamburg's public-transportation system, operates an extensive network of buses, ferries, and subways (the U-Bahn and S-Bahn). The **Tageskarte** (day pass; DM 9.20) is not valid on night buses or first-class S-Bahn; the **Hamburg-CARD** (*see* Visitor Information *in* Basics, *above*) is also a good deal. One-way tickets (DM 2.50–DM 4) are available at the orange ticket-dispensing machines located in subway stations and at most bus stops. For a **taxi,** dial 040/211211 or 040/611061.

WHERE TO SLEEP

Because of its proximity to the Hauptbahnhof, St. Georg is the most convenient area in which to spend the night (look on Bremer Reihe). It has a prominent drug and prostitution scene but is safe enough if you keep your wits about you, look like you have a purpose, and don't get offended if someone asks how much you cost an hour. St. Pauli is similarly sleazy yet safe, and has plenty of cheap hotels in the Reeperbahn area. The *Mitwohnzentrale* at Schulterblatt 112 (tel. 040/19445) finds private rooms for DM 50 per person per night (finding fee included).

ST. GEORG

Hotel Alt Nürnberg. Doubles start at DM 130 in this classy 160-year-old hotel with a beautiful reception area and clean rooms. *Steintorweg 15, tel. 040/246023. Closed Dec. 24–Jan. 1.*

Hotel Amsterdam. Close to the historic Dammtor area you'll find this small, intimate hotel full of old-fashioned but comfortable rooms. Doubles start at at DM 149. *Moorweidenstr. 34, tel. 040/441–1110.*

Hotel Terminus. One of the best options in town, rooms here have TV and telephone. Doubles are DM 100, triples DM 150, quads DM 180. *Steindamm 5, tel. 040/280–3144.*

Hotel Wedina. Rooms at this small hotel are neat, compact, and recently renovated. They are adorned with Tuscany-style furniture. Doubles are DM 77.50 (a person). *Gurlittstr. 23, tel. 040/243011.*

ST. PAULI

Hotel Inter-Rast. This noisy but fun 208-room hotel is at the end of Reeperbahn on Große Freiheit. Doubles cost DM 76–DM 110, triples DM 120 (including breakfast). *Reeperbahn 154–166, tel. 040/311591. S-Bahn to Reeperbahn. Cash only.*

Weller's Hotel. This standard Reeperbahn pit at top of creaky old stairs, has doubles for DM 65. *Reeperbahn 36, tel. 040/314838. U3 to St. Pauli or S-Bahn to Reeperbahn.*

HOSTELS

Hamburg "Auf dem Stintfang" (HI). A great location overlooking the harbor is the big draw here, but the place is almost always full; call ahead or come before 6 PM. There's a 1 AM curfew. Beds are DM 29. *Alfred-Wegener-Weg 5, tel. 040/313488. U3, S1, or S3 to St.-Pauli Landungsbr.*

Jugendgästehaus Hamburg "Horner Rennbahn." A quick trip from downtown on public transit drops you at the door of this high-quality accomodation with modern rooms for a decent price: DM 35, includ-

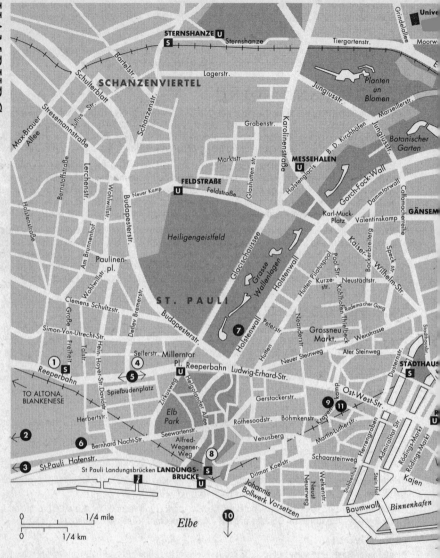

Sights ●

Deichstraße, **14**

Ernst-Barlach-Haus, **2**

Erotic Art Museum, **6**

Fischmarkt, **3**

Hamburger Freihafen, **10**

Krämeramts-wohnungen, **11**

Kuntshalle, **15**

Michaeliskirche, **9**

Museum für Hamburgische Geschichte, **7**

Museum für Kunst und Gewerbe, **20**

Rathaus, **12**

Reeperbahn, **5**

Speicherstadt, **16**

Lodging ○

Hotel Alt Nürnberg, **17**

Hotel Amsterdam, **13**

Hotel Inter-Rast, **1**

Hotel Terminus, **19**

Hotel Wedina, **18**

Jugendgästehaus Hamburg "Auf dem Stintfang" (HI), **8**

Jugendgästehaus Hamburg "Horner Rennbahn", **21**

Weller's Hotel, **4**

KEY

AE American Express Office

i Tourist Information

Rail Lines

U U-Bahn

S S-Bahn

N

Außenalster

Binnenalster

ST. GEORG

Fontenay

Rothenbaumchaussee

niversity

13

orweidenstr.

E-Siemers Allee

Mittelweg

Neue Rabenstr.

Warburgstr.

Alsterufer

Theodor-

S Heuss-

pl.

DAMMTOR

Dammtor-Damm

Alsterglacis

Kennedybrücke

An der Alster

Gurlittstr.

18

Koppel

Lange Reihe

Stephanspl.

Esplanade

DAMMTOR U

Lombardsbrücke

Holzdamm

Rautenbergstr.

St. Georg-str.

Kirchen-allee

Spadeich

Baumeisterstr.

SEMARKT
U

Gänse-markt.

Colonnaden

Neuer Jungfernstieg

Ballindamm

Glockengiesserwall

Ferdinandstr.

Brandsende

Ernst-Merck-Str.

Hachmannpl.

Kirchen-allee

Ellmenreichstr.

Bremer Reihe

Hohe Bleichen

Poststr.

Gr. Bleichen

Jungfernstieg

Hermannstr.

Alsterstr.

Raboisen

Rossenstr.

Kurze Mühren

HOF
NORD

15

U

Haupt-bahnhof

i

HOF
SUD

U

17

Steintor-pl.

19

Steindamm

Steintorwall

Adenauerallee

Bleichenbr.

Heuberg

N E U S T A D T

Bergstr.

Gerh Hauptm Pl.

Spitalerstr.

Mönckebergstr.

MÖNKEBERGSTR.

Lange Mühren

Steintor Wall

20

Kurt-Schumacher-Allee

Munzstr.

Neuerwall

Adolfsbr.

Rathausmarkt

12

Gr. Johannisstr.

RATHAUS U

Rathausstr.

Schmiede

Steinstr.

Johannis-wall

Klosterwall

Amsinckstraße

AUSBRÜCKE

Alterwall

Mönkedamm

Gr. Burstah

Domstrasse

Speersort

Pelzerstr.

Burchard Pl.

Burchardstr.

Deichtor-pl.

Graskeller

Gr. Burstah

Kl. Reichenstr.

Pumpen

RÖDINGSMARKT U

Rödings Markt

Burstah

Ost-West-Str.

A L T S T A D T U

14

Deichtstraße

Katharinenstr.

Dovenfleet

Oberbaumbrücke

Deichtor-str.

Altländer Str.

Stadtdeich

Banksstr.

Cremon

Matten Tw.

Mühren

Zippelhaus

Alter Wandrahm

Oberhafen

Neuen Krahn

Brook

Neuer Wandrahm

Brooktorkai

21

Zollkanal

Kehrwieder

Pickhuben

16

327

ing sheets and breakfast. Call ahead or come early. The curfew is 1 AM. *Rennbahnstr. 100, tel. 040/651–1671. U3 to Horner Rennbahn; walk 10 min north. Lockout 9–1. Closed Feb.*

CAMPING

City Camp Tourist. Renowned for its high security and good organization, this site is just off busy Kieler Straße, so don't expect to hear the birds singing. Sites are DM 12–DM 18 per tent plus DM 7 per person, showers included. *Kieler Str. 650, tel. 040/570–4498. U2 to Schlump; then Bus 182 to Reichbahnstr.; walk 33 ft farther.*

FOOD

For the cheapest seafood, check out the small restaurants in the port area. On Reeperbahn, you'll find a hefty number of ethnic restaurants (especially Turkish, Greek, and Italian) offering cheap, delicious meals. Downtown has mostly expensive restaurants; an exception is **Gestern & Heute Treff** (Kaiser-Wilhelm-Str. 55, tel. 040/344998), open 24 hours a day; pizza is DM 10, steak DM 12–DM 18.

The most celebrated—and tangy—local dish is probably *Aalsuppe* (eel soup). Smoked eel, called *Räucheraal,* is a particularly fatty Hamburg specialty. Other specialties to try are *Birnen, Bohnen, und Speck* (pears, beans, and bacon) and the sailor's favorite, *Labskaus,* a pickled meat, beetroot, and potato dish. Wash it all down with an *Alsterwasser* (or just "Alster"), a mix of beer and clear lemon soda.

DOWNTOWN

Avocado. The imaginative vegetarian menu at this trendy, modern restaurant is a bargain. If you're up to it, try one of their four- to six-course surprise dinner meals (DM 44–DM 66 per person). *Kanalstr. 9, tel. 040/220–4599. Closed Mon. U2 to Mundsburg.*

bon appetit. At this busy stand-up café near the train station, try the *Bauernfrühstück* (farmer's breakfast; DM 7.90) or one of the meat-and-potato dishes (DM 10). *Rathausstr. 4, behind Mönckebergstr., tel. 040/324570. Closed dinner.*

Daniel Wischer. Situated on pedestrian-only Spitalerstraße, you should expect to share tables during busy lunch hour at this busy eatery. Try their salmon fillet with potato salad or fries (DM 11.50) or salads from DM 5.50. *Spitalerstr. 12, tel. 040/382343.*

ST. GEORG

Cafe Gnosa. Check out the local gay scene gathered about the tables here and get some fantastic meals while you're at it. The vegetarian *Auflauf* casserole (DM 11.50) is a mixture of zucchini, cauliflower, carrots, and cheese. *Lange Reihe 93, tel. 040/243034.*

Max & Consorten. Conversation buzzes through smoke and music at his little restaurant, which is perfect for a quick beer (DM 4) or cheap meal. Salads are DM 8–DM 13. *Spadenteich 7, tel. 040/245617.*

ST. PAULI

Fischerhaus. Always busy, this waterfront establishment favors time-honored Hamburg fish specialties, including a delicious eel soup. It's hardly haute cuisine but the standards are ultrareliable. *Fischmarkt 14, tel. 040/314053.*

Medusa. This family-run Italian restaurant is known for its good value, quality pasta: Lasagna, tortellini, and fettuccine are only DM 13 each. Open late. *Spielbudenpl. 21, tel. 040/313503. Closed lunch.*

Schindlers. Stop here for a down-to-earth pub-restaurant with good pasta (try spinach noodles with gorgonzola sauce) and casseroles for DM 10–DM 15, and breakfasts (around DM 7) served weekend mornings. *Taubenstr. 23, just off Reeperbahn, tel. 040/315092.*

WORTH SEEING

The tourist office organizes a variety of **tours** (DM 20–DM 30) of the city and harbor, with English commentary. If you plan to pack a lot of sightseeing into a day, the Hamburg-CARD (*see* Visitor Information in Basics, *above*) is a great deal.

Hamburg's Freihafen (harbor), a case study in modernity and efficiency, is also the focal point of the city's oldest and liveliest area. The HADAG line organizes trips around the port (DM 15), lasting about one hour and taking in several docks. There's usually a fresh breeze, so dress warm. Harbor tours run from Piers 1–7 at Landungsbrücken. In summer they depart every ½ hr; in winter whenever a boat is full. *St. Pauli Landungsbrücken, tel. 040/564523 for information on an English-language tour.*

Check out the enormous, Gothic-influenced brick **Speicherstadt warehouses**; though warehouses usually don't elicit oohs and aahs, you'll admit that their daring architecture is special. If you can get up early enough, don't miss the **Fischmarkt** (Sunday 5 AM–10 AM), a tumultous bazaar of fish 'n' fowl and wily street vendors. And to get a dose of old Hamburg, spend some time on **Deichstraße,** which has been a peaceful residential street for the past 600 or so years.

KUNSTHALLE
Three thousand paintings, 400 sculptures, and coin and medal collections present European artistic life from the 14th century to the present. With the addition of a new wing in 1996 the museum doubled in size, and now also shows works by Andy Warhol, Joseph Beuys, Georg Baselitz, and David Hockney. *Glockengießerwall 1, near Hauptbahnhof, tel. 040/2486–2612. Admission: DM 10 (admission free with Hamburg-CARD). Open Tues.–Wed. and Fri.–Sun. 10–6, Thurs. 10–9.*

MICHAELISKIRCHE
The baroque St. Michael's Church (fondly nicknamed *Michel*) is Hamburg's most famous and best-loved landmark. Its copper-covered spire makes a distinct mark on Hamburg's already stately skyline, and the restored interior is lavishly elegant. Standing in its shadow are the **Krameramtswohnungen** (Krayenkamp 10–11), a cluster of tiny old courtyard houses that contain galleries and a museum that replicates the setup of a typical 15th-century house. *Krayenkamp 4c, tel. 040/3110–2624. S-Bahn to Stadthausbrücke. Open Tues.–Sun. 10–5.*

> *Hamburg has more than 2,400 bridges—more than London, Amsterdam, and Venice combined.*

RATHAUS
The town hall presides over the city-state of Hamburg in neo-Renaissance, Nordic hugeness. When neither city council nor state government is in session, you can tour the interior. In front of the Rathaus is a work by renowned German expressionist sculptor, Ernst Barlach, depicting a sorrowful mother hugging her child. The original was removed by the Nazis and replaced with an eagle to demonstrate Germany's strength. Later, the work was reconstructed as a warning against war. *Rathausmarkt, tel. 040/3681–2470. U3 to Rathaus. English-language tours (DM 2) Mon.–Thurs. 10:15–3:15, Fri.–Sun. 10:15–1:15.*

REEPERBAHN/ST. PAULI
The Reeperbahn may have a well-deserved reputation as "the wickedest mile in the world," but most of St. Pauli is residential and quiet. Still, the Reeperbahn—and sidestreets like **Herbertstraße** (off-limits to women and children)—beckon those who will pay to have sex, to watch someone else have sex, or to watch someone else pretend to have sex. The **Erotic Art Museum** (Bernhard-Nocht-Str. 69, off Davidstr., tel. 040/317–4757; admission DM 15) offers a lighter look at Hamburg's sinful side, with one of the largest collections of erotic art—displaying S&M art, peeing fountains, and numerous penis sculptures (including a 2-ft specimen right next to the entrance).

MUSEUMS AND GALLERIES
Built in 1876 as a museum and school, the **Museum für Kunst und Gewerbe** (Steintorpl. 1, near Hauptbahnhof, tel. 040/2486–2630; admission DM 12; open Tues.–Wed. and Fri.–Sun. 10–6, Thurs. 10–9) now contains an impressive collection of handicrafts from all over the world. If you liked the Ernst Barlach sculpture near the Rathaus, check out the **Ernst-Barlach-Haus** (Baron-Voght-Str. 50a, tel. 040/826085; S1 to Klein Flottbek; admission DM 6; open Tues.–Sun. 11–5) in Jenisch-Park. The **Museum für Hamburgische Geschichte** (Holstenwall 24, tel. 040/3504–2360; U3 to St. Pauli; admission DM 6; open Tues.–Sat. 10–5, Sun. 10–6) documents Hamburg from the 800s to the present. Inside, the Historic Emigration Office has records of the 5 million Germans who passed through Hamburg on their way to the New World during the 19th century.

AFTER DARK
Most of Hamburg's pubs and discos are clustered in St. Pauli, especially in the eastern parts of the Reeperbahn, Valentinskamp downtown, and Feldstraße in Schanzenviertel; also take a look around Altona. Spitalerstraße, the pedestrian zone near the Hauptbahnhof, usually has a mix of street musi-

cians, from Peruvian folk musicians to rockers to violinists to accordion players. *Prinz* (DM 5), *Szene* (DM 5), or *OK-Pur* (free at the tourist office) have good listings of pubs and discos; *Hinnerk* (free) covers the gay scene.

The **Freiluftkino auf dem Rathausmarkt** (open July–Aug.; admission free) shows movies on a big screen in front of the Rathaus Thursday–Sunday nights. There are usually a few films in English with German subtitles. Germany's biggest fair, the **Frühlingsdom** (Spring Fest), takes place at the Heiligengeistfeld, near the Reeperbahn, from late March through late April and again in July (when it's renamed the **Hummelfest**).

BARS AND LIVE MUSIC

Hans Albers Eck (Friedrichstr. 26, at Davidstr., no phone; cover DM 6; closed Sun. and Mon.) is a popular and crowded disco/bar near the Reeperbahn. An international crowd meets in **Shamrock** (Feldstr. 40, tel. 040/439–7678), Hamburg's leading Irish pub. For consistently good jazz, check out Hamburg's oldest club, **Cotton Club** (Alter Steinweg 10, tel. 040/343878; S-Bahn to Stadthausbr.); the cover varies.

DANCING

Madhouse (Valentinskamp 46a, tel. 040/344193; cover DM 6–DM 12, women free) is super-popular and always crowded, playing a wide variety of tunes. Dark and cavernous, **Kaiserkeller** (Gr. Freiheit 36, tel. 040/319–3649; cover DM 6–DM 10), former haunt of the Beatles in their earliest days, occasionally has live music also. The **After Shave** (Spielbudenplatz 7, tel. 040/319–3215, covers vary) is one of the biggest clubs in Hamburg, packed with young (and very trendy) locals dancing to funk.

VARIETY THEATERS

The **Schmidt Theater** and **Schmidts Tivoli** (Schmidt Theater, Spielbudenpl. 24; Schmidts Tivoli, Spielbudenpl. 27-28; tel. 040/3177–8899 for both) have become Germany's leading variety theaters. Their shows are televised nationally. The classy repertoire of live music, vaudeville, chansons, and cabaret in both houses is hilarious.

NORTH COAST

Germany's northern coast—largely comprised of the two states of **Schleswig-Holstein** and **Mecklenburg-Vorpommern**—is governed by the stormy moods of an ever-changing sea. Schleswig-Holstein joins Germany with Denmark and has been tossed back and forth between the two for centuries, leaving behind much Danish influence. Prior to 1989, the mostly rural Mecklenburg-Vorpommern was part of the German Democratic Republic (GDR).

The Hanseatic League, a powerful block that dominated trade on the Baltic from the 13th to 17th centuries, helped shape—if not create—most of the port and harbor towns on the north coast. This past wealth is visible today in striking Gothic brick churches and half-timbered merchants' homes, even in cities in the former GDR. Outside of the towns, remote fishing villages, hidden coves, and white-sand beaches are the area's real treasures.

BREMEN

Bremen, along with its deep-water harbor at Bremerhaven, is the smallest *Land* (state) in Germany. Once a Hanseatic League leader, Bremen may carry a thousand-year legacy of successful mercantile trade and industry—seen today in major names like Beck's beer and Eduscho coffee. Touring Bremen is largely a matter of soaking up the atmosphere of various neighborhoods, notably the **Schnoorviertel,** a cobblestone patchwork of cramped, labrynthine lanes, and steep-roofed medieval dwellings on the river south of the Dom.

Follow the river north to **Böttcherstraße,** a short, narrow pedestrian-only alley. In the 1920s, local coffee nabob Ludwig Roselius transformed the lane—originally a barrel makers' street—into a jumble of playful brick constructions, now occupied by shops and galleries. Follow Böttcherstraße away from the river to Bremen's stately **Markt,** bordered by a 16th-century guild hall, a modern glass-and-steel parliament building, and the imposing 900-year-old **Rathaus,** worth checking out for its opulent interior. At the northwest corner of the Rathaus stands Gerhard Marck's bronze of the **Bremen Town Musicians**—the dog, cat, donkey, and rooster from the Grimms' fairy tale. Ogle the great doors before entering the ochre-, sandstone-, and slate-color interior of the Markt's **St. Petri Dom** (open weekdays 10–5, Sat. 10–noon,

Sun. 2–5; shorter hrs off season). Inside, a museum (admission DM 2) exhibits flotsam and jetsam from the church's past. Get the lowdown on all of Bremen's colorful districts at the large **tourist office** (Hillmannpl. 6, tel. 0421/308000; open weekdays 9:30–6:30, until 8:30 Thurs., Sat. 9:30–2, Sun. 9:30–3:30), in front of the Hauptbahnhof.

COMING AND GOING

Trains leave Bremen's neoclassical Hauptbahnhof, just north of the city center, twice hourly for Hamburg (1¼ hrs, DM 31) and Bremerhaven (1 hr, DM 15). Most tram and bus lines (DM 1.50) pass by the Bahnhof; from here, walk south down Bahnhofstraße and Herdentor onto pedestrian-only Sögestraße to the Markt. Bremen is also very bikeable: **Fahrrad Station** (to left of Bahnhof; open Mon. and Wed.–Fri. 9:30–5; June–Sept., also weekends 9:30–noon) rents one-speeds for DM 15 per day.

WHERE TO SLEEP AND EAT

Jugendgästehaus Bremen (HI) (Kalkstr. 6, tel. 0421/171369; beds DM 32) has the cheapest and most central lodging, and a view of the Beck's brewery across the river. From the Hauptbahnhof, take Tram 6 or Bus 26 to Am Brill and follow the riverbank to the right. **Hotel Enzenspenger** (Brautstr. 9, tel. 0421/503224) is perched above a restaurant near the river. Small, lace-curtained doubles start at DM 70 (cash only). From the Altstadt, cross the Wilhelm-Kaisen bridge, go right on Osterstraße, and right on Brautstraße.

Stylish **Engel** (Ostertorsteinweg 31–33, tel. 0421/76615) serves good food for DM 13–DM 19 and excellent lunch deals for about DM 12. Or spoil yourself at **Schröter's** (Schnoor 13, tel. 0421/326677), favored by tourists and locals alike for its "new" German cuisine. Entrées run DM 16–DM 35. **Markets** brighten up the cathedral area on Tuesday and Saturday until 2 PM.

LUBECK

The medieval downtown district of Lübeck, founded by Henry the Lion in 1173 and relatively untouched by the scars of war, is a museum in itself. A seemingly endless procession of church spires dots the skyline, and you can't help but be impressed by the **Holstentor** gate: It welcomes you to the old town (protected by UNESCO as a World Heritage Site) with a pair of pointy towers. Lübeck offers modern diversions as well, and its young people are surprisingly hip and politically active.

Lübeck's dramatic **Dom** (end of Parade) is guarded by a lion statue, in honor of Henry. **Marienkirche,** Germany's third-largest church, looms ominously over the Marktplatz. The church bells remain embedded in the floor, exactly where they fell in a 1942 air raid. The tower of the **Petrikirche** (Kolk, off Holstenstr.; admission DM 3), another of Lübeck's Gothic landmarks, has the best views of the city. A bit farther down Breitestraße, prepare to be stunned by the stained glass and paintings in **Heiligen-Geist-Hospital** (Gr. Burgstr. 9; closed Mon.), which for 700 years has cared for the elderly and ailing—the tiny rooms in back re-create bygone living arrangements. The **tourist office** at Beckergrube 95 (tel. 0451/122–8109; open weekdays 8–4) is the most helpful office, but there is also a branch in the Hauptbahnhof.

COMING AND GOING

Lübeck is 40 minutes by train from Hamburg (DM 16). To reach the old town, walk past the Holstentor. You can rent bikes at **Leihcycle** (Schwartauer Allee 39, near Hauptbahnhof, tel. 0451/42660) for DM 12 per day.

WHERE TO SLEEP AND EAT

Lübeck has oodles of hostels: **CVJM-Haus** (Gr. Petersgrube 11, tel. 0451/71920; beds DM 40, doubles DM 25) is like a YMCA. To reach the hip and *umweltfreundliche* (eco-friendly) **Hotel Rucksack** (Kanalstr. 70, tel. 0451/706892; beds DM 21–DM 26), turn left on Königstraße after the city gate, then right on Glockengießerstraße. The **Jugendgästehaus** (Mengstr. 33, tel. 0451/702–0399; closed noon–1 and 6–7) has beds in single rooms for DM 40 and DM 37.50 in larger rooms, respectively.

The city center is jam-packed with food stands and semi-elegant restaurants. At **Hieronymus** (Fleischhauerstr. 81, tel. 0451/706–3017), you'll find local students nursing beers and munching on fresh gourmet pizzas (about DM 8) or excellent lunch specials. Attached to Hotel Rucksack, **Café Affenbrot** (tel. 0451/72193) serves soy burgers, salads, and assorted sandwiches, such as goat-cheese and tomato. The local café/bar scene is clustered around Fleischhauerstraße and Häxterstraße in the northeast corner of town.

RHINELAND

COLOGNE

The people of this large and diverse city—famous for its art museums and galleries, Roman ruins, and magnificent cathedral—are Kölners first and foremost. Being German or European is a distant second. Locals hypothesize that the legacy of Italian blood and culture in Cologne (Köln in German), colonized by the Romans more than 1,500 years ago, explains their warmth and wit. The gregarious locals let loose at **carnival,** which officially starts at the 11th minute of the 11th day of the 11th month. But the real debauchees arrive at the end of February with Rose Monday (the last Monday before Lent), when the parades and processions march down Cologne's streets, and costumed revelers scream, dance, kiss, and drink with beer-fueled passion.

VISITOR INFORMATION

Tourist office. *Unter Fettenhennen 19, across from Dom, tel. 0221/221–3345. Open Apr.–Oct., Mon.–Sat. 8 AM–10:30 PM, Sun. 9 AM–10:30 PM; shorter hrs off season.*

American Express. *Burgmauerstr. 14, across from Dom, tel. 0221/925–9010. Open weekdays 9–5:30, Sat. 9–noon.*

COMING AND GOING

Train destinations from Cologne include Berlin (6 hrs, DM 151), Paris (6 hrs, DM 96), and Amsterdam (2½ hrs, DM 75). Cologne is the northernmost German point on the Rhine for **Köln-Düsseldorfer ferries** (tel. 0221/208–8318), which go as far south (upstream) as Mainz. Eurailpass holders get free passage; otherwise, it's DM 82 Cologne–Koblenz and another DM 82 Koblenz–Mainz. Yet another understaffed public-service office, the **Mitfahr Büro** (Saarstr. 22, tel. 0221/19444) can get you to any major city in Germany with a day or two's notice. From U-Bahn Eifelplatz walk north on Am Duffesbach and turn left on Saarstraße.

GETTING AROUND

Only the city center, the museums, and sights directly around the Dom, and **Hohe Straße** and **Schildergasse** (Cologne's major *Fußgängerzonen,* or pedestrian zones) are accessible by foot. Luckily, Cologne has an incredibly extensive subway/tram system. Almost all of the subway lines, which become tram lines outside the city center, pass underneath the Hauptbahnhof (follow the blue-and-white U signs). For a taxi, dial 0221/2882 or 0221/19410.

WHERE TO SLEEP

Much of the year the city is flooded with people visiting trade fairs (less so in summer); you can often negotiate a lower price if there is no fair in progress. Even if the hotels are full, you can usually get a room in a hostel or pension outside the city center.

Hotel Berg. Only a five-minute walk from Hauptbahnhof, this little hotel has doubles from DM 90. *Brandenburger Str. 6, tel. 0221/912–9162. Exit rear of Hauptbahnhof, cross to Johannisstr., left on Brandenburger Str.*

Hotel Buchholz. This small, quaint hotel, with the Rhine and cathedral just around the corner, has been recently renovated. The owner is an Englishwoman, Carole Ann Buchholz. Doubles are 120. *Kunibertgasse 5, tel. 0221/121824. Walk (five minutes) north from the main train station.*

Hotel Im Kupferkessel. An ornate spiral staircase leads to the kitchen, where all the guests breakfast together at this elegant-for-the-price accomodation. Doubles cost from DM 110. *Probsteigasse 6, tel. 0221/135338. From Hauptbahnhof, follow Dompropst-Ketzer-Str. (which becomes Gereonsstr. then Christophstr.); right on Probsteigasse.*

Pension Jansen and **Pension Kirchener.** These two pensions are in the same building. Rooms are comfortable but small. The cost of doubles is DM 80–DM 120. *Richard-Wagner-Str. 18, tel. 0221/251875 (Jansen) or 0221/252977 (Kirchener). From Hauptbahnhof, U-Bahn to Neumarkt; transfer upstairs to Tram 1 (toward Junkersdorf) or Tram 2 (toward Benzelrath) to Rudolfpl.; left around Holiday Inn to Richard-Wagner-Str.*

HOSTELS • Jugendgästehaus Köln-Riehl. Within 15 minutes of the Hauptbahnhof, rooms at this modern hostel are clean, functional, and efficient (luggage storage available)—like any good production-line factory. Beds DM 32.50, including breakfast and sheets. There's no curfew. *An der Schanz 14, tel. 0221/767081. From Hauptbahnhof, U16 (toward Wiener Pl.) to Boltensternstr.; walk 33 ft in same direction as train. Reception open 24 hours.*

Jugendherberge Köln-Deutz (HI). A little cheaper and more central than other hostels, this place is also a little dirtier and louder, and has a 12:30 AM curfew. Beds are DM 26–DM 31. *Siegesstr. 5a, tel. 0221/814711. From Hauptbahnhof, cross bridge over the Rhine to Ottopl. (15 min on foot). Or, S-Bahn one stop to Bahnhof Deutz; cross Ottopl. to Neuhöflerstr., turn right on Sieggesstr. Reception open 24 hours. Closed 1 week at Christmas.*

CAMPING • Campingplatz Poll. This manicured field next to the Rhine is easy to get to, but car campers predominate. DM 5 per spot, DM 5.50 per person. *Weidenweg, tel. 0221/831966. From Hauptbahnhof, U16 (toward Hersel/Bonn) to Marienburg; then cross Rodenkirchener bridge and follow signs.*

FOOD

The best places to go for everyday Kölner food are the breweries. For groceries, stroll along Hohe Straße and Schildergasse. If you do only one thing in town besides see the Dom, sample some Kölsch beer, brewed by more than 40 different houses and served everywhere.

Alcazar. Crowds of university students pack this place, known for outstanding and healthy food (they have tons of salad and creative pasta dishes). Expect to pay DM 12–DM 15 for a meal. *Bismarckstr. 39, tel. 0221/515733. U-Bahn to Friesenpl.; walk down Venloer Str., turn left on Bismarckstr.*

Borsalino. Hearty portions are served at student prices. Capricciosa salad (tuna, egg, tomatoes, and olives) is DM 8.50; tortellini with spinach is DM 11. *Zülpicherstr. 7, tel. 0221/248852. U-Bahn or Tram to Zülpicher Pl.; walk 1 block down Zülpicher Str.*

WORTH SEEING

Most of Cologne's sights are in the old town, outlined by the Hohenzollernring, which marks the former site of the medieval city wall. A walk from the Dom to Friesenplatz or Rudolfplatz, whether on a sightseeing or a beer-drinking tour, is a good way to explore the inner city.

DOM • Towering over the train station and city center is Germany's finest Gothic cathedral, the **Kölner Dom.** It was not actually completed until 1880, with construction taking seven centuries (there were 300 years' worth of interruptions). Repairing and refurbishing the Dom, scarred by bombs in World War II and eroded even now by acid rain, is a permanent endeavor. Climb the 509 steps of the **Südturm** (South Tower; admission DM 3) for a great view of the Rhine. More spectacular, however, is the **Glockenstube,** 400 steps up, where the Dom's nine bells are housed, including the Petriglocke—the world's heaviest working bell.

WALLRAF-RICHARTZ-MUSEUM AND MUSEUM LUDWIG • In the same building right behind the Dom, these two museums form the core of Cologne's art scene. The collections are medieval through the Renaissance, plus a massive collection of 20th-century art. *Bischofsgartenstr. 1, behind Dom, tel. 0221/221–2372 for Wallraf-Richartz or 0221/221–2372 for Ludwig. Admission: DM 10. Open Tues.–Fri. 10–6, weekends 11–6.*

ROMISCH-GERMANISCHES MUSEUM • The museum was built around an enormous mosaic depicting the adventures of Dionysus, the Greek god of wine, that was uncovered there during the construction of an air-raid shelter in 1941. The mosaic once covered the dining-room floor of a wealthy Roman trader's villa. Roman tombs, memorial tablets, and spectacular collections of ancient glassware and jewelry are among the museum's other exhibits. *Roncallipl. 4, tel. 0221/221–4438. Admission DM 5. Tues.–Fri. 10–4, weekends 11–4.*

EL-DE-HAUS • This building served as headquarters for Cologne's Gestapo. Today it is a museum devoted to the memory of Holocaust victims and a tribute to Nazi-era resistance groups. *Appellhofpl. 23–25, tel. 0221/221–6331. U-Bahn to Appellhofpl. Admission DM 4. Open Tues.–Fri. 10–4, weekends 11–4.*

IMHOFF-STOLLWERCK-MUSEUM • Stollwerck, the owner of a local chocolate company of the same name, has created a Charlie-and-the-Chocolate-Factory experience with a chocolate fountain, greenhouses where cocoa is grown, demonstrations on production, and, of course, a gift shop at the end. *Rheinauhafen 1a, tel. 0221/931–8880. U-Bahn to Heumarkt; cross Pipinstr. and head down Paradiesgasse to the riverfront, turn right on Am Leistapei, and cross drawbridge just past the tower. Admission: DM 10. Open weekdays 10–6, weekends 11–7.*

AFTER DARK

You can dance all night in turn-of-the-century decor beneath the train station in the **Alter Wartesaal** (Johannisstrasse 11, tel. 0221/912–8850; admission DM 5). For summer biergarten atmosphere, go to the **Stadtgarten** (Venloer Str. 40, tel. 0221/516037; open daily noon–1 AM). **Museum** (Zülpicher Pl. 9, tel. 0221/232098) serves 10-liter minikegs of Kölsch outdoors under the protection of a two-story tall dinosaur. **Hallmackenreuthur** (Brüsseler Pl. 9, tel. 0221/517970) embraces the cheesy art deco style of the late '60s and early '70s. **Osho's** (Hohenzollernring 90, north of Friesenpl., tel. 0221/574–9725) is one of Cologne's best discos: The **One World** disco upstairs complements the **Petit Prince** downstairs. Both places have covers (DM 5–DM 12). The Prince's musical theme varies: jazz on Monday, reggae on Friday, and salsa or other Latin music most other nights. On Friday night, One World becomes the **Pink Triangle,** a gay-and-lesbian club.

NEAR COLOGNE

DUSSELDORF

In Düsseldorf you'll see beautiful, stylish women and men with chiseled jaws wearing tortoise-shell glasses and driving BMWs—but they probably won't see you. Ironically, while Düsseldorfers are considered snobby because of their wealth (incomes in Düsseldorf are 25% higher than the rest of the country), the city is also written off as a dumping ground for partying blue-collar workers from the Ruhrgebiet, the big industrial region northeast of the city. But Düsseldorf is well worth a visit—for its well-preserved and extensive Altstadt, food that is surprisingly cheap, art museums and galleries worthy of any urban center, and a spicy, diverse nightlife.

Bordered by the serene **Hofgarten Park** to the north and east and by the Rhine to the west, Düsseldorf's Altstadt and its maze of small alleys is home to more than 200 bars and restaurants, as well as the major art museums. It's only about 12 blocks long and 5 blocks wide, but to navigate the Altstadt, you'll need a walking map from the **tourist office** (Immermanstr. 65b, across from Hauptbahnhof, tel. 0211/17020). If you forget the next day where you were the previous night, go to the top of the 770-ft **Rheinturm** (Stromstr. 20), and glance down at the sprawling city. Then make your way to the star of the city's museums—the **Kunstsammlung Nordrhein-Westfalen** (Grabbepl. 5, tel. 0211/83810; admission DM 8), which specializes in modern art, featuring works by Pablo Picasso and Marc Chagall, and one of the finest Paul Klee exhibits anywhere.

WHERE TO SLEEP AND EAT • Conventions and trade fairs in Düsseldorf bring droves that fill hotels and raise the price of rooms. Try **Komet** (Bismarckstr. 93, tel. 0211/178790; doubles DM 85) or **Diana** (Jahnstr. 31, tel. 0211/375071; doubles from DM 80) for the cheapest rooms. Beds at the **Jugendherberge und Jugendgästehaus Düsseldorf (HI)** (Düsseldorf Str. 1, tel. 0211/557310) are DM 37. From the Hauptbahnhof take U70, U74, U75, U76, or U77 (toward Krefeld or Neuss) to Luegplatz and walk south on Kaiser-Wilhem-Ring to Rheinkniebrücke. **Füchschen** (Ratinger Str. 28/30, tel. 0211/137470) is a traditional beer tavern holding its own against time; guests rub elbows on the long wooden tables and quaff the *Altbier* fresh from the tap. It has its own butcher and feeds its carnivorous clientele very well. To eat and drink with twentysomethings, head to up the street to trendy **Zur Uel** (Ratinger Str. 16, tel. 0211/325369), which isn't exactly your traditional brew house.

AACHEN

Aachen, connected twice hourly by train with Cologne (1 hr, DM 19), is also known as Bad Aachen because of its hot springs (*Bad* means baths), and as Aix-la-Chapelle (place of the chapel) because of Charlemagne's 8th-century, 16-side chapel that now supports the rest of the city's **Dom** (Cathedral). Aachen is also called "Rome North" because Charlemagne and the next 32 Holy Roman emperors were crowned here. The golden shrine in the cathedral contains Charlemagne's remains, and the **Domschatzkammer** (Cathedral Treasury) displays an ivory diptych from Charlemagne's time, as well as an astonishing array of riches. Across from the Dom, is the regal 14th-century **Rathaus.** To the northeast of the Rathaus, the **Kurbad Quellenhof** (Monheimsallee 52, tel. 0241/180–2922) is an elegant spa offering rejuvenating soaks for DM 16.

WHERE TO SLEEP • There are two affordable hotels within walking distance of the Hauptbahnhof: **Hotel Dusa** (Lagerhausstr. 5, tel. 0241/403135; doubles DM 90) and **Hotel am Bahnhof** (Bahnhofpl. 8, tel. 0241/35449; doubles from DM 80). To get to the **youth hostel** (Maria-Theresia-Allee 280, tel. 0241/71101; beds DM 22—DM 26.50), take any bus west from the Hauptbahnhof one stop to Finanzamt, then cross to the opposite bus stop, and take Bus 2 to Ronheide or Bus 12 to Colynhof/Jugendherberge.

BONN

It's hard to say what Bonn will be like in the year 2000, when the government has packed up and left for Berlin. But it will still have the university; three bright, new museums of history and art; and its old claim to fame as the birthplace of Ludwig van Beethoven. If you choose to do the Beethoven tour, start at **Münsterplatz,** which is centered around a stoic statue of the composer. The maestro was born in the **Beethoven-Haus** (Bonngasse 20, tel. 0228/635188; admission DM 8), which has displays illustrating his entire intense and tormented life.

VISITOR INFORMATION • *Münsterstr. 20, tel. 0228/773466. From Hauptbahnhof, follow* STADT-MITTE *signs onto Poststr., then left on Münsterstr. Open weekdays 9–6:30, Sat. 9–5, Sun. 10–2.*

WHERE TO SLEEP • Both hostels have a 1 AM curfew and charge DM 37. **Jugendgästehaus Bonn-Venusberg** (Haager Weg 42, tel. 0228/289970) should be on the cover of *Better Youth Hostels and Gardens*. From Busbahnhof platform A2, take Bus 621 to Jugendherberge. To get to **Jugendgästehaus Bonn-Bad Godesberg** (Horionstr. 60, tel. 0228/317516), take U16 or U63 to Bahnhof Bad Godesberg, then Bus 615 to Jugendherberge.

Near Koblenzer Tor, under the university's castle wall, is **Blau** (Franziskanerstr. 5, tel. 0228/650717), a café and restaurant serving green salad (DM 4) and penne with pesto (DM 6.50) to students busy talking, reading, and studying.

WORTH SEEING • From Marktplatz, follow Stockenstraße to Regina-Pacis-Weg to reach the **Kurfürstliches Schloß,** a castle turned university administration building. From the Heussallee/Bundeshaus U-Bahn station, walk down Heussallee towards the Rhine and make a left on Görrestraße for the **Bundeshaus** (tel. 0228/162–2152; open weekdays 9–4, weekends 10–4). It's the home of the **Bundestag,** the 664-member Parliament

An unusually large number of Kölners celebrate their birthdays in November, ostensibly because nine months earlier, the city's carnival is at its most intense.

that makes most of Germany's laws and elects the chancellor and president. Call ahead for a spot on the mandatory 30-minute tour (English tour Tuesday at noon), and bring a passport.

Bonn is also home to two important modern-art museums, most especially the **Kunst-und Ausstellungshalle der Bundesrepublik Deutschland** (Federal Art and Exhibition Hall) and its neighbor, the **Kunstmuseum Bonn** (Bonn Art Museum). *Friedrich-Ebert-Allee 2 and 4, tel. 0228/917–1200 (Ausstellungshalle) or 0228/776260 (Kunstmuseum). Combined admission: DM 10. Both open Tues.–Sun. 10–7.*

The **Haus der Geschichte der Bundesrepublik Deutschland** documents the history of Germany since World War II. The very thorough coverage here requires the better part of a day. You can rent English-language cassette tours, or simply let the impressive audio-visual exhibits enlighten you about everything from concentration camps to early German television. *Adenauerallee 250, tel. 0228/91650. Admission free (except for special exhibits). Open Tues.–Sun. 9–7.*

RHINE AND MOSEL VALLEYS

The Rhine is the undisputed king of Germany's many rivers. Often called *Vater Rhein* (Father Rhine) in German, the river flows 1,355 km (833 mi) from its source in the Swiss Alps to the North Sea. The most glorious stretch of the Rhine is between **Mainz** and **Koblenz;** the Rhine's beautiful tributary, the **Mosel River,** is also a worthwhile area to explore. If you're short on time, don't try to visit both the Rhine and Mosel valleys—choose one. The Rhine is a willful, major waterway, which over the years has carved a dramatically beautiful valley. The Mosel is the quiet sibling, and the hills around it roll gently off into the green distance.

Rail lines run along both sides of the Rhine, but the best views are from the west side. Because of the Mosel Valley's peculiar geography, trains often bypass smaller towns. **Bus** trips are cheap, extensive, and scenic, but hot in summer and always bumpy and slow. Slower still is **boat** travel—the most peaceful and scenic way to see the Rhine Gorge. The major ferry operator is **Köln-Düsseldorfer Deutsche Rheinschiffahrt** (tel. 0221/258–3011), known as the KD Rhine Line; you can use your Eurailpass or Deutsche Bundesbahn (DB) pass, or get 50% off with your InterRail pass. If you don't have a pass, check out KD's combined river-rail tickets, which allow you to get off the boat at any stop and continue onward by train.

MAINZ

Mainz, gateway to the castle-studded Rhine Gorge, is worth checking out in its own right. Mainz's most famous son is Johannes Gutenberg (1390–1468), inventor of movable type. The central **Gutenberg-**

Museum (Liebfrauenpl. 5, tel. 06131/122640; admission DM 5), dominated by displays on Gutenberg, has a priceless copy of the 550-year-old Gutenberg Bible, the first book printed using movable type. Mainz's Altstadt was bombed in World War II but the city has managed to resurrect it. Dominating the Marktplatz in the center of the Altstadt is the **Martinsdom,** a mammoth Romanesque cathedral, begun during the 11th century. Also in the heart of the old town is **Stefanskirche** (Stefansberg); Marc Chagall designed the stained-glass windows of this otherwise ordinary church. **KD boats** dock in front of Mainz's Rathaus (Rheinstr.), and the helpful **tourist office** (Bahnhofstr. 15, tel. 06131/286210) gives out free maps.

WHERE TO SLEEP

The run-down and seedy **hostel** (Am Fort Weisenau, tel. 06131/85332; beds DM 21) is your only shot at a cheap sleep. **Terminus Hotel** (Alicenstr. 4, tel. 06131/229876) and **Pfeil Continental** (Bahnhofstr. 15, tel. 06131/232179) have decent doubles for DM 100–DM 120. **Campingplatz Rheinufer** (Rheinufer, tel. 06131/86852; reception open 3:30 PM–9 PM) charges DM 10 per person. From the Hauptbahnhof, take Bus 21 (30 min) to Laubenheim, then turn right and walk 1½ km (¾ mi) along the Rhine; the last bus is at around 10 PM.

KOBLENZ

Koblenz is not too pretty, yet oddly charming, sort of like its **Schängelbrunnen** (Scalawag Fountain), a bronze fountain with a statue of a young boy that spits water every three minutes or so at unsuspecting passersby. Looking down on Koblenz from **Festung Ehrenbreitstein** (to get here, take Bus 7 or 8 to Bahnhof Ehrenbreitstein, Bus 9 or 10 to Charlottenstraße, or a ferry across the Rhine), a 19th-century castle perched on a hill across the river, you'll see a modern city scattered with a few old buildings at the majestic confluence of the Rhine and the Mosel. Apart from a photogenic Altstadt, dominated by the spitting Schängelbrunnen fountain and the bulky Romanesque **Liebfrauenkirche** (Church of Our Lady), Koblenz gets big points for its proximity to the Rhine and Mosel valleys.

Maps, boat schedules, hotel listings, and reservations (DM 2) can all be had at the main **tourist office** (tel. 0261/31304), across from the Hauptbahnhof. If you're overnighting, try the **Hotel Jan van Werth** (Van Werth Str. 9, tel. 0261/36500; doubles DM 85), a five-minute walk from the train station. The spic-and-span **Jugendherberge (HI)** (Auf der Festung, tel. 0261/73737; beds DM 22.50) is inside Festung Ehrenbreitstein, with great views of the Rhine and Mosel.

TRIER

The ancient city of Trier, which claims to be Germany's oldest, is full of surprises. Greeting you as you enter from the station is **Porta Nigra** (Black Gate), which formed part of the 2nd-century Roman wall that once encircled the city. Other Roman monuments are the **Römische Palastaula** (Roman Basilica), the largest surviving single-hall structure of the ancient world, the ruins of the **Kaiserthermen** (Imperial Baths, admission DM 4), among the largest public baths in the Roman Empire and an **Amphitheater** (admission DM 4), where gladiators fought before crowds of 20,000. The **Rheinisches Landesmuseum** (Rhineland Archaeological Museum, admission DM 2) houses a huge collection of Roman antiquities, including a recently discovered pot of Roman gold coins.

Of the many centuries-old structures surrounding Trier's **Hauptmarkt,** the most notable is the 16th-century **Petrusbrunnen** (St. Peter's Fountain) on the southeast corner. Just down Stirnstraße from the Hauptmarkt is Trier's light, airy Romanesque **Dom** (cathedral)—the oldest Christian church north of the Alps, built and rebuilt over 15 centuries. Behind the front altar you can peek through locked doors at the eerily encased *Tunica Christi* (Robe of Christ), supposedly the garment worn by Jesus Christ at his trial by Pontius Pilate. Next to the Dom stands one of the first purely Gothic churches erected in Germany, the 13th-century **Liebfrauenkirche** (Church of Our Lady).

WHERE TO SLEEP

The **Jugendherberge Trier (HI)** (An der Jugendherberge 4, tel. 0651/29292) has beds in doubles (DM 35.50) and quads (DM 26.30); from the Hauptbahnhof, walk down Theodor-Heuss-Allee, turn right on Paulinstraße, and left on Maarstraße (which becomes An der Jugendherberge). Doubles at **Hotel zur Glocke** (Glockenstr. 12, tel. 0651/73109), just off Simeonstraße between the Hauptmarkt and Porta Nigra, are DM 80.

GREAT BRITAIN

N ever mind whether you've been to Great Britain before—for the English-speaking traveler, to go there is to go *back*. If there is a sense of tradition many Brit-bound visitors share, vague and nostalgic or bitter and mocking, it was born in large part here. Romantic poetry, the King James Bible, Adam Smith's vision of capitalism, Charles Darwin's revolution, and that darned Puritan work ethic are all legacies of the Commonwealth, elements of the parent culture from which an empire sprang. Whether filled with enthusiasm or misgivings, many of us come to Britain seeking our historical roots; still others arrive to explore the powerful cultural, political, and historical ties linking Britain and other countries around the world.

The sense of history is indeed palpable. Stone circles off the main roads hint at prehistoric civilizations and ways of life we can only guess about. Westminster Abbey's worn stone floors have seen just about every kind of human footwear, from noble slippers to running shoes. Some pubs even have signs over their doors saying "Rebuilt 1618" and "Founded AD 1400." Yet if these places inspire an eerie sense of déjà vu, it's because we've seen them before, courtesy of William Shakespeare, Charles Dickens, Charlotte Brontë, Dylan Thomas, Oscar Wilde, and a great host of others. Their stories and fairy tales have been handed down to many of us since we were tots, and here they are—or at least, here are their remains.

One of the benefits of the 20th century is that official histories of warring kings and clans, of manners and those to-the-manor-born, are no longer taken at face value. A new history, the story of those who did not win, is being told: working-class Welsh, Irish bricklayers, and ex-colonials. Alongside museum displays of royal pomp and pageantry, there are now exhibits about coal miners and crofters. Even more telling, there's a vibrant culture thriving outside Britain's traditional centers. For years now, London's club scene has shared the spotlight with its counterparts in northern cities like Manchester and Leeds, which have generated their own burgeoning cultures, far from the shadow of assumed chic produced by the capital. Despite the uncertain welcome extended to immigrants from India, Pakistan, the Caribbean, and Hong Kong, these groups have also done much to infuse new life into these cities. The most obvious evidence is culinary and musical, though the trend towards multiculturalism has taken root everywhere, forcing the stodgier elements of Britain to the periphery, like it or not.

But don't expect the keepers of Britain's cultural flame to roll over and play dead. When you come right down to it, many Brits are passionate about their homeland and convinced of their innate superiority to the rest of the world. You only have to see the Brits abroad to realize that, despite their long experience of

GREAT BRITAIN AND NORTHERN IRELAND

KEY
- Rail Lines
- Ferry Lines

N

0
50 km
50 miles
100 km
100 miles
150 km

REPUBLIC OF IRELAND

Armagh

Dublin

Cork

Rosslare

St. George's Channel

Irish Sea

Isle of Man

Holyhead
Caernarfon
Isle of Anglesey
Llandudno
Betws-y-Coed

Llŷn Peninsula

Aberystwyth

WALES

Pembroke
St. David's
Fishguard
Cardigan
Tenby
Gower
Swansea
Brecon

Cardiff
Newport

Liverpool
Blackpool
Lancaster

Chester
Stoke-on-Trent
Shrewsbury

Birmingham
Stratford
Coventry

ENGLAND

Manchester
Bradford
Leeds
York

Sheffield

Derby
Nottingham
Leicester
Stamford

Lincoln
Boston
Skegness
The Wash
Grimsby
Kingston-upon-Hull

Cromer

Bristol Channel
Ilfracombe
Barnstaple
Bude

Newquay
St. Ives
Penzance
Scilly Isles
Land's End
Lizard
Falmouth

Bodmin
Princetown
Plymouth
Torquay

Exeter

Bournemouth
Dorchester

Glastonbury
Bath
Bristol

M5
M4
Swindon

Gloucester
Cheltenham

Oxford
Reading
Salisbury
Stonehenge
Winchester
Southampton

Isle of Wight
Portsmouth
Arundel

Northampton
Cambridge
Ely

Norwich
Great Yarmouth

Ipswich
Harwich
Colchester

M6

M62

A1

Windsor
LONDON
Reigate
Brighton
Rye
Maidstone
Canterbury
Dover
Strait of Dover
Boulogne
Calais

English Channel

FRANCE

TO LE HAVRE

TO HOEK VAN HOLLAND

338

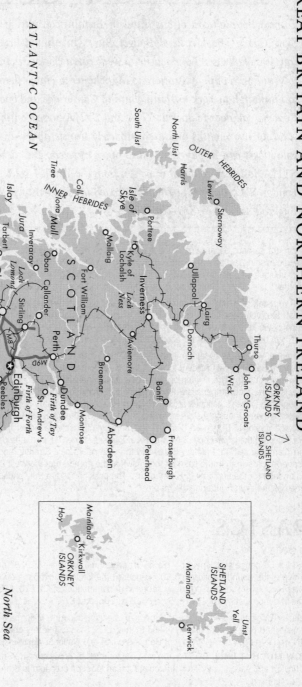

GREAT BRITAIN AND NORTHERN IRELAND

ATLANTIC OCEAN

NORTHERN IRELAND

Derry
Portadown
Ballycastle
Portrush
Lorne
M1
Belfast
Bangor
Stranraer
Campbeltown
Giant's Causeway

Islay
Jura
Tarbert
Arran
Ayr
Inveraray
Oban
Loch Lomond

Tiree
Coll
Iona
Mull
INNER HEBRIDES

Isle of Skye
Mallaig
Portree
Kyle of Lochalsh
Loch Ness

South Uist
North Uist
Harris
Lewis
Stornoway
OUTER HEBRIDES

SCOTLAND

Fort William
Callender
Stirling
Glasgow
Kilmarnock
M8
Lanark
Dumfries
Kirkcudbright
Keswick
Kendal
Carlisle
Windermere
Peebles
Edinburgh
M90
Perth
Dundee
St. Andrew's
Firth of Forth
Firth of Tay
Jedburgh
Berwick-on-Tweed
Newcastle-upon-Tyne
Durham
Whitby
A690
A696

Inverness
Aviemore
Braemar
Montrose
Aberdeen
Peterhead
Fraserburgh
Banff
Ullapool
Lairg
Dornoch
Wick
John O'Groats
Thurso

ORKNEY ISLANDS
TO SHETLAND ISLANDS

North Sea

Mainland
Hoy
Kirkwall
ORKNEY ISLANDS

Mainland
Yell
Unst
SHETLAND ISLANDS
Lerwick

THE SLOW COACH

To beat the high cost of bus travel in Britain, consider spending £99 on The Slow Coach (Backpackers' Budget Bus), an around-Britain bus service for travelers of all ages. Four coaches a week run a clockwise circuit—from London to Windsor to Bath to Stratford to Manchester to Haworth and the Lake District to Edinburgh to York to Nottingham to Cambridge and back again to London. Coaches call door-to-door at YHA and SYHA hostels on the route. Tickets are valid for two months and are completely transferable—any unused portion of your ticket can be given or sold to other travelers. Buy tickets from YHA and SYHA hostels en route, or in person from the Youth Hostel, 38 Bolton Gardens, London SW5, or write to The Slow Coach (71 Bradenstoke, Wiltshire SN15 4EL, England, tel. 01249/891–959).

Empire (or perhaps because of it), they feel the British way is the right way. There's still a sad but, thankfully, diminishing faction of the narrow-minded who mope if they can't get an English breakfast, chips, and a pint of bitter, and get into a terrible snit if the locals don't speak the King's English. Buy them a pint, in fact, and they'll tell you why your country's got it all wrong and how the Brits could do it a damn sight better.

Yet if you make the mistake of coming up with generalizations about how uptight and closed-minded the British are, you deserve to have an uptight and closed-minded experience. Britain is about ordinary, everyday workers as much as it is about Beefeaters—about burly sheep farmers as much as it is about the Rasta hawking Eddie Grant bootlegs in a London street market.

Of course, you'll have to take in the classic sights. From London's Bloody Tower to Canterbury Cathedral, from Bath's Royal Crescent to Yorkshire's Castle Howard, the country is a lode of cultural treasures that never runs dry. Then, again, a peek at the spoils of empire housed within London's British Museum reveals more about imperialism than a stack of history books ever could. By the same token, a look through the Queen's galleries at Buckingham Palace gives a better sense of royal wealth, power, and influence than a thousand stories printed in the *Sun*. On the other hand, don't get sucked into the tour-package version of Britain—a Disneyesque montage of busbied sentries and kilted bagpipers. Don't be afraid to grab the latest copy of *New Musical Express, Time Out,* and a thermos full of strong Earl Grey, and plant yourself on Trafalgar Square in the wee hours of a Sunday morning. Or go and see what inspired Wordsworth in the Lake District, gawk at the grandeur of the West Country coast, and eat Balti Indian food for the first time in Birmingham. The possibilities are truly endless and are as peculiar and varied as the towns cluttering the map.

BASICS

MONEY

US$1 = 60 pence and 1 pound = $1.68 (at press time, summer 1997). The unit of currency in Great Britain is the pound, broken into 100 pence. In the United Kingdom, pound (nicknamed the "quid") notes (not "bills") come in colorfully designed denominations of £5, £10, £20, and £50. Coins are available in denominations of 1p, 2p, 5p, 10p, 20p, 50p, and £1.

British ATMs can usually access an American checking account. Major bank chains like National Westminster and Barclays are usually linked to the PLUS, Star, or Internet chains. If your credit card has a PIN, you can draw money from it at Barclays (Visa) and National Westminster (MasterCard).

HOW MUCH IT WILL COST • You will be astounded by how expensive Britain can be. Even if you stay in hostels and eat only pub grub and cheap Indian food, be prepared to drop at least $50 a day. Lodging will be your greatest expense. Expect to pay around £9–£13 for a bed in a hostel, £12–£18 per person in a bed-and-breakfast (although prices vary widely), and £50 and up for a hotel. Campsites, bless 'em, can cost as little as £3. Foodwise, you can subsist quite easily on £10 a day, if you don't mind fish and chips or pub grub. Although trains are often the most convenient form of transportation, they also can be hideously expensive. Local transportation is pricey, too; it costs £1.10 just to go one stop on the Underground in London (although, of course, the same fare can take you from one end of the city to the other). As for tipping, leave about 10% for restaurant service (unless the menu or check indicates that service is included), 10% for taxi drivers, and nothing for pub bartenders unless you really like the service.

COMING AND GOING

BY FERRY • Ferries aren't always the most pleasant way of getting around, but they are the cheapest means of coming from France, Belgium, and the Netherlands. (The recent opening of the Channel Tunnel linking England with the Continent does nothing to alter this situation; the very cheapest one-way fare for a London–Paris train trip, booked at least two weeks in advance, is £69.) Ferries arrive at **Dover, Folkestone,** and **Portsmouth** from Calais, Boulogne, and Le Havre; there are many special offers on fares for day round-trips, starting in the off season from £5; with a car, fares begin around £15 (plus a small extra charge per person). However, these will cost you considerably more in the summer. Holland, northern Germany, and Scandinavia are best accessed from the East Anglia port of **Harwich** by ferries bound for Hoek van Holland (Hook of Holland). The Welsh port of **Holyhead** is the best town from which to catch ferries to Dublin (£20–£60 one-way), although there's also service from the Welsh port of **Fishguard** to the Irish port of **Rosslare,** from **Swansea** to **Cork,** and from **Stranraer** (Scotland) to **Belfast** (Northern Ireland).

BY PLANE • London has two enormous airports, **Heathrow** and **Gatwick,** that are burdened with the majority of England's international traffic; upstart **Stansted Airport,** halfway between London and Cambridge on the M11, recently opened as a more pleasant alternative, and **London City Airport** handles mostly European commuter flights. Manchester, Edinburgh, and Glasgow have airports serving some international destinations, primarily on the European continent. Although **British Airways** (from U.S., dial 800/247–9297) is considered the national airline, international carriers like Delta, United, Virgin, American, and Air France fly to Britain from the Continent and America.

GETTING AROUND

In the United Kingdom, say "single" instead of "one-way," and "return" instead of "round-trip," when inquiring about bus and train tickets.

BY BUS • Buses (often called coaches here) take much longer than trains, but tickets often cost half as much. Although many regional, long-distance bus companies exist, **National Express** (Caledonian Express in Scotland) has the most comprehensive coverage of towns and cities in England, Wales, and Scotland. The **Tourist Trail Pass** allows unlimited bus travel in England for 3 consecutive days (£49), 5 days in 10 (£79), 8 of 16 days (£119), and 15 of 30 days (£179). In the United States, the **British Travel Associates** (tel. 540/298–2232) sells passes over the phone and can quote you the latest price in dollars. In Britain, you can get passes at any National Express office or at the Heathrow or Gatwick bus stations. You'll get a 20% discount on these passes with the **Young Person's Coach Card** (£8), available to students age 16–25, or the **Student Coach Card** (£8), available to anyone who can prove they're a student. These cards are available at any National Express office.

BY TRAIN • Despite Britain's shifty allegiance to a unified Europe, it *still* does not accept the Eurailpass. Nonetheless, most budget travelers get around Britain by train. In the summer and autumn of 1996 **BritRail** was broken up and sold off to private companies. The old Intercity rail system (the track and stations, etc., now run by Railtrack), still links Britain's major cities via high-speed rail. The train service and service to towns within London's commuter belt are extremely frequent. However, as you get farther out into the countryside, off the main routes, service drops off dramatically, and it's important to plan your itinerary carefully. This is particularly true on Sundays, more especially so in the remote areas of northern and western England, Scotland, and Wales. The *Great Britain Passenger Railway Timetable* (£7), issued every May and October, contains details of all national rail services; pick one up at any major train station.

If you plan to do a lot of traveling, it's probably worth investing in a **BritRail Pass** (which still does exist), because full-price tickets (especially single) can be absurdly expensive, especially at rush hours. Remember that most rail passes cannot be purchased in the United Kingdom—you must get them *before* you leave home. Passes allow unlimited travel over the entire national rail network, which encompasses almost all lines you're likely to need. An adult **second-class pass** costs $249 for eight days, $379 for 15 days, $485 for 22 days, and $565 for one month. If you're 16–25 years old, consider a **BritRail Youth Pass.** It allows unlimited second-class travel in the following increments: $199 for eight days, $305 for 15 days, $389 for 22 days, and $450 for one month. Passes are available from most travel agents or from the **BritRail Travel Information Office** (1500 Broadway, New York, NY 10036, tel. 800/677–8585).

If you want to explore a specific part of Britain in greater detail, unlimited travel tickets offer excellent value. Now that British Rail has been broken up and sold off, there are 25 different rail operating companies. A main station, such as Waterloo, Paddington, or Victoria, will give price details and time restrictions of the different ticket schemes covering the various regions.

WHERE TO SLEEP
HOTELS AND B&BS

When it comes to hotels, expensive is practically the rule in Britain. You can pay an arm and a leg for a night's lodging if you don't watch out. We have included some moderately priced hotels along the way (along with some guest houses masquerading under the name "hotel," but none the worse for that). You have to make a decision. Do you want to pay a fair amount of money for a night's oblivion in chintz-adorned, antiques-bedecked surroundings, or would you rather spend your money while *conscious*. Every so often, in fact, we think you should allow yourself a splurge. A night or two in a classy hotel can make your bargain-cutting all the easier to bear. As for bargains, needless to say, B&Bs will help salvage your budget. Bed-and-breakfasts, which generally cost £12–£15 per person at the low end, are usually private homes that owners open to travelers. In general, expect to share bathrooms, although many rooms have their own washbasins. Breakfast—anything from soggy toast to the full splendor of bacon, sausage, eggs, tomato, and cereal—is included in the rates. Local Tourist Information Centres can be good sources on the best accommodation options out there.

HOSTELS • Hostelling International (HI) hostels in Great Britain are run by the **Youth Hostel Association of England and Wales (YHA)** (Trevelyan House, 8 St. Stephen's Hill, St. Albans, Herts AL1 2DY, England, tel. 01727/855–215) or the **Scotland Youth Hostel Association (SYHA)** (7 Glebe Crescent, Stirling FK8 2JA, Scotland, tel. 01786/891–400). You can write or call for detailed pamphlets. Most hostels also carry a guide to all of Britain's hostels, including prices, dates open, and directions. Most HI hostels have basic kitchen facilities and serve meals (breakfast starts at £3, dinner at £4). Hostels not affiliated with HI charge about the same rates as HI hostels and vary greatly in quality.

You can purchase a Hostelling International membership card at any hostel for £9.30 (£3.20 under 18). Nonmembers must pay an extra £1.55 per night for a guest stamp; after accruing six stamps you're granted full membership. Students between the ages of 18 and 26 and in possession of an ISIC card are given a £1 discount on hostel accommodations in England; be sure to ask.

To double check your accommodation plans, we advise you **telephone the hostel in advance—certain hostels close during off-season months.** While we note if any hostel is closed during off season (this can often occur in northern England and Scotland), it's best to inquire by phone as your arrival date approaches to **get the latest update.** Most HI hostels have sex-segregated dormitories. They ususally have an 11 PM curfew (except in major cities), daytime bedroom lockouts (usually 10–4), check-in times between 8–11 AM and 5–9 PM, and check-out by 10:30 AM.

STUDENT HOUSING

Many university residence halls rent out their rooms to travelers during the summer months. When inquiring about reservations by phone, be sure to ask if there is any minimum amount of stay—some places require at least a three-night booking. In addition, some halls only offers rooms to students and not to the general public, so you'll want to check when calling.

CAMPING • If you're planning to camp, keep the following in mind: (1) You're likely to get wet no matter where you are, (2) campgrounds in rural areas are often poorly served by public transportation, and (3) many campgrounds are closed except during summer months. For more information on Britain's more than 2,000 campsites, contact the British Tourist Authority for their free "Freedom" brochures on caravan and camping parks.

FOOD

Britain probably conquered half the world for no other reason than that they wanted some decent food. But Britain is far from being the culinary wasteland it was just two decades ago. London is undergoing a food revolution and its restaurant scene is currently the hottest in Europe. The trickle-down effect of what they are calling "Modern British" cuisine is being felt throughout the country. In larger cities, ethnic—Indian, Thai, Chinese—is always a nifty and tasty way to go. These family-run places have filtered out and most small towns have a Chinese takeout that doubles as a fish-and-chips. Otherwise, you may do best eating a pub meal. The old traditional stodgy pies and puddings have given way to basket meals—fried chicken or fish pieces with the ubiquitous chips—and in some places, quite adventurous meals, particularly in the south, west, and east of the country. Many also offer vegetarian options. Pub Sunday roast dinners can often be the cheapest and the best in town.

If you carry on like most Britons, you'll spend a considerable amount of time in pubs. The beer of choice among Britons is **bitter,** a lightly fermented beer with an amber color that gets its bitterness from hops. **Real ale,** served from wooden kegs, is flatter than regular bitters. **Stouts,** like Guinness, are a meal in themselves and something of an acquired taste—they have a burnt flavor and look like thickened flat Coke with a frothy top. **Lagers,** most familiar to American drinkers, are light-colored and carbonated. Designer and American beers are also making their way to bars across the country.

BUSINESS HOURS

Standard business hours are Monday–Saturday 9–5:30. Some shops observe an early closing day once a week, often Wednesday or Thursday. In small villages, many shops also close for lunch. Pubs are traditionally open Monday–Saturday 11–11, and Sunday noon–10:30, though some may close Sunday between 3 and 7 PM. Most banks are open 9:30–3:30; some have extended hours on Thursday evenings, and a few are open on Saturday mornings. Every other type of business is supposed to be closed on Sunday, but there has been a resurgence in out-of-town shopping malls staying open. Most villages even have an eight-till-late store open seven days a week.

FESTIVALS AND HOLIDAYS

In general, most annual events, such as festivals and races, take place in the spring and summer. The following are public holidays in Great Britain: January 1, January 2 (in Scotland only), Good Friday, Easter Sunday, Easter Monday (in Scotland, the Monday after Easter is not a holiday), December 25 and 26 (Boxing Day). Additionally, the first Monday in May, the last Monday in May, and the last Monday in August (in Scotland, it's the first Monday in August) are bank holidays. From mid-August to early September, the **Edinburgh International Festival,** one of the world's largest arts festivals, features exhibits, plays, concerts, films, and more. Plan months in advance if you want to attend.

EMERGENCIES

In the event of serious injury, dial **999** for the fire brigade, police, or ambulance. England has socialized medicine, and, happily, travelers can take advantage of this.

PHONES

Country code: 44. British Telecom (BT) is the major phone company operating in England, Scotland, and Wales. BT pay phones are easy to find throughout the United Kingdom; the ones with a red stripe around them accept coins, while those with a green stripe require a phone card, available at newsstands, train and bus stations, and tourist offices.

Local calls cost 10p. Public phones return any unused coins, but they don't make change, so think twice about using a £1 coin for a local call. To dial long-distance within the United Kingdom, dial the area code (including the "0") and number, and get ready to pay through the nose. If you're calling the United Kingdom from abroad, drop the "0" from all area codes. To dial another country direct from the United Kingdom, first dial "00," then the country code, then the area code and phone number. Calls to Northern Ireland from England, Scotland, or Wales can be dialed without the international codes.

Many travelers now use the convenience of access codes thanks to private telephone card numbers of the ATT, MCI, and Sprint systems. For **AT&T USADirect™** (tel. 0800/890011 or 0500/890303), if you're in Great Britain and wish to dial a telephone number in the U.S, first dial 0800–013–0011. A USA Direct operator will then log on to ask you for the U.S. area code and number plus your private telephone card number for billing. For **MCI** Call USA (tel. 0800/890222), access the U.S. from the U.K. by dialing 0800–89–0222. A World Phone operator will then come on the line, request your private telephone card number for billing, and will then access the number you wish to call in the U.S. For **Sprint** Express (tel. 0800/890877), access the U.S. from the U.K. by dialing 0800–89–0877. A Sprint Global 1 operator will then come on line to ask you for your card number and the U.S telephone number you wish to access. In all cases, by using a touch-tone phone, access to the U.S. will be done automatically.

To place an incredibly expensive collect call, dial 155. Directory assistance in Great Britain is 192.

MAIL

Nearly every city, town, village, or cluster of houses in the middle of nowhere has a post office—be it inside the butcher shop, liquor store ("off-license"), or pharmacy ("chemist"). Stamps may be bought at some grocery stores, at newsstands with stamp machines, or, after sometimes waiting in a long line, at the post office. Rates from the United Kingdom are from 43p (then more according to the weight) for an international airmail letter, 36p for an international aerogram, and 43p for an international postcard.

LONDON

London's history is a rich one, evident in the jumbled layers of its buildings. Rough 12th-century fortifications are juxtaposed with sleek 20th-century office towers, and Victorian churches contrast with remains of Roman city walls. Everywhere you look you'll see a confusion of ages, as well as countless symbols of the city that have become ingrained in the global subconscious, whether by the likes of Defoe, Fielding, and Dickens, or by the Beatles, the Stones, and the Sex Pistols. Even people who have never set foot in London have vivid images of Big Ben, Tower Bridge, red double-decker buses, and people wearing raincoats and holding black umbrellas aloft.

But London is more than a historical pop-up book; it is a living, thriving entity. As empire faded into commonwealth, former subjects relocated to the capital, bringing their traditions and beliefs. The presence of so many international influences is changing the very essence of what it is to be British. With a population of almost 7 million, London is both quintessentially English and eccentrically aberrant. For every traditional pub serving bangers and mash, there's a Bengali, Vietnamese, or Caribbean restaurant vying for tourist dollars. And, for every patriotic Londoner ranting about the importance of the monarchy, there are impassioned activists pressing for its abolishment. London has become far more diverse and complex than Dickens could ever have imagined.

With all its current problems and the turbulent centuries of the past, London tends to inspire extreme reactions. American novelist Henry James felt that people could be divided into London lovers and London haters, and this is even more true today—though your feelings may change from love to hate day-by-day or even moment-by-moment. And if one morning you decide you're down on the city, remember that it is ever-changing. As James put it, "Out of [London's] richness and its inexhaustible good humour it belies the next hour any generalisation you may have been so simple as to make about it."

BASICS

VISITOR INFORMATION

The **London Tourist Information Centre** provides details on tube and bus tickets; theater, concert, and tour bookings; and lodgings. *Victoria Station, SW1, no phone. Tube: Victoria. Open Easter–Oct., daily 8–7; Nov.—Easter, Mon.–Sat. 8–6, Sun. 9–4.*

Other information centers are located in **Waterloo International Station, Liverpool St. Station, Harrods** (Brompton Rd.; Tube: Knightsbridge), **Selfridges** (Oxford St.; Tube: Marble Arch or Bond Street), **Heathrow Airport** (Terminals 1, 2, and 3), and **Gatwick Airport** (International Arrivals Concourse).

The **British Travel Centre** provides details about travel, lodging, and entertainment for the whole of Britain. *12 Regent St., SW1, no phone. Tube: Piccadilly Circus. Open May–Sept., weekdays 9–7, weekends 10–4; off season weekdays 9–6:30.*

AMERICAN EXPRESS

Main office: 6 Haymarket, SW1Y 4BS, tel. 0171/930–4411. Tube: Charing Cross or Piccadilly Circus. Open weekdays 9–5:30, Sat. 9–4 (until 6 for currency exchange), Sun. 10–6 (currency exchange only).

Other full-service American Express locations in London include: **The City** (111 Cheapside, tel. 0171/600–5522; Tube: Bank or St. Paul's); **Knightsbridge** (78 Brompton Rd., tel. 0171/584–6182; Tube: Knightsbridge); **Mayfair** (89 Mount St., tel. 0171/499–4436; Tube: Bond Street); and **Victoria** (102–104 Victoria St., tel. 0171/834–5555; Tube: Victoria).

DISCOUNT TRAVEL AGENCIES

If you're looking for discount flights or cheap train, ferry, and bus tickets, you may want to scout the discounted fares advertised in the *Evening Standard* and *Time Out*—they're often cheaper than what travel agencies will quote you. Some of the most reliable agencies scrounging up discount fares are **Campus Travel** (52 Grosvenor St., SW1 and branches, tel. 0171/730–8111; Tube: Victoria); **Council Travel** (28A Poland St., W1, tel. 0171/437–7767; Tube: Oxford Circus); **STA Travel** (38 Store St., WC1 and branches, tel. 0171/361–6262); **Travel CUTS** (295A Regent St., W1, tel. 0171/255–1944; Tube: Oxford Circus); and **Trailfinders** (42–50 Earl's Court Rd., W8, tel. 0171/938–3366 or 0171/937–5400; Tube: Earl's Court or Kensington High St.).

CHANGING MONEY

Although you'll find exchange booths everywhere in London, using them is like flushing money down the drain—they offer exchange rates 10%–15% worse than banks. **Thomas Cook,** which has travel offices all over town, and **American Express** (*see above*) are the exceptions, charging bank rates for their respective checks. If you're desperate for cash after-hours, **Chequepoint** has six 24-hour branches; check the phone book for the closest location.

EMBASSIES

Australian High Commission: *Australia House, The Strand, WC2B 4LA, tel. 0171/379–4334. Tube: Temple. Open weekdays 9–3:30.* **Canadian High Commission–Consular Section:** *McDonald House, 1 Grosvenor Sq., W1X 0AB, tel. 0171/258–6600. Tube: Bond Street. Open weekdays 9–4 (visas issued weekdays 9–11).* **New Zealand High Commission:** *New Zealand House, 80 Haymarket, SW1Y 4TQ, tel. 0171/930–8422. Tube: Charing Cross or Piccadilly Circus. Open weekdays 9–5.*

United States Embassy. Passports are handled weekdays 8:30–11 (also Mon., Wed., and Fri. 2–4) around the corner at the **Passport Office** (55 Upper Brook St.). Visas are handled by appointment only. *Main Embassy Offices: 24 Grosvenor Sq., W1A 1AE, tel. 0171/499–9000. Tube: Bond Street or Marble Arch. Open weekdays 8:30–5:30.*

EMERGENCIES

The general emergency number for **ambulance, police,** and **fire** is 999. The **Rape Crisis Line** (tel. 0171/837–1600) provides counseling 10–10. For serious injuries, the following hospitals have 24-hour emergency wards: **Guy's Hospital** (St. Thomas St., SE1, tel. 0171/955–5000; Tube: London Bridge); **Royal Free** (Pond St., Hampstead, NW3, tel. 0171/794–0500; Tube: Belsize Park); **University College London Hospital** (Gower St., WC1, tel. 0171/387–9300; Tube: Euston Square or Warren Street). The pharmacy chain **Boots** has stores all over London, and their central stores are often open until 7 or 8 PM.

LUGGAGE STORAGE

If you're coming from Heathrow or Gatwick airports, the best place to store luggage is in **Victoria Station** (*see* Coming and Going, *below*). It costs £2.50–£5 per piece per day. **Abbey Self-Storage** (tel. 0800/622–244), with warehouses near Victoria, Earl's Court, and King's Cross, will store your stuff for £5 per item per week.

PHONES AND MAIL

London has two area codes: 0171 for inner London and 0181 for outer London. Look for **post offices** set up in general stores in the countryside as well as an actual post office, indicated by POST OFFICE signs bearing a red oval with yellow lettering. You can receive those dear letters from home via poste restante at any post office—or, if you have an AmEx card, at one of their offices (*see above*). A good post office to have your mail sent to is the **Post Office** (24–28 William IV St., WC2N 4DL, tel. 0171/930–8565; Tube: Charing Cross). They hold mail for up to one month.

COMING AND GOING

BY BUS

The main terminal for all long-distance bus companies is **Victoria Coach Station** (Buckingham Palace Rd., tel. 0990/808–080 or 0171/730–3466), just southwest of Victoria Station. **Economy Return** bus tickets are 30%–50% cheaper than train tickets; the catch is that they're only good Sunday–Thursday. Expect to pay about 20% more for **Standard Return** fares, allowing travel on Friday and Saturday. You can also buy cheap **APEX** tickets if you book seven days in advance and adhere to exact times and dates for departure and return. Tickets on **National Express** (tel. 0990/808–080) buses can be booked at Victoria Coach Station, or at one of their branch offices at 52 Grosvenor Gardens or 13 Regent Street.

BY PLANE

Heathrow International Airport (tel. 0181/759–4321) handles the vast majority of international flights to the United Kingdom. There are tourist information counters in each of its four terminals, along with banks and accommodations services. **Gatwick** (tel. 01293/535–353) accommodates a steady stream of commercial flights from the United States and the Continent. **Stansted** (tel. 01279/680–500) and **London City Airport** (tel. 0171/474–5555) serve mainly European destinations, plus some international and charter flights.

Getting into London from Heathrow is a piece of cake: the tube's Piccadilly Line makes a loop through the airport before heading back to central London. The hour ride into London costs £3.20. If you have lots of heavy baggage, consider taking London Transport's shiny red wheelchair-accessible **Airbuses** (tel. 0171/222–1234 or 0181/897–2688), which make 29 stops in central London. Airbuses run daily 6 AM to around 8 PM, at 15- to 30-minute intervals, and for this 1–1¼-hour voyage to the city center you pay a reasonable £6. From Heathrow, Airbuses make pickups at all four terminals—just follow the AIRBUS or BUSES TO LONDON signs. British Rail's **Gatwick Express** (tel. 0990/301530) is your best bet for getting from Gatwick to Victoria Station in central London. The 35-minute ride costs £8.90. Coming from Stansted, catch the **Stansted Skytrain** to Liverpool Street Station. Trains run every 30 minutes and cost £10. From **London City Airport,** take London Transport's Bus 473 (80p), which takes you to the Stratford tube station.

BY TRAIN

London has eight major train stations, each serving a specific part of the country (or the Continent). All eight stations have tourist information booths, rip-off bureaux de change, and luggage storage (£2–£5 per day). All are served by tube, so it's easy to get around after you arrive in London. The **British Travel Centre** (*see* Visitor Information, *above*) can provide you with train schedules, ticket prices, and other information. For nationwide 24-hour train information, dial 0345/484–950 (from the United Kingdom only).

Charing Cross (Strand, WC2) serves southeast England, including Canterbury, Dover, and Folkestone ferry ports. **Euston** (Euston Rd., NW1) serves the Midlands, northern Wales, northwest England, and western Scotland. **King's Cross** (York Way, N1) serves northeast England and Scotland. **Liverpool Street** (Liverpool St., EC2) serves East Anglia, including Cambridge and Norwich. **Paddington** (Praed St., W2) sends trains to southern Wales and the West Country, as well as Reading, Oxford, and Bristol. **St. Pancras** (Pancras Rd., NW1) serves Leicester, Nottingham, and Sheffield. **Victoria** (Terminus Pl., SW1) serves southern England, including Brighton, Dover, and the south coast. Train service for virtually all Europe-bound ferries leaves from Victoria or **Waterloo** (York Rd., SE1), which serves southeastern destinations, including Portsmouth and Southampton.

GETTING AROUND

Fares for both buses and the Underground (commonly called the tube) are based on zones. **London Transport (LT)** has divided London into six concentric rings, labeled Zones 1–6. With few exceptions, everything you want to see will be within Zones 1 and 2. Get your hands on LT's free *Tube Map* and *Travelling in London* map (which shows tube stops and bus lines) when you get into town. The best deal for getting around London is the **Travelcard,** available at the "Tickets and Assistance" windows of most tube stations and at some newsstands. It's good for unlimited travel on both buses and the tube for periods ranging from one day to one year. Your best bet is to get a Travelcard for Zones 1 and 2 (£3.20 for a day, £15.70 for a week); if you're buying a Travelcard for a week or more you'll need a passport-type photo and a local address (a hostel is fine). Get a **Carnet,** a book of 10 tickets for zipping around zone 1 (£10), and you'll make a saving. When you board an LT bus, just show your pass to the driver or conductor. On the Underground, feed your pass into the horizontal slot at the front of the turnstiles leading into the tube station. For more bus and tube information dial 0171/222–1234.

BY BUS

Riding on the top deck of one of London's red double-deckers has a lot more sentimental appeal than riding the tube, and offers considerably better views of the city. As with the tube, bus fares are based on zones: fares start at 90p (or 60p for a trip of less than ¾ mile). Pick up the free *Central London Bus Guide* at an LT Travel Information Centre.

Unlike the tube, buses run all night. From 11 PM to 5 AM, **Night** buses add the prefix "N" to their route numbers, although they don't come as often or operate on as many routes as day buses. You'll probably have to transfer at one of the night bus nexuses like Victoria, Westminster, and especially either Piccadilly Circus or Trafalgar Square (the main transfer points for late-night buses). Note that weekly and monthly Travelcards are good for Night buses, but one-day and weekend Travelcards are not. Night bus single fares are also a bit more expensive than daytime ones.

BY TAXI

Traditional "**black cabs**," which are not always black, are the most reliable. Fares start at £1.40 and go up 20p every 770 ft or 56 seconds, and are higher on weekends and evenings. **Radio Taxis** (tel. 0171/272–0272) is open 24 hours, but, like most companies, charges a "collection fee" depending on where you're getting picked up and where you're going. Minicabs (regular-looking cars run by private companies) usually don't have meters—agree on a price with the driver before stepping in. It's customary to tip cab drivers 10% of your fare.

BY UNDERGROUND

London is served by 11 different Underground lines, each color-coded, as well as by Docklands Light Railway (DLR) and Network Southeast. Fortunately, most visitors need concern themselves only with the Circle, District, Central, Piccadilly, and Victoria lines. Service is reliable; waiting more than 10 minutes for a train is unusual. Fares are £1.20–£3.20 one-way (single), depending on distance. Keep your ticket once you board a train; you'll need it at the exit. The Underground is fairly safe—probably because it closes around midnight. If you plan to party late, it pays to figure out the Night buses (*see above*) in advance.

WHERE TO SLEEP

London entirely deserves its reputation as an expensive city, with lodging costs a special bummer. Unless you're lucky enough to be staying in the guest bedroom of a London friend, the most expensive part of your trip can be your accommodations. We've listed a full range of value-for-the-money options, ranging from several splurge hotels (£50 and up) to dorm beds in hostels for £15–£25 per night. There are several bargain B&B havens in the center city, around the **Bloomsbury** area, on the streets around **Victoria** and **King's Cross** stations, and the less attractive **Earl's Court** and hipper-than-thou **Notting Hill Gate** areas. All in all, finding a tolerable double room for less than £40 is a major coup. Hard-core penny-pinchers can camp on the outskirts of London (about 30–45 minutes from town by bus or tube) for £5–£6 a night. The **Tourist Information Centre** at Heathrow Airport and Victoria Station (tel. 0171/824–8844) offers an accommodations booking service. They can book a bed in the £15–£25 range for a £5 fee and, rest assured, all accommodations are inspected before it goes on their books.

BAYSWATER AND NOTTING HILL GATE

Bars and cheap eateries on Bayswater cater to the budget and middlebrow travelers who pack the neighborhoods' innumerable hotels. If you're looking for a more sedate environment, Kensington Gardens and Hyde Park are just across Bayswater Road. Notting Hill is practically London's hottest neighborhood these days—a trendsetting square-mile favored by style-watchers and many of London's hippest youth.

UNDER £40 • Hyde Park House. One of the nicer hotels in the area, close to the Bayswater and Queensway tube stations and a short walk from Hyde Park. Simple singles £26, doubles £38, including continental breakfast. *48 St. Petersburgh Pl., W2, tel. 0171/229–9652. Tube: Queensway.*

Lords Hotel. Rooms are basic and a bit shabby, although some have wide windows and balconies. Singles from £26, doubles from £38. *20–22 Leinster Sq., W2, tel. 0171/229–8877, fax 0171/229–8377. Tube: Bayswater.*

UNDER £50 • The Gate Hotel. Tiny B&B at the top of Portobello Road with reasonably sized rooms. Rooms come equipped with refrigerators, TVs, and phones. Singles from £55, doubles from £58. *6 Portobello Rd., W11, tel. 0171/221–2403, fax 0171/221–9128. Tube: Notting Hill Gate.*

Norfolk Court and St. David's Hotel. The Regency-style Norfolk Court joined the neighboring St. David's hotel a few years ago; the result is a simple, comfortable art deco–style guest house. Singles £30, doubles £44. *16–20 Norfolk Sq., W2, tel. 0171/723–4963, fax 0171/402–9061. Tube: Paddington.*

St. Charles Hotel. If you book one of the cheaper rooms here (bathrooms have showers, no tubs), you can still enjoy the lovingly kept, old-world ambience—sumptuous wood paneling and molded ceilings—

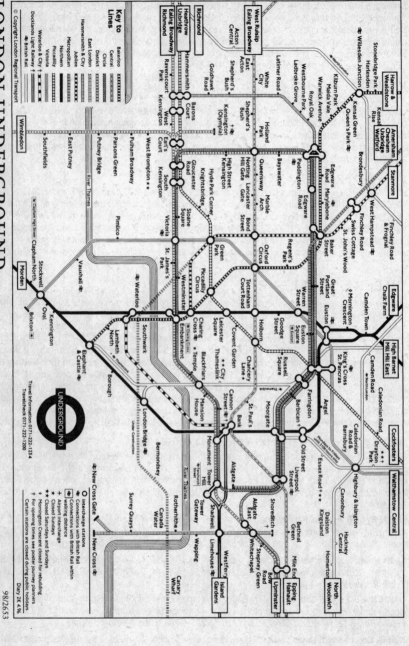

LONDON UNDERGROUND

© Copyright London Regional Transport

98/2653
Diary 2K 4.96

of this hotel. Singles £44, doubles £50. *66 Queensborough Terrace, W2 3SH, tel. 0171/221–0022. Tube: Queensway.*

UNDER £70 • Commodore. This peaceful hotel of three converted Victorians is deep in the big leafy square known as Lancaster Gate. It's another find of a very different stripe, as you'll notice on entering the cozy, carpeted lounge. There are some wonderful split-level rooms, with sleeping gallery, all large, all different, all with something special—like a walk-in closet with its own stained-glass window. It's getting very popular here, so book ahead. Singles go for £56, doubles for £69. *50 Lancaster Gate, W2 3NA, tel. 0171/402–5291, fax 0171/262–1088. Tube: Lancaster Gate.*

BLOOMSBURY

Just north of Soho is this neighborhood with a large number of private hostels and B&Bs. The British Museum, the University of London, and dozens of bookstores contribute to the quiet, academic atmosphere.

UNDER £40 • The Alhambra Hotel. Definitely the best B&B bargain in Bloomsbury, this place has clean and spacious rooms, decorated in either blue or red. Singles from £27, doubles from £36. *17–19 Argyle St., WC1, tel. 0171/837–9575, fax 0171/916–2476. Tube: King's Cross.*

Jesmond Dene Hotel. Possibly the smartest decor in London—a real gem, and well-priced to boot. Singles cost £25, doubles £36, and every room has a sink and TV. *27 Argyle St., WC1, tel. 0171/837–4654, fax 0171/833–1633. Tube: King's Cross.*

UNDER £50 • The Ridgemount Private Hotel. The kindly owners make you feel right at home, and the public areas have a friendly, cluttered, Victorian feel. Ask for a room that overlooks the garden. Singles from £29, doubles from £42. *65–67 Gower St., WC1, tel. 0171/636–1141, fax 0171/636–2558. Tube: Goodge Street.*

St. Athans Hotel. A simple but appealing Edwardian guest house close to Russell Square, St. Athans has charming sloping walls and sagging staircases. Singles from £36, doubles from £46, triples from £60. *20 Tavistock Pl., WC1, tel. 0171/837–9140, fax 0171/833–8352. Tube: Russell Square.*

UNDER £75 • The Morgan. This is a family-run Georgian row-house hotel with charm and panache. Rooms are small and functionally furnished, yet friendly and cheerful overall, with phones and TVs. The five newish apartments are particularly pleasing: three times the size of normal rooms (and an extra £15/night), complete with eat-in kitchens. The tiny, paneled breakfast room (rates include the meal) is straight out of a doll's house. The back rooms overlook the British Museum. Singles are £48, doubles £70. *24 Bloomsbury St., WC1B 3QJ, tel. 0171/636–3735. Cash only. Tube: Russell Square.*

EARL'S COURT

The area around the Earl's Court and Gloucester Road tube stations has the highest concentration of inexpensive lodgings in London.

UNDER £40 • The Albert Hotel. Inviting, inexpensive haven for London travelers, the Albert is just down the street from Kensington Gardens. Singles £35, doubles from £35, four- to six-person rooms £13–£14 per person, and 9- to 11-bed dorm rooms £10 per person. This is a first-come, first-served sort of place. *191 Queen's Gate, SW7, tel. 0171/584–3019, fax 0171/823–8520. Tube: Gloucester Road.*

VICTORIA

Victoria has a billion cheapish hotels; the farther from the station you go, the cheaper the rooms become. Because competition for customers is stiff, a good strategy is to walk down **Belgrave Road** or **Warwick Way,** offer everybody £10 less than they're asking, and see who makes the best counteroffer.

UNDER £40 • Georgian House Hotel. This tidy hotel offers several "student rooms": singles £19, doubles £32, triples £45, and quads £54. You don't have to be a student to qualify, but you do have to be able to hike up to the third and fourth floor. Regular singles £39, doubles £55, triples £68, and quads £75, all with TVs and private baths or showers. *35 St. George's Dr., SW1, tel. 0171/834–1438, fax 0171/976–6085. Tube: Victoria.*

Luna & Simone Hotel. Probably one of the best Belgrave Road hotels, this place features immaculate, comfortable rooms, complete with TVs and phones. Singles from £25, doubles from £40, triples from £60. *47–49 Belgrave Rd., SW1, tel. 0171/834–5897, fax 0171/828–2474. Tube: Victoria.*

UNDER £50 • Elizabeth House (YWCA). One of the nicest places to bed down near Victoria Station, the Elizabeth House is coed, clean, and cheery, with a heavenly garden patio. Handsome singles £22,

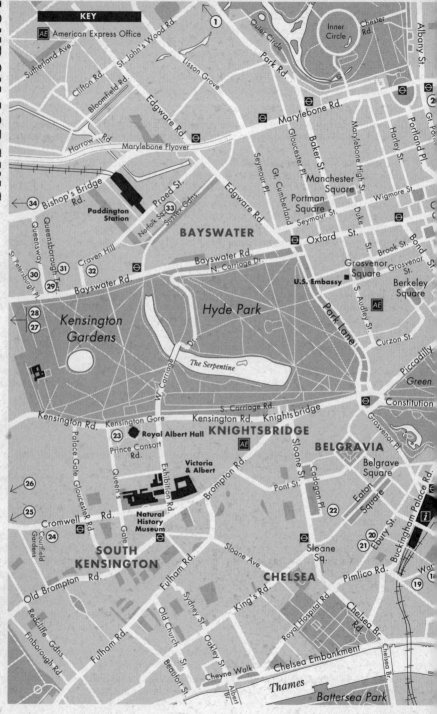

KEY

AE American Express Office

①

Inner
Circle

Chester
Rd.

Albany St.

Gt. Portland St.

②

Sutherland Ave.

Clifton Rd.

St. John's Wood Rd.

Lisson Grove

Park Rd.

Outer Circle

Bloomfield Rd.

Edgware Rd.

Marylebone Rd.

Marylebone High St.

Harley St.

Portland Pl.

Wigmore St.

Harrow Rd.

Marylebone Flyover

Gloucester Pl.

Baker St.

Manchester
Square

Bishop's Bridge Rd.

③④

Praed St.

③③

Norfolk Sq.

Sussex Gdns.

Seymour Pl.

Gt. Cumberland Pl.

Portman
Square

Duke St.

Brook St.

Bond St.

Paddington
Station

BAYSWATER

Seymour St.

Oxford   St.

Grosvenor
Square

Grosvenor
St.

Berkeley
Square

Queensway

Queensborough Ter.

Craven Hill

③①

③②

Bayswater Rd.

N. Carriage Dr.

U.S. Embassy ■

S. Audley St.

AE

St. Petersburgh Pl.

③⓪

②⑨

Bayswater Rd.

Hyde Park

Park Lane

Curzon St.

Piccadilly

②⑧

②⑦

Kensington
Gardens

Dr.

The Serpentine

Green

Constitution

Kensington Rd.

Kensington Gore

W. Carriage Dr.

S. Carriage Rd.

Kensington Rd.   Knightsbridge

Grosvenor Pl.

②③

● Royal Albert Hall

KNIGHTSBRIDGE

AE

BELGRAVIA

Prince Consort
Rd.

Victoria
& Albert

Sloane St.

Belgrave
Square

②⑥

Palace Gate

Gloucester Rd.

Queen's

Exhibition Rd.

Brompton Rd.

Pont St.

Cadogan Pl.

Eaton
Square

②⑤

Cromwell   Rd.

Natural
History
Museum

②②

Buckingham Palace Rd.

②④

Courtfield Gardens

Gate

Sloane Ave.

②⓪

②①

Ebury St.

i

Wa

SOUTH
KENSINGTON

CHELSEA

Sloane
Sq.

Pimlico Rd.

①⑨

Old Brompton

Rd.

Fulham Rd.

Sydney St.

Old Church

King's Rd.

Royal Hospital Rd.

Chelsea Br. Rd.

Redcliffe Gdns.

Finborough Rd.

Fulham Rd.

St.

Oakley St.

Beaufort St.

Cheyne Walk

Chelsea Embankment

Chelsea Br.

Albert Br.

Thames

Battersea Park

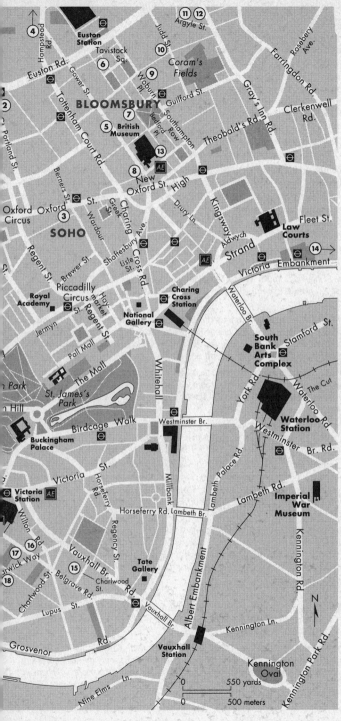

The Albert Hotel, **23**
The Alhambra, **12**
Campbell House, **6**
Chelsea Hotel, **26**
City of London
Hostel (YHA), **14**
College Hall, **7**
Collin House, **20**
Commodore
Hotel, **32**
Curzon House
Hotel, **24**
Earl's Court
(YHA), **25**
Elizabeth Hotel, **17**
The Gate Hotel, **27**
The Generator, **10**
Georgian House
Hotel, **18**
Hampstead Heath
(YHA), **1**
Highgate Village
(YHA), **4**
Hyde Park
House, **30**
International
Students House, **2**
Jesmond Dene
Hotel, **11**
Lord's Hotel, **34**
Luna and Simone
Hotel, **16**
Lynton House
Hotel, **21**
Melita House
Hotel, **15**
Morgan, **8**
Museum Inn
Hostel, **13**
Norfolk Court/St.
David's Hotel, **33**
Oxford Street Hostel
(YHA), **3**
Palace Hotel, **28**
Quest Hostel, **31**
Ridgemont, **5**
St. Athans
Hotel, **9**
St. Charles
Hotel, **29**
Wilbraham, **22**
Windermere
Hotel, **19**

351

doubles from £44; dorm beds £15 per person. *118 Warwick Way, SW1, tel. 0171/630–0741, fax 0171/630–0740. Tube: Victoria.*

Melita House Hotel. A comfortable, family-run hotel, the Melita is fitted out with strictly garage-sale furniture, but the small rooms are clean and have TVs. Singles start at £30, doubles at £50; triples at £60, quads £80. *33–35 Charlwood St., SW1, tel. 0171/828–0471, fax 0171/932–0988. Tube: Victoria.*

UNDER £60 • Collin House. The friendly owners of this spotless Victorian B&B maintain a quiet, nicely conservative atmosphere. The top-notch singles (£38), doubles (£52, £65 with shower), and triples (£80, £85 with shower) each have a sink and handsome wood-frame bed. *104 Ebury St., SW1, tel. and fax 0171/730–8031. Tube: Victoria. Cash only.*

Lynton House Hotel. This cozy B&B has a common terrace and excellent security. Comfy singles (£30–£40) and doubles (£50–£55) come equipped with TVs and washbasins. *113 Ebury St., SW1, tel. 0171/730–4032, fax 0171/730–9848. Tube: Victoria. Cash only.*

Windermere Hotel. A two-minute walk from Victoria Station, this spot has impeccably furnished rooms with TVs, phones, and high ceilings. Singles from £51, doubles from £64. *142–144 Warwick Way, SW1, tel. 0171/834–5163, fax 0171/630–8831. Tube: Victoria Station.*

UNDER £80 • Wilbraham Hotel. A lovely grandmother of a hotel, this trio of 19th-century row houses is near swanky Sloane Square. Doubles run about £75–£80. *1–5 Wilbraham Pl., SW1, tel. 0171/730–8296, fax 0171/730-6815. Tube: Sloane Square. Cross square to Sloane St., take 2nd right off Sloane.*

HOSTELS

Besides the private hostels, England's **Youth Hostel Association (YHA)** (tel. 0171/248–6547, fax 0171/236–7681) operates seven hostels in central London (some are more central than others). These tend to be clean to the point of sterility.

Chelsea Hotel. This huge, worn, Earl's Court hostel is incredibly popular with backpackers. Dorm rooms £10, singles £18, doubles £28–£30, triples £36, and quads £44. Free transportation from Victoria Station. *33–41 Earl's Court Sq., SW5, tel. 0171/244–6892, fax 0171/244–6891. Tube: Earl's Court. Walk south 3 blocks on Earl's Court Rd., turn right on Earl's Court Sq.*

City of London Hostel (YHA). This hotel has a great location, but zip for character. Dorm beds are £18.50–£23.50, depending on the number of beds in the room. *36–38 Carter Ln., EC4, tel. 0171/236–4965, fax 0171/236–7681. Tube: Blackfriars. Walk east on Queen Victoria St., turn left on St. Andrew's Hill, right on Carter Ln. Laundry.*

Curzon House Hotel. Clean and with a quiet, friendly atmosphere, the Curzon House has a great location in Earl's Court. Dorm beds £15, singles from £28, doubles from £36, and triples from £54. *58 Courtfield Gardens, SW5, tel. 0171/581–2116, fax 0171/835–1319. Tube: Earl's Court. Walk south on Earl's Court Rd., turn left on Barkston Gardens (which becomes Courtfield Gardens). Kitchen.*

Earl's Court (YHA). They really pack 'em in at this joint—rooms are often stuffed with up to a dozen travelers. There's a bureau de change here. Beds £18. *38 Bolton Gardens, SW5, tel. 0171/373–7083, fax 0171/835–2034. Tube: Earl's Court. Walk south on Earl's Court Rd., left on Bolton Gardens. Kitchen, laundry.*

The Generator. Easily the grooviest hostel in town, with a friendly, funky vibe, lots of young people, and vibrant decor. On site you'll even find a bar and a cafeteria. Rooms are simple but clean; singles £38, twins £23.50 per person, dorm beds £18.50–£20. *MacNaghten House, Compton Pl., WC1, tel. 0171/388–7666, fax 0171/388–7644. Tube: Russell Square. Turn right on Bernard St., left on Marchmont St., right on Tavistock Pl., left on Compton Pl.*

Hampstead Heath (YHA). One of the best hostels in London, this place is set on beautiful grounds right on Hampstead Heath. Doubles are £37, dorm beds £15. You can exchange money here. *4 Wellgarth Rd., NW11, tel. 0181/458–9054, fax 0181/209–0546. Tube: Golders Green. Walk southeast on North End Rd., turn left on Wellgarth Rd. Kitchen, laundry.*

Highgate Village (YHA). Dorm beds in this attractive Georgian house are a mere £12.50, but it's a serious uphill trek from the Archway tube station, and there is a midnight curfew. Reserve in advance. *84 Highgate West Hill, N6, tel. 0181/340–1831, fax 0181/341–0376. Tube: Archway. Walk north up Highgate Hill, left on South Grove. Kitchen.*

The Museum Inn Hostel (Astor). A great base for exploring Bloomsbury, the West End, and the British Museum (across the street), this place will book you only if you're 18–30 years old. Dorm beds £14–£15, twins £17 per person. *27 Montague St., WC1, tel. 0171/580–5360, fax 0171/589–1590. Tube: Tottenham Court Road. Walk north on Tottenham Court Rd., right on Great Russell St., left on Montague St. Kitchen.*

Oxford Street Hostel (YHA). In the center of hip Soho, this hostel has beds at £18, twins at £19.50 per person. You can exchange money here. *14 Noel St., W1, tel. 0171/734–1618, fax 0171/734–1657. Tube: Oxford Circus. Walk east on Oxford St., right on Poland St., left on Noel St. Kitchen.*

Palace Hotel. Situated on a pleasant street lined with redbrick buildings and close to a tube stop, this hostel features clean rooms, a newly renovated kitchen, and bathrooms with sparkling new loos. Dorm beds £12. Reservations advised. *31 Palace Ct., W2, tel. 0171/221–5628, fax 0171/243–8157. Tube: Notting Hill Gate. Walk east on Notting Hill Gate (which becomes Bayswater Rd.), turn left on Palace Ct. Kitchen.*

Quest Hostel. A fun place to stay near the happening Queensway tourist strip—but you can only book into here if you're between 18 and 30 years old. Dorm beds £14; the lone double is £34. *45 Queensborough Terr., W2, tel. 0171/229–7782, fax 0171/727–8106. Tube: Bayswater. Turn right on Queensway, left on Bayswater Rd., left on Queensborough Terr. Kitchen.*

STUDENT HOUSING

Many college residence halls try to earn a few extra pounds by throwing open their doors during vacations—usually late June through early September and also around Easter. Most student housing is in northwest Bloomsbury, an easy 10-minute walk from the West End. Reservations are a must.

Campbell House. Large rooms and excellent kitchen facilities make this a great place to settle in for a while. Singles £16.25, doubles £29. *5–10 Taviton St., WC1, tel. 0171/391–1479, fax 0171/388–0060. Tube: Euston Square. Walk east on Euston Rd., turn right on Gordon St., left on Endsleigh Gardens, right on Taviton St. Kitchen, laundry. Cash only.*

College Hall. This place offers easy access to university pubs and facilities, a library, and is smack dab in the center of London's student ghetto. Students can stay in singles for £15 with breakfast, £18 with breakfast and dinner. Nonstudents pay £20 with breakfast, £25 with breakfast and dinner. *Malet St., WC1, tel. 0171/580–9131. Tube: Goodge Street. From Goodge St. turn left on Tottenham Court Rd., right on Torrington Pl., right on Malet St. Laundry. Open mid-June–mid-Aug.*

International Student House. Reserve ahead for a berth in this fun, monstrously huge establishment at the southeast corner of Regent's Park. A fitness center and restaurant are two top amenities. A dorm bed in a three- or four-bunk room costs £16, a bed in an "economy" dorm with six or more beds is £10. Singles are £27, twins £19.50 per person. *229 Great Portland St., W1, tel. 0171/631–8300, fax 0171/636–8315. Tube: Great Portland Street. Laundry.*

CAMPING

If you don't mind a commute of 30 minutes or more, camping is practical, and certainly cheap. Both of the following sites are inside the public transit Zones 1 and 2—great for Travelcard holders.

Tent City Acton. This West London institution has 450 cots in 14 large tents spread across Wormwood Scrubs. Choose from men's, women's, and mixed tents, or pitch your own tent for the same daily price of £6. A fun and friendly crowd comes here, and all profits go to charity. *Old Oak Common Ln., W3, tel. 0181/743–5708, fax 0181/749–9074. Tube: East Acton. Walk NE on Erconwald St., turn left on Wulfstan St. (which merges with Old Oak Common Ln.). Toilets, showers. Closed Sept.–May.*

Tent City Hackney. This huge park on the outskirts of London is ideal for cheap sleeping in a small enclosed grove. BYOT (bring your own tent) and camp for a mere £5 per person, or call ahead and try to get one of the 30 dorm beds. *Millfields Rd., E5, tel. 0181/985–7656. Tube: Liverpool Street. From station, Bus 22A to Millfields and Mandeville Sts., cross bridge, and follow signs. Toilets, showers. Closed Sept.–May.*

FOOD

Once upon a time, eating in London was an experience to be endured rather than enjoyed. Not anymore. Today, the city has the most-talked-about dining scene in Europe, and everyone—even at the cheaper options—is talking turkey, literally. Of course, you can always find a yummy fish-and-chips, or bangers and mash, or any other of the other indigenous options in British budgetland. A lot of this diet, however, is changing, as health consciousness replaces the Church of England—by now good sandwich

RESTAURANT CHAINS

If the thought of dining in a chain restaurant makes you break out in a rash, relax—we're not suggesting you eat at McDonald's. The places listed below all have great food, decent prices, attractive decor, and, hey, they just happen to have more than one location. Maybe there's one near you.

Dôme. One of the best deals in town is the £5 three-course meal available all day long at this string of hip, French bistros. 32 Long Acre, Covent Garden, WC2, tel. 0171/379–8650; 35A Kensington High St., W8, tel. 0171/937–6655; 289–291 Regent St., W1, tel. 0171/636–7006; 354 King's Rd., SW3, tel. 0171/352–2828; 57–59 Charterhouse St., EC1, tel. 0171/336–6484.

Pizza Express. Pies arrive at your table hot and tasty, and the prices (£3.40 and up) are pretty cheap. Some of the branches even host live jazz. Approximately 25 locations throughout London.

Pret A Manger. For quick sandwiches (£1.20–£2), salads (£1.50–£2.80), and even sushi (£5–£5.85), Pret A Manger cannot be beat. Everything is prepared hourly on the premises, with the emphasis on fresh, natural ingredients (no grease, no preservatives). Approximately 40 locations throughout London.

The Stockpot. Count on these old-time café/diners for inexpensive English and Continental fare like soups (80p), omelets (£2.50), and casseroles (£2.75). 6 Basil St., SW3, tel. 0171/589–8627; 273 King's Rd., SW3, tel. 0171/823–3175; 40 Panton St., SW1, tel. 0171/839–5142; 18 Old Compton St., W1, tel. 0171/287–1066; 50 James St., W1, tel. 0171/486–1086.

bars are more ubiquitous in central London than the old greasy spoons. A Londoner with *nouse* (British for savvy), when starving and not rich, always heads to the city's fabulous ethnic eateries. Along the way, we also suggest a few jacket-and-tie splurge places to have a blow-out meal.

As for most sit-down cheapo grub, it usually runs £6–£9, while a decent meal usually costs £8–£14, not including VAT (value-added tax) and the cover charge (50p–£1) that some restaurants add to the bill. Some restaurants also include a mandatory service charge; otherwise the standard tip is 10%. London has an endless array of ethnic restaurants. Wander along **Gerrard Street,** in Soho, for Chinese; you'll find Bengali on Spitalfields's **Brick Lane** (Tube: Aldgate East), Indian on Bloomsbury's **Drummond Street** (Tube: Euston Square), and Vietnamese on **Lisle Street** (Tube: Piccadilly Circus).

BLOOMSBURY
Once London's literary slum, Bloomsbury is now better known for its thriving Asian and Indian communities.

UNDER £5 • Diwana Bhel Poori House. A popular spot for fresh southern Indian cuisine on big plates. Try the *thali,* a set meal with rice, dal, vegetables, chapatis, and pooris (£3.80–£6.50), or come noon–2:30 daily for their all-you-can-eat buffet (£4). *121–123 Drummond St., NW1, tel. 0171/387–5556. Tube: Euston.*

Greenhouse. A subterranean veggie heaven located beneath a gay and lesbian cultural center, the Greenhouse offers main courses like lentil stew with rice for £4; salads range from £1.10 to £3.70. Monday nights are "women only." *16 Chenies St., WC1, tel. 0171/637–8038. Tube: Goodge Street.*

UNDER £10 • Chutney's. On everybody's short list for London's best vegetarian Indian restaurant, Chutney's offers a £5 buffet (Mon.–Sat. noon–2:30, Sun. noon–10) that is one of the city's few culinary steals. *124 Drummond St., NW1, tel. 0171/388–0604. Tube: Euston.*

CAMDEN TOWN

There's no shortage of food in Camden, with dozens of stalls in the markets selling all kinds of cheap grub. **Camden High Street,** surprise, is the main drag, interspersed with stands selling kebabs, pizza, and sausage, and the odd café. **Inverness Street, Parkway,** and **Bayham Street** have eateries that are slightly less clogged with Camden shoppers.

UNDER £5 • Cactus. Halfway between Camden Town and Hampstead this funkily decorated basement restaurant serves up the best-value all-you-can-eat deal in the city. For just £4.88 there's a massive spread of 15 freshly cooked, hot Central American dishes plus loads and loads of salads and dips. Booking is essential. *83 Haverstock Hill, NW3, tel. 0171/722–4112. Tube: Chalk Farm or Belsize Park. From Chalk farm, walk up Haverstock Hill; from Belsize Park, walk downhill. Closed Mon.*

UNDER £10 • Thanh Binh. Just north of Camden Lock, Thanh Binh is deservedly a long-time *Fodor's* favorite. Sit down and enjoy the delicate Vietnamese prawns (£5.80) or finger-licking-good Mongolian lamb (£4). They also sell hot-meal lunch boxes to go. *14 Chalk Farm Rd., NW1, tel. 0171/267–9820. Tube: Chalk Farm. Walk southeast on Chalk Farm Rd. Closed Mon.*

CHELSEA

If you're looking to dine on a budget, stick to Chelsea's restaurants at the top of **King's Road,** or try **Fulham Road,** where the pace is less frenetic and the prices more reasonable.

UNDER £5 • Chelsea Bun Diner. Damn good breakfasts (not to mention terrific lunches and dinners) pack locals into this oddly named diner. *9A Limerston St., SW10, tel. 0171/352–3635. Tube: Earl's Court or Sloane Square.*

UNDER £10 • Ambrosiana Crêperie. This hip, attractive Chelsea restaurant dishes out a variety of both sweet and savory crêpes. Start with a savory one like salami, ratatouille, and cheese (£5.50), or chicken, spinach, tomato, and cheese (£5.80). Or hey, why not skip straight to a dessert crêpe, like pears and cinnamon (£3.50). Serious crêpeophiles dine on Mondays and Thursdays, when all crêpes are half-price. *194 Fulham Rd., SW10, tel. 0171/351–0070. Tube: South Kensington. Walk southwest on Old Brompton Rd., turn left on Sumner Pl., right on Fulham Rd.*

KNIGHTSBRIDGE, BAYSWATER, NOTTING HILL GATE

Knightsbridge is a ritzy area, featuring restaurants priced way beyond budget range. Bayswater, across Hyde Park, is Knightsbridge's complete opposite: a neighborhood full of kebab joints, chippies, and delis. Notting Hill Gate has a high concentration of ethnic restaurants. Marble Arch is the place to go for Middle Eastern eateries, particularly on **Edgware Road.**

UNDER £5 • La Barraca. The menu at this mellow, attractive place features tons of *tapas* (Spanish appetizers) like calamari with white beans, garlic chicken, and steamed mussels, all for around £4. Weekends, La Barraca is popular with young Londoners as a late-night watering hole. *215 Kensington Church St., W8, tel. 0171/229–9359. Tube: Notting Hill Gate. Walk east on Notting Hill Gate, turn right on Kensington Church St.*

Manzara. A nice option for tasty Turkish food, like grilled lamb with pine nuts on hummus, and grilled chicken skewers with rice. After 7 PM, splurge on their buffet (£6), where you pick what you want from an array of ingredients and the chef cooks it while you watch. *24 Pembridge Rd., W11, tel. 0171/727–3062. Tube: Notting Hill Gate.*

Norman's. For simple café food in a friendly environment, Norman's is a top spot. Full English breakfast staples like omelets with chips cost around £3, while sandwiches and spaghetti bolognese (£3.85) round out the menu. *7 Porchester Gardens, W2, tel. 0171/727–0278. Tube: Bayswater.*

UNDER £10 • Churchill Thai Kitchen. An excellent Thai restaurant, this spot is hidden in an enclosed patio at the rear of a traditional British pub. Chow on spicy *khao rad na ga prao* (rice with a choice of chicken, prawn, or meat sauce) or *kwaitiew pad thai* (Thai noodles with prawns), and other choices that all cost between £4.95 and £5.25. *Churchill Arms, 119 Kensington Church St., W8, tel. 0171/727–1246. Tube: Notting Hill Gate.*

Curry Inn. A tiny, tastefully decorated contender for the city's best Indian food, the Curry Inn offers up biryanis and curries (£4.50–£7) that are generous and expertly prepared. *41 Earl's Court Rd., W8, tel. 0171/937–2985. Tube: High Street Kensington. Closed Sun. lunch.*

Paradise by Way of Kensal Green. This converted Victorian pub may be a little off the main drag but is worth hunting out for superb-value Modern British dishes. Among the specialties are roast cod with green salsa and saffron mash (£6.50) and rack of organic lamb with a herb and garlic crust (£7.50) that come in generous portions. Vegetarian dishes (£5.80) are highly rated and the clientele is a lively bunch of music industry people. *19 Kilburn Ln., W10, tel. 0181/969–0098. Tube: Notting Hill. Then take Bus 52 and get off at the stop after Sainsbury's supermarket. Open Mon.–Sat. 7:30 PM–midnight, Sun. 12:30–3:30 and 7–11:30.*

SOHO, PICCADILLY, AND COVENT GARDEN

London's best Asian restaurants are in Soho's small Chinatown, on **Lisle Street** and **Gerrard Street** between Leicester Square and Shaftesbury Avenue. Despite the tourist crowds, a few gems still exist in Covent Garden and Piccadilly as well. **Denman Street** (in the latter) is a solid bet for sandwich shops and cafés.

UNDER £5 • Café Sofra. This is a cozy café with Middle Eastern snacks and light meals, like mixed mezze or lentil casserole (both £3.50), plus standard sandwiches and desserts. *10 Shepherd St., W1, tel. 0171/495–3434. Tube: Green Park.*

Food for Thought. You'll find large portions of fresh, inventive vegetarian and vegan food at this snug basement café. Roast pepper and almond soup (£2.20), pasta with mushrooms and sage (£3.50). *31 Neal St., WC2, tel. 0171/836–9072. Tube: Covent Garden. Closed Sun. dinner.*

Govinda's. This is the place for tasty vegetarian grub at rock-bottom prices. Baked potato with cheese, spinach lasagna, and vegetable curry are some of the offerings. Every night from 7:30, it's all you can eat for £4; Sunday at 5 PM the food is free. *9–10 Soho St., W1, tel. 0171/437–4928. Tube: Tottenham Court Road.*

New World. A huge Chinese dim-sum-o-rama with paper tablecloths, schlocky Chinese lanterns, and tacky Muzak, the New World offers a variety of dumplings, noodles, steamed buns, and even chickens' feet, all for around £1.50. *1 Gerrard Pl., W1, tel. 0171/734–0677. Tube: Leicester Square.*

Pollo. At this jovial, noisy Soho institution, you can pick from an extensive menu of incredibly cheap pastas: Basic spaghetti runs £3.30, with chicken £4.65. *20 Old Compton St., W1, tel. 0171/734–5917. Tube: Leicester Square.*

Poons. Try the special "wind-dried" duck with rice (£4.80), hotpot (soup with stuffed bean curd; £3.50), or deep-fried oysters (£5.80) at this smart restaurant. *27 Lisle St., WC2, tel. 0171/437–4549. Tube: Leicester Square.*

The Rock & Sole Plaice. Cross between your basic fish-and-chips bar and a pretheater bistro. Traditionally British options like cod and chips and chicken mushroom pie (£4). *47 Endell St., WC2, tel. 0171/836–3785. Tube: Covent Garden.*

UNDER £10 • Belgo Centraal. Don't ask why the waiters are dressed like Trappist monks in this Belgian diner—it's just one of those things. Belgo's specialty is mussels, on platters (£9) or in pots (£11). At lunchtime try their wild-boar sausage with mash and a beer (£5). *50 Earlham St., WC2, tel. 0171/813–2233. Tube: Covent Garden.*

Calabash. Lively African restaurant with terrific food. Go for lamb couscous (£7.50), or hearty groundnut stew with peanut sauce (£6.25). *38 King St., Africa Centre, WC2, tel. 0171/836–1976. Tube: Covent Garden. Closed Sun.*

Mars. Mars is definitely on a planet of its own: it's got funky blue and orange walls, broken-china mosaics, and strangely named, vaguely French food. The ever-changing menu features specialty soups (£3.50) and an entrée list (£6–£10) that always has some interesting veggie options as well as meat and fish. *59 Endell St., WC2, tel. 0171/240–8077. Tube: Covent Garden. Walk right on Long Acre, turn left on Endell St. Closed Sun., Mon. lunch.*

Wagamama. London's taken to noodles in a big way, and this place features a staggering variety, including *yaki udon* (pan-fried noodles with shitake mushrooms, eggs, prawns, and chicken, £5) and the spicy chili chicken ramen (£5.90). *10A Lexington St., W1, tel. 0171/292–0990. Tube: Oxford Circus. Other location: 4 Streatham St., WC1, tel. 0171/323–9223.*

UNDER £45 • Mezzo. The 700-seater Mezzo isn't only London's biggest glamour restaurant; it's the most gigantic eatery in all of Europe. Downstairs is the restaurant proper (dinners here can top £45), with its huge glass-walled kitchen. Upstairs, the bar overlooks a canteen-style operation called Mezzonine. Finally, a late-night café/patisserie/newsstand has a separate entrance next door. The prices in the canteen and café are reasonable, with meals going for £10 to £30. The place was a London landmark from day one, with a see-and-be-seen bustle, despite its low celebrity count. Wear your spiffiest threads. *100 Wardour St., W1, tel. 0171/314–4000.*

Rules. Come, escape from the 20th century. Almost 200 years old, this gorgeous London institution has welcomed everyone from Dickens to Charlie Chaplin. The menu is historic and good, even if some food critics feel it's "theme park–like"; try the noted steak and kidney and mushroom pudding. Happily, the decor is even more delicious: with plush red banquettes and lacquered Regency-yellow walls, which are festively adorned with 19th-century oil paintings and dozens of framed engravings, this is probably the most beautiful dining salon in London. If you're going to splurge, do it here. This is jacket-and-tie territory. *35 Maiden La., WC2, tel. 0171/836–5314.*

WORTH SEEING

Like any great city, London can't be done in a couple of days, or even in a couple of weeks. As the fountainhead of English-speaking culture for a sizable chunk of this millennium, London offers layer upon layer of sights, from royal bastions to literary landmarks to flourishing, diverse neighborhoods. Happily, the city's most famous sights, including Parliament, Westminster Abbey, and many of the palaces, are all within walking distance of one another. Still, a street map like *London A to Z* (sold at newsstands and W.H. Smith newsagents) is an invaluable investment.

If you *must* see the city in half a day, a huge mass of tour companies are begging for your money. **The Original London Sightseeing Tour** (tel. 0181/877–1722), **The Big Bus Company** (tel. 0181/944–7810), and **London Pride Sightseeing Company** (tel. 01708/631–122) all offer frequent open-top, double-decker bus trips past the major sights of central London. They charge £12 for a 24-hour ticket and allow you to hop on and off the company's buses all day long. If it's a sunny day, a boat along the Thames offers an interesting perspective on the city. **Thames Passenger Service Federation** (tel. 0171/930–4097) has downriver trips to Greenwich (£6.70 return) leaving every 30 minutes. **Westminster Passenger Service Association (WPSA) Upriver** (tel. 0171/930–2062) makes the trip from Westminster Pier to Kew (1½ hrs; £10 return) and Hampton Court Palace (3 hrs; £12 return) five times daily, Easter–October. The best of the walking tours is **The Original London Walks** (tel. 0171/624–3978), with funny, informative guides and reasonably good rates (£4.50).

BIG BEN AND VICTORIA TOWER

The clock tower on the north end of the Palace of Westminster, perhaps the most enduring symbol of London and Britain, has come to be known as Big Ben. This is actually the name of the 13½-ton bell, not the clock tower (officially named St. Stephen's Tower). At the other end of the complex is the 323-ft-high **Victoria Tower,** reputedly the largest square tower in the world. A Union Jack flies from the top of Victoria Tower whenever Parliament is in session.

BRITISH MUSEUM

The British Museum's collection of artifacts numbers into the millions, and on display within its 2½ mi of galleries is the golden hoard of 2½ centuries of empire, the booty bought—or flat-out stolen—from Britain's far-flung colonies. The collection spans the centuries as well as the globe, featuring artifacts from the prehistoric era, ancient Egypt, and Assyria, right on through to the Renaissance and contemporary times. It's an astonishing collection, full of goodies of world-historical importance: the Rosetta Stone, the Dead Sea Scrolls, the Magna Carta, the Lindow Bog Man—and that only begins the list.

One visit won't be enough to see it all. A good strategy is to take the 1½-hour tour (£6; ask at the information desk for times) and come back later to whatever intrigued you the most. The Library Reading Room, which will close at the end of 1998, is historically important in its own right; Marx wrote *Das Kapital* in it. *Great Russell St., WC1, tel. 0171/412–7111. Tube: Tottenham Court Road. Admission free. Open Mon.–Sat. 10–5, Sun. 2:30–6.*

BUCKINGHAM PALACE

This, of course, is the official London home of Queen Elizabeth II (a flag bearing the Royal Standard flies above the palace whenever the queen is at home (usually on weekdays), but back when, it was the abode of the duke of Buckingham. George III (the tea-taxing king that the United States revolted against) bought the place in 1762 for a mere £28,000. George IV, who ascended to the throne in 1820, decided that the mansion looked far too middle class, and set about remodeling with a vengeance with the help of the architect John Nash. Its great gray bulk sums up the imperious splendor of so much of

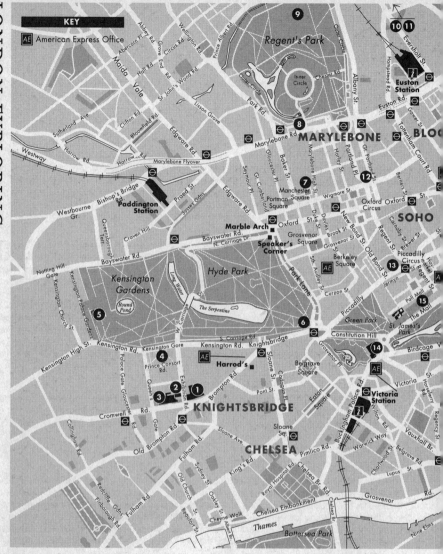

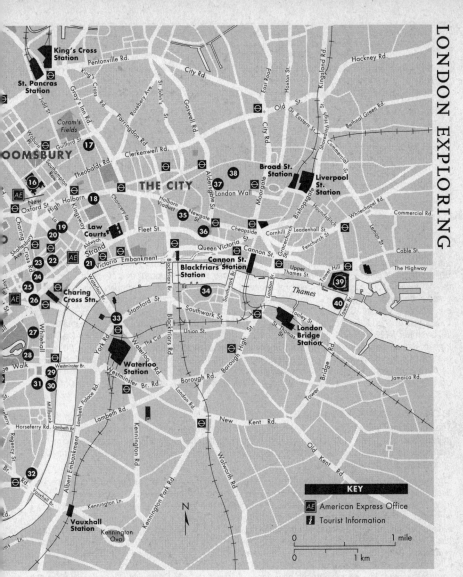

KEY

AE American Express Office

i Tourist Information

0   1 mile

0   1 km

Shakespeare's
Globe, **34**

Sir John Soane's
Museum, **18**

Somerset House, **21**

South Bank
Centre, **33**

St. Paul's
Cathedral, **36**

Tate Gallery, **32**

Tower Bridge, **40**

Tower of
London, **39**

Trafalgar
Square, **26**

Victoria and Albert
Museum, **1**

Wallace
Collection, **7**

Westminster
Abbey, **31**

CHANGING OF THE GUARD

The biggest tourist show in town, the Changing of the Guard—the ritual in which soldiers guarding the queen hand over their duties to the next watch—starts daily at 11:30 AM April–July (every other day only Aug.–Mar.), but if you're not there by 10:30, forget about getting a decent frontal view of the grand show. Early birds should grab a section of the gate facing the palace, since most of the ceremony takes place inside the fence. Latecomers can still get good views from the side along Constitution Hill, the thoroughfare leading to Hyde Park corner. For more information, tel. 0891/505–452.

the city: stately, magnificent, and ponderous. The palace contains some 600 rooms, including the State Ballroom and, of course, the Throne Room. During summer months, various rooms are open to the public, but forget about poking into medicine cabinets—only the state rooms are open. Here you'll find pomp and circumstance, but little else: these salons are where much of the business of royalty is played out—investitures, state banquets, receptions, lunch parties for the famous, and so on. Buckingham Palace was opened to visitors in 1993 to help pay for the restoration of Windsor Castle damaged by fire in November 1992. The work on Windsor is scheduled to be finished by the end of 1997, but the Buckingham Palace state rooms will be thrown open each August and September until the year 2000, when the situation will be reviewed. *Queen's Gardens, SW1, tel. 0171/839–1377. Tube: Green Park or St. James's Park. From Green Park, walk ½ mile south on Queen's Walk. From St. James's Park, walk north on Queen Anne's Gate, turn left on Birdcage Walk. Admission £9. Open Aug.–beginning Oct. daily 9:30–4:30.*

HOUSES OF PARLIAMENT

The Empire may be dead, but it's still fascinating to explore the site from which Britain once ruled with imperial impunity. The Houses of Parliament are actually one large building sprawling along the Thames, and home to the chambers of the House of Commons and the House of Lords, who meet on opposite sides of the octagonal Central Lobby.

The **House of Commons,** with 659 elected members, is where the real power lies. Incendiary bombs destroyed the original chamber in the Blitz of 1941, but some of the traditional touches were restored in reconstruction. A pair of red lines running the length of the floor dates back to more turbulent times when debate really raged—the lines are exactly two sword lengths apart, and all members must still remain behind them. The **House of Lords,** the "upper" body of Parliament, is composed of both the **lords spiritual**—archbishops and senior bishops of the Church of England—and the **lords temporal**—British peers and peeresses who inherited their titles. As a nonelected body, the Lords wield little parliamentary power: they may amend or delay bills, but what the House of Commons decides becomes law. Their chamber, however, is a sumptuous affair, with lots of wood paneling, gilt, and leather. The adjacent Royal Gallery features frescoes by Daniel Maclise depicting scenes from British history.

Sitting in on a session of Parliament is one of the best cheap thrills in London. Getting into the **Stranger's Galleries** is tough unless you get one of the few tickets available at your country's embassy; if you don't have a ticket, you're more likely to get in after 5:30 PM for an evening session—look for the light shining at the top of Big Ben to see if Parliament is sitting. The most exciting sessions are the prime minister's **Question Time** on Wednesdays from 3:00 to 3:30, when the PM defends himself against the slings and arrows of his "right honourable friends." Line up at St. Stephen's Hall Entrance (on the left for the Commons, on the right for the Lords). Admission is free. *Tel. 0171/219–4272. Tube: Westminster. Stranger's Galleries: House of Commons, open Mon., Tues., and Thurs. 2:30–late, Fri. 9:30–3; House of Lords, open Mon.–Wed. 2:30–late, Thurs. 3:30–late, Fri. 11 AM–late.*

HYDE PARK AND KENSINGTON GARDENS

Contiguous Hyde Park and Kensington Gardens together form a 634-acre park—the biggest in London. It's not that different from other large urban parks throughout the world; it's crowded (especially on weekends), but still a great no-hassle way to find a little greenery. Small boats cruise on the **Serpentine,** a long, thin lake that arcs through the middle of the two parks. You can rent a rowboat at the boathouse for £6.50 an hour. Don't miss **Speakers' Corner** in the northeast corner of Hyde Park: since 1873, this has been hallowed ground for amateur orators burning to make a point—originally, speakers mounted soapboxes, now they climb aboard aluminum stepladders. It really hits full swing by about 2 or 3 PM on weekends, as spielers spiel, hecklers heckle, and free speech dovetails into street theater. In 1996 Speakers' Corner became a sparring ground for Islamic extremists and Christian evangelists who still make appearances on a regular basis. *Kensington Gardens, W8. Tube: Lancaster Gate, Marble Arch, or South Kensington.*

NATIONAL GALLERY AND NATIONAL PORTRAIT GALLERY

After acquiring the private art collection of a wealthy banker early in the 19th century, Parliament felt compelled to start amassing some culture with a capital "C." To accommodate the growing collection, Parliament bought a plot of land on the edge of Trafalgar Square in 1828 and began to build the National Gallery, a bland classical structure best known for its tall, sandy-brown columns. If you can get past the legions of pigeons guarding the front doors, you'll find one of the world's most impressive collections of Western European art inside; the walls are virtually wallpapered with masterpieces by Van Eyck, Tintoretto, da Vinci, Caravaggio, della Francesca, Michelangelo, Monet, Titian, Rubens, Van Dyck, Goya, Rembrandt, Constable, Turner, Gainsborough, Seurat, et cetera, et cetera. Ready yourself for a staggering number of Virgins and Sons. The last few rooms of the National Gallery offer a tantalizing nibble of the impressionists and postimpressionists, including a room full of Picassos. Terrific free lectures (weekdays at 1 PM, Sat. at noon) and guided tours are available. *Trafalgar Sq., WC2, tel. 0171/747–2885. Tube: Charing Cross or Leicester Square. Admission free. Open Mon.–Sat. 10–6, Sun. noon–6.*

Next door is the National Portrait Gallery, featuring painted faces, sculpted faces, drawn faces, photographed faces—five floors of the visages of those who made British history and influenced British culture, including the only portrait of Shakespeare made in his lifetime. *St. Martin's Pl., WC2, tel. 0171/306–0055. Tube: Charing Cross. Admission free. Open Mon.–Sat. 10–6, Sun. noon–6.*

ST. PAUL'S CATHEDRAL

Right in the heart of the City, St. Paul's is instantly recognizable by its huge dome, towering 365 ft above street level. St. Paul's is also the symbolic heart of the City; unlike Westminster Abbey, which is seen as a royal and national church, St. Paul's is really a church for *Londoners.* The present structure, the third in a series of cathedrals erected on the site, was built by Christopher Wren between 1675 and 1710, shortly after the Great Fire ravaged London. Miraculously, the cathedral escaped major damage during World War II, when the rest of the city was reduced to little more than blazing rubble. The interior of the inner dome's base is encircled by the **Whispering Gallery**; once you've caught your breath from the 259-step climb, whisper into the wall and you'll be heard 100 ft away on the other side of the gallery. Continue 116 more steps up the dizzying staircase to the **Stone Gallery** outside the dome and the final 141 steps to the **Golden Gallery** at the top of the dome, and you'll be rewarded with amazing views of London. The cathedral's **crypt** is full of famous dead people, including military demigods Nelson and Wellington. *Tel. 0171/236–4128. Tube: St. Paul's. Admission: cathedral £3.50, galleries £3. Open Mon.–Sat. 8:45–4:15; galleries open Mon.–Sat. 9:30–4:15.*

TATE GALLERY

The Tate is well known for annually rearranging its permanent collection into brilliant and thought-provoking exhibits. The artwork is divided into two collections: the British collection, which features British painting from the 16th century to the present, and the modern collection, featuring contemporary European and American works; its superstar works include those by Monet, Dalí, and Kandinsky, along with an entire wing of oils and watercolors by British artist J. M. W. Turner. Twentieth-century masterpieces by Picasso, Ernst, and Johns round out the collection. Most unforgettable work? Sir John Everett Millais' Pre-Raphaelite vision of *Ophelia. Millbank, SW1, tel. 0171/887–8000. Tube: Pimlico. Admission free, special exhibits £1–£6. Open daily 10–5:50.*

TOWER BRIDGE

The instantly recognizable twin pillars of the Tower Bridge, a short walk from the Tower of London, house exhibitions on the bridge's history and engineering, as well as the history of London's bridges from

CHEAP DEALS IN CAMDEN TOWN—FLEA MARKET HEAVEN

Probably the most bohemian and diverse neighborhood in London, Camden becomes a serious mob scene on the weekend when tens of thousands of people flock to the Camden markets, particularly Camden Lock (Tube: Camden Town), the funky granddaddy of London flea markets. Get your bootleg tapes, incense, Doc Martens, leather jackets, silver jewelry, and used clothing right here. Camden High Street is the heart of the district, with the requisite cafés and record stores. From the Camden tube station walk north up Camden High Street.

Roman times onward. The two gangways across the top of the towers afford views second only to those from St. Paul's. *Tel. 0171/403–3761. Tube: Tower Hill. Admission £5.70. Open Apr.–Oct., daily 10–6:30 (last admission at 5:15); shorter hrs off season.*

TOWER OF LONDON

Home to the Bloody Tower, the Crown Jewels, the Beefeaters, and Larry, Hardy, George, Hugin, Mumia, and Rhys—the Tower Ravens—the Tower of London is one of the city's most famous sights. Besides serving as the residence of every British sovereign from William the Conqueror in the 11th century to Henry VIII in the 16th century, the Tower of London has performed a variety of other roles as fortress, jewel safe, armory, and garrison. It's probably most famous, though, as the prison and place of execution for some of England's most notable people, including Henry VIII's wives, Anne Boleyn and Catherine Howard (the chapel of St. Peter ad Vincula, adjacent to the Tower Green execution site, houses their headless skeletons). With its winding staircases, tunnels, bridges, and narrow passages, the Tower is much more than its name implies—20 towers make up the fortress (the largest in medieval Europe), which covers 18 prime acres on the banks of the Thames. The **Crown Jewels,** housed in the **Jewel House** north of the White Tower, are the star attraction. The Sovereign Sceptre boasts the largest cut diamond in the world, the 530-carat monster from the Cullinan diamond. Because shiny objects tend to attract huge crowds, it's best to visit immediately after the Tower opens or just before it closes.

Southwest of the White Tower is the **Bloody Tower,** one of the possible locations where the so-called Little Princes, Edward V and his brother, were murdered in the 15th century, probably by henchmen of either Richard III or Henry VII. Sir Walter Raleigh's prison cell (where he wrote the immodestly titled *History of the World*) is reconstructed as well. Great tours (free with admission) of the Tower of London, led by Beefeaters, leave from just inside the main entrance every half hour until 3:30 (2:30 in winter), but they don't go in bad weather. *Tel. 0171/709–0756. Tube: Tower Hill. Admission £8.50. Open Mar.–Oct., Mon.–Sat. 9–6, Sun. 10–6 (last admission 1 hr before closing, last entry to exhibits 30 mins before closing); shorter hrs off season.*

WESTMINSTER ABBEY

A fabled monument of hallowed splendor, Westminster Abbey is where Britain's monarchs have been crowned (and buried) since William the Conqueror assumed the English throne on Christmas Day, 1066. Among the deceased sovereigns buried here are Edward the Confessor, Elizabeth I, Mary Queen of Scots, Richard II, and Henry VII. Behind the altar, the **Chapel of St. Edward the Confessor** is home to the Coronation Chair, which is used during the crowning of Britain's kings and queens. In recent years, hooligans have managed to etch graffiti all over the wooden chair; when or if Prince Charles is crowned, his royal derriere will rest on incisive comments like "C loves S forever" and "smoke dope." The chair was built in 1300 to enclose the Stone of Scone (pronounced "skoon"), which Edward I swiped from Scotland in 1296. Scottish nationalists stole back the stone in 1950, but Scotland Yard (a misnomer) recovered it six months later. In an attempt to appease the Scottish nationalists, John Major announced in 1996—the 700-year anniversary of its removal—that the stone should indeed be returned to Scotland. **Poets' Corner,** in the south transept, houses the remains (or, more likely, memorial plaques) of nearly all the greats of English literature, including Chaucer, Shakespeare, Browning, Tennyson, Dylan Thomas, and Oscar Wilde. *Dean's Yard, SW1, tel. 0171/222–5152. Tube: Westminster. Admission free. Open Mon.–Sat. 7:30–6 (Wed. until 7:45), Sun. briefly between services at 10 AM, 3 PM, and 5:45 PM.*

NEIGHBORHOODS

THE CITY

Taking up more than a square mile in east London, the City is London's equivalent of Wall Street: it's home to the stock exchange, the Bank of England, Lloyd's, and a host of large trading firms. The City rests on the original Celtic settlement that the Romans conquered and built up into Londinium; vestiges of this ancient heritage pop up all over the City, but most of the buildings are ugly modern blobs. Until a decade ago, **Fleet Street,** which runs eastward from The Strand, was synonymous with newspapers and journalists. Most of Britain's major papers had their offices here, and the Fleet Street pubs were the lairs of hoary old journalists and their sources. Though the newspapers are all gone now, scattered to cheaper neighborhoods with lower overheads, "Fleet Street" remains the general term for the British press.

You can't beat the drama (it's all for real) or the price (it's free) of watching a trial at the **Old Bailey** (Old Bailey at Ludgate Hill; Tube: St. Paul's; closed weekends), officially known as Central Criminal Court. Just line up outside and scan the offering of trials—they're posted on a sort of legal menu du jour at the Newgate Street entrance. The juiciest trials happen in Courts 1–3; Oscar Wilde was convicted of homosexuality here in 1895. No bags or cameras are allowed in the building.

A large complex of residential towers and cultural venues built between 1959 and 1981 in an ill-fated attempt to resurrect central London as a living city instead of merely a place of work, the **Barbican Centre** (Silk St., tel. 0171/638–4141; Tube: Barbican) is an ugly amalgam of concrete blocks. Nevertheless, the Barbican has evolved into one of the city's principal cultural institutions, and houses the **Museum of London** (tel. 0171/600–3699; admission £4; closed Mon.), with fascinating exhibits on the history of the city, from the Stone Age to the present day. The Barbican Centre also hosts a variety of musical performances (*see* After Dark, *below*).

COVENT GARDEN

Just east of Soho lies Covent Garden, a nest of narrow streets, arcades, and pedestrian malls. The area's pubs and restaurants are expensive, but this is one of the best places in London for free entertainment—musicians, buskers, jugglers, and comics regularly perform in the streets and squares. The original Covent Garden was a plot of land used to grow fruit and veggies for the 13th-century Abbey of St. Peter at Westminster. In the 18th century, it evolved into London's principal produce market, a bustling maze of stalls and shops selling everything from tulips to taters. The original **Central Market building** has been completely renovated and is now filled with boutiques and trendy restaurants.

On the southeast corner of the square is the **London Transport Museum** (39 Wellington St., tel. 0171/836–8557; admission £4.50) where dozens of buses, trams, and trains from the early 1800s are displayed in the museum's exhibits on the development of mass transportation in London. The nearby **Theatre Museum** (1E Tavistock St., tel. 0171/836–7891; admission £3.50) has all sorts of theatrical goodies, from historical props and scripts to circus artifacts and Mick Jagger's jumpsuit.

East of the market is Bow Street, famous for the **Royal Opera House,** home to the Royal Ballet and the Royal Opera Company. Unfortunately, the theater is now closed until 1999 for a massive renovation, so the resident troupes will be appearing elsewhere for a while (*see* After Dark, *below*). Opposite the opera house stands the **Bow Street Magistrates' Court** (28 Bow St., WC2, tel. 0171/379–4713), established in 1749. Attend a session in London's oldest magistrate court weekdays 10:30–1 and 2–4:30, Saturdays 10:30–noon.

KENSINGTON AND KNIGHTSBRIDGE

The state rooms of the large (and somewhat gloomy) **Kensington Palace** (Kensington Gardens, tel. 0171/937–9561; Tube: Queensway; admission £5.50) are open to the public. On the grounds is the Orangery, a pretty and pricey place for a cuppa.

A major-league concert venue, the **Royal Albert Hall** (tel. 0171/589–8212; Tube: Knightsbridge) comes into its own during the summer, when it hosts the Promenade Concerts (*see* After Dark, *below*). The interior, a huge theater done up in wine red and gold, marks the height of Victorian imperial architecture. Known as the V&A, the **Victoria and Albert Museum** (Cromwell Rd., tel. 0171/938–8500; Tube: South Kensington; admission £5) features 7 mi of treasures weird and wonderful, like the snuff box believed to have been a gift to Nell Gwyn from Charles II; the great Mughal emperor Shah Jahan's jade cup; or the 12-sq-ft, solid oak, four-poster Great Bed of Ware, immortalized by Shakespeare in *Twelfth Night*. The **Art and Design Galleries** exhibit everything from Indian art to Italian Renaissance sculpture. The **Fakes and Forgeries Gallery** (Room 46) has a glorious collection of honest-to-goodness bogus art. There's also a very important vintage couture collection. All in all, the V&A remains the favorite museum for London's style mavens, budding fashion designers, and other extremely decorative types.

The six-floor **Science Museum** (Exhibition Rd., tel. 0171/938–8111; Tube: South Kensington; admission £5.50, free after 4:30) is chock full of groovy, user-friendly exhibits about science, technology, industry, and medicine. The fun **Natural History Museum** (Cromwell Rd., tel. 0171/938–9123; Tube: South Kensington; admission £6, free weekdays after 4:30, weekends after 5) has fossils, dinosaur skeletons, and stuffed (the taxidermic variety) animals from every corner of the earth, as well as amazing interactive exhibits. Kids adore the museum's Creepy Crawlies Gallery.

MARYLEBONE AND REGENT'S PARK

Marylebone may be boring and crowded, but it does have a few redeeming features, including the pleasant cafés along Marylebone High Street and its proximity to Regent's Park. For reasons unknown, people have been flocking to **Madame Tussaud's Wax Museum** (Marylebone Rd., tel. 0171/935–6861) for eons. Madame Tussaud's is full of dummies: both the waxy kind and the sort who were willing to pay £8.95 to get in. Don't say we didn't warn you. The **London Planetarium** (same building as Tussaud's; admission £5.65) is less hokey, and their virtual-reality effects are pretty good.

Developed in the early 19th century by the prince regent as an elite residential development for his aristocratic buddies, **Regent's Park** today contains the beautiful and amazingly varied **Queen Mary Gardens,** and the **London Zoo** (tel. 0171/722–3333; Tube: Baker Street; admission £8). The zoo's reptile house is extensive, as is the aquarium.

You need to book in advance for the **BBC Experience** (Broadcasting House, Portland Pl., W1, tel. 0870/603–0304; outside U.K., 01222/57771. Tube: Oxford Circus; admission free), a brand new exhibition set up by Britain's most noted TV company. Try your skills as a weather forecaster or sports commentator and take a look into the future of television and radio.

MAYFAIR

Mayfair is an ultraritzy residential neighborhood lined with beautiful 18th-century redbrick town houses and mansions. The May Fair, the market that gave its name to the neighborhood, moved here in 1686 from the Haymarket and was famed for its ribald entertainment; later, the area became a popular haunt of prostitutes. Today, **Shepherd's Market** is a charming nest of pedestrian-only alleys loaded with cafés, wine bars, pubs, and expensive restaurants. Perpendicular to Oxford Street, **Bond Street** may be the most expensive shopping street in London. The street is divided into New Bond and Old Bond, but prices are very, very expensive wherever you go. Running parallel to Bond Street is **Cork Street,** the center of London's art trade, with a number of contemporary galleries between Burlington Gardens and Clifford Street open to the public. The **Royal Academy of Arts** (Burlington House, W1, tel. 0171/439–7438; Tube: Green Park; admission £5) is the oldest institution in London devoted to the fine arts, with rotating exhibits throughout the year.

Two historic mansions are open here, both offering dazzling looks in the palatial Lifestyles of the Rich and Titled, 19th-century version. The first is the **Wallace Collection** (Hertford House, Manchester Sq., tel. 0171/935–0687; Tube: Bond St.; admission free)—a grand museum stuffed with famed Old Masters and the sort of furniture Marie Antoinette adored. Don't forget to say hello to Frans Hals's *Laughing Cavalier* in the Big Gallery. The other is the fabled abode of the Duke of Wellington, **Apsley House** (149 Piccadilly, tel. 0171/499–5676; Tube: Hyde Park Corner; admission £3). Once known, quite simply, as No. 1, London, this was built by Robert Adam in the 1770s and inhabited by the "Iron Duke." Highlights are the sumptuous Waterloo Gallery and Canova's gigantic statue of a nude (but fig-leafed) Napoléon, Wellington's archenemy.

SOHO AND BLOOMSBURY

Long one of the leading bohemian neighborhoods of London, Soho today is an amalgam of hip clothing stores, hair salons, sex shops, used-record stores, and trendy cafés. The area has an international flavor lacking in many of central London's neighborhoods. French Huguenots arriving in the 1680s were the first foreigners to settle the area en masse, followed by Germans, Russians, Poles, and Greeks—

though in recent times Soho displays more Chinese and Italian influences. Soho's **Chinatown** crowds around Gerrard and Lisle streets in the area between Leicester Square and Shaftesbury Avenue. **Leicester Square** (pronounced "Lester") is often compared to New York's Times Square, but it isn't as big, as bright, or as sleazy. Huge movie houses—many converted from grand old theaters—surround the square, tacky tourist attractions line some of the side streets, and weird street theater is often staged on the pedestrian mall at the western edge of the square.

To the northwest of Soho is Bloomsbury—the district that gave its name to the famed literati set (you know, Virginia Woolf, E. M. Forster, et al). Little is left of their haunts, but the University of London and lovely little streets continue to lure scholars, old and new. Best treat in Bloomsbury is **Sir John Soane's Museum** (13 Lincoln's Inn Fields, tel. 0171/405–2107; Tube: Chancery Lane; admission free), a must for any art connoisseur. Stuffed with antique busts and myriad Regency-era decorative delights, this is the most eccentric, smile-inducing 19th-century collection of art and artifacts around. Literature lovers, of course, will head first for the **Dickens House Museum** (48 Doughty St., tel. 0171/405–2127; Tube: Russell Square; admission £3), which looks just as it did when the beloved author lived here.

THE SOUTH BANK

Many visitors never venture across the Thames unless they're heading to or from Waterloo Station, but that's all changing: Some of London's most celebrated new attractions—including **Shakespeare's Globe** and the **London Aquarium**—have recently opened along the south bank of the river. The South Bank was bombed flat during World War II and is fairly industrial, but the area is on the rise. A sprawling, multitier monument to poured concrete, the **South Bank Centre** (Tube: Waterloo) takes its role as cultural beacon seriously, and is as progressive a complex as you could hope for from any quasi-official institution. Thick brochures listing the month's attractions at the center are available in the complex's various buildings. In addition to housing the **National Theatre,** the **National Film Theatre,** and the **Royal Festival Hall** (*see* After Dark, *below*), the center also has the **Hayward Gallery** (Belvedere Rd., tel. 0171/960–4242; admission £5), which is known for assembling thorough retrospectives of modern artists such as Magritte and Jasper Johns. Also in the center is the cool **Museum of the Moving Image (MOMI)** (tel. 0171/401–2636; admission £5.95), an impressive though somewhat kitschy TV and film museum.

That long-missing Exhibit A of Elizbethan-era England—**Shakespeare's Globe** theater (Bear Gardens, SE1, tel. 0171/401–9919; Tube: Mansion House, then walk across Southwark Bridge and along the riverbank)—finally has returned from the mists of history, thanks to this grand reconstruction of the arena where Shakespeare premiered many of his peerless dramas. The "Wooden O" is an amazing place to take in a play; the audience—500 of whom stand in the pit as "groundlings" (at a great bargain price)—is as much a part of the show as the on-stage drama (yes, you can boo Iago). The arena is open to the skies, so if clouds threaten, bring an umbrella! Even when the theater is closed it can be viewed on guided tours, which also take in a permanent Shakespeare exhibition. The theater's repertory season is May through September; performances are Tuesdays–Saturdays at 2 and 7:30, and Sundays at 7:30. Tickets run from £5 to £20.

The **London Aquarium** (County Hall, Westminster Bridge Rd., SE1, tel. 0171/967–8000) stands just across from the Houses of Parliament. It has 40-plus attractions including display tanks and schools of sharks, and is rather claustrophobic and dimly lit.

ST. JAMES'S

When Whitehall Palace burned down in 1698, all of London turned its attention to St. James's Palace (closed to the public), the new royal residence. In the 18th and 19th centuries, the area around the new palace became the place to live, and many of the estates surrounding the palace disappeared in a building frenzy as mansions were built, streets were laid out, and expensive shops sprang up. Today St. James's is one of London's most elegant and fashionable addresses.

The red-tarmac **Mall** cuts a wide swath all the way from Trafalgar Square to Buckingham Palace. It was laid out in 1904, largely because it was believed that the British monarchy needed a processional route in keeping with its imperial status. **Admiralty Arch** (built in 1911), a triumphal arch bordering Trafalgar Square, marks the start of the Mall; it continues past St. James's Park and **Carlton House Terrace,** a stately 1,000-ft-long facade of white stucco arches that is the home of the **Institute of Contemporary Arts (ICA)** (The Mall, tel. 0171/930–6393; admission £2.50). Lectures, avant-garde films, and rotating exhibits of photography, painting, sculpture, and architectural drawings by international and home-grown talent make ICA the headquarters for lusty cultural bolshevism. The Mall ends in front of Buckingham Palace at the **Queen Victoria Memorial,** to some an irritatingly didactic monument to the glory of Victorian ideals.

STRAND AND EMBANKMENT

Strand, which turns into Fleet Street about ½ mi from Charing Cross, is smelly, noisy, and dirty—a lot of cars in a boring concrete canyon with crowded sidewalks. The Embankment, on the other hand, is a bit more intriguing. Constructed between 1868 and 1874 by Sir Joseph Bazalgette (the same man who designed London's sewers), the Embankment, which runs all the way from Westminster to the City, was designed to protect the city from flooding (a job now handled by the Thames Barrier).

Somerset House, constructed between 1776 and 1786 by William Chambers, is home to Inland Revenue (the British equivalent of the IRS) and the **Courtauld Institute Galleries** (Strand, tel. 0171/873–2526; Tube: Temple; admission £4: unfortunately, this gallery will be closed for renovation until fall 1998), a gallery housing a collection of oils from the 15th to 20th centuries. The impressionists and postimpressionists are the best represented; Manet's *Bar at the Folies-Bergère* hangs here, and the collection of Cézannes is the best in London.

WHITEHALL

Whitehall is both the name of a street and a vast, faceless bureaucracy. Whitehall the street runs from Trafalgar to Parliament Square through the heart of tourist London. Whitehall the bureaucracy can't be so easily demarcated. Essentially, the term applies to the central British government, whose ministries fill many of the buildings on Whitehall and around Carlton Terrace. The long, low **Horse Guards** building (constructed 1745–1755) is the backdrop for a smaller version of Buckingham Palace's Changing of the Guard: at 11 each day (10 on Sun.), a mounted contingent of the Household Cavalry clops its way down the Mall from Hyde Park Barracks to Whitehall, arriving here 30 minutes later to relieve the soldiers standing in sentry boxes facing the Banqueting House.

Churchill, the Cabinet, and the Chiefs of Staff coordinated Britain's war effort from the **Cabinet War Rooms** (King Charles St., tel. 0171/930–6961; Tube: Westminster; admission £4.20), a fortified basement in a civil-service building. An audiotape tour guides you through rooms reconstructed to look as they did at the close of World War II.

SHOPPING

Name your poison, because London rivals any place in the known universe when it comes to shopping. Funky street markets that roar to life on weekends, swank department stores, music stores for the most discriminating ears, shoe stores for the least discriminating feet—it's all here.

The granddaddy of London stores and magnet for every traveler on the planet is **Harrods** (87–135 Brompton Rd., SW1, tel. 0171/730–1234). Don't come here to shop—it's incredibly expensive—but rather to browse. First stop: the incredibly lavish food halls, the best free show in town. Chic central is **Harvey Nichols** (109 Knightsbridge, SW1, tel. 0171/235–5000), a.k.a. *Absolutely Fabulous's* Patsy and Edina's home-away-from-home. Another popular department store is **Marks & Spencer** (458 Oxford St. tel. 0171/935–7954); Dukes and dustmen come here for underwear, among other things. **Charing Cross Road, Tottenham Court Road, and Cecil Court** have oodles of secondhand bookstores. Top chains, such as **Waterstone's** (121 Charing Cross Rd., tel. 0171/4344–4291) are also here. London has some of the biggest record stores around, including **HMV** (150 Oxford St., tel. 0171/631–3423) and **Virgin** (14 Oxford St., tel 0171/631–1234). Best of all are London's amazing street markets, where you can find everything from chipped Chippendale to cutting-edge frocks. **Portobello Road Market** (take the tube to Ladbroke Grove or Notting Hill Gate) is open Saturdays 6–4 and is a mile in length. It's a top place for antiques. **Petticoat Lane** (Middlesex Rd.; tube to Aldgate East or Liverpool Street) is open Sundays 9–2 and has lots of groovy bric-a-brac and bargain clothing. Best and busiest of all is **Camden Lock** (Camden Lock Place, take the tube to Camden Town), open weekends 10–6. The several different markets here make up for a totally fun London afternoon out.

AFTER DARK

London has a raging after-hours scene that's been setting global trends for decades. Rock music, jazz, raves, you name it—London probably did it first and often does it best but rarely does it cheap. A pint of beer runs £2, movie tickets are £4–£9, and clubs charge covers of £6 and up, up, up. Clubs, first-run cinemas, jazz joints, and big-name theaters are concentrated around Soho and Covent Garden, but you'll find hip, alternative clubs and theaters all over London. For the latest entertainment options, check out *Time Out* (£1.70), which is invaluable to travelers and locals for listing and reviewing the ever-evolving night scene. *What's On* and *The Evening Standard* are cheaper and less comprehensive.

CLASSICAL MUSIC, OPERA, AND DANCE

Tickets for classical concerts, ballet, and opera range anywhere from £2.50 to more than £100 for special performances. Most venues offer way-cheap **standby tickets** to students with valid ID, available an hour or so before curtain (call first to check on availability). For eight weeks from July to September, the **Royal Albert Hall** (Kensington Gore, SW7, tel. 0171/589–8212; Tube: Knightsbridge) hosts the **Promenade Concerts.** Tickets start at a very reasonable £3, but could cost up to £30 for special performances or really good seats. For the rest of the year the Royal Albert is home to the acclaimed **Royal Philharmonic Orchestra** (tickets from £3). **The London Coliseum** (St. Martin's Ln., tel. 0171/632–8300; Tube: Leicester Square) is the home of the **English National Ballet** troupe and attracts talented dance companies from around the world. Sharing the stage is the **English National Opera Company (ENO).** It's well known for English-language operas and offers lower prices than the Royal Opera Company. One hundred balcony seats go on sale the day of the performance at 10 AM for £5. The famous London Symphony Orchestra plays at the **Barbican Centre** (Silk St., EC2, tel. 0171/638–8891; Tube: Barbican). Although the emphasis is on classical music, everything from brass bands to jazz and world music is performed. Tickets cost £5–£45; ask about student standby tickets.

Royal Festival Hall. This incredible concert hall in the South Bank Arts Centre is home to the London Philharmonic Orchestra. Tickets cost £2.50–£30; student standby tickets are available two hours before the show. *Tel. 0171/960–4242. Tube: Waterloo.*

Royal Opera House. This fabled theater will be closed for the next two years for a grand-scale renovation. During this time, the resident troupes will be performing elsewhere. The **Royal Ballet** will be appearing at the Labatt's Apollo Theatre in Hammersmith and Festival Hall, while the **Royal Opera** will present full opera productions at the Barbican Theatre, the Shaftesbury Theatre, and Royal Albert Hall, and give concert versions elsewhere. For complete information, call the Royal Opera House Box Office. *Tel. 0171/240–1066.*

DANCE CLUBS

Every night of the week, scores of clubs spin contemporary dance music (jungle, drum and bass, *every* variety of house and techno), old R&B hits, '70s funk and disco, and the occasional indie platter. One-nighters (nomadic "theme" nights that take place at particular clubs on the same night every week, or move around from club to club) are very popular, but tend to confuse matters with erratic opening and closing times—always check the daily listings in *Time Out* for current information. Throughout London, clubs typically open by 10 PM and close around 3 AM; though some after-hours clubs *open* at 3 AM and run until sunrise. Cover charges usually cost £5–£7 in midweek and rise to a tenner and way beyond at the weekend.

The Astoria/LA2. A major rock venue in the early evening, the Astoria also hosts a variety of one-nighters both in its main hall and in its Siamese twin LA2. The *very* popular "G.A.Y." alternates between the two halls, playing trashy disco and funk. Friday brings the aptly named "Popscene" at LA2 and "Rockscene" at the Astoria. *157 Charing Cross Rd., tel. 0171/434–0403. Tube: Tottenham Court Road. Cover: free–£8.*

Blue Note. Quite possibly the best variety of music in London is trotted out at this club's one-nighters. The hottest night of the week must be Sunday's "Metalheadz," featuring jungle guru Goldie and his crew. "Magic Bus" pulls up on Fridays with a mix of acid jazz, soul, funk, and old school hip-hop. *1 Hoxton Sq., tel. 0171/729–8440. Tube: Old Street. Cover £3–£8.*

The End. The Shamen's Mr. C set up this place to be a club for clubbers run by clubbers. The C guy takes over the decks himself a couple of nights a week along with big name techno-DJs and the best homegrown drum-n'-bass groups. *16A West Central St., WC1, tel. 0171/419–9199. Tube: Tottenham Court Road. Walk west on New Oxford St., turn right on West Central St. Cover £3–£15.*

Heaven. This massive club turns into London's largest lesbian and gay party spot several nights a week. "Garage" (Friday) attracts a mixed gay/straight clientele, "Heaven" (Saturday) brings in a throbbing gay and lesbian crowd, and "Fruit Machine" (Wednesday) is mainly gay men. *Under The Arches, Villiers St., tel. 0171/930–2020. Tube: Charing Cross or Embankment. Cover £3–£8.*

LIVE MUSIC

ROCK, REGGAE, AND WORLD BEAT • Barfly Club. This is the finest and most eclectic small club in the capital, though the little square back room often gets crammed with people eager to see the newest flavor of the month. There are three bands seven nights a week with events regularly sponsored by the NME, Melody Maker, and Kerrang! publications. *Falcon Pub, 234 Royal College St, NW1, tel. 0171/482–4884. Tube: Camden Town. Cover £3–£6.*

Borderline. When record companies want to try out new bands, they send 'em to this hip Soho establishment. Who knows, maybe you'll see the next big thing. *Orange Yard, Manette St., tel. 0171/734–2095. Tube: Tottenham Court Road. Cover £5–£10.*

Garage. Clear views of the stage and a killer sound system make this a good place to see live rock and indie acts. *20–22 Highbury Corner, tel. 0171/607–1818. Tube: Highbury & Islington. Cover £4–£9.*

JAZZ • Jazz Café. Lines can be long, but the JC is a great relaxed place to see big-name jazz talents (Gil Scott-Heron, Abdullah Ibrahim) as well as some of the best eclectic new sounds (The Egg, Jimi Tenor). Admission and drink prices do lean toward the high end. *5 Parkway, NW1, tel. 0171/916–6060. Tube: Camden Town. Cover £6–£20.*

Ronnie Scott's. This legendary Soho club, opened in the early '60s, is the leading venue for jazz in London—if they're the best, they play here. Book in advance or get in line early. *47 Frith St., tel. 0171/439–0747. Tube: Tottenham Court Road. Cover £12–£14.*

PUBS

Most pubs are open Monday–Saturday 11–11 and Sunday noon–10:30. Bartenders don't get tipped in pubs. If you want to show appreciation for exceptional service, buy the bartender a drink; after placing an order say, "and one for yourself." For late-night drinking, try wine bars (which charge handsome prices to subsidize their expensive after-hours liquor licenses).

Coach & Horses. A historic hard-drinking place, with bright orange lights and lots of Naugahyde. Local character Jeffrey Barnard (a British Bukowski) spent the 1950s pissed at this bar, observing Soho's "Low Life" for *Spectator* magazine. *29 Greek St., off Shaftesbury Ave., tel. 0171/437–5920. Tube: Leicester Square.*

The Dog House. This little hole-in-the-wall has the hippest divey scene in Soho, full of young and friendly urban funkies. It's cramped, smoky, and loud. *187 Wardour St., tel. 0171/434–2118. Tube: Tottenham Court Road. Closed Sun.*

French House. The unofficial Resistance headquarters during World War II maintains a distinctly French aura. The wine selection is easily the best, as well as one of the cheapest, of any London pub. *49 Dean St., tel. 0171/437–2799. Tube: Leicester Square.*

Lamb & Flag. "The oldest tavern in Covent Garden" used to hold bare-knuckle boxing matches upstairs, prompting the pub's nickname, "Bucket of Blood." *33 Rose St., between Long Acre and Flora St., tel. 0171/497–9504. Tube: Covent Garden.*

Orange Brewery. Many champion Chelsea's solid, clubby, Victorian-era Orange as the "best pub in London." It makes its own brews. *37 Pimlico Rd., off Lower Sloane St., tel. 0171/730–5984. Tube: Sloane Square.*

Princess Louise. Wooden banisters, molded ceilings, and stained glass give this spacious, popular Bloomsbury pub a genuine turn-of-the-century feel. *208 High Holborn, tel. 0171/405–8816. Tube: Holborn. Closed Sunday.*

WKD. One of Camden's trendiest bars, with a wide range of clientele and music. During happy hour (Tues.–Sat. noon–9:30, Sun. noon–7), jugs of cocktails are £5.50 and beers £1.50. After 9 PM, there's live music and a £2–£5 cover. *18 Kentish Town Rd., tel. 0171/267–1869. Tube: Camden Town. Closed Mon.*

The Yard. Thanks to its courtyard at the end of a short alley, this gorgeous—almost idyllic—mixed gay bar and restaurant seems miles away from the noise of Soho. *57 Rupert St, off Shaftesbury Ave, W1, tel. 0171/437–2652. Tube: Piccadilly Circus. Closed Sun.*

Ye Olde Cheshire Cheese. One of the oldest pubs in London (*rebuilt* after the Great Fire of 1666) and a one-time haunt of Fleet Street journalists. Charles Dickens, once a parliament reporter for the *Morning Chronicle*, slammed down pints here. *145 Fleet St., tel. 0171/353–6170. Tube: Blackfriars.*

THEATER

Theater in London falls into two categories: the West End (London's equivalent of Broadway) and the fringe. The principal West End theaters are centered around Shaftesbury Avenue in Soho, the Haymarket in St. James's, and around Covent Garden. Half-price, same-day tickets are sold from the **Society of West End Theatres kiosk** (open Mon.–Sat. noon–30 mins before matinees, 2:30–6:30 for evening shows) in Leicester Square, but lines are always long; tickets run £3–£10. Fringe shows are even cheaper. Royal Shakespeare Company productions come to **The Barbican** (tel. 0171/638–8891) regularly. The **National Theatre** (South Bank Arts Centre, tel. 0171/928–2252; Tube: Waterloo; tickets £10–£24) puts on anything from cutting-edge stuff to imaginative interpretations of old standbys. Shakespeare fans won't want to miss the recently reconstructed **Globe Theatre** (Bear Gardens, SE1, tel. 0171/401–9919; Tube: London Bridge; tickets £5–£20) that stages plays twice daily between May and September.

NEAR LONDON

WINDSOR

Windsor, west of central London along the Thames, is the sort of place where rowboats roll gently upriver, where geese noisily lap up crumbs along the riverbank, and where families stroll with ice cream. Of all the day trips you could make from London, this is one of the nicest. The 11th-century, dirt-and-wood fort built here by William the Conqueror was later rebuilt in stone by Henry II; the brawny complex eventually evolved into **Windsor Castle**. Before a fire in 1992 heavily damaged 100 or so rooms, the queen spent most of her weekends here, and the entire castle closed to the public whenever she rolled into town. These days, it's open more often than not, but dial 01753/831–118 for the latest opening times and to complain about the staggering £8.80 castle admission fee. The castle is divided into Lower, Middle, and Upper wards. The principal structure of the Lower Ward is the 15th-century **St. George's Chapel,** where many of England's kings and queens are buried. The Middle Ward is where you'll find the **State Apartments,** the **Gallery,** and **Queen Mary's Dolls' House** (admission £1). The Dolls' House, measuring 8 ft by 5 ft, is a fully functional marvel of miniature engineering—teeny faucets even exude rivulets of water. Hours vary, but these places tend to be open 10–5 in summer, until 3 or so in winter. The **Changing of the Guard** takes place Monday–Saturday at 11 AM. BritRail makes the 50-minute trip (£5.50 return) to Windsor from London's Waterloo and Paddington stations every half hour. **Green Line** (tel. 0181/668–7261) Buses 700 and 702 also travel from the Colonade, near Victoria Station, to Windsor (1 hr, £6 return).

THE SOUTH

The South of England is like London's rich, plump, self-satisfied mother-in-law. It is the wealthiest—and consequently the most resented—and most conservative region in England, though the Tories did lose a significant number of seats in the last local elections. However, the wealth of the region—coupled with its proximity to London—ensures that any revolution in English pop culture will soon make its way down to the South. Plus, the scenery in the South is consistently impressive—not to say such legendary sights as Canterbury Cathedral and Brighton's Royal Pavilion; If crowds get you down, flee the towns and take long walks through the forests, or go for bike rides through the placid countryside.

CANTERBURY

The path between London and Canterbury has long been one of the most well-trod in Europe; unlike the modern BritRailer, though, medieval pilgrims had to go on horseback or on foot through bad English weather and terrain to visit the shrine of martyr Thomas à Becket. Canterbury's sights—essentially the cathedral and the crooked medieval streets—are an easy day trip from London, though the town makes a perfect pre-London stop for those just crossing the English Channel. The **Tourist Information Centre** (34 St. Margaret's St., tel. 01227/766–567) books beds for a 10% deposit.

COMING AND GOING

Frequent trains leave London's Victoria Station (1½ hrs, £15.60 five-day return) for **Canterbury East** (Station Rd. E, off Castle St., tel. 01732/770–111). The second station, Canterbury West, mostly serves destinations in Kent. Enter the **bus station** (tel. 01227/766–151) at the corner of St. George's Lane and St. George's Place. Buses leave about every two hours for London's Victoria Coach Station (£5).

WHERE TO SLEEP

Abundant B&Bs line New Dover, London, and Whitstable roads; most are tiny, so reserve ahead. Two pleasant choices are the **Dar-Anne** (65 London Rd., tel. 01227/760–907; doubles £28) and the **Courtney Guest House** (4 London Rd., tel. 01227/769–668; doubles £30–£38). The **Canterbury YHA** (54 New Dover Rd., tel. 01227/462–911) has beds for £9.40 (£6.30 under 18) and is usually full during summer; reserve ahead. From Canterbury East, turn right on Station Road East, veer right on Rhodaus Town (which becomes Upper Bridge Street), then turn right on St. George's Place (which turns into New Dover Road).

FOOD

A lovely option is **Alberry's Wine Bar** (38 St. Margaret St., tel. 01227/452–378). This popular bistro makes a good place to sit and recharge your batteries. Easy to find (on the same street as the tourist office), Alberry's offers a wide, daily-changing selection of inexpensive and hearty soups, salads, and pies. Less expensive places are mostly along the smaller lanes and alleys off High Street. The **Green Court Cafe** (17–18 The Borough, tel. 01227/458–368) serves tasty sandwiches and jacket (stuffed) potatoes. With an enormous menu and low prices, **August Moon** (49A St. Peter's St., tel. 01227/786–268) packs in the university crowd—try Kung Po Chili Chicken or the Vegetarian Feast (£5.90 for two). **Simple Simon's** (St. Radigund Hall, 3 Church Ln., off The Borough, tel. 01227/762–355), in a 14th-century hall, serves game, poultry, steaks, and fish, but specializes in pies, like lamb and apricot (£5.95). Each of the four colleges of the **University of Kent** has its own bar; **Woody's** is the most fun, with a sociable, young crowd. Take Bus 604 up St. Dunstan's Street and ask the driver for the university.

WORTH SEEING

Canterbury's small size means it's easy to see everything in one day. The hub of the English Church, the **Canterbury Cathedral,** is a wonder of Norman and Gothic architecture. The northwest transept was the site of Thomas à Becket's murder in 1170; this dissident priest disagreed with King Henry II's meddling in the church's business, and was silenced by four of Henry's knights. The assassins probably entered from the cloisters, which contain amazing vaults. The dazzling cathedral entrance was built to commemorate Henry V's 1415 victory at Agincourt. *Corner of Sun and St. Margaret's Sts. Admission £2.50, free Sun. Open Mon.–Sat. 9–7 (Oct.–Easter until 5), Sun. 12:30–2:30 and 4:30–5:30 (open all day Sun. for worship). Access may be restricted on Sat. afternoons when evensong is performed.*

Canterbury's attempt to re-create a historically accurate, multisensory version of Chaucer's stories resulted in **The Canterbury Tales** (St. Margaret's St., tel. 01227/454–888; admission £4.85; open July–Aug., daily 9–6; shorter hrs off season)—perfect for children, but insulting to a more mature intellect. Multilingual radio-controlled headphones guide you from room to room, where excerpts from the tales are illustrated by moving plywood cutouts. The stories are funny, but it's less expensive (and more fulfilling) to read the book. The popular **Canterbury Heritage Museum** (Stour St., tel. 01227/452–747; admission £1.90; open Mon.–Sat. 10:30–5; June–Oct., also Sun. 1:30–5) exhibits a collection of local artifacts left by pilgrims at Canterbury.

DOVER

Dover's role in the English tourism industry is unique: it's the closest city to the Continent, and visited largely because of its ferry port. In addition to a brutal recession, Dover and its ferries now face competition from the Eurotunnel's underwater technology, leaving the city with an uncertain future. If you're stuck here awaiting a boat, check out the **Old Town Gaol** (Biggin St., tel. 01304/202–723; admission £3.40; open Tues.–Sat. 10–4:30, Sun. 2–4:30; Oct.–May, closed Tues.) with creepy wax figures and vivid images of torture, confinement, and lunacy illustrating life in this Victorian prison. The impressive **Dover Castle** (Castle Hill Rd., tel. 01304/201–628; admission £6; open Easter–Oct., daily 9:30–6 or dusk if earlier; Nov.–Easter, daily 10–4) overlooks the coast with some first-rate views; don't miss the 45-minute tour of **Hellfire Corner,** a maze of tunnels the British dug into the cliffs beneath the castle to defend themselves against Napoléon. Dover's surroundings—the famous chalky seacliffs, or **White**

Cliffs—made the town an ideal fortress in the past, and now inspire lovers and travelers. Stop by the **tourist office** (Townwall St., tel. 01304/205–108) for the free pamphlet *White Cliffs Trails* outlining the best walks in the area.

COMING AND GOING

Stena Line (tel. 01233/647–047) and **P&O** (tel. 0990/980–980) ferries depart regularly from the Eastern Docks for Calais, France (70–90 mins, £24–£48 return). Call the tourist office for schedules. **Hoverspeed and SeaCat** (tel. 01304/240–241) runs speedy hovercrafts and catamarans: hovercrafts leave the Western Docks for Calais, while SeaCats leave from Folkestone for Boulogne; the fare for either is £20 (five-day return). **National Express** coaches run every hour from Dover's bus station on Pencester Road to London's Victoria Coach Station (£11). **Trains** leave at least once an hour from Dover's Priory Station to London's Victoria and Charing Cross stations (£16.80).

WHERE TO SLEEP AND EAT

Ask to see your room before money changes hands; some Dover B&Bs are lousy. **Clare House** (167 Folkestone Rd., tel. 01304/204–553; £12.50 per person) is a well-kept family home with extra-soft mattresses; the clean, comfortable **Number One** guest house (1 Castle St., tel. 01304/202–007; £18–£20) is almost luxurious. Dover's hostel, **Charlton House YHA** (306 London Rd., tel. 01304/201–314; beds £9.40, £6.30 under 18) is the best deal in town; from Priory Station, go left to the roundabout, turn left onto Priory Road (which becomes London Road), and continue 1 mi. It's hard to find a decent restaurant in Dover, but lace tablecloths give **Riviera Coffee House** (9–11 Worthington St., tel. 01304/201–303) a fancy feel, and sandwiches or tea and scones are cheap.

For information on gay events or referrals to other resources, contact the Gay Switchboard (tel. 01273/690–825) or the University of Sussex's Lesbian, Gay, and Bisexual Society (c/o Room 232, Falmer House, Brighton BN1 9QF).

BRIGHTON

The back-to-back palatial hotels along Brighton's waterfront attest to its status as England's premier beach resort, though it's changed a great deal since its 19th-century heyday. Brighton is now the liberal hole in the conservative belt of the South, and home to Britain's largest, most vibrant gay community outside London. If you can avoid the city's usual seaside tourist trappings, you'll find that it's a fine place to blow off steam before heading on to another quaint, medieval town.

Intended to be a simple seaside villa, the **Royal Pavilion** (corner of North St. and Old Steine, tel. 01273/290–900; admission £4.10; open June–Sept., daily 10–6; Oct.–May, daily 10–5), completed by John Nash in 1822, looks more like the Taj Mahal—note the extravagant Indian architecture and Chinese decor. During summer, the lawn becomes a venue for musical performances. Perhaps the most spectacular monument of the Regency era, Nash's Xanadu remains a must for art historians and decorative arts buffs. Nearby, the free **Brighton Museum and Art Gallery** (Church St., at Marlborough Pl., tel. 01273/290–900; open Mon., Tues., Thurs.–Sat. 10–5, Sun. 2–5) contains exhibits of armor, Art Deco glass, archaeological finds, fashion, and costume. Gaudy, beloved **Palace Pier** (Old Steine, at Grand Junction Rd., tel. 01273/609–361) has the requisite amusement rides, arcade, and slot machines; at night, a seedier crowd emerges, but it's still reasonably safe. **The Lanes,** a maze of narrow lanes near the ocean, have Brighton's most interesting and expensive shops, while **North Laine** draws a young crowd to its cafés and trendy stores.

BASICS

The **Tourist Information Centre** (10 Bartholomew Sq., across from town hall, tel. 01273/323–755) books accommodations (£1), and has maps and pamphlets. **American Express** (82 North St., tel. 01273/321–242) offers the usual services to cardholders.

For information on gay events or referrals to other resources, contact the **Gay Switchboard** (tel. 01273/690–825) or the University of Sussex's **Lesbian, Gay, and Bisexual Society** (LGB), which currently meets Tuesdays at 6:30 PM in the LGB room on the campus (write first, c/o Room 232, Falmer House, Brighton BN1 9QF). Money-changing offices in the train station are a rip-off, so head to one of the banks along North Street; **Lloyd's Bank** (171 North St., tel. 01273/324–971) has good rates for traveler's checks. The **post office** (51 Ship St., BN1 1BA, tel. 01273/573–209) is open Monday–Saturday 9–5:30.

COMING AND GOING

Trains leave Brighton's **rail station** (Queen's Rd., tel. 0345/484–950) twice hourly for London's Victoria Station (£13.30). National Express Bus 64 leaves for London every 1½–2 hours from the **bus station** (Pool Valley, tel. 01273/674–881) near the waterfront. General information on public transport in the Brighton area can be had by calling 01273/474–747.

WHERE TO SLEEP

One of the charming Brighton hostelries is **Topps** (17 Regency Sq., tel. 01273/729–334). Two Regency houses have been turned into a hotel run by Paul and Pauline Collins (remember her as the maid in *Upstairs, Downstairs*?). Topps is a right-on Brighton splurge (rooms are around £60 to £80), with attractive and well-equipped rooms with lush bathrooms. The atmosphere is relaxed and friendly, the owners are always ready with useful advice, and there's a fine restaurant in the basement. The cheapest places are on the east side of town, on Madeira Place, Charlotte Street, and Upper Rock Gardens. **Chester Court** (7 Charlotte St., tel. 01273/621–750; doubles £40–£44), near the seafront, is one of the best. The independent **Brighton Backpacker's Hostel** (75–76 Middle St., tel. 01273/777–717; beds £9, £40 per week) is fun, funky, and a half-block from the waterfront; from Brighton station, walk down Queen's Road to the seafront, turn left, then left again on Middle Street. Down the street, **Friese-Green** (20 Middle St., tel. 01273/747–551) has the same rates as Backpacker's but is more spacious.

FOOD

The Lanes, off North Street, and North Laine have restaurants aplenty. **Food for Friends** (17A–18 Prince Albert St., tel. 01273/736–236), is right off The Lanes, and serves up Chinese stir-fry or Sussex shepherdess pie for £3.35–£3.95. A great place is **English's Oyster Bar** (29–31 East St., tel. 01273/327–980). Buried in the Lanes, this 200-year-old restaurant is one of the few old-fashioned seafood havens left in England. You can either eat succulent oysters and other seafood dishes at the counter or have a table in the restaurant section, where there's a two-course set-price menu for £6.95.

AFTER DARK

The backbone of local nightlife is, unquestionably, the clubs, and travelers of any sexual orientation can enjoy a very hedonistic weekend here. Pick up *The Essential Guide* (£1) or *The Latest* (30p) at newsstands. Popular with students, **Smuggler's Pub** (Ship St.) has a dance club (tel. 01273/328–429) and a jazz club (tel. 01273/328–439), and **Leek and Winkle** (39 Ditchling Rd., tel. 01273/698–276) plays good music and has a beer garden. Club kids come from all over Britain to hang out at **Zap** (King's Rd. Arches, tel. 01273/821–588) and **Event II** (West St., tel. 01273/732–627).

WINCHESTER

Winchester, the "ancient capital of England," really takes the historical cake. The first king of England, Egbert, was crowned here in AD 827, and even William the Conqueror thought it prudent to restage his crowning here after his "official" ceremony in London. With dozens of walking and hiking trails crisscrossing the nearby fields, streams and rivers flowing through town, and centuries-old bells stirring the air on Sunday mornings, the longer you stay, the less you'll want to leave. The **tourist office** (Broadway, tel. 01962/840–500) is one of England's best stocked. The **train station** is on a direct BritRail line from London (70 mins, £17.70); buy tickets at the kiosk on Station Road (tel. 0345/484–950 for information). **National Express** (tel. 0990/808–080) buses run every 2 hours from the **Winchester bus station** (across from the tourist office) to London (2 hrs, £9–£11); buy tickets from the driver.

WHERE TO SLEEP

Several B&Bs are southwest of the cathedral, especially along Christchurch Road and its side streets. **Mrs. N. Basset** runs a great B&B (64 Middle Brook St., tel. 01962/862–222; £16–£18 per person) in the center of town. **The City Mill YHA** (1 Water Ln., tel. 01962/853–723; beds £8.50; closed Dec. 21–mid-Feb.), an 18th-century mill on an island in the middle of River Itchen, is a tourist attraction by day, hostel by night. It's definitely one of Britain's best, but it's small, so book way ahead. From the tourist office, turn right on Broadway and cross the bridge.

WORTH SEEING

Most of Winchester's sights are clustered near the **Winchester Cathedral** (5 The Close, tel. 01962/853–137; £2.50 donation requested; open daily 7:15–6:30), England's center of religion until Canterbury's rise to power in the 13th century. With magnificent stained-glass windows and sky-high pointed arches, the cathedral (1079) is one of the most remarkable and massive edifices of the Christian world. Look for Jane Austen's tomb south of the nave. The church's **library** (admission £1.50) houses an illuminated 12th-century copy of the Winchester Bible and a copy of Bede's 8th-century *Historia Ecclesiastica.* The **Great Hall** (Upper High St., at Castle Hill, tel. 01962/846–476; admission free; open daily 10–5, closes at 4 winter weekends) has been the site of crucial historical events, such as Parliament's first meeting (1246) and Sir Walter Raleigh's trial and sentencing for treason (1618), but most visitors come to see the painted wooden disk purported to be King Arthur's Round Table.

THE WEST COUNTRY

England's southwestern counties, known collectively as the West Country, are a patchwork quilt of thatched-roof houses, fishing villages, boggy moorland, eroded castles, and enigmatic stone structures that continue to evoke myths, legends, and speculation. To many, the mystery of the West Country is embodied by the legend of King Arthur, who is thought to have been born in Tintagel, to have battled with Mordred at Bodmin Moor, and to be buried in Glastonbury. The weather here can be surprisingly beautiful, and you may have to remind yourself that you're still in

Jane Austen's novel, "Persuasion," much of which is set in Bath, is useful for an insight into the town's history and high-society past.

England as you stare at the palm trees, white beaches, and turquoise waters of Cornwall. Extensive coastal paths ring the coasts of Devon and Cornwall, and England's warmest waters lap the shores of the surfing enclaves of Penzance and Newquay. Many visitors don't get beyond a visit to Bath—a shame, considering these many other worthwhile diversions. If you're going to be traveling extensively, consider buying the **Freedom of the Southwest** rail pass (£57–£64 according to season).

BATH

Immortalized in the novels of Jane Austen, Bath is perhaps the most elegant city in Britain. Its history extends, however, well back before the 18th century. Bath's fame was originally a result of its hot springs (which pour out of the earth at a steady 116°F). In the 1st century AD, the Romans built an intricate series of baths and pools and named the town Aquae Sulis. Queen Elizabeth I brought a certain prestige to the baths with her visit in 1574, while Queen Anne's visits in 1702 and 1703 established the "Bath season." In subsequent years, architect John Wood (1704–1754) gave Bath its distinctive, harmonious look: Using the yellowish "Bath stone" cut from nearby quarries, he created a city of crescents, terraces, and Palladian mansions, curving through the city like scalloped paper cutouts. These days, Bath is nearly equal to Stratford as a tourist draw, so lodging and food are expensive. If you want to stay over, the efficient **tourist office** (Abbey Chambers, Abbey Churchyard, tel. 01225/477–101) books rooms for a £2.50 fee. The office holds an **American Express** office (tel. 01225/424–416), which cashes all traveler's checks free of charge, as does the branch at 5 Bridge St. (tel. 01225/444–747).

COMING AND GOING

Great Western (tel. 0345/484–950 for information) makes the 1¼-hour trip from London's Paddington Station to **Bath Spa Station** for £35.50 return. **National Express** (Manvers St., tel. 0990/808–080) coaches from London (£19 return) arrive 10 times daily. Less frequent but cheaper are **Turner's** (0117/955–5333; £7.50 single, £13.50 return) and **Bakers Dolphin** (tel. 01934/616–000; £8.95 single, £14.25 return). Both leave from Marble Arch; tickets can be purchased on board or by phone with a credit card at least a day in advance.

WHERE TO SLEEP AND EAT

Woodville House (4 Marlborough Ln., tel. 01225/319–335) is ideally positioned if you want to be near Victoria Park and the Royal Crescent. Basic rooms cost £30, even if you're alone, though they don't take in solo travelers during summer. The no-smoking rule is absolutely rigid. All rooms at **Bathurst Guest House** (11 Walcot Parade, tel. 01225/421–884; doubles £36–£40), only a seven-minute walk north of Bath

Abbey in the city center, are nonsmoking and tastefully decorated. The friendly proprietors at **The Gardens** (7 Pulteney Gardens, tel. 01225/337–642; doubles £40) make you feel like family here and at their other guest house (check in at The Gardens); walk up Manvers Street, turn right and across bridge at North Parade, and left on Pulteney Road. Bath's **YMCA** (Broad St. Pl., tel. 01225/460–471; beds £10, singles £14.50, doubles £26) is in the center of town. **Bathwick Hill YHA** (tel. 01225/465–674; beds £9.40) is the cheapest lodging option; take Bus 18 or 418 (50p) from the train station to avoid walking up the steep hill.

The town's cheap eats center around the Theatre Royal, Sawclose, and Kingsmead Square areas. Enjoy a large range of sandwiches and lunches (£2.50–£4.50) at **The Crystal Palace** (Abbey Green, tel. 01225/423–944), a very English pub with garden patio. **The Canary Restaurant** (3 Queen St., tel. 01225/424–846) serves pasta and vegetarian dishes (£4–£6) to chamber music accompaniment.

WORTH SEEING

You can't soak your feet at the **Roman baths** (Abbey Churchyard, tel. 01225/477–000; admission £6), but you can join hordes of latter-day invaders and tour the well-preserved, sulfurous-smelling complex, built between the 1st and 5th centuries AD. Sample some vile-tasting mineral water at the overpriced Pump Room, above the baths. If you have extra time, visit the elegant Assembly Rooms (1771) and the **Museum of Costume** (Bennett St., tel. 01225/477–785; combined admission with baths £8), a prestigious collection of 400 years of fashion. One of the best examples of Bath's famous Georgian architecture is the **Royal Crescent,** a semicircle of 30 houses overlooking Victoria Park—the interior of No. 1 Royal Crescent (tel. 01225/428–126; admission £3.50) is decorated in period style. Gothic, 15th-century **Bath Abbey** (High St., tel. 01225/422–462) sits on the site of a previous Norman church. It is best known for its spindly, fan-vaulted ceiling.

NEAR BATH

GLASTONBURY

Glastonbury is England's hippie capital and spiritual center, where the Christian mixes with the Druidic, the ancient with New Age. Legend has it that Glastonbury is the mythical Isle of Avalon, where King Arthur died around AD 516. The chalice used during the Last Supper is reputedly buried in the hill next to **Glastonbury Tor,** a tall upcropping of land once used as a Druid congress, and the town itself is aligned most auspiciously on ley lines (invisible lines of spiritual energy that supposedly run across England). Among the healing establishments and aromatherapy dens, **Glastonbury Abbey** (Magdalene St., tel. 01458/832–267; admission £2.50) replaced an earlier church said to have been visited by Jesus; it's also Arthur's reputed burial site. Those who don't come seeking Jesus, Arthur, or Guenevere flock to the almost annual (late June) **Glastonbury Festival** for the hundreds of MTV-friendly bands who descend on town. Tickets (£77) include everything but food. The **tourist office** (9 High St., tel. 01458/832–954) sells festival tickets for a small booking fee. **Buses** (£6.65 return, or £4.80 on Day Rambler ticket) leave from Bath (change in Wells) once every hour.

SALISBURY

Salisbury ("SAULS-burr-ee") is swamped by hype from nearby Stonehenge—you can't walk 2 blocks without seeing leaflets and posters pointing you there. But if you overlook all the 'henge mania, you'll find Salisbury's Gothic cathedral, Tudor buildings, and walkable city center worth a gander themselves. Most Britons, however, equate Salisbury with its great Gothic **Cathedral** (The Close, tel. 01722/323–273; £2.50 donation requested), which its builders decreed "so great a church to the glory of God that those who come after us will think us mad even to have attempted it." The spire and tower, supported by stone columns bending underneath, weigh 6,400 tons. Inside the octagonal **Chapter House** (admission 35p) is one of the original copies of the Magna Carta. Opposite the main entrance, the **Salisbury and South Wiltshire Museum** (65 The Close, tel. 01722/332–151; Sept.–June, closed Sun.) is home to prehistoric, Roman, and Saxon artifacts. The **tourist center** (Fish Row, tel. 01722/334–956) has the complete scoop on Salisbury.

COMING AND GOING

South West trains (tel. 0345/484–950) serve Salisbury direct from London's Waterloo (£28.90 one-month return). The town center is five minutes west on Fisherton Road. National Express **buses** arrive in the center of town and cost £14.50 return from London.

WHERE TO SLEEP AND EAT

Pick up a list of B&Bs from the tourist office or check Salt Lane and Belle Vue Road. From the bus station, turn left on Endless Street and left on Milford Street for the **Milford Hill YHA** (Milford Hill, tel. 01722/327–572; beds £9.40). In the center of town, **Matt & Tiggy's** (51 Salt Ln., tel. 01722/327–443; beds £9; sheets 80p; showers 20p) is essentially a private hostel. **The Bacon Sandwich Café** (129–131 South Western Rd., next to the rail station, tel. 01722/339–655) is the place for meat lovers; try their megabreakfast (£3.75).

OUTDOOR ACTIVITIES

The **Wiltshire Cycleway** covers the entire county, the Vale of Pewsey, and the Wylye Valley. The shortest loop is from Salisbury to Horningsham (70 mi), and the longest is the County Route (160 mi). Salisbury's tourist office has free maps. Rent **mountain bikes** (£7.50 per day, £45 per week, £25 deposit) at Hayball Cycles (The Black Horse Chequer, Winchester St., tel. 01722/411–378).

NEAR SALISBURY

STONEHENGE

This Neolithic monument has been blamed on everything from druids to UFOs, but all anyone knows for sure is it was started around 2800 BC, expanded between 2100 and 1900 BC, and has long been used for religious and astronomical purposes. The fence around the monument was installed in 1978, as a defense against graffiti and the destruction of the stones by human traffic. These days you can get a better view of Stonehenge from some points on the A344 highway than

For £2.50–£3.50, squeeze through Exeter's historic underground passages (High St., near pharmacy; closed Sun., also Mon. Sept.–June).

from the paid area (tel. 01980/624–715; admission £3.70; open daily June–Aug., 9–7; mid-Mar.–May and Sept.–mid-Oct., 9:30–6; mid-Oct.–mid-Mar., 9:30–4). Still, the stones do have a mystical quality early in the morning, when the sun peeks over the horizon. Wilts & Dorset Bus 3 (£4.40 return) departs hourly from Salisbury's bus and train stations.

STOURHEAD HOUSE AND GARDENS

Close to the village of Stourton lies one of Wiltshire's most breathtaking sights, Stourhead, a country-house-and-garden combination that has few parallels for beauty anywhere in Europe. Most of Stourhead was built between 1721 and 1725 by "Henry the Magnificent," a wealthy banker by the name of Henry Hoare. While the house is a monument to the age of elegance, it must take second place to its adjacent gardens, the most celebrated example of the English 18th-century taste for "natural" landscaping. The estate is literally a three-dimensional Old Master painting. Stourhead (tel. 01747/841152. admission to house £4.30; gardens £4.30. House open mid-Mar.–Oct., Sat.–Wed. noon–5:30 or dusk; gardens daily 9–7 or sunset) is 9 mi northwest of Shaftesbury (follow B3081 to B3092), 30 mi west of Salisbury.

EXETER

During World War II, the German *Luftwaffe* thumbed through a *Baedeker's* travel guide looking for targets and found this southwestern cathedral city. The "Baedeker raids" were designed to hit England's jewel cities and erode citizen morale. But despite the devastation visited upon the city, Exeter still has plenty to offer. Seamlessly restored after the raids, **Exeter Cathedral** (Cathedral Close, off High St., tel. 01392/214–219; £2 donation requested) is still one of the finest examples of English Gothic architecture, with the longest unbroken Gothic vault of any building in Europe. The best parts of the **Royal Albert Memorial Museum** (Queen St., tel. 01392/265–858; admission free; closed Sun.) are the local and natural history rooms. The **tourist office** (Paris St., tel. 01392/265–700), opposite the bus station, sells maps and guides to Exeter and nearby Dartmoor National Park.

COMING AND GOING

Most **South West Trains** from London Waterloo (£34.70 single, £48 return) or **Great Western** trains from London Paddington (£39.50 single, £35–£79 return) arrive at Exeter Central (Queen St.). Some trains stop at St. David's Station (Bonhay Rd.); take Bus N or cut through the Clement's Lane pedestrian walk and turn right on St. David's Hill. **National Express buses** from London (4 hrs, £25 return) arrive at the central bus station (Paris St., tel. 01392/427–711).

WHERE TO SLEEP

Exeter YHA (47–49 Countess Wear Rd., tel. 01392/873–329; beds £9.40) is in the suburbs, amid thatched-roof houses and a contingent of sheep; take Bus K, T, J, or 57 to the Countess Wear post office, and follow the signs. July–September, **Exeter University** (Birks Hall, New North Rd., tel. 01392/211–500) offers private rooms for £12.50–£19. Many B&Bs are on St. David's Hill and Blackall Road near the train stations; **Highbury B&B** (89 St. David's Hill, tel. 01392/434–737; singles £12.50, doubles £25) has big comfortable rooms and an easygoing proprietor.

FOOD

High Street and its extensions have cheap chippies, some good ethnic eateries, pubs, and expensive hotel restaurants. The atmospheric **Coolings Wine Bar** (11 Gandy St., tel. 01392/434–184), which includes a cocktail bar in the low-slung cellar, serves lasagna (£4.75) or beef in Guinness with vegetables and sautéed potatoes (£5). **The Gallery Café and Centre Bar** (Gandy St., tel. 01392/493–287) serves filled rolls (£2) and ever-changing main courses (£3–£4.60), featuring pies, casseroles, and vegetable-filled pancakes. **Herbie's Whole Food Restaurant** (15 North St., tel. 01392/58473; closed Mon. evening and Sun.) serves healthy meals for under £5, though the organic ice cream will tempt you to bump up the bill.

NEAR EXETER

DARTMOOR NATIONAL PARK

This 25-sq-mi patch of land between Exeter and Plymouth preserves England's most extensive prehistoric ruins—from stone monuments to burial mounds to hut circles, all dating back to around 4000 BC. Near the town of Haytor is **Hound Tor**, a geological phenomenon that from certain angles looks like a hunter and a pack of hounds bounding over the moor. **Lydford Gorge**, while not exactly the Grand Canyon, is nevertheless impressive: a deep, wooded ravine cut by the River Lyd. For real wilderness, head for the north moor, which contains the highest peaks in the park. Farmland predominates in the west, and the northeast corner is a mix of high moor and more farms. Hikers should remember that Dartmoor gets 2½ times more rain than nearby Exeter. The park's two most central information centers are in **Princetown** (Tavistock Rd., tel. 01822/890–414; open daily year-round) and **Postbridge** (on the B3212, tel. 01822/880–272; closed Nov.–Mar.). Note: The Ministry of Defense does occasional target practice in the northwest corner of the park. Firing times rarely occur in high season, and the area is marked by warning notices, red flags, and lights. For recorded information, dial 01752/501–478.

COMING AND GOING • From Exeter, **buses** have scattershot service into the park. Pick up the free and indispensable *Dartmoor Bus Services* guide at any tourist office around the park. Several bus companies serve the towns surrounding the park, but only the **Transmoor Link** Bus 82 goes straight through the park, from Exeter through Plymouth (three to four buses per day, May–Sept.). The **Devon County Council** (in Exeter, tel. 01392/382–800) has comprehensive bus information.

WHERE TO SLEEP • The cheaper B&Bs in the park cost about £14–£15 per person. **Bellever YHA** (Bellever, Postbridge, tel. 01822/880–227; beds £8.50) shares a farmyard with the Forestry Commission. Besides its own pub and country inn, Princetown's **Plume of Feathers Inn** (tel. 01822/890–240) has bunks for £4.50–£5.50, doubles for £31, and campsites for £2.50 per person. Reserve ahead on summer weekends. Most campgrounds in the park are closed from the end of November until February. Near Exeter is **Clifford Bridge Park** (Clifford, near Drewsteignton, tel. 01647/24226), charging £7–£11 per twosome with a tent.

CORNWALL COAST

The Cornish simply do not smile enough. It's not that they lack in congeniality or a collective sense of humor, but with the abundance of lush, blue-green seascapes, Iron Age artifacts, the best of English weather, and a prosperous tourism industry, you'd think they'd be grinning 24 hours a day. The region's economic troubles have a lot to do with the dour dispositions; the local fishing industry is in decline and is being replaced by ever-expanding tourism, making it increasingly easy for travelers to visit the area, but more difficult for them to discover the *true* Cornwall. **Falmouth** and **Penzance** are good bases for exploring the south coast's sandy beaches. In the north, the landscape is more austere and the coast craggy, although **Newquay** serves as the nation's surfing capital.

COMING AND GOING • Train tracks to Cornwall end at Penzance, with lines branching off to Newquay, Falmouth, and St. Ives. **National Express** (tel. 0990/808–080) has regular bus service to all the main towns. For regional bus information, call **Western National** (tel. 01208/79898 or 01209/719–988).

FALMOUTH

With its harbor and dockyards, Falmouth has long been famous in maritime circles and rests comfortably below Tudor-era **Pendennis Castle** (tel. 01326/316–594; admission £2.70). The town has a number of **beaches,** including popular Gyllyngvase Beach and less-crowded Maenporth Beach. Falmouth is a great base for exploring the lush and lovely **Lizard Peninsula,** the southernmost point of mainland Britain. The South West Coastal Path winds along the Lizard shore, meandering past some of England's rarest and most beautiful flora and fauna; the best cliff walks are around Mullion Cove. From Falmouth, take Western National Bus 2 to Helston and transfer to Bus T1 to The Lizard, the peninsula's most southerly town.

WHERE TO SLEEP • B&Bs line Melvill Road and its offshoots, three minutes from the Falmouth Dell station. **Pendennis Castle YHA** (tel. 01326/311–435; beds £8.50) is near the castle, a 20-minute walk from town. From Falmouth Docks station, follow the road to Castle Street, climb the hill to the left, and follow the signs to the castle and hostel. By taxi, the trip costs around £3. The hostel is closed Dec.–mid-Feb. and Sun. and Mon. in Oct.–Nov.

PENZANCE

The pirate history of Penzance is common knowledge throughout Cornwall—apparently in the old days everyone was in on it, luring ships to its rocky shoals. Today, Penzance is a great place to explore, thanks to its seaside promenade and quiet town center, and makes a good base for most of Cornwall—get information at the **Tourist Information Centre** (Station Rd., tel. 01736/362–207). One nearby destination is **Land's End,** the westernmost point in England. Much of the beauty has been compromised by the crowds—witness the parking lot and tacky amusement-park playground (inclusive ticket for amusements £7.95).

WHERE TO SLEEP • For a hearty breakfast and teatime chitchat, try **Lynwood Guest House** (41 Morrab Rd., tel. 01736/365–871; doubles £24–£31), a comfy B&B with TVs and coffeemakers in every room. **Penzance YHA** (Castle Horneck, Alverton, tel. 01736/362–666; beds £9.40; closed Jan.) is a refurbished 18th-century mansion. Take Bus 5B, 6B, or 10B to the Pirate Inn and walk from there. The impeccably clean **Penzance YMCA** (The Orchard, Alverton Rd., tel. 01736/365–016; beds £8.50) books a lot of groups—call ahead for space.

ST. IVES AND NEWQUAY

St. Ives combines an appeal for both beach-bums and art buffs; the water is deep aqua, and the yellow lichen covering the town's rooftops looks like magic gold dust. The tiny town has long been popular (Virginia Woolf incorporated her experiences here into *To the Lighthouse*), and it gets crammed with families seeking sand, sun, and surf—especially in July and August. The excellent **Barbara Hepworth Museum** (Barnoon Hill, tel. 01736/796–226; admission £3), the home and studio of Cornwall's premier 20th-century sculptor, now houses a small museum run by the Tate Gallery, whose brand new building on Porthmeor Beach also merits a visit (tel. 01736/796–226; £3.50, joint ticket with Hepworth Museum £5.50). Strolling and bathing are popular at Porthmeor and Porthminster beaches. And although some people hate **Newquay,** clucking over its rampant commercialism and lack of Cornish charm, others thrive on the prime surf and crowds. The busy **Information Centre** (Marcus Hill, tel. 01637/871–345) is across the street from the bus station.

WHERE TO SLEEP • In St. Ives, Tregenna Terrace, Carthew Terrace, Channel View, and Bedford Road have many B&B options; **Garlands** (1 Belmont Terr., tel. 01736/798–999) and **Horizon Guest House** (Carthew Terr., tel. 01736/798–069) have rooms for £12–£16 per person. Sites at **Ayr Holiday Park** (tel. 01736/795–855), a 15-minute uphill walk on Higher Ayr Street, cost £7.50 for two people with a tent, £9.50 in July–August (closed Oct.–Easter). Pricewise, the best places to stay are at Newquay's laid-back **Towan Backpackers Hostel** (16 Beachfield Ave., tel. 01637/874–668; beds £6–£6.50) or **Rick's Hostel** (8 Springfield Rd., tel. 01637/851–143; beds £5–£8).

EAST ANGLIA

The landscape of East Anglia, northeast of London, can be summed up in a single word: flat. Especially in north Norfolk, nothing punctuates the smooth countryside except the stray farmhouse or cathedral. East Anglia's changing economic status has mirrored that of the textile industry over the past millennium. The evidence of the area's onetime prosperity is concrete: textile money built many of the cathedrals and so-called wool churches in the region. Most towns have experienced enormous population growth but fortunately haven't become polluted and depressed urban nightmares like some of the Midlands' larger cities. On the downside, because East Anglia is still predominantly a rural region, the public transportation system is primitive. Most towns are linked to long-distance walking paths that have been used since medieval times by merchants. If you're into pensive walks, look for **Peddar's Way,** which runs diagonally across Norfolk (in the northeast), and **Weaver's Way,** a 56-mi walking path along the Norfolk coast.

CAMBRIDGE

Even the most jaded dropout won't be able to resist the lure of Cambridge's stone walls, massive libraries, and robed fellows strutting about town. Cambridge is best known for producing some of the world's finest scientists (Stephen Hawking, author of *A Brief History of Time,* today occupies the same faculty chair Sir Isaac Newton once held), although the register of literary alumni includes John Milton and Virginia Woolf. For all the grandeur of ancient academia, Cambridge has plenty of life left: Today, progressive-thinking students swarm the streets with their three-speed bikes; death rockers and gray-bearded deans down pints in the town's pubs; tourists swarm the tea shops; sunbathers pack the banks of the River Cam; and occasionally some studying gets done.

BASICS

The staff of the **Cambridge Tourist Information Centre** (Wheeler St., tel. 01223/322–640; open Apr.–Oct., weekdays 9–6 (Wed. from 9:30), Sat. 9–5, Sun. 10:30–3:30; Nov.–Mar., weekdays 9–5:30 (Wed. from 9:30), Sat. 9–5) leads guided walking tours (£5.75) of the town. **American Express** (25 Sidney St., tel. 01223/461–410; closed Sun.) offers the usual AmEx services.

COMING AND GOING

The **train station** (Station St., tel. 0345/484–950) is a half-hour walk from the city center—walk down Station Road, turn right on Hills Road, and continue straight—or you can grab a Cityrail Link bus at the station. Trains leave twice hourly for London (1 hr, £15.20 day return, £17.30 standard return). The **bus station** (tel. 01223/423–554) is at the end of Drummer Street. **National Express** (tel. 0990/808–080) buses to London are £9 return; the trip takes about two hours. Buy tickets to local destinations on board; the driver often gives special fares the station's office doesn't list.

WHERE TO SLEEP

A slew of B&Bs and the youth hostel are about 3 blocks from the train station; walk down Station Road, turn right on Tenison Avenue, and continue for a block or 2. For a 10% deposit (plus a £3 fee), the tourist office can also book you a room.

Aaron Guest House. Lovely location near the park and river, with the atmosphere of an English country house. Singles £25, doubles £38. *71 Chesterton Rd., tel. 01223/314–723. From train station, Bus 3 or 5. From bus station, walk across Jesus Green.*

Antoni's Bed & Breakfast. A friendly and centrally located B&B. The proprietor is helpful and the rooms (singles £15–£20, doubles £30–£40) are clean and comfortable. *4 Huntingdon Rd., tel. 01223/357–444. From bus station, turn right on Emmanuel St., right on St. Andrews St.*

Belle Vue House. The good location and spacious rooms with TVs make this B&B a deal. The lone single is £22, and the two doubles go for £35. Reserve ahead. *33 Chesterton Rd., tel. 01223/351–859. Follow directions to Aaron Guest House (see above).*

HOSTELS • Cambridge YHA. Only 3 blocks from the train station, this hostel has clean beds, powerful showers, and an international crowd. Book ahead. Beds £10.30 (£7 under 18). *97 Tenison Rd., tel. 01223/354–601.*

CAMPING • Toad Acre Caravan Park. Well-equipped and bordered by apple trees, this camping park is frequented by motor homes. Sites £4.50–£5.50 per person. *Mills Ln., tel. 01954/780–939. Take Bus 155 or 157 (hourly) to Longstanton.*

FOOD

Although the students generally eat within their colleges, there are plenty of cafés and restaurants to tempt your taste buds. **Brown's** (23 Trumpington St. opposite the Fitzwilliam Museum, tel.01223/461–655) is a Cambridge classic. This huge, airy, brasserie-diner is the place where students take their parents when they're in town. Call in for the daily pasta dishes, house hamburgers (£6.45–£7.55) or even breakfast (11 AM–noon) or afternoon tea (3–5.30 PM). It's very busy on weekends, when you may have to wait in line. Another Cambridge tradition is the open-air produce market in the middle of town on **Market Hill**—every day but Sunday. **Clown's** (52 King St., tel. 01223/355–711) coffee bar is great for its sandwiches, quiches, strong coffees, and attractive, young clientele. **7A Jesus Lane** (7A Jesus Ln., tel. 01223/324–033) serves up individual gourmet pizzas (most under £6) in the snazzy former dining room of one of Cambridge's most uptight eating clubs. The cheap-and-cheerful **Eraina** (2 Free School Ln., off Bene't St., tel. 01223/368–786) taverna serves up monster portions of Greek food, as well as pizzas, salads, and curries. A terrific basement vegetarian restaurant with only 10 tables, **Rainbow** (9a King's Parade, tel. 01223/321–551) serves a good breakfast for £3.75, while the varied main dishes weigh in at under £6.

WORTH SEEING

Cambridge University has no exact center but is spread over many residential colleges scattered around town. The granddaddy of all colleges is **Peterhouse,** with some structures dating from the 13th century, when a disgruntled monk from Oxford's Merton College decided to begin a little school of his own. King Henry VI founded **King's College** (King's Parade, tel. 01223/350–411) in 1441 and five years later began constructing its greatest monument, **King's College Chapel** (tel. 01223/331–447; admission £2.50). Completed in 1536, the 289-ft-long Gothic structure features the world's longest expanse of fan-vaulted ceiling and is probably England's most sublime monument of the Perpendicular Gothic style. Rubens's *Adoration of the Magi* hangs behind the altar, and on Christmas Eve a festival of carols performed in the chapel is broadcast worldwide.

The huge rivalry between Oxford and Cambridge comes to a head at two annual sporting events: the Boat Race, where their rowing eights race each other down the Thames near Putney, and the rugby match, played at Twickenham in London.

The largest and richest of Cambridge's colleges, **Trinity College,** counts Lord Byron, Isaac Newton, William Thackeray, and Prince Charles among its graduates. The impressive **Wren Library** (tel. 01223/338–488; closed Sun.), designed entirely by Christopher Wren down to the bookshelves and reading desks, contains an astonishing display of valuable books. Though the list is hard to whittle down, other colleges worth a visit include **Queens', St. John's, Emmanuel, Magdalene,** and **Christ's.** The grounds of most colleges close during final exams, from the fourth week of May until mid-June.

The **Fitzwilliam Museum** (Trumpington St., tel. 01223/332–900; admission free, but £3 donation requested; closed Mon.) houses a first-rate permanent art collection—paintings and prints from the Renaissance (Leonardo da Vinci included) through impressionism. **The University Botanic Garden** (Bateman St., tel. 01223/336–265; admission £1.50, free Wed. and weekdays Nov.–Feb.) is the perfect place to kill time while waiting for a train; among its many delights are a glass igloo, a limestone rock garden, and flowers, flowers, flowers.

AFTER DARK

The Anchor (Silver St., tel. 01223/353–554) is filled with locals day and night, with an outdoor deck right on the River Cam. The **Eagle** (Bene't St., tel. 01223/301–286) is a traditional pub, frequented both by scientists Watson and Crick, who announced their discovery of DNA in a back room, and by British and Allied airmen during World War II—the ceiling still bears names and squadron numbers written in candle smoke. **The Junction** (Clifton Rd., near the train station, tel. 01223/511–511) is a music fan's version of one-stop shopping—it's a dance floor, jazz joint, and rock club all in one building. In the summer Cambridge gets festival fever, beginning with the **Cambridge Beer Festival** in May, the **Midsummer Fair** in June, and the **Film Festival, Fringe Festival,** and **Cambridge Folk Festival** in July. Plays are also staged in the gardens of some of the colleges during the month of June.

NEAR CAMBRIDGE

NORWICH

The wool and weaving trade once supplied Norwich's wealth, and local merchants built so many churches (30, to be exact) that subsequent city planners have allowed businesses to take them over instead of knocking them down—look for the latest camping equipment displayed in the stained-glass window of a so-called wool church. Norwich is also home to a more politically and culturally progressive populace than most cities north of London, thanks to a large environmental movement and the nearby University of East Anglia. Construction on the absurdly tall **Norwich Cathedral** (tel. 01603/767–617) began in 1096; it remains one of England's great cathedrals. **Norwich Castle** (Castle Meadows, tel. 01603/223–624; admission £2.30) dates back to the 12th century; tours (£1.50) of the dungeon and battlements—which offer great views over Norwich—run hourly and last 45 minutes. The **tourist office** (Guildhall, Gaol Hill, tel. 01603/666–071) is in the marketplace in the center of town.

COMING AND GOING • Norwich's **train station** (Thorpe Rd., tel. 0345/484–950) serves as a major hub for the East Anglia region, and is a 10-minute walk from the center of town. Trains to Cambridge cost £14 return. The **bus station** (Surrey St., tel. 01603/613–613) is a little closer to the center.

WHERE TO SLEEP AND EAT • Norwich YHA (112 Turner Rd., tel. 01603/627–647; beds £8.50, £5.70 under 18) is about a mile from the city center; take Bus 37 or 38 and ask for Earl of Leicester (say LESS-ter) stop. Near the train station, along Riverside Road and its side streets, are a bunch of small B&Bs that charge from £15 per person—**Aspland House** (6 Aspland Rd., tel. 01603/628–999) has smart en-suite doubles for £35, with color TV and tea- and coffee-making facilities in each room. Or try the coed **YMCA** (48 St. Giles St., tel. 01603/620–269; dorm beds £7 without breakfast, otherwise £8.50; doubles £25), which is extremely conveniently located in the center of town. **Pinocchio's** (11 St. Benedict St., tel. 01603/613–318) is a lavish, yupscale place with off-white walls and murals. Italian food is the house specialty, of course, with pastas for about £6, and meat or fish entrées for £8–£9. **The Treehouse** (14 Dove St., tel. 01603/763–258), a co-op vegetarian restaurant, has flyers on town happenings. **Pizza One and Pancakes Too** (24 Tombland, tel. 01603/621–583) has a great name, which tells you all you need to know about what it offers. Neither specialty costs much over a fiver, and it's a nice place to hang out.

THE HEART OF ENGLAND

The Heart of England is a swath of agricultural central England featuring some incredibly popular sights. Its accessibility from London makes it easy to visit while on a short tour of England, and although that means it's crowded with tour buses and tea shops, there are still plenty of reasons to go. If you're staying in London for more than a week, leave England in shame if you can't manage a trip to **Oxford,** the region's finest city. **Stratford-upon-Avon** is the birthplace of Shakespeare and tourist hell. We don't recommend ignoring Stratford, but prepare yourself for crowds, kitsch, and sometimes crass commercialism. Anyone want to buy a Shakespeare-head egg-timer?

OXFORD

Home of the world's first English-language university, Oxford today is bustling and crowded, a vast conurbation expanding ever outward from the university at its center. Once upon a time, cattle herders led their flocks over this shallow junction of the Thames and Cherwell rivers. These days, however, the horde of buses and foot traffic in the city center is more comparable to Piccadilly Circus. Contrary to the way it looks in movies, Oxford is not nearly as small and idyllic as Cambridge, England's other ivory tower. Even so, street performers and flying troops of bone-rattlers (those shaky bicycles associated with English academics) make Oxford a loud and engaging city. You'll also find that the food and nightlife rank far above that of quiet, sylvan Cambridge.

BASICS

Don't expect much help from the very commercial **tourist office** (The Old School, Gloucester Green, tel. 01865/726–871). The **American Express** office (4 Queen St., OX1 1EJ, tel. 01865/792–066) offers the usual cardholder services. **STA Travel** (36 George St., tel. 01865/792–800) provides a wide variety of services for budget travelers.

COMING AND GOING

Direct BritRail service to **Oxford Station** (Botley Rd., tel. 01865/722–333) from London's Paddington Station takes about an hour and costs £13.10 day return. There are frequent buses from London's Victoria Coach Station (£7 day return, £9 open return) to Oxford's **Gloucester Green Station.**

WHERE TO SLEEP

Finding budget accommodations in Oxford may remind you of the New York dating scene: there are some good ones out there, but they're usually taken. With two hostels now open, prospects are improving; however, try to book ahead whenever possible. Peak season lasts from May to August, and arriving unprepared could lead to heartache and serious wallet damage.

Brown's Guest House. Brown's is heartily recommended by the hostel staff, who often send overflow backpackers here for the comfortable beds, plush rooms, and yummy breakfasts. Try to get a room that doesn't face noisy Iffley Road. Singles are £25, doubles £42 (£48 with bath). There's a 5% surcharge added to bills paid with credit card. The place has 9 rooms, 2 with bath. *281 Iffley Rd., tel. 01865/246–822. From Carfax, take Oxford Bus 4 or Thames Transit Bus 3 toward Rose Hill and alight at Howard Street.*

Oxford University is where Percy Bysshe Shelley was unceremoniously expelled only a few months after arriving—and where Hugh Grant perfected his "nervous Englishman" look.

Falcon Private Hotel. This hotel really is a home away from home and definitely worth the splurge. The staff is friendly and the attractive rooms have luxuries such as satellite TV and hair dryers. Singles are £28, doubles £49, triples £66. *88–90 Abingdon Rd., tel. 01865/722–995. From Carfax, walk south on Abingdon Rd, or take Bus X3, 16, or 35.*

Mrs. O'Neil. This is one of Oxford's true lodging bargains, but there are only two rooms (one single, one double), so make reservations now. Bed and breakfast costs £12.50 per person. *15 Southmoor Rd., tel. 01865/511–205. From Carfax, walk north on Cornmarket St., turn left on Beaumont St., right on Walton St., left on Southmoor Rd.*

Nanford Guest House. The rooms are small and the decor a little busy, but this is a fine place to rest your weary head. Singles cost £23, doubles £35. *137 Iffley Rd., tel. 01865/244–743. From Carfax, any bus toward Rose Hill and alight at Addison Crescent.*

HOSTELS • **Oxford YHA** (32 Jack Straw's Ln., tel. 01865/762–997) is on a quiet street 1 mi from the city center. Try to reserve a bed (£9.40) a few days ahead. The newly opened **Oxford Backpacker's Hostel** (9A Hythe Bridge St., tel. 01865/721–761) has a central location, friendly staff, and dorm beds for £9 (£10 June–Sept.), plus £1 for sheets.

FOOD

Oxford has great food, with all ethnicities and price ranges represented. So popular is **Browns** (5–11 Woodstock Rd., tel. 01865/511–995) with both undergraduates and local people that you may have to wait for a table. The wide choice of informal dishes includes steak-mushroom-and-Guinness pie and hot chicken salad. Potted palms and mirrors give the otherwise plain rooms a cheery atmosphere. Hidden on a little side street inside the Museum of Modern Art, **Café MOMA** (30 Pembroke St., tel. 01865/722–733; closed Mon.) serves large salads (£3) and a vegan "Nutroast," a baked loaf of ground nuts and onions (£4.25). **Chang Mai Kitchen** (130A High St., tel. 01865/202–233) is Oxford's best Thai restaurant; most dishes cost £6–£7. For delicious hummus, breads, cheeses, and desserts visit **Gluttons Delicatessen** (110 Walton St., tel. 01865/553–748), or slip into **Heroes** (8 Ship St., tel. 01865/723–459) for fresh-baked breads and Italian-style subs (£2–£3). Right outside Oxford is Godstow, where you can repair to the vine-covered **Trout** (Godstow, tel. 01865/554–485), a historic, and still excellent, Thameside pub on the northern edge of Oxford. Its interior, adorned with sporting prints by "Phiz" and engravings of Oxford by Turner, is remarkable in itself. Come in the evening for a meal or a drink and watch its peacocks strutting back and forth beside the weir. Lewis Carroll considered this eatery one of his favorites.

WORTH SEEING

The 29 undergraduate colleges, six graduate colleges, five permanent halls, and All Souls College that make up the university are scattered around town. Many colleges charge a small admission fee to roaming visitors. Student-run **Oxford Student Tours** arranges guided walks (about £3) on summer afternoons. Official walking tours leave daily from the tourist office.

A handful of literary big shots (including Lewis Carroll and John Locke) did time at **Christ Church College,** which has an 800-year-old chapel (admission £3)—one of the smallest, most ornate cathedrals in the country. Pretty **Magdalen** (pronounced "maudlin") **College** opened its doors in 1458 and boasts Oscar Wilde and Dudley Moore as alumni. **Magdalen Tower** (admission £2) is one of Oxford's most recognizable landmarks. As the first college built after the bloody St. Scholastica's Day Riot in AD 1215, **New College** (officially called St. Mary College of Winchester in Oxenford) incorporated new design features—such as the first enclosed quad—to protect gownies in the event of another riot. **University College** is best known for expelling Percy Bysshe Shelley after he wrote *The Necessity of Atheism.*

The **Ashmolean Museum of Art and Archaeology** (Beaumont St., tel. 01865/278–000; admission free; closed Mon.), Britain's oldest public museum, boasts masterworks ranging from drawings by Michelangelo to Bronze Age weapons to the death mask of Oliver Cromwell. The **Museum of the History of Science** (Broad St., tel. 01865/277–280; admission free; closed Sun. and Mon.) has artifacts like Einstein's blackboard. The **Pitt Rivers and University Museums** (Parks Rd., tel. 01865/270–927; closed Sun.), one of the greatest natural history complexes in the world, share a building a 20-minute walk north of the town center. There are hundreds of exhibits on just about every facet of nature, but the local dinosaur finds attract the most attention. The collection also includes the head and left foot of a dodo, a large, flightless bird that has been extinct since the mid-17th century.

Punting—propelling a flat, long boat with a giant, metal-tipped stick—is one of the great Oxford experiences. Just head down to the river to hire one: boats cost £8–£10 per hour (plus a £25 deposit) at Folly and Magdalen bridges.

AFTER DARK

What's On In Oxford, available free at the tourist office, is an invaluable guide to clubbing in Oxford. **The Old Fire Station** (40 George St., tel. 01865/794–490) is a one-stop spot, with a restaurant, theater, bar, and art museum. The biggest "activity" pub in Oxford, **The Head of the River** (Abingdon Rd., tel. 01865/721–600) has barbecues, snooker playoffs, mechanical bucking bronco contests, and even bungee jumping on summer Saturday nights. Tiny, low-ceilinged **Turf Tavern** (4 Bath Pl., tel. 01865/243–235) is one of England's coziest pubs; if you come in winter, try the mulled wine—cinnamon-spiced and guaranteed to lift even the most discouraged traveler's spirits.

STRATFORD-UPON-AVON

To go, or not to go, that is the question. Do you really want to spend time in a town that has no cafés, no movie theaters, and nothing to do at night other than see a (usually sold-out) play? Stratford is suffocatingly overcrowded—a tourist trap, even—and its soul has been sucked dry by mercenary hucksters looking to make a few quid off Shakespeare's good name. If you're really that keen on saying you've "done" Stratford, you won't mind the crowds or the lack of other forms of cultural life beyond the theater. And while the **Royal Shakespeare Company (RSC)** stages frequent productions in Stratford, equally prestigious productions run in London—minus the hype. That said, the RSC is the best thing going for Stratford, and we unabashedly recommend it.

BASICS

American Express (Bridgefoot, tel. 01789/415–856) shares an office with the crowded **tourist office** (tel. 01789/293–127). **Guide Friday** (14 Rother St., tel. 01789/294–466), a local bus tour company, also has free tourist information, and the lines are much shorter.

COMING AND GOING

Stratford is easily accessible by public transportation—buses and trains come regularly from Birmingham, London, and most other major cities. To reach Stratford's **train station** (Alcester Rd., tel. 0345/484–950; Oct.–May, closed Sun.) from London's Paddington (2½ hrs, £21 return), take the train north to Royal Leamington Spa and change to the Stratford line. Buses stop on Bridge Street at Waterside, either directly in front of the McDonald's or across the street. Buses to London (£14–£17 return) leave throughout the day.

WHERE TO SLEEP AND EAT

Since nearly every tourist over the age of 40 is hypnotically drawn to Stratford, the town has no shortage of B&Bs; the hard part is finding an inexpensive one. One of the best and priciest options is the **Victoria Spa Lodge** (Bishopton La., Bishopton, tel. 01789/267–985). This rather grand B&B lies just outside town, within view of the canal. Draped with clematis, the listed building dates from 1837 and sports Queen Victoria's coat of arms in two of its gables. The lounge/breakfast room is a pleasure, with huge windows and sofas and chairs for relaxing. The spacious rooms—some with fireplaces—are tastefully decorated and go for £52, or ask for the lone smaller one for £45. Concentrated pockets of less expensive B&Bs are on Grove Road and Evesham Road, near the train station, and on Shipston Road, across the river from the center of town. **Newlands** (7 Broad Walk, tel. 01789/298–449) is a wonderfully quiet B&B, and the rooms (£19–£21 per person) are surprisingly large. **Stratford YHA** (Hemmingford House, tel. 01789/297–093; beds £12.95, £9.65 under 18) is about 2 mi outside Stratford in the village of Alveston; from Stratford, catch Bus 18. Clean rooms and especially helpful management make this one of the best hostels in England (closed mid-Dec.–early Jan.). **Elms Camp** (Tiddington Rd., tel. 01789/292–312; £2.75–£3.50 per person; closed Nov.–Mar.) is cheap and close to town; catch Bus 18 to Tiddington.

Locally called the Dirty Duck, the **Black Swan** (Southern La., tel. 01789/297–312) is one of Stratford's most celebrated pubs, attracting actors since Garrick's days. It has a little veranda overlooking the theaters and the Avon. Along with a pint of draft beer, enjoy English grill specialties on its fairly pricey menu. Make reservations for this popular place. Another crowd-pleaser is the **River Terrace** (Royal Shakespeare Theatre, Waterside, 01789/293–226). At this informal cafeteria, the meals and snacks include lasagna and shepherd's pie. **The Slug and Lettuce** (38 Guild St., tel. 01789/299–700)—don't let the name put you off—a pine-paneled pub, serves excellent meals that are worth splurging for. Another popular place is the **Wholefood Café** (Greenhill St., tel. 01789/415–741; closed Sun.), a vegetarian restaurant with simple dishes like quiche and stuffed potatoes (£2.50–£2.75) for lunch. **The Vintner Café and Wine Bar** (5 Sheep St., tel. 01789/297–259) is one of the few cool hangouts in town; chow on fish pie and the vegetarian dish of the day.

WORTH SEEING

The Shakespeare sights are the only reason to visit Stratford. Conveniently, the Shakespeare Birthplace Trust (tel. 01789/204–016) sells an **all-inclusive ticket** (£8.50) to the five major sights listed below. Shuffle through **Shakespeare's Birthplace** (Henley St., admission £3.60), heavily restored from its original state and displaying Bard-related paraphernalia. Adjacent to the house is the **Shakespeare Centre,** with an exhibit of costumes used in BBC productions of Shakespeare's plays. Shakespeare kicked the bucket at **Nash's House** (Chapel St., admission £2.20) in 1616 at the age of 52, after living here for 19 years. The museum within depicts Stratford life in the 16th and 17th centuries, but the adjacent garden is much more interesting. One of the least-visited sights on the Shakespeare trail, **Hall's Croft** (Old Town, admission £2.20) was the home of Shakespeare's daughter, Susanna, and her husband, Dr. John Hall. Of the 17th-century antiques on display, Dr. Hall's medical instruments are the coolest. **Mary Arden's House** (admission £3.50), outside Stratford in the burg of Wilmcote, is said to be the home of Shakespeare's mother, although it's probably not authentic. Preferable is the delightful 15-minute walk from Stratford to **Anne Hathaway's Cottage** (admission £2.50) in Shottery. The home of Shakespeare's wife (before marriage, of course) today holds a fine collection of Tudor furniture.

AFTER DARK

The **Royal Shakespeare Company** (Southern Ln., tel. 01789/295–623) holds performances on its two main stages Monday–Saturday at 7:30 PM, with additional matinees on Thursday and Saturday at 1:30 PM; in any given week, about five or six different plays—not all of which are by Shakespeare—are performed. If you don't mind standing during a performance, you can buy tickets for as little as £5; balcony seats start at about £9. If the show hasn't sold out, students can buy discount tickets at 7:15 PM for about £11 (£14 on Saturdays). Or, to be safe, arrive at the box office at 9 AM and hope to get one of the 20 or so tickets held for day-of-performance sales. **Backstage tours** (£4) and **postperformance tours** (£3) are also offered at both theaters.

THE NORTH

Londoners consider the North anything just beyond the city limits, but most English define the region as beginning just above the Midlands. The area contains the sprawling industrial cities of Birmingham, Manchester, and Liverpool; the bountiful walking and hiking paths of Yorkshire; the pastoral landscape of the Lake District; and coal-mining Northumbria near the Scottish border. BritRail's main London–Edinburgh line runs through towns like York and Durham but skips the Lakelands and the northwest, although they're easily accessible on other rail lines.

BIRMINGHAM

Birmingham, England's second-largest city, is a big, industrial place with all the problems that status entails. There are crowds, traffic, and blocky buildings. That said, the city also reaps the benefits of its size, with two strong art collections, an extensive and efficient bus system, and three universities whose student populations keep the cultural scene sharp. After an overdose of quiet, quaint towns, you might even enjoy a couple of days in Birmingham.

BASICS

The **main tourist office** (City Arcade, tel. 0121/643–2514; open Mon.–Sat. 9–5:30) is about 50 yards from the AmEx office, right near New Street Station. An unrelated **civic tourist office** (Chamberlain Sq., tel. 0121/236–5622; open weekdays 9–8, Sat. 9–5) sells theater tickets but does not book rooms.

American Express. *17 Martineau Sq., off Union St., tel. 0121/233–2141. Open weekdays 8:30–5:30, Sat. 9–5.*

COMING AND GOING

Getting in and out of Birmingham is simple; the main rail station is in the center of town, and the coach station isn't far away. Although there are three rail stations, **New Street Station** is the biggest and most useful. From here, trains run frequently to London (1¾ hrs, £12.50–£20 return), Manchester (1¾ hrs, £16.90 return), and Liverpool (1¾ hrs, £14.80 return), among other cities. You'll only need the commuter-friendly **Moor Street Station** or **Snow Hill Station** if you're heading to the suburbs or to Stratford-upon-Avon (45 mins, £3.30 single, £3.40 day return, traveling off-peak). For train information call BritRail (tel. 0345/484–950). The **Digbeth Coach Station** is a few blocks away from the New Street Rail Station via Bull Ring and Digbeth roads. **National Express** (tel. 0990/808–080) coaches regularly serve London (2¾ hrs, £12 return) and Manchester (2½ hrs, £11 return).

WHERE TO SLEEP

A good area to look for budget accommodations is Edgbaston, where one of the best deals is **Woodville House** (39 Portland Rd., Edgbaston, tel. 0121/454–0274), just a short ride from the city center via Bus 128 or 129. Rooms cost £16 per person. Over in Acocks Green, another B&B-rich neighborhood southeast of the center, try **Ashdale House** (39 Broad Rd., Acocks Green, tel. 0121/706–3598), where singles are £20, doubles £32 (£25 and £38 for rooms with bath), and good vegetarian and organic breakfasts are offered. It's a 10-minute train ride from Moor Street or Snow Hill stations on the Stratford line: get off at Spring Road station, then walk 3–4 minutes.

HOSTELS • YMCA/YWCA. Four coed Ys open their doors year-round to travelers over 18. The two YMCAs (300 Reservoir Rd., tel. 0121/373–1937; 200 Bunbury Rd., tel. 0121/475–6218) charge £15.50 per person. To reach the one on Reservoir Road, take Bus 102, 104, 105, or 115 from the center; for Bunbury Road, take Bus 61, 62, or 63 from the center. The main YWCA (5 Stone Rd., tel. 0121/440–2924) charges £9.50 per night for a bed in a single room; take Bus 61, 62, 63, or 64 from the center. A second YWCA (27 Norfolk Rd., tel. 0121/454–8134) usually rents beds only by the week (£47), but they will rent for a night (£7) if there's space available; take Bus 9 or 19 from the city center.

STUDENT HOUSING • Within walking distance of the city center, the University of Birmingham rents out students' lodgings July–early September. Single rooms in six-bedroom flats with shared kitchens go for £8.50–£17.50 per night. Write ahead to reserve space. *Housing Service, University of Birmingham, Edgbaston, Birmingham B15 2TT, tel. 0121/414–3344.*

FOOD

Birmingham is known for its cheap Balti—an Indian specialty of pan-fried vegetables cooked in curry—restaurants on Stoney Lane and Ladypool Road in Sparkbrook, just southeast of the city center; take Bus 5, 6, or 12 from the city center. Gorge yourself on first-rate curries and vindaloos—as well as on the largest nan bread you've ever seen—at the stupendous **I Am the King Balti** (230 Ladypool Rd., tel. 0121/449–1170), one of a dozen or so Balti options along busy Ladypool Road. The gaudily bedecked **King's Paradise** (321 Stratford Rd., tel. 0121/753–2212) earns points for being open midday—overload on the £4.95 lunch special. Full dinners run £6–£8. For vegan and vegetarian food in a totally different part of town, **The Warehouse Café** (54 Allison St., Digbeth, tel. 0121/633–0261; closed Sun.) serves big, cheap meals like tofu or herb burgers and eggplant curry with bread and salad (£5.75). It's on the second floor of the Friends of the Earth building, Birmingham's green center. Come by for excellent food and to find out the latest happenings in town.

WORTH SEEING

In addition to visiting the places below, you could spend a couple of hours browsing the enormous **Birmingham Museum and Art Gallery** (Chamberlain Sq., tel. 0121/235–2834), which houses an eclectic collection of insects, sarcophagi, stained glass, and watercolors. Take a break in the museum's exquisitely decorated **Edwardian Tea Room.**

It may come as a surprise that Birmingham has more canals in its city center than Venice does. In fact, using waterways from Birmingham, it's still possible to reach the Irish Sea, the Thames, and the Bristol Channel.

The University of Birmingham's **Barber Institute of Fine Arts** may be the finest small art museum in England. The gallery includes works by canonical artists like Rubens, Hals, and Bellini, but the real strength is the 19th- and 20th-century collection, including high-profile works by Degas, van Gogh, Léger, and Magritte. *University of Birmingham, off Edgbaston Park Rd., near the university's East Gate, 0121/414–7333. Take Bus 44, 61, 62, or 63 from the city center, get off at Edgbaston Park Rd., cross the street, and walk up the small hill toward the university. Admission free. Open Mon.–Sat. 10–5, Sun. 2–5.*

Cadbury World, a shrine to chocolate about 4 mi south of Birmingham, tells the story of chocolate's origins (the Aztecs liked to drink it) before moving through the factory, where visitors must don paper hats while viewing the chocolatiers at work. More interesting than the factory tour is the town of **Bournville,** a community created especially for Cadbury workers in the late 1870s. *Linden Rd., Bournville, tel. 0121/451–4180 or 0121/451–4159. Take the train from New St. Station to the Bournville Station and follow signs. Admission £6. Open mid-Apr.–Oct., daily 10–5:30 (last entry at 4); shorter hrs off season.*

If you want to see the English legal system in action and don't mind being frisked, waltz right into the **Victoria Law Courts** and sit in on some hearings. Just about every type of local criminal—from juveniles to murderers—passes through the 25 courts on any given day. *Corporation St., tel. 0121/212–6600. From New St. Station, turn right on New St., left on Corporation St., continue past Old Sq., and look for it on the left. Admission free. Open weekdays from 9:45.*

AFTER DARK

For a useful rundown of the town's cultural calendar, pick up the free brochure entitled *What's On Birmingham* at the tourist office. Hipper, more underground papers list the latest alternative hangouts; look for them at pubs and record stores around town. If you're looking for good live theater, the **Crescent Theatre** (Brindley Pl., off Cumberland St., tel. 0121/643–5858; tickets from £7) performs a wide selection of plays. If you enjoy fine music, Birmingham is the home of the **City of Birmingham Symphony Orchestra** (as of June 1998, however, its famous conductor, Sir Simon Rattle, takes off for other pastures). The International Convention Centre has plenty of concerts, but availability of tickets (£5.50–£31) depends on the event. Dial 0121/212–3333 for ticket information.

The tourist office sells symphony and theater tickets. For an arty cinematic experience, visit **Mac** (Cannon Hill Park, tel. 0121/440–3838), Birmingham's home for alternative films, stageworks, and exhibitions.

Bobby Brown's (52 Gas St., off Broad St., tel. 0121/643–2573) is in an expansive converted warehouse with tons of intimate nooks and crannies. **Ronnie Scott's** (Broad St., across from the convention center, tel. 0121/643–4525), an offshoot of the pioneering London jazz club of the same name, hosts outstanding jazz, blues, and world-music performers every night but Sunday. The third-largest pub in

England is Birmingham University's **Old Varsity Tavern** (56 Bristol Rd., tel. 0121/472–3186); it's not cozy, but you get variety with four separate bars.

NEAR BIRMINGHAM

SHREWSBURY

Shrewsbury (pronounced "Shrose-bur-ee" or "Shroos-bur-ee") is one of England's most important medieval cities, filled with 16th-century half-timbered houses, narrow passageways, a multitude of churches, and a wonderful castle. The River Severn cradles the city in a horseshoe shape, and many of the streets within the "island" are now reserved for pedestrians only. Unlike many other towns in central England, Shrewsbury has not yet been milked by industry; the town has always been wealthy, and its citizens keep things in beautiful shape.

Perhaps the best way to experience the town's natural character is to walk the **Frankwell Riverside Trail** (it's signposted around town), which wraps around Shrewsbury parallel with the river. Otherwise, spend some time in **Quarry Park,** a huge green expanse south of the city center; from the tourist center, turn left on Swan Hill, make a right on Murivance, and look for the big park on the left. The romantic, refined **Cornhouse** (59A Wyle Cop, tel. 01743/231–991) serves excellent dinners (£8–£10; lunches from £4), and there's live jazz in the wine bar on Sundays. The town's main draw is **Shrewsbury Castle** (Castle Foregate, next to train station, tel. 01743/358–516; admission £4), begun in the 11th century as a stronghold from which the Normans could keep an eye on Wales. For maps and the like, head to the **tourist office** (Music Hall, The Square, tel. 01743/350–761; open Mon.–Sat. 10–6, Sun. 10–4; shorter hrs off season). The local **American Express** office (27 Claremont St., tel. 01743/236–387) changes money and issues traveler's checks.

COMING AND GOING • There's no direct service from London to Shrewsbury's **train station** (Castle Foregate, tel. 0345/484–950); take the train from London's Euston and change at Birmingham or Wolverhampton. Trains to Birmingham (£4.90–£9.70 return) and Manchester (£11.40–£16.90 return) run about once an hour all day.

WHERE TO SLEEP • There is a string of B&Bs on Abbey Foregate, across the River Severn from the center of town (take the English Bridge east across the river). Make sure you look at the rooms before dishing out money because many rooms face the noisy street. Try the friendly **Berwyn House** (14 Holywell St., tel. 01743/354–858; £14 per person). **Shrewsbury YHA** (Abbey Foregate, tel. 01743/360–179; beds £8.50, £5.70 under 18; closed Jan.–mid-Feb.) is only a few blocks farther than the cluster of B&Bs on Abbey Foregate.

MANCHESTER

Despite giving the world Morrissey and Ian Curtis, Manchester is not the world's most depressing place. Sure it can be dirty and grimy, but it's also as ethnically diverse as any city in Britain, has one of the largest gay and lesbian communities in the country, and fosters an overpowering music scene. The students at Manchester University—the largest university in Europe—play a large part in Manchester's social scene and contribute to the city's progressive image. That image dates back a long way: England's suffragette movement was born here, as were Britain's first labor unions, not to mention the world's first computer. Manchester was even the first city to be declared a nuclear-free zone, in 1980.

Despite its aesthetic shortcomings, Manchester does have many worthwhile neighborhoods within easy reach of the city center. Right along Charlotte Street near Chorlton Bus Station is **Chinatown,** an honest-to-goodness Chinese neighborhood with busy markets and restaurants. Behind the bus station is Manchester's **Gay Village,** the largest gay and lesbian hangout north of London. Down Oxford Road past the university is **Rusholme,** home to a large Asian community—there's not much to see, but you shouldn't miss a meal in one of the memorable curry houses.

BASICS

The **Manchester Visitor Centre** (Town Hall Extension, Lloyd St., tel. 0161/234–3157; open Mon.–Sat. 10–5:30, Sun. 11–4) is just north of St. Peter's Square. They carry the very useful *City Guide* (£1), with a city-center map. Manchester's **American Express** (10–12 St. Mary's Gate, tel. 0161/833–0121; closed Sun.) has a travel service and bureau de change. The busy but well-organized **STA Travel** (75 Deansgate, tel. 0161/834–0668), open weekdays 9:30–5:30 and Saturday 10–3:30, has information on cheap travel deals and sells the ISIC card.

COMING AND GOING

There are three train stations in town: the main one is **Piccadilly Station** (London Rd.), serving London's Euston Station (£36 return, £45 on Fridays) and the south. The other large station is **Victoria Station** (New Bridge St.), serving the north and west, including Liverpool (£6.10–£8.70 day return depending on time of travel). The **Metrolink** tram service runs between these two stations. National Express buses leave from **Chorlton Street Coach Station** (Chorlton St., tel. 0990/808–080) for London (£20.50 return) and all other major cities. Most local buses converge at **Piccadilly Gardens Bus Station** (Piccadilly, by Portland and Mosley Sts.). Call 0161/228–7811 for route and timetable information.

WHERE TO SLEEP

The Manchester YHA makes life a lot easier for the budget traveler. Since virtually no one lives in the city center, B&Bs, especially the cheaper ones, are a bus ride away. Lace curtains and embossed wallpaper adorn the comfortable Victorian **Green Gables Guest House** (152 Barlow Moor Rd., tel. 0161/445–5365; singles £16, doubles £36); Bus 11 or 143 from the city center stops out front. The centrally located, gay-owned **Rembrandt** (33 Sackville St., tel. 0161/236–1311) has rooms for £30–£40 double (the latter price for en-suite facilities). **Manchester YHA** (Potato Wharf, off Liverpool Rd., tel. 0161/839–9960; beds £9–£12.50) is a traveler's dream come true in the beautifully redeveloped Castlefield area. In summer, the University of Manchester residence halls sometimes open cheap rooms (£10–£16 per person, even cheaper for students); call the University Accommodation Office (tel. 0161/275–2888) ahead of time for a list of halls that may have space.

FOOD

If you're looking for some late-night Indian grub, head to the **Rusholme** area (take Buses 40–45 or 48)—pop into one of the simple BYOB places, or a more upmarket restaurant like **Sangam** (13–15 Wilmslow Rd., tel. 0161/225–5785). At **Café Pop** (34–36 Oldham St., tel. 0161/237–9688; closed Sun.) nostalgic Americans ought to try the Scooby Snax—a huge sandwich "for vegetarian truck drivers." **Dmitri's** (1 Campfield Arcade, off Liverpool Rd., tel. 0161/839–3319) is a relaxed tapas haunt with everything from chicken satay sandwiches to moussaka (£7.45). **On the Eighth Day** (109 Oxford Rd., tel. 0161/273–4878; closed Sun.), a vegetarian restaurant next to Manchester Metropolitan University's student union, serves soups, stews, bakes, and salads, along with vegetarian lasagna.

WORTH SEEING

The **City Art Galleries** (Mosley St., tel. 0161/236–5244; admission free) reflect Manchester's diversity: the galleries display a traditional collection of British art by Gainsborough alongside progressive multimedia exhibits by artists such as the late Derek Jarman. Don't miss the hands-on **Museum of Science and Industry** (Liverpool Rd., Castlefield, tel. 0161/832–2244; admission £5), set on 7 acres on the site of the world's first passenger rail station (opened 1830). More of the city's industrial heritage is explored at the **Pumphouse People's History Museum** (Left Bank, off Bridge St., tel. 0161/839–6061; admission £1, free on Fri.), which details English labor history of the last 200 years: daily life, strikes, cooperatives, and the recent Yorkshire coal miners' protests. The **Pankhurst Centre** (60–62 Nelson St., tel. 0161/273–5673; admission free) celebrates Manchester's suffragette movement in the home of two of its leaders, Sylvia and Christabel Pankhurst.

AFTER DARK

Manchester's nightlife is endless. Grab a copy of _City Life,_ an essential biweekly guide. **The Lass O'Gowrie** microbrewery (36 Charles St., off Oxford Rd., tel. 0161/273–6932) has great beer and a mellow atmosphere. **The Haĉienda** (13 Whitworth St. W, by Princess Pkwy., tel. 0161/236–5051) helped launch The Smiths, Joy Division, and The Fall. Linger over a cappuccino at the **Cornerhouse Café** (70 Oxford St., tel. 0161/228–2463), part of a trendy arts center-cinema complex.

LIVERPOOL

Like the rest of the northwest, Liverpool reached its zenith in the 18th and 19th centuries when it became Britain's major port for products of the Industrial Revolution as well as for emigrants heading to the New World. In World War II, Liverpool suffered serious damage when the Germans bombed the city in an attempt to interrupt convoys ferrying material from the United States. Still, the architecture here is incredible—it is second only to London for historically listed buildings and has more Georgian buildings than Bath. Since World War II Liverpool has been struggling, with little to cheer about in recent years except their soccer club and those fabulous Beatles. But corny as it may sound, the humor of the people and the large university population keep Liverpool from becoming just another industrial casualty.

COMING AND GOING
Lime Street Station (Lime St., tel. 0345/484–950) sends trains to Manchester (£6.10–£8.70 day return depending on time of travel) and London's Euston (£36 off-peak return, £45 on Fridays). The **bus station** (Norton St., tel. 0990/808–080) serves most destinations, including London (4 hrs, £20.50) and Manchester (1 hr, £5.50).

WHERE TO SLEEP
The new youth hostel near Albert Dock may, or may not, be operational for 1998—check with the Merseyside Welcome Centre (*see* Worth Seeing, *below*). If you arrive late, your best bet is the row of reasonable B&Bs on Lord Nelson Street near the train station, although you should expect to spend at least £17 for a bed. The rowdy **Embassie Youth Hostel** (1 Falkner Sq., tel. 0151/707–1089; £9.50 per person) is cheap but *very* noisy. From Lime Street Station, turn left on Lime Street/Renshaw Street, veer left on Leece/Hardman/Myrtle streets, cross over Hope Street, turn right at the stoplights and right again at Falkner Square. The **YWCA** (1 Rodney St., at Mt. Pleasant, tel. 0151/709–7791) has beds for £11 per person, and men can often stay in the summer.

FOOD
The Indian and Middle Eastern restaurants on Renshaw Street and the Chinese eateries in Chinatown (along Nelson St.) are your best bets for affordable meals. For whole-food groceries and take-out items, try **Holland & Barrett Health Food Store** (17 Whitechapel, tel. 0151/236–8911). The intimate **Largo Bistro** (20 Colquitt St., at Seel St., tel. 0151/707–2030) serves huge dishes (from £2.25–£3.15) all day before transforming itself into a small venue for live music Wednesday–Saturday. There's also great-value food in the **Everyman Bistro** (9 Hope St., tel. 0151/708–9545; closed Sun.), including lots of veggie options, for under £5. Down at Albert Dock, a range of cafés, snack bars, and restaurants sell their stuff, some with outdoor seating overlooking the dock. **Est Est Est** (Unit 6, Edward Pavilion, tel. 0151/708–6969) is the top budget choice in the Albert Dock complex, a lively spot for lunch. The restaurant makes good use of the old warehouse brickwork, though tables are a bit cramped. Still, the Italian menu is strong, the service is brisk, the atmosphere bubbling, and the coffee good.

WORTH SEEING
The Merseyside Welcome Centre (Clayton Sq. Shopping Centre, tel. 0151/708–8838; open Mon.–Sat. 9:30–5:30, Sun. 10–5), near the train station, and **The Atlantic Pavilion** (tel. 0151/708–8838; open daily 10–5:30), along **Albert Dock** near the museums, both sell maps that cover every conceivable Beatles sight. The cheesy **Beatles Story** (Britania Vaults, Albert Dock, tel. 0151/709–1963; admission £5.45) doesn't tell you much you didn't already know, via cardboard cutouts and re-creations of haunts like the Cavern Club. Art exhibitions at the **Tate Gallery** (Albert Dock, tel. 0151/709–0507; admission free) instead are more improving, though it won't reopen until mid-1998. Also spare time for the **Merseyside Maritime Museum,** the **H.M. Customs and Excise Museum,** and the **Museum of Liverpool Life** (all at Albert Dock, tel. 0151/207–0001; admission to all three £3), which between them reveal the history of the city seen through the lenses of trade, social life, culture, and political revolt.

AFTER DARK
Nightlife in Liverpool is a big deal. During the school year, call the University of Liverpool's **Student Entertainment Office** (tel. 0151/794–4143) or stop by the university on Mount Pleasant to hear about the latest student goings-on; the student union bulletin board also posts information. Those looking for some nonplasticized Beatles trivia may want to find the cozy, friendly **Ye Cracke** (Rice St., tel. 0151/709–4171) on a skinny street off to the west of Hope Street; John Lennon hung out here before and during his Beatles days. However, best pub by far in the city is the **Philharmonic** (36 Hope St., tel. 0151/709–1163), a Victorian-tiled extravaganza, with comfortable barrooms and ornate, over-the-top rest rooms. For a totally different scene, check out **Baa Bar** (43–45 Fleet St., tel. 0151/708–0610), a pre-clubbing hotspot. **Garlands** (8–10 Eberle St., off Dale St., tel. 0151/236–3307; admission £3–£4) hosts a gay-friendly crowd (both men and women). **Cream/Nation** (Wolstenholme Sq., tel. 0151/709–1693; cover £8–£12), open Friday and Saturday, is one of England's top-rated clubs.

PEAK DISTRICT NATIONAL PARK

The Peak District, a hiker's paradise of rolling hills, brooding moors, and limestone cliffs, is England's most popular and accessible national park—all only one hour from Manchester. You won't find any "peaks"—the highest point is only 2,100 ft. You will, however, find more than 4,000 mi of beautiful walking trails. The northern portion is known as the **Dark Peak,** an area of rugged moors and looming escarpments. To the south, **White Peak** is a bucolic region of rolling hills, crumbling stone walls, and tiny villages sheltered in swales and valleys. To get a look at the difficulty and length of the hikes, buy maps and guides at **tourist offices** in the following villages: Bakewell (tel. 01629/813–227), Castleton (tel. 01433/620–679), Edale (tel. 01433/670–207), and Fairholmes (tel. 01433/650–953). The **Pennine Way,** all 256 mi of it, starts in Edale and offers amazing views along largely uninhabited territory. There are 17 hostels and numerous B&Bs along the trail between Edale and the trail's end in Kirk Yetholm, Scotland.

Besides wilderness, the Peak District is also full of charming villages. You can buy self-guided tours (20p) of many such block-long outposts at local information centers. Among them, **Bakewell** is an appealing village on the banks of the River Wye and the best spot from which to explore the White Peak area of the park (many hiking trails begin here). Nearby, **Chatsworth House** (tel. 01246/582–204; admission £5.90; closed Nov.–Mar.), home to the duke and duchess of Devonshire, has a remarkable collection of paintings plus some spectacular gardens; ask Bakewell tourist center which bus to take on any given day to Edensor village and walk the remaining 15 minutes on the marked path to Chatsworth. **Castleton** and the nearby village of **Edale** are both excellent places from which to explore the northern Peaks. Castleton is dominated by magnificent **Peveril Castle** (tel. 01433/620–613; admission £1.60), founded in 1066 by one of William the Conqueror's knights. However, it's best known for its various limestone caverns, notably **Speedwell Cavern** (Winnats Pass, Castleton, tel. 01433/620–512; admission £5), where motorized boats take tourists through claustrophobic water-filled caves, and nearby **Treak Cliff Caverns** (tel. 01433/620–571; admission £4.50) which sport crystals, veins of the local Blue John stone, and an amazing array of stalactites.

COMING AND GOING

Surrounded as it is by major cities, the Peak District is very accessible, especially by bus. The major entry towns to the Peaks are Bakewell and Matlock in the east, Ashbourne in the south, Buxton (on the London–Manchester train line) in the west, and Glossop in the north. The comprehensive *Peak District Bus and Train Timetables* (60p, available from all local tourist offices) is indispensable—if there's a route you can't figure out, then calling National Rail Enquiries (tel. 0345/484–950) is the answer. The most direct route into (and through) the Peaks is the **Trent Trans Peak** Bus TP (tel. 01298/23098), which runs from Manchester through the Peaks (Buxton, Bakewell, Matlock, and other villages) to Nottingham.

WHERE TO SLEEP

There are 19 YHA/HI hostels in the Peaks; many are on major walking trails and are easier to reach on foot than by public transportation. Almost every hostel charges £7–£10 for members 18 and older and £5–£7 for members under 18. Among the Peaks' hostels, the following are some of the best: super-quiet **Bakewell** (Fly Hill, tel. 01629/812–313; open Apr.–Oct., Mon.–Sat.; Nov.–Mar., weekends only); **Castleton** (Castleton Hall, tel. 01433/620–235), wonderfully located at the base of Peveril Castle; **Edale** (Rowland Cote, Nether Booth, tel. 01433/670–302); and **Matlock** (40 Bank Rd., tel. 01629/582–983). If you haven't booked ahead at a hostel, you can usually find a room at one of the area's plentiful B&Bs, where prices start at around £15 per person.

LINCOLN

Lincoln is fraught with history—medieval monuments dominate the narrow lanes tumbling down Steep Hill to the River Witham, and everywhere are reminders of the Romans and the Danes, former inhabitants of this site. As you approach Lincoln by train, the first feature visible over the mounds of rusting scrap metal is imposing **Lincoln Cathedral** (Exchequer Gate, tel. 01522/544–544; £2.50 donation requested) high atop Steep Hill. The massive, triple-tower Gothic structure is one of the most impressive in Europe. An earthquake in 1185 destroyed most of the original Norman building, but the 13th-century restoration is nothing to sneeze at. Stop by the cheeky 15-inch gargoyle perched on a pillar in the rear of the cathedral—no one, not even the priests, claims to know its origin. The sight of William the Conqueror's impenetrable **Lincoln Castle** (Castle Hill, tel. 01522/511–068; admission £2) next to the gargantuan cathedral served the purpose of informing ancient serfs just who was boss. West of the castle lies the **Lawn** (tel. 01522/560–306), a former lunatic asylum that now offers a 5,000-sq-ft greenhouse filled with tropical plants, an archaeological display, and a shopping center. Lincoln's **tourist office** (9 Castle Hill, behind the castle and cathedral, tel. 01522/529–828) has informative pamphlets on the town.

COMING AND GOING

London's King's Cross Station sends trains (2 hrs, £32) regularly to Lincoln's **Central Station** (St. Mary's St., tel. 0345/484–950). Directly across the street is Lincoln's **bus station** (St. Mary's St., tel. 01522/534–444).

WHERE TO SLEEP AND EAT

Many B&Bs line West Parade, Carholme, and Yarborough roads. The location of **Bradford Guest House** (67 Monks Rd., tel. 01522/523–947; singles £16, doubles £30–£35) can't be beat—it's an easy 10-minute trek from the stations and a short (but steep) walk to the cathedral and castle. Neither the hearty breakfast nor the gracious managers will disappoint. **Lincoln YHA** (77 South Park, tel. 01522/522–076; beds £8.50, (£5.70 under 18) is right in the middle of town. Unfortunately, it's closed most Sundays in spring and fall. To reach it from the train station, turn right out of the main entrance, then right again over Pelham Bridge; after the first roundabout turn right at South Park (not South Park Avenue).

Enormously popular **Brown's Pie Shop** (33 Steep Hill, tel. 01522/527–330) has sweets and meat- or veggie-filled pies for £2–£8. The **Wig and Mitre** (29 Steep Hill, tel. 01522/535–190) is a locally renowned pub/café/restaurant that stays open until 11 PM, offering an extremely wide range of food from breakfast to full evening meals. The grooviest pub in town is **Cornhill Vaults** (The Cornhill Exchange, tel. 01522/535–113), a Roman wine cellar that has been converted into an underground pub decorated with freakish caricatures of regular patrons.

YORK

York's capricious medieval streets, teeming with tea shops and tourists, ensure that you will lose your way and find something delightful: a hidden courtyard, a tranquil shrine, or a perfect pub. York's richly layered history is manifest in its magnificent architecture, from its ancient Roman foundations and Norman city walls, to its towering Gothic Minster. York has several first-rate museums, but its many handsome buildings and narrow, winding "snickleways" are historic treasures in their own right. On a busy day, it may seem that York has a million visitors and only about 40 residents, but as heavily beaten paths go, York ranks with the best in Britain. Even if schlepping from one museum to another bores you, the pleasure of drinking a pint in a perfectly preserved 17th-century pub makes a visit to York worthwhile.

BASICS

The **York Visitor and Conference Bureau** (6 Rougier St., tel. 01904/620–557; open Mon.–Sat. 9–6, Sun. 10–4; Nov.–Mar., closed Sun.) will exchange money for a flat £2.50 fee and book bus tickets. There are also perpetually crowded visitor information desks run by the tour company **Guide Friday** (tel. 01904/621–756) at the train station and at the **De Grey Rooms** (Exhibition Sq.). **American Express** (6 Stonegate, tel. 01904/670–030; open weekdays 9–5:30, Wed. from 9:30, Sat. 9–5; also Apr.–Oct., Sun. 10:30–4:30) works its magic in the center of town.

COMING AND GOING

Trains run from **York Central Station** (tel. 0345/484–950), just outside the city walls, to London's King's Cross about twice an hour (2 hrs, £40 off-peak return, £51–£59 standard return). Buses converge on Rougier Street, between the train station and Lendal Bridge; buy tickets directly from the bus driver. Call **National Express** (tel. 0990/808–080) for information; they send three buses daily to London (4½ hrs, £25.50 return).

WHERE TO SLEEP

A B&B bonanza lines Bootham and its side streets just north of the city walls. If you don't book ahead, you may end up looking farther out in The Mount area, along Scarcroft and Southlands roads. **Abbey Guest House** (14 Earlsborough Terr., Marygate, tel. 01904/627–782; £17 per person) is a pretty, no-smoking, terraced house just a 10-minute walk from the town center, overlooking the river. Another good B&B is **Queen Anne's Guest House** (24 Queen Anne's Rd., off Bootham, tel. 01904/629–389; £13–£17 per person), a 10-minute walk from the Minster. For a particularly grand splurge, consider **The Judge's Lodging** (9 Lendal, tel. 01904/638–733), easily the prettiest hotel in York. Past the elegant gates and charming front yard, you mount an imposing staircase to enter a Georgian town house. The main salon is a cozy cocoon of Queen Mum pastels, overstuffed chairs, and gilded mirrors. Upstairs, the decor continues in the same note; one room is even called the Queen Mother, and another grand suite, the Prince Albert (who actually stayed here) is a special treat. Doubles run about £90 to £135. At the other end of the price scale, on the camping front, **Poplar Farm Caravan Park** (Acaster Malbis, tel. 01904/706–548), near the River Ouse, has 30 sites. It costs £8 for two people and a tent, and is closed November–March. Take **Sykes** (01904/774–231) Bus 192 to Acaster Malbis from Skeldergate Bridge in central York.

HOSTELS • The **York YHA Hostel** (Water End, tel. 01904/653–147), an easy 20-minute walk from the city center, is one of England's best, although it's not cheap (beds £13.85, £10.30 under 18). The charmless **Youth Hotel** (11–13 Bishophill Senior, tel. 01904/625–904) has the atmosphere of a Dickensian orphanage, but it's cheap: dorm beds start at £9, and doubles are £24.

FOOD

Tucked behind an excellent bookstore, the **Blake Head Vegetarian Café** (104 Mickelgate, tel. 01904/623–767; closed Sun.) is a paradise for health-conscious eaters. Serious salads run £3.50–£5. At the opposite end of Stonegate from the Minster, **Betty's** (6–8 St. Helen's Sq., tel. 01904/659—142) has been a York institution since 1912, known for its teas, served with mouth-watering cakes. It can be pricey, but make a meal of it by grabbing a table on the upper floor, next to the ceiling-to-floor picture windows. Budget pizzas (£4.95) and pasta are served at the friendly **La Piazza** (45 Goodramgate, tel. 01904/642–641).

WORTH SEEING

Sightseeing in the morning or late afternoon is the surest way to avoid crowds. The *York Out 'n' About Chequebook* (£1), available at tourist offices and some museums, has discount coupons most useful for two or more people. The best way to explore is to buy a good map, walk the 2-mi circuit of the walls and gates, and then storm the old city. Be prepared to get lost in the labyrinth of twisting lanes that change names at nearly every intersection.

Crumbling **Clifford's Tower** is all that remains of York Castle and has an often macabre history. The original tower was wooden and was the site of a massacre of 150 Jews in 1190, during which the tower was burned to the ground. The walkway along the tower walls affords splendid views of the city. *Tower St., tel. 01904/646–940. Admission £1.80. Open Apr.–Sept., daily 10–6; shorter hrs off season.*

One of York's most picturesque streets, **The Shambles** once served as butchers' row, replete with open sewers. Today, its leaning homes and cobblestone streets brim with buskers, peddlers, and shoppers. Shops on the street are open Monday–Saturday 9–5. To get here from the Minster, follow Low Petergate down Colliergate.

Austere, imposing, and glorious, **York Minster** is the largest medieval cathedral in northern Europe. The exterior, crowned by Gothic spires and supported by amazing flying buttresses, makes the Minster famous, but the wealth of stained glass in the interior makes it wondrous. Don't miss the 15th-century **Great East Window,** the world's largest expanse of medieval stained glass. You can compare the constructions of Roman, Norman, and medieval engineers in the **foundations** (admission £1.80), underneath the Minster. The **central tower** (admission £2) offers tip-top views of York for those who don't mind the 200-plus stairs. The **crypt** (admission 60p) shows skeleton-faced devils, a Madonna without a head, and the shrine of St. William of York. *Duncombe Place, tel. 01904/624–426. Admission to Minster free, but £2 donation requested. Open daily 7–5 (during summer 7 AM–8:30 AM).*

The **National Railway Museum** (Leeman Rd., tel. 01904/621–261; admission £4.50) traces 200 years of train history. The **York City Art Gallery** (Exhibition Sq., tel. 01904/551–861; admission free) houses a collection of paintings from the 14th to 18th centuries. The **Yorkshire Museum** (Museum St., tel. 01904/629–745; admission £3) contains local archaeological artifacts and 10 acres of botanical gardens.

AFTER DARK

Allegedly the most haunted city in Europe, York offers a variety of guided ghost walks. **Haunted Walk** (tel. 01904/421–737; tours £3) will give you a gruesome account of local lore. The **Original Ghost Walk** (tel. 01759/373–090; tours £3.50) features master thespian Ray Alexander's atmospheric and amusing narrative. Ghost tours are spookiest in fall and winter. York's oldest pub, **Ye Olde Starre Inn** (40 Stonegate, tel. 01904/623–063), opened in 1644 and still rates high with locals. With outdoor tables along the River Ouse, **King's Arms** (Kings Staith, tel. 01904/659–435) gets packed with crowds during the summer.

NEAR YORK

CASTLE HOWARD

Castle Howard, well known to PBS junkies as the setting of *Brideshead Revisited* and *The Buccaneers,* is Yorkshire's best example of sheer opulence. Built as a hideaway for the third earl of Carlisle over a 60-year span beginning in 1699, this spectacular estate was designed by Sir John Vanbrugh, author of some bawdy morality plays, as his first architectural project. Without question he drew better plans than plots. A baroque-era extravaganza, the house is complete with massive dome, sculpted figures, a plethora of Palladian pilasters, and any number of obscenely gorgeous rooms (still housing the Howard family, once bearers of the Carlisle title). Better, the house is set in a true 18th-century fantasyland, studded with marble temples, pyramids, a spectacular fountain of Atlas, a lake, and formal rose gardens. Believe it or not, this magical destination can be done as a day trip from London—catch the 8 AM super-express train from King's Cross to York, get one of the tour buses (Yorktour, tel. 1904/641737; Guide Friday, tel. 1904/640896; call to confirm their daily schedules) to arrive at the house at noon, then do the trip in reverse around 4 PM, arriving back in London around 7 PM. *Coneysthorpe, tel. 01653/648333, 15 mi from York. From York's train station, if you have time, take Yorkshire Coastliner Bus 840 or 842 toward Pickering/Whitby (2 daily, £3.50 day return); otherwise opt for one of the daily tour bus excursions (see* tour guides *in* Basics, *above). Admission £7. Open mid-Mar.–Oct., daily 11–4:30.*

NORTH YORK MOORS NATIONAL PARK

About 25 mi north of York, the North York Moors contain some of the most varied and dramatic landscape in England. Throughout the park are wind-worn plateaus cut by steep gorges, sloping valleys carved from stone by ancient lakes, ruins of castles and abbeys, and lots of hilly moors—an experienced walker's paradise. The less avid trekker may find the inevitable rain, fog, mist, and bogs a distinct drawback. *Waymark Walk* pamphlets (30p each) cover more than 40 trails that crisscross the park. The **Cleveland Way,** Britain's second-longest footpath, meanders for 110 mi in a loop along the outskirts, but there are good walks from nearly every village within the park.

Pickering, right on the A169 (the main north–south highway through the moors) is a good base for exploring the park. Pickering's **tourist office** (Eastgate parking lot, tel. 01751/473–791) has a heap of information on park walks. The dramatic cliffs above coastal **Whitby** offer an amazing backdrop to the town's narrow cobblestone streets. Sitting on a tall headland above Whitby's beach, **Whitby Abbey** (admission £1.80) has a majestic silhouette. The stone three-tier choir and the north transept survive, brooding over the lively harbor and town. **St. Mary's Church,** a humble structure made frightening by the tilting gravestones in front, shares the cliff top.

COMING AND GOING • Transportation from York to the North York Moors is fast and frequent, and cheaper by bus than train. Pickering and Whitby are the best launchpads for trips into the moors, since bus connections to these towns are particularly good. The bus carrier **Yorkshire Coastliner** (tel. 01653/692–556) runs from York to Pickering every hour; three or four a day continue to Whitby. The free *Moors Connection* bus schedule, available at Whitby's **tourist office** (Langborne Rd., tel. 01947/602–674) and most other local tourist offices, is essential.

WHERE TO SLEEP • **Pickering** has several cheap sleeps: **Bennett Guest House** (4 Westgate, tel. 01751/476–776; £14 per person) and **White Lodge** (54 Eastgate, tel. 01751/473–897; £17 per person) are among the best. In **Whitby,** B&Bs line Hudson Street and Normanby Terrace; most cost £15–£20 per person and are within a 10-minute walk of the beach. Several campgrounds lie just outside town. **Whitby Holiday Park** (Saltwick Bay, tel. 01947/602–664) is on the Cleveland Way, about a mile south of Whitby near Whitby Abbey. **The Lansbury Guest House** (29 Hudson St., tel. 01947/604–821), a charming Victorian with a fireplace in the lounge, costs £15 per person. Next to Whitby Abbey at the top of 199 steps, the **Whitby YHA** (East Cliff, tel. 01947/602–878; beds £6.95, £4.75 under 18) offers incredible views of the abbey and the town, although it's only open Fridays and Saturdays in winter.

LAKE DISTRICT

The Lake District National Park contains remarkably varied features. Scafell Pike, England's highest peak at 3,210 ft, and other nearby mountains are steep and craggy enough to make for challenging hikes, and the views of the valleys, fells, and 100-plus lakes certainly capture the romantic imagination. Perhaps that's why the area's best-known writers and critics—from Wordsworth and Coleridge to Beatrix Potter—are famous for their celebrations of nature. The area is divided into the heavily visited villages around **Lake Windermere** and **Coniston Water** in the south and the less-explored areas to the north (around **Keswick**). **Lancaster** and **Kendal** in the south and **Carlisle** in the north are the major points of entry to the Lake District. From here, it's easy to reach **Windermere,** a scenic but heavily touristed outpost, or one of a dozen smaller villages that serve as trailheads for a variety of hikes.

The larger tourist offices stock heaps of useful information, including the *A–Z Visitor's Map of the Lake District* (£3.90). If you're camping, get *The Caravan and Tent Guide* (£1.50). Paul Buttle's *The 12 Best Walks in the Lake District* is a good buy at £2. *Where to Stay in South Lakeland, Where to Stay in Eden,* and *Keswick on Derwentwater and the Northern Lakes* (£1 each) list each town's B&Bs. There are about 30 (and the number is growing) youth hostels scattered about—the Southern Lakes are particularly well supplied. Reservations are always a good idea in summer and fall. In winter and spring, you'll be limited by sparse public transportation, closed tourist offices and hostels, and, of course, wet weather.

COMING AND GOING

Trains from London's Euston Station (£49 off-peak return) and Manchester (£17.40–£21.50 return) arrive daily at **Windermere.** Trains also join Windermere with Kendal and Oxenholme; from the latter you can rejoin the mainline InterCity network. Once you reach these towns, it's best to use buses. Local buses converge about 3 mi north of Windermere in **Ambleside,** making this a good spot to base yourself. An **Explorer Pass** (£5.20 for 1 day, £13 for 4 days) buys a day travel on all local lines and is a good deal if you're going to more than two towns. You can buy the pass on any bus. **Stagecoach Cumberland** (tel. 01946/63222 for information) runs extensive routes throughout the region. Bus 555 runs from **Carlisle** to Ambleside and Windermere four times daily between 9 AM and 4 PM. Bus 555 also runs from **Lancaster** to Ambleside and Windermere every hour.

SOUTHERN LAKES

WINDERMERE AND BOWNESS

Commercialized Windermere and nearby Bowness are best used as stopovers to grab some food and equipment before moving on. The Bowness-on-Windermere **tourist office** (Glebe Rd., off A5074, tel. 015394/42895) has so much information that you'll definitely need the assistance of the enthusiastic people behind the counter. The 3-mi round-trip climb from Windermere's tourist office to **Orrest Head** is the simplest hike in the area and offers a fine panorama of the lake and villages along the shore.

WHERE TO SLEEP • In Windermere, the **Windermere Hostel (YHA)** (Bridge Ln., tel. 015394/43543; closed Nov.–Dec.) has gorgeous views, but the 60p bus ride (Bus W1 or 555 to Troutbeck Bridge) and the ¾-mi uphill walk are a bummer. For more of a splurge, consider the B&Bs that line Beech, Birch, Oak, and Broad streets, off Crescent Road. **The Haven** (Birch St., tel. 015394/44017) is near the train station and charges £15 per person. Nearby Bowness doesn't have a hostel, only a slew of B&Bs on Lake Road (the main road from Windermere).

AMBLESIDE

Equally busy but less schlocky than Windermere, Ambleside makes an excellent base for touring the Southern Lakes. Most regional buses make connections in Ambleside, and cheap accommodations abound; get the lowdown from the town's helpful **tourist office** (Church St., tel. 015394/32582). Ambleside has some of the region's best—and most difficult—hikes. The best are highlighted in the Footprint Guides' *Walks Around Ambleside* (£3), available at the tourist office. The 6½-mi circular walk from Ambleside north to **Loughrigg Tarn** goes right by Wordsworth's home in **Rydal.** Near Loughrigg Fell, you'll get a breathtaking 360° view of Lake Windermere, Rydal Water, and Ambleside. **The Langdale Pikes,** offering some incredible views from their high ridges, are accessed from Ambleside via steep paths through rocky crags. The loop stretches almost 5 mi and ascends nearly 2,400 ft. The three- to five-hour hike begins at the New Dungeon Ghyll Hotel, located on the B5343 (take Bus 516 from Ambleside to Dungeon Ghyll).

WHERE TO SLEEP • Some cheap B&Bs surround Ambleside's tourist office at Church Street and Compston Road. Try **Linda's B&B** (Compston Rd., tel. 015394/32999), where singles and doubles are £11 (breakfast is £2–£3 extra). From the bus stop, go right on Kelsick Road and turn right on Compston Road. At **Ambleside YWCA** (Old Lake Rd., tel. 015394/32340; closed mid-Nov.–mid-Feb.) beds aren't any cheaper than at a regular B&B, but the dining room is classy and the rooms are clean. Singles, doubles, and dorm beds go for £13.50 per person. In the heart of town, **3 Cambridge Villas** (Church St., tel. 015394/32307) has bright, charming rooms from around £14.50 per person, English or vegetarian breakfast included.

GRASMERE

A ghost town in the winter, Grasmere metamorphoses into a hive of buses and duty-bound poetry students in the summer. This is Wordsworthland, the poet's home during his most creative periods, and let's just say it was a lot more remote and untrammeled when he actually lived here. Join the crowds on a pilgrimage to **Dove Cottage and Wordsworth Museum** (tel. 015394/35544; admission £4.25), Wordsworth's homestead during his "lyric years" (1799–1808). **Rydal Mount** (tel. 015394/33002; admission £3), between Grasmere and Ambleside on the A591, was Wordsworth's home from 1813 through 1850. Take Bus 555 from Grasmere and get off at the first stop. Unless you're staying at the **Thorney How Hostel** (tel. 015394/35591), with its lovely log fire and sticky toffee pudding (sigh), Grasmere makes a better day trip than overnight stay. Pick up information on hiking in the area from the **Grasmere National Park Information Centre** (Redbank Rd., tel. 015394/35245).

NORTHERN LAKES

The northern Lake District's largest town is **Keswick,** which also has the biggest and most convenient **information center** (Market Sq., tel. 017687/72645; open year-round). For park-specific information, check out the **Keswick National Park Visitor Centre** (31 Lake Rd., tel. 017687/72803; open Mar.–Nov., daily 10–4). If you don't like climbing, the long but easy hike from Keswick to **Seatoller** (9 mi) along Derwentwater's east shore will reward you with a view of Borrowdale Valley, one of the most beautiful spots in the Lake District. Dreamlike settings of green glens, rivulets, and pastures make this a pleasant, peaceful stroll. The cheaper B&Bs in Keswick cluster around the corner of Southey and Blencathra streets. The mellow **Keswick YHA** (Station Rd., tel. 017687/72484) is your best bet, as long as you book ahead.

The highest peaks in England, **Scafell Pike, Scafell, Great Gable,** and **Green Gable,** are accessed best from **Seathwaite** (a 1½-mi walk from the town of Seatoller, accessible on Bus 79). This largely volcanic area west of the major villages has a stark character that brings out serious hikers. **Ullswater** is the area's largest lake north of Lake Windermere and fortunately has yet to be destroyed by the crowds. Bus 108 connects the area's major villages. For directions to waterfalls in the area, pick up the handy *Walks to Lakeland Waterfalls* (60p).

DURHAM

Despite its long mining history and its location midway between the industrial cities of Darlington and Newcastle, Durham remains one of England's most arrestingly beautiful cities. Situated on a promontory created by an almost circular loop in the River Wear, the city has an idyllic quality. **Durham Cathedral** (Palace Green, tel. 0191/386–4266) is probably the finest piece of Norman architecture in Britain. The detailed, impressive exterior influenced many subsequent Gothic structures, and the cathedral's choir features the earliest use of rib vaulting in Western architecture—admission to the cathedral is free but a £2 donation is suggested; entrance to the tower and treasury costs £2 each. **Durham Castle** (Palace Green, tel. 0191/374–3800; admission £2.50), on the town's highest hill, served as the palace of Durham's prince-bishops for 800 years until 1832, when it became Durham University's University College. The **tourist office** (Market Pl., tel. 0191/384–3720) distributes free city maps.

COMING AND GOING

Durham's **train station** (North Rd., tel. 0345/484–950) is on the main north–south line, three hours north of London (£59 off-peak return) and two hours south of Edinburgh (£27.50–£38 return). Durham's **bus station** (North Rd., tel. 0191/384–3323) sends frequent buses to London (£25.50 return) and Edinburgh (£19 return).

WHERE TO SLEEP

Most of the town's cheap B&Bs are on Claypath/Gilesgate and its side streets, a 10-minute walk northeast of the city center. At **Mr. and Mrs. Himmins** (14 Gilesgate, tel. 0191/384–6485), you'll get a spacious double and a four-poster bed for £16 per person. **Mrs. M. C. Frisby** (1 Mayorswell Close, Gilesgate, tel. 0191/386–1987; £16 per person) runs a homey B&B within easy striking distance of the town center. The nearest year-round hostel is in Newcastle (*see below*); however, another possibility is staying at the colleges that rent rooms from July to September. The tourist office can supply you with a free list of the colleges, which you must call yourself. If you can, try to score a spot in **University College** (tel. 0191/374–3863; £18.50 per person), which is actually housed within the medieval stones of Durham Castle. Another option is **Grange Camping & Caravan** (Meadow Ln., Carrville, tel. 0191/384–4778), a quiet campground 2 mi from town via Bus 220 from Durham's North Road Station (ask to be dropped at the Grange Pub). Sites are £3.50 per person.

FOOD

You'll have no trouble finding a bakery on one of Durham's cobblestone streets; the town's pies, puddings, and pastries are excellent. Enjoy a variety of meat and vegetarian entrées at the centrally located **Vennel's Courtyard Cafe** (Saddler's Yard, tel. 0191/386–0484). For first-rate pizza and pasta and happy hour specials for £3 try **Pizzeria Venezia** (4 Framwellgate Bridge, tel. 0191/384–6777; closed Sun.). Of the pubs, the **Brewer & Firkin** (58 Saddler St., tel. 0191/386–4134) features live music two or three nights a week (jazz and blues a specialty), as well as weekend disco nights.

NEAR DURHAM

NEWCASTLE-UPON-TYNE

There's nothing subtle about Newcastle, a lively industrial city of angry rock bands and in-your-face fashion statements. One resident proudly declared Newcastle the loudest city in northern England: the buses shriek and rattle, conversation in any pub resembles a shouting match, and the nonstop noise of crowds on the streets could wake the dead. Newcastle's hard-working, hard-playing residents enjoy a varied nightlife, and the campuses of the University of Northumbria and the University of Newcastle keep the city young—you can't miss the youthful atmosphere if you take a walk along the River Tyne. As the last big city before the Scottish border, Newcastle serves as the major transportation hub for the region and is a frequent stop on the Edinburgh–London rail line.

In an effort to win Welsh loyalty, Edward I is said to have presented his newborn son in 1284 as the "first native-born Prince of Wales who speaks no English." The tradition of the monarch's firstborn son becoming the Prince of Wales continues to this day.

COMING AND GOING • Trains to Durham, York, and London depart every 30 minutes from Newcastle's **Central Station** (Neville St., tel. 0345/484–950), and trains to Edinburgh depart every hour. **National Express** (tel. 0990/808–080) runs to London and Edinburgh every two hours and to York twice a day.

WHERE TO SLEEP • Defiantly sporting a '60s theme with square burnt-orange sofas and Formica tables is **Newcastle YHA** (107 Jesmond Rd., tel. 0191/281–2570; beds £7.70, £5.15 under 18; closed Dec.–Jan.), conveniently located near the Jesmond metro stop.

AFTER DARK • Every second building in the city center is a pub, or so it seems. The **Crown Posada** (31 The Side, tel. 0191/232–1269) is a classic Newcastle pub, near the quayside, which wears its 19th-century decor well—Pre-Raphaelite stained glass, coffered ceiling, and Victorian lamps. Underground and indie folk will feel at home at the near-legendary **Riverside** (57–59 Melbourne St., tel. 0191/261–4386).

HADRIAN'S WALL

A 173-mi-long fortification spanning England at its narrowest point, Hadrian's Wall is Britain's most important Roman monument. The emperor Hadrian began construction of the wall in AD 122 to help the Roman legions control the various warring tribes in the area. The ravages of time—as well as wars between the English and Scots over the territory—have left the wall a shambles. Nevertheless, sizable ruins of forts and long stretches of a reduced wall give a sense of its original magnitude. In its heyday, the wall stood 15 ft high and was 9 ft thick, and a ditch 30 ft wide and 10 ft deep lay in front of it.

WALES

Most visitors flock to England or Scotland when traveling in Britain, ignoring Wales, one of the best off-the-beaten-track destinations in Europe. There's lots of undiscovered territory here, although the coastal resorts cram in crowds of British tourists, and busy **Mt. Snowdon** is being loved to death. If you want

THE LANGUAGE OF CYMRU

The Welsh revere their native language, and although everyone speaks English, signs in Cymru (Wales) are in both languages. You'll hear Welsh spoken on Radio Cymru and on television programs on Channel 4 Wales. Unfortunately for English speakers, the words with their disproportionate number of consonants look impossible to pronounce. Of all Welsh constructions—from "dydd" to "bws" to "fawr"—the most unfamiliar sound may be the "ll." To pronounce this, put your tongue on the ridge behind your upper teeth (as if pronouncing the "l" in hello), and let out a sharp burst of air. If this comes easy to you, look into a career in speech therapy.

more breathing room, pick your way among the sheep droppings at **Brecon Beacons National Park** or enjoy the seascapes along the **Pembrokeshire Coast Path.** In a country that still reveres Owain Glyndŷr, a revolutionary who fought to wrest Wales from English control, it's no surprise to find a strong sense of patriotism bordering on Anglophobia, especially in the north. South Wales, which has been industrialized and increasingly anglicized for the past few centuries, maintains Welsh traditions less staunchly, but no matter where you go in Wales, you'll find friendly people—and bilingual signs to remind you that this is *not* England.

BritRail basically covers only the top and bottom edges of Wales. From London, trains depart Paddington Station for Cardiff in the south and from Euston Station to Bangor, Aberystwyth, and Holyhead in the north. Once you're in Wales, regional railways take over. The **Freedom of Wales Rover** ticket (£57–£64 depending on season; £37.65–£42.25 with Young Person's Railcard), available at BritRail travel centers, gives you a week of unlimited rail travel. **National Express buses** (tel. 0990/808–080) depart from London's Victoria Coach Station for several points in Wales. Once you arrive in Wales, you must hook up with one of the many regional bus services.

CARDIFF

Despite its Welsh street signs, Cardiff feels like just another British town filled with modern buildings and souvenir shops. It was an important coal-shipping port during the Industrial Revolution and has been the Welsh capital since 1955, but the city lacks the full urban bustle of Britain's other capital cities. Stop for a day or two to tour the castle, museums, and watering holes, but move on if you're at all interested in seeing the "true" Wales.

BASICS
Cardiff Central Station conveniently houses the local **Tourist Information Centre** (tel. 01222/227–281; open Mon.–Sat. 9–6:30, Sun. 10–4). Near Cardiff Castle is **American Express** (3 Queen St., tel. 01222/668–858).

COMING AND GOING
Hourly trains run to the well-located **Cardiff Central Station** (tel. 0345/484–950 for all train inquiries, tel. 01222/228–000 station) from London's Paddington Station (2 hrs, £43.50 return). The **bus station** (Wood St., tel. 01222/344–751) next door sends frequent buses to London's Victoria Coach Station (3 hrs, £21.50, but £26 on Fridays). To see the sights just beyond the city center (like the Museum of Welsh Life at St. Fagans), take one of the orange **Cardiff Buses (Bws Caerdydd)** from the stop outside the train station. Rides are 35p–£1.30, depending on the distance and time of travel.

WHERE TO SLEEP AND EAT

The best place to find an affordable B&B is along Cathedral Road; take Bus 32 or 62 from the train station. **Amberley Guest House** (22 Plasturton Gardens, tel. 01222/374–936; singles £15, doubles £28) is cheap and quiet, and some of the spacious rooms overlook a small park. The bargain rates make up for the dreary rooms at **Rosanna House** (175 Cathedral Rd., tel. 01222/229–780; singles from £12.50, doubles £25). **Cardiff YHA** (Wedal Rd., tel. 01222/462–303; closed Dec.) is the only cheap sleep in town but requires a 30-minute bus ride. Beds are £9.40 (£6.30 under 18). Take Bus 78, 80, 80B, or 82 from the train station. On the food front, many small eateries and stands line St. Mary and High streets. The delicious **Celtic Cauldron** (47–49 Castle Arcade, tel. 01222/387–185) offers traditional Welsh lunches for around £5. A friendly family from Campobasso runs **Luciano's Zio Pin** (74 Albany Rd., tel. 01222/485–673), one of Cardiff's more affordable sit-down restaurants. Dim lighting and checkered tablecloths complement individual pizzas (from £3.80), pasta dishes (£5 and up), and specialties like garlic chicken (£7.20).

WORTH SEEING

Cardiff's main sights are within 20 minutes or so of one another in the city center. In the mid-19th century, the third marquess of Bute, faced with a drafty old castle on her hands and a pile of pounds in her pocket, went all out to renovate **Cardiff Castle** (Castle St., tel. 01222/878–100; admission to grounds £2.40, £4.80 with guided tour of castle). William Burges, an architect obsessed with whimsical flights of fancy, redesigned the castle's interior. The huge **National Museum of Wales** (Cathays Park, tel. 01222/397–951; admission £3.25; closed Mon.) has paintings and sculpture by Rodin, Cézanne, Rembrandt, and Welsh artists Richard Wilson and Augustus John. For a quiet, relaxing afternoon, take Bus 78, 80, 80B, or 82 northeast to **Roath Park,** with a riotous rose garden, a conservatory (70p), and a lake where you can rent rowing skiffs and paddleboats.

AFTER DARK

Pick up the free *Buzz* magazine at the tourist office for the latest entertainment information. **Philharmonic** (76 St. Mary St., tel. 01222/230–678) overflows with students drinking, dancing, and chatting each other up. **Four Bars In Sandy's** (Castle St., tel. 01222/374–962) is Cardiff's busiest watering hole. For something uniquely Welsh, try **Clwb Ifor Bach** (Womanby St., tel. 01222/232–199), which plays a mix of Celtic, acid jazz, trance, and techno. Classic and artsy films play at **Chapter Arts Centre** (Market Rd., tel. 01222/399–666).

NEAR CARDIFF

CAERPHILLY

Caerphilly is Wales's largest fortress and possibly its most impressive, with 30 acres of grounds that lord over the tiny village of Caerphilly and the surrounding patchwork of farms. The original 13th-century Norman fortress was largely destroyed over the years; some walls have toppled while others lean haphazardly, adding to the eerie stillness of the place. Exhibits inside trace the history of this 700-year-old ruin. Of all the sights near Cardiff, Caerphilly ranks among the very best. To reach the castle, catch a bus or train from Cardiff Central Station; the trip takes 30 minutes and costs £1.90–£2.30 return. *Tel. 01222/883–143. Admission £2.20.*

BRECON BEACONS NATIONAL PARK

If you want to see some of Wales's most awe-inspiring scenery—sheep-flecked hillsides, gently sloping valleys, and rural villages—you shouldn't miss Brecon Beacons National Park, even if you're only in Wales for a couple of days. Arm yourself with trail maps at park centers and flip through the innumerable choices of hikes and long walks. The **Waterfall Region** (Ystradffelte), accessible from the town of Merthyr Tydfil, has a number of spectacular falls, including the park's tallest, 90-ft-high **Nant Lech.**

The town of **Brecon** is the largest in the park and makes an excellent place to stock up on groceries, rent equipment, and clue into the region's best walks. The town itself is also worth a short visit to stroll the riverside promenade. Pick up information about the town at **Brecon Tourist Information Centre** (Cattle Market Car Park, tel. 01874/623–156). The park's main visitor center, **Brecon Beacons Visitor Centre**

(Libanus, tel. 01874/623–366; open daily year-round), is in the middle of nowhere. One of the park's best paths follows the **Monmouthshire and Brecon Canal** from Brecon through Abergavenny to Ponty-pool, 37 mi away. Many people cover the easy 20-mi Abergavenny–Brecon leg over two days, staying at a B&B or campsite near Llangynidir.

COMING AND GOING

You can reach Abergavenny, on the eastern edge of the park, from both London and Cardiff. You can-not go directly to the town of Brecon without hopping on a bus at some point, usually from Cardiff. The other option is to catch an hourly train from Cardiff to Merthyr Tydfil (50 mins, £3.40 single) and then hop on Bus 43 to Brecon from the station. **Stagecoach Red & White** (tel. 01633/266–336) is a major provider of bus services throughout the park.

WHERE TO SLEEP

In Brecon, look for B&Bs in the Llan Faes area, along Orchard, Church, and St. David's streets. **Tir Bach Guest House** (13 Alexandra Rd., tel. 01874/624–551; singles £15–£16, doubles £28–£30), 1 block from the tourist office, is better than average, with antiques-decorated rooms and mountain views. **Ty'n-y-Caeau YHA** (tel. 01874/665–270; beds £7.70, £5.15 under 18; closed Dec.–mid-Feb.) is near the Mon-mouthshire and Brecon Canal, 2 mi from Brecon. Counting sheep will take on new meaning at the rural **Llwyn-y-Celyn YHA** (tel. 01874/624–261; beds £6.95, £4.75 under 18; closed Dec.–mid-Feb.), 10 mi from Brecon. Hop on the bus toward Merthyr Tydfil and ask the bus driver to let you off at the hostel.

Within the park, campsites (£2.50–£5 per person) are everywhere. Although it's against the rules to camp randomly in the park, some people do it anyway. Most hostels are more convenient to hiking trails than to towns. **Capel-y-Ffin YHA** (tel. 01873/890–650) is north of Abergavenny near Hay-on-Wye. **Ystradfellte YHA** places you near the waterfall region near Merthyr Tydfil (tel. 01639/720–301; closed weekdays Dec.–Mar., and some Thurs. year-round; call ahead). **Llanddeusant YHA** (tel. 01550/740–619) is the park's westernmost hostel.

PEMBROKESHIRE COAST

This dramatic corner of Wales, bounded by the 168-mi **Pembrokeshire Coast Path,** encompasses both wild coast and popular resort towns cluttered with ice-cream huts. There's still a lot of untouched coastal wilderness here, especially in the "North Pembs," where smaller communities keep their rural roots. The free *Coast to Coast* newspaper, available at tourist information centers and newsstands, is crammed with useful information on the region.

The affable coastal town of **Tenby** makes for a good base. Women aren't allowed in the Cistercian monastery on nearby **Caldey Island,** but the rest of the island is a neat place to explore, with cliffs, sandy beaches, and an old priory church. Tenby's busy **tourist office** (The Croft, tel. 01834/842–402) is open late by British standards—until 9 PM in July and August (5:30 PM the rest of the year).

A tiny town named after the patron saint of Wales, **St. David's** is the home of the oldest and most beau-tiful **cathedral** in Wales. Behind the cathedral are the 14th-century ruins of **Bishop's Palace.** Nearby is **St. Non's Well,** where St. David was born. The town is convenient to stretches of the Pembrokeshire Coast Path; youth hostels and towns are all within a day's walk of each other, making it easy to plan a hiking tour of the area. The **tourist office** (City Hall, tel. 01437/720–392; open daily 9:30–5:30), also a national park center, can help map out your next hike.

COMING AND GOING

The regional railway swooshes from Cardiff through Tenby (£14 return) on its way across the southern coast, but most of this area is best seen by bus. Buses 358 and 359 run hourly from Haverfordwest to Tenby. Bus 411 heads north from Haverfordwest to St. David's. The tourist offices carry schedules of all the region's buses.

WHERE TO SLEEP

TENBY • There are plenty of affordable B&Bs around the train station. **Boulston Cottage** (29 Trafalgar Rd., tel. 01834/843–289) offers rooms for £13–£15 per person. **Hereford House** (Sutton St., tel. 01834/843–223) has basic rooms for £14–£15. The nearest campsite is **Meadow Farm** (Northcliffe, tel. 01834/844–829; £3 per person), a 15-minute walk uphill from the tourist office. On the coast at Skrin-kle Haven, about 20 minutes south of town along the Tenby–Pembroke bus line, is **Manorbier YHA** (tel. 01834/871–803), with beds for £8.50 (£5.70 under 18).

ST. DAVID'S • St. David's YHA (tel. 01437/720–345; beds £6.25, £4.25 under 18) is a 2½-mi walk from town toward the sea. Anyone in town can point you to this happy hostel; you may even be offered a ride if you're lucky.

ABERYSTWYTH

Home to one of the first universities in Wales, Aberystwyth is small and casual, mingling the permissive ambience of a Victorian seafront town with the rarefied air of higher learning. Geographically, Aberystwyth is the bridge between northern and southern Wales. The seafront heats up in the evening as pubs draw rowdy crowds of students, and the gay scene in town is the most open in Wales. The free **National Library of Wales** (Penglais Hill, tel. 01970/623–816) houses many of Wales's important documents and rare books. Since 1896 the **Electric Cliff Railway** (Cliff Terr., tel. 01970/617–642; £2 return) has been hauling visitors to the top of Constitution Hill to the free camera obscura observatory. The **tourist office** (Terrace Rd., tel. 01970/612–125) is a five-minute walk from the train station.

COMING AND GOING

From London's Euston Station, trains travel to Aberystwyth via Shrewsbury (5 hrs, from £35 return). Bus 701 makes two runs a day from Cardiff (4 hrs, £9.50). Local lines connect the town with the rest of Wales.

WHERE TO SLEEP

Walk down South Road to New Promenade and the side streets behind the castle and look for the unobtrusive B&B signs. On a pleasant street 1 block from the train station, **Llwynhaf** (26 Cambrian St., tel. 01970/624–826) offers pastel-colored rooms for £15 per person. The bright, friendly **Sunnymead Guest House** (34 Bridge St., tel. 01970/617–273) asks £15 per person. **Borth YHA** (Morlais, Cardiganshire, tel. 01970/871–498) is one train stop away from Aberystwyth, with beds for £8.50 (£5.70 under 18). The nearest campground is **Aberystwyth Holiday Village** (tel. 01970/624–211; sites £7.50–£9 per twosome), about a ¼ mi outside town.

FOOD

Try Pier Street, or shop for produce and baked goods on Chalybeate Street, east of Great Darkgate Street. Whole-food lovers should come to eclectic **Y Graig** (34 Pier St., tel. 01970/611–606) to feast on prawns, cockles, mussels, and local mackerel with organic brown rice, all for about £4. **Eastgate Fish Restaurant** (36A Eastgate St., tel. 01970/625–321) is a busy fish and chips joint where all things fried cost well under £5.

AFTER DARK

The favorite student watering hole is the fun and lively **Glengower Hotel** on Marine Terrace, with jostling crowds and loud music. **The Coopers Arms** (Northgate, tel. 01970/624–050) has a distinctly Welsh clientele. **Rummers Wine Bar** (tel. 01970/625–177), the last building before Trefechan Bridge, is usually packed with students and locals chatting over pints. On summer weekends, come here for live music and no cover.

SNOWDONIA NATIONAL PARK

Snowdonia National Park is one of the most beloved patches of land in Wales. The southern section near Dolgellau features glowering **Cader Idris**; craggy **Mt. Snowdon** is in the northwest; the northeast near **Betws-y-Coed** has fir and larch forests; sail-flecked **Llyn Tegid** (Bala Lake) defines the east; and castles and seascapes run along the coast south of Porthmadog. Unfortunately, everyone and his or her dog vacations here, making Snowdonia something of a Welsh Yellowstone Park. This isn't always a drawback; facilities include wheelchair-accessible trails in **Dolgellau** and descriptive signs in braille at the **Garth Falls Walk** at the west end of Betws-y-Coed. Most people, though, head straight to Mt. Snowdon, which has six main paths to the summit. Park offices carry 40p leaflets describing each of them.

The most popular path, the 6-mi round-trip **Llanberis Path,** is often crowded with families. It starts in Llanberis and parallels the railway up to Pen-y-Pass. **Miners' Track** is another easy trail crossing the northeast section of Llyn Llydaw Lake, where King Arthur supposedly threw his sword, Excalibur, after he was mortally wounded while slaying the giant Rhita Fawr at the summit of Mt. Snowdon. The **Snowdon Ranger Path** is the shortest trail, but it does have a few steep spots. **Pitt's Head Track** meets **Rhyd**

Ddu Path from the south, forming one faint trail that climbs up the face of Llechog and offers some spectacular views. Only experienced hikers armed with the right gear and weather information should think about hiking the **Horseshoe Path.** If you want to try it, talk to a park ranger first and get briefed on (and maybe dissuaded from) this 14-mi endeavor with its 2,000-ft drops. Before any excursion, contact **Mountaincall Snowdonia** (tel. 0891/500–449) for weather conditions.

In an attempt to reduce erosion and to keep hikers safe, Mt. Snowdon's bridleways operate a voluntary ban on bicycles daily 10–5. The roads are always fair game, though. The best cycling route is the 22-mi haul up **Llanberis Pass** to Pen-y-Gwrd. In Betws-y-Coed, **Beics Betws** (behind the post office off the A5, tel. 01690/710–766) rents bikes for £14 per day.

VISITOR INFORMATION

There are five National Park Visitor Centres in Snowdonia. The main administrative office is the **Snowdonia National Park Office** near Porthmadog (Penrhyndeudraeth, tel. 01766/770–274). The visitor centers are in **Aberdyfi, Betws-y-Coed, Dolgellau, Harlech,** and **Llanberis** (*see below*).

COMING AND GOING

BritRail (tel. 0345/484–950) has two lines running into Snowdonia National Park, the Conwy Valley Line to Betws-y-Coed and Blaenau Ffestiniog in the north, and the Cambrian Coast Line from Machynlleth in the south, through Aberdyfi and along the northern shore of Cardigan Bay. Betws-y-Coed is a good base from which to explore the eastern park. **Buses** will be your best bet, however, especially for getting to Llanberis. Companies that serve the Snowdonia area include **Crosville** (Bangor, tel. 01248/351–879) and **Williams Deiniolen** (Llanberis, tel. 01286/870–484).

GETTING AROUND

BY GREAT LITTLE TRAIN • Snowdonia is famous for the many narrow-gauge railways that putter through the park, providing a scenic and convenient way of getting around. The **Ffestiniog Railway** (01766/512–340) is a 13½-mi track linking Blaenau Ffestiniog with Porthmadog (where you can catch a southbound BritRail train along the coast). The trains wind their way for an hour through some of Snowdonia's most spectacular scenery. The full trip costs £12.40. Other little trains include **Bala Lake Railway** (tel. 01678/540–666), which chugs along the southeast side of narrow Bala Lake; **Llanberis Lake Railway** (tel. 01286/870–549), which covers part of the northwest perimeter of Llyn Padarn; and **Talyllyn Railway** (tel. 01654/710–472), connecting the coastal town of Tywyn with the village of Abergynolwyn. Most trains cost about £4–£12, but you can buy a **Wanderer Ticket** for unlimited travel on Wales's Little Trains (except the Snowdon Mountain Railway). The ticket is available at the railways and costs £26 for four days in eight, £34 for eight days in a 15-day period.

The other handy train is the **Snowdon Mountain Railway** (tel. 01286/870–223), which carries passengers up the mountain. During summer, trains are scheduled to run every half hour 8:30–5, though weather and the number of passengers dictate when and how often the trains actually depart. The round-trip fare is £14.

BY SHERPA • Sherpas are inexpensive buses that run regularly around Mt. Snowdon June–late October, schlepping walkers to the trailheads of all six paths to the summit and stopping on request at any point in the park. Easy pickup points are at Bangor, Betws-y-Coed, Caernarfon, Llandudno Junction, Llanrwst, and Porthmadog. For more information, contact the National Park Office (tel. 01766/770–274), pick up a **Snowdon Sherpa** leaflet at a tourist information center, or check the free *Snowdonia* newspaper.

WHERE TO SLEEP

Plenty of youth hostels dot the park; ask at the tourist office for the closest ones. If you're looking for atmosphere, try **Snowdon Ranger YHA** (Rhyd Ddu, Caernarfonshire, tel. 01268/650–391; beds £8.50, £5.70 under 18), next to Lake Cwellyn with its own beach and scenic location. **Capel Curig YHA** (Plas Curig, Betws-y-Coed, tel. 01690/720–225; beds £8.50, £5.70 under 18) is 5 miles from Pen-y-Pass, but the Snowdon Sherpa stops at the front door. Book ahead for **King's YHA** (King's, Penmaenpool, tel. 01341/422–392; beds £6.95, £4.75 under 18), 4 mi from Dolgellau in a wooded, peaceful valley. Crosville Cymru's Bus 28 from Dolgellau to Tywyn passes within a mile—get off a mi west of Penmaenpool.

LLANBERIS

At the foot of Mt. Snowdon, Llanberis is well rehearsed in the art of dealing with Snowdonia fun seekers. The town is small, but there's nothing particularly provincial about it. Its two lakes, Padarn and Peris, and its position as the lower terminus of the Snowdon Mountain Railway, attract hordes of hikers. Come here to stock up on food and outdoor gear. The town is only 7 mi from Caernarfon and 9 mi from Bangor and is easily accessible by bus from these cities. As Llanberis is the town closest to Mt. Snowdon, it's not surprising that its **Tourist Information Centre** (41A High St., tel. 01286/870–765) has more comprehensive information about Snowdonia than any other.

WHERE TO SLEEP AND EAT
You'll be in the thick of things at **Llanberis YHA** (Llwyn Celyn, Caernarfonshire, tel. 01286/870–280; beds £7.70, £5.15 under 18), only a short distance from the Llanberis Path up Mt. Snowdon. In town, a friendly proprietor and simple inviting rooms make **Beech Bank Guest House** (High St., tel. 01286/870–414; £13.50 per person) one of the better options in the High Street cluster of B&Bs. **Pete's Eats** (40 High St., tel. 01286/870–358) is a smoky, funky place filled with hikers and bikers. Pore over hiking maps while slurping a bowl of soup (£1.40) or munching on the daily vegan special (£4.30).

BALA

As you walk down the town trail—a walking trail devised by city fathers to cover the significant and historic aspects of the town—you can see the old Bala of knitters, whisky distillers, printers, and cattle drivers. At times, the 20th century seems like a veneer; the Henblas Garage on High Street, for instance, has its old-fashioned gas pumps on the sidewalk (you can fill 'er up from the parking lane). Today, Bala is best known for its 4-mi-long lake, the largest natural lake in Wales. It's a mecca for those into canoeing, sailing, and windsurfing. Powerboats are forbidden, making it one of the best sailing lakes in Britain.

The friendly staff at Bala's **Tourist Information Centre** (High St., tel. 01678/521–021) will tell you whatever you need to know. The foyer is papered with flyers advertising everything from music to laundry services to church hours. Other than by car, your only way into this town at the eastern edge of Snowdonia is by Bus 94, which runs back and forth between the west coast and the English border, starting at Barmouth with stops at Dolgellau, Bala, Llangollen, and Wrexham.

WHERE TO SLEEP
Abraham Lincoln's great-grandmother Sarah once lived at **Fferm Fron-Goch** (tel. 01678/520–483; £17–£19 per person), about 3 mi northeast of Bala toward Fron-Goch. Now a young Welsh family inhabits this 17th-century farmhouse and B&B, which lies tucked away in beautiful countryside. Very friendly, very Welsh Mrs. Jones runs **Traian Bed and Breakfast** (95 Tegid St., tel. 01678/520–059; £13–£15 per person), a short walk from Bala Lake.

BETWS-Y-COED

The Lledr, Llugwy, and Conwy rivers converge at Betws-y-Coed, tumbling over rocky outcroppings and through the tall trees of the Gwydyr forest. The town has been a popular inland resort since the last century; busloads of senior citizens still come here for day trips, and the shops and restaurants are predictably upscale. Still, several major walking trails and bike routes cross the area. The busy **Tourist Information Centre** (Royal Oak Stables, tel. 01690/710–426) can steer you in the right direction.

WHERE TO SLEEP AND EAT
Lodging is expensive here; your best bet is to hop on the train to the Pont-y-Pant stop and bed down amid trees, fields, and sheep at **Lledr Valley YHA** (tel. 01690/750–202; beds £7.70, £5.15 under 18; closed Nov.–Feb.). Ask the BritRail ticket taker to let you off at Pont-y-Pant, then walk left up the lane, cross the bridge, turn left on the main road, and walk about 15 minutes. The town's restaurants and cafés tend to be pricey. **Dil's Diner** (next to the train station, tel. 01690/710–346) fries up a mean veggie burger (£1.90) and serves a full English breakfast (until noon) for £4. **Siop a Popty Tondderwen** (Holyhead Rd.) has produce, groceries, and a bakery.

LLYN PENINSULA

The peaceful and untrammeled Llŷn Peninsula juts out from North Wales toward the Irish Sea, separating the Caernarfon and Cardigan bays. Fields and farms dominate the landscape inland, while sandy beaches attract the cognoscenti to the coast. Some 55 mi of the peninsula's coastline have been designated "Heritage Coast," meaning they won't be built up any further.

PORTHMADOG

The center of action on the peninsula, Porthmadog served as the primary port for the North Wales slate trade until the Cambrian Railway arrived in 1867. But the town definitely doesn't have an abandoned feel: in summer, its main street is clogged with cars and tour buses heading to nearby **Black Rock Golden Sands** beach. The city serves as the crossroads of the peninsula and Snowdonia, making it a good place to base yourself. By far the easiest way to get to the town is to come from the south via the Aberystwyth rail line; buses also head here from all over northern Wales. The Porthmadog **Tourist Information Centre** (High St., tel. 01766/512–981) is a 10-minute walk from the train station. **Mrs. Jones** (57 East Ave., off Cambria Terr., tel. 01766/513–087) runs a B&B minutes from the train station with rooms for £14 per person. Campers should head for the sites at **Tyddyn Llwyn Farm & Caravan Park** (tel. 01766/512–205; sites £6), 2 mi from Porthmadog and near the beach.

PORTMEIRION

This delightful Italianate village is the jewel in the Cambrian coast's crown and inspires an enthusiasm for architecture even in the most unlikely visitors. Popular with fans of the '60s cult TV series *The Prisoner*, which was filmed here (the annual *Prisoner* convention is held in August), and devotees of Portmeirion pottery, there are plenty willing to pay the £3.40 admission charge to the village. This place is curious, but charming, and well worth a visit. A local bus runs from Porthmadog, otherwise it's a 25-minute walk from Portmeirion train station.

CAERNARFON

The Welsh weren't too crazy about Edward I, who took the throne in 1272, so he built some fortresses to protect his men from the people of Cymru. **Caernarfon Castle** (tel. 01286/677–617; admission £3.80) is one of the results. The battlements offer great views of the Menai Strait, while the displays inside clue you in to castle lore. Down Pool Street is the **Segontium Roman Fort** (Beddgelert Rd., tel. 01286/675–625), where a Roman governor lodged garrisons of soldiers when he invaded Britain in AD 383. Today you can see artifacts on display in the museum. The **Tourist Information Centre** (Castle St., tel. 01286/672–232) sells maps for nearby Snowdonia, including a macabre little guide about airplane crashes in the park. The only way into town is via bus; No. 701 comes from the south, with stops in Porthmadog, while a zillion others head east from Bangor.

Most B&Bs are clustered on Church Street and along North and St. David's Roads. Two minutes from the castle is **Tegfan** (4 Church St., tel. 01286/673–703; £13–£16 per person), a B&B with thick carpets and British bric-a-brac. **Rhiw** (Constantine Rd., tel. 01286/673–612) is a cozy place with rooms for £13.50 per person. **Snowdonia Guest House** (Dinas Dinelle, tel. 01286/831–198; doubles are £28) is close to the beach. The nearest campground is **Llanberis Road Caravan Park** (tel. 01286/673–196; open Mar.–Oct.), with sites for £5.90–£7.30 for a small tent; it's a 20-minute walk from town. There are several decent restaurants along Hole-in-the-Wall Street. **Pigs and Stones Bistro** (Hole-in-the-Wall St., tel. 01286/671–152; closed Sun. and Mon.) dishes out generous helpings of their specialty, Welsh lamb (£9.85). **Just Pancakes** (34 High St., at Palace St., tel. 01286/672–552) serves up scrumptious savory pancakes like tuna and sweetcorn in spicy mushroom sauce.

SCOTLAND

With more than 130 windswept islands surrounding a mainland where even the lowlands are covered with hills, Scotland is a country that defies easy definition. The one thing that Scots can agree on, however, is that Scotland is nothing like England. The two were completely separate countries until 1603, when James VI of Scotland, son of Mary, Queen of Scots, succeeded the childless Elizabeth I of England and became King James I of England and Scotland. The tenuous bonds between the two countries broke down during the English Civil War, and after the execution of Charles I in 1649, Scotland was conquered by Oliver Cromwell. When the monarchy was restored, the two countries were once again ruled by the same king, but remained separate kingdoms. During England's Glorious Revolution of 1688, William of Orange took the crown with the understanding that he would allow the Scottish parliament to take more control of affairs than did his predecessor. Nevertheless, friction increased between the two countries, each of which maintained its own parliament, until the controversial Act of Union in 1707, in which the two parliaments were merged into one, and the United Kingdom of Great Britain was born.

The Scots are proud of their heritage, and not all are happy to be lumped under the generic heading of Great Britain or the United Kingdom. Although tourist boards may try to exploit the image of the tartan-clad bagpiper for every pence it's worth, to the Scots the image represents a once-outlawed way of life. Ironically, many of the things considered typically Scottish—tartan dress, misty glens, bagpipes, shady lochs, tightly knit clans—are remnants of a northern Highland way of life, which suffered a devastating blow after the British troops defeated the clan armies at Culloden in 1746. The English government out-lawed tartans, bagpipes, and clan armies—stripping clan chiefs of their power, and in many cases, land. Yet these images fashionably resurfaced in the 19th century after the threat of Scottish rebellion was long dead, when several royals, notably George IV and Queen Victoria, fell in love with the country. These images have proliferated and charmed tourists ever since, in the form of woolen shops, kilted bagpipers busking alongside touristed lochs, and tartan-covered shortbread tins.

Geographically, Scotland is divided into three primary regions. The **Uplands** along the southern border are much like North-ern England, with rolling moors interrupted by rivers; the fer-tile **Lowlands** are spread around the Firths of Forth and Clyde; and the rugged **Highlands,** covering much of the west and north of the country, are punctuated with mountains and deep lochs—a drop-dead panorama that in itself justifies a trip to Scotland. But whether you spend a few days in the cities of **Edinburgh** and **Glasgow,** only an hour apart and together home to one third of the population, or several months explor-ing the diverse landscape of the north coast and islands, Scot-land will not disappoint. Though the often harsh weather and sparse public transportation in some parts of Scotland can be challenging, the breathtaking scenery, rare landscapes and wildlife, and helpful locals reward every effort.

In recent years, Scottish nationalists have been enjoying increasing popularity, and though full independence remains a distant dream it is no longer unimaginable—a new Edinburgh Parliament is, in fact, now in the works.

EDINBURGH

In contrast to much of the rest of Scotland, Edinburgh is often thought of as a white-collar city of well-to-do citizens with lilting accents and a stunning history of intellectual and artistic enlightenment—which is all true. Other cities may go in and out of vogue, but Edinburgh will always command a place among the beautiful tourist meccas of the world. The city's foremost feature is **Edinburgh Castle,** loom-ing authoritatively from the crags of an ancient volcano; getting lost in the streets, *wynds* (winding, nar-row streets and walkways), and *closes* (medieval alleyways that connect the twisting streets) that spill from its ramparts is one of the best ways to explore the city. On gloomy, misty days, several excellent free (or cheap) galleries and museums can provide shelter, while on balmy afternoons, the hills surrounding the city, notably Arthur's Seat and Calton Hill, offer beautiful views of the city and surrounding country-side, as well as a chance to escape the hordes in summer. Almost unbelievably, crowds double during Edinburgh's famous **International Festival,** held from mid-August through the first week of September.

BASICS

VISITOR INFORMATION
The **Edinburgh Information Centre,** above Waverley Train Station and shopping complex, changes money and charges £3 to book rooms. *3 Princes St., tel. 0131/557–1700. Open Mon.–Sat. 9–6 (Apr.– Oct., also Sun. 11–6).*

AMERICAN EXPRESS
139 Princes St., across from St. John's Church, tel. 0131/225–7881. Open weekdays 9–5:30 (Thurs. from 9:30), Sat. 9–4.

EDINBURGH

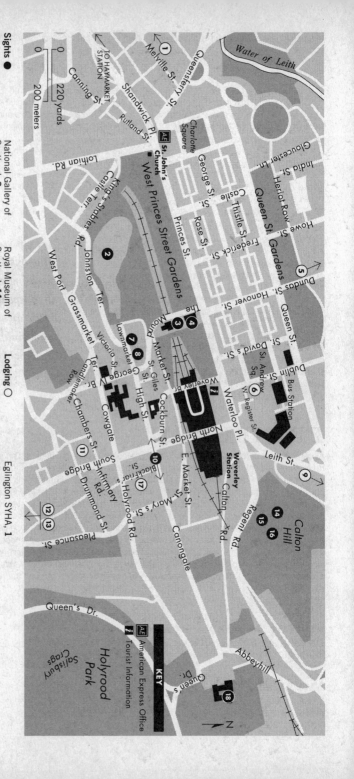

Sights ●

City Observatory, **14**
Edinburgh Castle, **2**
Gladstone's Land, **7**
Holyrood Palace, **18**
Lady Stair's
House, **8**

National Gallery of
Scotland, **3**
National
Monument, **16**
Nelson's
Monument, **15**
Royal Mile, **10**

Royal Museum of
Scotland, **11**
Royal Scottish
Academy, **4**

Lodging ○

Ardenlee Guest
House, **5**
Balmoral Guest
House, **9**
Crion Guest
House, **12**

Eglington SYHA, **1**
High Street
Hostel, **17**
Iolaire, **13**
Princes Street
Hostel, **6**

DISCOUNT TRAVEL AGENCIES

The **Edinburgh Travel Centre** has budget travel and student-discount information. *3 locations: 3 Bristo Sq., Edinburgh University, tel. 0131/668–2221; 196 Rose St., tel. 0131/226–2019; 92 South Clerk St., tel. 0131/667–9488. Open weekdays 9–5:30, Sat. 10–1:30.*

EMERGENCIES

The **Royal Infirmary of Edinburgh** is open 24 hours; you won't be charged for consultation for minor medical problems. *1 Lauriston Pl., tel. 0131/536–1000. Walk south on George IV Bridge to Lauriston.*

MAIL

You can receive poste restante mail at the main post office, relocated from its grand building at Waterloo Place to the more pedestrian **St. James Shopping Centre** at the far east end of Princes Street. *8/10 St. James Shopping Centre, EH1 3SR, tel. 0131/536–0478. Open weekdays 9–5:30, Sat. 9–6.*

COMING AND GOING

BY BUS

Long-distance coaches arrive at **St. Andrew Square** (tel. 0990/505–050), 2 blocks north of Princes Street next to the Royal Bank of Scotland. The bus is the cheapest way to reach Edinburgh from London, but the trip takes nine hours. The main carriers are **Scottish CityLink** (tel. 0131/332–2283) and **Caledonian Express** (tel. 0131/452–8777); both sell various discounts and passes, including the **Discount Coach Card** (£8), which offers a 30% discount on all fares.

For a truly gourmet haggis (tidbits of sheep's lungs, liver, and heart, seasoned with spices and onions and tucked into a sheep's stomach), head to Charles MacSween & Son (130 Bruntsfield Pl.). They also make a vegetarian version for the organ-shy.

BY TRAIN

Edinburgh's main rail hub, **Waverley Station,** lies at the east end of Princes Street. Trains to cities throughout Scotland and England, including London (5–6 hrs, £62 return), serve this busy hub. Trains from the smaller **Haymarket Station** (Haymarket Sq.), in the West End of Edinburgh, travel to points west, including Glasgow (50 mins, £13 return). For all train information, dial 01345/484–950.

GETTING AROUND

Edinburgh is a compact, walkable city. **Princes Street Gardens,** which runs east–west along the southern edge of Princes Street, roughly divides Edinburgh into two areas: the winding, nonsensical streets of **Old Town** to the south, and the orderly, Georgian **New Town** to the north. Buses to every part of the city run along **Princes Street.** Always ask whether you need to catch a bus on the "shop" side (north side) or "garden" side (south side). Maroon and white **LRT** (tel. 0131/555–6365) buses and green **SMT** (tel. 0131/558–1616) buses provide extensive service. Fares range from 45p to £1.10 for short rides. **One-day passes** are £2.20; **Ridecards,** good for one week, cost about £10. These and other passes are available at the **LRT office** on the corner of Waverley and Market streets.

WHERE TO SLEEP

Hostels are the cheapest choice in Edinburgh, although the many B&Bs and private houses provide a reasonable alternative; *always* book ahead. The **accommodations desk** in Waverley Station books rooms for £3. Edinburgh's SYHA hostels accept fax bookings from other hostels; ask for the "Book-A-Bed Ahead" service (70p). Telephone bookings can also be made no more than one week in advance between 5 PM and 10 PM. If you don't have a reservation, a good place to look is **Minto Street,** south of the east end of Princes Street; take Bus 3, 7, 8, 18, 31, 69, or 80 from the shop side of Princes Street. You can also try **Pilrig Street,** northeast of the city center; take Bus 7, 10, 11, 14, 16, 17, 22, 25, or 87 from the shop side of Princes Street.

UNDER £25 • Ardenlee Guest House. Run by David and Judy Dinse, this is a cozy, well situated home, just off Dundas Street. Breakfasts are good, and there are two family cats to keep you company. Expect to pay £26 per person. *9 Eyre Place, EH3 5ES., tel. 0131/556-2838. 8 rooms. Cash only.*

Crion Guest House. Newly renovated, family-run home about 1 mi from the train station. Doubles are £25 per person. Reserve at least two weeks in advance. *33 Minto St., tel. 0131/667–2708. Cash only.*

Iolaire. Quiet B&B on a residential street near a large park. Doubles £20, triples and quads £9 per person. *14 Argyle Pl., off Melville Dr., tel. 0131/667–9991. From Princes St. (garden side), take Bus 40, 41, or 41A.*

UNDER £35 • Balmoral Guest House. The proprietors pamper guests silly. Doubles from £34 including a substantial breakfast (with several vegetarian choices). Book ahead. *32 Pilrig St., tel. 0131/554–1857. Cash only.*

HOSTELS

Eglinton SYHA. Well-run hostel in the West End, near shops and pubs. Popular with large groups of devilish schoolchildren. Beds £10.75. *18 Eglinton Crescent, tel. 0131/337–1120. Bus 3, 4, 12, 13, 31, 33, or 44 from Princes St. (garden side) to Palmerston Pl. Kitchen, laundry. Cash only. Closed Dec.*

High Street Hostel. This friendly hostel is in the middle of the Royal Mile, just off High Street, and it's the perfect base for exploring pubs and clubs in Old Town. Beds start at £8.90, including linen. *8 Blackfriars, tel. 0131/557–3984. From Waverley Station, walk south on North Bridge Rd., turn left on High St., right on Blackfriars. Cash only.*

Princes Street Hostel. Close to the St. Andrew Square bus station, behind Burger King on Princes Street. The winding hallways and stairs make it seem like a modern castle. Squeaky dorm beds £8.50. *5 West Register St., tel. 0131/556–6894. Kitchen, laundry.*

CAMPING

Silverknowes Caravan Park. The lack of sheltered space means brutal winds may chill your bones or take your tent on an unexpected journey out to the North Sea. Sites £5.25–£6.60. *Marine Dr., tel. 0131/312–6874. Bus 8A or 14A from North Bridge. Closed Oct.–Mar. Cash only.*

FOOD

An inexpensive lunch at a pub or café usually runs £3–£5, and quite a few pubs in the **Grassmarket** area offer discount lunches for students. Dinner is always the most expensive meal, so sample Edinburgh's restaurants at lunch when prices are almost 50% what they are at night. Supermarkets and street grocers are an inexpensive alternative to eating out. The centrally located **Marks & Spencer** (54 Princes St., tel. 0131/225–2301) has a good food hall downstairs.

UNDER £5 • Café Byzantium. This huge place serves fresh, cheap, and delicious food in comfortable surroundings. Order the vegetarian buffet (£3.90) and get a plate piled high with rice and your choice of dishes like curry, spinach with cheese, and lentils. *9 Victoria St., between George IV Bridge Rd. and Grassmarket, tel. 0131/220–2241. Closed Sun. Cash only.*

The Cornerstone Café. Dine among the dead at this café, which once served as the catacombs for St. John's Church. Meals cost about £3. *Corner of Lothian Road and Princes St., under St. John's Church, tel. 0131/229–0212. Cash only.*

Henderson's. An excellent selection of cheap salads, hot dishes, and desserts is served cafeteria-style at this great dining option in New Town. Try lentil stew with potatoes (£2.60). Live folk or jazz every evening. *94 Hanover St., tel. 0131/225–2131. Closed Sun. Cash only.*

Suzy's Diner. Warm and folksy student hangout; legendary for its freshly baked brown bread. Cheap and filling vegetarian and vegan meals start at £3. *53 W. Nicolson St., tel. 0131/667–8673. Cash only.*

UNDER £10 • Chez Jules. This small and homey restaurant is like a French country kitchen. Entrées run £7–£10 and are worth every pound. You can also bring your own wine which makes the check at the end of the meal eminently reasonable. *2 locations: 1 Craig's Close, tel. 0131/225–7007; 61 Frederick St., tel. 0131/225–7983. Cash only.*

Indigo Yard. One of Edinburgh's more recent, and hippest, ventures with a good menu and an even better interior. An upstairs gallery provides good views of the action below while you tuck into your Thai fish cakes in spicy cucumber sauce, or just enjoy one of the fresh salads on offer. Brunch on Sunday is a particular joy. *7 Charlotte La., tel. 0131/220–5603. Open daily 8:30 PM–1 AM.*

Maison Hector. Very Now—at least, for a while—and often crowded with media types during the Edinburgh Festival, Maison Hector's is most worth visiting for Sunday brunch. The unusual decor of the men's rest rooms, alone, merits a detour. *47 Deanhaugh St., 0131/332–5328.*

UNDER £20 • (Fitz)Henry. Arty without being intimidating, (Fitz)Henry has recently received several awards, a tribute to a wonderfully eclectic menu. Dinner is around £22 for three courses, but worth every pound. Top off a meal with chocolate mousse with a saffron sauce. *19 Shore Pl., tel. 0131/555-6625. Closed Sun.*

WORTH SEEING

Edinburgh's foremost feature is its medieval castle, which broods authoritatively over the city from the crags of an ancient volcano. Many parts of **Old Town** date to the 16th century; the more orderly gridded streets of **New Town** offer a perfect example of what the Enlightenment did for urban planning.

EDINBURGH CASTLE

The castle has a few fine attractions inside, but the real reason to spend £5.50 is the mind-bending views—of Edinburgh and the entire Firth of Forth—from the castle's towering ramparts. Most of the battlements date to the 14th and 16th centuries, but the oldest building, **St. Margaret's Chapel,** dates to the 11th or 12th century (no one's sure which). The Scottish Regalia (the jeweled crown, scepter, and sword of Scotland) sparkle in the castle's **Crown Room.** *Top of the Royal Mile, tel. 0131/244–3101. Admission £5.50. Open daily 9:30–6; shorter hrs off season.*

ROYAL MILE

Divided into four sections (Castlehill, Lawnmarket, High Street, and Canongate) as it heads down the hill from the castle, the main street of Old Town stretches from Edinburgh Castle to Holyrood Palace. Pubs, shops, pubs, historic attractions, and pubs line its cobblestone length. Since so many 16th- to 18th-century city dwellers wanted to live as close to the castle's walls as possible, many five- and six-story buildings went up in this prime real-estate area; **Gladstone's Land** (tel. 0131/226–5856; admission £2.50) is a six-story tenement on Lawnmarket that reflects typical decor of a 17th-century merchant's house. **Lady Stair's House** (tel. 0131/529–4901; closed Sun.), another 17th-century building, now houses free exhibits on Scotland's literary greats—Sir Walter Scott, Robert Louis Stevenson, and Robert Burns among them. The 16th-century **Holyrood Palace** (tel. 0131/556–1096; admission £5), at the east end of the Royal Mile, is still used by the queen when she visits Edinburgh, so it's only accessible by guided tour.

CALTON HILL

The cylindrical tower, **Nelson's Monument** (admission £1), wasn't built so much to honor naval hero Admiral Nelson as to serve as a reminder to the sons of Edinburgh that they are to die for their country when duty requires it. The nearby **National Monument,** a half-completed Greco-Roman colonnade, wasn't left that way for aesthetic reasons: funding ran out and it was never finished. Also unfinished is the **City Observatory**; once built, there was no more money for a telescope. Despite its motley collection of monuments, the hill is worth climbing for its views of the city.

THE MOUND

Bisecting Princes Street Gardens, this walkway between the Old Town and New Town contains two of Edinburgh's best galleries. **The Royal Scottish Academy** (tel. 0131/225–6671; admission £1.50) features an annual exhibit of both established and amateur Scottish artists. The **National Gallery of Scotland** (tel. 0131/556–8921; admission free) sits right behind the academy and houses the national collection of Scottish art as well as works by Continental greats like Velásquez, El Greco, Rembrandt, Degas, Monet, and van Gogh. *Both open Mon.–Sat. 10–5, Sun. 2–5.*

ROYAL MUSEUM OF SCOTLAND

You can probably find something of interest at this museum, which has everything from stuffed animals and insects to Chinese art and a fantastic collection of telescopes. The museum makes a fine place to while away the time, especially since it's free. *Chambers St., tel. 0131/225–7534. Admission free. Open Mon.–Sat. 10–5, Sun. noon–5.*

AFTER DARK

Edinburgh has lots to do after the sun sets, from well-known pub crawls to the pas de deux of Europe's finest ballet companies. *The List* (£1.80), available at any newsstand, is indispensable for finding out what's going on. Old Town, especially High Street and the area around the University of Edinburgh, features a good selection of music clubs and theaters. New Town is best known for its Rose Street pubs.

A BRIEF HISTORY OF GOWF

Like most games that involve hitting a ball with a stick, golf evolved during the Middle Ages and found its way to Scotland, where it came to be known as both "gowf" and "goff." The first written reference to the sport appeared in 1457, when James II of Scotland decreed that both golf and soccer should be banned because they distracted his subjects from their archery practice. The world's first golfing clubs were the Honourable Company of Edinburgh Golfers (1744) and the Royal and Ancient of St. Andrews (1754). The first golf balls, called "featheries," were made of leather and stuffed with boiled feathers.

The huge annual **International Arts Festival** (tel. 0131/473–2000 to book tickets by phone, after Apr. 22) is usually held in the last three weeks of August. The **Fringe Festival** (tel. 0131/226–5257), held during the same three weeks, is a fantastically sprawling affair that just about takes over every cupboard space in the city, but for all its energy and verve it's increasingly less alternative than its older sibling.

PUBS AND CLUBS

The Black Bull (12 Grassmarket, tel. 0131/225–2236) is a groovy student hangout, with a late happy hour (midnight-1 AM), DJs every Friday and Saturday, and live music (mostly rock and folk) Sunday–Thursday. As you stumble along your Rose Street pub crawl, stop in at **Rose Street Brewery** (57 Rose St., tel. 0131/220–1227) for a home brew at the only spot in Edinburgh that makes its own beer. **Kitchen** (235 Cowgate, tel. 0131/225–5473) is a small and crowded, loud and smoky disco. If you feel like dancing, the grooves last until 3 AM, and there's no cover. There's a mesmerizing range of flavored vodkas to choose from at **Bar Kohl** (54 George IV Bridge, tel. 0131/225–6939) and a selection of brews to make your head spin at **The Malt Shovel** (11–15 Cockburn St., tel. 0131/220–1227), but the in place to be seen at the moment is **Po-Na-Na** (43b Frederick St., tel. 0131/226–2224), a souk bar featuring a tented ceiling and long queues.

NEAR EDINBURGH

ST. ANDREWS

According to legend, St. Andrews was founded in the 4th century by St. Regulus, who was shipwrecked here while toting the relics (a few bones and whatnot) of St. Andrew. Another version of the legend has these relics arriving around the 8th century when the Culdees, a strict Christian sect, founded a settlement here. Either way, St. Andrews emerged as the religious center of Scotland by the 12th century; the strong religious influence ultimately gave rise to **St. Andrews University,** the oldest university in Scotland, founded by Bishop Henry Wardlaw in 1412. But some visitors heed a call higher than academia—golf's holiest of holy shrines, **Old Course,** is here in St. Andrews. You must be a bona fide golfer to set a cleated foot on this sanctum sanctorum: you will need a current official handicap certificate and/or a letter of introduction from your home golf club, and reservations should be made up to a year in advance for summer play. These people are serious. Of course, if the ritual of golf makes you cringe, then St. Andrews is all about long rocky shores and the brooding ruins of a 13th-century castle.

Although **St. Andrews Cathedral** (at the end of North and South Sts.) was once a magnificent building, structural faults caused the 13th-century monument to collapse twice; it wasn't sturdy enough to withstand the wicked weather that blows in from the North Sea. Today, only the twin spires of the east and west ends remain, but they and the grounds are still impressive. Also still intact is **St. Rule's Tower** (admission £1.50), built between 1127 and 1244 to honor the founder of St. Andrews. The on-site museum helps visitors interpret the remains. Directly north of the cathedral stand the ruins of **St. Andrews Castle** (tel. 01334/477–196; admission £2), strategically situated upon a rocky cliff that is now home to hundreds of seagulls. Although St. Andrews isn't a big town, the folks at the **tourist office** (70 Market St., tel. 01334/472–021) have maps and will book you a room for free.

COMING AND GOING • From Edinburgh, **ScotRail** only goes as far as Leuchars (£8), about 8 mi north of town. From Leuchars, catch Bus 94, 95, or 96 (£1) to the St. Andrews bus station (City Rd., tel. 01334/474–0238). Or you can hop on **Fife Scottish** (tel. 01592/261–461) Bus X59 from Edinburgh (2 hrs, £7 return).

WHERE TO SLEEP AND EAT • The tourist office books rooms at B&Bs in the £12–£15 (per person) range. For a few pounds less, you can usually book into B&Bs outside the city center. The guest houses on **Murray Place** and **Murray Park** average a pricey £20–£25 for a single, but they're just off The Scores (the street that runs along the sea cliffs) and near the sights. Ten minutes from the town center on foot is **Mrs. Haston's B&B** (8 Nelson St., tel. 01334/473–227; £12 per person). **Pennington's Bunkhouse** (West Pitkierie, tel. 01333/310–768; beds £7.50), 11 mi from St. Andrews on the B9131 just outside of Anstruther, occupies a peaceful 13th-century farm. The friendly wardens will gladly pick you up from Anstruther, although Bus 61 from St. Andrews can drop you directly at the door.

The very popular **Kinness Fry Bar** (79 Bridge St., tel. 01334/473–802) serves fish and chips, some of the best pizza in town, and excellent kebabs. University students pull late-night study sessions at **All-Night Bakery** (4 Abbey St., tel. 01334/476–016), probably Scotland's only all-night anything. **The Victoria Café** (1 St. Mary's Pl., tel. 01334/476–964), on the upper floor of an old Victorian hotel, has good pub grub and all-day breakfasts for £4. If you're looking for a casual student pub, check out **Burt's Bar** (South St.).

GLASGOW

This sprawling industrial and technological center on the banks of the River Clyde is often dismissed as just another large city, but Glasgow has a vitality that makes Edinburgh seem stodgy by contrast. Home to two large universities, several good museums, beautiful parks, a thriving downtown area, and the country's best nightlife, Glasgow is truly representative of modern Scotland. The city was once considered the country's urban dumping ground, but extremely successful city planning in the last decade has brought many companies to town and rebuilt some of the more dilapidated areas. Highlights of any trip to Glasgow include one of the few medieval cathedrals to avoid destruction during the Reformation, a Victorian cemetery, and several buildings by the 19th-century architect Charles Rennie Mackintosh.

BASICS

A 10-minute walk from Central Station, the **Tourist Information Centre** (35 St. Vincent Pl., tel. 0141/204–4400; open June, Mon.–Sat. 9–7, Sun. 10–6; July–Sept. Mon.–Sat. 9–8, Sun. 10–6; shorter hrs off season) books rooms and sells maps and tickets for local events. Across from Central Station is **American Express** (115 Hope St., tel. 0141/221–4366; open weekdays 8:30–5:30, Sat. 9–noon). The **General Post Office** (St Vincent Street, G2, tel. 0141/204-3688; open weekdays 8:30–6, Sat. 9–1) will hold mail marked "poste restante." For a cheap flight or information on rail and ferry passes, stop by **Campus Travel** (11 George St., tel. 0141/553–1818).

COMING AND GOING

BY BUS • **Buchanan Bus Station** (N. Hanover and Killermont Sts., tel. 0141/332–7133), 2 blocks north of Queen Street Station, is the central depot for all destinations in Scotland and England. Express bus service to and from London (9 hrs) costs around £25 with a Discount Coach Card.

BY TRAIN • **Central Station,** between Hope and Union streets, handles southwest Scotland and England, with many direct trains to London (5 hrs, £55 return). **Queen Street Station,** at the corner of West George and Queen streets, serves all northern destinations. Both stations are in the center of town, only a few blocks from one another and connected Monday–Saturday by a frequent shuttle bus (50p). Both also have dozens of daily trains to Edinburgh (50 mins, £13 return). For rail information in Glasgow, dial 0141/204–2844.

GETTING AROUND

The free *Visitors' Transport Guide,* available at the tourist office, makes sense of Glasgow's complicated public transit system. So, too, does the **Strathclyde Transport Travel Centre** (St. Enoch Square, tel. 0141/226–4826). Most of Glasgow's bus routes are covered by orange-and-white buses, but some private companies use the same stops and charge about the same fares. Either way, most trips around the city cost about 65p. Glasgow's **Underground** (tel. 0141/226–4826; single fare 60p) connects the center with the suburbs south of the River Clyde but does not serve ScotRail depots.

WHERE TO SLEEP

You can book a B&B through the tourist office or at the small kiosk inside the Buchanan Bus Station. In a pinch, try **Alamo Guest House** (46 Gray St., G3 7SE, tel. 0141/339–2395; singles £18, doubles £20 per person), with a great location by Kelvingrove Park, the art gallery, and several good pubs. The **University of Strathclyde Campus Village** (Weaver St., tel. 0141/553–4148) almost always has a spartan dorm room to rent during summer.

HOSTELS • Glasgow Backpackers Hostel. In the University of Glasgow's Kelvin Lodge dorm, this hostel has spacious rooms, a large kitchen, two lounges, a super staff, and a kick-back atmosphere. Beds cost £9.50. *8 Park Circus, tel. 0141/332–5412. Take the Underground to St. George's Cross, walk south on St. George's Cross, turn right on Woodlands Rd., left on Lynedoch St., and continue to Park Circus Pl. (which becomes Park Circus). Open June–late Sept. Cash only.*

Glasgow SYHA. Fine if empty, a nightmare when large student groups arrive. Set in the lovely Kelvingrove Park—an excellent base for exploring Glasgow. Beds cost £11.95–£13.45. *7 Park Circus, G3 6BY, tel. 0141/332–3004. Follow directions to Glasgow Backpackers Hostel. Cash only.*

FOOD

Glasgow has the best variety of restaurants in Scotland, with everything from Caribbean joints to 1950s-style American diners. You can have a cheap and filling café or pub meal along **Byres Road** and the Hillhead area flanking the northern side of Glasgow University. **Bay Tree Café** (403 Great Western Rd., tel. 0141/334–5898) is a vegan workers' cooperative with a Middle Eastern slant on its dishes. The dark oak and red velvet chairs at **The Glasgow Tea Room** (38 Bath St., near Queen St. Station, tel. 0141/353–2361) create a comfortably wealthy feel, but the eats are cheap, especially the sandwiches (£1.60–£2.75). For those who love Latin food, **Chimmy Chungas** (499 Great Western Rd., near Kelvin Bridge Underground station, tel. 0141/334–0884) is an oasis in a desert of bland food. Before 7 PM you can get two dishes for £5. All around town there are numerous Indian eateries that are excellent value for the money.

WORTH SEEING

Glasgow is extremely committed to high art and low prices, something that's immediately apparent from the array of excellent and largely free museums. One of Glasgow's finest sights is the exquisitely preserved architecture of the Victorian West End. Walk about the crescents of the Kelvinbridge area (near the SYHA hostel) for the best examples.

GLASGOW CATHEDRAL • One of the few Scottish cathedrals to escape destruction during the Reformation, the small, dark, and weathered structure is everything you could want from a 12th-century cathedral. From Queen Street it's a 15-minute walk. Behind the cathedral is the hilltop **Necropolis,** *the* place to be buried in Victorian Glasgow. Families used to compete for the highest plot and the most elaborate monument to underscore their social position. *Castle St., tel. 0141/552–3205. Admission free. Open Apr.–Sept., Mon.–Sat. 9:30–1 and 2–6, Sun. 2–5; shorter hrs off season.*

GLASGOW SCHOOL OF ART • Architects and designers come from all over the world to admire the masterpiece of Glasgow-born architect Charles Rennie Mackintosh. Since it's a working school of art, visitor access is limited unless you take one of the excellent tours; call ahead for times and to reserve a space. *167 Renfrew St., tel. 0141/353–4526.*

GLASGOW UNIVERSITY • The main building on campus is an enormous, dark, Gothic structure with a 300-ft-high tower that dominates the skyline above Kelvingrove Park. The university has produced some of Scotland's leading thinkers, including Adam Smith, the famed economist, and James Watt, who made substantial improvements on the steam engine and coined the term "horsepower." The **Hunterian Museum** (tel. 0141/330–4221) and the more interesting **Hunterian Art Gallery** (tel. 0141/330–5431) are on University Avenue, in the center of campus. Along with a major group of works by James McNeill Whistler, the gallery houses prints and drawings by Reynolds, Rodin, Rembrandt, and Tintoretto, as well as a famous collection of furniture and decorative arts designed by Charles Rennie Mackintosh. *Admission free. Both open Mon.–Sat. 9:30–5.*

KELVINGROVE ART GALLERY AND MUSEUM • The architectural plans of this huge turn-of-the-century building were mistakenly turned around, and the error wasn't discovered until its massive foundation had already been laid. The museum had to be built back to front, and the architect was so distraught over this folly that he committed suicide. The collection inside includes 17th-century Dutch art, the work of French impressionists, Scottish art, and Egyptian artifacts. *West end of Sauchiehall St., Kelvingrove Park, tel. 0141/357–3929. Admission free. Open Mon.–Sat. 10–5, Sun. 11–5.*

POLLOCK COUNTY PARK • This large park is about 3 mi southwest of the city center, off Paisley Road. Within the park, you'll find the **Burrell Collection** (tel. 0141/649–7151), once the private collection of Sir William Burrell and his wife. Scotland's finest art collection, it consists of a hodgepodge of 8,000 pieces ranging from an ancient Assyrian iron bridle to Rodin bronzes. *Take train from Central Station to Pollokshaws West Station. Admission free. Open Mon.–Sat. 10–5, Sun. 11–5.*

AFTER DARK

The List (£1.80) lists every public event in Glasgow and Edinburgh, from opera to thrash bands to museum exhibits; buy it at any newsstand. **The Brewery Tap** (1055 Sauchiehall St., tel. 0141/339–8866) is a large pub, with several cozy rooms, heaps of dark wooden tables, and a gazillion beers—including many small Scottish brewery ales—and live music from jazz to techno depending on the night. **Uisge Beatha** (232–246 Woodlands Rd., tel. 0141/332–0473) is Gaelic for "water of life," which isn't a bad way to describe Scotch whisky. The bartenders wear their kilts well. Different mood grooves play throughout the week at **Volcano** (15 Benalder St., at Byres and Dumbarton Rds., tel. 0141/337–1100). The interior is dark and minimalist, the attitude fun. **Bennet's** (80–90 Glassford St., tel. 0141/552–5761) is the most popular gay and mixed club in town, but **Club Xchange** (25 Royal Exchange, 0141/226–5468) is gay trashy and seriously fun.

CENTRAL SCOTLAND

The accessible towns of **Perth** and **Stirling** are the gateways to the scenic Central Highlands, which stretch north of Glasgow along the jagged western coast. The slopes of the region's lochs and hills are forested with shaggy birch, oak, and pine—some of the most rugged and spectacular land in Scotland. The tops of the hills are high but not too wild for most travelers to tackle. Ben Lawers, near Killin, is the ninth-highest peak in Scotland, and the moor of Rannoch is as bleak and empty a stretch as can be seen anywhere in the north.

STIRLING

Stirling is a smaller, less-crowded version of Edinburgh. Stirling's castle, built on a steep-sided rock, dominates the landscape, and the building's Esplanade offers views of the surrounding valley-plain of the Forth River. It's as impressive as Edinburgh's castle, but instead of finding Edinburgh's ragged crowds, you'll find picnic tables set inside the castle's walls, inviting you to linger and enjoy the views of the tree-covered hills and cultivated fields of the Forth Valley. If you've got wanderlust, Stirling makes a good base for trekking in the central Highlands. Ask the helpful folks at the **Stirling and Trossachs Tourist Board** (41 Dumbarton Rd., tel. 01786/475–019) for a free map of the city.

COMING AND GOING

Trains from Stirling travel to Edinburgh (£4.60 single) and Glasgow (£4 single). **Buses** are a bit cheaper and not much slower. Check at the **bus station** (Gooscroft Rd., tel. 01786/473–763) for information on local lines serving the area; a bus to Glasgow costs £6 return.

WHERE TO SLEEP AND EAT

Queen Street, in the town center, has several reasonable B&Bs, including **Mrs. Cosgrove's** (32 Queen St., FK8 1DN, tel. 01786/463–716) rooms for £16–£18. The **Stirling SYHA** (St. John St., tel. 01786/473–442) is a 10-minute walk uphill from the train station on the way to the castle. There are plenty of places for a bite around the pedestrian streets in the commercial center of town and along Murray Place and Barnton Street, north of the city center. **Darnley Coffee House** (18 Bow St., tel. 01786/474–468), a pleasant and low-key café that's open daily 10–5, is a simple, cheap option. Stirling pubs also serve good grub; try **Behind the Wall Too** (61 King St., tel. 01786/461–041) or **Stirling Café and Brasserie** (Baker St.).

WORTH SEEING

Just below the southwestern ramparts of the castle lies the curious, geometrically shaped **King's Knot**, known locally as the "Cup 'n' Saucer," which was originally a terraced garden built by William III. Now it serves as a grassy park for letting children run themselves to exhaustion. Next to the castle are several buildings dating back to the 16th century. The unfinished house of **Mar's Wark** stands on Castle Hill Wynd in front of the **Church of the Holy Rude** and its adjoining cemetery. The cemetery contains an intriguing monument: a deteriorating glassed-in shrine of a marble angel standing over two young marble girls who have lost their marble heads. Along **Broad Street,** which was once the center of trade for old Stirling, is the 18th-century **Tolbooth,** the former town hall, with a traditional Scottish steeple and gilded weathercock. For centuries, the Burgh court handed down sentences here; the jail was next door.

THE TROSSACHS

Technically speaking, the name Trossachs refers to a short gorge linking lovely **Loch Katrine** with the much smaller **Loch Achray** to the east. Sir Walter Scott put this area on the map by setting *The Lady of the Lake* here. Victorians predictably flocked to the region to see what inspired him, and visitors continue to flock today, especially during the summer. Despite the crowds, the Trossachs remain pristine and lush in a rugged sort of way. Loch Achray, for instance, should fulfill your expectations of a Scottish loch: sparkling waters surrounded by meadows, rhododendron thickets, and richly wooded hills. Aberfoyle in the south and Callander in the northeast are the gateway towns, but as soon as you arrive, you'll see that time is best spent in the hills rather than in these towns. **Midland Bluebird** (tel. 01360/440–224 or 01786/473–763) runs buses between Stirling and Callander and between Glasgow and Aberfoyle. **Postbuses** (tel. 01877/382–231 or 01877/330–267) cover most of the interior routes. **Rover tickets** that cover most of the area routes are available for £3.50 per day (£5.50 including Stirling, £6.50 including Glasgow).

Unabashedly commercial, **Aberfoyle** is a blur of woolens shops with the occasional sheep show. Luckily, Aberfoyle is in the heart of the **Queen Elizabeth Forest Park,** just south of Loch Katrine and wedged between the Trossachs and Loch Lomond. The park is as royally scenic as its name implies, with a little more emphasis on "forest" than "park." Many dirt hiking and mountain-bike trails cross the 75,000 acres of pine forest. Stop by Aberfoyle's **Forestry Commission Visitor Centre** (tel. 01877/382–383), 1 mi north of town, for detailed information on hiking, biking, and camping within the park. The **tourist office** (Main St., tel. 01877/382–352) in town will help you out spring–fall. **Cobleland Campsite** is 2 mi south of town on an unclassified road off the A81 (ask someone at the tourist office to draw you a map); tent sites are £3.75 each. In Aberfoyle, stay at **Mayfield** (Main St., FK8 3UG, tel. 01877/382–845) for £17 per person or at **Old Coach House Inn** (Main St., FK8, tel. 01877/382–822) for £15–£18 per person.

Callander sits at the east end of the Trossachs, a few miles from Loch Vencachar. From here, you can hike out to two different waterfalls. The **Bracklinn Falls** can be reached via the short, 25-minute trail at the top of Golf Course Road at the east end of town. The **Falls of Leny,** by the Pass of Leny, are just north of Callander on the A84. Rent a bike for £8–£12 at **Wheels Cycle Hire** (Manse Ln., tel. 01877/331–100) and hit the road. The **tourist office** (Main St., tel. 01877/330–342) can provide more detailed information about biking and hiking in the area, as well as lodging. **Mrs. Collier's** (Ancaster Rd., tel. 01877/330–908) is open all year with beds £14–£16 in a relatively modern home.

LOCH LOMOND

Many hikers are attracted to the "bonnie, bonnie banks of Loch Lomond" and the hills rising above its banks. The southern end of the loch, Britain's biggest freshwater lake, is wide and island-studded; the north side is more enclosed. The thick-skinned swim, waterski, and windsurf in the loch's cold, peat-darkened waters, and all types take advantage of the many hiking trails around the loch. One great trail is the 97-mi **West Highland Way,** which winds along the eastern side of the Loch from Milngavie north to Glen Nevis.

COMING AND GOING

Trains from Glasgow travel to **Balloch** (1 hr, £2.50 single), at the south end of the loch, and to **Tarbet** (1½ hrs, £6.50 single) and **Ardlui** (1¾ hrs, £8.50 single) in the north. Balloch isn't especially interesting and doesn't offer much for backpackers, although it does have a seasonal **tourist office** (Balloch Rd., tel. 01389/53533). Less expensive **CityLink** buses (0990/505–050) go from Glasgow's Buchanan Street Station up the western side of the loch toward Oban and Fort William, and they will drop you off at any Loch Lomond hostel (*see* Where to Sleep, *below*). From Inverberg, you can catch a ferry (about three times daily in summer) to Rowardennan, at the base of the popular trail up Ben Lomond. Call the Rowardennan youth hostel for information on ferry schedules.

WHERE TO SLEEP

Several SYHA hostels in the area are perfect for hikers, at least from March to October when they're all open. **Rowardennan SYHA** (by Dryman, tel. 01360/870–259; beds £8.05, £6.85 under 18) has a stunning view of the loch. If you don't have a car, take the ferry from Inverbeg Bay. The best hostel in the area is **Loch Lomond SYHA** (Arden, tel. 01389/850–226; beds £8.05, £6.85 under 18), 3 mi north of Balloch on the A82. It occupies a former duke's hunting lodge and has yet another superb view of the loch. CityLink buses from Glasgow's Buchanan Street Station to Oban or Fort William will drop you off in front of the hostel.

HIGHLANDS AND NORTHERN ISLANDS

The most romantic images of Scotland—tartan dress, misty glens, bagpipes, shady lochs, tightly knit clans—are all drawn from the Highlands, without question Scotland's most breathtaking scenery. Many travelers headed for the north of Scotland make it only as far as Fort William or Inverness. Although they are both pleasant enough, they lack the drama of the rest of the region and are best used as entrances to the rural hinterlands—Fort William to the Inner and Outer Hebrides, and Inverness to the western and northern Highlands.

Population is sparse among the mountains and moorlands here, and, not surprisingly, public transportation is spotty. Still, you'll find a number of southerners who have moved here to escape the rat race and bask (or shiver) in the natural beauty. Venture to the Isle of Skye, famous for its misty Cuillin Mountains, or the Outer Hebrides, featuring some of Scotland's finest beaches, and you, too, might feel like staying in the northern Highlands, at least until winter sets in.

FORT WILLIAM

Fort William has almost enough interesting sights to compensate for its less-than-picturesque setting. But the main reason to visit is to stock up for a trip to the western Highlands. If you've got an afternoon to kill, check out the **West Highland Museum** (Cameron Sq., tel. 01397/702–169), a few doors down from the tourist office. This museum explores the theme of the 1745 Jacobite rebellion, with a "secret" portrait of Bonnie Prince Charlie that is only recognizable when viewed in a mirror. Helpful folks staff the **tourist office** in Cameron Centre (tel. 01397/703–781), a five-minute walk from the train station.

If you're ready for some exercise, head east toward **Ben Nevis,** the United Kingdom's highest mountain at 4,406 ft. A heavily traveled path goes from Fort William to the peak. The round-trip takes about four to six hours on a steep, steep path. Ask at the tourist office for information about less-touristed paths, but don't attempt anything without a map, plenty of food and water, and rain gear.

COMING AND GOING

Frequent trains travel from Glasgow to Fort William (£22 single) before heading north to Mallaig. **CityLink** (tel. 0990/505–050) buses travel to Glasgow, Edinburgh, and Skye. From Fort William, take **Highland Omnibuses** (tel. 01397/702–373) around the area.

WHERE TO SLEEP AND EAT

Fort William has more cheap sleeps than just about any other town this far north. The best option, **Fort William Backpackers** (Alma Rd., tel. 01397/700–711) has beds for £8.90. It is a 5-minute walk from the train station; walk left on Belford Road, turn right on Alma Road and veer left at the fork. Alma Road and nearby Fassifein Road are filled with B&Bs. Highly recommended is the **Rhu Mhor Guest House** (Alma Rd., tel. 01397/702–213). Host Ian MacPherson has an 11:30 PM curfew, but polices it with grace and charm, and his boarding house is full of gorgeous idiosyncrasies and character. He specializes in vegetarian and vegan cuisine, and can cater to any diet, given notice. A bed will cost you £17 with breakfast included. Picnic packers can find some reasonable deals at the **Safeway** behind the rail station.

INVERNESS

One of Scotland's major shipping ports, Inverness, on the Moray Firth, is best known as the town from which visitors launch their search for Scotland's beloved beast, the Loch Ness Monster. Inverness itself is relatively small, but it is the last substantial town as you head north into the sparsely populated regions of northernmost Scotland. The city center isn't particularly interesting; the real beauty of the town lies in the miles of trails along the quietly dark waters of the Caledonian Canal leading to Loch Ness. B&B bookings, information on travel to the Hebrides, and Loch Ness tours can be arranged at the **tourist office** (Castle Wynd, tel. 01463/234–353).

COMING AND GOING

The **train station** on Academy Street (tel. 01463/238–924) has several daily trains to Glasgow (£28 single) and the Kyle of Lochalsh for the Isle of Skye (£13.80 single). **CityLink** buses follow the same routes from the depot a few blocks from the train station, on Academy Street; the trip to Edinburgh costs £11.60 single.

WHERE TO SLEEP

Inverness gets crowded during the summer, so book ahead. Head across the river to Fairfield Road or Kenneth Street, both hotbeds of cheapish B&Bs. Or try the Crown District at the top of Castle Street behind the hostels. **Abermar Guest House** (25 Fairfield Rd., tel. 01463/239–019) has rooms for £16–£17 per person. The lovely and welcoming **Mary Ann Villa** (Mary Ann Ct., at Ardross Pl., tel. 01463/230–187), next to St. Andrews Cathedral, has £16 singles and £28 doubles. The relaxed, international **Inverness Student Hotel** (8 Culduthel Rd., tel. 01463/236–556; beds £8.50) overlooking the River Ness is reason enough to make the journey to Inverness. From the bus or rail station, follow Academy Street, turn right on High Street, left on Castle Street and head uphill.

LOCH NESS

This most famous of Scottish lakes—23 mi long and 1 mi wide—is supposedly inhabited by the Loch Ness monster, a shy beast that makes occasional appearances to observers only when they least expect it. Whether or not Nessie lurks in the depths—highly in doubt after the 1994 deathbed confession of a man who took one of the most convincing photos of Nessie (it was a fake)—plenty of camera-toting, sonar-wielding, submarine-traveling scientists and curiosity seekers haunt the loch looking for a glimpse of the elusive monster. **Urquhart Castle** (2 mi southeast of Drumnadrochit, tel. 0131/244–3101; admission £3) gives you the best views over the deep, ice-cold loch. This plundered fortress, begun in the 13th century and destroyed in the 17th to prevent the Jacobites (followers of James II) from using it, stands on a promontory overlooking the loch. The cheesy **Official Loch Ness Monster Exhibition** (A831, tel. 01456/450–573; admission £4.50) has photographs and unexplained sonar contacts of Nessie, along with the earnest testimony of eyewitnesses. Buses make the 20-minute trip between Inverness and Drumnadrochit daily. Boats also leave from Inverness and glide along the loch.

ISLE OF SKYE

Forty-five miles long and 25 mi across at its widest point, the Isle of Skye is the largest of the Inner Hebrides. It's also the most popular, thanks to the ease of the five-minute crossing from the mainland. Rugged mountain peaks, forested glens, and dramatic waterfalls pack the dense interior, rural villages dot the coast, and the formidable peaks of the Cuillins rise in the center. Some of the best climbing in Britain can be found in the domed, granite **Red Cuillins** and spiky, jagged **Black Cuillins** that will challenge both beginners and experts. To the north are **Macleod's Tables,** two flat-topped hills that are popular with hikers, and the dramatic **Trotternish Peninsula** hanging off the northern tip. For less-rugged exploring, head to the **Sleat Peninsula** on the southeast edge of the island. The lush vegetation is a dramatic contrast to the rocky terrain of the north.

With the completion of the highly controversial **Skye Bridge,** for which there is a vastly-inflated £5.40 toll in each direction, the ferries connecting Kyleakin with Kyle of Lochalsh were discontinued by government decree. The toll is included in your bus ticket from Fort William or Glasgow. **Highland Omnibus** (01478/612–622) runs to and from Fort William; **Skye-Ways** (01599/534–328) travels between the island and Glasgow, stopping in Oban along the way. The fares around Skye are extraordinarily high, but **Skye-Ways** offers a **Student Day-Rover** pass for £7.50. **Postbuses** cover less-traveled territory, and hitching is relatively easy throughout the island. Rent cars in Broadford from **Skye Car Rental** (tel. 01471/822–225) or in Kyleakin from **Kyleakin Car Hire** (01599/534–472), which charges only £3 per hour, making it a good deal when split among friends.

KYLEAKIN

This town's only real sight is the remnants of the 12th-century **Castle Moil,** which overlooks the town. Its **Kyleakin SYHA** (tel. 01599/534–585; beds £7.10, £6.50 under 18), the best in Skye, is just a few minutes from the ferry dock. The cozy **Backpackers Guesthouse** (tel. 01599/534–510) is just a few minutes farther.

PORTREE

The only serious town on Skye, Portree welcomes visitors with brightly painted houses, a beautiful setting on a small and sheltered bay, frequent buses to the rest of the island, and festivals of all kinds during the summer months. Nearby places of interest include the Storr Mountains, featuring the **Old Man of Storr,** a black monolith reaching 160 ft high. Farther on the A855 is **Quiraing,** with its spectacular lava formations. **Uig SYHA** (Uig, tel. 01470/542–211; beds £5.50; £4.60 under 18; open Mar.–Oct.), 2 mi from the pier on Portree Road, is a friendly place well situated for local walks. For more information, contact the **tourist office** (Meall House, tel. 01478/612–137).

GREECE

12

O ne of the best things you can do when you arrive in Greece is take your watch off. Service is slow, schedules are often erratic, and stores open and close according to a complicated program that varies with the kind of store, the day of the week, and the season. If you can't resign yourself to the Greeks' sense of time, you may just go mad here. But only in a country where time is not money and deadlines are fluid can you contentedly stare at the sea for days (or even months) and marvel anew at each approaching dusk.

It is the ancient Greece of Plato's philosopher-king that has formed most foreigners' perceptions of the country: myths and oracles, brilliant seas and sacred mountains, and a rich culture that became the cradle of Western Civilization. Greece boomed during the age of Pericles (495 BC–429 BC), with flourishing drama, poetry, and art, establishing principles of independent thought and aesthetic achievement that have defined Western culture ever since. However, the Peloponnesian Wars (431 BC–404 BC) soon led to the fall of Athens, the decline of the city-state, and centuries of invasions and subjugation by foreign powers.

In AD 324, Roman emperor Constantine built the new capital of Constantinople on the site of the ancient city of Byzantium, ushering in what we know as the Byzantine era. The legacy of the Byzantine Empire can be seen today in Greek art and architecture, most poignantly in the ruins of the last Byzantine capital, Mistrás. In 1453, the Ottoman Turks captured Constantinople (and renamed it İstanbul), a major step in occupying all the lands of the Byzantine Empire. After the Turks occupied Athens in 1456 and Mistras in 1460, the country lay under Ottoman Turkish rule for almost 400 years.

The Greek revolution against the Ottoman Turks broke out in 1821. Many Westerners supported the Greek struggle, which was actually decided by the naval victory of the combined English, French, and Russian fleets at Navarino in 1827. The independent Kingdom of Greece was formally recognized in 1833, but it did not reach its present size until after the Balkan Wars of 1912–13.

In 1981, Andreas Papandreou, leader of the socialist PASOK party, was elected prime minister, bringing a center-left government to power for the first time in modern Greek history. Despite personal scandals and considerable financial corruption under the PASOK government, Papandreou remained the dominant political figure in Greece until his death in 1996. Costas Simitis, the "conservative socialist" who succeeded him, has a monumental task. Economic austerity measures imposed to meet EU standards have reduced inflation but disgruntled many workers, as taxes, unemployment, and the costs of services have risen.

Greece continues to face difficulties from across its borders as well. Albanians are currently flooding the country in search of work. Many work hard and well for low pay, particularly in agricultural regions, but many others have indulged in vandalism and crime, engendering anti-Albanian sentiment among the Greeks. When the Yugoslav Republic dissolved in 1991, the former Yugoslav province of Macedonia, bordering northern Greece, became an independent country calling itself "Macedonia," and many Greeks took offense at the appropriation of this historically Greek name by this largely Slavic country. Ancient Macedonia was the ancient home of Alexander the Great and the seat of his Hellenic empire, and the new nation's name, combined with its newly minted bill depicting the White Tower of Thessalonaki, struck Greece as claims on Greek Macedonia. For the most part, this issue has blown over, and Greece now has normal diplomatic and economic relations with the new country, which most Greeks refer to by the name of its capital, Skopje. To the east, there was until recently considerable tension between Greece and Turkey due to some Turkish interest in expanding Turkey's border west into Greek territory.

Travelers have long been drawn to the Greek dream world of extended siestas and all-night parties. The islands beguile most visitors with their endless beaches, sparkling blue waters, Mediterranean sunshine, and Dionysian revelry; weathered locals throughout the country may invite you to their secluded villages and offer you wine, figs, and pungent cheeses; and the country as a whole (the Peloponnese in particular) recalls a time of gods, centaurs, and other ancient wonders.

BASICS

MONEY

US$1 = 270 drachmas and 100 drachmas = 37¢. The best exchange rates are at ATMs, which take Visa, MasterCard, AmEx, Cirrus, and Plus cards. The National Bank of Greece and the Commercial Bank of Greece, found in all but the smallest towns, are linked with these systems. Other than that, your credit cards will be pretty useless, since budget hotels and restaurants rarely accept them. American Express offices have the best rates for changing traveler's checks into drachmas; banks (usually open Mon.–Thurs. 8–2, Fri. 8–1:30) and post offices offer competitive rates, but they also charge a commission (about 300dr). Bureaux de change are convenient but have ridiculously high commissions and low rates.

HOW MUCH IT WILL COST • Prices differ dramatically from season to season: You can live on about $35–$40 a day September–June; in July and August, tack on an extra $10 a day, a little more on the islands. If you avoid touristy spots, a meal in a taverna with beer or wine will run you about 2,000dr. Transportation in Greece can be costly if you are in a hurry; planes and hydrofoils are expensive. The large ferries cost far less, particularly if you travel on deck. Buses are the cheapest way to cover long distances.

COMING AND GOING

The ferry is the only way to get all the way to Greece using your Eurailpass, but you'll still have to pay a supplement in high season.

BY BUS • You can bus it directly into Greece through Albania, Bulgaria, Hungary (get a Serbian visa before boarding; inquire your local tourist office) Romania, Turkey, and Italy (including ferry). Private coaches and buses, run by the **Hellenic State Railways (OSE)** (in Athens, 1–3 Karolou, tel. 01/52–22–491; 6 Sina St., tel. 01/36–24–402; or 17 Filelinon St., tel. 01/32–36–747), leave from the Laríssis train station in Athens. Prices vary greatly, so ask at any discount travel agency for specifics.

BY FERRY • Frequent ferries link Italy to Greece. Several companies, such as Anek Lines, Marline, and Med Link, offer 10% discounts on the return leg of a round trip. In summer, at least seven ferries sail daily to Pátra from Brindisi (15 hrs, 7,500dr), and about two each arrive from Bari (19 hrs, 10,000dr), Ancona (30 hrs, about 15,000dr), and Trieste (33 hrs, 17,600dr). All ferries continue to Corfu (Kérkira) and sometimes Igoumenítsa. Ferry companies generally have competitive prices, but ask around to find the cheapest. Eurailpasses are accepted only on the Adriatica and Hellenic Mediterranean ferries from Brindisi, and holders pay a 4,500dr supplement in high season. Ferries travel frequently between Turkey and the eastern Aegean islands, such as Sámos and Rhodes, but both Turkey and Greece levy huge port taxes: 3,000dr and 4,000dr, respectively.

BY PLANE • Planes are the priciest but easiest way to get here. **Olympic Airways** soars directly to Athens from Rome (2½ hrs, 107,000dr), Paris (2 hrs, 85,000dr), and London (2½ hrs, 75,000dr), but you can get much cheaper charter flights and budget rates from discount travel agencies all over Athens. Charter flights go from Athens to Paris for about 49,500dr and to Cairo for about 40,000dr. The many charter flights to London usually run about 42,000dr, but you may find a ticket for as low as 25,000dr.

GREECE

FORMER YUGOSLAV
REPUBLIC OF
MACEDONIA

BULGARIA

ALBANIA

Sta

Sidirókastro
Séres

Philipp

Kilkis

Eleftheroúpoli
Amfipoli

Kava

E86

Edessa

Thessaloniki

Florina

Alexandria

Néa
Apolonia

Thérmi
Polygyros

Kastoria

Ormylia

Vatopedic

Ptolemaïda

Veria

Ivirior

Kozani

Katerini

Dafni

Siatista

Gulf of
Thermaikos

Athos

Kónitsa

Grevena

Mount
Olympus

Litóhoro

Kalithéa

Kastráki

Metéora

Palioúri

Vória Pindos

Kérkira
Town

Agia

Aegea

Tirnavos

Corfu

Ioánnina

Kalambáka

Larissa

Paramythia

Trikala

Zagora

SPORÁDE

Igoumenítsa

Karditsa

Pontraria

Vizítsa

Válos

Parga

Stavros

Farsala

Skíathos

Arta

Almiros

Trikeri

Skópelos

Aliki

Lamia

Preveza

Karpenissi

Skyros

Lefkas
Vassiliki

Agrínio

Orhomenós

Kymi

ÉVIA

Kephalonia

Ithákí

Delfi

Livadia

Itea

Lixouri

Sami

E55

Nefpaktos

Galaxidi

Halkida

Messolongi

Pátra

Thebes

Kárystos

Gulf of Corinth

Diakofto

Loutráki

Megara

Killíni

Athens

Loutra

Nemea

Kórinthos

Pireaus

Zákinthos
Town

Amalias

Mikines

Egina

Vouliagméni

Pírgos

Argos

Náfplio

Poros

Lavrio
Soúnio

Zákinthos

Olympía

Tripoli

Toló

Kéa

Kaiafas

Ermioni

Kythnos

Andritsena

Ydra

Kyparissia

PELOPÓNNISOS

Spetses

Serifos

Ionian Sea

Messini

Sparta

Leonidio

Gargaliani

Kalamáta

Mistrás

Geraki

Pilos

Kyparíssi

Methoni

Koroni

Skala

Areopoli

Yithio

Monemvassía

Milos

Agía Pelagia

Kythira

Kythira

Mediterranean Sea

Khaniá

Soudha

0   100 miles
0   150 km

CRETE

418

Black Sea

THRAKI TURKEY

stavroúpoli
Xanthi
Kástanies
Didymótiho
ppi
vala
Avdira
Mákri
Alexandroúpolis

Istanbul

Sea of
Marmara

Thassos

Kamariótisa
Samothráki

dia
ion

Limnos

ean Sea

■ **Troy**

TURKEY

E S

Mithimna
Lésvos
Mitilíni

Plomari

Aegean

Híos
Híos
Mésta
Pirgí
Town
Cesme
Izmir

Sea

Andros
Andros
Sámos
■ **Ephesus**
Vathi
Pithagória

i
éa
Ikaria
Ermoupoli
Tinos
Tinos
Agios
Kirykos
Syros
Míkonos
Delos
Pátmos

Páros
Náxos
Léros
Bodrum

CYCLADES *Amorgós*
Kós
Kós

Íos
Astypalea
Nissyros
Symi
Rhodes
Town

Thira
Tilos
Kámiros
Santoríni *Anafi*
Halki
Lindos
Rhodes

DODECANESE

Sea of Crete

Kárpathos

ha
Réthimnon
Iráklion
Bali
Mallia
Kassos
Knossos

Phaestos
Ierapetra

KEY	
├──┼──┤	Rail Lines
⛴	Ferry Lines

THE GREEK ABG'S

Many proper names in this chapter are transliterated versions of the Greek name, so when you come upon signs written in the Greek alphabet, just use this list to decipher them.

Greek	Roman	Greek	Roman	Greek	Roman
Α, α	*a*	Ι, ι	*i*	Ρ, ρ	*r*
Β, β	*v*	Κ, κ	*k*	Σ, σ, ς	*s*
Γ, γ	*g or y*	Λ, λ	*l*	Τ, τ	*t*
Δ, δ	*th, dh, or d*	Μ, μ	*m*	Υ, υ	*i*
Ε, ε	*e*	Ν, ν	*n*	Φ, φ	*f*
Ζ, ζ	*z*	Ξ, ξ	*x or ks*	Χ, χ	*h or ch*
Η, η	*i*	Ο, ο	*o*	Ψ, ψ	*ps*
Θ, θ	*th*	Π, π	*p*	Ω, ω	*o*

GETTING AROUND

Scooting around a Greek island on a **motorbike** is liberating—especially since many beaches and small villages are not accessible by bus—but it's not terribly safe. Greek drivers can do crazy things, roads are rocky, bikes can be creaky, and helmets are rare. Most rental agencies offer only third-person/collision insurance, so get personal insurance before leaving home. The cheapest one-person scooters cost about 1,500dr per day; sturdier, two-person scooters are about 4,000dr per day.

BY BUS • The national bus system, **KTEL**, is efficient and comprehensive. In large towns, it's wise to buy tickets in advance at the bus station. In smaller towns, ask a local where the bus stop is (sometimes it's a sign, sometimes a tree, sometimes in front of a taverna) and how often buses pass; then flag one down, climb on, and tell the driver your destination. Drivers usually sell tickets.

BY FERRY • Huge, slow boats connect most islands and mainland coastal cities frequently during summer, less often off season. The cheapest tickets are in deck (D) class. **Hydrofoils** are twice as fast and twice the price. Buy tickets at the ferry docks or at any travel agency; you'll pay 20%–30% more if you buy them on board. Beware: Ferries are often late.

BY TRAIN • Greek trains are wretched. They're cheaper than the bus, but they're also slow, crowded, dirty, and useful only along the eastern coast (from Athens to Thrace), and on the Peloponnese. Make reservations to avoid long hours in the station waiting for openings. The clean and efficient **Intercity trains** between Athens and Thessaloniki are a welcome exception. The ride to Thessaloniki costs about 8,000drs (about one-fourth the airfare) and takes six hours; buy tickets at stations or at any one of the three Hellenic State Railways offices (*see* Coming and Going, *above*). From Athens, the train between Kifissia and Piraeus is the cheapest (about 75dr) way to get to the harbor.

WHERE TO SLEEP

Dhomatia (rooms) or *pansiyons* (pensions) are the best places to sack out at night; doubles start at 5,000dr–6,000dr. They're usually clean and in or near a private home, and the proprietors may be willing to bargain if you stay for more than one night. On the islands, you'll often find the best and cheapest beds through the hawkers who meet the arriving ferries; their rooms are usually in family homes and their prices negotiable, except in high season. **Hotel** quality varies widely from one region to the next, but doubles generally start around 6,000dr. **Hostels** are cheaper, at 2,500dr per bed (sometimes including breakfast), but lockouts and curfews force guests onto a rather un-Greek schedule. **Campgrounds,** usually only a short bus ride away, vary dramatically in price, ranging from 500dr to 1,000dr, per tent plus 1,000dr–2,000dr per person. Pitching a tent on public ground is prohibited but may be tolerated in untouristed coves or forested areas. On the islands, you can often stargaze and sleep for free on isolated beaches. Finally, ask at reception desks about unadvertised **rooftop** spaces, which cost about 2,000dr when available. Lodging reviews in this chapter are based on *high-season* rates, which can sometimes be as much as double the low-season rates. The high season varies from place to place, but it generally lasts from mid-June through August.

FOOD

Eating out in Greece is often the event of the night, with multiple courses, free-flowing wine, laughter, and music. Lunch is generally served 1–3, dinner 9–midnight. Budget travelers dine mostly in **tavernas,** casual, inexpensive restaurants that are often at least as good as more formal venues. Your bill will include a tip, but if you like the waiter, you can round the bill up a few hundred drachmas. For daytime snacks or a quick, cheap meal, street stalls sell gyros (sliced meat roasted on a spit) and souvlaki (skewered cubes of meat), both often served in píta bread with tomatoes; spanakopita (spinach pie); *tirópita* (cheese pie); *dolmádes* (stuffed grape leaves); and *tzatzíki* (yogurt, cucumber, and garlic dip). Common Greek dishes include moussaka (layered eggplant and ground meat, topped with white sauce and cheese) and *domátes yemistés* (tomatoes stuffed with rice and/or minced meat). Her-
bivores can try *patátes sto foúrno* (potatoes baked with olive oil, lemon, and oregano), *fasoládha* (oven-cooked beans with to-mato sauce and onions), and a plethora of other veggies dressed in oil and spices. On the islands, make a beeline for the *psaro-tavérnas,* which specialize in fresh seafood. *Ouzerí* (ouzo bars) are also great places to chow, especially for *mezédhes* (appetiz-ers) and the national hard drink of choice, ouzo (anise liqueur), which is usually diluted with water and served on the rocks. Retsina (wine flavored with pine resin) is an acquired taste; for some it's Dionysus incarnate, for others it's chilled turpentine. In summer, people sip frappés (whipped Nescafé on ice).

The ubiquitous períptera (kiosks) in Greece stock just about everything: newspapers, magazines, cigarettes, mosquito coils, aspirin, tampons, cookies, religious paraphernalia, condoms, laxatives—puts 7-Eleven to shame.

BUSINESS HOURS

Business hours are consistent throughout Greece, but in heavily visited areas, businesses often stay open through the siesta (roughly 2:30–6) and later at night. Generally, stores operate Monday, Wednes-day, and Saturday from 8:30 to 2:30 or 3; Tuesday, Thursday, and Friday from 8:30 to 2:30 or 3 and 5:30 to 8:30 or 9; and close Sunday. Travel agencies, which often double as tourist offices, operate daily 8 AM–9 PM, and sometimes until midnight.

VISITOR INFORMATION

The national tourist organization, **EOT,** has helpful offices in nearly every town. Some book rooms, and all provide maps, transport schedules, and general information. In smaller towns, most offices are open weekdays 8–4; in larger cities, weekdays 8–8 and Saturday 8:30–2.). In towns without EOT offices, or if the EOT office is closed, get visitor information at **tourist police offices** (open after hours).

PHONES

Country code: 30. The national phone company is **OTE.** All towns and most villages have an OTE office for telegram services and metered, collect, and calling-card calls. Telecard phone booths cover the cities and are moving into smaller towns; buy cards worth 100 units (1,500dr) at kiosks. Get the larger-unit cards (500 units, 6,500dr; 1,000 units, 11,500 drs) at OTE offices. Local calls cost one unit. Press the "i" button on telecard phones for instructions in English. Metered phones at news kiosks cost about 20dr per unit; OTE offices charge 17dr per unit. Before calling from a metered phone in a hotel or travel agency, find out what it charges per unit; the rate is often a rip-off. To call outside Greece, dial 00 + country code + number. To reach a U.S. operator (one unit) from any phone, dial 00–800–1311 for **AT&T** Direct Access[SM]; 00–800–1211 for **MCI**; or 00–800–1411 for **Sprint.** Regular calls to the United States from telecard phones or the OTE office cost 294dr (17.3 units) per minute. Between 11 PM and 3 AM, calls to the US cost 13.5 units per minute.

MAIL

The Greek mail system is fairly efficient; your postcards and letters home should arrive within a week. Sending postcards and letters up to 20 grams to Europe costs 120dr, to the United States and Australia 150dr. Buy stamps at post offices or kiosks. Post offices are normally open weekdays 7:30–2 but may have extended evening hours in larger towns. They're all supposed to hold poste restante for a month, but they may not always do it. Mailboxes are yellow contraptions with a picture of Hermes inside a horn. Drop international mail in the boxes marked EXWTERIKOY, domestic mail in boxes labeled ESWTERIKOY.

CRIME AND PUNISHMENT

If your pocket's been picked, contact the **tourist police,** present in most towns. Drugs, even "soft" drugs like marijuana, are not tolerated in Greece, and the average sentence for possession of a joint is five years plus a big fine. Greek cops are no Barney Millers; cross them and they'll give you a difficult time.

EMERGENCIES

Dial 100 for the **police** and 166 for a **medical emergency**; both calls cost 20dr from pay phones.

STAYING HEALTHY

Tap water is generally safe, but it's iffy on some islands; play it safe with bottled water, which is cheap and readily available. Watch out for cheap alcoholic drinks on the more touristy islands, where some clubs use grain alcohol instead of tequila or vodka. For non-emergency medical problems, you can try a **pharmacy** (one is open 24 hrs in each neighborhood in the large cities), labeled FAPMAKEÍON and marked with a green cross; pharmacists have near-doctor status and can prescribe medicine.

LANGUAGE

Greek is a passionate language, involving hand gestures, exaggerated facial expressions, and sudden exclamations. Most Greeks speak a bit of English, but they may not like having to do so, and will appreciate your efforts to learn Greek. Some useful phrases include: *yá sas* (hello, polite) or *yá soo* (hello, informal), both of which can also mean goodbye; *neh* (yes); *ókhi* (no); *efkharistó* (thank you); *parakaló* (please); *signómi* (excuse me); *poso káni?* (how much does it cost?); *ékhis . . .?* (do you have . . .?); *poo íneh to lootró/to bánio?* (where is the bathroom?); and *milateh Angliká?* (do you speak English?). Also try a friendly *kaliméra* (good morning), *kalispéra* (good evening), or *kaliníkhta* (good night). You are likely to hear the word *malákas* at some point—literally, masturbator, i.e., ineffective fool. Avoid the temptation to use this word yourself; spoken by anyone other than a lifelong Greek-speaking friend in jest, it is extremely offensive and can generate a harsh response.

CULTURE

The Greek Orthodox religion plays a central role in Greek life. Many Greeks cross themselves every time they pass a church and make frequent trips to kiss the icon of their favorite saint. When visiting a church, make sure you cover your legs and shoulders (many Greek churches will lend you a skirt). When using your fingers to designate numbers, keep your palm pointed toward you—an outward palm with the fingers stretched is a highly offensive gesture—and extending your thumb to indicate the number one. Remember that Greeks nod their heads down to one side to mean "yes," and lift their chin, raise their eyebrows, and click their tongue to mean "no." Women traveling solo may face some unpleasant challenges here; while Greek men aren't likely to be dangerous, they are collectively likely to proposition, leer at, and sometimes grab women travelers, as well as offer drinks, dinners, or motorcycle tours of the city. Use sound judgment when considering these sometimes well-intentioned offers.

ATHENS

Athens (Athínai in Greek), the political and intellectual center of ancient Greece, is the capital of modern Greece. Virtually a village when designated the capital in 1834, Athens now houses more than 4 million people, almost half the population of Greece. It is crowded, polluted, and ugly. Still, if you can see beyond the smog, Athens's concentration of culture and history will enchant you for days. When modern Greece was wrested from the Turks, Western European powers were enamored with the idea of turning the ancient home of Socrates and Pericles into the seat of a modern democratic government, and Danish and German architects reintroduced Greek architecture to the Greeks through the neoclassical University, Art Academy, National Library, and Royal Palace (now the parliament building). Twentieth-century Athens is a confusing place, a vast sprawl of concrete apartment buildings, narrow streets, bumper-to-bumper traffic, and imposing government offices, as well as the occasional stunningly beautiful 19th-century building or ancient ruin.

BASICS

VISITOR INFORMATION

The EOT office near Syntagma Square (Platía Syntágmatos) has good information on transportation and cultural events for all of Greece. *2 Amerikís, tel. 01/32–22–545. Open weekdays 9–7, Sat. 9–2.*

AMERICAN EXPRESS

Athens's only AmEx office is on Syntagma Square. The staff exchanges all traveler's checks fee-free and makes travel arrangements. Members can also receive mail and faxes here. *2 Ermou, Box 332, Athens 10225, tel. 01/32–44–975. Open weekdays 8:30–4, Sat. 8–1:30.*

CHANGING MONEY

The major banks are located on or around Syntagma Square. The **National Bank of Greece** (2 Karageórgis Servías; open weekdays 8–2; Fri. until 1:30) has a 24-hour currency-exchange machine with good rates. The 24-hour ATM machines around Syntagma Square take Visa, MasterCard, and most American bank cards, including those on the Cirrus, Plus, and Star systems. Don't change money on the street; you'll get ripped off.

DISCOUNT TRAVEL AGENCIES

Discount agencies have some amazing deals on charter flights; do your homework and check a few different places to find the best fare. The **International Student and Youth Travel Agency (I.S.Y.T.S.)** (11 Nikis St., 2nd floor, tel. 01/32–21—267 and 32—33–767; open weekdays 9–5, Sat. 9 AM–1 PM), STA's Greek representative, finds reasonable air- and boat fares for more than just students. The helpful folks at **Sotiríou Travel** (28 Nikis, tel. 01/32–20–503 or 01/32–38–177; open weekdays 9–5, Sat. 9–1) find good bus and ferry fares and book charter flights.

Learn to say "efkharistó" (thank you) in Greek and you'll earn a smile and a "parakaló" (you're welcome) from even the huffiest toilers in the tourist industry.

EMBASSIES AND CONSULATES

Australia: *37 Dimitríou Soútsou, tel. 01/64–47–303. Open weekdays 8:30–12:30.* **Canada:** *4 Genadíou, tel. 01/72–54–011. Open weekdays 8:30–12:30.* **New Zealand:** *24 Xenías, tel. 01/77–10–112. Open weekdays 8:30–12:30.* **United Kingdom:** *1 Ploutárchou, tel. 01/72– 36–211. Open weekdays 8–1.* **United States:** *91 Vasilíssis Sofías, tel. 01/72–12–951. Open weekdays 9–3.*

EMERGENCIES

Take Trolleybus 1, 5, 9, or 18 from Amalías Street on Syntagma Square to the **tourist police** office (77 Dimitrakopoúlou, tel. 171; open 24 hrs). Dial 106 for a **24-hour hospital,** 166 for an **ambulance.**

ENGLISH-LANGUAGE BOOKS

Compendium Books (28 Nikis, tel. 01/32–21–248; open weekdays 9–5, Sat. 9–3) has a good selection of books on Greece and a hit-or-miss secondhand section. The new flagship of **Eleftheroudákis** has five stories of English books, though not at bargain prices. **The Book Nest,** in the stoa (arcade) across from the university on Panepistimíou Street, has the best current academic work on Greece.

PHONES AND MAIL

Two **OTE** phone offices operate in the city center, one at the southeast corner of Syntagma Square (at Stadíou; open 7 AM–10 PM) and the other nearby at 15 Stadíou (at Ladá, tel. 01/32–31–899; open 24 hrs).

The **central post office** (tel. 01/32–62–53) on Syntagma Square, at the corner of Mitropóleos, has more windows than the one at 100 Eólou, just southeast of Omonia Square. Both are open weekdays 8:30–8, Saturday 8:30–2, and Sunday 9–1:30, and hold mail. Have letters addressed to the Omonia Square post office as follows: Your Name, Poste Restante, Central Post Office, GR-10200, Athens, Greece. Letters to the Syntagma Square office should be labeled: Your Name, Poste Restante, Syntagma Square, DR-10300, Athens, Greece.

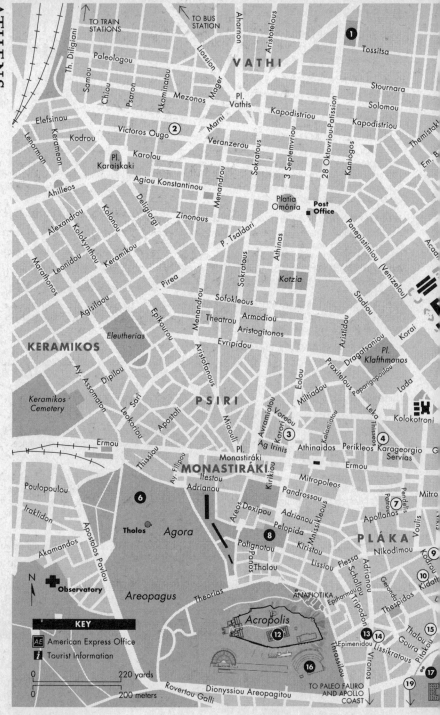

ATHENS

TO TRAIN STATIONS

TO BUS STATION

VATHI

1

Tossitsa

Th. Diligianni

Paleologou

Samou

Chiou

Psaron

Akominatou

Mezonos

Mager

Liossion

Acharnon

Aristotelous

Stournara

Solomou

Pl. Vathis

Kapodistriou

Kapodistriou

Elefsinou

Lenorman

Kerameon

Kodrou

Victoros Ougo

2

Karolou

Marni

Veranzerou

Sokratous

3 Septemvriou

28 Oktovriou-Patission

Kaniogos

Themistokl

Em. B.

Pl. Karaiskaki

Agiou Konstantinou

Menandrou

Platía Omónia

Post Office

Panepistimiou (Venizelou)

Acad

Ahilleos

Alexandrou

Kolokynthou

Kolonou

Deligiorgi

Zinonous

P. Tsaldari

Athinas

Stadiou

Marathonos

Leonidou

Keramikou

Pirea

Sokratous

Kotzia

Agisilaou

Epikourou

Eleutherias

Menandrou

Sofokleous

Theatrou

Armodiou

Aristogitonos

Evripidou

Praxitelous

Dragatsaniou

Pl. Klafthmonos

Papanigopoulou

Lada

KERAMIKOS

Ay. Assomaton

Dipilou

Sari

Aristofanous

Eolou

Miliadou

Kalamiotou

Leka

Korai

Aristidou

Keramikos Cemetery

Leokoriou

Apostoli

Miaouli

PSIRI

Avramiotou

Voreou

3

Kirott

Ag Irinis

Kalanerou

Thisseos

Kolokotroni

G

4

Ermou

Poutopoulou

Iraklidon

Apostolou Pavlou

Akamandos

Thissiou

Ay. Filipou

Pl. Monastiráki

MONASTIRÁKI

Ifestou

Adrianou

Kirikiou

Mitropoleos

Pandrossou

Athinaidos

Perikleos

Karageorgio Servias

Pendelis

Patroou

7

Apollonos

Mitro

Tholos

Agora

Areos

Dexipou

Pelopida

Adrianou

Manissikleous

Kiristou

Lissiou

Flessa

PLÁKA

Nikodimou

Voulis

Gerionda

Kidatt

9

N

✚ **Observatory**

Polignotou

8

Tholou

Panos

Nikis

10

Kidatt

Areopagus

Theorias

ANAFIOTIKA

Epiharmou

Tripodon

Adrianou

Schaliou

Thespidos

KEY

AE American Express Office

i Tourist Information

0   220 yards

0   200 meters

Rovertou Galli

Dionyssiou Areopagitou

Acropolis

12

13

14

Epimenidou

Vironos

Lissikratous

Goura

Thalou

Pitakou

15

16

Throssilou

19

17

TO PALEO FALIRO AND APOLLO COAST

424

Sights ●
Arch of Hadrian, **17**
Jewish Museum, **11**
Monument to
Lysikrates, **13**
National
Archaeological
Museum, **1**
Nicolas P.
Goulandris Museum
of Cycladic Art, **5**
Parthenon, **12**
Roman Agora, **8**
Temple of Olympian
Zeus, **18**
Theater to
Dionysus, **16**
Hephaisteon, **6**

Lodging ○
Dioskouri House, **15**
Hotel Kouros, **9**
Hotel Tempi, **3**
International Youth
Hostel (HI), **2**
John's Place, **7**
Phaedra Hotel, **14**
Student-Travelers
Inn, **10**
Thisseus Hostel, **4**
Voula Camping, **19**
Youth Hostel #5, **20**

Map labels:
Strefi
NEAPOLIS
Pl. Exarhion
Voulgaroktonou
Vatatzi
Lastareos
Tsimiski
Issavron
Smolentski
Methonis
Eressou
Dervenakou
Arachevis
Benaki
Zoodhou Pigis
Harilaou Trikoupi
Mavromihali
Ipokratous
Novarinou
Kallidromiou
N. Ouranou
Dafnomilis
Sarantopichou
LIKAVITOS
Lykabettos
Ayios Giorgias
Asklepiou
Municipal Cultural Center
Skoufa
Massalias
Solonos
Sina
Omirou
Didotou
Chesonos
Anagnostopoulou
Taskalof
Aristipou
Kleomenous
Loukianou
Xenokratous
Spefsipou
Haritos
Marasli
Pl. Dexameni
Amerikis
Dimokritou
Lykavitou
Voukourestiou
Pindarou
KOLONÁKI
Patriarhou Ioakim
Alopekis
Karneadou
Ploutarchou
Schliemann's Mansion
Kanari
Merlin
Pl. Filiks Eterias
Kapsali
Neof. Douka
Irodolou
Ypsilantou
Koumbari
Georgiou I
Vasilissis Sofias
Pl. Sindagma
Post Office
Xenofóntos
Filelinon
Sourt
Amalias
National Gardens
Herodes Atticus
Rigilis
Vasileos Georgiou II
President's House
Záppion
Vassileos Konstandinou
Pafsaniou
Eratosthenous
Arianou
Peta
Dedalou
Amalias
Vasilissis Olgas
Pl. Stadiou
Agras
Ardittos Hill
Panathenaic Stadium
Plastira

COMING AND GOING

BY BUS

The KTEL **Terminal A** at 100 Kifissoú (tel. 01/51–24- -910) serves most of Greece, with daily connections to Corinth (1½ hrs, 1,450dr), Ioánnina (7 hrs, 6,750dr), Zákinthos (6 hrs, 5,800dr), and Thessaloníki (6 hrs, 7,700dr). Buses leave from **Terminal B** at 260 Liossíon (tel. 01/83–17–096) for Delphi (3 hrs, 2,600dr), Vólos (6 hrs, 4,650dr), and Larissa (5½ hrs, 4,750dr). To reach the Kifissoú station, take Bus 051 from the corner of Zínonos and Menándrou, three blocks east of Omonia Square. For the Liossíon station, take Bus 024 from Syntagma Square. Pick up buses to places south of Athens, including Soúnion (2 hrs, 1,050dr), at **Platía Egiptou** or on **Mavromateon**, at the Pedíou tou Areos Park (north of Omonia Square at 28 Oktovriou-Patission). The **Greek Railway Organization (OSE)** (tel. 01/51–35–768 or 01/51–35–769) operates buses to Albania, Bulgaria, and Turkey; these leave from adjacent to the Peloponnísou train station and are actually cheaper, if slower, than the corresponding train connections.

BY FERRY

Ferries ship out from **Piraeus** (port authority tel. 01/45–11–311) for spots all over the Aegean and eastern Mediterranean. Some of the most popular destinations are Crete (10–11 hrs, 5,000dr), Náxos (6–7 hrs, 3,550dr), Íos and Santoríni (8–10 hrs, 4,280dr), and Míkonos (6 hrs, 3,450dr). You can reach Piraeus by Metro (from Monastiraki station, 75dr), which terminates near the docks for the Aegean Islands, the Dodecanese, and Crete. From Omonia Square, the Metro or Bus 049 drops you off near the docks for the Saronic Gulf islands; from Syntagma Square, the green Bus 040 goes to the docks for departures abroad. Buy ferry tickets at any travel agent or at the kiosks by the ferry docks.

BY PLANE

Athens's **Ellinikón Airport** is 9 km (6 mi) southeast of town. Foreign airlines use the east terminal; Olympic Airlines occupies the west terminal. Express Bus 091 links the airport to Syntagma and Omonia Squares in Athens every half-hour during the day (170dr) and every hour 11:30 PM–5:30 AM (200dr). Bus 019 (170dr) also connects Ellinikón with Piraeus roughly every hour 5 AM–10:20 PM. For domestic and international flights call **Olympic Airways** (tel. 01/93–63–363).

BY TRAIN

Two train stations serve Athens, both northwest of Omonia Square and connected to each other by a bridge over the tracks. The major northern cities are served by both regular and the faster Intercity trains from **Laríssis station** (Theodórou Deligiánni St., tel. 01/52–40–646 or 01/52–40–647). Times and rates for regular trains: Kalambáka (6½ hrs, 2,800dr), Vólos (6 hrs, 2,900dr), Thessaloníki (7½ hrs, 3,750dr). For Intercity trains: Kalambáka (5½ hrs, 5,500dr), Vólos (4½ hrs, 5,400dr), Thessaloníki (6 hrs, 7,700dr). Trains continue through Thessaloniki to Sofia (18 hrs, 10,100dr) and İstanbul (23 hrs, 19,600dr). Regular trains from the grand, Victorian **Peloponnísou station** (Konstantinoupóleos St., tel. 01/51-31-601) head south to Corinth daily at 2½ hrs and 800dr, Pátra at 5 hrs and 1,600dr. Intercity trains go to Corinth at 1½ hrs and 1,200 dr, Pátra at 3½ hrs and 2,600dr. To reach the center of town, take Trolleybus 1 from the Laríssis station to Syntagma or Omonia squares. From the Peloponnísou station, take Bus 057 to Panepistimíou Street, or cross the tracks to the Laríssis station and catch Trolleybus 1.

GETTING AROUND

The current Metro consists of a single, north–south line running from Kifisiá to Piraeus. Tickets are dispensed at vending machines outside stations and cost 75d–200dr. A new Metro is under construction, but Athens is also navigable on foot and by trolleybus, bus, and taxi, all of which are cheap. The city is laid out on a grid, except for the rambling streets of the **Pláka**, Athens's oldest continually inhabited area. The Pláka spreads southwest from Syntagma Square to the Acropolis and contains many of the major sights (and tourists). Northeast of Syntagma Square is the affluent neighborhood of **Kolonáki,** full of boutiques and fabulous hairdos; west of Syntagma Square is **Monastiráki**, adjacent to the ancient Greek and Roman *agoras* (marketplaces) and current home of the flea market. Head north from Monastiráki to **Omonia Square,** a somewhat dilapidated area with cheap lodging.

BY BUS

Athens has three different bus systems, all of which take the same 75dr ticket. The white kiosks near stations have unpredictable hours, so stock up on tickets at newsstands whenever possible. Crowded **yellow trolleybuses** serve the central district; routes are marked on the EOT city map. Trolleybus 1 goes from

Omonia Square to Syntagma Square, and from there you can walk to the Pláka; in fact, most buses that run down Stadíou Street from Omónia serve Syntagma and other stops near the Pláka. **Blue buses** stop more frequently, en route to the suburbs; the EOT map deciphers their complicated routes. **Orange buses** leave from 28 Mavromatéon Street, by the Pedíou tou Areos park, and shoot straight out to the 'burbs.

BY TAXI

Athens has some of the cheapest taxis in Europe: 200dr plus 62dr per km (⅗ mi) within the city, 120dr on the periphery. If you phone for a taxi, you pay 300dr extra; from the airport, you pay 400dr extra plus 50dr for each bag over 22 lbs. After midnight, the rates per km (⅗ mi) double, and there is also an extra charge on major holidays. Don't just accept a quoted price from the driver as you get in; go by the book or you might get shafted. Often an occupied taxi will stop for more riders; just shout the name of the neighborhood you want and jump in.

WHERE TO SLEEP

Athenian hotels aren't great, but they'll do for a night or two. Make reservations at least a day in advance July–August. Most budget travelers turn to the touristy **Pláka,** though some stay closer to **Omonia Square,** a grungier, cheaper area that can get loud and sleazy at night. Unless you have an early ferry out, there's no reason to stay in Piraeus, as it's only 30 minutes from central Athens. If you need a bed in Piraeus, **Hotel Acropole** (7 Gounari, 4 blocks east of Akti Possidonos Metro, tel. 01/41–73–313) has clean doubles for 8,000dr.

PLAKA

UNDER 10,000DR • Dioskouri House. This large, ghostly, 19th-century neoclassic building has a quiet patio and clean, somber rooms without bath. Doubles are 9,000dr. *6 Pitákou, at Periandrou near Hadrian's Arch, tel. 01/32–48–165.*

Phaedra Hotel. Facing the monument to Lysikrates, the Phaedra has friendly management, large, clean rooms, and 24-hour hot water. Doubles are 8,500dr without bath. *16 Herefontos, at Lissikratous, tel. 01/32–27–795.*

Student-Travelers Inn. This popular and well-run hotel in the heart of the Pláka features a bar and a vine-covered patio. Spotless doubles go for 9,000dr, dorm beds (four to a room) for 3,500dr. Breakfast is 1,000dr, and luggage storage is available. *16 Kidathineon, tel. 01/32–44–808.*

Hotel Kouros. Here you have placid, sunny patios, inspiring views of the Acropolis, and clean, simple rooms. There's no curfew, but Giorgos will shake his finger at you if you come home too late. Doubles range from 8,500dr to 9,500dr. *11 Kodrou, at Kidathinéon, tel. 01/32–27–431.*

MONASTIRAKI/PLATIA SINDAGMA

UNDER 10,000DR • John's Place. It's a bit run-down, but it's functional and clean. Rooms in the front get their share of street noise. The common rooms have tables, perfect for catching up on those postcards. Doubles cost 8,000dr. *5 Patróou, off Mitropóleos, tel. 01/32–29–719.*

Thisseus Hostel. The dingy entrance belies the backpacker's treasure within. Rooms are large and clean, some have balconies or fans, and there's a spacious kitchen. Doubles are 5,500dr, single beds in shared rooms (with 2–5 beds) 2,500dr. *10 Thisséos, tel. 01/32–45–960.*

UNDER 10,000DR • Hotel Tempi. About two blocks northeast of the Monastiráki flea market, Tempi overlooks a square filled with flower stands and kids. Some balconies have views of the Acropolis, and there's a roof balcony where you can make your offering to Helios or hang your laundry. Doubles are 7,000dr, 8,500dr with bath, and they'll store your luggage while you're out. *29 Eolou, at Ermou, tel. 01/32–13–175. Café/snack bar, laundry.*

NEAR VICTORIA TRAM STATION

Hostel Aphrodite. Friendly and clean, this small hotel is a pleasure. A double room with adjacent bath costs 5,600dr. They have hot water, a safe, a roof for sunning, free luggage storage, and a boat pass (11,500dr), all worthwhile. A few blocks northwest of the Victoria tram station in a residential area. *12 Einardou (Corner Michail Voda), tel. 01/88—10—589 or 01/88—39—249.*

HOSTELS

International Youth Hostel. A mecca for world travelers, this hostel has compact rooms with four beds, bath, and sunny balcony. Luggage storage is available. Beds 1,500dr, 2,000dr nonmembers. *16 Victor*

Hugo, tel. 01/52–34–170 or 01/52–34–015. From Omonia Square head up 3 Septemvríou and turn left on Veranzérou (becomes Victor Hugo).

Youth Hostel #5. Old ladies walk their dogs on streets lined with bitter-orange trees, giving this hostel a comforting neighborhood feel within hectic Athens. The walls are peppered with "philosophy of life" one-liners. Dorm beds are 1,500dr, doubles are 5,000dr, breakfast is 600dr, and luggage storage is 150dr. There's also a TV room. *75 Damaréos (corner Prínis) with large green door, tel. 01/75–19– 530. From Omónia or Syntagma square, take Trolleybus 2 or 11 (toward Pangrati) to Filolaou; walk SE 1 block. Kitchen, laundry.*

CAMPING

Voula Camping. About 45 minutes from Athens by bus, Voula is on the beach and boasts a bar, restaurant, and swimming pool. Small tents cost 880dr plus 1,250dr per person plus tax. *2 Alkionídon St., Voula, tel. 01/89–52–712, 01/89–53–249, or 01/89–51–648. Bus A2 (75dr) from Syntagma Square, Filelínon St., or Pl. Academias along Apollo Coast. Bus stops at entrance.*

FOOD

Despite noise, pollution, and lethargic waiters, dining in Athens can be highly gratifying. When you stumble upon a hidden taverna enveloped in the scent of retsina, you'll feel like you've traveled back in time. The ambience adds to the pleasure of the meal, and you're likely to experience some friendly banter with your waiter. Avoid Kidathinéon and Adrianoú streets in the Pláka, where waiters jump out and pressure passersby; you'll find better food and values elsewhere. Food kiosks and small sandwich and souvlaki shops abound, providing cheap, quick chow. The **market** around Monastiráki Square has plenty of fruit and vegetable stands for the economical. The **bakery** at 2 Níkis (open Mon.–Sat. 7:30–7) has spanakopita and *tirópita* for 300dr, and a nice selection of baked goods.

PLAKA

Eden. Indulge in moderately priced vegetarian delights such as eggplant stuffed with cheese and nuts or soya souvlaki with brown rice and *tzatzíki*, both 1,500dr. There's also a nonsmoking section, a rarity in smoke-happy Greece. *12 Lissíou, on corner of Mnissikléous, tel. 01/32–48–858. Closed Tues.*

Ouzeri Kouklas. The seats are crammed together on a vine-covered patio with views of Mt. Lykavitós, and waiters show up with salad and liters of house wine (which later show up on your bill) before you even order. 3,000 vegetarian dr buy enough fried eggplant, green salad, bread, and wine for two. *14 Tripódon, at Epihármou, tel. 01/32–47–605.*

MONASTIRAKI/SYNTAGMA SQUARE

Vangélis Taverna. Here's a deal: 2,500dr per person for salad and a grilled or oven-cooked entrée, including fish. *Evripídou 63, below the fruit-and-vegetable market, in an arcade, tel. 01/32–51–513. Closed August.*

Savas. This Middle Eastern restaurant specializes in beef kebab for 1,300dr and serves a variety of gyros for under 1,700dr. Greek salads are 700dr. Take your chicken-souvlaki pitas (500dr) on the road, or eat under the umbrellas at *86 Mitropóleos, just before Monastiráki Square, tel. 01/32–45–048.*

BETWEEN MT. LYKAVITTOS AND STREFI HILL

Lefka. This typical Greek taverna has a vine-covered garden lined with giant barrels of retsina. It's a bit out of the way, but worth the effort for its festive atmosphere. Salad, meat, potatoes, and wine for two won't run you more than 4,500dr. *121 Mauvromiháli, at Arianítou, tel. 01/36–14–038.*

KOLONAKI

Taverna Philípou. Scarf cheap dishes in central Athens's wealthiest district. Salads are 700dr; chicken with rice and potatoes is 1,200dr; and bean, pea, or eggplant dishes are 900dr. Lunch prices are cheaper still, and the bathroom is surprisingly opulent. *19 Xenokrátous, at Ploutárhou, tel. 01/72–16–390. Closed Sun.*

CAFES AND OUZERIA

The muddled distinction between *kafenía* (cafés) and *ouzería* (ouzo bars) is almost invisible in Athens. Both serve slender glasses of the anise-based ouzo along with beer, wine, frappés, and Greek coffee. Both are also bastions of Greek male culture, where older men spend their days drinking, smoking, and playing backgammon. The pub-like **Cafe Pláka** (corner of Fléssa and Tripódon) serves milkshakes (standing 600dr, sitting 1,100dr), fruit juices (standing 300dr, sitting 800dr), and crêpes (standing 600dr, sitting 2,500dr) from both its street window and its rooftop garden patio. One of Athens's best *ouzeria,* **O Glykós** (Géronda, at Hatzimiháli), is hidden from tourists on a side street in the center of the Pláka. Greek families, intellectuals, and young bohemians assemble here to enjoy frappés (500dr), beers (500dr), and *mezédhes* (900dr). From Filelínon, head down Kidathinéon and turn right on Géronda.

WORTH SEEING

The center of Athens is littered with splendidly decrepit monuments to the city's golden age (the 5th century BC) and its subsequent decline under Christian Rome. The AD 131 **Arch of Hadrian** (corner of Amalías and Vasilíssis Olgas) marks the boundary between ancient Athens and the newfangled Roman section. Greece's capital of both politics and culture, Athens has a disproportionate number of the nation's historic and artistic treasures, most of which are clustered in its older parts. A pet project of the first queen of modern Greece, the **National Gardens** (open daily dawn–dusk) provide a shady reprieve from the relentless bustle of downtown Athens. Solo women: Beware of men with hands down their pants here.

ACROPOLIS

Towering over the modern city of 4 million much as it stood over the ancient capital of 50,000, the **Acropolis** ("above the city") is perpetually Athens's most spectacular attraction. Although there was a settlement on the Acropolis around 5,000 BC and a palace during the Mycenaean Period, the Acropolis was a religious center long before Athens became a major city-state in the 6th century BC. It has been associated with Athena ever since the city's mythical founding, but virtually all of the city's other religious cults had temples or shrines here as well. As Athens became the dominant city-state in the 5th century BC, Pericles led the city in making the Acropolis the crowning symbol of Athenian power and successful democracy. Under his direction, the buildings within the

With the exception of a disastrous 1678 explosion of munitions stored in the Parthenon, it is said that the Acropolis has suffered more damage in the last 50 years from environmental pollution than it sustained in its previous 2,000 years of existence.

Acropolis's walls (dating back to the 13th century BC) were designed to be as visually harmonious as they were enormous, and they remain supremely elegant, even in their fragmented states. The entrance to the Acropolis is through the monumental **Propylaia,** a Doric and Ionic gateway built between 437 BC and 432 BC. Flanking the Propylaia is the Ionic temple of **Athena Nike,** or Temple of the Wingless Victory. The temple's marble balustrade, whose carvings of Athena receiving gifts adorned three of its sides, is now housed in the Acropolis Museum (*see below*). The **Erechtheion** is the site of the mythical contest between Athena and Poseidon to decide who would be Athens's patron god; the olive tree in front was Athena's victorious gift to the city. Facing the Parthenon is the **Porch of the Maidens,** where reproductions of six graceful caryatids (columns carved into a female form) support a stone architrave; the surviving originals are in the British Museum and the Acropolis Museum. The **Parthenon,** the Acropolis's largest temple, is considered a perfect example of the Doric order: Its careful proportions of height, width, breadth, column, and open space create a balance that belies the structure's massive size. *Tel. 01/32–10–219. Admission: 2,000dr. Open weekdays 8–6:30, weekends 8:30–2:30.*

The **Acropolis Museum** has an excellent collection of carvings and pottery, including many of ancient Greece's best-known reliefs and statues. *Tel. 01/32–36–665. Admission free with Acropolis ticket.*

Just below the Acropolis, the **Theater of Dionysus,** opened in 534 BC by Peisistratus, is where Sophocles, Aristophanes, and Euripides first presented their works to 13,000 Athenians and the high priests of Dionysus. Roman additions to the theater include the circular stage and marble railing, installed when the theater became an arena for gladiatorial bouts. To the east of the theater lies the foundation of Pericles' **Odeon,** once considered the best concert hall in Greece. *D. Areopagitou, tel. 01/32–24–625. Admission: 500dr. Open daily 8:30–2:30.*

ANCIENT GREEK AGORA

The ancient Greek Agora was the economic, social, and political center of Athens. Here Socrates and Plato discoursed, and occasionally scored excellent deals on figs. Founded in the 6th century BC, the Agora passed through several stages of glory and decline before the Romans showed up, and finally fell into disuse when the Byzantine empire eliminated the philosophical academies that had once sprouted here. Today the site is a motley collection of ruined Classical, Byzantine, and Turkish foundations. Dominating one side is the meticulous 1950s reconstruction of the **Stoa of Attalus,** originally built during the 2nd century BC by Attalus, King of Pergamon, to express gratitude for the education he received in Greece. Facing the Panathenaic Way, this long, arcaded building houses the Agora's **museum** (tel. 01/32–10–185; admission free with Agora ticket). On the opposite side of the Agora, the reconstructed 5th-century BC **Hephaisteion**—the best-preserved Greek temple in the world, with many fully intact columns and friezes—sits on a small hill. The 34 columns still hold up the original roof. *Admission: 1,200dr. Open Tues.–Sun. 8:30–2:45.*

JEWISH MUSEUM

This museum offers a comprehensive history of the Jewish diaspora in Greece, which dates back at least to the 3rd century BC. On display are traditional costumes, religious artifacts, a reassembled synagogue, and a photographic history of the Greek Jews' experience during World War II (almost 90% of Greece's prewar Jewish population was lost during the war, mostly to Auschwitz). *36 Amalías, tel. 01/32–315–77. Open Sun.–Fri. 9–1. Note: The museum was scheduled to move to Nikis 33, a few blocks away, in fall 1997.*

MONUMENT OF LYSIKRATES

Still intact despite years of abuse, this proud cylindrical monument is the oldest known building (335 BC) with Corinthian columns. It was once a library and the poet Byron's study when he stayed at the then-adjacent Capuchin Convent; today, it sits amid ruined foundations in the center of a café-rimmed platía. *Corner of Víronos (Byron) and Lissikrátous, 1 block south of Kidathinéon.*

NATIONAL ARCHAEOLOGICAL MUSEUM

This museum is one of the world's premier repositories of ancient Greek art. The rooms of *stelae* (carved-relief grave markers), *kouri* (idealized statues of young men), *amphorae* (decorated terra-cotta vases for wine or oils), and friezes are almost overwhelming. *44 28 Oktovríou-Patissíon, tel. 01/82–17–717. From Syntagma Square, take Bus 2, 4, 9, or 15; or walk 20 min. Admission: 2,000dr. Open Mon. 12:30–7, Tues.–Fri. 8–7, weekends 8:30–3.*

NICHOLAS P. GOULANDRIS MUSEUM OF CYCLADIC ART

From 2600 to 1000 BC, artists on the Cycladic Islands produced the first known life-size statues of the female body, as well as countless fertility statuettes. This museum holds the world's finest gathering of these smooth marble sculptures, long a misunderstood and undervalued Greek form of art. *4 Neofítou Doúka, tel. 01/72–28–321. Admission: 400dr. Open Mon. and Wed.–Fri. 10–4, Sat. 10–3.*

ROMAN AGORA

The Roman Agora, built in part by emperors Augustus and Hadrian, is a small, well-preserved collection of columns and monuments. The hollow, 1st-century **Tower of the Winds** was a hydraulic clock with a sundial and a weathervane; the tower's octagonal form corresponds to the eight winds, represented by winged figures on the frieze. The other standing structure on-site is a 16th-century **Fethiye mosque,** built by the sultan who conquered Constantinople; it has been variously used as a school, a bakery, and barracks and is now used by the Greek Archaeological Service as a storeroom. Next to the entrance to the Agora are the foundations and benches of a Roman public toilet. *Corner of Pelopída and Eólou, east of the Ancient Greek Agora, tel. 01/32–45–220. Admission: 500dr. Open Tues.–Sun. 8:30–2:45.*

TEMPLE OF OLYMPIAN ZEUS

Vying with the Acropolis for distinction as Greece's best-illuminated archaeological site at night, this temple was the largest in Greece when it was finally completed during the 2nd century BC. Only 15 of the original 114 massive Corinthian columns still stand. *Corner of Vasilíssis Olgas and Amalías, tel. 01/92–26–330. Admission: 500dr. Open Tues.–Sun. 8:30–3.*

CHEAP THRILLS

The **Evzónes,** unmistakable in tassled hats and pom-pommed shoes, guard the President's House (just east of the National Gardens) and the Parliament building on Syntagma Square. Every hour on the hour, they act out a traditional changing of the guard that falls somewhere between discipline and comedy.

For a bird's-eye view of Athens, go to the top of **Mt. Likavittós,** looming over Kolonáki. Bring a few beers and cherish this rare angle on the city—when you can't see the smog, Athens actually looks pretty. The cheapest way up is to walk the 15–20 minutes from Kolonáki. Otherwise, take Minibus 060 from Kanári and Akademías to the end of the road. A funicular (400dr) runs to the top until midnight.

At around 6 AM every morning, Athens's liveliest grandmas and grandpas invade the beach at **Palió Fáliro** for their morning constitutional. Take it from them—the water is revitalizing and the beach serene, especially at sunrise and sunset. Bus 126 from Syntagma Square or any bus heading down Singroú will have you there in about 30 minutes. Evenings, men brood over intense chess games played on boards drawn along the boardwalk—watch them literally wrestle with the life-size pieces as they heave them from square to square.

FESTIVAL

Best known for its staging of ancient Greek plays in the very theaters where they premiered, the **Athens Festival** also covers a broad spectrum of music, dance, and more recent drama. The shows are all beautiful—even awkward choreography is gorgeous in an ancient amphitheater. Performances are scheduled early June–mid-September. Purchase tickets (2,000dr–20,000dr, depending on the event) at the ticket office in the arcade at 4 Stadíou (open weekdays 8:30–2 and 5–7, Sat. 8:30–2, Sun. 10–1). Get schedules here or at the tourist office, or dial 01/32–21–459 for more information.

AFTER DARK

BARS

Around **Syntagma Square,** beware of overly friendly Greek men with offers of wine, women, and song. They lure hapless male tourists into bars, order them a few drinks, and then stick them with exorbitant checks. Bars and *ouzeria* proliferate in the **Pláka**; explore the winding side streets to find the perfect spot. Pretentious types besiege the bars around **Kolonáki Square,** but a wade through the Armani and the cell phones reveals a more relaxed crowd. Try **Jackson Hall Spirits** (4 Milióni, at Kanári, tel. 01/36–160–546) for 41 kinds of European beer. **Platía Exarhion,** in Exárhia, has several happening bars; favorites include **Double Coffee** (77 Themistokléous, on the platía, tel. 01/33–011–77) and **Café Floral** (81 Themistokléous, tel. 01/33–009–38).

Athens's flea market (which begins in Monastiráki on Ermoú; open daily early morning–early afternoon) erupts into pandemonium on Sunday morning. This is the place to experience the city's often obscured ethnic and cultural diversity.

DANCING

Like its tourism, Athens's club scene is seasonal. City clubs migrate to the coast in summer; most move to Glyfada on the Apollo Coast, which can mean expensive cab rides back to the city. In addition to high covers (about 3,000dr on weekends) and drink prices (1,000dr–2,000dr), many clubs exercise "face control," leaving entry up to the whims of the doorperson. Popular clubs du jour include **Avant-garde** (19 Lembéssi, tel. 01/92–427–37 in winter, Glyfada in summer) for ambient and trance; **Aerodhromio** (behind the east terminal of the airport) for techno; and **Amfitheatro** (Glyfada) for house. In the center of town, **Odyssia** (116 Ermoú; cover 1,500dr) is an intimate lesbian club where scores of beautiful women drink, smoke, dance, and make merry. **City** (4 Korizí, off Singroú, 01/92- -40–740; cover 2,500dr; closed Mon.–Wed.) claims a flamboyant gay and transvestite crowd, though anyone's welcome to grind. Consult the staff at **Metropolis Records** (54 Panepistimíou (Venizélou, tel. 01/38–085–49) for event flyers and the most current club information. Final note: Most clubs are mere ideas before 11 PM.

CINEMA

The audience talks and the projectors are often flicked off for intermission, but Athens's outdoor summer cinema/cafés are a blast. Films (1,700dr) are always shown in the original language, subtitled in Greek, with two screenings nightly at 9 and 11. In the Pláka, **Cine Paris** (22 Kidathinéon) caters to a mainstream crowd, while **Cine Refresh** (Pl. Dexameni, Kolonáki) sometimes shows first-run European art films.

NEAR ATHENS

APOLLO COAST

Masses of Athenians engulf the Apollo Coast in summer, but if you circumvent the full-blown resorts, like Glyfada, you will find some tranquil places to commune with the sea. The coast stretches from Piraeus to Soúnion, in the southeast; the first 27 km (17 mi) are accessible by Athens city buses. The town of **Vouliagméni** offers the best combination of space and sea; just outside it, blissful expanses of beach are broken only by the occasional nude sunbather. From Akademias or Filelinon, take Bus 122 (1 hr, 75dr); buy your return ticket before leaving Athens.

DELPHI

According to myth, Zeus released one eagle from the east and one from the west, and at the point where they met, he threw down a sacred stone to mark the "navel of the world" at what would later become Delphi. Dating back at least to the 2nd century BC, the famous oracle at Delphi is centered around a cave where Apollo kept his great sacrificial altar. Here the priestess Pythia would purify herself in the Kastalian fountain, eat a laurel leaf, and, in ecstasy, receive divine visions, perhaps inspired by the hallucinogenic vapors seeping through the crevice under the sacred stone. Questions presented to her received strange and garbled answers, which were then translated into verse by a priest. The Delphi **museum** houses all kinds of objects from the Sanctuary of Delphi, including restructured pediments, the famous bronze Charioteer, the Sphinx of the Naxians (550 BC), and a bust of Dionysus. The Doric Temple of Apollo commands the center of the site, where you can also visit (among other things) the Sanctuary of Athena and the Treasuries, where the erstwhile city-state kept votive offerings and religious vessels. The highway to modern Delphi cuts through the middle of the site; be sure to explore both sides. *Tel. 0265/82313. Admission to site 1,200dr; to the museum, another 1,200dr. Open weekdays 7:30–7:15, weekends 8:30–2:45; museum closed Mon. morning.*

KTEL buses serve Delphi from Athens's Liossíon station (3 hrs, 2,600dr). The bus stops at the site, but if you want to ensure a seat on the bus, walk the 2 km (1½ mi) back from the ruins to the "bus station" (a table in a taverna) on the far side of modern Delphi. To crash in modern Delphi, call ahead for one of the clean doubles (8,500dr) at **Hotel Athini** (55 Vasileon Pavlou, tel. 0265/82239). **Apollon Camping** (1½ km/1 mi south of town, on road to Itea, tel. 0265/82762 or 0265/82750, fax 0265/82639; 1,200dr per person plus 600dr per tent) has a pool, kitchen, laundry, restaurant, and market and panoramic views of the mountains.

TEMPLE OF POSEIDON

In a fit of ego, the poet Byron carved his name on one of this temple's columns, and thousands of less illustrious visitors have followed his lead. Happily, they haven't effaced the beauty of the structure, which is idyllically positioned on a rocky point overlooking the Aegean. (It was from these rocks that King Aegeus met his tragic end. Aegeus's son, Theseus had gone off in a boat with black sails to battle the Minotaur on Crete, promising that if he were successful he would rig the boat with white sails, and if not, his companions would return with the black sails. In the flush of his success, Theseus forgot his promise and left the black sails on, causing Aegeus to hurl himself into the water in grief just as his son returned home.) Only 12 of the temple's Doric columns are in their original positions, but the temple is still awe-inspiring, framed by the deep blue sky and the mystical sea. Bring your own food, if possible; the kiosk and café are expensive. Orange KTEL buses (2 hrs, 1,050dr) leave for Soúnion from the Mavromateon station (28 Oktovriou, at Platía Egiptou) and Platía Klafthmonos (on Odos Stadiou, between Syntagma and Omonia Squares. Take a *paraliakó* (coastal) rather than a *mesoyiakó* (inland) bus, as they're faster and more scenic. *Tel. 0292/39363. Admission: 800dr. Open Mon.–Sat. 9–sunset, Sun. 10–sunset.*

THE ISLANDS

Once you've oohed and ahhed your way through the relics of ancient culture on the mainland, hop on a boat to find out why the Greek isles enjoy near-legendary status. Stunning clusters of islands encircle the Greek peninsula and bridge the waters between Greece and Turkey, enticing travelers to such infamous party resorts as Míkonos and more remote getaways, such as Lésvos. The islands offer everything from hard partying to secluded coves where you can gaze at the tranquil Aegean. Privacy is much harder to find during the summer, when hordes of vacationing Europeans drive prices up and an unoccupied patch of sand becomes a hot commodity. Fortunately, "vacationers" don't care about ruins.

PELOPONNESE

"Pelopónnisos" means "Island of Pelops" (whose story is told in Olympia's sculptures), though only the narrow Kórinthos Canal separates it from the mainland. Composed of seven different prefectures, the Pelopónnese is the Greece of history and myth. At the northern tip of the peninsula, Korinthia contains the impressive ruins of ancient Corinth, while Argolis harbors the major sites of Mycenaean civilization (1600 BC–1100 BC). Untouristed Arcadia, the central prefecture, is lush and mountainous. Further south, Laconia and Messinia are home to a proud and individualistic people, especially on the Mani peninsula. In the northwest is Eleia, the site of ancient Olympia, and further north in Achaia is the busy port Pátra.

CORINTH

Corinth was an economic and maritime powerhouse in ancient Greece. Though most of its ruins are from the Roman period, some remains are older still, such as the 6th-century BC **Temple of Apollo** (one of Greece's oldest), seven of whose 38 thick columns still stand. The ruins of the temple overlook the ancient marketplace, or **Agora,** which contains several small temples, and ruins of fountains and baths. Next to the Temple of Apollo, the **museum** houses the city's famous Archaic pottery along with terra-cotta sphinxes, mosaics, and statues whose heads were lopped off by righteous Christians in their zeal to destroy all images of Hellenic and Roman worship. *Tel. 0741/31207. Admission to site and museum: 1,200dr. Open daily 8:45–7.*

Hanging 1,900 ft over ancient Corinth is a huge rock supporting the classical and then medieval fortress **Acrokórinth** (open weekdays 8–7, weekends 8:30–3), supposedly the largest and oldest fortress on the Pelopónnese. Within its walls are monuments from the Byzantine, Venetian, and Turkish eras. The ruins and spectacular views are well worth the hour's hike up to the fortress, but there is also a vehicle road. Admission is 500dr. On a nearby peak was the **Temple of Aphrodite,** which got rich off its 1,000 sacred prostitutes.

The main appeal of **modern Corinth** is its proximity to ancient Corinth. As modern Peloponnesian cities go, though, it's not bad, thanks to a central park with fountains and birds. Nightfall brings out strolling families and waiters maneuvering through pedestrian traffic along the café-filled waterfront street. Corinth is an easy day trip from Athens, but if you stay at the central **Hotel Belle-Vue** (41 Damaskinou, near the waterfront, tel. 0741/22088; doubles from 4,000dr), you'll get 15% off next door at **Kanita Restaurant** (tel. 0741/28834). Filling, veggie-stuffed tomatoes are 800dr, and pizzas run 1,200dr–1,600dr. The friendly **tourist police** (51 Ermou, on SE side of park near Athens bus stop, tel. 0741/72793; open daily 7:30 AM–9 PM) have tons of brochures and maps.

COMING AND GOING

Modern Corinth's **train station** (Dimokratias, tel. 0741/22523) sends daily trains to Athens (2 hrs, 780dr), Pátra (2½ hrs, 980dr), and Olympia (5 hrs, 1,780dr). The **main bus station** at Ermou and Koliatsou (tel. 0741/72793) sends buses to Athens (1½ hrs, 1,350dr), Mikínes (1 hr, 650dr), and Loutráki (20 min, 250dr). The bus stop for ancient Corinth (30 min, 190dr) is on Koliatsou; from the main bus station, walk through the central park, and the stop is on the right on the second block. Buses depart on the hour daily 7:10 AM–9:10 PM.

MIKINES

Once upon a time, Mikínes (or Mycenae, which Homer calls "rich in gold") was the mightiest city of the mightiest people in Europe, who ruled from the plains of Argos to the Saronic Gulf, including Crete. After 1200 BC, however, the city began to decline, and in 1100 BC, it was decimated by fire during the so-called Dorian invasions, after which Greece lapsed into chaos. The **Lion Gate,** the main entrance to the citadel (whose discovery in 1841 ignited a worldwide Mycenaean craze), remains one of the best-known ruins at this ancient site. The **Treasury of Atreus,** or Tomb of Agamemnon (1250 BC), is the largest of the renowned *tholos* (beehive) tombs. *Tel. 0751/76585. Admission: 1,500dr. Open daily 8–6.*

Uninteresting **Modern Mikínes** is a convenient, if generic, base for exploring the ruins 2 km (1½ mi) away. Famous archaeologist Heinrich Schliemann crashed in the welcoming rooms of **La Belle Helene** (main road, at bus stop, tel. 0751/76225; doubles 6,000dr) after long days of excavation in the 1870s. The **hostel** (main road, tel. 0751/76224; beds 1,500dr) here is dingy; check in at the restaurant Iphigenia (under hostel, tel. 0751/76255). **Camping Mycenae** (off main street, tel. 0751/76121; 1000dr per person plus 700dr per tent) is a peaceful, family-run campground with clean bathrooms and big sinks for laundry. Nearby, **Dassis Tours** (tel. 0751/76123; open daily 7:30 AM–10 PM) provides tourist information and rents rooms (doubles from 8,000dr). Mamma cooks delicious traditional dishes and veggie omelettes (900dr) at **Point** (main road, between La Belle Helene and hostel).

COMING AND GOING

Most buses from Athens (2 hrs, 1,750dr) and Corinth (1 hr, 650dr) stop in **Fihti.** From here, it's a 1½-km (1-mi) walk to the ruins at Mikínes, but with luck you can catch the bus (160dr) from Argos zipping through Fihti on its way to the site.

NEAR MIKINES

Today, people visit **Epidavros** to see its amazingly well-preserved **theater.** Built during the 4th century BC, the 14,000-seat theater still has perfect acoustics—from the 55th row, you can hear a coin drop in the center. Every year, the theater also puts on ancient drama during the month-long **Festival of Epidavros,** starting the third week of June. Buy festival tickets at the site office (open Thurs.–Sat. 9:30–1); Bourtzi Tours (Syngrou, six doors down from KTEL station, tel. 0752/22691) in Nafplio (*see below*); or the Athens Festival box office (*see* Cheap Thrills *in* Athens, *above*). In the 4th century BC, disciples of Asclepius, god of healing, came to Epidavros for treatment and respite at the **Sanctuary of Asclepius,** a kind of sanatorium, hotel, and hospital rolled into one; cures often came in dreams here. To put the scattered remains of the sanctuary in perspective, visit the on-site **museum,** which contains surgical instruments, votive statues, and a partial reconstruction of the *tholos* (circular building), whose cult remains a mystery. *Tel. 0753/22009. Admission to site and museum: 1,500dr. Site open Mon. noon–6, Tues.–Fri. 7:30–7:30.*

Since the one hotel in Epidavros is prohibitively expensive, most visitors day-trip here from the charming coastal town of **Nafplio,** to the southwest. Modern Greece's first captital, Nafplio is topped by a Venetian fortress. In the old part of town, try Staïkopoulou Street for a wealth of rooms (doubles from 5,000dr). In the new part of town, 15 minutes away, **Hotel Economou** (22 Argonafton, at Asklipiou, tel. 0752/23955) has doubles for 9,000dr. The deservedly popular **Kelari Restaurant** (16 Staïkopoulou, tel. 0752/24731) has friendly service and a varied menu (*dolmádes* with egg and lemon sauce 900dr). From Nafplio's **bus station** (8 Syngrou, tel. 0752/27323), four buses run to Epidavros daily (45 min, 480dr). Buses also go to Athens (3 hrs, 2,250dr) and Mikínes (30 min, 400dr).

MONEMVASSIA

Perched on a huge rock jutting out into the sea, the medieval fortress town of Monemvassia ("single entrance") has been conquered by Normans, Venetians, and Turks. Though now beseiged by tourists, its medieval character endures; to enter the old town through the narrow tunnel is to enter another time. The buildings here owe much to the Venetians, but the town's nearly 40 churches, some with beautiful architecture, reflect the Byzantine period. The 10th-century **Agia Stephanos** and the 13th-century **Church of Christ Elkomenos** are well preserved, but don't miss the haunting 13th-century **Agia Sophia,** clinging precariously to a cliff among the ruins of the upper town. For a truly eerie experience, stand inside and listen to the urgent winds howl around you.

A 1-km (⅔-mi) causeway connects Monemvassia to the pleasant seaside town of **Yéfira** ("bridge") on the mainland. You'll find all the tourist amenities here; **Malvasia Travel** (140 23rd Iouliou, tel. 0732/61752; open Mon.–Sat. 7 AM–9:30 PM, Sun. noon–2:30 PM) provides bus and ferry information and arranges car or scooter rentals.

COMING AND GOING

The **bus stop** is in the center of Yéfira. Most buses to and from Yéfira pass through Molai (20 min, 400dr). From Molai, you can get to other points on the Pelopónnese via Sparta (2 hrs, 1,600dr). Check with **Miras Ferries** (near Mobil station, in Yéfira, tel. 0732/61219; open daily 8 AM–9 PM) for details on its irregular ferry service to Crete (8 hrs, 3,050dr) and Piraeus (6 hrs, 3,600dr).

WHERE TO SLEEP AND EAT

Lodging in Monemvassia costs a fortune (doubles from 10,000dr), so head across the causeway to Yéfira. Signs reading ROOMS TO LET abound; or try **Hotel Acrogiali** (23rd Iouliou, across from National Bank, tel. 0732/61360), for immaculate doubles with bath (8,000dr), or **Derziotis** (249 23rd Iouliou, tel. 0732/67784), for pleasant 6,000dr doubles with views of Monemvassia and the sea. **Camping Paradise** (4 km/2½ mi south of Yéfira, tel. 0732/61123; 850dr per tent plus 1,000dr per person) has a beach, restaurant, bar, and minimart; call ahead to get picked up in their minivan. For excellent seafood (swordfish 1,900dr), head to **Restaurant Aktaion** (in Yéfira, before causeway, tel. 0732/61797).

SPARTA AND MISTRAS

To enhance their sons' military prowess, ancient Spartans fed them black-bean gruel and tossed the weak off a nearby mountain. Unfortunately for today's tourists, the Spartans spent more time building muscles than architectural wonders; the city wasn't impressive then, and not much of it remains. Modern Sparta isn't much to cheer about, either. As you pass through here on your way to Byzantine Mistrás, just 5 km (3 mi) away, take a look at the skeletal remains of the **Acropolis,** overlooked by the snowcapped Tayetos mountains, and the 1st- or 2nd-century hillside theater, whose marble was removed for the construction of **Mistrás.** Sparta's **Archaeological Museum** (Likourgou, tel. 0731/28575; admission 500dr; open Tues.–Sun. 8:30–3) is also worthwhile; from the bus station, turn left on Paleologou, continue one block, and turn left again on Likorgou. The highlight is the marble statue of heroic Leonidas, who led 300 unblinking Spartans to their deaths against the Persians; also of interest are Roman mosaics and prehistoric dedications from Laconia. The local **tourist police office** (8 Hilonos, 1 block east of museum, tel. 0731/26229; open daily 8 AM–10 PM) provides information for both Sparta and Mistrás.

Of all the 14th- and 15th-century Byzantine remains on the Pelopónnese, Mistrás is the most significant; it flourished even after Constantinople fell. Buses now run from one level of the site to the other, but a three-hour walk around the grounds offers more rewarding views of the ancient churches, monasteries, and palaces. From the 13th-century **citadel,** where the only signs of life are stubborn flowers and buzzing bees, a beautiful panorama of olive groves and misty mountains unfolds. The **Peribleptos** church has magnificent frescoes. Also visit the 15th-century **Pantanassa Convent,** the only fully occupied religious complex in Mistrás (dress: no shorts or bare shoulders). *Tel. 0731/93377. Admission: 1,200dr. Open daily 8:30–7 (until 3 off season).*

The tiny, attractive town of modern Mistrás exists mainly to facilitate visits to Byzantine Mistrás, 2 km (1 mi) to the north. Drop your pack off in **Christina Vahaviolou**'s plush, colorful rooms (from bus stop, take main road toward Agion Ioannis, tel. 0731/83432; doubles 5,000dr); Christina's husband serves homemade specials in the restaurant downstairs. On the road to Sparta, 300 yds from Mistrás's main square, **Camping Castle View** (tel. 0731/83303; 700dr per tent plus 1,100dr per person) is built among the olive groves, with a bus stop across the street.

COMING AND GOING

Daily buses connect Sparta to Athens (4 hrs, 3,300dr) and Corinth (2½ hrs, 2,050dr). Buses leave from the corner of Likourgou and Leonidou in Sparta almost hourly for Mistrás (10 min, 180dr). You can also catch a bus to Mistrás from Athens (4 hrs, 3,600dr) or Corinth (2½ hrs, 2,200dr).

OLYMPIA

The first recorded Olympic Games consisted of a 660-ft race across the stadium at Olympia in 776 BC. Soon the games were in full swing, happening every four years and eventually attracting athletes from the entire Greek world, from Sicily to Asia Minor. In AD 393, the Roman emperor Theodosius banned the Games, calling them unchristian. The huge **Temple of Zeus,** one of the Seven Wonders of the Ancient World, is in the center of Aldis, a sacred precinct where the games were originally held. The ancient **stadium,** which at one time held up to 20,000 spectators, is at the far end of the site, and enough of it remains for even the unimaginative to picture crowds and athletes. The site is big, shady, and pleasant. If you have only a day or two on the Pelopónnese, make Olympia a priority. To get to the site from Olympia village, head to the entrance of town and walk 500 yds up the road to your left. *Tel. 0624/22517. Admission: 1,200dr. Open weekdays 8–7, weekends 8:30–3.*

Across the street from the site is a new **Archaeological Museum,** which holds the massive pediments of the Temple of Zeus and Praxiteles' graceful *Hermes with the Infant Dionysus* (330 BC). You can also see the signed bronze helmet of Miltiades, Marathon's victorious general. *Tel. 0627/22742. Admission: 1,200dr. Open Mon. 12:30–7, Tues.–Fri. 8–7, weekends 8:30–3.*

COMING AND GOING

In modern Olympia, the **EOT** (on main street Kondili, tel. 0624/23100; open daily 9–9) also serves as the local bus station, with service to Athens (6 hrs, 5,000dr), Corinth (5hrs, 3,800dr), and Pátra (2 hrs, 1,600dr) via Pírgos.

WHERE TO SLEEP AND EAT

Olympia's **HI hostel** (18 Kondili, 1 block from bus stop, tel. 0624/22580; beds 1,400dr) has bunks in basic rooms and breakfast for 400dr. To reach the spacious, spotless 5,000dr doubles at **Hotel Praxiteles** (7 Spiliopoylou, tel. 0624/23570) from the bus stop, head down Kondili, make a left at the National Bank, and make another left one block up. The **restaurant** on the ground floor is good for a peaceful meal of rabbit stew (1,000dr), baked chicken (1,000dr), and baked beans (800dr).

PATRA

Pátra (Patras in English), transport hub of the Pelopónnese, has just enough sights to keep you occupied for an hour or two between ferries. To escape the ruckus of the port, walk from Platía Trion Simahon, the main square, up Agiou Nikolaou to the end. Climb the decrepit stairs and wander around the Venetian **Kástro**, built from Classical to Baroque. If you're dressed right (no shorts), you can make a pilgrimage to the church **Agios Andreas** (at southern end of Othonos Amalias, on Pl. Agiou Andreou), where the head of St. Andrew rests peacefully in a gold reliquary.

BASICS

The **EOT** (international ferry port, tel. 061/453–358; open Mon.–Sat. 7:30 AM–9:00 PM, Sun. 2:30–9) will point you to the appropriate ferry company. **Alpha Credit Bank** (9 Ag. Nikolaou, tel. 061/277–447; open weekdays 8–2), offers cash advances on American Express cards and charges a small commission for cashing AmEx traveler's checks. The **tourist police** (tel. 061/451–833; open daily 7:30 AM–11 PM) and **OTE** (open daily 8:30 AM–9 PM) are also at the international ferry port.

COMING AND GOING

Daily **ferries** run to and from Ancona, Italy (20 hrs, 20,800dr); Bari, Italy (12 hrs, 13,000dr); and Brindisi, Italy (15 hrs, 9,900dr), sometimes with a stop in Corfu (10 hrs, 5,300dr). The prices above include the 1,500dr port tax. Eurailers and InterRailers pay only a 4,500dr supplement (including port tax) if they come from Brindisi on **Adriatica** (across from Gate 6, between train station and international ferry port, tel. 061/421–995; open daily 9 AM–10 PM) or **Hellenic Mediterranean Lines** (1 km/⅔ mi from international ferry port, tel. 061/452–548; open daily 9 AM–11 PM).

The main **bus terminal** (Othonos Amalias, catercorner from train station, tel. 061/277–556) serves Athens (3 hrs, 3,200dr), Corinth (1¼ hr, 2,150dr), and Delphi via Itea (2½–4 hrs, 2,150dr). **Trains** (tel. 061/273–694) arrive from Athens (4 hrs 20 min, 1,580dr), Corinth (2 hrs 10 min, 980dr), and Pírgos (2 hrs, 820dr). Eurailers ride free.

WHERE TO SLEEP AND EAT

Hotels here are expensive and depressing, but if you get stranded overnight, there's a hospitable little **HI hostel** (68 Iroon Politehniou, tel. 061/427–278; beds 1,500dr) in an old mansion on the waterfront, a 10-minute walk from the port. **Pension Nicos** (3 Patreos, at 121 Ag. Andreou, tel. 061/623–757; doubles 6,000dr–7,000dr) has functional rooms and a rooftop bar. **Salt and Sugar** (54 Ag. Andreou, tel. 061/623–606) serves filling crêpes (500dr–1,000dr) 24 hours a day.

IONIAN ISLANDS

With fertile lands, forested peaks, and wide expanses of welcoming beach, the Ionian islands have been inhabited since the Stone Age, and their location on East–West trade routes has tempted many an occupier. The islands changed hands for centuries—from the Romans, Byzantines, and Venetians to the French, Russians, Turks, and British—before joining modern Greece in 1864. Though an earthquake rattled Zákinthos, Kefalonia, and Itháki in 1953, destroying much of the traditional architecture, the isles' beauty and tranquility remain. Corfu is the most heavily visited, Kefalonia is the largest, Zákinthos may be the most beautiful, and Itháki is rocky and secluded.

CORFU

Over the centuries, Corfu (Kérkira in Greek) has been ruled by many foreign powers, but it's the Venetians who have left the most visible relics, especially in Kérkira Town. Modern-day raiders content themselves by staking out little pieces of the island: At times you may feel surrounded by the British,

Scandinavians, Americans, Australians, and Germans who come to party and sunbathe amid Corfu's woodsy interior, diving cliffs, romantic architecture, sleepy coastal towns, and seaside villages.

Kérkira Town repays a day spent sightseeing, but Corfu's real charm lies in its world-class beaches. Hard-core partyers might appreciate wild nights at the depraved Pink Palace and touristy Glifada beach; for a mellower Corfu experience, head to the quiet north-side towns of Sidari and Roda.

BASICS

The **tourist information** booth (open daily 9:30–9) on the Spianáda (Esplanade), at Dousmani, has maps (500dr), camping information, and an inaccurate bus schedule. **American Express** services are handled by Greek Skies Travel (20A Kapodistriou, Box 24, 49100, tel. 0661/30883; open weekdays 9–2 and 5:30–8, Sat. 9–2), just south of the tourist booth; they have the best exchange rates in summer.

COMING AND GOING

Boats shuttle between Corfu and Pátra (10 hrs, 5,300dr) and Igoumenítsa (2 hrs, 850dr). Eurailers and InterRailers get free trips on **Adriatica** (tel. 061/421–995) and **Hellenic Mediterranean Lines** (tel. 061/652–548), from Brindisi, Italy (8 hrs, 9,500dr), though a 4,500dr supplement is charged during high season. You can also sail from Bari, Italy, in six hours, but rail passes aren't accepted.

GETTING AROUND

Kérkira Town itself is walkable; visitors spend most of their time wandering the old alleys between the Spianáda and Platía Sanrocco (a.k.a. Platía Theotoki). To get outside the town, however, you'll have to take a bus. From Platia Sanrocco, **blue buses** serve nearby destinations, such as the Achillion (20 min, 155dr). **Green buses** (station at Avramiou, just west of the New Fort) serve various towns on the rest of the island, including Glifada (45 min), Paleokastritsas (1 hr), and Kasiopi (1 hr); trips never cost more than 350dr. Renting a **scooter** (from 3,000dr) can be exciting, but traffic makes it pretty dangerous.

WHERE TO SLEEP

If you're too bushed to walk far from the ferry, **Hotel Europa** (Kérkira Town, tel. 0661/39304; doubles from 4,500dr) is passable if you don't mind cold showers. From the Pátra port, cross the street, take a right onto Venizeloi, and follow the signs; it's 50 yards ahead on the left. On the west side of the island, in Agios Gordios, lies the infamous **Pink Palace** (½ hr west of town, tel. 0661/53103; beds 4,500dr), whose pushy minions will take you straight from the ferry to their den of iniquity. Check your inhibitions and good taste at the door; every drunken night at this haven for North Americans echoes the one before. Once sober, visit the beautiful beach nearby.

Among Corfu's countless beach towns are easygoing hamlets, such as **Sidari** and **Roda** in the north, where you can just show up and bargain for a room to let (doubles from 4,000dr); most of these are on or near the water. The more famous **Paleokastritsa** and **Glifada** beaches are heavy on tourists and amenities and packed with hotels and rooms to let. Enjoy a bit of luxury at the beachfront **Golden Beach** (Glifada, tel. 0661/94258: doubles from 5,000dr); the hotel restaurant serves a mean vegetable crêpe (900dr) and features live traditional music on weekends. Nearby are the equally beautiful, and more relaxed, **Pelekas** and **Kontogiálos** beaches. If you can give up the sound of the waves lulling you to sleep, **Pelekas village,** a 10-minute walk from both beaches, has loads of slightly cheaper rooms to let (doubles 3,000dr–4,000dr).

WORTH SEEING

Before you've burned yourself to a crisp, take a day to check out the cool stuff in and around Kérkira Town. Perched precariously on the edge of the island, the crumbling **Old Venetian Fortress** (admission 800dr; open Tues.–Sun. 8:30–3) and the more intact 16th-century **New Venetian Fortress** (entrance on east side; admission 400dr; open daily 10–4) are Italian legacies; both have picturesque grounds, decaying walls, and panoramic views of Albania. Just west of the old fortress is the **Spianáda,** a leisurely park with a field where you might spy a cricket match. Off the Spianáda are the narrow streets of a flourishing tourist market with too many worry beads and Corfu t-shirts. About half an hour south by bus (220dr), the late-19th-century **Achillion** (admission 700dr; open daily 9:00–4:30), a palace built by Austrian royalty, sits high on a hill, surrounded by neatly landscaped and forested grounds that stretch to the water. Its highlights are the two statues of Achilles, to whom the residence is dedicated. The marble one, an amazingly beautiful work, depicts the great warrior crying out in pain as he tries to pull Paris's fatal arrow from his heel.

ITHAKI

No wonder Odysseus, king of Itháki (Ithaca in English), yearned for home so badly throughout Homer's *Odyssey*: This island has few tourists, little noise, and tiny, untouched coves. The northern and southern parts of Itháki are connected by a strip of land less than 900 yds wide. **Vathí,** in the south, is the capital town, and **Kioni,** in the north, is the island's charmer, built on hillsides around a small bay. The illuminated **Cave of the Nymphs** is where Odysseus supposedly hid his booty. To get there, head northwest along the coast from Vathí; at the top of the hill, turn left at the dirt road marked with a sign for the caves, and continue uphill about 4 km (2½ mi). One kilometer (⅔ mile) from the village of **Stavrós,** in the northern part of the island, is **Pilikata,** a hill where archaeologists have found Mycenaean ruins from the 3rd millennium BC, feeding rumors that this was the site of Odysseus's palace. Itháki's beaches are short on sand but long on peaceful, azure waters. Some of the best accessible beaches are on the 4–5 km (2½–3 mi) of coastline between Kioni and Frikes. Take a scooter or taxi to **Filiatro Beach,** 4 km (2½ mi) east of Vathí, or rent a motorboat (6,000dr at Dexa Beach) and head to the gorgeous, secluded **Gidaki Beach.** There's no tourist office in Itháki, but **Polyctor Tours** (in Vathí, south side of platía, tel. 0674/33120) has tourist information and makes travel arrangements.

COMING AND GOING

From Pátra, one **ferry** sails daily to Vathí (4 hrs, 2,950dr). On Itháki, a **bus** infrequently connects Vathí and Kioni (50 min, 500dr), leaving from the pharmacy on the southeast side of the platía. You can also take a **scooter**; the ride offers breathtaking views of the sea and Kefalonia, but it's not for the faint of heart—the narrow, winding road has sheer drops on one side and is sometimes blocked by resting goats.

WHERE TO SLEEP AND EAT

Vathí has only two hotels but plenty of rooms to let; expect to pay 5,000dr per double. Owners will greet you at the ferry dock. If that fails, the tour agencies also book rooms. **Dexa Beach** (tel. 0674/32855), a half-hour walk northwest of Vathí, offers free camping, showers (350dr), a bar/restaurant, deck chairs (500dr), and boat rentals. **To Trexantari** (Vathí, Doursiou Ippou, behind platía; dinner only) serves black-tail fish (1,000dr) and salads (450dr–800dr) to a crowd of boisterous locals. At night, walk along the east side of the bay to find **Scala,** the liveliest bar on Itháki, with a cool stone interior and a DJ playing a wide mix of music.

ZAKINTHOS

The Venetians, who occupied Zákinthos for 300 years, called this island *Fiore di Levante* (Flower of the East). Verdant with olive trees and vineyards, Zákinthos deserves the name. Birthplace of famous Greeks, such as the 19th-century poets Dionysios Solomos (author of the national anthem) and Andreas Kalvos, it was also headquarters for the anti-Ottoman revolutionary group *Filiki Etairia* (Friendly Society) before 1821. The island now hosts masses of British and German tourists, who gather at such noisy resorts as Laganas. **Zákinthos Town** lost its traditional architecture in the big 1953 quake; the coastal beach villages, a bus ride away, are prettier. The village of **Vasilikos** is near the island's best beaches, including **Pórto Róma,** and is speckled with signs advertising rooms to let. In sandy **Lagana Bay,** at the south end of the island, the endangered loggerhead sea turtle (*Caretta caretta* in Latin) lays its eggs between June and August. In summer, loads of tourists come here on turtle-spotting trips, perhaps unaware that they pose a threat to the turtle population, which prefers solitude. A nasty fight goes on here between environmentalists and developers; avoiding these beaches may help protect the species.

Travel agencies in Zákinthos Town run **boat tours** (around 5,000dr), showing off such wonders as the fantastic colors of the **Kianóu (Blue) Caves** on the island's northern tip at Skinari. They also highlight **Navagio,** a cove with a white-sand beach and bright turquoise waters right out of a desert-island fantasy; it's home to a suspiciously well-situated shipwreck from the 1970s.

Get information from the **tourist police** (tel. 0695/27367; open daily 8 AM–10 PM) in the Town Hall (corner of Lombardou and Tzoulati).

COMING AND GOING

Boats come into the Zákinthos Town port (tel. 0695/28117) daily from Killíni (1½ hrs, 1,350dr). **KTEL buses** (Filita, at K. Xenon, tel. 0695/22255) get ferried to Killíni, from which they head to Pátra (3 hrs, 1,235dr) and Athens (7 hrs, 4,235dr); the ferry ticket to Killíni is not included in the price. **Buses** (190dr–240dr) also serve the island's main towns.

WHERE TO SLEEP AND EAT

Cheap rooms are common in the small villages but scarce in Zákinthos Town. However, if a short, mustachioed man named **Fotis Giatras** (tel. 0695/23392) approaches you when you get off the ferry, go with him to Tsilivi, about 2 km (1⅓ mi) north of town. For 6,000dr, he'll put you in a double room with private bath, cooking facilities, and scooter. Otherwise, try the generic rooms at **Hotel Dhiethnes** (Agiou Lazárou, tel. 0695/22286; doubles 5,000dr). From the port, turn right down the waterfront, head left on Laskareos, and go right on Agiou Lazárou. Locals munch on such traditional Greek dishes as moussaka (900dr) at **Restaurant Zohios** (Psaron, behind the post office, tel. 0695/27575).

CYCLADES

The approximately 2,200 islands, islets, and rocky formations of the Cyclades create a dazzling ring of sorts around Delos island, which, according to myth, rose from the waves to become the birthplace of Apollo, god of light and music. Appropriately, the dry Cyclades are blessed with a brilliant sunlight that warms the islands' pristine beaches, and a famous conglomeration of raging bars and discos.

MIKONOS

Míkonos's golden sands dazzle under the brilliant sun, and its stark white Cycladic houses are in stunning contrast to the barren landscape and deep-blue waters. The island attracts hordes of international tourists and celebrities yearly and is a mecca for Europe's gays and lesbians, but its popularity also

According to Greek mythology, Míkonos is so rocky because it's where Heracles buried all the giants he slaughtered.

makes it Greece's most expensive island. **Míkonos Town,** Míkonos's capital and port, is a picturesque maze of small whitewashed houses, cobblestone streets, red- and blue-domed churches, and windmills catching sea breezes. The town's main activity is concentrated on the waterfront and just north of Platía Manto (named for the revolutionary-war heroine of 1821). In and around the famous **Venetia** quarter are restaurants, cafés, bars, and dance clubs blasting music over the innocent sea all night. The **Kastro,** the town's medieval quarter, is filled with gorgeous churches (the **Paraportiani** church is a much-photographed example of traditional Cycladic architecture), and is the perfect place to drink in the sunset and a bottle of wine.

The Tourlós/Agios Stéfanos bus (190dr) from Míkonos Town's northern bus station (*see* Coming and Going, *below*) will take you to the long stretch of sandy beach between **Tourlós** and **Agios Stéfanos.** Or take a bus from the southern bus station (*see* Coming and Going, *below*) to Platis Yialos (190dr), where boats leave regularly for **Paradise Beach,** carpeted with tanning backpackers and a short boat ride (300dr) away from the famous **Super Paradise Beach,** popular with celebrities, nudists, and gays (the gay area is on the west side of the beach). The quiet beaches around **Ormos Ai Yiannis** have fewer crowds and a more peaceful atmosphere; take a bus (190dr) from the southern bus station. For a change of pace, hop a boat (30 min, 1,600dr round-trip) west to the island of **Delos,** the most significant archaeological site (tel. 0289/22259; admission 1,200dr; open Tues.–Sun. 8:30–3) in the Cyclades. Believed to be the birthplace of Apollo, Delos was so sacred in the 5th century that births and deaths were forbidden there as impurities.

BASICS

At the port, the **tourist police** (Bldg 4, tel. 0289/22482; open daily 8 AM–10 PM) and **Rooms and Apartments** (Bldg. 2, tel. 0289/24860; open daily 8:30 AM–10 PM) offer information about the island and accommodations. Delia Travel Ltd. (tel. 0289/22322; open daily 9–9) is the **American Express** agent.

COMING AND GOING

Daily **ferries** (tel. 0289/22218) shove off from Míkonos Town to Páros (2 hrs, 1,640dr), Náxos (2 hrs, 1,570dr), Íos (5 hrs, 2,800dr), and Santoríni (6½ hrs, 3,000dr). Crete (9 hrs, 5,100dr) is serviced twice a week. Catch **local buses** (tel. 0289/23360) at one of two stations: From the docks, head straight up Agios Stéfanos for the **northern station** (corner of Agios Stéfanos and Agiou Ioannou); for the **southern station** (corner of Agiou Ioannou and Xenias), take Matoyianni away from the waterfront and turn right on Enoplon Dynameon, left on Laka Ipirou (which turns into Agiou Louka), and left again on Xenias.

WHERE TO SLEEP AND EAT

Rooms on Míkonos cost two to three times more than on other islands. High season prices *start* at 8,000dr–9,000dr. Reserve ahead in summer. Rent basic rooms at **Hotel Drafaki** (5 min north on Agiou

Ioannou from southern bus station, tel. 0289/22116; doubles 8,000dr) or from **Mrs. Sykiniotou** (4 km/2½ mi away in Agios Stéfanos, tel. 0289/25648; doubles 8,000dr–9,000dr); call and they'll come pick you up. In summer, camping is really the only affordable option. Two good 'grounds are **Mykonos Camping** (under the trees of Paraga Beach, a 10-minute walk from Platis Yialos, tel. 0289/24578; 1,500 per person, closed off season), and **Paradise Beach Camping** (at Paradise Beach, tel. 0289/22852; 1,500dr per person, bungalows 3,000dr per person; closed Nov.–Mar.). Paradise Beach, 6 km (4 mi) from Míkonos Town, has all amenities, sandy campsites, and sleeping-bag areas, and is served by public buses until 4:30 AM; you can also take the campground's own shuttle from the port.

Head straight up from the Delos port and join the Greek crowd at **Ta Kioupia** (tel. 0298/22866) for tasty, affordable food. In the midst of fancy restaurants, down-to-earth **Jiacomo de Latto** (tel. 0289/23235) serves an extremely tasty gyro (300dr). Go straight up from the Delos port, turn right at the Scandinavian Bar, and make a quick left. Míkonos Town is also filled with cheap, late-night souvlaki and gyro stands and even has a homemade-ice-cream shop, **Snowstorm** (Mitropoleous Georgoui St., tel. 0289/24995).

After dinner, throw yourself into Greek dancing at the **Famous Mykonos Dance Bar** (Venetia quarter, tel. 0289/23529; cover 900dr, including drink; open daily 7 PM–3:30 AM). Nearby is the waterfront **La Mer** (cover 1,000dr, including drink; open daily 7 PM–3:30 AM), where Greeks get down to bouzouki music. In the same area, the small cocktail bar **Galieraki** blares techno music as gyrating bodies spill out into the alley. **Montparnasse** (Venetia, tel. 0289/23719) has Lautrec posters and a superb sunset view, and often presents carabet music late at night. Mikonos's best-known gay bar, **Piero's** (Matoyianni, no phone), is always crowded after midnight.

PAROS

The waterfront in **Parikía,** Páros's main town, is lined with cafés, car-rental shops, bars, hotels, and travel agencies. In the last two years, gentrification has brought the town some marble pavement, plazas, and a park. Behind this thin slice of development, Paros remains graceful and pristine. Both Parikía and the fishing village of **Náousa,** 10½ km (6½ mi) northwest, are cheaper and quieter in the off season, but in peak season, prices and glitz mirror those of Mikonos. The **tourist office** (tel. 0284/22079; open daily 8:30 AM–midnight) sometimes operates across from the windmill at the Paríkia port. For travel tips, seek out the diminutive Mrs. Popi, who reigns at **Polos Travel** in the evenings (tel. 0284/22333; open 8 AM–11 PM; next to OTE near the dock).

For a dose of culture, visit **Ekatontapyliani Church** (Our Lady of the Hundred Doors; 100 yds northeast of port; open daily 7–2 and 5–8), a Byzantine church from the 4th century and perhaps the oldest church in Greece. Look for bits of mosaic floor and reused classical pieces. Note that you'll need to cover your legs and shoulders here. Behind the church, the **Archaeological Museum** (tel.0284/21231, 500 dr; Tues.–Sun. 8–2:30) has several fine "new" pieces to replace some that were stolen a few years ago. If you're lucky, you may catch an art show at the American-run **Aegean Center for the Fine Arts** (0284/23287), one block in from the waterfront's Hibiscus restaurant. From Parikía, the **Valley of the Butterflies** (20 min, 270dr), where myriads of colorful moths alight on the lush greenery every summer, is an easy bus ride (toward Aliki) or 4-km (2½ mi) walk away. Also easily accessible by bus from Parikía is **Golden Beach** (45 min, 500dr), a mile-long stretch of sand. From **Náousa** (20 min, 220dr from Parikía), boats run to the small and secluded beaches of **Monastiri** (20 min, 500dr round trip) and **Kolimbithres** (15 min, 420dr round trip), where you'll find a campground (tel. 0284/51595; 1,000dr per person plus 200dr per tent).

To experience Páros's boisterous night scene, follow your ears south of the port to **Irish Bar Stavros** (cover 500dr, including drink; open daily 9 PM–4:30 AM), a wild place packed with toping Hibernians. Farther down the road, 500dr buys you a drink and admission to a cacaphonous complex that includes **The Dubliner, Down Under,** and the **Páros Rock Club** (9 PM–4:30 AM). **Evinos** and **Pebbles,** on the Castro hill, are more civilized, with jazz, classical music, and sunset views. In Náousa the scene is on the picturesque harbor; **Leonardo's** is popular late at night.

COMING AND GOING

Many daily **ferries** (tel. 0284/21240) go to Piraeus (5–6 hrs, 3,900dr), Náxos (1 hr, 1,350dr), Íos (2–3 hrs, 2,320dr), and Santoríni (3½–4 hrs, 2,660dr). Ferries also go to Crete (7–8 hrs, 4,370dr), Míkonos (2 hrs, 1,600dr), Tinos (3 hrs, 2,000dr), and Samos (7 hrs, 3,700dr). The KTEL **bus station** (tel. 0284/21133 or 0284/21395), on the waterfront 100 yds north of the port, sends buses all over the island.

WHERE TO SLEEP AND EAT

In the off season, you'll easily find rooms for around 5,000dr (the same rooms can cost 9,000dr in high season) in one of the hotels or pensions near the Ekatontapyliani Church (*see* Páros, *above*) in Parikía. Downstairs doubles with private bath at **Festos Pension** (tel. 0284/21635) cost 6,000dr; from the port, head north and make a right after the windmill and another right after the church. For cleanliness, friendliness, and comfort, seek out Voula Maounis's **Pension Evangelistria** (tel.0284/21482; 10,000dr for a double with bath and fridge, 14,000dr for an apartment, much cheaper in June and Sept.); it has an ancient ruin in the cellar and is often filled with returnees. Turn right at Ekatontapyliani Church, then make a quick left to the through street and a right at the Paros restaurant. **Parasporos Camping** (15 min south of Parikía, tel. 0284/22268; 200dr tent plus 1,000dr per person), a 25-minute walk south from Parikía, is just five minutes from the beach, has a bar and restaurant, and rents tents; there's bus service to and from the port. To get away from it all (except from windsurfers), head to the **Santa Maria Beach** campsites (tel. 0284/524916; 200dr per tent plus 1,000dr per person); take the free bus from the port or a KTEL bus (30 min, 400dr).

For cheap eats in Parikía, try the traditional taverna **H Paros** (open daily 8:30 AM–3 AM, tel. 0284/23574)—excellent meatballs in sauce go for 950dr, *horta* (greens) for 600dr, and spit-roasted chicken for 850dr. Make a right at the Ekatontapyliani Church, then make a quick left and follow the street until you see the restaurant. On the alley behind the National Bank on the market street (turn right at Mam), the vegetarian **Happy Green Cow** is fresh and healthy; falafel in pita costs 800dr.

NAXOS

Fertile lands, colorful buildings covered with chipped paint, and warm, welcoming locals set Náxos apart from the other Greek islands. Soon you'll start to feel like a real live person, not passenger #689 from the four-o'clock ferry. The island's bounty—free-flowing wines, rich cheeses, potatoes, and olives—only adds to its allure.

In tiny **Náxos Town,** the relatively deserted **Kastro** district, enclosed by the **Venetian Castle** walls, was once inhabited by Venetian nobles, who ruled the Cyclades for 300 years starting in the 13th century. The **Archaeological Museum** (in Kastro, signposted from waterfront, tel. 2822/2275; admission 600dr; open Tues.–Sun. 8–3) holds findings from Mycenaean settlements, Cycladic goods from the 3rd millennium BC, and a 4th-century-BC marble funerary lion. Despina Kitini's excellent **Tourist Information Center** (on the waterfront near the dock, tel. 0285/22993; open daily 8 AM–11 PM) can tell you more; buy the local hiking guide for directions to the Hellenistic tower, preclassical cemetery, and Cave of Zeus. **Ciao Travel** (from port, take first left past bus station, tel. 0285/24398; open daily 8:30 AM–11 PM) will find you cheap lodging. For Náxos's most popular beach, head to **Agios Giórgios,** a 15-minute walk south of town; continue south by bus, and you'll hit the increasingly developed, partly nudist beach **Agia Anna** (15 min, 250dr), with 6 km (4 mi) of magnificent coastline. Or take a bus to the island's lush and mountainous interior: Náxos has the best hiking in the Cyclades, and marble-paved Apíranthos (45 min, 400dr), Filóti (30 min, 320dr), and Halkí (25 min, 280dr), in the Cyclades' biggest olive grove, are all excellent base villages.

COMING AND GOING

Daily **ferries** (tel. 0285/22300) chug between Náxos and Piraeus (6–7 hrs, 4,030dr), Íos (1½ hrs, 1,980dr), Santorini (3 hrs, 2,400dr), and Míkonos (3 hrs, 1,500dr). **KTEL buses** (at port, tel. 0285/22291) run frequently all over the island. **Mike's Bikes** (tel. 0285/24975; open daily 9–2 and 6–9), near Agios Giórgios, rents mountain bikes (1,800dr per day) and scooters (3,000dr per day). Náxos is big and mountainous, so watch it.

WHERE TO SLEEP AND EAT

Hotel Dionyssos (tel. 0285/22331; dorm beds 1,500dr, doubles 3,000dr) is a bit run-down but has a very sociable atmosphere. It's in the old market area below the Kastro, near hotels Panorama and Anixis; the tourist office (*see* Náxos, *above*) can direct you. The similar **Hotel Okeanis** (on east side of waterfront, tel. 0285/22931) has 5,000dr doubles. **Náxos Camping** (tel. 0285/23500 or 0285/23501; 800dr per tent), close to town, sends a minivan to meet the ferries. **Maragas** (tel.0285/24552; same prices as Náxos Camping) is on Agia Anna.

Have a good basic meal at **Meltemi** (tel.0285/22654). The selection is large; *dolmádes,* for example, are 1,000dr, and so is chicken with potatoes. At **O Tsitas** (tel. 0285/25362; open daily 10 AM–midnight) you can feast on salads (400dr–700dr), baked fish (1,200dr), or pasta with octopus (1,100dr) and wash it all down with retsina (500dr) or ouzo (250dr). From the ferry docks, walk west along the waterfront and make a left at Zas Travel. For better or worse, Náxos has developed quite a nightlife in recent years. **Veggera** (on the waterfront near Agios Giorgios, tel. 0285/23567) is loud and popular, and **Greek Bar** (on the same waterfront, tel. 0285/24675) features Greek music and dancing.

IOS

Twenty years ago, Ios was small, pure, white, and lovely; off season, it still is. But in August, it resembles Fort Lauderdale at spring break. If you're seeking the secluded sublime, stay on the ferry, and if you get off, get ready to party—even Homer, supposedly buried by the sea here, has a hard time sleeping. The 2-km (1½-mi) road from **Íos Town** (a.k.a **Hora**) to the sprawling, white **Milopotas Beach** would be almost picturesque if not for the graffitied discotheque signs, beer bottles, and loiterers; try the enchanting **Manganari Beach** (45 min, 500dr by bus from Ios Town) instead. Or, for snorkeling and fishing, head to **Agia Theodoti**, 12 km (7 mi) from Yialós port. For more ideas, contact **Acteon Travel and Tours** (by port bus stop, tel. 0286/91318; open daily 8 AM–11 PM).

The liveliest bars are around the platía in Íos Town, including **Dubliner** and **Sweet Irish Dream,** which get going around 11. Late nights, the action shifts to the road to Milopotas Beach: **Scorpions** (cover 1,000dr, including drink) attacks you with psychedelic lights and thumping techno from 11 PM to 4 AM.

COMING AND GOING
Daily **ferries** (tel. 0286/21264) motor to Íos from Santoríni (1½ hrs, 1,600dr), Páros (3 hrs, 2,465dr), Míkonos (5 hrs, 2,925dr), and Piraeus (8½ hrs, 4,760dr deck class). Íos Town lies between Yialós Port and Milopotas Beach. Every 15 minutes until midnight, a **bus** (190dr) travels along the main road connecting all three; wave your arms if you want it to stop.

WHERE TO SLEEP AND EAT
There are remote rooms to let all over Íos, but the easiest place to stay is in Íos Town or near Milopotas Beach. Pensions line the main road and are clustered behind the village bus stop. **Mrs. Ioannis** (tel. 0286/91494) has "very clean, very quiet, very fresh" 6,000dr doubles; from the National Bank, head right, then take your first left. On Milopotas Beach, **Far Out Camping** (tel. 0286/92301; 850dr per person) is a backpacker's Club Med, with a café (sandwiches from 400dr), a dive center, two pools, volleyball and basketball courts, pool tables, a minimarket, a bar, and a money exchange.

It's easier to find food at night, but if you crave a square meal in broad daylight, try **Restaurant Íos** (at Yialós port, tel. 0286/91134; open daily noon–midnight) for sea views and swordfish kebabs (1,600dr) or salads (500dr). In Íos Town, **Iliotropion** (just past platía) has good breakfasts (800dr–1300dr) and excellent spaghetti with mushrooms and cream sauce (800dr).

SANTORINI

Around 1500 BC, a huge volcanic eruption blew off Santoríni's center, creating the famous caldera bay and leaving the island moonscaped with pumice, glass, and black-and-red beaches. The explosion caused massive tidal waves that flooded surrounding islands and, according to some, caused the disappearance of Atlantis. Today every street corner in Santoríni's main town of **Firá** claims an Atlantis Tavern, Atlantis Dry Cleaner, Atlantis Paperclip Shoppe . . . . Because of the spectacular views, the cost of living here is high, but don't pass Santoríni up. The backpacking crowd has adopted black **Périssa Beach,** which has a good hostel and campground, but the **red beach** is the island's most fantastic; it's at the base of the red and black cliffs, near the Akrotíri archaeological site (*see* Worth Seeing, *below*). Photographs of beautiful small town of **Oia,** 12 km (7 mi) northwest of Firá, decorate half the advertisements for Greece. For a breathtaking, leisurely half-day walk, wander along the bay from Oia to Firá.

BASICS
Pelikan Travel (main platía in Thíra, tel. 0286/22478; open daily 8 AM–midnight) has visitor information and touring options, such as trips to the harbor's volcanic islets. There's a branch office in Périssa Beach. Also on the main platía is **American Express** (tel. 0286/23601; open daily 8:30 AM–9:30 PM).

COMING AND GOING
Ferries (tel. 0286/22239) from Íos (1½ hrs, 1,600dr), Náxos (3 hrs, 2,590dr), Páros (4 hrs, 2,800dr), and Míkonos (7 hrs, 3,090dr) dock here daily. Boats also leave a few times a week for Crete (5 hrs,

2,950dr) and Ródos (14 hrs, 5,670dr), and several times a day for Piraeus (9 hrs, 5,000dr). Crowded **KTEL buses** (tel. 0286/23812) serve most of the island. The central stop is on the platía **Theotokopoulou** (below main platía); other stops are at Périssa Beach (40 min, 350dr), Akrotíri (30 min, 330dr), Oia (20 min, 240dr), and the main port, Athinos (30 min, 300dr). In the small alley directly behind the AmEx office, **Kostás** (tel. 0286/22801; open daily 8 AM–7 PM) rents scooters (3,000dr per day). The rental cost includes limited insurance, tax, and sometimes a helmet.

WHERE TO SLEEP AND EAT

The two main areas for cheap lodging are up from the Firá bus stop: to the right, and to the left. Also, two hostels—**HI Kamares Hostel** (tel. 0286/24472; beds 900dr–1,000dr) and the **Youth Hostel Thíra** (tel. 0286/22387; nicer beds 1,200dr)—are 300 yds from the bus terminal; walk up the main street, past Pelikan Travel, until you see signs. Rooms in the dramatic, dazzling **Hotel Leta** (tel. 0286/22540 or 0286/23903; doubles 6,000dr) have walls of cool, underwater blue; vans come to the port to meet boats. Shady **Santoríni Camping** (tel. 0286/22944; 600dr per tent plus 950dr per person) features a saltwater pool and a view of the sea. From the bus station, walk straight up, turn right at Pelikan Travel, and follow the signs.

Steer clear of the overpriced eateries on or near the cliff. Try the old town favorite, **Nicolas Taverna** (two streets in from cliffside, open daily noon–11 PM), for excellent moussaka (1,200dr) and other traditional Greek fare. From the bus station, go left at Pelikan Travel, then take the first right. Next door to **Hotel Leta** (*see above*), a small, family-run restaurant serves savory roasted chicken (750dr) and Santorini's own tomato pancakes (520dr).

WORTH SEEING

In 1930, archaeologist Spyros Marinatos discovered a Minoan village (ca. 1500) buried and preserved by volcanic ash at **Akrotíri**. Though fleeing inhabitants had taken their gold, Marinatos's team unearthed utensils, furniture, houses, streets, and even a water-supply system. The village's beautiful frescoes and pottery are in the Athens Archaeological Museum, but the site offers a fascinating look at the excavation process and a hint of the ancient small town itself. *Tel. 0286/81366. From Theotokopoulou, bus (25 min, 280dr) to Akrotíri. Admission: 1,200dr. Open daily 8:30–3.*

At the turn of the century, German archaeologists discovered the classical capital **Ancient Thíra** (admission free), dating from the 9th century BC. Phoenicians, Dorians, Romans, and Byzantines all settled here at one time or another, leaving behind government buildings, public baths, theaters, and sanctuaries. The best way to get here is to rent a car or scooter and ride almost to Kamari, then up the cobbled mountain road. Or, from Theotokopoulou, take the bus (20 min, 175dr) to Kamari and start the long, hot hike. There is also a shorter path from Périssa Beach.

CRETE

The largest Greek island, Crete (Kríti in Greek) has a character and history all its own. Europe's first civilization, the graceful bronze-age Minoan, and the long Venetian presence (1210–1669), which inspired native El Greco, both left their legacies. The landscape is especially rugged, its blue-gray mountains split by deep gorges and fertile valleys. The southern part of the island, facing Africa, harbors secluded stretches of warm sea, Europe's only indigenous palm grove, and traditional villages.

IRAKLION

Until Crete was incorporated into Greece in 1913, Greeks had little control of this metropolis: Arabs built it in 824, Venetians took over from 1210 to 1669, and Turks ruled it until Crete became an independent state in 1898. Traces of these civilizations remain, and bits and pieces of the old Venetian fortress walls peek out from between modern buildings. For a view of it all, climb high above the city to the **Tomb of Kazantzakis**; the author of *Zorba the Greek,* forbidden a church burial, rests here in a tomb inscribed, "I fear nothing. I hope for nothing. I am free."

People in this full-fledged city move at a faster pace than on the other islands, and big, dirty buildings project into the sky. But while Iráklion may not be a visual dessert, it does pack a historical punch. If you visit only a few museums in Greece, make one of them the **Archaeological Museum** (from port road, take Ikarou to Pl. Eleftherías, tel. 081/224630; admission 1,500dr; open Mon. 12:30–7, Tues.–Sun. 8–7).

Nearly all surviving Minoan art is here, from Europe's first wheel-thrown pottery, to statuettes of snake-wielding-priestesses, to delicate frescoes of birds, bull-leapers, and chatting bare-breasted women.

BASICS

The main **tourist office** (tel. 081/244–462; open weekdays 7:30 AM–2:30 PM) is opposite the Archaeological Museum. **Poulios Travel** (35 Sof. Venizelou, at Handakos, tel. 081/284696; open daily 8:30 AM–9 PM) has information on sights, flights, and ferries. Adamis Tours (23 25th Avgoustou, tel. 081/246202; open Mon.–Sat. 9–9) is the **American Express** agent.

COMING AND GOING

Most **ferries** (081/244–912) to Crete land at Iráklion. Overnight ferries from Piraeus (12 hrs, 5,850dr) arrive daily, and boats from Santoríni (4 hrs, 2,950dr), Páros (8 hrs, 4,550dr), and Ródos (11 hrs, 5,745dr) dock several times a week. **KTEL buses** (tel. 081/245020) traverse the island; buses from the stations east of the main port head to Réthimnon (1½ hrs, 1,250dr), Bali (45 min, 800dr), and Haniá (2½ hrs, 2,400dr).

WHERE TO SLEEP

There's no compelling reason to stay in Iráklion. It's quite easy to leave your backpack at the bus station, check out the museum and Knossos (*see* Near Iráklion, *below*), then jump a bus to one of the nicer towns. But there's a nest of pensions off Handakos, as well as two local **HI hostels**: One (5 L. Vironos, off 25th Avgoustou, tel. 081/286–281; beds 1,500dr) has a midnight curfew, and the other (24 Handakos, off Sof. Venizelou, tel. 081/280–858; beds 1,000dr) is open 24 hours.

NEAR IRAKLION

The **Palace of Knossos** is the site of Europe's first high civilization. Knocked down by an earthquake around 1900 BC, it was quickly rebuilt by the Minoans, but the place was doomed; a series of natural disasters, including the volcanic explosion of Santorini, leveled it repeatedly. Its remaining faded red pillars and dusty beige walls are haunted by mystery: Was this the site of legend's labyrinth, where the Minotaur feasted on Athenian youths, or where Minos presided over rites in a bull mask? Be sure to visit the **Queen's Suite** and her bathroom, complete with flushable toilet. Other highlights are the **Throne Room** off the courtyard and the **theater** in the northwestern corner of the palace. *Tel. 081/231940. From terminal on Sof. Venizelou, Bus 2 to Knossos (20 min, 200dr). Admission: 1,500dr. Open daily 8–5.*

Knossos is over-restored, but its contemporary, the **Phaistos** palace (tel. 0892/91315; 1200 dr), is not; remembering its gorgeous art in the museum, you must recreate its splendors yourself. A 1½-hour bus ride (1150dr) south through the famously fertile Messara plain, Phaistos rests on a lovely low hill facing snow-capped Mt. Ida. A 20-minute bus ride further south (200dr) is **Matala,** hippie haven of the '60s, its high seacliffs pocked with habitable caves.

BALI

Five rocky coves, a handful of buildings, and locals who like foreigners make up this treasure caught between the mountains and the coast. Here, sounds of Balinese gamelan music and boats rocking in the small port replace disco tunes and rattling scooters. Though it's no longer Crete's best-kept secret, this tiny town is still one of the quaintest in Greece. Even residents of Iráklion will sigh when you mention Bali.

Both **Mary's Market** (on left side of main road 5 min before port, tel. 0834/94229) and **Hristhanís** (on left side of road closer to port, tel. 0834/94128), have 5,000dr doubles. Above the small port, **Panorama Restaurant** (tel. 0834/94217) serves a mean Greek salad (750dr). Buses traveling between Iráklion and Réthimnon stop about 2½ km (1¼ mi) above Bali (45 min, 1,000dr from either town)—it's a long walk down, but you can take a cab (500dr–800dr).

RETHIMNON

Old Réthimnon: A Venetian fortress rests above the city, cobblestone alleys squirm behind Turkish and Venetian houses, and old men sit outside cafés playing backgammon and sipping coffee. Glued to the old town, however, is a new one of high-rise hotels, pricey restaurants, bureaux de change, and tourists. Réthimnon is one of the most touristy spots on Crete, and Bermudas-clad yahoos do their best to detract from the town's appeal. Happily, they only half succeed.

The 16th-century **Venetian Fortezza** (tel. 0831/28101; admission 300dr; open Tues.–Sun. 8–7) includes the ruins of officers' houses, barracks, and a mosque. On summer evenings, music and theater festivals (admission 2,500dr) are held inside; schedules are posted all over town. To get here, take the dirt path at the waterfront all the way up. To escape the heat, head behind the old town to the tree-filled **Public Garden,** site of the annual Cretan Wine Festival (the second to fourth weeks of July), with free-flowing wine and music. Stroll also to the town's **Venetian Harbor** (north of the port, near the fortress), which is packed with expensive but atmospheric cafés, shops, and nightlife. Get maps and lists of accommodations at the **tourist office** (E. Venizelou, on western waterfront, tel. 0831/29148; open weekdays 8–2:30), in the same building as the **tourist police** (tel. 0831/28156; open 8 AM–10 PM).

COMING AND GOING

Ferries (tel. 0831/22276) arrive daily from Piraeus (10 hrs, 6,000dr). Daily **buses** (tel. 0831/22212) from Iráklion (1½ hrs, 1,250dr) and Haniá (1 hr, 1,200dr) come into the main terminal on Dimokratias Street, about a 20-minute walk from the town center.

WHERE TO SLEEP AND EAT

Budget places are in the old town, and private homes also rent rooms near the Fortezza. **Café Bar 67** (67 E. Venizelou, at waterfront, tel. 0831/51283) offers sparkling 5,000dr rooms in a 300-year-old house. But the best value is the tidy **HI hostel** (41 Tombazi, tel. 0831/22848; beds 1,200dr), with restaurant and laundry basins. From the bus station, go north on Dimokratias, left on Kountouri, and right on Tombazi. **Camping Elizabeth** (3 km/2 mi east of town, tel. 0831/28694; 1,000dr per tent plus 1,300dr per person) is on the beach. Take the bus to Misseria (departs every 20 minutes) and tell the driver to stop at the university; then walk straight up, go left at the fork, take your first left, then take your first right.

At **Maria's Restaurant** (31 George Papandreou, tel. 0831/23262), a small hangout for local students, Maria whips up amazing lamb with pasta (1,100dr) and other dishes (500dr–700dr). Go east on the waterfront, turn right on George Papandreou, and ask for Maria (there's no sign).

HANIA

The city that booms today with the second-highest population in Crete has been struggling for years to keep its buildings and character intact. Mentioned in Minoan times, burned to bits in 1266, rebuilt by Venetians in 1336, besieged by the Turks in 1645—normally this kind of history leaves three scorched stones, a pillar or two, and a modern sign denoting what used to be. But somehow Haniá has stuck through it all, even managing a comfortable small-town feel that makes it hard to leave. The **Archaeo-logical Museum** (Halidon, tel. 0821/90334; admission 500dr) in the old Venetian Church of San Francesco has an okay collection of statues, coins, and mosaics from the late Neolithic to Roman eras. The **EOT** (40 Kriari, off Pl. 1866 at Halidon, tel. 0821/92624) is open weekdays 7:30–3.

COMING AND GOING

From Piraeus, you can take daily **ferries** (tel. 0821/43052) to Soudha (10 hrs, 5,100dr), the nearest port to Haniá. From there, jump on a 185dr blue bus (tel. 0821/23024) to Haniá's marketplace. Or take a green bus all the way from Iráklion (2½ hrs, 2,400dr) or Réthimnon (1 hr, 1,200dr). The **bus station** (tel. 0821/93306) is on Kidonias, one block from Platía 1866.

WHERE TO SLEEP AND EAT

The rooms above **Cosy Cafe** (next to cathedral, off Halidon, tel. 0821/41213; doubles 3,000dr) are fairly spartan. Better rooms and gorgeous views await at **Pension Monastiri** (18 Agiou Markou, tel. 0821/54776; doubles 5,000dr), housed in the former Sainte Marie de la Coeur Monastery. Where Hali-don hits the waterfront, make a right on Kanevaro and a left on Agiou Markou.

The **market** (on Hatz Michali, 2 blocks east of Halidon; open daily 8–2, Tues. and Fri. also 6 PM–9 PM) has plenty of cheese, vegetable, bread, and fruit stalls. **Tamam** (Zambeliou 51, 1 block from water, tel. 0821/96080) serves excellent Greek and Turkish food; try the delicious *hoonkiar beyenti* (chicken with tomato and eggplant sauce; 1,400dr).

NEAR HANIA

Stretching 16 km (10 mi), the spectacular **Samarian Gorge** is Europe's longest. The six-hour hike through the gorge starts 1,300 yds up on the Omalos Plateau in Yloskala, 44 km (27 mi) south of Haniá. The gorge varies in width from 500 ft to a mere 11½ ft (at the famous "Iron Gate"), and ends at the Libyan Sea. Along the way, you'll encounter wildflowers, streams (which can close the gorge in early spring), vultures, and maybe a *kri-kri* (the Cretan wild goat). Wear sturdy shoes and bring sunscreen and food (there's plenty of water). To get here, catch the 6:15 AM bus from Haniá (1½ hrs, 1,000dr). At the end of the day, ferries meet exhausted hikers at the small beach town, Agia Roumelia, and take them east to Chora Sfakion (1,300dr) or west to Sougia (850dr), where buses (2 hrs, 1,200dr) bring them back to Haniá. You can also stay in these towns.

DODECANESE

RODOS

Though the crusading Knights of the Order of St. John are long gone, the Visa-wielding Order of the Holy Camcorder now besieges Ródos Town, capital of Ródos. The walled old town is dominated by the magnificent 14th-century **Palace of the Knights** (tel. 0241/23359; admission 1,200dr; open Mon. 12:30–7, Tues.–Fri. 8–7, Sat. 8–3, Sun. 8:30–3). These crusaders dominated Ródos until the Ottomans showed up in 1522, adding a library, several mosques, and **Turkish baths** (tel. 0241/27739; admission 500dr, 300dr Wed. and Sat.; open Tues.–Sat. 11–7) into which you can dip your dusty self; from the entrance to the old town, walk up Sokratous, make a left on Menekleous, and continue to Platía Arionos.

Even with all the turnover, Ródos has held onto some of its ancient Greek sites. As you enter Mandráki Harbor, you'll spot two ancient columns with bronze deer on top. They mark the spot where the **Colossus of Rhodes** (one of the Seven Wonders of the Ancient World), a massive bronze statue of the sun god Helios, supposedly stood until an earthquake leveled the city in 227 BC. Greek and Roman finds, notably two alluring statues of Aphrodite, are now housed in the **Archaeological Museum** (near palace, tel. 0241/75674; admission 800dr; open Tues.–Sun. 8:30–3).

Definitely make the one-hour trip east to beautiful **Líndos,** a town of winding cobblestone streets leading up to the **Acropolis of Ancient Líndos** (tel. 0241/21954; admission 1,200dr; open Mon. 12:30–7, Tues.–Fri. 8–7, weekends 8:30–3). In addition to the Temple of Athena Lindia, Byzantine treasures, and ancient ruins, the Acropolis boasts awe-inspiring views of southern Ródos, the coast of Turkey, and the brilliant white houses of Líndos below. Southwest of Ródos Town, the ancient town of **Kamiros** (tel. 0241/219454; admission 800dr; open Tues.–Sun. 8:30–3) showcases ruins of a Doric temple, a monastery, and a proto-Christian catacomb. To reach either site, catch a bus (tel. 0241/27706) from Platía Rimini (1 hr, 800dr).

Between June 20 and September, take a bus (tel. 0241/26300) southwest of Ródos Town to the **Valley of the Butterflies** in Petaloudes (40 min, 800dr) to see millions of winged creatures in a lush, green valley. Admission to the valley (open daily 7:30 AM–6:30 PM) is 300dr; catch the bus behind the marketplace in town.

BASICS

The **tourist office** (tel. 0241/35945; open Mon.–Sat. 8 AM–9 PM, Sun. 8–3) is north of the harbor on Platía Rimini, and the **tourist police** (tel. 0241/27423; open daily 7 AM–10 PM) is a few blocks up the street at 31 Papagou. In the old town, the helpful **Castellania Travel Service** (1 Euripidou, on Pl. Ippokratus, at Sokratous, tel. 0241/75860; open daily 8:30 AM–11 PM) offers 15% off ferries to Turkey.

COMING AND GOING

Plenty of daily **ferries** (tel. 0241/22220) hit Ródos, including those from Piraeus (14–15 hrs, 7,100dr) via Kos (4 hrs, 3,000dr) or Pátmos (8 hrs, 4,680dr), and from Marmaris, Turkey (45 min, 9,500dr including port tax in Marmaris). Boats come less frequently from Páros (18 hrs, 5,900dr) and Iráklion (12 hrs, 5,500dr). The **KTEL bus station,** located on Platía Rimini, sends buses to the east side of the island; the bus station around the corner serves points in western Ródos, such as the Valley of the Butterflies, ancient Kamiros, and Paradissi.

WHERE TO SLEEP AND EAT

Most of the island's cheap accommodations are in Ródos's old town. For pensions, check around the main drag, Avenue of the Knights. **Pension Apollo** (28C Omirou, tel. 0241/32003; doubles 3,500dr) is a backpacker magnet with a breezy patio, a kitchen, and spotless rooms. Next door, the French contingent sacks out at **Hotel Andrea** (28D Omirou, tel. 0241/34156; doubles 8,000dr), with large, comfy rooms, laundry, terrace, bar, and TV. To get to Omirou from Sokratous, take a right on Pithagora; Omirou is on the left. **Ródos Youth Hostel** (12 Ergiou, tel. 0241/30491; open May–Sept.) has 1,400dr dorm beds in an old, spooky building. From Sokratous, go left on Agiou Fanourio and right on Ergiou.

When your stomach starts grumbling, don't fall prey to the touristy cafés and restaurants on Sokratous or Avenue of the Knights. Head instead to **Café Bar Oasis** (12 Dorieos) for cheap breakfasts (omelettes 650dr) and decent dinners (grilled chicken 850dr); from Sokratous, go left on Agiou Fanouriou and then right on Platía Dorieos. The renovated Turkish bathhouse, **Café Xaman** (on Pl. Sofocleous, tel. 0241/33242; open daily noon–3 AM), is a mellow place to sip your frappé (500dr) and fantasize about ancient Ródos; from Sokratous, go left on Pithagora, right on Platanos, and left to Platía Sofocleous.

KOS

To experience the decline of Western civilization, visit Kos Town during the high season. The old town, which was once quite attractive, has been malled (or mauled) into an endless line of shops hawking tourist schlock. At night, the bars and discos pump retro music and overpriced drinks to the eager throngs. Fortunately, Kos native Hippocrates, father of Western medicine, seems to have immunized the rest of this mountainous island against tourists; the rest of the landscape is crowded only with bleating goats. Reminders of Hippocrates cover the island, starting right near the port: Supposedly the oldest tree in Europe, the **Plane Tree of Hippocrates,** which once shaded the great doctor and his students, stands—well, sort of stands—across from the castle.

The **Archaeological Museum** (Pl. Eleftherias, tel. 0242/28326; admission 800dr; open Tues.–Sun. 8:30–2:30) holds fine Hellenistic and Roman sculpture by Koan artists, including a 4th-century BC statue of Hippocrates. From the port, walk west down the waterfront and make a left on Agios Ioannidi. At the port, the **Knight's Castle** (tel. 0241/75674; admission 800dr; open Tues.–Sun. 8:30–2:30) dates from around 1450, when the Knights of St. John built it with the marble and stone left over from the ancient city destroyed in the earthquake. The best thing to do here is walk around the walls for a bird's-eye view of town.

Take the bus or bike the peaceful road to **Thermi,** where you can soak your weary bones in the hot water that trickles from rocks down into the sea. The 49°C (120°F) sulfurous water, whose odor has all the allure of rotten eggs, is supposedly good for arthritis, rheumatism, and skin ailments. For a truly soothing experience, dry off and enjoy the sunset from Thermi or the cliffs above it. The route to Thermi takes you past secluded stretches of sand, but the most beautiful (and most popular) beach on Kos is **Paradise Beach**; from the bus station at the back of town, take a green bus headed for Kéfalos. The **tourist office** (tel. 0242/24460; open weekdays 7:30 AM–8:30 PM, weekends 8:30–3) is to the right of the port as you face the water.

The **Asclepion,** 4 km (2½ mi) southwest of Kos Town, was the renowned medical school where Hippocrates' legacy was carried on. He planned the school, but it wasn't built until later that century, after he had died; it was then dedicated to Asclepius, the god of medicine. On your way in, take a peek at the Roman baths at the front of the building. *Tel. 0242/28763. From waterfront, take Asclepion bus (130dr). Admission: 800dr. Open Tues.–Sun. 8:30–6:30.*

COMING AND GOING
Ferries (port, tel. 0242/26594) from Piraeus (12–14 hrs, 6,550dr), Ródos (4 hrs, 3,000dr), and Pátmos (4 hrs, 2,400dr) dock daily. Intermittent boats also connect with Sámos and Iráklion. The ride to Bodrum, Turkey (10,000dr including port tax), takes only an hour. The best way to cover Kos Town is by pedaling. Rent bikes for 300dr per day at **Moto Holidays** (21 Alexandrou, tel. 0242/28676); walk west from the port and left on Alexandrou. You can catch a blue bus at the **local bus station** (on waterfront, west of castle, tel. 0242/26276; tickets 130dr–200dr) to get around town, or a green one at the **KTEL station** (Cleopatras, tel. 0242/22292) to other parts of the island.

WHERE TO SLEEP AND EAT
Hotels on Kos are ridiculously expensive, but **Pension Alexis** (9 Irodotou, at Omirou, tel. 0242/28798) has airy doubles for 6,500dr. Head west from the port down the waterfront, turn left on Alexandrou, and turn right on Irodotou. **Kos Camping** (across from Psalidi beach, tel. 0242/23910; 1,300dr per person including tent; closed mid-Oct.–mid-Apr.) is a nice, shady escape 2½ km (1½ mi) from town. Take the bus (130dr) toward Agios Fokás and ask for the campground; or take the shuttle from the ferry.

For delicious *kofta* (mince meat) sandwiches (350dr) or plates of *kofta, tzatzíki,* fries, and salad (1,000dr), stand in line with Greek families at **O Rasuboulos** (4 Amerikis, tel. 0242/26945); head west from the port, turn left on Alexandrou, and right on Irodotou, which becomes Amerikis. On Platía Eleftherias, the **marketplace** sells fresh veggies, bread, and cheese.

PATMOS

Sometimes called the Jerusalem of the Aegean, the little island of Pátmos is as peaceful as it must have been when St. John lived here. Its spiritual mystique grants it a calm that most islands in the Dodecanese cannot approach, and its natural beauty and still waters will revitalize you for the rest of your trip. The island's four main villages are the port towns of Skála, Hóra, Kábos, and the tiny Gríkos, which hoards a delightful little beach all to itself.

Make your pilgrimage to the village of Hóra to see the **cave** and the surrounding **Monastery of the Apocalypse** (both open Mon., Wed., Fri., and Sat. 8–1:30, Tues. and Thurs. 8–1 and 4–6, Sun. 10–noon and 4–6). According to tradition, St. John wrote the text of Revelation in the cave. A bit further uphill in Hóra is the **Monastery of St. John** (same hours), built in the 11th century; check out the 13th-century murals in the chapel of the Virgin. Inside the monastery, the **treasury** and **library** (tel. 0247/31398; admission 1,000dr) display relics, elaborately embroidered vestments, illuminated manuscripts, and codices containing parts of the Gospel of St. Mark and the Book of Job. To get to Hóra from the main town of Skála, take a bus (10 min, 130dr) or walk half an hour.

VISITOR INFORMATION

The **tourist office** in Skála offers maps, bus and ferry schedules, and brochures. *Right off main platía, tel. 0247/31666. Open weekdays 8:30–2:30 and 4–10.*

COMING AND GOING

Ferries (tel. 0247/31231) from Piraeus (10 hrs, 5,740dr), Kos (3½ hrs, 2,500dr–4,000dr), and Ródos (10 hrs, 4,770dr) arrive daily. Boats go to Sámos (3 hrs, 2,500dr) three times a week and to other islands in the northeast Aegean less frequently. Pick up local **buses** (130dr–200dr) at the port.

WHERE TO SLEEP AND EAT

A mob of residents hawking rooms will meet you at the port. For only 6,000dr per bathless double you can stay in **Irini Grilli's** (tel. 0247/31852) clean, well-tended rooms; walk north of the port along the water, make a left at the Beach Boys gelateria, and look for the ROOMS TO LET sign. **Stefanos Camping** (at Méloi Beach, tel. 0247/31821; 650dr per tent plus 1,200dr per person; closed mid-Oct.–mid-Apr.) is a good place to pitch your tent and do laundry while gazing at Méloi Beach. Walk north of the port along the water about 1½ km (1 mi), or call the campground and get picked up. At **Grigoris Grill and Fish Tavern** (tel. 0247/31515; open daily 6 PM–midnight) you can savor swordfish souvlaki (1,400dr), stuffed eggplant (950dr), or rice with seafood (900dr); walk south of the port to where the waterfront meets the paved road to Hóra.

NORTHEAST AEGEAN

Reaching from Macedonia down to the Dodecanese along the coast of Asia Minor, the islands of the northeast Aegean are a diverse bunch. Seductive Sámos was home to some of Greece's greatest thinkers; Híos is known for its stimulating architecture, with buildings dressed in geometric patterns; and Lésvos spawned some important artists and writers, much of whose work was inspired by the island's beauty. About the only thing these islands share is their proximity to Turkey; from their shores, you can see the very houses and fields of Greece's age-old neighbor and rival.

SAMOS

Sámos native Pythagoras was the first to note the mathematical relations in music and the beauty of proportions—ideas that aided in the development of classical architecture. Imagine the guest list for a Sámos block party: Pythagoras, Epicurus, Aristarchus (the first to note that the earth orbits the sun), and fabulous Aesop were the island's brightest stars. Sámos's great tyrant, Polycrates, who reigned from 540 BC–522 BC, made Samos the cultural center of the eastern Aegean, partly with money from piracy. Polycrates was long invincible at sea, but the Persians eventually made him parley, and promptly crucified him. One of his legacies is the huge **Temple of Hera** (tel. 0273/95277; open Tues.–Sun. 8:30–2:30), now a splendid ruin, where the Samians worshipped their patron goddess. To get here from the island's main town, **Vathí,** take a bus from the main station to Iraion (40 min, 400dr); the temple is 8 km (5 mi) from Pythagorio. Polycrates's slaves also created an amazing km- (⅔-mi-) long underground aqueduct, known as the **Efpalinion tunnel** (tel. 0273/61400; admission 500dr; open Tues., Wed., Fri., and Sun. 9–2, Thurs. 11:30–2, Sat. 10–2). With primitive tools and no means for measuring, the tunnelers simply dug toward each other every day until, 15 years later, they met in the middle. Today you can walk 1,000 ft into the slippery, dimly lit tunnel near the Pithagório bus stop. (Wear sturdy shoes and bring a flashlight.) From here there is also a footpath to pretty Pithagório, where you can visit the ruined **Logothetis Castle** of 1824, glance at some unimpressive ancient ruins, and gaze at nearby Turkey's Mt. Mykale from an expensive waterfront café.

Greek monumental sculpture first got going in Sámos, so check out the newly refurbished **Vathi Museum** (0273/27469; admission 400dr; walk up from waterfront at sign, then to the back of the public gardens) for an Archaic statue of Hera, a group of graceful maidens, and a thrice-lifesize kouros.

Sámos is a great place to rent a scooter and escape the crowds. **Tsamadou Beach,** 8 km (5 mi) from Vathí and served by bus, is one of the most beautiful (nude) beaches anywhere, but **Limnionas Beach,** on the southwestern edge of the island, is pure, isolated relaxation. Southwest of Tsabou, the village of **Manolates** also remains largely unafflicted by the onslaught of tourism. Beaches near the main towns are often pretty grungy, though **Psilí Amos,** near Vathí, is well kept. For more information, contact the **EOT** (from dock, second alley on left before Pl. Pithagora, tel. 0273/28530; open weekdays 8:30–2:30) or, in Pithagório, the **tourist office** (Lykourgou Logetheti, 1½ blocks from water; open daily 8 AM–10 PM).

COMING AND GOING

Most **ferries** (tel. 0273/27318) dock at Vathí. Daily connections link Sámos with Piraeus (12 hrs, 5,530dr), and go almost daily to Páros (6 hrs, 3,670dr), Híos (3½ hrs, 2,370dr), and Kos (8 hrs, 3,330dr). There are daily departures from Sámos to Kuşadası, Turkey (1½ hrs, 7,000dr plus a 5,000dr Greek tax, $10 Turkish port tax, and $20 for a Turkish visa), but you'll have to submit your passport a day in advance. The main **bus station** (tel. 0273/27262) is in Vathí, at the corner of I. Lekati and Kanari.

WHERE TO SLEEP AND EAT

Pithagório is prettier, costlier, and duller than Vathí. In Vathí, friendly Costas Diamantopoulos runs his mother's **Pension Dreams** most efficiently (9 Areos St; tel. 0273/24360; doubles 5,000dr–6,000dr, all with luxurious bathrooms, half with fridge and harbor-view balcony; open year-round). Walk from the dock along the waterfront, turn left after Café Europe, and go up the high stairs. In Pithagório's **Pension Arokaria** (tel. 0273/61287; doubles from 6,000dr), the elderly proprietors will set you up in a cozy chamber surrounded by gardens and vines. From the bus stop, walk toward the water and make a right on Metamorfiseos; it's the last house on the right before the church. Pithagório's picturesque waterfront is chock-a-block with eateries, but Sámos's best restaurant is in Vathi: **Katoï** (0273/23890) feels expensive, but isn't. You can get an excellent meal with several courses and wine for 3,000dr or less. Turn up the waterfront by the public gardens and head for the museum; Katoï is a block past it on the left.

HIOS

Until now, Greece has probably made you feel pretty important, what with store owners and hotel proprietors clamoring for your business. All that changes in Híos. The island depends on the sea, not tourists, for its livelihood, so locals go about their daily business without giving you a second glance. The island itself is a stunning blend of pristine shores, craggy (Homer's word) mountains, indigenous mastic trees (try a glass of local *mastíxa*), and a rough, desolate landscape. Visitors arrive in **Híos Town,** a pleasant enough place with a long taverna- and café-lined harbor, a bustling marketplace, and a spacious central park at Platía Plastira. **Pirgí Town,** 24 km (15 mi) southwest of Híos Town, is the island's most visually enticing community—the facades of all the houses are covered with *xistá* (geometric designs). Beaches to check out are the black-pebble, volcanic-rock **Emborió,** 5 km (3 mi) from Pirgí Town, and **Nagós,** near the beautiful coastal town of **Kardhámila.** Catch buses from Híos Town.

The most impressive sight on Híos is the 11th-century **Monastery of Néa Moní** (tel. 0271/27507; open daily 8–1 and 4–sunset). Here, an image of the Virgin Mary prophesied that Constantine Monomachos would one day become emperor of Byzantium. In turn, Constantine promised that if the prophecy came true, he would build a monastery. Six months later the throne was his, and up went the monastery, with an icon of Mary and luminous mosaics inside. Near the monastery, **Anávatos,** an ancient town on a plateau, has been eerily deserted ever since hundreds of residents, faced with Turkish reprisal, opted for death and jumped off the cliff in 1822. From Híos Town, take one of the buses (30 min, 1,500dr) heading to the monastery and Anávatos; they leave Tuesday and Friday at 9 AM and return at 12:30 PM. You can also rent a scooter from **Katsikadelis** (46 Livanou Mich., tel. 0271/41437; about 4,000dr per day). Ask at the **tourist office** (18 Kanari, in Híos Town, tel. 0271/44389; open weekdays 7–2:30 and 6:30–9:30, weekends 10 AM–1 AM, with possible break in the afternoon; shorter hrs off season) about other sights on the island.

COMING AND GOING

NEL Lines (16 Aigaiou, at port, tel. 0271/41319; open daily 7 AM–11 PM) has daily connections to Piraeus (9 hrs, 4,660dr) and Lésvos (3 hrs, 2,900dr) and regular ferries to Thessaloníki (16 hrs, 7,300dr). **Miniotis Lines** (12 Aigaiou; open weekdays 7 AM–11 PM, Sat. 7 AM–2 PM) serves Sámos (3½ hrs, 2,475dr), Pátmos (6 hrs, 4,415dr), and Çesme, Turkey (40 min, 8,000dr plus 5,000dr Greek port tax, $10 Turkish port tax, $20 Turkish visa). Efficient buses serve Híos: Local **blue buses** depart from the north side of the central park and Platía Plastira; long-distance **green buses** (tel. 0271/27505) leave the south side on Vlatarias. Destinations include Nagos (1¾ hrs, 750dr), Kardhámila (1½ hrs, 650dr), and Pirgí (1¼ hrs, 55dr).

WHERE TO SLEEP AND EAT

Híos Town is costly, but the central, homey **Savvas Rooms to Let** (34 Rodokanaki, tel. 0271/41721; doubles 4,000dr–5,000dr) is a good deal. **Rooms to Let "Alex"** (29 Livanou Mich., tel. 0271/26054) has pleasant doubles for 5,000dr–6,000dr and an amiable owner. **Camping Chios** (12 km/7 mi north of Híos toward Kardhámila, in Agios Isidoros, tel. 0271/74111; 800dr per tent plus 1,200dr per person) has good facilities and a beach view of Turkey. Rooms are scarce in Pirgí; at the main square, ask for **Rita** (tel. 0271/72523; doubles from 5,000dr), who exchanges Greek lessons for tutoring in English. For breakfast or lunch at the harbor, try the thick sheep's yogurt with honey (a big plate for 1,000dr) at the authentic **dairy shop** (no name) on the Corner of Roihou and Venizelou. For a full meal (about 2,000dr), try the **Two Brothers Taverna** (tel.0271/21313; 36 Livanou Street, a block in from the waterfront); it's open late.

LESVOS

The erotic songs of poet Sappho (6th century BC) immortalized her island. Lésvos still reveres women; rarely will you see so many statues of female leaders, such as Manto Mavroyennis, heroine of the 1821 War of Independence (alas, her rep was ruined by a love affair). The island is huge and varied—you could easily spend a glorious week exploring its beaches and villages, traipsing through its petrified and living forests, and hiking its rocky mountains.

Lesvos' vibrant capital, **Mitilíni,** makes few concessions to tourism yet offers much to the visitor. The **Archaeological Museum** (Arg. Eftalioti, 50 yds northeast of port, tel. 0251/28032; admission 500dr; open Tues.–Sun. 8:30–3) has an excellent display of mosaics from the Roman period and artifacts from the Neolithic to classical times. Also check out the **Kástro** (the highest point in town), built in 1373 by Genovese duke Francesco Gatteluso, and the ancient **theater** (to the left on the road leading to Thermi), which, in its day, was as esteemed as that of Epidavros (*see* Near Mikínes, *above*). In **Varia**, 4 km (2½ mi) south of town, there are two delightful little museums: the **Theophilos Museum** (tel. 0251/41644; admission 500dr; open Tues.–Sun. 9–1 and 4:30–8), with works by folk artist Theophilos Papamichail (1866–1934, but he walked about in ancient garb), and the adjacent **Teriade Museum** (tel. 0251/23372; same admission and hours), with lithographs by Picasso, Miró, and Chagall. Mitilíni's **tourist office** (6 James Aristardiou, 50 yds north of port exit, tel. 0251/42511; open weekdays 8:30–3) dispenses tons of information, including hiking maps and directions to hot springs.

Míthimna (Mólivos), on the northern coast, is Lésvos's touristy resort and artist haven, where cobblestone streets, small shops, and rooms to let overlook a nice stretch of beach. Towering above the town is a 14th-century Byzantine castle, the site of cultural events in the summer. The **tourist office** (tel. 0253/71347; open daily 9:30–4), on the main road, has information on all types of accommodations in Míthimna. Both the **Archaeological Collection** (tel. 0253/28032) and the **Fortress** (tel. 0253/71803) are free and open Tues.–Sun. 8:30–3.

COMING AND GOING

Ferries (0251/28647) head into Mitilíni several times a week from Piraeus (14 hrs, 5,540dr), less frequently from Thessaloníki (12 hrs, 7,100dr). Boats also leave Thursday at 8 AM for Ayvalık, Turkey (3 hrs, 12,000dr plus 5,000dr port tax). Buy tickets at **Nel Lines** (corner of Tenedou and Kondouriotou, tel. 0251/28480 or 0251/22220; open daily 6 AM–8 PM). The **bus station** (on waterfront, tel. 0251/28725) serving Mitilíni and neighboring villages is in the middle of the harbor, and the **main bus terminal** (tel. 0251/28873) for the whole island is right by the park off the waterfront; from the waterfront, make a right on Platía Konstantinoupoleos.

WHERE TO SLEEP AND EAT

The few rooms in Mitilíni are expensive, but cozy doubles (5,500dr–7,000dr) await at **Salina's Garden** (Fokeas 7, tel. 0251/42073). Follow the signs from the old Turkish mosque on Adramytíou. The freshest food (stuffed tomatoes 1,000dr) in town is at **To Fanari** (tel. 0251/214948), at the southern end of the modern harbor. **The Hott Spott** (northern end of harbor, tel. 0251/62274; open daily 8 AM–2 AM) lives up to its name as *the* place for Lesvians to sip frappés and listen to an excellent mix of music.

To camp in Míthimna, ask at the tourist office (*see above*) or pitch a tent at **Camping Míthimna** (1½ km/1 mi north of town, tel. 0253/71169; 550dr per tent plus 800dr per person; closed Nov.–Apr.). Freelance camping is also tolerated over most of the island. In Petra, 5 km (3 mi) south of Míthimna, the **Women's Co-operative** (tel. 0253/41238; closed Nov.–Feb.) arranges rooms in village homes. The price of a double (4,500dr–6,000dr) includes breakfast and possibly some quality time with the locals.

SPORADES

The fertile lands of the Sporádes ("scattered ones"), covered with olive trees and pines, hug the edges of red-clay cliffs, magnificent sand and pebble beaches, and the turquoise sea. Though overrun by tourists in high season, the smaller villages and lesser-known islands manage to maintain their traditional character.

SKIATHOS

The 5,000 residents of this island are eclipsed by the 50,000 visitors who come here each year for clear blue waters and scores of beaches. Gyro stands and suntan-lotion shops in the center of **Skíathos Town** cater unabashedly to tourists. The island's most popular beach is **Koukounariés** ("pine-nut trees"), a golden, horseshoe-shape beach surrounded by emerald pines; take a bus (220dr) from the shelter on the north end of the waterfront in Skíathos Town. The small, quiet beach at **Agia Eléni,** one bus stop before Koukounariés, is one of Skíathos' nicest. Hundreds of sandy inlets, accessible only by climbing and swimming, surround the beaches; try to find an empty one, as the nude sunbathers can be like territorial dogs.

BASICS

Papadiamántis Street (named after Greece's greatest fiction writer) hosts several **banks** and the **tourist police** (tel. 0427/23172; open daily 8 AM–9 PM). **Mare Nostrum Holidays** (21 Papadiamántis St., Box 16, 37002 Skíathos, tel. 0472/21463; open Mon.–Sat. 8–2 and 5–10:30, Sun. 9:30–1 and 5–10:30) is the **American Express** agent.

COMING AND GOING

Skíathos is regularly served by **ferries** (tel. 0427/22017) from Vólos (2¾ hrs, 2,450dr), Agios Konstandinos (3 hrs, 3,000dr), Skópelos (1½ hrs, 1,350dr), and Athens (5½ hrs, 5,650dr including bus ride) via Agios Konstandinos. **Nomicos Lines** (tel. 0427/22209) sends ferries Saturday and Monday to Míkonos (4,450dr), Paros (5,000dr) and several other Cycladic islands, and to Crete (8,000dr); buy tickets at Itas, across from the port. The **main bus station,** at the north end of the port, sends public buses all along the southern coast of the island.

WHERE TO SLEEP AND EAT

Expensive hotels and rooms to let (doubles from 6,000dr) abound. **Filitsa Asvesti** (tel. 0427/21185) and her sisters rent rooms (doubles 5,000dr–6,000dr) in pastures among grazing horses and goats; take the ring road toward Koukounariés and turn right on the road to Cinema Paradiso; the rooms are on the right, 50 yds before the cinema. The best **campground** (tel. 0427/49312; 1,400dr per tent plus 400dr per person) is on Aselinós Beach, far from town and near the sea; take the campground's private bus from the port, or public-bus it to Troulos (stop #9) and walk. Above a secluded inlet on the water is **Tarsanas** (tel. 0427/23768; closed lunch), a taverna worth the steep, five-minute climb through the old town's beautiful streets: Follow the path above Jimmy's Bar up the stairs, down an incline, and under bougainvillea to the blue menu stand; the taverna is next to Plakes, a rocky vista point.

SKOPELOS

Robed in magnificent jade pines, Skópelos is more peaceful and less touristy than neighboring Skíathos. **Skópelos Town**'s narrow hillside lanes overflow with whitewashed buildings, mellow cafés, balconies draped in fragrant flowers, and 123 churches, most notably the 11th-century **Ayios Athanasios.** Take the bus south of town to several beautiful beaches running west along the coast: The closest (8 km/5 mi) is popular **Stafilos Beach**; from here, go up the dirt path to the tranquil, nude **Velanios Beach.** Farther along the bus route, you'll hit the wide, sandy **Panormos Beach,** which wraps around a gorgeous bay with waters as still as glass, and **Milia,** the largest beach on Skópelos. You can rent rooms (6,000dr–10,000dr) at any of these beaches. For absolute peace and tranquility, head to the small town of **Glóssa,** 32 km (19 mi) from Skópelos on the northwestern side of the island.

VISITOR INFORMATION

In Skópelos Town, the **tourist information office** (tel. 0424/23220; open weekdays 8–2:30) is located in the town hall on the northwest side of the port. If you can't find what you need there, try the small information agency run by **Mayou Sp. Gerakou** (tel. 0424/22473), across from the port; it also sells ferry and hydrofoil tickets.

COMING AND GOING

Daily **ferries** (tel. 0424/22180) arrive in Skópelos Town from Skíathos (1½ hrs, 1,350dr), Vólos (4 hrs, 2,950dr), and Agios Konstandinos (4½–5 hrs, 3,560dr). From the station on the east side of the port, regular **buses** head to Stafilos (15 min, 190dr), Milia (30 min, 440dr), and Glóssa (1 hr, 770dr). You can also sail directly to Glóssa from the port at Loutráki, 3 km (2 mi) south of Skópelos town.

WHERE TO SLEEP AND EAT

Hotels in Skópelos Town are pricey, so you're best off following one of the women who meet the ferry screaming, "Cheap rooms, very cheap!" to their 4,000dr–10,000dr doubles; otherwise, ask around the port. Food at the port is also expensive, so try **Sergiani's** (tel. 0424/23971) for filling starters (1,500dr for two) or fried squid (1,100dr); look for the big SERGIANI sign east of the Kástro. As part of its heritage program, Skópelos Town supports the **Demotiko Kafeneion** (on the waterfront), which makes Greek coffee rather than Nescafé. For a magical cultural evening, take the steps on the far west side of the port and climb past the churches to the Kástro, where you'll find **Ouzeri Anatoli,** owned by a famous *rembetiko* (a kind of bluesy bouzouki) artist who performs nightly in summer. You'll pay dearly for the experience, though—beer goes for 3,000dr, a bottle of wine for 10,000dr. In Glóssa, **Pension Platana** (tel. 0424/33602) has doubles with bath and kitchen for 5,000dr (low season) and 10,000dr (high season); call ahead. **Taverna Agnanti** (tel. 0424/33606), in the town center, has good veal in wine sauce (1,000dr) and great views; the owner, N. Stamatakis, also arranges rooms (doubles 5,000dr–7,000dr)

NORTHERN GREECE

Northern Greece is less visited than the south, and at first glance it's easy to see why. Travelers often pass through the transport hubs of Vólos or Alexandroúpolis and figure they've seen enough. You can be sure, though, that if they had explored the monasteries at Metéora, built on the heights of rock pinnacles rising more than 1,800 ft, they wouldn't have been so quick to move on. The north may not have as many miles of drop-dead-gorgeous coastline as the south, but if you've brought your hiking boots as well as your bathing suit, the sparsely populated mountains and lush valleys make up for it.

IPIROS

Stretching south from the Albanian border, along the Ionian Sea, the Pindos Mountains of Ipiros (or Epirus) are geographically isolated enough for wild goats, deer, bears, and wolves to roam. They're also extraordinarily beautiful, with at least two of the most impressive gorges in Europe (Aoós and Víkos). Isolation and rugged terrain was not enough, however, to keep out such foreign invaders as the Romans,

Slavs, Bulgars, Serbs, Normans, Albanians, and Ottoman Turks, the last of whom took over in the early 15th century. Beginning in 1788, Ali Pasha, Ottoman governor of Ioánnina, extended his control over much of Greece as a virtually independent ruler until Sultan Mahmud II decided that he had had enough, and dispatched an army to, um, reassert Ottoman authority in 1822. Ipiros only became part of modern Greece after an extraordinary battle during the Balkan Wars, in the winter of 1912–13.

IOANNINA

Situated at the foot of the Píndos Mountains on the shores of murky Lake Pamvótis, Ioánnina boasts an idyllic setting and a complex history. Despite the Greek distaste for all things Turkish, Ioánnina retains much of its former Turkish flavor. (482 years of Ottoman rule will do that to a town.) The helpful **EOT** office (SE corner of Pl. Pírrou, tel. 0651/25086) can give you tips on exploring the Píndos Mountains (*see* Near Ioánnina, *below*) and the local museums.

COMING AND GOING

Buses heading to points south and west, including Pátra (4 hrs, 4,050dr), leave from the station at 28 Bizaniou. Buses to everywhere else, including Athens (6 hrs, 6,750dr), Igoumenítsa (2 hrs, 1,800dr), Kalambáka (3 hrs, 2,150dr), and Thessaloníki (6 hrs, 5,650dr), leave from the station at 4 Zossimadón.

WHERE TO SLEEP AND EAT

The hotels in the heart of town are adequate. **Hotel Metropolis** (Avérof, at K. Kristálli, tel. 0651/25507 or 0651/26207; doubles 7,600) is clean and convenient, though it rarely has hot water. The **El Greco** (8 Tsirigoti, tel. 0651/30726 and 0651/30727; doubles 10,000dr) has wonderful, spacious rooms a two-minute walk from the Zossimadón bus station. If you need help finding a place to stay and the EOT office is closed, go to the **tourist police** (tel. 0651/25673), on October 28 Street across from the central post office. Platía Mavíli, on the lakefront next to the Kastro, is full of café/bar/restaurants. Prices here are somewhat higher than elsewhere in town; the best deal is further along the lakefront at **Sin 2** (28 Papagou, tel. 0651/78695). Forget your waistline and order the pork with white sauce (950dr) or the fried feta cheese (500dr).

WORTH SEEING

The main street, Avérof (it changes names along the way), is jammed with vendors of jewelry and metalwork, traditional crafts that have flourished since the early 13th century, when many craftsmen left Constantinople after its fall to the Crusaders. At the southeast end of Avérof, where the town juts into the lake, is Ioánnina's main sight, the **Kastro** (castle), surrounded by the city's defense walls. Within the walls are two mosques: One houses the **Municipal Museum,** with artifacts from this millennium's three main Greek communities—Christians, Muslims, and Jews—and next to the other is the **Byzantine Museum.**

It's worth taking the ferry (leaves every half-hour from Pl. Mavíli, 200dr) out to the island of **Nissí,** with narrow cobblestone streets and whitewashed stone houses. Legend has it that the island's 500 residents trace their ancestry back to Máni, in the southern Peloponnese. Two of the island's five monasteries are open to the public: **Filanthropínon** displays dramatic and well-preserved frescoes; and the guest house at the 17th-century **Panteleímon** is where Ali Pasha was assassinated.

NEAR IOANNINA

Dodoni, 22 km (13 mi) southeast of Ioánnina, was first used in the worship of the Earth Goddess; later, in the second millenium BC, Hellenic tribes came to worship Zeus and hear the prophecies revealed by the rustling leaves of a sacred oak tree. This oracle was second only to Delphi in sacredness, and during the 4th century BC a temple and other buildings were erected around it. The 3rd-century BC amphitheater is still almost entirely intact and provides a stunning view of the mountains across the valley. Now an archaeological site, Dodoni is not often visited, so you can enjoy a nearly private exploration. *Tel. 0652/82287. Admission: 500dr. From Ioánnina, catch bus (3–4 times daily), at 28 Bizaniou. Open daily 8–7.*

NORTHERN PINDOS • The northernmost stretch of the Píndos Mountains, Vória Píndos, is home to Greece's second-highest peak and 46 traditional villages known as the **Zágoria.** Though these villages boast some unique and surprisingly grand stone architecture, the area's real draw is the stunning **Víkos Gorge,** which slices dramatically through the mountains. The village of **Monodéndri** is the usual trailhead for the trek through the ravine; from here, Trail 03 runs 13 km (8 mi) along the Voidomátis River to the beautiful village of **Megálo Pápingo. Mikró Pápingo,** which lies farther along on the trail at the base of a rock cliff, is just large enough to have a couple of tavernas and guest houses. If you're not planning to spend the night, the six- to seven-hour hike through the beautiful gorge makes a possible, though strenuous, day trip from Ioánnina; take the *early*-morning bus (1½ hrs, 1,000dr) from the Zossimadon station to Monodéndri, then return to Ioánnina from Mikró Pápingo on the mid-afternoon bus. Get bus schedules and a free trail map at the Ioánnina EOT office (*see* Ioánnina, *above*).

THESSALIA

A fairly mundane stretch of farmland bounded by the mountains of Ipiros to the west and the Aegean Sea to the east, Thessalía is usually passed through rather than visited, and with reason: The region's main towns of Lamía, Vólos, and Larissa are pretty concrete. The magnificent monasteries of the Metéora and the historic villages of the Pílion, however, are spectacular cultural enclaves in some seriously beautiful settings.

VOLOS

As the transportation center for northern Greece, Vólos usually sees tourists only when they pass through en route to the gorgeous Pílion peninsula and the Sporádes Islands. But this port town isn't a terrible place to make a pit stop; the pleasant, mile-long waterfront overflows with bars and restaurants, perfectly situated for a leisurely afternoon of people-watching. At the east end of the waterfront, the **Archaeological Museum** (next to hospital; admission 500dr; open Mon.–Sat. 8:30–3) has a diverse regional collection, with artifacts from the Neolithic to the Roman periods. The collection includes grave stelae, tomb reconstructions, pottery, and jewelry.

If you're stuck here for the night, the **EOT tourist office** (Grigoriou Lambraki, on south side of park, 10-min walk east of stations, tel. 0421/23500 or 0421/37417) has some good dope on local lodging. The spotless, comfy **Pension Roussas** (1 Tzaanou, near museum, tel. 0421/21732; doubles from 5,000dr) has a helpful proprietor and a great location on the waterfront. Or try **Camping Hellas** (17 km/11 mi SE of Vólos toward Kala Nera and Visitsa, tel. 0423/22278; 720dr per tent plus 960dr per person), on the Pagasitic Gulf; take any of the coastal buses and ask to be dropped off at the campground.

COMING AND GOING

The **bus** and **train** stations are 200 yds apart on Grigoríou Lambráki, just west of the waterfront. Frequent buses connect Vólos with Athens (5 hrs, 4,900dr), Thessaloníki (3 hrs, 3,300dr), Kalambáka (3 hrs, 2,800dr), and Litohóro (2 hrs, 2,000dr). Trains serve Athens (5 hrs, 2,830dr), Thessaloníki (3½ hrs, 1,720dr), and Kalambáka (3½ hrs, 1,140dr). For bus schedules, dial 0421/35555 or go to the information window at the bus station. For trains, dial 0421/24056.

Ferries to the Sporádes dock at the western end of the waterfront. Schedules change frequently, but you can expect three or four boats daily to Skíathos (3½ hrs, 2,450dr), with continuing service to nearby Skópelos and Alónissos.

PILION MOUNTAINS

The low Pílion range, mythical home of centaurs, stretches from Vólos along a lush, slender peninsula. Once you rise past the olive trees that skirt the mountains, you'll be greeted by the sound of running water, which springs magically from fountains and crevices, flowing along cobblestone paths and across roads. All access to the Pílion is by KTEL bus from Vólos. Once you're in the mountains, getting around is difficult, for though the range is small, it's rugged and not easily explored.

Just across the peninsula from Vólos, **Zagora** is a good base for hikes to the tiny villages and churches hidden in the mountains. The Vólos tourist office (*see* Vólos, *above*) has a decent hiking map of the area. Ten kilometers (6 miles) down the road from Zagora, the touristy **Horefto** beach offers a welcome respite from your hiking, with lots of hotels and a nearby camping area (Siagos D., tel. 0426/22180 or 0426/22806). Buses to Zagora (2 hrs, 750dr) depart only twice daily from Vólos, usually in early morning and mid-afternoon; check the schedule at Vólos's station.

If you can't fit Zagora in, or you'd rather just enjoy amazing vistas from the hills above Vólos, take the bus (25 min, 260dr) up to **Makrinítsa,** an EOT-mandated landmark settlement—all tourists' dollars are dedicated to the town's upkeep. Makrinítsa has a pretty Byzantine church, steep winding paths, and a flagstone square, but the highlight of the town is its view of Vólos and the bay. Accommodations here are pricey, so most people stay in the cheaper but more touristy **Portaria,** a 20-minute walk away.

About an hour's bus ride (480dr) southeast of Vólos, **Visitsa,** a lovely old village of winding cobblestone streets and amazing views of the Pílion peninsula and Pagasitic Gulf, also makes a fine jaunt. Donkeys are still a viable means of transportation here, and the people grow much of their own food. If you're inclined to linger, the hospitable **Karagiannopoulou Guest House** (#108 on main road, tel. 0421/86447) has nice doubles for 10,000dr. Near the bus stop, **Café Oetis** has decent continental breakfasts for 1,100dr. Just above the bus stop, there are several reasonably priced tavernas on the tree-lined platía.

Another idyllic day trip is **Trikeri Island,** a tiny speck of land at the toe of the bootlike Pílion peninsula. Accessible by the Flying Dolphin hydrofoil (3,600dr round trip) from Vólos, Trikeri is not much more than a couple of peaceful olive grove–covered hills; the highest supports a former monastery, which is well worth the 15-minute walk up. The few dozen locals won't mind if you wander aimlessly among the isle's trails and the roaming sheep and goats, or lounge on the two beautiful beaches, both of which are near the only hotel, **Palio Trikeri** (tel. 0421/49402; doubles from 5,000dr).

METEORA

The surreal gray cliffs and tiny buildings of the Metéora could only have been created by a combination of earth and spirit. The organic-looking stone-and-timber monasteries seem to have sprouted from the land. The monasteries' inaccessibility (until recently, you could reach them only by scaling the rock face or being pulled up in a net) allowed the monks of the Metéora to worship unhindered by Greek and Turkish politics from the 13th to the 16th centuries. After the 16th century, the monasteries began a gradual deterioration that has been halted only recently by the fascination and money of visitors. Today, six are in operation as residences for monks and nuns, all pandering shamelessly to tourists. But the elegant frescoes and breathtaking views are worth the crowds and the 600dr admission to each. Wear suitable clothing to all of the monasteries: long pants for men, skirts below the knee for women, and covered shoulders for everyone.

You can visit all six monasteries in a full day of strenuous walking, but if time is limited, head first to **Metamórphosis** (open Sat.–Thurs. 9–1 and 3–6). It has a stunning library, well-preserved frescoes, and impressive views. Looming above from one of the most dramatic sites in the Metéora is **Roussánou** (open daily 9–1 and 3–6); frescoes cram an entire history of Christianity onto the walls of the small but overwhelming chapel.

COMING AND GOING

Five km (3 mi) down the road from the Metéora, **Kalambáka** is served by frequent trains from Vólos (4½ hrs, 1,140dr), Thessaloníki (6½ hrs, 2,220dr), and Athens (7½ hrs, 2,700dr) and by KTEL buses from Ioánnina (3 hrs, 2,050dr), Vólos (3 hrs, 2,600dr), and Athens via Tríkala (6 hrs, 5,110dr). A bus also leaves the KTEL station for Méga Metéoron (190dr one way) twice daily. To get to **Kastráki,** at the foot of the Metéora, walk the 2 km (1⅓ mi) from Kalambáka or take a taxi (500dr) or bus (150dr), which leaves the platía two blocks from the KTEL station.

WHERE TO SLEEP

If you arrive late in Kalambáka, follow the signs advertising rooms to let. Otherwise, the road to Kastráki is littered with hotels, campgrounds, and more rooms to let. **Hotel Kastráki** (tel. 0432/22286; doubles 5,000dr) is perfectly situated at the start of the road to the Metéora. (Don't confuse it with the new, expensive hotel further along the road.) **Camping the Cave** (tel. 0432/24802; 950dr per person) has an incredible location at the base of the rocks, which compensates for its somewhat cramped sites.

MACEDONIA

Despite its numerous archaeological treasures and remnants of the reign of Alexander the Great, Macedonía is rarely visited. Macedonians are fiercely proud of their legacy and only vaguely acknowledge their region's Byzantine and Ottoman history. Legend-enshrouded Mt. Olympus is one of the best reasons to come here, and Thessaloníki lends the region some cosmopolitan flair.

THESSALONIKI

Thessaloníki has always been a second city, playing a supporting role to Pélla in Macedonía's heyday, to Constantinople during the Byzantine Empire, to İstanbul during the Ottoman Empire, and to Athens in the modern era. Rather than wallow in this eternal shadow, Thessaloníki has excelled as a cultural and intellectual center. It was here that Aristotle taught young Alexander the Great in the 4th century BC, St. Paul wrote his epistles in the 1st century AD, and Jews fleeing persecution from their native Spain were taken in and protected by the Ottoman sultan after 1492.

With the largest port in the Balkans, Thessaloníki today is a wealthy, modern city, colored but not dwarfed by its ancient history. Visitors can expect both a jet-set stomping ground and a sweaty provincial port. Men draped in Armani crowd the chic shops, cafés, and platías, sipping their 1,000dr coffees while merchants in the bazaar erupt in their usual spirited bartering. Downtown, amid the pockets of Greek, Roman, Turkish, and Byzantine ruins, 20th-century excavations and restorations remind you that though the city revels in a vibrant present, it remembers its ancient glory as well. The European Union named Thessaloniki the Cultural Capital of Europe for 1997.

BASICS

The **tourist office** (8 Pl. Aristotélous, tel. 031/271–888) is open weekdays 8–8 and Saturday 8:30–2. **American Express** (19 Tsimiskí, tel. 031/221–672 or 031/239–797; open weekdays 8–2, Fri. until 1:30) has financial services but no travel office. Pick up poste restante at the **central post office** (45 Tsimiskí, tel. 031/264–208), postal code 54101.

COMING AND GOING

Thessaloníki has one of Greece's largest **train stations** (Monastiríou, 3 km/2 mi west of city center). It serves Athens (8 hrs, 3,720dr on regular train; 6 hrs, 7,700 drs on Intercity), Alexandroúpolis (7 hrs, 3,000dr on regular train; 5½ hrs, 4,900 dr on Intercity), Sofia (7 hrs, 5,300dr), and İstanbul (22 hrs, 11,600dr). Take Bus 3 from one of its stops along Tsimiski to the train station at the end of the line. Get train information at the **OSE** office (corner of Ermou and Aristotelous, tel. 031/276–382).

KTEL operates **bus service** from several stations, most of them near the train station. Buses split frequently for Athens (7 hrs, 7,700dr) from 65 Monastiriou (tel. 031/545–302); for Alexandroúpolis (6 hrs, 5,200dr) from 31 Koloniari (tel. 031/514–111); and for Katerini (1 hr, 1,150dr) from 10 Promitheos (tel. 031/519–101). Buses also leave for Halkidikí from 69 Karakassi (tel. 031/924–444); from the center, take Bus 10 to the corner of Egnatia Odos and Karakassi, and walk two blocks southwest on Karakassi.

GETTING AROUND

The focus of the lower city is the waterside combination of Platía Aristotélous and Tsimiskí Street, the center for shopping, banking, and socializing. The city is sprawling and hilly outside the center, but **buses** (75dr) cover it all; board single-length buses in the front and buy a ticket from the vending machine behind the driver, or board caterpillar buses through the rear door and pay the seated conductor. No **taxi** fare in town should run over 1,000dr; a taxi to the airport will cost about 2,000dr.

WHERE TO SLEEP

Budget hotels are concentrated on busy, grimy **Egnatia,** west of Venizelou. From the stations, go east on Monastiriou, which becomes Egnatia; from Platía Aristotelous, head north and turn left onto Egnatia. The cheapest deal here is **Hotel Argo** (1 E. Svoronu, tel. 031/519–770; doubles 7,000dr with bath), one block east of Platía Dimokratias, just north of Egnatia. Hotels on Komninón are quieter and better-located (two blocks off Platía Aristotelous, by the waterfront) but much pricier. An exception is the **Hotel Continental** (Komninón 5, tel. 031/277–553 or 031/228–917), where pleasant doubles with TV and fridge start at 7,000dr.

The **Youth Hostel Thessaloníki** (44 Svolou, tel. 031/225–946; beds 2,000dr; open Mar.–Nov.) is drab and dirty, but it's centrally located. From Platía Aristotélous, go north on Aristotelous Street and then east on Ermou, which becomes Svolou; or, from the train station, take Bus 10 to Kamara and head one block south on Ipodromiou.

FOOD

You'll find some horrifically expensive tavernas and restaurants around the waterfront streets. Among the trendy, overpriced cafés, the unassuming **Ariston** (Gounari 13, tel. 031/262–715) serves an above-average Greek meal for less than 2,000dr. Weekdays 7–4, there's a **bazaar** just west of Aristotelous and south of Ermou, offering fruit, cheese, bread, and olives. Inside, on the Komninón side, **Mirovolos Emirni** (tel. 031/274–170) is popular for its fresh seafood (800dr–1,200dr).

WORTH SEEING

Thessaloníki is not exactly brimming with must-see attractions. The mosaics at the **Agia Sofia** (Agias Sofias, at Ermou) church are worth a peek. For a spectacular crash course on the glitter and glory of ancient Macedonía, hit the **Archaeological Museum.** See the stunning gold larnax, discovered in 1978 and decorated with the Macedonian sun emblem; this box is believed to contain the bones of Phillip II, Alexander's father. *Corner of Tsimiski and Angelaki, tel. 031/830–538. Admission: 1,500dr. Open Mon. 12:30–7, Tues.–Fri. 8–7, weekends 8:30–3.*

The facade and setting of the **White Tower,** which once marked where the city walls met the waterfront, are more attractive than the modest exhibits inside. The six floors of the tower wind up to a tiny café and a terrace with a view of Thessaloníki and the sea. *Nikis, at Pavlou Mela. Admission: 800dr. Open Mon. 12:30–7, Tues.–Fri. 8–7, weekends 8:30–3.*

AFTER DARK

Thessaloníki is at its best after the sun sets, when the entire populace floods the trendy and expensive cafés on Nikis (along the waterfront) up to Platía Aristotelous. You'll also find a slew of upscale bars around Platía Morihovou, Thessaloníki's former red-light district. In summer, bars and discos line the airport road, 10 km (6 mi) outside of town; any taxi driver will know how to get there (2,000dr). Out this way, **Hantres** (tel. 031/475–469 or 031/475–470) puts on a wonderfully cheesy show of traditional Greek music, and gets really lively after 1 AM. Another popular nightspot, **Milos** (5 Korovagou, tel. 031/525–968 or 031/516–945; cover 1,000dr–1,500dr for music after 10 PM), is a café, restaurant, gallery, blues club, and bar all rolled into a complex of buildings centered around an old flour mill; a taxi here should run 1,000dr.

If you get stuck in Alexandroúpolis overnight, try Hotel Lido (K. Palaiológou 15, tel. 0551/28808; doubles from 6,000dr), one block north of the bus station.

MT. OLYMPUS

Mt. Olympus (Oros Olimbos in Greek) ascends dramatically from greenery to rock to cloud, with no bothersome rolling hills to muddle the effect. In summer, **Mytikas,** the mountain's highest peak (9,626 ft), is accessible to inexperienced and expert climbers alike; the winter climb requires considerable knowledge and equipment. Many visitors make the mistake of racing for the top; instead, consider shorter and mellower hikes that allow you time to soak up the views the gods enjoyed.

The most popular way to climb Mt. Olympus is in a succession of two- to three-hour hikes broken up by stays in refuges. The initial leg is from **Litóhoro** to the itsy-bitsy village of **Priónia**; this four-hour hike runs along a gorge (head up the road past the post office on the central platía in Litóhoro, and cross the little bridge; the way is marked from there), or you can take an equally adventurous taxi ride (6,000dr) along a skinny gravel road. From Priónia, the E4 trail leads from the 3,630-ft mark to the 6,930-ft **Refuge A** (tel. 0352/81800; beds 2,500dr; closed Nov.–Apr.), run by the Greek Alpine Club (EOS); reserve ahead to ensure your share of water, overpriced food, and sleep. From here, it's a 2½-hour hike along cliffs to the Mytikas peak. Closer to the summit are the privately run Christou Takálou and the Greek Climbing Club (SEO) refuges; for information on the dramatic routes to these higher-altitude refuges, check with either the municipal information office or the Greek Climbing Club (SEO) office in Litóhoro. Camping is verboten in this national park.

BASICS

In Litohóro, the **Litóhoro Municipality information office** (Ag. Nikoláou, in front of the Town Hall, tel. 0352/83100; open June–Sept., daily 9–8) hands out a map of the town and trails and has some information on private rooms. They can also guide you (and you'll see signs in the square) to the offices of both the **Greek Alpine Club (EOS)** (tel. 0352/81944; open weekdays 9–12:30 and 6:30–8:30, weekends 9–noon) and the **Greek Climbing Club (SEO)** (tel. 0352/82300). Both offices can radio your reservation to their refuge.

COMING AND GOING

Buses will try to drop you off as far from Litóhoro as possible—demand to be taken at least as far as the gas station by the turnoff to town. From here, it's 5 km (3 mi) on foot, or via the odd bus. Buses leave Litóhoro's central platía directly for Thessaloníki (1½ hrs, 1,500dr), often via Kateríni. For all other destinations, you'll first have to catch a bus north to Kateríni (½ hr, 380dr) to make connections.

WHERE TO SLEEP AND EAT

Unfortunately, Litóhoro offers few sleeping options. The only budget hotel is **Hotel Park** (Ag. Nikoláou 23, tel. 0352/81252), which has ordinary doubles with private bath for 7,000dr. **Ashtarti Travel** (28 Oktovrion 3, near the platía, tel. 0352/82690) may be able to set you up with a private room for about 3,000dr per person. There's no dearth of tavernas, though, on the main street, Agiou Nikoláou.

THRACE

Thrace (Thráki), comprising the far northeast corner of the country, has only been part of Greece since 1922, when it was formally ceded by Turkey. With a large population of Turks and Bulgarians, this region has one of Greece's most diverse religious and cultural populations—so alas, it has its share of problems and resentments. The borders with Turkey and Bulgaria, though certainly traversable by train or bus, are heavily militarized and make for a highly charged atmosphere.

SAMOTHRAKI

Rising 5,283 from the surface of the Aegean on the island of Samothráki, the peak of Mt. Fengári gave Poseidon the perfect vantage point for watching the siege of Troy, across the water in Asia Minor. Aside from German hippies at the hot springs and grazing sheep and goats, the island is a largely uninhabited mass of imposing wilderness, punctuated by a handful of remote hamlets.

Samothráki's one road fails to circumnavigate the island; only the northwestern half is accessible by car. Here, the port town of **Kamariótisa** is a busy strip of cafés, rooms to let, and other tourist services. About 5 km (3 mi) inland is the quaint capital town **Samothráki (Hora),** nestled on the slope of Mt. Fengári. To the north, the road hooks up with **Thérma,** home of hot springs and package tourists. From here, hike along the small river, with waterfalls and swimming holes; the **Gria Vathra** waterfall is about 30 minutes along, and the walk gets a little steeper after that. The lovely beach **Pahía Amos** is at the end of the road on the island's south side; rent a moped for the hilly but scenic half-hour jaunt.

Samothráki's claim to fame is the **Sanctuary of the Great Gods** (admission 500dr), one of the most mysterious and revered sites of ancient Greece. Little is known of the cult worship here because initiates were sworn to secrecy. In the 15th century, the Venetians disassembled the sanctuary to build fortifications; the remaining ruins and five reconstructed Doric pillars give you an idea of its original glory. An English-friendly map at the entrance explains the excavated site. French archaeologists liberated the famed **Nike of Samothrace** statue from the top of the amphitheater here, and, after installing it in the Louvre, sportingly sent back a plaster copy to the site's **museum** (admission 500dr), which is otherwise devoted to real finds from the sanctuary. The site and museum (both open Tues.–Sun. 8:30–3) are in **Paleópoli,** a village-like clump of hotels halfway between Kamariótisa and Therma on the north shore. Take a bus or moped; or, from Hora, walk 3 km (2 mi) on the hilly path.

BASICS

In Kamariótisa, you can rent mopeds (4,000dr) across from the ferry dock. **Buses,** headquartered just north of the dock, travel hourly to the north of the island and less frequently to Hora. The closest thing you'll find to **tourist information** is Saos Tours (across from bus stop, tel. 0551/41505), which has bus and ferry schedules and a fairly useless 500dr map.

COMING AND GOING

The easiest way to get here is from the transport hub of Alexandroúpolis; buses run regularly from Athens (12 hrs, 12,000dr) and Thessaloníki (6 hrs, 5,000dr) to Alexandroúpolis's **bus station** (38 Venizelou), a few blocks north of the port. Trains also serve Alexandroúpolis from Athens (14 hrs, 6,800dr) and Thessaloníki (7 hrs, 3,000dr); the **train station** is just east of the ferry dock. From there, **ferries** leave for Samothráki (3 hrs, 2,100dr) twice daily Monday–Thursday and thrice daily Friday–Sunday. Get schedules at the Thessaloníki (*see* Basics *in* Thessaloníki, *above*) tourist office.

WHERE TO SLEEP AND EAT

Just about every *zimmer ist frei* (room is available) in Kamariótisa—for 6,000dr–7,000dr per room. If that's too rich for your blood, make tracks to the wonderful, waterfront **campground** (400dr per tent plus 600dr per person) 1 km (½ mi) from Therma. From Kamariótisa, take the coastal road east and stay to the left at the turnoff for Therma, following the signs. Don't confuse this campground with the more expensive trailer-park type farther along the road.

HUNGARY

Western visitors to Eastern Europe may want to start their travels in Hungary. The culture shock is far less pronounced here than in some other Eastern European countries, in part because Hungary is comparatively unscarred by the legacy of Communism. Even during the height of the Cold War, Hungary attempted a kinder, gentler totalitarianism, which encouraged certain types of private enterprise and rejected the collectivization of the land. This "goulash communism," as it came to be called, wasn't freedom, but it sure wasn't Romania.

As Hungarian Communism differed from the other Eastern European models, so Hungarians as a people differ from other East Europeans. Whereas most of this part of the world is Slavic, the 10.2 million Hungarians are Magyars, descendants of an Asian tribe that arrived in Europe during the 9th century. Hungarians' closest relatives are the Finns, the Estonians, and the Vogul and Ostiak peoples of Siberia. The most obvious reminder of this unusual genealogy is the language, a tongue so unlike any other in the world that even its closest relative, Finnish, is less similar to it than Italian is to German. Their language gives the Hungarians a sense of national identity—and national isolation—that helps insulate them from the tensions that have ripped apart more ethnically diverse Eastern European nations.

When the Eastern European economy collapsed in the late 1980s, it dragged the Hungarian Communist party down with it. Hard-line leaders were removed in May 1988, a multiparty system was introduced in October 1989, and Hungary's first free elections in more than 40 years were held in 1990. Free elections don't automatically put food on the table, however, and Hungary remains beset by such woes as unemployment and inflation. On the bright side, its economic growth ranks third (behind Poland and the Czech Republic) among former Soviet-bloc nations. It was invited to join NATO in July 1997, and membership in the European Union also seems likely in the next several years. For travelers, Hungary provides the opportunity to witness a society in transition to democratic capitalism. What will emerge from the clash of Eastern heritage and Western aspirations remains to be seen.

BASICS

MONEY

At press time, US$1 = 185 forints and 100 forints = 54¢. The Hungarian forint (Ft.) is divided into 100 fillér, though these days fillér coins are rare and totally useless. Most Hungarian cities have plenty of

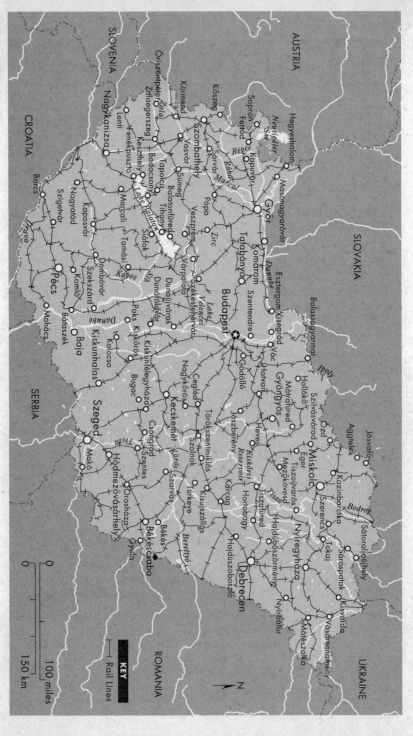

HUNGARY

SLOVENIA

CROATIA

AUSTRIA

SLOVAKIA

SERBIA

ROMANIA

UKRAINE

Őriszentpéter
Zalaegerszeg
Lenti
Nagykanizsa
Barcs
Szigetvár
Nagyatád
Kaposvár
Pécs
Komló
Szekszárd
Bátaszék
Mohács
Baja
Kalocsa
Kiskunhalas
Bugac
Szeged
Makó
Hódmezővásárhely
Orosháza
Békéscsaba
Gyula
Békés

Zalai
Zala
Keszthely
Fenékpuszta
Tapolca
Badacsony
Sümeg
Magcali
Tamási
Dombóvár

Körmend
Vasvár
Szombathely
Sárvár
Kőszeg
Sopron
Fertőd
Hegyeshalom
Neusiedler See

Répce
Rábca
Marcal
Pápa
Zirc
Veszprém
Balatonfüred
Tihany
Siófok
Várpalota
Kapos
Lake Balaton

Kapuvár
Mosonmagyaróvár
Győr
Tatabánya
Komárom
Danube

Esztergom
Kisvisegrád
Szentendre
Vác
Budapest
Gödöllő
Hatvan
Ercsi
Dunaújváros
Dunaföldvár
Paks
Kiskőrös
Kiskunfélegyháza
Nagykőrös
Cegléd
Kecskemét
Csongrád
Szentes
Szarvas
Szolnok
Törökszentmiklós
Jászberény
Mezőkövesd
Kiskörei Reservoir
Heves
Szolnok
Kunszentmárton
Túrkeve
Kisújszállás
Karcag
Hortobágy
Hajdúszoboszló
Debrecen
Hajdúböszörmény
Hajdúnánás

Székesfehérvár
Velencei Lake
Tata

Balassagyarmat
Ipoly
Hollókő
Mátrafüred
Gyöngyös
Szilvásvárad
Ózd
Aggtelek
Jósvafő
Kazincbarcika
Eger
Miskolc
Tiszaújváros
Szerencs
Tokai
Bodrog
Sátoraljaújhely
Sárospatak
Nyíregyháza
Nyírbátor
Kisvárda
Mátészalka
Vásárosnamény
Tisza
Berettyó
Körös

Tisza
Körös
Dráva
Danube

KEY
— Rail Lines

N

0
100 miles
0
150 km

ATMs, which will get you the best exchange rates. Otherwise, travel agencies and bureaux de change will change traveler's checks into forints (and occasionally even provide credit-card advances), but at lousy rates—you're better off going to a bank. The amount you may change back at the end of your trip is officially limited to 50% (up to US$100 worth) of the total amount of currency you have changed into forints, and you must have the exchange receipts.

HOW MUCH IT WILL COST • Hungary is not cheap, and with the forint's devaluation and raging inflation, prices are on the rise. Overall, it's on par with the Czech Republic and slightly more expensive than other Eastern European countries. Staying in budget hotels and pensions (doubles 2,500 Ft.– 4,000 Ft.) and eating all your meals in restaurants, you can expect to pay about $40 per day. You'll spend much less if you stay in private homes (1,500 Ft.–2,500 Ft. per person), university dorms and youth hostels (500 Ft.–1,000 Ft. per person), or campgrounds (1,200 Ft.–2,600 Ft. per two-person campsite), and buy some of your meals in produce markets. Prices in Budapest and Lake Balaton are much higher than elsewhere in the country (hotel and hostel prices in Budapest are double the norm). Throughout Hungary, prices shoot up at least 20% during July and August.

VISA AND ENTRY REQUIREMENTS

Travelers with a valid U.S., Canadian, or British passport do not need visas to visit Hungary for less than 30 days. Australians and New Zealanders need visas and should contact the Hungarian Consulate in Australia (Suite 405, Edgecliff Centre, 203–233 New South Head Rd., Edgecliff NSW 2027, Sydney, tel. 02/328-7859).

COMING AND GOING

Eurailpasses, European East passes, and InterRail passesare valid throughout Hungary. Express **trains** depart daily from Budapest's Keleti Station for major European cities such as Vienna (3 hrs, 4,200 Ft.), Prague (8 hrs, 8,800 Ft.), and İstanbul (31 hrs, 17,900 Ft.). It's wise to make reservations (600 Ft.) for *nemzetközi gyorsvonat* (international express) trains at least 24 hours in advance, either through a travel agency or at the train station. From Budapest, you can also catch **buses** to most major European cities. Prices are 30%–50% cheaper than trains, but your journey will be longer and less comfortable. Hungary's only airport is **Ferihegy Airport** (*see* Coming and Going *in* Budapest, *below*).

During the off season (winter and early spring or late fall), lodging rates in Hungary can dip very low. If approached politely, hotel managers are often willing to bargain rather than leave a room empty.

GETTING AROUND

Thanks to the national railway, **MÁV,** train travel to and from Budapest is fast, efficient, and cheap. Travel between other towns is more difficult—you'll often get sent back to Budapest to change trains. To avoid confusion, ask, "*Át kell szállnom?*" ("Do I have to change trains?"). If the town you're traveling to is on the *gyorsvonat* (express) route, definitely go express; *személyvonat* (local trains) can be painfully slow. Reservations are 300 Ft. for InterCity trains, 80 Ft. for Expressz trains. All ticket prices are calculated by distance, approximately 500 Ft. per 100 km (60 mi); also, all tickets are **csak oda** (one-way) unless you request *oda-vissza* (round-trip). Buy train tickets before you board or you'll pay a surcharge (400 Ft.). The 7- and 10-day **discount train passes** (7,000 Ft. and 9,000 Ft. respectively), good for unlimited domestic travel, are worthwhile only if you plan to see the entire country. A final note: Hungarian **buses** are only better than trains for short hops from village to village, such as along the Danube Bend—otherwise, they're more crowded and far less comfortable.

WHERE TO SLEEP

A **panzió** (pension) is slightly cheaper and more homey than a hotel. But you can't get much homier than one of your cheapest options—a room in a private house. **Private rooms** are usually booked through tourist offices, or you can walk around looking for signs that say SZOBA KIADO (room to rent) or ZIMMER FREI. Breakfast is usually available for a small extra fee at most pensions and private houses in the countryside, and this gives you a chance to meet your hosts and get their inside advice on what to see and do in the area. Though **hostels** are uncommon outside Budapest, some towns open their **university dorms** to travelers during July and August; inquire at the local tourist office. The atmosphere and price at a student dorm is about the same as in a hostel. Camping is the cheapest, most scenic way to go, and many **campgrounds** rent tents and let bungalows. Every town has a campground; for a complete list, pick up the free booklet "Camping" at any Tourinform office.

FOOD

Hungarian dishes tend to be greasy, with lots of sour cream, grated cheese, and shimmering globs of fat. Though this kind of food might take years off your life, it sure tastes good. Some slightly lower-cholesterol options in the land of deep-fried meats include *gulyás* (goulash), a soup or stew with meat, potatoes, small noodles, and plenty of paprika; *paprikás csirke* (chicken paprika); and *halászlé* (fish soup). Many restaurants now also have a few vegetarian options—usually deep-fried cheese and vegetables served with tartar sauce. Even dishes that look meatless are frequently cooked with lard; strict vegetarians should double-check when ordering to avoid disappointment. A full meal in a decent restaurant, including wine or beer, costs around 1,100 Ft. You can eat well for less by choosing the prix-fixe "menü" offered in many restaurants.

BUSINESS HOURS

Shops are generally open weekdays 10–6 and Saturday 9–1. Banks, post offices, and other businesses tend to keep shorter hours, Monday–Thursday 9–5 and Friday 9–1. Restaurants are typically open daily noon–10 PM, though some shut briefly during the late afternoon hours. Food markets are usually open weekdays 7–6 and Saturday 7–1. Museum hours are generally Tuesday–Sunday 10–6. "Nonstops" are convenience stores open 24 hours, or at least until the clerk decides it's bedtime.

VISITOR INFORRMATION

The national tourist agency is **Tourinform,** which dispenses free information on lodging, transportation, and sights. Offices, with English-speaking staff, are in all the major Hungarian cities. For information before you go, write the head office in Budapest (Sütő u. 2, H-1024 Budapest), send an email (tourinform@hungary.com), or visit the Tourinform Web site (http://www.hungary.com/tourinform); you can request to have brochures sent to you by mail.

The leading travel agency, **IBUSZ,** has more than 700 locations throughout the country. Services range from Budapest's 24-hour Welcome Hotel Service to minor operations in the countryside that open only when the people in charge feel so inspired. IBUSZ offices can usually book private rooms and pensions, exchange money, and load you up with local maps and brochures.

PHONES AND MAIL

Country code: 36. Hungary's phone lines are old and often unreliable. Give the party you're calling your phone number, as it's common to be disconnected. Blue public phones are coin-operated; silver ones take phone cards, available at post offices, Telefon centers, and shops displaying a sticker reading TELEFONKÁRTYA ÁRUSÍTS (PHONE CARDS SOLD HERE). For long-distance calls within Hungary, wait for the tone, dial 06, wait for another tone, then dial the area code and number. For international calls, dial 00, wait for the strange tone, then dial the country code + area code + number. To reach a U.S. long-distance carrier, dial 00, wait for a tone, then dial 800–01–111 for **AT&T** Direct Access[SM], 800–01–411 for **MCI,** or 800–01–877 for **Sprint.**

Sending a postcard via airmail costs 70 Ft.; letters start at around 100 Ft. Unless your mail has a blue LEGIPOSTA sticker or "Airmail" printed on it, it will arrive home after you do. Airmail letters usually arrive in about a week.

LANGUAGE

The Hungarian language, Magyar (MADJ-yar) is one of the world's most difficult. Struggling with the pronunciation may often seem embarrassing, but Hungarians will be flattered if you try. Some helpful phrases: jo napot kivánok (YO NUP-oat KEE-vah-noak; good day [formal]); szervusz (SAIR-voose; hello); kérem (KAY-rem; please); köszönöm (KUH-suh-num; thank you); hol van . . .? (hole vun; where is . . .?); szeretnék . . . (SAIR-et-neck; I would like . . .); igen/nem (EE-gen/nem; yes/no); beszél angolul? (BESS-el ON-goal-ool?; do you speak English?); bocsánat (BOH-cha-not; excuse me); mennyibe kerül (MEN-yibe kair-ULE?; how much is it?).

BUDAPEST

Budapest is divided by the Danube River into hilly, historic **Buda** and the commercial flatlands of **Pest.** It is Hungary's capital and largest city, with a population of around 2 million. A castle built in the hills,

Roma (Gypsy) folk musicians, and paprika-spiced cuisine are some of the attractions that will draw you to Budapest; plenty of cheap accommodations, an excellent public transportation system, interesting museums, and eminently wanderable streets will make it hard to leave.

Budapest was settled during the 9th century by Magyar tribes, who built on the Roman military camp of Aquincum. Since then, this ancient city has been the locus of foreign oppression and Hungarian resistance. Burned to the ground in 1241 by the Mongols, the city rose from ashes to Renaissance glory under King Mátyás, was conquered by the Turks in 1568, and then conquered again by the Hapsburgs in 1699. Budapest became the second city of the Hapsburg empire and prospered in this role; unfortunately, this alliance with Austria put it on the wrong side of both world wars. At the end of World War II, a six-month battle for Budapest between the Nazis and the Red Army left all the bridges destroyed and the severed halves of the city in ruins. The cycle of occupation and revolt continued through the Cold War: Stalinist hardliners kept the city in fear until Imre Nagy's reforms left the door open for the anti-Soviet uprising of 1956, which was quickly crushed by Russian tanks. Subsequent "goulash communist" governments stirred a little capitalism into Hungary's eastern-bloc socialism, setting Budapest up to be the charming "Western city with Eastern flavor" that it is today.

BASICS

VISITOR INFORMATION

Among dozens of agencies in town advertising "free tourist information," the best is the government-sponsored **Tourinform.** Its English-speaking staff doles out brochures, maps, and the monthly *Programme,* which lists concerts and festivals nationwide. *Sütő u. 2, tel. 1/117–9800. Metro: Deák tér; walk south ½ block on Sütőd u. Open weekdays 9–7, weekends 9–4.*

Another agency offering reliable tourist information and accommodation services is **IBUSZ,** which has dozens of branches throughout the city. The largest office is open 24 hours (*see* Where to Sleep, *below*), but there are also offices in each train station.

AMERICAN EXPRESS

The office in downtown Pest offers a variety of services, including an AmEx-linked ATM. *Deák Ferenc u. 10, Budapest H-1052, tel. 1/266–8680, fax 1/267–2029. Metro: Deák tér. Open June–Sept., weekdays 9–6:30, Sat. 9–2; shorter hrs off season.*

The smaller **Castle Hill AmEx** in Buda offers most of the same services, but no ATM. *Szentháromság tér, inside Hilton Hotel, tel. 1/214–6446. Metro: Moszkava tér. Open mid-Apr.–mid-Oct., daily 9–8; shorter hrs off season.*

DISCOUNT TRAVEL AGENCY

Vista Travel Agency (Andrássy út 1, tel. 1/267–8600 or 1/267–8602; Metro: Bajcsy-Zsilinszky) specializes in cheap international airfares.

EMBASSIES

Australia: *Királyhágó tér 8–9, tel. 1/201–8899. Metro: Déli pu. Open Mon.–Thur. 8–4:30, Fri. 8–1:30.* **Canada:** *Zugligeti út 51–53, tel. 1/275–1200. Metro: Déli pu. Open weekdays 8–noon and 2–4.* **United Kingdom** (citizens of New Zealand may also use this embassy): *Harmincad u. 6, tel. 1/266–2888. Metro: Deák tér. Open weekdays 9–noon and 2–4.* **United States:** *Szabadság tér 12, tel. 1/267–4400. Metro: Kossuth tér. Open Mon.–Tues. and Thurs.–Fri. 2–4.*

EMERGENCIES

Dial 04 for **ambulance,** 07 for **police,** 05 for **fire,** and 118–8212 for 24-hour **emergency assistance** in English. There are **24-hour pharmacies** (*gyógyszertár*) at Teréz körut 41, tel. 1/111–4439 (Nyugati Metro), and Rákóczi út 39, tel. 1/114–3694 (Blaha Lujza tér Metro).

ENGLISH-LANGUAGE BOOKS AND NEWSPAPERS

Bestsellers Bookshop. *Október 6 u. 11, tel. 1/312–1295. Metro: Deák tér. Open Mon.–Sat. 9–6.*

PHONES AND MAIL

The crowded **main post office** (Petőfi Sándor u. 13; open weekdays 8–8, Sat. 8–2) is near the Ferenciek tere Metro station. Adjacent to it is the **telephone center** (Petőfi Sándor u. 17), where you can place

TO OBUDA

Margit-sziget
(Margaret
Island)

TO ÁRPÁD
BUS STATION

Lehel
tér

Frankel Leó út

Rómer Flóris u.

Margit híd
(Margaret Br.)

Újpesti rakpart

Pannónia u.

Katona József

Visegrádi u.

Váci út

Ferdinánd h.

Nyugati
(West)
Station

Szent István körút

Balassi Bálint u.

Pálfy György

Markó u.

Nyugati tér

Podmaniczk

Bem József u.

Kis Rokus u. Margit körút

Bem rakpart

Bem u.

Szemere u.

Bihari u.

Bajcsy-Zsilinszky út

Teréz körú.

Jókai u.

Varsányi Iren u. Kacsa u.

Fő u.

Nagymező u

Hajós u.

Csalogány

Moszkva Hattyú u.
tér

Batthyány u.

Batthyány
tér

Kossuth
Lajos tér

Alkotmány u.

Báthory u.

American
Embassy

Zoltán u.

Szabadság
tér

Andrá

Lázár u.

Donáti u.
Szabó Ilonka u.

Táncsics M. u.
Fortuna u.

Szentháromság
tér Hunyadi János út

BUDA

Arany János u.

Nádor u.

PEST

Paulay Ede u.

Király u.

Tóth Árpád sétány

Úri utca

Lovas út

Roosevelt tér

Várhegy
(Castle
Hill)

Vérmező

Déli
(South)
Station

Logodi u.

Attila út

Disz
tér

Clark
Ádám
tér

Széchenyi
lánchíd
(Chain Br.)

József Attila u.

Erzsébet
tér

Erzsébet
Bus Station

Deák
tér

Deák F. u.

Károly krt.

Alagút u.

Vigadó
tér

Belgrád

Vörösmarty
tér

IBUSZ
(24 hr.)

Petőfi Sándor u.

Váci utca

Astori

Mészáros u.

Krisztina körút

Naphegy u.

Lisznyai u.

Groza P. rakpart

Széchenyi rakpart

Danube

Ferenciek
tere

Kossuth L.

Múzeum krt.

Avar u.

Tigris u.

Hegyalja út

Orom u.

Döbrentei
tér

Erzsébet híd
(Elizabeth
Br.)

Veres Pálné u.

Váci utca

Molnár u.

Csörsz u.

Hegyalja út.

Bérc u.

Szirtes u.

Sz. Gellért rakpart

Fővám tér

Vámház krt.

Lónya

Somlói út

Kelenhegyi u.

Gellért-hegy
(Gellért
Hill)

Szent
Gellért
tér

Ménesi út

Somlói út

Kelenhegyi út

Budafoki út

Müegyetem rakpart

Danube

Budaörsi út

Alsóhegy u.

Villányi út

Karolina u.

Szüret u.

Ménesi út

Móricz
Zsigmond
körtér

Bartók Béla u.

Bertalan L. u.

Kruspér u.

Szabadság híd
(Liberty Br.)

Egry József u.

Bocskai út

Rómer Flóris út

Kó

464

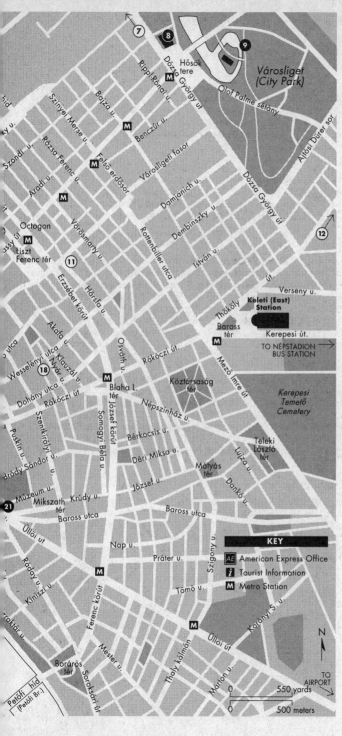

Sights ●

Fine Arts Museum, **8**

Gellért Hill, **20**

Great Synagogue, **17**

Margit-Sziget (Margaret Island), **3**

Matthias Church, **15**

Nemzeti Múzeum, **21**

Parliament, **5**

St. Stephen's Basilica, **16**

Vajdahunyad Castle, **9**

Lodging ○

Backpack Guest House, **22**

Bánki (TYH), **6**

Büro Panzió, **4**

Diáksport (TYH), **7**

Dominik Panzió, **12**

Elm, **11**

Hill (TYH), **24**

Hotel Citadella, **19**

Hotel Kulturinnov, **14**

KEK, **23**

Marco Polo (U), **18**

Medosz Hotel, **10**

Római Camping, **1**

Rózsa, **25**

Sirály, **2**

Zugligeti Niche Camping, **13**

international calls and send faxes. There are smaller post offices throughout the city; look for signs that say POSTA.

COMING AND GOING

BY BUS

Buses depart from downtown Pest's **Erzsébet tér Station** (tel. 1/117–2966; Metro: Deák tér) for major Western cities and many domestic stops. You can also catch the airport shuttle bus (*see* By Plane, *below*) here. North of downtown Pest, **Árpád híd Station** (tel. 1/120–9229; Metro: Ápád híd), is the terminal for buses to the Danube Bend. Eastern Pest's **Népstadion Station** (tel. 1/252– 4496; Metro: Népstadion) serves towns in northern Hungary.

BY CAR

If you can afford it, the best way to see Hungary—especially the countryside and smaller towns—is by car. The big international rental agencies charge US $75–$100 per day; you'll score a small discount for making reservations before arriving in Hungary. Rates at **Americana Rent-a-Car** (Dózsa György út 65, tel. and fax 1/120–8287) start at $65 per day (US $110 per weekend), insurance and unlimited mileage included.

BY PLANE

Hungary's one and only commercial airport, **Ferihegy Airport** (tel. 1/296–9696, or 1/296–7155 for same-day flight information), lies 22 km (13 mi) southeast of the city. Terminal 2 is served by Lufthansa and Malév Hungarian Airlines; Terminal 1 is served by all other airlines. **Minibuses** marked LRI CENTRUM–AIRPORT–CENTRUM (40 min, 500 Ft.) run between the airport and Platform 1 of the Erzsébet tér bus station on the hour and half hour, daily 5:30 AM–9:30 PM. In the airport, buy tickets at the LRI counter in the Arrivals hall. For 1,000 Ft., the **LRI Airport Minibus Service** (tel. 1/296–8555 or 1/296–6283) will pick you up anywhere in Budapest and bring you to the airport; make reservations at least one day in advance, and allow at least one hour travel time.

BY TRAIN

Budapest has three main train stations, each with its own Metro station. **Keleti pályaudvar** (Eastern Station; tel. 1/313–6835), in eastern Pest, runs express trains to Győr (1½ hrs, 800 Ft.), Sopron (2½ hrs, 1,300 Ft.), and many international destinations. **Nyugati pályaudvar** (Western Station; tel. 1/149–0115), north of downtown Pest, runs express trains to Debrecen (2½ hrs, 1,300 Ft.), Kecskemét (1 hr 10 min, 700 Ft.), and select international destinations. In Buda, **Déli pályaudvar** (Southern Station; tel. 1/175–6293) runs express trains to Pécs (2 hrs 40 min, 1,300 Ft.) and other towns in southern Hungary. For more information on trains to international stations, *see* Coming and Going *in* Basics, *above*.

GETTING AROUND

The fastest and easiest way to get around the city is on the **Metro,** which stops near most of the major sights and at all of Budapest's train and bus stations. The three color-coded lines run daily 5 AM–11:30 PM; all meet at Deák tér, in the heart of downtown Pest. Reliable *villamos* (trams) and **buses** serve the parts of the city that the Metro misses, and after midnight, **night buses** (marked by an "É") still provide access to many areas. Pick up Budapest Transport's **city map** (150 Ft.) at any Metro station.

Budapest's mass transit services all use the same purple tickets, available at any Metro station's *pénztár* (ticket booth), a *hírlap* (newsstand), and most hostels. A single ticket (*jegy,* pronounced "yedge") costs 70 Ft. Discount tickets are available for Metro trips shorter than 30 minutes or those involving transfers between two Metro lines; get information at any ticket window. However, if you plan to use mass transit for more than just a few isolated trips, the least-complicated and most economical option is to buy tickets in 10- or 20-ticket booklets—called *gyűjtőjegy*—or to spring for an unlimited one- or three-day pass, around 600 Ft. and 1,100 Ft., respectively. Cancel your ticket yourself in one of the ticket-punching contraptions as you board the bus or the tram, and at the row of orange machines as you enter the Metro. Failure to do so could net you an 800 Ft. fine (undercover inspectors often target tourists).

WHERE TO SLEEP

No one should have trouble finding a bed in Budapest. The problem is deciding what kind, where, and how much you'd care to spend. Hotels tend to be outrageously overpriced or depressingly dirty; hostels are open to all, and many offer clean, cheap doubles with private baths, in addition to their bargain, bazillion-bed dorms. The 24-hour **IBUSZ Welcome Hotel Service** (Apáczai Csere Jáns u. 1, across from Marriott Hotel, tel. 1/118–4848, fax 1/117–9099; Metro: Vörösmarty tér), in downtown Pest, books private rooms as well as less expensive hotels and pensions in the city's outer districts. This service is free.

Private rooms cost 1,500 Ft.–2,800 Ft. per person per night. You can book them through the dozens of travel agencies in Budapest's train stations, but **IBUSZ** and **Budapest Tourist** tend to be the most helpful and reliable. If you're considering an "invitation" from one of the room-hawkers roving the train stations, use caution. First check the location on a map, and don't pay until you see the room. The one drawback to private rooms: Most folks require a minimum stay of two (or more) nights; any fewer and you'll pay a hefty surcharge. Wherever you stay, reservations are a good idea in summer, and absolutely essential if you desire a single room.

HOTELS

Hotels in Pest are much shabbier than the ones in Buda, but they're closer to nightlife and sights.

BUDA • Büro Panzió (Dékán u. 3, tel. 1/212– 2929, fax 1/212–2928; doubles 8,400 Ft.) has 10 conveniently located rooms with TVs and phones. From Moszkva tér, cross Margit körút and walk north on Dékán utca. At **Hotel Citadella** (Citadella sétány, tel. 1/166–5794, fax 1/186–0505; dorm beds 1,150 Ft., doubles 6,000 Ft.—6,600 Ft.; cash only) you can sleep on top of Gellért Hill in a hunting lodge. From Nyugati Station, take Tram 6 to Móricz Zsigmond körtér, then take Bus 27 from Villányi út to the last stop. The spotless **Hotel Kulturinnov** (Szentháromság tér 6, tel. 1/155–0122, fax 1/175–1886; doubles 10,000 Ft., breakfast included) inhabits one wing of a 1902 neobaroque building in the center of the Castle Hill district, across the street from the Mátyás Templom. The location makes it worth the price.

PEST • The less expensive hotels are along seedy **Rákóczi út,** near Keleti Station, and on truck- and bus-clogged **Ferenc körút,** between Petőfi bridge and Üllői út. Otherwise, your best bet is **Dominik Panzió** (Császár András u. 3, tel. and fax 1/343– 7655) with clean, bright doubles (4,000 Ft., breakfast included; cash only) on a residential street near Keleti Station. Take Bus 7 two stops east. The **Medosz** (Jókai tér 9, tel. 1/153–1700; doubles 6,300 Ft.; cash only) offers a fantastic location on lovely Andrássy út, near the Opera House. The rooms are clean but depressingly worn, small, and institutional. From Oktogon Metro, walk southwest (towards the Danube) on Andrássy út.

HOSTELS

Hostels have no age limits or membership requirements, and they offer a 10% discount to HI cardholders on the prices listed below. Reception desks are open 24 hours, and there are no curfews, but you usually have to check out by 9 AM. Most of Budapest's hostels are in university dorms, and open only when school is not in session (typically July and August). Prices listed below are all per person rather than per room.

Almost all of Budapest's hostels are associated with one of two companies: **Universum Ltd. (U)** (Báthory László u. 18, H-1029 Budapest, tel. and fax 1/275–7046) and **Travellers' Youth Hostels (TYH)** (Reservation Center, Dózsa György út 152, Budapest H-1134, tel. 1/140–8585 or 1/129–8644, fax 1/120–8425). Both companies promise an array of amenities (free bedding, hot showers, and laundry, to name a few) and offer free shuttles to and from Budapest's train stations. For shuttle service, look for a representative in the appropriate T-shirt at the station when you arrive. Book ahead (essential in summer months) through travel agencies like IBUSZ or Budapest Tourist, or contact the company directly.

YEAR-ROUND • Backpack Guest House. Tons of activities (bike rentals, rock climbing, windsurfing, fishing) and friendly staff give this independent Buda hangout a summer-camp feel. Cramped but clean dorm rooms (all with lockers) cost 1,100 Ft. per bed; homey doubles cost 1,400 Ft. per person. Reservations are advised. *Takács Menyhért u. 33, tel. 1/185–5089. From Keleti Station, Bus 7 or 7A west to Tétenyi u. (after rail bridge); walk back under bridge, turn left, and follow tracks for 3 blocks (watch for green signs). Kitchen. Cash only.*

Diáksport (TYH). This loose and lively place in northern Pest has a 24-hour bar that fuels its reputation as Budapest's "party hostel." A "never-full" policy means there's always space for one more. Doubles cost 1,900 Ft.–2,500 Ft. per person, dorm beds 1,300 Ft. There is a bureaux de change on the premises. *Dózsa György út 152, tel. 1/140–8585. Metro: Dósza György. Kitchen, laundry.*

Marco Polo (U). The first hostel in Eastern Europe built specifically as a hostel is a sparkling six-story building with a great downtown Pest location. Dorms (2,700 Ft. per bed) were designed and furnished to provide privacy; the hostel also has doubles (4,500 Ft.) and quads (3,600 Ft.). Rates include breakfast. Extras include email access, bike rentals, pub, TV and game room, and a pool. *Nyár u. 6, tel. 1/342–9586. Between Blaha Lujza tér and Astoria metro stops. Kitchen, laundry.*

SUMMER ONLY • Bánki (TYH). Walk across the street from Pest's Nyugati Station and you're home. Doubles cost 1,880 Ft. per person, dorms 1,500 Ft.–1,900 Ft. *Podmaniczky u. 8, tel. 1/112–5268. From Nyugati pu. Metro, walk 1 block SE on Teréz krt. and turn right. Closed Sept.–mid-July.*

Elm (TYH). A step up from most hostels: Clean doubles (3,300 Ft.) share toilet, shower, and kitchen with one other room. Near Pest's grand shopping boulevard. *êžêHársfa u. 59B, tel. 1/322–3292. Tram 4 or 6 to Király u.; walk 1 block NE on Király u. and turn right. Closed Sept.–June.*

Hill (TYH). This hotelesque hostel near Buda's Gallért Hill has immaculate, air-conditioned doubles for 3,300 Ft. For 3,800 Ft. you get breakfast, plus access to the hostel's sauna, swimming pool, tennis courts, and gym. *Ménesi út 5, tel. 1/185– 2122. Tram 6 or Bus 7 to Móricz Zsigmond krt.; walk 1 block north on Himfy u. then 10 min west on Ménesi út. Closed mid-Sept.–June.*

KEK (TYH). This relaxing, quiet hostel is in a tree-lined neighborhood beside Gellért Hil. Doubles are 2,300 Ft. with shower. *Szüret u. 2–18, tel. 1/371–0066. Tram 6 or Bus 7 to Móricz Zsigmond krt., then Bus 27 for 2 stops. Closed Sept.–June.*

Rózsa (U). Score one for privacy: This small, recently renovated hostel offers only doubles (2,200 Ft.– 2,700 Ft. per person). It's in Buda, near a pizzeria and large supermarket. *Bercsényi u. 28–30, tel. 1/166–6677. From Kálvin tér Metro, Tram 47 or 49 to Móricz Zsigmond krt.; walk 2 blocks east on Karinthy Frigyes út to Bercsényi u. Closed Sept.–June.*

Sirály. This friendly, independent hostel on wooded Margaret Island has a sprawling terrace and great views. Clean 12-person dorms cost 950 Ft. per bed. *Behind Casino Margitsziget, tel. 1/302–3952. From Nyugati pu. Metro, Bus 26 west across Margit Bridge to island. Closed Nov.–mid-Apr. Cash only.*

CAMPING

Római Camping. Budapest's largest campground is north of the city in the Obuda suburb. Tent sites are 700 Ft. plus 600 Ft. per person; three- and four-person bungalows start at 2,00 Ft. The campground has all of the luxuries of town, including its own restaurant, general store, bureaux de change, pool, and post office. *Szentendrei út 189, tel. 1/168–6260. From Batthyány tér Station, HÉV train north (20 min) to Rómaifürdő Station. Showers. Cash only. Closed mid-Oct.–Mar.*

Zugligeti Niche Camping. For camping close to the city center, try Zugligeti Niche in the gorgeous Buda Hills. The English-speaking staff provides maps and arranges tours. Tent sites cost 250 Ft. plus 550 Ft. per person, and have access to super-clean bathrooms, restaurant, and 24-hour snack bar. *Zugligeti út 101, tel. 1/156–8641. From Moszkva tér Metro, Bus 158 to last stop. Showers. Closed mid-Sept.–mid-Mar. Cash only.*

FOOD

Unlike the rest of Hungary, Budapest offers plenty of dining options—so when you tire of gorging on goulash, indulge your every Tex-Mex, Japanese, or vegan craving. **Acapulco** (Erzsébet krt. 39, tel. 1/322–6014; Tram 4 or 6 to Király u.) serves Mexican food (under 1,500 Ft.) that makes homesick Americans cry. **New York Bagels** (Bajcsy-Zsilinszky út 21, tel. 1/111–8441; Metro: Arany János) does credible bagels (60 Ft. each); in Buda, look for their shop below Castle Hill (Hattyú u. 2). **Ramen House Miyako** (Visegrádi u. 1, tel. 1/111–3023; Metro: Nyugati pu.) serves authentic Japanese soba noodles.

For a true Hungarian experience, sample the goodies at the city's ubiquitous *lángos* (deep-fried potato-puff pancakes), *goffri* (waffles), and *pékaru* (pastries and small sandwiches) stands. Vendors sell produce from small street stands and huge open-air markets; the **Vásárcsarnok** (Central Market; Vámház körút 1–3; closed Sun.) is on the Danube in the 19th-century Customs House. It's a banquet of food (and crafts) to see, smell, and taste. If none of the restaurants listed here appeal to your picky palate, take a peek at the *Budapest Sun* or *Budapest Week* (both cost around 100 Ft.). Most restaurants listed below provide English-language menus on request.

BUDA

Buda's affordable restaurants cluster below Castle Hill and in areas surrounding the Moszkva tér and Batthány tér Metro stations. Buda's prices are generally higher than Pest's.

UNDER 500 FT • Marxim. At this communist theme spot, decent pizzas are named after the old hard-liners whose photos line the walls. The alternative rock music and young crowds can get pretty loud. *Kisrókus u. 23, tel. 1/212–4183. Metro: Moszkva tér. No lunch Sun.*

Söröző a Szent Jupáthoz. The city's only 24-hour diner dishes up mountains of hearty Hungarian fare. *Retek u. 16, tel. 1/212–2928. From Moszkva tér Metro, walk north on Vérmező út to Széna tér, turn left onto Retek u. Cash only.*

UNDER 1,000 FT • Tabáni Kakas. Located just below Castle Hill, this cozy restaurant specializes in traditional poultry dishes, particularly goose. Some dishes are priced under 750 Ft. A pianist entertains every evening except Sunday and Monday. *Attila út 27, tel. 1/175–7165. Bus 5 or 78 to Szarvas tér. No breakfast.*

Kikelet. This cozy restaurant on Rozsa-domb (Rose Hill) serves top-notch Hungarian dishes (650 Ft. and up), though with emphasis on lower cholesterol and fat. It offers outdoor dining in summer, with views of the Buda hills. *Fillér u. 85, tel. 1/212– 5444. Bus 49 from Moszkava tér. Cash only.*

PEST

In recent years, Pest has become overrun with American fast-food joints. They lurk on every corner near Kálvin tér, Deák tér, and on the pedestrian-only streets of downtown.

UNDER 500 FT • Bohémtanya. You'll need to be patient to secure a table at this lively, crowded hangout. The reward: heaping plates of stuffed cabbage, fried pork chops filled with goose liver, and other Hungarian specialties. The quadrilingual menu is arranged by price. *Paulay Ede u. 6, tel. 1/268– 1453. Metro: Deák tér. Cash only.*

Kádár Étkezde. This fun, frenetic place with shared tables and topnotch fare is in the city's historic Jewish district. Chicken soup with matzo balls and other favorites fill the menu. Sadly, it's open for lunch only. *Klauzál tér 9, tel. 1/321–3622. Tram 4 or 6 to Wesselényi u.; walk 3 blocks SW on Wesselényi u., right on Klauzál u., and continue 1 block. Cash only.*

Korona Passage. For a quick, cheap meal, order a palacsinta (dessert crêpe) at this sparkling cafeteria-style joint. Prices for hefty savory and sweet crêpes depend on the filling, from berry jam to ham and cheese. *Hotel Mercure Korona, Kecskeméti út 14, tel. 1/117–4111. From Kálvin tér Metro, walk NE on Kecskeméti út. Cash only.*

Semiramis. Excellent Middle Eastern fare such as gyros, hummus, and falafel is served in an airy loft. *Alkotmány u. 20, tel. 1/111–7627. From Nyugati pu. Metro, walk 3 blocks south on Bajcsy-Zsilinszky út and turn right. Cash only. No breakfast. Closed Sun.*

Tüköry Söröző. Courageous carnivores can sample the beefsteak tartar (topped with a raw egg) at this bustling traditional eatery. Prix-fixe lunch specials cost under 300 Ft., but are gobbled up quickly. *Hold u. 15, tel. 1/269–5027. Metro: Arany János. Cash only. Closed weekends.*

UNDER 1,000 FT • Café Kör. For excellent service and elegant surroundings, visit this lovely Pest restaurant. Hungarian and Continental fare is prepared with less grease than elsewhere. *Sas u. 17, tel. 1/111–0053. From Arany János Metro, walk west on Arany János u., then left at Sas u. Closed Sun.*

Vegetárium Étterem. This "vegetarian" restaurant bends the rules a bit by serving fish and poultry as well as macrobiotic vegetarian dishes. It's a lively place with sake, beer, and organic wine on the menu, plus live guitar most evenings. *Cukor u. 3, tel. 1/267–0322. From Ferenciek tere Metro, walk south across square to Cukor u. No breakfast.*

CAFES

In Budapest there's a *cukrászda* (sweet shop) or *kávéház* (café) every few blocks, tempting passersby with excellent, inexpensive treats. **Művész Cukrászda** (Andrássy út 29, tel. 1/267–0689; Metro: Opera) is a mellow, old-time spot, great for people-watching. **New York Kávéház** (Erzsébet krt. 9–11, tel. 1/322–1648; Metro: Blaha Lujza tér), open since 1894, is totally over-the-top, grand, and gilded. Both **Bécsi** (Hotel Intercontinental, Apáczai Csere János u. 12–14, tel. 1/328–3333; Metro: Vörösmarty tér) and **Gerbeaud** (Vörösmarty tér 7, tel. 1/118–1311; Metro: Vörösmarty tér) are expensive, but the former serves possibly the best pastries in town, and the latter has been a Budapest institution since 1835. **Talk Talk** (Magyar u. 12–14, tel. 1/266–7521; Metro: Astória) is a 24-hour café serving sandwiches and good coffee. For a coffee break while sightseeing on Castle Hill, head to hip little **Miró** (Úri u. 30, tel. 1/175–5458).

WORTH SEEING

Budapest presents a mind-boggling array of sightseeing opportunities; what you'll find below is a great-est-hits package. Gallery and museum special exhibitions are listed in the English-language weeklies *Budapest Week* and *Budapest Sun* (both cost around 100 Ft.), available at newsstands.

CASTLE HILL

Várhegy (Castle Hill) is the historic center of Buda, and boasts many of the city's tourist attractions. There are three easy ways to get here: by Vár minibus from Moszkva tér; on Bus 16 from Deák tér to Disz tér; or by *sikló* (funicular car; 150 Ft. one way; operates Tues.–Sun. 7:30 AM–10 PM) from the base of Széchenyi lánchíd (the bridge with the lions). Alternately, you can walk up any of the stone stairways along Hunyadi János út. After hitting the major sights, cool off with a 30-minute, guided **labyrinth walk** (Úri u. 9, tel. 1/175–6858; admission 700 Ft.; open daily 9:30–8) through the maze of ancient pas-sageways underneath Castle Hill. The damp, hand-hewn tunnels were used by the Turkish military dur-ing the 16th century, and later as a German military headquarters and wartime hospital.

BUDAPEST HISTORY MUSEUM • For anyone interested in the city's past, the Budapesti Történeti Múzeum (Budapest History Museum) is a must. It's housed in the southern wing (Building E) of the grandiose **Királyi Palota** (Royal Palace). On display are palace artifacts from the Romanesque, Gothic, and Renaissance periods, as well as videos and photos examining the transformation of Budapest's landmarks over the centuries. *Buda Castle (Wing E), Szent György tér 2, tel. 1/175–7533. Admission: 200 Ft. Open Apr.–Oct., Wed.–Mon. 10–6; shorter hrs off season.*

HUNGARIAN NATIONAL GALLERY • Also in the Királyi Palota (wings B, C, and D in the main building) is the prestigious Magyar Nemzeti Galéria (Hungarian National Gallery), displaying the work of the country's finest painters from the 15th to 19th centuries. The Hungarian impressionists, especially Pál Szinyei Merse and Kosztka Tivadar Csontváry, are worth a special trip. Ask at the front desk for English-language guidebooks (400 Ft.) and guided tours (1,000 Ft. per person, maximum 5 people). There's a 200 Ft. surcharge to bring a camera into the museum, 400 Ft. for a video camera. *Disz tér 17, tel. 1/175– 7533. Admission: 150 Ft., free Wed. Open mid-Mar.–mid-Dec., Tues.–Sun. 10–6; shorter hrs off season.*

MATTHIAS CHURCH • The 13th-century Mátyás Templom (Matthias Church) has an interior like a riotously painted Easter egg—every square inch is decorated. It was originally named the Church of the Blessed Virgin in Buda, but the 15th-century king Matthias Corvinus, who was married here twice, had other ideas. If you're here in the evening, stick around for the frequent organ recitals (some are free). *Szentháromság tér 2, next to Hilton Hotel, tel. 1/155–5657. Open daily 7 AM–8 PM.*

Behind Matthias Church is a restored turn-of-the-century turreted wall and lookout tower called **Halászbástya** (Fisherman's Bastion), built so that residents of Castle Hill could keep an eye on what was once a thriving fishing settlement. A 328-ft **promenade** stretches along the wall, with stunning views of the Országház (Parliament). On the other side of Szentháromság tér sits Budapest's oldest dessert shop, **Ruszwurm Cukrászda** (Szentháromság u. 7, tel. 1/175–5284). The building has housed a bakery for 500 years—as good an excuse as any to try their delectable pastries.

CITY PARK

Városliget (City Park), 1 square km of greenery in northeast Pest, is home to a zoo, a circus, a famous bathhouse (*see box, below*), and an amusement park (Vidámpark; Állatkerti krt. 14–15; open Apr.–Sept. daily, 10–7:30; shorter hrs off season) with a creaky ferris wheel and rickety wooden roller coaster. The row of statues of Hungarian heroes in **Hősök tere** (Heroes' Square), the gateway to the park, was erected in 1896 as part of the millennial celebration of Magyar settlement. For a crash course in Hun-garian architecture, investigate **Vajdahunyad Castle** near the lake, also built for the 1896 celebration. Few people know that all of Hungarian history was shifted forward a year to accommodate the building's tardy construction schedule; the Magyars really came to the area in AD 895. Nearby, the **Petőfi Csarnok Recreation Center** hosts frequent concerts and dance productions, and a great flea market most week-ends. To reach the park, take the Metro to Hősök tere.

FINE ARTS MUSEUM • Flanking one side of Hősök tere at the entrance to Városliget, Budapest's acclaimed Szépművészeti Múzeum (Fine Arts Museum) has the largest collection of works by Spanish masters outside Spain. The Modern Gallery features all the French giants: Monet, Cézanne, Gauguin, you name it. In 1983, two skilled thieves made off with seven Old Masters (later recovered and returned), in the greatest art robbery of the century. *Dózsa György út 41, tel. 1/343–9759. Admission: 250 Ft. Open Apr.–Nov., Tues.–Sun. 10–5:30, shorter hrs off season. Metro: Hősök tere.*

GELLERT HILL

From Szabadság híd (Freedom bridge), follow the tree-lined walkways up, up, up steep Gellért Hill to the **Citadella** (admission 80 Ft.), a fortress built so the Imperial armies could better spy on the city after the failed Hungarian Revolution of 1849. Its old stone walls now enclose a beer garden, souvenir shop, and the Hotel Citadella (*see* Where to Sleep, *above*). Also atop Gellért is the huge **Szabadság Szobor** (Liberation Monument), highly visible from any point in Budapest. This Hungarian "Statue of Liberty" was erected in 1947 to commemorate the Soviet victory over Nazi Germany. To avoid the steep 30-minute hike uphill, catch Bus 27 from Móricz Zsigmond körtér. Reward yourself at the end of your odyssey with a splash in the refreshing **mineral water pools** of the ritzy Gellért Hotel (*see box, below*).

GREAT SYNAGOGUE

After years of extensive reconstruction and restoration, the Byzantine Moorish–style Nagy Zsinagóga (Great Synagogue), built in 1859, is open again. The largest synagogue in Europe, it can accomodate nearly 3,000 worshipers, and its 140-ft onion dome is visible blocks away. In the garden behind the synagogue, a **Holocaust Memorial** stands over a mass grave. Next door, the **Zsidó Múzeum** (Jewish Museum; tel. 1/342– 8949; admission 300 Ft.) has a collection of medieval Torahs and prayer books and a powerful display on concentration camps and the deportation of Hungarian Jews. *Dohány u. 2–8, tel. 1/342–1335. Donation suggested. Synagogue and museum open weekdays 10–2:30, Sun. 10–1. Metro: Deák tér.*

Budapest's lush, tree-covered Gellért Hill was named after the unlucky 11th-century Saint Gerard, who was stuffed into a barrel and pushed from its peak after trying to convert local pagans to Christianity.

JANOS-HEGY CHAIRLIFT
AND BUDA HILLS

For an afternoon of fresh air and stunning views, head to the Buda Hills, just west of Castle Hill. Take Bus 158 from Moszkva tér to Zugliget, then ride the János-hegy chairlift (tel. 1/176–3764 or 1/395–6494; admission 150 Ft.; open mid-May–mid-Sept., daily 9–5; shorter hrs off season) to the top of the hills. Well-marked **hiking trails** cut through forests thick with beech and oak.

MARGARET ISLAND

Set serenely in the middle of the Danube, Margit-Sziget (Margaret Island) is a popular recreation spot, and on weekends it fills with strolling families. For 1,000 Ft. you can rent *sétacikli* ("walkcycles"; altered bikes that seat up to four people) to cruise along the island's many paths. Along with plenty of snack stands and beer gardens, the island has two pools: **Hajós Alfréd Nemzeti Sportuszoda** (tel. 1/111–4046; admission 200 Ft.; open Apr.–Sept., daily 6–5) for swimming laps and, on the island's northwest end, the **Palatinus Strand** (tel. 1/112–3069; admission 200 Ft.; open May–Sept., daily 8–5) for splashing around on a waterslide. **Margit híd** (4 blocks west of the Nyugati Metro station), the main bridge linking the island to Buda and Pest, brings back painful memories for Budapest's older residents: During rush hour in November 1944, the Germans blew it up, killing hundreds.

NATIONAL MUSEUM

The Nemzeti Múzeum (National Museum) walks you through Hungary's history and culture, with exhibits updated in 1996 to include the end of Communism and the exodus of Russian troops. The biggest attractions are the royal crown and the crown jewels, both of which were smuggled into the United States after World War II and returned by President Carter in 1978. The crown was reputedly given to St. Stephen by the pope in about AD 1000 (making it one of the oldest royal crowns around) and has been stolen a number of times since; the cross was bent during one such escapade. *Múzeum krt. 14–16, tel. 1/138–2122. Admission: 250 Ft. Open mid-Mar.–mid-Oct., Tues.–Sun. 10–6; shorter hrs off season. Metro: Kálvin tér.*

PARLIAMENT

The huge, neo-Gothic Országház (Parliament) building is the most impressive structure on Budapest's left bank. It was designed by Hungarian architect Imre Steindl and took 1,000 workers 17 years (1885–

BUDAPEST: CITY OF BATHS

Budapest, fondly known as the "City of Baths," harbors within its city limits over 120 natural hot springs. These springs' medicinal properties are thought to relieve arthritis, chronic back pain, and (if you believe the brochures) certain "feminine troubles." Of course, thermal baths are also excellent places to simply relax and splash around. One of the most popular and beautiful is the art-nouveau bathhouse adjoining the grand Gellért Hotel (Kelenhegyi út 4–6, tel. 1/166–6166; open May–Sept., daily 6 AM–7 PM and 8–midnight; Oct.–Apr., daily 6–6). On the premises are separate-sex thermal baths, coed indoor and outdoor swimming pools, and a state-of-the-art outdoor wave pool (also coed), priced 400 Ft. for one hour or 1,200 for a full day. Pay a bit more and you'll be pampered from head to toe, with a facial, massage, and even a pedicure. Take Tram 47 or 49 to Szent Gellért tér. The Turkish-style sunken pools of Király Fürdő (Fő u. 84, tel. 1/202–3688; open weekdays 6:30–6, Sat. 6:30–noon; admission 300 Ft.), also called the "Bath of Kings," allows men on Monday, Wednesday, and Friday, and women on Tuesday, Thursday, and Saturday. Take the Metro to Batthyány tér and walk north on Fő utca. In City Park (see Worth Seeing, above) is one of the largest bathhouses in Europe, the coed Széchenyi Baths (Állatkerti krt. 11–14, tel. 1/121–0310; admission 300 Ft.; open daily 6–6). It's a popular spot for fierce water-chess competitions, played on splash-proof chessboards.

1902) to build. The outside is lined with 90 statues of heroes from Hungarian history. Inside are 691 rooms, 10 courtyards, and 29 staircases; some 88 pounds of gold were used to gild the staircases and halls. English-language **tours** (700 Ft.) are given daily at 10 AM whenever Parliament is not in session; dial 1/268–4457, 1/268–4437, or 1/268–4811 for more information. To reach the building, take waterfront Tram 2, or the Metro to Kossuth tér Station.

Opposite the Országház, the **Néprajzi Múzeum** (Ethnographic Museum; Kossuth Lajos tér 12, tel. 1/332–6340; admission 200 Ft.; open mid-Mar.–Nov., Tues.–Sun. 10–6; shorter hrs off season) displays colorful folk costumes and folk art. The grand, neo-Renaissance palace that houses it is worth a visit in itself.

ST. STEPHEN'S BASILICA
Szent István Bazilika (1905), Budapest's largest church, holds as many as 8,500 people. No doubt the massive structure would have pleased St. Stephen, Hungary's first king, who made Christianity the national religion. A statue of the man himself is behind the main altar, and his mummified right hand is displayed in a small room off the nave. On clear days, the dizzying climb up to the **cupola tower** (admission 150 Ft.; open May–Aug., daily 9–6; shorter hrs off season) affords excellent views of the city. *Szent István tér, tel. 1/117–2859. Donation suggested. Open Mon.–Sat. 7–7, Sun. 1–7. Metro: Arany János u.*

STATUE PARK
The Szoborpark (Statue Park) is filled with the icons of Communism that, since 1989, have been removed from perches and plazas across the city. *Balatoni út, tel. 1/227–7446. From Kosztolányi Dezső*

tér, take Volánbusz from Stand 6 (20 min, 60 Ft.) and ask driver for Szoborpark. Admission: 150 Ft. Open mid-Apr.–Oct., daily 10–dusk; weekends only off season.

AFTER DARK

Every night in Budapest you'll find everything from slick, see-and-be-seen dance clubs to dark, smoky bars featuring sizzling local bands. If you're looking for something more highbrow, you can choose from opera, ballet, classical and choral music, folk dance, and live jazz. Best of all, cover charges and tickets, even at exclusive discos, cost far less than what you'd pay in Paris, Berlin, or New York, and almost universally beers cost 200 Ft. and cocktails 400 Ft. For up-to-the-minute listings, check *Budapest Week* or the *Budapest Sun*.

Most public transportation shuts down between 11:30 PM and 5 AM, but Night Bus 6E runs around the Nagykörút (ring road), starting at Moszkva tér and ending at Móricz Zsigmond körtér. It can get you to and from almost all of the happening areas, including Jászai Mari tér, Nyugati tér, and Ferenc körút. Packed on weekends with young revelers, the night bus can sometimes be a form of entertainment in and of itself.

BARS AND CLUBS

There are numerous bars along Pest's Erzsébet, Teréz, and Szent István körút, especially near the Nyugati and Oktogon Metro stations. Bars typically stay open until 2 AM, while nightclubs often keep going until 3 or 4 AM.

Angel Bar and Disco. This hot gay nightspot draws drag queens, gym bunnies, and a growing number of appreciative straights. *Szövetség ut 33, no phone. Tram 74 to Almássy tér. Closed Mon.–Wed.*

Becketts. The most popular of Budapest's Irish pubs is a favorite expat watering hole that proudly pours Guinness. *Bajcsy-Zsilinszky út 72, tel. 1/111–1035. Metro: Nyúgati tér.*

Big Mambo. The bohemian crowd comes to this dark cellar bar to smoke, think, argue, smoke some more, and drink good, cheap beer. *Mária ut 48, tel. 1/134–4277. Metro: Ferenc krt.*

Fél 10 Jazz Club. Fél 10 is a stylish but unpretentious jazz spot with a dance floor and two bars on three levels. The decor is a mix of wrought iron and maroon velvet. *Baross u. 30, tel. 1/133–772. Metro: Kálvin tér.*

Franklin Trocadero Café. Salsa and Latin jazz have come to Budapest. This airy, split-level club offers dancing, billiards, and frequent concerts. *Szent István krt. 15, near Margit bridge, tel. 1/111–4691. Tram 4 or 6 to Jászai Mari tér. Cover: 200 Ft. and up.*

Picasso Point. A dark, DJ'd dance floor awaits downstairs at this popular, long-running Budapest nightspot. It has a hip, coffeehouse feel and Picasso-theme decor. *Hajós u. 31, tel. 1/269–5544. From Arany János Metro, walk north on Bajcsy-Zsilinszky út, then right on Desseuffy u. to Hájós u.*

PERFORMING ARTS

Budapest's exquisite 1884 Magyar Állami Operaház (Andrássy út 22, tel. 1/153–0170; Metro: Opera) is home to high-quality, affordable opera and ballet performances. It's worth the 200 Ft.–2,000 Ft. ticket price just to marvel at its polished marble stairs, crystal chandeliers, and the magnificent fresco ceiling of its 1,300-seat main hall. Guided tours (600 Ft.) in English are available daily at 3 and 4. The box office is open Tuesday–Saturday 11–1:45 and 2:30–6:30, Sunday (only if there is a performance) 10–3 and 4–7.

Liszt Ferenc Zeneakadémia (Liszt Ferenc tér 8, tel. 1/342–0179), usually referred to as the Zeneakadémia (Music Academy), is Budapest's premier classical concert venue, hosting orchestra and chamber music concerts in its ornate main hall. The sparkling 1896 **Vígszínház** (Szt. István krt. 14, tel. 1/269–5340) is another grand old arts palace; today, it hosts primarily musicals.

TANCHAZ • For a unique experience, visit a **táncház** (dance house), where Hungary's master folk musicians play traditional tunes and spectators are encouraged to get up and dance. These are not tourist attractions, but venues where locals celebrate their Magyar heritage. **Marczibányi téri Művelődési Központ** (Marczibányi tér 5/a, tel. 1/212–5789), **Almássy tér Szabadidő Központ** (Almássy tér 6, 2 blocks from Blaha Lujza Metro, tel. 1/342–0387), and the **Belvárosi Ifjúsági és Művelődésiház** (Molnár u. 9, tel. 1/117–5928) are three good options; check the English-language papers for current schedules.

DANUBE BEND

For a hassle-free break from Budapest's urban pace and pollution, escape north along the Danube River. You'll find tiny, quaint villages where the preferred vehicle is a bicycle and the preferred speed is slow. Don't worry about getting bored—Danube Bend towns have plenty of worthy museums, castles, and churches, too. Many Danube Bend museums, restaurants, and hotels close up tight during the frigid months of January and February.

COMING AND GOING

Frequent **trains** go from Budapest's Nyugati Station to Esztergom (1 hr 45 min, 300 Ft.), and the **HÉV suburban railway** runs daily every 10 to 20 minutes between Budapest's Batthyány tér and Szentendre (40 min, 140 Ft.). **Buses** (100 Ft. and up) depart hourly from Budapest's Árpád híd Station for villages along the Danube, and are the quickest way to travel from town to town. If you have the time, though, the most enjoyable way to cruise up the Danube is by ferry. Three times daily May–September (once daily during off season), **MAHART ferries** (tel. 1/118–1704 or 1/118–1586) depart from Budapest's Batthyány tér and Vigadó tér for Szentendre (1½ hrs, 420 Ft.), Visegrád (3½ hrs, 460 Ft.), and Esztergom (5 hrs, 500 Ft.).

SZENTENDRE

The baroque town of Szentendre (SEHNT-ahn-drey) is a thrill, as long as you don't mind that it's recently been recast as a destination for tourists. Its charming cobblestone streets and Serbian-built brick houses drew artists by the dozens in the 1920s, who settled and made the town a flourishing artists' colony. There are still many art galleries, but they are unfortunately now outnumbered by a tsunami of tourist traps hawking T-shirts and giant wooden pencils, and swarms of visitors triple Szentendre's population in peak season. You can pick up a list of art galleries at the Tourinform office (see Where to Sleep and Eat, below). The **Kovács Margit Múzeum** (Vastagh György u. 1, between Görög u. and Futó u., below Fő tér, tel. 26/310–244; admission 200 Ft.; open May–Sept., Tues.–Sun. 10–6; shorter hrs off season) explores the life and work of the celebrated ceramist Margit Kovács (1902–1977). The **Szabadtéri Néprajzi Múzeum** (Skanzen) (Szabadforrás út, tel. 26/312–304; admission 150 Ft.; open Apr.–Oct., Tues.–Sun. 9–5) is an open-air museum that re-creates 18th- and 19th-century village life. Skanzen is 5 km (3 mi) northwest of town; take a local bus from the Szentendre bus terminal (adjacent to the HÉV station).

The center of town is **Fő tér,** lined with immaculate 18th- and 19th- century burghers' houses. Adjacent to Fő tér, **Templom-domb** (Church Hill) is home to several of the village's churches. The 18th-century **Beograda** (Orthodox Episcopal Cathedral), on Alkotmány utca, has a lavish interior and a small garden filled with gravestones as old as the hills. Crowning the hill just north of Templom-domb are the handsome crimson **Serbian Orthodox Cathedral** (1740s) and the **Serbian Orthodox Collection of Religious Art** (Pátriárka u. 5, tel. 26/312–399; admission 50 Ft.; open May–Sept., Wed.–Sun. 10–6; shorter hrs off season). The museum displays exquisite artifacts relating to the history of the Serbian Orthodox Church in Hungary from the 15th to 19th centuries. On the northeast corner of Fő tér stands the tiny **Blagovestenszka Templom** (Serbian Orthodox Annunciation Church; admission 40 Ft.; open Apr.–Oct., Tues.–Sun. 10–5; closed Jan.–Feb.). One of the town's most cherished pieces of rococo art is this church's 18th-century *iconostasis* (the screen running before the sanctuary), painted by a Serbian artist from Buda.

WHERE TO SLEEP AND EAT

The friendly **Tourinform** (Dumtsa Jenő u. 22, at Jókai u., tel. 26/317–965; open weekdays 10–4, weekends 10–2) arranges private rooms (1,750 Ft.–2,500 Ft.) and sells maps. The centrally located **Ilona Panzió** (Rákóczi Ferenc u. 11, tel. 26/313–599; cash only) has four doubles for 3,500 Ft., breakfast included. From the HÉV station, walk north on Kossuth Lajos utca to Fő tér and turn left. At the delightful **Villa Apolló** (Méhész u. 3, tel. 26/310–909; doubles 2,400 Ft., breakfast included; cash only) you can take breakfast in the charming garden. From the HÉV station, take a northbound bus to the third stop, turn right, and walk a half-block. **Pap-sziget Campground** (tel. 26/310–697; closed Oct.–Apr.; cash only) has a pool and restaurant; to reach it, take any northbound bus. Tent sites for two cost 1,500

Ft., beds in three-bed bunkrooms are 900 Ft., and double-occupancy bungalows with kitchen, private bathroom, and shower cost 5,000 Ft. All rates include admission to the nearby pool complex.

Sellers of gourmet goulash abound in this tourist town. Sadly, culinary bargains don't. **Vidám Szerzetesek** (Bogdányi u. 3–5, just north of Fő tér, tel. 26/310–544; closed Mon.; cash only), or "Gay Monks" restaurant, has shaded outdoor tables and hefty house specials like "Monk's Pleasure" (pork and potato casserole) and "Farmer's Bundle" (pork chop stuffed with spinach and mushrooms; 780 Ft.). Less expensive, though not exactly nutritious, are the deep-fried *lángos* (salty bread sticks) drizzled with sour cream or brushed with garlic from **Piknik Büfé** (Dumtsa Jenő u. 22, next door to the Tourinform, no phone; cash only).

VISEGRAD

Placid, enchanting Visegrád (VISH-ah-grod), Hungary's capital during the 14th–16th centuries, sits on a gorgeous, mountainous stretch of the Danube Bend, 23 km (14 mi) north of Szentendre. In Slavic, the name means "High Castle," and though the town's 4th-century Roman fortress is long gone, there's still plenty to see. At the center of town are the ruins of the 350-room **Királyi Palota** (Royal Palace; Fő u. 29, tel. 26/398–026; admission 100 Ft.; open Tues.–Sun. 9–4:30), said to have been Europe's finest royal residence after top-to-bottom renovations by King Matthias Corvinus and Queen Beatrice in the 15th century. It was destroyed by the Turks in 1543, then dynamited in 1702, but parts of the grounds and courtyard have since been restored. Looming in the hills above is the massive, 13th-century **Salamontorony** (Solomon's Tower); inside is the **Mátyás Múzeum** (admission 100 Ft.; open May–Sept., Tues.–Sun. 9–4:30), which displays precious artifacts unearthed at the royal palace. To get here walk up Salamon-torony utca from the MAHART ferry pier. Past Solomon's Tower, continue upward (a 30-minute hike) on the trail marked FELLEGVÁR to the **Citadel** (admission 200 Ft.; open mid-Mar.–late-Sept., daily 8–6, shorter hrs off season), then follow signs to the Nagy-Villám lookout tower (admission 100 Ft.; open Tues.–Sun. 9–6) for spectacular views of the entire Danube Bend. If this sounds like too much hiking, you can opt for the city **shuttle bus** (about 1,000 Ft. for transportation to all Visegrád sights), which operates May–Sept.; inquire at the tourist office.

Once you've seen the sights, head to the **Pilis nature reserve**—just follow the well-marked trail (3½ km/2¼ mi one way) from Salamon-torony utca. **Visegrád Tours** (Rév u. 15, at Rte. 11, tel. 26/398–160; open Apr.–Oct., daily 9–6, weekdays only off season) rents bikes (1,000 Ft. per day) and sells maps. The whole town comes alive for the annual **Visegrád Palace Games** (second weekend in July), featuring jousts, knights in armor, and general medieval *joie de vivre*.

WHERE TO SLEEP AND EAT

Walk along Visegrád's main street, **Fő utca** (parallel to and inland from Route 11), and look for ZIMMER FREI signs; private rooms are typically 1,500 Ft.–2,000 Ft. per person. Otherwise, the tidy **Haus Honti** (Fő u. 66, just south of Rév u., tel. 26/398–120; cash only) has doubles for 3,400 Ft. The best of Visegrád's handful of restaurants is tiny, candlelit **Gulás Csárda** (Nagy Lajos u., at Fő u., no phone; cash only), with hearty Hungarian dishes for less than 600 Ft. During summer, they often serve a delicious cold raspberry soup.

ESZTERGOM

Follow the Danube to the Slovakian border and you'll reach Esztergom (ES-ter-gohm), the religious capital of Hungary. It's also the birthplace of Hungary's beloved first king, St. István I, who, in addition to uniting the Magyar tribes, established Christianity as the national religion and built the country's first cathedral. Esztergom's blockbuster sights are all on Castle Hill, where you'll find the ruins of the **Royal Palace,** home to Hungarian royals until the mid-13th century (in the 14th they split for a bigger palace in Buda). Twelve of the palace's rooms have been carefully restored and are now part of the **Vármúzeum** (Castle Museum; Szent István tér 1, tel. 33/315–986; admission 120 Ft.; open Tues.–Sun. 9–5), including the room where some believe King István was born in AD 975, a Gothic chapel, and a hall with 15th-century frescoes of the Virtues. Next door to the palace is Esztergom's 19th-century **basilica** (Szent István tér 2, tel. 33/311–895; open Apr.–Oct., daily 6–6; shorter hrs off season), the largest in the country. Look for its Italian frescoes, spooky crypt, the all-marble **Bakócz Chapel,** and the largest altarpiece in the world. The **treasury** (admission 100 Ft.) houses 1,000-year-old bejeweled relics. Make the steep,

406-step climb up to the basilica's copper-domed **kupola** (admission 40 Ft.) and reward yourself with awe-inspiring views.

On the streets below Castle Hill, signs direct you to the **Keresztény múzeum** (Christian Museum; Mindszenty tér 2, tel. 33/313–880; admission 150 Ft.; open mid-Mar.–Sept., Tues.–Sun. 10–6; shorter hrs off season), which contains priceless medieval and Renaissance paintings. Or kick back at a café on bustling **Rákóczi tér,** the city's main square. The much quieter **Széchenyi tér,** the heart of town in medieval days, is surrounded by beautiful baroque buildings.

Esztergom's **ferry terminal** is on tiny **Primate Island,** separated from the rest of Esztergom by the Kis Duna (Little Danube), which is more like a narrow, muddy canal. And the island has nothing to do with hairy apes—"primate" is a religious title. You can reach the town center by crossing at one of two small bridges and walking east on Lőrinc utca. The **train station** is a 20-minute walk south of Rákóczi tér; follow Kossuth Lajos utca to Baross Gábor út.

WHERE TO SLEEP AND EAT
IBUSZ (Kossuth Lajos u. 5, tel. 33/312–552; open June–Aug., weekdays 8–5, Sat. 8–noon; weekdays only off season) assists with private rooms (1,000 Ft. per person) that are usually on the town's outskirts. **Gran Tours** (Széchenyi tér 25, tel. 33/413– 756; open weekdays 8–4, Sat. 9–noon) books rooms closer to the center of town, and sells a city map. **Platán Panzió** (Kis-duna sétány 11, just south of Lőrinc u., tel. 33/311–355; doubles 2,500 Ft.; cash only) has institutional-looking rooms on the street bordering Kis Duna. **Alabárdos Panzió** (Pázmány Péter u. 49, tel. 33/312–640; doubles 5,800 Ft.–6,300 Ft., breakfast included; cash only) has large rooms with TVs and a view of the basilica. Just up the street, **Csülök Csárda** (Batthyány u. 9, tel. 33/312–420; cash only) dispenses reasonably priced Hungarian home-cooking, such as roast pork with cheese and apples. The town's daily **produce market** is on Simor János utca, beginning at Rákóczi tér.

LAKE BALATON

Landlocked Hungary has but one great body of water, Lake Balaton, known affectionately as the "Hungarian Sea." It's the third-most-popular tourist destination in Hungary, behind Budapest and the Danube Bend. Sadly, Eastern Europe's largest freshwater lake is not all it's cracked up to be. In fact, it's tepid, silty, and scarcely 6½ ft deep—so shallow that motorboats are not allowed—which explains the lake's other nickname, the "People's Puddle." For decades, Hungarian, German, and Czech party animals turned the whole lake into a communist's Club Med. At the height of summer, Balaton towns—particularly the south shore's **Siófok**—are still crammed with tourists, and lodging prices all around the lake skyrocket in July and August. The northern shore is a bit more subdued and far more scenic, and towns like **Balatonfüred** and **Tihany** are loaded with history and class. Since most visitors stay close to shore, even a nominal foray into the surrounding countryside will reward you with picturesque scenery and a break from the summer crowds. The most scenic way to travel here is by **MAHART ferry** (tel. 84/310–050, in Siófok), which offers frequent service to some 22 towns around the lake mid-April–October. Fares average 250 Ft.–400 Ft. **Trains** are about the same price, but speedier, and you'll find train stations at all towns except Tihany. Less frequent **buses** duplicate most train routes.

SIOFOK

Siófok, on Balaton's south shore, has nonstop glitzy nightlife, acres of narrow beachfront, and zillions of tourists. The busiest of the Balaton towns, it's regularly pegged as "cheesy" and a "meat market." Like it or not, your Balaton vacation may include a few hours here, as it's also the main stopping point for ferries and trains around the lake. The two major streets run parallel: **Petőfi sétány** lines the beach, passing large hotels and strip joints; **Fő utca,** a few blocks inland, runs along the train tracks, through **Szabadság tér** (the main square), and across the Sió Canal. The **train** and **bus** stations are next to each other on Fő utca. Trains run daily from Budapest's Déli Station (1 hr 40 min, 690 Ft.). **Ferries** depart several times daily for Tihany (1 hr 20 min, 380 Ft.), Balatonfüred (1 hr, 380 Ft.), and a dozen other towns on the north and south shores; the pier is at the west end of Petőfi sétány. The friendly staff at **Tourinform** (Fő u., in water tower west of train station, tel. 84/310–117 or 84/315–355; open July–Aug.,

Mon.–Sat. 8–8, Sun. 10–noon; Sept.–June, Mon.–Thur. 9–noon and 1–4, Fri. 9–2) can help with all your needs.

WHERE TO SLEEP AND EAT

The key to a low-budget excursion to Siófok is to come anytime but high season (July–Aug.). To rent a private room (2,100 Ft.–2,600 Ft.), look for ZIMMER FREI signs on Erkel Ferenc utca and Szent László utca, or book through Tourinform. The **Hotel Korona** (Erkel Ferenc u. 53, tel. 84/310–471; doubles 8,000 Ft.) offers clean, simple doubles with balconies, and it's on a quiet side street about 300 ft from the lake shore. Restaurants in town are similarly high-priced, but **Csárdás** (Fő u. 105, tel. 84/310–642) has an English menu with plenty of inexpensive Hungarian food. The main discos are **Flőrt** (Mártirok u., south of Fő u.) and **Paradiso** (Mártirok útca 15, at Petőfi sétány). Frolic with caution; gangs of prostitutes have been known to bully tourists and steal valuables.

BALATONFURED

The north-shore town of Füred (natives tend to drop the prefix) is the unofficial capital of the "Hungarian Sea." The oldest and most aristocratic Balaton settlement, it boasts sailing regattas, a world-famous hospital for cardiology, and a dozen medicinal springs with allegedly healthful, albeit pungent, waters. You can have a taste from the spring flowing in the center of Füred's main square, Gyógy tér. Also on tap in Füred are windsurfing, sailing, tennis, cycling, fishing, and horseback riding. For more information on these sports, check with **Balatontourist** (Tagore sétány 1, tel. 87/342–822), on the waterfront promenade next to the MAHART ferry pier. When you tire of the sporting life, spend an afternoon sipping vino (from 150 Ft. per liter) at the wine warehouse **Badacsonyi Pincegazdaság** (Zrínyi u. 11, tel. 87/343–513; open weekdays 7:30–noon and 12:30–4:30, Sat. 8–noon); Füred is famous for its *olasz-rizling,* a type of white wine. The warehouse is next door to the **train** and **bus** stations—from the ferry pier, take Jókai Mór utca inland, turn left on Horváth Mihály utca, and walk three blocks. Trains run to Budapest's Déli station (2 hrs, 800 Ft.) 11 times daily.

Brochures may swoon about the "Nation's Playground," but it's wise to realize that Lake Balaton is just a lake, not an ocean. The wind occasionally whips up a wave or two, but nobody's going to hang ten here.

WHERE TO SLEEP AND EAT

Balatontourist arranges private rooms (doubles 2,500 Ft.). Best of the cheap hotels, the **Blaha Lujza Hotel** (Blaha Lujza u. 4, tel. 87/343–094; doubles 4,900 Ft.; cash only) has spotless, bright rooms in a 19th-century building. The hotel's **restaurant** gets raves for its Hungarian edibles (400 Ft. and up) and frequent live music at night. **Széchenyi Ferenc Kertészeti Szakközépiskola** (Hősök tere 1, Balatonarács, tel. 87/342–651; beds 1,000 Ft.; closed Sept.–June; cash only), just outside Füred, has pleasant dorm rooms. Take Bus 4 or 4A from Füred to the neighboring town of Balatonarács. At the deluxe **Füred Camping** (Széchenyi u. 24, tel. 87/343–823; closed mid-Nov.–mid-Mar.) one of its 3,800 tent sites costs 2,000 Ft.–2,500 Ft. (three-person maximum) in low season; June 25–August 26 prices nearly triple. From the ferry pier, walk 2 km (1 mi) west on Széchenyi utca, or take Bus 1 or 2.

TIHANY

Tiny Tihany is perched at the tip of a hilly, 5½-km (3¼-mi) peninsula that juts from the north shore like a hitchhiker's thumb. At the peninsula's center is a nature reserve and the small, secluded **Belső-tó** (Inner Lake). On the western side of the peninsula you'll find deep-water **beaches.** Totally unmissable (even from Balatonfüred) are the twin towers of Tihany's stately 18th-century **Bencés Apátsági templom** (Benedictine church), one of the finest monuments to the baroque in a country that eventually overdosed on the style. In the adjacent AD 1055 Benedictine monastery is the **Bencés Apátsági Múzeum** (Első András tér 1, tel. 87/448–650; admission 180 Ft.; open May–Sept., 9–5:30, Sun. 11–5:30; shorter hrs off season). Don't skip the basement lapidarium, which has tombstones and statues dating from the 2nd century AD. The staff at **Tihany Tourist** (Kossuth út 11, tel. 87/448–481; open June–Aug., daily 9–9; shorter hrs off season) rents bikes (200 Ft. per hour, 1,000 Ft. per day) and doles out hiking maps.

For a scenic two-hour hike, follow the marked trail from the monastery to the peak of **Csúcs Hill.** Tihany is accessible only by bus or ferry; buses depart hourly from Balatonfüred (30 min, 150 Ft.).

WHERE TO SLEEP AND EAT

The Tihany Tourist office can help you find a private room, but a peaceful night by the lake costs 2,500 Ft.–3,500 Ft. per double. Hotels and pensions are twice the price, so consider sleeping in Balatonfüred. The restaurant **Kakas-Csárda** (Batthyány u. 1, tel. 87/448–541; closed mid-Nov.–Feb.), across from Tihany Tourist, has an English menu featuring grilled chicken and such for 880 Ft. and up.

BADACSONY

A combination of excellent wine and striking rock formations may sound dangerous, but they're what make the north shore's Badacsony (BAD-a-chone) region so attractive—the wine, great hiking, and 700-ft basalt columns draw outdoorsy types and snooty wine connoisseurs alike. A party-minded crowd hangs out at the **beach,** and every other structure is a borozó (wine bar) or söröző (beer hall). To sample some wine, knock on the front door of any vineyard/cellar marked BOROZÓ or WEIN—many line **Római út,** southwest of town. You can view Balaton landscapes by a famous local painter at the eponymous **Egry József Memorial Museum** (Egry sétány 12, tel. 87/431–140; admission 80 Ft.; open May–Oct.,Tues.–Sun. 10–6). For hiking, hit the dozens of trails that ribbon flat-topped **Badacsony Hill.** Pick up a trail map at **Balatontourist** (Park u. 10, in Il Capitano mall, tel. 87/431–292), or check the map inside the **train station** (Balatoni út, near ferry pier).

WHERE TO SLEEP AND EAT

Private rooms booked through Balatontourist start at 2,000 Ft. per double. Just around the corner from the tourist office is the tidy **Hársfa Panzió** (Szegedi Róza u. 1, tel. 87/431–293; doubles 2,000 Ft.; closed Oct.–Apr.), with a **restaurant** that serves tasty *cigánypecsenye* (roast pork) and other traditional Hungarian dishes. Splash out at **Óbester Fogadó** (Római út 177, tel. 87/431–648; doubles 5,000 Ft., breakfast included), a charming, homey pension in a 350-year old residence. It's on the lower slopes of Badacsony Hill, surrounded by vineyards.

KESZTHELY

Keszthely, 70 km (42 mi) west of Balatonfüred, is the second-most-touristed town on Lake Balaton, but its well-preserved Renaissance and baroque buildings give it an old-time, uncommercial feel. **Kossuth Lajos utca,** the main street, runs north to the whopping 101-room, renovated **Festetics Palace** (Kastély u. 1, tel. 83/312–190; admission 600 Ft.; open July–Aug., daily 9–6; Sept.–June, Tues.–Sun. 10–5). The palace was built in 1745 with a fascinating room of mirrors; in summer, musical and theatrical performances fill the palace's courtyards. Other nearby attractions include the **Helikon strand** beach and the mud baths of Europe's largest hot-water lake, **Lake Héviz.** For more information on these sights, check with **Tourinform** (Kossuth Lajos u. 28, tel. 83/314–144) or **IBUSZ** (Kossuth Lajos u. 27, tel. 83/314–320). The **train** and **bus** stations are about 10 minutes south of town, and just south of the ferry pier (Kazinczy u., at Mártirok u.)—follow Mártirok utca to Kossuth Lajos utca.

WHERE TO SLEEP

For private rooms (doubles 2,500 Ft. and up), check with the tourist offices (*see above*) or knock on any door marked ZIMMER FREI. At **Zalatour Camping** (Balatonpart, near Helikon Strand, tel. 83/312–782; closed Oct.–Apr.; cash only), 20 minutes south of the train station on Kossuth Lajos utca, two-person tent sites run 2,200 Ft.–2,600 Ft.; two-bed bungalows 2,800 Ft.

TRANSDANUBIA

The mighty Danube divides Hungary into eastern and western regions that differ substantially in character and history. The western region, known as Transdanubia (Dunántúl in Hungarian), is characterized by mountains and hills, broken up by tracts of flat, open countryside, and acres of sunflower fields. The region gracefully bears signs of Roman occupation and 150 years of Turkish rule. The Austrian influence, too, is more visible here than elsewhere in Hungary. Architecturally striking **Győr** and **Sopron** are heavily touristed, but medieval **Kőszeg** and the hills around **Pécs** remain relatively unknown to foreigners.

GYOR

Győr (pronounced DJUR) is called the "City of Balconies" for its gracious railed windows, the "City of Rivers" for the three that meet here (the Danube, Mosoni, and Raba), and the "City of Belching Smokestacks" for its tremendous number of factories. Fortunately, all the smoke and noise is well south of Győr's lovingly preserved, pedestrian-only town center. Narrow streets lead up to historic **Káptalan-domb** (Chapter Hill), where the town's oldest church, the **Episcopal cathedral** (admission free; open Mon.–Sat. 10–noon and 2–6, Sun. 2–6) rises from 11th-century foundations. An adjoining **Gothic chapel** houses the gilded bust of King St. Ladislas; the medieval masterpiece is rumored to contain part of the saint's skull. Across the square from the cathedral is the overgrown garden of the **Püspökvár** (Bishop's Palace).

The town's main square is postcard-perfect **Széchenyi tér.** At its northeast corner is the **Xantus János Múzeum** (admission 80 Ft.; open Apr.–Sept., Tues.–Sun. 10–6; shorter hrs off season), with historical artifacts and contemporary Hungarian paintings. East of Széchenyi tér is **Bécsi kapu tér,** lined with baroque houses and a few open-air cafés; its main feature is an 18th-century Italianate-baroque **Carmelite church.** Also on the square are 16th-century fortifications built to repel the Turks, who were evicted (after four years of occupation) in 1598. For a free town map, drop by **Tourinform** (Árpád u. 32, tel. 96/311–771; open May– Sept., Mon.–Sat. 9–9, Sun. 10–2; shorter hrs off season).

Though it now looks like any other serene, well-kept public building, Győr's 19th-century Town Hall (across from the railroad station) was the site of anti-Soviet protests during Hungary's 1956 revolt.

COMING AND GOING
Express trains depart daily for Budapest's Keleti Station (1½ hrs, 800 Ft.) and Vienna (1½ hrs, 3,400 Ft.). The **train station** (Révai Miklós u.) and adjacent **bus station** (connected by an underground passageway) are 10 minutes from the historic center; walk north on Aradi vértanúk útja or Baross Gábor utca.

WHERE TO SLEEP AND EAT
IBUSZ (Kazinczy u. 3, ½ block east of Bécsi kapu tér, tel. 96/311–700; open May– Sept., weekdays 8–5:45, Sat. 8–noon; shorter hrs off season) arranges private rooms (2,250 Ft.) outside the town center. **Széchenyi Istvan Főiskola Kollégiuma** (KTMF, Hédarvái u. 3, tel. 96/429–722; beds 1,800 Ft. per person; cash only) offers three-bed dorm rooms. From Széchenyi tér, walk north on Jedlik Ányos utca, cross Kossuth bridge, and turn left on Kálóczy tér. The dorm is at the far end of the KTMF parking lot. The central **Arany Panzió** (Arany Janos u. 7, tel. 96/322–171; doubles 4,200 Ft.) offers four immaculate rooms with TVs and fans; walk four blocks north from the train station on Aradi vértanúk útja and turn right.

At the popular, central **Komédiás** restaurant (Csuszor G. u. 30, tel. 96/319–050; closed Sun.), you can fill up on *pörkölt* (stew) and other hearty fare for about 300 Ft. per plate. For excellent Hungarian-style pizza, join the hip crowd at **Wansör** (Király u. 9, tel. 96/320–455; open daily noon–2 AM; cash only), a former wine cellar. The entry's in an alley, down a steep flight of stairs: From the northeast corner of Bécsi kapu tér, walk along Király utca and look for a sign to your left.

NEAR GYOR

FERTOD
Dominating the small town of Fertőd is the magnificent baroque **Eszterházy Palace** (1720)—its large French-style park and hall of mirrors inevitably invite comparisons with Versailles. Music lovers will enjoy the occasional concerts held here, as well as the exhibit on composer Joseph Haydn (who composed many of his famous pieces during a 30-year stay here). You, too, can overnight in the palace (doubles 2,175 Ft.), but tour groups tend to fill it; call ahead for reservations. From Győr, trains depart daily for **Fertőszentmiklós** (40 min, 370 Ft.); take a local bus the final 4 km (2½ mi) to the palace. Bartók Béla út 2, tel. 99/370–971. Admission: 500 Ft. Open May–Sept., daily 9–5; closed Sat. off season.

PANNONHALMA ABBEY

The Benedictine abbey of Pannonhalma, perched dramatically atop the Mons Sacer Pannoniae (Holy Mount of Pannonia) in the Sokorói Mountains, was one of Eastern Europe's premier political and religious power centers during the Middle Ages. Now 1,002 years old, it's still pretty important—it is, after all, where the Pope lunched during a 1996 visit to Hungary. Among its many wonders is a 13th-century crypt and a library with more than 300,000 priceless medieval documents. Unfortunately, you must take a hasty guided tour (tours in English cost an extra 200 Ft.) to see them. The abbey is 21 km (12½ mi) from Győr; **buses** (45 min, 170 Ft.) leave from Platform 11 of Győr's station. Vár 1, tel. 96/570–191. Admission: 300 Ft. Tours depart June–Sept., daily 9–5 (in English at 11 and 1); mid-Mar.–May and Oct.–mid-Nov., Tues.–Sun. 9–4 (in English at 11 and 1); mid-Nov.–mid-Mar., Tues.–Sun. 10–3 (no English tours).

SOPRON

The town of Sopron (SHOH-prahn) was never sacked by Mongol or Turkish invaders, and its winsome Renaissance, baroque, and Roman buildings are beautifully intact. Its pristine, fairyland air makes it one of the most visited—and expensive—towns in all of Hungary. Everything touristy is clustered around the tiny main square, **Fő tér,** and can be seen in a single afternoon: The **Bencés-templom** (Goat Church; Fő tér, at Templom u.; open daily 10–noon and 2–5) acquired its unusual name from a grateful goatherder who paid for its construction with gold unearthed by his animal. Across from the church is the 215-ft **Tűztorony** (Fire Tower; admission 100 Ft.; open Tues.–Sun. 10–5:30), symbol of Sopron. Climb to the top for views of the forested Lővér foothills. At the tower's base is **Loyalty Gate**; local legend has it that if an adulterous woman walks through, its bells will ring (unfaithful men, however, can slip right by). Side by side are two worthwhile museums: The Római kőtár in the **Fabricus-Ház** (Fő tér 6; admission 100 Ft.; open May–Sept., Tues.–Sun. 10–6; shorter hrs off season) displays Roman statues unearthed from beneath Fő tér in 1988, while **Storno-Ház** (Fő tér 8; admission 100 Ft.; open May–Sept., Tues.–Sun. 10–6; shorter hrs off season) displays furniture and decorative arts. Sopron's Jews were expelled in 1526, but one of the town's original **synagogues** (Új u. 22, 1 block south of Fő tér, tel. 99/311–327; admission 200 Ft.; open May–Aug., Wed.–Mon. 9–5; shorter hrs off season) has been converted to a museum of Judaica.

Practically the only affordable eatery in town is **Gyógygödör Borozó & Weinstube** (Fő tér 4, tel. 99/311–280), where you can complement your meal with a liter of *soproni kékfrankos* (extra-strength Sopron red wine; 210 Ft.; cash only). Sopron is connected by **train** to Győr (1 hr, 500 Ft.), Budapest's Keleti Station (2½ hrs, 1,300 Ft.), and Vienna (1 hr 10 min, 3,000 Ft.). To reach Fő tér from the train station, walk north on Mátyás király utca, turn left at Széchenyi tér, and then right on Templom utca.

KOSZEG

This enchanting little fortress town lies in the easternmost foothills of the Alps, at an elevation of 3,000 ft. Kőszeg (KO-seg, meaning "stone top") was designed with an eye for defensibility, a strategy put to the test in 1532, when a few hundred Hungarian soldiers turned back 200,000 Turks, keeping the invaders from pillaging Vienna. The fortress, **Jurisics-vár** (Rájnis u. 9; admission 100 Ft.; open Tues.–Sun. 10–5), now resembles a slightly organized pile of rocks. Still, the tower affords a spectacular view, and the history museum inside is engaging. In the town center, **Jurisics tér** is packed with historical buildings, including a red-and-yellow-stripe town hall. **Szent Jakáb-templom** (St. James Church) is a magnificent structure with a baroque exterior and Gothic interior; it's next to the 17th-century **Szent Imre-templom** (St. Emerich's Church). Three tourist offices are located close to where Fő tér meets Városház utca. The best of the lot is **Savaria Tourist** (Várkör u. 69, tel. 94/360–238; weekdays 8–5, Sat. 8–noon), where you can change money and get a map.

COMING AND GOING

From Budapest's Keleti or Déli stations, take a train to Szombathely (3 hrs, 1,350 Ft.) and transfer to Kőszeg (30 min, 100 Ft.). The **train station** (Vasutállomas u., tel. 94/360–053) is about 10 minutes south of the town center; head north along Rákóczi Ferenc utca, or grab Bus 1A or 1Y to Fő tér. The **bus station** (Liszt Ferenc u., off Kossuth u.) is one block southeast of the town center.

WHERE TO SLEEP AND EAT

Don't count on booking a private room (2,000 Ft. and up) at Savaria Tourist (*see above*), as the few that are available tend to go quickly. The popular **Aranystrucc Hotel** (Várkor u. 124, at Rákóczi u., tel.

94/360–323; doubles 4,000 Ft.; reservations advised) has housed visitors for more than 300 years, but the recently upgraded guest rooms each include modern private bathrooms, telephones, and TVs. Breakfast is served in the hotel restaurant. The best deal in town is **West Camping & Turistaszálló** (Strand sétány 1, tel. 94/360–981; closed Nov.–Mar.; cash only). Dorm housing runs about 650 Ft. per bed (bedding included), and the shaded, riverside tent sites are 300 Ft. plus 275 Ft. per person. From Fő tér, follow Várkör to Kiss Janos utca, turn right, continue to the first bridge, go right on the gravel path, and left on the footbridge. The friendly folks at **Bécsikapu Söröző** (Rájnis u. 5, off Jurisics tér near castle, tel. 94/360–297) serve delicious cottage cheese and yogurt *palacsinta* (dessert crêpes), each puffed up like a soufflé. Ibrahim Kávézó (Fő tér 17, tel. 94/360–854) offers excellent venison (800 Ft.; cash only) with potato dumplings.

PECS

Pécs (pronounced PAYCH), southern Transdanubia's most interesting destination, reflects a rich 2,000-year history. Many of the town's eclectic buildings—including two mosques, a synagogue, and several cathedrals—have recently been restored, augmenting the pleasant atmosphere created by Péc's warm climate, red-tile roofs, rambling streets, and surrounding vineyards. Pécs has long served as an outpost of art and learning; Hungary's first university was established here, though nothing remains of it today. The town has also produced several noteworthy artists, including humanist poet Jánus Pannonia, and the Zsolnay family, whose ceramics are widely admired. Entertainment here tends to be refined, with more than a dozen museums and many art galleries to visit, along with excellent ballet and symphony performances at the national theater.

Tourinform (Széchenyi tér 9, tel. 72/213–315; open Mar.–Oct., weekdays 8–6, weekends 9–2; Nov.–Feb., weekdays 9–4), on the main square, dispenses maps and brochures. **IBUSZ** (Apáca u. 1, 1 block SW of Széchenyi tér, tel. 72/211–011; open May–Aug., weekdays 8–6, Sat. 8–noon; Sept.–Apr., Mon.–Thur. 8:30–4:30, Fri. 8:30–3:30) books private rooms (about 1,000 Ft. per person).

COMING AND GOING

Pécs is a large city with a small, walkable center. Trains run regularly from Budapest's Déli Station (2 hrs 40 min, 1,300 Ft.). Pécs's **train station** is 20 minutes south of town. To reach the city center, walk to the far right (east) end of the station and continue straight (north) up Jokai utca north to Széchenyi tér; or take Bus 36 or 37. The **bus station** is near the market on Zóyom utca.

WHERE TO SLEEP AND EAT

Pécs's only drawback is its lack of cheap accommodations. **Hotel Főnix** (Hunyadi János út 2, 2 blocks north of Széchenyi tér, tel. 72/311–680; doubles 4,800 Ft., breakfast included) has clean rooms with cable TV, refrigerators, and showers. **Motel Centrum** (Szepesy Ignác u. 4, tel. 72/311–707; doubles 3,900 Ft.; cash only) is a quiet six-room pension, 150 ft north of the northeast corner of Széchenyi tér. **Szalay László Kivalo College** (Universitas u. 2, tel. 72/324–473; closed Oct.–June; cash only) charges 400 Ft. per person for basic three-bed rooms. **Toboz Panzió** (Fenyves sor 5, tel. 72/325–232; doubles 5,600 Ft.; cash only) is nestled among the pines of the Mecsek hills that rise above the city. Each of the handsome rooms is equipped with a skylight.

Pubs and restaurants line two of Pécs's busiest pedestrian-only streets, Ferencesek utcaja and Király utca, both of which intersect Széchenyi tér. **Fiáker Etterem** (Felsőmalon u. 7, tel. 72/327–859; closed Sun.; cash only) may be the best budget restaurant within a 100-mile radius; hearty Hungarian standards cost under 600 Ft. **Barbakán Borozó** (Klimó G. u. 18, tel. 72/324–930; dinner only), built into the old town wall, serves traditional Hungarian fare (up to 1,200 Ft.) and *palacsinta* (dessert crêpes). From Széchenyi tér, walk west on Ferencesek utca to Kórház tér, then north on Klimó G. utca. The cheerful **Cellárium** (Hunyadi u. 2, tel. 72/314–453) serves up Hungarian classics like roast duck with steamed cabbage (550 Ft.), as well as more adventurous fare like "Hungarian stew with the comb and balls of cockerel."

WORTH SEEING

Pécs's central square, Széchenyi tér, is crowned by the 16th-century **Belvárosi plébánia templom,** also known as Gazi Khassim Pasha Inner City Parish Church (open mid-Apr.–mid-Oct., weekdays 10–4, weekends 11:30–4; weekdays only off season). It's the largest and finest relic of Turkish architecture remaining in Hungary. When the Turks occupied Pécs from 1543 to 1686, they destroyed St.

Bartholomew's Church and recycled its stone to build this mosque. Muslim and Christian elements are combined not only in its name but also on its dome, where a cross shares space with a gilded crescent.

From the northwest corner of Széchenyi tér, walk west along central Káptalan utca, accurately dubbed "The Street of Museums" by locals. The first stop is the impressive **Csontváry Museum** (Jánus Pannonius u. 11, off Káptalan u.; admission 160 Ft.; open Apr.–Oct., Tues.–Sun. 10–6; shorter hrs off season) exhibits the work of pharmacist-turned-expressionist painter Mihály Csontváry Kosztka (1853–1919). Lots of Bible scenes are showcased in its five small rooms. You won't need your 3-D glasses to be astonished by the works of Victor Vasarely, founder of op art, at the excellent **Vasarely Museum** (Káptalan u. 3; admission 160 Ft.; open Tues.–Sun. 10–6). Across the street is the **Zsolnay Museum** (Káptalan u. 2; admission 160 Ft.; open Tues.–Sun. 10–6), with a good display of Zsolnay ceramics crafted from 1853 to the present, along with helpful explanatory notes. The building itself is a gorgeous 14th-century Gothic landmark.

A few hundred feet west is Pécs's austere four-tower **cathedral** (Dóm tér; admission 120 Ft.; open Apr.–Oct., weekdays 10–1 and 2–5, Sat. 9–1, Sun. 1–5; shorter hrs off season). Inside, no stone has been left unpainted, and the frescoes and mosaics practically explode with color—however, to get the full effect, you must pay the caretaker an additional 200 Ft. to turn on the lights. Built by Hungary's patron saint and first king, István, the building still has some of its original parts, including an 11th-century crypt.

Pécs's **synagogue** (Kossuth tér, 3 blocks south of Széchenyi tér off Irgalmasok u.; admission 50 Ft.; open Apr.–Sept., Sun.–Fri. 10–11:30 and noon–5; shorter hrs off season), built in 1865, used to have a congregation 4,000 members strong prior to World War II. Today the 300-person congregation is a poignant reminder of the Nazi era, as are the names of Holocaust victims inscribed in the entryway.

SHOPPING

Pécs is the birthplace and center of the Zsolnay porcelain craft, and is the best place to purchase exquisite Zsolnay pieces. The **Zsolnay Márkabolt** (Jókai tér 2, tel. 72/310–220) is the factory's outlet store, and offers quality merchandise at the best prices.

NORTHERN HUNGARY

Don't make the mistake of skipping northern Hungary just because it doesn't get much attention from Hungarian tourist offices. This temperate, hilly region produces excellent wines, and in the towns of **Eger** and **Tokaj** you'll have plenty of opportunities to taste them. Three mountain ranges—the Bükk, Mátra, and Cserhát—provide ample opportunities for horseback riding, hiking, and mountain biking. Spelunking enthusiasts need look no further than **Aggtelek National Park,** which boasts the largest cave system in Europe.

EGER

Pastel rococo buildings and outdoor cafés line the narrow, banner-hung streets of Eger (EH-gair). It's a startlingly good-looking town, so clean you'll swear that the Eger Sanitation Department takes toothbrushes to the cobblestones each night. Just outside town, cellars churn out casks of the famed **Egri Bikavér** (Bull's Blood), a hair-raising, cheek-warming blend of red wine. Add a hefty dose of baroque churches, a striking citadel, thermal baths, and frequent open-air classical concerts, and you'll see why this "City of Wine and Grape" is the great charmer of Northern Hungary. The main square, **Dobó tér,** is arguably one of the most stunning in the entire country. Make your first stop **Tourinform** (Dobó tér 2, tel. 36/321–807; open May–Sept., weekdays 9–6, weekends 9–2; shorter hrs off season), at the square's southwest corner, and pick up a free map.

COMING AND GOING

There are four express trains daily from Budapest's Keleti Station (2 hrs, 920 Ft.) to Eger's **train station** (Állomás tér 1, tel. 36/314–264). To reach the center of town, take Bus 10, 11, or 14. The 20-minute walk is pleasant: Go west on Vasút utca, turn right onto Deák Ferenc út, right onto Kossuth Lajos utca, and left onto Jókai Mór utca. The main square, **Dobó tér,** will be on your right. Buses make the trip from Budapest's Népstadion Station to Eger (3 hrs, 650 Ft.). The **bus station** (Pyrker tér) is just west of the town center, behind the Egri Bazilika.

WHERE TO SLEEP AND EAT

Eger's lodging tends to be expensive, and books solid in summer. **IBUSZ** (Széchenyi u. 9, 1 block west of Dobó tér, tel. 36/312–526; open May–Sept., weekdays 8–noon and 1–6, Sat. 9–noon; Oct.–May, weekdays 8–noon and 1–4:30) can set you up in a private room (doubles 2,200 Ft. and up) or pension (doubles 3,500 Ft.–6,000 Ft.). Your bargain-basement option is a college dorm: Ask for a list at Tourinform (*see above*) or try the dorms of the **Wégner Jenő Műszaki Informatikai Szakközépiskola** (Rákóczi út 2, tel. 36/311–211; beds 670 Ft. per person; open mid-June–Aug.; cash only). From the town center walk north (5 min) on Szécheny István utca, which becomes Rákóczi út. **Vénusz Panzió** (Pacsirta u. 49, tel. 36/411–421; doubles 4,500 Ft., breakfast included; cash only), with a sauna, solarium, and lush garden terrace, is 20 minutes from the center: Follow Deák Ferenc út south, turn right on Arpád utca, then left on Pacsirta utca.

Talizmán (Kossuth Lajos u. 19, tel. 36/410–883; reservations required), near the gate to Eger Castle, is one of the region's most popular restaurants for its top-notch Hungarian cuisine. Main dishes start at around 450 Ft., with many good choices in the 600 Ft.–700 Ft. range.

WORTH SEEING

Towering above town is **Eger Castle** (Dózsa György tér; admission to castle and exhibits 250 Ft.; castle entry only 70 Ft.), reduced to ruins by the Turks during their second invasion and occupation (1596–1690) of Eger. It's now interesting for its art gallery—with Italian and Dutch Renaissance works—and its casemates (artillery vaults) in a labyrinth of partially excavated underground tunnels. The castle **museum** (open Mar.–Oct., Tues.–Sun. 9–5; shorter hrs off season) displays ancient weapons, coins, and utensils from the excavations, and the **Panoptikum** exhibit (admission 200 Ft.) features wax figures of grimacing Turks and noble Hungarian warriors. On Dobó tér, two statues commemorate the Hungarian army's historic defeat of Turkish forces in 1552 (the first Turkish invasion), despite being outnumbered six to one. Another relic from the Turkish occupation is a lonely **minaret** (admission 50 Ft.; open daily 10–6) at the corner of Knézich Károly utca and Torony utca. From this 100-ft tower the town's muezzin once called the Islamic faithful to prayer five times a day.

Two of Eger's churches are worth a look: The 1771 **Minorite Church** (Dobó tér; admission 50 Ft.; open daily 10–5) is one of the finest examples of Baroque architecture in Eastern Europe. The imposing 19th-century **Egri Bazilika** (Szabadság tér, opposite Eszterházy Teacher Training College; open daily 7–7), Hungary's second-largest cathedral, hosts organ recitals in summer (Mon.–Sat. 11:30 AM, Sun. 12:45). Across from the Bazilika is the impressive late-baroque **Lyceum** (Szabadság tér; admission 150 Ft.; open mid-Mar.–mid-Dec., Tues.–Sun. 9:30–12:30; weekends only off season), built in 1776 as one of Hungary's first post-secondary schools. These days it's part of the city's Teacher Training College, and its **library** holds one of the most valuable book collections in the country, including the first Latin edition of Dante's *Divine Comedy*. On the ninth floor an amazing view of the city is reflected through the lens of a **camera obscura.**

SZEPASSZONY VOLGY • Pass an afternoon sampling the famous Egri Bikavér (Bull's Blood) and other regional wines in **Szépasszony völgy** (Valley of the Beautiful Women), a 30-minute walk from the center of town. In all, there are about 320 hand-hewn stone cellars here, though only 40 are open at any given moment. Each is centuries old—Hungarian villagers built and lived in them during the 16th- and 17th-century Turkish occupation. For maximum enjoyment just stroll along and stop in whichever ones catch your fancy; wines average about 40 Ft. per glass. Legend has it that if you manage to stick a coin into the mildew of the cool cellar walls, you will someday return. *From Egri Bazilika, walk 1 block south on Deák Ferenc u., turn right on Telekesy István u. to Király u. (becomes Szépasszony völgy u.). Cellars open daily until midnight.*

NEAR EGER

SZILVASVARAD

North of Eger in the Bükk Mountains, the village of Szilvásvárad (SIL-vash-vah-rahd) is great for horseback riding, hiking, and mountain biking. The town has been a famous breeding center of prized Lippizaner horses since the late 15th century, and is the center of the region's horse culture. A huge **stable** and equestrian arena are at the center of town; rides through the Bükk are about 1,500 Ft. per hour. Hiking and biking enthusiasts should head to **Kölcsönző** (at entrance to Bükk National Park in the Szilvásvárad-Szalajka Valley, tel. 60/352–695), which rents bikes by the hour (300 Ft.) or by the day (1,150 Ft.), and sells regional map *No. 30A Bükk* (200 Ft.–300 Ft.). The most traversed route is the 4-km (2½ mi) hike (beginning near the equestrian arena) along a stream through **Szalajka Valley.** Hiking past the modest **Veil Waterfall,** you'll find the upper terminus of the cog railway (120 Ft. one way) in a large meadow; the lower terminus is by the trailhead. The cheapest of the many reasonably priced pensions in town is the lovely **Szalajka Fogadó** (Egri út 2, tel. 36/355–257; doubles 2,700 Ft., breakfast included). From Eger, catch the Szilvásvárad-bound **bus** (1 hr, 140 Ft.) or one of seven daily **trains** (1 hr, 190 Ft.).

AGGTELEK NATIONAL PARK

The remote Aggtelek National Park, 150 km (90 mi) north of Eger on the border with Slovakia, is home to rugged, densely forested mountains ribboned with miles of hiking trails, and the **Baradla Caves,** the largest stalactite system in Europe, with 24 km (14½ mi) of limestone passageways. This isn't the easiest place to visit in Hungary (there's no direct train service), but it's worth the effort. From Budapest's Keleti Station, take the **train** to Miskolc (2 hrs, 1,150 Ft.); from there, take one of seven daily trains to Jósvafő–Aggtelek (1½ hrs, 230 Ft.), then hop a shuttle bus for the final 15 km (9 mi). **Buses** travel directly to the park from Budapest (5 hrs, 850 Ft.), Eger (3½ hrs, 450 Ft.), or Miskolc (2 hrs, 150 Ft.), but each makes only one round trip daily, so plan ahead.

There are three entrances (all stocked with hiking maps) to the Baradla Caves. The main entrance is **Aggtelek,** a short walk from Aggtelek town. The **Vörös-tó** and **Jósvafő** entrances are 6 km (4 mi) east of town; hike to them by marked trail, or catch a shuttle bus at the Cseppkő Hotel (*see below*). Guided tours depart several times daily from each entrance; the best one, a 1½-hour tour (350 Ft.) starting at Vörös-tó, features fabulous stalactite and stalagmite formations like the "Fairy Castle" and "Leaning Tower of Pisa," plus a short concert in the cavernous, acoustically perfect "Concert Hall." For information on longer, in-depth cave tours (500 Ft.–2,700 Ft.), call the park office (tel. 48/350–006). A final note: Temperatures inside the caves get down to 10°C (50°F), so dress appropriately.

WHERE TO SLEEP AND EAT

Facilities around the park are limited, restaurants nearly nil. Stock up on snacks and such at the **ABC market** at the center of Aggtelek town. A block away (about 700 ft from the Aggtelek cave entrance), the **Cseppkő Hotel** (Külterület, tel. 48/343–075; doubles 4,900 Ft.) has clean rooms (breakfast included), a restaurant, sauna, and terrace bar. Downhill from the Cseppkő, the **Baradla Turistaszállás & Camping** (Baradla oldal 1, tel. 48/343–073; campground closed mid-Oct.–Apr.; cash only) offers dorm-style beds (500 Ft.), tent sites (700 Ft. for two persons), and four-bed bungalows (3,200 Ft.). HI members receive a 10% discount.

TOKAJ

At the junction of the Bodrog and Tisza rivers, beneath the volcanic Zempléni Hills, sleepy Tokaj (TOH-kay) is the pearl of the Hegyalja wine-producing region. Vineyards here have been fermenting grapes since the Middle Ages; satisfied 18th-century customer King Louis XIV of France called Tokaj "the wine of kings and the king of wines." Wine-tasting costs around 30 Ft. per glass; don't forget to sample *Tokaji aszú,* the legendary dessert wine. *Pincék* (wine cellars) dot the hillside along **Rákóczi út,** the town's main road, and signs point to 600-year-old **Rákóczi Pince** (Kossuth tér 13, tel. 47/352–408; open July–Aug., daily 10–8; shorter hrs off season), Europe's largest cellar. It was here that Hungarian hero Ferenc Rákóczi II was chosen to lead the War of Independence against the Hapsburg Empire (1703–1711). A standard cellar tour with a tasting of six different wines costs around 700 Ft. Make reservations at least one day in advance. To reach town from the **train station** (Baross Gábor u.), walk 15 minutes north on Bajcsy-Zsilinszky utca, which becomes Rákóczi út. Trains from Budapest's Keleti Station (3 hrs, 1,300 Ft.) often require a transfer at Szerencs.

WHERE TO SLEEP AND EAT

Private rooms in Tokaj start around 1,500 Ft. per person; look for ZIMMER FREI signs around town or inquire at Tokaj Tours (Serház u. 1, tel. 47/352–259). The 600-site, riverfront **Tisza Camping** (Tisza-part, tel. 47/352–012; closed Oct.–Mar.) offers tent sites (600 Ft. for two persons; cash only) and four-bed bungalows (900 Ft. per person). From Rákóczi út, cross the bridge near the Tokaj Hotel and follow signs. The recently remodeled, ultra-spiffy **Makk Marci Panzió** (Liget Köz 1, at Rákóczi út, tel. 47/352–336; doubles 3,500 Ft., breakfast included) has laundry service, a bar, and a restaurant serving 300 Ft. entrées.

GREAT PLAIN

Like, say, Nebraska, the Nagyalföld (Great Plain) rarely wins applause as a fun vacation spot. It's flat. It's hot. It's empty. When asked what he thought of the region, one local said, "I call it the Big Nothing." On its seemingly endless sunbaked fields roam sheep, Magyar longhorns, and their attendant *csikós* (cowboys). As luck would have it, though, you can whiz through the truly arid parts of the Great Plain in an air-conditioned train and land in the surprisingly vital, colorful cities of **Debrecen** and **Kecskemét.**

DEBRECEN

If any Hungarian city can claim to be almost as important as Budapest, it's Debrecen (DEB-ret-sen), capital of the Great Plain and the nation's second-largest city. The 16th-century Hungarian Protestant movement was born and remains centered here, earning Debrecen the nickname "the Calvinist Rome." In the succeeding 400 years, it has continued to be the epicenter for many Hungarian revolts, protests, and counter-protests—and in 1944, the Soviets set up a provisional government here rather than in Budapest to curb rioting. These days the city's home to the largest per-capita student population in Hungary.

At the center of town is **Kalvin tér,** where you'll find two important monuments: a neoclassical barn known as the Protestant **Great Church** (open mid-Mar.–mid-Oct., daily 9–4; shorter hrs off season; admission 40 Ft.), built 1805–1827, and across a statue-laden garden, the **Reformed College** (Kalvin tér 16; admission 70 Ft.; open Tues.–Sat. 9–5, Sun. 9–1), which houses a small historical museum that has frescoes depicting moments in Hungarian history, and some religious art. Hungarian hero Lajos Kossuth declared Hungary's independence from Austria on the steps of the Great Church in 1849, and convened the first modern Hungarian National Assembly in the College.

The **Déri Museum** (Déri tér 1, tel. 52/417–577; admission to first-floor exhibits 90 Ft., second-floor exhibits 100 Ft.; open Nov.–Apr., Tues.–Sun. 8–4) houses the collection of a wealthy Hungarian silk manufacturer; exhibits run the gamut from Egyptian archaeology to modern Hungarian art. From Kalvin tér, walk west on Museum utca. Behind the museum, the **Kölcsey Cultural Center** (Hunyadi J. u. 1–3, tel. 52/419–647) is your best resource for concerts and events; Friday–Sunday evenings, films are shown here in their original language. The **Csokonai Theater** (Kossuth u. 10, tel. 52/417–811) presents operas, operettas, musicals, and dramas September through early June. For information on Debrecen's several summer festivals, drop by the helpful **Tourinform** office (Piac u. 20, tel. 52/316–419; open June–Aug., daily 8–8; Sept.–May, weekdays 8:30–4:30).

The **Tímárház** (Tanner House; Gál István u. 6, tel. 52/368–857; open May–Sept., Tues.–Sun. 10–6; closed Sun. off season; admission 80 Ft.) is dedicated to preserving and maintaining the ancient folk arts and crafts of Hajdú-Bihár county. Here you can admire exquisite pieces and watch the artisans at work in their workshops.

On the city's outskirts is the **Great Forest,** Debrecen's sprawling park, where you can spend an afternoon splashing around in the indoor and outdoor thermal baths at **Nagyerdei Gyógyfürdő** (Nagyerdei Park 1, tel. 52/346–000; admission 260 Ft.; open daily 8–noon and 1–6:30). From Kalvin tér, take Tram 1 north.

COMING AND GOING

Trains run frequently from Budapest's Nyugati Station (2½ hrs, 1,300 Ft.) to the Debrecen **train station** (Petőfi tér, tel. 52/346–777). To reach the center of town, walk north on Piac utca about 20 minutes, or take Tram 1 (50 Ft.). Debrecen's **bus station** (Külső vásártér u. 1, tel. 52/413–999) is southwest of town. To get to Kalvin tér, walk east on Arany Janos utca to Piac utca, then walk four blocks north.

WHERE TO SLEEP AND EAT

IBUSZ (Révész tér 2, tel. 52/415–555; open Apr.–Aug., weekdays 8–6, Sat. 8–noon; Sept.–Mar., weekdays 8–4) arranges private rooms (1,500 Ft.). The **Kossuth Lajos University** (Egyetem tér 1, tel. 52/316–666; doubles 1,500 Ft.; closed Sept.–June; cash only) dorms are just north of town near the Great Forest; take Tram 1 from the train station. **Hotel Főnix** (Barna u. 17, at Piac u., tel. 52/413–355), a five-minute walk from the train station, has well-kept doubles (2,600 Ft.–4,200 Ft.). **Thermal Camping** (Nagyerdei krt. 102, tel. 52/412–456), in the Great Forest near Debrecen's thermal baths (*see above*), has tent sites (350 Ft. plus 450 Ft. per person). Reserve ahead during summer festivals. **Sörpince a Flaskához** (Miklos u. 4, at Piac u., tel. 52/414–582) serves outstanding Hungarian soups, stuffed pancakes, and an array of spiced and stuffed pork hocks (450 Ft. and up). **Gilbert Pizzeria** (Kálvin tér 5, tel. 52/343–681; cash only) serves delicious pizzas and pastas.

KECSKEMET

If you've only got a few days in Hungary and want a quick glimpse of the Great Plain, head for Kecskemét. This small, charmed town, about an hour south of Budapest, was spared the ravages of 16th-century Ottoman invaders and has since grown to become the prosperous capital of the biggest wine-growing region in Hungary. Skirted by acres of vineyards and apricot orchards, Kecskemét is also a favored stomping-ground for artists, and some of the funkiest mini-museums in the country are here.

On the town's main square, **Szabadság tér,** you'll find crowded cafés and bars stocking the region's famous *barack pálinka* (apricot brandy). At the square's southwest corner stands the Hungarian art nouveau (i.e., lots of turrets and colorful tiles) **Town Hall,** built in 1893; listen for the hourly chime of the hall's bells. At the square's northern end is the classic art nouveau **Cifra Palota** (Fancy Palace), which houses the **Kecskeméti Képtár** (Rákóczi út 1, tel. 76/480–776; admission 110 Ft., free Thur.; open Tues.–Sun. 10–5), exhibiting works by István Farkas and other Hungarian artists. To reach Szabadság tér from the **train** and **bus** stations, walk south past József Katona Park and then west on Rákóczi út. Trains travel north to Budapest (1 hr 10 min, 700 Ft.).

WHERE TO SLEEP AND EAT

Drop by **Tourinform** (Kossuth tér 1, tel. 76/481–065; open June–Aug., weekdays 8–6, weekends 9–1; shorter hrs off season) for tips on lodging, museums, and other town sights, including a handful of nearby thermal pools. **IBUSZ** (Kossuth tér 3, tel. 76/486–955; open June–Aug., weekdays 8:30–4:30, Sat. 9–noon; closed Sat. off season) arranges private rooms from 2,000 Ft. per room. **Caissa Panzió** (Gyenes tér 18, tel. 76/481–685; doubles from 2,700 Ft.; cash only) has gorgeous fifth-floor rooms with TVs. From Szabadság tér, walk north on Minály/Móricz Zsigmond utca, then left at Jokai tér. The sirloin steak (1,300 Ft.) and stuffed turkey breast astound at **H.B.H. Bajor Söröző** (Csányi u. 4, near Szabadság tér, tel. 76/481–945). Vegetarian dishes are available on request, and the menu is in English.

NEAR KECSKEMET

BUGAC AND THE KISKUNSA NATIONAL PARK

Huge, flat, grassy **Kiskunság National Park** takes up some 87,000 acres surrounding Kecskemét. Both the park and the area around it are a great place for long, leisurely strolls; the biggest and most famous chunk of Kiskunság is easily accessible from the village of Bugac. Buses go from Kecskemét to Bugac (40 min, 250 Ft.) five times daily; ask the driver to drop you off at the park entrance, at the end of Pustal út, due west of town. The 700 Ft. admission to the park includes a half-hour **horse show,** held April–October daily at 1 PM. During the performance, adrenaline-charged Hungarian cowboys stand on the backs of racing steeds and perform all manner of slapstick comedy. There's a restaurant and a campground (sorry, no bungalows) at the park's entrance.

IRELAND

14

B efore 1492 and all that, Ireland was on the very edge of the European universe. To the merchants and explorers who chanced upon this storm-battered isle, Ireland was a wild, indomitable place, mysterious and brooding; a land that, viewed from afar, appeared to rise in defiance from the water. To the medieval mind, Ireland was only a short sail away from oblivion.

The history of Ireland is the history of its many conquerors: the Celts, Vikings, Anglo-Normans, and British. The arrival of the Celts, a Continental tribe of warriors, in the 6th century BC began a fabled period in Irish history, a time when Druids (the Celts' priests and teachers) spread their wisdom, bards recited epic poetry, and ferocious warriors roamed in search of honor, glory, and heads. The Christians appeared around the 4th century AD with Latin and learning, and while continental Europe languished in the so-called Dark Ages, Ireland became a beacon of enlightenment. Christianity and the Catholic church are still pervasive forces in Ireland, though a wave of modernism has recently swept across the nation, best illustrated by a growth in anti-clericalism; a recent referendum made divorce legal in some cases.

The most serious threat to the Christians was the Vikings, who began their conquest of the coast around 800. The Vikings established many of Ireland's greatest cities, including Dublin, and dominated the area well into the 11th century. In 1155, English-born Pope Adrian IV boldly granted dominion over Ireland to his fellow Englishman King Henry II. By the time the last of Ireland's Gaelic kings lost his land to the British in 1603, Ireland had become a servile colony lorded over by English nobles. Conquered and subdued, Celtic Ireland faded slowly into oblivion, its culture and traditions relegated to imagination, myth, and fairy tale.

Following King Henry VIII's conversion to Protestantism in 1534, Ireland was divided not only along political lines but also along religious ones. Under charter from Elizabeth I, Scottish Presbyterians settled on the lands of defeated Ulster chieftains, sowing the seeds of a sectarian conflict that haunts Northern Ireland to this day. Later in the 17th century, the religious schism became the focus of renewed animosity in the aftermath of the English Civil War, in which the pro-Catholic Charles I was deposed by the vigorously Protestant Oliver Cromwell. Intent on making Ireland a Protestant country, Cromwell arrived with his troops in 1649, launching a campaign of persecution against the already bitter Irish Catholics.

Worse was still to come in the wake of Cromwell's Act of Settlement (1652), which called for the forced migration of all Catholics west of the River Shannon. If they removed themselves from the anglicized and

IRELAND

ATLANTIC OCEAN

North Channel

Malin Head
Fanad Head
Tory Island

Portrush
Giant's Causeway
Coleraine
Cushendall
TO CAIRNRYAN, STANRAER
Larne

Aranmore Island
Gweebarra Bay
Letterkenny
Derry
DERRY
NORTHERN IRELAND (Great Britain)
ANTRIM
Belfast
TO LIVERPOOL, ISLE OF MAN

DONEGAL

Glencolumbkille
Donegal
Omagh
TYRONE
Lisburn
DOWN

Kilcar
Killybegs
Enniskillen
Lower Lough Erne
FERMANAGH
Upper Lough Erne
Armagh City
ARMAGH
Lough Neagh
Newcastle

Donegal Bay

Killala Bay
Killala
Sligo Bay
Sligo Town
SLIGO
LEITRIM
Monaghan Town
MONAGHAN
Newry

Belmullet
Bangor
Lough Conn
MAYO
ROSCOMMON
CAVAN
Cavan
LOUTH
Dundalk

Achill Island
Clare Island
Castlebar
WESTMEATH
MEATH
Drogheda

Irish Sea

Westport
Lough Mask
Cong
Mullingar

Inishbofin
Cleggan
Lough Corrib
GALWAY
Athlone
TO LIVERPOOL, HOLYHEAD, DOUGLAS

Clifden
Galway City
REPUBLIC OF IRELAND
Dublin
DUBLIN

Rossaveal
Galway Bay
OFFALY
Bray
TO HOLYHEAD

Aran Islands
Doolin
Kilfenora
CLARE
Portlaoise
KILDARE
Glendalough
Dun Laoghaire

Cliffs of Moher
Rosecrea
LAOISE
WICKLOW
Wicklow Town

Kilkee
Ennis
Limerick City
CARLOW
Arklow

Listowel
Shannon
LIMERICK
Rock of Cashel
Cashel
TIPPERARY
KILKENNY
Kilkenny Town
WEXFORD
Wexford Town

Mouth of the Shannon
Tralee
Cahir
Clonmel
Waterford City
Rosslare Harbour
TO FISHGUARD, LE HAVRE, CHERBOURG, PEMBROKE

Dingle
Dingle Peninsula
KERRY
Mallow
WATERFORD
Tramore

Blasket Islands
Dingle Bay
Killarney
CORK
Cork City
Youghal

Cahirciveen
Iveragh Peninsula
Kenmare
Blarney
Cobh
Kinsale

Valencia Island
Skellig Rocks
Glenbeigh
Beara Peninsula
Kenmare Bay
Bantry
Clonakilty

Mizen Head Peninsula
Baltimore
Cape Clear and Sherkin Island
Bantry Bay

St. George's Channel

N

KEY
—⊢— Rail Lines
🚢 Ferry Lines

0   40 miles
0   60 km

TO ROSCOFF, LE HAVRE

488

increasingly commercialized east, the Gaels were welcome to go, in Cromwell's words, either "to Hell or Connaught." To this day, many in Ireland feel bitter animosity toward the British, whom they blame for more than one grim chapter in their country's history.

But Ireland has effected its own sweet form of revenge: the development of an identity that is rooted in shared suffering, in the subtle twist of a phrase, and—perhaps most important of all—in the realization that time and an unhurried lifestyle are the luxuries of the vanquished. In the words of Oliver Goldsmith, one of Ireland's great Anglo-Irish authors: "The natives are peculiarly remarkable for their gaiety . . . and levity; English transplanted here lose their serious melancholy and become gay and thoughtless, more fond of pleasure and less addicted to reason." To the Irish, these are the highest of compliments.

BASICS

MONEY

US$1 ł = 64 pence and 1 pound ł = US$1.55. The Irish currency is technically known as the punt, but nearly everyone calls it the Irish pound. Notes come in denominations of £5, £10, £20, £50, and (rarely seen) £100; coins come in denominations of 1p, 2p, 5p, 10p, 20p, 50p, and £1. Remember that Irish and English pounds are *not* interchangeable. Exchanging money in Ireland is rarely a problem; nearly every backwater town has a Bank of Ireland or Allied Irish branch. In general, Irish banks are open weekdays 10–12:30 and 1:30–3. For weekend exchanges, try gift shops (which extort large commissions) or, in larger towns, post offices.

The Virgin Mary is Ireland's true queen. She appears in the unlikeliest of places—in glass-enclosed shrines, in run-down Dublin apartments, at the intersections of country roads, along stone quarries, and carved into green hillsides.

HOW MUCH IT WILL COST • Ireland is by no means cheap. Hostels cost about £7–£12 a night, a double in a B&B will run £26–£35, cheap grub can be found for £3–£5, and decent sit-down meals are £8 and up. If you stay in hostels and generally watch your budget, you can probably get by on $40–$45 a day.

COMING AND GOING

BY FERRY • Dublin has two main ferry ports for passengers from Britain, one at the docks and one in nearby Dún Laoghaire. **Irish Ferries** (tel. 01/679–7977) and **Stena Sealink** (tel. 01/204–7700) are the carriers; both sail from Holyhead, in Wales, and the trip takes 3½ hours. One-way fares begin at about £25. Irish Ferries also runs a service from Le Havre and Cherbourg in France to Cork and Rosslare, respectively. The journey from France to Ireland costs £68–£95 but is free for those with a Eurailpass, and all ferries are discounted 20%–50% for all Eurail, InterRail, ISIC, and Travelsave-stamp holders (*see* Getting Around, *below*).

BY PLANE • Ireland has two principal airports, **Dublin International** and **Shannon International,** near Limerick in southwest Ireland. Some flights originating in the United States land and clear customs in Shannon, where you can catch any one of a dozen daily connections to Dublin; others fly directly to Dublin. Ireland's major carriers are **Aer Lingus** (tel. 01/844–4777) and **Ryanair** (tel. 01/677–4422).

GETTING AROUND

Ireland's trains and express buses (which serve major cities) are free or discounted for all InterRail and Eurailpass holders. The **Irish Explorer** pass allows unlimited train and bus travel on 8 out of 15 consecutive days for £90. Both the Travelsave stamp and the Fair Card are available from **Bord Fáilte,** the Irish Tourist Board; **USIT,** Ireland's excellent student-run travel organization (with offices for all travelers in Dublin, Cork, and Galway); and most Bus Éireann depots.

BY BIKE • Ireland is a cyclist's paradise. The roads are flat and uncrowded, the scenery is phenomenal, and the distance from one village to the next is rarely more than 10 mi. On the down side, foul weather and rough roads are all too common, so rain gear and spare parts are essential. You can rent bikes from **Raleigh Rent-A-Bike,** with dealers throughout Ireland; the going rate is £7 per day or £30 per week, plus a refundable deposit of £40. For a list of Raleigh Rent-A-Bike shops, contact any Bord Fáilte tourist office or dial 01/626–1333.

BY BUS • Bus Éireann (Busáras, Store St., Dublin, tel. 01/836–6611), Ireland's national bus service, provides reasonably priced, comfortable service to nearly every town in Ireland. Bus fares are generally £5–£10 cheaper than the equivalent train fare, and since Ireland's rail network only covers the large hubs, you'll probably end up taking a bus at least once. Expressway routes (discounted to Eurailpass holders) are listed in yellow in the Bus Éireann timetable (70p), available at any depot or at the Dublin office. Bus Éireann also issues **Rambler** tickets, good for bus travel in the Republic for 3 out of 8 days (£28), 8 out of 16 days (£68), and 15 out of 30 days (£98).

BY TRAIN • Ireland's rail network is modern and comfortable, but it only serves major cities. Trains generally run between 5 AM and midnight, making it impossible to sleep on trains. Reservations are a good idea on the popular Dublin–Galway, Dublin–Cork, and Dublin–Wexford routes, especially on summer weekends. Irish trains are operated by **Iarnród Éireann** (Irish Rail), the state-owned rail company. Stop by any depot or their Dublin office (35 Lower Abbey St., tel. 01/836–6222) for a timetable (50p).

HITCHING • Ireland seems to be one of the world's few bastions of easy and (relatively) safe hitchhiking. Everyone does it: schoolgirls in frocks and pigtails; twentysomethings heading to the nearest dole office; retired couples going to town for groceries; and, of course, backpackers. If you're traveling between big cities, head to the appropriate highway and stake your claim either well before or well after a roundabout. Of course, safety requires common sense, and everyone—especially women traveling solo—should carefully consider the risks. Avoid hitching at night and into and out of big cities, and refuse a ride with anyone who gives you the creeps.

WHERE TO SLEEP

Without exception, Irish hotels charge £30–£60 *per person* for a night's accommodation, so get used to sleeping in hostels or, for about an extra £10, in cozy B&Bs. Ireland also has hundreds of campgrounds, which typically charge £3–£5 per tent site plus an additional 20p–£1 per person. Many are only open from April through September or October, and in summer the majority are quite crowded. Reserve ahead whenever possible.

Youth hostels offer the cheapest beds in Ireland—generally between £6 and £10 per person. Despite their name, youth hostels welcome all guests, regardless of age. There are two main youth-hostel associations in Ireland. **An Óige,** the "official" association, is affiliated with Hostelling International. If you have an HI card, you do not need a separate An Óige pass; if not, you must purchase a "welcome stamp" (£7.50) from An Óige's Dublin office or any member hostel. Almost all An Óige hostels have 11 PM curfews, daytime bedroom lockouts, and check-in between 8 AM–11 AM and 5 PM–8 PM only. Unless you bring your own sleep sheet or sleeping bag, you must rent one (85p). A better bet is hostels overseen by the **Independent Holiday Hostels** (Doolin, Co. Clare, tel. 065/74006), a friendly organization that boasts nearly 90 hostels throughout Ireland. At IHH hostels, you don't need a membership card, you can check in whenever you like, and there are no curfews or daytime lockouts. Many IHH hostel also have camping facilities. Try to reserve ahead; they are often booked solid in summer.

VISITOR INFORMATION

Bord Fáilte, the umbrella organization for Ireland's seven regional tourist boards, will fill your pockets with maps, brochures, and pamphlets, including a number of helpful lodging guides. Their main office (Baggot St. Bridge, Dublin) makes lodging reservations for the whole country; dial 01/602–400.

PHONES

Country code: 353. Within Ireland, the cost of a three-minute local call is 20p. If you run into trouble, dial 10 to speak with an Irish operator (free). For free **directory assistance,** dial 1190. To place collect and credit-card calls to the United States, call **AT&T** Direct Access^{SM} (tel. 800/550–000), **MCI** (tel. 800/551–001), or **Sprint** (tel. 800/552–001) from any phone. If you're calling Ireland from abroad, drop the "0" from all area codes.

MAIL

The Irish mail service is known as **An Post.** Post offices and smaller substations (generally housed in the backs of shops or newsagents) are located in every block-long town in Ireland. All offices sell stamps—52p per letter and 38p per postcard for international destinations, 32p per letter and 28p per postcard for domestic and EU destinations. Larger offices offer competitive currency exchange and are usually open Monday–Saturday 9–1 and 2:15–5:30.

DUBLIN

James Joyce provided a detailed map of turn-of-the-century Dublin in *Ulysses*, and, except for a few name and street changes, not much has changed. The dirty lanes, soot-covered flats, dockside slums, and smoky pubs are all still here. Many of the people, too, seem to be from a distant era: portly grand-mums complaining about the price of tea in Bewley's Café, gruff pubflies soaking themselves in stout while triple-checking the horse sheets between hellos and handshakes. But Dublin in the late 1990s is in the midst of great change. European Union funds and an economic upswing have inspired a modernization program, resulting in new construction on every second street. In the wake of this boom the yuppie has truly come to Dublin, armed with the ubiquitous cell phone; don't be surprised if you pass a few sushi bars and espresso cafés on the streets of the old capital.

The capital of modern Ireland, Dublin was first settled by Celtic traders during the 2nd century AD. The Celts named it *Baile Atha Cliath,* or City of the Hurdles, a name still used by Gaelic speakers. Dublin's convenient location by the River Liffey, however, meant that it was only a matter of time before the Vikings got wind of the settlement and descended en masse in their dreaded longboats; by AD 850, Dublin, known then by the Norse name *Dubh Linn* (Black Pool), was firmly under Viking control.

The Vikings remained the major force in Dublin for 200 years, often marrying into and assuming the native culture. During the early Middle Ages, Dublin was thoroughly refashioned as political ties between Ireland and England were strengthened. Under the guidance of the English—who provided the money, artisans, and urban planners—the city grew into a modern capital. Over time, the English influence also led to Trinity College (founded in 1591) and to the city's Victorian and Georgian architecture. But despite their English flavor, places like Merrion Square and northside appear uniquely Irish, if only because they're hemmed in by the grimy tenements of working-class Dublin. Despite recent growth in employment, the jobless rate hovers around 40% in some parts of the city, so don't be surprised to see beggars and ragged drunks, even horse-drawn carts pulling loads of trash or coal. The tourist board does its best to suppress such images of Ireland's "cosmopolitan capital," but you'll probably find that this grittiness and the constant play between the ancient and modern are at the heart of Dublin's appeal.

BASICS

AMERICAN EXPRESS

116 Grafton St., directly across from Trinity College, tel. 01/677–2874. Open weekdays 9–5, Sat. 9–noon.

DISCOUNT TRAVEL AGENCIES

USIT. Besides offering currency exchange and heaps of information on budget travel in Ireland, this neon agency can book you on any rail, plane, or boat tour imaginable. Arrive early to avoid hour-long lines. *19 Aston Quay, west of O'Connell Bridge, tel. 01/677–8117. Open weekdays 9–6 (Thurs. until 8), Sat. 11–4.*

MAIL

Towering over O'Connell Street, two blocks north of the River Liffey, is the majestic **General Post Office** (GPO). For currency exchange, walk inside, turn left, and follow the signs. *1 Prince's St., at O'Connell St., tel. 01/705–7000. Open Mon.–Sat. 8–8, Sun. 10–6:30.*

VISITOR INFORMATION

An Óige, the Irish Youth Hostel Association, provides maps and listings of its hostels as well as tons of information on sights, tours, transportation, and the like. *61 Mountjoy St., tel. 01/830–1766 or 01/830–4555, fax 01/830–5808. Open weekdays 10–5.*

The best **Dublin Tourism** office is the new one-stop branch on Suffolk Street: Gray Line tours, Bus Éirrean, AmEx, and Irish Ferries all have offices inside. At any office you can book a room (£1 fee, plus 10% deposit), pick up train and bus schedules, and buy walking-tour guides. *2 Suffolk St., tel. 01/605–7777. Open July–Aug., Mon.–Sat. 9–8:30, Sun. 11–5:30. Other locations: Baggot St. Bridge, facing Grand Canal; Dublin Airport, main terminal; Dún Laoghaire Ferry Terminal.*

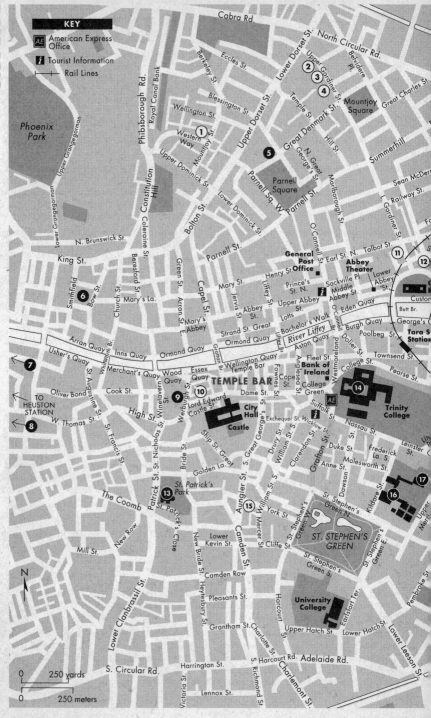

KEY

AE American Express Office

i Tourist Information

⊢⊣ Rail Lines

Phoenix Park

Cabra Rd.

North Circular Rd.

Eccles St.

Berkeley St.

Blessington St.

Wellington St.

Lower Dorset St.

Upper Gardiner St.

Belvedere Pl.

Great Charles St.

Mountjoy Square

Summerhill

Sean McDermott

L. Gardiner St.

Railway St.

Phibsborough Rd.

Royal Canal Bank

Western Way

Upper Dorset St.

Temple St.

Great Denmark St.

Hill St.

N. Great George's St.

Marlborough St.

Upper Dominick St.

Lower Dominick St.

Constitution Hill

Upper Grangegorman

Lower Grangegorman

Parnell Sq. W.

Parnell Square

Parnell Sq. N.

Parnell St.

O'Connell St.

Earl St. N.

Talbot St.

General Post Office

Abbey Theater

Henry St.

Prince's St. N.

Sackville Pl.

Lower Abbey St.

N. Brunswick St.

King St.

Bolton St.

Capel St.

Green St.

Beresford St.

Church St.

Mary's La.

Mary St.

Liffey St.

Jervis St.

Abbey St.

Upper Abbey St.

Middle Abbey St.

O'Connell St.

Eden Quay

Custom

Butt Br.

George's

Tara S Station

Smithfield

Bow St.

Arran St.

Mary's Abbey

Strand St. Great

Lotts

Bachelor's Walk

Burgh Quay

Poolbeg

Arran Quay

Inns Quay

Ormond Quay

River Liffey

Ormond Quay

Grattan Br.

Aston Quay

Westmoreland St.

D'Olier St.

Townsend St.

Usher's Quay

Whitworth Br.

Merchant's Quay

Wood Quay

Essex Quay

Wellington Quay

Temple Bar

Fleet St.

Anglesea St.

Copeland St.

College St.

Pearse St.

Oliver Bond

St. Augustine St.

Cook St.

Winetavern St.

TEMPLE BAR

Dame St.

Bank of Ireland

College Green

AE

Suffolk St.

Trinity College

TO HEUSTON STATION

W. Thomas St.

High St.

Lord Edward St.

City Hall

Castle

Exchequer St.

George's St.

i

Nassau St.

Wicklow St.

Frederick La. S.

Leinster St.

St. Francis St.

St. Nicholas St.

Bride St.

Ship St. Great

Werburgh St.

Drury St.

William St.

Clarendon St.

Grafton St.

Duke St.

Anne St.

Molesworth St.

The Coomb

Patrick St.

St. Patrick's Close

St. Patrick's Park

Golden La.

Dawson St.

Kildare St.

Upper Merri

New Row

Patrick St.

Lower Kevin St.

Camden St.

Mercer St.

York St.

William St. S.

Aungier St.

St. Stephen's Green N.

St. Stephen's Green

ST. STEPHEN'S GREEN

St. Stephen's Green E.

Mill St.

Lower Clanbrassil St.

New Bride St.

Heytesbury St.

Camden Row

Pleasants St.

Cliffe St.

St. Stephen's Green S.

Upper Merri

University College

Harcourt St.

Upper Hatch St.

Lower Hatch St.

Lower Leeson St.

Pembroke St.

Grantham St.

Charlotte St.

Camden St.

Eastfort Ter.

N

S. Circular Rd.

Harrington St.

Victoria St.

S. Harcourt Rd.

Adelaide Rd.

Richmond St.

Charlemont St.

Lennox St.

0   250 yards

0   250 meters

① ② ③ ④ ⑤ ⑥ ⑦ ⑧ ⑨ ⑩ ⑪ ⑫ ⑬ ⑭ ⑮ ⑯ ⑰

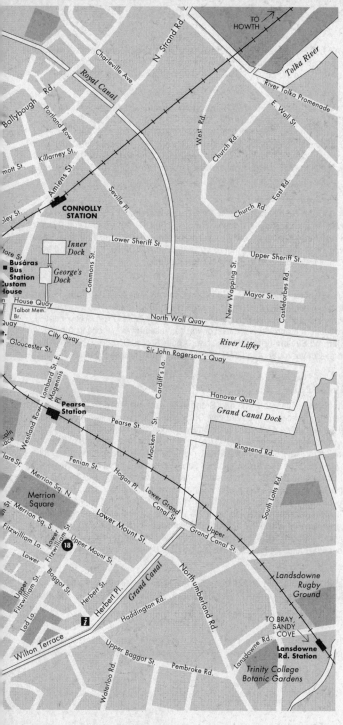

Sights ●

Christ Church Cathedral, **9**

Dublin Writers Museum, **5**

Guinness Brewery, **8**

Irish Museum of Modern Art (Kilmainham Hospital), **7**

Irish Whiskey Corner, **6**

National Gallery of Ireland, **17**

National Museum of Ireland, **16**

Number 29, **18**

St. Patrick's Cathedral, **13**

Trinity College, **14**

Lodging ○

Avalon House (IHH), **15**

Dublin International Youth Hostel (An Óige), **1**

Fatima House, **3**

Globetrotters Tourist Hostel (IHH), **11**

Isaac's (IHH), **12**

Kinlay/USIT House (IHH), **10**

Marian Guest House, **4**

Stella Maris, **2**

COMING AND GOING

BY BUS

Busáras (pronounced bus-AR-us), Bus Éireann's sole Dublin depot, is in the city center, around the corner from Connolly Station. You can reach nearly every town in Ireland from here, but Expressway service is offered only to hub cities. *Store St., tel. 01/836–6111. Information desk open daily 8:30–7.*

BY FERRY

Irish Ferries (16 Westmoreland St., tel. 01/679–7977) and **Stena Sealink** (15 Westmoreland St., tel. 01/204–7700) offer regular ferry service to Dublin from Wales (Holyhead). Irish Ferries (2 per day, £20–£25 one way) sails directly into Dublin Harbour; Stena Sealink (4 per day, £26–£35 one way) docks in Dún Laoghaire, 6 mi south of the city center. Prices and schedules vary according to season, so call the companies to confirm. Make reservations in summer. From Dún Laoghaire, a DART train is the most convenient way to reach the city center; from Dublin Harbour, take a bus (£1.10) or taxi (*see below*).

BY PLANE

Dublin Airport (tel. 01/844–4900) is 6½ mi north of town. Daily flights to and from Britain and the Continent are offered by Irish carriers **Aer Lingus** (41 Upper O'Connell St., tel. 01/705–6705) and **Ryanair** (3 Dawson St., tel. 01/677–4422). Between 6 AM and 11 PM express buses (£2.50) run directly between the airport and Busáras depot. You can save some money by taking Bus 41 (£1.10) to the airport from Eden Quay (immediately east of O'Connell Bridge, facing the River Liffey).

BY TRAIN

Dublin has two train stations, **Heuston** (tel. 01/836–6111) and **Connolly** (tel. 01/703–2359), located across town from one another but connected by frequent shuttle buses (90p). Buses leave for Heuston from outside USIT's downtown office; from Heuston Station, take any bus labeled AN LÁR (city center). Connolly Station is a short walk from a number of hostels, or you can take any AN LÁR bus to Trinity College and O'Connell Street. **Iarnród Éireann** (Irish Rail, 35 Lower Abbey St., tel. 01/836–6222) provides information on all domestic passenger routes and DART (Dublin Area Rapid Transport) trains.

GETTING AROUND

Dublin's **northside** (once the home of James Joyce and Brendan Behan), with its disheveled facades and unkempt streets, is the place to soak up the pure city. O'Connell Street, which stretches between the River Liffey and **Parnell Square,** is the northside's main artery, filled to overflowing with cheap tourist shops and neon fast-food outlets. **Henry Street** runs off O'Connell Street and leads into one of the city's main shopping districts, including the glorious **More Street** markets; you're sure to hear the Dublin accent here in all its rough splendor. The area around Parnell Square has a well-deserved reputation for being dangerous at night. Dublin's **southside,** with its smart shopping avenues and rowdy pubs and cafés in the **Temple Bar** district, is where you'll probably want to spend most of your time. **Trinity College** and the adjacent **Bank of Ireland,** a block south of the Liffey from O'Connell Bridge, are the area's most famous landmarks. Any bus labeled CITY CENTER or AN LAR will eventually deposit you somewhere near here. Dublin's meager excuse for a subway is **DART** (Dublin Area Rapid Transport), an aboveground train that connects central Dublin with some of the suburbs. DART trains run daily between 6:30 AM and 11:30 PM. Single (one-way) fares range between 65p and £1.60.

BY BUS

Buses run between 6 AM and 11:30 PM. Fares range from 35p to £1.25, and all drivers make change. **Bus Atha Cliath** (Dublin Bus, 59 Upper O'Connell St., tel. 01/873–4222; closed Sun.) stocks free maps and timetables.

BY TAXI

There's no shortage of taxis in Dublin, but at £1 per mi, you may do better to explore the city center on foot. If you don't see any cabs, call **Castle Cabs** (tel. 01/831–9000) or **City Cabs** (tel. 01/872–7272). Tipping is optional.

WHERE TO SLEEP

The city center is peppered with B&Bs and hostels. The majority lie just north of the River Liffey near the bus station and Parnell Square—Talbot and Gardiner are good streets to try—and south of the river near Trinity College. Reserve in advance during the summer. Tourist offices have lodging guides and will book rooms; there are also **automated reservation kiosks** at the airport and the Suffolk Street tourist office. With a Visa card, you can book a room at these machines, which will then spit out your confirmation, a map of Dublin, and directions to the lodging.

Fatima House. For £22 per person (£18 off season), you'll get a simple, comfortable room in a plain northside house. The thickly fried breakfast can't be beat. *17 Upper Gardiner St., tel. 01/874-5292.*

Marian Guest House. Here's a clean, quiet home run by a friendly woman who'll talk your ear off. Beds £15 per person. *21 Upper Gardiner St., tel. 01/874-4129.*

Stella Maris. High ceilings and an oak staircase grace this beautiful old house. Airy and bright rooms cost £20-£25 per person, depending on the room. The snug common room is littered with antiques and books. *13 Upper Gardiner St., tel. 01/874-0835.*

HOSTELS

Avalon House (IHH). This hostel is an elegant Georgian relic with dorm beds (£7.50, £10.50 in summer) and doubles (£28-£30). *55 Aungier St., tel. 01/475-0001. From city center, Bus 16, 16A, 19, or 22 to front door. Kitchen, laundry.*

> *To blend in with locals, eat only when faint, scorn all fruits and vegetables, and drink plenty of stout.*

Dublin International Youth Hostel (An Oige). Housed in a 19th-century convent, this enormous hostel is centrally located and the first to fill up in summer. Beds cost £7.50 (£9.50 in summer). *61 Mountjoy St., tel. 01/830-4555. From bus station walk north on Lower Gardiner St.*

Globetrotters Tourist Hostel (IHH). The wonderful Globetrotters has an outdoor courtyard, comfortable rooms, and an all-you-can-eat breakfast. You're within walking distance of the city center, one block from the bus station, and two blocks from the train station. Beds cost £11-£12 (£14 July-Sept.). *46 Lower Gardiner St., near Lower Abbey St., tel. 01/873-5893. Luggage storage.*

Isaac's (IHH). This noisy northside hostel caters to good-natured vagabonds and international students. Dorm rooms are large and institutional (beds £6.25-£8.50). *2-5 Frenchman's La., around corner from Busáas depot, tel. 01/874-9321. Lockout 11 AM-5 PM.*

Kinlay/USIT House (IHH). In southside Dublin, this hostel is like something from a Dickens novel, with red masonry and wrought-iron fixtures. Musty but comfy dorm beds are £8.50, doubles £25; both rates include breakfast. The staff will also change money and store luggage. *2-12 Lord Edward St., tel. 01/679-6644. From Trinity College, walk west on Dame St. Kitchen.*

FOOD

Budget dining in Dublin is not a transporting experience. Get used to dull sandwiches, bags of greasy chips, eggs and bacon, Cadbury chocolate, and Guinness. Besides local chains like **Abrakebabra** (whose lamb-filled pita pockets are a Dublin staple) and **Beshoff's** (fast-food fish), Dublin's essential eateries are chippers—grungy holes-in-the-wall that serve burgers, chips, chicken, and sausage and eggs for £2-£4.

UNDER £5 • Alpha Restaurant. Popular with Dubliners who hold quantity and fair prices above quality, Alpha serves eggs and beans or roast and potatoes for under £4. It's hard to find; look for a shop with a small neon sign in the window, and go up two flights. *37 Wicklow St., off Grafton St., tel. 01/767-0213. Closed Sun.*

Leo Burdock's Traditional Fish and Chips. U2, Liam Neeson, Mick Jagger, and Rod Stewart are regulars at this popular take-away. For £2.50, try the fresh cod, haddock, whiting, or plaice with a side of tomato and tartar sauce. *2 Wherburgh St., tel. 01/497-3177. Closed Sun.*

Munchies. The ultimate sandwich shop fills thick slabs of freshly baked bread with your choice of meat (tandoori chicken, tuna, roast turkey) for about £3.50. *2 locations: 146A Lower Baggot St.; 2 S. William St.*

Cornucopia. A pioneer among Dublin vegetarian eateries, Cornucopia still serves a menu of fine soups (try the spicy spinach) and sandwiches for £3–£4. The Vegetarian Fry Breakfast includes excellent meatless sausages. *19 Wicklow St., tel. 01/677–7583. Closed Sun.*

UNDER £10 • Cleary's Restaurant. Popular with the older locals, the famous Cleary's department store on O'Connell Street is a well-kept secret on Dublin's budget-food scene. Its third-floor restaurant has a standard, meat-and-two-veg dining room, an elegant tea room with a full lunch menu, and a coffee shop with pastries and sandwiches. *O'Connell St., tel. 01/878–6000. Open Mon.–Sat. 9–5.*

Elephant & Castle. In the heart of Temple Bar, the Elephant & Castle is one of Dublin's most accessible upscale restaurants, filling up daily with wealthy businesspeople and ragged Trinity students. Try the huge, delicious hamburgers (£6) or the Chinese chicken salad (£9.50). *18 Temple Bar, tel. 01/679–3121.*

La Mezza Luna. Enjoy reasonably priced Italian food, like salads (£3–£5) and daily pasta specials (£7), in a hip, eclectic setting. The Death by Chocolate cake (£3) should not be attempted alone. *Temple Ln., corner of Dame and S. Great Georges Sts., tel. 01/671–2840.*

COFFEEHOUSES

The **Winding Stair Café and Bookshop** (40 Lower Ormonde Quay, tel. 01/873–3292) has a fabulous view of the River Liffey. Dubliners spend a good deal of the day at one of three **Bewley's Café**s, the city's oldest (founded in 1847) and most famous coffeehouse. *3 locations: 78 Grafton St., tel. 01/677–6761; 13 S. Great George's St., tel. 01/679–2078; 12 Westmoreland St., tel. 01/677–6761.*

WORTH SEEING

Dublin Tourism offices offer several snazzy walking guides (£2.50) highlighting particular aspects of the city, such as the "Rock and Stroll" guide to the fave hangouts of Irish rock stars. Writers who like to drink, or drinkers who like to write, can go on the **Jameson Dublin Literary Pub Crawl** (no phone; £6), a guided performance tour of pubs with literary associations. A couple of Dublin bit players act and sing various texts for two hours while everyone gets loopy on Guinness. Tours leave nightly at 7:30 PM from Easter to Oct. 2 (Thurs.–Sat. only from Nov. to Mar.), and at noon on Sunday year-round, from the Duke pub on Duke Street. **Historical Walking Tours of Dublin** (tel. 01/845–1241) nabs some of the city's most knowledgeable guides for its two-hour rambles (£5). Meet outside Trinity College. **Gray Line Tours** (tel. 01/605–7705) runs popular three-hour bus tours (£6.50) that allow you to get off the bus and check out Dublin's main sights.

CHRIST CHURCH CATHEDRAL

Christ Church, the Church of Ireland's flagship, is also Dublin's oldest standing monument, founded in 1038 by the mead-swilling Sitric, king of the Dublin Norsemen. Check out the lavishly detailed fenestration and gallery-level carvings and the famous "leaning wall of Dublin." The crypt contains some fine religious relics and a set of 17th-century punishment stocks. *Christ Church Pl., tel. 01/677–8099. Admission: £1. Open daily 10–5.*

DUBLIN WRITERS MUSEUM

Rare manuscripts, personal effects, and a rich collection of portraits and publicity posters commemorate Ireland's most famous writers in this splendid Georgian house. Ireland's four Nobel Prize winners (Shaw, Yeats, Beckett, and Heaney) are especially well represented, along with Wilde, O'Casey, Behan, Swift, Joyce, and Synge. *18 Parnell Sq. N, tel. 01/872–2077. From O'Connell Bridge, walk north on O'Connell St. to Parnell Sq. Admission: £2.90. Open Mon.–Sat. 10–5, Sun. 11:30–6.*

GUINNESS BREWERY

Located in the heart of the Liberties—an area filled with empty warehouses and redbrick tenements that used to house Guinness employees—the Guinness Brewery is the most popular tourist destination in town. The brewery itself is off-limits, but the part-museum, part–gift shop **Hop Store** (lined with vats, barley roasters, and Guinness memorabilia) is open year-round. After a brief tour and film, enjoy a free glass of what's generally considered the best Guinness in the world, poured straight from the adjoining brewery. Afterward, spend some time walking the perimeter of the 65-acre brewery, which has changed little since Arthur Guinness opened it in 1759. *Crane St., tel. 01/453–6700. From Trinity College, walk west on Dame St./Lord Edward St./High St./Thomas St., turn left on Crane St. Admission: £3. Open Mon.–Sat. 9:30–5, Sun. 10:30–4:30.*

IRISH MUSEUM OF MODERN ART (KILMAINHAM HOSPITAL)

The Royal Hospital of Kilmainham, built in 1684 to house retired soldiers in style, is itself one of the best examples of aristocratic, 17th-century Dublin architecture. Restored and converted by the Irish government in 1986, it now houses an excellent collection of works by Rembrandt, Dürer, Manet, and Hogarth, along with temporary exhibits. *Corner of Steven's La. and James's St., tel. 01/671–8666. Walk west along Liffey and turn left on Steven's La.; or take Bus 68, 68A, 69, 78A, 79, or 90. Admission free. Open Tues.–Sat. 10–5:30, Sun. noon–5:30.*

NATIONAL GALLERY OF IRELAND

Established by Act of Parliament in 1854, this museum is a visitors' must, with a permanent collection of more than 3,000 paintings, sculptures, and etchings. Feast on numerous examples of the 17th-century Italian, French, Spanish, and Irish schools and a small collection of Dutch Masters. *Merrion Sq. W, tel. 01/661–5133. From Trinity College, walk east ½ mi on Nassau St., turn right at Merrion Sq. Admission free. Open Mon.–Sat. 10–5:30 (Thurs. until 8:30), Sun. 2–5.*

NATIONAL MUSEUM OF IRELAND

When a work crew unearths the odd Viking tool or Celtic brooch, it gets shipped to this outstanding museum for display. The glorious Ardagh Chalice is the star of the collection. *Kildare St. and Merrion Row, tel. 01/677–7444. Admission free. Open Tues.–Sat. 10–5, Sun. 2–5.*

NUMBER 29

Everything in this exquisite Georgian town house has been meticulously refurbished to the taste of the period 1790–1820. Hand-painted trunks and porcelain dolls are strewn about the attic, and hairbrushes and jewelry sit expectantly on lace-covered dressers. *29 Lower Fitzwilliam St., opposite Merrion Sq., tel. 01/702–6165. Admission: £2.50. Open Tues.–Sat. 10–5, Sun. 2–5.*

St. Stephen's Green, at the south end of Kildare Street, is a magnificent southside park lined by Georgian houses and filled with lakeside paths, gardens, duck ponds, and statues. Several buildings on the south side of the square used to house the Catholic University of Ireland, where Stephen Dedalus studied in "Portrait of the Artist as a Young Man."

ST. PATRICK'S CATHEDRAL

*A hot new monument in 1190, St. Patrick's stands on the oldest Christian site in Dublin. Jonathan Swift (1667–1745), poet, author, wit, and dean of St. Patrick's from 1713 to 1745, is generously remembered with monuments and plaques. *Patrick's Close, tel. 01/475–4817. Admission: £1.20. Open weekdays 9–6, Sat. 9–5, Sun. 10–4; shorter hrs off season.*

TRINITY COLLEGE

The oldest university in Ireland, Trinity College was established in 1592 by a grant from Queen Elizabeth I of England. Historically, Trinity was Dublin's strongest pro-Brit enclave; the university opened its doors to all creeds at the turn of the century, but as recently as 1966, Irish Catholics faced excommunication for attending classes here. These days nearly 70% of Trinity students are Catholic.

Trinity has produced an impressive list of alumni over the years, including Dracula creator Bram Stoker, writer and deadly satirist Jonathan Swift, and Nobel Prize winner Samuel Beckett. For an excellent overview, catch the **Guided Tour of Trinity** (£4.50, including admission to the Book of Kells exhibit). Try to secure Joseph, resident fop and wit, as your guide; his hourly tours (May–Sept., daily 10:15–3) are notoriously wry. Meet under the main arches and keep your eyes peeled for the gentleman sporting tweed and a pocket kerchief.

In Trinity Library's **Long Room** (admission £3.50; open Mon.–Sat. 9:30–5, Sun. noon–4:30) look for the *Book of Kells*, considered one of the most striking illuminated manuscripts ever produced. This 682-page gospel was obsessively illustrated by monks with a penchant for iconographic doodling and frantic spirals. Equally impressive is the smaller and older *Book of Durrow*, essentially a 7th-century coloring book punctuated now and again with religious verse. Also on display are manuscripts by Beckett, Joyce, and Wilde.

IRISH WHISKEY CORNER

*Learn just how Irish whiskey is made at this small northside museum housed in a former distiller's warehouse. The best part of the compulsory guided tour is—you guessed it—the tasting at the end, when you're free to sample two Irish whiskeys at your leisure. *Bow St., tel. 01/872–5566. Admission: £3. Tours given May–Oct., weekdays at 11, 2:30, and 3:30, Sat. at 2:30 and 3:30; Nov.–Apr., weekdays at 3:30. Reservations advised.*

AFTER DARK

Whether you're up for a staggering pub crawl or a quiet chat over a pint of plain, head to any one of Dublin's 1,000 public houses. If your head is still throbbing from last night's sing-along, stagger to the theater or to any one of a dozen music pubs in the city center. If you're stuck for inspiration, pick up Dublin's excellent weekly magazine, *The Big Issue* (£1), from one of the many street vendors who make their living selling it.

PUBS

As a general rule, the area between Grafton and South Great George's streets is a gold mine for locally popular pubs. Another good bet is the Temple Bar district, sandwiched between Dame Street and the River Liffey.

The Brazen Head. Dublin's oldest pub (built in 1688) served as the headquarters for the rebellious United Irishmen during the late 18th century. Loaded with character and friendly drunks, the Brazen Head has live traditional music nightly. *20 Lower Bridge St., tel. 01/677–9549.*

The George. Across the street from The Globe, this gay/lesbian pub is dimly lit, smoky, and laid-back. The crowd—a good mix of locals and out-of-towners of all ages—wraps itself around the long bar. *89 S. Great George's St., tel. 01/478–2983.*

The Globe. This is *the* pub for the young and progressive, with massive oak tables, old posters, and ambient sounds. Downstairs is the dance club, Rí-Rá, whose atmosphere changes nightly; Thursday is "Funk Off," a debauched evening of '70s-style clothes and hair. *11 S. Great George's St., tel. 01/671–1220.*

The Lincoln Inn. The Lincoln is a fine pub in all respects: dark, quiet, sufficiently ancient, and frequented by Trinity students and leathery locals. Standard pub grub is available for less than £4. *19 Lincoln Pl., by Trinity College, tel. 01/676–2978.*

McDaid's. Most nights you'll hear jazz, blues, or Irish folk music in the upstairs lounge at this popular student pub. *3 Harry St., off Grafton St., tel. 01/679–4395.*

Mulligan's of Poolbeg Street. Journalists, locals, and students flock here for what some argue is the "Best Pint of Guinness on Earth." *8 Poolbeg St., off Pearse St., tel. 01/677–5582.*

Stag's Head. No visit to Dublin is complete without lunch (around £4) at the Stag's Head, the city's most impeccably preserved pub. On weekend nights it's packed with Trinity students. *1 Dame Ct., 1 block south of Dame St., tel. 01/679–3701.*

Toner's. Built in the early 1800s, Toner's still retains its original furnishings and flavor (old men nursing pints, antique books and bottles on the walls). Cheap grub is available daily. *139 Lower Baggot St., tel. 01/676–3090.*

MUSIC

Dublin's music scene is thriving, riding the international wave of U2, Sinead O'Connor, and the Cranberries. Grab a copy of *The Big Issue* for current listings, or take a walk down Grafton Street and keep your ears open. A number of city-center pubs double as independent-music venues: Try **Baggot Inn** (143 Baggot St.), one of the better clubs on the fringe of the city center; the northside club **Slattery's** (129 Capel St.); the rocking **Wexford Inn** (26 Wexford Street); or **The Kitchen** (E. Essex St.), a dance club owned by U2.

THEATER

Dublin's theater scene is impressive even by New York and London standards. Especially popular (with tourists) are the Irish classics staged every summer. If you're in the mood for low-key entertainment with some good-natured song and dance thrown in, **Olympia Theatre's** (73 Dame St., tel. 01/677–7744)

"Midnight at the Olympia," a raucous, cabaret-like mix of music and theater staged on Friday and Saturday nights, is an excellent choice. Shows cost around £7–£10. Contact some of Dublin's better-known theaters for showtimes: **Abbey Theatre** and **Peacock Theatre** (Lower Abbey St., tel. 01/878–7222), **Project Arts Centre** (39 Essex St., tel. 01/671–2321), and **The Gate Theatre** (Parnell Sq., tel. 01/874–4045).

NEAR DUBLIN

GLENDALOUGH

Glendalough, one of Ireland's premier monastic sites, is nestled in the rugged Wicklow mountains among trees, lakes, and acres of heather. Glendalough flourished as a monastic center from around 400 until 1398, when English soldiers plundered the site, leaving it in the ruins you see today. Highlights include **St. Kevin's Cell,** a hive-shaped rock pile by Upper Lake; the perfectly preserved, 108-ft-tall **Round Tower,** built in the 11th or 12th century; the shell of **St. Mary's Church**; and the impressive graveyard.

Sadly, Glendalough has been ruthlessly exploited by the national tourist board, making it one of the most visited sights in eastern Ireland. To make the most of Glendalough, you'll need to arrive early and/or spend the night. Most everyone goes home around 6 PM, when the parking lot and **visitor center** (tel. 0404/45325; admission £2) close for the evening.

COMING AND GOING • Bus Éirrean and **Gray Line Tours** (*see* Worth Seeing *in* Dublin, *above*) organize bus excursions to Glendalough for around £10 per person including admission. A cheaper option is **St. Kevin's** bus service (tel. 01/281–8119; £8 round-trip), which departs daily at 11:30 AM and 6 PM from in front of the Royal College of Surgeons, on St. Stephen's Green in Dublin.

WHERE TO SLEEP • Pick one of the many B&Bs on the road between the ruins and the nearby town of Laragh, or try **Lilac Cottage** (Laragh, tel. 0404/45574), which has tiny rooms for £14 per person. **Gleann Dá Loch** (tel. 0404/45342) youth hostel, a five-minute walk from Glendalough, has dorm beds in spartan rooms for £6.

SOUTHEAST IRELAND

With few typically Irish attractions (romantic coastlines, wild bogs, etc.), the southeast is one of the least visited parts of the country. One of the main reasons for coming, in fact, is strictly practical: Rosslare Harbour, near Wexford, is one of only three ferry ports in the country and is perhaps the most convenient hub for Eurail and InterRail pass holders headed for the Continent.

KILKENNY

Dubbed "Ireland's Medieval Capital" by the tourist board, Kilkenny is a 900-year-old Norman citadel 75 mi southwest of Dublin. Unfortunately, with a wide load of tourist kitsch and roaring traffic, the town won't whisk you easily back to the Middle Ages. Kilkenny does have a lively pub and traditional-music scene, though, and in August, **Kilkenny Arts Week** showcases Irish film, theater, and music; for schedules call the Arts Council (tel. 056/63663) or the **tourist office** (Rose Inn St., opposite Kilkenny Castle, tel. 056/51500). From **McDonagh Station** (Dublin Rd., tel. 056/22024 for trains, 051/79000 for buses), the joint bus and rail depot, buses travel frequently to Dublin (£7 one-way), Waterford, Cork, and Galway. Kilkenny is also on Irish Rail's Dublin (Heuston Station)–Waterford line (£10 one way).

WHERE TO SLEEP AND EAT

Most of Kilkenny's B&Bs are on Waterford Road. **Beaupre House** (Waterford Rd., tel. 056/21417) and **Ashleigh House** (Waterford Rd., tel. 056/22809) are both family-run establishments with large, airy rooms (£14–£16 per person). In town, **J&K Dempsey B&B** (26 James St., tel. 056/21954) has small, frilly rooms for £15 per person. The best hostel in town is the large, high-ceiling **IHH Kilkenny Tourist**

Hostel (35 Parliament St., tel. 056/63541; beds £7), in the city center. From McDonagh Station, turn left on John Street, cross the River Nore, and turn right on Kieran Street.

Lautrec's (9 Kieran St., tel. 056/62720) is an elegant wine bar and café that serves vegetarian crêpes (£3), steak fajitas (£4), and apple burritos with cream (£2.45). It stays open until 12:30 AM Monday–Saturday. Cluttered, homey **M. Dore** (Kieran St., at High St., tel. 056/63374) serves coffee (65p), warm fruit scones (60p), and tasty sandwiches (£1.45).

WORTH SEEING

In summer, **Tynan Walking Tours** (tel. 056/52066) organizes excellent guided walking tours of Kilkenny (£2.50). If you'd rather tour independently, pick up Joseph O'Carroll's *Historic Kilkenny* (£3) at the tourist office.

Kilkenny Castle has been the seat of the earls and dukes of Ormond, one of the more powerful clans in Irish history, since 1391. Two-thirds of the castle has been meticulously restored. Most impressive is the Long Room, a refined hall with a nicely carved ceiling. *The Parade, opposite tourist office, tel. 056/ 21450. Admission: £3. Open June–Sept., daily 10–7; Oct.-May, daily 10:30–5 (Sun. 11–5).*

Rothe House is a typical Tudor-era home, built in 1594 by merchant and beer brewer John Rothe. Recent renovations have restored the rooms to their original splendor. There is a motley collection of Bronze Age artifacts, smithy tools, and coal-mining gear. *Parliament St., tel. 056/22893. Admission: £2. Open Apr.–Oct., Mon.–Sat. 10:30–5, Sun. 3–5; Nov.–Mar., weekends 3–5.*

Kilkenny's most famous cathedral, **St. Canice's Cathedral,** is also the second-longest in Ireland (212 ft). St. Canice's was founded in 1197 and later used to store volumes of the Irish Annals and other one-of-a-kind religious manuscripts. The interior has been blandly restored; the complex's biggest attraction is the 102-ft-tall **Round Tower** (admission 70p), built in 847 by King O'Carroll of Ossory. *Coach Rd., at northern foot of Parliament St., tel. 056/64971. Open June–Sept., Mon.–Sat. 9–1 and 2–6, Sun. 2–6; Oct.–May, Mon.–Sat. 10–1 and 2–4, Sun. 2–4.*

AFTER DARK

If you're looking for a pint, browse the pubs along Parliament and High streets. **Kyteler's Inn** (Kieran St., tel. 056/21064) is the oldest in town. **John Cleare's Pub** (28 Parliament St.) and **Widow MacGrath's** (29 Parliament St.) feature traditional music. On nearby John Street, **Langton House** (69 John St., tel. 056/ 65133), voted "Best Pub of the Year" by the locals for five years in a row, has four bars and a classy restaurant.

ROSSLARE HARBOUR

If you're traveling to Ireland from England or the Continent, chances are you'll end up on a ferry bound for Rosslare Harbour. The two ferry companies—**Irish Ferries** and **Stena Sealink**—serving Rosslare Harbour have small information kiosks in the terminal building, adjacent to the full-service **tourist office** (tel. 053/33622). You can purchase tickets at the terminal, but try to reserve a space in advance at the companies' Cork or Dublin offices to avoid the frequent sellouts. Reservations are also a must if you're traveling by car or motorcycle, as on-board parking space is at a premium.

Irish Ferries (tel. 053/33158 or 01/610–511) makes the 3¾-hour crossing to Pembroke, Wales, at 8:30 AM and 8:30 PM; tickets are £25–£30 one way. Irish also makes the 24-hour journey to Cherbourg and Le Havre, France, once daily for £68–£95 one way; call for current prices and schedules. **Stena Sealink** (tel. 053/33115 or 01/280–8844) sails at 9 AM and 9:40 PM to Fishguard, Wales; the journey takes approximately three hours and costs £22–£33 one way. The new high-speed *Stena Lynx* makes the same trip in 99 minutes for £26–£35 one way.

From Rosslare's **train station** (tel. 053/33162), next to the ferry terminal, there are frequent trains to Dublin's Connolly Station (£10 one way) and Cork (£12 one way). For most other destinations, you have to change in Dublin. From the **bus depot,** next to the train station, Bus Éireann runs buses to Dublin (£9 one way) and Galway (£16 one way), among other places. If you're stuck in town overnight, there's an 82-bed **An Óige youth hostel** (Goulding St., tel. 053/33399; beds £6).

CASHEL

Cashel owes its fame to the surrounding **Rock of Cashel,** a ragged outcrop of limestone that several centuries of religious orders have fashioned into church towers and elaborately carved crosses. The rock must have inspired awe in generations of devout peasants, but today's tourist coaches make it feel like a theme park. Still, the religious architecture is breathtaking: Set atop the limestone hill are a completely restored Romanesque church, a mostly complete round tower, a buttressed medieval cathedral, the 15th-century Hall of Vicars, and the remnants of two priories. *Admission: £2.50. Open mid-June–mid-Sept., daily 9–7:30; shorter hrs off season.*

Most tourist buses arrive after noon, so come as early as possible. The **tourist office** (Town Hall, Main St., tel. 062/61333) runs hourly guided tours in the summer. Cashel's unstaffed **bus stop** is located outside O'Reilly's shop, on Main Street. From Cashel, Bus Éireann serves Dublin (£11 round-trip), Cork (£8 one way), and Clonmel (£4.80 one way). The closest train station is in Cahir, with trains to Tralee, Killarney, Waterford, and Rosslare Harbour.

WHERE TO SLEEP
Cashel Holiday Hostel (John St., near tourist office, tel. 062/62330) has dorm beds for £6.50 and doubles for £18. Another option is the IHH **Lisakyle Hostel** (tel. 052/41963)—11 mi south of Cashel, outside the village of Cahir—which offers beds for £6, doubles for £16s, and tent sites for £4. Pick up free transportation to the hostel at IHH's office (Church St.) across from the post office in Cahir.

SOUTHWEST IRELAND

The southwest, which encompasses all of County Kerry and much of County Cork, is by far the most heavily visited part of Ireland. Its principal attractions are Cork, Ireland's second-largest city, and Killarney, a market town that attracts an upscale breed of tourists—mostly retired Americans who happily pay an inflated £90 for a real Irish sweater. Killarney is the best base for exploring the adjacent Ring of Kerry, a 110-mi coastal loop that encircles the rugged Iveragh Peninsula. Cyclists are the real winners in this part of Ireland; freed from the tourist crunch, they can penetrate the remotest stretches of the equally spectacular Dingle Peninsula, where rural pubs and Irish music soften the roughest of roads.

CORK

Dublin is home to more than half of Ireland's 3.5 million people. With a population of only 175,000, Cork comes in a very distant second, and "distant" is certainly how Dubliners view this outpost. For them, a trip to Cork is a trip to the country, a place to retreat for hurling, Gaelic football, and televised plowing contests.

Cork has few crucial attractions, but that's not the point. It has a formidable pub scene and some of Ireland's best traditional and modern music; it has a respected and progressive university, University College Cork (UCC); it has art galleries and offbeat cafés; and, like Galway, it nurtures an active community of artists, musicians, and poets. This progressive spirit is best seen along Cork's South Mall, or along the lanes that fan northward from Patrick Street—areas that mark the historic and modern centers of Cork. Numerous bridges and quays make Cork confusing at first, but they also add character to this ancient port town.

BASICS
VISITOR INFORMATION • Cork Kerry Tourism. *Grand Parade, near Washington St., tel. 021/273–251. Open Mon.–Sat. 9:15–5:30.*

The student-run **USIT,** with two Cork locations, has the best prices for rail, bus, and plane tickets in town and is open to all. *10–11 Market Parade, tel. 021/270–900. UCC Travel, Boole Library, tel. 021/273–901. Both open weekdays 9:30–5:30, Sat. 10–2.*

Sights ●
Bishop Lucey
Park, **7**
Crawford Art
Gallery, **5**
Murphy's Brewery, **3**
Shandon Church, **1**

Lodging ○
Campus House
(IHH), **4**
Isaac's (IHH), **8**
Kent House, **9**
Kinley House, **2**
Oakland's, **10**
Sheila's Cork
Tourist Hostel, **6**
Tara House, **11**

KEY

i Tourist Information

0   440 yards
0   400 meters

MAIL • The **General Post Office** has a bureau de change, phone cards, and a stamp kiosk. *Oliver Plunkett St., at Pembroke St., south of the River Lee, tel. 021/272–000. Open Mon.–Sat. 9–5:30.*

COMING AND GOING

Cork's **Kent Station** (Lower Glanmire Rd., tel. 021/506–766) is on the north side of the River Lee, ½ mi east of the city center. Rail destinations from here include Dublin (£29–£32 one way), Killarney (£13.50 one way), and Limerick (£13.50 one way). All local and Bus Éireann buses depart from **Parnell Place Station** (Parnell Pl., tel. 021/508–188), on the south side of the River Lee.

Cork's ferry port is in **Ringaskiddy** (tel. 021/378–401), an industrial complex 10 mi south of town. Frequent buses shuttle passengers from the bus station to the ferry port (45 min, £3). **Brittany Ferries** (42 Grand Parade, next to tourist office, tel. 021/277–801) sails for Roscoff, France (£40–£61 one way); **Swansea-Cork Ferries** (52 South Mall, tel. 021/271–166) sails every second day in summer to Swansea, Wales (£21–£30 one way); and **Irish Ferries** (9 Bridge St., tel. 021/551-995) sails in summer to Le Havre, France (£76–£92 one way, £5 for Eurailpass holders).

WHERE TO SLEEP

Cork is rarely short of cheap beds, but reservations are imperative during the insanely crowded October Jazz Festival. Cork's B&Bs are clustered mainly around the train station on Lower Glanmire Road and near Cork University on Western Road. The cheapest is **Kent House** (47 Lower Granmire Rd., tel. 021/504–260), with beds for £12–£15. **Oakland's** (51 Lower Granmire Rd., tel. 021/500–578) has doubles for £15–£16.75, and **Tara House** (52 Lower Granmire Rd., tel. 021/500–294) charges £13.50–£20 per person.

HOSTELS • Isaac's (IHH) (48 MacCurtain St., tel. 021/500–011; dorm beds £6.25–£8.50, doubles £56), in a stately four-story Georgian town house, is Cork's best-looking hostel. **Campus House (IHH)** (3 Woodland View, Western Rd., tel. 021/343–531; beds £6), a 20-minute walk from the city center, is the smallest and most relaxed hostel in town. If these are full, try the large, modern **Kinlay House/USIT**

(Bob and Joan Walk, Shandon, tel. 021/508–966; dorm beds £7.50, doubles £22) or **Shelia's Cork Tourist Hostel** (Belgrave Pl., Wellington Rd., tel. 021/505–562; dorm beds £7–£7.50, doubles £19).

CAMPING • Cork Camping Park. These sites, 2½ mi southwest of Cork University, are nothing special, but they're only £5 each, plus £1 per person. *Togher Rd., tel. 021/961–866. Bus 14 from Parnell Station. Open May–Oct.*

FOOD

For breakfast and afternoon snacks, snag an outdoor table at **GingerHouse** (10 Paul St., tel. 021/276–411), famous for its cappuccinos and buttery croissants. Cork's slackers and longhairs tend to gather at **The Other Side** (South Main St., between Castle and Washington Sts., tel. 021/278–470), where they sip coffee and fill up on cheap vegetarian salads and soups (£1–£3). For pub grub and solid pints, try **The Lobby** (1 Union Quay, tel. 021/319–307) or **Dan Lowrey's** (13 Mac Curtain St., tel. 021/505–071), both famed for their old-fashioned decor and high-quality bar food.

New Maharajah. Here is the best and cheapest Indian food in Cork. The prix-fixe lunch menu (appetizer, tandoori dish, dessert) is a steal at £5; or you can choose from the à la carte tandoori menu (£6.50). *19 Cook St., off Patrick St., tel. 021/276–576. Closed Sun.*

Quay Co-op. This is Cork's most happening vegetarian hangout. Linger over breakfast with coffee and the paper, or lunch on sandwiches, soups, and salads with a veggie twist (from £2). *24 Sullivan's Quay, 1 block south and across river from tourist office, tel. 021/317–660. Closed Sun.*

Triskel Arts Café. This quiet tearoom on the top floor of the Triskel Arts Centre serves simple but delicious salads (£3–£4) and hearty soups and sandwiches. *S. Main St., off Washington St., tel. 021/272–022. Closed Sun.*

WORTH SEEING

Bishop Lucey Park, one block north of the tourist office, was opened in 1985 to celebrate the 800th anniversary of the town's charter. Next to the site is the 16th-century **Christ Church,** where Edmund Spenser married the Irishwoman Elizabeth Boyle while writing *The Faerie Queene. Grand Parade. Park open daily sunrise–sunset.*

Crawford Art Gallery. This is Ireland's most active and respected provincial art gallery, with regular exhibitions of modern Irish and foreign works. *Emmet Pl., tel. 021/273–377. Admission free. Open Mon.–Sat. 10–4:45.*

Murphy's Brewery. Murphy's began brewing here in 1856, but the company's purchase by Heineken in 1983 has led diehards to moan that the it hasn't been the same since. The brewery isn't open to the public, but you can taste the goods for yourself at the Brewery Tap Pub across the road. *Lady's Well, Leitrim St., tel. 021/503–371.*

Shandon Church. This Cork landmark is on the north side of town atop a steep hill. The steeple's motley red-sandstone and bleached-limestone faces have become Cork's official city colors—red and white. After a treacherous climb to the top of the 170-ft tower, ring Shandon's famous bells for 50p. *Church St., off Shandon St., tel. 021/505–906. Church admission: £1. Open daily 10–5:30.*

AFTER DARK

One of the most popular stops is **Union Quay,** on the south side of town opposite the South Mall and River Lee. Here three excellent pubs stand side by side: **An Phoenix** (tel. 021/964–275), famed for its nightly traditional-music sessions; **The Lobby** (tel. 021/319–307), a rock-and-roll pub packed with yuppies and middle-aged slackers; and **Donkey Ears** (tel. 021/964–846), home to drunken bikers and youthful fashion slaves. The only gay pub in town is **Loafers** (Douglas St., tel. 021/311–612), which is papered with gay and lesbian community information.

NEAR CORK

BLARNEY CASTLE

Five miles northwest of Cork, Blarney Castle is one of Ireland's most famous historical sites—in other words, it's plagued by herds of tourists and nearly impossible to enjoy. That said, it's hard to deny the allure of the **Blarney Stone,** set in a wall below the castle's battlements. Tradition holds that all who kiss the Blarney Stone will receive the gift of "the Blarney": eloquence and a crafty tongue. To receive this blessing, you lean backward from the second-story parapet and stick your head through a small opening, grasping an iron rail for support. Despite the difficulty, there's generally a long line of portly retirees waiting to scale the skeletal remains of the castle. From Cork's bus station, Bus Éireann offers 15 daily coaches (£2.60 round trip) to Blarney Square. You can also walk (2 hrs) or hitch from Cork by following the N8 highway past the train station. *Admission: £3. Open daily 9–6:30; slightly shorter hrs in winter and on Sun.*

KILLARNEY

Killarney is the most visited city in southwestern Ireland. Its proximity to Shannon Airport ensures a constant flow of wealthy foreigners, and most coach companies use Killarney as a base for their bus tours. Another reason this prim tourist village is at the top of everyone's to-do list is its location on the eastern fringe of the **Ring of Kerry** (*see below*). If you're planning to explore the Ring by bicycle or tourist coach, you will inevitably find yourself stranded in Killarney for at least one night.

Killarney National Park (tel. 064/31440), a pristine 25,000-acre wood whose principal entrance is 1 mi east of town, is yet another reason to visit. Much of the park straddles **Lough Leane** (Lower Lake), a windswept lake that's littered with rocky islets and dozens of hard-to-reach waterfalls. It would take days and a good map to explore the park fully, but a few good day hikes are signposted at each of the park's entrances. The gates are open daily 9–6, and admission is free.

BASICS

Besides booking B&B rooms for £1, the **tourist office** (New Town Hall, south end Main St., tel. 064/31633) arranges tours of the Ring of Kerry through the dozens of coach companies that have offices across the street.

COMING AND GOING

The **train station** (E. Avenue Rd., tel. 064/31067) is 30 yards from the **bus station** (tel. 064/34777); turn left from either station and follow East Avenue Road as it curves past the tourist office. Four trains per day go to both Dublin (£33.50 one way) and Tralee (£5.50 one way). Expressway bus destinations from Killarney include Cork (£8.80 one-way), Dublin (£14 one-way), and Tralee (£4.40 one-way).

WHERE TO SLEEP

City-center accommodations fill up quickly in summer, so reserve in advance. Muckross Road has the largest selection of B&Bs; try **Innisfallen House** (Muckross Rd., tel. 064/34193) or **Killarney View Guest House** (Muckross Rd., tel. 064/33122); both charge £16.50–£18 per person. **The Arch House** (E. Avenue Rd., near train station, tel. 064/32184) has rooms with bath starting at £16 per person.

HOSTELS • The Súgán (IHH) (Lewis Rd., tel. 064/33104; beds £7) is the nicest hostel in town, with 18 beds spread throughout a two-story stone cottage. From the train station, turn left on Park Road, then right on Lewis Road. **Four Winds (IHH)** (43 New St., tel. 064/33094; beds £6–£7) is large and generally crowded, but is right in the center of town and has a fire-warmed common room. Turn left from the train station and follow East Avenue Road as it curves past the tourist office, then turn left on New Street. **Neptune's** (Bishop's La., off New St., tel. 064/35255; dorm beds £6–£9.50) is large and hotel-like, but it rarely fills up.

FOOD

The Súgán (*see* Hostels, *above*) serves delicious three-course meals for £10 (£7 for hostel guests) in its intimate dining room. The restaurant is open May–October 6 PM–9:30 PM and closed Monday; on summer weekends there's often live traditional music. **Mayflower Chinese Restaurant** (Church La., off Plunkett St., tel. 064/32212) serves chow mein (£4–£6) and tofu dishes (£5) daily until midnight. At the other end of town, **Grunts** (New St., off E. Avenue Rd., tel. 064/31890) has good soups and sandwiches for less than £3.

AFTER DARK

For information on current Kerry events, pick up the free *Killarney Advertiser* at the tourist office. Most of Killarney's pubs are unabashedly devoted to the tourist trade. **The Laurels** (Main St., tel. 064/31149) charges a scandalous £3 cover for the privilege of singing "Danny Boy" with a choir of drunken foreigners. **O'Connor's** (High St., tel. 064/31115) is a worn 1960s pub that mixes large crowds of tourists with solid pints and frequent traditional music. In summer, a sure bet for nightly traditional music is **Fáilte Bar** (College St., tel. 064/31893).

RING OF KERRY

The Ring of Kerry is one of Ireland's most famous—and heavily visited—attractions. The circular, 110-mi Ring can be accessed at any number of places, although Killarney (*see above*) is the most practical starting point. On sunny days, the two-lane highway that handles the bulk of traffic is choked with rental cars, tourist coaches, and cyclists all engaged in the vain struggle to find the real, rural Ireland promised by the tourist board. Many are disappointed to find that the Ring is one of the country's busiest roads, overflowing with cars, buses, fumes, gift shops, restaurants, and other tourists.

If you don't mind sharing the road, you will encounter some truly stunning coastal and mountain views. To do the Ring justice, you'll need a minimum of two days on a bike, more if you're traveling by bus or hitching. Allow some time for detours on winding back roads, or to do the 22½-mi **Skellig Loop**, a scenic circuit ignored by most luxury coaches. Most people prefer to tackle the Ring in a counterclockwise direction, starting from Killarney, then pausing for a night in Glenbeigh, Cahirciveen (also spelled Cahirsiveen), Valentia Island, Ballinskelligs, Waterville, or Kenmare.

One pub that shouldn't be missed is Dick Mack's, on Green Lane in Dingle Town, which appears not to have changed since it opened in 1899. The snug (antechamber) at the end of the bar was where local women, not allowed into the pub proper, used to gather and wait for their husbands to finish getting sloshed.

GETTING AROUND

Hostels every 20 mi or so and the mostly flat terrain mean that even wimps can tackle the Ring by bike. If you're short on time, one of the best ways to see the Ring is on Bus Éireann's **Ring of Kerry Service** (tel. 064/34777), which departs Killarney twice daily in summer, stopping at Killorglin, Glenbeigh, Cahirciveen, Waterville, and Kenmare before returning to Killarney. The entire loop costs £9.70 (£12.20 if you want to get off once and then continue on in the next bus). Other options are private coach tours arranged by several companies in Killarney—the going rate is £10–£16 for a full-day tour. Ask the tourist office to recommend a private carrier.

WHERE TO SLEEP

CAHIRCIVEEN • Sive Hostel (IHH) (15 East End, tel. 066/72717; beds £6.50, tent sites £3.50 per person), three blocks from Cahirciveen's small square, arranges day trips to the Skellig Islands.

VALENTIA ISLAND • Ring Lyne Hostel (Chapeltown, tel. 066/76103; beds £6–£7, tent sites £3) is an immensely comfortable hostel within a stone's throw of Chapeltown's pubs and chippers. More intimate is **Royal Pier Hostel** (Knightstown, tel. 066/76144; dorm beds £6.50, tent sites £3), in a brooding manor house.

WATERVILLE • Peter's Place (no phone; beds £6, tent sites £3) is an amazingly mellow town house 300 yards west of town. **Waterville Leisure House** (tel. 066/74400; dorm beds £6.50) is generally packed with families and school groups. The best B&B is **Clifford's** (Main St., tel. 066/74283; £15 per person; closed Nov.–Feb.).

KENMARE • Kenmare's Fáilte Hostel (IHH) (Henry St., tel. 064/41083; dorm beds £6.50) is in a beautifully restored town house with a pleasant courtyard. If it's full, try **Riverside House** (Killarney Rd., tel. 064/41316; closed Nov.–Mar.) or **Ardmore House** (Killarney Rd., tel. 064/41406; closed Dec.–Feb.), with doubles for £26 and £32–£36, respectively.

DINGLE PENINSULA

The Dingle Peninsula stretches for 30 mi between Tralee in the east and Slea Head in the west. Its small size makes it one of Ireland's most accessible summer retreats, especially for cyclists who don't have time to cover the larger Mizen, Beara, or Ring of Kerry circuits. Despite its size, the Dingle Peninsula is diverse and brazenly scenic, encompassing the rugged Slieve Mish Mountains in the east, the Brandon Mountains in the west, and smooth, rolling hills on either side.

Dingle Town is a small fishing village that makes an excellent base for exploring the surrounding peninsula. Although many expect Dingle to be undeveloped, it's actually a haven for pricey seafood restaurants and a handful of luxury hotels. Still, it has the peninsula's only **tourist office** (Main St., tel. 066/51241) and **Foxy John Moriarty Bikes** (Main St., tel. 066/51316), which rents bikes by the day (£5–£7) and week (£25); just bring a passport or driver's license.

From Dingle, an excellent walk or bike ride away is **Ventry,** a small outcrop of pubs and newsagents 2 mi west. If you keep to the R559 coastal road from Ventry, you'll soon end up on the 20-mi **Slea Head Loop,** an incredible circuit that skirts the foot of Mt. Eagle (1,692 ft) and eventually curves north past Dunmore Head and Dunquin. This road is treacherous for cyclists, but the views of the coast and the Blasket Islands are unforgettable. **Dunquin** itself is a loose collection of fields and isolated, peat smoke–spouting cottages. Here you can stop for lunch at **Kruger's Pub** (tel. 066/56127) and catch the **Blasket Island Ferry** (Dunquin Pier, tel. 066/56455). After the 20-minute ferry ride (£7), spend the day exploring Blasket Island, where you'll find the ruins of a few 15th- and 16th-century monasteries and dozens of good hiking trails. Depending on the weather, the ferry will collect you two to three hours later.

COMING AND GOING

The town of Tralee makes a good springboard for exploring the Dingle Peninsula. Although **Irish Rail** does not serve the Dingle Peninsula, it does have daily service to Tralee from Killarney (£5.50 one way), Cork (£17 one way), and Dublin (£35 one way). From Tralee, **Bus Éireann** offers year-round Expressway service to Dingle (£8 round-trip); buses drop passengers in the center of town. In the summer, service is slightly more frequent to the Dingle, Dunquin, and the peninsula's smaller towns.

WHERE TO SLEEP

Dingle has the largest selection of cheap accommodations. The incredibly friendly people at **Avondale House** (Dykegate and Avondale, tel. 066/51120) offer cozy rooms and an amazing breakfast for £15–£16.50 per person. The best hostel is **Rainbow** (The Wood, tel. 066/51044; beds £6, tent sites £3), a 15-minute walk west of town; a free shuttle will whisk you to and from the bus stop. An Óige's **Dunquin Hostel** (tel. 066/56121) has a superb location, overlooking the coast and Blasket Islands, but the room lockout, shower lockout, and strict midnight curfew make this place hard to love. Beds cost £5.50 (£6.50 June–Sept.). The hostel's saving grace is its proximity to **Kruger's Pub** (tel. 066/56127), down the road, with its views of the frothy Blasket Sound. Kruger's also offers comfortable rooms (£14 per person) from March through October.

WESTERN IRELAND

The west embodies all the stereotypes generally associated with Ireland—whitewashed cottages, sheep, rugged seascapes, misty bogland, and firelit country pubs, all processed through a filter of Guinness and traditional music. Fortunately, these characterizations hold more truth than many cynics might expect, which helps to explain why the west is the second-most-visited part of the country, and often the highlight of a trip to Ireland. Even with the heavy influx of summertime travelers, a few areas—notably Doolin—balance accessibility with an authentic take on rural Ireland.

DOOLIN AND THE CLIFFS OF MOHER

Despite its large population of presumably tone-deaf sheep, Doolin is *the* place for traditional music. Its three pubs—**McGann's, McDermott's,** and **O'Connor's**—host first-rate music sessions nightly throughout the year. All three pubs habitually defy Ireland's puritanical 11:30 PM closing time by bolting the doors and drawing the curtains.

Doolin's other main draw is its proximity to the **Cliffs of Moher.** The preferred way to see the Cliffs of Moher is to hike the 2½-mi **Burren Way** from Doolin. This rugged dirt trail (walk past the Doolin Hostel, cross the riverbed, and continue straight) keeps entirely to the coast, providing great views of the sea and clusters of thatched cottages. At some points, the only thing separating you from the ocean, 700 ft below, is a patch of slippery heather that may or may not offer a last-chance handhold. For other walks and a good rundown of the area's history, pick up Martin Breen's *Doolin Guide & Map* (£1.50) in shops and at the Doolin Hostel.

BASICS

You can exchange money or buy maps at the **tourist desk** in Doolin Hostel, which also serves as the local Raleigh Rent-A-Bike outlet and **Bus Éireann** depot. Express buses run twice daily Monday–Saturday (once on Sunday) between Doolin and Dublin (£12 one way), and also to the Cliffs of Moher.

WHERE TO SLEEP

Of Doolin's three hostels, **Aille River** (tel. 065/74260; dorm beds £6.50, doubles £15, tent sites £3.50 per person; closed mid-Nov.–mid-Mar.) is the most comfortable. Up the road, **Rainbow Hostel** (tel. 065/74415; beds £6.50) has slightly cramped and damp bedrooms, but there's a cozy common room and farmyard facilities for camping (£3 per person). At the other end of town, **Doolin Hostel** (tel. 065/74006; beds £6) is large and rather light on character.

GALWAY

Ireland's third-largest city is a progressive student town with a flair for the hip and offbeat. The small city center has the atmosphere of a bustling market town, especially in the streets that lead from the River Corrib to **Eyre Square,** the city's main social hub. Galway is also western Ireland's most prominent music and arts center. Because of its proximity to the surrounding *Gaeltacht* (communities where Irish is still commonly spoken), Galway's music scene is happily and predominantly traditional. Lacking large numbers of historic sites, Galway seems to cherish its traditional-music pubs with a vengeance, recognizing their importance to the town's cultural (and tourist) appeal. Civic pride also stems from the city's famed academic institution, the University College Galway (UCG), a center of Irish-language and Celtic studies. The annual **Galway Arts Festival** (tel. 091/563–800), in late July, showcases Irish and international drama in a dozen city-center venues. Book a bed in advance, and get to the pub early if you want a seat.

From Doolin you can ferry to the beautiful, forbidding, very traditional Aran Islands. Doolin Ferries (tel. 065/74455) makes the 30- to 90-minute trip to Inisheer (£15 round trip) and Inishmore (£20 round-trip) twice daily April–September.

BASICS

The **tourist office** (Victoria Pl., tel. 091/563–081) arranges city tours and can book ferry tickets to the nearby Aran Islands. Student-run **USIT** (New Science Bldg., UCG, tel. 091/524–601) works miracles finding cheap transport tickets for travelers of any age.

COMING AND GOING

Ceannt Station (tel. 091/562–000 or 091/561–444), on the corner of Eyre Square, doubles as the rail and bus depot. Galway exchanges six trains daily with Dublin (£13 one way), but for any other destination you'll have to change in Athlone. **Bus Éireann** Expressway buses make daily hauls to Dublin (£8 one way), Donegal (£13 one way), Sligo (£10.50 one way), and Cork (£12 one way). To reach the hostels and pubs from the station, turn left at Eyre Square, right on Victoria Place, and left on Williamsgate Street.

WHERE TO SLEEP

Although Galway has more than 150 B&Bs and many hostels, you'll want to reserve ahead in July and August. What **Corrib Villa** (4 Waterside, tel. 091/562–892; beds £6.50–£7.50) lacks in modernity, it makes up for in character. Take Williamsgate Street from Eyre Square, turn right on Eglinton Street, and follow it to the end. The clean kitchen and dining room at convenient **Galway City Hostel** (25–27 Dominick St., tel. 091/566–367; beds £5.50–£7) make it one of the best options in town. Dorm rooms at the cozy **Salmon Weir Hostel** (3 St. Vincent's Ave., tel. 091/561–133; dorm beds £5–£7, doubles £20) are small but well-kept, and the happy staff organizes Monday-night pub crawls.

FOOD

Galway has an abundance of cheap restaurants and cafés, most of which are located south of Eyre Square between Abbeygate Street and the River Corrib. **Fat Freddy's** (Quay St., tel. 091/567–279) does good pizzas and pastas in the £5–£6 range and is about the only cheapish sit-down place that's open on Sunday. Unpretentious **Food for Thought** (Lower Abbeygate St., no phone) serves homemade soups, sandwiches, and veggie casseroles for less than £3. The **Round Table** (6 High St., tel. 091/564–542) serves hearty pork, beef, and chicken specials and tasty desserts in a pleasant, 16th-century dining room with a 15-ft-high stone fireplace. The huge breakfast is also worth a try.

WORTH SEEING

Your first impression of Galway is likely to be **Eyre Square,** opposite the bus and train station in the center of town. Formerly a green where livestock and produce were sold, it's not much to look at today (although the park in its center is a fine place for an afternoon snooze). From Eyre Square's southwest corner, Galway's main shopping artery (called Williamsgate, Williams Street, Shop Street, High Street, and Quay Street at different points) leads to the River Corrib. On nearby Market Street is the **Nora Barnacle House** (4 Bowling Green, tel. 091/564–743; admission £1), birthplace of James Joyce's wife. Joyce and Nora Barnacle first met in Dublin on June 16, 1904, a date known to most Joyce fans as Bloomsday. Inside the house is a mediocre collection of photographs and letters and a small gift shop.

AFTER DARK

Dozens of good pubs pepper Galway's eminently crawlable city center. For traditional music, **Taaffes** (19 Shop St., tel. 091/564–066) and **King's Head** (15 High St., tel. 091/566–630) are musts, though a recent deluge of green-sweater types threatens the authenticity of the summer sessions. Two summer options for unhyped, old-style music are **An Púcán** (11 Forster St., tel. 091/561–528) and **Crane Bar** (2 Sea Rd., tel. 091/567–419). **Lisheen Bar** (Bridge St., tel. 091/563–804) and **Sally Long's** (33 Upper Abbeygate St., tel. 091/565–756) are dependable for good jazz and folk.

The **Druid Theater Company** (tel. 091/568–660) has built its reputation on its revivals of Anglo-Irish classics and a slew of Irish-language plays. More touristy but no less entertaining, the Irish-language theater **An Taibhdhearc** (Middle St., tel. 091/562–024) is famous for its bilingual productions of lesser-known Irish plays. Inquire at the tourist office for performance details.

NORTHWEST IRELAND

Northwest Ireland is the most rugged and wildly gorgeous part of the country. No matter where you're headed, the point is the landscape—harsh and satisfyingly empty, dotted with tiny villages and quiet rural pubs. It's said that in this part of Ireland sheep outnumber people by roughly 100 to 1. Thankfully, sheep also outnumber tourists by a large margin; outside Sligo or Donegal Town, the region's largest villages, few tourist buses travel the jagged 280-mi coastline. As a result, this region presents some transportation challenges. **McGeehan Coaches** (tel. 075/46150) and **Lough Swilly Buses** (tel. 074/22400) cover routes ignored by Bus Éireann.

SLIGO

Considering its location, straddling the mouth of Lough Gill, Sligo ought to be a picturesque and thoroughly enjoyable market town. Over the past 20 years, however, Sligo has fallen victim to its own prosperity. Companies from Dublin and the Continent persist in refashioning the small city center with bleakly modern shopping malls, and family-run shops have been replaced with fast-food restaurants. In other words, Sligo is little more than a functional stopover on the way to somewhere else, preferably County Donegal and its wonderful coastline. If you've got a few hours to kill, don't miss **Hargadon's** (4–5 O'Connell St., tel. 071/70933), Sligo's most famous pub, a dark place filled with sepia photographs and antique whiskey jugs.

The **tourist office** (Temple St., tel. 071/61201) stocks a full range of maps and brochures. Sligo's **County Museum, Municipal Art Gallery,** and **Yeats Museum** are all housed in the local library (Stephen St., tel. 071/42212; admission free; open Mon.–Sat. 10–12:30 and 2:30–4:30; shorter hrs off season). The art gallery has a small collection of Irish and Anglo-Irish canvases. The Yeats Museum displays a comprehensive collection of Yeats's writings from 1889 to 1936 and Yeats's 1923 Nobel Prize medal. If that doesn't quench your thirst, the **Yeats Memorial Building** (Hyde Bridge, at O'Connell St., tel. 071/45847) houses a Yeats gallery (admission free; open Mon.–Sat. 10–5) and the headquarters of the **Yeats Society** (tel. 071/42693). During the Yeats Summer School session in August, the society presents lectures and plays. Across the street is a sculpture of the poet, draped in a flowing coat overlaid with poetic excerpts.

COMING AND GOING

Trains and buses both stop at **McDiarmada Station** (Lord Edward St., tel. 071/60066 for bus information, 071/69888 for rail information), a 10-minute walk from the city center. Almost all trains, even those to nearby Galway or Belfast, go through Dublin, so take the bus unless you're Dublin-bound. Bus Éireann destinations from Sligo include Belfast (£11.50 one way), Cork (£16 one way), Derry (£10 one way), and Galway (£10.50 one way).

WHERE TO SLEEP

The only time when rooms may be tight is August, when the Yeats Summer School draws poets and Yeats fans from around the world. Most B&Bs are on Lower and Upper Pearse roads. **The Anchor Guest House** (Quay St., tel. 071/42904) offers standard private rooms with lovely fried breakfasts for £16–£18 per person. **White House (IHH)** (Markievicz Rd., tel. 071/45160; beds £6–£6.50), overlooking the river in the heart of the city center, is the best of Sligo's three hostels. From the station walk downhill, turn left, and follow Lord Edward Street until you cross the river. Opposite the train station is the damp, bland **Yeats Country** hostel (Lord Edward St., tel. 071/46876), where £6–£6.50 buys a bed but not much else.

DONEGAL TOWN

Donegal Town is a small outpost of pubs and shops overlooking the River Eske. The entire village can be walked in 10 minutes, and nearly everything of interest is centered around the **Diamond,** a former marketplace that's now a parking lot. The town was founded in AD 1200 by the O'Donnell clan; in 1474, Red Hugh O'Donnell commissioned a castle (now destroyed) and the **Donegal Monastery,** located on the riverbank south of the Diamond. The ivy-covered ruins are impressive considering that the complex was ransacked by the English three times between 1593 and 1607. If you're in the mood for a pint, try **Charlie's Star Bar** (Main St., tel. 073/21158) or **McGroarty's** (the Diamond, tel. 073/21049), both of which have live traditional music most summer nights. The **tourist office** (Quay St., tel. 073/21148) overlooks the water south of the Diamond.

COMING AND GOING

Lacking an official bus depot, all **Bus Éireann** coaches arrive and depart from the Diamond, usually outside the Abbey Hotel; pick up schedules at the tourist office. Express destinations from Donegal Town include Sligo (£6 single), Galway (£10 single), and Dublin (£10 single).

WHERE TO SLEEP

B&Bs are easy to come by. On Waterloo Place, just off Bridge Street, both **Riverside House** (tel. 073/21083) and **Castle View** (tel. 073/22100) offer spacious rooms for £16–£20 per person. Donegal's best youth hostel is the **IHH Donegal Town Independent Hostel** (Killybegs Rd., tel. 073/22805; beds £6). You can also camp (£3.50 per person) on the lawn surrounding the hostel, which is ¾ mi from the Diamond on the road to Killybegs. You can also take any Bus Éireann bus or hike 3 mi toward Killybegs to the peaceful, beachside **Ball Hill Hostel** (tel. 073/21174; beds £5.50–£6).

NEAR DONEGAL TOWN

KILCAR AND SLIEVE LEAGUE

The village of **Kilcar** would probably be forgotten were it not for the nearby **Derrylahan Hostel (IHH)** (Carrick Rd., tel. 073/38079; dorm beds £6, doubles £16, tent sites £3). The hostel is 2 mi north of Kilcar on the road to Carrick; if you call from either town, a staffer will come get you. From the hostel, you're within hiking distance of both **Slieve League** (2,972 ft) and the **Bunglass Cliffs,** the highest sea cliffs in the country. Don't worry about hyperbole—these two natural wonders are simply the most intense and beautiful places on earth. To access the mountain, hike from the hostel to Carrick, walk just under 1 mi south on the road to Teelin, then turn right and follow the signs for Bunglass. The hike is fairly easy, and the views are nothing short of incredible. From Bunglass, follow the few signs to Slieve League's summit (be extra careful on windy and rainy days). Once you reach the summit, take a well-anchored peep over the edge: 2,000 ft below, the ocean moves in slow motion, soundless. On the way down, head south for Cappagh and finally Teelin (follow the occasional sign), where you can grab lunch at **Rusty Mackerel Pub** (tel. 073/39101). The entire circuit from Carrick to Slieve League to Teelin takes five hours of medium-paced hiking, slightly more when heavy fog calls for vigilance.

ITALY

The turmoil that can pervade life in Italy may not be apparent when you first step foot on Italian soil. It's easy to be seduced by the country's beautiful and diverse scenery, incredible food and wine, warm people and climate, and stunning architecture and elegance—not to mention the most concentrated collection of artistic masterpieces in the world. It's when you confront the many contrasts of 20th-century life here—traffic jams and pollution, ancient ruins, curious stares from the locals, Baroque cathedrals, and Vespa drivers swerving through narrow streets as they debate on their cellular phones—that the downsides of Italy become evident. The country that gave us Fiat, fashion, and Fellini films is still searching to define itself as it approaches the Jubilee Year of 2000.

In a period spanning 3,000 years, the narrow peninsula and its islands have supported a series of peoples from a nearly endless variety of ethnic, religious, and philosophical backgrounds. Not even the seemingly impenetrable Roman Empire, founded in 27 BC, could manage to hold Italy together forever. Dynasties such as the Austrian Hapsburgs and the Spanish Bourbons eventually laid claim to parts of Italy, leaving behind a mixture of languages, architectural styles, and culinary treats (luckily, the English never conquered Italy). Finally, in 1861, Turinese nobleman Camillo Cavour, together with Giuseppe Garibaldi and his thousand-man army (the "Red Shirts"), unified the short-lived Kingdom of Italy. Ultimately, Italy's inability to organize itself paid off for the Allies in World War II. The Italian Fascist party under *Il Duce,* Benito Mussolini, fought countless bloody battles, first alongside the Axis powers, then the Allies, and finally the partisan revolutionaries. In the end, Mussolini was overthrown by his own compatriots and assassinated, his body left hanging in a piazza in Milan.

Since World War II, more than 50 governments have tried to comb Italy's unruly hair. As money poured into the north through companies such as Olivetti and Fiat, the money sent to the impoverished Mezzogiorno, the provinces south of Rome, took a detour into the pockets of organized crime and corrupt politicians. This disparity continues to affect Italians today: Many northerners consider those from the south to be ignorant, and southerners often complain of the northerners' coldness and obsession with money. Unpredictable Umberto Bossi, leader of the separatist Lega Nord (Northern League), has increased the animosity by advocating the creation of a "nation of the North" called Padania. But in 1996, Italians ushered in *L'Ulivo* (Olive Tree), a coalition of former communists and left-leaning centrists, and named economist Romano Prodi, a political outsider, their prime minister. While many Italians are hopeful that L'Ulivo will augur an improved Italy, the coalition faces an uphill climb trying to cope with the chaos of the past and disillusioned citizens of the present.

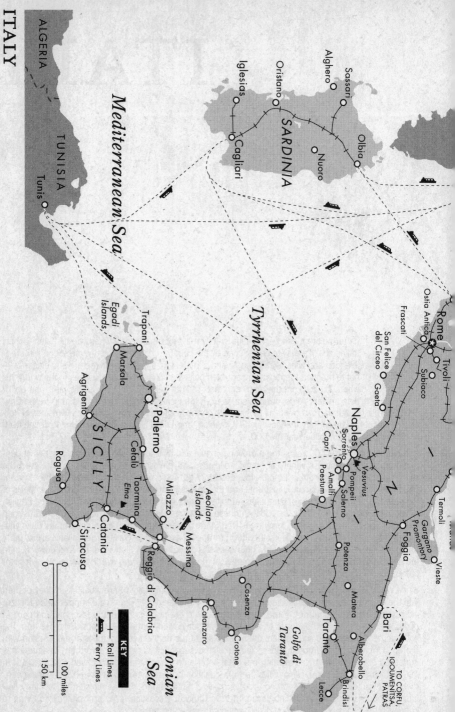

ALGERIA

TUNISIA

TUNISIA

Tunis

Mediterranean Sea

SARDINIA

Iglesias

Oristano

Alghero

Sassari

Nuoro

Olbia

Cagliari

Tyrrhenian Sea

Egadi Islands

Trapani

Marsala

Agrigento

SICILY

Ragusa

Cefalù

Palermo

Etna

Taormina

Milazzo

Aeolian Islands

Catania

Siracusa

Messina

Reggio di Calabria

Ionian Sea

Rome

Ostia Antica

Frascati

San Felice del Circeo

Gaeta

Subiaco

Tivoli

Naples

Sorrento

Capri

Amalfi

Pompeii

Salerno

Paestum

Vesuvius

Potenza

Cosenza

Catanzaro

Crotone

Golfo di Taranto

Matera

Taranto

Bari

Alberobello

Brindisi

Lecce

Foggia

Gargano Promontory

Vieste

Termoli

TO CORFU, IGOUMENITSA, PATRAS

KEY
Rail Lines
Ferry Lines

0   100 miles

0   150 km

FRANCE

SWITZERLAND

GERMANY

AUSTRIA

SLOVENIA

CROATIA

HUNGARY

BOSNIA AND HERZEGOVINA

MONTENEGRO

Corsica

Ligurian Sea

Adriatic Sea

Golfo di Venezia

N

A L P S

A L P I

THE DOLOMITES

T U S C A N Y

U M B R I A

L A Z I O

Mt. Blanc

Mt. Aosta

Turin

Asti

Novara

Stresa

Lago Maggiore

Lago di Orta

Lago di Como

Lugano

Tremezzo

Cannobio

Como

Bellagio

Varenna

Lago di Lecco

Milan

Pavia

Genoa

Final Ligure

San Remo

Monterosso

Cinque Terre

La Spezia

Rapallo

Piacenza

Parma

Modena

Bologna

Ferrara

Ravenna

Rimini

San Marino

Arezzo

Gubbio

Assisi

Perugia

Spoleto

Orvieto

Viterbo

Terni

Rieti

L'Aquila

Ascoli Piceno

Macerata

Urbino

Ancona

Pescara

Vasto

Tivoli

Rome

Civitavecchia

Grosseto

Elba

Siena

San Gimignano

Florence

Pistoia

Lucca

Pisa

Livorno

Bastia

Bergamo

Brescia

Desenzano

Gardone

Torbole

Riva del Garda

Lago di Garda

Lago d'Iseo

Trento

Bolzano

Cortina d'Ampezzo

Verona

Mantua

Padua

Vicenza

Venice

Treviso

Udine

Trieste

Tremiti Islands

Termoli

Po

Adige

Arno

Tiber

513

Ironically, the most stable aspect of Italy is crime. Known as the *'ndragheta* in Calabria, *la camorra* in Naples, and Mafia—or preferably La Cosa Nostra—in Sicily, organized crime has been documented in graphic movies, novels, and news reports for decades. The Mafia proves ever-resilient, as evidenced by their devastating, brutal bombings/assassinations in the early 1990s of judges Giovanni Falcone and Paolo Borsellino, hardline Mafia prosecutors in Sicily. In May 1996, top Mafia boss Giovanni Brusca, the man charged with detonating the bomb that killed Falcone, was caught. Wearing masks to protect their identity, the arresting officers demonstrated the still-pervasive fear of the Mafia, whose contacts penetrate to the highest echelons of Italian government and finance.

While the Italy that approaches the millennium may not have a clear direction or purpose, even the most jaded cynic cannot mistake Rome, Florence, Naples, or Venice for anything other than what they are— at once extravagant, dilapidated, and quintessentially Italian. Those whose images of Italy range from frescoed villas to chronically late trains agree: The reasons for coming here are as compelling as ever. Despite the political and economical woes of their homeland, Italians know how to make the most of everything—and lucky for us, their passion and appetite for life is contagious.

BASICS

MONEY

US$1 = 1817 lire and 1000 lire = 55¢. Lire (plural) come in notes of 1000, 5000, 10,000, 50,000, 100,000, and 500,000. Coins come in denominations of 50, 100, 200, and 500. The best place to change money in Italy is usually the bank. Always ask banks or exchange bureaus if they charge a commission; some places take up to 5% off the top, though 2%–3% is more common. Most banks in Italy now have cash machines—the only problem is getting them to give you money.

HOW MUCH IT WILL COST • Thanks to its unsteady economy and faltering lira, travel in Italy has become cheaper in the last few years. For the most part, the north is more expensive than the south. You can travel in Italy on $60–$70 or so a day, if you're careful—and on even less if you're really frugal.

GETTING AROUND

Usually clean, affordable, and surprisingly punctual, Italian trains are the way to travel, but towns in the hills and mountains are likely to be served by bus only.

BY BUS • Long-distance buses can be complicated; you often have to get off in an obscure town to switch lines, and sometimes you'll have to suffer ungodly long waits. Buses, however, often cost less, run more frequently, and go more places than trains. Buy tickets at *tabaccherie* (marked TABACCHI), at bars near bus stops, at the bus station (if the town has one), or on the bus.

BY TRAIN • The fastest Italian train service, called *pendolino,* runs between major cities only and is prohibitively expensive. *InterCity* (IC) is the next fastest, followed by *rapido.* You pay a *supplemento* (extra charge) of up to 50% for IC and Rapido service, although the supplement is waived for Eurailpass holders. *Espresso* and *diretto* trains make a few more stops and are usually a little slower, and *locale* trains are slow as molasses. A new toll-free **train information** (tel. 1478/88088 toll-free within Italy) number has been instituted; local train station numbers are slowly being phased out.

Italian trains are relatively cheap, and it might not be worth your while to buy a rail pass. The Italian train system offers three main types of passes, available at train stations throughout Italy. All prices were in effect at press time. The **Italy Flexi Railcard** costs $135 for four days of second-class ($189 for first-class) travel taken within one month; $199/$291 for eight days of travel within one month; and $244/$365 for 12 days of travel within one month. The **Italy Railcard** allows unlimited use of all trains for eight days ($172/$254), 15 days ($213/$320), 21 days ($248/$371), and 30 days ($297/447). The **Italian Kilometric Ticket** is valid for two months and can be used by as many as five people to travel a total of 3,000 km (1,860 mi) second class (you'll have a hard time using it up unless you're traveling with at least two companions). This pass costs $156 (first-class) and $264 (second-class). The **Carta Verde** saves those under 26 years 20%–30% for first- or second-class rail travel within a year, so it isn't worthwhile for short-term travel. It's about L40,000, and must be purchased in Italy. For information about and to purchase Italian State Railways rail passes, call **CIT** (15 West 44th St., 10th fl., 10036 New York, NY, tel. 212/730–2888 and 800/CIT–RAIL, fax 212/730–4544).

WHERE TO SLEEP

Hotels in Italy are classified by the government in categories ranging from one to five stars. Most hotels reviewed in this chapter are one- and two-star establishments. One-star hotels vary from gross to charming, with most falling into the "clean-but-generic" category. Two-star establishments are usually a little nicer and have more rooms with private baths. The words *albergo, pensione,* and *locanda* all basically mean hotel and are interchangeable for your purposes.

Hostels are generally the best budget choice if you're traveling alone—beds cost L15,000–L25,000. **Associazione Italiana Alberghi per La Gioventù** (V. Cavour 44, Rome 00184, tel. 06/4871152, fax 06/4741256), the official Italian hostel organization, puts out a complete guide to HI (Hostelling International) hostels in the country. Independent hostels, sometimes run by religious organizations, offer alternatives to expensive hotels and full hostels, but they're usually single-sex and specify a score of rules to follow.

Campgrounds near cities are often big, ugly affairs. Camping is usually the cheapest option at L7000–L15,000 per person, though some big campgrounds charge as much as L20,000 for a site. Be prepared for long bus rides in and out of town. **Federazione Italiana del Campeggio**, a.k.a. Federcampeggio (Calenzano, Florence 50041, tel. 055/882391) issues a free, complete list of campgrounds and a map.

The Dolomites and other mountain groups are scattered with huts called **rifugi**. Rifugi are sometimes free; most, however, cost about the same as a hostel or a cheap hotel (L20,000–L50,000). Definitely inquire about availability before trudging up a mountain to find all the beds are taken. Amenities are generally few, although running water is almost always provided. Tourist boards in the towns at the base of the mountains will provide you with a list of rifugi and usually call them for you. **Club Alpino Italiano** (V. Ugo Foscolo 3, 20122 Milan, tel. 02/8056971) owns hundreds of these huts and publishes a free annual guide with information on access, prices, and equipment.

Thirteen years prior to his brutal assassination, Mussolini told a companion, "Everybody dies the death that corresponds to his character."

FOOD

Italian food is all about yummy plates of pasta, cheap local wine, and frothy cappuccino—a delectable triumvirate that even backpackers can enjoy without breaking the bank. However, think twice before entering a *ristorante* (restaurant), often more expensive and stuffy than a family-run, neighborhood *trattoria* or *tavola calda* (Italy's version of fast food). Faster and cheaper still are places that sell squares of pizza *al taglio* (sold by the piece or weight), to be eaten while standing. An *osteria* can either be an expensive, touristy restaurant or an unassuming wine shop that serves food. *Paninoteche* serve simple *panini* (sandwiches). *Gastronomie* dish out prepared food to be taken out. Find bread at a *panificio* or a *forno*, which also sell pizza, and pastries and sweets at a *pasticceria*. There are also *rosticcerie* that roast and sell meat and poultry.

The easiest way to keep costs down at restaurants is by *not* ordering a full, three-course meal. The *primi piatti*, or *primi* (first courses), plates of pasta, risotto, or soup, are usually so filling that you won't need to order the more expensive *secondi* (second courses), usually chicken, beef, or fish accompanied by a *contorno* (side dish) of vegetables or salad. Of course, don't skip out on a pre-dinner trip to the *antipasti* table for appetizers. Bread is usually included in the cover charge, and bottled water costs L2000–L3000. If you don't want to pay extra for water, ask for tap water, called *acqua semplice*, instead. Bottled wine can double your bill, so stick with the house red or white, which is usually decent. It's almost always cheaper to go to a bar or a *gelateria* for dessert and coffee.

Throughout Italy, lunch is served roughly 1–3, dinner 8–10, sometimes later in summer months. Both meals are meant to be lingered over with wine, coffee, and conversation—Italians don't like to rush a meal. Most restaurants serve the same menu for lunch and dinner, so don't expect lunch to be much cheaper. At lunch, though, waiters are less likely to sneer at you for not ordering a secondo.

BUSINESS HOURS

Business hours in Italy will inevitably irritate and confound you. The average business is open Monday–Friday or Monday–Saturday from around 9 AM to about 7:30 PM. Many businesses shut down for a few hours between noon and 4. All shops close on Sunday. Banks have the most absurd hours of all: weekdays 8:30–1 and around 3:30–4:15.

FESTIVALS AND HOLIDAYS

Most businesses close for the following dates: January 1 (New Year's Day), January 6 (Epiphany), Easter Monday, April 25 (Liberation Day), May 1 (Labor Day), August 15 (Assumption of the Virgin), November 1 (All Saints' Day), December 8 (Feast of the Immaculate Conception), December 25 (Christmas Day), and December 26 (St. Stephen's Day). In addition, many cities and towns also close down on the day of their patron saint. In August, it seems every Italian closes up shop for at least two weeks during *ferragosto,* the unofficial national holiday.

Two of the biggest celebrations in this festival-happy nation are **Siena**'s II Palio (July 2 and August 16), a fiercely competitive bareback horse race dating from the Middle Ages, and **Venice**'s Carnevale, in late February or early March.

VISITOR INFORMATION

Even the dinkiest town will usually have a tourist office, often run by the **Azienda di Promozione Turismo (APT)** or **Ente Provinciale per II Turismo (EPT).**

PHONES

Country code: 39. It's best to make long-distance calls from telephone offices labeled TELECOM. In some towns you can use an AT&T or similar phone card to charge your call. In phone offices, sometimes found in train stations, you can buy *carte telefoniche*—phone cards in denominations of L5000, L10,000, and L15,000. Phones that accept coins are being phased out; you should pick up a phone card if you plan on being in the country for a while. A local call costs L200. To use a credit card or call collect from a pay phone, you have to deposit L200, which you get back when you finish the call. To call collect, dial 170 to get an English-speaking operator; or call **AT&T** USA Direct (tel. 1721011), **MCI** (tel. 1721022), or **Sprint** (tel. 1721877).

MAIL

Italian mail is slow and not too reliable, so don't send valuables in the mail. Stamps, available at post offices and tobacco shops everywhere, cost L1300 for a letter up to 20 grams and L1100 for a postcard to the United States. The main post offices in cities and major towns all accept *fermo posta* (held mail). American Express cardholders can receive mail at local offices for free.

EMERGENCIES

For first aid and the *polizia* (local police), dial 113; to report a fire, dial 115. The general toll-free emergency number is 167/355920.

LANGUAGE

Italians will be impressed by and receptive to your attempts to speak their language. While most people who work in the tourist industry speak English, the average person on the street probably does not. A few helpful Italian words and phrases never hurt: *buon giorno* (hello/good morning); *arrivederci* (goodbye); *per favore* (please); *grazie* (thank you); *dov'è/dove sono . . .?* (where is/where are . . .?); *quanto costa . . .?* (how much is . . .?); *lei parla inglese?* (do you speak English?).

GAY AND LESBIAN TRAVELERS

Because Italians are affectionate in general, some hand-holding and hugging won't attract attention. But Italy's population is mostly Catholic, with a strong dose of machismo, and obvious displays of homosexual affection could get you in trouble—with the police in some places. Be subtle in small towns and in the south, and live it up in the thriving gay scenes of Bologna, Milan, Florence, and Rome.

VENICE AND THE VENETO

For hundreds of years, the cities of the Veneto came when Venice whistled. But the Veneto, the stretch of land that sprawls east–west between Venice and Verona and reaches far north to the Dolomites, is much more than a suburb of The Canaled One. While the Venetian Republic was busy becoming a maritime bully, the rest of the Veneto cities were forming civic centers, universities, and distinct cultural identities. Today the region is an expensive place to travel through and residents are notoriously closed to outsiders—but that doesn't deflect the annual flood of travelers, who come to ponder Palladian villas, peaceful green hill towns, and paintings by locals Titian and Tintoretto. The extensive hostel network, the allure of Venice, and the all-around cultural appeal make the Veneto one of the most touristed provinces in Italy.

VENICE

Pink palazzi, green canals, the blue Adriatic Sea, yellow signs pointing to Piazza San Marco, and too many red-face tourists swirl together to form Venice—no wonder the city's artists were into color over form. Ethereally beautiful, culturally vigorous, grossly overpriced, and infuriatingly crowded, Venice (Venezia) prods you into forming a strong opinion. Built on 100-some islands crisscrossed by canals, Venice thrived as a port town for many centuries, dominated at first by the Byzantine Empire. You can see the Byzantine thumbprint everywhere, especially in the onion-shape domes and opulent gold mosaics of the Basilica di San Marco. Venice hit its peak during the 13th–15th centuries, when rich merchants commissioned scores of ostentatious Venetian-Gothic palazzi, which still line the Grand Canal today. The city has been dependent on tourism for more than a century, and you're just going to have to adjust to paying at least L50,000 or more per person to sleep, and not much less for an edible dinner.

BASICS

VISITOR INFORMATION

APT (San Marco 71/G, tel. 041/5226356; open June–Sept., Tues.–Sun. 9:30–12:30 and 2–5; Oct.–May, Tues.–Sun. 9:40–3:20) also runs a small office in the train station (tel. 041/5298727; open daily 8:10–6:50). The main office on Piazza San Marco is less hectic.

AMERICAN EXPRESS

The office (San Marco 1471, on Salizzada San Moisè, tel. 1678/72000; open Mon.–Sat. 9–5:30) is two minutes from Piazza San Marco on the Ponte dell'Accademia path.

CHANGING MONEY

Try to change your money in Padova or wherever else you came from—Venice's rates are atrocious. Banks cluster on the San Marco side of the Ponte di Rialto, and on Calle Larga XXII Marzo on the path from Piazza San Marco to the Ponte dell'Accademia.

CONSULATE

United Kingdom (Dorsoduro 1051, near the Accademia, tel. 041/5227207). The nearest U.S. and Canadian consulates are in Milan (*see below*).

DISCOUNT TRAVEL AGENCY

Try the **Centro Turistico Studentesco** (CTS; Dorsoduro 3252, on Fondamenta Tagliapietra, tel. 041/5205660; open weekdays 9–12:30 and 3:30–7). From Ca' Foscari, take Calle Larga Foscari; take left on Fondamenta Tagliapietra before the bridge.

LAUNDRY

Lavaget (Cannaregio 1269, on Fondamenta Pescaria, tel. 041/715976) costs L15,000 per load, soap included. To get there, take the train station–Piazza San Marco route, cross first bridge, and take left on Fondamenta Pescaria.

PHONES AND MAIL

The **main post office** (San Marco 5555, facing Canal Grande north of Ponte di Rialto, tel. 041/5289317; open weekdays 8:15–7) is just north of Ponte Rialto. In the same building you'll find the **Telecom** office (open weekdays 8:30–12:30 and 4–7), where you can make calls and buy phone cards.

COMING AND GOING

BY BUS

You probably won't use buses in and out of Venice, but **ACTV** (P. Roma, tel. 041/5287886) Buses 2, 4, or 7 run to Mestre (L1200).

BY PLANE

International flights into Venice don't always cost more than flights to Milan. **Aeroporto Marco Polo** (tel. 041/2609260) is on the lagoon north of Venice. To get to and from **Piazzale Roma** (Venice's parking lot), your two cheapest options are to ride on the **ATVO** blue bus (20 min, L5000) or on the poky orange **ACTV** Bus 5 (30 min, L1200).

Canale
delle Sacche

Pte. della
Libertà

Tronchetto

Canale di S. Chiara

Bacino
Stazione Marittima

Canale Scomenzera

Canale di S. Maria Maggiore

Rio d. S. Maria Maggiore

Rio di S. Nicola

Sacca Físola

Canale d. Lauraneri

Canale delle Sacche

Rio del Battello

Canal Cannaregio

Rio di S. Girolamo

Rio d. Sensa

Rio d. Madonna dell'Orto

F. della Misericordia

Rio della Misericordia

Rio d. S. Fosca

R. di Noale

Campo del
Ghetto
Nuovo

R. t. S.
Leonardo

Stazione
Santa Lucia

Lista di Spagna

Riva di Biasio

Canal Grande

Lista di Bari

C. Riello

Rio d. S. Cassiano

C. d. Tintor

Campo Larga/
Fond. Megio

Bus
Station

Piazzale
Roma

C. d. S. Andrea

F. d. S. Simeon Piccolo

S. S. Simeon Piccolo

Corte
Canal

C. d. Lacca

Rio Marin

R. di
Zan Degola

Campo dei Frari

Campo
S. Polo

Rio terra dei Pensieri

Rio
Nuovo

F. Minotto

S. S.
Pantalon

Rio della
Frescada

Rio Foscari

Campo di
S. Margherita

Rio terrà
Canal

Rio d. S. Margherita

Rio d. S. Barnaba

Campo
S. Barnaba

Calle
Avogaria

Calle de
Toletta

Rio d. Ognissanti

Fondamenta delle Zattere

Canal Grande

C. d.
Carrozze

Campo
S. Stefano

C. Morosini

Riva

C. d.
Mandola

Campo
S. Angelo

C. Lga
22 Marzo

Campo
della
Carità

R. d. S. Viu

Rio d. Fornace

Canale Giudecca

Fond. S. Biagio

Rio d. S. Biagio

R.d. Convertite

Isola della Giudecca

Fond. S. Eufemia

Sights ●

Basilica di
San Marco, **25**

Ca' d'Oro, **7**

Collezione Peggy
Guggenheim, **22**

Gallerie
dell'Accademia, **20**

Isola di San Giorgio
Maggiore, **27**

Museo Civico
Correr, **24**

Museo Communitá
Ebraica, **1**

Palazzo Ducale, **26**

Ponte di Rialto, **12**

Santa Maria
della Salute, **23**

Santa Maria
Gloriosa dei
Frari, **10**

Scuola di San
Giorgio degli
Schiavoni, **18**

Scuola Grande di
San Rocco, **9**

Lodging ○

Albergo Bernardi-
Semenzato, **8**

Albergo Rossi, **3**

Alloggi Trattoria
Nuova, **5**

Caneva, **13**

Casa Bettina, **17**

Casa Gerotto, **6**

Domus Cavanis, **21**

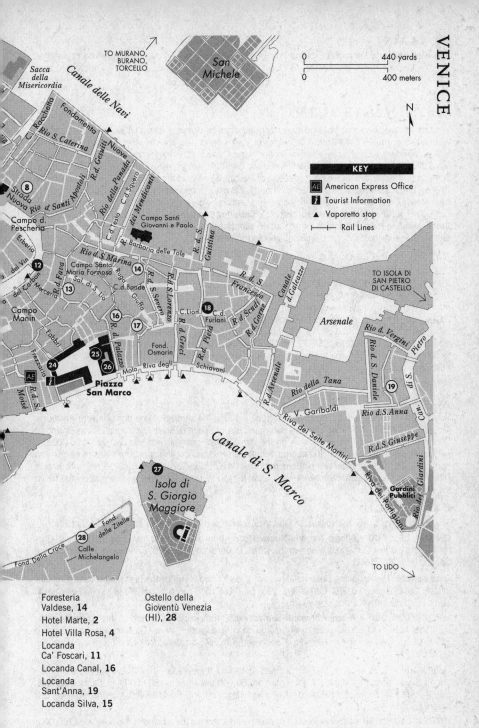

TO MURANO,
BURANO,
TORCELLO

Sacca
della
Misericordia

San
Michele

| 0 | | 440 yards |
| 0 | | 400 meters |

Canale delle Navi

KEY

AE American Express Office

i Tourist Information

▲ Vaporetto stop

╽─┼─┤ Rail Lines

Fondamenta Nuove

R.d. Gesuiti

R. dei Mendicanti

Campo Santi
Giovanni e Paolo

Rio S. Caterina

R. della Panada

C.d. Savero

Ca' Testa

(8)
Strada
Nuova
Rio d' Santi Apostoli

Campo d.
Pescheria

Erberio

del Vin

(12)

Mercaria

C. del Carbon

R.d. Fava

(13)

Campo
Manin

Fabbri

Frezzaria

(24)

AE
i

R.d. S.
Moise

Freicuaria

(25)

(26)

Molo
Riva degli

**Piazza
San Marco**

R. Barbaria delle Tole

Rio d.S. Marina

Campo Santa
Maria Formosa

Ruga

Sal. di S. Lio

C.d. Bande

R.d. S. Severo

(14)

R.d. Palazzo

(16)

(17)

R.d. Greci

R.d. Pietà

Fond.
Osmarin

C.Lion

C.d
Furlani

(18)

Schiavoni

Guistina

R. d. S.

R. d. S.
Francesco

R. d. Scudi

R.d. Corne

Canale d.Galeazze

Canale d'Arsenale

R.d. Arsenale

Arsenale

TO ISOLA DI
SAN PIETRO
DI CASTELLO

Rio d. Vergini

Rio d. S. Daniele

di S. Pietro

(19)

Can.

Rio della Tana

V. Garibaldi

Rio d.S.Anna

Riva dei Sette Martiri

R.d.S.Giuseppe

Rio del Giardini

**Gardini
Pubblici**

Riva dei partigiani

Rio del

Canale di S. Marco

(27)

**Isola di
S. Giorgio
Maggiore**

ci

(28)

Fond
delle Zitelle

Calle
Michelangelo

Fond. Della Croce

TO LIDO

Foresteria
Valdese, **14**

Hotel Marte, **2**

Hotel Villa Rosa, **4**

Locanda
Ca' Foscari, **11**

Locanda Canal, **16**

Locanda
Sant'Anna, **19**

Locanda Silva, **15**

Ostello della
Gioventù Venezia
(HI), **28**

BY TRAIN

The **Venezia-Santa Lucia train station** (tel. 1478/88088 toll-free) is in Venice proper; don't get off at Venezia-Mestre. Trains go to Milan (3–4 hrs, L22,000), Rome (5 hrs, L47,000), Padova (30 min, L3500), and Florence (3 hrs, L22,000).

GETTING AROUND

Venice's narrow alleys and close-quartered buildings can be dizzying. Invest L4000 in a map from any tobacco shop (the APT offers two maps—they're always out of one, and the other a shameless waste of a tree), wander about and pay attention to landmarks—and try to enjoy getting lost. At least the yellow signs all over town pointing you to San Marco and the Rialto are great navigational tools. The train station and bus station are on the northwest end of the city; San Marco is south/central. The **Canal Grande** (the big one that makes a backwards "S" through the city), is bridged by the Ponte di Scalzi (near the train station), the Ponte di Rialto (in the center), and the Ponte dell'Accademia. For orientation purposes, get to know the six *sestieri* (districts): **Castello, Cannaregio, San Marco, Dorsoduro, Santa Croce,** and **San Polo.** To confuse things further, addresses usually don't include a street name but contain the name of the district and a seemingly random number.

BY VAPORETTO

The *vaporetto* (water bus) is the only way to get to the hostel on Giudecca, or to any of the other islands. It's also a scenic, but pricey, way to get around without getting lost. **Vaporetto 1** docks at every stop along the Grand Canal; **82** makes fewer stops. The **52** makes a huge loop of the island. Vaporetti marked LIMITATO only make a loop between two major stops. You buy tickets for the vaporetti at the kiosks by the *fermate* (stops) or onboard if the kiosk is closed (you pay an extra L800). A one-way ticket bought beforehand is L4500, round-trip L9000, though some trips out in the lagoon cost a bit more. You can also get 24-hour tickets (L15,000), 72-hour tickets (L30,000), and one-week tickets (L55,000). Be sure to stamp your ticket in the yellow boxes by the stops before boarding. If you're caught without a validated ticket, you could be fined L30,000.

WHERE TO SLEEP

You'll need a miracle to find cheap digs in Venice during the summer if you don't have reservations. Most budget hotels are in Cannaregio (along the Lista di Spagna), scattered through Castello, and in Dorsoduro (near the university). A one- or two-star hotel will generally run you L30,000–L65,000 per person; breakfast is usually included. You can stay in Padova, but the commute takes more than an hour. For L15,000, the **hotel reservations desk** (tel. 041/715288; open daily 8 AM–10 PM, until 9 PM in winter) at the train station will make a reservation for you in a one-star hotel and then apply the fee to the price of your room.

CANNAREGIO

This neighborhood near the station isn't the most scenic part of town, but it's chock-full of hotels.

UNDER L65,000 • Alloggi Trattoria Nuova. Rooms here are dark and fairly ugly, but clean. Register and the get key at the trattoria down the street. Doubles cost L60,000. *Cannaregio 189, on Lista di Spagna, tel. 041/716005.*

Casa Gerotto. This spanking clean hotel has hot showers and is run by the best mother-and-son team in Italy. Doubles are L60,000. *Cannaregio 283, tel. 041/715361. From Lista di Spagna, left on Campo San Geremia and look for CALDERAN sign.*

UNDER L95,000 • Albergo Bernardi-Semenzato. The *dipendenza* (annex) of this otherwise unremarkable hotel is in an old palazzo with some canal and garden views. Doubles with breakfast are L90,000. Luggage storage is available. *Cannaregio 4363/66, on Calle dell'Oca off Strada Nuova, tel. 041/5227257.*

Hotel Marte. Rooms are comfortable in a chain-motel way. If they're full, they'll send you to the similarly priced **Biasin** across the canal. Doubles start at L60,000 low season, L80,000 high. *Cannaregio 338, tel. 041/716351. From Lista di Spagna, follow San Marco signs to Ponte delle Guglie and turn right just before bridge.*

UNDER L110,000 • Albergo Rossi. Impeccably clean rooms are a bit noisy. Doubles are L100,000. *Cannaregio 262, on Calle delle Procuratie off Lista di Spagna, tel. 041/715164.*

Hotel Villa Rosa. Here you don't get ambiance, just mass-produced furniture and bare walls. But L90,000 does buy you hot water, clean bathrooms, and breakfast. *Cannaregio 389, tel. 041/716569. From Lista di Spagna, turn left on Calle della Misericordia.*

DORSODURO

The university is in this district, which means you'll find students and several casual cafés in this neighborhood.

UNDER L85,000 • Domus Cavanis. This place is a steal at L80,000 for well-kept doubles in a prime location between the Accademia and the Zattere. *Dorsoduro 912, tel. 041/5287374. From Ponte dell'Accademia, turn right on Rio Terrà Foscarini. Cash only. Closed Oct.–mid-May.*

UNDER L100,000 • Locanda Ca' Foscari. A friendly, English-speaking manager and good location are among the perks at this hotel. Spacious, pleasant doubles run L95,000, including breakfast. Reception is open until 10 PM. *Dorsoduro 3887/B, on Calle della Frescada, tel. 041/710401. Cash only.*

CASTELLO

The edge of Castello closest to San Marco is predictably expensive, but you'll find good deals further into the district.

UNDER L55,000 • Casa Bettina. Large doubles with wood floors go for L50,000. *Castello 4388, on Campo San Giovanni Novo, tel. 041/5239084. Cash only.*

UNDER L100,000 • Caneva. Airy rooms are the cheapest you'll find close to San Marco. Doubles are L90,000, but prices fall considerably in the off-season. *Castello 5515, on Ramo dietro la Fava, tel. 041/5228118. From Ponte di Rialto, walk past Campo San Bartolomeo to Calle Stagnieri, cross bridge to Campo della Fava; Ramo della Fava is on the right. Cash only first two nights.*

Locanda Canal. Here you'll find bright, big rooms with rickety furniture. Doubles cost L90,000, including breakfast. *Castello 4422/C, on Fondamenta Remedio, tel. 041/5234538. From Campo Santa Maria Formosa, walk behind church to Campiello Querini, veer right to Fondamenta Remedio. Cash only.*

Locanda Sant'Anna. In a working class neighborhood past the Arsenale, this hotel has a courtyard conducive to relaxing. Doubles are L95,000, including breakfast. Expect a curfew of 12:30. *Castello 269, on Corte del Bianco, tel. and fax 041/5286466. From west end of V. Garibaldi, veer right on Fondamenta Sant'Anna, left on 2nd bridge, right on Corte del Bianco.*

Locanda Silva. The staff is bored but helpful and some of the L90,000 doubles have canal views; all are clean. *Castello 4423, 30122, on Fondamenta Remedio, tel. 041/5227643. Cash only.*

HOSTELS

Venice has one perennially packed HI hostel, but there are enough dormlike places (often called *foresterie*) to ensure that you get a cheap bed for the night. If the places below are full, try **L. Murialdo** (Cannaregio 3512, tel. 041/719933), **Patronato Salesiano Leone XIII** (Castello 1281, tel. 041/5287299), **Ostello Santa Fosca** (Cannaregio 2372, tel. 041/715775), or the basic dorm beds at **Casa Gerotto** (*see* Cannaregio, *above*). For a taste of strict convent life at L19,000, women can try **Istituto Canossiano** (tel. 041/5222157).

Foresteria Valdese. Basic dorms are L28,000 the first night, L27,000 thereafter. One large room has a kitchen and is great for groups of three to six. *Castello 5170, tel. 041/5286797. From Campo Santa Maria Formosa, walk down Calle Lunga Santa Maria Formosa to the end, and cross bridge to Protestant church; it's on the right.*

Ostello della Gioventù Venezia (HI). Good luck trying to get a bed here in summer; phone reservations are only accepted October-May. Beds fetch L24,000, breakfast included. There's an 11:30 curfew. Only HI members can stay here; they'll sell you a card for L30,000. *Giudecca 86, on Fondamenta della Croce, tel. 041/5238211. Vaporetto 82 to Zitelle/Ostello stop and turn right. Lockout 10–6.*

FOOD

It's just not right that the pigeons eat better than you do. Food in Venice tends to be both bland and overpriced. Stay away from the restaurants in San Marco, unless you want to sample the most expensive and unappealing food in town. One exception to the rule is **Vino, Vino** (San Marco 2007/A, Ponte delle Veste, tel. 041/5237027; cash only for bills under L30,000), where you can sip wine as you wait for a table, and then sup on pasta dish like gnocchi with arugula sauce. If you wander through the back streets of

THE GREAT CORPSE ROBBERY

A symbol of Venetian prowess, the lions all over town and parts of the Veneto have a wacky tale behind them. In AD 828, two Venetian merchants on business in Alexandria spirited off with St. Mark's body and smuggled it back to Venice in a shipment of pork so that Muslim customs officials wouldn't inspect it. Mark was instated as the new patron saint of the city, and both the city officials' and the sneaky merchants' consciences were clear—apparently an angel had once told Mark that his body would be buried here. The angel's message is written on all winged lion statues, which symbolize St. Mark.

Dorsoduro and San Polo, you can find excellent meals at relatively low prices. When you're ready to splurge, try some of the city's famous seafood, like *seppia con polenta* (squid in its ink, served on polenta) and spaghetti *alle vongole* (with clams). If you're short on cash, put together a meal of your own at the **Mercato di Rialto** on the San Polo side of the Rialto Bridge.

CANNAREGIO
Avoid eating anywhere near the train station and push on into the narrow streets north of Strada Nuova.

UNDER L10,000 • Iguana. This is the only place for hundreds of miles where you can get a burrito (L9500) smothered in fresh guacamole (L3000)—washed down with a Corona (L5000). *Cannaregio 2515, on Fondamenta della Misericordia, tel. 041/716722. Closed Tues.*

UNDER L15,000 • Ristorante L'Arca di Noè. Imagine, a macrobiotic restaurant in Venice. Primi are healthy versions of already healthy Italian dishes, like tagliatelle with *seitan* (wheat gluten). *Cannaregio 5401, on Calle Larga Giacinto Gallina, tel. 041/5238153. From Campo SS Giovanni e Paolo, cross bridge leading into Calle Larga. Cash only. Closed Sat. lunch and Sun.*

SAN POLO AND SANTA CROCE
Not many tourists make it into the winding streets of San Polo and Santa Croce—good news for you as food tends to be better and cheaper here. You'll have to do some tricky navigating to find the neighborhoods' restaurants.

UNDER L10,000 • Alle Oche. You'll have to choose from 50 different kinds of gargantuan pizzas, such as the Inferno, with spicy salami, hot peppers, and mozzarella. *Santa Croce 1552/A, tel. 041/5241161. From Campo San Polo, take Calle Bernardo, cross bridge, 1st left on Rio Terrà Secondo, right on Rio Terrà Primo Perrucchetta, cross first bridge, left on Calle delle Oche. Closed Sun.*

Due Colonne. This is considered the best pizza in Venice—look for seasonal toppings like buffalo mozzarella, tomatoes, and fresh arugula (L12,000). *San Polo 2343, on Campo San Agostin, tel. 041/5240686. Closed Sun.*

DORSODURO
The university crowd demands a lot of cheap, honest food, though a few places do cater to discriminating palates.

UNDER L10,000 • Al Profeta. Above-average pizzas range from L5000 to L28,000, size depending. There's a garden in back. *Dorsoduro 2671, Calle Lunga San Barnaba, tel. 041/5237466. From SE corner of Campo San Barnaba, take Calle Lunga San Barnaba. Closed Mon. in winter.*

Crepizza. This friendly family-run place does pasta, but pizzas—starting at L4000—like *biancaneve* (mozzarella and basil) are your best bet. *Dorsoduro 3757/3761, on Calle San Pantalon, tel. 041/5229189. Closed Tues.*

UNDER L15,000 • Taverna San Trovaso. The best modestly priced restaurant in all of Venice serves exquisite secondi for L10,000–L16,000. Try the spaghetti *alla pirata*, with sweet peppers, tomatoes, and mussels. Reservations are recommended. *Dorsoduro 1016, on Fondamenta Priuli near Accademia, tel. 041/5203703. Closed Mon.*

UNDER L25,000 • L'Incontro. Treat yourself—the dishes here are creative, fresh, and excellent. Primi include some interesting pasta variations, and the selection of secondi (around L20,000) depends upon which fish were brought in that morning. Make reservations. *Dorsoduro 3062/A, Rio Terrà Canal, tel. 041/52222404. On edge of Campo Santa Margherita towards Ponte dell'Accademia. Closed Mon., 2–3 wks in Jan, and 1 wk in Aug.*

CASTELLO

As long as you stay away from the back side of Piazza San Marco, you'll do okay in Castello. Via Garibaldi has lots of little places with reasonable fixed-price menus of varying quality.

UNDER L15,000 • Trattoria alla Fonte. If you're starving in San Marco, take a short walk to this trattoria for pizza or pasta, like the gnocchi *ai quattro formaggi* (with four cheeses; L10,000). *Castello 3820, on Campo Bandiera e Moro, tel. 041/5238698. Closed Wed.*

WORTH SEEING

You could easily argue that Venice is the most beautiful city in the world, and without marathon distances or car traffic, almost every inch of the city is open to exploration. During the madness of summer, it's not a bad idea to visit a museum at lunchtime, when the crowded streets are at their most miserable. Note that last admissions are generally an hour before closing.

During the Risorgimento, those who backed Italy conspired in Caffè Florian, on the Procuratorie Vecchie, while supporters of Austria plotted in Quadri, on the Procuratorie Nuove. Now they seem to plot together to ream tourists, charging L8,500 for caffè when the bands are playing.

SAN MARCO

The center of cultural life in Venice, the *sestiere* of San Marco is dominated by the tourist-clogged Piazza San Marco and the spectacular Basilica di San Marco, but it's also home to some slightly less-hyped attractions. **Teatro La Fenice** (San Marco 1965, tel. 041/5210161), once one of the world's finest opera houses, is now a web of scaffolding and charred innards after suffering its second fire in 1996 (it was rebuilt in 1837 after the first fire). During restoration, performances are being held in **Pala La Fenice,** a temporary outdoor tent in Tronchetto (take Vaporetti 4 or 82 or the *FeniceBus* from P. Roma); get tickets at Cassa di Risparmio (Campo San Luca, near San Marco, tel. 041/5210161).

PIAZZA SAN MARCO • San Marco is the single most-visited spot in Italy, and nobody's denying it. Prepare to be overwhelmed, both by the outlandish majesty of the buildings and the gaudy tourist fanfare. The huge, hallucinatory **Basilica di San Marco** (open Mon.–Sat. 9:45–5, Sun. 2–5) was reconstructed in 1094 after the original was burned down in an uprising against a new doge. The builders of the church were obviously smitten with Byzantine architecture: Domes and gold mosaics abound. The interior is a confusing and wonderful jambalaya of Byzantine, Gothic, and Renaissance styles. Take a free guided tour, with explanations of the mosaics' biblical significance, at 11 AM or 3 PM weekdays; tours start at the entrance hall. Don't bother with the treasury, but the **Pala d'Oro** is worth the L3000 admission; this altar screen is covered with more than 2,000 jewels and lots of gold—all proof of Venetian dominance in the 12th–14th centuries.

In addition to being a religious center, the piazza has been the seat of the municipal government since the 9th century. The pink-checkered **Palazzo Ducale** (tel. 041/5224951; admission L14,000, includes Museo Civico Correr; open daily 8:30–7; last tickets 5:30), next to the basilica, was the doges' private home and the seat of courts, prisons, and political intrigues. It's also a perfect example of Venetian Gothic architecture. Inside, the rooms are covered with paintings by Tintoretto, Veronese, Tiepolo, Titian, and other Venetian masters. From the Great Council Hall, walk down to the **Ponte dei Sospiri** (Bridge of Sighs), which leads to part of the prisons. On the other end of the piazza, the **Museo Civico Correr** (tel. 041/5225625; admission L14,000, includes Palazzo Ducale; open daily 9–7) provides a thorough history of the city and helps put all those paintings, palazzi, and canals into context. The display includes a room of portraits by the Bellini brothers and a sinister-looking chastity belt.

The two long buildings stretching out from the basilica are the **Procuratie,** were the offices of the procurators tended to the more mundane aspects of running the city while the doge was out a-conquering. The Procuratie Vecchie start at the **Torre dell'Orologio** (Clock Tower), where bronze "Moors" strike the hour on the roof. The Procuratie Nuove stand opposite. After 11 centuries of standing strong as a watch-tower and lighthouse, the 328-ft **Campanile di San Marco** (elevator admission L5000; open daily 10–6) suddenly collapsed into a pile of rubble in 1902. (An exact replica was rebuilt within 10 years.) The view from the breezy belfry is the tower's best feature.

DORSODURO

The site of the university and two of Venice's greatest museums, the Galleria dell'Accadema and the Collezione Peggy Guggenheim, Dorsoduro is also a mellow residential district. The fantastically fes-tooned **Santa Maria della Salute** (Campo della Salute; donation L2000; open daily 9–noon and 3–6:30), at the tip of Dorsoduro, was built during the 17th century as thanks to the Virgin Mary for saving Venice from yet another plague, even though half of the city's population died anyway. The main draw of the church is its **sacristy,** home to some of Titian's major works and Tintoretto's *The Wedding at Cana.*

GALLERIE DELL'ACCADEMIA • This collection is the single most stunning and extensive gathering of Venetian art, from 14th-century gold-gilt altarpieces to 18th-century bucolic fantasies. Don't miss the enigmatic *Tempest* by Giorgione and Veronese's enormous *Feast in the House of Levi. Dorsoduro, at foot of Ponte dell'Accademia, tel. 041/5222247. Admission: L12,000. Open Mon.–Sat. 9–7, Sun. 9–2.*

COLLEZIONE PEGGY GUGGENHEIM • In 1949 American heiress Peggy Guggenheim came to Venice to escape the New York City art scene. She died 30 years later, leaving behind her 18th-century palazzo and the 300 or so works that make up Italy's most important modern art collection. You may have seen these artists before—Pollock, Klee, Picasso, Man Ray, Giacometti, and Kandinsky—but you haven't seen this collection, and Peggy had a hell of a nose for art. *Dorsoduro 701, on Fondamenta Venier dai Leoni, tel. 041/5206288. Admission: L12,000. Open Wed.–Mon. 11–6.*

CANNAREGIO

This neighborhood of extremes covers both the salty area around the Misericordia and Fondamente Nuove and the upscale Strada Nuova, a commercial street lined with shops and gelaterie. Cannaregio also holds the **Jewish Ghetto** and several thousand churches within its northern bulge.

CA' D'ORO • Called the "House of Gold" because the facade once had gilded carvings, this Gothic palazzo is no longer golden, but it's still an amazing example of Venetian Gothic palatial architecture. Inside, the Galleria Giorgio Franchetti displays *St. Sebastian* by Mantegna and *Venus* by Titian. *Cannare-gio 3932, from train station, Vaporetto 1 to Ca' d'Oro stop, tel. 041/5238790. Admission: L4000. Open daily 9–2.*

GHETTO EBREO • A symbol of oppression, and at times, tolerance, the Jewish Ghetto tells an uneasy story of Venice's history. Jews were first welcomed to the city in 1381, when Venice badly needed funds to defend the lagoon against invaders; by 1516, Jews were shunted to the ghetto, forced to wear iden-tifying clothing, and denied equal economic opportunity. As you walk under the underpass leading to the ghetto, you can see the grooves where bars were placed to keep the residents in at night. The **Museo Comunità Ebraica** houses a small collection of Torah screens and the like; more interesting is the museum's hourly tour (L10,000) of the five beautiful synagogues still in use. *Cannaregio 2902/B, on Campo del Ghetto Nuovo, tel. 041/715359. Near Fondamenta di Cannaregio. Admission: L4000. Open Sun.–Thurs. 10–4:30, Fri 10–3:30. Closed Jewish holidays.*

CASTELLO

The more-touristed part of Castello—the streets and canals extending eastward out of San Marco—holds in store grand palazzi; stunning churches, like the 15th-century **San Zaccaria;** and tacky souvenir stands. By the time you've wandered out by the **Arsenale,** once the most important ship factory in Europe, anybody not Venetian is either lost or a serious explorer. On **Via Garibaldi** you can still find old folks who seem to do nothing but smoke, chat, shop, and drink wine all day.

SCUOLA DI SAN GIORGIO DEGLI SCHIAVONI • Once a guild for Venice's large Slavic commu-nity (which Venice subsidized in the hopes of getting a piece of the eastern Adriatic coast), the Scuola di San Giorgio degli Schiavoni houses Carpaccio's painting cycle about St. George and the Dragon and St. Jerome and the Lion. The building itself has barely been touched since the 1600s. *Castello, on Ponte dei Greci, tel. 041/5228828. Admission: L5000. Open Tues.–Sat. 9:30–12:30 and 3:30–6:30, Sun. 9:30–12:30.*

SAN POLO AND SANTA CROCE

Quiet streets and tiny canals characterize this area near the center and surrounded by a curve of the Canale Grande. San Polo has a handful of palazzi on Campo San Polo and some of the largest and most luscious gardens in Venice. The neighborhood around the little church of San Giacomo dell'Orio is strictly local. The bulky brick exterior of the church **Santa Maria Gloriosa dei Frari** (Campo dei Frari, tel. 041/5222637; admission L2000; open daily 9–11:45 and 2:30–6) is balanced by the delicate art inside, including some works by Titian, Bellini, and the Florentine Donatello. The link between the commercial heart of the city and San Marco since 1172, the **Ponte di Rialto** is now full of souvenir hawkers and gawking tourists. The marble bridge was designed by Antonio da Ponte (whose name happened to mean "of the bridge") after he beat out Sansovino, Michelangelo, and Palladio in a 1551 competition.

SCUOLA GRANDE DI SAN ROCCO • Tintoretto was a busy, busy guy: His paintings are plastered all over Venice, but this former guild—originally formed to exalt San Rocco, another anti-plague saint—contains some of his best work. The most interesting paintings are in the Mary cycle on the ground floor. *San Polo 3052, tel. 041/5234864. On Campo San Rocco, behind I Frari's apse. Admission: L8000. Open daily 9–5:30.*

FESTIVALS

Venice's weeklong **Carnevale** features parades and performances more or less daily, during which participants don traditional Venetian *commedia dell'arte* masks and costumes. The date varies, but it's always at the end of February or beginning of March, right before the start of Lent. On the third Sunday in July, Venice holds the **Festa del Redentore,** an offer of thanks to Jesus for ending a plague back in the 1500s. The real fun comes at night, when an unbelievable fireworks display explodes over thousands of partying Venetians clamoring from streamer-covered cargo launches and trash barges turned into floating dinner parties. In late August and September, Venice's **International Film Festival** is *the* film industry party, second only to Cannes; for information, call the Biennale office (tel. 041/5218711).

After visiting Venice's Basilica di San Marco, catch Vaporetto 1, 5, or 82 at San Zaccharia to Isola di San Giorgio Maggiore to see the beautiful Church of San Giorgio Maggiore. The bare white Palladian walls are the best antidote for Byzantine overload.

AFTER DARK

You love the nightlife. You've got to boogie. Not in this town, baby. If you want to go clubbing in summer, you have to go to Mestre or the Lido; if you're looking for classical music, check with the APT for a list of current concerts. **Le Bistrot de Venise** (San Marco 4685/86, Calle Fabbri, tel. 041/5236651) tries really hard to be French, with crepes and café-art on the walls. It's a good place to grab a late bite and sometimes hear live music until 1 AM. **Paradiso Perduto** (Cannaregio 2540, on Fondamenta della Misericordia, tel. 041/720581; closed Wed.) will immediately become home base for traveling hipsters, though it becomes much more mellow in winter.

NEAR VENICE

Murano is most famous for its production of glassware and really has little else to offer. From the vaporetto stop, walk over the bridge to the Fondamenta Venier to get good deals on glass goods, but expect salespeople to grab you by the arm and try to steer you into their shop. Pay L8000 admission at the **Museo Vetrario di Murano** (Fondamenta Giustinian 8, tel. 041/739586; closed Wed.) to see a nifty exhibit of glass through the ages.

The lace-making island of **Burano** is a pretty and tranquil old fishing community, with brilliantly painted houses. Deserted, swampy **Torcello** was once the most populated island in the lagoon—about 200,000 people lived here in its heyday—but today only a handful remain. The **Cattedrale di Torcello** (tel. 041/730084; admission L1500) was built during the 7th century, and the building's interior reveals astonishing 11th- and 12th-century mosaics. According to legend, Lucifer himself can be seen at the **Devil's Bridge,** which earned its name when drunkards fell from it, later claiming, "the devil made me do it!"

The tragic elegance of the *Lido* in Thomas Mann's *Death in Venice* is now the tragic scuzziness of too many people, too much pollution, and not enough sand. Nevertheless, many Venetians come here in summer to escape the tourists. If looking at water all day has made you desperate for a swim, the **free public beach** (down Viale Santa Maria Elizabetta from the vaporetto stop) is less toxic than the canals.

COCKTAILS
VENETIAN STYLE

Forget that martini or cosmopolitan and see how it's done in Venice. The Bellini, peach juice with champagne or Prosecco, is heavenly at Harry's Bar (Calle Vallaresso 1323, tel. 041/5285777), where it was perfected by bartender Claudio Ponzio, or Ai Sportivi (Campo di Santa Margherita, tel. 041/5211598). Fragolino is a Veneto specialty—a sweet, spicy, nectarlike wine, usually red. After dinner, indulge in an exquisite sgroppino, a whip of lemon sorbet and vodka, at Haig's American Bar (San Marco 2477/B, tel. 041/5232368). But the true Venetian drink is the spritzer, white wine and seltzer water ordered bitter (with Campari) or all'aperol, with orange bitters. You haven't lived the good life until you've sipped a spritz at Bar Rosso (Dorsoduro 2963, on Campo di Santa Margherita, tel. 041/5287998).

The wineshop Casa Mattiazzi Vini e Spumanti sells excellent, cheap wine by the liter. Grab an empty bottle, jar, or laundry tub and bring it in; they'll fill it up with red, white, or sparkling wines from their wooden vats. There are locations in Campo di Santa Margherita (tel. 041/5231979), in Castello (on V. Garibaldi, tel. 041/5224893, and at Castello 5179 (on Calle Lunga near Santa Maria Formosa, tel. 041/5237592).

You can rent bikes at **Lazzari Bruno** (Gran Viale Santa Maria Elisabetta 21/B, tel. 041/5268019) for about L5000 an hour.

PADUA

Most people use Padua (Padova) as a place to stay while visiting Venice—they see Giotto's beautiful Cappella degli Scrovegni and then skedaddle. If you come in August, when Padua is hotter than hell, this reaction might be justified. A city of both high-rises and history, it's not as beautiful, but it's cheaper, more convenient, and mellower than other Veneto towns. Student restaurants, lame theme bars, and English-language bookstores are everywhere. The **APT** tourist office (open summer, Mon.–Sat. 9–7, Sun. 8:30–12:30; winter Mon.–Sat. 9:15–5:45, Sun. 9–noon) in the train station stocks the most comprehensive source of information, the free booklet *Padova Today*.

COMING AND GOING

The large **train station** (P. Stazione Ferrovia, tel. 1478/88088) has frequent trains to Venice (30 min, L3500) and Milan (3 hrs, L19,400). The **SITA** bus station (V. Trieste 42, tel. 049/8206811) has buses to small towns in the Veneto like Bassano del Grappa (1 hr, L5700). From the train station, walk up Corso del Popolo and turn left on Via Trieste. Corso del Popolo runs from the train station to town center, changing its name many times along the way.

WHERE TO SLEEP AND EAT

Most cheap hotels lie southeast of the university. "Holiday houses" pop up July–September; try **Antonianum** (V. Donatello 24, tel. 049/651444), which has doubles with bath for L25,000 per person. Tiny, spotless doubles with bath at **Al Santo** (V. del Santo 147, ½ block north of P. Santo, tel. 049/8752131) cost L75,000. **Albergo-Locanda La Perla** (V. Cesarotti 67, tel. 049/8758939) has clean doubles for L55,000. At the hostel, **Ostello Città di Padova** (V. Aleardi 30, tel. 049/8752219), you get a bed and breakfast for L20,000. The price is reduced if you reserve for three or more nights.

Your food budget goes pretty far in Padua. One money-saver is the daily **open-air market** in twin Piazzas Erbe and Frutte. **Trattoria al Pero** (V. Santa Lucia 72, 1 block north of P. dei Signori, tel. 049/8758794; closed Sun. and Aug.) serves authentic Veneto food at low prices. After dinner, head to **Lucifer Young** (V. Altinate 89, tel. 049/8752251), an imaginative bar based on Dante's *Inferno*. To get here, walk down Corso del Popolo and turn left on Via Altinate, just after Piazza Garibaldi.

WORTH SEEING

The APT office (*see above*) sells an all-inclusive ticket to Padua's sights for L15,000. The tiny **Cappella degli Scrovegni** (P. Eremitani, tel. 049/8204550; open daily 9–7; winter, 9–6) is home to Giotto's New Testament fresco cycle, which is regarded as marking the end of medieval art and the beginning of the Renaissance. The captivating frescoes display an individual human expression and three-dimensional space unseen before in medieval art. The admission ticket (L10,000) also gets you into the other museums in the Eremitani complex. At the bizarre, grab-bag Gothic-Byzantine-Renaissance **Basilica di Sant'Antonio** (P. del Santo; open daily 6:30 AM–7 PM), you'll find everything from artwork by Donatello, including the equestrian monument to *Gattamelata* outside, to the morbid remains of the saint's tongue and jaw in the apse. People come from all over the world to request help or give thanks to the patron saint of lost and found objects. **Caffè Pedrocchi** (P. Pedrocchi; closed at press time for restoration), the most elaborate place in Padua to sip coffee, was a Risorgimento haven for students and intellectuals. On February 8, 1848, it was the seat of a nationalist insurrection.

VERONA

A collection of stone-lined streets, stagelike piazzas, and sidewalks paved with characteristic pink marble, Verona is one of the oldest, best-preserved, and most beautiful cities in Italy. It hit its first peak during the 1st century BC, when the Romans used it as a pit stop on the trade route to the rest of Europe. In the Middle Ages, the Scaligeri clan built the city up as a prestigious family domain, and during the 15th century, Venice came west and sucked the city into its empire. Instead of challenging Venice's power, Verona decided to turn all its aspirations inward, restoring Roman ruins and building up its cultural cache (ie: Shakespeare placed Romeo, Juliet, and a couple of gentlemen here). Tourism is very big here, and you might detect a snide attitude from the monied locals. But unlike Venice, in Verona it feels like some of the people in the streets might actually *live* here.

BASICS

APT has tourist offices in the train station (tel. 045/8000861; open Mon.–Sat. 8–7:30, Sun. 9–noon; winter Mon.–Sat. 9–6) and on Piazza Brà (V. Leoncino 61, tel. 045/592828; open Mon.–Sat. 8–8). The *Passport Verona* brochure comes with a map and a list of cheap hotels, plus up-to-date information on concerts and festivals. Two blocks south of Piazza Brà, the **Fabretto Viaggi e Turismo** (C. Porto Nuovo 11, tel. 045/8009045; open weekdays 8:30–7, Sat. 9–noon), is an American Express agent. Bring your debit card; there are ATMs all over town.

COMING AND GOING

The main station is **Verona Porta Nuova** (P. XXV Aprile, tel. 1478/88088). Trains run to Milan (1¾ hrs, L12,100), Venice (2 hrs, L10,100), Rome (5 hrs, L42,000), and Florence (2¾ hrs, L18,800). Get an **APT bus** (P. XXV Aprile, tel. 045/8004129) for the less-visited towns of the region. From either station, walk down Corso Porta Nuova to Piazza Brà in the town center.

WHERE TO SLEEP AND EAT

The center has a few budget hotels. Call in advance to get a room in sunny, central **Locanda Catullo** (V. Valerio Catullo 1, tel. 045/8002786; doubles L70,000). The **Albergo Arena** (Stradone Porta Palio 2, tel. 045/8032440) isn't that cheap—doubles without bath are L85,000—but you wanted to sleep central. At least it's clean. The central **Armando** (V. Dietro Pallone 1, tel. 045/8000206) has doubles without bath for L80,000–L90,000; beyond location, you don't get a lot for your money, and it's often full. **Cancellata** (V. Colonnello Fincato 4, tel. 045/532820) has functional, unexciting, but clean and quiet rooms. Doubles with bath fetch L80,000–L90,000; it's five minutes from the center by bus. **Ostello della Gioventù** (Villa Francescati (Salita Fontana del Ferro 15, across Ponte Nuovo and Ponte Pignolo, Bus

72 or 90 Sun. and nights, tel. 045/590360), a 16th-century villa adorned with frescoes, lets beds for L20,000; camping in the garden costs about L8000.

Cross the river into the Veronetta (university) district and you'll find better food at better prices than in the center. The vegetarian restaurant **Il Grillo Parlante** (Vicolo Seghe San Tommaso 10, off P. Isolo, tel. 045/591156; closed Thurs. dinner and Mon.) serves filling secondi and spinach croquettes for about L9000 to anarchist types. Locals go to **Trattoria dal Ropeton** (V. San Giovanni 46, tel. 045/8030040; closed Tues.) for delicious pasta and secondi (L12,000). From the hostel, walk down Salita Fontana del Ferro and turn left on San Giovanni.

WORTH SEEING

The center is jammed with Austrian, Venetian, and Roman buildings, all within easy walking distance of each other. Roman arches mark the entrance to Piazze Brà and Dante and the beginning of Corso Porta Borsari. The cavernous, pink 1st-century **Arena** (admission L6000), right smack in the middle of Piazza Brà, is a testament to both the ingenuity of the Romans and the meticulous upkeep of Verona by its inhabitants. Rock stars occasionally play at the arena, but it's more famous for opera. The opera season is late June to August. For tickets, dial 045/8005151. Walk to the end of Via Roma from Piazza Brà to reach the seriously fortified **Castelvecchio** (C. Cavour 2, tel. 045/594734; admission L5000), next to a dramatic bridge crossing the Adige River. The museum features works by Titian, Veronese, Tintoretto, Pisanello, and Rubens, as well as a startling number of breast-feeding Madonnas.

The Romanesque Gothic **Duomo** (admission L4000; open daily 7–noon and 3–7) on Piazza Duomo was built on the site of an ancient spa where early Christian architectural remnants have been found. A fresco by Titian, *The Assumption,* is in the first chapel on the left. Beautiful Romanesque **San Zeno Maggiore** (P. San Zeno, tel. 045/8006120; admission L4000; open daily 8:30–noon and 3–8) has bronze doors with biblical scenes and Andrea Mantegna's glorious triptych, Madonna and Saints, on the high altar. The arch-lined 12th-century cloister of the adjoining Benedictine abbey is thick with atmosphere. Most of Verona's sights are free the first Sunday of every month and closed Monday, but the city is now cashing in on its churches by charging a L4000 admission fee. You can buy one pass (inside any church) for all of the city's churches for L9000.

THE NORTHEAST

Many travelers to northern Italy aren't aware that the country stretches east and north of Venice. Perhaps that's because the provinces of **Trentino–Alto Adige** (north of the Veneto) and **Friuli–Venezia Giulia** (northeast of Venice) are the least "Italian" regions. Before the 20th century, neither even belonged to Italy. Trentino–Alto Adige was part of Austria's South Tyrol region for centuries, and its inhabitants generally prefer speaking German to Italian and eating schnitzel rather than pasta. Many of the residents of **Trieste,** the main city in Venezia Giulia, are Slavic in origin, some of them recent refugees from the former Yugoslavia. Besides sharing a schizoid cultural identity, both regions are renowned for their natural beauty. The jagged limestone peaks of the Dolomites beckon climbers, and the white cliffs overlooking the deep blue Adriatic near Trieste inspired poet Rainier Maria Rilke to write his passionate *Duino Elegies.*

TRENTO

The breezy, frescoed town of Trento isn't quite the bustling metropolis one would expect from a province's capital city. Trento's 15 minutes of fame came during the 16th century, when it hosted the famous Counter Reformation showdown, the **Council of Trent.** The 18-year-long council may not have stopped the spread of Protestantism in Europe, but it did wonders for the city—most of the palazzi, porticoes, and frescoes date from this era. Mellow Trento is the bus hub for the surrounding mountains and a good place to relax and shower before tackling the Brenta mountain range (*see* Near Trento, *below*) and the nearby Parco Naturale Paneveggio. The **APT** (V. Alfieri 4, tel. 0461/983880), across Piazza Dante from the station, provides oodles of helpful information on the city and Parco Naturale Paneveggio. For ski and rifugi information in English, head for **APT Trentino** (V. Romagnosi 3, tel. 0461/839000), which covers the entire region.

COMING AND GOING

The **Stazione di Trento** (P. Dante, tel. 1478/88088) sends trains to Venice (3 hrs, L14,000) and Verona (1 hr, L8200). To the right of the train station is the **bus station** (V. Pozzo 6, tel. 0461/983627). Hourly buses run to Paneveggio (2 hrs 20 min, L9400) and Riva del Garda (1¼ hrs, L4800). **Ferrovia Trento-Malè** (V. Secondo da Trento 7, tel. 0461/238350) runs electric trains to Malè (1½ hrs, L6000) and other mountain destinations. To get to the station from Stazione di Trento, turn left onto Via Dogana, veer left around the curve to Via Segantini, and walk straight ahead; it's at the end of the street and to the left.

WHERE TO SLEEP

Trento is short on budget hotels; the ones listed here are *it*. It's worth the 15-minute train ride south on the Verona line to reach **Ostello Città di Rovereto** (Viale delle Scuole 16/B, Rovereto, tel. 0464/433707; beds L20,000, including breakfast). Rooms (holding two to six beds) have baths, and some have terraces. Good, nourishing meals are served at dinner (L14,000). The large doubles at **Al Cavallino Bianco** (V. Cavour 29, tel. 0461/231542; L92,000) have showers and sinks. At the **Ostello Giovane Europa** (V. Manzoni 17, tel. 0461/234567; beds L20,000), most rooms have baths. From the train station, turn left on Via Dogana, right on Via Romagnosi, and left on Via Manzoni.

FOOD

In general, run from things called currywurst and go for the *strangolapreti* (literally "to strangle the priests"), a pasta specialty similar to spinach gnocchi with a Gorgonzola or butter sauce. The best salad bar for miles is at **Ristorante Al Giulia** (V. Gazzoletti 15, tel. 0461/984752), in an alley behind Piazza Dante's Banco di Roma. The **Birreria-Pizzeria Pedavena** (V. Santa Croce 15, tel. 0461/986255; open Wed.–Mon. 8:30–midnight) has pizzas for L6000–L9200.

WORTH SEEING

The **Castello di Buonconsiglio** (V. Bernardo Clesio 5, tel. 0461/233770; admission L7000; open Apr.–Sept., Tues.–Sun. 9–noon and 2–5:30; shorter hrs off-season) is really two buildings: the **Castelvecchio,** a 14th-century hunk of stone renovated in the 15th century to give it that trendy Venetian-Gothic look; and the **Magno Palazzo,** a 16th-century Renaissance palace. The real reason to visit is to see the **Aquila Tower** (ask the friendly staff for a peek), which houses the wonderful Gothic fresco *Cycle of the Months,* detailing everyday life for both the plebs (all work) and aristocrats (all play). The **Duomo** (P. Duomo; open daily 6:45–12:15 and 2:30–7:30), site of most Council of Trent meetings, is a dark, gloomy cathedral. Underneath are the remains of the **Basilica Paleocristiana** (admission L2000), a musty pre-Christian basilica-turned-crypt.

NEAR TRENTO

DOLOMITI DI BRENTA

The Brenta Dolomites are jagged, stark peaks that look—and are—forbidding. Hiking their trails sometimes requires climbing metal ladders hooked onto rock or gliding over glaciers; to get through, you'll need alpine know-how, climbing equipment, water, and a *Kompass Wanderkarte* map (L8500–L9000), available in bookstores and some tourist offices. Skiers pack this area in winter; the best slopes are on **Monte Paganella,** accessible by chair lift from Andalo, a stop on the Trento–Molveno rail line. Inquire at the **Skipass Paganella-Brenta** office (V. Paganella, Andalo, tel. 0461/585869) about equipment.

The resort town, **Molveno,** a L5000 bus ride from Trento (1¾ hrs), is the best base for hiking in the Brenta Dolomites. The **APT** (P. Marconi 7, tel. 0461/586924) offers a hiking and biking map, and can place you in one of Molveno's overpriced hotels. **Garnì Camping** (V. Lungolago, tel. 0461/586169), actually a hotel, has large, boring doubles for L90,000–L100,000. RVs go to **Camping Spiagga Lago di Molveno** (V. Lungolago 25, tel. 0461/586978) to breed and die. In high seasons, camping costs L11,500 per person plus L18,000 per tent; in the off-season, prices go down exponentially.

TRIESTE

Squashed between the Adriatic and Slovenia in the eastern corner of Italy, Friuli–Venezia Giulia's largest city lies across the water from Slovenia's shadowy hills. Slavic languages are often heard in Trieste's streets. Most of the city's older architecture was razed by Austrians in the 19th century, when neoclassic architecture was considered the apex of taste. But the Roman ruins of **Capitoline Hill** will remind you that Trieste was a Roman settlement. The hilltop ruins offer captivating views of the city and sea. Also worth a peek is the **Museo Revoltella** (V. Diaz 27, at P. Venezia, tel. 040/300938), especially the modern annex, designed by the innovative architect Carlo Scarpa. Also from Trieste, you can hike the beautiful, craggy limestone cliffs known as **Il Carso**, or visit **Aquileia**, a well-preserved Roman ghost town, a short bus ride away. Stop by the **APT** (train station, tel. 040/420182; open Mon.–Sat. 9–7, Sun. 10–1 and 4–7) for information.

COMING AND GOING

Stazione Centrale (P. della Libertà 8, tel. 1478/88088) runs trains to Venice (2 hrs, L14,000) and Udine (1½ hrs, L7400). From the adjacent bus station, **SAITA** buses (tel. 040/425001) run to Aquileia (1 hr, L5500) and the nearby beach town Grado (45 min, L5500). To reach the center from either station, veer right down Corso Cavour to Piazza Unità d'Italia.

WHERE TO SLEEP AND EAT

There are some decently priced rooms in the center. **Locanda Marina** (V. Galatti 14, tel. 040/369298; doubles L60,000) has the three c's down—clean, central, and cheap. Trieste's cheapest place is the beachfront **Ostello Tergeste** (Viale Miramare 331, tel. 040/224102), where L18,000 gets you a bunk, breakfast, and a chance to hang in the bar with locals on summer nights. Take Bus 36 catercorner from the train station and ask the driver where to get off; the last bus is at 9 PM. James Joyce's old stomping ground, **Osteria da Libero** (V. Risorta 7; closed Wed.), offers a lunch of soup, bread, and wine for L5000; particularly tasty is the Trieste specialty *polpi alla trestiana* (octopus marinated in paprika and olive oil) for only L8000.

LOMBARDY

Despite the apparent drawbacks—the pollution, the high prices, and the somewhat unwelcoming population—the beauty of the Lombardy lakelands, the miles of wooded hiking trails, and the high culture of cosmopolitan Milan attract thousands of visitors. Be prepared to encounter the vacationing masses during the summer, when you may end up feeling as if you, too, are on a package tour. Worst of all, the influx of well-heeled tourists has driven prices up, making budget travel a real challenge. Though the residents may strike you as a bit snobbish, persist if you want to experience the refined pleasures of Italy's best-dressed region.

MILAN

In no way will Milan (Milano) satisfy your yearnings for the laid-back, beautiful, and charmingly disorganized Italy; it's faster, more serious, and more expensive than the rest of the country. It also lacks the visual appeal of other Italian cities. Still, Milan does have the cultural buzz and amenities of an international metropolis. It offers excellent shopping and people-watching, a glitzy nightlife, and one of the few gay scenes in Italy. Though Milan is home to some of Italy's finest artistic masterpieces (its Gothic Duomo and Leonardo da Vinci's *Last Supper* to name a few), it's not a living museum in the same sense as Venice, Florence, or Rome. Milan is a place to visit not only for what it was in centuries gone by but for what it is today.

BASICS

VISITOR INFORMATION

APT tourist offices are at Stazione Centrale (tel. 02/6690532; open Mon.–Sat. 8–7, Sun. 9–12:30 and 1:30–6) and in Palazzo del Turismo (V. Marconi 1, tel. 02/72524300; open weekdays 8:30–7, weekends 9–1 and 2–5). Be sure to pick up the indispensable free publications *Hello Milano* and *Milano Mese* for more information on nightlife and cultural events. Another good source of arts information is **Comune di Milano** (Galleria Vittorio Emanuele, tel. 02/878363; open Mon.–Sat. 8–8).

AMERICAN EXPRESS

You'll find the Amex office behind La Scala (V. Brera 3, tel. 02/72003694; open Mon.–Thurs. and Sat. 9–5:30, Fri. 9–5. Postal code: 20121).

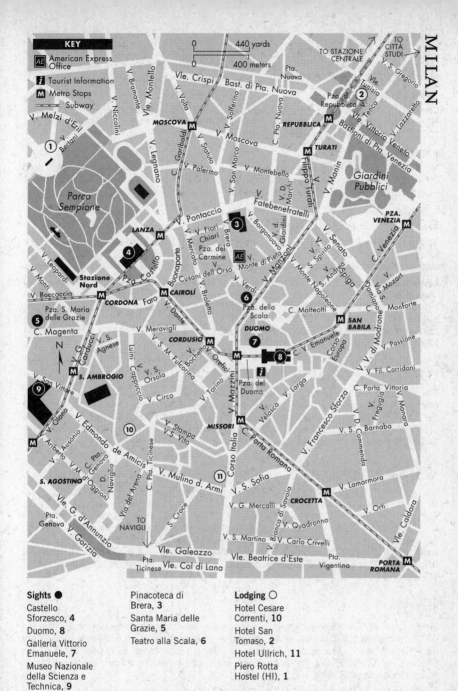

KEY

AE	American Express Office
i	Tourist Information
M	Metro Stops
	Subway

0 — 440 yards
0 — 400 meters

TO STAZIONE CENTRALE

TO CITTÀ STUDI

V. S. Gregorio

V. Melzi d'Eril

Vle. Crispi

Bast. di Pta. Nuova

Pta. Nuova

V. S. Regani

MOSCOVA

V. Moscova

REPUBBLICA

Pza. d. Repubblica

Vle. Tunisia

Vle. Tenca

Vle. Vittorio Veneto

Vle. Lazzaretto

V. Bramante

V. Montello

V. Volta

V. Staleo

V. Palermo

C. Garibaldi

V. Legnano

V. Niccolini

V. San Marco

V. Montebello

TURATI

Filippo Turati

V. Manin

Bastioni di Pta. Venezia

Parco Sempione

V. Pontaccio

V. Fatebenefratelli

V. D. Marchi

Giardini Pubblici

PZA. VENEZIA

LANZA

V. Fiori Chiari

Pza. del Carmine

V. Brera

V. Mercato

V. Borgonuovo

V. di Pietro

Giardini

V. Senato

V. Venezia

Stazione Nord

Pza. Castello

V. Buonaparte

Cusani

Cusani dell'Orso

V. Monte di Pietà

V. Manzoni

V. S. Spirito

V. S. Andrea

V. Piga

V. Mozart

V. Leopardi

V. Monti

V. Boccaccio

CORDONA

Faro

CAIROLI

V. Dante

V. Broletto

V. Verdi

Pza. della Scala

C. Matteotti

V. Monte Napoleone

Via Mozart

V. Damiano

Monforte

Pza. S. Maria delle Grazie

C. Magenta

V. Carducci

V. S. Agnese

V. Meravigli

CORDUSIO

DUOMO

Galleria Vittorio Emanuele

C. V. Emanuele

Corso Europa

SAN BABILA

V. di Modrone

V. V. di Passione

C. Porta Vittoria

S. AMBROGIO

V. San Vittore

V. Luini

V. Cappuccio

V. S. M. Fulcorina

V. Bocchetto

V. Orefici

Pza. del Duomo

V. Larga

C. Europa

V. Fil. Corridoni

V. S. Barnaba

V. D. Commenda

Fregiaria

V. Manara

V. Olona

V. Ariberto

V. S. Orsola

V. Circo

V. Torino

V. Mazzini

MISSORI

C. Italia

C. Porta Romana

Velasca

V. Francesco Sforza

C. Porta Vittoria

V. Edmondo de Amicis

V. Ausonio

V. M. d'Oggioni

V. J. Genova

D. Naviglio

V. Stampa

V. S. Vito

C. Pta. Ticinese

V. della Arena

V. Mulino d. Armi

S. Croce

V. S. Sofia

Corso Italia

V. Velasca

V. S. Barnaba

V. Lamarmora

V. Orti

Vle. Caldara

CROCETTA

S. AGOSTINO

Vle. G. d'Annunzio

Pta. Genova

V. Gorizia

TO NAVIGLI

Vle. Galeazzo

Vle. Col di Lana

Pta. Ticinese

Vle. Beatrice d'Este

V. G. Mercalli

Bianca di Savoia

V. Quadronno

V. S. Martino

V. Carlo Crivelli

Pta. Vigentina

PORTA ROMANA

Sights ●

Castello Sforzesco, **4**

Duomo, **8**

Galleria Vittorio Emanuele, **7**

Museo Nazionale della Scienza e Technica, **9**

Pinacoteca di Brera, **3**

Santa Maria delle Grazie, **5**

Teatro alla Scala, **6**

Lodging ○

Hotel Cesare Correnti, **10**

Hotel San Tomaso, **2**

Hotel Ullrich, **11**

Piero Rotta Hostel (HI), **1**

CHANGING MONEY

Change cash and traveler's checks for a 1%–2% fee at the information office in Stazione Centrale or at Malpensa and Linate airports. Or head to **Banca Commercacle** (try the branch at Stazione Centrale), which does not charge commissions.

CONSULATES

Canada (V. Vittor Pisani 19, tel. 02/67581; open weekdays 9–noon). **United Kingdom** (V. San Paolo 7, tel. 02/723001; open weekdays 9:15–12:15 and 2:30–4:30). **United States** (V. P. Amedeo 2/10, tel. 02/290351; open weekdays 9–noon and 2–4).

PHONES AND MAIL

Make long-distance collect or cash calls from either of **Telecom**'s central offices: in the Galleria Vittorio Emanuele and in Stazione Centrale. Both offices are open daily 8 AM–9:30 PM. The **main post office** (V. Cordusio 4, tel. 02/8692136) is open weekdays 8:15–7:40, Saturday 8:15–5:40.

COMING AND GOING

Stazione Centrale (tel. 1478/88088), on Metro lines M2 and M3, handles trains to Venice (4–5 hrs, L21500), Florence (3 hrs, L25,000), and Rome (5–7 hrs, L49,200). Long-distance buses depart from outside the **Autostradale** office (P. Castello, tel. 166/845010; open daily 6:30 AM–9:30 PM).

Linate Airport, 10 km (6 mi) southeast of Milan, and **Malpensa Airport,** 50 km (31 mi) northwest of Milan, both handle domestic and international flights. For general information about both Malpensa and Linate, dial 02/74852200. **STAM** buses (tel. 02/717106) connect Linate (20–30 min, L4500) and Malpensa (1 hr, L13,000) with Stazione Centrale. The cheaper city service route 73 runs every 10–15 minutes between Linate and Piazza San Babila (L1500), in the center, and STAM buses also connect Malpensa and Linate.

GETTING AROUND

The city resembles a bull's-eye, with three concentric thoroughfares encircling **Piazza del Duomo.** Milan's main attractions generally lie within the two most central rings. Within the center circle, **Cerchia dei Navigli,** are the majority of Milan's attractions. Tickets good for the Metro, buses, and trams cost L1500; 10-ticket packs cost L14,000. Buy reduced-fare passes at offices marked ABBONAMENTI in the Cadorna, Romolo, San Donato, and Centrale Metro stations.

WHERE TO SLEEP

The best hotels near the station are around the Giardini Pubblici. Your best bet, however, is in the center near the Duomo and most museums, as prices are uniformly high in Milan, regardless of location. The clean **San Tomaso** (V. Tunisia 6, 4th floor, tel. 02/29514747) offers doubles, all with bath, for L70,000–L90,000. Ask for discounts on longer stays. A tidy hotel in the center, **Hotel Cesare Correnti** (V. Cesare Correnti 14, tel. 02/8057609), rents doubles with TVs for L70,000. One of the best in Milan, **Hotel Ullrich** (C. Italia 6, tel. 02/86450156) has spotless doubles for L70,000. The **Piero Rotta Hostel** (**HI,** V. Martino Bassi 2, tel. 02/39267095), on the outskirts of town, has beds for L23,000 per person. There's an 11:30 curfew and a lockout 9 AM–5 PM.

FOOD

Though Milan does not cater to budget diners, there are a few affordable places out there. Check out one of the many fast-food and self-service chains such as **Brek.** Cheaper still are Milan's *latterie* (dairy markets), and the very cheapest meals are best assembled at a supermarket; try **La Coloniale** (V. Cesare Correnti 6, tel. 02/72000067). For sweets, bread, or pizza by the kilo, try **Il Forno dei Navigli** (Alzaia Naviglio Pavese 2, tel. 02/8323372).

Latteria Unione (V. Unione 6, tel. 02/874401; closed Sun.) serves dependable food; L15,000 will get you pasta, wine, and coffee. Stop at **L'Osteria del Pallone** (C. Garibaldi 46, tel. 02/8051865) for a quick sandwich or salad (L8000–L10,000). With no menu, the wait staff at **Quicosì** (V. Poma 6, tel. 02/733849; closed Mon.) keeps bringing plates of food until you burst. You'll get appetizers, two pastas, two secondi, cheese, sweets, liqueur, wine, and coffee for L30,000; at lunch stick to one course and coffee for L10,000–L12,000.

WORTH SEEING

Most of the "main" attractions lie within Milan's two innermost ring roads. Definitely make a stop at the glass-arch **Galleria Vittorio Emanuele,** the best people-watching spot in Milan. Another must-see is the imposing **Castello Sforzesco** (P. Castello, tel. 02/62083940; admission free; closed Mon.). Bramante designed the castle's *rocchetta* (fortress), and Leonardo da Vinci had his hand in the interior. It's currently an important venue for Renaissance art—the **Pinacoteca** contains Arcimbaldi's *Spring* and works by Bellini, Bembo, Mantegna, and Foppa. The castle's **Museo d'Arte** features Michelangelo's haunting, unfinished *Rondanini Pietà*. Reigning serenely over the city center, Milan's **Duomo** is one of the most ornate cathedrals in the world. Not surprisingly, it took centuries to complete this odd but mesmerizing mix of Gothic and Baroque. The vast interior is softly colored by stained-glass windows, and the central crucifix, which hangs from a suspension device, was designed by da Vinci. Architecture enthusiasts will want to check out the **Museo del Duomo** (P. del Duomo 14, tel. 02/860358; admission L8000; closed Mon.).

The **Pinacoteca di Brera** (V. Brera 28, tel. 02/722631; admission L8000; closed Mon.) is Milan's most important museum, housing such masterpieces as Piero della Francesca's *Urbino Altarpiece,* Raphael's *Marriage of the Virgin,* Mantegna's *Dead Christ,* Giovanni Bellini's *Pietà,* and Caravaggio's *Supper at Emmaus.* Inside the refectory of **Santa Maria delle Grazie** (tel. 02/4987588; admission L12,000; closed Mon.) is Leonardo da Vinci's coveted *Last Supper.* Since Leonardo's death in 1519, the Last Supper has suffered innumerable attacks, including abuse by Napoléon's troops, a World War II bombing that nearly destroyed the church, and disastrous restoration attempts. However, it's still a striking example of Renaissance individualism, with each apostle expressing his own unique emotion. Housed in a former Benedictine monastery, the **Museo Nazionale della Scienza e Tecnica** (V. San Vittore 21, tel. 02/485543; admission L10,000; closed Mon.) is one of the world's foremost museums of science and technology. Inside, the **Galleria Leonardo** has a collection of models based on technical designs by the man himself.

From December to May, make an effort to see anything Milan's Teatro alla Scala, a sacred pilgrimage site for opera buffs and Verdi lovers. Discounted tickets on performance days cost as little as L10,000, standing room only.

AFTER DARK

Milan's nightlife is hoppin' but costly. Ticket prices for concerts, theater, and even movies tend to be exorbitant. The newspapers *Il Corriere della Sera* and *La Repubblica* regularly list cultural events and club schedules. Hot spots ice over in a manner of minutes, but if you cruise the **Navigli canal** near Porta Ticinese, you're sure to stumble on *the* place of the week. For information on Milan's gay scene, call **ARCI Gay** (V. Torricelli 19, tel. 02/89401749).

Coquetel (V. Vetere 14, tel. 02/8360688; closed Sun.) is the place to be in Milan. All kinds of cocktails are served, none cheap. **Nuova Idea** (V. de Castiesa 30, tel. 02/69007859) is Italy's largest gay disco. The cover (L25,000) includes one drink. **Capolinea** (V. Lodovico Il Moro 119, tel. 02/89122024; closed Mon.) remains the preeminent jazz club in Milan, featuring big-name Italian and international performers.

NEAR MILAN

BERGAMO

Skip charmless Bergamo Bassa (Lower Bergamo) and head straight up to majestic Bergamo Alta (Upper Bergamo), where you'll find Bergamo's main attractions. Bernard Berenson, Le Corbusier, and Frank Lloyd Wright considered Bergamo's **Piazza Vecchia** to be one of Italy's loveliest squares. **Accademia Carrara** (P. dell'Accademia, tel. 035/399527; admission L5000) has an exceptional collection that Raphael, Mantegna, Bellini, Tiepolo, and Titian. **Piazza del Duomo** features both the frothily decorated Duomo and the impressive pink-and-white marble **Cappella Colleoni,** designed by Giovanni Antonio Amadeo. The **APT** office (Vicolo Aquila Nera 2, off P. Vecchia, tel. 035/232730) has more information on sights. If you want to stay the night, **Hostel Bergamo (HI,** V. Galileo Ferraris 1, tel. 035/361724) charges L25,000 for a bed and breakfast. **Trains** run hourly between Milan and Bergamo's train station (P. Marconi, tel. 035/247624); the one-hour trip costs L5100.

MANTOVA

A city rich in art, history, political intrigue, and that amorphous quality called atmosphere, Mantova was essentially created by the Gonzaga family and their preferred artists: Leon Battista Alberti, Andrea Mantegna, and Giulio Romano. The Gonzaga family's **Palazzo Ducale** (P. Sordello, tel. 0376/320283; admission L12,000) is a 500-room extravaganza housing excellent artwork by Rubens, Mantegna, Romano, Pisanello, Fancelli, and Titian. The pleasure palace, **Palazzo Te** (V. Te, tel. 0376/323266; admission L12,000; closed Mon.), is a study in Mannerist excess. The town's 11th-century **Duomo** (P. Sordello) reveals a distinctive carved ceiling. Skip Alberti's poorly renovated San Sebastiano (V. N. Sauro), but definitely check out his austere **Chiesa Sant'Andrea** (P. Mantegna), where painter Andrea Mantegna is buried. The **APT** (P. Mantegna 6, tel. 0376/328253; closed Sun.) provides tons of information. For overnight visitors, **Hotel ABC** (P. Don Leoni 25, tel. 0376/323347) has doubles for L75,000–L110,000. The cheapest lunchtime option is **Speedy's Spizza** (V. Grazioli 12, tel. 0376/224540). Mantova's small **train station** (P. Don Leoni) has frequent service to Milan (2 hrs, L14,000).

THE LAKES

The lakes of northern Italy denote a vast region spread over the middle third of the borderlands and on into Switzerland. Each of the lakes have a distinct personality: among them are **Garda,** the so-called party lake; **Como** and **Maggiore,** the posh where-do-I-park-my-Ferrari lakes; and **Orta** and **Iseo,** the small and serene lakes. Unfortunately, one unifying trait is industrial pollution. Even so, tourists flock to the lakes for their sports (you're in prime windsurfing territory) and beauty. If you're lucky enough to have a car, the region's small mountain roads definitely rank among the world's most beautiful and challenging.

LAGO DI GARDA

This is Italy's largest lake, combining grand-hotel ritz with RV camper culture. Garda has hosted its fair share of famous people, including the poet Gabriele d'Annunzio, who built his extravagant home **Il Vittoriale** (P. Vittoriale, tel. 0356/20130; admission L16,000) in **Gardone.** Throughout the year you can enjoy sailing, diving, and windsurfing in towns such as **Torbole** and **Riva del Garda.** The **tourist office** (V. Repubblica 35, tel. 0365/20347) in Gardone gives out information on lake activities. Camping is always possible, but for indoor accommodations the **Benacus Youth Hostel** (P. Cavour 10, tel. 0464/554911; closed Nov.–Feb.), in Riva del Garda, has beds for L20,000. Reach Lago di Garda's resorts from **Desenzano,** on the lake's southern tip. Desenzano's **train station** (V. Cavour 48, tel. 1478/88088) serves Milan via Brescia (1½ hrs, L10,100).

LAGO DI COMO

Long a favorite escape for artists, jet-setters, and wealthy Italians, Lago di Como remains an alluring spot even for budget travelers, with its sumptuous villas and peaceful small towns. **Como** is a pretty little city with some impressive architecture and reasonably priced accommodations. It's hard not to be enchanted by the 14-acre gardens of Villa Carlotta in **Tremezzo.** The ancient fishing village of **Varenna** is best for an afternoon of purposeless wandering. Iron-balconied homes looking out onto the narrow streets of **Bellagio** make this town a sight in and of itself. Como's **APT** office (P. Cavour 17, tel. 031/269712; closed Sun. in winter) offers information on train and ferry travel, hotels, and sports. Also in Como, the **Villa Olmo Youth Hostel** (V. Bellinzona 2, tel. 031/573800; closed Dec.–Feb.) charges L15,000 for breakfast and a bed; bike rental is L15,000 per day. Trains run frequently (30–45 min, L4300) from Milan to Como's **Stazione S. Giovanni** (P. S. Gottardo, tel. 1478/88088). Daily **ferries** depart from Como to lakeside towns.

THE RIVIERA

The Italian Riviera of the flashy '60s postcard—absurdly long yachts and beach goddesses in gold-plated bikinis—is a hazy delusion for people wearing expensive sunglasses and Bain de Soleil suntan oil. Such luxury does exist here, but only for those who don't carry their own luggage. The rest of us have to settle for sprays of bougainvillea and honeysuckle flowers, balmy air, hot focaccia, and hostel beds. **Finale Ligure** to the west and **Santa Margherita Ligure** in the east both beckon the budget traveler, but **Cinque Terre**'s cliff-clinging seaside villages offer small-town atmosphere, cozy accommodations, and adventurous hikes. **Genoa,** the fascinating but weathered port town in the center of the Riviera, doesn't attract many tourists except as a transportation hub, but it merits some exploration.

GENOA

The central town of the Italian Riviera is a composite of extremes. The people seem to mimic the geographic highs and lows of mountains and sea as they vacillate between wild gesticulation and melancholic reserve. Visibly, Genoa (Genova) has come down in the world since its Renaissance glory days of commerce and conquest. Though the city is soiled from neglect, you don't have to look hard to see its former splendor—artistic spoils procured from the Crusades, the colonial era, and foreign occupation are everywhere. The best way to understand Genoa is to surrender to its mood swings: Get lost in back alleys, feast on regional cooking, and take in the view from high on a hill.

BASICS

The exchange bureaus in the two major train stations, **Stazione Principe** and **Stazione Brignole** (for both, tel. 1478/88088), offer the best rates and charge no commission. Make long-distance calls at the main **phone office** (V. XX Settembre 139; open Mon.–Sat. 8 AM–10 PM). The **post office** (V. d'Annunzia 34, tel. 010/591762; open Mon.–Sat. 8:15–7:40) is just off Piazza Dante. You'll find one **EPT** visitor information office near Piazza Corvetto (V. Roma 11, tel. 010/541541; open weekdays 8–1:30 and 2–5, Sat. 8–1:15) and one at Stazione Principe (tel. 010/262633; open Mon.–Sat. 8–8, Sun. 9–noon).

Lest you fall prey to unsavory characters, stay away from Genoa's centro storico after dark—with your alien look fanny pack screaming "mug me"—unless you know exactly where you are going.

COMING AND GOING

Genoa has two main train stations, **Stazione Principe** (P. Acquaverde) and **Stazione Brignole** (P. Verdi); for both, use toll-free tel. 1478/88088. Both stations are on the same line, but sometimes trains scheduled to pass through both will only stop at one, so ask the conductor when you board. Trains run to Milan (2 hrs, L14,000) and Rome (6 hrs, L42,000) from both stations. The **Tigullio** bus line (tel. 010/313851) runs frequently from Piazza Vittoria (near Stazione Brignole), linking Genoa with towns on the eastern Riviera Levante. **Tirrenia Navigazione** (Ponte Colombo, tel. 010/2758041) offers ferry service to Sardinia. **Corsica Ferries** (Ponte Andrea Doria, tel. 010/593301) offers service to Bastia and Corsica. Schedules and prices vary drastically from season to season.

GETTING AROUND

Stazione Principe is on the west end of town, Stazione Brignole on the east; in between lies the mazelike *centro storico* (historic center), where most of the interesting sights are. City bus tickets are sold at any tabaccheria and at the train stations. One ticket (L1500) is good for 90 minutes. Bus 33 travels between the train stations; Buses 37 and 41 will take you into the city center and Bus 31 goes to the waterfront. A series of *funicolari* (trams) and *ascensori* (elevators) will help truck you up and down the hills.

WHERE TO SLEEP

The best choice for affordable lodging is near Stazione Brignole. The inconvenient but heavenly **Ostello per La Gioventù** (V. Costanzi 120, tel. 010/2422457) charges L22,000 (including breakfast) for a dorm bed or L23,000 per person for a family room with bath. Take Bus 40 from Stazione Brignole to the top of the hill. **Albergo Carletto** (V. Colombo 16/4, off P. Verdi, tel. 010/561229) has spacious, clean doubles (L80,000) with mosaic floors. Charming doubles at **Albergo Fiume** (V. Fiume 9/R, tel. 010/591691) go for L75,000–L80,000. If you want to camp, the excellent **Villa Doria** (V. al Campeggio Villa Doria 15, tel. 010/6969600), in the suburb of Pegli, costs L6000 per person plus L9000 per tent, or you can stay in a bungalow for two–six people for L50,000–L100,000. Take the local train to Pegli, then catch Bus 93.

FOOD

Genoa is the home of pesto, so don't leave town without indulging in some of it over *trennette* (a potato-based pasta) or on a pizza with delicious Stracchino cheese. The food here is among the cheapest in any big Italian city, and the centro storico, a good place for daytime meals only, and the lido overflow with trattorias and pizzerias. **Caffè degli Specchi** (Salita Pollaioli 43/R, off P. Matteotti, tel. 010/2468193) serves coffee and sandwiches downstairs and has a sit-down restaurant upstairs, where you can get a plate of cold specialties (L12,000) that includes *la farinata,* a torte made with garbanzo beans. At **Trattoria da Maria** (Vico Testadoro 14/R, off V. XXV Aprile, tel. 010/581080), you eat at big tables side by side with everyone from toothless salty dogs to chic execs. A full meal including wine costs L13,000. At the **Trattoria Ugo** (V. Guistiniani 86/R, tel. 010/2469302; closed Sun.–Mon.) the proprietor will tell you what's on the menu and then proceed to order for you.

WORTH SEEING

The centro storico, extending west from Piazza de Ferrari to Piazza Caricamento, south to Piazza Sarzano, and north to Piazza Nunziata, is where you find most of the good stuff. The **Porta Soprana,** an entrance to the district off Piazza Dante, leads to a maze of convents and monasteries and to Piazza Sarzano. It's next to Casa Colombo—Christopher Columbus's father was actually the gatekeeper of the Porta Soprana. You'll see traces of the city's Baroque past on the palace-packed **Via Garibaldi,** though the buildings suffer from centuries of sooty neglect. **Palazzo Bianco** (V. Garibaldi 11; admission L6000; open Tues., Thurs.–Fri., Sun. 9–1, Wed. and Sat. 9–7) is not so *bianco* anymore, but it houses a collection of outstanding paintings by Ligurian, Dutch, and Flemish masters. The exterior of **Cattedrale San Lorenzo** (V. San Lorenzo, off P. Matteotti, tel. 010/296469; open daily 7–noon and 3–8), built in 1118, is made of the signature Genovese black-and-white striped marble. Inside, the beautiful **Chapel of St. John the Baptist** contains St. John's 13th-century sarcophagus.

CINQUE TERRE

The cluster of five tiny villages called Cinque Terre is the Cinderella of the Italian Riviera. In their rugged simplicity, the five old fishing towns seem to mock the caked-on artifice of neighboring resorts. Pastel houses are layered and propped up on sheer cliffs, and rocky mountains rise precipitously to gravity-defying vineyards and olive groves. The geography here prevents expansion, and the small towns retain their enchanting intimacy. **Monterosso al Mare** is the biggest, least attractive, and most expensive of the towns, but it does have the sandiest beaches; **Vernazza, Corniglia,** and **Riomaggiore** are far more appealing. **Manarola,** the runt of the litter, is perched on a steep cliff. In Vernazza, climb the octagonal bell tower of the 14th-century church dedicated to Santa Margherita, on a hill overlooking the piazza and the water.

Train service to Cinque Terre is good: Take the hourly local train from either Genoa or La Spezia, which stops at each town. The towns are only a few minutes apart (L1500) by local train, but the best way to enjoy the scenery is to hike—it takes less than five hours from one end to the other. The **Pro Loco** (V. Fegina 38, tel. 0187/817506; open Mon.–Sat. 10–noon and 5–7:30, Sun. 10–noon; shorter hrs off-season), just outside the Monterosso train station, has hiking maps as well as lots of information about hotels and boat rides.

WHERE TO SLEEP AND EAT

Cinque Terre is the latest backpackers' "discovery," so you should definitely make reservations. *Affita-camere* (private rooms for rent) abound here, especially in tiny Riomaggiore; look for signs posted on homes or ask the first matronly person you encounter. In Vernazza, **Pensione Barbara** (P. Marconi 23, tel. 0187/812201; closed Dec.–Jan.) has swell doubles overlooking the port for L70,000. **Rifugio Mamma Rosa** (P. Unità 2, Riomaggiore, tel. 0187/920050; beds L25,000) should have been condemned long ago; it has somewhat crowded dorms and a decidedly feline odor from the rampant cats, but there is no curfew or lockout.

In Monterosso, locals frequent **Focacceria Il Frantoio** (V. Gioberti 1, tel. 0187/818333) and the **open-air market** along the waterfront, which offers fresh cheeses, produce, and deep-fried seafood. **Mister D&G** (V. Columbo 237, Riomaggiore, tel. 0187/920820) creates some of the most delicious and innovative pasta sauces in Liguria. The tourist menu (L20,000), with pasta, fresh seafood, and a salad, is a bargain. For a hangout, head to **Caffè Cagliari** (V. Roma 13, tel. 0187/817164); it gets packed around midnight.

BOLOGNA AND EMILIA-ROMAGNA

Stretching between the flat northern plains of the Padana, the foothills of the Apennines, and the Adriatic Coast, Emilia-Romagna, known as the heartland of Italy, has something for everyone. Composed of Emilia to the west and Romagna to the east, Italy's most prosperous region is a tranquil place where life slowly cruises by. In the region of Emilia, the peacefulness of stately Renaissance towns, such as **Parma, Modena,** and **Piacenza,** is interrupted only by the metropolitan decadence of one of central Italy's most beautiful cities: Bologna. East of Bologna lies Romagna, with mosaic-filled **Ravenna** and super party-resort **Rimini.**

BOLOGNA

Renaissance architects went to great lengths to distinguish Bologna from Florence, and the result is one of the most spectacular skylines in Italy, with a sea of red rooftops interrupted only by towers and domes rising skyward. But appearances aside, Bologna truly has spirit: It's crowded, it's cosmopolitan, and with 80,000 students attending its 900-year-old university (the oldest in Europe), it's truly alive. Bologna is known in Italy as a great eating town, with more than its fair share of *osterie* (wine bars or taverns) and restaurants, and also thought to be more than a little left-leaning. Priests, pundits, poets, communists, gluttons, lesbians, and nuns pass each other nonchalantly on the street, earning the city its well-known moniker: *la Dotta, la Grassa, e la Rossa* (the Learned, the Fat, and the Red).

Gelateria Ugo (V. San Felice 24, tel. 051/263849; closed Mon. and Tues. and Nov.–Feb.) concocts the dreamiest ice-cream sandwich: gelato stuffed in a warm raisin focaccia, topped with whipped cream.

BASICS

APT tourist offices book rooms and are at the train station (tel. 051/246541; open Mon.–Sat. 9–12:30 and 2:30–7) and the airport (tel. 051/6472036, 8:30–3 and 4–8), and at Piazza Maggiore (No. 6, tel. 051/239660; open Mon.–Sat. 9–7, Sunday 9–2). For international phone calls head to the **phone office** (P. VIII Agosto 24, no phone), open daily 7 AM–10:30 PM. The **post office** (P. Minghetti; tel. 051/223598) is open weekdays 8:15–6:30 and Saturday 8:15–12:20.

COMING AND GOING

Bologna's **train station** (P. della Medaglie d'Oro, tel. 1478/88088) is a major rail hub. Over 20 trains depart daily to Milan (2 hr 20 min, L26,900) and to Rome (3½ hrs, L39,900), via Florence (50 min, L13,200). For urban and suburban bus information and tickets, head to the **ATC bus station** (P. XX Settembre 1, tel. 051/248374; open weekdays 7–7, Sat. 9–1). Purchase tickets, good for one hour, at tobacco shops (L1400). Buses run 5:30 AM–12:30 AM or 5:30 AM–8:30 PM depending on the line; check posted schedules at stops.

WHERE TO SLEEP

Albergo Panorama (V. Livraghi 1, tel. 051/221802, fax 051/266360) is Bologna's best deal, with red-rooftop views and immaculate doubles without bath for L85,000. Centrally located **Pensione Marconi** (V. Marconi 22, tel. 051/262832) has doubles with bath for L92,000, but you'll have to put up with street noise. Just a block from the Duomo, **Albergo Centrale** (V. della Zecca 2, tel. 051/225114) has remodeled doubles with TVs for L100,000–L130,000, some with great views.

Far from the town center but housed inside a former villa, **Ostello per La Gioventù San Sisto (HI**; V. Viadagola 14, San Sisto, tel. 051/519202; closed Dec. 20–Jan. 19) has beds for L18,000 per night, breakfast included. From the train station, walk two blocks south to Via dei Mille/Via Irnerio and take Bus 93 or 21B to Località San Sisto. North of the center, **Camping Città di Bologna** (V. Romita 12/4A, tel. 051/325016, fax 051/325318) costs about L15,000 plus L5500–L7500 per person; bungalows for two start at L110,000. From the train station, take Bus 21 or 25 and ask the driver where to get off.

FOOD

East of Due Torri, **Clorofilla** (Strada Maggiore 64, tel. 051/235343; closed Sun.) is a meat-free haven serving sandwiches and monster salads. At **L'Osteria Il Cantinone** (V. del Pratello 56/A, tel. 051/553223; closed Wed.) you'll sit on warped benches and eat off sticky tables stained with years of spilled wine. Try penne *cantinone* (with a creamy saffron sauce). A great place for a late-night snack, **Osteria del Montesino** (V. del Pratello 74/B, tel. 051/523426; closed Mon.) serves Sardinian wine (L7000) and great *crostini* (toasted bread with a variety of toppings; L9000). One of Bologna's oldest and best gourmet food shops, **Tamburini** (V. Caprarie 1, tel. 051/234726; closed Sun.) opens its dining room at lunch and dishes out top-rate sandwiches (L2000–L5000) from 10 AM to closing. To pick up your own supplies, head to the **Mercato delle Erbe** (V. Ugo Bassi 2; open Mon.–Wed. and Fri. 7:15–1 and 5–7, Sat. 7:15–1).

WORTH SEEING

You might be content strolling under the Bologna's shady porticoes or people-watching in the shadow of the Duomo, but don't get so swept away that you miss Bologna's architectural and artistic treasures. In late July and August, Bologna can be hellishly hot: Beware of scalding afternoon sun and plan on an post-lunch siesta, as the locals do.

The plans for the 14th-century **Basilica di San Petronio** on Piazza Maggiore were so ambitious that its construction was curtailed by papal decree to prevent it from surpassing St. Peter's in size. Noteworthy features include the Gothic arches, Parmigianino's *San Rocco,* and frescoes by Giovanni da Modena. Across the piazza is Giambologna's **Fontana del Nettuno**; the original version of this monument—a fantasia of monumental endowment, highly erotic cherubim, and breast-clenching sirens—was initially rejected by the Catholic church as indecent, so the artist had to manipulate Neptune's left arm in the interest of modesty.

Inside **Palazzo Ghilisardi-Fava,** the **Museo Civico Medievale** (V. Manzoni 4, tel. 051/228912; admission L8000; open Mon. and Wed.–Fri. 9–2, Sat. and Sun. 9–1 and 3:30–7) includes a fabulous collection of 13th- and 14th-century sepulchers depicting masters with their sleeping or otherwise distracted students, along with medieval and Renaissance ceramic, glass, and bronze instruments. The painting collection at the **Pinacoteca Nazionale** (V. delle Belle Arti 56, tel. 051/24322; admission L8000; open Tues., Wed., and Fri. 9–2, Thurs. and Sat. 9–6:30, Sun. 9–1) ranges from Byzantine to Baroque.

Santo Stefano (V. Santo Stefano 24, tel. 051/223256; open 9–noon and 3:30–6:30), a hodgepodge of four adjoining churches, grows more amazing around every corner. The Romanesque **Crucifix Church** has been restored to its medieval Lombard style after a series of alterations. The **Chiesa dei Santi Vitale e Agricola** is the oldest church in the group, built from bits and pieces of Roman artifacts. The **Holy Sepulchre Church,** containing St. Petronio's remains, is thought to have been a pagan temple in the 1st century AD. Don't overlook **Pilate's Courtyard,** with its sepulchers and *St. Peter's Cock,* a stone rooster whose presence is a reminder of St. Peter's denial of Christ. Inside the fourth church, the **Trinità,** is an underwhelming but free museum.

AFTER DARK

Unless you're here in August, you can count on one of the best scenes for miles around. Pick up the indispensable *Zero in Condotta* (L4000) at any newsstand for an extensive listing of nightlife options. For information on gay and lesbian events, call **ARCI Gay** (tel. 051/6447054).

From July to September the city hosts **Bologna Sogna** (Bologna Dreams), a series of free events ranging from classical concerts and live jazz in palace courtyards to DJs spinning dance grooves in parks and on hillsides. Just off Via San Vitale, the bar **Vicolo Bolognetti** serves up beer and free outdoor concerts every night from mid-May to September. Outside of summer Bologna's nightlife is found in the city's many osterie, where friends meet to drink and snack at long wooden tables. Between 7:45 PM–8:45 PM only, try the charmingly squalid **Osteria del Sole** (Vicolo Ranocchio 2/B, no phone) for an incredibly cheap glass of wine (L2500). **Cassero** (P. di Porta Saragozza 2, tel. 051/6446902) is a dance place catering to a mostly gay crowd. Movies in English are played nightly at **Adriano d'Essai** (V. San Felice 52, tel. 051/555127) for L12,000.

RAVENNA

On the surface, Ravenna is much like other Italian cities, its narrow streets spiraling out from a palazzo-lined central piazza, bell towers poking into the sky. But Ravenna's treasure—what makes this city unique—is its mosaics. Griffins and peacocks and ships sailing for the Crusades glimmer on the walls and ceilings of Ravenna's basilicas, baptisteries, and tombs. Though not quite as brilliant as the mosaics, the town's unconventional, cylindrical campaniles, are also worth a look. Trains arrive in Ravenna from Bologna (1 hr 20 min, L7200), Ferrara (15 daily, 1 hr 10 min, L6500), and Rimini (hourly, 1 hr, L4200). For the usual tourist information, head to Ravenna's **tourist office** (V. Salara 8, near P. del Popolo, tel. 0544/35404; open Mon.–Sat. 8:30–6, Sun. 9–noon and 3–6).

A special L10,000 ticket, available at the Basilica di San Vitale, Basilica di Sant'Apollinare Nuovo, and the Neonian Baptistry, will get you in to all of Ravenna's mosaic attractions. The nave of **Basilica di Sant'Apollinare Nuovo** (V. Roma, tel. 0544/497629; admission L5000; open Apr.–Sept., daily 9:30–6:30; Oct.–Mar., daily 9–4:30) is blanketed by glittering mosaics; this effect is achieved by carefully placing *tesserae* (bits of glass or calcareous rock) at uneven levels in the plaster base so different colors catch the light at different angles. The first scene on the men's side is the earliest-known artistic depiction of the *Last Supper*. One of the most glorious examples of Byzantine art in the West, the **Basilica di San Vitale** (V. San Vitale, tel. 0544/34266; admission L6000; open daily 9–7, 9–4:30 in winter) is illuminated by brilliant mosaics depicting Christ, the Byzantine emperor Justinian, bishop Maximillian (who consecrated the church), and the empress Theodora—said to be where East meets West in Ravennese mosaic art. Just behind the basilica, the **Tomba di Galla Placidia** (V. Fiandrini, same hours and ticket as San Vitale) is adorned with vibrant, ornate mosaics displaying an earlier Roman style. A few km (2 mi) outside Ravenna, **Basilica di Sant'Apollinare in Classe** (V. Romea Sud, Classe, tel. 0544/527004; admission free; open daily 8–noon and 2–6) is decked out with lustrous gold mosaics representing Ravenna's patron saint, St. Apollinare, in a pastoral scene. The upper portion, in lustrous gold achieved by applying real gold leaf to glass tesserae, portrays the transfiguration of Christ on Mt. Tabor. The four mythical creatures flying toward Christ in the apse are the Evangelists.

To catch a glimpse of Bologna's red-roof splendor, climb up the city's most conspicuous point of reference, the Torre degli Asinelli (P. di Porta Ravegnana; admission L3000; open daily 9–7).

Adjacent to the **Battistero Neoniao** (open Oct.–Mar., daily 9:30–4:30, Apr.–Sept., 9:30–6:30), Ravenna's oldest monument, the **Museo Arcivescovile** (tel. 0544/33696; admission L5000; same hours as the Battistero) contains a marvelously decorated private chapel of the bishops. The **Tomba di Dante** (open Apr.–Sept., daily 9–7, Oct.–Mar., daily 9–noon and 2–5) and neighboring **Museo Dantesco** (V. Dante Alighieri 4, tel. 0544/30252; admission L3000, free Sun.; open Apr.–Sept., Tues.–Sun. 9–noon and 3:30–6; Oct.–Mar., 9–noon only) are must-sees for fans of Italy's most famous poet.

WHERE TO SLEEP AND EAT

All of Ravenna's budget hotels are a two-minute walk from the train station and a 10-minute walk from the town center. **Albergo al Giaciglio** (V. Brancaleone 42, tel. 0544/39403) has pleasant doubles for L50,000 (L65,000 with bath). **Albergo Ravenna** (V. Maroncelli 12, tel. 0544/212204, fax 0544/212077) rents immaculate doubles with bathrooms for L70,000—L100,000; from Piazza Farini, turn right down Via Maroncelli. Big, noisy, friendly, clean, the **Ostello Dante** (HI, V. Aurelio Nicolodi 12, tel. and fax 0544/421164) lets beds for L22,000, including a morning roll and coffee that may or may not be hot and strong. From the train station, take Bus 1 to the corner of Via Molinetto and Via Aurelio Nicolodi.

Ravenna's **Mercato Coperto** (P. Costa) gets going Monday—Saturday 7–2, and Friday extra hours are 4:30–7:30. Never will you feel more tragically hip than while sitting next to Dante's tomb in the beautiful **Ca' de Ven** (V. C. Ricci 24, tel. 0544/30163; closed Mon.), munching on cheap *piadine* (unleavened bread filled with meats, cheeses, or veggies; L5000) or *crescioni* (flaky pastries; L3800) and drinking excellent wine by the glass.

FLORENCE

Michelangelo's *David* and Botticelli's *Birth of Venus* may be the most famous works of art in Florence (Firenze), but the city's attitude toward visitors is best represented in Donatello's *St. George*: Valiant but cautious, the saint surveys an approaching dragon with a slightly worried eye. During the early 15th century the study of antiquity—the glory that was Greece, the grandeur that was Rome—became a Floren-

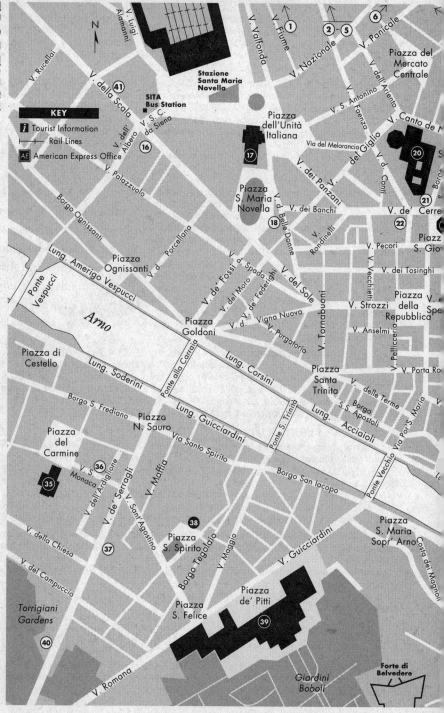

KEY

i Tourist Information

Rail Lines

AE American Express Office

N

V. Luigi Alamanni

V. Fiume

V. Vallonda

Stazione
Santa Maria
Novella

SITA
Bus Station

V. della Scala

(41)

V. Rucellai

V. dell'
Albero

V. S. C.
da Siena

(16)

V. Palazzuolo

Borgo Ognissanti

Piazza
Ognissanti

V. d. Porcellana

Ponte
Vespucci

Lung. Amerigo Vespucci

Piazza di
Cestello

Lung. Soderini

Borgo S. Frediano

Piazza
del
Carmine

V. S.
Monaca

(36)

(35)

V. dell'Ardiglione

V. de' Serragli

V. Sant'Agostino

Piazza
N. Sauro

Via Santo Spirito

V. Maffia

(37)

V. della Chiesa

V. del Campuccio

Torrigiani
Gardens

(40)

V. Romana

Piazza
S. Felice

Borgo Tegolaio

(38)

Piazza
S. Spirito

V. Maggio

Arno

Piazza
Goldoni

Ponte alla Carraia

Lung. Corsini

Lung. Guicciardini

Ponte S. Trinità

Piazza
de' Pitti

(39)

Giardini
Boboli

(1)

V. Nazionale

(2) (5)

(6)

V. Panicale

Piazza del
Mercato
Centrale

V. dell'Ariento

V. S. Antonino

V. Faenza

V. d. Conti

Via del Melarancio

del Giglio

(17)

Piazza
dell'Unità
Italiana

V. dei Panzani

Piazza
S. Maria
Novella

(18)

V. di Bella Donne

V. dei Banchi

Rondinelli

(20)

Canto de i

(21)

V. de' Cerre

(22)

Piazz
S. Gio

V. Pecori

V. dei Tosinghi

V. Vecchietti

Piazza
della
Repubblica

V. Strozzi

V. Anselmi

Pellicceria

V. Spe

V. Porta Ro

V. de' Fossi

V. d. Spada

V. del Moro

V. de' Federighi

V. del Sole

Vigna Nuova

V. Purgatorio

V. d.

V. Tornabuoni

Piazza
Santa
Trinita

V. delle Terme

Borgo
S.S. Apostoli

Lung. Acciaioli

Via Por S. Maria

Borgo San Iacopo

Ponte Vecchio

Piazza
Guicciardini

V. Guicciardini

Piazza
S. Maria
Sopr' Arno

Costa dei Magnoli

Forte di
Belvedere

tine passion, and with it came enlightenment in art and architecture, mostly fueled by the Medici clan. A long list of painters, sculptors, architects, poets, and essayists brought about a return to classical esthetics, styles, and techniques. As a result, Florence contains a phenomenal array of Renaissance art and architecture within its compact, vibrant center. The massive onslaught of tourists knows no season, but there is plenty of Florence to go around, and when the going gets too tough, get going to the hill towns of **Fiesole, San Gimignano,** and **Siena.**

BASICS

VISITOR INFORMATION
The best **visitor center** (V. Cavour 1r, tel. 055/290832; open Mon.–Sat. 8:15–7:15, Sun. 8:15–1:30; off-season, daily 8:15–2) is right next to the Palazzo Medici-Riccardi. Other offices are just off Piazza della Signoria (Chiasso de' Baroncelli 17r, tel. 055/2302124; open Mon.–Sat. 8:15–5:15), and next to the train station, across from Track 16 (P. della Stazione, tel. 055/212245; open Mon.–Sat. 8:15–7:15, Sun. 8:15–2). **ARCI Gay/ARCI Lesbica** (V. del Leone 5r–11r, tel. 055/288126) is the local gay resource center, where you can pick up a copy of *Quir,* a monthly Italian/English magazine with listings of gay and lesbian events.

AMERICAN EXPRESS
To get to the Amex office (V. Dante Alighieri 22r, tel. 055/50981; open weekdays 9–5:30, Sat. 9–12:30) from the Duomo, walk south on Via de' Calzaiuoli, turn left on Via dei Tavolini, which becomes Via Dante Alighieri.

CHANGING MONEY
There is no shortage of money exchanges, though as usual, banks are your best bet. If you brought your ATM card you'll find plenty of machines to put it in. For those who arrive without a lira in hand, head to the money exchange (no commission but lousy rates) at the information counter by Track 5.

CONSULATES
United Kingdom (Lungarno Corsini 2, north bank of Arno, tel. 055/212594; open weekdays 9:30–12:30 and 2:30–4:30). **United States** (Lungarno Vespucci 38, tel. 055/2398276, on north bank of Arno; open weekdays 8:30–noon and 2–4).

DISCOUNT TRAVEL AGENCIES
Centro Turistico Studentesco Giovanile (CTS; V. de' Ginori 25r, tel. 055/289570; open weekdays 9–12:45 and 2:30–5:45, Sat. 9–noon).

ENGLISH-LANGUAGE BOOKS AND NEWSPAPERS
Florence is one of the rare Italian cities with good English bookstores. **After Dark** (V. dei Ginori 47r, tel. 055/294203) and **The Paperback Exchange** (V. Fiesolana 31r, tel. 055/2478154) have the best selections.

LAUNDRY
Launderette (V. Guelfa 55r) costs about L10,000 to wash and dry one load—the cheapest deal in town.

PHONES AND MAIL
Telecom offices are scattered throughout the city (there's one at V. Cavour 21r) and usually offer both operator-assisted and phone-card calling. The **main post office** (V. Pellicceria, off P. della Repubblica, tel. 055/213384) is open weekdays 8:15–5:30 and Saturday 8:15–12:30.

COMING AND GOING

BY BUS
Florence's long-distance bus system takes you to the hilly areas where trains don't go. **SITA** (V. Santa Caterina da Siena 15r, tel. 055/483651 on weekdays or 055/483651 on weekends; open daily 6:40 AM–7 PM) is the most comprehensive, with service to Siena (1¼ hrs, L8200) and San Gimignano (1½ hrs, L8100; change at Poggibonsi), which are better reached by bus than by train. To reach SITA from the train station, walk out the doors by Track 5, cross Via Luigi Alamanni and go left, then make a right on Via Santa Caterina da Siena.

BY TRAIN

The huge **Stazione Santa Maria Novella** (tel. 1478/88088) has luggage storage (L5000 per 12 hrs), information counters (open daily 7 AM–8 PM), a reservations desk for international trains (open 7 AM–8:30 PM), a 24-hour pharmacy, and an office that books hotel rooms for a small fee. Trains go to Rome (2½ hrs, L36,200), Milan (3 hrs, L36,200), and Venice (2 hrs, L31,600; change in Bologna), as well as Pisa's airport (1 hr, L6500).

GETTING AROUND

Most of Florence's sites are in the **centro storico,** a virtual open-air Renaissance museum. To follow the changing street names, it's essential to arm yourself with a map. One major headache: Each street has two numbering systems—blue numbers for hotels and residences, and red numbers (denoted here by an "r") for businesses. Two main routes are helpful to know: To the north is the permanently crowded **Piazza del Duomo,** jammed with tourists and Italian pickup artists. The main artery Via Calzaiuoli runs from the Duomo south to the **Piazza della Signoria,** which is lined with important Medici buildings. Intersecting this north–south runway starting from the train station and moving east are **Piazza Santa Maria Novella, Piazza della Repubblica,** and **Piazza di Santa Croce.**

Many streets in the center of town are open only to pedestrians, so it's usually faster to walk than to take a lumbering bus. If you need to reach places farther out like Fiesole, the HI hostel, or the campgrounds, you can get a free route map from the **ATAF** at the train station (*see* Visitor Information, *above*). A L1400 ticket good for an hour can be purchased at machines or tobacco shops, and most buses stop running around midnight. **Alinari** (V. Guelfa 85r, tel. 055/280500) rents bikes (L20,000 per day) and mopeds (L45,000 per day).

WHERE TO SLEEP

There are plenty of budget hotels and hostels within easy walking distance of the major sights. Reservations are not a bad idea, as Florence gets a steady flow of visitors through the year. **Consorzio ITA** (tel. 055/282893; open daily 8:30 AM–9 PM) in the train station books rooms for a small service fee (from L3000).

NEAR STAZIONE SANTA MARIA NOVELLA

You'll find a bunch of moderately priced hotels just outside the train station along **Via Faenza, Via Fiume,** and **Via Nazionale.** The Duomo is only a 10-minute walk away, but keep in mind that at night Piazza Santa Maria Novella and the area around the station become rather seedy.

UNDER L75,000 • Albergo Merlini. Great views of the hills surrounding Florence from tastefully decorated doubles with comfy beds cost just L70,000. A 1-AM curfew is set. *V. Faenza 56, tel. 055/212848, fax 055/283939.*

Albergo La Romagnola. This friendly but musty hotel has 37 rooms (6 with bath), making it less likely to fill up than other budget lodgings. Doubles start at L70,000. There's a midnight curfew. *V. della Scala 40, tel. 055/211597. Cash only.*

UNDER L90,000 • Hotel Il Bargellino. This meticulously clean hotel features Mediterranean tile and a gorgeous garden terrace. Doubles start at L85,000. *V. Guelfa 87, tel. 055/2382658, fax 055/2382698. Exit train station at Track 16 and turn left, then right on V. Cennini, left on V. Faenza, right on V. Guelfa. Cash only.*

Pensione Indipendenza. Next to green Piazza Indipendenza, this tiny pension has doubles for L80,000 with a bathroom down the hall. *P. Indipendenza 8, tel. 055/496630. Cash only.*

UNDER L100,000 • Albergo Montreal. Mellow managers charge L90,000 for a bright double with a bathroom and require a 1:30 AM curfew. *V. della Scala 43, tel. and fax 055/2382331. Cash only.*

Pensione Ferretti. Each room in this quiet, family-run inn has a distinct character. Doubles start at L96,000. *V. delle Belle Donne 17, tel. 055/2381238, fax 055/219288.*

UNDER L120,000 • Albergo Azzi. The cheery young staff here makes you feel welcome. Doubles run L110,000, breakfast included. Rates drop significantly in off-season. The curfew is 2 AM. *V. Faenza 56, tel. and fax 055/213806.*

UNDER L150,000 • Albergo Fiorita. This roomy top-floor inn (with elevator) is just one block from the train station. Cheerful bathless doubles run a hefty L147,000. *V. Fiume 20, tel. 055/283189, fax 055/283693.*

SPLURGE • Hotel Monica. The pastel colors in the lobby and hallways here feel like Southern California, but the view from the terrace reminds you you're in Italy. Clean, bright doubles without bath run L100,000–L140,000, L170,000 with bath. *V. Faenza 66, 50123, tel. 055/283804, fax 055/281706.*

CENTRO

As usual, you pay a bit more as you get a little farther from the train station and a little closer to what you want to see.

UNDER L80,000 • Locanda Orchidea. Seven small, comfortable rooms open onto pleasantly neglected gardens. Bathless doubles run L75,000. *Borgo degli Albizi 11, tel. and fax 055/2480346. Cash only.*

Albergo Soggiorno Bavaria. This renovated inn atop an old palazzo has enormous, sunny top-floor rooms with views. The cheapest double is L75,000. *Borgo degli Albizi 26, tel. and fax 055/2340313. Cash only.*

UNDER L90,000 • Hotel Cristina. This is one block from the Uffizi. Large doubles, redecorated and featuring new mattresses, run L80,000, and rooms for four–five people go for L150,000. *V. della Condotta 4, tel. 055/214484, fax 055/215518. Cash only.*

UNDER L100,00 • San Giovanni. Very clean, big, spartan rooms overlook the Duomo and the Battisero. Doubles run L80,000–L95,000. *V. de' Cerretani 2, tel. 055/288385, fax 055/213580.*

UNDER L125,000 • Albergo Firenze. Rooms are clean but short on charm in this Best Western-esque, American-style hotel. Doubles with bath will set you back L100,000, including breakfast. *P. dei Donati 4, off V. del Corso, tel. 055/214203, fax 055/212370. Cash only.*

Albergo Il Perseo. Stunning views and very helpful management are among the perks. Doubles go for L105,000 (L120,000 with bath), breakfast included. *V. de' Cerretani 1, tel. 055/212504, fax 055/28377.*

PIAZZA SAN MARCO AND THE UNIVERSITY QUARTER

You'll get a bit more value for your money around **Via Cavour, Via de' Ginori,** and **Via San Gallo.** The farther down **Via degli Alfani** from the station you go, the more student cafés and restaurants pop up. Prepare yourself for a long walk from the station with your luggage, or take Bus 7 to Piazza San Marco.

UNDER L90,000 • Hotel Tina. A happy-go-lucky manager maintains 16 spotless rooms; some have showers, two with full bathrooms. Doubles start at L80,000. *V. San Gallo 31, tel. 055/483519, fax 055/483593. Cash only.*

UNDER L110,000 • Albergo Mirella. This is a solid deal, but a 25-minute walk from the train station. Enormous, pleasant doubles cost L100,000. *V. degli Alfani 36, 50121. tel. and fax 055/2478170. Cash only.*

UNDER L130,000 • Hotel San Marco. This hotel just off Piazza San Marco is a cut above the norm. Doubles with bath are L120,000, without bath L85,000, breakfast included. *V. Cavour 50, tel. 055/281851, fax 055/284835.*

SPLURGE • Hotel Casci. This is the place to indulge. Immaculate, comfortable rooms in a renovated 14th-century palazzo have modern bathrooms and TVs. Prices in the low season start at L110,000 for doubles; in the high season they go up to L160,000. *V. Cavour 13, 50129. tel. 055/211686, fax 055/2396461.*

HOSTELS

Florence's hostels are a great bargain, but they fill up fast, so reserve if you can. If the hostels listed below are full, you can show up early in the morning at the **Ostello Archi Rossi** (V. Faenza 94r, tel. 055/290854, L22,000 per bed), since they don't take reservations. A bed in the large and clean rooms of **Pensionato Pio X** (V. de' Serragli 106, tel. and fax 055/225044) costs L22,000. They don't take reservations, but if you arrive between 8 AM–10 AM or call from the train station, you'll probably get a spot.

Istituto Gould. This glorious hostel has room for only 80 people. Reserve ahead or show up at 9 AM. Thoroughly scrubbed doubles with big windows start at L33,000 per person, triples L32,000 per person, quads L30,000 per person. *V. de' Serragli 49, tel. 055/212576. Reception open weekdays 9–1 and 3–7, Sat. 9–1. Cash only.*

Ostello Santa Monaca. The sexes are strictly segregated here, but they do have a deal with a local trattoria that provides slightly reduced-price meals. Beds are L21,000 per person, shower included. Reservations are possible by fax. *V. Santa Monica 6, off V. de' Serragli, tel. 055/268338, fax 055/280185. Curfew 12:30 AM. Cash only.*

Ostello Villa Camerata (HI). This excellent megahostel is far from town in a villa surrounded by green acres. Reserve ahead by mail, fax, or through computers at HI hostels in Rome, Naples, and Venice. Check-in begins at 2 PM (3 in winter). Beds cost L23,000 and are only available with a hostel card. *Viale Augusto Righi 4, tel. 055/601451, fax 055/610300. Take Bus 17. Curfew 11:30, lockout 9–2 (9–3 in winter). Cash only.*

FOOD

Good food town that Florence is, you shouldn't plan on skipping too many meals. Produce comes straight from the nearby countryside, and excellent local olive oil is drizzled on everything from the otherwise flavorless bread to the seasoned *fave* or *fagioli* (white beans) that appear in delicious, filling soups. The crown of Florentine cuisine is the expensive *bistecca alla Fiorentina,* a grilled T-bone, usually big enough for two. The best place to look for authentic local cuisine and atmosphere is south of the Arno in the Oltrarno. If you just want a cheap, filling meal, the tourist menus posted everywhere are both a blessing and a curse: You get a multi-course meal without paying the service charge and standard L2000 *coperto* (cover), but you're often getting the dregs of the menu.

NEAR THE STATION

UNDER L15,000 • Il Latini. Everything here is excellent, from chopped-liver crostini to thick and rich soups to savory roast meats (about L18,000). An assortment of primi costs L9000. Arrive early to avoid waiting in line. *V. dei Palchetti 6r, tel. 055/210916. From P. Santa Maria Novella, walk down V. de' Fossi, turn left on V. della Spada, right on V. de' Federighi, left on V. dei Palchetti. Cash only. Closed Mon. and two wks in Aug.*

To stock up on provisions, head to the Mercato Centrale (open Mon.– Sat. 8–2), in an restored 19th-century iron building just north of San Lorenzo. Downstairs you'll find bread, cheese, and butcher shops; fresh produce is upstairs.

Trattoria da Giorgio and **Trattoria Il Contadino.** Just across the street from each other, these two places serve similar food at the exact same price: pasta, meat, a vegetable, and bread, water, and wine for L16,000. *Giorgio: V. Palazzuolo 100r, no phone. Contadino: V. Palazzuolo 69r–71r, tel. 055/2382673; both closed Sun.*

CENTRO

The center is home to horrendously expensive tourist traps, terrific little take-out stands, and everything in between. Near Santa Croce you'll find the most tantalizing options on **Via dei Neri** and the streets branching off to the north.

UNDER L10,000 • Antico Noè. The best panini counter in Florence has fresh turkey and roast beef sandwiches, *Volta di San Piero 6r, tel. 055/2340838. From Duomo, walk east on V. dell'Oriuolo; take covered passageway on right. Closed weekends June and July.*

Il Nilo. This cheap take-out counter, popular with North African immigrants, serves great veal *shawarma* (broiled marinated meat served in a pita with veggies) and falafel (L5000 each). The fine selection of bottled beers is a treat. *Volta di San Piero 9r. Across from Antico Noè. Closed Sun.*

UNDER L15,000 • La Maremmana. Splurge on roasted-meat dishes and seafood, like the delicious *scoglio,* a big plate of pasta with seafood for three people (L32,000). *V. de' Macci 77r, tel. 055/241226. From Santa Croce, take V. dei Pepi, right on V. Ghibellina, and left on V. de' Macci. Closed Sun.*

Trattoria Che C'è C'è. Despite its touristy look, you've found one of the best trattorias in the area. Try Tuscan specialties like large bowls of *ribollita* (thick bean and bread soup) or bistecca alla fiorentina (L45,000 per kilo, which feeds several). *V. de' Magalotti 11r, tel. 055/216589. Closed Mon.*

Trattoria Pallottino. This is what you envisioned: handwritten menus, big tables, and hearty Tuscan fare. For L13,000 you get a first and second course, and coffee or dessert. *V. Isola delle Stinche 1r, tel. 055/289573. From P. Salvemini, take V. M. Palmieri south, which becomes V. Isola delle Stinche. Closed Mon.*

PIAZZA SAN MARCO AND THE UNIVERSITY QUARTER

In the small area bordered by Piazza San Marco, Piazza Santissima Annunziata, and café-lined **Via degli Alfani,** neighborhood joints cater to the university population. Northwest toward Piazza della Indipendenza, along **Via Guelfa** and **Via XXVII Aprile,** narrow side streets offer reasonably priced restaurants.

SMASHING MUSES

The Pietà in Museo dell'Opera del Duomo was a source of great frustration for Michelangelo. The 80-year-old genius hacked off Christ's left arm and leg in a fit of anger over his failure to achieve perfection. A servant stopped him and the arm was reattached, but the back leg is still missing. When a nutcase tried to smash David in the Galleria dell'Accademia five years ago, he only succeeded in pulverizing a big toe. Good samaritans tackled the culprit, others scrambled for the marble shards as mementos. Museum guards had to strip-search everyone and successfully retrieved all the pieces.

UNDER L10,000 • Rosticceria. Labeled only with an unassuming ROSTICCERIA sign, this tiny eatery has delicious Arabic sandwiches and salads (all around L4000). In addition to the wide range of vegetarian choices, it's a nice change from pizza. *V. Guelfa 40r, no phone. Closed Sun.*

Rosticceria Alfio e Beppo. Delicious lasagna, ravioli, and tortellini (L4000 per serving) vie for your attention with salads and roasted chicken. *V. Cavour 118r, near P. San Marco, tel. 055/214108. Closed Sat. Cash only.*

UNDER L15,000 • Trattoria San Zanobi. Enjoy an authentic Italian trattoria serving rich and filling pastas (around L9000) among gleaming brass and linen. *V. San Zanobi 33r, tel. 055/475286. A block off of P. Indipendenza. Closed Sun.*

THE OLTRARNO

You'll have no problem eating well south of the Arno. Just one block away from the river, **Borgo San Jacopo/Via Santo Spirito/Borgo San Frediano** (one long street that changes names) is packed with restaurants.

UNDER L15,000 • I Tarocchi. Tarot cards are the theme, and your fate is to eat pizza in the midst of locals. The menu also includes pastas and daily specials, but it's the thin-crust pizzas that make the trek worthwhile. *V. de' Renai 12r–14r, tel. 055/2343912. Cross river at Ponte alle Grazie and make 2nd left on V. de' Renai. Closed Sat. lunch and Sun.*

Trattoria La Casalinga. In short, this place is very large, very crowded, and very informal. But, you'll savor solid, traditional Tuscan fare. *V. dei Michelozzi 9r, just off P. Santo Spirito, tel. 055/218624; closed Sunday. Cash only.*

WORTH SEEING

With Renaissance masterpieces everywhere, where to begin? Florence is compact, but densely packed with things to see. Your best bet is to hit the main museums—the Uffizi, Pitti Palace, and Accademia—later in the afternoon, when the crowds thin out. Spend mornings in the city's voluminous churches or at smaller museums. Keep in mind that most museums close on Monday, and it's worth getting an updated schedule of opening times and prices from the tourist office. If you're watching your lire, know that all together, tickets to Florence's sights can really add up. Churches are still free, but even then you may have to pay to enter their cloisters, chapels, towers, or domes. Museum hours can change drastically from season to season.

PIAZZA DEL DUOMO

Even the thousandth glimpse of the **Duomo,** officially called Santa Maria del Fiore, will make your jaw drop. Brunelleschi's huge dome is offset by the rest of the exterior's heavily patterned green, white, and pink marble. Construction of the cathedral was fitful during the 14th century because traditional building methods could not support the dome's size. In 1418, Brunelleschi created an adaptation of a perfectly hemispherical Roman dome—slightly taller than it is wide, with an interior and exterior shell linked by an elaborate system of hidden ribs and supports. A beautiful **cupola** (admission L8000; open summer, Mon.–Sat. 9:30–6; winter, 10–5) creates a central supporting axis, which you can climb for a supreme view of Florence. Giotto's **campanile** (admission L8000; open Apr.–Sept., daily 8:30–6; Oct.–Mar, 9–5:20) may be more bang for your buck because it has more look-out points along the way. Look for tables when you enter to sign up for tours of the cathedral in English (daily 10:30 and 3).

After the dazzling exterior, the interior (open daily 9–6) inevitably disappoints. Paolo Uccello's unusual equestrian portrait of John Hawkwood (1436), to the left as you enter, approaches the subject from two geometric angles. Above the entrance, Uccello's intriguing clock moves counterclockwise, counting down the hours from the last sunset until the next one. The Duomo's best artistic works have been moved to the excellent **Museo dell'Opera del Duomo** (P. del Duomo 9, tel. 055/2302885; admission L8000; open Mon.–Sat. 9–6:50, until 5:30 in winter), which exhibits Michelangelo's delicate *Pietà*, Donatello's haggard *Mary Magdalene,* some of Ghiberti's panels from the Baptistry doors, and Luca della Robbia's wonderful celebration of youth, *Cantoria.*

Just opposite the Duomo's entrance, the **Battistero** (tel. 055/2302885; admission free; open Mon.–Sat. 1:30–6, Sun. 9–1:30) is the city's oldest standing building, originally built during the 6th or 7th century. Inside you'll find opulent, Byzantine-looking medieval mosaics, including a portrait of Jesus and five levels of unusual biblical allegories. Look for the wacky, macabre depiction of the Apocalypse over the west door. The Baptistry's eastern doors are the most famous sculptural panels in Renaissance art. Ghiberti beat out Donatello and Brunelleschi in a contest to redesign them, creating a survey of the Old Testament from Adam and Eve to Solomon and Sheba with a depth and emotion unprecedented in this medium. The panels here are copies—some of the originals are in the Museo dell'Opera del Duomo (*see above*), and some are being restored.

Caffelatte (V. degli Alfani 39r; closed Sun.) invites long sessions with a newspaper, tea, and piece of homemade cake. It's probably the only place in town you can get a bowl of yogurt topped with fresh fruit or muesli—and a huge bowl of caffè latte.

PIAZZA DELLA SIGNORIA

Now a major loitering spot and recognizable from Merchant-Ivory's *A Room With a View,* Florence's principal piazza was designed in part as a celebration of Medici power. The family dominated the piazza: They lived in the Palazzo Vecchio and funded the Loggia della Signoria and the Palazzo degli Uffizi. The **Palazzo Vecchio** (tel. 055/2768965; admission L10,000; open Mon.–Wed., Fri., and Sat. 9–7, Sun. 8–1), a fortresslike rusticated brick structure at the piazza's southeast corner, was the city hall in medieval times and is so again today. The exterior is an irregularly shaped combination of palazzo and crenellated castle; inside is a wide array of artwork, including Michelangelo's *Victory* sculpture, Mannerist pieces by Vasari and Bronzino, and statues by Giambologna. The **Loggia della Signoria,** a porch on the square's south side, contains Cellini's bronze *Perseus* carrying Medusa's head and Giambologna's twisted *Rape of the Sabines,* both 16th-century masterpieces.

GALLERIE DEGLI UFFIZE • Vasari was commissioned by the Medici family in 1560 to design the Uffizi as an office for local government, but the top floor was reserved for the family's fantastic art collection, donated to the city of Florence in 1737. Anyone with even a passing interest in Renaissance art will be amazed at the number of recognizable works inside, representing just about every breakthrough of the period. Key works include three masterful Madonna altarpieces by Cimabue, Duccio, and Giotto; Piero della Francesca's coolly detailed portraits of Federico da Montefeltro and his wife Battista Sforza; Paolo Uccello's *Battle of San Romano* (1456), with wild perspective effects like dramatically foreshortened horse legs; Botticelli's *Birth of Venus, Primavera,* and *Adoration of the Magi; The Annunciation,* for which Leonardo da Vinci painted the angel (and perhaps more); and Michelangelo's only nonfresco painting, the *Doni Tondo. Loggiato degli Uffizi 6, tel. 055/2768965. Admission: L12,000. Open Tues.– Sat 9–7, Sun. 9–2.*

BARGELLO • Florence's police headquarters and jail during the Renaissance, the Bargello is now Italy's foremost museum of Renaissance sculpture. On the ground floor are some of Michelangelo's early works, several small bronze statues of Perseus by Cellini (studies for the Loggia della Signoria), and a few of Giambologna's major works. Upstairs, look for Donatello's effete bronze *David,* his watchful *St. George,* and Verrochio's skirted version of *David. V. del Proconsolo 4, tel. 055/210801. Admission: L8000. Open Tues.–Sun. 9–2.*

A SUBURB WITH A VIEW

Enchanting Fiesole, a 20-minute ride on Bus 7 from Florence's train station, or a nice moped jaunt, has an ancient Roman theater, excellent museum of Etruscan ruins, and a magnificent view of Florence to boot. If you have a couple hours to spare, it's definitely worth the trip up the olive-groved hill to get a different angle on the local scene. In summer, the town is home to the spectacular Estate Fiesolana (tel. 055/597277), a music, dance, theater, and film festival many consider the region's richest cultural event.

PIAZZA SANTA MARIA NOVELLA

It may get seedy at night, but this piazza is the best free grassy space in the center of Florence during the day. A complex facade enlivens the church of **Santa Maria Novella** (tel. 055/210113; open daily 7–11:30, and 3:30–6), which you can gaze at for hours as you nurse a beer in one of the piazza's cafés. The circles and scrolls on the upper level, designed by Alberti, were purely ornamental additions to a more somber Gothic lower level. The interior of the church features the black-and-white striped marble characteristic of the early Renaissance. Massaccio's luminescent fresco *Trinity* (1428), important for its strict compositional patterning, dominates the left-hand wall along the nave. The **Strozzi Chapel** holds Filippino Lippi's melodramatic frescoes. You can check out Uccello's excellent frescoes in the adjoining cloister **museum** (tel. 055/282187; admission L5000; open Mon.–Thurs., Sat. 9–2, Sun. 9–1).

PIAZZA SAN LORENZO

Standing literally and figuratively in the shadow of the Duomo, **San Lorenzo** (tel. 055/216634; open daily 7–noon and 3:30–5:30) is one of the city's most elaborate churches. The Medici wanted it to equal the Duomo in beauty and prestige, but because the exterior Michelangelo designed was never built, it appears lonely and unimpressive from the outside. Brunelleschi's interior, however, is sumptuous, with monumental pillars and arches forming a Latin cross. On the right side of the transept is the **Sagrestia Vecchia** (Old Sacristy), which features sculpture by Donatello (who's buried here).

The church cloisters, upstairs off the left aisle, contain the **Biblioteca Laurenziana** (tel. 055/210760; open Mon.–Sat. 9–1), the only place in Florence where you can see for free something Michelangelo had a hand in designing. The artist's famous convex staircase, a pun on the Renaissance exactitude of architects like Brunelleschi, pushes outwards for no other reason than because it looks cool. Medici ostentation is apparent in the **Cappelle Medici** (admission L10,000; open Tues.–Sun. 9–2), a set of chapels accessible from the back end of the church. The **Cappella dei Principi,** built to house the family's remains, is a dizzying mess of green, black, and pink marble. Escape to Michelangelo's much more subtle **Sagrestia Nuova** (New Sacristy), with the sculpted tombs of two minor members of the Medici clan. The unusual poses of the four stages of day confirm—not that you doubted it—Michelangelo's total mastery of the human form (but his women look like men with silicone implants).

The area around San Lorenzo is congested, but not with churchgoers: Shoppers crowd dozens of leather stands near the church, and the city's premier food market, the **Mercato Centrale,** is just a block away. The nearby **Palazzo Medici-Riccardi** (V. Cavour 1, tel. 055/2760340; open Mon., Tues., Thurs.–Sat. 9–12:30 and 3–6, Sun. 9–noon), the former Medici headquarters, ushered in a new age of Florentine civic architecture with its solemn but unimposing brick facade. The second-floor chapel holds the exquisite *Procession of the Magi* by Benozzo Gozzoli. Unfortunately, the cost to enter the small chapel is L6000, and the frescoes, though delightful, are all you get.

PIAZZA SAN MARCO AND
PIAZZA SANTISSIMA ANNUNZIATA

These neighboring squares north of the Duomo are hangouts for coeds (the university is nearby). In Piazza San Marco, the **Museo di San Marco** (tel. 055/210741; admission L8000; open Tues.–Sun. 9–

2) was once the city's Dominican convent, where the devout Renaissance painter Fra Angelico spent years as a friar. It's now one of Florence's best museums, with a gallery containing Fra Angelico's oil paintings and altarpieces, including a *Last Judgment*. In the **Sala Capitolare** is his wall-size *Crucifixion*, and at the top of the stairs you'll find his most famous *Annunciation,* with sparkling colors in a geometrically balanced space. On the same floor are 44 monks' cells, each with its own small fresco by Fra Angelico and his students.

Piazza Santissima Annunziata contains the **Ospedale degli Innocenti** (Foundling Hospital), whose portico, designed by Brunelleschi, is considered by some the first manifestation of true Renaissance style in architecture. Begun in 1419 by the master, it was completed in 1445 by Francesco della Luna. The simple columns topped by perfect half-circle arches seem standard today, but they mark the beginning of Brunelleschi's infatuation with perfect mathematical equilibrium.

GALLERIA DELL'ACCADEMIA • The L12,000 entrance fee is awfully steep to see essentially one statue, but Michelangelo's magnificent *David* is worth it. The artist began the monumental work in 1501 from a single block of discarded marble. Designed to stand outdoors on the Piazza della Signoria and to be viewed from a distance, the statue is larger than life, with proportions a bit off: The head seems slightly large for the body, and the hands are enormous. The surrounding gallery holds a series of *Slaves* by Michelangelo from the 1520s, figures that just barely free themselves from solid stone. *V. Ricasoli 60, tel. 055/214375. Admission: L12,000. Open summer, Tues.–Sat. 9–7, Sun. 9–2; winter, Tues.–Sat. 9–2, Sun. 9–1.*

Pass up the gelato shops selling technicolor synthetic gelato pumped up with air and get the real thing at Carabè (V. Ricasoli 84r), where the lemons, almonds, and hazelnuts come from Sicily, just like the gelato maker, who only uses real ingredients.

PIAZZA SANTA CROCE

Piazza Santa Croce marks the southeastern edge of the Florentine tourist triangle. Here the city's main Franciscan church, the late-13th-century **Santa Croce** (tel. 055/244619; open Mon.–Sat. 8–6:30, Sun. 3–6; shorter hrs in winter), has an all-star line-up with the tombs of Michelangelo, Galileo, Ghiberti, and Machiavelli and monuments to Dante, da Vinci, and Raphael (the last three are buried elsewhere). Giotto's fresco cycles of St. Francis in the **Cappella Bardi** near the altar and his *John the Baptist* in the adjacent **Cappella Peruzzi** helped prod painting out of stiff medieval conventions and into more imaginative and psychologically complex compositions.

On the right-hand side of the facade is the entrance to the cloisters, containing the church **museum** and Brunelleschi's justly famous **Cappella dei Pazzi** (combined admission L3000; open Thurs.–Tues. 10–12:30 and 2:30–6:30; shorter hrs in winter). Luca della Robbia and friends did the terra-cotta tondi of the apostles, as well as the evangelists above the door. The museum boasts Donatello's massive bronze *San Ludovico d'Angio* (1423), Domenico Veneziano's ravaged John the Baptist and St. Francis, and Cimabue's *Crucifixion,* damaged by the 1966 flood.

Built in the 1870s in Moorish-Byzantine style, Florence's enormous **Sinagoga** (V. Farini 4, tel. 055/245252; admission L5000; open Sun.–Thurs. 10–1 and 2–5, Fri. 10–1), a few blocks north of Santa Croce, is both delightful and garish. Ornate, hand-painted arabesques cover the walls, and Turkish-style domes decorate the exterior. Upstairs, the small, worthwhile **Museo Ebraico** depicts the history of Florence's Jewish population.

OLTRARNO

On the way to the south side of the Arno you cross the **Ponte Vecchio,** Florence's oldest bridge, rebuilt in the 14th century from a wooden structure dating to Roman times. In the 16th century, Ferdinando I installed jewelry merchants on the bridge, and today the tradition continues. From the Ponte Vecchio, a street leads to the massive **Palazzo Pitti,** designed as a home for businessman Luca Pitti and bought by the Medici in 1549. You could spend more than L20,000 visiting the palace's museums and gardens, but save your dough for the most substantial museum, the **Galleria Palatina** (tel. 055/210323; admission L12,000; open Tues.–Sun. 9–7), with works by Rubens, Caravaggio, Titian, Raphael, and Van Dyck. Outside, the luxurious **Giardini Boboli** (tel. 055/213440; admission L4000; open summer, Tues.–Sun. 9–8:30; closes 1 hr before sunset in winter) were the Medicis' vision of an idyllic retreat. When the park was made into free public space in the last century, Florentines visited regularly. Then the city imposed an entrance fee, and now almost all visitors are tourists.

You wouldn't guess it from the unadorned yellow exterior, but the nearby church of **Santo Spirito** (P. Santo Spirito, tel. 055/210030; open Thurs.–Tues 8–noon and 3:30–6:30), another mathematically precise Brunelleschi project, was one of the most ambitious creations to come out of the Renaissance. Unfortunately, Brunelleschi died before completing the church, and the original design was modified to a more traditional style. In the right transept is Filippino Lippi's *Madonna and Child with Saints,* and off the left aisle of the nave sits a harmonious sacristy designed by Giuliano da Sangallo.

Perhaps the most important and moving fresco cycle in Florence is the one in the tiny **Cappella Brancacci** (P. del Carmine, behind church of Santa Maria del Carmine, tel. 055/2382195; admission L5000; open Mon., Wed.–Sat. 10–5, Sun. 1–5). The chapel is best known for Massaccio's brilliant frescoes *Expulsion from Eden* and *The Tribute Money.* Adam and Eve's expulsion is perhaps the most wrenching artistic image of the Renaissance, and Massaccio, who died at the age of 27, painted it in less than a month.

AFTER DARK

The Italian-language *Firenze Spettacolo* (L2700), available at local newsstands, lists films, discos, music, and cultural goings-on. Also look for *Quir,* the bilingual gay magazine listing local events at English-language bookstores (*see* Basics, *above*). For a good old-fashioned Irish bar, try **The Fiddler's Elbow** (P. Santa Maria Novella 7r); beers aren't cheap at L6000 a pint. Locals congregate at the outdoor cafés on **Piazza Santo Spirito. Cabiria Café** (P. Santo Spirito, tel. 055/215732) is the hippest place in town, busy all afternoon and evening. In the student area near Piazza San Marco, try the happening **Cadillac Caffè** (V. degli Alfani 57r, tel. 055/2344455), which hosts a gay and lesbian night Friday.

Admission to discos costs around L15,000–L20,000, but women often get in free, and discount passes are handed out on Piazza del Duomo, Piazza della Repubblica, and Via de' Calzaiuoli. Two of the better discos are the cavernous **Yab Yum** (V. Sassetti 5r, tel. 055/282018; closed Mon. and summer), and **055** (V. Verdi 57, tel. 055/244004; closed Mon.). Locals are much keener on places outside the center, where there's space to dance outdoors during summer. The wildest dancing heats up at **Meccanò** (Viale degli Olmi 1, on the south edge of Cascine Park, tel. 055/331371). You can get here on Bus 17, but the area is sketchy and the bus stops running around midnight. Gay discos come and go, and the scene is much more accommodating for gay men than for lesbians. **Tabasco** (P. Santa Cecilia 3, just off P. della Signoria, tel. 055/213000; closed Mon.), traditionally men-only, has recently become popular with lesbians as well. **Piccolo Café** (Borgo Santa Croce 27, tel. 241704; closed Mon.) offers a casual mixing ground for gays and lesbians where late-night coffee and art exhibits are all a part of the scene.

The only screen in town that shows English-language films full-time is **Cinema Astro** (P. San Simone, across from Gelateria Vivoli, no phone; closed mid-July–mid-Aug.). American hits from three months ago are interspersed with frequent showings of the unavoidable *Room with a View.*

NEAR FLORENCE

Replete with small vineyards, dusty olive groves, and sunflowers stretching out to the horizon, Tuscany's countryside radiates an allure that has attracted wave after wave of artists. In addition to providing the birthplace for the Renaissance, the vibrant and verdant area inspired the Romantic poets. What's surprising is that Tuscan cities have changed so little since their glory days—many, like San Gimignano, still stand within their original walls with populations smaller than they were in the Middle Ages and the Renaissance. As one might expect of the home of the Leaning Tower of Pisa, Tuscany is subject to a year-round tourist invasion, which peaks in the summertime. If you don't have a car, it can be difficult getting around the more rural areas, but larger cities like Pisa and Siena are well-connected by train and bus to Florence.

PISA

Thanks to an engineering mistake, Pisa's name is instantly recognized worldwide. Most visitors stop in Pisa only long enough to catch a glimpse of the famous Leaning Tower, and maybe the remarkable Duomo and Battistero, between connecting trains. Many of Pisa's secondary sights are mediocre, it's true, but the city does have some redeeming qualities: Lodging is more affordable than in nearby Siena and Florence, and a university gives the city character. If possible, arrive in the late afternoon, when the main drag quiets down. The **visitor center** at the train station (tel. 050/42291; open summer, Mon.–Sat.).

8–8, Sun. 9–1; shorter hrs in winter) runs out of maps early in the day but will gladly point you in the right direction. A better office (tel. 050/560464) is just north of the Leaning Tower on **Piazza del Duomo.**

COMING AND GOING

Trains to Florence (1 hr, L7200) leave hourly from busy **Pisa Centrale** (P. Stazione, tel. 1478/88088), as do trains to Siena (1 hr, L9800; change at Empoli). Most **city buses** (L1200) stop in front of the train station. Bus 1 runs to the Duomo, Battistero, and Leaning Tower. Pisa's **Galileo Galilei Airport** (P. d'Ascanio, tel. 050/500707) is 1 km (½ mi) from the train station. The train from Florence continues past Pisa's central station to the airport, and Bus 7 heads there from the central station.

WHERE TO SLEEP AND EAT

At **Albergo di Stefano** (V. Sant'Appollonia 35, tel. 050/553559), large, clean doubles (some with outdoor terraces) go for only L55,000. Rooms in the ideally located **Albergo Gronchi** (P. Arcivescovado 1, tel. 050/561823, doubles L50,000) are big and comfortable, and the place emanates a patina of fading elegance. **Ostello Madonna dell'Acqua** (V. Pietrasantina 15, tel. 050/890622), a church-run hostel, charges only L20,000 for a bed but is tainted by the stench of a nearby canal. Bus 3 will take you here; the reception doesn't open until 6 PM. **La Grotta** (V. San Francesco 103, near P. San Paolo all'Orto, tel. 050/578105; closed Sun.) is the old eatery in town, with excellent food and late hours.

WORTH SEEING

Contrary to popular belief, Pisa isn't just a mundane town with one major sight—it's a mundane town with three major sights: the Leaning Tower, the Duomo, and the Baptistry, all in the Campo dei Miracoli. The **Leaning Tower** (Torre Pendente) is one of the world's most famous buildings because of its amazing tilt, about a 13-ft discrepancy between top and bottom. Unfortunately, the tower has been closed for the past six years, and you can't even get within spitting distance of it. The six blind arcades are in the same style as the cathedral's facade, and a wondrous belfry by Tomasso di Andrea da Pontedera

Work began on Pisa's Leaning Tower in 1173, but the soil under the site began to shift by the time the third tier had been built. The original architect, Pisano, fled the city fearing for his life, and architects have tried to correct the tilting ever since.

crowns the top. Galileo, a professor at the University of Pisa, utilized the angle and conducted his famous gravitation experiments from the tower. The black-and-white striping on the nearby **Duomo** (tel. 050/560547; open Mon.–Sat. 10–7:40, Sun. 1–7:40; shorter hrs off-season) is perhaps the church's most famous trait, although time has eroded the black marble. Inside, have a look at Giovanni Pisano's eight-side pulpit, which outdoes the pulpit built by his father, Nicola Pisano, for the circular **Battistero** (tel. 050/560547; admission L7000; open Apr.–Oct., shorter hrs off-season) next door. The baptistry is known for its perfect acoustics and irregularly shaped dome. The long, low, white edifice on Piazza del Duomo is the **Camposanto,** a cemetery that looks more mysterious from the outside than the inside; think twice before paying to enter. Legend holds that the soil here is from the hill on which Jesus was crucified.

SAN GIMIGNANO

When you're high on a hill surrounded by crumbling towers in silhouette against the blue sky, it's difficult not to fall under the medieval spell of San Gimignano. Fourteen towers dot the skyline, which is what brings in all the tour groups at midday. Escape them by heading outside the city walls for a hike, and return to explore town in the late afternoon, when things quiet down and the shadows cast by the towers take on fascinating shapes. The **Torre Grossa** (P. Duomo, tel. 0577/940340; admission L8000; open daily Mar.–Oct. 9:30–7:30; shorter hrs off-season) is the only tower you can climb; at least it's the biggest in town. The nearby Palazzo del Popolo, built in the late 13th century, houses the **Museo Civico** (L7000), which features Taddeo di Bartolo's celebratory *Bethroned San Gimignano and His Miracles.* On the same piazza, the **Duomo Collegiata** (tel. 0577/940316; chapel admission L3000) has a treasure trove of well-preserved frescoes.

If you're creeped out by the words "rectal," "impale," or "emasculate," avoid the **Museo di Criminologica Medievale** (V. del Castello, off P. della Cisterna, tel. 0577/942243; admission L10,000; open daily 10–1 and 2–7), with its extensive and thoughtfully presented displays of medieval torture devices.

To reach San Gimignano, catch a bus (L2400) from Poggibonsi, about 12 km (7 mi) away. Poggibonsi's **train station** (tel. 0577/936462) is on the Florence–Siena line; trains from the former cost L6800 (1 hr

THIS AIN'T NO RODEO

Siena's Palio horse race takes place July 2 and August 16, but its spirit lives all year long. Three laps around Il Campo earn participants the respect or scorn of the other contrade, and almost nothing is too underhanded to be against the rules.

Like the Spanish bullfight, the tradition is criticized for its violence and inhumanity. Horses are frequently injured, and bribery, brutality, and kidnapping of the jockeys occurs. But if you can stand being mobbed by a hot sea of fans (the faint of heart get carried out on stretchers), by all means catch the Palio; it's a spectacle you won't soon forget.

20 min), from the latter L3000 (30 min). The **tourist office** (P. Duomo 1, tel. 0577/940008; open daily 9–1 and 3–7, winter 2–6) has lists of *affittacamere* (private rooms in homes) for great prices. The way-above-average **San Gimignano Youth Hostel** (V. delle Fonti 1, tel. 0577/941991; beds L20,000; closed Nov.–Feb.) is right in the center. There's lots of meat on the menu, a smooth *ribollita*, and good wines at **Osteria delle Catene** (V. Mainardi 18, tel. 0577/941966; closed Wed. and Jan.).

SIENA

Once a world leader in art, banking, and commerce, Siena stopped growing about 600 years ago, but it never stopped flourishing. Unlike many of the hill towns that surround it, Siena has aged well, retaining its traditional charm while integrating the conveniences of modern life. Fourteenth-century palazzi now house laundromats and pastry shops, and residents still gather on the central piazza, Piazza del Campo. The town's character is largely defined by its 17 medieval *contrade* (neighborhoods), each with its own church and symbol. For information on the contrade and hotel and restaurant listings, stop at the **APT** (P. del Campo 56, tel. 0577/280551; open Apr.–Sept., Mon.–Sat. 8:30–7:30; Oct.–Mar., Mon.–Sat. 9–12:30 and 3:30–7).

COMING AND GOING

Siena's **train station** (P. Fratelli Rosselli, tel. 1478/88088) sends trains to Florence (1½ hrs, L7800), but buses are more frequent. Trains to and from Rome (2½ hrs, L19,900) require a switch at Chiusi. The **bus station** (P. San Domenico, tel. 0577/204245) sends **TRA-IN/SITA** buses every half hour to Florence (1¼ hrs, L10,500) and San Gimignano (1¼ hrs, L7900; change at Poggibonsi). TRA-IN also sends orange buses (not to be confused with blue long-distance buses) around the perimeter of town (L1300 for an hour ticket). Buses going to the center empty around **Piazza Gramsci.** To get to Il Campo from here, take Via Malavolti through Piazza Matteotti to Via delle Terme, which empties into Il Campo.

WHERE TO SLEEP AND EAT

Hotels in Siena get away with charging a pretty penny, and prices skyrocket when the Palio (*see box, below*) comes to town on July 2 and August 16. The ultra-clean **Ostello Guidoriccio** (V. Fiorentina 89, tel. 0577/52212, fax 0577/56172) charges L22,000 per person, breakfast included. It's 4 km (2½ mi) from town, an easy ride on Bus 15 (Bus 10 weekends and evenings). A series of staircases from Il Campo leads to **Tre Donzelle** (V. delle Donzelle 5, tel. 0577/280358, fax 0577/223933), the best deal in Siena. Sizable, worn doubles with views and breakfast cost L66,000, with bath L83,000. If you've always dreamed of throwing open your bedroom shutters to a postcard panorama, **Bernini** (V. della Sapienza 15, 1 block from the bus station, tel. 0577/289047) is for you. Doubles are L100,000, with bath L120,000, and much less in the off-season.

For good vegetarian pizza and spectacular focaccia (about L2000 per huge slice), come to **Forno Indipendenza** (P. Indipendenza 27, tel. 0577/280295; closed Sun.), Siena's premier bakery. **Osteria dell'Artista** (V. Stalloreggi 11, tel. 0577/40064; closed Thurs.) has some of the cheapest sit-down meals in town, with grilled chicken for L8000 and amazing pasta for L10,000. **Antica Pizzicheria al Palazzo del Chigiana** (V. di Città 93–95, tel. 0577/289164) is a great place to pick up panini to go, but never mind the bespectacled hog's head peering down from the entryway or the butcher in his blood-splattered apron.

WORTH SEEING

The southeast corner of Il Campo is dominated by the stupendous **Palazzo Pubblico** (Town Hall). Built during the late 13th and early 14th centuries, the building features the crenellated cornices and three-part arches that define Sienese architecture. Inside, the **Museo Civico** (P. del Campo 1, tel. 0577/292263; open Mon.–Sat. 9–6:15, Sun. 9–12:45, admission L8000) has frescoes and paintings by Siennese greats Simone Martini, Lorenzetti, and Duccio. The **Sala della Pace** features the famous frescoes *Allegories of Good and Bad Government,* by Ambrogio Lorenzetti, who wasn't very subtle in his messages to the ruling council that used to hold meetings right below the frescoes. The Palazzo Pubblico's most distinctive feature is the famous **Torre del Mangia** (tel. 0577/292263; open in good weather, winter 10–12:45, summer 9:30–7:30, admission L5000), a 335-ft tower built in 1334. It offers the greatest possible view of Siena—only right, since you'll climb more than 400 stairs to get there.

A quizzical combination of Gothic and Romanesque architecture, Siena's **Duomo** (P. del Duomo; open 9–7:30 in summer, 7:30–1:30 and 2:30–5) makes all other Tuscan cathedrals appear underadorned. Both outside and in, the vivid black-and-white color scheme prevails. The marble floors loudly depict an array of biblical subjects, and the arched vaulting is covered with stars. Don't miss Nicola Pisano's carved pulpit. Next door, the **Museo dell'Opera del Duomo** (tel. 0577/283048; open summer 9–7:30, shorter hrs in winter, admission L6000) houses Duccio's ambitious

Siena is built on hills made of red clay—a color so distinctive that a "Siena" found its way into every Crayola crayon box.

Maestà (1310). Behind the cathedral in the **Battistero** (admission L3000; same hrs as Museo dell'Opera del Duomo) Donatello's famous *Feast of Herod* decorates the rear right-hand side of the font. The **Pinacoteca Nazionale** (V. San Pietro 29, tel. 0577/281161; admission L8000; open Tues.–Sat. 9–7, Sun. 8:30-1:30, shorter hrs in winter) has a memorable collection of Madonna-and-child paintings and Simone Martini's unlabeled *St. Augustine and His Miracles* (1324).

UMBRIA AND MARCHE

Central Italy does not begin and end with Tuscany—the pastoral, hilly provinces of Umbria and Marche pick up where the well-traveled route between Florence and Rome leaves off. Medieval towns, orchards, vineyards, and olive groves cover the landscape, which, unlike Tuscany, hasn't been trampled by tourists. The only hill town with heavy tourist traffic is **Assisi,** home of the ascetic St. Francis (1181–1226) and an important pilgrimage site since medieval times. **Perugia** is the Umbria's provincial capital, a university town known for its cultural vivacity and its chocolate. Also worth a visit are **Orvieto,** built atop a volcanic outcropping; **Spoleto,** with its international arts festival; and **Gubbio,** one of Italy's best-preserved medieval cities. Marche, to the east, offers a long coastline full of resorts, breathtaking mountain scenery, and cities bursting with magnificent art. Its main port town, **Ancona,** is a gateway to Greece; **Urbino** is Marche's most spectacular city. Captivating **Ascoli Piceno** offers access to the **Sibillini Mountains,** the most beautiful section of the Apennines.

PERUGIA

Much of Umbria's lifeblood courses through Perugia, its bustling capital. A hill town that has endured barbarian conquests and medieval chaos, Perugia today, with its 1604-ft-high location, massive city gates, and grand palaces and churches, still bears the mark of a much-coveted dwelling spot. Though its panoramic views are spectacular, many are drawn to Perugia because of its importance as an intellectual and cultural center. A thriving international student population and a world-renowned jazz festival make this town's joints really jump.

VINO FANTASTICO

Orvieto sits atop a circular plateau of tufa stone shoved up from the valley floor by volcanic movements. Its natural defenses eliminated the need for medieval walls, making it something of an anomaly among Umbrian hill towns.

Excavations have revealed a network of over 1,200 Etruscan wells and storage caves, but Orvieto's big attraction is its stunning Duomo. Shops along the narrow streets sell the town's export: Dry, white Orvieto Classico, or "liquid gold." Trains arrive from Rome (1 hr 20 min, L12,500) and Florence (1½ hrs, L16,200); a funicular (L1400) carries you the centro storico.

BASICS

The **tourist office** (P. IV Novembre 3, tel. 075/5736458) is open daily 8:30–1:30 and 3:30–6:30, Sun. 9–1. To find out what's going on, pick up a copy of *Perugia What, Where, When* (L1000) from a newsstand.

COMING AND GOING

The **main train station** (P. Vittorio Veneto, tel. 1478/88088) is below the town. Trains go to Rome (17 daily, 3 hrs, L17,200; change in Foligno), Florence (14 daily, 2 hrs, L15,500), Assisi (hourly, 30 min, L2700), and Spoleto (17 daily, 1 hr, L5700). From the station, Bus 20, 26, 27, 28, or 29 will get you to **Piazza Italia,** and Buses 33 and 36 go to **Piazza Matteotti. Long-distance buses** depart from Piazza dei Partigiani, just beyond Piazza Italia.

WHERE TO SLEEP AND EAT

The hostel **Centro Internazionale di Accoglienza per la Gioventù** (V. Bontempi 13, off P. Dante, tel. 075/5722880) has beds for L15,000 a night; sheets are L2000 extra. **Pensione Anna** (V. dei Priori 48, 06123, off Corso Vannucci; tel. and fax 075/5736304) feels more like a home than a hotel. Doubles without bath are L58,000. On Piazza Matteotti you'll find food specialty shops and the **Mercato Coperto** (open weekdays 7–1:30, Saturdays 7–1:30 and 4:30–7:30) for fruit and veggies. Head for **Osteria Il Gufo** (V. della Viola 18, tel. 075/5734126), and eat and drink like a Perugino.

WORTH SEEING

Perugia's main street, Corso Vannucci, runs from Piazza Italia to Piazza IV Novembre, where two key monuments, the Palazzo dei Priori and the Duomo, face each other across the **Fontana Maggiore** (1275). The facade of the 15th-century **Duomo** was never finished, but the marble design on the lower wall hints at how it might have looked. Inside is Federigo Barocci's *Deposition*—his finest work—and the Virgin's wedding ring, a hunk of onyx Mary is supposed to have worn in her earthly marriage to Joseph. The enormous **Palazzo dei Priori,** Perugia's town hall since the 13th-century, holds the **Galleria Nazionale dell'Umbria** (tel. 075/5741247; admission L8000; open Mon.–Sat. 9–7, Sun. 9–1, closed the first Mon. of the month). The 33-room collection is rich with religious artwork, among them an altarpiece by Pinturicchio and early Renaissance paintings by Fra Angelico, Agostino di Duccio, and Piero della Francesca.

The church of **San Domenico** (P. Bruno, off C. Cavour), Perugia's largest, contains one of Italy's largest stained-glass windows (75 ft tall), and the handsome tomb of Pope Benedict XI (first chapel on the right), who died in Perugia after eating poisoned figs in 1324. The **Museo Archeologico Nazionale dell'Umbria** (P. Bruno, off C. Cavour, tel. 075/5727141; admission L4000; open Mon.–Sat. 9–1:30 and 2:30–6, Sun. 9–1), inside the cloister to the left of the double staircase, displays a solid collection of Etruscan and Roman artifacts illustrating Perugia's ancient origins. Beside the large church of San Francesco al Prato, now just an attractive facade, shines the Oratorio di San Bernardino (P. San Francesco, off Via dei Priori; open daily 8–noon and 4–7). Its marvelous facade (1461) is the work of Florentine sculptor Agostino di Duccio.

ASSISI

The legacy of St. Francis, champion of humility and asceticism and founder of the Franciscan order, surrounds the rose-colored hill town of Assisi. Each year, thousands of pilgrims make the trek here to pay homage to the man who made God accessible to commoners. But don't let that scare you away—not even a steady, massive flow of tourists and the trinket shops they necessitate can spoil the singular beauty of Umbria's religious center or its magnificent church. No other town speaks so much about one person, and to get to know a bit about Francis is reason enough to stop here for a day. The **tourist office** (P. del Comune 12, tel. 075/812534) is open weekdays 8–2 and 3:30–6:30, Saturday 9–1 and 3:30–6:30, and Sunday 9–1.

COMING AND GOING

Trains run to Perugia (30 min, L2700). To get to Florence, transfer at Terontola; for Rome or Ancona transfer at Foligno. A bus labeled ASSISI-SANTA MARIA DEGLI ANGELI travels between the station and town (4 km/2½ mi). **Long-distance buses** leave from Piazza Matteotti, Largo Properzio, and Piazza Unità d'Italia.

WHERE TO SLEEP AND EAT

Ostello Fontemaggio (V. Eremo delle Carceri 7, Fontemaggio, tel. 075/813636) is a combination hostel, campground, and restaurant. Beds cost L17,000 a night, breakfast included. From Piazza Matteotti, exit town through Porta Cappuccini and follow Via Eremo delle Carceri 1 km (½ mi) uphill to the Fontemaggio turnoff on the right. **Ostello La Pace** (HI; V. Valecchie 177, tel. and fax 075/816767) is cleaner and better maintained, with beds for L20,000, showers and breakfast included. Set up on one of the town's terraces, the **Hotel La Rocca** (V. Porta Perlici 27, tel. 075/816467, fax 075/812284) has spacious doubles—many with balconies and views—for L70,000 (L53,000 without bath).

Perugia's claim to fame is the chocolate Bacio (kiss), wrapped in paper inscribed with multilingual love messages. Chocoholics can visit the museum at the Perugina factory in San Sisto (Viale San Sisto 207, tel. 075/52761; open Mon.–Fri. 9–noon).

For a rundown on regional goodies, stop at **La Bottega dei Sapori** (P. del Comune 34, tel. 075/812294), where proprietor Fabrizio might give you a tour of his deli-market-*enoteca* (wine shop). **Ristorante Spadini** (V. Sant'Agnese 6, off C. Mazzini, tel. 075/813005; closed Mon.) cooks up regional specialties.

WORTH SEEING

The Piazza del Comune, Assisi's main square, shelters the **Pinacoteca** (Palazzo del Priori, tel. 075/812579; admission L4000; open 10–1 and 3–6), a survey of Umbrian art. The **Tempio di Minerva,** with a classical facade and corrugated columns supporting a tympanum, and the **Foro Romano** (V. Portica), a museum of Roman remains under the piazza, are both nearby. Stop by the little **Chiesa Nuova** (take V. Arco dei Priori out of the piazza) atop St. Francis's family home.

In a city full of churches, the glorious **Basilica di San Francesco** (tel. 075/813061) is stellar. This celebration of Italy's patron saint is actually two structures in one: a Gothic church built atop a Romanesque basilica, both remarkably beautiful and decorated floor to ceiling with perhaps the finest collection of frescoes in the world. Dress codes are strictly enforced: no bare legs or shoulders.

URBINO

It's not hard to understand why Urbino is held by many to be the surviving example of the Renaissance utopia, true in architecture and art to the harmony and balance exemplified in the mysterious painting *Città Ideale* (Ideal City), which hangs in Urbino's Galleria Nazionale. Isolated in the sharp foothills of the Sibillini Mountains, the cobblestone-and-brick town with its skyline of towers and domes has changed little since Il Castiglione based his *Cortegiano* (The Courtier)—the definitive book on Renaissance etiquette—on Urbino's Duke Federico da Montefeltro. With a popular university and summer programs that attract students from all over the world and a Jazz Festival every June, little Urbino is still very much alive. The **tourist office** (P. Rinascimento 1, tel. 0722/2613) is open Monday–Saturday 9–1 and 3–6, Sunday 9–1 (in winter daily 9–1, closed Sun.).

COMING AND GOING

There are no trains to Urbino, so get the bus at Pesaro (50 min, L3500) or Rimini (1 daily, 1 hr, L5500). The **information booth** (open July–Aug., daily 9–1 and 3–7) beneath Palazzo Ducale has a schedule; buy tickets onboard.

WHERE TO SLEEP AND EAT

Albergo Italia (C. Garibaldi 32, tel. 0722/2701), just off Piazza della Repubblica, has spacious rooms, some with panoramic views. Doubles cost L60,000, with bath L85,000. **Pensione Fosca** (V. Raffaello 67, tel. 0722/2542, fax 0722/329622) lets airy doubles with brand new bathrooms down the hall for L59,000. The offbeat vegetarian **Un Punto Macrobiotico** (V. Pozzo Nuovo 4, tel. 0722/329790; closed Sun.) serves a L4000 menu, including soup, rice, beans, and salad. Try **Ristorante Agripan** (V. del Leone 11, tel. 0722/327448, closed Wed.) for locally grown organic vegetables, free-range chickens, and smoke-free dining.

WORTH SEEING

Inside the sublime Renaissance **Palazzo Ducale** is Duke Federico's library and the **Galleria Nazionale delle Marche** (P. Duca Federico, tel. 0722/2760; admission L8000; open daily 9–7, Sun. and Mon. 9–2), which houses the *Città Ideal* and paintings by Titian and della Francesca. The **Oratorio di San Giovanni** (Scala di San Giovanni 31, off V. Mazzini, tel. 0722/320936; admission L3000) and the Oratorio di San Giuseppe (L2000) next door are Renaissance chapels containing important frescoes and paintings; they're open 10–noon and 3–5:30. **Raphael's House** (V. Raffaello 57, tel. 0722/320105; admission L5000; open daily 9–1 and 3–7, closed Sun. afternoon) looks a lot like it did in 1483 when he lived here, but there are only a few original works by the artist.

ROME

The currents of time run deep in Rome: 2,500 years of history are piled on top of each other, a study in contrasts as the modern metropolis grows over them like a vine. Modern offices in Renaissance buildings with dirty and worn Baroque facades look out over ancient ruins at a bus stop, and proud Romans chat on cell phones, driving along the same paths their ancestors once walked. These layers are a large part of the capitol's enigmatic charm and make Rome a continually unfolding city. Undoubtedly, the home of the Colosseo, the Fontana di Trevi, the Pantheon, Basilica di San Pietro, *and* the Cappella Sistina demands a lot of sightseeing, but despite its cultural treasures, Rome is no museum. The city (and it is *definitely* a city) bears its history with what is at best an offhand grace, at worst, an erratic carelessness. Careening motorists, blaring televisions, stylish café-goers, all manner of worker, politician, immigrant, tourist, and thief keep modern Rome in constant, vibrant motion around, over, and through the decaying remains of civilizations gone by.

According to legend, Rome was founded in 753 BC by Romulus and Remus, twin brothers nursed by a she-wolf in a cave below the Capitoline Hill. The city prospered and grew, eventually defeating its Etruscan rulers and for a millennium was the heart and soul of the nation that bore its name, which reached across Europe to the British Isles, and spanned the Mediterranean from Gibraltar to Constantinople. As Rome was rebuilt after centuries of looting and sacking, medieval churches were constructed over ancient temples and early Christian basilicas. In the Renaissance (1350–1600) and Baroque (1600–1750) periods, the elite-sponsored papacy commissioned extravagant additions to existing structures, ensuring that by the modern era much of Rome's architecture bore the mark of one papal dynasty or another. During the early 20th century, Mussolini tried his hand at renovating the Eternal City, bulldozing neighborhoods to make way for neo-Imperial boulevards intended, along with government reforms, to make Rome a model of efficiency and a city of the future.

In the last few years the city has begun to reap the rewards of ambitious restoration projects, with freshly cleaned facades emerging from behind the scaffolding. And there is much more to come as the city readies itself for the *Giubileo* (Jubilee) in the year 2000, when more than 30 million people are expected to visit.

BASICS

VISITOR INFORMATION

Look for the small **EPT** tourist office branch opposite Track 2 in **Stazione Termini** (tel. 06/4824078), or trek three blocks northwest of the station to the **main office** (V. Parigi 5, tel. 06/48899255). Both are open Monday–Saturday 8:15–7. **Enjoy Rome** (V. Varese 39, tel. 06/4451843; open weekdays 8:30–1 and 3:30–6, Sat. 8:30–1), 3½ blocks from Stazione Termini, is a good stop for maps, accommodation listings, free room bookings, updated event schedules, and advice in English. **Hotel Reservation Service** (Stazione Termini, opposite Track 10, tel. 06/6991000; service daily 7 AM–10 PM), books hotel rooms free of charge.

AMERICAN EXPRESS

The office is on Piazza di Spagna (P. di Spagna 38, tel. 06/67641; 1678/74333 for lost or stolen cards; 1678/72000 for lost or stolen traveler's checks after hrs; open weekdays 9–5:30, Sat. 9–12:30).

CHANGING MONEY

For instant gratification try the sketchy-looking office in **Stazione Termini** (south side of information office; open daily 8–1:30 and 3–7:30) displaying the cardboard NO COMMISSION sign. Banks change money weekdays 8:30–1:30 and 2:45–3:45 and usually charge a flat fee of L5000, but their rates are typically the best. The rates at **Thomas Cook** (P. Barberini, 21A, tel. 06/4828082; or Via della Conciliazione 23, near the Vatican, tel. 06/68300435) aren't great, but you can draw money from some credit cards. The Barberini office is open every day: daily Monday–Saturday 8:30–7 and Sunday 9–1:30.

CONSULATES AND EMBASSIES

Australia (C. Trieste 25/C, tel. 06/852721; open Mon.–Thurs. 9–noon and 1:30–5, Fri. 9–noon). **Canada** (V. Zara 30, tel. 06/445981; open weekdays 8:30–12:30 and 1:30–4). **New Zealand** (V. Zara 28, tel. 06/4402928; open weekdays 8:30–12:45 and 1:45–5). **United Kingdom** (V. XX Settembre 80/A, tel. 06/4825441; open weekdays 9:30–1:30). **United States** (V. Veneto 121, tel. 06/46741; open weekdays 8:30–noon).

EMERGENCIES

The general emergency number for **first aid** or **police** is 113. If you have to file the all-too-routine theft report, an English speaker is usually on staff at the **Ufficio Stranieri** (Foreigners' Office, V. Genova 2, off V. Nazionale, tel. 46862235; open weekdays 8–8, Sat. 8–6). **Rome American Hospital** (V. Emilio Longoni 69, tel. 06/22551) has English-speaking doctors and dentists on hand. For pharmaceutical needs, the **Farmacia Piram Omeopatia** (V. Nazionale 228, tel. 06/4880754) and **Farmacia della Stazione** (P. Cinquecento 51, tel. 06/4880019) are both open 24 hours.

ENGLISH-LANGUAGE BOOKS

You'll find good selections at **Feltrinelli International** (V. V.E. Orlando 84, tel. 06/4827878; open Mon.–Sat. 9–8, Sun. 10–1:30 and 4–7:30). **The Anglo-American Bookstore** (V. della Vite 102, near P. di Spagna, tel. 06/679522.; open Mon.–Sat. 9:30–1:30 and 3:30–7:30) is well stocked, good for cookbooks, novels, and history books.

MAIL

Post offices are located all around town and are open mornings Monday–Saturday; some are also open in the afternoons. The **main post office** (P. San Silvestro, 1 block east of V. del Corso) is open 9–6 every day, and you can change money and pick up held mail (*fermo posta* there—articles should be addressed to "Your Name, Fermo Posta San Silvestro, 00187 Roma." If you just need to buy stamps, go to a tobacco shop, marked TABACCHI.

COMING AND GOING

BY BUS

Rome does not have a central bus terminal. Instead, blue **COTRAL** (tel. 06/5915551) buses leave from different points around town. Get details from the EPT office, or call COTRAL directly. Private coaches—most with plush seats and air-conditioning—serve destinations throughout Italy. Get information and buy tickets at **Eurojet Tours** (P. della Repubblica 54, tel. 06/4817455; Open weekdays 9–7, Sat. 9–1).

KEY

AE American Express Office

i Tourist Information

M Metro Stops

Metro Lines

Rail Lines

N

| 0 | 880 yds |
| 0 | 800 m |

Sights ●

Santa Maria degli Angeli, **22**	
Santa Maria della Concezione, **18**	
Santa Maria Maggiore, **36**	
Santa Maria del Popolo, **9**	
Santa Maria Sopra Minerva, **50**	
Scalinata di Spagna, **14**	
Villa Farnesina, **55**	

Lodging ○

Albergo del Sole, **53**
Albergo Fiorella, **10**
Fawlty Towers, **31**
Giuggioli Hotel, **2**
Hotel Cervia, **29**
Hotel Cisterna, **56**
Hotel Erdarelli, **20**
Hotel Fuggetta, **30**
Hotel Germano, **25**
Hotel Giuggiù, **23**

Hotel Montreal, **35**
Hotel Margutta, **11**
Hotel Parlamento, **13**
Hotel Pensione Selene, **24**
Hotel Perugia, **41**
Hotel Sweet Home, **32**
Hotel Teti, **33**
Ostello del Foro Italico, **1**

Pensione Carmel, **58**
Pensione Katty, **27**
Pensione Monaco, **28**
Pensione Panda, **12**
Pensione Stella Elsa, **34**
Pensione Virginia, **26**
YWCA, **37**

BY PLANE

Leonardo da Vinci International Airport (tel. 06/65951), 30 km (19 mi) southwest of the city center, is usually referred to as **Fiumicino,** after the suburb where it's located. Inside the terminal, there's currency exchange, luggage storage (L4100 per bag per day) and an **information office** (tel. 06/65953038). Trains leave roughly every 20 minutes for Rome's Trastevere, Ostiense, and Tiburtina stations. More expensive express trains to Stazione Termini run hourly 7:50 AM–10:05 PM.

BY TRAIN

Rome's principal rail depot is the low-lying, marble-clad **Stazione Termini.** Other Rome stations include **Ostiense,** with all-night service to Genoa, Naples, Palermo, and Nice. Rome's **Tiburtina** station has buses to towns in Lazio, as well as Naples and Palermo.

Trains from **Stazione Termini** (P. dei Cinquecento, tel. 06/47307996 for station information, toll-free 1478/88088 for toll-free rail information for all of Italy) serve major Italian and European cities and many points in between. On the left as you leave the station, there's an information window that serves exclusively Eurailpass holders. Downstairs an *albergo diurno* (day hotel) charges L10,000 for showers.

GETTING AROUND

"All roads lead to Rome," but then they leave you confused, disoriented, befuddled. Luckily, Rome has gobs of landmarks with which to orient yourself. Bear in mind that the **Tiber River** runs north–south through the city, making a backwards S-curve that separates the Vatican to the west from the **centro storico** to the east. Brown-and-white signs are posted throughout the center, directing pedestrians to major sights along the most direct routes.

BY BIKE

In good weather you will find bike rental stands on Piazzas Popolo, San Silvestro, Spagna, and Augusto Imperatore. **Collalti Bici** (V. del Pellegrino 80–82, near Campo dei Fiori, tel. 06/68801084) is open all year round. **Scoot-a-Long** (V. Cavour 302, tel. 06/6780206; open daily 9–8) rents both bikes and scooters.

BY BUS AND METRO

Rome's easily spotted orange ATAC buses go just about everywhere you'll want to go. Stops are marked by yellow or green posts and labeled FERMATA, and most list the main destinations along each route and lines with night service. Tickets (L1500) are sold at cafés, tobacco shops, newspaper kiosks displaying the ATAC emblem, and at the ATAC booth in front of Stazione Termini; be sure to validate them in the orange boxes at the back of buses for 75 minutes of travel on buses, urban trains, and one Metro ride.

The red **Metro Line A** runs between Ottaviano and Anagnina, hitting Piazzas Repubblica, Barberini, and Spagna. The blue **Line B** runs between Laurentina and Rebibbia and is useful for reaching the Colosseo (Colosseum) and the Ostiense train station. Entrances are marked by M signs above ground and in Stazione Termini, the only point where the two lines intersect. The Metro runs daily 5:30 AM–11:30 PM. Tickets (L1500), validated in the turnstile as you enter the station, are good for bus rides or a combination of one metro ride and bus rides within 75 minutes.

WHERE TO SLEEP

If you're not too picky, a clean double in a no-nonsense pension can be had for L60,000–L80,000. In the L90,000–L130,000 range you'll get ambience, a private bath, and a somewhat central address. Stick to the area around Stazione Termini if price is more important than location. Rome's centro storico is the most convenient and atmospheric place to sleep, but prices here start around L90,000. Finally, be wary of solicitors in Stazione Termini offering a place to sleep: many are not legit.

NEAR STAZIONE TERMINI

UNDER L105,000 • Hotel Cervia. Spartan doubles ranging from L80,000 to L100,000 may not be homey, but they're clean; 28 rooms means that vacancies are common. *V. Palestro 55, tel. 06/491057, fax 06/491056.*

Hotel Germano. New, airy rooms (doubles starting at L75,000, with bath L95,000) with modern furniture, hairdryers, and phones speak of a more expensive hotel. Reservations are a must. *V. Calatafimi 14/A, 00185, tel. 06/486919.*

Hotel Giuggiù. Sunny, comfy rooms (doubles L65,000—L95,000) are big enough to pitch a tent in. *V. del Viminale 8, tel. and fax 06/4827734. Cash only.*

Hotel Pensione Selene. Bright and clean, Selene is like someone's beach house. Recently redone doubles run L95,000. There's a curfew of 12:30 AM. *V. del Viminale 8, 00184, tel. 06/4744781, fax 06/47821977. Cash only.*

Pensione Katty. Rooms here have high ceilings and mosaic floors, and cots doubling as beds. Doubles cost L75,000, with bathroom L95,000. *V. Palestro 35, 00185, tel. 06/4441216. 14 rooms, 2 with bath. Cash only.*

Pensione Virginia. Inexpensive rooms pleasantly decorated with faux frescoes are in store for you here. Doubles L75,000, with bathroom L85,000. *V. Montebello 94, tel. 06/4457689. Cash only.*

UNDER L125,000 • Hotel Perugia. You'll find this on a quiet alleyway two blocks from the Foro Romano and the Colosseo. Plain rooms (doubles L70,000) come with phones. *V. del Colosseo 7, tel. 06/6797200.*

Pensione Stella Elsa. A hospitable couple makes sure that the renovated rooms here (doubles start at L60,000; with bath L120,000) are spotless; all have either a sink or a shower. *V. Principe Amedeo 79/A, tel. and fax 06/4460634. Cash only.*

UNDER L150,000 • Hotel Fuggetta. Live it up: rooms come with showers, minibars, and TVs, and will run you L110,000—L140,000. *V. Palestro 87, 00185. tel. 06/4456821, fax 06/4959254. Cash only.*

Hotel Montreal. Another simple, cleaner-than-average hotel in the south of Termini area, this time on a tree-lined street across from Santa Maria Maggiore. Doubles are billed at L150,000. *V. Carlo Alberto 4, tel. 06/4465522, fax 06/4457797.*

Hotel Teti. This small, no-nonsense hotel between the station and Santa Maria Maggiore is clean and fresh looking. Rooms have firm beds and ample closet space. Doubles with bath cost L140,000. *V. Principe Amedeo 76, tel. 06/4825240. Cash only.*

SPLURGE • Hotel Sweet Home. Cute hotel with sunny, immaculate doubles (with bath L180,000; without L120,000), all with TVs and phones. *V. Principe Amedeo 47, tel. 06/4880954.*

CENTRO STORICO

UNDER L70,000 • Pensione Monaco. At this simple, very clean, family-run place between the train station and Villa Borghese, doubles without bath run L65,000. *V. Flavia 84, 00187, tel. 06/4744335. Cash only.*

UNDER L100,000 • Albergo Fiorella. A cross between the Brady's house and your grandmother's, this hotel charges L89,000 for a good-size double. There's a 1-AM curfew. *V. del Babuino 196, tel. 06/3610597.*

UNDER L150,000 • Hotel Margutta. This gem hidden away on a charming sidestreet between Piazza di Spagna and Piazza del Popolo commands L147,000 for its double rooms. *V. Laurina 34, tel. 06/3223674, fax 06/3200395.*

Pensione Panda. This friendly, quiet, renovated pension has wrought-iron fixtures, terra-cotta tiles, and marble sinks throughout. Doubles start at L95,000, L130,000 with super-clean bathrooms. *V. della Croce 35, tel. 06/6780179, fax 06/69942151.*

SPLURGE • Albergo del Sole. This is a worthwhile splurge right near Campo dei Fiori. Antique-filled common rooms and a beautiful sunset view from fifth-floor terrace justify the cost. Doubles fetch L100,000–L170,000. *V. del Biscione 76, tel. 06/68806873.*

Hotel Erdarelli. Halfway between the Spanish Steps and the Trevi Fountain, the Erdarelli has comfy doubles for L150,000, with bath L180,000. Ask for a room on the inner courtyard to avoid street noise. *V. Due Macelli 28, tel. 06/6791265.*

Hotel Parlamento. If this hotel an elevator, you'd be paying a lot more. Schlep your bags up the stairs and reap the rewards: a roof terrace where you can eat breakfast. Doubles with bath cost L150,000. *V. delle Convertite 5, tel. 06/69921000. Cash only.*

WEST OF THE TIBER

Except for the area surrounding the Vatican, this is probably the least tourist-oriented part of Rome.

UNDER L110,000 • Pensione Carmel. At the edge of Trastevere, this pension has average-size doubles (L100,000) with mountain-lodge flair. *V. Mameli 11, tel. 06/5809921.*

UNDER L140,000 • Giuggioli Hotel. Grand, high-ceiling rooms (doubles L110,000–L130,000) here are full of stately antiques. *V. Germanico 198, tel. 06/3242113.*

Hotel Cisterna. In lively mid-Trastevere you'll be free to enjoy this hotel's small rooftop patio plus a courtyard in back. Doubles run L130,000. *V. della Cisterna 79, tel. 06/5817212.*

HOSTELS

Fawlty Towers. In this hostel steps away from Stazione Termini, beds in semiprivate rooms run L30,000–L35,000. Best of all, there's no curfew or lockout. *V. Magenta 39, tel. 06/4450374. Luggage storage. Cash only.*

Ostello del Foro Italico (HI). A flat rate of L23,000 per person includes sheets, hot showers, and breakfast. Hostel cards are required but can be issued on the spot for L30,000. Three-day maximum stay in summer. Luggage storage is available. *V. delle Olimpiadi 61, tel. 06/3236267. From Stazione Termini take Bus 32 2 stops past V. Maresciallo Giardino; entrance is around building to the right. Midnight curfew, lockout 9–2. Cash only.*

YWCA. If you can handle the midnight curfew and segregation of unmarried guests, the YWCA is unbelievably posh. Sexes mix in the TV room, the sitting room, and the peaceful library. Doubles are L80,000, L100,000 with bathroom, breakfast included. *V. Cesare Balbo 4, tel. 06/4880460. Midnight curfew. Reception open 7 AM–11 PM. Cash only.*

FOOD

If you're looking to eat on the cheap, the answer is pizza, either on your feet from a by-the-slice shop (actually al taglio—by the cut and sold by weight) or sitting down in a boisterous pizzeria, where your pie comes plate-size and wafer thin and out of a wood-burning oven. But don't miss the opportunity to eat like the Roman's do, which is to say well and at table for a good long time.

NEAR STAZIONE TERMINI AND THE COLOSSEO

Stazione Termini is surrounded by cheap pizza al taglio shops and snack bars. **Caffè dell'Orologio** (V. Cavour 77/79, 3 blocks south of Stazione Termini, tel. 06/4740491) is good for killing time and grabbing a panini if waiting room at Termini isn't your style. Two good wine bars with great food are **Cavour 313** (V. Cavour 313, tel. 06/6785496; closed Aug. and Sun. in July and Sept.) and **Trimani** (V. Cernaia 37/B; closed Sun.). There's good pizza at **Alle Carrette** (Vicolo delle Carrette 14, tel. 06/6792770; closed Mon.) tucked into an alley at the bottom of Via Cavour.

UNDER L10,000 • Da Bruno e Romana. Amid friendly atmosphere and assorted country-style pots, clocks, and keys, feast on *stracciatella alla romana* (egg drop soup) and cannelloni filled with spinach and ricotta. Thursday is gnocchi day. *V. Varese 29, tel. 06/490403. Cash only. Closed Sun.*

UNDER L15,000 • Donati. You'll find a decidedly flashy look in the pink tablecloths and polished granite tiles. *Uova strapazzate* (scrambled eggs) and requisite pasta dishes are the drill. *V. Magenta 20, tel. 06/491868. Corner of V. Marghera, 1 block north of Stazione Termini. Cash only. Closed Sat. in winter.*

UNDER L20,000 • Osteria Nerone. Sumptuous antipasti, *fettuccine alla Nerone* (fresh pasta with peas, salami and mushrooms), and other fresh pastas are the specialties at this family-run trattoria. *V. Terme di Tito 96, tel. 06/4745207. Closed Sun. and mid-Aug. Cash only.*

Pommidoro. The long walk or short ride to this typical of Roman trattoria is rewarded: hearty pasta dishes and grilled meats and game. Reservations are a good idea. *P. dei Sanniti, 44, tel. 06/4452692. Bus 492 from Stazione Termini. Closed Sun. and Aug. Cash only.*

CENTRO STORICO

You can still eat on the cheap within view of a great church if you're careful. Campo dei Fiori, home of the open-air market (Mon–Sat. 8–1) is unbeatable for raw materials. For primo pizza, head to **Pizza alla Pala** (V. del Pellegrino 11. tel. 06/68804557; closed Sun.) or **Pizzeria Il Leoncino** (V. Leoncino 28, tel. 06/6876306; closed Wed. and Aug.). Try Roman Jewish pastries from **Forno del Ghetto** (V. di Portico d'Ottavia 2, tel. 06/6878637; closed Sat.). Fast, cheap, and light snacks can be put together at any *alimentari*.

UNDER L10,000 • Al Piccolo Arancio. Even though it's been in a dozen guidebooks, this back-alley trattoria still manages cheap, tasty meals. *Vicolo Scanderbeg 112, near Trevi Fountain, tel. 06/6786139. Closed Mon. and middle 2 wks of Aug.*

L'Ambramarina. Narrow, homey, and surprisingly stylish, this pizzeria also has soups, salads, and vegetarian tarts. *Campo dei Fiori 48, tel. 06/68802474. Cash only.*

Crêperie Damiano. The crêpes at this take-out hole-in-the-wall can be sweet and savory. There's a long list to choose from, or create your own for L8000. *V. Tor Millina 8, 2 blocks west of P. Navona, tel. 06/6861091. Cash only.*

Da Tonino. Tonino cooks a lot of things—spaghetti alla carbonara, meatballs, roasted potatoes—and charges very little. Hence the crowds. *V. del Governo Vecchio 18. Cash only. Closed Sun.*

Insalata Ricca. This low-cal, low-budget restaurant offers a dozen meal-size salads, pastas, and secondi in a jovial atmosphere. *Largo dei Chiavari 83, off C. Vittorio Emanuele II, tel. 06/68803656. Cash only. Closed Wed.*

UNDER L15,000 • Il Filettaro di Santa Barbara. This is the closest you'll get to fish and chips in Rome. Wash fillets of salt cod (baccalá) down with half a liter of Frascati. *Largo dei Librari 88, just off of V. dei Giubbonari, tel. 6864018. Cash only. Closed Sun.*

Orso 80. You'll be blown away by the antipasto spread in this old-style trattoria near Piazza Navona. There's lots of pasta dishes—if you're still hungry. *V. dell'Orso 33, tel. 6864904. Closed Mon. and mid-Aug.*

UNDER L25,000 • Il Bacaro. This tiny, pretty bistro close to the Pantheon prepares traditional dishes with a creative touch. Specialties include stuffed homemade pasta. Reservations are recommended. *V. degli Spagnoli 27, tel. 06/6864110. Closed lunch, Sun., and Aug.*

Margutta. A vegetarian place harking back to the '70s, Margutta just got a facelift. But, the food is still a solid reworking of Italian standards in meatless fashion. Save room for dessert. *V. Margutta 119, tel. 06/36001912. Closed Sun.*

Il Gelato di San Crispino (V. della Panetteria 64, tel. 06/6991243) serves Rome's (maybe Italy's) best gelato, made without artificial colors or flavorings. Go taste the difference.

TRASTEVERE

At night the streets and restaurants of Trastevere fill with people—it could almost be a different place. Check out one of the city's oldest and best **bakeries,** where you can get bread and pizza by the slice, at Via del Moro (no sign, opposite the Corner Bookstore).

UNDER L10,000 • Il Vicolo. This intimate restaurant, hidden on a backstreet, serves typical hearty fare. Specialties are risotto with radicchio and tarot readings Monday evening. *Vicolo dei Cinque 27, near P. Trilussa, tel. 06/5810250. Closed Tues.*

UNDER L15,000 • Da Lucia. Choose from a short list of Roman dishes like *spaghetti cacio e pepe* (spaghetti with black pepper and pecorino cheese) inside this old-style trattoria. *Vicolo del Mattonato 2/B, tel. 06/5803601. Cash only. Closed lunch, Mon., and Aug.*

Trattoria da Augusto. The old man outside this family restaurant assures that *qui si mangia bene e si paga poco* (here you'll eat well and pay little), and it's true: you'll enjoy pasta, homemade ravioli, and savory meat dishes. *P. de' Renzi 15, tel. 06/5803798. From P. Trilussa, walk 1 block on V. del Moro, turn right on V. de' Renzi. Closed Sat. dinner and Sun.*

WORTH SEEING

Rome wasn't built in a day, and you can't see it all in a day, either. Beyond the list of postcard monuments, Rome is also home to a bevy of tiny neighborhood churches, quirky museums, and long-forgotten treasures. As if the sheer number of sites was not enough, you also have to contend with the hassles of a big city and other (Italian) impediments: endless restoration projects and erratic opening hours. Be a little flexible, have alternatives, and don't try to see more than you have time for.

ANCIENT RUINS

Begin where Rome began, in the valley between the Colle Palatino and the Campidoglio (Palatine and Capitoline hills; to the south of P. Venezia). This was the political, social, and religious center of Rome for its first thousand years, and featured elaborately decorated villas, stately buildings, impressive temples, and triumphal arches. Unfortunately, another thousand years of looting, sacking, and decay means that the remains are often a bit scarce so you'll have to use your imagination. The Foro Romano deserves at least a few hours of exploring and is a good place for a discreet picnic.

ARCO DI CONSTANTINO • Back in ancient Rome, emperors built triumphal arches to celebrate and remember great victories. This one commemorates Constantine's victory over rival Maxentius in 312 AD, and is decorated with sculptures recycled from earlier structures, linking the contemporary victories to the glories of old. *Next to the Colosseo.*

COLOSSEO • The single most evocative symbol of Rome, the Colosseum is equal parts glory and gore. Completed in AD 80, the elliptical four-story structure held 50,000 people. A moveable canopy protected spectators from the sun, and a vast underground network of tunnels was used to move wild beasts and combatants. See what's left from the ground floor for free, or view the upper level for L8000. *Metro B to Colosseo, tel. 06/7004261. Open 9–7, Wed. and Sun. until 1.*

FORO IMPERIALE • By the end of the Roman Republic (1st-century BC), the forum could no longer accommodate all the trials and discussions that it took to run Western civilization, so Caesar built a new forum. Over the next 200-plus years Emperors Augustus, Domitian, Vespasian, and Trajan all followed suit. The **Foro di Traiano** (admission L3,750; open Tues.–Sat. 9–7, Sun. 9–1:30) is most well preserved. Built in the 2nd century AD, the hemispherical structure at one end was a multilevel marketplace—the ancient world's main shopping mall—and across the way stands the incredibly intricate **Colonna di Traiano,** a masterpiece of ancient sculpture that commemorates a great Roman battle and conquest.

FORO ROMANO AND COLLE PALATINO • Here is where ancient Rome began, and you can still walk along Roman streets, passing the remains of temples, public buildings, and shops. Among the myriad ruins, the vaulted ceiling of the massive **Basilica di Massenzio** demands attention. Figuring out what's what can be pretty tough, so you might want to consider investing in a little guidebook from one of the many stands nearby that has some renderings of how the buildings might have looked, according to archaeologists.

Don't miss the Colle Palatino (Palatine Hill), where emperors built their palaces that once covered the whole hill. Shady spots and impressive views make it choice picnic grounds, and a good place for an afternoon snooze after a long tramp through the Forum. To reach Palatine Hill, head uphill from the Arch of Titus through the Roman Forum. *Entrance to Roman Forum and Palatine Hill on V. dei Fori Imperiali. Metro B to Colosseo. Admission: L12,000 including museum. Open Mon.–Sat. 9–6, Sun. 9–1.*

SAN PIETRO IN VINCOLI • Although this church houses the very chains that bound the imprisoned St. Peter, the hordes of tourists who descend upon it every day are usually snapping pictures of Michelangelo's magnificent *Moses. P. San Pietro in Vincoli, between Colosseum and V. Cavour. Admission: Free. Open daily 7–12:30 and 3:30–7.*

TERME DI CARACALLA • These gigantic thermal baths give some indication of the size, scope, and engineering genius of ancient Roman architects. More than just a place to wash, the baths were the center of recreation and social life for all social classes in the ancient era. They included sports facilities, gardens, and libraries, as well as several chambers with hot, warm, and cold water. *V. Terme di Caracalla. Metro B to Circo Massimo; or, from P. Venezia, Bus 160. Admission: L8000. Open Tues. 9–6, until 3 in winter, Sun. and Mon. 9–1.*

CAMPIDOGLIO

Once the political and religious epicenter of ancient Rome, the Campidoglio (Capitoline Hill) was home to a big temple, the state archives, treasury, and mint. In 1537, Michelangelo was called in to redesign the square and bordering palazzi, and left the piazza a miracle of Renaissance harmony and balance. Today you'll find the town hall—mustard color Palazzo Senatorio—and the matching Musei Capitolini on the freshly restored, majestic square. The huge equestrian statue of Emperor Marcus Aurelius in the middle of the square is a new, high-tech copy that stands in place of the original, on display in the Museo Capitolino. Head to the top of Palazzo Senatorio's stairway to get a look at the symmetrical pavement, then head around either side of the building for commanding views onto the Roman Forum and Palatine Hill. Inside the plain brick **Basilica Santa Maria in Aracoeli** (open daily 7–noon and 4–7) are colorful 16th-century frescoes.

MUSEI CAPITOLINI • One single ticket gets you into the museums in the matching buildings on the Campidoglio. In the **Museo Capitolino,** you'll find one of the most extensive collections of Roman sculpture in the world, including over a hundred busts of Roman emperors, poets, and philosophers. Across the way in the richly decorated **Palazzo dei Conservatori,** there's more sculpture and a good bunch of 17th-century paintings. Even if you skip the museums, don't miss the courtyard of Palazzo dei Conservatori, lined with the gigantic head and assorted body parts that remain from the mammoth sculpture of Constantine. *P. del Campidoglio, tel. 06/67102071 or 06/67101244. Admission: L10,000, free last Sun. of the month. Open Tues.–Sun. 9–7.*

FONTANA DI TREVI

From the narrow end of Piazza di Spagna, take Via due Macelli past Largo Tritone and turn left at Via in Arcione; follow the sound of crashing water, and there you have it—the justly famous Trevi Fountain. The fantastic Baroque arrangement of Neptune atop dolphins, sea creatures, and boulders is still fed by a 1st-century BC Roman aqueduct, named the *Acqua Vergine* after a virgin who led a group of thirsty soldiers to a spring outside the city. Legend had it that the water made men faithful, and women dragged their hubbies here to drink. Today the area is a hunting ground for Italian men on the prowl; brave the lechery long enough to toss a coin over your left shoulder, ensuring your return to the Eternal City.

PIAZZA DELLA REPUBBLICA AND PIAZZA BARBERINI

Chances are you'll pass through Piazza della Repubblica on the way from Stazione Termini to the centro storico. Take a look at the nearby museums, then head northwest from the square on Via Orlando and veer left onto Via Barberini. This leads to Piazza Barberini, a heavily trafficked square sporting Bernini's graceful Fontala Tritone (Fountain of the Triton), designed in 1637 for Pope Urban VIII. From here, it's a short walk up Via delle Quattro Fontane to Rome's excellent Galleria Nazionale d'Arte Antica.

GALLERIA NAZIONALE D'ARTE ANTICA • This first-rate art museum inside the 17th-century Palazzo Barberini leads you from the 13th to the 18th century with paintings by the likes of Fra Filippo Lippi, Raphael, Perugino, El Greco, and Caravaggio. *V. delle Quattro Fontane 13, tel. 06/4814591. Admission: L8000. Open Tues.–Sat. 9–2, Sun. 9–1.*

Did Romans invent snow cones, too? Romans line up to beat summer heat with grattachecca, ice shaved by hand from a big block, topped with colorful sweetened syrups, sometimes spiked with a little alcohol. Look for street stands on the Tiber.

SAN CARLO ALLE QUATTRO FONTANE • This small, yet sumptuous church got its name from the four fountains—each representing a season—that stand on the corners of the intersection. Designed by Bernini's main rival, Francesco Borromini, it is one of the first experiments in a pure Baroque style. Later Baroque works in town are indebted to Borromini's heavily curved walls and fluted decorations. *V. del Quirinale, at V. delle Quattro Fontane, tel. 06/7676531. Open daily 7–noon and 4–7.*

SANTA MARIA DEGLI ANGELI • If this doesn't look like most churches, it's because Michelangelo—at age 86—designed the basilica within the ruins of the 4th-century Terme di Diocleziano. *P. della Repubblica. Open daily 7–12:30 and 4–6:30.*

SANTA MARIA DELLA CONCEZIONE • Tourists climb the stairs of the church of the Cappuccin monks to visit their creepy and bizarre "cemetery" in which the remains of 4,000 priests and monks have been arranged. Fluted arches made of collarbones, arabesques of shoulder blades, and spirals of dusty vertebrae are humorously macabre. *V. Vittorio Veneto 27, tel. 06/462850. Donation requested. Open Fri.–Wed. 9–noon and 3–6.*

PIAZZA DEL POPOLO

At one end of three of the centro storico's most important streets—Via del Babuino, Via del Corso, and Via di Ripetta—Piazza del Popolo once served as the gateway to visitors from the north. Today it's a meeting and mingling spot for teenagers on Vespas, grandmothers on park benches, and businessmen on cell phones. Take in the commotion from the Egyptian obelisk of Ramses II (a mere 3,200 years old) at the center of the piazza, and check out the symmetry of the twin 17th-century churches. For a view from above, walk up the steps (east side of the piazza) to the **Pincio.** Down Via di Ripetta from Piazza del Popolo, the moss-covered circular brick **Augusteum** once held the remains of the Emperor Augustus, who commissioned the **Ara Pacis,** or Peace Altar, in order to exalt his role in ending the empire's civil wars.

SANTA MARIA DEL POPOLO • Not much from the outside, but this church is packed with great artwork, including two stunning Caravaggio paintings depicting the martyrdoms of St. Peter and St. Paul, delicate frescoes by Pinturricchio, cherubs by Bernini that hang from the ceiling, and a lot of marble all around. *P. del Popolo. Open daily 8–1:30 and 4:30–7.*

PIAZZA DI SPAGNA

The **Scalinata di Spagna** (Spanish Steps) have been a magnet for sightseers and visitors ever since a diplomatic visit from the King of Spain inspired the glitzy makeover still evident today. The famous steps were constructed in 1723 by architect Francesco de Sanctis to link the Church of the **Trinità dei Monti** at the top with **Via Condotti** below. In the 19th century this was the heart of bohemian Rome, especially

PAPAL POMP AND CEREMONY

"Private" papal audiences are held for the masses every Wednesday at 11 AM in the Papal Audience Hall (and at 10 AM when it is unbearably hot). Free tickets are available Monday and Tuesday 9 AM–1 PM and Wednesday 9 AM–10 AM through the bronze doors on the west side of Piazza San Pietro. For advance tickets write to: Prefettura della Casa Pontifici, 00120 Città del Vaticano; indicate the date and language you speak. Or, you can stand with 200,000 others on Piazza San Pietro every Sunday at 11 AM, when the pope appears at the Vatican Palace window to bless the public.

popular with American and British writers. Keats, Byron, and Shelley all made their homes in the neighborhood. Keats died at No. 26, which today is home to the **Keats Shelley Museum** (P. di Spagna 26; admission L5000; open weekdays 9–1 and 3–6, 2:30–5:30 in winter), with a collection of Romantic-era books, letters, pictures, locks of hair, antique roller skates, and old furniture.

VILLA BORGHESE

Rome's largest park is filled with fountains, sculptured gardens, and Roman pines. Stretches of green and plenty of leafy pathways make this a great place for wandering, biking, or just hanging out. It is also home to several art museums, including the magnificent Galleria Borghese.

GALLERIA BORGHESE • With five of Bernini's most celebrated sculptures downstairs and paintings by Raphael, Caravaggio, Titian, and Carracci upstairs, you could call this collection the greatest hits of the 17th century. But instead, just say Borghese. Relentlessly assembled (a few pieces even stolen) by the avaricious Cardinal Scipione Borghese, the collection is on display again in its original setting——the stunning **Palazzo Borghese**—which recently underwent a 14-year restoration. *P. Scipione Borghese 5, tel. 06/8548577. Metro A to Piazza di Spagna; follow signs to park and then museum. Admission: L10,000. Open Tues.–Sat. 9–7, Sun. 9–1.*

GALLERIA NAZIONALE D'ARTE MODERNA • Rome's modern art museum, in an immense neoclassical building on the north side of Villa Borghese, houses an interesting collection of Italian Impressionist and Romantic art, as well as works by Klimt, Degas, van Gogh and Cézanne. *Viale delle Belle Arti 131, tel. 06/322981. Admission: L8000. Open Tues.–Sat. 9–7, Sun. 9–1.*

MUSEO NAZIONALE DI VILLA GIULIA • The villa of Pope Julius III on the northwest edge of Villa Borghese houses one of the world's most important and exhaustive collections of artifacts left by the Etruscans, who dominated Lazio and Tuscany from the 8th until the 5th century BC, when their city-states were finally swallowed by the growing Roman state. The villa's display of sculpture, earthenware water jugs, terra-cotta bowls, bronze figures, and jewelry demonstrates the high artistry attained by the culture. A highlight is the *Sarcofago degli Sposi*, a double tomb built so the deceased couple could cling eternally. *P. di Villa Giulia 9, tel. 06/3201951. Admission: L8000. Tues.–Sat. 9 AM–7 PM, Sun 9–1.*

CENTRO STORICO

Rome's historic center—bordered by the Augusteum to the north, Via del Corso to the east, and the Tiber River to the south and west—is where many of the blockbuster historical sights are located, and where narrow alleyways and outdoor cafés are alive with people, particularly in the area surrounding **Campo dei Fiori,** site of Rome's oldest outdoor market (open Mon.–Sat. 8–1). If you spend only one day in Rome, this is the place to do it.

CHIESA DEL GESU • After St. Peter's Basilica, Il Gesù is the most colorful church in Rome—every inch is covered with red, green, gold, and pink marble. The elaborately frescoed ceiling and altar to St. Ignatius of Loyola (the founder of the Jesuits), slathered in silver and gold, always gets a gasp from the crowd. *V. del Plebiscito. Open daily 6–12:30 and 4–7:15.*

MONUMENTO DI VITTORIO EMANUELE II • When Vittorio Emanuele II, the first king of Italy, died in 1878, a contest was held to construct a monument befitting the "Father of Italy." Nicknamed the "wedding cake" because of its enormous white-marble facade, this monument is commonly thought of as pretentious and overbearing compared to the treasured remains of ancient Rome that surround it. *P. Venezia.*

PANTHEON • This ancient temple-cum-church, the best preserved ancient Roman structure, was built by Hadrian in AD 119–128, after the destruction of an earlier square version by Agrippa (whose name is still visible on the facade). The spherical dome measures 141 ft across at it widest and highest points, and was the largest ever built until this century (St. Peter's is a close second). The oculus at the top has always been open, allowing light and rain to pour in. The Pantheon avoided some of the looting and neglect suffered by other ancient monuments only because it was converted from a shrine to all gods into a Catholic church in AD 608. Still, much of the roof was stripped of its bronze in 667, and Barberini Pope Urban VIII snatched what was left to recycle into the baldachino in St. Peter's. *P. della Rotonda, tel. 68300230. Admission: Free. Follow signs posted all over. Open Mon.–Sat. 9–6:30, Sun. 9–1.*

PIAZZA NAVONA • The queen of all piazzas and the crown jewel of the centro storico, Piazza Navona showcases Bernini's extravagant **Fontana dei Quattro Fiumi,** whose statues represent the four corners of the world and, in turn, the world's great rivers. Emperor Domitian's stadium once stood on this site, hence the piazza's unusual oval shape. In more recent centuries, wealthy Romans imitated their ancient predecessors (who had staged boat battles in the stadium and Colosseum) by flooding the piazza and riding their carriages through the water for fun. Today, Navona's attractions are more subdued: Surrounding the piazza are flowered balconies, colored palazzi, requisite sidewalk cafés, and every sort of street artist and musician. If you ever pull an all-nighter at Rome's discos, be sure to visit this normally packed piazza at dawn, when only the sound of your footsteps and the squawks of pigeons echo through the vast space.

> *If you go inside one building in Rome, make it the Pantheon. The effect of walking in through the massive front portico is breathtaking, and you will see why it is said to be the world's only architecturally perfect building.*

SANTA MARIA SOPRA MINERVA • Rome's only Gothic church has a serene, exquisite interior instead of the usual Baroque excesses, and is full of great art, including the **Cappella Carafa,** with a brilliant fresco cycle by Filippino Lippi depicting the *Annunciation,* and Michelangelo's sculpture *The Redeemer.* The elephant supporting the small obelisk in the piazza out front was designed by Bernini. *P. della Minerva, 1 block south of Pantheon. Open daily 7–noon and 4–7.*

GHETTO EBRAICO

Jews have lived in Rome continuously since the 1st century BC, and their living conditions have always followed the vicissitudes of whoever ruled Rome. One of the worst periods began in 1555, when Pope Paul II established a ghetto in Rome, in which Jews were forced to live and abide by restrictive laws. The area quickly became Rome's most squalid and densely populated neighborhood. At one point, Jews were limited only to the sale of used clothing as a trade. Dismantled around the time of the Risorgimento, not much remains of the ghetto as it was, but some of Rome's 15,000 Jews still live in the area, which lies between the Portico d'Ottavia, the Tiber, and Via Arenula. Among the most interesting sights is the **Fontana delle Tartarughe** (Fountain of the Turtles) on Piazza Mattei, with turtles thought to be added by Bernini.

MUSEO EBRAICO AND SINAGOGA • The **Museo Ebraico** contains decorative objects and tapestries dating from the 17th century, most donated by prominent Jewish families whose ancestors once lived in the ghetto. It's refreshing to see precious metals and marble crafted into something other than saints and angels. One of the more haunting displays is a prayer book that literally saved its owner's life during the 1982 attack on the synagogue—bullet holes and bloodstains tell the tale. One ticket grants you entrance to both the museum and adjacent **Sinagoga,** but the latter can only be toured with a guide (inquire at the museum). *Lungotevere Cenci, near Ponte Fabricio, tel. 06/6875051. Admission: L8000. Open Mon.–Thurs. 9:30–2 and 3–5, Fri. 9:30–2, Sun. 9:30–12:30.*

COLLE GIANICOLO

If you're crowd-weary from the Vatican or feeling frayed by urban chaos, take a walk up the Colle Gianicolo (Janiculum Hill) for a shady respite and a chance to view Rome at a quiet distance. Leaf-strewn **Via Garibaldi** winds up the hill, passing the late 15th-century church of **San Pietro in Montorio** (full of great paintings and home to Bramante's Tempietto) and the **Acqua Paola,** a gushing early 17th-century fountain, to the **Porta di San Pancrazio.** From there go right along tree-lined **Passeggiata del Gianicolo.**

FOR THAT
SPECIAL BISHOP
IN YOUR LIFE

If you've come to the Eternal City looking for ecclesiastical garb or religious doodads, you've hit gold. The shops on Via dei Cestari, north of Largo Argentina, specialize in ornate liturgical vestments with a sideline in Christian-theme knickknacks, and shops near the Vatican on Via Porta Angelica offer a celestial array of Pope portraits, postcards, figurines, and even snow globes for low, low prices (many times what they're worth). The devout can have the loot blessed at a papal audience; blasphemers can put Pope stickers on their cars. Lay shoppers may want to stick to the windows.

TRASTEVERE

So maybe it's not the neighborhood it once was, no longer full of working-class folks, no longer the city within a city. And so what if it's been discovered by tourists and guidebooks and real estate agents. There's still plenty of reasons to cross the river and enjoy charming, cool Trastevere: great walks day or night through narrow crumbling streets with little *trattorie* and bars at every turn. The heart of the neighborhood is **Piazza Santa Maria in Trastevere,** with its namesake 12th-century church (open daily 8–1 and 4–6).

VILLA FARNESINA • What would you do if you were one of the wealthiest bankers in Renaissance Rome in the early 1500s? Build a villa outside town on a choice piece of land overlooking the River. Call on the leading artist of the day, Raphael, to oversee the decoration of the walls and ceilings, a master of trompe l'oeil like Peruzzi to make the second floor walls disappear, and get Il Sodoma to come in and put some rather suggestive imagery on the bedroom walls. *V. della Lungara 230, tel. 06/650831 or 06/6540565. Admission: L8000. Open Mon.–Sat. 9–1.*

VATICAN CITY AND CASTLE SANT'ANGELO

The world's second-smallest nation, The Vatican is Europe's last remaining absolute monarchy, currently ruled over by Pope John Paul II. It has its own postal system, radio, newspaper, and military force (the Swiss Guards), and still exercises a great deal of influence over Italian politics. A 10-minute walk from Vatican City toward the Tiber will deposit you at the imposing Castel Sant'Angelo, for centuries used as a fortress to guard the Pope and his riches.

BASILICA DI SAN PIETRO • St. Peter's is a must on any Rome itinerary, no matter what your religion is. The original church was built in 319 AD by Constantine on the site of St. Peter's grave, and later Italy's greatest Renaissance artists and architects—including Bramante, Bernini, Raphael, Peruzzi, Sangallo the Younger, and Michelangelo—all contributed to a total rebuilding. Highlights inside—besides the sheer vastness of the space—feature Michelangelo's famous **Pietà** (behind lunatic-proof glass on the right) and Bernini's huge baldachino. To the right of the Pietà is the Holy Door, which the Pope will ceremoniously open with a hammer to mark the beginning of the holy year 2000. Take the elevator or a laborious hike up the stairs to the top of St. Peter's **cupola** (admission L6000 via elevator, L5000 via stairs; open daily 8–5, until 6 in summer) for glorious views over Vatican City and central Rome. *Open daily 7–7. Dress code strictly enforced: no bare shoulders or bare knees.*

CASTEL SANT'ANGELO • The unusual, impressive round structure was originally built in AD 135 as a mausoleum for the Emperor Hadrian and his successors. Gradually built up over the centuries, it was used alternatively as a fortress, prison, warehouse, and often as a hideout for the popes, since it is connected to the Vatican by a passageway inside the wall that runs between the two. Wandering around the many winding ramps and courtyards—more interesting than the art, armor, and cannonballs on display—is a great way to chill out after a morning at the Vatican. Grab a snack at the bar and enjoy the great views. The statue-lined **Ponte Sant'Angelo** spans the Tiber directly in front of the castle. *Lungote-*

vere Castello 50, tel. 06/6875036. Admission: L8000. Open Apr.–Sept., Mon.–Sat. 9–2; Oct.–Mar., Mon. 2–7, Tues.–Sat. 9–1, Sun. 9–noon.

MUSEI VATICANI

You would have to walk about 7 km (4½ mi) just to cover the dozen or so different museums containing artifacts and artwork from every corner of the world. Once inside, four color-coded trails lead through the labyrinthine palace, lasting two, three, four, and six hours, respectively. Choose your poison or venture through on your own. Either way, the recorded English-language commentary is definitely worth the L3000 rental fee.

First among the galleries, you'll come to the **Egyptian Museum** filled with hieroglyphic tablets, jewelry, and mummies. The **Pio Clementino Museum** holds some of the world's most notable sculptures, among them the *Laocoön, Belvedere Torso,* and *Apollo Belvedere,* all works from the 1st century BC that had a tremendous influence on Renaissance artists. The superb **Gallery of Tapestries** leads to the **Gallery of Maps,** a stunning display of late 16th-century cartographic ingenuity and accomplishment. Next are the **Raphael Stanze,** decorated with biblical scenes by the Urbino-born Raphael (1483–1520). One of these rooms, the *Stanza della Segnature,* contains the artist's *School of Athens* (1511), a painting whose balance of geometric composition and harmonies of color exemplifies the Renaissance visual ideal. The faces of Plato, Aristotle, and other philosophers of antiquity are portraits of Raphael's contemporaries—note Leonardo da Vinci posing as Plato. The next stop is the cramped **Chapel of Nicholas V,** painted floor-to-ceiling with frescoes by Fra Angelico, followed by the **Borgia Apartments,** with ceiling mosaics by Pinturicchio.

The highlight, of course, is the **Cappella Sistina,** always packed with neck-craning tourists. Just about every great Renaissance artist in Rome had a hand in its decoration—Pinturicchio, Signorelli, Botticelli, Cosimo Rosselli—before Michelangelo, much to his dismay, was cajoled by Pope Julius II to paint the barrel-vaulted ceiling, an artist's nightmare. The result of Michelangelo's labors, recently restored to brilliant colors, has been called the most sublime example of artistry in the world. Twenty years later, Michelangelo was commissioned to paint the *Last Judgment* on the wall behind the simple altar. *Viale Vaticano, tel. 06/69883333. Admission: L15,000, free last Sun. of month. Open Nov.–Feb. and mid-June–Aug., Mon.–Sat. 8:45–1:45 (last admission 1 PM); Mar.–mid-June and Sept.–Oct., Mon.–Sat. 9–4:45 (last admission 4 PM); also last Sun. of every month 9–1:45. Closed Jan. 1, Jan. 6, Feb. 11, Mar. 19, Easter Sun. and Mon., May 1, Ascension Thurs. and Corpus Christi, June 29, Aug. 14–15, Nov. 1, and Dec. 25–26.*

VIA APPIA AND THE CATACOMBS

Via Appia (Appian Way) was the most important of all Roman roads. Completed in 312 BC, it crossed the peninsula to the Adriatic. It's best known today for the miles of underground cemeteries that lie beneath. Since burial was forbidden within Rome's city limits, residents buried their dead just outside the walls, digging elaborate, multi-level tunnels in the soft tufa rock. Most of the remains are long gone, so you'll have to make do with eerie subterranean passageways and lots of Christian graffiti. Although the catacombs themselves stretch for miles, there are only three official entrances: **San Callisto** (V. Appia Antica 110, tel. 06/5136725; closed Wed.), **Domitilla** (V. delle Sette Chiese 283, tel. 06/5548766; closed Tues.), and **San Sebastiano** (V. Appia Antica 136, tel. 06/7887035; closed Thurs.). Each charges L8000 admission and guided tour, and is open 8:30–noon and 2:30–5.

SHOPPING

Shopping and browsing are as much social pastimes in Rome as anywhere else in the country. Unfortunately, the designer shoes and clothes that Italy is famous for don't come cheaper here, especially at the celebrated shops along **Via Frattina** and **Via dei Condotti.** Lower-rent Roman fashion can be had along **Via del Corso, Via Nazionale,** and **Via dei Giubbonari** (off Campo dei Fiori), where clothes tend toward the trendy and funky, and where good-quality shoes—miracle of miracles—cost less than in the United States. Clearly, however, Rome isn't just about clothes and shoes. Before you exhaust your credit cards on a whole new wardrobe, take a look at what else can be had in the stores and *botteghe* of modern Rome. Religious articles are plentiful near the Vatican and on Via dei Cestari, behind the Pantheon.

MARKETS

The Sunday morning **Porta Portese flea market** (7 AM–2 PM, along Via Portuense in Trastevere) has mainly used or second-rate new clothing, though there are still some deals to be had on old furniture

CREEPY CAPPUCCINI

Entombed within the Catacombe dei Cappuccini (V. Cappuccini, Bus 389 from C. Vittorio Emanuele; donation L1000; open daily 9–noon and 3–5) are over 8,000 ghostly mummies displayed behind flimsy mesh screens. From the early 16th–late 19th centuries, the Capuchin monks dried and embalmed cadavers, which were then dressed and inserted upright into individual wall niches. The Capuchins took their job pretty seriously, dividing the mummies according to earthly occupation, gender, and social class. You'll need a strong stomach to view the glass-encased, mummified small children.

and interesting junk. Bargaining is the rule here, as are pickpockets; beware. The market is immense, and without official beginning or end. If you go, go early, while there's still a lot of choice and room to move around. To get there, hop on any bus going up Viale Trastevere and ask the driver to drop you at the market, or just follow the crowd. A less frenetic and crowded version of the Porta Portese market is the set of stands on **Via Sannio** (Mon.-Sat. 8 AM–2 PM; take Metro Line A San Giovanni).

SPECIALTY STORES

For gift ideas, check out the two coolest shops for designer household items and furniture: **Spazio Sette** (V. dei Barbieri 7, near Largo Argentina, tel. 06/6869708) and **Stock Market** (V. dei Banchi Vecchi 51, near P. Navona, tel. 06/6864238). Pottery and handicrafts at reasonable prices can be found at **Myricae** (V. Frattina 36, tel. 06/6795335). Cheeses and salami will be thrown away (or eaten) at the airport by the customs folks, but there's no problem with most other things, and **Castroni** (V. Cola di Rienzo 196, near P. Risorgimento, tel. 06/6874383) is a great place to find that special something. The little **Lattoniere** (P. de' Renzi 22, in Trastevere, tel. 06/5806737) has tons of great tools and decorations all made right there by one of Rome's last tinsmiths, who might make something for you to order.

AFTER DARK

When Romans go out on the town, they literally head outside to the streets and piazzas, where so much of Italian social life takes place. As long as the weather is good, you'll find many Romans out on an after-dinner passeggiata, enjoying the night air and perhaps a cup of gelato. If you have something a bit more active in mind, read on. **Campo dei Fiori** and the streets around **Piazza Navona** and the **Pantheon,** are all good places to hang out, usually full of people and bars, pubs, *birrerie,* and clubs to check out. **Trastevere** is home to dozens of night spots, and nearby **Testaccio** is packed with discos for serious grooving. In summer, the majority of discos move to the beach, so if you want to shake it to techno, your options will be better there.

Indispensable for anyone with an after-dark agenda is *Romac'e'* (L1500), a weekly guide to what's happening in town; it comes out every Thursday at newsstands. There is a short summary in English at the back, but the lists in Italian of clubs, concerts, and events are easy to decipher.

Be prepared to pay for a *tessera* (membership card) at many clubs without public licenses that are forced to operate as *associazioni culturali* (cultural associations). Membership lasts from a month to a year and costs L5000–L20,000. Just think of it as a cover charge, which most real clubs charge anyway. If you want a simple beer and don't care about atmosphere (or even sitting down), head for one of Rome's innumerable cafés, where beer *alla spina* (on tap) or a glass of wine cost L2500–L3500.

BARS, CLUBS, AND NIGHTSPOTS

Angelo Azzurro. This is a funky underground Trastevere disco, awash in black lights and mirrors. Women only on Friday, men only on Saturday. *V. C. Merry del Val 13, off Viale di Trastevere, Buses 56, 60. tel. 06/5812081. Cover: L10,000–L20,000, includes 1 drink. Closed Mon.*

Antico Caffè della Pace. On an elegant, ivy-clad street behind Piazza Navona, this is perhaps Rome's most civilized caffè-bar. By day you can have tea. It's worth the price just to sit outside in the midst of it all. *V. della Pace 3, tel. 06/6861216.*

Bar del Fico. Decidedly hip and cool, this large bar has tables outside on the piazza, even in winter. *P. del Fico 26/28, near P. Navona. tel. 06/6865205.*

Bossa Nova. Hear live Brazilian music and dance until way, way into the night in this simply decorated club. Tuesday is lesson night, well worth the L10,000 and one drink minimum. *V. Orti di Trastevere 23, tel. 5816121. Closed Mon.*

Circolo degli Artisti. This warehouse space and bar blasts everything from ragamuffin and hip-hop to electrowave. In summer expect the occasional live band and performance art piece. The *tessera* costs L7,000. *V. Lamarmora 28, tel. 06/4464968. Metro A to Vittorio Emanuele; V. Lamarmora is 1 block south. Closed Mon.*

Fiddler's Elbow. Maybe you recognize the Elbow, because the owners have identical pubs in Florence and Venice. You'll find the usual: Irish beers, cider, and gab. *V. dell'Olmata 43, near Metro B Cavour, tel. 06/4872110. Take night Buses 122N, 20N, 21N.*

Jonathan's Angels. This bar is famous for its eclectic decoration that includes murals and paintings, mirrors and statues, and yes . . . the grooviest toilet in town. *V. della Fossa 16, tel. 06/6893426.*

Miscellanea. During lunch and afternoon tea this tavern fills with Italians who happily line-up for generous salads and panini. At night it's geared toward a university crowd, a mix of Italians and expatriate internationals. *V. delle Paste 110/A, no phone. From NE corner of P. della Rotonda, take V. de' Pastini to V. delle Paste.*

Oasi della Birra. As the name suggests, this is the oasis for beer; where else can you choose from a list of almost 600 different beers from all over the world. *P. Testaccio 41, tel. 5746122. Closed Sun. and Mon.*

Vineria. This so-so wine shop on Campo dei Fiori becomes a popular wine bar after hours: From 7 PM it's popular with the after-work crowd, from 10 PM with youthful Romans. They serve about 50 different wines available by the glass and panini. *Campo dei Fiori 15, tel. 06/68803268. Closed Sun.*

CLASSICAL MUSIC

Check signs around town or *Romac'e'* listings for free (or inexpensive) concerts, usually in churches. Rome's main classical music associations are the **Accademia di Santa Cecilia** (V. della Conciliazione 4, tel. 06/3611064), **Accademia Filarmonica Romana** (usually at Teatro Olimpico, V. Gentile da Fabriano 17, tel. 06/3234890), and the **Istituzione Universitaria dei Concerti** (Lungotevere Flaminio 50, tel. 06/3610051). Opera season runs November–May in the **Teatro dell'Opera** (P. B.Gigli, tel. 06/481601), then moves to Piazza di Siena in the Villa Borghese for the outdoor summer opera series (with very cheap bleacher seats).

CINEMA

Rome's lone English-only theater is Trastevere's **Pasquino** (Vicolo del Piede 19, tel. 06/5803622), with four daily screenings starting around 4; call for times and programs. **Alcazar** (V. Mario del Val 14, off Viale Trastevere, tel. 06/5880099) and **Cinema Majestic** (V. S.S. Apostoli 20, off V. del Corso, tel. 06/6794908) show films in English on Monday.

NEAR ROME

FRASCATI

Huddled on a hillside 40 km (25 mi) to the southeast, Frascati is like a balcony overlooking Rome and its rural suburbs. If you need an excuse for a day trip, consider checking out the sweeping views, which on clear days extend to the sea. Although a welcome escape from the big city, Frascati lacks the charm of a Tuscan or Umbrian hill town, and there are fewer historic sights; the reason for coming here has always been to drink the local wine and to eat yourself immobile. So do like the locals do and buy picnic supplies from the market (open daily 8–1, closed Sun.) or the stands on **Piazza del Mercato** before heading to any of the numerous local *cantine* on nearly every street in the old part of town, where you can sit and quaff cheap local wine. Halfway up the stairs from the train station is the loud and chaotic **Cantina Gomandini** (V. Emanuele Filiberto 1, tel. 06/9420307; open Mon.–Sat. 4–8), where long picnic tables play well with crowds of tourists. To toast Bacchus a bit more off the beaten track, pull up a chair and order a liter (L4000 to stay, L2500 to go) at **Cantina da Santino** (V. P. Campana 17, up the stairs from P. Marconi). The **AAST** (P. Marconi 1, tel. 06/9420331; open Mon.–Sat. 9–2 and 4–7:15, in winter 3:30–6:45) has a detailed map marked with wine-tasting spots in Frascati and nearby villages.

COMING AND GOING

Trains from Rome's Stazione Termini (26 min, L2700) drop you off at Frascati's tiny depot and pick you up for the trip back up until 10 PM. To reach the center, climb the hillside stairs to Piazza Marconi; Piazza San Pietro is two blocks to the left, and Villa Aldobrandini is straight ahead along Via Catone. **COTRAL buses** leave from Rome's Metro A Anagnina station (every 20 min until 10:50 PM from Rome, until 9:50 PM from P. Marconi, 1 hr, L1500) and drop you in Piazza Marconi. In Frascati, buy tickets a few doors down from the bus stop at Piazza Marconi 16 (open daily 8–1 and 4–8).

TIVOLI

Tivoli has been equated with "getting away" since ancient times, when just about anybody who was anybody had a villa here, including Cassius, Trajan, Hadrian, Horace, and Catullus. Nowadays, Tivoli is a small but vibrant town with exquisite views of the surrounding countryside and easy access to its main attractions: **Villa d'Este** (tel. 0774/312070; admission L8000; open Tues.–Sun. 9–6:30, until 4 in winter), with its 500 sumptuous fountains, and the lush greenery of **Villa Gregoriana** (admission L2500; open daily 9–7, until 3 in winter). Tivoli's **AAST** tourist office (Largo Garibaldi, tel. 0774/311249; open 9–6, Sun. 9–1, shorter hrs off-season) has free maps and listings of the town's food and lodging options.

If the villas in Tivoli have left you wanting more, take Bus 4 from Tivoli's Piazza Garibaldi to the astoundingly grand 2nd-century AD **Villa Adriana** (15 min, L1500), commissioned by the emperor Hadrian (he gets credit for the Pantheon, too). It took the best architects in Rome 13 years to design and build temples, baths, living quarters, and gardens, many of which are still intact. Don't miss the swimming pool and the **Museo Didattico** (open sporadically) at the villa's entrance. Before trekking into the unknown, fill up your water bottle at the spring by the entrance. *Tel. 0774/530203. Admission: L8000. Open daily 9–6:30, until 4 in winter.*

COMING AND GOING

Buses are by far your best bet. From Rome's Metro B Rebibbia station, COTRAL buses run every 15–20 minutes (5 AM–midnight) to Tivoli (45 min, L6000 round-trip). You'll be dropped off at Piazza Garibaldi, a.k.a. Largo Garibaldi, across from the tourist office.

OSTIA ANTICA

Ostia Antica, like Pompeii, is an ancient city preserved in its entirety—only without the volcano and hordes of visitors; even in the summer it's possible to have the place to yourself. The once port city is far more than a pile of ruins, with intact theaters, apartment buildings, baths, temples, and even ancient pubs to explore (all overgrown with ivy and shaded by lofty trees, many filled with murals, mosaics, and sculptures), there's plenty to see. Plus, directly accessible by Rome's Metro and Lazio's regional rail system, it's hands-down Rome's most convenient day trip.

The main street, **Decumano Massimo,** leads to the **Terme di Nettuno,** one of 18 bath complexes with ornate mosaics depicting the robust Neptune frolicking with all manner of scaly beasts. Next door lies the *palestra,* where Ostia residents came for a workout. Further along is the *teatro,* which held 2,700 spectators. Beyond the stage is the **Piazzale delle Corporazioni,** where traders and merchants did their business. A fascinating series of mosaics encircles the piazza, recounting maritime scenes and Ostian daily life, and declarations and titles of each office. Within the piazza is a *tempio,* thought to be dedicated to Ceres, goddess of grain and abundance, to whom Ostia owed a great deal of thanks for trade surpluses. From the Decumano, turn right on Via dei Molini to find an ancient **bakery** with stone mills and ovens. The nearby **Casa di Diana** was an ancient low-cost housing project with communal toilets. On Via di Diana, you'll see the *thermopolium,* a local bar where clients once ate, drank, and made merry. Notice the huge wine vats and the painted menu on the wall.

Ostia's **Foro** served as the city's civic center, dominated by the imposing **Capitolium,** dedicated to Juno, Jupiter, and Minerva. Other remains of the Forum include the **Curia** (headquarters of the town council), the **Basilica** (seat of the tribunal), and the temple to Rome and Augustus opposite the Capitolium. Currently undergoing restoration, the **Insula delle Muse** was once the opulent home of a bourgeois family. Though faded, the extensive wall paintings are of a similar style to those found in Pompeii. The nearby **Dumus dei Dioscuri** showcases two striking mosaics. Climb to the second-story terraces to catch a bird's eye view.

Off the Decumano, the **Museum of Ostia** is definitely worth a gander. It mostly contains Ostian sculpture, including remarkable marble reliefs documenting scenes of town life. There are also beautifully preserved sarcophagi and an exquisite altar to the 12 gods of Olympus. Adjacent to the museum is a **bookstore** that stocks guides, slides, and postcards.

COMING AND GOING

Take Rome's Metro B to Magliana and change to a Lido train to the Ostia Antica stop. A day-pass (*biglietto integrato giornaliero*; L6000) costs the same as a round-trip ticket but is valid for unlimited Metro travel. To reach the site from the station, walk across the pedestrian overpass, continue straight, and follow the signs to the left.

CAMPANIA

More travelers visit Campania than any other region south of Rome, and it's no wonder. The region has the balmy climate and vistas, bougainvillea-draped architecture, and mouth-watering cuisine that can't help but draw ferryloads of pleasure-seekers. Some of the oldest ruins this side of Constantinople are also here, like the famed archaeological sites of **Herculaneum** and **Pompeii**—both with views of menacing Mt. Vesuvius. In between history lessons, you can flit from island to island in the Bay of Naples and lie beneath cliffs on the beaches of the **Amalfi Coast.** Then, of course, there's Naples, whose bad reputation keeps the tourist crowds away—all the better for those who are willing to discover its innumerable fascinations.

NAPLES

Approaching Naples (Napoli) from the water at sunset, as the moon rises over Mt. Vesuvius, you may be moved to agree with the assertion of lifelong Neapolitans that theirs is the most beautiful city on Earth. Once assailed by the murderous traffic of the city, however, you may think you have tumbled from *Paradiso* to *Inferno.* Naples's energy, chaos, and (seeming) lawlessness rival anything in Europe, and little effort has been made to soften the city's hard edges for foreigners. As a result, too many visitors flee the city for the inviting islands and the ancient ruins that surround Naples on all sides. It's a pity, because it only takes a little patience and an open mind to adapt to the unique pace of Neapolitan life—an effort well rewarded by the city's numerous monuments, churches, and museums, not to mention its world-renowned pizza and seafood.

BASICS

VISITOR INFORMATION

There's an **EPT** office (tel. 081/268779; open Mon.–Sat. 8:30–8, Sun. 9–2) in Stazione Centrale, but the main office is in Piazza dei Martiri (tel. 081/405311; open weekdays 8:30–3:45). An **AACST** (tel. 081/5523328; open Mon.–Sat. 9–7, Sun. 9–2) in Piazza Gesù Nuovo specializes in information on Old Naples. Look for the brochure *Qui Napoli* for helpful bilingual listings of museums and transport schedules. **Changing money** is convenient at the **Ufficio di Cambio** (open daily 7:15 AM–8:30 PM) inside Stazione Centrale, but you'll get more for your money at one of the banks around Piazza Municipio.

EMERGENCIES

The **police station** (V. Medina 75, tel. 081/7941111) has an *ufficio stranieri* (foreigners' office) that usually has an English speaker on staff.

PHONES AND MAIL

Make long-distance calls at **Telecom** (V. A. Depretis 40). The main **post office** is at Piazza Matteotti (tel. 081/5511456; open weekdays 8:15–7:20, Sat. 8:15–1:30); the postal code is 80100.

COMING AND GOING

Stazione Centrale (tel. 1478/88088) sends trains to Rome (2½ hrs, L18,000), and Milan (7 hrs, L64,000). One floor under the station, the **Ferrovia Circumvesuviana** commuter line has trains to Herculaneum, Pompeii, and Sorrento. For ferry rides, the major long-distance carriers are **Tirennia** (tel. 081/7201111) and **Linee Lauro** (tel. 081/5513352). Boats leave occasionally for Tunisia, Sardinia, Palermo, and the Aeolian Islands. Look up departure times in *Qui Napoli*. For trips around the Bay of Naples, the main port is **Molo Beverello**, below Castel Nuovo. Carriers include **Linee Lauro** and **Caremar** (tel. 081/5513882).

GETTING AROUND

Naples stretches along the Bay of Naples with its back to the Vomero Hills. Most visitors arrive at Stazione Centrale, on Piazza Garibaldi. From here, Corso Umberto I heads southwest to the downtown area of **Piazzas Bovio, Municipio,** and **Trieste e Trento.** To the north is the historical center of Old Naples; to the south is the port. Farther west are the more fashionable districts of **Santa Lucia** and **Chiaia.**

Important **bus** lines include **R1,** from Piazza Bovio up into the hills; **R2,** between Piazza Garibaldi and Piazza Trieste e Trento; and **R3,** between Piazza Dante and Mergellina. The **Metropolitana** is an efficient subway system with a stop at Stazione Centrale. The **Giranapoli** ticket (L1200) works on all public transportation and is good for 90 minutes. Tickets are available at tabbachi and newsstands.

WHERE TO SLEEP

Considering how divey the dives can be in Naples, you may want to shell out the extra lire for a little cleanliness and security. In general, the farther you stray from Piazza Garibaldi, the more palatable (and pricey) the accommodations become.

DIRT CHEAP • Albergo Aurora. This is a cut above most of the low-end places nearby. Doubles run about L32,000. *P. Garibaldi 60, tel. 081/201920.*

UNDER L65,000 • Pensione Teresita. These clean rooms by the bay—some with balconies—are almost always full. Doubles are L55,000–L60,000, including the use of decent showers down the hall. *V. Santa Lucia 90, 2nd floor, tel. 081/7640105. From Stazione Centrale, Bus R2 to P. Trieste e Trento.*

Il Soggiorno Imperiale. Tidy, secure budget accommodations are run by a friendly couple in a great area in Old Naples. Doubles are L50,000. *P. Miraglia 386, 3rd floor, tel. 081/459347. Metro: P. Cavour, then walk south to V. Tribunali, turn right; V. Tribunali leads into P. Miraglia.*

UNDER L80,000 • Hotel Casanova. This is the best deal near Piazza Garibaldi, with small, clean doubles for L60,000, L75,000 with bath. *C. Garibaldi 333, tel. 081/268287, fax 081/269792.*

HOSTEL

Ostello Mergellina (HI). On the western edge of town. HI members pay L22,000–L25,000 per person; nonmembers pay L5000 extra a night. Luggage storage is available. *V. Salita della Grotta 23, tel. 081/7612346. Metro: Mergellina; leave station to the right, go back under tracks and follow signs. Lockout 9–4. Cash only.*

FOOD

Neapolitans like their architecture Baroque but their cuisine classic and simple. **Open-air food markets** line Via Tribunali, between Piazza Dante and the Duomo. Most of the restaurants around Piazza Garibaldi serve mediocre food in a rushed atmosphere. Venture into Old Naples or down to the harbor for the real thing. Local specialties include mozzarella *di bufalo* (buffalo's milk cheese), spaghetti *alle cozze* (with sweet tomatoes and mussels), and *zuppa di pesce* (fish stew). Pizza was born here—don't leave town without trying a fresh-baked Neapolitan pie.

UNDER L10,000 • Trianon da Ciro. If you haven't yet tried a Neapolitan pizza, head to this esteemed old-style pizzeria, where pies range from L5500 to L12,500. *V. P. Colletta 44–46, tel. 081/5539426.*

UNDER L15,000 • Dante e Beatrice. Justifiably one of the most famous spots in the city, this tasteful and elegant trattoria whips up Neapolitan specialties. *P. Dante 44–45, tel. 081/5499438. Closed 3 weeks in Aug. or Sept.*

UNDER L20,000 • Amici Miei. At this family-run trattoria on a quiet street, dishes run about L10,000. *V. Monte di Dio 78, tel. 081/7646063. From P. del Plebiscito, go down V. Chiaia to arched city gate, ascend stairs inside gate's building (not through the arch), and turn left on V. Giovanni Nicotera, which becomes V. Monte di Dio.*

Ristorante Marino. Loud Neapolitans crowd this ultratypical local spot with boisterious waiters. First courses begin at L4000. *V. Santa Lucia 118, tel. 081/7640280. From Castel dell'Ovo, turn right on V. Partenope, left on V. Santa Lucia.*

WORTH SEEING

Naples has a numbing array of churches and museums, especially in Old Naples, near Piazza Dante and the Duomo. To get a handle on them all, pick up the tourist office brochure describing different tours of medieval, Renaissance, Baroque, and Rococo churches. Naples's **Duomo,** the Cathedral of San Gennaro (V. Duomo; open daily 7:30–noon and 5–7:30), was built at the end of the 13th century. The Duomo's big moment comes each year on September 19, when it hosts the celebration of San Gennaro, Naples's patron saint. On that day, if the two vials of the saint's blood kept in the cathedral don't liquefy, Naples is in for it. Cholera epidemics and volcanic eruptions have been known to follow ceremonies when Gennaro's blood remains congealed.

If you work up an appetite walking along the bay in Naples, stop at any of the stands between Santa Lucia and Mergellina for a tarallo con mandorle e pepe, a savory almond pastry that makes a great quick snack.

Old Naples centers around the Spaccanapoli neighborhood, where electric-candle shrines pay homage to the Madonna, kids play soccer in piazzas, and clotheslines crisscross narrow passageways. In the middle of Piazza Gesù Nuovo, the **Guglia dell'Immacolata,** a prickly looking Spanish spire, exemplifies the square's Baroque design. The spire faces the Trinità Maggiore, popularly referred to as the **Gesù Nuovo.** In 1601, this former palace was turned into a Jesuit church, with a brilliant Baroque interior that contrasts with the grim facade. Locals come to the huge, lofty **Santa Chiara** (V. Benedetto Croce, tel. 081/5526280; open daily 7–7) to hear morning mass, but you should come for the exquisite **cloister** (open 8:30–12:30 and 4–6:30). Its antique blue tiles and columns, painted with fanciful 18th-century landscapes, are graced by grapevines and a very large family of cats. The **Cappella Sansevero** (V. Francesco de Sanctis 19, near P. San Domenico Maggiore, tel. 081/5518470; admission L6000; open Tues. and Sun. 10–1:30, Mon. and Wed.–Sat. 10–6) is a ghoulish Baroque chapel overflowing with cherubs, melancholic Madonna images, and richly colored frescoes. Most spectacular is the center-piece sculpture, known as the Veiled Christ. Downstairs, two cadavers with supposed preserved cardio-vascular systems add to the macabre atmosphere.

The incredible **Museo Archeologico Nazionale** holds one of the most extensive collections of Greek and Roman antiquities in the world, including the famous Farnese collection and most of the mosaics and paintings taken from the ruins at Pompeii and Herculaneum. *P. Museo Nazionale 19, tel. 081/440166. Metro: P. Cavour. Admission: L12,000. Open Tues.–Sat. 9–2, Sun. 9–1.*

Huge, gray **Palazzo Reale** casts a heavy shadow on Piazza del Plebiscito. The facade is flanked by statues of some of the city's many international conquerors. Just past the entrance, the space is dominated by a sweeping marble stairway, and upstairs, the living apartments stretch endlessly—all gold, mirrors, and family portraits. The **Biblioteca Nazionale,** at the rear of the palazzo, has changing exhibits of old books and manuscripts. *P. del Plebiscito, tel. 081/413888. Admission: L8000. Open Tues.–Sun. 9–1:30.*

The **Castel dell'Ovo** (literally "Egg Castle") juts into the Bay of Naples from the Santa Lucia port with a backdrop of Vesuvius. Built in the 12th century, this beige monster has housed many different VIPs in Naples, including the Basilican monks, Normans, and a few Swabians. These days, the castle hosts art exhibits, concerts, and other cultural events. *V. Partenope, tel. 081/7648311. Open Mon.–Thurs. 10:30–8. Fri.–Sun. 10:30 AM–11 PM.*

Broad switchback ramparts lead to the **Castel Sant'Elmo,** built under the Bourbon king Robert of Anjou, who chose the site for its strategic vantage point. Ascend to the broad roof and check out the outdoor bar and the astounding view. *Entrance on V. Tito Angelini, tel. 081/5784030. Admission: L4000. Open Tues.–Sun. 9–2.*

Set in a large wooded park, the 18th-century **Museo e Gallerie di Capodimonte** was built as a Bourbon homestead. It now houses an important collection of Italian, Spanish, and Dutch Renaissance paintings. Don't miss Masaccio's *Crucifixion* and the wonderful cartoons by Michelangelo. *Parco di Capodimonte, tel. 081/7441307. From Stazione Centrale, Bus 110 or 127R; or, from P. Dante, Bus 160. Admission: L8000. Open Tues.–Sat. 10–6, Sun. 9–2.*

AFTER DARK

Naples gets going after dark, with outdoor bars in **Piazza Bellini,** plenty of live music clubs, and nocturnal Neapolitan theatrics on the streets. Look in *Qui Napoli* and the local newspaper *Il Mattino* for information on free summertime concerts, club events, theater, and movies.

Duded up in '50s Americana, **Le Rock** (V. Bellini 9, next to P. Dante) features U.S. rock and blues played by local musicians. A young crowd flocks to the outdoor **Club 1799** (P. Bellini 71, tel. 081/294483) and at the many other cafés on the square, where it doesn't cost much more for a table on the piazza than for an espresso at the bar. In Old Naples, **Riot** (V. San Biagio dei Librai 39, up staircase in the back of courtyard, tel. 081/7663228) will give you insight into the Neapolitan avant garde. Jazz groups jam throughout the evening in front of young leftist intellectual types. **Via G. Paladino,** also in Old Naples, is home to several popular bars, including **Il Mattone, Frame Café,** and **La Vineria.**

NEAR NAPLES

POMPEII

There is probably nothing in the world like the massive ghost town of Pompeii, an imposing and haunting testament to a long-vanished civilization. With more than 20,000 inhabitants, the city had everything: outdoor theaters, banks, bars, working-class and wealthy districts, public baths, health clinics, and brothels. It was a hub of commercial activity in the region, until Mt. Vesuvius destroyed it all in the big bang of AD 79. Today, tourists come in droves to see the incredibly well-preserved buildings, a few pornographic mosaics, and some of the eruption's carbonized victims: Their death screams, flailing arms, and tortured poses are cast permanently in plaster. The ruins are open daily from 9 AM until one hour before sunset; admission is L12,000. Pick up a free map at the **tourist office** (near Porta Marina, tel. 1670/13350).

As you enter the ruins at Porta Marina, make your way to the **Forum,** which served as Pompeii's cultural, political, and religious center. The **House of the Tragic Poet** is believed to be the home of the Latin poet Glaucus, but it's more famous for the black and white mosaic of a dog at the entrance, with the message "cave canem" (beware of the dog). The **House of the Vettii** boasts a lovely garden and a small room of well-preserved Roman paintings, but most people remember it for its depictions of Priapus, who shows off with absurdly swollen pride why he is the god of fertility. For more raunchy frescoes, make a stop at the two-story brothel **Lupanar.** Illustrations of various sex acts adorn the entry to each prostitute's room, rooms just large enough for an uncomfortable-looking stone bed. Farther down Via Stabiana lie the **Stabian Baths,** Pompeii's largest bathhouse, which had a variety of hot and cold baths, steam rooms, a swimming pool, and even boxing rings. Continue along Via Stabian to the **Teatro Grande,** which held 5,000 ancient Pompeiians, with box seats for bigwigs. Today, the theater hosts weekend music performances in the summer and early fall (ask at the tourist office for more information). Finally, the large **amphitheater** near the east entrance to the site seated 20,000 spectators in its day, and was one of the most raucous (and egalitarian) social spots in town.

COMING AND GOING • From Naples's Stazione Centrale or Vesuviana, the Sorrento line of the Circumvesuviana railway system runs trains to the Pompeii Scavi stop (35 min, L2700), which is about halfway to Sorrento (do not go to any other stop named "Pompei").

CAPRI

Capri has long been the life of the party in the Bay of Naples, outshining its sister islands in both glamour and scenery. In summer it seems a zillion tourists swarm the island, and the towns of Capri and Anacapri can feel like ant farms. Despite the towns' high population density, the island abounds with chances to climb mountains that suddenly drop off into the sea, wander through Roman ruins, and swim in the clear blue water off beautiful, rocky beaches. The only real drawback to Capri is that it's much more expensive than the rest of the region.

With such beautiful surroundings it's no wonder that everyone from the Greeks to the Phonecians partied here. Emperor Augustus had his vacations on Capri, and Tiberius littered the island with 12 villas, including the impressive, crumbling **Villa Jovis** (V. Tiberio; admission L4000; open daily 9–2 hrs before sunset). In the 19th and early 20th centuries, a new wave of foreign expats started building villas here. Maxim Gorky headed a school for communist revolutionaries here, and Swedish doctor and humanitarian Axel Munthe built the lovely **Villa San Michele** (V. Axel Munthe, tel. 081/8371401; admission L5000; open daily 9:30–6; shorter hrs off-season). It houses an eclectic collection of ancient art, most of which he dug up from his own backyard (his villa was built on the ruins of one of Tiberius's villas). **Anacapri**'s most popular sight is the **Grotta Azzurra,** a large cavern lit up from underwater by sunlight reflecting off the submerged limestone walls. It glows an eerie blue, but boatloads of tourists popping flashbulbs detract from the dazzle. From 9 until 5 (earlier in winter), the only way in is to pay L14,000 for a brief peek from a rowboat. To get there, you can take a boat from Marina Grande (L7600 round-trip) or a 10-minute bus ride from Anacapri. It's technically illegal, but many people swim into the Grotta Azzurra before 9 or after closing.

VISITOR INFORMATION • You'll find an **AACST** information office at Marina Grande (tel. 081/8370634), in the center of Capri Town (P. Umberto I, tel. 081/8370686), and off Piazza Vittoria in Anacapri (V. Orlandi 59/A, tel. 081/8371524).

COMING AND GOING • The carriers that serve Capri are **Alilauro** (tel. 081/8376965), **Caremar** (tel. 081/8370700), **SNAV** (tel. 081/8377577), and **Navigazione Libera del Golfo** (tel. 081/8370819). Frequent hydrofoils run to both of Naples's ports, Sorrento, and Amalfi; service is less frequent to Positano, Salerno, and Ischia. Ferries run to Naples and Sorrento and are cheaper and slower than hydrofoils. All the ticket offices are on the waterfront by the port. A **funicular** connects Marina Grande to the center of Capri every 15 minutes (L3000 round-trip), and **buses** (L1500) run every 20 minutes between Capri and Anacapri.

WHERE TO SLEEP AND EAT • Even the barest rooms are costly in swank Capri, but you can try to talk down the price in the off-season. In Capri Town, **Stella Maris** (V. Roma 27, across from the main bus stop, tel. 081/8370452), a friendly, family-run pension with views of the sea, has doubles for L100,000. **La Tosca** (V. D. Birago 5, tel. 081/8370989) has some doubles with bath for L95,000. At **Il Girasole** (V. Linciano 47, tel. 081/8373620) in Anacapri, the cheapest doubles start at L50,000; call ahead and the friendly owners will pick you up at the port.

Buying groceries from bakeries and markets is the best way to eat cheaply and well, but there are a few restaurants worth trying. On the waterfront in Marina Grande, the best option is **Buonocuore** (tel. 081/8370384), a tavola calda with good, cheap panini and small pizzas. The owners also run **Da Peppino,** a restaurant on the same block with pizzas and simple dishes like lasagna. In Anacapri, you can eat cheap pizza and sandwiches at popular **Aumm Aumm** (V. Caprile 18, tel. 081/8372061). If you want to splurge, take Via Migliera out of Anacapri to Belvedere Migliera to find **Da Gelsomina** (V. Migliera 72, tel. 081/8371499), which serves excellent food at high but fully justified prices.

SORRENTO

Most of Sorrento stretches across a plateau that ends abruptly at a steep tufa cliff 100 ft above the sea. Hotels and villas monopolize most of the cliff's edge and the bay views that inspired artists like Richard Wagner, Maxim Gorky, and Henrik Ibsen. At the base of the cliff are beaches blanketed with sunbathers. Sorrento's manageable size and secure feel, combined with its location and good transportation connections, make it a fine base for exploring the Bay of Naples and the Amalfi Coast to the south. For aquatic action, the narrow stretches of breakwater beach along **Marina Piccola** and **Marina San Francesco** are the most convenient. Sorrento's only museum, **Museo Correale di Terranova** (V. Correale 48, 5 min from P. Tasso, tel. 081/8781846; admission L5000; closed Tues. and Sun. afternoon) has Greek, Byzantine, and Roman statues, as well as later Italian art and Sorrentine inlaid woodwork.

BASICS

Follow the yellow signs from the train station to the **tourist information office** (V. Luigi de Maio 35, tel. 081/8074033). The **American Express** representative (P. Lauro 12, tel. 081/8072363; open weekdays 9–1 and 3–7, Sat. 9–1, Sun. 10–12:30) in Campania is in Acampora Travel.

TRULY COOL TRULLI

In the heart of the Murge Hills, between Bari and Taranto, Alberobello has a dense concentration of trulli, some of the oddest dwellings in Europe. One legend has them dating from the 13th century, another claims they date from a 16th-century decree forbidding the use of mortar in building a roof. The necessary result was the construction of squat, small, one-story houses with steep, conical roofs of flat stones. If you see an ENTRATA LIBERA sign, have a peek inside, but there may be pressure to buy. Alberobello is a 1½-hour train ride from Bari (L5700).

COMING AND GOING

The private trains on the **Circumvesuviana** line (tel. 081/7792144) make frequent trips between Sorrento and Naples's Stazione Centrale (1 hr, L4200), stopping along the way at Pompeii (30 min, L2600) and Herculaneum. **SITA** (tel. 081/5522176) sends buses to towns on the Amalfi Coast from the train station. Between **Alilauro** (tel. 081/8781430) and **Caremar** (tel. 081/8073077) there is frequent hydrofoil service to Naples (30 min, L12,000) and Capri (20 min, L8000); there are also a few departures for Ischia (40 min, L16,000) and Amalfi (45 min, L20,000). Ferries also go to Capri (50 min, L5300).

WHERE TO SLEEP AND EAT

Reserving a room in advance is key in Sorrento. Every room in small **Hotel City** (C. Italia 221, tel. 081/8772210) has a patio or a terrace, but all face busy Corso Italia. Doubles cost L65,000–L90,000. From the station, turn left on Corso Italia. Comfortable and homey **Hotel del Corso** (C. Italia 134, tel. 081/8073157; closed Nov.–mid-Feb.) has sunny doubles (L90,000 with bath, L70,000 without). **Pensione Linda** (V. degli Aranci 125, tel. 081/8782916) has an ugly exterior, but the beds are firm and the bathrooms are spacious. Doubles are L60,000–L80,000. From the station, turn left, then left again above the tracks, and left one more time on Via degli Aranci.

For cheap nutrition, seek out the delis and produce stands along car-free **Via San Cesario,** toward the bay. Corso Italia is a locus for cheap pizzerias, and a **Standa** supermarket (C. Italia 223) provides the basic loot. **Gigino** (V. degli Archi 15, tel. 081/8781927; closed Tues.) serves excellent local specialties, with a fixed-price menu at lunch.

PUGLIA

Puglia forms the heel of the Italian boot. The region's defining characteristic is its long stretch of coastline, extending for hundreds of miles along the Adriatic and Ionian seas. Puglia has a hot, semiarid climate and plenty of spectacular coastline. But Puglia isn't all beach; though little public transportation penetrates the mountains and trees in the interior, with a car the pristine wilderness is absolutely worth exploring. Puglia's largest and most important cities, Bari and Brindisi, are known for crime, congestion, and convenient ferry service to Greece. Don't skip Lecce, an important center of Baroque architecture, or the small town of Otranto that feels more like Greece than Italy. Getting around Puglia can be tricky, but it's worth the time and the effort.

BARI

This thriving business and commercial center is responsible for shuttling goods and tourists throughout the eastern Mediterranean. Most people just pass through Bari on their way to someplace else, but if you have time, wander through the bewildering array of cobblestone streets and medieval homes in the old quarter. Check out the remains of St. Nicolas in the **Basilica di San Nicola** (P. San Nicola, tel. 080/5211205), or stop by the beautiful **Cattedrale di San Sabino** (P. Odegitria, tel. 080/5210605).

VISITOR INFORMATION

The ubiquitous **Stop-Over in Bari** stands help budget travelers under age 30. Look for their "magic bus," open daily 8:30–8:30, outside the main train station. No matter what you need, go here first. The **EPT** (P. Aldo Moro 32/A, tel. 080/5242244) is unhelpful by comparison.

COMING AND GOING

The **FS railway** (tel. 1478/88088) at the main station in **Piazza Aldo Moro** handles seven daily trains to Milan (8½ hrs, L67,500) and five to Rome (5½ hrs, L38,500). Orange **local buses** and blue **SITA** buses leave from Piazza Aldo Moro. Buy tickets at the main train station at window 1.

Bari's **Stazione Marittima** has cheaper and better ferry connections to Greece and the eastern Mediterranean than Brindisi. Keep in mind, however, that Eurailpasses are not good for ferry travel out of Bari. Ferries leave Bari for Patras (16–18 hrs), Igoumenitsa (11–13 hr), and Corfu (10–12 hrs), and should cost L75,000–L115,000 for *poltrone* (reclining chairs) inside. To reach the ferries from the train station, take Bus 20 to the port, or the more frequent Buses 18, 21, and 22, which go to Piazza Massari, 10 minutes away.

WHERE TO SLEEP AND EAT

The Stop-Over in Bari people have set up a free campsite in the large **Pineta San Francesco Park** (take Bus 3 or 5 from the station). If you don't have a tent they'll provide one for you, and if camping isn't your style, they'll call around to find you a hotel. At press time, the **HI Ostello del Levante** (Lungomare Nicola Massaro 33, tel. 080/5300282) is scheduled to reopen in summer '97; call before you make the trek. To get here, take Bus 1 from the Teatro Petruzzelli on Corso Cavour.

At **Cuba Libre** (V. Imbriani 40, tel. 080/5243937; closed Mon.) you get the works—a plate of pork, chicken, beef, fish, octopus, or eggplant, and fries, rice and beans, a drink, dessert, and live Cuban music for L25,000. For a good self-service meal (L16,000) head to **El Pedro** (V. Piccinni 152, tel. 080/5211294; closed Sun.).

BRINDISI

Think of Brindisi as the backpacker's rite of passage into the big league of budget travel. Exchange offices, ticket agents, and café-bars have multiplied like rabbits on the Americanized strip that leads from the train station to the docks, where ferries depart for Albania, Greece, and beyond. To avoid lines and crowds, it's best to buy your ferry ticket from a travel agency in another Italian city. There are more than 20 lines, so shop around for the best price. It's also a good idea to buy a warm shirt for the crossing, and a cushion or mat to sit on while you wait . . . and wait, and wait.

BASICS

The **visitor information office** (Lungomare R. Margherita 12, no phone) is open weekdays 8:30–1:30. To change money, stop at any of the banks on Corso Umberto or Corso Garibaldi.

COMING AND GOING

Three trains leave daily for Rome (6½ hrs, L56,900), six for Milan (9½ hrs, L81,000). Trains leave hourly for Bari (1½ hrs, L9800). **FSE** buses depart from the main train station for major Puglian towns.

If you're a Eurailpass holder, you'll be taking a ferry to Greece from Brindisi, as Eurailpasses are not valid for trips out of Bari. Ferry rates vary month to month, company to company. Generally, you can expect Greek companies to charge less than Italian ones. **Adriatica** (C. Garibaldi 85, tel. 0831/523825) and **Hellenic Mediterranean Lines** (C. Garibaldi 8, tel. 0831/528531) are the companies you'll be doing business with if you have a **Eurail** or **InterRail** pass. **Fragline** (C. Garibaldi 88, tel. 0831/590334) has regular service to Corfu (6–10 hrs), Igoumenitsa (7–10 hrs), and Patras (18–19 hrs). *Posta ponte* (deck seat) tickets cost L30,000–L60,000; inside seats will cost at least L35,000–L66,000.

SICILY

Sicily (Sicilia), the largest island in the Mediterranean, is a place of contrasts. Salty old farmers, widows in black veils, dry mountains, and clear seas can all be found, but so can poverty, backwardness, and the Mafia. Though recent progressive movements by the government and the Sicilian people themselves have provided hope that the region will one day get out from under its feudalistic thumb, the Mafia continues to be a real presence in the everyday lives of Sicilians.

Over the centuries, the island's location, fertile soil, and warm climate encouraged every great Mediterranean civilization to invade it—from the Phoenicians to the Greeks, Romans, Arabs, Normans, and Bourbons. In spite of its millennia-long economic and political instability, or perhaps because of it, much of Sicily retains its traditional flavor. Some of the best Greek ruins in the world are in the ancient cities of **Siracusa** and **Agrigento**, and the capital, **Palermo,** is a quagmire of cathedrals and exotic palaces and gardens. When you're not at historic sites improving yourself, beaches call out for sunbathing, and volatile Mt. Etna beckons to be climbed. Best of all, after a long day in the sun, you'll have the chance to sample some of Italy's best seafood, prepared with a delicate mix of Arab, Greek, and Spanish spices.

COMING AND GOING

Messina, on the northernmost tip of the Ionian coast, is the main gateway to Sicily and is serviced by frequent trains, hydrofoils, and ferries. It's also possible to ferry from Genoa and Naples to Palermo, and from Reggio di Calabria to Siracusa.

PALERMO

Palermo will not charm you at first glance. Sicily's capital has been undergoing a steady decline since the 14th century. It's certainly noisy, chaotic, and occasionally dangerous, but its rich heritage makes it too intriguing a place to ignore. The exotic influence of the city's Arab and Norman conquerors is apparent as you wander its winding medieval streets, with their dilapidated but beautiful palaces and palm-filled gardens. Though the city is known as the home of Italy's most powerful dons, you probably won't see burly men kissing each other and exchanging suitcases, or even armor-plated Alfa Romeos. What you may witness, however, are adept pickpockets and Vespa-riding bag snatchers. That said, there's no reason to be paranoid, and travelers who make the effort to chat with locals will be rewarded with a friendliness rarely found in large Italian cities.

BASICS

The only **tourist office** (P. Castelnuovo 34, tel. 091/6058351; open weekdays 8–8, Sat. 8–2) is on the opposite side of town from the train station; take Bus 101 or 107 to Piazza Castelnuovo. The local **American Express** representative is G. Ruggieri e Figli (V. Emerico Amari 40, tel. 091/587144; open weekdays 9–1 and 4–7, Sat. 9–1). From Piazza Castelnuovo, follow Via Emerico Amari toward the port.

COMING AND GOING

Stazione Centrale is at the southern end of Via Roma near Palermo's medieval districts. Destinations include Messina (3½ hrs, L19,000) and Agrigento (2¼ hrs, L11,700). Most bus companies make a stop at the train station. **Cuffaro** (tel. 091/6161510) travels to Agrigento (2 hrs, L10,500), **Segesta** to Siracusa (4 hrs, L20,000). All ferries and hydrofoils dock at Palermo's **Stazione Marittima** (V. Francesco Crispi 118); from Stazione Centrale, take Bus 118. **Tirrenia** (Calata Marinai d'Italia, tel. 091/333300) has service to Naples and Genoa.

WHERE TO SLEEP

Palermo's cheapest hotels are squashed between **Via Maqueda, Via Roma, Corso Vittorio Emanuele,** and Stazione Centrale. To avoid crime, head to the modern part of Palermo near Piazza Castelnuovo and keep out of La Kalsa district. **Albergo Orientale** (V. Maqueda 26, tel. 091/6165727) is housed in a decaying, 18th-century palace with a courtyard. Some doubles (L40,000) are quite large, but all are a little dusty. **Albergo Luigi** (Salita Santa Caterina 1, off C. Vittorio Emanuele, tel. 091/585085) is central, with clean if slightly seedy rooms (doubles L50,000), some with a view. **Hotel Petit** (V. Principe di Belmonte 84, off V. Roma near P. Castelnuovo, tel. 091/323616) is in Palermo's most congenial neighborhood, offering balconies and sparkling bathrooms, making it worth the L65,000 for doubles.

FOOD

Seafood fans should try *pesce spada* (swordfish) and *polpo* (octopus)—a local specialty that's more appetizing than it sounds—and everyone should try olives and vegetable dishes from the city's well-stocked antipasto tables. The atmosphere at blue-collar **Osteria al Ferro di Cavallo** (V. Venezia 20, off V. Roma, tel. 091/331835) is hectic and lively. A lunch of salad, pasta, bread, meat or fish, and a drink costs only L7000–L12,000. **Trattoria Primavera** (P. Bologni 4, tel. 091/329408) has gotten stellar international press, and it's downright shocking that its prices are still affordable. The squid-ink spaghetti lives up to its reputation. **Trattoria Stella** (V. Alloro 104, tel. 091/6161136) is one of the best places to eat cheaply and well in the old district of Palermo, in the palm-filled courtyard of a seemingly abandoned palazzo. Penne with ricotta is a full meal. In Palermo's main open-air market, **Mercato della Vucciria** (between C. Vittorio Emanuele and P. San Domenico), watch boisterous guys holding aloft heads of lettuce and freshly butchered swordfish while you grab a picnic.

WORTH SEEING

Palermo's attractions are scattered among the labyrinthine streets and alleyways of its four medieval quarters. Near the waterfront, **Galleria Regionale di Sicilia** (V. Alloro 4; admission L2000; open Mon.–Sat. 9–1:30; also Tues. and Thurs. 3–5:30; Sun. 9–12:30) displays a spectacular collection of paintings and sculpture from the 11th to 17th centuries. The **Museo Internazionale delle Marionette** (V. Butera 1, tel. 091/328060; admission L5000; open weekdays 9–1 and 4–7, Sat. 9–1) has a spooky and vibrant display of thousands of puppets, marionettes, and shadow figures from around the world. Founded in 1143, **La Martorana** chapel (P. Bellini 3, off V. Maqueda; open Mon.–Sat. 9:30–1 and 3:30–5:30) was refurbished in 1688; the interior houses some 12th-century Byzantine mosaics.

Palazzo dei Normanni (P. Indipendenza), a former Saracen castle, was transformed into a royal palace by Sicily's 11th-century Norman king Roger de Hauteville. Today it houses the Sicilian Parliament and is closed to the public. Fortunately, its chapel, the **Cappella Palatina** (open weekdays 9–noon and 3–5; Sat. 9–noon; Sun. 9–10 and noon–1), remains open. Constructed between 1130 and 1143, every inch of the chapel's interior sparkles with brilliant Byzantine mosaics. To the right of the palace entrance, **San Giovanni degli Eremiti** (V. dei Benedettini 3; open Mon.–Sat. 9–1; Mon. and Thurs. also 3–5; Sun. 9–12:30) was designed by Norman-employed Arab architects and built on the foundations of a mosque in the 12th century. It's recognizable by its five pink domes, but the ruined cloisters and peaceful gardens inside are the real attraction. The imposing 12th-century **Duomo** (C. Vittorio Emanuele; open Mon.–Sat. 7–noon and 4–7, Sun. 8–1:30 and 4–7) is a grab bag of architectural styles. Inside, notice the numerous saint sculptures, the 15th-century portal, and the tombs of Roger II and Frederick II. The **Museo Archeologico Regionale** (P. Olivella 4, off V. Roma; admission L2000; open Mon.–Sat. 9–2; also Tues. and Fri. 3–7; Sun. 9–1) is one of the best archaeological museums in Italy, with artifacts dredged from the Mediterranean. The museum's most famous exhibits are in the **Salone di Selinunte.** From Stazione Centrale, take Bus 191, 107, or 122.

AFTER DARK

As in most of Italy, Palermo's bars tend to be fashionable spots for socializing rather than venues for unabashed boozing. Via Principe di Belmonte (off V. Roma) is lined with outdoor tables where you can gawk at the beautiful people. **Liberty Pub** (V. N. Cozzo 20, tel. 091/329385) is a cool place to grab a cheeseburger and a beer while contemplating the latest Italian disco hits.

TAORMINA

Taormina's meandering stairways, bougainvillea-covered palazzi, and dazzling vistas have seduced travelers since Goethe's time, but if you come during summer today, you can barely see the sights for all the video cameras. Once you escape the crowds, which is possible, wandering around the city is still enchanting. The buildings on Corso Umberto I between the **Porta di Mezzo** and **Porta Catania** date to the Middle Ages, though almost all have been rebuilt since World War II. The **Teatro Greco** (tel. 0942/23220; admission L2000; open daily 9–6:30) is the second-largest amphitheater in Sicily, famous for its breathtaking backdrop of Mt. Etna and the sea. First built during the 3rd century BC by the Greeks, the Romans added holding pens (for animals and warriors) and drainage gutters (for what was inside the animals and warriors). Perched above the city on Monte Tauro, **Castello di Taormina** (open daily 9 AM–1 hr before sunset) was once a proud fortress but is now home to a jumble of ruined

AEOLIAN ISLANDS

The seven Aeolian Islands (Isole Eolie) have been inhabited for more than 3,000 years, and the Aeolian natives have understandably developed a fearful reverence for their temperamental, volcanic homeland. The threat of fiery ruin has neither stemmed the tide of tourists, nor stopped the outcrop of ritzy beach and health resorts. With its hoppin' nightlife, resorts, and good hiking, Vulcano is a fun but expensive island—a definite day trip unless you're loaded with cash. Lipari, the main island, is a lot cheaper but more crowded, so you may have to fight for bed in summer. Panarea is one of the least touristed and most Grecian of the islands, with whitewashed houses and smooth black-sand beaches. If you're a snorkeling or scuba diving enthusiast, come hither. There's not much to do on Salina, Filicudi, or Alicudi except hike or bask in the sun. On Stromboli, you can hike to the calderas of active volcanoes. Ferries and hydrofoils to the islands leave most frequently from the town of Milazzo on Sicily's Tyrrhenian Coast. SNAV (hydrofoils only, V. Luciano Rizzo 14, Milazzo, tel. 090/9284509) and Siremar (both hydrofoils and ferries, V. dei Mille 33, Milazzo, tel. 090/9283242) are the two largest carriers, with offices on every island.

walls and wildflowers. To enjoy the water and sun you see around you, take a bus or moped to Giardini-Naxos, the Bay of Mazzarò, or the Gole dell'Alcantara, an inland gorge. The **ASST** (C. Umberto I, near Porta Messina, tel. 0942/23243; open Mon.–Sat. 8–2 and 4–7) has maps, lodging, and transportation information.

COMING AND GOING

The **Taormina-Giardini** station (tel. 1478/88088) sits uncharitably far below town, with trains to Siracusa (2 hrs, L11,700), Catania (45 min, L4200), and Messina (1 hr, L4200). Leave your luggage and hike 30 minutes up the hill or take a sporadic bus until 10:25 PM (until 7:30 PM Sun.). **SAIS** long-distance buses aren't as speedy or scenic as the train, but they drop you off in the center, serving Messina (1½ hrs, L5100) and Giardini-Naxos (20 min, L1500). The **bus terminal** is on Via Pirandello, five minutes downhill from Porta Messina. **California Motonoleggio** (V. Bagnoli Croce 86, tel. 0942/23769) rents Vespas at L47,000 a day with a credit-card deposit.

WHERE TO SLEEP

Consider making Taormina a day trip, or if you decide to stay, call ahead for reservations. The best deal in town is **Locanda Diana** (V. di Giovanni 6, tel. 0942/23898), which has homey rooms just a heartbeat from Piazza Vittorio Emanuele II. Some of the doubles (L40,000) have views. **Il Leone** (V. Bagnoli Croci 126, tel. 0942/21182) has tiny but functional rooms and a stunning rooftop terrace, with doubles at L60,000. At **Camping San Leo** (tel. 0942/24658; L7000 per person) sites fill up fast in summer because of the bayside setting, but it's also right near the highway. Take any bus between the train station and town, and ask driver to drop you halfway at "il camping."

FOOD

Most restaurants aren't as expensive as you might imagine, and many have pleasant outdoor terraces, but the town suffers from culinary mediocrity. The best out of dozens of similar eateries, **La Botte** (P. Santa Domenica, tel. 0942/24198) serves up *spaghettini alle sarde* (thin spaghetti with sardines) on its lantern-lit patio. Scrappy old Salvatore boasts of his *pennette alla vecchia Taormina* (pasta with pesto, cream, mushrooms, and garlic) at the restaurant under his hotel, **Il Leone** (*see* Where to Sleep, *above*). If you'd rather fend for yourself, head downtown to the inexpensive shops and fruit carts on the side streets leading to Via Roma.

SIRACUSA

During the glorious millennium of Greco-Roman domination, Siracusa rivaled Athens as one the most powerful and influential cities in the western world. The temples and amphitheaters built during this ancient age of splendor have been well maintained—add that to the temperate seaside climate, and you've got hordes of archaeology buffs and shutterbugs. But even the crowds can't completely diminish the allure of Siracusa. Though most of the population today lives in bulky concrete apartment blocks, if you cross the bridge to the island of **Ortigia** you'll find an interesting web of alleyways lined with Arab, Norman, Baroque, and 19th-century buildings. South of Siracusa you'll find great beaches, although in summer you'll probably have to pay a small access fee. For maps and lodging listings, head to **AAST** (V. Maestranza 33, 1½ blocks east of P. Archimede, tel. 0931/464255) or **APT** (V. San Sebastiano 45, tel. 0931/67710).

COMING AND GOING

Stazione Centrale (V. Francesco Crispi, NW of the mainland) serves Messina (3 hrs, L15,500), Catania (1½ hrs, L7200), and Taormina (2 hrs, L11,700). **AST** (Riva delle Poste 13, tel. 0931/462711) buses make trips to nearby towns like Noto (45 min, L2700) and Ragusa (2 hrs, L7500). **SAIS** buses (V. Trieste 28, tel. 0931/66710) leave one block behind Riva delle Poste, serving Palermo (4 hrs, L20,000).

WHERE TO SLEEP

Beds at **Ostello della Gioventù** (V. Siracusa 7, Belvedere, tel. 0931/711118), 6 km (4 mi) from town, cost L25,000, including breakfast. To get here, it's a 20-minute ride from Corso Umberto on Bus 9 or 11. **Hotel Centrale** (C. Umberto 141, tel. 0931/60528; doubles L40,000) is cheap and close to the station, with rooms that resemble monks' cells. **Hotel Milano** (C. Umberto 10, tel. 0931/66981; doubles L50,000), near the bridge to Ortigia, has rooms that are big and sparse.

FOOD

Corso Umberto on the mainland sports a handful of cheap take-away pizza joints. Every day until 10:30 PM, the salumeria **Cassia Ionario** (SE corner of P. Marconi) does a boisterous job of making panini. The place of the moment, **Spaghetteria do Scogghiu** (V. Domenico Scina 11) is friendly, chaotic, and authentic. Choose from 20 varieties of spaghetti, each only L6000. Bust out the velvet for **La Nottola** (V. Gargallo 61, off V. Maestranza, tel. 0931/60009; L15,000 cover), the elegant megaplex of disco, piano bar, jazz club, and restaurant in the former stables and courtyard of a centuries-old country estate.

WORTH SEEING

On Ortigia, the **Museo Nazionale di Palazzo Bellomo** (V. Capodieci 16, tel. 0931/69511; admission L2000; open Mon.–Sat. 9–2, Sun. 9–1) is filled with the usual hodgepodge of Madonnas and period costumes, but it also houses a masterpiece by Caravaggio. Ortigia's oblong central **Piazza del Duomo** sports several fine Baroque palazzi, including the 18th-century **Palazzo Beneventano del Bosco,** with an inviting courtyard and elegant winding staircase. The Duomo is an opulent concoction of Norman and Baroque buildings on the site of a 5th-century BC temple to Athena. Some of the original Doric columns are now incorporated into the church's walls.

The bulk of Greek Siracusa's artifacts are hidden among the towering apartment blocks of the mainland. The **Museo Archeologico** (V. Teocrito 66, tel. 0931/464022; admission L2000; open Tues.–Sat. 9–1, sometimes Sun. 9–1) documents the majority of Sicily's ancient Greek artifacts in painstaking detail. Across from the museum, the **Santuario della Madonnina** (tel. 0931/64077; open daily 6–12:30 and 4–7:30) holds a plaster bust of the Virgin Mary that supposedly cried for five miraculous days in 1953. The sanctuary itself is the massive, 262-ft upside-down ice cream cone you can see from all over the city.

The **Parco Archeologico** (admission L2000; open daily 9 AM–1 hr before sunset) is the only section of the ancient city—founded in 275 BC—left uninhabited since Roman times. The most famous ruin is the cave called the **Ear of Dionysius,** named for its lobe-shape entrance. Because of the cave's acoustics, Siracusa's most tyrannical leader could stand at the entrance to the cave and eavesdrop on the conversations of his enemies incarcerated inside. Inside the park you can also visit the **Teatro Greco** (Greek Theater), with room for 15,000 spectators, where Aeschylus presented his plays. Hold on to your ticket to gain

MONTE ETNA

With soft ridges and gradual slopes, snowcapped Mt. Etna only pretends to be sleeping. At 11,256 ft, the temperamental lout has exploded more than 140 times in recorded history. Despite the dangers, veteran travelers often say it's the highlight of a trip to Sicily. Getting to the top is a complex process, so ask for guidance at the helpful AAPIT office on track 1 of the Catania train station (tel. 095/531802) or the Grupo Guide Alpine (tel. 095/914141).

From Catania, a bus leaves at 8:15 for Nicolosi Nord. From here, you can reach the Rifugio Montagnola (8,200 ft) by foot (2 hrs), Jeep (15 min, L9500), or cable car (10 min, L14,000). Then the caldera is an additional two-hour hike. The easiest hiking path follows the roads that start behind the SITAS building in Nicolosi Nord. No matter when you make it up the volcano, it will be cold. Rifugio Montagnola rents puffy down jackets and uncomfortable rubber boots. Nothing really compares to staring into the crater's abyss after a long day's hike, but the privately owned Ferrovia Circumetnea (FCE) runs a 71-mi, four-hour circuit around the base of the mountain. You can catch the train from either end of its circuit in Catania or Giarre-Riposto, by train from Messina, or by bus from Taormina.

entrance to the adjacent **Anfiteatro Romano,** a 2nd-century arena carved almost entirely out of an existing hillside. From Corso Gelone or Corso Umberto, take Bus 1, 4, 5, 8, or 10W to the park's entrance.

AGRIGENTO

It is not too difficult to see how beautiful Agrigento must have been at one time. Built on a broad open field that slopes gently to the sun-baked Mediterranean, the Greek poet Pindar called ancient Akragas "the most beautiful city among mortals." What's left of the ancient city is called the **Valle dei Tempi,** a showpiece of temples erected to flaunt a victory over Carthage. Today these temples are considered to be, along with the Acropolis in Athens, the finest Greek ruins in the world. The medieval and modern city center of Agrigento is great for wandering, the views of the sunset over the Mediterranean are amazing, and the city is visitor-friendly, but besides the temples, there isn't much to keep you here. It's pretty much impossible to make in a day trip, however, because whether you come by bus or train, getting in and out of Agrigento is slow at best, and agonizing at worst.

COMING AND GOING

Agrigento's **Stazione Centrale** (P. Marconi, tel. 1478/88088) sits just downhill from Piazza Vittorio Emanuele. Trains head to Palermo (2 hrs, L11,700) and Ragusa (3½ hrs, L15,500; change at Canicatti). Agrigento's long-distance **bus station** (P. Fratelli Rosselli) is just east of Piazza Vittorio Emanuele II. **SAIS** (V. Ragazzi del '99 12, tel. 0922/595620) offers infrequent service to Catania (3 hrs, L6000; change at Canicatti). The most helpful **AAST** office (V. Cesare Battisti 15, tel. 0922/20454; open Mon.–Sat. 8:30–1:40 and 4–7) is in the center of town.

WHERE TO SLEEP AND EAT

Agrigento gets packed in summer—you must call ahead for a room. **Hotel Belvedere** (V. San Vito 20, tel. 0922/20051; doubles L60,000) has comfy double beds, clean bathrooms, and a rather-wilted, though lovely, garden, where you can drink a beer as evening rolls into dinnertime. Take Via Pirandello from Piazzale Aldo Moro to reach **Hotel Concordia** (P. San Francesco 11, tel. 0922/596266), the closest hotel to the train station. While small, the rooms are clean and comfortable (doubles L70,000), but ask for a room with a shower, because the communal bathroom doesn't have one.

Most of the restaurants in the center of town cater to tourists, so your best bet may be the grocery stores on the side streets below Via Atenea. You probably won't be the only foreigner at **Trattoria Black Horse** (V. Celauro 8, tel. 0922/23223), but the food is excellent. Sit at a quiet outdoor table and try an immense platter of roasted calamari. The menu changes according to what's fresh at **Trattoria La Forchetta** (P. San Francesco, tel. 0922/596266), but there's bound to be penne-with-something-good on the menu.

WORTH SEEING

The most interesting attraction in the medieval quarter is the 13th-century **Chiesa Santa Maria dei Greci,** which was built by the Normans on the site of a 5th-century BC Doric temple. Inside are some original columns and partially preserved 14th-century frescoes. You can see the **Valle dei Templi** from the train station. To get here, it's either an easy 40-minute walk (start below the train station on Via Crispi, then follow the signs) or a short ride on TUN Bus 1, 1/, 2, 2/, or 3 (L1000). On your way to the valley, stop by the **Museo Archeologico** (Contrada San Nicola, tel. 0922/49726; open daily 8–12:30) for a good overview of the site. If you head east at Piazzale dei Tempi, you'll see three of the major temples; the lesser ones are to the west. The 6th-century BC **Tempio di Ercole** (Temple of Hercules), the oldest structure in the valley, was dedicated to the favorite hero of the often-warring citizens of Akragas. Farther up Via Sacra is the 5th-century BC **Tempio di Concordia** (Temple of Concord), thought to be the best-preserved Greek temple in the world. The final and easternmost structure is the **Tempio di Giunone** (Temple of Juno), a 5th-century BC cleric temple. From here you can see all along the ruins, over the olive groves, and to the sea.

LUXEMBOURG

This morsel of land was conquered by just about every major power in European history before finally gaining independence in 1839. Since then, the people of Luxembourg have worked to create their own utopia in the heart of Europe. While favorable tax laws have transformed the capital into a center of international banking and finance, the country-side, with its tranquil valleys and charming villages, remains the kind of place where cars stop for pedestrians and stores close for a two-hour lunch. Usually overlooked as a travel destination, the Grand Duchy of Luxembourg is well worth a visit, with Roman villas, medieval castles, World War II monuments, excellent hiking, and mellow, meandering rivers easily explored in a kayak.

BASICS

MONEY

US$1 = 34 Luxembourg francs and 10 Luxembourg francs = US29¢. The Luxembourg franc (LF) is locked into the same exchange rate as the Belgian franc. All Belgian currency is accepted in Luxembourg, but Belgians are less keen on LFs. Banks, generally open weekdays 9–noon and 12:30–4:30, offer the best exchange rates, but the American Express office in Luxembourg City is also a good bet. In bigger cities you'll find ATMs that accept MasterCard, Visa, and bank cards on the Cirrus and PLUS systems.

HOW MUCH IT WILL COST • Luxembourg is a little more expensive than Belgium. If you don't eat at too many sit-down restaurants, you can get by on $45–$50 a day, maybe $10 less if you sleep in hostels and really scrimp. Gas and alcohol are less heavily taxed than elsewhere in Europe and are thus a comparative bargain.

GETTING AROUND

Train travel in Luxembourg is cheap because trips are always so short. Buy an **Oeko-Billjee** for 160LF at any train or bus station and you can travel all day on the country's trains and buses. When taking trains, make sure you validate your ticket at the orange box *before* you board. Eurailpasses and the Benelux Tourrail Pass (*see* Basics *in* Chapter 4) are also accepted on trains.

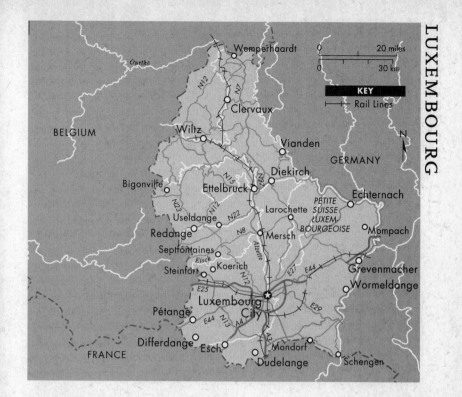

WHERE TO SLEEP

Hostels provide the cheapest bed-and-breakfast deals in Luxembourg (about 345LF; 425LF for non-members), and some occupy buildings of historical interest. There are 120 campgrounds in this Rhode Island–size country, many with scenic views. Hotel doubles with breakfast go for about 1,600LF; expect to pay about 200LF more for a room with a bath.

PHONES AND MAIL

Country code: 352. There are no area codes. Five-digit numbers are being phased out, and will be history by the fall of 1998. To make an old, five-digit number new, insert a zero between the 2nd and 3rd digits. The telephones and postal service in Luxembourg are efficient and reliable. Send mail at the ubiquitous yellow post boxes attached to walls in every city. Most post offices are open weekdays 9–noon and 2–5. Telephones take both phone cards and coins, but the smallest-value phone cards (available at post offices and train stations) cost 250LF, so use coins unless you plan to stay a while. To reach **AT&T** Direct Access[SM], dial 0800–0111 from any phone; for **MCI,** dial 0800–0112; and for **Sprint,** dial 0800–0115. A 10-minute call to the United States is 370LF, to Australia 560LF, and to the United Kingdom 200LF.

EMERGENCIES

The central emergency number is **112.**

LUXEMBOURG CITY

You once had to brave a shower of cannonballs and gunfire to enter this fortress. In recent years Luxembourg's tiny capital has thrown its doors wide open, attracting the world's major financial institutions as well as young Europeans coveting jobs and the country's high standard of living. Some of the European Union's major institutions are here, and well-heeled "Eurocrats" have helped drive up the cost of

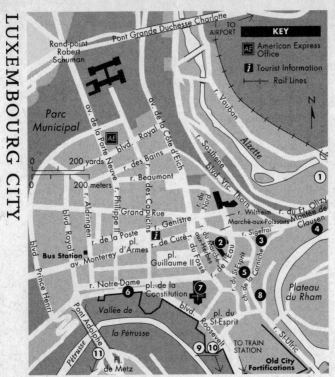

LUXEMBOURG CITY

KEY

- **AE** American Express Office
- **i** Tourist Information
- Rail Lines

Sights ●

Bock Casemates, **4**
Casino de Luxembourg, **6**
Cathédrale Notre-Dame, **7**
Eglise St-Michel, **3**
Grand Ducal Palace, **2**
Musée d'Histoire de la Ville de Luxembourg, **5**
Natur Musée au Grund, **8**

Lodging ○

Auberge de Jeunesse Luxembourg (HI), **1**
Italia, **11**
Le Papillon, **9**
Touring, **10**

living. Tourists will enjoy clean streets, restored historical sights, and pristine public squares edging up to the deep gorges that cut through the city. But Luxembourg City does have two big downers: expensive restaurants (finding a meal for less than 400LF is cause for celebration) and hills so steep that you'll wish you'd emptied half your backpack at home.

BASICS

The **Office National du Tourisme,** inside the train station, has free maps and tourist information for the entire country, and handles room reservations as well. *Gare Centrale, tel. 48–11–99. Open mid-July–Aug., daily 9–7, rest of year daily 9–noon and 2–6:30. A satellite office at Findel Airport offers the same services (open after flight arrivals).*

The **city office,** just 2 blocks east of the Aldringen bus depot in the old city, dispenses city information, helps with hotel reservations, and hands out free maps. *Pl. d'Armes, tel. 22–28–09. Open Apr.–Oct., Mon.–Sat. 9–7 and Sun. 10–6; shorter hrs off season.*

You'll find phones at the two main **post offices,** one near the train station (28 pl. de la Gare, tel. 4–08–81; open weekdays 6–7 and Sat. 6–noon), and the other in the city center (25 rue Aldringen, tel. 4–76–51; open weekdays 7–8 and Sat. 7–7). Poste restante goes to the city-center office; have it sent to Your Name, Poste Restante, L–1118 Luxembourg City, Luxembourg. The **American Express** office (34 av. de la Porte Neuve, tel. 22–85–55; open weekdays 9–5:30, Sat. 9:30–noon) makes hotel reservations, changes money, sells traveler's checks, and handles MoneyGrams.

COMING AND GOING

The travel-information booth at the train station, **Gare Centrale,** is open daily 4 AM–1 AM, and the exchange office (open weekdays 8:30 AM–9 PM, weekends 9–9) offers decent rates. Trains zip to Brussels (3 hrs, 782LF) almost every hour, and to Amsterdam (6 hrs, 1,900LF) and Paris (4 hrs, 1,484LF) less frequently. **CFL intercity buses** (tel. 49–24–24) leave from the **bus depot,** to the left as you exit the train station. Bus schedules are posted outside the depot.

Findel Airport (6 kms/4 mi from downtown) is where all those cheap Icelandair flights arrive. This is also the base of Luxair, the local airline, which flies to many European destinations. Bus 9 to the city center and train station costs 40LF.

GETTING AROUND

Luxembourg City is tiny, and if it were flat it would be easy to cover on foot. But just to make matters difficult, the city is built on four high plateaus overlooking steep gorges, at the bottom of which flow the scrawny Pétrusse and Alzette rivers. Take a bus if you're lugging a pack. All buses (except Bus 12) go from the train station to the main bus depot on rue Aldringen, in front of the central post office. You'll find maps detailing routes and hours at both the train station and the bus depot. Buses generally run 6 AM–10 PM and charge 40LF (plus an extra 40LF for large luggage). Dial 47–96–29–75 for bus information.

WHERE TO SLEEP

All but the most expensive hotels are near the train station. Generally speaking, a double without bath should cost about 1,700LF. Singles are rarely less than 1,150LF.

Le Papillon. Narrow, creaky stairs lead to rooms painted flamingo pink. There are only 10 rooms, so reserve ahead. Doubles, all with bath, go for 1,700LF. *9 rue Jean Origer, tel. 49–44–90. From Gare Centrale, right on av. de la Gare, left on rue Jean Origer.*

Touring. Charming Italian women run this hotel and the restaurant below. Rooms are large, and all were recently renovated. Doubles, some with bath, are 1,800LF. *4 rue de Strasbourg, tel. 48–46–29. From Gare Centrale, take av. de la Liberté, left on rue de Strasbourg.*

SPLURGE • Italia. This is a find: a former apartment house converted into hotel rooms, with some of the plaster details and cabinetry left in place. Rooms are solidly furnished and have tile bathrooms. Doubles start at 2,800LF. The downstairs restaurant is one of the best Italian eateries in the city—and there are many. *Rue d'Anvers 15–17, tel. 48–66–26, fax 48–08–07. From Gare Centrale, right on av. de la Gare, left on av. de la Liberté, left again on Pl. de Paris.*

> *So few outsiders speak Lëtzeburgesch, Luxembourg's native language, that residents have had to become multilingual. In addition to French, the official language, most people speak German and at least a bit of English.*

HOSTEL • Auberge de Jeunesse Luxembourg (HI). This major party zone is a short downhill hike from the city center. Unfortunately, the showers are an extra downhill hike to the basement. A pathetic breakfast (included in price) is served until 8:30, and dinner (260LF) is served at the in-house bar. Another bonus includes bike rental. Doubles cost 1,100LF; dorm beds 500LF (sheet rental 110LF), 415LF if you're under 26. Nonmembers pay 100LF more. Curfew is 2 AM. *2 rue du Fort Olizy, tel. 22–68–89, fax 22–33-60. From Gare Centrale, Bus 9 (tell driver where you're going). Reception open 1:30–7 and 7:30–10, lockout 10–1:30. Kitchen, laundry.*

CAMPING • Camping Kockelscheuer. This is the closest campground to the city, but it's still a bus ride away. Trailers get the nicest spots, while tents are crowded into an open, grassy area. Tent sites are 120LF plus 110LF per person, and you can launder your rags for 50LF. There's also a food store. *22 rte. de Bettembourg, tel. 47–18–15. From Gare Centrale, Bus 2 toward Kockelscheuer and tell driver where you're going (last bus 10:15 PM). Closed Nov.–Easter.*

FOOD

Hope you didn't actually want to eat in Luxembourg City. Natives will look dumbfounded if you ask about cheap restaurants, but don't despair—there's always pizza. Most restaurants are downtown near the place d'Armes and around the Gare Centrale. For something quick, try **Créole** (34 pl. de la Gare, across from train station, tel. 48–52–52), which has pizza by the slice for 75LF–95LF. Lots of little grocery stores dot the city: **Supermarché Primavera** (downstairs in Galleria Kons, across from station; open Mon.–Sat. 8–8, Sun. 8 AM–12:30 PM) has some good deals.

Ems. Across the street from the train station, this vinyl-booth joint draws a loyal crowd for its vast portions of mussels in a wine-and-garlic broth, accompanied by a cold, sharp, and inexpensive bottle of local white wine. *Pl. de la Gare 30, tel. 48–77–99. Closed Sat. lunch.*

Giorgio. Fun, laid-back waiters sing when they're in a good mood, which seems to be often. Pizza goes for 245LF, and pasta, piled high, goes for 290LF. *11 rue du Nord, 1 block north of Grand Rue, tel. 22–38–18. Closed Sun.*

Pizzeria Bacchus. This sleek, modern, almost art-deco eatery a few steps from the Grand Ducal Palace serves pizzas for 300LF. Grungy travelers may feel underdressed. *32 rue du Marché-aux-Herbes, tel. 47–13–97. Closed Mon.*

WORTH SEEING

One of the city's best attractions is the **Bock Casemates** (Montée de Clausen, tel. 22–28–09), a huge complex of tunnels, staircases, and gun turrets carved into the Bock, a rock promontory on the east side of town. Built during the 17th and 18th centuries, the casemates were used most recently as bomb shelters during the two world wars. About 17 km (11 mi) of tunnels are still intact, and you can explore some of them for 70LF. Near the Bock Casemates, the tiny **Eglise St-Michel** (rue Sigefroi; open daily 10–noon and 2–6) dates from the 11th century, but owes its present appearance to a restoration in 1688. Check out the baroque organ and the interesting altarpiece depicting the Assumption of the Virgin. The original half of the **Cathédrale Notre-Dame** (rue Notre-Dame; open daily 10–noon and 2–6) was built during the early 17th century, and the half with the extravagant altar was added in 1938; check out the shiny burial vault of the Grand Ducal family in the crypt. Nearby, the **Grand Ducal Palace** (rue du Marché-aux-Herbes), with its pointy turrets and gilded balconies, is a showpiece of Spanish Renaissance ornamentation.

The **Musée d'Histoire de la Ville de Luxembourg** (Luxembourg City Historical Museum) is an exciting addition to modern museum architecture (opened 1996). Its interactive, multimedia collection traces the development of the city over 1,000 years. Models of the city fortress at various stages of development are supplemented by 1,000 exhibits. The museum begins at ground level in four converted old town houses, then plunges down five levels to show the town's ancient stonework. A panoramic elevator provides a wonderful view of the ravine from the upper floors. *Rue du St-Esprit 14, tel. 22–90–50–1. Admission 150LF. Open Tues.–Sun. 10–6 (Thurs. until 8).*

CHEAP THRILLS

From the Bock Casemates follow signs for the **Wenzel Walk,** a self-guided tour (get the descriptive leaflet from the City Tourist Office) through the oldest part of the fortifications, once known as the Gibraltar of the North; keep an eye out for the turrets of the old city wall. The Luxembourg fortress and old town have been declared part of the World Heritage by UNESCO, and the tour is exceptionally well designed. The walk ends in a valley below the old city fortifications, where an elevator inside the cliff takes you back up to the city plateau; look for the ASCENSEUR sign. There are guided walks Saturday at 3 PM in summer (240LF); call 4796–2709 for reservations. If you're up for more walking, stay below the city and continue into the **Vallée de la Pétrusse.** Nestled between high cliffs and blanketed with willow and cherry trees, this is one of Europe's most beautiful city parks. Spend some time exploring it; finding your way in and out is half the fun.

AFTER DARK

Melusina (rue de la Tour Jacob 145, tel. 43–59–22) is basically a disco, with pop and techno on weekends, but it also draws aspiring local musicians and touring guests for the occasional jazz concert. Grab a beer and climb onto the bunk bed at **The Playground** (8 rue Sigefroi, tel. 22–12–36), where baby pictures of the regulars decorate the walls. **Café des Artistes** (Montée du Grund, tel. 46—13–27) is a friendly old pub where a mostly middle-aged clientele makes the chandeliers ring on sing-along evenings.

DIEKIRCH

To reach the town of Diekirch, take the train to Ettelbruck (35 mins, 120LF) and continue by bus (5 min, 40LF) or walk the 5-km (3-mi) path along the Sûre River. Diekirch has been inhabited since before Roman times, and you can still see the remains of early civilizations. Parts of the **Vieille Eglise St-Laurent** (pl. de la Libération; not to be confused with the modern church of the same name) date back to the 1st century AD; ask to be taken down to the church's 1,000-year-old crypt, which holds a collection of sarcophagi—one of them still contains an intact skeleton, resting in full view. Also check out the delicate mosaic floors of a 3rd-century Roman villa at the **Musée Mosaïques Romaines** (pl. Guillaume II; admission 20LF). The oldest monument in town is a dolmen (a small Stonehenge-like monument) called the **Deiwelselter.** Nobody knows for sure why it was built, so decide for yourself whether it was a Celtic sacrificial altar or just the work of stone-age pranksters. To find it, follow signs for hiking path D from route de Larochette in the south of town. The town's **tourist office** (1 Esplanade, tel. 80–30–23; open daily 10–noon and 2–4), across from the *newer* Eglise St-Laurent, hands out free maps and sells detailed hiking guides (80LF).

WHERE TO SLEEP AND EAT

Doubles range from 1,200LF to 2,200LF at the centrally located **Hotel Ernzbach** (av. de la Gare 4, tel. 80–36–36, fax 80–28–88). Nearby, at the Tivoli (av. de la Gare 53, tel. 80–88–51), a pizza is yours for 240LF.

VIANDEN

Despite the hordes of tourist who pour in to see Vianden's beautiful hilltop castle, cobblestone streets, meandering river, and lush forests, the town manages to retain an authentic feel. Free maps and information on sights are available at the **tourist office** (37 rue de la Gare, tel. 8–42–57; open daily 9:30–noon and 2–6). Buses run from Ettelbruck to Vianden daily (30 min, 80LF). The **bus stop** is just south of town on rue de la Gare.

The big attraction here is the **Château de Vianden** (tel. 8–41–08; admission 120LF, 100LF students; open daily 10–6), visible from all over town. Restorations completed in 1983 added facilities for exhibitions and concerts while preserving the pile's medieval appearance. Your entrance fee buys you a small English guidebook to the entire building, including the colorfully painted chapels and the tapestried Count's Hall. For a dramatic aerial view of the town and château, take a ride on the **chairlift** (tel. 8–43–23; 90LF one-way) from 39 rue du Sanatorium.

Yes, steak cheval on your menu does mean horse meat. It's a regional specialty that usually costs 500LF.

WHERE TO SLEEP AND EAT

The upbeat **HI hostel** (3 Montée du Château, tel. 8–41–77; dorm beds 345LF) is about a 20-minute uphill hike north of the bus station; lockout is from 10 to 5. **Camping Op dëm Deich** (tel. 8–43–75), 1 km (½ mi) south of town on the Our River, charges 390LF for two people with a tent. Campground amenities are minimal; you'll have to walk into town for food.

Heintz. The hallways in this four-generation family inn are filled with local antiques, the rooms with oak furniture. This was the site of a major World War II snafu: U.S. intelligence, billeted in the hotel, were informed of a German buildup in December 1944, but before the report had reached Eisenhower, the Battle of the Bulge had begun. Vianden was the last bit of Luxembourg territory to be liberated a second time. Doubles from 1,700LF to 2,800LF. *Grand-rue 79, in the center of town, tel. 8–46–16, fax 84–92–30.*

Most restaurants lie along rue de la Gare or the Grand Rue. If you avoid the overpriced hotel restaurants, you can find meals for 300LF–350LF. At **City Corner** (1 rue du Vieux Marché, tel. 8–47–97), the menu includes everything from sandwiches and omelettes to finer and more expensive French fare. You'll fork over about 380LF for a meal. For about 20LF more, you can eat on a terrace overlooking the river at **Café du Pont** (near the bridge). **Cheng Bao** (rue Victor Hugo 13, tel. 8–43–48) features Shanghai cuisine and Mongolian barbecue for 250LF–500LF.

ECHTERNACH

This tiny town in eastern Luxembourg is 1,300 years old, having been founded in 968 by the Anglo-Saxon missionary Willibrord. Although bombed heavily during the 1944 Battle of the Bulge, it has since been so well restored that few scars remain. Dominating the town is the rebuilt **Basilique de St-Willibrord**; in the crypt below, you can see the neo-Gothic tomb of the basilica's patron saint. To this day, thousands of people gather for a unique dancing procession in his honor on the Tuesday after Pentecost. Another worthy religious sight is the **Eglise Sts-Pierre-et-Paul,** on a hill in the center of town. Parts of this church date from the 7th century, and some remains even go back to the Roman era, when a fort stood on the site. At the ruins of the **Villa romaine,** try to imagine the feasts and orgies that once took place here—you showed up 2,000 years too late. The ruins are a 10-minute walk south of town: Follow the signs for walking path R, which veers off from rue de Luxembourg. If you're feeling lazy, lounge in the lush **Parc** at the east end of town; here you can sit on the banks of the Sûre and literally throw a stone across the river into Germany.

The helpful **tourist office** (Porte St. Willibrord, tel. 72–02–30), across from the basilica, sells maps (80 LF) of hiking trails in the Petite Suisse and Basse-Sûre regions of Luxembourg. With rocky cliffs and gorges, castles, cool streams, and roaming deer, these forested regions to the west of town are excellent hiking turf.

COMING AND GOING

CFL buses serve the town daily from Luxembourg City (1 hr, 160LF). Echternach's **bus station** (tel. 72–90–09) is in the northwest corner of town, within easy walking distance of everything. Rent mountain bikes (600LF per day) at **Irisport** (31 rte. de Luxembourg, tel. 72–00–86).

WHERE TO SLEEP AND EAT

All beds in town are just five minutes from the bus stop. The **HI hostel** (9 rue Andre Duchscher, tel. 72–01–58; beds 345LF, 425LF nonmembers) is in a cool stone building just off the main square; lockout is 10–5. The rooms at **Hotel Aigle Noir** (54 rue de la Gare, tel. 72–03–83) have wooden floors; doubles cost 1,350LF–1,500LF. **Camping Officiels** (rte. de Diekirch, tel. 72–02–72), south of town on the River Sûre, charges 360LF for two people with a tent.

Rue de la Gare and the area around the place du Marché brim with restaurants. On the terrace of **Beim Lange Veit** (pl. du Marché 39, tel. 72–00–81), next to the 15th-century arcaded law courts, you have a ringside seat on the busy, attractive square; snacks start at 320LF. Another good deal is at **La Coppa** (22 rue de la Gare, tel. 72–73–24), where you can sip a tropical cocktail (150LF) while scarfing a giant *salade mexicaine* (330LF). For your hikes in the surrounding area, grab some groceries from **Match** on rue de Luxembourg.

MOROCCO 17

S ix dynasties, two protectorates, scads of foreign powers, and two kings have left Morocco with a remarkably intricate cultural heritage. The population is largely Muslim, but other faiths are also practiced, and cathedrals and synagogues dot the urban landscape. While much of northern Morocco bustles with tourism and trade, the south is home to nomadic Berbers, the indigenous Moroccans who were assimilated into Arab tribes during the 11th century. Today, 60% of Moroccans claim Berber heritage, and three main dialects of the Berber language are still spoken. The country's human and physical diversity is astounding, ranging from white Andalusian villages to pink Portuguese ramparts; from the dramatic Todra and Dades gorges to the ice-tipped peaks of the High Atlas Mountains; and from silent, rose-hued expanses of the Sahara to undiscovered surfing beaches on the Atlantic coast.

Though all of this is a boon for the hardy budget traveler, there *is* a downside—in a word, Tangier. Almost all of the difficulties tourists suffer in Morocco occur in this notorious northern city. Hasslers, hustlers, faux guides, con men, officials, and "friends" send many visitors scurrying back to Spain. But if you head south immediately, you'll find an enormously different Morocco. Long popular with tourists, the imperial cities of Fès and Marrakech provide a necessary reprieve, as well as a wealth of Islamic architecture and dazzling street scenes. As you negotiate the serpentine byways of medieval medinas, you'll hear the call to prayer echoing from mosques, and you'll smell everything from the fresh scent of mint, sold by the armful, to the regal indifference of a herd of camels roaming unattended by the side of the road.

King Hassan II's ancestors, the 'Alawites, who trace their lineage back to the prophet Mohammed, have ruled as sultans of Morocco for more than 300 years. Hassan's father, Sultan Mohammed V, dubbed himself king in 1956, when the state won its independence from France and Spain; since then, the king and his son have been virtually deified. Today, Hassan II is "commander of the faithful," head of the army, unchallenged big cheese of the government, and all-around nice guy; you'll see his picture hanging in nearly every Moroccan business.

Poised precariously between Middle Eastern politics and the tumultous Western Sahara, and tied to the United States—and, controversially, Israel—Morocco is a nation of many contradictions. Today, Morocco is attempting (unsuccessfully) to join the EU and struggling to boost tourism. There has been some discussion about building a bridge from Morocco to Spain, but until then Morocco is a world— perhaps a century—away from Europe.

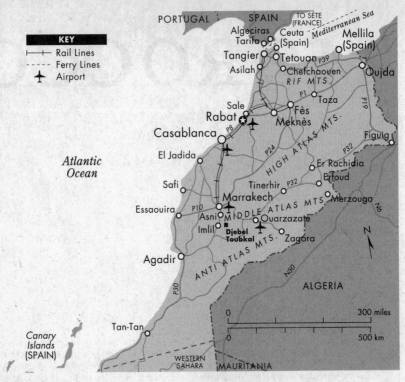

KEY
├┼─┼ Rail Lines
------ Ferry Lines
✈ Airport

BASICS

MONEY

US$1 = 8.61 dirhams and 1 dirham = 12¢. The dirham (dh) is divided into 100 centimes. Credit cards (Visa, MasterCard, American Express), Eurocheque traveler's checks, and, increasingly, American Express traveler's checks are accepted at upscale hotels and restaurants and at most expensive shops, though some will charge *you* the 5%–6% transaction fee. Pay in cash whenever possible, as credit-card fraud is a problem here.

When exchanging currency, stick to banks—they offer the government-set rate and don't charge commissions. In big cities, exchange windows at the ubiquitous Banque Marocaine du Commerce Extérieur (BMCE) are open daily 8–8. ATMs at larger banks (Banque Al-Maghrib, BMCE, Banque Populaire) usually accept Visa, Cirrus, and sometimes Plus, and the rates (including those for cash advances) are often more favorable than those for exchanging checks. Try to spend all your dirhams before leaving Morocco; to reconvert them into your own currency, you'll have to show original exchange receipts, and even then you can only exchange up to 5,000dh. Outside Morocco, you can't exchange dirhams at all.

HOW MUCH IT WILL COST • Compared to Europe, Morocco is dirt cheap. The price of souvenirs is negotiable (vendors usually accept 20%–40% of the original asking price), and innkeepers will sometimes cut you deals. Simple hotel doubles start at 60dh, beds in hostels at about 25dh, but lodging prices can jump 40%–50% in July and August and around Christmas and Easter. At restaurants, cheap entrées cost about 15dh–25dh. Morocco's trains are inexpensive even without a rail pass, and travel will be much cheaper here than in Europe even if you lay down a few extra dirhams for a *grand taxi* (*see* Getting Around, *below*).

VISA REQUIREMENTS

North Americans and Europeans (except for Dutch and Belgian citizens) can stay for up to 90 days without a visa. To stay longer, reset the timer by going to Spain or Gibraltar for a few days and, to be safe, reentering at a different border post; or inquire at a police station about a residency permit.

COMING AND GOING

BY FERRY • From the Spanish port of **Algeciras,** the ferry to Tangier (2½ hrs, 3,150 Spanish ptas) is ultimately more convenient and comfortable—even though it takes longer and is more expensive—than the ferry to the Spanish-owned port of **Ceuta** (1½ hrs, 2,000 Spanish ptas), from which you have to take a local bus to the Moroccan border, a taxi to Tetouan, and another bus if you want to hook up with Morocco's train system. Change money on board before docking in Tangier. Once you disembark, head next door to the train station, where regular and overnight trains can get you (unscathed and unhustled) into Marrakech or Rabat that day or the next morning. Another good thing about the Tangier ferry: Inter-Rail holders (but *not* Eurailpass holders) receive a 30% discount. For more information on ferry companies *see* Coming and Going *in* Tangier, *below.*

BY PLANE • **Royal Air Maroc** (**RAM**) (tel. 212/750–6071 or 800/344–6726) has weekly flights from New York to Casablanca; the basic round-trip fare is $1,160, but prices fluctuate seasonally and youth fares are available. RAM also has round-trip flights to Casablanca from Paris ($720), Madrid ($477), and London ($796).

Remember to watch all transactions carefully. Tourist-industry proprietors in Morocco are not yet famous for their honesty.

GETTING AROUND

Public transportation is cheap, even if you spend a few extra dirhams on first-class upgrades. Trains cost slightly more than buses (especially on long-distance trips), but they're often faster and offer more legroom. Trains, however, travel only from Tangier to Asilah and Casablanca/Rabat, and from Casablanca to Fès and Marrakech. For all other routes take a bus or, for about 15% more, a *grand taxi* (collective taxi). The latter are privately owned Mercedes that travel between major (and not-so-major) towns for a sometimes negotiable fee, and they're faster and more comfortable than trains. To find *grands taxis,* look for clusters of white Mercedes at vaguely defined "stands."

BY BUS • **CTM,** the national bus company, has regular service to larger towns. Buses are relatively comfortable and fast; the slightly more expensive deluxe coaches offer air conditioning and badly dubbed American films. Buses run by **private lines** aren't air-conditioned, but they're usually 10%–15% cheaper and more of an adventure. Some differences between the two: (1) While CTM usually indicates when buses are full, private lines will gladly sell you a spot *in* the aisle, and (2) While CTM charges only a small baggage fee (2dh–4dh per bag), private lines usually demand 5dh–10dh per bag just to open the storage compartment and watch you stuff it in yourself. Your bags are safe once they're in the compartment; just *do not* give them to anyone but a uniformed (blue coat) attendant. Buy tickets at the station's *guichet* (ticket office)—get there three–four hours early for popular CTM routes—or on board (private lines only).

BY TAXI • Six-passenger **grands taxis** are ideal for short treks between towns. Ask any local to point you toward a stand. If you hail a taxi on the street, you may get a lower fare than at stands, where drivers conspire to secure the highest fares for their colleagues. *Grands taxis* generally follow specific routes, so for longer journeys you may have to change cars. The price should be the same regardless of the number of passengers, but make it clear that you want to pay for only *one* seat in the taxi. Check at your hotel or compare with bus fares to estimate a fair price to your destination. If there are no Moroccans in your taxi, agree on the price before leaving; otherwise, wait until arrival and pay what the locals pay. *Grands taxis* usually fill up and depart in about 15 minutes, though occasionally you'll have to wait two–three hours. There's no need to tip drivers or pay for luggage. The smaller **petits taxis** can carry as many as three passengers on trips within a city's limits. Most rides are 15dh–20dh; ask the driver to turn on the meter, or negotiate the price in advance.

BY TRAIN • Second-class is the most popular way to travel on **ONCF,** the national rail company, but first-class offers air conditioning for only a few dollars more. For long trips, consider paying the 50dh–93dh supplement for a sleeper; these cabins lock from the inside, and the entire couchette section is locked with a chain and padlock and guarded by a full-time attendant. This attendant (and no one else) will take your ticket at the start of the trip and return it at the end. If you prefer traveling with families and their livestock, get a spot in E (*économique*) class. Trains denoted "*rapide*" cost one-third more than regular tickets but aren't really so rapid. Purchase tickets (several days ahead for popular routes) at the station's *guichet*; otherwise you'll probably be charged a 10% supplement for buying them on board. Also remember that *only* InterRail passes are accepted on Moroccan trains.

WHERE TO SLEEP

Some Moroccan **hotels** are government-regulated (*classé,* or classified), but most are of the cheaper, *nonclassé* (nonclassified) sort. The latter, typically found in a town's medina (old quarter), are either great finds (sunny, clean, and charming) or utter disasters (dirty and vermin-ridden, with atrocious plumbing); you can always ask to see a room before you sign on the dotted line. Across the board, sinks and toilets (Turkish-style) in *nonclassé* hotels are inadequate, and hot water is rare; but many have ter-races (20dh) where you can sleep under the stars on sweaty summer nights. *Nonclassé* rates may rise sharply during peak periods (July, August, Christmas, and Easter). *Classé* hotels, listed at tourist offices and often on city maps sold at kiosks, are generally twice as expensive as the others, but you're paying for cleanliness, superior plumbing, and linens. Many also offer laundry services (open to non-guests as well), which may come in handy, as you won't find any laundromats around; for only 15dh–20dh, the hotel's maid might hand-wash your clothes. Don't be afraid to ask. Morocco's HI-affiliated **hostels** cost 10dh–25dh per night—have your HI card handy or fork over the 3dh–5dh surcharge for nonmembers. Campers will pay 10dh per person plus 10dh per tent to stay at simple **campgrounds,** about twice that to camp at fancier places with swimming pools and nightclubs.

FOOD

Though Moroccan restaurants cater to tourists, they do serve fairly authentic dishes. Look for *tajine,* a sweet-and-spicy vegetable-and-meat stew; *harira,* a thick, chickpea-based soup with beans and a bit of meat thrown in; *brochettes,* small pieces of skewered steak; *kefta,* balls of spicy ground meat; and grilled *poulet* (chicken), *viande* (beef), or *agneau* (lamb). A staple Moroccan dish is *couscous,* a bowl of steamed semolina grain, onions, beans, and other vegetables, often topped with meat. Vegetarians should stick with veggie tajine, vegetable couscous, and bean soups prepared without meat—ask for your food *sans viande.* Other veggie options include salads, *leben* (a yogurt drink), and munchies like olives, almonds, dates, carefully washed fruit, and French-style bread and pastries. For bottled water, request a brand like Sidi Ali or Sidi Harazem. The cheap food stalls in the souks (markets) are pretty safe—if food is lukewarm, not thoroughly cooked, or smells off, try the next stall. To tip, just round up; in more expensive, Western-style places, add 10%.

BUSINESS HOURS

Moroccan shops, bazaars, and banks are open weekdays 9–noon and 2:30–6; many close on Friday afternoon. Restaurants often close from 3–6. Tourist sights are open daily, except for museums (closed Tuesday) and some houses of worship (closed Friday for prayer).

FESTIVALS AND HOLIDAYS

The most important holiday on the Moroccan calendar is the month-long **Ramadan,** when eating, drink-ing, and smoking are forbidden during daylight hours. (Between sunset and dawn, the country goes wild.) Other holidays are the feast-filled **Mouloud,** the birthday of the prophet Mohammed, usually cel-ebrated in September or October, and **Aïd el Kebir** (around June), which is followed shortly by **Moharem,** the Muslim New Year. The best and biggest event of the year is Marrakech's tourist-oriented **Folklore Festival** (early June), which draws performers from around the country; book a room weeks in advance.

VISITOR INFORMATION

Most towns have at least one tourist office, called either **Syndicat d'Initiative** or **ONMT** (Office National Marocain de Tourisme); some towns have both. Each has a stash of cheesy brochures and vague maps, and a French- and Arabic-speaking staff (some also speak a little English) who can set you up with offi-cial tour guides or refer you to hotels that supply them.

PHONES

Country code: 212. For domestic operator assistance, dial 16. Ten-minute local calls from pay phones cost about 1.75dh. Some pay phones take only phone cards, which are sold at **PTT** (post and tele-phone) offices; a 50-unit card costs 68.50dh and buys you 500 minutes of local phone time, or one minute to the United States. *Do not* buy phone cards from hustlers waiting by the phone booths. When-ever possible, use the more modern pay phones at the **Téléboutique** phone centers. PTT offices (found in Rabat and most other large cities) are the most convenient places to make long-distance calls. For direct and collect calls, write down your name and the phone number, city, and country you want to call, hand it in at the counter, and wait (anywhere from 10 to 45 minutes) until your name is called. In larger cities, some PTT offices are open 24 hours. To call long-distance from pay phones, dial 00, wait for the tone, then dial the country code and number. Per-minute rates are about 70dh to the United States and Canada and about 40dh to western Europe. You can also reach **AT&T** Direct Access[SM] (tel. 002–11–0011), **MCI** (tel. 002–11–0012), or **Sprint** (tel. 002–11–0014) for collect and credit-card calls to the United States.

MAIL

Morocco's generally efficient postal system will get your letters to North America for about 10dh and to Europe for about 5dh; postcards are 2dh less. Stamps are sold at post offices (open weekdays 8–noon and 3–6:30) and at some *tabacs* (tobacco shops). Travelers can receive mail at larger hotels and main post offices. For the latter, have mail addressed to Your Last Name (underlined), First Name, Poste Restante, PTT Centrale, City name, Morocco. Postal codes are unnecessary.

CRIME AND PUNISHMENT

Smoking *kif* (a hash derivative, a.k.a. hash, *chocolaté*, or *parfumé*) is a widespread pastime among Moroccans, who just offer a small bribe if the police even bother to notice. However, tourists caught with drugs are in a much worse situation, facing a definite fine and possible jail time. Dealers sometimes double as police informers; in some cases, after you're arrested, the *kif* is returned to the dealer for resale to another foreign-looking stooge. In 1996, the government aggressively cracked down on people (tourists *and* Moroccans) smuggling hash into Europe, so don't be stupid—leave it in Morocco.

Moroccan men sometimes hold hands or kiss in public, but this reflects only fraternity; gays are not open about their sexuality in Morocco. Foreign men traveling alone are often presumed to be looking for male prostitutes. You may be propositioned.

EMERGENCIES

For an **ambulance,** dial 15; for emergency **police** action, dial 19. You'll find pharmacies in every town, but only in larger cities are they open 24 hours. If you somehow land in jail or a hospital, immediately call your local consulate (*see* Casablanca, Rabat, and Tangier, *below*); the staff can arrange local assistance and contact someone back home.

LANGUAGE AND CULTURE

Morocco's official language is Arabic, though most people also speak French. Three Berber dialects prevail in much of rural Morocco, and Spanish is widely spoken in Tangier and Tetouan. English is becoming more common, but most Moroccans truly enjoy hearing Westerners grapple with their native tongue. Some handy Arabic phrases are *as-salaamu alaykoom,* a hello that is answered with *wa alaykoom-assalaam*; *la bas* (a less formal hello); *m'aslamah* (goodbye); *'afaak* (please); *shookrun* (thank you); *na'am* (yes); *lah* (no); *smahh leeya* (excuse me); *bee-shahhal . . .?* (how much is . . .?); *wash 'and kum . . .?* (do you have . . .?); *fain . . .?* (where . . .?), as in *fain mir had?* (where is the bathroom?); *tatakalem ingleezee?* (do you speak English?), and *ma afham* (I don't understand). The common expression *inshallah* (if God wills it) can mean "maybe" or "I hope." Other terms you'll hear are *medina qedima,* referring to the oldest part of a town, usually composed of winding alleyways and tightly packed shops and apartments; and *ville nouvelle,* the "new city," built by the occupying colonial power (France), with wide streets, banks, and big hotels. Sights include the *kasbah* (fortress or castle), *bab* (gate or archway), *souk* (market), and *medersas* (Koranic schools housing students, attached to a mosque).

Except on the beach, long pants are a good idea for both sexes. When visiting mosques, dress according to Islamic custom: Men should wear long sleeves and pants, and women must wear long sleeves and pants or a long skirt (ankle-length) and must cover their hair. Although many Moroccans drink, alcohol is forbidden to Muslims, and some medinas are officially dry. Most upscale hotels and restaurants stock beer for foreigners, and every ville nouvelle has bars and liquor stores; still, you'll want to be sensitive about drinking around Moroccans. Also keep in mind that in Morocco the left hand is used in the toilet, *not* for eating or shaking hands.

WOMEN TRAVELERS

Foreign women have a tarnished reputation here. Be forewarned: If you go somewhere alone with a Moroccan man, onlookers will imagine the worst, and you may be hassled. To avoid harassment, wear long pants and long sleeves; the next-best thing is a long skirt. Less bundling is necessary in a city's ville nouvelle and in resort towns, and swimsuits are okay on the beach. If you get caught in a sticky situation, yelling in the presence of many bystanders will usually bring assistance.

STAYING HEALTHY

You don't need any inoculations to visit Morocco. The only truly dangerous water comes from streams and still lakes or pools, which are often infected with harmful bacteria. Tap water is quite safe in big cities, but elsewhere it may raise hell in your stomach; protect yourself by drinking and brushing your teeth only with bottled water (make sure the bottle is sealed and wrapped in plastic). A touch of diarrhea may be inevitable if you drink tap water, eat at food stalls, or ingest unwashed or prepeeled fruits and vegetables. The best cure is to consume only yogurt, bread, plenty of water, and mint tea—or do what the Berbers do and down a hearty cup of opium tea (available at any grocery store). Bringing along rehydration tablets is also a good idea.

Moroccan summers are hot as hell. You must drink *a lot* of water to avoid heatstroke, which sometimes causes only headaches and nausea but can also result in death. Always carry water with you when traveling by train or bus; it will be overpriced on board. If you stay in campgrounds, wear sandals in the showers to avoid picking up fungal infections from the wet, dirty floors. Morocco's pharmacies are usually well-stocked, and every marketplace has *souks* dedicated to herbal cures that Moroccans swear by. Large hotels and tourist offices sometimes provide lists of English-speaking doctors.

TANGIER

"Tangier is a foreign land if ever there was one," wrote Mark Twain upon his visit to Morocco's most notorious city, and indeed it still feels that way after the short ferry ride from Spain. With its lucid skies; azure bay; long, lovely beach; and swell views across the Strait of Gibraltar, this city has played a fascinating role in modern Western culture. Tangier entered the European imagination in the years following 1912, when the major European powers settled all claims on its strategic importance by granting it international status (i.e., it was now *everyone's* doormat). Until Moroccan independence in 1956, Tangier was home to an unprecedented gay scene, shadowy financiers, musicians, artists, and expatriate writers— Tennessee Williams, Paul Bowles, William Burroughs, and Edith Wharton, to name a few.

Amazing though Tangier is, you may be better off catching the first train out of here; the Morocco you came for lies farther south. The hustlers at Tangier's train and ferry stations are among Morocco's most intimidating—reports of travelers being kicked, punched, spit on, and even threatened with knives are common. From the moment you step off the ferry, prepare to be hassled by unofficial guides and "friends" intent on showing you the medina, their favorite restaurant, or a carpet shop. If you walk purposefully and avoid eye contact, you may be left alone. Still, Tangier does have a lot to offer those visitors who can endure the initial hassles of arriving. Its stunning kasbah and dizzying medina are worth a peek, so if you've got some time to kill, grab a map and a bottle of water, and explore.

To reach the city from the waterfront avenue d'Espagne, walk northwest on Zankat Salah Eddine el Ayoubi. You'll emerge onto **Grand Socco** (also called place de 19 Avril 1947), once Tangier's central market. On the square's east side are two arches, and between them is a narrow, crowded lane, rue es Siaghin, which curves right toward the 19th-century market **Souk el-Dakhil** (sometimes referred to as the Petit Socco). The left-hand arch, Bab Fahs, opens onto rue d'Italie. About (328 ft) beyond the arch, you'll reach rue de la Kasbah; follow the signs up this street to the town's former center of government, the **place de la Kasbah** (you'll go through a tunnel, a small square, and a second tunnel, then up a steep hill). If you continue up avenue Mohammed Tazi, you'll find the **Forbes Museum** (tel. 09/93–36–06; admission 10dh; open daily 9–1 and 3–7), where 115,000 little tin soldiers quietly fight world history's biggest battles. The museum's gardens are beautiful. To the left of the square is the gate **Bab Hahr,** which has amazing views of Spain's coast. Hidden in an opposite corner of the square is the entrance to the old **Dar el Makhzen** (Royal Palace), which now houses a **museum** (tel. 09/93–20–97; admission 10dh; open Wed.–Mon., 9–1 and 3–6) with pottery, clothing, daggers, and a room of archaeological finds from the Roman site of Volubilis, near Meknès. **Rue des Almohades,** a popular shopping street, snakes into the medina from the Hotel Mauritania's entrance on the Souk el-Dakhil. As a rule, save your dirhams for cheaper, better-quality goods in cities further south.

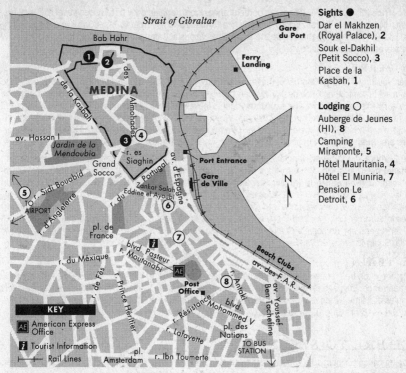

Sights ●
Dar el Makhzen
(Royal Palace), **2**
Souk el-Dakhil
(Petit Socco), **3**
Place de la
Kasbah, **1**

Lodging ○
Auberge de Jeunes
(HI), **8**
Camping
Miramonte, **5**
Hôtel Mauritania, **4**
Hôtel El Muniria, **7**
Pension Le
Detroit, **6**

BASICS

VISITOR INFORMATION

The friendly staff at **ONMT** speaks English and has mediocre maps. For better city maps, go to the large tobacco shop (look for the white sign with three blue circles) across the street from the central post office (*see* Phones and Mail, *below*). *29 blvd. Pasteur, tel. 09/93–82–39. Open weekdays 8:30–noon and 2:30–6:30.*

Ask about **American Express** services at Voyages Schwartz; otherwise, cash your checks at the BMCE up the street (open 8:30–2:30 in summer, 8–3 in winter). *54 blvd. Pasteur, tel. 09/93–34–59. Open weekdays 9–12:30 and 3–7, Sat. 9–12:30.*

CONSULATES

United Kingdom. *Rue d'Angleterre, tel. 09/93–58–95. Open summer, Mon.–Thurs. 9–noon and 2–5, Fri. 9–noon; off season, Mon.–Thurs. 9–12:30 and 2:30–5:30, Fri. 9–noon.*

PHONES AND MAIL

Central post office. *33 blvd. Mohammed V, tel. 09/93–25–18. Open weekdays 8–6:30. Phone room around corner open 8 AM–9 PM.*

COMING AND GOING

Most of Tangier is walkable, but if you're foot-weary or headed to the bus station, hail a blue *petit taxi*. Most trips cost 15dh–20dh.

BY BUS

The **main bus station** (Sahat Al Jamia Al Arabia, tel. 09/94–66–82) is 2 km (1⅓ mi) from the city center (7dh by taxi). Luggage storage is 2.50dh. CTM buses leave from both the main bus terminal and the

CTM office (tel. 09/93–24–15) at the port entrance. From Tangier, daily CTM buses travel to Fès (6 hrs, 79dh), Marrakech (12 hrs, 160dh), Casablanca (6 hrs, 100dh), Rabat (5 hrs, 80dh), and Tetouan (1¼ hrs, 16dh). Private companies serve the same destinations at competitive prices; get to the station early and ask at the various windows.

BY FERRY

When you buy a ticket in Morocco, the ferry company will give you a departure form, which you need to fill out and take to the police desk. This can proceed at whatever pace the attendant wants. Get to the ferry early in case of delays, and expect the boat to leave late anyway. Upon inspection of your form and passport, you'll be allowed through customs. When planning your trip, remember that Morocco sets its clocks two hours behind Spain in summer, one hour behind the rest of the year. All arrivals and departures are listed in Moroccan times; pick up ferry schedules at most travel agencies.

The 2½-hour trip between Tangier and Algeciras, Spain, costs 210dh on the **Transmediterranea** and **Limadet** (tel. 09/93–36–26) ferry lines. Together, the companies offer up to 18 departures daily in summer, eight daily in winter. In Tangier, buy ferry tickets at the port entrance or from any travel agency on boulevard Pasteur or avenue d'Espagne; InterRail holders get a 30% discount. If you're pressed for time, Transmediterranea's hydrofoil to Algeciras is quicker (45 min, 210dh); there are two daily departures in summer (8:15 AM and 3 PM, and sometimes another at 5 PM), usually one daily off season (3 PM), and generally no service at all in January. **Transtour** (tel. 09/93–40–04) sends one daily ferry to Tarifa, Spain (55 min, 210dh).

BY TRAIN

Tangier's main train station, the **Gare de Ville** (Place de la Marché Verte, tel. 09/93–45–70), is by the port entrance. Luggage storage (2.50dh) is open from 6 AM until 10 PM (closing intermittently, for a few minutes at a time, when receiving packages from incoming trains). Destinations include Meknès (5 hrs, 80dh), Fès (6 hrs, 90dh), Casablanca (6½ hrs, 125dh), and Marrakech (9 hrs, 145dh).

WHERE TO SLEEP

Lodging can get tight in July and August; reservations are an excellent idea. You'll find a bunch of cheap pensions in the Souk el-Dakhil and on Zankat Salah Eddine el Ayoubi.

Hôtel Mauritania. Here, right on the Souk el-Dakhil, are more than 30 of the largest, cleanest, and cheapest rooms in the medina. Doubles cost 100dh (60dh in winter). *2 rue des Almohades, tel. 09/93–46–77. From Grand Socco, walk downhill on rue es-Siaghin, then turn left after reaching Souk el-Dakhil.*

Hôtel El Muniria. Fully furnished, El Muniria has loads of charm and a friendly atmosphere, but the area is seedy at night. Bill Burroughs wrote *Naked Lunch* in Room 9. The bar downstairs is open 9 PM–1 AM. Doubles with (hot) shower are 120dh; ask for a room with an ocean view. *Rue Magellan, tel. 09/93–53–37.*

Pension Le Detroit. Cheap and right off avenue d'Espagne by the port, Le Detroit is usually booked in late summer, so call the friendly manager a week ahead. Doubles are 60dh, hot showers 8dh. *130 Zankat Salah Eddine el Ayoubi, around corner from Hotel Valencia, tel. 09/93–48–38.*

HOSTEL

Auberge de Jeunes (HI). The place is clean, bright, and close to the beach, and the beds are 33dh for members, 35dh for nonmembers. Hot showers are 5dh extra. *8 rue Antaki, tel. 09/94–61–27. Laundry (10–20dh).*

CAMPING

Camping Miramonte. This small, shaded camping area is 3 km (2 mi) west of the kasbah, near a somewhat uninspiring beach. Keep an eye on your stuff. Sites are 17dh per person plus 15dh per tent. There's also an overpriced hotel (rooms 120dh–150dh), a pool (50dh per day), a restaurant, and a supply shop. *Rte. Marshan, tel. 09/93–71–33. From stop on rue Sidi Bouabid (1 block west of Grand Socco).*

FOOD

For cheap restaurants, look in the alleys on the east side of Souk el-Dakhil and on rue Méxique, behind the Royal Air Maroc office on place de France. A couple of great cafés are **Café de Paris** (1 pl. de

France, tel. 09/93–84–44), a hotbed of political intrigue during World War II, and **Restaurant Detroit** (1 rue Riad Sultan, tel. 09/93–80–80), which has good views of the bay. If you're on the go, the streets south and west of the Grand Socco are packed with fruit and vegetable **markets.**

Hamburgers Al Izdihar. Scarf cheap beef fillets and *frites* (french fries; 15dh) with the locals. *23 rue es-Siaghin, between Grand Socco and Souk el-Dakhil, tel. 09/93–61–83.*

Restaurant La Marsa. The best value in Tangier, this is *the* place for pizza (served 11–11), whether it's plain cheese (23dh), the topping-heavy house special (42dh), or any of the 19 varieties in-between. Try the Moroccan salad (19dh), perfect hot-weather fare. Despite tablecloths and uniformed waiters, the atmosphere is laid-back. *92 av. d'Espagne, tel. 09/93–19–28.*

NEAR TANGIER

CEUTA

Ceuta is a Spanish military town with some duty-free shopping thrown in; there's really no reason to linger here. If you're Morocco-bound, take the bus marked CENTRO (75 Spanish ptas) from Ceuta's ferry terminal to Plaza de la Constitución. Get some dirhams from a nearby exchange bank, then take Bus 7 (75 Spanish ptas) to the *frontera* (border), about 10 minutes away in Fnidek. At the border, ignore all those who want to fill out your *débarquement* form for a hefty tip. Pick up the form yourself from a customs window, then wait in line (sometimes an hour or more during late summer and holidays). Once you're through, you can catch a *grand taxi* (6 people maximum; 2dh–4dh) to a nearby bus stop and hop on a bus to Tetouan or Tangier. Although it's quicker and more comfortable to take a *grand taxi* straight to Tetouan (20dh), Tetouan's hustlers send their "recon units" to the border, so waiting for the taxi to fill up is about as pleasant as a case of body lice. Don't be talked into buying anything; everything is a rip-off here.

The **Patronato Municipal de Turismo** (Alcalde J. Victori Goñalons, tel. 956/51–40–92), on the main plaza, has ferry schedules and a list of Ceuta's hotels and restaurants. If you must stay in Ceuta, the refreshingly refined hostel **Residencia de la Juventud** (27 Pl. Rafael Gibert, near Pl. de la Constitución, tel. 956/51–51–48; dorm beds 1,825 Spanish ptas) is up the stairs next to a mediocre Chinese restaurant. Reserve at least five days ahead.

ASILAH

This mellow beach town is an easy one-hour bus (11.50dh) or train (15dh) ride from Tangier—well worth the effort if Tangier's hustlers are getting you down. Especially in the low season, beautiful and breezy Asilah is the best deal in Morocco; light tourism and a heavy sunshine seem to be the rules. Asilah follows a pattern often repeated farther south: plentiful sand, plentiful seafood, and a Portuguese medina that dates from the 16th century (when Portugal controlled Morocco's western coast). Walking through the medina from an entrance off **avenue Hassan II** (Asilah's main drag), you'll reach a terrace overlooking the sea. Nearby is **Palais de Raisuli,** built in 1908 by its namesake, a legendary bandit who ruled the Berber tribes of the western Rif Mountains and was briefly the govenor of Tangier. The palace is open only in July, when it hosts an annual festival of art and music (and lodging in town becomes hard to find). Asilah has a few Berber carpet shops with decent prices, but your dirhams are better spent on a donkey trek (1½ hours, three hours by foot) to nearby **Paradise Beach,** a clean, laid-back spot where local burners like to smoke hash and watch the sunset. Ask at the Hotel Asilah (*see below*) for information on guides, and don't pay more than 30dh per person. Also, be wary of locals who offer cheap home-stays; they're unregulated and not recommended.

COMING AND GOING • If you arrive at the **train station** (tel. 09/91–73–27), take a shuttle (5dh) to the Central Plaza Mohammed V; or walk south for about 2 km (1⅕ mi), turning right at the first street that splits from the highway (look for the RABAT sign). If you fancy the nearby Paradise Beach, head straight for the water when you get off the train. Don't take *grands taxis* from the station; they'll charge you 40dh–50dh for the trip. Everything in Asilah is grouped around the main plaza; the **bus station** (tel. 09/91–73–54) is a few blocks north, and the medina, restaurants, and beaches are a few blocks west. The train (6 hrs, 56dh) and bus (5 hrs, 46dh) also connect Asilah with Fès.

WHERE TO SLEEP AND EAT • The central **Hôtel Asilah** (79 av. Hassan II, tel. 09/91–72–86) has simple, clean doubles with hot shower (120dh, 10% off for *upCLOSE Guide* readers); ask for one on the terrace. **Camping as-Saada** has quiet but unshaded sites (10dh per tent plus 12dh per person) on the beach; head left out of the train station. Restaurants along avenue Hassan II offer feasts of fresh fish, clams, or squid. If you can afford them, the seafood dishes (40dh–50dh) are *enormous* at **El Espigón**

(rue Yacoub el Mansour, tel. 09/91–71–57), at the end of the tiled promenade, by the beach north of the medina.

TETOUAN

With its awe-inspiring views of the coast and Rif Mountains, Tetouan is a popular summertime resort with Moroccans—and especially with hustlers, reputedly the worst in Morocco. This university town also has a distinct Spanish feel, as it was capital of the Spanish Protectorate from 1913 to 1956. Prior to that, it had been so isolated that when the Spaniards arrived in 1912, they found a small community still speaking Medieval Castilian. To tour the wide lanes of the blue-and-white–walled medina, follow the road next to the Royal Palace, then enter through **Bab er-Rouah** (Gate of the Wind). Turn left at the first fork and follow the main lane (go as straight as possible) to the T-shape intersection, then bear right. A little farther on is the entrance to a large cemetery (closed Friday). Climb the hill inside for picturesque views of Tetouan.

If you turn right at that first fork, you'll pass through the *souks* before reaching a fish-and-poultry market. Savor the pungent aroma, then exit the medina by heading east through the **Bab Okla** city gate (on your right). The **Museum of Moroccan Arts** (admission 10dh; open weekdays 8:30–noon and 2:30–6), on the far eastern edge of the medina just outside Bab Okla, has a collection of traditional crafts and tools. Skip the **tourist office** (30 blvd. Mohammed V, tel. 09/96–19–16) unless you're staying in town for a while; you can easily navigate Tetouan alone in a few hours.

COMING AND GOING • Tetouan is 1½ hours from Tangier; the easiest way to get here is by bus (the closest train station is near Asilah). From Tetouan's bus depot (Calle Ayuntamiento), **CTM** (tel. 09/96–16–88) serves Fnidek (across the border from Ceuta; 30 min, 7.50dh), Tangier (15dh), Chefchaouen (1½ hrs, 16.50dh), and Fès (5½ hrs, 61dh). **Supratours/ONCF** (18 rue Achra Mai, tel. 09/96–75–59) sells combined tickets that include bus fare (to the train station near Asilah) and train fare to your final destination—perhaps the best bet for those headed to or from Casablanca (8 hrs, 182dh). To reach Supratours/ONCF from Tetouan's bus station, turn left and walk about four blocks to place de Moulay el Mehdia.

WHERE TO SLEEP AND EAT • Don't stay too close to the medina or let Tetouan's hustlers show you a hotel. Try **Hôtel Príncipe** (20 rue Youssef Ibn Tachfine, tel. 09/96–27–95), well-located on the path between the bus station and place de Moulay el Mehdia, northeast of the station. Good-size doubles cost 95dh. Just up the street from here are several cheap snack bars.

CHEFCHAOUEN

Tucked away in the cannabis-forested Rif Mountains, an hour's *grand taxi* ride (24dh) south of Tetouan, Chefchaouen (a.k.a. Chaouen) offers cool alpine breezes, a wonderfully relaxed atmosphere, white-washed walls, and the cheapest hashish in Morocco. Originally a base for 15th-century raids on the Portuguese, and then a haven for Muslim refugees from Spain, Chefchaouen has maintained an air of rebelliousness and Andalusian architectural grace. Because the region has never really seemed Moroccan, popular politics predict its eventual secession. But life flows gently here, as a mellow haze of *kif* shrouds the usually frenetic hustlers—some claim that the entire town (aged 12 and up) is stoned.

The 17th-century **kasbah** on Plaza Uta el-Hammam harbors an elegant garden and an **Ethnographic Museum** (admission 10dh; open Mon.–Sat. 9–1 and 3–6:30), with traditional clothes and weapons. Climb the kasbah walls for a good view of the city. From the Plaza Uta el-Hammam, walk east toward the Hôtel Parador, ascend a staircase before the hotel parking lot, and continue 650 ft east through the medina until you cross the rushing Oued Laou river. Hike up the opposite side of the valley to reach a bombed-out (courtesy of the Spanish in the 1920s) **mosque** for amazing valley vistas.

BASICS • To reach the Plaza Uta el-Hammam, the center of town, from the new **bus station,** take a *petit taxi* (10dh) or walk uphill for 20 minutes, bearing right 490 ft up from the station. **CTM** and private lines have daily service to Fès (3 hrs, 42dh) and Tetouan (1½ hrs, 17dh). **Grands taxis** from Fès and Tetouan drop you off below Plaza Mohammed V. From here head east on avenue Hassan II, passing the **post office** on your right, and ascend through the medina to Plaza Uta el-Hamman.

WHERE TO SLEEP AND EAT • Of the many cheap hotels sprinkled throughout the medina, **Pension Mauritania** (15 Kadi Alami, tel. 09/98–61–84; doubles with lukewarm showers 40dh) has the prettiest courtyard and great breakfasts (10dh). Restaurants surround Plaza Uta el-Hammam; try **Restaurant Marbella** (40 rue Granada Hay Andalouss, tel. 09/98–71–20), 330 ft above the plaza, for excellent brochettes (20dh).

FES

In Fès el Bali (Old Fès), the streets are thick with narrow shops and smells that range from pungent to putrid to just plain mysterious. In a way, this is Morocco at its best—a place where dead chickens and spices, street merchants and hustlers, and donkeys bearing cartons of Tide and crates of Coca-Cola form a street scene you won't soon forget. Almost the quintessential Moroccan city, the only thing conspicuously missing in Fès is that vexing, indefatigable hustler endemic to the rest of the country. Hustlers are in fact everywhere, but now so are the police—busily condemning just about any suspected unofficial guide to two months in Fès's notoriously awful prison.

It's said that in the ancient Islamic world, only Cairo could rival the opulence of 14th-century Fès; the same could probably be said of Fès's religious and academic traditions. The Kairaouine Mosque, one of the world's oldest universities (AD 859), educated generations of Fassis (Fès residents), not to mention Christians and Muslims from all over the world. As the Catholic reconquest of Spain gained momentum, Fès attained further prestige and influence in North Africa; after the fall in 1492 of Granada (the last Muslim kingdom on the European continent), persecuted Jews and Muslims fled here from southern Spain, and Fès was made heir to almost 800 years of Andalusian culture.

BASICS

VISITOR INFORMATION

To get free (but useless) maps or hire friendly official guides (120dh half-day, 150dh full day), stop by the multilingual **Syndicat d'Initiative** (pl. Mohammed V, no phone). **ONMT** (pl. de la Résistance, 05/62–47–69) has lots of pamphlets. *Both open weekdays 8:30–noon and 2:30–6:30, Sat. 9–noon.*

PHONES AND MAIL

The **main post office,** in the ville nouvelle, is at the corner of avenue Hassan II and boulevard Mohammed V. The **phone annex,** open daily 8:30 AM–9 PM, has a separate entrance on boulevard Mohammed V. *Post office open weekdays 8:30–6:45, Sat. 8–11.*

COMING AND GOING

BY BUS

Both CTM and private buses pull into the **bus station** (tel. 05/62–20–41; av. Mohamed V), across the street from Bab el Mahrouk and Bab Boujeloud. Buses head to Rabat (3½ hrs, 52dh), Casablanca (5 hrs, 75dh), Tangier (6 hrs, 79dh), and Marrakech (8 hrs, 118dh).

BY TRAIN

The **Gare de Fès** (av. des Almohades, tel. 05/93–03–33), on the ville nouvelle's western edge, is a long haul from Fès el Bali and the main medina sights. You can store luggage (2.50dh) here; just follow the signs that say CONSIGNE. Take a metered taxi (10dh) to your hotel or Bus 10 (1.80dh) from the station to place des Alaouites (in Fès el Jdid) or Bab Boujeloud (in Fès el Bali). From Fès, trains go to Meknès (1 hr, 18dh), Rabat (4 hrs, 70dh), Casablanca (4 hrs 40 min, 95dh), and Tangier (6 hrs, 112dh). The slow ("*nonrapide*") train to Marrakech (11–12 hrs, 165dh) travels via the coast—a long, tedious journey.

GETTING AROUND

Fès el Bali (Old Fès) is the dense network of tiny streets northeast of the train station; this is where you'll find the **medina,** best accessed via the Bab Boujeloud gate. **Fès el Jdid** (New Fès) is split by the market street Grande Rue de Fès el Jdid. The train station is in the **ville nouvelle,** which starts at place de la Résistance and continues down avenue Hassan II. Metered taxis are best for shuttling between the ville nouvelle and the medina.

BY BUS

All buses within the city cost 2dh. The most useful is Bus 9, which serves the Syndicat d'Initiative, youth hostel (if you ask the driver), and Fès el Bali. Bus 10 stops at the train station, Bab el Mahrouk (near the bus station and Bab Boujeloud), and near the Merenid Tombs.

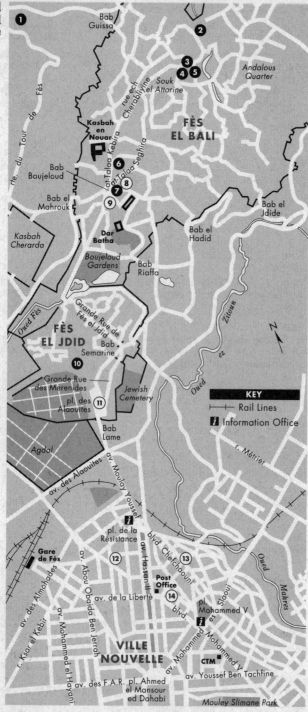

FES

Sights ●

Attarine Medersa, **4**

Bou Inania Medersa, **6**

Dar el Makhzen, **10**

Hammam, **7**

Kairaouine Mosque, **3**

Merenid Tombs, **1**

Place Seffarine/ Seffarine Medersa, **5**

Tanneries, **2**

Lodging ○

Association des Auberges de Jeunesse de Fès (HI), **13**

Hôtel Cascade, **8**

Hôtel du Commerce, **11**

Hôtel du Jardin Public, **9**

Hôtel Kairouan, **12**

Hôtel Olympic, **14**

WHERE TO SLEEP

Most cheap hotels are just inside Bab Boujeloud in Fès el Bali. Expect noisy nights, lukewarm showers, and poor lighting.

UNDER 75DH • Hôtel Cascade. The terrace here has a view of the busy gateway. Bright rooms have pretty tile floors but get noisy; ask the friendly manager to show you several before you choose. Doubles are 75dh; a bed on the terrace is 20dh. *26 Serrajine Bab Boujeloud, tel. 05/63–84–42.*

Hôtel du Commerce. This is the best choice in Fès el Jdid, opposite the Royal Palace. Some of the clean, comfy rooms share a large terrace with views of the Merenid Royal Palace. Expect clamor from the nearby market. Doubles cost 65dh. *Pl. des Alaouites, tel. 05/62–22–31.*

Hôtel du Jardin Public. The rooms here are clean and cool but a bit dark, and the mattresses have seen better days. The friendly staff (who will trade English books with you) and reliable plumbing (including hot showers) mean that this place is often full. Doubles 70dh. *153 Kasbah Boujeloud, tel. 05/63–30–86.*

UNDER 150DH • Hôtel Kairouan. This clean, stark refuge is in a quiet neighborhood between the train station and the ville nouvelle's place de la Résistance, near a couple of restaurants. Hot water? No problem. Doubles are 111dh, 129dh with bath. *84 rue Soudan, tel. 05/62–35–90.*

Hôtel Olympic. Centrally located in the ville nouvelle, these comfortable rooms, with snazzy bedspreads and small balconies, overlook a noisy street. There's scads of hot water, and a restaurant (meals 75dh) and bar below. Doubles are 110dh, 129dh with bath. Breakfast is 18dh. *Blvd. Mohammed V, at rue 3, tel. 05/62–45–29.*

HOSTEL

HI Association des Auberges de Jeunesse de Fès. The hostel's in the *ville nouvelle*, an easy 1-km (⅗-mi) trek from the train station. Expect bunk beds and cold showers. HI members receive priority and pay 25dh; nonmembers pay 30dh. *18 rue Abdeslam Seghrini, tel. 05/62–40–85. Taxi from train station (5dh–7dh). Lockout 9–noon and 3–6. Kitchen.*

CAMPING

Diamant Vert. Campers get free use of the water slides here in the Ain Chkef forest, 5 km (3 mi) southwest of town, and there's also a restaurant and free hot showers. Sites cost 15dh per tent plus 20dh per person. Beware that the area near the disco is noisy, and remember to keep an eye on your stuff. *Tel. 05/60–83–68. Take Bus 17 or 218 (20 min, 2.20dh) from avenue de la Liberté (stop is near post office).*

FOOD

There's a good selection of restaurants near Bab Boujeloud, in the medina, but watch out for restaurants that have two menus—same food, different prices. In Fès el Jdid, look for places at the southern end of Grande Rue de Fès el Jdid. If cleanliness is a serious concern, try the restaurants along boulevard Mohammed V in the ville nouvelle.

Al Khozama Fast Food. Sit inside, or garnish your meal with ville-nouvelle traffic fumes. Choose from kefta kebab (28dh) or French dishes like mushroom crêpes (40dh). *23 av. Mohammed es Slaoui, ½ block west of blvd. Mohammed V, tel. 05/62–23–77.*

Restaurant du Centre. Eat with Moroccans right on the main drag in this dark place with first-rate chicken *tajine* (45dh). Prix-fixe meals start at 60dh. *105 blvd. Mohammed V, tel. 05/62–05–04.*

Restaurant des Jeunes. Just inside Bab Boujeloud on your right, this place serves good couscous (25dh) and *pastilla* (30dh). *16 Serrajine Bab Boujeloud, tel. 05/63–49–75.*

WORTH SEEING

If you're courageous enough to explore the medina without a guide, remember that Talaa Kebira is one of two main streets that run northeast from Bab Boujeloud through the heart of Fès el Bali. The only "official" sight in Fès el Jdid is the mammoth **Dar el Makhzen** (Royal Palace)—the largest palace in Morocco. Its seven doors, commissioned by King Hassan II in the late 1960s, represent the doors to the seven heavens of Islam. It's closed to the public, but you get a decent view of it from place des Alaouites. The ville nouvelle, although comfortable and busy, doesn't offer any noteworthy sights.

THE HAMMAM EXPERIENCE

Moroccans bathe at hammams (public bathhouses). Foreigners can use the baths as well, but they should be prepared for an intense cultural experience, some direct stares, and a lot of nudity. Bring soap, shampoo, and a towel (plus a swimsuit if you're modest). Admission is rarely more than 7dh, plus 15dh–20dh for a massage. The baths are open noon–8 PM for women, 8 AM–noon and 8 PM–1 AM for men. Only Muslims can enter on Thursday and Friday. In Fès el Bali, there's a hammam adjacent to Hôtel Cascade; it's near Bab Boujeloud, on the first street to your right.

MUSEE DAR BATHA

Between Fès el Jdid and Fès el Bali is the palace Dar Batha, built in 1873 by Hassan I in an effort to unify the two towns. It's now a museum of traditional Moroccan crafts, including 13th-century pottery and wall-size Berber rugs. *Pl. Istiqlal, 5 min around corner (left) from Bab Boujeloud, tel. 06/63–41–16. Admission: 10dh. Open Wed.–Mon. 9–noon and 3–6.*

TALAA KEBIRA AND BOU INANIA MEDERSA

Enter Bab Boujeloud and take the first left onto **Talaa Kebira,** which leads through the medina toward Kairaouine Mosque. Walking this cramped, aromatic lane is what Fès el Bali is all about: Dodging donkeys and vulturous merchants, you pass scores of stalls laden with mint, baby chickens, bunnies, and mountains of olives and exotic fruits. A hundred meters from your entry point, on the right, is the 14th-century **Bou Inania Medersa** (admission 10dh), the largest and most beautiful of the Koranic schools built in Fès by the Merenid dynasty. *Medersas* were chiefly dorms for poor students who studied at nearby mosques, and their construction was at once an act of charity, a proof of religious devotion, and a monument to the builder. This medersa was built by Merenid Sultan Abou Inan, who is said to have fathered 325 sons and married a prostitute. Notice the medersa's densely decorated walls, its cedar ceilings, the ablution fountain in the courtyard, and the oratory (no admittance). Students once lived in the small, bare rooms upstairs, which are sometimes open for a peek. The medersa is open daily (Sat.–Thurs. 9–7, Fri. 11–1), but visitors are kept out during the five daily times of prayer.

KAIRAOUINE MOSQUE AND ENVIRONS

Talaa Kebira eventually becomes **rue ech-Cherabliyine** (Slipper Makers' Street). Shortly thereafter, look for Cherabliyine Mosque on your right and Fès's central market, the **Souk el Attarine** (Spice Sellers' Market), beyond an arched gateway. Linger a while in this visually enticing center of the medina before continuing to the giant **Kairaouine Mosque,** ahead on your right, at the street's end. This one of the Arab world's most prestigious mosques, and one of more than 365 mosques in the medina. Founded in AD 859, Kairaouine has long been one of Islam's chief intellectual centers, drawing students from Europe and beyond. The university was moved to the ville nouvelle in 1947, and Kairaouine is now used exclusively for prayer. Non-Muslims aren't allowed in, but tour groups continually cluster at the main door to gawk. Despite its size, the mosque is hard to find: The encircling street is narrow and looks like any other medina lane, densely packed with people and animals.

It's harder to miss the large bronze door of **Attarine Medersa** (admission 10dh; open Mon.–Thurs. 9–noon and 2–6, Fri. 9–noon), across Souk el Attarin from the mosque. This smaller, slightly older structure rivals the workmanship of Bou Inania, especially with Attarine's complicated floor tiling, patterned with stars and other celestial shapes. Non-Muslims may enter the oratory, which is not used for prayer; and the roof, if open, offers a spectacular view of Karaouine Mosque. Circumnavigate the mosque until you reach the small **place Seffarine,** where brass workers share stalls. Every guided tour of the neighborhood also visits the **tanneries** near Oued Fès (Fès River), accessed by an unmarked lane on place Seffarine's northeast corner. If you're lost, follow the stench of the cow, sheep, goat, and camel skins that have been laid out to dry. These medieval tanneries can be an intense and unforgettable experience, particularly their networks of round dye pits, some bright yellow and blue, some murky brown and blood-red, some filled with pigeon poop and slithery entrails. You'll probably see child laborers here, too, despite protests by local activists; contact with the chemicals leaves many kids ridden with cancer and other diseases.

CHEAP THRILLS

Late one afternoon, climb the hill above the medina for an inspiring view. Your first stop should be the posh **Hôtel Les Merenides,** where you can sit on the terrace sipping a real beer (this is a European, air-conditioned hotel, so let loose). Your next stop should be the nearby **Merenid Tombs,** which overlook Fès's ochre walls and white rooftops. To get here from Bab Boujeloud, walk through the local-bus and *petit taxi* square and turn right, exiting through Bab el Mahrouk. Follow the road to your right, past the Department de Transport building, and climb the hill.

RABAT

Nicknamed "the most complicated square mile on earth," Old Fès is a maze of streets, each no more than 2 feet wide. If you get lost, just remember that uphill is out, and downhill is deeper into the medina.

Once a launching point for the Muslim conquest of Spain, then an autonomous port noted for its mercenary pirate fleets, Rabat ultimately emerged as Morocco's capital (though Casablanca is the country's real financial and industrial leader). The primary residence of King Hassan II, attractive Rabat has much less of the hustle and bustle characteristic of other Moroccan towns; a stop here can be a welcome break from the rigors—or just the excitement—of traveling in Morocco. In fact, if it weren't for the North African architecture, palm trees, and Arabic street signs, you might think you were in a prosperous city on the Swiss Riviera. And thanks to Rabat's laid-back atmosphere, you can talk to people on the street without the constant worry of being hustled. After a day or two of hassle-free strolling, you'll probably be ready to return to Morocco's more exotic side.

BASICS

VISITOR INFORMATION
Syndicat d'Initiative. For 20dh you get as many brochures as you want, although the maps of Rabat are pretty bad. *25 rue Patrice Lumumba, (no phone.) Open Mon.–Sat. 8:30–noon and 3–6:30.*

EMBASSIES
Canada: Aussies and New Zealanders should inquire here as well. *13 rue Jaafar Assadik (Agdal), tel. 07/77–28–80. Open Mon.–Thurs. 8–noon and 1:30–5:30, Fri. 8–1:30.* **United Kingdom:** *17 blvd. Tour Hassan, tel. 07/72–09–06. Open in summer, weekdays 8–12:30 and 2–5:30; off season, weekdays 8–2.* **United States:** *2 av. de Marrakech, tel. 07/76–22–65. Open weekdays 8:30–noon and 1:30–5:30.*

PHONES AND MAIL
The **post office** is two blocks left of the train station (as you exit); the 24-hour **poste restante** and **phone annex** are across the street. *Av. Mohammed V, at rue Soékarno. Open weekdays 8:30–noon and 2:30–6:30.*

COMING AND GOING

BY BUS
The bus depot, **Gare Routière,** is 4½ km (2¾ mi) southwest of Rabat on the road to Casablanca; to get there, take a *petit taxi* (15–20dh) or Bus 30 (3dh) from the medina entrance at boulevard Hassan II. From Rabat, **CTM** (tel. 07/79–51–24) serves Tangier (5 hrs, 82dh), Fès (4 hrs, 55dh), Casablanca (1 hr, 25dh), and loads of nearby villages. *Grands taxis* bound for Casablanca and Marrakech also

NECESSARY EVILS

Guides are an unfortunate necessity in Fès el Bali: necessary because the medina is so labyrinthine and confusing, unfortunate because they cost money. Official guides booked through the tourist office make peanuts from the half-day fee (120dh); the real money comes from commissions, which is why you'll spend most of the day trekking from carpet warehouse to pottery store to engraving shop. Since the average monthly income in Morocco is less than US$100, you can understand the guides' zeal. Still, be firm in refusing to enter shops if you don't want to buy. The unofficial guides, who congregate around Bab Boujeloud and charge about half as much, are a hit-or-miss option—some are greedy bloodsuckers, but some are genuinely friendly students.

depart from Gare Routière; prices are negotiable but usually end up 10%–15% higher than the corresponding bus fares.

BY TRAIN
Don't get off the train at Rabat-Agdal (also called Rabat-Salé); if you're headed into Rabat proper, you want the **Rabat-Ville station,** in the center of town. Inside the station, you can store luggage (5dh per day; locked luggage only) and exchange money at the BMCE booth. Trains head to Aéroport Mohammed V (1¾ hrs, 48dh), Fès (4 hrs, 70dh), Marrakech (4 hrs, 75dh), and Tangier (5 hrs, 84dh). *Av. Mohammed V, tel. 07/70–73–63.*

WHERE TO SLEEP
Hotels along avenue Mohammed V are safe bets, but the best deals are in or just outside the medina, along rue Souika and rue des Consuls. That said, hotels get cheesier farther into the medina.

Hôtel d'Alsace. It's a bit dusty and noisy on the outside, but the lime-green interior is quiet and pleasant. For 70dh (doubles), you get comfy beds, steaming-hot showers, and a real sit-down toilet. *9 Derb Guessous, at av. Hassan II, tel. 07/72–26–11.*

Hôtel Dorhmi. Located above a café just outside the medina, this charming hotel with velvet sleigh beds is chic and clean, and has friendly management. Bonus: Use of the laundry machine is free. Doubles cost 100dh, hot showers 7dh. *313 av. Mohammed V, tel. 07/72–38–98.*

Hôtel Kasbah. These clean, neon-blue rooms and their sunny, colorful courtyard have an excellent location in the medina. Doubles are 62dh. *22 Zankat Sidi M'hamed el Ghazi, no phone.*

HOSTELS
Auberge de Jeunesse (HI). The gardens are surprisingly elegant, but the bathrooms are grim and the showers teeth-chatteringly cold. Beds are 26dh, 31dh for nonmembers. *43 rue Marassa, Bab el Had, tel. 07/72–57–69. Lockout 9:30–noon and 3–6.*

FOOD
For affordable eateries, try avenue Allal ben Abdallah, parallel to and one block east of avenue Mohammed V. As a rule, you can eat cheaply in the medina, but for a beer you should venture outside (medinas are generally dry) to the more upscale joints.

La Clef. Lounge on couches and plush pillows while you enjoy Moroccan specialties like crispy, cinnamon-dusted chicken *pastilla* (42dh); there's also a daily prix-fixe menu (55dh). From noon to 3, when the restaurant upstairs closes, try the café downstairs. *On small lane off av. Moulay Youssef, tel. 07/70–19–72.*

Restaurant de L'Union. This one stands apart from other medina cheapies—it's friendlier, cleaner, and serves tastier chow. Good basic choices are *brochettes* (22dh) and *tajine de kefta* (25dh). *260 rue Mohammed V, tel. 07/73–06–54.*

Restaurant Saadi. This is culinary heaven—seriously. Try the delicious couscous *au poulet* (with chicken; 80dh), big enough for two. *23 av. Allal ben Abdallah, at rue le Caire (a.k.a. Kahira on some maps), tel. 07/73–10–28.*

WORTH SEEING

Rabat's layout is easy to grasp: Boulevard Hassan II runs east–west along the medina walls, while avenue Mohammed V runs south–north past the train station, then intersects boulevard Hassan II and slices through the medina (where it's renamed "rue"). The city's sights are pretty spread-out, so bring extra dirhams for *petits taxis* or be prepared to hoof it.

KASBAH DES OUDAIAS

Originally the site of a 10th-century *ribat* (fortified camp), in 1146 the kasbah became the launching-point for the newly established *jihad* (religious war) against Catholic Spain. Three centuries later, the Spanish monarchy expelled most Muslims from the Iberian peninsula, and some sought refuge here, imparting an Andalusian feel to the white-washed kasbah and its surrounding cobble streets. The fortress's main attraction is the impressive **Bab Oudaïa** (at the top of the outside steps), a masterpiece of Almohad architecture. From the gate, the kasbah's short main street leads to a large platform with breathtaking views of the sea and the Bou Regreg river. The lower kasbah entrance opens onto the **Andalusian Gardens,** beautifully landscaped and redolent with jasmine and orange blossoms. There's also an outdoor café overlooking the Bou Regreg and the beach at Salé. Don't bother with the guides at the entrance; the kasbah is small and accessible. *From rue Mohammed V in medina, take rue Souika almost to end, and turn left on rue des Consuls. Open daily 8 AM–sunset.*

> *Look for women feeding eels in the Chellah's reflecting pool. Legend holds that doing so will make a woman conceive.*

HASSAN TOWER AND MOHAMMED V MAUSOLEUM

The Almohad sultan Yacoub el Mansour celebrated his conquest of North Africa and Spain by initiating construction of the giant **Hassan Mosque,** designed to hold 20,000 people. Upon the sultan's death in 1199, however, work stopped permanently. All that remain are the 170-ft-tall minaret and the sand-worn support columns, staring forlornly over the city. The **Mohammed V Mausoleum,** resting-place of the current king's father, who died in 1961, is decorated with valuable stones donated by Islamic countries the world over; it's an ornate Moroccan version of Napoléon's tomb in Paris, complete with stern-faced royal guards in cream-colored capes. *Follow blvd. Hassan II east to river, then look right. Admission free. Open daily 8 AM–sunset. Appropriate dress required.*

CHELLAH

The Merenid sultan Abou el Hassan built the fortified walls of the necropolis Chellah in the early 14th century, yet the site was inhabited much earlier: There is archaeological evidence of a Phoenician settlement dating from 700 BC, and visible remains of ancient Rome's southernmost African colony. The place now belongs to the storks and the thousands of white birds that nest in trees on the grounds. *Outside Bab Zaër, at south end of av. Yacoub el Mansour. Admission: 10dh. Open daily 8–6.*

BEACHES

Nearby Temara's impressive beaches put Rabat's small stretches of sand to shame. From the bus stop on Hassan II, take Bus 17 to **Harhoura** (3dh). From there, you can catch a *grand taxi* to an even better beach at **Sable D'Or.**

NEAR RABAT

CASABLANCA

Morocco's biggest city is hardly its most exciting, though it does boast the kingdom's best surfing. Except to see the Hassan II mosque (*see below*), the world's second-largest after Mecca's, Casablanca is definitely not worth a special trip. If you happen to fly into its Aéroport Mohammed V, do yourself a favor and take the bus or train directly to Rabat for a gentler introduction to Morocco. That said, if you're stuck here, don't be afraid to dip quickly into the city's Westernized urban crush. To reach Casablanca's most formidable sight, the **Hassan II mosque,** turn right out of the Casa Port station and walk 20 minutes along boulevard des Almohades. Completed in 1993 with $600 million "solicited" by the king from the Moroccan people, the mosque holds up to 100,000 people and sports the world's highest minaret, which towers 656 ft over a rocky bay. For 100dh, non-Muslims may enter Saturday–Thursday at exactly 9, 10, 11, or noon. To escape the city's smoggy confusion, go to **place Mohammed V,** a large, fountain-filled square where millions of pigeons work the crowd amid smart-looking French-colonial buildings. Rick's Café is nowhere to be found, but you didn't come all the way to Morocco to see that, did you?

BASICS

For general information and a booklet packed with phone numbers and maps, stop by the English-speaking **Syndicat d'Initiative** (98 blvd. Mohammed V, next to post office, tel. 02/22–15–24; open Mon.–Sat. 8:30–noon and 3–6:30, Sun. 9–noon). The **American Express** office (Voyages Schwartz, 112 av. du Prince Moulay Abdullah, tel. 02/27–80–54; open weekdays 8:30–noon and 2:30–6:30, Sat. 8:30–noon) is hard to find; look for the palm-lined promenade near the McDonald's (yep, there's one here, too) on place Mohammed V.

CONSULATES • United Kingdom: *60 blvd. d'Anfa, tel. 02/22–16–53. Open in summer, daily 8–2; in winter, daily 8–12:30 and 2–5:30.* **United States:** *8 blvd. Moulay Youssef, tel. 02/26–45–50. Open weekdays 8:30–noon and 1:30–5:30.*

COMING AND GOING

Most international flights to Morocco land at **Aéroport Mohammed V** (tel. 02/33–91–00), 30 km (18 mi) southwest of Casablanca. From the airport, an hourly shuttle (28dh, exact change required) heads to Casablanca's main bus station; from the train station below the airport, trains roll into Casablanca (30 min, 26dh) and Rabat (1¼ hrs, 45dh). If you're headed to Casablanca by train, stay on until you reach the centrally located **Casa Port station** (tel. 02/22–30–11), at the north end of boulevard Houphouët-Boigny. From here you can catch a train to Rabat (1 hr, 25.50dh), Marrakech (3 hrs, 70dh), Fès (4 hrs 40 min, 95dh), or Tangier (6½ hrs, 110dh).

Casablanca's main bus station, **CTM Gare Routière** (23 rue Léon l'Africain, tel. 02/44–81–27), is a five-minute walk east of place Mohammed V. Buses go to Rabat (1½ hrs, 25dh), Marrakech (4½ hrs, 60dh), and Fès (5 hrs, 75dh). Private bus lines operate from the **Dar Ben Jdia** station, off rue de Strasbourg. A *petit taxi* to Dar Ben Jdia from the CTM should cost less than 20dh.

WHERE TO SLEEP AND EAT

The **Auberge des Jeunes (HI)** (6 pl. Admiral Philbert, tel. 02/22–05–51) has cool, clean rooms (beds 40dh, skimpy breakfast included) and is centrally located in the Old City, near everything. Of the several safe, cheap hotels near the CTM bus station, try **Hôtel Mon Rêve** (tel. 02/31–14–39; doubles 76dh), at 7 rue Colbert (Chaoui). Also explore rue Colbert for cheap restaurants, scattered throughout the city's back alleys. Grab a sandwich from **Alaska Snack** (48 rue Foucault, next to Cinema Rif on pl. Mohammed V, tel. 02/27–47–24), or hit one of the ubiquitous cheap snack stands.

MARRAKECH

With a population of nearly 1.5 million, Marrakech is the second-largest city in the country, and with its *tabia* (red-mud) walls, desert-bound camel caravans, and oceans of sand, it's easily one of the most interesting. Marrakech's roller-coaster history has dragged it from 12th-century imperial splendor under Sultan Yacoub el Mansour to economic stagnation in the 19th century to its current status as a burgeoning industrial metropolis, attracting everyone from rural Berber farmers to world superpowers (for the 1994 GATT negotiations). Still, many people come to Marrakech not just for the city itself, but for what's around it. The High Atlas Mountains, south of Marrakech and just out of sight, have kept the harsh Sahara at bay for centuries, yet Marrakech remains the main gateway to North Africa's torpid, sun-baked interior. It's not quite *Lawrence of Arabia,* but this crowded desert town seems to validate even the most romantic images of North Africa.

BASICS

VISITOR INFORMATION

ONMT in Gueliz (Marrakech's ville nouvelle) can arrange official guides (120dh half-day, 150dh full day) and has the usual poor maps. Better orange city maps (10dh–13dh) are sold at most kiosks. *Pl. Abdelmoumen Ben Ali, tel. 04/43–31–61. On av. Mohammed V, at rue de Yougoslavie, behind beige telecommunications booth. Open weekdays 8:30–noon and 2:30–6:30, Sat. 9–noon and 3–6.*

AMERICAN EXPRESS

For emergency check-cashing and traveler's-check refunds, go to **Credit du Maroc** (215 av. Mohammed V, around corner from Voyages Schwartz, tel. 04/43–48–51; open weekdays 8:15–11:15 and 2:45–4:45).

PHONES AND MAIL

The **main post office** (pl. du 16 Novembre, tel. 04/44–14–71; open weekdays 8:30–6:45, Sat. 8:30 AM–11:30 AM) is in Gueliz at the corner of Mohammed V and Hassan II. The phone office here is open daily 8:30 AM–9 PM. In the medina there's another **post office** (tel. 04/44–14–17), in the southwest corner of place Jema'a el Fna, next to place de Foucauld. The **phone annex** (open weekdays 8:30–12:15 and 2:30–6:45), around the corner and down a flight of stairs, is much larger than the one at the main post office.

COMING AND GOING

BY BUS

The place Mourabiton **bus station** is at the medina's northwest gate (Bab Doukkala); walk 20 minutes or take Bus 3 (2.40dh) from place Jema'a el Fna. Buses to the train station also depart from in front of the bus depot. From place Mourabiton, **CTM** (tel. 04/43–44–02) serves Casablanca (4 hrs, 60dh) and Fès (9 hrs, 118dh).

BY PLANE

Marrakech's **airport** (rte. de l'Aéroport, tel. 04/44–78–62) is 5 km (3 mi) southwest of the city, past the Menara Gardens. For most destinations, you'll have to change planes in Casablanca. From the airport, take a taxi (40dh–50dh) to the medina. Bus 11 also goes into town (3.10dh); to reach the unmarked stop, leave the terminal parking lot, turn left, and walk about 10 minutes to the main road (cross the road and flag a bus). Contact **RAM** (av. Mohammed V, tel. 04/44–64–44) or the airport for flight information.

BY TRAIN

The **train station** (av. Hassan II, tel. 04/44–77–68) is on the far side of Gueliz, five minutes from the hostel and 30 minutes from the medina. Catch Bus 3 (2.40dh) or Bus 8 (2dh) across the street for the bus station and place Jema'a el Fna. Trains from Marrakech serve Casablanca (3 hrs, 75dh), Tangier (9 hrs 40 min, 180dh), and Fès (8 hrs, 165dh).

GETTING AROUND

In the medina, everything radiates from the triangular place Jema'a el Fna, Morocco's most intriguing open-air square; it's bordered by cheap hotels to the south and souks to the north. Local buses stop a block from the square's west side, on the tree-filled place de Foucauld. From place Jema'a el Fna, rue Bab Agnaou heads south to the Sa'adi Tombs and other sights, and avenue Mohammed V, Marrakech's principal street, runs northwest into Gueliz. At place du 16 Novembre, avenue Mohammed V intersects avenue Hassan II, which eventually leads to the train station. Although some of Marrakech is explorable on foot, you'll need the bus or a *petit taxi* to reach place du 16 Novembre and the gardens, hostel, campsite, and bus and train stations.

BY BUS AND TAXI

Bus 1 (2.40dh) runs up and down avenue Mohammed V, between place de Foucauld and Gueliz. *Petits taxis* are your best bet for the Agdal and Menara gardens. Trips between the medina and the train station should cost 15dh–20dh; rates increase 50% after dark.

BUT FOR YOU, MY FRIEND . . .

Lavish carpets, exquisite pottery, slick leather—it's all cheap here, but not for the impatient. It's possible to pay only 20%–40% of the original asking price, but you may have to haggle for hours to get there. Start by bargaining aggressively. Be sure to express your lack of funds; if it seems feasible, tell the merchant you're only a student. If you still can't get the price you want, try walking away in an uninterested huff, claiming that you saw the same goods in another store for half the price. Always examine goods carefully and take claims of "old," "authentic," and "Berber" with a grain of salt. Final note: Bargain only if you're actually prepared to buy; otherwise, don't bargain at all.

BY CALECHE

Horse-drawn carriages charge 30dh for half-hour jaunts through the medina, 60dh for longer, more leisurely tours. Carriages line up on the street between Koutoubia Minaret and place Jema'a el Fna.

WHERE TO SLEEP

Cheap, nearly identical hotels lie just south of place Jema'a el Fna, about 250 ft east of Hotel CTM. Another clump of cheap hotels is on rue de Bab Agnaou, just west of Hotel CTM. Whichever you choose, be wary of alleyway "friends" eager to unload their hash.

UNDER 75DH • Hôtel CTM. Suffer this hotel's great location on place Jema'a el Fna with roaches and saggy mattresses. There's hot water—at times. Have breakfast on the terrace for 16dh. Doubles are 71.50dh, 99.50dh with shower. *SW corner of pl. Jema'a el Fna, next to hotel arch, tel. 04/44–23–25.*

Hôtel Eddakhla. The ambitious, eager-to-please management draws both foreigners and Moroccans. The sheets are clean, and there's a kitchen and a large terrace. Doubles start at 60dh. *43 Sidi Bouloukate, tel. 04/44–23–59.*

Hôtel Essaouira. At this gem of a place next to Hôtel Medina (which also has nice doubles, from 60dh), the first-rate café on the rooftop terrace offers sweeping views of Koutoubia Minaret and the distant High Atlas Mountains. Some rooms are spacious; ask to see several before choosing. Doubles cost 70dh, hot showers 5dh extra. Call a week ahead in peak summer months. If your Arabic is rusty, ask for the English-speaking Mohamed Araban. *3 Derb Sidi Bouloukate, tel. 04/44–38–05.*

Hôtel Restaurant Café de France. These clean rooms overlook the noisy place Jema'a el Fna. Doubles cost 70dh, triples 75dh. *Pl. Jema'a el Fna, tel. 04/44–23–19. Laundry 10dh (negotiable).*

UNDER 100DH • Hôtel Ali. Make a beeline here for spotless sheets and well-priced breakfasts and buffet dinners served on a terrace. Reception helps organize trekking, 4x4, and ski expeditions. Doubles with bath run 90dh. *Rue Moulay Ismael, tel. 04/44–49–79. 165 ft from pl. Jema'a el Fna, just off pl. de Foucauld.*

HOSTEL

HI Auberge de Jeunesse. It's in a quiet Gueliz neighborhood near the train station, but far from medina sights. Evening arrivals are fine here, as there's always space. Hot showers are 5dh, but toilets are seatless. Beds in dorms are 20dh. When it's slow, HI cards are not strictly necessary. *70 rue el Jahed, tel. 04/44–77–13. Lockout 9–noon and 2–6.*

FOOD

As the day fades into dusk, countless food stands set up shop in the middle of place Jema'a el Fna, offering a variety of dishes for about 15dh–20dh. If you prefer your *brochettes* without hustlers, thank you, the restaurants on rue Bani Marine, west of the plaza through an arch next to the post office, are good for an oily, 30dh meal. For a breakfast of fried eggs, onions, bread, and mint tea (5dh), walk from place de Foucauld along the southern wall of Koutoubia Minaret (on rue Ibn Khaldoun); at the first square, you'll encounter the scent of sizzling onions wafting from a handful of food stands.

UNDER 40DH • Café Toubkal. If you'd rather starve than eat at a food stand, try this quick, efficient, clean café by the hotel arch on place Jema'a el Fna; look for the red awning and white tables. Salad (5dh) is a good prelude to steak or *brochettes* (25dh) and fries (5dh). *Bab Riad Zitoun, tel. 04/22–44–62.*

Chez Chegrouni. This is the best cheap eatery on place Jema'a el Fna, but the flies are wicked. Try the excellent chicken *tajine* (20dh) followed by a cup of sweetened yogurt (2dh). *Pl. Jema'a el Fna. Walk east from hotel arch past Café de France.*

UNDER 100DH • Hôtel de Foucauld. Tourists flock to this beautiful restaurant for the friendly waiters, thick *harira*, wine, and beer. Almond-chicken *pastilla* is 70dh; prix-fixe meals start at 100dh. *Av. el Mouahidine, on pl. de Foucauld (about 250 ft south of Koutoubia Minaret), tel. 04/44–54–99.*

The name Jema'a el Fna means "Assembly of the Dead," recalling a time when freshly decapitated heads were displayed here as a warning to would-be thieves.

Restaurant Café de France. Standard Moroccan fare is served on a terrace overlooking place Jema'a el Fna. It's enchanting at twilight. The prix-fixe menu starts at 75dh. *Pl. Jema'a el Fna, tel 04/44–23–19.*

CAFES

Watch the famous rosy sunsets of Gueliz at **Cafeteria le Jet de l'Eau** (pl. de Liberté, no phone), halfway up avenue Mohammed V, where the avenue hits the large, inoperative fountain. **Patisserie des Princes** (32 rue Bab Agnaou, tel. 04/44–30–33) is the best place for continental pastries; try the *chausson d'amandes* (almond Danish; 3.50dh) or the *mille feuille* (layered pastry; 5dh).

WORTH SEEING

The best way to explore Marrakech is to wander aimlessly in place Jema'a el Fna and the surrounding souks, which are extensive but still manageable without a guide. If you're pressed for time or don't want to deal with hustlers, hire an official guide from ONMT in Gueliz (*see* Visitor Information, *above*).

PLACE JEMA'A EL FNA

By day, this exotic, triangular plaza is filled with photogenic snake charmers, acrobats, card-tricksters, and trained monkeys. Chocolate sellers peddle unwrapped gobs of fly-covered goo, and itinerant merchants hawk daggers, fried fish, hash pipes, Koranic texts, steamed sheep heads (whole), and popcorn. Beggars beat their palms for money, while water carriers negotiate the thick crowds and hissing orange-juice vendors vie for your 2.50 dirhams. As the sun rises higher and the heat becomes unbearable, the crowds begin to melt away. When dusk approaches, the square livens up with fortune-tellers, traditional musicians, amateur boxers, and animated storytellers. A tip: Rather than stopping at each spectacle (leaving yourself prey to relentless requests for money), circle each crowd of onlookers continuously until you're ready to move to the next. Also, when exploring the medina, stay alert, withdraw money from your wallet discreetly, and hide all your valuables or wear your pack in front.

Lording over the plaza is the 220-ft **Koutoubia Minaret,** visible from nearly every approach. Construction of the tower began in about 1158, and was completed in 1190 under Yacoub el Mansour, the same Almohad sultan who commissioned Rabat's (permanently unfinished) Hassan Mosque. Non-Muslims may not enter.

SOUKS

To explore the labyrinthine network of *souks* north of place Jema'a el Fna, move to the eastern side of the square and, with your back to the white HÔTEL RESTAURANT CAFÉ DE FRANCE sign, walk straight ahead down rue Souk Smarine, the medina's main thoroughfare. Further down, the street splits into two: Souk Attarine is to the left, and Souk el Kebir is straight ahead. Before the split, look on your right for the entrance to **Rahba Qedima,** a small square where medicinal and supposedly magical herbs are sold. An alley at the far (north) end of the herb market opens onto the **Criée Berbère** (Berber Carpet Market), which caters mostly to tourists (prices here are only so-so).

Back at the split, continue straight on Souk el Kebir. After it turns 90° to the left, take the first right and continue straight. To the left (in the open-air square) is the entrance to **Koubba al Baroudiyine** (admission 10dh; open daily 8:30–noon and 2:30–5:45), a modest, 12th-century, Amoravid-dynasty mosque that, despite the city's many sackings, has survived a millennium largely intact. It may be the only Amoravid structure left in Marrakech.

Even more interesting is the nearby **Ali Ben Youssef Medersa** (admission 10dh; open daily 8:30–noon and 2:30–6); from the Koubba's entrance, continue straight down the street with the grillwork on the windows. Founded in the 14th century by Abu el Hassan, the "Black Sultan," who built many of Marrakech's mosques and Koranic schools, this *medersa* is noted for its stunning decorative detail. Go upstairs and duck into some of the tiny rooms where students once lived; you enter via a long, dark corridor, which leads to a courtyard filled with tile mosaics. An intriguing detour from here is the cluster of **tanneries** east of the *medersa* (go past the entrance, then right at the first fork, then straight for 10 minutes). You know you're close when kids eager to be your guides accost you; offer no more than 10dh.

SA'ADI TOMBS

The diminutive but marvelously artistic Sa'adi cemetery is strewn with the narrow graves of some 166 princes and members of the elite who were buried facing Mecca; all were interred between 1557 and 1792 and rediscovered in 1917. Most of the Andalusian-Moroccan structures around the graves were built by Sultan Ahmed el Mansour, who is remembered mainly for getting rich in the 16th-century conquest of Timbuktu (whose trade routes were most lucrative). He also built the **El Badi Palace** (admission 10dh; open 8:30–noon and 2:30–6), now a ruin. You can still see the palace's pools and wander its small maze of underground prisons. *Tombs: From pl. Jema'a el Fna, walk south on rue Bab Agnaou and turn left through gate Bab Agnaou; tombs are straight ahead, to right of mosque. El Badi Palace: Turn left through Bab Agnaou gate, then right at first street to pl. des Ferblantiers; walk across parking lot and through arch in wall, then turn right.*

GARDENS

The many gardens in this city provide a refreshing change from the noise and grit. The subtropical **Marjorelle Gardens** (admission 10dh; open in summer, Tues.–Sun. 8–noon and 3–7; in winter, Tues.–Sun. 8–noon and 2–5) were designed by French artist Louis Marjorelle. The **Agdal Gardens** (rue de Bab Ahmar; admission free; open daily sunrise to sunset) were built in the 12th century by the Almohads and later converted to a farm. The orange and olive groves supposedly inspire professions of love from young Moroccans; try your luck.

NEAR MARRAKECH

ESSAOUIRA

This peaceful seaside resort was a Portuguese stronghold (then called Mogador) during the 16th century, a Moroccan commerical powerhouse during the 18th century, and Jimi Hendrix's favorite hangout in the 1960s. Though it gets touristy in the summer, the rest of the year you'll share Essaouira with only the fishermen, some windsurfers, and the occasional dredlocked stoner. If you can tear yourself away from the beach for a moment or two, sip a coffee on the central place Moulay Hassan, browse Essaouira's many art galleries, or catch the sunset from the terrace at Hôtel Les Ramparts, on the left-hand alley behind place Moulay Hassan.

BASICS • The **Syndicat d'Initiative** (rue du Carré; open weekdays 8–10 and 3–6:30) is east of place Moulay Hassan, through the medina wall. To get to place Moulay Hassan from the **bus station,** take a *petit taxi* (5dh) or walk west 1 km (⅔ mi), go through the Bab Doukkala into the medina, and bear left toward the plaza. Buses to Essaouira from Marrakech (3½ hrs, 35dh) and Agadir (4 hrs, 36.50dh) are considerably cheaper than the *grands taxis* (60dh) from Marrakech.

WHERE TO SLEEP AND EAT • One of several cheapies in the medina, the **Hôtel Central** (no phone; doubles 60dh), off rue Sidi Ben Abdallah, has antique furniture and psychedelic pink rooms. Get back to nature at the **camping municipal** (blvd. Mohammed V, tel. 04/47–21–00) for 9dh per person (plus 8dh for "hot" showers). For seafood, grab a picnic table on the fishing pier, point to the object of your desire (plucked from the ocean that morning), and watch them cook it up (35dh–45dh). A little further down the dock, **Chez Sam** (tel. 04/47–35–13) serves a superb 65dh menu.

HIGH ATLAS MOUNTAINS

Travelers to the High Atlas Mountains are rewarded with spectacular vistas of rolling desert foothills giving way to ice-capped peaks. **Djebel Toubkal,** North Africa's highest peak (13,750 ft), is a popular two-day trek from Marrakech. Serious hikers should bring their own equipment—tent, sturdy boots, cooking gear, food, and water—but you don't have to be Hannibal to make this trek; people have done it with some water, a pair of Nikes, and not much else. A word of caution: In spring and summer, the weather is hot and windy, but in winter, nighttime temperatures drop far below freezing. If you're interested in longer treks (5–10 days) from Marrakech, most cheap hotels in the city will arrange a guide. Hôtel Essaouira (*see* Where to Sleep *in* Marrakech, *above*) can contact Amerda Omar, in Imlil, (*see below*) to lead a trek, and Hôtel Ali (*see* Where to Sleep *in* Marrakech, *above*) also arranges trips.

Getting to Toubkal is a delightful hassle. From Marrakech, take a *grand taxi* (from outside the gate Bab er Robb, at the south end of rue Bab Agnaou) to **Asni** (1 hr, 13dh per person). It's a stomach-churning trip on a narrow mountain road that overlooks a long, treacherous drop. (A word to the wise: Run like hell from the taxi stand if rain looks imminent—this hiking trip in a downpour is more like a rafting expedition.) If you need to stay overnight here, Asni's large **HI youth hostel** (no phone) has plenty of 20dh dorm beds; head through the market arch on the right hand side of the square, walk about 328 ft, and turn left.

From Asni, head as quickly as possible to **Imlil,** a good base for the Toubkal climb. By *grand taxi,* the trip costs around 100dh per person or 400dh per car, but it's only 15dh by *camionette* (pickup truck); catch one at the market arch, 328 ft from the *grand taxi* stand. Although the asphalt disappears halfway through the hour-long trip, the roadside waterfalls, the cows grazing by the stream below, and the cool mountain breezes more than make up for the bumps. Once in town, drop your pack off at the hostel **Refuge d'Imlil,** run by the Club Alpin Français (CAF). This low stone structure next to the main parking lot has clean rooms (beds 30dh, 32dh nonmembers), a kitchen, squat toilets, cold showers, and no bedding (bring your own sleeping bag or blanket); it's popular with European backpackers in the summer. The government-operated **Bureau des Guides et des Accompagnateurs** (open daily 7–6), across the street from the hostel, provides guides and information on Toubkal. To reach the peak itself from Imlil, first walk five to six hours to CAF's **Toubkal Refuge** (39dh, 52dh nonmembers); spend the night here (again, bring your own bedding, food, water, and supplies) and start the three-hour ascent to the summit as early as possible in the morning. The easiest "path" is marked by piles of stones—do *not* take shortcuts. If you're very clear on the route, a guide isn't mandatory; but if you have any doubts at all, hire one of the officially qualified guides pictured on the bulletin boards outside Asni's and Imlil's hostels, or one of the pesky youths milling about the refuge. The official guide rate is 200dh per day, more if you need supplies, boots, snow equipment, or mules (75dh).

ERG CHEBBI

If you've ever fantasized about the life of a haggard but hearty explorer trudging across the vast, windswept Sahara, the arduous but astoundingly scenic two-day jaunt from Marrakech (1½ days from Fès) to **Merzouga** might just be for you. This mellow town is home to Morocco's only true *erg* (massive shifting dune), the Erg Chebbi; at 264–330 ft tall (depending on the wind), it's Morocco's largest dune, and a popular destination for backpackers. For the most dramatic views of the horizon, climb the erg (pronounced "ark") at both sunset and sunrise. During the rest of the sweltering day—which encourages no activity more strenuous than breathing—hang out with the elderly rheumatics, who come in droves from around the world to bury themselves in the healing power of the hot, amber sand.

COMING AND GOING • From Marrakech, take CTM's morning bus to **Ouarzazate** (5 hrs, 46dh), then catch the private bus to **Er-Rachidia** (8 hrs, 60dh); the private buses leave from the station 328 ft up the street, to the right of the CTM station. If you have enough energy and luck, you might be able to catch the night bus (coming from Fès) to **Erfoud** (12dh), your next stop on the journey to the dune. Or, take a breather and crash in Er-Rachidia at one of the greasy hotels (about 30dh per person) by the *grand taxi* stand; then catch an early *grand taxi* to Erfoud (1 hr, 13.50dh). Upon arrival, look for Sayeed, who drives the red Mercedes van that will take you to Merzouga (1 hr, 15dh), and ask him to drop you off at the Hotel-Auberge Merzouga (*see below*), which lies at the foot of Erg Chebbi.

WHERE TO SLEEP • If you can't get a room at **Hôtel-Auberge Merzouga** (about 35dh per person), or you're in search of the consummate vista, try the **Erg Chebbi Auberge** (no phone), which opens onto the dune. Doubles are 80dh (20–25dh more July–August). To get here from Merzouga, catch a taxi (5–10dh).

TODRA AND DADES GORGES

One of Morocco's most mind-boggling natural wonders, the massive **Todra Gorge** appeals to daring climbers and casual hikers alike. Nearly 990 ft high but only a few yards wide at its widest, this giant crevice gets hotter than hell in summer, and should be explored early in the morning. Don't forget to bring water, and ask the tourist office how to check the plastic wrapping on bottles you buy here; this area is notorious for bottled-water scams. To get here from Marrakech, catch a bus to Ouarzazate (3 hrs), then take a bus (2½ hrs, 40dh) or taxi (50dh) to Tinerhir, where *petits taxis* (5dh–20dh) travel the final 15 km (10 mi) up the beautiful valley. Stay overnight at **Café Hôtel les Roches** (tel. 04/83–48–14; breakfast 30dh), a fun, touristy place near the gorge. Doubles are 60dh (90dh with shower), and beds under the large tent are 20dh. No formal trekking organizations operate here, but if you ask around at various hotels, you can often secure transport (i.e., a truck) through the gorge to **Imilchil** (4 hrs, 60dh per person in group of 7–10), where treks depart.

You can also venture east and south to the **Dades Gorge,** which has spectacular, colorful rock formations; it's a 30-minute taxi ride (15dh) from Todra. **Auberge des Gorges du Dadès** is a lively place with nightly Berber music (Berber teens on drums), good food, and a wonderful morning view from the terrace. Doubles with bath are 140dh, including breakfast.

THE NETHERLANDS

Travelers used to come to the Netherlands in search of windmills, picturesque canals, fields of tulips, and Dutch denizens in wooden shoes. Tulips do grow in abundance in some rural areas, and windmills are still pumping water from the marshy land; but since World War II, the Netherlands has developed into an urbane, happening, culturally rich place to hang out. Many of today's budget travelers are attracted by the country's reputation for political, social, and cultural progressivism and its anything-goes social scene; Amsterdam in particular is probably more famous now for hash and hookers than for windmills and wooden shoes. The country's liberal bent goes all the way back to its open-door policy of the 17th century, when religious refugees arrived here from all over Europe.

Of course, there's more to the Netherlands than hedonism and horticulture. The paintings of Rembrandt are a legacy of the Netherlands' Golden Age, the 17th century, when the country was one of the world's leading political, military, and cultural powers. When the Dutch weren't busy pumping water out of their tiny patch of lowland, they were busy exploring the seas, and they became a major player in global imperialism. Today the Dutch government occupies a pragmatic middle ground between Thatcheresque capitalism and strictly regulated social-welfare programs. This so-called polder model has been praised by world leaders, and has made the Netherlands one of the world's strongest economies. The gap between poor and rich is relatively small, and the government continues to subsidize all sorts of educational and artistic pursuits. The Netherlands has one of the most diverse populations in Europe, and gained an even greater reputation for liberalism when it passed the world's least restrictive laws on euthanasia, in 1993. Many members of the country's ethnic minorities, however—mostly Indonesians, Surinamese, Turks, and Moroccans—argue that things aren't as rosy as they seem. Job prospects are dim for many of them, forcing them to live in rapidly growing ghettos.

The Dutch are unfailingly courteous and helpful, though they may not seem like the warmest bunch at first. They are vigilant about their privacy—only half the size of Maine, the Netherlands is home to more than 15 million people. To get to know the Dutch better, try hanging out at neighborhood bars and cafés, where locals of all ages take pleasure in each other's company (an idea embodied by the Dutch word *gezellig*, loosely translated as "convivial"); they usually don't mind if a few visitors join in.

THE NETHERLANDS

North Sea

Schiermonnikoog

Ameland

Delfzijl

Terschelling

Dokkum
Groningen
Winschoten

West-Terschelling

Leeuwarden
Drachten
Assen

Vlieland
Harlingen
Bolsward
Grouw

Texel
Sneek
Emmen

Waddenzee
Hoogeveen

Den Helder

IJsselmeer
Meppel

Enkhuizen
Zwolle
Almelo

Hoorn
Hengelo

Alkmaar
Lelystad
Enschede

Purmerend
Apeldoorn
Deventer

Velsen
Zaandam
Amsterdam

Haarlem
Bussum
Winterswijk

Zandvoort
Hilversum
Doetinchem

Amersfoort
Arnhem

Hoge Veluwe National Park

Leiden
Utrecht
Oosterbeek

Kijkduin
Gouda
Rhine

Rijn
Tiel
GERMANY

The Hague
Delft
Nijmegen

Hoek van Holland
Oss

Rotterdam
's Hertogenbosch
Veghel

Haringvliet
Dordrecht

Overflakkee
Breda
Tilburg
Eindhoven

Schouwen Duiveland
Steenbergen
Weert
Roermond

Tholen
Bergen op Zoom

Oosterschelde
Goes

Walcheren
Beveland
Middelburg

Vlissingen
Westerschelde
Sittard
Aachen

Breskens
Terneuzen
Vaals

Antwerp
Maastricht

BELGIUM
Liège

Brussels

KEY

—†— Rail Lines

⛴ Ferry Lines

0 — 40 miles

0 — 60 km

BASICS

MONEY

US$1 = 1.9 guilder and 1 guilder = 52¢. The guilder, written as Dfl, fl, or just f, is divided into 100 cents. Banks generally offer the best exchange rates and charge about f5 commission for changing cash or traveler's checks. **GWK** offices, in most train stations, offer similar rates. GWK offices are generally open Monday–Saturday 8–8 and Sunday 10–4, and offices in major cities or at border checkpoints are open 24 hours. Try to avoid changing money at tourist offices and bureaux de change.

HOW MUCH IT WILL COST • Compared with other Western European countries, the Netherlands is fairly inexpensive. You can spend as little as US$35 a day if you stay in hostels and scrimp, $50–$55 if you stay in budget hotels and eat out now and then. Doubles in an average budget hotel will set you back about f75–f95, but camping is usually only f12. Fast food will fill you for f7, while you'll pay about f15 to dine in a cheap restaurant, f20–f25 in a nicer one. Train trips come cheap; you can travel about 40 km (24 mi) on f6. Admission to museums is rarely more than f10.

COMING AND GOING

Most travelers arrive by **train** at Amsterdam's busy Centraal Station (tel. 020/620–2266 for international information). The new **Thalys** (tel. 0900/9228) train service to Brussels and Paris has reduced journey times there by 75 minutes. **Eurolines** (see Basics in Amsterdam, below) runs buses from Amsterdam's Amstel Station to destinations all over Europe. The Netherlands' main **ferry** ports are the Hoek van Holland (Rotterdam) and Vlissingen. **Stena Line** has an ultramodern High Speed Service (HSS) between Hoek van Holland and Harwich (tel. 0900/8123). **Hoverspeed UK** (tel. 0181/554–

Technically, "Holland" refers to only two provinces in the Netherlands. Calling the collective Dutch provinces "Holland" is akin to calling Great Britain "England" and offends most residents.

7061, in London) and Eurolines go from London to Amsterdam via the Dover–Calais ferry. New services include the **Scandinavian Seaways** (tel. 0255/534–546) overnight ferry from IJmuiden, just 20 km (12 mi) west of Amsterdam, and Newcastle-upon-Tyne, in northern England. Many bus companies offer cheap **bus-ferry-bus** combinations; a quicker option is the new **Eurostar** rail service, which goes from Brussels-Zuid to London via the Channel Tunnel. International **flights** land at the sleek Schiphol Airport, one of Europe's finest, just 15 minutes from Amsterdam (see Basics in Amsterdam, below); flights from the United States generally cost the same as flights to Paris or Frankfurt.

GETTING AROUND

Because the Netherlands is so small, travel within the country is relatively inexpensive. Trains are frequent, efficient, and cheap. Most cities are served by rail, and the nationalized bus system, charging comparable rates, is a good alternative for getting to more remote places. For information on buses and trains, call the national transportation line (tel. 0900/9292, 75¢ per min). The flat Netherlands are naturally ideal for biking; even the unfit can pedal from town to town with ease. Rent a bike, or *fiets,* at train stations in larger towns for f8–f9 a day with a f100–f200 deposit or ID. (To take your bike on the train you'll have to pay an extra f10–f15.)

You can use a *strippenkaart*—a card with 2–45 strips—on all local buses, trams, and Metro lines. The number of strips you use depends on how many zones you cross; a typical trip within a city's central zone requires two strips. Tell bus and tram drivers where you want to go, and they'll cancel the appropriate number. On the Metro, use the yellow machines to cancel strips, but ask an attendant for help to figure out how many strips you'll need. If you don't cancel the strips and an inspector apprehends you, you'll be hit with a hefty f60 fine plus the price of the ticket. A 15-strip card is f11.25, a 45-strip card f32.50. Two people can share a card; just have it punched twice. You can buy *strippenkaarts* at train stations, post offices, and tobacconists. If you don't have one, you'll pay the driver f3–f4.50 per zone.

BY TRAIN • The Eurailpass and InterRail pass are valid on all train trips. Even without a rail pass, you won't have to dig too deeply into your pockets for city-to-city fares. In fact, the Benelux Tourrail Pass (see Belgium in Chapter 4) isn't really worth the cost unless you plan on traveling from one end of the country to the other every day. You don't need reservations for trains within the Netherlands; just buy your ticket and show up at the appropriate *spoor* (platform). Note that there are no standard return tickets, but there are special rates for day and weekend returns. **Nederlandse Spoorwegen (NS),** the national railway, runs trains between major cities every 15 minutes and between smaller towns every half-hour.

HEAD FOR THE . . . HILLS?

Despite their many battles for naval supremacy, the Dutch have never faced a greater threat than the North Sea itself. More than half of this flat country has an altitude of less than 16 ft, making it extremely vulnerable to flooding; indeed, half the country was under water until just a few centuries ago. To keep the sea out, the Dutch have dikes along all major rivers and the entire north coast. Windmills have long been used to drain lakes and keep the reclaimed lands (known as polders*) dry, though today they're aided by sophisticated pumping systems that suck excess water right from the ground.*

If you plan to cover a lot of the Netherlands by train, you can buy a **Holland Domino** rail pass, valid for three days (f90, f65 under age 26), five days (f140, f99 under 26), or 10 days (f250, f165 under 26) of unlimited travel within a month. For an extra f5 per day you can get a pass for travel on all public transport. Unlimited day tickets are another option (f97.50 1st class, f65 2nd class), but it's nearly impossible to travel enough in one day to make them worth the investment. From June–August there is also the **Zomertoer** ticket, covering 3 days of travel within a period of 10 days (f89, or f119 for two people).

WHERE TO SLEEP

With the exception of Amsterdam, most cities in the Netherlands are short on cheap sleeps. A double room in a budget hotel starts at about f80, and a single is about 75% the price of a double. To reserve rooms before you leave home, contact the **Netherlands Reservation Center** (Box 404, 2260 AK Leidschendam, tel. 070/320–2500, fax 070/320–2611). Once in the country you can book a room at any tourist office (VVV; *see* Visitor Information, *below*) for a small fee as soon as you walk into town. The VVV is also a good place to book rooms in private homes or B&B's, which usually cost f30–f40 per person.

If you don't mind sacrificing privacy, you'll save a bundle by staying in any of the **HI hostels,** run by the Nederlandse Jeugdherberg Centrale (NJHC). Most hostels charge members f22–f27 for a dorm bed, including breakfast; sheets usually cost an extra f6.50. Prices given in this chapter are high-season (July and August) member rates; nonmembers pay about f5 more, and prices generally drop a few guilders in the off season. For a complete list of hostels, contact the NJHC (Prof. Tulpstr. 4, 1018 HA Amsterdam, tel. 020/551–3155), or ask for a free copy of the *Herberggids* at any hostel. Unofficial hostels charge about as much as NJHC hostels, but they're often shabbier and dirtier.

FOOD

Traditional Dutch food is wholesome but basic. *Eetcafés* (which are what they sound like—cafés where you can eat) serve traditional food, usually at reasonable prices: meat or fish with potatoes and a few vegetables or salad. Dutch specialties include *erwtensoep,* (a thick pea soup with pieces of tangy sausage or pigs' knuckles) and *stamppot,* mashed potatoes and greens with *worst* (sausage). Lunch is often a well-filled *broodje* (sandwich) from a great selection of bakeries, delicatessens, or cafés. The Dutch usually eat their main meal in the early evening; many restaurants will not take orders after 10 PM. Brown cafés (*see* After Dark *in* Amsterdam, *below*) are like pubs; they serve alcoholic drinks and sometimes simple food. Penny-pinchers will rely on Dutch fast food, such as *patat* (french fries), served with tangy mayonnaise, and *broodjes. Shoarmas* (spit-roasted lamb in pita bread) are available at takeout stands everywhere, and vegetarians can nosh on falafel.

There are as many foreign restaurants here as elsewhere: Italian pizzerias, Tex-Mex, and all the rest. Since Indonesia was once under the Netherlands' thumb, you'll find immigrant-run Indonesian restaurants everywhere. Surinamese food, which is somewhat like Chinese and Indonesian cuisines, is also abundant. For an Indonesian blowout, treat yourself to a *rijsttafel* (from about f30), an assortment of meat, poultry, and vegetarian dishes served with peanut, curry, and coconut sauces.

BUSINESS HOURS

Stores, banks, post offices, supermarkets, and many restaurants are closed most Sundays, and the Dutch are in no hurry to get the work week started; many places don't open until late morning or early afternoon on Monday. The rest of the week, expect shops to be open 10–6, museums 10–5, and banks 9–5. Many towns have late-night opening hours one night during the week, usually Thursday or Friday.

FESTIVALS AND HOLIDAYS

Koninginnedag (Queen's Day) is celebrated every April 30th with a "free market" (i.e., anyone can set up a stall and sell whatever they like), parties, parades, and other festivities, and is definitely a bigger deal in Amsterdam than elsewhere (*see* Cheap Thrills *in* Amsterdam, *below*). The nation also observes *Pinksteren,* or Whit Monday, 40 days after Easter, and *Hemelsvaart,* or Pentecost, soon after that; the Dutch have wisely merged these long weekends into a fortnight's holiday, which has become known as the "tulip break." Except for restaurants and bars, most businesses close for each holiday, but some museums do remain open.

VISITOR INFORMATION

You'll find a tourist office, or **VVV**, in almost every town with even the teeniest of tourist attractions. These offices sell maps (f2–f4) and reserve rooms (f5–f10); some also change money when the GWK (*see* Money, *above*) is closed. If you're a serious museum hound, take a passport-size picture and f47.50 (f17.50 under age 24) to the VVV and buy the Museumjaarkaart, a year-long pass to all municipal and state museums (*see* Museums *in* Amsterdam, *below*).

PHONES AND MAIL

Country code: 31. Most of the neon-green public phone booths take only phone cards (f5–f25), which are sold at post offices and train stations. Dial 0900/8008 for national directory enquiries, 0900/0412 for international directory enquiries. Long-distance calls are cheapest between 8 PM and 8 AM. To dial an international call directly, dial 00 + country code + phone number. For an international operator, dial 0900/0410; for **AT&T** Direct Access℠, 0800/022–9111; for **MCI,** 0800/022–9122; and for **Sprint,** 0800/022–9119.

Post offices are open weekdays 9–5. A few are open until 8 on Thursday, and some main branches are also open Saturday 10–noon. Most branches hold poste restante, sell postcards, and exchange money. To send mail abroad, put it in the OVERIGE slot at the post office.

CRIME AND PUNISHMENT

Contrary to popular belief, marijuana is *not* legal here, but it is tolerated by police and residents alike, and the Dutch government has stubbornly resisted attempts by other European Community countries to force a change in this policy. Still, the police do differentiate between hard and soft drugs, so be careful with street dealers. Don't even think about taking drugs across the border; tourists are favorite targets of customs officials and their sniffer-dogs.

EMERGENCIES

The national emergency number for the police, fire department, and ambulances is 112. Health care isn't free for travelers; make sure you bring your health-insurance card.

LANGUAGE

It's easy to feel linguistically inferior in the Netherlands, where even dogs seem to understand English. Most Dutch speak German, French, and flawless English, though they appreciate visitors' attempts to speak their own language. Here are a few words to facilitate friendly relations: *dag* (hello); *tot ziens* (good-bye/see you later); *alstublieft* (please/you're welcome); *dank u wel* (thank you); *ja* (yes); *nee* (no); *spreekt U Engels?* (do you speak English?); *waar is . . .?* (where is . . .?); *hoeveel kost . . .?* (how much is . . .?).

AMSTERDAM

Amsterdam is a city with a split personality. This refined, museum-packed metropolis is also one of the most progressive and hedonistic cities in the world. There is an incomparable romance in the city's concentric canals lined with stately gabled houses, especially at night; but even the city's oldest church has to compete for attention with the prostitutes in the windows across the street.

During the Dutch Golden Age, Amsterdam became the political and economic center of the Netherlands, which was at that time the world's leading trading power. Although the city has remained worldly,
wealthy, and influential, its modern reputation is inevitably linked to its tradition of free thinking and tolerance. Today many visitors come to Amsterdam out of simple curiosity. They've heard about the pot
sold in cafés, the prostitutes on display, the uninhibited gay scene—and it's all here.

If you're hell-bent on seeing the sleaze, stick to the Red Light District and you'll get more than an eyeful—possibly a stomach full—of vice. If, on the other hand, you're looking for a little tranquility, head for
the Jordaan, the area west of Dam Square, to find locals relaxing in the brown cafés along some of the
city's many beautiful canals. (Amsterdam has more canals than Venice.) You can also spend a lazy
afternoon picnicking among the lakes and lawns of Vondelpark, just south of the city center, or join the
crowds of in-line skaters for a spin; you can rent skates right in the park. Whatever your pleasure, you're
guaranteed to understand why residents love this crazy and beautiful city.

BASICS

VISITOR INFORMATION

Amsterdam's main **VVV,** in the Old Dutch Coffee House just outside Centraal Station, has a good selection of maps for f3.50–f7.50 and will book accommodations for f5. There's a less crowded branch at the
Leidseplein. Alas, nothing, not even a cheesy brochure, is free here, and the bureau de change is a rip-
off. You can also phone for tourist information (tel. 0900/3403–4066), but note that you'll be kept waiting in an electronic line, and it will cost you f1 a minute. *Main office: Stationspl. 10; open daily 9–5.
Other locations: Leidseplein 1; open daily 9–7, summer 9–9.*

AMERICAN EXPRESS

The main office holds client mail and gives cardholders the best exchange rate in town, but it's perpetually crowded. Cardholders can also use the cash machine outside. The smaller office, near Museumplein, doesn't hold mail. *Main office: Damrak 66, 1012 LM, tel. 020/520–7777; open weekdays
9–5, Sat. 9–noon. Branch office: Van Baerlestr. 39, tel. 020/673–8550 or 020/671–4141; open weekdays 9–5, Sat. 9–noon.*

CHANGING MONEY

Damrak, Leidsestraat, and Rokin runneth over with rip-off bureaus de change. Don't be deceived by ads
for excellent rates; many charge a 10% commission. Banks offer good rates and generally charge a
much smaller commission but are closed weekends. Besides American Express (*see above*), the best
bureau is **GWK,** whose offices at **Centraal Station** (tel. 020/627–2731), and **Schiphol Airport** (tel. 020/
601–0507) are open 24 hours.

CONSULATES

Consulates for Australia, Canada, and New Zealand are in The Hague (*see* Basics *in* the Hague, *below*).

United Kingdom: *Koningsln. 44, south side of Vondelpark, tel. 020/676–4343 or 020/675–8121 for
visa information. Open weekdays 9–noon and 2–3:30.* **United States:** *Museumpl. 19, tel. 020/664–
5661. Open weekdays 8:30–noon, 1:30–3:30 for passport information.*

DISCOUNT TRAVEL AGENCIES

Budget travelers in the know head to **NBBS** (Rokin 38, tel. 020/624–0989) and its sister concern, **Budget Air** (Rokin 34, tel. 020/626–5227), for cheap plane and train tickets, even though they don't accept
credit cards. Up the road, **Eurolines** (Rokin 10, tel. 020/627–5151) sells bus tickets for destinations like
London (10 hrs, f75), Prague (23 hrs, f135), and Brussels (3 hrs, f35). Inside the office is an **Airtech**
desk (tel. 020/421–2738), where you can arrange standby flights to the United States and Canada.

EasyJet offers cheap one-way tickets (from f99) to its hub at London Luton airport, from which it serves
other European destinations; call them directly to book tickets (tel. 023/568–4880). Call **KLM Call&Go**
(tel. 023/567–4567) between 1 and 10:30 PM for a list of next-day departures at considerably reduced
prices.

PHONES

Public phone booths are plentiful on main tourist drags; note that they only take phone cards. Avoid private phone centers, which sting tourists with steep rates.

MAIL

The main post office, west of Dam Square off Raadhuisstraat, holds poste restante. Have your pen pal address mail as follows: Your Name, Poste Restante, Main Post Office, 1016 AB Amsterdam, The Netherlands. *Singel 250, tel. 020/556–3303. Open weekdays 9–6, Sat. 10–1:30.*

COMING AND GOING

If you arrive at Schiphol Airport, frequent trains (f6.75) can whisk you to Centraal Station, a 15-minute ride away.

BY TRAIN

Amsterdam's **Centraal Station** is a major hub for European trains as well as local buses, trams, and the Metro. For schedules and bookings on domestic trains, call 0900/9292; for international information call 0900/9296. Both calls cost f1 per minute.

RIDES

For a f10 subscription fee plus a f10–f20 processing fee, the **Liftcentrale** (Oudezijds Achterburgwal 169, tel. 020/622–4342) will hook you up with drivers heading to cities all over Europe. Once matched, you pay the driver about 6¢ per km (⅔ mi).

GETTING AROUND

Amsterdam can be terribly confusing at first. One canal looks like another, and street names change every few blocks. If you'll be around for more than a few days, get yourself a big map from the VVV or GVB (*see below*) office and consider taking an hour-long cruise on one of the many **glass-topped boats** that chug around the city offering a unique perspective. Whole flotillas are moored close to Centraal Station, and a basic cruise costs only f10–f12.

With your back to Centraal Station, the Red Light District is to the left, the Jordaan is to the right, and the Damrak, which leads to the Dam, half a mile away, is straight ahead—past the redbrick geometrical shapes of the Beurs van Berlage (Berlage's Stock Exchange). Carrying on past the Dam in the same direction takes you along the Rokin, at the end of which is another useful landmark, the Munttoren (Mint Tower). Running parallel to the Damrak and Rokin is the pedestrianized Kalverstraat, the main shopping street. Leidsestraat, another shopping paradise, cuts through Singel, Herengracht, Keizersgracht, and Prinsengracht, the four canals that form concentric semicircles around the station. Trams 1, 2, and 5 cut through the city from Centraal Station along Leidsestraat to Vondelpark. Raadhuisstraat is a main thoroughfare lined with bureaux de change and hotels, running west from the Dam.

Once oriented, you can easily conquer the city by foot or bike, but **trams** also cover the city extensively and efficiently. Amsterdam's official public transportation company, **GVB** (Stationpl. 15; open weekdays 7 AM–10:30 PM, weekends 8 AM–10:30 PM), sells maps (f2.50) and the *strippenkaart* (*see* Basics *in* the Netherlands, *above*), accepted on all public transport. A recent addition to the tram system is the **Circle Tram 20,** offering 30 different stops where you can hop on and off to see the sights; it runs every 10 minutes in both directions from 9–6. The ticket includes a printed guide and is valid on all other forms of public transport (1 day, f10; 2 days, f15; 3 days, f19; 4 days, f23).

Wherever the trams don't go, the **buses** do. The area across the canal north of the train station, where you'll find a campground, is reachable only by bus. (Taking the ferry involves a long walk.) After midnight, buses are the only form of public transportation, but routes are limited and service infrequent. The GVB has a pamphlet with the night-bus details. **Taxis** (tel. 020/677–7777) are an option if you're in a jam; the rate is f2.85 per km (⅔ mi), plus an initial charge of about f6. You cannot officially hail a cab on the street, but there are yellow taxi stands throughout the city. You can catch the **Metro** at Centraal Station, but the Nieuwmarkt and Waterlooplein stops are the only useful ones for visitors; the Metro mainly serves the modern suburbs and business districts. Remember to cancel strips ahead of time at the yellow machines.

The cheapest bike rental is at the train station's **Take-A-Bike** (Koenders Jr. Stationpl. 12, tel. 020/624–8391); with a f200 deposit, it's f8 per day (f32 per week). With a train ticket, it's even cheaper; a f100 deposit plus f6 per day (f24 per week). **MacBike** throws friendly service and helpful maps in with the bike at a number of handy locations ('s-Gravesandestr. 49, near the Arena; Mr. Visserplein 2, near the Waterlooplein; and Marnixstr. 220, tel. 020/620–0985).

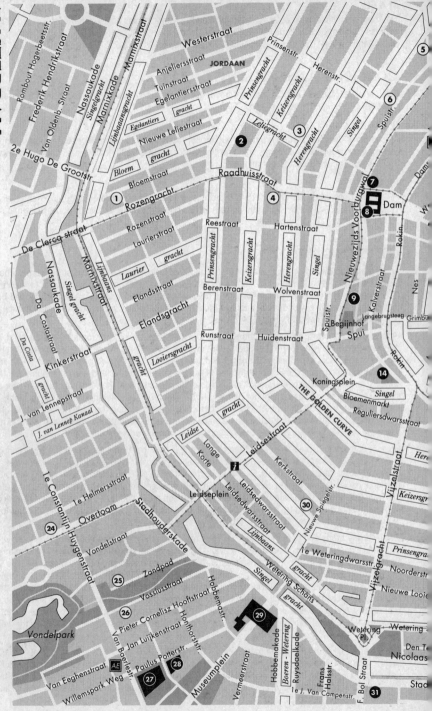

AMSTERDAM

JORDAAN

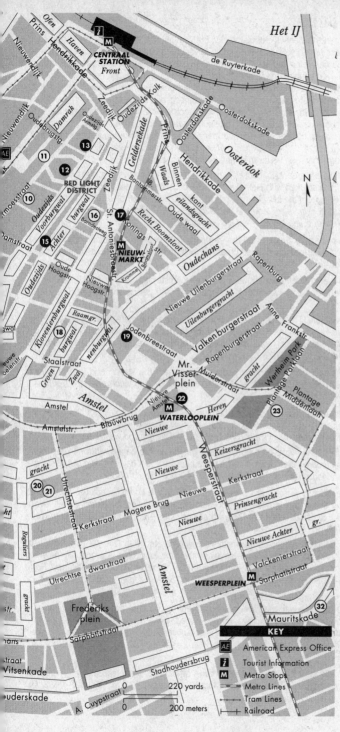

Het IJ

de Ruyterkade

CENTRAAL
STATION
Front

Oosterdokskade

Oosterdok

RED LIGHT
DISTRICT

N

Oosterdoksade

Hendrikkade

NIEUW
MARKT

Oudechans

Rapenburg

Nieuwe Uilenburgerstraat

Uilenburgergracht

Jodenbreestraat

Valkenburgerstraat

Anne Frankstr.

Rapenburgerstraat

Wertheim Park

Plantage Parklaan

Plantage
Middenlaan

Mr.
Visser-
plein

Muiderstraat

gracht

Amstel

Amstel

Blauwbrug

WATERLOOPLEIN

Heren

Amstelstr.

Nieuwe

Keizersgracht

gracht

Nieuwe

Kerkstraat

Nieuwe

Prinsengracht

Utrechtsestraat

Kerkstraat

Magere Brug

Nieuwe

Nieuwe Achter

gr.

Valckenierstraat

Utrechtse dwarsstraat

Amstel

Sarphatistraat

WEESPERPLEIN

gracht

Frederiks
plein

Sarphatistraat

Mauritskade

Stadhoudersbrug

A. Cuypstraat

American Express Office

Tourist Information

Metro Stops

Metro Lines

Tram Lines

Railroad

0   220 yards
0   200 meters

Amsterdam Historisch Museum, 9
Anne Frankhuis, 2
De Waag, 17
Hash Marihuana/ Hemp Museum, 15
Heineken Brewery, 31
Joods Historisch Museum, 22
Koninklijk Paleis, 8
Munttoren, 14
Museum Amstelkring, 13
Museum Het Rembrandthuis, 19
Nieuwe Kerk, 7
Rijksmuseum, 29
Ouede Kerk, 12
Stedelijk Museum, 27
Van Gogh Museum, 28

Lodging ○

Aspen, 4
Bill's Residence, 3
Eben Haëzer, 1
Flying Pig, 26
Hans Brinker Budget Hotel, 30
Hortus, 23
Hotel Abba, 24
Hotel Beursstraat, 11
Hotel Brian, 6
Hotel Winston, 10
Jeugdherberg Stadsdoelen (HI), 18
Jeugdherberg Vondelpark (HI), 25
Liberty Hotel, 5
Lucky Mothers, 21
Seven Bridges, 20
The Shelter, 16
SleepInn Arena, 32

WHERE TO SLEEP

Accommodation isn't cheap in this densely populated city, but you can find beds in plenty of hostels for about f25. The hostel scene is pretty lively, especially at the private hostels, where curfews are either very late or nonexistent, and you can relax and socialize with fellow travelers. Official hostels and Christian hostels are a bit more prim, with earlier curfews and a ban on drugs. Doubles in the cheapest hotels run f80–f100. The area southeast of the train station, around the Warmoesstraat and the Red Light District, is crammed with hostels and budget hotels. To avoid the drug dealers and seedy alleys, reach your hotel by walking west, toward the Jordaan, on Nieuwendijk (which becomes Haarlemmerstraat), Nieuwezijds Voorburgwal, or Prins Hendrikkade, or by taking a tram south toward Vondelpark. In July, August, and other holiday periods, most hotels, hostels, and even campgrounds are fully booked; reserve as far ahead as possible, or try to arrive at Centraal Station by about 10 AM to start making phone calls. If everything's full, try getting a room through VVV (*see* Visitor Information *in* Basics, *above*).

DIRT CHEAP • Hortus. This is a great backpacker hangout—the lounge comes complete with bongs, stereo, cable TV, soda machine stocked with Heineken, and soccer paraphernalia. Rooms are spotless, if a good 15- to 20-minute walk from the city center. Beds in singles, doubles, triples, and quads are f40 per person, breakfast included. *Plantage Parkln. 8, tel. 020/625–9996. From station, Tram 9 to Artis Zoo; walk west on Plantage Middenln., left on Plantage Parkln. Cash only.*

Hotel Brian. The lounge is pleasantly chaotic, and the young owners keep rooms and showers nice and clean. Doubles–quads are f40 per person, cooked breakfast included. Call a few weeks ahead in summer. *Singel 69, tel. 020/624–4661. Cash only.*

Liberty Hotel. The young, friendly staff here knows what's up in Amsterdam. The lounge has bongs, a stereo, and free tea and coffee all day. Two- to five-bed rooms run f40 per person. *Singel 5, tel. 020/620–7307. Cash only.*

UNDER F80 • Bill's Residence. The canal-side location is dreamy, and a mere 10-minute walk from the station. Cake and coffee are delivered to your room each morning by a charming old proprietor, who's been looking after backpackers for more than 25 years. Reserve a week ahead. Doubles without bath are f75. *Leliegr. 18, tel. 020/622–3109. Cash only.*

Hotel Beursstraat. These clean rooms, with firm beds, are near both the station and the Red Light scene. Doubles without bath are f85. *Beursstr. 7, tel. 020/626–3701. Reception open 24 hrs. Cash only.*

Lucky Mothers. The owners and the atmosphere are both groovy at this small hotel. Doubles cost f60–f110, and apartments are also available by the week or month. Reserve a few weeks in advance. *Keizersgr. 705, tel. 020/420–6466. From station, take Tram 16, 24, or 25 to Keizersgr. and walk 1 block east.*

UNDER F100 • Aspen. The front rooms face a busy street, but the double-paned windows keep them pretty quiet, and all rooms are large and clean. There's no lounge, so you'll have to head out to socialize. Doubles are f80–f100. *Raadhuisstr. 31, tel. 020/626–6714, fax 020/620–0866.*

Hotel Abba. These simple, slightly worn rooms near the Leidseplein are comfy, spacious, and bright. There's a great lounge, and the price (doubles f90–130) includes an excellent breakfast buffet. *Overtoom 122, tel. 020/618–3058, fax 020/685–3477. From station, take Tram 1 to 1e Constantijn Huygensstr.*

UNDER F150 • Seven Bridges. All rooms are meticulously decorated with Oriental rugs, art-deco lamps, and marble sinks. Top-floor rooms are the smallest; the first-floor room is practically palatial. Doubles cost f125–f230, including breakfast delivered to your room. Reserve a month in advance. *Reguliersgr. 31, tel. 020/623–1329. From station, Tram 16, 24, or 25 to Keizersgr.; walk 1 block east to Reguliersgr.*

Hotel Winston. Newly refurbished—with real, live artists contributing paintings and decor ideas to each room—the Winston is popular with a young crowd; its well-priced, clean accommodations are right in the center of town. The bar has regained its reputation as a vibrant venue for live performances and late-night music. Doubles start at f130, breakfast included. *Warmoesstraat 123, tel. 020/623–1380, fax 020/639–2308.*

Hans Brinker Budget. Ideally located for all of Amsterdam's attractions, this clean and lively budget hotel offers doubles with shower for f117, dorm beds for f40.50. *Kerkstraat 136, tel. 020/622–0687, fax 020/638–2060.*

NJHC HOSTELS

Jeugdherberg Stadsdoelen (HI). Centrally located on a leafy canal, this hostel boasts a bar with a pool table and the cheapest pints of beer in town, served until 1 AM. Dorm beds are f29.75 (sheets f6.25 extra), breakfast included. Happy hour is 8–9. *Kloveniersburgwal 97, tel. 020/624–6832, fax 020/639–1035. Reception open 7 AM–12:30 AM. Kitchen, laundry.*

Jeugdherberg Vondelpark (HI). In a picturesque location at the edge of the Vondelpark, this joint is currently undergoing extensive renovation and should emerge in January 1998 with a completely new wing. Doubles cost f90–f100, dorm beds f34, and sheets f6.25, breakfast included. They'll store your luggage with a f10 deposit. *Zandpad 5, tel. 020/683–1744, fax 020/616–6591. From station, Tram 1, 2, 11, or 5 to Leidsepl.; walk 5 min SW to Vondelpark. Lockout 10:45–2:30.*

PRIVATE HOSTELS

Flying Pig Vondelpark. It's a bit on the grungy side, but it's close to the serenity of Vondelpark and the madness of the Leidseplein. Dorm beds are f23.50–f31, blankets f4.50 extra. They'll store your luggage with a f15 deposit. *Vossiusstr. 46–47, tel. 202/400–4187, fax 020/400–4105. From station, take Tram 1, 2, or 5 to Leidseplein and walk south toward Vondelpark. Kitchen.*

Arena. This beautiful complex, with 400 dorm beds, is also home to the International Centre for Youth Culture and Tourism and a lively music venue with restaurant, bar, and dance floor. Doubles (f100) are on the top floor, away from most of the revelry. Dorm beds are f22.50, sheets f5. *'s Gravesandestr. 51, tel. 020/694–7444. From station, Tram 9 or Bus 22 to Oosterpark; or Metro to Weesperpl. Lockout 11–3.*

> *Some hostels may ask for your passport as a key deposit. Offer a cash deposit instead—the word on the street is that passports sometimes disappear.*

CHRISTIAN HOSTELS

Eben Haëzer. These large, well-lit rooms have a nice, quiet location in the Jordaan. Beds are f20, breakfast included. They'll watch your luggage for a f10 deposit. *Bloemstr. 179, tel. 020/624–4717, fax 020/627–6137. From station, take Tram 13, 14, or 17 to Westermarkt; walk north on Prinsengr., then turn left on Bloemstr. Lockout 10–2.*

The Shelter. The beds are cheap, and the smoke-free café and quiet courtyard are a nice change of pace. Lockout is 10 AM–1 PM, but common rooms are always open. There's an optional dinner for f8.50, and the bed charge of f20 includes breakfast. Drop your luggage off for f1, plus a f10 deposit. *Barndesteeg 21, tel. 020/625–3230, fax 020/623–2282. Reception open 7:30 AM–midnight.*

CAMPING

Gaasper Camping. The countryside location is nice, and although it's an inconvenient 15 km (9 mi) southeast of the city, you can get here on the Metro for four strips. Tent sites are f8 plus f6 per person, and the premises include a grocery and a laundromat. *Loosdrachtdraas 7, tel. 020/696–7326. From station, take Gaasperplas Metro line to last stop; follow signs. Closed Jan.–mid-Mar.*

Vliegenbos. The closest campground to Centraal Station (near a residential area 2 km/1 mi to the north), Vliegenbos is popular with young, international backpackers. Tent sites in a grassy, tree-lined field are f9.25 per person, shower included. Small, four-person cabins are f63. The grocery and laundromat come in handy. *Meeuwenln. 138, tel. 020/636–8855. From station, take Bus 32 or 36. Closed Oct.–Mar.*

FOOD

Budget travelers needn't starve in Amsterdam. If you're really scrounging, you can always head for the ubiquitous snack bars and **FEBO** self-serve snack bars, where you can get *patat* for f2, chicken drumsticks for f2, and burgers for f4. Pick up groceries at **Albert Heijn** stores throughout the city; the most central locations are on the Nieuwezijds Voorburgwal, behind the Royal Palace on the Dam, or at Koningsplein 4–6. Some of the best values in Asian cuisine are along the Zeedijk, around the Nieuwmarkt, in the Red Light District, and around Albert Cuypstraat. For more traditional local cuisine head for any *eetcafé*, most of which double as brown cafés (*see* Bars, *below*).

UNDER F10 • Gary's Muffins. Those craving fresh-baked muffins, brownies, or bagels with gourmet toppings can now stuff themselves at branches throughout the city. A bagel with cream cheese is f3.75, a huge cup of coffee with a warm muffin f4. *Prinsengr. 454, off Leidsestr., tel. 020/638–0186; also*

Marnixstraat 121; Jodenbreestraat 15 (near Waterlooplein); Reguliersdwarsstraat 53. Open daily 8–6; the Reguliersdwarsstraat branch is open late.

Maoz Falafel. There's only one item on the menu here—falafel (f5)—but you can load it up with lots of veggie toppings and hot sauces. *Reguliersbreestr. 45, west of Rembrantspl. and overlooking the Munttoren, tel. 020/624–9290.*

Toscana. People pack this place for its cheap pizzas and pasta dishes. It's the most popular pizzeria—and there are many—on this busy shopping street. Spaghetti with tomato sauce is f8, pizza with ham and mushrooms f8.50, but watch out; you may be tempted by expensive side dishes as well. *Haarlemmerstr. 130, tel. 020/622–0353. Open daily 4 PM–11:30 PM.*

UNDER F15 • Originally a soup kitchen, the **Keuken Van 1870** (Spuistr. 4, 5 min SW of station, tel. 020/624–8965) specializes in standard, hearty, meat-and-potato Dutch meals for around f12.

Amigo. The decor is plain, but the filling plates of Surinamese cuisine are delicious. Try the *roti* (savory pancake) dishes with lightly spiced meat and vegetables. *Rozengracht 5 (just west of the Dam), tel. 020/623–1140.*

De Vliegende Schotel. You get more for less in this vegetarian restaurant, hidden away in the Jordaan. Choose from a fine selection of soups, filling main courses for as little as f10, and desserts. *Nieuwe Leliestr. 162, tel. 625–2041*

Pannekoekenhuis "Upstairs." Owner Gerrit prepares a multitude of crêpes right before your eyes in the tiny kitchen. Soup is f4, savory crêpes start at f10, and sweet crêpes with powdered sugar are f6.50. *Grimburgwal 2 (just east of Rokin), tel. 020/626–5603. Closed Mon.*

UNDER F20 • Song Kwae. This cheap Thai restaurant near the Nieuwmarkt is the best in its class. Green or red curries with beef or chicken cost a mere f12.50, and most other main courses are under f20. Enthusiastic diners often spill onto the terrace. *Kloveniersburgwal 14A, tel. 624–2568.*

Bojo. Despite its proximity to the touristy Leidseplein, Bojo is the best value in town for Indonesian food. The tasty and filling fried-rice special is f12.50; other entrées are f14–f18. Empty at lunch but packed at dinner, Bojo is perfect for late-night munchies—you're welcome until 1 AM Sunday through Thursday and 4:30 AM Friday and Saturday. *Lange Leidsedwarsstr. 51, tel. 020/622–7434.*

Goodies. This excellent sandwich shop recently expanded its repertoire to become a "spaghetteria" in the evenings. Tasty risottos and fresh pastas cost just f15, meat dishes a bit more. Make a reservation. *Huidenstraat 9, tel. 020-625 6122.*

"COFFEE SHOPS"

In Amsterdam, coffee shops are synonymous with smoking pot, a pastime as acceptable as drinking a beer when indulged in the right place. At the **Hash Marihuana/Hemp Museum** (Oudezijds Achterburgwal 148, tel. 020/623–5961; admission f6), you'll find educational pamphlets on the benefits and uses of marijuana plants. Try to avoid the numerous rip-off shops, especially around the Red Light District and the main tourist drags. Most coffee shops are open daily from about 10 AM to midnight or 1 AM; if you fancy some stuff, ask for the menu, which lists prices and descriptions of the wares. Some coffee shops still sell "space cake," made with cannabis oil, but the dosage and effects are unpredictable, and have led to the hospitalization of some unsuspecting users.

De Dampkring. This place is a bit hard-core, but it's convenient to Leidseplein. The pot counter looks like a fast-food express window. There's a microscope on hand so patrons can inspect the density of the sparkling THC crystals. Alcohol is also served. *Handboogstr. 29, off Heiligeweg, no phone.*

Global Chillage. This big hangout is too cool for chairs—everyone sits on pillows on the floor. There's a good selection of imported hash and local grass, as well as dope on the local rave and ambient scenes. *Kerkstr. 51, tel. 020/639–1154.*

The Greenhouse. Every connoisseur in Amsterdam will tell you that it doesn't get any better than this. Both locations, though one of them is quite far from the center, have unique and changing decor—look for the fountain made from bat dung in the Waterlooplein shop. They also serve alcohol. *Waterloopl. 345, tel. 020/622–5499; Tolstr. 91, tel. 020/673–7430. To Tolstr., take Tram 4 from Rembrandtpl.*

Tweede Kamer. Named after the Dutch parliament's lower house, Tweede Kamer makes for a pleasantly dreamy afternoon with gentle hash highs (they don't sell weed). Draughts, chess, and backgammon make for a convivial, civilized atmosphere. *Heisteeg 6, just off the Spui, no phone.*

WORTH SEEING

Before you head off to Amsterdam's blockbuster museums, get to know the city by wandering around Dam Square, the Wallen, and the Jordaan.

AROUND DAM SQUARE

Dam Square is a crowded meeting-place for tourists, street performers, and thousands of pigeons. The **Koninklijk Paleis,** or Royal Palace (Nieuwezijds Voorburgwal 147, tel. 020/624–8698; admission f5; open daily 12:30–5 in summer, call for information off season), was completed in 1665, but its glamorous touches (like the crystal chandeliers) were added in 1808, when Louis Napoléon moved in. The **Nieuwe Kerk** (New Church), next door, is a bright, spacious, 15th-century church used mainly for temporary exhibitions, most notably the disturbing images of the annual World Press Photo (photojournalism competition), and the occasional coronation. A few blocks south of the Dam is the informative **Amsterdam Historisch Museum** (Nieuwezijds Voorburgwal 357, tel. 020/523–1822; admission f5), a museum documenting the history of Amsterdam from the 13th century to the present day. Follow the galleried walkway from the museum's inner courtyard and you'll find yourself in one of Amsterdam's most idyllic spots, the **Begijnhof** (Beguine Court), also accessible from the Spui. The houses lining this tranquil, grassy square were once the homes of the Beguines, an order of lay nuns founded in the 13th century. No. 34 is one of only two wooden medieval structures in the city.

THE RED LIGHT DISTRICT (WALLEN)

Tourists, drug dealers, drug addicts, and men seeking prostitutes converge on the "Wallen" between the Warmoesstraat and the Zeedijk, two of the city's oldest streets. These "walls" were once the city's embattlements, but they're now tree-lined canals lined by somewhat disheveled old houses. The district is a notorious hangout for pickpockets, so despite a strong police presence (both uniformed and plainclothed), take good care. The **Oude Kerk** (Oudekerksplein 1, tel. 020/625–8284; admission f5; open Apr.–Oct., Mon.–Sat. 11–5, Sun. 1-5, Nov.–Mar., Fri.–Sun. 1–5), just off the Warmoesstraat, is Amsterdam's oldest standing monument, dating from 1325. The Romanesque single nave was extended to three naves of the same height in 1336, but because it was only supported by sandstone pillars (rather than granite), the builders mixed in as much glass as possible to keep the construction light. Some 15th-century frescoes are still visible. Just up the Oudezijds Voorburgwal is the **Museum Amstelkring** (*see* Museums, *below*), and a few canals further east is the Zeedijk, once a notorious haunt for unwholesome sailors but now the thriving heart of Chinatown. Hang a right along the Zeedijk and you'll find yourself at the **Nieuwmarkt,** full of cafés and terraces. The imposing turreted building is the **Waag,** or weigh-house for incoming cargo, dating from 1488; the lofty, beamed interior has been converted into a grand café and restaurant.

THE JORDAAN

Head west from the Damrak across the main ring of canals to the **Jordaan** area, a maze of narrow streets and bridges lined with workshops, brown cafés, and quirky stores. Once Amsterdam's working-class district, the Jordaan has become quite trendy, yet it still feels like an artisans' neighborhood. The intriguing specialty shops feature everything from secondhand clothes and 1950s *objets d'art* to Dutch high fashion and kitchen utensils.

MUSEUMS

Many of Amsterdam's biggest museums are conveniently clustered around the Museumplein, just south of the city center. If you're under 24, haul your photo to the VVV and buy a **Museumjaarkaart** (f17.50), which gets you free admission to most museums (though not the Anne Frankhuis) for a whole year. If you're over 24, the card costs f47.50, which is probably not worth spending unless you're determined to visit every museum in town.

ANNE FRANKHUIS

The young Jewish girl whose diary led to her posthumous international fame hid here, in the secret annex, with her family from 1942 to 1944. All were eventually discovered and sent to Auschwitz. The house also has a small exhibition on the Holocaust. *Prinsengr. 263, tel. 020/556–7100. Admission: f10. Open Sept.–Apr., Mon.–Sat. 9–5, Sun. 10–5; May–Aug., daily 9–7.*

THE GOLDEN CURVE

This stretch of the Herengracht extends from the Leidsegracht to the Vijzelstraat and contains some of Amsterdam's most opulent 18-century architecture. Built by wealthy merchants, the buildings are faced with expensive sandstone and are wider than most canal houses, blessed with a grandeur befitting their cost. Most notable are numbers 475 (designed by Hans Jacob Husly in 1703), 485 (Jean Coulon, 1739), 493 and 527, both in the Louis XVI style (1770), and 284 (Van Brienen House, 1728) another ornate Louis XVI facade.

MUSEUM AMSTELKRING

It looks like a typical canal house from the outside, but hidden away upstairs is a church, complete with altar, pulpit, seats hanging from the roof, rows of pews, and an organ. The church dates from 1663, when Roman Catholics were forbidden to hold public services but were allowed to build clandestine churches. This one, nicknamed "Our Lord in the Attic," was built in the attics of three adjoining houses and is the last such church still standing. The winding staircases and aura of secrecy are an eerie parallel to the Anne Frank house. *Oudezijds Voorburgwal 40, tel. 020/624–6604. Admission: f7.50. Open Mon.–Sat. 10–5, Sun. and holidays 1–5.*

MUSEUM HET REMBRANDTHUIS

This was the old master's home from 1639 to 1660. The art collection is not so spectacular, but you'll be entertained by Rembrandt's self-portraits, which capture his many moods, hairdos, and hats. *Jodenbreestr. 4–6, tel. 020/624–9486. Admission: f7.50. Open Mon.–Sat. 10–5, Sun. and holidays 1–5.*

RIJKSMUSEUM

This immense and beautiful building houses an extensive collection of paintings and applied art, mostly by 17th-century Dutch artists. Rembrandt's *Nightwatch* may get top billing, but the four small paintings by Vermeer, including his beautiful *Kitchen Maid,* are the real highlights. The exterior, designed by the same architect who came up with Centraal Station, is worth a close look for its montage of sculptures, tilework, and reliefs paying homage to the movers and shakers of Dutch art. *Stadhouderskade 42, at north end of Museumpl., tel. 020/673–2121. Admission: f12.50. Open Mon.–Sat. 10–5, Sun. 1–5.*

VAN GOGH MUSEUM

The first floor features a permanent collection of works by such 19th-century painters as Gauguin and Émile Bernard; the second floor is devoted entirely to Van Gogh. It's the *Best of Van Gogh* album—all the sunflowers, irises, and manic self-portaits your heart desires. Take a good look at *Wheatfield with Crows,* one of the last paintings VG completed before killing himself. NOTE: From Sept. '98–May '99, the museum will be closed for renovation. Part of the collection will be on display in the Rijksmuseum's South Wing. *Paulus Potterstr. 7, tel. 020/570–5200. Admission: f12.50. Open daily 10–5.*

STEDELIJK MUSEUM

Amsterdam's museum of modern art is right next door to the Van Gogh Museum. Along with some far-out work by Dutch artists, the Stedelijk has Picassos, Matisses, and a sprinkling of impressionist and post-impressionist work. *Paulus Potterstr. 13, tel. 020/573–2911. Admission: f9. Open Apr.–Sept., daily 10–6; Oct.–Mar., daily 10–5.*

JOODS HISTORISCH MUSEUM

The Jewish Historical Museum is housed in a series of 17th- and 18th-century synagogues near the Waterlooplein. On display is a well-organized history of Jews in Amsterdam and the Netherlands plus occasional visiting exhibitions. There is also a non-smoking (!) kosher restaurant. *Jonas Daniel Meyerplein 2–4, tel. 020/626–9945. Metro to Waterlooplein or Tram 9. Admission: f7. Open daily 11–5.*

CHEAP THRILLS

CYCLING

If you find yourself craving green pastures and bodies of water, take yourself there on two wheels. One of the most scenic tours is the **Waterland route.** Starting from the back of Centraal Station, take the ferry across the North Sea Canal, then bear east toward the picturesque village of Broek-in-Waterland. You can then head north to the former fishing villages of Volendam and Marken on the IJsselmeer, and return to Amsterdam via Durgerdam. The routes vary from 20 km to 40 km (12 mi to 24 mi); maps are available from the VVV or bike-rental shops.

SHOPPING

Amsterdam hosts several bazaar-type street markets every day except Sunday. The lively **Waterlooplein flea market** (Mon.–Sat. 9:30–4), next to the Muziektheater, is the ideal place to rummage for second-hand clothes, cheap antiques, and all manner of other curiosities. The bustling covered market **Antiek-markt de Looier** (Elandsgracht 109; Sun.–Wed. 11–5, Thurs. 11–9) is great for antiques, especially silver and toys. The **Nieuwe Spiegelstraat** is a particularly good haunt for curiosa and art, from antique navigation instruments and Dutch dressers to the colorful, primitivist paintings of the CoBrA group. In the summer, art lovers can scrutinize contemporary work at the Sunday **art markets** on Thorbeckeplein and the Spui.

Suffering from museum fatigue? The best place to picnic in Amsterdam is on the lawns of the Vondelpark. In July and August, the outdoor stage hosts free concerts and plays.

The **Albert Cuyp market,** south of the Heineken Brewery on Albert Cuypstraat, has an intercontinental mix of fresh produce, as well as cheap new clothes. On Saturday the **Noordermarkt** and **Nieuwmarkt** feature **organic farmers' markets** (10–4), with purveyors of biodynamic foods, essential oils, and other wholesome fare. The **flower market,** floating on the Singel canal between the Koningsplein and Vijzelstraat, will brighten any gray day and remind you that Holland is still the land of tulips.

FESTIVALS

Expect things to get truly out of hand on **Koninginnedag** (April 30), the birthday of the late Queen Juliana. Markets, live music, and parties fill the streets, blocking all traffic, and the entire city basically becomes a Dutch Mardi Gras. Most businesses close for the day, and nearly everyone sports traditional orange clothing.

AFTER DARK

Most of Amsterdam's nightlife is concentrated around Leidseplein and Rembrandtsplein. The fortnightly **Queer Fish** (f2.50) has the most detailed listings of events and nightlife (straight and gay) and is available at most newsstands. Discos and jazz clubs can be expensive, so many locals fall back on the quieter pleasure of downing a few beers in a café, brown or otherwise. Amsterdam is something of a gay mecca, with fashionable bars in the Regulierdwarsstraat, casual bars in the Kerkstraat and along the Amstel, and late-night leather bars in the Warmoesstraat; the **Gay and Lesbian Switchboard** (tel. 202/623–6565; open daily 10–10) can help you find your bearings.

BROWN CAFES AND GRAND CAFES

Brown cafés are traditionally characterized by a predominance of wood and yellowish walls stained by years of cigarette smoke. However, recent years have seen the burgeoning of designer culture, and many bars have been refitted in chrome and glass. You'll find the best selection of these hangouts in the Jordaan and the Wallen (*see above*), where they occupy almost every street corner.

De Jaren. A mere minute's walk from the Munt, De Jaren is the largest of grand cafés, with high ceilings and two wonderful terraces overlooking the Amstel. There's a fine salad bar and an international array of daily newspapers. Dinner is served upstairs. *Nieuwe Doelenstr. 20, tel. 020/625–5771.*

Café Ebeling. A nice escape from the sensory overload of the Leidseplein, this brown café provides an inviting environment with alternative music, a pool table, and a good selection of imported beer. Sandwiches, omelettes, and salads are served noon–6; dinner is served 6 PM–10 PM. *Overtoom 52, tel. 020/689–4858. Tram 1 to Overtoom.*

(ALMOST) FREE BEER

Down the road past the Rijksmuseum, the now defunct Heineken Brewery gives informative tours on Heineken history and the brewing process. Afterwards, they throw you munchies and all the beer you can drink in half an hour, and your admission fee goes to charity. Get here early—tours sell out by about 11:30 AM. Stadhouderskade 78, tel. 020/523–9666. Admission: f2. Tours June–mid-Sept., weekdays at 9:30, 11, 1, and 2:30 (also Sat. at noon and 2 in July and Aug.); mid-Sept.–May, weekdays at 9:30 and 11.

't Gasthuys. Close to the busy Rokin but on a quiet side street overlooking a canal, this is a popular student hangout during the academic year. A tomato-and-brie sandwich is f5. In the evening you can feast on handsome portions of traditional Dutch home cooking, with excellent fries and piles of salad, for about f15. *Grimburgwal 7, tel. 020/624–8230.*

CLUBS

Amsterdam has no shortage of dance clubs. Depending on the night of the week, covers range from f5 to f15, and beer costs f3.50–f4.50. **Mazzo** (114 Rozengr., tel. 020/626–7500) is about as hip as it gets, but the biggest club in Amsterdam is **iT** (Amstelstr. 24, tel. 020/625–0111; closed Mon.–Wed.), famous for its gay Saturday night. **ROXY** (Singel 465–467, tel. 020/620–0354; closed Mon. and Tues.) and **Escape** (Rembrandtplein 11, tel. 020/622-1111) also draw huge crowds on weekends, and ROXY hosts the **Pussy Lounge,** an all-lesbian party, every third Sunday 6–midnight. Casual garb is okay at Mazzo, but you'll want to doll up for ROXY, Escape, and iT.

SQUATS

The recent Eurotop summit in Amsterdam brought alternative political groups out of the woodwork for 1960s-style demonstrations. Squatting is still a popular way to nab some of Amsterdam's elusive cheap housing, and the communities that have grown up around the squats often host some of the more interesting arts events and dance parties. Two established squats hold dance nights on weekends. The **Vrankrijk** (Spuistr. 216, no phone) throws a popular Saturday-night party with cheap drinks, alternative music, and arty visuals. On Sunday night the **Trut** (corner of Bilderdijkstr./Kinkerstr., no phone) hosts a disco exclusively for lesbians and gays. Folks start queueing 20 minutes before the 11 o'clock opening.

LIVE MUSIC

Tickets for nearly all cultural events in Amsterdam are available from the **UitBuro** (Leidsepl. 26, under the Stadsschouwburg theater, tel. 020/621-1211). Closer to Amsterdam's center, **Melkweg** (Lijnbaansgr. 234, tel. 020/624–8492; cover f17.50–f30) and **Paradiso** (Weteringschans 6–8, tel. 020/626–4521; cover f15–f30) are two popular forums for big-name artists. The **Arena** and **Winston Kingdom** (*see* Where to Sleep *above*) also host live bands, poetry evenings, and comedy. Major-league international artists usually play the new, Metro-accessible **ArenA** stadium, in the Bijlmer.

Alto. One of the more popular jazz clubs around Leidseplein, the Alto is small but jammin', and full of locals. Music kicks in at 9:30, and there's no cover. *Korte Leidsedwarsstr. 115, tel. 020/626–3249.*

Café Meander. This popular venue has live music every night, everything from trad jazz to the latest in hip-hop. Cover is f5, though it can expand if a big name is playing. *Voetboogsteeg 5, tel. 020/625–8430).*

Maloe Melo. When Eurodisco overload sets in, head straight for this rock and blues bar. Nightly music starts at 11. Cover is free or f5–f10, depending on who's playing. *Lijnbaansgr. 163, tel. 020/420–4592.*

THE CLASSICS

Amsterdam's world-famous **Concertgebouw** (Concertgebouwpl. 2-6, tel. 020/671–8345), whose neo-classical facade overlooks the Museumplein, offers free lunchtime concerts at 12:30 every Wednesday, sometimes featuring a top orchestra as an appetizer for its concert in the evening (if not the renowned

Concertgebouw Orchestra itself). Get there early if you want a good seat. In July and August, tickets to orchestral concerts are just f25. You can also catch free organ and carillon concerts during the summer months at churches throughout the city.

THE RANDSTAD AND AROUND

The Dutch refer to the area encircled by Amsterdam, The Hague, Rotterdam, and Utrecht as the Randstad (Round City). The megalopolis is also called "the West" by young, provincial Randstad wanna-bes who see it as the place to hit the big time. In addition to harboring the capital of international justice (The Hague) and the world's largest port (Rotterdam), the 10 small and medium-size cities in this tiny area are home to more than 40% of the country's residents—and that's not counting the tulip growers and vegetable and dairy farmers who fill in what little open land remains here.

HAARLEM

Haarlem was once a thriving artists' colony, home to such painters as Frans Hals, Judith Leyster, and Claus Sluter, who put their works on the block at the weekly market. After the decline of the Golden Age, however, the artists packed up their easels and headed for Amsterdam, so their legacies are enshrined in Haarlem's museums, the main attractions in this quiet town. The much-hyped Saturday and Monday outdoor markets still take place, but they're fairly small.

Chill out warmly at the Fenomeen Sauna (Eerste Schinkelstr. 16, tel. 020/671–6780; open daily 1–11, women only Mon., closed July–mid-Aug.), near the southernmost exit of the Vondelpark. Steam, sweat, and snooze all day for just f12.50.

If you're lucky enough to score a cheap room here (usually booked through the VVV), Haarlem is a great base for exploring Kennemerduinen National Park (*see* Near Haarlem, *below*), local beaches, the nearby resort of Zandvoort, and the surrounding countryside. Haarlem's **VVV** (Stationspl. 1; tel. 0900/3202–4043, f1 per minute), next to the train station, books rooms (f9) and sells maps (f3) and accommodation lists (f1.50). There is a **GWK** office inside the train station.

COMING AND GOING
Haarlem is a 15-minute train ride (f6.25) from Amsterdam. All trains pull into **Haarlem Station NS** (Stationspl. 11), at the north end of town, an art-deco monument from 1908. **Grote Markt,** the main square, is just a 10-minute walk from the station; head south on Kruisweg. **Buses** stop at the train station on their way through the city.

WHERE TO SLEEP AND EAT
Haarlem's few budget hotels aren't all that "budget." The **Carillon** (Grote Markt 27, tel. 023/531–0591, fax 023/531–4909; doubles from f120), just off the northern end of Grote Markt, is attached to a relaxed outdoor café. In a turn-of-the-century building a few minutes west of Grote Markt, the **Stads Café** (Zijlstr. 56, tel. 023/532–5202, fax 023/532–0504; doubles from f80) rents large rooms over the restaurant; just pop downstairs for a f10 main course. For a cheaper private room (f60–f70 for a double), aim for a B&B through the VVV, or find a pension or B&B in the nearby seaside resort of Zandvoort. The HI hostel, **Jeugdherberg Jan Gijzen** (Jan Gijzenpad 3, tel. 023/537–3793, fax 023/537–1176), in a bucolic setting 3 km (2 mi) north of the train station, charges f22.50, but remember to figure in the three strips it costs to get here. Take Bus 2 from the station.

Do-it-yourselfers can seek sustenance at the **Albert Heijn** supermarket (Grote Houtstr. 178). **Jacobus Pieck** (Warmoesstr. 18, tel. 023/532–6144) is a stylish but well-priced *eetcafé* just off the Grote Markt, where a main course costs about f15. **Donatello's** (Gierstr. 66, tel. 023/531–7581) sells generous portions of pizza and pasta for f8.75, but they're open for dinner only. **Maple Forest** (Zijlstr. 77, tel. 023/531–0471) has a huge selection of Chinese food; dim sum starts at f7, vegetarian dishes at f17.

WORTH SEEING

Haarlem's focal point is the **Grote Markt,** surrounded by Flemish-influenced architecture from the Renaissance, such as the **Vleeshal,** from 1603, and the **Stadshal** (closing off the west corner), which dates mainly from the 14th century. Market stalls fill the square on Monday and Saturday. The colossal, Romanesque **Grote Kerk** (also known as the **St. Bavo),** built between 1400 and 1550, towers over the square (tel. 023/532–4399; admission f2.50; open Mon.–Sat. 10–4); its highlight is the monumental Müller organ, whose 5,068 pipes were played by the young Mozart and Handel. As well as the biannual international organ festival (held the first week of July in even-numbered years), there are free weekly concerts on Thursday at 3 PM (mid-June–August) and Tuesday at 8:15 PM (mid-May–October).

The historic **Vleeshal** and **Verweyhal** have fine collections of modern art (Grote Markt; admission f4). Three blocks south of the church is Haarlem's pride and joy, the **Frans Hals Museum** (Groot Heiligland 62, tel. 023/516–4200; open Mon.–Sat. 11–5, Sun. 1–5; admission Apr.–Sept. f7.50, Oct.–Mar. f6.50). A former almshouse for old men, built in 1607–1610, it now boasts a collection of old-master paintings from the late 16th to 17th centuries, many by Frans Hals himself. Two blocks east of Grote Markt along the broad Spaarne canal is the **Teylers Museum** (Spaarne 16, tel. 023/531–9010; admission f7.50; open Tues.–Sat. 10–5, Sun. noon–5), reputed to be the oldest public museum in the Netherlands; it was founded in 1778 by the wealthy merchant, Pieter Teyler van der Hulst, to further the arts and sciences. The collections are an unusual admixture of art, old scientific gadgets, and rock and mineral samples. You have to peek behind curtains to see the light-sensitive Renaissance drawings. The **Corrie ten Boomhuis** (Barteljorisstr. 19, just off Grote Markt, tel. 023/531–0823; admission free; open Apr.–Nov., Tues.–Sat. 10–4; Nov.–Mar., Tues.–Sat. 11–3) looks like an ordinary clock shop—and that's exactly the point. During World War II the Ten Boom family hid Jewish refugees above their store before they themselves were imprisoned by the Gestapo.

If you're not in the mood to museum-hop, spend your day enjoying the quiet, pedestrian-only cobblestone streets and the Flemish architecture around and to the south of Grote Markt, and popping into the inner courtyards of the *hofjes* (former almshouses or hospices).

NEAR HAARLEM

NATIONAL PARK DE KENNEMERDUINEN

Biking through this park (tel. 023/525–7653; admission f1.75), about a 10-minute ride west of Haarlem, is one of the cooler things to do around here, both literally and figuratively. Dirt paths wind through the forest, paved paths cut through the dunes, and you can feel the air get cooler as you approach the North Sea. Originally preserved for its huge, underground, fresh-water reservoir, the park is now cherished as one of the last undeveloped areas in the Netherlands, with deer and foxes scampering through the forests. You can rent bikes for f8 per day, plus a f100 deposit, in the **Rijwiel Shop** (tel. 023/531–7066) at the train station. Stop by the **visitors' center** (tel. 023/527–1871), at the southeast corner of the park, for trail maps. If you prefer an old-fashioned ramble, bus 81 goes to the park from the Haarlem train station; the trip costs three strips.

ZANDVOORT

Ten minutes from Haarlem by train, this former fishing village is now a budding Atlantic City, complete with large casino, luxury hotels, race-car track, and crowded beaches. To avoid the glare of the commerce, you can walk 10–15 minutes south from the main boulevard to the nude beach, popular with straights and gays alike. Happily, cheap pensions abound in Zandvoort, though in high season they're no cheaper than elsewhere. Hogeweg and Brederodestraat, south of the train station, are lined with pensions and small hotels. One of the cheaper family-run hotels is **Hotel Faber** (Kostverlorenstr. 15, tel. 023/571–2825, fax 023/571–6886; doubles with shower or bath f60, breakfast included), just a few minutes' walk from the beach.

Frequent trains serve Zandvoort from Amsterdam (30 min, f8), with additional direct service in the summer; otherwise, change trains at Haarlem. Zandvoort's **VVV** (Schoolpl. 1, tel. 023/571–7947, closed Sun.) has a list of pensions and books rooms for f5.25.

LEIDEN

Leiden first landed in history books during the Eighty Years' War with Spain. On October 3, 1574, after the town had faced starvation for weeks under a Spanish siege, Prince William the Silent broke through the dikes and whisked in his fleet to save the day. October 3 is thus reserved for the **Relief of Leiden Celebration,** when the townsfolk drink beer, make merry, and eat the white bread and herring that were brought to their starving forebears. Prince William then established the University of Leiden as a reward for the city's endurance, and the town became a center of Protestant learning. Leiden has gorgeous architecture and street-lined canals, and the students at its prestigious university hang about as if they had nothing better to do than row boats or, in winter, skate on the canals. The idyllic atmosphere, amazing museums, and luxurious botanical gardens make Leiden worth several days' attention.

GETTING AROUND

Trains roll into Leiden from Amsterdam (35 min, f12.75) and Rotterdam (30 min, f12.75); the train station is north of the town center. The **VVV** (Stationspl. 210, across from train station, tel. 071/514–6846) sells maps (f2.50) and hands out free lodging lists. The best map of Leiden's confusing streets is in the brochure "Leiden Museumstad." **Haarlemmerstraat,** the main pedestrian street, is lined with shops and cheap eateries.

WHERE TO SLEEP

Cheap accommodations are an endangered species in Leiden. The best deals are at the **Lits-Jumeaux Youth Hotel** (Lange Scheistr. 9, tel. 071/512–8457), where doubles overlooking Langegracht are f75, and beds in the quieter dorm are f25; breakfast is an extra f12.50 (cash only). Doubles at the few pensions listed at the **VVV** start at f80. The **Hotel Witte Singel** (Witte Singel 80, tel. 071/512–4592; doubles from f85) is next to a gorgeous canal at the south edge of the town center. **The Rose** (Beestenmarkt 14, tel. 071/514–6630) is ideally located, overlooking a pleasant square near the station, but f100 is a bit pricey for doubles with a private shower but shared toilet. Consider upgrading for one night to enjoy the **Hotel De Doelen**'s superb situation overlooking a broad, gracious canal just outside the town center (Rapenburg 2, tel. 071/512–0527, fax 071/512–8453); here doubles with bath and TV are f130, including breakfast.

FOOD

Locals line up for a quick lunchtime fix at pastry shops and snack bars; Haarlemmerstraat is full of them. **Edah** (Stationweg), a few steps from the train station, has cheap picnic fixings. **Annie's Verjaardag** (Hoogstr. 1A, tel. 071/512–5737; cash only), which means "Annie's Birthday," has a floating patio at the fork of the Oude Rijn and Nieuwe Rijn canals; the extensive menu includes such cheap options as Greek salad for f9 and filling lasagna for f14. For a typical Dutch treat, try the **Pannekoekenhuysje** (Steenstr. 51, tel. 071/513–3144; closed Sun.), where your sweet, savory, and cheap pancakes are prepared in the kitchen of the more formal **Oudt Leyden,** next door. **Koetshuis de Burcht Café** is a characterful *eetcafé* housed in a former stable at the foot of **De Burcht,** a fortified mound left over from the city's medieval fortification system. (Burgsteeg 13, tel. 071/512–1688). After dinner, the cafés along the Nieuwe Rijn canal and the broad Rapenburg fill up with the fashionable.

WORTH SEEING

Almost all of Leiden's 15 museums are in the western half of the city, between Lange Mare and Witte Singel. Pick up the free handout "Leiden Museumstad" at the VVV for a complete listing. The **Rijksmuseum van Oudheden,** or National Museum of Antiquities (Rapenburg 28, tel. 071/516–3163; admission f5; open Tues.–Sat. 10–5, Sun. noon–5), has comprehensive exhibits on classical, Near Eastern, Egyptian, and Dutch archaeology; the highlight is the complete 1st-century Temple of Taffeh, donated by the Egyptian government. The **Museum De Lakenhal** (Oude Singel 28, tel. 071/516–5353, admission f5; open Tues.–Sat. 10–5, Sun. noon–5), once a 17th-century guildhouse, houses a variety of old-master and contemporary Dutch art and presents a history of the town's textile industry and medieval guilds. The cavernous **Pieterskerk** (Pieterskerkhol, tel. 071/512–4319; open daily 1:30–4), dating from 1428, is where the Pilgrim Fathers worshiped (remember their Dutch detour?). The **Hortus Botanicus** (Rapenburg 73, tel. 071/527–7249; admission f5; open Apr.–Sept., Mon.–Sat. 9–5, Sun. 10–5; Oct.–Apr., weekdays 9–4:30, Sun. 10:30–3, closed Sat.) is one of Europe's oldest botanical gardens; the first seeds were planted in 1587. The brick paths are lined with exotic plants, trees, and brilliantly colored flowers. Don't miss the sensual tropical greenhouse, with its wonderfully overwhelming humidity and hanging vines.

THE HAGUE

The Hague (Den Haag or 's Gravenhage in Dutch) is a worthwhile day trip for a glimpse of the Netherlands' royal history and political structure. Although Amsterdam is the nation's constitutional capital, The Hague is the seat of the Dutch government and the International Court of Justice (World Court), where war criminals from former Yugoslavia are currently being tried. The Hague is also the home of the Dutch royal family, headed by Queen Beatrix. The city center near Centraal Station is dominated by postmodern high-rise towers and theater complexes. The ritzy dwellings of the royals and international diplomats are in the exclusive northern suburbs, while to the south and west are much poorer neighborhoods.

BASICS

The **VVV** (Koningin Julianapl. 30, in front of Centraal Station, tel. 06/3403–5051, f1.4 per minute) sells local maps (f2.75) and books rooms (f3.50 per person). Cash traveler's checks and pick up client mail at **American Express** (Venestr. 20, tel. 070/370–1100, or toll-free 0800/022–0100 for 24-hour assistance with lost or stolen checks), in the heart of the shopping district between Grote Markt and the Binnenhof. The most convenient **post office** (Koningin Julianapl. 6, tel. 070/347–3872) is across from Centraal Station.

CONSULATES • Australia: *Carnegieln. 4, tel. 070/310–8200. Open Mon.–Thurs. 8:30–5, Fri. 8:30–1.* **Canada:** *Sophialn. 7, tel. 070/361–4111. Open weekdays 9–1 and 2–5:30.* **New Zealand:** *Carnegieln. 10, tel. 070/346–9324. Open weekdays 9–12:30 and 1:30–5:30.*

COMING AND GOING

Trains from Utrecht (40 min, f16) stop at **Centraal Station** (Koningin Julianapl., tel. 070/385–3235), but direct trains from Amsterdam (40 min, f14.50) and Rotterdam (15 min, f7.25) stop at **Den Haag HS** (Stationspl., tel. 070/389–0830), 20 minutes south of the sights. Trams 9 and 12 scoot between the stations regularly, but if you really want to roll directly into Centraal Station from Amsterdam, you can change trains at Leiden.

The Hague's major museums and palaces are about a 10-minute walk northwest of Centraal Station, making them perfect for day-trippers. If, however, you plan to spend the night, you'll definitely have to contend with local **buses** and **trams.** Otherwise, you can rent **bikes** at the train stations or the Kijkduinpark campground (*see* Where to Sleep and Eat, *below*) for f10 per day.

WHERE TO SLEEP AND EAT

Most hotels in The Hague cater to diplomats and business travelers. If you really want an affordable private room in the city, ask the tourist office to book you a room in a private home (f50–f60 per person). There are some relatively inexpensive hotels near the Den Haag HS station; the best one is **Hotel Astoria** (Stationsweg 139, tel. 070/384–0401, fax 070/354–1653, cash only) which has comfortable doubles with shower from f100, breakfast included. The **HI Jeugdherberg Ockenburgh** (Monsterseweg 4, tel. 070/397–0011, fax 070/397–2251; beds f26.50) is in a beautiful park, but the busloads of rowdy pubescents here guarantee you'll hear slamming doors and clunky footsteps all evening. To get here from Centraal Station, take Bus 122 or 123 to Ockenburgh. Campsites at **Kijkduinpark** (Wijndaelerweg 25, tel. 070/325–2364, closed Nov.–Feb.) are f10 plus f7.50 per person; the site has a small supermarket and is just 10 minutes from the beautiful beach at Kijkduin (*see* Near the Hague, *below*).

You'll find reasonably priced restaurants west of the Centraal Station, along Herengracht, Plein, and Grote Marktstraat. In the summer, most put tables outside so you can enjoy the city air while you eat. **Tin-On** (Herengr. 54, tel. 070/364–8545) is one of the cheaper Chinese/Indonesian restaurants in town; most dishes are in the f10–f25 range. At the corner of the Plein square, off Korte Poten, the *eetcafé* **La Perroquet** (Plein 12A, tel. 070/363–9786) has daily specials for f16–f25. The **Sinbad Shoarma Grillroom** (Oude Molstr. 15, just south of Paleis Noordeinde, tel. 070/364–9892; open noon–3 AM) is one of the few late-night restaurants in the city center, serving *shoarmas* (kebabs) and the like for f7 and up. For picnic supplies, hit the **Dagmarkt** (Raamstr. 2) off Grote Markt Straat, the street with the huge department stores.

WORTH SEEING

Most of The Hague's major sights encircle the **Hofvijver,** a lily-covered lake that was originally a moat to protect the **Binnenhof** (Inner Court), with its gracious Parliament buildings. The complex is a few blocks northwest of Centraal Station, a short walk along the Herengracht and Lange Poten (which converge). You can visit the **Riddershal** (Knight's Hall) and either the first or the second chamber of parliament (when not in use) by guided tour only; 50-minute tours are given in Dutch, with an English transcript (Binnenhof 8A, tel. 070/365–4779; admission f6; Mon.–Sat. 10–4). The **Vredespaleis** (Carnegiepl. 2, tel. 070/346–9680; admission f5; open June–Sept., weekdays 10–4; Oct.–May, 10–3), home of the **International Court of Justice,** is a 10-minute walk northwest; to visit, you must take a guided tour, given in English and Dutch at 10, 11, 2, and 3. Tours for both the Vredespaleis and the Binnenhof are popular, so call a few days ahead to reserve a space.

If you visit more than one of the town's museums on a single day, you can get a f1 discount by showing a ticket from another museum. The 1644 **Mauritshuis** (Korte Vijverberg 8, tel. 070/346–9244; admission f10; open Tues.–Sat. 10–5, Sun. 11–5), formerly a royal palace, houses a wonderful collection of 17th-century paintings, including Rembrandt's *Anatomy Lesson of Professor Tulp* and three fine works by Vermeer. Andy Warhol's pop rendition of Queen Beatrix has the dubious honor of hanging in the locker area. If you crave yet more 17th-century art, visit the **Museum Bredius** (Lange Vijverburg 14, tel. 070/362–0729; admission f6; open Tues.–Sun. noon–5), which houses the substantial art collection of Abraham Bredius in a grand and patrician 18th-century mansion. The paintings of unrenowned artists (with a handful of masters thrown in), natural lighting, and Bredius's own furnishings warm the place up. West of the Hofvijver is the **Rijksmuseum Gevangenpoort** (Buitenhof 33, tel. 070/346–0861; admission f5), built during the 13th century as a gatehouse and used as a prison from 1420 to 1828. Visitors must take the guided tour (in Dutch), which leaves hourly (weekdays 10–4, Sun. 1–4). A 20-minute walk or short tram ride northwest brings you to the **Haags Gemeentemuseum** (Stadhouder-sln. 41, tel. 070/338–1111; admission f8; open Tues.–Sun. 11–5), which holds the world's largest collection of works by Piet Mondrian, illustrating his gradual progress from figurative art to abstraction. Also on display is a diverse collection of Delftware (exquisite china from the Dutch town of Delft), rare musical instruments, and other modern art.

Every second weekend in July, more than 60,000 people swarm into The Hague for the North Sea Jazz Festival (tel. 015/215–7756 for information), a three-day whirlwind of jazz, blues, and gospel acts from around the world. Day tickets cost about f80.

Common folk aren't allowed inside the three **royal palaces,** but if you make a reservation at the VVV and fork over f25, you can join the **Royal Tour** for a 2½-hour bus ride from palace to palace. Better yet, take a gander at the palaces yourself; the VVV has a pamphlet —"An Historic Walk Around The Hague" (f3)—that describes them at length. **Noordeinde Palace** (Noordeinde 68), the most interesting, has a small garden and is still used by Queen Beatrix; **Kneuterdijk Palace** (Kneuterdijk 20) was once the home of Princess Juliana; and **Lange Voorhout Palace** (Lange Voorhout 74) is where Queen Emma, Beatrix's great-grandmother, lived until her death in 1934.

NEAR THE HAGUE

KIJKDUIN
Just north of The Hague is the tiny beach resort of Kijkduin. If you forget your swimsuit, feel free to loll around in the buff. Kijkduin is much quieter than the other resorts on this coast, such as the popular **Scheveningen,** to the north, but it's far from an isolated getaway. You can rent a bike at Kijkduinpark (*see* Where to Sleep and Eat *in* The Hague, *above*) and pedal a pleasant 10 or 15 minutes to Kijkduin, then follow a number of bike trails through the dunes and shrubbery. If all that pedaling sounds like too much work, Bus 4 goes to Kijkduin, and Bus 22 goes to Scheveningen; both buses leave The Hague's Centraal Station and cost 3 strips.

ROTTERDAM

Rotterdam was nearly annihilated in the German blitzkrieg of 1940. Almost everything in the town's center was destroyed except for the **Stadhuis** (Town Hall; Coolsingel 40, tel. 010/417–9111), and the port suffered the same destruction in 1944. In rebuilding their city, the ever-resilient Dutch abandoned their traditional brick structures and canals in favor of hastily constructed steel-and-concrete monstrosities, but many of these have since been replaced by newer, more architecturally ambitious creations, whose quirky shapes and colors are an intriguing departure from traditional European architecture. A prime example is the **Kijk-Kubus** (Overblaak 70, tel. 010/414–2285; admission f3.50; open daily 11–5; Nov.– Feb., closed Mon.), a massive structure reminiscent of a Rubik's Cube; one of its unique apartments is open to the public, though the surrounding cubic houses are all occupied. What remains of historical Rotterdam is in **Delfshaven,** where you'll find rows of gabled canal houses and trendy shops and restaurants. Take the Metro to Delfshaven station.

Perched at the delta formed by the Meuse, Rhine, and Waal rivers, Rotterdam has been an important port since the 14th century and is now the world's busiest and largest. The massive Europoort complex is an important center of heavy industry and has drawn immigrant workers from all over the world, rendering Rotterdam one of the most cosmopolitan cities in the country. The city also has several art and historical museums, several of which are conveniently clustered in the **Museumpark,** a short walk from the Eendrachtsplein Metro station. The most impressive is the **Boymans–van Beuningen Museum** (Museumpark 18–20, tel. 010/441–9400; admission f7.50; open Tues.–Sat. 10–5, Sun. 11–5), which displays well-known old masters as well as surrealists such as Dali and Magritte. The temporary exhibits, such as French-impressionist retrospectives, draw the biggest crowds. If museum fatigue strikes, relax on the lawns of the adjoining sculpture garden. Across from the Boymans museum is the **Netherlands Architectuurinstituut** (Museumpark 25, tel. 010/440–1200; admission f7.50; open Tues.–Sat. 10–5, Sun. 11–5), with exhibits on architecture, urban development, and interior design. At the southern end of the park is the **Kunsthal,** a vacuous 1992 pile that hosts major exhibits of contemporary art and intriguing installations.

The **Maritiem Buitenmuseum** (Leuvehaven 50–72, tel. 010/404–8072; admission free; open weekdays 10–4, weekends noon–4) is an open-air maritime museum where you can see ship engines, port cranes, and steamships in action. Every Sunday from May to September, there are tugboat tours of the harbor (f7.50) starting at the museum itself. For a more extended tour, take the **Spido** (Leuvehoofd, tel. 010/413–5400) 1¼-hour cruise (f14.50) around the city's docks and waterways. In the summer, Spido also offers an eight-hour trip (f45) to the Delta Expo, an array of massive dikes that prevents the southwest section of the country from being swallowed by the sea.

BASICS

Rotterdam's **VVV office** (Coolsingel 67, tel. 0900/3403–4065, 75¢ per min) hands out free maps, books rooms for f2.50, and sells tickets to plays and concerts for a f3.50 fee. **American Express** (Meent 92, tel. 010/433–0300) offers the usual cardholder services. The **post office** (Coolsingel 42, tel. 010/454–2349) is just south of the Stadhuis.

COMING AND GOING

Rotterdam has several train stations. The most convenient to the city center and all forms of public transportation is **Centraal Station** (Stationspl.), where you can catch frequent trains to Amsterdam (1 hr, f22.25) and The Hague (15 min, f7.25).

Rotterdam's sprawling urban landscape is well-served by tram, Metro, and bus, but most travelers will walk or use only the Metro, which stops near all major sights. Buy a *strippenkaart* and get a free transit map at the city's public-transportation office, **RET** (Stationspl., in front of Centraal Station).

WHERE TO SLEEP AND EAT

The central **HI City Hostel Rotterdam** (Rochussenstr. 107–109, tel. 010/436–5763, fax 010/436–5569) has dorm beds for f31. Take the Metro to Churchillplein and transfer to the Dijkzigt line; the hostel is above the Dijkzigt station. Rotterdam's budget digs are in a rather grungy part of town; women traveling alone may wish to break out the plastic and stay in a more expensive hotel near the city center. If seedy is okay with you, **'s Gravendijkwal** has a bunch of budget motels (the neighborhood is also full of topless nightclubs). **Roxane** ('s Gravendijkwal 14, tel. 010/436–6109, fax 010/436–2944) is one of the nicer motels, with clean doubles starting at f70. Back in the center, **Hotel van Walsum** (Mathenesserlaan 199–201, tel. 010/436–3275 fax 010/436–4410), within walking distance of the Museumpark, continually redecorates its rooms; doubles with bath start at f135.

In Delfshaven, **Hiernaast** (Havenstr. 9, tel. 010/476–4516) and its attached café, **Oude Sluis** (tel. 010/477–3068), have outdoor tables overlooking the historic harbor; a lively crowd gathers on warm evenings. The daily special is f15. **Betty Beer** (Blaak 329, tel. 010/412–4741) is part of a chain of local restaurants named after different bears; the restaurant serves traditional Dutch specials on weekdays for f13.50–f16.50. Get groceries at **A and P** (Nieuwe Binnenweg 30a, tel. 010/436–1805).

GOUDA

This tiny town between Rotterdam and Utrecht gets lots of attention, mostly because of its namesake cheese. Every Thursday morning from mid-June to late August you'll find mild Gouda cheese galore at the **cheese market,** 9:30–12:30. Farmers weigh their cheese at the **Waag,** or weighhouse, which has been in use since the 17th century and now also holds an informative exhibit on all manner of dairy products (Markt 35–36, tel. 0182/52–99–96; admission f5; open Apr.–Oct., 10–5). The Gothic **Stadhuis** (Markt 1, tel. 0182/58–84–75; open to the public weekdays 9–noon and 2–4, when not in use) stands on the southern side of the square; built in 1449, it's the oldest town hall in the Netherlands. Further south, it's hard to miss the ornate clock tower of **Grote St. Janskerk** (Achter de Kerk 16, tel. 0182/51–26–84; admission f3; open Mar.–Oct., Mon.–Sat. 9–5; Nov.–Feb., Mon.–Sat. 10–4). St. Janskerk was originally a Catholic church, but when the Reformation hit Gouda in 1572, the Protestants took possession of this Gothic treasure. They kept the original stained-glass windows, which depict biblical scenes, but added a few of their own, many representing events in Dutch history.

Once the town hospital, the **Stedelijk Museum Het Catharina Gasthuis** (Oosthaven 10, tel. 0182/58–84–44; admission f4; open Mon.–Sat. 10–5, Sun. noon–5) now houses a little bit of everything, from 16th- and 17th-century paintings to a torture chamber and a gory operating theater. The **Zuidshollands Verzetsmuseum** (Turfmarkt 30, tel. 0182/52–03–85; admission f3; open Apr.–Sept., Tues.–Fri. 10–5, weekends noon–5; Oct.–Mar., Tues.–Fri. 1–5, weekends noon–5) documents resistance of German occupying forces during World War II. Everything is in Dutch, but you can request a booklet in English.

English-speakers' attempts to pronounce "Gouda" provide the natives of this town with hours of family fun. Pronounce the name "HOW-dah," with a guttural "h."

The **train station** (Stationspl.) has frequent trains to and from Rotterdam (15 min, f7), Utrecht (20 min, f8.75), and Amsterdam (40 min, f16). The **VVV** (Markt 27, tel. 0182/51–36–66), 10 minutes south of the station, books rooms for f3.50 per person and hands out free maps and a lodging list.

WHERE TO SLEEP AND EAT

At **Hotel De Utrechtse Dam** (Geuzenstr. 6, 3 minutes SE of Markt, tel. 0182/52–79–84), doubles are f74.50–f92.50, breakfast included. There's also the nonsmoking **Hotel-Restaurant Het Blauwe Kruis** (Westhaven 4, 5 min south of Markt, tel. 0182/51–26–77), where doubles are f90. Less than 10 minutes south of Markt, **Hotel Het Trefpunt** (Westhaven 46, tel. 0182/51–28–79, fax 0182/58–51–86) has doubles with private showers for f111.50, and a bar and restaurant below.

If you don't feel like hauling a Gouda cheese wheel to your next destination, you can buy it by the slice at **Albert Heijn** (Markt 50), 165 ft west of the Waag. For inexpensive Surinamese and Indonesian food, try **Warung Blauwgrond** (Wijdstr. 22, south end of Markt, tel. 0182/58–21–58), a modest restaurant/snack bar serving rice dishes for f9.50–f15.50. The friendly staff at **Cafeteria de Scherf** (Korte Groenendaal 6, tel. 0182/51–36–23) serves everything from soup (f3.25) and pancakes (f5) to Wiener schnitzel (f11).

UTRECHT

This heart-of-Holland city was established in Roman times and flourished to become an important academic and religious center, though you might notice a subtle tension between students at the prestigious university (who sometimes call locals "ordinary people") and locals (who, in turn, sometimes find students uppity). The power of Utrecht's medieval prince-bishops extended beyond the low countries, and the city still has a charming medieval flavor: an abundance of Gothic churches, a smattering of museums, and a thoroughly confusing network of streets and tree-lined canals all make for great exploring.

Utrecht's must-see sight is also the tallest and hardest to miss. Tours of the **Dom Tower** (Dompl., tel. 030/286–4540; admission f5.50) involve a climb up its 465 steps (on the hour; Apr.–Oct., weekdays 10–4, weekends noon–4; Nov.–Mar., weekends noon–5). The Gothic **Domkerk** (Dompl., tel. 030/231–0403; admission free; open May–Sept., weekdays 10–5, Sat. 10–3:30, Sun. 2–4; shorter hrs Oct.–May), next door, was once connected to the tower by a nave, but the nave collapsed during a storm in 1674; you can see its outline on the paving stones between the church and tower. Appropriately located in a late medieval convent, the **Museum Catharijneconvent** (Nieuwegr. 63, tel. 030/231–7296; admission f7; open Tues.–Fri. 10–5, weekends 11–5) tells the story of Christianity in the Netherlands; the museum's collection of medieval art, including illustrated manuscripts, religious relics, and robes, is the largest in the country. Utrecht's most entertaining museum, the **Nationaal Museum Van Speelklok tot Pierement** (Buurkerkhof 10, tel. 030/231–2789; admission f7.50; open Tues.–Sat. 10–5, Sun. 1–5), has a huge collection of elaborate music boxes, street organs, and nickelodeons, some of which date to the 19th century. The hourly tours are festive and informative affairs.

BASICS

To get to the **VVV** (Vredenburg 90, tel. 0900/340–4085) from the train station, emerge into the monstrous Hoog Catharijne shopping mall and attempt to follow the signs around this ugly and depressing labyrinth. The office hands out a free brochure, complete with map and lodging list, and books rooms for a f3.50 fee. There's a convenient **GWK** office (tel. 030/231–7872; open Mon.–Sat. 8 AM–9 PM, Sun. 9–9) in Centraal Station.

GETTING AROUND

The **train** and **bus stations** are located in the Hoog Catharijne shopping complex, in the western part of the city center. Utrecht is a major international rail hub, with trains leaving for Budapest, Vienna, and Zürich, to name just a few. To make reservations and buy international tickets, call or visit **NS International** (tel. 0900/9296), in the train station. Utrecht also has direct lines to Amsterdam (30 mins, f11), Rotterdam (35 mins, f14.50), and Maastricht (2 hrs, f40.50). If you plan to take a bus from Centraal Station, remember that *Stadsbussen* cover only the city, while *Streekbussen* go to neighboring towns. In general, the center of town and the major sights are easily walkable.

WHERE TO SLEEP AND EAT

Utrecht's cheap sleeps are outside the city center. The **HI Rhijnauwen** (Rhijnauwenseln. 14, tel. 030/656–1277; beds f26) is an old country house in the middle of a peaceful pasture in Bunnik, a 15-minute ride from Utrecht. Take Streekbus 41 and follow the HI signs down a dirt road, about a 10-minute walk. The canal-side **Parkhotel** (Tolsteegsingel 34, tel. 030/251–6712, fax 030/254–0401) is a well-maintained residence in a leafy setting about 10 minutes' walk from the Dom Tower; the terrace adjoining the breakfast room is a great place to wind down. Doubles with bath cost f95. From Centraal Station take Bus 2 or 22 to Ledig Erf, cross the bridge on Tolsteegburg, and hang a left. **Hotel Ouwi** (F.C. Dondersstr. 12, tel. 030/271–6303; cash only) is a pleasant family hotel; doubles with bath go for f122, breakfast included. Take bus 11 from Centraal Station to the end of the street. The closest campground is **De Berekuil** (Ariënsln. 5, tel. 030/271–3870; f6 per person plus f8 per tent), on the east edge of town near a forest; the site has laundry facilities and a restaurant. To get there, take Bus 57 to Blitse Rading.

There are plenty of picturesque picnic spots in Utrecht; pick up supplies at **Albert Heijn** (Voorstr. 38). The city also has lots of cafés and restaurants, some in the 13th-century cellars along Oude Gracht. Daily specials from the Burgundian kitchen at **Tantes Bistro** (Oudegracht 61, tel. 030/231–2191) cost about f15. **De Soepterrine** (Zakkendragerssteeg 40, tel. 030/231–7005) serves some 10 seasonal soups and salads with crispy bread. The collectively run **De Baas** (Lijnmarkt 8, tel. 030/231–5185; open Wed.–Sun. 5:30–8:30) serves scrumptious vegetarian, fish, and meat dishes for under f15. The celebrated student cafeteria **Veritas** (Kromme Nieuwegracht 54, tel. 030/231–6754) serves meals for about f7 after 5 on weeknights; on Sunday evening around 11, it turns into a student disco. The Nobelstraat bars just north of the Dom, such as **De Kneus** (Nobelstr. 303), are generally packed with students; **De Zotte** (Nobelstr. 243) is open latest, until about 4:30 AM. Domplein and 't Wed, the tiny street off Oude Gracht, have several bars with outdoor tables.

ELSEWHERE IN THE NETHERLANDS

Despite the Netherlands' small size and relatively flat terrain, its countryside is quite diverse. In the northern provinces of Friesland, Groningen, and Drenthe, more than 25,000 acres of lakes and cow-filled pasture extend as far as the eye can see. Groningen itself is a culturally rich university town with lots of street life and a blissful lack of cars. Much of the central Netherlands is covered with forests, but an important art museum is hidden deep in the 13,000-acre De Hoge Veluwe nature reserve (*see* Near Arnhem, *below*). The southern border provinces are a mixture of windswept peninsulas, riverside industrial areas, and gentle hills dotted by half-timbered farmhouses. Maastricht, the oldest city in the Netherlands, is in the southernmost corner of the country, squeezed between Germany and Belgium.

FRIESLAND AND THE FRISIAN ISLANDS

Friesland is a bilingual province where 75% of the population still speaks Fryske, an ancient West Germanic language with close ancestral ties to English. Friesland is famous for the sprawl of woods in its southeast corner, the bird sanctuaries and cliffs of Gaasterland, and the prime sailing waters of Grouw. The Frisian islands, a favorite Dutch getaway, are dotted along the North Sea coast.

Leeuwarden is the capital of Friesland and has some charming historic sections, particularly around the canals and quiet streets. If you plan to explore Friesland, the **Fries Museum** (Turfmarkt 11, tel. 058/212–3001; admission f6.50; open Mon.–Sat. 11–6, Sun. 1–5) explains the history of the province through archaeological finds, traditional home interiors, and Frisian arts and crafts. In the attic is a well-designed exhibit on Frisian resistance activities during World War II.

The traditional Frisian sport fierljeps (cross-canal pole vaulting) picks up steam in various northern towns during the summer. For competition sites and dates, call the Friese Fierljeppersbond (tel. 0514/58–17–79); admission is usually free.

BASICS

Before heading off to one of the Frisian islands, find out all you need to know at the Friesland-Leeuwarden **VVV** (Stationspl. 1, tel. 0800/3202–4060, 75¢ per minute), which also sells maps and guides, and reserves rooms for a small fee. Since there's no GWK office at the station, change money at **Rabobank,** next to the VVV office.

COMING AND GOING

Trains from Amsterdam (2½ hrs, f46) arrive and depart every half-hour. The central shopping district is only a five-minute walk from the station.

WHERE TO SLEEP AND EAT

For a short stay, use the handy **Hotel De Pauw** (Stationsweg 10, tel. 058/212–3651 fax 058/216–0793), right across the street from the station. Clean and simple doubles start at f80, including breakfast in the cozy restaurant. **Hotel 't Anker** (Eewal 69, tel. 058/212–5216) has a quieter setting in the center and basic doubles for f77. The closest campground, **De Kleine Wielen** (De Groene Ster, 14 km/8½ mi NE of town, tel. 0511/43–16–60, f5 per tent plus f6 per person), has a small grocery store and can be reached via Buses 51, 57, and 62.

The broad **Nieuwestad** is lined with restaurants, most with daily specials for less than f20. Cheaper snack-bar options hover around the **Grote Hoogstraat,** a buzzing area filled with student bars and music clubs.

TERSCHELLING

This windswept island off the country's northern coast is a favorite Dutch vacation spot, good for hiking, biking, surfing, sailing, and sunning. The biggest town is **West-Terschelling,** a remnant of the island's past as an important whaling outpost. Urban sights include a handful of museums devoted to the history and ecology of the island, and the **Brandaris,** a 16th-century lighthouse. The rest of Terschelling is a nature reserve, with 30 km (18 mi) of beautiful dunes and endless beaches ideal for lazy cycling. At the southeast end of the island is the **Boschplaat bird sanctuary,** off-limits to wingless visitors from mid-March to mid-August unless you take a guided tour.

Between May and September, **ferries** run from **Harlingen** to West-Terschelling (1¾ hrs, f36 return) thrice daily. There's also a hydrofoil, which is quicker but costs a bit more (f45). For information, call the ferry company, **Rederij Doeksen** (tel. 0562/44–21–41) during business hours. Trains run twice hourly from Leeuwarden to Harlingen (30 min, f9) and hourly from Groningen to Harlingen (1½ hrs, f12.25). The ferry terminal is a five-minute walk from the station.

West-Terschelling's **VVV** (Willem Barentszkade 19a, tel. 0562/44–30–00; open weekdays 9–5, Sat. 9–1) sells maps (f6.50) and books rooms for a f8 fee. The hostel **HI Terschelling** (Burgemeester Van Heusdenweg 39, tel. 0562/44–31–15, fax 0562/44–33–12) has dorm beds for f28, a few doubles for f83, and incredible views of the harbor. The mellower **Pension De Holland** (Molenstr. 5, tel. 0562/44–23–02, cash only) has doubles for f80, breakfast included. **Camping Cnossen** (Hoofdweg 8, tel. 0562/44–23–21; closed Nov.–Mar.) is 2 km (1⅓ mi) east of town; you'll have to walk or bike there, but they'll transport your bags to and from the ferry landing for free. Tent sites are f5.25 plus f7 per person.

GRONINGEN

This large university town is the capital of its province. The surrounding countryside is mainly land reclaimed from the sea, with farmsteads on mounds dotting the otherwise flat plains; farmers used to retreat here with their livestock when floods threatened. Successful farmers and traders consolidated their power during the Middle Ages by joining the Hanseatic League, a medieval forerunner of the EC based on collaborative trade; nowadays, the city's wealth comes from its exploitation of nearby natural-gas reserves.

Despite considerable local damage during World War II, many of Groningen's beautiful 16th- and 17th-century mansions survived unscathed. The city center's broad arteries are laid out in a rough grid, with smaller interconnecting streets. A radical move by city elders banned cars from the city center over 15 years ago, so people go about their business on foot or bike. Once the shops shut, the bars have plenty of room to spread out their terraces; sit back and relax in one of the most sophisticated cities in the Netherlands.

BASICS

There is a small **VVV** office at the train station, but the main office is in town (Gedempte Kattendiep 6, at east end of Gedempte Zuiderdiep, tel. 0900/3202–3050); they sell local maps and book rooms at hotels or B&Bs for a small fee. Change money at the **GWK** in the station or at banks in the center.

COMING AND GOING

Groningen is served by trains to and from Amsterdam (2½ hrs, f48.50) every hour. You can also leave to and from Amsterdam on the half-hour, but you'll need to change in Amersfoort. Trains divide at Zwolle, so don't relax until you know you're in the correct section. The **train station** is less than five minutes' walk from the town center—take the footbridge leading through the modern Groninger Museum and go straight. Much of the city center is pedestrian-only, so taking a bus makes little sense. If you fancy cycling around town, you can hire a bike from the station depot, to your right as you leave the station.

WHERE TO SLEEP AND EAT

There's a fair selection of budget hotels in the town center. On a quiet side street in the heart of the city, **Hotel Friesland** (Kleine Pelsterstr. 4, tel. 050/312–1307) has small doubles for f77.50, breakfast included. **Hotel Weeva** (Gedempte Zuiderdiep 8, tel. 050/312–9919) is a former working man's hotel with doubles from f80; insist on a room away from the busy street. The hostel option is the **Simplon Jongerenhotel** (Boterdiep 73, tel. 050/313–5221), just north of the town center; dorm beds cost f25, and the place also serves handily as a major pop-music venue. At the other end of the scale, you might want to stretch your budget to crash at the **Schimmelpenninck Huys** (Oosterstr. 53, tel. 050/318–9502), an 18th-century mansion with spacious doubles from f185. Decor in the grand café is Art Nouveau.

Raucous student restaurants and their terraces line the Grote Markt, Poelestraat, and Peperstraat. Happily, the large student population helps keep prices down. **Het Binnenhof** (Oosterstr. 7A, tel. 050/312–3697), in a courtyard setting just around the corner from the hubbub, is ideal for a quiet meal. Dishes du jour, including imaginative veggie options, are less than f15. On Saturday, dinner at **De Twee Dames** (Gedempte Zuiderdiep 64, tel. 050/314–2052) is accompanied by a visiting cabaret act: The menu changes weekly, and you can eat for less than f20 while being royally entertained. The idea has wide appeal, so be sure to reserve.

WORTH SEEING

The **Grote Markt** is the city's focal point and is filled with stalls almost every day. Here you'll find the classical **Stadshuis** (1810), and just behind it the **Goudkantoor** (1635), with its fine step gable. These are surrounded by the new Waagstraat shopping and apartment complex, just completed in 1996. The **Martinikerk** (Martinikerkhof, tel. 050/311–1277; open Jun.–mid-Sept., Tues.–Sat. noon–5), with the 317-ft tower, was originally a Romano-Gothic basilica; it was extended to its present form during the 15th century. The world-famous organ dates from 1480, the fading frescoes in the choir loft from about 1545. The **Prinsenhoftuin** (Turfsingel; open Apr.–mid-Oct.) is a formal hedged garden just behind the church. The **A-kerk** (tel. 050/312–3569 for hrs), built during the 13th–15th centuries, is situated behind the **Korenbeurs** (Corn Exchange), at the western end of the Vismarkt.

Revel in your bewilderment at the unusual architecture of the **Groninger Museum** (Museumeiland 1, tel. 0900/821–2132; admission f10; open Tues.–Sun. 10–5), just across from the train station. Alessandro Mendini oversaw the work of "guest" architects here: Michele De Lucchi's red-brick block, containing archeological finds, is the base of Philippe Starck's aluminium pavilion, which houses the decorative-arts collection. Coop Himmelb(l)au's gravity-defying, deconstructivist glass and steel balance precariously on Mendini's own multicolored mass; both house temporary exhibitions. With each block connected by galleries below the water level, the building is an experience in itself.

ARNHEM AND THE GREEN HEART

What's in Arnhem isn't nearly as interesting as what lurks on its outskirts (*see* Near Arnhem, *below*). Not much has gone down here since World War II, when, during the Operation Market Garden campaign, British and Polish troops were slaughtered after trying to take control of the **John Frost** bridge. The bridge is about 1 km (⅔ mi) south of the town center; today you can sit on the riverbanks and envision the battle. West of Arnhem in Oosterbeek is the **Airborne Museum** (Utrechtsweg 232, tel. 026/333–7710; admission f5; open Mon.–Sat. 11–5, Sun. noon–5), which gives fascinating, detailed accounts of the 1944 Battle of Arnhem. Arnhem's other main attraction, the **Museum voor Moderne Kunst** (Utrechtseweg 87, tel. 026/351–2431; admission free; open Tues.–Sat. 10–5, Sun. 11–5), west of the station, has 20th-century silver, ceramics, and paintings by Dutch realists, and awesome views of the Rhine River from the sculpture garden. Arnhem's **VVV** (Stationspl. 45, tel. 026/442–0330), east of the train station, has the usual brochures and books rooms for f3.50.

In Leeuwarden, take in the excellent National Museum of Ceramics (Grote Kerkstr. 11, tel. 058/212–7438; admission f6.50; open Mon.–Sat. 10–5, Sun. 2–5), with tiles from North Africa, Spain, and Persia; early Asian ceramics; and Art Deco.

COMING AND GOING

Arnhem's train station, northwest of the town center, has frequent **trains** to Amsterdam (1 hr, f24), Rotterdam (70 min, f29.25), and Maastricht (2 hrs, f34.50). City buses leave from in front of the station, regional buses from the west side.

WHERE TO SLEEP AND EAT

The VVV directs everyone to **HI Alteveer** (Diepenbrockln. 27, tel. 026/442–0114, fax 026/351–4892; dorm beds f28, a few doubles from f77), north of the city in a green suburb. From the station, take Bus 3 to Gemeente Ziekenhuis (a big hospital), head away from the hospital on Wagnerlaan, turn left on Catterpoelseweg, and walk about half a block. The **HI De Zilverberg** (Kerklaan 50, tel. 026/333–4300; beds f27) is nestled in the woods about 8 km (5 mi) west of town, in Doorwerth. Take Bus 50, 80, 81, or 88 to Kerklaan, a three-strip trip. **Hotel-Pension Parkzicht** (Apeldoornsestr. 16, tel. 026/442–0698) offers comfortable doubles for f95; it's a 15-minute walk east of the station, across from Arnhem's PTT Telecom headquarters. **Hotel Blanc** (Coehoornstr. 4, tel. 026/442–8072) is close to the station and has comfortable doubles with bath for f140. The huge **Camping De Bilderberg** (Sportln. 1, tel. 026/333–2228; f3.50 per tent plus f4.85 per person) is open year-round and surrounded by forests with meandering paths. It's 5 km (3 mi) west of town, in Oosterbeek; take Bus 50, 80, 81, or 88 to d'Oude Herbergh and walk north on Valkenburglaan.

You won't have any problems finding cheap snack bars or french fries at **Korenmarkt,** the shopping area around Jansstraat. For a reasonable sit-down dinner, **Daleone** (Korenmarkt 1, tel. 026/442–6964) offers create-your-own pizzas (f9.75) and pasta (f10–f18). **Café Meijers** (Beekstr. 2, tel. 026/442–3807), on the eastern edge of the shopping district, is popular with the lunch crowd; sandwiches start at about f4, and there are plenty of sidewalk tables. For picnic supplies, pop into **Albert Heijn** (Ir. J.P. van Muijlwijkstr. 23, off Velperpl.). If you're staying at HI Alteveer, **Manders Super** (Beethovenln. 59–63, off Catterpoelseweg) is even closer.

NEAR ARNHEM

The green, forested hills outside Arnhem are a great place to catch a glimpse of the rural Netherlands, past and present. The **Nederlands Openluchtmuseum** (Schelmseweg 89, tel. 026/357–6100; admission f16; open Apr.–Oct.) reconstructs 19th-century rural Dutch life in the form of working farmhouses, taverns, windmills, and even a tram system. Demonstrations show you how bread and cheese were made, and the working paper mill is an interesting example of how some farmers earned a second income. Everything made in the demos is sold on the spot. Take Bus 3 (or Bus 13 in July and August) from Arnhem station.

HOGE VELUWE NATIONAL PARK

The Hoge Veluwe National Park is the country's largest, with more than 13,000 acres of heath, woodland, sand dunes, and grassy fields, and such fauna as deer, foxes, badgers, and wild boar. Although access to much of the park is restricted, game-observation points in the southern half of the park allow you to watch for wildlife. The f7.50 entrance fee covers the whole estate, including admission to museums.

Besides the animals, the real highlight of the park is the huge (and free with park admission) **Kröller-Müller Museum** (tel. 0318/59–12–41; open Tues.–Sun. 10–5), which houses an impressive collection of modern art, including works by Picasso, Mondrian, and Gris, and a Van Gogh collection so vast that only a fraction of the works can be shown at any given time. Outside, the beautifully conceived sculpture garden is filled with works by such artists as Rodin, Jacques Lipchitz, and Henry Moore. About 5 km (3 mi) north of the museum is **St. Hubertus,** a 1920s art-deco hunting lodge designed by Hendrik Berlage, the Netherlands' "father of modern architecture." From April to October, park visitors can take a free guided tour of the interior; the rest of the year, you'll have to content yourself with walking around the beautiful garden and the artificial lake.

The best way to see all of this is by bike. Once you pay the park-entrance fee, you can help yourself to one of hundreds of bikes at the park entrances or at **De Aanschouw visitor's center** (tel. 0318/59–16–27; open Apr.–Aug., daily 9–5; Sept.–Mar., daily 10–5), a 15-minute walk north of the museum, next to the Koperen Kop restaurant. The **Museonder** is an underground museum dedicated to subterranean phenomena. The simulated volcano and the exhibit on the stratification of the earth's surface are popular with schoolkids from around the globe. *Park office: Apeldoornseweg 250, tel. 055/378–1441. Park open Apr.–Aug., daily 8 AM–sunset; Sept. and Oct., daily 9 AM–sunset; Nov.–Mar., daily 9–5.*

COMING AND GOING

The easiest and cheapest option is to buy an *Er-op-Uit*—a round-trip day ticket including all travel plus admission to the Hoge Veluwe National Park and the Kröller-Müller Museum—at any train station. From Amsterdam it costs f43.50. During the day from late June to early August, Bus 12 runs hourly from the Arnhem train station. If you stay past 5 PM, hop a bike west to the Otterlo entrance, and walk 15 minutes into the town of Otterlo to catch Bus 107 back to Arnhem.

MAASTRICHT

Limburg, the southernmost province of the Netherlands, differs from the rest of the country in many ways. For one, the rolling hills and dense forests resemble the landscape of close neighbors Belgium and Germany. The Romans took control of this strategic ford on the Maas River more than 2,000 years ago, and the city's medieval ramparts are a later legacy of its ongoing desirability. Literally out on a limb, Maastricht has been subjected to many a conflict; most recently, it was the site of the much-contested signing of the 1992 Treaty of European Union (a.k.a. the Maastricht Treaty), an important step in the formation of the EU. The region is also a devout Catholic stronghold in an otherwise Protestant nation, celebrating feast days with grand processions that have more in common with southern Europe than the discreet Calvinism of the North. The milder southern climate does its share to contribute to Maastricht's exuberant and sophisticated street life.

BASICS

Maastricht Station (Stationspl.), on the eastern edge of town, has a **VVV** outlet that books rooms for a f3.50 fee and sells a guide (f1.75) with a map and list of accommodations. The **main VVV office** (Kleine Staat 1, 043/325–2121), in the town center, is a 15-minute walk west of the train station.

COMING AND GOING

Since Maastricht is so far south, you can easily catch trains to Cologne (Köln), Germany (2½ hrs, f50), and Liège (Luik), Belgium (30 min, f14). Trains also go to Amsterdam (2½ hrs, f48.50) via Utrecht.

Maastricht is divided by the River Maas. Most of the sights are on the west bank, and you can easily walk from the eastern edge of town (where the train station is) to the western edge (past the shopping district and museums) in less than 30 minutes. You'll need a bus if you want to crash at the youth hostel; the bus station is to your left as you exit the train station. The town's main square, **Vrijthof,** is surrounded by cafés and two churches. The main shopping area is around the **Markt**; the more exclusive boutiques cluster around the **Stokstraat,** the site of the original Roman settlement along the Maas.

WHERE TO SLEEP AND EAT

The VVV has a list of rooms in private homes (which run f35–f40 per person). **De Poshoorn** (Stationsstr. 47, tel. 043/321–7334) is a cheerful little hotel above a café, conveniently situated between the Old Town and the train station. Doubles with shower are a hefty f135. The unique **Hotelboot** (Maasblvd. 95, tel. 043/321–9023), a converted boat anchored along the west bank of the river, has cramped but clean cabins; doubles are f85. Maastricht's **HI De Dousberg** (Dousbergweg 4, tel. 043/346–6777, fax 043/346–6755; beds f26.50–f31.50) is a massive, modern hostel that caters to preadolescent sports teams. In the same building, the **Budget Hotel** has nicer private accommodations, with doubles for f97.50 (f10 extra for breakfast). Take Bus 55 or 56 from the train station; if you need a lift from the station between 7 PM and 10:20 PM, dial 043/329–2566, and ask to have Bus 28 pick you up there and drop you off at the hotel.

Maastricht is a culinary paradise, if you can afford it. Dress up a notch from "casual" if you decide to try one of the many renowned gourmet restaurants here. Some patient searching will reveal three-course dinners for under f50, but you'll want to reserve a table in advance. Try the French-influenced **La Ville** (O.L. Vrouweplein 28, tel. 043/321–9889), overlooking an idyllic square. If you're holding fast to your wallet, make a beeline for **De Preuvery** (Kakeberg 6, tel. 043/325–0903), a five-minute walk south of the Vrijthof, which dishes out hearty meals (f10) and huge baguette sandwiches (f3.75) until 2 AM. **Falstaff** (Amerspl. 6, no phone) is a popular bar with a great selection of specialty draught beers and simple food. At **t'Pothuiske** (Het Bat 1, tel. 043/321–6002), the lunchtime patio is transformed by twinkling strings of lights for dinner. Sandwiches start at f5.50, and chili con carne is just f11. Stuff your pack with groceries from **Dagmarkt** (Grote Staat 5–15).

WORTH SEEING

Maastricht's main sights are all within 10 minutes of each other. A leafy walk along the remaining **city walls** provides an excellent overview of the city's history; pick up the "Maastricht Fortifications Walk" guide (f1) from the VVV, or just walk down to Onze Lieve Vrouwe Wal and along the walls as they turn west. The oldest part of the wall, near the western bank of the river along Maasboulevard, was built in 1229; extensions and reinforcements were added in the 16th century during the war with Spain. If you have time, join a guided tour of the labyrinthine corridors of the sandstone mines in the nearby **St Pietersberg,** a wooded hill rising to the west of the city; the VVV has details.

The 7th-century Romanesque **St. Servaasbasiliek** (Vrijthof, tel. 043/321–2082; admission f3.50; open July and Aug., daily 10–6; off-season, daily 10–4) dominates the Vrijthof and houses the remains of Maastricht's first bishop, St. Servaas, who died in AD 384. The church was enlarged during the 14th and 15th centuries. Don't forget to look up at the richly colored, vaulted ceiling. The smaller, Gothic church next door is the Protestant **St. Janskerk** (Vrijthof, open Apr.–Sept., Mon.–Sat. 11–4; closed Mon. off season). Admission is free, but to climb the tower for a bird's-eye view of the city will cost you f2. The **Onze Lieve Vrouwebasiliek** (O.L. Vrouweplein 20, tel. 043/325–1851), near the river on a quiet, shady square, was begun around 1000, but it may be on the site of a former Roman temple. The side chapel at the entrance has been a pilgrims' destination for centuries.

STEAMING SPA

Valkenburg is a small, tourist-filled town 10 km (6 mi) west of Maastricht by train. To escape the hullaballoo (or anything else that's on your nerves), spoil yourself with a day's relaxation at the ultramodern Thermae 2000 (Cauberg 27, Valkenburg aan de Geul, tel. 043/601–9419; admission ƒ28.50 for 2 hrs, ƒ52.50 per day; open 9 AM–11 PM), perched at the top of a hill overlooking gladed valleys. It's a massive suite of saunas, outdoor whirlpools, and swimming pools filled with warm spring water.

The exhibits at the modern **Bonnefanten Museum** (Av. Ceramique 250, on the east bank of river, tel. 043/329–0190; admission ƒ10; open Tues.–Sun. 11–5) include prehistoric finds, Roman artifacts, medieval religious art, and contemporary installations—a strange mix, but it works. Take Bus 2, 5, or 17, or the pleasant 5-minute walk south along fortified east bank of the river Maas on Stenenwal, which turns into Maaspuntweg.

NORWAY 19

amuel Beckett once called Norway "a daughter of the Sea." Indeed, the people who live in this rugged country, which has some 3,400 km (2,108 mi) of meandering coastline, have always relied on the sea for their livelihood. A thousand years ago, Vikings in wooden ships set sail from Norway's ragged coast to plunder distant shores. Today, luxury liners roll up to Norway's ports to disgorge armies of tourists, eager for a glimpse of breathtaking fjords, the midnight sun, or the magical northern lights.

As the the birthplace of notables such as artist Edvard Munch, composer Edvard Grieg, and playwright Henrik Ibsen, Norway is celebrated as much for its cultural achievements.as for its physical beauty. This wild land and the fertile Norwegian imagination have also given rise to countless fairy tales; most involve trolls who sulk around at night wreaking havoc on fishermen and farmers but turn to stone if caught in a ray of sunlight. Equally impressive, if less lauded, are Norway's social accomplishments. Its citizens enjoy one of the world's highest standards of living, longest life expectancies, and a literacy rate of almost 100%. Then again, its population density is only 13 people per square kilometer—compare that to 228 per square kilometer in Great Britain.

The Norwegians' best-known ancestors were the Vikings, an unruly bunch of explorers who terrorized Europe in the 9th century and are believed to have landed on the American continent long before Columbus was born. By the 11th century, Viking king St. Olav had converted his pagan subjects to Christianity, and it was shortly afterward that many of Norway's unique *stave churches* (churches lavishly decorated with dragon heads and icons from Viking mythology) were built. Norway has spawned a number of modern-day adventurers as well: Explorer Roald Amundsen was the first man to reach the South Pole, and ethnologist Thor Heyerdahl, of **Kon Tiki** fame, sailed across the Pacific and Atlantic oceans in reconstructions of balsa-and-reed rafts to lend credence to his theories of early migration.

Norway was part of Denmark and Sweden for part of its long history, but the country gained independence in 1905 and has guarded it fiercely ever since. Hitler's army invaded in 1940 and stayed for five years, but Norwegian resistance was strong. In 1945 the Germans surrendered, Norwegian Nazi leader Vidkun Quisling was executed, and King Håkon VII's exiled Norwegian government triumphantly returned. Now a constitutional monarchy, Norway is enjoying the independence it fought so long to gain, and Norwegian voters have overwhelmingly rejected proposals to join the European Union.

Most visitors come to Norway in the summer, when days are long, hostels are open, and train and bus departures frequent. But Norway is equally beautiful in winter, when it becomes an uncrowded won-

200 miles

300 km

KEY
Rail Lines

ATLANTIC
OCEAN

*Norwegian
Sea*

**LOFOTEN
ISLANDS**
Austvågøy
Svolvær
Vestvågøy
Stamsund
Moskenesøy
Å
Vestfjorden

NORDKAPP
Honningsvåg
Vardø
Vadsø
Hammerfest
Kirkenes
FINNMARK
Alta
Karasjok
Masi
Kautokeino
Tromsø

FINLAND

Bardu
Narvik

Bodø
Fauske

Arctic Circle

Mo-i-Rana
Umbukta

Sandnessjøen
Møsjøen

Brønnøysund

E6

S W E D E N

Gulf of Bothnia

Vikna
Namsos
Steinkjer

Meråker
Trondheim
Støren

Kristiansund N.
Geirangerfjord
Ålesund
Andalsnes
70
Oppdal
Røros
Tynset

Geiranger
Maløy
Stryn
Hellesylt
Dombås
Otta
9
Koppang

Nordfjord
Florø
JOSTEDALSBREEN
Jotunheimen
Rena
Balestrand
Fjærland
Lillehammer
Sognefjord
Flåm
Myrdal
Finse
*Lake
Mjøsa*
Hamar
Voss
Eidsvoll
Bergen
Geilo
40
Hønefoss
Oslo
Hardangerfjord
11
Kongsberg
Drammen
Sarpsborg
Fredrikstad
Haugesund
Skien
SØRLANDET
Larvik
Porsgrunn
Stavanger
Sandnes
Evje
Arendal
36
Grimstad
Mandal
Kristiansand
Skagerrak

Kattegat

Baltic Sea

N

derland of snow-covered mountains, glowing under the northern lights. Thanks to the Gulf Stream, which flows along the Norwegian coast, the winters here are surprisingly mild for such a high latitude. The one big drawback for visitors is the cost—Norway is incredibly expensive. That first glimpse of the fjords, however, is usually enough to make visitors forget how quickly the kroner are flying out of their pockets.

BASICS

MONEY
US$1 = 7 kroner and 1 krone = 100 øre = 17¢. Post offices are convenient places to change money because most are open on Saturday. Banks are generally open weekdays 9–4 in summer, 9–5 in winter. Banks and post offices both charge a service fee of 10kr per traveler's check, with a 20kr minimum fee, so avoid excess charges by carrying checks in large denominations. Banks and post offices offer better exchange rates for traveler's checks than for cash.

HOW MUCH IT WILL COST • Norway is one of Europe's most expensive countries. Hotel doubles for less than 450kr are practically nonexistent, a basic sit-down meal will usually cost more than 70kr, and a drink at a bar will run you 40kr–60kr. Transportation costs are also high in this vast nation, because everything is so spread out. If you insist on staying in hotels and dining out, expect to spend upward of $90 a day; if you camp, buy groceries, and only travel to the areas covered by your Eurailpass, you can see the Great White North for about $50 less per day.

The distance from northern to southern Norway (2,826 km/1,752 mi) is the same as the distance from southern Norway to Rome.

COMING AND GOING
Most travelers reach Norway by **train,** riding north to Copenhagen, crossing to Sweden, and eventually arriving in Oslo. Eurail, InterRail, and Scanrail passes (*see* Getting Around, *below*) cover the short ferry ride that carries the train across the water from Denmark to Sweden. International **ferries** also connect Norway with England, Germany, and Iceland. Service, frequency, and price increase in summer. For ferry specifics, *see* Oslo, Kristiansand, Stavanger, and Bergen, *below*.

If you want to reach Norway from elsewhere in Europe and don't have a Eurailpass, **flying** is a better option than you might think, as Oslo and Bergen are hubs for international flights. Fares from London (2 hrs) to Oslo are about $380; and from Paris (2 hrs) about $760. Many flights into Norway are handled by the Scandinavian airline **SAS.**

GETTING AROUND
Norway's transportation system is a complex web of trains, planes, ferries, and buses. It's fully detailed in the massive *Rutebok for Norge,* available in Norwegian bookstores and train stations for 210kr. Most tourist offices and travel agencies keep a copy on hand, and the staff will often photocopy relevant information for you. The free pocket-size train schedule (available at the same places) is usually sufficient for the typical traveler, but be aware that some service is cut back or canceled in winter, when mountain roads are covered by snow.

BY BUS • Buses are the only way to hop fjords and are just about the only option for land travel north of Bodø. **Norway Bussekspress** (tel. 23–00–24–00) publishes a free timetable that lists routes and prices for buses throughout Norway. Most tourist offices distribute copies. A few routes offer discounts to travelers using InterRail or Scanrail passes—always ask.

BY FERRY • Ferries stop at all major ports and often, in the fjords, provide service between roads that dead-end at the water's edge. Hydrofoils also serve popular destinations in the fjords and the Lofoten Islands, considerably faster than ferries but at least twice as expensive; rail-pass holders sometimes get a 50% discount. A plush alternative is the **Hurtigrute,** a coastal steamer that departs daily from Bergen on a six-day journey to Kirkenes, stopping at ports along the way. Prices are steep, but overnight travelers save a little money by purchasing deck-class tickets and passing nights in the sleeping-bag room or anywhere in the lounge. In Northern Norway, Hurtigrute tickets are comparable in price to full-fare bus tickets, but the trip is more scenic by ferry, especially through the fjords and in the Lofoten Islands.

BY PLANE • Flying is a viable travel option within Norway, given the country's large size and expensive land-transportation system. Contact **Kilroy Travel** (*see* Oslo and Tromsø, *below*) for information on flights with **Widerø** (tel. 67–59–66–00), **Braathen SAFE** (tel. 67–59–70–00), and **SAS** (tel. 81–00–33–00). Widerø's four-flight, south-to-north air passes (valid June 1–Aug. 31) cost 1,640kr.

BY TRAIN • Eurail and InterRail passes are good for free travel on all Norwegian trains. If you plan to stay in Norway or Scandinavia for any length of time, consider buying a **Scanrail** pass, which gives you five days of travel in a 15-day period (1,380kr second-class), or three weeks of unlimited travel (2,130kr second-class). Scanrail also offers many ferry and bus discounts not available to Eurailpass holders. Another discount option is the **minipris,** a discount of up to 50% on tickets bought at least one day in advance for special "green" departure times, which are usually on weekdays; check train schedules for more details. Norway's train system goes only as far north as Bodø, but trains from Sweden cross the border farther north at Narvik. Seat reservations, mandatory on certain long-distance trains and on all Oslo–Bergen trains, cost 20kr.

WHERE TO SLEEP

Hotels are prohibitively expensive, but tourist offices in many towns book rooms in **private homes** for 100kr–200kr per person. Norway also maintains an excellent network of well-located **hostels,** used by people of all ages. Most hostels serve excellent breakfasts—a hearty all-you-can-eat spread of cereal, bread, cold cuts, soft-boiled eggs, and coffee—for 45kr–60kr. Many also have kitchens, though few provide pots, pans, and utensils. Prices range from 75kr to 175kr for a dorm bed (member prices are listed in this chapter; nonmembers always pay 25kr more). *Vandrerhjem i Norge,* a valuable book available free to HI members (40kr for nonmembers) from **Norske Vandrerhjem** (Dronningens gate 26, Oslo, tel. 22–42–14–10), details every hostel in the country, with descriptions in Norwegian, German, and English. **Campgrounds** are scattered across the Norwegian countryside, but most cater to the motorhome crowd. You'll pay 50kr–150kr for a tent spot, and sometimes an extra 10kr–15kr per person. Most campgrounds also have cabins, starting at about 200kr for four beds (BYO sleeping bag). **Camping rough** is perfectly legal—just make sure you're 470 ft from buildings and the road, and you stay only one night. **Den Norske Turistforening (DNT)** (*see* Visitor Information, *below*) runs a network of mountain *hytter* (huts) in the main wilderness areas. Prices start at 70kr for members, 120kr nonmembers.

FOOD

This will be a big expense. When considering the price of a room, figure in whether breakfasts are included—those all-you-can-eat smörgåsbords can save you money for the rest of the day. If you plan to stick to a budget, supermarkets will probably provide the bulk of your nourishment, and the kitchens in almost all budget lodgings give you a chance to whip up something warm now and then. Beer is available in supermarkets, but wine and hard liquor are sold only in government liquor stores, which usually close at about 4:30 weekdays, 1 PM Saturday.

Many cafeteria-style restaurants offer a *dagens rett* (daily special) for 45kr–80kr, especially at lunch. Norway is a meat-and-potatoes kind of place, not very friendly to vegetarians, but if you eat fish, you'll have lots of options. The exorbitant food prices will probably keep you from sampling local delicacies on a daily basis, but travelers able to splurge may get to try reindeer steak, cod tongues, or the much-heralded minke-whale steak.

BUSINESS HOURS

Most businesses are open weekdays 9–4, and grocery stores often stay open as late as 10 PM, 6 PM on weekends. Post offices in larger cities have additional hours Saturday 9–1. In July, most Norwegians go on vacation and many shops are closed.

VISITOR INFORMATION

Every tiny settlement with any tourist trade whatsoever has a tourist information office, often open only in summer. Be sure to pick up local guides, which list accommodations, restaurants, and outdoor activities. Norway's mountain-touring association, **Den Norske Turistforening (DNT)** (Storgaten 3, Oslo, tel. 22–82–28–00), is the best place to go for help when planning a hiking or climbing trip. A year-long membership (315kr) will reduce the cost of staying in DNT's rural huts (*see* Where to Sleep, *above*).

PHONES

Country code: 47. Pay phones accept 1kr, 5kr, 10kr, and 20kr coins but don't give change; calls costs a minimum of 2kr. Phone cards (starting at 35kr), available at telephone offices in most towns, are useful for calling long distance. Dial 00 to make direct international calls (almost impossible without a phone card). To reach an **AT&T** Direct Access[SM] operator dial 800–19–011; for **MCI** dial 800–19–912; and for **Sprint** dial 800–19–877.

LANGUAGE

Norway's under-40 crowd is generally quite good at English; schools here start teaching it from age 10. Some helpful Norwegian words and phrases are: *hei* (hello); *ha det bra* (goodbye); *ja* (yes); *nei* (no); *var så snill* (please); *takk* (thank you); *snakker du engelsk?* (do you speak English?); *hvor mye koster dette?* (how much is this?); *hvor er . . .?* (where is . . .?).

OSLO

What sets Oslo apart from other European cities is not so much its cultural tradition or internationally renowned museums as its spectacular natural beauty. What other world capital has subway service to stunning forests and lakes, or hiking trails within city limits? And where else but Oslo could you get lost in the woods while making the rounds of city museums? Norwegians will be quick to remind you, though, that Oslo is as cosmopolitan as any major capital city (or at least any Scandinavian capital). It has a brain-numbing collection of museums, a well-established theater scene, and a varied, vibrant nightlife. And like other big metropolises, Oslo also has modern architectural monstrosities, traffic problems, and even a hint of urban sprawl.

Founded by Harald Hardråde in 1048, Oslo is the oldest Scandinavian capital. After the original city on the eastern side of the Oslo fjord was repeatedly destroyed by fire, the 17th-century Danish king Christian IV moved it to its present site and renamed it Christiania. (The original name Oslo was readopted in 1925.) The city grew up around the Oslo fjord and into the surrounding woodlands, and an extensive public transit network connects all the major (and minor) sights, most of them just outside the city center. **Akershus** and **Nordmarka,** the wilderness areas surrounding Oslo, are full of hiking, boating, rafting, biking, fishing, and skiing opportunities. Check with the DNT or tourist offices (*see* Visitor Information *in* Basics, *below*) for details, or just take Tunnelbanen (T-bane) 15 to Frognerseteren and go for a hike.

BASICS

VISITOR INFORMATION

Oslo's main **Information Center** sells the Oslo Card, good for free admission to museums, unlimited travel on public transit, and discounts at shops and restaurants. It comes in one-day (130kr), two-day (200kr), and three-day (240kr) versions. The center also distributes the *Oslo Guide* and *What's On in Oslo* (both free) with up-to-date information on the city's sights. A smaller office in the Sentralstasjon (no phone; open daily 8–5) provides the same services and also books rooms in private homes for a 20kr fee. *Vestbaneplassen 1, tel. 22–83–00–50. Open May–June, Mon.–Sat. 9–5; July–Aug., daily 9–8; shorter hrs off season.*

Den Norske Turistforening (DNT) is your one-stop hiking-information warehouse, with maps, brochures, and keys for Norway's extensive mountain-hytter network. *Storgaten 3, tel. 22–82–28–00. Open weekdays 10–4 (Thurs. until 6), Sat. 10–2.*

Use It has heaps of information for budget travelers. Its free, annual magazine *Streetwise* is a comprehensive guide to cheap eats, sleeps, and activities in and around Oslo. The staff can also book rooms in private homes at no charge. *Møllergata 3, tel. 22–41–51–32. Open mid-June–Aug., weekdays 7:30–6, Sat. 9–2; Sept.–mid-June, weekdays 11–5.*

AMERICAN EXPRESS

This AmEx office offers the usual cardmember services, as well as exchanging currency and selling traveler's checks. *Karl Johans gate 33, tel. 22–98–37–20. Open weekdays 8:30 AM–9 PM, Sat. 10–7, Sun. 1–7. Other location: Fritjof Nansens pl. 6, near City Hall, tel. 22–98–37–35; same hours.*

DISCOUNT TRAVEL AGENCY

Kilroy Travel specializes in budget travel. Check here for summer and standby flight specials. *Nedre Slottsgata 23, tel. 22–42–01–20.*

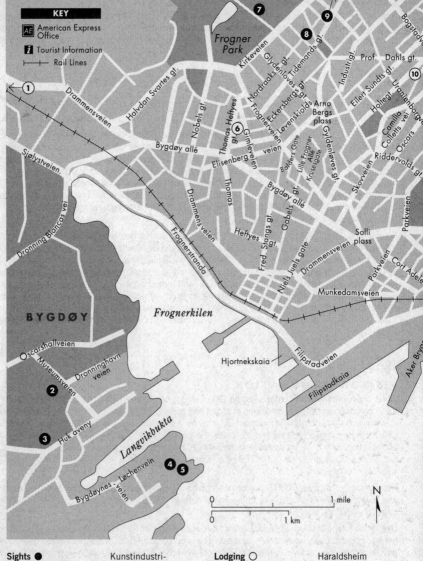

OSLO

KEY

AE American Express Office

ℹ️ Tourist Information

├──┼── Rail Lines

Frogner Park

Drammensveien

Sjelystveien

Dronning Blancas vei

BYGDØY

Oscarshallveien

Museumsveien

Dronninghavn veien

Huk aveny

Langvikbukta

Bygdøynes – Løchenvein

Frognerkilen

Hjortnekskaia

Filipstadveien

Filipstadkaia

Aker Brygge

Halvdan Svartes gt.

Bygdøy allé

Nobels gt.

Thomas Heftyes

Elisenberg

Gimleveien

Drammensveien

Frognerstranda

Thomas

Heftyes

Fred. Stangs gt.

Niels Juels gate

Gabels gt.

Bygdøy gt.

Bygdøy allé

Kirkeveien

Nordraaks gt.

Gyldenløves gt.

Eckersbergs gt.

Frognerveien

Løvenskjolds

veien

Balders Gate

Lille Frogner Allé

Kruses gate

Gyldenløves gt.

Arno Bergs plass

Skovveien

Drammensveien

Solli plass

Munkedamsveien

Parkveien

Cort Adelers

Tidemands gt.

Industrigt.

Prof. Dahls gt.

Eilert Sundts gt.

Holtegt.

Uranienborgveie

Camilla

Colletts vei

Oscars

Rid28dervolds

Parkveien

Bogstadveie

0 ───── 1 mile
0 ───── 1 km

N ↑

Sights ●

Akershus Slott and Norges Hjemmefront-museum, **20**

Barnekunst-museet, **8**

Fram-museet, **5**

Holmenkollen, **9**

Kon-Tiki Museum, **4**

Kunstindustri-museet, **13**

Munchmuseet, **17**

Nasjonal-galleriet, **12**

Norsk Folkemuseum, **2**

Oslo Domkirke, **16**

Vigelands Sculpture Park, **7**

Vikingskips-museet, **3**

Lodging ○

City Hotel, **19**

Cochs Pensjonat, **11**

Ekeberg Camping, **21**

Ellingsen's Pensjonat, **10**

Frogner Pensjonat, **6**

Haraldsheim (HI), **15**

Holtekilen Sommerhotell (HI), **1**

Hotel Fønix, **18**

KFUM InterRail Point (YMCA), **14**

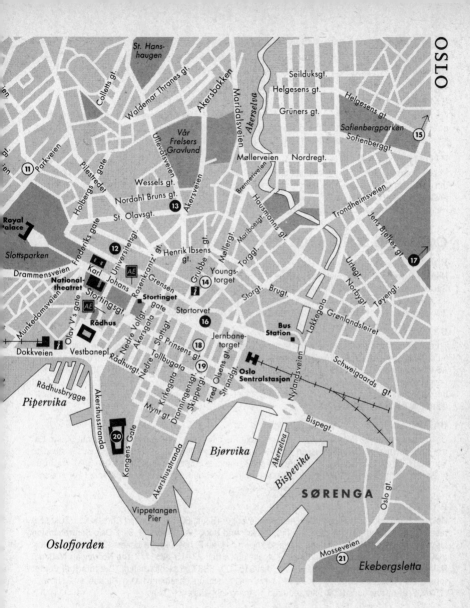

EMBASSIES

Canada: *Oscarsgata 20, tel. 22–46–69–55. Open weekdays 8–3:30.* **United Kingdom:** *Thomas Heftyesgata 8, tel. 22–55–24–00. Open weekdays 9–12:30.* **United States:** *Drammensveien 18, tel. 22–44–85–50. Open weekdays 9–noon.*

EMERGENCIES

For a **fire** or major accident dial 110, for the **police** 112, and for an **ambulance** 113. For non-emergency police matters, stop by or call the police station (Grønlandsleiret 44, tel. 22–66–90–50). Jernbane-torvets Apotek, a **24-hour pharmacy** (tel. 22–41–24–82), is across from Sentralstasjon.

PHONES AND MAIL

Phone cards are sold at the telephone office **Telehuset** (Universitetsgata 7, tel. 22–77–86–00), or at the ubiquitous Narvesen kiosks, which sell newspapers and tobacco. Pick up poste restante at the **main post office** (Dronningens gate 15, tel. 22–40–78–02). Address mail as follows: Your Name, Poste Restante, Dronningens gate 15, N-0101 Oslo, Norway.

COMING AND GOING

BY BUS

Norway Bussekspress (Schweigaards Gate 8, tel. 23–00–24–00), northeast of the train station in the Galleri Oslo, operates an extensive bus network with service to all of Norway, including Fjaerland (8 hrs, 410kr), Kristiansand (6 hrs, 270kr), and Stockholm (8 hrs, 310kr). Some northbound buses give a 50% discount to rail-pass holders, so be sure to ask. Buses do not require reservations.

BY FERRY

Three ferry companies link Oslo with Germany, Denmark, and England. Call **Color Line** (Hjortneskaia, tel. 22–94–44–70), **Scandinavian Seaways** (Vippetangen Pier 2, tel. 22–41–90–90), or **Stena Lines AS** (Jernbanetorget 2, tel. 23–17–90–00) for the latest schedules and prices. Prices are seasonal and hover around 600kr per trip. Color Line ferries dock at Hjortneskaia; take Tram 10, 11, 12, or 13 from the train station. All other ferries dock at Vippetangen Pier near Akershus castle; from the train station, take Bus 29 or walk 20 minutes.

BY PLANE

Oslo has two airports: **Fornebu,** 7 km (4½ mi) from the city center, and **Gardermoen,** about 50 km (30 mi) from town. The **SAS Flybussen** connects both airports to Oslo's bus terminal. Buses head to Fornebu (20 min, 50kr) every 10 minutes (every 20 minutes on weekends) from 6 AM to 9:40 PM. Buses to Gardermoen (50 min, 70kr) leave the bus terminal two hours before flight departures. For informa-tion on airport shuttle buses, call 67–58–38–00.

BY TRAIN

Oslo is the rail hub for Norway. Trains head to Stavanger (8 hrs, 600kr), Bergen (7 hrs, 500kr, 20kr seat reservation required), Åndalsnes (5–7 hrs, 490kr), and Bodø (20–24 hrs, 910kr). **Oslo Sentralstasjon** (Jernbanetorget 1, tel. 22–17–14–00), also known as Oslo S, has luggage lockers (20kr), tourist infor-mation, a currency exchange, and a lost-luggage office (tel. 23–15–40–47). The **Norwegian National Railway** (NSB) has an office in the station; dial 815–00–888 for rail information. The **InterRail Center** (open mid-June–mid-Sept., daily 7 AM–11 PM) in the station basement has a kitchen and showers (15kr). Seat reservations (20kr) are required on many long-distance trains.

GETTING AROUND

Oslo's city center is easily navigated on foot. **Karl Johans gate,** the main street, runs east–west from the train station to the Royal Palace and the **Nationaltheatret,** a local transport hub. Beyond the city cen-ter, Oslo disolves into suburban sprawl, though subways, local trains, buses, trams, and ferries link even the most remote suburbs. To figure out which mode of transport to take, ask or use the maps at **Trafikanten** (Jernbanetorget, in front of Sentralstasjon, tel. 22–17–70–30 or tel. 177 within Oslo). Here you can buy a 24-hour transport pass (40kr), good for citywide buses, trams, subways, and ferries, and pick up a free copy of *Sporveiskart for Oslo,* a valuable map of greater Oslo and its complex web of pub-lic transportation. Ride the entire network for free with the one-, two-, or three-day Oslo Card (*see* Visitor Information, *above*). Individual tickets (18kr) are good for an hour on all of the city's public transportation; buy them from bus or tram drivers, or from machines in the subway stations.

Most **buses** stop at Sentralstasjon or the Nationaltheatret, and run until about 12:30 AM Sunday–Thursday. Friday and Saturday nights, buses and trams run until 4 AM or 5 AM but are a rip-off at 36kr; it would probably be cheaper to share a taxi. Oslo's subway, the **Tunnelbanen** (T-bane), has a hub at Stortinget in the city center from which eight lines set out for the suburbs. The system starts up daily at 6 AM and runs until about 12:30 AM. **Tram** hubs are Stortorvet and Jernbanetorget, in front of the Sentralstasjon. **Local trains** run from Sentralstasjon and the Nationaltheatret.

Ferries connect the city center with the Bygdøy peninsula, the fjord islands, and outlying districts along the Oslo fjord. **Ferries** leave for Bygdøy from the docks outside the Rådhus, and for the islands from Vippetangen Pier behind Akershus castle. Oslo is a great city for **biking** and bikes are allowed on the subway, so you can get a head start up to the excellent mountain trails. **Den Rustne Eike** (Vestbaneplassen 2, next to main tourist office, tel. 22–83–72–31) rents mountain bikes starting at 95kr for three hours, with a 1,000kr or credit-card deposit.

WHERE TO SLEEP

Cheap summer rooms in Oslo are about as easy to find as snow in a sauna, so plan ahead. For the best lodging deal in town, rent a room in a private home through Use It (*see* Visitor Information, *above*); rooms (100kr–130kr) fill up fast in high season, though, and can be some distance from the center. The tourist information center at Sentralstasjon also books rooms in private homes, but these start at 150kr per person in a double, require a 20kr fee, and must be arranged in person. If you really must stay in a hotel, you'll find a few "cheap" options west of the palace around Frogner Park.

UNDER 400KR • Ellingsen's Pensjonat. This place on a tree-lined street on the central west side has an enthusiastic proprietress and a homey feel. The smallish, tidy doubles are 380kr. *Holtegata 25, tel. 22–60–03–59. From Sentralstasjon, Tram 1 (toward Majorstuen) to Uranienborgveien. Cash only.*

Frogner Pensjonat. The pink walls are on the tacky side, but it's reasonably cheap. Doubles cost 400kr. *Thomas Heftyesgata 41, tel. 22–55–37–82. 3 blocks south of Frogner Park tram stop. Cash only.*

UNDER 550KR • Cochs Pensjonat. Behind the palace on the central west side is this establishment with spacious, almost antiseptic rooms. Doubles cost 420kr, 513kr with shower; quads with showers (680kr) are a good deal for groups. *Parkveien 25, tel. 22–60–48–36. From Sentralstasjon, Tram 17 (toward Majorstuen) to Dalsbergstien, or Tram 11 (same direction) to Welharens gate. Cash only.*

UNDER 750KR • City Hotel. The City Hotel offers clean, basic rooms and convenient, central location. Its charming lobby/reception area comes complete with antique furniture and a nonsmoking section. Doubles without bath are 680kr, breakfast included. *Skippergata 19, tel. 22–41–36–10. Off Karl Johans gate near Sentralstasjon.*

Hotel Fønix. The small rooms here are decorated with matching wood furniture. Breakfast (included in price) is served next door in a dining room that doubles as a bar. Doubles without bath are 750kr. *Dronningens gate 19, off Karl Johans gate, tel. 22–42–59–57. Bar, laundry.*

HOSTELS

Haraldsheim (HI). A no-frills hostel near public transportation, the Haraldsheim offers views of the Oslo fjord. Reservations are essential in summer; call at least a week ahead. Beds cost 155kr, breakfast included. *Haraldsheimveien 4, tel. 22–22–29–65. From Sentralstasjon, Tram 10 (toward Disen) to Sinsenkrysset; walk up right side of field and look for hostel signs. Lockout 10–3. Laundry.*

Holtekilen Sommerhotell (HI). Figure 40kr round-trip bus fare into the price of a bed here, as it's far enough outside Oslo that passes aren't valid. Dorm beds cost 155kr; doubles 400kr, 450kr nonmembers; breakfast is included. *Michelets vei 55, Stabekk, tel. 67–53–38–53. From Sentralstasjon, Bus 151 to Kveldsroveien; walk across highway overpass, go left down hill, and look for signs. Reception open 24 hrs. Closed late Aug.–mid-May.*

KFUM InterRail Point (YMCA). The pluses here are cheap 100kr beds, a central location, and special cultural events on Thursday evenings. If you arrive here when reception is closed, take a number at the Use It office next door to reserve a spot. *Møllergata 1, entrance on Grubbegata, tel. 22–20–83–97. Reception open daily 8 AM–11 AM and 5 PM–midnight. Kitchen. Closed mid-Aug.–June. Cash only.*

CAMPING

Travelers with tents will never be without a place to sleep in Oslo. You can pitch yours anywhere in the forest—just remember to stay at least 470 ft from any dwelling. If you're traveling without a tent, talk to **Den Norske Turistforening** (*see* Visitor Information, *above*) about wilderness huts.

Ekeberg Camping. Only 3 km (2 mi) from the center are campsites with some great views of the city and fjord (although some sites overlook only a trailer parking lot). Sites cost 110kr, 130kr with a car. *Ekebergveien 65, tel. 22–19–85–68. From Sentralstasjon, Bus 24, 45, or 46 toward Ekeberg. Kitchen, laundry. Closed Sept.–late-May.*

FOOD

You'll find the cheapest hole-in-the-wall restaurants and small grocery stores in the immigrant areas of Grønland and Tøyen, northeast of the Sentralstasjon. Also look for produce markets at Jernbanetorget, Grønlands torg, and Youngstorget. **KIWI MiniPris** (corner of Storgata and Brugata) is the most centrally located grocery store.

UNDER 50KR • Café Sekel. Floral drapes and wooden tables evoke the atmosphere of a country home. The friendly staff serves heaping portions of typical Norwegian fare. You get a solid meal for 35kr–70kr. *Tollbugata 6, at Skippergata, tel. 22–42–42–12. Closed Sun. Cash only.*

Punjab Sweet House. Indian specials are served in a spartan setting here in the Grønland district. Choose from *nan* (Indian flat bread), rice, or *dal* (cooked lentils) to go with chicken curry (35kr) or *samosas* (fried dumplings stuffed with vegetables or meat). *Grønlandsleiret 24, tel. 22–17–20–86. T-bane: Grønland. Cash only.*

UNDER 75KR • Krishnas Cuisine Vegetarian Restaurant. One of the city's best bargains is Krishnas's all-you-can-eat special (70kr): salad, soup, rice, *pakora* (deep-fried vegetables), and two entrées. Mouth-watering curries and other Indian dishes are also served. *Kirkeveien 59B, tel. 22–60–62–50. T-bane: Majorstuen. Closed weekends. Cash only.*

Teddy's Soft Bar. Teddy's super-cool interior remains unchanged since 1958. For typical Norwegian diner fare order the 55kr *pytt i panne* (two eggs, coffee, and bread). *Brugata 3A, tel. 22–17–64–36. A few blocks north of Sentralstasjon, near Vaterlands parken. Cash only.*

UNDER 120KR • Vegeta Verthus. This vegetarian restaurant has a buffet with hot entrées, pizza, and salad fixings; a small plate costs 69kr, a large one 79kr, and all-you-can-eat is 108kr. Each comes with your fill of bread and cheese. *Munkedamsveien 3B, tel. 22–83–40–20. Just south of Nationaltheatret bus stop. Cash only.*

WORTH SEEING

The great outdoors is the main attraction in Oslo, but the city also has many first-class museums to keep you occupied. Open hours vary drastically by season, so call before you go or consult the *Oslo Guide* (*see* Visitor Information *in* Basics, *above*).

CITY CENTER

You can explore interesting dungeons and courtyards at **Akershus Slott** (tel. 23–09–39–17; admission 20kr). The castle, first built in the 13th century and converted into a Renaissance palace by Christian IV in the 17th century, is infamous for having served as a Nazi prison during World War II. The castle's resistance museum, the **Norges Hjemmefrontmuseum** (tel. 22–40–31–38; admission 15kr), documents the episode in an eerie collection of photographs, papers, and recordings. Also in the city center, the **Kunstindustrimuseet** (St. Olavs gate 1, tel. 22–20–35–78; admission 25kr; closed Mon.) displays Norwegian handicrafts, tapestries, and royal costumes dating from the 7th century.

To celebrate its 300th anniversary, the city's cathedral, **Oslo Domkirke** (Stortorvet 1, tel. 22–41–27–93; open weekdays 10–3, Sat. 10–1), was carefully restored in 1997. The underground crypts are fascinating if you've a morbid curiosity: Decaying wood coffins line the walls of two chambers, while another houses an ornate marble tomb containing the remains of the richest man in 18th-century Oslo. Call the cathedral to arrange a tour of the crypts; generally tours are given only to groups of at least five.

BYGDOY

This peninsula has its share of museums, but they're a far cry from the usual staid collections of paintings. You can wander the forests and explore reconstructed buildings and farms dating from the middle ages at **Norsk Folkemuseum** (Museumsveien 10, tel: 22–12–37–00; admission 50kr). The museum also has exhibits on Norwegian folk art and traditional costumes, as well as information about the Sami—the traditionally nomadic people of northern Scandinavia, whose culture is centered around herding reindeer.

On the opposite side of the peninsula, the **Kon-Tiki Museum** (Bygdøynesveien 36, tel. 22–43–80–50; admission 25kr) displays the original *Kon Tiki* raft that ethnologist Thor Heyerdahl took across the Pacific in 1947, and *Ra II*, the reed boat that he sailed across the Atlantic. The vessel Roald Amundsen used in his 1911 Antarctic odyssey is beached at the **Fram-museet** (Bygdøynesveien, tel. 22–43–83–70; admission 20kr; closed Jan.–Feb.); to get a true sense of what it's like to be an adventurer, step on board and check out the explorers' cramped living quarters. At the **Vikingskipsmuseet** (Huk Aveny 35, tel. 22–43–83–79; admission 30kr), you can see three 9th-century Viking burial ships, along with the tools found inside them. For a break from so much museum-hopping, head to **Huk Beach,** through the woods behind the Vikingskipsmuseet. From late April to late September, ferries travel between the Rådhusbrygge and the Bygdøy peninsula every 30 minutes 7:45–5:45; year-round Bus 30 makes the trip from Jernbanetorget.

If you're in Oslo on a sunny summer day, take T-bane 4 to Sognsvann, in the hills north of the city center. Here you'll find a lake that will make you forget you're in a European capital.

ART MUSEUMS

Local-boy-made-good Edvard Munch is idolized in Oslo, and the museums here hold all of this 20th-century expressionist's best work. The **Munchmuseet** (Tøyengata 53, tel. 22–67–37–74; admission 40kr) focuses on Munch, but the **Nasjonalgalleriet** (Universitetsgaten 13, tel. 22–20–04–04; admission free) has a large collection of Norwegian and European art, as well as a room dedicated entirely to Munch. Because Munch painted multiple copies of his paintings so he could always keep a copy for himself, both museums display some of the same works, including *The Scream*. The **Barnekunstmuseet** (Lille Frøens vei 4, tel. 22–46–85–73; Frøen T-bane; admission 30kr) is an international museum of children's art with works by youngsters from 180 countries. This may be the only museum in Europe where you're asked to put your shoes in cubbyholes before entering.

VIGELANDS SCULPTURE PARK

At the turn of the century, Oslo city officials handed over Frogner Park to sculptor Gustav Vigeland, letting him fill it with all the sculptures he could produce before his death. He brought Oslo its first fountain and eventually completed 212 sculptures that dramatically depict the cycle of human life. His most famous and impressive sculpture is an obelisk of seething human forms that thrusts 65 ft into the sky. Admission is free; take Tram 12 or 15 to Vigelandsparken.

Gustav wasn't the only artist in the family, however. His brother Emanuel painted his own version of the life cycle as a fresco on the wall of his own tomb at the **Emanuel Vigeland Museum** (Grimelundsveien 8, tel. 22–14–93–42; admission free; open Sun. noon–3). Hundreds of writhing bodies, some laughing skulls, and a pair of skeletons making whoopee make this more interesting than your average tomb. Take the T-bane to Slemdal and head south on Frognerseterveien.

HOLMENKOLLEN

You get a nice view of Oslo from the base of this world-famous ski jump, but to catch the view from the top, you have to pay admission to the ski museum, which is actually pretty interesting. *Tel. 22–92–32–00. T-bane 1 (toward Frognerseteren) to Holmenkollen. Museum admission: 50kr.*

OSLOFJORDEN

In summer, hardy Norwegians enjoy dipping into the cold waters of Oslo's inner fjord. The islands here make for a relaxing day trip in pleasant weather: **Hovedøya,** the closest to town and most crowded, has an old monastery that's open to visitors (admission free). **Langøyene,** to the south, is known for its nude beaches, and often hosts all-night beach parties. Ferries to the islands leave from Vippetangen Pier.

SHOPPING

Oslo is the best place to buy anything Norwegian, as you'll have a wide selection to choose from. However, as with everything in the country, prices are high. Look for signs advertising sales and specials—*salg* and *tilbud* are the key words. **Husfliden** (Møllergt 4, tel. 22–42–10–75) sells pewter, ceramics, knits, handwoven textiles, furniture, handmade felt boots and slippers, hand-sewn loafers, sweaters, national costumes, wrought-iron housewares, Christmas ornaments, and wooden kitchen accessories with such obscure and ancient forms that even your Norwegian grandmother wouldn't know what to do with them. Everything at Husfliden is made in Norway. **Norway Designs** (Stortingsgt. 28, tel. 22–83–11–00) specializes in glass crafted by Norwegian and Scandinavian folk artists and jewelers. The shops at **Basarhallene,** behind the cathedral, also sell glass and ceramics. For information on the city's sporadic flea markets, pick up a copy of *Aftenposten*.

AFTER DARK

Pick up the free *Natt & Dag* anywhere in town for the whole story on Oslo's nightlife; the listings are helpful even if you don't understand Norwegian. Of the city's plentiful bars and pubs, those in east Oslo are the cheapest. Many bars have happy hours before 9, with half-liters of beer for about 25kr. After 9, prices rise to about 36kr (or even more, in the pricier outdoor cafés). Oslo's loudest nightlife takes place in the streets off Karl Johans gate; just follow the blasting music that you like best. **Head On** (Rosenkranz' gate 11, tel. 22–33–52–64) plays '70s funk mixes and attracts a mellow alternative crowd. **Blitz** (Pilestredet 30, tel. 22–11–01–09), off the northwest corner of Slottsparken, is a punk hangout that hosts primarily underground bands. **Club Castro** (Kristian IVs Gt. 7, tel. 22–41–51–08) is Oslo's premier gay hangout. Cover for the disco is 50kr on Saturday; no cover on Friday.

North of the Sentralstasjon, beyond downtown, is another great selection of cheap bars. Beers are 27kr at **Café Fiasco** (in Galleri Oslo, above bus station, tel. 22–17–66–50). The **Afro International Night Club** (Brenneriveien 5, tel. 22–36–07–53) features jazz, blues, reggae, and disco for a 50kr cover. For some Scandinavian-style salsa, head to **Caramba Nattklubb** (Storgata 25, tel. 22–41–34–85; 50kr cover). Don't show up in sneakers and rumpled clothes, or you'll get snubbed at the door.

SORLANDET

In summer, Oslo's residents migrate to the southern coast to soak up some sunshine while the rest of the country endures incessant rain. Unfortunately, unless you have plenty of time or your own set of wheels, you'll probably catch only glimpses of the spectacular Sørlandet region through a train window. The international ferry ports of Kristiansand and Stavanger are easy to reach, but there's no reason to make a special effort to see them. Your best bet for exploring Sørlandet is to pick a remote youth hostel or mountain hut and then slowly make your way there.

KRISTIANSAND

In June and July, Kristiansand becomes a madhouse as thousands of sun-seeking Norwegians arrive with beach blankets and paperbacks in hand. The rest of the year you should have plenty of room to enjoy the area's "beaches," most of which are actually jumbles of big, smooth rocks sloping gently into the sea. The **tourist information office** (Dronningens gate 2, tel. 38–12–13–14) has information on the best beaches and sells area maps (30kr). To get there from the train station, go right on Vestre Strandgate to Dronningens gate. At the north end of town is the **Baneheia recreation area,** with a beautiful lake, hiking trails, and a nice view of the city.

COMING AND GOING

Trains from Oslo (6 hrs, 395kr) stop right next to the bus and ferry terminals at the southwestern edge of town. **Color Line** (tel. 38–07–88–88) runs ferries to Hirtshals, Denmark (6 hrs; 97kr–360kr, depending on the season). The streets of Kristiansand form a grid, with the Domkirke (cathedral) in the center and the old town in the northeast corner. **City buses** (16kr) converge at the bottom of Henrik Wergelands gate; pay the driver when you board.

WHERE TO SLEEP AND EAT

The **HI hostel** (Skansen 8, in southeast corner of town, tel. 38–02–83–10, fax 38–02–75–05; beds 150kr) has plenty of beds, except in June and July, when it's generally booked solid; the only problem is that it's not on a bus route, so it's a 25-minute hike to get there. **Roligheden Camping** (Framnesveien, tel. 38–09–67–22) is more than twice as far away, but is easily reached by Bus 15 or 16. Beachfront rooms with four beds go for 550kr and tent spaces are 60kr plus 20kr per person.

Pizzerias line Markens gate, and there's always **MEGA**, a big supermarket across from the train station. For some Norwegian cuisine, head to **Nellas Hus** (corner of Gyldenløves gate and Kirkegata, tel. 38–02–22–93), where lunch specials include fish soup (32kr) and fried mackerel.

STAVANGER

The main reason to visit Stavanger is to see the **Lysefjord,** one of Norway's most spectacular fjords. By far the most popular destination here is **Preikestolen** (Pulpit Rock), a massive granite precipice, looming 2,000 ft above the fjord. The quick and lazy way to see Lysefjord is to take the boat tour (3 hrs, 190kr) run by **Rødne Clipper Fjord Sightseeing** (tel. 51–89–52–70). During summer, boats leave from Skagenkaien at 10:30 AM every day except Wednesday and Sunday, and stop at all the major sights. Another way to see it is to hike to the top of Preikestolen and then wave at the less adventuresome tourists huddled in the boats down below. To get to Preikestolen, take the 8:20 AM ferry to Tau (40 min, 25kr), and then the summer-only bus through Jørpland to the trailhead (37kr). From there, it's a two-hour haul to the top. The bus returns from the trailhead at 4 PM, but if you want to stay, sleep at the **Preikestolen Youth Hostel** (330 ft from trailhead, tel. 94–53–11–11, fax 51–84–02–14; beds 105kr), located in a little farmhouse on the shores of a stunning mountain lake. For information on longer hikes, including treks to the dramatic Kjeragbolten (another natural rock ledge), head to **Stavanger Turistforening** (in underpass just upstairs from train station, tel. 51–84–02–00); they have free maps and firsthand advice about trails and hiking conditions. For general tourist information, pick up the free *Stavanger Guide* at the **tourist information office** (next to fish market on wharf, tel. 51–89–62–00; open June–Aug., daily 10–8).

COMING AND GOING

Trains from Oslo (8 hrs, 600kr) arrive at the **train station** (tel. 51–56–96–00), south of the town center next to the bus station, where you can catch the express bus to Bergen (6 hrs, 355kr). **Color Line** (Strandkaien, tel. 51–52–45–45) ferries run to and from Newcastle, England (19 hrs, fares from 460kr in June, 880kr in July, less off season) and on to Bergen. For a quick trip to Bergen, take the express ferry **Hurtigbåt** (4 hrs, 470kr) from the bottom of Kirkegata. Travelers with hostel cards or rail passes get substantial discounts. Dial 51–89–50–90 for information.

WHERE TO SLEEP AND EAT

Both the **HI hostel** (H. Ibsens gate 21, tel. 51–87–29–00, fax 51–87–06–30; beds 100kr) and **Mosvangen Camping** (Tjensvoll 1, tel. 51–53–29–71; tents 55kr plus 10kr per person, 4-bed cabins 340kr; closed Sept.–May) are inconveniently located 2½ km/1½ mi south of town. Take Bus 97 or 130 (15kr) from the cathedral if you don't want to walk. **Rogalandsheimen Bed and Breakfast** (Muségata 18, tel. 51–52–01–88; doubles 450kr late June–mid-Aug.; less off season) is a charming, old wood home. It's upstairs behind the train station and under the highway.

The best meal deal in town is a 89kr all-you-can-eat taco bar served Sundays from 11:30 AM to 5 PM at **Restaurant Mexico** (Skagenkaien 12, tel. 51–89–15–55). Otherwise, head to the **RIMI 1000** supermarket in the bus station next to the train station, where you can buy cans of sardines or mackerel that were canned right here in Stavanger.

CENTRAL NORWAY AND THE FJORDS

The Norwegian fjords (long, narrow, deep inlets from the sea, bracketed by steep cliffs and slopes) extend all along the coastline, from the Russian border in the far north all the way to the country's southern tip. In spectacular fjords like Sognefjord and Geirangerfjord, sheer rock walls rise straight up from the water, jagged snowcapped peaks and massive glaciers seem to rake the sky, and turquoise rivers turn to frothing waterfalls as they plummet down mountainsides.

Unfortunately, you may not often be able to enjoy the fjords' beauty in solitude. After a tough three-hour hike to the top of a mountain, it can be discouraging to look down the other slope at an armada of tour buses chugging your way. Campgrounds are plentiful in the region, but they're often packed with trailers. The strategically placed youth hostels are a good bet, and you'll encounter mountain hytter regularly. If you travel in a group, you'll expand your options considerably—almost every campground has four-bed cabins for 250kr–500kr. Camping rough is also an option here, but you should first check with the locals whose property you may be invading. The dining scene is very basic in all the fjord towns except Bergen, which is large and offers greater variety. Most towns have cafeterias with specials for about 60kr–80kr, but for anything else prepare to play chef in the hostel kitchens.

BERGEN

Eurailpass holders who make it as far as Norway often bypass Oslo and barrel straight ahead to Bergen, where they find hundreds of other people who have had the same idea. Despite the fact that it's the second-largest city in Norway and is swamped by thousands of cruise-ship tourists each summer, Bergen, the gateway to Norway's gorgeous fjords, has managed to keep an intimate, small-town feeling.

Founded in 1070 by Olaf Kyrre, this former capital of Norway was most important as a center of trade for the Hanseatic League, a federation of north German merchant-cities that held sway in medieval days. A physical legacy of this era survives today in the buildings lining **Bryggen,** Bergen's famous wharf. Each year the town celebrates during the **Bergen International Music Festival** (tel. 55–31–21–70), with 12 days of music, drama, and dance performances. The town also hosts an international **jazz festival** (tel. 55–32–09–76), which has attracted such big acts as James Brown and Dave Brubeck. Both festivals are held in late May.

BASICS

The hectic **tourist office** changes money at generally lousy rates (banks are a better option), but their free *Bergen Guide* is indispensable. *Corner of Bryggen and Lodin Leppsgata, tel. 55–32–14–80. Open May–Sept., Mon.–Sat. 8:30–9, Sun. 10–7; Oct.–Apr., weekdays 9–4.*

The Bergen **DNT** can help you arrange trips to the fjords and recommend hikes in the nearby mountains; they also have maps and information about mountain hytter. *Tverrgaten 4–6, down Marken from train station, tel. 55–32–22–30. Open weekdays 10–4, Thurs. until 6.*

Take care of postal needs or change money at the main **post office** (tel. 55–54–15–00; open Mon.–Wed. 8–5, Thurs.–Fri. 8–6, Sat. 9–3) on Småstrandgaten, in the green building with the clock. The **Telegraph Building** (Starvhusgaten 4, next to post office, tel. 55–96–80–00; open weekdays 9–4) is the best place to make long-distance calls.

COMING AND GOING

The Oslo–Bergen train (7 hrs, 500kr, 20kr seat reservation required) travels from lush pine forests through the bleak tundra of the Hardangervidda and into the fjords. The Bergen **train station** (tel. 55–96–60–00) is on the corner of Strømgaten and Kaigaten, at the south end of town near the big fountain and pond. Long-distance buses leave from the **bus station** (tel. 55–32–67–80), next to the train station on Strømgaten. Buses are most useful for trips north through the fjords, such as to Stryn (7hrs, 317kr), and for going south to Stavanger (6 hrs, 355kr) without returning to Oslo.

International ferries from England, Iceland, Denmark, Scotland, and the Faroe Islands dock at **Skoltegrunnskaien,** on the east side of the harbor. **Color Line** (Skuteviksboder 1–2, tel. 55–54–86–60) runs to Stavanger and on to Newcastle, England (24 hrs); fares fluctuate drastically by season. **Fjord Line** (Slottsgaten 1, across from Bryggens Museum, tel. 55–32–37–70) runs to Hirtshals, Denmark (16½ hrs, 850kr in summer, 435kr off season). Domestic ferries leave from **Strandkai Terminal** on the west side of the harbor. Dial 55–23–87–80 for information on express boats to Stavanger and Hardangerfjord, or 55–32–40–15 for information on boats to Sognefjord and Nordfjord. The **Hurtigrute** luxury coastal steamer leaves from **Frieleneskaien,** behind the Natural History Museum.

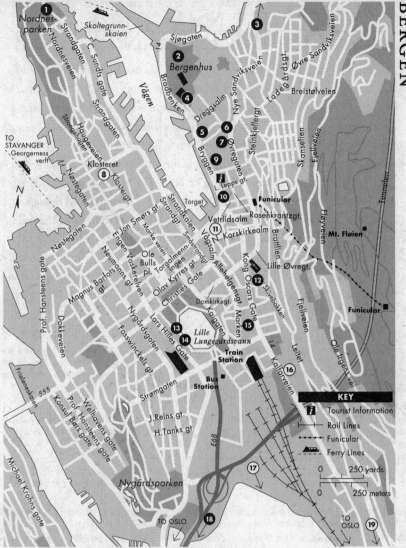

KEY

- 🛈 Tourist Information
- ⋯ Rail Lines
- ⋯⋯ Funicular
- 🚢 Ferry Lines

| 0 | 250 yards |
| 0 | 250 meters |

Sights ●

Bergen Akvariet, **1**
Bryggens Museum, **5**
Domkirke, **12**
Gamle (Old) Bergen, **3**
Håkonshallen, **2**
Hanseatisk Museum, **10**
Leprosy Museum, **15**

Mariakirken, **6**
Municipal Art Museum/ Stenersen's Collection, **13**
Rasmus Meyer's Samlinger, **14**
Rosenkrantztårnet, **4**
Schøtstuene, **7**
Thetamuseum, **9**
Troldhaugen, **18**

Lodging ○

Fagerheim Pensjon, **19**
Intermission, **16**
Kloster Pensjon, **8**
Montana Vandrerhjem (HI), **17**
YMCA InterRail Center, **11**

HIKING THE
OSLO—BERGEN LINE

The stunning mountains between Bergen and Oslo are filled with forested dells and snowy peaks that will take your breath away. Many travelers whiz through the region by train, but the rewards are great for those who disembark. Geilo, a winter ski center, offers summer hiking and a youth hostel (tel. 32–09–03–00; beds 145kr; closed May, Oct.–mid-Jan.). Finse village is on the snowy Hardanger plateau. From here you can trek through the Aurland Valley to Flåm (see below), then catch the train to Bergen or Oslo. The three- to five-day journey from Finse to Vassbygdi relys on DNT-operated hytter, evenly spaced throughout the valley. Check the weather first; Finse can be snowed in until July. Mjølfjell is popular with skiers; in summer its youth hostel (tel. 56–51–81–11; beds 95kr; closed Oct.–Mar. and May–mid-June), in an old farmhouse, is nearly deserted. Take the Bergen–Myrdal train, ask the conductor to stop at Ørnaberget, and follow the short (but steep) trail down into the valley.

GETTING AROUND

Bergen's center is walkable, and only a few attractions will force you onto the bus (about 14kr for a one-hour ride). Most everything is located near the harbor, with the **Bryggen** area on the east shore and **Strandkaien** on the west shore; **Torget,** the fish market, is at the southern end. Most local buses converge on **Småstrandgaten,** behind the post office on Olav Kyrres gate, and at Torget.

WHERE TO SLEEP

Bergen has a good selection of cheap accommodations, but rooms fill up fast in high season. The DNT (*see* Visitor Information, *above*) operates hytter on Mt. Ulriken and Mt. Fløien. Another option is to pay the tourist office 20kr to book you a double (270kr–320kr) in a private home.

UNDER $450 • Fagerheim Pensjon. Though it's fairly far from town, this funky old mansion will charm you with its fantastic views. Doubles cost 400kr; breakfast 45kr. *Kalvedalsveien 49A, tel. 55–31–01–72. From train station, walk south 1½ km/¾ mi on Kalfarveien; or from town center, Bus 2, 4, 7, or 11. Kitchen. Cash only.*

Kloster Pensjon. Here's a centrally located pension with a mountain-cabin ambience. Doubles are 450kr, simple breakfast included. *Strangehagen 2, tel. 55–90–21–58. Cash only.*

HOSTELS • Intermission. This family-run, coed dorm offers 40 beds in an 18th-century home. A friendly staff and homey atmosphere make it the best deal in town. The no-reservations policy means no groups of noisy schoolchildren. Talk to the manager about staying out past the midnight curfew. Beds cost 95kr breakfast 25kr. *Kalfarveien 8, tel. 55–31–32–75. Behind train station, near big, white gatehouse; from town center, Bus 2, 4, or 11. Lockout 11–5. Kitchen, laundry. Cash only. Closed mid-Aug.–mid-June.*

Montana Vandrerhjem (HI). At the foot of Mt. Ulriken—5 km (3 mi) from town—is this massive youth hostel with a somewhat sterile, institutional feeling. It offers gorgeous views and is a great base for hiking. Beds in quads cost 155kr, dorm beds 125kr, breakfast included; sheets cost 35kr. *Johan Blyttsvei 30, tel. 55–29–29–00. From town center, Bus 4; tell driver to let you off at the hostel. Lockout 10–4:30. Laundry (20kr). Cash only.*

YMCA InterRail Center. They squeeze as many people as they can into this centrally located hostel, with a sauna. Bring your own sleep sheet. Beds are 100kr; breakfast 20kr. Curfew is 1 AM. *Nedre Korskirkealmenning 4, tel. 55–31–73–32. Lockout 11–5. Kitchen. Cash only. Closed Sept.–mid-June.*

CAMPING • Bergenshallen Camping. The only official camping spot within city limits, Bergenshallen is a 10-minute bus ride north of the center. Tent sites go for 40kr; there are no cabins. *Vilh. Bjerknesvei 24, tel. 55–27–01–80. From town center, Bus 3. Cash only. Closed Oct.–June.*

FOOD

Look for restaurants with a *dagens rett* (daily special); most cafeterias have one for 45kr–70kr. Seafood is plentiful here and cheaper than you'd expect: Warm, smoked herring is a treat at 5kr, and the **Torget** fish market sells ready-to-eat boiled shrimp, crab, and salmon *rundstykke* (open sandwiches). Also try the local specialty *schillingsbolle,* a sugar-and-cardamom bun. Some of the cheapest food in town is at **EPA,** a grocery store conveniently located between the bus and train stations.

Den Gode Klode Vegetar Kafé. This café offers superb vegetarian food and a pleasant, bright interior. The dagens rett is 65kr. *Fosswinckelsgata 18, tel. 55–32–34–32. Cash only. Closed some Sun.*

Pasta Sentral. At one of Bergen's cheapest restaurants, less than 50kr gets you basic pasta with sauce and bread or a daily pasta special with soda. *Vestre Strømkai 6, tel. 55–96–00–37. Walk under bus station, turn right into tunnel near gate 20, and look for Pasta Sentral behind you as you exit tunnel. Cash only.*

USF Kulturhuset. This former United Sardine Factory is now a bohemian enclave featuring a movie theater, dance club, art gallery, and café/pub. Daily meat, fish, and pasta specials cost 49kr. Sip a beer and savor the barbecue (sunny days only) while enjoying pleasant views of Bergen's fjord. *Georgernes verft 3, tel. 55–91–55–70. Cash only.*

WORTH SEEING

Bergen has almost as many museums as Oslo. For a complete list and for information on seasonally changing opening hours, pick up the *Bergen Guide* at the tourist office. Other attractions include the 16th-century **Rosenkrantztårnet** (tel. 55–31–43–80) and, next to it, the 13th-century **Håkonshallen** (tel. 55–31–60–67), aptly named after its royal resident, King Håkon Håkonsson. Masons were summoned all the way from Scotland to build the Rosenkrantztårnet, a defensive tower that stands at the entrance to Vågen harbor. Admission to each is 15kr. Bergen's aquarium, **Bergen Akvariet** (Nordnesbakken 4, tel. 55–23–85–53; admission 45kr), has seals, penguins, exhibits on fishing in Norway, and of course, lots of fish.

AROUND BRYGGEN • The gabled, wooden warehouses lining Bryggen, the wharf on the northeast side of Bergen's harbor, were rebuilt in their original medieval style after a fire destroyed them in 1702. Although Bryggen has its share of tacky souvenir stands, it also possesses some excellent museums. The **Hanseatisk Museum** (on Bryggen, across from fish market, tel. 55–31–41–89; admission 35kr) re-creates the living quarters of a Hanseatic merchant in a well-preserved, wooden building. Check out the intricate wall paintings. The same admission ticket gets you into the **Schøtstuene** (Øvregaten 50, tel. 55–31–60–20), which also documents the lifestyle of Hanseatic merchants. The **Theta Museum** (Enhjørningsgården; admission 15kr; open late May–mid-Sept., Tues. and weekends 2–4) has moving exhibits detailing resistance to the 1940–1945 Nazi occupation of Norway. To get to the museum from Bryggen, turn into the alley under the sign with the unicorn, walk to the end, and take the staircase on the right. Reaching further into history, the **Bryggens Museum** (Dreggsalmenningen 3, tel. 55–31–67–10; admission 20kr) displays archaeological finds from around Bergen, including the foundations of some 12th-century buildings unearthed when the museum was under construction. Behind the Bryggens Museum is the city's oldest building, the 12th-century **Mariakirken** (Dreggsalmenningen, tel. 55–31–59–60; open mid-May–mid-Sept., weekdays 11–4; off season, Tues.–Fri. noon–1:30), a lovely baroque church. If you're in the mood for yet another church, check out the **Domkirke** (Kong Oscars gate and Domkirkegaten, tel. 55–31–04–70; open May–Aug., weekdays 11–2). This poor church has burned down and been rebuilt many times since it was first constructed in the 12th century.

OTHER MUSEUMS • You'll find a string of art museums on Rasmus Meyer's allé. The **Rasmus Meyer's Samlinger** at No. 7 has haunting landscapes by I.C. Dahl and portraits by Munch, while the **Municipal Art Museum** houses the Stenersen Collection, which features modern works by less well-known artists as well as works by Munch, Picasso, and Klee. Admission (35kr) is good for both museums, which are open Monday to Saturday 11–4 and Sunday noon–3 in summer, and Tuesday to Sunday noon–3 off season. For information about either museum, dial 55–56–80–00.

You can wander around outside in **Gamle (Old) Bergen** (tel. 55–25–78–50; open mid-May–Aug., daily 11–6) for free, but a guided tour (45 min, 40kr) is required to go inside the 18th- and 19th-century wood houses. However, the tour is worth the price, as it gives you a chance to view some fascinating period antiques: toys, furnishings, scary medical equipment, and even scarier beauty supplies. English-language tours depart hourly. To get here from the city center, take Bus 1 or 9 and get off after the second tunnel.

Composer Edvard Grieg's home, **Troldhaugen** (tel. 55–91–17–91; admission 40kr; open May–Sept., daily 9:30–6; shorter hrs off season), has been turned into a museum as lovely as his music. During summer, concerts are held here on Wednesday and weekends. The house is in the town of Hop, 8 km (5 mi) south of Bergen: Catch any bus from Platform 19, 20, or 21 at the bus station, get off in Hop at Hopsbroen, turn right, walk about 200 yards, turn left on Troldhaugsveien, and follow the signs; the walk takes about 20 minutes.

Bergen's most macabre attraction is the **Leprosy Museum** (Kong Oscars gate 59, no phone; open May–Aug. daily 11–3). The displays at this former leper hospital chronicle Norwegian doctors' struggle against the disease, and other exhibits include some truly creepy drawings. At 15kr, it's a must-see for the curious and a must-miss for the squeamish.

SHOPPING

Kløverhuset (Strandkaien 10, tel. 55–21–37–90), between Strandgaten and the fish market, has 40 shops under one roof. You'll find outlets for Dale knitwear, souvenirs, and leathers. Galleriet, on Torgalmenningen, is the best of the downtown shopping malls.

AFTER DARK

Bergen is a university town with lively nightlife. Concerts, performances, and film screenings happen frequently at the **USF Kulturhuset** (*see* Food, *above*). **Café Opera** (Engen 24, tel. 55–23–03–15) offers no-cover acid jazz on weekends and live jams on Tuesday. **Maxime** (Ole Bulls plass, near National Theater, tel. 55–90–22–23) gets "big" rock 'n' roll acts and features Latin music on Tuesday. The cover varies, but admission to the patio area is always free. The **Ugla Café** (Olav Kyrres gate, between Våskerelven and Nygårdsgaten; cover 50kr) hosts bands seven days a week, and attracts appreciative crowds for beers that are priced 27kr until 10 PM. **Fincken** (Nygårdsgatan 2A, tel. 55–32–13–16), a comfortable café/bar, is the only gay and lesbian hangout in town.

OUTDOOR ACTIVITIES

Two of Bergen's mountains have transportation to the top for those who don't like to sweat their way up to the viewspots. **Mt. Fløien**'s famous funicular (30kr round-trip) leaves from the big, ivy-covered building about 500 ft east of the fish market. To get to the top of **Mt. Ulriken** you can take a cable car (25kr each way), accessible by frequent buses (25kr round-trip) from the Bryggen tourist office. Once on top, you'll have endless miles of hiking trails to explore. To get advice on the best trails, talk to the folks at DNT (*see* Basics, *above*).

SOGNEFJORD

Water cascades down a 3,300-ft rock face into Sognefjord, Norway's longest and deepest fjord, which is also its most accessible. The area is eminently explorable, as several towns have youth hostels, and hytter are everywhere. If you have a tent, this is the place to use it; you can sleep next to a rushing river or beside the still fjord water. For details on the area, pick up a free *Sognefjorden Guide* from local tourist offices.

The best towns to use as a base for exploring the fjord are Flåm and Balestrand (*see below*), but if you can't leave the trappings of civilization, head to **Sogndal,** the closest thing around to a teeming metropolis. From here a three-hour bus ride will take you to Nigardsbreen, the most popular section of the Jostedalsbreen glacier (*see below*), or you can head for the Jotunheimen mountains to the east. To get to Sogndal's **HI hostel** (tel. 57–67–20–33; beds 90kr; cash only; closed mid-Aug.–mid-June), walk up the main street from the bus stop, turn right on Gravensteinsgata, and continue to just south of the bridge. Stop by the **tourist office** (in Kulturhuset, next to post office, tel. 57–67–30–83; open June–Aug., weekdays 9–8, Sat. 10–1, Sun. 1–6; shorter hrs off season) to rent bikes (100kr per half-day), plan day trips, or book a room in a private home (100kr–160kr per person).

COMING AND GOING

The easiest ways to approach Sognefjord are by train from Bergen to Flåm; by bus from Voss to Gudvangen (1½ hrs, 48kr) or Vangsnes (1½ hrs, 95kr); or by hydrofoil from Bergen. From mid-May to mid-

September, **Fylkesbaatane** (tel. 55–32–40–15) operates a daily 8 AM hydrofoil service from Bergen to Flåm with stops along the way (5 hrs, 410kr). The scenic Flåm railroad, or Flåmsbanen (*see below*), also carries masses of tourists to Flåm from the town of Myrdal (2 hrs, 160kr, 180kr express from Bergen). Buses run to Sogndal from Otta (*see* Jotunheimen National Park, *below*) and Oslo in the east and to Balestrand from many points north. Pick up the free *Sogn og fjordane* timetable at local tourist offices.

FLAM AND THE FLAMSBANEN

The steepest and one of the most scenic train routes in Europe, the Flåmsbanen slowly rolls from Myrdal to Flåm. Along the way, you'll see waterfalls plunging down sheer valley walls and follow the path of a raging emerald-green river as it snakes through narrow gorges. Take comfort in knowing that the train is equipped with not one, not two, but five sets of brakes.

Hundreds of tourists pour off the 8:45 AM train from Bergen to Myrdal (*see above*) and cram into the railroad cars that make the 50-minute journey to Flåm (85kr). If you're looking for solitude (and a long walk), skip the train ride and instead hike the 20 km (12 mi) from Myrdal to Flåm (about 5 hrs). You can send your pack down on the train for 40kr; ask the conductor or the ticket agent where the baggage car is and pick up your pack at the Flåmsbanen luggage counter in Flåm (tel. 57–63–21–00; open June–mid-Sept., daily 8–9; shorter hours off season).

Flåm's waterfront district swarms with day-trippers who stream off of the Flåmsbanen at noon, have lunch in the cafeteria, and sweep out of town again at about 3. After they leave, a peaceful stillness descends on Flåm, made all the more profound by the nearby towering fjord walls. The friendly folks at the **tourist information office** (in train station, tel. 57–63–21–06; open June–Aug., weekdays 8:30–8:30, weekends 10–5; shorter hrs off season) have maps and transportation schedules—avoid visiting during the midday rush, if at all possible. **Flåm Camping and Youth Hostel** (tel. 57–63–21–21) is across the river, a short walk from the train station; it sits under a massive peak with views of a waterfall. Beds are 85kr, and a campsite for two is 75kr. The hostel accepts cash only.

The Hopperstad Stave Church, near the village of Balestrand, is believed to be the oldest church in Norway. It has a rare intact canopy, a wooden roof painted with scenes from the life of Mary.

BALESTRAND

Balestrand has been Sognefjord's main resort town since the 19th century, and it's still extremely popular with aging Brits. Still, this village, which lies beneath snowy peaks that soften into rolling hills and farmland before hitting the water, feels less like a tourist center than a place where people actually live. The **Viking burial mounds** on the waterfront are the only real sights in town, but the 12th-century **Hopperstad Stave Church** (admission 40kr; closed mid-Sept.–mid-May), believed to be the oldest church in Norway, is in nearby Vik. Take a bus to Dragsvik (20kr), a ferry from Dragsvik to Vangsnes (18kr), then a bus to Vik (14kr), and walk the final 1 km (⅔ mi) to the church. The journey takes about three hours each way. For more information call Balestrand's **tourist information office** (at harbor, tel. 57–69–16–17; open mid-June–mid-Aug., weekdays 7:30–9, Sat. 7:30–6:30, Sun. 7:30–5:30; shorter hrs off season).

COMING AND GOING

The **hydrofoil** from Bergen to Flåm (*see above*) stops at Balestrand twice daily; most other ferries go to Dragsvik instead of Balestrand. For a more scenic route from Bergen, take the **train** to Voss (1¼ hrs, 105kr, 125kr express) and transfer to a bus that travels through the snow-capped Vika mountains to Vangsnes (1 hr 40 min, 85kr), a short ferry (18kr) or hydrofoil hop from Dragsvik. In summer, hourly **buses** travel between Balestrand and Dragsvik (10 min, 30kr), though you can walk the 8 km (5 mi) if you have time.

WHERE TO SLEEP

The **Balestrand Youth Hostel** (Kringsjå Hotel, tel. 57–69–13–03, fax 57–69–16–70; beds 145kr; closed mid-Aug.–mid-June) has private baths and balconies with stupendous fjord views. At **Sjøtun Camping** (tel. 57–69–12–23), cabins start at 200kr, and campsites are 55kr plus 15kr per person, all cash only. To get here, walk south along the main street past the school.

JOSTEDALSBREEN GLACIER

Blanketing the entire inner Nordfjord and Sognefjord regions is the 5,000-year-old Jostedalsbreen gla-cier, the largest ice field in Europe. Guided tours of the blue ice are absolutely worth the cost; prices cor-respond to distance and difficulty (1½-hour walks start at 80kr). *Never, ever* climb a glacier on your own, as fresh snow often conceals crevasses hundreds of yards deep that could swallow you whole. You can gaze at icy arms of the glacier from any of 24 valleys: **Nigardsbreen,** one of the most popular (i.e., crowded) of Jostedal's arms, is the site of the **Jostedal Glacier Center** (tel. 57–68–32–50). The center is near the village of Gjerde, at the foot of the ice. Daily buses to the site leave Sogndal at 9 AM.

FJAERLAND

The **Norsk Bremuseum** (tel. 57–69–32–88; admission 65kr) in Fjærland is a good place to glean gla-cier facts, and to view a short panoramic film and a model that re-creates the feeling of walking through a glacier tunnel. Fjærland makes an easy day trip from Balestrand: Ferries run up the fjord daily at 9 and 12:30 (also at 5 PM June–Aug.) and connect with handy buses that transport you to the museum and then to Flatbreen for a look at the glacier itself. Balestrand's tourist office arranges the whole excursion (273kr round trip, museum admission included). For **guided walks** (6–8 hrs, 250kr) in the area, con-tact mountaineer Jostein Øygard (tel. 57–69–32–92), or arrange a walk through a nearby tourist office.

BODALSBREEN

From the rustic cluster of huts at Bødalseter, you can ascend the fractured ice of Bødalsbreen or attempt the 12-hour climb to Lodalskåpa, Jostedal's highest peak (6,921 ft). Tour buses never get this far, so if you're up for some adventure, call Eivind Skjerven (tel. 57–87–12–00) of **Stryn Fjell-og Bre-førarlag** to arrange a walk. A 10- to 12-hour walk will get you to the peak (400kr). Shorter hikes (4–5 hrs, 250kr) are available for less ambitious hikers, but be warned: This isn't a stroll in the woods—even the so-called "easy" walk is demanding. Walks are available June–August only; call Eivind a day or two in advance to arrange transportation from Stryn (*see* Nordfjord, *below*).

NORDFJORD

This isn't the most interesting part of the fjord region, but cliff roads along the water make for pleasant viewing, as do the mountain peaks that rise up to cradle the monstrous Jostedalsbreen glacier. Summer skiing, hiking, and glacier visits (*see* Jostedalsbreen Glacier, *above*) are the Nordfjord's main attractions, and the water, colored blue-green by glacial silt, is gorgeous. Although it has little character, **Stryn** is the best town to use as a base in the inner Nordfjord, with cheap lodging and bus connections to Oslo (8 hrs, 475kr), Bergen (7 hrs, 315 kr), Balestrand (4½ hrs, 249kr), Geiranger (1½ hrs, 120kr), and Trond-heim (8 hrs, 425kr). Stryn's **tourist information office** (Perhusvegen 19, tel. 57–87–23–33) has plenty of information on local activities. It also rents bikes (100kr per day) and hands out the useful *Guide for Stryn* and *Nordfjord Guide.* Hydrofoils and the coastal steamer from Bergen stop at **Måløy** (5 hrs, 445kr) at the Nordfjord's mouth; from here, buses to Stryn (2 hrs, 150kr) will bring you into the fjord.

WHERE TO SLEEP

Stryn's hostel **Stryn Vandrerhjem** (tel. and fax 57–87–11–06; beds 90kr; closed mid-Sept.–mid-May), 2 km (1 mi) up the hill behind the bus station, has a nice view and is usually inhabited by skiers, hik-ers, and glacier explorers. **Stryn Camping** (tel. 57–87–11–36; 65kr per tent minimum), in the center of town, is full of caravans. Ask at the tourist office for assistance if you'd like to visit some of the region's most scenic sites. The quiet town of **Byrkjelo** (1 hr 10 min, 70kr from Stryn), a bit south of the Nordfjord in a spectacular valley on the bus route between Stryn and Sognefjord, also has a modest **hostel** (tel. 57–86–73–21; beds 75kr; cash only; closed mid-Sept.–mid-May).

GEIRANGERFJORD

The narrow Geirangerfjord is one of Norway's most impressive, most visited attractions. Roiling rivers hurtle down the mountains and rush through the towns of Geiranger and Hellesylt, which offer spectacular scenery and hiking. The two towns (which are at opposite ends of the fjord) are similar, but Geiranger has steeper cliffs, more waterfalls, and larger numbers of tourists. Both **Geiranger Tourist Information** (at dock, tel. 70–26–30–99; open mid-June–mid-Aug., daily 9–6; shorter hrs off season) and **Hellesylt Tourist Information** (at dock, tel. 70–26–50–52; open June–Aug., daily 9:30–5:30) distribute free hiking maps. Several daily ferries make the trip (70 min, 30kr) from Hellesylt to Geiranger and back, and each includes a taped travelogue that points out (in six languages) abandoned farms and famous waterfalls along the way.

COMING AND GOING

Hellesylt is a one-hour journey (57kr) from Stryn (*see above*) on the bus to Ålesund. You can reach Geiranger from Stryn in two hours (120kr), or from Otta (*see* Jotunheimen National Park, *below*) in three (196kr); both trips require that you switch buses in Langevatnet. One of Norway's most scenic bus rides follows the **Golden Route**, which stretches between Geiranger and Åndalsnes. The Ørneveien (Eagle's Highway) from Geiranger to the top of the fjord cuts a seemingly impossible path, winding its way up one of the fjord walls to the first of many five-minute photo stops. Just when you've recovered from the last breathtaking view, the bus plunges over Trollstigen (Troll's Path) and clings to the face of a vertical wall, traversing teeth-clenching, hairpin switchbacks. A one-way journey on the Golden Route costs 110kr and takes about three hours; buses leave Geiranger twice a day during the summer.

To experience the power of the 500-square-km (193-square-mi) Jostedalsbreen glacier, take a guided walk through the yawning chasms and listen to the thunder as blue ice grinds over buried rock.

WHERE TO SLEEP

The only **hostel** on the fjord is in Hellesylt (up path next to waterfall, tel. and fax 70–26–51–28; beds 100kr, 4-bed cabins 250kr; closed Sept.–May) and has a tremendous fjord view. In Geiranger you'll find a whopping 10 campgrounds. The centrally located **Geiranger Camping** (tel. 70–26–31–20; 40kr per tent plus 10kr per person) has a nine-hole mini-golf course. Four-bed cabins at **Dalen Camping** (about 7 km/4½ mi up road from tourist office, tel. 70–26–30–70) start at 300kr. All accept cash only.

JOTUNHEIMEN NATIONAL PARK

Norwegians love the mountains, and the Jotunheimen range in the center of the country is one of their most popular year-round playgrounds. Elk roam this boulder-strewn range, Europe's highest mountain chain north of the Alps. It's also home to Norway's highest peak, Galdhøpiggen (2,469 m/8,100 ft); the neighboring Glittertind mountain is only slightly smaller. Hostels dot the area around Jotunheimen and the nearby Rondane and Dovrefjell ranges; consult your handy *Vandrerhjem i Norge* (*see* Basics, *above*) for details. **Otta,** on the Oslo–Trondheim railway, is an important transport hub in the area, and its **tourist information office** (in train station, tel. 61–23–03–65) has maps (60kr–98kr) and timetables. You can stay overnight at **Sagatun Gjestgiveri** (Ottekra 1, behind Otta Hotel, tel. 61–23–08–14), where doubles are 250kr, or at **Killis Overnatting** (Ola Dahlsgate 35, tel. 61–23–04–92), where doubles go for 220kr.

West of Otta the massive peaks of Jotunheimen National Park loom like giants above the rest of Norway. Walking trails crisscross the park, with hytter at day-hike intervals. Make sure you've got the proper gear before setting off into the mountains, and remember that a Norwegian "six-hour hike" often takes closer to eight or nine hours.

ANDALSNES

For the average traveler, Åndalsnes is merely the northern gateway to the fjords. Rock-climbers, though, are hip to Åndalsnes because of nearby **Trollveggen** (Troll Wall), the highest vertical face in Europe. The **Tindemuseum** (on road to Åndalsnes Camping, tel. 71–22–12–74; admission 30kr; open mid-June–mid-Aug., daily 1–5) is a museum with information about Trollveggen. Or, you can practice on the 36-ft indoor climbing wall (2 hrs for 40kr) at **Aak Fjellsport Senter** (behind Fina station, tel. 71–22–71–00; wall closed May–Aug.), which arranges lots of outdoor activities. Hikers will want to tackle the steep climb (about 2 hrs) to the top of **Mt. Nesaksla,** behind town. The tourist information office (adjoining train station, tel. 71–22–16–22) hands out guides, sells walking maps (50kr–80kr), and books private rooms (from 300kr) for a 20kr fee.

COMING AND GOING

Åndalsnes, at the end of a **rail** line that splits off the main line in Dombås, is the northern jumping-off point for the western fjord region. The **bus** to Geiranger (3 hrs, 110kr), which runs mid-June–August, takes you up and over the practically vertical Trollstigen (*see* Geirangerfjord, *above*), which boasts 11 hairpin turns.

WHERE TO SLEEP

Most of the cheap lodging is in the countryside outside Åndalsnes. The **HI hostel** (cross Rauma River on E9 to Ålesund, tel. 71–22–13–82, fax 71–22–68–35; cash only; closed mid-Sept.–mid-May) has beds for 100kr and breakfast for 55kr. From the train station (2 km/1 mi away), follow the tracks to the intersection of Vollan and Jernbanegata and look for the signs; if you're arriving by bus, ask the driver to drop you off. To reach the riverside **Åndalsnes Camping** (tel. 71–22–16–29; tents 45kr plus 15kr per person, cabins 130kr–550kr), head toward the hostel and turn left on the road just after the bridge.

NORTHERN NORWAY

A narrow but immensely long strip of land stretches between the towns of Trondheim and Kirkenes in northern Norway. Finnmark, one of the northernmost regions, is by itself the size of Denmark, though its population density is comparable to Siberia's. In the vast northern territory, you'll encounter dramatically different ways of life and a great variety of geographical features, from the craggy peaks of the Lofoten Islands to the sprawling, barren stretches of the Finnmarksvidda. Students dominate the university towns of Trondheim and Tromsø, but elsewhere the region is populated by the Sami people, some of whom live as nomads and rely on reindeer herding for their livelihood.

A large portion of northern Norway lies above the Arctic Circle, where the sun shines nonstop for two to three months in summer and then disappears completely for several months in winter. Seeing the midnight sun in the north is an unforgettable experience—it's not every day that you descend a mountain at 1 AM and find your path bathed in the pink and orange glow of the sun.

Budget travelers usually skip the narrow stretch of Norway between Trondheim and Tromsø. Most head straight for the Lofoten Islands or to Nordkapp at Finland's northernmost tip, stopping only briefly in **Bodø,** the northern terminus of Norway's rail line. If you get stuck in Bodø, there's a **hostel** (Sjøgate 55, tel. and fax 75–52–11–22; beds 140kr; cash only) above the train station. Bodø's major tourist attraction is **Saltstraumen,** the world's largest maelstrom, where the water from two fjords churns and dashes in a narrow strait at high tide. Even at its most powerful the sight isn't that impressive, but if you want to see it, daily buses (78kr round trip) make the trip from Bodø to Saltstraumen. Check the tide tables in Bodø before you go.

Buses bound for the far north depart from **Fauske,** about 45 minutes before the Bodø stop. The town's **hostel** (Nyvegen 6, tel. 75–64–67–06, fax 75–64–59–95; beds 100kr; closed mid-Aug.–May) will do if you're stuck for the night. **Narvik,** to the north, is also an important transit point, especially for trains from Sweden. If you're staying over, head for the **hostel** (Havnegate 3, tel. 76–94–25–98, fax 76–94–29–99; beds 140kr, breakfast included; cash only; closed Christmas) about 1 km (½ mi) south of the train station; call ahead Sept.–May.

TRONDHEIM

Norway's third largest city, Trondheim can trace its history back to AD 997, when Viking king Olav Tryggvason founded the city as the country's first capital. Only 33 years after the town's birth, King Olav Haraldson (St. Olav to future generations) fell at the battle of Stiklestad and was buried beneath what is now **Nidaros Domen** (*see below*). For centuries, Norway's kings were crowned in Trondheim's Gothic behemoth, giving the town a special place in Norwegian history and politics. If you're heading north, you'll probably take a rest stop in this lively university town, since it's on the rail line between Oslo and Bodø.

BASICS

Trondheim has an enthusiastic **tourist information office** (Market Sq., tel. 73–92–93–94; open mid-May–Aug., Mon.–Sat. 8:30–8, Sun. 10–8; shorter hrs off season) that rents bikes (80kr–100kr per day plus 200kr deposit), changes money after hours, and books rooms in private homes for a 20kr fee. To get there from the train station, walk down Sødregate, turn right on Kongensgate, and continue to Market Square. The **DNT** office (Munkegata 64, 2nd floor of Idrettens Hus, tel. 73–52–38–08; open weekdays 9–4, Thurs. until 6), near the wharf, hands out maps and helps plan hiking trips. You can send mail at the **main post office** (Dronningengate 10, tel. 73–95–84–00) and call home at the **telephone office** (Kongensgate 8, tel. 73–54–30–11).

COMING AND GOING

Trondheim lies almost halfway between the beginning of the **rail** line in Oslo (6½–8 hrs, 580kr) and the end of the line in Bodø (10 hrs, 670kr). The **Hurtigrute** (see Getting Around in Basics, above) stops twice daily at the big dock north of the train station. Long-distance buses leave from the train station (tel. 73–57–20–20), and city buses (15kr, exact change required) leave from the corner of Munkegata and Dronningensgate. Most budget lodging is across the Nidelva River, which loops through town.

WHERE TO SLEEP

There's no shortage of cheap beds in Trondheim—in fact, the fierce competition for customers often drives some places out of business, so call ahead. To reach the comfortable **Singsaker Sommerhotell** (Rogertsgate 1, tel. 73–89–31–00; doubles 345kr, dorm beds 125kr, breakfast included; closed Sept.–May) take Bus 63 from the train/bus station or from Munkegata between Olav Tryggvasonsgate and Dronningensgate. The **HI Rosenborg Youth Hostel** (Weidemannsvei 41, tel. 73–53–04–90, fax 73–53–52–88; beds 160kr; cash only) is sterile, but open almost year-round; take Bus 63 from Munkegata to the end of the line. **HI Jarlen** (Kongensgate 40, tel. 73–51–32–18; closed Sept.–May; cash only) has 175kr beds and a convenient downtown location.

Approximate dates for viewing the Midnight Sun: Alta, May 21–July 23. Bodø, June 4–July 8. Nordkapp, May 14–July 30. Stamsund (Lofoten), May 28–July 17. Tromsø, May 21–July 23.

FOOD

Unless you're willing to splurge, eating out in Trondheim is not an exciting experience. A decent, all-you-can-eat pizza dinner comes to 54kr at **Pizzakjelleren** (Fjordgate 7, tel. 73–51–38–38; open daily until midnight; cash only). The **Peking House Restaurant** (Kjøpmannsgate 63, tel. 73–51–29–01; cash only) serves its 48kr lunch special daily from 2 to 4. At night, join the artsy crowd at **Café Ni Muser** (Bispegata 9A, at Prinsensgate), where they serve a *dagens rett* (daily special; 65kr) and the most affordable wine in town (135kr for a bottle). **Banzara** (Ørjaveita 4, tel. 73–52–21–08; cash only) has Indian specials (79kr) and African dance music on Friday and Saturday nights.

WORTH SEEING

Trondheim is dominated by the impressive Gothic **Nidaros Domen** (Nidaros Cathedral; on Kongsgårdsgate; tel. 73–52–52–33; open weekdays 9–5:30, weekends 9–2), the site of Norwegian coronations for a thousand years. Though Norway no longer holds coronations, an official blessing of each new king or queen still takes place here. This cathedral, Scandinavia's largest medieval building, was erected over the grave of St. Olav, the Viking king who shepherded Norway's conversion from paganism to Christianity. It is now home to the crown jewels. Admission is 20kr; for an additional 5kr you can climb up a twisting, narrow staircase (170 steps) to the top of the tower.

At the **Ringve Museum of Music History** (Lade Allé 60, tel. 73–92–24–11; admission 40kr; closed Oct.–May), which lies within the Ringve Botanical Gardens, music students demonstrate many of the instruments on display. You're not allowed to wander around on your own, but English-language tours, which are offered several times a day throughout the summer, are included in the admission price. To get here, take Bus 4 (toward Lade) to Fagerheim. The **Trøndelag Folkemuseum** (Sverresborg, tel. 73–53–14–90; admission 40kr) has exhibits of a stave church from Haltdalen, and re-created rooms from the turn of the century, including an old dentist's office and grocery store. The **Nordenfjeldske Kunstindustrimuseum** (Munkegata 5, tel. 73–52–13–11; admission 30kr), a decorative-arts museum, has period rooms from the Renaissance to the present. If the sun is out, hop a ferry (30 kr round trip) to the island of **Munkholmen,** the setting for an ancient, abandoned monastery.

LOFOTEN ISLANDS

Sawtooth, glacier-carved peaks form the Lofoten island chain, Norway's most popular destination after Bergen and the fjords. Seaside fishing villages hug the shores and extend over the water on wooden boardwalks, though these days more tourists than fishermen pack the old fishing *rorbuer* (shanties). Most people stop in Stamsund and Å (*see below*), but the more ambitious also head to the tiny, southern islands of **Værøy** and **Røst** to watch colonies of puffins, terns, razorbills, and guillemots, as well as the rare sea eagle. Svolvær is an important transportation hub on the island of Austvågøy, but it's a soulless city in the midst of this arctic paradise; the nearby **hostel** (in Kabelvåg, Vågan Folkenhøgskole, tel. 76–07–81–03, fax 76–07–81–17; beds 130kr; open mid-June–mid-Aug.; cash only), 5½ km (3¼ mi) south of Svolvær's center on E10, is equally bleak. The town's best-known attraction is a weird, two-horned rock formation called the **Svolværgeita** (Svolvær goat). Thrill seekers leap from side to side, knowing that if they don't make it, they'll end up with the folks buried in the graveyard below.

COMING AND GOING

Lofoten's four main islands—Moskenesøy, Flakstadøy, Vestvågøy, and Austvågøy—are connected to each other and the mainland by bus and ferry. The cheapest and easiest way to get to the islands is on one of several daily **ferries** from Bodø on the mainland to the town of Moskenes on Moskenesøy (4 hrs, 102kr). The 11 AM boat makes a good connection with the night train from Trondheim. A few ferries per week travel from Bodø to Værøy (4 hrs, 94kr) and Røst (5 hrs, 112kr). Ask at the Bodø tourist information kiosk inside the train station for other bus and ferry options. More than twice as expensive but twice as fast, **express boats** run during summer from Bodø to Leknes on Vestvågøy, from Bodø to Værøy, and from Skutvik to Svolvær on Austvågøy. The luxury **Hurtigrute** coastal steamer makes daily stops in Stamsund on Vestvågøy and in Svolvær. The ride from Tromsø to Stamsund (22 hrs) costs 560kr.

MOSKENESOY

The island of Moskenesøy has some of Lofoten's most picturesque fishing villages—you've proably seen them on postcards sold all over Norway. **Å**, one of the prettiest and most popular villages, is where you'll find the island's cheapest accommodations. Å's boardwalk, lined with red *rorbuer* (boathouses), is an open-air museum flanked by buildings preserved since the 19th century. The **Norske Fiskevgermuseum** (tel. 76–09–14–88; admission 35kr) contains odds and ends from Lofoten's colorful past, when fearless Norwegians would set out into the dead-cold January waters of the North Sea to fish for cod from 20-ft open wooden boats. The **Moskenestraumen,** a powerful whirlpool between Værøy and the southern tip of Moskenesøy, moved both Jules Verne and Edgar Allan Poe to literary excess. Boat trips (290kr per person) arranged through the tourist office skirt the whirlpool and explore caves containing ancient petroglyphs. For more adventure, rent bikes from the town's hostel (*see below*) for 100kr per day and head for the fairy-tale villages of **Reine** and **Hamnøy.** The tourist information office (tel. 76–09–15–99; open mid-June–mid-Aug., daily 10–7; off season, weekdays 10–5) is at the ferry dock in the town of Moskenes. From here it's a 5-km (3-mi) walk or bus ride (15kr) to Å.

Å has a **hostel** (tel. 76–09–11–21, fax 76–09–12–82), with beds (95kr) inside museum buildings. If it's full, try **Å-Hamna Rorbuer** (tel. 76–09–12–11; cash only), with 80kr beds in a rustic, old house, and 500kr–700kr rooms in the 19th-century seafront shanties. Or hike around the lake outside town to find a secluded camping spot.

VESTVAGOY

From **Leknes,** Vestvågøy's sleepy capital, you can catch a bus (30 min, 23kr) to the town of **Stamsund,** one of those places budget travelers come for a day, only to find themselves still loafing weeks later. The main reason is the town's rustic seaside **hostel** (Stamsund 8340, tel. 76–08–93–34, fax 76–08–97–39; beds 75kr; closed mid-Oct.–mid-Dec.; cash only), about 1 km (½ mi) from the business center of Stamsund (ask the bus driver to drop you off). The low-key caretaker, Roar Justad, lends rowboats and fishing lines for free, contributing to the hostel's close-knit, communal atmosphere. Like everyone else, you might prefer to lie around all day on the hostel's sun-drenched dock, but you'll have to drag yourself up the precarious, two-hour climb from the hostel to the peak of **Steinetinden** to catch the most spectacular view of the midnight sun. The **tourist office** (tel. 76–08–97–92) has maps. If a leisurely bike ride is more your pace, rent a bike from the hostel (75kr per day) and cruise the scenic 4 km (2½ mi) from Stamsund to Steine. If the hostel's full, try the friendly **Nordbakk Overnatting** (around bend from hostel toward town, tel. 76–08–97–43; beds 75kr; cash only), where showers and coffee are free.

TROMSO

Tromsø, the world's northernmost university city, is home to the world's northernmost brewery. It's an attractive town, bathed in summer by the midnight sun and in winter by the northern lights. Snow-covered mountains encircle Tromsø, and spectacular hiking trails lie just a bus ride away. Perhaps because of its large student population, or perhaps because of those long, sunless winter nights, the town has more bars per capita than any other Norwegian city.

BASICS

The **tourist information office** (Storgata 61, near cathedral, tel. 77–61–00–00) is open weekdays 8:30–6 and weekends 10–5 from June to mid-August; weekdays 8:30–4:30 in winter. The **post office** (Strandgata 41, tel. 77–62–40–00; open weekdays 8:30–5, Sat. 10–2) doubles as a currency exchange, and the **Telesenter** (Sjøgata 2, tel. 81–07–70–00), or the bank of phones in front, is the place to make phone calls. **Kilroy Travel** (Breivikasenter, near university, tel. 77–67–58–20), which operates out of a Unireiser office, excels at budget, summer, and standby flight specials.

COMING AND GOING

From Bodø the **Hurtigrute** coastal steamer takes 24 hours and costs 758kr; from Honningsvåg it takes 18 hours and costs 702kr. **Long-distance buses** depart from the cathedral and the tourist office, near the docks. One bus runs south to Narvik (5 hrs, 263kr), an access point for the railway, and the other runs once daily at 4 PM to Alta (7 hrs, 298kr) in Finnmark. Call **AS TIRB** (tel. 77–61–08–70) for bus information. Tromsø is the air hub for northern Norway, and **air travel** is surprisingly cheap; book tickets through **Kilroy Travel** (*see* Basics, *above*). City buses (22kr for 3 zones) stop on Havnegata at Stortorget and on Storgata at Fr. Langesgate. Get schedules and routes from the tourist office.

WHERE TO SLEEP

Tromsø is no mecca of cheap lodging, and the **HI Tromsø Vandrerhjem Elverhøy** (Gitta Jønsons vei 4, tel. 77–68–53–19, fax 77–06–63–03; beds 95kr; closed mid-Aug.–mid-June) is a depressing monstrosity about 2 km (1 mi) uphill from town; from Fr. Langesgate take Bus 24 toward Åsgård. Even the closest campground, **Tromsdalen Camping** (tel. 77–63–80–37), on the mainland 3 km (2 mi) from central Tromsø, is expensive with tent sites for one to six people at 100kr, and two-person cabins from 250kr. To get there from Stortorget, take Bus 30, 31, or 36 over the bridge. **Kongsbakken Pensjonat** (Skolegata 24, tel. 77–68–22–08; follow Fr. Langesgate and walk through park) is the cheapest hotel near the center, with doubles for 480kr. The central **Skipperhuset Pensjonat** (Storgata 112, past Stortorget, tel. 77–68–16–60; doubles 498kr, breakfast included) is a comfortable place with friendly management. For a 25kr fee, the tourist office will get you a room (from 250kr) in a private home.

FOOD

Stock up on groceries at **Domus** (Stortorget 1). For a hot meal, try **Prelatten** (Sjøgata 12, tel. 77–68–20–85), a pub with filling dagens rett from 50kr. **Paletten** (Storgata 51, tel. 77–68–05–10) has two rooftop patios and a 67kr salad bar. **Café Panorama** (Sjøgata 39, tel. 77–68–81–00; cash only), above Henne's boutique on the third floor, offers a 55kr lunch special daily between 11 and 1:30. Bars on practically every corner serve the tasty local brew, Mack Beer. The **Blå Rock Café** (Strandgata 14–16, tel. 77–61–00–20) is a multilevel, postmodern nightspot with band memorabilia on the walls and 35kr beer. The outdoor patio at the more upscale **Verthuset Skarven** (Strandtorget 1, tel. 77–61–01–01) is a perfect place to soak up the midnight sun. The cheapest beer here will cost you 45kr.

WORTH SEEING

Across the bridge on the mainland, the white, angular **Ishavskatedrale** (Arctic Cathedral; tel. 77–63–76–11; admission 10kr), open June through August, Monday–Saturday 10–5 and Sunday 1–5 (during other months by appointment only), dominates the skyline. Its architecture is meant to mimic a snow-covered mountain, symbolizing northern Norwegian nature, culture, and faith. The cathedral also contains one of the largest stained-glass windows in Europe—an almost cubist rendition of the Crucifixion. During July, organ concerts (10kr) are held Wednesday–Friday. From Stortorget take Bus 30 or 31.

Learn about the northern lights from a 360° panoramic film at the **Northern Lights Planetarium** (Breivika, at university, tel. 77–67–60–00; admission 50kr); call for reservations. From Sjøgata take

THE STRUGGLE
OF THE SAMI

The Sami of Norway have struggled to preserve their culture for much of the 20th century. Until the 1960s, those who couldn't speak Norwegian were barred from buying land, and school instruction was only in Norwegian. It wasn't until 1988 that the Sami gained their civil rights. Since then, efforts have been made to preserve their legends, yoik (traditional music), and duodji (handicrafts). Today, three Sami languages are still spoken by some 20,000 people in northern Norway.

Bus 25. While you're on campus, wander around 4 acres of alpine and arctic shrubs at the world's northernmost **botanical gardens** (Breivika, tel. 77–67–01–97). Learn about Arctic geology, zoology, archaeology, and Sami ethnography at the **Tromsø Museum** (Lars Thøringsvei 10, in Folkeparken, tel. 77–64–50–00; admission 20kr); to reach the museum from Storgata, take Bus 27.

FINNMARK

The vast, windswept tundra of the Finnmarksvidda is home to Norway's Sami, some of whom still live as nomadic reindeer herders and wander freely across the open borders of Lapland, which stretches across all the Scandinavian countries and into Russia. Although many Sami still live in traditional tents and dress in colorful costumes, you're most likely to experience their culture through roadside souvenir stands and tourist exhibits. The desolate expanses of the Finnmarksvidda are a popular trekking destination, and you're almost guaranteed an encounter with reindeer herds, as well as helicopter-size mosquitoes—bring lots of bug repellent.

The region stretches from the rugged cliffs at Nordkapp (North Cape) to the lush river valleys below the Finnmarksvidda, encompassing the towering, gray-slate mountains near Alta and the Russian border at Kirkenes. Unfortunately, travel here is neither convenient nor cheap. **Buses** never run overnight, so be sure to check timetables for the night stop, often in **Alta**—a town that doesn't offer much to do, but does have a **hostel** (Midtbakken 52, tel. and fax 78–43–44–09; beds 115kr; cash only; closed mid-Aug.–mid-June). Ask your bus driver for directions. ScanRail-pass holders get 50%–60% off most bus fares (Eurailpass holders get no discounts). North of Bodø, the **Hurtigrute** coastal steamer is a viable travel option, with fares that are often comparable to full-price bus tickets. **Flying** is also a good way to travel in Finnmark. Call **Kilroy Travel** (*see* Basics *in* Tromsø, *above*) for the best deals.

NORDKAPP

So you finally arrive at the northern edge of the continent, the tip of Europe, only to find what you came to escape—a great big shopping mall. Nordkapp, a rugged piece of rock jutting into the Arctic Ocean at 71°11′21″, is Europe's northernmost point (well, almost—Knivskjelloden, a peninsula to the west, reaches 71°11′48″). Nordkapp is invaded daily by an army of tourists, pushing and shoving their way through **Nordkapp Hall** (tel. 78–47–22–33; admission 175kr), an underground exhibit center where you can view the midnight sun from inside the cliff instead of from the top of it. You're likely to be socked in by round-the-clock fog, but on sunny evenings a walk along the cliffs, which plunge more than 1,000 ft into the Arctic Ocean, is almost worth the trip and the expense.

In summer, regular public buses run from Honningsvåg (1 hr, 100kr round-trip) to Nordkapp, and the **Hurtigrute** from Tromsø stops in Honningsvåg (17 hrs, 702kr). **Buses** from Bodø to Nordkapp (tel. 77–84–04–33) take two days and cost 793kr; to Narvik (tel. 75–52–50–25) it's 7½ hours and 322kr. **Widerøe** flies to Honningsvåg from Tromsø (510kr late June–mid-Aug.; 250kr off-season), and there's also an express boat from Hammerfest (2 hrs, 248kr). Honningsvåg's **hostel,** the Nordkapp Vandrerhjem (8 km/5 mi toward Nordkapp at Skipsfjorden, tel. 78–47–33–77, fax 78–47–11–77; beds 100kr; closed mid-Sept.–mid-May), is a spartan hut on a barren plateau in front of the huge, luxury Rico hotel; take an outbound bus (10 min, 15kr) to get here.

KARASJOK AND KAUTOKEINO

Karasjok and Kautokeino are the two major Sami settlements in Norway. Both towns explode with activity during the Sami **Easter celebration,** the best time to visit. Traditional concerts, mass weddings and confirmations, and reindeer sled races are all part of the fun. Karasjok, in a lush river valley below the Finnmarksvidda, is the seat of the independent Sami Parliament. The **tourist information office** (tel. 78–46–73–60) is in the Sámelandssenteret (Sami Cultural Center), which also has a Sami camp exhibit, a slide show, and handicraft shops. Kautokeino, famous for the Sami artisans who craft unique, silver folk art, sits atop the wide-open Finnmarksvidda; the **tourist information office** (tel. 78–48–65–00), in the Duodji Siida shopping center, can direct you to the Kautokeino museum (tel. 78–48–58–00) and help with hiking itineraries.

COMING AND GOING

Buses run from Alta (4 hrs 10 min, 272kr) and Kirkenes (5½ hrs, 352kr) to Karasjok. Buses also travel to Kautokeino from Hammerfest (4¾ hrs, 307kr) and Alta (4 hrs 10 min, 153kr). Infrequent buses run between Karasjok and Kautokeino (1 hr¾, 147kr).

WHERE TO SLEEP AND EAT

Karasjok's **hostel** (Kautokeinoveien, tel. 78–46–61–35, fax 78–46–66–23; beds 115kr; cash only), 1 km (½ mi) from the tourist office, is on the road to Kautokeino in the midst of a mosquito-infested forest. The reception area has a small kiosk that sells food, and there are plenty of cafeterias and groceries back in town. Ask at the Kautokeino tourist office about cheap *fjellstue* (mountain cabins), where beds run about 120kr.

POLAND

20

Throughout its 1,000-year history, Poland has expanded, been ripped apart completely, and shifted its borders often enough to bewilder even the most cynical historian. The result is a national character equally fraught with tensions: Poles are by turns capricious, crafty, gruff, generous, warm-hearted, high-minded, and anxious to a fault about their Polishness. In addition, their long history of rebellion against foreign masters, culminating in 1989 with the inclusion of the Solidarity trade union in the government, appears to have produced in them a need for remaining at odds with the powers that be—which may explain the December 1995 election of former Communist apparatchik Aleksander Kwaśniewski to replace Lech Wałesa as president of Poland.

There are, however, no more lines at ill-stocked grocery stores, nor is there mandatory currency exchange at artificial rates. Poland is well on its way down the primrose path of capitalism; however, although slick ad campaigns, Pizza Huts, and IKEA home furnishings give Poland the commercial landscape of a Western nation, you can still live well here on less than $35 a day, making it a perfect destination for the budget traveler. The best reason to come to Poland, however, isn't politics or history or even the low prices; rather, it's the abundance of natural and cultural attractions, from haunting Baltic seascapes to excellent hiking and skiing in the Tatra Mountains; from Warsaw's bustling, postsocialist charm to the beautifully restored old Hanseatic town of Gdańsk; from the 4,000 unspoiled lakes in the Mazurian region to the vaulted cellar pubs of Kraków, where vodka, *Żywiec* beer, and jazz flow freely; from a romantic midnight walk along the Vistula to a rambling train ride past factory smokestacks, vivid mustard fields, and the ruins of a castle on a hill . . .

BASICS

MONEY

US$1 = 3.20 złoty and 1 złoty = 30¢. The złoty (zł) is divided into 100 groszy (gr). You'll get the best exchange rates at *kantory* (exchange booths), which are open until 7 or 8 PM; after that, try hotels. You can exchange traveler's checks at banks and some hotels.

HOW MUCH IT WILL COST • Cheap hotels charge 80 zł–100 zł a night for a double. Hostels charge 12 zł–15 zł, or a bit less with an HI card. You'll rarely spend more than 15 zł for a complete meal in an inexpensive restaurant, and it would be hard to spend more than 60 zł on a train trip within Poland.

KEY
├─┼─┤ Rail Lines

0 ——————— 100 miles
0 ——————— 150 km

N

(Keep in mind, though, that inflation runs about 20% a year, and thus outstrips published prices very quickly.) If you forgo first-class hotels and taxis, you can easily live for less than $35 a day.

VISA AND ENTRY REQUIREMENTS

U.S. and British citizens don't need a visa to enter Poland for stays of up to 90 days. Canadians and citizens of other countries that have not abolished visas for Poles must have visas, which cost the equivalent of US$34 (more for multiple-entry visas). Apply at Polish consulates before travel and allow several weeks for processing. Visas can be extended in Poland through the local Police headquarters.

COMING AND GOING

LOT Polish Airlines (500 5th Ave., New York, NY 10017, tel. 212/869–1074) has the cheapest student fares to Warsaw; round-trip fares from New York hover around $750 in peak season. Check with Delta and American Airlines also. Warsaw and Kraków are the major travel hubs; there are daily trains from Berlin to Warsaw (7 hrs), from Prague to Warsaw (10 hrs), and from Berlin to Kraków (8 hrs).

GETTING AROUND

Buses are generally crowded and uncomfortable, and renting a car is expensive. This leaves you with the train. Eurail and InterRail passes aren't valid in Poland; **Polrail,** Poland's national rail pass, available through Orbis, costs $50 (eight days) or $90 (one month). The **European East Pass** covers Poland, the Czech Republic, Slovakia, Hungary, and Austria but isn't much of a bargain given Eastern Europe's low train fares. The pass costs $195 for five days' travel in a 30-day period, plus $21 for each additional day of travel. Call **Rail Europe** (tel. 800/438–7245) for details.

PKP is the Polish national train service. Trains run at three speeds: *ekspres* (express), *pośpieszny* (fast), and *osobowy* (slow); avoid slow trains at all costs. Both fast and express trains have first- and second-class cars; for long trips it's worth the few extra złoty for first-class, as second-class gets crowded. For the faster *InterCity* trains, which travel between larger cities, you'll pay an additional 5 zł–10 zł. Seat assignments are required on express trains; make them when you buy your ticket. To decipher timetables in the stations, look for *odjazdy* (departures) on the yellow posters and *przyjazdy* (arrivals) on the white posters. Roman numerals indicate the platform.

WHERE TO SLEEP

In peak season, choose among hotels, private rooms, university housing, and campgrounds. Many hostels are on campuses, so they're only open in summer. Look for homeowners offering POKOJE (ROOMS) or NOCLEGI (LODGING).

FOOD

Food is hearty and cheap but can also be heavy and fatty. *Bar mleczne* (milk bars) are great for home-made (and cheap!) food. Polish cuisine offers a wide variety of soups, delicious starch-based (usually noodle or potato) dishes, and pastries. Common types of soup include *flaki* (tripe), *barszcz* (beet), *kartoflanka* (potato), and *żurek* (sour cream and rye). Main courses include *kotlet schabowy* (pork cutlet), *bigos* (hunters' stew), and *pierogie* (dumplings with meat, cabbage, or cheese fillings). Dessert is a Polish passion—try *lody* (ice cream; Lody Zielonabudka is the best brand), *naleśniki* (crêpes with sweet cheese or fruit), and *makowiec* (poppy-seed cake). Wash it all down with *kawa* (coffee) or *herbata* (tea). Most restaurants are affordable, and you should generally tip 10%.

BUSINESS HOURS

Banks are usually open weekdays 8–5; some are also open Saturday 10–2. Most central post offices are open weekdays 7 AM–8 PM, Saturday 9–2, and Sunday 9 AM–11 AM. Shops are generally open weekdays 10–6 and Saturday 9–2. Grocery stores are open weekdays 8–6, with scaled-back hours on Saturday; most are closed Sunday, but many towns have 24-hour "nonstop shops" that never close. Museums are generally closed Monday but have longer hours in summer; schedules can be unpredictable, so call before you go.

VISITOR INFORMATION

Orbis, the state-owned tourist agency, sometimes doubles as an AmEx office, changes traveler's checks, gives credit-card cash advances and train information, and has English-speakers. **PTTK** has general information offices, runs youth hotels, and has budget-lodging information. **Almatur,** the Polish student-travel organization, also has lodging information, particularly on dorms. **IT** is helpful with everything from lodging to travel arrangements to bike rentals.

PHONES

Country code: 48. Pay phones increasingly take only *kartki magnetyczne* (magnetic cards), available at kiosks and post offices for 4 zł (25 units) to 15 zł (100 units); local calls generally cost one unit. For international calls, dial direct, or go to the post office, where you pay after the call. For an international operator, dial 901. To reach **AT&T,** dial 00–800–111–1111. For **MCI,** dial 00–800–111–2122; for **Sprint,** dial 00–800–111–3115.

MAIL

Airmail letters to North America cost 1.40 zł; postcards 1zł.

WARSAW

The geographical and political center of Poland since 1595, Warsaw (Warszawa) may depress first-time visitors with its bleak, socialist appearance. The better you understand this city's history, however, the more you'll appreciate it. During August and September 1944, while Nazi soldiers systematically plundered, then razed Warsaw, the Soviet army watched from across the Vistula before "liberating" the remaining 20,000 inhabitants (out of a prewar 1.2 million). Poles are convinced that the Soviets waited so that the Nazis could "finish off" the Polish Home Army, thus clearing the way for the Sovietism of Poland. After the war, Warsaw was literally rebuilt from the ashes.

Although Warsaw does not gleam, it is a bustling metropolis, with all the cultural offerings, crime, and attitude of other large European cities. Its greatest charms are its acres of parks, and even amid the urban drabness there are some architectural attractions. After the war, Warsaw's Stare Miasto (Old Town) was painstakingly reconstructed, using old prints and paintings as a guide. Closed to all traffic except horses and carriages, the beautiful, cobblestone Rynek Starego Miasta (Old Town Square) is an impressive reproduction of the original marketplace. The Royal Palace, which houses a museum, is the greatest of the rebuilt monuments.

BASICS

VISITOR INFORMATION

Centrum Informacji Turystycznej (pl. Zamkowy 1/13, tel. 022/635–1881; open Mon.–Sat. 9–6, Sun. 11–6) is the best place for tourist information; they have maps and can point you toward affordable digs. **Almatur** (ul. Kopernika 23, tel. 022/826–3512; open weekdays 9–6, Sat. 10–2) specializes in student travel and has the scoop on student hotels.

Orbis is a good place for information on travel within Poland. You can change cash and traveler's checks and buy train tickets here. *Ul. Marszałkowska 142, tel. 022/827–3673. Also: ul. Bracka 16, tel. 022/826–0271. Open weekdays 8–7, Sat. 9–2.*

AMERICAN EXPRESS

Two full-service AmEx offices cash personal and traveler's checks, hold mail for cardholders, reserve rooms, and provide transit information. The Krakowskie branch has a 24-hour ATM that accepts AmEx cards. *Ul. Krakowskie Przedm. 11, opposite Europejski Hotel, tel. 022/635–2002. Open weekdays 9–6. Al. Jerozolimskie 65/79, Marriott Hotel lobby, tel. 022/630–6952. Open weekdays 8–8, weekends 10–6.*

EMBASSIES

Australia: *Ul. Estońska 3/5, tel. 022/617–6081. Open weekdays 9–1.* **Canada:** *Ul. Matejki 1/5, tel. 022/629–8051. Open weekdays 9–noon and 1–4.* **Great Britain/New Zealand:** *Al. Róż, tel. 022/628–1001. Consular office: Ul. Emilii Plater 28. Open weekdays 9–noon and 2–4.* **Ireland:** *Ul. Humańska 10, tel. 022/496–633. Open weekdays 9–1 and 2–5.* **United States:** *Ul. Piękna 12 (off Al. Ujazdowskie), tel. 022/628–3041. Open weekdays 8:30–5.*

ENGLISH-LANGUAGE BOOKS

For the latest Warsaw happenings, pick up the *Warsaw Insider* (5 zł), the *Warsaw Voice (4 zł),* or the *What, Where, When* and *Welcome To Warsaw* magazines (both free), which include maps. All of these, as well as same-day English-language papers, are available at major hotels. Most larger bookstores have a small selection of English books; the **American Bookstore** (Krakowskie Przedmieście 45, tel. 022/826–0161) has one of the better stocks.

PHONES AND MAIL

You can pay for operator-assisted long-distance calls 24 hours a day at the **main post office** (ul. Świętokrzyska 31/33, near ul. Marszałkowska), or at the post office at Warszawa Centralna.

WARSAW

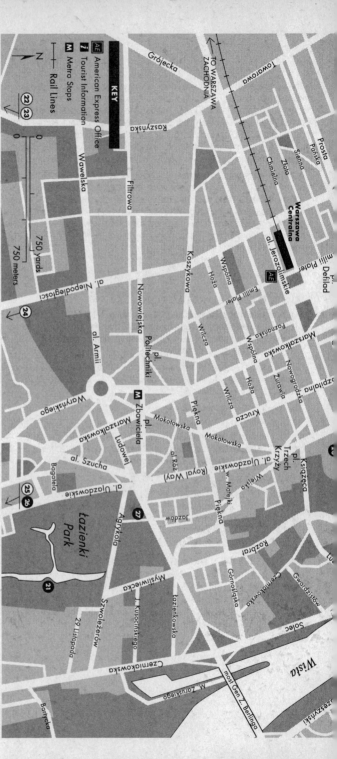

KEY

AE American Express Office

i Tourist Information

M Metro Stops

Rail Lines

N

0   750 meters
0   750 yards

Sights ●

Archikatedralna
Bazylika św. Jana, **5**
Centrum Sztuki
Współczesnej, **27**
Jewish Cemetery, **2**
Kościół Sakramentek, **1**
Kościół św. Anny, **9**

Kościół św. Krzyża, **15**
Kościół Wizytek, **13**
Łazienki Palace, **21**
Muzeum Historyczne, **4**
Muzeum Narodowe, **20**
Nożyks Synagogue, **16**
Pałac Kultury i
Nauki, **18**

Polish Military
Museum, **19**
Pomnik Bohaterów
Getta, **3**
Wilanów, **26**
Zamek Królewski, **8**
Żydowski Instytut
Historyczny, **10**

Lodging ○

Bursa Szkolnictwa
Artystycznego, **6**
Dom Nauczyciela
Belfer, **19**
Dom Studencki, **24**
Dom Turysty
Harenda, **14**

Federacja Metalowcy, **7**
Gromada Camping, **22**
Gromada Dom
Chłopa, **17**
Hotel Hera, **25**
Hotel Saski, **12**
S.S.M.(Karolkowa), **11**

S.S.M. (Smolna), **18**
Warsaw University
Dorms, **23**

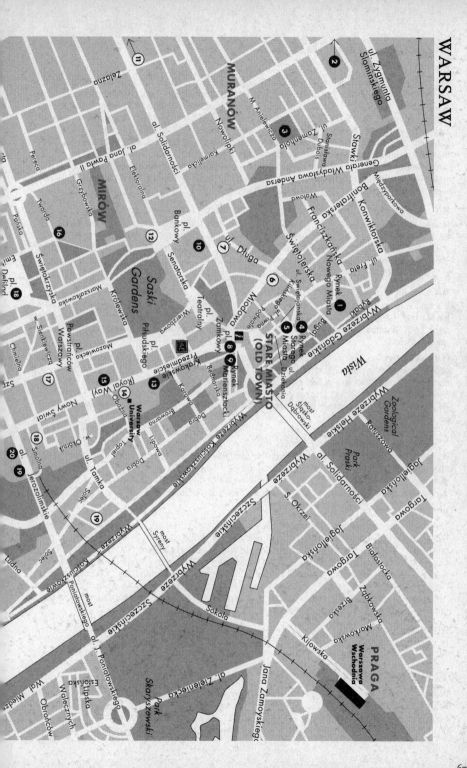

COMING AND GOING

BY BUS

The best way to travel by bus to major Polish cities is by **Polski Express** (tel. 022/620–0330. This private company has a kiosk right outside Warszawa Centralna on Jana Pawła II (near the Holiday Inn) and at the arrivals terminal at the airport; you can buy tickets at either. **Centralny Dworzec PKS** (Al. Jerozolimskie 144, tel. 022/620–0330), 10 minutes on Bus 172 from Warszawa Centralna, serves most long-distance express routes and cities to the west; **Dworzec PKS Stadion** (ul. Targowa, at ul. Zamoyskiego and Al. Zieleniecka) serves northeastern destinations; **Dworzec PKS Marymont** (ul. Marymoncka, at ul. Żeromskiego) serves primarily local destinations. Tickets for all destinations can be purchased at Centralny Dworzec PKS or at the PKS window in Warszawa Centralna. Buses are very cheap—tickets for most domestic destinations cost 10 zł–35 zł. The buses generally stop for 30 minutes every four hours; overnight buses have bunk beds.

BY PLANE

Modern **Okęcie Airport** (tel. 022/650–4220) is 6½ km (4 mi) south of the city center. To reach the center, hop on the Airport City bus (5 zł), which leaves Terminal 1 from platform 4 about every 20 minutes, or Bus 175, which leaves every 15 minutes. These hit the train station, major hotels, and main drags. Avoid taxi drivers who approach you in the arrival hall. Call 919 for a radio taxi; expect to pay about 50 zł to town, depending on the final destination.

BY TRAIN

Warszawa Centralna, the main station, is in the heart of the city, surrounded by the Palace of Culture, the Marriott Hotel, and the Holiday Inn. Be on your guard here—it's a mecca for criminals. Most trains also stop at **Wschodnia** (ul. Kijowska), the eastern station, or **Zachodnia** (Al. Jerozolimskie 144), the western station.

Warszawa Centralna has four levels. The first contains all the train platforms; the second holds the baggage-check area, information kiosks, and exits to Al. Jerozolimskie; the third has ticket offices for domestic trains, a timetable, a post office, a bus (PKS) information booth, a tourist-information booth, and a Wasteels student-ticket counter; and the fourth has an international ticket office. *Al. Jerozolimskie 54, tel. 022/620–4512 for international information, or 022/620–0361 for domestic information.*

GETTING AROUND

Warsaw is flat except for the ravine carved by the Wisła River, which runs north to south through the city. Most sights, attractions, and hotels are west of the river. Major thoroughfares include Aleje Jerozolimskie, which runs east–west, and Nowy Świat/Krakowskie Przedmieście, which runs north–south through a main shopping district, passes the university, and ends at the Old Town.

BY BUS AND TRAM

The new subway system, which opened in 1995, runs 17½ km (11 mi) from the southeastern suburb of Kabaty to Politechnika, near pl. Zbawicila. Buses and trams operate 5 AM–11 PM; less-frequent night buses run 11 PM–5 AM. Buy tickets for all three systems at kiosks (*ruch*) for 1.40 zł. You'll find transit routes on most city maps. To get to the Old Town, take Bus 175 from outside the west entrance of Warszawa Centralna. All trams that stop in front of the Marriott Hotel (across the street) will take you to the junction with Nowy Świat. From the corner of Al. Jerozolimskie and ul. Marszalkowska, Tram 4 heads toward plac Zamkowy, and any south-bound trams will drop you off at plac Zbawiciela, a block from the first Metro stop. Beware of pickpockets.

BY TAXI

Dial 919 or 022/644–444 for a reliable **Radio Taxi.** A few kilometers usually cost less than 10 zł.

WHERE TO SLEEP

Warsaw's shortage of budget hotels means you may want to consider alternatives, like the centrally located **Gromada Camping** (ul. Żwirki i Wigury 32, tel. 022/254–391; closed Oct.–Apr.; 9 zł per person; bring your own tent). To get there, take Bus 175 from Warszawa Centralna toward the airport, and get off at ul. Banacha. Another alternative is staying in a private room; **Syrena** (ul. Krucza 17, 2 tram stops east of Warszawa Centralna, tel. 022/628–7540, fax 022/629–4978; open weekdays 8–7, Sat. 8–5, Sun. 9–5) arranges doubles for 53 zł.

UNDER 75 ZŁ • Bursa Szkolnictwa Artystycznego. Open in July and August, this music school is the best overnight deal in Warsaw, with an excellent location on the north side of Stare Miasto. Rooms are clean, simple, and a bargain at 25 zł per person (30 zł with bath), and the cafeteria serves cheap meals. *Ul. Miodowa 24a.; tel. 022/635–4174. From Warszawa Centralna take Bus 175. Entrance to the school is around the block—go right on ul. Długa past the church, take your first right, and go right again in front of the SEAT store. Cash only.*

Federacja Metalowcy. As long as you don't mind supporting an old Communist trade union, this small, simple hotel is a bargain and only a five-minute walk from Rynek Starego Miasta. Doubles with sinks are 56 zł (showers are in the hall). *Ul. Długa 29, tel. 022/831–4021. From Warszawa Centralna take Bus 175 to ul. Miodowa. Cash only.*

UNDER 100 ZŁ • Dom Nauczyciela Belfer. Right on the river, this hotel (also an old Communist trade-union property) gives priority to teachers, but there's often plenty of space. Clean and spartan but comfortable doubles cost 84 zł (126 zł with bath). *Ul. Wybrzeże Kościuszkowskie 31/33, a few blocks north of Al. Jerozolimskie, tel. 022/625–0571.*

Hera. Taken over by Warsaw University from the Central Committee of the Communist Party in 1990, Hera gives priority to University guests but often has space for tourists, especially in the summer. Try to get a room in the back overlooking Łazienki Park. Doubles are 93 zł (183 with bath and TV). *Ul. Belvederska 26-30, tel. 022/410–245. Take Bus 131 from Warszawa Centralna or Bus 195 from downtown.*

Saski. Experience one of Warsaw's few remaining pre–World War II hotels, albeit one in desperate need of renovation. Doubles without bath are 100 zł (breakfast included). *Pl. Bankowy 1, tel. 022/620–4611. Take Bus 175 from Warszawa Centralna.*

UNDER 125 ZŁ • Dom Turysty Harenda. Well located near the Old Town and the university, this hotel has been renovated but retains a Communist-era feel. Doubles cost 110 zł (165 zł with bath). *Krakowskie Przedm. 4/6, tel. 022/826–0071.*

HOSTELS

Dom Studencki. The triples in this southern-Warsaw hostel are clean, but the bathrooms are *not.* Cost is 13 zł per person. *Ul. Smyczkowa 5/7, tel. 022/438–621. From pl. Zbawiciela, Tram 4, 36, 19, or 33. Closed Oct.–June.*

Szkolne Schronisko Młodziezowe (HI). The place is clean, friendly, and central, but the 11 PM curfew may put a damper on your nightlife. Beds are 15 zł, 17 zł for nonmembers. Reserve a few days ahead. *Ul. Smolna 30, tel. 022/278–952. Near corner of ul. Nowy Świat and Al. Jerozolimskie. From Warszawa Centralna take any tram three stops east. Lockout 10–4.*

Szkolne Schronisko Młodziezowe (HI). These digs are not centrally located, but they're clean, comfortable, and friendly, and there's a café. Although the curfew is not strictly enforced, it is at 11 PM. Beds are 16 zł, 18 zł for nonmembers. *Ul. Karolkowa 53a, tel. 022/632–8829. From Warszawa Centralna take Tram 24 to big department store (seven stops west). Kitchen.*

STUDENT HOUSING

Warsaw University Dorms. Two dorms with a total of 1,350 rooms are open to tourists from July through September. The communal bathrooms are relatively clean, but you'll need to bring your own toilet paper. Each floor has a kitchen, and the front desk is open 24 hours. Beds in triples are 13 zł. Reservations are advised. *Ul. Żwirki i Wigury 95/99, tel. 022/668–6307 or 022/668–6329 (weekdays 9–5). Take Bus 175 from Warszawa Centralna to ul. Banacha. Kitchen.*

FOOD

Warsaw has a great variety of eateries. For a cheap snack, hit the food stands near Warszawa Centralna and the Palace of Culture. Restaurants open at about 11 AM.

UNDER 15 ZŁ • Czytelnik. This cafeteria-style lunch spot is a hangout for intellectuals and for politicians who drop in from Parliament, next door. *Ul. Wiejska 12a, tel. 022/628–1441. Cash only.*

Giovanni. Vegetarians will love the Hawaiian pizza—it's topped with bananas. *Ul. Krakowskie Przedm. 37, tel. 022/826–2788.*

Między Nami. The cafeteria, known for its *Kawa na mleku* (coffee in milk), turns into a bar at night. It's behind the Smyk department store; look for the GAULOISE sign. *Ul. Bracka 20, tel. 022/827–9441.*

UNDER 30 ZŁ • Pod Samsonem. Located between the Stare and Nowe Miasta, this restaurant is popular with locals for its wide variety of fish and seasonal fresh veggies at low prices. You can also try traditional Polish and Jewish dishes here, and luxuriate in the English menu. *Ul. Freta 3/5, tel. 022/831–1788.*

CAFÉS AND BAKERIES

Warsaw is filled with *Kawiarnia* (cafés), serving coffee and pastries. One of the oldest and best bakeries in the city is **Blikle** (Nowy Świat 33). If you can pronounce *kawa z śmietanką,* you'll get coffee with whipped cream. **Sklep z Kawą Pożegnanie z Afryką** (Out of Africa Coffeeshop; ul. Freta 4) serves a great variety of coffees and has a pleasant outdoor café in summer. **Nowy Świat** (Nowy Świat 63), **Nowe Miasto** (Nowego Miasta 13–15), and **Batida Piekarnia Francuska** (The French Bakery, but actually run by Belgians; ul. Nowogrodzka 1/3) are great places to grab a meal and a sweet.

WORTH SEEING

Most museums and churches are in or near the **Stare Miasto** (Old Town). Parks and little patches of greenery are scattered throughout the city, especially south of Al. Jerozolimskie and on the east bank of the Wisła.

STARE MIASTO

After the war, the city restored this area to its original style, sparing it from "brutalist" architecture. The result is both a welcome respite from the rest of the city and a glimpse of Warsaw's former grandeur.

AROUND PLAC ZAMKOWY • You'll probably enter Stare Miasto through plac Zamkowy, the square on the southern border of the district. In the center of the square is a **statue** of King Zygmunt III Wasa, the Swedish-Polish monarch who moved the capital from Kraków to Warsaw in the early 17th century.

North of the Zygmunt III statue is the 14th-century **Zamek Królewski** (Royal Castle), which was the royal residence and seat of Polish parliament until the end of the 18th century. Destroyed by the Nazis, the castle was meticulously re-created from old plans and photos in the 1970s. Today it gleams as it did in its glory days, with gilt, marble, and murals. English-speaking guides are available for 30 zł every day but Sunday. *Pl. Zamkowy 4, tel. 02/657–2170. Admission 8 zł (buy tickets around corner at ul. Świętojan-ska 2). Open Tues.– Sun. 10–2:30.*

RYNEK STAREGO MIASTA • In its long heyday from the 13th to the 19th centuries, the Rynek Starego Miasta (Old Town Square) bustled with traders and merchants. Though it's now closed to traffic and hosts no formal market, the square is as busy as ever. Artists and artisans sell their wares, and concerts both scheduled and impromptu go on constantly. Traces of original Gothic and Renaissance architecture still remain in the mansions lining the square; the **Muzeum Historyczne (Historical Museum of Warsaw)** (Rynek Starego Miasta 42, tel. 022/635–1625; admission 3 zł; open Tues. and Thurs. noon–7, Wed. and Fri. 10–3, weekends 10:30–4:30) is spread throughout several of these mansions, and its film about the history of Warsaw is a must (shown in English Mon.–Sat. at noon).

ARCHIKATEDRALNA BAZYLIKA SW. JANA • Once a coronation site for Poland's elected kings, the Cathedral of St. John began as a parish church in the 13th century, then grew to its present proportions through centuries of renovations, the most recent following its destruction in World War II. *Ul. Kanonia 6. Open Mon.–Sat. 10–6, Sun. 2–6.*

JEWISH GHETTO

The neighborhoods of Mirów and Muranów, which now contain mostly drab apartment buildings, were once home to Europe's largest Jewish population: about 380,000 Jews lived here at the outbreak of World War II. In November 1940, German forces sealed off the area, creating the Warsaw Ghetto. Jews from other parts of Poland were relocated here, and the ghetto became increasingly congested, declining rapidly as its occupants succumbed to starvation and disease. Between July and September of 1942, some 300,000 ghetto inhabitants were deported to the death camp at Treblinka, prompting the Jewish Combat Organization (ZOB) to launch the Ghetto Uprising in April 1943. After four weeks of Jewish resistance—during which even children threw homemade bombs at tanks—the Nazis razed the entire ghetto and killed all those who had not fled or died fighting.

The Uprising is memorialized by the **Pomnik Bohaterów Getta** (Monument to the Heroes of the Warsaw Ghetto; ul. Zamenhofa, near ul. Anielewicza). Using materials that Hitler intended for a monument to his own anticipated victory, sculptor Natan Rappaport created this monument in 1948, on the fifth anniversary of the uprising. The **Nożyk Synagogue** (ul. Twarda 6, behind theater) is the only Ghetto synagogue that survived the war. The **Żydowski Instytut Historyczny** (Jewish Historical Institute; Al. Tłomackie 3/5, near pl. Bankowy, tel. 022/827–1843; normally open weekdays 9–3 but closed until late 1998 for renovations) houses a library, a research institute, and a museum displaying photographs, memorabilia, and a model of the bunker used by Warsaw Jews during the uprising. A visit to the vast **Jewish Cemetery** (ul. Okopowa 49; open Sun.–Thurs. 9–3, Fri. 9–1) provides a glimpse at the extent and significance of Warsaw's pre–World War II Jewish population.

NOWE MIASTO

Though Nowe Miasto (New Town) is primarily a residential district, it contains many restaurants and galleries. The cool, white **Kościół Sakramentek** (Church of the Sisters of the Blessed Sacrament) was built on the quiet **Rynek Nowego Miasta** (New Town Square) to commemorate King Jan Sobieski's victory over the Turks in 1683; it was used as a hospital during the Warsaw Uprising, and more than 1,000 people died when it was bombed.

LAZIENKI PARK AND PALACE

In 1939, about 380,000 Jews lived in Warsaw. Just six years later, only 300 or so remained.

If Warsaw isn't your idea of paradise, head to beautiful Łazienki Park, stretching to the east of Al. Ujazdowskie. In the late 18th century, Poland's last king, Stanisław August Poniatowski, turned the grounds into an English-style garden. The star of the park is the neoclassic Łazienki Palace (admission 4 zł, open Tues.–Sun. 9:30–3). The palace, which boasts impressive collections of art and period furniture, was so faithfully reconstructed after the war that there is still no electricity—visit when it's sunny or you won't see a thing. On Sundays in summer, classical **concerts** and other performances are held at noon and 4 PM near the park entrance on Al. Ujazdowskie, at the foot of the Chopin Monument, or in the wooden theater of the 18th-century orangery. On the park's northern edge is the reconstructed, 18th-century Zamek Ujazdowski (Ujazdów Castle), home of the **Centrum Sztuki Współczesnej** (Center for Contemporary Art; Al. Ujazdowskie 6, tel. 022/628–1271; open Tues.–Sun. 11–5), which displays interesting new work by Polish and international artists. Around the back of the castle is a wonderful view of the Wisła and a great restaurant with reasonably priced nouvelle cuisine.

MUZEUM NARODOWE

The National Museum has an amazing collection of contemporary Polish and European paintings and Gothic icons. Also on display are some famous paintings by Bernardo Bellotto (a.k.a. Canaletto), which were used as references in the rebuilding of Warsaw after the war. Allow a good couple of hours to see the whole museum. For military buffs, the **Polish Military Museum** (Wed.–Sun. 10–4) is next door. *Al. Jerozolimskie 3, tel. 022/621–1031. Admission: 5 zł, free Thurs. Open Tues., Wed., Fri.– Sun. 10–4, Thurs. 11–6.*

PALAC KULTURY I NAUKI

The Palace of Culture and Science (PKiN) was "donated" to the city by Josef Stalin in 1955. Strangely enough, the money for its construction came from Polish coffers. Towering ominously over downtown, it houses the Zoological and Technical Museums, the Polish Academy of Science, four cinemas, four theaters, a nightclub, a bookstore, restaurants, exhibit halls, a swimming pool, and even a casino. Varsovians joke that the observation deck is the best place to view the city, since it's the only place from which you can't see the monstrosity itself. *Admission to observation deck 7 zł. Open daily 9–4, Sun. 10–4.*

CHURCHES

One of the few buildings that survived World War II unscathed is the beautiful baroque **Kościół Wizytek** (Church of the Nuns of the Visitation; ul. Krakowskie Przedmieście 34, near the university), where Frederic Chopin used to play the organ. Generally, this church is open to the public only during or immediately between masses; otherwise, you might be able to peer effectively through the grille, or go to the side gate and ask a nun to let you in. Farther down the street, at ul. Krakowskie Przedmieście 68, is the resplendent **Kościółśw. Anny** (St. Anne's Church), founded in the mid-16th century; its gilded baroque and rococo interior is laden with sculptures and paintings. The 18th-century **Kościółśw. Krzyza** (Holy

Cross Church; ul. Krakowskie Przedmieście 1) houses the largest organ in Warsaw. Check out the second pillar to the left of the nave, where an urn holds Chopin's heart.

WILANOW

Just 10 km (6 mi) south of Warsaw on the Royal Road, Wilanów is well worth a visit. This small town dates back to 1677, when King Jan III Sobieski began to expand a manor to create his ideal summer residence—a project that went on for 20 years, even after his death. The end result was a magnificent baroque palace. Tours of the palace interior are 8 zł; pay an extra 2 zł to walk around the grounds. The palace is open Wed.–Mon. 9:30–2:30; the park stays open until dark. Wilanów is served by several buses; the most convenient is Bus 180 from ul. Marszałkowska, near Warsaw's Palace of Culture. Alternately, hop on the Metro to Wilanowska, then take Bus 165 south to the palace.

AFTER DARK

Warsaw's nightlife is rich, but it's not easy to track down. Pick up the *Warsaw Insider* or *Gazeta Wyborcza* from a kiosk or hotel desk before setting out. During the school year (October–May), student clubs are a great option for budget travelers; try **Riviera Remont** (ul. Waryńskiego 12, tel. 022/257–497) and the trendy **Pwinica Architektów** (ul. Koszykowa 55, tel.022/660–5206). A former bomb shelter, **Ground Zero** (ul. Wspólna 62, tel. 022/625–4380) is a hot spot for dancing. There's also the small, quiet bar **Pasieka** (ul. Freta 7/9, no phone), near Stare Miasto.

MUSIC

You can hear just about any kind of live music in Warsaw. The spread of Western jazz has given rise to a large and talented population of Polish jazz musicians; they haunt the city's jazz clubs and participate in the citywide **Jazz Jamboree** each October. The hottest jazz spot by far is **Akwarium** (ul. Emilii Plater 49, near Palace of Culture, tel. 022/620–5072; cover 20 zł), where top Polish players and foreign groups jam.

Classical concerts are a craze in Warsaw, and tickets are incredibly cheap. In the last hour before a performance, most theaters sell *wejśiówka* (entry tickets) for a few złoty, which allow you to take an empty seat or sit on the floor. The **National Philarmonic** (ul. Sienkiewicza 10, tel. 022/826–5712; closed in summer) is the best place for classical music. The **Royal Castle** (Plac Zamkowy 4, tel. 022/657–2170) holds concerts in its stunning Great Assembly Hall. The **Towarzystwo im. Fryderyka Chopina** (Chopin Society; Pałac Ostrogskich, ul. Okólnik, tel. 022/827–5471) stages delightfully Chopin-heavy recitals and chamber concerts in its beautiful palace. **Wielki Teatr/Naradowy** (pl. Teatralny, tel. 022/826–3288) stages spectacular productions of classic operas and ballets. Order concert and theater tickets through **Zasp** (Al. Jerozolimskie 25, tel. 022/621–9454), your hotel, or the theater itself.

KRAKOW

There once was a dragon who for many years terrorized a certain riverside village—until an enterprising fellow called Krak came along, slew the beast, erected a fortress on the hill above its cave, and named the newly delivered town Kraków. Home to Eastern Europe's second-oldest university, and the seat of the Polish monarchy from the 11th to 16th centuries, Kraków has long been a center of Central European culture. Though it lost much during World War II—including all but 1,000 of its 65,000 Jews to nearby Auschwitz—a surprise Red Army appearance saved the city from destruction by the Germans. Today, Kraków is culturally rich and visitor-friendly; with its medieval spires, baroque facades, and winding cobblestone streets, it remains the picture of a fairy-tale city.

BASICS

VISITOR INFORMATION

Get maps and brochures at **Sport Tourist** (ul. Pawia 8, tel. 012/229–510; open weekdays 9:30–5, Sat. 9–2), across from plac Kolejowy. **Jordan Tours** (ul. Florianska 37 or ul. Pawia 12) specializes in budget-travel information.

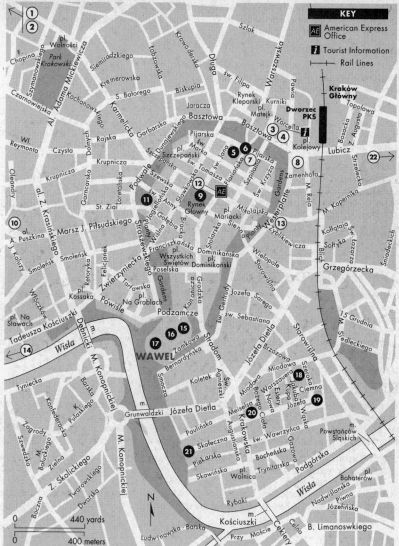

KEY

AE American Express Office

i Tourist Information

Rail Lines

Sights ●

Brama Floriańska, **6**

Centrum Kultury Żydowskiej, **20**

Dragon's Cave, **17**

Katedra Wawelska, **16**

Pauline Church and Monastery, **21**

Remu'h Synagogue, **18**

Stara Synagoga (Museum), **19**

Sukiennice, **9**

Uniwersytet Jagielloński (Collegium Maius), **11**

Zamek Wawelski, **15**

Zbiory Czartoryskich, **5**

Lodging ○

Camping Krak, **1**

Dom Studencki Piast, **2**

Europejski, **8**

Letni Summer Hostel, **22**

Polonia, **3**

Polski, **7**

PTSM (Kościuszki) (HI), **14**

PTTK Dom Turysty, **13**

Saski, **12**

Studencki Zaczek, **10**

Warszawski, **4**

Orbis. The Rynek branch has information on southern Poland and arranges half-day tours to Auschwitz and Birkenau and a bus tour of Kraków (45 zł). *Rynek Główny 41, tel. 012/224–035. Open weekdays 8–7, weekends 8–3 (closed Sun. in winter).*

AMERICAN EXPRESS

The main AmEx office is a booth in the Rynek Orbis office (*see above*). *Mailing address: AMEX F.E.S. KRAKÓW, 41 Rynek, 31–013 Kraków. Tel. and fax 012/229–180. Open June–Sept., weekdays 8–7, weekends 8–1; Oct.–May, weekdays 8–7, Sat. 9–1.*

CONSULATES

United States. *Ul. Stolarska 9, tel. 012/221–294 or 221–400 Off ul. Sienna, 1 block east of Rynek. Consulate open weekdays 8:30–5. Library, which has English-language newspapers and magazines, is open Tues. 1–4:45.*

PHONES AND MAIL

Poczta Główna offers fax, telegram, and telex services and, around the corner, a 24-hour phone office. Lines are shortest in late afternoon and longest after 7 PM. Have poste restante sent to LAST NAME (underlined), first name, Poste Restante, Poczta Główna, 31–045 Kraków 1. *Ul. Wielopole 2, fax 012/231–900 or 012/223–606. Open weekdays 7:30 AM–9 PM, weekends 9 AM–11 AM.*

The **post office** in the large building opposite the train station has fax, telegram, and 24-hour phone services. *Ul. Lubicz 4, tel. 012/229–168, fax 012/229–468.*

COMING AND GOING

East of the city center is the main train station, **Kraków Główny** (pl. Kolejowy 1, tel. 012/224–182). Finding your way around this station can be confusing, so remember: all tracks can be reached via an underground passageway just north of the rear of the station. Express buses depart from the main bus station, **Dworzec PKS** (pl. Kolejowy 2, opposite train station, tel. 012/939; open daily 4 AM–11 PM). Lot and several other international airlines fly into **Balice Airport** (tel. 012/116–700). Bus D goes from the center of town to the airport (30 mins, 1.50 zł).

GETTING AROUND

To reach the center of town from the train station, go left as you exit the station and grab a tram; most run along ul. Basztowa and ul. Lubicz. To walk the 10 minutes to **Stare Miasto,** head straight out of the station, go through the pedestrian underpass on the other side of the market, and turn right. The **MPK booth** off Platform 1 has local bus information.

The **Planty Gardens** encircle Stare Miasto. Buses and trams follow the ring road there, leaving the central streets and main square to pedestrians. Pick up the handy transit map, *Plan Miasta,* at kiosks and bookstores on the Rynek. Tickets cost 1.50 zł for either the bus or tram and can be purchased at MPK or kiosks; punch both sides when you board. From 11 PM to 5 AM, buses run twice an hour for double the fare. Taxis are available at Kraków Główny and are especially convenient after 11 PM; expect to pay 4 zł plus 2 zł per kilometer.

WHERE TO SLEEP

Tourists flock to Kraków each summer, and hotel space is very limited. Make reservations at least one week in advance—no kidding. Accommodations near the stations are an easy walk from the main sights; if you stay at a hostel or campground, you'll need a bus or tram to get around. **Waweltur** (ul. Pawia 8, across from stations, tel. 012/221–921; open weekdays 8 AM–9 PM, Sat. 9–3) arranges stays in private homes; most are outside the city center. **Almatur** (Rynek 7/8, tel. 012/226–352; open weekdays 9–5) provides information on summer-only student hostels, most of which are a good 20 minutes away.

Europejski. Here is one of the better options near the station, with comfortable doubles for 110 zł (with bath 159 zł), triples for 185 zł, and quads for 195 zł. *Ul. Lubicz 5, south of station, tel. 012/232–510, fax 012/232–529.*

Polonia. Doubles in this faded hotel, complete with chandeliers and faux marble, cost 109 zł (with bath 159 zł), triples 120 zł (with bath 182 zł). Rooms in front are noisier but have balconies. *Ul. Basztowa 25, tel. 012/221–233, fax 012/221–621.*

Polski. Across the street from the Brama Floriańska, the Polski offers simple, clean doubles for 125 zł (210 zł with a modern bathroom), including breakfast. Streetside rooms are noisy in the summer. *Ul. Pijarska 17, tel. 012/221–144, fax 012/221–426.*

PTTK Dom Turysty. Perfectly serviceable doubles in this Communist-era motel (now privately owned) go for 125 zł; beds in an eight-bed dorm are 23 zł. *Ul. Westerplatte 15, 10 mins south of station, tel. 012/229–566, fax 012/225–719.*

Saski. A stupendous pre–World War II elevator takes you up to your room in this centrally located Old World hotel. Doubles go for 100 zł (140 zł with bath). *Ul. Sławkowska 3, tel. 012/214–22, fax 012/214–830.*

Warszawski. The Warszawski is a bit run-down, but it's cheap and opposite the station. Doubles cost 100 zł (145 zł with bath). *Ul. Pawia 6, tel. 012/220–622.*

HOSTELS AND STUDENT HOUSING

Dom Studencki Piast. Clean doubles with bath are a mere 34 zł here, and they come with a cheap cafeteria, cheap laundry service, and a post office. This place is popular, so book a few weeks ahead. *Ul. Piastowska 47, tel. 012/374–933. From station, Bus 238 or 208. Laundry.*

Letni Summer Hostel (HI). From late June through mid-September only, doubles with bath and balcony are 30 zł. *Al. Jana Pawła II 82, tel. 012/480–207. From station take Tram 4, 5, 10, or 40 east seven stops.*

PTSM (Kościuszki) (HI). Ten blocks from the city center on the Wisła, this quiet, clean, nonsmoking building above an Augustine convent rents bunk beds for 5.5 zł and sheets for 2 zł. There's an 11 PM curfew. *Ul. Kościuszki 88, tel. 012/221–951. From station take Tram 2 west to terminus or Bus 100 to convent. Lockout 10–5.*

Studencki Żaczek. Mingle with Polish students in this busy dorm, which arranges tours to Auschwitz and the Wieliczka Salt Mine and has its own jazz club. Doubles go for 42 zł and include use of the kitchen. *Al. 3 Maja 5, tel. 012/335–477. Take Tram 15 or Bus 119 from the station to Hotel Cracovia; go 1 block down Al. 3 Maja. Kitchen.*

CAMPING

Krak. A 25-minute bus ride northwest of town, Krak has excellent amenities and all the charm of a truck stop. Sites are 8 zł per person. The motel next door has a bar, café, disco, and restaurant. *Ul. Radzikowskiego 99, tel. 012/372–122. From station take Bus 173 or 238 to Motel Krak. Kitchen. Closed Oct.–Apr.*

FOOD

Snack bars and restaurants are scattered along ul. Floriańska and ul. Sienna, off the Rynek, as well as in the university district along ul. Szewska and plac Szczepański. And the Rynek, like any large European plaza, is teeming with cafés. Kraków's most famous café is the Art Nouveau **Jama Michalika** (ul. Floriańska 45, north of Rynek), home to generations of avant-garde Poles; in the evening it hosts a great satirical musical show. **Kabaret Loch Camelot** (ul. Tomasza 17, right off the main square) is a good place to sip a glass of wine, hear a recital (Fri. and Sat. 8 PM), or have a coffee in the morning. The popular **Lody u Jacka i Moniki** (ul. Sławkowska, 1 block north of Rynek) serves great ice cream and cappuccino. The self-reliant will find a **market** (closed Sun.) at ul. Poselska 7/9. There's also a 24-hour market just outside the train station and a "nonstop" shop at ul. Szewska 10.

UNDER 10 ZŁ • Bistro Piccolo. This popular joint serves traditional Polish dishes like *kotlet schabowy* (pork cutlet dipped in egg and bread crumbs and fried). *Ul. Szczepańska 4, across from Stary Teatr, tel. 012/221–739.*

Chimera Salad Bar. Choose from more than 15 types of salad at this vegetarian's dream. *Ul. św. Anny 3, 1 block west of Rynek.*

UNDER 25 ZŁ • Balaton. Small and crowded, Balaton serves the best Hungarian food outside Budapest; try the goulash or the *placki ziemnaczane po węgiersku* (potato pancakes, Hungarian-style). *Ul. Grodzka 37, 2 blocks south of Rynek, tel. 012/220–469.*

UNDER 50 ZŁ • Hawełka. Considered by many the finest in Kraków, this renovated turn-of-the-century restaurant serves delicious żurek and a hearty kotlet. The restaurant on the ground floor is casual and far cheaper than the one upstairs, which is one of the priciest in town. *Rynek Główny 34, tel. 012/220–631.*

Pod Aniołami (Under the Angels). In summer, the Pod Aniołami serves in a courtyard; in winter it moves into a cozy cellar. It's a favorite lunch place with Kraków's diplomatic corps. The salads and homemade bread are especially good. *Ul. Grodzka 35, tel. 012/213–999.*

SPLURGE • Wierzynek. This stylish, nationally known restaurant served its first meal in 1364, when Cracovian Mikołaj Wierzynek prepared a banquet for King Kazimierz and his royal guests. The fresh perch and pheasant are especially good. Downstairs, the café serves delicious miód (mead). Be prepared to spend a small fortune; a meal here runs about 200 zł. The interior is opulent, and you should be too. Reservations advised in summer. *Rynek Główny 15, at Grodzka, tel. 012/221–035.*

WORTH SEEING

Kraków's **Stare Miasto** (Old Town) is a historical gold mine, a vast and lovely living museum of historic buildings and churches. For a break from all the history, hike to the top of nearby **Kopiec Kościuszki** (Kościuszko Mound), where the views are excellent, or head to the eastern suburb of **Nowa Huta** for an honest-to-Stalin look at a Soviet-era factory town.

UNIWERSYTET JAGIELLONSKI

Nicolaus Copernicus and Pope John Paul II are graduates of this university, established in 1364. From a tiny doorway on ul. Jagiellońska, you can enter the courtyard of the oldest surviving university building, the 15th-century Gothic **Collegium Maïus,** and check out its peculiar, spiral brick chimney. Inside is the **University Museum,** which boasts the first globe (1510) depicting the New World. *Ul. Jagiellońska 15, tel. 012/220–549. Admission 5 zł. Open weekdays 11–2:30, Sat. 11–1:30.*

KAZIMIERZ

Kazimierz became the Jewish quarter in 1494, when King Jan Olbracht ordered the Jews out of what is now the university district. For more than 400 years, it flourished as a center of Jewish culture, religious study, and trade, as Jews from all over Europe, drawn by Poland's reputation for ethnic tolerance, came to settle here. Under Austrian rule, the ghetto walls came down in 1818, and the residents were free to move into all parts of Kraków. By 1938, about 65,000 Jews lived in the metropolitan area, roughly a quarter of Kraków's total population. In 1941 the Nazis forced the Jews into a ghetto in Podgórze, south of the Wisła; shortly thereafter, they transported them to the Auschwitz and Birkenau death camps. Today the city's scant Jewish population numbers in the hundreds, and Kazimierz has the arid feel of a museum exhibiting the remnants of a vanished community.

The **Stara Synagoga** (Old Synagogue; ul. Szeroka 24, tel. 012/220–962) was built in the mid-15th century, reconstructed in 1557, looted and destroyed by the Nazis, and renovated in the 1950s; it now houses the **Museum of History and Culture of Kraków Jewry** (admission 4 zł; open 1st Mon. and Tues. each month plus Wed. and Thurs. 9–3:30, Fri. 11–6, weekends 9–3 (except 1st weekend of month). Down the street from the Stara Synagoga is the 400-year-old **Remu'h Synagoga** (ul. Szeroka 40, tel. 012/221–274; donation requested; open weekdays 9–4), which still serves Kraków's Jewish community. Ironically, this building escaped destruction during the occupation by serving as a storehouse for Nazi munitions. Behind the synagogue is the restored **Orthodox Cemetery,** from which the Nazis removed many of the gravestones to pave the streets during World War II. Remnants were later retrieved and used to construct a **Wailing Wall,** visible to the right as you enter the cemetery. Male visitors must wear a yarmulke (provided by the caretaker) in the synagogue and cemetery. The nearby **Centrum Kultury Żydowskiej** (Center for Jewish Culture; ul. Meiselsa 17, tel. 012337–058; open daily 10–6) sponsors lectures, concerts, and exhibits and has a pleasant café.

PAULINE CHURCH AND MONASTERY ON THE CLIFF

Famous as the site of the martyrdom of Stanisław, bishop of Kraków, the current baroque church is actually the third to be built on this cliff overlooking the Wisła. Although the bishop's remains were buried in Wawel Cathedral (*see below*), he is remembered here by a statue outside the church, marking the spot of his death. Below the church, the **Crypt of Honor** (admission 1 zł) holds the remains of gifted Polish artists, composers, and playwrights. *Ul. Skałeczna. Admission to church 1 zł. Open daily 8–noon and 2–5.*

RYNEK GLOWNY

Northern Europe's largest medieval marketplace, the magnificent Rynek Główny (Main Market Square) is dominated by the arcaded Gothic and Renaissance **Sukiennice** (Cloth Hall), where merchants once gathered to trade goods and tourists now flock to buy souvenirs. The top floor houses the National Museum's **Gallery of Polish Painting** (tel. 012/221–166; admission 3 zł, free Sun.; open Tues.–Sun. 10–3, Thurs. 10-5:30), with an impressive collection of 19th-century works, including Jan Matejko's *Hołd Pruski* (*The Prussian Allegiance*).

BRAMA FLORIANSKA AND PLAC JAN MATEJKI

St. Florian's Gate (1307) was the starting point for royal processions (kings' coronations, burials, and the like) that led to Wawel Hill. An effigy of the Roman knight and martyr St. Florian sits on the side of the gate that faces away from **Planty Gardens,** a ring of green parkland that lies where the city's walls, 47 defensive towers, and eight medieval entrance gates once stood. North of the gate is plac Jan Matejki, named for the famous historical painter and professor, where you'll find **St. Florian's Church,** the resting-place of the saint's holy relics.

WAWEL

Wawel Hill is the symbolic heart of Poland and one of its most popular tourist destinations. This threefold attraction is worth battling the torrent of schoolchildren and other tour groups to explore.

The Pauline Church honors the martyred Bishop Stanisław, who was hacked to bits by King Bolesław the Bold in 1079. According to legend, the parts of Stanisław's body were reunited by two eagles, an act seen as a metaphor for Poland: from many parts, one nation.

Katedra Wawelska (Wawel Cathedral), the Polish equivalent of Westminster Abbey, was long the site of royal coronations and burials. The remains of Polish Romantic poets Mickiewicz and Słowacki rest in the **crypt** downstairs. The cathedral was built in 1364, but 19 adjoining chapels were added over the centuries to form a striking mix of Gothic, Renaissance, and baroque styles. The most famous of these, the **Kaplica Zygmuntowska** (Sigismund Chapel), is the finest Italianate chapel north of the Alps; climb the narrow, wooden bell-tower stairway to the nine-ton Dzwon Zygmunt (Sigismund Bell), cast in 1520. *Admission to cathedral free. Admission to crypt or bell 2 zł (buy tickets across street). Cathedral open Mon.–Sat. 9–5, Sun. 12:15–5.*

Down toward the river, a spiral staircase descends to the depths of the **Smocza Jama** (Dragon's Cave), legendary lair of Prince Krak's dastardly foe. On the Wisła's bank, a cast-iron dragon will greet you. *Admission 1 zł. Open daily 9–5.*

Zamek Wawelski (Wawel Castle) was originally built in the 11th century, but a 16th-century fit of royal Italophília, after a 15th-century fire, resulted in renovations in late-Renaissance Tuscan style. Subsequent fires and destruction by various foreign armies led to further reconstruction, giving the castle its haphazard appearance. The **Royal Chambers** contain an impressive collection of Flemish tapestries, and the **Royal Treasury** exhibits what's left of the Polish crown jewels. *Tel. 012/225–747. Admission to castle, chambers, or treasury 4 zł. Two-day pass to all sites (including cathedral and Dragon's Cave) 7 zł. Open Tues.–Sat. 10–6, Sun. 10–3.*

ZBIORY CZARTORYSKICH

The oldest branch of the National Museum and one of the best art collections in Poland is the **Czartoryski Collection,** which grew out of the collection held by Princess Izabella Czartoryska at the family palace in Puławy. Although some pieces were lost during the Nazi occupation, two masterpieces— Leonardo da Vinci's delicate *Lady with Ermine* (1485) and Rembrandt's moody *Landscape with the Good Samaritan* (1638)—are still on display. *Ul. św. Jana 19, tel. 012/225–566. Admission 2 zł, free Sun. Open Tues.–Sun. 10–3:30, Fri. 10–5:30.*

AFTER DARK

Kraków may seem quiet at night, but that's because everyone has retreated into a courtyard or *ogródek* (small garden) bar, or into the depths of a smoky *piwnica* (beer cellar). Follow suit in the enormous vaulted cellar of the **Free Pub** (ul. Sławkowska 4), the hippest bar in town, or the **Black Gallery** (ul.

Mikołajska 22), a patio café and favorite haunt of Kraków's young glitterati. Student clubs are also good places to hang—try **Pod Jaszczurami** (Rynek 7, tel. 012/220–902) and **Rotunda** (ul. Oleandry 1, tel. 012/333–538) for films, jazz, and dancing.

Kraków hosts a variety of musical events; look for the monthly schedule, *Karnet*, in hotel lobbies and tourist offices, or inquire at the **Cultural Information Centre** (ul. św. Jana 2, tel. 012/217–787; open daily 10–7). On weekends, head to **Krzysztofory** (ul. Szczepańska 2, ½ block from NW corner of Rynek, tel. 012/229–360), a brick cellar (under an art gallery) that hosts jazz, rock, and techno shows. Tickets go on sale one hour before show time. Trendy **U Muniaka** (ul. Floriańska 3, tel. 012/231–205) features live jazz (15 zł) Thursday–Saturday.

NEAR KRAKOW

Don't let Kraków's enchanting atmosphere blind you to the many attractions a few hours away. Both the best and worst of Poland are nearby, from the natural wonders of the stunning Tatra Mountains surrounding Zakopane to the concentration camps at Oświęcim (Auschwitz) and Brzezinka (Birkenau).

WIELICZKA SALT MINES

Carved into the walls of the underground tunnels within the **Kopalnia Soli Wieliczka** are chapels, a museum, and ingenious sculptures. This UNESCO World Heritage Site was first mined in AD 1044; today the mines stretch more than 150 km (90 mi) and reach depths of 330 ft. Tours take you deep into the ground, down 53 flights of stairs and along 3 km (2 mi) of corridors and galleries carved out by generations of miners. Highlights—all underground—include the 180-ft-long **St. Kinga's Chapel,** where five salt-crystal chandeliers illuminate a 17th-century carved-salt altar; the 148-ft-high **Staszic Chamber,** where the Germans manufactured airplane parts during World War II; and the **Warsaw Chamber,** complete with a bar and sports facilities for the miners, and a salt statue of a gnome—kiss it if you want to be married within a year. Official tours last two to three hours and are only in Polish, but English guides and guidebooks are available. Organized tours and transportation can be arranged in Krakow through Orbis. Frequent minibuses (Lux Bus, 1.50 zł) make the 13-km (8-mi) trip to the mine from outside the Kraków train station. *Ul. Daniłowicza 10, tel. 012/787–334. Admission 17 zł. Open daily 8–4.*

OJCOW NATIONAL PARK

Just 25 km (15 mi) northwest of Kraków, on the way to Częstochowa, **Ojców Park Narodowy** (Ojców National Park) sits in a densely wooded canyon of sculpted gorges, rocky needles, and white limestone caves carved by the Prudnik River. More than 180,000 years ago, prehistoric communities lived in the caves, now home to numerous species of wildlife. The park map details hiking trails that fan out across the valley from the Ojców bus stop. Among other options, you can hike 9 km (5½ mi) north of Ojców village to the 16th-century castle **Pieskowa Skała** (Dog's Rock; admission 2 zł; open daily 9–3). To get to Ojców, take a bus from Kraków's Dworzec PKS; buses run hourly every day until noon (10 zł).

AUSCHWITZ AND BIRKENAU

The small town of Oświęcim, 55 km (33 mi) west of Kraków, is better known by its German name, Auschwitz. Between 1940 and 1945, upwards of 1.5 million people (some historians calculate close to 4 million), primarily Jews, died at the Nazis' concentration camp here. When this camp became overcrowded, Birkenau (Brzezinka) was built nearby; their combined gas chambers were capable of killing 60,000 people a day. Among the dead were thousands of children, but young voices do not disturb the silence of Auschwitz today; children under the age of 13 are not admitted.

The barracks at **Auschwitz** have been completely restored and made into a museum that survivor Primo Levi described as "something static, rearranged, contrived." With that in mind, begin with the movie (1 zł) filmed by Soviet troops on January 27, 1945, the day they liberated the few prisoners left behind by the retreating Nazis. Buy an English guidebook and walk through the notorious gate marked ARBEIT MACHT FREI (WORK BRINGS FREEDOM). The most provocative exhibits—"pitiful relics," in Levi's words—are the huge piles of belongings confiscated from victims, as well as the two tons of human hair intended for use in German industry. The execution wall, prison block, and reconstructed crematorium are particularly sobering. *Ul. Więźniów Oświęcimia 20, tel. 033/4321–33. Admission free. Museum open daily 8–4.*

Three kilometers (2 miles) away are the far more affecting, unaltered barracks, electric fences, and blown-up gas chambers of the enormous **Birkenau** camp, which has been preserved as it stood after the Nazis abandoned it. This is where the greatest number of prisoners lived and died, hundreds of

Pick up
the phone.

Pick up
the miles.

Calling Card

415 555 1234 2244
J.D. SMITH

WorldPhone

Use your MCI Card® to make an international call from virtually anywhere in the world and earn frequent flyer miles on one of eight major airlines.

Enroll in an MCI Airline Partner Program today. In the U.S., call **1-800-FLY-FREE.** Overseas, call MCI collect at **1-916-567-5151.**

1. To use your MCI Card, just dial the WorldPhone access number of the country you're calling from.
   (For a complete listing of codes, visit www.mci.com.)
2. Dial or give the operator your MCI Card number.
3. Dial or give the number you're calling.

# Austria (CC) ♦	022-903-012		# Netherlands (CC) ♦	0800-022-91-22
# Belarus (CC)			# Norway (CC) ♦	800-19912
From Brest, Vitebsk, Grodno, Minsk	8-800-103		# Poland (CC) ⋅:⋅	00-800-111-21-22
From Gomel and Mogilev regions	8-10-800-103		# Portugal (CC) ⋅:⋅	05-017-1234
# Belgium (CC) ♦	0800-10012		Romania (CC) ⋅:⋅	01-800-1800
# Bulgaria	00800-0001		# Russia (CC) ⋅:⋅ ♦	
# Croatia (CC) ★	99-385-0112		To call using ROSTELCOM ■	747-3322
# Czech Republic (CC) ♦	00-42-000112		For a Russian-speaking operator	747-3320
# Denmark (CC) ♦	8001-0022		To call using SOVINTEL ■	960-2222
# Finland (CC) ♦	08001-102-80		# San Marino (CC) ♦	172-1022
# France (CC) ♦	0-800-99-0019		# Slovak Republic (CC)	00-421-00112
# Germany (CC)	0130-0012		# Slovenia	080-8808
# Greece (CC) ♦	00-800-1211		# Spain (CC)	900-99-0014
# Hungary (CC) ♦	00▼800-01411		# Sweden (CC) ♦	020-795-922
# Iceland (CC) ♦	800-9002		# Switzerland (CC) ♦	0800-89-0222
# Ireland (CC)	1-800-55-1001		# Turkey (CC) ♦	00-8001-1177
# Italy (CC) ♦	172-1022		# Ukraine (CC) ⋅:⋅	8▼10-013
# Kazakhstan (CC)	8-800-131-4321		# United Kingdom (CC)	
# Liechtenstein (CC) ♦	0800-89-0222		To call using BT ■	0800-89-0222
# Luxembourg	0800-0112		To call using MERCURY ■	0500-89-0222
# Monaco (CC) ♦	800-90-019		# Vatican City (CC)	172-1022

Is this a great time, or what? :-)

thousands of them taken directly to the gas chambers from boxcars where they had been locked up for days. At the back of the camp is the **Monument to the Glory of the Victims,** designed by Polish and Italian artists and erected in 1967. Behind the trees to the right of the monument lies a farm pond, its banks still silted with human ashes and bone fragments. The staff at the reception office in the main guardhouse can provide a tape of the camp's history, in English. *Admission free. Open daily until dark.*

COMING AND GOING • Buses depart hourly for Oświęcim from Kraków's **Dworzec PKS** bus station (1½ hrs, 5 zł). Direct trains also run three times daily from **Kraków Główny** to the camps (1 hr, 4.50 zł). The way from the train station to the camps is poorly marked; turn right in front of the station, then take the next left on ul. Więźniów Oświęcimia. Or, you might want to take the **Orbis** (*see* Basics *in* Visitor Information, *above*) tour from Kraków (65 zł).

ZAKOPANE

Surrounded by the rocky peaks of the magnificent Tatra Mountains, the highest range of the Carpathians, Zakopane is the perfect base for hiking some of the finest trails in Europe. Ornate highland architecture decorates this village, which has emerged as Poland's leading mountain resort. Despite the onslaught of skiers and hikers, the highland culture remains largely intact, especially on market day (Wednesday) and during the **International Song and Dance Festival** in late August. Before you set out on your hike, pick up a *Tatry Polskie: Słowackie* or *Tatrzański Park Narodowy* trail map at a kiosk or PTTK. To reach the cable car to the impressive peak of Kasprowy Wierch, or the hiking trails on Mt. Giewont, head to the suburb of **Kuźnice,** a 3-km (2-mi) bus ride from downtown Zakopane.

BASICS • **Orbis** (ul. Krupówki 22, tel. 0165/12–238; open July–Sept., weekdays 9–5, Sat. 9–3; off season, closed Sat.) sells train and cable-car tickets, arranges rafting excursions on the Dunajec River, books private rooms, and represents AmEx. **PTTK** (ul. Krupówki 12, tel. 0165/12–429; open weekdays 8–4 and Sat. 8–12; off season, closed Sat.) knows all about sleeping in mountain huts along Tatra hiking trails.

COMING AND GOING • Buses are by far the fastest, most convenient transport to and from Kraków (2½ hrs, 9 zł); they depart hourly from outside the train station in Kraków and from **Zakopane's Dworzec PKS** (ul. Kościuszki 25, tel. 0165/14–603). For an even cheaper bus trip to Zakopane (7 zł one way), contact **Waweltur** (in Kraków, tel. 012/221–921). Direct trains also run from Warsaw to Zakopane. Zakopane's bus and train stations are across from one another, on ul. Kościnszki, 1 km (½ mi) northeast of the town center.

WHERE TO SLEEP • PTTK and Orbis both arrange rooms in private homes for 23 zł per person, but Orbis charges double in July and August. Beds in mountain huts cost 10 zł–15 zł per person; you can also hunt down POKOJE (ROOMS FOR RENT) signs in windows. Highland-style **Dom Turysty PTTK** (ul. Zaruskiego 5, off ul. Krupówki, tel. 0165/63–281) has doubles for 54 zł (84 zł with bath) and 14 zł bunk beds. **Radowid** (ul. Sienkiewicza 3, off ul. Kościuszki, tel. 0165/66–835) is a clean *pensjonat* (pension) close to the station; beds start at 14 zł (40 zł with three meals) and fill up quickly. **Camping Pod Krokwią** (ul. Żeromskiego, tel. 0165/12–256) rents bungalows for 25 zł per person, with shower, campsites for 7 zł per person, and tents for 7 zł; to get there, take any Kuźnice-bound bus and get off at the *Rondo,* the roundabout at the edge of town.

FOOD • Walk along ul. Krupówki for your pick of restaurants and snack bars. For late-night snacks to disco music, **Snake Restauracja** (ul. Krupówki 12) opens at 9 PM. Sample traditional fare at **Karczma Obrochtówka** (ul. Kraszewskiego 10A, off ul. Zamoyskiego); their crispy potato pancakes *à la Obrochtówka* (with Hungarian goulash) are excellent. If you're staying at Camping Pod Krokwią or heading south of town, try **Kolibecka,** a mountain hut at the Rondo which serves cheap Polish food.

CZESTOCHOWA

As a Catholic pilgrimage site, Częstochowa ranks with Lourdes and Santiago de Compostela. Every year 5 million devotees flock to this small industrial town north of Kraków to see Poland's holiest shrine, the monastery on **Jasna Góra** (Light Hill). Inside is one of the most revered icons in Poland, a Black Madonna—legend has it that this "Queen of Poland" was painted by St. Luke on a plank from Jesus' home, but it's probably a copy of a Byzantine-era icon from Istanbul's Hagia Sophia.

The **train station** (ul. Piłsudskiego, tel. 034/241–337) is on the eastern side of town, a block from the **bus station.** Express trains run frequently to Kraków (2½ hrs, 11 zł) and Warsaw (3½ hrs, 24 zł). A 25-minute walk or short bus ride west brings you to the foot of the monastery.

WESTERN POLAND

Western Poland has always been the country's traditional heartland, despite spending about 60 of the past 200 years under German control. **Poznań** and **Toruń** stand out as vibrant historic cities, and **Rogalin,** with its 1,000-year-old oaks, makes a great excursion from Poznań.

POZNAN

Despite centuries of German and Soviet domination, heavy damage during World War II, and a subsequent industrial buildup, Poznań has retained the look and feel of an elegant historic city. Closer to Berlin than to Warsaw, Poznań is a gateway to Western Europe and has been an important trading post between East and West since the Middle Ages; it is now a center of publishing, manufacturing, and international trade fairs. With boutiques, restaurants, and a lively market square, Poznań is also a great place to just hang out.

BASICS

Buy a copy of *IKS* at a kiosk; it's mostly in Polish but has a calendar of events in English. **Almatur** (ul. Fredry 7, tel. 061/520–344; open weekdays 9–6) can set you up in a university dorm; from the station, take Tram 8 to the corner of Gwarna and ul. Fredry and turn left. **Glob-Tour** (in Dworzec Główny, tel. 061/660–667; open daily 24 hrs) changes money and arranges accommodations. **Orbis** (pl. Andersa 1, in Hotel Poznań, tel. 061/330–941; open Mon.–Sat. 8–4) offers AmEx services; from the Rynek, go south on ul. Szkolna and down ul. Półwiejska.

COMING AND GOING

Trains run frequently from **Dworzec Główny PKP** (ul. Dworcowa 1, tel. 061/661–212 or 061/693–499) to Toruń (2½ hrs, 14.20 zł) and Warsaw (2½ hrs, 24.60 zł). Store your bag (5 zł per day) on the main floor—look for the PRZECHOWALNIA BAGŻY sign. From the central platform, take the stairs to street level and turn right to reach downtown or the bus station, **Dworzec PKS** (ul. Towarowa 17, tel. 061/331–212). Tram 5 will get you to the Old Town.

WHERE TO SLEEP AND EAT

There aren't many cheap rooms here, especially during international trade fairs (monthly except for July and August), when prices often double. **Biuro Zakwaterowania Przemysław** (ul. Głogowska 16, opposite train station, tel. 061/663–560) arranges private rooms (37 zł per double), flats, and villas. To get to the **hostel** (ul. Berwińskiego 2/3, tel. 061/664–040), walk west from the train station 20 minutes down ul. Głogowska, or take any tram from the city center to Woodrow Wilson Park. Another cheap option is the **Wojewódzki Ośrodek Metodyczny** (Al. Niepodległości 34, tel. 061/532–251), with dorm beds for 17 zł; take Tram 11 from the train station to ul. Nowowiejskiego, walk 3 blocks east, and turn right on ul. Niepodległości. A first-class joint, **Wielkopolska** (ul. św. Marcin 67, tel. 061/527–631) has 100 zł doubles (124 zł with bath) and room service. In an old mansion on the Rynek, **Dom Turysty** (Stary Rynek 91, tel. 061/528–893) has doubles for 100 zł (180 zł with bath) and dorm beds for 35 zł. Camp at **POSir** (ul. Koszalińska 15, tel. 061/483–129) for 6 zł per person plus 4 zł for tent rental. From Dworzec Główny, take Tram 2 to Ogrode, then take Bus 95 to Strzeszynek.

Cheap food is easy to find. The milk bar **Bistro Apetyt** (Pl. Wolności 7, tel. 061/521–339) serves tasty Polish grub. For cheap pizza, head to crowded **Tivoli** (ul. Wroniecka 13, tel. 061/523–916), 2 blocks north of Rynek, or dial 061/336–252 for delivery.

WORTH SEEING

Despite its grim industrial environs, Poznań's Old Town is one of the most charming in Poland. At its heart lies **Stary Rynek,** the main market square. The imposing clock tower on the arcaded Renaissance **Ratusz** (Town Hall) is famous for its goats, which appear every day at noon to butt heads. The tower also houses the **Muzeum Historii Miasta Poznania** (Historical Museum of Poznań; Stary Rynek 1, tel. 061/525–613; open Mon., Tues., and Fri. 10–4, Wed. noon–6, Sun. 10–3). At the **Muzeum Instrumentów Muzycznych** (Musical Instrument Museum; Stary Rynek 45, tel. 061/520–857; open Tues. and Sat. 11–5, Wed. and Fri. 10–4, Sun. 10–3), you can see an 18th-century gilded harpsichord, Chopin's piano, and a plaster cast of the composer's hands. **Muzeum Narodowe** (National Museum; Al.

Marcinkowskiego 9, tel. 061/528–011; open Tues. noon–6, Wed.–Sat. 10–4, Sun. 10–3) has a collection of Polish art, including some stunning pieces by symbolist painters Jacek Malczewski and Stanisław Wyśpiański. *Admission to each museum 1 zł, free Fri.*

Northeast of the Rynek, **Ostrów Tumski,** an islet in the Warta River, is the oldest part of Poznań and the birthplace of modern Poland—it was here that the Polanie tribe first settled. The 10th-century **Poznań Cathedral** was originally constructed by Poland's first king, Mieszko I, and rebuilt after World War II. The portal has a bronze door depicting the lives of Sts. Peter and Paul. To get here, take Tram 8 from Dworzec Główny PKP or Stare Miasto.

NEAR POZNAN

ROGALIN

Just 45 minutes south of Poznań, Rogalin is well worth a day trip for its combination of natural and architectural beauty. The baroque **Palace at Rogalin** (tel. 061/138–030), built in 1786 for the Raczyński family, is now part of the National Museum in Poznań. Don't miss the collection of 19th-century German and Polish art or the double piano, with keyboards at both ends. The **English Garden** out back contains some of the oldest oak trees in Europe (1,000 years and counting), three of which—Lech, Czech, and Rus—are named for the legendary founders of the Slavic nations. Buses to Rogalin leave Poznań's Dworzec PKS frequently.

TORUN

You'll glimpse Toruń's medieval turrets and spires as soon as you begin the approach from across the Wisła River. Once in the town center, you'll see the word *Kopernik* everywhere—especially on ulica Kopernik—in tribute to native son Mikołaj Kopernik (a.k.a. Nicolaus Copernicus), the astronomer who argued that the sun, not the earth, was the center of the solar system.

Because Toruń was relatively undamaged by World War II, most of its ancient buildings are still intact. Three areas have distinct historical features: **Stare Miasto** (Old Town) was once a neighborhood of merchants' homes and now contains most of the museums and churches; **Nowe Miasto** (New Town) originally housed artisans and craftsmen; and the **Ruiny Zamku Krzyżackiego** (Ruins of the Teutonic Knights' Castle) once housed—you guessed it—Teutonic Knights, when they dominated the region from the 13th to the 15th century.

BASICS

IT (Rynek Staromiejski 1, tel. 056/10–931; open Mon. and Sat. 9–4, Tues.–Fri. 9–6, Sun. 9–1), in the town hall, has information in English and arranges cheap accommodations. **Orbis** (ul. Żeglarska 31, tel. 056/26–130; open weekdays 9–5) sells train tickets and has a cash-only exchange desk (no traveler's checks).

COMING AND GOING

Trains from Warsaw (3 hrs, 19 zł) roll into **Dworzec Główny PKP** (tel. 056/27–222), south of the city across the Wisła. From there, Bus 11, 12, 14, 22, 27, 34, or 103 will get you to Stare Miasto. The bus station, **Dworzec PKS** (tel. 056/22–842), is a few minutes northeast of Stare Miasto, on ulica Dałbrowskiego.

WHERE TO SLEEP AND EAT

Toruń has a number of hotels, most in or around Rynek Staromiejski (Old Town Square). Reservations are essential in summer. On the outskirts of town, **Dom Wycieczkowy PTTK** (ul. Legionów 24, north of bus station, tel. 056/23–855; beds 18 zł, doubles 42 zł) has clean, modest rooms and a friendly staff; take Bus 10 north from the entrance to Stare Miasto. The charming **Hotel Pod Czarną Różą** (ul. Rabiańska 11, tel. 056/621–9637), where antique-furnished doubles cost 125 zł (breakfast included), is a trip in itself. For a more homey experience, head to **Polonia** (pl. Teatralny 5, tel. 056/23–028; doubles 38 zł), 2 blocks north of Rynek Staromiejski. Toruń's only **hostel** (ul. Rudacka 15, tel. 056/27–242) is far from town but charges only 9 zł (7 zł with HI card); take Bus 13 south from the Rynek. A short walk from the station, **Tramp** (ul. Kujawska 14, tel. 056/24–187) has bungalows for 15 zł–25 zł and tent sites for 4 zł.

Stroll over to Rynek Staromiejski for the widest variety of restaurants. The Italian owner of **Staromiejska** (ul. Szczytna 2/4, tel. 056/26–725) serves great meals and killer cappuccinos. Delis with international specialties line ul. Szeroka, off the Rynek; **Hania** (ul. Chelminska 22/24) is open 24 hours. In the evening, hang out with students in the dusky cellars of **Pod Aniołem** (beneath the Town Hall).

WORTH SEEING

Rynek Staromiejski (Old Town Square) is home to most of Toruń's museums, churches, and other important sights, while **Rynek Nowomiejski** (New Town Square) contains an outdoor market, shops, and a few churches. One of the largest and oldest buildings of its kind in northern Poland, the 14th-century **Ratusz** (Town Hall) dominates Rynek Staromiejski. The Ratusz has 365 windows, and its four pinnacles correspond to the four seasons. Concerts and poetry readings are occasionally held inside (inquire at IT). Also in the Town Hall is a gallery with rotating exhibits, an excellent collection of Gothic art, and the **Muzeum Okręgowe** (Regional Museum; tel. 056/27–038; admission 3 zł, open Wed.–Sun. 10–4), with regional artifacts and works by local artisans. For 3 zł, you can go up into the Ratusz's tower (open Tues.–Sun. 10–4) for a view of the entire city.

For a better sense of Toruń's geography and history, check out the **Dom Kopernika**, where Copernicus was born and where he lived until he was 17. The museum has period furnishings, some of the astronomer's instruments, and a miniature model of Toruń with an accompanying slide show. *Ul. Kopernika 17, tel. 056/26–748. Admission 3 zł. Open Mon. and Wed.–Fri. 9–3, Tues. and weekends 10–5.*

The **Muzeum Etnograficzne** (Ethnographic Museum) has fishing paraphernalia from northwestern Poland, and examples of regional crafts and architecture. On the grounds outside the museum, brightly decorated Polish farmhouses have been restored and filled with antiques. *Ul. Wały gen. Sikorskiego 19, tel. 056/28–091. Open Mon., Wed., and Fri. 10–4, Tues., Thurs., and weekends 10–6.*

NORTHERN POLAND

Stretching from the beaches of Pomerania to the lakes of Mazuria to the borders of Lithuania and Belarus, where bison still roam Europe's last expanse of old-growth forest, Northern Poland holds many attractions. Few areas in Europe are as unspoiled *and* accessible. If nature's not your thing, you'll find plenty of excitement in Gdańsk, the birthplace of Solidarity and the hometown of both Lech Wałęsa and Günter Grass.

SWINOUJSCIE

Most of Usedom Island lies within Germany, but on its easternmost edge is the Polish town of Świnoujście, a fishing port, seaside resort, and gateway to Scandinavia. The train and bus stations are on ul. Dworcowa, across the river from the town. To reach the town, take a free 10-minute ferry ride across the river; ferries depart every 20 minutes from the dock next to the train station. Hotels, restaurants, and tourist information are near the small port and beach; take Bus 1 from the corner of plac Słowiański and ul. Armii Krajowej.

The folks at **Almatur** (ul. Żeromskiego 17, tel. 097/321–5850; open weekdays 9–5, Sat. 9–2) have tourist information and arrange tours to nearby **Woliński National Park.** You'll find them inside **Almatur Hotel,** a cheap place to crash (doubles 40 zł) 1 block from the beach; take Bus 1 from the port to ul. Słowackiego, then walk 3 blocks north toward the sea. The **Hotel Albatros** (ul. Kasprowicza 2, tel. 097/321–2335) has doubles from 65 zł (but prices double in high season). **Relax** (ul. Słowackiego 1, tel. 097/936–3912) has tent sites for 4 zł (plus 3 zł per person) and three-person cabins for 55 zł (95 zł in summer). **Wolin Tours** (ul. Armii Krajowej 14, tel. 097/321–2394) has a Polferries counter, where you can arrange travel to Sweden and Denmark.

GDANSK

Maybe it's the Baltic air; maybe it's the Hanseatic architecture and commercial traditions; or maybe it's the Gdańsk Shipyard, where the **Solidarność** (Solidarity) movement began in 1980. Whatever the reason, Gdańsk, along with its "Tri-City" neighbors Sopot and Gdynia, ranks with Kraków as one of Poland's most vibrant cities. Known as Danzig before World War II, Gdańsk was reduced to rubble by the Soviet army in 1945, and its largely German population was replaced with refugees from Poland's eastern provinces. Today, the carefully restored old town hums with commercial and cultural activity.

BASICS

IT (ul. Długa 45, tel. 058/319–327; open daily 9–6) is the best tourist office, but it's not as well-located as **Gdańsk Tourist** (ul. Heweliusza 8, tel. 058/314–816), across from the train station. Both arrange private rooms for a fee (up to 46 zł). The AmEx representative is at **Orbis** (ul. Heweliusza 22, tel. 058/314–944; open weekdays 9–5, Sat. 9–2), which also has the scoop on ferries to Scandinavia. **Gdańsk Główny** (ul. Podwale Grodzkie, tel. 058/310–051), the main RR station, has excellent connections to the rest of Poland; the bus station **Dworzec PKS** (ul. 3 Maja, tel. 058/321–532) is in back.

WHERE TO SLEEP

Even in summer—the high season for German tourists who flock to Gdańsk—finding budget lodgings is not difficult. Rooms can be arranged through Orbis or **Maria Macur** (ul. Beethovena 8, tel. 058/324–170), who speaks English and arranges private lodgings over the phone for 36 zł per person. **Dom Harcerza** (ul. Za Murami 2/10, tel. 058/313–621; doubles 97 zł) is conveniently in the heart of the old town.

HOSTELS • Gdańsk's five hostels vary little in terms of facilities and cost; expect to pay 8 zł per night with an HI card, 10 zł without. However, the hostel at ul. Wałowa 21 (tel. 058/312–313) has the best location; it's a 10-minute walk from the station, near the shipyards. Reserve ahead in summer. Your next-best option is the hostel at ul. Kartuska 245b (tel. 058/324–187); from the train station, take Bus 161 or 167.

FOOD

When hunger strikes, stroll along ul. Długa and Długi Targ, the center of activity in Gdańsk, and choose from a broad range of pleasant eateries. For pizza or Greek salad, try **Napoli** (Długa 62/63). **Neptun** (Długa 33/34) is a great milk bar with homemade food.

CAFÉS • Cafés lurk in every other corner; some of the better ones are on Długi Targ and ul. Mariacka or along the riverfront. **Piekarnia Pellowski** (ul. Podwale Staromiejskie 82, near St. Catherine's Church; no phone) has the best pastries in town. For jazz, try the **Cotton Club** (ul. Złotników 25/26), popular with students, or **Żak** (Wały Jagiellońskie 1). Żak is in the basement of the beautiful building that housed the League of Nations between the wars and now contains Lech Wałesa's office. The **Ratusz Staromiejski** (Old City Hall) is an architectural gem (ul. Korzenna, no street number) with a café and bookstore on the ground floor and an Irish pub in the basement.

WORTH SEEING

The streets of the **Główny Miasto** (Main Town) have been lovingly restored since their near-destruction in World War II. Stroll along **Długi Targ** (Long Market), shady **ul. Mariacka,** with its gallery scene, and the **waterfront walkway** along the Motława River; and stop at the **marketplace** on the northern edge of the Main Town for anything from wild mushrooms to Madonna tapes.

In the Old Town, visit **St. Catherine's Church** (ul. Katarzynki), one of the oldest in the city. Next door is **Św. Brigida** (St. Bridget's); once a locus of Solidarity opposition, St. Bridget's legendary priest, Father Henryk Jankowski, has fallen from grace because of his controversial political activities, but the church retains a sense of Solidarity's drama. The 14th-century **Kościół Mariacki** (Church of Our Lady), the largest church in Poland and the largest brick church in the world, can accommodate 25,000 people. Its 500-year-old astronomical clock tracks solar and lunar phases and features signs of the zodiac, an anomaly in a Catholic church. Clamber up the 256-ft-high tower for a breathtaking view of the city (ul. Piwna. Admission to tower 2 zł).

The heavily symbolic **Pomnik Słoczniowców** (Monument of the Shipyard Workers; ul. Jana Z. Kolna) consists of three towering steel crosses standing outside the gates of the **Stocznia Gdańska** (Gdańsk Shipyards). It was erected by Solidarity in 1980 to commemorate workers killed during the brutally quelled worker protests of 1970. The shipyard is now on the brink of bankruptcy.

At the head of Długi Targ is one of the city's most distinctive landmarks, the 17th-century **Fontanna Neptuna** (Neptune Fountain), which is illuminated every day after dusk. Nearby, **Gdańsk's Ratusz Główny** (Main Town Hall), which was reconstructed after the war, houses the **Muzeum Historii Miasta** (City History Museum; ul. Długa 47, tel. 058/314–871; admission 4 zł; open 11–4, closed Mon. and

Fri.). The **Muzeum Narodowe** (ul. Toruńska 1, tel. 058/317–061; admission 3 zł; open Tues.–Sat. 10–3, Sun. 10–4) contains Gothic sculptures and Hans Memling's amazing *Last Judgment*.

MALBORK

The stupendous **Castle of the Teutonic Knights** is the central feature of Malbork, 40 km (24 mi) southeast of Gdańsk. In 1230 the Teutonic Knights arrived on the banks of the Wisła River and aimed to establish their own state on the conquered Prussian lands. After the castle underwent a post–World War II face lift, the EU adopted it as a major restoration project. Exhibits are annotated in English. Don't miss the book display in the Middle Castle, with handwritten mass liturgies, a medieval medical book, some works by Cicero, and a collection of amber. *Ul. Hiberna 1, tel. 055/723–364. From the station take Bus 9. Admission 10 zł. Open Oct.–Apr., Tues.–Sun. 9–3; May–Sept., Tues.–Sun. 9–5. Grounds open daily until 6.*

The **train** and **bus stations** are next to each other on the eastern side of town. For tourist information, maps, a good meal, and cheap rooms, check out **Hotel Zbyszko** (ul. Kościuszki 43, tel. 055/723–394; doubles 50 zł–75 zł); from the station, go right on ul. Dworcowa and cross over to ul. Kościuszki, to your right. A large **hostel** (ul. S. Żeromskiego 45, tel. 055/722–408; beds 9 zł) is only a short walk from the castle; make reservations well in advance. Refuel at **Café Zamkowa** (ul. Starościńska 14, tel. 055/722–738), just east of the castle gates in Hotel Zamek.

MAZURIAN LAKES

With a network of more than 4,000 crystalline lakes and rivers winding through its forests and hills, Mazuria is one of Poland's most beautiful regions. It's also a popular vacation spot for Poles and Germans, especially in July and August, when rooms fill up fast. Opportunities for swimming, sailing, fishing, and kayaking abound, and the dense forests, inhabited by elk and wild boar, offer excellent hiking. Mazuria is also home to the **Wolf's Lair** (near Kętryzn), a bunker that served as Hitler's main headquarters during World War II; it's now in ruins, but still worth a visit. The town of Mrągowo hosts a country-western music festival in July.

Giżycko, on the north shore of Lake Niegocin, is a great base for exploring the area. Midway between Olsztyn and Białystok, it is situated on one of the most picturesque stretches of rail in Poland; numerous daily trains run from either of those towns as well as from Warsaw (6 hrs, 20 zł). The lakeside **Dom Wycieczkowy PTTK** (ul. Nadbrzeżna 11, tel. 087/282–905; open May–Oct.) has doubles for 40 zł; upstairs, you can rent sailboats (60 zł–200 zł per day) or arrange trips downstream to the charming village of **Mikołajki** (45 zł one way). For more information on water sports and hiking, drop in at **Centrum Informacji Turystycznej** (ul. Warsawska 7, tel. 087/285–760).

PORTUGAL

ortugal's diverse landscape may surprise you. In a single day, you can frolic in the snow of the Serra da Estrela, cross the arid Alentejo, and end up on a sun-drenched beach in the Algarve. Farther north, the wine-growing Minho and Douro regions are cool, wet, and unbelievably green, whereas Trás-os-Montes is a rugged, mountainous hinterland. This variety is reflected in the Portuguese people, who fill the entire spectrum between the agricultural, left-leaning south and the industrial, conservative north. Urban and rural cultures differ as well; although cities such as Lisbon and Oporto are not exactly cosmopolitan, they (along with the resorts of the southern coast) are accustomed to foreign travelers. Small towns in Portugal are about as far off the beaten track as you'll get in Western Europe, and most rural villages remain much as they were a hundred years ago.

Although it may seem somewhat provincial today, Portugal's distinctive character is the product of centuries of intense contact with other cultures. More than 2,000 years ago, the Lusitanians of Western Iberia were conquered by none other than Julius Caesar. Five centuries of Roman rule ended with the fall of the Empire, leaving a vacuum soon filled by Germanic invaders, whose relatively brief rule established a Christian community in the north that managed to survive the Islamization of Iberia that followed the arrival of the Moors (Arabs and Berbers) in the 8th century. The Moors brought sophisticated agricultural and building techniques and a civilization that remained the dominant power in the area until the 12th-century Christian Reconquest. During the next four centuries, this small, seafaring nation became a major empire in its own right, leading the European age of expansion with bloody land grabs and slave trading in Africa, the Americas, and the Far East. It was unable, however, to maintain its own autonomy, which by the end of the 16th century was lost to Spanish "unification."

Portugal regained its independence in 1640, but its power declined in the colonial period, largely because of an extremely draining economic relationship with England, which provided naval protection and a market for Portuguese goods. After a host of insurrections and power struggles, the country became a republic in 1910, only to be subjected to more than four decades of intellectual and social isolation under dictator António Salazar, who took increasing control of the country after his appointment as Finance Minister in 1928. Salazar's regime outlawed Communism, jailed labor organizers, and dispatched secret police to infiltrate and suppress student protests. Salazar's successor, Marcello Caetano, was overthrown on April 25, 1974, by a group of military captains fed up with the colonial war and a state that had all the trappings of fascism. The resulting democracy allowed Portugal to join the European Community in 1986 and cleared the path for great social, political, and intellectual growth.

Portugal has been left behind the rest of Europe in many ways—its reputation as the Third World of Western Europe derives as much from its somewhat fastidious conservatism as from its modest, agriculturally based economy. Young Portuguese have many worries. They face serious levels of unemployment, and the perception that refugees streaming in from the former colonies of Cape Verde and war-torn Angola are hurting the job situation has led to increased racial tension and even violence. Still, most Portuguese maintain a carefree attitude, rivaling their Spanish neighbors in the art of staying out all night. Don't expect France's or Italy's glamour here; instead, you'll find the lowest prices in Western Europe, truly stunning natural beauty, and a culture that brings its traditions into the present in unique and intriguing ways.

BASICS

MONEY

US$1 = 172 escudos and 100 escudos = 57¢. The dollar sign is also the escudo sign. You can exchange cash and traveler's checks at banks, which are generally open weekdays 8:30–3, but commissions run upwards of 500$ per transaction. Bureaux de change offer lower rates but lower commissions. Larger cities and tourist areas have 24-hour exchange machines that accept cash (i.e., dollars, marks, and pounds) and charge lower commissions, but can be fussy about crumpled bills. **Multibanco** ATMs take bank cards affiliated with the Cirrus network, as well as MasterCard and Visa. Portuguese ATMs often run out of money on weekends, and occasionally refuse foreign bank cards for no apparent reason. In either case, just keep trying at other machines.

HOW MUCH IT WILL COST • Portugal is cheaper than Spain and much cheaper than France or England. A double in a pension can usually be had for no more than 4,000$, and a full restaurant meal including wine and bread goes for less than 2,000$ almost anywhere but Lisbon. The tip in a restaurant is usually 10%, unless it has already been included (if the IVA listed is more than 7%, it has). Transport, especially on second-class trains, is very cheap—you can easily traverse half the country for less than 2,000$. All in all, you should be able to get by on US$40 a day if you live simply. If you are under 26 and will be spending any length of time in Portugal, buy a **Cartão Jovem** for 1,800$ from **Movijovem** (Av. Duque D'Àvila 137, tel. 01/355–90–81) in Lisbon. Cardholders receive discounts of up to 40% on museum admissions, bus and train tickets, and tons of other goods and services. Other European youth cards and the ISIC card will sometimes substitute, but their discounts are often smaller.

GETTING AROUND

Before you do anything drastic, like getting into a car, know that Portugal's best drivers are Europe's worst—accident rates here are the highest on the continent. To make matters worse, gasoline is expensive (about US$4/gallon), as are highway tolls. If you're still undeterred, rental rates start at about 4,500$ per day for unlimited mileage.

Long-distance biking hasn't really caught on in Portugal. If you bring your wheels, carry extra tubes and tools and be prepared for long stares as you pedal by. You can rely on getting bicycle parts only in Lisbon, Oporto and other large towns, and rentals only in the touristed Algarve coast to the south. If you want to transport your bike by train (350$), show up early to register it as baggage.

BY BUS • Buses are usually more comfortable and often faster than trains, and tickets are only slightly more expensive. All buses are air-conditioned, and bus stations are nearly always centrally located. The biggest bus company, **Rede Expressos** (see Coming and Going in Lisbon, below), serves nearly all of Portugal and can direct you to regional companies for out-of-the-way destinations. **Intercentro** (see Coming and Going in Lisbon, below) connects Lisbon with major European cities and offers youth discounts of 20%–30% to those under 25.

BY TRAIN • **Caminhos de Ferro Portugueses (CP),** Portugal's national railroad, runs three classes of trains: regional (very cheap but painfully slow trains that seem to stop at every street corner); interregional (somewhat more expensive and twice as fast, stopping only in important cities); and intercidades (express trains between cities; these require a seat reservation). Eurailpasses are valid on any train (300$ supplement if you reserve), though you may want to pay the fares and save your pass for countries where rail travel is more expensive. Only Alfas—ultra-fast, first-class-only express trains—require supplements to Eurail. Buy your ticket before boarding or you'll be subject to a fine of at least 10,000$.

WHERE TO SLEEP

The **pensão** is the budget traveler's mainstay in Portugal. Rooms usually offer a sturdy bed, a tiny sink, and a bidet; a private bath will bump the price of a double to more than 3,000$. Prices posted on the door of each room are the maximum allowed by law. You can often get a room in a **private home** for the same price or less. People with rooms to let generally approach travelers at train and bus stations or advertise with small QUARTOS signs in their windows.

There are 21 official **Pousadas de Juventude** (HI hostels) in Portugal. These are administered by Lisbon's **Movijovem** (Av. Duque D'Àvila 137, tel. 01/313–88–20). Get your hostel card before you leave for Portugal; Movijovem sells them only to Portuguese. Officially, holders of non-Portuguese hostel cards must pay an extra 300$ (100$ for those under 25) per night for the first five nights, but this is generally ignored. Hostels are cheaper by 200$–400$ from October to mid-June. All hostels serve guests free breakfast, and some serve dinner for 900$. **Campgrounds** are more expensive than you might think; they tend to have lots of facilities (i.e., feel more like malls than the wilderness) and charge a base price for a tent space (usually around 400$) plus a higher charge per person. *Roteiro Campista,* a comprehensive guide to Portuguese campgrounds, is available at tourist offices—buy it for 650$, or just consult it for free. Camping rough is officially illegal in most places and can be dangerous; inquire at the tourist office.

FOOD

Portuguese meals are hearty, usually based around a large portion of meat or fish, and taken late. Breakfast is all but nonexistent, consisting of little more than a quickly gulped cup of espresso and maybe a pastry eaten while standing at the *balcão* (counter) of a snack shop. Specialties include *bacalhau* (cod that's been salted, dried, and soaked in water before cooking), *lulas* (squid), *arroz de marisco* (shellfish and rice stew), and *açorda de gambas* (a garlicky prawn-and-bread-crumb porridge). *Caldo verde,* a potato-based soup with kale and sausage, is a national staple. Note that in restaurants a *dose* often serves two—for a single serving, order a *meia-dose.* Also keep in mind that appetizers (bread, cheese, olives) set on your table are not free; touch them and you'll be charged for them. They are listed on the menu as the *couvert.*

If you shun animal flesh, you can often get a cheese omelet, but your staples are likely to be mixed salads, french fries, and bread. Lunch places called **snacks** serve *salgados*—seasoned items, such as pastries filled with meat, fish, or chicken—plus alcohol or coffee. Order a *café* or a *bica* and you'll get an espresso. A *galão* or *meia de leite* is café au lait. *Cerveja* (beer) in Portugal tends to be strong, with an alcohol content around 5.5%. Be sure to sample the famous *Dão* and port wines from the north, the light, sparkling *vinho verde* (young wine), and *amendôa amarga,* an almond liqueur from the southern coast.

BUSINESS HOURS

Most businesses are open weekdays 9–12:30 and 2–6, Saturday 9:30–2. Museums are often closed on Mondays and free on Sunday or Tuesday.

PHONES AND MAIL

Country code: 351. You'll find public phones everywhere. Local calls cost 20$ for three minutes (less before 10 AM and after 6 PM). Long-distance calls will gobble up your change; **Credifone** and **Telecom** cards, available in 850$ and 1,600$ denominations from newspaper kiosks and post offices, are accepted in more than half the public phones. Larger cities have phone offices, and post offices usually have pay-after-you-call phones. It costs around US$2 per minute to call the United States, with no night or weekend discounts. To make an international call, dial 00 followed by the country code, area code, and phone number. Dial 098 to talk to an English-speaking operator. For **AT&T** Direct Access℠, dial 05017–1–288; for **Sprint,** 05017–1–877; for **MCI,** 05017–1–234.

You'll pay 140$ to mail a letter or a postcard to the States, 80$ within the European Community. All post offices accept poste restante mail; envelopes should be addressed NAME, a/c Posta Restante, Postal Code, City, Portugal. Letters will end up at the main post office of that city; look for the window labeled ENCOMENDAS.

EMERGENCIES

The national emergency number is **115.** For medical problems, call the English-speaking staff at Lisbon's **hospital** (Rua Saraiva de Carvalho 49, tel. 01/395–50–67), or try the nearest *farmacia* (pharmacy), which can dispense drugs and send you in the right direction if the problem seems serious. In large cities, the address of the 24-hour pharmacy is posted on the doors of all other pharmacies.

LANGUAGE

Even natives admit that Portuguese is a difficult language to learn, with its irregular verb conjugations, odd slang, and rapid-fire, slurred speaking style. Many people hearing Portuguese for the first time think it sounds Slavonic, though it somewhat resembles Spanish on paper. A knowledge of any Romance language helps. You will generally get a better response using English than Spanish, since the Portuguese aren't wild about their Spanish neighbors. English is spoken widely, especially by young people, who have grown up on American TV, movies, and pop music. A few helpful Portuguese phrases: *bom dia* (good morning); *boa tarde* (good afternoon); *boa noite* (good night); *adeus* (good-bye); *obrigado/a* (thank you, as spoken by men/women); *fala inglês?* (do you speak English?); *cuanto é . . .?* (how much is. . . ?); *onde fica . . .?* (where is. . . ?).

LISBON

Portugal's capital city—Lisboa to Lusophones—is an unassuming mix of local tradition and worldly modernity. The narrow cobblestone streets lined with stately old buildings are now frequently blocked by construction, as Lisbon prepares to host the 1998 World Expo and take its place, at least for a moment, at the center of the international stage. And although its citizens appear modest and respectable by day, Lisbon's bars and nightclubs heat up after dark with a frenetic, all-night crowd. The city also has its share of problems—locals complain of pollution, traffic, unemployment, and racial tensions between white Europeans and African-Portuguese immigrants—but, all things considered, Lisbon is a relatively safe city that hasn't yet grown bored of its foreign visitors.

In 1755, a huge earthquake nearly wiped Lisbon out, killing 40,000 and destroying many monuments and historical buildings. Fortunately, the layout of the old Moorish and medieval quarter known as the Alfama survived, and the neighborhood retains its mazelike character. The riverfront commercial area was rebuilt in a grid pattern; other neighborhoods were built in the forms of steep stairways and alleys winding over the city's many hills. Despite the catastrophic damage the city suffered in the 18th century, remnants of Portugal's 15th- and 16th-century heyday as a seafaring empire live on in the city's Manueline architecture, named after King Manuel I (1469–1521) and marked by nautical motifs. But Lisbon's main appeal lies away from the museums and monuments—in quiet parks where old folk doze on the benches, in bustling shops and markets, and in cafés and bars à la mode.

May and June are big festival months in Portugal. May brings the Queima das Fitas to university towns—a week or two of parties, concerts, and cultural events culminating in a ceremonial burning of departmental ribbons by university graduates. June contains many of the most important saints' days, and cities celebrate their patrons with wild street parties. The biggest are Santo António in Lisbon (early June) and São João in Oporto (late June).

BASICS

VISITOR INFORMATION
The busy, English-speaking staff at the central **posto de turismo** (tourist office) in Restauradores Square will research bus and train schedules for you, book rooms (no fee, though they tend to push the more expensive hotels), and provide free maps and listings of local events. *Palácio Foz, Pr. dos Restauradores, tel. 01/346–36–58 or 01/346–36–43. Metro: Restauradores. Open daily 9–8.*

AMERICAN EXPRESS
The friendly folks at **Top Tours,** Lisbon's American Express representative, cash AmEx traveler's checks, make travel reservations, handle emergency check refunds and card replacements, and hold client mail for two months. *Av. Duque de Loulé 108, Lisboa 1000, tel. 01/354–05–90. Metro: Rotunda. Open weekdays 9:30–1 and 2:30–6:30.*

CHANGING MONEY
Most banks (many with ATMs or 24-hour exchange machines) are along **Rua Augusta,** in the Baixa, but charge astronomical commissions. Exchange machines are abundant; look for them in central plazas and commercial areas.

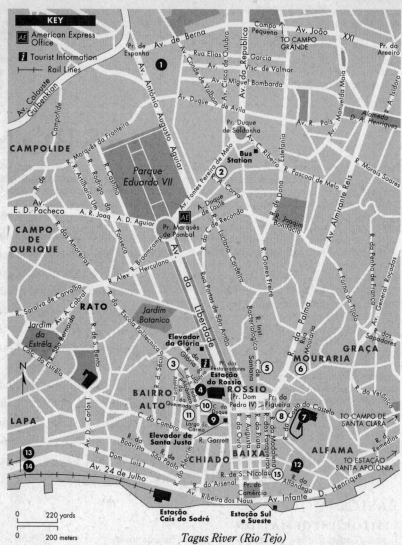

KEY

- AE American Express Office
- i Tourist Information
- ⊢┼┤ Rail Lines

CAMPOLIDE

Pr. de Espanha

Av. de Berna

Rua Elias

Av. Cinco de Outubro

Campo Pequeno

Av. João XXI

TO CAMPO GRANDE

Pr. do Areeiro

Garcia

Visc. de Valmor

Av. Miguel Bombarda

Alameda D. A. Henriques

Av. Duque de Ávila

Pr. Duque de Saldanha

Av. R. Pais

R. Morais Soares

Parque Eduardo VII

Bus Station

R. Pascoal de Melo

CAMPO DE OURIQUE

Av. E. D. Pacheco

Pr. Marquês de Pombal

A. Duque de Loulé

R. Joaquim Bonifácio

Av. Almirante Reis

R. da Penha de França

RATO

Jardim da Estrêla

Jardim Botanico

Elevador da Glória

GRAÇA

MOURARIA

BAIRRO ALTO

Estação do Rossio

ROSSIO
(Pr. Dom Pedro IV)

LAPA

CHIADO

Elevador de Santa Justa

BAIXA

ALFAMA

Castelo de São Jorge

TO CAMPO DE SANTA CLARA

TO ESTAÇÃO SANTA APOLÓNIA

Av. 24 de Julho

Av. Infante D. Henrique

Estação Cais do Sodré

Estação Sul e Sueste

| 0 | 220 yards |
| 0 | 200 meters |

Tagus River (Rio Tejo)

Sights ●

Castelo de
São Jorge, **7**

Convento do
Carmo, **9**

Fundação Calouste
Gulbenkian, **1**

Igreja de
São Roque, **4**

Mosteiro dos
Jerónimos, **13**

Museu Nacional de
Arte Antiga, **14**

Sé, **12**

Lodging ○

Casa de Hóspedes
Duque, **10**

Grande Pensão
Alcobia, **8**

Pensão A
Moderna, **6**

Pensão Estrela da
Serra, **15**

Pensão Globo, **3**

Pousada de
Juventude-Lisboa, **2**

Residencial
do Norte, **11**

Residencial
Nossa Senhora
do Rosário, **5**

EMBASSIES

Canada: *Av. da Liberdade 144–56, 4th floor, tel. 01/347–48–92. Open Mon.–Thurs. 8:30–12:30 and 2–5, Fri. 8:30–12:30.* **United Kingdom:** *Rua São Bernardo 33, next to Jardim da Estrela, tel. 01/392–40–00. Bus 9 from Pr. dos Restauradores. Open weekdays 10–noon and 3–4:30.* **United States:** *Av. das Forças Armadas 16, tel. 01/727–33–00. Open weekdays 8:30–12:30 and 1:30–5.*

PHONES AND MAIL

Pick up poste restante weekdays only at Lisbon's **main post office** (Pr. do Comércio, tel. 01/346–32–31; open Mon.–Sat. 8:30–6; postal code 1100) from the window on Rua do Arsenal 25. The branch across from the tourist office is also open Sunday. Both offices have international telephone and fax services. The main **Telecom** office (Pr. Dom Pedro IV 68), around the corner from the Rossio train station, is open daily 8 AM–11 PM.

COMING AND GOING

BY BUS

Lisbon's main **bus station** (Av. Casal Ribeiro 18, tel. 01/577715) is near the Saldanha metro stop. **Intercentro** (tel. 01/571765) serves international destinations such as Seville (8 hrs, 4,850$), Madrid (12 hrs, 6,550$), Paris (23 hrs, 14,490$), and Amsterdam (40 hrs, 16,000$). **Rede Expressos** (tel. 01/545–439) covers all of Portugal.

BY PLANE

The **Aeroporto de Lisboa** (tel. 01/802060) is a 20-minute bus ride north of the city center. The airport has an irregularly staffed **tourist office** (tel. 01/849–36–89; open daily 6 AM–2 AM), a 24-hour exchange office (a rip-off), and cash-exchange machines. The express **Aerobus** (430$) is the fastest way into town, and your ticket is valid on any bus, trolley, or funicular all day long. A **taxi** (around 900$) is your only option after 9 PM. **TAP** (Pr. Marquês do Pombal 3, tel. 01/386–10–20) is Portugal's national airline and does not, contrary to popular belief, stand for "Take Another Plane."

BY TRAIN

Lisbon has four train stations. International and long-distance trains from Paris (24 hrs, 21,000$), Madrid (9 hrs, 8,000$), and northern Portuguese towns like Oporto (4½ hrs, 1,760$) arrive at **Estação Santa Apolónia** (tel. 01/888–40–25), on the riverfront about 2 km (1 mi) east of Lisbon's center. This station has a bureau de change. Buses 9, 39, 46, and 90 head from there to Praça dos Restauradores, in the center of town. Central **Estação do Rossio** (tel. 01/346–50–22) sends trains to Sintra (35 mins, 185$). Commuter trains to Cascais (30 mins, 180$) leave from the waterfront **Estação Cais do Sodré** (tel. 01/347–01–81); to get there, take Trolley 15 or 17 from Praça da Figueira or Bus 35 from Santa Apolónia. If you're Algarve-bound, use **Estação Sul e Sueste** (tel. 01/877092), sometimes called Estação Fluvial, just east of the Praça do Comércio. This station is merely a ticket window and ferry dock; trains depart from the town of Barreiro, on the other side of the river. The ferry fare is an extra 160$ and is sold separately. All stations have **luggage lockers** (250$–400$) with a 24-hour limit.

GETTING AROUND

North of the Tagus River (Rio Tejo) estuary, Lisbon spreads out over a string of hills. The center of town is formed by three adjacent squares, which mark the northern limits of the Baixa: the **Rossio** (its formal name is Praça Dom Pedro IV), **Praça da Figueira,** and **Praça dos Restauradores.** The **Bairro Alto** (Upper Town), the **Baixa** (Lower Town), and the **Alfama** (the old Moorish and medieval quarter) constitute the heart of Lisbon and are all within walking distance of each other.

BY BUS

Carris (tel. 01/363–20–16) buses and trolleys can take you almost anywhere in Lisbon, though service is limited after midnight. One-trip tickets (bought from the driver) cost 150$. **Carris passes** (430$ for 1 day, 1,000$ for 3 days) are available from the kiosk on Praça da Figueira, as is the **Bilhete Único de Coroa (BUC),** which gets you two trips for 150$. Another option is the LisboaCard (*see* Worth Seeing, *below*). Most buses stop at Praça da Figueira or Praça do Comércio.

BY METRO

Lisbon's Metro, open 6:30 AM–1 AM, is clean, fast, and cheap, but it has limited stops. Individual tickets (70$) are sold at machines and ticket booths at each Metro stop; books of 10 cost 500$. If you're caught without a ticket, expect a fine of at least 7,500$. The main stops near the tourist office and budget digs are Restauradores and Rossio.

BY TAXI

Taxis rarely cost more than 500$ for a ride within the city, though there are small surcharges for luggage and rides after midnight. Make sure the driver resets the meter when you enter the taxi, and tip small change. Taxis are in great demand after dark, so call **Rádio-Táxis de Lisboa** (tel. 01/815–50–61).

BY TROLLEY

Eléctricos (trolleys) have traveled Lisbon's steep, narrow streets since the 1800s, and they're still a nifty way to tour the city. Eléctricos run every 10–15 minutes until around 12:30 AM; weekend hours are reduced. *Elevadores* (funiculars) take on Lisbon's two steepest hills. The **Elevador de Santa Justa** (really an elevator, not a funicular) climbs to Largo do Carmo from the corner of Rua Aurea (commonly called Rua do Ouro) and Rua de Santa Justa in less than a minute. The **Elevador da Glória** whisks passengers from the west side of Avenida da Liberdade to the Bairro Alto and a wonderful viewpoint overlooking the castle and city; the **Elevador da Bica** clanks up the same hill from Rua de São Paulo, near the river. The **Elevador de Lavra** climbs the hill on the other side of Praça dos Restauradores, starting at Largo da Anunciada.

WHERE TO SLEEP

Pensions are scattered throughout Lisbon, almost invariably on the upper floors of buildings—be prepared to haul your luggage up at least two flights of poorly lit stairs. Street noise can be a problem, so try to get a back room. The cheapest rooms are in the Rossio, east of Rua Madalena, just up from the Praça do Comércio. To find a room in the historic neighborhoods of Bairro Alto or Alfama, set out early in the day. In a pinch, the Praça da Figueira is lined with slightly sleazy pensãos where you can often get a double for about 3,000$.

UNDER 3,000$ • Casa de Hóspedes Duque. Here on a quiet street in the Bairro Alto, the rooms are small but clean and comfy, and the managers genuinely like their clientele. Singles cost 2,200$, doubles 2,500$. *Calçada do Duque 53, tel. 01/346–34–44. Take Elevador de Santa Justa and turn right up the stairs.*

Pensão Estrela da Serra. The singles here, from 1,500$, are about as cheap as a lone traveler can get; doubles, from 2,500$, are a less stunning value. Rooms are clean and basic, but because the place is small, it fills quickly. *Rua dos Fanqueiros 122, a busy shopping street just off Rua Madalena, near Praça do Comércio, tel. 01/887–42–51.*

Residencial Nossa Senhora do Rosário. This huge old building in the Rossio has small rooms and a TV lounge. The friendly owner speaks several languages—usually all at the same time. Singles start at 2,000$, doubles at 4,000$. *Calçada de Santana 198, tel. 01/885–36–50. From Pr. da Figueira, east on Rua Portas de São Antão behind theater and climb steps to right.*

UNDER 4,000$ • Pensão A Moderna. These rooms, below the charming Mouraria district, are about as close to perfect as your budget will allow: set back from the street, clean, quiet, nicely furnished, and congenially managed. Singles cost 2,000$, doubles 3,000$. *Escadinhas da Saúde 10, at Ruas da Mouraria and da Palma, tel. 01/886–38–00.*

UNDER 5,500$ • Grande Pensão Alcobia. Every room in this centrally located, impressive old pension has a phone, and the more expensive rooms have TVs. Singles are 3,500$, doubles 5,000$. *Poço do Borratém 15, where Madalena turns into Poço do Borratém, tel. 01/886–51–71.*

Pensão Globo. Right behind the Port Wine Institute in the Bairro Alto, this mom-and-pop joint is beautiful and super-friendly. Singles range from 2,000$ to 2,500$; doubles are 4,500$. *Rua da Teixeira 37, tel. 01/346–22–79. Take Bus 100 from Praça da Figueira or ride up Elevador da Glória and walk 1 block west.*

Residencial do Norte. You'll climb lots of stairs to reach this one; it's above a disco in the Bairro Alto. There's a sun porch, a TV room, and—hallelujah—laundry facilities. Singles begin at 2,500$, doubles at 5,500$. *Rua do Norte 123, tel. 01/346–50–68. From Elevador da Glória, go west on Travessa da Queimada, then left on Rua do Norte.*

HOSTELS

Pousada de Juventude-Lisboa (HI). The hostel is a bit out of the way, but it's near a Metro stop and has a ride board and a popular bar to make up for the midnight curfew. Dorm beds cost 2,350$ (1,900$ Oct.–June), doubles with bath 5,700$ (4,500$ Oct.–June), breakfast included. Pensions are cheaper. *Rua Andrade Corvo 46, tel. 01/353–26–96. Metro: Picoas. Lockout 2 PM–6 PM.*

CAMPING

Parque de Campismo Monsanto. You'll find this campground about 6 km (4 mi) west of the city center in the Parque Florestal Monsanto, next to the freeway. It's partially closed for restoration through mid-1998, but foreign tourists can still camp if they don't mind the temporary lack of amenities. There is a café and grocery store on the premises. One person with tent pays 1,170$; if two share the tent, each pays 1,150$. *Tel. 01/760–20–61. Take Bus 43 from Praça da Figueira.*

FOOD

Lisbon's restaurants tend to serve large, cheap, and almost exclusively Portuguese meals featuring fish, chicken, fish, or chicken. Try some of Portugal's famed pastries at the tiny, unpretentious **Pastelaria A Tentação** (Pr. da Figueira 12, tel. 01/886–87–31), where coffee and the sticky sweet of your choice will cost about 300$. The **Mercado da Ribeira Nova** (market; open Mon.–Sat. 8–1), which almost faces the Estação Cais do Sodré, is prime hunting ground for cheap fruits and vegetables. **Celeiro** (Rua 1° de Dezembro 81, near Estaç ão do Rossio, tel. 01/342–75–41; closed Sat. afternoon and Sun.) has groceries, ready-made food, cold drinks, and an extensive selection of wines. **Celeiro Dieta,** just up the street, is its health-food sister store.

Come nighttime, the otherwise quaint Bairro Alto fills with young, stylish hipsters spilling out of the district's bars and discos. Lisbon's youth parties with the fervor of those who have no home to go to but their parents; they're still arriving at the clubs at 6 AM.

UNDER 1,000$ • Café Geronte. The classy lunch counter (with full bar) makes great coffee and cheap sandwiches (350$–850$), including freshly grilled meats on chewy homemade bread. *Rua de São Pedro de Alcântara 33, at top of Elevador da Glória, no phone. Closed Sun.*

Espiral. This homey, vegetarian, health-food cafeteria hosts meditation and yoga workshops and presents free jazz and ethnic music on Saturday nights. Food is cheap (around 800$), delicious, and filling. There's a health-food grocery in back and a New Age bookstore next door. *Pr. Ilha do Faial 14A–B, tel. 01/573585. From Saldanha Metro, go south on Av. Casal Ribeiro and make a hard left.*

Restaurante Flor do Jasmim. The *bacalhau* and *lulas* (both around 800$) are grilled outdoors at this tiny hole-in-the-wall deep in Mouraria. Good food, good wine, and good company. *Beco do Jasmim 18, no phone. Follow Rua do Capelão up from the Rua da Mouraria. Closed daily 4 PM–7 PM and Sun.*

UNDER 1,500$ • Arroz Doce. Close to bars and clubs in the Bairro Alto, Arroz Doce gets especially lively and crowded after 10 PM. The grilled trout (900$) and grilled chicken (850$) are not small. *Rua da Atalaia 119, no phone. From top of Elevador da Glória, go 2 blocks west.*

Costa do Castelo. Stop here for a beer (200$) on your way up to the Castelo de São Jorge (*see* Worth Seeing, *below*). The food is African and Portuguese, the view of the city is fantastic. Chicken with rice is 800$. *Calçada do Marcos Tancos 1B, off Rua da Costa do Castelo, tel. 01/886–70–08.*

Majong. Sweet-and-sour chicken (850$) and veggie chop suey (800$) have a nouveau-Asian slant and a fresh, nongreasy taste at this hangout for twentysomething locals. After 11 PM, they break out the Foosball table. *Rua da Atalaia 3, tel. 01/342–10–39. From Elevador da Glória, go 2 blocks west, turn right.*

WORTH SEEING

The most appealing thing about Lisbon's central neighborhoods is that they're entirely lived-in. With the exception of the Baixa, urban flight has not emptied the older parts of town; a large portion of the city's population lives, shops, and works in the vicinity. Lisbon's commercial center is the **Baixa,** which stretches inland from the large, riverside Praça do Comércio. Wiped out by the 1755 earthquake and tidal wave, it was rebuilt in a modern grid of parallel streets. Bankers and shoppers crowd the district by day, but the southern end between the Rossio and the river is deserted after sunset; in contrast, the northern end, with its large plazas and pedestrian streets lined with outdoor restaurants, stays alive well through happy hour. Just east of the Baixa lies the **Alfama,** the old Moorish quarter that survived the earthquake; this labyrinth of narrow streets and stairways seems unchanged by time. To reach the **Bairro Alto,** to the west, you could climb an endless series of stairways, but it's more fun to ride one of the elevadores (*see* Getting Around, *above*) up the steep hill. Another historic neighborhood, the **Mouraria,** lies just north and east of the Praça da Figueira. The Mouraria is poorer than the Alfama and much less touristed, but its narrow, black stone walkways and steep stairways make for a satisfying afternoon wander. Southeast of the Bairro Alto, the **Chiado** is the most affluent of Lisbon's neighborhoods. It was wiped out by a 1988 fire and is being rapidly rebuilt with expensive boutiques, trendy cafés, and secondhand bookshops. The **LisboaCard** (1,200$ for 24 hrs, 2,000$ for 48 hrs), available at the tourist office, grants free transportation and free entrance to most museums.

Lisbon is the place to see the normally reserved Portuguese let loose. Bullfights are held all summer long at **Campo Pequeño,** the big arena near the Metro station of the same name; soccer games, held at the **Luz** and **Alvalade** stadiums (near Metro stops Colegio Militar and Campo Grande, respectively), are equally passionate displays. A big victory is cause for huge celebration, usually involving hours of driving up and down main streets honking horns and waving team colors.

CASTELO DE SAO JORGE

The restored medieval battlements of St. George's Castle, on a hill above the Alfama, more or less enclose the site where Lisbon was founded. The Romans, Visigoths, Moors, and medieval Christians are long gone—you'll find only a pricey restaurant and a few peacocks roaming the well-kept gardens—but there is a sense of their presence. There are plenty of places to wander and climb, and the views of Lisbon are excellent. *Rua do Chão da Feira. Take Bus 37 from Pr. da Figueira or Trolley 28 from Rua do Arsenal. Admission free. Open daily 9–7.*

CONVENTO DO CARMO

Largely destroyed by the 1755 earthquake, this derelict convent's remaining arches reach toward the sky, lending a haunting, skeletal feel. Currently undergoing restoration, it should be safe and open for visitors "soon," according to the tourist office. Even if it isn't, this eerily beautiful ruin is worth a peek. *Largo do Carmo, at top of the Elevador Santa Justa.*

FUNDACAO CALOUSTE GULBENKIAN

Armenian oil magnate Calouste Gulbenkian (1869–1955) donated his extensive art collection to the Portuguese people in return for tax concessions, and set up a huge foundation to support literary and cultural activity throughout the country. The Lisbon headquarters, a 10-minute subway ride north of the city center, has two museums. The **Museu Gulbenkian** houses Egyptian, Greek, Roman, Islamic, and Asian, and European art; look for prints by 19th-century Japanese artist Katsushika Hokusai, Van Dyck's *Portrait of a Man,* early Rodin sculptures, and Degas's self-portrait. The **Centro de Arte Moderna** displays works by contemporary Portuguese artists along with rotating international exhibitions. Check out the surrealist works of Fernando de Azevedo and Marcelino Vespeira and the powerful art of Paula Rego. At both museums you'll find good cafés and dirt-cheap posters. The complex has a sculpture garden with duck ponds, shady spots ideal for picnics, and a large amphitheater that hosts occasional free concerts. *Av. de Berna 45, tel. 01/795–02–36. Metro: São Sebastão or Palhavã; walk east. Admission to each museum 500$, free Sun. Open Tues., Thurs., Fri., and Sun. 10–5, Wed. and Sat. 2–7:30.*

IGREJA DE SAO ROQUE

Unremarkable outside but remarkable inside, the Renaissance Church of São Roque has a number of side chapels; the Capela de São João Baptista, for one, has rare stones and mosaics that resemble oil paintings. *Largo Trinidade Coelho, just south of Elevador da Glória. Admission free. Open daily 10–6.*

MOSTEIRO DOS JERONIMOS

This gorgeous Hieronymite monastery in the Belém district has come to symbolize Portugal's seafaring empire and is the single most important example of the Manueline decorative style. Begun in 1496 and finished in the 1600s, the monastery was inspired (and funded) by the voyages of Vasco da Gama, whose tomb is here. The expansive spaces in the main church and cloister represented the growing empire and the riches that the colonies were to provide. The Portuguese Hieronymite order acted as guardians of sailors' souls and prayed for their safe (and profitable) return. Notice the sailor's rope-and-knot motifs in the stonework tracery—the same knots are still used by Portuguese sailors. *Pr. do Império, tel. 01/363–91–45. Trolley 15 or Bus 27, 28, 49, or 51 to Belém, about 30 mins from Pr. da Figueira. Admission 400$; 200$ in winter. Open Tues.–Sun. 10–5.*

Across from the monastery at the water's edge, the **Padrão dos Descobrimentos** (Monument to the Discoveries; admission 310$; open Tues.–Sun. 9:30–6) marks the departure point for many historic voyages. The plaza in front of the monument has an immense compass and map commemorating the Portuguese discoveries. Several hundred feet west is the **Torre de Belém** (admission 400$; open Tues.–Sun. 10–5), constructed in the early 1500s as a defense against pirates and such, and another marvel of Manuelite decoration. The tower, which contains a tiny maritime museum, was once surrounded by water, but the gradual silting of the river has nearly connected it with the land.

CENTRO CULTURAL DE BELEM

This huge complex of concert halls and galleries stands imposingly on the same square as Mosteiro dos Jerónimos. It should stand further back, according to some critics of its austere lines, but it hosts some of Lisbon's most interesting cultural events. *Praça do Imperio, tel. 01/361–24–44. Open daily 1–7:30.*

MUSEU NACIONAL DE ARTE ANTIGA

The National Museum of Art features an extensive collection of 15th-century paintings by Portuguese artists, of whom Nuno Gonçalves is the most famous. His masterpiece, the six-paneled *St. Vincent Altarpiece,* shows the saint receiving the homage of king, court, and citizens. In the general collection, check out Bosch's fanciful *Temptation of St. Anthony* and Dürer's *St. Jeronimo,* with his trademark signature on the lower left side of the bookmark. *Rua das Janelas Verdes 9, tel. 01/396–41–51. Trolley 18 or Bus 40 from Praça da Figueira to Parque 9 de Abril. Admission 500$, free Sun. morning. Open Tues. 2–6, Wed.–Sun. 10–6.*

All day Saturday and every Tuesday morning, the feira da ladra (literally, "thieves' market") fills the Campo de Santo Clara, in the Alfama east of the Castelo de São Jorge. Cheap eats, lots of junk, and goods of questionable origin turn up here.

SE

To commemorate the Christian army's victory over the Moors in 1147, Alfonso Henriques, Portugal's first king, ordered the construction of this *sé* (cathedral) on the site where Lisbon's main mosque once stood. Romanesque in style, the church is formidable and austere, except for its dual rose windows; the 1755 earthquake destroyed its rococo decorations. Your ticket for the 13th-century cloisters and sacristy of treasures also lets you peek at the Roman ruins being unearthed beneath the church. *Largo da Sé. Trolley 28 from Rua do Arsenal. Admission to cloisters 80$. Open daily 9–noon and 2–5.*

AFTER DARK

Lisbon's nightlife is colorful and varied, but generally trendy and somewhat exclusive. This is doubly true of the **Bairro Alto,** one of the centers of the action—restaurants fill up around 10 PM, bars fill up at around 11, and discos start thumping after midnight. Throngs with disco fever head down to **Avenida 24 de Julho,** which extends east along the river from the Cais do Sodré train station, or to the nearby dockside scene at Doca de Santo Amaro. The clubs here tend to have high covers, long lines, and fashion-conscious bouncers who occasionally refuse admittance to the insufficiently attractive. These venues are usually packed until the wee hours.

If for some reason techno doesn't slake your thirst for Portuguese culture, you have plenty of other options. Check out posters around the main plazas for live music at large venues; Lisbon often attracts Brazilian and African groups that don't tour in the States. Tickets to these shows are available at the BAFA kiosk on Praça dos Restauradores. The tourist office hands out *Agenda Cultural,* a free monthly listing of cultural events; for weekly listings of film, theater, and other events, try the Friday edition of *Público* (140$) or **Diario de Noticias** (140$), both available at newspaper kiosks throughout the city.

BARS

The Bairro Alto is filled with trendy bars serving up stiff drinks (400$–800$) and loud music. **Lugar da Rosa** (Rua da Rosa 136, no phone) is lively, as is **Nova** (Rua da Rosa 261, tel. 01/346–28–34), down the street. For no-frills drinking and a less-pretentious student crowd, try **Lua Nova Bar** (Travessa da Queimada 6, tel. 01/642365), across from the Igreja de São Roque (*see* Worth Seeing, *above*). You can take your pick of bars on the Avenida 24 de Julho, but at **Restaurante Francês** (Av. 24 de Julho 110, tel. 01/397–24–21), beers cost half the usual price.

DANCING

The discos in the Bairro Alto tend to be less frenzied and more casual than their counterparts on Avenida 24 de Julho. **3 Pastorinhos** (Rua da Barroca 111, tel. 01/346–43–01) and **Keops** (Rua da Rosa 157, tel. 01/342–87–73) are two favorite bars whose dance floors pick up around 2 AM. That said, Avenida 24 de Julho is the place to go for guaranteed hours of sweaty gyration. Among the most popular places are **Kapital** (Av. 24 de Julho 68, no phone) and **Cargo** (Av. 24 de Julho 84A, tel. 01/600760), both of which have lines, 1,500$ covers, and loud techno.

LIVE MUSIC

The Bairro Alto is home to many tourist-oriented *fado* restaurants, where visitors can experience Portugal's traditional soulful, bluesy singing, accompanied by two guitars. **Restaurante Nó Nó** (Rua do Norte 47, tel. 01/342–99–89) is somewhat less cheesy than the others, though it charges a 2,000$ food/drink minimum per person. Sets start at 11 PM and run continuously until 4 AM. Live Brazilian acts play infectious rhythms nightly at **Pé Sujo** (Largo São Martinho 6–7, tel. 01/886–56–29), in the Alfama near the Sé (*see* Worth Seeing, *above*). A tiny basement in the Bairro Alto, **Hot Clube de Portugal** (Pr. Alegria 39, north of Estação do Rossio, tel. 01/346–76–39; cover 1,000$; closed Mon.), comes to life when the jazz starts. Sets begin at 11 PM and 12:30 AM. Lisbon's largest African club is the **Ritz Club** (Rua da Glória 55, tel. 01/342–51–40; cover 1,000$–2,000$), which has a good house band and special guests.

GAY NIGHTLIFE

Lisbon's gay scene is not strictly separate from the rest of the nightlife; most of the bars and clubs are mixed. There's a late-night pickup scene at **A Brasileira** (Rua Garrett 120–122, tel. 01/346–95–41), in the center of the Chiado. **Frágil** (Rua da Atalaia 126, tel. 01/346–54–31), in the Bairro Alto, is a hopping postmodern techno place with no cover and a mixed clientele.

NEAR LISBON

CASCAIS

Commuter trains leave Lisbon's Estação Cais do Sodré daily every 20 minutes between 5:30 AM and 2:30 AM for the seaside suburb of Cascais (30 mins, 180$). Although mostly unspectacular, this little resort town is a pleasant spot for a day by the sea; its modest patches of sand are connected by a long, stone boardwalk and slope down to beautiful, blue-green waters dotted with fishing boats and pleasurecraft. (There are far better beaches at other train stops nearby, in towns such as Carcavelos and Estoril.) Cascais is full of good pubs, bars, and restaurants, but they're crowded and somewhat pricey in summer, as many Cascais residents are wealthy locals and expats. You may want to pack a picnic.

SINTRA

By far the best day trip from Lisbon, this cool, green mountain town 27 km (16½ mi) west of Lisbon was once a summer playground for European aristocrats. Described by Lord Byron as a "glorious Eden," Sintra enchants with its verdant landscapes and its exotic palaces dating from the 15th to the 19th centuries. A day's hike will bring you past several of these and allow you to explore the fabulous **Pena Park**—a green, hilly expanse worthy of only the highest praise—and the romantic remains of a Moorish castle.

The 14th-century **Paço Real** (Royal Palace), with its huge, conical twin chimneys, sits in the center of the *vila velha* (old town) and flaunts a combination of Moorish, Gothic, and Manueline architecture. To see the interior, with its fabulous *mudéjar* (Moorish-style) tilework, you have to join the guided tour. *Pr. da República, tel. 01/923–00–85. Tours 400$; 200$ Oct.–May. Open Thurs.–Tues. 10–1 and 2–5.*

From the steps of the palace you can see the ruins of the 8th-century **Castelo dos Mouros** (Moorish Castle; Estrada da Pena, tel. 01/923–51–16; open daily 10–7). For a romp through its ruins (admission free) and some overgrown gardens with spectacular views, follow the signs for a 1½-hour climb up the steep road. Backtrack along the same road to find the entrance to Pena Park and the **Palácio da Pena** (tel. 01/923–02–27; open Tues.–Sun. 10–1 and 2–5); this fantastic castle, complete with turrets, ramparts, and domes, was created in 1839 out of the ruins of a 16th-century monastery. The interior is furnished with turn-of-the-century furniture and trimmings owned by Portugal's last royal family, who fled the country in 1910. Admission 400$; 200$ October–May.

Trains leave for Sintra every 12 minutes between 6 AM and 2 AM from Lisbon's Estação do Rossio (45 mins, 180$). Sintra's **train station** (Av. Miguel Bombarda, tel. 01/346–50–22) has a small **tourist office** (open daily 9–8) where you can get a free map and other information. As you exit the station, the old town is to your left, and the *vila nova* (new town), where the town lives its own life, is to your right. The walk to the center of the old town winds uphill on a tree-lined road and takes about 15 minutes. If the thought of fighting gravity overwhelms you, **buses** run every half hour from near the train station. All-day tickets cost 500$. The **post office** (Praça da República 26, tel. 01/924–15–90) doubles as a phone office and is open weekdays 9–12:30 and 1:30–6.

WHERE TO SLEEP AND EAT • On top of a wooded mountain in Pena Park, Sintra's **HI hostel** (Santa Eufémia, tel. 01/924–12–10; beds 1,750$) is the best in Portugal, and since everyone knows it, you'll want to make reservations. The rooms have incredible views of the woods and castles. Restaurants in the old town can be pricey, so try **Restaurante Dom Pedro** (Av. Miguel Bombarda 15, 1 block west of train station), with grilled fish and meat dishes (850$–1,000$) in a friendly, local atmosphere.

SOUTHERN PORTUGAL

In contrast to the lush north, most of southern Portugal is open, dry, rolling land interspersed with vineyards, wheat fields, cork and olive groves, and expanses of sunflowers. The people of the rural Alentejo region are, on the whole, poorer than their northern counterparts and often subject to the whims of powerful *monte* (farm) owners, who control nearly all the land and resources. Despite the hardships of life here, the southern Portuguese are extremely friendly, and you may find yourself becoming a bit friendlier, too, after a few days of heady Alentejo wine, hot sun, and slow living. This timeless atmosphere changes dramatically once you hit the Algarve, Portugal's southern coast and most heavily visited region. Here, plantations and fishing villages are giving way to luxury hotels and time-share condos. Not to worry; there are still some pockets of tranquility, and plenty of outstanding beaches. Consider buses for long-distance trips in the south—they're faster than trains, they sometimes show movies, and, most important, they're air-conditioned.

EVORA

The principal city of the Alentejo region, southeast of Lisbon, Évora's abundance of historic buildings and monuments has won it a UNESCO designation as a World Heritage Site. Throughout the small city, mixtures of Roman, Moorish, Gothic, and Manueline buildings surround serene plazas. Revenue from the upscale tourist trade has established a higher standard of living and higher prices here than in most of the surrounding region, but Évora is not exclusive; students from the centuries-old university liven things up considerably when they emerge from their daily heat-induced hibernation to join the old men and pigeons in the Praça do Giraldo.

BASICS

Free illustrated city maps are available at the centrally located **posto de turismo** (Pr. do Giraldo 73, tel. 066/22671; open weekdays 9–7, weekends 9–12:30 and 2–5:30). Just outside is a 24-hour exchange machine. Cash traveler's checks at one of the banks (many with ATMs) around Praça do Giraldo. The **post office** (Rua de Olivença, at Pr. de Sertorio, 2 blocks north of Pr. do Giraldo, tel. 066/29250; open weekdays 8:30–6:30, Sat. 9–12:30) doubles as a phone office. The postal code is 7000.

COMING AND GOING

The **bus station** (Rua da República, at Rua de Cisioso, tel. 066/22121), 4 blocks downhill from the Praça do Giraldo, has regular service to Lisbon (1¾ hrs, 1,350$) and Faro (4½ hrs, 1,600$). The **train station** (Largo da Estação, tel. 066/221225) is about 1 km (½ mi) farther from the center in the same direction. The trip to Lisbon (3 hrs) costs 965$–1,105$, but you may have to change trains in Casa Branca. To reach the town center, head right out of the station and take your first left onto Avenida de Dr. Barahona; you'll cross a fairground and pass under a set of arches, where the road turns into Rua da República and leads to the center. If you arrive in Évora in the brutal midday heat, however, do yourself a favor and grab a cab (500$). Neither station has luggage storage.

WHERE TO SLEEP

Évora's pensions are a bit nicer and more expensive than those in most other Portuguese cities. Your cheapest option in the center is a room in a private home, booked through the tourist office; a double should be about 4,000$ in the off season. Two reasonably priced options are **Residencial O Alentejo** (Rua Serpa Pinto 74, downhill from church on Praça do Giraldo, tel. 066/22903), which charges 6,500$ for a classy double with bath, breakfast, and TV, and **Pensão Policarpo Residencial** (Rua Freiria de Baixo, 16, tel. 066/22424), which has doubles with bath for 4,500$ and up. You can camp 2 km (1 mi) from town at the well-equipped **Parque de Campismo** (tel. 066/25190), where you'll pay 550$ per person and 450$ per tent. Follow Rua do Raimundo to the highway and look for signs, or take the bus (200$) towards Valverde, which leaves the bus station at 1 PM and 5:30 PM—tell the driver you want to get off at *o campismo* (the campground).

FOOD

Most of the restaurants near the Praça do Giraldo are tourist traps. A notable exception is **Café Alentejo** (Rua do Raimundo 5–7, tel. 066/20640), where basic dishes such as grilled fish with potatoes and salad cost around 900$. The dining room closes at 11 PM, at which point the bar in the next room starts filling up with a talkative local crowd. A bit further afield, cafeteria-style **Restaurante Jovem** (Pátio do Salema, tel. 066/22426) serves cheap meals like fish and rice (750$) and grilled lamb (800$) to a student crowd and doubles as a nightspot, with a huge pool hall next door and occasional performances by local rock and jazz bands. To get here, go up the stairs from Rua Miguel Bombarda, then follow the signs toward Residencial Diana. **Adega do Alentejano** (Rua Gabriel Vitor do Monte Pereira, 21 A, tel. 066/744447) serves excellent, hearty regional fare in a huge, old Alentejo wine cellar. A meal with wine from the barrel will run you 800$–1,200$. For coffee and homemade ice cream, head back down the hill to **Gelataria Zoka** (Rua Miguel Bombarda 14, tel. 066/22652). If you prefer to fend for yourself, you'll find great produce and cheese at a little unnamed **market** at Travessa do Sertorio 15, on the way to the post office from Praça do Giraldo.

WORTH SEEING

Évora's main sights are marked on the illustrated map provided by the tourist office, but you'll find most of them just walking around town. (Note that most of Évora's museums are closed Mondays.) Local legend holds that the 2nd-century **Templo Romano** (Largo da Conde Vila Flor, uphill from post office) was dedicated to the adoration of the goddess Diana, but the site, a series of granite columns on a stagelike platform, was used as a slaughterhouse until the 19th century. Steps away, the **Museu de Évora** (Largo da Conde Vila Flor; admission 200$; open Tues.–Sun. 10–12:30 and 2–5) has a rich collection of paintings and Roman artifacts. Around the corner, the 12th-century Romanesque and Gothic **Sé** (Rua 5 de Outubro; open Tues.–Sun. 9–noon and 2–5) houses the **Museu de Arte Sacra.** The 350$ admission buys you a peek at the cathedral's wooden high choir and its cloister, where spooky winding staircases lead to great rooftop views of the Alentejo countryside.

The main attraction of the grand 16th-century **Igreja de São Francisco** is the singularly gruesome **Capela dos Ossos** (Chapel of Bones), the walls of which are lined with the skulls and bones of 5,000 people. The rhyming welcome inscribed over the entrance translates roughly as "Here we bones are, waiting for yours." In case you miss the point, a plaque hanging in the chapel begins "Where are you going, walking so fast?" *Pr. 1 de Maio, 1 block uphill from bus station, tel. 066/24521. Admission 100$, 50$ more to take pictures. Open Mon.–Sat. 8:30–1 and 2:30–6, Sun. 10–11:30 and 2–6; shorter hrs off season.*

THE ALGARVE

Visitors flock to Portugal's sunny southern coast to enjoy a year-round mild climate, spectacular beaches, warm waters, and cheap seafood. Some never leave—the Algarve is home to hundreds of expatriates (mainly British and Dutch) who have either retired here or opened up pubs and restaurants to serve those who have. Unfortunately, development has left its mark on the region in the form of pricey five-star hotels and concrete high-rise apartment buildings. Your best bet for relative privacy is either edge of the region: **Tavira** to the east and **Sagres** at the western tip. If you want the company of bronzed, beery backpackers, try **Lagos.** Whatever your inclinations, be sure to savor the local specialties, including the hearty *cataplana* (a tomato-based stew of fish and prawns), tasty *lulas recheias* (fried and stuffed), and delicate *amendôa amarga.*

Once a mellow fishing village, **Faro,** the capital of the Algarve, has been transformed into a bustling commercial center and is the transport hub for the rest of the region. Arriving in Faro from Lisbon (5½ hrs by bus, 2,000$; 5 hrs by train, 1,950$), you'll probably want to leave as soon as possible. Getting around the Algarve is cheap and easy: Several trains run daily from Lagos, in the west, to **Vila Real de Santo António,** in the east. Several trains run daily along the route, which takes three to four hours to complete (some of the faster trains don't stop at every station). The transfer point for northbound trains is **Tunes,** roughly halfway between Lagos and Faro—you can buy a long-distance ticket at any station, but you'll probably need to change trains here. Buses follow roughly the same route as trains, and some continue west to Sagres. August is the Algarve's busiest month, but crowds start drifting in around July and don't thin out until September. Local tourist offices can be an invaluable asset in this region, especially during the busiest months. Most have English-speaking personnel who can make reservations at pensions (essential in August at nicer places), locate rooms in private homes, and provide bus and train schedules. If at all possible, visit the Algarve off season, when the crowds disappear and prices decrease by a third to half.

TAVIRA

Tavira, 30 km (18 mi) east of Faro, is an enormously friendly and pleasant little town. Though justly popular with travelers, it has yet to sell its briny soul to tourism, as its primary income is still derived from farming, fishing, and salt. Tavira's tourist attractions include the requisite churches and a crumbling castle, but you'll probably want to focus on the long white beaches of the **Ilha de Tavira** (Tavira Island), just outside town. To get to the island, follow the palm-lined Rua do Cais along the Gilão River for 2 km (1 mi) to the Quatro Aguas ferry landing (100$ round-trip; operates 8 AM–9 PM, weekends until 10 PM), or, in July and August, take a bus from the Praça da República, just outside the cinema. Off season, the ferry runs less regularly, but local fishermen will take passengers for about the same price as the ferry. The **posto de turismo** (Rua da Galeria 9, tel. 081/22511; open daily 9:30–7:00 June–Sept; 9:30–5:30 Oct.–May), just up the stairs off the Praça da República, has free maps and transport schedules and can call around for a room if you need help.

Sintra is famous for its queijadas (small, floury cheesecakes). The best are reputed to come from Queijadas da Sapa, at Volta do Duche 12, between the Câmara Municipal and the center of the vila velha.

COMING AND GOING

Tavira's **train station** (tel. 081/22354), about 1½ km (1 mi) from the center of town, is a minor stop on the Algarve line, with fairly frequent service to Lagos (2½ hrs, 860$) and Faro (35 mins, 280$). Taxis meet trains at the station, but the walk to town only takes about 15 minutes. You'll see three roads as you leave the station; the middle one leads straight to the Praça da República. The **bus station** (Rua dos Pelames, tel. 081/22546) is by the river, a few blocks west of the main plaza; it serves Lisbon (5 hrs, 2,500$) and Évora (5 hrs, 1,800$), among other destinations, but you might have to change buses in Faro for northbound trips.

WHERE TO SLEEP

During high season, try to arrive early in the day, as rooms fill up quickly. **Pensão Almirante** (Rua Almirante Cândido dos Reis 51, tel. 081/22163) is the best pension value around, with tiny doubles for 4,000$ and very friendly service. Cross the river, go up 1 block, and turn right. The sunny, plant-filled **Pensão Mirante** (Rua da Liberdade 83, tel. 081/22255) has 4,500$ doubles just 2 blocks from the main plaza. From May through September, you can pitch a tent (580$ for a single or 630$ for a double, plus 370$ per person) at the **Parque de Campismo Ilha de Tavira** (tel. 081/324455)—it's an unspectacular sandy expanse surrounded by a fence, but it's close to the beach and has well-maintained showers (100$ for a hot one, nothing for a cold), laundry, phones, and a minimarket.

FOOD

Tavira has many good, inexpensive seafood restaurants. In the gardens along the river, **Restaurante América** (Rua José Pires Padinha 2, tel. 081/23330) offers cheap daily specials (750$–900$) and cheesy decor; swordfish steak with all the fixings is just 900$. **Restaurante Bica** (Rua Almirante Cândido dos Reis 22, tel. 081/23843), below Residencial Lagões, has an ever-changing menu of marvelous seafood and other dishes typical of the Algarve, such as the mountain of clams in garlic sauce for 800$. Pick up fresh produce at the **mercado** on Rua do Cais, near the garden.

LAGOS

Few cities on the Algarve are more popular—or rowdier—than Lagos. Situated at the western end of the Algarve rail line, Lagos attracts a mix of young foreign and Portuguese travelers. High season turns the train station into a sea of dusty rucksacks, the beaches into a mass of sunburn victims, and the nights into a scene from a spring-break movie. The main draw, of course, is the spectacular coast, with post-card-perfect beaches, multihued rock formations, and brilliant waters.

Long before it became a hotspot for tourists, Lagos was a critical naval center. In the 15th century, Por-tuguese ships returning from the coast of Africa unloaded cargoes of gold, ivory, and slaves here. The **Mercado Antigo dos Escravos** (on the northeast corner of Pr. Dom Henriques) was one of Europe's first African slave markets. The **João Cutileiro** statue in Praça Gil Eanes depicts Dom Sebastião, a boy king who led nearly 8,000 Portuguese to their (and his) deaths on a failed 1578 crusade to Morocco. (Poorly led and inappropriately dressed for the African heat, Sebastião's army was easily slaughtered by the more numerous Moors; the boy went on to become a legendary figure who would one day return to lead his people.) Lagos's most unusual attraction is the **Museu Municipal** (Rua General Alberto da Silveira 1, tel. 082/762301; admission 320$; open Tues.–Sun. 9:30–12:30 and 2–5), where an eclectic collection of pottery, guns, animal fetuses, and mannequins are assembled in an attempt to illustrate the town's history. The adjacent **Igreja de Santo António** is adorned with rich, gilded wood carvings. Many of the central streets are pedestrian walks packed with strolling musicians, street artists, human statues, and the like. The new **Centro Cultural** (Cultural Center, Rua Lançarote de Freitas 7; tel. 082/763403) hosts exhibitions, film and music festivals, and other cultural events.

If you'd rather stick to sun, sand, and salt water, there's a nice beach just down the street from the Praça Infante Dom Henrique, at the foot of the **Forte do Pau da Bandeira,** a former battlement. The long beach you see across town is actually in the town of Meia Praia; it's exposed and blustery here, so expect a bit of a sandstorm. A 1½-hour hike roams along the cliffs past a number of accessible beaches, great vistas, and small snack bars to the **Ponta da Piedade lighthouse.** The beaches become more secluded the farther you go, and the last grotto before the lighthouse shelters a tiny nude beach, acces-sible via a steep but manageable trail over what appears to be the edge of the cliff. Though the beach is barely visible from the clifftop, it is quite exposed to boats taking tourists on grotto tours. Past the light-house, you'll find more grottoes and the popular beaches **Praia Canavial** and **Praia do Mós,** both well equipped with bars and bathers. To reach the trailhead, follow the main road to Sagres south for about five minutes and look for signs to **Praia do Pinhão;** you'll see the trail to your right at the entrance to the beach. If you don't feel like hiking to the beaches, hop a bus from the center of town.

BASICS

The **posto de turismo** (Largo Marquês de Pombal, just west of Pr. Gil Eanes, tel. 082/763031; open daily 9–7:30) has a message board and plenty of transport information. The staff books rooms for free and hands out free but lame city maps—leaf through the mountains of brochures to find a better one, or hunt one down in the tourism office at the **Camara Municipal** (Town Hall) in Pr. Gil Eanes. Most **bureaux de change** in Lagos stay open until 10 PM or later, and all will exchange traveler's checks commission-free. The **post office** (Rua das Portas de Portugal, at Pr. Gil Eanes; open weekdays 9–6; postal code 8600) doles out poste restante 9–noon. You can make phone calls here or at the adjacent **Telecom Por-tugal** (open daily 8:30–7).

COMING AND GOING

The **train station** (tel. 082/762987) is less than a 10-minute walk from the town center, just over a foot-bridge that crosses a small channel. Ten trains a day run east to Tavira (2½ hrs, 820$) and Faro (3 hrs, 700$). The **bus station** (Rossio de São João Bautista, tel. 082/762944) is just 1 block inland from the channel. Buses leave frequently for Sagres (50 mins, 445$), Évora (5 hrs, 1,700$), and Lisbon (4½ hrs, 2,100$). Buses also serve Seville, Spain (5 hrs, 2,050$) Thurs.–Sun. The **private buses** (Mundial de Turismo and Sol Expresso) in the same station are slightly more expensive, but they're faster and more comfortable. The Avenida dos Descobrimentos, a wide, palm-lined promenade, runs along the channel and leads to the yacht harbor and the central Praça Gil Eanes.

If you want to explore remote stretches of coastline, **Motöride Aluguermoto** (Rua José Alfonso 23, tel. 082/761720) rents dinky scooters for 2,000$ a day. Their lot is west of the youth hostel, just outside the old city wall. Bring your passport and a 5,000$ deposit.

WHERE TO SLEEP

Pensions and hotels are often booked for the entire summer and are usually expensive. Your best bet is the youth hostel or a room in a private home. Local residents with spaces to let will accost you in the train and bus stations, the tourist office, and the main squares. Competition has driven room prices down to about 1,000$–1,500$ per person, and you can often find four-person apartments with kitchens for 6,000$–10,000$ a night.

The modern **HI Pousada de Juventude Lagos** (Rua Lançarote de Freitas 50, tel. 082/761970) is centrally located and has a kitchen, but beware—it's often full. There is no curfew or lockout, and you might be able to squeak by with a passport if you don't have an HI card. Beds are 1,800$; 1,400$ Oct.–June. From the train station, cross the bridge, walk down Avenida dos Descobrimentos to Praça da República, and follow the signs. The most reasonable pension in town is **Rubi Mar** (Rua da Barroca 70, tel. 082/763165), where clean, pleasant doubles are 4,500$ (3,500$ Oct.–June) and include a good breakfast. **Pensão Caravela** (Rua 25 de Abril 16, tel. 082/763361) offers a double with breakfast from 4,500$. Lagos has two campgrounds. **Trindade** (Rua Dona Ana, tel. 082/763165) is cramped and ugly but comes cheap: 450$ per person and 450$ per tent (350$ and 370$ off season). From Avenida dos Descobrimentos, take the first right west of town and follow the signs. Much nicer is the enormous **Imulagos** (Estrada do Porto de Mós, tel. 082/760031), west of town (follow the signs) overlooking the water. The good life—which here includes pool access (500$ extra), laundry, a minimarket, a disco, and transport to and from the train station—is yours for a hefty 890$ per person and 500$ per tent (595$ and 295$ off season).

If traditional souvenirs seem too tame, try The Body Shock (Rua Vasco da Gama, across from bus station), where you can bring home your very own tattoo, nipple piercing, or eyebrow ring.

FOOD

Lagos is filled with tourist-oriented restaurants and cafés, many with outdoor seating, especially along Rua 25 de Abril and Rua Silva Lopes. Prices are almost uniform: expect to pay 600$–900$ for pizza, 850$–1,100$ for seafood dishes, and 250$–350$ for beer. Just south of the hostel, **Restaurante-Bar Primavera** (Rua Lançarote de Freitas 11, tel. 082/764226) serves tasty meals like grilled mackerel (900$) in an elegant atmosphere. For Portuguese dishes such as *feijoada á portuguesa* (bean stew, 800$) or *ensopado de lulas* (squid stew, 750$), go to **Churrasqueira O Franguinho** (Rua Prof. Luis de Azevedo 25, no phone). The small meat, cheese, and apple pies (150$–300$) at **Borley's Fresh Foods** (Rua Marreiros Neto 16, tel. 082/762353) make excellent beach snacks. Cheap fruits and vegetables abound at the **mercado** (Av. dos Descobrimentos, 1 block west of Pr. Gil Eanes).

AFTER DARK

Lagos is a party town. Scouts working on commission will fill your pockets with flyers offering free shots and cheap drinks. They find no shortage of willing customers, and the bars fill up quickly with a young, hard-drinking international crowd. The infamous **Joe's Garage** (Rua de Maio 78, tel. 082/761720) tries hard to be the alternative hangout, but it's essentially just another boozy pickup spot. **Mullens** (Rua Cândido dos Reis 86, tel. 082/761281), directly opposite, has a friendly atmosphere and serves stiff drinks at average prices. **Tribes & Vibes** (Rua Marreiros Neto 52) plays hip-hop to a mellower crowd and serves slices of pizza (200$) until 2 AM. The only dance place in town is **Phoenix** (Rua de S. Gonçalo de Lagos 29, no phone; cover 1,800$), a techno disco just around the corner from the hostel; it starts to fill up around 2 AM, when the bars close.

SAGRES

Rocky, windswept Sagres, with its edge-of-the-earth atmosphere, is the most dramatic place on the Algarve. Strong winds stir the Atlantic here, and relentless waves beat against awesome, sheer cliffs as high as 500 feet. Remote Sagres attracts no package tours; it's popular with backpackers, motorcyclists, vagabonds, and bohemians inspired by the desolate beauty and vast ocean vistas. The train doesn't even come this far west; catch a bus from Lagos (50 mins, 400$), or be a true road warrior and rent a scooter (*see* Coming and Going *in* Lagos, *above*). On the way, you'll pass a number of roads leading to gorgeous, semideserted beaches where windsurfers practice their moves.

The town's layout is simple: a long street connects the fishing harbor, bus stop, and sheltered **city beach** on one end with the earthquake-damaged *fortaleza* (fortress) and an abandoned museum project on the other. West of town lie several prime beaches. The wide, golden beach next to the fortress is often impossibly windy and its waters unsafe for swimming, but **Praia do Beliche,** 4 km (2½ mi) farther down the road, is both safe and beautiful. **Cabo de São Vicente,** at the west end of the road, is a rugged cape with a beautiful lighthouse and even more stunning cliff-top views. To explore the area, rent a mountain bike (1,200$ for 4 hrs, 1,900$ for 8 hrs) from **Turinfo** (Pr. da República, tel. 082/64520), a private tourist service in what passes for the center of Sagres, or hop on the campground's free bus.

WHERE TO SLEEP AND EAT

Your best bet for a bed in Sagres is a private home. You'll probably be accosted at the bus stop by people offering doubles for around 2,500$ in the low season, 3,000$ in summer. Otherwise, walk along the road in either direction and inquire at places with QUARTOS signs. Turinfo tends to push the pricier places. The **Parque de Campismo Sagres** (tel. 089/64371) is in a wooded expanse about halfway between the fortress and Cabo de São Vicente. Rates are 500$ per person and 500$ per tent (300$ and 350$ off season), and the campground has a restaurant, a market, a laundromat, and hot showers (100$). Free shuttles run from the bus stop to the campground six times daily between 10 and 5.

Pick up inexpensive sandwiches and picnic supplies at small markets on the main drag. The cafés and restaurants on Praça da República serve decently priced meals; **Café Conchinho** (Praça da República, no phone) has good seafood at great prices (500$–800$). There are a number of sleepy bars here as well. Most popular is **Rosa dos Ventos** (Pr. da República, tel. 089/64480), where folks gather to celebrate being on the edge of the continent.

NORTHERN PORTUGAL

In the northern Minho, Douro, and Trás-os-Montes regions, bald and rocky mountain ranges are separated by rich, green river valleys. The northern Portuguese, whether rural wine-grape growers or industrious city dwellers, have a reputation for conservative attitudes and a deep respect for traditional religious, social, and political values. Their rural areas are some of the most remote and least visited in Portugal, especially the northeast, which sees very little tourism. There are some important cities here, however, including **Coimbra,** a lively university town; **Oporto,** an industrial capital famous for the fortified wine of the same name; and **Braga,** home to some spectacular ecclesiastical architecture and the transport hub to the northern and northeastern corners of the country.

COIMBRA

Coimbra is a lively university city with a rich past. It was erected on the site of a Roman city called Aeminium and was the capital of Portugal for more than a hundred years, beginning in the 12th century. The university, founded in 1290, wasn't permanently installed here until 1537, but today, perched on a hill above the Mondego River, it is the distinguishing feature of the city's social and physical landscape. The student population dominates this part of town, which, with its churches, monuments, and parks, is also the area of most interest to visitors. In late May, the whole place bursts into activity for the **Queima das Fitas** (Burning of the Ribbons), the students' end-of-the-year bash, which is celebrated with Coimbra's unique brand of *fado* and large amounts of beer and champagne.

The upper town and the university contrast sharply with the commercial district down the hill, which is basically a maze of winding cobbled walkways packed with shoppers. Modern Coimbra is a no-nonsense city that seems to value content over form—its streets are crowded; its restaurants are cheap, cavernous cafeterias or holes-in-the-wall serving regional food; and its residents always seem en route to somewhere important. The beautiful old buildings dotting the cityscape, however, attest to a monumental past. The combination bodes well—you've got all the distractions of a modern city along with enough culture and history to satisfy the most ardent shutterbug.

BASICS

Get free maps and transport information at Coimbra's **main tourist office** (Largo da Portagem, at foot of Ponte Santa Clara, tel. 039/23886; open weekdays 9–7, weekends 9–1 and 2–5:30), in the commercial district 3 blocks east of the Coimbra A train station. Two other branches are in the upper town: on Praça da República (tel. 039/33202; open weekdays 10–6:30) and on the university grounds (Pr. Dom Dinis, tel. 039/32591; open weekdays 9–6, weekends 9–12:30 and 2–5:30). **Banks** along Rua Ferreira Borges, which separates the upper and lower towns, are open weekdays 8–3. **Montepio Geral** (Largo do Portagem, tel. 039/28031; open weekdays 8–3) is just behind the main tourist office and charges no commission for transactions under 10,000$. The **main post office** (Av. Fernão Magalhães 223, tel. 039/28181; open weekdays 8:30–6:30) is halfway between the Coimbra A train station and the bus station. Poste restante should be addressed to the Estação Central; the postal code is 3000. Another convenient post office is next to the market (Rua Olímpio Nicolau Rui Fernandes, tel. 039/24356; open weekdays 8:30–6:30, Sat. 9–12:30).

COMING AND GOING

Coimbra has three train stations: **Coimbra A** (Av. Fernão Magalhães, at Largo da Portagem), in the heart of the city; **Coimbra B,** 7 km (4½ mi) north of the center; and **Coimbra Parque**—next to Parque Manuel de Braga, a 5-minute walk from the center—with trains to Central Portugal. Trains from Lisbon (2½ hrs, 1,390$) and Oporto (1¾ hrs, 940$) arrive at Coimbra B, where a free shuttle train heads into Coimbra A. Schedules and information area available at either station, or call **CP** (tel. 039/34998). The **bus station** (Av. Fernão Magalhães, tel. 039/27081) is 1 km (9½ mi) north of Coimbra A and offers express service to Lisbon (2½ hrs, 1,350$) and Oporto (1 hr, 1,200$) and local service to Leiria (1 hr, 850$), Fátima (1 hr, 1,100$), Batalha (1½ hrs, 1,000$), and Luso (45 mins, 405$), among other destinations.

GETTING AROUND

Coimbra is not large, but it is hilly. The main business promenade, **Rua Ferreira Borges,** runs northwest from the main bridge, **Ponte Santa Clara.** Bus 5 passes both train stations and the Terminal Rodoviária every 15 minutes until midnight, running through the commercial district and up to the **Praça da República** (near the university) and continuing on to the campground. Most other buses run up the hill to the Praça da República; just ask the driver. Individual tickets, purchased on the bus, are 205$, or you can buy a book of 10 at any newspaper kiosk for 620$.

WHERE TO SLEEP

The commercial district practically overflows with affordable, but mediocre, pensions. From Coimbra A, go 1 block up from the river and turn left to reach the friendly **Pensão da Sota** (Rua da Sota 41, tel. 039/22732), which is slightly less dingy than it looks from the outside and is the cheapest in the area: doubles are 2,500$. The immaculate **Pensão Residência Gouveia** (Rua João de Ruão 21, tel. 039/29793; doubles 3,000$) is in the busy shopping area—a great place to stay if you don't want to be too far from either the sights or the train station. If you prefer calm, stay near the university. **Residência Santa Cruz** (Rua Castro Matoso 4, tel. 039/23657) has spotless doubles with bath for 3,000$ (4,000$ July–Aug.); in its other excellent location, in front of the 12th-century monastery Church of Santa Cruz (Praça 8 de Maio, tel. 039/26197), doubles with private bath, TV, and balcony run 4,500$. An **HI Pousada de Juventude** has been under construction in Praça 25 de Abril; the tourist-office types promised a late-1997 opening. The uninspiring **Parque de Campismo** (Rua General Humberto Delgado, tel. 039/701497), 2 km (1 mi) southeast of the center, charges 231$ per person and 153$ per tent. Bus 5 will get you here from the bus/train stations or the Praça da República.

FOOD

Coimbra is a university town, and students demand cheap meals. Several cantinas near the university do the trick. The **Cantina Central** (Rua Dr. Oliva Matos 22, tel. 039/26748; open weekdays 8 AM–9:30 PM), in an unmarked building at the foot of the stairs leading up to the university, serves full meals for under 500$, though sometimes they ask for a student ID (any student ID will do). **UC Cantina,** across the street, has cheap daily selections, such as grilled chicken or pizza, for about 250$ and stays open seven days a week until 3 AM. Alternatively, try the workers' cafés along **Rua Ferreira Borges,** which stay full all day and have cheap snacks, or the places on **Rua des Azeiteiros,** off Praça do Comércio. For excellent fruits, vegetables, cheeses, and sausages, hit the **mercado** (Rua Olímpio Nicolau Rui Fernandes; open Mon.–Sat. 9–3), a few blocks above Praça 8 de Maio. If the market's closed, head downhill to the massive **Pingo Doce** supermarket (Rua João de Ruão 25, across from Pensão Residencial Gouveia).

WORTH SEEING

Coimbra's principal sights are clustered in the historical city center, which crowns a large hill above the commercial district. If you enter the old city through the **Arco de Almedina** (Rua Ferreira Borges), a steep, winding flight of steps called *quebra costas* (backbreaker) will lead you to the 12th-century **Sé Velha** (Largo da Sé Velha; open daily 9–6:30). This musty cathedral houses Portugal's oldest cloisters (admission 100$) and beautiful *azulejos* (decorative tiles) brought from Seville in 1503. Above the cathedral, the **Museu Nacional Machado Castro** (Largo de Dr. José Rodrigues, tel. 039/23727; open Tues.–Sun. 10–12:30 and 2–5; admission: 250$) houses paintings, sculpture, and furniture in what was formerly the bishop's palace. Under the museum is the cryptoportico, three tiers of spooky rooms used as storerooms for the Roman forum that originally stood on the site.

At the crest of the hill is the **Universidade de Coimbra,** whose central complex, **O Pátio,** is as much a museum as an institution of higher learning. The courtyard is dominated by an 18th-century clock and bell tower, Coimbra's most recognized landmark. The **Sala dos Capelos** (Ceremonial Hall; literally, "Hall of the Hoods"), which you're allowed to view only from a balcony, oozes pomp, with its wood-paneled ceiling and intricately painted tiles. The **Biblioteca Joanina** (King João's Library; ring bell to left of door), an exercise in baroque opulence, contains rosewood-and-ebony tables and richly inlaid bookshelves—not the kind of place to put your feet up with a paperback. The "marble" columns and arches are actually made of wood, as are the curtains around the portrait of King João (1730). Also included in the 500$ admission is the **Museum of Sacred Art.**

Across the bridge, on the other side of the river, are some other gems: **Portugal dos Pequenos,** a miniature city with Portugal's most outstanding historic buildings and monuments; the 12th-century **Santa Clara Velha** convent; and the convent's 17th-century version, **Santa Clara Nova.** Take Bus 46 from Largo da Portagem.

AFTER DARK

Mild evenings find the student population knocking back beers and coffees at the outdoor bars and cafés of the Praça da República. The **Café-Galeria Almedina** (Rua Ferreira Borges, at Arco de Almedina), at the border between the upper and lower towns, is also popular and occasionally hosts live acoustic music (no cover). Dancing fools can join the masses at crowded **Via Latina** (Rua Almeida Garrett 1, just off Pr. da República, tel. 039/33034), where the cover runs 500$–1,000$. For special events, check the bulletin boards in university buildings and around the student cantinas.

OUTDOOR ACTIVITIES

Any day between April 1 and October 15, you can spend several hours kayaking the Mondego River (3,000$) or mountain biking in the nearby Penacova hills (3,000$) with the student-run **O Pioneiro do Mondego** (tel. 039/478385). For information and reservations, call the English-speaking staff 1 PM–3 PM or 8 PM–10 PM at least a day in advance—they'll come pick you up near the main tourist office. **Oda Barca** offers 1-hour boat trips on the Mondego during the summer, daily except Monday. The boats leave from Dr. Manuel Braga Park, on the river.

NEAR COIMBRA

FOREST OF BUCACO

This 250-acre wooded park, 25 km (15 mi) from Coimbra, was once a silent retreat for barefoot Carmelite monks, who imported hundreds of trees here from all over the world. The shady expanse is an enchanting place to spend a day following the monks' footsteps along tangled, but well-maintained, forest paths. The Coimbra tourist office can supply a map showing springs, tiny chapels, and panoramic lookouts in the forest. To get here, take an RBL bus (destination: Guimaraes) from the bus station to the sleepy spa town of Luso (45 mins, 400$) and walk five minutes to the southern park entrance, or catch one of the two daily Luso/Buçaco trains from Coimbra A or B (215$). Though the entire park can be seen in a day, consider spending the night in one of Luso's beautiful and affordable pensions. The **Pensão Choupal-Residencial** (Largo Poeta Cavador, tel. 031/939628) has huge, elegant doubles for 4,600$, including breakfast. Luso's **tourist office** (Rua Emidio Navarro, tel. 031/939133) can help with transport and lodging information.

CONIMBRIGA

The ruins of this Roman city overlook a deep, idyllic valley with shaded walks and picnic grounds. Conimbriga's buildings, aqueduct, and walls date from the beginning of the 2nd century to the end of the 4th century, and the adjoining modern museum has objects from the Roman and Visigoth periods. Bonus: the snack bar overlooking the ruins is clean, airy, and cheap. Direct buses run by **AVIC** (Rua João de Ruão 18, tel. 039/23769) leave Coimbra at 9:35 AM and return from Conimbriga at 1 PM or 6 PM (250$ round trip); the ride takes half an hour. Admission to the site (ruins and museum) is 350$.

BATALHA

This vast monastery (officially called Santa Maria da Vitória Batalha) is both Portugal's most important Gothic site and a symbol of the country's independence from Spain. It was built at the behest of King João I, who, while taking abuse from the Spaniards in a 1385 battle at nearby Aljubarrota, made a vow to build the Virgin Mary a monument if he prevailed. God helped out, João won, and Mary got her monastery. Construction began in 1388 and was finished in 1533—except for the "unfinished chapels."

Flying buttresses, grimacing gargoyles, and impossibly detailed sculptures on the exterior belie the uncluttered magnificence of the interior. The **cloisters** (admission 400$, 250$ in winter; open daily 9–6) show the early development of Manueline architecture and house the jealously guarded **Túmulo do Soldado Desconhecido** (Tomb of the Unknown Soldier). Still more tombs line the cathedral's small mausoleum, including that of Prince Henry the Navigator, whose 15th-century naval enterprises down the coast of Africa culminated in the discovery of the sea route to India. The unfinished chapels in back, left roofless because of lack of funds, were intended as a royal mausoleum. Behind the unfinished chapels is a small **tourist office** (open daily 9–12:30 and 2–6). Buses to Coimbra (1¼ hrs, 1,100$) and Fátima (25 mins, 275$) leave frequently from the bus stop a block away.

All the hype about the Fátima miracle has given rise to new lows in religious entrepreneurialism. Here you can buy your very own glow-in-the-dark apparition, Ave Maria thermometer, or Virgin Mary shot-glass set, and at night, a light show reenacts Mary's descent from the sky.

FATIMA

Theological students and flocks of believers make the pilgrimage to Fátima to worship at its **Basílica.** The story holds that in 1917, three young children—Lúcia, Jacinta, and Francisco—were shepherding their flock when the Virgin Mary came from the heavens and spoke to them. She offered visions of heaven and hell, threw in three prophesies, and asked them to return on the 13th day of every month for the next five months. Not many believed the children at first, but increasing numbers of people turned out each month until 70,000 were on hand to witness the "great miracle of the sun," in which the cloudy skies cleared and beams of colored light radiated to earth. The cult of Fátima has grown exponentially, and devotion runs deep. An enormous esplanade, reminiscent of a mall parking lot, has been built to accommodate the masses, and tons of cheap restaurants have appeared to sustain them. There's always a crowd of pilgrims here; they come to pray in one of several chapels, make offerings of candles and wax replicas of body parts (if the original is ailing), and visit the tombs of Francisco and Jacinta inside the basilica. The main pilgrimages are in May and October, in commemoration of the first and last appearances of the Virgin Mary. The complex is about a five-minute walk up the main street from the bus stop, which has frequent buses to Coimbra (1½ hrs, 1,000$) and Batalha (25 mins, 275$).

OPORTO

The traveler's first impression of Oporto, from the window of a train or bus approaching from the south, is a knockout. A series of graceful bridges span the broad Douro River, lined with disorderly rows of brightly colored houses and red roofs rising on either bank. The de facto capital of northern Portugal and the second-largest city in Portugal, Oporto has been designated a World Heritage Site by UNESCO. Once you arrive in Oporto's midst, however, you may lose sight of some of this grandeur; Oporto is industrial and polluted, and the summer heat can be oppressive. Still, it has a lot to offer if you're willing to dig beneath the surface. The historic district, **Ribeira,** contains medieval streets, grubby *tascas* (bar-restaurants), and the former Jewish quarter. Across the river, the neighborhood of **Vila Nova de Gaia** has been the headquarters of the Portuguese wine trade since the late 17th century; port wine was born here in the 1730s, when British wine merchants began to lace the best Douro wines with brandy. The most lively time to visit is during the late June festival honoring São João, a week's worth of dancing, drinking, fireworks, and boat races. A good place to get your bearings and escape the hubbub of downtown is the **Torre dos Clérigos** (Rua dos Clérigos, tel. 02/200–17–29; admission 100$; open 10:30–noon and 3:30–5; adjacent church closed Wed. afternoon)—after an exhausting 225 steps, you are rewarded with an unparalleled view of the city, bridges, and river.

BASICS

The **main tourist office** (Rua Clube dos Fenianos 25, at north end of Av. dos Aliados, tel. 02/312740; open July–Sept., weekdays 9–5:30, weekends and holidays 10–5; shorter hrs off season) has free maps and a monthly cultural calendar. Ask for a map to the wineries and for brochures on special tours (baroque, medieval, neoclassical, and tile). There is another **tourist office** in the Ribeira (Rua Infante Dom Henrique, 63, tel. 02/2009770, open weekdays 9–7, weekends and holidays 10–5). Oporto also has an **American Express** office (Top Tours, Rua Alferes Malheiro 96, tel. 02/208–27–85; open weekdays 9–12:30 and 2:30–6:30). **Banks** are concentrated around Praça da Liberdade and Avenida dos Aliados and will change money weekdays 9–3. **Banco Espirito Santo** (Av. dos Aliados 45–69, tel. 02/200–87–26) and several other banks have 24-hour cash-exchange machines.

Portugal Telecom's phone office (Pr. da Liberdade) is open Monday–Saturday 9–7. The main **post office** (Av. dos Aliados 320, tel. 02/208–02–51) is open weekdays 8 AM–9 PM, weekends 9–6. Oporto's postal code is 4000.

COMING AND GOING

Most long-distance trains from Lisbon (4 hrs, 1,890$) and Paris (20 hrs, 22,000$) arrive at the main **Estação de Campanhã** (Rua de Estação, tel. 02/564141), about 9 km (5½ mi) east of the center. Free shuttle trains connect Campanhã every 20–30 minutes with **Estação de São Bento** (Pr. Almeida Garrett, tel. 02/200–27–22) in the heart of the city. São Bento has an information office for train travel, and local and northbound trains leave directly from here. The trip to Braga (360$) takes 1½ hours. Of the two **Rede Expressos terminals,** the one at Praça Filipa de Lencaster 178 (tel. 02/200–31–52) serves cities to the north and east, such as Braga (1 hr, 620$); the one on Rua Alexandre Herculano 364 (tel. 02/200–69–54) sends buses to Lisbon (4 hrs, 1,800$) and southern Portugal.

GETTING AROUND

Oporto lies on a steep hillside above the Douro River. The São Bento train station is near **Praça da Liberdade,** the heart of downtown Oporto, from which the broad **Avenida dos Aliados** stretches north toward the tourist office. The two-tiered **Ponte Dom Luis I,** the middle of three bridges that span the Douro, leads from the riverfront Ribeira district to Vila Nova de Gaia.

Oporto sprawls, and you'll probably want to use buses to get around. Nearly all city buses stop at Praça da Liberdade, which has an **STP** kiosk (tel. 02/606–82–28) where you can get information and tickets. Individual tickets cost 160$; a one-day pass is 350$. Taxis are indispensable if you go out at night. They're easy enough to catch on the main streets, or you can call **Radio-Taxi Porto** (tel. 02/522693).

WHERE TO SLEEP

Oporto has many affordable pensions. The cheapest are concentrated west of Avenida dos Aliados and Praça da Liberdade, on the other side of the square as you exit the São Bento train station. The barren and overpriced **Parque de Campismo Prelada** (Rua Monte dos Burgos, in Quinta da Prelada, tel. 02/812616) lies within the city limits, 3 km (2 mi) north of the Praça da Liberdade. You'll pay 530$ for a tent site plus 550$ per person; hot showers are an extra 140$. Take Bus 6 or 54 from Praça da Liberdade, or 50, 87, or 85 from Praça do Carmo.

Pensão Europa. These large, spartan but quiet rooms with bath sit atop a cheap restaurant and are near lots of other eateries, as well as the tourist office. Singles are 2,000$, doubles 3,500$. *Rua do Almada 396, tel. 02/200–69–71. 1 block west of tourist office.*

Residencial Porto Chique. The homey atmosphere's the thing here: run-down hallways, friendly manager, and perfectly nice rooms. The neighborhood can be noisy at night, so choose a room away from the street. Singles are 2,500$, doubles (all with bath) 3,500$. *Rua Conde de Vizela 26, tel. 02/208–00–69. From Pr. da Liberdade, take Rua Clérigos and turn right on Rua Conde de Vizela.*

Residencial Santa Luzia. This is not one of Oporto's cheapest stays, but it's central, cheerful, and clean. A double with bath will run you 4,000$–5,000$ *Rua da Alegria 147, tel. 02/200–11–19.*

HOSTEL • Pousada de Juventude do Porto (HI). This spic-and-span new hostel looks out on the river and sea. There's a kitchen, a TV room, pool tables, and a bar, and they're open 24 hours a day every day but Christmas. Beds are 2,350$ in the high season, 1,750$ in the low, breakfast included. *Rua Paulo da Gama 551, tel. 02/617–72–57. Take Bus 35 in Largo dos Loios, near Praça da Liberdade.*

FOOD

Workers' cafés in the streets west of Avenida dos Aliados serve simple, filling lunches for around 750$, but the action dies after sunset, so you'll have to look elsewhere for dinner. There are plenty of cheap restaurants southeast of the São Bento train station. **Café Restaurant Brazuca** (Rua das Flores 100, tel. 02/200–31–15) serves tasty chicken dishes (500$) and an excellent Brazilian feijoada (900$) in a casual atmosphere.

Restaurants in the Ribeira are more expensive but offer outside seating and lively atmosphere. At both **Café Cardoso** (Rua da Fonte Taurina 58, tel. 02/318644; closed Sun.) and **Restaurante São Nicolau** (Rua São Nicolau 1, at end of Rua da Fonte Taurina, tel. 02/200–82–36) you'll find attractive surroundings, formal waiters, and tasty seafood dishes (1,000$–1,200$) that feed two small appetites. For a break from Portuguese food, seek and ye shall find **Take Away Istanbul** (Pr. Carlos Alberto 83, 4 blocks west of Pr. da Liberdade along Rua Fábrica), where excellent lamb or chicken kebabs (700$), dolmas (300$), and pizzas on Turkish bread (300$–700$) will jump-start your taste buds. Despite the name, you can eat inside as well. Buy your own staples at the immense **Mercado de Bolhão** (Rua Sá da Bandeira, at Rua Formosa).

WORTH SEEING

Oporto's most important church is the **Sé** (Terreiro da Sé; admission free; open daily 10–12:30 and 2:30–6), a somber 12th-century cathedral on the site of a former Roman temple. The adjoining cloister (closed Sun.; admission 200$) has some impressive azulejos and artwork. A few minutes' walk downhill to the west brings you to the even more memorable **Igreja de São Francisco** (Rua Infante Dom Henrique 1, tel. 02/200–64–93; admission to museum 500$; open daily 9–5:30). This late-14th-century church is Gothic on the outside, but the inside was redone in the 1700s with ornate gilt carvings. Next door, the museum's cellar contains an *osseria* (bone room), where you can view the earthy remains of long-dead Oportans.

The poor man's sightseeing tour of Oporto is a ride on the city's one and only eléctrico (80$), which runs from Praça Gomes Teixera along the Douro, past the Foz (Estuary) district and the beaches, and back to the center along Avenida da Boavista, stopping at Praça Mouzinho de Albuquerque, more commonly known as Rotunda da Boavista.

West of the city center, visit the **Quinta da Macierinha** (Rua de Entre-Quintas 220, tel. 02/697793), which contains both the **Museu Romântico** (admission 100$, weekends free; open Tues.–Sun. 10–noon and 2–5) and the **Solar do Vinho do Porto** (open weekdays 10 AM–11:45 PM, Sat. 11–10:45). The former contains 19th-century art; the latter is a very civilized bar, run by the Port Wine Institute, where you can sample hundreds of local ports. Most are about 150$ a glass, though you can pay as much as 2,000$. The bar's rose garden offers great views of the Douro, and the gardens next door—on the grounds of the **Palácio de Cristal** (Rua Dom Manuel II, tel. 02/609–99–41; admission free) sports arena—are even more beautiful. Also nearby, the **Museu Nacional Soares dos Reis** (Rua D. Manuel II, tel. 02/208–19–56; admission 350$; open Tues.–Sun. 10–12:30 and 2:30–5:30) has a collection of painting and sculpture, Portuguese and otherwise. To get here, take Bus 3, 6, 20, 35, 37 or 52 from Praça da Liberdade. From the museum, take Bus 78 for 20 min. and you'll end up at the outstanding **Fundação Serralves** (Rua de Serralves 977, tel. 02/617524; open Tues.–Fri. 2–8, weekends 10–8; shorter hrs off season), one of the best modern-art museums in Portugal.

From the center of town, a stroll across Ponte Dom Luis I (take the lower level) leads to the suburb of Vila Nova de Gaia, home of the **port-wine cellars** (open Mon.–Sat. 9:30–12:30 and 2:30–5:30). As their names (such as **Cockburn's, Graham's,** and **Osborne**) suggest, most of the wineries are still owned by the British, who have controlled the port-wine trade since its inception. The cellars, which advertise with large white lettering on their roofs, are within a few minutes' walk of one another and offer tours, detailed explanations of the port-making process, and, best of all, free tastings. The tourist office has schedules and a good map.

Oporto is the launch pad for several short boat trips up the Douro. **Turisdouro** offers a 50-minute "Bridges Cruise" in a *barco rabelo*, the traditional Douro wine boat, leaving the Cais Amarelo quay in Vila

Nova de Gaia, near the Sandeman lodges, six times daily (Rua Machado dos Santos 824, Vila Nova de Gaia, tel. 02/306389). **Endouro Turismo** runs a 50-minute "Four Bridges and Douro Mouth Tour" from the Ribeira quay six times every weekday (Rua da Reboleira 49, tel. 02/324236). A ticket for either boat is 1,500$.

AFTER DARK

Oporto's nighttime meeting place is *o cubo,* a failed piece of modern art that now serves as an unmistakable reference point on the **Praça da Ribeira.** You can often catch live music and dancing here, and there are at least a dozen bars along the river and back streets of the Ribeira, crowded any night of the week. For dancing, try **Cosa Nostra** (Rua de São João 76, tel. 02/208–66–72), a fairly ritzy joint with so-called alternative music and a 300$ drink minimum. For more serious techno dancing until 7 or 8 AM, cab it (about 600$) to **Indústria,** just outside Oporto, near the sea in Foz de Douro (Avenida Brasil 843, tel. 02/617–68–06); or head to **Swing** (Rua Julio Dinis 766), a student hangout in Boavista. Most discos have a 1,000$ drink minimum and high prices. Doormen tend not to look kindly on the unescorted, particularly women.

BRAGA

Portugal's northernmost major city, Braga prides itself on its long alliance with the Roman church, dating back to the establishment of a Braga bishopric in the 6th century. Today, this large, commercial city is growing rapidly, but the historical quarter remains an oasis of 16th-century churches and a center of theological research. Braga holds Portugal's most impressive Easter celebration; during **Holy Week** churches are decorated with flowers, and hooded penitents bearing torches form midnight processions through town. Braga is also attractive as a jumping-off point for Peneda-Gerês, Portugal's largest national park (an hour north, near the Spanish border).

At the center of the old town is the huge **Sé** (Largo Dom João Peculiar, at Rua Dom Diego de Sousa), originally Romanesque but now representing a blend of styles, and home to a stunning gilded pipe organ. Nearby, the former **Paço dos Arcebispos** (Archbishop's Palace), parts of which date from the 14th century, houses the local university faculty, the district archives, and the substantial **public library** (Largo do Paço 1, tel. 053/612234; open weekdays 9–noon and 2–5:30). The baroque **Palácio dos Biscainhos** (Rua dos Biscainhos 46, tel. 053/217645; admission 250$; open Tues.–Sun. 10–12:15 and 2–5:30) belonged to Portuguese nobility for four centuries, but it's now a small furniture museum with manicured gardens. The **posto de turismo** (Av. da Liberdade 1, tel. 053/22550; open weekdays 9–7, Sat. 9–12:30 and 2–5, Sun. 9–12:30 and 2–6) is right on the Praça da República and hands out useful city maps. Braga's **post office** (Av. da Libertade, at Rua Gonçalves Sampião, tel. 053/22331; open weekdays 8:30–6, Sat. 8:30–12:30; postal code 4700) also houses a **Telecom** telephone office.

COMING AND GOING

The **train station** (tel. 053/22166), a 15-minute walk west of the central Praça da República, has direct trains to Oporto (1½ hrs; 330$), Lisbon (4½ hrs, 2,500$), and Faro (11 hrs, 3,000$). From the station, follow Rua Andrade Corvo past the Sé—the street changes names a few times, but keep going straight and you'll hit the Praça. The **bus station** (Av. General Norton de Matos, tel. 053/616080), about a five-minute walk uphill from the center, sends buses to all points in northern Portugal, as well as express lines to Oporto (1 hr, 620$) and Lisbon (5½ hrs, 2,000$).

WHERE TO SLEEP

Arrive early in the day or call ahead to secure the most affordable options. Conveniently located just off the Praça da República, the **Francfort** (Av. Central 7, tel. 053/22648) is almost 100 years old and has large rooms and a breezy sitting room. Doubles are 5,000$. **Residencial São Joã** (Rua Monsenhor Airoso 66, tel. 053/75204) doesn't have much character, but it's clean, modern, and conveniently located in the center of town. Doubles with private bath and breakfast go for 5,900$. **Residencial Inácio Filho** (Rua Francisco Sanches 42, tel. 053/23849) has decent rooms, but it's a bit musty and not quite worth the 5,000$ price. The bright, cheery **HI Pousada de Juventude** (Rua de Santa Margarida 6, tel. 053/616163), with beds for 1,550$ (1,300$ Oct.–June), has a kitchen and serves free breakfast. This is a popular place, so you'd best reserve in the high season. Reception is open 8–noon and 6–midnight; ask for a key to stay out past midnight. From the tourist office, walk east on Avenida Central until the park turns into a rose garden, then make a left on Rua de Santa Margarida. Braga's **Parque de Campismo** (tel. 053/73355) is 3 km (2 mi) south of the center and charges 330$ per person and 250$

per tent. It's not exactly nature, but it's grassy and quiet and has free hot showers. Take the bus labeled ARCOS (175$) from Avenida da Liberdade, between Rua do Raio and Rua 25 de Abril.

FOOD

Braga's culinary scene is rather barren, though several places along Avenida Central serve typical Portuguese food at decent prices. **A Grulha** (Rua Biscainhos 95, tel. 053/22883) is family-run and serves old-fashioned regional food cooked over an open wood fire, at prices that won't set you back a week (main dishes around 800$). **Restaurante Moçambicana** (Rua Andrade Corvo 8, uphill from train station, tel. 053/613228) specializes in African food, particularly grilled kid (1,500$) and stuffed haddock (1,500$)—in portions that can feed two. Buy produce, cheese, bread, and sausage at the **mercado** (Praça do Comércio; open Mon.–Sat. until 3 PM). The cafés on atmospheric Praça da República also serve as the town's nightspots, staying open until 2 AM (earlier on Sundays); **A Brasileira** (Rua de São Marcos 1) is the oldest and classiest of the lot, with excellent coffee and a dignified clientele.

NEAR BRAGA

PARQUE NACIONAL DA PENEDA-GERES

In the northern reaches of the country, next to the Spanish border, Portugal's largest national park contains a stunning array of granite mountains, freshwater lagoons, and rivers and streams. The park is divided into the peripheral "rural environment area," containing some 115 highly traditional villages, three campgrounds, some tourist developments, a youth hostel, and the protected "natural environment area," which provides sanctuary for wild ponies, boar, wolves, golden eagles, and the Gerês iris, unique to the region. FAPAS, a large ecological organization, runs a nature school and tree farm in the park and has the formidable task of instilling conservation ideas in villagers who employ centuries-old grazing and farm-

Braga's Teatro Circo (Av. da Liberdade, across from post office, tel. 053/22403) is a gorgeous cinema and performance space, with red leather chairs and a luxurious balcony. Make it a point to see something here—just dress for the lack of air conditioning.

ing techniques. Before setting out, visit the **park headquarters** in Braga (Quinta das Parretas, Rodovia, tel. 053/600–34–80), where you can buy a topographical map of the park (530$) and get camping and hiking information. Unfortunately, no trail map is available, and due to the mountainous terrain, distances can be deceiving.

The park is best accessed from Braga. **EH Gerês** (tel. 053/615896) runs buses from the terminal to several villages within the park that can serve as base camps or jumping-off points. The bus to Gerês (1½ hrs, (537$) brings you to the **Parque de Campismo Vidoeiro** (Vilar da Vega, tel. 053/391289), where you can camp for 350$ per tent plus 400$ per person. The Rodoviario Entre Douro e Minho bus to Campo de Gerês (1¼ hrs, 515$) drops you off at the **HI Pousada de Juventude Vilarinho das Furnas** (Terras de Bouro, tel. 053/351339), perched high on a mountain overlooking a tiny village and a swimmable reservoir. The hostel is large, but it's swarmed with student groups in the summer, so do make reservations; beds are 1,600$ (1,300$ Oct.–June). You can't use the kitchen, but the cafeteria serves breakfast (free) and a substantial dinner (900$), for which you must reserve before noon.

BOM JESUS

A pleasant weekend-retreat town has sprung up around the pilgrimage site of Bom Jesus, a religious edifice built by a wealthy archbishop in 1893. The site itself consists mainly of an incredible baroque staircase. The first several landings hold tiny chapels that depict the agonies of Christ before his crucifixion, while the next five have fountains, each of which represent one of the five senses. At the top are a large church and several more small chapels. Particularly during Holy Week, the staircase is packed with pilgrims making the climb on their knees. On weekends, you'll see wedding processions and picnickers. For the slothful, a funicular (100$) makes the almost 1,000-ft climb, but you'd be foolish to miss the walk. To get here from Braga, catch a bus marked BOM JESUS (15 mins, 175$), which leaves every half hour from the stop on Largo Carlos Amarante; from the tourist office, take Avenida da Liberdade downhill and turn right on Rua Gonçalves Sampião. The site is open daily from sunrise to sunset, and admission is free.

CITANIA DE BRITEIROS

One of the few accessible pre-Roman sites in Portugal, the **Citânia de Briteiros** (admission 200$; open daily 9–6) is an Iron Age Celtic hill settlement thought to be some 2,500 years old. The plan of the ancient site is remarkably urban: two main cobbled pathways and a network of smaller roads lead to water sources, public spaces, and some 150 distinct dwellings, all of which are surrounded by a double set of fortified walls. Two of the huts have been rebuilt, allowing you to see a hypothetical version of the Celts' digs. Alas, getting here from Braga is something of a chore. The best way is to take the bus from Braga to Bom Jesus and get off at Lageosa Sobre Post; from there it's a 2-km (1-mi) hike. Alternatively, all buses to Guimarães pass through the spa town of Caldas das Taipas (45 mins, 275$), 9 km (5½ mi) from Citânia de Briteiros; from Caldas, local buses heading toward Póvoa de Lanhoso (200$) can drop you 4 km (2½ mi) downhill from the site. Once here, you're almost sure to find visitors with cars heading back to Braga or Guimarães.

ROMANIA

T o most Westerners, Romania is as remote and mysterious today as it was a century ago, when it fired the imagination of *Dracula* author Bram Stoker. Only in the last decade has Romania emerged from behind the veil of more than 40 years of Communist rule. Marking the end of dictator Nicolae Ceauşescu's reign, the 1989 revolution was as bloody as Romania's folklore is dark: During the seven short days of the revolution, more than 1,000 people were gunned down or crushed to death by armored vehicles. The violence culminated in the hasty "trial" and Christmas-day executions of Ceauşescu and his wife, Elena, whose corpses were then televised.

Romania is currently suffering a painful transition to a market economy and liberal democracy. In the autumn of 1996, the Romanian people finally ousted the remnants of the former communist leadership and elected a new government, under the direction of President Emil Constantinescu. This administration has announced a commitment to change, and has implemented stringent economic policies under the direction of the International Monetary Fund (IMF), including reducing the money supply and allowing exchange rates to fluctuate freely. In the long run these policies should bear fruit, but as yet they have not shortened Romania's long list of social problems, which includes high unemployment, inflation, a crumbling social-welfare system, and a stubbornly low standard of living. Romanians have long accepted daily hardships as a matter of course, and they continue to wait patiently for change to affect their individual lives.

Many of the country's tourist sites show signs of neglect. They are slowly improving, but the tourist industry as a whole lacks both knowledge and resources. To get the most out of your visit to Romania, avoid the smoke-belching, industrial cities. Moldavia, in the remote north, keeps vibrantly painted monasteries hidden in the Carpathian mountains, while Transylvania reveals its Hungarian and Saxon heritage in well-preserved medieval castles and fortified villages.

BASICS

MONEY

US$1 = 6,000 lei and 100 lei = 6¢ The value of the Romanian leu (plural lei) fluctuates wildly; we give prices in dollars so that you can budget with some confidence. If you plan to stay here a while, bring

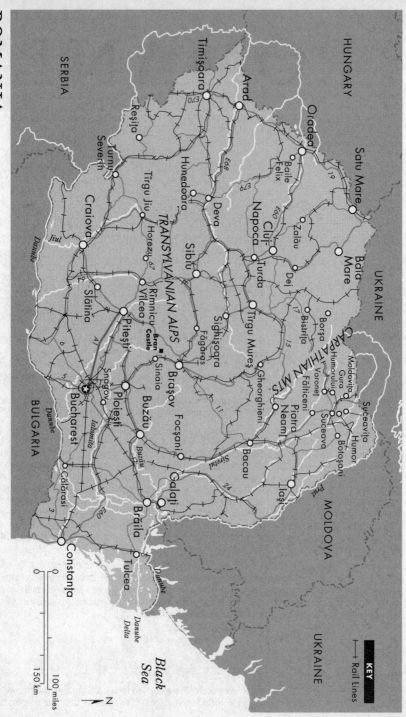

ROMANIA

HUNGARY

SERBIA

UKRAINE

Satu Mare

Baia Mare

Oradea

Baile Felix

Zalău

Cluj Napoca

Dej

Turda

Bistrița

Borșa

Humorului

Gura

Moldovița

Suceavița

Voroneț

Fălticeni

Suceava

Botoșani

Piatra Neamț

Iași

MOLDOVA

UKRAINE

Timișoara

Arad

Reșița

Hunedoara

Deva

Sibiu

Sighișoara

Făgăraș

Târgu Mureș

Gheorghieni

TRANSYLVANIAN ALPS

CARPATHIAN MTS

Turnu Severin

Târgu Jiu

Horezu

Craiova

Râmnicu Vâlcea

Bran Castle

Pitești

Sinaia

Brașov

Buzău

Focșani

Bacău

Slatina

Snagov

Ploiești

Bucharest

Câlărași

Brăila

Galați

BULGARIA

Constanța

Tulcea

Black Sea

Danube Delta

Jiul

Danube

Olt

Ialomița

Buzău

Siretul

KEY

Rail Lines

N

0

100 miles

150 km

American dollars in small bills (British pounds and German marks are useful, too), and exchange them in small amounts so you can take advantage of any decline in the value of the leu. You can change currency at any *casa de schimb valutar* (exchange bureau) for little or no commission. Traveler's checks are gaining acceptance in Bucharest (though you still need hard currency at train stations and in the countryside); you can exchange them at banks, better hotels, and some *casa de schimb valutar* (commissions are 1.5%, 5%, and 10%, respectively). Credit cards are now accepted at more upscale establishments, and you can get cash advances (lei only) at some banks and *casa de schimb valutar* (15% commission). Keep exchange receipts to reconvert lei into dollars. Whatever you do, don't change money on the street; the rates aren't much better, and you'll probably get robbed.

HOW MUCH IT WILL COST • Romania is no longer the great deal that it once was, especially in Bucharest. Inflation and new economic policies are driving prices up to Western levels. With some effort, you may be able to eat and sleep in Bucharest for under $50 per day (less in the countryside). Count on at least $30 per night for lodging and $5 to $10 for a good meal. Alcohol is still a good deal at about $3 for an imported beer. Tipping at restaurants isn't necessary, but 10% is nice.

VISAS AND ENTRY REQUIREMENTS

Americans can enter Romania for up to 30 days visa-free; border guards may try to extort money from you, but be firm. Brits, Canadians, Australians, and Kiwis must purchase a 30-day visa ($30 at the border, less at a Romanian embassy at home). To extend your visa, go to the **Romanian Passport Office** (Str. Nicolai Iorga 27, in Bucharest; open weekdays 9:30–2 and 5–8, Sat. 9:30–2; closed Wed.) across from the Canadian embassy, 1 block west of Piaţa Romană. If you are carrying expensive-looking electronic equipment or jewelry, your passport will be stamped; show the items again at departure or pay a hefty fine. You must also present receipts for any pricey items you pick up in Romania.

It was actually a Hungarian who instigated the '89 revolution: When Ceauçescu tried to exile dissident pastor László Tökés, both Romanians and Hungarians rose in protest, igniting revolutionary urges across the country.

COMING AND GOING

Most budget travelers arrive in Bucharest from Budapest by **train**; you can save money on the return to Budapest (12 hrs, $45) by paying in lei. Regular trains connect Bucharest to Sofia (12 hrs, $26) and İstanbul (17 hrs, $20). The national airline, **TAROM** (tel. 212/687–6013 in U.S.), flies to Bucharest from Chicago and New York several times a week, and also from major European cities, such as Milan (3 hrs, $200). Most major international airlines now fly to Bucharest as well. **Buses** to Bucharest are frequent from İstanbul, though infrequent from western Europe; they're as cheap and fast as the trains, but are usually crowded, smoky, and uncomfortable. In Bucharest, call **Toros** (Gara de Nord, tel. 01/638–2424) or check out the sketchy-looking bus companies around the station. One reputable Romanian bus company is **Double T** (C. Victoriei 2, tel. 01/613–3642), with frequent service from Bucharest to Rome (36 hrs, $170) and Frankfurt (40 hrs, $185).

GETTING AROUND

Unless you have a car (and the parts and know-how to fix it yourself), you'll spend most of your travelling time on trains. Trains will take you anywhere you want to go (cross-country rides cost no more than $12), so you'll probably never need to take the grimy, crowded, and slow intercity buses. TAROM has extensive domestic flights, but airfare is more costly: A ticket from Bucharest to Timisoara (1 hr) is $60. Hitchhiking in Romania is neither practical nor safe.

BY TRAIN • Romanian trains accept InterRail passes and the new Eurail-Romania pass. The latter is so new, however, that conductors are hard-pressed to accept it, and given how cheap trains are, they're probably not worth the trouble. There are four categories of color-coded train service: *InterCity* (yellow), *rapide* (green), *accelerat* (red), and *personal* (blue), in descending order of price and speed. Trains are often overbooked, so make reservations. You can buy domestic tickets the day of departure at the *gara* (train station) or anytime at a **CFR** (Romania's national train company, pronounced chay-fay-ray) office. Domestic couchettes, which sell out quickly, cost only a few dollars; buy tickets at the station before noon the day of departure, or at a CFR office up to nine days in advance. Purchase international tickets and couchettes at the station up to two hours before departure or anytime at a CFR office. Domestic tickets from the Bucharest train station look like regular old tickets; tickets from the CFR office or other Romanian train stations are a scribbled-on piece of cardboard. If you upgrade or make a seat reservation, which you should do, you'll be given another piece of cardboard with the updated information. Timetables at the station list *sosira* (arrivals) and *plecari* (departures). Whenever possible, ride *clasa întii* (first-class), since it costs only a few dollars more for domestic tickets. Ask at CFR offices for the most recent **Mersul Trenurilor** (railway timetable), usually $1. Always pack food and toilet paper for long train rides.

WHERE TO SLEEP

Avoid the expensive state-run hotels—they charge foreigners higher rates and may demand hard currency. Private homes are your best bet, followed by private hotels. **Private hotels** are rated according to the standard star stystem. One-star hotels provide the basic amenities, are clean with good plumbing, and are relatively inexpensive. Two- and three-star hotels are, of course, nicer but much more expensive. We list mostly one-star digs. **Private rooms,** as cheap as $5–$15 a night, can be tricky to find; if you don't run across any locals hawking rooms at the train station, inquire at the local tourist office. **Camping** is by far the cheapest option. Tent spaces usually run $5 a night, two-person bungalows about $10 per night. **Hostels** don't yet exist in Romania.

FOOD

In summer, good, cheap produce is plentiful, and you'll see produce stands on all the streets. In winter, fresh produce is scarcer, but you won't go hungry. Tap water isn't safe here, so buy bottled water, which is cheap and always available. For other refreshments, try beer, wine, or *tzuicâ,* a Romanian plum brandy taken at the beginning of a meal. *Cotnari, Murfatlar,* and *Tirnave* are good Romanian wines.

Typical restaurant entrées include *porc* (pork), *biftec* (steak), *pui* (chicken), *miel* (ground lamb), *cîrnaţi* (sausages), and *ficat de porc* (pork liver). Slightly lighter and healthier are *nişte ouâ* (omelettes), *orez şi tăiţei* (rice and pasta), *fasole* (beans), *supă de pasăre* (chicken soup), and *borş* (meat and vegetable soup). Most meals are served with *pîine* (bread). If you're a vegetarian, specify *fără carne* (without meat) when ordering—you'll probably have the best luck with *ciorba* (soup) and pizza. Note: Always double-check the math on your bill.

BUSINESS HOURS

Outside big cities, standard business hours are weekdays 8–4:30 and Saturday 8–1; everything tends to stay open later in cities. Restaurants and beer halls usually open at 11 and stay open all day; some close on Sunday. Many grocery stores, restaurants, and bars are open 24 hours. Casa de schimb valutar are generally open weekdays 9–5 and Saturday 9–2, but many banks are open only weekday mornings 8:30–11:30. Most museums are open Wednesday–Sunday 10–5.

PHONES AND MAIL

Country code: 40. The phone system in Romania has improved vastly over the past few years. Place local calls from blue or gray phones with 50-lei or 100-lei coins, or from orange phones with phone cards, available at post and phone offices in denominations of 5,000 lei, 10,000 lei, and 20,000 lei. You can also place direct-dial international calls from any of those phones. To access U.S. operators from blue phones, deposit 50 lei or 100 lei and dial 01/800–4288 for **AT&T** Direct Access℠; 01/800–1800 for **MCI**; or 01/800–0877 for **Sprint.** Dial 01/800–4444 for a direct connection to the United Kingdom and 01/800–5000 for calls to Canada. As a last resort, you can always go to a *telefon/fax* office (open 24 hours) at train stations and post offices; here, the attendant at the front desk will place your call for you, often for a $2 fee. **Mail** within Europe takes one week; overseas mail takes two weeks. The price of international stamps changes regularly, so check before mailing. Deposit your mail in any yellow box marked POSTA.

CRIME AND PUNISHMENT

Compared to the United States, Romania is relatively safe; violent crime is rare, and the biggest threats to tourists are theft and scheming money-changers. Always keep your valuables on you (hidden in a money belt) and don't change money on the street. Watch out for pickpockets (particularly on buses or in train stations)—often groups of young men or children will crowd around you, distracting you long enough to snatch your cash. Streets are dark at night, and women traveling solo should use common sense.

EMERGENCIES

All cities have hospitals with 24-hour emergency rooms. Foreigners are charged a nominal fee, usually around $20. Bigger cities also have at least one 24-hour pharmacy, but don't count on being able to fill a foreign prescription.

LANGUAGE

Of all the romance languages, Romanian remains closest to Latin. It also borrows from Slavic, and was actually written in Cyrillic until the 19th century. If you know any romance languages, you'll probably understand basic signs and restaurant menus but not spoken Romanian. Fortunately, English is widely spoken (especially by younger Romanians), as are French and German. Hungarian is also common in Transylvania. The following Romanian words should help you out: *bună* (hello); *la revedere* (goodbye); *vă rug* (please); *mulţumesc* (thank you); *mă scuzaţi* (excuse me); *căt costă?* (how much?); *unde?* (where is . . .?); *ba/no* (yes/no); *nu înţeleg* (I don't understand); *unu* (one); *doi* (two); *trei* (three); *patru* (four); *cinci* (five); *şase* (six); *şapte* (seven); *opt* (eight); *nouă* (nine); *zece* (10); *o sută* (100); *o mie* (1,000); *milion* (1,000,000).

CULTURE

Especially in rural Romania, Africans, Asians, and other ethnic minorities will find themselves stared at (then again, Romanians stare at everybody, including each other), but will likely encounter no animosity. Gays and lesbians should be careful about showing affection in public. Shortly after the fall of communism the legal ban on homosexuality was lifted, but due to strong feelings, it was recently reinstated.

BUCHAREST

Once upon a time, Bucharest (Bucureşti) was called the Paris of the East, and even after 50 years of malaise, it seems possible that the city might someday regain the title. Though Ceauşescu did his best to destroy the oldest and most picturesque neighborhoods, some of the Parisian architecture remains, and it's still possible to stroll down shady boulevards lined with mansions, imagining the city that was.

BASICS

VISITOR INFORMATION

Downtown, the friendly staff at **ONT Carpaţi S.A.** will give you maps and brochures, help you find private rooms and hotels, and exchange money at official rates. But they'll charge you an exorbitant 10% to change traveler's checks to lei, and 15% to get lei from a credit card. *B-dul. G. Magheru 7, 3 blocks south of P. Romană, tel. 01/614–5160. Open weekdays 8–4:30, Sat. 8:30–2.*

AMERICAN EXPRESS

The full-service AmEx office at **Marshal Tourism Ltd.** holds client mail, replaces cards and traveler's checks, offers traveler's checks against a personal check or an AmEx card, and helps with travel arrangements and lodging. *B-dul. G. Magheru 43, just south of P. Romană, tel. 01/659–6812. Open weekdays 9–5, Sat. 10–2.*

CHANGING MONEY

The professional staff at **Romanian Commercial Bank** will cash your traveler's checks (1.5% commission) for dollars or lei and get you lei from your MasterCard or Visa for no fee. Better still, the ATM outside accepts Visa, MasterCard, Cirrus, and PLUS. For more information on changing money, *see* Money in Basics, *above. B-dul. Republicii 12–14, 1 block west of P. Universităţii, tel. 01/312–4104. Open Mon.–Thurs. 9–6, Fri. 9–2.*

EMBASSIES AND CONSULATES

Australia, New Zealand, and United Kingdom: *Str. Jules Michelet 24, off B-dul. G. Magheru, tel. 01/312–0303. Metro: Romană. Open weekdays 9–5, 9–noon on Friday.* **Canada:** *Str. Nicolae Iorga 36, near P. Romană, tel. 01/222–9845. Open weekdays 9–5.*

United States. Personnel at the **embassy** probably won't see you without an appointment. However, the friendly staff at the American Services window of the **Consular Section** will register you as an American abroad, give you helpful information on banking services, and fill you in on the do's and don'ts of visiting Romania. *Embassy: Str. Tudor Arghezi 7–9, near Inter-Continental Hotel, tel. 01/210–4042. Consular Section: Str. Nicolae Filipescu (formerly Snagov) 26, at Str. Batiştei, diagonally behind embassy, tel. 01/210–4042 or 01/210–6384 for emergencies. Open Mon.–Thurs. 8–11:30 and 1–3, Fri. 8–11:30. Metro: Universităţii.*

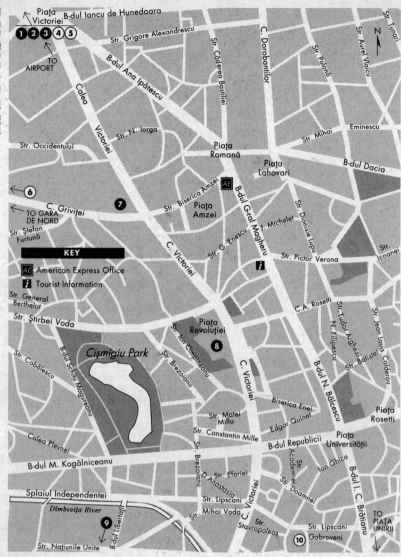

Piaţa
Victoriei → B-dul Iancu de Hunedoara

① ② ③ ④ ⑤

TO
AIRPORT

Str. Grigore Alexandrescu

B-dul Ana Ipătescu

Str. N. Iorga

Str. Occidentului

Calea Victoriei

Str. Căderea Bastiliei

C. Dorobanţilor

Str. Polonă

Str. Aurel Vlaicu

Str. Tunari

N

Eminescu
Str. Mihai

Piaţa
Romană

Piaţa
Lahovari

B-dul Dacia

AE

B-dul G-ral Magheru

Str. Biserica Amzei

Piaţa
Amzei

Str. Dionisie Lupu

Str. G. Enescu J. Michelet

Str. Pictor Verona

Str.
Icoanei

⑥

C. Griviţei

⑦

TO GARA
DE NORD

Str. Ştefan
Furtună

i

KEY

AE American Express Office

i Tourist Information

Str. General
Berthelot

Str. Ştirbei Voda

Str. Cobălcescu

B-dul Schu Magureanu

Cişmigiu Park

Str. Ion Cîmpineanu

Str. Brezoianu

Piaţa
Revoluţiei

⑧

C. Victoriei

C.A. Rosetti

Str. Tudor Arghezi

N. Filipescu

Str. Batiştei

Str. Jean Louis Calderon

Piaţa
Rosetti

B-dul N. Bălcescu

Biserica Enei

Edgar Quinet

Piaţa
Universităţii

Str. Matei
Millo

Str. Constantin Mille

Calea Plevnei

B-dul M. Kogălniceanu

B-dul Republicii

Str.
Academiei

Str.
Doamnei

Ion Ghica

B-dul I. C. Brătianu

Splaiul Independenţei

Dîmboviţa River

⑨

Str. Naţiunile Unite

B-dul Libertăţii

Str.
Brezoianu

D. Anastasia

Str. Eforiei

Str. Lipscani

Str. Mihai Voda

Str.
Stavropoleos

Str. Lipscani
⑩ Gabroveni

TO
PIAŢA
UNIRII

Sights ●

Casa Republicii, **9**

Hěrastrău Park, **1**

Muzeul Colecţilor
d'Arta, **7**

Muzeul National
d'Arta, **8**

Muzeul Satului, **2**

Muzeul Taranului
Roman, **3**

Lodging ○

Casa Victor, **5**

Cerna Hotel, **6**

Hanul Lui Manuc
Inn, **10**

Triumf, **4**

EMERGENCIES

Dial 961 for an **ambulance.** For 24-hour emergency hospital care, go to **Spitalul de Urgenta** (C. Flore-asca 8, tel. 01/212–0107, 01/212–0170; Stefan Cel Mare Metro). For medications, try **Pharmacy #5** (B-dul. G. Magheru 20, near P. Universităţii, tel. 01/659–6115), open 24 hours. **American Express** (*see* Visitor Information, *above*) gives medical referrals and advances emergency funds for cardmembers through the Global Assist service (call collect in U.S. 202/783–7474).

ENGLISH-LANGUAGE BOOKS AND NEWSPAPERS

The library **Information USA** (American Center, Str. Jean-Louis Calderon 7, tel. 01/210–1602; open Tues.–Fri. 1–4), near Piaţa Universităţii, has reference books, computers with Internet access, current editions of the *New York Times,* and an amazing array of magazines. **Librăria Noi** (B-dul. G. Magheru 18, near P. Universităţii, tel. 01/614–3786; open weekdays 9–8, weekends 10–4) has a fantastic mix of new and used books. Check in the Inter-Continental Hotel for the English-language dailies *România Liberia, Romanian Economic Observer, Nine O'Clock,* and *Romanian Business Journal.*

PHONES AND MAIL

Avoid the zoolike **main post office** (C. Victoriei, at Str. Matei Millo); head instead to the mellow **PTTR** (Post, Telephone, Telegraph, Radio; Str. Ion Cimpineanu 23, 2 blocks NW of main post office; open weekdays 8–8, Sat. 9–2) for all your postal needs. Have poste restante sent to Your Name, Office Postale Bucarest 45, Romania. Make international calls at the outdoor **phone arcade** (½ block down Str. Matei Millo from main post office), where you can dial direct from the blue phones; for more information, *see* Phones and Mail *in* Basics, *above.*

COMING AND GOING

BY PLANE

Bucharest's main airport is **Otopeni International.** To get there, take a cab ($20) or a Bus 783 (50¢), which runs every half hour from Piaţa Unirii through the center of town. The airport has restaurants, luggage storage, car rentals, and a 24-hour information desk. Buy plane tickets at one of the many travel agencies in Bucharest. *Sos. Bucareţi-Ploieţi 40, tel. 01/212–0138.*

Domestic flights leave from **Băneasa Airport** (tel. 01/633–0030), on the way to Otopeni from Bucharest. Take Bus 131 from Piaţa Romană or Bus 783 (*see above*), which stops across the street from Băneasa on its way to Otopeni.

BY TRAIN

The **Gara de Nord** (west of downtown, between C. Griviţei and B-dul. Golescu) receives 98% of Bucharest's rail traffic. For international tickets and domestic InterCity tickets, head to the wing marked CASELE DE BILETE CL. 1; ticket offices are closed 1:30 AM–4 AM. Domestic tickets are also available at the **main CFR office** (Str. Eforiei, at Str. Brezoianu), and international tickets and couchettes are sold at the CFR office outside the Piaţa Unirii II Metro; both offices are open weekdays 7:30–7, Saturday 7:30–noon. For more information on buying train tickets, *see* Coming and Going *in* Basics, *above.* The Gara de Nord has a 24-hour luggage desk, a 24-hour telefon/fax office, direct-dial phones, restaurants, a post office, and a travel agency. Downtown hotels are a 20-minute walk or a short metro ride east of the train station; after 11 PM (when the Metro and buses stop), definitely spring for a taxi ($5) to the center of town.

GETTING AROUND

Bucharest is mostly a sprawling mess of curving streets and identical cement apartment blocks. Bucharest's *centrum* (downtown) has more character, and it's easier to get your bearings here; the Inter-Continental Hotel on **Piaţa Universităţii** towers above everything around it and marks the exact center of town. Most sights, lodging, and restaurants are near **Bulevardul General Magheru** and **Bulevardul Nicolae Bălcescu,** the main street that runs between the downtown Metro stops Piaţa Romană and Piaţa Universităţii, or on **Calea Victoriei,** which basically runs parallel. **Bulevardul Kogălniceanu,** which runs through Piaţa Universităţii, is lined with restaurants and cafés. Take Bulevardul Brantianu south from Piaţa Universităţii to reach **Piaţa Unirii,** and head northwest of the Metro stop to the run-down but vibrant oldest section of Bucharest, where children play in the rubble and *Ţigan* (Gypsies) hawk goods on the street.

BY BUS AND TRAM

Overcrowded trams and buses run 5 AM–11 PM and cover the city extensively, but their routes are very confusing. Each stop has a sign indicating which lines stop there. Trams and buses take the same ticket (700 lei), which can be purchased at most stops from kiosks marked RAŢ TICHETE or SI BILETE. Validate your ticket as you board the bus.

BY METRO

The Metro (which runs 5:30 AM–11:00 PM) is the best way to reach the centrum. The four lines—blue (M2), orange (M3), red (M1), and yellow (also M1)—are fairly comprehensive. However, only three stations—**Piaţa Unirii, Piaţa Universităţii,** and **Piaţa Romană,** all on the blue M2 line—serve the downtown area. As a rule of thumb, work your way toward Piaţa Universităţii to reach the heart of town. Buy tickets (800 lei for two rides, though regular increases are expected) at any station.

BY TAXI

Taxis, easily hailed on the street, are a convenient and relatively inexpensive way to get around; fares within the city shouldn't go above $5. Cabbies may try to rip you off, though, especially if you're going far, such as to the airport or an outlying area, so agree on the fare before getting in. You can also call cabs from home: Try **Cobalcescu** (tel. 945) or **Perazzi** (tel. 941), or dial 953 for the main switchboard that handles all taxi companies. Most drivers speak English.

WHERE TO SLEEP

Staying with a Romanian family is the cheapest option ($5–$15 per person). The tourist office (see Visitor Information in Basics, above) can arrange for a place to stay, and people will probably approach you at the Gara de Nord with room offers. Look at a map so you know what you're getting into, and never pay until you see the room. A few reasonably cheap hotels lie near the Gara de Nord—not a great neighborhood, but convenient if you're fleeing town early the next morning.

UNDER $40 • Cerna Hotel. Spacious rooms are within a stone's throw of Gara de Nord at the Cerna, the new kid in a neighborhood, where comfort and cleanliness are usually in short supply. Doubles are $25–$33. B-dul. Dinicu Golescu 29, south of Gara de Nord, tel. 01/637–4087. Cash only.

UNDER $60 • Hanul Lui Manuc Inn. This excellent villa-style inn has doubles ($60) overlooking a central courtyard, and a superb restaurant. You'd best reserve ahead. Iuliu Maniu 62, tel. 01/613–1415. From NW entrance of Unirii Metro, take immediate right and turn left before red church.

Triumf. This grand turn-of-the-century building offers doubles ($60) on a small park near the Arcul de Triumf. Şoseaua Kiseleff 12, tel. 01/2223172. Take metro to Piaţa Victoriei and walk north on Kiseleff almost 1 mi.

SPLURGE • Casa Victor. A simple and clean alternative to the former communist-style hotels, this pension offers double ($70) rooms and small apartments ($80). Reserve ahead if possible. Str. Campia Turzii 44, tel. 01/2225723. Take metro to Piaţa Charles De Gaulle (formerly Aviatorilor) and walk west 2 blocks toward the Arcul de Triumf, then left.

FOOD

Though Bucharest has a surprisingly good selection of restaurants, most Romanians can't afford to eat out very often; you're more likely to find a true Romanian atmosphere at cafés and beer gardens. Try **Bulevardul Kogălniceanu** for a full day's worth of cafés and pastry shops. You can buy fresh produce at the **open-air market** (P. Amzei, between C. Victoriei and B-dul. G. Magheru) near Piaţa Romană.

Bradet. Vegetarians shouldn't leave Bucharest before trying this Lebanese restaurant. Menu standouts include stuffed eggplant ($2), calamari ($2), and shish kebabs ($5). Make reservations. Str. Dr. Carol Davila 60, tel. 01/638–6014. 3 blocks SW of Eroilor Metro, off B-dul. Eroilor. Open daily noon–midnight.

Cafe de la Joie. It's just that: joyful. Unwind with good French food (green salad $1, chicken breast $4) accompanied by tasteful music. Str. Lipscani 80, tel. 01/312–2910. North of Unitii Metro, off B-dul. Brătianu. Open daily 6 PM–midnight.

Caru Cu Bere. The "Cartful of Beer" serves traditional Romanian sarmale (meat and rice wrapped in grape leaves; $3) and tocană (stew; $5). There's live traditional folk music and dancing nightly. Str.

Stravropoleos 5, tel. 01/613–7500. From Universității Metro, walk SW on B-dul. Kogălniceanu, left on C. Victoriei, and left on Str. Stravropoleos. Open daily 11 AM–midnight.

Scala International. This lovely, spacious café with marble tables is perfect for people-watching. You can also order real food, such as pasta ($3) or a delicious Greek salad ($3). But the real attraction is the restroom: It's clean *and* has toilet paper. *C. Rosetti 14, at B-dul. G. Magheru, tel. 01/614–8977.*

WORTH SEEING

The most interesting sights aren't on any map: peculiar back alleys, ornate but dusty 19th-century mansions, overgrown gardens, and inebriated workers contemplating half-liters of beer. Tourist offices can arrange guided tours, or you can arm yourself with an up-to-date map and strike out alone from Piața Universității. **Herăstrău Park,** north of Piața Victoriei on Bulevardul Aviatorilor, is a good place to rest, rent a rowboat (next to the village museum), or take a stroll. Also check out the **Muzeul Colectilor d'Arta** (C. Victoriei 111, tel. 01/650–6132; admission 1,000 lei; open Wed.–Sun. 10–5), with Romanian and foreign 19th-century art culled from private collections. From the Romană Metro, take Bulevardul Dacia west.

CASA REPUBLICII

The second-largest government building in the world (after the U.S. Pentagon), the House of the Republic was Ceaușescu's most ambitious project, complete with a secret Metro stop and a vast underground bomb shelter. The 1,000-plus rooms can only be seen through arrangements with a tour guide (Medair Travel and Tourism, tel. 01/311–3190 or 01/311–1801). *B-dul. Libertătii, near P. Națtiunile Unite. Metro: Unirii.*

MUZEUL NATIONAL DE ARTA

Many of Ceaușescu's Securitate forces took refuge inside this former palace during the '89 revolution, only to be shot and thrown from the second-story windows. Unfortunately, most of the museum is closed to the public, as it's still recovering from all the excitement; but the temporary exhibits featuring Romanian artists of the 19th and 20th centuries are worth a trip. Across the street is the **University Library,** which the Securitate set ablaze in 1989 in hopes of quelling the revolution. *Str. Stirbei Vodă 1, near C. Victoriei, tel. 01/614–9774. Admission: 1,500 lei. Open Wed.–Sun. 10–5.*

MUZEUL SATULUI

The open-air Village Museum sprawls over 20 acres and contains more than 80 replicas of Romanian peasant homes and churches. Most of the full-scale homes are inhabited by "peasants" (museum workers) in traditional dress, allowing you to see what life in 16th-century Moldavia and Transylvania was really like. On the occasional Sunday, dancers put on live folk performances. *C. Soseaua Kiseleff, near Lake Herăstrău, tel. 01/222–9110. Metro: Aviatorilor. Admission: 1,000 lei. Open fall–spring, daily 9–8; winter, daily 9–5.*

Muzeul Țaranului Român (Museum of the Romanian Peasant). This museum has costumes, icons, carpets, and other artifacts from rural life, including reconstructed interiors from two 19th-century wooden churches. *Șoseaua Kiseleff 3, just off Piața Victoriei, tel. 01/650–5360. Admission: 1,000 lei. Open Tues.–Sun. 10–6.*

CHEAP THRILLS

Not all of Bucharest's churches were destroyed during Ceaușescu's reign. As you wander around town, keep an eye out for tiny Orthodox churches tucked away on side streets and alleys. They may be crumbling and covered in dust, grime, and scaffolding, but their insides are still resplendent with medieval icons. On Calea Victoriei, at Strada George Enescu, you'll find the dainty **Biserica Alba.** On Iuliu Maniul, next to Palatul Voievodul, is the well-preserved, 16th-century **Old Princely Court Church.** A couple of blocks away, climb over the rubble to peer into the 18th-century **Biserica Stavropoleos** (corner of Str. Stavropoleos and Str. Poștei). A few blocks north is the imposing **Russian Church** (Str. Ion Ghica).

If your stay in Romania is unfortunately limited to Bucharest, you can still take home a taste of Moldavia: Buy folk art, handmade musical instruments, and tailored clothes at **Romartia** (Str. Gabroveni 22). On the surrounding streets, and along Strada Lipscani—the narrow, crooked street that winds from Bulevardul Brătianu to Calea Victoriei—you'll find a big **open-air bazaar** filled with Turkish, Polish, Bulgarian, and Romi merchants selling their wares and haggling over the price of sunflower seeds.

AFTER DARK

Nightlife in Bucharest begins as soon as people leave work. In summer, the outdoor cafés fill quickly and stay that way until about midnight, when the club scene gets going. Most bars are open until at least 3 AM. **Club Indigo** (Str. Eforie 2, off C. Victoriei, near Universităţii Metro, tel. 01/312–6556) is a dark, mellow place to talk and listen to live jazz; American movie classics (in English) are shown for less than $1 at the adjoining **cinema.** Various jazz and blues bands perform at the hip Bohemian enclave **Lăptăria Enarche-Prima Club** (B-dul. Bălcescu 2, on roof of Teatrul National, tel. 01/615–8508; cover $2).

Dance clubs usually cost $2 on Friday and $3 on Saturday, and drinks run about $3–$5. For Euro-techno, head to the large, crowded, and stylish **Vox Maris** (Str. Buzesti 155, just south of Victoriei Metro, tel. 01/311–1994). To hear some Greek dance tunes, try the more down-to-earth, Greek-owned **Vogue** (Str. George Enescu 25, 2 blocks south of Romană Metro, tel. 01/613–9077).

The **Ateneul Român** (corner of Str. Stirbei Voda and C. Victoriei, tel. 01/615–6875) hosts classical music each Friday and Saturday night for $2–$4 per ticket, as does the **Teatrul National** (B-dul. Bălcescu 2, tel. 01/615–4746), near the Universităţii Metro. Stop by during the day to purchase a ticket (50¢) and check the schedule. The **Romanian Opera House** (B-dul. Kogălniceanu 70, at Eroiler Metro, tel. 01/613–1857) has an excellent reputation for its renditions of domestic and foreign works. Tickets ($3) do sell out, so try to buy in advance.

NEAR BUCHAREST

LAKE SNAGOV

The **monastery** at Lake Snagov may or may not be the final resting place of the 15th-century prince of Wallachia, Vlad Tepeş, alias Count Dracula. Legend has it that Vlad was captured by Turks, barely escaped execution, and fled to Snagov; he then ordered the monastery built on one of Lake Snagov's islands for protection. Today, the monastery contains an empty church and a dusty, marble-covered coffin. You can get here easily by taking a boat from the nearby village of Snagov, which has a **campground** ($5 per tent; open May–Sept.), a basic **hotel** (singles $10), and a **restaurant** with an adjoining beer patio. On weekdays, a train leaves Bucharest's Gara de Nord for Snagov (1½ hrs, 50¢) at 7:30 AM, returning at 4:30 PM; on weekends, trains leave at 7:25 AM and 8:25 AM, returning at 6:17 PM and 8:30 PM. To reach the lake itself, walk out of the train station, turn right, and follow signs (1 km/½ mi to lake). Otherwise, you can take a taxi from Otopeni airport to Snagov for $10 each way. Be sure to set the price beforehand, or you'll get ripped off.

CONSTANTA

Despite the vulturous hustlers and pickpockets, Constanţa, the major town on the Black Sea coast, attracts a large summer crowd. The medieval-looking town center is filled with beer patios, stately hotels, elegant restaurants, and several museums—not to mention Roman-era walls, baths, and battlements, remnants from the days when Constanţa was known as Tomis. Two must-see museums are the **Muzeul National de Istorie şi Archeologie** (National History and Archeology Museum; P. Ovidiu 12; admission 3,000 lei; open Tues.–Sun. 10–6) with an impressive collection of Greek busts and Roman coins, and the **Muzeul De Arte Populare** (Museum of Folk Art; B-dul. Tomis 32, at Str. Karatzali, tel. 041/616–133; admission 1,000 lei; open daily 9–8), with Romanian pottery, paintings, jewelry, textiles, and costumes from the 18th and 19th centuries. Walk down Strada Karatzali, on the east shore, to find the public beaches—they're crowded (expect lots of families with bare-bottomed children) but friendly and clean, and the water is refreshing. **Bulevardul Carpaţi,** a marble-covered boardwalk, winds along the south shore.

BASICS

ONT Carpaţi (B-dul. Tomis 66, tel. 041/614–800; open Mon.–Sat. 8–5) and the **Agentia de Turism Littoral** (B-dul. Tomis 48, tel. 041/615–777; open daily 8–7) can help you with hotels and private rooms ($10–$15). **Gara Feroviăra** (P. Victoriei 1, tel. 041/616–725) is a major transport hub, with trains to and from Bucharest (2½ hrs, $3), Braşov (4½ hrs, $6) and Cluj (8 hrs, $8); from the station, walk 20 minutes on Bulevardul Ferdinand to **Victoria Park** (the city center) or take Bus 40 or 43 from in front of the station (where there's a transit map and ticket kiosk). **Danubius Tours** (P. Ovidiu, near Archaeological Museum, tel. 041/619–481) runs ferries between Constanța and İstanbul (7 hrs, $60 one-way, $100 round-trip) three times per week, May through October.

WHERE TO SLEEP AND EAT

Make reservations, as Constant stays booked all summer. **Hotel Intim** (Str. Titulescu 9, at Str. Dianei, tel. 041/617–814) is a palatial old place with beautiful rooms (doubles $50)—you'll have to shell out some cash no matter what, so you might as well enjoy it. Otherwise, settle for the super-clean but unspectacular **Hotel Tineretului** (B-dul. Tomis 20/26, 3 blocks east of Victoria Park, tel. 041/613–590), with doubles for $40 (you can try bargaining down to the price of a single).

You'll find snack stands and some cheap restaurants on Bulevardul Tomis. Just past Strada Sulmona is **Pizzeria Italiana,** where ham-and-mushroom pizzas are $2. At the popular, waterfront **Restaurant Cazino** (B-dul. Carpati 2, tel. 041/617–416), you can sit outdoors and enjoy *sole meuniére* (sautéed sole, $6) or chateaubriand ($5).

TRANSYLVANIA

The name Transylvania (Latin for "across the forest") conjures up scenes from B movies about bloodthirsty vampires, Gothic castles, and the walking undead. But many of Transylvania's Dracula-related tourist attractions are well-preserved towns in their own right, easily reached by rail on the route from Budapest to Bucharest. The ominous **Bran Castle** of Count Dracula legend draws visitors to **Brașov**; the Hungarian stronghold of **Cluj** affords a glimpse of Magyar culture; and the old fortified Saxon settlements at **Sibiu** and **Sighişoara** are impressive legacies of German economic power. Aside from these medieval towns, though, most of Transylvania remains undeveloped.

BRASOV

Set against the lush backdrop of Mts. Tîmpa and Postăvarni, Brașov still has its medieval fortifications, erected by 12th-century Saxon merchants. The town is worth a visit if only for the small alleys, squat battlements, and ornate facades of its historic center. Brașov also hosts the **Golden Stag Folk Festival** in July and August, attracting such names as Boy George, Ray Charles, and James Brown, as well as a **Jazz Festival** in September and an **Octoberfest** in early October. The staff at the **ONT** office (B-dul. Eroilor 27, in lobby of Hotel Aro-Palace, tel. 068/142–840, fax 068/150–427; open weekdays 8–4) books hotel rooms and hands out maps.

COMING AND GOING

Brașov's **train station** (B-dul. Gării) serves Bucharest (3 hrs, $3), Cluj (7 hrs, $5), and other major cities. To get to town, take Tram 4 to Parcul Central, or walk 20 minutes: Head southwest on Bulevardul Victoriei, turn right on Strada Kogălniceanu, right on Bulevardul 15 Novembrei, and right again on Bulevardul Eroilor. Buy international tickets at the **CFR** office (Str. Republicii 53, tel. 068/142–912; open weekdays 7 AM–7:30 PM).

WHERE TO SLEEP AND EAT

The big hotels are overpriced (from $40), and the tourist office doesn't arrange private rooms. Fortunately, locals offering rooms will greet you at the station. The private accommodations office **Exo** (Str. Postăvarul 6, tel. 068/144–591, fax 068/143–975; open Mon.–Sat. 11–8, Sun. 11–2) sets you up in the city center for about $10 a night. From Piața Sfatului, walk north on Strada Postăvarul and look for the video store (Exo's inside). Well-known to seasoned travelers, **Maria Bolea** (tel. 068/311–962) rents nice rooms with kitchen facilities and shared baths for $10 a night. Call at any hour and she'll pick you up at the train station.

Strada Republicii has plenty of food stands and cafés, and Piața Sfatului is lined with good, cheap restaurants. For some great pizza ($3) in a comfortable atmosphere, try **Stradivari** (Piața Sfatului 2, tel. 068/151–165; closed Wed.).

WORTH SEEING

On the southern edge of Piaţa Sfatului, the impressive **Black Church** (open Mon.–Sat. 10–6:30) is a rare Protestant stronghold in the Balkans. Completed in 1477, it took nearly a century to build; by the time the Saxon founders got around to erecting the bell tower, they ran out of money, which is why it's so small. On Piaţa Unirii (from SE corner of P. Sfatului, walk down Str. Hirscher 1 block and turn right on Str. Porta Schei) lies the spired **St. Nicholas's Church** (Sun. mass at 7 AM and 6 PM) and the **First Romanian School Museum,** where you can see what a 15th-century classroom looked like (they haven't changed much in 500 years). To get perspective on all of Braşov and beyond, head to the summit of **Mt. Tîmpa** and take the winding trail (1 km/½ mi) or a three-minute ride on the cable car (10,000 lei round-trip; open Tues.–Fri. 10–7, weekends 10–8). From Piaţa Sfatului, walk southeast on Strada Hirscher, turn right on Strada Castelului, and turn left on Strada Brediceanu (a promenade that runs the length of town); the cable car is located halfway down the promenade.

NEAR BRASOV

CASTELUL BRAN

Looming in the shadow of Mt. Bucegi, 28 km (17 mi) southwest of Braşov, Bran Castle looks like one of those gruesome fortresses you'd find in a Poe story. Built in 1377 by Braşov's Saxon merchants, the castle was intended to protect the town's stalwart citizens from bandits and Turkish raiders. Although it's known as "Dracula's Castle" because of Vlad Tepeş's periodic raids on Braşov, Vlad's ferocious armies never conquered the fortress itself, and it's likely that the count never even set foot inside. You can tour the fortress on your own; with whitewashed walls and 19th-century furniture left over from the castle's stint as Romanian Queen Marie's country home, the interior is hardly spooky. To get here from Braşov, catch the bus marked BRAN (60¢), directly in front of Braşov's University of Transylvania (B-dul. Eroilor, at Str. Mureşenilor); the bus runs daily about every hour 6:30 AM–11:00 PM. *Admission: 8,000 lei. Open Tues.–Sun. 9–4:30.*

SINAIA

Tiny Sinaia remained peacefully isolated in the lush Prahova Valley until 1870, when King Carol fell in love with the countryside and decided to build the ornate **Peleş Castle** (admission 10,000 lei; open Wed.–Sun. 9–3:30) nearby. Today, Sinaia maintains its reputation as a resort town and boasts skiing and extensive hiking in the nearby Bucegi Mountains. Pick up trail maps at the **Montana Hotel** (B-dul. Carol 24, tel. 044/312–751). Behind the Montana Hotel is the **Teleferic** (gondola station), which whisks you to the top of the bluff; in winter, it drops you off at the ski runs. Sinaia is easily reached by several daily trains from Braşov (45 min, $1) and Bucharest (2 hrs, $2). From the station, walk directly up the stone steps to Bulevardul Carpaţi and Bulevardul Carol, both lined with banks, shops, and hotels. The tele-feric is to the left, and Peleş Castle and the monastery are way up the hill to the right. If no one approaches you at the station to offer a private room ($5–$10), try the decrepit but charming **Hotel Intim** (Str. Furnica 1, next to monastery, tel. 044/311–754) where doubles are $19.

SIGHISOARA

The medieval village of Sighişoara juxtaposes multicolor 16th-century houses and cobblestone streets with jagged mountains, lush forests, and a peaceful river. In the heart of a quiet, old neighborhood sits the legendary birthplace of Vlad Tepeş, now the popular **Restaurantul Berarie** (P. Muzeului 5).

Sighişoara's main draw is its medieval **citadel,** in the hills above the modern city. The fortress has three concentric walls and 14 towers, including the 14th-century **clock tower,** which also houses a fine history **museum** (admission 500 lei; open Tues.–Sun. 9–3:30). Climb to the top of the tower for spectacular views of Sighişoara's red-tile roofs and the green mountains beyond. Across the way, the 16th-century **monastery church** is worth a look. Atop Castle Hill, the Gothic **Bergkirche,** built by the Saxons in 1345, adjoins a 14th-century cemetery. The park here is perfect for an afternoon lunch, and a few hiking paths meander south. To reach the church, walk to the south end of Strada Scolii and climb the **Covered Stairway** (1650).

COMING AND GOING

Sighişoara's **train station** (Str. Libertăţii 51, north of downtown, tel. 065/771–886) is on the Cluj–Bucharest line, and all trains running between Budapest and Bucharest via Oradea stop here. To reach downtown, turn right on Strada Libertaţii, turn left on Strada Gării, cross the Tîârnava Mare River at the bridge next to the Orthodox Church, and turn left on Strada Morii to Strada 1 Decembrie. Buy international tickets at the **CFR** office (Str. 1 Decembrie 2, tel. 065/771–820; open weekdays 7:30–7:30) at least one day in advance.

WHERE TO SLEEP AND EAT

The **ONT** office (Str. 1 Decembrie 10, tel. 065/771–072; open weekdays 8–3, Sat. 10–noon) helps find private rooms ($5–$10). The **Hotel Steaua** (Str. 1 Decembrie 12, tel. 0950/771–594) has $25 doubles with baths. At the remote **Dealul Gării** (Str. Dealul Gării 1, tel. 065/771–046; closed Nov.–Apr.), camping costs almost nothing, with double cabins at $10; it's a short cab ride ($1) away. For more than 15 varieties of pizza, head to one of two outposts of **4 Amici** (Str. Morii 7 or Str. Goga 12, tel. 065/772–569 for either).

SIBIU

Of the seven original *sedes* (seats) settled by the Saxons in Transylvania during the 12th century, Sibiu was for many centuries the wealthiest and most powerful. Few Romanian cities have remained as pleasant, and after a few days you may understand why some residents call this the city of "mystical sadness and impossible beauty." Sibiu has two levels: the upper citadel, a historic district; and the lower citadel, a charmless wasteland. In the northern upper section is **Piaţa Mare,** with shops, cafés, and, right around the corner at Piaţa Mica, a cool bookstore (next to Dori's Bistro) with English titles. **Strada N. Bălcescu,** the main promenade, meanders south from Piaţa Mare to Piaţa Unirii.

BASICS

The **Prima Ardeleana S.A.** office (P. Unirii 1, tel. 069/211–788; open weekdays 8–4) offers maps, books hotel rooms, and exchanges traveler's checks. The **Trans-Europa** office (Str. N. Bălcescu 41, upstairs, tel. 069/215–057; open weekdays 9–5, Sat. 9–noon) also exchanges traveler's checks at a good rate for almost no commission. Sibiu's **train station** (P. 1 Decembrie 1918, tel. 069/211–139) is northeast of the town center; walk 10 minutes on Strada General Magheru from Piaţa Mare, or cab it for $1. Going to Cluj (4 hrs, $4), you'll change trains in Copşa Mică; to Bucharest (6 hrs, $3.50), you'll change in Braşov. Buy international tickets at the **CFR** office (Str. N. Bălcescu 6, tel. 069/212–085; open weekdays 7 AM–7:30 PM).

WHERE TO SLEEP AND EAT

Try the **Hotel La Podul Minciunilor** (Str. Azilului 1, tel. 069/217–259), a converted house with funky furnishings and five $15–$20 rooms; make reservations. From Piaţa Gării, walk up Bulevardul 9 Mai and turn left on Strada Azilului.

There are cafés and food stands along Strada N. Bălcescu, and at the northern end of Strada Mitropoliei where it hits Piaţa Griviţei. **Împăratul Romanilor** (Str. N. Bălcescu 4; open daily 7 AM–midnight) serves excellent meat dishes, such as lamb with polenta (about $2); vegetarians can try the pasta ($1) or a variety of veggie salads ($1).

WORTH SEEING

Near Piaţa Mare sits the **Brukenthal Museum** (admission 2,000 lei; open Tues.–Sun. 10–4:30), with its excellent collection of regional silver and paintings by Romanian—especially Transylvanian—artists; and the **Catholic Cathedral,** with an elaborate interior. Piaţa Griviţei is dominated by the imposing **Evangelical Cathedral** (open weekdays 9–1), a Lutheran church rumored to shelter the tomb of Dracula's son, Mihnea the Bad. South on Strada Mitropoliei is the **Orthodox Cathedral,** a miniature of İstanbul's Hagia Sophia.

BUKOVINA

In the northeastern corner of the country, Bukovina is one of Romania's most isolated and pristine provinces. This stunningly wild land teems with medieval-looking villages and anachronistic farming settlements. If you don't mind roughing it a bit and foraging for food in the occasional market, you'll discover a part of the world untainted by cement or technology. Even better, you'll get the chance to explore Bukovina's painted monasteries, considered some of Romania's outstanding artistic treasures.

SUCEAVA

Suceava's lavishly adorned churches and relic-filled treasuries have tempted European fortune-hunters since the Middle Ages. The wily Hapsburgs invaded and conquered the town in 1775, and it remained part of Austria and Germany until the end of World War I. Much of Suceava was destroyed during World War II, so most of the architecture that remains is from the communist era. Still, the town has nice parks, and the surrounding fir-covered mountains are always visible. More important, Suceava makes a great base from which to explore Bukovina's spectacular monasteries.

BASICS

The **ONT** office (Str. N. Bălcescu 2, tel. 030/221–297) will hand out maps, help you find a driver to the monasteries (which costs upwards of $30 per day), and exchange cash at good rates, but it doesn't deal in private rooms. Go to **Banca Comerciala Romana S.A.** (Str. Stefan Cel Mare, just past Parcul Central, tel. 030/221–112; open weekdays 8:30–1, weekends 9–2) to cash traveler's checks or get lei from a credit card.

COMING AND GOING

Suceava has two train stations: **Gara Suceava** (Str. N. Iorga 6) and **Gara Nord** (Str. Gării 4), both 3 km (2 mi) from the city center. Express trains run to Bucharest (7 hrs, $6), Iaşi (3 hrs, $2), Cluj (6 hrs, $5), and Timişoara (8 hrs, $7); local trains head north to Bukovina five times daily. From Gara Suceava, take Trolleybus 2 (across the street from the train station) to the city center; from Gara Nord, take Bus 1 or Trolleybus 5 eight stops.

WHERE TO SLEEP AND EAT

Sixty-eight-dollar doubles await at the comfortable hotels **Suceava** (Str. N. Bălcescu 2, north side of piaţa, tel. 030/521–080) and **Arcaşul** (Str. Mihai Viteazul 4/6, behind church, tel. 030/210–944). Each has a good restaurant with the usual soup, meat, and potatoes ($3). Oddly enough, the **Lacto-Vegetarian Restaurant** (Str. N. Bălcescu 4, on piaţa behind Hotel Suceava, tel. 030/225–458) serves mostly meat dishes (delicious roast chicken, potatoes, and salad, $3).

WORTH SEEING

The 1522 **Sfintu Ioan Cel Nou Monastery** (Monastery of St. George; Str. I. V. Viteazu 2; admission free; open daily 8–9) has immense but badly faded exterior frescoes. If you can't make it to any of Bukovina's monasteries, come here to get a small sense of what you'll be missing. From Piaţa 22 Decembrie, head south on Bulevardul Ana Ipătescu, turn left on Strada Mitropoliei, and turn left on Strada Ioan Vodă Viteazu. On the east side of the city, **Parcul Cetătii** is one of northern Romania's most expansive and beautifully overgrown attractions, encompassing some 20 square km (8 square mi) of lush forests and meandering rivers on a hill. At the top of the hill is a sprawling cemetery with massive, ornate vaults and elaborate tombs. If you get caught in the park after sunset, you'll have a heck of a time finding your way out. To reach the park (a half-hour walk), follow Strada Mitropoliei out of town, staying to the left and following the road uphill another 5–10 minutes.

NEAR SUCEAVA

The Bukovine monasteries seem far beyond the reach of modern civilization, but most have small hotels and restaurants nearby. If you miss your return train to Suceava, you can arrange lodging at any point along the so-called monastery trail. The closest and least dramatic monastery is **Putna,** which has undergone so many renovations it feels more like a modern building than a 500-year-old relic. Three daily trains from Suceava run through unblemished countryside to Putna; turn right out of the train station, bear left when the road forks, and continue about 2 km (1 mi) to the monastery. On the way, you'll pass a tourist complex (doubles $22) with a cheap restaurant. Or, stay at the nice hotel (outside monastery; doubles $16, diminutive cabins $5; open June–Aug.) run by monks.

MOLDOVITA MONASTERY

Built in 1532, Moldoviţa is Bukovina's largest and best-preserved monastery. On its exterior is the famed *Siege of Constantinople,* a massive fresco cycle divided into cartoonlike panels. Styles in this series range from gruesomely realistic (see the panel of Turkish cavaliers forging through a sea of crushed bodies) to stylized and allegorical (see the infant Jesus tipping the scales of justice against the Turks).

To reach Moldoviţa, take the Suceava–Cluj' train to **Vama** and transfer for Vatra Moldovitei; the train station is 1 km (½ mi) from the monastery. Three daily trains (in early morning, mid-afternoon, and evening) run between Suceava and Vama. Trains between Vama and Vatra Moldavitei run less frequently, so check the train schedule for transfer times. Nuns at the monastery may set you up with a local family, especially if you're traveling solo. Otherwise, **Hotel Mărul de Aur** (tel. 030/336–201; doubles $20, $14 off season) is a charming hostelry with spacious rooms and a restaurant; reserve ahead. Follow the paved road past the turn-off to the monastery a few hundred yards.

VORONET MONASTERY

Perched on the cusp of a forested ridge, Voroneţ Monastery is one of Bukovina's best, known for its well-preserved murals. Erected by Stefan the Great in 1488 (illuminated in 1546–57), Voroneţ was considered in its day to be the flagship of the monastery fleet. Its west wall contains the strikingly detailed *Last Judgment* fresco, a masterpiece that depicts believers being saved and "sinners" (i.e., non-Christians) going to Hell. Note the intense shade of blue used in the background of Voroneţ's frescoes—this pigment, which has not been found in any other fresco, is now known as Voronet blue.

Voroneţ is tough to reach without a car. If you're up for a journey, take a bus or train from Suceava to **Gura Humorului,** and catch one of the buses (about four per day 7 AM–4 PM) to the monastery, 4 km (2½ mi) south of town. Or, walking from the Gura Humorului train station, turn left onto the main road, follow it about 10 minutes, take the first left leading out of town, and continue to the monastery (about an hour). Ask at the monastery and around the village of Voroneţ for private rooms. For tips on staying in Gura Humorului, *see* Humor Monastery, *below*.

HUMOR MONASTERY

The Humor Monastery was built in 1530 by Toader Bubuoig and Petru Rareş and painted in 1534 by an artist named Toma, one of the few to sign his name on a Bukovine fresco (look for the soldier coming out of a Moldovan stronghold with the "Toma" written on his head). Little is known about Toma, but his work at Humor speaks volumes—check out the 20 panels dedicated to St. Nicolae on the southern wall. Also note the "funny devil," as he's known by the monks, depicted not as a horrifying monster but as a fat, old woman with an infectious belly laugh.

To reach Humor Monastery, take the train from Suceava to Gura Humorului, where buses run to Humor about seven times a day. If you'd rather walk, the road leading to the monastery runs through a beautiful stretch of wide, sweeping valleys. Come nightfall, ask at the monastery about a private room or head back to Suceava. Otherwise, try **Hotel Carpaţi** (Str. 9 Mai, tel. 030/231–103; doubles $22), which also has a decent restaurant.

SLOVAKIA

S lovakia doesn't have the name recognition of its neighbors. Not only is it the newest country on the continent, but the last time it conquered anyone was during the 10th century, when it was part of the Great Moravian Empire. For the next millenium the region was controlled by Hungarian kings and emperors, and only in the past century did the concept of Slovak nationhood emerge as a tangible political reality. Slovakia's "Velvet Divorce" from the Czech Republic on January 1, 1993, was quick, mutually acceptable, and bloodless— thereby drawing little Western notice.

What has pricked Western ears, though, has been the circuslike battle between the two main poltical camps to govern the country. Slovakia has had five governments since 1989, and the current prime minister, Vladimir Meciar, has been elected to the premier's post on three separate occasions. Since the last election in 1994, when Meciar came back for the third time, his government has been accused of the kidnapping and deporting of the president's son, whose father is a bitter enemy of Meciar's. Those opposed to Meciar's Movement for a Democratic Slovakia will remember such incidents come election time in autumn 1998.

Despite the politics, the good news for travelers is that hardly anyone knows Slovakia exists, which makes it a delightful, inexpensive destination, especially for those who love the outdoors. The people will actually welcome you, and you'll find some of the most varied (and cheap) vacation spots in Europe, from medieval towns like Banská Bystrica to the Vysoké Tatry (High Tatras), a stunning alpine range interwoven with superb hiking trails and ski resorts and populated by chamois and golden eagles. Bratislava, the capital, is a surreal mix of architectural styles brushed by the heavy hand of Communist aesthetics. It's hard to get a sense of Slovak identity in Bratislava, so close to the borders of the Czech Republic, Hungary, and Austria, but that changes as you move east through the country. Insulated by increasingly rugged terrain, the villages become more and more timeless and Western influences less apparent.

BASICS

MONEY

US$1 = 33 Slovak crowns and 3 Slovak crowns = 10¢. Since the breakup of Czechoslovakia, Slovakia has been phasing in its own new money, the Slovak crown (Sk), which is divided into 100 hellers. You

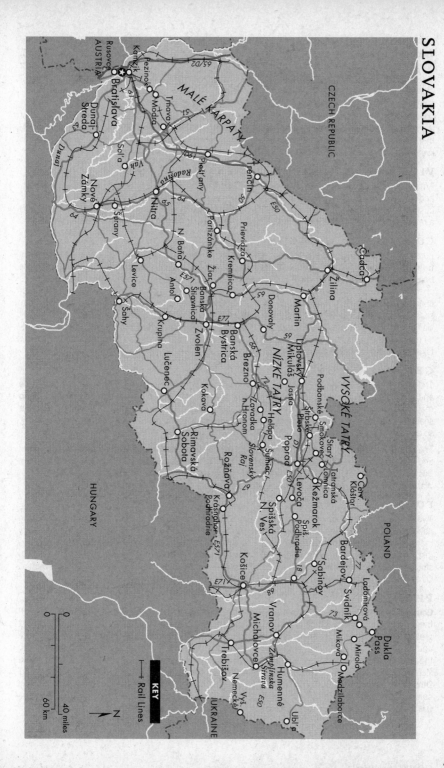

SLOVAKIA

CZECH REPUBLIC

AUSTRIA

Rusovce
Karloves
Pezinské
Bratislava
Dunaj-
Streda
Dunaj
Modra
Trnava
Sol'a
Váh
Nové
Zámky
Šúrany
Nitra
Levice
Antol
Šahy
Krupina

MALÉ KARPATY

Piešt'any
Radošná
Trenčín

N Baňa
Partizánske
Žiar
Kremnica
Banská
Štiavnica
Banská
Bystrica
Zvolen
Lučenec
Kokava
Rimavská
Sobota

E50

Čadca
Žilina

Martin
Donovaly
Liptovský
Mikuláš
Jasná
Brezno
Zavadka
n.Hronom
Helpa
Slovenský
Raj
Šuňiac
Rožňava
Krásnohor.
Podhradie

NÍZKE TATRY

VYSOKÉ TATRY

Podbanské
Smokovec
Štrbské
Pleso
Starý
Smokovec
Tatranská
Lomnica
Poprad
Levoča
Kežmarok
Spiš
Podhradie
Spišská
N. Ves

Košice

Červ
Kláštor

POLAND

Bardejov
Sabinov
Svidník
Ľadomírová
Mirolа
Dukla
Pass
Mikova
Medzilaborce

Vranov
Michalovce
Trebišov
Nemecké
Humenné
Zemplínska
Šírava
Vyš.
Nemecké
Ubl'a

HUNGARY

UKRAINE

E65/D2
E50
E57
E77

KEY
Rail Lines

0   40 miles
0   60 km

N

739

can now change cash or traveler's checks at several banks, and ATM machines dot the city center. **Všeobecná úverová** is the largest Slovak bank; look for its blue "B" symbol. There are also solid foreign banks like Tatra Banka, whose branch on Františkanske namestie contains the American Express office, and Ludova Banka, where you can make just about any transaction. Keep your exchange receipts to change Slovak crowns upon departure.

HOW MUCH IT WILL COST • If you stay in budget accommodations, you can still eat well and spend under $35 per day. Bus and train services are reasonably priced (under 250 Sk from one end of the country to the other), and cheap hotels are around 500 Sk. The best deal, however, is eating out; there's little financial difference between living off groceries and eating at restaurants. Even skiers can live cheaply in Slovakia: Lift tickets and ski rentals each cost about 200 Sk per day.

VISA AND ENTRY REQUIREMENTS

Americans can stay visa-free for up to 30 days; Canadians for 90 days; Brits for 6 months. Australians, and Kiwis, however, need a visa (US$46), available at Slovak consulates or at the border. Upon entry, customs officials may ask you to show sufficient funds for each day you plan to stay in the country, and a return ticket or enough money to leave.

COMING AND GOING

Eurail and InterRail are not accepted in Slovakia, but most people still arrive (usually in Bratislava) by **train** from Budapest (3 hrs, 300 Sk round trip), Prague (5 hrs, 500 Sk round trip on regular express trains, 700 Sk on EC or IC trains), or Vienna (1 hr, 220 Sk round trip). Round trip tickets are always cheaper, so be sure to ask for them (*Spiatočy listok* in Slovak). You don't need reservations for international trains, but you may want to make them to ensure yourself a seat on longer trips or during holiday seasons. Bratislava's growing **M. R. Štefánik International Airport** now serves most of the world, mainly via British Airways, Swiss Air, and Czech Air (CSA). Flying into Vienna is still convenient, though; a shuttle runs six times a day between Schwechat Airport in Vienna and Bratislava's main bus station. The trip takes an hour and costs 74 Austrian schillings.

GETTING AROUND

Though the mountainous terrain limits them to a small number of lines, the **ŽSR** trains cost the same and are faster, less crowded, and far more comfortable than buses. Look for express trains between major destinations (they're printed in red on the schedules). You can upgrade to first class (comfier seats and cleaner bathrooms) by paying the conductor 50% of the basic ticket price. Trains are timely, so don't be late for your connection.

The **ČSAD** bus network (newer signs indicate its new Czech-less name, **SAD**) has been raising prices and cutting service over the past few years, but it's still fairly cheap. Avoid traveling on weekends, when bus frequency drops drastically. Express-bus schedules are printed in red on station schedule boards. Warning: Buses are often early, so make sure you are, too, if your connection is important.

FOOD

Two words: pork and potatoes. Almost every menu includes a *bravčovy rezeň* (pork chop), and the national dish is *bryndzové halušky* (potato dumplings with sheep cheese and bacon fat). Almost every major town has a veggie restaurant; if yours doesn't, you can still find egg- or cheese-based dishes— just make sure you say "*bezmäsité jedlá*" (without meat). Slovak *potraviny* (grocery stores) seem to stock approximately half their shelf space with sweets, and few of them are open much later than 7. Other words you should know: *káva* (coffee), *čaj* (tea), and *pivo* (beer).

PHONES

Country code: 421. Public phones (both coin- and card-operated) can be difficult to find in Slovakia. If there's only one in town, it'll be in front of the post office. Local calls cost 2 Sk. Phone cards (100 Sk) greatly reduce the risk of being disconnected during international calls. Otherwise, go to a post office and pay the clerk to place your long-distance call. For collect and credit-card calls from pay phones to the United States, insert 6 Sk or a phone card and dial **AT&T Direct Access**ˢᴹ (tel. 0042100101), **MCI** (tel. 0042100112), **Sprint** (tel. 0042107187), **Canada Direct** (for Canada; tel. 0042100151), or **BT Direct** (for the U.K.; tel. 0042104401). Your money or card will (usually) be returned after the call is completed. About area codes: If you're calling from outside Slovakia, drop the 0 from the area code. The 0 is for long-distance calls within Slovakia.

LANGUAGE

The national language, **Slovenčina,** is similar to Czech (*see* Basics *in* Chapter 6). German is widely spoken, English less so, and in Bratislava a fair number speak French. Some common terms that differ from Czech are *d'akujem* (thank you), *dobrý den* (good day), *do videnia* (good-bye), *nie* (no), *kol'ko stojí . . .?* (how much is . . .?), *nerozumiem* (I don't understand), and *nehovorím po slovenský* (I don't speak Slovak—probably evident by this point).

BRATISLAVA

Slovakia's capital, Bratislava, stands at the juncture of four countries—Slovakia, the Czech Republic, Hungary, and Austria—testifying to both the historical forces that have shaped Central Europe and the lingering presence of the former Soviet Union.

The brooding **hrad** (castle), once a fortress protecting the Hungarian Empire's frontier, dwarfs modern high-rises and the neo-Gothic **Dóm sv. Martina** (St. Martin's Cathedral), topped with a Hungarian crown. The **Staré Mesto** (Old Town) is charming, with remnants of city walls built during the 13th–18th centuries surrounding a few stately palaces. Not that Bratislava hasn't had architectural growing pains: Petržalka, the huge housing project across the Danube River, was inspired by Communist-era concrete aesthetics, and towering above town is **Most SNP TV tower,** a dubious tribute to modernity.

BASICS

AMERICAN EXPRESS • Tatratour, next to a Tatra Banka, holds cardholder mail, deals with lost or stolen traveler's checks, and changes money at fair rates. *Františkánske nám. 3, tel. 07/533–5536, fax 07/533–5538. Open weekdays 9–5:30.*

EMBASSIES • Canada (consulate only): *Kolárska 4, tel. 07/361–277 or 07/361–220. Open Mon. and Wed. 3–5.* **United States:** *Hviezdoslavovo námestie 4, tel. 07/333–338 or 330–861. Open weekdays 8:30–noon and 2–4.*

Great Britain. Aussies and Kiwis can seek help here, but those with complicated problems will be directed to their nearest embassies—in Vienna and Bonn, respectively. *British Panska 16, tel. 07/531–2313, 07/531–9633, or 07/531–9632.*

MAIL AND PHONES • The main post office (nám. SNP 34–35; open weekdays 7 AM–8 PM, Sat. 7–6, Sun. 9–2) is on Bratislava's main square. Its **phone office** is open weekdays 7 AM–9 PM.

VISITOR INFORMATION • Bratislava Information Service (BIS) (Klobučnícka 2, tel. 07/533–3715; open weekdays 8–7, Sat. 9–2) arranges hotel rooms, private rooms, and, in July and August, dorm rooms for 20 Sk. Pick up a city map for 20 Sk. There's also a BIS branch in the train station (tel. 07/204–4484; open weekdays 8:30–6:30, weekends 9–6). Try to go there in person, because the person answering the phone probably won't speak English.

COMING AND GOING

Trains leaving from the **main train station** (Predstaničné nám., tel. 07/204–4484) serve most major European destinations, including Budapest (3 hrs, 290 Sk), Prague (5 hrs, 500 Sk), and Vienna (1 hr, 220 Sk); from the station, Tram 1 heads to town. The long-distance **bus depot** (tel. 07/211–2222—but beware that the operator will not speak English) is on Mlynské nivy. Allow plenty of time to purchase a ticket before you board. From the depot take Bus 217, 216, or 215 to town. The **M. R. Štefánik International Airport** (tel. 07/522–0036), east of the city, serves Prague (7,000 Sk) and Warsaw (13,000 Sk). The **ČSA** office (Štúrova 13, tel. 07/361–038; open weekdays 9–5) has student airfares. To reach downtown from the airport, take the ČSA bus or a taxi.

WHERE TO SLEEP

Clubhotel (Odbojárov 3, tel. 07/256–369) is in a student area northeast of the center; doubles go for 880 Sk. Take tram 2, 4, 6, or 10 to Odbojárov and turn right. Also close to the center, and near the city's largest outdoor market, is **Hotel Dukla** (Dulovo nam. 1, tel. 07/526–9318 or 07/526–9815), where doubles range from 1,590–2,350 Sk; take bus 23 from the train station or bus 38 from the Novy Most. **Hotel Junior** (Drienova 14, tel. 07/238–000), in outlying Ružinov, is right next to a small lake; doubles are 1,700 Sk. Take tram 8, 9, or 12 east to Ružinov. **Hotel Sorea** (Kralovske udolie 6, tel. 07/531–4442), with doubles for 1,540 Sk, is the fairest of them all—modern and friendly—but it's small, so reserve ahead.

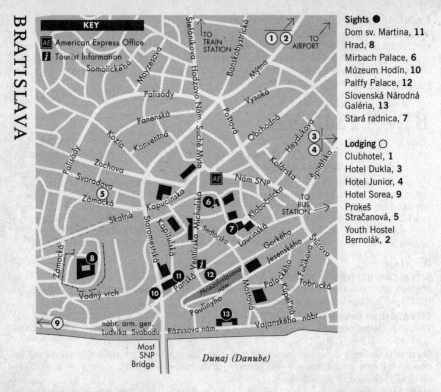

KEY

AE American Express Office

i Tourist Information

Sights ●
Dom sv. Martina, **11**
Hrad, **8**
Mirbach Palace, **6**
Múzeum Hodín, **10**
Palffy Palace, **12**
Slovenská Národná
Galéria, **13**
Stará radnica, **7**

Lodging ○
Clubhotel, **1**
Hotel Dukla, **3**
Hotel Junior, **4**
Hotel Sorea, **9**
Prokeš
Stračanová, **5**
Youth Hostel
Bernolák, **2**

Dunaj (Danube)

HOSTELS AND STUDENT HOUSING • Prokeš Stračanová.
Clean, cheap, and central, it functions both as a hotel and a hostel. Lay your head down in the hotel year-round; all doubles (720 Sk) have baths. The hostel is open from July 15 through August, with doubles and triples for 300 Sk. *Svoradova 13, tel. 07/531–5386. Tram 1, 5, or 9 to Kapucínska; cross bridge (toward castle) and turn right on Židovská, then left on Svoradova.*

Youth Hostel Bernolák. From June to mid-September, you can crash here in a single (300 Sk) or a dorm bed (270 Sk) in a quad, breakfast included. A hostel card will save you 20 Sk. Bonus: There's a pool. *Bernolákova 1, tel. 07/397–721. Tram 2, 8, 9, 10, or 11 to Vazovova; go left on Blumentálska, left on Bernolákova, and enter under STUDENTSKY DOMUV JURA HRONCA sign.*

FOOD
Bratislava was the capital of Hungary for centuries, and the spicy preferences of the Magyar palette still linger. Recent privatization has opened the doors of all kinds of ethnic restaurants. **Food Market,** a passageway off Gorkeho, at Hviezodslavovo námestie, is home to several cheap fast-food eateries, with French, Italian, Chinese, British, and Mexican options.

Chez David. Make this gourmet kosher spot (with an English menu) your one splurge. Try the roasted salmon with asparagus sauce (177 Sk) or the turkey breast with apples (137 Sk). *Zámocká 13, near castle, tel. 07/531–3824. Open Sun.–Thurs. 11:30–10, Fri. 11:30–3.*

Vegetariánska Jedáleň. Order and pay as you enter this crowded vegetarian place. Dishes combine fruits, vegetables, yogurt, tofu, and salad, all for less than 50 Sk. *Laurinská 8. Open weekdays 11–3.*

WORTH SEEING
The center of Bratislava, on the northern bank of the Danube, is bordered by the massive *hrad* (castle) on the hill and the space-age **Most SNP** bridge just below it. What's left of the capital's **Staré Mesto** (Old Town) is huddled to the east of the castle. At the center of **Staré Mesto** is the 15th-century **Stará radnica** (Old Town Hall; Hlavné nám.), with a sunny courtyard and a **museum** (admission 20 Sk; open

Tues.–Sun. 10–5) that offers a history of the city and a display of various torture devices with graphic depictions of their use. Ask about the summer concerts and plays.

Slovakia's central repository of art, the **Slovenská Národná Galéria** (Slovak National Gallery; Riečna 1, tel. 07/533–4276; admission 25 Sk), is on the north bank of the Danube, downriver from Most SNP. In the 1970s, the sober 18th-century building grew an astonishingly awkward red-metal wing, a crippling aesthetic blow. Pop inside anyway to see the small collection of modern Slovak works. Two other Slovakian collections are on display in Staré Mesto: **Mirbach Palace** (Františkánske nám. 11; open 10–5), with 18th- and 19th-century art, and the renovated **Palffy Palace** (Panská 19; open Tues.–Sun. 10–5), with an intriguing exhibit dedicated to the founders of modern Slovak art.

One look at Bratislava's **hrad** and you'll understand why locals refer to this squat, square building as an upturned table. The castle dominates the hill above the city, leaving a firm imprint on its skyline. Three impressive gates lead into the grounds, which offer good views, pleasant lawns, and summer concerts. The main building houses a museum with some interesting exhibits on the history of the region; the temporary exhibits are generally excellent. *Tel. 07/531–1444. Trolleybus 216 or 217 to rear entrance; or cross under Most SNP and climb the winding cobblestone streets. Open year-round Tues.–Fri. 9–5, Sat. and Sun. 10–6.*

Separated from the castle by the new highway is **Dóm sv. Martina.** As the tiny gold crown atop its tower testifies, this 15th-century Gothic church served as the coronation site for Hungarian monarchs from 1563 to 1830. Roughly between the castle and cathedral, the narrow **Múzeum Hodín** (Clock Museum; Zidovská 1, tel. 531–1940, admission 20 SK; open Wed.–Mon. 10–5) is mentioned in many architecture textbooks as one of Central Europe's best remaining examples of rococo architecture. It was built on such a small lot that it's only 7 ft wide at the base, making it the narrowest building in Europe. Inside are three floors of clocks.

For a glimpse of the recent past, check out **Slavin,** a gray marble monument celebrating the Russians' liberation of Slovak territory in 1945; you'll see Soviet soldiers waving a flag. From here the view of the city is actually better than the view from the castle, and you can visit the graves of fallen Russian soldiers, their ranks noted in Cyrillic.

For serious hrad-watchers, the little fortress at **Devin** is the area's real jewel. A lone tower stands watch over the timeless mingling of the Danube and Morava rivers, and makes for a fantastic photo at sunrise or sunset. Recently opened for the first time is the section of the castle perched on a craggy ridge. On July 5, Devin welcomes hundreds of pilgrims who come to celebrate Saints Cyril and Methodius, the codifiers of the erstwhile Slavonic language. *Take bus 29 from underneath Novy Most.*

AFTER DARK

Bratislava brims with cinemas showing subtitled American films. Look for CESKE TITULKY (Czech subtitles) or SLOVENSKE TITULKY (Slovak subtitles) signs; otherwise, films are dubbed (you have been warned). Some of the hipper cinemas are **Charlie Centrum** (Špitálska 6, tel. 07/363–396), **Kino Hviezda** (Nam. 1 Maja 11, tel. 07/367–471), which also shows movies outside in the *Zahrada* (Garden), and the **Kino Tatra** (Nam. 1 Maja 7, tel. 07/368–994). In summer, check out the amphitheater on ulica Búdková, which holds movies and concerts outdoors; check the schedule at BIS (*see* Basics, *above*). Beware that theaters will change films at a moment's notice; call the cinema ahead of time if you're dying to see a particular pic. You can also call 145 to get (in Slovak) the day's movie listings.

Nightmare (Františkánske nám. 10, tel. 07/533–3073) is *the* place for blues or jazz on Thursday; other nights the hip, English-speaking bartenders offer suggestions. **Stará Sladovňa** (Cintorínska 32, tel. 532–2111) is a fixture of Bratislava nightlife: *"Mamut"* (Mammoth), as it's been dubbed, maintains a festive crowd in a typical Central European beer-hall atmosphere. The **Gremium** (Gorkého 11, tel. and fax 07/533–0653) is an art gallery/café/pension/restaurant popular with Bratislava's gay crowd. Tackle the dance floor to the tune of Western pop music and techno at **Charlie Centrum** (below the movie theater), open 'til the wee hours.

BANSKA BYSTRICA

Locals will tell you that Banská Bystrica (BAN-skuh bis-TREE-tzuh) is at the geographic center of Europe. Whether or not this is true, Banská Bystrica, encircled by hills and mountains, is certainly at the heart of Slovakia. The town prospered during the Middle Ages as a mining center (*banská* means "mine") but is best known as the home of the Slovak National Uprising (SNP) against the Nazis in 1944.

This unsuccessful movement was a two-month-long, grassroots call to arms by rural residents to push fascist Germany westward. Now bustling, Banská Bystrica is filled with restaurants, bars, students, and, as the government moves more bureaus outside Bratislava, civil servants. The fine central square, a beautifully remodeled plaza lined with churches, pastel "burgher" houses, and outdoor cafés, is one place where you can get a real feeling for what Slovakia is.

BASICS

Kultúrne-informačné stredisko (KIS) is run by a young staff that gives advice about music, cultural events, and lodging. *Nám. Moyzesa 1, tel. 088/543–69, fax 088/535–92. Open weekdays 9–7.*

Satur. Located between the stations and town, Satur will arrange private rooms (from 300 Sk per person) if you plan to stay a few nights; otherwise, they can book more expensive hotel rooms. **Tatra Banka** (tel. 088/742–572), the local AmEx agent, shares the Satur office; change cash and traveler's checks (1% commission) here. *Nám. Slobody 4, tel. 088/742–569, fax 088/742–568. From train or bus station, head west toward town, take first right (Kukucínova), and continue 100 yds to nám. Slobody.*

COMING AND GOING

The **train** and **bus stations** are next to each other just east of town. Most train trips require a change in Zvolen (22 min, 12 Sk), and trains stop here hourly; total fare from Banská Bystrica to Bratislava is 128 Sk; to Prague, 500 Sk. Stash your bags in the station, 24 hours a day, for 15 Sk. Buses serve the region more thoroughly, but study the departure board carefully: Distant destinations are listed according to which small nearby town they stop at first. To reach downtown, turn left on Duklianskych hrdinov (the busy street in front of the stations) and turn right when you see the spires marking Námestie SNP (the main square)—about 10 minutes by foot.

WHERE TO SLEEP

Banská Bystrica's classiest spot, **Hotel Národný Dom** (Národná 11, tel. 088/723–737, fax 088/725–786; doubles 600 Sk), is just a block from the main square. Nearby is **Hotel Passage** Urpin (J. Cikkera 5, tel. 088/724–556, fax 088/723–831; doubles 680 Sk). The cheapest place in town is **BPM Prevádzka** (Podhaj 51, tel. 088/761–626; 150 Sk per person), part of a cluster of dreary high-rises. From the stations, take Trolleybus 2 (buy the 6 Sk ticket from the driver) to the PODHAJ stop; continue walking in the trolley bus's direction, take the first right, and walk uphill to the second street on the left. The only indication of the hotel's existence is a small sign on the door: TURISTICKA UBYTOVNA.

Hotel Lux (Nové námestie 2, tel. 088/724–141), a short walk from the central square, is the tallest building in the city; doubles are 1,620 Sk. The newly built **Arkadia** (Namestie SNP 5, tel. 088/702–111 or 088/702–500; doubles 2,190 Sk.) is a real treat if you can nab a room.

FOOD

Banská Bystrica has amazing restaurants, especially on the square; even the fast food is good. The main square is beautifully lit up at night, and many of the bars and restaurants (and ice-cream stands) stay open late. **Copaline Baguette,** at the lower end of námestie SNP, makes a mean submarine sandwich for less than 35 Sk, and it's open daily until midnight. **Fishman** (Dolná 5, tel. 088/725–105; open daily 11–midnight), a short walk from the lower end of Namestie SNP, has fresh seafood and Mexican-inspired meals (tacos—very exotic for Slovakia). **Quatro** (Horná ulica 18, entrance through courtyard; no phone) and **Pub 21** (Dolná 12, tel. 088/724–535) draw frenetic youths.

WORTH SEEING

Pay homage to the SNP by visiting the engaging **Múzeum SNP** (Kapitulska 23, 1 block south of main square tel. 088/723–258, admission 10; open Tues.–Sun. 9–6), in a remarkable split building that locals describe as a potato cut in half. **Námestie SNP** features a number of interesting houses, including that of the Thurzo family; the graffiti on the outside was lopped on in the 16th century, when the family's wealth was at its height. Today the building houses the **Stredoslovenske muzeum** (nám. SNP 4; tel. 088/725–896, admission 10 Sk adults; open Sun.–Fri. 8–noon and 1–4). Across the street is the **Benický House,** now an art gallery. At the top of the square, **Dóm Panny Márie** (Cathedral of the Virgin Mary), built in 1255, features a carved-wood altar and remaining bits of the city fortifications. For a spectacular view of the valley in which Banská Bystrica sits (as well as the concrete high-rises that litter its suburbs), head up to **Urpín,** the hill that looms immediately south of town. On the hill's grassy crest, locals like to spread out blankets and, well. . . . It's a half hour to the summit and another half hour to **Vartovka,** an observatory in the woods. For information on longer hikes, ask at KIS (*see* Basics, *above*).

OUTSIDE BANSKA BYSTRICA

SPANIA DOLINA

Nestled in the foothills of the **Nizke Tatry** (Low Tatras), this tranquil little village seems suspended in time. Its centerpiece is a white church with an onion-shape, wood-paneled spire that has yet to bow to age. Drop by on a Sunday morning and you'll see some of this hamlet's 150 residents making their way to Mass, the women in black and some of the men in traditional dress. You'll be sure to pique the locals' interest by presenting yourself in the town's *krčma* (bar) for a drink. Half a day will do the job; just take a local bus from the Banska Bystrica bus station, and remember to catch the last bus back at 4.

VYSOKE TATRY (HIGH TATRAS)

Ask the average Slovak what you should see in her country, and she will invariably say Vysoké Tatry (High Tatras). The mountains' main ridge comprises 20 jagged peaks (Mount Gerlach is the highest at 8,758 ft) and stretches 26 km (16 mi) along the Polish border, making it the shortest alpine range in the world. Tucked within are several ski resorts (lift tickets cost 250 Sk), miles of excellent hiking, impenetrable pine forests, and 35 glacial lakes that, according to legend, can bestow X-ray vision upon anyone who bathes in them. **Harmanec** publishes two indispensable maps (50 Sk each): one for the mountains themselves and the other for the towns at the southern foot of the range.

You can't camp in **Tatran National Park** (TANAP), so base yourself at one of the three resorts—Štrbské Pleso to the west, Starý Smokovec in the middle, and Tatranská Lomnica to the east—or commute from Poprad (*see below*). You can also stay in mountain *chaty* (huts) within the park for about 400 Sk per person, but you must reserve in advance. Contact Satur in Starý Smokovec (*see below*) or AIA in Poprad. **Buses** and **ŽSR trams** connect all the towns.

POPRAD

Think of Poprad as a hub. The square **námestie sv. Egídia** makes for a pleasant stroll, but the real draws are cheap hotels, *potraviny, lekáreň* (pharmacies), and the information office. Your first stop should be the extremely helpful **AIA office** (nám. sv. Egídia 114, tel. 092/721–394; open weekdays 9–5, Sat. 9–1). The English-speaking staff sells maps and brochures on the Tatras and books private rooms and mountain chaty. **Hotel Satel** (Mohelova 826/5, tel. 092/721–306) is the classiest of the middling hotels; doubles are 1,960 Sk, and it's all less than five minutes from the train station. **Klub Olympia** (Partizanska ul, tel. 092/657–55), with doubles for 1,100 Sk, and **Gerlach** (Hviezdoslavova 2, tel. 092/721–945), doubles 850 Sk, are fine if you don't mind aging carpets or walls that could use a fresh coat of paint.

Poprad's **train station** (Wolkerova, tel. 092/721–829) is well connected with the rest of the country, and the **bus station** across the street serves all surrounding towns. To reach downtown, take a bus from Platform 4 or walk south 10 minutes away from the tracks, and cross the river. Motorky (electric trains) run from the upstairs platform in the train station to Tatry resorts. From Poprad you can reach the base of the Vysoké Tatry in 30 minutes.

SMOKOVCE

Starý Smokovec (Old Smokovec) was the first Tatry resort, founded in 1793. It's now surrounded by Nový (new), Horný (upper), and Dolný (lower) Smokovec, known collectively as **Smokovce.** Starý Smokovec has the most accommodations, shops, and services, making it the best place to stay. More important, it's also the starting point for some of the best hikes in the Tatras, and as the tourist industry grows, so does the quality of the service here. **Satur** (Starý Smokovec, next to the train station, tel. 0969/2417; open weekdays 8–4) changes money and arranges accommodations. Next door, the guys at **Tatrasport Adam** (tel. and fax 0969/3255; open daily 8–8; off season, daily 9–6) rent mountain bikes (249 Sk per day) and skis (199 Sk per day). Tatranska informacna sluzba (tel. 0969/3440) also has the skinny on accommodations. For maps and advice on hiking or skiing, follow the green signs from above the train station to **Združenie Cestovného Ruchu** (tel. and fax 0969/3127; open weekdays 8–6, weekends 9–5; shorter hrs off season).

WHERE TO SLEEP AND EAT

Junior (Horný Smokovec, tel. 0969/2661; doubles from 400 Sk) is in the forest, two stops east by electric train; showers and toilets are in the hall. Follow your nose to **Pekáren Wolf** (Nový Smokovec 10), a bakery with unbelievable pastries at unbelievably low prices. Cross the street and follow the signs to **Restaurant Siríbanka,** where the protein-deprived can chow on the Misa Siribanka, 1,000 grams of meat for 450 Sk. Or try a more modest plate, such as trout (81 Sk).

TATRANSKA LOMNICA

In this most picturesque and peaceful Tatry town, *penzióny* (pensions) and hotels abound, and campgrounds are an easy trek downhill. Frequent trains (regular and electric) arrive here from Starý Smokovec. In the Hotel Renomal, **Polńobanka** can change money, and **Tatrasport Adam** (tel. 0969/967–365) has a branch as well. After a day of hiking, head to the **TANAP museum** (admission 10 Sk; open weekdays 8:30–noon and 1–5, weekends 8–noon), which has a thorough display of the region's fauna (including humans); or picnic in the botanical gardens, filled with Tatry flora. Then crash in one of the clean, comfy rooms (170 Sk per person) at **Bělín** (tel. 0969/967–778), a small family-run pension. From the train station, walk uphill to the main road and continue uphill on the road that intersects near Slalom Restaurant, past the parking lot. Cheap eateries cluster around the train station.

STRBSKE PLESO

This westernmost of the Tatry resorts has excellent facilities and offers the best access for an ascent to Rysy Peak, one of the most memorable Tatry hikes. Head directly to **Tatranska Informačná Sluzba** (tel. 0969/3440; open weekdays 9–5, Sat. 9–noon), by the big green "I" just north of the train station, for marvelous resources on both accommodations and outings. Lodging is seriously expensive here. If you're really on a budget, take the train down to nearby Tatranská Štrba and look for PRIVAT and ZIMMER FREI signs. **Stavbár** (tel. 0969/924–56, fax 0969/924–82) is cheaper than the adjacent Nezábudka for rooms with balconies and bath (doubles 600 Sk); from the Tatranská Štrba train station, walk five minutes uphill toward Štrbske Pleso.

SPAIN

24

pain and its exuberant way of life have much to teach the astute traveler. Listen up and loosen up: These southern European and Mediterranean peoples are direct descendants of the ancient Greeks and Romans, born to *carpe diem*. *A vivir que son dos días* (live it up; life is short) is Spanish for Horace's "Seize the day," and indeed, it often seems that Spaniards are intent on seizing two at a time. Pleasure and passion are at least as imperative as profession here—people work to live rather than live to work. Aesthetic values tend to eclipse practical ones, dinners and conversations last as long as they need to, and sleep is just a chance to gather strength for a new assault on living fully. Why are dinner and bedtime so late? There's too much to do! Don't fight it—take a leisurely walk with no destination in mind, linger with a glass of wine over your midday meal, and dance until dawn.

Spain is more than a place to savor paella and sip heady Rioja wine, however; a real appreciation for the country and its people requires an understanding of its turbulent history. Centuries of foreign influence and domination left an astounding array of architecture and ruins from the Celts, Iberians, Romans, Visigoths, Moors, and Jews. In 1492, with Ferdinand and Isabella waging their Inquisition, Catholicism finally triumphed. But the resulting nation, which was for a time one of the richest and most powerful in the world, was in many ways an artificial alliance, forged from disparate kingdoms and "united" only through stategic royal marriages, the expulsion of the Moors and Jews, and the subjugation of other kingdoms to the Crown of Castile.

When General Francisco Franco took power following the Spanish Civil War (1936–1939), he sought to strengthen this fragile unity through centralization and the suppression of regional languages and identities. When Franco died in 1975, he left Spain injured, but not demoralized. In the wake of his death—and 36 years of repressive dictatorship—the sweetness of democracy gave rise to 17 autonomous regions, each with its own flag, president, legislative assembly, and judicial system. The Spanish now harbor a fierce liberalism, and their regional languages—Catalan, Basque, and Galician—once banned under Franco's regime, flourish today alongside Castilian (Spanish). But old wounds run deep, and the Basques (and some Catalans) still struggle, with words and with bombs, for the independence that has eluded them for centuries. While Spain now strives for unity with its European neighbors, its greatest challenge remains within—to bridge the cultural and political barriers between its own factions.

COSTA DE LA MUERTE
COSTA VERDE
Golfo Vizcaya

Ferrol
A Coruña
Ribadeo
Luarca
Gijón
Ribadesella
Santander
Villalba
Oviedo
Fisterra
Santiago de
Compostela
Lugo
Mieres
Cangas
de Onís
PICOS DE
EUROPA
B
Muros
CANTABRIAN MTS.
Pontevedra
Ponferrada
León
Burgos
Logr
Vigo
Astorga
Palencia
So
Tui
Orense
Benavente
Tordesillas
Valladolid
Duero
Zamora
Salamanca
Adanero
Segovia
SIERRA DE GUADARRAM
La Granja
Ciudad
Rodrigo
Avila
Guad
El Escorial
MADRID
PORTUGAL
Plasencia
SIERRA DE GREDOS
Toledo
Tajo
Talavera
de la Reina
Aranjuez
Ta
Guadalupe
Alcáz
San J
Cáceres
Trujillo
Guadiana
Mérida
Abenójar
Ciudad
Real
Valdep
Almadén
Badajoz
Jerez de los
Caballeros
Zafra
Linares
Fregenal
de la Sierra
SIERRA MORENA
Córdoba
Bailén
Ubec
Jaén
Baeza
Guadalquivir
Baena
Ayamonte
Sevilla
Ecija
Lucena
Granada
Guad
Carmona
Bobadilla
SIERRA
Huelva
Loja
*Gulf of
Cadiz*
Sanlúcar de
Barrameda
Ronda
Antequera
Nerja
COSTA DE LA LUZ
Jerez de
la Frontera
Torremolinos
Málaga
Motril
Cádiz
Estepona
Fuengirola
COSTA DEL SOL
*ATLANTIC
OCEAN*
Algeciras
Marbella
Tarifa
Gibraltar (U.K.)
Straits of Gibraltar
TO CANARY
ISLANDS

748

FRANCE

San
Sebastián Fuenterrabia
Bilbao
Vitoria   Roncesvalles   Sabiñanigo
                Pamplona   Torla   Parque
roño   Nacional   Vielha/
        Tudela   Jaca   de Ordesa   Viella
                                    Boi   La Seu   Puigcerdà
            Huesca   d'Urgell   Ripoll Olot
                Barbastro   El Pont   Sort   Vich/
Calatayud   de Suert   Llavorsi   Vic
                Zaragoza   La Pobla   Manresa
Medinaceli   Daroca   de Segur   Montserrat
                Caminreal   Alcañiz   Lleida
Monreal   Lérida   Barcelona
del Campo   Tarragona   Sitges
        Teruel
Cuenca   Tortosa
rancón   La Jana   Vinaròs
                                Castellón
Sagunto   de la Plana
        Requena   Valencia   Golfo de
Albacete   Valencia
Alcaraz   Gandia
eñas   Hellín   Piles
        Alicante   Benidorm
Murcia   Elche   Villajoyosa
Lorca   Orihuela
                Manga del
                Mar Menor
        Cartagena
                COSTA
NEVADA   CALIDA
Almería
        COSTA DE ALMERIA

Parque
Nacional
d'Aiqüestortes

ANDORRA

Figueres/
Figueras
Port Bou
Cadaqués
Empúnes
Girona/Gerona
Tossa de Mar

COSTA BRAVA

COSTA DORADA

Balearic
Sea

TO
MENORCA →

Palma

Mallorca

Ibiza

BALEARIC
ISLANDS

Ibiza
Formentera

Menorca
Ciudadela   Mahón

KEY
├──┤ Rail Lines

Mediterranean
Sea

N

ALGERIA

0   100 miles
0   150 km

749

BASICS

MONEY

US$1 = 145 pesetas and 100 pesetas = 69¢. Traveler's checks can be exchanged in banks, *casas de cambio* (exchange offices), or El Corte Inglés, a large department-store chain found in major cities throughout Spain; all three have competitive rates. Banks are usually open weekdays 9–2, and also Saturday 9–1 in winter. Major credit cards such as Visa, MasterCard, and American Express are widely accepted in Spain, except at some cheap restaurants and hotels. If you're desperate, you can also use your credit card to draw money from Spanish ATMs (rates are typically poor); check with your credit-card company before you leave home.

HOW MUCH IT WILL COST • Although the cost of traveling in Spain keeps creeping up, travel here is still much cheaper than in many other European countries. Expect to pay about 750 ptas–1,000 ptas for a filling *menú del día* (daily menu) at an inexpensive eatery; 2,500 ptas–3,000 ptas for a double in a cheap pensión; about 2,000 ptas on a typical night out; and about 850 ptas for a one-hour bus ride. Frugal travelers can live on $35–$40 a day. Tips are welcome, but not compulsory; the norm is 10%–15% for good service in restaurants, 5% for taxi drivers.

GETTING AROUND

Most towns you'll want to visit are on the rail lines. Occasionally, you may have to use buses, which are usually faster and more expensive than trains for short distances, but slower and much cheaper for longer distances.

BY BUS • Without a rail pass, taking the bus is often the cheapest and most convenient way to go—especially if you can get a discount from a youth-oriented travel agency such as **TIVE.** There's no national bus line, but instead a vast number of private bus companies. You'll have to call individual companies for information; buses often depart from different locations in a city, even when a central bus depot exists. Plan ahead, because service is reduced—and sometimes nonexistent—on Sunday and holidays.

BY PLANE • With growing service from major companies, such as **Iberia** (tel. 91/411–10–11) and **Air Europa** (tel. 91/542–73–38), prices continue to drop. For special youth deals, contact your local **TIVE** office. The cheapest tickets often restrict you to a five-day advance reservation and a weekend stay.

BY TRAIN • The national train company, **RENFE**, which operates most trains in Spain, accepts Eurail and InterRail passes; the smaller, private companies—**FEVE** (which runs trains mostly in the north) and **ET** (in the Basque region)—do not. RENFE has several varieties of trains. The fastest and most luxurious are the *electro, talgo,* and *AVE* trains, but these cost up to 70% more than standard trains, and rail-pass holders usually have to pay a *suplemento* (supplement) to take them. Regular trains are called *expresos* or *rápidos* and are comparable in speed and price to buses. *Semi-directos, tranvías,* and *correos* (mail trains) are the cheapest, but also the slowest (*correos* appear to move backward). You can buy tickets and make reservations—recommended for *largo recorrido* (long-distance) trains—at RENFE stations, travel agents displaying the RENFE logo, and RENFE offices. Buy tickets for *cercanías* (commuter trains traveling short distances) from ticket machines in larger stations to avoid long lines at the windows. RENFE gives a 20% discount to students and the under-26 crowd on all their trains—always ask. The cheapest times to travel are late at night, early in the morning, and on *días azules* (blue days, or nonpeak days); get schedules indicating peak and nonpeak days at any RENFE station.

WHERE TO SLEEP

In Spain, budget travelers aren't condemned exclusively to youth hostels. **Fondas, casas de huéspedes, pensiónes, hostales, hospedajes,** and **hostal-residencias** all offer basic accommodations—usually with a bed, desk, sink, and shared bath—often for little more money than a hostel bed. You can usually get a double for 2,500 ptas–3,000 ptas. **Hoteles** (hotels), considerably more plush, charge at least 5,000 ptas for a double. Most places jack up their prices for the *temporada alta* (high season), usually July–September. Especially in touristy areas, book a few weeks ahead in high season, a week ahead off season, and a month ahead during festivals.

Hostels, or **albergues juveniles,** are run by the HI-affiliated REAJ. Buy the requisite HI card (1,000 ptas; 500 ptas under age 26) at REAJ offices, some travel agencies, some hostels, and TIVE student-travel offices, found in most large cities. Beds cost 1,200 ptas–2,100 ptas, 900 ptas–1,300 ptas if you're under 26; breakfast is normally included. Unfortunately, hostels tend to be taken over by herds of schoolkids in summer, and most enforce heartless midnight curfews, which means you're locked in just when the nightlife is heating up. Ask at larger tourist offices for a free guide to all of Spain's HI hostels, or contact the REAJ office (C. Alcalá 31, Madrid, tel. 91/580–42–16, fax 91/580–42–15) for information and reservations. Tourist offices and bookstores also sell *Guía de Campings* (700 ptas), which lists all of Spain's **campgrounds.** The cheapest sleeps of all, campgrounds charge about 550 ptas–700 ptas per person.

FOOD

You can eat both well and cheaply in Spain, thanks in large part to the national custom of eating tapas (appetizers). This kind of casual grazing is perfect for Spain's highly social lifestyle: You stand at the bar with your friends, chug a *cerveza* (beer), and munch on little plates of delicious *gambas al ajillo* (shrimp in garlic), *calamares* (squid), *alcachofas* (artichokes), or *jamón serrano* (smoked ham). Almost every bar and café offers tapas, usually costing 150 ptas–350 ptas. *Raciones* are simply entrée-size servings of tapas, and *pinchos* are small tapas.

Spaniards eat lunch between 1 and 4; afterward, Spain slows down for the siesta (more commonly called *descanso*), and supper doesn't roll around until 9–11. The midday meal is the most substantial of the day, typically consisting of an appetizer, a main course, bread, wine, and dessert. The *menú del día* offered in most restaurants is usually the best bargain for a full meal; you get the above dishes plus a drink for 800 ptas–950 ptas. Another cheap option is the *plato combinado* (combination plate), which includes a filling main course (usually meat, fish, or eggs) and a couple of side dishes. The classic budget staple is the hearty *bocadillo* (sandwich), served in almost any bar; take pains to ask for a *bocadillo*, not a *sandwich*, as the latter is usually just a thin slice of meat on dry bread. Hardcore penny-pinchers will have to hunt down grocery stores (called *supermercados* and *alimentaciones*), which usually close during the siesta. The El Corte Inglés department stores (generally open 9–8), found in most major cities, have giant supermarkets inside.

Each region has its own culinary specialties, but Spanish cooks generally make good use of garlic and olive oil, and agree that *tortilla española* (potato omelette), gazpacho (cold vegetable soup), and paella (saffron rice with meat and seafood) are among the tastiest staple dishes. Vegetarianism hasn't really caught on here, so if you don't eat meat you're in for countless tortillas or *bocadillos con queso* (cheese sandwiches). You'll see *sangría* (red wine served cold with fruit) everywhere, but this is hardly the best Spanish libation; Spain produces some world-class wines (*vino blanco* is white, *tinto* is red), particularly the reds of La Rioja and the sherries of Jerez, in Andalucía.

BUSINESS HOURS

Banks and businesses usually open around 8, museums at 10. Stores generally open for Saturday morning and close on Sunday, and many stores also close for a few weeks in late summer. Post offices are open weekdays 8 AM–9 PM and Saturday 9–2. The great Spanish tradition of the afternoon siesta, or *descanso*, is still very much alive, so expect shops, museums, churches, and tourist offices to be closed weekdays 2–4. Take a nap, take a walk, or down a beer—hotels and bars usually stay open. Businesses eventually reopen around 4 and stay open until 7:30 or 8. Aside from fast-food joints, restaurants normally close 4–8.

FESTIVALS AND HOLIDAYS

Major festivals to plan your schedule around include Semana Santa (the entire week before Easter), Corpus Christi (early June), Carnaval (late February), Los San Fermines (the running of the bulls, in the second week of July) in Pamplona, and Las Fallas (the third week of March) in Valencia. Innumerable smaller festivals celebrate favorite local saints and miracles. Come and join the fun by all means, but reserve ahead for trains and hotels. Also, expect most businesses to close on national holidays: Epiphany (Jan. 6), Good Friday, Easter Sunday and Monday, Labor Day (May 1), St. John's Day (June 24), St. James's Day (July 25), Assumption Day (Aug. 15), National Day (Oct. 1), Christmas, and New Year's Day.

PHONES

Country code: 34. When calling Spain from the U.S., omit the 9 from the area code. Telephones in Spain are operated by **Telefónica.** The ubiquitous blue phone booths accept coins, credit cards (American Express and Diners Club only), and Telefónica cards. Phone cards, available at post offices and *tabacs* (tobacco shops), come with values of 1,000 ptas or 2,000 ptas; local calls start at 20 ptas. For international calls, head to a Telefónica office and use a pay-after-you-phone booth (credit cards are sometimes accepted). A three-minute call to most European countries costs about 310 ptas, to the United States about 545 ptas, and to Australia a whopping 1,000 ptas; rates drop 20% daily 10 PM–

8 AM and all day Sunday. Private telephone offices, known as *locutorios,* offer similar services at similar rates. To call another country directly, dial 07, wait for the tone, then dial the country code, area code, and phone number. To make an international collect call (*cobro revertido*) from any phone in Spain, dial 900–9900 followed by 11 (**AT&T** Direct Access^{SM}), 14 (**MCI**), or 13 (**Sprint**) for the United States; 15 for Canada; 44 for the United Kingdom; or 61 for Australia. Dial 008 for an English-speaking operator, 003 for the Spanish operator.

MAIL

You can receive mail at *correos* (post offices) or American Express offices (for check- or cardholders only). Poste restante should be marked LISTA DE CORREOS and include the name of the town and province, as well as the local five-digit postal code. A letter to the United States or Canada takes about 10 days to arrive and costs 90 ptas; letters within Europe take about five days and cost 62 ptas. You can buy stamps at *tabacs,* post offices, and some hotels.

LANGUAGE AND CULTURE

Spain's four official languages serve as a constant reminder of its past life as a collection of diverse kingdoms and peoples: Castellano (Castilian, or Spanish); Gallego (Galician), a cross between Portuguese and Castilian, spoken in the far northwest; Catalán (Catalan), the language of eastern regions including Catalunya (Catalonia); and Euskera (Basque), the unrelated language spoken in Euskadi, the Basque region. Spanish is almost universally understood throughout the country, however, due in no small part to Franco's official ban on all languages other than Castilian. Awareness of this linguistic suppression and the fierce regional pride of the different communities is imperative: Try to speak the regional language and never, ever refer to Catalan or Galician as a "dialect" of Castilian, or refer to Castilian as "Spanish" in these regions. Here are a few helpful Castilian phrases to tide you over while you're brushing up on your Catalan or Galician: *hola* (hello); *adiós* (goodbye); *por favor* (please); *gracias* (thank you); *sí/no* (yes/no); *perdóneme* (excuse me); *¿dónde están los servicios/aseos?* (where is the bathroom?); *¿tiene . . . ?* (do you have . . .?); *¿cuánto vale . . .?* (how much does . . . cost?); and *¿habla inglés?* (do you speak English?).

WOMEN TRAVELERS

The Spaniards' legendary machismo can be problematic for foreign, especially light-complected, women. Most women traveling solo in Spain do not run into problems, but some report catcalls, persistent Don Juans, and obnoxious groping at night. To minimize your risk, keep your legs covered in the evenings and ignore any hissing from leering men—if they see that it bothers you, they'll only persist.

GAY AND LESBIAN TRAVELERS

Ever since Franco passed on, Spaniards have been coming out in droves. The Spanish are generally tolerant, but public displays of affection tend to draw heckling from youths. **COGAM,** a gay and lesbian organization, has an office at Calle Carretas 12 in Madrid; if you speak Spanish, call them at 91/522–45–17 to find out about their branches in other cities. Also based in Madrid is **GAI INFORM** (tel. 91/523–00–70), a gay-and-lesbian hotline. Check out **Librería Bercona** (C. la Palma 39, Madrid), a gay-oriented bookstore in Madrid, and look for the magazine *Entiendes* (500 ptas), widely sold in kiosks.

MADRID

The intense smells of Madrid—from tangy cheddar to rosy champagne—arrest the first-time visitor. With its hectic streets and gritty atmosphere, it's not an unusually graceful city by European standards, nor does it have a particularly colorful history. Madrid dates back to ancient times, but it did not gain prominence until 1561, when Felipe II crowned it Spain's new capital, determined to use the city's central location to increase and consolidate his power over the country. Still the political center of Spain, Madrid is also the focus of Spain's economic and cultural energies; it is home to some of the greatest art museums in the world and hosts a constant stream of cultural events. But as those who have taken the time to appreciate Madrid will tell you, the real spirit of this city lies in the lifestyle of its people and the passion with which they pursue the pleasurable. In Madrid you can drink in more bars, dance in more clubs, and stay out later than just about anywhere else in the world. Forget about grand squares, beautiful buildings, and impressive monuments—this may be the only town in the entire country where you won't feel obligated to visit a single church.

BASICS

VISITOR INFORMATION

The municipal tourist office is conveniently located at Plaza Mayor 3. *Tel. 91/366–54–77. Metro: Sol. Open weekdays 10–2 and 4–8, Sat. 10–2.*

Most of the national tourist offices are open weekdays 9–7 and Saturday 9–1. *Torre de Madrid, Pl. de España, tel. 91/541–23–25; Metro: Pl. de España. Duque de Medinaceli 2, tel. 91/429–49–51; Metro: Banco de España. Chamartín train station, tel. 91/315–99–76; Metro: Chamartín. Barajas Airport, tel. 91/305–86–56.*

AMERICAN EXPRESS

Members can change traveler's checks or cash, replace lost or stolen cards, receive mail, and get tourist information. *Pl. de las Cortes 2, tel. 91/322–54–40, or 900/99–44–26 for traveler's-check refunds. Metro: Banco de España. From C. de Alcalá, take C. del Marqués de Cubas south. Open weekdays 9–5:30, Sat. 9–noon.*

CHANGING MONEY

American Express offers a competitive exchange rate and charges no commission. The same goes for **El Corte Inglés** department stores (Madrid has 10), most of which are open until 9 weekdays and Saturday, 8 on Sunday; the most central store is at Calle Preciados 3, at Puerta del Sol. For larger transactions, you're better off at banks like **Banco Central, Central Hispano,** or **Caja de Madrid,** all of which charge a commission (500 ptas–1,000 ptas), but offer significantly better rates. ATMs, which accept most credit cards and some bank cards (including Cirrus and STAR), are also plentiful. After hours, try the smaller cambios along **Gran Vía** and **Sol**; they're a rip-off, but some stay open all night.

DISCOUNT TRAVEL AGENCIES

TIVE specializes in student and youth discounts. *C. de Fernando el Católico 88, tel. 91/543–02–08. Metro: Moncloa. Open weekdays 9–2, Sat. 9–noon.*

EMBASSIES

Australia: *Paseo de la Castellana 143, tel. 91/579–04–28. Open Mon.–Thurs. 9–1 and 2–4:30, Fri. 9–2.* **Canada:** *C. Núñez de Balboa 35, tel. 91/431–43–00. Open weekdays 9–12:30.* **Great Britain:** *C. Fernando el Santo 16, tel. 91/319–02–00. Open weekdays 9–1:30 and 3–6.* **Ireland:** *C. Claudio Coello 73, tel. 91/576–35–00. Open weekdays 10–2.* **United States:** *C. Serrano 75, tel. 91/577–40–00. Open weekdays 9–12:30 and 3–5.*

EMERGENCIES

Dial 091 for the **police,** 080 for the **fire department,** and 91/479–93–61 for an **ambulance.** Dial 003 or 098 or check the newspaper under *farmacias de guardia* to find a 24-hour pharmacy.

PHONES AND MAIL

There are two **Telefónica** offices in Madrid, one at Paseo de Recoletos 37–41 (Banco de España Metro), the other at Gran Vía 30 (Metro: Gran Vía). Both are open Monday–Saturday 9 AM–midnight, Sunday 10 AM–midnight.

Palacio de Comunicaciones. They'll meet your every postal need. *Pl. de las Cibeles, tel. 91/536–01–10. Metro: Banco de España. Open weekdays 8 AM–9:30 PM or 10 PM, Sat. 8:30–2, Sun. 10–1. Postal code: 28070.*

COMING AND GOING

BY BUS

Though private bus companies launch buses from various points, Madrid's main station is **Estación Sur de Autobuses** (C. Canarias 17, tel. 91/468–42–00; Metro: Palos de la Frontera). From here, buses will take you to Seville (6 hrs, 2,680 ptas) and Granada (5½ hrs, 1,875 ptas). Other important points of departure include **Auto Res** (Fernández Shaw 1, tel. 91/551–89–00; Metro: Conde de Casal), where you can hop a bus to Valencia (4½ hrs, 2,745 ptas), and **La Sepulvedana** (Paseo de la Florida 11, tel. 91/547–52–61; Metro: Norte), where buses leave for Salamanca (3 hrs, 740 ptas).

C. del Rey
Francisco
① C. Evaristo San Miguel
C. Luisa Fernanda
C. Ventura
Rodríguez
C. Martín de
los Heros
C. Juan Álvarez
Mendizábal
C. Ferraz

③ ②
Conde Duque
C. del Limón
Travesía Conde Duque

VENTURA
RODRÍGUEZ

C. de la Princesa

Parque
del
Oeste

Pl.
España

C. Amaniel

C. de
⑤ Pl. Dos
de Mayo

C. de
Ruíz
C. de
San Andrés
C. del
Divino Pastor

C. de la Palma

C. de S. Vicente Ferrer

TRIBUNAL

NOVICIADO

C. del Pez

C. San Bernardo

PL. DE ESPAÑA

Gran Vía

C. de la Luna

TO ESTACIÓN
DEL NORTE

Cuesta San Vicente

Pl. de la
Marina
Española

STO DOMINGO

C. de la Bola

Pl. Santo
Domingo

Pl. de
Callao

Gonzalo Jiménez
de Quesada

GRAN VÍA

⑨ Red de
San Luis

C. del Barco
C. de Valverde
C. Fuencarral
C. de

CALLAO

C. del Carmen
C. Preciados

C. Jardines

C. de Bailén

Pl. de
Oriente

Pl. de
Isabel II

OPERA

C. Arenal

Pl. San
Martín

Pl.
Descalzas

C. de
Tetuán

⑧

Coloreros

C. de la Montera

①

C. de Alcalá
C. de Sevilla

Campo
del
Moro

④

SOL

Puerta
del Sol

C. de San

Victoria
Y Mina

Espoz
Y Mina

Matheu

⑫ C. Príncipe
⑬
Pl.
Santa

⑥

C. de Bailén

Calle Mayor

C. de Sacramento

Pl.
San Miguel

C. de Segovia

Pl. del
Cordón

C. de
Segovia

Pl. de
la Paja

Pl. de
Puerta
Cerrada

Pl.
Humilladero

C. Felipe III

Pl.
Mayor

C. Cuchilleros

C. Maqués
Viudo de
Pontejos

⑦

C.
Santo
Tomás

C. Jerónima

Espárteros

C. Carretas

C. Ramanones

C. de la Cruz

C. Núñez de Arce

Pl. Jacinto
Benavente

Jardines
Vistillas

C. de Segovia

Redondilla

Puerta de
Moros

C. de San Francisco

C. Toledo

Duque de Alba

TIRSO DE
MOLINA

Pl. Tirso
de Molina

C. de Magdalena

Cabeza

C. Atocha

Ronda de
Segovia

G. V. de
San Francisco

LA LATINA

Pl. de la
Cebada

Pl. de
Cascorro

C. Encomienda

C. Lavapié
C. Jesús y María
C. del Amparo

LA

Ribera de Curtidores

C. de Embajadores

C. Mesón de Paredes

Pl.
Lavapié

KEY

C. Toledo

Mira el Río Alto

EL RASTRO

C. Miguel Servet

AE American Express Office

i Tourist Information

Ⓜ Metro Stops

PUERTA DE
TOLEDO

0   1/4 mile
0   1/4 km

Gta. Puerta
de Toledo

Campillo del
Mundo Nuevo
Rda. de Toledo

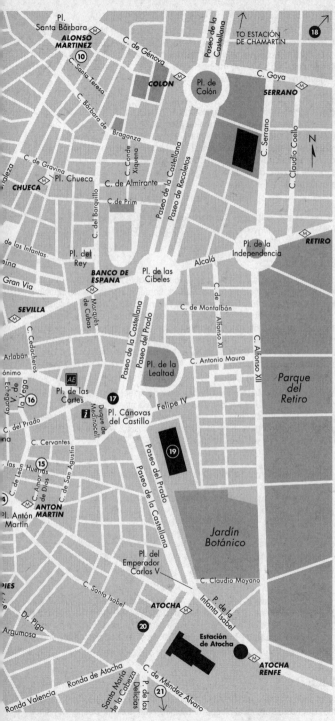

Sights ●

Centro de Arte
Reina Sofia, **20**

Museo de
la Ciudad, **18**

Museo de la Real
Academia de Bellas
Artes de San
Fernando, **11**

Museo del
Prado, **19**

Museo Thyssen-
Bornemisza, **16**

Palacio Real, **4**

Lodging ○

Albergue Juvenil
Richard Schirrmann
(HI), **6**

Albergue Juvenil
Santa Cruz de
Marcenado, (HI), **3**

Hostal Alfaro, **16**

Hostal Alicante, **8**

Hostal Castilla, **10**

Hostal
Encarnita, **7**

Hostal Lopez, **15**

Hostal Lucense/
Pensión Poza, **13**

Hostal Oxford, **2**

Hostal Villar, **12**

Hostal-Residencia
Alegría, **21**

Hostal-Residencia
Conde de Alba, **1**

Hostal-Residencia
Flores, **9**

Jemasaca, **5**

Pensión Pacios, **14**

BY PLANE

Barajas Airport (Carretera N-11, tel. 91/305–83–44) is 16 km (10 mi) northeast of Madrid. Round-trip tickets to Malaga cost about 16,500 ptas; check prices with several travel agencies and airlines before you buy. Buses (tel. 91/401–99–00) run between the airport and the bus terminal at Plaza de Colón in Madrid's center every 12–30 minutes 4:45 AM–1 AM; the ride costs 360 ptas and takes about 40 minutes. Bus 101 (130 ptas) connects the airport to the Canillejas Metro station.

BY TRAIN

Madrid's two main train stations, both of which offer luggage storage (200 ptas; look for CONSIGNIA signs), are **Estación de Chamartín** (Metro: Chamartín) and **Estación de Atocha** (Metro: Atocha RENFE); many trains stop at both. Some popular destinations are Barcelona (7½ hrs, 5,900 ptas), Valencia (4 hrs, 3,800 ptas), Granada (6 hrs, 5,600 ptas), and Paris (14 hrs, 17,500 ptas). **Estación de Norte** (Metro: Norte) serves destinations in north and northwest Spain, such as Burgos (4 hrs, 2,900 ptas). Buy tickets at stations, travel agents, or the **RENFE office** (C. de Alcalá 44, tel. 91/532–06–32; Metro: Banco de España). For rail information, dial 91/328–90–20.

RIDES

To skip town for the price of a tank of gas, call **Autos Compartidos** (C. Carretas 33, tel. 91/522–77–72; open weekdays 10–2 and 4:30–8); their staff will try to hook you up with someone driving your way.

GETTING AROUND

In the very center of Madrid is **Puerta del Sol** (a.k.a. Sol), a large roundabout fed by major avenues and pedestrian streets. The surrounding area is the oldest part of Madrid, bordered on the east by the city's main park, **Parque del Retiro,** and on the west by the **Manzanares River** and **Casa de Campo,** another sprawling park. South of Sol, you'll find the traditionally working-class neighborhoods **La Latina** and **Lavapiés,** which stretch south of Plaza Mayor and Calle Atocha. North of Sol is Madrid's major east–west artery, **Gran Vía,** and north of Gran Vía is **Chueca,** a gritty but interesting area. Further north the neighborhood is sprawling and gentrified, especially along **Paseo de la Castellana,** the major north–south artery. East of Paseo de la Castellana, the **Salamanca** neighborhood contains wealthy residential areas and upscale shops.

Though you can walk almost everywhere in Madrid, the city has clean, efficient Metro and bus (EMT) systems; one Metro or bus ride costs 130 ptas. Ten-ride tickets are only 665 ptas—for the Metro, buy a *billete de diez viajes* (10-trip ticket) from any station attendant, and for the bus, get a *bonobus* pass at any newspaper kiosk. A monthly pass covers travel on both systems and costs 2,790 ptas–7,295 ptas, depending on your age and how many zones you want to cover.

BY BUS

The bus system is more comprehensive, more complicated, and slower than the Metro. If you want to stay above ground, pick up a bus map and schedule at the tourist office, or, if you speak Spanish, dial 91/401–31–00. Bus service begins at 5:45 AM or 7 AM, depending on the line, and ends at midnight. A few buses (marked with an N) run all night long.

BY METRO

No address lies far from one of the Metro's many stops. Nine of the 10 Metro lines run daily 6 AM–1:30 AM; Line 6 to the university, however, runs weekdays 7 AM–10 PM and not at all in August. You can get a Metro map at any ticket window.

BY TAXI

Taxis are a pretty good deal in Madrid. The rate is 170 ptas plus 75 ptas per km (⅗ mi), but surcharges for traveling to the airport (350 ptas) or between 11 PM and 7 AM on Sunday (150 ptas) may make the price you pay very different from what you see on the meter. Hailing a cab in the city should be no problem, but if you can't find one, call **Tele-Taxi** (tel. 91/445–90–08). Ask for a receipt if you think you've been cheated, and the driver might recant.

WHERE TO SLEEP

The overwhelming advantage of avoiding the youth hostels is that you can stay out as late as you like— a vital consideration in Madrid. But hostels are ideal places for meeting other travelers, especially since

Spanish *hostales* are usually small, mellow, and family-run. Contact **REAJ** (C. Alcalá 31, tel. 91/580–42–16, fax 91/580–42–15) or individual hostels for reservations.

SOUTH OF GRAN VIA

The center of Madrid, from Gran Vía south to Calle Atocha, is near most main sights and some intense nightlife. It's also home to many inexpensive *hostales, pensiones,* and *casas de huéspedes*; the best places to poke around are **Puerta del Sol, Plaza Mayor, Santa Ana, Tirso de Molina, Antón Martín,** and **Estación de Atocha.**

UNDER 3,000 PTAS • Hostal Encarnita. This peaceful haven between Sol and Plaza Mayor sports big windows over sturdy beds and squeaky-clean tile floors. Doubles are 2,600 ptas (2,900 ptas with shower). *C. Marqués Viudo de Pontejos 7, tel. 91/531–90–55. Metro: Sol. From C. Mayor, turn left on C. Esparteros, then take first left.*

Hostal Lucense. Book at least a week ahead for cozy doubles (2,400 ptas, 2,800 ptas with bath). Showers are an extra 200 ptas. Also try **Pensión Poza** (C. Núñez de Arce 9, tel. 91/522–48–71), down the street—same owner, same great deal. *C. Núñez de Arce 15, tel. 91/522–48–88. Metro: Sol or Sevilla.*

UNDER 3,500 PTAS • Hostal Alfaro. Amid funky restaurants and pubs, the Alfaro is also in a great location for museum junkies. Most doubles are 4,000 ptas (3,500 ptas with shower); the one really classy double is 5,500 ptas. *C. Ventura de la Vega 16, tel. 91/429–61–73. Metro: Sol or Sevilla.*

Hostal-Residencia Alegría. Near Estación de Atocha, these tidy but stark rooms are perfect for the weary traveler too tired to decipher the Metro map. Doubles cost 3,000 ptas. *C. de Rafael de Riego 8, tel. 91/528–76–82. From station and Pl. del Emperador Carlos V, take C. de Méndez Alvaro and turn right on Rafael de Riego.*

Hostal-Residencia Flores. It's right on Gran Vía, but it's also eight floors up, so nice and quiet. You'll find art in the hallways and plants in the bathrooms, and the friendly hostess will hand-wash—free!—that shirt that's just not going any further. Doubles cost 3,500 ptas (4,200 ptas with bath). *Gran Vía 30, tel. 91/522–81–52. Entrance on G. J. Quesada. Metro: Gran Vía.*

Hostal Villar. Come to these posh rooms (most with satellite TV and phone) to escape that caged-refugee feeling at the hostels, or to drink yourself into oblivion at one of the many nearby bars. Doubles go for 3,300 ptas (4,200 ptas with bath). *C. Príncipe 18, tel. 91/531–66–00, fax 91/521–50–73. Metro: Sol.*

Pensión Pacios. A very friendly older couple runs these small, quiet rooms with high ceilings and immaculate bathrooms (down the hall). Stumble one block from Plaza Santa Ana and Calle Las Huertas. Doubles are 3,000 ptas. *C. Atocha 28, tel. 91/239–11–12. Metro: Antón Martín.*

UNDER 4,000 PTAS • Hostal Alicante. With flower-laden balcony windows practically overlooking Sol, cushy easy chairs, and an array of postmodern furniture, the Alicante is relatively luxurious. Clean doubles cost 4,000 ptas (4,400 ptas with bath). *C. Arenal 16, tel. 91/531–51–78. Metro: Sol.*

Hostal López. This little *hostal* is smack in the middle of the happening night scene and five minutes from Madrid's three main museums. Doubles cost 3,700 ptas (4,500 ptas with bath). *C. Huertas 54, tel. 91/429–43–49. Metro: Antón Martín.*

NORTH OF GRAN VIA

As you move north from the center of Madrid—around **Argüelles, Malasaña,** and **Plaza Santa Bárbara**—rooms get prettier, quieter, and cheaper. If you're in search of the ultimate bar, stay around Malasaña; if you're after a good night's sleep, stay near Santa Bárbara or Argüelles.

UNDER 3,500 PTAS • Hostal Castilla. These cheap rooms are in a fun neighborhood near Plaza Santa Bárbara. Rooms vary widely, but some are very pretty. Doubles are 3,500 ptas (3,900 ptas with bath). *C. Santa Teresa 9, tel. 91/310–21–76. Metro: Alonso Martínez.*

Hostal-Residencia Conde de Alba. The halls are dark, but the rooms are quiet and bright, the courtyard is sunny, and the water is hot. Doubles go for 3,000 ptas (3,200 ptas with shower). *C. Juan Alvarez Mendizabal 44, tel. 91/542–28–39. Metro: Ventura Rodriguez. Take C. de la Princesa north, turn left on C. Evaristo San Miguel, then right on C. Juan Alvarez Mendizabal.*

UNDER 4,000 PTAS • Jemasaca. The water-stained facade of this hotel hides a well-kept interior. It's on the more tranquil periphery of the rocking Malasaña evening scene, with lots of restaurants and little markets nearby. Book at least a week ahead. Doubles are 3,000 ptas–4,000 ptas. *C. de la Palma 61, tel. 91/532–70–11. Metro: Noviciado.*

Hostal Oxford. This small, charming *hostal* offers newly refurbished rooms and a friendly hostess. Doubles cost 3,900 ptas (4,700 ptas with shower). *C. Guzman el Bueno 57, 1 centro, tel. 91/544–13–02. Metro: Argüellas.*

HOSTELS

Albergue Juvenil Richard Schirrmann (HI). This friendly hostel is a 20-minute walk from the nearest Metro, in a large park where you can swim. There's no curfew, but it's a ways from the nightlife. Beds are 1,300 ptas (950 ptas under 26), and perks include a bar, a library (!), laundry facilities, and lockers. HI members only. *Casa de Campo, tel. 91/463–56–99. From Lago Metro, turn left, then left again on first main road, continue about 20 min.*

Albergue Juvenil Santa Cruz de Marcenado (HI). Only HI members can exploit this great bargain in a great location. Check in 9 AM–10 AM for one of the 72 beds in four- to eight-person rooms. Beds cost 1,300 ptas (950 ptas under 26). There are laundry facilities and lockers, but there's also a 1:30 AM curfew, and the entire hostel closes Sunday noon–5. *C. Santa Cruz de Marcenado 28, tel. 91/547–45–32. From Argüelles Metro, take C. de la Princesa south, turn left on C. Serrano Jover, right on C. Santa Cruz de Marcenado.*

CAMPING

Osuna. This campground features a hopping bar, parties, bands, and good food—all next to beautiful El Capricho Jardín. Sites are 600 ptas per person and car plus 600 ptas per tent; hot showers are free. Bungalows for two with bath are 4,200 ptas. *Av. de Logroño, tel. 91/741–05–10. From Canillejas Metro, cross pedestrian bridge, take road that cuts through 2 parking lots, turn right just past* BURGOS *sign, and look for campground's* BAR RESTAURANT COKE *sign.*

FOOD

Madrid's myriad tapas bars and *cervecerías* (beer bars) are concentrated around Sol and Plaza Mayor; by Estación de Atocha, between the La Latina and Embajadores Metro stops; and in the student area around the San Bernardo, Noviciado, Argüelles, and Moncloa Metro stops. For ethnic restaurants, check out Malasaña. Cheapest of all are Madrid's many indoor markets, such as the one at **Plaza San Miguel** (open Mon.–Sat. 9–2 and 5:30–8:30), a few blocks west of Plaza Mayor, or **Galería Comercial** (C. de Quintana, at C. J. A. Mendizabal; open Mon.–Sat. 9–1:30 and 5–8; Argüelles Metro). There are also supermarkets in almost all **El Corte Inglés** department stores.

UNDER 750 PTAS • Cervecería la Vega. A great place to be Sunday afternoon after shopping at El Rastro (*see* Cheap Thrills, *below*), this restaurant is so packed that people resort to sitting on the sidewalk with their generous portions of paella (350 ptas), cheap beers (120 ptas), and guitars. *C. Encomienda 2, tel. 91/467–56–16. Metro: Lavapiés or Tirso de Molina. Open daily.*

El Maragato. Perpetual darkness envelops this dingy, nearly windowless eatery, but remember to thank the smiling, toothless waiter for one of the best *menús* (700 ptas) you had in Madrid. *C. de San Andrés 14, on Pl. Dos de Mayo, tel. 91/53–23–073. Metro: Bilbao or Tribunal.*

Restaurante Magumar. The student bustle, the smell of garlic, and wonderful *champiñones* (mushrooms) more than make up for the lack of formal ambience. The food is very tasty and very cheap—combination plates start at 550 ptas. *C. San Bernardo 69, tel. 91/532–84–55. Meals served 1 PM–8:30 PM, tapas until midnight. Metro: San Bernardo.*

Restaurante Manacor. It's touristy, but the paella and *ternera* (veal) are fantastic, and the 650-ptas *menú del día* could feed an army. *Pasaje de Matheu 2, off C. Espoz y Mina near Sol, tel. 91/522–22–93. Metro: Sol.*

UNDER 1,000 PTAS • El Campero. Down a delicious salad (350 ptas) or a *menú del día* (900 ptas; weekdays only) at this cozy, friendly eatery. *C. Pilar de Zaragoza 67, tel. 91/356–11–09. From Diego de León Metro, go SE on C. de Francisco Silvela, turn left on C. de Alonso Heredia, then left on C. Pilar de Zaragoza.*

La Caserola. Right off Puerta de Sol, lively locals mix with tipsy tourists in a chummy, publike atmosphere. The myriad seafood specialties start at 1,000 ptas. *C. Echegaray 3, tel. 91/429–39–63. Metro: Sol or Sevilla.*

El Granero de Lavapiés. Vegetarian and macrobiotic food is served amid Japanese lampshades and '60s love beads; the menu features vegetable cream soups, gazpacho, paella, and great carrot juice

(320 ptas). All entrées are 715 ptas–850 ptas. *C. Argumosa 10, tel. 91/467–76–11. Open Sun.–Fri. 1 PM–4 AM. Metro: Lavapiés.*

Pizzería Mastropiero. This trendy but intimate pizzeria serves 16 varieties of thin-crust pizza. Slices cost 210 ptas, small pies start at 800 ptas. *C. de San Vicente Ferrer 34, at C. Dos de Mayo, no phone. Metro: Noviciado or Tribunal.*

UNDER 1,500 PTAS • La Biotika. Here's a vegetarian oasis for those who refuse to eat another cheese sandwich. Gazpacho is 380 ptas, the *menú del día* 1,100 ptas. *C. Amor de Dios 3, no phone. Metro: Sol or Antón Martín. From Pl. Santa Ana, turn right on C. Príncipe, left on C. Las Huertas, then right on C. Amor de Dios.*

Restaurante del Palacio de Anglona. Full of beautiful young people, this hip, boisterous, circa-1561 palace-cum-restaurant is a fail-safe date impresser, but class doesn't come cheap (entrées from 1,300 ptas, pizzas 785 ptas–855 ptas). *C. de Segovia 13, tel. 91/366–37–53. Open daily. Metro: Sol or La Latina.*

Puebla. True, the fake-wood beams fool no one, but you'd be hard-pressed to find better food at such affordable prices anywhere in Madrid. Puebla opened in 1992 and is always crowded with bankers and politicians. The *menú del día* is either 1,100 ptas or 1,400 ptas. *Ventura de la Vega 12, tel. 91/429–67–13. Closed Sunday.*

Kick your shoes off and join the Hare Krishnas (Espíritu Santo 19, tel. 91/521–30–96) for a hearty vegetarian meal at a mere 200 ptas. Come early for mantra and meditation.

WORTH SEEING

If you think Madrid's food and drink are amazing, wait until you see the art. Don't leave this city before checking out the Prado, the Centro de Arte Reina Sofía, and the Museo Thyssen-Bornemisza—a trinity of stellar museums.

MUSEO DEL PRADO

The Prado is dizzying. Exhibits range from the ecstatic (El Greco) to the dark and romantic (Goya) to the downright trippy (Bosch), and extend to thousands of works by artists such as Mantegna, Raphael, Titian, Dürer, Brueghel, and Botticelli. This museum alone is reason enough to come to Madrid—and stay for a long while. The Prado's masterpieces (remember those slides in art history class?) include Fra Angelico's *La Anunciación* (The Annunciation); Bosch's *El Jardín de las Delicias* (The Garden of Earthly Delights), a triptych of creation, hell, and the earthly delights in between; Peter Paul Rubens's *Las Tres Gracias* (The Three Graces), sensual and ample nudes; Velázquez's *Las Meninas* (The Maids of Honor), which depicts the artist himself painting a most unusual royal portrait; and Goya's *El Tres de Mayo* (The Third of May), in which Napoléon's soldiers execute Spaniards. Don't miss Goya's *pinturas negras* (black paintings), downstairs, especially *Saturno devorando a un hijo* (Saturn Devouring One of His Children). *Paseo del Prado, tel. 91/330–28–00. Admission: 500 ptas. Open Tues.–Sat. 9–7, Sun. 9–2. Metro: Atocha RENFE, Banco de España, or Retiro.*

CENTRO DE ARTE REINA SOFIA

With sparkling white walls and a pleasant courtyard, this building belies the radical spirit of its first-class collection of modern art. A ride up the futuristic exterior elevator might be a more fitting prelude to the works by such Spanish greats such as Picasso, Dalí, and Miró. The surrealism room is breathtaking and leads to the most shattering painting of all, Picasso's *Guernica*, painted in the month following the Franco-sponsored, German-executed bombing of the town of Guernica. The Dalís in the next room will further challenge your equilibrium. *C. Santa Isabel 52, tel. 91/467–50–62. Metro: Atocha RENFE. Admission: 400 ptas (free Sat. after 2:30 and Sun.). Open Mon. and Wed.–Sat. 10–9, Sun. 10–2:30.*

MUSEO DE LA CIUDAD

With high-tech exhibits and flashing digital displays, this museum is a fun way to learn about Madrid's history and culture. Check out the exhibit explaining how ancient Roman aqueducts are still used today, and stroll past the miniature bullring—a model of Madrid's own Plaza de Toros—complete with *toros* (bulls) and *toreros* (bullfighters), as well as an explanation of what gets those bulls so steamed. *C. del Príncipe de Vergara 140, tel. 91/588–65–99. Admission free. Open Tues.–Fri. 10–2 and 4–6, weekends 10–2. Metro: Cruz del Rayo.*

MUSEO DE LA REAL ACADEMIA DE BELLAS ARTES DE SAN FERNANDO

This intimate fine-arts museum has an excellent collection and beautiful interior without being as physically demanding as the Prado. It features works by El Greco, Goya, Veronese, Caravaggio, Tintoretto, and Rubens, in addition to Giuseppe Arcimboldo's *La Primavera* (Spring) and Ribera's *Ecce Homo*. *C. de Alcalá 13, tel. 91/522–14–91. Admission: 200 ptas. Open Tues.–Fri. 9–7, Sat.–Mon. 9–2:30. Metro: Sol or Sevilla.*

MUSEO THYSSEN-BORNEMISZA

It may seem like the height of arrogance to display one's private art collection right across from the Prado, but Baron Heinreich's collection warrants the audacity. The museum's works, arranged chronologically and illuminated by skylights, span seven centuries of Western painting. A helpful guide (1,800 ptas) from the bookstore can aid those who skipped their art-history lectures. The collection's emphasis is squarely on modern and German art, including works by Hans Holbein, Max Ernst, Max Beckmann, and Paul Klee. *Paseo del Prado 8, tel. 91/369–01–51. Admission: 600 ptas. Open Tues.–Sun. 10–7. Metro: Banco de España.*

PALACIO REAL

Visiting the Royal Palace should be high on your list of things to do. Its extravagant interior detail and political and historical importance—it was home to the Spanish monarchs from 1764 to 1931—make it source of Madrileño pride. Today King Juan Carlos, who lives in the far less ostentatious Zarzuela Palace outside Madrid, uses it for official state functions. Tours (100 ptas) are available for groups of at least five. *C. de Bailén, tel. 91/542–00–59. Admission: 850 ptas. Open Mon.–Sat. 9:30–5, Sun. 9–3. Metro: Opera.*

PARQUE DEL RETIRO

This is where it's at on Sunday, when thousands of Madrileños, with kids and dogs in tow, come to play ball, relax, rap over a drink at one of several outdoor cafés, and browse at the annual book fair (in June). Take it easy, but don't take your eyes off your backpack—cunning thieves may be camouflaged in the masses. The formal heart of this park is the **estanque** (pond), presided over by a grand statue of the 19th-century monarch Alfonso XII. Rent a rowboat (500 ptas for 45 min) and paddle around, or just hang out and watch the sunset on the surrounding steps. *Metro: Retiro.*

PLAZA MAYOR

Once the place to watch bullfights, the canonization of saints, and the burning of heretics, these days Plaza Mayor (Sol Metro) is the place to watch tourists, pigeons, and political rallies. Originally designed by Juan de Herrera, the architect who built El Escorial (*see* Near Madrid, *below*), this spacious plaza was inaugurated in 1620 during the reign of Felipe III, whose statue stands in the center. Under the arcades that ring the square, expensive cafés set up hundreds of outdoor tables in summer. The cheaper and less touristy cafés lie just off the plaza, especially around Calle Marqués Viudo de Pontejos.

CHEAP THRILLS

You can graze at outdoor food stands, get your hair wrapped by hippies, and buy tacky, imported knick-knacks and local street art the world over, but Madrid's famous flea market is special. **El Rastro** (Metro: La Latina), historically the thieves' market, is gigantic. Roughly framed by Calle Toledo, Calle Ribera de Curtidores, and Ronda de Toledo, the market is packed every Sunday from 10 to 3 with everyone from sleepless party animals to old bargain-hounds with sharp elbows. Here you can buy leather bags (from 2,000 ptas), secondhand Levis (800 ptas), and even small animals.

Just as compelling are two of Madrid's oldest neighborhoods, **La Latina** and **Lavapiés,** which stretch south from Plaza Mayor. Centuries ago, before the Inquisition, this area housed Madrid's Jewish community. Today it's the most racially diverse area of Madrid, embracing immigrants from Africa, Asia, and South America. Despite attempts to gentrify the area, Lavapiés's character remains intact; if you walk through the narrow, twisting streets, you'll see that it's still an authentic and dynamic neighborhood, and you might even catch an impromptu concert.

Join tourists and die-hard Spaniards at **Los Toros** (bullfights). During the main season (March–October), bulls face the *toreros* every Sunday and Thursday at 7 PM at the stadium **Plaza Monumental de Las Ventas** (Metro: Ventas). The cheap tickets cost about 500 ptas—you might not be able to see all the details, but then again, you might not want to. Buy tickets at the stadium; for more information, dial 91/356–22–00.

AFTER DARK

What makes Madrid's nightlife—considered by many the best in the world—so exceptional is not just the city's countless bars, pubs (bars with music and dancing), and discos, but also the fervid energy of the revelers within them. Pick up the weekly *Guía del Ocio* (125 ptas) at a newsstand for the most comprehensive list of nocturnal activities.

There is a distinct rhythm to nightlife in Madrid. Having emerged refreshed from your siesta and primping no earlier than 10, you might start with drinks and some tapas at a bar or cueva (*see* Bars, *below*). Next, you'll want to hit the discos, but don't even think about arriving before 2 or 3; any earlier and they'll be empty or, worse, full of teenagers. Giants on the *discoteca* scene are **Joy Eslava** (*see below*); **¡Oh Madrid!** (C. La Coruña, tel. 91/307–86–97; Metro: Estrecho); **Pachá** (C. Barceló 11, tel 91/447–01–28; Metro: Tribunal); and **Kapital** (C. Atocha 125, tel. 91/420–29–06; Metro: Atocha). All charge a cover of about 1,500 ptas–2,000 ptas. Take a break at 5 to refuel, then return for more drinking and dancing, and take your final leave at around 8, in time for a breakfast of *churros con chocolate* (crullers with chocolate).

The areas around Plaza Santa Ana and nearby Calle Las Huertas, and calles Echegaray and Ventura de la Vega, are bursting with great pubs and small discos, many of which have no cover. Lavapiés, Madrid's oldest quarter, is also crammed with bars, pubs, and discos. From Plaza Mayor, wander down Calle Cuchilleros, making your way to Calle de Segovia, Calle Constanilla San Pedro, and Plaza de la Villa. For a more alternative scene, head north to Malasaña; for Madrid's thriving gay scene, head to the bars and pubs around Plaza Chueca.

If the scorching summer heat is getting to you, take a plunge in the Piscina de Comunidad (Avenida de Angel, across from Lago Metro; admission 475 ptas; open daily 10:30–8), where you can laze in a lounge chair or write postcards at the poolside café.

BARS

Cuevas (caves), clustered around Plaza Mayor, are cozy little places with low ceilings and dim lights; each serves drinks and specializes in a certain type of *tapa*. Go down Escalerilla de la Piedra and around the corner to the right to Cava de San Miguel, which houses about six cuevas, including **Meson de Champiñones** (17 Cava de San Miguel, tel. 91/559–67–97). Not immune to tourists, the *cuevas* nonetheless retain a distinctively local feel and clientele. Sangría and tapas cost about 600 ptas per person (don't forget to tip the musicians).

Cervecería de Santa Ana. Nestled in a row of happening bars, this place has indoor and sidewalk seating and is a great place to scope out good-looking Madrileños. Whiskey costs 600 ptas, brandy 200 ptas. *Pl. Santa Ana 10, tel. 91/429–43–56. Metro: Sol.*

Chocolatería San Gines. Your early-morning stop for *churros con chocolate* (400 ptas), this sweetery looks like an ice-cream parlor, but there's a full bar inside and techno vibes from the disco next door. *C. de Coloreros 2, off C. Arenal, tel. 91/365–65–46. Metro: Sol.*

Las Cuevas de Sesamo. A muted exterior diguises the cavernous dungeons within. Enjoy Bohemian piano music, extract wisdom from the inscribed walls, and revel in the "pitchers only" of sangría (700 ptas). *C. Príncipe 7, tel. 91/429–65–24. Metro: Sevilla or Sol.*

La Escondida. Sit on little stools in the cozy nooks of this cool, unpretentious bar and listen to its great jazz collection. Beer and wine are each 150 ptas. *Pl. de Puerta Cerrada 6, tel. 91/365–34–19. Metro: Sol.*

Eucalipto. Sit at a sidewalk table, order a *mojito* (550 ptas; made with mint, white rum, and lemon), and absorb the Afro-Caribbean music at this funky bar. *C. Argumosa 4, tel. 91/530–07–94. Metro: Lavapiés.*

Los Gabrieles. With Spain's cultural history colorfully inscribed on its tile walls, this bar was Franco's natural choice for a cold one after trouncing Morocco. Local flamenco fans and tourists imbibe sangría (300 ptas) and beer (500 ptas); after 7 PM, drink prices rise 200 ptas. *C. Echegaray 17, tel. 91/429–62–61. Metro: Sol or Sevilla.*

Galería d'Arte. An explosion of green plants and artsy artifacts bedeck this cozy café. Couples make out in corners while club-hoppers down beer (300 ptas) and wine (225 ptas) before hitting Joy Eslava (*see below*) around the corner. *C. Coloreros 5, tel. 91/366–35–19. Metro: Sol.*

Medina Magerit. This groovy joint hosts great music, magic shows, board games, and poetry readings. Hang with Fernando, the owner, and sip fancy coffees (600 ptas) and *horchatas* (sweet rice-based drinks; 300 ptas) on couches in the dim, smoky back room or basement. *C. del Divino Pastor 21, at C. de Ruiz, tel. 91/594–37–51. Metro: Bilbao.*

El Pirata. This popular watering hole, which is the inside of an actual ship, caters to a twentysomething crowd. Whiskey (700 ptas) and beer (275 ptas) are served on the gangplank, and toilets are in the hold. Caribbean-salsa motifs abound, and the funky artwork changes monthly. *Conde de Xiquena 2, at C. de Prim, no phone. Closed Sunday. Metro: Chueca.*

PUBS AND CLUBS

Café del Mercado. The lights don't get much brighter—or hotter—at everybody's favorite place to drink (sangría 500 ptas) and dance. Thursdays are free. *Ronda de Toledo 1, tel. 91/365–87–39. Metro: Puerta de Toledo. Cover: 1,000 ptas.*

Daniels. Madrid's gay scene explodes at Daniels, where flashing neon lights, intense disco music, and erotic videos precede the main attraction: muscle shows nightly at 1 AM. Beers are 450 ptas, rum-and-Cokes 650 ptas; all drinks are half-price until 11. *C. Hortaleza 43, tel. 91/531–86–14. Metro: Chueca.*

El Jardín de las Delicias. This beautiful pub is ringed by plants, sculptures, and big windows. On the outside terrace, students dance to everything from feminist jazz to R&B to Celtic folk and funky blues. Shows begin at midnight; drinks begin at 500 ptas. *Pl. Christino Martol 5, tel. 91/542–44–99. Open weekends until 5 AM. Metro: Pl. de España.*

Joy Eslava. Shake your booty with ritzy celebs, unwinding politicos, and hip youngsters alike at this late-19th-century theater-turned-disco in the heart of the city—*about* the coolest place in Madrid. Disco, hip-hop, and techno pulsate on three dance floors. The cover (1,500 ptas weekdays, 2,000 ptas weekends) buys you a drink. *C. Arenal 11, tel. 91/366–37–33. Metro: Sol.*

No Se Lo Digas a Nadie, Nadie, Nadie. This is the club for everyone, everyone, everyone. Body-rocking techno-pop blares on the smoky dance floor below, while serious shooters test their skills on the pool tables above (1,200 ptas per hour). Whiskey and rum are 600 ptas. *C. Ventura de la Vega 7, tel. 91/420–29–80. Open weekdays 6 PM–2 AM, weekends until 5 AM.*

Soniquete. Kick up your heels Spanish-style: Zealous but patient native dancers teach flamenco nightly 9 PM–1 AM. Classes are free; sangría is 600 ptas. *C. Felipe III 4, tel. 91/366–30–01. Metro: Sol.*

Stella. Straight and gay bunches alike pound beers (400 ptas), bowl, and dance to sexy salsa. The crowd thickens after 2 AM. *C. Arlabán 7, tel. 91/522–41–26. Cover: 1,000 ptas (includes drink). Open Thurs.–Sun. midnight–6 AM. Metro: Sevilla.*

NEAR MADRID

Surrounded by dazzling landscapes and steeped in fresh air, the small cities around Madrid will take you back several eras. Here you can gaze at cathedrals, contemplate Moorish architecture, and admire a wealth of paintings by the likes of El Greco. Ancient Toledo (Spain's former capital), the great palace-monastery of El Escorial, tranquil Cuenca, and elegant Segovia, all within a few hours of Madrid, are all worth extended visits.

EL ESCORIAL

The main attraction of El Escorial, an elegant town on the slopes of the Guadarrama Mountains, is the enormous **Real Monasterio de San Lorenzo de El Escorial,** an imposing gray-cinder structure stabbed into the hilly verdure. El Escorial, as the monastery is called, was founded by Felipe II in the 16th century for two reasons: to thank God for Spain's victory over France on the feast day of San Lorenzo, and to honor his father Carlos V's wish that a pantheon be built to house his earthly remains and those of his descendants. It's a massive complex with beautiful views, containing not only a functioning monastery and church, but also a school, library, royal palace, mausoleum, and museums. *Tel. 91/890–59–03. Admission: 850 ptas. Open Tues.–Sun. 10–6. Tours (950 ptas) 10–1:30 and 4–6.*

El Escorial is organized into two zones, with the biggest attractions concentrated in Zone A. The **Museo de Pintura,** a dramatic collection of paintings mostly from the 16th–18th centuries, features religious works by artists such as Tintoretto, José Ribera, Francisco Zurbarán, and El Greco. The **Sala Capitular** contains several paintings by Ribera, two by El Greco, and, best of all, Bosch's triptych *La Creación* (Creation). The **Royal Apartments** contain old paintings, royal beds, and royal treasures, and their elegant decor and beautiful tiles give them a distinctly Spanish character. Finally, there's the mausoleum, which has two parts: the **Panteón de los Reyes,** a seductively creepy room containing the sarcophagi of all but two Spanish monarchs since Carlos V, and the **Panteón de los Infantes,** where those royalty who never made it to adulthood are enshrined. To see all of Zone A on a 45-minute tour, join one of the groups clustered around a Spanish-speaking guide. (Sometimes the groups are as large as 300 people, so you may not see or hear much.) They'll also give tours in English for groups of 40 or more.

In Zone B, you'll see the **basilica**'s amazing altar, flanked by gold statues and topped with a crucified Jesus cast in gold. You'll also want to visit the **library,** filled with rare manuscripts, codices, and ancient books. On the painted ceiling is Tibaldi's representation of the seven liberal arts, with Filosofía and Teología facing off at opposite ends of the room.

VISITOR INFORMATION

C. Floridablanca 10, tel. 91/890–15–54. Open weekdays 10–2 and 3–5, Sat. 10–2.

COMING AND GOING

Trains for Escorial (1 hr, 370 ptas–430 ptas) leave hourly from Madrid's Estación de Atocha; some continue to Ávila. El Escorial's **train station** (tel. 91/890–04–13) sits at the bottom of the hill; Bus L-1 (10 min, 80 ptas) will take you to the monastery from here. **Buses** (tel. 91/543–36–45 for information) leave roughly every half-hour from Madrid (from C. Fernández de los Rios, at Isaac Peral; Metro: Moncloa) and stop at Bolera Pub, near the monastery. The trip takes 50 minutes and costs 380 ptas; buy your ticket as you board.

For an amazing view of Toledo, cross the Tagus River and follow Carretera de Circunvolación upward.

TOLEDO

Majestic Toledo's labyrinthine cobblestone streets, colorful facades, and spire-charged skyline make it almost unbelievably wondrous. Only an hour from Madrid, this ancient city rises high above the banks of the Tagus River, which almost completely encircles the city, creating a sort of natural moat. Thousands of tourists cruise through Toledo's narrow streets, but it would take more than exhaust-spewing buses or a bunch of t-shirt vendors to bring down this little city on a hill. Strategic Roman stronghold, site of the Visigoths' court, capital of Christian Spain until 1561, and onetime location of Spain's chief military outpost, Toledo wears the marks of its turbulent history beautifully—buildings and artifacts remain from all of these periods. If you can elbow your way through the crowds, you'll also find Mudéjar (Spanish Muslim) architecture, tile doorways, and even the occasional Toledano.

VISITOR INFORMATION

The **tourist office** (Puerta de Bisagra, tel. 925/22–08–43; open weekdays 9–2 and 4–6, Sat. 9–3 and 4–7; Sun. 9–3) is in the southeast corner of Paseo de Merchán park. A satellite **kiosk** (tel. 925/22–14–00; open Mon.–Sat. 10–6, Sun. 10–3) is in Plaza de Zocodover, the main plaza. Toledo is small, but not easy to navigate. Pick up a *plano callejero* (street map) gratis at the tourist office or kiosk, or for 350 ptas at a newsstand.

COMING AND GOING

Toledo's **train station** (Paseo de la Rosa, tel. 925/22–30–99) is just east of the city's main attractions, across the Río Tajo. Several trains leave daily for Madrid (1¼ hrs, 605 ptas); most go to Estación de Atocha, and a few go to Estación Chamartín. To get to the center of Toledo from the station, walk 20 minutes uphill or take Bus 5 or 6 (110 ptas); the buses leave just to the right of the station (as you exit) and end up at Plaza Zocodover. Buses run between Toledo's **bus station** (Av. de Castilla–La Mancha, tel. 925/21–58–50) and Madrid's Estación Sur (1 hr, 570 ptas) every half hour. Toledo's bus station is about a 15-minute walk north up Ronda de Juanelo (east of Plaza Zocodover), or a short ride on Bus 5 or 6.

WHERE TO SLEEP

Don't count on finding a cheap room without a written reservation in the summer; book a week ahead.

Fonda Segovia. Nine comfortable, plain rooms with big beds go for 2,500 ptas (doubles) or 3,500 ptas (triples). *C. Recoletos 2, tel. 925/21–11–24. From top of C. Real del Arrabal, go up stairs and around corner.*

Pensión Virgen de la Estrella. With stern owners and a collection of religious artifacts, this place is not ideal for unmarried couples or party types, but the price is right: doubles are 3,000 ptas. *C. Real del Arrabal 18, tel. 925/25–31–34. From Pl. Zocodover bus stop, walk north up C. Real del Arrabal.*

Posada del Estudiante. These 12 rooms are near the cathedral, and some have views of the Posada's tile courtyard. The restaurant below dishes out home-cooked meals (650 ptas) faster than you can say *gazpacho andaluz.* Doubles cost 3,000 ptas. *Callejón de San Pedro 2, off C. Cardenal Cisneros, tel. 925/21–47–34. From Pl. Zocodover bus stop, take C. Armes south, veer right on C. Comercio, left on Tornerias, around cathedral, then left on Callejón de San Pedro.*

HOSTEL • San Servando (HI). You won't live like royalty in this medieval castle; you're locked out from 10:30 AM to 5:30 PM and turned into a pumpkin at midnight, when the curfew clangs. Still, it's pleasant and has a TV room, a pool, and laundry facilities (300 ptas). Come early for one of the 46 beds; the hostel opens daily at 7 AM. Beds are 1,200 ptas, or 945 ptas if you're under 26, but you need to be an HI member. *Tel. 925/22–45–54. From train station, go right (west) on Paseo de la Rosa, left at Puente de Alcántara bridge, and uphill toward castle.*

CAMPING • Circo Romano. This place has blackberry bushes, a patio restaurant-bar, tennis courts (600 ptas per hour), a huge pool (400 ptas per day), and a minimarket, all just a 15-minute walk from the center of Toledo. Sites are 450 ptas–500 ptas plus 550 ptas per person. *Av. Carlos III 19, tel. 925/22–04–42. From Pl. Zocodover bus stop, take C. Real del Arrabal north to Puerta de Bisagra, turn left, then turn onto Carlos III at traffic circle.*

FOOD

Toledanos generally eat at home, so it's slim pickings for the poor and hungry traveler. You can save money if you pack it in at lunchtime and have tapas for dinner. **El Corralito** (Corral de Don Diego 10, 2 blocks south of Pl. Zocodover, at Tornerías, tel. 925/21–50–24; closed Tues. and daily 4–7) serves a tapa of *croquetas* (croquettes) with a *caña* (glass) of beer for 250 ptas. There are several cheap eateries on the main road between Plaza Zocodover and Puerta de Bisagra. **Restaurante Cafetería Bisagra** (C. Real del Arrabal 14, tel. 925/22–06–93) has combination plates for 500 ptas–900 ptas. **La Abadia** (Pl. San Nicolás 3, tel. 925/25–11–40) is a café-bar-restaurant with lots of students, good German beer (350 ptas), and tapas (300 ptas–400 ptas). Shop for groceries at the **Mercado Municipal** (Pl. Mayor 2; open weekdays 8:30–2 and 4:30–7:30, Sat. 8:30–2).

WORTH SEEING

Toledo's art and architecture were deeply influenced by its large Jewish and Muslim populations, and by El Greco, who lived here during the Renaissance.

EL ALCAZAR • Lording over Toledo and the surrounding region, the Alcázar is a monument to Spain's former military glory. Despite such cheesy displays as a room filled with *photocopies* of important documents and regiments of toy soldiers, this museum offers a fascinating glimpse of Spain's military history. The former fortress, thrice burned and rebuilt, was most recently thrashed in 1936, during the Spanish Civil War—Nationalist troops, led by Colonel Moscardó, barricaded themselves inside and withstood a 70-day siege by the Republican army. You can hear the dramatic telephone conversation between Colonel Moscardó (whose son had been taken hostage in Madrid) and the Republican representative reenacted in four different languages. *Cuesta de Carlos V, tel. 925/22–30–38. From Pl. Zocodover, take C. Armas south to Cuesta de Carlos V. Entrance on other side of building. Admission: 125 ptas. Open Tues.–Sat. 9:30–1:30 and 4–6:30, Sun. 10–1:30 and 4–6:30 (until 5:30 Oct.–Mar.).*

CATEDRAL • Because its construction spanned over 250 years (from 1226 to around 1492), the cathedral embodies a hodgepodge of Gothic, Renaissance, and Mudéjar styles. In the middle of the ambulatory, the Transparente—a dizzying example of baroque architecture—depicts angels reaching toward heaven, sometimes ethereally illumined by light streaming through a hole in the roof. The sacristy houses a kind of miniature Prado, with works by El Greco, Goya, Velázquez, Titian, and Raphael. *Pl. de Ayuntamiento, tel. 925/22–22–41. From Pl. de Zocodover, take C. Comercio to C. Chapinería, turn right at Catedral, enter on C. Arco de Palacio. Admission: 500 ptas. Open Mon.–Sat 10:30–1 and 3:30–7, Sun. 10:30–1:30 and 4–7 (4–6 Oct.–Mar.).*

EL GRECO'S TOLEDO • Toledo owes some of its fame to Domenikos "El Greco" Theotokopoulos, Greek artist of the late 16th and early 17th centuries. El Greco's thought-provoking visions have a temporal relevance in Toledo, where El Greco spent the latter part of his life. View the artist's allegorical representation of the city, *Vista y Plano de Toledo* (View and Plan of Toledo), at the **Casa del Greco** (C. Samuel Levi 3, SW of Pl. Zocodover, tel. 925/22–40–46; open Tues.–Sat. 10–2 and 4–6, Sun. 10–2). Admission is 400 ptas weekdays, free Saturday afternoon and Sunday morning. One of the artist's most famous works, *El Entierro del Conde de Orgaz* (The Burial of the Count of Orgaz), is the only painting housed in the modest **Iglesia de Santo Tomé** (Pl. del Conde 4; admission 150 ptas; open daily 10–1:45 and 3:30–6:45; shorter hrs Oct.–Mar.). The 16th-century church and hospital-cum-museum **Museo de Santa Cruz de Toledo** (C. Miguel de Cervantes 3, east of Pl. Zocodover, tel. 925/22–10–36; open Mon. 10–2 and 4:30–6:30, Tues.–Sat. 10–6:30, Sun. 10–2) features many a crucifix, some beautiful tapestries, an outstanding collection of El Grecos, and numerous 19th-century sketches of the city. Admission is 200 ptas, free Saturday after 2:30 PM.

JEWISH TOLEDO • Before the Spanish Inquisition, Toledo was the home of Spain's largest and most prominent Jewish community. Today, only 2 of an estimated 10 synagogues remain. The 1203 **Sinagoga de Santa María la Blanca** (C. de los Reyes Catolicos 2, at C. de la Judería, tel. 925/22–72–57; admission 150 ptas; open daily 10–2 and 3:30–7) was a synagogue until 1405, when it became a church—which explains the name. Inscriptions of JHS (for Jesus Christ), combined with Mudéjar arches and woodwork, make this a seemingly un-Jewish synagogue. The other synagogue, **El Tránsito** (C. Samuel Levi, tel. 925/22–36–65; open Tues.–Sat. 10–2 and 4–6, Sun. 10–2), which also functions as a **Sephardic Museum,** was completed in 1357 and endured as a synagogue until 1492, after which it served various military purposes. Today it's but a shell of an elegant synagogue, with mosaics, tapestries, and delicate marble etchings of biblical quotations. The museum exhibits cultural artifacts and provides an excellent history of the Jewish tradition in Spain.

Whether it's the unusually flashy Mudéjar ceiling, the mannequins behind the armored masks, or the electric candelabras, there's something surreal about Segovia's Alcázar.

MUSLIM TOLEDO • Nearly three centuries of Muslim rule ended when Alfonso VI seized Toledo for the Christians in 1085, and the local Muslims became known as "Mudéjares," or "subjected ones." Churches then replaced mosques, but traditional architectural styles endured. Muslim influence on Toledo's buildings can be seen today in the geometric tiles framing doorways, Mudéjar arches on street corners, and the cathedral and monastery **San Juan de los Reyes** (C. de los Reyes 17, SW of Pl. de Zocodover; admission 150 ptas; open daily 10–1:45 and 3:30–6:45, until 5:45 Oct.–Mar.). Only one wholly Muslim building remains—the beautiful 10th-century mosque now called **El Cristo de la Luz** (C. Cristo de la Luz, above Puerta del Sol); but you can only admire it from the outside.

SEGOVIA

With its gorgeous, late-Gothic cathedral, Roman aqueduct, and beautiful buildings decorated with sculpted geometric shapes, Segovia draws tourists like moths to a flame. Nonetheless, the town maintains its identity and integrity, celebrating every Sunday with music, small parades, and dancing in the streets. Plaza Mayor contains some elegant cafés and the **oficina de turismo** (Pl. Mayor 10, tel. 921/46–03–34; open daily 10–2 and 5–8), which hands out free maps.

COMING AND GOING

The **train station** (C. Obispo Quesada, tel. 921/43–66–66) dispatches about eight trains a day to Madrid (2 hrs, 735 ptas); buses from the sleazy **bus station** (C. Ezequiel González, tel. 921/44–30–10) also travel to Madrid (1½ hrs, 765 ptas). Both stations are in the newer part of Segovia, and buses 2, 3, and 4 (85 ptas) stop in front to take you to Plaza Mayor, in the historic center of town. Otherwise, it's a 15- to 20-minute walk; follow the CENTRO HISTÓRICO signs.

WHERE TO SLEEP AND EAT

Huespedaje Cubo (Pl. Mayor 4, tel. 921/46–09–17), in the middle of town, is the cheapest option, with doubles for 2,400 ptas; reserve ahead. A block from Plaza Mayor, **Pensión Ferri** (C. Escuderos 10, tel. 921/43–05–44) has doubles for 2,200 ptas–2,750 ptas. A 10-minute walk southeast of Plaza Mayor, **Residencia Tagore** (C. Santa Isabel 13, tel. 921/42–00–35) is more expensive (doubles 4,000 ptas–5,500 ptas) and is sometimes flooded with student groups, but it may be the best deal in Segovia. It's a kind of budget resort, with pool, TV room, library, restaurant, and laundry facilities.

Restaurants in the *centro histórico* cater to tourists with money to burn; it's hard to find a *menú del día* for less than 2,000 ptas. But **La Cueva de San Esteban** (C. Valdelaquila 15, tel. 921/46–09–82) serves up tasty *menús* for 900 ptas, including two glasses of wine. Try the paella (650 ptas) at **La Catedral,** where the full *menú* is 1,200 ptas. (C. Marqués del Arco 32, tel. 921/46–05–51; closed daily 4:30–8:30).

WORTH SEEING

The last Gothic cathedral built in Spain, Segovia's **catedral** (Pl. Mayor; open Apr.–Sept., daily 9:30–7; Oct.–Mar., daily 9–6) has a sumptuous facade and a warm, golden interior kissed by light streaming through 16th-century Flemish windows. The cathedral's museum and cloister (tel. 921/43–53–25; admission 250 ptas) display Flemish tapestries and lots o' gold.

Since the 12th century, the **Alcázar** has served as a fortress, royal palace, military school, and the original emblem of Segovia—so when it was gutted by fire in 1862, the city took pains to reconstruct it. The Alcázar may lack authenticity, but it compensates by indulging romantic myths of medieval knights and castles, and by offering amazing views of seemingly endless plains. *Pl. de la Reina Victoria Eugenia, tel. 921/46–07–59. Admission: 375 ptas. Open Apr.–Oct., daily 10–7; Nov.–Mar., daily 10–6. From Plaza Mayor, take C. Marqués del Arco past Catedral and follow signs.*

Below the Alcázar and across the Río Eresma stands a clump of holy houses, all worth the trek even for the seriously churched-out. **Iglesia de la Vera Cruz** (admission 175 ptas; open June–Sept., Tues.–Sun. 10:30–1:30 and 3:30–7; shorter hrs off-season) is especially fascinating. Originally designed for the crusading Knights Templar, it was built to resemble the Church of the Holy Sepulchre in Jerusalem. If you aren't claustrophobic, climb to the top of the Mudéjar bell tower for a view of the Alcázar and surrounding plains. *From Alcázar, turn left on C. del Pozo de la Nieve, walk 300 ft, turn left onto winding footpath to Paseo de Santo Domingo, right on Carretera de Zamarramala, and continue for ½ km (⅓ mi).*

Built in 1721 for the Bourbon king Felipe V, the perfectly symmetrical **Palacio Real de la Granja** and adjoining gardens actually deserve their comparison to Versailles and attract far fewer tourists than that French behemoth. The grounds rest on the northern slopes of the Guadarrama range, in the town of La Granja de San Ildefonso, 9 km (6 mi) southeast of Segovia. The highlights of the palace are the tremendous tapestry room and the handblown crystal chandeliers. About 12 buses leave daily from the bus station in Segovia (105 ptas). *Tel. 921/47–00–20. Admission: 650 ptas. Open June–Sept., Tues.–Sun. 10–6; Oct.–May, Tues.–Sat. 10–1:30 and 3–5, Sun. 10–2.*

CUENCA

As you stand at the top of Cuenca's *ciudad vieja* (old city), surrounded by deep canyons and the rivers Huécar and Júcar, with ruins, grand churches, and a Mudéjar tower unfolding below, it's hard not to be overcome by the town's dramatic tranquility. **Plaza Mayor,** the charming central square of the *ciudad vieja,* is dominated by the 12th-century Gothic **catedral** (tel. 969/21–24–63; admission 200 ptas; open Tues.–Fri. 9–2 and 4–6, Sat. 9–2 and 4–7, Sun. 9–2). From the Gothic and Renaissance chapels below, you can hear the songbirds nested in the rafters. Around the corner and to the left as you exit the cathedral, the **Museo Diocesano** (C. Obispo Valero 3, tel. 969/22–42–10; admission 200 ptas; open Tues.–Fri. 11–2 and 4–6, Sat. 11–2 and 4–8, Sun. 11–2) seems at first glance a bland rug shop, but some of these rugs, which represent Flemish and local styles, date from the 16th century; one depicts Jesus motioning you to come hither. Pop downstairs to see three El Grecos. Across the street, the **Museo de Cuenca** (C. Obispo Valero 12, tel. 969/21–30–69; admission 200 ptas; open Tues.–Fri. 10–2 and 4–7, weekends 10–2), traces the region's history, covering everything from the Stone Age to Cuenca's Roman period and the Visigoth conquest. Cuenca's most unique and celebrated museum is the labyrinthine **Museo de Arte Abstracto Español** (SE of Pl. Mayor, tel. 969/21–29–83; admission 300 ptas; open Tues.–Fri. 11–2 and 4–6, Sat. 11–2 and 4–8, Sun. 11–2), featuring works by the remarkable 1950s generation of Spanish abstract artists, including Fernando Zobel, Antonio Saura, and Manuel Rivera. The museum is in one of Cuenca's famed **Casas Colgadas** (Hanging Houses), built on steep rocks almost over the town's eastern precipice. For more information, hit the **tourist office** (Pl. Mayor 1, tel. 969/23–21–19; open weekdays 10–2 and 4–6, Sat. until 7, Sun. until 6:30).

COMING AND GOING

Cuenca is connected by train with Madrid's Estación de Atocha (3 hrs, 1,300 ptas) and by bus with Madrid's Auto Res (3 hrs, 1,300 ptas). From Cuenca's **train station** (C. Mariano Catalina 10, tel. 969/22–07–20) or **bus station** (C. Fermín Caballero 20, tel. 969/22–11–84), on the south edge of town, buses 1, 2, and 7 zip up to Plaza Mayor for 80 ptas. Otherwise, turn left when exiting either station and walk uphill 15 to 20 minutes, following the CASCO ANTIGUO signs.

WHERE TO SLEEP AND EAT

The only reason to spend more than 15 minutes in Cuenca's *ciudad nueva* (new city) is to save a few hundred pesetas on food and lodging. You'll find several budget *hostales* on Calle Ramón y Cajal, which starts 160 ft to the left of the train station, then bears right and turns into Calle las Torres. Here, **Pensión Marín** (Ramón y Cajal 53, tel.969/22–19–78) has bright, airy double rooms for 2,400 ptas. In the *ciudad vieja*, lodging and restaurants are concentrated north of Plaza Mayor. **Posada de San José** (C. Julián Romero 4, tel. 969/21–13–00), uphill from the cathedral, has firm, comfy beds and spacious rooms; summer rates for doubles are 3,800 ptas–8,400 ptas (add about 500 ptas Friday and Saturday). One of the best places to stay in Cuenca is also one of the best places to eat: **Pensión Tabanqueta** (Pl. Trabuco 13, tel. 969/21–12–90) has attractive doubles (4,000 ptas), and the **Mesón-Bar Tabanqueta,** below, serves excellent tapas, a 1,000-pta *menú del día,* and an amazing view of the Júcar River. Though in a student dormitory, **UIMP** (C. Julian Romero 18, tel. 969/22–09–25) is an elegant *comedor* (dining room) overlooking the Júcar, and the *menú* (1,000 ptas) is one of the cheapest meals on the hill. Unfortunately, it's only open in July and September–November.

OLD CASTILE

Castellano, Spain's dominant language, derives from the area known as Old Castile, which encompasses Castile y León and cities such as Burgos, León, Logroño, and Valladolid. Castile was so christened for the *castillos* (castle fortresses) built here more than 1,000 years ago to thwart attacks by the ruling Moors. This relatively small region, north of Madrid, is historically and sentimentally the cradle of modern, unified Spain, as it was the seat of the first successful resistance of the Muslims.

In **Old Castile,** known for its dry, scorching summers and bitter winters, you are in the heart of religious and militaristic Spain. These high plateaus were the birthplace of both the fanatical brand of Catholicism that would become the country's hallmark, and many famous Spaniards. El Cid, one of Spain's celebrated Moor-battlers, was born just outside Burgos. St. James, Spain's patron saint (later dubbed Santiago Matamoros, or James the Moorslayer), also figures prominently in the region's history; his tomb in Galicia remains a popular stop on the famous Camino de Santiago pilgrimage route through the regions of Castilla and León. The legacy of such fervent religion mixed with military might has resulted in some of the most impressive cathedrals in the land, especially in León, Burgos, and Salamanca.

SALAMANCA

The home of Spain's first university, Salamanca has a long intellectual history. Despite its violent history of Moorish domination and Christian conquest, Salamanca's magnificent cathedrals, austere convents, and stunning palaces, glowing with the gold of aged sandstone, make Salamanca a showpiece of the Spanish Renaissance. The essence of life here today is to be found in the elegant **Plaza Mayor,** completed in the 18th century by architect Alberto Churriguera. Under the plaza's grandiose arches, young mingle with old, vendors bargain with tourists, and *tunas* drop by to make folkloric music.

BASICS

The **Oficina Regional de Turismo** (Rúa Mayor, in Casa de las Conchas, tel. 923/26–85–71; open weekdays 10–2 and 5–8, Sat. 9–2 and 5–7, Sun. 11–2) specializes in regional information. For Salamanca tips, go to the **Oficina Municipal de Turismo** (Pl. Mayor 10, tel. 923/21–83–42; open Mon.–Sat. 9–2 and 4:30–6:30, Sun. 10–2 and 4:30–6:30). Both offices hand out free maps. To fax or phone, head to the *locutorio* **Sabera** (Pl. Mayor 11; open daily 9:30 AM–11:30 PM). The main post office, **Correos y Telégrafos** (Gran Vía 25, tel. 923/26–06–07; open weekdays 9–2 and 4–6, Sat. 9–2; postal code 37008), holds poste restante.

COMING AND GOING

The **train station** (Pl. de la Estación, tel. 923/12–02–02) sits at the north end of town; to get to Plaza Mayor, take Paseo de la Estación west to Plaza de España, then walk west on Calle Azafranal. Bus L1 (50 ptas) leaves the station every half hour for Plaza del Mercado, adjoining Plaza Mayor. Trains go directly to Ávila (2 hrs, 805 ptas), Madrid (3½ hrs, 1,560 ptas), Barcelona (14 hrs, 6,500 ptas), and

Paris (16 hrs, 15,185 ptas). Get tickets and information at the **RENFE office** (Pl. de la Libertad 10, tel. 923/21–24–54; open weekdays 9–2 and 5–8), just northwest of Plaza Mayor.

It's generally fastest to take the bus into Salamanca. The **bus station** (Filoberto Villalobos 71, tel. 923/23–67–17) is a 25-minute walk west of Plaza Mayor. Otherwise, take Bus L4 to Plaza de España and walk 10 minutes up Calle Toro. Buses travel to Ávila (1½ hrs, 820 ptas), Madrid (3¼ hrs, 1,690 ptas), and Barcelona (11½ hrs, 6,250 ptas).

GETTING AROUND

Plaza Mayor, dominated by the *ayuntamiento* (town hall), is in the heart of Salamanca. The university and most other sights lie to the south, toward the Río Tormes. Gran Vía, a boulevard loaded with great bars, runs along the modern part of the city, to the north.

WHERE TO SLEEP

A popular destination for budget travelers, Salamanca has lots of places to crash, especially around Plaza Mayor and on Rúa Mayor, Calle Meléndez, and their side streets.

Fonda San José. Clean, newly renovated rooms go for 1,300 ptas (singles) or 2,200 ptas (doubles), but if you stay a while, the owner might cut you a deal. Rooms don't have baths, but you can shower for 100 ptas. *C. Jesús 24, south of Pl. Mayor, tel. 923/21–27–24.*

Pensión Estefanía. These rooms have the works—dresser, desk, curtains, even out-of-date movie posters. Doubles are 2,600 ptas, 3,400 ptas with bath. *C. Jesús 3–5, south of Pl. Mayor, tel. 923/21–73–72.*

Pensión Las Vegas. It's a great deal, but there are only five rooms, and they'll take a reservation only with first night's rent. Doubles are 2,400 ptas, 3,000 ptas with bath. *C. Meléndez 13, SW of Pl. Mayor, tel. 923/21–87–49. Laundry (700 ptas).*

Pensión Los Angeles. Smack in the middle of the action, the Los Angeles is a bargain if you don't mind the noise. There's a great view of Plaza Mayor from most doubles (3,000 ptas). *Pl. Mayor 10, tel. 923/21–81–66.*

Albergue Juvenil Salamanca. Five minutes from the Plaza Mayor, this brand-new youth hostel gives priority to those under 26; but if there's room, everyone else sleeps for the same price (beds 1,500 ptas, 1,750 ptas with breakfast). *C. Escoto 13-15, tel. 923/ 26–91–41, fax 923/21–42–27.*

FOOD

Salamanca does have cheap food, but you'll have to search for it. Take advantage of the university cafeterias for generous portions at student prices. Look for the black-iron gate of Anaya University's **Las Caballerizas** (C. Tostado 1–9, east of Pl. Mayor, tel. 923/29–44–45; closed weekends), where you can feast on pork-and-egg combos (under 475 ptas) and gulp java (80 ptas) in the cool brick-and-mortar cellar. **Le Mans Cervecería** (C. Sánchez Barbero 13, at Rúa Mayor, tel. 923/27–07–84) is the perfect place to sate that late-night hunger; try grilled sandwich No. 18 (375 ptas). There's also an **indoor market** (open weekdays 9–2) in Plaza del Mercado, just past the east arch of Plaza Mayor.

Cafetería Rue. This bustling sidewalk eatery in the middle of Rúa Mayor has good meat and veggie combos for 800 ptas, including wine and bread. *Rúa Mayor 46, SE of Pl. Mayor, tel. 923/21–73–33.*

Mesón de Cervantes. The cozy atmosphere and down-to-earth prices make this mesón anything but touristy, despite its Plaza Mayor location. Tapas are 100 ptas; beer is 150 ptas. Outside seating is about 200 ptas extra. *Pl. Mayor 15, tel. 923/21–72–13.*

Plus Ultra. This Salamancan institution serves up elaborate *pinchos* (like tapas, but generally smaller). Two big tapas and wine cost 425 ptas; combination plates are 650 ptas–800 ptas. *C. del Consejo 4, north of Pl. Mayor, tel. 923/21–72–11.*

WORTH SEEING

All over Salamanca, gorgeous buildings stand embellished with the patterns of plateresque architecture. Popularized in the 16th century, this style got its name from the word *platero* (silversmith) and was based on Italian Renaissance forms, with some Gothic and Moorish designs thrown in for good measure. For a close look at the designs, stroll down and around **Calle Ramón y Cajal,** where you'll see the Colegio Fonseca, Casa de las Muertes, and Palacio Monterrey. The Universidad and Escuelas Menores, on **Calle de Libreros,** are considered some of the greatest representations of the plateresque style.

UNIVERSIDAD • The reputation of Spain's oldest university, established in the 13th century by Alfonso IX, was somewhat diminished by 19th-century decadence and Nationalist repression, but its mystique persists, in no small part because of its beautiful plateresque buildings. Somewhere on the intricate facade of the main building is a little frog on top of a skull; legend says that if you find it without help, you'll be married within a year—or do well on your exams, or something of the sort. The lecture hall, **Sala de Fray Luis de León,** looks the same as it did when de León coolly returned after five years of Inquisition torture and began, "As we were saying yesterday . . . " In the **Escuelas Menores,** on the other side of the patio by the same name, the **Sala de Exhibiciones** holds photo exhibits (usually black-and-white), and the **Museo de la Universidad** contains the 15th-century fresco *El Cielo de Salamanca* (The Sky of Salamanca), by Fernando Gallego. *C. de Libreros, SW of Pl. Mayor, tel. 923/29–44–00. Admission to all: 200 ptas. University and museum open June–Sept., Mon.–Sat. 9:30–1:30 and 4–7, Sun. 10–1; Oct.–May, Mon.–Sat. 9:30–1:30 and 4–6, Sun. 10–1.*

CATEDRAL • When Salamanca's 12th-century Romanesque cathedral became too small for the town's growing population during the 16th century, the **Catedral Nueva** (New Cathedral) was added on. The Gothic facade is incredibly grand, but the golden-stone interior makes this an unusually warm cathedral. The adjacent **Catedral Vieja** (Old Cathedral; admission 300 ptas; open daily 10–12:30 and 4–5:30) is much smaller and less ornate—so much the better for its amazing paintings and altarpiece. *Pl. de Anaya, tel. 923/21–74–76. Admission free. Open daily 10–1 and 4–6.*

CONVENTO DE SAN ESTEBAN • The ornate plateresque facade of this 16th-century church was designed in 1524 by Juan de Alava, architect of the Catedral Nueva (*see above*). Inside, the baroque gold altarpiece by José Churriguera attests to the riches brought from the Americas by Christopher Columbus. (San Esteban's monks were among the first to support the explorer.) *Pl. Dominicos, at south end of Gran Vía, tel. 923/21–50–00. Admission: 200 ptas. Open daily 9–1 and 4–8.*

Though the regions of Castile and León have been united politically since the 11th century, the area still reflects the aggressive regionalism of much of modern Spain; graffiti on city walls demands "León Solo" ("León Alone").

Across the street from San Esteban, you'll find the Dominican **Convento de las Dueñas,** founded in 1419. With five sides and unusual angles, the 16th-century plateresque cloister is far from typical. Check out the columns up on the balcony: They're decorated so that as you walk by, children's faces turn to skulls, men become birds, and horses become dragons. *Tel. 923/21–54–42. Admission: 200 ptas. Open daily 10:30–1 and 4:30–7.*

CLERECIA • With its heaven-reaching towers, this monument—the headquarters of the Pontifical University—exemplifies classic baroque architecture. Academics here staunchly defended the principle of Immaculate Conception in the 17th century, and the church's pristine walls and vaulted ceilings still impress solemnity and modesty upon all who pass through. *C. San Isidro, off Rúa Mayor, tel. 923/26–46–60. Admission free. Closed for mass weekdays at 1:15 and 7:30 PM, Sun. at 12:30 PM.*

The **Casa de las Conchas** (House of Shells), across the street, was constructed by Dr. Rodrigo Arias around 1500. As the new chancellor of the Order of Santiago, Arias adorned the place with hundreds of shells, the Order's symbol. Legend holds that he placed a huge gold nugget under one of them, hence the chips in the house's lower shells. *Tel. 923/26–93–17. Admission to cloister free. Open weekdays 9–9, Sat. 9–2 and 4–7, Sun. 10–2 and 4–7.*

AFTER DARK

Throngs of university students keep Salamanca's nightlife hopping. Partying Salamanca-style means loading up at a pub and then heading to a disco. A good starting point is the central **Pub Oba-Oba** (Pl. Corrillo 9, just past SE arch of Pl. Mayor, tel. 923/26–99–79); pass through the Candyland of its red-and-white arches to chug beer (250 ptas) and sink into beanbag chairs. Ditch the tourist hordes and join locals at **El Callejón** (Gran Vía 68, NE of Pl. Mayor, tel. 923/26–54–67), where you'll find reasonably priced drinks (rum is 500 ptas) and infectious Spanish music that just may get you moving. **Submarino** (Pl. de San Justo, NE of Pl. Mayor, tel. 923/26–02–64; open until 5), shaped like a submarine, has a dance floor on the bottom deck and a gay bar up top. **Camelot** (C. Boraderos 3, south of Pl. Mayor) is also worth a boogie, as long as you don't mind the kitschy medieval exterior and faux royal tapestries; beers are only 300 ptas, and the party lasts 'til 5 AM. **Abadia** is a good place to spend a mellow few hours talking (C. Rua Mayor 40, no phone).

BURGOS

Redolent with the faded glory of Old Castile, Burgos was a conservative military stronghold for centuries; most recently, it served as the center of Franco's operations during the Spanish Civil War. During the Middle Ages and into the Reconquista, Burgos was the Cabeza de Castilla, the political and familial center of the Castilian royalty; most of Burgos's sights, such as the huge cathedral, are vestiges of this era. The city's chilly and insular atmosphere contrasts starkly with the open spontaneity of other Spanish cities, but for all its traditionalism, Burgos is still striking, with looming, gray stone buildings, graceful plazas, and tranquil river banks.

BASICS

Two convenient **tourist offices** (C. Asunción de Nuestra Señora 3, tel. 947/27–94–32; Arco de Santa María, tel. 947/26–53–75) lie just south and west of the cathedral plaza. Both have free maps and are open daily 9–2 and 5–7. For maps and information on other cities, try the **regional tourist office** (Pl. Alonso Martínez, tel. 947/20–31–25; open weekdays 9–2 and 5–7, weekends 10–2 and 5–8), west of the cathedral, down Calle Lain Calvo. The **TIVE** office (Av. General Yaque 20, tel. 947/20–98–81; open weekdays 9–2), which distributes hostel cards and tips on cheap travel, is in the business district, east of Plaza España. The **Correos** (Pl. del Conde de Castro 1, tel. 947/26–27–50; open weekdays 8:30–8:30, Sat. 9:30–2; postal code 09080) faces the river at Puente de San Pablo. There's also a **telephone office** (C. de la Paloma 41; open weekdays 9 AM–11 PM, weekends 10:30–3 and 4–9) just across the street from the cathedral.

COMING AND GOING

The **RENFE station** (Av. Conde de Guadalhorce s/n, tel. 947/20–35–60) is a 10-minute walk south of the town center. Trains zip to Madrid (4 hrs, 3,300 ptas), León (2 hrs, 2,000 ptas), Pamplona (2 hrs, 1,900 ptas), and San Sebastián (4 hrs, 2,800 ptas). You'll find a handy **RENFE office** (C. Moneda 21, tel. 947/20–91–31; open weekdays 9–1 and 4:30–7:30, Sat. 9:30–1:30) off Plaza Primo de Rivera.

The **bus station** (C. Miranda 4, tel. 947/26–55–65) is east of the train station, just off Plaza de Vega. Buses head to Barcelona (8 hrs, 4,800 ptas), Madrid (3 hrs, 2,000 ptas), San Sebastián (3¼ hrs, 1,950 ptas), and León (3½ hrs, 1,800 ptas).

GETTING AROUND

Burgos is split in half by the lovely **Río Arlanzón.** On the north side, the historic section surrounds the cathedral and Plaza del Rey Fernando; in a newer area to the south are the bus and train stations. As you exit the train station, walk straight up Calle Conde de Guadalhorce to the river, then head right until you reach **Puente Santa María.** Cross the bridge to reach the cathedral, or head right onto Plaza de Vega for cheap lodging.

WHERE TO SLEEP

You should have no problem finding good, relatively inexpensive lodging; check around Plaza de Vega and in the commercial districts west of the cathedral. Avoid the cheap pensions closest to the cathedral, as some are popular with prostitutes. **Hostal Joma** (C. San Juan 26, tel. 947/20–33–50) has bright, homey doubles for 2,600 ptas (2,900 ptas in summer). Near the bus station, **Pensión Boston** (C. San Pablo 13, tel. 947/26–13–41) has spacious doubles for 3,400 ptas. Otherwise, there's a bland, antiseptic youth hostel, **Albergue Juvenil Gil de Siloé** (Av. General Vigón, tel. 947/22–03–62; beds 1,500 ptas, 1,300 ptas under age 26; closed Sept.–June) out in the 'burbs; from Plaza España, take Bus "Río Vena" (85 ptas) to the first stop on Avenida General Vigón. About 3½ km (2¼ mi) east of town along the river, wooded **Camping Fuentes Blancas** (tel. 947/22–10–16; closed Oct.–Mar.) charges 500 ptas per tent plus 550 ptas per person; to get here, take Bus "Fuentes Blancas" (100 ptas) from Plaza Primo de Rivera, near the El Cid statue.

FOOD

The best hunting ground for cheap bars and restaurants is in and around the squares west of the cathedral, an area known as **Las Llanas.** A great spot for cheap *bocadillos* (300 ptas–400 ptas) and *raciones* (450 ptas–650 ptas) is **Bar Espejos** (C. Cardenal Segura 11, off Pl. Huerto del Rey, tel. 947/26–07–36; closed Aug.), where everyone packs in like sardines to admire the burly barmen. Or treat yourself to **Ristorante Prego** (C. Huerto del Rey 4, tel. 947/26–04–47), a cozy Italian with lots of veggie options, like spinach ravioli (950 ptas). For tapas, try **Mesón de los Herreros** (C. San Lorenzo 20, off Pl. Mayor, tel. 947/20–24–48). For supplies, try **Mercado Municipal de Abastos** (open Mon.–Sat. 7:30–3), half a block from the bus station, or **Mercado Norte** (open Mon.–Thurs. and Sat. 7:30–3, Fri. 5:30 PM–8 PM), just off Plaza España. After dinner, join every other randy young person in town and cruise Plaza Huerto del Rey, where jam-packed bars and discos disgorge merrymakers onto the square and teenyboppers flirt on the benches. Here, **Kiss** (C. Huerto Del Rey 8) has 275-pta beers and thumping dance music.

WORTH SEEING

Burgos's biggest draw is its 13th-century **cathedral** (Pl. del Rey Fernando, tel. 947/20–47–12; open daily 9:30–1 and 4–7), a masterpiece of Gothic design and an important stop on the pilgrimage route to Santiago de Compostela. Entrance to the **museum** (admission 400 ptas) includes access to chapels overflowing with treasures, such as ornate works by Diego de Siloé, and a peek at the tomb of El Cid and his wife, Ximena. For a more secular panoply, peruse the paintings, tombstones, and archaeological pieces at the **Museo de Burgos** (C. Miranda, just east of Pl. de Vega, tel. 947/20–16–30; admission 250 ptas; open Tues.–Fri. 9:45–1:50 and 4:15–7, weekends 10–2), housed in a magnificent Renaissance mansion.

Two monasteries lie on the outskirts of town, both worth the hike. West of the town center, the **Real Monasterio de las Huelgas** (tel. 947/20–16–30; admission 650 ptas, free Wed.; open Tues.–Sat. 10:30–1:15 and 4–5:45, Sun. 10:30–2:15), founded in 1187, once housed the virginal daughters of some of Spain's wealthiest families. The main church holds tombs of Castilian royalty, and the grounds include a Romanesque cloister with lovely rose gardens and a fountain. To get here, follow the signs along the south side of the river for about 20 minutes. The **Cartuja de Miraflores** (Carretera a Cartuja; open Mon.–Sat. 10:15–3 and 4–6; Sun. 11:20–12:30, 1–3, and 4–6), a gorgeous Gothic monastery still in use today, was commissioned by Isabela la Católica to house the remains of her parents, Juan II and Isabel of Portugal. To get here, take the wonderful 45-minute walk east along the river on Paseo de la Quinta; or take Bus "Fuentes Blancas" to the nearby campground, from which the Cartuja is a 10-minute walk uphill.

Burgos was home to one of Spain's greatest heroes, the Moor-slaying El Cid. In Plaza General Primo de Rivera is a statue of El Cid pointing grandly toward the sea of infidels he's about to mow down— or just pointing out the post office.

LEON

Another legacy of Spain's Moor-Christian clashes, modern León is at once dignified and prosperous. The old town surrounding the cathedral is a maze of winding streets and cobbled, café-filled plazas, where lively crowds gather at night. The wide avenues of the newer commercial district, which extends west toward the Bernesga River, are nearly as pleasant. León really picks up in July, when pilgrims stream through on their way to Santiago de Compostela—look for the pilgrim's symbol, the scallop shell, along the city sidewalks.

BASICS

Get free maps at the **tourist office** (Pl. de Regla 3, tel. 987/23–70–82; open daily 10–2 and 5–7:30, shorter hrs off season), which faces the cathedral. The **TIVE** office (C. Arquitecto Torbado 4, off C. Santa Nonia, tel. 987/20–09–51; open Mon.–Sat. 9–2) sells hostel cards and discounted transport. South of the old town, the **post office** (Jardín de San Francisco, tel. 987/23–42–90; postal code 24080) is open weekdays 8:30–8:30 and Saturday 9:30–2. The **Telefónica** (open weekdays 9–2:30 and 4–10:30, Sat. 9–2 and 4–9) is on Calle Burgo Nuevo, just past Plaza Cortes.

COMING AND GOING

The **RENFE station** (C. Astorga 2, tel. 987/27–02–02) sends trains to Madrid (4:30 hrs, 3,150 ptas), Oviedo (2 hrs, 1,600 ptas), and Barcelona (10 hrs, 5,800 ptas). The town center is a 15-minute walk from the station: Follow Avenida de Palencia west across the bridge and continue up Avenida de Ordoño II into the old city. You can also take Bus 4 to Plaza Santo Domingo, at the edge of the old city, where Bus 8 takes you to the hostel.

Several companies serve the **bus station** (Cardenal Lorenzana, s/n, tel. 987/21–10–00), five minutes west of the train station. **ALSA** (tel. 987/20–47–52) goes to Oviedo (2 hrs, 1,200 ptas) and Seville (10 hrs, 4,800 ptas); **Fernández** (tel. 987/26–05–00) goes to Madrid (4½ hrs, 2,550 ptas).

WHERE TO SLEEP

Finding cheap lodging in León is easy except during the last week of June, when tourists flood in for festivals in honor of various saints. The national celebration of San Juan, for example, usually starts around June 24. Many cheap sleeps lie along Avenida de Roma and on Avenida de Ordoño II, between the train station and the old town. In summer, try the large, well-kept rooms at **Hotel Riosol** (Avda de Palencia 3, 987/21–66–50), near the train station, or **Hostal España** (C. Carmen 3, off Av. de Ordoño II, tel. 987/23–70–14; doubles 2,700 ptas). **Hostal Oviedo** (Av. de Roma 26, tel. 987/22–22–36) is a friendly, family-run place with slightly dark but clean doubles for 2,900 ptas. If it's full, **Hostal Europa** (tel. 987/22–22–38), just downstairs, has doubles for 2,500 ptas. Two hostels, both charging 1,200 ptas (850 ptas under age 26), lie slightly to the south of the city center. The better of the two is the often-full **HI Residencia Juvenil Infanta Doña Sancha** (C. de La Corredera 2, tel. 987/20–34–14; closed Sept.–June), a five-minute walk south of the post office. Continue south down this street past the Plaza de Toros to find the hostel **Consejo de Europa** (Paseo Parque 2, tel. 987/20–02–06; closed Sept.–June), generally filled with pilgrims heading to Santiago. Bus 8 from Plaza Santo Domingo swings by both hostels.

FOOD

The liveliest areas for food and drink are near the plazas Mayor, the heart of León's old town, and San Martín, where most of the tapas bars are located; this area is called the Barrio Húmedo (Wet Neighborhood). Seek out more cozy places for food and drink along Calle del Cid on the north side of Avenida Generalísimo Franco. **Pizzería Rocco** (Pl. San Martín, tel. 987/20–13–27; closed Mon. and Tues. lunch) has outdoor tables in the summer, great for surveying the scene on the plaza and enjoying salads, pastas, and vegetarian dishes for 600 ptas–800 ptas. Next door at **Bar Chivani** (tel. 987/25–60–61), the whistling proprietor will set you up with fried calamari or sardine tapas for 250 ptas–350 ptas. After 11 PM, the streets around Plaza San Martín fill with barhopping youth. **Mesón Cordero** (Travesía de Recoletas, off C. del Cid, tel. 987/20–18–36) serves *cortos* (cheap beers; 125 ptas) and tapas (200 ptas).

WORTH SEEING

The city's major sights are on the east side of the river north of avenidas de Ordoño II and Generalísimo Franco.

CATEDRAL • This Gothic masterpiece of the 13th and 14th centuries is one of Spain's most beautiful buildings, thanks mainly to its famous stained-glass windows. Try to visit at different times of day to see the sun's rays penetrate the vibrantly colored glass at different angles. Your ticket to the **museum** (admission 450 ptas; open Mon.–Sat. 9:30–1:30 and 4–7), containing medieval sculptures and an assortment of ivory crucifixes, also gets you into the **cloisters.** *Pl. de la Regla, off Av. Generalísimo Franco, tel. 947/23–00–60. Admission to cathedral free. Open daily 8:30–2 and 4–7:30.*

BASILICA DE SAN ISIDORO AND EL PANTEON REAL • This Romanesque complex contains a 12th-century church, built to house the remains of St. Isidore, and the 11th-century Pantheon of Kings. The church is dark and imposing, but the ceilings of the mausoleum are painted with scenes from the life of Christ and the agricultural calendar. The guided tour (in Spanish only) takes you through the library, filled with moldy manuscripts and Bibles, and the treasury, which contains art and desiccated body parts of saints. *Pl. de San Isidoro, off C. del Cid, tel. 987/22–96–08. Admission and tour of Pantheon: 350 ptas. Open Mon.–Sat. 10–1:30 and 3–8, Sun. 9–2.*

MONASTERIO DE SAN MARCOS • This was the 12th-century home of the Knights of St. James, a monastic order dedicated to protecting pilgrims (i.e., battling Moors) on the often perilous journey to Santiago. The building's ornate plateresque facade and baroque relief of St. James the Moorslayer were both added much later. Inside, the **museum** displays an eclectic collection that includes the famous 11th-century Cristo del Monasterio de Carrizo, an ivory Christ with haunting eyes and strangely proportioned limbs. The monastery itself is now a five-star hotel; have a drink in the café and you're automatically rich and famous. *Pl. San Marcos, near river off Av. Suero de Quiñones, tel. 987/24–50–61. Admission: 200 ptas. Open Tues.–Sat. 10–2 and 5–8:30, Sun. 10–2.*

ANDALUCIA

Andalucía, the province bordered by Portugal to the west and the Atlantic to the south, is a large and diverse region, encompassing the ancient Moorish cities of Granada and Seville, the snow-peaked

Sierra Nevada, the tacky tourist meccas along the Costa del Sol, and endless groves of olive trees and sunflowers. The area's cultural landscape has been shaped in large part by its neighbors from North Africa: The Moors arrived in 711 and established an emirate that would flourish for centuries. By the 12th century, the tide turned, and Christian knights flocked to al-Andalus to rid the area of Christendom's enemies. By the 15th century, the Moors were driven out, leaving their tremendous architecture—bridges, castles, palaces, and mosques—as evidence of their rich and powerful civilization. Try as they might, Christian conquerors never could outdo the the Moors' beautiful granite structures, with their endless patios, arches, and cupolas and their lavishly colored marquetry and tilework.

SEVILLE

Seville, one of the most beautiful and romantic cities in Europe, conforms to every Spanish stereotype you've ever heard, from raucous celebrations, flamenco, and bullfighting to placid winding lanes, white-washed buildings, orange trees, and bougainvillea. The setting for Bizet's *Carmen,* Molière's *Don Juan,* and Mozart's *Figaro,* Seville is the quintessential Spanish city. The stunning Alcázar, a Moorish palace rebuilt by Pedro the Cruel during the 14th century, remains the city's foremost tourist attraction, but you'll also find some newer additions to this Moorish city, such as the development of the Cartuja Island, a public area for concerts and shows; the newly renovated Maestranza opera house; and new rail and bus stations. The swinging nightlife, stemming partly from the infamous heat (in summer, it doesn't begin to cool down until midnight), and partly from the large number of university students here, is another major draw. If you stay in Seville long enough, you might pick up the locals' infectious good humor and casual attitude and never want to leave.

BASICS

VISITOR INFORMATION
Av. de la Constitución 21B, 2 blocks south of cathedral, tel. 95/422–14–04. Open Mon.–Sat. 9–7, Sun. 10–2.

AMERICAN EXPRESS
This office cashes AmEx checks free and replaces cards, but it has no travel services. *Pl. Nueva 7, tel. 95/421–16–17. Open weekdays 9:30–1:30 and 4:30–7:30, Sat. 10–1.*

CHANGING MONEY
The best rates and lowest commissions are at the kiosk inside the train station and at **Banco Español de Crédito** (Av. de la Constitución 1; open weekdays 8:30–2). You'll also find plenty of ATMs and 24-hour exchange machines along Avenida de la Constitución.

CONSULATES
Australia: *C. Federico Rubio 14, tel. 95/422–02–40. Open weekdays 10–noon.* **Canada:** *Av. de la Constitución 302-304, 2nd floor, tel. 95/422–94–13. Open weekdays 9:30–1.* **Great Britain:** *Pl. Nueva 8B, tel. 95/422–88–75. Open weekdays 8–3.* **United States:** *Paseo de las Delicias 7, tel. 95/423–18–83. Open weekdays 10–1.*

DISCOUNT TRAVEL AGENCIES
The **Wasteels** (tel. 95/442–50–65) kiosk inside the train station sells bargain international train and plane tickets and makes hotel reservations.

ENGLISH-LANGUAGE BOOKS AND NEWSPAPERS
Librería Beta (Av. de la Constitución 27, tel. 95/456–07–03) has a good selection of contemporary literature. **El Giraldillo** (C. San Fernando 7, tel. 95/422–8643) sells the classics for a song; look downstairs for the best deals.

PHONES AND MAIL
Telefónica (open weekdays 10–2 and 5–9, Sat. 10–2:30) is at Calle Sierpes 11. The **Correos** (tel. 95/421–95–85; open weekdays 8 AM–8:30 PM, Sat. 9–2; postal code 41001) is at Avenida de la Constitución 32, across from the cathedral.

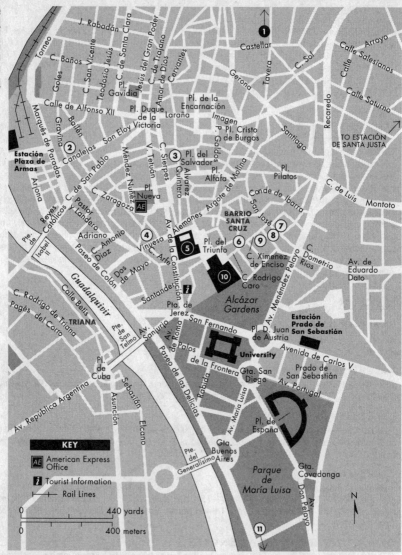

KEY

AE American Express Office

i Tourist Information

⊢⊣⊢ Rail Lines

| 0 | | 440 yards |
| 0 | | 400 meters |

Sights ●

Alcázar, **10**

Basílica de
la Macarena, **1**

Catedral, **5**

Lodging ○

Albergue Juvenil-
Sevilla (HI), **11**

Hostal Monreal, **6**

Hostal Nuevo
Suizo, **3**

Hostal-Residencia
Cataluña, **4**

Hostal-Residencia
Gala, **2**

Hostal San Benito
Abad, **7**

Murillo, **9**

Pensión
San Pancracio, **8**

COMING AND GOING

BY BUS

Seville has two bus stations: Most long-distance buses use the **Estación Plaza de Armas** (Cristo de la Expiración, near east end of Puente del Cachorro, tel. 95/490–80–40), including those headed to Madrid (5 hrs, 2,750 ptas), Lisbon (8 hrs, 4,450 ptas), and Lagos, Portugal (5 hrs, 1,900 ptas). The **Estación Prado de San Sebastián** (Prado de San Sebastián s/n, tel. 95/441–71–11), on the north side of the Plaza de San Sebastián, serves most regional destinations as well as Barcelona (15 hrs, 9,300 ptas).

BY PLANE

The **Aeropuerto Internacional de San Pablo** (tel. 95/444–90–00), about 12 km (7 mi) northeast of the city center, is served by **Iberia** (tel. 95/451–06–77) and **Air France** (tel. 95/492–43–88). Amarillos Tour (tel. 95/441–93–62) runs an **airport shuttle** (30 min, 750 ptas) from Seville's Hotel Alfonso XIII (San Fernando 2, tel. 95/422–28–50); the shuttle stops at the train station en route. Otherwise, grab a cab.

BY TRAIN

Seville is the rail hub for southwestern Spain; unfortunately, the **Estación de Santa Justa** (Av. Kansas City, tel. 95/454–02–02) is more than 3 km (2 mi) east of downtown Seville. Take Bus 27 to Plaza de la Encarnación, or Bus C2 to the Prado de San Sebastián; both are near budget lodging and the center of town. High-speed AVE trains serve Seville from Madrid's Estación de Atocha (3½ hrs, 6,800 ptas) and Córdoba (40 min, 2,400 ptas).

GETTING AROUND

Seville is a confusing maze; be sure to pick up the tourist office's excellent map (100 ptas). Fortunately, a few central landmarks facilitate navigation somewhat. The city is centered around the cathedral and **Plaza del Triunfo,** on **Avenida de la Constitución,** the main street running north from the Puerta de Jerez to **Plaza Nueva.** The **Barrio Santa Cruz,** full of twisting lanes, extends east of the cathedral. The sights are clustered in a walkable area on the east side of Guadalquivir River, and two bridges cross the river to the neighborhood of **Triana,** on the west side.

Tussam (tel. 95/441–11–52) local buses can get you anywhere in the city for 125 ptas. Buses run every 10–20 minutes from about 6 AM to midnight, when less frequent night service begins. If you'll be staying a while, get a 10-ride Bonobus ticket from any tobacco shop, the automatic dispenser in front of the Correos (*see* Basics, *above*), or the orange kiosk on Plaza Nueva, which also hands out free route maps. Most buses stop at Plaza Nueva, at the north end of Avenida de la Constitución, or Plaza Encarnación, about seven blocks northeast of Plaza Nueva. To explore the river, Triana, and Parque de María Luisa (*see* Worth Seeing, *below*), consider renting a bike: **BiciSevilla** (C. Alvaro de Bazán 5, tel. 95/490–63–34) rents by the day (1,500 ptas) or the half-day (1,000 ptas).

WHERE TO SLEEP

You'll only face stiff competition for a room during Seville's popular festivals (*see below*). Look for *pensiones* and *hostales* in the neighborhoods north and west of Plaza Nueva and the Barrio Santa Cruz.

UNDER 3,000 PTAS • Hostal Residencia Gala. In a quiet neighborhood at the northern end of Calle Zaragoza, this place has small, sparse rooms with good beds. Doubles (most with bath) are 3,500 ptas. *C. Gravina 52, tel. 95/421–45–03.*

Hostal San Benito Abad. The rooms are beautifully decorated here, in a quiet alley on the eastern edge of Barrio Santa Cruz. Doubles are 3,200 ptas. *C. Canarios 4, off C. San José Santa María La Blanca, tel. 95/441–52–55.*

Pensión San Pancracio. These nice, cool rooms are set in a serene plaza in the Barrio Santa Cruz. Doubles cost 3,000 ptas. *Pl. de Las Cruces 9, off C. Ximénez de Enciso, tel. 95/441–31–04.*

UNDER 4,000 PTAS • Hostal Nuevo Suizo. Hidden on a side street near a shopping district, this *hostal* resembles a 19th-century French apartment building. Doubles cost 4,000 ptas (5,000 July–August). *C. Azofaifo 7, off C. Sierpes, tel. 95/422–91–47.*

Murillo. This picturesque hotel in the heart of the Barrio Santa Cruz has small, simple rooms, but the setting is a virtue. Doubles cost 4,500 ptas (more during festivals and summer). (Lope de Rueda 7, tel. 95/421–9616).

Hostal Residencia Cataluña. In a primo locale near Plaza Nueva, it's reminiscent of a Spanish church: dark, quiet, and clean. Doubles are 3,000 ptas–3,500 ptas (4,000 ptas–4,500 ptas July–Aug.). *C. Doña Guiomar 1, off C. Zaragoza, tel. 95/421–68–40.*

Hostal Monreal. The rooms are airy and tiled, and there's a small, social bar downstairs. Doubles cost 4,000 ptas. *C. Rodrigo Caro 8, tel. 95/421–41–66. 2 blocks east of Pl. del Triunfo in Barrio Santa Cruz.*

HOSTEL

Albergue Juvenil-Sevilla (HI). Beds in modern doubles, triples, or quads are just 1,200 ptas (900 ptas under age 26). Flop down in the TV lounge. *C. Isaac Peral 2, tel. 95/461–31–50. From Pl. Nueva, Bus 34 toward Heliopolis.*

FOOD

Avoid the expensive tourist traps along Avenida de la Constitución across from the cathedral—the posted prices usually don't include the 15%–20% service charge. Small bars, especially those away from the central shopping district, often serve the cheapest meals; wander the streets between the cathedral and the river, or north of Plaza Nueva, to find good ones. Another good bet is the neighborhood of Triana, across the river; it's bordered by Avenida San Jacinto to the north and Avenida República Argentina to the south. Stock up on groceries at **Cobreros** (C. Alfafa 5, open Mon.–Sat. 9–2 and 5:30–9).

Las Escobas. A few steps from the Giralda, this atmospheric restaurant claims to have first opened in 1386 and served the likes of Cervantes and Lord. Today it serves inexpensive Sevillian dishes such as gazpacho (300 ptas) and *pescaíto frito sevillano* (700 ptas). *Álvarez Quintero 62, tel. 95/421–4479.*

Baguetteria La Merienda. This bright place with an outdoor patio serves sandwiches (225 ptas–375 ptas), pizzas (700 ptas), and salads (450 ptas) to a student crowd. Nota bene: Beer is free during important soccer games. *C. San Fernando 27, across from university, no phone.*

Bar Manolo. This lively, informal bar offers plenty of cheap tapas (150 ptas–200 ptas). Make a point of trying the *caracoles* (snails; 300 ptas) when they're in season. *Pl. de Alfafa, no phone. Closed Sun.*

Bar Tobias. Down combos of fried squid and salad (700 ptas) or gazpacho and paella (750 ptas) and soak up the bar's Sevillian-bullfighting aesthetic. *C. Arfe 26, no phone. Closed Mon.*

Doña Carmen. This friendly bar is full of locals and serves excellent food. Specialties include *raciones* of spinach and garbanzo beans (200 ptas), grilled red peppers (200 ptas), and whiskey-marinated pork (725 ptas). *C. San Eloy 19, tel. 95/456–07–21. From Pl. Nueva, go north on C. Mendez Nuñez to C. San Eloy. Closed Sun.*

La Trastienda. This traditional bar has the best seafood tapas in Seville. Try the oysters (300 ptas) or king prawns (800 ptas) with a *tinto de verano* (red wine and lemon soda; 150 ptas). *C. Alfafa 8, no phone. Closed Sun.*

WORTH SEEING

Though the cathedral and palace take center stage, Seville's lesser attractions are worth seeking out: On the northern edge of town, the **Basílica de la Macarena** (Calle Béquer 1, tel. 95/490–18–00; open daily 9–1 and 5–9) houses a stunning *azulejo* (tile) portrait of the Virgin Mary; catch Bus 13/H from Plaza Duque de la Victoria. Save some time to wander the **Barrio Santa Cruz,** the old Jewish quarter, with twisting alleyways past some of Seville's most beautiful mansions and patios. For another outdoor excursion, visit **Plaza de España,** a graceful brick and blue-tile edifice built for the Spanish Americas Fair in the 1920s. The adjacent **Parque de María Luisa** is a shady expanse of formal gardens, perfect for escaping the heat and bustle of the city.

ALCAZAR

The high, fortified walls of Seville's Alcázar belie the delicacy of the royal palace's intricate interior. Though it's been occupied by various groups since the Roman era, the current site became a Mudéjar masterwork *after* the Christians' conquest of the Moors—during the 14th century, Pedro the Cruel brought in Moorish artisans and sculptors from Granada to rebuild it. The stately **Patio de las Doncellas** (Court of the Damsels) served as the center of official functions, while the **Patio de las Muñecas** (Court of the Maidens) was the royals' private rec room. The grandest room is the **Salón de Embajadores** (Hall of the Ambassadors), featuring a cedarwood cupola of green, red, and gold. Today, the

Alcázar is the official Seville residence of the king and queen of Spain. *Pl. del Triunfo, tel. 95/422–71–63. Admission: 600 ptas. Open June–Sept., Tues.–Sat. 10–1:30 and 5–7; Sun. 10:30–1; Oct.–May, Tues.–Sat. 10:30–5, Sun. 10:30–1.*

CATEDRAL

If you were thinking, "Man, that church is *big!*" you were right; according to the *Guinness Book of World Records,* it's the world's largest Gothic church. The Catedral was built during the 17th century on the site of a former mosque; the **Giralda** bell tower was originally the mosque's minaret. In the dim interior, look for the beautiful virgins painted by Murillos and Zurbarán. *Pl. Virgen de los Reyes, tel. 95/421–49–71. Admission: 600 ptas. Open Mon.–Sat. 11–6, Sun. 10:30–1:30 and 2–4.*

AFTER DARK

Seville is renowned for its indefatigable nightlife, and though many of its bars and discos can be pricey, the budget-conscious have plenty of options. Head just north of the cathedral to **Antigüedades** (C. Argote de Molinas 1, no phone) for tapas, *fino* (dry) sherry (150 ptas), and chic Sevillians. Nearby, **Pico-lagarto** (C. Hernán de Colón 5, no phone) has occasional live music. At the north end of the **Alameda de Hércules,** about a 20-minute walk from the cathedral, several more bars compete for young attention. The three small bars on **Plaza del Salvador** serve cheap beer (125 ptas) and tapas to a lively crowd, and in the Barrio Santa Cruz, the **Bodega Santa Cruz** (C. Rodrigo Caro 1, no phone) has superior tapas and yet more beer (125 ptas). To find out what's on in Seville, pick up *El Giraldillo,* the free monthly guide to events, at the tourist office.

The original capital of flamenco, Seville has some lively flamenco clubs, albeit patronized more by tourists than by locals. In the heart of the Barrio Santa Cruz, **Los Gallos** (Pl. Santa Cruz 11, tel. 95/421–69–81) is intimate; the steep 3,000-ptas admission to the nightly shows (at 9 and 11:30) includes a drink. If you'd rather not part with the cash, head to Plaza del Salvador or Plaza Alfafa, where you can catch spontaneous Spanish guitar music for free.

FESTIVALS

Every Spanish town celebrates **Semana Santa** (Holy Week), but Seville's processions are considered the most elaborate in the country. Every evening during the week before Easter Sunday, thousands gather in the streets for these solemn processions, which have been organized by *cofradías* (religious brotherhoods) since the 16th century. Some members of the *cofradías* dress as penitents, wearing hoods, masks, and capes and carrying candles or heavy crosses; others carry huge platforms with statues representing scenes of the Passion of Christ. In addition to the processions, the whole city gives itself up to celebrating in the streets—eating, singing, and enjoying the spectacle of it all. The city again erupts in celebration for the more secular **Feria de Abril** (April Festival), six days of bullfights, parades, flamenco performances, and fireworks.

NEAR SEVILLE

An hour and a half south of Seville by train (850 ptas), laid-back **Jerez de la Frontera** is a great place to spend a day tasting sherry. This region is famous for its sweet and dry sherries, and this tiny town's six *bodegas* (wine cellars) offer tasting tours. **Domecq** is good (C. San Idelfonso 3, tel. 956/15–15–00; admission 350 ptas); call ahead for reservations. Remember that most of the bodegas shut down in August for the *cosecha* (harvest). After your tour, sober up with an excellent meal (800 ptas) at **Mesón Alcazaba** (C. Medina 19, tel. 956/33–29–60), or sleep off your buzz at **Hostal San Andrés** (C. Moreno 12, tel. 956/34–09–83), where doubles cost 2,500 ptas. For more information, visit the **tourist office** (C. Larga 39, tel. 956/33–11–50), about eight blocks west of the **train station** (Pl. de la Estación, tel. 956/34–23–19) and **bus station** (C. Cartuja, tel. 956/34–10–63).

CORDOBA

Occupied by Romans, then occupied by Visigoths, then the seat of the Moorish caliphate, Córdoba is made of 2,000 years of cultural fusion. The city's most famous landmark is its Moorish mosque, the Mezquita, which now houses a cathedral and is truly one of the gems of Iberian Moorish architecture.

In **La Judería,** the medieval Jewish quarter that surrounds the mosque, you'll see one of the few syna-gogues in Spain to survive demolition or conversion to a Christian church. Córdoba's historic quarter is bordered by the Guadalquivir River to the southeast and the narrow city parks along Avenida Conde Val-lellano and Avenida de la República Argentina to the southwest; the newer part of the city spreads north-east above Plaza Tendillas.

BASICS

Two blocks northeast of the Mezquita, the **municipal tourist office** (Pl. Juda Leví, tel. 957/20–05–22; open Mon.–Sat. 8:30–2:30, Sun. 9–2) has free maps and knows the drill on buses and trains. For snazzier maps (100 ptas) and tips on other Andalusian destinations, get thee to the **regional tourist office** (C. Torrijos 10, tel. 957/47–12–35; open Mon.–Sat. 9–2 and 5:30–7:30), just across from the southern wall of the Mezquita. The **Telefónica office** (Pl. Tendillas 7, at C. Diego León; open weekdays 9:30–2 and 5–11, Sat. 9:30–2) is three blocks east of the **post office** (C. José Cruz Conde 15, tel. 957/ 47–81–02; open weekdays 8 AM–9 PM, Sat. 9–2; postal code 14003).

COMING AND GOING

High-speed AVE trains connect Córdoba's **train station** (Av. de América, near Av. de Cervantes, tel. 957/ 49–02–02) with Madrid (2 hrs, 5,500 ptas), Málaga (2 hrs, 2,000 ptas), and Seville (¾ hr, 2,100 ptas). Buses run frequently from the **bus station** (Av. de Medina Azahara, tel. 957/23–64–74) to Seville (1¾ hrs, 1,150 ptas), Málaga (3½ hrs, 1,460 ptas), and Granada (2–3 hrs, 1,680 ptas).

The train station is a 30-minute walk west of La Judería. For 110 ptas, Bus 12 will take you to La Jud-ería from the stop on Avenida de América just north of Avenida del Gran Capitán, about five minutes from the train station. From the bus station (10 minutes south of the train station), walk northeast on Avenida de Medina Azahara and cross the park to Avenida de Cervantes, where Bus 3 will take you to the Puente Romano just east of the Mezquita.

WHERE TO SLEEP

A number of pensions are scattered among the old homes in La Judería. **Hostal El Portillo** (C. Cabezas 2, SE of Mezquita, off C. de San Fernando, tel. 957/47–20–91), has spacious doubles (2,800 ptas) with ceiling fans. **Hostal Trinidad** (C. Cardenal Gonzales 58, SE of Mezquita, tel. 957/48–79–05; doubles 2,500 ptas) is a small, family-run place with friendly service. The convenient **HI Albergue Juvenil Cór-doba** (Pl. Juda Leví, tel. 957/29–01–66; beds 1,490 ptas over age 26, 1,177 ptas under, plus 300 ptas extra for nonmembers) has an antiseptic atmosphere but great amenities: double rooms, good showers, a backyard, and no curfew. From the northwest corner of Mezquita, go west on Calle Herreros and turn left on Calle Manriquez.

FOOD

Avoid the extravagant traps near the Mezquita; two blocks away you'll find better prices and quality. The mellow **Bodega Taberna Rafaé** (C. Deanes 1, 1½ blocks north of Pl. Juda Leví, no phone) is a good place to try Córdoba's traditional local specialties, such as *salmorejo* (cold vegetable soup; 450 ptas) and *rabo de toro* (bull's tail; 725 ptas). Or get drinks and tortilla *bocadillos* (175 ptas) to go at **Bodeguilla Bocadil-los** (C. Zapatería Vieja 12, off C. Luís de la Cerda, no phone).

WORTH SEEING

Though it's no longer used as a place of worship, Córdoba's medieval **synagogue** (C. Judíos, tel. 957/20–29–28; admission 50 ptas; closed Mon.) was the only one in Andalucía to survive the expulsion of the Jews in 1492. A remnant of Roman rule, the **Puente Romano** (Roman bridge) still spans the Guadalquivir. At the eastern end of the bridge is the **Torre de la Calahorra** (tel. 957/29–39–29; admis-sion 400 ptas; open daily 10–1 and 5:30–8:30), built in 1369 to guard the entrance to Córdoba; it's now a spiffy audiovisual museum outlining the three major cultures that flourished here. To return to modern Spanish passions, peruse the surprisingly tasteful display of vintage bullfighting paraphernalia and posters at the **Museo Municipal Taurino** (Pl. Maimónides 5, tel. 957/20–10–56; admission 400 ptas, free Thurs.; closed Mon.).

MEZQUITA • For centuries, Córdoba's great mosque was a renowned center of Muslim practice, serv-ing the religious needs of an immense and wealthy empire. Soon after gaining control of most of Iberia, in the 8th century, Abd ar-Rahman I began construction of the mosque on the site of a 6th-century Visigothic Christian church. Archaeological remains from the site, some dating back to the 1st century, are on display inside the mosque. As the wealth and power of the emirate of al-Andalus grew, so did the mosque; by the beginning of the 11th century, subsequent emirs had more than doubled the size of the original structure and built a new *mihrab,* the prayer niche that's supposed to face Mecca. Due to an error in construction, Córdoba's mihrab faces more south than east.

In the center of the elegant mosque is a Gothic cathedral, added in 1523 despite the objections of the church council and the entire town. It was King Carlos V who originally sanctioned construction of the **Cathedral Coro,** which obscures the *mihrab;* he later regretted the addition, and admitted to the local bishop that he had "destroyed something that was unique in the world." *Corner of C. Torrijos and C. Cardenal Herrero, tel. 957/47–05–12. Admission: 750 ptas (free Sun. 10–1:30). Open Apr.–Sept., daily 10–7; Oct.–Mar., daily 10–1:30 and 2:30–7.*

ALCAZAR DE LOS REYES CRISTIANOS • Córdoba's Mudéjar-style royal palace has the dubious distinction of having been the headquarters of the Inquisition from 1428 to 1821. Today it contains ancient archaeological finds, a modern re-creation of a Roman bath, several large Roman mosaics, and an ornate garden littered with fallen oranges. *Pl. Campo Santo de los Mártires, tel. 957/42–01–51. Admission: 300 ptas (free Fri.). Open Tues.–Sat. 10–2 and 6–8 (5–7 in winter), Sun. 9:30–3.*

MUSEO ARQUEOLOGICO • When Roman mosaics were discovered on the walls of what everyone thought was a 16th-century mansion, the whole place was converted into a museum. The collection contains an impressive array of Roman statuary, tombstones, mosaics, and glassware, as well as Moorish artifacts. *Pl. de Jerónimo Páez 7, tel. 957/47–40–11. Admission: 250 ptas. Open Tues.–Sat. 10–1:30 and 6–8 (5–7 in winter), Sun. 10–1:30.*

GRANADA

If every city were as beautiful as Granada, people would never travel. They would stay home and enjoy their own fountains, plazas, and parks, and their castle on a hill against a backdrop of snowcapped mountains. When Muslim Granada surrendered in 1492 to Ferdinand and Isabella's seven-month siege, the city became the final jewel in their Catholic crown, completing the Christian Reconquista (reconquest) of Spain. Granada's importance to the Catholic royalty, and particularly to Ferdinand and Isabella, is evident in the massive cathedral; the adjoining Capilla Real, which contains their tombs; and the statue of Isabella with Christopher Columbus in the center of town. The Moors left their architectural mark with the fantastic Alhambra, a palace that lives up to its legendary reputation. Today Granada is home to several universities, including a large medical school, making for lively nightlife and a casual, friendly atmosphere.

BASICS

The **regional tourist office** (Corral del Carbón, just south of Pl. de Isabel la Católica, tel. 958/22–59–90; open Mon.–Sat. 9–7, Sun. 10–2) has maps (100 ptas) and hefty English-language booklets (400 ptas) detailing hiking, skiing, and mountain-biking options in the Sierra Nevada. The smaller **municipal office** (Pl. Mariana Pineda, tel. 958/22–66–88; same hours) has free city maps.

American Express operates out of Viajes Bonal (C. Mariá Luisa de Dios, off Av. de la Constitución, tel. 958/27–63–12). They're open weekdays 9:30–2 and 5–8 (4:30–7:30 in winter) and Saturday 10–1, but exchange money on weekday mornings only. The **Telefónica** office (C. Reyes Católicos 54, SW of Pl. de Isabel la Católica) is open Monday–Saturday 9–2 and 5–10. The **Correos** (Puerta Real, tel. 958/22–48–35; postal code 18080) is open weekdays 8:30–8:30 and Saturday 9:30–2.

COMING AND GOING

RENFE trains connect Granada to Madrid (6–9 hrs, 2,500 ptas), Barcelona (12 hrs, 7,000 ptas), and Seville (4 hrs, 2,235 ptas). In addition to the information window in the **train station** (Av. Andaluces, off Av. de la Constitución, tel. 958/27–12–72), there's a **ticket office** (C. Reyes Católicos 63, tel. 958/22–31–19; open weekdays 9–1:30 and 5–7:30, Sat. 9–1:30) by Plaza de Isabel la Católica.

The **Alsina-Graells bus terminal** recently moved to the new bus station just outside Granada. Bus #3 can take you to and from the city center (Av. de Madrid, tel. 958/18–50–10 or 958/18–50–11). Buses also leave here for Madrid (5 hrs, 1,900 ptas) and most Andalucian cities, including Málaga (2 hrs, 1,165 ptas) and Seville (3 hrs, 2,710 ptas). The **Enatcar-Bacoma bus terminal** is also part of the new bus station (tel. 958/15–75–57) and serves Alicante (12 hrs, 3,335 ptas), Valencia (14 hrs, 4,855 ptas), and Barcelona (19 hrs, 7,805 ptas).

GETTING AROUND

The train station is a 20-minute hike west from the center of town; you may want to take one of the many buses that stop nearby (*see below*). Happily, the rest of the city is walkable, centering around the series of plazas leading southwest down Calle Reyes Católicos from **Plaza Nueva** to the central **Puerta Real.** From the train station, **Avenida de la Constitución** leads southeast toward the center of town and feeds into **Gran Vía de Colón,** which continues south past the cathedral to **Plaza de Isabel la Católica.**

Autocares Rober (tel. 958/81–37–11) buses cover every inch of Granada. You can get a schedule and free route map at any tourist office (*see* Basics, *above*). Buses cost 100 ptas, or you can buy a 10-ride Bonobus passe (670 ptas) at a *tabac.* To get to the center of town from the train station, catch Bus 3, 4, 7, 8, 9, or 11 from Avenida de la Constitución at Avenida Andaluces, and get off at Gran Vía 1, near the cathedral.

WHERE TO SLEEP

Dozens of cheap pensions are clustered in Granada's commercial district, which begins southwest of the cathedral and extends east of Puerta Real. At run-down **Pensión Castil** (C. Darrillo de la Magdalena 1, off C. de la Alhóndiga, tel. 958/25–95–07), doubles cost only 2,000 ptas. For rooms overlooking a tree-lined plaza, try the fancier **Hostal Zurita** (Pl. de la Trinidad 7, tel. 958/27–50–20), with doubles for 4,500 ptas. Rooms closer to the Alhambra usually cost more; even the dumpiest *pensión* there will charge around 3,000 ptas for a double. One exception to the Dumpy rule is the **Hostal Viena** (C. Hospital de Santa Ana 2, off C. Cuesta de Gomerez, tel. 958/22–18–59), just off the street leading up to the Alhambra; snag a big double and a helpful staff for 3,500 ptas.

The **HI Albergue de la Juventud** (C. Ramón y Cajal 2, off Camino de Ronda, tel. 958/27–26–38; beds 1,600 ptas, 1,300 ptas under age 26), overlooking the Estadio de la Juventud sports field, is short on character, but it has a TV lounge and doubles with private baths. From the train station, go left on Avenida de la Constitución, left at the fork, left on Camino de Ronda, then right on Calle Ramón y Cajal. **Sierra Nevada** (Av. de Madrid 107, tel. 958/15–00–62; open Mar.–Oct.), the nearest campground, has a pool and real, honest-to-gosh trees; sites are 535 ptas per tent plus 535 ptas per person. Take Bus 3 (about 20 min) east from the town center; the last one leaves town around 11 PM.

FOOD

You'll find plenty of cheap restaurants in the areas northwest of Plaza Nueva and west of the cathedral, near the university. The extravagantly decorated **Casa de Wu** (C. San Juan de Dios 10, tel. 958/27–57–56) serves up great *sopa de Wan-tu* (wonton soup; 315 ptas), lemon chicken (625 ptas), and a *menú del día* (695 ptas). Several Middle Eastern restaurants line Calle Calderería Nueva, west of Plaza Nueva; one of the cheapest is **Medina Zahara** (C. Calderería Nueva 12, tel. 958/22–15–41; open daily until 1 AM), a tiny place serving scrumptious lamb kebabs (100 ptas), falafel (200 ptas), and lots of veggie options. Try **Torres Bermejas** (Plaza Nueva 6, tel. 958/22–31–16) for a typical Spanish restaurant with deals on such standards as paella (900 ptas). Every weekday morning there's an open-air **mercado** on Plaza Romanilla, southwest of the cathedral; follow Calle Pescadería northwest past Plaza Bib-Rambla.

WORTH SEEING

Granada's historic neighborhoods are as interesting as the city's major sights. The old Moorish quarter, **El Albaicín,** is an alluring maze of tiny lanes, dilapidated white houses, and immaculate private villas enclosed by high walls. Here, **Plaza San Miguel Bajo** offers spectacular nighttime views of the Alhambra bathed in light. You'll find dozens of *cuevas de flamencos* (flamenco cellars) in the old gypsy quarter, **Sacromonte,** up the hill north of the city center; take Bus 12 from Gran Vía.

Granada is also a good base for hiking in the **Sierra Nevada** range; **Autocares Bonal** (tel. 958/27–31–00) plies the mountain route daily at 9 AM, returning to Granada at 5. Before setting off, get a good hiking map (500 ptas) at **Librería Continental** (C. Acera de Darro 2, near Puerta Real, tel. 958/26–35–86).

ALHAMBRA • This massive Moorish palace attracts thousands of visitors daily; arrive early to avoid the tour-bus herds. The **Alcazaba,** the oldest segment of the compound, is the least interesting except for the amazing views from the fortress's dilapidated towers. Far more elaborate is the **Alcázar,** the former residence of Moorish emirs; several of its halls are decorated with delicate tilework and wall carvings. Among the palace's more notable chambers are the **Palacios Nazaries,** covered in Arabic script carvings (many reading "There Is No Conqueror But God"), and the **Palacios de los Leones,** the ceiling of which looks like a natural formation of stalactites. Finally, there are the heavenly gardens of the **Generalife,** featuring roses, fountains, and fab views. *Tel. 958/22–75–27. From Pl. Nueva, take C. Cuesta* uphill, go through gate, and ascend dirt footpath on left. Admission: 725 ptas. Open Apr.–Sept., Mon.–Sat. 9–8, Sun. 9–6; Tues., Thurs., and Sat. also 10 PM–midnight; Oct.–Mar., daily 9–6; Sat. also 8 PM–10 PM. Closed Christmas, New Year's Day.

CAPILLA REAL • Ferdinand and Isabella's son Carlos V built this Gothic chapel to house his folks' remains. A recess in the floor allows you to view the coffins of the monarchs and their kin, arranged in a chamber below marble tablets. Next door is the **cathedral** (admission 200 ptas; open Mon.–Sat. 10:30–1:30 and 4–7), built in the 16th century in a Gothic-Renaissance fusion. *Gran Vía de Colón, tel. 958/22–92–39. Admission: 200 ptas. Open daily 10:30–1 and 4–7 (3:30–6 in winter).*

AFTER DARK

Students flock to bars along **Calle Pedro Antonio,** south of the town center, for cheap beer and decent tapas. For excellent seafood tapas, head to **Bar Arco Iris** (C. Serrano, at C. Elvira, no phone), near Plaza Nueva; or try **Pub Eshaceín** (C. Postigo de la Cuna 4) for live jazz and flamenco shows. For *authentic* flamenco, check out **Reina Mora** (Mirador de San Cristobal, tel. 958/27–22–28). To taste Granada's *ambiente* (gay nightlife), cruise the western bank of the Río Darro. The boys at **Fonda Reservada** (Pl. de Santa Inez, near C. Cobertizo de Santa Inez) grind to '80s pop 'til the sun comes up.

COSTA DEL SOL

The rich, the bohemian, and everyone in between rubs elbows on the Sun Coast, Spain's Riviera. After several decades of frenzied development, the Costa del Sol is now a nearly unbroken chain of high-rise concrete resorts, but some of the beaches are still clean, and the nightlife in the larger towns is worth a few all-nighters. If the commercialism of the coastal resorts gets to you, head inland to the beautiful hilltop *pueblos blancos* (white towns), or take a day trip to Gibraltar or to Tangier, in northern Morocco.

Near the cathedral, gypsy women are likely to thrust aromatic herbs into your hands and read your palms: "You are on a long journey. You will have two children. That will be five hundred pesetas." Give them 100 ptas and learn to keep your hands in your pockets.

MALAGA

Welcome to the capital of the Costa del Sol, a bland port city with a decent beach and good transport connections to other coastal destinations. Towering above town, the **Alcazaba** (C. Alcazabilla, tel. 95/222–00–43; admission 30 ptas; closed Mon.) is a fortress begun in the 8th century, when Málaga was Spain's principal Moorish port. The inner palace was built between 1057 and 1063, when the Moorish emirs took up residence here. Inside is the **Museo Arqueológico,** with a collection of Moorish art and pottery. Further up the hill, through the Alcazaba gardens, is the ruined **Castillo de Gibralfaro** (admission free), part of a fractured wall that may once have encircled the Alcazaba; the views of the Alcazaba and the city below are spectacular from here. Also notable is the **Museo de Bellas Artes** (C. San Agustín 8, tel. 95/221–83–82; admission 225 ptas; closed Mon.), which has a room dedicated to Malagüeño Pablo Picasso.

BASICS

The regional **oficina de turismo** (Pasaje de Chinitas 4, at Pl. de la Constitución, tel. 95/221–34–45) has tips and maps for other Costa del Sol destinations. The **Viajes Wasteels** (C. Cuarteles 54, tel. 95/231–48–66; open summer only, weekdays 9–1:30 and 5–8, Sat. 9–1) office, in the mall across the street from the train station, sells discounted train and plane tickets.

COMING AND GOING

A 15-minute walk southwest from the center of town, the **train station** (Explanada de la Estación, tel. 95/236–02–02) serves Córdoba (2 hrs, 2,150 ptas) and Madrid (4½ hrs, 7,250 ptas). The **bus station** (Paseo de los Tilos 21, tel. 95/235–00–61), two blocks west of the train station, serves Ronda (2 hrs, 1,200 ptas), Algeciras (2½ hrs, 1,300 ptas), and La Linea/Gibraltar (3 hrs, 1,700 ptas). As you exit the RENFE train station, you'll see the entrance to the **Cercanías Málaga train station,** which provides local train service to the airport (15 min, 145 ptas) and nearby resort towns, such as Torremolinos (20 min, 145 ptas) and Fuengirola (45 min, 225 ptas). If you're planning to stay in the hostel or use the local buses frequently, get a 10-ride Bonobus ticket (675 ptas) at a *tabac*; otherwise, each ride is 125 ptas.

Bus 3 will take you from Málaga's train station to the **Alameda Principal,** near budget lodging. From the central **Plaza de la Marina,** which overlooks the port, the park-lined Paseo del Parque leads to Málaga's beaches. Paseo del Parque is also where you catch Bus 11 to **Pedregalejo,** a touristy fishing village with a nice beach, humming nightlife, and cheap seafood restaurants.

WHERE TO SLEEP AND EAT

Unfortunately, Málaga's lodging scene is rather bleak; rooms tend to be expensive and dreary. If you need to crash near the train station, your best bet is **La Hispanidad** (Exp. Estación Terminal 5, tel. 95/331–11–35), where clean doubles go for 3,200 ptas. The more central **Avenida** (Alameda Principal 5, tel. 95/221–77–28) has clean doubles for 2,900 ptas, and the **Hostal Larios** (C. Marqués de Larios, tel. 95/222–54–90), has quiet, cool doubles with TVs for 3,600 ptas. **HI Albergue Juvenil-Málaga** (Pl. Pío XII 6, tel. 95/230–85–00; beds 1,450 ptas, 1,200 ptas under age 26) is in a sterile modern building; to get there from the bus or train station, take Bus 18 to Carranque.

There are plenty of eateries north and east of Plaza de la Constitución, but many are expensive. Try **Cafetería La Traviata** (C. Salvago 3, tel. 95/222–00–49), where the *menú* is only 700 ptas and the *bocadillos* 200 ptas–325 ptas. The mellow **La Tetería** (C. San Augustín 9) serves specialty teas and coffees (200 ptas–300 ptas) and delicate crêpes with fruit (250 ptas) or chocolate (300 ptas). For groceries, roam the **mercado** (C. Ataranzas), two blocks north of the Alameda Principal. Afterward, head to the popular Irish bar **O'Neill's** (C. Luis de Velázquez 3, tel. 95/260–43–33) for good beer (250 ptas–400 ptas).

MARBELLA

This fashionable resort town is a favorite with middle-aged British couples and road-weary backpackers. Fortunately, prescient town planners saw the potential appeal of their home to tourists and restricted development, so Marbella's picturesque *casco antiguo* (old quarter), with its narrow lanes and its whitewashed houses covered in bougainvillea, has been spared the ugly development that consumed so much of the Costa del Sol. High fortress walls built by the Moors during the 9th century still encircle part of the old quarter, which is centered around **Plaza de los Naranjos,** a beautiful square filled with flowers, orange trees, and pricey cafés. While Marbella itself has abundant charm, most people come for the beaches and resorts stretching 16 km (10 mi) or so on either side of town.

BASICS

You'll find an **oficina de turismo** in Plaza de los Naranjos (tel. 95/282–35–50; closed Sun.) and another one on the beach boardwalk (Miguel Cano 1, at end of Av. Arias Maldonado, tel. 95/277–14–42; open weekdays 9:30–8, Sat. 10–2). **American Express** (Av. Arias Maldonado 2, tel. 95/282–14–94) offers the usual cardholder services.

COMING AND GOING

There's no train station in Marbella, but the **bus station** (Av. Ricardo Soriano 21, tel. 95/277–21–35) has connections to Málaga (1 hr, 565 ptas), Ronda (1½ hrs, 600 ptas), and Córdoba (4½ hrs, 2,150 ptas). The old quarter is a 10-minute walk east from the bus station.

WHERE TO SLEEP AND EAT

There's plenty of budget lodging in the old quarter. The best digs are in **Hostal del Pilar** (C. Mesoncillo 4, off C. Peral, tel. 95/282–99–36; beds 1,500 ptas–3,000 ptas), run by a hospitable British couple who have turned the place into a funky travelers' haven with laundry service and real English breakfasts. If Pilar is full, the small **Hostal Internacional** (C. Alderete 7, no phone) has doubles for 2,750 ptas. The **HI Albergue Juvenil Marbella** (C. Trapiche 2, tel. 95/277–14–91; dorm beds 1,550 ptas, 1,200 ptas under age 26) is a 10-minute walk north up Calle Ancha from Plaza de los Naranjos.

Just one block north of the beach, **Restaurante Cortés** (Av. Antonio Belón 19, tel. 95/277–70–33; closed Tues.) serves beautiful dishes like curry chicken (675 ptas) and paella (1,600 ptas for two) in a romantic setting. Cozy **Vinacoteca Riojana** (C. Peral 8, tel. 95/282–99–07) dishes up tasty *raciones* (600 ptas–1,000 ptas) and excellent *tinto de Rioja* (red wine; 150 ptas). The macrobiotic **Salvia** (Pl. de la Victoria 3, tel. 95/282–38–02) features miso soup (250 ptas) and vegetarian ravioli (700 ptas).

RONDA

Ringed by mountains, the small town of **Ronda** is perched on a sheer, 425-ft cliff above the Guadalevín River, overlooking a valley of farms. Because of its strategic position, Ronda was the last stronghold of the legendary Andalusian bandits and the scene of the last great rising of the Moors against Ferdinand and Isabella. El Tajo, Ronda's dramatic ravine, divides La Ciudad, the old Moorish town, from El Mercadillo, the newer town that developed after the Christian reconquest.

The few sights within town are eclipsed by the beauty of the surrounding countryside, the dramatic layout of the town itself, and the old quarter, where residents have maintained their neighborhood's medieval charm. For a good look at the old quarter, head south from Plaza de España across the remarkable **Puente Nuevo** (New Bridge) and then east down Calle Santo Domingo to the **Puente Arabe** (Arab Bridge) and the 13th-century **Arab baths** (admission free), some of the best-preserved in all of Spain. From here, follow the stone steps leading south to the **Puerta de la Exijara**, the old gate to the Jewish quarter, and go on to the **Puerta de Almocabar**, the 13th-century gate to the city at the southern edge of town. The **oficina de turismo** (Pl. de España, tel. 95/287–12–72) has maps for 100 ptas.

COMING AND GOING

A 10- to 15-minute walk northeast from the town center, the **train station** (Av. Alférez Provisional, tel. 95/287–16–73) has direct service to Algeciras (2 hrs, 855 ptas); for other Andalusian destinations, transfer at Bobadilla (1 hr, 575 ptas). The **bus station** (Pl. Concepción García Redondo 2), southwest of the train station down Avenida de Andalucía, is home to several companies, including **Portillo** (tel. 95/287–22–62), which travels to Marbella (1½ hrs, 575 ptas). To explore the countryside, rent a mountain bike at the campground **El Sur** (*see below*) for 200 ptas per hour or 1,500 ptas per day.

WHERE TO SLEEP AND EAT

Most *pensiónes* are near Carrera Espinel, a five-block pedestrian shopping street. For small, bright rooms, try **Hostal Ronda Sol** (C. Almendra 11, tel. 95/287–44–97; doubles 2,700 ptas). Ronda's fancy campground, **El Sur** (Carretera a Algeciras, tel. 95/287–59–39), is well worth the uphill walk 2 km (1½ mi) south of town; for 550 ptas per person, you get tent space, use of the pool, and an amazing view of town. They also rent small log cabañas with kitchenettes (doubles 3,000 ptas). The cheapest place in town to drink and scarf light tapas is **Bodega La Giralda** (C. Nueva 19, no phone); try *patatas con alcachofas* (potatoes with artichoke; 80 ptas) or *langostinos* (king prawns; 150 ptas). Join locals at the lively **Cafetería Casa Eugenio** (C. Sevilla 6, tel. 95/287–01–86) for tasty three-course *menús* (900 ptas). Stop at **Supermarquez** (C. Molino 36, 5 blocks NW of Car. Espinel) for groceries.

ALGECIRAS

The only reasons to come to this seedy port city are: (1) you want to go to Morocco; (2) you want to go to Gibraltar. If neither of these describes you, turn back now. If you need to stay a night before catching the ferry, there are cheap beds near the bus station, train station, and port. The **oficina de turismo** (C. Juan de la Cierva s/n, tel. 956/57–26–36; open Mon.–Sat. 9–2) lies between the the port and the **train station** (Carretera a Cádiz, tel. 956/65–44–07). Daily high-speed *talgo* trains zoom in from Málaga (4½ hrs, 1,800 ptas) and Madrid (12 hrs, 5,700 ptas). The **Comes bus terminal** (Car. a Cádiz, tel 956/65–34–56), half a block east of the train station, serves La Línea/Gibraltar (¾ hr, 225 ptas) and Marbella (1½ hrs, 765 ptas). For buses to Málaga (3 hrs, 1,300 ptas), plant yourself at the **Bus Málaga terminal** (Av. de la Marina 15, tel. 956/65–10–55), across the street from the port.

Ferries and hydrofoils leave several times daily for Tangier (2½ hrs, 2,960 ptas) and Ceuta, Morocco (1½ hrs, 1,850 ptas); oddly, the prices are the same for the ferry and the faster hydrofoil. During the summer, ferries leave almost hourly, but there's only one daily hydrofoil, at 9:30 AM. Tickets are available at the ferry port, but Eurailpass holders can buy discount tickets to Tangier at **Wasteels** (tel. 956/63–23–32), in the train station.

WHERE TO SLEEP AND EAT

If you're headed for Tangier and it's already late, you're better off spending a night in Algeciras and catching an early ferry. There are plenty of budget digs northeast of the train station. Otherwise, the **HI hostel** (Barriada El Pelayo, tel. 956/67–90–60; beds 1,300 ptas, 950 ptas under age 26) is 8 km (5 mi) southwest of the town center; take the bus toward Tarifa and ask to be let off at the *albergue*. Get snacks for the ferry at the colorful **mercado** (Pl. Palma, 1 block west of port), but watch out for pickpockets.

GIBRALTAR

The British colony of Gibraltar is a curiosity, both geographically and politically. The Brits invaded the strategic peninsula in 1704, and today it is the last British colony on mainland Europe. The tiny town—known locally as "Gib"—is an English-speaking amalgam of pubs, fish-and-chip shops, and a deteriorating military complex, all dwarfed by the dramatic limestone Rock. A cable car (£4.90 or 1,090 ptas round trip) will take you up 1,350 ft to the so-called Top of the Rock, with spectacular views of Africa on clear days. From here, you can explore the weird interior of St. Michael's Caves, where stalactites and stalagmites are lit by green and red lights and spooky organ music plays in the background. The cable car also stops at The Ape's Den, home to a bunch of tailless macaques, who wander unfazed among hordes of tourists. Catch the cable car back down or hike the steep, poorly maintained Mediterranean Steps, which lead down the east side of the rock; the descent takes about 45 minutes. For more information on the Rock, visit the main tourist office (Main St., tel. 9567/74950), near the cathedral, or the booth just outside Customs.

Gibraltar is not accessible by train, but Comes buses make the trip from most Andalusian cities, including Algeciras (3/4 hr, 225 ptas) and Málaga (2½ hrs, 1,650 ptas). The bus drops you at the bus terminal (Poligano San Felipe, tel. 956/10-00-93) in the Spanish border town La Linea; from here it's a 15-minute walk south to Gibraltar. Gibraltar's official currency is the pound sterling, but pesetas are widely accepted, generally at a slightly poorer rate. The airport's bureau de change (tel. 9567/42390; open daily 9–9) is convenient but doesn't exchange traveler's checks. American Express (Cloister Bldg., corner of Irish Town Rd. and Market La., tel. 9567/79200) operates out of Bland Travel.

Often filled to capacity, Miss Serruya's Guest House (92/1a Irish Town Rd., tel. 9567/73220) is the cheapest sleep in town, with doubles for £12–£18 (2,500–3700 ptas). Down the street, the wood-paneled Clipper Pub has good beer and tasty fish and chips (£4.35 or 950 ptas).

MEDITERRANEAN COAST

The stretch of coast reaching south from Valencia nearly to Cartagena is known as the *Costa Blanca* (White Coast) because of its fine, powdery beaches. Fortunately, with a few notable exceptions, these beaches have been spared the overdevelopment that plagues the Costa del Sol. Although the beaches at Valencia and Alicante are of your basic crowded, dirty, and urban variety, the town of **Gandía,** halfway between the two, more than makes up for them. The Costa Blanca's nighttime playground is **Benidorm,** dominated by an admittedly beautiful beach, but marred by countless high-rise eyesores and discos with names like Penelope and Star Garden. Just 10 km (6 mi) south of Benidorm is the small, ancient village of **Villajoyosa,** a pristine village sporting multicolored window shutters, funky old buildings, and lots of aging fishermen.

ALICANTE

About 100 km (62 mi) south of Valencia on the Costa Blanca, Alicante provides a welcome respite for those who need a vacation from their vacation. Never mind that its beaches aren't up to par with those of its coastal neighbors, or that the city boasts few attractions; this is the place to sleep off a five-day tour of every late-night club in Barcelona—unless, of course, you come in June, when people throng the streets for the **Festival of San Juan** (June 20–24). Elaborately constructed effigies are set afire during the ceremonies, and then, during the much-anticipated *banyá,* the fire brigade turns on their hoses for a merciless dousing of the crowd.

Alicante's only real sight is the **Castillo de Santa Bárbara** (tel. 96/526–31–31), perched on a hill at the eastern edge of town. An elevator on Calle Virgen del Socorro, along the hill's southern face, will whisk you up for 200 ptas (though if you walk up—a good 45 minutes—you can ride down for free). The castle houses two free museums. The **Museo de Armas** (open Tues.–Sat. 10–2 and 5–8, Sun. 10–2) features copies of weapons spanning three centuries, and the **Museo Cerámica** (same hours) has a small collection of ancient pottery. Though the castle itself is a bit of a disappointment, its view of the coast is incredible.

VISITOR INFORMATION

Both the **municipal tourist office** (C. Portugal 17, in front of bus station, tel. 96/592–98–02; open July–Sept., weekdays 9–9, Sat. 9–2; Oct.–June, weekdays 9–2) and the **regional tourist office** (Explanada de España 2, tel. 96/520–00–00; open Mon.–Sat. 10–8) provide free maps.

COMING AND GOING

RENFE trains connect Alicante to Madrid (4 hrs, 3,800 ptas) and Valencia (2 hrs, 1,400 ptas). There's an information window at the **train station** (Av. de Salamanca, tel. 96/592–02–02), but the lines are shorter at the **RENFE travel office** (Explanada de España, at C. Cervantes, tel. 96/521–13–03; open weekdays 9–1:30 and 5–7, Sat. 9–1:30).

The center of Alicante is Plaza de los Luceros, a huge roundabout a few blocks east of the train station. The old district, **Alicante Antiguo,** also referred to as **El Barrio,** is southeast of Luceros and bordered by the waterfront promenade. To get to the pretty, clean beach **Playa de San Juan,** 8 km (5 mi) farther east, catch Bus C-1 (125 ptas) from Plaza del Mar. In summer, the bus serves the beach's discos all night. Alternatively, you can take **FGV local trains** (Avda. Villajoyosa, at the east end of Playa de Postiguet, tel. 96/526–27–31) to Playa de San Juan (100 ptas), Benidorm (410 ptas), and Villajoyosa (475 ptas).

WHERE TO SLEEP AND EAT

Most of the cheap sleeps are on calles San Francisco and San Fernando, between Avenida Doctor Gadea and Rambla de Méndez Núñez. **Hostal San Fernando** (C. San Fernando 34, tel. 96/521–36–56) has doubles with big balconies for 3,800 ptas June–September, 3,000 ptas off season. You'll find cheap doubles (3,200 ptas) at **Hostal Olimpia** (C. San Francisco 62, east of Pl. de los Luceros, tel. 96/520–53–11), though the 30 rooms vary from cramped closets to comfy chambers; ask to see one first. The modern **HI Albergue Juvenil la Florida** (Av. Orihuela 59, tel. 96/511–30–44) opens large singles, doubles, and triples (1,400 ptas per person; 1,000 ptas under age 26) to HI members June–August. From the bus-station entrance, take Bus G to the end.

Avoid the pricey cafés and restaurants lining the Explanada de España; instead, wander around El Barrio and the streets west of Rambla de Méndez Núñez. You'll also find cheap tapas behind the cathedral, particularly on calles Labradores, San Isidro, and San Pascual. Chug more than 30 kinds of beer and chow on *pollo a la cerveza* (beer-marinated chicken; 700 ptas) and a great variety of salads (500 ptas–700 ptas) at **La Abadia Cervezas** (Pl. San Cristobal 7, off Rambla de Méndez Núñez, tel. 96/521–08–42; closed Sun.). Buy supplies at the huge **Mercado Central** (Av. Alfonso X El Sabio, at Av. Constitución; open Mon.–Sat. 7–3).

AFTER DARK

The few discos and bars in Alicante are high-tech, modern, expensive, and empty in summer. People hang out at cafés in El Barrio until around midnight or 1 AM before heading to Playa de San Juan (*see* Coming and Going, *above*). Here, **Escola Bruselas,** between avenidas de la Costa Blanca and Niza, is densely packed with bars.

VALENCIA

Spain's third-largest city (after Madrid and Barcelona), Valencia is suprisingly graceful, with fountains, plazas, blue-dome churches, baroque buildings, and stylish shops. Though generally left-leaning, in 1981 Valencia was the site of an attempted military coup by neo-Francoist forces, who held the parliament hostage until smooth-talking King Juan Carlos defused the situation. These days you'll find a bustling, highly livable city with a large gay scene and a lively university—not bad for a town once known only for its oranges and as the birthplace of paella. Many of the city's cosmopolitan residents speak the Valencian dialect, a cross between Catalan and Castilian.

BASICS

The **regional oficina de turismo** (C. La Paz 48, north of Pl. Ajuntament, tel. 96/394–22–22; open weekdays 9–6:30, Sat. 10–2) has information on the surrounding regions, including the Balearic Islands. Get free maps at the **local oficina de turismo** (tel. 96/351–04–17; open weekdays 8:30–2:15 and 4:15–6:15, Sat. 9:15–12:45) in Plaza Ajuntament, or at the **tourist information office** (tel. 96/352–85–73; open daily 9–2 and 3–5) inside the train station.

AMERICAN EXPRESS • *Viajes Duna, Cirilo Amorós 88, tel. 96/374–15–62. Open June–Aug., weekdays 10–2 and 5–8, Sat. 10–1; Sept.–May, weekdays 9:30–1:30 and 4:30–7:30.*

PHONES AND MAIL • **Correos** *Pl. Ajuntament 24, tel. 96/394–20–59. Open weekdays 8:30–8:30, Sat. 9:30–2. Lista de Correos open weekdays 8–8. Postal code: 46004.*

Locutorio Rovi. This private company offers phone, fax, and copy services (Pasaje Rex 7, off Av. Marqués de Sotelo. Open Mon.–Sat. 9–3 and 4–9).

CONSULATE • **United States.** *C. de la Paz 6, tel. 96/351–69–73. Open weekdays 9–2.*

COMING AND GOING

The main train station, **Valencia Término** (C. Xátiva 24, next to the bullring, tel. 96/352–02–02), in the town center, has daily service to Alicante (2 hrs, 1,815 ptas), Tarragona (4 hrs, 2,400 ptas), and Barcelona Sants (5 hrs, 2,750 ptas).

The main **bus station** (Av. Menéndez Pidal 13, tel. 96/349–72–22) is a 30-minute walk northwest from the center of town. **Auto Res** (tel. 96/349–22–30) runs buses to Madrid (4½ hrs, 3,000 ptas); **Ubesa** (tel. 96/340–08–55) goes to Barcelona (4 hrs, 2,850 ptas); and **Bacoma** (tel. 96/347–96–08) goes to Andalusian destinations, such as Granada (9 hrs, 4,940 ptas) and Algeciras (13 hrs, 7,250 ptas). To get into town, catch Bus 8 (90 ptas) to Plaza Ajuntament.

Trasmediterránea (Estación Marítima, southeast corner of university district, tel. 96/367–65–12) runs ferries to Ibiza (8 hrs, 2,850 ptas) and Palma, Mallorca (8 hrs, 5,100 ptas). During high season (July 25–Sept 5), prices are as much as 2,000 ptas higher.

GETTING AROUND

Plaza Ajuntament is at the center of town. The train station is south of the plaza, and the *Ciutat Vella* (Old Town), home to most tourist sights, is to the north. The city is large but walkable—just be aware of the confusing differences between Castilian and Valencian street names. You'll likely need a bus only for the beaches and the port. Local buses run by **Empresa Municipal de Transportes de Valencia (EMT)** (tel. 96/352–83–99) cost 115 ptas per ride; get a 10-ride Bonobus card (610 ptas) from newsstands and *tabacs*. Every bus in the system stops at Plaza Ajuntament, Calle Xátiva near the train station, or on the two streets on either side of the train station. Bus 8 goes between the train and bus stations; buses 20, 21, 23, 31, 91, and N-1 go to the beach; buses 3, 4, and 30 go to the ferry port; and buses 1, 2, and 19 serve both the beach and port. Not to worry—maps are posted at nearly every stop.

WHERE TO SLEEP

There's no shortage of affordable beds here. You'll find a few cheap places on Calle de Bailén and Calle de Pelayo, next to the train station, but this area can be a bit scuzzy. If all of the following are full, your best bet is to wander the streets of the old town between the Mercado and Plaza de la Virgen.

Hostal Residencia del Pilar. You money is well spent on these homey rooms and immaculate baths. The sincerely friendly owner rents doubles for 2,600 ptas (3,600 ptas with bath). *Pl. del Mercado 19, tel. 96/361–66–00. From Pl. Ajuntament, walk north on Av. María Cristina to Pl. del Mercado. Reception open 24 hrs.*

Hostal Residencia del Rincón. The beds are firm in this huge place; doubles are 2,800 ptas. Ask for a room on the second or third floor, away from the street noise. *C. Carda 11, tel. 96/391–79–98. From Pl. Ajuntament, walk north on Av. María Cristina, through Pl. del Mercado, then left on C. Carda. Reception open 24 hrs.*

Pensión Paris. A young, friendly staff keeps bathrooms spotless and beds spiffy in the bright, if boring, rooms. Doubles without bath cost 3,000 ptas. *C. Salvá 12, tel. 96/352–67–66. From Pl. Ajuntament, east on C. Barcas, left on C. Poeta Querol, right on C. Salva. No reservations.*

HOSTEL • Albergue Juvenil-Valencia (HI). The hostel is in the new university district, far from the sights. Beds are 1,400 ptas, 1,000 ptas under age 26; sheets are 500 ptas. *Av. del Puerto 69, tel. 96/361–74–59. From Pl. Ajuntament, Bus 19 over Puente de Aragón to Av. de Puerto. Midnight curfew, lockout 10–5. Closed Oct.–June.*

In March, people converge on Valencia for Las Fallas, a festival celebrating the rites of spring. Huge papier-mâché figures satirizing current events are torched, lighting up the sky.

FOOD

Paella is Valencia's passion, and restaurateurs squeeze every peseta (usually about 1,000) they can get out of you for paella *de mariscos* (seafood), *carne* (meat), or *mixta* (mixed). A number of eateries line calles de Bailén and Pelayo, west of the train station. The area around the Plaza del Carmen is also full of possibilities, particularly along Calle Roteros. For supplies, hit **Mercado Central** (Av. Barón de Carcer; open Mon.–Thurs. 6–2:30, Fri. 6–8, Sat. 6–3), or try **J. Navarro Herbolario** (C. de Padilla 5; open Sun.–Fri. 9–1:30 and 4–8, Sat. 9–1:30), a local health-food store.

Cafetería Roma. This unpretentious, quiet outdoor café is popular with both tourists and locals. *Raciones* of calamari (500 ptas) are perfect for smaller appetites; the ravenous can try a meat combo for 700 ptas. *Pl. de la Virgen 4, tel. 96/392–24–74. From Pl. Ajuntament, walk north, veer right onto C. San Vicente Mártir, go through Pl. de la Reina, then right on C. Micalet to Pl. de la Virgen.*

La Cuca Fera. This homey place with checkered tablecloths has a wood-fire oven that bakes up yummy pizzas (675 ptas–900 ptas), grilled vegetables (550 ptas), and other vegetarian options. *C. Roteros, off Pl. del Carmen, tel. 96/392–31–31. Closed Mon.*

La Utielana. It's worth the wait for a table in this small, blue-tile dining room—the food is cheap, tasty, and truly traditional. Gazpacho (250 ptas) and *fabadas asturias* (pork-and-bean stew with sausage; 350 ptas) make a good combo, and the excellent Valencian paella is 825 ptas. *Pl. Picadero Dos Aguas 3, tel. 96/352–94–14. From Pl. Ajuntament, west on C. Las Barcas, left on C. Poeta Querol, left on C. Vilaragut, leading to tiny alley Pl. Procide. Closed daily 4–9.*

WORTH SEEING

Many of Valencia's 18 museums and seven gardens are free. The **Museo de Bellas Artes** (C. San Pío V, tel. 96/360–57–93; admission 350 ptas; open Tues.–Sat. 10–2 and 4–6, Sun. 10–2) and the **Centro de Artesana Comunidad Valenciana** (C. Hospital 7, tel. 96/351–30–90; admission free; open Tues.–Sat. 10–2 and 5–8, Sun. 10–2) are both worth a visit. The former is a treat for Goya fans; the latter is a haven for sociologists, ethnologists, and anyone else interested in folk art. Work your imagination at the two **IVAM** (Valencian Institute of Modern Art) museums. The **Centre Julio González** (C. Guillém de Castro 118, SE of Pl. Ajuntament, tel. 96/386–30–00; admission 350 ptas, free Sun.; open Tues.–Sun. 11–8) features Gonzalez's avant-garde fusion of iron and sculpture; the **Centre del Carmen** (C. Museo 2, SE of Pl. Ajuntament, tel. 96/386–30–00; admission free; open Tues.–Sun. noon–2:30 and 4:30–8) hosts temporary exhibits of up-and-coming artists. In Valencia's 14th-century **catedral** (Pl. de la Reina, tel. 96/391–81–27; open June–Sept., Mon.–Sat. 10–1 and 4:30–7; shorter hrs off season), a side chapel contains a purple agate chalice said to be the Holy Grail. The **Museo de la Catedral** (admission 250 ptas; same hours as cathedral) contains two Goya paintings, various chalices, and a 1,300-kilogram gold, silver, and platinum *custodia* encrusted with diamonds, used to carry the host through the streets during the Semana Santa parade. If you climb the 207 steps of the cathedral's 230-ft tower, **El Miguelete** (admission 250 ptas), you can watch the hammer hit the 1,100-kilogram Miguel-Vicente bell on the hour and enjoy great views of the city.

To feast your eyes on trees, bushes, ferns, cacti, and feral cats, go to the **Jardín Botánico** (C. Beato Gaspar Bono 6, 1 block SE of Puente Glorias Valencianas, tel. 96/391–16–57; admission 100 ptas; closed Mon.). The most bizarre sight in town is the **Parque Gulliver** (in Túria riverbed park, at Puente Angel Custodio, tel. 96/337–02–04; closed Mon.), with a huge, climbable sculpture of the guy that makes Kareem Abdul-Jabbar look Lilliputian.

AFTER DARK

Shortly after the sun sets, unbridled partying commences. Theme bars and discos in **Barrio del Carmen** (NW of Pl. Ajuntament) feature everything from Brazilian drums to the tropical fanfare at the multilevel **Café Bolsería** (C. Bolsería 41, at corner of C. Conquista, tel. 96/391–89–03), where the beautiful congregate to drink and, on Saturday, dance. **Plaza Xuquer,** in the new university district, swarms with students around 11 PM. *Chupitos* (shots) are the current craze; knock one back at the standing-room-only **Sabor** (Pl. Xuquer 9, tel. 96/369–27–10) or the more intimate **Squalo** (Pl. Xuquer 3). The gay scene centers around Calle Quart; the most popular disco is **Balkiss** (C. Dr. Montserrat 23, off C. Quart, tel. 96/391–70–81). Film freaks should go to the **Rialto Theatre** (Pl. Ajuntament 17, tel. 96/351–23–36; admission 300 ptas) for frequent, undubbed screenings of arty independent films. To see what's on in Valencia, pick up the weekly *Qué Y Dónde* (175 ptas) at any newsstand.

NEAR VALENCIA

Along the 250 km (150 mi) of coastline of the Costa Blanca, you'll discover some of the cleanest, most unspoiled beaches on the east coast. Towns like **Elche,** famous for its ancient palm trees, and **Oriheula,** with its ornate seaside exposition of Gothic, Renaissance, and baroque architecture, contrast with the serene beauty of smaller villages like **Piles,** 10 km (6 mi) southeast of Gandía (*see below*). Piles's unbelievably well-located HI hostel, **Mar I Vent** (C. Doctor Fleming, tel. 96/283–17–48; beds 1,100 ptas, 900 ptas under age 26; closed Dec.), is right on the beach—open the door, and there's the sand. To get to Piles (95 ptas) from Gandía, catch one of the regular **Autobuses Amistad** (Marqués de Campo 9, tel. 96/287–44–10) buses Monday–Saturday; they stop in front of Bar La Amistad, across from Gandía's train station.

GANDIA

Ever since this sleepy village received a 1992 European Community Commission award for having the most pristine continental beach, tourists have been arriving by the busload. Luckily, these sun-baskers have yet to ruin the place; the sand remains so fine and clean that the beach appears blanketed in snow. The town of Gandía and its beach are separated by a 3-km (2-mi) stretch of farmland traversed by a single bus, which departs from in front of the **tourist office** (C. Marqués de Campo, across from train station, tel. 96/287–77–88; open July–Sept., weekdays 10–2 and 4:30–7:30; shorter hrs off season). The **train station** (C. Marqués de Campo s/n, tel. 96/286–54–71) in town serves Valencia (1 hr, 470 ptas, 535 ptas weekends) every half-hour.

WHERE TO SLEEP • Gandía has only a handful of cheap places to stay. **Requena** (Tirso de Molina 30, 3 blocks north of train station, off C. Perú, tel. 96/286–58–63; open June–Sept.) has mushy beds in doubles for 2,500 ptas. A better choice is **Hostal Residencia Duque Carlos** (C. Duque Carlos de Borja 34 and 36, tel. 96/287–28–44), a cushy place with fancy bedspreads and large doubles (3,745 ptas). **L'Alquería** (Carretera Gandía–Playa de Gandía, km 2, tel. 96/284–04–70), along the main road to the beach, is one of three campgrounds near the waterfront; sites are 550 ptas per tent plus 490 ptas per person.

BARCELONA

Catalan poet Joan Maragall dubbed Barcelona *la gran encisera* (the great enchantress), and most visitors to this gorgeous city do fall quickly under its intoxicating spell. From the cool, dark dampness of

Barcelona's Barri Gòtic (Gothic Quarter) and the breezy splendor of the broad, geometric avenues of the Eixample (which means "widening" or "enlargement") to La Rambla, Barcelona's famous, flower-lined pedestrian street, you're bound to find what you seek here.

Madrileños have long competed with their counterparts in 2,000-year-old Barcelona for economic, cultural, and political supremacy. By the Middle Ages, Barcelona was riding on the riches generated by brisk worldwide trade. With the conquest of the New World, however, and Madrid's newfound wealth from plundering it, as well as the switch in central importance from the Mediterranean to the Atlantic, Barcelona eventually lost economic primacy.

During the 19th century, the Industrial Revolution found a home in Barcelona, and the city became the industrial capital of an overwhelmingly agrarian Spain. The Industrial Revolution also set the stage for the launching of the *Renaixenca* (Renaissance), a golden age in Barcelona's (and Catalonia's) history. As artists and architects began to redesign the burgeoning city, the growing spirit of *Catalanisme*, Catalan nationalism, was reflected in the ornate Art Nouveau artistic movement known here as *modernisme*; this style emphasized traditional Catalan building techniques incorporating stained glass, tilework, and iron grills. Today, the city aggresively maintains its edge in architectural design. With new buildings cropping up daily and structures constantly under renovation, it's no wonder that architecture students from around the world come to Barcelona to study (and play) in this unique, open-air classroom.

BASICS

VISITOR INFORMATION
Barcelona has several tourist offices, all of which hand out free maps. If you arrive by train, go to the **oficina de turisme** (tel. 93/491–44–31; open daily 8–8) at Estació Sants. The **Catalunya oficina de turisme** (Gran Via Corts Catalanes 658, tel. 93/301–74–43; open weekdays 9–7, Sat. 9–2) has loads of information on Barcelona and Catalonia. There's also an information **kiosk** at Port Vell (open June–Sept., daily 9–8). From June 24 to September 24, city-sponsored **tourist guides** (decked out in red-and-white uniforms) hang out in key locales, such as La Rambla and the Barri Gòtic. For information on Barcelona's gay and lesbian scene, head to **Zeus** (C. Riera Alta 20, tel. 93/442–97–95), a gay shop and information center that doles out advice and maps.

AMERICAN EXPRESS
Pg. de Gràcia 101, at C. Rosselló, tel. 93/217–00–70. Open weekdays 9:30–6, Sat. 10–noon. Metro: Diagonal.

CHANGING MONEY
There are several commission-free *casas de cambio* on La Rambla, but their rates are worse than banks' rates, and the area is a mecca for pickpockets and thieves. The only advantage to using the *casas de cambio* is that they stay open late—until 11 PM or midnight. **Exact Change** (La Rambla 85 and 130, tel. 93/302–23–51; open daily 9 AM–10 PM) has slightly better rates than the others.

DISCOUNT TRAVEL AGENCIES
For tips on transport, stop by the main **Centre d'Informació i Assessorament per a Joves** (C. Ferran 32, at C. Avinyó, tel. 93/402–78–00; open weekdays 10–2 and 4–8), or the **branch office** (C. Ciutat 4, tel. 93/402–71–48; open early June–mid-Aug., weekdays 10–2 and 4–8, Sat. 11–2); guide yourself through their vast collections of maps, travel guides, and brochures, or talk to the peppy staff. **Unlimited**—previously TIVE (C. Rocafort 116-122, tel. 93/483–83–83)—arranges youth travel of all kinds. Another good source of budget-travel wisdom is **Nouvelles Frontières** (C. Balmes 8, tel. 93/318–68–98; open weekdays 9:30–7:30, Sat. 10–6).

The best spot for cheap bus, train, and plane tickets is the **Viva** youth-travel office inside the Catalunya Jove complex. In addition to a ride-sharing bulletin board, they have tickets, hostel cards, and general advice on budget travel. Come early to avoid the lines. In the evening, they're open for information but not tickets. *C. Calàbria 147, tel. 93/483–83–78. From Rocafort Metro, walk 2½ blocks north on C. Calàbria, past C. Consell de Cent. Open weekdays 10–8, Sat. 10–1:30.*

EMBASSIES
Australia: *Gran Via Carles III 98, tel. 93/330–94–96. Open weekdays 10–noon.* **Canada:** *C. Travessera de Les Corts 265, tel. 93/410–66–99. Open weekdays 9–1.* **Great Britain:** *Av. Diagonal 447, tel. 93/419–90–44. Open in summer, weekdays 9–2; in winter, also 4–5.* **Ireland:** *Gran Via Carles III 94, tel.*

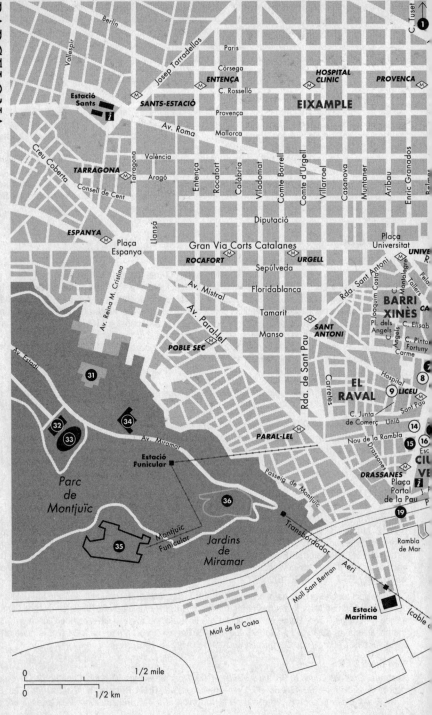

BARCELONA

Berlin
Vallespir
Josep Tarradellas
Paris
Còrsega
ENTENÇA
C. Rosselló
HOSPITAL
CLINIC
PROVENÇA

Estació
Sants
SANTS-ESTACIÓ
EIXAMPLE
Av. Roma
Provença
Mallorca

Creu Coberta
València
Tarragona
TARRAGONA
Aragó
Consell de Cent
Entença
Rocafort
Calàbria
Viladomat
Comte Borrell
Comte d'Urgell
Villarroel
Casanova
Muntaner
Aribau
Enric Granados
Balmes

ESPANYA
Plaça
Espanya
Llançà
Diputació
Plaça
Universitat
UNIVE
R

Gran Via Corts Catalanes
ROCAFORT
Sepúlveda
URGELL
Rda. Sant Antoni
C. Montalegre
Tallers
Pela
CA

Av. Mistral
Floridablanca
C. Joaquim Costa
BARRI
XINÈS
Av. Paral·lel
Tamarit
Pl. dels
Àngels
C. Elisab

SANT
ANTONI
Manso
Àngels
C. Pinto
Fortuny
Carme

POBLE SEC
Rda. de Sant Pau
EL
RAVAL
Hospital
LICEU

31
Carretes
C. Junta
de Comerç
Unió
Sant Pau

34
SANT
Av. Miramar
PARAL-LEL
Nou de la Rambla
14
32
Esc
33
Estació
Funicular
Drassanes
15
16
CIU
VE

Parc
de
Montjuïc
Passeig de Montjuïc
DRASSANES
Plaça
Portal
de la Pau

Av. Estadi
36
19

35
Montjuïc
Funicular
Jardins
de
Miramar
Rambla
de Mar

Transbordador
Aeri

Moll Sant Bertran
Estació
Marítima
(cable

Moll de la Costa

0 ———— 1/2 mile
0 ———— 1/2 km

GRÀCIA

SAGRADA FAMÍLIA

DIAGONAL

Rosselló

Provença

VERDAGUER

Plaça Sagrada Família

Mallorca

Av. Diagonal

València

PASSEIG DE GRÀCIA

Aragó

Estació Apeadero de Gràcia

Consell de Cent

GIRONA

Diputació

TETUAN

Plaça Tetuán

Gran Via Corts Catalanes

MONUMENTAL

RSITAT

Casp

Casp

Onda Universitat

Plaça de Catalunya

Fontanella

URQUINAONA

Ausiàs Marc

Ronda S. Pere

TALUNYA

Santa Anna

BARRI GÒTIC

ARC DE TRIOMF

Arc de Triomf

Estació del Nord (Bus Station)

Av. Vilanova

MARINA

Canuda

S. Pere Més Alt

Almogàvers

La Rambla

Cardenal Casañas

Av. Catedral

S. Pere Més Baix

Plaça St. Agustí Vell

LA RIBERA

Passeig Pujades

Ferran

JUAME I

Parc Ciutadella

Jaume I

Princesa

Vigatans

Wellington

Marina

Plaça Palau

Ample

Plaça Antoni López

Av. M. de l'Argentera

Estació França

BARCELONETA

CIUTADELLA

asseig Colom

Clavé

Moll Bosch i Alsina (Moll de la Fusta)

Moll Espanya

BARCELONETA

Plaça Poeta Boscán

C. Sant Carles

Mediterranean Sea

KEY

American Express Office

Tourist Information

Metro Stops

Rail Lines

Funicular/ Cable Car

93/491–50–21. Open weekdays 10–1. **United States:** *Pg. Reina Elisenda 23–25, tel. 93/280–22–27. Open weekdays 9–12:30 and 3–5.*

EMERGENCIES

The 24-hour **police station** at La Rambla 43 (across from Pl. Reial) offers visitor-assistance and counseling services in English. In spring and summer, the special **tourist-police** number is 93/301–90–60. The **central police office** is at Via Laietana 43. In an emergency, dial 092 (Municipal Police) or 091 (National Police).

ENGLISH-LANGUAGE BOOKS AND NEWSPAPERS

Get reacquainted with your native tongue at **Happy Books** (C. Pelai 20, tel. 93/317–07–68; Pg. de Gràcia 77, tel. 93/487–30–01), **Crisol** (C.Consell de Cent 341, tel. 93/215–31–21; Rambla de Catalunya 81, tel. 93/215–27–20), or **The Bookstore** (C. La Granja 13, tel. 93/237–95–19).

PHONES AND MAIL

The **Telefónica** office (open daily 8 AM–10:15 PM) is inside Estació Sants. The main post office, **Correos** (Pl. Antoni López s/n, tel. 93/318–38–31; Jaume I or Barceloneta Metro; open Mon.–Sat. 8–8), has telegram services, sells stamps, and holds mail. Have it sent to Your Name, Lista de Correos, 08002 Barcelona Central.

COMING AND GOING

BY BUS

The bus system is complicated. Visit the nearest tourist office to find out which of the many bus companies serves your destination, then go to a travel agency or the bus company itself to purchase tickets. Within Barcelona, you can also dial 010 for information on all bus routes, prices, and hours. Most buses arrive and depart from the central bus station, **Estació del Nord** (Av. Vilanova; Arc de Triomf Metro). Several companies operate from this station: **Enatcar** (tel. 93/245–25–28) goes to Madrid (8 hrs, 2,950 ptas) and Valencia (4½ hrs, 2,850 ptas); **Bacoma** (tel. 93/231–38–01) to Granada (14 hrs, 7,950 ptas) and Seville (16 hrs, 8,600 ptas); **Irbarsa** (tel. 93/265–60–61) to San Sebastián (6 hrs, 2,650 ptas) and Pamplona (5 hrs, 2,450 ptas); **Sarfa** (tel. 93/265–65–08) to towns along the Costa Brava, such as Cadaqués (2½ hrs, 2,000 ptas); and **Alsina-Graells** (tel. 93/265–68–66) to Andorra (4 hrs, 2,505 ptas) and La Seu d'Urgell (3½ hrs, 2,450 ptas). Estació del Nord's information booth is open daily 8 AM–10 PM.

Carrer Viriato (C. Viriato, tel. 93/490–40–00), to the left as you exit Estació Sants, has buses to Paris (15½ hrs, 12,500 ptas) and London (21 hrs, 14,450 ptas) and offers a 10% discount to travelers under 26. **Iberbus-Linebus** (Av. Paral-lel 116, tel. 93/329–64–06) serves international destinations, such as Milan (17½ hrs, 11,100 ptas) and London (25 hrs, 13,000 ptas), and also shaves prices for everyone under 26 and students under 29.

BY FERRY

Ferries for the Balearic Islands arrive and depart from **Estació Marítima** (tel. 93/412–2524), at the port south of La Rambla (Drassanes Metro). **Trasmediterránea** (tel. 93/317–7211) has the monopoly on ferries; in summer, their boats leave daily for Palma, Ibiza, and Menorca, usually at around 10 or 11 PM. Expect to pay 6,900 ptas for a seat on the eight- to nine-hour trip during high season (late July–early Sept.), 5,750 ptas off season, and about 3,750 ptas more for a bed. Travelers under 26 can get a 10% break if they reserve tickets in advance at the Oficina de Turisme Juvenil (*see* Discount Travel Agencies, *above*).

BY PLANE

Barcelona's airport is 12 km (8 mi) south of the city, in the suburb of El Prat de Llobregat. Trains (335 ptas) head to **Estació Sants** every half-hour 6 AM–10:45 PM, and from there you can get on the Metro. After 11 PM, a bus heads to Plaça de Catalunya (475 ptas) until 3:15 AM, but it only runs hourly, so you may want to splurge on a taxi into town (about 3,000 ptas). For airport information, dial 93/478–50–00. **Iberia Airlines** (Pg. de Gràcia 30, tel. 93/412–56–67) has round-trip youth fares to Paris (29,400 ptas) and London (31,200 ptas) for the under-26 crowd.

BY TRAIN

Most trains arrive at Barcelona's main train station, Estació de Sants, northwest of the city center. Some trains, especially those to or from France, arrive and depart from the Estació França, near the port and

Barri Gòtic. There are also RENFE stations at the intersection of Passeig de Gràcia and Carrer Aragó and at Plaça Catalunya. For rail information, dial 93/490–02–02.

Estació Sants (Pl. Paisos Catalans, tel. 93/411–44–31), the larger of the two stations, serves most national and international destinations. Trains rumble daily to Madrid (9–10 hrs, 4,400 ptas–6,600 ptas), Tarragona (1½ hrs, 675 ptas), and Valencia (7 hrs, 3,200 ptas). The station's ticket office is open 7 AM–10 PM, luggage storage (450 ptas–650 ptas per day) 5:30 AM–11 PM, and currency exchange 7 AM–11 PM. To get to La Rambla, hop on the Metro (Line 3 toward Montbau) inside the station and get off at Liceu or Drassanes. For late-night arrivals, night buses N2, N12, and N14 will whisk you to Plaça de Catalunya.

Estació França (Av. Marqués de l'Argentera, tel. 93/319–68–10) has trains to Paris (11 hrs, 17,500 ptas), Geneva (9½ hrs, 10,500 ptas), and Milan (13 hrs, 12,100 ptas); tickets are sold 6:30 AM–10 PM. França is a short walk from the budget lodging in the Barri Gòtic: from the station, head southwest (toward the Columbus monument) on Avinguda Marquès de l'Argentera and turn right onto Via Laietana, or, further down, onto La Rambla. The closest Metro stop (Barceloneta) is just behind the station, toward the port.

Ferrocariles Catalanes (C. Diputació 239, tel. 93/205–15–15), the local rail system, connects with the Metro at several places. From Plaça Catalunya, it sends trains to Terrassa (40 min, 375 ptas); from Plaça Espanya, trains leave for the Montserrat aerial station (1 hr, 650 ptas).

RIDES

Barnastop (Carrer San Ramon 29, off Carrer Nou de la Rambla; tel. and fax 93/443–06–32; open weekdays 11–2 and 5–8, Sat. 11–2) arranges shared rides.

GETTING AROUND

Many of Barcelona's attractions and hotels are within easy walking distance of La Rambla, but the city also has an excellent public-transportation system. Alas, the Metro closes at 11 PM on weekdays, but buses continue to run. Taxis are also plentiful and relatively cheap. Dial 93/412–00–00 for information about public transport.

BY BUS

The bus will take you wherever the Metro won't; night buses run from 11 PM to 4 AM, long after the Metro shuts down. The yellow night buses (day buses are red) usually start or finish in Plaça de Catalunya. Use your T-2 card (*see above*) or pay 140 ptas per ride. For free brochures with route information, drop in at the tourist office.

BY METRO

Five Metro lines cover most of the city quickly and efficiently; you'll never have to wait more than five minutes for a train. Single tickets cost 140 ptas. If you're going to be here a few days, get the multiride T-2 (Tarjeta Multiviatge) card (790 ptas), good for 10 rides on the bus, Metro, or local train (Ferrocariles Catalanes), or the T-1 card (700 ptas), good for 10 rides on the Metro only. If you plan to cover a *lot* of ground in a day, you can buy a one-day pass (600 ptas), good for unlimited travel on public transport. Buy tickets and pick up free maps at any Metro station.

BY TAXI

You can hail yellow-and-black taxis from most key spots in the city; the rate is 295 ptas plus 114 ptas per km (⅗ mi). Watch out when taking a late-night taxi from Estació Sants—they'll probably try to rip you off. If you think you're getting shafted, ask for a *recibo* (receipt) and the driver might back down. Dial 93/225–00–00 or 93/490–22–22 for a taxi.

WHERE TO SLEEP

The great thing about cheap sleeps in Barcelona is that they're concentrated around La Rambla and the Barri Gòtic—an area brimming with sights. The only problem is that the Barri Xinès, the hangout for prostitutes, heroin addicts, and other lost souls, lies adjacent to these central areas. If the darker side of urban life makes you nervous, search for a room away from the port, toward the Eixample and the newer parts of town. If you roll into Estació França late at night and don't feel like walking far, just cross the street to **Hostal Orleans** (Av. Marquès de l'Argentera 13, across from Estació França, tel. 93/319–73–82), with basic doubles (4,800 ptas, 5,400 ptas with bath).

UNDER 2,500 PTAS • Hostal New-York. The place has a dark, gloomy, Addams Family air, but the prices are rock-bottom, the owners are friendly, and you really aren't likely to run into Lurch in the halls. Doubles are 2,300 ptas. *C. Gignàs 6, off C. Avinyó, tel. 93/315–03–04. Metro: Jaume I.*

Pensión Aviñó. It's not well marked, but it's in a very welcoming corner of Barri Gòtic. Flash your *upCLOSE Guide* for 2,700-pta doubles (2,950 ptas with bath). *C. Avinyó 42, just west of C. Escudellers, tel. 93/318–79–45, fax 93/318–68–93. Metro: Drassanes or Jaume I.*

UNDER 3,500 PTAS • Hostal-Residencia Europa. Friendly management runs these quiet, small rooms near La Rambla. Showers are a mixed bag: hot water but low pressure. Doubles are 3,300 ptas (3,700 ptas with bath). *C. Boqueria 18, tel. 93/318–76–20. Metro: Liceu.*

Pensión Alamar. Staying here with owner Josefa Jimínez is like visiting your Spanish aunt—you get a homey atmosphere and full use of a kitchen and washing machine (1,000 ptas to wash and dry). It's a tiny place, so call two weeks ahead in the summer. Doubles are 3,300 ptas. *C. Comtessa de Sobradiel 1, tel. 93/302–50–12. From Liceu or Drassanes Metro, take C. Escudellers, off La Rambla, to C. Avinyó; C. Comtessa de Sobradiel is at intersection.*

Pensión Macarena. This convenient place is just off La Rambla and has a beautiful, plant-filled patio where you can hang laundry. Rooms are basic, tidy, and small. Doubles go for 3,000 ptas (3,750 ptas with bath). *C. Unió 9, ½ block from La Rambla, tel. 93/412–56–95. Metro: Liceu.*

Pensión Venecia. Sparkling bathrooms, nice owners, and quiet nights await off La Rambla, near the Liceu Metro. Doubles cost 2,800 ptas (3,700 ptas with bath). *C. Junta de Comerç 13, tel. 93/302–61–34. From Liceu Metro, take C. Hospital to C. Junta de Comerç.*

UNDER 4,500 PTAS • Hostal Campi. It's very secure (you buzz for entry both at the front door and on your floor) and in a primo locale right near Plaça de Catalunya. Spacious doubles are 3,700 ptas (4,750 ptas with bath). *C. Canuda 4, tel. 93/301–35–45. Metro: Plaça de Catalunya.*

Hostal Paris. Overlooking La Rambla at Plaça Boqueria, this large place has clean, commodious rooms. Check out the groovy TV room with questionable oil paintings of Catalonia. Doubles go for 4,000 ptas (5,000 ptas with bath). *C. Cardenal Casañas 4, on Pl. Boqueria, tel. and fax 93/301–37–85.*

Pensión Las Flores. For clean, well-kept rooms in a great location right on La Rambla, you'll have to endure embarrassing jaunts to the shower, which is right next to the front desk. Doubles are 3,500 ptas (5,300 ptas with bath). *La Rambla 79, tel. 93/317–16–34. 8 rooms. No reservations. Metro: Liceu 11.*

Pensión Nueva Orleans. Most of these near-spotless rooms have flowery bedspreads and TVs, and they're right behind the post office on Carrer Ample, with easy access to Estació França. Doubles cost 4,300 ptas (5,200 ptas with bath). *C. Ancha 53, tel. 93/310–18–75. From Barceloneta or Estació França Metro, take C. Fusteria away from port to C. Ample. Reception open 24 hrs.*

UNDER 5,500 PTAS • Hostal Oliva. This uptown address, on Passeig de Gràcia near Plaça de Catalunya, is most respectable, and it buys you a beautiful courtyard and an old wooden elevator adorned with cut glass. Doubles are 5,550 ptas (6,650 ptas with bath). *Pg. de Gràcia 32, tel. 93/488–01–62. Reservations taken with one night's deposit. Metro: Plaça de Catalunya.*

HOSTELS

Albergue Palau (HI). Fancy this: coed dorm rooms, with baths, that won't give you the willies, and a big dining room, perfect for socializing or just vegging in front of the TV. Bed and breakfast will cost you 1,400 ptas, sheets 200 ptas. Present yourself at 9:30 AM to get a bed, as they don't take reservations; and make sure you're in by the 3 AM curfew. *C. Palau 6, tel. 93/412–50–80. From Jaume I Metro, go west on C. Jaume I, turn left at C. Ciutat, right at C. Templaris, then left at C. Palau. Kitchen.*

Albergue Verge de Montserrat (HI). In this beautiful, Moorish-style building out near Parc Güell, a dorm bed and breakfast will run you 2,250 ptas, 1,750 ptas with HI card (they'll sell you one) or under age 25; sheets are 375 ptas. Only groups can reserve, so come between 8 AM and 9 AM to get a spot. The bell tolls at midnight, but doors open again at 1 AM, 2 AM, and 3 AM sharp. Store your luggage here after checkout. *Pg. Mare de Déu del Coll 41–51, tel. 93/210–51–51. From Vallcarca Metro, take Av. República Argentina over bridge, right to Pg. Mare de Déu del Coll (a 15-min walk). Lockout 10 AM–2 PM. Laundry (500 ptas). Closed Christmas.*

Hostal de Joves (HI). Across the street from Parc Ciutadella, and minutes from Estació França, Joves offers dorm beds including breakfast and hot shower for 1,450 ptas, sheets for 250 ptas, and blankets for 150 ptas. There's a midnight curfew, but doors open again at 1 AM and 2 AM sharp. It gets busy in summer, so come before 10 AM and be persistent. There's a safe (100 ptas) for your many valuables.

Pg. Pujades 29, tel. 93/300–31–04. From Arc de Troimf Metro, walk south on C. Nàpols, turn left on Pg. Pujades. Lockout 10–3. Checkout 9:30 AM. Kitchen, laundry (1,000 ptas).

Kabul Youth Hostel (HI). This privately owned hostel on Plaça Reial is friendly, casual, and a great place to socialize—their ads even boast of a "great party atmosphere," and there are pool tables on-site. There's no breakfast, but there's no curfew or lockout either, and they'll store your luggage for you. Dorm beds are 1,550 ptas, sheets 250 ptas. Come at 10:30 AM to get a spot. *Pl. Reial 17, tel. 93/318–51–90. Laundry (800 ptas). Metro: Drassanes or Liceu.*

Pensión Colóm 3 (HI). Centrally situated on noisy Plaça Reial, Colóm offers dorm beds for 1,650 ptas (sheets 250 ptas) and private rooms (doubles with shower 5,400 ptas). Come and go as you please—there are no curfews or lockouts. Be here at 10:30 AM to get a spot; you can reserve for private rooms only. *C. Colóm 3, tel. 93/318–06–31. Laundry (750 ptas). Metro: Drassanes or Liceu.*

CAMPING

To reach the campgrounds south of the city, take Bus 94 (which runs 8:45 AM–9:45 PM) from Plaça Universitat; most 'grounds are either on the main highway, Autovia Castelldefels, or just off it. The closest is **El Toro Bravo** (Aut. Castelldefels, Viladecans, 11 km (7 mi) south of Barcelona, tel. 93/637–34–62), which have a bar, restaurant, supermarket, pool, laundry, and currency exchange. Sites cost 750 ptas per tent plus 700 ptas per person. For general camping information, call **Asociación de Campings de Barcelona** (Gran Via Corts Catalanes 603, 3rd floor, tel. 93/415–59–55), or drop by the tourist office for a list of nearby campgrounds.

Estrella de Mar. It's cheap, intimate, and a stone's throw from the beach, *and* it has an on-site bar, restaurant, supermarket, pool, and laundromat. Sites cost 650 ptas per tent plus 650 ptas per person. *Aut. Castelldefels, 16.7 km (10 mi) south of Barcelona, tel. 93/633–07–84. Take Bus 95 (every 30 min) from Ronda Universitat 33.*

FOOD

People dine here in characteristic Catalan style: late into the night and with gusto. Although prices here tend to be higher in Barcelona than in other parts of Spain, you can eat well on a budget. You'll find the largest concentration of cheap bars and restaurants around La Rambla, the Barri Gòtic, and the hip neighborhood of Gràcia. Another wallet-friendly option is a visit to one of Barcelona's excellent open markets. The best is **Mercat Sant Josep, a.k.a. La Boqueria** (La Rambla 91, tel. 93/318–25–84; open Mon.–Sat. 8–8), housed in a grand *modernista* structure. If you're not faint of heart, venture into the meat section, where bloody slabs of meat, eyeballs, and innards are enthusiastically displayed. Vegetarians should look to the self-service restaurant **Self Naturista** (C. Santa Anna 11–17, tel. 93/318–23–88; closed Sun.). For a quick bite, try the top-notch falafel/gyro stand on Plaça Reial.

UNDER 750 PTAS • La Cova Fumada. This small, popular hole-in-the-wall in Barceloneta (*see* Worth Seeing, *below*) has no sign, but finding it is half the fun: Look for the big wooden doors on the south side of Plaza Poeta Boscán. Try *bombas* (stuffed potato croquettes; 145 ptas) or the fabulous *calamari plancha con ajo* (calamari with garlic; 380 ptas) with cheap beer. *C. Baluard 56, tel. 93/221–40–61. From Barceloneta Metro, walk south on Pg. Joan de Borbó, turn left on C. Sant Carles, then left on C. Baluard. Closed weekdays 3–5:30 and Sun.*

Velodromo. First opened in 1909, this vast, lofty-ceilinged joint is the perfect stop for a quick game of pool (200 ptas), a beer (300 ptas), and tapas while you're out exploring the Eixample. Grilled octopus, artichokes, sardines, tortilla, and other tapas run 250 ptas–500 ptas. *C. Muntaner 213, tel. 93/230–60–22. Closed daily July 26–Aug. 26. Metro: Diagonal.*

El Xampanyet. This popular tapas bar, just down the street from the Picasso Museum, is famous for its seafood tapas and *cava*, the local champagne (110 ptas a glass). *C. Montcada 22, tel. 93/319–70–03. Metro: Jaume I. Closed Sun. night, Mon., and Tues.–Sat. 4–6:30.*

UNDER 1,000 PTAS • L'Hórtet. A down-to-earth vegetarian restaurant that resembles Grandma's house: checkered tablecloths, fruit baskets, and a ban on smoking. The savory *menú del día* is 850 ptas. *C. Pintor Fortuny 32, tel. 93/317–61–89. Open daily 1 PM–4 PM. Metro: Catalunya or Liceu.*

Gran Bodega. In the Eixample, not far from Passeig de Gràcia, this atmospheric bar is renowned for its tapas. Model airplanes hover overhead, and pics of the original owner with celebrities line the walls—check out the one where he and Muhammad Ali are pretending to box. The lunch *menú* costs 950 ptas. *C. València 193, tel. 93/453–10–53. Metro: Universitat.*

UNDER 1,500 PTAS • Flash Flash. Offers more than 60 variations on that Spanish staple, *tortilla de patatas* (potato omelette; 500 ptas–1,000 ptas). The slick, white plastic decor must be seen to be believed—Andy Warhol meets Cher in a room from Kubrick's *A Clockwork Orange.* It's near Avinguda Diagonal, just east of the Eixample. *C. de la Granada de Penedes 25, tel. 93/237–09–90. From Diagonal Metro, go west on Av. Diagonal, turn right on C. Tuset, then right on C. Granada de Penedes. Closed daily 5–8:30.*

La Fonda. This chic, airy restaurant is less expensive than it looks, with generous, reasonably priced portions of fantastic Catalan and Spanish specialties (*menú del día* 1,000 ptas). They don't take reservations, so come before 9 PM or stand in line. *C. Escudellers 10, north of Pl. Teatre, tel. 93/318–87–29. Closed daily 3:30–8:30. Metro: Drassanes.*

Restaurant Borràs. This beautifully tiled, busy lunch spot near Parc Ciutadella is known as "Económico" to its diverse clientele. The superb *menú del día* (1,050 ptas) includes beef stew, grilled chicken, and soups and salads. If you fancy liver, order the *hígado de ternera* (veal) prepared with garlic. *Pl. Sant Agustí Vell 13, tel. 93/319–64–94. Head north off C. Princesa to C. Tantarantana, then to Pl. Sant Agustí Vell. Open weekdays 12:30–4:30.*

La Llesca. A friendly eatery above Plaça del Sol in Gràcia, La Llesca has a checkered tile floor and a collection of old radios in the back room. Specialties include grilled meats, such as *butifarra* (thick, Catalan sausage; 650 ptas) and *conejo* (rabbit; 950 ptas). *C. Terol 6, tel. 93/285–02–46. From Fontana Metro, walk south on C. Gran de Gràcia, left on C. Ros de Olano (becomes C. Terol). Other location: Trav. de Gràcia 86, tel. 93/416–05–03. From Fontana Metro, walk south on C. Gran de Gràcia, right on Trav. de Gràcia. Both closed daily 4:30–8:30.*

CAFES

With its long, tree-lined Rambla, countless plaças, and fundamentally social denizens, Barcelona revels in café culture. One reliable option is the popular **Café de l'Opera** (La Rambla 74, across from Gran Teatre del Liceu; open daily until 3 AM), a classy place to gulp your morning coffee (160 ptas) or a late-night beer. Another turn-of-the-century spot, **Café Valenciana** (C. Aribau 1, tel. 93/453–11–38), overlooks Plaça Universitat and specializes in wonderfully refreshing *horchatas* (sweet, grain-based drinks; 250 ptas) and *granizados* (granitas, or Slurpee-like drinks, usually flavored with lemon; 225 ptas). Out in Gràcia, head to **Café del Sol** (Pl. del Sol 29), the most happening of several cafés and bars that line the plaça.

WORTH SEEING

Barcelona is spread out along the Mediterranean, hemmed in by the Collserola hills and punctuated by two promontory parks—Montjuïc, to the south, and Tibidabo, to the north. Many of the city's major sights are centrally located near La Rambla and in the **Ciutat Vella** (Old Town). Take advantage of Barcelona's great transportation system to see some of the further-flung highlights, such as Parc Güell and the Sagrada Familia (*see below*).

LA RAMBLA

La Rambla is Barcelona's throbbing heartbeat. Technically, it's not one street but a series of five connected streets, collectively called Las Ramblas, leading up from the port to the Plaça de Catalunya. All along its sweeping, shady expanse you'll see café waiters whisking glasses off outdoor tables while flamenco dancers, mimes, bird and flower vendors, folk singers, tourists, pickpockets, and cops compete for attention. As you're strolling, keep an eye out for a few particularly deserving sights. **Palau Güell** (C. Nou de la Rambla 3, tel. 93/317–39–74, just off La Rambla), originally the Güell family's private residence and now a museum, was built around 1888 by Barcelona's beloved Antoni Gaudí. Restorations should be completed by 1998; give the luxurious interior and high vaulted ceilings a look. Nearby is the graceful **Plaça Reial,** designed according to Napoleonic city plans, with several entrances on side streets and La Rambla; its palm trees and central fountain, not to mention the lofty balconies of adjacent buildings, make the square quite lovely, despite the seedy characters hanging around. Lively clubs and bars (*see* After Dark, *below*) line the plaça, and on Sunday and holidays the square hosts a flea market where you can buy anything from old coins and stones to postcards and books. Off La Rambla is Barcelona's central food market, **La Boqueria** (*see* Food, *above*), a sensory overload of edibles; remember to stop and admire the tile design by Joan Miró at the entrance to the market (La Rambla, at Plaça Boqueria).

BARCELONETA AND THE HARBOR

La Rambla empties into the port at the **Monument a Colom,** which depicts Columbus pointing prophetically (if mistakenly) out to sea toward, oh, Naples. Stroll down the waterfront boardwalk, **Moll de la Fusta,** to get to the former fishing village of **Barceloneta.** Most of the port has been renovated with newly planted trees, pristine stretches of lawn, and a lot of cement (for good measure), but Barceloneta retains its small-neighborhood feel, at least once you're off the main drag, Passeig Joan de Borbó. When you get hungry, explore the side streets, where you'll find some great little seafood restaurants. The sea itself begins just behind this strip of land, and though Barcelona's crowded beaches are not the best in Spain, they're appealing enough on a hot day. If you can't muster up the energy to walk, let someone else haul you around the scenic harbor: **Las Golondrinas al Rompeolas** launches boat tours (450 ptas) from Portal de la Pau, near the Columbus statue. Tours run May to late September, daily 11–8:45, and October–April, daily 11–5.

PARC DE LA CIUTADELLA

This large city park near Estació França has lots of trees (all labeled by variety) and lots of grass—perfect for sprawling out and chilling. The Catalan Parliament meets here in a building that also houses the **Museu d'Art Modern** (Pl. Armes, tel. 93/319–57–28; admission 500 ptas; open Tues.–Sat. 10–7, Sun. 10–2), with a great collection of works from the *modernisme* period; find out what other Catalan artists (Fortuny, Casas, and Rusinyol) were doing while Gaudí's star rose. At the other end of the park is a monumental fountain, one of young Gaudí's first projects in Barcelona; note the extravagant organic forms that would later become a hallmark of his work.

PARC DE MONTJUIC

Montjuïc is another idyllic park that manages to thrive amid Barcelona's congestion and chaos. This one allows you to escape the city by literally rising above it. Montjuïc's prime location overlooking Barcelona and the port has made it a favorite spot for the military: The fortresslike **Castell de Montjuïc** is where Franco's troops executed the president of the Catalan Generalitat. Today the castle houses the **Museu Militar** (tel. 93/329–86–13; admission 250 ptas; open Tues.–Sun. 9:30–1:30 and 3:30–7:30), with an extensive collection of weapons, uniforms, and medals. On the lighter side, the **Parc d'Attraccions de Montjuïc** (tel. 93/441–70–24; admission to grounds 700 ptas; open late June–early Sept., Tues.–Fri. 5 PM–10 PM, Sat. 6 PM–1 AM, Sun. noon–11; off-season, weekends 11:30–8) is an amusement park with your basic nausea-inducing rides. Montjuïc also has claims to Olympic fame, and you'll find both the renovated **Estadi Olímpic** (tel. 93/426–06–60; open Sun. 10–2, Tues.–Sat. 10–2 and 4–7; until 8 Apr.–Sept.) and the modern **Palau Sant Jordi** (Pg. Olímpic, tel. 93/426–20–89) just off Avinguda Estadi, a major road cutting through Montjuïc. Inside the Palau Nacional (National Palace), you'll find the **Museu Nacional d'Art de Catalunya** (National Museum of Catalan Art) (tel. 93/423–71–99; admission 650 ptas; open Tues.–Sat. 10–7, Thurs. until 9, Sun. 10–2:30), featuring what is generally considered the world's best collection of Romanesque art—frescoes, murals, and altarpieces saved and restored from chapels throughout the Catalan Pyrenees. To get to Montjuïc from Plaça de Catalunya, take Metro Line 1 to Plaça Espanya and walk uphill toward the Palau Nacional. You can also hop on Bus 61 from Plaça Espanya or take the funiculars from near the Paral-lel Metro or near the port.

FUNDACIO JOAN MIRO • This beautifully designed building on Montjuïc houses the most important works of renowned 20th-century Catalan artist Joan Miró. The collection—much of which was donated by Miró himself—traces the development of his distinctive style, laden with abstract symbols and bright colors. *Pl. Neptú, on Av. Miramar, tel. 93/329–19–08. Admission: 750 ptas. Open Tues.–Sat. 11–7, Thurs. until 9:30, Sun. 10:30–2:30.*

TIBIDABO

If it's a supernaturally clear day, you might hop up to this promontory for a bird's-eye view of Barcelona. Otherwise, give it a miss; the amusement park (tel. 93/211–79–42; admission 1,950 ptas; open June, Tues.–Sun. noon–8; until 10 July and Aug.) is noisy, tacky, and expensive. To get up here, take Ferrocarriles Catalanes to Avinguda del Tibidabo; then from Plaça JFK, take Bus "Tramvia Blau" (150 ptas–250 ptas) to the funicular (400 ptas one way) for the final ascent. On your way up or down, stop at the bar **Mirablau** (tel. 93/418–58–79), where you can down a beer (350 ptas) and admire the amazing view.

BARRI GOTIC

Most of Barcelona's oldest and most-visited sights are packed into the tiny, winding streets of the Barri Gòtic (Gothic Quarter). The area centers around the **Catedral** (*see below*) and **Plaça Sant Jaume,** home to the impressive **Ajuntament** (Town Hall) and the even more impressive Generalitat, seat of the Cata-

MODERNISME AND ANTONI GAUDÍ

Thanks to the homegrown genius of architect and visionary Antoni Gaudí, wandering around Barcelona can be a surreal experience—Gaudí's wavy, elaborate, fantastical buildings are everywhere. During the Catalan Renaissance of the late 19th and early 20th centuries, Gaudí helped popularize modernisme *in art and architecture. Other brash Catalan architects and designers of the period include Domènech i Muntaner and Puig i Cadafalch, but Gaudí, who was killed at the age of 75 when hit by a streetcar in 1926, lives on as the city's favorite son.*

Wander the Eixample and Gràcia to study the majority of Barcelona's modernista *works. A required stop on the Gaudí route is the Casa Milà, a.k.a. La Pedrera (Pg. Gràcia 92, tel. 93/488–35–92; tours Tues.–Sat. at 10, 11, noon, and 1), a city-block–sized apartment building built between 1905 and 1910 as Gaudí's last civil project. The building's nickname means "rock quarry," owing to its organic, chipped-rock exterior. Inside, all the normally mundane details of a building—railings, chimneys, columns, doors—have been transformed into a fusion of the functional and the surreal. Espai Gaudi (C. Provença 261, tel. 93/484–59–95); open Tues.–Sun. 10–8, admission: 650 ptas), the Gaudí museum in the building's attic, is the best study of the architect ever assembled for public consumption, and the rooftop is as spectacular as anything in town. Casa Batlló just down Passeig de Gràia below Carrer Aragó is another urban fantasy. Casa Vicens (C. Carolines 22; Fontana Metro), a colorful brick-and-tile Mudéjar-style building in Gràcia, was Gaudí's first project. To sniff out the other* modernista *works scattered about town, pick up the free "Discovering Modernist Art in Catalonia" at the tourist office.*

lan government. The Barri Gòtic proper is bordered by La Rambla, to the south, and Via Laetana, to the north. Crossing Via Laietana, you enter **La Ribera.** Here you'll find the Museu Picasso (*see below*) and the elegant church of **Santa María del Mar** (Pg. del Born 1, tel. 93/310–23–90; open daily 8:30–12:30 and 4:30–8:15), a superlative example of Mediterranean-Gothic architecture featuring unusual (in Barcelona) symmetry, simplicity, and integrity of design.

LA CATEDRAL • Construction of this impressive Gothic structure began in 1298, but the main facade wasn't completed until 1890. The otherwise gloomy interior is illuminated by candles blazing away in the 20-odd chapels—one of them contains a replica of the famous Black Virgin icon found in Montserrat (*see* Near Barcelona, *below*). Enter the museum (admission 300 ptas; open daily 11–1) from the lovely, tropical cloister, where geese waddle among the palm trees and fountains. *Pl. de la Seu. Open daily 8–1:30 and 4–7:30.*

MUSEU FREDERIC MARES • Downstairs you'll find an extensive collection of sculptures of Christ, particularly of the Crucifixion. Look for the unusual 14th-century carving of Christ and Joseph of Arimathea. It's a wonderful collection, if a bit heavy. The delightful upstairs section provides some comic relief in the form of the eccentric personal collection of local sculptor Frederic Marès. This guy was a collector extraordinaire, hoarding turn-of-the-century keys, watches, photographs, cigarette cases, pipes, cards, stamps, shells, and more. *Pl. St. Iu 5, near cathedral, off C. Comptes, tel. 93/310–58–00. Admission: 350 ptas. Open Tues.–Sat. 10–5, Sun. 10–2.*

MUSEU PICASSO • This museum's two medieval palaces contain one of the world's best collections of Picasso's work. Picasso spent many of his formative years in Barcelona, including his Blue and Rose periods (1901–06), and this collection is particularly representative of his earlier work. If you're expecting black outlines and tortured lovers, you may be in for a beautiful and educational surprise. *C. Montcada 15, off C. Princesa, tel. 93/319–63–10. Admission: 600 ptas (free first Sun. of month). Open Tues.–Sat. 10–8, Sun. 10–3.*

TEMPLE EXPIATORI DE LA SAGRADA FAMILIA

You'll visit innumerable cathedrals in Spain, but you'll never see anything like this. This fantastical, Dr. Seuss-ish building was Gaudí's all-consuming project until he died in 1926; he left it unfinished, and cranes still hover over various parts of the cathedral. The architect's design involves complex symbolism, including 18 towers, of which only four (representing the Apostles, the Evangelists, the Virgin, and Christ) are completed. Climb the stairs if you want a view of the unfinished interior; otherwise, take the elevator for 200 ptas. A small museum chronicles the work on the building. *Pl. Sagrada Familia, tel. 93/455–02–47. Admission: 800 ptas. Open daily 9–8. Metro: Sagrada Familia.*

PARC GUELL

Commissioned by Eusebi Güell in 1900 as a kind of garden city intended for single-family residences, Parc Güell ended up instead as a whimsical city park with fine views and a curvy wonder of a park bench adorned with colorful ceramic tiles. A *modernista* house (once Gaudí's residence) on the premises is now a museum, **Casa Museu Gaudí** (tel. 93/219–38–11; admission 350 ptas; open Apr.– Oct., Sun.–Fri. 10–2 and 4–7, until 6 off season), with furniture that has the same imaginative flair as the building. *C. Olot. From Pg. de Gràcia, Bus 24.*

CHEAP THRILLS

The tradition of campy drag performance (in a Pedro Almodóvar/John Waters vein) flourishes in Barcelona. The best place to see a free, fun-for-the-whole-family drag show is at **Marsella** (C. Sant Pau 65, no phone; Liceu Metro), Thursday and Sunday nights at 12:30 AM. Unfortunately, the shows break for July and August. Just a few blocks away, toward the port, is **El Cangrejo** (C. Montserrat 9, tel. 93/ 301–85–75; closed Mon.), which serves up its own tacky and flashy drag show, also free, Thursday– Saturday nights at 12:30 AM.

FESTIVALS

Barcelona lives to socialize. Tons of festivals, both secular and religious, pack crowds into the streets. Big ones to look out for are **Sant Jordi's Day,** on April 23, when lovers exchange books and roses in celebration of Catalonia's patron saint and the nearly simultaneous deaths of Cervantes and Shakespeare on 23 April, 1616; and **La Verbena de Sant Joan** (Midsummer's Eve), on June 23, when all-night partying is accompanied by firecrackers and bonfires in the street. On August 15, dancing, fireworks, and street decorations enliven the neighborhood of Gràcia during its annual fiesta. The week of September 24, the **Festa de la Mercè** (Our Lady of Mercy) calls forth music, fireworks, and parades of papiermâché giants. In June and July, the state-sponsored **Grec Summer Festival** puts on a series of cultural events ranging from rock concerts to opera to theater; get the program at **Palau de la Virreina** (La Rambla 99, tel. 93/301–77–75).

AFTER DARK

Take advantage of the midday siesta (especially since it's fading slowly into history); you may need some extra sleep to do as the natives do—start late, and stay out until dawn. Locals head out for drinks around 11:30 PM or midnight, then eventually wander over to a club or disco. The only real difference between a bar and a disco is that the former stays open until around 2, while the latter stays open until 5 AM or later. Some discos and music clubs charge a cover, though enforcement depends entirely on the whims of the doorperson.

Generally speaking, you'll find the posh spots out near Avinguda Diagonal in the Eixample, in Gràcia, and along Carrer de Marià Cubí, just off Via Augusta; the funky, shabby places are mostly in and around the Barri Xinès. Check *Guía del Ocio* (200 ptas), sold at newsstands, for music, film, and theater listings.

BARS

Casa Quimet. Also known as the "Guitar Bar," this famous old joint in Gràcia features guitars galore hanging from the ceiling. You're free to play them, so spontaneous jam sessions often erupt. Beer is 400 ptas. *C. Rambla del Prat 9, off C. Gran de Gràcia, no phone. Metro: Fontana.*

The Clansman. This traditional Scottish alehouse has eight different beers on tap (300 ptas), and you might even catch a live bagpipe concert. *C. Vigatans 13, tel. 93/319–71–69. Closed Sun. Metro: Jaume I.*

London Bar. This famous drinking hole was once the hangout (so to speak) of circus performers, which explains the trapeze over the bar and the occasional acrobatic. There's a stage in back for performances—anything from jazz to drag shows. Beers are 350 ptas; mixed drinks 700 ptas. *C. Nou de la Rambla 34, tel. 93/318–52–61. Closed Mon. Metro: Drassanes.*

Punto BCN. Barcelona's thriving gay scene starts here. Knock back a few beers (350 ptas) at this barn-like bar from midnight to 1:30 AM, then head around the corner to **Este Bar** (C. Consell de Cent 255, no phone; beer 350 ptas) and ogle the prettiest guys in town. *C. Muntaner 63–65, tel. 93/451–91–52. Metro: Universitat.*

LIVE MUSIC AND CLUBS

Most of Barcelona's clubs start their engines after midnight.

La Boîte. If you can find this underground, mirrored club in the Eixample, you're in for some great live jazz and blues. On weekends after 2 AM, a DJ plays funk, and everyone grooves until 6 AM. The cover (1,500 ptas–2,000 ptas) includes a drink. *Av. Diagonal 477, in shopping plaza behind Bank Santander, tel. 93/419–59–50. Metro: Diagonal.*

Karma. If you just want to dance and aren't concerned with atmosphere or attitude, come to this thumping disco on Plaça Reial. The 1,500-pta cover isn't usually collected. A beer is 500 ptas. *Pl. Reial 10, tel. 93/302–56–80. Closed Mon. Metro: Liceu.*

Pipa Club. You don't have to smoke a pipe to get in; just ring the buzzer and enter dim lighting, comfy chairs, and live blues, jazz, and tango music (nightly at 10). *Pl. Reial 3, next to Cervecería Glaciar, tel. 93/302–47–32. Cover: 500 ptas.*

Marten's Disco. After you've made your rounds, you may well end up here—Barcelona's biggest gay disco. Shake it until 5 AM. *Pg. Gràcia 130, tel. 93/218–71–67. Metro: Diagonal.*

Daniel's. Barcelona's lesbian scene is small and underground, but it does have cool joints like this low-key women's club. There's no cover, snacks are free, and the dance floor is groovin'; ring the buzzer for entry. *Pl. Cardona 7, between C. Marià Cubí and C. Laforja, tel. 93/209–99–78. Metro: Gràcia.*

NEAR BARCELONA

MONTSERRAT

Barcelona may be the undisputed cultural and political capital of Catalonia, but the region's spiritual home is the monastery of Montserrat, perched high atop bizarre rock formations. Poet Joan Maragall wrote that "Montserrat is the Catalan miracle," and the mountain truly seems miraculous until you read the brochures' dry, scientific explanations of limestone and ocean drainage some 10 million years ago. The monastery dates back to the early 11th century and has long been associated with the preservation of the Catalan language and identity. During Franco's reign, when Catalan was officially banned, the monastery was one of the few places allowed to hold mass in that language. As well as being a breathtaking symbol, Montserrat is famous beyond Catalonia for the Black Virgin icon housed in the **basilica** (open weekdays 8–10:30 and noon–6:30, weekends 7:30 PM–10:30 PM). The Black Virgin sits high on a silver throne, encased in a protective Plexiglas shield (one hand has thoughtfully been left exposed for pilgrims to kiss). Try to time your visit to the basilica so that you can hear the heavenly **Montserrat Boys'**

Choir sing *Salve Regina* (daily at 1 PM; no performances July or Christmas). The **Museo de Montserrat** (tel. 93/835–02–51 ext. 1502; admission 500 ptas; open daily 10–5) exhibits works by El Greco, Mir, Rusiñol, and other Catalan artists.

Hiking around this mountain can be a religious experience in itself, with truly awesome views of the plains below and the rocks above. You can walk to the hermitage of Sant Jeroni, or, for 750 ptas round trip, take the **funicular** (tel. 93/835–04–80; open daily 10–7) to the hermitage of Sant Joan, near the summit. The mountaintop **tourist booth** (Pl. de la Creu, tel. 93/835–02–51 ext. 586; open daily 9–2:15 and 3:15–6), across from the funicular station, has free brochures and maps.

Though Montserrat makes a fine day trip, it's pretty inspiring to wake up here. You can stay in the dorm rooms adjoining the monastery at **Cel·les de Montserrat** (Monestir de Montserrat, tel. 93/835–02–51 ext. 630) for 5,500 ptas per person, or 7,000 ptas for two. **Hostelería de Montserrat** (Plaça de Monestir, tel. 93/835–02–01, fax 93/828–10–06) has doubles for 4,000 ptas, and **Marcel Millet** (tel. 93/835–02–51), a five-minute hike toward Sant Jeroni from Sant Joan, will set you up with a campsite at 450 ptas per tent plus 400 ptas per person.

COMING AND GOING

Ferrocarriles Catalanes trains (C. Diputació 239, Barcelona, tel. 93/205–15–15) leave Barcelona's Plaça Espanya for the Montserrat rail station, where you can take the cable car, **Montserrat Aeri** (tel. 93/835–00–05), on a hair-raising ride to the monastery. The entire trip takes 1½ hours and costs 1,550 ptas round trip. If dangling over the mountain makes you nervous, shell out for a guided **Julia Tours** bus (Ronda Universitat 5, tel. 93/317–64–54) from Barcelona's Estació Sants. The trip takes 1 hour and costs 5,750 ptas round trip; reserve a day ahead.

SITGES

In Sitges, a small beach resort 36 km (22 mi) south of Barcelona, you can relax on beautiful, quiet beaches by day and join the frenetic hedonists on their bar-and-disco route by night. There are fine beaches all along the main Passeig Marítim, but if you prefer a bit more seclusion, walk up behind the church and city hall to the smaller **Platja de Sant Sebastià**; continue 2 km (1⅓ mi) south to **Platja del Muerto** for sunbathing in the buff. Carrer Primer de Maig, dubbed "The Street of Sin," is packed with bars; all night long the tanned masses parade hither and yon while music thumps in the background. Carrer San Francisco and Carrer San Buenaventura are also great troves of bars and clubs, whether straight, mixed, or gay. If you're here in late February, you'll soon learn that **Carnaval,** in Sitges, is one of the wildest anywhere; it's like a miniature Rio de Janeiro, with nonstop partying and lots of men in high-style drag.

Trains from Barcelona's Estació Sants to Sitges take half an hour and cost 300 ptas. The **train station** (Pl. E. Maristany, tel. 93/894–98–89) is a 10-minute walk north from the center of town and the beach. The **oficina de turisme** (C. Sínia Morera 1, tel. 93/811–76–30; open July–mid-Sept., daily 9–9; off-season, weekdays 9–2 and 4–6:30, Sat. 10–1) is down the hill (west on C. Salvador Mirabent Paretas) as you exit the station.

WHERE TO SLEEP AND EAT

Cheap lodging can be scarce in July and August, when most rates jump by about 500 ptas. Your best bet is to scour the streets in the center of town; from the oficina de turisme, head down Passeig de Vilafranca. **Hostal Casa Bella** (Av. Artur Carbonell 12, tel. 93/894–32–43; low-season doubles 5,500 ptas) has rooms reminiscent of summer camp: spartan, yet homey. You can also find affordable digs at **Hostal Internacional** (Carrer Sant Francesc 52, tel. 93/894–26–90), which has low-season doubles for 4,500 ptas (5,000 ptas with bath). Camp at **El Rocà** (Av. de Ronda s/n, tel. 93/894–00–43) for 575 ptas per site plus 575 ptas per person (585 ptas July and August), or at **Sitges** (Carretera Comarcal 246, km 38, tel. 93/894–10–80) for 600 ptas per site plus 525 ptas per person (675 ptas per site plus 550 ptas per person July and August). The cozy **Bar Barón** (C. Sant Gaudenci 17, no phone; closed daily 3–6 and mid-Dec.–mid-Jan.) is a good spot for *bocadillos* (350 ptas), tapas (350 ptas–500 ptas), and a cup of *malvasìa* (sweet cherry wine; 225 ptas). For a real meal, head to **La Vina** (C. Sant Francesc 11, tel. 93/811–01–25), where combo platters are 550 ptas–1,000 ptas.

AROUND CATALONIA

Don't limit your stay in Catalonia to Barcelona; this autonomous region has other charms. Its Mediterranean beaches have drawn travelers for thousands of years—the Greeks were here a good 2,000 years ago and left behind fascinating ruins at **Empúries.** Wherever the Greeks went the Romans were sure to follow, and cities like **Tarragona** offer impressive evidence of their civilization as well. If hiking is your bag, head to the spectacular Pyrenees mountain range; for information on the Catalan Pyrenees, *see* the Pyrenees *in* Northern Spain, *below.*

COSTA BRAVA

This rugged stretch of coastline between the French border and Barcelona is Catalonia's most overvisited attraction. The hotel-building spree of the 1960s may have marred the natural beauty of the more established resorts, but fear not; a number of small fishing villages have successfully maintained their traditional appearance.

PORT BOU

A tiny fishing village before the international rail barreled through in 1878, Port Bou, which nudges the French border, still has some of that old-fashioned flavor. Here you can enjoy characteristic Costa Brava scenery—small, pebbly cove beaches encased by dramatic cliffs—without having to share it with too many tourists. Hourly trains connect Port Bou with Barcelona's Estació França (2–3 hrs, 2,000 ptas). The **train station** (tel. 972/39–00–99 for RENFE information) sits above the town; head down any street from the station and you'll end up downtown. When you reach Carrer Miguel Cabre, turn left and you'll run into the **tourist-office kiosk** (Pg. Lluis Companys, tel. 972/12–51–61; open mid-June–mid-Sept., daily 9–2 and 3–8), where you can get a map of the town and surrounding area. Passeig Sardana, the beach boardwalk, is just to the right.

WHERE TO SLEEP AND EAT

Fortunately, lodging in Port Bou is less expensive than in some of the showier beach resorts. **Hostal Juventus** (Av. Barcelona 3, tel. 972/39–02–41), just half a block off Passeig Sardana, has large, airy doubles for 3,500 ptas. The cheaper **Hostal Comercio** (Rambla Catalunya 16, tel. 972/39–00–01) is also near the boardwalk but isn't as nice. In July and August, doubles are 3,750 ptas (3,850 ptas with bath); off season, doubles are 3,250 ptas (3,500 ptas with bath). On the boardwalk, you'll find cafés and restaurants with cheap *menús del día* (about 1,000 ptas); hordes of waiters serve up tasty food at **Restaurant Espanya** (Pg. de la Sardana 4, tel. 972/39–00–08). For cheaper fare and quiet tapas bars, head up Carrer Miguel Cabre and veer left. **Bodega Antonio** (Federico Marés 14, tel. 972/12–52–33) serves tasty *sepia* (fried cuttlefish with spices) for 500 ptas.

FIGUERES

The spirit of Figueres's favorite son, Salvador Dalí (1904–1989), permeates life in this pleasant, relatively unvisited town. In 1974 the artist opened the **Teatre-Museu Dalí** (Pl. Gala-Salvador Dalí 5, tel. 972/51–18–00; open July–Sept., daily 9–7:15; shorter hrs off season) on the site where he held his first public exhibition in 1918. One of the most popular museums in all of Spain, it's a fantastical building full of the whimsical and macabre. Admission to the museum in the high season (July–Sept.) is 1,300 ptas; off season it's 900 ptas. During the high season, you can also come at night for 1,200 ptas (daily 8 PM–midnight). Also worth a visit is the **Castle Sant Ferran,** where Dalí did his time in the military. You can't go inside, but the views from the hill are wonderful.

BASICS

The **American Express office** is at **Viatges Figueres** (C. Perelada 28, tel. 972/50–91–00; open Mon.– Sat. 9–1 and 5–8). Just past the Rambla, up Carrer Lasuca, you'll find the well-stocked **oficina de**

turisme (Pl. del Sol, tel. 972/50–31–55; open weekdays 8:30 AM–9 PM, Sat. 9–1:30 and 3:30–9 in summer; shorter hrs off season), and behind it the **post office** (postal code 17600) and **telefónico** office.

COMING AND GOING

Figueres is the transfer point for most Costa Brava destinations, as well as the gateway to the Pyrenees. Unfortunately, bus service is somewhat infrequent and connections are ill-timed; plan accordingly. The train and bus stations are a 15-minute walk from the town center. From the stations, go straight up Carrer Sant Llàtzer to Carrer Nou and turn right toward the Rambla and the museum. The **train station** (tel. 972/50–31–55, or tel. 972/50–46–61 for RENFE information) sends trains to Barcelona (2 hrs, 1,250 ptas) and Port Bou (½ hr, 350 ptas). The **bus station** (tel. 972/30–06–23; luggage storage 350 ptas) is just west of the train station. **SARFA** (tel. 972/67–42–98) runs buses to Barcelona (1½ hrs, 1,500 ptas), Cadaqués (1½ hrs, 650 ptas), and other Costa Brava destinations. **Teisa** (rel. 972/50–31–75) has buses to Olot (1 hr, 750 ptas) and connections to Ripoll (45 min, 430 ptas from Olot). Purchase RENFE tickets in town at **Viajes dal Sol** (C. Lasauca 20, tel. 972/50–86–00; open weekdays 9–1:30 and 4–8, Sat. 9–1:30 and 5–8).

WHERE TO SLEEP AND EAT

The best options for budget travelers are on the streets around the Dalí museum. There are two cheap hotels right off Carrer del Castell: **Pensión Mallol** (C. Pep Ventura 9, tel. 972/50–22–83), with large, nicely tiled doubles for 3,250 ptas; and, next door, **Hostal La Venta del Toro** (C. Pep Ventura 5, tel. 972/51–05–10), with sparse but clean doubles for 2,900 ptas. Splurge on the **Hotel Los Angeles** (C. Barceloneta 10, tel. 972/51–06–61; doubles 4,400 ptas, 5,450 ptas in Aug.) if big bathrooms, comfy beds, and Dalí prints in the hallway sound appealing. The centrally located **HI hostel** (C. Anicet Pagès 2, tel. 972/50–12–13, fax 972/67–38–08; beds with breakfast 2,400 ptas, 1,750 ptas under age 26; closed Oct.–mid-Nov. and Christmas) has a midnight curfew,

At night, go to L'Hostal, a bar on Passeig Marítim, and try to imagine the scene on that night sometime in the '70s when Dalí brought Mick Jagger in for a drink.

but the doors open for 10 minutes on every hour between 1 AM and 4 AM. Cheap restaurants line Carrer de la Jonquera, behind the museum. The **Costa Brava Grill** (C. de la Jonquera 10, tel. 972/50–00–75; open daily 11–11) serves tasty paella for 1,100 ptas.

EMPURIES

A 45-minute bus ride from Figueres takes you back in time to ancient Empúries, or at least to what's left of it. Greek sailors first set up camp here in Emporion ("market" in Greek) early in the 6th century BC, but less than 500 years later the Romans came to town, took it over, and built their own bustling city above it. The Romans ultimately gained control of this entire strip of Mediterranean coastline and dotted it with thriving cities and trading posts. While some of these—like Barcino (Barcelona) and Tarraco (Tarragona)—became fat and prosperous, old Empriae was abandoned by the 3rd century AD. Now you can stroll around the well-preserved archaeological **ruins** (open daily 10–6, until 8 Apr.–Sept.) of both the Greek and the Roman cities and visit the on-site **museum** (admission to ruins and museum 500 ptas; open daily 10–2 and 3–7 in summer; shorter hrs off season), which contains such everyday items as medical instruments, jewelry, and ceramics. The ruins are on a fine sandy beach with pine trees and a promenade leading to another former Greek colony, **Sant Martí D'Empúries,** a 20-minute walk away. With beautiful, ivy-covered stone buildings, this is now a walled village with a group of bars and restaurants centered around the Plaza Major. **Bar Casa Coll** (tel. 972/77–09–81; open Mar.–Oct., daily 8 AM–1 AM), is one of the cheaper ones, serving tasty grilled sardines for 650 ptas. If you want to sleep near the ruins, there's a **youth hostel** (Los Coves 41, tel. 972/77–12–00; beds with breakfast 2,275 ptas, 1,700 ptas under age 26) right on the beach; reserve a month ahead in summer. You can rent a bike at the hostel (500 ptas per hr, 1,350 ptas per half-day) and pedal the road from the beach to Sant Martí. Most of the road from Empúries is lit at night, but the roads to the hostel and the boardwalk are not; bring a flashlight. To get to Empúries from Figueres, take the bus toward L'Escala (545 ptas) and ask the driver to drop you off at "la cruz de las ruinas," a two-minute walk from the hostel.

CADAQUES

A picturesque town of whitewashed houses and cobblestone streets, Cadaqués is a place to savor both natural beauty and the legacies of Dalí, Picasso (who lived here briefly in 1911 while developing his

ANDORRA

Andorra is a tiny principality of 62,000 people and approximately 190 square mi, squeezed into the scenic Pyrenees mountains on the border between France and Spain. Its official language is Catalan, but most residents also speak Castilian and French. Andorra first celebrated independence when it was liberated from the Moors in the early 9th century. In the 13th century, Andorra was divided between the Spanish bishops of Urgel and the French counts of Foix. Today it remains under the dual suzerainty of France and the Bishop of Urgell, though it has its own constitution and government. Apart from its ski resorts and mountainous terrain, Andorra's claim to fame is its shopping—it levies virtually no taxes on luxury items such as booze, cigarettes, perfume, and electronic gear, and thus has a cheesy shopping district in its capital, Andorra la Vella. Fortunately, the older part of the capital has been spared much of the madness, and a walk through this quarter gives you an idea of what was, until recently, a charming little town.

You can stay in Andorra la Vella, but frequent buses journey to the less developed towns of Ordino, Canillo, and El Serrat, all just 20 minutes away, and all good bases for hiking the Pyrenees. In the capital, most cheap lodging is centered on the main streets of Avinguda Meritxell and its continuation, Avinguda Princep Benlloch. Just off Plaça Guillemó, where the bus from La Seu d'Urgell drops you off, is Residència Benazet (C. la Llacuna 19, tel. 376/82–06–98), whose bright doubles (2,600 ptas) have lacy curtains and firm beds.

With its jagged mountains, verdant hills, and wild rivers, Andorra offers great hiking. Get trail maps and tips on lodging, mountain biking, skiing, fishing, and rock climbing from the main tourist office (C. Dr. Vilanova, tel. 376/82–02–14) in Andorra la Vella. The travel agency Viatges Relax (C. Roc dels Escolls 12, tel. 376/82–20–44) offers AmEx services. You can reach Andorra by bus from Barcelona (4 hrs, 2,750 ptas) with the Alsina-Graells bus company (Av. Riberaygua, Andorra la Vella, tel. 376/82–73–79) and from La Seu (½ hr, 450 ptas) with La Hispano-Andorrana (Av. Sta. Coloma 85–87, Andorra La Vella, tel. 376/82–13–72). To reach the tourist office from the central bus station, walk west on Avinguda de Tarragona, cross the bridge, then turn right on Carrer Doctor Vilanova and continue up the hill.

Cubist style), and García Lorca. The beach here is small and pebbly, but the hiking around the coast and in the surrounding hills is excellent. Dalí groupies should pay a visit to his house (soon to be converted into a museum), about 1 km (⅔ mi) northeast in Port Lligat. Also worth a stop is the **Museu Perrot Moore** (C. Vigilant, tel. 972/25–80–76; admission 750 ptas; open Mon.–Sat. 10:30–1:30 and 4:30–8:30, Sun. 10:30–1:30 in summer; shorter hrs off season), boasting Dalí's earliest painting, completed when he was 8 years old, as well as 42 studies and sketches for Picasso's famous painting *Guernica*. Cadaqués's **oficina de turisme** (C. Cotxe 2, tel. 972/25–83–15; open Mon.–Sat. 10–1 and 4–7 in summer; shorter hrs off season), just off Plaça de Federico Rahola, has maps, accommodation lists, and information on scuba diving. There's no train service to Cadaqués, but **SARFA** (C. Sants Vicens, tel. 972/25–87–13) runs three daily buses (five daily mid-July–Aug.) to Figueres (1 hr, 550 ptas). The bus stop is a five-minute walk from the center, just off Avenida Roses, the main road into town.

WHERE TO SLEEP AND EAT

Finding a cheap room in the high season can be tough—call at least a month ahead in July and August. If everything's booked when you get here, ask a local shopkeeper about rooms for rent. Try the 3,500-pta doubles (3,750 ptas July–Aug.) at the small, family-run **Fonda Encarna** (C. Tórtola 5, tel. 972/25–80–19), or the 4,500-pta doubles at the centrally located **Hostal Cristina** (C. Riera, at the Plaça de Federico Rahola, tel. 972/25–81–38). The steep 20-minute hike up to **Camping Cadaqués** (tel. 972/25–81–26; reception open daily 10–1:30 and 4–9) is worth it; for 700 ptas per site plus 575 ptas per person, you can use the pool to your heart's content. From the bus stop, walk toward town, turn left on Sol d'Engirol just before the gas station, then keep walking uphill and follow the signs to the campground. Once you've stashed your pack, take a walk along Carrer Miguel Roset, a small street that runs one block behind Passeig Marítim and has a number of cheap eateries. Or, for delicious *platos combinados* (950 ptas), try **Restaurant ix!** (C. Horta Sanés 1, tel. 972/25–87–33), just east of the crowded waterfront restaurants.

TARRAGONA

South of Barcelona and the popular Costa Brava resorts, the oft-overlooked Tarragona is a former Roman stronghold with some well-preserved Roman ruins, a pretty beach, and a massive and magnificent cathedral. Ancient Roman sites are clustered in the upper part of town, bordered by the remains of Roman walls on three sides, while the newer section of town, the beach, and the port spread out below.

To do as the Romans did, visit the **Amfiteatre** (Parc del Miracle, tel. 977/24–25–79; admission 500 ptas; open June–Sept., Tues.–Sat. 9–8, Sun. 9–3; Oct.–May, Tues.–Sat. 10–1 and 3–7, Sun. 10–2). It dates from the 1st century AD and affords fine views of **Platja Miracle,** Tarragona's main beach. Dating from the 1st–3rd centuries AD, the mosaics at the **Museu Arquelógic** (Pl. del Rei 5, tel. 977/23–62–09; admission 400 ptas; open June–Sept., Tues.–Sat. 10–1 and 4:30–8, Sun. 10–2; shorter hrs off season) are well worth a peek. The **Museu d'Art Modern** (C. Santa Anna 8, tel. 977/23–50–32; admission 100 ptas; open Tues.–Sat. 10–8, Sun. 11–2) holds neoclassical sculptures by Catalan artist Julio Antonio, as well as a large, multicolor tapestry by Joan Miró, a thank-you note to the Tarragona Red Cross for their help when Miró's daughter was in a car accident here. The **Catedral** (Pl. de la Seu, tel. 977/23–86–85; admission 400 ptas; open July–mid-Oct., Mon.–Sat. 10–7; shorter hrs off season) is a magnificent hulking monster designed in a mix of architectural styles. Inside, the chapels are elaborately decorated, and tapestries hang in the naves. Check out the big, bad organ, one of the largest in Catalonia.

BASICS

Get free maps at the **Oficina de Turisme de la Generalitat** (C. Fortuny 4, just off Rambla Nova, tel. 977/23–34–15; open daily 9–3 and 4–7) or the satellite office at Carrer Major 39 (tel. 977/24–50–64; open July–Sept., Mon.–Sat. 9:30–8:30, Sun. 9:30–2; shorter hrs off season). Do your postal duties at the **post office** (Pl. Corsini; open weekdays 8:30–8:30, Sat. 9:30–2; postal code 43001). You can exchange money at the **banks** and **bureaux de change** lining La Rambla; banks have slightly better rates but usually charge a commission of 500 ptas.

COMING AND GOING

Frequent trains arrive from Barcelona (1½ hrs, 825 ptas) and Valencia (3 hrs, 2,575 ptas); the **train station** (Pg. d'Espanya, tel. 977/24–02–02) is a 10-minute walk southeast of Rambla Nova. There's a bus stop to your left as you exit the station. The main **bus station** (Pl. Imperial Tárraco, tel. 977/22–91–26) serves Barcelona (1½ hrs, 950 ptas) and Valencia (3 hrs, 2,410 ptas) daily; from here, you can walk to the hostel or take Bus 9 to Rambla Vella, in the heart of town.

GETTING AROUND

Most sights are clustered in and around the old part of the city. The Circular A and Circular B buses circle the city, stopping at the train and bus stations, the port area of El Serrallo, and Rambla Nova. To get to the beach, walk a short distance down Via Augusta from Rambla Viella, or take Bus 9 or 1. Most buses (100 ptas) run until about 10:30 PM in the high season (July–Sept.), until 9:30 off season.

WHERE TO SLEEP

Budget lodging is concentrated in front of the train station and in the old part of town around Plaça de la Font. A five-minute walk from the train station, off Carrer Barcelona, is **Habitaciones Mariflor** (C. General Contreras 29, tel. 977/23–82–31), where doubles are 3,300 ptas in the high season, 2,600 ptas off season. Though not in the most picturesque part of town, the small rooms (doubles 3,500 ptas) at **Pensión Marsal** (Pl. de la Font 26, tel. 977/22–40–69) have ceiling fans and bathrooms, and some even overlook the plaza. Reminiscent of a vacation resort, **Sant Jordi Hostel (HI)** (Av. President L. Companys 5, at C. Marquès de Guad-el-Jelu, tel. 977/24–01–95) has dorm beds with breakfast (Apr.–Aug. 2,275 ptas, 1,700 ptas under age 25; off season 1,950 ptas, 1,475 ptas under age 25). Curfew is 11 PM, but doors open on the hour throughout the night. To get to the hostel, walk northwest up Avinguda President L. Companys from Plaça Imperial Tárraco. You can **camp** north of the city along the beach. **Tárraco** (C-340, tel. 977/23–99–89; 600 ptas per person; closed Oct.–Mar.), 2 km (1 mi) north of town, is the closest; take Bus 1 or 9 to La Playa Rabassada.

FOOD

There aren't many inexpensive restaurants in Tarragona, but a few cheapies dot the streets leading away from the train station. A bunch of restaurants in the port neighborhood of El Serallo serve the fresh catch of the day at moderate prices. Try the unmarked **El Varado** (corner of C. Santa Andreu and C. Trafalgar, no phone) for delicious *pulpito en salsa* (octopus; 950 ptas). Closer to the center of town, **Cafe Cantonada** (C. de Reding 16, at C. de Fortuny, tel. 977/21–35–24; closed Sun. in July and Aug.) serves up *menús del día* (1,000 ptas) and *chocolate con churros* (450 ptas). Plaça de la Font, just above Rambla Vella, yields cheaper options. Try the café **Can Peret** (Pl. de la Font 6, tel. 977/23–76–25; closed Sun. and daily 3:30–6) for scrumptious croissants (150 ptas). Join Tarragona's beautiful people for a drink at **El Cau** (C. del Trinquet Vell 2, just off Pl. de la Font, no phone), a Roman-era underground cave-turned-bar.

BALEARIC ISLANDS

For most Europeans, the Balearic Islands represent the height of hedonistic vacationing. The natives don't take much offense at this narrow perception of their islands, as the summer disruption brings in big bucks. But after the mass exodus of tourists every September, prices go down, bars close, and the islanders take refuge once more in their intimate seashore communities. Los Baleares form an autonomous Spanish province, where the islanders' version of Catalán, the language that dominated before Franco banned its use, is rapidly replacing Castellano. All the islands share the same near-perfect Mediterranean climate—warm with lovely sea breezes—and arguably the prettiest beaches in Spain. **Ibiza** is the wildest and most expensive of the four islands. Cross-dressers, hippies, the too-cool, the utterly normal, and all others meet on the streets of Ibiza's main town every night. Off Ibiza's southern tip, **Formentera** is the smallest and most isolated island, with spectacular beaches and nature trails. Palma, the capital of the archipelago, is on **Mallorca,** the largest, best-known, and most heavily visited of the islands. **Menorca,** the easternmost island, has the sedate charm of a place not yet fully discovered.

Your greatest challenge as a traveler to the Balearic Islands is finding a place to stay. Rooms are sometimes booked weeks in advance, and even if they're available, you'll have to pay through the nose. The rugged traveler will rent a moped and crash on a deserted beach. Camping in unofficial campsites is forbidden, but in practice few people ever get shooed away from obscure beaches. Your second-greatest challenge is transportation between islands and to the mainland; the small number of ferry companies conspire to keep prices high. Flying is a little more expensive, but the 25-minute flights beat the slow, uncomfortable ferry rides.

IBIZA

Everything you've heard about Ibiza's decadent partying is probably true. But look beyond the flashing lights and you'll find that the island offers more than just intense nightlife. Picturesque hiking trails twist along hillsides, and peaceful villages overlook the chaotic tourist meccas. For travelers who want to get their feet wet, Ibiza (known locally as Eivissa) presents ample opportunities, from diving to sailing; get information at the tourist office (*see below*).

The best way to escape the madness of the town of **Ibiza** is to hop on a bus to the tranquility of the island's endless stretches of sand. The nearest beaches are **Playa d'En Bossa** and **Ses Salines**; further away, the beach at **Santa Eulàlia** (northeast of Ibiza) is lined with hotels but is not nearly as frenetic or developed as the resort of **Sant Antoni de Portmany,** on the west coast. **Portinatx,** along the island's north coast, is a series of small coves with sandy beaches, of which the first and last, Cala Xarraca and Caló d'Es Porcs, are the best. If you tire of the crowds at any of these places, you can hop on a boat that circles the island and hop off at any beach along the way—some are only accessible by water. Boats leave from the ferry port in Ibiza, and most companies charge around 1,000 ptas one way.

BASICS

Ibiza Town greets visitors with a **tourist office** (Pg. de Vara del Rey 13, tel. 971/30–19–00; open weekdays 9:30–1:30 and 5–7, until 8 July and Aug., Sat. 10:30–1) and an **American Express office** (C. Vicente Cuervo 9, tel. 971/31–11–11; open weekdays 9–1:30 and 4:30–8, Sat. 9–1).

COMING AND GOING

Trasmediterránea (Estación Marítima, at the port, tel. 971/31–50–50) ferries serve Barcelona (3–6/week, 8 hrs, 6,300 ptas), Valencia (5/week, 8 hrs, 4,400 ptas), and Palma (1/week, 5 hrs, 3,150 ptas). Also at the port, **Trasmapi-Sercomisa-Flebasa** (Puerto Marítimo, tel. 971/31–40–05) has about 15 daily ferries to Formentera (1 hr, 1,350 ptas) and two weekly ferries to Dénia, north of Alicante (8 hrs, 3,500 ptas with 48 hrs' advance purchase; otherwise 5,475 ptas). **Inserco** (C. del Carmen, next to Estación Marítima, tel. 971/31–11–57) serves Formentera several times daily (1 hr, 1,100 ptas). The two major carriers at Ibiza's **airport** (tel. 971/30–03–00) are **Iberia/Aviaco** (tel. 971/30–03–00) and **Lufthansa/Condor** (tel. 971/30–33–90). An hourly bus connects the airport to Ibiza Town (15 min, 105 ptas); catch it a block east of the bus station on Avinguda Isidoro Macàbich.

GETTING AROUND

If you're planning to disco- or beach-hop, rent a bike (1,200 ptas), scooter (2,900 ptas), or car (4,600 ptas) for the day at **Extra Rent** (Av. Santa Eulàlia 27, tel. 971/19–17–17); buses and ferries can get expensive and are often overcrowded. If you opt for public transport, several bus companies operate out of the small station on Avinguda Isidoro Macàbich. **H.F. Vilas** (tel. 971/31–21–17) goes to local beaches (250 ptas) such as Santa Eulàlia and Portinax. **Autobuses San Antonio** (tel. 971/31–20–75) runs a 24-hour "Disco Bus" (225 ptas) with hourly service to San Antonio and Playa d'En Bossa.

WHERE TO SLEEP AND EAT

Reservations are a must in the summer—book a month ahead July–September, two weeks ahead April–June. On the streets just parallel to Passeig de Vara de Rey are a number of *casas de huéspedes,* identifiable by the standard blue sign with the cH. The nice man who owns **La Peña** (C. de la Virgen 76, tel. 971/19–02–40; doubles 2,900 ptas; open May–Oct.) is proud of his large rooms, some of which have balconies. Another place right in the thick of things is **Hostal La Marina** (Andenes del Puerto 4, tel. 971/31–01–72; doubles 3,200–4,700 ptas; open June–Aug.), sporting firm beds in clean rooms, some overlooking the harbor, others facing the wild street scene. The popular backpacker hangout **Hostal Residencia Sol y Brisa** (Av. Bartolomé Vicente Ramón 15, tel. 971/31–08–18) has comfortable doubles (4,000 ptas June–Sept., 3,000 ptas Oct.–May).

There is no shortage of fast-food places in the old town, south of the marina. For regional specialties (500 ptas–700 ptas), go to **Bar San Juan** (C. Montgri 8, tel. 971/31–07–66; closed daily 3:15–8); try the *greixonera* (a creamy cheese pastry; 150 ptas) for dessert. The busy **Restaurant Victoria** (C. Riambau 1, off Av. Ramón y Tur, tel. 971/31–06–22; closed Mon.–Sat. 4–8:30 and Sun.) serves tasty entrées (500 ptas–700 ptas). The big, indoor **Mercado Ibiza** (C. Extremadura; open weekdays 7–2, Sat. 7–3) is near the bus station, south of Avinguda Isidoro Macàbich.

AFTER DARK

If you're easily turned off by wanton displays of wealth, flesh, and sequins, Ibiza may not be the place for you. If not, tease your hair, squeeze into that slinky skirt (girls *and* guys), and hit the streets. The first thing everyone does here is go to the bars. From 10 PM to midnight, the old town/marina area is jam-packed with people clinging to tables and checking each other out. Most bars see a very mixed crowd. **Liberty Bar** (Pl. Gradigo 12, no phone), a British-owned hole-in-the-wall near the lighthouse at the eastern end of the marina, plays a good selection of modern rock. At around 2 AM, people head for the discos. These charge roughly 4,000 ptas for admission, but if you pick up discount coupons in bars you can save a few pesetas; any number of slick, young hawkers plant themselves outside the bars along the marina to dole out these cards, which usually throw in the first drink for free (expect to pay at least 1,000 ptas per drink after that). The big five discos are: **Pachà** (Paseo Marítimo, Ibiza, tel. 971/31–09–59), **Amnesia** (Carretera San Antonio, tel. 971/19–80–41), **Es Paradis Terreneal** (Av. Dr. Fleming, tel. 971/34–66–00), **Discoteca Anfora** (Carrer Sant Carles 5, tel. 971/30–28–93), and **Privilege** (Carretera San Antoni, tel. 971/19–81–60). All of these are on the Disco Bus line—except Pachà, which is a 20-minute walk north of the Estación Marítima—and all are replete with fly girls and guys, bizarre murals, and great sound and lights. Calle de la Virgen has a cluster of gay bars, including **JJ Bar** (C. de la Virgen 79; open May–Oct.) and **Bar Teatro** (C. de la Virgen 83; open May–Sept.).

NEAR IBIZA

FORMENTERA

Just 30 km (18 mi) south of Ibiza is the tiny, unassuming island of Formentera, home to only about 500 permanent residents. Less than 20 km (12 mi) from east to west, Formentera makes a perfect day trip. The main port is **La Savina,** at the north end of the island; ferries from Ibiza come every hour (1 hr, 1,250 ptas), hydrofoils every two hours (½ hr, 1,800 ptas). Buy your ticket on board. The **oficina de turismo** (Edificio Junta Puertos, tel. 971/32–20–57; open weekdays 10–2 and 5–7, Sat. 10–2) is at the port. The best way to get around the island is by bike, but if you're not up for the hills, rent a moped. Several outfits in front of the port, including **Moto Rent Mirada** (tel. 971/32–83–29), rent bikes (400 ptas–1,000 ptas) and mopeds (1,000 ptas–2,000 ptas). **Autocares Paya** (tel. 971/32–30–85) runs the sole, infrequent bus service around the island. Take diving lessons or rent equipment at the **Vellmarí Diving Centre** (Av. del Mediterraneo 90, tel. 971/32–21–05; open weekdays 10–2 and 5–7, Sat. 10–2).

MALLORCA

The grand island of Mallorca attracts a hodgepodge of visitors—from the Germans, who rent homes in villages in the north and west, to the British, who descend on the west-coast town of Peguera, to the French, who flood the port town of Alcúdia. Visitors to this horse-head–shaped island eventually wind up in the capital city of **Palma,** whose old town, despite the general hustle and bustle, maintains an air of antiquity. The impressive Gothic **cathedral** (C. Palau Reial; admission 400 ptas; open weekdays 10–6, Sat. 10–2:30) is notable for its lack of a *coro,* the standard choir found in the center of Spanish cathedrals, and also for the striking detail work by Antoni Gaudí.

Tourists may outnumber inhabitants in Palma during the summer, but you can easily escape to a remote beach or trail when the crowd becomes a bit much. The tourist offices (*see below*) have information on water activities and scenic hikes, including the difficult but breathtaking 10-km (6 mi) trek through the mountains that once inspired Chopin. To reach the trailhead, take the **Bus Nort Balear** (C. Arxiduc Lluis Salvador, north of Pl. Espanya, tel. 971/20–21–25) line to the Valldemossa bus stop (40 min, 175 ptas), walk 80 ft further along the crazy, winding road, and look closely for the marked trail to Deía off to the right.

BASICS

There are two principal **tourist offices** in Palma, one in the Plaça Espanya (tel. 971/71–15–278), the other at Carrer Sant Domingo 11 (tel. 971/72–40–90). Both provide free maps and accommodation lists and are open weekdays 9–8, Saturday 9–1:30. There's an **American Express office** (Pg. d'es Born 16, tel. 971/72–67–43; open weekdays 9–1:30 and 4:30–7:30, Sat. 9:30–1) in Viajes Iberia.

COMING AND GOING

Most people come here by air, since plane fares are comparable to (or even cheaper than) ferry tickets. **Iberia/Aviaco** (tel. 971/716410) has daily flights between Palma's airport (tel. 971/26–46–56) and Barcelona (7,500 ptas), Madrid (7,950 ptas), Valencia (7,500 ptas), Ibiza (5,900 ptas), and Mahón (5,300 ptas). Bus 17 (½ hr, 265 ptas) runs between Palma's airport and the bus station at Plaça Espanya. **Trasmediterránea** (Estación Marítima 2, tel. 971/40–50–14) runs ferries to Mallorca from Barcelona (7–10/week, 9 hrs, 6,300 ptas), Valencia (6/week, 8 hrs, 6,300 ptas), and Ibiza (2/week, 6 hrs, 3,200 ptas). From the ferry terminal, take Bus 1 to Plaça Reina and cheap lodging.

GETTING AROUND

Buses are the cheapest way to explore Mallorca. **Transports a Palma** (tel. 971/71–13–93) runs local buses (165 ptas, 750 ptas for a 10-ride Bonobus ticket) from Plaça Espanya; ask the tourist office for information on bus service around the island. Mallorca has two railway lines, one a modern metropolitan train to the leather-industry town of **Inca** (40 min, 235 ptas), the other an antique wooden train that winds through the mountains to **Sóller** (1½ hrs, 380 ptas). Both services come and go from the railroad station at Plaça Espanya. The train ride to Soller is particularly beautiful, whisking you through mountain gorges and fruit orchards. If you want to rent a car, the cheapest rates are at **Hasso** (Av. Bartolomé Riutort 100, tel. 971/26–10–05), in Ca'n Pastilla, 15 minutes east of Palma on Bus 100. Prices start at 2,550 ptas per day, but rates are lower if you rent for more than four days or pay in cash up front. Reserve a week ahead for the best selection.

WHERE TO SLEEP

As on the other islands, your biggest challenge is finding cheap lodging. The few cheap *hostales* in Palma are just west of Plaça Reina, in the narrow lanes of the old town. **Hostal Pons** (C. General Barceló 8, tel. 971/72–26–58; doubles 3,000 ptas–4,000 ptas) has huge antique beds and a bizarre but friendly, Spanish, Fawlty Towers–esque staff. The British proprietress at the **Hostal Ritzi** (C. Apuntadores 6, tel. 971/71–46–10) charges 3,300 ptas–4,500 ptas for roomy doubles and will also fix a full English breakfast for 600 ptas. Splurge on the large, well-furnished rooms—some with balconies—at **Hostal Brondo** (C. Brondo 1, off Pl. Rei Joan Carles I, tel. 971/71–90–43); doubles are 3,800 ptas mid-July–October, 3,500 ptas off season. The only HI hostel on the island is near the beach, a 20-minute bus ride southeast of Palma, and usually full; take Bus 15 from Plaça Espanya to **Playa de Palma** (C. Costa Brava 13, tel. 971/26–08–92; beds 1,200 ptas). Take the Port Alcúdia bus from Plaça Espanya to the campground **Club Picafort** (Carretera Artá–Puerto Alcúdia, km 23.4, tel. 971/53–78–63), where sites are 2,375 ptas plus 525 ptas per person, or drive to the cheaper **Club San Pedro** (Cala dels Camps, Colonia San Pedro, tel. 971/58–90–23; open mid-Apr.–mid-Oct.), where sites are 1,350 ptas plus 550 ptas per person.

FOOD

Finding tasty food, on the other hand, is no problem—just remember that most restaurants close at midnight. West of Plaça Reina, calles Apuntadores and Vallseca are rife with restaurants of all shapes and sizes. For a slice of the good life without a big slice to your wallet, head to **Giovanini Pizzería** (C. Apuntadores 4, tel. 971/72–85–89; closed Tues.); try the fiery Diablo Pizza (850 ptas). For excellent tapas (175 ptas–275 ptas), stop in at the friendly bar **Pica Pica** (C. Dels Paraires 21, tel. 971/71–00–86). For a little more money, try the fresh, delicious food at **La Cueva** (C. Apuntadores 5, tel. 971/72–44–22; closed daily 3:30–7:30), where 1,000 ptas will get you a huge, scrumptious combo platter of *raciones* like *boquerones vinagre* (fresh, anchovylike fish), *calamares salsa* (squid in tomato sauce), or *champignons al ajillo* (garlic mushrooms). Buy supplies at **Supermercado SYP** (C. Bonaire 6, off Av. Jaime III; open weekdays 9–2 and 5:30–8:30, Sat. 5:30–8:30).

AFTER DARK

Pop into Palma's **Centre de Cultura** (C. Concepció 12, tel. 971/72–52–10) for free nightly poetry readings, concerts, and other arty events starting at 8 PM. Near the marina, the bars and clubs along **Passeig de Sagrera**, between Plaça Llotja and Plaça Reina, get crowded around midnight. Try the laid-back **Blues Ville** (C. Ma d'es Moro 3, off C. Apuntadores) for nightly live blues and soul; there's no cover, but drinks are about 400 ptas during the shows. Poke your head into **Abaco** (C. Sant Joan 1, tel. 971/71–49–39) to gawk at the opulence within: candelabras, marble columns, and rich, tanned people sipping pricey drinks.

MENORCA

Not long ago, word got out that Menorca was an isolated paradise, and every middle-class British family with a few pounds to spare got on the next plane south. By August, the locals in **Mahón** (the east-coast capital town also known as **Maó**) and **Ciutadella** (the west coast's largest town) tend to be pretty fed up with English-speaking guests. If you know any Spanish at all, use it. Package tours notwithstanding, however, Menorca is a relatively quiet haven of small, pretty beaches and quiet country roads. As on all the islands, the best beaches are as far from the towns as possible. If you have a scooter, hit the beaches west of **Fornells,** on the north coast, or those east of **Cala Morell,** in the northwest. Rent a bike for access to **Punta Prima,** the largest of an attractive series of beaches south of Mahón.

VISITOR INFORMATION

Mahón's **tourist office** (tel. 971/36–37–90; open weekdays 9–2 and 5–7, Sat. 9:30–1) is at Plaça Explanada 40, and **American Express** (tel. 971/36–28–45; open weekdays 9–1:30 and 4:30–7:30, Sat. 9–2:30) is at Carrer Nou 35.

COMING AND GOING

Trasmediterránea (tel. 971/36–60–50) ferries go from Mahón to Valencia (15 hrs, 6,300 ptas), Barcelona (11 hrs, 6,300 ptas), and Palma (8 hrs, 3,150 ptas). **Flebasa** (tel. 971/48–00–12) connects Ciutadella to the port of Alcúdia (3½ hrs, 3,245 ptas), on Mallorca. In general, **buses** stick to the main road connecting Mahón and Ciutadella (45 min, 450 ptas); you'll need your own wheels to seek out more remote areas, like the north-coast beaches. The cheapest scooter rentals (about 2,500 ptas per day) are at **Valls** (Pl. Espanya 13, tel. 971/36–28–39, fax 971/35–42–39); call two days before you arrive for the best selection. You can rent sturdy mountain bikes from **Just Bicicletas** (C. Infanta 19, at the Hostal Orsi, tel. 971/36–47–51) for 800 ptas per day, or 2,250 ptas for three days.

WHERE TO SLEEP AND EAT

Finding a place to stay in Mahón can be a challenge, especially if you arrive without a reservation. The best affordable place is the inviting **Hostal Residencia Orsi** (C. Infanta 19, tel. 971/36–47–51; doubles 3,200 ptas–3,800 ptas), run by an incredibly helpful British couple. At **Hostal La Isla** (C. Santa Caterina 4, 4 blocks east of Pl. de la Miranda, tel. 971/26–31–51) doubles with bath are 4,000 ptas in the summer, 3,500 ptas off season. There are two official campgrounds: **S'Atalaia** (Carretera Cala Galdana, km 4, tel. 971/37–30–95) and **Torre Soli Nou** (Carretera Torre Soli Nou, km 5, tel. 971/37–27–27). Each charges around 1,000 ptas per night, and both lie just off the main Mahon-Ciutadella road. The Mahon-Cala Galdana bus stops within a kilometer of S'Atalaia, but the Torre Soli Nou site is a hard slog from the main road.

The beige-and-orange cafeteria setting belies the incredible variety of tasty food at **La Tropical** (C. Luna 36, tel. 971/36–05–56), where a whopping plate of sautéed veggies goes for 500 ptas. Pick up groceries at the **mercado** (open Mon.–Sat. 8–1:30) inside the cloister of the church of El Carmen, near Plaza de la Miranda.

NORTHERN SPAIN

Spain's lush and verdant north is dominated by rolling hills that rise up from fields of sunflowers and climax in the stunning Pyrenees, bordering France, and the Picos de Europa, running parallel to the north coast. This is not Spain's most easily traveled region, especially off the beaten path, but its variety makes it worth the effort—dedicated travelers will experience everything from beautiful beaches to pristine mountain trails, from raging bulls in Pamplona to the tranquility of isolated villages, from the political fervor in the Basque provinces to the religious devotion of pilgrims en route to Santiago de Compostela.

THE PYRENEES

The Pyrenees mountains, stretching 450 km (270 mi) from the Atlantic to the Mediterranean, form an imposing natural barrier between Spain and France. Along with other geographical, political, and cul-

tural factors, the Pyrenees have contributed to the Iberian Peninsula's historical tendency toward isolation. Today, rather than isolating Spain, these mountains draw foreigners to some of the best hiking, skiing, and river rafting in Europe. Once here, you'll discover that the fine old monasteries, Romanesque
buildings, and small, friendly towns can be as compelling as the natural beauty. Take time to venture to
Ordesa or Aigüestortes National Parks and Vall d'Aran, all remote but infinitely rewarding sections of the
range. Before hitting the trails, get Editorial Alpina's excellent hiking map (600 ptas), available in most
bookstores in mountain towns and in some tourist offices.

The only drawback to exploring these breathtaking mountains (other than sporadic summer rains) is
getting to, from, and around them. Buses tend to be few and far between, and schedules are erratic; if
you've got the bucks, consider renting a car. The two final rail connections to the Catalan Pyrenees are
Puigcerdà, accessible from Barcelona and France, and La Pobla de Segur, accessible from Lleida. Bus
hubs, of a sort, include La Seu d'Urgell and El Pont de Suert (*see below*).

PUIGCERDA

The furthest mountain stop on the rail from Barcelona is Puigcerdà, the capital of the Cerdanya Valley
and the first Spanish stop on the Toulouse–Barcelona line. The town is on a hill (*puig*, in Catalan; *cerdà*
derives from Cerdanya); the **train station** (tel. 972/88–01–65), unfortunately, is not. If your luggage is
weighty, it's a grim walk up the stairs that lead to town and the **tourist office** (C. Querol, at Pl. Ajuntament, tel. 972/88–05–42; open daily 9–2 and 3–9). If you're stuck here, crash at **Pensió Cerdanya** (C.
Ramon Cosp 7, tel. 972/88–00–10; 2,750 ptas per person, 2,500 ptas off season). Five trains arrive
here daily from Barcelona (3 hrs, 1,140 ptas) via Ripoll (1 hr, 450 ptas). Alsina-Graells **buses** (tel. 973/
35–00–20) depart from the Restaurante Terminus, on Plaça de Barcelona (in front of the train station),
for La Seu d'Urgell (1 hr, 650 ptas) at 7:30 AM, 2:30 PM, and 5:30 PM (Sun. at 5:30 PM only); and for
Lleida (4 hrs, 2,350 ptas) at 2:30 PM. Buses to Puigcerdà leave La Seu at 9:30 AM, 12:30 PM, and 7 PM
daily (Sun. at 9:30 AM only), and leave Lleida at 9:30 AM and 4 PM daily.

LA POBLA DE SEGUR

For a small town, Pobla de Segur packs a wallop. The **oficina de turisme** (Av. Verdaguer 35, tel. 973/
68–02–57; open summer, Mon.–Sat. 10–2 and 6–8, mornings only off season) has plenty of rafting and
hiking information. If you need to stay the night, nothing's cheaper than **Cán Fasérsia** (C. Major 4, tel.
972/68–02–27; doubles 3,000 ptas–4,500 ptas, 3,000 ptas–3,750 ptas off season). Sleep under the
stars at **Camping Collegats** (N-260, km 306, tel. 973/68–07–14; 575 ptas per tent plus 575 ptas per
person), 3 km (2 mi) from town on the road to Gerri de la Sal. Unfortunately, there's no bus service
here—you'll have to hoof it.

COMING AND GOING • La Pobla de Segur is the last stop on the train from Lleida. Make bus connections here to Viella (2½ hrs, 1,550 ptas), El Pont de Suert (1 hr, 550 ptas), and other pretty towns
along the river, such as **Sort** and **Llavorsí** (both renowned whitewater-rafting spots in spring). June
through October, two daily buses head to Viella, in the Vall d'Aran (the 9:30 AM bus goes through the tunnel via El Pont de Suert; the 11:40 AM bus heads north via Sort and Llavorsí), and one daily bus leaves
Pont de Suert for La Pobla de Segur at 2:45 PM. Buses also go to Barcelona (4 hrs, 2,550 ptas). The **train
station** (Av. Estació, tel. 973/68–04–80; open 8 AM–2 PM) is a 10-minute walk from the **bus station** (Av.
Verdaguer 1, tel. 973/68–03–36), which is near the center of town. Buy train tickets on board.

EL PONT DE SUERT

In El Pont de Suert, situated in the lush, green Ribagorza River valley, you really start feeling the call of
the great outdoors. The **tourist office** (Pl. Mercadal 7, tel. 973/69–06–40; open July–Sept., daily 10–
1:30 and 4:30–7:30) is in the square behind the church. The family-run **Pensión Isard** (C. de Sant
Aventi 29, tel. 973/69–01–39) has doubles for 2,750 ptas (3,750 ptas with bath) and serves a hearty
menú del día (1,550 ptas) in the dining room.

Pont de Suert is near **Vall de Boí,** a secluded valley harboring several beautiful Romanesque churches,
and **Aigüestortes Park,** with magnificent lakes, glaciers, waterfalls, and river otters and other wildlife.
The park office (in the town of Boí, tel. 973/69–61–89; open daily 9–1 and 3:30–7) has trail maps and
a list of *refugios* in and around the 25,500-acre park. You can drive from Boí to **La Ruta de la Llúdriga,**
a 5-km (3-mi) nature walk to Llebreta Lake and the park entrance, or you can take a four-wheel-drive
taxi (750 ptas per person, 2-person minimum) directly to the entrance; taxis leave every 30–60 minutes
from the lot behind the park office. A beautiful place to stay while exploring your options is the **Hostal
Pascual** (25528 Pont de Boí, tel. 973/69–60–14; doubles 3,800 ptas), on the river at the turnoff to Boí
from the main valley road.

WET AND WILD

There's some excellent whitewater rafting in the Spanish Pyrenees, especially on the Río Noguera Pallaresa in Catalonia (near Sort and Llavorsí), the Río Ara and Río Cinca (near Torla and Aínsa), and the Río Gállego (near Reglos). The Río Ara is the most challenging, with class IV rapids in the high-water season (May and June). The rafting season generally runs from April through September, and day trips generally cost 4,500 ptas—6,500 ptas. To arrange trips, contact Natura Actividades (Av. Rgto. Galicia 3, tel. 974/36–08–90) in Jaca, or Sport L'Aventura (Av. Pas d'Arro 5, tel. 973/64–24–44) in Viella.

COMING AND GOING • Buses leave El Pont de Suert for Viella (1 hr, 520 ptas), in the Vall d'Aran, at 11 AM and 7 PM and for Lleida (1 hr, 1,565 ptas) and Barcelona (5 hrs, 3,415 ptas) at 6:30 AM and 2:30 PM. A bus leaves El Pont de Suert for the Vall de Boí at 11 AM, returning at 2 PM; it will drop you at the turnoff to Boí (1 km/⅗ mi away).

VALL D'ARAN

The big payoff for all of these bus shenanigans is the gorgeous valley of Vall d'Aran, where the Garonne River rushes though a postcard-perfect mountain landscape. The valley is formed by a break in the Pyrenees, which have long kept it removed from its French and Catalan neighbors; indeed, until 1948 when a tunnel was hacked 6 km (4 mi) through the mountains in the direction of Lleida, the Vall d'Aran was snowbound and cut off from the rest of Catalonia during winter. The remote valley even has its own language, Aranés, an odd mix of Gascon, Catalan, and Basque.

If you don't want to stay in touristy **Viella** (Vielha in Catalan), the largest town in the Vall d'Aran, hop on a bus to **Les** and the valley's other smaller towns. Along the trails leading out of Viella are several refuges where you can stay for free. Get information on hiking and skiing at the **tourist office** (C. Sarrieléra 10, tel. 973/64–01–10; open weekdays 10–1 and 4:30–7:30); send postcards from the **post office** (open weekdays 8:30–2:30, Sat. 9:30–1; postal code 25530) across the street. Just off Avinguda Castiero, **Pension Puig** (C. Reiau 6, tel. 973/64–00–31; 1,250 ptas per person in summer, 1,350 ptas in winter) has wonderful cabinesque rooms. The rooms at **Habitacions de Miguel** (Av. Castiero 1, tel. 973/64–00–63; doubles 3,750 ptas–4,250 ptas) aren't quite as cozy, but they're big. **Camping Artigane** (Carretera Francia/Viella, tel. 973/64–03–38; 550 ptas each per person, car, and tent; closed Oct.–May) is 2½ km (1¼ mi) north of town on the road to France; from Viella catch the local bus toward Les. The **HI hostel** (C. de Viella, tel. 973/64–52–71; beds 2,475 ptas, 1,750 ptas under age 26; sheet rental 375 ptas) is in nearby Salardú, near a ski resort. The bus from Pobla de Segur (via Sort) passes Salardú; ask the driver to drop you off at the hostel. Better yet, try the cozy **Refugio Montaña** (C. Nacionál, just before the southern entrance to Viella tunnel, tel. 973/64–28–90), where rooms are 1,475 ptas per person.

COMING AND GOING • Alsina-Graells (tel. 973/27–14–70) runs buses in and out of Vall d'Aran. One daily bus in winter (9 AM) and two in summer (9 AM and 5 PM) leave Lleida for Viella (2½–3½ hrs, 2,100 ptas), passing through the town of El Pont de Suert roughly midway. In summer, daily buses for Viella leave La Pobla de Segur at 7:30 AM, 9:30 AM, and noon, and Barcelona (7 hrs, 3,750 ptas) at 6:30 AM and 2:30 PM. Three daily buses (5:30 AM, 11 AM, and 1:45 PM) leave Viella for Barcelona and Lleida. Beware: These buses don't always stick to their schedules.

PARQUE NACIONAL DE ORDESA

Even if you don't have much time to spend in the Pyrenees, you shouldn't miss this unbelievably beautiful park, with its mountain goats, marmots, and 16,000 acres of alpine meadows, forests, waterfalls, crystal-clear rivers, and sheer peaks covered year-round by snow. Though Ordesa is sometimes crowded—the varied terrain is popular with both serious hikers and families packing small children and picnic supplies—it's still possible to blaze your own trail. Call the main **ICONA park-information center** (tel. 974/24–33–61) for more information.

You can hike into the park from Torla (*see below*) on a trail that starts just to the left of the Hostal Bella Vista, on the main road into town from Sabiñánigo (*see below*). Cross the bridge and follow the dirt road left along the river for an easy, beautiful, two-hour hike. The trail eventually deposits you at a parking lot and the Restaurante-Bar La Pradera. The **park information center** (no phone; open July–Oct., daily 10–1 and 4–8:30; shorter hrs off season), where you can get free maps of the park's hiking trails, is five minutes further up the main road. One steep trail leads up to the **Refugio Góriz** (tel. 974/50–02–45; beds 1,200 ptas), the only place to sleep in the park and a four-hour hike from the parking lot; call a month ahead for reservations in summer. There are several other *refugios* surrounding the park, but most are open only June–September and on weekends in spring. You're free to **camp** at elevations above 7,000 ft, and around the grounds of the Refugio Góriz if it's full.

TORLA

The bus from Sabiñánigo (*see below*) lets you off in this pretty town, the closest (8 km/5 mi) you can get to the park by public transport, and your best base for outdoor exploration . The **tourist information office** (no phone; open daily 10–1 and 4–8:30), across the plaza at the far end of Calle Francia, has basic trail maps and a list of accommodations and campgrounds. You'll find cheap beds at the rustic **Refugio L'Atalaya** (C. Francia, tel. 974/48–60–22; beds 1,250 ptas; by reservation only Nov.–Easter), whose French owners serve some of the town's best food at the attached restaurant (*menú* 1,375 ptas). Beds at the newer **Refugio L'Briet** (C. Francia, tel. 974/48–62–21) also cost 1,200 ptas. To reach the *refugios,* head up the street across from the bus stop. Further along Calle Francia and up the hill to the right, you'll find the **Fonda Ballarín** (C. Capuvita 11, tel. 974/48–61–55), where cozy, clean doubles are 4,000 ptas in winter, 5,000 ptas–6,000 ptas in summer. You can camp and take hot showers at **Camping Río Ara** (tel. 974/48–62–48; 425 ptas each per person, tent, and car; closed Nov.–Mar.); just after the bridge on the way to Ordesa, walk up the paved road to the right. **Camping Ordesa** (tel. 974/48–61–46; 525 ptas per person plus 550 ptas for each tent and car; closed Dec.–Easter), about 1 km (2//3 mi) past Torla on the main road, also has hot showers. In July and August, buses leave Sabiñánigo for Torla (1 hr, 355 ptas) daily at 11 AM and 6:30 PM, returning at 3:30 PM and 8:05 PM; the rest of the year, only one bus leaves Sabiñánigo for Torla daily at 11 AM, returning at 3:30 PM.

SABINANIGO

This town is little more than a transportation junction. If you get stuck here, the cheapest beds are at **Fonda Laguarta** (C. Serrablo 21, tel. 974/48–00–04; doubles 4,400 ptas with bath), and the attached restaurant serves *menús* for 1,250 ptas. Three daily trains (20 min, 155 ptas) and buses (15 min, 205 ptas) go to Jaca, and two daily buses go to and from Huesca (1hr, 650 ptas), the transfer point for buses to Lleida.

JACA

This town at the base of the beautiful Aragonese Pyrenees is one of the stops on the long Christian pilgrimage from France to Santiago de Compostela. Jaca also makes a good pit stop for nature worshipers on their way into the wilderness of the Pyrenees and the awe-inspiring Parque Nacional de Ordesa (*see above*). The town itself, with its hopping bars and cafés, is not so serene. Perhaps it's all the testosterone in the air—this is where many young Spanish army recruits are stationed for training in the mountainous terrain.

Jaca has a number of worthwhile sights, reflecting its history as both a pilgrims' stopover and a military base. The **cathedral** isn't particularly stunning, but it's historically and architecturally significant as one of the first Romanesque churches built in Spain (it went up around AD 1060). The **Museo Diocesan** (inside the cathedral, tel. 974/35–63–68; admission 200 ptas; open Tues.–Sun. 11–1:30 and 4–6:30) houses well-preserved Romanesque frescoes from the area. On the western edge of town, **La Ciudadela** (admission 150 ptas; daily tours at 11 and 5), built in 1590, is a testament to Jaca's former military importance as one of the first defenses of the Spanish frontier. Five of its bastions are still intact.

VISITOR INFORMATION

The **oficina de turismo** (Av. Regimiento Galicia 2, tel. 974/36–00–98; open Apr.–Oct., weekdays 10–2 and 4–8, Sat. 10–2 and 5–8, Sun. 10–2; shorter hrs off-season), tucked into a row of shops just below the Paseo Generalísimo Franco, has skiing and hiking tips. The **post office** (Av. Regimiento Galicia; postal code 22700) is open weekdays 8:30–2:30 and Saturday 9:30–1.

RUN FOR YOUR LIFE

To see the encierro (running of the bulls), get a spot behind the fences at the beginning of the course, near the Plaza Santo Domingo, or near the end of it, just before the bullring. This means dragging yourself out of bed around 6 AM. To see the end of the run into the ring (through the narrow entrance known as the "tunnel of death"), nab one of the free spots reserved on the lower level (arrive by 6:30 AM), or pay 2,000 ptas or more for a seat higher up. The advantage of being inside the ring itself is that you can check out the action at greater length, as the actual running through the streets lasts only about three minutes from start to finish, and it all flashes by in a blur of scared runners and thundering bulls. After the encierro, the action moves to Plaza del Castillo and the streets of the old section, where the party continues day and night.

Make sure you watch a run and know the course before you decide to tempt fate and try it yourself. It's always dangerous—many people (13 this century) have died doing it—but it's much less dangerous when the bulls stay together and run as a pack. When they get separated, they get aggressive and start goring their way through the crowd. Another factor to keep in mind is when to run; try to avoid the huge weekend crowds, when all the extra bodies add an additional hazard. On one weekend in 1993, a bottlenecked wall of flesh formed; no one was able to move, and the bulls plowed through and over the crowd. Women are traditionally barred from running, but every year some do it anyway; just keep a low profile and avoid contact with officials at the beginning of the course. You can see the same bulls that ran in the morning at the bullfights that take place each night at 6:30. Seats start at about 2,000 ptas. After the fights, you can buy tickets for the following day from the windows at the bullring; if you wait until the last minute, scalpers will demand more (4,000 ptas and up).

COMING AND GOING

The **bus station** (Av. Jacetania, tel. 974/35–50–60) sends buses to Sabiñánigo (15 min, 250 ptas), Huesca (1¼ hrs, 1,120 ptas), Pamplona (1½ hrs, 985 ptas), and Barcelona (6½ hrs, 3,000 ptas). The ticket window opens half an hour before each departure. From the **RENFE station** (end of Av. de Juan XXIII, tel. 974/36–13–32), northeast of town, you can rail it to Huesca (2 hrs, 975 ptas), via Sabiñánigo (20 min, 175 ptas), and to Madrid (6½ hrs, 3,850 ptas). Half an hour before every departure, you can catch a bus to the train station (50 ptas) from the front of the **Ayuntamiento** (City Hall), on Calle Mayor, or around the left corner of the bus station; buses leave the train station for the city center 10 minutes after each arrival.

If you're itching to splurge on a rental car, Jaca is a good place to do it. **Don Auto** (C. de Correos 4, tel. 974/35–50–27; open daily 9:30–1:30 and 4–8) rents four-wheel-drives (13,500 ptas per day; discounts for longer rentals) and will supply you with maps and travel tips.

WHERE TO SLEEP AND EAT

You should have no problem finding cheap and decent lodging here; look along Calle Mayor and around the cathedral. The cheapest rooms are at **Hostal Paris** (Pl. San Pedro 5, tel. 974/36–10–20; doubles 3,500 ptas, 3,800 ptas with bath), near the cathedral. At the HI hostel, **Albergue Juvenil de Vacaciones** (Av. Perimetral 6, tel. 974/36–05-36; closed Oct.–Nov.), beds are 1,800 ptas, 1,550 ptas under age 26 (200 ptas more for nonmembers). Take a bus from the train station to the *pista de hielo* (skating rink); the hostel is just to the right. The closest campsite is **Camping Victoria** (Llano la Victoria, tel. 974/36-03–23; 475 ptas for each tent, car, and person), a 1½-km (1-mi) walk from the town center toward Pamplona.

The young *soldados* (soldiers) stationed here keep the bars and restaurants pretty lively, especially around Calle Mayor. **El Viejo Rancho** (C. Bellido II, tel. 974/36–10–52) has a large selection of *raciones* (450 ptas–700 ptas); try the spinach or Roquefort pie. One of the best deals in town is at the homey **Meson La Fragua** (C. Gil Berges, tel. 974/36–06–18; closed Wed.), where a *plato combinado* of grilled meats will set you back 750 ptas–950 ptas.

PAMPLONA

Pamplona (Iruña in the Basque language), a quiet city in the Basque region of northern Navarre, positively explodes every year from noon on July 6 through midnight on July 14 in the world-famous—or infamous—festival of **San Fermín**. Everyone wraps a traditional red-and-white *bañuclos* (bandanas) around his or her neck, and all mundane matters are abandoned for the nonstop party in the streets. The main event, the running of the bulls, or *encierro*, takes place every morning at 8 AM sharp, when huge, lethal fighting bulls are unleashed into the street behind an adrenaline- and alcohol-infused crowd of runners. You'd think this reckless tradition was dreamed up after one too many, but it's actually a festival honoring Pamplona's patron saint, who died a martyr after being dragged through the streets by bulls.

Even if you don't take part in any of the bull-related antics, the nine-day, citywide party—with parades of gigantic papier-mâché figures, dancing, bands, and spectacular fireworks—is reason enough to stop by. The rest of the year, Pamplona upholds its usual dignity, attracting tourists with its charming old town and its churches: **San Saturnino** (Pl. Consistorial; open daily 8:15–noon and 6:30–7:30) and **San Nicolás** (Pl. San Nicolás; open daily 8–12:45 and 6–7:30), both dating from the 13th century, and the **Catedral de Santa María** (Pl. San Jose, tel. 974/22–74–00; open daily 9 AM–10 AM and 6–8), with a beautiful Gothic cloister. The city park, **Parque de La Taconera,** is surrounded by a moat and houses deer, rabbits, chickens, turkeys, and peacocks.

BASICS

The small **oficina de turismo,** near the Plaza de Toros, has schedules of events, a list of accommodations, and maps indicating the route of the *encierro*. *C. Duque de Ahumada 3, tel. 948/22–07–41. Open June–Sept., daily 10–2 and 4–7; off season, weekdays 10–2 and 4–7.*

DISCOUNT TRAVEL AGENCY • TIVE's friendly staff will find you the cheapest ways to leave town. *C. Paulino Caballero 4, 5th floor, between C. Arrieta and C. Roncesvalles, tel. 948/21–24–04. Open weekdays 9–1:30, 10–12:30 during San Fermínes.*

PHONES AND MAIL • The **Telefónica** (C. Cortes de Navarre, tel. 948/22–86–02; open Mon.–Sat. 9–2 and 4–9; longer hrs during San Fermínes) is across the street from the bull ring. The main **post office** (Paseo de Sarasate 9, tel. 948/22–12–63; postal code 31002) sells stamps weekdays 8 AM–9 PM and Saturday 9–2. Pick up *poste restante* around the corner at Calle Estella 10.

COMING AND GOING

Pamplona is better (and more cheaply) connected to the outside world by bus than by train. The **bus station** (Av. Conde Oliveto 8, tel. 948/22–38–54) is centrally located near the Parque de la Ciudadela (neither a particularly safe nor appealing place), about a 10-minute walk from the tourist office and Plaza del Castillo. From the station, walk down Conde Oliveto, take the second left at the roundabout onto San Ignacio, and walk straight to reach the Plaza. **Conda** (tel. 948/22–10–26) runs buses to Madrid (5 hrs, 3,450 ptas); **Ibarsa** (tel. 948/22–09–97) has buses to Barcelona (5½ hrs, 2,435 ptas); and **Roncalesa** (tel. 948/22–20–79) sends buses to San Sebastián (1½ hrs, 950 ptas).

EUSKADI TA ASKATASUNA

Isolated in mountainous southern France and northern Spain, the residents of the País Vasco (Basque Country) are perhaps the last remnants of Europe's indigenous population, who preceded the vast waves of migration from the East over 3,000 years ago. The Basques' complex language, called Euskera or Euskara, is not known to be related to any other language on Earth. Even their blood types distinguish them genetically from other Europeans—they have high proportions of types B and Rh+.

The Basques have always fiercely resisted foreign influence. They were the last people in this corner of Europe to convert to Christianity, and even when they were incorporated into the Spanish state in the 16th century, they maintained an enviable level of autonomy. Basque nationalism resurged early in the 20th century but was interrupted by the Spanish Civil War, in which the Basque provinces of Guipúzcoa and Vizcaya defended the Republic while Alava and Navarra sided with Franco. The brutal punishment of Viscaya and Guipúzcoa set the stage for the organized resistance to Franco's regime by ETA (Euskadi ta Askatasuna, Basque Homeland and Freedom) in the early '60s. ETA has now organized terrorist activities for over 30 years, from the 1972 assassination of Franco's chosen successor, Admiral Carrero Blanco to the 1987 bombing of a supermarket in Barcelona to the 1993 detonation of two car bombs in Madrid. These attacks, coupled with increased autonomy for the Basques since Franco's death in 1975, have greatly eroded support for ETA, and fear of terrorism has kept investment out of the region. The July 1996 arrest of ETA member Daniel Deguy, the alleged mastermind of the 1993 bombings, hasn't stemmed the organized violence—at least five Spanish coastal resort towns were bombed in the summer of 1996, and there seems no end in sight.

You don't need to trek all the way to the train station for reservations; just go to the **RENFE office** (C. Estrella, tel. 948/13–02–02; open weekdays 9:30–1 and 4:30–7:30, weekends 9:30–1), around the corner from Paseo Sarasate. The **train station** (Av. San Jorge s/n, tel. 948/13–02–02), northwest of the city center, has connections to Barcelona (7–8 hrs, 4,100 ptas), Madrid (5 hrs, 3,850 ptas–4,200 ptas), and San Sebastián (2 hrs, 1,700 ptas).

GETTING AROUND

Pamplona's old section centers around the Plaza del Castillo, with the two large city parks, Parque de la Taconera and Parque de la Ciudadela, bordering the city center to the west. From the train station, take Bus 9 to Paseo Sarasate, near budget lodging and the city center. City buses (tel. 948/12–93–00; 125 ptas) normally run until 11 PM, but they run all night long during San Fermín.

WHERE TO SLEEP

For the week of San Fermín, Pamplona's rooms are booked a year in advance, and generally at more than double their usual rates. Still, there are plenty of alternative lodging options. Ads for beds in *casas particulares* (private homes) are often posted around the bus station and listed in the local paper, *Diario de Navarra*. Some older folks hang around outside the tourist office offering rooms in their homes; expect to pay 4,000 ptas–10,000 ptas for one of these. To get to the closest official campground, **Ezcaba** (tel. 948/33–03–15; 475 ptas per tent and per person), 7 km (4½ mi) north of town, take the "La Montañesa" bus from Calle Arrieta, near the Plaza de Toros. During San Fermín, a free campground is set up next to the official campsite, but there's no security there—check your pack and valuables (350 ptas per bag for the duration of your stay) at the special 24-hour luggage-storage office set up at the bus station during the festival. If all else fails, you may want to stash your bags and do as many others do— camp in the parks and streets of Pamplona.

The rest of the year, look for cheap *pensiónes* and *hostales* around Plaza San Nicolás, especially along Calle San Nicolás and Calle San Gregorio. Plan B: Try those on Calle Estafeta and the streets near the cathedral. The **Angeles Arrondo Lizarraga Pensión** (C. Estafeta 23, tel. 948/22–18–16; 1,750 ptas per person) has balconies overlooking the bull route. Brave your way past the dark entrance of **Pensión Santa Cecilia** (C. Navarrería 17, tel. 948/22–22–30; doubles 3,300 ptas) to the nice rooms inside.

FOOD

Other than the usual *bocadillos,* there's a frustrating lack of cheap food in Pamplona. If you feel like sitting down to eat, try the places along Calle Jarauta and its continuation, Calle San Lorenzo. **Mesón Pírineo** (C. Estafeta 41, tel. 948/22–20–45; closed Wed.) looks like the cellar of a monastery but hosts an extraordinarily merry crowd; they've got a *menú* for 1,350 ptas and other specialties for about 800 ptas. San Nicolás is lined with lively bars, some serving tapas. Just off Plaza San Nicolás, **Casa Paco** (C. Lindachiquia 20, tel. 948/22–51–05) serves salads and entrées (600 ptas–950 ptas) and a tasty *menú* (1,300 ptas). The **market** is just behind Plaza de los Burgos.

SAN SEBASTIAN

Simply put, San Sebastián (Donostia, in the Basque language), the capital of the Basque province of Guipúzcoa, is a gorgeous town. Unlike other beach resorts, the city hasn't wrecked its beaches or its aesthetics to cater to tourists. Part of the city's self-assured beauty comes from its hundred-year status as the playground of the rich and famous. Beautiful fountains, gardens, trees, and parks abound, and you can practically smell the money when you get off the train. Not surprisingly, San Sebastián is not cheap; you may find yourself dropping painful sums of money on lodging in July and August. A night or two shouldn't clean you out entirely, though, as you can find cheap eats in literally hundreds of tapas bars.

BASICS

The **main tourist office** (Blvd. Reina Regente, at Paseo de Republica Argentina, tel. 943/48–11–66; open Mon.–Sat. 8–8, Sun. 10–1), on the river near the older part of town, provides maps and a list of accommodations; to get there from the RENFE station, cross Puente María Cristina, turn right, and walk along the water—it's on the left just before Puente Zurriola. A second tourist office operates out of a booth on the bay at Paseo de Mollard. The **Basque government tourist office** (Fueros 1, tel. 943/48–11–66), also on the river, has maps and information on the entire Basque region. You can get hostel cards and cheap bus and plane tickets at the **TIVE office** (C. Tomás Gros 3, tel. 943/27–69–34; open summer, weekdays 9–2; shorter hrs off season), on the east side of the river, near Plaza de Euskadi off Calle Miracruz; unfortunately, the office sometimes closes for a month in the summer. The **post office** (C. Urdaneta, tel. 943/46–49–14; postal code 20080) is just behind the cathedral; the **Telefónica** (C. San Marcial 29; open Mon.–Sat. 9:30 AM–11 PM) is a few blocks away toward Avenida de la Libertad.

COMING AND GOING

A major point of entry from the rest of Europe, San Sebastián hosts an **airport** (tel. 943/64–22–40), two train stations, and numerous private bus companies.

BY BUS • The **Estación de Autobuses** (Pl. de Pío XII; luggage storage 350 ptas per day) is a 15-minute walk south of the city center; from here you can follow the river north to the tourist office, or take Bus 28 to Alameda del Boulevard and the old quarter. Various bus companies sell tickets nearby along Paseo

IT'S NO USE CRYING OVER SPILLED CIDER

Asturian bartenders are excellent marksmen, pouring sidra *(hard cider) from bottles high above their heads into glasses held far below their waists. The real pros don't even look. Funnily enough, the cider often misses the glass, but no matter—the real purpose of this ritual is to oxygenate the cider and give it a good head. When you order cider, you get three shots (about 200 ptas each), each of which you're supposed to polish off in one swig. Don't drink the last few drops—dump them on the ground. And never pour the cider yourself; that's the waiter's or bartender's job.*

de Bizkaia and Avenida de Sancho el Sabio, which leads north from the station straight into town. **Continental Auto** (Av. de Sancho el Sabio 31, tel. 943/46–90–74) buses go to Madrid (7–8 hrs, 4,100 ptas) and Burgos (4 hrs, 2,125 ptas); **La Roncalesa** (Av. Berriozar 14, tel. 943/46–10–64) buses go to Pamplona (50 min, 950 ptas); **Ibarsa** (Paseo de Bizkaia 16, tel. 943/45–75–00) buses go to Barcelona (6 hrs, 2,750 ptas); and **Pesa** (Av. de Sancho el Sabio 33, tel. 902/10–12–10) buses go to Bilbao (1¼ hrs, 1,300 ptas).

BY TRAIN • The main RENFE station, **Estación del Norte** (Av. Francia, tel. 943/28–35–99; luggage storage 450 ptas), is on the east side of the river at Puente María Cristina, 10 minutes from the old quarter. Trains leave for Madrid (7½ hrs, 5,300 ptas), Barcelona (9 hrs, 5,600 ptas) via Pamplona (2 hrs, 1,800 ptas), and Burgos (3–4 hrs, 2,700 ptas), and Paris (11 hrs, 13,000 ptas). For trains to Bilbao (3–4 hrs, 650 ptas) and the surrounding region, go to the **Estación de Amara** (Pl. Easo 9, tel. 943/45–01–31), also known as ET; to get there from the bus station, walk four blocks north to where Avenida de Sancho el Sabio splits. These trains aren't part of RENFE, so InterRail and Eurailpasses aren't valid.

GETTING AROUND

San Sebastián wraps itself around the pretty La Concha bay, and the Urumea River snakes through the city. You'll spend most of your sightseeing time west of the river, and your eating, drinking, and snoozing will probably happen in the old quarter, which is squeezed into the strip of land between the bay and the river, near Monte Urgull. The town is easily navigated by foot or by the plentiful city buses (100 ptas) that zip around town until about 10 or 11 PM; for city-bus information, dial 943/28–71–00. You can also rent mountain bikes at **Comet** (Av. de la Libertad 6, tel. 943/42–66–37) for a steep 3,000 ptas for the first full day, 2,000 ptas per day thereafter.

WHERE TO SLEEP

Fierce competition for rooms in July and August means that even hovels can charge ridiculously high prices. Most of the cheaper places cluster around the cathedral and in the small, busy streets in the old town. **Pensión Aussie** (C. San Jerónimo 23, tel. 943/42–28–74), near Iglesia Santa María, has darling doubles for 4,400 ptas–5,500 ptas in summer (3,500 ptas off season). **Pensión Urkia** (C. Urbieta 12, near cathedral, tel. 943/42–44–36) has spotless doubles for 5,000 ptas July–September, 3,200 ptas off season. **Pensión San Juan** (C. San Juan 13, 3rd floor, tel. 943/42–63–45) has nice, airy doubles (5,500 ptas July–Aug., 4,000 ptas off season) and dorm beds (2,400 ptas July–Aug., 1,750 ptas off season). In July and August, beds at the great **HI hostel** (El Paseo de Igueldo 25, tel. 943/31–02–68) are 2,400 ptas, 2,100 ptas under age 26; off-season beds cost 1,975 ptas, 1,675 ptas under age 26. To reach the hostel, take Bus 24 (direction Antiguo) from the RENFE station, or Bus 16 (toward Igueldo) from Alameda del Boulevard to Playa de Ondarreta. Walk about 10 minutes up Avenida de Satrustegui to Paseo de Igueldo and turn left. **Camping De Igueldo** (Igueldo Village, tel. 943/21–45–02; 2,000 ptas per site for 2 people) is near Monte Igueldo, about 4 km (2½ mi) from the town center. Take Bus 16 (toward Igueldo) from Alameda del Boulevard.

FOOD

Nearly every bar you stumble upon will have tapas (150 ptas–350 ptas). **Bar Aralar** (C. Puerto 10, tel. 943/42–63–78), a noisy, popular bar and restaurant, serves *pimientos rellenos* (red peppers stuffed with cod) for 300 ptas. You should try the Basque specialty *chipirones en su tinta* (squid in their ink) at least once; **Casa Vergara** (C. Mayor 21, tel. 943/43–10–73; closed Thurs. Sept.–June) serves them for 1,900 ptas.

WORTH SEEING

The lively, narrow streets of the **old quarter,** bordered by the Alameda to the south, Monte Urgull to the north, and the bay and ocean to the west, contrast markedly with the wide, regal boulevards in the rest of town. Bars pack the streets, encouraging noisy crowds and lots of drinking, eating, and general carousing. But before hitting the bars, you should venture into the baroque church of **Santa María** (corner of C. Mayor and C. Treinta y Uno de Agosto). Sugary cherubs mark the outside, but the interior is more subdued. Also check out San Sebastián's beautiful Gothic cathedral, **El Buen Pastor,** a kilometer directly east of Santa María.

An easy climb up the hill **Monte Urgull,** behind the old town, will take you to an enormous statue of Jesus Christ and commanding views of both the bay and sea. Up top, you can see the vestiges of Monte Urgull's strategic importance in some old cannons and the remains of a castle fortress. At the foot of the hill, the **San Telmo Museum** (Pl. Zuloaga 1, tel. 943/42–49–70; admission free; open Tues.–Sat. 9:30–1:30 and 4–7:30, Sun. 10–1:30) houses an interesting collection of artwork in a 16th-century monastery. The view from **Monte Igüeldo** is even better than the view from Monte Urgull, but the climb is more of an effort. The road starts just to the left of the tennis courts, at the bottom of the mountain near the west end of Playa de Ondaretta. If you're feeling lazy, a **funicular** (tel. 943/21–05–64; 125 ptas one-way) hauls tourists to the top every 15 minutes between 11 AM and 10 PM.

OVIEDO

Oviedo is the capital of the Asturias region—the only Spanish kingdom never conquered by the Moors, thanks mostly to the Picos de Europa range, an imposing and beautiful natural barrier. It was here that the Reconquista of Spain began, inspiring a tradition of spirited resistance that has continued into this century, highlighted during the Spanish Civil War when feisty Asturian miners lobbed dynamite at Franco's forces. Today, Oviedo is a polluted industrial center, and although the city's unique churches and **casco antiguo** (old quarter) are worth a look, the region's true appeal lies in the surrounding mountains. A handful of organizations run excursions, including **Montañeros de Rivayaqüe** (C. Menéndez Pelayo 2, tel. 98/528–47–04), located northwest of the train station. Before setting out on your own, pick up "El Cornion" (580 ptas), an excellent booklet of maps and hiking information available at most local bookstores.

Oviedo is known for a unique architectural style: Asturian Pre-Romanesque. As Europe groped its way out of the Middle Ages, Asturians were designing truly innovative buildings with mixed elements of Visigothic, Muslim, and early Romanesque architecture. Two churches within walking distance of the city are perfect examples of this style. **Santa María del Naranco** (tel. 98/529–67–55; admission 200 ptas, free Mon.) was originally built as a royal residence for King Ramiro I but was eventually consecrated. It sits on a hill 3 km (2 mi) northwest of the city and offers beautiful views from its high, arched windows, which are bordered by a ropelike design called *sogueado*. A five-minute walk further up the Avenida de los Monumentos brings you to the 9th-century **San Miguel de Lillo** (free entry with ticket from Santa María), a church with a graceful yet unusual sense of proportion—the height is three times the width of the nave. Its windows are decorated with beautiful, delicate latticework, and the door jamb at the entrance features unusual carvings of circus performers. To get to the churches, take Bus 6 (85 ptas) from Calle General Yagüe (near the park), or walk up Calle Nicolás Soria (under the bridge between the two train stations), turn left on Calle de Lorenzo Abruñedo, then turn right on Avenida de los Monumentos—a pleasant, well-marked, 45-minute jaunt. Back in town, visit the Gothic **cathedral,** with its *Cámara Santa* (Holy Chamber), built by Alfonso II to house holy relics when this was the only spot safe from the Moors. On Thursday, admission is free to the Cámara Santa, museum, and cloister (tel. 98/522–10–33; admission 300 ptas; open summer, weekdays 10–7, Sat. 10–6:30; off season, weekdays 10–1 and 4–8, Sat. 10–1 and 4–6).

BASICS

The **tourist office** (Plz.de la Catedral 6, tel. 98/521–33–85; open weekdays 9:30–1:30 and 4:30–6:30, Sat. 10–2), on the plaza in the front of the cathedral, has free maps and information on hiking in the Picos de Europa. The **American Express office** (C. Uría 6, tel. 98/522–52–17) is open weekdays 9:30–1 and 4:30–7, Saturday 9:30–1.

COMING AND GOING

The cathedral and surrounding old quarter are east of the strollable, fountained city park, **Campo de San Francisco.** The RENFE and FEVE train stations and the bus station are all within spitting distance of one another, a 5- to 10-minute walk northwest of the park. The underground **bus station** (Pl. Primo de Rivera 1, tel. 98/528–12–00) is hard to find; look for the shopping center with a big electronics store. The station serves León (2 hrs, 1,200 ptas), Madrid (6 hrs, 3,695 ptas), and Santiago (6 hrs, 3,395 ptas). Buses run by **Económicos Easa** (tel. 98/529–00–39) will take you to Picos de Europa jumping-off points such as Covadonga (750 ptas) and Arenas de Cabrales (925 ptas). The **RENFE station** (C. Uría, at Av. de Santander, tel. 98/525–02–02) has trains to León (2 hrs, 1,500 ptas), Madrid (6 hrs, 4,200 ptas), Burgos (4 hrs, 2,600 ptas), and Barcelona (11 hrs, 5,050 ptas). One block northeast of the RENFE station, the **FEVE station** (Av. de Santander, tel. 98/529–01–04) sends trains to Santander (4½ hrs, 1,610 ptas), where you can connect for eastern destinations such as Bilbao and San Sebastián.

WHERE TO SLEEP AND EAT

Rooms are relatively cheap and plentiful. Most budget lodging is near the train stations, around Calle Uría, or around the nearby commercial district by Calle Pelayo. **Pensión Oriente** (C. Melquiades Alvarez 24, tel. 98/521–22–82; doubles 2,500 ptas) has unadorned but clean rooms, some with balconies. Plunk down a little more cash for the pleasant rooms with rugs, fluffy beds, and gleaming bathrooms at **Pensión Pilar** (C. Nueve de Mayo 11, tel. 98/521–77–45; doubles 3,000 ptas). West of the town center, you can crash at the **HI Residencia Juvenil R. M. Pidal** (C. Julián Clavería 14, tel. 98/523–20–54; beds 1,000 ptas, 720 ptas under age 26). Take Bus 2 from Plaza Primo de Ribera or from the corner of Avenida Santander and Calle Nicolás Soria, and get off at the last stop. For cheap meals head northwest of the cathedral, where you'll find dozens of *sidrerías* (cider houses) serving *menús del día* (1,000 ptas), and, of course, Asturian ciders; **Sidrería Villaviciosa** (C. Gascona 7, tel. 98/522–70–61) is a good bet. Get supplies at **Mercado El Fontán** (C. Fierro, near Pl. Constitución; open weekdays 8–8, Sat 8–2:30), an open-air market in the heart of the *casco antiguo*. To sample the best *fabada* at a reasonable price (1,000 ptas–1,500 ptas), head 6 km (4 mi) outside the city on the road to Avilés until you see a farmhouse called **La Máquina** (Avda. De Santa Bárbara 59, tel. 98/526–0019) —it's the one with the miniature locomotive out front.

GALICIA

Brushing aside the raindrops as you hike through a forest, savoring ribeira wine and fresh octopus, or lying on a beautiful Atlantic beach, you may begin to understand why Gallegos, the Galician natives, don't have much use for the foreigner's idea of Spain as dusty roads, bullfights, and flamenco. Galicia is green and mountainous, and its independent character depends heavily on the sea—the source of both its most important industry, fishing, and its sense of connection to the rest of the world. Much is made here of the area's ancient cultural links to the Celts, whose influence can be heard in traditional Galician music, based on the *gaita*, or Gallego bagpipe. Galicia's geographic separateness is augmented by its regional language—Gallego is a bit like Portuguese and is a point of regional pride—though most people do speak Castilian as well. The area's draws include its remarkable countryside; great seafood (local specialties include *navajas*, or razor clams, and about a million recipes for octopus); beaches, such as **Baiona, O Grove,** and **Noia**, still unspoiled by international tourism; and the usual mind-boggling array of churches and monuments, including the cathedral in Santiago de Compostela, one of the most important pilgrimage sites in the Christian world.

SANTIAGO DE COMPOSTELA

The name *Compostela* derives from the Latin for "field of stars." The region was so named because it was here that, in the 9th century, a great light appeared, leading the hermit Pelayo to the tomb of St. James (Santiago). As if this weren't enough, Santiago then rose from the dead, disguised himself as a knight on a white horse, and led the Catholics to victory over the Moors. The city soon became known as one of Christendom's holiest places and continues to attract thousands of pilgrims annually, from all over the world. Today, Santiago is an alluring combination of the sacred and the profane. It became a university town during the 15th century, with the foundation of the Colegio de San Xerome, which became the Universidad de Santiago 100 years later; and the strikingly well-preserved historic center contains churches, religious museums, and monuments as well as tons of lively bars and restaurants catering to a festive student crowd. Santiago's enormous festival, the Feast of St. James, takes place here every year on July 25.

VISITOR INFORMATION

The **main tourist office** (Rúa do Vilar 43, tel. 981/58–40–81; open weekdays 10–2 and 4–7, Sat. 10–1:30) is two blocks south of the cathedral. There's a smaller **regional tourist office** (tel. 981/57–39–80; open weekdays 10–2 and 5–8, Sat. 11–2 and 5–8, Sun. noon–2 and 5–7) on Praza Galicia, just outside the old town. The main **post office** (Travesa de Fonseca, at Rúa do Franco, tel. 981/58–12–52) is open weekdays 8:30–8:30, Saturday 9:30–2. For **currency exchange** there are banks and *casas de cambio* all over the center. The banks close on weekends and at 2 PM weekdays, while *casas de cambio* are open daily until 10 PM or so but offer terrible rates. **American Express** services are provided at **Ultratur** (Av. de Figueroa 6, tel. 981/58–70–00; open weekdays 9:30–2:30 and 4:30–7, Sat. 10–12:30), at the edge of the historic center.

COMING AND GOING

The **train station** (Pr. Estación, tel. 981/52–02–02) is a 15-minute walk south of the old city, along Rúa do Hórreo. Trains travel to La Coruña (1½ hrs, 600 ptas), Vigo (2 hrs, 750 ptas), Madrid (9 hrs, 5,700 ptas), Pamplona (10 hrs, 5,800 ptas), and other destinations in northern Spain and Portugal. The **bus station** (San Cayetano, tel. 981/58–77–00) is a half-hour hike east of the town center; Bus 10 (125 ptas) runs between the station and the Plaza de Galicia. **Intercar** (tel. 981/58–61–33) buses serve Madrid (9 hrs, 5,440 ptas), and **Castromil** (tel. 981/58–97–00) buses serve Galician destinations such as La Coruña (50 min, 780 ptas).

GETTING AROUND

Santiago is very walker-friendly. To the south are the sprawling newer districts, to the north is the compact and largely pedestrianized old town, to the west is the pretty Alameda park, and wedged in-between is **Plaza de Galicia,** a good point of reference. The old city is dominated by the cathedral and several large plazas. The most important streets in the old city are those leading up to the cathedral from the south, such as Rúa do Vilar and Rúa do Franco (named for the tax that pilgrims entering Santiago once had to pay, not for the dictator).

WHERE TO SLEEP

It's fairly easy to find a room here. Rúas da Raiña, do Franco, and do Vilar have plenty of *hostales* and *hospedajes,* many of them above bars and restaurants. **Hostal-Restaurante El Rápido** (Rúa do Franco 22, tel. 981/58–49–83) has large doubles, all with bath, for 3,500 ptas. In the heart of the action, **Hospedaje Fonseca** (Calle Fonseca 1, across from cathedral, tel. 981/58–24–04) has immaculate doubles for 3,000 ptas. **Hospedaje Viño** (Pr. de Mazarelos 7, tel. 981/58–51–85), in the quieter northern section of the old town, has clean, comfortable doubles for 3,000 ptas. From Praza de Galicia, walk up Fuente de San Antonio (toward the bus station) and go left through the Arco de Mazarenos.

FOOD

Marvelous sweets (including the traditional, almond-based *tarta de santiago*), homemade bread, artfully displayed fruit, local ribeira wines, dark sausages, and breast-shaped cheeses called *tetillas* beckon the hungry from windows all over the city. By no means deprive yourself of these treats, but be aware that prices in the little shops can be high. See what you can pick up at the **market** (Pl. de Abastos; open Mon.–Sat. 8–1), in the northern part of the old town. The streets south of the cathedral are filled with bars and restaurants, but most tend to be pricey. Try **Café-Bar Platerias** (Rúa da Raiña 1), which serves

ON THE
BEATEN PATH

According to tradition, the body of St. James the Apostle was brought from Palestine by his disciples to rest in the lonely lands of Galicia. Much later, a 9th-century archbishop discovered the shrine and thus established the pilgrimage site that became known as Santiago de Compostela, named for the saint and for the field of stars that miraculously lit the way for early pilgrims. For centuries, believers of every class and occupation streamed through, making Santiago the most visited shrine in the Christian world, above even Rome and Jerusalem.

Today, as centuries ago, the most popular route to Santiage de Compostela is the so-called French Route, which leads from the Pyrenees through the Catholic strongholds of Burgos and León and continues into Galicia. Historically, pilgrims made the journey on horseback or on foot, and were sheltered and fed by devout citizens. Today's pilgrims travel by bike or on foot, and dozens of pilgrim's refuges have been established to provide inexpensive or free lodging. Bookstores sell pilgrim's guides describing the the route, most of which include a passportlike booklet to be stamped at lodges and shrines along the way.

fresh *mejillones* (clams) in oil and vinegar; a plateful, plus bread and a glass of wine, costs only 500 ptas. For a sit-down meal, head north of the cathedral. **Cafetería Viño** (Pr. Mazarelos 7, below the *hospedaje* of the same name, tel. 981/50–86–33) serves a complete *menú del día* for 675 ptas; Tuesday's special is paella. **Cuatro Vientos** (C. de Santa Cristina 21, at C. de Algilia de Arriba, no phone) is popular for cheap dishes (200 ptas–300 ptas) and a *menú del diá* for just 600 ptas. Once the hangout of Galician poets, **Café Derby** (C. Orfas 29, near Pr. Galicia, tel. 981/58–65–71) remains a serene place for coffee and pastries.

WORTH SEEING

With a map from the tourist office, die-hard sightseers can take the endless walking tour of Santiago's historical buildings, parks, and monuments, but some might prefer to wander around and enjoy the sights in a less thorough manner. In any case, don't miss the **catedral** (Pr. del Obradoiro; open daily 7 AM–9 PM). At night, when its baroque facade is lit, the building seems a miracle itself. It's not hard to believe that it was here in AD 813 that hermit Pelayo saw the great light, leading him and Bishop Teodoro to the tomb of the apostle St. James, buried beneath the undergrowth. Pilgrims have been trekking here since the 10th century to embrace the statue of the apostle in the chancel and kneel before his mortal remains in the crypt. The 12th-century **Pórtico de la Gloria** depicts the resurrection of Christ; the central marble column bears a deep handprint, worn by the touch of centuries of devoted pilgrims. Originating in the Middle Ages, the **Botafumeiro** ceremony is breathtaking (and a little scary)—at the end of the daily midday pilgrim's mass (around 12:45), huge urns of flaming, smoking incense suspended on chains fly wildly through the cathedral. The **Museo de la Catedral** (admission 400 ptas; open daily 10–1:30 and 4–7:30) holds tapestries based on works by Goya and Rubens.

The **Palacio de Xelmírez,** a magnificent work of 12th- to 15th-century civic architecture, was built as the palace of the first archbishop of Compostela. Because it was built onto the cathedral during the 12th century, you can see parts of the cathedral's original Romanesque shell from its entrance. Inside the main hall, the sculptures seem to be moving, playing music, and indulging in Galician food and wine. *Pr. Obradoiro. Admission: 200 ptas. Open daily 10–1:30 and 4:30–7:30.*

AFTER DARK

Santiago's students and summertime pilgrims keep the nightlife rocking year-round. Within the old town, bars and pubs are concentrated around Vía Sacra and the streets branching off from Praza de Cervantes. Competitive drinkers join in "Paris to Dakar," starting out at **Paris** (Rúa dos Bautizados 11, at the southern end of Rúa do Franco, tel. 981/58–59–86) and drinking a *copa* (cup) at every bar (there are about 30) on the way to **Cafetería Dakar** (Rúa do Franco 13, tel. 981/57–81–92). Those with less strenuous inclinations can sit down to a big bowl of *queimada,* a potent Galician brew of *aguardiente* (brandy), coffee, fruit, and sugar that is set on fire and stirred for several minutes before being consumed. This has the double effect of heating the mixture and banishing any evil spirits that may be lurking about. The *queimada* at **Los Caracoles** (Rúa da Raiña 14, tel. 981/56–14–98) is a local favorite and serves four to six people for 2,000 ptas. When school is in session, the discos in the new sections of town thump with fun-lovers. **Ruta 66** (Rúa Perez Constantini 4, tel. 981/58–60–53) plays cheesy American music, but there's no cover and the kids love it.

NEAR SANTIAGO DE COMPOSTELA

You'll need to venture out of Santiago de Compostela to discover Galicia's most beautiful beaches. **Castromil** (tel. 981/58–97–00) buses travel from Santiago to breathtaking beaches such as **Noia** (1 hr, 375 ptas) and **O Grove** (2 hrs, 540 ptas), both among the Rías Bajas, a series of inlets piercing the western Costa de la Muerte (Coast of Death).

LA CORUNA

The northern city of La Coruña (A Coruña in Gallego) is a bright, cheerful metropolis with popular surfing beaches on its edges. The **bus station** (C. Caballeros, tel. 981/23–90–99) and the **train station** (Av. Joaquín Planelles, tel. 981/15–02–02) are both south of the marina, across the highway from each other. Buses 21 and 24 serve the center of town. The **tourist office** (Dársena de la Marina, tel. 981/22–18–22) has free maps and information on nearby beaches. There's plenty of cheap food and lodging in the shopping district north of the marina. Even though it's above a McDonald's, **Hostal Castelo** (C. Real 14, tel. 981/22–29–06) is a delightful place with gorgeous doubles (3,000 ptas). Nearby **Café-Bar La Viña** (C. Real 28) has seafood *raciones* for about 500 ptas.

VIGO

This industrial port city makes a good, inexpensive base for exploring nearby beaches and the Islas Cíes, a pair of islands in the Ría de Vigo (Vigo Estuary). Vigo's **train station** (Pr. de la Estación, tel. 986/43–11–14) is southwest of the port; follow Rúa Urzáiz to Rúa Principe to get to the center of town. There's a **municipal tourist office** (tel. 986/43–05–77; open daily 9:30–1:30 and 5–9) in the train station, and a **regional tourist office** (Las Avenidas, tel. 986/81–01–44; open weekdays 10–2 and 5–9) south of the port, near Praza do Rei. Both offices have free maps and information on beaches such as **Samil** and **Canido,** west of town. Buses to more distant beach towns such as **Baiona** (40 min, 300 ptas) leave from the **bus station** (Av. Madrid, tel. 986/37–34–11), south of town. Buses 7, 12, and 21 run between the station and the port. Cheap *hostales* line **Rúa Carral,** which runs from the Monumento al Marqués de Elduayen on the waterfront up to the Porta do Sol. A little nicer than these is **Hospedaje Peña** (Pr. de Compostela 24, tel. 986/22–84–12; doubles 3,000 ptas), which overlooks a pretty, café-lined promenade. For cheap seafood, head down to the waterfront and the **Mercado da Pedra,** where women prepare plates of fresh octopus (500 ptas) while you wait. **Restaurante Chino Shanghai** (Pr. de Compostela 27, tel. 986/22–58–88) has a wide selection of veggie, tofu, and rice dishes for 500 ptas–700 ptas, and meat dishes are only slightly more expensive. For provisions, try **Spar Super** (open Mon.–Sat. 10–2 and 5–9) on Garcia Olloqui 9, just up from the waterfront.

Vapores de Pasaje (Estacíon Marítima de Ría, tel. 986/43–77–77) runs ferries to the gorgeous Islas Cíes (2,000 ptas round-trip). If one day isn't enough, you can stay over at **Camping Isla Cíes** (tel. 986/43–46–55; open June–Sept.), where sites are 525 ptas per tent plus 515 ptas per person, but do reserve, as it's often full.

SWEDEN

S weden was a power to be reckoned with in the Nordic region long before the United States was even a twinkle in Uncle Sam's eye. The Vikings pillaged their way through Russia as far south as Turkey, then decided to take a look at Europe and the United Kingdom. Ravenous 17th-century kings fought to take over all of Scandinavia. Since the 1800s, though, Sweden has been a neutral country and has focused on tending to its own population. Sweden is known for its generous social welfare and medical systems; despite cutbacks in the past few years, it's still one of Europe's most munificent setups. But to pay for it, Swedes have to part with 50%–60% of their paychecks.

Sweden is bottom-heavy in population: most people live in the south; in the north, nature reigns supreme. Throughout the country, though, the two are invariably integrated. From the parks of Stockholm to the dense forests of the north, green spaces are respected, well tended, and actively appreciated. No one can say the Swedes haven't produced their fair share of cultural notables, either; the cast includes Alfred Nobel, Carl von Linné (Linnaeus), ABBA, August Strindberg, Ingmar Bergman (Woody Allen's favorite filmmaker), Ingrid Bergman, Greta Garbo, and Anders Celsius.

The '90s haven't been kind to Sweden. The country went through a rough, six-year recession and is only now beginning to recover. Austerity measures have meant that Sweden's lavish foreign-aid program (traditionally 1% of its GNP—compare that to 0.1% for the United States in 1995) and domestic welfare programs have faced drastic cuts. The Swedes voted "Ja" to joining the European Union by only a slim margin, and their recent economic troubles had many wishing they had voted "Nej." However, the economy is beginning to look up, even if this has little to do with the decision makers in Brussels; Swedish exporting companies have helped to pull the country out of the financial doldrums. Despite the setbacks from a Swede's point of view, it's not likely you will notice the negative effects on the Swedish lifestyle, thanks to a favorable exchange rate, a remarkably high standard of living, and a relatively low crime rate.

BASICS

MONEY

US$1 = 7.2 kroner and 1 kronor = 14¢. The krona (SKr) is divided into 100 öre. Most banks charge 3% or SKr 50 per exchange, whichever is greater, making them the least preferable option. **Forex** or **Valu-**

KEY
⊢⊣ Rail Lines
······· Hiking Trail

*Norwegian
Sea*

ARCTIC CIRCLE

Abisko
Kebnekaise ▲
Kiruna
Kungsleden
Kvikkjokk
Gällivare
Luleälven
Jokkmokk
Haparanda
Ammarnäs
Arjeplog
Boden
Töre
Kalix
E12
Sorsele
Arvidsjaur
Luleå
Storuman
95
Piteå
Lycksele
Skellefteå
342
Åsele
90
Strömsund
Umeälven
92
Umeå
Åre
Östersund
E14
Ljungan
Sundsvall
Fjällnäs
84
*Gulf
of
Bothnia*
Idre
Sälen
70
Bollnäs
Hudiksvall
Mora
62
Söderhamn
Klarälven
Leksand
Falun
Gävle
Borlänge
80
Fagersta
Avesta
Karlstad
E4
Uppsala
E18
Mellerud
Västerås
Mälaren
Stockholm
Örebro
Vänern
Strömstad
Nynäshamn
*Gotska
Sandön*
Uddevalla
Trollhättan
Norrköping
Vättern
Linköping
Göteborg
*Baltic
Sea*
Borås
Jönköping
40
Falkenberg
Nässjö
Visby
E6
Värnamo
E22
Oskarshamn
Gotland
Halmstad
Växjö
23
Kalmar
Öland
Helsingborg
Karlskrona
Malmö
Kristianstad
Luna
Trelleborg
Ystad

N

NORWAY

FINLAND

Gulf of Finland

ESTONIA

*Gulf of
Riga*

LATVIA

LITHUANIA

DENMARK

DALARNA

LAPLAND

400

0   50 miles
0   75 km

taspecialisten exchange offices, usually found at the airport or near the train station, generally offer the best rates; they only charge SKr 20 per exchange, and they buy back Swedish kronor. You can change money at post offices, but the SKr 35 fee encourages large exchanges.

HOW MUCH IT WILL COST • Sweden can be expensive. One of the reasons for this is the 25% *moms* (value-added tax) charged on almost everything. If you're thinking about renting a car, you should know that gasoline is a serious cash-eater. Hostelling International hostels are pretty reasonable at around SKr 100 a night. Hotels in summer run about SKr 450 per double. A decent lunchtime meal can be had for around SKr 65. Service is included in restaurant and taxi bills, but taxi drivers expect some sort of tip (about SKr 15), especially if you have luggage.

COMING AND GOING

If you don't have a Eurail or ScanRail pass, you might want to consider flying to Sweden. There are flights from many European cities that cost no more than taking the train or ferry. Those under 26 generally get 30% discounts on trains and similar discounts on buses.

BY BUS AND TRAIN • Eurolines (tel. 020/987–377 in Stockholm) is the major international bus company, with service to France, Germany, the Netherlands, and England. Trains from major European cities head to Stockholm via Hamburg and Copenhagen (trains and buses are loaded right onto the ferries). Some train routes, especially from Finland and Norway, are supplemented by buses; in such cases, rail passes are honored by the bus line.

BY FERRY • There are numerous ferry routes to and from Sweden and a variety of ferry lines competing for your kronor. The major carriers are **Silja Line** (tel. 08/222–140) and **Viking Line** (tel. 08/452–4000). (Eurailers ride Viking free and receive a 50% discount on Silja; ScanRail pass holders get a 50% discount on both lines; and those under 26 get 30% off Viking Line ferries). **Stena Line** (tel. 031/750–000) and **Scandinavian Seaways** (tel. 08/679–8880) operate to and from the United Kingdom, as well as to the Netherlands, Denmark, Germany, and Norway.

BY PLANE • Traveling by plane may be a better deal than you think. If you're under 25, it's possible to receive discounts of 50%–70%. **SAS** (tel. 020/727–000 for domestic flights or 020/727–555 for international flights) provides regular service to Stockholm and Göteborg from most European cities. The discounts normally apply to off-peak flights and are often of a last-minute nature, though it is occasionally possible to get them even when booking ahead. Just remember that parental adage: it never hurts to ask.

GETTING AROUND

Most **trains** in Sweden are state-run by **Statensjärnvägar** (SJ); dial 020/757–575 toll-free for information on all domestic trains (wait for recorded message to end for operator assistance). In major cities there are also local **Stockholms Lokaltrafik** (SL) services to nearby suburbs. Eurailpasses are generally valid only on SJ trains, so seriously consider the **ScanRail** pass, which gives you unlimited train travel throughout Sweden, Denmark, Finland, and Norway, plus limited ferry passage in and beyond Scandinavia. The pass is available for five days of travel within 15 days; 10 days within a month; or one month. In the United States, call **RailEurope** (tel. 800/438–7245), or **DER** (tel. 800/782–2424), which also offers a 21-day pass. The *Reslustkort* (SKr 150) gives you a 25% discount only on trains leaving Tuesday–Thursday and Saturday, and a 50% discount on some *röda avgånger* ("red," or off-peak, departures) listed on train schedules.

Buses are sometimes cheaper than trains and are equally as comfortable. Discounts and specials vary according to season and day of the week; the cheapest fares are on weekdays September–May. **Swebus** (tel. 031/103–800) and **Svenska Buss** (tel. 020/676–767) are the major carriers in the south. Buses are essential in the north (there are no train services to speak of); dial 020/470–047 toll-free for information in basic English on the routes offered by the various companies. Bus stations are usually situated conveniently next to or within train stations. In the far north, postal buses delivering mail to remote areas also carry passengers, providing an offbeat, inexpensive journey. You can ask at a local post office about this, but catching one is mostly a stroke of luck.

WHERE TO SLEEP

Hotels are pricey, even on weekends and in summer when discount rates apply. Far and away the cheapest places to stay in Sweden are **hostels** (*vandrarhem*) and **campgrounds** (*campingplatser*); luckily, these two options shouldn't be a hardship. Swedish hostels are superior to most in Europe; they're normally more modern and tend to have better facilities, even in out-of-the-way places. Best of all, they're *clean*. Most are run by **Svenska Turistföreningen** (STF; tel. 08/463–2100), a member of Hostelling International (HI), and have fully equipped kitchens, laundry facilities, TV rooms, and luggage storage. Doubles are usually available if you reserve in advance (a couple of weeks for city hostels, a day or two for hostels in more remote areas). Don't forget to check the calendar, since festivals, holidays, and such can make beds scarce. Prices listed in this chapter are for HI members; nonmembers pay between SKr 35 and SKr 50 extra. Sheets can be rented at most hostels for around SKr 40.

Campers rejoice: *Allemansrätt* (every man's right) is the law in Sweden, so you can pitch a tent practically anywhere in the open for one night, as long as you are 500 ft from the nearest dwelling. Official campgrounds (costing roughly SKr 150 per night near the southern cities, and roughly SKr 80 in the northern countryside) are usually clean and well-equipped, and draw a ton of family vacationers with their ensuing cars, caravans, and barbecues. Sites are generally open between June 1 and September 1, although some stay open year-round. A free, abbreviated list of sites is published in English by the **Sveriges Campingvårdernas Riksforbünd** (Swedish Campsite Owners' Association, Box 255, 451 17 Uddevalla, tel. 0522/642–440, fax 0522/642–430).

FOOD
The cheapest time to eat out in Sweden is midday, when many restaurants offer a *dagens rätt* (daily special) consisting of a main dish, salad, bread, light beer or soda, and coffee for around SKr 65. Most places offer several choices: *biff* (beef), *fläsk* (pork), *vegetarisk* (vegetarian), and some sort of pasta. Fish and potatoes are the true Swedish staples; the legendary Swedish *smörgåsbords* have become hard to find except in fancy restaurants and during Christmastime. In the north, *renskav* (reindeer) is served in a variety of ways, especially smoked, and usually with potatoes. Pizzerias are everywhere, with tasty versions at prices ranging from SKr 30 to SKr 50. Just about every bar and café offers a full meal of some kind, largely to satisfy Swedish licensing laws; luckily, these meals tend to be a cut above greasy-spoon numbers, and they're generally quite reasonably priced. Coffee, about SKr 20, is served in small portions, but *patår* (refills) usually cost only a few kronor extra. **ICA** and **Konsum supermarkets** will come to the rescue of budget travelers, but in small towns their weekend hours might be very short.

> *The Swedes may seem a bit standoffish at first, but give them time. As the Swedish saying goes, "A Swede is like a bottle of ketchup: first comes nothing, then comes nothing, then comes everything."*

BUSINESS HOURS
Swedish stores are usually open weekdays 9–6 and Saturday 9–1 or 9–4. Banks are open 9:30–3 (sometimes until 5 in bigger cities), and post offices are almost always open weekdays 9–6 and Saturday 10–1. Museum hours vary widely, but most are open weekdays 10–4 or 10–5, weekends 11–4; sometimes they close on Mondays. The off-season runs from September through mid-May; expect reduced hours at museums and tourist offices and most open-air museums, except Skansen, to be closed.

FESTIVALS AND HOLIDAYS
Midsommar (Midsummer) is Sweden's biggest festival. On the summer solstice, usually the third weekend of June, revelers dance around maypoles, just as their ancestors did, while others just waddle drunkenly in circles. The few trains that operate are crowded, many stores close early on Friday, and virtually everything is closed on Saturday and Sunday while the Swedes recover from a nationwide hangover. Dalarna is the most popular region in which to celebrate because of its tradition-heavy festivities.

VISITOR INFORMATION
Swedish tourist offices, called *turistbyrån* or *turist information* and marked with green signs with a big white I, are usually found near the train station and always have an English-speaking staff. Most stock information about the entire country, sell tickets to local events, and arrange guided tours.

Swedes tend to have a liberal yet reserved attitude towards homosexuality, and just about every sizable town has a **Riksförbundet För Sexuellt Likaberättigande** (National Association for Sexual Equality, usually listed in phone books under RFSL), which happily provides information to gay and lesbian travelers. **De Handikappades Riksförbund** (Katrinebergsvägen 6, 11743, Stockholm, tel. 08/189–100) has a brochure in English to assist travelers with disabilities that is invaluable—the government makes recommendations for accessibility, but getting businesses to follow them is another matter.

PHONES
Country code: 46. If you're calling from outside the country, drop the first zero in the regional area code. You can make an international call from any pay phone in Sweden via an international operator. For

AT&T Direct Access[SM], dial 020/795–611; for **MCI,** dial 020/795–922; and for **Sprint,** dial 020/799–011. To dial directly to United States or Canada dial 009, then the country code, then the number. Pay phones use either coins (SKr 1, SKr 5, or SKr 10) or *telefonkort* (phone cards), which you can buy at a *Telebutik* (telephone retail outlet), hospital, or *Pressbyrån* (newsstand) for SKr 35 for 30 units, SKr 60 for 60 units, or SKr 100 for 120 units). One krona buys you one unit of phone credit in all pay phones. Local calls cost SKr 2, and domestic long-distance calls take an additional krona every 25 seconds. Some of the nationwide Telebutiker have phone booths where you can pay after placing a call; prices are the same as at pay phones. For free directory information (in English) within Sweden from a pay phone, dial 07975. For international directory assistance, dial 07977.

MAIL

Letters to North America cost SKr 8 and take about a week. For the rest of Europe, letters cost SKr 7 and take four working days. You can buy stamps everywhere postcards are sold, at all *Pressbyrån* newsstands, and, of course, at the post office. Have your poste restante mail addressed as follows: Poste Restante, Central Post Office, postal code, City, Sweden. American Express offers a poste restante service free to cardholders and for a small fee to others.

EMERGENCIES

Dial 112 for all emergencies anywhere in the country. *Nattapotek* (night pharmacies) are few and far between (check the local telephone directory), so for late-night emergencies go to the local *vårdcentral* (medical center) or *sjukhuset* (hospital).

LANGUAGE

Apart from Swedish, Finnish and Sami are also spoken in parts of northern Sweden. Virtually everyone speaks at least a little English, and many people have some basics in German, too. Knowledge of a few essential words in Swedish won't hurt, however, and addressing locals in their native tongue will make most people far more willing to use yours. These phrases may help: *hej* (hello); *hejdå* (good-bye); *var snäll* (please); *tack* (thank you); *var finns . . .?* (where is . . .?); *hur mycket . . .?* (how much is . . .?); *talar du Engelska?* (do you speak English?).

STOCKHOLM

Stockholm is one of Europe's most beautiful cities. The wealthy Birger Jarl knew what he was doing when he founded the city as a trading port in 1252; its location on Sweden's southeast coast means access to the Baltic and protection by the vast *skärgården* (archipelago) made up of 24,000 islands, now used by Stockholmites as their own private natural playground.

The Stockholm City Council works hard to maintain the pristine beauty of their environment; they have commissioned art for the subways, cleaned the waterways to make them safe for swimming and fishing, and set aside tracts of land as an Eco Park, which can't be built on (or under) for all eternity. These measures are heartily approved by the local populace, who, despite their cosmopolitan appearance, spend much of their free time sunbathing by the water, walking through the woods, and basically enjoying the nature that is an integral part of their urban environment. Spend some time in Gamla Stan (the Old Town), wooded Djurgården, or Södermalm, with its casual cafés and galleries, and you'll agree that it's a combination of urban and natural pleasures that gives Stockholm its special character.

BASICS

VISITOR INFORMATION

Stockholm This Week (it actually covers a whole month), available free from tourist offices and most hotels, has a good, if not overly detailed, map and lots of information on museums, sights, and things to do. It appears at the end of each month. The helpful **Sverigehuset** (Sweden House) has an in-house Forex currency exchange desk. *Hamng. 27, across from NK shopping center, tel. 08/789–2490. Open June–Aug., weekdays 9–9, weekends 9–5; Sept.–May, weekdays 9–6, weekends 9–3.*

The **Hotellcentralen,** on the main level of the train station, doles out information and will reserve beds at hostels (SKr 15 per person booking fee) and hotels (SKr 40 per room booking fee, plus deposit). Best of all, if you make a personal appearance at their office, they'll book you a room for free. *Central Station, Vasag., tel. 08/789-2425. Open Oct.-Apr., daily 9-6; May and Sept. daily 8-7, June-Aug. daily 7-9.*

AMERICAN EXPRESS
Birger Jarlsg. 1, tel. 08/679-7880, 24-hr toll-free hotline 020/795-155. Open weekdays 9-5, weekends 10-2. Mailing address: Box 1761, 11187 Stockholm.

CHANGING MONEY
Forex has offices in the train station, airport, Silja ferry terminal, and Sverigehuset (*see* Visitor Information, *above*).

EMBASSIES
Australia: *Sergels Torg 12, tel. 08/613-2900. Open weekdays 8:30-12:30 and 1:30-4:30.* **Canada:** *Tegelbacken 4, tel. 08/453-3000. Open weekdays 9:30-12:30 and 2-4.* **United Kingdom:** *Skarpög. 6, tel. 08/671-9000. Open weekdays 9:30-12:30 and 2-4.* **United States:** *Strandv. 101, tel. 08/783-5300. American Citizens' Services open weekdays 9-11.*

EMERGENCIES
For the police, an ambulance, or the fire department, dial 112. The emergency medical center, **City Akuten** (tel. 08/411-7177) always has doctors on duty. **C.W. Scheele** (tel. 08/454-8130) is a 24-hour pharmacy.

PHONES AND MAIL
The main **Telebutik** (open daily 8 AM-9 PM) is in the train station. The main **post office** is an enormous brick building at the corner of Vasagatan and Mäster Samuelsgatan, across from the train station; the postal code is S-101 10. If you want to send an e-mail, get on line at **Cafe Access** (Sergels Torg 3, tel. 08/700-0100; open Mon. 11-6, Tues. 10-6, Sat. 10-4, and Sun. noon-4) in the Kulturhuset (*see* Stockholm Museums, *below*); they charge SKr 20 per half hour and SKr 2 per message printed. Word processing is also available.

COMING AND GOING

BY TRAIN
Trains head from Stockholm's **Central Station** (Vasag., tel. 020/757-575) to Paris (24 hrs, SKr 1,880 for second class), Copenhagen (9 hrs, SKr 630), Amsterdam (20 hrs, SKr 1,444), and Frankfurt (21 hrs, SKr 1,592). An extra SKr 125 reservation charge is often required. Underneath the train station is a T-bana station (*see* Getting Around, *below*), several grocery stores, and some cafeterias, which are usually open until 10 PM.

BY BUS
The main bus station, **Cityterminalen** (Klarabergsviadukten 72, tel. 020/640-640 for bookings and information) is in the World Trade Center across from the train station. Buses are generally cheaper than trains. Prices for one-way trips are SKr 1,275 (27 hrs) to Paris, SKr 1,125 (27 hrs) to Amsterdam, and SKr 420 (15 hrs) to Copenhagen.

BY FERRY
Five ferry companies operate along Stockholm's waterways; each has its own terminal. Three of them are **Viking Line** (tel. 08/452-4000) with daily boats to Turku (Åbo), Finland (12 hrs, SKr 220) and Helsinki (Helsingfors, 15 hours, SKr 420), which depart from the terminal on Södermalm; take the T-bana to Slussen and then a free Viking Line bus. **Estline AB** (tel. 08/667-0001) has boats to Tallinn, Estonia (16 hrs, SKr 455) that leave from Frihamnen. **Silja Line** (tel. 08/222-140) goes daily to Helsinki (15 hrs, SKr 450) and Turku, Finland (12 hrs, SKr 310), and leaves from Frihamnen; take the T-bana to Ropsten and catch a free Silja bus.

BY PLANE
Arlanda International Airport is 40 minutes from Stockholm via Flygbuss airport buses (SKr 60). The buses leave City Terminalen every 10-15 minutes until 10 PM, and leave from the airport until 11 PM. The local airline is **SAS** (*see* Coming and Going *in* Sweden Basics, *above*).

Tegnér-lunden

Tegnérgatan
Vasagatan
Dalagatan
Kammakargatan
Wallingatan
Barnhusgatan
Olof Palmes Gata
Kungsgatan
Vasagatan
Bryggargatan
Drottninggatan

HÖTORGET
Hötorget

Brunnsgatan
Kungsgatan

Humlegården
ÖSTERM.

Östermalmstorg
Humlegårdsgatan
Sturegatan
Nybrogatan
Sibyllegatan
Sture Plan

Malmskillnadsgatan
Sveavägen
Mäster Samuelsgatan
Smålandsgatan
Birger Jarlsgatan
Biblioteksgatan

Norr Malmstorg
Nybroplan

Karlbergssjön

Klarastrandsleden
Kungsbro Strand
Kungsholmsgatan

T-CENTRALEN
NORRMALM

Sergels Torg
Kulturhuset 11
Regeringsgatan
Hamngatan

Kungsträdgården

Flemming-gatan

Klarabergsviadukten
Klarabergsgatan
Train Station

Vattugatan
Herkulesgatan
Jakobsgatan
Fredsgatan
Gustav Adolfs Torg
Karl XII's Torg
Strömgatan
Arsenalsgatan
Nybrokajen

KUNGS-HOLMEN

Hantverkargatan
Stadshusbron
Stadshuset 12

Norr Mälarstrand
Klara Mälarstrand
Tegel Backen
Gångbron
Centralbron
Vasabron

HELGEANDS-HOLMEN

Södra Blasieholmsh.
Skeppsbron
Skeppsholms-bron

Riddarfjärden

RIDDAR HOLMEN

Myntgatan
Storkyrkobrinken
Riddarhus Torget
Stortorget
Köpmang.
Brunnsgr.
GAMLA STAN
Kungliga Slottet 13

Riddarholmskyrkan 14

GAMLA STAN

Västerlånggatan
Stora Nygatan
Lilla Nygatan
Kornhamnstorg
Österlånggatan
Skeppsbron
Strömmen

Centralbron
Slussen

Söder Mälarstrand

SÖDERMALM

Bastugatan
Tavastgatan
Brännkyrkagatan
Hornsgatan
Blekholmsgränd
Bellmansgatan
Götgatan

Söderm. Torg
Stadsgården
Katarinavägen

Sights ●
Kulturhuset, 11
Kungliga Slottet, 13
Millesgarden, 5
Moderna Museet, 3
National Museet, 10

Nordiska Museet, 7
Riddarholms-kyrkan, 14
Skansen, 6
Stadhuset, 12
Vasamuseet, 8

Lodging ○
af Chapman and Skeppsholmen's Vandrarhem (STF), 9
Café Bed and Breakfast, 2
Columbus Hotell, 17
Gustav af Klint, 18

Hotell Danielson, 1
Hotell Östermalm, 4
Långholmen (STF), 15
Zinkens (STF), 16

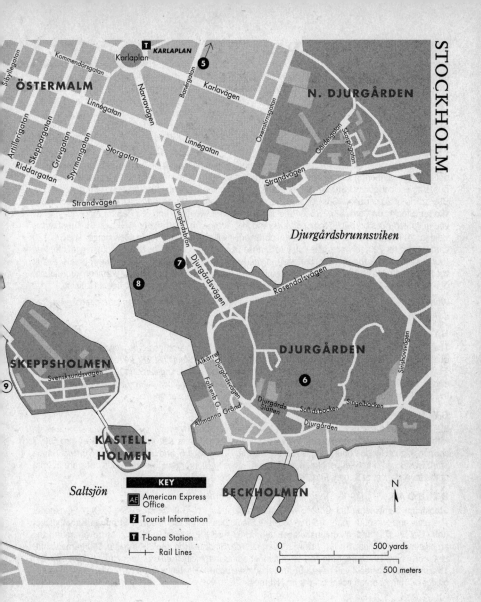

ÖSTERMALM

Sibyllegatan
Kommendörsgatan
Karlaplan

Narvavägen
Banérgatan
Karlavägen

N. DJURGÅRDEN

Linnégatan

Artilerigatan
Skeppargatan
Grevgatan
Styrmangatan
Storgatan

Linnégatan

Oxenstiernsgatan

Gardesgatan
Skarpögatan

Riddargatan

Strandvägen

Strandvägen

Djurgårdsbron

Djurgårdsbrunnsviken

Djurgårdsvägen

Rosendalsvägen

Sirishovsvägen

SKEPPSHOLMEN

DJURGÅRDEN

Svensksundsvägen

Alkärret
Djurgårdsvägen
Folkenb G.

Djurgårds
Slätten

Sollidsbacken

Singelbacken

Allmanna Gränd

Djurgården

KASTELL-
HOLMEN

Saltsjön

BECKHOLMEN

N

KEY		
AE	American Express Office	
i	Tourist Information	
T	T-bana Station	
⊢—⊢	Rail Lines	

0 ——————— 500 yards

0 ——————— 500 meters

GETTING AROUND

Stockholm is built on 14 islands, seven of which make up the city center. The train station is on the western edge of the biggest island, **Norrmalm**; the eastern part of the island, called **Östermalm,** has fancy shops and luxury apartments. Next in size is **Södermalm** to the south, traditionally an artsy working-class neighborhood. Between Östermalm and Södermalm, from west to east, are **Riddarholmen,** punctuated by the lacy spire of Riddarholm church; **Gamla Stan,** home to the old royal palace; **Skeppsholmen,** marked by the masts of the 17th-century ship (now a hostel) af Chapman; and **Djurgården,** dominated by the Wasa Museum and the amusement park, Gröna Lund. **Kungsholmen,** west of the train station, has the massive brick tower of the Stadshuset on its southeastern tip.

The T-bana (subway) and buses can tote you around town in no time at all. Local trains run from the city outskirts to neighboring towns; their routes are marked on the T-bana map. The T-bana, local trains, and buses all use coupons at SKr 14 per zone and valid for one hour; many trips cost two or three coupons. Buy a strip of 20 coupons (SKr 95) at Pressbyrån, tourist offices, and T-bana stations. The **Stockholmskortet** (Stockholm Card, SKr 185 for one day, SKr 350 for two days, and SKr 425 for three days) gives you unlimited rides on public transportation and free admission to 70 sights. A SKr 60 **SL Turistkort** is valid for 24 hours on all forms of local transportation; it will pay for itself within a few hours. The SKr 120 card is good for 72 hours and gets you into Skansen (see Worth Seeing, below) and other sights for free (but not as many as the Stockholmskortet). All cards are available at tourist offices, many hotels, and at the Hotellcentralen office (see Visitor Information, above). For general public transportation information, dial 08/600–1000 for the Stockholm Transit Authority; you should be able to get help in English.

When wandering by foot, the basic street sign terms you'll come across are gatan (street, abbreviated to g.), vägen (abbreviated to v.) and gränd (shortened to gr.).

BY T-BANA

The T-bana system is convenient for both short hops and for longer trips across town; trains come frequently, and it sure beats waiting for the bus in bad weather. Tickets cost SKr 14 for travel within Zones 1 and 2, and an additional SKr 7 for Zone 3. Zones are arranged in rings around the city; be sure to get a map, available at most T-bana stations. Tickets are available in each station. All four T-bana lines run through T-Centralen at the Central Station (see Coming and Going, above).

BY BUS

SL's red buses cruise the city from 5 AM to 11 PM, stopping at nearly every corner. (Look for a square sign with a red-and-white background, marked SL BUSS.) The drivers sell tickets (SKr 14 or two SKr 7 coupons), good for one hour and also on the T-bana. Buses 48, 55, and 59 go to Södermalm via Gamla Stan, Bus 65 goes to Skeppsholmen, and Bus 47 goes to Djurgården. The main bus hubs are in front of the train station, at Sergels Torg, and at Slussen on Södermalm.

BY BOAT

Stockholm Sightseeing (tel. 08/240–470) has various tours (1–3 hrs, SKr 90–SKr 250) of Stockholm. The one- and two-hour tours are free with the Stockholmskortet (see above). **Strömma Kanalbolaget** (tel. 08/233–375) and **Waxholmsbolaget** (tel. 08/679–5830) both have boats that travel around the archipelago (see Cheap Thrills, below), departing from Stadhusbron and Strömgatan. **Djurgården** shuttles scurry between Djurgården and several other points in the city from 6 AM to midnight. They cost SKr 15 a shot, but are free if you have a SL Turistkort (see above). Boat information is available at the tourist offices or in front of the ticket booths on Nybroplan.

WHERE TO SLEEP

Stockholm has a veritable slew of hotels and hostels in all price categories. Hotel prices can drop dramatically on weekends and in summer, and some hotels have large double rooms they are willing to rent to groups of three or four. Hostels are usually excellent. **Hotellcentralen** (see Visitor Information, above) books rooms in both hotels and hostels and publishes a useful hotel guide. If you don't stick close to the city center, your bus and T-bana fares will add up. You must reserve ahead during the Stockholm Water Festival (Aug. 8–16).

Gustav af Klint. A hotel ship moored at Stadsgården quay, near Slussen subway station, the Gustav af Klint is divided into two sections—a hotel and a hostel. The hotel section has 4 single-bunk and 3 two-bunk cabins with bedsheets and breakfast included. The hostel section has 18 four-bunk cabins and

10 two-bunk cabins; a 14-bunk dormitory is also available from May through mid-September. Rates are about SKr 120 per person in a four-bunk room, and SKr 140 per person in a two-bunk room. All guests share common bathrooms and showers. There is a cafeteria and a restaurant, and you can dine on deck in summer. *Stadsgårdskajen 153, S–116 45, tel. 08/640–4077, fax 08/640–6416. 7 hotel cabins, 28 hostel cabins, 28 dormitory beds.*

Hotell Danielson. Rooms here are spacious, clean, and high-ceilinged. Doubles cost SKr 520 with shower, SKr 420 without; three- and four-bed rooms run SKr 200 per person with shower and SKr 175 without; all include breakfast. *Walling. 31, tel. 08/411–1076. From train station, walk 6 blocks north on Vasag., turn left at City Conference Center.*

Hotell Östermalm. This elegant building, within walking distance of city center and near the T-bana, has that well-cared-for atmosphere without being too pricey. Doubles will set you back SKr 550, SKr 640 with bath. *Karlv. 57, tel. 08/660–6996. From Stadion T-bana, walk east 1 block on Karlv.*

HOSTELS

Af Chapman and **Skeppsholmen's Vandrarhem (STF).** The *af Chapman,* an 18th-century sailing rig, and the adjacent Skeppsholmen, an old military building, have both been converted into very cozy hostels. You'll shell out just SKr 95 per person for a double, or SKr 100 for dorm beds; breakfast is an extra SKr 45. It's a great place for meeting other travelers. Reserve several weeks in advance. *Af Chapman: Skeppsholmen, tel. 08/679–5015. 120 beds. Closed Dec.–Mar. STF: tel. 08/679–5017. 155 beds. From the train station, take Bus 65 to Skeppsholmen. Lockout 11–3.*

Café Bed and Breakfast. Once a dance studio, this space is now an intimate basement hostel run by a friendly couple. It's a stone's throw from the Hard Rock Cafe in the university area. Doubles cost SKr 320, dorm beds SKr 125; breakfast costs an extra SKr 30. You'll have to wash your socks elsewhere; there are no laundry facilities. *Rehnsg. 21, tel. 08/152–838. Just off Sveav., catercorner to Rådmansg. T-bana. 30 beds. Kitchen facilities.*

The **Columbus Hotell** and **Gustaf af Klint** (*see above*) also offer dorm rooms at reasonable rates. The Columbus Hotell is near the Medborgarplatsen T-bana station; the rooms are nothing fancy, but they're nothing to wince at, either. Hotel doubles run SKr 315 per person; hostel doubles are Skr 165, plus a small fee for sheets and towels. *Tjärhovsgatan 11, tel. 08/644–1111. Kitchen, laundry.*

Långholmen (STF). Put one over on the Establishment by staying in this former prison—now an extraordinarily well-maintained hostel (though as you might expect, the windows are practically nonexistent). It's a little far from city center, but the calm island locale is a nice respite from hectic Eurotouring. Beds, most in doubles, cost SKr 180. *Kronohäktet, tel. 08/668–0510. From Hornstull T-bana, go left on Högalidssg., then turn right across the Långholmsbron bridge. 254 beds in summer, 26 in winter. Kitchen facilities, laundry.*

Zinkens (STF). This woodsy spot on Södermalm just outside the city center attracts huge tour groups. It has a TV room, and you can even rent bikes at SKr 80 per day. Beds run SKr 160, and there's no curfew. *Zinkens Väg 20, tel. 08/616–8100. From Zinkensdamm T-bana, walk south on Ringv. and turn right. 280 beds. Kitchen, laundry.*

CAMPING

Bredäng Camping. This site is 10 km (6 mi) south of Stockholm, squished between Lake Mälaren and high-rise apartments. Luckily it has a café/store, is near hiking and beaches, and is a five-minute walk from the T-bana and a supermarket. Tent sites cost SKr 150; next to the marked sites is an open field for overflow. There is also a hostel with 64 beds. Call for more information. *Stora Sälskapets Väg, tel. 08/977–071. From Bredäng T-bana, go left under tunnel and head straight. 115 sites. Kitchen facilities, laundry. Campground closed Sept.–May.*

FOOD

Stockholm offers a wide variety of dining choices—both Swedish and international. Lunch time eating generally costs around SKr 70. Look out for signs saying *dagens rätt* for about SKr 65. Take advantage of hostel breakfasts (SKr 30–SKr 40) and supermarkets (like ICA, Konsum and Vivo) to cut costs. Most cheap restaurants are found outside the city center, especially south in Södermalm and north along Drottninggatan and Odenplan, where you'll find lots of ethnic restaurants.

UNDER SKR 70 • Herman's Vegetarian Restaurants. These are godsends for vegetarians suffering on the cheese pizza diet. Lunch specials (SKr 65) include lasagna and paella. Make sure you try the spicy Yogi tea. *Stora Nygatan 11, tel. 08/411–9500. Hornsg. 87, tel. 08/669–7727. Fjllg. 23 A, tel. 08/643–9480. Katarina Bang. 17, tel. 08/640–3010.*

Indira. Don't forget to order *nan* (flat bread) so you can soak up the remnants of your beef-in-coconut-milk (SKr 65) or *Polak Ponir* (bean curry, SKr 65). There is also a selection of SKr 55 lunches at the counter. *Bondeg. 3B, tel. 08/641–4046. From Medborgarplatsen T-bana, take Götg. south, left on Bondeg.*

Silverhästen. This late-night postparty hangout near Sergels Torg looks like a typical counter-service café, but it serves up heaping hot dishes of lasagna, salmon, or roast beef (SKr 60–SKr 70), all with salad and unlimited bread. It's open 'til 11 PM on weekdays, 2 AM on weekends. *Mäster Samuelsg. 21, tel. 08/202–374. From T-Centralen T-bana, west on Mäster Samuelsg.*

Stortorgets Kaffestuga. *The* breakfast spot in Stockholm (read: crowded), with coffee/tea, juice, a sandwich, and an egg or yogurt for SKr 35—for SKr 10 more, you can get porridge instead of the egg/yogurt. *Stortorget 22, tel. 08/205–981. In Gamla Stan, 1 block south of Storkyrkan. Cash only.*

UNDER SKR 150 • Hot Wok Café. Stare at psychedelic graffiti art while eating enormous Asian meat or vegetarian lunches (SKr 65–SKr 75). A filling half-portion of à la carte dishes is SKr 50–SKr 75. *Hantverkarg. 78, west of Fridhemsplan T-bana, tel. 08/654–4202. Other locations: Kungshallen, tel. 08/209–444; Nytorgsg. 33, tel. 08/640–8018.*

Saigon Bar. To really discombobulate yourself, visit this 70s-inflected, quasi-American GI-in-Saigon restaurant. The food is an interesting mix of Swedish and Asian, with single dishes starting from SKr 90 (but they're big). For something a little cheaper, try the wok for SKr 35. There's no lunch. *Tegnerg. 19–21, tel. 08/203–887. From Rdmandsgatan T-bana, east along Tegnerg. Closed last 2 wks of July.*

CAFÉS

Café Art. This vaulted, candlelit café in a former wine cellar is one of the few survivors of a massive fire that nearly destroyed Stockholm in 1624. Devour crêpes, pastas, and enchilada lunches (each SKr 55) with pricey coffee (SKr 20) and an array of pastries (SKr 25–SKr 30). Come late (it's open until 11) to avoid tourists. *Västerlångg. 60, tel. 08/411–7661. From Gamla Stan T-bana, walk east on Kåkbrinken.*

Mosebacke. This spot may be an upscale restaurant and dance club at night, but during the day the SKr 18 coffee seems cheap considering the million-dollar view of the city. *Mosebacke Torg 3, tel. 08/642–4130. From Slussen T-bana, take Katarinahissen elevator to top of hill, cross footbridge, turn left, and follow signs.*

WORTH SEEING

At first glance, Stockholm seems to be all water, spires, historic buildings, and breathtaking sights (from the right vantage points). It is also rife with small museums, such as **Musikmuseet** (Sibylleg. 2, tel. 08/666–4530; admission SKr 30; open Tues.–Sun. 11–4), showcasing 18th-century musical instruments, and the **Almgrens Sidenväveri & Museum** (Almgren's Silk-Weaving Mill and Museum; Repslagarg. 15A, tel. 08/642–5616; admission SKr 45; open Mon.–Thurs. 2–5, Fri. 9–4, Sat. 10–4), with everything you always wanted to know about silk and how it becomes a fabric. The thorough *Stockholm's Museums,* available from the tourist office, will help you choose; it's in Swedish, but decipherable.

MUSEUMS

Stockholm's museums are dotted all over the city. Student discounts run between 30% and 50%; the Stockholmskortet (*see* Getting Around, *above*) gives you free admission to all the spots listed below.

KULTURHUSET • There's always something brewing at the huge House of Culture, which features contemporary Swedish art in changing exhibits, a packed art library, and galleries with superfluous artsy objects for sale. At press time, the Kulturhuset was, fittingly, being renovated for 1998s cultural celebrations, so call ahead for hours. *Sergels Torg 3, tel. 08/700–0100. Admission SKr 40.*

MILLESGARDEN • Just a few kilometers north of Stockholm, the enchanting house and garden of Swedish sculptor Carl Milles are filled with his own dreamy, symbolic works and the private collection of classical Greek and Italian pieces from which he drew inspiration. From the Ropsten T-bana, take any bus to the first stop across the bridge and follow signs. *Carl Milles Väg 2, tel. 08/731–5060. Admission SKr 50. Open May–Sept., Tues.–Sun. 10–5; Oct.–Apr., Tues.–Sun. 11–4.*

MODERNA MUSEET • Now back in its renovated old/new building this is one of Stockholm's best museums. Its world-class collection includes works by Picasso, Duchamp, Pollock, and Rauschenberg. Shutter-bugs can sate themselves with a great photography selection. *Skeppsholmen, tel. 08/666–4250. Admission SKr 50. Open Tues.–Thurs. 11–8, Fri.–Sun. 11–6.*

NATIONAL MUSEET • The marble building is a masterpiece in itself, housing artwork from the 17th century to the present, with an emphasis on Swedish artists like Zorn, Larsson, and Eriksson. Lots of floral landscapes and angst. *Södra Blasieholmshamnen, just before bridge to Skeppsholmen, tel. 08/666–4250. Admission SKr 40, free on Fri. Open Wed., Fri.–Sun. 11–5, Tues., Thurs. 11–8.*

NORDISKA MUSEET • This palatial museum celebrates the history of Sweden, with displays so saturated with props, films, and visual aids that you almost forget they're all in Swedish. The top floor has life-size models of typical 18th-century Swedish houses. *Djurgårdsv., tel. 08/666–4600. From Norrmalmstorg take Bus 47. Admission SKr 50 (including 45-min tour in English at 3:30). Open Tues.–Sun. 11–5, Thurs. 11–8.*

SKANSEN • This open-air folk museum has about 150 reconstructed traditional buildings from all over Sweden. There's also a zoo, with native Scandinavian lynxes, wolves, and elks, plus an aquarium and an old-style *tivoli* (amusement park). *Djurgårdsslätten 49–51, tel. 08/4428000. Admission Sept.–Apr., SKr 30 weekdays, SKr 40 weekends; May–Aug., SKr 50. Open Sept.–Apr., daily 9–5; May–Aug., daily 9–10.*

VASAMUSEET • After sinking in 1628, only 20 minutes into her maiden voyage, the intricately carved flagship *Vasa* sat on the bottom of the inlet to Stockholm for 333 years until she was lifted in one piece, restored, and put on display. It's a must-see for anybody who has ever dreamed of being a pirate. From Norrmalmstorg take Bus 47; or take the Djurgården ferry. *Galärvarvet, Djurgården, tel. 08/666–1800. Admission SKr 50. Open Thurs.–Tues. 10–5, Wed. 10–8. Tours in English hourly.*

PALACES AND CHURCHES

DROTTNINGHOLM PALACE • One of the more rewarding excursions from the city is to Drottningholm on the island of Lovön in Lake Mälaren; it's been the permanent residence of the Swedish royal family since 1981. The sections open to the public were mostly decorated in the 17th century, and there's also an enormous baroque garden, a Chinese pavilion, and plenty of lawn space for picnics. There's also an 18th-century theater which has a pretty dramatic history—and we're not talking curtain calls. It was originally a wedding present for Gustav III from his mother; the ill-fated Gustav, however, was assassinated at a masked ball in 1792 (dramatized in Verdi's opera *Un Ballo in Maschera*). The boat ride (50 mins, SKr 60) from Stadhusbron to the palace will give you a glimpse of Stockholm's beautiful surroundings; or take the T-bana to Brommaplan and transfer to one of the many buses heading south to the palace. *Tel. 08/759–0310. Admission SKr 40; free admission to gardens. Open June–Aug., daily 11–4; Sept.–May, daily 1–3.*

GRIPSHOLM SLOTT • On the southern side of Lake Mälaren about 64 km (38½ mi) from Stockholm, is Gripsholm Slott (Gripsholm Castle); its drawbridge and four massive round towers make it one of Sweden's most romantic castles. It now houses the state portrait collection, some 3,400 paintings, making it one of the largest portrait galleries in the world. If you're visiting between mid-June and late August, dust yourself off and get on the elegant vintage steamer **Mariefred,** the last coal-fired ship on Lake Mälaren (you can also take the train). The boat leaves from the quay next to City Hall; the ride costs SKr 160 round trip. Call 08/669–8850 for information. *Tel. 0159/10194. Admission SKr 40. Open Apr.–Sept., Tues.–Sun. 10–3.*

KUNGLIGA SLOTTET • The Royal Palace was built in 1760 and has been used mainly for formal royal affairs (and by scores of tourists) ever since the royal family relocated. The palace is divided into three separate sections. The **Representationsvän** (State Apartments; admission SKr 45) offer a peek at the royal living arrangements. The **Livrustkammaren** (Royal Armory; admission SKr 55) has a collection of armor, weapons, and stagecoaches. The **Skattkammaren** (Royal Treasury; admission SKr 40) has a dazzling display of crowns, orbs, and scepters. Call for times, as they're subject to change. *Slottsbacken, tel. 08/587–71000. From Gamla Stan T-bana, head uphill to northeast corner of island.*

RIDDARHOLMSKYRKAN • With its ironwork spire and a floor covered with the graves of more than 200 Swedish kings and nobility, this is Stockholm's most distinctive church. Originally a monastery, dating from 1270, it is also one of Stockholm's oldest structures. *Riddarholmen, tel. 08/402–6130. From Gamla Stan T-bana, head west across Centralbron. Admission SKr 20. Open May–Aug., Mon.–Sat. 11–4, Sun. noon–4; shorter hrs off-season.*

STADSHUSET • Stockholm's gigantic brick city hall is most famous as the site of the annual Nobel Prize award dinner on December 10. Equally impressive is the labyrinthine staircase that takes you to the top of the 350-ft tower for a sparkling view of the city. To see the rest of the building you have to take one of the daily 50-minute guided tours (SKr 30). *Hantverkarg. 1, tel. 08/508–29000. Across Stadhus-bron bridge from train station. Tower open May–Sept., daily 10–4:30. Admission to tower SKr 15. Tours June–late Aug., daily at 10, 11, noon, and 2; Sept., daily at 10, noon, and 2; Oct.–May, daily at 10 and noon.*

AFTER DARK

Stockholm has become a night-owl's paradise; places are staying open later than in years past. Sture-plan is the place to be on a Friday and Saturday night. Wherever you're going, get there early to avoid the queues. Södermalm is where you'll find SKr 40 beers (before the prices go up at 9 PM). The university area around Odenplan and Sveavägen is dotted with cheap student bars. Look for posters or check out *Nöjesguiden,* a free monthly paper that lists local happenings in theater, music, and film; they're in Swedish, but decipherable.

Glenn Miller Café. Musical instruments and photos of jazz greats line the walls of this offbeat side-street pub. Traditional Swedish meals cost SKr 60–SKr 90. Score the table in the corner by the record player and play DJ for the night. *Brunnsg. 21, tel. 08/100–322. 1 block north of Kungsg.*

Hus¹. Pronounced "Hus-et," this high-end gay dance club has mirrored walls, weekend drag shows, and a whopping SKr 60 cover (SKr 40 before 10). *Sveav. 57, tel. 08/315–533. T-bana: Rådmansgatan.*

Pelikan. High, painted ceilings, a tiled floor, and carved wood furniture are reminiscent of a 1920s beer hall; the place attracts a fairly bohemian crowd. If you're suddenly famished, you're in luck; Swedish meals (fish and potatoes) go for SKr 47. *Blekingeg. 40, tel. 08/743–0695. From Medborgarplatsen T-bana, walk south on Götg. and turn left.*

CHEAP THRILLS

Take time to find your favorite Stockholm view on leisurely strolls through the city center and the outlying areas. The harbor at **Nybroplan** hosts a constant flow of nautical activity, and **Djurgården,** once the royal hunting grounds, has many explorable parks and trails. The island's paths, flanked by trees, ambassadors' mansions, and great views of the Feather Islands, make for some of the most beautiful walks in Europe. Take Bus 47 from Sergels Torg to Waldemarsudde or Bus 69 from the Central Station to Blockshusudden (the very tip of Djurgården). For the most dramatic view over Stockholm, go to Södermalm and up onto **Fjällgatan.**

Stockholm's **archipelago** consists of more than 24,000 islands extending about 70 km (42 mi) into the *Östersjon* (Baltic Sea). Pack some clothes and purchase the *Båtluffarkortet* (boat-bum pass; SKr 250) from **Waxholmsbolaget** (on Sodra Blasieholmsh wharf, tel. 08/679–5830), entitling you to 16 days of unlimited ferry travel. Bring bikes free of charge. Hiking opportunities and beaches are plentiful on the lush islands, and hostels aren't too hard to find.

FESTIVALS

Stockholm will be the Cultural Capital of Europe in 1998, hosting events of all kinds; their tourist brochures claim it will be a sort of cultural renaissance. You'll have a whole year to determine if they can reach such heights, since events and exhibits will be mounted throughout the year. Best of all, admissions will be low or entirely free. Among the planned events are an international dance and ballet series, an exhibit of current Swedish artists in Kungsträdgården, guest circus performances, a jubilee exhibit of Orrefors glass at the National Museum, a music festival at Ulriksdal's Castle, a photographic festival, and a theater festival with a whole host of European theaters taking part (you can count on some shows in English). Contact the tourist office at Sverigehuset (*see* Visitor Information, *above*) for more information.

The **Stockholm Water Festival** (tel. 08/459–5500 for information) is a very big deal in Stockholm. People from all over the world come for the concerts, races, fireworks competition, and general partying that takes place here August 8–16. July 5–7 is the **Skansen Jazz and Blues Festival** (SKr 150 per night), where big names play on outdoor stages. Book lodging well in advance during both festivals (dates given are for 1998).

NEAR STOCKHOLM

UPPSALA

The Middle Ages seem to seep through the walls of Uppsala's 600-year-old university and the cafés where Carl von Linné (a.k.a. Linnaeus, originator of the modern binomial system of scientific nomenclature) and Olof Rudbeck (inventor of the anatomical theater) used to get their caffeine fixes. From the Domkyrkan, Scandinavia's largest church, to Ofvandahl's Konditori, which supplied bread to kings and queens at the turn of the century, Uppsala is steeped in history. Strangely, the town doesn't *feel* old, probably because of the 25,000 students hanging out in cafés, sitting on the grass, or hurrying to class. Even the Viking burial mounds outside of town in Gamla Uppsala (Old Uppsala) don't look so ancient with half-naked picnickers on their slopes and joggers and bikers cruising around their base. Hard-core sightseers can make Uppsala a day-trip from Stockholm (one hour by train), but it deserves an overnight stay.

BASICS

The main **tourist office** (Fyris Torg 8, tel. 018/274–800; open weekdays 10–6, Sat. 10–3) is just south of the cathedral. The main **post office** (Svavagallerien, tel. 018/179–630), across from the train station on the second floor of the Svava mall, changes money for a SKr 35 fee.

COMING AND GOING

The **train station** (tel. 018/652–210, wait for end of Swedish messages for operator assistance) is on the east side of town, a block east of the shopping district. All trains south from Uppsala go through Stockholm (1 hr, SKr 70), and all trains north go through Gävle (1 hr, SKr 120). The **bus station** (tel. 018/141–414) is next to the train station, but buses are generally necessary only for journeys to Arlanda airport (35 mins, SKr 70).

GETTING AROUND

The heart of town is divided by the tree-lined **Fyris canal,** crossed by seven bridges. The train station, bus station, and modern shopping centers are on the east side, while the historic sites are mostly huddled around the cathedral on the west side. **Bredgrändgatan** runs southwest from the train station, across the canal, and into the old part of town. The center of town is easily walkable.

All city buses leave from **Storatorget,** the big square on the corner of Drottninggatan and Kungsängsgatan. You can also catch a bus on any of Uppsala's major thoroughfares; keep your eyes peeled for square green-and-white signs that indicate the stops. Tickets, available from the driver, cost SKr 14 weekdays 9 AM–3 PM and all weekend, SKr 16 all other hours except after 11:30 PM, when the fare goes up to SKr 25.

WHERE TO SLEEP

You will find that some hotels close for the entire summer, or on weekends. Hotels that stay open, however, have very cheap rates. Places outside town tend to be nicer and cheaper than those in the center, but the SKr 15 bus fare and limited weekend service to the suburbs make them a bum deal. **Samariterhemmets Gästhem** (Sameritergränd 2, tel. 018/103–400), near the train station, offers singles with shared bath for SKr 410, doubles for SKr 650. There are also single and double rooms with their own bathroom (you still have to share showers); singles run SKr 490, and doubles cost SKr 750. Weekend prices for all rooms dip a bit; breakfast is always included. From the train station, walk left on Kungsgatan and take a right after the hospital.

Plantan (Dragarbrunnsg. 18, tel. 018/104–300) offers large doubles with private bath for SKr 400 and dorm beds for SKr 125–SKr 150. From the train station, head right on Kungsgatan and make a left on St. Olofsgatan. **STF Sunnersta Herrgård** (Sunnerstav. 24, tel. 018/324–220; closed Sept.–Apr.) is a bit of a tradeoff. The building is a gorgeous villa, but the rooms aren't exactly spic-and-span. It's 8 km (5 mi) south of town with pocket-sized two- and four-person rooms for SKr 120 per person; breakfast is SKr 50 and bike rentals are SKr 50. From the train station, take Bus 20 (the nighttime bus is Bus 50). Neither of these spots has kitchen or laundry facilities.

FOOD

Pizzerias here are among the cheapest in Sweden; try along Sysslomansgatan. In summer, pubs and bars often have menus that include the daily special and a beer for around SKr 70. The velvet-lined Victorian elegance of **Ofvandahl's Konditori** (Sysslomansgatan 5 tel. 018/134–204), just north of the cathedral, is a perfect backdrop for lasagna, baked potato, or salad lunches (SKr 55). Pick up picnic supplies in the old-fashioned market **Saluhallen** (St. Eriks Torg, across from cathedral; closed Sun.) or the grocery store **ICA City** (Plaza St. Per, 3 blocks northwest of train station).

WORTH SEEING

Medical students in particular will be thrilled by the **Gustavianum** (Akademig. 3, behind cathedral, tel. 018/185–500), a rare anatomical theater. It was built in 1663 to accommodate 200 eager spectators during a human dissection. Admission is SKr 10; it's open June–September, weekdays 11–3. Also worth a once-over is the **Universitet** (University Building; behind the cathedral, open late June–Aug., daily 11–3:30). Built in 1887 to commemorate the university's 400th anniversary, it displays a collection of paintings and sculptures in formally decorated rooms. Tours are offered in summer at noon, 1, and 2. Strategically positioned atop a hill, the impressive **Uppsala Slott** (Uppsala Castle; Borggarden, tel. 018/544–810) was built during the 1540s by King Gustav Vasa. Having broken his ties with the Vatican, the king was eager to show who was actually running the country; he even arranged to have the cannons aimed directly at the archbishop's palace. The castle is open mid-April to mid-June, daily 11–3, and mid-June to mid-August, daily 10–5. The **Uppsala Art Museum** (in Uppsala Castle, tel. 018/272–482) has a permanent collection of modern and classical art. Admission is SKr 20; it's open daily 11–4.

CAROLINA REDIVIVA • Finished in 1841, this is the oldest university library in Sweden. The display hall has manuscripts by the likes of Charles Darwin, Linné, and Marie Curie; texts dating back to the 9th century; and the much-glorified Silver Bible, written in 895 on silver and gold leaf. *At south end of Drottningg., next to Uppsala castle, tel. 018/183–900. Admission free (SKr 10 weekend afternoons). Open weekdays 9–5, Sat. 9–6, Sun. 1–3:30.*

DOMKYRKAN • Sweden's oldest coronation church, Domkyrkan was completed in 1435 after 175 years of construction. It looks pretty new following a thorough cleaning with white bread supplied by Ofvandahl's Konditori in 1976—apparently, something in the bread removes the dirt but leaves the old paint unharmed. Among those laid to rest here are King Gustav Vasa, Johan III, Linné, and St. Erik. The spot where King Erik's head was removed by a Dane in battle (1160) is marked by the tall green water pump just outside the church. As the story goes, water gushed forth from the spot where Erik was decapitated. *Domkyrkoplan, tel. 018/187–201. Admission free. Open daily 8–6.*

GAMLA UPPSALA • In 1874, excavators confirmed that these mounds 4 km (2½ mi) north of Uppsala were the final resting place of the crematorium urns of three kings who ruled over Svea (ancient Sweden) around AD 500. The 12th-century **church** next to the mounds is thought to have been built on the former site of a pagan temple, where every nine years pagans sacrificed nine people during their Fröblot festival. A leisurely stroll around the site shouldn't take more than 20 minutes; explanatory displays are in Swedish. Thirsty? Try some mead, brewed from a 14th-century recipe, at the adjacent Odinsborg Restaurant (tel. 018/323–525). To make instant friends, ask a passerby for assistance with translation. *From train station take Bus 24 or 20 (Bus 54 at night). Admission free.*

LINNETRADGARDEN • These botanical gardens, planted in 1650, are today arranged according to the plan of their most famous caretaker, Carl von Linné, inventor of the binomial system of scientific nomenclature for plants and animals. This is a botanist's Graceland, but the variety of plants (1,300 species) is impressive even to the taxonomically challenged. The adjoining museum—Linné's former home—is dull except for the terrifyingly lifelike stuffed animals upstairs. From the train station, head north on Kungsgatan, then turn left at Linnegatan. *Svartbäcksg. 27, tel. 018/109–490. Admission to gardens: SKr 10; museum: SKr 10. Gardens open daily 9–9; museum open May–Aug. 9 AM–9 PM, Sept. 9–7.*

AFTER DARK

Even in summer, when most university towns are dead, Uppsala has a busy nightlife—which gets even busier if you're a student. Student bars called **nations** (each one represents a different "nation" or region of Sweden) take over libraries and school buildings to serve cheap beer and food and host live music. To enjoy the fun you have to buy a student guest card (available only to students with a valid school ID—not an ISIC—for SKr 40) from the **student union** (Ovre Slottsg. 7; Thurs. 5 PM–9 PM). You can get a list of all 13 nations when you buy the guest card; some of the more popular ones are **V-Dala,** on Sysslomansgatan, and **Smålandsnation** and **Snörkes nation,** both behind the university off St. Olofsgatan. For a traditional bar, head to **StenSture** (Nedre Slottsg. 3, just east of Uppsala Castle, tel. 018/124–030), featuring local rock bands. During the day, the outdoor café serves a large SKr 70 lunch.

SOUTHERN SWEDEN

Once a major battleground in the territorial conflicts between Denmark and Sweden, much of southern Sweden was actually Danish until 1658, when the Peace of Roskilde was signed. Listen closely and you'll hear a bit of Danish in the local dialect (a fact northerners tease them about). And though it's less stereotypically Swedish than the northern regions, this is the home of Sweden's oldest towns (Lödöse and Küngalv, to name but two) and much of its richest history—and the countryside is mighty picturesque, to boot. Considering its proximity to the Continent, the South is the easiest place to visit in Sweden, and according to the locals, you'd do just fine spending your whole trip here and avoiding those Stockholm snobs up north.

GOTEBORG

Life in Göteborg has always revolved around the sea. Rather, you could say life here is rooted *in* the sea. With technical assistance from the Dutch (the world's canal engineering experts at the time), the city was built on wetlands in 1621. Before that, it was a departure point for Viking raiding parties; later, in the 17th century, Swedes of a less violent, though no less mercenary, inclination decided to annex the city to avoid paying Danish tolls on cargo traveling the Göta canal. Today, Göteborg is Scandinavia's largest port and home to Stena Line, the world's largest ferry company. On top of that, Göteborg is also home to Nordstan, Europe's largest indoor shopping mall; Liseberg, Scandinavia's biggest amusement park; and Scandinavium, one of Europe's biggest indoor arenas.

Bag the touristy ferry excursions and join Göteborg locals for a day-trip to the archipelago southwest of the city. Take Tram 4 to Saltholmen, show the ferry captain your tram ticket, and sail free to the islands of Asperö and Köpstadsö.

Although it can't match Stockholm's museums and sights, Göteborg makes up for it as the friendlier of Sweden's two big cities. Lots of young university types reside here, making for diverse youth culture and raucous nightlife. This isn't picture-postcard Sweden, but in many ways Göteborg is typical of where most modern Swedes live. It's safe, has good public transportation, and is close to the beautiful southern archipelago, a 15-minute ferry ride to the west.

BASICS

The main **tourist office** (Kungsportsplatsen 2, tel. 031/100–740; open July–Aug., daily 9–8; shorter hrs off-season) books private rooms (doubles from SKr 300) for a SKr 60 fee. You can change money at the **American Express** office (Ostra Hamng. 35, tel. 031/130–712; open weekdays 9–6, Sat. 10–2) or, for slightly better rates, at the **post office** (Götg. 13, in Nordstan shopping center, tel. 031/623–911). **STF Resebyrå** (Drottningtorget 6, tel. 031/150–930; open weekdays 10–6) also books hotel rooms, sells ScanRail passes, and makes boat, bus, and plane reservations.

COMING AND GOING

You can get anywhere from Göteborg's central **train station,** (Drottningtorget; Nils Eriksson Platsen, northeast of city center, tel. 031/104–445), including Oslo (4 hrs, SKr 485), Stockholm (4½ hrs, SKr 520), and Berlin (14 hrs, SKr 845). **Swebus** (tel. 020/640–640) and **Eurolines Scandinavia** (tel. 020/987–377) bus companies share an office in the train station.

The STF Resebyrå near the train station (*see* Basics, *above*) has mounds of information on all the ferry lines. Most prices double on weekends. **Stena Line** (tel. 031/775–0000) has services to Frederikshavn, Denmark (3 hrs, SKr 85), from the Danmarksterminal and Kiel, Germany (14 hrs, SKr 415–SKr 610), from the Tysklandsterminal. Take Tram 3 or 9 to Masthuggstorget for Frederikshaven, or Chapmans Torg for Kiel. **Scandinavian Seaways** (tel. 031/650–650) has ferries to Harwich (24 hrs, SKr 995 one-way) and Newcastle (20 hrs, SKr 1,095 one-way); prices to Harwich drop to SKr 695 mid-August–early June. Ferries depart from the northern side of the Göta Canal. A shuttle (SKr 40) leaves from in front of the train station two hours before each ship's departure.

GETTING AROUND

Almost everything is within walking distance or an easy tram ride. Göteborg has three main centers of activity: Nordstan shopping center, Kungsportsplatsen (the tourist office is here), and Götaplatsen (the cultural hub, where you'll find the university, theaters, and the Röhsska Museum). The five streets (particularly Kungsgatan) that run perpendicular to Östra Hamngatan/Kungsportsavenyn make up the city's main shopping and strolling area.

Efficient **trams** run Sunday–Thursday 5 AM–12:55 AM, Friday and Saturday until 2:15 AM. Tickets cost SKr 16 from the driver. A good map of the seven main tram routes is available in the tourist office brochure. Be careful when using the **buses** (SKr 16); they often head directly out of the city. The main bus information center is at Tidpunkten on Drottningtorget (near the train station). For SKr 40 you can get a 24-hour pass for all forms of public transportation, but if you're doing the tourist thing full force, think about buying the **Göteborgkortet** (one day, SKr 125; two days, SKr 225; three days, SKr 275), which covers public transportation and museum admissions. You can purchase either card from the tourist office, Pressbyrån kiosks, and hotels.

WHERE TO SLEEP

There are several good, cheap sleeps scattered around town, and the hostels and pensions lurking on the edges of the city are all easily reached by tram or bus. In the heart of Göteborg, **Aveny Turist Hotel** (Södra Vägen 2, tel. 031/205–286) is a real find, with crystal chandeliers, Oriental rugs, and fresh flowers. Call ahead for their SKr 495 doubles or SKr 395 singles. Rooms don't have private baths, but at least the price includes breakfast. Take Tram 4 or 5 to Berzeliigatan. Old, but ideally located just off Kungsportsavenyn, **City Hotel** (Lorensbergsg. 6, tel. 031/180–025) has 50 doubles for SKr 420, including breakfast; bathrooms and showers are in the corridor. Take Tram 1, 4, 5, 6, or 8 to Valand and walk a block east on Vasagatan.

Kärralund Vandrarhem (STF) (Olbersg. 1, tel. 031/840–200) is like a woodsy summer camp, with a hostel, campground, trailer park, general store, and lots of rowdy teenagers. From late June to mid-August, dorm beds are SKr 110, four-bed cabins SKr 615, and campsites SKr 170; prices drop the rest of the year. Take Tram 5 to Welandergatan and walk up the small hill past the Mat Dax market. The **M/S Seaside** (Packhuskajen, next to Maritime Center, tel. 031/105–970), an old boat-cum-youth hostel with a café, is moored in Göteborg's harbor. The three-bed cabins (SKr 175 per bed) are small but comfy; dorm beds run SKr 100, while single cabins go for SKr 250. It's closed between October and March. Take Tram 5 to Lilla Bommen, walk to the harbor, and go left.

FOOD

The best place to find budget restaurants is close to the university at the southern end of Kungsportsavenyn. **Tien Tsin** (Engelbrektsg. 34B, tel. 031/162–647) serves daily Cantonese lunch specials (SKr 55) from 11 to 4. Try the *biff i satesås* (beef with spicy sauce). **Café Krasnapolsky** (Storg. 41, tel. 031/711–1836) is a great place for a cup of coffee (SKr 16) and a little conversation. While there, ask about the owner's ride-sharing program, which provides travelers with rides to places all over Europe at unbeatable prices.

WORTH SEEING

In this seafaring town, a stroll down by the **harbor** can turn into an all-day excursion. The **Maritima Centrum** (Maritime Center; Packhuskajen 8, tel. 031/105–950; admission SKr 45; open May–June, daily 10–6; July–Aug., daily 10–9; shorter hrs off-season), the largest maritime museum in Europe, has a variety of boats, from tugs and freighters to a U-boat and a missile-ready destroyer—inspect all 13. Göteborg's main art museum, the **Konstmuseet** (Götaplatsen, tel. 031/612–980; admission SKr 35; open May–Aug., weekdays 11–4, weekends 11–5; shorter hrs off-season) has a huge collection of works by Sweden's most famous painters and sculptors; don't miss the deep blues of Jansson's *Nocturne* on the top floor. Take Tram 4 or 5 to Berzeliigatan. The **Röhsska Museum** (Vasag. 37–39, tel. 031/613–850; admission SKr 40; open weekdays noon–4, weekends noon–5) is the only museum in Sweden to specialize in arts and crafts and industrial design. The permanent exhibit of furniture, glass works, and art from the Renaissance to the present features a decade-by-decade history of 20th-century design, including some furniture from the 1970s that the Salvation Army might be ashamed to sell.

AFTER DARK

Fueled by the university, Göteborg's nightlife, especially on Kungsportsavenyn (known to locals as "the avenue"), is pretty darn good. The blue walls of **Smaka** (Vasaplatsen 3, at Storg., tel. 031/132–247) echo with soul, pop, and conversation. **Bistro Chez Amis** (Vasaplatsen 2, at Parkg., tel. 031/711–4404) serves lunch (SKr 65) before becoming a crowded student hangout at night. You won't have to go far to find a disco in Göteborg; after all, it is Ace of Base's home town. **Sommar Trägårn** (Trädgårdsföreningen, tel. 031/133–170; cover SKr 25 before 9, SKr 80 after) is one of the more popular spots, but you'll find places to dance the night away anywhere along Kungsportsavenyn; cover charges are hefty (SKr 60–SKr 90). Or try **Bacchus** (Bellmansg. 7, tel. 031/132–043), a comfortable gay disco.

MALMO

Look up as you ride or sail into Malmö and you'll see an unusual skyline—the bulky steel of massive cranes at the loading docks, the modern glass structure of Malmö's navigation center, and lots of domes and spires. But it seems like every other building in the city is only two stories high. As Sweden's third-largest city, Malmö comes complete with fast-food chains, shopping malls, beggars, and, as evidenced by public service announcements, urban violence.

Just a short ferry ride away from Copenhagen, it is the capital of the province of Skåne. The city boasts a comprehensive **history museum** that tells the tale of southern Sweden. This museum, along with the city's art collection, a natural-history museum, an aquarium (an extra SKr 40), and a nocturnal animal exhibit, is in **Malmöhus Slott** (Malmöhusv., basic admission SKr 40, museums SKr 30; open daily noon–4), a moated castle built in the 16th century. An old power plant houses the wonderful **Rooseum Center for Contemporary Art** (Gasverksg. 22, tel. 040/121–716; admission SKr 30; open Tues.–Sun. 11–5). To get an eyeful of Swedish architecture, check out **St. Petri Kyrka,** a Gothic church behind Stortorget, the main square, and **Rådhuset,** the city hall on the northeast corner of Stortorget.

BASICS

The **tourist office** (tel. 040/300–150; open June–Aug., weekdays 9–8, Sat. 9–5; shorter hrs off-season) is in the train station. Head to **Forex** (in train station [*see below*], open daily 8 AM–9 PM) to change cash (SKr 20 commission), or to the **main post office** (Skeppsbron 1, across from train station, tel. 040/149–000; open weekdays 8–6, Sat. 9:30–1) to change traveler's checks. **STF** (in post office building, tel. 040/302–600; open weekdays 10–5) books hotel rooms and makes train and ferry reservations.

COMING AND GOING

Malmö is 25 km (15 mi) across the Öresund from Copenhagen. The **Flygbåtarna hydrofoil** (tel. 040/103–930) will whisk you across in 45 minutes for SKr 99 one-way, but **Pilen Line** (tel. 040/234–411) ferries are just as fast, and cost only SKr 30 one-way (SKr 40 Thurs.–Fri. and Sun., SKr 50 Sat.). Both lines depart from the ferry terminal north of the train station on Skeppsbron. Those with a Scan-Rail pass might prefer the roundabout, but free route: two trains and a ferry (3 hrs). Inquire at the train station.

Malmö has daily trains to Göteborg (4 hrs, SKr 395) and Stockholm (5–7 hrs, SKr 685). The purple regional trains run from an adjoining station and make trips to Lund (15 mins, SKr 30) and Helsingborg (48 mins, SKr 70). All trains leave from the **train station** (Lunds Järnvägstation; Bang., tel. 040/202–100) at the northern edge of town.

GETTING AROUND

Malmö is easily manageable on foot or by bus. Heading south from the train station, you'll cross the canal via the **Mälar bridge** to **Stortorget,** the main square. **Lilla Torg** ("Little Square"), lined with 16th-century half-timbered houses, branches off from the southwest corner of Stortorget. **Södergatan,** leading away from the southeast corner, is the main pedestrian street.

City buses leave from the south side of the train station and cost SKr 12. Bus 21 goes to Gustav Aldophs Torget and Trianglen. Bus 20 runs to Malmöhus Slott, west of the train station via the busy Norra Vallgatan. For a view of the city by boat, try the canal boat tour (45 mins, SKr 75), which leaves every hour across from the south side of the train station.

WHERE TO SLEEP AND EAT

The conveniently located **Pallas Hotell** (Norra Vallg. 74, tel. 040/611–5077, fax 040/409–799–00) has relatively elegant singles (SKr 280) and doubles (SKr 380) without bath. Those with an early train to catch will be happy to know it's just three blocks west of the station. The **STF Youth Hostel Malmö** (Backav. 18, tel. 040/822–200; beds SKr 100) has spacious rooms, but it's as industrial and impersonal as the part of town it's in. From the train station, take Bus 21 to Vandrarhemmet, follow Fosievägen south past Eriksfältsgatan, and turn right on Backavägen. Considering the SKr 12 bus ride out here, it might be cheaper (if you have a rail pass) to stay at the hostel in Lund, a 15-minute train ride away (see Where to Sleep and Eat in Lund, below). The friendly staff at the **City Youth Hostel** (Västerg. 9, tel. 040/235–640) offers doubles (SKr 250) or dorm beds (SKr 100) in a student dormitory (never fear, those without a report card—it's open to everyone). It's only open during the summer, but it is conveniently located a few blocks away from the train station.

Malmö isn't exactly a pleasant surprise in terms of culinary options (or prices), but for lunch you can always grab a quick fix at one of the hot dog or falafel stands on Sodra Forstadsgatan. For a tad more atmosphere, try **Saluhallen** (northwest corner of Lilla Torget), an indoor market with a host of groceries, prepared food, and even a Filipino fast-food bar; it's open weekdays 10–6 and Saturdays 10–2. Near the train station, the **Olympus Pub and Restaurant** (Norra Vallg. 78, tel. 040/239–792) serves Greek dishes and pasta for SKr 70–SKr 90.

LUND

The university town of Lund can be a fun stop for a night or two. It's filled with a ton of historical buildings and museums to keep you busy during the day, and hopping student-fed nightlife to amuse you at night. Its proximity to Malmö and Copenhagen makes it a perfect spot to visit if you want to get a glimpse of Sweden, but are short on time and cash.

The **Domkyrkan** (Kyrkog.; open weekdays 8–6, Sat. 9–5, Sun. 9:30–6) still acts as a center of social and religious activity in Lund. Consecrated in 1145, the cathedral is declared (by the town of Lund, tooting its own horn) to be "the finest Romanesque building in Scandinavia." It's a claim few would contest, since Scandinavia has no other Romanesque buildings on this scale. Try to visit at noon or 3 PM (1 PM on Sunday) to watch the 14th-century astronomical and astrological (with Mary standing in for Virgo) clock play *In dulci jubilo.* To traipse through Lund's history, wander behind the cathedral to **Kulturen** (Tegnérsplatsen, tel. 046/350–400; admission SKr 40; open May–Sept., daily 11–5; shorter hrs off-season). The beautifully arranged temporary exhibits and the huge courtyard containing replicas of Swedish houses are impressive. North of the cathedral is the **Skissernas Museum** (Museum of Sketches; Finng. 2, tel. 046/222–7283; open Tues.–Sat. noon–4, Sun. 1–5), which will give nonartists an idea of the hours of sketching and model-making required to produce a finished work of art. It's absolutely worth the SKr 20 admission.

BASICS

The **tourist office** (Kyrkog. 11, tel. 046/355–040; open May–Aug., weekdays 10–6, weekends 10–2; shorter hrs off-season) doles out helpful information. The **post office** (Knut den stores torg 2, across from train station; open weekdays 8–6, Sat. 9–1) changes money, but charges SKr 35 per transaction. **Forex** (Bang. 8, tel. 046/323–410; open weekdays 8–7, Sat. 8–5), across from the train station, charges less (SKr 20) and has better rates.

COMING AND GOING

Local trains run to Copenhagen (change to ferry in Malmö; 2½ hrs, SKr 175), Helsingborg (45 mins, SKr 60), and Malmö (15 mins, SKr 40). For longer trips, pick up the national SJ trains in Malmö. All trains leave from the **train station** (Lunds Järnvägstation, Bang., tel. 046/312–500) on the western edge of town.

GETTING AROUND

Life in Lund centers around three main areas: the university and Domkyrkan, Stortorget, and Mårtenstorget, which all form an easily walkable triangle. There's also the Stadstraffiken bus system (tel. 046/141–450); light-blue, square signs indicate a bus stop. The main station is on Botulfsplatsen, and tickets cost SKr 10 each.

WHERE TO SLEEP AND EAT

It's almost worth coming to Lund just to stay in the **STF Vandrarhem Tåget** (Vävareg. 22, tel. 046/142–820), an old wooden train that has been converted into a youth hostel (beds for SKr 100). The amiable staff, fully equipped kitchen, and cheap bike rentals (SKr 30 per day, third day free) make up for the extra-close quarters and spotty showers. Ask at the train station for directions. Call ahead; the reception desk is open 8AM–10 AM and 4 PM–8 PM.

With relatively large student and immigrant populations (from Iran, the former Yugoslavia, and Eritrea), Lund offers many international cuisines, mostly around Stortorget. One of the spiciest meals in Sweden is the *vegetarisk tallrik* (vegetarian plate; SKr 55) at **Falafel Kungen** (Kungsg. 2A, tel. 046/141–950; open 24 hrs), just south of the cathedral. **El Dorado** (St. Söderg. 17, tel. 046/145–050) serves good pizza (SKr 45) and a burrito du jour (SKr 50).

GOTLAND

Five hours by ferry from the Swedish mainland lies the island of Gotland, hailed as the Swedish version of a Mediterranean resort. Locals will be quick to inform you that it never rains here in the summer—and they're almost telling the truth. Even if rain clouds do show up, stiff ocean breezes ensure that they don't stick around. Roughly 150 km (90 mi) long, Gotland boasts archaeological finds, limestone rock formations, reconstructed Viking settlements, and kilometer upon kilometer of rocky cliffs and sandy beaches. Linking the whole shebang together is an amazing system of bicycle trails, hostels, and campgrounds. Highlights for those who want to do some exploring include the 12th-century monastery of **Roma,** in the middle of the island; **Torsburgen,** the largest fortification in Scandinavia, on the east side of the island; and the limestone cliffs and rock formations of **Stora Karlsö,** a little island off the southwest coast of Gotland, with an isolated but excellent **hostel** (tel. 0498/240–500). The ferry (*see* Coming and Going *in* Visby, *below*) to Gotland is decently affordable.

VISBY

Visby, the main town on Gotland, is the kind of storybook-perfect place where cobblestone streets wind crookedly under vaulted passageways, through ancient church ruins, and past small cottages whose gardens burst with color in spring. The city wall, built in the 13th century to protect the town from angry farmers protesting against rich landowners, is one of Europe's largest relics from the Middle Ages; its history is described on placards set into the wall. The history of Visby and of Gotland is presented in the **Gotlands Fornsal** (Historical Museum of Gotland; Strandg. 14, tel. 0498/247–010; admission SKr 30; open mid-May–Aug., daily 11–6; shorter hrs off-season); the exhibits include part of a reconstructed house from the Middle Ages. Check out the **Silversmederna** (Silversmith Shop; Strandg. 28, tel. 0498/212–889; open weekdays 2–6, Sat. 10–1), where artists create silver and gold jewelry in a merchant's house built in 1250. The **Domkyrkan St. Maria** (Cathedral of St. Maria; Västra Kyrkog. 5) is the only one of Visby's 17 medieval churches that isn't in ruins; dial 0498/212–633 for information about organ recitals.

If you're feeling claustrophobic, take a moped (*see* Getting Around, *below*) northeast up Route 149 toward **Fårö Island**; on the way, stop to explore the caves of **Lummelundagrottan** (30-minute tour SKr 40; open late June–Aug., daily 9–6; shorter hrs off-season), or the dramatic cliff of **Lickershamn.** A 10-minute free ferry from Fårösund brings you to Fårö itself, home of introverted filmmaker Ingmar Bergman. If you're tempted to linger, see if there's room at the inn, the inn here being the peaceful **Fårögarden hostel** (Fårösund, tel. 0498/223–639; beds SKr 80, doubles SKr 200). Remember to watch the fuel gauge on your moped; a roundabout one-way trip (2½ hrs) will empty the tank, and gas stations are rarer than brunettes.

BASICS

Pick up bus schedules at one of Visby's tourist offices, **Gotlands Turistförening & Visby Turistcenter** (Hamng. 4, tel. 0498/201–700). Down the street is the **Turistcenter** (Korsg. 2, tel. 0498/279–095; open daily 10–6), where you can make ferry reservations for SKr 40 and book private rooms; doubles cost SKr 400 (outside Visby's wall) or SKr 445 (inside the wall). The best exchange rates are at either of the two **post offices** (Norrahanseg. 2A, outside Österport; Söderväg 6, inside ICA market); they're open Monday through Friday 9:30–6 and Saturday 10–1.

COMING AND GOING

Gotlandslinjen (tel. 0498/293–000 or 08/520–640–00) has a monopoly on the ferry business. Boats from Nynäshamn (south of Stockholm) run nightly at 11:30 PM (6 hrs, SKr 135 adult one-way). On weekends, prices rise to SKr 175. From early June to mid-August, additional boats head out at 12:30 PM and 5 PM. Also, a "fast ferry" runs spring to autumn in less than half the time, but it more than doubles the student fare (SKr 210 weekdays); adult prices stay the same. Reservations are a must in summer.

Buses leave **Visby Busstation** (Kung Magnusväg 1, tel. 0498/214–114), just outside the city wall of Söderport (South Gate); rides cost anywhere from SKr 25 to SKr 90. Pay drivers when you board—they even make change. Bus 11 goes to Roma (20 mins, SKr 35); Bus 41 to Torsburgen (get off in Hardö and ask the driver for directions; 40 mins, SKr 35); and Bus 31, 32, or 33 to Klintehamn, where you can catch a ferry to Stora Karlsö (which takes 1½ hrs, at SKr 170).

GETTING AROUND

Even if it's a relatively small place, you can get lost in Visby's complex street system. But remember, you're never far from the city wall. Generally, if you're within it and it's on your left, you're heading south. For those who want to head straight out of town or go to the hostel, buses meet your ferry for the short ride up to the bus station. Otherwise, head north from the ferry terminal and make a right on Hamngatan to get to the tourist office.

Biking is a big draw all over Gotland, and bikes are widely available in Visby for SKr 60–SKr 75 per day. **Team Sportia** (Österväg 17, across from Österport post office, tel. 0498/210–986) has a large selection; mountain bikes go for SKr 90 per day. **Bil & Mc-Uthyrningen** (Inre Hamnen, tel. 0498/211–116) rents mopeds (SKr 190 per day plus SKr 350 deposit).

WHERE TO SLEEP AND EAT

Accommodations in the center of town are expensive, but buses to lodgings on the outskirts are also costly (SKr 20 and up). At the centrally located **Hamnhotellet** (Färjeleden 3, Visby, tel. 0498/201–250; closed mid-Aug.–early Apr.) rooms go for SKr 420–SKr 660 from mid-April to mid-May; between mid-May and August, the prices are jacked up to SKr 495–SKr 690. Rooms are small (and no-smoking), but they have bathrooms with showers, and breakfast is included in the rates. The best bet is the **STF Vandrarhem** (Hus 55, tel. 0498/269–842; closed early Aug.–early June); beds cost SKr 80–SKr 110, doubles SKr 200. To get here from the bus station, walk east up Artillerigatan, past the cemetery and soccer field; the hostel will be on your right. **Norderstrands camping** (tel. 0498/212–157), 1 km (½ mi) north of town and right on the water, has tent spots for SKr 95 and four-bed cabins for SKr 395 per night; there are bathroom, shower, and laundry facilities. And if you're discreet, you can camp for free in the grassy expanses 3 km (2 mi) northeast of the city wall.

Most of the budget pizza joints and falafel stands are down by the harbor and along Adelsgatan just inside Söderport. At **St. Hans Konditori** (St. Hansplan 2, tel. 0498/210–772), have a full lunch (SKr 69) or just coffee among spectacular church ruins.

AFTER DARK

Nightlife in Visby centers around **Skeppsbron** along the harbor and **Stora torget,** with clubs on Strandgatan absorbing the spillover. The hottest spot is **Munkkällaren** (Lilla Torggrand 2, in Stora torget, tel. 0498/271–400; cover SKr 50 after 10), which was built in 1150 and has been a pub since 1600. In summer, it features live bands several times a week, dancing after midnight (you can start earlier in the salsa section), and a "vinyl room" where you can peruse an eclectic collection of LPs and devise your own play list.

NORTHERN SWEDEN

Most Swedes consider everything north of Dalarna to be Northern Sweden. This just underscores the fact that most southern-dwelling Swedes have never been to this part of the country, for if they had, they would realize that the difference between Dalarna and Norrland (the true north) is extreme. Dalarna, the country's most stereotypically Swedish area, is home to plenty of red and white houses, that little wooden flower-painted horse you see on every Swedish brochure, and some of the most picturesque villages you'll find, complete with maypoles and quiet churchyards. Once in Norrland, however, Dalarna's coziness will seem a world removed. Here, the winter (during which the sun doesn't rise for a month) gives way to a summer of *long* (sometimes 24-hour) days and billions of bloodthirsty mosquitoes and blackflies. But be not dismayed, for the lakes, mountains, and forests of the north are the Sweden you'll fall in love with.

DALARNA

According to tourist brochures, people in the region of Dalarna paint flowers on everything from clogs and wooden horses to grandfather clocks and candlesticks. During the Midsommar festival, everybody puts flowers in their hair, holds hands, and dances around maypoles covered in . . . flowers. The amazing thing is that it's all for real, or at least it was about 100 years ago. Nowadays, Dalarnians keep up the old traditions mainly to draw Scandinavian tourists by the busload. Despite the cloying commercialization, there are still plenty of reasons for heading this far north: the area is historically interesting and the landscapes, particularly around Lake Silja, are breathtaking. The **Siljasleden** trail circling Lake Silja is ideal for hiking, biking, and cross-country skiing, but is also a great place to simply relax and enjoy the countryside.

Dalarna's major towns—Rättkiv, Mora, Leksand, and Orsa—are each about three hours from Uppsala by train (SKr 170), and several trains a day (about 20 mins, SKr 30) connect the smaller towns. Dalatrafik buses cost the same as the train but run more frequently between towns. Campgrounds are plentiful, and RUM (ROOM) signs mean a cheap bed and hearty breakfast in someone's house.

MORA

As the terminus for Sweden's Vasaloppet, the world's largest cross-country ski race, Mora is easily Dalarna's most famous town. The first race was held in 1922 and it is now something of a Swedish Super Bowl—nearly half of Sweden watches TV coverage of the 35,000-skier-strong race, which begins in Sälen, close to the Norwegian border, and 90 km (54 mi) later ends in Mora amid cheers, tears, and huge parties. The current Swedish King has even been known to participate. At the **Vasaloppsmuseet** (Vasag., tel. 0250/39225; admission SKr 30; open daily 10–6), memorabilia and a video give a good explanation of the race's significance. Except during the week of the race (held the first Sunday in March), the race's namesake Gustav Vasa, hometown hero and founder of modern Sweden, takes a back seat to the impressionist painter Anders Zorn, Mora's most acclaimed citizen. You'll have to book at least one day in advance to get inside his house, called **Zorngården** (Vasag.; admission SKr 30; open Mon.–Sat. 10–4:15, Sun. 11–4:15), but you can wander through his gardens for free or go next door to the **Zornmuseet** (tel. 0250/16560; admission SKr 25; open May 15–Sept. 15, Mon.–Sat. 9–5, Sun. 11–5; Sept. 16–May 14, Mon.–Sat. noon–5, Sun. 1–5) and see many of his oils and watercolors. Guided tours (in Swedish) of Zorngården happen every half hour.

BASICS • The tourist office (Ångbåtskajen, tel. 0250/26550; open summer, weekdays 9–8, weekends 10–8; off-season, weekdays 9–5, Sat. 10–1) is on the lake about 2,600 ft from the **train station** (Järnvägstation Mora; Stationsv., tel. 0250/94515). You can change money at the **post office** (Kyrkog. 25, tel. 0250/16030).

WHERE TO SLEEP AND EAT • The centrally located St. Mikael (Fridhemsg. 15, tel. 0250/15900) is definitely no-frills, but it's neat and clean, and there's a restaurant in the building. Doubles with a bathroom and TV go for SKr 560, breakfast included. Another spot to lay your weary head is the **Hotel Kung Gösta** (Kristinebergsv. 1, tel. 0250/15070), which is just a wee bit cheaper—SKr 529 for a double room with bathroom, plus breakfast. The rooms are your basic pastel-and-wood decor. Another thing to keep in mind if you can't get to the exchange office—both these places take all the major credit cards. The **STF Vandrarhem** hostel (Vasag. 19, tel. 0250/038–190) has sparkling, clean rooms in the center of town for SKr 100 per person. The reception is open 8 AM–10 AM and 5 PM–8 PM. **Mora Camping** (Hantverkarg. 30, tel. 0250/15352) is across from Zorn's house and has tent spots for SKr 70 and double cabins for SKr 260; bathrooms and showers are available. The cheapest eats are at the grocery stores, cafés, and pizzerias lining Kyrkogatan. There's also the intimate **Cousin Vitamine** (Lisselby Torg., just west of Zornmuseet, tel. 0250/17488), in a wooden house, serving SKr 90–SKr 130 meals ranging from pork fillet to broccoli pie to ostrich.

LEKSAND

One of Lake Siljan's most picturesque towns, Leksand also has an excellent *gammelgård* (open-air museum), **Hembygdsgården** (open in summer daily 11–5). In this re-created 17th-century village, you can see locals baking bread and weaving birch baskets. The **Kulturhuset** (Cultural Center; Norrsg. 29, tel. 0247/80243; admission free; open weekdays 11–5, Sat. 11–4, Sun. 1–4) displays local art. Outdoor activities in Leksand range from hiking, biking, and canoeing to cross-country skiing and hang gliding. Stop by the **tourist center** (Norrsg., tel. 0247/80300; open summer, Mon.–Sat. 9–8, Sun. 11–8; shorter hrs off-season) to get information on the various sport outfitters, and to pick up a map of **Siljansleden,** the 340-km (211-mi) trail around Lake Silja; choose among treks that take you over rolling hills and

THE KUNGSLEDEN

Discussions about hiking in Scandinavia inevitably turn to the Kungsleden (the King's Trail). Roughly 500 km (300 mi) long, this popular pilgrimage for European hikers is clearly labeled and user-friendly, with foot bridges and wooden boards for crossing brooks, streams, and marshes, and conveniently placed rowboats for crossing larger bodies of water. Hikers can leisurely meander manageable distances each day with minimal gear since STF mountain stations and huts are placed every 15–20 km (9–12 mi). Mountain huts are basic, outfitted only with beds, stoves, and cooking supplies; at mountain stations, however, you can also rent equipment and stock up on provisions. The entire trail runs from Abisko in the north to Hemavan in the south, and it can be hiked in stretches. Above the Arctic Circle, the northern section (Abisko to Kvikkjok) passes mountain valleys, and is especially popular for its connection to Kebnekaise, Sweden's highest mountain (6,944 ft). To reach Kvikkjokk, take a bus from Jokkmokk (see Jokkmokk, above); to reach Abisko, take a train from Kiruna (1 hr, SKr 80). The trail's southern section from Hemavan to Ammarnäs traverses flatter and wetter terrain: moors, swamps, lakes, and waterfalls. To reach Ammarnäs, take a train to Sorsele, then a bus to Ammarnäs (call the Sorsele Tourist Office at 0952/14090 for information). The weather is warm and least muggy in August and September. Call STF in Stockholm (tel. 08/4632–100) to find out which mountain station is closest to you for equipment rental.

along brooks. It's a fairly easy hike, and the trail is well-traveled, but keep in mind that the whole thing will take about 2–3 weeks. Alternatively, you can do a segment of the trail and then take a train or boat back to your starting point. The **train station** (Leksand Tågstation; Stationsg., tel. 0247/10115) is on the eastern edge of town. If you need to change money, head to the **post office** (Torget Posten, tel. 0247/10045).

WHERE TO SLEEP AND EAT • You can sleep in your very own log cabin at the **STF Vandrarhem** (Parkgården, tel. 0247/15250). To get here, go south through town, cross the bridge, and turn left on Insjövagen (about 3 km (2 mi) total), or take Bus 58 and tell the driver where you're headed. Beds go for SKr 100, and you can also rent a bike (SKr 60). **Resturang Bosporen** (Torget 1, tel. 0247/13280) is the local pizzeria/bar; their daily lunch special is SKr 65.

NORRLAND

The inhabitants of Sweden's northernmost provinces are a fairly diverse mix, including a large contingent of Samis, Sweden's only indigenous population, as well as a sizable Finnish community. Happily, there's plenty of room for everyone in this region—it's one of Europe's most sparsely populated areas. The province's small towns are separated by huge forests and thousands of lakes, but the real wilderness begins in the mountains about 120 km (72 mi) west of most towns. Once here, purists will want to walk the *Kungsleden* (*see box, below*), a 500-km (300-mi) hiking trail that ends in Abisko, at the northern tip of the country. **Norbotten AB** (tel. 020/470–047) buses go to the mountains from most towns for about SKr 70. You'll undoubtedly hear a lot about the *Inlandsbana,* a slow, tourist-oriented train with numerous local stops (taking two days to travel from Mora to Gällivare). But even if you're starting in Dalarna, your best bet is to head to Gävle, where you can transfer to the night train from Stockholm to Gällivare (15 hrs, SKr 580); the train goes through Boden, where **Hotell Standard** (Stationsg. 5, across from train station, tel. 0921/16055) has SKr 100 beds for nights when trains and buses don't coordinate. Don't worry about missing prime countryside while you sleep; the scenery is pretty constant from just north of Uppsala to Gällivare, and as mentioned above, if you want scenery, you'll want to head west to the mountains anyway.

OSTERSUND

Östersund's bustling, shop-lined streets snuggle up to the northeast side of Storsund (Big Sound), and its small harbor and lakeside park make for beautiful 11 PM sunset strolling. Try to visit in late July when the town lights up with its annual **Storsjöyran** festival. The open-air museum of **Jamtli** (Museiplan; admission SKr 60; open June–Aug., daily 11–5) has farms and cabins from the 18th and 19th centuries where people go about their daily chores as if the 20th century were still a futuristic farce. You can wander around and watch (and maybe feel lazy). For sea lovers, the SS *Thomée,* Sweden's oldest steamboat still in regular service, leaves from the harbor at the west end of Biblioteksgatan for one- to four-hour cruises (SKr 50–SKr 80). About 1,000 ft across the water, the mountainous island of **Fröson,** where Viking gods held court 1,000 years ago, is now home to loads of skiing and hiking trails, as well as the *sommarhagen* (summer home, no address but signposted; admission SKr 30; open daily 11–3; July, until 6 PM) of composer Wilhelm Peterson-Berger. There's also the 12th-century wooden Frösö Church, which is still in use. Take Bus 3 or 4 to get to the island. For more information, talk to the **tourist office** (Rådhusg. 44, tel. 063/144–001; open June–Aug., Mon.–Sat. 9–9, Sun. 10–7; shorter hrs offseason). You can change money at the **post office** (Kyrkg., tel. 063/141–610).

COMING AND GOING • Östersund is a convenient stopping point before heading west to Trondheim, Norway (6 hrs, SKr 340), or south to Stockholm (9 hrs, SKr 595) if you're coming from Norway. There are two train stops in Östersund: The first is 1 km (½ mi) south of the town center and the second, Östersunds Järnvägstation, is two blocks west of the town center (take Samuel Permans Gata). Get off at the first only if you're headed for STF Vandrarhem (*see below*). Local buses leave from Gustav III's Torg, on Rådhusgatan, and cost SKr 12 (SKr 30 after 11 PM).

WHERE TO SLEEP AND EAT • All the cheap options are here: hostels, camping, pensions, and small hotels. The **tourist office** books rooms for a SKr 40 fee, but you're better off checking the list of places on the tourist map and calling them yourself. The centrally located **STF Vandrarhem** (Södra Gröng. 34, tel. 063/139–100; beds SKr 100) is only open June–August; it's just northeast of the train station. **Vandrarhemmet Jamtli** (Museiplan, tel. 063/105–984) has doubles for SKr 280 and dorm beds for SKr 160, including free use of their washer and dryer. At lunchtime, stroll down Storgatan and Prästgatan for sit-down eateries with SKr 55 daily specials. If you're wondering why the streets are empty after 7 PM, it's because everybody is at **Brunkullans Krog** (Postgränd 5, tel. 063/101–454) having dinner and a beer.

JOKKMOKK

If you can visit only one town in the north, Jokkmokk, a 1½-hour bus trip south of Gällivare (SKr 84), is a good choice. Located on the Arctic Circle near Maddus, Sarek, and Padjelanta National Parks, it's something of a gateway to Lapland. Long a winter meeting place for Sami reindeer herders, the town was officially founded in 1602 as part of a trading chain meant to expand population and, more importantly, taxation northward. Jokkmokk's Wintermarket, held the first Thursday–Saturday in February, has been held every year since 1605. For a four-hour canoe tour (SKr 350 per person and yes, you'll be paddling) of the area lit by the midnight sun, contact **Jokkmokk Guiderna** (tel./fax 0971/12220). The town's biggest attraction is the **Ájtte Swedish Mountain and Sami Museum** (Kyrkog. 3, east of tourist office, tel. 0971/17070; admission SKr 40; open weekdays 9–6, until 8 Wed., weekends 11–6), where hands-on displays and exhibitions teach you about Sami culture past and present. If you're interested in hiking, the National Park representative in the museum will help you plan treks in the area. The nearby town of Kvikkjokk (1½ hrs, SKr 105 by bus) is a good place for the adventurous hiker, as you can hike between the two towns via Muddus National Park's historic 45-km (27-mi) Gällivare–Porjus trail. In 1910, workers each carried as much as 70 kilograms (150 pounds) of materials over the trail to build the electric power station on the Porjus falls. Get maps of the trail at the Gällivare tourist office. Jokkmokk's **main tourist office** (Stortorget 4, tel. 0971/12140; open daily 9–7) is two blocks south of the **train station** (Jokkmokks Järnvägsstation, on north edge of town).

WHERE TO SLEEP AND EAT • As you head south on Stationsgatan from the station, the first two houses on your right—**Wikström** (Stationsg. 5, tel. 0971/10553) and **Eriksson** ("Yellow House"; Stationsg. 7, tel. 0971/35026)—have cozy double rooms starting at SKr 120 per person. At Eriksson, you can also get breakfast. The **STF Vandrarhem** (Åsg. 20, tel. 0971/55977; beds SKr 100) is the red house on the hill behind the tourist office; it features a self-serve kitchen and a free sauna. Dinner at the town pizzeria, **Restaurang Milano** (Foreningsg. 3, tel. 0971/96232), will cost about SKr 70.

GALLIVARE

It's ironic that in the middle of such pristine wilderness, the first thing you hear about in Gällivare is **Aitik,** Europe's largest copper mine. From mid-June to August you can shell out SKr 150 for a three-hour bus tour into the mine, where a guide will show you one of the world's largest mechanical shovels. Tours leave at 2 PM from the tourist office (*see below*), which also conducts tours (SKr 160) of the 2,800-ft deep iron mine daily at 10 AM. Between late June and early August, some tours are given in English. For a more old-fashioned excursion, follow the signs marked KULTURSTIGAN (CULTURE PATH), which leads you on a 2-km (1-mi) tour around town. The path starts at the school building, winds back toward the train station, crosses the railway station bridge, and heads along the water past an 18th-century church. It finally reaches the **Hembygdsområdet** (open June–Aug., daily 11–6), a collection of old buildings, including a Sami camp, bakery cottage, and Sweden's northernmost windmill. For another fine outdoor excursion, head 2½ km (1½ mi) up Dundret Mountain to the outdoor museum **Vägvisaren** (tel. 0970/55560; admission SKr 40; open daily 10–6), where, if you call in advance, an English-speaking Sami guide will show you around a hand-built Sami village, talk about reindeer herding, and offer you coffee that's been prepared over an open fire inside a hut. Continue up the mountain to find prime spots for basking in the glow of the midnight sun. To meet other trekkers, join the hiking tour (SKr 150) that leaves the **tourist office** (Storg. 16, tel. 0970/16660; open June–Aug., daily 9–8; Sept.–May, weekdays 9–4) daily at 11 PM in summer. The beautiful 19th-century wooden **train station** (Gällivare Järnvägstation, tel. 0970/75200) is on the southwest edge of town.

WHERE TO SLEEP AND EAT • The useful *Guld Guiden,* handed out by the tourist office, has a list of private homes with rooms (SKr 100 per person). The **STF Vandrarhem** (tel. 0970/14380; reception open 8 AM–10 AM and 5 PM–10:30 PM), across the bridge from the train station, has beds in spacious cabins, each with its own bathroom and kitchen. You won't exactly be barraged with dining options, so try the *husmanskost* (home-cooking) at **Cafe Forell** (Hantverkarg. 7, tel. 0970/10112), which serves lots of fish—especially trout.

SWITZERLAND

I t's a wonder that Switzerland's trademark orderliness and efficiency developed amid its chaos of languages, religions, and impassable mountain ridges. In this land of fresh alpine meadows, sparkling blue lakes, and dizzying peaks, where four languages—German, French, Italian, and Romansch—rub shoulders, the Swiss transform order and hard work into an art form, as evidenced by their efficient trains and immaculate city centers. In the process, though, they forfeit a certain amount of spontaneity and creativity. As Orson Welles said in *The Third Man,* "Hundreds of years of peace, and what did it [Switzerland] produce? The cuckoo clock." But don't expect the Swiss to rend their garments in disgrace over this—their self-restraint and discipline have earned them one of the highest standards of living in the world.

At first glance, Swiss history also seems a bit uneventful. But when you realize that other countries' official histories are mostly chronicles of war and egomaniacal rulers, you gain a new admiration for Switzerland's 700-year-old democratic tradition. In medieval times, a nation of peasants, monks, and small-time lords began to take shape; then, in the 13th century, when the Hapsburgs threatened to interfere in Swiss affairs, a handful of Swiss convened in the Rütli meadow near Lake Luzern and formed an alliance. Since then foreign powers have been shut out almost completely, an extraordinary feat considering Switzerland's location in the rich belly of Europe. Still, the Swiss haven't remained disinterested in foreign conflicts (more than a million Swiss fought as mercenaries from the end of the 14th century until 1859), nor have they been immune to internal conflicts (the Reformation, sparked by Zwingli in Zürich and Calvin in Geneva, led to vicious religious wars during the 16th and 17th centuries). Though regionalism certainly persists—Switzerland's last civil war ended in 1847—hostilities have mostly been resolved with the creation of a decentralized political system. The federal government takes care of international affairs, but local administrations handle schools, road construction, taxation, and town planning. Sovereign power, at least in theory, rests with the people, who can vote on everything from the official color of trash cans to whether Switzerland should join the European Union (they voted "nay").

As the country's countless museums and music festivals attest, the Swiss enjoy the arts at least as much as any other Europeans. Granted, Switzerland itself has produced only a few famous artists, such as Paul Klee, Alberto Giacometti, and novelist Max Frisch; but the country's neutrality during World War II attracted many talented refugees, among them James Joyce, Hermann Hesse, Thomas Mann, and Max Beckmann. That said, don't expect to overload on high culture on your visit to Switzerland. What you *will* find are loads of bucolic charm, mountain scenery that astounds, and peaceful lakeside cities that could lull you into staying for months . . . if this weren't one of the most expensive countries in Europe.

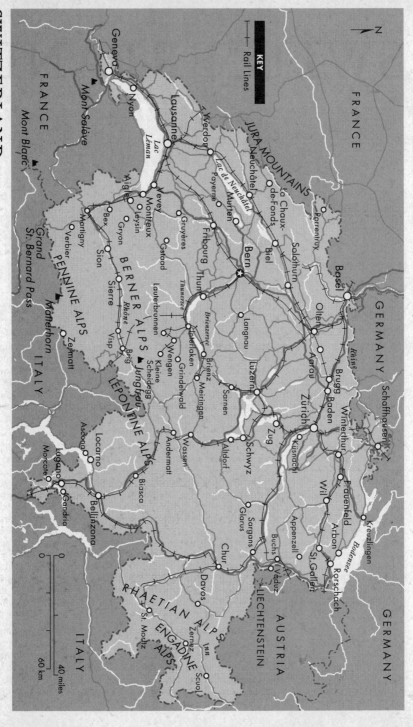

SWITZERLAND

N

KEY

━━┿━━ Rail Lines

FRANCE

Geneva
Nyon
Mont Salève
Mont Blanc
FRANCE
Lausanne
Lac Léman
Vevey
Montreux
Aigle
Bex
Gryon
Leysin
Martigny
Verbier
Sion
Sierre
Visp
Brig
Grand St. Bernard Pass
Zermatt
Matterhorn
PENNINE ALPS
ITALY
BERNER ALPS
Gstaad
Gruyères
Fribourg
Thun
Thunersee
Lauterbrunnen
Wengen
Kleine Scheidegg
Jungfrau
Grindelwald
Interlaken
Brienz
Meiringen
Briezersee
Sarnen
LEPONTINE ALPS
Andermatt
Wassen
Altdorf
Ascona
Locarno
Morcote
Lugano
Gandria
Bellinzona
Biasca
Chur
Davos
St. Moritz
Zernez
Scuol
RHAETIAN ALPS
ENGADINE ALPS
ITALY
Yverdon
Lac de Neuchâtel
Payerne
Murten
JURA MOUNTAINS
Neuchâtel
la Chaux-de-Fonds
Biel
Solothurn
Bern
Langnau
Luzern
Schwyz
Zug
Glarus
Sargans
Buchs
Vaduz
LIECHTENSTEIN
AUSTRIA
Porrentruy
Basel
Olten
Aarau
Brugg
Baden
Zürich
Küsnacht
Winterthur
Wil
Frauenfeld
Appenzell
St. Gallen
Arbon
Rorschach
Schaffhausen
Kreuzlingen
Bodensee
Rhine
GERMANY
GERMANY
Rhône

0
20 km
40 miles
60 km

The most refined way to fly to Switzerland.

ADVICO YOUNG & RUBICAM

With Swissair you can fly to over 130 destinations worldwide. And you don't have to say good-bye to having fun.

A sophisticated infrastructure makes enticing Switzerland the ideal place for work and play. So when will you next combine business with pleasure? For reservations or information contact your travel agent or call Swissair at 1-800-221-4750. http://www.swissair.com

swissair ✚ **world's most refreshing airline.**

Partner in the Delta Air Lines, Midwest Express, US Airways and Air Canada frequent flyer programs.

TAKE OUR TRAINS THROUGH EUROPE AND WE'LL EVEN LET YOU DRIVE

Arrive in one of Europe's exciting cities by rail, then take off and explore charming, old-world villages by rental car. Our *Europass Drive* combines two great ways to see five of the most popular European countries - *France, Germany, Italy, Spain and Switzerland* - at one low price.

For information or reservations call your travel agent or Rail Europe:

1-800-4-EURAIL(US)

1-800-361-RAIL(CAN)

Your one source for European travel!

www.raileurope.com

UST**O**A
INTEGRITY IN TOURISM

BASICS

MONEY

US$1 = 1.45 Swiss francs and 1 Swiss franc = 69¢. The Swiss franc (SFr) contains 100 centimes. You can change money at banks, usually open weekdays 8–noon and 2–6:30 and sometimes Saturday morning. Bureaux de change at train stations (look for CHANGE signs) offer rates nearly as good as the banks' and have longer hours. ATMs that accept Visa, MasterCard, and Cirrus cards can be found just about anywhere there's a bank, which is to say, just about everywhere. ATMs accepting Plus cards are at The Swiss Bank Corporation in St. Moritz, Zürich, and Basel.

HOW MUCH IT WILL COST • A lot, but just about everything in Switzerland is of high quality. Food is especially pricey: A meal at a cheap sit-down restaurant runs at least SFr15, and even a sandwich or slice of pizza often costs SFr5. Cover charges are SFr10–SFr30, a beer in a bar SFr3.50–SFr5, and mixed drinks SFr10–SFr20. Hostels average SFr25, and the cheapest hotels, SFr100 per double. Trains are expensive, so get a Eurailpass, Swiss Pass, or Swiss Card (*see* Getting Around, *below*) if you plan to stay long. If you sleep in hostels, pack lunches, and live like a monk, you can probably get by on less than $60 a day. Budget extra for any outdoor activities that require more than a pair of hiking boots.

GETTING AROUND

BY BIKE • Train stations rent **bikes** for SFr22 per day, SFr88 per week (mountain bikes SFr30 per day, SFr120 per week), and you can pick up from one station and return to another for a fee (SFr2 if you inform them ahead of time, SFr12 otherwise). Reserve the bike at 6 PM the day before you want it.

Although they declared their neutrality 300 years ago, the Swiss remain ready for war, with extensive underground airports and enough food reserves to feed the entire country for six months.

BY BUS • Yellow **PTT postal buses** link cities with off-the-beaten-track villages not reachable by train. Swiss Passes are good on many buses, but Eurailpasses aren't. Get free timetables at post offices.

BY TRAIN • The rail system is quintessentially Swiss: clean, orderly, and punctual. *Schnellzuge* (express trains, often designated IC for Intercity) race between major cities, while *Regionalzuge* (local trains) chug slowly from town to town. Official timetables (called "Kursbuch" or "Horaire") covering all rail and bus lines cost about SFr16 at train stations, but you can also get free blue-and-white booklets listing schedules for specific routes. For train information, dial 157–22–22 (SFr1.19 per minute). Eurailpasses are good on most trips, but not on private mountain railways.

The **Swiss Pass,** available inside or outside Switzerland, buys you travel on most trains, buses, trams, and ferries and a 25%–50% discount on certain mountain railways and cable cars. It's available for 4 days (SFr210), 8 days (Sfr264), 15 days (SFr306), or one month (SFr420). A **Swiss Flexipass** (SFr210) gets you three days of travel within a 15-day period. Unless you move quite fast, it may not be worth the price. The **Swiss Card** (SFr140) gets you a 50% discount on trains, buses, and boats for one month and a free round trip to the airport or border. Regional passes, most valid for either 3 days of travel within 7 days, or 5 days within 15, are useful if you're exploring one part of the country in depth. Swiss Passes and Swiss Cards get you a 20% discount on regional passes.

WHERE TO SLEEP

Hostels (called Jugendherbergen, Auberges de Jeunesse, or Alberghi per la Gioventú), which range from new and clean to brand-new and spotless, are the most affordable option, and they usually welcome all ages, from families with small children to retirees. Buy a membership card (good for one year) for SFr25 at your first stop; otherwise you'll pay SFr5 extra per night. Hostels often have strict curfews and lockouts (some will give you a key if you ask) and can be overrun with organized tour groups. Beds average SFr25 nightly (SFr2 less for longer stays) and include sheets. For a small fee, your hostel can reserve you a room at another hostel. **Camping** opportunities abound in the spectacular Swiss outdoors. Many campgrounds close between October and April; the higher the altitude, the shorter the season. Prices average SFr4–SFr6 per person plus SFr6–SFr9 per tent.

For names of good budget **hotels,** ask a tourist office for a copy of the free *E&G Hotel Guide,* which specializes in cheap but atmospheric inns outside major cities. In rural areas, **privatzimmer** (rooms in private homes) are plentiful; book them through local tourist offices.

FOOD

Bountiful supermarket/restaurant combos like **Migros, Manora,** and **Coop** provide the cheapest and healthiest meals. In small towns, the supermarket half closes between noon and 2 (just when your tummy starts to rumble) and all day Sunday, so pick up your picnic supplies early. Some other department stores house popular buffet-style restaurants with tasty meals at good prices. Otherwise, stick to produce markets and street stands, unless you want to leak Swiss francs at a frightening rate. Your main fallbacks will be burgers and pizza, as well as *Wurst* (sausage) in German-speaking areas. Other German specialties include *Geschnetzeltes* (veal in cream and white-wine sauce) and *Rösti* (fried potatoes, similar to hash browns, usually topped with cheese or baked ham). Restaurants are quite expensive, though you can make a filling lunch of fondue for a barely affordable SFr18–Sfr20. Keep your eyes peeled for blackboard lunch specials (Sfr12–Sfr16). French Switzerland boasts famous cheese fondues and *raclettes* (melted cheese and potatoes), and the Ticino region rarely strays from standard Italian cuisine. Vegetarian restaurants are beginning to pop up more often in this land of meat and cheese, giving vegetarian travelers options besides cheese pizza.

BUSINESS HOURS

The larger the city, the longer the business hours. Many businesses close for lunch. Banks are generally open weekdays 8–5:30 (but many close noon–2) and sometimes Saturday morning. Most museums are open Tuesday–Sunday 10–5; most stores are open weekdays 9–6 and Saturday morning. Post offices are open weekdays 7:30–noon and 2–6, Saturday 7:30–noon; main post offices stay open longer and sometimes on Sunday.

PHONES AND MAIL

Country code: 41. You'll need to deposit at least 60 centimes for all calls from pay phones, which also take PTT phone cards (SFr5–SFr20), available at post offices and train stations. Make international calls from phone booths or the post office, which accepts cash and credit. Dial 111 for directory assistance, 191 or 114 for an English-speaking operator. Deposit at least 60 centimes (which gets returned) and dial 0–800–550011 for **AT&T** Direct Access℠, 155–02–22 for **MCI,** or 155–97–77 for **Sprint.** Calling the United States costs about SFr1.50 per minute.

You can receive poste restante (or *postlagernde*) at any post office in Switzerland. Have it sent to Your Name, Poste Restante, 1 [city name] Hauptpost, Switzerland.

EMERGENCIES

Dial 117 for the **police,** 144 for an **ambulance.**

LANGUAGE

German (or rather Swiss German, which barely resembles High German) is spoken by 64% of the population, French by 19% (in the west), Italian by 8% (in the south), and Romansch by less than ½% (in the southeast). Romansch, a relic from Roman times, is spoken in parts of the Graubünden (Grisons in French), but it has been steadily replaced by German. Rumantsch Grischun, as written Romansch is called, has recently been promoted to semi-official status, though in fact no real unified dialect exists. Most German and French speakers also speak English and have no hang-ups about doing so.

GAY AND LESBIAN TRAVELERS

The Swiss are a pretty progressive people, and homophobia is rare. Zürich in particular has a fairly open gay population. In typical Swiss fashion, there is an organized network of centers for gay men, and you'll find one in just about every major city. The *Pink Guide* lists all centers, bars, and other meeting places for gays. No such network exists for lesbians, though some women's centers can provide information.

GERMAN SWITZERLAND

In most respects, the Swiss more closely resemble their efficient German neighbors to the north than the French or Italians to the south. The country's notorious coziness is everywhere tempered by strict control and state-of-the-art technology—you'll see liquor measured with scientific precision into 2-centiliter glasses, and miniaturized stereo speakers concealed behind oversize cowbells. Switzerland's fastidious side is especially apparent in its German-speaking regions. Bern, for example, preserves its medieval arcades and towers to an eerie perfection, and Zürich's strict Protestant work ethic shaped it into one of the world's best-organized financial centers. Even quirky Basel moves 27,500 French and German commuters into Switzerland every day with clockwork precision.

ZURICH

Straddling the banks of the Limmat River and Lake Zürich (Zürichsee), Zürich is Switzerland's largest city (population: 363,000 at last count) but is hardly overwhelming. In fact, its genteel tearooms, mellow coffeehouses, and friendly bars lend the city a surprisingly intimate feel. Zürich has been the capital of international banking since World War II, and it continues to bring in almost one-fifth of Switzerland's income. The days when you could walk into any bank, plunk down a suitcase full of cash, and anonymously open an account are over, but Zürich is still saturated with money; even the street musicians make a decent living. The city's wealth is most conspicuous in the impeccable style of its residents, who seem determined to prove that Zürich is the best-dressed town in the world. Despite its capitalist preoccupations, however, Zürich is no stuffed shirt. Lenin and Joyce once lived here, and it's still Ground Zero for nightlife in Switzerland.

BASICS

At the train-station **tourist office** (Bahnhofbrücke 1, tel. 01/215–40–00; open Nov.–Mar., weekdays 8:30–7:30, weekends 8:30–6:30; Apr.–Oct., weekdays 8:30 AM–9:30 PM, weekends 8:30–8:30), you can pick up *Züri News* and *Zürich Next,* free publications listing concerts, bars, restaurants, cinemas, and exhibits. The **American Express** office (Bahnhofstr. 20, tel. 01/211–83–70) is open weekdays 8:30–5:30, Saturday 9–noon. The **post office** (Kasernenstr. 95–99, tel. 01/245–41–11; open weekdays 6:30 AM–10:30 PM, Sat. 6:30 AM–8 PM, Sun. 11–10:30) holds poste restante (*see* Phones and Mail *in* Basics, *above*). If you're in need of a **consulate,** the U.S. office recently closed here, but the U.K. office (Dufourstr. 56, tel. 01/261–15–20) is open weekdays 9–noon and 2–4.

COMING AND GOING

Trains arrive at the **Hauptbahnhof** (tel. 01/157–22–22) in the city center. Zürich has express connections to Basel (1 hr, SFr30), Geneva (3 hrs, SFr74), Bern (1 hr 10 min, SFr42), and Lugano (3 hrs, SFr59) at least once an hour from 6 AM to midnight. **Kloten** (tel. 01/812–12–12) is Switzerland's main airport. A train terminal beneath the airport has direct service into the Hauptbahnhof (10 min, SFr5.10).

GETTING AROUND

Nearly all the sights are within walking distance of the Altstadt (Old Town), which stretches to the Hauptbahnhof in the north, Zürichsee in the south, Bahnhofstrasse in the west, and Rämistrasse in the east. Zürich's **trams** and **buses** are a breeze to use; get a system map from the tourist office. Single rides cost SFr3.60, so a day pass is a good deal at SFr7.20. You can buy tickets at any of the blue machines. Watch out for lines that change routes at night, and be aware that all lines stop at midnight.

WHERE TO SLEEP

Prices in the center of town are no worse than those out in the boonies; doubles generally cost SFr100–SFr130. Women, married couples, and families can stay at the cozy **Foyer Hottingen** (Hottingerstr. 31, 3 blocks from Kunsthaus, tel. 01/261–93–15; dorm beds SFr25–SFr30, doubles SFr95). The nuns who run it impose a midnight curfew. From the Hauptbahnhof, take Tram 3 to Hottingerplatz.

The hippest hotel in Zürich is the centrally located **Hotel Otter** (Oberdorfstr. 7, tel. 01/251–22–07; doubles SFr120; SFr100 Nov.–Mar.). All rooms come with TV and minifridge, and there's a great bar downstairs. **Martahaus** (Zähringerstr. 36, tel. 01/251–45–50), in the Altstadt, has a cool breakfast room and dorm beds for only Sfr32; doubles are SFr80. You may think **Hotel Splendid** (Rosengasse 5, tel. 01/252–58–50; doubles SFr96) is a misnomer when you see its run-down hallways, but the rooms and bathrooms themselves look brand-new. **Hotel Poly** (Universitätstr. 63, tel. 01/362–94–40; doubles SFr80) is a cozy place a bit off the beaten track, though just a short tram ride uphill from the town center. Pricier rooms here (doubles SFr110) have better amenities, which vary by room.

HOSTELS • The City Backpacker/Hotel Biber. Opened in 1994, this hostel still feels new and has an unbeatable location, smack in the center of the Altstadt. It offers kitchen facilities, comfortable common rooms, and no curfew. Dorm beds cost SFr30 (sheets SFr3), doubles SFr85. *Niederdorfstr. 5, tel. 01/251–90–15. From Hauptbahnhof, cross Bahnhofbrücke and go right on Niederdorfstr.*

ZURICH

Zürich-Wollishofen (HI). In exchange for a removed location, you get lots of amenities here (e.g., game room, movies, patio). A filling breakfast is included, and hearty dinners are SFr11. Beds are SFr29, SFr36 for nonmembers. Reserve ahead for doubles (SFr40, SFr44 with bath). *Mutschellenstr. 114, tel. 01/482–35–44. From Hauptbahnhof, Tram 7 to Morgenthal; walk north on Mutschellenstr. 10 min. Reception open 24 hours.*

FOOD

Eating out in Zürich will eat a hole through your wallet; meals in restaurants start at SFr12 and go way up. Don't despair; just pack a lunch from **Metzgerei Traiteur** (Hirschenpl., near east side of Rathausbr.) or the **Coop Super-Center** (Bahnhof-Br., by the train station), and settle down to a picnic. Some places in the Altstadt sell pizzas for around SFr12, and in cafés you can get a small *schinken und käse* (ham-and-cheese) sandwich for about SFr9 or a bowl of soup with bread for SFr7. **Berner**

(Hottinger-Str. 33, 3 blocks from Kunsthaus), open every weekday, has pizza slices, quiche, and sandwiches for around SFr4. Also open weekdays, the cafeteria at the **Universität Zürich** (Rämistr. 71) serves up typical cafeteria fare (menu about SFr5); students linger all day in the large, glass-covered atrium.

Blockhus. The friendly owner of this Altstadt favorite serves delicious Mediterranean meals (SFr15–SFr29). The cozy, calm atmosphere draws locals. *Schifflände 4, at Krug-Gasse, near corner of Limmatquai and Rämistr., tel. 01/252–14–53.*

Gran Café. Tables line the sidewalk outside this loud café. Hot sandwiches with salad are only SFr11. *Limmatquai 66, tel. 01/252–31–19.*

Hiltl Vegi. Vegetarians will love this elegant, lively place. A meal will cost you the better part of SFr20. *Sihlstr. 28, 2 blocks from Bahnhof-Str., tel. 01/221–38–70.*

WORTH SEEING

A walk through Zürich should provide your recommended daily allowance of churches and museums. For a taste of the former, head to **Peterskirche** (St. Peter's Church), on a tranquil medieval square west of the river. It's most famous for its 16th-century clock, the largest in Europe—the minute hand alone is 12 ft long. Directly to the south is the elegant copper spire of the **Fraumünster,** which was founded in the 9th century, though constructed mostly in the 11th. Marc Chagall created the choir's impressive stained-glass windows in the 1970s. Competing for attention across the Münsterbrücke, the **Großmünster,** with its two distinctive towers, features modern stained-glass windows by Giacometti. The interior, courtesy of the original Protestant reformers, is somewhat austere. The Grossmünster is dedicated to Zürich's patron saints (Felix, Regula, and Exuperantius), who, after drinking molten lead and being beheaded (goes the legend), mustered enough energy to carry their heads uphill and bury themselves to the right of the church. Check the entertainment guides at the tourist office for information on concerts in city churches; the acoustics in some are superb.

Bahnhofstrasse, the fanciest shopping street in Switzerland, is loaded with boutiques selling clothes, jewelry, and watches—a feast for the eyes, but an insult to the wallet. If the sartorial riches leave you feeling deprived, treat yourself to a **boat cruise** (summer only). A one-hour tour on the Limmat River is only SFr3.60 and leaves from the Landesmuseum (*see below*). Tours of Zürichsee leave from Bürkliplatz (1½-hr trip, SFr5.10; 4- to 5-hr trip, SFr27.20). Or head up to the university: The **Polyterrasse,** in front of the Eidgenössische Technische Hochschule offers an excellent view of the city, with a plaque pointing out all the sights. On warm days, **Uto-Quai,** a park along the lake, south of Bellevueplatz, fills with everyone from Rastas and in-line skaters to nude sunbathers and businesspeople playing hooky. Head all the way to the south end for more grass and a swimming spot in cold, clean Lake Zürich.

KUNSTHAUS • This eclectic museum has it all: works by such famous Swiss artists as Ferdinand Hodler; big, bright spaces filled with constructivist art; a serene upper room displaying Giacometti's works; and some Matisse and Rodin sculptures thrown in for good measure. The Edvard Munch collection is one of the largest outside Norway, and Marc Chagall is well represented. *Heimpl. 1, tel. 01/251–67–65. Admission: SFr5. Open Tues.–Thurs. 10–9, Fri.–Sun. 10–5.*

SCHWEIZERISCHES LANDESMUSEUM • In an eccentric 19th-century building behind the train station, the Swiss National Museum holds the country's most important national treasures. The collection starts with Stone Age relics and doesn't quit until it reaches modern times. Along the way, you'll see costumes, furniture, early Swiss watches, and thousands of toy soldiers reenacting battle scenes. *Museumsstr. 2, tel. 01/218–65–11. Admission free. Open Tues.–Sun. 10:30–5.*

AFTER DARK

Zürich has plenty of dance clubs and live music (mostly jazz) venues, but the club of the moment can vary from week to week; check *Zürich Next* for listings. The most popular nightspot is **Kaufleuten** (Pelikanstr. 18), packed with the well-to-do. Duck the SFr15 cover by hanging out in the bar. The Altstadt is filled with bars and cafés; one of the better bars is **Würste** at Hotel Otter (*see Where to Sleep, above*). An alternative crowd hangs out at **Café Zähringer** (Spitalgasse 14, off Niederdorfstr.), which offers live music—from Latin to funk—every Wednesday. Next door, **Barfüsser** has a gay clientele. Walk toward Bellevueplatz to reach the gorgeous Art Nouveau **Bar Odeon** (Limmatquai 2). Lenin hung out here while sitting out World War I.

BASEL

Although Basel lies at the convergence of France, Germany, and Switzerland, its personality is firmly its own. The town prides itself on being different from "Züri," mocks the French during Carnival, and revels in its reputation as a center for art. From Jean Tinguely's great mechanical sculpture at the train station and the huge Hammering Man at Aeschenplatz to the modern pieces hidden in parks, Basel's mania for the arts is obvious. Residents even take pride in the colorful graffiti that covers the walls along the train route from Zürich. Switzerland's oldest university (where Friedrich Nietzsche once taught) also fuels this artistic interest. But if the arts aren't your thing, you may be unimpressed with Basel, as it lacks Zürich's style and Geneva's grace.

BASICS

The small information office in the Hauptbahnhof (tel. 061/271–36–84) books rooms for Sfr10. The **main tourist office** (Schifflände 5, near Mittlere-Br., tel. 061/268–68–68; open weekdays 8:30–6, Sat. 10–4) is more centrally located on the Rhine; pick up a free calendar of live music and other cultural events. From the Hauptbahnhof, take Tram 1 or 8 to Schifflände. The **American Express** office (Steinenvorstadt 33, tel. 061/281–33–80) in the Altstadt is open weekdays 9–6:30 and Saturday 10–4.

COMING AND GOING

Basel is a transportation hub, with French, German, and Swiss train stations. Be sure to get off at the Swiss station **Schweizerische Bundesbahnen (SBB)** (Centralbahnstr., tel. 157–22–22); many a weary traveler has walked an hour from the German side of town. **Klein-Basel** (Small Basel), east of the Rhine in German territory, is an industrial center; the more affluent **Gross-Basel** (Greater Basel) on the western side contains most of the sights and the **Altstadt** (Old Town). To reach the Altstadt from the SBB, head north (left) on Heuwaage-Viadukt, turn right on Steinenvorstadt and continue until you reach the central square, Barfüsserplatz. To reach outlying areas, take the **tram**. Tickets cost SFr2.60, and a day pass is SFr7.20.

WHERE TO SLEEP

Basel's hotels are clean and charming, but they don't come cheap. The least-expensive doubles usually cost SFr120–SFr150. Because Basel is a prime convention town, however, many slick business hotels offer bargain rates during their quieter periods—weekends and July/August—and some other places have terrific deals for travelers under 26. If you want to live it up, try **Steinenschanze Garni** (Steinengraben 69, tel. 061/272–53–53), near the train station, where doubles with bath and breakfast start at SFr140. Make a left outside the station (on Viadukstr.), a right on Steinentorberg, and a left on the main drag. Across from the Bahnhof, the pricey, four-star **Victoria** (Centralbahnpl. 3–4, tel. 061/271–55–66) has come up with a creative student discount: They charge you SFr2 for every year you've been alive. Everyone else should pursue the weekend and summer specials, which offer doubles without breakfast for SFr111. The homey, spotless **Hotel Rochat** (Petersgraben 23, tel. 061/261–81–40), next to the university, is outstanding; doubles start at SFr140. The dry restaurant downstairs serves good meals sans booze for SFr13–SFr20. Take Tram 3 to Lyss and walk downhill.

Your typical spotless Swiss hostel, **HI Jugendherberge** (St. Alban-Kirchrain 10, tel. 061/272–05–72; dorm beds SFr26.80, doubles SFr76) lies beside a shady stream, a short walk from the town center. From the train station, take Tram 2 to Kunstmuseum, then walk down St. Alban-Vorstadt and turn left on Mühlenberg Castellio, following the signs. About 6 km (4 mi) outside the city, **Camp Waldhort Basel** (Heideweg 16, tel. 061/711–64–29; open Mar.–Oct.) has a grocery store, warm showers, and a swimming pool. Sites are SFr6.50 per person, SFr4 per tent. From Aeschenplatz, take Tram 11 to Landhof and make a left at the Landhof Restaurant.

FOOD

Most students find refuge from Basel's expensive restaurants at the self-service joints in **Migros Market** (Unt. Rebgasse 11, near Clarapl.) or the ever-present **Coop** grocery stores. Pick up pizza slices and great pastries at **Ziegler Bakery** (Freiestr. 8). On Marktplatz, a big daily **market** sells fruit, veggies, bread, cheese sandwiches, and even egg rolls. If you come here, stop in at Basel's oldest tearoom (open since 1870—but closed Sunday and Monday), the **Schiesser Café.** You can buy beautiful chocolates (about SFr8.50 for 100 grams) downstairs, then down coffee and a sumptuous pastry or cold lunch with a polite local crowd upstairs.

Restaurant Fischerstübe (Rheingasse 45, tel. 061/692–66–35), a block from the river in Klein-Basel, brews its own Ueli beer and serves typical Swiss meals and fresh fish for SFr12–SFr16. At night it becomes a beer hall. **Café Pfalz** (Münsterberg 11, tel. 061/272–65–11), below the cathedral, is a bookish little self-service café, with veggie specials, salad bar, juicer, and muësli. **Gleich** (Steinenvorstadt 23, tel. 061/281–82–86; closed weekends), a haven for vegetarians, has Rösti with fried egg and apple pancakes (each about SFr14).

WORTH SEEING

The Altstadt's three main plazas—Münsterplatz, Marktplatz, and Barfüsserplatz—offer the best sights and the most action. The colorful **Marktplatz,** in the middle of the pedestrian zone, is dominated by the bright red, fancifully overdone **Rathaus** (Town Hall). The front of the building is covered with colorful frescoes; the interior courtyard features more frescoes and a gilded statue of Basel's founder, Munatius Plancus. Several blocks south of Marktplatz, people and trams jam the small **Barfüsserplatz** (Barefoot Plaza), home to businesses and restaurants. Bordering the square, the **Historisches Museum** (tel. 061/271–05–05; admission SFr5, free first Sun. of month; open Wed.–Mon. 10–5), in a former Franciscan church, outlines Basel's history with archaeological finds, medieval relics, and mementos of Erasmus, who died here in 1536.

Basel's extensive list of museums can satisfy anyone's appetite for art. In addition to the Kunstmuseum (*see below*), the **Kunsthalle** (Steinenberg 7, near Theatrepl., tel. 061/272–48–33; admission SFr9; open Tues.–Sun. 11–5, Wed. 11–8:30) merits a visit; it was the first European gallery to show American abstract expressionists, and continues to display experimental work by major contemporary artists. The macabre mechanical whimsy of Basel's favorite sculptor is showcased in the spectacular new interactive **Museum Jean Tinguely,** in Solitude Park (entrance on Grenzacherstrasse, tel. 061/681–93–20; admission SFr5; open Wed.–Sun. 11–7), devoted to the work of this surrealist rebel and his wife, Niki de Saint Phalle. Press a pedal on one of a hundred works and a suspended montage of, say, a horsetail, fox pelt, cafeteria tray, hinged leg with moth-eaten sock, and blood-soaked nightgown will dangle and dance on command.

Basel celebrates its Carnival (Fasnacht) with fifes, drums, and fabulous oversize masks. You'll spot the stock characters year-round: Ueli the clown; the Vogel Gryff (griffin); and the Lälle-König, who sticks out a mechanical tongue.

KUNSTMUSEUM • In the courtyard outside this museum are Rodin's *Burghers of Calais* and sculptures by Alexander Calder—only a preview of the incredible art inside. The ground floor is rich in Giacomettis, Klees, Mondrians, Chagalls, and Kandinskys, as well as Braques, Picassos, and Légers. The second floor features local artist Konrad Witz and the world's largest group of paintings by Hans Holbein the Younger. You'll also find modern art by the likes of Degas, Van Gogh, Gauguin, Renoir, and Rodin, a room full of Cézanne sketches, and world-class traveling exhibitions. *St. Alban-Graben 16, tel. 061/271–08–28. Admission: SFr7, free first Sun. of month. Open Tues.–Sun. 10–5.*

MUNSTER • Basel's main attraction sits over the Rhine, on Münsterplatz. The relief-covered facade and marvelous north portal of this red sandstone cathedral date from the 12th century and are worth the visit in themselves. Inside you'll find some illustrious dead folk, including Erasmus and the Hapsburg Queen Anna. You can view the square and a good chunk of Basel from the Gothic towers for SFr3. *Open weekdays 10–5, Sat. 10–noon and 2–5, Sun. 1–5.*

AFTER DARK

Nightlife centers around Barfüsserplatz, where the **Rio Bar** is an established local hangout. On warm nights, crowds gather on the stairs of Theatreplatz, where the busy outdoor **Kunsthalle Restaurant** (Steinenberg 7, 061/272–42–33) bubbles over with Basel's literati. **Atlantis** (Klosterberg 13, behind Theatrepl., tel. 061/272–20–38) is popular with students and often has live music; the cover ranges from nothing to SFr40 for big-name acts. **Elle et Lui** (Rebgasse 39, tel. 061/692–54–79) in Klein-Basel hosts a mostly gay and lesbian clientele.

LUZERN

With its peaceful lake, stunning mountains, and quaint bridges, Luzern (Lucerne in French) is as picturesque as any Swiss city. Unfortunately, such attributes are irresistible to tourists, and in summer Luzern sells its soul to mobs of camcorder-toting sightseers. The city's Altstadt in particular has a sterile, made-for-tourists feel, and the sights and museums are nothing to rave about. Head for the mountains, or to Luzern's beautiful lake for one of Switzerland's best boat rides. The **tourist office** (Frankenstr. 1, 1 block from station, tel. 041/410−71−71) offers two-hour guided tours for SFr15. The *City Guide* (available at tourist office), when stamped by your hotel, gets you discounted admission to most sights. **American Express** (Schweizerhotquai 4, tel. 041/410−00−77) is open weekdays 8−6, weekends 8:30−noon.

COMING AND GOING

Express trains run to Luzern from Zürich (50 min, SFr19.40) and Geneva (4 hrs, SFr65). The **Bahnhof** (train station) is on Zentralstrasse on the lake, near the Reuss River. Everything in Luzern is accessible on foot. Most sights are north of the river and south of Museggmauer, the old fortified walls. To get to the hostel and a few faraway sights, take the **bus**; tickets (SFr1.50−SFr2, day pass SFr10) are available at automated machines at each stop.

WHERE TO SLEEP

If you have a sleeping bag, the best deal in town is a dorm bed (SFr15) or a campsite (SFr3 per tent, SFr6 per person) at the lakeside **campground** (Lidostr., tel. 041/370−21−46). From the Bahnhof, take Bus 2 to Verkehrshaus or walk a half-hour along the lake. The friendly, centrally located **Tourist Hotel** (St. Karliquai 12, tel. 041/410−24−74) has dorm beds for SFr36 and doubles for SFr104. The hotel is on the northern riverbank, about 15 minutes' walk west of the Bahnhof; they'll collect groups of three or more at the station. The new hostel, **Backpackers** (Alpenquai 12, tel. 041/360−04−20), is also 15 minutes from the Bahnhof, across the street from the lake. Dorm beds are SFr21.50 (sheets SFr2), doubles SFr53. Follow Inseliquai (it will turn into Werfftestrasse then Alpenquai); the hostel is in the student dormitory.

FOOD

Entrées at **Movie Restaurant** (Metzgerrainle 9, tel. 041/410−35−31), named after your favorite flicks, are a bit pricey (SFr18 and up), but lunch specials (SFr16.50−SFr19.50 with soup or salad and drink) aren't a bad deal. Lenin pondered and Mata Hari danced at the landmark **Odéon** (Am Bellevue, tel. 01/251−16−50); nurse a coffee and read one of the house's daily papers amid the unfiltered smoke, or dine on pasta, sandwiches, and dessert for less than SFr30. The food at the cavernous **Zeughauskeller** (Bahnhofstrasse 28, tel. 01/211−2690) is what the Swiss call *gutbürgerlich*—simple local stuff, big portions, no frills. For the cheapest in chow, hit supermarkets like **Migros** (Hertensteinstr. 40), or try **Bell Market,** just outside the Bahnhof to the left, which has salads, meats, and pizza slices for SFr5. Most nightspots are scattered in the new town, just beyond the tourist's eye. Enjoy the view from the **Penthouse Bar** (Pilatusstr. 22, tel. 041/210−22−44), on the 7th floor of the Hotel Astoria; once a month it throws a full-moon party. **Piranha** (Bundespl., no phone), with a tile interior apparently inspired by Gaudí, provides your basic dance music. Drinks are half-price before 11, and there's no cover on weekdays (weekends SFr10).

WORTH SEEING

Begin a quick walk around town at **Kornmarkt,** site of the old grain market and the bakers' guild, a white building with a mural of a baker's family tree. The nearby **Picasso Sammlung** (Furrengasse 21, tel. 041/410−35−33; admission SFr6; open Apr.−Oct., daily 10−6; shorter hrs off season), housed in the 17th-century Am Rhyn Haus, has a collection of Picasso's paintings and drawings, primarily from his later years. A bit farther east, you can cross the wooden **Kapellbrücke,** built in 1333. Partially destroyed by fire in 1993, it has been restored to its original form. The Heinrich Wagmann paintings along the bridge were added during the 17th century to teach illiterate townspeople about Swiss history. The south side of the bridge ends at the **Jesuitenkirche** (1666), built by the Jesuits with a light, cheery interior to lure wayward Catholics to mass.

The Renaissance **Hofkirche** (St. Leodegarstrasse), dedicated to the town's patron saint, Léger, houses a famous 4,950-pipe organ. The church is a well-known city symbol, as is the **Löwendenkmal** (Lion of Luzern), a massive lion sculpted into the side of a mountain; this piece is dedicated to the Swiss soldiers who died defending Louis XVI and Marie Antoinette in Paris. Just above the lion, the **Gletschergarten** (Denkmalstr. 4, tel. 041/410−43−40; admission SFr7; open May−mid-Oct., daily 8−6; shorter hrs off season) is a group of potholes—the largest 31 ft in diameter—dramatically etched 20,000 years ago by the glacier that formed the Reuss River. Amazingly, the potholes prove that Luzern was a subtropical beach some 20 million years ago; the information area has details.

The **Verkehrshaus** (Lidostr. 5, tel. 041/370−44−44; admission SFr16; open Apr.−Oct., daily 9−6; shorter hrs off season) is a knockout survey of every type of transportation imaginable, from stagecoaches to spaceships. The **Richard Wagner Museum** (Wagnerweg 27, tel. 041/360−23−70; admission SFr5; open Apr.–Oct., Tues.–Sun. 10–noon and 2–5; shorter hrs off season) displays letters, pictures, Wagner's piano, and some original music in the house on the lake where he lived and composed from 1866 to 1872. From the Bahnhof, catch Bus 6, 7, or 8, or walk 45 minutes southeast along Alpenquai and go left across the park to the head of the small peninsula.

OUTDOOR ACTIVITIES

Boating is one of Luzern's best activities, and boat trips are free with a Eurailpass (from SFr20 without). Lasting anywhere from one to four hours, some go to lakeside resorts, some into the Alpine ranges. **Mt. Pilatus** (7,036 ft), supposedly haunted by the spirit of Pontius Pilate, offers outstanding views, and you can reach the peak on the world's steepest cog rail (a special train for mountains). Take the ferry to Alpachstad and transfer to the train. You can descend by cable car and take Tram 1 back to town, or brave the 4½-hour walk from Pilatus to the town of Kriens. If you don't walk, the round trip from Luzern costs SFr40 with a Eurailpass, SFr75 without.

Some find the view from **Mt. Rigi** (5,940 ft) as beautiful as the view from Pilatus. Mark Twain trekked up here, but he slept through the sunrise once on top. You can make the trip more easily: From Luzern, take a boat to Vitznau and transfer to the cog rail, or take the boat to Weggis and transfer to the cable car. The whole trip costs SFr39 with a Eurailpass, SFr78 without. Both peaks have restaurants, but you'll save money if you pack a lunch.

INTERLAKEN

The first thing to do when you get to Interlaken is leave. Get out into the mountains, or blow some money on the multitude of outdoor activities offered in the area, including paragliding, mountain biking, rock climbing, river rafting, and bungee jumping. There's not much to the town itself except some bustling nightspots, but its location at the foot of the mighty Jungfrau (see Near Interlaken, below) makes it an excellent entryway to some of the country's most beautiful landscape. The **tourist office** (Höheweg 37, tel. 033/822–21–21; open weekdays 8–noon and 2–6, Sat. 8–noon) at Hotel Metropole can give you the scoop on planning trips. The cheerful guys at **Alpin Raft** (Hauptstr. 7, by Balmer's, tel. 033/823–41–00) can set you up with any activity from rafting (SFr83) and rock climbing (SFr95) to canyoning (riverbed hiking in wetsuits; SFr68), and ice climbing (SFr125). For something completely different, try rappelling down the sky-scraping Hotel Metropole (SFr65). The more activities you elect, the better the package deal.

COMING AND GOING

Two train stations serve Interlaken: **Westbahnhof** (Bahnhofstr.) and **Ostbahnhof** (Allmendstr.), at opposite ends of the major street, Höheweg. Trains run hourly from Geneva (2¾ hrs, SFr60) and Bern (50 min, SFr24), sometimes with a change in Spiez. The scenic trip from Zürich (SFr42) through Luzern takes about two hours. The action centers around the Westbahnhof; you'll probably use the Ostbahnhof only to catch trains into the mountains.

WHERE TO SLEEP

The easiest way to find lodging is to peruse the boards listing rooms and prices at the train stations; the phone near the board links you directly to the hotels for free. The **Alp Lodge** (Marktgasse 59, tel. 033/822–47–48) has bright rooms, many decorated by local artists. Doubles are SFr54 and include a hearty breakfast. The **Happy Inn Lodge** (Rosenstr. 17, off Centralpl., tel. 033/822–32–25) offers straightforward doubles for SFr72. **Hotel Aarburg** (Beatenbergstr. 1, tel. 033/822–26–15; doubles SFr100) is a beautifully sited, if musty, chalet on the river.

You'll join a raucous American horde at **Balmer's Herberge** (Hauptstr. 23, tel. 033/822–19–61; doubles SFr56). If the beds are full, they'll put you on a spare mattress or send you down the road to the huge tent. From the Westbahnhof, take Bus 5; from the Ostbahnhof, turn right on Höheweg, left onto Jungfraustrasse, and follow the signs. For a more tranquil experience, try **HI Jugendherberge Böningen** (Aareweg 21, tel. 033/822–43–53; beds SFr25.30; reception open 7 AM–10 AM and 5 PM–midnight) on the Brienzersee. From either station, take Bus 1 to Bönigen.

FOOD

Grab a picnic for your excursion at **Migros,** across the street and to the right of the Westbahnhof. **Laterne** (Obere Bönigstrasse 18, tel. 033/822–11–41) serves locals Rösti combos (sausage, egg, steak) for SFr12–SFr18 in a rustic atmosphere complete with televised sports. **Vegetaris Restaurant** (Höheweg 14, tel. 033/822–27–33) serves tasty vegetarian entrées for around SFr15.

TREKKING FROM INTERLAKEN

Strike out in just about any direction from Interlaken and you're guaranteed some awesome sights. The trip outlined here offers dramatic views of the Alps, good hiking, and a visit to the incredible Trümmelbach Falls. From Interlaken's Ostbahnhof, take the train to Lauterbrunnen (SFr6); you can gaze at waterfalls, snowy mountains, and the rock walls of the Lauterbrunnen Valley as the train snakes its way through the trees. From Lauterbrunnen, a funicular (SFr8.40) heads up to Mürren, where you'll see the dramatic Eiger, Mönch, and Jungfrau peaks rising nearly 11,880 ft above sea level. From Mürren, walk about 45 minutes to Gimmelwald for even more superb views of the rocky monsters. You can stay overnight here in the excellent Mountain Hostel (tel. 033/855–17–04; beds SFr15), but bring food to cook, as meals are not part of the deal. From Gimmelwald, take the gondola (SFr7.20) to Stechelberg, then walk 20 minutes to the tremendous Trümmelbach Falls (admission SFr10; open daily 8:30–6), which cut a stormy path through the rocks. Take the postal bus or walk 3 km (2 mi) from Trümmelbach back to the Lauterbrunnen train station. If you're thinking of spending the night in Lauterbrunnen, the Matratzenlager Stocki (tel. 033/855—17–54; dorm beds SFr12), a charming hostel with spectacular mountain views, is reason enough. From the back of the train station, cross the bridge and take a right to get to the hostel. Reservations are a good idea.

NEAR INTERLAKEN

Eurailers and Swiss Pass holders can take free boat cruises on Thunersee and Brienzersee, the lakes immediately west and east of Interlaken. **Thunersee** (SFr31.20) is the more popular of the two excursions; besides great views, a round-trip ride buys you visits to the **castles** at Thun and Spiez. Keep a schedule in your pocket, and get on and off at will. You can also stop at Beatushöhlen, where a 20-minute walk from the landing leads to the eerie stalagmites and stalactites of the **St. Beatus caves** (admission SFr12; open Apr.–Oct., daily 9:30–5). On the **Brienzersee** (SFr24.80), stop at the tranquil town of **Brienz,** worth a stay if you want to relax by the lake or take a bus to the **Freilichtmuseum Ballenberg** (tel. 033/951–11–23; admission SFr12; open Apr.–Oct., daily 10–5), an open-air museum featuring an impressive collection of traditional Swiss buildings and crafts. The boat can also drop you at a starting point for a memorable hike to the beautiful **Giessbach Falls.**

JUNGFRAUJOCH

You can't see the whole continent from the Jungfraujoch, the plateau on Europe's highest accessible peak, but it sure seems like you can. The train from Interlaken's Ostbahnhof passes through Grindelwald or Lauterbrunnen before arriving at Kleine Scheidegg, just below the mountain. Here you can transfer to the famous **Jungfraubahn,** which winds its way slowly uphill through a rock tunnel, stopping twice for views from lookout windows. There's not much to do at the top, but the lack of oxygen and the blinding white landscape will make you feel like you've left Earth. For the real adventurer, there's a hut where you can spend the night when the weather's right; ask at regional tourist offices for more information. Unfortunately, prices for the entire trip are as high as the peak itself: SFr153, or SFr115 if you catch the 6:34 AM train from Interlaken, the 7:05 AM train from Lauterbrunnen, or the 7:18 AM train from Grindelwald (a Eurailpass gets you a 25% discount on certain lines). If you plan to spend some time in the area, look into purchasing a regional rail pass. The tourist office (Höheweg 37, tel. 033/822–21–21) can help explain the options. Dial 855–10–22 for climatic conditions; bad weather will ruin the trip. At 11,338 ft there's always snow, so dress warmly.

GRINDELWALD

The tiny town of Grindelwald is framed by the sculpted edges of the Eiger peak. From here, you can hike past lakes and waterfalls or through icy glaciers and precipitous gorges. The town consists of a single street of touristed shops and a smattering of wood-timbered houses and finely trimmed farms. Most hostels offer amazing views—you might have a hard time getting your bum off the back porch, as it usually faces the mountains. Still, you should motivate yourself to take a gondola ride; you'll see overwhelming mountain vistas set to a symphony of cowbells. Thanks to the wonders of Swiss engineering—cog-wheel trains, gondolas, and buses—visitors can reach the most remote points near Grindelwald without sweating a drop. The **tourist office** (Hauptstr., in Sportzentrum, tel. 033/854–12–12; open weekdays 8–noon and 2–6, Sat. 8–noon and 2–5) is your source for hiking and gondola information; get a map here before you attempt any hikes. In winter, the tourist office can give you the lowdown on skiing (lift tickets SFr50 per day), snowboarding, sledding, and hiking. Grindelwald's sport shops have similar rental prices— SFr28–SFr38 for skis or snowboards, SFr15–SFr19 for boots, and SFr7 for toboggans.

One popular hike leads from the **First** ski area back to town. The Firstbahn (about a 10-minute walk up the main road from the Grindelwald station) will take you up for SFr27. From First you can hike straight down to Grindelwald or take a detour to the vantage point at **Faulhorn.** A comfortable two-hour hike from First leads to the village of Grosse-Scheidegg, with striking views the entire way. If you travel before July, you're bound

What do you get when you cross a force-fed cow, a number wheel marked in chalk, and a bunch of enthusiastic gamblers encouraging the cow to do its thing on their lucky number? Cow Pie Bingo, a tradition at Grindelwald's Country Music Festival.

to hit snow (and slushy trails), so bring your best hiking boots. To avoid paying for a gondola ride, hike from the Grindelwald station uphill to Grosse-Scheidegg (3 hrs) on a paved road through wildflower meadows, or take a bus (40 min, SFr15) to the town and walk back. You can also hike from Grindelwald to the **Oberer Gletscher** (1 hr), a fast-moving glacier, accessible by steep stairs (15 min). The glacier houses the **Blause Eisgrotte** (Blue Ice Cave), famous for its spectacular ice sculptures (admission SFr5; open mid-May–Oct., daily 9–6). If you have energy left over once you get here, walk up a steep incline to the base of **Mt. Schreckhorn** (1½ hrs from Oberer Gletscher); from there, about two hours of scenic strolling will take you back to Grindelwald.

For a dramatic zoom-lens view of the mountains, take a gondola ride (SFr27 one-way) from Grund (15-min walk from Grindelwald station) to Männlichen. From here, it's an hour's walk to **Kleine Scheidegg,** where you'll come face to face with the Eiger, Mönch, and Jungfrau peaks. From Kleine Scheidegg, you can catch the Jungfraubahn up to Jungfraujoch for SFr94 round-trip (*see above*).

WHERE TO SLEEP AND EAT • HI Jugendherberge die Weid (Terrassenweg, tel. 033/853–10–09; beds SFr29.50) is an inviting wooden house with a comfy common room and a deck facing the mountains. From the Bahnhof, cross the street and follow the signs that begin behind the post office; it's a steep 20-minute climb. The crowd is slightly older, the hikers a little more serious at **Naturfreundehaus** (tel. 033/853–13–13; beds SFr32, SFr28 HI members; doubles SFr64), en route to the hostel (again, follow the signs). You'll find clean, wood-paneled dorm rooms, friendly sitting rooms, and a small garden out back where smokers and beer drinkers (beer SFr3) congregate after dinner to take in the views. The Hotel **Wetterhorn,** sited above town at the base of the Oberer Gletscher, offers simple doubles with bath (SFr 98–SFr104), good home cooking, and a sprawling terrace café with glacier views.

Pick up supplies at **Coop,** three minutes southeast of the Bahnhof. Restaurants are generally expensive, most offering a similar variety of sausages, fondue, and Italian dishes. The Hotel Spinne (tel. 033/853–23–41) houses the **Espresso Bar,** a nighttime hot spot, and **Mercato,** which serves a fantastic vegetarian pizza (SFr15). Across the street and down the block a bit, the terrace of the **Ringgenberg Tea Room** (tel. 033/853–10–59) is a popular place to munch on a sandwich (SFr5.50–SFr9) and watch tourists wander by. The pretty, chic **Swiss Bistro,** in the Hotel Fiescherblick (up the Hauptstrasse, tel. 033/853–

44–53), serves creative twists on local standards—potato pancakes with chives, or wild garlic sausage with onion sauce—for SFr15–SFr18.

BERN

Sophisticated Zürichers say that Bern (Berne in French) is too much like its mascot, the slow, clumsy bear. Bern is the capital of Switzerland, but it's a modest place: The president of the Swiss Confederation takes the tram to work, and the city's annual fair celebrates the onion. (In gratitude for neighboring town Fribourg's assistance after the great fire of 1405, Bern granted Fribourg the right to sell onions in the town center.) With old men playing chess on cobblestone streets and vendors hawking fruit beneath the spires of 13th-century towers, the town has an almost medieval character; only when you check out the interesting museums and the university do you remember that Bern has been the seat of the modern Swiss government since 1848. Who can resist a place where residents farm small gardens in the town center while well-behaved heroin addicts shoot up on the terrace of the parliament building?

BASICS

The **tourist office** (tel. 031/311–66–11; open May–Oct., daily 9–8:30; Nov.–Apr., Mon.–Sat. 8–6:30, Sun. 10–5) is in the train station. **American Express** (Bubenbergpl. 11, tel. 031/311–00–22) is open weekdays 8:30–6, Saturday 9–noon. The **Schanzenpost** (Schanzenstr. 4, behind station, tel. 031/386–61–11) holds poste restante (*see* Phones and Mail *in* Basics, *above*).

COMING AND GOING

Since there is no bus service to other cities from Bern, the **train station** (Baunhofpl., tel. 031/157–22–22) is your only option for getting to or from such destinations as Zürich (1 hr 10 min, SFr42) and Geneva (1¾ hrs, SFr48). Yellow **postal buses** (tel. 031/386–65–65 for information), which leave from the train station, are useful for short trips to nearby towns.

GETTING AROUND

Bern is easy to navigate. From the station, the main shopping street, **Spitalgasse,** leads straight through **Bärenplatz;** this square and the adjacent **Bundesplatz** mark the center of town. Most sights are on or near Spitalgasse, which becomes Marktgasse, Kramgasse, and Gerechtigkeitsgasse. **Trams** and **buses** (tel. 031/321–88–88) are handy for getting outside the Altstadt. Before boarding, buy a SFr7.50 ticket, good for 24 hours, at the machines near each stop. Single-ride tickets cost SFr1.50–SFr2.40.

WHERE TO SLEEP

As usual in Switzerland, hotel rates are awful. The run-of-the-mill **HI Jugendherberge** (Weihergasse 4, tel. 031/311–63–16; beds SFr18, breakfast SFr6) is near the river, below the Bundeshaus; from the station, head down Christoffelgasse; when you hit the park, go down the steps on your left, then follow the signs. **Camping Kappelenbrücke** (Wohlenstr. 62C, Hinterkappelen, tel. 031/901–10–07; SFr6.20 per person plus Sfr6.30–Sfr11.60 per tent) is a beautiful new campground on the shores of Wohlensee; from the station, take the yellow postal bus marked WOHLEN/AARBERG to Eymatt. Smack-dab in the Old Town in a historic building, **Hospiz zur Heimat** (Gerechtigkeitgasse 50, tel. 031/311–04–36) offers plain doubles without bath for SFr96, with bath for SFr128. A bit removed from the town center, **Martha-haus** (Wyttenbachstr. 22A, tel. 031/332–41–35) has quiet, tasteful rooms (doubles SFr95); from the station, take Bus 20 (toward Haltestelle) to Gewerbeschule.

FOOD

Supermarket **Migros** (Bubenbergpl., at Schanzenstr.) is near the station; **Coop** is on Spitalgasse near Bärenplatz; and **Vatter,** a health-food store, is across from the Coop. **Bell Market** (Spitalgasse 34) has such goodies as tofu salad, corn salad, and chicken. Locals flock to **Restaurant Manora** (Bubenbergpl. 5A, at Bahnhofpl., tel. 031/311–37–55) for pastries, cheap coffee (SFr2), pasta (SFr7.90), and an extensive salad bar (SFr9.40); look for the sign with the green alligator. **Restaurant Marzilibrücke** (Gasstr. 8, around corner from hostel, at Brückenstr., tel. 031/311–27–80) is popular with Bern's Generation X; it serves relatively cheap meals (chicken SFr7.50, veggie dishes SFr12.50) on an outdoor terrace. **Kornhauskeller** (Kornhauspl. 18, tel. 031/311–11–33), in a huge, barrel-vaulted hall, is a throwback to earlier centuries. Have a full meal for SFr15–SFr35, or just grab a drink in the well-known wine gallery.

WORTH SEEING

Bern's most famous landmark, the 16th-century **Zeitglockenturm** (Clock Tower), puts on a little show four minutes before every hour. Originally at the western gate of the city, the clock tower now marks the western boundary of **Zähringerstadt,** the oldest part of town, first built by the German duke of Zähringer in the 12th century. (Most of the buildings you see today date from the 16th and 17th centuries.) Tours (SFr6) daily at 4:30 show you what makes the clock tick.

Legend has it that Duke Zähringer named Bern after the first animal he killed in a hunt. Five bears cavort at the **Bärengraben** (Bear Pits; across Nydeggbrücke bridge to right), clowning around for snacks.

The Gothic **Münster** (Münsterpl.; open Tues.–Sat. 10–5, Sun. 11–5; shorter hours off season), built between 1421 and 1893, was conceived as a Catholic church but became Protestant during its rather lengthy construction. The main portal vividly illustrates what awaits the damned in hell and the elect in heaven (notice which side has the majority of the women). A climb up the tower leaves you SFr3 poorer, but you get a great view. The cathedral holds concerts at 8 PM every Tuesday in the summer; admission varies, and is sometimes free. The tourist office has details.

More than 40 oil paintings and 2,000 drawings at the **Kunstmuseum** (Hodlerstr. 8–12, tel. 031/311–09–44; entry SFr6; open Tues. 10–9, Wed.–Sun. 10–5) allow you to trace Paul Klee's development from draftsman to abstract artist. You'll also find works from the 14th–16th centuries by Italian painters, Impressionists, and surrealists. The small **Einstein-Haus** (Kramgasse 49, tel. 031/312–00–91; admission SFr2; open Tues.–Fri. 10–5, Sat. 10–4), where Einstein scraped together his theory of relativity in 1905, has some interesting exhibits, including the scientist's secondary-school report card and an advertisement in which he appeals for work.

A whole slew of museums lines Helvetiaplatz. The **Kunsthalle** (No. 1, tel. 031/351–00–31; admission SFr6; open Tues. 10–9, Wed.–Sun. 10–5) gives up-and-coming artists a chance to strut their stuff. The **Bernisches Historisches Museum** (No. 5, tel. 031/350–77–11; open Tues.–Sun. 10–5), housed in a 16th-century castle, displays booty from Swiss victories over Burgundy; admission is SFr5, free Saturday. The **PTT Museum** (Helvetiastrasse 16, tel. 031/338–77–77; admission SFr2; open Tues.–Sun. 10–5) has one of the largest and most valuable stamp collections in the world.

CHEAP THRILLS

On a clear day, treat yourself to a great SFr3 cup of coffee at the **Bellevue Hotel** (Kochergasse 3, at Theaterpl., tel. 031/311–45–45) and join diplomats in gazing at the Alps from a beautiful terrace overlooking the Aare River. Don't linger too long, though; at night the price of coffee goes way up. Take a jump into the Aare River at the free **River Bath Marzili** swimming pools (open weekdays 8:30–8, weekends 8:30–7) on Aarstrasse, one block from Brückenstrasse. A quick hike up the steep cobblestone path on your left after you cross Nydeggbrücke takes you to the **Rosengarten**—a perfect example of Swiss fastidiousness. This tranquil garden is perfectly manicured, offering gorgeous roses and irises, as well as a priceless view of the city.

AFTER DARK

Nightlife centers around **Bärenplatz,** where locals gather for beer (SFr4–SFr5) at outdoor cafés. **Bar Big Ben** (Zeughausgasse 12, tel. 031/311–24–28), around the corner from Bärenplatz, is packed with international English-speakers. The **Reitschule** (Schützenmatte, near Lorrainebr., tel. 031/302–63–17), almost a town in itself, is an alternative-art center housed in a 100-year-old riding school. The event schedule varies, but you'll usually find live music (cover SFr5–SFr15) Thursday–Sunday. The women's center here occasionally hosts events and is a source of information for lesbians. The restaurant and cafeteria serve some of the cheapest meals in town (daily menu SFr5). **Anderland** (Mühlepl. 11, 5th floor, near Schifflaube, tel. 031/311–11–97) can give you the lowdown on the Bernese gay scene.

ST. MORITZ

St. Moritz (San Murezzan in Romansch) is one of the world's ritziest ski resorts. You can expect the train ride from Chur, the main transport hub for southeastern Switzerland, to be a highlight of your visit: The route, known as the **Rhätische Bahn,** takes you past lush green valleys, golden fields with round haystacks, and ravines spanned by arched bridges. The town itself may seem tranquil after such a sensational ride; it's a mix of traditional Engadine buildings, stone churches, boxy modern hotels, and glam-

POCKET PAL

It's hard to imagine how you would slice your Gruyère, trim your toenails, or perform emergency tracheotomies on your friends (yes, it's been done) without a Swiss Army Knife. The knife got its legendary versatility from Charles Elsener, a Swiss nationalist so rankled by Swiss soldiers' defending their fatherland with German knives that he invented his own in 1897, the Officer's Knife. By using just two springs for every six blades, Elsener found that he could include more utensils without increasing the size of the handle—so he added a corkscrew, a vital piece of equipment for army officers. When American soldiers returned from Europe after World War II and showed these pocket companions around, they caught on immediately, and the United States is now the largest consumer of the knife. The Swiss Army orders about 30,000 knives annually (sans corkscrew), and the German Army orders them as well, with one minor alteration: A German eagle replaces the Swiss cross. Wenger and Victorinox are the two official manufacturers of the knife, both recognized diplomatically by the Swiss government; but imitators now number in the thousands worldwide. Who says that all Swiss civilization has produced is the cuckoo clock?

orous shops. Tourists converge here from everywhere, but unless you've got deep pockets, you'll need to brace yourself for the steep prices. Despite its location in the Engadine region, within the Graubünden, St. Moritz doesn't contain many Romansch-speakers; you'll hear mostly German and some Italian. One of the town's cultural attractions is the **Engadine Museum** (Via dal Bagn, tel. 081/833–43–33; admission SFr5), whose elegant rooms are loaded with traditional furniture. For more information on the town and the region, head to the tourist office, **Kur-Und Verkehrsverein** (Via Maistra 12, tel. 081/837–33–33; open weekdays 9–noon and 2–6, Sat. 9–noon).

The skiing aristocrats clear out of St. Moritz in summer, leaving the town peacefully empty. You may want to follow their lead and take off for some hiking in the Engadine and Bregaglia valleys. Ride the gondola from **Surlej** to **Piz Corvatsch** (SFr21 one way, SFr30 round trip), where the seemingly infinite white peaks make you feel like you've hit the top of the world; or take the funicular (SFr21 one way, SFr32 round trip) from Via Stredas to glorious **Piz Nair** and walk back down (3 hrs). If you get off the funicular at the second stop, Corviglia (SFr14 one way, SFr21 round trip), the hike is only two hours. For a longer hike (6 hrs) past lakes and mountains, take **Via Engadina** to the town of Maloja. You can also rent a bike from the train station, or a mountain bike (SFr30) from any sports shop, and ride along the lake to **Sils**, the town where Nietzsche spent his summers from 1881 to '88. The locals have turned his house into an eclectic **museum** (tel. 081/826–61–88; open Tues.–Sun. 3–6; admission SFr4).

GETTING AROUND
St. Moritz Lake (Lej da San Murezzan in Romansch) divides the town into two parts: swanky St. Moritz-Dorf and modern, ugly St. Moritz-Bad. Blue-and-white local buses connect the two parts of town. Yellow regional buses stop at the **train station,** which is along the lake on the St. Moritz-Dorf side.

WHERE TO SLEEP
The **HI Jugendherberge** (Via Surpunt 60, tel. 081/833–39–69; beds SFr41.50, doubles SFr108; closed Nov.–mid-Dec.) is across the lake from the train station. Fortunately, the high price includes breakfast and dinner; sadly, it's the best deal in town. To get here, take the yellow postal bus (toward Sils, Corvatsch, or Maloja) to Hotel Sonne and follow the signs to the left. Next to the train station,

Hotel Bellaval (Via Grevas 55, tel. 081/833–32–45; SFr60 per person) has pleasant rooms with views of the lake. Pontresina, a charming village just 20 minutes by bus or 10 minutes by train (both SFr4.20), has a low-key **HI Jugendherberge** (tel. 081/842–72–23; beds SFr29, SFr40 with dinner) next to the train station. Don't miss the daily morning concert in Tais Woods. For relatively uncrowded camping, go to **Camping Plauns Morteratsch** (tel. 081/842–62–85; SFr7.50 per person, SFr13 per tent), a 15-minute walk along a well-marked path from the train station in Morteratsch (30 min, SFr7.20).

FOOD

Food is expensive in this upscale resort, so you may want to pack picnic lunches—there's a **Coop** (Hauptstrasse) for subsistence fare, and a good meat market, **Fleisch**, in Piazza de Scoula. One of the cheaper restaurants in town, **Au Reduit** (Piazza Mauritius, in St. Moritz-Dorf, tel. 081/833–66–57) has an upstairs terrace with mountain views. Pizzas start at SFr14, and a big *Aelpler-Rösti* (potato with ham, eggs, and cheese) will fill you up for SFr20.

FRENCH SWITZERLAND

The French Swiss differ noticeably from their German-speaking compatriots—in their elegant dress, their easy sense of humor, and the unexpected flashes of joie de vivre that liven up their calm and orderly towns. French Switzerland centers around romantic Lac Léman (Lake Geneva), whose hazy blue grandeur has inspired many a poet. Stravinsky wrote *The Rite of Spring* in Montreux, on the east side of the lake, and it's now the site of one of the world's hottest jazz festivals. To the west, Geneva, head-quarters of the International Red Cross, has established itself as a humanitarian center, though even the city lets down her *chignon* once a year to celebrate the Escalade, a 17th-century battle that ended with a pot of soup dumped on the enemies' heads, on December 11.

GENEVA

The first image that will probably strike you as you arrive in Geneva (Genève in French) is a harbor filled with slender sailboat masts, backed by the white mists of the Jet d'Eau fountain. You'll find plenty of sights to match it, from the opulent mansions and flowery promenades that wrap around Lac Léman, to the copper spire of the cathedral at the apex of the old town. Placid Geneva may look prototypically Swiss, but the town is French at the core—not until 1815, after the collapse of the Napoleonic empire, did Geneva join the Swiss Confederation. As the second seat of the United Nations (after New York), it is one of Europe's more cosmopolitan cities. Rousseau and Voltaire are two of many famous residents who have left their marks here, but their influence is slight compared to Calvin's. The Protestant reformer preached here against theater, dancing, and wine consumed for pleasure, but his exhortations were only half-successful—you'll still find a few things to do here at night.

BASICS

The **tourist office** (3 rue du Mont-Blanc, tel. 022/909–70–00; open mid-June–Aug., daily 8–8; Sept.–mid-June, Mon.–Sat. 9–6) also maintains small offices at the train station and at 4 place du Molard on the left bank; all provide maps and brochures. Pick up *Geneva Agenda* for a list of museums, restaurants, and clubs. The **Centre d'Accueil et de Renseignements (CAR)** (30 rue du Mont-Blanc, tel. 022/731–46–47) also has an information kiosk outside the station that helps travelers daily 8 AM–11 PM June 18–September 15. If you're a member, have your mail sent to **American Express** (7 rue du Mont-Blanc, Box 859, Geneva 1, CH-1208, tel. 022/731–76–00; open weekdays 8:30–6, weekends 9–noon); they'll hold it for two months. Otherwise, the **main post office** (18 rue du Mont-Blanc; open weekdays 7:30–6, Sat. 8–11) is a block from the station in the Hôtel des Postes. Have poste restante sent to Your Name, Poste Restante, Hôtel des Postes, CH-1208, Geneva 1, Switzerland.

COMING AND GOING

Most trains arrive at the **Gare de Cornavin** (between pl. de Cornavin and rue de Montbrillant, tel. 157–22–22), on the northern edge of town; a few, mostly from the French Alps, arrive at the **Gare Genève**

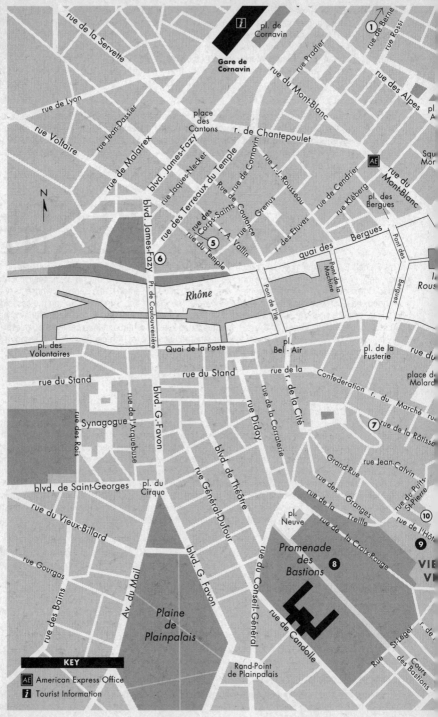

GENEVA

pl. de
Cornavin

Gare de
Cornavin

rue de Berne

rue de Rossi

rue de la Servette

rue Pradier

rue du Mont-Blanc

rue des Alpes

pl.
A

rue de Lyon

rue Jean-Dassier

place
des
Cantons

r. de Chantepoulet

Squ
Mor

rue du
Mont-Blanc

rue Voltaire

rue de Malatrex

blvd. James-Fazy

rue Jaques-Necker

rue des Terreaux du Temple

Rue de rue de Cornavin

Rue de Coutance

rue J.-J.-Rousseau

rue de Cendrier

rue Kléberg

pl. des
Bergues

rue des
Corps-Saints

F.-A. Vallin

Grenus

r. des Etuves

blvd. James-Fazy

rue du Temple

Bergues

Pont des
Bergues

I.
Rous

quai des

Rhône

Pt. de Coulouvrenière

Pont de
la Machine

Pont de l'Ile

pl. des
Volontaires

Quai de la Poste

pl.
Bel - Air

pl. de la
Fusterie

rue du

rue du Stand

rue du Stand

rue de la

r. de la Cité

Confederation

r. du Marché

place d
Molard

rue des Rois

blvd. G.-Favon

rue de l'Arquebuse

rue Diday

rue de la Corraterie

rue du

rue de la Rôtisse

Synagogue

Grand-Rue

rue Jean-Calvin

blvd. de Saint-Georges

pl. du
Cirque

blvd. de Théâtre

rue des

Granges

Treille

rue du Puits
St-Pierre

rue de l'Hôt

rue du Vieux-Billard

rue Général-Dufour

pl.
Neuve

rue de la Croix-Rouge

rue Gourgas

blvd. G.-Favon

Promenade
des
Bastions

VIE
V

rue des Bains

Av. du Mail

rue du Conseil-Général

rue de Candolle

Plaine
de
Plainpalais

Rond-Point
de Plainpalais

Rue St-Léger

r. de

Cours
des Bastions

KEY

American Express Office

Tourist Information

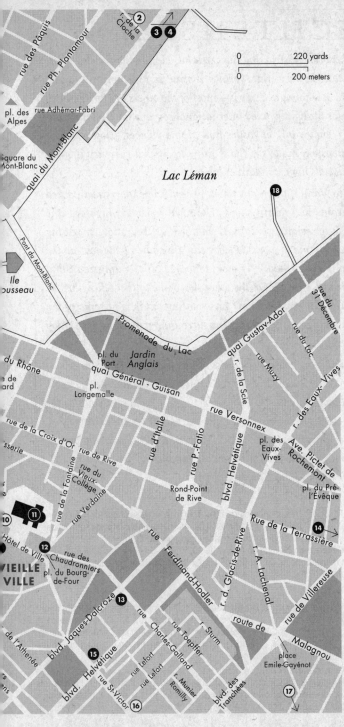

Sights ●

Cathédrale
St-Pierre, **11**

Hôtel de Ville, **9**

Jet d'Eau, **18**

Musée d'Art et
d'Histoire, **13**

Musée de
l'Horlogerie, **14**

Musée du Petit
Palais, **15**

Musée International
de la Croix-Rouge et
du Croissant-
Rouge, **4**

Palais de
Justice, **12**

Palais des
Nations, **3**

Promenade des
Bastions/Monument
de la Réformation, **8**

Lodging ○

Auberge de
Jeunesse (HI), **1**

Cité
Universitaire, **17**

Hôme St-Pierre, **10**

Hôtel Central, **7**

Hôtel de la
Cloche, **2**

Hôtel des
Tourelles, **6**

Hôtel St-Gervais, **5**

Pension
St-Victor, **16**

LIECHTENSTEIN

A dot on the map between Austria and Switzerland, Liechtenstein is one of the smallest sovereign states in the world. A prince, a princess, and a measly 30,000 residents (only 60% of whom are citizens—most of the others are foreign businessmen who work for the lightly taxed international corporations) share about 164 square km (63 square mi) of castles and alpine villages. Closely tied to Switzerland, Liechtenstein made the Swiss franc its official currency in 1924 and shares Switzerland's high standard of living.

There's not much to Vaduz, the main town, except a one-lane street packed with terrace restaurants and tourist shops. The royal residence, high over the city and inaccessible to visitors, contains a valuable art collection, including some of Rubens' most famous works. Plebes can see some of the loot at the Staatliche Kunstsammlung (Städtle 37, next to tourist office; admission SFr5; open daily 10–noon and 1:30–5). On the other side of the tourist office, the free Briefmarkenmuseum (Stamp Museum) has rotating exhibits of some of the country's most famous stamps. Head into the surrounding mountains to enjoy the area's natural beauty.

Liechtenstein has no trains; to get here, catch a bus from the train stations in Switzerland's Sargans or Buchs. If you've come just to collect another passport stamp, the tourist office (Städtle 37, tel. 075/232–14–43) will give you one for SFr2, but if you're looking to stay overnight, the bucolic HI Jugendherberge (tel. 075/232–50–22; beds SFr26.30) in Schaan is an ace facility. The Städtlemarkt (Äulestr. 20) has a Denner Discount for picnic supplies; or try Azzurro (tel. 075/232–48–18) for pizzas from SFr7.50.

Eaux-Vives (tel. 022/736–16–20), on the city's eastern edge. Trains depart every hour for Bern (1¾ hrs, SFr48), Basel (2¾ hrs, SFr34), and Zürich (3 hrs, SFr42). The international **bus station** (pl. Dorciere, off rue des Alpes, tel. 022/732–02–30) offers transportation comparable to trains in both price and duration. The **Compagnie Générale de Navigation (CGN)** (tel. 022/311–25–21) runs boat trips to and from Geneva free with a Eurailpass. Boats depart from the quai du Mont-Blanc for Lausanne (3½ hrs, SFr47 round trip) and Montreux (5 hrs, SFr54 round trip).

GETTING AROUND

The Rhône River divides Geneva into two parts: the **Rive Gauche** (Left Bank) and the **Rive Droite** (Right Bank). The Rive Gauche, to the south, comprises the *vieille ville* (old town), the Jardin Anglais, and the university. The Rive Droite includes the St-Gervais district, the quai du Mont-Blanc, and the important parks. Pont du Mont-Blanc, the main bridge, connects the two areas. From the bridge, you can see the copper steeple of Cathédrale St-Pierre, in the old town.

BY BUS AND TRAM • Geneva has an extensive public transportation system, but you won't need it to see most sights. If you want to take buses or trams, vending machines at each stop spit out tickets good for one hour (SFr2.20). All-day tickets, available from agents listed on the signs at the stops, cost SFr5. Tickets must be validated at automatic machines. Fares are higher once you leave the city center.

WHERE TO SLEEP

Geneva has decent hotel rooms at reasonable prices—for Switzerland, at least. But with all the international organizations centered here, they fill up fast, and you're taking a risk if you show up without reservations. Student-housing options are plentiful and cheap, though not always very comfortable. If the places below are full, **Hôtel des Tourelles** (2 blvd. James-Fazy, tel. 022/732–44–23) offers comfy, sunny doubles for SFr85; most rooms have hardwood floors and river views. **Hôtel Central** (rue de la Rôtisserie 2, tel. 022/818–81–00) offers private tile bathrooms in all rooms and bargain rates (doubles for SFr80).

Hôtel St-Gervais (rue des Corps-Saints 20, tel. 022/732–45–72), in one of the city's oldest buildings, has beams, antiques, and cute, tiny rooms (doubles SFr78 without bath, SFr105 with bath). Just 10 minutes from the station, off quai du Mont-Blanc, **Hôtel de la Cloche** (6 rue de la Cloche, tel. 022/732–94–81) is a find—most rooms have garden balconies—with doubles for SFr75. Probably the best deal in Geneva, however, is the tidy and dependable **Pension St-Victor** (1 rue Lefort, tel. 022/346–17–18; doubles SFr90, breakfast included), in a quiet residential neighborhood two minutes from the vieille ville; make reservations. From the station, take Bus 8 or 3 to the Museum stop, then walk down boulevard des Tranchées, turn right on rue Charles-Galland, and left on rue Lefort.

HOSTELS • Auberge de Jeunesse (HI). This hostel is clean, modern, and well equipped, even for Switzerland—and that's saying a lot. Great doubles with shower and balcony are SFr70, without shower SFr60. Dorm beds are SFr23. The SFr14 hot evening meal includes drink and dessert. There's a midnight curfew. *30 rue Rothschild, tel. 022/732–62–60. From station, walk 10 min on rue de Lausanne, turn right on rue Rothschild. Reception open 6:30 AM–10 AM and 5 PM–11 PM. Lockout 10–4. Kitchen, laundry.*

Hôme St-Pierre. In the center of the old town, facing the cathedral that sponsors it, this hotel is a great place to stay, but it only accepts women under age 35. Rooms are a little cramped, but there's a common room and a rooftop sitting area with a view of the lake. Dorm beds are SFr22, singles SFr35, the rare double SFr50, and breakfast SFr7.50. *4 cour St-Pierre, tel. 022/310–37–07. Reception open 9–1 and 4–8. Kitchen, laundry.*

FOOD

Cosmopolitan Geneva offers a refreshing variety of cuisines. If you find yourself craving Indian, Korean, or Thai food, you're in the right place, provided you're padded with cash. Even produce markets are incredibly pricey, often twice as expensive as ordinary grocery stores. The vieille ville has diversity and atmosphere aplenty; but those who just want a good deal can choose from 17 different **Migros** self-service restaurants. You'll find a free restaurant guide to all areas at the tourist office or CAR. **Taverne de la Madeleine** (rue Toutes-âmes 20, tel. 022/310–60–70), run by the Women's Temperence League and thus dry, passes its liquor-license savings on to you in the form of cheap daily specials and good fruit tarts.

Les Armures. Geneva's oldest café, around the corner from the cathedral, has arms and armor inside, outdoor seating in a picturesque alley outside. Savor *longeole* sausage and chicken fricasee (both local specialties) and cheap pizza (praised by Jimmy Carter and Bill Clinton). *1 rue du Puits-St-Pierre, tel. 022/310–34–42.*

Le Café du Grütli. This hip café and restaurant in the Maison des Arts is a haven for resident artists, photographers, and filmmakers. It offers chic lunches (Gruyère carpaccio with dried fruit, grilled duck) and late snacks (quiche, hot chèvre salad). *16 Général-Dufour (next to Victoria Hall), tel. 022/329–44–95. Cash only. Closed Sun.*

Chez Leo. Next door to his dad's upscale landmark, Roberto's, Leo serves homemade pastas and fruit tarts in this tiny, charming bentwood bistro. *12, rue Pierre-Fatio, tel. 022/311–53–07. MC, V. Closed Sat. evening, Sun.*

WORTH SEEING

You could easily spend an afternoon watching the boats sail across Lac Léman. Along quai du Mont-Blanc, on the lake's north bank, hotels, shops, and cafés vie for space with impressive mansions. Across Pont du Mont-Blanc in the **Jardin Anglais,** the **Horloge Fleurie** (Flower Clock), on a neatly sculpted bed of flowers, keeps accurate time, in the good Swiss fashion. Next to the Jardin Anglais, along quai Gustave Ador, the impressive **Jet d'Eau** shoots 132 gallons of water per second 460 ft into the air. The fountain has become Geneva's premier landmark, and you can see its misty sprays shooting up above rooftops all around the city. On a hot day, walk underneath the fountain and let the spray revive you.

Also worth exploring is the **vieille ville,** with its cobblestone hills and narrow streets. The busiest area here is place du Bourg-de-Four, originally a Roman forum and later a medieval town square. Outdoor cafés, a fountain covered with flowers, historic buildings, and art galleries make this a popular hangout for tourists and dapper Genevois. The **Palais de Justice** was built on the south side of the square in 1707. A short walk up rue de l'Hôtel de Ville will bring you, appropriately enough, to the **Hôtel de Ville** (Town Hall), the site of the first Red Cross convention in 1864. Across from here, the **Arsenal** shows off cannons and colorful mosaic murals. On the other side of the Hôtel de Ville, rest your weary bones on the world's longest bench. If you can't get enough of the chronological thing, head east to the free **Musée de l'Horlogerie** (15 rte. de Malagnou, tel. 022/418–64–70; open Wed.–Mon. 10–5), where you'll find hourglasses, sundials, and loads of watches from the 17th and 18th centuries.

CATHEDRALE ST-PIERRE • This cathedral, constructed mostly during the 12th and 13th centuries, radiates plain Swiss strength and common sense. But like the Genevois themselves, it displays a little unexpected zest, especially in the colorful Gothic chapel on the south side, built in the 15th century, and in the neoclassical facade, added in the 18th century. Underneath the church is an impressive archaeological site, the **Site Archéologique de St-Pierre** (admission SFr5), complete with a baptistry, a crypt, 4th-century mosaics, and sculptures covering more than 2,000 years of history. *Cour St-Pierre, tel. 022/29–75–98. Admission to tower: SFr3. Site open Tues.–Sun. 10–1 and 2–6. Cathedral open June–Sept., daily 9–7; Mar.–May and Oct., daily 9–noon and 2–6; Nov.–Feb., daily 9–noon and 2–5.*

MUSEE D'ART ET D'HISTOIRE • In a posh residential neighborhood next to the vieille ville, this museum displays an impressive bunch of archaeological finds from Egypt, Greece, and Rome. The best works in the painting collection are the powerful landscapes by Swiss artist Ferdinand Hodler, which capture the luminous mountains. The museum also has a good collection of period weapons. *2 rue Charles-Galland, tel. 022/418–26–00. From station, Bus 3. Admission free. Open Tues.–Sun. 10–5.*

The **Musée d'Art Moderne et Contemporain** is a gritty new venue for stark, mind-stretching art works, all post-1965. They're mounted in a former factory amid concrete floors and fluorescent lighting. *Rue des Vieux-Grenadiers 10, tel. 022/320–61–22. Admission: SFr9. Open Tues.–Sun. noon–6.*

PALAIS DES NATIONS • The imposing United Nations building, beautiful in its stark features, sits in a garden filled with gifts from different countries (the United States donated a bronze sphere in honor of President Wilson; Russia, an obelisk commemorating space travel). The interior is worth a visit for its works by international artists and for the famous assembly rooms, but you have to take an exhausting tour to see it all (call ahead for the schedule). *14 av. de la Paix, tel. 022/907–45–39. From the station, Bus 8 to Appia. Admission: SFr8.50. Open Apr.–Oct. daily 10–noon and 2–4; July–Aug., daily 9–6; Nov.–Mar., weekdays 10–noon and 2–4.*

Across from the Palais des Nations lies the impressive **Musée International de la Croix-Rouge et du Croissant-Rouge,** where high-concept, often emotionally jarring exhibits, films, and slides chronicle the history of human kindness in the face of disaster, both natural and man-made. Jean-Henri Dunant, a local businessman, founded the Red Cross after witnessing the inhumane treatment of prisoners and the wounded in the 1859 Battle of Solferino. *17 av. de la Paix, tel. 022/733–26–60. Admission: SFr8.*

PROMENADE DES BASTIONS • Below the walls of the vieille ville stands the impressive, unadorned **Monument de la Réformation.** Forbidding sculptures of four local Protestant reformers— Calvin, Farel, Bèze, and Knox—and other reliefs flank this 300-ft wall. The surrounding park, Promenade des Bastions, contains the university. It's a nice daytime hangout, with students and life-size sidewalk chess games.

CHEAP THRILLS

Gardens galore make Geneva a great place for picnicking, strolling, and admiring finely pruned flower beds. **Parc Mon Repos, Parc Perle du Lac,** and **Parc Villa Barton** are three connecting parks that form an extensive green area north of the train station, at the end of quai Wilson. Wander here and around the botanical gardens next door to see a multitude of plants, a rock garden, a deer pen, and an aviary. **Parc de la Grange,** on the opposite bank, has a rose garden that's especially colorful in June. In early August, look for the **Fêtes de Genève,** which bring fireworks, live music, and flower parades to the city. For a dip in the lake or a pool, head to **Genève Plage** (tel. 022/736–24–82; admission SFr6; open mid-May–mid-Sept.); take Bus 2 from Bel-Air or place Eaux Vives.

AFTER DARK

Place du Bourg-de-Four and surrounding alleys are full of cafés and bars. **Café la Clémence** takes up a large chunk of the plaza, and a handsome international crowd lounges here day and night. **Post Café** (7 rue de Berne, tel. 022/732–96–63), off rue du Mont Blanc near the train station, draws a lively, mostly English-speaking crowd into its two small rooms. Drinks are cheaper during happy hour (5 PM–8 PM). **Au Chat Noir** (13 rue Vautier, tel. 022/343–49–98; cover SFr10), in the charming and posh neighborhood of Carouge, has live music nightly, from jazz to Swiss hip-hop. Take Tram 12 or 13, but beware: The last Tram 12 leaves Carouge before midnight, and Tram 13 leaves before 9. Sharing the block with a strip joint, **Club 58** (15 rue de Glacis de Rive, tel. 022/735–15–15; drinks SFr18) will keep you dancing to the best hip-hop and funk. Lesbians should contact **Centres Femmes** (tel. 022/789–26–00); gay men, **Dialogai** (tel. 022/340–00–00), for listings of gay clubs.

NEAR GENEVA

From Geneva you can take boat rides to nearby towns, including beautiful **Yvoire** (1¾ hr; SFr30 round-trip), loaded with restaurants, flowers, and tourists. Eurailpasses are valid on all cruises run by **CGN** (*see* Coming and Going *in* Geneva, *above*).

MONT SALEVE

In France, 6 km (4 mi) south of Geneva, Mont Salève makes a great half-day excursion. From this 3,960-ft ridge you can see Geneva on one side and the fabulous French Alps and Mont Blanc on the other. Take time to wander under soaring parasailers, or hang out with some contented cows. *From Geneva, Bus 8 to Veyrier, go through passport control, then cable car (SFr19 round trip) to peak.*

LAUSANNE

Lausanne is not quite the city it was when heavyweight writers like Voltaire, Rousseau, Byron, and Victor Hugo waxed passionate about its beauty—Hugo described the graceful tiered city as "a staircase where my thoughts climbed step by step and broadened at each new height." You'll still find beautiful sights here and there—a burnt-orange jumble of medieval rooftops, shuttered windows with flower boxes, misty Lac Léman and the Alps—but much of the town is just a maze of modern buildings. Atmospheric alleys and narrow streets that once filled the town were mostly demolished after World War II for the sake of progress and hygiene. Though less cosmopolitan than Geneva, Lausanne warrants a brief sojourn for its lively arts scene and its occasionally rowdy social life. The **tourist offices** in the train station and near the water in the Ouchy district (2 av. de Rhodanie, tel. 021/613–73–73) can help you get your bearings.

COMING AND GOING

Lausanne lies on a major **train** route between Bern (1 hr, SFr30) and Geneva (30 min, SFr19.40), with express trains running from Basel and Zürich. Make reservations for high-speed **TGV** trains to Paris (3 hrs 40 min, SFr89). **CGN boats** (tel. 021/617–06–66) leave from place du Port, behind the Château d'Ouchy, for Montreux (1½ hrs, SFr18 one-way), Vevey (1 hr, SFr14 one-way), and Geneva (3 hrs, SFr30 one-way). All trips are free with a Eurailpass.

Lausanne is divided into the **haute ville** (upper town), which contains the vieille ville, and the **basse ville** (lower town), which contains Ouchy, the lakeside resort area. The vieille ville and Ouchy are easily seen on foot, but you'll need the bus or Metro to traverse the steep streets from one to the other. Buy **bus** tickets at the slot machines before boarding. Fares (from SFr1.30), based on zones, are posted at stops. Get 24-hour tickets (SFr6.50) at major stops. The **Metro** (most trips SFr2.20) swooshes from place St-François, just below the heart of the vieille ville, through the train station and down to place de la Navigation at the Ouchy port. A one- to two-hour walking tour (tel. 021/321–77–66) costs SFr10 and leaves at 10 AM and 3 PM from the Hôtel de Ville. Call ahead to reserve.

WHERE TO SLEEP

The clean **Pension Bienvenue** (2 rue du Simplon, behind station, tel. 021/616–29–86; doubles SFr70) rents to women of all ages. The elderly proprietress at **Hôtel le Chalet** (49 av. d'Ouchy, tel. 021/616–52–06; doubles SFr85 without breakfast) keeps a beautiful garden and offers big, sunny rooms in a 19th-century house. **Hotel Regina** (rue Grand St-Jean 18, tel. 021/320–24–41) offers mix-and-match decor and bare-bones comfort, but it's in a great vieille ville location; doubles without bath are SFr85–SFr120, with bath SFr115–160.

Jeunotel (36 chemin du Bois-de-Vaux, tel. 021/626–02–22; doubles SFr74–SFr98), a big new complex with spotless rooms around a courtyard, is a great alternative if you're traveling with a friend or two (or 10—dorm beds are SFr27 for groups of 10 or more). Take Bus 2 to Bois-de-Vaux, then backtrack and turn right toward the water on chemin du Bois-de-Vaux.

FOOD

The laid-back and urban-hip **Bleu Lézard** (rue Enning 10, tel. 021/312–71–90) offers cheap chic in its daily lunch specials (say, aubergine carpaccio), its found-object art, its flannel-shirted waiters, and its evening cocktails and jazz. The vast, clamorous **Café Romand** (Place St-François 2, tel. 021/312–63–75) draws rowdy crowds of artistes for mussels, *choucroute,* (sauerkraut) sausage, or fondue. **Manora Crocodile** (Place St-François 17, tel. 021/320–92–93) is a bright, clean self-service joint with fresh, varied salad bars and hot specials cooked before your eyes. The barrel-vaulted **Pinte Besson** (rue de l'Ale 4, tel. 021/312–72–72) offers a dark, smoky, local contrast, with fondue, slabs of ham heaped with potato salad, and local wines for toasting your friendly neighbors.

WORTH SEEING

Medieval charm blends with modern commerce on the hills of the vieille ville, whose cobblestone streets teem with wandering pedestrians, shoppers, and café seekers. Place de la Palud, a center of activity, contains the 17th-century **Hôtel de Ville** and the **Fontaine de la Justice** (1726). Examine the facade on the building next to this fountain; animated clock figures perform on the hour 9 AM–7 PM.

On Place de la Riponne, just north of Place de la Palud, the early 20th-century **Palais de Rumine** once housed the university and now contains a host of free museums. The **Musée Cantonal des Beaux-Arts** (6 pl. de la Riponne, tel. 021/312–83–32; open Tues. and Wed. 11–6, Thurs. 11–8, Fri.–Sun. 11–5) has paintings by Swiss artists of the 18th–20th centuries as well as works by Matisse, Degas, Bonnard, and Utrillo. In summer, most of the permanent display makes way for temporary exhibits.

CATHEDRALE DE NOTRE-DAME • The doors of Switzerland's most famous Gothic cathedral are ornamented with fanciful reliefs, while the stunning 13th-century rose window, *Imago Mundi,* depicts the elements, seasons, and, oddly enough, signs of the zodiac. It's worth a climb up the 232 steps (admission SFr2) for a view of the town, Lac Léman, and the Alps. From June to mid-October, free concerts are held here every Friday evening (perfomance times vary). Next door, the Ancien-Evêché, the former bishop's palace, now houses the **Musée Historique de Lausanne** (4 pl. de la Cathédrale, tel. 021/312–13–68; admission SFr4; open Tues.–Sun. 11–6, Thurs. until 8), with fascinating exhibits on the history of Lausanne that include a remarkable scale model of the city itself.

COLLECTION DE L'ART BRUT • This tantalizing and disturbing collection of "outsider art," gathered by painter and sculptor Jean Dubuffet, is kept in the former stables of the 18th-century Beaulieu Château. The collection consists of imaginative and individualistic works by people on the fringes of society—schizophrenics, the criminally insane, and reclusive eccentrics, *11 av. des Bergières, NW of vieille ville, tel. 021/647–54–35. Admission: SFr6. Open Tues.–Fri. 11–1 and 2–6; closed weekends.*

OUCHY • At this lakeside resort area, you can rent boats, stroll along the river on quai d'Ouchy and quai de Belgique, or walk west to the **Bellerive Beach and Pool** (23 av. de la Rhodaine, tel. 021/617–81–31; admission SFr4.50). The International Olympic Committee has been based in Lausanne since 1915, and the modern **Musée Olympique** (1 quai d'Ouchy, tel. 021/621–65–11; open May–Sept., daily 10–7, Thurs. until 8; Oct.–Apr., Tues.–Sat. 10–6, Thurs. until 9:30) shows the history of the Olympics from antiquity to the present. Videos of famous Olympic moments will bring tears to your eyes, as will the SFr14 admission.

AFTER DARK

Lausanne has enough students to keep the place hopping (at least on weekends). Most of the action is in the vieille ville, where lively youth fill up on tequila drinks at **La Factoria** (av. du Tribunal-Fédéral, at rue Étraz)—try the *sangrita* (SFr4), a shot of tequila with a spicy tomato-juice chaser. A slightly older crowd fills the dark, wine cellar–like **Treizième Siècle** (10 rue Cité-Devant, behind cathedral; no cover), with a D.J. and a crowded dance floor. In Ouchy, you can't miss the stylish crowd packing the terrace at **MGM** (av. de Rhodanie).

MONTREUX

Spilling down steep hillsides into a sunny bay, Montreux has maintained its dignity in the face of considerable development. This scenic town has been a resort for wealthy tourists since its casino opened in 1883, but these days, with a SFr5 maximum bet, you won't find many Vegas-style high rollers here. Montreux is usually very tranquil—except in early July, when the **Jazz Festival** (tel. 021/963–82–82) heats it up. Standing-room tickets cost SFr29–SFr69; reserved seats are SFr59–SFr129. Tickets generally sell out early. If you miss out, take a trip to the vineyards that surround the town; ask for more information at the **tourist office** (pl. du Débarcadère, at Grand-Rue, tel. 021/963–84–84; open Oct.–Mar., weekdays 9–6, Sat. 9–noon; Apr.–Sept.. Mon.-Sat. 9–6, Sun. 9–noon). The **train station** (tel. 021/157–22–22) is between rue de La Gare and avenue des Alpes.

Montreux's must-see sight is the **Château de Chillon,** an awe-inspiring 13th-century castle on the shore of Lac Léman less than 3 km (2 mi) from the city (take Bus 1). Check out the festival hall, with a roof in the form of an inverted ship's hull, and the elaborate bedrooms, some of which were used as torture chambers in the 17th century. The underground vaults were once the prison that held François de Bonivard, who was chained to a pillar for four years after trying to introduce the Reformation in Geneva. Inspired, Lord Byron immortalized the reformer's travails in *The Prisoner of Chillon,* after carving his name on the pillar to which Bonivard was chained. *Tel. 021/963–39–12. Admission: SFr6.50. Open July–Aug., daily 9–6:15; shorter hrs off season.*

> *If you're near the cathedral 10 PM–2 AM, you may hear le guet (town crier) shouting the hour from the bell tower. Centuries old, this tradition started when the town was made of wood—the crier was assuring everyone that there was no sign of fire.*

WHERE TO SLEEP AND EAT

The **HI Montreux** (8 passage de l'Auberge, tel. 021/963–49–34; beds SFr27, doubles SFr72) is a bit out of the way, but its modern facilities and lovely view of the lake make it a worthwhile option. From town, walk 30 minutes along the lake; or take Bus 1 to Territet, continue down the road, and go right at passage de l'Auberge. **Hotel Elite** (25 av. du Casino, tel. 021/966–03–03), in the center of town, has remodeled doubles (SFr100–SFr160) with private bath, TV, and phone; from the station, walk down avenue des Alpes and head right on avenue Nestlé. **Hostellerie du Lac** (12 rue du Quai, tel. 021/963–32–71), right on the lake, has cheap rooms (doubles from Sfr85) and a lakefront terrace restaurant; make reservations. Montreux's restaurants are super-expensive, but if you've got cash to burn, try **La Rouvenaz** (1 rue de Marché, at Grand-Rue near tourist office, tel. 021/963–27–36), where the smell of gnocchi beckons. For something different, **Kim Long's** (5 av. de la Gare, next to train station, tel. 021/961–22–47) serves up chicken fried noodles and shrimp fried rice. The financially challenged can forage for groceries at the **Coop** (80 Grand Rue) or **Migros** (45 av. du Casino).

NEAR MONTREUX

If even Montreux is too metropolitan for your mood, take the train southeast to nearby **Aigle** (SFr4.80). From here, another train (SFr9) makes the steep climb to the hilltop village of **Leysin,** and you can walk back to the right of the tracks toward Aigle (2–3 hrs) past woods, vineyards, and meandering cows. Amid the vines, the **Château d'Aigle** (tel. 024/466–21–30; admission SFr6; open Apr.–Oct., Tues.–Sun. 10–12:30 and 2–6; July and Aug., 10–8) houses the **Musée de la Vigne et du Vin,** with labels, goblets, information on the wine-making process, and impressive wooden contraptions used for pressing grapes.

Past Aigle is **Gryon,** a charming 800-year-old village perched high in the Alps. This quiet town is a haven for lovers of the great outdoors, with hiking, rock climbing, paragliding, mountain biking, skiing, and endless breathtaking views. To get here, take a train from Montreux to Bex (30 min, SFr7.80) and transfer to the red tram (30 min, SFr5.40) that chugs up the mountain. Once here, stay with the exuberantly friendly Australian-Swiss couple at the **Chalet Martin** (follow backpacker signs from station, tel. 024/498–33–21; beds SFr17 first night, 15 SFr thereafter, doubles SFr42 first night, SFr40 thereafter), a clean, homey hostel in a newly restored building. You can rent all necessary outdoor gear right here, including warm clothes. Full use of the kitchen and a **Coop** down the street make meals easy.

ITALIAN SWITZERLAND

Newcomers to Switzerland might hear the names Lugano, Locarno, and Ascona and assume they're in Italy. The photos in the tourist brochures for this region, which is called Ticino (or Tessin in German), certainly wouldn't set them straight: Nearly every publicity shot shows palm trees, red roofs, and Renaissance architecture. But behind the wavering date palms are the telltale signs: the surgical neatness, the fresh paint, the timely trains, the well-behaved men, and the exorbitant prices. There's no mistaking Ticino—it's a little bit of Italy, but Swiss at heart.

LUGANO

Wedged between the gently rounded peaks of Mt. Bré and Mt. San Salvatore, the Italian Swiss city of Lugano offers hot weather, densely wooded slopes, and sparkling water that begs you to take a boat ride to a neighboring village. The **main tourist office** (Palazzo Civico, tel. 091/921–46–64) can help you plan your visit; take almost any bus to Piazza della Riforma in the town center. A booth at the train station also gives hotel information and directions.

COMING AND GOING

Trains arrive here from Zürich (3 hrs, SFr59) and Milan (1½ hrs, SFr14). From the **train station,** a funicular runs to Piazza Cioccaro, north of **Piazza della Riforma,** the main square; it's worth the SFr.90 if you're carrying a heavy bag. The central quay, the departure point for many boat trips, is just south of Piazza della Riforma. **Buses** are useful for reaching accommodations, many of which are just outside town. Fares are posted at stops; a SFr4.40 day pass will save you money if you're going to ride the bus more than twice.

WHERE TO SLEEP

As usual, the cheapest bed is at the hostel, **Albergo per la Gioventú** (Via Cantonale, tel. 091/966–27–28; beds SFr15, doubles SFr40, breakfast SFr6), whose ample grounds feature tropical plants and a swimming pool. What the hostel lacks in Swiss fastidiousness, it makes up threefold in charm; the only bummer is the ridiculous 10 PM curfew. Across from the station, take Bus 5 (toward Vezia) to Crocifisso and follow the signs up Via Cantonale (the street right before the stop). The hostel is closed November–mid-March.

There's no getting around it: Hotels here are expensive, especially if they're even slightly attractive. In the center of town, **Hotel San Carlo** (Via Nassa 28, tel. 091/922–71–07) has a friendly staff and offers doubles (SFr135) overlooking a cobblestone street. **Hotel Pestalozzi** (C. Pestalozzi, tel. 091/921–46–46), across from the Palazzo dei Congressi and 2 blocks from Parco Civico, has doubles for SFr96. The restaurant downstairs serves reasonably priced meals (lasagna with salad SFr8.50, Rösti with eggs and salad SFr12.80). The view of the lake from the cheerful **Hotel Victoria au Lac** (Via Guisan 3, tel. 091/994–20–31; doubles SFr140; closed Nov.–Mar.) is worth the long, albeit scenic, walk to get there. Take Bus 1 (toward Paradiso) to Riva Paradiso and turn right at Via Guisan. The SFr20 beds at the modern **Casa delle Giovane** (C. Elvezia 34, tel. 091/922–95–53; breakfast Sfr4.50) are for women only.

FOOD

Piazza della Riforma has lots of popular cafés, but you'll get more for your money around the corner, on Piazza Cioccaro. **Restaurant INOVA** (P. Dante 2, tel. 091/921–38–88), in the Innovations department store, serves huge plates of pasta (SFr7.90) and has a great salad bar (SFr4.20–SFr10.50). Another location, with windows overlooking the lake, is on Via Canove near Piazza della Riforma, in the Inno Lago boutique. The colorful corner of Via Pessina and Piazza Cioccaro has a meat store, a bakery, and a fruit-and-vegetable market—pick up some wurst (SFr4.50) or a delicious torte (SFr2) for a picnic. **Arlecchino** (P. Cioccaro 8) offers a *piatto del giorno* (daily special) for SFr15.80 and tasty pizzas and pasta from SFr10.80. Full meals at the popular **La Salista** (C. Elvezia 22, tel. 091/922–03–65; open 8 PM–1AM) are expensive, but you can always grab some snack-size burritos (SFr12) or quesadillas (SFr8).

WORTH SEEING

The **Cattedrale di San Lorenzo** (Via Cattedrale), with its copper dome, greets you as you exit the train station. Its main attractions are three Renaissance portals, an elegant facade and baroque interior, and a 16th-century tabernacle. The terrace has a good view of both Lugano and the lake. The **Chiesa di Santa Maria degli Angeli** (P. Luini, at Via Nassa) is a simple, elegant church with two beautiful frescoes by Bernardino Luini, the 1529 *Crucifixion* and *The Lord's Supper*; they've been compared to Leonardo da Vinci's work. **Museo Cantonale d'Arte** (Via Canova 10, tel. 091/910–47–80; admission SFr10; open Tues. 2–5, Wed.–Sun. 10–5) has works by Klee, Renoir, and the early 20th-century Russian painter Alexei von Jawlensky. Once you've done your cultural duty, plop down under a tree in **Parco Civico,** on Lake Lugano. The **lido** (admission SFr6), a swimming area with lots of grass, heated pools, and a small beach, is right next to the park.

NEAR LUGANO

VILLA FAVORITA

This lakeside villa (tel. 091/971–61–52; admission SFr10; open mid-Apr.–Oct., Fri.–Sun. 10–5), surrounded by beautiful public gardens, houses the **Thyssen-Bornemisza art collection,** the private holding of a family of wealthy German industrialists. Unfortunately, the family recently carted its most famous works—including some by Raphael, Titian, and Rembrandt—to Madrid's Villahermosa Palace, but the museum still has an impressive bunch of 19th- and 20th-century paintings by cubists, dadaists, surrealists, American impressionists, German expressionists, and Russian constructivists. To get here, take a boat ride (30 min, SFr4 round trip) from Lugano's central quay near Piazza Manzioni, or take Bus 2.

GANDRIA

Your efforts to get here are amply rewarded—restaurants hover over the water, small cobblestone streets climb the hill, and lush vegetation is everywhere. Gandria is so attractive that many popular postcards of Lugano actually picture this town instead. You can pay SFr16 for a round-trip boat ride from Lugano's central quay, or buy a one-way ticket (SFr10) and then take a pleasant one-hour walk through gardens leading to Villa Favorita (*see above*); from there, it's SFr2 for a ticket back to Lugano. You can also walk to Castagnola, an attractive town along the lake, in less than half an hour—follow signs from Gandria.

MORCOTE

An excellent bike ride (1 hr) takes you from Lugano through small lakeside towns to the beautiful old fishing village of Morcote. When you arrive, you can climb the hill to the **Church of Madonna del Sasso** for a cool rest amid 16th-century frescoes and calming organ music. Walk through the cemetery next door—you'll be amazed by the pains they took to bury local bigwigs. The **Parco Scherrer** (tel. 091/996–21–25; admission SFr7; open Mar. 15–Oct., daily 10–5) contains colorful gardens and paths lined with sculpture, mostly neoclassical repros. Eat next door at **Ristorante Grotto del Parco,** or try one of the restaurants on the water; you can always find pasta for around SFr14. The cheapest bed in town, complete with balcony and breathtaking view of the lake, is at **Hotel Oasi** (Riva del Dreva, tel. 091/996–11–61), where doubles are SFr90; take a right from the boat dock. Boat fare from Lugano to Morcote is SFr24 round-trip, SFr14 one-way. You can also combine a visit to Morcote with a trip to the top of **Mt. San Salvatore**; take Bus 1 to Paradiso, just south of Lugano, where a funicular travels to the top of San Salvatore (SFr11 one way); check out the great view of the lakes and the Alps, then walk 2½ hours down the mountain to Morcote (the path is marked next to the self-service restaurant).

LOCARNO

Cooled by breezes from Lago Maggiore (Lake Maggiore), Locarno strikes a balance between resorty Ascona and citified Lugano. The town had its 15 minutes of fame in 1925, when it hosted the post–World War I Disarmament Conference; since then, Locarno has attracted German retirees, who hang out in cafés downing afternoon coffee and tortes. Unfortunately, Locarno's waterfront is not as appealing as Ascona's, and swimming spots in the lake are hard to find. A 20-minute climb up Via al Sasso, past lush greenery and craggy rocks, takes you to **Madonna del Sasso,** a 15th-century sanctuary that features a spectacular view of the lake and its surrounding towns. On the way there, detour down **Vicolo Cappuccini,** a stone path bordered by fragrant roses. You can also take a funicular from Via alla Romogna for SFr4.20.

In summer, Locarno hosts plenty of musical events and an international **film festival,** which dominates Piazza Grande for the first two weeks of August. Inquire at the **tourist office** (Largo Zorzi 1, off P.

Grande, tel. 093/751–03–33; open Apr.–Oct., weekdays 8–7, weekends 9–noon and 1–5; Nov.–Mar., weekdays 8–noon and 2–6). If you're staying, try to get a dorm room (SFr33 per person) at **Pensione Città Vecchia** (Via Torretta 13, tel. 093/751–45–54), north of Piazza Grande. Self-service **INOVA Restaurant** (Via Stazione 1) has an endless variety of dishes and a salad bar, all at reasonable prices.

ASCONA

Small Ascona is a resort town through and through, good for a day trip but not worth a long visit. Ice-cream stands, outdoor cafés, and pedestrians line the busy lakefront, with most of the activity centered around Piazza G. Motta. Colorful houses and cobblestone streets attract small crowds of wanderers. As you join them in shuffling along the lake, stop by **Piazza San Pietro,** just a block from the water, where street musicians take advantage of good acoustics; or visit the Renaissance courtyard of the **Collegio Pontificio Papio.** The church of **Santa Maria della Misericordia** next door has some admirable frescoes. Unfortunately, swimmers take a backseat to boats around here, so those with the urge to submerge have to get themselves to the south side of the lake. The **Ente Turistico di Ascona e Losone** (P. San Pietro, near San Pietro tower, tel. 093/791–00–90) dispenses visitor information Monday–Saturday 8–7. A **PTT** bus (20 min, SFr2.40)—but no trains—runs between Ascona and Locarno. Bus passengers disembark on Via Papio. You can also catch a boat (45·min, SFr5) at the Locarno ferry terminal every hour until 6:30 PM.

WHERE TO SLEEP AND EAT

Garni Silvia (Via Circonvallazione 7, tel. 093/791–13–14; doubles SFr90–SFr102) is pretty much the Motel 6 of Ascona, but the rooms are big, clean, and the cheapest in town. To live large, **Hotel La Perla** (Via Collina 14, tel. 093/791–35–77) rents rooms (SFr75–SFr90 per person) in quaint villas; most have lush flower gardens and an outdoor terrace. The cheerful, balconied rooms fill up quickly at the busy hotel/restaurant **Ristorante Belvedere** (Via Locarno 19, tel. 093/791–42–22; SFr60 per person). You can eat in an outdoor courtyard to the sound of jazz at **Al Torchio** (Contrada Maggiore 1, tel. 093/791–71–26), where spaghetti is a bargain at SFr12, but a full meal could run you SFr30. The most happening waterfront restaurant is **Osteria Nostrana** (P. G. Motta, tel. 093/791–51–58), where pasta and pizza start at SFr12. **Ristorante al Lago** (Via Moscia, tel. 093/791–10–65) has a disco downstairs, making it a popular nightspot.

TURKEY

Every morning the front page of the *Turkish Daily News* greets readers with the same headline: "Peace at Home, Peace in the World." The person credited is Mustafa Kemal Atatürk (1881–1938), founder of the modern Turkish Republic—the man who gave Turkish women the vote, latinized the Turkish alphabet, and in 1923 built a secular state out of the ashes of the Ottoman Empire. More than 70 years later, Turkey remains democratic, secular, and mostly peaceful—which is quite remarkable given that it shares its border with "troublemakers" like Syria, Iran, and Iraq, and has been waging a brutal internal war against the Kurdistan Worker's Party (PKK) since the 1980s. So far, the death toll from the civil strife is estimated at 20,000, rendering many parts of eastern Turkey off-limits for Turks and tourists alike. And don't forget about Greece, Turkey's neighbor to the west. The two governments are forever playing hardball, be it over Cyprus, Turkey's desire to join the European Union (EU), or the barren Aegean islands that both countries claim.

Turkey's political road has always been a rocky one. After three military coups in the 1970s and '80s, Turkey finally seemed poised for prosperity in the 1990s, with a booming tourist industry and economic ties to several Muslim republics of the former Soviet Union. But while the rich got richer, the poor got poorer, and an increasing number began to turn to religion. From 1987 to 1996 the pro-Islamic Welfare Party (RP) tripled its share of votes in general elections. In June 1996 RP leader Necmettin Erbakan became Turkey's first Islamic prime minister at the head of a shaky coalition. His appointment worried Turkey's staunchly secularist military leaders, who claimed that he was encouraging fundamentalist activities and forging closer links with states such as Libya and Iran at the cost of Turkey's traditional ties with the West. In February 1997 the military initiated a campaign to bring the government down, and by July 1997, Erbakan was gone, forced out of office under heavy pressure from the country's military commanders. The new prime minister, Mesut Yilmaz, appointed by Turkey's president, vowed to put an end to the nation's year-long experiment with Islamic leadership—but the Welfare Party is unlikely to remain gone for long. Experts predict that in the next elections (to be held by early 1998) the party will win an even larger share of the vote.

These recent rumblings have highlighted Turkey's age-old search for an identity. There is an old saying that "Turkey is a man running West on a ship heading East." In recent years it has looked as if the ship has been gathering steam. Yet the truth is that modern Turkey belongs neither to Europe nor Asia. It combines elements of both, and yet falls somewhere in between.

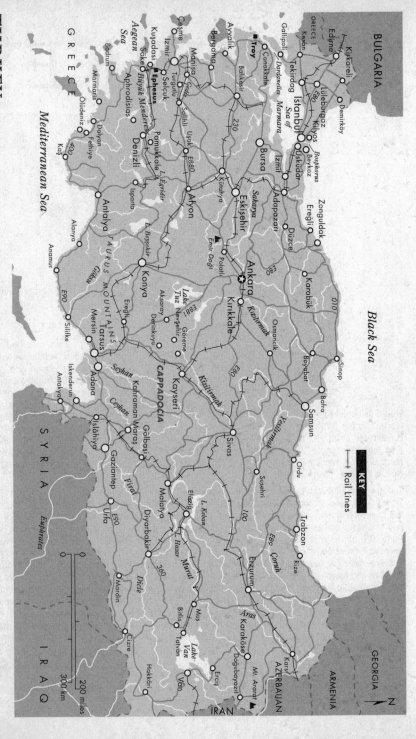

TURKEY

BASICS

MONEY

US$1 = 150,900 Turkish lira and 25,000 Turkish lira = 7¢. At press time, the yearly rate of inflation in Turkey was 80%, so don't hold on to too much currency; exchange money every week or so. In Turkey everyone is a multi-millionaire, thanks to bills that come in denominations of 5,000,000; 1,000,000; 500,000; 250,000; 100,000; 50,000; and 20,000. Coins come in denominations of 50 *bin* (thousand— i.e., 50,000); 25 bin; 10 bin; 5,000; 2,500; 1,000; and 500 (practically worthless). Get ready to do some math, because all prices quoted in this chapter are in U.S. dollars.

Banks, generally open weekdays 9–noon and 1:30–5, are everywhere, and you'll usually find at least one teller who speaks English. Almost all banks change cash and traveler's checks, although commissions vary between 2% and 7%. In most cities, **PTT** (Phones and Mail, *below*) offers competitive rates. In Istanbul and the big seaside tourist towns, the best cash rates can usually be found at foreign exchange agencies, which have electronic displays showing buying and selling rates—but not all take traveler's checks. Outside bank hours, nearly any hotel owner or merchant will change cash for a commission, at rates slightly worse than those offered by the banks.

Most Turkish banks and their ATMs give cash advances on Visa and MasterCard, and thousands of ATMs accept bank cards (with four-digit PIN codes) affiliated with PLUS, Cirrus, and EuroCard. The best bank to go to for Visa cash advances is **Türkiye İş Bank,** which doesn't charge for the service. Otherwise, expect to pay a 2%–5% commission plus $3 for a phone call to verify your credit.

HOW MUCH IT WILL COST • Turkey is the cheapest Mediterranean country; you can easily get by on $25 a day or less. Budget hotels are $4–$10 per person ($8 and up in Istanbul), and meals at budget restaurants cost about $3. A 100-km (60-mi)journey on a bus is usually no more than $1. Museums and archaeological sites charge $2–$5. Nightspots usually don't charge covers, and beer costs 50¢–$2. Tipping generally isn't necessary—except in the finest restaurants, and when someone goes out of their way for you. In these cases, tip 10%–15%.

VISA AND ENTRY REQUIREMENTS

Citizens of the United States, the United Kingdom, and Ireland are routinely issued 90-day visas ($20 for the United States and $10 for the United Kingdom and Ireland) upon entry to the country. Canadians, Australians, and New Zealanders don't need visas for stays of less than three months.

COMING AND GOING

Flying into Istanbul is expensive but will save you a long overland journey. Call **Turkish Airlines (THY)** (tel. 212/225–05–56 or 212/518–68–40) for fares. The flight from Paris is about $240 and from London $300. If you're coming by train, remember that **InterRail** is good throughout Turkey, but a **Eurailpass** will get you only as far as Istanbul. Clocked at 12 hours, the trip from Sofia, Bulgaria to Istanbul is a little better than the grim 23-hour ride from Athens. Sofia and Alexandroúpolis in Greece are popular points for picking up international **buses,** which may be faster than trains but are hardly enjoyable. If you're coming from Greece and you've got some time, island-hop your way to Turkey aboard the **ferry.** Frequent ferries sail from Lésvos to Ayvalık, from Khíos to Çeşme, from Sámos to Kuşadası, from Kós to Bodrum, and from Ródos to Marmaris. The ferries cost about $20–$30 each, plus $10–$15 for port taxes.

GETTING AROUND

The Turkish rail system, **Türkiye Cumhuriyeti Devlet Demiryollari (TCDD)** (tel. 212/527–00–50) connects all major cities and costs about 85¢ for every 100 km (60 mi); take advantage of the express service between Istanbul and Ankara (7½ hrs, $8.50). Though slightly cheaper than buses, trains are often painfully slow. Make reservations on weekends and in summer.

BY BUS • Buses travel so frequently and are so reliable that you don't need reservations, even in summer. Walk to the *otogar* (bus station), pick your destination, and hawkers will usually put you on a bus within the hour. You can also stop any bus on the road and pay the rate from the last stop—a good option for stranded hitchhikers. Buses are universally clean and modern with reclining seats, and although most don't have toilets, they all make regular pit stops. Many luxury lines offer air-conditioning, beverage service, and videos of American movies dubbed into Turkish. The pitfalls: Blaring Turkish pop music and clouds of cigarette smoke (only a few bus companies prohibit smoking, and you'll pay 20%–40% more for the privilege). Prices don't vary much between companies: about $1 for a 100-km (60-mi) trip.

BY DOLMUŞ • For shorter journeys between or within towns, wave down a *dolmuş* (shared taxi—often a Ford Transit or Mercedes van) on any main road; you needn't go to the station. Most journeys cost no more than 30¢. Destinations are displayed in the front window, and you pay on board the van.

WHERE TO SLEEP

Without a private shower, budget hotel rooms cost $4–$10 per person (sometimes more in İstanbul). *Pansiyons* (pensions) usually have cooking and washing facilities, but otherwise aren't substantially different from *otelis* (hotels). You can sleep on a mattress on a rooftop terrace at some hostels and pensions for as little as $2–$4, although on a breezeless night you may not be able to see the stars for all the mosquitoes. **Campsites** cost $3–$7; seek shade, or you'll wake and bake in your sleeping bag come dawn. In Turkey, the few HI **hostels** and scores of independent ones normally charge $4 a dorm bed.

FOOD

The language barrier shouldn't be a problem in restaurants; just peruse the trays of already cooked food and point at what you want. You can even go into the kitchen for a closer look. Restaurants usually charge $1 for cold starters in olive oil and $2 for warm entrées; at hyped-up resorts and in İstanbul you'll pay more. Budget standards include *kebap* (roasted meat, usually lamb), served with pita bread or salad; *pide* (pizzalike bread dough topped with butter, cheese, egg, or ground lamb); and *dolmaş* (vine leaves variously stuffed with eggplant, bell peppers, and lamb). Turkish pizza (not to be confused with pide), often topped with cheese and tomato, will bail out vegetarians, as will *meze* (assorted vegetable appetizers). But be careful of meat in disguise: Many meatless soups or entrées are cooked initially in meat stock. Play it safe by saying *"hiç et yiyemem"* ("I don't eat meat").

Pastanesis (bakery-cafés) serve trays of mouth-watering baklava, cakes, chocolate mousse, and *lokum* (Turkish delight), most for less than $1. Turkish *kahve* (coffee) is strong and fairly expensive ($1); sip your small cup slowly lest you ingest the gritty, bitter grounds that settle at the bottom. More common and less expensive (15¢–60¢) are the hundreds of varieties of Turkish *çay* (tea)—all highly caffeinated and served in little tulip-shape glasses invariably accompanied by a small spoon and two lumps of sugar.

Take advantage of pension cooking facilities by buying groceries. Fresh produce costs little, and the peaches, apricots, cherries, figs, bananas, eggplants, onions, and garlic for sale in local markets are excellent. A loaf of Turkish white bread is bland but cheap (30¢) and is also served with every meal (some tourist-oriented restaurants charge by the slice, so be sure to ask before tucking in). Efes Pilsen, a light lager, is the most widely available beer and costs $1–$2.50. The national cocktail is *rakı*, an aniseed liqueur that turns milky white when diluted with water.

BUSINESS HOURS

Normal business hours are Monday–Saturday 9–6, but shops will sometimes stay open until 10 when business is good. Many shops and restaurants also stay open Sunday, though some pious merchants close on Friday, the Muslim holy day. **Bakkals,** small grocery stores, are usually open daily 7 AM–9 PM. Museums are usually open daily 9–5, but sometimes close for lunch and on Monday.

VISITOR INFORMATION

All but the tiniest towns have a tourist office—sometimes called Turizm Danışma Bürosu—with free brochures in French, German, and English, plus local and regional maps. Offices are generally open May–September, daily 8:30–5:30; October–April (the off-season), weekdays 8:30–5:30. They often take an hour-long lunch break at about 12:30.

PHONES AND MAIL

Country code: 90. Go to any PTT—the combination post and phone office—for long-distance calls or to get a *telekart* (phone card) with which you can make national and international calls at orange phones scattered throughout most towns. Telekarts are sold in three denominations: 30 units ($2), 60 units ($3.50), and 100 units ($5). On average, calls to the United States are 38 units per minute during peak hours and 30 units per minute during off-peak hours. Otherwise, you'll have to use one of three *jetons* (tokens), available at PTTs, some stores, and newsstands. For calls within Turkey, deposit the token and dial the city code and phone number. A *küçük* (small) token costs 7¢ and is valid for one three-minute call; *normal* (standard) tokens cost 25¢ and are good for long-distance calls within Turkey; *büyük* (big) tokens cost 80¢ and are a must for dialing internationally. Note that no change is given, so don't use big tokens for local calls. Collect calls tend to get cut off every few minutes and cost about $10 for three minutes to the United States—more than double the direct-dial rate. For the local operator, dial 118. For international calls, dial the country code and the number; you'll usually get an immediate, clear connection. To reach English-speaking operators in America call **AT&T** Direct Access^{SM} (tel. 00–800–12277), **MCI** (tel. 00–800–15555), or **Sprint** (tel. 00–800–14477); for Canada, dial 00–800–16677; for the United Kingdom, dial 00–800–441177; for Australia, dial 00–800–611177.

Mailboxes are found outside PTTs, and you can buy stamps inside. The central branch in each city has **poste restante** (10¢ per item). Address letters: Your Name, Poste Restante, PTT, and the name of the city. Letters and postcards to Europe cost 60¢, to the United States 80¢.

CRIME AND PUNISHMENT

Turkey is not the place to break, or even bend, the law. Turks scoff when you bring up *Midnight Express*, but the police and penal system can be equally harsh today. In case of arrest, notify your consulate before all else—the staff can provide you with a list of lawyers. In general, theft is a problem only in heavily touristed areas, but you should watch for pickpockets in large bazaars.

EMERGENCIES

Police (tel. 155), **fire** (tel. 110), **ambulance** (tel. 112).

STAYING HEALTHY

Travelers to Turkey rarely report major health problems, but cautious doctors recommend that your diphtheria-tetanus, typhoid, gamma globulin, and polio vaccinations are up-to-date before you go. Anti-malarial pills are recommended for those heading to eastern Turkey. Tap water is chlorinated and generally safe, though if you'll only be in Turkey for a few days you might want to drink *su* (bottled water; 60¢ per liter). The food is almost always safe, particularly if you eat at restaurants rather than street stands; Turkish kitchens are very clean and open for your inspection. The biggest health risks are overexposure to the summer sun and the occasional scorpion or adder in rural areas, though especially in winter air pollution is a serious concern in İstanbul and other big cities, where coal is still burned.

LANGUAGE

English is widely spoken in the more touristed areas, but knowing a little German or French helps: German because a large number of Turks are former residents of Germany, and French because a few, particularly the better educated Turks, speak it. However, try to learn at least a few Turkish words, such as *merhaba* (hello), *lütfen* (please), *teşekkür ederim* (thank you), *evet* (yes), *hayır* (no), *tamam* (okay), *ingilizce biliyormusunuz?* (do you speak English?), *kaç para. . . ?* (how much is. . . ?), *nerede tuvalet?* (where is the bathroom?), as well as numbers to help you bargain in the bazaars: *bir* (one), *iki* (two), *üç* (three), *dört* (four), *beş* (five), *altı* (six), *yedi* (seven), *sekiz* (eight), *dokuz* (nine), and *on* (10). One hundred is *yüz*, 1,000 is *bin*, 50,000 is *elli bin*, 100,000 is *yüz bin*, and 1,000,000 is *bir milyon*.

CULTURE

Though many Turks consider themselves "secular" and "European," Turkey is 99% Muslim and very different from the rest of Europe. Visitors to mosques should always cover their arms and legs and avoid arriving during prayer times. Women should dress modestly to avoid unwanted attention; in resort towns, however, Western tourists can outnumber Turks, and shorts and bikinis are the norm. Gays are not likely to be hassled, but both gay and straight couples are advised to avoid public displays of affection, particularly in rural areas where customs are more conservative. That said, if you respect customs of modesty you'll find the Turks are deeply hospitable to foreigners.

ISTANBUL

İstanbul is in the midst of remaking itself, a process that has continued for the past 1,600 years. Originally settled by Mycenaean Greeks in the 5th century BC, it was known as Byzantium until AD 330, when Roman emperor Constantine moved the capital of his empire here; his minions, not surprisingly, began calling it Constantinople. Constantine died seven years later, but not before converting to Christianity and ushering in a major building campaign, culminating in the magnificent Hagia Sophia (AD 548). As the seat of Christendom for the next millenium, Constantinople became the object of Ottoman conquest—finally achieved in 1453. The sultans then recast the city, now called İstanbul, as the capital of a vast Islamic empire, lavishing it with palaces, pavilions, and mosques. İstanbul retained its function as the administrative center of a slowly crumbling empire until 1923, when Atatürk moved the capital to

HALICIOĞLU

Çakırbeyler Sok.

Kumbarahane Cad.

Kulaksız Cad.

Tay Sogaki

Hacıhüsrev Cad.

İplıç Sok.

Kurtulus C.

Yenişehir

YEN

HASKÖY

Hasköy Cad.

Okmeydanı Cad.

Kasımpaşa

KULAKSIZ
MEZARLIĞI

KASIMPAŞA

Bahriye Cad.

Tarlabaş

Sıraselviler Sok.

Turnacıbaşı Sok.

İstiklal

TEPEBAŞI

Aşmalı
Mescit
Sok.

Saydam Cad.

BEY

Yeniçarşı C.

İstanbul

Ayvansaray
Cad.

AYVANSARAY

Demirhisar Cad.

Bypass

Hasköy Yolu Melez Sok.

Evliya Çelebi
Cad.

Refik
Meşrutiyet Cad.

Postacılar S.

16

İstiklal

BALAT

Mürselpaşa Cad.

Haliç (Golden Horn)

Yolcuzade Cad.

THY
Galata
Tower

Tünel
Subway
Line

Kemeralı Cad

FENER

Draman Cad.

Tersane

Yoyvoda Cad.

Necatibey Cad.

Kemanke

EDİRNEKAPİ

Fevzipaşa Cad.

Yavuz Selim Cad.

Tabak Yunus Sok.

Haliç Caddesi

Karadeniz Cad.

Abdülezel Paşa Cad.

Salhpaşa Cad.

Cibali Cad.

Atatürk Bridge

GALATA

Galata Bridge

Eminönü
Ferry
Docks

Akşemsettin Cad.

UNKAPANI

Ragıp Gümüşpala Cad.

Yeni Postahane Cad.

2

EMİNÖNÜ

Ker

Akdeniz Cad.

Macar Kardeşler Cad.

İtfaiye Cad.

KÜÇÜKPAZAR

Aşır Efendi
Cad.

Sirkeci
Station

M

Vatan Cad.

Haliçlar Cad.

Atatürk Bulvarı

Kalipvefa Cad.

1
İstanbul
University

Uzun Çarşı Cad.

Fuatpaşa Cad.

PTT

SİRKECİ

CAĞALOĞLU

Vezirhan Cad.

Tourist
Police

Millet Cad.

T

Horhor Cad.

Şehzadebaşı Cad.

LÂLELI

3

Kalpakçılar Cad.

ALEMDAR

4

7

M
T

Ordu Cad.

BEYAZIT

Yeniçeriler Cad.

Tiyatro Cad.

Gedikpaşa Cad.

Divanyolu
Cad.

5

6

Namık Kemal Cad.

Mustafa Kemal Cad.

T

AKSARAY

Cerrahpaşa Cad.

Türkeli Cad.

Kadirgalimanı Cad.

Hippodrome

Alemdar Sok.

9

KUMKAPI

Kumkapı Cad.

Şifa
Hamamı
Sok.

Üçler Sok.

Kabasakal

10

11

Kennedy Cad.

Mehmet
P.Y.

SULTANAHMET

Kennedy Cad.

TO İSTANBUL
INTERNATIONAL
AIRPORT

Sea of

882

Sights ●

Arkeoloji Müzesi, **14**
Blue Mosque, **9**
Hagia Sophia, **8**
Kapalı Çarşı
(Grand Bazaar), **3**
Mısır Çarşısı
(Egyptian Bazaar), **2**
Süleymaniye
Mosque, **1**
Topkapı Palace, **15**
Yerebatan Sarnıcı, **6**

Lodging ○

Barut's Guesthouse/
Hotel Empress
Zoe, **13**
Çelik Guest
House, **10**
Hotel As, **17**
Hotel Ayasofya, **4**
Hotel Devran II, **16**
Interyouth Hostel
(HI), **7**
Orient Youth
Hostel, **12**
Özlem Pansiyon, **5**
Sultan Tourist
Hostel, **11**

KEY

AE American Express Office
i Tourist Information
T Tramvay Station
M Metro Station

N

0 440 yards
0 400 meters

TO PRINCES'
ISLANDS

Ankara. As evidenced by the onslaught of immigrants (some 50,000 relocate here every month) from the former Soviet Union and eastern Turkey, İstanbul remains an alluring regional crossroads.

Modern İstanbul may not live up to its grandiloquent history, but in many of the city's districts—Galata, Sirkeci, Beyazıt, and parts of Sultanahmet—life remains old-fashioned. From dawn to dusk, men bend under enormous crates and navigate narrow cobblestone alleys, while shops and cluttered bazaars host haggling merchants. Under a skyline of domes and minarets, this timeless scene contrasts with modern İstanbul, a city of high-rise offices and telecommunication towers. In some areas, *müezzins* (the Muslim criers who once beckoned the faithful to prayer) have been replaced by prerecorded broadcasts on public-address systems. But contradiction has always been one of İstanbul's defining characteristics—don't be disappointed if you end up sipping an espresso in a neon-lit café off Taksim Square rather than taking *çay* (tea) with merchants in a smoky teahouse. They're both equally authentic İstanbul experiences.

BASICS

VISITOR INFORMATION

Sultanahmet Tourism Information (Divanyolu Cad. 3, at far north end of Hippodrome, tel. 212/518–87–54; open daily 9–5), the government-affiliated tourist office, distributes brochures in various languages. There are other offices at the **Sirkeci train station** (tel. 212/511–58–88; open daily 9–5), the **Karaköy ferry docks** (tel. 212/249–57–76; open weekdays 9:30–5), and in the **Beyoğlu district** (Meşrutiyet Cad. 57, tel. 212/245–68–75; open weekdays 9–5). To reach the latter from İstiklâl Caddesi, turn left on Meşrutiyet Caddesi and left again at the British Consulate.

AMERICAN EXPRESS

Türk Ekspres holds mail and can help you with AmEx traveler's checks and credit cards. *Mailing address: Cumhuriyet Cad., İstanbul Hilton Hotel lobby, 80200 Harbiye-İstanbul, tel. 212/241–02–48, fax 212/241–04–31. From Taksim Meydanı, walk 500 yds north on Cumhuriyet Cad. From Eminönü, Bus 74 to Hilton. Open weekdays 9–5.*

CHANGING MONEY

Exchange agencies usually offer better rates than do banks, but unlike banks, they also charge a commission on traveler's checks (or refuse to change checks altogether). A better bet is drawing money on your ATM card; **Yapı Kredi 24, Pamukbank,** and **AkMatik** ATMs are plentiful throughout the city, giving you 24-hour access to your Visa and Cirrus- or PLUS-linked accounts.

CONSULATES

Consulates are generally open Monday through Friday 9 AM to 5 PM. Some consulates are closed on Friday afternoons during summer. **Australia:** *Tepecik Yolu Üzeri 58, Etiler, tel. 212/257–70–50.* **Canada:** *Büyükdere Cad. 107/3, Gayrettepe, tel. 212/272–51–74.* **United Kingdom:** *Meşrutiyet Cad. 34, off İstiklâl Cad., Beyoğlu, tel. 212/293–75–40.* **United States:** *Meşrutiyet Cad. 104–108, Tepebaşı, near Taksim tourist office, tel. 212/251–36–02.*

DISCOUNT TRAVEL AGENCIES

Backpacker's Travel Agency. This is a reputable agency offering cheap airfares, bus tickets, and car rentals. English is spoken. *Akbıyık Cad. 22, opposite Orient Youth Hostel, tel. 212/638–63–43, fax 212/638–14–83. Open daily 9–7.*

EMERGENCIES

Ambulance (tel. 112), **fire** (tel. 110), **police** (tel. 155). The **Tourist Police** (Yerebatan Cad. 6, tel. 212/527–45–03) can help out 24 hours a day with minor tourist catastrophes, such as theft and harassment; look for them in the pink house opposite the Yerebatan Sarnici 100 yds west of Hagia Sophia. All speak some English. For what ails you, İstanbul has plenty of modern, fully stocked **pharmacies**—take your pick along Divanyolu Caddesi. Contact the **American Hospital** (Güzelbahçe Sok., in Nişantasi district, tel. 212/231–40–50) for more serious medical problems.

PHONES AND MAIL

For information on making calls within Turkey, and for international access codes, *see* Basics, at the beginning of this chapter. At İstanbul's palatial **main post office** you can change money, buy stamps, make phone calls, and pick up poste restante. Address letters to: Büyük PTT, Yeni Postahane Caddesi, Sirkeci. To get here, follow Ankara Caddesi north as it winds its way toward Sirkeci, then take a left on Asir Efendi Caddesi. *Asir Efendi Cad. 25, tel. 212/526–12–00. Open Mon.–Sat. 8 AM–midnight, Sun. 9–7.*

COMING AND GOING

BY BUS

About 5 km (3 mi) northwest of the city center, the new and modern **Esenler Terminus** handles all domestic and international routes, with daily departures to Athens (20 hrs, $48), İzmir (9 hrs, $9), and dozens of other cities. It's easiest to buy your ticket at one of the travel agencies in Sultanahmet (there are many along Divanyolu Caddesi) or Taksim (there are many along Taksim Meydanı); though you'll pay an extra 20¢–$1, you'll usually get a free minibus ride from the agency to the station. Otherwise, take the Tramvay to Aksaray (if your tram doesn't stop at Aksaray, get off at Lâleli and walk 300 yds downhill along the tracks), transfer to the nearby Metro, and get off at the Otogar stop. The station is right outside—your bus will depart from the kiosk with its company name on it. All told, it takes 45 minutes to reach the station from Sultanahmet.

BY FERRY

Express catamarans travel frequently to Yalova, where they connect with buses to Bursa. Overnight ferries to İzmir (19 hrs, $11) also depart Istanbul frequently. For both routes schedules vary by season and prices fluctuate widely, so consult a travel agency for more information.

BY PLANE

Atatürk International Airport (Yeşilköy, tel. 212/663–64–00), 25 minutes by bus from the city center, has domestic and international flights through two terminals. The airport's **tourist desk** (tel. 212/663–07–93) is open daily 8 AM–10 PM. To reach central İstanbul, board the hourly bus ($2) operated by Turkish Airlines and get off at Aksaray, where you can catch the Tramvay (25¢) to Sultanahmet or Eminönü. Many Sultanahmet travel agencies—including Backpacker's (Discount Travel Agencies, *above*)—offer shuttle service to the airport ($3.50) May–September, six times daily.

BY TRAIN

İstanbul has two train stations. **Sirkeci** (tel. 212/527–00–50), on the Golden Horn in the Eminönü district, serves Europe and is an appropriately exotic terminus for the *Orient Express*. There's a tourist information booth here, as well as three ATMs (PLUS and Cirrus) in the front lobby. A train runs daily at 11:30 PM to Athens (23 hrs, $40). To reach Sultanahmet, walk outside and take the Tramvay for two stops (board by the sign marked GIRIŞ) or simply follow the Tramvay tracks 1½ km (¾ mi) on foot. A taxi should cost no more than $2. To reach Beyoğlu and Taksim, either take a cab ($2–$3) or walk across the Galata Bridge and catch the Tünel subway to Istiklâl Caddesi.

Haydarpaşa (tel. 216/336–20–63), across the Bosphorus, serves the east, with two express trains daily to Ankara (7½ hrs, $8.50). The quickest way to Haydarpaşa is via ferry from the Eminönü docks (150 yds northwest of Sirkeci) or the Karaköy docks (500 yds northeast of Galata Bridge).

GETTING AROUND

İstanbul is constantly on the move, but don't expect to reach your destination quickly—the city simply goes nowhere at a breakneck pace. The public transportation system is massively disjointed, with subways, buses, and trains working nearly but not exactly in sync with one another. Walking can be just as frustrating: Sidewalks narrow to about 1½ ft on busy throughways, and taxis refuse to slow down or swerve to avoid foot traffic. On the upside, İstanbul's narrow and often hilly streets are fascinating to explore, so don't be afraid to wander into the unknown. Detailed street maps ($2) are available at most every newsstand, and getting *really* lost is surprisingly difficult.

The **Boğaziçi** (Bosphorus) strait divides European İstanbul, where all the sights are, from Asian İstanbul. The **Haliç** (Golden Horn) waterway creates a peninsula where travelers spend most of their time. If you stay in **Sultanahmet,** the region nearest the tip of the peninsula, well-known sights are within easy walking distance. Another popular option is **Taksim,** a modern, bar- and restaurant-filled district north of the Haliç. Taxis become useful at night, when most public transport stops running. Be sure the driver turns on the meter. Expect to pay $4 to go from Taksim to Sultanahmet; fares double after midnight.

BY BUS

Buses are best for getting across the Haliç from Sultanahmet. The various stations, including Eminönü (200 yds west of Sirkeci) and Taksim, are recognizable by groups of people looking expectantly up the road. Buy tickets from the white kiosks at stations (40¢) or from a street vendor (50¢); routes and the final destination are listed by the bus door.

BY DOLMUS

Dolmuş, shared taxis traveling specified routes, are a convenient form of transport throughout most of İstanbul—that is, if you have a detailed city map or know the routes by heart. Otherwise, you'll have to ask a lot of questions, since routes are marked only at the first and last stops. Catch dolmuş at stops or hail them like taxis. They're especially useful at night for moving between clubs. Fares average about 50¢.

BY FERRY

İstanbul's ferry system moves tens of thousands of people between Europe and Asia daily but is of little use to budget travelers, since most sights are on the European side of the city. Most ferries depart from Eminönü, shipping out every few minutes from five separate terminals (destinations are spelled out at the dock terminals, so check to make sure you're at the right one). Single-ride tokens cost 50¢. If you're traveling more than one stop, you're supposed to get off at each station, buy a new token and then reboard. There are also ferry docks at Karaköy, across the Galata bridge from Eminönü, as well as in Beşiktaş and Ortaköy.

BY SUBWAY

The Eminönü–Topkapı **Tramvay,** which runs daily until 11 PM, is speedy and covers a wide range of districts, though it's most useful for traveling between Sirkeci station and Sultanahmet. In major stations you can purchase tickets (35¢) at kiosks by the turnstiles; at small stations you have to pay a street vendor 10¢ more. İstanbul's puny **Tünel** is a subway with two stops, using antique streetcars to bring tourists and a few locals from Tersane Caddesi (at the northern end of Galata Bridge) up to Istiklâl Caddesi. It's good for a quick zip up the hill in this part of town; purchase tokens (15¢) at either end. For budget travelers, İstanbul's **Metro** is only useful for traveling between the Aksaray Tramvay stop and the Esenler bus station; buy tickets (35¢) at kiosks or from street vendors.

WHERE TO SLEEP

If you prefer to stay close to the main sights, the **Sultanahmet** district is your best choice. It's loaded with cheap hotels, hostels, and pensions, most within a 15-minute walk of Hagia Sophia and Topkapı Palace. Another bonus is that many hotels in Sultanahmet have rooftop bars and terraces that overlook the Sea of Marmara; be sure to ask before paying. The **Taksim** and **Beyoğu** districts, on the other hand, are better bets if nightclubs and restaurants are your priorities. Either way, expect to pay about $4 for a dorm bed, $8–$15 for a double room in a hostel or budget pension, and upward of $25 for a double in a nicer hotel. Breakfast is generally included in the room price. In summer, many budget hotels offer rooftop accommodations—involving anything from a cement slab to chairs and cushions—for about $4. If this sounds awful, be sure to make reservations for the busy months of July and August. One final note: *Always* inspect a room before paying.

SULTANAHMET

If everything below is full, you'll pass a handful of true budget hotels by following the Tramway tracks from Sirkeci toward Sultanahmet.

UNDER $15 • Hotel Ayasofya. The Ayasofya is an all-around amazing deal: It's centrally located, it's clean, and the rooms are almost classy. Doubles cost $11. *Yerebatan Cad. 33, 1 block west of Tourist Police, tel. 212/522–71–26. Cash only.*

Özlem Pansiyon. This is a cramped but clean pension on busy Divanyolu Caddesi, with carpet shops and kebap stands all around. Look before paying: Some rooms are impossibly small. All beds cost $8. *Ticarethane Sok. 1, tel. 212/527–18–68. From Sultanahmet Tramvay station, head 1 block east on Divanyolu Cad., left on Ticarethane Sok. Cash only.*

UNDER $25 • Celik Guest House Pension. The Celik's surprisingly elegant rooms all have private bath, and there is a comfortable upstairs café/common room. It's centrally located, too. Doubles are

$24, quads $36. *Mimar Mehmetağa Cad. 22, tel. 1/518–96–75. From plaza in front of Blue Mosque, SE on Mimar Mehmetağa Cad.*

UNDER $45 • Barut's Guesthouse. Barut's is clean, friendly, efficient, and offers great views from its rooftop terrace. The owners are well-respected artists. Doubles cost $45, breakfast included. *İshak Paşa Cad. 8, tel. 212/517–68–41, fax 212/516–29–44. From Hagia Sophia, left on Kabasakal Cad., right on İshak Paşa Cad.*

UNDER $65 • Hotel Empress Zoe. This new and artful hotel is built inside an old stone cistern. Each room has a handwoven *kilim* (carpet) and marble bath. The hotel's terrace bar offers amazing views. Doubles cost $65, suite $95. *Adliye Sok. 10, near Hanedan Pension, tel. 212/518–25–04, fax 212/518–56–99.*

TAKSIM

On the other side of the Haliç from Sultanahmet, the Taksim district offers a vibrant nightlife and café scene, but the hotels here can be cramped, dirty, noisy, and overpriced. Still, it's second only to Sultanahmet for budget lodging.

UNDER $25 • Hotel As. If you're here to enjoy the nightlife, choose the plush Hotel As: It has a full bar and is located near Taksim's cafés and nightclubs. Doubles go for $21. *Bekar Sok. 26, tel. 212/252–65–24, fax 212/245–00–99. From Taksim Meydanı, walk south on Istiklâl Cad., right on Bekar Sok. Cash only.*

Hotel Devran II. All of the rooms at this large, snazzy hotel are quiet and orderly, but the best are those that face the sunny street. Doubles are $24. *Asmalı Mescit Sok. 4, tel. 212/243–36–51, fax 212/243–53–30. From Tünel subway, walk north on Istiklâl Cad., left on Asmalı Mescit Sok. Cash only.*

HOSTELS

Interyouth Hostel (HI). This well-run place boasts an incredible location, opposite the Hagia Sophia. Dorm beds cost $4, doubles $13, quads $24. There are no age restrictions. *Caferiye Sok. 6/1, tel. 212/513–61–50, fax 212/512–76–28. From Sultanahmet Tramvay stop, cross Alemdar Cad. and veer left on Caferiye Sok. Laundry. Cash only.*

Orient Youth Hostel. A large hostel, the Orient is favored by backpackers. Its top-floor café is a hip Sultanahmet hangout, with big beers ($1) and cable TV, plus dinner and breakfast items for $2–$5. Dorm beds cost $4, doubles $5 per person; luggage storage is available. There are no age restrictions. *Akbıyık Cad. 13, tel. 212/518–07–89, fax 212/518–38–94. From Ayasofya Sq., walk SE on Tevfikhane Sok., left on Kutlugün Cad., right on Adliye Sok., right on Akbıyık Cad. Cash only.*

Sultan Tourist Hostel. You'll find one of the best rooftop terraces in Sultanahmet at this upscale hostel. Dorm beds cost $6, doubles $9 person, triples $7 per person. There are no age restrictions, and they offer luggage storage for guests. *Terbıyık Sok. 3, near Orient Youth Hostel, tel. 212/516–92–60, fax 212/517–16–26. Laundry. Cash only.*

FOOD

You can find a cheap meal—especially from street stands, *pideçis* (pide stands), and *büfes* (minimarkets that sell groceries and hot snacks)—in practically every area of the city. Fresh produce abounds at street markets, held regularly in different districts of the city; on Tuesday there's an excellent outdoor market on Terbıyık Sokak, near Sultanahmet's budget hotels. İstanbul's finest restaurants are scattered behind the Blue Mosque in Sultanahmet and in Taksim, where a night out can be as expensive as one in Western Europe.

SULTANAHMET

Meals in Sultanahmet are usually hastily prepared and overpriced. The neon-lit places on **Divanyolu Caddesi** charge $1–$3 more than the nontouristy spots south of the Blue Mosque and surrounding the Grand Bazaar. In summer only, open-air restaurants on **Kumkapı Caddesi,** 2 km (1 mi) east of Sultanahmet, feature live music and late-night crowds.

UNDER $5 • Cennet Gözleme Manti. This place is strictly for tourists, with gimmicks like bread-making demonstrations and folk bands with dancing. The decor is like the interior of a mosque, with low-lying couches. Menu includes such traditional dishes as *shish kebap* (skewered roast meat) and meze. *Divanyolu Cad. 90, near Ankara Cad., tel. 212/513–14–16. Cash only.*

Doy-Doy. This is a favorite with budget travelers, but still not a tourist trap. It offers some of the cheapest, freshest Turkish food around, and you can stuff yourself for less than $3.50. *Sifa Hamamı Sok. 13, tel. 212/517–15–88. From south end of Hippodrome, south on Nakilbent Sok., veer left (east) on Sifa Hamamı Sok. Cash only.*

Underground Cafe. Come here for true British cooking: eggs 'n chips, fish 'n chips, and sausage 'n chips. Try the chicken sandwich for a lighter blast of grease. Happy hour (daily 5–8) means 50¢ beers and U2 on the stereo. *Akbıyık Cad. 14, opposite Orient Youth Hostel, tel. 212/575–12–53. Cash only.*

Vitamin Restaurant. The high grease content of the food at this place doesn't affect its popularity in the slightest. It's as close as İstanbul comes to a vegetarian restaurant, offering at least eight such plates (in addition to plenty for carnivores). A basic meat and potatoes meal costs $2.50. *Divanyolu Cad. 16, facing Blue Mosque, tel. 1/526–50–86. Cash only.*

TAKSIM/BEYOGLU

Taksim's **Istiklâl Caddesi** is loaded with restaurants, from Pizza Hut and Burger King to back-alley kebap stands. On **Sahne Sokak,** a covered market off Istiklâl Caddesi, search among the fish and produce sellers for **Mercan Cafe Birahane** (Sahne Sok. 13; closed Sun.; cash only), where you can feast on fried mussels and beer for $2.50.

UNDER $5 • Bereket Döner. Although this place is well-known by locals, its obscure location keeps it off the tourist track. The orthodox Muslims owners serve delicious food, including a good selection of vegetable and rice dishes. Fresh-squeezed O.J. is $1. *Hava Sok. 14, off Istiklâl Cad., tel. 212/249–82–50. Cash only.*

UNDER $10 • Peace & Nature. Here is a healthy vegetarian oasis in the Land of Kebaps. You pay a bit more for eggplant casserole or lentils with dill and feta ($5.50), but it's worth it. Prices are slightly lower at lunch. *Büyük Parmakkapı Sok. 27, off Istiklâl Cad., tel. 212/213–23–43. Closed Mon. Cash only.*

TEAHOUSES

The teahouses that in summer spill out onto the streets and courtyards immediately surrounding Sultanahmet's Blue Mosque and Hagia Sophia charge almost double the price of smaller, out-of-the-way places. Of course, this means your *çay* still costs less than 75¢. The penultimate Sultanahmet teahouse is **Erenler Nargile Salonu** (Yeniçeriler Cad. 36), an octagonal smoke-filled room where old men sip tea (30¢) and toke on water pipes loaded with strong, sweet tobacco. It's through a gate marked ÇORLULU ALIPAŞA MEDRESSI. During summer, you can opt to sit in the teahouse's pleasant, shaded courtyard, which is decorated with the kilims of surrounding rug merchants. **Sevenin Kiraathanesi** (Sifa Hamamı Sok. 13), near the Doy-Doy restaurant, is a no-frills teahouse with Turks playing cards around an iron stove or at a handful of outdoor tables. In Taksim, **Cafe Paris** (Hamalbaşı Cad. 12, opposite British Consulate) is part traditional teahouse, part billiards hall (50¢ a game). Teahouses welcome men and women alike.

WORTH SEEING

It can take weeks to even scratch the surface of İstanbul, a city with more than 100 museums and dozens of other star attractions. The following will get you started, but to do İstanbul justice, buy one of the full-color guides ($2–$5) sold at newsstands, on street corners, and by groups of eager children who stand outside Hagia Sophia. Tourist offices have little in the way of literature, but they do organize guided half-day tours ($5–$8).

BLUE MOSQUE

In the middle of Sultanahmet sits the Blue Mosque, or Sultan Ahmet Camii, a stone mountain of domes, half-domes, and minarets rising above the trees opposite Hagia Sophia. The structure was built during the early 17th century under the patronage of Ottoman ruler Sultan Ahmet, who wanted to prove that Islam could produce a building as beautiful and impressive as Christendom's Hagia Sophia. The mosque gained its name from the thousands of blue tiles covering the inside, which create a dazzling symphony of Arabic script and patterns. The mosque's interior is most graceful at night, when electric chandeliers cast dancing lights among severe shadows throughout the building. In summer, the grounds hosts an almost nightly outdoor light show with accompanying narration in Turkish, English, French, and German. During certain portions of the show, the mosque's exterior is lit with green, blue, and red lights—it's quite a sight.

To enter you'll have to don a muslin cloth at the door if you're wearing shorts or a short-sleeved shirt—this applies to men as well as women. You must also leave your shoes outside (give the shoe holder a 20¢–50¢ tip) and refrain from pointing your feet toward Mecca (the altar). On your way out, walk 50 yds west to the ruins of the **Hippodrome,** where the Byzantines once raced chariots. If you paid attention in Art History, you may remember that the Hippodrome's **Quadriga**—a famous bronze sculpture depicting a team of four horses—was stolen in the Fourth Crusade and now sits atop St. Mark's Church in Venice. *Sultanahmet. Admission free. Open daily 9–5; closed during daily prayers (held 5 times daily).*

HAGIA SOPHIA

One of the most magnificent buildings ever constructed, Hagia Sophia (*Aya Sofya* in Turkish) has been both the central church of Christendom and the major inspiration for the mosques of Islam. Completed in AD 532 under the patronage of Emperor Justinian, the Christian church was designed by the mathematician Anthemius and the scientist Isidorus, who managed to create a dome 106 ft in diameter—a size that remained unsurpassed until the construction of Michelangelo's dome at St. Peter's in Rome a millennium later. The seemingly impossible stability of Hagia Sophia awed the faithful; the unfaithful had their day when the dome partially collapsed in 558. The next dome was higher than the first, but stress caused by lateral pressure forced repairs in 989 and again in 1346. After that, the dome held up pretty well until recently, when it again underwent renovation—including the installation of scaffolding that ascends to the ceiling, over 15 stories from the ground. The spiraling steel structure is a useful aid for gauging the church's awesome size.

Once the Turks conquered Constantinople in 1453, the church was converted into a mosque. In the mid-15th century, its mosaics were plastered over in accordance with the Islamic belief that the human figure shouldn't be represented in religious art. Atatürk ended the religious career of the building in 1936, uncovering some of its original mosaics and turning it into a museum. *Sultanahmet, tel. 212/522–17–50. Admission: $4.25. Open Tues.–Sun. 9:30–5.*

SULEYMANIYE MOSQUE

The mosque of Süleyman the Magnificent dates from 1557 and is one of the finest examples of early Ottoman architecture. It was commissioned by Süleyman and his wife Hürrem Sultan—both of whom are buried on the grounds. The mosque was modeled after the Hagia Sophia, with a series of delicate domes offset by four towering minarets. Also note the graceful stained-glass windows and white-marble *mihrab* (prayer vestibule). When tour groups swarm Hagia Sophia and the Blue Mosque, you'll appreciate this mosque's relative calm. Part of the fun is simply getting here: Along the way you pass **İstanbul University** and dozens of cramped, shop-filled streets. *Enter off Prof. Sıddık Sami Ona Cad. Donation encouraged. Open daily sunrise–sunset; closed during daily prayers.*

TOPKAPI SARAYI

Overlooking the Sea of Marmara, **Topkapı Palace** is a sumptuous collection of landscaped courtyards and elegant buildings. Its construction began in the mid-15th century and continued for more than 400 years; at first the palace was enlarged according to the tastes of Ottoman sultans, but Sultan Abdül Mecit—in an attempt to please European royalty—abandoned it for the European-style Dolmabahçe Palace in 1853. Topkapı Palace contains a series of museum galleries that unfold over four courtyards. The **Harem** ("Forbidden"), a sort of gilded cage composed of hundreds of salons, baths, and bedrooms, held the sultan and his mother—the second most powerful person in the empire—as well as his wives, brothers (kept in virtual isolation lest they aspire to the throne prematurely), children, concubines, and female slaves. Although only a fraction of the Harem is open to the public (by guided tour only; admission $2), you'll see enough inlaid furniture and silk-lined domes to get a taste of its royal flavor.

The four courtyards of the palace are flanked by former kitchens and janissary quarters, now a museum of pocket watches and galleries containing ancient manuscripts. The **treasury** in the third courtyard holds such booty as an 86-carat diamond (mounted on a rotating velvet cushion to better catch the light), clippings from the beard of the prophet Mohammed, the occipital bone of St. John the Baptist, and a bucket of emeralds. The palace grounds make for a pleasant afternoon on their own, as does the adjacent **Archaeological Museum** (*below*). *Sultanahmet, tel. 212/512–04–80. From Ayasofya Sq., walk SE until street dead-ends, turn left, and continue 100 yds. Admission: $4. Open Wed.–Mon. 9:30–5.*

ARKEOLOJI MUZESI • One of the oldest ancient-art collections open to the public outside Western Europe and the United States, the Sultanahmet **Archaeological Museum** houses a stunning collection of Mediterranean and Near Eastern art. Under Ottoman intellectual Osman Hamdi Bey's direction, the museum unearthed what some believe is the tomb of Alexander the Great at an unmarked site in Egypt

ATATURK, FATHER OF THE TURKS

By now you've probably determined that the overly serious, steely-eyed fellow occupying the central square in every Turkish town is Mustafa Kemal Atatürk. Modern Turkey is largely the legacy of this one man, born in 1881 in what is now the Greek city of Thessaloníki. Mustafa Kemal first made a name for himself at the battle of Gallipoli (1915), which forced the Allies to postpone their conquest of the strategic Dardanelles Straits. After the war, Kemal fought the corruption of the Ottoman Empire in order to establish Turkey as a modern nation-state. Reaching power in the 1920s, he dismantled the caliphate, thus giving the government the secular emphasis that it maintains today (despite the shift to fundamentalism throughout the Muslim world), and ordered that written Turkish be latinized. In the 1930s, he gave women the right to vote, and took the new surname "Atatürk" (Father of the Turks). Most Turks revere him, and it's probably unwise to question his legacy in public unless a violent argument is your idea of a good time.

(others dispute its authenticity, claiming Alexander was buried in Alexandria, not Phoenicia). Along with the tomb, the museum's collection includes a lion from the mausoleum at Halicarnassus and an exceptional gathering of athletes, nymphs, poets, and soldiers immortalized in marble. *Inside Topkapı Palace grounds, tel. 212/520–77–40. Admission: $2. Open Tues.–Sun. 9:30–5.*

YEREBATAN SARNICI

Rumbling trams and carpet salesmen shouting in the streets contrast with the almost churchlike peacefulness of this underground sanctuary. The Yerebatan Sarnıcı is an immense subterranean reservoir built by Emperor Justinian during the 6th century to keep a steady water supply for imperial Constantinople. The cistern was used until the mid-1980s, when it was drained and opened to the public. Water continues to drip from the vaulted brick ceiling, cooling the dark, humid, column-lined vault and adding a soothing accompaniment to the piped-in arias. All in all, this is one of İstanbul's most romantic and memorable sights, and you can enjoy it further by lingering at the subterranean café near the exit. *Yerebatan Cad., opposite Tourist Police, tel. 212/522–12–59. Admission: $2. Open daily 9–4:30.*

ORTAKOY

Far removed from the city center and its attendant crowds of tourists is the tiny waterfront district of Ortaköy. In the shadow of the Boğaziçi Bridge, Ortaköy is a quaint 10-block area with cobblestone streets. Mellow during the day, the district fills up at night with İstanbul's bohemian crowd, thirsting for an alternative time in beautifully restored Ottoman houses that now serve as bars. Somehow, strains of the Gypsy Kings and John Lee Hooker don't sound out of place here. Sunday, the streets are overrun with an arts-and-crafts bazaar, drawing shoppers from all over the city. *Take Bus 22, 22A, or 22C from Eminönü, or Bus 23B from Taksim Meydanı; or catch the ferry from Eminönü to Beşiktaş and walk 15 min north (parallel to water) along Çırağan Cad./Muallim Naci Cad.*

CHEAP THRILLS

The most beautiful, cost-efficient way to İstanbul is from the deck of a city-transit **ferry** (Getting Around, *above*). Although the rush-hour crowds and smoke can be less than romantic, a sunset view of the city's minarets and parks is worth the minor discomfort. You can take any ferry (be sure to board one that makes a round-trip); the Eminönü–Kadıköy is usually the least crowded.

To get a sense of the immensity and complex geography of İstanbul, ascend the **Galata Tower,** built in 1348 by the Genoese. On a clear day, the panoramic view from the top is stunning. *Galata, tel. 212/245–11–60. Admission: $1. Open daily 9–8.*

BAZAARS

İstanbul has two incredible and exotic bazaars. The best known is **Kapalı Çarşı** (Grand Bazaar) in Beyazıt. The central market encompasses eight covered lanes that stretch for six long blocks, but since the 18th century the surrounding streets have been overtaken by merchants and artisans—creating a bazaar that today sprawls for nearly 2 km (1 mi). Inside you'll find tea, trinkets, carpets, jewelry, sweets, fabrics, leather ware, electronics, and the usual tourist junk. The Grand Bazaar's teahouses are fine, but think twice before sitting down to lunch at one of the overpriced restaurants. *Open Mon.–Sat. 8:30–7.*

Less hectic but no less interesting is the **Mısır Çarşısı** (Egyptian Bazaar), in Eminönü a few hundred yards west of Sirkeci station. Its nickname is "Spice Bazaar" in recognition of the many merchants selling henna, cinnamon, clove, saffron, and peppers. *Open Mon.–Sat. 8–7.*

BATHHOUSES

A Turkish bath—the ritual of being steamed, scalded, soaped, scrubbed, beaten, and cooled down, followed by a cup of tea or some fresh orange juice—is the most glorious torture you can inflict upon yourself. Most baths (*hamam* in Turkish) have separate sections for men and women, and all offer semi-secure rooms where you can leave your belongings. Nudity isn't generally acceptable, so keep your *peştemal* (bath towel) wrapped tightly.

The Grand Bazaar's covered markets hum with the daily drama of İstanbul: merchants clamor for attention, old men shoulder impossible loads, and young boys run from stall to stall delivering hot cups of tea.

Çemberlitaş Hamamı. It's the most stunning bathhouse in Sultanahmet, built in 1584 and lavished with marble. Stay and soak as long as you like. A standard bath is $5, a bath with massage $10. *Vezirhan Cad. 8, off Divanyolu Cad. near Çemberlitaş Tramvay stop, tel. 212/522–79–74. Open daily 6 AM–midnight.*

Tarihi Galatasaray Hamamı. This Taksim bathhouse is difficult to find; look for it down an alley off İstiklâl Caddesi (on the right opposite Burger King), one block past the Galatasaray high school (big building with iron gates). Cost for men is $20, women $22. *Turnacıbaşı Sok. 24, tel. 212/244–14–12. Open daily 7 AM–11 PM.*

AFTER DARK

Taksim has a few first-run and rep cinemas; the most popular is the **Alkazar** (İstiklâl Cad. 179, tel. 212/293–24–66), which shows films like *A Clockwork Orange* along with the latest from Hollywood. Movies cost $4 and are usually in English with Turkish subtitles—be sure to ask, though, as the billboards don't say which films are dubbed. The last showings are generally around 9:30 PM.

BARS

In Sultanahmet, the only decent bar besides the Underground Cafe (Food, *above*) is on the roof of the **Orient Youth Hostel** (Where to Sleep, *above*), where Dutch and Kiwis spend their nights drinking $1 beers. Taksim has a better and brighter selection of bars, mostly along the small streets off İstiklâl Caddesi. Among them is **Büyük Parmakkapı Sokak,** with kebap shops, clothing stores, and two good watering holes: the slightly sophisticated **Hayal Kahvesi** (No. 19), with frequent live music and the best martinis in İstanbul; and the popular **Asparagas** (No. 30), a modern, sleek cellar-bar bathed in blue neon and decorated with funky wrought-iron fixtures. Higher on the bohemian scale is Taksim's **Café Guitar** (Ayhan Işık Sok. 11/1), also off İstiklâl Caddesi. Join the long-haired rockers drinking Efes Pilsen ($1.50) and playing darts until the live music kicks in.

MUSIC AND CLUBS

A good resource for clubs is *The Guide,* an English-language magazine available at newsstands for $2.50. The famed **Andromeda** (dial 212/246–01–68 for current location), an almost grotesque mix of lasers, lights, and faux-marble columns, is touted as Europe's largest disco. Like most İstanbul clubs, Andromeda spends winter in Taksim and summer in larger outdoor quarters on the Boğaziçi—at all times of the year, taxi drivers know where to find it. Numerous rock bars line **Siraselviler Caddesi,** off Taksim Meydanı. The emphasis here is on heavy metal.

NORTHWESTERN TURKEY

The northwestern corner of Turkey isn't the most popular region for foreign travelers. Aside from the Gallipoli peninsula, the scenery isn't very compelling: Mountains or other landmarks rarely break up the horizon of endless, plowed fields. **Bursa,** however, nearly matches İstanbul in charm, and lacks its overcrowding and air of desperation. Most travelers, though, head straight for the small port of **Çanakkale,** a good base for day trips to **Gallipoli** and **Troy.** The town of **Edirne,** near the Bulgarian border, makes a good stopover on a journey from Greece or Bulgaria to İstanbul.

BURSA

Bursa, nestled below the northern slopes of the Uludağ mountains, is the sort of city you might like to live in—but not one that's especially interesting to visit. It's blessed with mild weather (except in winter, when it's c-c-c-cold), fresh mountain-spring water, cobblestone streets that wind up into the hills, an active university population, and plenty of well-stocked shops. If İstanbul overwhelmed you, mellow out in Bursa for a day or two, hike in the **Uludağ,** visit a historic bath, and view some early Ottoman buildings.

BASICS
There's one **tourist booth** (open in summer only) at the otogar and another (tel. 224/221–23–59; open weekdays 9–5) about 50 yds east of the **PTT office** beneath Atatürk Caddesi, in the sunken plaza opposite the luxurious Kent Hotel. Both booths can recommend hotels, but neither has a good city map.

COMING AND GOING
The hectic **otogar** is 2 km (1 mi) north of Heykel; from the bus stands, walk inside the station, turn left and exit, then catch any bus (20¢) or dolmuş (30¢) marked HEYKEL and get off at the impossible-to-miss PTT office on Atatürk Caddesi. From the otogar there are hourly buses to İstanbul (4½ hrs, $6), Çanakkale (5 hrs, $8), Ankara (7 hrs, $9), and İzmir (6 hrs, $8). Express **ferries** from İstanbul (3 hrs, $4) arrive five times each weekday. Bursa's dock is at **Yalova,** a 45-minute dolmuş ride ($2) from Heykel.

GETTING AROUND
Heykel, at the center of town near the intersection of Atatürk Caddesi and İnönü Caddesi, is where you'll find the obligatory Atatürk equestrian statue (*heykel* means "statue"). The best landmark here is the PTT office, 200 yds west of the statue. Walking is the best way to get almost everywhere except the thermal baths in **Çekirge,** a well-to-do neighborhood 3 km (2 mi) west; from Heykel catch any bus or dolmuş marked ÇEKIRGE.

WHERE TO SLEEP
Avoid the cheap hotels near the otogar and head instead to Heykel, where you'll be closer to all the restaurants and sights. Facing the PTT office, walk right (west) and make the first left; dead-ahead is the frumpy but endearing **Lâl Otel** (Maksem Cad. 79, tel. 224/221–17–10; doubles $12; cash only), the most comfortable budget option in Heykel, even if some rooms don't have running water. Again facing PTT, walk west two blocks and turn left (at the Alçelik appliance store) for the somewhat upscale **Hotel Çamlıbel** (İnebey Cad. 71, tel. 224/221–25–65, fax 224/223–44–05; doubles $23; cash only). Its greatest feature is a 24-hour supply of hot water.

FOOD
Bursa, a great town for carnivores, is famous for its *iskender* kebaps (with spicy tomato sauce, butter, and yogurt) and its *İnegöl köftesi* (savory meat patties). Try both at shops along Atatürk Caddesi. For fresh produce, cheeses, and breads, wander through the immense **open-air market** immediately north of the Atatürk Caddesi tourist office. For a simple sit-down meal, try one of the restaurants along Ünlü

Caddesi in Heykel: **Kebapçı İskender** (No. 7, tel. 224/221–46–16; cash only) claims to be the original home of the iskender kebap, while food at the nearby **Hacı Bey** (Yılmaz İş Han 14C, tel. 224/221–64–40; cash only) more than makes up for its tacky café-style decor. Expect to pay about $2.50 at each for a main course, salad, and soft drink.

WORTH SEEING

In 1326 Bursa became the first Ottoman capital, and remained so until Edirne assumed the title in 1402. The first six Ottoman sultans are buried in Bursa, and the town contains a few preserved examples of early Ottoman architecture. Most notable is the yet-unfinished **Yeşil Camii** (Green Mosque; admission free), covered with blue and green İznik tiles. Next door, **Yeşil Türbe** (Green Tomb; admission free; open daily 8:30–noon and 1–5) contains the enormous green-tile sarcophagus of Mehmet I. From the statue of Atatürk, walk east across the riverbed and turn left at the traffic circle, which is graced by a large tree. Bursa's 14th-century **Bedesten** (Covered Bazaar), 400 yds northwest of the tourist office, was carefully restored after a massive earthquake flattened it in 1855. Here you can find *ipek* (silk cloth), and camel-skin puppets used as props in a comic theatrical form called *Karagöz,* named after a legendary clown from the 14th century. Bursa's most famous baths are in the neighborhood of Çekirge; try **Eski Kaplucaları** (Çekirge Cad.; open daily until 10 PM), a restored ancient bath next to the Kervansaray Termal Hotel. An afternoon soaking costs $6, a scrub and massage $18. Down the street from Otel Çamlıbel is the **İnebey Hamamı** (İnebey Cad. 44; open daily until 10:30 PM), a nontouristy spot that charges $4 for the basics, $10 for the works.

NEAR BURSA

To picnic or camp in the **Uludağ Mountains,** take any dolmuş from Heykel marked TELEFERI; you'll be dropped at the base of the cable car that leaves every 30–45 minutes for **Sarialan** (35 min, $6 round-trip), a crowded and littered park midway up the slope. You'll find pretty lakes and hiking trails nearby and mediocre skiing December–March. If you want to ski ($25 per day for equipment and passes), it's best to book in advance with a travel agent in Bursa (many have offices on Atatürk Caddesi).

CANAKKALE

The naval town of Çanakkale (pronounced tchah-KNACK-ka-lay) sits strategically on the southern coast of the Dardanelles straits, guarding a narrow passage that's been fought over for centuries—most notably during the 1915 Gallipoli campaign (Near Çanakkale, *below*). These days, once you get past the 2-km (1-mi) sweep of blocky high-rises, Çanakkale is little more than a carefree port town with plenty of pensions, bars, and waterfront restaurants. In summer, legions of tourists on their way to nearby Troy (plus all the Aussies, Kiwis, and Brits on pilgrimage to Gallipoli) pump life into the discos and souvenir shops. The rest of the year, "pleasantly sleepy" best describes Çanakkale.

BASICS

Change money at the 24-hour **PTT** (İnönü Cad., tel. 286/217–10–00) or access your PLUS- or Cirrus-linked account at the two 24-hour ATMs by the docks in the center of town. Only 20 yds from the ATMs is the helpful, map-dispensing **tourist booth** (Cumhuriyet Meydanı 67, tel. 286/217–11–87; open daily 8–5).

COMING AND GOING

Buses from Bursa (5 hrs, $8), İstanbul (5 hrs, $6.50), İzmir (6 hrs, $9), Ayvalık (3½ hrs, $6), and other towns arrive at the **otogar** on Atatürk Caddesi, about a 15-minute walk from the town center. Turn left out of the station and, at the first set of traffic lights, turn right onto busy Cumhuriyet Meydanı. You'll soon pass a monumental cannon, Anzac House, the tourist office, and the clock tower (on your left) before the road dead-ends at the docks. For the ferry to Eceabat (30¢, every 30 min) and the Gallipoli battlefields, hang a left at the dead end and continue for 30 yds.

WHERE TO SLEEP

Around April 25 (Anzac Day) and during mid-August (when the Troy Festival is held), reserve ahead. Most budget hotels are clustered in the streets surrounding the clock tower. The "in" choice is the newly remodeled **Anzac House** (Cumhuriyet Meydanı 61, tel. 286/217–01–56, fax 286/217–29–06; doubles $8 per person; cash only). The rooms are clean and comfortable and the water in the communal showers is hot. Another good choice is the **Yellow Rose Pension** (Yeni Sok. 5, tel. 286/217–33–43; doubles $6 per person; cash only); facing the clock tower, make your first left onto Kemal Yeri Sokak and turn right onto Yeni Sokak. If you want more privacy and peace, **Hotel Kervansaray** (Fetvane Sok. 13, tel. 286/217–69–64; doubles $6.50 per person; cash only) has high ceilings and a leafy garden—it was once a Turkish pasha's mansion. From the clock tower, bear left at the fork and walk one block.

FOOD

For fresh seafood on the waterfront try **Yalova Liman Restaurant** (Gümrük Sokak 7, tel. 286/217–10–45; cash only). Across the street from Hotel Kervansaray, **Gaziantep** (Kemalpaşa Mah. Fetvane Sok. 8, tel. 286/217–11–93; cash only) dishes out excellent iskender kebap and pide, costing under $3 for a meal. **Aussie and Kiwi Restaurant** (Yalı Cad. 32, tel. 286/212–17–22; cash only) is owned by Kemâl, a hospitable Turk who serves up mackerel and fried eggplant for less than $4, and is a great resource for travel information to boot.

WORTH SEEING

At the docks, turn left and walk 200 yds to **Cimenlik** castle, which houses the interesting naval museum **Askeri ve Deniz Müzesi** (tel. 286/217–17–07; closed Mon.). The grounds contain a large collection of artillery guns from the Gallipoli campaign, plus a replica of the mine-laying ship *Nusrat,* which single-handedly stopped the Allied flotilla by laying mines in the dead of night on March 15, 1915. The small **Archaeological Museum** (Atatürk Cad., tel. 286/217–32–52; admission $1.50; closed Mon.), 2 km (1 mi) south of the town center, has precious jewelry and gold laurel wreaths dating back to the 4th century BC. To get here, look for a dolmuş marked SEHIRICI by the cannon monument, or wave down a dolmuş marked KEPEZ along Atatürk Caddesi. If you have time, take a ferry to Eceabat and visit **Kilitbahir** (closed Mon.), the fortress opposite Cimenlik. Both were built by Fatih Sultan Mehmet in 1451 to control the passage of ships into İstanbul (*kilitbahir* means "padlock on the sea").

NEAR CANAKKALE

GALLIPOLI

The Gallipoli peninsula (called Gelibolu in Turkish) saw some of the World War I's fiercest, bloodiest fighting: Between them, the attacking Allies and defending Turks suffered a half-million casualties during the nine-month campaign in 1915. The plan was for the Allies to sweep through the area, establish a bridgehead, and knock Turkey out of the war by conquering Constantinople (modern İstanbul). But at the attack's outset, the marker that General George Hamilton's scouts had placed at **Brighton Beach** (an ideal landing point) was moved during the night by the Turks to **Anzac Cove,** a shallow beach with steep, steep cliffs. Tragically, Allied forces followed Hamilton's beacon and landed in full view of the Turks; more than 1,500 Allied soldiers were slaughtered on the first day alone. Lieutenant Colonel Mustafa Kemal (better known as Atatürk) led the Turkish force, telling his men: "I order you not just to fight, but to die." Aside from testifying to the idiocy of war, the area has hot, pebbly beaches and sweeping views of the Greek island **Samothráki** and Turkish **Gökçeada**.

COMING AND GOING • The peninsula is too large to see on your own, so either arrange a four-hour minibus tour ($8–$10 per person) through Anzac House or the Yellow Rose Pension (*see* Where to Sleep, *above*), or ask Kemâl at the Aussie and Kiwi Restaurant (*see* Food, *above*). He'll have a taxi meet you at the ferry in Eceabat, and you'll get a more intimate tour for $6–$8 per person.

TROY

If you come to Troy (Truva in Turkish) expecting to the great city of Homer's *Iliad,* you're bound to be disappointed by this small set of ruins. All that remains is the city wall's foundation and a small theater. In front of the archaeological site, a wooden Trojan horse appeases package tourists and gives the kids something to play on while adults look at the rubble. A short video in German and English covers the site's excavation, from the destructive treasure hunt of Heinrich Schliemann in 1871 to reverential dusting with toothbrushes by university students. As much damage as Schliemann did, his excavation was important: Previously, Troy was the only site in Homer's poems that archaeologists had been unable to locate, and the town was thought to exist in legend only. Dolmuş ($1.20) travel the 20 km (12 mi) to Troy from the cannon monument in the center of Çanakkale. *Tel. 286/283–10–61. Admission: $2. Open daily 8–5.*

EDIRNE

Edirne, home to the largest mosque outside Mecca, is incongruously also the world capital of the sport of *yağlı güreş* (grease wrestling). Even in summer, few Western tourists bother with this small, easy-to-navigate market town; it caters instead to Bulgarians and Romanians on shopping expeditions for clothes and electronics. Sadly, the historic market Semiz Ali Paşa Çarşısı has burned down and is now being rebuilt (but don't expect it to open before 1999). Remaining markets include **Arasta,** in front of Selimiye Camii, and **Bedesten,** in front of Eski Camii off Talatpaşa Caddesi. The market buildings are spectacular, but the merchandise within is cheap and poorly made.

Edirne's major mosque **Selimiye Camii,** designed by Mimar Sinan in 1569, has minarets 231 ft high and a dome that surpasses that of İstanbul's Hagia Sophia in diameter; it's easy to find 1 km (½ mi) east of Hürriyet Meydanı. Behind Selimiye Camii, the **Archaeological and Ethnographical Museum** and the **Turkish Islamic Art Museum** (both open Tues.–Sun. 9–5) store calligraphy, Greek artifacts, and photos on the history of grease wrestling. Each museum charges $1.50 admission. During Edirne's annual, four-day **Kırkpınar Festival,** held at the end of June or beginning of July, people pour into town to dance and listen to Gypsy music and watch—you guessed it—grease wrestling.

BASICS

Edirne's main street **Talat Paşa Caddesi** runs from the Tunca River east through town, crossing **Saraçlar Caddesi,** the biggest north–south street. There's a fountain and café in the central square **Hürriyet Meydanı,** near the intersection of the two streets. Also nearby is the small **tourist office** (Hürriyet Meydanı 17, tel. 284/225–15–18), with an annex at Talat Paşa Caddesi 76/A (tel. 284/213–92–08); both have maps and assist with hotels. Hours are Monday through Saturday 9–5.

The attack of the Light Horse regiment in the film "Gallipoli" took place at The Neck—a 65-ft stretch of land where, on August 15, 1915, more than 300 Australians were butchered in less than 30 minutes.

COMING AND GOING

Edirne lies on the major road and rail line from Istanbul to Bulgaria. Buses are the most efficient way to travel the 230 km (138 mi) east to İstanbul (4 hrs, $5); they leave from the **otogar,** 2 km (1 mi) southeast of town. Dolmuş (30¢) travel between the center and the otogar every 10 minutes during business hours. To reach the Bulgarian border, 18 km (11 mi) away, hop one of the buses that depart from behind Eski Camii and stop at Karaağac. From there it's a 3-km (2-mi) walk or $3 taxi ride to the border.

WHERE TO SLEEP

Açikgöz Otel (Tüfekçiler Çarşısı 74, tel. 284/213–19–44; doubles $10, cash only) has tidy rooms and a staff committed to TV-watching. From Saraçlar Caddesi, turn right on Balıkpazarı Caddesi, left on Tüfekçiler Çarşısı. **Saray Otel** (Eski İstanbul Cad. 28, tel. 284/212–14–57; doubles $11, cash only), left off Saraçlar Caddesi, is lit by neon and decorated in apple green.

AEGEAN COAST

During high season (July–August), travelers come here in droves to enjoy the sun and swim in the clear blue Aegean—but many are shocked to find out how overdeveloped and sleazy the resorts are, especially south of **İzmir,** the region's hub. If your plan is to day-trip from Greece to the Turkish port of **Kuşadası,** don't bother—it's an incredibly distasteful and crowded resort. You're better off in **Ayvalık,** which is a short (but expensive—$70 round-trip) ferry ride from Lésvos. No matter where you go, though, you're bound to encounter party-minded hordes in summer. On the plus side, in addition to great beaches the Aegean Coast has some of the country's most famous archaeological sites, notably **Ephesus** and **Pergamon.**

AYVALIK

The town of Ayvalık comes as a great relief if you're traveling south from İstanbul. Entering it, you see a tidy waterfront resort fit for a tourist brochure, with strolling crowds, ice cream stands, and expensive seafood restaurants. Head for the streets immediately behind the waterfront, however, and you're in a different Ayvalık: genuinely friendly locals, colorful Ottoman houses, and a maze of cobbled lanes winding uphill to olive groves and pine forests overlooking the Greek island of Lésvos. The best view is from **Sıeytan Sofrası** (Satan's Table), a point high on the rocks south of the town center (take a dolmuş there for 25¢). Besides walking the streets and the waterfront, there's not much to do here—except maybe to take a 30¢ ferry to **Alibey Adası** (Cunda Island), home to a small fishing community of Greek descent.

BASICS

The town's **tourist office** (Yat Limanı Karşısı, tel. 266/312–21–22; open daily 9–noon and 1–5) is on the waterfront 2 km (1 mi) south of the main square—a serious inconvenience. Banks and ATMs crowd the central square near the statue of Atatürk.

COMING AND GOING

If you're unlucky, İzmir- and İstanbul-bound buses will drop you at a gas station 5 km (3 mi) from Ayvalık. Any taxis that swing by will charge $6 to reach the main square, or you can hitchhike. Slightly more convenient is the **otogar**, 2 km (1 mi) north of town. Either walk due south on İnönü Caddesi, or buy a 35¢ ticket at the station and catch any city bus marked AYVALIK BELEDIYESI. The otogar offers buses to Çanakkale (3½ hrs, $6), İzmir (2 hrs, $3), and Bursa (5½ hrs, $8). Going to Bergama (1½ hrs, $1.50) is easier since minibuses stop hourly in front of **Barbaros Çay Bahçesi**, a waterfront teahouse 300 yds south of Ayvalık's main square. Ferries to Lésvos are expensive (2 hrs, $30 one-way) and, to make matters worse, they usually don't sail unless enough passengers show up. When they do operate, **Yeni Shipping Agency** (Talatpaşa Cad. Gümrük Meydanı 9, tel. 266/312–61–23) has service Tuesday, Thursday, and Saturday from mid-April to October. Port tax is about $14.

WHERE TO SLEEP

Prices nearly double July–early September, but bargains are available at other times of year. A popular spot for budget travelers is **Kıyı Motel** (Gümrük Meydanı, tel. 266/312–66–77; doubles $16, cash only), a short walk from the Atatürk statue: Facing the water, walk right (north) one block and make the first left onto Talat Paşa Caddesi. Immediately opposite is the somewhat upscale **Hotel Ayvalık Palace** (Gümrük Meydanı, tel. 266/312–10–64, fax 266/312–10–46; doubles $23, breakfast included; cash only).

FOOD

Tiny restaurants and *birahanesi* (pubs) fill the Teneke Kalayı (Tinmaker's Alley) district, one block east of İnönü Caddesi. You'll also find fresh bread and produce. **Arkadaşımın Yeri** (Helvacılar Sok., tel. 266/312–75–88; cash only) has a full selection of meze ($1) and a side room done up in the old Turkish fashion. Nearby, **Avçılar Birahanesi** (Gümrük Cad. 3, no phone; cash only) has pungent köfte (meat patties) and, for the bold, *deniz karadikan* (sea urchin meze). Each costs under $1 apiece.

BERGAMA (PERGAMON)

During the 4th century BC, the ancient city of Pergamon was a base for Lysimachus, a general under Alexander the Great. At the time, the town was a trade center and home to many artists, but it fell into ruin after a Goth invasion in AD 262 and wasn't rediscovered until 1873, when German engineer Karl Humann carted its well-preserved Altar of Zeus back to Berlin. These days, in addition to extensive remains (which rival the more famous ones of Ephesus), you'll find some attractive old neighborhoods with blue and white houses, reminders that a Greek community flourished here until 1923, when it was expelled from Anatolia during the creation of the Turkish Republic.

BASICS

The **tourist office** (İzmir Cad. 54, tel. 232/633–18–62 has simple maps and sometimes arranges transportation to the Acropolis. The office, open daily until 7 in summer, is in the modern building 50 yds right (north) of the Arkeoloji Müzesi.

COMING AND GOING

Buses arrive at the **otogar** (İzmir Cad., in town center) from İstanbul (6 hrs, $10), İzmir (2 hrs, $2), and Ayvalık (1½ hrs, $1.50). The main road changes names every 300 yds or so: At the otogar it's called **İzmir Caddesi**, then **Bankalar Caddesi**, and finally **Istiklâl Caddesi** as it zigzags its way up to the Acropolis. Since taxi drivers extort $10 round-trip to drive you to the ruins, it's worth making the 4-km (2½-mi) trek on foot: Follow the multinamed main road north and look for the yellow traffic signs marked AKROPOL. To get to the Asclepion, either walk along the twisting narrow streets behind the Arkeoloji Müzesi and up a steep incline, or follow the main road 1½ km (¾ mi) south of the otogar and turn right at the well-sign-posted turnoff (from which it's another 1 km/½ mi to the site). The former route takes about 35 minutes but is more scenic than the latter.

WHERE TO SLEEP

There are plenty of budget hotels near the otogar, but the pensions in the secluded old town at the foot of the Acropolis are quieter and more winsome. The best of the bunch is **Nike Pension** (Talat Paşa Mah., Tabak Köprü Çıkmazı 2, tel. 232/633–39–01; $5.50 per person; cash only), with well-kept rooms and free homemade maps of the Acropolis, complete with easy-to-follow directions. However, if convenience is key, turn left (south) out of the otogar, cross to the far side of İzmir Caddesi, and within 200 yds you'll pass a pair of pensions: **Sayin Pension** (No. 32, tel. 232/633–24–05) and **Pension Gobi** (No. 26, tel. 232/633–25–18). Both charge $5–$7 for doubles, cash only; the Sayin is preferable.

FOOD

Expensive restaurants along the main road are used to dealing with (and conning) tourists; check your bill carefully. The best is **Meydan Restaurant** (İstiklâl Meydanı 4, tel. 232/633–17–93; cash only), where you can feast on stuffed bell peppers, rice, eggplant salad, and beer for $3. The adventurous may gorge on *ciğer sarma* (sheep's liver, raisins, and rice stuffed into pastry shell) at **Sen Kardeşler Lokantası** (Bankalar Cad. 105, tel. 232/633–11–14; cash only).

WORTH SEEING

The **Arkeoloji Müzesi** (İzmir Cad., between otogar and tourist office; admission $2.50; open Tues.–Sun. 9–5:30) has a variety of jewelry, swords, old costumes, ornate rifles, and a fine bust of Zeus. The dramatic **Kızıl Avlu** (Red Basilica; admission $1.50; open daily until 7 PM), built as a pagan temple and later dedicated to St. John, is famous for being referred to in the Book of Revelations as the throne of the devil; the basilica is located at the intersection of the river and İzmir Caddesi.

The ancient health spa **Asclepion** attracted moneyed Greeks in search of a hedonistic holiday. Much of the medical treatment at the Asclepion consisted of dream analysis, but patients would also be instructed to run barefoot, eat particular foods, take mud baths, or soak in mineral waters to cure their ills. These days you enter the site from the **Sacred Way,** a sunken street overgrown with grass. Nearby, the **Temple of Telesphorus** is linked by an underground corridor to the **Sacred Spring.** What were once mud baths are now algae-covered pits, home to a group of turtles. Above the ancient theater, a shaded walkway offers a view of the site and the surrounding hills. Unfortunately, the site is near military buildings, and the original theater is being converted into a modern concert arena due to reopen in 1998. *Admission: $2.50. Open daily 8:30–5:30.*

The **Acropolis,** the windswept home of the ancient kings of Pergamon, looms majestically upon the mountain above the town. Most of the **Altar of Zeus,** the site's main attraction, was carted to Germany during the 19th century, but the chalky white pillars remain, overlooking a **theater** dug into the hill—one of the finest sights this side of Ephesus. It's a long walk up here, but definitely worth it. *Admission: $1.50. Open daily 9–6.*

İZMIR

İzmir, Turkey's third-largest city, is a congested urban sprawl—characterless buildings dominate the business district, and blocks of concrete apartments seem to extend as far as the eye can see. The waterfront here is industrial and bland, but don't write off İzmir just yet: Its stunning bazaar is alone worth the trip. And, if you climb the hills, you'll find twisting alleyways and older houses hugging **Mt. Pagos,** where each turn reveals scenes of children constructing kites out of newspaper and old men settled comfortably with their water pipes, as the inevitable call to prayer rings across the city.

BASICS

Of the four **tourist offices,** the one by the clock tower in Konak (tel. 232/482–11–70; open weekdays 9–6) is most central. There's another branch on Gaziosmanpaşa Bulvarı (tel. 232/484–21–47; open daily 9–6), near Cumhuriyet Meydanı. There's also a small, clearly marked information booth at the otogar.

COMING AND GOING

If possible, arrive in İzmir by train—you'll have an easier time getting your bearings from **Basmane train station,** just south of the Kültürparkı. From here there's daily service to Ankara (16 hrs, $8) and İstanbul

(10 hrs, $6). The main **otogar,** a confusing 4 km (2½ mi) from the center, has service to Ankara (9 hrs, $8), İstanbul (9 hrs, $9), Bergama (2 hrs, $2), and Selçuk (2 hrs, $2.50). Another option is the overnight **ferry** to İstanbul (19 hrs, $11), which leaves Sunday at 2 PM, arriving in İstanbul at 9 AM. Show up two hours prior to departure at Feribot İskelesi in the Alsancak District; a taxi from Basmane costs $4–$5.

GETTING AROUND

İzmir's byzantine layout bewilders the best minds; study a city map before you set out. From Basmane station, walk west down **Fevzi Paşa Bulvarı;** the first 1½ km (¾ mi) will take you past streets (on your left) that funnel into the bazaar and, about 1 km (½ mi) farther, the road dead-ends at **27 Mayıs Meydanı,** a traffic circle just a stone's throw from the waterfront. From here veer left and continue straight, toward the neighborhood of **Konak,** with its clock tower and tourist office. If you've arrived in town at the otogar, walk past the tourist booth, turn right at the busy street, buy a 30¢ ticket, and catch Bus 51 toward Basmane. After a few minutes you'll pass Alsancak train station; wait another 5–10 minutes and get off at the traffic circle **9 Eylül Meydanı** (look for the Kâmil Koç bus office to your left, the massive facade of the "IEF" Kültürpark to your right). From 9 Eylül Meydanı, walk one block south along **Anafartalar Caddesi** and you'll pass Basmane station. Or, you can save yourself some trouble by taking a taxi ($2.50) from the otogar directly to Basmane station.

WHERE TO SLEEP

Just west of Basmane station, hundreds of near-identical hotels charge $2–$6 per person for noisy, often bedraggled rooms. **Otel Saray** (Anafartalar Cad. 635, tel. 232/483–69–46; $7 per person; cash only) is one of the friendliest places in the area and has clean, quiet rooms that open onto an inner courtyard. From Basmane station, walk left (south) down Anafartalar Caddesi and follow it when it turns 90° to the right (two blocks past the mosque). A big step up, the **Hotel Baylan** (1299 Sok. 8, tel. 232/483–14–26, fax 232/483–38–44; doubles from $40; cash only) offers rooms loaded with all the amenities and absolutely worth the expense. From Basmane station, walk left (south) 1½ blocks and turn right on 1299 Sokak (this hard-to-find side street is directly across from the mosque).

FOOD

The cheapest eateries lie near the budget hotels: Take your pick along Anafartalar Caddesi and Fevzi Paşa Bulvarı. The smell of frying fish will lead you to **Güneş Lokantası** (Anafartalar Cad. 769, tel. 232/421–05–02; cash only), with fried sardines smothered in lemon and onions for 80¢. Don't leave İzmir without having at least one meal in the massive **bazaar;** let your nose be your guide, as you'll quickly become lost in its twisting passageways. Choose a place that looks busy, clean, and stocked with fresh fixings, and you can't go wrong.

WORTH SEEING

İzmir, formerly known as Smyrna, is believed by some to have been home to the epic poet Homer in about 850 BC. Some centuries later, Alexander the Great left a permanent mark on the city: He dreamed that he should build a fortress here, and with the oracle of Apollo at Claros chiming in agreement he constructed **Kadifekale** (the Velvet Fortress) on the flat top of Mt. Pagos, on the southern edge of the city. Only the western and southern walls remain, but the fortress's view of the Aegean and Khíos and Lésvos is spectacular. Take a 30¢ dolmuş here from Basmane or, better yet, splash out on a $3 taxi.

As foreign merchants and foreign ideas began to flow through İzmir during the 1500s, the port became known as the City of the Infidel. İzmir is still a center for merchants, as witnessed by its renowned and perplexing **bazaar. Anafartalar Caddesi,** with the most important stores and all of the banks, curves along the area's southern edge to **Konak** and its clock tower. From the tower, head left (south) along the grassy gardens and veer left when you hit the first big traffic circle; about 200 yds ahead in Turgutreis Parkı is the mediocre **Arkeoloji Müzesi** (Konak Birlişmiş Milletler Cad., tel. 232/484–83–24; open Tues.–Sun. 8:30–5:30), with a colossal statue of the emperor Domitian. Adjoining it is the **Etnoğrafya Müzesi,** with quirky displays on folk arts and daily life. Admission to each is $2.50.

SELCUK

As tourist towns go, Selçuk is better than average, with a splendid natural setting (it's surrounded by mountains) and a hilltop castle to explore. And the town makes a perfect base for visiting Pamukkale and Ephesus (Near Selçuk, *below*); however, Selçuk also has a few of its own great ancient sites, an intriguing Ephesus-related museum, and the easy-to-miss remains of the **Temple of Artemis,** one of the Seven Wonders of the Ancient World. Great beaches are a short dolmuş ride away.

BASICS

The **tourist office** (Agora Çarşısı 35, tel. 232/892–63–28; open May–Sept., daily 8:30–5), on the corner of Atatürk Caddesi, doles out maps and Ephesus brochures.

COMING AND GOING

Highway E24 divides the small market town. On the east side are the otogar, train station, and bazaar. From the **otogar,** catch a bus to Kuşadası (20 min, 80¢), İzmir (2 hrs, $2.50), or Bodrum (2½ hrs, $3), or a dolmuş to Efes (Ephesus; 10 min, 75¢). To reach the tourist office, walk right (west) out of the otogar, cross busy Atatürk Caddesi, and continue 20 yds. The **train station** is 1 km (½ mi) northeast, on the edge of Selçuk's *centrum* (business center). Walk left (south) out of the station and turn right when you feel like it; Atatürk Caddesi is 100 yds ahead (turn left for the tourist office). All trains stop first in İzmir (1½ hrs, $1.50), where you can make onward connections.

WHERE TO SLEEP

Selçuk has more than 50 pensions, and competition is fierce: You'll undoubtedly be greeted at the otogar with "Hello, my friend, where are you staying? . . ." Ask if hot water is available and don't pay more than $5–$6 per person. If you'd rather find your own accommodations, cross Atatürk Caddesi, walk through the pretty park, and continue 20 yds to **Pansiyon Kirhan** (1045 Sok. 28, tel. 232/892–22–57; doubles $12, cash only), which has a swell patio overlooking the town. Or walk the other direction and follow the weathered signs for **Homeros Pension** (Asmali Sok. 17, tel. 232/892–39–95; $6 per person, cash only), which has a carpeted, covered rooftop—a great place to enjoy the breeze on hot afternoons.

FOOD

The shaded restaurants in the park across from the otogar are refreshing on a hot afternoon. But the real action takes place in the four-block-long **centrum,** loaded with dozens of bars, pide stands, and sit-down eateries. From the otogar, walk north on Atatürk Caddesi and turn right when you the shop-lined streets; **Seiburg Caddesi** is a good place to start hunting. At the centrum's north end, **Namik Kemal Caddesi** is equally packed with places, notably **Ephesus Restaurant** (No. 26, tel. 232/892–32–67; cash only), which delivers a fine rendition of moussaka ($1.75) and a salad made with yogurt with carrots. For fresh fruits and vegetables, hit the **bazaar** directly behind the otogar. On Sunday, hundreds of farmers descend upon Selçuk and set up stands due south of the otogar.

WORTH SEEING

Penis pendants hung on wires get giggles from Japanese tourists at the **Ephesus Museum** (Agora Çarşısı, no phone; admission $2; open daily 8:30–6:30), directly behind the tourist office. A famous Priapus statue (which gets star billing on Turkish postcards) is a disappointing few inches high, but two interesting statues of Artemis are decorated with eggs (or breasts, or testicles, depending on your interpretation). Just south of the otogar, **St. John's Basilica** (St. Jean Sok.; admission $2; open daily 8–5), where St. John is said to be buried, is also well worth a peek. The barrel-vaulted roof collapsed long ago, but a few walls have been heaved back into place. The adjacent mosque, **İsa Bey Camii** (St. Jean Sok.; open daily 9–5), is an architectural hodgepodge, built of marble blocks with Latin inscriptions, chunks of the altar from the Temple of Artemis, and black granite columns from Ephesus.

NEAR SELCUK

EFES (EPHESUS)

This ancient city, built on a bay where the Küçük Menderes River once met the sea, is the most visited place in Turkey after İstanbul. The first settlers were the Ionians, who came during the 11th century BC. Like most Ionian cities in Asia Minor, Ephesus later became a Roman city and eventually a Christian one. It remained an important commercial center even after the river silted up and cut off direct access to the sea. Local tradition claims that St. John, St. Paul, and the Virgin Mary all set up camp here and left behind churches and tombs that attest to their presence (although the historical record only verifies that of St. Paul, who preached against the Cult of Artemis during his AD 51–52 sojourn here). Despite the crowds of tourists, Ephesus is amazing, and it's worth buying a guidebook ($5) to learn about its intricate history. A hint: Try to arrive early in the day or as the sun sets, when the stone turns pink and the crowds thin out. To get here, either take a dolmuş (10 min, 75¢) from Selçuk's otogar or walk 3½ km

(2¼ mi) from town along the dusty, well-signposted road. *Admission: $3.50. Open May–Sept., daily 8–6; Oct.–Apr., daily 8–5:30.*

PAMUKKALE

No doubt about it—the landlocked cliffs at Pamukkale (Cotton Castle) are unique. What looks like a landslide from far away and like powdery snow close up is actually solidified calcite, blooming from natural terraces that rise 330 ft above the plain. The cliffs were formed when a calcium-rich spring flowed downhill and then evaporated. You can still sit under a small waterfall that runs over the cliffs, or wade knee-deep through milky pools. Pamukkale's beauty, unfortunately, has recently been marred by development and the cliffs are eroding under tourists' feet. Air pollution and overuse by tourists has also turned some of the terraces a dirty brown. Most people leave slightly disappointed, especially if they got their first impression from a glossy tourist brochure.

The **museum** (tel. 258/272–20–34; admission $1.50; closed Mon.) at the top of the cliffs houses a meager collection of finds from **Hierapolis** (admission $4), the archaeological site just behind the museum. Hierapolis was a Roman spa where the rich bathed in mineral waters, thought to cure various ailments. The ruins of this vast ancient city are definitely worth a look, but the waters, instead of flowing freely over the cliff, are now channeled into swimming pools belonging to the overpriced cliff-top resort hotels. The well-marked **tourist office** (near museum, tel. 258/272–20–77) gives out a useless map and brochure showing you what the place must have looked like before it became so touristed.

COMING AND GOING • Pamukkale may be easy to navigate, but it is not easy to reach. First you must take a bus to Denizli from Selçuk (3 hrs, $5) or Antalya (5 hrs, $8). From Denizli, about 12 km (7 mi) from Pamukkale, it's a 30-minute, $1.20 dolmuş ride to Pamukkale Köyü (the village at the bottom of the cliffs) or the cliff-top resorts.

WHERE TO SLEEP • All of the affordable accommodations, most charging $5–$6 per person, are in the village at the bottom of the cliffs. **Arkadaş Pansiyon** (at top of main road, tel. 258/272–21–83; $5 per person, cash only) has a central fountain and comfortable rooms with bath. Farther down the street, **Motel Mustafa** (tel. 258/272–22–40; $6 per person, cash only) throws in a swimming pool—an important amenity in hot Pamukkale—for an extra $1 a night.

BODRUM

Bodrum, known as Halicarnassus in antiquity, is Turkey's most exclusive and expensive Aegean resort. Though filled with the usual resort shops and discos, the town itself is undeniably gorgeous; a building code ensures that hotels don't rise over a few stories and that all are coated in the same shade of white paint, blindingly bright in midday sunshine. But physical beauty notwithstanding, there's not much here for the budget traveler. Spend a few hours in the Crusader castle and its museum, take 10 minutes at the mausoleum, enjoy a tea on the waterfront, and you'll be done. Bodrum is so pretty that it's a shame there's so little to do—in fact, many people come simply to catch a ferry to the Greek island of **Kos.**

BASICS

The **tourist office** (next to castle on waterfront, tel. 252/316–10–91; open May–Sept., daily 8–7:30) has a town map and a list of hotels. The 24-hour **PTT** (tel. 252/316–15–60) is on Cevat Şakir Caddesi.

COMING AND GOING

The **otogar** on Cevat Şakir Caddesi, Bodrum's main road, has frequent connections to Selçuk (2½ hrs, $4), Marmaris (3 hrs, $3.50), and Fethiye (5 hrs, $7). Dolmuş leave from the otogar and pick up passengers along the road to Bodrum's peninsula resorts. To reach town from the station, walk 400 yds south down Cevat Şakir Caddesi; you'll pass the PTT and then end at the waterfront. You can book a ferry to the Greek island of Kos from the agency next to the tourist office. Ferries leave May–September, daily at 9 AM; October–April, departures are every Monday, Wednesday, and Friday. The cost is $13 one-way, $20 round-trip, plus $8–$10 for port taxes. For more information dial 252/316–10–86.

WHERE TO SLEEP

The most convenient options are on **Türkkuyusu Caddesi**: From the otogar, walk south down Cevat Şakir Caddesi and make a 180° right turn at the mosque near the water. Of the pensions along Türkkuyusu Caddesi, **Sevin Pension** (No. 11, tel. 252/316–83–61; doubles $11, cash only) wins praise for its comfort and cleanliness. Another option is to walk south down Cevat Şakir Caddesi from the otogar and turn left just before the PTT onto **Atatürk Caddesi.** The best choices here are **Elvan Pansiyon** (No. 24, tel. 252/316–24–90; doubles $15, cash only) and, just uphill from the Elvan, **Dilek Pension** (No. 32, tel. 252/316–38–91; doubles $15, cash only).

FOOD

Local produce is pricey, restaurants even worse. The kebap house behind the otogar, **Hilal Restaurant** (Ali Aydınlıoğlu İshanı, Kölçü Sok., Yokuşbaşı, tel. 252/316–57–90; cash only) is an exception, with excellent pizza or kebaps for $1.50. In town, you're better off scouting the shop-lined streets 200 yds east of the castle, where you'll find no fewer than 50 restaurants and overpriced bars. A good bet here is the 24-hour **Pizzeria Vivaldi** (Dr. Alim Ekinci Cad. 33, tel. 252/316–71–79; cash only), which serves vegetarian pizza for $2.50.

WORTH SEEING

Bodrum (the name means "dungeon") is most famous for its Crusader-era **St. Peter Castle,** built around AD 1410 by the Knights of St. John of Jerusalem (who were subsequently expelled by the Ottomans in the 1430s). The **Glass Wreck Hall** (open Tues.–Fri. 10–11 and 2–4) of the castle's excellent **Underwater Archaeology Museum** displays the oldest shipwreck ever recovered as well as treasures from Ionian, Greek, and Roman ships that foundered off the Aegean Coast. The castle also has an extensive display of *amphorae* (elongated clay vessels for storing wine and other ancient treasures). And be sure to check out the **English Tower,** where you can relax with a glass of wine while listening to recorded medieval chants. *Tel. 252/316–10–95. Admission: $3. Castle open Tues.–Sun. 8–noon and 1–5.*

On the other side of the harbor on Turgutreis Caddesi lies the **Tomb of Mausolus,** one of the Seven Wonders of the Ancient World, but these days just a pile of rubble hardly worth the $2.50 admission.

MEDITERRANEAN COAST

Stretching 1,025 km (615 mi) from the resort town of **Marmaris** in the west to the Syrian border in the east, the Mediterranean Coast has some of Turkey's best beaches and is an easy ferry ride from Greece. You won't find as many slick, sleazy resorts here as on the Aegean, but this is by no means uncharted tourist territory, especially in the west. **Fethiye** and **Kaş** are developed vacation towns, used primarily as bases from which to explore nearby beaches. Avoid **Alanya,** a singularly unappealing resort overrun by German package tourists.

FETHIYE

Fethiye is too large to be quaint, too small to be overdeveloped. It has a large harbor and plenty of snazzy yachts with foreign registries, not to mention discos that throb into the wee hours every single summer night (bring ear plugs). On the other hand, the waterfront setting is stunning, its Lycian tombs (carved into the cliffs above town) are mesmerizing, and there are plenty of locals simply going about their business in the tiny shops and bazaars of the **Pasbatur** (old town). It's definitely a two-day town, especially if one of those days is spent sailing to the islands and beaches offshore. Just walk down to the harbor by 8:30 or 9 AM, hand over $11–$14 to any of the waiting boats, and you'll return to Fethiye by 5 or 6 PM—just in time to hit the bars or join the locals promenading along the harbor at sunset.

BASICS

The waterfront **tourist office** (İskele Meydanı 1, tel. 252/614–15–27; open daily 8–5:30) distributes an excellent map and a comprehensive hotel list. Facing the water, the office is left (south) next to the Otel Dedeoğlu. The 24-hour **PTT** (tel. 252/614–24–64) is on Atatürk Caddesi, between town and the otogar.

COMING AND GOING

The **otogar** is 1½ km (¾ mi) from Fethiye's waterfront. Turn left out of the station and left again at the traffic circle. This will put you on **Atatürk Caddesi,** the main drag—and 400 yds farther you want to veer right at the fork in the road (veer left and you'll pass the **dolmuş station** before landing at the waterfront).

You're going in the right direction (i.e., following Atatürk Caddesi) if you pass the museum and the PTT office. Or, just catch a dolmuş (30¢) across the street from the otogar's main driveway and get off at the water. From Fethiye there are frequent buses to Kaş (2 hrs, $2.50), Antalya (7 hrs, $8), and Ankara (10 hrs, $12.50).

WHERE TO SLEEP

The cheapest places are right in town: Walking down Atatürk Caddesi from the otogar, turn left at the Hotel Plaza and continue straight for 3½ blocks. You'll signs for both **Öztürk Pansiyon** (Çarşısı Cad., Deppoy Sok. 16, tel. 252/614–14–18; cash only) and, a few twisting alleys away, **Ülgen Pension** (Mevkii Merdiven 3, tel. 252/614–34–91; cash only). Both charge $5–$6 per person for clean, standard doubles. **Hotel Plaza** (Atatürk Cad. 2, tel. 252/614–90–31), opposite the Atatürk statue, is a step up in comfort, with air conditioning and 24-hour hot water. Doubles from $25.

FOOD

The cheapest restaurants are on Atatürk Caddesi and its side streets. On **Çarşı Caddesi,** two blocks inland and parallel to Atatürk Caddesi, there are plenty of pizzerias and fancy sit-down restaurants. **Meğri Lokantası** (Çarşı Cad. 13/A, tel 252/614-4047) serves simple Turkish food and has a selection of vegetarian dishes. Expect to pay about $3 for a main course and salad. One block farther inland is **Karagözler Caddesi,** home to the **Ottoman Cafe** (No. 3, tel. 252/612–11–48), where you can sip wine ($1.20 per glass) or tea, groove to Whirling Dervish music, and toke on your very own water pipe ($3.50). On the waterfront, popular **Pizza 74** (İskele Meydanı, tel. 252/614–18–69) has a variety of appetizers and delicious goulash ($3). Put away your plastic; none of these joints take credit cards.

WORTH SEEING

Besides strolling the waterfront and taking a boat trip to nearby islands, the main attraction is the **Tomb of Amyntas** (open daily 8–6:30; admission $1.25), a 4th-century BC tomb carved into the cliffs above town. It looks most impressive from a distance; up close erosion and graffiti almost ruin the effect. Still, it's a popular place to watch the sun dip below the mountains. From town, walk east on Atatürk Caddesi toward the otogar and follow the yellow road signs; all told it's a 25-minute walk, the last section up a steep hill. On the way back, turn east (right) on Atatürk Caddesi and walk two blocks toward the otogar. You can't miss the yellow signs leading to the **Fethiye Museum** (Atatürk Cad., tel. 252/614–41–50; open Tues.–Sun. 8–noon and 1–5, admission $2), full of artifacts found in the region. The main attractions are a trilingual inscription (in Lycian, Persian, and Greek) on a block of stone dating from the 4th century BC, and a beautifully carved church door.

NEAR FETHIYE

KAYAKOY

In 1923, the 3,000 Greek residents of Kayaköy were (forcibly) repatriated to Greece following Atatürk's creation of the Turkish Republic. They left behind more than 2,000 perfectly preserved stone houses, inhabited today by a handful of Turkish farmers. Pack your camera, a bottle of water, and go to the dolmuş station in Fethiye; it's an 8-km (5-mi), 50¢ ride. You can also walk: The Kayaköy road intersects Atatürk Caddesi near the museum, but you can only the sign coming from the otogar into town. Make a day of it and follow the rural, three-hour trail from Kayaköy to Ölüdeniz, and then catch a dolmuş back to Fethiye.

OLUDENIZ

In the last six years, this once-secluded lagoon—with a pebbly 2½-km- (1¼-mi-) long beach and great swimming—has been ruthlessly developed with hotels and holiday villages. Many remain half-built, waiting for some German or British tour group that will never show up. Still, Ölüdeniz's beach is unabashedly beautiful and worth the trip, especially if you crave nothing more than a day splashing in the warm, clear Mediterranean. A dolmuş from the station in Fethiye (75¢) takes 25 minutes. When you reach the water, head west (right) for the lagoon, the rope swing, and **Bambus Kamp** (near Motel Meri Önü, no phone; cash only), which has comfortable bungalows for $7 per person. If they're full, pitch a tent next door at **Genç Camping** ($3 per person, cash only). A raucous assortment of travelers and Turks congregate nightly at Genç's **Rucksnack Bar** for $1 beers.

KAS

This tiny Mediterranean town may have sacrificed itself to tourism, but it's still exceptionally lovely. Kaş's harbor is a knockout, fronted by narrow cobblestone streets that snake up into the rocky hills. Summer evenings in Kaş are warm and breezy, and you can linger late into the evening at waterfront restaurants, gazing across the bay at the Greek island of Kastellorizo. There are no major sights here, except perhaps for the Lycian **rock tombs,** a short walk northeast of the PTT, and, on the opposite side of town about 1 km (½ mi) west of the main square, a restored 6th-century BC **theater,** the last remnant of the ancient town of Antiphellos. Otherwise, visitors to Kaş spend their days lounging in the sun and browsing for trinkets in tiny shops. Another option is an eight-hour boat trip to **Kekova** (an untouristed village), with stops at **Üçağız** (an even smaller untouristed village) and at ancient ruins now submerged under the sea. Walk down to the harbor by 10 AM and pay one of the waiting boat captains $10–$14 (lunch costs $2–$3 extra) to take you out to Kekova.

BASICS

The **tourist office** (Cumhuriyet Meydanı 5, tel. 242/836–12–38; open Mon.–Sat. 9–5) is conveniently situated on the main square, overlooking the harbor. The **PTT** (Cukurbağli Cad., tel. 242/836–14–30; open daily 8:30–5:30) is a few blocks north along Sube Caddesi.

COMING AND GOING

The **otogar** is a five-minute walk northwest from the center of town; turn right out of the station, follow Cukurbağli Caddesi downhill, and turn left at the harbor to reach the main square. From the otogar, buses run to Fethiye (2 hrs, $2.50) and Antalya (4 hrs, $5).

WHERE TO SLEEP

Kaş is packed with pensions; the standard rate is $7–$9 per person. Many are clustered around the otogar (you'll pass a few on the short walk to the harbor) and in the whitewashed buildings east of the main square. For the latter, follow the road that snakes east (left) along the harbor until it starts climbing. Pick and choose among the dozens of pensions and hotels, or walk another 80 yds and turn left up the steep steps that lead to **Hotel Kayahan** (Küçük Çakil Meyvkii, tel. 242/836–13–13; doubles $25; cash only), a clean, well-furnished place with a friendly staff. Back at the main square, walk five minutes west (right) for **Otel Andifli** (Hastane Cad., tel. 242/836–10–42; doubles $15; cash only), which has a stellar sea view. Just beyond the Antiphellos theater along the sea, **Kaş Camping** (tel. 242/836–10–50; $7 per person, $15 double in a bungalow; cash only) has a rock platform for sunbathing and an on-site bar.

FOOD

Chief among Kaş's dining gems is **Smiley's Restaurant** (Gürkoy Sok., tel. 242/836–28–12; cash only), in the alley behind the tourist office. It offers two tasty meze, garlic pide, and an entrée all for $4. For cheaper meals try the three adjacent, self-service restaurants in the **bazaar** two blocks north of the harbor; at **Babani Yeri,** a large plate of lentils, meat, potatoes, and salad costs $3.

ANTALYA

Antalya is a vast city of 250,000, and on its outskirts dirty beaches and grim, low-income apartments line the coast for miles. But attractive **Kaleiçi,** the historic harbor district, makes up for the city's blight. It's packed with restored Ottoman houses, cramped shops, and shady courtyards that double as bars and teahouses. Antalya is exceedingly popular with older Europeans and Israelis, who contribute to the beastly crowds here in July and August. One last caveat: Skip the boat trips from Antalya. The going rate is $15–$20 per person for a mediocre three-hour ride.

BASICS

The main **tourist office** (Cumhuriyet Cad., tel. 242/241–17–47; open daily 8–6) is next to the Turkish Airlines office; facing the clock tower and Fluted Minaret, walk west (right) on Cumhuriyet Caddesi for 500 yds. More convenient (but harder to find) is **Kaleiçi Tourist Information** (Selçuk Mah., Mermerli Sok., tel. 242/247–50–42; open Mon.–Sat. 9–5), in the heart of Kaleiçi by the Hotel Aspen. A 24-hour **PTT** is near Kalekapısı Square; head west about 500 yds on Cumhuriyet Caddesi, then right on Anafartalar Caddesi.

COMING AND GOING

The **otogar** is 1 km (½ mi) north of Kaleiçi; turn left out of the station onto busy **Kazım Özalp Caddesi** and walk straight ahead. Along the way it becomes a pedestrian-only shopping street before dead-ending at the clock tower and Fluted Minaret. Frequent buses leave for Fethiye (7 hrs, $8), Konya (6½ hrs, $7), and Ankara (10 hrs, $11).

WHERE TO SLEEP

Head directly to the Kaleiçi district for a plethora of pensions—many with sweeping harbor views—charging $8–$15 for a double. Facing the clock tower with your back to the otogar, veer slightly left (east) and walk into the heart of Kaleiçi via **Uzun Çarşı.** For Antalya's cheaper pensions, face the clock tower and walk east (left) one block on Cumhuriyet Caddesi and make the first major right onto traffic-congested **Atatürk Caddesi.** About 200 yds farther, on your right, towers Hadrian's Gate; walk beneath it and turn left onto **Hesapçı Sokak,** which leads past dozens of pensions. Watch for signs pointing to the **Garden Pension** (Hesapçı Sok. 35, tel. 242/247–19–30; doubles $10, cash only), a large walled garden surrounded by bungalows. Around the corner is **Kleopatra Pansiyon** (Kaledibi Sok. 6, tel. 242/243–47–21; doubles $20, cash only), with a large roof terrace and great views of the bay.

FOOD

In Kaleiçi, you could eat at a different restaurant every night for a year. The problem is that you'd run out of money very fast, especially if you choose from the romantic terrace restaurants overlooking the harbor. A better bet is **Eski Sebzeciler İçi Sokak,** a covered pedestrian street lined with hard-sell restaurants, most offering kebaps for about $4; facing the clock tower, walk east (left) for one block and turn right just before Atatürk Caddesi. For reasonable prices, a fine sunset view, and delicious eggplant kebaps, walk to Hıdırlı Park and search out **Villa Park Restaurant** (tel. 242/248–63–09; cash only).

WORTH SEEING

Everything worth seeing is in historic Kaleiçi, except for the **Antalya Müzesi** (tel. 242/241–45–28; admission $3; open Tues.–Sun. 9–6), 1 km (½ mi) west of the main tourist office and accessible by a westbound dolmuş from the city center. The museum has an overwhelming assortment of statuary and attention-grabbing, human-size amphorae. Back toward the main square is the **Yivli Minare** (Fluted Minaret), a 13th-century tile tower commissioned by Seljuk sultan Alaeddin Keykubat; these days it's home to a small **art gallery** (admission free). A short walk west is the squat **clock tower,** the most recognizable landmark in Antalya. At the eastern entry to Kaleiçi, **Hadrian's Gate,** built in honor of the Roman emperor in AD 130, is most picturesque at night when the floodlights are turned on. At the southern edge of Kaleiçi, the tower **Hıdırlık Kulesi** overlooks the bay, beside a grassy knoll perfect for sunset strolls.

CENTRAL TURKEY

A triangle 200 km (120 mi) on each side—with Konya in the south, Cappadocia to the east, and Ankara in the north—encompasses the central Anatolian plateau. **Ankara** has one of the best museums in Turkey but little else of interest. You can usually avoid a stop in the city if you're traveling by bus, although it's a transport hub for many trains. **Konya** is worth a stop for its Whirling Dervish monastery; it also breaks up the long journey between the Mediterranean and **Cappadocia,** the region's undisputed highlight.

ANKARA

A backwater village until 1923 when Atatürk made it the capital of Turkey, Ankara fails to make much of an impression today. There's little reason to visit, though you might get stuck here for a night waiting for a train or bus connection to someplace more interesting. The **Kızılay** district is new and posh, with lush, well-maintained parks, but the historic **Ulus** district, north of the train tracks, has most of the sights. At the top of a hill 500 yds east of Ulus Meydanı, the main square, the crumbling, 1,100-year-old Hisar citadel is one of the remnants of ancient Ankara. Within the walls you'll find a rambling, old-fashioned Turkish town with bits of broken columns from Roman ruins now adapted to household use. Immediately south of the citadel is Ankara's **bazaar**; walk downhill from here and follow the signs to **Ankara**

Anadolu Medeniyetleri Müzesi (Museum of Anatolian Civilizations; Kadife Sok., tel. 312/324–31–60; admission $3; open Tues.–Sun. 8:30–5:30), a must-for its unrivaled collection of Hittite artifacts. Modern Ankara's only blockbuster sight is the mausoleum **Anit Kabir** (tel. 312/231–79–75; open Tues.–Sun. 9–5:30), in a park 3 km (2 mi) southwest of Ulus (take Bus 63). Enter respectfully: This massive colonnaded building holds the remains of Turkey's national hero Kemal Mustafa Atatürk in a 40-ton sarcophagus.

BASICS

For the essential city map, try the **tourist offices** at the otogar or the airport. The **American Express** office (Cinnah Cad. 9/4, , tel. 312/467–73–34; closed Sun.) is on the southern end of Atatürk Bulvarı; from Ulus Meydanı, walk 3½ km (2¼ mi) south down Atatürk Bulvarı, past the German and Italian embassies. Each district has its own PTT office, but 24-hour **Ulus PTT** (Atatürk Bulvarı, just south of Ulus Meydanı, tel. 312/488–57–56) is the main one.

COMING AND GOING

Ankara's main artery is **Atatürk Bulvarı,** which runs 4 km (2½ mi) from Ulus Meydanı (a traffic circle graced with a statue of Atatürk) in the north, past Gençlik Park, and south through the adjacent districts of **Kızılay, Bakanlıklar,** and **Kavaklıdere,** which constitute "modern" Ankara. Buses (25¢) cruise up and down the street, and a taxi from Ulus to Bankanlıklar costs $3–$4.

Ankara's new **Aşti Yenı Otobüs Terminal** (Söğütözü, tel. 312/224–10–00) is about 3 km (2 mi) from Ulus. Catch a cab to Ulus Meydanı ($3) or, from the main entrance, cross over the elevated concrete archway and, on the opposite side of the street, catch a 30¢ dolmus to Ulus (heading left). From the Ulus domuş station, walk past the Hotel Suna and turn right onto busy Atatürk Bulvarı (Ulus Meydanı is 100 yds ahead). Buses go just about everywhere from the otogar, including İstanbul (8 hrs, $7), Antalya (10 hrs, $11), and Nevşehir (4 hrs, $7). Ankara's **central train station** (Hipodrum Cad., tel. 312/311–06–20) has express trains to İstanbul (7½ hrs, $8.50) and trains to İzmir (16 hrs, 8). From the station, walk east (right) through the park and the first main street you hit is Atatürk Bulvarı; walk 500 yds north (left) for Ulus Meydanı. **Esenboğa Airport** is 33 km (20 mi) north of town. Havaş buses ($2.50) leave the Turkish Airlines office (Atatürk Bulvarı 125, Bakanlıklar, tel. 312/419–28–25) 1½ hours before flight departures, but you should call to confirm. There are regular flights to İstanbul (45 minutes, $55 oneway), most other major Turkish cities, and some European capitals.

WHERE TO SLEEP

Most hotels—from cheap pensions to $20-a-night, upscale affairs—are in Ulus. From Ulus Meydanı, walk 200 yds south down Atatürk Bulvarı and look on the left for comfy **Otel Akman** (Kosova Sok. 6, tel. 312/324–41–40; doubles $17; cash only); it's set off from the main road, past the red-and-blue modern sculpture. Continue down the street for cheaper hotels. Back at Ulus Meydanı, walk 150 yds due east toward the castle for noisy, central **Hisar Oteli** (Hisarpark Cad. 6, tel. 312/311–98–89; $6 per person, cash only). The rooms have sinks, but the locked showers encourage you to use the adjacent bathhouse, Hisar Hamam ($3).

FOOD

Ulus has the cheapest kebap stands and sit-down restaurants, with full meals for about $3. **Madencioğlu Pasta ve Piknik** (Anafartalar Cad. 25/B, near Hisar Oteli, tel. 312/312–39–54; cash only) makes great *peynir börek* (cheese pastry; 50¢) and is packed in the morning. For a wider selection of bars, cafés, and restaurants—not to mention McDonald's and Wimpy's—hasten to Kızılay. As you walk south down Atatürk Bulvarı, turn left past the Kızılay PTT office and make the first major right onto **Karanfil Sokak,** a street loaded with food and drink options.

CAPPADOCIA

With its underground cities and bizarre rock formations, Cappadocia is like another planet. Three now-extinct volcanoes are largely responsible for the rocky landscape, spewing ash that over 60 million years was carved by the elements into deep canyons and tall spires of malleable rock. As early as 1000 BC, humans discovered that the rock was easy to cut, easy to defend, and a sound protection from winter's fierce cold and summer's blistering heat. By the 8th century AD entire subterranean cities had been built into the landscape—complete with ventilation systems that let smoke out and air in, as well as massive rounded stones to block the entrances in case of attack (a wise precaution, considering that Cappadocia has been traversed by many of history's great conquerors, including the Hittites, Romans, Persians, Mongols, and Turks). Today some farming families still live in these ancient rock structures, existing as their ancestors did—without electricity or running water—though in many Cappadocian villages, hotels and pensions have refurbished the bare rock with all the tourist amenities. Along with tourism, farming is the mainstay of the region: The desolate-appearing land is actually very fertile, and Cappadocian wine is justly world-renowned.

Cappadocia stretches 150 km (90 mi) from **İhlara Gorge** in the west to the 5,000-room underground city of **Derinkuyu** in the east. With so much to cover, you need at least three full days to do Cappadocia justice. Nearly all buses stop in **Nevşehir,** the dreary transport hub from which you should immediately make a connection to **Göreme,** the best base for day trips.

GOREME

Göreme is only 9 km (5½ mi) east of barren Nevşehir (dolmuş depart every 45 minutes), but it may as well be 900 km (540 mi), so stunning is its landscape. You'll want to spend one day hiking, biking, or taking a guided tour of Cavuşin and Zelve (*below*); one day biking or taking a dolmuş to Kaymaklı and Derinkuyu (*below*); and another day checking out the **Açık Hava Müzesi** (Open-Air Museum; admission $3.50; open daily 9–5:30), a walkable 1 km (½ mi) east of Göreme (look for the yellow road signs), then hiking to **Uçhisar,** a small village 5 km (3 mi) southwest (and uphill) from Göreme, with mostly uninhabited rock houses to explore and a thrilling ancient hilltop **castle** (admission $1.50; open daily 9–5:30). The Open-Air Museum itself has more than 30 rock churches decorated with weathered 1,000-year-old Byzantine frescoes. It's on every package-tour itinerary, so arrive as early as possible.

BASICS • Göreme hasn't any official tourist office; try **Haybil Tours** (tel. 384/271–22–11), **Gulliver's Travels** (tel. and fax 384/271–22–28), or any of the other travel agents clustered in the center of this tiny town. Most offer daily tours of Cappadocia ($10–$15 per person, lunch included), but it's far more interesting to venture out on your own. The one thing these agencies do have, however, is free walking maps—absolutely imperative if you're planning a trek that's off the region's paved roads. There are no ATMs in Göreme, but you can change traveler's checks at the **PTT** (tel. 384/271–28–81), on the north side of town toward Avanos.

GETTING AROUND • The small **otogar** at the center of town has frequent direct service *to* most places in Turkey, including Ankara (4 hrs, $7) and Konya (3 hrs, $5). Yet on your way *from* these places, you'll probably have to change buses or catch a dolmuş in Nevşehir (20 min, 75¢). Once in Göreme, your free walking map is all you need to get around. The only exceptions are Kaymaklı and Derinkuyu, which are too far to reach on foot. You'll have to catch a dolmuş, join a guided tour, or rent a mountain bike ($5–$8 per day) or moped ($13–$16 per day) from one of the shops in the center of Göreme.

WHERE TO SLEEP • Göreme has plenty of great pensions, many built into the hillside; most cost around $5 per person. For the ever-popular **Ottoman House** (tel. 384/271–26–16; $10 per person; cash only), a plush hotel that's worth every penny, walk 160 yds north from the otogar along the dry riverbed. Even if you don't stay here, check out its **Harem Bar** for drinks in a very cool, very Ottoman setting. Another option is **Keleş Cave Pension** (tel. 384/271–21–52; $5 per person; cash only), which has four floors of rooms with windows carved into the rock. Like all rock rooms, they're cold, damp, and have little natural light, but the experience of sleeping in a cave is unique. From the otogar, cross the canal and walk due south up the tiny main road, past the huge portrait of Kemal Mustafa; 300 yds farther you'll spot signs for Keleş. There are also several pensions on the way to the Open-Air Museum—from the otogar, walk 50 yds west (toward Avanos) and look for the yellow museum sign.

FOOD • Food isn't cheap in Göreme, so introduce yourself to its markets and kebap stands. If you want to indulge, walk 50 yds southeast from the otogar to **Göreme Restaurant** (tel. 384/271–21–83; fairly authentic meals $3–$5, cash only), adorned with low couches and comfy pillows. Across the road, **Sedef** (tel. 384/271–12–23; cash only) serves a staggering range of Turkish appetizers, salads, and entrées for slightly more.

CAVUSIN AND ZELVE

In the mood for a moderate 17-km (10½-mi), seven-hour hike? Grab a free walking map (*see* Basics, *above*) and follow the paved road 4 km (2½ mi) east from Göreme to **Cavuşin** (the road is clearly marked). Beyond a few carpet shops, a teahouse, and some restaurants, there's not much to Cavuşin. Take a quick peek at **Cavuşin Kilisesi,** a rock church at the town's crossroads, then follow the weathered yellow signs for 200 yds to the **old town,** where you could easily spend an hour exploring the hundreds of houses carved into the cliffs. Afterwards, either walk back to the main road and continue 3 km (2 mi) to Zelve or—a much better plan—return to the café at the base of Cavuşin's old town, and then walk back up the hill keeping to your right at every fork. Once you clear the rock houses, small footpaths lead northeast (left) for 2 km (1 mi) along the base of the mountains. This is Cappadocia at its best: herds of goats, vineyards, and the occasional farmer tilling his fields. Though you may think you're lost, nearly every footpath winds in the same direction around the mountain, and you'll rejoin the paved road—which is always easy to spot—about 500 yds from the entrance to Zelve. As long as you don't climb *over* the mountain, you're fine.

Zelve (admission $3; open daily 9–6) is not a town or a village, but rather an open-air collection of rock houses and churches spread over three valleys. Many were built more than 1,000 years ago, and some churches retain their simple red-painted frescoes. Bring a flashlight if you want to explore the nooks and crannies, particularly the pitch-black, 99-ft-long **tunnel** that joins Valley 2 with Valley 1. At the restaurants by the front gate lunch will cost $2–$3.

To head back to Göreme, follow the paved road 1 km (½ mi) to the cluster of roadside souvenir stands. This is your cue to hike into the small valley on the left, following the footpaths that wind past fields and odd plumes of volcanic rock. The valley parallels the paved road and eventually leads to Cavuşın. If you're tired, rejoin the paved road and continue 3 km (2 mi) to Göreme. Otherwise, on the fringe of Cavuşın there's a small (often bone-dry) **canal**; turn left and follow it. Dirty and dull for the first 800 yds, it then enters a small forest and runs through a cliff-encircled valley. The trail can be easy to lose, so make sure you have plenty of daylight left (at least three hours). Most walking maps are not detailed enough to give precise directions, but the idea is to follow the canal/creek for 3 km (2 mi). The creek often turns to a trickle and flows through arched tunnels in parts. Along the way you'll pass weathered signs for various rock churches, though if you take one of these detours be sure to backtrack to the creek—it's your best guide. The creek finally disappears at the end of the valley, where a few footpaths ascend and eventually meet a paved road. This happens to be the road to Göreme's Open-Air Museum, so turn west (right) and walk 1½ km (¾ mi) back to Göreme.

KAYMAKLI AND DERINKUYU

Make every effort to visit these two underground cities. **Kaymaklı,** 28 km (17 mi) northeast of Göreme, is a farm town seemingly oblivious to the **Yeraltı Şehri** (uninhabited underground city; admission $2; open daily 9–5:30) in its midst. The damp caverns dip 248 ft into the earth, connecting long-abandoned chapels, wineries, and living areas via a network of cramped walkways and tunnels. Bring a flashlight since many of the best caverns are unlit, though perfectly safe to explore. **Derinkuyu,** 10 km (6 mi) south of Kaymaklı, has its own **Yeraltı Şehri** (admission $2.50; open daily 9–6:30), with 5,000 rooms spread over about ½ acre. The eight excavated levels contain a crucifix-shape church, a wine press, dining areas, and 52 ventilation shafts that allowed air down and smoke up. During the 12th–14th centuries, Derinkuyu actually *was* a subterranean city, housing upwards of 8,000 people. To get to these cities, you can take a guided tour, a moped, or a dolmuş (via Nevşehir).

KONYA

Although Konya is one of the world's oldest cities and of great importance to Islam, it attracts surprisingly few tourists. One reason is geography: It's stuck on a beautiful but out-of-the-way plateau and is a half-day journey from most anywhere else in Turkey. The other reason is that Konya, with its wide boulevards and drab office buildings, is not especially alluring. But if you're heading for Cappadocia from the Mediterranean Coast, a daylong break in Konya makes good sense, and you'll get a crash course in Turkish culture besides.

BASICS

The **tourist office** (Mevlâna Cad. 65, tel. 332/351–10–74; open daily 8:30–5) is opposite the Mevlâna Müzesi.

COMING AND GOING

The **otogar** is 1 km (½ mi) north of town on Ankara Caddesi, and dolmuş shuttle people to the center for 20¢. Look for one marked HÜKÜMET ALANI or KONAK and, after you pass **Alaaddin Tepesi** (a large, circular, raised park) you'll turn east (right) onto **Alaaddin Caddesi,** Konya's main street. Have the dolmuş stop 300 yds farther at **Hükümet Alanı** (the main square), in front of the PTT. From here, the bazaar is due south (behind the PTT), the tourist office ½ km (¼ mi) farther east along Alaaddin Caddesi (which gets renamed Mevlâna Caddesi). From the otogar there are buses to Antalya (6½ hrs, $7), Nevşehir (3 hrs, $5), and Ankara (4 hrs, $5.50).

WHERE TO SLEEP AND EAT

From the dolmuş stop on Alaaddin Caddesi, walk 20 yds south to the PTT, then turn left and walk to the corner (past the shoeshine stalls). If you make a right turn, a 30-yd walk will bring you to comfortable **Otel Petek** (Çıkrıcılar Cad. 40, tel. 332/351–25–99; doubles $13–$15), in the heart of Konya's bazaar and on a street well-known for its cheap kebap stands. Most restaurants in Konya close early, usually at 9 or 10 PM, and don't serve alcohol. An exception is **Damla Restaurant** (Hükümet Alanı, tel. 332/351–37–05), behind Otel Şahin off the main square, with great appetizers and a range of Turkish entrées. Both establishments accept cash only.

WORTH SEEING

Nobody leaves Konya without visiting the **Mevlâna Müzesi** (Mevlâna Meydanı, tel. 332/350–64–61; admission $2; open daily 9–5), catercorner to the tourist office. This active mosque with a slender bright-green minaret is dedicated to the Whirling Dervishes, a group of Sufi Muslims famous for conical red hats, haunting pipe music (buy the $3 cassette at the gift shop), and dizzying dances. The group's original leader, Celaleddin Rumi (AD 1207–73), known as Mevlâna, wrote the 25,000-verse poem *Mesnevi* and initiated a ritual dance symbolizing union with God; dervishes spin for Allah but encourage people of all faiths to join in. Both robe and hat are draped over symbolic tombs in the museum, which also contains 8th-century Korans and 17th-century carpets. The best times to catch a dance are late December (when Konya hosts a big dervish festival) and on Monday evenings in summer. **Selimye Camii** (Selim Mosque), in front of the museum, is worth a look for its glass windows and decorative carpets. From here, follow the yellow signs for ½ km (¼ mi) to **Koyunoğlu Müzesi** (admission 75¢; open Tues.–Sun. 9–5), which has a collection of antique carpets and Roman and Ottoman coins, and a restored Ottoman house on the grounds, decked out with 19th-century period furniture.

INDEX

WHEREVER YOU TRAVEL, *H*ELP IS NEVER FAR AWAY.

From planning your trip to

providing travel assistance along

the way, American Express®

Travel Service Offices are

always there to help

you do more.

American Express Travel Service
Offices are found in central locations
throughout Europe.